175 YEARS OF DICTIONARY PUBLISHING

Collins

175 YEARS OF DICTIONARY PUBLISHING

Canadian English Dictionary & Thesaurus

HarperCollins Publishers
2 Bloor Street East,
20th floor,
Toronto,
Ontario,
Canada M4W 1A8

Third edition 2011

Reprint 10 9 8 7 6 5 4 3 2 1 0

ISBN 978-0-00-739849-2

Collins ® is a registered trademark of HarperCollins Publishers Limited

www.harpercollins.ca

A catalogue record for this book is available from the British Library

Typeset by Market House Books Ltd, Aylesbury, Great Britain

Printed in Great Britain by Clays Ltd, St Ives plc

Acknowledgements

We would like to thank those authors and publishers who kindly gave permission for copyright material to be used in the Collins Word Web. We would also like to thank Times Newspapers Ltd for providing valuable data.

CONTENTS

List of Contributors vi

Foreword vii

Using This Dictionary and Thesaurus viii – xi

Abbreviations xii

Collins Canadian English Dictionary & Thesaurus 1 – 972

Supplement: Reports and Presentations

LIST OF CONTRIBUTORS

Consultant Editor
Jessica de Villiers

Senior Editor
Robert Pontisso

Editors
Gerry Breslin
Lorna Gilmour
Robert Groves

For the Publisher
Lucy Cooper
Kerry Ferguson
Elaine Higgleton

FOREWORD

This book is an immensely practical and helpful language resource. It provides two kinds of language help, arranged on the same page for quick and easy look-up. In the top section of each page you will find a dictionary text which gives help with spellings and meanings, while the lower section of each page provides a matching thesaurus with a choice of synonyms.

The dictionary includes spelling help for all irregular forms of words. Pronunciation help is also given for words considered difficult or confusing.

The synonyms of the thesaurus text are arranged in order of frequency of usage in actual Canadian English. In addition, the most useful synonym for each sense is given first and highlighted in bold type. This is particularly helpful when a main entry word has a number of different senses. It also gives you an idea of which synonym is the closest alternative to the word you have looked up.

The thesaurus text also includes key opposites (antonyms) at many of the main entry words. These opposites provide you with another way of expressing yourself. For instance, if you want to say that something is *difficult*, it can sometimes be effective to use a negative construction and, using the word's opposite, you may think of a phrase such as "*by no means easy*".

The symbol Ⓣ appears after the headword of every dictionary entry which has matching thesaurus text, to draw the user's attention to the fact that additional synonym help is included for that entry.

The Reports and Presentations Supplement will help you to write reports and give presentations in a style that will smoothly communicate your message to your audience.

This book is thus a uniquely helpful reference tool, providing spelling, meaning, language help, a wide choice of alternatives and opposites, and a report writing guide, all based on actual Canadian English and brought together in a single source. This makes it an invaluable language resource, and an ideal companion for anyone who wants to increase their command of English.

USING THIS DICTIONARY AND THESAURUS

DICTIONARY AND THESAURUS

Main entry words are printed in large bold type. All main entry words, including abbreviations and proper names on the dictionary side, appear in one alphabetical sequence, eg

Aalto
aardvark
AB
aback

Variant spellings are shown in full, eg

adrenalin, adrenaline

When a main entry word on the dictionary side is also a main entry word on the thesaurus side, the Ⓣ symbol follows the dictionary entry word, eg

abbreviate Ⓣ

Parts of speech are shown in italics as an abbreviation, eg

afflict *v*

In the dictionary, when a word can be used as more than one part of speech, the change of part of speech is shown after an empty arrow, eg

aim Ⓣ *v* **1** point (a weapon or missile) or direct (a blow or remark) at a target **2** propose or intend ▷ *n* **3** aiming

In the thesaurus, the change of part of speech is shown after a black arrow, eg

aim *v* **1 = intend**, plan, attempt, propose, strive, aspire • *The company aims to sign up a million customers within the next five years.* ▶ *n* **2 = intention**, plan, goal

Parts of speech may be combined for words, eg

afloat *adv, adj*

Meanings of the word in the dictionary and thesaurus are separated by sense numbers, eg

> **absorb** Ⓣ *v* **1** soak up (a liquid) **2** take in **3** engage the interest of (someone)

> **absorb** *v* **1** = **soak up**, digest, take in • *Plants absorb carbon dioxide.* **2** = **preoccupy**, engage, fascinate...

Examples illustrate certain meanings of the main entry words, and follow the meaning to which they apply. In the dictionary, these are shown in italics, preceded by a colon, eg

> **apiece** Ⓣ *adv* each: *they were given two apples apiece*

In the thesaurus, examples are preceded by a black dot, eg

> **ability** *n* = **skill**, talent, capability, expertise, competence • *the ability to get along with others*

Phrases and idioms are included within the main entry. In the dictionary, they follow the meanings of the main entry word and are preceded by a black arrow, eg

> **head** Ⓣ *n...adj...*
> ▶ **go to someone's head** make someone drunk or conceited
> ▶ **head over heels** very much in love

In the thesaurus, phrases and idioms come at the end of the part of speech to which they apply, and are preceded by an empty arrow, eg

> **head** *n...*
> ▷ **go to one's head** = **excite**, intoxicate, make conceited, puff up...
> ▷ **head over heels** = **uncontrollably**, completely, thoroughly

Cross references refer the user to another entry. These are shown in bold, and are preceded by explanatory text, eg

> **alto** *n, pl* **-tos** *music* **1** short for **contralto**

> **accommodation** *n* = **housing**, house, digs...
> *See also*: **space**

DICTIONARY

Pronunciations are given in square brackets for words that are difficult or confusing; the word is respelled as it is pronounced, with the stressed syllable in bold type, eg

> **aegis** [**ee**-jiss]

Irregular parts or confusing forms of verbs, nouns, adjectives, and adverbs are shown in bold black, in smaller type than the main entry word, eg

> **begin** Ⓣ *v* **-ginning, -gan, -gun**
> **regret** Ⓣ *v* **–gretting, -gretted**
> **anniversary** Ⓣ *n, pl* **-ries**
> **busy** Ⓣ *adj* **busier, busiest**
> **well**[1] Ⓣ *adv* **better, best**

Derived forms are shown in the same paragraph as the main entry word, eg

> **abuse** Ⓣ *n* **1** prolonged ill-treatment of someone...**abuser** *n* **abusive** *adj* **abusively** *adv* **abusiveness** *n*

Derived forms that require a definition are preceded by a black arrow, eg

> **accelerate** Ⓣ *v* (cause to) move faster
> **acceleration** *n*
> ▸**accelerator** *n* pedal in a motor vehicle to increase speed

Compound words formed from the main entry word are shown in alphabetical order at the end of the entry, preceded by a black arrow, eg

> **ash**[1] *n*...
> ▸**ashtray** *n* receptacle for tobacco ash and cigarette butts
> ▸**Ash Wednesday** first day of Lent

THESAURUS

Synonyms are shown in order of appropriateness to the meaning of the main entry word. Synonyms are separated by commas, with the best, or 'key', synonym for that particular meaning listed first in bold type, eg

> **abate** *v* = **decrease**, diminish, wane, lessen, subside, ebb

Antonyms are words which have the opposite meaning to a certain meaning of the main entry word. These are preceded by 'OPPOSITE' in small capital letters, and follow the meaning to which they apply, eg

> **abrupt** *adj* ... **2** = **curt**, short, rude, terse • *He was taken aback by her abrupt manner.* OPPOSITE: polite

Related words follow the heading 'RELATED WORD' or 'RELATED WORDS', and are preceded by a word in italics explaining their relation to the main entry word, eg

> **alcohol** *n* = **drink**, liquor, booze (*informal*), spirits ... RELATED WORD *like*: dipsomania

Context labels indicate when the main entry word or a synonym is commonly used with another word or phrase (a 'collocate'). The main entry word or synonym is indicated by a tilde (~), and the collocate appears in italics, within round brackets, eg

> **break** *v*... **6** (~ *a record, etc.*) = **beat**, top, surpass, exceed, better

ABBREVIATIONS

AD	anno Domini	meteorol	meteorology
adj	adjective	mil	military
adv	adverb	n	noun
anat	anatomy	N	North
archit	architecture	naut	nautical
astrol	astrology	Nfld	Newfoundland
Aust(ral)	Australia(n)	NZ	New Zealand
BC	before Christ	orig.	originally
biol	biology	photog	photography
Brit	British	pl	plural
Canad	Canadian	prep	preposition
chem	chemistry	pron	pronoun
conj	conjunction	psycho	psychology
E	East	Queb	Quebec
eg	for example	®	Trademark
esp.	especially	RC	Roman Catholic
etc.	et cetera	S	South
fem	feminine	S Afr	South Africa(n)
foll.	followed	Scot	Scottish
geom	geometry	sing	singular
hist	history	US	United States
interj	interjection	usu.	usually
lit	literary	v	verb
masc	masculine	W	West
med	medicine	Zool	Zoology

DICTIONARY

Aa

a *adj* indefinite article, used before a noun being mentioned for the first time
A1 *adj informal* first-class, excellent
AA **1** Alcoholics Anonymous **2** Automobile Association
Aalto *n* **Alvar**. 1898–1976, Finnish architect and furniture designer, noted particularly for his public and industrial buildings, in which wood is much used. He invented bent plywood furniture (1932)
aardvark *n* S African anteater with long ears and snout
AB **1** Alberta **2** able-bodied seaman
aback *adv* **taken aback** startled or disconcerted
abacus [**ab**-a-cuss] *n* beads on a wire frame, used for doing calculations
abalone [ab-a-**lone**-ee] *n* edible shellfish yielding mother-of-pearl
abandon Ⓣ *v* **1** desert or leave (one's wife, children, etc.) **2** give up (hope etc.) altogether ▷ *n* **3** freedom from inhibition **abandonment** *n*
▶ **abandoned** *adj* **1** deserted **2** uninhibited
abase *v* humiliate, degrade (oneself) **abasement** *n*
abashed Ⓣ *adj* embarrassed and ashamed
abate Ⓣ *v* diminish in strength **abatement** *n*
abattoir [**ab**-a-twahr] *n* slaughterhouse
Abba *n* Swedish pop group (1972–82): comprised Benny Andersson (born 1946), Agnetha Faltskog (born 1950), Anni-Frid Lyngstad (born 1945), and Bjorn Ulvaeus (born 1945); numerous hit singles included "Waterloo" (1974), "Dancing Queen" (1977), and "The Winner Takes It All" (1980)
abbess *n* nun in charge of a convent
abbey Ⓣ *n* dwelling place of, or a church belonging to, a community of monks or nuns
abbot *n* head of an abbey of monks
Abbott *n* Sir **John**. 1821–93, Canadian Conservative politician; Prime Minister (1891–92)
abbr., abbrev abbreviation
abbreviate Ⓣ *v* shorten (a word) by omitting some letters
▶ **abbreviation** *n* shortened form of a word or words
ABC *n* **1** alphabet **2** rudiments of a subject
abdicate Ⓣ *v* give up (the throne or a responsibility) **abdication** *n*
abdomen *n* part of the body containing the stomach and intestines **abdominal** *adj*
abduct Ⓣ *v* carry off, kidnap **abduction** *n* **abductor** *n*
Abdullah II *n* born 1962, King of Jordan from 1999, son of King **Hussein**
Abelard *n* **Peter**, French name *Pierre Abélard*. 1079–1142, French scholastic philosopher and theologian whose works include *Historia Calamitatum* and *Sic et Non* (1121). His love for Héloïse is recorded in their correspondence
Aberdeen *n* **1** **George Hamilton-Gordon**, 4th Earl of. 1784–1860, British statesman. He

THESAURUS

abandon *v* **1** = **leave**, desert, maroon, forsake, jilt, leave behind, leave in the lurch, bail on *slang* • *He abandoned the car and walked home.* **2** = **give up**, surrender, yield, relinquish ▶ *n* **3** = **wildness**, recklessness • *He began to laugh with abandon.* OPPOSITE: control
See also: **cancel**
abandoned *See* **derelict**
abandonment *n* = **leaving**, dereliction, desertion, forsaking
abashed *adj* = **embarrassed**, ashamed, dismayed, chagrined, disconcerted, humiliated, mortified, shamefaced, taken aback
abate *v* = **decrease**, diminish, wane, lessen, subside, ebb • *The four-day flood at last abated.*
See also: **ease, moderate**
abbey *n* = **monastery**, convent, friary, nunnery, priory
abbreviate *v* = **shorten**, cut, contract, reduce, compress, summarize, condense, abridge
abbreviation *n* = **shortening**, reduction, summary, contraction, synopsis, abridgment
abdicate *v* = **give up**, resign, quit, abandon, renounce, relinquish, step down (*informal*)
abdication *n* = **giving up**, retirement, surrender, resignation, abandonment, renunciation, quitting
abduct *v* = **kidnap**, seize, snatch (*slang*), carry off
abduction *n* = **kidnaping**, seizure, carrying off

DICTIONARY

was foreign secretary under Wellington (1828) and Peel (1841–46); became prime minister of a coalition ministry in 1852 but was compelled to resign after mismanagement of the Crimean War (1855) **2 John Campbell Gordon**, 1st Marquess of Aberdeen and Temair. 1847–1934, British statesman. Governor General of Canada (1893–98)

Aberdeen Angus *n* breed of cattle, orig. Scottish

aberration Ⓣ *n* **1** deviation from what is normal **2** mental lapse

▸**aberrant** *adj* showing aberration **aberrance** *n*

abet Ⓣ *v* **abetting, abetted** assist or encourage in wrongdoing **abettor** *n*

abeyance Ⓣ *n* state of not being in use

abhor Ⓣ *v* **-horring, -horred** dislike strongly **abhorrence** *n*

▸**abhorrent** *adj* hateful, loathsome

abide Ⓣ *v* **1** endure, put up with **2** *obsolete* stay or dwell: *abide with me*

▸**abiding** *adj* lasting

▸**abide by** *v* obey (the law, rules, etc.)

ability Ⓣ *n, pl* **-ties 1** competence, power **2** talent

abject Ⓣ *adj* **1** utterly miserable **2** lacking all self-respect **abjectly** *adv* **abjectness** *n*

abjure *v* deny or renounce on oath **abjuration** *n*

ablative [**ab**-lat-iv] *n* case of nouns in Latin and other languages, indicating source, agent, or instrument of action

ablaze Ⓣ *adj* burning fiercely

able Ⓣ *adj* capable, competent **ably** *adv*

▸**able-bodied** *adj* strong and healthy

ablutions *pl n* act of washing

ABM antiballistic missile

abnegate *v* give up, renounce **abnegation** *n*

abnormal Ⓣ *adj* not normal or usual **abnormally** *adv* **abnormality** *n*

aboard *adv, prep* on, in, onto, or into a ship, train, or aircraft

abode Ⓣ *n* home, dwelling

abolish Ⓣ *v* do away with **abolition** *n*

▸**abolitionist** *n* person who wishes to do away with something, esp. slavery

abominate *v* detest or hate **abomination** *n*

▸**abominable** *adj* detestable, very bad **abominably** *adv*

▸**abominable snowman** large apelike creature said to inhabit the Himalayas

aborigine [ab-or-**rij**-in-ee], **aboriginal** *n* original inhabitant of a country or region **aboriginal** *adj*

▸**Aborigine** *or* **Aboriginal** original inhabitant of Australia

abort Ⓣ *v* **1** terminate (a pregnancy) prematurely **2** give birth to a dead fetus **3** end prematurely and unsuccessfully

THESAURUS

aberration *n* = **oddity**, defect, irregularity, lapse, abnormality, quirk, anomaly, peculiarity

abet *v* = **help**, support, assist, aid, connive at

abeyance *n* ▹ **in abeyance** = **shelved**, suspended, hanging fire, on ice (*informal*), pending

abhor *v* = **hate**, loathe, detest, abominate, shrink from, shudder at

abhorrence *See* **horror**

abhorrent *adj* = **hateful**, offensive, horrid, distasteful, abominable, repulsive, disgusting, hated, loathsome, scuzzy (*slang*)

abide *v* = **tolerate**, stand, bear, suffer, accept, endure, put up with

abide by *v* = **obey**, follow, observe, agree to, comply with, conform to, submit to

abiding *adj* = **everlasting**, permanent, persistent, lasting, enduring, unchanging, continuing

ability *n* = **skill**, talent, capability, expertise, competence • *the ability to get along with others* OPPOSITE: inability
See also: **capacity, gift, potential, qualification**

abject *adj* **1** = **miserable**, deplorable, hopeless, wretched, forlorn, pitiable **2** = **servile**, submissive, cringing, degraded, fawning, grovelling

ablaze *adj* = **on fire**, burning, fiery, flaming, aflame, lighted, alight, blazing, ignited

able *adj* = **capable**, expert, efficient, skilled, talented, accomplished, first-rate • *She proved herself to be an able politician.*
See also: **proficient, skilful**

able-bodied *adj* = **strong**, healthy, sound, fit, robust, sturdy

ably *See* **well**

abnormal *adj* = **unusual**, odd, extraordinary, strange, exceptional, irregular, uncommon, atypical, peculiar

abnormality *n* = **oddity**, exception, irregularity, deformity, peculiarity, singularity, strangeness

abode *n* = **home**, house, pad (*slang, dated*), residence, habitat, lodging, dwelling, habitation, domicile, quarters

abolish *v* = **do away with**, overturn, annul, put an end to • *Their objective was to abolish the new tax.*

abolition *n* = **ending**, end, destruction, cancellation, elimination, termination, extermination, wiping out

abominable *adj* = **terrible**, horrible, despicable, lousy (*slang*), hateful, vile, horrid, repulsive, disgusting, detestable, revolting, scuzzy (*slang*)

abort *v* **1** = **terminate** (a pregnancy),

DICTIONARY

▸**abortion** *n* **1** operation to terminate a pregnancy **2** *informal* something grotesque
▸**abortionist** *n* person who performs abortions, esp. illegally
▸**abortive** *adj* unsuccessful
abound Ⓣ *v* **1** be plentiful **2** overflow
abounding *adj*
about Ⓣ *prep* **1** concerning, on the subject of **2** in or near a place ▹ *adv* **3** nearly, approximately **4** nearby
▸**about to** **1** intending to **2** on the point of: *about to give up hope*
▸**about turn** *v mil* turn to face the opposite direction
▸**about-turn** *n* **1** turn to the opposite direction **2** complete change of attitude
above Ⓣ *adv, prep* **1** over or higher than **2** greater than **3** superior to
▸**above board** in the open, without dishonesty
abracadabra *n* supposedly magic word
abrade *v* rub or scrape away
abrasion Ⓣ *n* scraped area on the skin
▸**abrasive** *adj* **1** harsh and annoying in manner **2** causing abrasion ▹ *n* **3** substance for cleaning or polishing by rubbing
abreast Ⓣ *adj, adv* side by side
▸**abreast of** up to date with
abridge Ⓣ *v* shorten by using fewer words
abridgment *or* **abridgement** *n*
abroad Ⓣ *adv* **1** to or in a foreign country **2** at large
abrogate *v* cancel (a law or agreement) formally **abrogation** *n*
abrupt Ⓣ *adj* **1** sudden, unexpected **2** blunt and rude **abruptly** *adv* **abruptness** *n*
abs *pl n informal* abdominal muscles
abscess *n* inflamed swelling containing pus
abscond Ⓣ *v* leave secretly
abseil [**ab**-sale] *v esp. Brit* rappel
absent Ⓣ *adj* **1** not present **2** lacking **3** inattentive ▹ *v* **4** keep (oneself) away
absently *adv*
▸**absence** *n* **1** being away **2** lack
▸**absentee** *n* person who should be present but is not
▸**absenteeism** *n* persistent absence from work or school
▸**absent-minded** *adj* inattentive or forgetful
absent-mindedly *adv*
absinthe *n* potent green aniseed-flavoured liqueur
absolute Ⓣ *adj* **1** complete and utter **2** not limited, unconditional **3** pure: *absolute alcohol*

THESAURUS

miscarry **2 = stop**, end, arrest, fail, check, halt, axe (*informal*), terminate, call off
abortion *n* **= termination**, miscarriage, deliberate miscarriage
abortive *adj* **= failed**, unsuccessful, useless, vain, futile, fruitless, ineffectual, miscarried
abound *v* **= be plentiful**, swell, thrive, flourish, swarm, teem, proliferate
abounding *adj* **= plentiful**, full, rich, prolific, abundant, bountiful, copious, profuse
about *prep* **1 = regarding**, on, concerning, relating to • *anxiety about his sick son* **2 = near**, nearby, beside, circa (of a date), adjacent to, close to ▸ *adv* **3 = nearly**, around, almost, roughly, approximately • *The procedure takes about 30 minutes.*
above *prep* **1 = over**, higher than • *above the clouds* OPPOSITE: below RELATED WORDS *prefixes*: super-, supra-, sur- **2 = greater than**, beyond, exceeding • *The temperature is above 30°.*
above board *adj* **= honest**, straight, fair, square, legitimate, genuine
abrasion *n* (*Medical*) **= graze**, scratch, scrape, chafe, scuff, surface injury
abrasive *adj* **1 = unpleasant**, sharp, rough, cutting, caustic, galling, grating, irritating **2 = rough**, scratchy, grating, chafing, scraping
abreast *adv* **= alongside**, beside, side by side ▹ **abreast of = informed about**, acquainted with, *au courant* with (*French*), *au fait* with (*French*), conversant with, familiar with, in the picture about, in touch with, keeping one's finger on the pulse of, knowledgeable about, up to date with, up to speed with
abridge *v* **= shorten**, cut, reduce, decrease, summarize, abbreviate, condense
abroad *adv* **= overseas**, in foreign lands, out of the country
abrupt *adj* **1 = sudden**, unexpected, unforeseen • *the abrupt resignation of the prime minister* **2 = curt**, short, rude, terse • *He was taken aback by her abrupt manner.* OPPOSITE: polite
See also: **sharp**
abscond *v* **= flee**, escape, disappear, clear out, make off, run off, steal away
absence *n* **1 = nonattendance**, absenteeism, truancy **2 = lack**, want, need, deficiency, omission, unavailability
absent *adj* **1 = missing**, away, elsewhere, gone • *absent from work* OPPOSITE: present **2 = absent-minded**, blank, vacant, vague, oblivious, distracted, inattentive, preoccupied ▸ *v* ▹ **absent oneself = stay away**, withdraw, keep away, play truant
absent-minded *adj* **= vague**, distracted, forgetful • *Her absent-minded stepfather left the camera in the taxi.*
absolute *adj* **1 = complete**, total, pure, utter,

DICTIONARY

▸**absolutely** *adv* **1** completely ▹ *interj* **2** certainly, yes
▸**absolutism** *n* government by a ruler with unrestricted power
absolve Ⓣ *v* declare to be free from blame or sin **absolution** *n*
absorb Ⓣ *v* **1** soak up (a liquid) **2** take in **3** engage the interest of (someone) **absorption** *n*
▸**absorbent** *adj* able to absorb liquid **absorbency** *n*
abstain Ⓣ *v* **1** choose to refrain **2** choose not to vote **abstainer** *n*
▸**abstention** *n* abstaining, esp. from voting
▸**abstinence** *n* abstaining, esp. from drinking alcohol **abstinent** *adj*
abstemious Ⓣ [ab-**steem**-ee-uss] *adj* sparing in the consumption of food or alcohol **abstemiously** *adv* **abstemiousness** *n*
abstract Ⓣ *adj* **1** existing as a quality or idea rather than a material object **2** theoretical **3** (of art) using patterns of shapes and colours rather than realistic likenesses ▹ *n* **4** summary **5** abstract work of art **6** abstract word or idea ▹ *v* **7** remove **8** summarize
▸**abstracted** *adj* preoccupied **abstraction** *n*
abstruse Ⓣ *adj* not easy to understand
absurd Ⓣ *adj* incongruous or ridiculous **absurdly** *adv* **absurdity** *n*
abundant Ⓣ *adj* plentiful **abundantly** *adv* **abundance** *n*
abuse Ⓣ *n* **1** prolonged ill-treatment of someone **2** insulting comments **3** wrong use

THESAURUS

thorough, sheer, downright • *He is talking absolute nonsense.* **2 = supreme**, dictatorial, tyrannical • *an absolute ruler*
See also: **final, perfect, rank**
absolutely *adv* = **totally**, completely, fully, entirely, perfectly, wholly, utterly, one hundred per cent
absolutely not *See* **no**
absolution *n* = **forgiveness**, release, pardon, mercy, exoneration, deliverance, exculpation
absolve *v* = **forgive**, release, deliver, excuse, pardon, exculpate, let off, set free
absorb *v* **1 = soak up**, digest, take in • *Plants absorb carbon dioxide.* **2 = preoccupy**, engage, fascinate, captivate, rivet, engross
See also: **busy, grasp**
absorbed *adj* **1 = preoccupied**, lost, involved, captivated, engrossed, fascinated, immersed, rapt, riveted, wrapped up **2 = digested**, incorporated, assimilated, received, soaked up
absorbent *adj* = **permeable**, receptive, porous, spongy
absorbing *adj* = **fascinating**, interesting, captivating, engrossing, gripping, intriguing, riveting, spellbinding
absorption *n* **1 = soaking up**, consumption, digestion, assimilation, incorporation, sucking up **2 = concentration**, involvement, fascination, preoccupation, immersion, intentness
abstain *v* = **refrain**, avoid, forgo, deny oneself, give up • *The patient had to abstain from food for several hours.*
See also: **decline, refuse**
abstemious *adj* = **self-denying**, moderate, sober, austere, frugal, temperate, ascetic
abstention *n* = **refusal**, abstinence, avoidance, self-control, self-restraint, abstaining, forbearance, refraining, self-denial
abstinence *n* = **self-denial**, moderation, avoidance, self-restraint, abstemiousness, forbearance, soberness, teetotalism, temperance
abstinent *adj* = **self-denying**, moderate, sober, temperate, abstaining, abstemious, forbearing, self-controlled
abstract *adj* **1 = theoretical**, general, indefinite, hypothetical, abstruse, notional, recondite ▸ *n* **2 = summary**, outline, digest, synopsis, epitome, abridgment, précis, résumé ▸ *v* **3 = summarize**, outline, shorten, digest, epitomize, abbreviate, condense, abridge, précis **4 = remove**, separate, withdraw, isolate, extract, detach, take away, take out
abstraction *n* **1 = idea**, thought, theory, formula, concept, notion, hypothesis, generalization, theorem **2 = absent-mindedness**, absence, preoccupation, inattention, remoteness, dreaminess, pensiveness, woolgathering
abstruse *adj* = **obscure**, deep, complex, vague, enigmatic, arcane, unfathomable, esoteric, recondite
absurd *adj* = **ridiculous**, crazy (*informal*), ludicrous, illogical, nonsensical • *an absurd waste of money*
See also: **impossible, incredible, irrational, silly, stupid**
absurdity *n* = **ridiculousness**, joke, nonsense, stupidity, farce, folly, foolishness, silliness, incongruity
abundance *n* = **plenty**, bounty, affluence • *an abundance of wildlife* OPPOSITE: shortage
See also: **lot, lots, wealth**
abundant *adj* = **plentiful**, full, ample, copious • *an abundant supply of fuel* OPPOSITE: scarce
See also: **generous, rich**
abuse *n* **1 = ill-treatment**, hurt, harm, exploitation, oppression • *the prevention of*

DICTIONARY

▷ *v* **4** use wrongly **5** ill-treat violently **6** speak harshly and rudely to **abuser** *n* **abusive** *adj* **abusively** *adv* **abusiveness** *n*
abut *v* **abutting, abutted** adjoin, border on ▶**abutment** *n* end support of a bridge or arch
abuzz *adj* noisy, busy with activity etc.
abysmal Ⓣ *adj informal* extremely bad, awful **abysmally** *adv*
abyss Ⓣ *n* very deep hole or chasm
AC alternating current
a/c account
acacia [a-**kay**-sha] *n* tree or shrub with yellow or white flowers
academy *n, pl* **-mies 1** society to advance arts or sciences **2** institution for specialized training **3** *Scot* secondary school ▶**academic** *adj* **1** of an academy or university **2** of theoretical interest only ▷ *n* **3** lecturer or researcher at a university **academically** *adv* ▶ **academician** *n* member of an academy
acanthus *n* **1** prickly plant **2** ornamental carving in the shape of an acanthus leaf
accede Ⓣ *v* **1** consent or agree (to) **2** take up (an office or position)
accelerate Ⓣ *v* (cause to) move faster **acceleration** *n* ▶**accelerator** *n* pedal in a motor vehicle to increase speed
accent Ⓣ *n* **1** distinctive style of pronunciation of a local, national, or social group **2** mark over a letter to show how it is pronounced **3** stress on a syllable or musical note ▷ *v* **4** place emphasis on
accentuate Ⓣ *v* stress, emphasize **accentuation** *n*
accept Ⓣ *v* **1** receive willingly **2** consider to be true **3** agree to **acceptance** *n* ▶**acceptable** *adj* **1** satisfactory **2** tolerable **acceptably** *adv* **acceptability** *n*
access Ⓣ *n* **1** means of or right to approach or enter ▷ *v* **2** obtain (data) from a computer ▶**accessible** *adj* easy to approach or enter **accessibility** *n*

THESAURUS

animal abuse **2 = insults**, censure, derision, invective • *I was left shouting abuse as the car sped off.* **3 = misuse,** misapplication ▶ *v* **4 = insult**, curse, scold • *The baseball umpire was vally abused by the hometown fans.* **5 = ill-treat,** damage, injure, hurt, harm, exploit, misuse, maltreat, take advantage of
See also: **impose on, mistreat, wrong**
abused *See* **oppressed**
abusive *adj* **1 = insulting**, offensive, scathing, rude, disparaging • *abusive language* **2 = harmful**, rough, brutal, cruel, destructive, hurtful, injurious
abysmal *adj* **= terrible**, bad, dire, awful, appalling, dreadful
abyss *n* **= pit**, void, fissure, gorge, chasm • *He crawled forward to peer over the edge of the abyss.*
See also: **hell**
academic *adj* **1 = scholarly**, literary, bookish, erudite, highbrow, learned, studious **2 = hypothetical**, abstract, speculative, theoretical, impractical, conjectural, notional ▶ *n* **3 = scholar**, professor, fellow, master, don, lecturer, tutor, academician
accede *v* **1 = agree**, endorse, accept, admit, grant, comply, concede, consent, concur, assent, acquiesce **2 = inherit**, assume, succeed, attain, come to, enter upon, succeed to (of an heir)
accelerate *v* **= speed up**, hurry, quicken, step up (*informal*) • *She accelerated away from the curb.*
accelerated *See* **fast**
acceleration *n* **= speeding up**, hastening, hurrying, quickening, stepping up (*informal*)
accent *n* **1 = pronunciation**, tone, inflection, articulation, brogue, enunciation, intonation, modulation **2 = emphasis**, force, beat, pitch, stress, rhythm, cadence, timbre ▶ *v* **3 = emphasize**, stress, underscore, underline, accentuate
accentuate *v* **= emphasize**, stress, highlight, underscore, underline, accent, foreground, draw attention to
accept *v* **1 = receive**, take • *She accepted the award on his behalf.* OPPOSITE: refuse **2 = agree to**, acknowledge, concur with, consent to • *All those invited to next week's conference have accepted.*
See also: **admit, assume, believe, grant, resign oneself, tolerate**
acceptable *adj* **= satisfactory**, fair, adequate, tolerable, passable, all right, good enough • *an acceptable standard of living*
See also: **correct, okay, right, suitable**
acceptance *n* **1 = accepting**, receipt, taking, acquiring, gaining, getting, obtaining, securing **2 = agreement**, approval, recognition, admission, consent, adoption, cooperation, acknowledgment, assent, acquiescence, concurrence
accepted *adj* **= agreed**, common, traditional, normal, conventional, established, customary, acknowledged, approved, recognized
access *n* **= entrance**, road, approach, entry, path, passage, admission, admittance
accessibility *n* **1 = handiness**, possibility, availability, readiness, nearness **2 = approachability**, friendliness, informality, affability, cordiality **3 = openness**, susceptibility

a

DICTIONARY

accession *n* taking up of an office or position
accessory Ⓣ *n, pl* **-ries 1** supplementary part or object **2** person involved in a crime although not present when it is committed
accident Ⓣ *n* **1** mishap, usu. one causing injury or death **2** event happening by chance ▸**accidental** *adj* **1** happening by accident ▷ *n* **2** *music* symbol indicating that a sharp, flat, or natural note is not a part of the key signature **accidentally** *adv*
acclaim Ⓣ *v* **1** applaud, praise ▷ *n* **2** applause ▸**acclamation** *n* **1** acclaim **2** election without opposition to a public position
acclimatize Ⓣ *v* adapt to a new climate or environment **acclimatization** *n*
accolade Ⓣ *n* **1** award, honour, or praise **2** award of knighthood
accommodate Ⓣ *v* **1** provide with lodgings **2** have room for **3** do a favour for **4** get used to (something)
▸**accommodating** *adj* obliging
▸**accommodation** *n* house or room for living in
accompany Ⓣ *v* **-nying, -nied 1** go along with **2** occur with **3** provide a musical accompaniment for
▸**accompaniment** *n* **1** something that accompanies **2** *music* supporting part that goes with a solo **accompanist** *n*
accomplice Ⓣ *n* person who helps another to commit a crime
accomplish Ⓣ *v* **1** manage to do **2** finish
▸**accomplished** *adj* expert, proficient
▸**accomplishment** *n* **1** personal ability or skill **2** completion
accord Ⓣ *n* **1** agreement, harmony ▷ *v* **2** fit in with

THESAURUS

accessible *adj* **1 = handy**, near, available, nearby, achievable, attainable, reachable, at hand, obtainable **2 = approachable**, available, friendly, informal, cordial, affable **3 = open**, vulnerable, liable, susceptible, wide-open, exposed
accessory *n* **1 = addition**, extra, supplement, decoration, attachment, adjunct, trimming, accompaniment, appendage, adornment **2 = accomplice**, partner, associate, colleague, assistant, helper, abettor, confederate
accident *n* **1 = misfortune**, disaster, mishap, misadventure, calamity **2 = collision**, crash, wreck, hit-and-run **3 = chance**, fate, hazard, luck, fortune, fluke, fortuity
accidental *adj* **= unintentional**, chance, random, casual, inadvertent • *The fire was accidental*. OPPOSITE: deliberate
accidentally *adv* **= unintentionally**, randomly, inadvertently, unwittingly, incidentally, haphazardly, by accident, by chance, fortuitously
acclaim *v* **1 = praise**, approve, celebrate, cheer, hail, applaud, salute, honour, commend, clap, exalt ▸*n* **2 = praise**, approval, celebration, applause, honour, kudos, commendation, acclamation
acclamation *n* **= praise**, approval, tribute, ovation, acclaim, plaudit, adulation
acclimatization *n* **= adaptation**, adjustment, habituation, inurement, naturalization
acclimatize *v* **= adapt**, adjust, accommodate, accustom, naturalize, inure, get used to, habituate
accolade *n* **= praise**, approval, tribute, recognition, ovation, applause, acclaim, compliment, commendation, props (*informal*)
accommodate *v* **1 = house**, shelter, put up • *a hotel built to accommodate many guests* **2 = help**, serve, assist, aid, oblige **3 = adapt**, settle, fit, adjust, comply, modify, reconcile, conform, harmonize
accommodating *adj* **= helpful**, kind, considerate, hospitable, obliging • *his polite, accommodating manner*
accommodation *n* **= housing**, house, digs (*informal*), lodgings, quarters • *Travel and overnight accommodation are included in the price.*
See also: **space**
accompaniment *n* **1 = supplement**, accessory, companion, complement **2 = backing music**, backing
accompany *v* **1 = go with**, conduct (*formal*), escort, usher • *Children must be accompanied by an adult*. **2 = occur with**, come with, go together with • *severe pain accompanied by fever*
See also: **guide**
accompanying *adj* **= additional**, related, attendant, complementary, supplementary, associated, attached
accomplice *n* **= helper**, partner, associate, colleague, assistant, ally, accessory, collaborator, henchman, abettor
accomplish *v* **= do**, complete, manage, achieve, fulfill, bring about • *We could accomplish a lot by working together.*
See also: **carry out**
accomplished *adj* **= skilled**, expert, talented, gifted, polished, proficient, masterly, practiced
accomplishment *n* **1 = completion**, performance, execution, conclusion, finishing, fulfillment, bringing about, carrying out **2 = achievement**, act, stroke, triumph, coup, exploit, feat, deed

DICTIONARY

accordance *n* **in accordance with** in conformity with
according *adv* **according to 1** as stated by **2** in conformity with
▸ **accordingly** *adv* **1** in an appropriate manner **2** consequently
accordion *n* portable musical instrument played by moving the two sides apart and together, and pressing a keyboard or buttons to produce the notes **accordionist** *n*
accost Ⓣ *v* approach and speak to
account Ⓣ *n* **1** report, description **2** business arrangement making credit available **3** record of money received and paid out with the resulting balance **4** person's money held in a bank **5** importance, value ▷ *v* **6** judge to be
▸ **on account of** because of
▸ **accountable** *adj* responsible to someone or for something **accountability** *n*
accounting *n* skill or practice of maintaining and auditing business accounts
▸ **accountant** *n* person who maintains and audits business accounts **accountancy** *n*
accoutrements [ak-**koo**-trem-ments] *pl n* clothing and equipment
accredited Ⓣ *adj* authorized, officially recognized
accretion [ak-**kree**-shun] *n* **1** gradual growth **2** something added
accrue Ⓣ *v* **-cruing, -crued** increase gradually **accrual** *n*
accumulate Ⓣ *v* gather together in increasing quantity **accumulation** *n* **accumulative** *adj*
▸ **accumulator** *n* rechargeable electric battery
accurate Ⓣ *adj* exact, correct **accurately** *adv* **accuracy** *n*
accursed Ⓣ *adj* **1** under a curse **2** detestable
accusative *n* grammatical case indicating the direct object
accuse Ⓣ *v* **1** charge with wrongdoing **2** blame **accused** *n, adj* **accuser** *n* **accusing** *adj* **accusation** *n* **accusatory** *adj*
accustom Ⓣ *v* make used to
▸ **accustomed** *adj* **1** usual **2** used (to)

THESAURUS

accord *n* **1 = agreement**, sympathy, correspondence, harmony, unison, rapport, conformity ▸ *v* **2 = fit**, agree, match, suit, tally, correspond, conform, harmonize
▸ *adv* ▷ **according to = as stated by**, as believed by, as maintained by, in the light of, on the authority of, on the report of; **= in keeping with**, after, after the manner of, consistent with, in accordance with, in line with, in compliance with, in the manner of
accordingly *adv* **1 = appropriately**, properly, suitably, correspondingly, fitly **2 = consequently**, so, therefore, thus, hence, as a result, ergo, in consequence
accost *v* **= approach**, hail, greet, confront, buttonhole
account *n* **1 = description**, report, statement, story, version, tale, explanation, narrative **2** (*Commerce*) **= statement**, charge, score, bill, register, balance, tally, invoice, reckoning, books **3 = importance**, note, value, worth, standing, consequence, significance, honour ▸ *v* **4 = consider**, think, rate, judge, value, estimate, count, regard, reckon ▷ **account for = explain**, justify, clarify, illuminate, rationalize, answer for, clear up, elucidate
accountability *n* **= responsibility**, liability, culpability, answerability, chargeability
accountable *adj* **= responsible**, liable, amenable, answerable, charged with, obligated, obliged
accountant *n* **= auditor**, bean counter (*informal*), book-keeper
accredited *adj* **= authorized**, official, licensed, certified, appointed, empowered, endorsed, guaranteed, recognized
accrue *v* **= increase**, follow, grow, collect, flow, arise, accumulate, amass, enlarge, be added, build up
accumulate *v* **= collect**, increase, store, gather, amass, hoard, accrue, build up, pile up
accumulation *n* **= collection**, increase, stock, store, mass, gathering, pile, stockpile, stack, hoard, heap, build-up
accuracy *n* **= exactness**, precision, authenticity, correctness, closeness, veracity, fidelity, truthfulness, accurateness, carefulness, strictness
accurate *adj* **= exact**, right, true, correct, strict, faithful, precise • *Quartz watches are very accurate.* OPPOSITE: inaccurate
accurately *adv* **= exactly**, strictly, closely, truly, correctly, precisely, faithfully, authentically, scrupulously, to the letter, unerringly
accursed *adj* **1 = cursed**, unfortunate, doomed, ill-fated, damned, unlucky, hopeless, wretched, bewitched, condemned, ill-omened, jinxed **2 = hateful**, horrible, despicable, lousy (*slang*), abominable, detestable, hellish, execrable, scuzzy (*slang*)
accusation *n* **= charge**, allegation, complaint, indictment, denunciation, recrimination, incrimination
accuse *v* **= charge**, blame, cite, denounce, censure • *He accused me of cheating.*
accustom *v* **= adapt**, train, exercise,

DICTIONARY

3 in the habit (of)
ace Ⓣ *n* **1** playing card with one spot on it **2** *informal* expert **3** *tennis* unreturnable serve ▷ *adj* **4** *informal* excellent
acerbic [ass-**sir**-bik] *adj* harsh or bitter **acerbity** *n*
acetate [**ass**-it-tate] *n* **1** *chem* salt or ester of acetic acid **2** Also **acetate rayon** synthetic textile fibre
acetic [ass-**see**-tik] *adj* of or involving vinegar
▸ **acetic acid** colourless liquid used to make vinegar
acetone [**ass**-it-tone] *n* colourless liquid used as a solvent
acetylene [ass-**set**-ill-een] *n* colourless flammable gas used in welding metals
ache Ⓣ *n* **1** dull continuous pain ▷ *v* **2** be in or cause continuous pain
achieve Ⓣ *v* gain by hard work or ability
▸ **achievement** *n* something accomplished
Achilles heel [ak-**kill**-eez] *n* small but fatal weakness
▸ **Achilles tendon** cord connecting the calf to the heel bone
achromatic *adj* **1** colourless **2** *music* with no sharps or flats
acid Ⓣ *n* **1** *chem* one of a class of compounds, corrosive and sour when dissolved in water, that combine with a base to form a salt **2** *slang* LSD ▷ *adj* **3** containing acid **4** sour-tasting **5** sharp or sour in manner **acidic** *adj* **acidify** *v* **acidity** *n*
▸ **acidulous** *adj* **1** sharp **2** caustic
▸ **acid rain** rain containing acid from atmospheric pollution
▸ **acid reflux** regurgitation of stomach acid, causing heartburn
▸ **acid test** conclusive test of value
ack-ack *n mil* anti-aircraft gunfire or arms
acknowledge Ⓣ *v* **1** admit, recognize **2** indicate recognition of (a person) **3** say one has received **acknowledgment** *or* **acknowledgement** *n*
acme [**ak**-mee] *n* highest point of achievement or excellence
acne [**ak**-nee] *n* pimply skin disease
acolyte *n* **1** follower or attendant **2** *Christianity* person who assists a priest
aconite *n* **1** poisonous plant with hoodlike flowers **2** poison obtained from this plant
acorn *n* nut of the oak tree
acoustic *adj* **1** of sound and hearing **2** (of a musical instrument) not electronically amplified **acoustically** *adv*
▸ **acoustics** *n* **1** science of sounds ▷ *pl n* **2** features of a room or building determining how sound is heard within it
acquaint Ⓣ *v* make familiar, inform **acquainted** *adj*
▸ **acquaintance** *n* **1** person known **2** personal knowledge

THESAURUS

discipline, acquaint, acclimatize, familiarize
accustomed *adj* **1 = used**, adapted, familiar • *I've become accustomed to his poor performance*. OPPOSITE: unaccustomed **2 = usual**, common, regular, traditional, normal, conventional, ordinary, everyday, established, customary, habitual, expected
ace *n* **1** (*Cards, dice, etc.*) **= one**, single point **2** (*Informal*) **= expert**, champion, star, master, wizard (*informal*), virtuoso
ache *v* **1 = hurt**, suffer, pain, pound, smart, throb, twinge ▸ *n* **2 = pain**, hurt, suffering, soreness, pang, pounding, throbbing
achieve *v* **= accomplish**, do, complete, perform, nail (*sports*), fulfill, carry out • *She has achieved her best tournament result yet*.
See also: **gain, win**
achievement *n* **= accomplishment**, exploit, feat, deed • *His presence here is an achievement in itself*.
See also: **act, action, qualification**
aching *See* **painful, tender**
acid *adj* **1 = sour**, tart, acerbic, pungent, acrid, vinegary **2 = sharp**, bitter, harsh, cutting, vitriolic, caustic, biting, trenchant
acidity *n* **1 = sourness**, acerbity, pungency, tartness **2 = sharpness**, bitterness, harshness, hurtfulness
acknowledge *v* **1 = accept**, allow, own, admit, declare, recognize, grant, concede, yield, confess, profess **2 = greet**, address, recognize, notice, hail, salute **3 = reply to**, return, answer, recognize, notice, react to, respond to
acknowledged *adj* **= accepted**, approved, accredited, confessed, declared, professed, recognized, returned
acknowledgment *n* **1 = acceptance**, declaration, confession, admission, profession, realization, allowing, yielding **2 = greeting**, notice, hail, recognition, salute, salutation, addressing, hailing **3 = appreciation**, return, credit, response, answer, reaction, reply, recognition, gratitude, kudos, thanks, props (*informal*)
acquaint *v* **= tell**, reveal, disclose, inform, notify, divulge, enlighten, familiarize, let (someone) know
acquaintance *n* **1 = associate**, contact, colleague **2 = knowledge**, experience, relationship, understanding, awareness, familiarity, fellowship
acquainted with *adj* **= familiar with**, alive to, apprised of, *au fait* with (*French*), aware of,

DICTIONARY

acquiesce ⓣ [ak-wee-**ess**] *v* accept without complaining **acquiescence** *n* **acquiescent** *adj*
acquire ⓣ *v* gain, get **acquirement** *n*
▸**acquisition** *n* **1** act of getting **2** thing acquired
▸**acquisitive** *adj* eager to gain material possessions **acquisitiveness** *n*
acquit ⓣ *v* **-quitting, -quitted 1** declare innocent **2** conduct (oneself) in a particular way **acquittal** *n*
acre *n* measure of land, 4840 square yards
▸**acreage** [**ake**-er-rij] *n* land area in acres
acrid ⓣ [**ak**-rid] *adj* pungent, bitter **acridity** *n*
acrimony ⓣ [**ak**-rim-mon-ee] *n* bitterness of speech or manner **acrimonious** *adj*
acrobat *n* person skilled in gymnastic feats requiring agility and balance **acrobatic** *adj*
▸**acrobatics** *pl n* acrobatic feats
acronym *n* word formed from the initial letters of other words, such as NATO
acropolis [a-**crop**-pol-liss] *n* citadel of an ancient Greek city
across *adv, prep* **1** from side to side (of) **2** on or to the other side (of)
▸**across the board** applying equally to all
acrostic *n* word puzzle in which the first or last letters of each line spell a word or saying
acrylic *n, adj* (synthetic fibre, paint, etc.) made from acrylic acid
▸**acrylic acid** strong-smelling corrosive liquid
act ⓣ *n* **1** thing done **2** law or decree **3** section of a play or opera **4** one of several short performances in a show **5** pretended attitude ▹ *v* **6** do something **7** behave in a particular way **8** perform in a play, film, etc.
▸**act of God** unpredictable natural event
▸**acting** *n* **1** art of an actor ▹ *adj* **2** temporarily performing the duties of
▸**actor** (**actress**) *n* person who acts in a play, film, etc.
actinium *n* radioactive chemical element
action ⓣ *n* **1** process of doing **2** thing done **3** operating mechanism **4** lawsuit **5** minor battle
▸**actionable** *adj* giving grounds for a lawsuit
▸**action replay** rerun of an event on a television tape

THESAURUS

conscious of, experienced in, informed of, knowledgeable about, versed in
acquiesce *v* = **agree**, allow, approve, accept, submit, comply, yield, consent, conform, concur, assent, accede, give in, go along with
acquiescence *n* = **agreement**, approval, consent, submission, compliance, acceptance, assent, obedience, conformity, giving in, yielding
acquire *v* = **get**, gain, secure, obtain, attain, procure, pick up • *I have recently acquired a digital camera.*
See also: **buy, earn, possess**
acquisition *n* **1** = **possession**, buy, gain, purchase, property, prize **2** = **acquiring**, procurement, attainment, gaining
acquisitive *adj* = **greedy**, avid, predatory, avaricious, covetous, grabbing, grasping, rapacious
acquit *v* **1** = **clear**, release, free, discharge, liberate, vindicate **2** = **behave**, bear, perform, conduct, comport
acquittal *n* = **clearance**, release, relief, discharge, liberation, vindication, exoneration, absolution, deliverance
acrid *adj* = **pungent**, sharp, bitter, harsh, vitriolic, caustic
acrimonious *adj* = **bitter**, testy, caustic, irascible, rancorous, petulant, spiteful, splenetic
acrimony *n* = **bitterness**, virulence, harshness, ill will, irascibility, rancour
act *v* **1** = **do**, work, operate, perform, function • *The bank acted properly in the best interests of the depositors.* **2** = **perform**, play, portray, act out, play the part of, characterize, personify • *He acted at the Stratford Festival in Ontario.*
▹ **act against** *See* **counteract** ▹ **act for** = **stand in for**, represent, replace, cover for, deputize for, fill in for, substitute for, take the place of ▹ **act on** *See* **affect** ▹ **act out** *See* **act** ▹ **act toward** *See* **treat**
▹ **act up** (*Informal*) = **make a fuss**, misbehave, have a fit, horse around, raise Cain, raise hell ▸ *n* **3** = **deed**, achievement, accomplishment, feat, undertaking • *an act of disloyalty to the king* **4** = **law**, bill, measure, resolution, decree, statute, ordinance, edict, enactment **5** = **performance**, show, turn, routine, sketch **6** = **pretense**, show, front, performance, pose, attitude, posture, affectation
See also: **appear, behave, conduct yourself**
acting *n* **1** = **performance**, portrayal, theatre, characterization, impersonation, performing, playing, stagecraft ▸ *adj* **2** = **temporary**, interim, substitute, provisional, surrogate, pro tem
action *n* **1** = **activity**, operation, process • *He had to take evasive action to avoid being hit.* **2** = **deed**, achievement, exploit, accomplishment, feat • *He did not like his actions questioned.* **3** = **lawsuit**, case, suit, prosecution, proceeding, litigation **4** = **energy**, force, activity, spirit, vitality, vigour, liveliness, vim **5** = **battle**, fight, contest, conflict, clash, combat, encounter, engagement, skirmish, sortie

a

DICTIONARY

active ⓣ *adj* **1** busy, energetic **2** moving, working **3** *grammar* (of a verb) in a form indicating that the subject is performing the action, eg *threw* in *Kim threw the ball* **actively** *adv*
▸**activity** *n* **1** active behaviour **2** leisure pursuit
▸**activate** *v* make active **activation** *n* **activator** *n*
▸**activist** *n* person who works energetically to achieve political or social goals **activism** *n*
actual ⓣ *adj* existing in reality **actuality** *n*
▸**actually** *adv* really, indeed
actuary *n, pl* **-aries** statistician who calculates insurance risks **actuarial** *adj*
actuate *v* activate (a device) **actuation** *n*
acuity [ak-**kew**-it-ee] *n* keenness of vision or thought
acumen ⓣ [**ak**-yew-men] *n* ability to make good judgments
acupuncture *n* medical treatment involving the insertion of needles at various points on the body **acupuncturist** *n*
acute ⓣ *adj* **1** severe or intense **2** keen, shrewd **3** sharp, sensitive **4** (of an angle) less than 90° ▹ *n* **5** accent (´) over a letter to indicate the quality or length of its sound, as in *café* **acutely** *adv* **acuteness** *n*
ad ⓣ *n informal* advertisement
AD anno Domini
adage ⓣ [**ad**-ij] *n* wise saying, proverb
adagio [ad-**dahj**-yo] *adv music* slowly and gracefully
Adam *n* **1 Adolphe**. 1803–56, French composer, best known for his romantic ballet *Giselle* (1841) **2 Robert**. 1728–92, Scottish architect and furniture designer. Assisted by his brother, **James**, 1730–94, he emulated the harmony of classical and Italian Renaissance architecture ▹ *adj* **3** in the neoclassical style made popular by Robert Adam
adamant ⓣ *adj* inflexibly determined **adamantly** *adv*
Adams *n* **1 Bryan**. born 1959, Canadian rock musician. His recordings include "Run to You" (1984) and "(Everything I Do) I Do It For You" (1990) **2 Gerry**, full name *Gerrard Adams*. born 1948, Northern Ireland politician; president of Sinn Féin from 1983: negotiated the Irish Republican Army ceasefires in 1994–96 and 1997 **3 Henry (Brooks)**. 1838–1918, US historian and writer. His works include *Mont Saint Michel et Chartres* (1913) and his autobiography *The Education of Henry Adams* (1918) **4 John**. 1735–1826, second president of the US (1797–1801); US ambassador to Great Britain (1785–88); helped draft the Declaration of Independence (1776) **5 John Coolidge**. born 1947, US composer; works include the operas *Nixon in China* (1987) and *The Death of Klinghoffer* (1991) **6 John Quincey**. son of John Adams. 1767–1848, sixth president of the US (1825–29); secretary of state (1817–25) **7 Samuel**. 1722–1803, US revolutionary leader; one of the organizers of the Boston Tea Party; a signatory of the Declaration of Independence

THESAURUS

activate *v* = **start**, move, stir, initiate, energize, mobilize, arouse, galvanize, rouse, set in motion
active *adj* **1 = energetic**, lively, restless, vivacious, sprightly • *Having an active child around the house can be exhausting.* **2 = busy**, enthusiastic, involved, hard-working, occupied, industrious, engaged • *people who are active in local politics* **3 = in operation**, working, operative, acting, at work, effectual, in action, in force
See also: **alive, healthy, vital**
activist *n* = **militant**, organizer, partisan
activity *n* **1 = action**, energy, bustle, liveliness • *There is an extraordinary level of activity in the office.* **2 = hobby**, interest, pursuit, pastime • *sports and other leisure activities*
See also: **excitement, exercise**
actor *n* = **performer**, actress, player, Thespian
actress *n* = **performer**, player, actor, starlet, leading lady, Thespian
actual *adj* = **real**, true, realistic, genuine, authentic, verified • *That is the estimated figure. The actual figure is much higher.*
See also: **precise**
actually *adv* = **really**, truly, indeed, literally, as a matter of fact, in fact, in point of fact, in reality, in truth
acumen *n* = **judgment**, intelligence, insight, ingenuity, astuteness, cleverness, perspicacity, shrewdness
acute *adj* **1 = serious**, great, critical, severe, intense, extreme, grave • *an acute shortage of supplies* **2 = perceptive**, quick, alert, sharp, bright, keen, shrewd, astute • *an acute mind* **3 = sharp**, powerful, violent, severe, intense, shooting, fierce, piercing, excruciating
See also: **brilliant, intelligent, uncommon**
acuteness *n* **1 = seriousness**, importance, severity, gravity, urgency **2 = perceptiveness**, discrimination, insight, sharpness, astuteness, cleverness, perspicacity
ad *See* **advertisement**
adage *See* **saying**
adamant *adj* = **determined**, firm, stubborn, resolute, uncompromising,

DICTIONARY

Adam's apple *n* projecting lump of thyroid cartilage at the front of the throat
adapt ⓣ *v* alter for new use or new conditions **adaptable** *adj* **adaptability** *n*
▸**adaptation** *n* **1** adapting **2** thing produced by adapting something
▸**adaptor** *or* **adapter** *n* device for connecting several electrical appliances to a single socket
add ⓣ *v* **1** combine (numbers or quantities) **2** join (to something) **3** say further
addendum ⓣ *n, pl* **-da 1** an addition **2** appendix to a book etc.
adder *n* **1** any of various harmless American snakes **2** *Brit* small poisonous snake
addict ⓣ *n* **1** person who is unable to stop taking drugs **2** *informal* person devoted to something **addicted** *adj* **addiction** *n*
▸**addictive** *adj* causing addiction
Addington *n* **Henry**, 1st Viscount Sidmouth. 1757–1844, British statesman; prime minister (1801–04) and Home Secretary (1812–21)
Addison *n* **Joseph**. 1672–1719, English essayist and poet who, with Richard Steele, founded *The Spectator* (1711–14) and contributed most of its essays, including the *de Coverley Papers*
addition ⓣ *n* **1** adding **2** thing added **additional** *adj* **additionally** *adv*
▸**in addition** besides, as well
▸**additive** *n* something added, esp. to foodstuffs
addle *v* make rotten or muddled
address ⓣ *n* **1** place where a person lives **2** direction on a letter **3** location **4** formal public speech ▷ *v* **5** mark the destination, as on an envelope **6** speak to **7** give attention to (a problem, task, etc.)
▸**addressee** *n* person addressed
adduce *v* cite as proof
adenoids [**ad**-in-oidz] *pl n* mass of tissue at the back of the nose
▸**adenoidal** *adj* having a nasal voice caused by swollen adenoids
adept ⓣ *adj, n* very skilful (person)
adequate ⓣ *adj* **1** sufficient, enough **2** not outstanding **adequately** *adv* **adequacy** *n*

THESAURUS

fixed, obdurate, unbending
adapt *v* = **adjust**, change, convert, modify, alter • *The TV series was adapted from a movie.* *See also*: **fit**
adaptability *n* = **flexibility**, resilience, versatility, changeability
adaptable *adj* = **flexible**, plastic, versatile, resilient, easy-going, compliant, adjustable, changeable, pliant
adaptation *n* **1** = **acclimatization**, familiarization, naturalization **2** = **conversion**, change, version, variation, adjustment, transformation, modification, alteration
adapted *See* **accustomed**
add *v* **1** = **include**, supplement, attach, augment, affix, append, adjoin • *Add the grated cheese to the sauce.* **2** = **count up**, total, add up • *Banks add all the interest and other charges together.* OPPOSITE: subtract ▷ **add to** = **increase**, raise, boost, advance, extend, spread, expand, supplement, strengthen, escalate, intensify, enhance, heighten, inflate, multiply, magnify, augment, amplify, enlarge, proliferate, step up (*informal*) ▷ **add up** = **count up**, add, total, count, compute, reckon, tot up ▷ **add up to** *See* **total**
added *See* **extra, more**
addendum *n* = **addition**, extra, extension, supplement, attachment, appendage, appendix, postscript
addict *n* **1** = **junkie** (*informal*), freak (*informal*), fiend (*informal*) **2** = **fan**, enthusiast, follower, nut (*slang*), buff (*informal*), devotee, adherent
addicted *adj* = **hooked** (*slang*), dependent, dedicated, devoted, absorbed, accustomed, habituated
addiction *n* = **dependence**, habit, obsession, craving, enslavement
addition *n* **1** = **increase**, supplement, addendum, adjunct, appendage • *recent additions to their CD collection* **2** = **inclusion**, extension, attachment, enlargement, augmentation, amplification, adding, increasing **3** = **counting up**, computation, adding up, totalling, totting up ▷ **in addition, in addition to** = **as well** *or* **as well as**, also, too, besides, moreover, additionally, into the bargain, over and above, to boot *See also*: **extra**
additional *adj* = **extra**, new, other, further, fresh, spare, added, supplementary
address *n* **1** = **location**, home, house, situation, residence, whereabouts, dwelling, abode **2** = **speech**, talk, lecture, sermon, discourse, dissertation, oration ▸ *v* **3** = **speak to**, approach, hail, greet, talk to ▷ **address (oneself) to** = **concentrate on**, apply (oneself) to, attend to, devote (oneself) to, engage in, focus on, take care of
adept *adj* **1** = **skilful**, expert, able, skilled, accomplished, proficient, adroit, practiced, versed ▸ *n* **2** = **expert**, master, genius, hotshot (*informal*)
adequacy *n* = **sufficiency**, capability, fairness, competence, suitability, tolerability
adequate *adj* = **enough**, acceptable, sufficient, ample, satisfactory • *an adequate*

DICTIONARY

adhere ⓣ *v* **1** stick to **2** be devoted to
adherence *n*
▶**adherent** *n* devotee, follower
▶**adhesion** *n* **1** adhering **2** abnormal sticking together of parts of the body, as after surgery
adhesive ⓣ *adj* **1** able to stick to things ▷ *n* **2** substance used to stick things together
ad hoc *adj, adv* for a particular occasion only
adieu ⓣ [a-**dew**] *interj* farewell, goodbye
ad infinitum *adv Latin* endlessly
adipose *adj* of fat, fatty
adj. adjective
adjacent ⓣ *adj* **1** near or next to **2** having a common boundary **3** *geom* (of a side in a right-angled triangle) lying between a specified angle and the right angle
adjective *n* word that adds information about a noun or pronoun **adjectival** *adj*
adjoin ⓣ *v* be next to **adjoining** *adj*
adjourn ⓣ *v* **1** close (a court) at the end of a session **2** postpone temporarily **3** *informal* go elsewhere **adjournment** *n*
adjudge *v* declare (to be)
adjudicate ⓣ *v* **1** decide on (a dispute) **2** judge (a competition) **adjudication** *n*
adjudicator *n*
adjunct *n* subordinate or additional person or thing
adjure *v* **1** command to do **2** appeal earnestly
adjust ⓣ *v* **1** adapt to new conditions **2** alter slightly so as to be suitable **adjustable** *adj*
adjuster *n* **adjustment** *n*
adjutant [**aj**-oo-tant] *n* army officer in charge of routine administration
Adler *n* **Alfred**. 1870–1937, Austrian psychiatrist, noted for his descriptions of overcompensation and inferiority feelings
ad-lib ⓣ *v* **-libbing, -libbed 1** improvise a speech etc. without preparation ▷ *n* **2** improvised remark
admin *n informal* administration
administer ⓣ *v* **1** manage (business affairs) **2** dispense (justice) **3** give (medicine or treatment)
administrate *v* manage (an organization)
administration *n* **administrative** *adj*
administrator *n*
admiral *n* highest naval rank
admire ⓣ *v* regard with esteem and approval **admirable** *adj* **admirably** *adv*
admiration *n* **admirer** *n* **admiring** *adj*
admiringly *adv*

THESAURUS

diet OPPOSITE: insufficient
See also: **all right, decent, tolerable**
adequately *See* **well**
adhere *v* = **stick**, fix, attach, paste, cling, glue, fasten, cleave, hold fast ▷ **adhere to** *See* **obey**
adherent *n* = **supporter**, fan, follower, admirer, devotee, disciple, upholder
adhesive *adj* **1** = **sticky**, tenacious, cohesive, gluey, clinging, glutinous ▶ *n* **2** = **glue**, gum, paste, cement
adieu *n* = **good-bye**, farewell, parting, leave-taking, valediction
adjacent *adj* = **next**, close, near, beside, touching, adjoining, bordering, cheek by jowl, neighbouring, next door ▷ **adjacent to** *See* **beside, near**
adjoin *v* = **connect**, link, border, join, touch
adjoining *adj* = **connecting**, adjacent, touching, abutting, bordering, neighbouring, next door
adjourn *v* = **postpone**, delay, suspend, interrupt, defer, discontinue, put off
adjournment *n* = **postponement**, delay, suspension, recess, interruption, discontinuation, putting off
adjudicate *v* = **judge**, decide, determine, settle, referee, mediate, umpire, arbitrate, adjudge
adjudication *n* = **judgment**, decision, ruling, settlement, finding, verdict, conclusion, arbitration, pronouncement
adjust *v* = **alter**, modify, adapt, accustom, make conform
adjustable *adj* = **alterable**, flexible, adaptable, movable, malleable, modifiable
adjustment *n* **1** = **alteration**, regulation, adaptation, modification, redress, tuning **2** = **acclimatization**, orientation, settling in
ad-lib *v* = **improvise**, busk, extemporize, make up, speak off the cuff, wing it (*informal*)
administer *v* **1** = **manage**, run, control, direct, command, supervise, be in charge of • *people who administer large companies* **2** = **carry out**, deal, perform, impose, execute, inflict, dispense • *He administered most of the punishment.*
See also: **handle, rule**
administration *n* = **management**, government, control, conduct, application, direction, supervision, running
administrative *adj* = **managerial**, executive, regulatory, directorial, governmental, organizational, supervisory
administrator *n* = **manager**, official, executive, organizer, bureaucrat, supervisor
admirable *adj* = **excellent**, fine, wonderful, worthy, exquisite, commendable, laudable, praiseworthy
admirably *See* **well**
admiration *n* = **regard**, respect, approval, appreciation, esteem • *I have always had the greatest admiration for him.*
See also: **worship**
admire *v* **1** = **respect**, value, appreciate,

DICTIONARY

admissible Ⓣ *adj* allowed to be brought in as evidence in court **admissibility** *n*
admission Ⓣ *n* **1** permission to enter **2** entrance fee **3** confession
admit Ⓣ *v* **-mitting, -mitted 1** confess, acknowledge **2** concede the truth of **3** allow in
▸**admittance** *n* permission to enter
▸**admittedly** *adv* it must be agreed (that)
admixture *n* **1** mixture **2** ingredient
admonish Ⓣ *v* reprove sternly **admonition** *n* **admonitory** *adj*
ad nauseam [ad **naw**-zee-am] *adv Latin* to a boring or sickening extent
ado *n* fuss, trouble
adobe [ad-**oh**-bee] *n* sun-dried brick
adolescence Ⓣ *n* period between puberty and adulthood
▸**adolescent** *n, adj* (person) between puberty and adulthood
adopt Ⓣ *v* **1** take (someone else's child) as one's own **2** take up (a plan or principle) **adoption** *n*
▸**adoptive** *adj* related by adoption
adore Ⓣ *v* **1** love intensely **2** worship **adorable** *adj* **adoration** *n* **adoring** *adj* **adoringly** *adv*
adorn Ⓣ *v* decorate, embellish **adornment** *n*
Adorno *n* **Theodor Wiesengrund.** 1903–69, German philosopher, sociologist, and music critic. His writings include *The Philosophy of the New Music* (1949) and *Negative Dialectics* (1966)
ADP automatic data processing
adrenal [ad-**reen**-al] *adj* near the kidney
▸**adrenal glands** glands covering the top of the kidneys
adrenalin, adrenaline *n* hormone secreted by the adrenal glands in response to stress
adrift Ⓣ *adj, adv* **1** drifting **2** without clear purpose
adroit Ⓣ *adj* quick and skilful **adroitly** *adv* **adroitness** *n*
adsorb *v* (of a gas or vapour) condense and form a thin film on a surface **adsorbent** *adj* **adsorption** *n*
ADT Atlantic Daylight Time
adulation Ⓣ *n* uncritical admiration
adult Ⓣ *adj* **1** fully grown, mature ▹*n* **2** adult person or animal **adulthood** *n*

THESAURUS

look up to • *All those who knew him admired his work.* OPPOSITE: scorn **2 = marvel at**, appreciate, delight in, take pleasure in, wonder at
See also: **approve, praise**
admirer *n* **1 = suitor**, lover, boyfriend, sweetheart, beau, wooer **2 = fan**, supporter, enthusiast, follower, partisan, devotee, disciple
admissible *adj* **= permissible**, acceptable, allowable, tolerable, passable
admission *n* **1 = entrance**, access, entry, introduction, acceptance, initiation, admittance, entrée **2 = confession**, disclosure, declaration, revelation, allowance, acknowledgment, divulgence
admit *v* **1 = accept**, grant, acknowledge • *I admit that your actions were justified.* OPPOSITE: deny **2 = let in**, receive, accept, take in • *He was admitted to university.* OPPOSITE: exclude **3 = confess**, own, reveal, declare, acknowledge, disclose, divulge, fess up (*informal*)
admonish *v* **= reprimand**, rebuke, scold, berate, chide, slap on the wrist, tell off (*informal*)
adolescence *n* **1 = youth**, minority, boyhood, girlhood, teens **2 = youthfulness**, immaturity, childishness
adolescent *adj* **1 = young**, teenage, youthful, juvenile, immature, boyish, girlish, puerile ▸*n* **2 = youth**, teenager, minor, youngster, juvenile
adopt *v* **1 = foster**, take in **2 = choose**, follow, accept, maintain, assume, espouse, take up
adoption *n* **1 = fostering**, adopting, taking in **2 = choice**, selection, endorsement, assumption, appropriation, embracing, espousal, taking up
adorable *adj* **= lovable**, attractive, cute, dear, charming, appealing, pleasing, delightful, fetching
adoration *See* **love, worship**
adore *v* **= love**, admire, honour, revere, worship, glorify, cherish, esteem, idolize, exalt, dote on, put on a pedestal (*informal*)
adored *See* **beloved**
adoring *adj* **= loving**, fond, devoted, affectionate, admiring, doting
adorn *v* **= decorate**, array, embellish, festoon
adornment *n* **= decoration**, supplement, accessory, ornament, trimming, embellishment, festoon, frill, frippery
adrift *adj* **1 = drifting**, afloat, unanchored, unmoored **2 = aimless**, goalless, directionless, purposeless ▸*adv* **3 = wrong**, astray, amiss, off course
adroit *adj* **= skilful**, expert, skilled, clever, neat, adept, masterful, deft, proficient, dexterous
adulation *n* **= worship**, fawning, fulsome praise, servile flattery, sycophancy
adult *n* **1 = grown-up**, man, woman • *I'd like tickets for three children and two*

DICTIONARY

adulterate *v* make impure by addition **adulteration** *n*
adultery *n, pl* **-teries** sexual unfaithfulness of a husband or wife **adulterer** (**adulteress**) *n* **adulterous** *adj*
adumbrate *v* give a faint indication of **adumbration** *n*
adv. adverb
advance Ⓣ *v* **1** go or bring forward **2** further (a cause) **3** propose **4** lend (a sum of money) ▷ *n* **5** forward movement **6** improvement **7** loan **advances 8** approaches to a person with the hope of starting a romantic or sexual relationship ▷ *adj* **9** previous
▸ **in advance** ahead
▸ **advanced** *adj* **1** at a late stage in development **2** not elementary ▷ *n* **3** green flashing traffic signal that allows left turn
▸ **advancement** *n* promotion
advantage Ⓣ *n* **1** more favourable position or state **2** benefit or profit **3** *tennis* point scored after deuce **advantageous** *adj* **advantageously** *adv*
▸ **take advantage of 1** use (an opportunity) **2** use (a person) unfairly
advent Ⓣ *n* **1** arrival **2 Advent** season of four weeks before Christmas
▸ **Adventist** *n* member of a Christian sect that believes in the imminent return of Christ
adventitious *adj* added or appearing accidentally
adventure Ⓣ *n* exciting and risky undertaking or exploit **adventurous** *adj*
▸ **adventurer** (**adventuress**) *n* **1** person who seeks adventures **2** person who unscrupulously seeks money or power
adverb *n* word that adds information about a verb, adjective, or other adverb **adverbial** *adj* **adverbially** *adv*
adversary Ⓣ [**ad**-verse-sair-ree] *n, pl* **-saries** opponent or enemy
adverse Ⓣ *adj* **1** antagonistic or hostile **2** unfavourable **adversely** *adv*
▸ **adversity** *n* affliction or hardship
advertise Ⓣ *v* **1** present or praise (goods or services) to the public in order to encourage sales **2** make (a vacancy, event, etc.) known publicly **advertiser** *n* **advertising** *adj, n*
▸ **advertisement** *n* public announcement to sell goods or publicize an event

THESAURUS

adults. OPPOSITE: child ▸ *adj* **2 = fully grown**, mature, ripe, grown-up, full grown, fully developed, of age
adulterous *See* **unfaithful**
advance *v* **1 = progress**, proceed, make inroads, press on • *Rebel forces are advancing on the capital.* **2 = benefit**, improve, further, prosper **3 = suggest**, offer, present, submit, proffer, put forward **4 = lend**, pay beforehand, supply on credit ▸ *n* **5 = progress**, step, gain, development, breakthrough • *a scientific advance* **6 = forward movement**, development, progress, advancement, headway, inroads, onward movement **7 = loan**, credit, deposit, retainer, prepayment, down payment ▷ **advances = overtures**, approach, proposition, approaches, moves, proposals ▸ *adj* **8 = prior**, early, forward, beforehand, in front ▷ **advance warning** *See* **notice**
▷ **in advance = beforehand**, ahead, previously, earlier
See also: **develop, go, improvement, payment, produce, raise**
advanced *adj* **= foremost**, forward, ahead, higher, progressive, cutting-edge, avant-garde, precocious, leading
advancement *n* **= promotion**, rise, gain, progress, improvement, betterment, preferment
advantage *n* **= benefit**, dominance, superiority, ascendancy • *We have a competitive advantage.* OPPOSITE: disadvantage
See also: **beauty, merit, value, virtue**
advantageous *adj* **1 = beneficial**, valuable, useful, profitable, helpful, convenient, worthwhile, expedient, of service **2 = superior**, dominant, win-win (*informal*), favourable, dominating
advent *See* **appearance**
adventure *n* **= escapade**, experience, incident, venture, exploit, enterprise, occurrence, undertaking
adventurer *n* **1 = mercenary**, gambler, rogue, speculator, opportunist, charlatan, fortune-hunter **2 = hero**, daredevil, heroine, traveller, knight-errant, voyager
adventurous *adj* **= daring**, bold, reckless, daredevil, intrepid, enterprising
adversary *n* **= opponent**, rival, competitor, enemy, contestant, foe, antagonist
adverse *adj* **= unfavourable**, negative, contrary, hostile, detrimental, inopportune, opposing
adversity *n* **= hardship**, trouble, disaster, reverse, distress, misfortune, affliction, bad luck, hard times
advertise *v* **= publicize**, push, promote, plug (*informal*) • *They advertise their products on television.*
See also: **announce**
advertisement *n* **= notice**, ad (*informal*), commercial, plug (*informal*) • *She recently placed an advertisement in the local newspaper.*

DICTIONARY

advice Ⓣ *n* recommendation as to what to do
▸**advise** *v* **1** offer advice to **2** notify (someone)
adviser *or* **advisor** *n*
▸**advisable** *adj* prudent, sensible
advisability *n*
▸**advisory** *adj* giving advice
▸**advised** *adj* considered, thought-out: *ill-advised*
▸**advisedly** *adv* deliberately
advocaat *n* liqueur with a raw egg base
advocate Ⓣ *v* **1** propose or recommend ▹ *n* **2** person who publicly supports a cause **3** *Scot* barrister **advocacy** *n*
adze *n* tool with an arched blade set at right angles to the handle
aegis [**ee**-jiss] *n* sponsorship, protection
aeolian harp [ee-**oh**-lee-an] *n* musical instrument that produces sounds when the wind passes over its strings
aeon *n* same as **eon**
aerate *v* put gas into (a liquid), as when making a fizzy drink **aeration** *n*
aerial *adj* **1** in, from, or operating in the air **2** relating to aircraft ▹ *n* **3** metal pole or wire for receiving or transmitting radio or TV signals
aerie *n* same as **eyrie**
aerobatics *pl n* stunt flying **aerobatic** *adj*
aerobics *pl n* exercises designed to increase the amount of oxygen in the blood **aerobic** *adj*
aerodrome *n* small airport
aerodynamics *pl n* (study of) air flow, esp. around moving solid objects **aerodynamic** *adj*
aerofoil *n* part of an aircraft, such as the wing, designed to give lift
aerogram *n* airmail letter on a single sheet of paper that seals to form an envelope
aeronautics *n* study or practice of aircraft flight **aeronautical** *adj*
aeroplane *n Brit* airplane
aerosol *n* pressurized can from which a substance can be dispensed as a fine spray
aerospace *n* earth's atmosphere and space beyond
Aesop *n* ?620–564 BC, Greek author of fables in which animals are given human characters and used to satirize human failings **Aesopian** *or* **Aesopic** *adj*
aesthetic, esthetic [iss-**thet**-ik] *adj* relating to the appreciation of art and beauty **aesthetically** *or* **esthetically** *adv*
aestheticism *or* **estheticism** *n*
▸**aesthetics** *or* **esthetics** *n* study of art, beauty, and good taste
▸**aesthete** *or* **esthete** [**ess**-theet] *n* person who has or affects an extravagant love of art
aether *n* same as **ether**
aetiology *n* same as **etiology**
afar Ⓣ *adv* from or at a great distance
affable Ⓣ *adj* friendly and easy to talk to
affably *adv* **affability** *n*
affair Ⓣ *n* **1** event or happening **2** sexual relationship outside marriage **3** thing to be done or attended to **affairs** **4** personal or business interests **5** matters of public interest
affect[1] Ⓣ *v* **1** act on, influence **2** move (someone) emotionally
▸**affecting** *adj* moving the feelings
▸**affection** *n* fondness or love

THESAURUS

See also: **announcement**
advertising *See* **publicity**
advice *n* = **guidance**, opinion, counsel (*formal*), suggestion • *Take my advice and stay away from him!*
See also: **help, hint**
advisability *n* = **wisdom**, fitness, prudence, suitability, expediency, appropriateness, desirability, aptness, propriety
advisable *adj* = **wise**, appropriate, recommended, fitting, prudent, desirable, sensible, politic, expedient, seemly
advise *v* **1** = **recommend**, caution, suggest, urge, counsel • *They advised him to leave as soon as possible.* **2** = **inform**, notify, make known • *I think it best that I advise you of my decision to quit.*
See also: **brief**
adviser *n* = **consultant**, aide, guru, mentor, counsellor, tutor, consigliere • *The premier and her advisers spent the day in meetings.*
advisory *adj* = **advising**, consultative, counselling, helping, recommending
advocate *v* **1** = **support**, back, endorse, champion, promote, recommend, favour, uphold • *She advocates better conditions for prisoners.* ▸ *n* **2** = **supporter**, spokesman, champion, defender, promoter, proponent, campaigner, counsellor, upholder **3** (*Law*) = **lawyer**, attorney, counsel, barrister
See also: **suggest**
afar *See* **far**
affable *adj* = **friendly**, pleasant, cordial, amicable, courteous, sociable, amiable, genial, approachable, congenial, urbane
affair *n* **1** = **event**, issue, business, question, matter, situation, subject • *The funeral was a sad affair.* **2** = **relationship**, romance, fling, liaison • *He had an affair with someone he met on vacation.*
See also: **concern, experience, occasion, undertaking**
affect[1] *v* **1** = **influence**, change, alter, act on, impinge on • *More than 7 million people have been affected by the drought.* **2** = **move**, touch, upset, overcome, stir, disturb, perturb

DICTIONARY

▸**affectionate** *adj* loving **affectionately** *adv*
affect[2] ⓣ *v* **1** put on a show of **2** wear or use by preference
▸**affectation** *n* show, pretence
▸**affected** *adj* **1** full of affectation **2** pretended
affianced [af-**fie**-anst] *adj old-fashioned* engaged to be married
affidavit [af-fid-**dave**-it] *n* written statement made on oath
affiliate ⓣ *v* (of a group) link up with a larger group **affiliation** *n*
affinity ⓣ *n, pl* **-ties 1** close connection or liking **2** close resemblance **3** chemical attraction
affirm ⓣ *v* **1** assert, declare **2** uphold or confirm (an idea or belief) **affirmation** *n*
▸**affirmative** *n, adj* (word or phrase) indicating agreement
▸**affirmative action** provision of special opportunities in employment for a disadvantaged group
affix ⓣ *v* **1** attach or fasten ▹ *n* **2** word or syllable added to a word to change its meaning
afflict ⓣ *v* give pain or grief to **affliction** *n*
affluent ⓣ *adj* wealthy
▸**affluence** *n* wealth
afford ⓣ *v* **1** have enough money to buy **2** be able to spare (the time etc.) **3** give or supply **affordable** *adj*
afforest *v* plant trees on **afforestation** *n*
affray *n* noisy fight, brawl
affront ⓣ *v, n* insult
Afghan *adj* of Afghanistan or its language
▸**afghan hound** large slim dog with long silky hair
aficionado [af-fish-yo-**nah**-do] *n, pl* **-dos** enthusiastic fan of something or someone
afield *adv, adj* **far afield** far away
aflame ⓣ *adv, adj* burning
afloat *adv, adj* **1** floating **2** at sea
afoot ⓣ *adv, adj* happening, in operation
aforesaid *adj* referred to previously
aforethought *adj* premeditated: *with malice aforethought*
Afr. Africa(n)
afraid ⓣ *adj* **1** frightened **2** regretful

THESAURUS

See also: **concern, infect**
affect[2] *v* = **put on**, adopt, assume, pretend, simulate, imitate, feign, aspire to, contrive
affectation *n* = **pretense**, show, act, pose, artificiality, assumed manners, façade, insincerity, pretentiousness
affected *adj* = **pretended**, artificial, phony (*informal*), contrived, unnatural, feigned, insincere, mannered, put-on
affecting *adj* = **moving**, sad, pathetic, poignant, touching, pitiful
affection *n* = **fondness**, love, attachment, warmth, liking • *She thought of him with affection*. OPPOSITE: dislike
See also: **friendship**
affectionate *adj* = **fond**, tender, loving, caring • *She gave me a long and affectionate hug*. OPPOSITE: cold
See also: **friendly, warm**
affiliate *v* = **join**, link, associate, combine, ally, unite, incorporate, amalgamate, band together
affiliation *n* = **association**, link, tie, union, league, connection, relationship, coalition, combination, alliance, amalgamation, confederation, incorporation, banding together, joining, merging
affinity *n* **1** = **attraction**, sympathy, fondness, inclination, leaning, liking, rapport, partiality **2** = **similarity**, connection, relationship, correspondence, likeness, resemblance, closeness, analogy, kinship
affirm *v* = **declare**, state, confirm, maintain, testify, swear, pronounce, assert, certify
affirmation *n* = **declaration**, statement, testimony, certification, confirmation, assertion, oath, pronouncement
affirmative *adj* = **agreeing**, positive, favourable, approving, assenting, concurring, confirming, consenting, corroborative
affix *See* **attach, connect**
afflict *v* = **torment**, hurt, pain, trouble, plague, grieve, distress, harass, oppress
affliction *n* = **suffering**, disease, trial, trouble, plague, woe, ordeal, curse, hardship, scourge, adversity, misfortune, torment
affluence *n* = **wealth**, plenty, fortune, prosperity, abundance, riches, opulence
affluent *adj* = **wealthy**, rich, prosperous, loaded (*slang*), well-heeled (*informal*), opulent, well-off, well-to-do, moneyed
afford *v* **1** = **have the money for**, stand, bear, manage, sustain, spare **2** = **give**, offer, provide, produce, supply, yield, render
affordable *adj* = **inexpensive**, cheap, moderate, modest, reasonable, low-cost, economical
affront *n* **1** = **insult**, slight, outrage, slur, offence, provocation, slap in the face (*informal*) ▸*v* **2** = **offend**, anger, insult, provoke, slight, outrage, annoy, displease
aflame *adj* = **burning**, fiery, ablaze, flaming, alight, blazing, lit, on fire
afoot *adv* = **going on**, up (*informal*), current, abroad, brewing, happening, in preparation, in progress, on the go (*informal*)
afraid *adj* **1** = **scared**, nervous, fearful, frightened, apprehensive • *I was afraid of the*

DICTIONARY

afresh Ⓣ *adv* again, anew
African *adj* **1** of Africa ▷ *n* **2** person from Africa
▶ **African violet** house plant with pink or purple flowers and hairy leaves
Afrikaans *n* language used in S Africa, related to Dutch
Afrikaner *n* White S African whose mother tongue is Afrikaans
Afro *n, pl* **-ros** frizzy bushy hair style
Afro- *combining form* African: *Afro-Caribbean*
aft *adv* at or towards the rear of a ship or aircraft
after Ⓣ *prep* **1** following in time or place **2** in pursuit of **3** in imitation of ▷ *conj* **4** at a later time than ▷ *adv* **5** at a later time
▶ **afters** *pl n Brit informal* dessert
afterbirth *n* material expelled from the womb after childbirth
aftercare *n* **1** support given to a person discharged from a hospital or prison **2** regular care required to keep something in good condition
aftereffect *n* effect occurring some time after its cause
afterglow *n* **1** glow left after a source of light has gone **2** pleasant feeling left after an enjoyable experience
afterlife *n* life after death
aftermath Ⓣ *n* aftereffects collectively
afternoon *n* time between noon and evening
aftershave *n* lotion applied to the face after shaving
afterthought *n* **1** idea occurring later **2** something added later
afterwards, afterward Ⓣ *adv* later
Ag *chem* silver
again Ⓣ *adv* **1** once more **2** in addition
against Ⓣ *prep* **1** in opposition or contrast to **2** in contact with **3** in readiness for
Aga Khan IV *n* Prince **Karim**. born 1936, spiritual leader of the Ismaili sect of Muslims from 1957
agape *adj* **1** (of the mouth) wide open **2** (of a person) very surprised
agaric *n* fungus with gills on the underside of the cap, such as a mushroom
Agassi *n* **Andre**. born 1970, US tennis player: won the Wimbledon men's singles in 1992 and the US Open in 1994 and 1999
Agassiz *n* **Jean Louis Rodolphe**. 1807–73, Swiss natural historian and geologist, settled in the US after 1846
agate [**ag**-git] *n* semiprecious form of quartz with striped colouring
age Ⓣ *n* **1** length of time a person or thing has existed **2** time of life **3** latter part of human life **4** period of history **5** long time ▷ *v* **ageing** *or* **aging, aged 6** make or grow old
ageing *or* **aging** *n, adj*
▶ **aged** *adj* **1** [**ay**-jid] old **2** [rhymes with **raged**] having the age of
▶ **ageless** *adj* **1** apparently never growing old **2** timeless
▶ **age-old** *adj* very old
agenda Ⓣ *n* list of things to be dealt with, esp. at a meeting
agent Ⓣ *n* **1** person acting on behalf of another **2** person or thing producing an effect
▶ **agency** *n* **1** organization providing a service **2** business or function of an agent **3** *old-fashioned* power or action by which something happens
▶ **agent general** diplomat who represents a Canadian province
agent provocateur [**azh**-on prov-vok-at-**tur**] *n, pl* **agents provocateurs** [**azh**-on prov-vok-at-**tur**] person employed by the

THESAURUS

large dog. OPPOSITE: unafraid **2 = sorry**, unhappy, regretful
afresh *adv* = **again**, newly, anew, once again, once more, over again
after *adv* = **later**, following, afterwards, subsequently • *Shortly after, police arrested five suspects*. OPPOSITE: before RELATED WORD *prefix*: post-
aftermath *n* = **effects**, wake, outcome, sequel, upshot, aftereffects, consequences, end result, results
afterwards *See* **after, next**
again *adv* **1 = once more**, anew, afresh • *He told the story again*. **2 = also**, besides, moreover, furthermore, in addition
against *prep* **1 = in opposition to**, versus, averse to, hostile to • *I am against animal cruelty*. RELATED WORDS *prefixes*: anti-, contra-, counter- **2 = in preparation for**, in anticipation of, in expectation of • *precautions against fire* **3 = beside**, on, upon, touching, facing, abutting, in contact with, opposite to
age *n* **1 = time**, day *or* days, period, date, generation, era, lifetime, span, duration, epoch **2 = old age**, decline, majority, maturity, seniority, advancing years, senescence, senility ▶ *v* **3 = grow old**, decline, mature, deteriorate, mellow, ripen
aged *adj* = **old**, elderly, ancient, antique, grey, antiquated, getting on
agency *n* **1 = business**, office, organization, department, bureau **2** (*Old-fashioned*) = **medium**, activity, means, mechanism
agenda *n* = **list**, plan, program, schedule, timetable, calendar, diary
agent *n* **1 = representative**, envoy, negotiator, rep (*informal*), surrogate, go-between **2 = worker**, author, operator, performer, doer, mover **3 = force**, cause, power, agency, vehicle, instrument, means

DICTIONARY

authorities to tempt people to commit illegal acts and so be discredited or punished

agglomerate *v* **1** gather into a mass ▷ *n* **2** confused mass **3** rock consisting of fused volcanic fragments ▷ *adj* **4** formed into a mass **agglomeration** *n*

agglutinate *v* stick with or as if with glue **agglutination** *n* **agglutinative** *adj*

aggrandize *v* make greater in size, power, or rank **aggrandizement** *n*

aggravate Ⓣ *v* **1** make worse **2** *informal* annoy **aggravating** *adj* **aggravation** *n*

aggregate Ⓣ *v* **1** gather into a mass ▷ *adj* **2** gathered into a mass **3** total or final ▷ *n* **4** total **5** rock consisting of a mixture of minerals **6** sand or gravel used to make concrete **aggregation** *n*

aggression Ⓣ *n* **1** unprovoked attack **2** hostile behaviour
▸ **aggressive** *adj* **1** full of anger or hostility **2** forceful or determined **aggressively** *adv* **aggressiveness** *n* **aggressor** *n*

aggrieved Ⓣ *adj* upset and angry

aggro *n slang* aggression

aghast Ⓣ *adj* amazed or shocked

agile Ⓣ *adj* **1** nimble, quick-moving **2** mentally quick **agilely** *adv* **agility** *n*

agitate Ⓣ *v* **1** disturb or excite **2** stir or shake (a liquid) **3** stir up public opinion for or against something **agitation** *n* **agitator** *n*

aglow *adj* glowing

AGM annual general meeting

Agnes *n* **Saint**. ?292–?304 AD, Christian child martyr under Diocletian. Feast day: Jan 21

Agnesi *n* **Maria Gaetana**. 1718–99, Italian mathematician and philosopher, noted for her work on differential calculus

Agnew *n* **Spiro Theodore**. 1918–96, US Republican politician; vice president (1969–73)

agnostic *n* **1** person who believes that it is impossible to know whether God exists ▷ *adj* **2** of agnostics **agnosticism** *n*

ago *adv* in the past

agog Ⓣ *adj* eager or curious

THESAURUS

aggravate *v* **1** = **make worse**, increase, worsen, intensify, exacerbate, inflame, exaggerate, magnify **2** (*Informal*) = **annoy**, provoke, bother, irritate, get on one's nerves (*informal*), nettle

aggravation *n* **1** = **worsening**, increase, exaggeration, intensification, exacerbation, heightening, inflaming, magnification **2** (*Informal*) = **annoyance**, grief (*informal*), provocation, hassle (*informal*), irritation, gall, exasperation

aggregate *n* **1** = **total**, body, amount, whole, mass, collection, combination, pile, bulk, sum, accumulation ▸ *adj* **2** = **total**, mixed, combined, composite, cumulative, accumulated, collected ▸ *v* **3** = **combine**, collect, mix, pile, assemble, accumulate, amass, heap

aggression *n* **1** = **hostility**, antagonism, belligerence, destructiveness, pugnacity **2** = **attack**, injury, assault, offensive, raid, invasion, onslaught

aggressive *adj* **1** = **hostile**, quarrelsome • *These fish are very aggressive.* OPPOSITE: peaceful **2** = **forceful**, militant, bold, energetic, dynamic, vigorous, assertive, enterprising, pushy (*informal*)
See also: **fierce**

aggressor *n* = **attacker**, assailant, invader, assaulter

aggrieved *adj* = **hurt**, injured, unhappy, distressed, disturbed, afflicted, harmed, wronged

aghast *adj* = **horrified**, shocked, amazed, awestruck, appalled, astonished, astounded, confounded, startled, stunned

agile *adj* **1** = **nimble**, supple, lithe, sprightly • *as agile as a cat* OPPOSITE: clumsy **2** = **acute**, alert, sharp, bright (*informal*), clever, lively, quick-witted

agility *n* = **nimbleness**, quickness, litheness, liveliness, suppleness, swiftness

agitate *v* **1** = **campaign**, push, protest, demonstrate • *They began to agitate for better conditions.* **2** = **upset**, bother, **distress**, worry, trouble, disturb, faze (*informal*), perturb • *Everything she said was beginning to agitate me.* **3** = **stir**, beat, shake, toss, disturb, rouse, convulse
See also: **excite** ▷ **agitate for** *See* **incite**

agitated *adj* = **upset**, troubled, nervous, anxious, excited, distressed, worried, uneasy, edgy, shaken, disturbed, alarmed, rattled (*informal*), unsettled, unnerved, antsy (*informal*), angsty, disconcerted, worked up, ruffled, perturbed, on edge, in a flap (*informal*), ill at ease, hot under the collar (*informal*), hot and bothered (*informal*), flustered, fazed, distracted, disquieted, discomposed, all of a flutter (*informal*) OPPOSITE: calm

agitation *n* **1** = **turmoil**, trouble, confusion, excitement, disturbance, upheaval, clamour, commotion, ferment **2** = **turbulence**, disturbance, convulsion, shaking, stirring, tossing

agitator *n* = **troublemaker**, revolutionary, instigator, firebrand, agent provocateur, rabble-rouser, stirrer (*informal*)

agog *adj* = **eager**, curious, enthusiastic, excited, avid, impatient, expectant, enthralled, in suspense, wired (*slang*)

agonize *v* = **suffer**, struggle, worry, strain,

DICTIONARY

agony Ⓣ *n, pl* **-nies** extreme physical or mental pain
▶ **agonize** *v* **1** (cause to) suffer agony **2** worry greatly **agonizing** *adj*
▶ **agony column** newspaper or magazine feature offering advice on personal problems
agoraphobia *n* fear of open spaces **agoraphobic** *n, adj*
Agostini *n* **Giacomo.** born 1944, Italian racing motorcyclist: world champion (500 cc. class) 1966–72, 1975; (350 cc. class) 1968–74
agrarian *adj* of land or agriculture **agrarianism** *n*
agree Ⓣ *v* **agreeing, agreed 1** be of the same opinion **2** consent **3** reach a joint decision **4** be consistent **5** (foll. by *with*) be suitable to one's health or digestion
▶ **agreeable** *adj* **1** willing **2** pleasant **agreeably** *adv*
▶ **agreement** *n* **1** agreeing **2** contract
Agricola *n* **Gnaeus Julius.** 40–93 AD, Roman general; governor of Britain who advanced Roman rule north to the Firth of Forth
agriculture Ⓣ *n* raising of crops and livestock **agricultural** *adj* **agriculturalist** *n*
agronomy [ag-**ron**-om-mee] *n* science of soil management and crop production **agronomist** *n*
aground Ⓣ *adv* onto the bottom of shallow water
ague [**aig**-yew] *n* periodic fever with shivering
ahead Ⓣ *adv* **1** in front **2** forwards
Ahmadinejad *n* **Mahmoud.** born 1956, Iranian politician; President from 2005
ahoy *interj* shout used at sea to attract attention
AI 1 artificial insemination **2** artificial intelligence
aid Ⓣ *v, n* help, support
aide Ⓣ *n* assistant
aide-de-camp [**aid**-de-kom] *n, pl* **aides-de-camp** [**aid**-de-kom] military officer serving as personal assistant to a senior
AIDS acquired immunodeficiency syndrome, a viral disease that destroys the body's ability to fight infection
ail *v* **1** trouble, afflict **2** be ill
▶ **ailing** *adj* sickly
▶ **ailment** *n* illness
aileron [**ale**-er-on] *n* movable flap on an aircraft wing which controls rolling
aim Ⓣ *v* **1** point (a weapon or missile) or direct (a blow or remark) at a target **2** propose or intend ▷ *n* **3** aiming **4** intention, purpose
▶ **aimless** *adj* without purpose **aimlessly** *adv*

THESAURUS

labour, be distressed, be in agony, be in anguish, go through the mill
agony *n* = **suffering**, pain, torture, distress, misery, anguish, torment, throes
agree *v* **1** = **concur**, assent, be of the same opinion, see eye to eye • *So we both agree there's a problem?* OPPOSITE: disagree **2** = **match**, accord, square, tally, conform, jibe (*informal*) • *Her second statement agrees with facts as stated by the other witnesses.* ▷ **agree to** *See* **accept** ▷ **agree with** *See* **side with**
See also: **correspond, settle, submit, suit**
agreeable *adj* **1** = **pleasant**, nice, lovely, enjoyable, delightful, pleasurable • *I found it a most agreeable experience.* OPPOSITE: disagreeable **2** = **willing**, game, ready, happy, prepared • *She said she was agreeable to this plan.*
agreement *n* **1** = **arrangement**, deal (*informal*), contract, pledge, settlement, treaty, pact, covenant • *The two countries have signed agreements on fishing and oil rights.* **2** = **assent**, union, consent, compliance, harmony, unison, agreeing, concord, concurrence **3** = **correspondence**, similarity, compatibility, consistency, conformity, congruity
See also: **approval, bond, understanding**
agricultural *adj* = **farming**, country, rural, rustic, agrarian
agriculture *n* = **farming**, culture, cultivation, husbandry, tillage
aground *adv* = **beached**, ashore, stuck, foundered, grounded, high and dry, on the rocks, stranded
ahead *adv* = **in front**, before, winning, cutting-edge, at an advantage, at the head, in advance, in the lead, leading, to the fore
ahead of time *See* **early**
aid *n* **1** = **help**, service, support, benefit, relief, assistance, promotion, favour, encouragement ▶ *v* **2** = **help**, support, serve, assist, promote, encourage, sustain, subsidize, favour
aide *n* = **assistant**, second, supporter, attendant, helper, right-hand man, consigliere
ailing *adj* = **ill**, weak, sick, poorly, unwell, infirm, indisposed, under the weather (*informal*)
ailment *n* = **illness**, disease, complaint, disorder, sickness, malady, affliction, infirmity
aim *v* **1** = **intend**, plan, attempt, propose, strive, aspire • *The company aims to sign up a million customers within the next five years.* ▶ *n* **2** = **intention**, plan, goal, target, objective, ambition • *Our main aim is to offer a superior product.*
See also: **cause, focus, mean, object,**

DICTIONARY

ain't *not standard* **1** am not **2** is not **3** are not **4** has not **5** have not

air ⓘ *n* **1** mixture of gases forming the earth's atmosphere **2** space above the ground, sky **3** breeze **4** tune **5** quality or manner **airs 6** affected manners ▷ *v* **7** expose to air to dry or ventilate **8** make known publicly

▸ **on the air** in the act of broadcasting on radio or television

▸ **airy** *adj* **1** well-ventilated **2** jaunty, nonchalant **airily** *adv* **airiness** *n*

▸ **airless** *adj* stuffy

▸ **airing** *n* **1** exposure to air for drying or ventilation **2** exposure to public debate

▸ **air base** centre from which military aircraft operate

▸ **air bed** inflatable mattress

▸ **airborne** *adj* **1** carried by air **2** (of aircraft) in flight

▸ **air brake** brake worked by compressed air

▸ **airbrush** *n* atomizer spraying paint by compressed air

▸ **air conditioning** system that controls the temperature and humidity of the air in a building

▸ **aircraft** *n* any machine that flies, such as an airplane

▸ **aircraft carrier** warship from which aircraft operate

▸ **airfield** *n* place where aircraft can land and take off

▸ **air force** branch of the armed forces responsible for air warfare

▸ **air gun** gun discharged by the force of compressed air

▸ **airlift** *n* **1** transport of troops or cargo by aircraft when other routes are blocked ▷ *v* **2** transport by airlift

▸ **airline** *n* company providing scheduled flights for passengers and cargo

▸ **airliner** *n* large passenger aircraft

▸ **airlock** *n* **1** air bubble obstructing the flow of liquid in a pipe **2** airtight chamber

▸ **airmail** *n* **1** system of sending mail by aircraft **2** mail sent in this way

▸ **airman** (**airwoman**) *n* member of the air force

▸ **airplane** *n* powered flying vehicle with fixed wings

▸ **airplay** *n* broadcast performances (of a record) on radio

▸ **airport** *n* airfield for civilian aircraft, with facilities for aircraft maintenance and passengers

▸ **air raid** attack by aircraft

▸ **airship** *n* lighter-than-air flying machine with means of propulsion

▸ **airsick** *adj* nauseated from travelling in an aircraft

▸ **airspace** *n* atmosphere above a country, regarded as its territory

▸ **airstrip** *n* strip of ground where aircraft can take off and land

▸ **airtight** *adj* not allowing the passage of air

▸ **airworthy** *adj* (of aircraft) fit to fly **airworthiness** *n*

Airedale *n* large rough-coated terrier dog

aisle ⓘ [rhymes with **mile**] *n* passageway separating seating areas in a church, theatre, etc., or row of shelves in a supermarket

ajar ⓘ *adj, adv* (of a door) partly open

Akhenaten, Akhenaton *n* original name *Amenhotep IV.* died ?1358 BC, king of Egypt, of the 18th dynasty; he moved his capital from Thebes to Tell El Amarna and introduced the cult of Aten

Akhmatova *n* **Anna**, pseudonym of *Anna Gorenko.* 1889–1966, Russian poet: noted for her concise and intensely personal lyrics

Akihito *n* born 1933, Emperor of Japan from 1989

akimbo *adv* **with arms akimbo** with hands on hips and elbows outwards

akin ⓘ *adj* similar, related

THESAURUS

point, purpose, seek

aimed *See* **calculated**

aimless *adj* = **purposeless**, random, stray, pointless, directionless

aimlessly *See* **at random**

air *n* **1** = **atmosphere**, sky, heavens **2** = **wind**, draft, breeze, zephyr **3** = **manner**, look, appearance, atmosphere, mood, impression, aura, demeanour **4** = **tune**, song, lay, melody, aria ▸ *v* **5** = **publicize**, reveal, express, display, voice, exhibit, circulate, give vent to, make known, make public **6** = **ventilate**, expose, freshen, aerate

airborne *adj* = **flying**, floating, gliding, hovering, in flight, in the air, on the wing

airing *n* **1** = **ventilation**, aeration, drying, freshening **2** = **exposure**, display, expression, circulation, publicity, vent, dissemination, utterance

airless *adj* = **stuffy**, close, heavy, oppressive, sultry, muggy, stifling, suffocating

airs *pl n* = **affectation**, arrogance, haughtiness, hauteur, pomposity, pretensions, superciliousness

airy *adj* **1** = **well-ventilated**, open, light, fresh, spacious, uncluttered **2** = **light-hearted**, lively, cheerful, jaunty, blithe, high-spirited, sprightly

aisle *n* = **passageway**, path, passage, lane, alley, corridor, gangway

ajar *See* **open**

akin *See* **like**

alacrity *n* = **eagerness**, speed, enthusiasm,

DICTIONARY

Al *chem* aluminum
alabaster *n* soft white translucent stone
à la carte *adj, adv* (of a menu) having dishes individually priced
alack *interj obsolete* cry of grief or sorrow
alacrity ⓣ *n* speed, eagerness
à la mode *adj* fashionable
Alaric *n* ?370–410 AD, king of the Visigoths, who served under the Roman emperor Theodosius I but later invaded Greece and Italy, capturing Rome in 410
alarm ⓣ *n* **1** sudden fear caused by awareness of danger **2** warning sound **3** device that gives this **4** alarm clock ▷ *v* **5** frighten **alarming** *adj*
▸ **alarmist** *n* person who alarms others needlessly
▸ **alarm clock** clock which sounds at a set time to wake someone up
alas *adv* unfortunately, regrettably
Alban *n* **Saint**. 3rd century AD, the first English martyr. He was beheaded by the Romans on the site on which St Alban's Abbey now stands, for admitting his conversion to Christianity. Feast day: June 17
albatross *n* large sea bird with very long wings
albeit *conj* although
Albéniz *n* **Isaac**. 1860–1909, Spanish composer; noted for piano pieces inspired by folk music, such as the suite *Iberia*
Albers *n* **Josef**. 1888–1976, US painter, designer, and poet, born in Germany. His works include a series of abstract paintings entitled *Homage to the Square*
Albert *n* **Prince**, full name *Albert Francis Charles Augustus Emmanuel of Saxe-Coburg-Gotha*. 1819–61, Prince Consort of Queen Victoria of Great Britain and Ireland
Alberti *n* **Leon Battista**. 1404–72, Italian Renaissance architect, painter, writer, and musician; among his architectural designs are the façades of Sta. Maria Novella at Florence and S. Francesco at Rimini
albino *n, pl* **-nos** person or animal with white skin and hair and pink eyes **albinism** *n*
Albinoni *n* **Tomaso**. 1671–1750, Italian composer and violinist. He wrote concertos and over 50 operas
album *n* **1** book with blank pages for keeping photographs or stamps in **2** long-playing record
albumen *n* egg white
albumin, albumen *n* protein found in blood plasma, egg white, milk, and muscle
albuminous *adj*
alchemy *n* medieval form of chemistry concerned with trying to turn base metals into gold and to find the elixir of life
alchemist *n*
Alcock *n* Sir **John William**. 1892–1919, English aviator who with A.W. Brown made the first nonstop flight across the Atlantic (1919)
alcohol ⓣ *n* **1** colourless flammable liquid present in intoxicating drinks **2** intoxicating drinks generally
▸ **alcoholic** *adj* **1** of alcohol ▷ *n* **2** person addicted to alcohol
▸ **alcoholism** *n* addiction to alcohol
Alcott *n* **Louisa May**. 1832–88, US novelist, noted for her children's books, esp. *Little Women* (1869)
alcove ⓣ *n* recess in the wall of a room
aldehyde *n* one of a group of chemical compounds derived from alcohol by oxidation
alder *n* tree related to the birch
alderman *n* member of a municipal council
Aldiss *n* **Brian W**(**ilson**). born 1925, British novelist, best known for his science fiction. His works include *Non-Stop* (1958), *Enemies of the System* (1978), *The Helliconia Trilogy* (1983–86), *Forgotten Life* (1988), and *The Detached Retina* (1995)
ale *n* kind of beer
aleatory *adj* dependent on chance
alert ⓣ *adj* **1** watchful, attentive ▷ *n* **2** warning of danger ▷ *v* **3** warn of danger **4** make (someone) aware of

THESAURUS

willingness, readiness, zeal, quickness, alertness, promptness
alarm *n* **1 = fear**, scare, panic, anxiety, apprehension, nervousness, fright • *The cat sprang back in alarm*. OPPOSITE: calm **2 = danger signal**, distress signal, warning, siren • *a burglar alarm* ▸ *v* **3 = frighten**, scare, panic, distress, startle, unnerve • *We could not see what had alarmed him*. OPPOSITE: calm
See also: **horror**
alarmed *See* **frightened**
alarming *adj* = **frightening**, shocking, daunting, startling, distressing, disturbing, scaring, unnerving
alcohol *n* = **drink**, liquor, booze (*informal*), spirits • *There wasn't any alcohol at the party*. RELATED WORD *like*: dipsomania
alcoholic *n* **1 = drunkard**, drunk, drinker, wino (*informal*), inebriate, dipsomaniac, tippler, toper ▸ *adj* **2 = intoxicating**, strong, hard, distilled, brewed, fermented
alcove *n* = **recess**, corner, bay, niche, compartment, cubicle, nook, cubbyhole
alert *adj* **1 = watchful**, wary, vigilant, attentive, observant, on guard • *apprehended by alert security staff* OPPOSITE: unaware ▸ *v* **2 = warn**, inform, notify, forewarn • *I was*

DICTIONARY

(a fact) **alertness** *n*
▸**on the alert** watchful
A level *n* (pass in a subject at) the advanced level of the GCE
Alexander *n* **Harold** (**Rupert Leofric George**), Earl Alexander of Tunis. 1891–1969, British field marshal in World War II, who organized the retreat from Dunkirk and commanded in North Africa (1943) and Sicily and Italy (1944–45); governor general of Canada (1946–52); British minister of defence (1952–54)
Alexander I *n c.* 1080–1124, king of Scotland (1107–24), son of Malcolm III
Alexander II *n* 1198–1249, king of Scotland (1214–49), son of William (the Lion)
Alexander III *n* **1** 1241–86, king of Scotland (1249–86), son of Alexander II **2** original name *Orlando Bandinelli.* died 1181, pope (1159–81), who excommunicated Barbarossa
Alexander the Great *n* 356–323 BC, king of Macedon, who conquered Greece (336), Egypt (331), and the Persian Empire (328), and founded Alexandria
Alexandra *n* 1844–1925, queen consort of Edward VII of Great Britain and Ireland
alfalfa *n* kind of plant used as fodder
Alfred the Great *n* 849–99, king of Wessex (871–99) and overlord of England, who defeated the Danes and encouraged learning and writing in English
alfresco *adv, adj* in the open air
algae [**al**-jee] *pl n* plants which live in or near water and have no true stems, leaves, or roots
algebra *n* branch of mathematics using symbols to represent numbers **algebraic** *adj*
ALGOL *n computers* computer programming language designed for mathematical and scientific purposes
Algonquin, Algonkin *n* member of a North American Indian people formerly living along the St Lawrence and Ottawa Rivers in Canada
algorithm *n* logical arithmetical or computational procedure for solving a problem
Ali *n* **1** ?600–661 AD, fourth caliph of Islam (656–61 AD), considered the first caliph by the Shiites: cousin and son-in-law of Mohammed **2 Mehemet.** See **Mehemet Ali** **3 Muhammad.** See **Muhammad Ali**
alias Ⓣ *adv* **1** also known as: *William Bonney, alias Billy the Kid* ▹ *n* **2** false name
alibi Ⓣ *n* **1** plea of being somewhere else when a crime was committed **2** *informal* excuse
Alice band *n* band worn across the head to hold the hair back from the face
alien Ⓣ *adj* **1** foreign **2** repugnant (to) **3** from another world ▹ *n* **4** foreigner **5** being from another world
▸**alienable** *adj law* able to be transferred to another owner
▸**alienate** *v* cause to become hostile **alienation** *n*
alight[1] Ⓣ *v* **1** step out of (a vehicle) **2** land
alight[2] Ⓣ *adj* **1** burning **2** lit up
align Ⓣ [a-**line**] *v* **1** place in a line **2** make or bring (a person or group) into agreement with the policy of another **alignment** *n*
alike Ⓣ *adj* **1** like, similar ▹ *adv* **2** in the same way
alimentary *adj* of nutrition
▸**alimentary canal** food passage in the body
alimony *n* allowance paid under a court order to a separated or divorced spouse
A-line *adj* (of a skirt) slightly flared
aliquot *adj* **1** of or denoting an exact divisor of a number ▹ *n* **2** exact divisor

THESAURUS

hoping she'd alert the police. ▸*n* **3 = warning**, signal, alarm, siren
See also: **acute, alive, astute, scare, sharp**
alertness *n* **= watchfulness**, vigilance, attentiveness, heedfulness, liveliness
alias *adv* **1 = also known as**, otherwise, also called, otherwise known as ▸*n* **2 = pseudonym**, assumed name, nom de guerre, nom de plume, pen name, stage name
alibi *n* **= excuse**, reason, plea, explanation, defence, justification, pretext
alien *adj* **1 = foreign**, strange, exotic, unfamiliar, incongruous ▸*n* **2 = foreigner**, stranger, newcomer, outsider
alienate *v* **= set against**, estrange, disaffect, make unfriendly, shut out, turn away
alienation *n* **= setting against**, separation, remoteness, estrangement, disaffection, turning away
alight[1] *v* **1 = get off**, descend, disembark, dismount, get down **2 = land**, light (*archaic*), settle, descend, perch, come down, come to rest, touch down
alight[2] *adj* **1 = on fire**, burning, fiery, ablaze, flaming, aflame, lighted, blazing, lit **2 = lit up**, bright, brilliant, illuminated, shining
align *v* **1 = ally**, agree, join, side, associate, affiliate, cooperate, sympathize **2 = line up**, order, range, regulate, straighten, even up
alignment *n* **1 = alliance**, agreement, union, association, sympathy, affiliation, cooperation **2 = lining up**, order, arrangement, adjustment, evening up, straightening up
alike *adj* **1 = similar**, close, identical, analogous, the same • *You and your father are so alike.* OPPOSITE: different ▸*adv* **2 = similarly**, equally, uniformly, in the same

DICTIONARY

alive Ⓣ *adj* **1** living, in existence **2** lively
▸ **alive to** aware of
▸ **alive with** swarming with
alkali [**alk**-a-lie] *n* substance which combines with acid and neutralizes it to form a salt **alkaline** *adj* **alkalinity** *n*
▸ **alkaloid** *n* any of a group of organic compounds containing nitrogen
all Ⓣ *adj* **1** whole quantity or number (of) ▹ *adv* **2** wholly, entirely **3** (in the score of games) each ▹ *n* **4** whole **5** everything, everyone
▸ **all-Canadian** *adj* composed exclusively of Canadians
▸ **all in** *adj* **1** exhausted **2** (of wrestling) with no style prohibited ▹ *adv* **3** with all expenses included
▸ **all right** *adj* **1** adequate, satisfactory **2** unharmed ▹ *interj* **3** expression of approval or agreement
▸ **all-rounder** *n* person with ability in many fields
▸ **all-terrain vehicle** motor vehicle with large tires for travel over rough land
Allah *n* name of God in Islam
allay *v* reduce (fear or anger) or relieve (pain or grief)
allege Ⓣ *v* state without proof **alleged** *adj* **allegedly** *adv*
▸ **allegation** *n* thing alleged
allegiance Ⓣ *n* loyalty to a person, country, or cause
allegory Ⓣ *n, pl* **-ries** story with an underlying meaning as well as the literal one **allegorical** *adj* **allegorically** *adv* **allegorize** *v*
allegretto *adv music* fairly quickly or briskly
Allegri *n* **Gregorio**. 1582–1652, Italian composer and singer. His compositions include a *Miserere* for nine voices
allegro *adv music* in a brisk lively manner
Allen *n* **Woody**, real name *Allen Stewart Konigsberg*. born 1935, US film comedian, screenwriter, and director. His films as an actor and director include *Annie Hall* (1977), *Manhattan* (1979), *Hannah and Her Sisters* (1986), *Bullets over Broadway* (1994), and *Anything Else* (2003)
Allende *n* **1 Isabel**. born 1942, Chilean writer, born in Peru; her works include *Eva Luna* (1989), *Paula* (1995), and *Daughter of Fortune* (1999) **2 Salvador**. 1908–73, Chilean Marxist politician; president of Chile from 1970 until 1973, when the army seized power and he was killed
allergy Ⓣ *n, pl* **-gies** extreme sensitivity to a substance, which causes the body to react to any contact with it
▸ **allergic** *adj* **1** having or caused by an allergy **2** *informal* having an aversion (to): *allergic to work*
▸ **allergen** [**al**-ler-jen] *n* substance capable of causing an allergic reaction

THESAURUS

way • *I punish all players alike who break the rules.* *See also*: **like, same**
alive *adj* **1 = living**, breathing, animate • *The lost skier was found alive.* OPPOSITE: dead **2 = lively**, alert, active, animated, energetic, vivacious, full of life • *I never expected to feel so alive in my life again.* OPPOSITE: dull **3 = in existence**, active, operative, existing, extant, functioning, in force
See also: **live**
all *pron* **1 = the whole of**, each, everything, every one, the whole amount, the (whole) lot (*informal*) • *Why did you have to say all that?* RELATED WORDS *prefixes*: pan-, panto- ▸ *adj* **2 = the whole of**, every bit of, the complete, the entire, the sum of, the totality of, the total of, the whole schmear (*informal*), the whole enchilada (*slang*) **3 = every**, each, each and every, every one of, every single **4 = complete**, full, total, perfect, entire, utter, greatest
▹ **all right = acceptable**, average, fair, OK (*informal*), adequate • *It was all right, but nothing special*; **= O.K.** *or* **okay** (*informal*), well, safe, healthy, sound, whole, unharmed, uninjured
See also: **okay, satisfactory** ▹ **all-out = total**, complete, full, maximum, full-scale, exhaustive, undivided, unrestrained, thoroughgoing, unremitting ▸ *adv* **5 = completely**, fully, totally, entirely, altogether, wholly, utterly ▸ *n* **6 = whole amount**, total, everything, aggregate, utmost, entirety, totality, sum total
See also: **whole**
allegation *n* **= claim**, charge, statement, accusation, declaration, assertion, affirmation
allege *v* **= claim**, charge, state, declare, maintain, assert, affirm
alleged *adj* **1 = stated**, affirmed, asserted, declared, described, designated **2 = supposed**, so-called, purported, doubtful, dubious, ostensible, professed, unproved
allegiance *n* **= loyalty**, devotion, fidelity, obedience, constancy, faithfulness
allegorical *adj* **= symbolic**, emblematic, figurative, symbolizing
allegory *n* **= symbol**, story, tale, myth, symbolism, fable, parable
allergic *adj* **= sensitive**, susceptible, affected by, hypersensitive
allergy *n* **= sensitivity**, susceptibility, antipathy, hypersensitivity

DICTIONARY

alleviate Ⓣ *v* lessen (pain or suffering) **alleviation** *n*
alley Ⓣ *n* **1** narrow street or path **2** long narrow enclosure in which tenpin bowling or skittles is played
alley-oop *n basketball* high pass to a teammate who jumps to catch it and immediately attempts to score
alliance Ⓣ *n* **1** state of being allied **2** formal relationship between countries or groups for a shared purpose
alligator *n* reptile of the crocodile family, found in the southern US and China
alliteration *n* use of the same sound at the start of consecutive words **alliterative** *adj*
allocate Ⓣ *v* allot or assign **allocation** *n*
allophone *n* Canadian whose native language is neither French nor English
allot Ⓣ *v* **-lotting, -lotted** assign as a share or for a particular purpose
▶**allotment** *n* **1** distribution **2** portion allotted **3** small piece of public land rented to grow vegetables on
allotrope *n* any of two or more physical forms in which an element can exist **allotropic** *adj*
allow Ⓣ *v* **1** permit **2** acknowledge (a point or claim) **3** set aside **allowable** *adj*
▶**allow for** take into account
▶**allowance** *n* **1** amount of money given at regular intervals **2** amount permitted
▶**make allowances for 1** be lenient towards (someone) because he or she has special problems **2** take into account
alloy Ⓣ *n* **1** mixture of two or more metals ▷*v* **2** mix (metals)
allspice *n* spice made from the berries of a tropical American tree
Allston *n* **Washington.** 1779–1843, US painter and author, regarded as the earliest US Romantic painter. His paintings include *Elijah in the Desert* (1818) and *Moonlit Landscape* (1819)
allude Ⓣ *v* (foll. by *to*) refer indirectly to
▶**allusion** *n* indirect reference **allusive** *adj*
allure Ⓣ *v* **1** entice or attract ▷*n* **2** attractiveness **allurement** *n* **alluring** *adj*
alluvium *n* fertile soil deposited by flowing water **alluvial** *adj*
ally Ⓣ *n, pl* **-lies 1** country or person having an agreement to support another ▷*v* **-lying, -lied 2 ally oneself with** join as an ally **allied** *adj*
alma mater *n* one's former school, university, or college
almanac *n* yearly calendar with detailed information on anniversaries, phases of the moon, etc.

THESAURUS

alleviate *v* = **ease**, reduce, moderate, relieve, lessen, allay, lighten, soothe
alley *n* = **passage**, walk, lane, pathway, alleyway, passageway, backstreet
alliance *n* = **union**, agreement, league, connection, marriage, coalition, association, combination, partnership, treaty, pact, federation, affiliation, confederation
allied *adj* = **united**, combined, related, connected, affiliated, associated, in league, linked
allocate *v* = **assign**, allow, budget, designate, earmark, allot, mete, apportion, set aside, share out
allocation *n* = **assignment**, share, lot, portion, quota, allowance, ration, allotment
allot *v* = **assign**, budget, designate, allocate, earmark, mete, apportion, set aside, share out
allotment *n* **1** = **plot**, patch, tract, kitchen garden **2** = **assignment**, share, grant, portion, quota, stint, allowance, ration, allocation
allow *v* **1** = **permit**, let, approve, authorize, tolerate, stand for • *Talking will not be allowed during the exam.* OPPOSITE: forbid **2** = **set aside**, grant, assign, allocate, allot • *Allow four hours for the paint to dry.* **3** = **acknowledge**, own, admit, grant, concede, confess
See also: **sanction**
▷**allow for** = **take into account**, consider, make allowances for, make concessions for, make provision for, plan for, provide for, take into consideration
allowable *adj* = **permissible**, appropriate, acceptable, suitable, admissible, tolerable, all right
allowance *n* **1** = **portion**, share, lot, amount, grant, quota, stint, ration, allocation **2** = **concession**, reduction, discount, rebate, deduction
alloy *n* **1** = **mixture**, combination, compound, composite, hybrid, blend, amalgam, admixture ▶*v* **2** = **mix**, combine, compound, blend, fuse, amalgamate
allude *v* = **refer**, suggest, mention, hint, intimate, imply, touch upon
allure *n* **1** = **attractiveness**, appeal, lure, charm, attraction, temptation, glamour, persuasion, enchantment, enticement, seductiveness ▶*v* **2** = **attract**, lure, persuade, charm, entice, tempt, captivate, seduce, enchant, win over
alluring *adj* = **attractive**, glamorous, tempting, seductive, beguiling, captivating, come-hither, fetching
allusion *n* = **reference**, mention, hint, suggestion, implication, innuendo, insinuation, casual remark, intimation
ally *n* **1** = **partner**, friend, associate,

DICTIONARY

almighty ⓣ *adj* **1** having absolute power **2** *informal* very great ▷ *n* **3 the Almighty** God
almond *n* edible oval-shaped nut which grows on a small tree
almoner *n* person who distributes alms
almost ⓣ *adv* very nearly
alms [**ahmz**] *pl n old-fashioned* gifts to the poor
▸ **almshouse** *n* formerly, a house financed by charity, offering accommodation to the poor
aloe *n* **1** plant with fleshy spiny leaves **aloes 2** bitter drug made from aloe leaves
aloft *adv* **1** in the air **2** in a ship's rigging
alone ⓣ *adj, adv* without anyone or anything else
along *prep* **1** over part or all the length of ▷ *adv* **2** forward **3** in company with others: *come along for the ride*
▸ **alongside** *adv, prep* beside
aloof ⓣ *adj* distant or haughty in manner **aloofness** *n*
alopecia [al-loh-**pee**-sha] *n* loss of hair
aloud ⓣ *adv* in an audible voice
Aloysius *n* **Saint**, full name *Aloysius Luigi Gonzaga*. 1568–91, Italian Jesuit who died nursing plague victims; the patron saint of youth. Feast day: June 21
alp *n* high mountain
▸ **the Alps** high mountain range in S central Europe
alpaca *n* **1** Peruvian llama **2** its wool **3** cloth made from this
alpenstock *n* iron-tipped staff used by climbers
alpha *n* **1** first letter in the Greek alphabet **2** highest grade in an examination
▸ **alpha and omega** the first and last
▸ **alpha particle** positively charged particle emitted during some radioactive transformations
▸ **alpha ray** stream of alpha particles
alphabet *n* set of letters used in writing a language
▸ **alphabetical** *adj* in the conventional order of the letters of an alphabet **alphabetically** *adv*
▸ **alphabetize** *v* put in alphabetical order **alphabetization** *n*
alpine *adj* **1** of high mountains **2 Alpine** of the Alps ▷ *n* **3** mountain plant
already ⓣ *adv* **1** before this time **2** sooner than expected
Alsatian *n* large wolflike dog
also ⓣ *adv* **1** in addition **2** too
▸ **also-ran** *n* loser in a race, competition, or election
alt. *combining form informal* alternative: *alt. rock*
Alta. Alberta
altar *n* **1** raised structure on which sacrifices are offered and religious rites are performed **2** table used for Communion in Christian churches
▸ **altarpiece** *n* work of art above and behind the altar in some Christian churches
Altdorfer *n* **Albrecht**. ?1480–?1538, German painter and engraver: one of the earliest landscape painters
alter ⓣ *v* make or become different **alteration** *n*
altercation ⓣ *n* heated argument
alter ego *n* **1** second self **2** very close friend
alternate ⓣ *v* **1** (cause to) occur by turns ▷ *adj* **2** occurring by turns **3** every second one of a series: *alternate Fridays* **alternately** *adv* **alternation** *n*

THESAURUS

colleague, accomplice, collaborator, helper, homeboy (*slang*), homegirl (*slang*) ▸ *v* **2 = unite**, join, associate, combine, collaborate, unify, join forces
almighty *adj* **1 = all-powerful**, absolute, unlimited, supreme, invincible, omnipotent **2** (*Informal*) **= great**, severe, intense, terrible, loud, enormous, excessive
almost *adv* **= nearly**, about, approximately, practically, close to, not quite • *Over the past decade their salaries have almost doubled.*
See also: **barely**
alone *adj* **= by oneself**, single, separate, isolated, detached • *He was all alone in the middle of the hall.*
See also: **lonely, on your own**
alongside *See* **beside, near**
aloof *adj* **= distant**, remote, unfriendly, detached, haughty, standoffish, supercilious, unapproachable
aloud *adv* **= out loud**, audibly • *Our father reads aloud to us.*
already *adv* **= before now**, before, previously, at present, by now, by then, even now, heretofore, just now
also *adv* **= as well**, besides, furthermore, too, moreover, into the bargain • *The artist is also a well-known writer.*
alter *v* **= change**, turn, reform, convert, adjust, modify, revise, vary, adapt, transform, amend
alteration *n* **= change**, difference, amendment, conversion, variation, adjustment, adaptation, revision, transformation, modification, reformation
altercation *n* **= argument**, dispute, row, clash, controversy, contention, disagreement, squabble, wrangle, quarrel, bickering, discord, dissension
alternate *v* **1 = change**, substitute, rotate, fluctuate, interchange, act reciprocally, oscillate, take turns ▸ *adj* **2 = every other**,

DICTIONARY

▸**alternative** *n* **1** one of two choices ▹ *adj* **2** able to be done or used instead of something else **3** (of medicine, lifestyle, etc.) not conventional **alternatively** *adv*
▸**alternator** *n* electric generator for producing alternating current
▸**alternating current** electric current that reverses direction at frequent regular intervals
although Ⓣ *conj* despite the fact that
Althusser *n* **Louis**. 1918–90, French Marxist philosopher, author of *For Marx* (1965) and *Reading Capital* (1965): committed to a mental hospital (1981) after killing his wife
altimeter [al-**tim**-it-er] *n* instrument that measures altitude
altitude *n* height above sea level
Altman *n* **1 Robert**. 1925–2006, US film director; his films include *M*A*S*H* (1970), *Nashville* (1975), *Short Cuts* (1994), and *Gosford Park* (2001) **2 Sidney**. born 1939, US chemist born in Canada. Winner, with Thomas Cech, of the 1989 Nobel Prize for chemistry for their work on ribonuclease-P
alto *n, pl* **-tos** *music* **1** short for **contralto** **2** (singer with) the highest adult male voice **3** instrument with the second-highest pitch in its group
altogether Ⓣ *adv* **1** entirely **2** on the whole **3** in total
altruism *n* unselfish concern for the welfare of others **altruist** *n* **altruistic** *adj* **altruistically** *adv*
aluminum, aluminium *n* light nonrusting silvery-white metal
alumnus [al-**lumm**-nuss] *n, pl* **-ni** [-nie] graduate of a college **alumna** [al-**lumm**-na] *n fem, pl* **-nae** [-nee]
always Ⓣ *adv* **1** at all times **2** for ever
Alwyn *n* **William**. 1905–85, British composer. His works include the oratorio *The Marriage of Heaven and Hell* (1936) and the *Suite of Scottish dances* (1946)
alyssum *n* garden plant with small yellow or white flowers
am *v* see **be**
AM amplitude modulation
a.m. before noon
amalgam *n* **1** blend or combination **2** alloy of mercury and another metal
amalgamate Ⓣ *v* combine or unite
amalgamation *n*
amanuensis [am-man-yew-**en**-siss] *n, pl* **-ses** [-seez] person who writes from dictation
amaranth *n* **1** imaginary flower that never fades **2** lily-like plant with red, green, or purple flowers
amaryllis *n* lily-like plant with large red or white flowers
amass Ⓣ *v* collect or accumulate
amateur Ⓣ *n* **1** person who performs a sport or activity as a pastime rather than as a profession **2** person unskilled in something ▹ *adj* **3** not professional
▸**amateurish** *adj* lacking skill
amateurishly *adv*
Amati *n* **1** a family of Italian violin makers, active in Cremona in the 16th and 17th centuries, esp. **Nicolò**, 1596–1684, who taught Guarneri and Stradivari **2** *pl* **Amatis** a violin or other stringed instrument made by any member of this family
amatory *adj* relating to romantic or sexual love
amaut, amowt *n* a hood on an Eskimo woman's parka for carrying a child
amaze Ⓣ *v* surprise greatly, astound
amazing *adj* **amazingly** *adv* **amazement** *n*

THESAURUS

alternating, every second, interchanging, rotating
alternative *n* **1 = choice**, other, option, selection, substitute, preference, recourse ▸ *adj* **2 = different**, other, second, another, alternate, substitute
alternatively *adv* **= or**, instead, otherwise, as an alternative, if not, on the other hand
although *conj* **= though**, while, albeit, notwithstanding, despite the fact that, even if, even though
altogether *adv* **1 = completely**, quite, fully, absolutely, totally, perfectly, thoroughly, wholly, utterly **2 = on the whole**, generally, collectively, all in all, all things considered, as a whole, in general **3 = in total**, all told, everything included, in all, in sum, taken together
altruistic *adj* **= selfless**, humanitarian, charitable, generous, philanthropic, unselfish, benevolent, public-spirited, self-sacrificing
always *adv* **= continually**, forever, invariably, perpetually, every time • *You're always moaning.*
amalgamate *v* **= combine**, ally, unite, merge, incorporate, blend, integrate, fuse, mingle
amalgamation *n* **= combination**, union, coalition, merger, compound, blend, mixture, fusion, joining
amass *v* **= collect**, gather, compile, assemble, accumulate, hoard, pile up
amateur *n* **= nonprofessional**, layman, dabbler, dilettante
amateurish *adj* **= unprofessional**, crude, amateur, clumsy, bungling, inexpert, unaccomplished
amaze *v* **= astonish**, surprise, shock, stun, stagger, astound • *He amazed us by his*

DICTIONARY

Amazon *n* **1** legendary female warrior **2** tall strong woman **Amazonian** *adj*
ambassador Ⓣ *n* senior diplomat who represents his or her country in another country **ambassadorial** *adj* **ambassadorship** *n*
amber *n* **1** yellowish translucent fossil resin ▷ *adj* **2** brownish-yellow
ambergris [**am**-ber-greece] *n* waxy substance secreted by the sperm whale, used in making perfumes
ambidextrous *adj* able to use both hands with equal ease
ambience *n* atmosphere of a place
ambient *adj* surrounding
ambiguous Ⓣ *adj* **1** having more than one possible meaning **2** uncertain **ambiguously** *adv* **ambiguity** *n*
ambit *n* limits or boundary
ambition Ⓣ *n* **1** desire for success **2** something so desired, goal **ambitious** *adj* **ambitiously** *adv* **ambitiousness** *n*
ambivalence [am-**biv**-a-lenss] *n* state of feeling two conflicting emotions at the same time **ambivalent** *adj* **ambivalently** *adv*
amble Ⓣ *v* **1** walk at a leisurely pace ▷ *n* **2** leisurely walk or pace
Ambler *n* **Eric.** 1909–98, English novelist. His thrillers include *The Mask of Dimitrios* (1939), *Journey into Fear* (1940), *A Kind of Anger* (1964), and *Doctor Frigo* (1974)
Ambrose *n* **Saint.** ?340–397 AD, bishop of Milan; built up the secular power of the early Christian Church; also wrote music and Latin hymns. Feast day: Dec 7 or April 4 **Ambrosian** *adj*
ambrosia *n* **1** *myth* food of the gods **2** anything delightful to taste or smell **ambrosial** *adj*
ambulance *n* motor vehicle designed to carry the sick or injured
ambuscade *n* ambush
ambush Ⓣ *n* **1** act of waiting in a concealed position to make an attack **2** attack from a concealed position ▷ *v* **3** attack from a concealed position
ameliorate [am-**meal**-lee-yor-rate] *v* make (something) better **amelioration** *n* **ameliorative** *adj*
amen *interj* so be it: used at the end of a prayer
amenable Ⓣ *adj* likely or willing to cooperate **amenability** *n*
amend Ⓣ *v* correct or improve (something) **amendment** *n*
amends Ⓣ *pl n* **make amends for** compensate for
Amenhotep III, Amenhotpe III *n* Greek name *Amenophis*. ?1411–?1375 BC, Egyptian pharaoh who expanded Egypt's influence by peaceful diplomacy and erected many famous buildings
amenity Ⓣ *n, pl* **-ties** useful or enjoyable facility
American *adj* **1** of the United States of America or the North, Central, or South American continents ▷ *n* **2** American person ▶ **Americanism** *n* expression or custom

THESAURUS

knowledge of sports history.
amazement *n* = **astonishment**, surprise, shock, wonder • *Much to my amazement, he arrived on time.*
amazing *adj* = **astonishing**, startling, astounding, staggering, stunning, surprising • *some of the most amazing stunts you're ever likely to see*
See also: **extraordinary, incredible, wonderful**
ambassador *n* = **representative**, minister, agent, deputy, diplomat, envoy, consul, legate
ambiguity *n* = **vagueness**, doubt, uncertainty, obscurity, equivocation, dubiousness
ambiguous *adj* = **unclear**, vague, obscure, indefinite, dubious, inconclusive, enigmatic, indeterminate, equivocal
ambition *n* **1** = **enterprise**, drive, desire, aspiration, longing, zeal, yearning, eagerness, striving **2** = **goal**, hope, aim, dream, wish, purpose, desire, intent, objective, aspiration
ambitious *adj* = **enterprising**, hopeful, intent, eager, avid, zealous, purposeful, aspiring, striving
ambivalent *adj* = **undecided**, uncertain, doubtful, contradictory, equivocal, in two minds, wavering
amble *v* = **stroll**, walk, wander, ramble, dawdle, meander, saunter, mosey (*informal*)
ambush *n* **1** = **trap**, lying in wait, waylaying ▶ *v* **2** = **trap**, attack, surprise, ensnare, bushwhack (*US*), waylay
amenable *adj* = **receptive**, open, susceptible, responsive, agreeable, able to be influenced, acquiescent, persuadable
amend *v* = **change**, improve, fix, repair, reform, correct, modify, revise, alter, remedy, mend
amendment *n* **1** = **change**, repair, reform, improvement, correction, remedy, revision, modification, alteration, emendation **2** = **alteration**, addition, attachment, clarification, addendum
amends *pl n* = **compensation**, satisfaction, redress, restitution, reparation, atonement, recompense
amenity *n* = **facility**, service, advantage, comfort, convenience

DICTIONARY

peculiar to people in the US
amethyst [**am**-myth-ist] *n* bluish-violet variety of quartz used as a gemstone
Amherst *n* **Jeffrey**, 1st Baron Amherst. 1717–97, British general who defeated the French in Canada (1758–60): governor general of British North America (1761–63)
amiable Ⓣ *adj* friendly, pleasant-natured **amiably** *adv* **amiability** *n*
amicable Ⓣ *adj* friendly **amicably** *adv* **amicability** *n*
amid, amidst Ⓣ *prep* in the middle of, among ▸**amidships** *adv* at or towards the middle of a ship
amino acid [am-**mean**-oh] *n* organic compound found in protein
Amis *n* **1** Sir **Kingsley**. 1922–95, British novelist and poet, noted for his novels *Lucky Jim* (1954), *Jake's Thing* (1978), *Stanley and the Women* (1984), *The Old Devils* (1986), and *The Folks that Live on the Hill* (1990) **2** his son, **Martin**. born 1949, British novelist. His works include *The Rachel Papers* (1974), *Money* (1984), *London Fields* (1989), *The Information* (1994), and *Yellow Dog* (2003)
amiss Ⓣ *adv* **1** wrongly, badly ▹ *adj* **2** wrong, faulty
▸**take something amiss** be offended by something
amity *n* friendship
ammeter *n* instrument for measuring electric current
ammonia *n* **1** pungent alkaline gas containing hydrogen and nitrogen **2** solution of this in water
ammonite *n* fossilized spiral shell of an extinct sea creature
ammunition Ⓣ *n* **1** any projectile that can be fired from or as a weapon **2** facts that can be used in an argument
amnesia *n* loss of memory **amnesiac** *adj, n*
amnesty Ⓣ *n, pl* **-ties** general pardon for offences against a government
amniocentesis *n, pl* **-ses** removal of amniotic fluid to test for possible abnormalities in a fetus
amniotic fluid *n* fluid surrounding a fetus in the womb
amoeba [am-**mee**-ba] *n, pl* **-bae, -bas** microscopic single-celled animal able to change its shape
amok Ⓣ *adv* **run amok** run about in a violent frenzy
among, amongst Ⓣ *prep* **1** in the midst of **2** in the group or number of **3** to each of: *divide it among yourselves*
amoral [eh-**mor**-ral] *adj* without moral standards **amorality** *n*
amorous Ⓣ *adj* feeling, showing, or relating to sexual love **amorously** *adv* **amorousness** *n*
amorphous *adj* without distinct shape
amortize *v* pay off (a debt) gradually by periodic transfers to a sinking fund **amortization** *n*
amount Ⓣ *n* **1** extent or quantity ▹ *v* **2** (foll. by *to*) be equal or add up to
amour *n* (illicit) love affair
amp *n* **1** ampere **2** *informal* amplifier
ampere [**am**-pair] *n* unit of electric current
Ampère *n* **André Mari**. 1775–1836, French physicist and mathematician, who made major discoveries in the fields of magnetism and electricity
ampersand *n* the character (&), meaning *and*
amphetamine [am-**fet**-am-in] *n* drug used as a stimulant
amphibian *n* **1** animal that lives on land but breeds in water **2** vehicle that can travel both on land and water

THESAURUS

amiable *adj* = **pleasant**, friendly, charming, engaging, lovable, likable *or* likeable, affable, agreeable, genial, congenial
amicable *adj* = **friendly**, civil, peaceful, cordial, courteous, sociable, amiable, harmonious, neighbourly
amid, amidst *prep* = **in the middle of**, among, amongst, in the midst of, in the thick of, surrounded by
amiss *adv* **1** = **wrongly**, mistakenly, improperly, incorrectly, inappropriately, erroneously, unsuitably ▸ *adj* **2** = **wrong**, faulty, incorrect, mistaken, awry, untoward ▹ **take (something) amiss** = **take as an insult**, take as offensive, take out of turn, take wrongly
ammunition *n* = **munitions**, shot, powder, armaments, explosives, rounds, shells
amnesty *n* = **general pardon**, immunity, reprieve, forgiveness, remission, absolution, dispensation
amok, amuck *adv* ▹ **run amok** = **go mad**, go berserk, go into a frenzy, go insane, lose control, turn violent, go wild
among, amongst *prep* **1** = **in the middle of**, amid, amidst, in the thick of, surrounded by • *The bike lay among piles of chains and pedals.* **2** = **to each of** • *The money will be divided among seven charities.* **3** = **in the group of**, in the class of, in the company of, in the number of, out of
amorous *adj* = **loving**, tender, passionate, erotic, impassioned, in love, lustful
amount *n* = **quantity**, volume, expanse • *I still do a certain amount of work for them.* *See also*: **figure, measure, price**
amount to *v* = **add up to**, become, mean, total, equal, come to, develop into

DICTIONARY

▸**amphibious** *adj* living or operating both on land and in water
amphitheatre *n* open oval or circular building with tiers of seats rising round an arena
amphora *n, pl* **-phorae, -phoras** two-handled ancient Greek or Roman jar
ample Ⓣ *adj* **1** more than sufficient **2** large **amply** *adv*
amplify Ⓣ *v* **-fying, -fied 1** increase the strength of (a current or sound signal) **2** explain in more detail **3** increase the size or effect of **amplification** *n*
▸**amplifier** *n* device used to amplify a current or sound signal
amplitude *n* **1** greatness of extent **2** breadth or scope
▸**amplitude modulation** method of sending information by varying the size of the peaks and troughs of the carrier wave to suit the input signal
ampoule *n* small sealed glass vessel containing liquid for injection
amputate Ⓣ *v* cut off (a limb etc.) for medical reasons **amputation** *n*
amuck Ⓣ *adv* same as **amok**
amulet *n* something carried or worn as a charm against evil
Amundsen *n* **Roald**. 1872–1928, Norwegian explorer and navigator, who was the first to successfully navigate the Northwest Passage (1903–06) and to reach the South Pole (1911)
amuse Ⓣ *v* **1** entertain or divert **2** cause to laugh or smile **amusing** *adj*
▸**amusement** *n* **1** state of being amused **2** something that amuses
an *adj* form of **a** used before vowels, and sometimes before *h*: *an hour*
anabolic steroid *n* synthetic steroid hormone used by athletes to stimulate muscle growth
anachronism [an-**nak**-kron-iz-zum] *n* person or thing placed in the wrong historical period or seeming to belong to another time **anachronistic** *adj*
anaconda *n* large S American snake which kills by constriction
anaemia *n* same as **anemia**
anaerobic *adj biol* not requiring oxygen
anaesthetic *n, adj* same as **anesthetic**
Anaglypta *n* ® thick embossed wallpaper, designed to be painted
anagram *n* word or phrase made by rearranging the letters of another word or phrase
anal [**ain**-al] *adj* of the anus
analgesic [an-nal-**jeez**-ik] *n, adj* (drug) relieving pain
▸**analgesia** *n* absence of pain
analogy Ⓣ [an-**nal**-a-jee] *n, pl* **-gies 1** similarity in some respects **2** comparison made to show such a similarity **analogical** *adj* **analogically** *adv*
▸**analogize** *v* use or show analogy
▸**analogue** [**an**-nal-log] *n* something that is analogous to something else ▹ *adj* displaying information by means of a dial
▸**analogous** [an-**nal**-log-uss] *adj* similar in some respects
analysis Ⓣ [an-**nal**-liss-iss] *n, pl* **-ses** [-seez] **1** separation of a whole into its components for study and interpretation **2** psychoanalysis **analytical** *or* **analytic** *adj* **analytically** *adv*
▸**analyse** [**an**-nal-lize] *v* **1** make an analysis of (something) **2** psychoanalyse

THESAURUS

ample *adj* = **plenty of**, enough, sufficient, abundant • *There is ample space for a good-sized kitchen.*
See also: **adequate, generous, handsome, plentiful, spacious**
amplify *v* **1** = **explain**, develop, expand, elaborate, enlarge, flesh out, go into detail **2** = **increase**, extend, expand, strengthen, widen, intensify, heighten, magnify, enlarge
amply *adv* = **fully**, completely, generously, richly, abundantly, profusely, copiously
amputate *v* = **cut off**, remove, separate, sever, curtail, lop, truncate
amuck see **amok**
amuse *v* = **entertain**, interest, please, cheer, charm, delight, tickle ▹ **amuse oneself** *See* **play**
amusement *n* **1** = **entertainment**, fun, cheer, pleasure, enjoyment, merriment, mirth **2** = **entertainment**, game, sport, joke, diversion, recreation, hobby, pastime
amusing *adj* = **funny**, enjoyable, humorous, witty, comical, interesting, droll, entertaining
analogous *adj* = **comparable**, like, similar, equivalent, related, parallel, alike, akin, corresponding, homologous, resembling OPPOSITE: different
analogy *n* = **similarity**, relation, comparison, parallel, correspondence, likeness, correlation, resemblance
analysis *n* = **examination**, test, investigation, inquiry, scrutiny, breakdown, dissection, perusal, sifting
analytic, analytical *adj* = **rational**, organized, investigative, logical, systematic, inquiring, inquisitive, problem-solving
analyze *v* **1** = **examine**, test, research, investigate, evaluate, work over **2** = **break down**, separate, resolve, divide, dissect, think through

DICTIONARY

▸**analyst** [**an**-nal-list] *n* person skilled in analysis
Ananda *n* 5th century BC, the first cousin, favourite disciple, and personal attendant of the Buddha
anarchy Ⓣ [**an**-ark-ee] *n* **1** lawlessness and disorder **2** lack of government in a state **anarchic** *adj*
▸**anarchism** *n* doctrine advocating the abolition of government
▸**anarchist** *n* person who believes in anarchism **anarchistic** *adj*
Anastasia *n* **Grand Duchess**. 1901–?18, daughter of Tsar Nicholas II, believed to have been executed by the Bolsheviks in 1918, although several women subsequently claimed to be her
anathema [an-**nath**-im-a] *n* detested person or thing
▸**anathematize** *v* curse (a person or thing)
anatomy Ⓣ *n, pl* **-mies 1** science of the structure of the body **2** physical structure **3** person's body: *a delicate part of his anatomy* **4** detailed analysis **anatomical** *adj* **anatomically** *adv*
▸**anatomist** *n* expert in anatomy
ancestor Ⓣ *n* **1** person from whom one is descended **2** forerunner **ancestral** *adj*
▸**ancestry** *n* lineage or descent
anchor *n* **1** heavy hooked device attached to a boat by a cable and dropped overboard to fasten the ship to the sea bottom ▷ *v* **2** fasten with or as if with an anchor
▸**anchorage** *n* place where boats can be anchored
▸**anchorman** *n* **1** broadcaster in a central studio who links up and presents items from outside camera units and other studios **2** last person to compete in a relay team
anchorite *n* religious recluse
anchovy [**an**-chov-ee] *n, pl* **-vies** small strong-tasting fish
ancien régime [**on**-syan ray-**zheem**] *n French* a former system, esp. the political and social system in France before the 1789 Revolution
ancient Ⓣ *adj* **1** dating from very long ago **2** very old ▷ *n* **3** person who lived long ago
ancillary Ⓣ *adj* **1** auxiliary, supplementary **2** subsidiary
and Ⓣ *conj* **1** in addition to **2** as a consequence **3** then, afterwards
andante [an-**dan**-tay] *adv music* moderately slowly
Andersen *n* **Hans Christian**. 1805–75, Danish author of fairy tales, including *The Ugly Duckling, The Tin Soldier,* and *The Snow Queen*
Anderson *n* **1 Carl David**. 1905–91, US physicist, who discovered the positron in cosmic rays (1932): Nobel prize for physics 1936 **2 Elizabeth Garrett**. 1836–1917, English physician and feminist: a campaigner for the admission of women to the professions
andiron *n* iron stand for supporting logs in a fireplace
André *n* **Brother**, original name *Alfred Bessette*. 1845–1937, Canadian monk to whom thousands of healings have been attributed by believers. Beatified in 1982
Andretti *n* **Mario**. born 1940, US racing driver: world champion (1978)
androgynous *adj* having both male and female characteristics
android *n* robot resembling a human
anecdote Ⓣ *n* short amusing account of an incident **anecdotal** *adj*
anemia, anaemia [an-**neem**-ee-a] *n* deficiency in the number of red blood cells
▸**anemic** *or* **anaemic** *adj* **1** having anemia **2** pale and sickly **3** lacking vitality
anemometer *n* instrument for recording wind speed
anemone [an-**nem**-on-ee] *n* plant with white, purple, or red flowers
aneroid barometer *n* device for measuring air pressure, consisting of a partially evacuated chamber in which variations in pressure cause a pointer on the lid to move
anesthetic, anaesthetic Ⓣ [an-niss-**thet**-ik] *n, adj* (substance) causing loss of sensation

THESAURUS

anarchic *adj* = **lawless**, chaotic, rebellious, disorganized, riotous, ungoverned
anarchist *n* = **revolutionary**, terrorist, rebel, insurgent, nihilist
anarchy *n* = **lawlessness**, disorder, riot, chaos, confusion, revolution, disorganization
anatomy *n* **1** = **examination**, study, investigation, inquiry, division, analysis, dissection **2** = **structure**, build, frame, framework, composition, make-up
ancestor *n* = **forefather**, parent, predecessor, forebear • *He could trace his ancestors back 700 years.*
ancestry *See* **origin, stock**
ancient *adj* = **old**, antique, old-fashioned, archaic, primordial, aged, primeval, timeworn
ancillary *adj* = **supplementary**, extra, additional, subsidiary, secondary, subordinate, auxiliary, supporting
and *conj* = **also**, plus, moreover, furthermore, along with, as well as, in addition to, including, together with
anecdote *n* = **story**, tale, sketch, yarn, reminiscence, short story, urban legend
anemic *adj* = **pale**, weak, feeble, sickly, pallid, wan, ashen, colourless
anesthetic *n* **1** = **painkiller**, narcotic,

DICTIONARY

▸**anesthesia** *or* **anaesthesia** [an-niss-**theez**-ee-a] *n* loss of sensation
▸**anesthetist** *or* **anaesthetist** [an-**neess**-thet-ist] *n* doctor trained to administer anesthetics **anesthetize** *or* **anaesthetize** *v*
aneurysm, aneurism [**an**-new-riz-zum] *n* permanent swelling of a blood vessel
anew Ⓣ *adv* **1** once more **2** in a different way
angel Ⓣ *n* **1** spiritual being believed to be an attendant or messenger of God **2** very kind person **angelic** *adj* **angelically** *adv*
angelica [an-**jell**-ik-a] *n* **1** aromatic plant **2** its candied stalks, used in cookery
Angelico *n* **Fra**, original name *Guido di Pietro;* monastic name *Fra Giovanni da Fiesole*. ?1400–55, Italian fresco painter and Dominican friar
Angelou *n* **Maya**, real name *Marguerite Johnson*. born 1928, African-American novelist, poet, and dramatist. Her works include the autobiographical novel *I Know Why the Caged Bird Sings* (1970) and its sequels
Angelus [**an**-jell-uss] *n* (in the Roman Catholic Church) **1** prayers recited in the morning, at midday, and in the evening **2** bell signalling the times of these prayers
anger Ⓣ *n* **1** fierce displeasure **2** extreme annoyance **3** rage, wrath ▹ *v* **4** make (someone) angry
▸ **angry** *adj* **1** full of anger **2** inflamed: *an angry wound* **angrily** *adv*
angina [an-**jine**-a] *n* heart disorder causing sudden severe chest pains (Also **angina pectoris**)
angle[1] Ⓣ *n* **1** space between or shape formed by two lines or surfaces that meet **2** divergence between these, measured in degrees **3** corner **4** point of view ▹ *v* **5** bend or place (something) at an angle
angle[2] Ⓣ *v* **1** fish with a hook and line **2** try to get by hinting **angler** *n* **angling** *n*
Anglican *n, adj* (member) of the Church of England **Anglicanism** *n*
anglicize *v* make English in outlook, form, etc.
▸**Anglicism** *n* expression or custom peculiar to the English
Anglo- *combining form* English or British: *Anglo-French*
▸**Anglo** *n* an English-speaking person
Anglophile *n* person who admires England or the English
Anglo-Saxon *n* **1** member of any of the W Germanic tribes which settled in England from the fifth century AD **2** language of the Anglo-Saxons ▹ *adj* **3** of the Anglo-Saxons or their language
angora *n* **1** variety of goat, cat, or rabbit with long silky hair **2** hair of the angora goat or rabbit **3** cloth made from this hair
Angostura Bitters *pl n* ® bitter tonic, used as a flavouring in alcoholic drinks
angst Ⓣ *n* feeling of anxiety
angstrom *n* unit of length used to measure wavelengths
Ångström *n* **Anders Jonas**. 1814–74, Swedish physicist, noted for his work on spectroscopy and solar physics
anguish Ⓣ *n* great mental or physical pain
anguished *adj*
angular *adj* **1** (of a person) lean and bony **2** having angles **3** measured by an angle
angularity *n*
anhydrous *adj chem* containing no water
aniline *n* colourless oily liquid obtained from coal tar and used for making dyes, plastics, and explosives
animadversion *n* criticism or censure
animal Ⓣ *n* **1** living creature having specialized sense organs and the power of voluntary motion, esp. one other than a human being **2** quadruped ▹ *adj* **3** of animals **4** sensual, physical
▸**animalcule** *n* microscopic animal
animate Ⓣ *v* **1** give life to **2** enliven

THESAURUS

sedative, opiate, analgesic, anodyne, soporific ▸ *adj* **2 = pain-killing**, sedative, analgesic, anodyne, deadening, dulling, numbing, soporific
anew *See* **again**
angel *n* **1 = divine messenger**, cherub, archangel, seraph **2** (*Informal*) **= dear**, beauty, treasure, jewel, gem, saint, darling, paragon
angelic *adj* **1 = pure**, beautiful, lovely, adorable, virtuous, entrancing, saintly **2 = heavenly**, celestial, ethereal, cherubic, seraphic
anger *n* **1 = rage**, outrage, wrath, fury • *We vented our anger at the umpire.* ▸ *v* **2 = enrage**, outrage, infuriate • *remarks that will anger his critics* OPPOSITE: calm
See also: **irritate, provoke, resentment**
angle[1] *n* **1 = intersection**, point, edge, corner, elbow, bend, crook, nook **2 = point of view**, side, position, approach, outlook, perspective, aspect, viewpoint, standpoint, slant
angle[2] *v* **= fish**, cast
angry *adj* **= furious**, cross, mad (*informal*), enraged • *She gets angry with me if I'm late.*
See also: **resentful**
angst *n* **= anxiety**, worry, apprehension, unease
anguish *n* **= suffering**, pain, woe, grief, distress, misery, sorrow, agony, torment, heartache
animal *n* **= creature**, beast • *attacked by wild animals* RELATED WORD *prefix*: zoo-
animate *v* **1 = enliven**, move, fire, inspire,

DICTIONARY

3 motivate **4** make a cartoon film of ▷ *adj* **5** having life **animated** *adj* **animator** *n*
▸ **animation** *n* **1** life, vigour **2** technique of making cartoon films
animism *n* belief that natural objects possess souls **animist** *n, adj* **animistic** *adj*
animosity Ⓣ *n, pl* **-ties** hostility, hatred
animus *n* hatred, animosity
anion [**an**-eye-on] *n* ion with negative charge
anise [**an**-niss] *n* plant with liquorice-flavoured seeds
aniseed *n* liquorice-flavoured seeds of the anise
ankle *n* joint between the foot and leg
▸ **anklet** *n* ornamental chain worn round the ankle
annals Ⓣ *pl n* yearly records of events **annalist** *n*
Annan *n* **Kofi**. born 1938, Ghanaian international civil servant; secretary-general of the United Nations (1997–2007): Nobel peace prize 2001 with the UN
Anne *n* **1 Princess**, the Princess Royal. born 1950, daughter of Elizabeth II of Great Britain and Northern Ireland; a noted horsewoman and president of the Save the Children Fund **2 Queen**. 1665–1714, queen of Great Britain and Ireland (1702–14), daughter of James II, and the last of the Stuart monarchs **3 Saint**. (in Christian tradition) the mother of the Virgin Mary. Feast day: July 26 or 25
anneal *v* toughen (metal or glass) by heating and slow cooling
annelid *n* worm with a segmented body, such as an earthworm
Anne of Bohemia *n* 1366–94, queen consort of Richard II of England
Anne of Cleves *n* 1515–57, the fourth wife of Henry VIII of England: their marriage (1540) was annulled after six months
Anne of Denmark *n* 1574–1619, wife (from 1589) of James I of England and VI of Scotland
annex Ⓣ *v* **1** seize (territory) **2** take (something) without permission **3** join or add (something) to something larger ▷ *n* **4** extension to a building **5** nearby building used as an extension **annexation** *n*
Annigoni *n* **Pietro**. 1910–88, Italian painter; noted esp. for his portraits of President Kennedy (1961) and Queen Elizabeth II (1955 and 1970)
annihilate Ⓣ *v* destroy utterly **annihilation** *n*
anniversary Ⓣ *n, pl* **-ries 1** date on which something occurred in a previous year **2** celebration of this
anno Domini *adv Latin* (indicating years numbered from the supposed year of the birth of Christ) in the year of our Lord
annotate *v* add notes to (a written work) **annotation** *n*
announce Ⓣ *v* **1** make known publicly **2** proclaim **announcement** *n*
▸ **announcer** *n* person who introduces radio or television programmes
annoy Ⓣ *v* irritate or displease **annoyance** *n*

THESAURUS

excite, stimulate, energize, invigorate, kindle ▸ *adj* **2** = **living**, live, alive, breathing, moving, alive and kicking
animated *adj* = **lively**, passionate, energetic, enthusiastic, excited, spirited, ebullient, vivacious, wired (*slang*)
animation *n* = **liveliness**, energy, spirit, passion, excitement, enthusiasm, zest, verve, ebullience, fervour, vivacity
animosity *n* = **hostility**, hatred, dislike, resentment, antagonism, malice, antipathy, ill will • *There is no animosity between these two players.*
See also: **hate**
annals *pl n* = **records**, history, archives, accounts, chronicles
annex *v* **1** = **seize**, acquire, appropriate, occupy, conquer, take over **2** = **join**, add, connect, attach, fasten, adjoin
annihilate *v* = **destroy**, eradicate, abolish, decimate, extinguish, obliterate, exterminate, wipe out
annihilation *See* **destruction**
anniversary *See* **festival**
announce *v* = **make known**, tell, reveal, advertise, proclaim • *He will annce tonight that he is resigning from office.*
See also: **declare**
announcement *n* = **statement**, report, broadcast, declaration, advertisement, bulletin • *There has been no formal anncement by either government.*
See also: **word**
announcer *n* = **anchor** *or* **anchorperson**, reporter, broadcaster, commentator, newscaster, newsreader, master of ceremonies
annoy *v* = **irritate**, bother, displease, plague, hassle (*informal*), vex, get on someone's nerves (*informal*), tee off (*slang*), piss off (*taboo slang*) • *Try making a note of the things that annoy you.*
See also: **pester, provoke**
annoyance *n* **1** = **irritation**, displeasure • *He made no secret of his annoyance.* **2** = **nuisance**, pain (*informal*), drag (*informal*), bore, pest, pain in the neck (*informal*) • *Snoring can be more than an annoyance.*
See also: **bother**
annoyed *See* **cross**
annoying *adj* = **irritating**, troublesome,

DICTIONARY

annual Ⓣ *adj* **1** happening once a year **2** lasting for a year ▷ *n* **3** plant that completes its life-cycle in a year **4** book published each year **annually** *adv*
annuity *n, pl* **-ties** fixed sum paid every year
annul Ⓣ *v* **-nulling, -nulled** make (something, esp. a marriage) invalid
annulment *n*
annular [**an**-new-lar] *adj* ring-shaped
Annunciation *n Christianity* angel Gabriel's announcement to the Virgin Mary of her conception of Christ
anode *n electricity* positive electrode in a battery, valve, etc.
▸ **anodize** *v* coat (metal) with a protective oxide film by electrolysis
anodyne *n* **1** something that relieves pain or distress ▷ *adj* **2** relieving pain or distress
anoint Ⓣ *v* smear with oil as a sign of consecration
anomaly Ⓣ [an-**nom**-a-lee] *n, pl* **-lies** something that deviates from the normal, irregularity **anomalous** *adj*
anon *adv obsolete* in a short time, soon
anon. anonymous
anonymous Ⓣ *adj* **1** by someone whose name is not known **2** having no known name **anonymously** *adv* **anonymity** *n*
anorak *n* waterproof hooded jacket
anorexia *n* psychological disorder characterized by fear of becoming fat and refusal to eat (Also **anorexia nervosa**)
anorexic *adj, n*
another Ⓣ *adj, pron* **1** one more **2** a different (one)
answer Ⓣ *v* **1** give an answer (to) **2** respond or react **3** be responsible to (a person) ▷ *n* **4** reply to a question, request, letter, etc. **5** solution to a problem **6** reaction or response
▸ **answerable** *adj* (foll. by *for* or *to*) responsible for or accountable to
▸ **answering machine** device for answering a telephone automatically and recording messages
ant *n* small insect living in highly organized colonies
▸ **anteater** *n* mammal which feeds on ants by means of a long sticky tongue
▸ **ant hill** mound built by ants around their nest
antacid *n* substance that counteracts acidity, esp. in the stomach
antagonist Ⓣ *n* opponent or adversary
antagonistic *adj*
▸ **antagonism** *n* open opposition or hostility
▸ **antagonize** *v* arouse hostility in, annoy
antalkali [ant-**alk**-a-lie] *n* substance that neutralizes alkalis
Antarctic *n* **1 the Antarctic** area around the South Pole ▷ *adj* **2** of this region
ante *n* **1** player's stake in poker ▷ *v* **-teing, -ted** *or* **-teed 2** place (one's stake) in poker
ante- *prefix* before in time or position: *antedate; antechamber*
antecedent *n* **1** thing coming before something else ▷ *adj* **2** preceding, prior
antedate *v* precede in time
antediluvian *adj* **1** of the time before the biblical Flood **2** old-fashioned
antelope *n* deerlike mammal with long legs and horns
antenatal *adj* during pregnancy, before birth
antenna *n* **1** *pl* **-nae** insect's feeler **2** *pl* **-nas** aerial
antepenultimate *adj* third last
anterior *adj* **1** to the front **2** earlier

THESAURUS

maddening, disturbing, exasperating
annual *adj* = **yearly**, yearlong, once a year
annually *adv* = **yearly**, by the year, once a year, per annum, per year
annul *v* = **invalidate**, cancel, retract, abolish, repeal, negate, nullify, declare null and void *or* render null and void
anoint *v* = **consecrate**, bless, hallow, sanctify
anomalous *adj* = **unusual**, odd, exceptional, abnormal, inconsistent, irregular, eccentric, peculiar, incongruous
anomaly *n* = **irregularity**, exception, oddity, abnormality, inconsistency, eccentricity, incongruity, peculiarity
anonymous *adj* = **unnamed**, unknown, unidentified, unsigned, nameless, incognito, unacknowledged, uncredited
another *See* **different**
answer *v* **1** = **reply**, respond, retort. OPPOSITE: ask ▷ **answer for** = **be responsible for**, be accountable for, be answerable for, be chargeable for, be liable for, be to blame for ▸ *n* **2** = **reply**, response, retort • *Without waiting for an answer, he left the room.* OPPOSITE: question
See also: **meet, reaction**
answerable *adj* (usually with *for* or *to*) = **responsible**, subject, accountable, liable, amenable, chargeable, to blame
antagonism *n* = **hostility**, opposition, conflict, rivalry, friction, discord, dissension, antipathy
antagonist *n* = **opponent**, rival, competitor, enemy, contender, foe, adversary
antagonistic *adj* = **hostile**, incompatible, conflicting, unfriendly, at odds, at variance, in dispute, opposed
antagonize *v* = **annoy**, anger, offend, irritate, hassle (*informal*), get on one's nerves (*informal*)

a

DICTIONARY

anteroom *n* small room leading into a larger one, often used as a waiting room
Antheil *n* **George**. 1900–59, US composer. His best known work is the controversial *Le Ballet Méchanique* (1924) for motor horns, bells, and airplane propellers
anthem Ⓣ *n* **1** song of loyalty, esp. to a country **2** piece of music for a choir, usu. set to words from the Bible
anther *n* part of a flower's stamen containing pollen
anthology Ⓣ *n, pl* **-gies** collection of poems or other literary pieces by various authors **anthologist** *n*
Anthony *n* **Saint**. ?251–?356 AD, Egyptian hermit, commonly regarded as the founder of Christian monasticism. Feast day: Jan 17
Anthony of Padua *n* **Saint**. 1195–1231, Franciscan friar, who preached in France and Italy. Feast day: June 13
anthracite *n* hard coal burning slowly with little smoke or flame but intense heat
anthrax *n* dangerous disease of cattle and sheep, communicable to humans
anthropoid *adj* **1** like a human ▷ *n* **2** ape, such as a chimpanzee, resembling a human
anthropology *n* study of human origins, institutions, and beliefs **anthropological** *adj* **anthropologist** *n*
anthropomorphic *adj* attributing human form or personality to a god, animal, or object **anthropomorphism** *n*
anti- *prefix* **1** against, opposed to: *anti-war* **2** opposite to: *anticlimax* **3** counteracting: *antifreeze*
anti-aircraft *adj* for defence against aircraft attack
antiballistic missile *n* missile designed to destroy a ballistic missile in flight
antibiotic *n* **1** chemical substance capable of destroying bacteria ▷ *adj* **2** of antibiotics
antibody *n, pl* **-bodies** protein produced in the blood, which destroys bacteria
Antichrist *n* **1** *New Testament* the antagonist of Christ **2** any enemy of Christ or Christianity
anticipate Ⓣ *v* **1** foresee and act in advance of **2** look forward to **3** expect **anticipation** *n* **anticipatory** *adj*
anticlimax Ⓣ *n* disappointing conclusion to a series of events
anticlockwise *adv, adj* in the opposite direction to the rotation of the hands of a clock
antics Ⓣ *pl n* absurd acts or postures
anticyclone *n* area of moving air of high pressure in which the winds rotate outwards
antidote Ⓣ *n* substance that counteracts a poison
antifreeze *n* liquid added to water to lower its freezing point, used in automobile radiators
antigen [**an**-ti-jen] *n* substance, usu. a toxin, causing the blood to produce antibodies
antihero *n, pl* **-roes** central character in a book, film, etc. who lacks the traditional heroic virtues
antihistamine *n* drug used to treat allergies
antimacassar *n* cloth put over a chair-back to prevent soiling
antimony [**an**-tim-mon-ee] *n* brittle silvery-white metallic element
antinuclear *adj* opposed to nuclear weapons or nuclear power
Antiochus IV *n* ?215–164 BC, Seleucid king of Syria (175–164), who attacked the Jews and provoked the revolt of the Maccabees
antipasto *n, pl* **-tos** appetizer in an Italian meal
antipathy Ⓣ [an-**tip**-a-thee] *n* dislike, hostility **antipathetic** *adj*
antiperspirant *n* substance used to reduce or prevent sweating
antiphon *n* hymn sung in alternate parts by two groups of singers **antiphonal** *adj*
antipodes [an-**tip**-pod-deez] *pl n* any two places diametrically opposite one another on the earth's surface **antipodean** *adj*
▶ **the Antipodes** Australia and New Zealand
antipyretic *adj* **1** reducing fever ▷ *n* **2** drug that reduces fever

THÉSAURUS

anthem *n* **1 = hymn**, chant, carol, psalm, canticle, chorale **2 = song of praise**, paean
anthology *n* **= collection**, selection, treasury, compilation, compendium, miscellany
anticipate *v* **= expect**, predict, await, foresee, foretell, hope for, look forward to, prepare for
anticipated *See* **likely**
anticipation *n* **= expectation**, expectancy, foresight, forethought, premonition, prescience, presentiment
anticlimax *n* **= disappointment**, letdown, bathos, comedown (*informal*)
antics *pl n* **= clowning**, mischief, escapades, horseplay, playfulness, pranks, tomfoolery, tricks
antidote *n* **= cure**, remedy, countermeasure
antipathy *n* **= hostility**, hatred, dislike, aversion, enmity, bad blood, ill will
antiquated *adj* **= obsolete**, antique, old-fashioned, archaic, dated, out-of-date, passé

DICTIONARY

antique Ⓣ *n* **1** object of an earlier period, valued for its beauty, workmanship, or age ▷ *adj* **2** made in an earlier period **3** old-fashioned
▸ **antiquarian** *adj* of or relating to antiquities or rare books
▸ **antiquary** *n* student or collector of antiques or ancient works of art
▸ **antiquated** *adj* out-of-date
▸ **antiquity** *n* **1** great age **2** ancient times **3** object dating from ancient times
antiracism *n* policy of challenging racism and promoting racial tolerance
antirrhinum *n* two-lipped flower of various colours
anti-Semitism *n* prejudice against Jews **anti-Semitic** *adj*
antiseptic Ⓣ *adj* **1** preventing infection by killing germs ▷ *n* **2** antiseptic substance
antisocial Ⓣ *adj* **1** avoiding the company of other people **2** (of behaviour) harmful to society
antistatic *adj* reducing the effects of static electricity
antithesis Ⓣ [an-**tith**-iss-iss] *n, pl* **-ses** [-seez] **1** exact opposite **2** placing together of contrasting ideas or words to produce an effect of balance **antithetical** *adj*
antitoxin *n* (serum containing) an antibody that acts against a toxin
antivirus *adj* protecting computers from viruses
antler *n* branching horn of male deer
Antonioni *n* **Michelangelo**. 1912–2007, Italian film director; his films include *L'Avventura* (1959), *La Notte* (1961), *Blow-Up* (1966), *Zabriskie Point* (1970), *Beyond the Clouds* (1995), and *Just To Be Together* (2002)
Antony *n* **Mark**, Latin name *Marcus Antonius*. ?83–30 BC, Roman general who served under Julius Caesar in the Gallic wars and became a member of the second triumvirate (43). He defeated Brutus and Cassius at Philippi (42) but having repudiated his wife for Cleopatra, queen of Egypt, he was defeated by his brother-in-law Octavian (Augustus) at Actium (31)
antonym *n* word that means the opposite of another
anus [ain-uss] *n* opening at the end of the alimentary canal, through which feces are discharged
anvil *n* heavy iron block on which a smith hammers metal into shape
anxiety Ⓣ *n, pl* **-ties** state of being anxious
anxious Ⓣ *adj* **1** worried and tense **2** intensely desiring **anxiously** *adv*
any *adj, pron* **1** one or some, no matter which ▷ *adv* **2** at all: *it isn't any worse*
▸ **anybody** *pron* anyone
▸ **anyhow** *adv* anyway
▸ **anyone** *pron* **1** any person **2** person of any importance
▸ **anything** *pron*
▸ **anyway** *adv* **1** at any rate, nevertheless **2** in any manner
▸ **anywhere** *adv* in, at, or to any place
Anzac *n* (in World War 1) a soldier serving with the Australian and New Zealand Army Corps
aorta [eh-**or**-ta] *n, pl* **-tas, -tae** main artery of the body, carrying oxygen-rich blood from the heart **aortic** *or* **aortal** *adj*
Aouita *n* **Saïd**. born 1960, Moroccan middle-distance runner: set new world records for the 1500 metres (1987–93), 2000 metres (1987–95), and 5000 metres (1987–94)
apace *adv lit* swiftly
apart Ⓣ *adv* **1** to or in pieces **2** to or at a distance **3** individual, distinct
apartheid *n* former official government policy of racial segregation in S Africa

THESAURUS

antique *n* **1 = period piece**, relic, bygone, heirloom ▸ *adj* **2 = vintage**, classic, antiquarian, olden **3 = old-fashioned**, outdated, obsolete, archaic
antiquity *n* **1 = old age**, age, ancientness, elderliness, oldness **2 = distant past**, ancient times, olden days, time immemorial
antiseptic *adj* **1 = hygienic**, clean, pure, sterile, sanitary, uncontaminated, germ-free ▸ *n* **2 = disinfectant**, purifier, germicide
antisocial *adj* **1 = unsociable**, reserved, unfriendly, alienated, misanthropic, retiring, uncommunicative, withdrawn **2 = disruptive**, hostile, disorderly, rebellious, belligerent, antagonistic, menacing, uncooperative
antithesis *n* **= opposite**, reverse, contrast, contrary, converse, inverse
anxiety *n* **= worry**, concern, fear, apprehension, nervousness, unease, misgiving • *our growing anxiety about their safety*
See also: **alarm, burden, care, strain, stress**
anxious *adj* **1 = worried**, troubled, nervous, concerned, fearful, uneasy, apprehensive, bothered • *He admitted he was still anxious about the situation.* **2 = eager**, intent, impatient, desirous, keen, yearning
See also: **tense**
any minute now *See* **soon**
apart *adv* **1 = to pieces**, asunder, in bits, in pieces, to bits **2 = separate**, away, alone, aside, isolated, by oneself, to one side ▷
apart from = except for, but, save, besides, aside from, excluding, not counting, other than

DICTIONARY

apartment Ⓣ *n* set of rooms for living in which are part of a larger building
apathy Ⓣ *n* lack of interest or enthusiasm **apathetic** *adj* **apathetically** *adv*
ape Ⓣ *n* **1** tailless monkey such as the chimpanzee or gorilla **2** stupid, clumsy, or ugly man ▷ *v* **3** imitate **apish** *adj*
Apelles *n* 4th century BC, Greek painter of mythological subjects, none of whose work survives, his fame resting on the testimony of Pliny and other writers
aperient [ap-**peer**-ee-ent] *adj* **1** mildly laxative ▷ *n* **2** mild laxative
aperitif [ap-per-rit-**teef**] *n* alcoholic drink taken before a meal
aperture *n* opening or hole
apex Ⓣ *n* highest point
APEX Advance Purchase Excursion: reduced fare for journeys booked a specified period in advance
aphasia *n* disorder of the central nervous system that affects the ability to speak and understand words
aphid [**eh**-fid], **aphis** [**eh**-fiss] *n* small insect which sucks the sap from plants
aphorism *n* short wise saying **aphoristic** *adj*
aphrodisiac [af-roh-**diz**-zee-ak] *adj* **1** arousing sexual desire ▷ *n* **2** aphrodisiac substance
apiary [**ape**-ee-yar-ee] *n, pl* **-ries** place where bees are kept
▸**apiarist** *n* beekeeper
▸**apiculture** *n* breeding and care of bees
apiece Ⓣ *adv* each: *they were given two apples apiece*
aplomb Ⓣ [ap-**plom**] *n* calm self-possession
apocalypse *n* **1** end of the world **2** event of great destruction **apocalyptic** *adj*
▸**the Apocalypse** book of Revelation, last book of the New Testament
Apocrypha [ap-**pok**-rif-fa] *pl n* **the Apocrypha** collective name for the 14 books of the Old Testament which are not accepted as part of the Hebrew scriptures
▸**apocryphal** *adj* (of a story) of questionable authenticity
apogee [**ap**-oh-jee] *n* **1** point of the moon's or a satellite's orbit farthest from the earth **2** highest point
apolitical *adj* politically neutral
Apollonius of Perga *n* ?261–?190 BC, Greek mathematician, remembered for his treatise on conic sections
Apollonius of Rhodes *n* 3rd century BC, Greek epic poet and head of the Library of Alexandria. His principal work is the four-volume *Argonautica*
apologia *n* formal written defence of a cause
apology Ⓣ *n, pl* **-gies** **1** expression of regret for wrongdoing **2** (foll. by *for*) poor example of **3** formal written defence of a cause
▸**apologetic** *adj* making an apology **apologetically** *adv*
▸**apologetics** *n* branch of theology concerned with the reasoned defence of Christianity
▸**apologist** *n* person who formally defends a cause
▸**apologize** *v* make an apology
apophthegm [**ap**-poth-em] *n* short wise saying
apoplexy *n med* stroke
▸**apoplectic** *adj* **1** of apoplexy **2** *informal* furious
apostasy [ap-**poss**-stass-ee] *n, pl* **-sies** abandonment of one's religious faith or other belief **apostate** [ap-**poss**-state] *n, adj*
a posteriori [**eh** poss-steer-ee-**or**-rye] *adj logic* involving reasoning from effect to cause
Apostle Ⓣ *n* **1** one of the twelve disciples chosen by Christ to preach the Gospel

THESAURUS

apartment *n* = **rooms**, flat, pad (*slang*), accommodation, lodging, penthouse, living quarters, bachelor pad (*slang*), bachelorette (*Canad*), bachelor apartment, studio apartment • *a two-bedroom apartment*
apathetic *adj* = **uninterested**, cool, indifferent, passive • *apathetic about politics* OPPOSITE: enthusiastic
apathy *n* = **lack of interest**, indifference, inertia, passivity, coolness, nonchalance, torpor, unconcern
ape *See* **copy, imitate**
apex *n* = **highest point**, point, top, summit, crown, peak, crest, culmination, pinnacle
apiece *adv* = **each**, respectively, separately, individually, for each, from each, to each
aplomb *n* = **self-possession**, confidence, poise, composure, self-confidence, calmness, level-headedness, sang-froid, self-assurance
apocryphal *adj* = **dubious**, legendary, questionable, doubtful, mythical, unsubstantiated, unauthenticated
apologetic *adj* = **regretful**, sorry, remorseful, contrite, penitent, rueful
apologize *v* = **say sorry**, ask forgiveness, beg someone's pardon, express regret • *I apologize for being late.*
apology *n* = **defence**, plea, excuse, confession, explanation, justification, acknowledgment ▷ **apology for** = **mockery of**, caricature of, excuse for, imitation of, travesty of
apostle *n* **1** = **evangelist**, herald, missionary, preacher, messenger **2** = **supporter**, champion, advocate, pioneer, proponent, propagandist

DICTIONARY

2 apostle ardent supporter of a cause or movement **apostolic** *adj*
apostrophe [ap-**poss**-trof-fee] *n* **1** punctuation mark (') showing the omission of a letter or letters in a word (eg *don't*) or forming the possessive (eg *Jill's coat*) **2** digression from a speech to address an imaginary or absent person or thing ▸**apostrophize** *v* address an apostrophe to
apothecary *n, pl* **-caries** *obsolete* pharmacist
apotheosis Ⓣ [ap-poth-ee-**oh**-siss] *n, pl* **-ses** [-seez] **1** elevation to the rank of a god **2** perfect example
appall Ⓣ *v* **-palling, -palled** dismay, terrify ▸**appalling** *adj* dreadful, terrible
apparatus Ⓣ *n* equipment for a particular purpose
apparel [ap-**par**-rel] *n old-fashioned* clothing
apparent Ⓣ *adj* **1** readily seen, obvious **2** seeming as opposed to real **apparently** *adv*
apparition Ⓣ *n* ghost or ghostlike figure
appeal Ⓣ *v* **1** make an earnest request **2** be attractive **3** request a review of a lower court's decision by a higher court ▹*n* **4** earnest request **5** attractiveness **6** request for a review of a lower court's decision by a higher court **appealing** *adj*
appear Ⓣ *v* **1** become visible or present **2** seem **3** be seen in public ▸**appearance** *n* **1** sudden arrival of someone or something **2** way a person or thing looks
appease Ⓣ *v* **1** pacify (a person) by yielding to his or her demands **2** satisfy or relieve (a feeling) **appeasement** *n*
Appel *n* **Karel**. 1921–2006, Dutch abstract expressionist painter
appellant *n* person who makes an appeal to a higher court
appellation *n* name, title
append *v* join on, add ▸**appendage** *n* thing joined on or added
appendicitis *n* inflammation of the appendix
appendix Ⓣ *n, pl* **-dixes, -dices 1** separate additional material at the end of a book **2** *anat* short closed tube attached to the large intestine
appertain *v* (foll. by *to*) **1** belong to **2** be connected with

THESAURUS

apotheosis *n* = **deification**, elevation, glorification, exaltation, idealization, idolization
appall *v* = **horrify**, shock, alarm, outrage, frighten, dismay, dishearten, unnerve, daunt
appalling *adj* = **horrifying**, horrible, shocking, awful, fearful, daunting, dreadful, frightful, alarming, terrifying
apparatus *n* **1** = **equipment**, device, tackle, gear, mechanism, appliance, machinery, contraption (*informal*), tools **2** = **organization**, system, network, structure, setup (*informal*), bureaucracy, hierarchy, chain of command
apparent *adj* **1** = **obvious**, visible, evident, distinct, marked, manifest, unmistakable, discernible **2** = **seeming**, superficial, outward, ostensible
apparently *adv* = **it appears that**, seemingly, ostensibly, it seems that, on the face of it, outwardly, superficially
apparition *n* = **ghost**, spirit, phantom, chimera, spectre, wraith
appeal *v* **1** = **plead**, request, pray, beg, implore, call upon, entreat • *The police appealed for witnesses to come forward.* **2** = **attract**, interest, please, fascinate • *The idea appealed to him.* ▹**appeal to** *See* **attract** ▸*n* **3** = **plea**, request, petition • *an appeal for peace* **4** = **attraction**, beauty, charm, allure, fascination
See also: **ask**
appealing *adj* = **attractive**, charming, desirable, engaging, alluring, winsome
appear *v* **1** = **come into view**, emerge, surface, crop up (*informal*), show up (*informal*), turn up • *A woman appeared at the far end of the street.* OPPOSITE: disappear **2** = **come into existence**, become available, be invented, come into being, come out • *small white flowers that appear in the spring* **3** = **perform**, play, act, play a part • *He is soon to appear in two more episodes.* **4** = **look**, **look like**, *or* **look as if**, seem, occur, strike one as
See also: **come**
appearance *n* **1** = **arrival**, debut, introduction, dawn, emergence, advent, coming • *the appearance of modern technology* **2** = **look**, image, bearing, looks • *I used to be so fussy about my appearance.* **3** = **impression**, front, image, illusion, guise, pretense, semblance, outward show
See also: **entrance, entry**
appease *v* **1** = **pacify**, quiet, calm, satisfy, soothe, placate, mollify, conciliate, de-stress **2** = **ease**, calm, relieve, alleviate, allay, soothe
appeasement *n* **1** = **pacification**, compromise, concession, accommodation, conciliation, mollification, placation **2** = **easing**, soothing, alleviation, lessening, relieving
appendage *n* = **attachment**, addition, supplement, accessory
appendix *n* = **supplement**, addition, adjunct, addendum, appendage, postscript

DICTIONARY

appetite Ⓣ *n* desire or inclination, esp. for food or drink
▸**appetizer** *n* **1** first course of a meal **2** thing eaten or drunk to increase the appetite
▸**appetizing** *adj* stimulating the appetite **appetizingly** *adv*
applaud Ⓣ *v* **1** show approval of by clapping one's hands **2** approve strongly
▸**applause** *n* approval shown by clapping one's hands
apple *n* round firm fleshy fruit that grows on trees
▸**apple-pie order** *informal* perfect order
▸**apple polisher** *informal* sycophant or toady
appliance Ⓣ *n* device with a specific function
appliqué [ap-**plee**-kay] *n* kind of decoration in which one material is cut out and attached to another
apply Ⓣ *v* **-plying, -plied 1** make a formal request **2** put to practical use **3** put onto a surface **4** be relevant or appropriate
▸**apply oneself** concentrate one's efforts
▸**applicable** *adj* relevant **applicably** *adv* **applicability** *n*
▸**applicant** *n* person who applies for something
▸**application** *n* **1** formal request **2** act of applying something to a particular use **3** concentrated effort **4** act of putting something onto a surface
▸**applied** *adj* (of a skill, science, etc.) put to practical use
appoint Ⓣ *v* **1** assign to a job or position **2** fix or decide: *appoint a time* **3** equip or furnish
▸**appointment** *n* **1** arrangement to meet a person **2** act of placing someone in a job **3** the job itself **appointments 4** fixtures or fittings
apportion Ⓣ *v* divide out in shares **apportionment** *n*
apposite Ⓣ *adj* suitable, apt **appositeness** *n*
▸**apposition** *n* grammatical construction in which two nouns or phrases referring to the same thing are placed one after another without a conjunction: *my son the doctor*
appraise Ⓣ *v* estimate the value or quality of **appraisal** *n*

THESAURUS

appetite *n* = **desire**, demand, taste, passion, stomach, hunger, relish, longing, craving, liking, yearning
appetizing *adj* = **delicious**, tasty, appealing, tempting, palatable, yummy (*informal*), succulent, inviting, mouthwatering
applaud *v* = **clap**, approve, encourage, praise, cheer, acclaim, compliment, commend, extol
applause *n* = **ovation**, hand, approval, praise, accolade, big hand, cheers, clapping
appliance *n* = **device**, tool, machine, implement, gadget, instrument, mechanism, apparatus
applicable *adj* = **appropriate**, useful, relevant, suitable, fitting, apt, pertinent
applicant *n* = **candidate**, claimant, inquirer
application *n* **1** = **request**, claim, appeal, inquiry, petition, requisition **2** = **effort**, industry, commitment, dedication, diligence, perseverance, hard work
applied *See* **practical**
apply *v* **1** = **request**, claim, appeal, petition, inquire, put in, requisition **2** = **use**, practise, exercise, implement, employ, exert, utilize, bring to bear, carry out **3** = **put on**, place, paint, smear, cover with, lay on, spread on **4** = **be relevant**, relate, refer, fit, pertain, be applicable, be appropriate, bear upon, be fitting ▹ **apply oneself** = **try**, concentrate, persevere, be diligent, buckle down (*informal*), commit oneself, dedicate oneself, devote oneself, work hard
appoint *v* **1** = **assign**, name, choose, commission, elect, select, nominate, delegate **2** = **decide**, set, choose, fix, establish, designate, arrange, assign, allot **3** = **equip**, provide, supply, furnish, fit out
appointed *adj* **1** = **assigned**, selected, elected, chosen, delegated, named, nominated **2** = **decided**, set, established, assigned, allotted, arranged, chosen, designated, fixed **3** = **equipped**, fitted out, furnished, provided, supplied
appointment *n* **1** = **meeting**, interview, date, rendezvous • *She has an appointment with her accountant.* **2** = **selection**, election, nomination, naming • *his appointment as manager* **3** = **job**, post, place, position, assignment • *He applied for a diplomatic appointment.* ▹ **appointments** = **fittings**, gear, outfit, paraphernalia, fixtures, furnishings, trappings
apportion *v* = **divide**, share, distribute, assign, allocate, dispense, allot, dole out, ration out
apportionment *n* = **division**, distribution, assignment, allocation, allotment, dispensing, doling out, rationing out, sharing
apposite *adj* = **appropriate**, relevant, suitable, fitting, applicable, apt, pertinent, to the point
appraisal *n* = **assessment**, estimate, opinion, judgment, evaluation, estimation
appraise *v* = **assess**, rate, review, judge, value, estimate, evaluate, gauge

DICTIONARY

appreciate Ⓣ *v* **1** value highly **2** be aware of and understand **3** be grateful for **4** rise in value
▸ **appreciable** *adj* enough to be noticed **appreciably** *adv*
▸ **appreciation** *n* act of appreciating
▸ **appreciative** *adj* feeling or showing appreciation
apprehend Ⓣ *v* **1** seize, arrest **2** understand
▸ **apprehension** *n* **1** dread, anxiety **2** arrest **3** understanding
▸ **apprehensive** *adj* fearful or anxious
apprentice Ⓣ *n* **1** someone working for a skilled person for a fixed period in order to learn his or her trade ▷ *v* **2** take or place (someone) as an apprentice **apprenticeship** *n*
apprise *v* make aware (of)
appro *n* **on appro** *informal* on approval
approach Ⓣ *v* **1** come near or nearer (to) **2** make a proposal or suggestion to **3** begin to deal with (a matter) ▷ *n* **4** approaching or means of approaching **5** approximation **approachable** *adj* **approachability** *n*
approbation *n* approval
appropriate Ⓣ *adj* **1** suitable, fitting ▷ *v* **2** take for oneself **3** put aside for a particular purpose **appropriately** *adv* **appropriateness** *n* **appropriation** *n*
approve Ⓣ *v* **1** consider good or right **2** authorize, agree to
▸ **approval** *n* **1** favourable opinion **2** consent
▸ **on approval** (of goods) with an option to be returned without payment if unsatisfactory

THESAURUS

appreciable *adj* = **significant**, substantial, obvious, considerable, evident, marked, pronounced, definite, noticeable, discernible
appreciate *v* **1** = **value**, respect, treasure, admire, prize, rate highly • *I appreciate fine food.* OPPOSITE: scorn **2** = **understand**, recognize, realize, perceive, be aware of • *I didn't appreciate the seriousness of it at the time.* **3** = **be grateful for**, be appreciative, be indebted, be obliged, be thankful for, give thanks for **4** = **increase**, rise, grow, gain, improve, enhance
See also: **comprehend, enjoy, grasp, like, love, see, take in**
appreciation *n* **1** = **gratitude**, obligation, acknowledgment, indebtedness, gratefulness, thankfulness, thanks **2** = **awareness**, understanding, recognition, perception, sympathy, sensitivity, admiration, realization, enjoyment, comprehension **3** = **increase**, rise, gain, growth, improvement, enhancement
appreciative *adj* **1** = **grateful**, thankful, indebted, beholden, obliged **2** = **aware**, sensitive, understanding, enthusiastic, sympathetic, respectful, responsive, admiring
apprehend *v* **1** = **arrest**, catch, capture, seize, take prisoner **2** = **understand**, recognize, realize, perceive, conceive, grasp, comprehend, get the picture
apprehension *n* **1** = **anxiety**, concern, fear, worry, alarm, suspicion, dread, trepidation, foreboding **2** = **arrest**, capture, seizure, taking, catching **3** = **awareness**, understanding, perception, grasp, comprehension
apprehensive *adj* = **anxious**, nervous, concerned, worried, uneasy, foreboding, wired (*slang*)
apprentice *n* = **trainee**, student, pupil, novice, beginner, learner, probationer
approach *v* **1** = **move towards**, reach, near, come close, come near, draw near **2** = **make a proposal to**, appeal to, apply to, make overtures to, sound out **3** = **set about**, undertake, commence, begin work on, embark on, enter upon, make a start ▸ *n* **4** = **coming**, advance, arrival, drawing near, nearing **5** (*often pl*) = **proposal**, offer, appeal, advance, application, invitation, proposition, overture **6** = **access**, way, road, passage, entrance, avenue **7** = **way**, style, method, technique, manner, means **8** = **likeness**, semblance, approximation
approachable *adj* **1** = **friendly**, open, cordial, affable, sociable, congenial **2** = **accessible**, attainable, reachable
approaching *See* **future, near**
appropriate *adj* **1** = **suitable**, correct, proper, fitting, apt • *Jeans are not appropriate clothing for some jobs.* OPPOSITE: inappropriate ▸ *v* **2** = **seize**, confiscate, commandeer, usurp, impound, take possession of **3** = **steal**, pocket, misappropriate, pilfer, embezzle, filch **4** = **set aside**, devote, assign, allocate, earmark, allot, apportion
See also: **relevant, right**
approval *n* **1** = **consent**, agreement, sanction, mandate, permission, blessing, endorsement, authorization, ratification, assent, green light (*informal*), imprimatur, endorsation (*Canad*) • *The plan will require approval from those in charge.* **2** = **favour**, praise, admiration, esteem, respect • *He wanted to gain his parents' approval.* OPPOSITE: disapproval
approve *v* **1** = **favour**, respect, praise, admire, think highly of • *Not everyone approves of his idea.* OPPOSITE: disapprove **2** = **consent to**, endorse, sanction, permit, authorize • *The*

DICTIONARY

approx. approximate(ly)
approximate Ⓣ *adj* **1** almost but not quite exact ▷ *v* **2** come close to **3** be almost the same as **approximately** *adv* **approximation** *n*
appurtenance *n* minor or additional feature
Apr. April
après-ski [ap-ray-**skee**] *n* social activities after a day's skiing
apricot *n* **1** yellowish-orange juicy fruit like a small peach. ▷ *adj* **2** yellowish-orange
April *n* fourth month of the year
▸ **April fool** victim of a practical joke played on April 1 (**April Fools' Day**)
a priori [**eh** pry-**or**-rye] *adj* involving reasoning from cause to effect
apron Ⓣ *n* **1** garment worn over the front of the body to protect the clothes **2** part of a stage in front of the curtain **3** area at an airport or hangar for manoeuvring and loading aircraft
apropos [ap-prop-**poh**] *adj, adv* appropriate(ly)
▸ **apropos of** with regard to
apse *n* arched or domed recess, esp. in a church
apt Ⓣ *adj* **1** having a specified tendency **2** suitable **3** quick to learn **aptly** *adv* **aptness** *n*
▸ **aptitude** *n* natural ability
APT Advanced Passenger Train
AQ al-Qaeda
aqualung *n* mouthpiece attached to air cylinders, worn for underwater swimming
aquamarine *n* **1** greenish-blue gemstone ▷ *adj* **2** greenish-blue
aquaplane *n* **1** board on which a person stands to be towed by a motorboat ▷ *v* **2** ride on an aquaplane **3** (of a motor vehicle) skim uncontrollably on a thin film of water
aquarium *n, pl* **aquariums, aquaria** **1** tank in which fish and other underwater creatures are kept **2** building containing such tanks
aquatic *adj* **1** living in or near water **2** done in or on water
▸ **aquatics** *pl n* water sports
aquatint *n* print like a watercolour, produced by etching copper
aqua vitae [**ak**-wa **vee**-tie] *n obsolete* brandy
aqueduct *n* structure carrying water across a valley or river
aqueous *adj* of, like, or containing water
aquiline *adj* **1** of or like an eagle **2** (of a nose) curved like an eagle's beak
Aquinas *n* **Saint Thomas**. 1225–74, Italian theologian, scholastic philosopher, and Dominican friar, whose works include *Summa contra Gentiles* (1259–64) and *Summa Theologiae* (1267–73), the first attempt at a comprehensive theological system. Feast day: Jan 28
Ar *chem* argon
Arab *n* **1** member of a Semitic people originally from Arabia ▷ *adj* **2** of the Arabs
▸ **Arabian** *adj* of Arabia or the Arabs
▸ **Arabic** *n* **1** language of the Arabs ▷ *adj* **2** of Arabic, Arabs, or Arabia
arabesque [ar-ab-**besk**] *n* **1** ballet position in which one leg is raised behind and the arms are extended **2** elaborate ornamental design
arable Ⓣ *adj* suitable for growing crops on
arachnid [ar-**rak**-nid] *n* eight-legged invertebrate, such as a spider, scorpion, tick, or mite
Arafat *n* **Yasser**. 1929–2004, Palestinian leader; cofounder of Al Fatah (1956), leader from 1968 of the Palestine Liberation Organization, president of the Palestinian National Authority from 1996: signed a peace agreement with Israel (1993); Nobel peace prize 1994 with Shimon Peres and Yitzhak Rabin
Aran *adj* (of sweaters etc.) knitted in a complicated pattern traditional to the Aran Islands, usu. with natural unbleached wool
Arany *n* **János**. 1817–82, Hungarian epic

THESAURUS

court approved the compensation plan. OPPOSITE: veto
See also: **allow**
approved *See* **formal**
approving *See* **favourable**
approximate *adj* **1 = rough**, estimated, loose, inexact • *We believe that an approximate figure of 20 per cent is more accurate.* OPPOSITE: exact **2 = close**, near ▸ *v* **3 = come close**, reach, approach, touch, resemble, border on, come near, verge on
See also: **broad**
approximately *adv* **= almost**, about, around, nearly, roughly, circa (of a date), close to, in the region of, just about, more or less
approximation *n* **= guess**, estimate, estimation, conjecture, guesswork, rough calculation, rough idea
apron *n* **= pinafore**
apt *adj* **1 = inclined**, likely, ready, prone, liable, given, disposed, of a mind **2 = appropriate**, relevant, suitable, fitting, pertinent, to the point **3 = gifted**, quick, sharp, smart, talented, clever
aptitude *n* **1 = tendency**, inclination, leaning, propensity, predilection, proclivity **2 = gift**, ability, intelligence, talent, capability, faculty, proficiency
arable *adj* **= productive**, fertile, fruitful, farmable

DICTIONARY

poet, ballad writer, and scholar
arbiter Ⓣ *n* **1** person empowered to judge in a dispute **2** person with influential opinions about something
▸**arbitrary** *adj* based on personal choice or chance, rather than reason **arbitrarily** *adv*
▸**arbitrate** *v* settle (a dispute) by arbitration
▸**arbitration** *n* hearing and settling of a dispute by an impartial referee chosen by both sides **arbitrator** *n*
arboreal [ahr-**bore**-ee-al] *adj* of or living in trees
arboretum [ahr-bore-**ee**-tum] *n, pl* **-ta** place where rare trees or shrubs are cultivated
arboriculture *n* cultivation of trees or shrubs
arbour *n* glade sheltered by trees
Arbus *n* **Diane**, original name *Diane Nemerov*. 1923–71, US photographer, noted esp. for her portraits of vagrants, dwarfs, transvestites, etc.
arc Ⓣ *n* **1** part of a circle or other curve **2** luminous discharge of electricity across a small gap between two electrodes ▹*v* **3** form an arc
arcade Ⓣ *n* **1** row of arches on pillars **2** covered passageway, usu. lined with shops **3** set of arches
arcane Ⓣ *adj* mysterious and secret
arch[1] Ⓣ *n* **1** curved structure supporting a bridge or roof **2** something curved **3** curved lower part of the foot ▹*v* **4** (cause to) form an arch
▸**archway** *n* passageway under an arch
arch[2] Ⓣ *adj* **1** superior, knowing **2** coyly playful **archly** *adv* **archness** *n*
arch- *combining form* chief, principal: *archenemy*
archaeology, archeology *n* study of ancient cultures from their physical remains **archaeological** *or* **archeological** *adj* **archaeologist** *or* **archeologist** *n*
archaic Ⓣ [ark-**kay**-ik] *adj* **1** ancient **2** out-of-date **archaically** *adv*
▸**archaism** [**ark**-kay-iz-zum] *n* archaic word or phrase **archaistic** *adj*
archangel [**ark**-ain-jell] *n* chief angel
archbishop *n* chief bishop
archdeacon *n* priest ranking just below a bishop **archdeaconry** *n*
archdiocese *n* diocese of an archbishop
archduke *n* duke of specially high rank **archduchess** *n fem*
▸**archduchy** *n* territory of an archduke or archduchess
archery *n* art or sport of shooting with a bow and arrow **archer** *n*
archetype Ⓣ [**ark**-i-type] *n* **1** original model **2** perfect specimen **archetypal** *adj*
archiepiscopal *adj* of an archbishop
Archimedes *n* ?287–212 BC, Greek mathematician and physicist of Syracuse, noted for his work in geometry, hydrostatics, and mechanics **Archimedean** *adj*
archipelago [ark-ee-**pel**-a-go] *n, pl* **-gos** **1** group of islands **2** sea full of small islands **archipelagic** *adj*
architect Ⓣ *n* person qualified to design and supervise the construction of buildings
▸**architecture** *n* **1** style of building **2** designing and construction of buildings **architectural** *adj*
architrave *n archit* **1** beam that rests on columns **2** moulding round a doorway or window

THESAURUS

arbiter *n* **1** = **judge**, referee, arbitrator, umpire, adjudicator **2** = **authority**, expert, governor, master, dictator, controller, ruler, pundit, lord
arbitrarily *See* **at random**
arbitrary *adj* = **random**, chance, personal, inconsistent, erratic, subjective, whimsical, capricious
arbitrate *v* = **settle**, judge, decide, determine, referee, mediate, umpire, adjudicate, pass judgment
arbitration *n* = **settlement**, decision, judgment, determination, adjudication
arbitrator *n* = **judge**, referee, umpire, adjudicator, arbiter
arc *n* = **curve**, bow, bend, arch, crescent, half-moon
arcade *n* = **gallery**, cloister, colonnade, portico
arcane *adj* = **mysterious**, secret, hidden, occult, esoteric, recondite
arch[1] *n* **1** = **curve**, span, vault, dome, archway **2** = **curve**, bow, bend, arc, hump, semicircle ▸*v* **3** = **curve**, bridge, bow, span, bend, arc
arch[2] *adj* = **playful**, mischievous, sly, saucy, frolicsome, pert, roguish, waggish
archaic *adj* **1** = **old**, ancient, antique, primitive, bygone, olden (*archaic*) **2** = **old-fashioned**, obsolete, antiquated, outmoded, behind the times, out of date, passé
archetypal *adj* **1** = **typical**, standard, model, classic, ideal **2** = **original**, prototypic *or* prototypical
archetype *n* **1** = **standard**, model, pattern, paradigm, prime example **2** = **original**, prototype
architect *n* = **designer**, planner, master builder
architecture *n* **1** = **design**, building, construction, planning **2** = **structure**,

a

DICTIONARY

archive ⓣ [**ark**-ive] *n* **1** *often pl* collection of records or documents **2** place where these are kept **archival** *adj*
▸**archivist** [**ark**-iv-ist] *n* person in charge of archives
Arcimboldo *n* **Giuseppe**. 1527–93, Italian painter, best remembered for painting grotesque figures composed of fruit, vegetables, and meat
Arctic ⓣ *n* **1** **the Arctic** area around the North Pole ▷ *adj* **2** of this region **3** **arctic** *informal* very cold
▸**arctic hare** large hare with white fur in winter
▸**arctic willow** low-growing shrub of Canadian tundra
ardent ⓣ *adj* **1** passionate **2** eager, zealous **ardently** *adv* **ardency** *n*
▸**ardour** *n* **1** passion **2** enthusiasm, zeal
arduous ⓣ *adj* hard to accomplish, strenuous **arduously** *adv* **arduousness** *n*
are[1] *v* see **be**
are[2] *n* unit of measure, 100 square metres
area ⓣ *n* **1** part or region **2** size of a two-dimensional surface **3** subject field **4** small sunken yard giving access to a basement
arena ⓣ *n* **1** seated enclosure for sports events **2** area of a Roman amphitheatre where gladiators fought **3** sphere of intense activity
Arendt *n* **Hannah**. 1906–75, US political philosopher, born in Germany. Her publications include *The Origins of Totalitarianism* (1951) and *Eichmann in Jerusalem* (1961)
aren't are not
areola *n*, *pl* **-lae**, **-las** small circular area, such as the coloured ring around the human nipple
argon *n* inert gas found in the air
argot [**ahr**-go] *n* slang or jargon
argue ⓣ *v* **-guing**, **-gued** **1** try to prove by giving reasons **2** debate **3** quarrel, dispute **arguable** *adj* **arguably** *adv*
▸**argument** *n* **1** point presented for or against something **2** discussion **3** quarrel
▸**argumentation** *n* process of reasoning methodically
▸**argumentative** *adj* given to arguing
aria [**ah**-ree-a] *n* elaborate song for solo voice, esp. one from an opera
Arias Sánchez *n* **Oscar**. born 1940, Costa Rican statesman; president (1986–90); Nobel peace prize 1987
arid ⓣ *adj* **1** parched, dry **2** uninteresting **aridity** *n*
aright *adv* rightly
arise ⓣ *v* **arising**, **arose**, **arisen** **1** come about **2** come into notice **3** get up
Aristarchus of Samos *n* 3rd century

THESAURUS

design, construction, style, framework, make-up
archive *n* = **record office**, museum, registry, repository ▷ **archives** = **records**, annals, chronicles, documents, papers, rolls
arctic *adj* (*Informal*) = **freezing**, cold, icy, frigid, chilly, glacial, frozen
Arctic *adj* = **polar**, far-northern, hyperborean
ardent *adj* **1** = **enthusiastic**, intense, keen, passionate, avid, devoted, fervent • *an ardent supporter of animal rights* **2** = **passionate**, intense, impassioned, hot-blooded, amorous, lusty
See also: **eager**
ardour *n* **1** = **passion**, spirit, intensity, warmth, fervour, vehemence **2** = **enthusiasm**, zeal, eagerness, avidity, keenness
arduous *adj* = **difficult**, rigorous, strenuous, onerous, gruelling, exhausting, fatiguing, laborious, punishing, taxing, tiring
area *n* **1** = **region**, zone, neighbourhood, district, locality • *a built-up area of the city* **2** = **size**, range, extent, footprint, expanse • *The islands cover a total area of 625 square kilometres.* **3** = **part**, sector, section, portion **4** = **field**, province, department, territory, domain, realm, sphere
See also: **place, stretch**
arena *n* **1** = **ring**, field, ground, stadium, bowl, enclosure, amphitheatre **2** = **sphere**, province, area, field, sector, territory, domain, realm
argue *v* **1** = **quarrel**, fight, disagree, feud, squabble, wrangle, bicker, fall out (*informal*) • *They argued over the cost of the taxi fare.* **2** = **claim**, reason, debate, maintain, assert • *She argued that her client had been wrongly accused.*
argument *n* **1** = **quarrel**, fight, dispute, row, clash, feud, squabble • *She got into an argument with the referee.* **2** = **reasoning**, case, logic, grounds • *There's a strong argument for lowering the price.* **3** = **discussion**, claim, debate, dispute, plea, assertion, questioning, remonstration
See also: **defence, disagreement**
argumentative *adj* = **quarrelsome**, contrary, contentious, combative, belligerent, opinionated, disputatious, litigious
arid *adj* **1** = **dry**, desert, torrid, sterile, barren, parched, waterless **2** = **boring**, dry, dull, dreary, tedious, tiresome, uninspired, uninteresting
arise *v* **1** = **happen**, start, begin, follow, result, occur, emerge, stem, ensue **2** = **get up**, rise, get to one's feet, go up,

DICTIONARY

BC, Greek astronomer who anticipated Copernicus in advancing the theory that the earth revolves around the sun
aristocracy ⓣ *n, pl* **-cies 1** highest social class **2** government by this class
▸**aristocrat** *n* member of the aristocracy
aristocratic *adj* **aristocratically** *adv*
Aristotle *n* 384–322 BC, Greek philosopher; pupil of Plato, tutor of Alexander the Great, and founder of the Peripatetic school at Athens; author of works on logic, ethics, politics, poetics, rhetoric, biology, zoology, and metaphysics. His works influenced Muslim philosophy and science and medieval scholastic philosophy
arithmetic *n* **1** calculation by or of numbers ▷ *adj* **2** of arithmetic **arithmetical** *adj* **arithmetically** *adv* **arithmetician** *n*
ark *n* **1** *Bible* boat built by Noah, which survived the Flood **2 Ark** *Judaism* chest containing the writings of Jewish Law
arm[1] ⓣ *n* **1** upper limb from the shoulder to the wrist **2** sleeve of a garment **3** side of a chair
▸**armful** *n* as much as an arm can hold
▸**armchair** *n* upholstered chair with side supports for the arms
▸**armhole** *n* opening in a garment through which the arm passes
▸**armpit** *n* hollow under the arm at the shoulder
arm[2] ⓣ *v* **1** supply with weapons **2** prepare (a bomb etc.) for use
▸**arms** *pl n* **1** weapons **2** military exploits **3** heraldic emblem
▸**armament** *n* **1** military weapons **2** preparation for war
armada ⓣ *n* large number of warships
armadillo *n, pl* **-los** small S American mammal covered in strong bony plates
Armageddon *n* **1** *Bible* final battle between good and evil at the end of the world **2** catastrophic conflict
armature *n* revolving structure in an electric motor or generator, wound with coils carrying the current
armistice ⓣ [**arm**-miss-stiss] *n* suspension of fighting
armour, armor ⓣ *n* **1** metal clothing formerly worn to protect the body in battle **2** metal plating of tanks, warships, etc.
▸**armourer** *or* **armorer** *n* maker, repairer, or keeper of arms or armour
▸**armoury** *or* **armory** *n* place where weapons are stored
▸**armorial** *adj* relating to heraldry
Armstrong *n* **1 Lance**. born 1971, US cyclist, winner of 7 Tour de France titles, 1999–2005 **2** (**Daniel**) **Louis**, known as *Satchmo*. 1900–71, US jazz trumpeter, bandleader, and singer **3 Neil** (**Alden**). born 1930, US astronaut; commanded Apollo 11 on the first manned lunar landing during which he became the first man to set foot on the moon on July 20, 1969
army ⓣ *n, pl* **-mies 1** military force that fights on land **2** great number
Arne *n* **Thomas** (**Augustine**). 1710–78, English composer, noted for his setting of Shakespearean songs and for his song *Rule Britannia*
Arnold *n* **1** Sir **Malcolm**. 1921–2006, English composer, esp. of orchestral works in a traditional idiom **2 Matthew**. 1822–88, English poet, essayist, and literary critic, noted particularly for his poems *Sohrab and Rustum* (1853) and *Dover Beach* (1867), and for his *Essays in Criticism* (1865) and *Culture and Anarchy* (1869)
aroma ⓣ *n* pleasant smell **aromatic** *adj*
aromatherapy *n* massage with fragrant oils to relieve tension

THESAURUS

stand up, wake up
aristocracy *n* = **upper class**, elite, nobility, gentry, patricians, peerage, ruling class
aristocrat *n* = **noble**, lady, peer, lord, grandee, patrician, peeress
aristocratic *adj* = **upper-class**, genteel • *He loves talking about his aristocratic family.*
arm[1] *n* = **upper limb**, limb, appendage
arm[2] *v* (Especially with weapons) = **equip**, provide, supply, array, furnish, accoutre, deck out, issue with
armada *n* = **fleet**, navy, squadron, flotilla
armaments *pl n* = **weapons**, ammunition, ordnance, weaponry, munitions, materiel, arms, guns
armed *adj* = **carrying weapons**, protected, equipped, fitted out, primed
armistice *n* = **truce**, peace, ceasefire, suspension of hostilities
armour *n* = **protection**, shield, covering, armour plate, sheathing
armoured *adj* = **protected**, bulletproof, ironclad, armour-plated, bombproof, mailed, steel-plated
arms *pl n* **1** = **weapons**, ordnance, weaponry, armaments, firearms, guns, instruments of war **2** = **heraldry**, crest, insignia, blazonry, escutcheon
army *n* **1** = **soldiers**, military, armed force, legions, military force, soldiery, troops **2** = **vast number**, host, pack, array, swarm, throng, multitude, horde
aroma *n* = **scent**, smell, perfume, fragrance, bouquet, odour, redolence, savour
aromatic *adj* = **fragrant**, balmy, spicy, pungent, perfumed, redolent, savoury, sweet-

DICTIONARY

arose *v* past tense of **arise**
around Ⓣ *prep, adv* **1** on all sides (of) **2** from place to place (in) **3** somewhere in or near **4** approximately
arouse Ⓣ *v* **1** awaken **2** stimulate, make active
Arp *n* **Jean** *or* **Hans**. 1887–1966, Alsatian sculptor, painter, and poet, cofounder of the Dada movement in Zürich, noted particularly for his abstract organic sculptures based on natural forms
arpeggio [arp-**pej**-ee-oh] *n, pl* **-gios** *music* notes of a chord played or sung in quick succession
arr. **1** arranged (by) **2** arrival **3** arrive(d)
arraign [ar-**rain**] *v* **1** indict (a person) on a charge **2** accuse **arraignment** *n*
arrange Ⓣ *v* **1** plan **2** agree **3** put in order **4** adapt (music) for performance in a certain way **arrangement** *n*
arrant *adj* utter, downright
arras *n* tapestry wall-hanging
array Ⓣ *n* **1** impressive display or collection **2** orderly arrangement, esp. of troops **3** *poetic* rich clothing ▷ *v* **4** arrange in order **5** dress in rich clothing
arrears *pl n* money owed
▸**in arrears** late in paying a debt
arrest Ⓣ *v* **1** take (a person) into custody **2** stop the movement or development of **3** catch and hold (the attention) ▷ *n* **4** act of taking a person into custody **5** slowing or stopping
▸**arresting** *adj* attracting attention, striking
arrive Ⓣ *v* **1** reach a place or destination **2** happen, come **3** *informal* be born **4** *informal* attain success
▸**arrival** *n* **1** arriving **2** person or thing that has just arrived
arrivederci [ar-reeve-a-**der**-chee] *interj* *Italian* goodbye
arrogant Ⓣ *adj* proud and overbearing
arrogantly *adv* **arrogance** *n*
arrogate *v* claim or seize without justification
arrow Ⓣ *n* **1** pointed shaft shot from a bow **2** arrow-shaped sign or symbol used to show direction
▸**arrowhead** *n* pointed tip of an arrow

THESAURUS

scented, sweet-smelling
around *prep* **1** = **surrounding**, about, encircling, enclosing, encompassing, on all sides of, on every side of **2** = **approximately**, about, roughly, circa (of a date) ▸ *adv* **3** = **everywhere**, about, throughout, all over, here and there, in all directions, on all sides, to and fro **4** = **near**, close, nearby, nigh (*archaic or dialect*), at hand, close at hand
arouse *v* **1** = **stimulate**, spur, provoke, excite, incite, instigate, stir up, summon up, whip up **2** = **awaken**, rouse, waken, wake up
arrange *v* **1** = **plan**, schedule, organize • *Why don't you arrange to meet him later?* **2** = **put in order**, group, order, sort, organize, classify, fix up • *He started to arrange the CDs in alphabetical order.* **3** = **agree**, determine, settle, adjust, compromise, come to terms **4** = **adapt**, score, instrument, orchestrate
See also: **fit, lay, position, set up, stage**
arranged *See* **set**
arrangement *n* **1** (*often pl*) = **plan**, schedule, organization, preparation, provision, planning **2** = **agreement**, deal, settlement, compromise, adjustment, compact, terms **3** = **order**, system, form, organization, structure, classification, alignment **4** = **adaptation**, score, version, interpretation, orchestration, instrumentation
array *n* **1** = **arrangement**, show, supply, display, collection, exhibition, parade, formation, line-up **2** (*Poetic*) = **clothing**, dress, clothes, apparel, attire, regalia, finery, garments ▸ *v* **3** = **arrange**, show, group, range, display, exhibit, parade **4** = **dress**, clothe, deck, decorate, adorn, attire, festoon
arrest *v* **1** = **capture**, seize, apprehend, take prisoner • *Police arrested five men in connection with the attack.* **2** = **stop**, end, delay, slow, block, interrupt, suppress, obstruct, inhibit **3** = **grip**, hold, engage, occupy, absorb, intrigue, fascinate, engross ▸ *n* **4** = **capture**, seizure, apprehension • *The police made two arrests.* **5** = **stopping**, end, delay, obstruction, interruption, blockage, suppression, hindrance
See also: **catch**
arresting *adj* = **striking**, cool (*informal*), impressive, remarkable, outstanding, engaging, noticeable, phat (*slang*), stunning, surprising
arrival *n* **1** = **coming**, appearance, entrance, occurrence, happening, advent, arriving, taking place **2** = **newcomer**, visitor, caller, entrant, incomer
arrive *v* **1** = **come**, reach, appear, enter, get to, show up (*informal*), turn up **2** (*Informal*) = **succeed**, become famous, make good, make it (*informal*), make the grade (*informal*)
arrive at *See* **reach**
arrogance *n* = **conceit**, pride, swagger, disdainfulness, haughtiness, high-handedness, insolence, superciliousness
arrogant *adj* = **conceited**, proud, high-handed, disdainful, haughty, overbearing, scornful, supercilious
arrow *n* **1** = **dart**, flight, bolt, shaft (*archaic*), quarrel **2** = **pointer**, indicator

DICTIONARY

arrowroot *n* nutritious starch obtained from the root of a W Indian plant
Arroyo *n* **Gloria Macapagal**. born 1948, Filipino stateswoman; president of the Philippines from 2001; vice-president (1998–2001)
arse *n taboo* buttocks or anus
▸**arsehole** *n taboo* **1** anus **2** stupid or annoying person
arsenal Ⓣ *n* place where arms and ammunition are made or stored
arsenic *n* **1** toxic grey element **2** highly poisonous compound of this **arsenical** *adj*
arson *n* crime of intentionally setting property on fire **arsonist** *n*
art Ⓣ *n* **1** creation of works of beauty, esp. paintings or sculpture **2** works of art collectively **3** skill **arts 4** nonscientific branches of knowledge
▸**artful** *adj* cunning, wily **artfully** *adv* **artfulness** *n*
▸**artist** *n* **1** person who produces works of art, esp. paintings or sculpture **2** person skilled at something **3** artiste **artistic** *adj* **artistically** *adv*
▸**artiste** *n* professional entertainer such as a singer or dancer
▸**artistry** *n* artistic skill
▸**artless** *adj* **1** free from deceit or cunning **2** natural, unpretentious **artlessly** *adv* **artlessness** *n*
▸**arty** *adj informal* having an affected interest in art
artefact, artifact *n* something made by man
arteriosclerosis [art-ear-ee-oh-skler-**oh**-siss] *n* hardening of the arteries
artery *n, pl* **-teries 1** one of the tubes carrying blood from the heart **2** major road or means of communication
▸**arterial** *adj* **1** of an artery **2** (of a route) major
artesian well [art-**tee**-zhan] *n* well bored vertically so that the water is forced to the surface by natural pressure
arthritis *n* painful inflammation of a joint or joints **arthritic** *adj, n*
arthropod *n* animal, such as a spider or insect, with jointed limbs and a segmented body
Arthur *n* **1** a legendary king of the Britons in the sixth century AD, who led Celtic resistance against the Saxons: possibly based on a historical figure; represented as leader of the Knights of the Round Table at Camelot **2 Chester Alan**. 1830–86, 21st president of the US (1881–85)
artic *n informal* articulated lorry
artichoke *n* thistle-like plant with a flower cooked as a vegetable
article Ⓣ *n* **1** item or object **2** written piece in a magazine or newspaper **3** clause in a document **4** *grammar* any of the words *the*, *a*, or *an*
▸**articled** *adj* bound by a written contract: *an articled clerk*
articulate Ⓣ *adj* **1** able to express oneself clearly and coherently **2** *zool* having joints **3** (of speech) clear, distinct ▹ *v* **4** speak or say clearly and coherently **articulately** *adv* **articulation** *n*
▸**articulated** *adj* jointed
artifice Ⓣ *n* **1** clever trick **2** cleverness, skill
▸**artificer** [art-**tiff**-iss-er] *n* craftsman
▸**artificial** *adj* **1** man-made, not occurring naturally **2** made in imitation of something natural **3** not sincere **artificially** *adv* **artificiality** *n*
▸**artificial insemination** introduction of semen into the womb by means other than sexual intercourse
▸**artificial intelligence** branch of computer science aiming to produce machines which can imitate intelligent human behaviour
▸**artificial respiration** method of restarting a person's breathing after it has stopped
artillery Ⓣ *n* **1** large-calibre guns **2** branch of the army who use these
artisan Ⓣ *n* skilled worker, craftsman

THESAURUS

arsenal *n* = **armoury**, store, supply, stockpile, storehouse, ammunition dump, arms depot, ordnance depot
art *n* = **skill**, craft, expertise, mastery, ingenuity, virtuosity
artful *adj* = **cunning**, smart, clever, wily, crafty, shrewd, sly
article *n* **1** = **piece**, story, feature, item • *There's an article about it in today's paper.* **2** = **thing**, item, object • *household articles* **3** = **clause**, point, part, item, section, portion, passage, paragraph
articulate *adj* **1** = **expressive**, clear, fluent, coherent, lucid, eloquent, well-spoken ▸ *v* **2** = **express**, say, talk, state, speak, voice, pronounce, utter, enunciate
artifice *n* **1** = **trick**, device, tactic, machination, manoeuvre, subterfuge, contrivance, stratagem **2** = **cleverness**, skill, ingenuity, inventiveness
artificial *adj* **1** = **synthetic**, plastic, man-made, manufactured, non-natural **2** = **fake**, counterfeit, mock, bogus, sham, simulated, imitation **3** = **insincere**, false, affected, phony (*informal*), forced, contrived, unnatural, feigned
artillery *n* = **big guns**, battery, cannon, ordnance, cannonry, gunnery
artisan *n* = **craftsman**, mechanic, technician, journeyman, skilled workman

DICTIONARY

arum lily [**air**-rum] *n* plant with a white funnel-shaped leaf surrounding a spike of flowers
Aryan [**air**-ree-an] *n* **1** (in Nazi Germany) non-Jewish person of the Nordic type **2** person supposedly of Indo-European descent ▷ *adj* **3** of Aryans
as Ⓣ *conj* **1** while, when **2** in the way that **3** that which: *do as you are told* **4** since, seeing that **5** for instance ▷ *adv, conj* **6** used to indicate amount or extent in comparisons: *he is as tall as you* ▷ *prep* **7** in the role of, being: *as a mother, I am concerned*
As *chem* arsenic
ASA Advertising Standards Authority
asafoetida *n* strong-smelling plant resin used as a spice in Eastern cookery
a.s.a.p. as soon as possible
asbestos *n* fibrous mineral which does not burn
▸**asbestosis** *n* lung disease caused by inhalation of asbestos fibre
ascend Ⓣ *v* go or move up
▸**ascension** *n* ascending
▸**ascent** *n* **1** ascending **2** upward slope
▸**ascendant** *adj* dominant or influential ▷ *n* **in the ascendant** increasing in power or influence
▸**ascendancy** *n* condition of being dominant
ascertain Ⓣ *v* find out definitely
ascertainable *adj* **ascertainment** *n*
ascetic Ⓣ [ass-**set**-tik] *n* **1** person who abstains from worldly pleasures and comforts ▷ *adj* **2** abstaining from worldly pleasures and comforts
ascetically *adv* **asceticism** *n*
ascorbic acid [ass-**core**-bik] *n* vitamin C
ascribe Ⓣ *v* attribute, as to a particular origin **ascribable** *adj* **ascription** *n*
aseptic [eh-**sep**-tik] *adj* germ-free
▸**asepsis** [eh-**sep**-siss] *n* aseptic condition
asexual [eh-**sek**-shoo-al] *adj* without sex
asexually *adv*
ash[1] *n* **1** powdery substance left when something is burnt **ashes 2** remains after burning, esp. of a human body after cremation
▸**ashen** *adj* pale with shock
▸**ashtray** *n* receptacle for tobacco ash and cigarette butts
▸**Ash Wednesday** first day of Lent
ash[2] *n* tree with grey bark
ashamed Ⓣ *adj* feeling shame
Ashe *n* **Arthur** (**Robert**). 1943–93, US tennis player: US champion 1968; Wimbledon champion 1975
ashlar *n* square block of hewn stone used in building
Ashley *n* **Laura**. 1925–85, British designer, who built up a successful chain of retail stores selling dresses and fabrics based on traditional English patterns
ashore Ⓣ *adv* towards or on land
ashram *n* religious retreat where a Hindu holy man lives
Asian *adj* **1** of the continent of Asia or any of its peoples or languages ▷ *n* **2** person from Asia or a descendant of one **Asiatic** *adj*
aside Ⓣ *adv* **1** to one side **2** out of other people's hearing: *he took me aside to tell me his*

THESAURUS

artistic *adj* = **creative**, beautiful, sophisticated, elegant, stylish, refined, aesthetic, tasteful, cultured
artistry *n* = **skill**, creativity, mastery, brilliance, finesse, proficiency, craftsmanship, virtuosity
artless *adj* **1** = **straightforward**, open, plain, frank, guileless **2** = **natural**, simple, pure, plain, unaffected, unpretentious, homey, unadorned
as *conj* **1** = **when**, while, at the time that, during the time that, just as **2** = **in the way that**, like, in the manner that **3** = **what**, that which **4** = **since**, because, considering that, seeing that **5** = **for instance**, like, such as ▸ *preposition* **6** = **being**, in the character of, in the role of, under the name of ▷ **as a result** *See* **therefore** ▷ **as a result of** *See* **by virtue of** ▷ **as a rule** *See* **on average** ▷ **as good as** *See* **nearly** ▷ **as one** *See* **together** ▷ **as well** *See also* **too**
ascend *v* = **move up**, climb, scale, mount, go up
ascendancy *See* **advantage, power**
ascent *n* **1** = **rise**, climb, rising, ascension, mounting, ascending, scaling, upward movement **2** = **upward slope**, rise, grade, ramp, incline, gradient, rising ground
ascertain *v* = **find out**, confirm, learn, discover, determine, establish
ascetic *n* **1** = **monk**, nun, recluse, hermit, abstainer ▸ *adj* **2** = **self-denying**, austere, frugal, celibate, puritanical, abstinent, self-disciplined
ascribe *v* = **attribute**, charge, credit, refer, assign, impute, put down, set down
ashamed *adj* = **embarrassed**, guilty, sorry, sheepish, humiliated • *He was not even ashamed of what he had done.* OPPOSITE: proud
ashen *adj* = **pale**, white, grey, pallid, wan, colourless, leaden, like death warmed up (*informal*)
ashore *adv* = **on land**, aground, landwards, on dry land, on the beach, on the shore, shorewards, to the shore
aside *adv* **1** = **to one side**, apart, privately, beside, separately, on one side, out of the

DICTIONARY

plans ▷ *n* **3** remark not meant to be heard by everyone present
Asimov *n* **Isaac.** 1920–92, US writer and biochemist, born in Russia. His science-fiction works include *Foundation Trilogy* (1951–53; sequel 1982) and the collection of stories *I, Robot* (1950)
asinine Ⓣ [**ass**-in-nine] *adj* stupid, idiotic **asininity** *n*
ask Ⓣ *v* **1** say or write (something) in a form that requires an answer **2** make a request or demand **3** invite
askance [ass-**kanss**] *adv* **look askance at** **1** look at with an oblique glance **2** regard with suspicion
askew Ⓣ *adv, adj* to one side, crooked
aslant *adv, prep* at a slant (to), slanting (across)
asleep Ⓣ *adj* **1** sleeping **2** (of limbs) numb
asp *n* small poisonous snake
asparagus *n* plant whose shoots are cooked as a vegetable
aspect Ⓣ *n* **1** feature or element **2** appearance or look **3** position facing a particular direction
aspen *n* kind of poplar tree
asperity [ass-**per**-rit-ee] *n* roughness of temper
aspersion *n* **cast aspersions on** make derogatory remarks about
asphalt *n* **1** black hard tarlike substance used for road surfaces etc. ▷ *v* **2** cover with asphalt
asphodel *n* plant with clusters of yellow or white flowers
asphyxia [ass-**fix**-ee-a] *n* suffocation
▶ **asphyxiate** *v* suffocate **asphyxiation** *n*
aspic *n* savoury jelly used to coat meat, eggs, fish, etc.
aspidistra *n* plant with long tapered leaves
aspirate *phonetics* ▷ *v* **1** pronounce with an *h* sound ▷ *n* **2** an *h* sound
aspire Ⓣ *v* (foll. by *to*) yearn (for), hope (to do or be)
▶ **aspirant** *n* person who aspires
▶ **aspiration** *n* strong desire or aim
aspirin *n* **1** drug used to relieve pain and fever **2** tablet of this
Asquith *n* **Herbert Henry**, 1st Earl of Oxford and Asquith. 1852–1928, British statesman; prime minister (1908–16); leader of the Liberal Party (1908–26)
ass Ⓣ *n* **1** donkey **2** stupid person
Assad *n* **1** **Hafiz al.** 1928–2000, Syrian statesman and general; president of Syria (1971–2000) **2** his son, **Bashar al.** born 1965, Syrian statesman; president of Syria (2000–)
assagai *n* same as **assegai**
assail Ⓣ *v* attack violently **assailant** *n*
assassin Ⓣ *n* person who murders a prominent person
▶ **assassinate** *v* murder (a prominent person) **assassination** *n*
assault Ⓣ *n* **1** violent attack ▷ *v* **2** attack violently
▶ **assault course** series of obstacles

THESAURUS

way, to the side ▶ *n* **2 = interpolation**, parenthesis
asinine *adj* **= stupid**, foolish, senseless, idiotic, moronic, fatuous, imbecilic
ask *v* **1 = inquire**, question, quiz, interrogate, query • *She asked me if I'd enjoyed my dinner.* OPPOSITE: answer **2 = request**, seek, demand, appeal, plead, beg, implore, beseech, entreat • *We had to ask him to leave.* **3 = invite**, bid (*lit*) • *Not everybody had been asked to the wedding.* ▷ **ask (for)** *See* **charge** ▷ **ask for advice** *See* **consult** ▷ **ask forgiveness** *See* **apologize** ▷ **ask oneself** *See* **wonder**
See also: **pose**
askew *adv* **1 = crookedly**, awry, obliquely, aslant, off-centre, to one side ▶ *adj* **2 = crooked**, lopsided, oblique, awry, cockeyed (*informal*), off-centre
asleep *adj* **= sleeping**, dormant, dozing, fast asleep, napping, slumbering, snoozing (*informal*), sound asleep
aspect *n* **1 = feature**, point, part, side, factor, element, consideration • *Test results are only one aspect of a school's success.* **2 = position**, view, situation, scene, prospect, outlook, point of view **3 = appearance**, look, air, condition, attitude, manner, expression, bearing, demeanour
See also: **detail, face, quality**
asphyxiate *v* **= suffocate**, choke, stifle, smother, strangle, throttle, strangulate
aspiration *n* **= aim**, goal, hope, dream, wish, desire, objective, ambition
aspire *v* **= aim**, long, hope, seek, dream, wish, desire, set one's heart on
aspiring *adj* **= hopeful**, would-be, eager, ambitious, longing, wannabe (*informal*)
ass *n* **1 = donkey** **2 = fool**, idiot, blockhead, dork (*slang*), halfwit, jackass, oaf, schmuck (*slang*)
assail *v* **= attack**, assault, fall upon, set upon
assailant *n* **= attacker**, invader, aggressor, assailer, assaulter
assassin *n* **= murderer**, killer, executioner, hatchet man (*slang*), hit man (*slang*), liquidator, slayer
assassinate *v* **= murder**, kill, hit (*slang*), eliminate (*slang*), slay, liquidate, take out (*slang*)
assassination *See* **murder**
assault *n* **1 = attack**, charge, offensive, invasion, onslaught ▶ *v* **2 = attack**, beset,

DICTIONARY

used in military training
assay *n* **1** analysis of a substance, esp. a metal, to ascertain its purity ▷ *v* **2** make such an analysis
assegai *n* slender spear used in S Africa
assemble ⓣ *v* **1** collect or congregate **2** put together the parts of (a machine)
▸ **assemblage** *n* **1** collection or group **2** assembling
▸ **assembly** *n* **1** assembling **2** assembled group
▸ **assembly line** sequence of machines and workers in a factory assembling a product
assent ⓣ *n* **1** agreement or consent ▷ *v* **2** agree or consent
assert ⓣ *v* **1** declare forcefully **2** insist upon (one's rights etc.) **assertion** *n* **assertive** *adj* **assertively** *adv*
▸ **assert oneself** speak and act forcefully
assess ⓣ *v* **1** judge the worth or importance of **2** estimate the value of (income or property) for taxation purposes **assessment** *n* **assessor** *n*
asset ⓣ *n* **1** valuable or useful person or thing **assets 2** property that a person or firm can sell, esp. to pay debts
asseverate *v* declare solemnly **asseveration** *n*
assiduous ⓣ *adj* diligent and persevering **assiduously** *adv* **assiduity** *n*
assign ⓣ *v* **1** appoint (someone) to a job or task **2** allot (a task) **3** attribute
▸ **assignation** [ass-sig-**nay**-shun] *n* **1** assigning **2** secret arrangement to meet
▸ **assignment** *n* **1** assigning **2** task assigned
assimilate ⓣ *v* **1** learn and understand (information) **2** absorb or be absorbed or incorporated **assimilable** *adj* **assimilation** *n*
assist ⓣ *v* give help or support **assistance** *n*
▸ **assistant** *n* **1** helper ▷ *adj* **2** junior or deputy
assizes *pl n* court sessions formerly held in each county of England and Wales

THESAURUS

fall upon, set about, set upon, strike at
assemble *v* **1 = gather**, mass, collect, convene, muster, congregate, come together • *a convenient place for students to assemble between classes* **2 = put together**, make, build, construct, erect • *Workers were assembling planes.*
See also: **form, manufacture, meet, piece together**
assembly *n* **1 = gathering**, company, group, conference, meeting, crowd, mass, collection, council, muster, congress **2 = putting together**, construction, connecting, building up, piecing together, setting up
assent *n* **1 = agreement**, approval, sanction, permission, consent, compliance, acceptance, concurrence ▸ *v* **2 = agree**, allow, approve, grant, permit, consent
assert *v* **1 = state**, declare, maintain, swear, pronounce, affirm, profess **2 = insist upon**, claim, defend, press, stress, uphold, put forward, stand up for ▷ **assert oneself = be forceful**, exert one's influence, make one's presence felt, put oneself forward, put one's foot down (*informal*)
assertion *n* **1 = statement**, claim, declaration, pronouncement **2 = insistence**, maintenance, stressing
assertive *adj* **= confident**, positive, aggressive, feisty (*informal*), forceful, emphatic, insistent, strong-willed, domineering, pushy (*informal*)
assess *v* **1 = judge**, rate, value, estimate, weigh, evaluate, appraise, size up (*informal*) **2 = evaluate**, rate, tax, value, fix, impose, levy
assessment *n* **1 = judgment**, estimate, rating, evaluation, valuation, appraisal **2 = evaluation**, charge, fee, toll, rating, levy, valuation
asset *n* **= benefit**, help, service, aid, advantage, resource, blessing, boon, feather in one's cap ▷ **assets = property**, money, capital, estate, wealth, funds, goods, possessions, resources
assiduous *adj* **= diligent**, persistent, hard-working, industrious, indefatigable, persevering, unflagging
assign *v* **1 = select**, name, choose, appoint, nominate, delegate, designate **2 = give**, grant, distribute, allocate, allot, consign, apportion, give out **3 = attribute**, accredit, ascribe, put down
assignation *n* **1 = secret meeting**, rendezvous, tryst, clandestine meeting, illicit meeting **2 = selection**, choice, nomination, appointment, delegation, assignment, designation
assignment *n* **= task**, post, job, mission, position, commission, duty, responsibility, appointment
assimilate *v* **1 = learn**, absorb, incorporate, digest, take in **2 = adjust**, adapt, mingle, blend in
assist *v* **= help**, support, serve, aid, cooperate, abet, lend a helping hand
assistance *n* **= help**, support, aid, backing, cooperation, helping hand
assistant *n* **= helper**, colleague, deputy, ally, aide, right-hand person • *His assistant took over while he was out of town.*
associate *v* **1 = connect**, link, couple, identify • *Poverty is sometimes associated with old age.* **2 = socialize**, mix, mingle, hang out (*informal*), run around (*informal*) • *I began associating with different crowds of people.* ▸ *n*

DICTIONARY

associate Ⓣ *v* **1** connect in the mind **2** mix socially ▷ *n* **3** partner in business **4** friend or companion ▷ *adj* **5** having partial rights or subordinate status: *associate member*
▸ **association** *n* **1** associating **2** society or club
assonance *n* rhyming of vowel sounds but not consonants, as in *time* and *light* **assonant** *adj*
assorted Ⓣ *adj* consisting of various types mixed together
▸ **assortment** *n* assorted mixture
assuage [ass-**wage**] *v* relieve (pain, grief, thirst, etc.)
assume Ⓣ *v* **1** take to be true without proof **2** pretend: *I assumed indifference* **3** take upon oneself: *he assumed command*
▸ **assumption** *n* **1** assuming **2** thing assumed
assumptive *adj*
assure Ⓣ *v* **1** promise or guarantee **2** convince **3** make (something) certain **4** insure against loss of life
▸ **assured** *adj* **1** confident **2** certain to happen
▸ **assuredly** *adv* definitely
▸ **assurance** *n* assuring or being assured
AST Atlantic Standard Time
Astaire *n* **Fred**, real name *Frederick Austerlitz*. 1899–1987, US dancer, singer, and actor, whose films include *Top Hat* (1935), *Swing Time* (1936), and *The Band Wagon* (1953)
aster *n* plant with daisy-like flowers
asterisk *n* **1** star-shaped symbol (*) used in printing to indicate a footnote etc. ▷ *v* **2** mark with an asterisk
astern *adv* **1** at or towards the stern of a ship **2** backwards
asteroid *n* any of the small planets that orbit the sun between Mars and Jupiter
asthma [**ass**-ma] *n* illness causing difficulty in breathing **asthmatic** *adj, n*
astigmatism [eh-**stig**-mat-tiz-zum] *n* inability of a lens, esp. of the eye, to focus properly **astigmatic** *adj*
astir *adj* **1** out of bed **2** in motion
astonish Ⓣ *v* surprise greatly
astonishment *n*
Astor *n* **1 John Jacob**, 1st Baron Astor of Hever. 1886–1971, British proprietor of *The Times* (1922–66) **2 Nancy (Witcher)**, Viscountess, original name *Nancy Langhorne*. 1879–1964, British Conservative politician, born in the US; the first woman to sit in the British House of Commons

THESAURUS

3 = colleague, co-worker • *the restaurant owner's business associates* **4 = friend**, ally, comrade, companion, homeboy (*slang*), homegirl (*slang*)
associate with *See* **identify with**
association *n* **1 = group**, company, body, club, league, society, institution, syndicate, confederation • *a research association* **2 = connection**, tie, relationship, bond, affiliation, attachment • *his association with an animal rights group*
See also: **fellowship, link, organization, union**
assorted *adj* **= various**, different, mixed, diverse, varied, miscellaneous, motley, sundry
assortment *n* **= variety**, choice, collection, selection, array, mixture, medley, jumble
assume *v* **1 = suppose**, think, believe, guess (*informal*), imagine • *I assumed that he would turn up.* **2 = take on**, accept, shoulder, undertake • *She will assume the position of chief executive officer.* **3 = put on**, affect, adopt, mimic, simulate, imitate, impersonate, feign, pretend to
See also: **expect, gather, reckon**
assumed *adj* **1 = false**, fake, counterfeit, bogus, fictitious, made-up, make-believe **2 = taken for granted**, hypothetical, presumed, accepted, supposed, expected, presupposed, surmised
assumption *n* **1 = presumption**, guess, belief, hypothesis, inference, conjecture, surmise, supposition **2 = taking on**, takeover, acquisition, adoption, acceptance, entering upon, putting on, shouldering, taking up **3 = taking**, takeover, acquisition, seizure, appropriation
assurance *n* **1 = assertion**, statement, promise, word, pledge, vow, guarantee, declaration, oath **2 = confidence**, conviction, poise, faith, nerve, certainty, self-confidence, boldness
assure *v* **1 = promise**, confirm, pledge, vow, guarantee, swear, certify, declare confidently, give one's word to **2 = convince**, encourage, persuade, comfort, reassure, embolden, hearten **3 = make certain**, confirm, complete, ensure, secure, guarantee, seal, clinch, make sure
assured *adj* **1 = confident**, positive, certain, self-assured, poised, self-confident, sure of oneself **2 = certain**, sure, secure, beyond doubt, confirmed, ensured, fixed, guaranteed, in the bag (*slang*), settled
astonish *v* **= amaze**, surprise, stun, stagger, astound, daze, bewilder, confound, dumbfound
astonishing *adj* **= amazing**, brilliant, sensational (*informal*), breathtaking, astounding, bewildering, staggering, stunning, surprising
astonishment *n* **= amazement**, surprise, wonder, confusion, awe, consternation, bewilderment, wonderment

DICTIONARY

astound ❶ *v* overwhelm with amazement **astounding** *adj*
astrakhan *n* **1** dark curly fleece of lambs from Astrakhan in Russia **2** fabric resembling this
astral *adj* **1** of stars **2** of the spirit world
astray ❶ *adv* off the right path
astride *adv, prep* with a leg on either side (of)
astringent ❶ *adj* **1** severe or harsh **2** causing contraction of body tissue **3** checking the flow of blood from a cut ▷ *n* **4** astringent substance **astringency** *n*
astrolabe *n* instrument formerly used to measure the altitude of stars and planets
astrology *n* study of the alleged influence of the stars, planets, and moon on human affairs **astrologer** *n* **astrological** *adj*
astronaut *n* person trained for travelling in space
astronautics *n* science and technology of space flight **astronautical** *adj*
astronomy *n* scientific study of heavenly bodies **astronomer** *n*
▸ **astronomical** *adj* **1** of astronomy **2** very large **astronomically** *adv*
astrophysics *n* science of the physical and chemical properties of stars, planets, etc. **astrophysical** *adj* **astrophysicist** *n*
Astroturf *n* ® artificial grass
astute ❶ *adj* perceptive or shrewd **astutely** *adv* **astuteness** *n*
asunder *adv* into parts or pieces
asylum ❶ *n* **1** refuge or sanctuary **2** old name for a mental hospital
asymmetry *n* lack of symmetry **asymmetrical** *or* **asymmetric** *adj*
asymptote [ass-im-tote] *n* straight line closely approached by but never met by a curve
at *prep* **1** indicating position in space or time **2** towards **3** engaged in **4** in exchange for: *it's selling at two pounds* **5** indicating the cause of an emotion: *shocked at his rudeness*
atavism [at-a-viz-zum] *n* recurrence of a trait present in distant ancestors **atavistic** *adj*
ataxia *n* lack of muscular coordination **ataxic** *adj*
at-bat *baseball* ▷ *n* **1** turn to bat resulting in the batter making an out or a hit ▷ *adv* **2** Also **at bat** (of a batter) about to bat
ate *v* past tense of **eat**
atheism ❶ [aith-ee-iz-zum] *n* belief that there is no God **atheist** *n* **atheistic** *adj*
Athelstan *n* ?895–939 AD, king of Wessex and Mercia (924–939 AD), who extended his kingdom to include most of England
atherosclerosis *n, pl* **-ses** disease in which deposits of fat cause the walls of the arteries to thicken
athlete ❶ *n* person trained in or good at athletics
▸ **athletic** *adj* **1** physically fit or strong **2** of an athlete or athletics **athletically** *adv* **athleticism** *n*
▸ **athletics** *pl n* track and field sports such as running, jumping, throwing, etc.
athwart *prep* **1** across ▷ *adv* **2** transversely
atigi *n* a type of parka worn by the Inuit
Atkins *n* **Robert C.** 1930–2003, US physician and nutritionist. An advocate of complementary medicine, he devised a widely-used diet (the Atkins diet) based on controlled intake of carbohydrates for weight management and disease prevention

THESAURUS

astound *See* **amaze, surprise**
astounding *adj* = **amazing**, cool (*informal*), impressive, brilliant, sensational (*informal*), breathtaking, astonishing, bewildering, phat (*slang*), staggering, stunning, surprising
astray *adj, adv* = **off the right track**, off, lost, adrift, amiss, off course, off the mark, off the subject
astringent *See* **bitter**
astute *adj* = **intelligent**, quick, alert, sharp, smart, keen, clever, shrewd, perceptive • *an astute judge of character*
See also: **acute**
asylum *n* **1** = **refuge**, safety, preserve, retreat, shelter, haven, sanctuary, harbour **2** (*Old-fashioned*) = **mental hospital**, hospital, institution, funny farm (*slang*), madhouse (*informal*), psychiatric hospital, psychiatric ward
asymmetrical *See* **irregular**
at an end *See* **over**
at ease *See* **comfortable, relaxed**
at fault *See* **responsible**
at hand, on hand *adj* = **nearby**, close, near, available, handy, within reach, at the ready, at one's fingertips
atheism *n* = **nonbelief**, skepticism, disbelief, infidelity, godlessness, heathenism, irreligion, paganism, unbelief
atheist *n* = **nonbeliever**, infidel, skeptic, pagan, heathen, disbeliever, unbeliever
athlete *n* = **sportsperson**, player, competitor, runner, contestant, gymnast, sportsman, sportswoman
athletic *adj* = **fit**, strong, powerful, active, energetic, muscular, sturdy, strapping
athletics *pl n* = **sports**, gymnastics, track and field events, contests, races, exercises
at home *See* **comfortable**
at large *See* **free**
at last *See* **finally**
at liberty *See* **free**

DICTIONARY

Atlantic Daylight Time *n* one of the standard times used in North America, three hours behind Greenwich Mean Time Abbreviation: **ADT**
Atlantic Standard Time *n* one of the standard times used in North America, four hours behind Greenwich Mean Time Abbreviation: **AST**
atlas *n* book of maps
Atleo *n* **Shawn A-in-chut**. National Chief of the Assembly of First Nations (2009–)
atmosphere Ⓣ *n* **1** mass of gases surrounding a heavenly body, esp. the earth **2** prevailing tone or mood (of a place etc.) **3** unit of pressure **atmospheric** *adj*
▸**atmospherics** *pl n* radio interference due to electrical disturbance in the atmosphere
atoll *n* ring-shaped coral island enclosing a lagoon
atom Ⓣ *n* **1** smallest unit of matter which can take part in a chemical reaction **2** very small amount
▸**atomic** *adj* **1** of atoms **2** of or using atomic bombs or atomic energy
▸**atomic bomb** *or* **atom bomb** bomb in which the energy is provided by nuclear fission
▸**atomic energy** nuclear energy
▸**atomic number** number of protons in the nucleus of an atom
▸**atomic weight** ratio of the mass per atom of an element to one twelfth of the mass of a carbon atom
▸**atomize** *v* reduce to atoms or small particles
▸**atomizer** *n* device for discharging a liquid in a fine spray
atonal [eh-**tone**-al] *adj* (of music) not written in an established key **atonality** *n*
atone Ⓣ *v* make amends (for sin or wrongdoing) **atonement** *n*
atop *prep* on top of
atrium *n, pl* **atria 1** upper chamber of either half of the heart **2** central hall extending through several storeys of a modern building **3** main courtyard of an ancient Roman house
atrocious Ⓣ *adj* **1** extremely cruel or wicked **2** horrifying or shocking **3** *informal* very bad **atrociously** *adv*
▸**atrocity** *n* **1** wickedness **2** act of cruelty
atrophy [**at**-trof-fee] *n, pl* **-phies 1** wasting away of an organ or part ▹ *v* **-phying, -phied 2** (cause to) waste away
attach Ⓣ *v* **1** join, fasten, or connect **2** attribute or ascribe: *he attaches great importance to his looks* **attachment** *n*
▸**attached** *adj* (foll. by *to*) fond of
attaché [at-**tash**-shay] *n* specialist attached to a diplomatic mission
▸**attaché case** flat rectangular briefcase for papers
attack Ⓣ *v* **1** launch a physical assault (against) **2** criticize **3** set about (a job or problem) with vigour **4** affect adversely ▹ *n* **5** act of attacking **6** sudden bout of illness **attacker** *n*

THESAURUS

atmosphere *n* **1 = air**, sky, aerosphere, heavens **2 = feeling**, climate, environment, character, spirit, tone, mood, surroundings, ambience
at no time *See* **never**
atom *n* **= particle**, spot, bit, trace, dot, molecule, speck
at once *adv* **1 = immediately**, now *or* right now, directly, instantly, forthwith, right away, straight away, this minute *or* this very minute **2 = simultaneously**, together, at the same time
atone *v* (usually with *for*) **= make amends**, compensate, redress, do penance, make redress, make reparation, make up for, pay for, recompense
atonement *n* **= amends**, compensation, redress, restitution, reparation, penance, recompense
atrocious *adj* **1 = cruel**, brutal, vicious, wicked, savage, barbaric, monstrous, fiendish, infernal **2** (*Informal*) **= shocking**, terrible, horrible, appalling, grievous, detestable, horrifying
atrocity *n* **1 = cruelty**, horror, brutality, savagery, viciousness, barbarity, fiendishness, wickedness **2 = act of cruelty**, crime, outrage, evil, horror, abomination
at someone's disposal *See* **available**
attach *v* **1 = connect**, link, join, couple, tie, fasten, affix • *The gadget can be attached to any surface.* OPPOSITE: separate **2 = put**, associate, connect, attribute, assign, ascribe
See also: **add, fix, hang, secure, stick**
attached *adj* **= spoken for**, married, engaged, accompanied, partnered
▹ **attached to = fond of**, affectionate towards, devoted to, full of regard for
attachment *n* **1 = fondness**, love, bond, affection, liking • *The puppies formed a close attachment to each other.* **2 = accessory**, part, unit, component, fitting, fixture • *The drill comes with a wide range of attachments.*
See also: **association, friendship, link**
attack *v* **1 = assault**, charge, storm, raid, invade, set upon • *I thought the dog was going to attack me.* **2 = criticize**, blast, censure, berate, lambaste, vilify (*formal*), put down (*informal*), revile • *She attacked the government's economic policies.* ▸ *n* **3 = assault**, charge, offensive, raid, invasion, onslaught • *a vicious attack on an unarmed person* **4 = criticism**,

DICTIONARY

attain ⓣ *v* **1** achieve or accomplish (a task or aim) **2** reach **attainable** *adj* **attainability** *n*
▸**attainment** *n* accomplishment
attar *n* fragrant oil made from roses
attempt ⓣ *v* **1** try, make an effort ▷*n* **2** effort or endeavour
Attenborough *n* **1** Sir **David**. born 1926, British naturalist and broadcaster; noted esp. for his TV series *Life on Earth* (1978), *The Living Planet* (1983), and *The Life of Birds* (1998) **2** his brother, **Richard**, Baron Attenborough. born 1923, British film actor, director, and producer; his films include *Gandhi* (1982), *Cry Freedom* (1987), and *Shadowlands* (1993)
attend ⓣ *v* **1** be present at **2** look after **3** pay attention **4** apply oneself (to)
▸**attendance** *n* **1** attending **2** number attending
▸**attendant** *n* **1** person who assists, guides, or provides a service ▷*adj* **2** accompanying
▸**attention** *n* **1** concentrated direction of the mind **2** consideration **3** care **4** alert position in military drill
▸**attentive** *adj* **1** giving attention **2** considerately helpful **attentively** *adv* **attentiveness** *n*
attenuate *v* **1** weaken **2** make or become thin **attenuation** *n*
attest *v* affirm the truth of, be proof of **attestation** *n*
attic ⓣ *n* space or room within the roof of a house
Attila *n* ?406–453 AD, king of the Huns, who devastated much of the Roman Empire, invaded Gaul in 451 AD, but was defeated by the Romans and Visigoths at Châlons-sur-Marne
attire ⓣ *n* **1** fine or formal clothes ▷*v* **2** clothe
attitude ⓣ *n* **1** way of thinking and behaving **2** posture of the body
Attlee *n* **Clement Richard**, 1st Earl Attlee. 1883–1967, British statesman; prime minister (1945–51); leader of the Labour party (1935–55). His government instituted the welfare state, with extensive nationalization
attorney ⓣ *n* person legally appointed to act for another, esp. a lawyer
attract ⓣ *v* **1** arouse the interest or admiration of **2** draw (something) closer by exerting a force on it

THESAURUS

blame, abuse, stick (*slang*), censure, denigration, vilification **5 = bout**, stroke, fit, seizure, spasm, convulsion, paroxysm
See also: **bomb, savage**
attacker *n* = **assailant**, intruder, raider, invader, aggressor, assaulter
attain *v* = **achieve**, get, reach, gain, complete, acquire, obtain, accomplish, fulfill
attainable *See* **possible**
attainment *n* = **achievement**, accomplishment, completion, feat
attempt *v* **1 = try**, seek, strive, endeavour, try your hand at • *They attempted to escape.* ▸*n* **2 = try**, go (*informal*), shot (*informal*), bid, crack (*informal*), stab (*informal*) • *one of his rare attempts at humour*
See also: **aim, effort**
attend *v* **1 = be present**, visit, appear, frequent, haunt, go to, put in an appearance, show oneself, turn up **2 = take care of**, nurse, tend, care for, look after, minister to **3 = pay attention**, note, hear, mark, listen, observe, heed, pay heed ▷**attend to = apply oneself to**, concentrate on, deal with, devote oneself to, get to work on, look after, occupy oneself with, see to, take care of
attendance *n* **1 = presence**, appearance, attending, being there **2 = turnout**, house, crowd, audience, gate, number present
attendant *n* **1 = assistant**, guard, aide, escort, servant, companion, follower, supporter, helper ▸*adj* **2 = accompanying**, related, connected, accessory, associated, consequent, concomitant
attention *n* **1 = concentration**, deliberation, heed, intentness, thought, scrutiny, thinking **2 = notice**, regard, recognition, consideration, awareness, observation, consciousness **3 = care**, concern, treatment, looking after, ministration
attentive *adj* **1 = intent**, alert, careful, awake, watchful, mindful, observant, concentrating, heedful, studious **2 = considerate**, kind, helpful, polite, respectful, thoughtful, courteous, obliging
at the last moment *See* **finally**
attic *n* = **loft**, garret
at times *See* **sometimes**
attire *n* = **clothes**, wear, dress, costume, outfit, apparel, garb, garments, robes
attitude *n* **1 = outlook**, position, perspective, stance, point of view • *negative attitudes to work* **2 = position**, pose, stance, posture
See also: **conduct, view, viewpoint**
attorney *See* **lawyer**
attract *v* = **appeal to**, pull (*informal*), draw, lure, entice, tempt • *The championship has attracted many leading skaters.* OPPOSITE: repel
See also: **appeal**
attraction *n* = **appeal**, pull (*informal*), lure, charm, temptation, allure, fascination, magnetism, enticement
attractive *adj* = **appealing**, pretty, lovely,

DICTIONARY

▸**attraction** *n* **1** power to attract **2** something that attracts **attractive** *adj* **attractively** *adv* **attractiveness** *n*
attribute Ⓣ *v* **1** (usu. foll. by *to*) regard as belonging to or produced by ▹ *n* **2** quality or feature representative of a person or thing **attributable** *adj* **attribution** *n*
▸**attributive** *adj grammar* (of an adjective) preceding the noun modified
attrition *n* constant wearing down to weaken or destroy: *war of attrition*
attune Ⓣ *v* adjust or accustom (a person or thing)
Atwood *n* **Margaret** (**Eleanor**). born 1939, Canadian poet and novelist. Her novels include *Lady Oracle* (1976), *The Handmaid's Tale* (1986), *Alias Grace* (1996), the Booker Prize-winning *The Blind Assassin* (2000), and *Oryx and Crake* (2003)
atypical [eh-**tip**-ik-al] *adj* not typical
Au *chem* gold
Auber *n* **Daniel François Esprit**. 1782–1871, French composer, who was prominent in the development of opéra comique. His works include 48 operas
aubergine [**oh**-bur-zheen] *n Brit* eggplant
aubrietia [aw-**bree**-sha] *n* trailing plant with purple flowers
auburn *adj, n* (of hair) reddish-brown
auction *n* **1** public sale in which articles are sold to the highest bidder ▹ *v* **2** sell by auction
▸**auctioneer** *n* person who conducts an auction
audacious Ⓣ *adj* **1** recklessly bold or daring **2** impudent **audaciously** *adv* **audacity** *n*
Auden *n* **W**(**ystan**) **H**(**ugh**). 1907–73, US poet, dramatist, critic, and librettist, born in Britain; noted for his lyric and satirical poems and for plays written in collaboration with Christopher Isherwood
audible Ⓣ *adj* loud enough to hear **audibly** *adv* **audibility** *n*
audience Ⓣ *n* **1** group of spectators or listeners **2** formal interview
audio *adj* **1** of sound or hearing **2** of or for the transmission or reproduction of sound
▸**audiotypist** *n* typist trained to type from a dictating machine
▸**audiovisual** *adj* (esp. of teaching aids) involving both sight and hearing
audit *n* **1** official examination of business accounts ▹ *v* **2** examine (business accounts) officially **auditor** *n*
audition *n* **1** test of a performer's ability for a particular role or job ▹ *v* **2** test or be tested in an audition
auditorium *n, pl* **-toriums, -toria** building for public gatherings or meetings
auditory *adj* of or relating to hearing
au fait [**oh fay**] *adj French* **1** fully informed **2** expert
auf Wiedersehen [owf **vee**-der-zay-en] *interj German* goodbye
Aug. August
auger *n* carpenter's tool for boring holes
aught *pron old-fashioned* anything
augment Ⓣ *v* increase or enlarge **augmentation** *n*
au gratin [**oh grat**-tan] *adj* covered and cooked with breadcrumbs and sometimes cheese
augur *v* be a sign of (future events)
▸**augury** *n* **1** foretelling of the future **2** omen
august *adj* dignified and imposing
August *n* eighth month of the year
Augustine *n* **1 Saint**. 354–430 AD, one of the Fathers of the Christian Church; bishop of Hippo in North Africa (396–430), who profoundly influenced both Catholic and Protestant theology. His most famous works are *Confessions*, a spiritual autobiography, and *De Civitate Dei*, a vindication of the Christian

THESAURUS

charming, handsome, fetching • *an attractive woman* OPPOSITE: unattractive
See also: **beautiful, cute**
attractiveness *See* **beauty**
attribute *n* **1 = quality**, feature, property, characteristic, trait • *a normal attribute of human behaviour* ▸*v* **2 = ascribe**, charge, credit, refer, assign, put down to, set down to, trace to
See also: **point, virtue**
attune *v* **= accustom**, regulate, adjust, adapt, harmonize, familiarize
at your fingertips *See* **handy**
audacious *adj* **1 = daring**, brave, bold, reckless, rash, courageous, fearless, intrepid **2 = cheeky**, defiant, brazen, shameless, presumptuous, impertinent, impudent, insolent
audacity *n* **1 = daring**, nerve, courage, bravery, recklessness, boldness, fearlessness, rashness **2 = cheek**, nerve, chutzpah (*informal*), effrontery, impertinence, impudence, insolence
audible *adj* **= clear**, distinct, detectable, discernible, hearable, perceptible
audibly *See* **aloud**
audience *n* **1 = spectators**, crowd, gallery, assembly, gathering, turnout, listeners, onlookers, viewers **2 = interview**, meeting, hearing, reception, consultation
augment *v* **= increase, add to**, boost, supplement, reinforce, complement, top up • *a good way to augment your income*
See also: **add**

DICTIONARY

Church. Feast day: Aug 28 **2 Saint**. died 604 AD, Roman monk, sent to Britain (597 AD) to convert the Anglo-Saxons to Christianity and to establish the authority of the Roman See over the native Celtic Church; became the first archbishop of Canterbury (601–604). Feast day: May 26 or 27 **3** a member of an Augustinian order

a

Augustus *n* original name *Gaius Octavianus;* after his adoption by Julius Caesar (44 BC) known as *Gaius Julius Caesar Octavianus.* 63 BC–14 AD, Roman statesman, a member of the second triumvirate (43 BC). After defeating Mark Antony at Actium (31 bc), he became first emperor of Rome, adopting the title Augustus (27 bc)
auk *n* northern sea bird with short wings and black-and-white plumage
Aung San Suu Kyi *n* born 1945, Burmese politician; cofounder (1988) and general secretary (1988–91; 1995–) of the National League for Democracy: Nobel peace prize 1991
aunt *n* **1** father's or mother's sister **2** uncle's wife
▸ **auntie** *or* **aunty** *n informal* aunt
▸ **Aunt Sally 1** figure used in fairgrounds as a target **2** target of abuse or criticism
au pair *n* young foreign woman who does housework in return for board and lodging
aura Ⓣ *n* distinctive air or quality of a person or thing
aural *adj* of or using the ears or hearing **aurally** *adv*
Aurelian *n* Latin name *Lucius Domitius Aurelianus.* ?212–275 AD, Roman emperor (270–275), who conquered Palmyra (273) and restored political unity to the Roman Empire
aureole, aureola *n* halo
au revoir [**oh** rev-**vwahr**] *interj French* goodbye
Auric *n* **Georges**. 1899–1983, French composer; one of *les Six.* His works include ballet and film music
auricle *n* **1** upper chamber of the heart **2** outer part of the ear **auricular** *adj*
Auriol *n* **Vincent**. 1884–1966, French statesman; president of the Fourth Republic (1947–54)
aurochs *n, pl* **aurochs** recently extinct European wild ox
aurora *n, pl* **-ras, -rae** bands of light sometimes seen in the sky in polar regions
▸ **aurora australis** aurora seen near the South Pole
▸ **aurora borealis** aurora seen near the North Pole
auscultation *n* listening to the internal sounds of the body, usu. with a stethoscope, to help with diagnosis
auspices [**aw**-spiss-siz] *pl n* **under the auspices of** with the support and approval of
auspicious Ⓣ *adj* showing signs of future success, favourable **auspiciously** *adv*
Aussie *n, adj informal* Australian
Austen *n* **Jane**. 1775–1817, English novelist, noted particularly for the insight and delicate irony of her portrayal of middle-class families. Her completed novels are *Sense and Sensibility* (1811), *Pride and Prejudice* (1813), *Mansfield Park* (1814), *Emma* (1816), *Northanger Abbey* (1818), and *Persuasion* (1818)
austere Ⓣ *adj* **1** stern or severe **2** ascetic **3** severely simple or plain **austerely** *adv* **austerity** *n*
Australasian *n, adj* (person) from Australia, New Zealand, and neighbouring islands
Australian *n, adj* (person) from Australia
autarchy [**aw**-tar-kee] *n* absolute power or autocracy
autarky [**aw**-tar-kee] *n* policy of economic self-sufficiency
authentic Ⓣ *adj* known to be real, genuine **authentically** *adv* **authenticity** *n*
▸ **authenticate** *v* establish as genuine **authentication** *n*
author Ⓣ *n* **1** writer of a book etc. **2** originator

THESAURUS

aura *n* = **air**, quality, feeling, atmosphere, tone, mood, ambience
auspicious *adj* = **favourable**, bright, hopeful, promising, encouraging, felicitous
austere *adj* **1** = **stern**, serious, severe, formal, strict, solemn, forbidding **2** = **ascetic**, strict, solemn, sober, puritanical, abstemious, self-disciplined, strait-laced **3** = **plain**, simple, harsh, spare, bleak, stark, Spartan, homey
austerity *n* **1** = **sternness**, severity, seriousness, stiffness, formality, rigour, inflexibility, solemnity, strictness **2** = **asceticism**, sobriety, abstinence, puritanism, self-denial, self-discipline, rigour **3** = **plainness**, simplicity, starkness
authentic *adj* = **real**, true, genuine, bona fide • *an authentic French recipe* OPPOSITE: fake *See also*: **actual, exact, realistic**
authenticity *n* = **genuineness**, certainty, legitimacy, accuracy, validity, purity, truthfulness, faithfulness
author *n* **1** = **writer**, creator, composer **2** = **creator**, producer, father, founder, designer, architect, inventor, originator
authoritarian *adj* **1** = **strict**, severe, autocratic, dictatorial, tyrannical, dogmatic, doctrinaire ▸ *n* **2** = **disciplinarian**, dictator, tyrant, despot, absolutist, autocrat
authoritative *adj* **1** = **reliable**, accurate,

DICTIONARY

or creator **authoress** *n fem* **authorship** *n*
authority Ⓣ *n, pl* **-ties** 1 power to command or control others 2 *often pl* person or group having this power 3 expert in a particular field
▸**authoritarian** *n, adj* (person) insisting on strict obedience to authority
▸**authoritative** *adj* 1 recognized as being reliable: *the authoritative book on Shakespeare* 2 possessing authority **authoritatively** *adv*
▸**authorize** *v* 1 give authority to 2 give permission for **authorization** *n*
autism *n psychiatry* disorder, usu. of children, characterized by lack of response to people and limited ability to communicate **autistic** *adj*
auto- *combining form* self-: *autobiography*
autobahn *n* German motorway
autobiography *n, pl* **-phies** account of a person's life written by that person **autobiographical** *adj* **autobiographically** *adv*
autocrat Ⓣ *n* 1 absolute ruler 2 dictatorial person **autocratic** *adj* **autocratically** *adv*
▸**autocracy** *n* government by an autocrat
autocross *n* motor-racing over a rough course
Autocue *n* ® electronic television prompting device displaying a speaker's script, unseen by the audience
autogiro, autogyro *n, pl* **-ros** self-propelled aircraft resembling a helicopter but with an unpowered rotor
autograph *n* 1 handwritten signature of a (famous) person ▷ *v* 2 write one's signature on or in
automate *v* make (a manufacturing process) automatic
automatic Ⓣ *adj* 1 (of a device) operating mechanically by itself 2 (of a process) performed by automatic equipment 3 done without conscious thought 4 (of a firearm) self-loading ▷ *n* 5 self-loading firearm 6 vehicle with automatic transmission
automatically *adv*
▸**automatic transmission** transmission system in a motor vehicle in which the gears change automatically
▸**automation** *n* use of automatic devices in industrial production
▸**automaton** *n* 1 robot 2 person who acts mechanically
automobile Ⓣ *n* motor vehicle designed to carry a small number of people
autonomy Ⓣ *n* self-government
autonomous *adj*
autopsy *n, pl* **-sies** examination of a corpse to determine the cause of death
autoroute *n* expressway
autosuggestion *n* process in which a person unconsciously influences his or her own behaviour or beliefs
autumn *n* fall **autumnal** *adj* **autumnally** *adv*
auxiliary Ⓣ *adj* 1 secondary or supplementary 2 supporting ▷ *n, pl* **-ries** 3 person or thing that supplements or supports
▸**auxiliary verb** verb used to form the tense, voice, or mood of another, such as *will* in *I will go*

THESAURUS

valid, definitive, authentic, dependable, trustworthy **2 = commanding**, assertive, imposing, imperious, self-assured, masterly
authority *n* **1 = power**, control, weight, influence, direction, command, sway, supremacy **2** (*usually pl*) **= powers that be**, government, police, management, administration, officialdom, the Establishment **3 = expert**, judge, professional, specialist, master, connoisseur
authorization *n* **= permission**, leave, approval, warrant, permit, licence, a blank check
authorize *v* **1 = empower**, commission, enable, entitle, accredit, give authority **2 = permit**, allow, approve, warrant, sanction, license, give authority for
authorized *See* **legal, official**
autocracy *n* **= dictatorship**, tyranny, absolutism, despotism
autocrat *n* **= dictator**, tyrant, despot, absolutist
autocratic *adj* **= dictatorial**, absolute, despotic, tyrannical, imperious, all-powerful, domineering
automated *See* **automatic**
automatic *adj* **1 = mechanical**, robotic, automated, self-propelled • *An ATM is an automatic teller machine.* **2 = involuntary**, natural, reflex, instinctive • *automatic body functions*
automobile *n* **= car**, vehicle • *the Japanese automobile manufacturer*
autonomous *adj* **= self-ruling**, free, independent, sovereign, self-determining, self-governing
autonomy *n* **= independence**, freedom, sovereignty, self-government, self-determination, self-rule, home rule
auxiliary *adj* **1 = supplementary**, reserve, emergency, subsidiary, secondary, substitute, back-up, fall-back **2 = supporting**, accessory, ancillary, aiding, assisting, helping ▸ *n* **3 = backup**, reserve **4 = helper**, supporter, associate, assistant, companion, subordinate
avail *v* **1 = benefit**, help, profit, assist, aid, be of advantage, be useful ▸ *n* **2 = benefit**,

a

DICTIONARY

avail Ⓣ *v* **1** be of use or advantage (to) ▷ *n* **2** use or advantage: *to no avail*
▶ **avail oneself of** make use of
available Ⓣ *adj* obtainable or accessible **availability** *n*
avalanche Ⓣ *n* **1** mass of snow or ice falling down a mountain **2** sudden overwhelming quantity of anything
avant-garde Ⓣ [av-ong-**gard**] *n* **1** group of innovators, esp. in the arts ▷ *adj* **2** innovative and progressive
avarice Ⓣ [**av**-a-riss] *n* greed for wealth **avaricious** *adj*
avast *interj naut* stop
avatar *n Hinduism* appearance of a god in animal or human form
Ave. Avenue
Ave Maria [**ah**-vay ma-**ree**-a] *n* same as **Hail Mary**
avenge Ⓣ *v* take revenge in retaliation for (harm done) or on behalf of (a person harmed) **avenger** *n*
avenue Ⓣ *n* **1** wide street **2** road between two rows of trees **3** way of approach
aver [av-**vur**] *v* **averring, averred** state to be true **averment** *n*
average Ⓣ *n* **1** typical or normal amount or quality **2** result obtained by adding quantities together and dividing the total by the number of quantities ▷ *adj* **3** usual or typical **4** calculated as an average ▷ *v* **5** calculate the average of **6** amount to as an average
Averroës *n* Arabic name *ibn-Rushd*. 1126–88, Arab philosopher and physician in Spain, noted particularly for his attempts to reconcile Aristotelian philosophy with Islamic religion, which profoundly influenced Christian scholasticism
averse Ⓣ *adj* (usu. foll. by *to*) disinclined or unwilling
▶ **aversion** *n* **1** strong dislike **2** person or thing disliked
avert Ⓣ *v* **1** turn away **2** ward off
avg. average
aviary *n, pl* **aviaries** large cage or enclosure for birds
aviation *n* art of flying aircraft **aviator** *n*
avid Ⓣ *adj* **1** keen or enthusiastic **2** greedy (for) **avidly** *adv* **avidity** *n*
avocado *n, pl* **-dos** pear-shaped tropical fruit with a leathery green skin and yellowish-green flesh
avocation *n old-fashioned* **1** occupation **2** hobby
avocet *n* long-legged wading bird with a long slender upward-curving bill
Avogadro *n* **Amedeo**, Conte di Quaregna. 1776–1856, Italian physicist, noted for his work on gases
avoid Ⓣ *v* **1** refrain from **2** prevent from happening **3** keep away from

THESAURUS

help, good, use, profit, aid, advantage
availability *n* = **accessibility**, readiness, attainability, handiness
available *adj* = **accessible**, free, handy, at someone's disposal, on hand • *There are three campsites still available for the long weekend.* OPPOSITE: unavailable
See also: **ready**
avalanche *n* **1** = **snow-slide**, landslide, landslip **2** = **flood**, barrage, deluge, torrent, inundation
avant-garde *adj* = **progressive**, experimental, innovative, unconventional, ground-breaking, pioneering
avarice *n* = **greed**, covetousness, meanness, miserliness, niggardliness, parsimony, stinginess
avaricious *adj* = **greedy**, cheap, stingy, miserly, parsimonious, covetous, niggardly, grasping
avenge *v* = **get revenge for**, get even for (*informal*), punish, repay, retaliate, hit back
avenue *n* = **street**, way, drive, road, course, approach, route, path, passage, boulevard
average *adj* **1** = **usual**, standard, regular, normal, typical • *the average Canadian teenager* **2** = **mean**, medium, middle, median, intermediate ▶ *n* **3** = **usual**, mean, medium, standard, normal, par, norm, midpoint ▷ **on average** = **usually**, generally, normally, as a rule, typically • *Men are, on average, taller than women.* ▶ *v* **4** = **make on average**, balance out to, be on average, do on average, even out to
See also: **all right, common, moderate**
averse *adj* = **opposed**, reluctant, hostile, unwilling, loath, disinclined, ill-disposed
aversion *n* = **hatred**, hostility, dislike, unwillingness, animosity, revulsion, antipathy, disinclination
avert *v* **1** = **turn away**, turn aside **2** = **ward off**, prevent, avoid, frustrate, forestall, preclude, fend off, stave off
aviator *n* = **pilot**, flyer, airman, aeronaut
avid *adj* **1** = **enthusiastic**, intense, eager, keen, passionate, devoted, zealous, ardent, fanatical **2** = **insatiable**, hungry, thirsty, greedy, voracious, ravenous, grasping, rapacious
avoid *v* **1** = **refrain from**, dodge, shirk, duck out of (*informal*) • *He avoids talking about unpleasant things.* **2** = **keep away from**, shun, elude, evade, dodge, sidestep, eschew (*formal*), steer clear of • *She thought he was trying to avoid her.* **3** = **prevent**, avert
See also: **abstain, escape**

DICTIONARY

avoidable *adj* **avoidance** *n*
avoirdupois [av-er-de-**poise**] *n* system of weights based on pounds and ounces
avow *v* **1** state or affirm **2** admit openly
avowal *n* **avowed** *adj* **avowedly** *adv*
avuncular *adj* friendly, helpful, and caring towards someone younger
await Ⓣ *v* **1** wait for **2** be in store for
awake Ⓣ *adj* **1** not sleeping **2** alert ▷ *v* **awaking, awoke, awoken 3** emerge or rouse from sleep **4** (cause to) become alert
awaken Ⓣ *v* awake
▶ **awakening** *n* start of a feeling or awareness
award Ⓣ *v* **1** give (something, such as a prize) formally ▷ *n* **2** something awarded, such as a prize
aware Ⓣ *adj* having knowledge, informed
awareness *n*
awash *adv* washed over by water
away Ⓣ *adv* **1** from a place: *go away* **2** to another place: *put that gun away* **3** out of existence: *fade away* **4** continuously: *laughing away* ▷ *adj* **5** not present **6** distant: *two miles away* **7** *sports* played on an opponent's ground
awe Ⓣ *n* **1** wonder and respect mixed with dread ▷ *v* **2** fill with awe
▶ **awesome** *adj* **1** inspiring awe **2** *slang* excellent or wonderful
▶ **awestruck** *adj* filled with awe
awful Ⓣ *adj* **1** very bad or unpleasant **2** *obsolete* inspiring awe **3** *informal* very great
▶ **awfully** *adv* **1** in an unpleasant way **2** *informal* very
awhile *adv* for a time
awkward Ⓣ *adj* **1** clumsy or ungainly **2** embarrassed **3** difficult to use, handle, or deal with **4** inconvenient **awkwardly** *adv* **awkwardness** *n*
awl *n* pointed tool for piercing wood, leather, etc.
awning *n* canvas roof supported by a frame to give protection against the weather
awoke *v* past tense of **awake**
▶ **awoken** *v* past participle of **awake**

THESAURUS

avoidance *n* = **evasion**, escape, dodging, eluding, keeping away, shunning, steering clear
avowed *adj* **1** = **declared**, open, self-proclaimed, professed, sworn **2** = **confessed**, acknowledged, admitted
await *v* **1** = **wait for**, expect, anticipate, abide, look for, look forward to, stay for **2** = **be in store for**, attend, be in readiness for, be prepared for, be ready for, wait for
awake *adj* **1** = **not sleeping**, aware, conscious, aroused, awakened, wakeful, wide- awake **2** = **alert**, alive, aware, vigilant, watchful, attentive, observant, heedful, on the lookout ▶ *v* **3** = **wake up**, wake, awaken, rouse **4** = **alert**, revive, provoke, stimulate, arouse, kindle, stir up
awaken *v* **1** = **awake**, wake, revive, arouse, rouse **2** = **alert**, provoke, stimulate, kindle, stir up
awakening *n* = **waking up**, revival, stimulation, rousing, arousal, stirring up
award *v* **1** = **give**, present, grant, bestow, confer, endow, hand out ▶ *n* **2** = **prize**, grant, gift, trophy, decoration ▷ **award-winning** *See* **prize**
aware *adj* ▷ **aware of** = **conscious of**, acquainted with, familiar with, mindful of • *She was acutely aware of the noise of the city*; = **informed**, knowledgeable, in the picture • *Keep me aware of any developments*. OPPOSITE: unaware
See also: **perceptive**
awareness *n* = **knowledge**, understanding, recognition, perception, consciousness, realization, familiarity
away *adv* **1** = **off**, elsewhere, abroad, hence, from here, from home **2** = **at a distance**, far, apart, remote **3** = **aside**, out of the way, to one side **4** = **continuously**, repeatedly, relentlessly, incessantly, interminably, uninterruptedly, unremittingly ▶ *adj* **5** = **not present**, out, elsewhere, abroad, absent, gone, not at home, not here
awe *n* **1** = **wonder**, fear, respect, terror, horror, dread, admiration, amazement, astonishment, reverence ▶ *v* **2** = **impress**, stun, intimidate, terrify, frighten, astonish, amaze, horrify
awesome *adj* **1** = **awe-inspiring**, cool (*informal*), amazing, impressive, formidable, breathtaking, astonishing, intimidating, phat (*slang*), stunning **2** (*Informal*) = **first-class**, choice, excellent, elite, superior, world-class, hand-picked, first-rate
awful *adj* = **terrible**, horrendous, appalling, dreadful, ghastly, frightful • *the same awful jokes*
See also: **horrible**
awfully *adv* **1** = **badly**, woefully, disgracefully, dreadfully, reprehensibly, unforgivably, unpleasantly, wretchedly **2** (*Informal*) = **very**, extremely, greatly, terribly, exceptionally, immensely, exceedingly, dreadfully
awkward *adj* **1** = **clumsy**, lumbering, ungainly, gauche, gawky, inelegant, uncoordinated **2** = **unmanageable**, difficult, inconvenient, troublesome, cumbersome, clunky (*informal*), unwieldy **3** = **embarrassing**, difficult, delicate, uncomfortable, inconvenient, ill at ease

DICTIONARY

AWOL *adj mil* absent without leave
awry [a-**rye**] *adv, adj* **1** with a twist to one side, askew **2** amiss
axe Ⓣ *n* **1** tool with a sharp blade for felling trees or chopping wood **2** *informal* dismissal from employment etc. ▷ *v* **3** *informal* dismiss (employees), restrict (expenditure), or terminate (a project)
axil *n* angle where the stalk of a leaf joins a stem
axiom Ⓣ *n* **1** generally accepted principle **2** self-evident statement
▶ **axiomatic** *adj* **1** containing axioms **2** self-evident
axis Ⓣ *n, pl* **axes 1** (imaginary) line round which a body can rotate or about which an object or geometrical figure is symmetrical **2** one of two fixed lines on a graph, against which quantities or positions are measured
axial *adj* **axially** *adv*
axle Ⓣ *n* shaft on which a wheel or pair of wheels turn
ayatollah *n* Islamic religious leader in Iran
aye, ay Ⓣ *interj* **1** yes ▷ *n* **2** affirmative vote or voter
Aykroyd *n* **Dan**, full name *Daniel Edward Aykroyd*. born 1952, Canadian film actor and screenwriter, best known for the television show *Saturday Night Live* (1975–80) and the films *The Blues Brothers* (1980), *Ghostbusters* (1984), and *Driving Miss Daisy* (1989)
azalea [az-**zale**-ee-ya] *n* garden shrub grown for its showy flowers
Azaña *n* **Manuel**. 1880–1940, Spanish statesman; president of the Spanish Republic (1936–39) until overthrown by Franco
Azikiwe *n* **Nnamdi**. 1904–96, Nigerian statesman; first president of Nigeria (1963–66)
azimuth *n* **1** arc of the sky between the zenith and the horizon **2** horizontal angle of a bearing measured clockwise from the north
Aztec *n, adj* (person) of the Indian race ruling Mexico before the Spanish conquest in the 16th century
azure *adj, n* (of) the colour of a clear blue sky

THESAURUS

awkwardness *n* **1** = **clumsiness**, gawkiness, inelegance, ungainliness **2** = **unwieldiness**, difficulty, inconvenience **3** = **embarrassment**, difficulty, inconvenience, delicacy
axe *n* **1** = **hatchet**, chopper, adze ▷ **the axe** (*Informal*) = **dismissal**, termination, the boot (*slang*), the chop (*slang*) ▶ *v* **2** (*Informal*) = **cut back**, fire (*informal*), remove, cancel, eliminate, dismiss, sack (*informal*), dispense with, get rid of
axiom *n* = **principle**, adage, maxim, truism, dictum, aphorism, precept
axiomatic *adj* = **self-evident**, certain, manifest, granted, accepted, given, assumed, understood
axis *n* = **pivot**, shaft, spindle, axle, centre line
axle *n* = **shaft**, pin, pivot, rod, axis, spindle
aye *See* **yes**

Bb

BA Bachelor of Arts
baa *v* **baaing, baaed 1** make the cry of a sheep ▷ *n* **2** cry made by a sheep
baba *n* small cake, usu. soaked in rum
Babbage *n* **Charles**. 1792–1871, English mathematician and inventor, who built a calculating machine that anticipated the modern electronic computer
babble Ⓣ *v* **1** talk excitedly or foolishly **2** (of streams) make a low murmuring sound ▷ *n* **3** incoherent or foolish talk
babe *n* baby
babel [**babe**-el] *n* confused mixture of noises or voices
babiche *n* thongs or lacings of rawhide
Babington *n* **Anthony**. 1561–86, English conspirator, executed for organizing an unsuccessful plot (1586) to assassinate Elizabeth I and place Mary, Queen of Scots, on the English throne
baboon *n* large monkey with a pointed face and a long tail
baby Ⓣ *n, pl* **-bies 1** very young child or animal **2** *slang* sweetheart ▷ *adj* **3** comparatively small of its type **babyish** *adj*
▶ **baby beef 1** young beef animal **2** its meat
▶ **baby carriage** small hand-pushed carriage for a baby
▶ **baby-sit** *v* take care of a child while the parents are out **baby-sitter** *n*
baccarat [**back**-a-rah] *n* card game involving gambling
bacchanalia *pl n* drunken revelry or orgy
Bach *n* **1 Johann Christian**, 11th son of J. S. Bach. 1735–82, German composer, called *the English Bach*, resident in London from 1762 **2 Johann Christoph**. 1642–1703, German composer: wrote oratorios, cantatas, and motets, some of which were falsely attributed to J. S. Bach, of whom he was a distant relative **3 Johann Sebastian**. 1685–1750, German composer: church organist at Arnstadt (1703–07) and Mühlhausen (1707–08); court organist at Weimar (1708–17); musical director for Prince Leopold of Köthen (1717–28); musical director for the city of Leipzig (1728–50). His output was enormous and displays great vigour and invention within the northern European polyphonic tradition. His works include nearly 200 cantatas and oratorios, settings of the *Passion according to St John* (1723) and *St Matthew* (1729), the six *Brandenburg Concertos* (1720–21), the 48 preludes and fugues of the *Well-tempered Clavier* (completed 1744), and the *Mass in B Minor* (1733–38) **4 Karl** (*or* **Carl**) **Philipp Emanuel**, 3rd son of J. S. Bach. 1714–88, German composer, chiefly of symphonies, keyboard sonatas, and church music **5 Wilhelm Friedemann**, eldest son of J. S. Bach. 1710–84, German composer: wrote nine symphonies and much keyboard and religious music
Bacharach *n* **Burt**. born 1928, US composer of popular songs, usually with lyricist Hal David
bachelor *n* **1** unmarried man **2** person who holds the lowest university degree
bacillus [bass-**ill**-luss] *n, pl* **-li** [-lie] rod-shaped bacterium
back Ⓣ *n* **1** rear part of the human body, from the neck to the pelvis **2** part or side of an object opposite the front **3** part of anything less often seen or used **4** *ball games* defensive player or position ▷ *v* **5** (cause to) move backwards **6** provide money for (a person or enterprise) **7** bet on the success of **8** (foll.

THESAURUS

babble *v* **1 = blabber**, chatter, gurgle, burble, gabble, jabber, prattle, gibber • *He babbled on and on.* **2** *See* **gurgle** ▶ *n* **3 = gabble**, drivel, burble, gibberish
See also: **ramble, rave**
babies *See* **young**
baby *n* **1 = infant**, child, newborn *or* newborn child, tot, babe, suckling, little one, babe in arms, neonate, rug rat (*informal*), ankle biter (*informal*) • *I've had a dimple since I was a baby.* **2 = sissy**, suck (*chiefly Canad*), coward, wimp, pansy (*offensive slang*), weakling, pussy (*taboo slang*), wuss (*slang*), milquetoast, pantywaist (*informal*) ▶ *adj* **3 = small**, minute, little, tiny, mini, miniature, wee, teeny-weeny
babyish *adj* **= childish**, juvenile, foolish, immature, infantile, puerile, sissy, spoiled
back *n* **1 = rear**, end, reverse, stern • *the back of a postcard* OPPOSITE: front ▷ **behind one's back = secretly**, surreptitiously, covertly, deceitfully, sneakily ▶ *v* **2 =**

DICTIONARY

by *onto*) have the back facing towards ▷ *adj* **9** situated behind **10** owing from an earlier date ▷ *adv* **11** at, to, or towards the rear **12** to or towards the original starting point or condition

▶ **back bacon** sweet pickled bacon cut from the loin

▶ **backbench** *adj Canad, Brit, Aust, & NZ* relating to a backbencher or backbenchers

▶ **backbencher** *n* Member of Parliament who does not hold office in the government or opposition

▶ **backbiting** *n* spiteful talk about an absent person

▶ **backbone** *n* **1** spinal column **2** strength of character

▶ **back channel** secret or unofficial intermediary or means of communication

▶ **backchat** *n informal* answering back, esp. impudently

▶ **backcheck** *v hockey* (of a forward) return to the defensive area and check attacking opponents

▶ **backcloth** *or* **backdrop** *n* painted curtain at the back of a stage set

▶ **backdate** *v* make (a document) effective from an earlier date

▶ **backer** *n* person who gives financial support

▶ **backfire** *v* **1** (of a plan) fail to have the desired effect **2** (of an engine) make a loud noise like an explosion

▶ **back forty 1** area of farm most remote from a farmhouse **2** any remote area

▶ **background** *n* **1** events or circumstances that help to explain something **2** person's social class, education, or experience **3** space behind the chief figures in a picture

▶ **backhand** *n tennis etc.* stroke played with the back of the hand facing the direction of the stroke

▶ **backhanded** *adj* sarcastic: *a backhanded compliment*

▶ **backhouse** *n* outhouse

▶ **backing** *n* **1** support **2** musical accompaniment for a pop singer

▶ **backlash** *n* sudden and adverse reaction

▶ **backlog** *n* accumulation of things to be dealt with

▶ **backpack** *n* rucksack

▶ **backside** *n informal* buttocks

▶ **backslide** *v* relapse into former bad habits
backslider *n*

▶ **backstage** *adv, adj* behind the stage in a theatre

▶ **backstroke** *n* swimming stroke performed on the back

▶ **backtrack** *v* **1** return by the same route by which one has come **2** retract or reverse one's opinion or policy

▶ **back up** *v* support

▶ **backup** *n* **1** support or reinforcement **2** reserve or substitute

▶ **backward** *adj* **1** directed towards the

THESAURUS

support, second, endorse, champion, promote, favour, encourage, advocate, espouse • *His friends are backing him.* OPPOSITE: oppose **3 = move back**, retire, withdraw, retreat, reverse, backtrack, back off, go back, turn tail ▷ **back away** *See* **retreat** ▷ **back down = give in**, withdraw, submit, surrender, concede, yield, cave *or* cave in, accede, admit defeat, back-pedal ▶ **back off** *See* **retreat** ▷ **back out** (often with *of*) **= withdraw**, cancel, resign, quit, abandon, retreat, excuse oneself, give up, go back on, wimp out (*slang*) ▷ **back up = support**, second, confirm, assist, aid, bolster, reinforce, substantiate, corroborate, stand by ▶ *adj* **4 = rear**, end, tail, hind, posterior, hindmost **5 = previous**, former, past, earlier, delayed, overdue, elapsed
See also: **finance, gamble, sanction**

backbiting *n* **= slander**, gossip, defamation, malice, bitchiness (*slang*), cattiness (*informal*), disparagement, scandalmongering, spitefulness

backbone *n* **1** (*Medical*) **= spinal column**, spine, vertebrae, vertebral column **2 = strength of character**, character, resolution, nerve, determination, courage, pluck, grit, fortitude

backbreaking *adj* **= exhausting**, hard, arduous, strenuous, gruelling, crushing, laborious, punishing

backer *n* **= supporter**, second, advocate, sponsor, subscriber, patron, promoter, angel (*informal*), benefactor

backfire *v* **= fail**, rebound, disappoint, flop (*informal*), miscarry, recoil, boomerang

background *n* **= social circumstances**, history, environment, culture, upbringing • *What is your family's background?*
See also: **foil, record, surroundings**

backing *n* **= support**, aid, sponsorship, assistance, endorsement, encouragement, patronage, moral support

backlash *n* **= reaction**, response, resistance, retaliation, repercussion, recoil, counteraction

backlog *n* **= build-up**, stock, reserve, supply, excess, hoard, accumulation

backside *See* **buttocks**

backslide *v* **= relapse**, slip, weaken, lapse, stray, revert, go astray, go wrong

backslider *n* **= relapser**, deserter, renegade, apostate, turncoat, recidivist, recreant

backward *adj* **= slow**, behind, dull,

DICTIONARY

rear **2** retarded in physical, material, or intellectual development **backwardness** *n*
▸ **backwards** *adv* **1** towards the rear **2** with the back foremost **3** in the reverse of the usual direction
▸ **backwash** *n* **1** water washed backwards by the motion of a boat **2** repercussion
▸ **backwater** *n* isolated or backward place or condition
▸ **backwoods** *pl n* remote sparsely populated area
backgammon *n* game played with counters and dice
bacon *n* salted or smoked pig meat
Bacon *n* **1 Francis**. 1909–92, British painter, born in Dublin, noted for his distorted, richly coloured human figures, dogs, and carcasses **2 Francis**, Baron Verulam, Viscount St Albans. 1561–1626, English philosopher, statesman, and essayist; described the inductive method of reasoning: his works include *Essays* (1625), *The Advancement of Learning* (1605), and *Novum Organum* (1620) **3 Roger**. ?1214–92, English Franciscan monk, scholar, and scientist: stressed the importance of experiment, demonstrated that air is required for combustion, and first used lenses to correct vision. His *Opus Majus* (1266) is a compendium of all the sciences of his age
bacteria Ⓣ *pl n, sing.* **-rium** large group of microorganisms, many of which cause disease **bacterial** *adj*
▸ **bacteriology** *n* study of bacteria **bacteriologist** *n*
bad Ⓣ *adj* **worse, worst** **1** of poor quality **2** lacking skill or talent **3** harmful **4** immoral or evil **5** naughty or mischievous **6** rotten or decayed **7** severe or unpleasant **badly** *adv* **badness** *n*
▸ **badlands** *pl n* barren, rocky region in western N America
bade *v* a past tense of **bid**
badge Ⓣ *n* emblem worn to show membership, rank, etc.
badger Ⓣ *n* **1** nocturnal burrowing mammal with a black and white head ▹ *v* **2** pester or harass
badinage Ⓣ [**bad**-in-nahzh] *n* playful and witty conversation
badminton *n* game played with a racket and shuttlecock, which is hit over a high net
Baeck *n* **Leo**. 1873–1956, German Jewish theologian: a leader of the German Jews during the Nazi period. His major work is *The Essence of Judaism* (1905)
Baez *n* **Joan**. born 1941, US rock and folk singer and songwriter, noted for the pure quality of her voice and for her committed pacifist and protest songs
baffle Ⓣ *v* perplex or puzzle **bafflement** *n*
bag Ⓣ *n* **1** flexible container with an opening at one end **2** *offensive* ugly or bad-tempered woman **bags** **3** *informal* (foll. by *of*) lots of ▹ *v* **bagging, bagged** **4** put into a bag **5** (cause to) bulge **6** capture or kill

THESAURUS

undeveloped, underdeveloped, retarded, subnormal
backwards, backward *adv* = **towards the rear**, behind, in reverse, rearward
bacteria *pl n* = **microorganisms**, bacilli, bugs (*slang*), germs, microbes, pathogens, viruses
bad *adj* **1** = **inferior**, poor, faulty, inadequate, defective, lousy (*slang*), substandard, unsatisfactory, imperfect • *bad roads* OPPOSITE: satisfactory **2** *See* **harmful** **3** = **evil**, mean, criminal, wrong, corrupt, wicked, immoral, sinful • *a bad person* OPPOSITE: good **4** = **naughty**, unruly, mischievous, disobedient **5** = **rotten**, decayed, mouldy, sour, rancid, putrid, spoiled **6** = **unfavourable**, troubled, unfortunate, adverse, grim, gloomy, unpleasant, distressing
See also: **serious**
badge *n* = **mark**, sign, device, brand, stamp, identification, token, emblem, insignia
badger *v* = **pester**, plague, bully, harass, hound, nag, torment, goad, importune
badinage *n* = **banter**, mockery, wordplay, teasing, repartee, pleasantry
badly *adv* **1** = **poorly**, wrongly, incorrectly, inadequately, carelessly, imperfectly, ineptly • *This essay is badly written.* OPPOSITE: well **2** = **unfavourably**, unfortunately, unsuccessfully OPPOSITE: well **3** = **severely**, seriously, extremely, deeply, greatly, desperately, intensely, exceedingly
bad-mouth *verb* (*Slang*) = **criticize**, abuse, insult, mock, deride, malign, slander
badness *See* **evil**
baffle *v* = **puzzle**, confuse, stump, mystify, bewilder, perplex, confound, flummox, nonplus
baffled *See* **confused**
baffling *adj* = **puzzling**, unclear, mysterious, strange, weird, confusing, elusive, enigmatic, incomprehensible, inexplicable, unfathomable, unaccountable, perplexing, bewildering, mystifying OPPOSITE: understandable
bag *n* **1** = **container**, sack, pouch, receptacle **2** = **handbag**, clutch *or* clutch bag, purse, shoulder bag, evening bag **3** = **luggage**, chest, baggage, backpack, trunk, suitcase, knapsack, crate, overnighter ▸ *v* **4** = **catch**, kill, shoot, land,

DICTIONARY

▸**baggy** *adj* (of clothes) hanging loosely
▸**bagman** *n informal* person who solicits money for a political party
bagatelle *n* **1** something of little value **2** board game in which balls are struck into holes
baggage Ⓣ *n* suitcases packed for a journey
bagpipes *pl n* musical wind instrument with reed pipes and an inflatable bag

b

bail[1] Ⓣ *n law* **1** money deposited with a court as security for a person's reappearance in court ▹*v* **2** pay bail for (a person)
bail[2], **bale** Ⓣ *v* (foll. by *out*) remove (water) from (a boat)
▸**bail on** *v slang* leave or abandon a person or thing
▸**bail out** *or* **bale out** *v* **1** *informal* help (a person or organization) out of a predicament **2** make an emergency parachute jump from an aircraft
bailey *n* outermost wall or court of a castle
Bailey *n* **1** **David**. born 1938, English photographer **2** **Donovan**. born 1967 in Jamaica. Canadian sprinter: winner of two gold medals at the Olympic Games
bailiff *n* **1** sheriff's officer who serves writs and summonses **2** court official **3** landlord's agent
bailiwick *n* bailiff's area of jurisdiction
bairn *n Scot* child
bait Ⓣ *n* **1** piece of food on a hook or in a trap to attract fish or animals ▹*v* **2** put a piece of food on or in (a hook or trap) **3** persecute or tease
baize *n* woollen fabric used to cover billiard and card tables
bake Ⓣ *v* **1** cook by dry heat as in an oven **2** make or become hardened by heat
▸**baker** *n* person whose business is to make or sell bread, cakes, etc.
▸**baker's dozen** thirteen
▸**bakery** *n, pl* **-eries** place where bread, cakes, etc. are baked or sold
▸**baking powder** powdered mixture used in baking instead of yeast
bakeapple *n* cloudberry
Baker *n* **1** Sir **Benjamin**. 1840–1907, British engineer who, with Sir John Fowler, designed and constructed much of the London underground railway, the Forth Railway Bridge, and the first Aswan Dam **2** Sir **Samuel White**. 1821–93, British explorer: discovered Lake Albert (1864)
baksheesh *n* (in some Eastern countries) money given as a tip
Bakunin *n* **Mikhail**. 1814–76, Russian anarchist and writer: a prominent member of the First International, expelled from it after conflicts with Marx
Balaclava, Balaclava helmet *n* close-fitting woollen hood that covers the ears and neck
Balaguer *n* **Joaquin**. 1907–2002, Dominican statesman; president of the Dominican Republic (1960–62, 1966–78, 1986–96)
Balakirev *n* **Mily Alexeyevich**. 1837–1910, Russian composer, whose works include two symphonic poems, two symphonies, and many arrangements of Russian folk songs
balalaika *n* guitar-like musical instrument with a triangular body
balance Ⓣ *n* **1** stability of mind or body **2** state of being in balance **3** harmony in the parts of a whole **4** something that remains **5** difference between the credits and debits of an account **6** weighing device ▹*v* **7** weigh on a balance **8** remain steady **9** equalize in weight, amount, etc. **10** consider or compare
Balboa *n* **Vasco Núñez de**. ?1475–1519, Spanish explorer, who discovered the Pacific Ocean in 1513
balcony Ⓣ *n, pl* **-nies** **1** platform on the outside of a building with a rail along the

THESAURUS

capture, acquire, trap
baggage *n* = **luggage**, equipment, gear, paraphernalia, accoutrements, bags, belongings, suitcases, things
baggy *adj* = **loose**, slack, floppy, ill-fitting, oversize, droopy, roomy, bulging, sagging
bail *n* (*Law*) = **security**, pledge, bond, guarantee, warranty, surety ▸*v* ▹**bail out** = **help**, aid, rescue, relieve, save (someone's) bacon (*informal*); = **escaped**, quit, withdraw, retreat, flee, recede, slip away
bait *n* **1** = **lure**, incentive, attraction, bribe, temptation, snare, inducement, decoy, allurement, enticement • *He isn't taking the bait.* ▸*v* **2** = **tease**, bother, harass, annoy, hound, irritate, hassle (*informal*), persecute, torment
See also: **pick on**
bake *See* **cook, harden**
baked *adj* = **dry**, torrid, arid, parched, sun-baked, desiccated, scorched, seared
balance *v* **1** = **stabilize**, level, steady • *Balancing on one leg is difficult.* **2** = **compare**, consider, estimate, weigh, assess, evaluate, deliberate **3** (*Accounting*) = **calculate**, total, settle, square, tally, compute ▸*n* **4** = **equilibrium**, parity, equity • *the chemical balance of the brain* **5** = **stability**, poise, composure, self-control, equanimity, self-possession, steadiness **6** = **remainder**, rest, difference, surplus, residue
See also: **compensate**
balcony *n* **1** = **terrace**, veranda **2** = **upper circle**, gallery, gods, peanut gallery (*informal*)

DICTIONARY

outer edge **2** upper tier of seats in a theatre or cinema
bald ⓣ *adj* **1** having little or no hair on the scalp **2** (of a tire) having a worn tread **3** without unnecessary words **baldness** *n*
▸**balding** *adj* becoming bald
▸**bald prairie** part of prairie without trees
balderdash *n* stupid talk
Baldwin *n* **1 James Arthur**. 1924–87, US Black writer, whose works include the novel *Go Tell it on the Mountain* (1954) **2 Stanley**, 1st Earl Baldwin of Bewdley. 1867–1947, British Conservative statesman: prime minister (1923–24, 1924–29, 1935–37)
bale[1] *n* **1** large bundle of hay or goods tightly bound together ▷ *v* **2** make or put into bales
bale[2] *v* same as **bail**[2]
baleful *adj* vindictive or menacing
balefully *adv*
Balfour *n* **Arthur James**, 1st Earl of Balfour. 1848–1930, British Conservative statesman: prime minister (1902–05); foreign secretary (1916–19)
Baliol, Balliol *n* **1 Edward**. ?1283–1364, king of Scotland (1332, 1333–56) **2** his father, **John**. 1249–1315, king of Scotland (1292–96): defeated and imprisoned by Edward I of England (1296)
balk, baulk ⓣ *v* **1** be reluctant to (do something) **2** thwart or hinder
Balkan *adj* of any of the countries of the Balkan Peninsula: Romania, Bulgaria, Albania, Greece, the former Yugoslavia, and the European part of Turkey
ball[1] ⓣ *n* **1** round or nearly round object, esp. one used in games **2** single delivery of the ball in a game **3** *baseball* ball pitched outside the strike zone and not swung at by the batter **balls** *taboo, slang* **4** testicles **5** nonsense ▷ *v* **6** form into a ball
▸**ball bearings** steel balls between moving parts of a machine to reduce friction
▸**ball cock** device with a floating ball and a valve for regulating the flow of water
▸**ballpoint** *or* **ballpoint pen** *n* pen with a tiny ball bearing as a writing point
ball[2] *n* formal social function for dancing
ballroom *n*
Ball *n* **John**. died 1381, English priest: executed as one of the leaders of the Peasants' Revolt (1381)
ballad *n* **1** narrative poem or song **2** slow sentimental song
Ballantyne *n* **R(obert) M(ichael)**. 1825–94, British author, noted for such adventure stories as *The Coral Island* (1857)
Ballard *n* **J(ames) G(raham)**. 1930–2009, British novelist, born in China; his books include *Crash* (1973), *The Unlimited Dream Company* (1979), *Empire of the Sun* (1984), *Cocaine Nights* (1996), and *Super-Cannes* (2000)
ballast ⓣ *n* substance, such as sand, used to stabilize a ship when it is not carrying cargo
Ballesteros *n* **Severiano**. born 1957, Spanish professional golfer: won the British Open Championship (1979; 1984; 1988)
ballet *n* **1** classical style of expressive dancing based on conventional steps **2** theatrical performance of this
▸**ballerina** *n* female ballet dancer
ballistics *n* study of the flight of projectiles, such as bullets
▸**ballistic missile** missile guided automatically in flight but which falls freely at its target
balloon ⓣ *n* **1** inflatable rubber bag used as a plaything **2** large bag inflated with air or gas, designed to carry passengers in a basket underneath ▷ *v* **3** fly in a balloon **4** swell or increase rapidly in size **balloonist** *n*
ballot ⓣ *n* **1** method of voting secretly **2** actual vote or paper indicating a person's choice ▷ *v* **-loting, -loted 3** vote or ask for a vote from **ballot box**
ballyhoo ⓣ *n* exaggerated fuss
balm ⓣ *n* **1** aromatic substance used for healing and soothing **2** anything that comforts or soothes
balmy ⓣ *adj* **balmier, balmiest 1** (of

b

THESAURUS

bald *adj* **1 = hairless**, baldheaded, depilated **2 = plain**, direct, blunt, straightforward, forthright, unadorned, unvarnished
baldness *n* **1 = hairlessness**, alopecia (*pathol*), baldheadedness **2 = plainness**, severity, simplicity, austerity, bluntness
balk *v* **1 = recoil**, refuse, resist, evade, hesitate, shirk, flinch, jib, shrink from **2 = foil**, defeat, prevent, check, frustrate, thwart, hinder, obstruct, counteract
ball *n* **= sphere**, drop, globe, pellet, orb, globule, spheroid • *a soccer ball*
See also: **lump**
ballast *n* **= counterbalance**, weight, balance, stability, sandbag, equilibrium, counterweight, stabilizer
balloon *v* **= swell**, expand, inflate, billow, dilate, blow up, distend, grow rapidly, puff out
ballot *n* **= vote**, election, poll, polling, voting
ballyhoo *n* **= fuss**, noise, racket, commotion, to-do, babble, hubbub, hue and cry, hullabaloo
balm *n* **1 = ointment**, cream, lotion, balsam, embrocation, emollient, salve, unguent **2 = comfort**, solace, consolation, palliative, restorative, curative, anodyne
balmy *adj* **= mild**, pleasant, temperate,

DICTIONARY

weather) mild and pleasant **2** same as **barmy**
baloney Ⓣ *n informal* nonsense
balsa [**bawl**-sa] *n* tropical American tree that yields light wood
balsam *n* **1** soothing ointment **2** flowering plant
baluster *n* set of posts supporting a rail
▸**balustrade** *n* ornamental rail supported by balusters
Balzac *n* **Honoré de.** 1799–1850, French novelist: author of a collection of novels under the general title *La Comédie humaine*, including *Eugénie Grandet* (1833), *Le Père Goriot* (1834), and *La Cousine Bette* (1846)
bamboo *n* tall treelike tropical grass with hollow stems
bamboozle Ⓣ *v informal* **1** cheat or mislead **2** confuse, puzzle
ban Ⓣ *v* **banning, banned 1** prohibit or forbid officially ▹*n* **2** official prohibition
banal Ⓣ [ban-**nahl**] *adj* ordinary and unoriginal **banality** *n*
banana *n* yellow crescent-shaped fruit
band[1] Ⓣ *n* **1** group of musicians playing together **2** group of people having a common purpose **3** community of Canadian Indians recognized by federal government
bandsman *n*
▸**bandstand** *n* roofed outdoor platform for a band
▸**band together** *v* unite
band[2] Ⓣ *n* **1** strip of material, used to hold objects together **2** *physics* range of frequencies or wavelengths between two limits
Banda *n* **Hastings Kamuzu.** 1906–97, Malawi statesman. As first prime minister of Nyasaland (from 1963), he led his country to independence (1964) as Malawi: president (1966–94)
bandage Ⓣ *n* **1** piece of material used to cover a wound ▹*v* **2** cover with a bandage
bandanna, bandana *n* large brightly coloured handkerchief
Bandaranaike *n* **1 Chandrika.** See Chandrika **Kumaratunga 2 Sirimavo.** 1916–2000, prime minister of Sri Lanka, formerly Ceylon (1960–65; 1970–77; 1994–2000); the world's first woman prime minister **3** her husband, **Solomon.** 1899–1959, prime minister of Ceylon (1956–59); assassinated
b. and b., B and B bed and breakfast
bandit Ⓣ *n* robber, esp. a member of an armed gang **banditry** *n*
bandoleer, bandolier *n* shoulder belt for holding cartridges
bandwagon *n* **climb on the bandwagon** *or* **jump on the bandwagon** join a party or movement that seems assured of success
bandy *adj* **-dier, -diest 1** having legs curved outwards at the knees ▹*v* **-dying, -died 2** exchange (words) in a heated manner **3** circulate (a name, rumour, etc.)
bane Ⓣ *n* person or thing that causes misery or distress **baneful** *adj*
bang Ⓣ *n* **1** short loud explosive noise **2** hard blow or loud knock ▹*v* **3** hit or knock, esp. with a loud noise **4** close (a door) noisily ▹*adv* **5** with a sudden impact **6** precisely
banger *n* **1** *slang* sausage **2** *informal* old decrepit automobile **3** firework that explodes loudly
bangle *n* bracelet worn round the arm or the ankle
banish Ⓣ *v* **1** send (someone) into exile

THESAURUS

clement, summery
baloney *n (Informal)* = **nonsense**, garbage, crap (*slang*), drivel, hogwash, claptrap (*informal*), poppycock (*informal*), trash, tripe (*informal*), balderdash, hot air (*informal*)
bamboozle *v (Informal)* **1** = **cheat**, trick, fool, con (*informal*), dupe, deceive, swindle, hoodwink **2** = **puzzle**, confuse, baffle, stump, mystify, perplex, confound, befuddle
ban *v* **1** = **prohibit**, bar, exclude, forbid, banish, outlaw, suppress, disqualify, proscribe • *The coach was banned from the game.* OPPOSITE: permit ▸*n* **2** = **prohibition**, embargo, suppression, disqualification • *a ban on smoking* OPPOSITE: permit
See also: **sanctions, veto**
banal *adj* = **unoriginal**, pedestrian, stale, mundane, trite, unimaginative, hackneyed, humdrum, stereotyped
band[1] *n* **1** = **group**, orchestra • *a singer in a rock band* **2** = **gang**, company, party, crowd, bunch, troupe • *a band of thugs*
See also: **body, ring, team**
band[2] *n* = **strip**, bond, chain, belt, cord, strap, ribbon
bandage *n* **1** = **dressing**, compress, Band-Aid (*trademark*), gauze ▸*v* **2** = **dress**, cover, bind, swathe
bandit *n* = **robber**, thief, outlaw, desperado, highwayman, marauder
bane *n* = **plague**, ruin, curse, pest, scourge, nuisance, torment, bête noire
bang *v* **1** = **hit**, beat, pound, slam, knock, hammer, thump • *a toddler banging a saucepan with a wooden spoon* **2** = **explode**, boom, thump, thunder, resound, clang ▸*n* **3** = **explosion**, boom, crack, thump, detonation • *The balloon exploded with a bang.* **4** = **blow**, knock, thump, whack • *a nasty bang on the elbow* ▸*adv* **5** = **hard**, abruptly, suddenly, noisily **6** = **straight**, slap, smack, precisely
See also: **bump, crash**
banish *v* **1** = **exile**, deport, expel, eject, evict • *banished to a distant island* **2** = **dispel**,

DICTIONARY

2 dismiss from one's thoughts **banishment** *n*
banisters Ⓣ *pl n* railing supported by posts on a staircase
banjo *n, pl* **-jos, -joes** guitar-like musical instrument with a circular body
bank[1] Ⓣ *n* **1** institution offering services, such as the safekeeping and lending of money **2** any supply, store, or reserve ▷ *v* **3** deposit (cash or cheques) in a bank **banking** *n*
▸ **banker** *n* manager or owner of a bank
▸ **bank machine** machine that allows users to withdraw or deposit money at a bank
▸ **banknote** *n* piece of paper money
▸ **bank on** *v* rely on
bank[2] Ⓣ *n* **1** raised mass, esp. of earth **2** sloping ground at the side of a river ▷ *v* **3** form into a bank **4** cause (an aircraft) or (of an aircraft) to tip to one side on turning (of an aircraft)
bank[3] Ⓣ *n* row of switches, keys, etc. on a machine
bankrupt Ⓣ *n* **1** person declared by a court to be unable to pay his or her debts ▷ *adj* **2** financially ruined ▷ *v* **3** make bankrupt **bankruptcy** *n*
Banks *n* Sir **Joseph**. 1743–1820, British botanist and explorer: circumnavigated the world with James Cook (1768–71)
banner Ⓣ *n* **1** long strip of cloth displaying a slogan, advertisement, etc. **2** placard carried in a demonstration or procession
Bannister *n* Sir **Roger** (**Gilbert**). born 1929, British athlete and doctor: first man to run a mile in under four minutes (1954)
bannisters *pl n* same as **banisters**
bannock *n* round flat cake made from oatmeal or barley
banns *pl n* public declaration, esp. in a church, of an intended marriage
banquet Ⓣ *n* elaborate formal dinner
banshee *n* (in Irish folklore) female spirit whose wailing warns of impending death
bantam *n* **1** small chicken ▷ *adj* **2** *sports* under 15 years of age
▸ **bantamweight** *n* boxer weighing up to 118lb (professional) or 54kg (amateur)
banter Ⓣ *v* **1** tease jokingly ▷ *n* **2** teasing or joking conversation
Banting *n* Sir **Frederick Grant**. 1891–1941, Canadian physiologist: discovered the insulin treatment for diabetes with Best and Macleod (1922) and shared the Nobel prize for physiology or medicine with Macleod (1923)
Bantock *n* Sir **Granville**. 1868–1946, British composer. His works include the *Hebridean Symphony* (1915), five ballets, and three operas
Bantu *n* group of languages of Africa
banyan *n* Indian tree whose branches grow down into the soil forming additional trunks
bap *n* large soft bread roll
baptism Ⓣ *n* Christian religious ceremony in which a person is immersed in or sprinkled with water as a sign of purification and acceptance into the Church **baptismal** *adj*
▸ **baptize** *v* perform baptism on
Baptist *n* member of a Protestant denomination that believes in adult baptism by immersion
bar[1] Ⓣ *n* **1** rigid length of metal, wood, etc. **2** solid, usu. rectangular block, of any material **3** anything that obstructs or prevents **4** counter or room where drinks are served **5** heating element in an electric fire

THESAURUS

remove, eliminate, dismiss, eradicate, discard • *to banish illness*
banishment *n* = **expulsion**, deportation, exile, transportation, expatriation
banisters *pl n* = **railing**, rail, handrail, balusters, balustrade
bank[1] *n* **1** = **store**, fund, stock, reserve, hoard • *a blood bank* **2** = **storehouse**, repository, depository ▸ *v* **3** = **save**, keep, deposit
bank[2] *n* **1** = **side**, edge, shore, brink • *He sat fishing on the bank.* **2** = **mound**, mass, banking, pile, heap, ridge, embankment ▸ *v* **3** = **pile**, mass, mound, amass, stack, heap **4** = **tilt**, pitch, tip, heel, slope, incline, cant, slant, camber ▷ **bank on** *See* **depend**
bank[3] *n* = **row**, group, file, series, line, rank, array, sequence, succession
banking *See* **finance**
bankrupt *adj* = **insolvent**, impoverished, broke (*informal*), destitute, in the red, ruined, wiped out (*informal*)
bankruptcy *n* = **insolvency**, failure, ruin, liquidation
banned *See* **illegal**
banner *n* = **flag**, standard, pennant, placard, streamer, colours, ensign
banquet *n* = **feast**, treat, dinner, meal, revel, repast
banter *v* **1** = **joke**, kid (*informal*), rib (*informal*), taunt, tease, jest ▸ *n* **2** = **joking**, wordplay, badinage, jesting, kidding (*informal*), repartee, teasing
baptism *n* (*Christianity*) = **christening**, purification, immersion, sprinkling
baptize *v* (*Christianity*) = **christen**, cleanse, purify, immerse
bar *n* **1** = **rail**, pole, shaft, rod • *bars across the windows* **2** = **obstacle**, stop, block, barrier, obstruction, barricade, deterrent, impediment, hindrance **3** = **pub**, tavern, canteen, saloon, counter, parlour (*Canad*), inn, brasserie (*Quebec*), watering hole

DICTIONARY

6 *music* group of beats repeated throughout a piece of music ▷ *v* **barring, barred** **7** secure with a bar **8** ban or forbid **9** obstruct ▷ *prep* **10** Also **barring** except for **barman** (**barmaid**) *n*
▸ **the bar** lawyers collectively
bar² *n* unit of atmospheric pressure
barachois *n* (in the Atlantic Provinces) a shallow lagoon formed by a sand bar
Barak *n* **Ehud**. born 1942, Israeli Labour politician, prime minister (1999–2001)
barb Ⓣ *n* **1** point facing in the opposite direction to the main point of a fish-hook etc. **2** cutting remark **barbed** *adj*
▸ **barbed wire** strong wire with protruding sharp points
barbarian Ⓣ *n* member of a primitive or uncivilized people
▸ **barbaric** *adj* cruel or brutal
▸ **barbarism** *n* condition of being backward or ignorant
▸ **barbarity** *n* **1** state of being barbaric or barbarous **2** vicious act
▸ **barbarous** *adj* **1** uncivilized **2** brutal or cruel
barbecue Ⓣ *n* **1** grill on which food is cooked over hot charcoal, usu. outdoors **2** outdoor party at which barbecued food is served ▷ *v* **3** cook (food) on a barbecue
barber *n* person who cuts men's hair
Barber *n* **Samuel**. 1910–81, US composer: his works include an *Adagio for Strings*, adapted from the second movement of his string quartet No. 1 (1936) and the opera *Vanessa* (1958)
barbiturate *n* drug used as a sedative
bard *n lit* poet **the Bard** William Shakespeare
Bardot *n* **Brigitte**. born 1934, French actress
bare Ⓣ *adj* **1** unclothed **2** without the natural or usual covering **3** unembellished, simple **4** just sufficient ▷ *v* **5** uncover **bareness** *n*
▸ **bareback** *adj, adv* (of horse-riding) without a saddle
▸ **bare-bones** *adj* basic, containing only the essential elements
▸ **barefaced** *adj* shameless or impudent
▸ **barefoot** *or* **barefooted** *adj, adv* with feet uncovered
▸ **barely** *adv* only just
bargain Ⓣ *n* **1** agreement establishing what each party will give, receive, or perform in a transaction **2** something bought or offered at a low price ▷ *v* **3** negotiate the terms of an agreement
▸ **bargain for** *v* anticipate or take into account
barge Ⓣ *n* **1** flat-bottomed boat used to transport freight ▷ *v* **2** *informal* push violently
▸ **barge in** *or* **barge into** *v* interrupt rudely
barista *n* person who makes and sells coffee in a coffee bar
baritone *n* (singer with) the second lowest adult male voice
barium [**bare**-ee-um] *n* soft white metallic element

THESAURUS

(*facetious slang*), booze can (*Canad*), beer parlour (*Canad*), beverage room (*Canad*) ▸ *v* **4 = obstruct**, prevent • *His bodyguards barred the way.* **5 = fasten**, secure, lock, bolt, barricade, latch **6 = exclude**, ban, prohibit, forbid, blackball, keep out
See also: **close**
barb *n* **1 = dig**, cut, insult, scoff, affront, sarcasm, sneer, gibe **2 = point**, spur, spike, bristle, thorn, prickle, prong, quill
barbarian *n* **1 = savage**, yahoo, brute **2 = lout**, bigot, boor, philistine
barbaric *adj* **1 = uncivilized**, wild, rude, primitive **2 = brutal**, crude, fierce, cruel, savage, inhuman, coarse, barbarous
barbarism *n* **= savagery**, coarseness, crudity
barbarity *See* **cruelty**
barbarous *adj* **1 = uncivilized**, wild, rough, rude, savage, primitive, barbarian, brutish, uncouth **2 = brutal**, vicious, cruel, ferocious, inhuman, barbaric, ruthless, monstrous, heartless
barbecue *See* **cook**
barbed *adj* **1 = cutting**, critical, nasty, hostile, scathing, pointed, hurtful, unkind **2 = spiked**, thorny, hooked, jagged, prickly, spiny
bare *adj* **1 = naked**, nude, exposed, uncovered, undressed • *bare legs* OPPOSITE: covered **2 = empty**, open, vacant, spartan • *a small bare office* **3 = plain**, simple, basic, stark, sheer, bald, unembellished
See also: **blank**
barefaced *adj* **1 = obvious**, open, transparent, blatant, flagrant, unconcealed **2 = shameless**, bold, brazen, audacious, brash, impudent, insolent
barely *adv* **= hardly**, just, almost, scarcely • *She is barely sixteen.*
barf (*Slang*) *v* **1 = vomit**, spew, heave, puke (*slang*), retch, throw up (*informal*), toss one's cookies (*slang*) ▸ *n* **2 = vomit**, puke
bargain *n* **1 = agreement**, contract, promise, pledge, pact, arrangement **2 = good buy**, purchase *or* cheap purchase, reduction, discount, giveaway, good deal, steal (*informal*), bargoon (*Canad slang*) ▸ *v* **3 = negotiate**, agree, contract, promise, stipulate, covenant, transact **4 = haggle**, deal, trade, sell, traffic, barter
barge *n* **= canal boat**, lighter, flatboat, narrow boat

DICTIONARY

bark[1] ⓣ *n* **1** loud harsh cry of a dog ▷ *v* **2** (of a dog) make its typical cry **3** shout in an angry tone
bark[2] ⓣ *n* tough outer layer of a tree
Barker *n* **William George**, known as *Billy*. 1894–1930, Canadian fighter pilot. He was credited with 53 air victories during World War I; awarded the VC in 1918
barley *n* tall grasslike plant cultivated for grain
bar mitzvah *n Judaism* ceremony marking the 13th birthday of a boy, who then assumes full religious obligations
barmy *adj* **-mier, -miest** *slang* insane
barn *n* large building on a farm used for storing grain
▸ **barnstorm** *v* tour rural districts putting on shows or making speeches in a political campaign
barnacle *n* shellfish that lives attached to objects under water
Barnard *n* **1 Christiaan** (**Neethling**). 1923–2001, South African surgeon, who performed the first human heart transplant (1967) **2 Edward Emerson**. 1857–1923, US astronomer: noted for his discovery of the fifth satellite of Jupiter and his discovery of comets, nebulae, and a red dwarf (1916)
Barnave *n* **Antoine Pierre**. 1761–93, French revolutionary. A prominent member of the National Assembly, he was executed for his royalist sympathies
Barnhart *n* **Gordon**. born 1945, Canadian politician; Lieutenant Governor of Saskatchewan (2006–)
barometer *n* instrument for measuring atmospheric pressure **barometric** *adj*
baron *n* **1** member of the lowest rank of nobility **2** powerful businessman **baroness** *n fem* **baronial** *adj*
baronet *n* commoner who holds the lowest hereditary British title **baronetcy** *n*
baroque [bar-**rock**] *n* **1** highly ornate style of art and architecture from the late 16th to the early 18th century ▷ *adj* **2** extremely complicated, rich, and elaborate
barque [**bark**] *n* sailing ship, esp. one with three masts
barrack *v* criticize loudly or shout against (a team or speaker)
barracks ⓣ *pl n* building used to accommodate military personnel
barracuda [bar-rack-**kew**-da] *n* predatory tropical sea fish
barrage ⓣ [**bar**-rahzh] *n* **1** continuous delivery of questions, complaints, etc. **2** continuous artillery fire **3** artificial barrier across a river
Barras *n* **Paul François Jean Nicolas**, Vicomte de Barras. 1755–1829, French revolutionary: member of the Directory (1795–99)
barrel *n* **1** cylindrical container with rounded sides and flat ends **2** tube in a firearm through which the bullet is fired
▸ **barrel organ** musical instrument played by turning a handle
barren ⓣ *adj* **1** (of land) unable to support the growth of crops, fruit, etc. **2** (of a woman or female animal) incapable of producing offspring **barrenness** *n*
▸ **Barren Lands** *or* **Barren Grounds** sparsely inhabited tundra region in Canada
barricade ⓣ *n* **1** barrier, esp. one erected hastily for defence ▷ *v* **2** erect a barricade across (an entrance)
Barrie *n* Sir **James Matthew**. 1860–1937, Scottish dramatist and novelist, noted particularly for his popular children's play *Peter Pan* (1904)
barrier ⓣ *n* anything that prevents access or progress
barrister *n* lawyer who pleads in court
barrister and solicitor *n Canad* lawyer empowered to plead in court, advise clients, draw up documents, etc.
barrow[1] *n* **1** wheelbarrow **2** movable stall, used esp. by street vendors
barrow[2] *n* mound of earth placed over a prehistoric tomb
Barry *n* **1** Sir **Charles**. 1795–1860, English architect: designer of the Houses of

THESAURUS

bark[1] *n, v* = **yap**, bay, howl, snarl, growl, yelp, woof
bark[2] *n* = **covering**, skin, crust, casing, cortex (*anat, botany*), rind, husk
barracks *pl n* = **camp**, garrison, encampment, billet, quarters
barrage *n* **1** = **torrent**, mass, hail, stream, burst, deluge, onslaught, plethora **2** (*Mil*) = **bombardment**, battery, gunfire, salvo, volley, cannonade, fusillade, shelling
barren *adj* **1** waste, dry, empty, desert, arid, unproductive, desolate • *a barren desert* OPPOSITE: fertile **2** = **infertile**, sterile, childless
barricade *n* **1** = **barrier**, blockade, fence, obstruction, rampart, bulwark, palisade, stockade ▸ *v* **2** = **bar**, protect, defend, block, blockade, fortify, obstruct, shut in
barrier *n* **1** = **barricade**, wall, fence, obstacle, obstruction • *The eager fans broke through the barriers.* **2** = **obstacle**, hurdle, impediment, handicap, hindrance • *trade barriers between Canada and the United States*
See also: **disadvantage, protection, safeguard**

DICTIONARY

Parliament in London **2 Comtesse du**. See **du Barry 3 John**, real name *John Barry Prendergast*. 1933–2011 , British composer of film scores, including several for films in the James Bond series

Bart *n* **Lionel**. 1930–99, British composer and playwright. His musicals include *Oliver* (1960)

barter Ⓣ *v* **1** trade (goods) in exchange for other goods ▷ *n* **2** trade by the exchange of goods

Barth *n* **Karl**. 1886–1968, Swiss Protestant theologian. He stressed man's dependence on divine grace in such works as *Commentary on Romans* (1919)

Barthes *n* **Roland**. 1915–80, French writer and critic, who applied structuralist theory to literature and popular culture: his books include *Mythologies* (1957) and *Elements of Semiology* (1964)

Bartholdi *n* **Frédéric August**. 1834–1904, French sculptor and architect, who designed (1884) the Statue of Liberty

Bartók *n* **Béla**. 1881–1945, Hungarian composer, pianist, and collector of folk songs, by which his music was deeply influenced. His works include six string quartets, three piano concertos, several piano pieces including *Mikrokosmos* (1926–37), ballets (including *The Miraculous Mandarin*, 1919), and the opera *Bluebeard's Castle* (produced 1918)

Barton *n* **Elizabeth**, known as the *Maid of Kent*. ?1506–34, English nun, who claimed the gift of prophecy. Her criticism of Henry VIII's attempt to annul his first marriage led to her execution

basalt [**bass**-awlt] *n* dark volcanic rock **basaltic** *adj*

bascule *n* drawbridge that operates by a counterbalanced weight

base[1] Ⓣ *n* **1** bottom or supporting part of anything **2** fundamental part **3** centre of operations, organization, or supply **4** starting point **5** *baseball* any of three corners of the baseball diamond which batters must reach before returning to home plate to score a run ▷ *v* **6** (foll. by *on* or *upon*) use as a basis (for) **7** (foll. by *at* or *in*) station, post, or place

▸ **base hit** hit that enables the batter to run to at least one base

▸ **baseless** *adj* **basement** *n* partly or wholly underground storey of a building

▸ **baserunner** *n baseball* member of the batting team who is on a base or running between bases

base[2] Ⓣ *adj* **1** dishonourable or immoral **2** of inferior quality **basely** *adv* **baseness** *n*

baseball *n* **1** N American team game played with a bat and ball **2** ball used for this

▸ **baseball diamond** part of the playing field delimited by home plate and the three bases

bash Ⓣ *informal* ▷ *v* **1** hit violently or forcefully ▷ *n* **2** heavy blow

bashful Ⓣ *adj* shy or modest **bashfully** *adv* **bashfulness** *n*

Basho *n* full name *Matsuo Basho*, originally *Matsuo Munefusa*. 1644–94, Japanese poet and travel writer, noted esp. for his haiku

basic Ⓣ *adj* **1** of or forming a base or basis **2** elementary or simple **basically** *adv*

▸ **basics** *pl n* fundamental principles, facts, etc.

BASIC *n* computer programming language that uses common English words

Basie *n* **William**, known as *Count Basie*. 1904–84, US jazz pianist, bandleader, and composer: associated particularly with the polished phrasing and style of big-band jazz

basil *n* aromatic herb used in cooking

Basil *n* **Saint**, called *the Great*. ?329–379 AD, Greek patriarch: an opponent of Arianism

THESAURUS

barter *v* = **trade**, sell, traffic, exchange, bargain, swap, haggle, drive a hard bargain

base[1] *n* **1** = **bottom**, stand, foot, bed, foundation, pedestal • *the base of the cliffs* OPPOSITE: top **2** = **centre**, post, station, camp, headquarters • *a military base* **3** = **basis**, heart, key, source, core, root, origin, essence ▸ *v* **4** = **ground**, build, found, derive, hinge • *The movie is based on a true story*. **5** = **place**, post, station, locate

base[2] *adj* **1** = **dishonourable**, evil, despicable, shameful, wicked, immoral, lousy (*informal*), sordid, contemptible, disreputable, scuzzy (*slang*) **2** = **counterfeit**, fake, fraudulent, alloyed, debased, forged, impure

baseless *adj* = **unfounded**, unjustified, unconfirmed, unsupported, unsubstantiated, groundless, uncorroborated, ungrounded

bash *v* (*Informal*) = **hit**, strike, smash, belt (*informal*), wallop (*informal*), sock (*slang*)

bashful *adj* = **shy**, timid, reserved, coy, reticent, blushing, diffident, retiring

bashfulness *See* **embarrassment**

basic *adj* = **fundamental**, key, central, necessary, primary, essential, vital, elementary, indispensable • *the basic requirements for the job*
See also: **straightforward**

basically *adv* = **essentially**, mostly, primarily, fundamentally, inherently, intrinsically, at heart, in substance

basics *pl n* = **essentials**, ABCs, brass tacks (*informal*), fundamentals, nitty-gritty (*informal*), nuts and bolts (*informal*), principles, rudiments

DICTIONARY

and one of the founders of monasticism. Feast day: Jan 2, June 14, or Jan 1
basilica *n* rectangular church with a rounded end and two aisles
basilisk *n* legendary serpent said to kill by its breath or glance
basin *n* **1** round open container **2** sink for washing the hands and face **3** sheltered area of water where boats may be moored **4** catchment area of a river
basis Ⓣ *n, pl* **-ses** fundamental principles etc. from which something is started or developed
bask Ⓣ *v* lie in or be exposed to (pleasant warmth)
basket *n* **1** container made of interwoven strips of wood or cane **2** *basketball* metal hoop with netting mounted on a tall pole, serving as the goal **basketwork** *n*
basketball *n* **1** game in which two teams of five players bounce a rubber ball and try to place it in a high hoop called the basket to score points **2** ball used for this
basque *n* tight-fitting bodice for women
Basque *n, adj* (member or language) of a people living in the W Pyrenees in France and Spain
bas-relief *n* sculpture in which the figures stand out slightly from the background
bass[1] Ⓣ [**base**] *n* **1** (singer with) the lowest adult male voice ▷ *adj* **2** of the lowest range of musical notes
bass[2] *n* edible sea fish
basset hound *n* smooth-haired dog with short legs and long ears
bassoon *n* large woodwind instrument
basswood *n* tall shade tree with heart-shaped leaves
bastard Ⓣ *n* **1** person born of parents not married to each other **2** *offensive* obnoxious or despicable person **bastardy** *n*
▸ **bastardize** *v* debase or corrupt
baste[1] *v* moisten (meat) during cooking with hot fat
baste[2] *v* sew with loose temporary stitches
bastion Ⓣ *n* **1** projecting part of a fortification **2** thing or person regarded as defending a principle
bat[1] Ⓣ *n* **1** any of various types of club used to hit the ball in certain sports ▷ *v* **batting, batted 2** strike with or as if with a bat
▸ **batting average** *baseball* number of hits divided by times at bat, expressed as a decimal with three places
bat[2] *n* nocturnal mouselike flying animal
batch Ⓣ *n* group of people or things dealt with at the same time
bated *adj* **with bated breath** in suspense or fear
bath Ⓣ *n* **1** large container in which to wash the body **2** act of washing in such a container **baths 3** public swimming pool ▷ *v* **4** wash in a bath
▸ **bathroom** *n* room with a bath, sink, and usu. a toilet
bathe Ⓣ *v* **1** swim in open water **2** apply liquid to (the skin or a wound) in order to cleanse or soothe **3** (foll. by *in*) fill (with): *bathed in sunlight* **bather** *n*
bathos [**bay**-thoss] *n* sudden change in speech or writing from a serious subject to a trivial one
bathyscaph, bathyscaphe *n* deep-sea diving vessel for observation
batik [bat-**teek**] *n* **1** process of printing fabric using wax to cover areas not to be dyed **2** fabric printed in this way
Batista *n* **Fulgencio**, full name *Batista y Zaldívar*. 1901–73, Cuban military leader and dictator: president of Cuba (1940–44, 1952–59); overthrown by Fidel Castro
baton Ⓣ *n* **1** thin stick used by the conductor of an orchestra **2** short bar transferred in a relay race **3** policeman's truncheon
battalion *n* army unit consisting of three or more companies

THESAURUS

basis *n* = **foundation**, heart, core, principle, fundamental, premise • *The same theme is the basis of several poems.*
See also: **cause, grounds**
bask *v* = **lie in**, relax, lounge, sunbathe, laze, loll, swim in
bass *adj* = **deep**, low, deep-toned, low-pitched, resonant, sonorous
bastard *n* **1** (*Informal, offensive*) = **rogue**, villain, miscreant, reprobate, scoundrel, wretch **2** = **illegitimate child**, love child, natural child
bastion *n* = **stronghold**, support, rock, prop, defence, mainstay, fortress, citadel, bulwark, tower of strength
bat *n*, *v* = **hit**, strike, bang, thump, smack, wallop (*informal*), whack, swat
batch *n* = **group**, set, lot, amount, crowd, collection, pack, bunch, quantity, assemblage
bath *n* **1** = **wash**, shower, soak, cleansing, scrubbing, douche **2** = **bathtub**, tub
bathe *v* **1** = **wash**, soak, cleanse, rinse **2** = **cover**, flood, steep, immerse, suffuse
bathroom *n* = **washroom**, lavatory, loo, latrine, toilet, convenience *or* public convenience, restroom, outhouse, powder room, water closet, W.C., commode
baton *n* **1** = **stick**, staff, rod, crook, wand, sceptre **2** = **club**, truncheon, mace, nightstick, billy club

DICTIONARY

batten[1] Ⓣ *n* strip of wood fixed to something, esp. to hold it in place
▸**batten down** *v* secure with a batten
batten[2] **batten on** *v* thrive at the expense of (someone else)
batter[1] Ⓣ *v* **1** hit repeatedly ▷ *n* **2** *baseball* member of the batting team who is currently at bat
▸**battering ram** large beam used to break down fortifications
batter[2] *n* mixture of flour, eggs, and milk, used in cooking
battery Ⓣ *n, pl* **-teries 1** device that produces electricity in a flashlight, radio, etc. **2** group of heavy guns operating as a single unit **3** series of cages for intensive rearing of poultry
battle Ⓣ *n* **1** fight between large armed forces **2** conflict or struggle ▷ *v* **3** struggle
▸**battle-axe** *n* **1** *informal* domineering woman **2** large heavy axe
▸**battleship** *n* heavily armoured warship
battlement *n* wall with gaps for shooting through
batty Ⓣ *adj* **-tier, -tiest** *slang* **1** crazy **2** eccentric
bauble Ⓣ *n* trinket of little value
Baudelaire *n* **Charles Pierre**. 1821–67, French poet, noted for his macabre imagery; author of *Les fleurs du mal* (1857)
baulk *v* same as **balk**
bauxite *n* claylike substance from which aluminum is obtained
bawdy Ⓣ *adj* **bawdier, bawdiest** (of writing etc.) containing humorous references to sex
bawdiness *n*
bawl Ⓣ *v* shout or weep noisily
Bax *n* Sir **Arnold** (**Edward Trevor**). 1883–1953, English composer of romantic works, often based on Celtic legends, including the tone poem *Tintagel* (1917)
bay[1] Ⓣ *n* wide curving coastline
bay[2] Ⓣ *n* **1** recess in a wall **2** area in which vehicles may park or unload
bay[3] Ⓣ *v* (of a hound or wolf) howl in deep prolonged tones
bay[4] *n* Mediterranean laurel tree
▸**bay leaf** dried leaf of a laurel, used in cooking
bay[5] *adj, n* reddish-brown (horse)
Bayle *n* **Pierre**. 1647–1706, French philosopher and critic, noted for his *Dictionnaire historique et critique* (1697), which profoundly influenced Voltaire and the French Encyclopedists
bayonet *n* **1** sharp blade that can be fixed to the end of a rifle ▷ *v* **-neting, -neted 2** stab with a bayonet
bazaar Ⓣ *n* **1** sale in aid of charity **2** market area, esp. in Eastern countries
bazooka *n* rocket launcher that fires a projectile capable of piercing armour
BB Boys' Brigade
BBC British Broadcasting Corporation
BC 1 before Christ **2** British Columbia
BD Bachelor of Divinity
be Ⓣ *v, present sing. 1st person* **am** *2nd person* **are** *3rd person* **is** *present pl.* **are** *past sing. 1st person* **was** *2nd person* **were** *3rd person* **was** *past pl* **were** *present participle* **being** *past participle* **been 1** exist or live **2** used as a linking between the subject of a sentence and its complement: *John is a musician* **3** forms the progressive present tense: *the man is running* **4** forms the passive voice of all transitive verbs: *a good film is being shown on television tonight*
beach Ⓣ *n* **1** area of sand or pebbles on a shore ▷ *v* **2** run or haul (a boat) onto a beach

THESAURUS

batten *v* (usually with *down*) = **fasten**, fix, secure, tighten, board up, clamp down, cover up, nail down
batter *v* = **beat**, pound, pummel, wallop (*informal*), clobber (*slang*), pelt, buffet, thrash
battery *n* = **artillery**, cannon, cannonry, gun emplacements, guns
battle *n* **1** = **fight**, attack, action, combat, encounter, engagement, skirmish, hostilities **2** = **conflict**, campaign, struggle, dispute, contest, crusade ▸ *v* **3** = **struggle**, fight, war, dispute, argue, strive, clamour, lock horns
battlefield *n* = **battleground**, field, front, combat zone, field of battle
battleship *n* = **warship**, gunboat, man-of-war
batty *adj* = **crazy**, absent-minded, bonkers (*informal*), daft (*informal*), mad, odd, eccentric, peculiar
bauble *n* = **trinket**, toy, plaything, trifle, bagatelle, gewgaw, gimcrack, knick-knack
baulk *See* **balk**
bawdy *adj* = **rude**, dirty, indecent, lewd, coarse, salacious, lascivious, lecherous, ribald, smutty
bawl *v* **1** = **cry**, weep, sob, wail, blubber **2** = **shout**, call, roar, yell, howl, clamour, bellow
bay[1] *n* = **cove**, sound, inlet, gulf • *the Bay of Fundy*
bay[2] *n* = **recess**, opening, niche, compartment, nook, alcove
bay[3] *v* = **howl**, cry, bark, yelp • *wolves baying in the moonlight*
bazaar *n* **1** = **market**, exchange, marketplace **2** = **rummage sale**, fair, carnival, garage sale, flea market
be *v* = **exist**, live, breathe, inhabit, be alive
beach *n* = **seaside**, coast, shore, sands,

DICTIONARY

▶**beachcomber** *n* **1** person who searches shore debris for anything of worth **2** (in British Columbia) person who is paid for salvaging loose logs for logging companies
▶**beachhead** *n* beach captured by an attacking army on which troops can be landed
beacon Ⓣ *n* fire or light on a hill or tower, used as a warning
bead Ⓣ *n* **1** small ball of plastic etc., pierced for threading on a string to form a necklace etc. **2** small drop of moisture **beaded** *adj*
▶**beading** *n* strip of moulding used for edging furniture
▶**beady** *adj* small, round, and glittering: *beady eyes*
beadle *n* **1** *Brit* (formerly) minor parish official **2** *Scot* church official who attends the minister
beagle *n* small hunting dog with short legs and drooping ears
beak Ⓣ *n* **1** projecting horny jaws of a bird **2** *slang* nose **beaky** *adj*
beaker *n* **1** large drinking cup **2** lipped glass container used in laboratories
beam Ⓣ *n* **1** broad smile **2** ray of light **3** narrow flow of electromagnetic radiation or particles **4** long thick piece of wood, metal, etc., used in building ▷*v* **5** smile broadly **6** divert or aim (a radio signal, light, etc.) in a certain direction
bean *n* seed or pod of various plants, eaten as a vegetable or used to make coffee etc.
bear[1] Ⓣ *v* **bearing, bore, borne 1** support or hold up **2** bring: *to bear gifts* **3** *passive* **born** give birth to **4** produce as by natural growth **5** tolerate or endure **6** hold in the mind **7** show or be marked with **8** move in a specified direction **bearable** *adj* **bearer** *n*
▶**bear out** *v* show to be truthful
bear[2] *n* large heavy mammal with a long shaggy coat
▶**bearskin** *n* tall fur helmet worn by some British soldiers
beard *n* hair growing on the lower parts of a man's face **bearded** *adj*
Beardsley *n* **Aubrey** (**Vincent**). 1872–98, English illustrator: noted for his stylized black-and-white illustrations, esp. those for Oscar Wilde's *Salome* and Pope's *Rape of the Lock*
bearing Ⓣ *n* **1** relevance (to) **2** part of a machine that supports another part, esp. one that reduces friction **3** person's general social conduct **bearings 4** sense of one's own relative position
beast Ⓣ *n* **1** large wild animal **2** brutal or uncivilized person
▶**beastly** *adj* unpleasant or disagreeable
beat Ⓣ *v* **beating, beat, beaten** *or* **beat 1** hit hard and repeatedly **2** move (wings) up and down **3** throb rhythmically **4** stir or mix vigorously **5** overcome or defeat ▷*n* **6** regular

b

THESAURUS

seashore • *building sandcastles on the beach*
beached *adj* = **stranded**, ashore, abandoned, aground, deserted, grounded, high and dry, marooned, wrecked
beacon *n* = **signal**, sign, flare, beam, bonfire, lighthouse, watchtower
bead *n* **1** = **ball**, pill, globe, pellet, pearl, sphere, orb, spherule **2** = **drop**, pill, bubble, dot, pellet, droplet, blob, globule
beady *adj* = **bright**, sharp, gleaming, glinting, glittering, shining
beak *n* = **bill**, mandible, nib
beam *n* **1** = **ray**, streak, stream, glow, shaft, gleam, glimmer, glint **2** = **rafter**, support, plank, spar, timber, girder, joist **3** = **smile**, grin ▶*v* **4** = **radiate**, shine, glow, glitter, glare, gleam **5** = **send out**, broadcast, transmit, emit **6** = **smile**, grin
bear *v* **1** = **carry**, take, support, shoulder, convey • *The ice wasn't thick enough to bear their weight.* **2** = **display**, have, exhibit, harbour • *The room bore the signs of a party.* **3** = **suffer**, endure, stomach, tolerate, abide • *He can't bear to talk about it.* **4** = **produce**, generate, yield, breed, engender, beget, bring forth, give birth to ▷**bear a resemblance to** *See* **resemble** ▷**bear in mind** *See* **consider** ▷**bear out** = **support**, confirm, endorse, prove, uphold, justify, vindicate, substantiate, corroborate
See also: **bring, put up with**
bearable *adj* = **tolerable**, sustainable, manageable, admissible, passable, endurable, sufferable, supportable
bearer *n* = **carrier**, agent, runner, servant, orderly, messenger, conveyor, porter, doorman
bearing *n* **1** (usually with *on* or *upon*) = **relevance**, connection, import, relation, application, reference, significance, pertinence **2** = **manner**, air, attitude, aspect, behaviour, posture, demeanour, deportment
bearings *pl n* = **position**, way, track, aim, situation, course, location, direction, orientation, whereabouts
beast *n* **1** = **animal**, creature, brute **2** = **brute**, monster, savage, swine, barbarian, ogre, fiend, sadist
beastly *adj* = **unpleasant**, mean, nasty, awful, rotten, horrid, disagreeable
beat *v* **1** = **hit**, strike, pound, batter, buffet, thrash • *He started to beat the poor dog.* **2** = **defeat**, overcome, overwhelm, outstrip, outdo, vanquish, surpass, master, conquer • *She was easily beaten in the race.* **3** = **throb**, pound, quake, thump,

DICTIONARY

throb **7** assigned route, as of a policeman **8** basic rhythmic unit in a piece of music **beater** *n*

▸**beat up** *v* injure (someone) by repeated blows or kicks

beatify [bee-**at**-if-fie] *v* **-fying, -fied** *RC Church* declare (a dead person) to be among the blessed in heaven **beatification** *n*

▸**beatific** *adj* displaying great happiness

▸**beatitude** *n* supreme blessedness

Beaton *n* Sir **Cecil** (**Walter Hardy**). 1904–80, British photographer, noted esp. for his society portraits

Beatrix *n* full name *Beatrix Wilhelmina Armgard*. born 1938, queen of the Netherlands from 1980

Beatty *n* **Warren**, full name *Henry Warren Beatty.* Born 1937, US film actor and director: his films include *Bonnie and Clyde* (1967), *Heaven Can Wait* (1978), *Reds* (1981, also directed), *Bugsy* (1991), and *Bulworth* (1998, also wrote and directed)

beau Ⓣ [**boh**] *n, pl* **beaus, beaux** dandy

Beaufort *n* **1 Henry**. ?1374–1447, English cardinal, half-brother of Henry IV; chancellor (1403–04, 1413–17, 1424–26) **2** Lady **Margaret**, Countess of Richmond and Derby. ?1443–1509, mother of Henry VII. She helped to found two Cambridge colleges and was a patron of Caxton

Beaufort scale *n* scale for measuring the speed of wind

Beauharnais *n* **1 Alexandre**, Vicomte de. 1760–94, French general, who served in the War of American Independence and the French Revolutionary wars; first husband of Empress Joséphine: guillotined **2** his son, **Eugène de**. 1781–1824, viceroy of Italy (1805–14) for his stepfather Napoleon I **3** (**Eugénie**) **Hortense de**. 1783–1837, queen of Holland (1806–10) as wife of Louis Bonaparte; daughter of Alexandre Beauharnais and sister of Eugène: mother of Napoleon III **4 Joséphine de**. See (Empress) **Josephine**

beauty Ⓣ *n, pl* **-ties 1** combination of all the qualities of a person or thing that delight the senses and mind **2** very attractive woman **3** *informal* something outstanding of its kind

▸**beautiful** *adj* **1** possessing beauty **2** very pleasant **beautifully** *adv*

▸**beautify** *v* make or become beautiful **beautification** *n*

▸**beautician** *n* person whose profession is to give beauty treatments

beaver *n* **1** amphibious rodent with a big flat tail **2 Beaver** Beaver Scout

▸**beaver away** *v* work industriously

▸**beaver lodge** rounded structure of mud, sticks, and stones built by beavers as a den

▸**Beaver Scout** member of a junior branch of the Boy Scouts

Beaverbrook *n* **1st Baron**, title of *William Maxwell Aitken*. 1879–1964, British newspaper proprietor and Conservative politician, born in Canada, whose newspapers included the *Daily Express*; minister of information (1918); minister of aircraft production (1940–41)

becalmed Ⓣ *adj* (of a sailing ship) motionless through lack of wind

became *v* past tense of **become**

because Ⓣ *conj* on account of the fact that

▸**because of** on account of

Bechet *n* **Sidney** (**Joseph**). 1897–1959, US jazz soprano saxophonist and clarinettist

Bechstein *n* **Karl**. 1826–1900, German piano maker; founder (1853) of the Bechstein company of piano manufacturers in Berlin

beck *n* **at someone's beck and call** subject to someone's slightest whim

THESAURUS

vibrate, pulsate, palpitate ▹ **beat up** (*Informal*) = **assault**, attack, pound, batter, thrash, pulverize, beat the living daylights out of (*informal*), knock around ▸ *n* **4** = **rhythm**, time, stress, metre, cadence, groove (*informal*), pace, swing, (*old-fashioned, informal*) • *the thumping beat of the music* **5** = **throb**, pulse, palpitation, pulsation **6** = **route**, way, course, path, circuit, rounds ▸ *adj* **7** *See* **exhausted**

See also: **bang, club, top**

beaten *adj* **1** = **stirred**, mixed, frothy, blended, foamy, whipped, whisked **2** = **defeated**, overcome, overwhelmed, cowed, thwarted, vanquished

beau *n* **1** (*Old-fashioned*) = **boyfriend**, lover, suitor, sweetheart, admirer, fiancé **2** = **dandy**, gallant, coxcomb, fop, ladies' man

beautiful *adj* = **attractive**, fine, lovely, gorgeous, exquisite, pleasing, delightful • *beautiful music* OPPOSITE: ugly

See also: **pretty**

beautify *v* = **make beautiful**, decorate, adorn, ornament, garnish, embellish, festoon, glamorize

beauty *n* **1** = **attractiveness**, charm, grace, glamour, elegance, loveliness, comeliness, exquisiteness, handsomeness • *a scene of outstanding beauty* OPPOSITE: ugliness **2** = **belle**, lovely (*slang*), stunner (*informal*), good-looker • *a dark-haired beauty with a great smile* **3** = **advantage**, benefit, asset, attraction • *The beauty of the deal is that everyone makes money.*

becalmed *adj* = **still**, motionless, stuck, settled, stranded

because *conj* = **since**, as, due to, owing

DICTIONARY

Becker *n* **Boris**. born 1967, German tennis player: Wimbledon champion 1985, 1986, and 1989: the youngest man ever to win Wimbledon
Becket *n* **Saint Thomas à**. 1118–70, English prelate; chancellor (1155–62) to Henry II; archbishop of Canterbury (1162–70): murdered following his opposition to Henry's attempts to control the clergy. Feast day: Dec 29 or July 7
Beckett *n* **Samuel** (**Barclay**). 1906–89, Irish dramatist and novelist writing in French and English, whose works portray the human condition as insignificant or absurd in a bleak universe. They include the plays *En attendant Godot* (*Waiting for Godot*, 1952), *Fin de partie* (*Endgame*, 1957), and *Not I* (1973) and the novel *Malone meurt* (*Malone Dies*, 1951): Nobel prize for literature 1969
beckon Ⓣ *v* summon with a gesture
become Ⓣ *v* **-coming, -came, -come 1** come to be **2** (foll. by *of*) happen to **3** suit
▸ **becoming** *adj* **1** attractive or pleasing **2** appropriate or proper
Becquerel *n* **Antoine Henri**. 1852–1908, French physicist, who discovered the photographic action of the rays emitted by uranium salts and so instigated the study of radioactivity: Nobel prize for physics 1903
bed Ⓣ *n* **1** piece of furniture on which to sleep **2** garden plot **3** bottom of a river, lake, or sea **4** layer of rock ▷ *v* **bedding, bedded 5** have sexual intercourse with **bedroom** *n*
▸ **go to bed with** have sexual intercourse with
▸ **bedding** *n* sheets and covers that are used on a bed
▸ **bed down** *v* go to or put into a place to sleep or rest
▸ **bedpan** *n* shallow bowl used as a toilet by bedridden people
▸ **bedridden** *adj* confined to bed because of illness or old age
▸ **bedrock** *n* **1** solid rock beneath the surface soil **2** basic facts or principles
▸ **bedsit** *or* **bedsitter** *n* furnished sitting room with a bed
BEd Bachelor of Education
bedaub *v* smear with something sticky or dirty
Bede *n* **Saint**, known as *the Venerable Bede*. ?673–735 AD, English monk, scholar, historian, and theologian, noted for his Latin *Ecclesiastical History of the English People* (731). Feast day: May 27 or 25. Latin name **Baeda**
bedeck *v* cover with decorations
bedevil Ⓣ [bid-**dev**-ill] *v* **-illing, -illed** harass or torment
bedlam Ⓣ *n* noisy confused situation
bedraggled Ⓣ *adj* untidy, wet, or dirty
bee *n* insect that makes wax and honey
▸ **beehive** *n* structure in which bees live
▸ **beeswax** *n* wax secreted by bees, used in polishes etc.
beech *n* European tree with a smooth greyish bark
Beecher *n* **Henry Ward**. 1813–87, US clergyman: a leader in the movement for the abolition of slavery
beef *n* **1** flesh of a cow, bull, or ox ▷ *v* **2** *informal* complain
▸ **beefy** *adj* **1** like beef **2** *informal* strong and muscular **3** *informal* fleshy, obese
▸ **beefalo** *n* cross between bison and other cattle
▸ **beefeater** *n* yeoman warder at the Tower of London
been *v* past participle of **be**
beep *n* **1** high-pitched sound, like that of an

THESAURUS

to, in that, on account of, owing to • *I went home because I was tired.* ▷ **because of** *See* **by virtue of**
beckon *v* = **gesture**, bid, motion, signal, nod, summon, gesticulate, wave at
become *v* **1** = **come to be**, be transformed into, change into, develop into, grow into, mature into, ripen into **2** = **suit**, fit, enhance, flatter, embellish, set off
becoming *adj* **1** = **appropriate**, proper, worthy, suitable, fitting, compatible, in keeping, seemly **2** = **flattering**, pretty, attractive, neat, graceful, tasteful, comely, enhancing
bed *n* **1** = **cot**, berth, crib, couch, cradle, bunk, divan, bedstead **2** = **plot**, area, border, row, strip, patch, garden **3** = **bottom**, base, foundation, groundwork
bedevil *v* **1** = **torment**, worry, trouble, plague, distress, harass, afflict, vex **2** = **confuse**, confound
bedlam *n* = **pandemonium**, chaos, confusion, turmoil, uproar, furor, commotion, tumult
bedraggled *adj* = **messy**, dirty, dishevelled, disordered, muddied, scuzzy (*slang*), unkempt, untidy
bedridden *adj* = **confined to bed**, confined, flat on one's back, incapacitated, laid up (*informal*)
bedrock *n* **1** = **bottom**, bed, foundation, rock bottom, substratum, substructure **2** = **basics**, basis, core, essentials, fundamentals, nuts and bolts (*informal*), roots
beefy *adj* (*Informal*) = **brawny**, muscular, bulky, sturdy, stocky, hulking, strapping, thickset

DICTIONARY

automobile horn ▷ *v* **2** (cause to) make this noise **beeper** *n*
beer *n* alcoholic drink brewed from malt and hops **beery** *adj*
▶ **beer parlour** tavern
Beerbohm *n* Sir (**Henry**) **Max**(**imilian**). 1872–1956, English critic, wit, and caricaturist, whose works include *Zuleika Dobson* (1911), a satire on Oxford undergraduates
beet *n* plant with an edible root and leaves
▶ **beetroot** *n* type of beet plant with a dark red root
Beethoven *n* **Ludwig van**. 1770–1827, German composer, who greatly extended the form and scope of symphonic and chamber music, bridging the classical and romantic traditions. His works include nine symphonies, 32 piano sonatas, 16 string quartets, five piano concertos, a violin concerto, two masses, the opera *Fidelio* (1805), and choral music
beetle *n* **1** insect with a hard wing cover on its back ▷ *v* **2** *informal* scuttle or scurry
befall Ⓣ *v old-fashioned* happen to (someone)
befit *v* be appropriate or suitable for **befitting** *adj*
before Ⓣ *conj* **1** earlier than the time when **2** rather than ▷ *prep* **3** preceding in space or time **4** in the presence of **5** in preference to ▷ *adv* **6** at an earlier time, previously **7** in front
▶ **beforehand** *adv* in advance
befriend Ⓣ *v* be a friend to
beg Ⓣ *v* **begging, begged 1** solicit (for money or food), esp. in the street **2** ask formally or humbly **beggar** *n* **beggarly** *adj*
began *v* past tense of **begin**
beget *v* **-getting, -got** *or* **-gat, -gotten** *or* **-got 1** cause or create **2** father
begin Ⓣ *v* **-ginning, -gan, -gun 1** start **2** bring or come into being **beginning** *n*
▶ **beginner** *n* person who has just started learning to do something
Begin *n* **Menachem**. 1913–92, Israeli statesman, born in Poland. In Palestine after 1942, he became a leader of the militant Zionists; prime minister of Israel (1977–83); Nobel peace prize jointly with Sadat 1978. In 1979 he concluded the Camp David treaty with Anwar Sadat of Egypt
begonia *n* tropical plant with waxy flowers
begrudge Ⓣ *v* grudge
beguile Ⓣ [big-**gile**] *v* **1** cheat or mislead **2** charm or amuse **beguiling** *adj*
begun *v* past participle of **begin**
behalf *n* **on behalf of** in the interest of or for the benefit of
behave Ⓣ *v* **1** act or function in a particular

THESAURUS

befall *v* = **happen**, fall, chance, occur, transpire (*informal*), come to pass, take place
befitting *adj* = **appropriate**, right, fit, proper, suitable, fitting, apposite, becoming, seemly
before *adv* **1** = **previously**, earlier, formerly, sooner, in advance • *Have you been to Greece before?* OPPOSITE: after **2** = **in front**, ahead ▶ *preposition* **3** = **ahead of**, in advance of, in front of **4** = **earlier than**, in advance of, prior to RELATED WORDS *prefixes*: ante-, fore-, pre- **5** = **in the presence of**, in front of
▷ **before long** *See* **soon**
beforehand *adv* = **in advance**, before, already, previously, earlier, sooner, ahead of time, in anticipation
befriend *v* = **help**, back, support, assist, aid, welcome, encourage, side with, stand by
beg *v* **1** = **plead**, petition, implore, beseech (*formal*) • *I begged him to come to the party.* **2** = **scrounge**, mooch, seek charity, solicit charity, sponge on, panhandle (*informal*) ▷ **beg someone's pardon** *See* **apologize**
See also: **appeal, ask, press, request, urge**
beggar *n* **1** = **panhandler** (*informal*), bum (*informal*), tramp, bag lady, pauper, down-and-out, vagrant **2** = **scrounger** (*informal*), supplicant, sponger (*informal*), mendicant, cadger
beggarly *adj* = **poor**, impoverished, needy, poverty-stricken, destitute, indigent
begin *v* = **start**, institute, originate, initiate, commence (*formal*), inaugurate, set about • *She began to move around the room.* OPPOSITE: end
See also: **proceed**
beginner *n* = **novice**, rookie (*informal*), starter, amateur, apprentice, trainee, intern, neophyte, learner, tyro, newbie, noob (*slang*) • *a course for beginners* OPPOSITE: expert
See also: **recruit**
beginning *n* **1** = **start**, birth, opening, origin, onset, outset, commencement (*formal*) • *the beginning of the city* OPPOSITE: end **2** = **seed**, root, germ, fount
See also: **head, source**
begrudge *v* = **resent**, envy, grudge, be jealous, be reluctant, be stingy
begrudging *See* **bitter**
beguile *v* **1** = **fool**, trick, mislead, cheat, dupe, deceive, delude, hoodwink, take for a ride (*informal*) **2** = **charm**, occupy, divert, entertain, distract, amuse, engross
beguiling *adj* = **charming**, attractive, alluring, bewitching, captivating, enchanting, enthralling, intriguing
behave *v* **1** = **act**, work, run, operate, perform, function **2** = **conduct oneself properly**, act correctly, keep one's nose clean,

DICTIONARY

way **2** conduct (oneself) properly **behaviour** *or* **behavior** *n*
behead *v* remove the head from
beheld *v* past of **behold**
behest *n* order or earnest request
behind Ⓣ *prep* **1** at the back of **2** responsible for or causing **3** supporting ▷ *adv* **4** in or to a position further back **5** remaining after someone's departure **6** in arrears **7** late ▷ *n* **8** *informal* buttocks
behold *v old-fashioned* look (at), observe **beholder** *n*
beholden Ⓣ *adj* indebted or obliged
behove *v old-fashioned* be necessary or fitting for
Beiderbecke *n* **Leon Bismarcke**, known as *Bix*. 1903–31, US jazz cornettist, composer, and pianist
beige *adj* pale brown
being Ⓣ *v* **1** present participle of **be** ▷ *n* **2** existence **3** something that exists or is thought to exist **4** human being, person
belabour, belabor *v* attack verbally or physically
belated Ⓣ *adj* late or too late **belatedly** *adv*
belch Ⓣ *v* **1** expel wind from the stomach noisily through the mouth **2** expel or be expelled forcefully: *smoke belched from the factory* ▷ *n* **3** act of belching
beleaguered Ⓣ *adj* **1** besieged **2** surrounded or beset
belfry *n, pl* **-fries** part of a tower where bells are hung
belie *v* show to be untrue
belief Ⓣ *n* **1** trust or confidence **2** opinion **3** principle etc. accepted as true **4** religious faith
▸ **believe** *v* **1** accept as true or real **2** think, assume, or suppose **3** (foll. by *in*) be convinced of the truth or existence of **believable** *adj* **believer** *n*
belittle Ⓣ *v* treat as having little value or importance
bell *n* **1** hollow, usu. metal, cup-shaped instrument that emits a ringing sound when struck **2** device that rings or buzzes as a signal
Bell *n* **1** **Acton**, **Currer**, and **Ellis**, pen names of the sisters Anne, Charlotte, and Emily **Brontë** **2** **Alexander Graham**. 1847–1922, scientist, inventor, and aviation pioneer, born in Scotland and active in Canada and the United States, he invented the telephone and many other devices, often related to sound transmission **3** (**Susan**) **Jocelyn**, married name *Jocelyn Burnell*. born 1943, British radio astronomer, who discovered the first pulsar **4** **Vanessa**, original name *Vanessa Stephen*. 1879–1961, British painter; a member of the

THESAURUS

mind one's manners ▷ **behave toward** *See* **treat**
behaviour *n* **1** = **conduct**, manner, bearing, demeanour, actions, deportment, manners, ways **2** = **action**, operation, performance, functioning
behind *prep* **1** = **after**, following, at the back of, at the heels of, at the rear of, later than **2** = **causing**, at the bottom of, initiating, instigating, responsible for **3** = **supporting**, for, backing, in agreement, on the side of ▷ **behind time** *See* **late** ▸ *adv* **4** = **after**, next, following, subsequently, afterwards, in the wake *or* in the wake of **5** = **overdue**, behindhand, in arrears, in debt ▸ *n* **6** (*Informal*) = **bottom**, butt, bum, posterior, buttocks
behold *v* = **look at**, survey, watch, view, witness, regard, observe, perceive
beholden *adj* = **indebted**, grateful, bound, obliged, owing, under obligation
being *n* **1** = **existence**, life, reality **2** = **nature**, substance, spirit, soul, entity, essence **3** = **creature**, individual, human being, living thing
belated *adj* = **late**, delayed, overdue, behindhand, behind time, late in the day, tardy
belch *v* **1** = **burp** (*informal*) **2** = **emit**, erupt, discharge, vent, disgorge, give off, spew forth
beleaguered *adj* **1** = **harassed**, badgered, hassled (*informal*), persecuted, pestered, plagued, put upon, vexed **2** = **besieged**, beset, assailed, blockaded, hemmed in, surrounded
belief *n* **1** = **opinion**, trust, view, confidence, conviction, judgment • *belief in reincarnation* **2** = **faith**, principle, ideology, doctrine, tenet, creed, dogma • *the culture and beliefs of ancient times*
See also: **idea, viewpoint**
believable *adj* = **credible**, likely, possible, probable, imaginable, plausible • *The book is full of believable characters.* OPPOSITE: unbelievable
believe *v* **1** = **accept**, trust, assume, swallow (*informal*), presume • *Don't believe everything you read in the papers.* OPPOSITE: doubt **2** = **think**, judge, gather, suppose, assume, imagine, speculate, presume, reckon
See also: **consider, expect, feel, suspect, understand**
believed *See* **supposed**
believer *n* = **follower**, supporter, convert, devotee, adherent, zealot, disciple, upholder
belittle *v* = **disparage**, deride, minimize, scorn, downgrade, undervalue, decry, denigrate, deprecate, scoff at, sneer at • *He belittles my opinions.* OPPOSITE: praise
See also: **put down**

DICTIONARY

Bloomsbury group, sister of Virginia Woolf and wife of the art critic Clive Bell (1881–1964)
belladonna *n* (drug obtained from) deadly nightshade
belle *n* beautiful woman
bellicose *adj* warlike and aggressive
belligerent Ⓣ *adj* **1** hostile and aggressive **2** engaged in war ▷ *n* **3** person or country engaged in war **belligerence** *n*
Bellini *n* **1 Giovanni**. ?1430–1516, Italian painter of the Venetian school, noted for his altarpieces, landscapes, and Madonnas. His father **Jacopo** (?1400–70) and his brother **Gentile** (?1429–1507) were also painters **2 Vincenzo**. 1801–35, Italian composer of operas, esp. *La Sonnambula* (1831) and *Norma* (1831)
Belloc *n* **Hilaire**. 1870–1953, British poet, essayist, and historian, born in France, noted particularly for his verse for children in *The Bad Child's Book of Beasts* (1896) and *Cautionary Tales* (1907)
bellow Ⓣ *v* **1** make a low deep cry like that of a bull **2** shout in a loud deep voice ▷ *n* **3** loud deep roar
Bellow *n* **Saul**. 1915–2005, US novelist, born in Canada. His works include *Dangling Man* (1944), *The Adventures of Angie March* (1954), *Herzog* (1964), *Humboldt's Gift* (1975), *The Dean's December* (1981), and *Ravelstein* (2000): Nobel prize for literature 1976
bellows *pl n* instrument for pumping a stream of air into something
belly Ⓣ *n, pl* **-lies 1** part of the body of a vertebrate which contains the intestines **2** stomach **3** front, lower, or inner part of something **4 go belly up** *informal* fail utterly; die ▷ *v* **-lying, -lied 5** (cause to) swell out
▶ **bellyful** *n slang* more than one can tolerate
Belmondo *n* **Jean-Paul**. born 1933, French film actor
belong Ⓣ *v* (foll. by *to*) **1** be the property of **2** (foll. by *to*) be a part of **3** have a proper or usual place
▶ **belongings** *pl n* personal possessions
beloved Ⓣ *adj* **1** dearly loved ▷ *n* **2** person dearly loved
below Ⓣ *prep, adv* at or to a position lower than, under
belt Ⓣ *n* **1** band of cloth, leather, etc., worn usu. around the waist **2** long narrow area **3** circular strip of rubber that drives moving parts in a machine **4** area where a specific thing is found ▷ *v* **5** fasten with a belt **6** *slang* hit very hard
bemoan Ⓣ *v* express sorrow or dissatisfaction about
bemused Ⓣ *adj* puzzled or confused
bench Ⓣ *n* **1** long seat **2** judge or magistrate sitting in court **3** long narrow work table
▶ **bencher** *n* governing member of a provincial law society
▶ **bench mark 1** mark on a fixed object, used as a reference point in surveying **2** criterion by which to measure something
bend Ⓣ *v* **bending, bent 1** (cause to) form a curve **2** (often foll. by *down* etc.) incline the body ▷ *n* **3** curved part **bends 4** *informal*

THESAURUS

belligerent *adj* **1 = aggressive**, hostile, combative, unfriendly, pugnacious, bellicose, warlike, warring ▶ *n* **2 = fighter**, combatant, warring nation
bellow *n, v* **= shout**, cry, scream, roar, yell, howl, clamour, shriek, bawl
belly *n* **1 = stomach**, abdomen, gut, tummy, insides (*informal*), paunch, potbelly ▶ *v* **2 = swell out**, spread, fill, swell, bulge, billow
bellyful *n* **= surfeit**, enough, plenty, excess, glut, satiety, plateful, too much
belong See **fit** ▷ **belong to = be the property of**, be at the disposal of, be held by, be owned by; **= be a member of**, be affiliated to, be allied to, be associated with, be included in
belonging *n* **= relationship**, association, acceptance, loyalty, attachment, inclusion, fellowship, affinity, rapport
belongings *pl n* **= possessions**, stuff, gear, paraphernalia, accoutrements, chattels, effects, goods, personal property, things
beloved *adj* **= darling**, precious, cherished, adored, dearest, treasured • *His beloved pet died last year.* OPPOSITE: despised
See also: **dear**
below *preposition, adv* **1 = under**, down, lower, beneath, underneath • *about 6 m below sea level* OPPOSITE: above ▶ *preposition* **2 = lesser**, subject, inferior, subordinate **3 = less than**, lower than
belt *n* **1 = waistband**, band, girth, sash, girdle, cummerbund **2** (*Geography*) **= zone**, area, region, stretch, district, strip, layer, tract
bemoan *v* **= lament**, mourn, regret, deplore, rue, bewail, grieve for, weep for
bemused *adj* **= puzzled**, confused, at sea, bewildered, flummoxed, muddled, nonplussed, perplexed
bench *n* **= worktable**, board, table, counter, trestle table, workbench ▷ **the bench = court**, tribunal, courtroom, judiciary, judges, magistrates
benchmark *n* **= reference point**, level, measure, standard, model, par, criterion, gauge, norm, yardstick
bend *v* **1 = curve**, turn, twist, buckle, warp • *Bend the bar into a horseshoe.* **2 = stoop**, bow, lean, incline, arch, crouch • *I bent over*

DICTIONARY

decompression sickness **bendy** *adj*
beneath Ⓣ *adv, prep* **1** below **2** not worthy of
Benedict *n* **Saint**. ?480–?547 AD, Italian monk: founded the Benedictine order at Monte Cassino in Italy in around 540 AD. His *Regula Monachorum* became the basis of the rule of all Western Christian monastic orders. Feast day: July 11 or March 14
Benedict XVI *n* original name *Joseph Alois Ratzinger*. born 1927, pope from 2005, born in Germany
Benedictine *n, adj* (monk or nun) of the order of Saint Benedict
benediction *n* prayer for divine blessing
benefit Ⓣ *n* **1** something helpful, beneficial, or advantageous **2** payment made by a government to a poor, ill, or unemployed person ▷ *v* **-fiting, -fited 3** do or receive good
▶ **beneficial** *adj* advantageous
▶ **beneficiary** *n* person who gains or benefits
▶ **benefactor** (**benefactress**) *n* someone who supports a person or institution by giving money **benefaction** *n*
▶ **beneficent** [bin-**eff**-iss-ent] *adj* charitable or generous **beneficence** *n*
benevolent Ⓣ *adj* kind and helpful **benevolently** *adv* **benevolence** *n*
Ben-Gurion *n* **David**, original name *David Gruen*. 1886–1973, Israeli socialist statesman, born in Poland; first prime minister of Israel (1948–53, 1955–63)
benighted *adj* ignorant or uncultured
benign Ⓣ [bin-**nine**] *adj* **1** showing kindliness **2** (of a tumour) not malignant **benignly** *adv*
Benjamin *n* **Arthur**. 1893–1960, Australian composer. In addition to *Jamaican Rumba* (1938), he wrote five operas and a harmonica concerto (1953)
Bennett *n* **1 James Gordon**. 1837–1931, US newspaper editor, born in Scotland. He founded (1835) the *New York Herald* and introduced techniques of modern news reporting **2 Richard Bedford**, 1st Viscount. 1870–1947, Canadian Conservative statesman; prime minister (1930–35) **3** Sir **Richard Rodney**. born 1936, British composer, noted for film music and his operas *The Mines of Sulphur* (1965) and *Victory* (1970)
bent Ⓣ *v* **1** past of **bend** ▷ *adj* **2** curved **3** *slang* dishonest ▷ *n* **4** personal inclination or aptitude
▶ **bent on** determined to pursue (a course of action)
Bentham *n* **Jeremy**. 1748–1832, British philosopher and jurist: a founder of utilitarianism. His works include *A Fragment on Government* (1776) and *Introduction to the Principles of Morals and Legislation* (1789)
bento, bento box *n* thin lightweight box divided into compartments, which contain small separate dishes comprising a Japanese meal
Benton *n* **Thomas Hart**. 1889–1975, US painter of rural life; a leader of the American Regionalist painters in the 1930s
benzene *n* flammable poisonous liquid used as a solvent, fuel, etc.
bequeath Ⓣ *v* dispose of (property) as in a will

THESAURUS

and picked up the loonie. ▷ **bend down** *See* **crouch** ▶ *n* **3 = curve**, turn, corner, twist, angle, loop, arc, arch • *a bend in the road*
See also: **fold**
beneath *prep* **1 = under**, below, underneath, lower than **2 = inferior to**, below, less than **3 = unworthy of**, unbefitting ▶ *adv* **4 = underneath**, below, in a lower place
benefactor *n* **= supporter**, donor, sponsor, patron, backer, philanthropist, helper
beneficial *adj* **= advantageous**, healthy, useful, helpful, wholesome, good for you • *Calcium is beneficial to the bones*.
See also: **favourable, valuable**
beneficiary *n* **= recipient**, receiver, heir, inheritor, payee
benefit *n* **1 = good**, advantage, help, use, profit, gain, asset, boon • *the benefits of relaxation* OPPOSITE: disadvantage ▶ *v* **2 = help**, profit, further, assist, aid, enhance • *The experience will benefit you*. OPPOSITE: harm
See also: **beauty, blessing, value**
benevolence *n* **= kindness**, charity, understanding, humanity, sympathy, tolerance, grace, compassion, goodwill, clemency, decency, goodness, generosity, altruism, indulgence, philanthropy, magnanimity, beneficence, kind-heartedness, kindliness, gentleness, fellow feeling OPPOSITE: ill will
benevolent *adj* **= kind**, charitable, benign, compassionate, humane, philanthropic, altruistic, beneficent • *a benevolent ruler*
benign *adj* **1 = kindly**, kind, friendly, sympathetic, amiable, genial, obliging **2** (*Medical*) **= harmless**, curable, remediable
bent *adj* **1 = curved**, twisted, crooked, arched, angled, bowed, hunched, stooped ▷ **bent on = determined to**, disposed to, fixed on, inclined to, insistent on, predisposed to, resolved on, set on ▶ *n* **2 = inclination**, ability, preference, tendency, penchant, leaning, propensity, aptitude
bequeath *v* **= leave**, will, give, grant, bestow, entrust, endow, impart, hand down, pass on
bequest *n* **= legacy**, settlement, gift, estate,

DICTIONARY

▸**bequest** *n* legal gift of money or property by someone who has died
berate Ⓣ *v* scold harshly
bereaved *adj* having recently lost someone close through death **bereavement** *n*
bereft Ⓣ *adj* (foll. by *of*) deprived
beret [**ber**-ray] *n* round flat close-fitting brimless cap
Berg *n* **Alban** (**Maria Johannes**). 1885–1935, Austrian composer: a pupil of Schoenberg. His works include the operas *Wozzeck* (1921) and *Lulu* (1935), a violin concerto (1935), chamber works, and songs
bergamot *n* small Asian tree with sour pear-shaped fruit
Bergman *n* (**Ernst**) **Ingmar**. 1918–2007, Swedish film and stage director, whose films include *The Seventh Seal* (1956), *Wild Strawberries* (1957), *Persona* (1966), *Scenes from a Marriage* (1974), *Autumn Sonata* (1978), and *Fanny and Alexander* (1982)
Bergson *n* **Henri Louis**. 1859–1941, French philosopher, who sought to bridge the gap between metaphysics and science. His main works are *Memory and Matter* (1896, trans. 1911) and *Creative Evolution* (1907, trans. 1911): Nobel prize for literature 1927 **Bergsonian** *adj, n*
beriberi *n* tropical disease caused by vitamin B deficiency
Berio *n* **Luciano**. 1925–2003, Italian composer, living in the US, noted esp. for works that exploit instrumental and vocal timbre and technique
Berkeley *n* **1 George**. 1685–1753, Irish philosopher and Anglican bishop, whose system of subjective idealism was expounded in his works *A Treatise concerning the Principles of Human Knowledge* (1710) and *Three Dialogues between Hylas and Philonous* (1713). He also wrote *Essay towards a New Theory of Vision* (1709) **2** Sir **Lennox** (**Randal Francis**). 1903–89, British composer; his works include four symphonies, four operas, and the *Serenade for Strings* (1939)
Berlin *n* **1 Irving**, original name *Israel Baline*. 1888–1989, US composer and writer of lyrics, born in Russia. His musical comedies include *Annie Get Your Gun* (1946); his most popular song is *White Christmas* **2** Sir **Isaiah**. 1909–97, British philosopher, born in Latvia, historian, and diplomat. His books include *Historical Inevitability* (1954) and *The Magus of the North* (1993)
Berlioz *n* **Hector** (**Louis**). 1803–69, French composer, regarded as a pioneer of modern orchestration. His works include the cantata *La Damnation de Faust* (1846), the operas *Les Troyens* (1856–59) and *Béatrice et Bénédict* (1860–62), the *Symphonie fantastique* (1830), and the oratorio *L'Enfance du Christ* (1854)
Berlusconi *n* **Silvio**. born 1936, Italian politician and media tycoon: prime minister of Italy (1994, from 2001)
Bermuda shorts *pl n* close-fitting shorts that come down to the knees
Bernadette of Lourdes *n* **Saint**, original name *Marie Bernarde Soubirous*. 1844–79, French peasant girl born in Lourdes, whose visions of the Virgin Mary led to the establishment of Lourdes as a centre of pilgrimage, esp. for the sick or crippled. Feast day: Feb 18
Bernard *n* **Saint**, known as *Bernard of Menthon* and the *Apostle of the Alps*. 923–1008, French monk who founded hospices in the Alpine passes. Feast day: Aug 20
Bernard of Clairvaux *n* **Saint**. ?1090–1153, French abbot and theologian, who founded the stricter branch of the Cistercians in 1115
Bernini *n* **Gian Lorenzo**. 1598–1680, Italian painter, architect, and sculptor: the greatest exponent of the Italian baroque
Bernstein *n* **Leonard**. 1918–90, US conductor and composer, whose works include *The Age of Anxiety* (1949), the score of the musical *West Side Story* (1957), and *Mass* (1971)
berry *n, pl* **-ries** small soft stoneless fruit
Berry *n* **1 Chuck**, full name *Charles Edward Berry*. born 1926, US rock-and-roll guitarist, singer, and songwriter. His frequently covered songs include "Maybellene" (1955), "Roll over Beethoven" (1956), "Johnny B. Goode" (1958), "Memphis, Tennessee" (1959), and "Promised Land" (1964) **2 Jean de France**, Duc de. 1340–1416, French prince, son of King John II; coregent (1380–88) for Charles VI and a famous patron of the arts
berserk Ⓣ *adj* **go berserk** become violent or destructive
berth Ⓣ *n* **1** bunk in a ship or train **2** place

THESAURUS

inheritance, endowment, bestowal
berate *v* = **scold**, criticize, rebuke, reprimand, censure, castigate, chide, upbraid, harangue, reprove, tell off (*informal*)
bereavement *n* = **loss**, death, deprivation, misfortune, affliction, tribulation
bereft *adj* = **deprived**, devoid, lacking, parted from, robbed of, wanting
berserk *adv* = **frenzied**, wild, mad, crazy, frantic, enraged, raging, amok • *The protester went berserk and started attacking the crowd.*
berth *n* **1** = **bunk**, bed, hammock, billet **2** (*Naut*) = **anchorage**, port, dock, haven, wharf, pier, harbour, quay ▸ *v* **3** (*Naut*) = **anchor**, land, dock, moor, drop anchor, tie up

DICTIONARY

assigned to a ship at a mooring ▷ *v* **3** dock (a vessel)
Bertolucci *n* **Bernardo**. born 1940, Italian director: his movies include *The Spider's Stratagem* (1970), *The Conformist* (1970), *1900* (1976), *The Last Emperor* (1987), *The Sheltering Sky* (1990), and *The Dreamers* (2003)
beryl *n* hard transparent mineral
beseech Ⓣ *v* **-seeching, -sought** *or* **-seeched** ask (someone) earnestly
beset Ⓣ *v* trouble or harass constantly
beside Ⓣ *prep* **1** at, by, or to the side of **2** as compared with
▶ **beside oneself** overwhelmed or overwrought
▶ **besides** *adv, prep* in addition
besiege Ⓣ *v* **1** surround with military forces **2** overwhelm, as with requests
besmirch *v* **1** dirty **2** dishonour
besom *n* broom made of twigs
besotted Ⓣ *adj* infatuated
besought *v* past of **beseech**
bespatter *v* **1** splash, esp. with dirty water **2** dishonour
bespeak *v* indicate or suggest
▶ **bespoke** *adj* (of clothes) made to the customer's specifications
best Ⓣ *adj* **1** most excellent of a particular group etc. ▷ *adv* **2** in a manner surpassing all others ▷ *n* **3** most outstanding or excellent person, thing, or group in a category
▶ **best man** groom's attendant at a wedding
▶ **best seller** book or other product that has sold in great numbers
Best *n* **Charles Herbert**. 1899–1978, Canadian physiologist: associated with Banting and Macleod in their discovery of insulin in 1922
bestial Ⓣ *adj* **1** brutal or savage **2** of or like a beast **bestiality** *n*
bestir *v* cause (oneself) to become active
bestow Ⓣ *v* present (a gift) or confer (an honour) **bestowal** *n*
bestrew *v* scatter or lie scattered over (a surface)
bestride *v* have or put a leg on either side of
bet Ⓣ *n* **1** agreement that money will be paid to someone who correctly predicts the outcome of an event **2** stake risked ▷ *v* **betting, bet** *or* **betted 3** make or place (a bet) **4** *informal* predict (a certain outcome)
beta *n* second letter in the Greek alphabet
▶ **beta-blocker** *n* drug used to treat high blood pressure and angina
▶ **beta particle** electron or positron emitted by a nucleus during radioactive decay or nuclear fission
betel [**bee**-tl] *n* Asian climbing plant, the leaves and nuts of which can be chewed
bête noire [**bet nwahr**] *n, pl* **bêtes noires** person or thing that one particularly dislikes
Bethune n **(Henry) Norman**. 1890–1939, Canadian physician and campaigner for socialized medicine. He pioneered the use of mobile medical units during the Spanish Civil War and in China during the second Sino-Japanese War
betide *v* happen (to)
Betjeman *n* Sir **John**. 1906–84, English poet, noted for his nostalgic and humorous verse and essays and for his concern for the preservation of historic buildings, esp. of the Victorian era; poet laureate (1972–84)

THESAURUS

beseech *v* = **beg**, ask, plead, pray, solicit, implore, call upon, entreat
beset *v* = **plague**, trouble, harass, bedevil, pester
beside *prep* = **next to**, near, alongside, adjacent to, close to • *In the photo, I'm standing beside my father and my uncle.* ▷ **beside oneself** = **distraught**, apoplectic, at the end of one's tether, desperate, frantic, frenzied, out of one's mind, unhinged
besides *adv* **1** = **too**, also, further, otherwise, moreover, furthermore, as well, in addition, into the bargain, what's more ▶ *preposition* **2** = **apart from**, without, barring, excepting, excluding, in addition to, other than, over and above
besiege *v* **1** = **surround**, blockade, encircle, hem in, lay siege to, shut in **2** = **harass**, plague, hound, nag, hassle (*informal*), badger, harry, pester
besotted *adj* = **infatuated**, doting, hypnotized, smitten, spellbound
best *adj* **1** = **finest**, principal, outstanding, foremost, supreme, pre-eminent, unsurpassed, leading, most excellent • *the best TV series I have seen in a long time* OPPOSITE: worst ▷ **best part** *See* **majority** ▶ *adv* **2** = **most highly**, extremely, greatly, most deeply, most fully ▶ *n* **3** = **finest**, top, pick, prime, cream, flower, elite, *crème de la crème* (*French*) • *Of all my presents, this is the best.* OPPOSITE: worst
See also: **senior**
bestial *adj* = **brutal**, savage, inhuman, barbaric, sordid, beastly, brutish
best-loved *See* **favourite**
bestow *v* = **present**, give, award, commit, grant, lavish, impart, hand out
bet *n* **1** = **gamble**, risk, stake, speculation, venture, wager, long shot ▶ *v* **2** = **gamble**, risk, chance, stake, venture, speculate, hazard, wager

DICTIONARY

betoken Ⓣ *v* indicate or signify
betray Ⓣ *v* **1** hand over or expose (one's nation etc.) treacherously to an enemy **2** disclose (a secret or confidence) treacherously **3** reveal unintentionally **betrayal** *n* **betrayer** *n*
betrothed *adj* engaged to be married **betrothal** *n*
better Ⓣ *adj* **1** more excellent than others **2** improved or fully recovered in health ▷ *adv* **3** in a more excellent manner **4** in or to a greater degree ▷ *pl n* **5** one's superiors ▷ *v* **6** improve upon
between Ⓣ *prep* **1** at a point intermediate to two other points in space, time, etc. **2** indicating a linked relation or comparison **3** indicating alternatives ▷ *adv* **4** between one specified thing and another
betwixt *prep, adv old-fashioned* between
Beuys *n* **Joseph**. 1921–86, German artist, a celebrated figure of the avant-garde, noted esp. for his sculptures made of felt and animal fat
Bevan *n* **Aneurin**, known as *Nye*. 1897–1960, British Labour statesman, born in Wales: noted for his oratory. As minister of health (1945–51) he introduced the National Health Service (1948) **Bevanite** *n, adj*
bevel *n* **1** slanting edge ▷ *v* **-elling, -elled** **2** cut a bevel on (a piece of timber etc.)
beverage Ⓣ *n* drink
▸ **beverage room** tavern
bevy Ⓣ *n, pl* **bevies** flock or group
bewail Ⓣ *v* express great sorrow over
beware Ⓣ *v* be on one's guard (against)
bewilder Ⓣ *v* confuse utterly **bewildering** *adj* **bewilderment** *n*
bewitch Ⓣ *v* **1** attract and fascinate **2** cast a spell over **bewitching** *adj*
beyond Ⓣ *prep* **1** at or to a point on the other side of **2** outside the limits or scope of ▷ *adv* **3** at or to the far side of something
Bhutto *n* **1 Benazir**. 1953–2007, Pakistani stateswoman; prime minister of Pakistan (1988–90; 1993–96); deposed and subsequently defeated in elections in 1997; assassinated in 2007 **2** her father, **Zulfikar Ali**. 1928–79, Pakistani statesman; president (1971–73) and prime minister (1973–77) of Pakistan: executed for the murder of a political rival
bi- *combining form* twice or two: *bifocal*
biannual *adj* occurring twice a year **biannually** *adv*
bias Ⓣ *n* **1** mental tendency, esp. prejudice **2** diagonal cut across the weave of a fabric **3** *bowls* weight on one side of a bowl that

THESAURUS

betoken *v* = **indicate**, suggest, promise, represent, signify, bode, denote
betray *v* **1** = **be unfaithful**, break your promise, double-cross (*informal*), inform on • *I was betrayed by someone I had thought was a friend*. **2** = **reveal**, show, expose, manifest • *My voice betrayed little emotion*.
betrayal *n* **1** = **disloyalty**, back-stabbing (*informal*), treason, deception, sell-out (*informal*), treachery, trickery, double-cross (*informal*) **2** = **giving away**, disclosure, revelation, divulgence
better *adj* **1** = **superior**, preferable, higher-quality, excelling, finer, greater, more desirable, surpassing • *Today was much better than yesterday*. OPPOSITE: inferior **2** = **well**, cured, fully recovered, on the mend (*informal*), recovering, stronger • *I hope you feel better soon*. OPPOSITE: worse ▷ **better part** *See* **majority** ▸ *adv* **3** = **in a more excellent manner**, in a superior way, more advantageously, more attractively, more competently, more effectively **4** = **to a greater degree**, more completely, more thoroughly ▸ *v* **5** = **improve**, raise, further, enhance
See also: **reform, senior, top**
between *prep* = **amidst**, among, mid, betwixt, in the middle of
beverage *n* = **drink**, liquid, liquor, refreshment
bevy *n* = **group**, company, crowd, band, collection, pack, gathering, bunch (*informal*), troupe
bewail *v* = **lament**, mourn, regret, bemoan, deplore, moan, cry over, grieve for
beware *v* = **be careful**, be cautious, be wary, guard against, look out, watch out • *Beware of the dog*.
bewilder *v* = **confound**, puzzle, confuse, baffle, mystify, perplex, flummox, bemuse, nonplus
bewildered *adj* = **confused**, at a loss, at sea, baffled, flummoxed, mystified, nonplussed, perplexed, puzzled
bewildering *See* **confusing**
bewitch *v* = **enchant**, entrance, charm, fascinate, captivate, hypnotize, beguile, enrapture
bewitched *adj* = **enchanted**, charmed, entranced, fascinated, mesmerized, spellbound, under a spell
bewitching *See* **magical**
beyond *prep* **1** = **past**, over, above, apart from, at a distance, away from **2** = **exceeding**, out of reach of, superior to, surpassing
bias *n* **1** = **prejudice**, bigotry, favouritism • *Some employers show bias against younger workers*. ▸ *v* **2** = **prejudice**, weight, influence, twist, sway, predispose, distort, slant, warp

DICTIONARY

causes it to run in a curve ▷ *v* **-asing, -ased** *or* **-assing, -assed 4** cause to have a bias **biased** *or* **biassed** *adj*
bib *n* **1** piece of cloth or plastic worn under a child's chin to protect his or her clothes when eating **2** upper front part of dungarees etc.
Bible *n* **1** sacred writings of the Christian and Jewish religions **2 bible** book regarded as authoritative **biblical** *adj*
bibliography *n, pl* **-phies 1** list of books on a subject **2** list of sources used in a book etc. **bibliographer** *n*
bibliophile *n* person who collects or is fond of books
bibulous *adj* addicted to alcohol
bicarbonate *n* salt of carbonic acid ▸**bicarbonate of soda** powder used in baking or as medicine
bicentenary *n, pl* **-naries** 200th anniversary
biceps *n* large muscle in the upper arm
bicker Ⓣ *v* argue over petty matters
bicultural *adj* having or relating to two cultures, esp. English and French **biculturalism** *n*
bicycle *n* vehicle with two wheels, one behind the other, pedalled by the rider
bid Ⓣ *v* **bidding, bade, bidden 1** offer (a sum of money) in an attempt to buy something **2** *past* **bid** say (a greeting etc.) **3** command ▷ *n* **4** offer of a sum of money **5** attempt **bidder** *n* ▸**biddable** *adj* obedient ▸**bidding** *n* command
bide *v* **bide one's time** wait patiently for an opportunity
bidet [**bee**-day] *n* low basin for washing the genital area
biennial *adj* **1** occurring every two years ▷ *n* **2** plant that completes its life cycle in two years
bier *n* stand on which a coffin rests before burial
Bierce *n* **Ambrose** (**Gwinett**). 1842–?1914, US journalist and author of humorous sketches, horror stories, and tales of the supernatural: he disappeared during a mission in Mexico (1913)
bifocals *pl n* pair of spectacles with each lens in two parts, the upper for distance and the lower for reading
bifurcate *v* fork into two branches
big Ⓣ *adj* **bigger, biggest 1** of considerable size, height, number, or capacity **2** important through having wealth etc. **3** elder **4** generous, magnanimous **5** (of wine) full-bodied, with a strong aroma and flavour ▷ *adv* **6** on a grand scale ▸**Bigfoot** *n* legendary hairy, human-like monster in Pacific NW of N America ▸**big league 1** highest league in a professional sport, esp. baseball **2** highest class in any sphere of activity ▸**big shot** *or* **bigwig** *n informal* important person
bigamy *n* crime of marrying a person while still legally married to someone else **bigamist** *n* **bigamous** *adj*
bight *n* long curved shoreline
bigot Ⓣ *n* person who is intolerant, esp. regarding religion or race **bigoted** *adj* **bigotry** *n*

THESAURUS

See also: **colour, injustice**
biased *adj* = **prejudiced**, partial, one-sided, weighted, slanted • *biased attitudes* OPPOSITE: neutral
See also: **narrow-minded**
bicker *v* = **quarrel**, fight, dispute, argue, disagree, squabble, wrangle
bid *v* **1** = **offer**, propose, submit, tender, proffer, counterbid **2** = **say**, call, tell, wish, greet **3** = **tell**, ask, order, require, direct, command, instruct ▸ *n* **4** = **offer**, price, advance, amount, proposal, tender, sum **5** = **attempt**, go (*informal*), try, effort, crack (*informal*), stab (*informal*)
bidding *n* = **order**, request, direction, command, instruction, summons, beck and call
big *adj* **1** = **large**, great, huge, massive, extensive, substantial, enormous, immense, supersize, vast • *a big house* OPPOSITE: small **2** = **important**, main, significant, powerful, prominent, influential, eminent, leading • *a big name in the world of hockey* OPPOSITE: unimportant **3** = **grown-up**, adult, mature, elder, grown **4** = **generous**, noble, gracious, unselfish, benevolent, altruistic, magnanimous, hospitable • *That's very big of him.* ▷ **big cheese** (*Informal*) = **manager**, alpha male, boss (*informal*), supervisor, superintendent, foreman, overseer, bossman (*slang*), head honcho (*slang*), muckymuck ▷ **big name** *See* **celebrity, personality**
bighead *n* (*Informal*) = **boaster**, know-it-all (*informal*), braggart
bigheaded *adj* = **boastful**, arrogant, cocky, overconfident, conceited, egotistic, immodest, swollen-headed
bigmouth *See* **braggart**
bigot *n* = **fanatic**, sectarian, racist, zealot
bigoted *adj* = **intolerant**, sectarian, opinionated, narrow-minded, dogmatic, biased, prejudiced
bigotry *n* = **intolerance**, discrimination, bias, prejudice, sectarianism, fanaticism, dogmatism, narrow-mindedness

DICTIONARY

bijou [**bee**-zhoo] *adj* small but tasteful
bike *n informal* bicycle or motorcycle
Bikila *n* **Abebe**. 1932–73, Ethiopian long-distance runner: winner of the marathon at the Olympic Games in Rome (1960) and Tokyo (1964)
bikini *n* woman's brief two-piece swimming costume
Biko *n* **Steven Bantu**, known as *Steve*. 1946–77, Black South African civil rights leader: founder of the South African Students Organization. His death in police custody caused worldwide concern
bilateral *adj* affecting or undertaken by two parties
bile *n* bitter yellow fluid secreted by the liver ▸**bilious** *adj* sick, nauseous
bilge *n* **1** *informal* nonsense **2** ship's bottom, where dirty water collects
bilingual *adj* speaking, or written in, two languages **bilingualism** *adj*
bill[1] Ⓣ *n* **1** statement of money owed for goods or services supplied **2** draft of a proposed new law **3** piece of paper money **4** poster **5** list of events, such as a theatre programme ▹ *v* **6** send or present a bill to **7** advertise by posters
▸**billable** *adj* referring to time worked, esp. by a lawyer, for which a client will be expected to pay
bill[2] *n* bird's beak
billabong *n Aust* stagnant pool in an intermittent stream
billboard *n* large outdoor board for displaying advertisements
billet Ⓣ *v* **-leting, -leted 1** assign a lodging to (a soldier) ▹ *n* **2** civilian accommodation for a soldier
billet-doux [bill-ay-**doo**] *n, pl* **billets-doux** love letter
billhook *n* tool with a hooked blade, used for chopping etc.
billiards *n* game played on a table with balls and a cue
billion *n* **1** one thousand million **2** *Brit* formerly, one million million **billionth** *adj*
billow Ⓣ *n* **1** large sea wave ▹ *v* **2** rise up or swell out
billy, billycan *n, pl* **-lies, -lycans** metal can or pot for cooking on a camp fire
billy goat *n* male goat
bimbo *n slang* attractive but empty-headed young person, esp. a woman
bimonthly *adv, adj* **1** every two months **2** twice a month
bin *n* container for garbage or for storing grain, coal, etc.
binary [**bine**-a-ree] *adj* **1** composed of two parts **2** *math, computers* of or expressed in a counting system with only two digits, 0 and 1
Binchy *n* **Maeve**. born 1940, Irish novelist and journalist; her bestselling novels include *Circle of Friends* (1990) and *Quentins* (2002)
bind Ⓣ *v* **binding, bound 1** make or become secure with or as if with a rope **2** place (someone) under obligation **3** enclose and fasten (the pages of a book) between covers ▹ *n* **4** *informal* annoying situation
▸**binder** *n* firm cover for holding loose sheets of paper together
▸**binding** *n* **1** book cover **2** strip of cloth used as edging
▸**bindweed** *n* flowering plant that twines around a support
binge Ⓣ *n informal* bout of excessive eating or drinking
bingo *n* gambling game in which numbers are called out and covered by the players on their individual cards
bin Laden *n* **Osama**. born 1957, Saudi-born leader of the al-Qaida terrorist network: presumed architect of the terrorist attacks on New York and Washington of September 11 2001
binoculars *pl n* telescope made for both eyes ▸**binocular** *adj* involving both eyes
binomial *n, adj* (mathematical expression) consisting of two terms

THESAURUS

bigwig *n* (*Informal*) = **important person**, celebrity, somebody, mogul, dignitary, big shot (*informal*), personage, V.I.P., muckymuck
bill *n* **1** = **charge**, statement, account, invoice • *a huge hotel bill* **2** = **proposal**, measure, piece of legislation, projected law **3** = **list**, program, schedule, card, inventory, agenda, roster, listing, catalogue **4** = **advertisement**, notice, poster, handout, bulletin, circular, leaflet, placard, handbill ▸ *v* **5** = **charge**, debit, invoice **6** = **advertise**, announce, slate, give advance notice of
billet *v* **1** = **quarter**, station, berth, accommodate ▸ *n* **2** = **quarters**, accommodation, lodging, barracks
billow *v* **1** = **surge**, roll, swell, balloon, belly, puff up, rise up ▸ *n* **2** = **wave**, surge, swell, tide, roller, crest, breaker
bind *v* **1** = **secure**, lash, hitch, fasten, tie, strap **2** = **oblige**, force, require, engage, compel, constrain, necessitate ▸ *n* **3** = **difficulty**, spot (*informal*), dilemma, quandary
binding *adj* = **compulsory**, necessary, mandatory, obligatory, irrevocable, indissoluble, unalterable
binge *n* (*Informal*) = **bout**, feast, spree, fling, orgy

DICTIONARY

bio- *combining form* life or living organisms: *biology, biography*
biochemistry *n* study of the chemistry of living things **biochemist** *n*
biodegradable *adj* capable of being decomposed by natural means
biography Ⓣ *n, pl* **-phies** account of a person's life by another **biographical** *adj* **biographer** *n*
biology *n* study of living organisms **biological** *adj* **biologist** *n*
bionic *adj* having a part of the body that is operated electronically
biopsy *n, pl* **-sies** examination of tissue from a living body
bioterrorism *n* use of viruses, bacteria, etc. by terrorists **bioterrorist** *n*
biped [**bye**-ped] *n* animal with two feet
biplane *n* airplane with two sets of wings
bipolar *adj* **1** having two poles **2** having two extremes **bipolarity** *n*
birch *n* **1** tree with thin peeling bark **2** birch rod or twigs used, esp. formerly, for flogging offenders
bird *n* **1** creature with feathers and wings, the female of which lays eggs **2** *slang* young woman
birdie *n golf* score of one stroke under par for a hole
biretta *n* stiff square cap worn by the Catholic clergy
birth Ⓣ *n* **1** childbirth **2** act of being born **3** ancestry
▸**give birth to** *v* bear (offspring)
▸**birth control** any method of contraception
▸**birthday** *n* anniversary of the day of one's birth
▸**birthmark** *n* blemish on the skin formed before birth
▸**birthright** *n* privileges or possessions that someone is entitled to as soon as he or she is born
biscuit *n* **1** small cake of bread made with soda or baking powder **2** *Brit* cookie or thin cracker
bisect Ⓣ *v* divide into two equal parts
bisexual *adj* sexually attracted to both men and women **bisexuality** *n*
bishop *n* **1** member of the clergy who governs a diocese **2** piece at chess
▸**bishopric** *n* diocese or office of a bishop
Bismarck *n* Prince **Otto** (**Eduard Leopold**) **von**, called *the Iron Chancellor*. 1815–98, German statesman; prime minister of Prussia (1862–90). Under his leadership Prussia defeated Austria and France, and Germany was united. In 1871 he became the first chancellor of the German Reich
bismuth *n* pinkish-white metallic element
bison *n, pl* **-son** large hairy animal of the cattle family
bisque *n* thick rich soup made from shellfish
bistro *n, pl* **-tros** small restaurant
bit[1] Ⓣ *n* small piece, portion, or quantity
▸**a bit** rather, somewhat
▸**bit by bit** gradually
bit[2] *n* **1** metal mouthpiece on a bridle **2** cutting or drilling part of a tool
bit[3] *v* past tense of **bite**
bit[4] *n* smallest unit of information held in a computer's memory, either 0 or 1
bitch Ⓣ *n* **1** female dog, fox, or wolf **2** *offensive* spiteful woman ▷ *v* **3** *informal* complain or grumble **bitchy** *adj* **bitchiness** *n*
bite Ⓣ *v* **biting, bit, bitten 1** cut off, puncture, or tear as with the teeth or fangs **2** take firm hold of or act effectively upon ▷ *n* **3** act of biting **4** wound or sting inflicted by biting **5** snack **biter** *n*
▸**biting** *adj* **1** piercing or keen **2** sarcastic
bitter Ⓣ *adj* **1** having a sharp unpleasant taste **2** showing or caused by hostility or resentment **3** extremely cold ▷ *n* **4** beer with a slightly bitter taste **bitters 5** bitter-tasting alcoholic drink. **bitterly** *adv* **bitterness** *n*
bittern *n* wading bird like a heron
bivalve *n* marine mollusc with a double shell

THESAURUS

biography *n* = **life story**, account, bio (*informal*), record, life, profile, memoir
birth *n* **1** = **childbirth**, delivery, nativity, parturition **2** = **ancestry**, stock, blood, background, pedigree, lineage, parentage, breeding
bisect *v* = **cut in two**, cross, separate, split, halve, intersect, cut across, divide in two
bit *n* = **piece**, part, grain, scrap, fragment, crumb, speck, iota, jot • *a bit of bread*
See also: **portion**
bitch *n* **1** = **vixen**, cow, dragon (*informal*), nag, scold, fury, spitfire, shrew, harridan, virago, termagant (*rare*), harpy, ballbreaker (*slang*), biach, biatch (*slang*) ▸ *v* **2** (*Informal*) = **complain**, object, lament, bemoan, grumble, gripe (*informal*), grouse
bitchy *adj* (*Informal*) = **spiteful**, mean, nasty, vindictive, catty (*informal*), snide, backbiting
bite *v* **1** = **nip**, chew, nibble, gnaw • *His cat bit me when I tried to pat it.* ▸ *n* **2** = **wound**, nip, pinch, prick, sting, tooth marks **3** = **snack**, food, piece, taste, mouthful, refreshment, light meal, morsel
See also: **savage**
biting *adj* **1** = **piercing**, sharp, bitter, harsh, cutting, penetrating **2** = **sarcastic**, scathing, cutting, vitriolic, caustic, incisive, mordant, stinging, trenchant
bitter *adj* **1** = **resentful**, sour, acrimonious,

DICTIONARY

bivouac *n* **1** temporary camp in the open air ▷ *v* **-acking, -acked 2** camp in a bivouac
bizarre Ⓣ *adj* odd or unusual
Bizet *n* **Georges**. 1838–75, French composer, whose works include the opera *Carmen* (1875) and incidental music to Daudet's *L'Arlésienne* (1872)
blab Ⓣ *v* **blabbing, blabbed 1** reveal (secrets) indiscreetly **2** chatter thoughtlessly
black Ⓣ *adj* **1** of the darkest colour, like jet or coal **2 Black** dark-skinned **3** without hope **4** angry or resentful: *black looks* **5** unpleasant in a macabre manner: *black comedy* ▷ *n* **6** darkest colour **7 Black** member of a dark-skinned race, esp. of African origin **8** complete darkness ▷ *v* **9** make black **blackness** *n*
▶ **blacken** *v* **1** make or become black **2** defame or slander
▶ **blackball** *v* exclude from a group
▶ **blackbird** *n* common American or European thrush
▶ **blackboard** *n* hard black surface used for writing on with chalk
▶ **blackhead** *n* small black spot on the skin
▶ **blacklist** *n* list of people or organizations considered untrustworthy etc.
▶ **black magic** magic used for evil purposes
▶ **blackmail** *n* **1** act of attempting to extort money by threats ▷ *v* **2** (attempt to) obtain money by blackmail
▶ **black market** illegal trade in goods or currencies
▶ **black out** *v* **1** extinguish (lights) **2** lose consciousness or memory temporarily
▶ **blackout** *n* **1** extinguishing of all light as a precaution against an air attack **2** momentary loss of consciousness or memory
▶ **black sheep** person who is regarded as a disgrace by his or her family
▶ **blacksmith** *n* person who works iron with a furnace, anvil, etc.
Black *n* **1 Conrad** (**Moffat**), Lord Black of Cross Harbour. born 1944, Canadian-born British newspaper owner. Convicted of fraud and obstruction of justice in a US court in 2007 **2 Joseph**. 1728–99, Scottish physician and chemist, noted for his pioneering work on carbon dioxide and heat
BlackBerry *n* ® hand-held wireless device incorporating e-mail, browser, and mobile-phone functions
Blackmore *n* **R**(**ichard**) **D**(**oddridge**). 1825–1900, English novelist; author of *Lorna Doone* (1869)
Blackwood *n* **Frederick Temple**, 1st Marquess of Dufferin and Ava. 1826–1902, British diplomat. Governor General of Canada (1872–78)
bladder *n* **1** sac in the body where urine is held **2** hollow bag which may be filled with air or liquid
blade *n* **1** cutting edge of a weapon or tool **2** thin flattish part of a propeller, oar, etc. **3** leaf of grass

THESAURUS

rancorous, begrudging, embittered • *a bitter argument* **2 = sour**, sharp, acid, tart, acrid, astringent • *the pill has a bitter taste* OPPOSITE: sweet **3 = freezing**, severe, intense, fierce, biting, stinging
See also: **cold**
bitterness *n* **1 = sourness**, acidity, sharpness, acerbity, tartness **2 = resentment**, hostility, grudge, animosity, sarcasm, acrimony, asperity, rancour
bizarre *adj* **= strange**, odd, unusual, extraordinary, fantastic, weird, curious, eccentric, ludicrous, peculiar, outlandish, zany, queer, freakish • *He has some bizarre ideas about gardening*. OPPOSITE: ordinary
blab *v* **= tell**, reveal, disclose, divulge, blurt out, give away, let slip, let the cat out of the bag, spill the beans (*informal*)
black *adj* **1 = dark**, jet, raven, dusky, ebony, sable, swarthy **2 = hopeless**, sad, dismal, gloomy, ominous, sombre, depressing, foreboding **3 = angry**, hostile, furious, sullen, resentful, menacing, threatening **4 = wicked**, bad, evil, nefarious, villainous, iniquitous • *a black day for the livestock industry* ▷ **black magic = witchcraft**, sorcery, wizardry, black art, diabolism, necromancy, voodoo ▷ **black sheep = disgrace**, dropout, bad egg (*old-fashioned informal*), renegade, outcast, prodigal, reprobate, wastrel
blacken *v* **1 = darken**, cloud, soil, dirty, smudge, befoul, begrime, make black **2 = discredit**, smear, defame, vilify, malign, slander, denigrate, smirch
blackguard *n* **= scoundrel**, bastard (*offensive*), rogue, villain, swine, rascal
blacklist *v* **= exclude**, ban, reject, bar, boycott, expel, snub, debar
blackmail *n* **1 = threat**, ransom, intimidation, extortion, hush money (*slang*) ▶ *v* **2 = threaten**, demand, squeeze, compel, intimidate, coerce, extort, hold to ransom
blackness *n* **= darkness**, gloom, duskiness, murkiness, swarthiness
blackout *n* **1 = power failure** *or* **power outage**, blown fuse, electricity failure **2 = unconsciousness**, coma, faint, oblivion, swoon, loss of consciousness **3 = noncommunication**,

DICTIONARY

Blair *n* **Tony**, full name *Anthony Charles Lynton Blair*. born 1953, British politician; leader of the Labour Party (1994–2007); prime minister (1997–2007)
Blake *n* **1** Sir **Peter**. born 1932, British painter, a leading exponent of pop art in the 1960s: co-founder of the Brotherhood of Ruralists (1969) **2 Quentin** (**Saxby**). born 1932, British artist, illustrator, and children's writer; noted esp. for his illustrations to books by Roald Dahl **3 William**. 1757–1827, English poet, painter, engraver, and mystic. His literary works include *Songs of Innocence* (1789) and *Songs of Experience* (1794), *The Marriage of Heaven and Hell* (1793), and *Jerusalem* (1820). His chief works in the visual arts include engravings of a visionary nature, such as the illustrations for *The Book of Job* (1826), for Dante's poems, and for his own *Prophetic Books* (1783–1804)
Blakey *n* **Art**, full name *Arthur Blakey*. 1919–90, US Black jazz drummer and leader of the Jazz Messengers band
blame Ⓣ *v* **1** consider (someone) responsible for ▷ *n* **2** responsibility for something that is wrong **blameless** *adj*
▸ **blameworthy** *adj* deserving blame
blanch *v* **1** become pale **2** prepare (vegetables etc.) by plunging them in boiling water
Blanche of Castile *n* ?1188–1252, queen consort (1223–26) of Louis VIII of France, born in Spain. The mother of Louis IX, she acted as regent during his minority (1226–36) and his absence on a crusade (1248–52)
blancmange [blam-**monzh**] *n* jelly-like dessert made with milk
bland Ⓣ *adj* dull and uninteresting **blandly** *adv*
blandishments *pl n* persuasive flattery
blank Ⓣ *adj* **1** not written on **2** showing no interest, feeling, or understanding ▷ *n* **3** empty space **4** cartridge containing no bullet **blankly** *adv*
▸ **blank verse** unrhymed verse
blanket Ⓣ *n* **1** thick covering for a bed **2** concealing cover, as of snow ▷ *v* **3** cover as with a blanket
blare Ⓣ *v* **1** sound loudly and harshly ▷ *n* **2** loud harsh noise
blarney *n* flattering talk
blasé Ⓣ [**blah**-zay] *adj* indifferent or bored through familiarity
blaspheme Ⓣ *v* speak disrespectfully of (God or sacred things) **blasphemy** *n* **blasphemous** *adj* **blasphemer** *n*
blast Ⓣ *n* **1** explosion **2** sudden strong gust of air or wind **3** sudden loud sound, as of a trumpet ▷ *v* **5** blow up (a rock etc.) with explosives
▸ **blastoff** *n* launching of a rocket
blatant Ⓣ [**blay**-tant] *adj* glaringly obvious **blatantly** *adv*
blaze[1] Ⓣ *n* **1** strong fire or flame **2** very bright light ▷ *v* **3** burn or shine brightly

THESAURUS

censorship, secrecy, suppression, radio silence, withholding news
blame *v* **1 = hold responsible**, charge, accuse • *Don't blame me for this trouble.* ▸ *n* **2 = responsibility**, fault, accountability, liability, culpability, incrimination • *I'm not going to take the blame for that!*
See also: **censure, condemn**
blameless *adj* **= innocent**, clean, perfect, impeccable, immaculate, unblemished, virtuous, above suspicion, faultless, guiltless, irreproachable
blameworthy *adj* **= reprehensible**, shameful, inexcusable, indefensible, discreditable, disreputable, iniquitous, reproachable
bland *adj* **= dull**, flat, boring, tasteless, vapid, humdrum, insipid, unexciting, uninspiring,
blank *adj* **1 = unmarked**, clear, clean, empty, plain, bare • *a blank sheet of paper* **2 = impassive**, empty, vacant, dull, deadpan • *a blank expression on his face* ▸ *n* **3 = empty space**, space, gap, void, vacuum, vacancy, emptiness, nothingness
See also: **ignore**
blanket *n* **1 = cover**, coverlet **2 = covering**, sheet, layer, coat, carpet, cloak, mantle ▸ *v* **3 = cover**, hide, mask, coat, cloak, suppress, conceal, obscure
blare *v* **= sound out**, blast, scream, roar, trumpet, resound, clamour, clang
blaring *See* **loud**
blasé *adj* **= indifferent**, lukewarm, apathetic, unconcerned, nonchalant, offhand
blaspheme *v* **= curse**, abuse, swear, damn, desecrate, profane, revile, execrate
blasphemous *adj* **= irreverent**, profane, sacrilegious, godless, impious, irreligious, ungodly
blasphemy *n* **= irreverence**, profanity, desecration, swearing, cursing, execration, impiety, sacrilege
blast *n* **1 = explosion**, crash, burst, bang, discharge, outburst, eruption, salvo, volley, detonation **2 = blare**, blow, scream, wail, honk, clang, peal, toot **3 = launch**, shot, firing, projection, discharge, liftoff, expulsion, launching ▸ *v* **4 = blow up**, destroy, explode, burst, ruin, shatter, demolish, break up, put paid to
blatant *adj* **= obvious**, brazen, flagrant, overt, glaring, conspicuous, obtrusive, ostentatious
blaze *n* **1 = fire**, bonfire, conflagration,

DICTIONARY

blaze² *n* mark made on a tree to indicate a route
blazer *n* lightweight jacket, esp. in the colours of a school etc.
blazon *v* proclaim publicly
bleach Ⓣ *v* **1** make or become white or colourless ▷ *n* **2** bleaching agent
bleak Ⓣ *adj* **1** exposed and barren **2** offering little hope
bleary Ⓣ *adj* **-rier, -riest** with eyes dimmed, as by tears or tiredness **blearily** *adv*
bleat *v, n* (utter) the plaintive cry of a sheep, goat, or calf
bleed Ⓣ *v* **bleeding, bled 1** lose blood **2** draw blood from (a person or animal) **3** *informal* obtain money by extortion
bleep *n* **1** short high-pitched sound made by an electrical device ▷ *v* **2** make a bleeping sound
blemish Ⓣ *n* **1** defect or stain ▷ *v* **2** spoil or tarnish
blench *v* shy away, as in fear
blend Ⓣ *v* **1** mix or mingle (components) **2** look good together ▷ *n* **3** mixture
▶**blender** *n* kitchen appliance for mixing food or liquid at high speed
bless Ⓣ *v* **1** make holy by means of a religious rite **2** call upon God to protect **3** endow with health, talent, etc.
▶**blessed** *adj* holy
▶**blessing** *n* **1** prayer for God's favour **2** happy event
blew *v* past tense of **blow**²
Bligh *n* **William**. 1754–1817, British admiral; Governor of New South Wales (1806–9), deposed by the New South Wales Corps: as a captain, commander of *H.M.S. Bounty* when the crew mutinied in 1789
blight Ⓣ *n* **1** withering plant disease **2** person or thing that spoils or prevents growth ▷ *v* **3** frustrate or disappoint
blighter *n informal* irritating person
blimp *n* small airship
blind Ⓣ *adj* **1** unable to see **2** unable or unwilling to understand **3** not determined by reason: *blind hatred* ▷ *v* **4** deprive of sight **5** deprive of good sense, reason, or judgment ▷ *n* **6** covering for a window **7** something that serves to conceal the truth **blindly** *adv* **blindness** *n*
▶**blinders** *pl n* leather flaps on a horse's bridle to prevent sideways vision
▶**blindfold** *v* **1** prevent (a person) from seeing by covering the eyes ▷ *n* **2** piece of cloth used to cover the eyes
▶**blind trust** arrangement in which a public official's personal wealth is managed by another person

THESAURUS

flames **2** = **glare**, light, flash, flare, beam, glow, glitter, brilliance, gleam, radiance ▶ *v* **3** = **burn**, fire, flame **4** = **shine**, flash, flare, beam, glow, glare, gleam
bleach *v* = **whiten**, fade, lighten, blanch, grow pale, wash out
bleached *See* **light**
bleak *adj* **1** = **bare**, exposed, barren, desolate, windswept, unsheltered, weather-beaten **2** = **dismal**, grim, gloomy, dreary, hopeless, sombre, cheerless, depressing, discouraging, joyless
bleary *adj* = **blurred**, misty, murky, dim, fuzzy, hazy, blurry, foggy, indistinct
bleed *v* **1** = **hemorrhage**, run, flow, spurt, gush, ooze, lose blood, shed blood **2** = **draw blood** *or* **take blood**, extract, leech **3** (*Informal*) = **extort**, milk, drain, squeeze, exhaust, fleece
blemish *n* **1** = **mark**, flaw, defect, fault, taint, stain, blot, smudge, imperfection, disfigurement ▶ *v* **2** = **stain**, mark, damage, injure, spoil, taint, impair, mar, tarnish, disfigure, sully
blend *v* **1** = **mix**, combine, merge, mingle • *Blend the butter with the sugar*. OPPOSITE: separate **2** = **harmonize**, match, suit, co-ordinate, complement, go well • *The colours blend with the rest of the decor*. ▶ *n* **3** = **mixture**, mix, combination, compound, alloy, fusion, amalgamation • *a blend of juice and sparkling water*
See also: **cross, union**
bless *v* **1** = **consecrate**, dedicate, hallow • *The priest blessed the congregation*. OPPOSITE: curse **2** = **grant**, give, provide, favour, grace, bestow
blessed *adj* = **holy**, sacred, divine, hallowed, adored, beatified, revered, sanctified
blessing *n* **1** = **benefit**, help, gift, boon, godsend • *Good health is a blessing*. OPPOSITE: disadvantage **2** = **approval**, leave, support, permission, consent, backing • *They got married with their parents' blessing*. OPPOSITE: disapproval **3** = **benediction**, dedication, grace, commendation, benison, consecration, invocation, thanksgiving
See also: **sanction**
blight *n* **1** = **curse**, pollution, corruption, contamination, plague, evil, woe, scourge, affliction, bane **2** = **disease**, fungus, infestation, pest, decay, rot, canker, mildew, pestilence ▶ *v* **3** = **frustrate**, disappoint, crush, ruin, spoil, wreck, mar, dash, undo
blind *adj* **1** = **visually impaired**, sightless, eyeless, unseeing, unsighted, visionless **2** = **unaware of**, ignorant, oblivious, careless, indifferent, insensitive, heedless, inattentive, inconsiderate, unconscious of **3** = **unreasoning**,

DICTIONARY

blink ⓣ *v* **1** close and immediately reopen (the eyes) **2** shine intermittently ▷ *n* **3** act of blinking
▸ **on the blink** *slang* not working properly
blip *n* small light which flashes on and off regularly on equipment such as a radar screen
bliss ⓣ *n* perfect happiness **blissful** *adj* **blissfully** *adv*
Bliss *n* Sir **Arthur**. 1891–1975, British composer; Master of the Queen's Musick (1953–75). His works include the *Colour Symphony* (1922), movie and ballet music, and a cello concerto (1970)
blister ⓣ *n* **1** small bubble on the skin **2** swelling, as on a painted surface ▷ *v* **3** (cause to) have blisters
▸ **blistering** *adj* **1** (of weather) very hot **2** (of criticism) extremely harsh
blithe ⓣ *adj* casual and indifferent **blithely** *adv*
blitz ⓣ *n* **1** violent and sustained attack by aircraft **2** *football* defensive charge on the quarterback **3** intensive attack or concerted effort ▷ *v* **4** attack suddenly and intensively
blizzard ⓣ *n* blinding storm of wind and snow
bloated *adj* swollen up with liquid or gas
bloater *n* salted smoked herring
blob ⓣ *n* **1** soft mass or drop **2** indistinct or shapeless form
bloc ⓣ *n* people or countries combined by a common interest
Bloch *n* **1 Ernest**. 1880–1959, US composer, born in Switzerland, who found inspiration in Jewish liturgical and folk music: his works include the symphonies *Israel* (1916) and *America* (1926) **2 Felix**. 1905–83, US physicist, born in Switzerland: Nobel prize for physics (1952) for his work on the magnetic moments of atomic particles **3 Konrad Emil**. 1912–2000, US biochemist, born in Germany: shared the Nobel prize for physiology or medicine in 1964 for his work on fatty-acid metabolism **4 Marc**. 1886–1944, French historian and Resistance fighter; author of *Feudal Society* (1935) and *Strange Defeat* (1940), an essay on the fall of France: killed by the Nazis
block ⓣ *n* **1** large solid piece of wood, stone, etc. **2** large building of offices, apartments, etc. **3** group of buildings enclosed by intersecting streets **4** obstruction or hindrance **5** *slang* person's head ▷ *v* **6** obstruct or impede by introducing an obstacle **blockage** *n*
▸ **blockhead** *n* stupid person
▸ **block heater** electrical device for keeping engine of motor vehicle warm
▸ **block letter** plain capital letter
blockade ⓣ *n* **1** action that prevents goods from reaching a place ▷ *v* **2** impose a blockade on
Bloc Québécois *n Canad* federal party advocating autonomy for Quebec

THESAURUS

indiscriminate, prejudiced ▸ *n* **4** = **cover**, front, screen, mask, cloak, camouflage, masquerade, façade, feint, smoke screen
blindly *adv* **1** = **thoughtlessly**, recklessly, carelessly, heedlessly, inconsiderately, senselessly **2** = **aimlessly**, indiscriminately, instinctively, at random
blink *v* **1** = **wink**, bat, flutter **2** = **flicker**, shine, flash, gleam, glimmer, wink, twinkle ▸ *n* ▷ **on the blink** (*Slang*) = **broken**, faulty, not working *or* not working properly, malfunctioning, out of action, out of order, playing up
bliss *n* = **joy**, happiness, heaven, paradise, ecstasy, euphoria, nirvana, rapture, beatitude, blessedness, blissfulness, felicity, gladness
blissful *adj* = **joyful**, happy, ecstatic, heavenly (*informal*), euphoric, elated, enraptured, rapturous
blister *n* = **sore**, boil, abscess, pimple, carbuncle, cyst, pustule, swelling
blithe *adj* = **heedless**, casual, careless, indifferent, thoughtless, unconcerned, nonchalant, untroubled
blitz *n* = **attack**, strike, campaign, assault, offensive, raid, bombardment, onslaught, blitzkrieg
blizzard *n* = **snowstorm**, storm, blast, squall, tempest, gale
bloat *v* = **puff up**, expand, swell, balloon, inflate, enlarge, dilate, blow up, distend
blob *n* = **drop**, bead, droplet, dab • *He had a blob of pudding on his tie.*
bloc *n* = **group**, union, league, coalition, alliance, faction, axis
block *n* **1** = **piece**, bar, brick, chunk, lump, ingot • *a block of wood* **2** = **obstruction**, bar, barrier, jam, obstacle, impediment, blockage, hindrance ▸ *v* **3** = **obstruct**, choke, plug, clog • *Mud blocked the river.* OPPOSITE: unblock **4** = **prevent**, stop, check, bar, halt, thwart, obstruct • *The committee blocked his plans.*
See also: **close, frustrate, hinder, impede**
blockade *n* = **stoppage**, block, restriction, barrier, obstacle, obstruction, siege, barricade, impediment, hindrance
blockage *n* = **obstruction**, block • *a blockage in the pipe*
blockhead *n* = **idiot**, fool, chump (*informal*), dork (*slang*), dunce, nitwit, schmuck (*slang*), thickhead, idiot, dummy, moron, half-wit, cretin, jackanapes, lemming, bozo

DICTIONARY

blog *n* **1** short for **weblog** ▷ *v* **blogging, blogged 2** write such a blog **blogger** *n*
Blok *n* **Aleksandr Aleksandrovich**. 1880–1921, Russian poet whose poems, which include *Verses about the Beautiful Lady* (1901–02) and *Rasput'ya* (1902–04), contain a mixture of symbolism, romanticism, tragedy, and irony
bloke *n informal* man
blond, blonde Ⓣ *adj, n* fair-haired (person)
blood Ⓣ *n* **1** red fluid that flows around the body **2** race or ancestry **bloodless** *adj*
▸ **in cold blood** done deliberately
▸ **bloody** *adj* **1** covered with blood **2** marked by much killing ▷ *adj, adv* **3** *slang* extreme or extremely ▷ *v* **4** stain with blood
▸ **bloody-minded** *adj* deliberately unhelpful
▸ **blood bath** massacre
▸ **bloodhound** *n* large dog used for tracking
▸ **bloodshed** *n* slaughter or killing
▸ **bloodshot** *adj* (of eyes) inflamed
▸ **blood sport** sport involving the killing of animals
▸ **bloodstream** *n* flow of blood round the body
▸ **bloodsucker** *n* **1** animal that sucks blood **2** *informal* person who extorts money from other people
▸ **bloodthirsty** *adj* taking pleasure in violence
bloom Ⓣ *n* **1** blossom on a flowering plant **2** youthful or healthy glow ▷ *v* **3** bear flowers **4** be in a healthy glowing condition
bloop *v baseball* **1** hit the ball just beyond the infield ▷ *n* **2** (as modifier): *a bloop single*
▸ **blooper** *n* **1** *informal* blunder or stupid mistake **2** *baseball* ball hit just beyond the infield
blossom Ⓣ *n* **1** flowers of a plant ▷ *v* **2** (of plants) flower **3** come to a promising stage
blot Ⓣ *n* **1** spot or stain **2** something that spoils or stains ▷ *v* **blotting, blotted 3** cause a blemish in or on **4** soak up (ink) by using blotting paper **blotter** *n*
▸ **blot out** *v* darken or hide completely
▸ **blotting paper** soft absorbent paper for soaking up ink
blotch Ⓣ *n* discoloured area or stain **blotchy** *adj*
blotto *adj slang* extremely drunk
blouse *n* woman's shirtlike garment
blow[1] Ⓣ *v* **blowing, blew, blown 1** (of air, the wind, etc.) move **2** move or be carried as if by the wind **3** expel (air etc.) through the mouth or nose **4** cause (a musical instrument) to sound by forcing air into it **5** burn out (a fuse etc.) **6** *slang* spend (money) freely **blower** *n*
▸ **blowy** *adj* windy
▸ **blow-dry** *v* style (the hair) with a hand-held dryer
▸ **blowout** *n* **1** sudden loss of air in a tire

THESAURUS

blond, blonde *adj* = **fair**, light, fair-haired, fair-skinned, flaxen, golden-haired, tow-headed
See also: **fair, light**
blood *n* **1** = **lifeblood**, gore, vital fluid **2** = **family**, birth, descent, extraction, ancestry, lineage, kinship, relations
bloodcurdling *adj* = **terrifying**, fearful, horrendous, appalling, dreadful, hair-raising, chilling, frightening, horrifying, scaring, spine-chilling
bloodshed *n* = **killing**, murder, slaughter, massacre, slaying, carnage, gore, blood bath, blood-letting, butchery
bloodthirsty *adj* = **cruel**, brutal, vicious, murderous, ferocious, savage, gory, barbarous, cut-throat, warlike
bloody *adj* **1** = **bloodstained**, raw, blood-soaked, bleeding, blood-spattered, gaping **2** = **cruel**, fierce, ferocious, savage, sanguinary
bloom *n* **1** = **flower**, opening (of flowers), blossom, bud, blossoming, efflorescence **2** = **prime**, health, beauty, glow, heyday, vigour, lustre, freshness, flourishing, radiance ▸ *v* **3** = **blossom**, open, blow, burgeon, bud, sprout **4** = **flourish**, grow, develop, succeed, thrive, wax, prosper, fare well
blooming *See* **well**
blossom *n* **1** = **flower**, bloom, bud, floret, flowers ▸ *v* **2** = **flower**, burgeon, bloom **3** = **grow**, develop, progress, mature, thrive, flourish, bloom, prosper
blot *n* **1** = **spot**, mark, patch, smear, speck, smudge, blotch, splodge **2** = **stain**, spot, flaw, defect, fault, taint, scar, blemish ▸ *v* **3** = **stain**, mark, spot, spoil, disgrace, tarnish, smudge, sully, smirch **4** = **soak up**, dry, absorb, take up ▷ **blot out** = **obliterate**, destroy, shadow, eclipse, obscure, darken, efface; = **erase**, cancel, expunge
blotch *See* **spot**
blow[1] *v* **1** = **gust**, drive, sweep, buffet, flutter, whirl, waft • *The wind blew his papers away.* **2** = **exhale**, breathe, pant, puff **3** = **play**, sound, mouth, pipe, trumpet, blare, vibrate, toot ▷ **blow out** = **put out**, snuff, extinguish; = **burst**, explode, erupt, shatter, rupture, fracture, break, split open ▷ **blow up** = **explode**, bomb, blast, burst, detonate, shatter, rupture, blow sky-high; = **inflate**, fill, expand, swell, enlarge, bloat, distend, puff up, pump up; (*Informal*) = **lose one's temper**, erupt, rage, become angry, fly off the handle (*informal*), hit the roof (*informal*), see red (*informal*)
See also: **sound**

DICTIONARY

2 escape of oil or gas from a well 3 *slang* filling meal
▶ **blow up** *v* 1 explode 2 fill with air 3 *informal* enlarge (a photograph) 4 *informal* lose one's temper
blow² Ⓣ *n* 1 hard hit 2 sudden setback 3 attacking action
blown *v* past participle of **blow²**
blowzy, blowsy *adj* fat, untidy, and red-faced
blubber *v* 1 sob without restraint ▷ *n* 2 fat of whales, seals, etc.
bludgeon Ⓣ *n* 1 short thick club ▷ *v* 2 hit with a bludgeon 3 force or bully
blue Ⓣ *n* 1 colour of a clear unclouded sky 2 short for **blue line** **blues** 3 feeling of depression 4 sad slow music like jazz ▷ *adj* **bluer, bluest** 5 of the colour blue 6 depressed 7 pornographic **bluish** *adj*
▶ **out of the blue** unexpectedly
▶ **bluebell** *n* flower with blue bell-shaped flowers
▶ **bluebottle** *n* large fly with a dark-blue body
▶ **blue-collar** *adj* denoting manual industrial workers
▶ **blue jay** N American bird with bright blue feathers
▶ **blue line** *ice hockey* line drawn midway between the centre of the rink and each goal
▶ **blueprint** *n* 1 photographic print of a plan 2 description of how a plan is expected to work
▶ **blue-sky** *v* theorize about something that may not lead to any practical application
bluff¹ Ⓣ *v* 1 pretend to be confident in order to influence (someone) ▷ *n* 2 act of bluffing
bluff² Ⓣ *n* 1 steep cliff or bank ▷ *adj* 2 good-naturedly frank and hearty
blunder Ⓣ *n* 1 clumsy mistake ▷ *v* 2 make a blunder 3 act clumsily
blunderbuss *n* obsolete gun with a wide muzzle
blunt Ⓣ *adj* 1 lacking sharpness 2 (of people, speech, etc.) straightforward or uncomplicated ▷ *v* 3 make less sharp
bluntly *adv*
blur Ⓣ *v* **blurring, blurred** 1 make or become vague or less distinct ▷ *n* 2 something vague, hazy, or indistinct **blurry** *adj*
blurb *n* promotional description, as on the jacket of a book
blurt Ⓣ *v* (foll. by *out*) utter suddenly and involuntarily
blush Ⓣ *v* 1 become red in the face, esp. from embarrassment or shame ▷ *n* 2 reddening of the face
bluster Ⓣ *v* 1 speak loudly or in a bullying way ▷ *n* 2 empty threats or protests
▶ **blustery** *adj* (of weather) rough and windy
Blyton *n* **Enid** (**Mary**). 1897–1968, British

b

THESAURUS

blow² *n* 1 = **knock**, bang, thump, smack, whack • *a blow to the head* 2 = **shock**, upset, setback, disappointment, jolt, catastrophe, bombshell, calamity, misfortune • *Our third loss in overtime was a major blow*.
See also: **hit**
bludgeon *n* 1 = **club**, truncheon, cudgel ▶ *v* 2 = **club**, beat up, strike, cudgel, knock down 3 = **bully**, force, coerce, railroad (*informal*), bulldoze (*informal*), steamroller
blue *adj* 1 = **azure**, navy, cobalt, sapphire, cerulean, cyan, sky-coloured, ultramarine 2 = **depressed**, low, sad, unhappy, dejected, melancholy, despondent, downcast 3 = **smutty**, obscene, indecent, lewd, X-rated (*informal*), risqué
blueprint *n* = **plan**, design, draft, outline, pattern, sketch, prototype, pilot scheme
blues *pl n* = **depression**, gloom, unhappiness, doldrums, melancholy, dumps (*informal*), low spirits
bluff¹ *v* 1 = **deceive**, fake, mislead, con, pretend, delude, feign, pull the wool over someone's eyes ▶ *n* 2 = **deception**, fraud, sham, deceit, pretense, bravado, bluster, subterfuge, humbug
bluff² *n* 1 = **precipice**, bank, peak, cliff, ridge, escarpment, headland, crag, promontory ▶ *adj* 2 = **hearty**, open, outspoken, blunt, good-natured, genial, blustering, plain-spoken
blunder *n* 1 = **mistake**, blooper (*informal*), foul-up (*slang*), faux pas, indiscretion 2 = **error**, slip, mistake, fault, oversight, inaccuracy, slip-up (*informal*), screw-up ▶ *v* 3 = **make a mistake**, err, botch, bungle, screw up, mess up, foul up (*slang*), slip up (*informal*) 4 = **stumble**, flounder, bumble
blunt *adj* 1 = **dull**, rounded, unsharpened • *blunt scissors* OPPOSITE: sharp 2 = **frank**, outspoken, straightforward, forthright, brusque • *a blunt speaker* OPPOSITE: tactful ▶ *v* 3 = **dull**, weaken, soften, dampen, numb, deaden, take the edge off, water down
See also: **candid, direct, straight**
blur *v* 1 = **make indistinct**, cloud, mask, obscure, darken, make hazy, make vague ▶ *n* 2 = **indistinctness**, confusion, fog, haze, obscurity
blurt *v* **blurt out** = **exclaim**, reveal, disclose, let the cat out of the bag, spill the beans (*informal*), tell all, utter suddenly
blush *v* 1 = **go red**, flush • *I felt myself blushing.* ▶ *n* 2 = **reddening**, colour, glow, flush, pink tinge, rosiness, rosy tint, ruddiness
bluster *v* 1 = **roar**, storm, bully, rant,

DICTIONARY

writer of children's books; creator of Noddy and the *Famous Five* series of adventure stories
BO *informal* body odour
boa constrictor *n* large snake that kills its prey by crushing
boar *n* **1** uncastrated male pig **2** wild pig
board Ⓣ *n* **1** long flat piece of wood **2** smaller flat piece of rigid material for a specific purpose: *ironing board* **3** group of people who administer a company, trust, etc. **4** meals provided for money **boards 5** wooden barrier around the surface of an ice hockey rink ▷ *v* **6** go aboard (a train, airplane, etc.) **7** cover with boards **8** receive meals and lodgings in return for money
▸ **on board** on or in a ship, airplane, etc.
▸ **boarder** *n* pupil who lives at school during the school term
▸ **boarding** *n ice hockey* illegal bodycheck of a player into the boards
▸ **boarding house** private house that provides meals and accommodation for paying guests
▸ **boardroom** *n* room where the board of a company meets
boast Ⓣ *v* **1** speak too proudly about one's talents etc. **2** possess (something to be proud of) ▷ *n* **3** boasting statement **boastful** *adj*
boat *n* small vehicle for travelling across water **boating** *n*
▸ **boater** *n* flat straw hat
▸ **boatswain, bo's'n,** *or* **bosun** [**boh**-sn] *n* ship's officer in charge of the equipment
bob¹ Ⓣ *v* **bobbing, bobbed 1** move up and down repeatedly ▷ *n* **2** short abrupt movement
bob² *n* **1** hair style in which the hair is cut level with the chin ▷ *v* **bobbing, bobbed 2** cut (the hair) in a bob
bobbin *n* reel on which thread is wound
bobble *n* small ball of material, usu. for decoration
bobby *n, pl* **-bies** *informal* policeman
bobsleigh *n* **1** sledge used for racing ▷ *v* **2** ride on a bobsleigh
Boccaccio *n* **Giovanni**. 1313–75, Italian poet and writer, noted particularly for his *Decameron*(1353), a collection of 100 short stories. His other works include *Filostrato* (?1338) and *Teseida* (1341)
Boccherini *n* **Luigi**. 1743–1805, Italian composer and cellist
bod *n informal* **1** person **2** body
bode Ⓣ *v* be an omen of (good or ill)
bodice *n* upper part of a dress
bodkin *n* blunt large-eyed needle
body Ⓣ *n, pl* **bodies 1** entire physical structure of an animal or human **2** trunk or torso **3** corpse **4** group regarded as a single entity **5** main part of anything **6** woman's one-piece undergarment
▸ **bodily** *adj* **1** relating to the body ▷ *adv* **2** by taking hold of the body
▸ **bodycheck** *sports* ▷ *n* **1** use of the body to block an opposing player ▷ *v* **2** make a bodycheck
▸ **bodyguard** *n* person or group of people employed to protect someone
▸ **body mass index** measure used to gauge whether a person is overweight: a person's weight in kilograms divided by the square of his or her height in metres
▸ **bodywork** *n* outer shell of a motor vehicle
Boer *n* descendant of the Dutch settlers in S Africa
Boethius *n* **Anicius Manlius Severinus**. ?480–?524 AD, Roman philosopher and statesman, noted particularly for his work *De Consolatione Philosophiae*. He was accused of treason and executed by Theodoric
bog Ⓣ *n* **1** wet spongy ground **2** *slang* toilet

THESAURUS

domineer, hector ▸ *n* **2 = hot air** (*informal*), bluff, bravado, bombast
blustery *adj* = **gusty**, violent, wild, stormy, windy, boisterous, inclement, tempestuous, squally
board *n* **1** = **plank**, panel, lumber, timber, slat, piece of timber **2** = **directors**, committee, panel, council, conclave, advisers, trustees **3** = **meals**, daily meals, provisions, victuals ▸ *v* **4** = **get on**, enter, mount, embark **5** = **lodge**, quarter, room, put up
boast *v* = **brag**, crow • *He boasted about his high marks.*
boaster *See* **braggart**
boastful *adj* = **cocky**, conceited, crowing, egotistical, swaggering • *a boastful skateboarder* OPPOSITE: modest
bob *v* = **bounce**, duck, nod, hop, wobble, wiggle, oscillate
bode *v* = **portend**, threaten, predict, signify, augur, foretell, forebode, be an omen of
bodily *adj* = **physical**, material, substantial, actual, tangible, corporal, carnal, corporeal
body *n* **1** = **physique**, build, figure, form, shape, frame • *My whole body hurts!* RELATED WORDS *adjs*: corporal, physical **2** = **corpse**, carcass, dead body, remains • *a body buried in the forest* **3** = **organization**, company, band, society, association, corporation, confederation • *local voluntary bodies* **4** = **torso**, trunk **5** = **main part**, matter, material, mass, substance, bulk, essence
bog *n* = **marsh**, swamp, mire, quagmire, slough, muskeg (*Canad*),

DICTIONARY

boggy *adj* **bog down** *v* **bogging, bogged** impede physically or mentally
bogan *n* sluggish side stream
Bogarde *n* Sir **Dirk**, real name *Derek Jules Gaspard Ulric Niven van den Bogaerde*. 1920–99, British movie actor and writer: his movies include *The Servant* (1963) and *Death in Venice* (1970). His writings include the autobiographical *A Postillion Struck by Lightning* (1977) and the novel *A Period of Adjustment* (1994)
Bogart *n* **Humphrey** (**DeForest**), nicknamed *Bogie*. 1899–1957, US film actor: his films include *High Sierra* (1941), *Casablanca* (1942), *The Big Sleep* (1946), *The African Queen* (1951), and *The Caine Mutiny* (1954)
bogey Ⓣ *n* **1** something that worries or annoys **2** *golf* score of one stroke over par on a hole
boggle Ⓣ *v* be surprised, confused, or alarmed
bogus Ⓣ [**boh**-guss] *adj* not genuine
bogy *n, pl* **-gies** same as **bogey**
bohemian Ⓣ *n, adj* (person) leading an unconventional life
Bohemond I *n* ?1056–?1111, prince of Antioch (1099–1111); a leader of the first crusade, he helped to capture Antioch (1098)
Bohr *n* **1 Aage Niels**. 1922–2009, Danish physicist, noted for his work on nuclear structure. He shared the Nobel prize for physics 1975 **2** his father, **Niels** (**Henrik David**). 1885–1962, Danish physicist, who applied the quantum theory to Rutherford's model of the atom to explain spectral lines: Nobel prize for physics 1922
boil[1] Ⓣ *v* **1** (cause to) change from a liquid to a vapour so quickly that bubbles are formed **2** cook by the process of boiling ▷ *n* **3** state or action of boiling
▶ **boiler** *n* piece of equipment which provides hot water
▶ **boilerplate** *v* incorporate standard material in a text automatically
boil[2] Ⓣ *n* red pus-filled swelling on the skin
boisterous Ⓣ *adj* noisy and lively
boisterously *adv*
Boito *n* **Arrigo**. 1842–1918, Italian operatic composer and librettist, whose works include the opera *Mefistofele* (1868) and the librettos for Verdi's *Otello* and *Falstaff*
Bokassa I *n* original name *Jean Bedel Bokassa*. 1921–96, president of the Central African Republic (1972–76); emperor of the renamed Central African Empire from 1976 until overthrown in 1979
bold Ⓣ *adj* **1** confident and fearless **2** immodest or impudent **boldly** *adv*
boldness *n*
Bolden *n* **Buddy**, real name *Charles Bolden*. 1868–1931, US Black jazz cornet player; a pioneer of the New Orleans style
bole *n* tree trunk
bolero *n, pl* **-ros 1** short open jacket **2** traditional Spanish dance
Bolivar *n* **Simon**. 1783–1830, South American soldier and liberator. He drove the Spaniards from Venezuela, Colombia, Ecuador, and Peru and hoped to set up a republican confederation, but was prevented by separatist movements in Venezuela and Colombia (1829–30). Upper Peru became a separate state and was called Bolivia in his honour
bollard *n* short thick post used to prevent the passage of motor vehicles
boloney *n* same as **baloney**
Bolshevik *n* Russian Communist
▶ **bolshie** *or* **bolshy** *adj informal* difficult or rebellious
bolster Ⓣ *v* **1** support or strengthen ▷ *n* **2** long narrow pillow
bolt Ⓣ *n* **1** sliding metal bar for fastening a door etc. **2** metal pin which screws into a nut **3** flash (of lightning) ▷ *v* **4** fasten with a bolt

THESAURUS

morass, fen, wetlands
bogey *n* = **bugbear**, nightmare, bête noire, bugaboo
boggle *See* **wonder**
bogus *adj* = **fake**, false, counterfeit, artificial, fraudulent, phony (*informal*), sham, imitation, forged
bohemian *adj* **1** = **unconventional**, alternative, artistic, unorthodox, offbeat, artsy *or* artsy-fartsy (*informal*), left bank, nonconformist ▶ *n* **2** = **nonconformist**, dropout, hippie, beatnik, iconoclast
boil[1] *v* = **bubble**, foam, froth, fizz • *The water is boiling.*
See also: **cook**
boil[2] *n* = **swelling**, tumour, blister • *a boil on my neck*
boiling *See* **hot**
boisterous *adj* = **unruly**, wild, loud, noisy, disorderly, rowdy, vociferous, unrestrained, riotous, rollicking
bold *adj* **1** = **impudent**, forward, confident, brazen, cheeky, brash • *a bold question* OPPOSITE: shy **2** = **fearless**, brave, daring, courageous, valiant, adventurous, intrepid • *a bold attempt* OPPOSITE: cowardly **3** = **bright**, strong, loud, striking, vivid, flashy • *bold colours* OPPOSITE: dull
boldness *n* = **daring**, bravery, impudence
bolster *v* = **support**, help, boost, strengthen, reinforce, augment, shore up
bolt *v* **1** = **run away**, fly, rush, escape, flee, dash, run off, take off • *I bolted toward the exit.* **2** = **lock**, bar, secure, latch,

DICTIONARY

5 eat hurriedly **6** run away suddenly
▸ **bolt upright** stiff and rigid
▸ **bolt hole** place of escape
Bolt *n* **Robert** (**Oxton**). 1924–95, British playwright. His plays include *A Man for All Seasons* (1960) and he also wrote a number of screenplays
Boltzmann *n* **Ludwig**. 1844–1906, Austrian physicist. He established the principle of the equipartition of energy and developed the kinetic theory of gases with J. C. Maxwell
bomb Ⓣ *n* **1** container fitted with explosive material ▷ *v* **2** attack with bombs **3** move very quickly
▸ **the bomb** nuclear bomb
▸ **bomber** *n* **1** aircraft that drops bombs **2** person who throws or puts a bomb in a particular place
▸ **bombard** *v* **1** attack with heavy gunfire or bombs **2** attack verbally, esp. with questions **bombardment** *n*
▸ **bombshell** *n* shocking or unwelcome surprise
bombastic Ⓣ *adj* using pompous language
bona fide Ⓣ [**bone**-a **fide**-ee] *adj* real or genuine
bonanza *n* sudden good luck or wealth
Bonaparte *n* **1** See **Napoleon I** **2** **Jérôme**, brother of Napoleon I. 1784–1860, king of Westphalia (1807–13) **3** **Joseph**, brother of Napoleon I. 1768–1844, king of Naples (1806–08) and of Spain (1808–13) **4** **Louis**, brother of Napoleon I. 1778–1846, king of Holland (1806–10) **5** **Lucien**, brother of Napoleon I. 1775–1840, prince of Canino
Bonaventura, Bonaventure *n* **Saint**, called *the Seraphic Doctor*. 1221–74, Italian Franciscan monk, mystic, theologian, and philosopher; author of a *Life of St Francis* and *Journey of the Soul to God* Feast day: July 14
bonbon *n* sweet
bond Ⓣ *n* **1** something that binds or fastens **2** feeling of friendship etc. that unites two people or a group of people **3** (*often pl*) something that restrains or imprisons **4** written or spoken agreement **5** *finance* certificate of debt issued to raise funds ▷ *v* **6** bind **bonded** *adj*
bondage Ⓣ *n* slavery
Bondar *n* **Roberta**. born 1945, Canadian neurologist and astronaut, first Canadian woman to go into space (1992)
Bondi *n* Sir **Hermann**. 1919–2005, British mathematician and cosmologist, born in Austria; joint originator (with Sir Fred Hoyle and Thomas Gold) of the steady-state theory of the universe
bone *n* **1** any of the hard parts in the body that form the skeleton ▷ *v* **2** remove the bones from (meat for cooking etc.) **boneless** *adj*
▸ **bony** *adj* **1** having many bones **2** thin or emaciated
▸ **bone-dry** *adj* completely dry
▸ **bone-idle** *adj* extremely lazy
bonfire *n* large outdoor fire
bongo *n, pl* **-gos, -goes** small drum played with the fingers
Bonhoeffer *n* **Dietrich**. 1906–45, German Lutheran theologian: executed by the Nazis
bonhomie [**bon**-om-ee] *n* happy friendliness
Boniface *n* **Saint**, original name *Wynfrith*. ?680–?755 AD, Anglo-Saxon missionary:

THESAURUS

fasten **3 = gobble**, stuff, wolf, cram, guzzle, devour, gorge, gulp, swallow whole ▸ *n* **4 = bar**, catch, lock, latch, fastener, deadbolt, sliding bar **5 = pin**, peg, rod, rivet
See also: **run**
bomb *n* **1 = explosive**, device, mine, rocket, missile, shell, grenade, firebomb, torpedo, projectile • *The bomb exploded near the city.* ▸ *v* **2 = bombard**, attack, destroy, shell, firebomb, torpedo, blow up • *London, England, was heavily bombed during World War II.*
bombard *v* **1 = bomb**, assault, pound, shell, blitz, strafe, fire upon, open fire **2 = attack**, harass, hound, assail, beset, besiege, pester
bombardment *n* **= bombing**, attack, assault, blitz, barrage, fusillade, shelling
bombastic *adj* **= grandiloquent**, inflated, grandiose, pompous, verbose, high-flown, wordy
bombshell *n* **1 = complete surprise**, shock, revelation, jolt, bolt from the blue **2** (*Slang*) **= beautiful woman**, beauty, knockout, babe (*informal*), hottie (*slang*), vixen, cutie, temptress, looker (*old-fashioned, informal*)
bona fide *adj* **= genuine**, real, true, actual, legitimate, honest, authentic, kosher (*informal*)
bond *n* **1 = tie**, link, union, connection, relationship, attachment, affinity • *a special bond between us* **2 = agreement**, contract, promise, word, pledge, obligation • *the bonds of marriage* **3 = fastening**, tie, chain, cord, shackle, fetter, ligature, manacle ▸ *v* **4 = fix**, tape, bind, paste, glue, fuse, fasten • *strips of wood bonded together*
See also: **association, relation, stick**
bondage *n* **= slavery**, imprisonment, confinement, captivity, enslavement, subjugation
bonds *See* **stock**
bonus *n* **= extra**, gift, reward, plus, dividend, premium, prize, icing on the cake
bony *adj* **= thin**, lean, skinny, gaunt, scrawny, emaciated, skin and bone

DICTIONARY

archbishop of Mainz (746–755). Feast day: June 5
bonk *v informal* **1** have sex with **2** hit
bonking *n*
bonkers *adj slang* crazy
bon mot [bon **moh**] *n, pl* **bons mots** clever and fitting remark
Bonnard *n* **Pierre**. 1867–1947, French painter and lithographer, noted for the effects of light and colour in his landscapes and sunlit interiors
bonnet *n Brit* **1** hood of automobile **2** hat which ties under the chin
bonny *adj* **-nier, -niest** *Scot* beautiful
Bonporti *n* **Francesco Antonio**. 1672–1749, Italian composer and violinist, noted esp. for his *Invenzioni* (1712), a series of short instrumental suites
bonsai *n, pl* **-sai** ornamental miniature tree or shrub
bonspiel *n* curling match
bonus Ⓣ *n* something given, paid, or received above what is due or expected
bon voyage *interj* phrase used to wish a traveller a pleasant journey
boo *interj* **1** shout of disapproval ▷ *v* **booing, booed 2** shout 'boo' to show disapproval
boob *n slang* **1** foolish mistake **2** female breast
booby *n, pl* **-bies** foolish person
▸ **booby prize** prize given for the lowest score in a competition
▸ **booby trap 1** hidden bomb primed to be set off by an unsuspecting victim **2** trap for an unsuspecting person, intended as a joke
boogie *v informal* dance quickly to pop music
book Ⓣ *n* **1** number of printed pages bound together between covers **2** written work **3** number of tickets, stamps, etc. fastened together **books 4** record of transactions of a business or society ▷ *v* **5** reserve (a place, passage, etc.) in advance **6** record the name of (a person) in a book or on a list
▸ **bookie** *n informal* short for **bookmaker**
▸ **booklet** *n* thin book with paper covers
▸ **book-keeping** *n* systematic recording of business transactions
▸ **bookmaker** *n* person whose occupation is taking bets
▸ **bookworm** *n* person devoted to reading
bookmark *v computers* store (a website) so that one can return to it easily
Boole *n* **George**. 1815–64, English mathematician. In *Mathematical Analysis of Logic* (1847) and *An Investigation of the Laws of Thought* (1854), he applied mathematical formulae to logic, creating Boolean algebra
boom[1] Ⓣ *v* **1** make a loud deep echoing sound **2** prosper vigorously and rapidly ▷ *n* **3** loud deep echoing sound **4** rapid increase **5** period of high economic growth
boom[2] *n* **1** pole to which the foot of a sail is attached **2** pole carrying an overhead microphone **3** barrier across a waterway
boomerang *n* **1** curved wooden missile which returns to the thrower ▷ *v* **2** (of a plan) recoil unexpectedly
boon Ⓣ *n* something helpful or beneficial
boondoggle *n informal* unnecessary work
Boone *n* **Daniel**. 1734–1820, American pioneer, explorer, and guide, esp. in Kentucky
boor *n* rude or insensitive person **boorish** *adj*
boost Ⓣ *n* **1** encouragement or help **2** increase ▷ *v* **3** improve **4** increase
▸ **booster** *n* small additional injection of a vaccine
boot[1] Ⓣ *n* **1** shoe that covers the whole foot and the lower part of the leg **2** *Brit* trunk of automobile **3** *informal* kick ▷ *v* **4** *informal* kick **5** start up (a computer)
▸ **bootee** *n* baby's soft shoe
boot[2] *n* **to boot** in addition
booth *n* **1** small partly enclosed cubicle **2** stall where goods are sold
Booth *n* **William**. 1829–1912, British

THESAURUS

book *n* **1 = work**, title, volume, publication, textbook, tome (*formal*) • *I'm reading a great book.* **2 = notebook**, album, pad, diary, exercise book, jotter, scribbler (*Canad*) ▸ *v* **3 = reserve**, schedule, organize, engage, charter • *The tickets for the cruise are booked.* **4 = note**, record, list, enter, register, log, mark down, put down, write down
booklet *n* **= brochure**, leaflet, pamphlet
boom *v* **1 = bang**, crash, blast, roll, explode, roar, rumble, thunder, resound, reverberate **2 = flourish**, increase, grow, develop, expand, strengthen, swell, intensify, thrive, prosper ▸ *n* **3 = bang**, crash, blast, explosion, burst, roar, rumble, thunder, clap **4 = expansion**, increase, growth, boost, jump, development, improvement, upswing, upsurge, upturn
boon *n* **= benefit**, advantage, favour, gift, blessing, windfall, godsend, manna from heaven
boorish *adj* **= loutish**, crude, vulgar, coarse, uncivilized, churlish, oafish, uncouth
boost *n* **1 = help**, praise, promotion, encouragement **2 = rise**, increase, jump, addition, expansion, improvement, increment ▸ *v* **3 = increase**, raise, develop, expand, heighten, amplify, enlarge, add to **4 = advertise**, further, promote, encourage, praise, foster, hype, plug (*informal*)
boot *v* **= kick**, drive, knock, punt, drop-kick, shove

DICTIONARY

religious leader; founder and first general of the Salvation Army (1878)
bootleg *v* **-legging, -legged 1** make, carry, or sell (illicit goods) ▷ *adj* **2** produced, distributed, or sold illicitly **bootlegger** *n*
booty Ⓣ *n, pl* **-ties** valuable articles obtained as plunder
booze Ⓣ *v, n informal* (consume) alcoholic drink **boozy** *adj*
▸ **boozer** *n informal* **1** person who is fond of drinking **2** pub
▸ **booze-up** *n informal* drinking spree
bop *v* **bopping, bopped** *informal* dance to pop music
borage *n* Mediterranean plant with star-shaped blue flowers
borax *n* white mineral used in making glass
Borden *n* Sir **Robert** (**Laird**). 1854–1937, Canadian lawyer and Conservative politician; Prime Minister (1911–20)
border Ⓣ *n* **1** dividing line between regions **2** band around or along the edge of something ▷ *v* **3** provide with a border **4** be nearly the same as: *his stupidity borders on madness*
bore[1] Ⓣ *v* **1** make (a hole) with a drill etc. ▷ *n* **2** (diameter of) the hollow of a gun barrel
bore[2] Ⓣ *v* **1** make weary by being dull or repetitious ▷ *n* **2** dull or repetitious person or thing **boredom** *n*
bore[3] *n* tidal wave in a narrow estuary
bore[4] *v* past tense of **bear**[1]
boreal *adj* northern
Borg *n* **Björn**. born 1956, Swedish tennis player: Wimbledon champion 1976–80
Borges *n* **Jorge Luis**. 1899–1986, Argentinian poet, short-story writer, and literary scholar. The short stories collected in *Ficciones* (1944) he described as "games with infinity"
Borgia *n* **1 Cesare**, son of Rodrigo Borgia (Pope Alexander VI). 1475–1507, Italian cardinal, politician, and military leader; model for Machiavelli's *The Prince* **2** his sister, **Lucrezia**, daughter of Rodrigo Borgia. 1480–1519, Italian noblewoman. After her third marriage (1501), to the Duke of Ferrara, she became a patron of the arts and science **3 Rodrigo**. See **Alexander VI**
Borglum *n* (**John**) **Gutzon**. 1867–1941, US sculptor, noted for his monumental busts of US presidents carved in the mountainside of Mount Rushmore
Bormann *n* **Martin**. 1900–45, German Nazi politician; Hitler's adviser and private secretary (1942–45): committed suicide
born *v* **1** a past participle of **bear**[1] ▷ *adj* **2** possessing certain qualities from birth: *a born musician*
borne *v* a past participle of **bear**[1]
Borodin *n* **Aleksandr Porfirevich**. 1834–87, Russian composer, whose works include the unfinished opera *Prince Igor*, symphonies, songs, and chamber music
boron *n* chemical element used in hardening steel
borough *n* town or district with its own council
Borromini *n* **Francesco**, original name *Francesco Castelli*. 1599–1667, Italian baroque architect, working in Rome: his buildings include the churches of San Carlo (1641) and Sant' Ivo (1660)
borrow Ⓣ *v* **1** obtain (something) temporarily **2** adopt (ideas etc.) from another source **borrower** *n*
borsch, borscht *n* Russian soup based on beetroot
borstal *n* prison for young criminals
borzoi *n* tall dog with a long silky coat
Bosch *n* **1 Carl**. 1874–1940, German chemist, who adapted the Haber process to produce ammonia for industrial use. He shared the Nobel prize for chemistry 1931 **2 Hieronymus**, original name probably *Jerome van Aken* (or *Aeken*). ?1450–1516, Dutch painter, noted for his macabre allegorical representations of

THESAURUS

booty *n* = **plunder**, haul, loot, prey, swag (*slang*), gains, spoils, takings, winnings
booze *See* **alcohol, drink**
border *n* **1** = **frontier**, line, boundary, borderline • *the border between two countries* **2** = **edge**, margin, rim, bounds, limits • *plain tiles with a bright border* ▸ *v* **3** = **edge**, trim, rim, fringe • *Tall trees bordered the fields*.
See also: **coast**
borderline *See* **border**
bore[1] *v* = **drill**, mine, sink, tunnel, penetrate, pierce, burrow, gouge out, perforate
bore[2] *v* **1** = **tire**, fatigue, weary, be tedious, jade, pall on, send to sleep, wear out ▸ *n* **2** = **nuisance**, pain (*informal*), geek (*slang*), nudnik (*informal*) **3** = **pain** (*informal*), yawn (*informal*)
bored *adj* = **fed up**, tired, uninterested, wearied • *I am bored with this movie.* OPPOSITE: interested
See also: **sick of**
boredom *n* = **weariness**, apathy, dullness, flatness, monotony, tedium • *the boredom of long trips* OPPOSITE: interest
boring *adj* = **dull**, flat, stale, tedious, tiresome, monotonous, humdrum, meh (*slang*), insipid, repetitious • *a boring job* OPPOSITE: interesting
See also: **dreary**
borrow *v* **1** = **take on loan**, mooch, scrounge (*informal*), use temporarily **2** = **steal**, take, adopt, copy, obtain, plagiarize, usurp

DICTIONARY

biblical subjects in brilliant transparent colours, esp. the triptych *The Garden of Earthly Delights*

Bose *n* **1** Sir **Jagadis Chandra**. 1858–1937, Indian physicist and plant physiologist **2 Satyendra Nath**. 1894–1974, Indian physicist, who collaborated with Einstein in devising Bose-Einstein statistics

bosh *n informal* empty talk, nonsense

Bosnian *n, adj* (person) from Bosnia

bosom Ⓣ *n* **1** chest of a person, esp. the female breasts ▷ *adj* **2** very dear: *a bosom friend*

boss[1] Ⓣ *n* person in charge of or employing others ▷ *v* **boss around** *or* **about** be domineering towards **bossy** *adj*

boss[2] Ⓣ *n* raised knob or stud

Boswell *n* **James**. 1740–95, Scottish author and lawyer, noted particularly for his *Life of Samuel Johnson* (1791) **Boswellian** *adj*

botany *n* study of plants **botanical** *or* **botanic** *adj* **botanist** *n*

botch Ⓣ *v* **1** spoil through clumsiness ▷ *n* **2** Also **botch-up** badly done piece of work

both *adj, pron* two considered together

Botha *n* **1 Louis**. 1862–1919, South African statesman and general; first prime minister of the Union of South Africa (1910–19) **2 P**(**ieter**) **W**(**illem**). 1916–2006, South African politician; defence minister (1965–78); prime minister (1978–84); state president (1984–89)

bother Ⓣ *v* **1** take the time or trouble **1** give annoyance or trouble to **2** pester ▷ *n* **4** trouble, fuss, or difficulty **bothersome** *adj*

Bothwell *n* **Earl of**, title of *James Hepburn*. 1535–78, Scottish nobleman; third husband of Mary Queen of Scots. He is generally considered to have instigated the murder of Darnley (1567)

Botticelli *n* **Sandro**, original name *Alessandro di Mariano Filipepi*. 1444–1510, Italian (Florentine) painter, illustrator, and engraver, noted for the graceful outlines and delicate details of his mythological and religious paintings

bottle Ⓣ *n* **1** container for holding liquids ▷ *v* **2** put in a bottle

▸ **bottleneck** *n* narrow stretch of road where traffic is held up

▸ **bottle up** *v* restrain (powerful emotion)

bottom Ⓣ *n* **1** lowest, deepest, or farthest removed part of a thing **2** buttocks ▷ *adj* **3** lowest or last **bottomless** *adj*

botulism *n* severe food poisoning

Boucher *n* **François**. 1703–70, French rococo artist, noted for his delicate ornamental paintings of pastoral scenes and mythological subjects

Boudicca *n* died 62 AD, a queen of the Iceni, who led a revolt against Roman rule in Britain; after being defeated she poisoned herself (Also **Boadicea**)

boudoir [**boo**-dwahr] *n* woman's bedroom or private sitting room

bouffant [**boof**-fong] *adj* (of a hairstyle) having extra height through backcombing

bougainvillea *n* climbing plant with red or purple flowers

bough *n* large branch of a tree

bought *v* past of **buy**

bouillon [**boo**-yon] *n* thin clear broth or stock

boulder *n* large rounded rock

boulevard *n* **1** wide street **2** grass strip between sidewalk and road

THESAURUS

bosom *n* **1** = **breast**, bust, chest ▸ *adj* **2** = **intimate**, close, confidential, boon, dear, cherished, very dear

boss[1] *n* = **head**, leader, director, chief, manager, employer, big cheese (*informal*) • *His boss insisted he get to work on time.* ▸ *v* ▷ **boss around** (*Informal*) = **domineer**, order, dominate, bully, oppress, push around (*slang*) *See also*: **superior**

boss[2] *n* = **stud**, point, tip, knob, protuberance

bosses *See* **management**

bossy *adj* = **domineering**, arrogant, authoritarian, dictatorial, imperious, overbearing • *a rather bossy little child* *See also*: **pushy**

botch *v* = **mess up**, mar, bungle • *a botched operation* ▷ **botch up** *See* **mess**

bother *v* **1** = **disturb**, concern, worry, trouble, upset, distress, harass, inconvenience, annoy, irritate, agitate, pester, get on someone's nerves (*informal*), piss off (*taboo slang*), tee off (*slang*) • *His lack of money bothers him.* ▸ *n* **2** = **trouble**, concern, worry, strain, difficulty, distress, inconvenience, fuss, hassle, nuisance, irritation, annoyance • *I hate the bother of shopping.*

bothered *See* **anxious, worried**

bottle *n* ▸ *v* **bottle up** = **suppress**, contain, check, restrict, trap, curb, keep back, shut in

bottleneck *n* = **hold-up**, block, jam *or* traffic jam, obstacle, obstruction, congestion, impediment, blockage

bottom *n* **1** = **base**, foot, floor, bed, depths • *the bottom of the stairs* OPPOSITE: top **2** = **underside**, sole, underneath, lower side **3** = **buttocks**, behind (*informal*), seat, butt, rear, informal, bum, backside, posterior, rump, tush (*slang*), buns ▸ *adj* **4** = **lowest**, ground, basement • *the bottom drawer* OPPOSITE: highest

bottomless *adj* = **unlimited**, deep, infinite, immeasurable, unfathomable, inexhaustible, boundless, fathomless

DICTIONARY

Boulez *n* **Pierre.** born 1925, French composer and conductor, whose works employ total serialism

bounce Ⓣ *v* **1** (of a ball etc.) rebound from an impact **2** *slang* (of a cheque) be returned uncashed owing to a lack of funds in the account ▷ *n* **3** act of rebounding **4** springiness **5** *informal* vitality or vigour

▶ **bouncer** *n* person employed at a disco etc. to remove unwanted people

▶ **bouncing** *adj* vigorous and robust

bound[1] Ⓣ *v* **1** past of **bind** ▷ *adj* **2** destined or certain **3** compelled or obliged

bound[2] Ⓣ *v* **1** move forwards by jumps ▷ *n* **2** jump upwards or forwards

bound[3] Ⓣ *v* **1** form a boundary of ▷ *pl n* **2** limit: *his ignorance knows no bounds*

▶ **boundary** *n* dividing line that indicates the farthest limit

bound[4] *adj* going or intending to go towards: *homeward bound*

bounty Ⓣ *n, pl* **-ties 1** generosity **2** generous gift or reward **bountiful** *or* **bounteous** *adj*

bouquet Ⓣ *n* **1** bunch of flowers **2** aroma of wine

bourbon [**bur**-bn] *n* whiskey made from corn

bourgeois Ⓣ [**boor**-zhwah] *adj, n offensive* middle-class (person)

Bourgeois *n* **Léon Victor Auguste.** 1851–1925, French statesman; first chairman of the League of Nations: Nobel peace prize 1920

Bourke-White *n* **Margaret.** 1906–71, US photographer, a pioneer of modern photojournalism: noted esp. for her coverage of World War II

bout Ⓣ *n* **1** period of activity or illness **2** boxing or wrestling match

boutique Ⓣ *n* small clothes shop

bouzouki *n* Greek stringed musical instrument

bovine Ⓣ *adj* **1** relating to cattle **2** rather slow and stupid

bow[1] Ⓣ *v* **1** lower (one's head) or bend (one's knee or body) as a sign of respect or shame **2** comply or accept ▷ *n* **3** movement made when bowing

bow[2] Ⓣ *n* front end of a ship

bow[3] *n* **1** knot with two loops and loose ends **2** long stick stretched with horsehair for playing stringed instruments **3** weapon for shooting arrows

▶ **bow-legged** *adj* bandy

Bow *n* **Clara,** known as the *It Girl*. 1905–65, US film actress, noted for her vivacity and sex appeal

bowdlerize *v* remove words regarded as indecent from (a play etc.) **bowdlerization** *n*

bowel *n* **1** intestine, esp. the large intestine **bowels 2** innermost part

Bowell *n* Sir **Mackenzie.** 1823–1917, Canadian Conservative politician, born in

THESAURUS

bounce *v* **1 = rebound,** jump, bump, bound, bob, ricochet • *I bounced a ball against the wall.* ▶ *n* **2** (*Informal*) **= life,** go (*informal*), energy, zip (*informal*), vigour, dynamism, liveliness, vivacity **3 = springiness,** give, spring, resilience, recoil, elasticity
See also: **glance, leap**

bound[1] *adj* **1 = tied,** secured, fastened, fixed, pinioned, tied up **2 = certain,** sure, doomed, destined, fated **3 = obliged,** committed, required, forced, beholden, compelled, constrained, duty-bound, pledged

bound[2] *v, n* **= leap,** jump, spring, bounce, skip, hurdle, vault, bob, gambol

bound[3] *v* **= limit,** surround, restrict, restrain, confine, enclose, encircle, demarcate, hem in

boundary *n* **= limits,** border, edge, margin, barrier, brink, fringe, frontier, borderline, extremity

boundless *adj* **= unlimited,** vast, endless, immense, infinite, untold, inexhaustible, incalculable, unconfined

bounds *pl n* **= boundary,** border, limit, edge, rim, verge, confine, extremity

bountiful *adj* (*Lit*) **1 = plentiful,** prolific, lavish, ample, abundant, exuberant, copious, bounteous, luxuriant **2 = generous,** liberal, magnanimous, open-handed, prodigal, unstinting

bounty *n* (*Lit*) **1 = generosity,** charity, kindness, largesse *or* largess, philanthropy, benevolence, liberality **2 = reward,** present, gift, bonus

bouquet *n* **1 = bunch of flowers,** spray, wreath, garland, buttonhole, corsage, nosegay, posy **2 = aroma,** scent, perfume, savour, fragrance, redolence

bourgeois *adj* **= middle-class,** traditional, conventional, materialistic, hidebound

bout *n* **1 = period,** term, turn, fit, spell, stint **2 = fight,** match, struggle, competition, contest, encounter, engagement, boxing match, set-to

boutique *See* **store**

bovine *See* **cow**

bow[1] *v* **1 = bend,** nod, bob, stoop, droop, genuflect **2 = give in,** submit, surrender, comply, concede, yield, defer, succumb, relent, acquiesce, kowtow ▶ *n* **3 = bending,** nod, bob, genuflexion, kowtow, obeisance

bow[2] *n* (*Naut*) **= prow,** head, stem, beak, fore

bowels *pl n* **1 = guts,** entrails, innards (*informal*), insides (*informal*), intestines, viscera, vitals **2 = depths,** inside, deep, core, interior, belly

DICTIONARY

England: Prime Minister (1894–96)
bower *n* shady leafy shelter
Bowie *n* **1 David**, real name *David Jones*. born 1947, British rock singer, songwriter, and movie actor. His recordings include "Space Oddity" (1969), *The Rise and Fall of Ziggy Stardust and the Spiders from Mars* (1972), *Heroes* (1977), *Let's Dance* (1983), and *Heathen* (2002) **2 James**, known as *Jim Bowie*. 1796–1836, US frontiersman. A hero of the Texas Revolution against Mexico (1835–36), he died at the Battle of the Alamo
bowl[1] ⓣ *n* **1** round container with an open top **2** hollow part of an object
bowl[2] *n* **1** large heavy ball **bowls 2** game played on smooth grass with wooden bowls ▷ *v* **3** *cricket* send (a ball) towards the batsman **bowler** *n*
▸ **bowling** *n* game in which bowls are rolled at a group of pins
bowler *n* stiff felt hat with a rounded crown
Bowles *n* **Paul**. 1910–99, US novelist, short-story writer, and composer, living in Tangiers. His novels include *The Sheltering Sky* (1949) and *The Spider's House* (1955)
box[1] ⓣ *n* **1** container with a flat base and sides **2** separate compartment in a theatre, stable, etc. **3** *informal* television ▷ *v* **4** put into a box
▸ **box office** place where theatre or cinema tickets are sold
box[2] ⓣ *v* fight (an opponent) in a boxing match
▸ **boxer** *n* **1** man who participates in the sport of boxing **2** medium-sized dog similar to a bulldog
▸ **boxing** *n* sport of fighting with the fists
▸ **boxer shorts** *or* **boxers** men's underpants shaped like shorts but with a front opening
box[3] *n* evergreen tree with shiny leaves
boy ⓣ *n* male child **boyish** *adj* **boyhood** *n*
▸ **boyfriend** *n* woman's male companion
Boyce *n* **William**. ?1710–79, English composer, noted esp. for his church music and symphonies
boycott ⓣ *v* **1** refuse to deal with or engage in ▷ *n* **2** instance of boycotting
Boycott *n* **Geoff(rey)**. born 1940, English cricketer: captained Yorkshire (1970–78); played for England (1964–74, 1977–82)
Boyd Orr *n* **John**, 1st Baron Boyd Orr of Brechin Mearns. 1880–1971, Scottish biologist; director general of the United Nations Food and Agriculture Organization: Nobel peace prize 1949
Boyle *n* **Robert**. 1627–91, Irish scientist who helped to dissociate chemistry from alchemy. He established that air has weight and studied the behaviour of gases; author of *The Sceptical Chymist* (1661)
BQ Bloc Québécois
Br *chem* bromine
bra *n* woman's undergarment for supporting the breasts
Brabham *n* Sir **John Arthur**, known as *Jack*. born 1926, Australian motor-racing driver: world champion 1959, 1960, and 1966
brace ⓣ *n* **1** object fastened to something to straighten or support it **2** appliance of metal bands and wires for correcting uneven teeth **3** pair, esp. of game birds **braces 4** *Brit* suspenders ▷ *v* **5** steady or prepare (oneself) for something unpleasant **6** strengthen or fit with a brace
▸ **bracing** *adj* refreshing and invigorating
bracelet *n* ornamental chain for the wrist
bracken *n* large fern
bracket *n* **1** pair of characters used to enclose a section of writing **2** group falling within certain defined limits **3** support fixed to a wall ▷ *v* **-eting, -eted 4** put in brackets **5** class together
brackish *adj* (of water) slightly salty
bract *n* leaf at the base of a flower
Bradbury *n* **1** Sir **Malcolm** (**Stanley**). 1932–2000, British novelist and critic. His novels include *The History Man* (1975), *Rates of Exchange* (1983), *Cuts* (1988), and *Doctor Criminale* (1992) **2 Ray**. born 1920, US science-fiction writer. His novels include *Fahrenheit 451* (1953), *Death is a Lonely Business* (1986), and *A Graveyard for Lunatics* (1990)
Bradlaugh *n* **Charles**. 1833–91, British radical and freethinker: barred from taking his seat in parliament (1880–86) for refusing to take the parliamentary oath

THESAURUS

bowl *n* = **basin**, vessel, dish
box[1] *n* = **carton**, case, container, chest, trunk • *All her possessions were packed in boxes.*
box[2] *v* = **fight**, spar, exchange blows
boxer *n* = **fighter**, pugilist, prizefighter, sparring partner
boy *n* = **lad**, fellow, schoolboy • *I knew him several years ago, when he was a boy.*
boycott *v* = **spurn**, reject, exclude, embargo, blacklist, proscribe, refrain from • *Some voters are boycotting the election.*
See also: **sanctions**
boyfriend *n* = **sweetheart**, man, date, lover, suitor, admirer, beau
boyish *adj* = **youthful**, young, adolescent, juvenile, childish, immature, puerile
brace *n* **1** = **support**, stay, bolster, prop, bracket, reinforcement, truss, buttress, strut ▸ *v* **2** = **support**, strengthen, steady, bolster, reinforce, fortify, buttress
bracing *adj* = **refreshing**, fresh, crisp, brisk, exhilarating, invigorating, stimulating

DICTIONARY

brag Ⓣ *v* **bragging, bragged** speak arrogantly and boastfully **braggart** *n*
Brahe *n* **Tycho**. 1546–1601, Danish astronomer, who designed and constructed instruments that he used to plot accurately the positions of the planets, sun, moon, and stars
Brahman, Brahmin *n* member of the highest Hindu caste
Brahms *n* **Johannes**. 1833–97, German composer, whose music, though classical in form, exhibits a strong lyrical romanticism. His works include four symphonies, four concertos, chamber music, and *A German Requiem* (1868)
braid Ⓣ *v* **1** interweave (hair, thread, etc.) ▷ *n* **2** length of hair, etc. that has been braided **3** narrow ornamental tape of woven silk etc.
Braille[1] *n* system of writing for the blind, consisting of raised dots interpreted by touch
Braille[2] *n* **Louis**. 1809–52, French inventor, musician, and teacher of the blind, who himself was blind from the age of three and who devised the Braille system
brain Ⓣ *n* **1** soft mass of nervous tissue in the head **2** intellectual ability ▷ *v* **3** hit (someone) hard on the head
▸ **brainless** *adj* stupid
▸ **brainy** *adj informal* clever
▸ **brainchild** *n* idea produced by creative thought
▸ **brainwash** *v* force (a person) to change his or her beliefs, esp. by methods based on isolation, pain, sleeplessness, etc.
▸ **brainwave** *n* sudden idea
braise *v* stew slowly in a covered pan
brake Ⓣ *n* **1** device for slowing or stopping a vehicle ▷ *v* **2** slow down or stop by using a brake
Bramante *n* **Donato**. ?1444–1514, Italian architect and artist of the High Renaissance. He modelled his designs for domed centrally planned churches on classical Roman architecture
bramble *n* prickly shrub that produces blackberries
bran *n* husks of cereal grain
branch Ⓣ *n* **1** secondary stem of a tree **2** offshoot or subsidiary part of something larger or more complex ▷ *v* **3** (of stems, roots, etc.) grow and diverge (from another part)
▸ **branch out** *v* expand one's interests
brand Ⓣ *n* **1** particular product **2** particular kind or variety **3** identifying mark burnt onto the skin of an animal ▷ *v* **4** mark with a brand **5** denounce or stigmatize
▸ **brand-new** *adj* absolutely new
brandish Ⓣ *v* wave (a weapon etc.) in a threatening way
Brando *n* **Marlon**. 1924–2004, US actor; his films include *On the Waterfront* (1954) and *The Godfather* (1972), for both of which he won Oscars, *Last Tango in Paris* (1972), *Apocalypse Now* (1979), *A Dry White Season* (1989), and *Don Juan de Marco* (1995)
brandy *n, pl* **-dies** alcoholic spirit distilled from wine
Branting *n* **Karl Hjalmar**. 1860–1925, Swedish politician; prime minister (1920; 1921–23; 1924–25). He founded Sweden's welfare state and shared the Nobel peace prize 1921
Braque *n* **Georges**. 1882–1963, French painter who developed cubism (1908–14) with Picasso

THESAURUS

brag *v* = **boast**, crow • *They never stop bragging about their achievements.*
braggart *n* = **boaster**, bigmouth (*slang*), bragger, show-off • *He's a braggart and a liar.*
bragger *See* **braggart**
bragging *See* **boastful**
braid *v* = **interweave**, weave, lace, intertwine, entwine, interlace, twine, plait
brain *n* **1** = **cerebrum**, mind, grey matter (*informal*) **2** (*Informal*) = **intellectual**, mastermind, scholar, sage, pundit, genius, intellect, prodigy, egghead (*informal*), highbrow, bluestocking (*usually derogatory*), brainbox RELATED WORD *adj*: cerebral
brainless *adj* = **stupid**, foolish, senseless, mindless, idiotic, thoughtless, inane, witless
brains *pl n* = **intelligence**, sense, understanding, intellect
brainteaser *See* **puzzle**
brainwave *n* = **idea**, thought, bright idea, stroke of genius
brainy *adj* (*Informal*) = **intelligent**, smart, bright, brilliant, clever
brake *n* **1** = **control**, check, curb, rein, restraint, constraint ▸ *v* **2** = **slow**, stop, check, halt, moderate, decelerate, slacken, reduce speed
branch *n* **1** = **bough**, shoot, arm, spray, limb, offshoot, sprig **2** = **division**, part, office, department, section, wing, chapter, subdivision, subsection
brand *n* **1** = **label**, sign, mark, stamp, symbol, marker, trademark, logo, hallmark, emblem **2** = **kind**, make, type, quality, class, cast, sort, variety, species, grade ▸ *v* **3** = **mark**, burn, label, stamp, scar, burn in **4** = **stigmatize**, mark, expose, denounce, disgrace, discredit, censure
brandish *v* = **wave**, raise, display, shake, exhibit, swing, parade, flourish, wield, flaunt

DICTIONARY

brash ⓣ *adj* self-confident and aggressive **brashness** *n*
brass *n* **1** alloy of copper and zinc **2** group of wind instruments made of brass
▸**brassy** *adj* **1** like brass, esp. in colour **2** insolent or brazen
brasserie *n* **1** restaurant specializing in food and beer **2** (in Quebec) pub
brassiere *n* bra
brat *n* unruly child
bravado ⓣ *n* showy display of self-confidence
brave ⓣ *adj* **1** having or showing courage, resolution, and daring ▹ *n* **2** North American Indian warrior ▹ *v* **3** confront with resolution or courage **bravery** *n*
bravo *interj* well done!
bravura *n* **1** display of boldness or daring **2** *music* brilliance of execution
brawl ⓣ *n* **1** rough fight ▹ *v* **2** fight noisily
brawn ⓣ *n* **1** physical strength **2** pressed meat from the head of a pig or calf **brawny** *adj*
bray *v* **1** (of a donkey) utter its loud harsh sound ▹ *n* **2** donkey's loud harsh sound
brazen ⓣ *adj* **1** shameless and bold **brazenly** *adv*
brazier [**bray**-zee-er] *n* container for burning charcoal or coal
brazil nut *n* large three-sided nut of a tropical American tree
breach ⓣ *n* **1** breaking or violation of a promise etc. **2** gap or break ▹ *v* **3** break (a promise etc.) **4** make a gap in
bread ⓣ *n* **1** food made of baked flour and water **2** *slang* money
▸**breadwinner** *n* person whose earnings support a family
breadth ⓣ *n* extent of something from side to side
break ⓣ *v* **breaking, broke, broken** **1** separate or become separated into two or more pieces **2** damage or become damaged so as to be inoperative **3** fail to observe (an agreement etc.) **4** disclose or be disclosed: *he broke the news* **5** bring or come to an end: *the good weather broke at last* **6** weaken or be weakened, as in spirit **7** cut through or penetrate **8** improve on or surpass: *break a record* **9** (of the male voice) become permanently deeper at puberty ▹ *n* **10** act or result of breaking **11** gap or interruption in continuity **12** *informal* fortunate opportunity
breakable *adj* **breakage** *n*
▸**breaker** *n* large wave
▸**break camp** *v* leave one's camping place
▸**break down** *v* **1** cease to function **2** yield to strong emotion **4** analyse

THESAURUS

brash *adj* = **bold**, rude, brazen, cocky, impertinent, impudent, insolent, pushy (*informal*)
bravado *n* = **swagger**, bluster, swashbuckling, boastfulness, boasting, bombast, vaunting
brave *adj* **1** = **courageous**, bold, heroic, daring, valiant, plucky, fearless, intrepid, valorous • *a brave attempt to stop the attack* OPPOSITE: cowardly ▸ *v* **2** = **face**, stand up to • *Fans braved the rain to hear him sing.*
bravery *n* = **courage**, pluck, valour, heroism, mettle, fortitude, boldness, fearlessness • *He deserves praise for his bravery.* OPPOSITE: cowardice
See also: **daring**
brawl *n* **1** = **fight**, dispute, clash, scuffle, skirmish, altercation, melee, fray, fracas, punch-up (*informal*), affray (*law*), rumpus ▸ *v* **2** = **fight**, scrap (*informal*), wrestle, scuffle, tussle
brawn *n* = **muscle**, power, might, beef (*informal*), strength, vigour, muscles
brawny *adj* = **muscular**, strong, powerful, hefty (*informal*), beefy (*informal*), sturdy, lusty, strapping, well-built
brazen *adj* = **bold**, defiant, audacious, shameless, brash, unabashed, barefaced, impudent, insolent, unashamed
breach *n* **1** = **infringement**, offence, violation • *a breach of confidence* **2** = **crack**, opening, hole, split, gap, rift • *the breach in the wall*
See also: **break, division**
bread *n* **1** = **food**, fare, nourishment, sustenance **2** (*Slang*) = **money**, cash, dough (*slang*)
breadth *n* **1** = **width**, spread, span, latitude, broadness, wideness **2** = **extent**, range, scale, scope, compass, expanse
break *v* **1** = **fracture**, destroy, crack, split, burst, smash, shatter, fragment, snap, disintegrate, separate • *I broke a plate.* **2** = **breach**, violate, infringe, contravene • *He broke his promise to attend.* **3** = **reveal**, tell, announce, disclose, inform, proclaim, divulge, impart, let out, make public **4** = **stop**, cut, rest, suspend, abandon, pause, interrupt, discontinue, give up **5** = **weaken**, undermine, subdue, tame, demoralize, dispirit **6** (*~ a record, etc.*) = **beat**, top, surpass, exceed, better, excel, outstrip, outdo, go beyond ▹ **break down** = **collapse**, stop, fail, malfunction, come unstuck, seize up, stop working; = **be overcome**, crack up (*informal*), go to pieces ▹ **break free** *See* **escape** ▹ **break into** *See* **raid** ▹ **break off** = **detach**, part, separate, divide, sever, splinter, pull off, snap off; = **stop**, end, finish, suspend, halt, cease, terminate, discontinue,

DICTIONARY

▸**breakdown** *n* **1** act or instance of breaking down **2** nervous breakdown **3** analysis
▸**break even** *v* make neither a profit nor a loss
▸**break-in** *n* illegal entering of a building, esp. by thieves
▸**breakneck** *adj* fast and dangerous
▸**break off** *v* **1** sever or detach **2** end (a relationship etc.)
▸**break out** *v* begin or arise suddenly
▸**breakthrough** *n* important development or discovery
▸**break trail** *v* force a path through snow or bush
▸**break-up** *n* thawing of ice in lakes and rivers in springtime
▸**break up** *v* **1** (cause to) separate **2** (of a relationship) come to an end **3** (of a school) close for the holidays
▸**breakwater** *n* wall that extends into the sea to protect a harbour or beach from the force of waves

breakfast Ⓣ *v, n* (eat) the first meal of the day

breast Ⓣ *n* **1** either of the two soft fleshy milk-secreting glands on a woman's chest **2** chest ▹*v* **3** meet at breast level: *she breasted the finishing line*
▸**breaststroke** *n* swimming stroke performed on the front

breath Ⓣ *n* **1** taking in and letting out of air during breathing **2** air taken in and let out during breathing **breathless** *adj*
▸**breathtaking** *adj* causing awe or excitement
▸**breathe** *v* **1** take in oxygen and give out carbon dioxide **2** whisper
▸**breather** *n informal* short rest

Breathalyzer *n* ® device for estimating the amount of alcohol in the breath **breathalyze** *v*

Brecht *n* **Bertolt**. 1898–1956, German dramatist, theatrical producer, and poet, who developed a new style of "epic" theatre and a new theory of theatrical alienation, notable also for his wit and compassion. His early works include *The Threepenny Opera* (1928) and *Rise and Fall of the City of Mahagonny* (1930) (both with music by Kurt Weill). His later plays are concerned with moral and political dilemmas and include *Mother Courage and her Children* (1941), *The Good Woman of Setzuan* (1943), and *The Caucasian Chalk Circle* (1955) **Brechtian** *adj, n*

bred *v* past of **breed**

breech *n* **1** buttocks **2** part of a firearm behind the barrel
▸**breech delivery** birth of baby with the feet or buttocks appearing first

breeches *pl n* trousers extending to just below the knee

breed Ⓣ *v* **breeding, bred 1** produce new or improved strains of (domestic animals or plants) **2** bear (offspring) **3** produce or be

THESAURUS

desist, pull the plug on ▹**break out = begin**, start, appear, happen, occur, emerge, arise, commence, set in, spring up ▹**break up = separate**, part, split, divorce, divide, dissolve, scatter, sever; **= stop**, end, suspend, dismantle, adjourn, terminate, disband ▹**break your promise** *See* **betray** ▸*n* **7 = interval**, rest, pause, intermission, recess, hiatus, respite, interlude • *I took a five-minute break from work.* **8 = division**, opening, hole, tear, split, crack, gap, fracture, fissure **9** (*Informal*) **= stroke of luck**, chance, opportunity, advantage, opening, fortune ▹**break-in = burglary**, robbery, breaking and entering
See also: **burst, dash, disobey, holiday, ruin**

breakable *adj* **= fragile**, delicate, frail, brittle, flimsy, crumbly, frangible, friable

breakdown *n* **= collapse**, failure, malfunction, disruption, stoppage, mishap, disintegration

breaker *See* **wave**

breakfast *See* **eat**

breakneck *See* **furious**

breakthrough *n* **= development**, find, advance, progress, discovery, invention, leap, quantum leap, step forward

breakup *See* **split**

breast *n* **= bosom**, front, bust, chest, udder, teat

breath *n* **= respiration**, pant, breathing, wheeze, inhalation, gasp, gulp, exhalation

breathe *v* **1 = inhale and exhale**, pant, wheeze, puff, gasp, gulp, draw in, respire **2 = whisper**, sigh, murmur

breather *n* (*Informal*) **= rest**, break, halt, pause, recess, respite, breathing space

breathing *See* **alive**

breathless *adj* **1 = out of breath**, spent, gasping, gulping, panting, short-winded, wheezing **2 = excited**, eager, open-mouthed, on tenterhooks, wired (*slang*), with bated breath

breathtaking *adj* **= amazing**, cool (*informal*), impressive, exciting, thrilling, sensational, magnificent, awe-inspiring, astonishing, phat (*slang*), stunning (*informal*)

breed *n* **1 = variety**, stock, kind, type, strain, species • *What breed of dog shall we get?* **2 = kind**, type, brand, sort, variety, stamp ▸*v* **3 = rear**, keep, raise, develop, nurture, cultivate • *They breed dogs at the farm.* **4 = reproduce**, produce, multiply, propagate • *Frogs can breed in most*

DICTIONARY

produced: *breed trouble* ▷ *n* **4** group of animals etc. within a species **5** kind or sort **breeder** *n*
▶**breeding** *n* result of good upbringing or training
breeze Ⓣ *n* **1** gentle wind ▷ *v* **2** move quickly or casually
▶**breezy** *adj* **1** windy **2** casual or carefree
Brel *n* **Jacques**. 1929–78, Belgian-born composer and singer, based in Paris. His songs include "Ne me quitte pas" ("If you go away")
Brentano *n* **Clemens** (**Maria**). 1778–1842, German romantic poet and compiler of fairy stories and folk songs esp. (with Achim von Arnim) the collection *Des Knaben Wunderhorn* (1805–08)
Bresson *n* **Robert**. 1901–99, French film director: his films include *Le Journal d'un curé de campagne* (1950), *Une Femme douce* (1969), and *L'Argent* (1983)
brethren *pl n old-fashioned* (used in religious contexts) brothers
Breton[1] *adj* **1** of Brittany ▷ *n* **2** person from Brittany **3** language of Brittany
Breton[2] *n* **André**. 1896–1966, French poet and art critic: founder and chief theorist of surrealism, publishing the first surrealist manifesto in 1924
Breuer *n* **Marcel Lajos**. 1902–81, US architect and furniture designer, born in Hungary. He developed bent plywood and tubular metal furniture and designed the UNESCO building in Paris (1953–58)
breve *n* long musical note
breviary *n, pl* **-aries** book of prayers to be recited daily by a Roman Catholic priest
brevity Ⓣ *n* shortness
brew Ⓣ *v* **1** make (beer, ale, etc.) by steeping, boiling, and fermentation **2** prepare (a drink) by infusing **3** be impending or forming ▷ *n* **4** beverage produced by brewing **brewer** *n*
▶**brewery** *n* **1** company that brews beer etc. **2** place where beer etc. is brewed
Briand *n* **Aristide**. 1862–1932, French socialist statesman: prime minister of France 11 times. He was responsible for the separation of Church and State (1905) and he advocated a United States of Europe. Nobel peace prize 1926
briar *n* wild rose with long thorny stems
bribe Ⓣ *n* **1** anything offered or given to someone to gain favour, influence, etc. ▷ *v* **2** give (someone) a bribe **bribery** *n*
bric-a-brac Ⓣ *n* miscellaneous small ornamental objects
Brice *n* **Fanny**, real name *Fannie Borach*. 1891–1951, US actress and singer. The movie *Funny Girl* was based on her life
brick Ⓣ *n* **1** (rectangular block of) baked clay used in building ▷ *v* **2** build, enclose, or fill with bricks
▶**bricklayer** *n* person who builds with bricks
bride *n* woman who has just been or is about to be married **bridal** *adj*
▶**bridegroom** *n* man who has just been or is about to be married
▶**bridesmaid** *n* girl who attends a bride at her wedding
bridge[1] Ⓣ *n* **1** structure for crossing a river etc. **2** platform from which a ship is steered or controlled **3** upper part of the nose **4** dental plate with artificial teeth that is secured to natural teeth **5** piece of wood supporting the strings of a violin etc. ▷ *v* **6** build a bridge over (something)
▶**bridgehead** *n* fortified position at the end

THESAURUS

ponds. **5 = produce**, cause, create, generate, arouse, bring about, give rise to, stir up
breeding *n* **1 = upbringing**, development, training, reproduction, nurture, cultivation, ancestry, raising, lineage, rearing **2 = refinement**, conduct, culture, courtesy, polish, cultivation, sophistication, urbanity
breeze *n* **1 = light wind**, air, draft, gust, waft, breath of wind, current of air, zephyr ▶ *v* **2 = move briskly**, pass, sweep, sail, hurry, glide, flit
breezy *adj* **1 = windy**, fresh, gusty, blustery, airy, blowy, squally **2 = carefree**, casual, lively, easy-going, light-hearted, jaunty, blithe, free and easy, sprightly
brevity *n* **1 = shortness**, briefness, impermanence, transience, transitoriness **2 = conciseness**, economy, crispness, curtness, pithiness, succinctness, terseness
brew *v* **1 = make** (beer), boil, soak, steep, stew, infuse (tea), ferment **2 = develop**, start, form, gather, foment, stir up ▶ *n* **3 = drink**, preparation, beverage, liquor, blend, mixture, infusion, concoction
bribe *v* **1 = buy off**, reward, corrupt, grease the palm of *or* grease the hand of (*slang*), pay off (*informal*), suborn ▶ *n* **2 = inducement**, kickback, backhander (*slang*), allurement, enticement, sweetener (*slang*), pay-off (*informal*)
bribery *n* **= buying off**, corruption, payola (*informal*), inducement, palm-greasing (*slang*)
bric-a-brac *n* **= knick-knacks**, baubles, curios, ornaments, trinkets
brick *See* **block**
bridal *adj* **= matrimonial**, marriage, wedding, marital, conjugal, connubial, nuptial
bridge *n* **1 = arch**, span, overpass, fixed link (*Canad*), ice bridge (*Canad*), viaduct ▶ *v* **2 = connect**, link, join, span

DICTIONARY

of a bridge nearest the enemy
bridge² *n* card game based on whist
Bridge *n* **Frank.** 1879–1941, English composer, esp. of chamber music. He taught Benjamin Britten
Bridget *n* **Saint. 1** Also **Bride, Brigid** 453–523 AD, Irish abbess; a patron saint of Ireland. Feast day: Feb 1 **2** Also **Birgitta** ?1303–73, Swedish nun and visionary; patron saint of Sweden. Feast day: July 23
bridle Ⓣ *n* **1** headgear for controlling a horse ▷ *v* **2** show anger or indignation **3** restrain
▶ **bridle path** path suitable for riding or leading horses
Brie [**bree**] *n* soft creamy white cheese
brief Ⓣ *adj* **1** short in duration ▷ *n* **2** condensed statement or written synopsis **3** set of instructions **briefs** **4** men's or women's underpants ▷ *v* **5** give information and instructions to (a person)
briefly *adv*
▶ **briefcase** *n* small flat case for carrying papers, books, etc.
brier *n* same as **briar**
brig *n* two-masted square-rigged ship
brigade Ⓣ *n* **1** army unit smaller than a division **2** group of people organized for a certain task
▶ **brigadier** *n* high-ranking army officer
brigand *n* bandit
brigantine *n* two-masted sailing ship
bright Ⓣ *adj* **1** emitting or reflecting much light **2** (of colours) intense **3** clever **brightly** *adv* **brightness** *n* **brighten** *v*
brilliant Ⓣ *adj* **1** shining with light **2** splendid **3** extremely clever **brilliance** *or* **brilliancy** *n*
brim Ⓣ *n* **1** projecting edge of a hat **2** upper rim of a cup etc. ▷ *v* **brimming, brimmed** **3** be full to the brim
brimstone *n obsolete* sulfur
brindled *adj* brown streaked with another colour
brine *n* salt water **briny** *adj* very salty
▶ **the briny** *informal* the sea
bring Ⓣ *v* **bringing, brought 1** carry, convey, or take to a designated place or person **2** cause to happen **3** *law* put forward (charges) officially
▶ **bring about** *v* cause to happen
▶ **bring down** *v* present (a budget) in a legislature

THESAURUS

bridle *n* **1 = curb**, control, check, rein, restraint ▶ *v* **2 = get angry**, bristle, be indignant, draw (oneself) up, get one's back up, raise one's hackles, rear up
brief *adj* **1 = short**, quick, swift, momentary, fleeting • *a brief appearance on television* OPPOSITE: long ▶ *v* **2 = inform**, prime, prepare, advise, instruct, fill in • *The press secretary briefed reporters.* ▶ *n* **3 = summary**, outline, sketch, abstract, digest, synopsis, epitome, abridgment, précis *See also*: **concise**
briefing *n* **= instructions**, conference, information, preparation, guidance, rundown, directions, priming
briefly *adv* **= quickly**, shortly, hastily, momentarily, hurriedly, concisely, in a nutshell, in brief
brigade *n* **= group**, company, team, force, troop, organization, unit, band, squad, corps, outfit
brigand *n* **= bandit**, robber, outlaw, gangster, desperado, freebooter, highwayman, marauder, plunderer
bright *adj* **1 = brilliant**, vivid, glowing, luminous, radiant, dazzling, shining • *a bright light* OPPOSITE: dull **2 = intelligent**, smart, brilliant, clever, ingenious, brainy • *my brightest student* OPPOSITE: dim **3 = cheerful**, happy, lively, merry, jolly, light-hearted • *a bright smile* **4 = sunny**, clear, fair, transparent, pleasant, lucid, translucent, cloudless, limpid, unclouded *See also*: **acute, astute, bold, colourful, gaudy, glossy, sharp**
brighten *v* **= make brighter**, shine, glow, illuminate, lighten, gleam, light up
brightness *n* **1 = shine**, light, intensity, glare, brilliance, incandescence, luminosity, radiance, vividness **2 = intelligence**, quickness, sharpness, acuity, cleverness, smartness
brilliance *n* **1 = brightness**, intensity, dazzle, sparkle, lustre, luminosity, radiance, vividness **2 = talent**, excellence, wisdom, distinction, genius, greatness, inventiveness, cleverness **3 = splendour**, glamour, grandeur, éclat, illustriousness, magnificence
brilliant *adj* **1 = bright**, sparkling, vivid, glowing, luminous, radiant, dazzling, gleaming • *a brilliant light* OPPOSITE: dull **2 = intelligent**, sharp, smart, bright, acute, clever, perceptive, sophisticated • *a brilliant student* OPPOSITE: stupid **3 = splendid**, famous, notable, celebrated, outstanding, glorious, magnificent, superb, illustrious *See also*: **colourful, glossy, keen, shining, witty**
brim *n* **1 = rim**, border, edge, margin, brink, lip, verge, skirt ▶ *v* **2 = be full**, fill, spill, overflow, fill up, hold no more, run over, well over
bring *v* **1 = take**, lead, carry, transport, convey • *Bring a friend to the party.* **2 = cause**, create, produce, effect, occasion, wreak,

DICTIONARY

▸**bring off** *v* succeed in achieving
▸**bring out** *v* **1** publish or have (a book) published **2** reveal or cause to be seen
▸**bring up** *v* **1** rear (a child) **2** mention **3** vomit (food)
brink Ⓣ *n* edge of a steep place
brisk Ⓣ *adj* lively and quick **briskly** *adv*
brisket *n* beef from the breast of a cow
bristle Ⓣ *n* **1** short stiff hair ▹ *v* **2** (cause to) stand up like bristles **3** show anger **bristly** *adj*
Brit *n informal* British person
British *adj* **1** of Great Britain or the British Commonwealth ▹ *pl n* **2** people of Great Britain
Briton *n* native or inhabitant of Britain
Britten *n* (**Edward**) **Benjamin**, Baron Britten. 1913–76, English composer, pianist, and conductor. His works include the operas *Peter Grimes* (1945) and *Billy Budd* (1951), the choral works *Hymn to St Cecilia* (1942) and *A War Requiem* (1962), and numerous orchestral pieces
brittle Ⓣ *adj* hard but easily broken **brittleness** *n*
broach Ⓣ *v* **1** introduce (a topic) for discussion **2** open (a bottle or barrel)
broad Ⓣ *adj* **1** having great breadth or width **2** not detailed **3** extensive: *broad support* **4** vulgar or coarse **5** strongly marked: *a broad Yorkshire accent* **broadly** *adv* **broaden** *v*
▸**broadband** *n* telecommunication transmission technique using a wide range of frequencies
▸**broadleaf** *n* evergreen tree with large glossy leaves
▸**broad-minded** *adj* tolerant
▸**broadside** *n* **1** strong verbal or written attack **2** *naval* firing of all the guns on one side of a ship at once
broadcast Ⓣ *n* **1** programme or announcement on radio or television ▹ *v* **2** transmit (a programme or announcement) on radio or television **3** make widely known **broadcaster** *n* **broadcasting** *n*
Broca *n* **Paul**. 1824–80, French surgeon and anthropologist who discovered the motor speech centre of the brain and did pioneering work in brain surgery
brocade *n* rich woven fabric with a raised design

THESAURUS

inflict, result in • *Bring the water to a boil.* ▹ **bring about** = **cause**, create, produce, generate, provoke, make happen • *Her suggestions brought about several big improvements.* ▹ **bring around** *See* **persuade, reason** ▹ **bring back to** *See* **remind** ▹ **bring down** *See* **overthrow, depress** ▹ **bring forward** *See* **produce** ▹ **bring in** *See* **earn** ▹ **bring off** = **accomplish**, perform, achieve, execute, succeed, carry off, pull off ▹ **bring out** *See* **publish** ▹ **bring to an end** *See* **end** ▹ **bring to a standstill** *See* **cripple** ▹ **bring to bear** *See* **employ** ▹ **bring to light** = **reveal**, show, discover, unveil, expose, disclose, uncover, unearth, show up, lay bare ▹ **bring up** = **rear**, support, raise, develop, form, train, teach, breed, educate, nurture; = **mention**, move, raise, propose, introduce, broach, allude to, put forward
brink *n* = **edge**, border, limit, margin, rim, lip, boundary, verge, skirt, threshold, fringe, frontier, brim
briny *See* **salty**
brisk *adj* **1** = **lively**, quick, active, busy, energetic, vigorous, spry, bustling, sprightly **2** = **invigorating**, fresh, sharp, keen, crisp, biting, stimulating, bracing, refreshing, exhilarating, nippy • *The breeze was cool, brisk and invigorating.*
briskly *adv* = **quickly**, rapidly, actively, promptly, readily, efficiently, smartly, apace, energetically
bristle *n* **1** = **hair**, spine, barb, thorn, stubble, whisker, prickle ▸ *v* **2** = **stand up**, rise, stand on end **3** = **be angry**, rage, seethe, bridle, flare up, see red
bristling *See* **thick**
bristly *adj* = **hairy**, rough, prickly, stubbly
brittle *adj* = **fragile**, delicate, crisp, frail, crumbly, breakable, crumbling, frangible, friable
broach *v* **1** = **bring up**, suggest, propose, introduce, mention, open up, raise the subject, speak of, talk of, touch on **2** = **open**, start, crack, tap, puncture, pierce, uncork, draw off
broad *adj* **1** = **wide**, large, extensive, vast, thick, ample, spacious, expansive • *His shoulders were broad and his waist narrow.* OPPOSITE: narrow **2** = **comprehensive**, general, wide, extensive, universal, wide-ranging, sweeping • *A broad range of issues was discussed.* **3** = **general**, rough, vague, approximate, non-specific, sweeping • *a broad outline of Canadian politics*
See also: **widespread**
broadcast *n* **1** = **transmission**, show, program, telecast, podcast, webcast ▸ *v* **2** = **transmit**, show, air, radio, cable, relay, beam, televise, put on the air **3** = **make public**, report, announce, publish, spread, advertise, circulate, proclaim
broaden *v* = **expand**, increase, develop, extend, spread, stretch, supplement,

DICTIONARY

broccoli *n* type of cabbage with greenish flower heads
brochure Ⓣ *n* booklet that contains information about a product or service
Brock *n* Sir **Isaac**. 1769–1812, British military commander and administrator in Canada, killed during the War of 1812
Brockhouse *n* **Bertram** (**Neville**). 1918–2003, Canadian physicist. Winner of the 1994 Nobel Prize for physics for his work on neutron-scattering techniques
broderie anglaise *n* open embroidery on white cotton etc.
Brodsky *n* **Joseph**, original name *Iosif Aleksandrovich Brodsky*. 1940–96, US poet, born in the Soviet Union. His collections include *The End of a Beautiful Era* (1977). Nobel prize for literature 1987
brogue[1] *n* sturdy walking shoe
brogue[2] *n* strong accent, esp. Irish
broil *v* grill
broke Ⓣ *v* **1** past tense of **break** ▷ *adj* **2** *informal* having no money
broken Ⓣ *v* **1** past participle of **break** ▷ *adj* **2** fractured or smashed **3** (of the speech of a foreigner) imperfectly spoken: *broken English*
▶ **brokenhearted** *adj* overwhelmed by grief
broker Ⓣ *n* agent who buys or sells shares, securities, etc.
brolly *n, pl* **-lies** *informal* umbrella
bromide *n* chemical compound used in medicine and photography
bromine *n* toxic liquid element
bronchus [**bronk**-uss] *n, pl* **bronchi** [**bronk**-eye] either of the two branches of the windpipe **bronchial** *adj*
▶ **bronchitis** *n* inflammation of the bronchi
bronco *n, pl* **-cos** wild or partially tamed pony
Brontë *n* **1 Anne**, pen name *Acton Bell*. 1820–49, English novelist; author of *The Tenant of Wildfell Hall* (1847) **2** her sister, **Charlotte**, pen name *Currer Bell*. 1816–55, English novelist, author of *Jane Eyre* (1847), *Villette* (1853), and *The Professor* (1857) **3** her sister, **Emily** (**Jane**), pen name *Ellis Bell*. 1818–48, English novelist and poet; author of *Wuthering Heights* (1847)
brontosaurus *n* very large plant-eating four-footed dinosaur
bronze Ⓣ *n* **1** alloy of copper and tin **2** statue, medal, etc. made of bronze ▷ *adj* **3** made of, or coloured like, bronze ▷ *v* **4** (of the skin) make or become brown
brooch *n* ornament with a pin for attaching to clothes
brood Ⓣ *n* **1** number of birds produced at one hatching **2** all the children of a family ▷ *v* **3** think long and morbidly
▶ **broody** *adj* **1** moody and sullen **2** (of a hen) wishing to hatch eggs
brook[1] Ⓣ *n* small stream
brook[2] *v* bear or tolerate
Brook *n* **Peter** (**Paul Stephen**). born 1925, British stage and movie director, noted esp. for his experimental work in the theatre
Brooke *n* **1 Frances** (née *Moore*). 1724–89, English writer, novelist, and translator who spent part of her life in Canada. Her epistolary *The History of Emily Montague* (1769) is regarded as Canada's first novel **2 Rupert** (**Chawner**). 1887–1915, British lyric poet, noted for his idealistic war poetry, which made him a national hero
Brooks *n* **1** (**Troyal**) **Garth**. born 1962, US country singer and songwriter; his bestselling records include *Ropin' the Wind* (1991) and *Scarecrow* (2001) **2 Mel**, real name *Melvyn Kaminsky*. born 1926, US comedy writer,

THESAURUS

widen, swell, enlarge
broad-minded *adj* = **tolerant**, liberal, unbiased, open-minded, indulgent, permissive, free-thinking, unbigoted, unprejudiced
broadside *n* = **attack**, assault, criticism, censure, bombardment, diatribe, denunciation, battering
brochure *n* = **booklet**, flyer, circular, leaflet, pamphlet • *a travel brochure*
broke *adj* (*Informal*) = **penniless**, short, bust (*informal*), impoverished, bankrupt, insolvent, down and out, down on one's luck (*informal*), in the red, ruined
broken *adj* **1** = **smashed**, burst, fractured, shattered, fragmented, demolished • *a broken window* **2** = **infringed**, violated • *a broken promise* **3** = **interrupted**, incomplete, erratic, intermittent, discontinuous, fragmentary, spasmodic **4** = **not working**, defective, imperfect, kaput (*informal*), on the blink (*slang*), out of order **5** = **imperfect**, disjointed, halting, hesitating, stammering
broken-down *See* **worn out**
brokenhearted *adj* = **heartbroken**, miserable, devastated, desolate, grief-stricken, inconsolable, wretched, disconsolate, sorrowful
broker *n* = **dealer**, agent, factor, negotiator, middleman, intermediary, go-between
bronze *adj* = **reddish-brown**, copper, tan, rust, chestnut, brownish
brood *n* **1** = **offspring**, family, issue, litter, clutch, progeny ▶ *v* **2** = **think upon**, ponder, muse, agonize, dwell upon, mope, mull over, ruminate
brook *n* = **stream**, creek, rill, rivulet, watercourse

DICTIONARY

actor, and director. His movies include *The Producers* (1968), *Blazing Saddles* (1974), *High Anxiety* (1977), and *Dracula: Dead and Loving It* (1996)
broom *n* **1** long-handled sweeping brush **2** yellow-flowered shrub
▸ **broomball** *n hockey* game similar to hockey, played with a large ball that the players hit with brooms
▸ **broomstick** *n* handle of a broom
Broonzy *n* **William Lee Conley**, called *Big Bill*. 1893–1958, US blues singer and guitarist
broth *n* soup, usu. containing vegetables
brothel *n* house where men pay to have sex with prostitutes
brother Ⓣ *n* **1** boy or man with the same parents as another person **2** member of a male religious order **brotherly** *adj*
▸ **brotherhood** *n* **1** fellowship **2** association, such as a trade union
▸ **brother-in-law** *n* **1** brother of one's husband or wife **2** husband of one's sister
brought *v* past of **bring**
brouhaha *n* loud confused noise
brow *n* **1** forehead **2** eyebrow **3** top of a hill
browbeat Ⓣ *v* frighten (someone) with threats
brown Ⓣ *n* **1** colour of earth or wood ▷ *adj* **2** of the colour brown ▷ *v* **3** make or become brown **brownish** *adj*
▸ **browned-off** *adj informal* bored and depressed
Brown *n* **1** Sir **Arthur Whitten**. 1886–1948, British aviator who with J. W. Alcock made the first flight across the Atlantic (1919) **2 Ford Madox**. 1821–93, British painter, associated with the Pre-Raphaelite Brotherhood. His paintings include *The Last of England* (1865) and *Work* (1865) **3 (James) Gordon**. born 1951, British Labour politician; Chancellor of the Exchequer (1997–2007); Prime Minister (2007–10) **4 James**. 1933–2006, US soul singer and songwriter, noted for his dynamic stage performances and for his commitment to Black rights **5 John**. 1800–59, US abolitionist leader, hanged after leading an unsuccessful rebellion of slaves at Harper's Ferry, Virginia
brownie *n* **1** elf said to do household chores at night **2** small square nutty chocolate cake
Brownie Guide, Brownie *n* junior Girl Guide
Browning *n* **1 Elizabeth Barrett**. 1806–61, English poet and critic; author of the *Sonnets from the Portuguese* (1850) **2** her husband, **Robert**. 1812–89, English poet, noted for his dramatic monologues and *The Ring and the Book* (1868–69)
browse Ⓣ *v* **1** look through (a book or articles for sale) in a casual manner **2** nibble on young shoots or leaves ▷ *n* **3** instance of browsing **4** shoots and leaves used as food by wild animals
▸ **browser** *n computers* software package that enables a user to read hypertext, esp. on the internet
Brubeck *n* **Dave**. born 1920, US modern jazz pianist and composer; formed his own quartet in 1951
Bruce *n* **1 James**. 1730–94, British explorer, who discovered the source of the Blue Nile (1770) **2 Lenny**. 1925–66, US comedian, whose satirical sketches, esp. of the sexual attitudes of his contemporaries, brought him prosecutions for obscenity, but are now regarded as full of insight as well as wit **3 Robert the**. See **Robert I**
Bruch *n* **Max**. 1838–1920, German composer, noted chiefly for his three violin concertos
Bruckner *n* **Anton**. 1824–96, Austrian composer and organist in the Romantic tradition. His works include nine symphonies, four masses, and a Te Deum
Brueghel, Bruegel, Breughel *n* **1 Jan**. 1568–1625, Flemish painter, noted for his detailed still lifes and landscapes **2** his father, **Pieter**, called *the Elder*. ?1525–69, Flemish painter, noted for his landscapes, his satirical paintings of peasant life, and his allegorical biblical scenes **3** his son, **Pieter**, called *the Younger*. ?1564–1637, Flemish painter, noted for his gruesome pictures of hell

THESAURUS

brother *n* **1 = sibling**, relative, relation, kin, blood brother, kinsman **2 = monk**, cleric, friar
brotherhood *n* **1 = fellowship**, camaraderie, companionship, friendliness, kinship, brotherliness, comradeship **2 = association**, order, community, union, league, society, alliance, guild, fraternity
brotherly *adj* **= kind**, friendly, sympathetic, cordial, neighbourly, affectionate, fraternal, amicable, philanthropic, benevolent, altruistic
browbeat *v* **= bully**, threaten, intimidate, coerce, badger, dragoon, hector, ride roughshod over, tyrannize
brown *adj* **1 = brunette**, bronze, chocolate, coffee, bay, tan, chestnut, auburn, dun, hazel, sunburned, tanned, tawny, umber ▸ *v* **2 = fry**, cook, grill, sear, sauté
browse *v* **1 = skim**, survey, scan, peruse, dip into, examine cursorily, flip through, glance at, leaf through, look around, look through **2 = graze**, eat, feed, nibble, chow down (*slang*)

b

DICTIONARY

bruise Ⓣ *n* **1** discoloured area on the skin caused by an injury ▷ *v* **2** cause a bruise on
▶ **bruiser** *n* strong tough person
brunch *n informal* breakfast and lunch combined
Brunelleschi *n* **Filippo**. 1377–1446, Italian architect, whose works in Florence include the dome of the cathedral, the Pazzi chapel of Santa Croce, and the church of San Lorenzo
brunette *n* girl or woman with brown hair
Bruno *n* **Giordano**. 1548–1600, Italian philosopher, who developed a pantheistic monistic philosophy: he was burnt at the stake for heresy
brunt Ⓣ *n* main force or shock of a blow, attack, etc.
brush[1] Ⓣ *n* **1** device made of bristles, wires, etc. used for cleaning, painting, etc. **2** brief unpleasant encounter **3** fox's tail ▷ *v* **4** apply, remove, clean, etc. with a brush **5** touch lightly and briefly
▶ **brush off** *v slang* dismiss or ignore (someone)
▶ **brush up** *v* refresh one's knowledge of (a subject)
brush[2] Ⓣ *n* thick growth of shrubs
brusque Ⓣ *adj* blunt or curt in manner or speech **brusquely** *adv* **brusqueness** *n*
Brussels sprout *n* vegetable like a tiny cabbage
brute Ⓣ *n* **1** brutal person **2** animal other than man ▷ *adj* **3** wholly instinctive or physical, like that of an animal **4** without reason
▶ **brutish** *adj* of or like an animal
▶ **brutal** *adj* cruel and vicious **brutally** *adv* **brutality** *n* **brutalize** *v*
Brutus *n* **1 Lucius Junius**. late 6th century BC, Roman statesman who ousted the tyrant Tarquin (509) and helped found the Roman republic **2 Marcus Junius** ?85–42 BC, Roman statesman who, with Cassius, led the conspiracy to assassinate Caesar (44): committed suicide after being defeated by Antony and Octavian (Augustus) at Philippi (42)
BSc Bachelor of Science
BSE bovine spongiform encephalopathy
bubble Ⓣ *n* **1** ball of air in a liquid ▷ *v* **2** form bubbles **3** move or flow with a gurgling sound
▶ **bubbly** *adj* **1** excited and lively **2** full of bubbles
▶ **bubble over** *v* express an emotion freely
Bublé *n* **Michael**. born 1975, Canadian pop jazz singer and pianist. His recordings include *Call Me Irresponsible* (2007) and *Crazy Love* (2009)
bubonic plague [bew-**bonn**-ik] *n* acute infectious disease characterized by swellings
buccaneer Ⓣ *n* pirate
Buchan *n* **John**, 1st Baron Tweedsmuir. 1875–1940, Scottish statesman, historian, and writer of adventure stories, esp. *The Thirty-Nine Steps* (1915) and *Greenmantle* (1916); governor general of Canada (1935–40)
Buchanan *n* **1 George**. 1506–82, Scottish historian, who was tutor to Mary, Queen of Scots and James VI; author of *History of Scotland*

THESAURUS

bruise *v* **1 = discolour**, mark, damage, injure, pound, mar ▶ *n* **2 = discoloration**, injury, mark, blemish, contusion, black mark, swelling
bruised *See* **tender**
brunt *n* **= full force**, force, violence, pressure, impact, stress, shock, strain, burden, thrust
brush[1] *n* **1 = broom**, sweeper, besom **2 = encounter**, conflict, clash, confrontation, skirmish, tussle ▶ *v* **3 = clean**, sweep, paint, wash, buff, polish **4 = touch**, sweep, stroke, kiss, flick, glance, scrape, graze ▷ **brush off** (*Slang*) **= ignore**, reject, dismiss, snub, scorn, disregard, spurn, disdain, repudiate, blow off (*slang*) ▷ **brush up = review**, study, cram, bone up (*informal*), go over, polish up, read up, refresh one's memory, relearn
brush[2] *n* **= shrubs**, scrub, thicket, brushwood, bushes, copse, undergrowth
brusque *adj* **= curt**, short, sharp, abrupt, terse, gruff, surly, discourteous, impolite
brutal *adj* **1 = cruel**, vicious, savage, inhuman, ruthless, heartless, bloodthirsty, uncivilized, animalistic **2 = harsh**, severe, rough, rude, insensitive, callous, gruff, impolite
brutality *n* **= cruelty**, atrocity, ferocity, savagery, inhumanity, viciousness, barbarism, bloodthirstiness, ruthlessness
brute *n* **1 = savage**, devil, monster, beast, swine, barbarian, fiend, sadist **2 = animal**, creature, beast, wild animal ▶ *adj* **3 = mindless**, physical, bodily, senseless, carnal, fleshly, instinctive, unthinking
bubble *n* **1 = air ball**, drop, bead, blister, droplet, blob, globule ▶ *v* **2 = foam**, boil, sparkle, froth, percolate, seethe, effervesce, fizz **3 = gurgle**, trickle, ripple, murmur, babble, burble
bubbles *See* **foam**
bubbly *adj* **1 = lively**, happy, animated, excited, merry, bouncy, elated, wired (*slang*) **2 = frothy**, sparkling, effervescent, carbonated, fizzy, foamy
buccaneer *n* **= pirate**, corsair, freebooter, privateer, sea-rover
buckle *n* **1 = fastener**, catch, clip, clasp, hasp ▶ *v* **2 = fasten**, close, secure, hook,

DICTIONARY

(1582) **2 James**. 1791–1868, 15th president of the US (1857–61)
buck[1] *n* **1** male of certain animals, such as the deer and hare ▷ *v* **2** (of a horse etc.) jump with legs stiff and back arched
▶ **buck up** *v* make or become more cheerful
buck[2] *n slang* dollar
buck[3] *n* **pass the buck** *informal* shift blame or responsibility onto someone else
bucket *n* open-topped round container with a handle **bucketful** *n*
▶ **bucket down** *v* **-eting, -eted** rain heavily
Buckingham *n* **1 George Villiers, 1st Duke of**. 1592–1628, English courtier and statesman; favourite of James I and Charles I: his arrogance, military incompetence, and greed increased the tensions between the King and Parliament that eventually led to the Civil War **2** his son, **George Villiers, 2nd Duke of**. 1628–87, English courtier and writer; chief minister of Charles II and member of the Cabal (1667–73)
buckle Ⓣ *n* **1** metal clasp for fastening a belt or strap ▷ *v* **2** fasten or be fastened with a buckle **3** (cause to) bend out of shape through pressure or heat
▶ **buckle down** *v* apply oneself with determination
buckram *n* coarse stiffened cloth
buckshee *adj slang* free
buckteeth *pl n* projecting upper front teeth **buck-toothed** *adj*
buckwheat *n* small black grain used for making flour
bucolic [bew-**koll**-ik] *adj* rustic
bud Ⓣ *n* **1** swelling on a tree or plant that develops into a leaf or flower ▷ *v* **budding, budded 2** produce buds **3** develop or grow: *a budding actor*
Buddhism *n* eastern religion founded by Buddha **Buddhist** *n, adj*
buddleia *n* shrub with purple or yellow flowers
buddy Ⓣ *n, pl* **-dies** *informal* friend
budge Ⓣ *v* move slightly
Budge *n* **Don**(**ald**). 1915–2000, US tennis player, the first man to win the Grand Slam of singles championships (Australia, France, Wimbledon, and the US) in one year (1938)
budgerigar *n* small brightly coloured Aust. bird
budget Ⓣ *n* **1** financial plan for a period of time **2** money allocated for a specific purpose ▷ *v* **-eting, -eted 3** plan the expenditure of (money or time) ▷ *adj* **4** cheap **budgetary** *adj*
budgie *n informal* short for **budgerigar**
buff[1] Ⓣ *adj* **1** dull yellowish-brown ▷ *v* **2** rub with soft material
▶ **in the buff** *informal* naked
buff[2] Ⓣ *n informal* expert on a given subject
buffalo *n* **1** type of cattle **2** bison
▶ **buffalo jump** (formerly) place where bison were stampeded over a cliff
Buffalo Bill *n* nickname of *William Frederick Cody*. 1846–1917, US showman who toured Europe and the US with his famous *Wild West Show*
buffer Ⓣ *n* something that lessens shock or protects from damaging impact, circumstances, etc.
buffet[1] [**buff**-ay] *n* **1** refreshment bar **2** meal at which guests serve themselves
buffet[2] Ⓣ [**buff**-it] *v* **-feting, -feted** knock against or about
Buffon *n* **Georges Louis Leclerc, Comte de**. 1707–88, French encyclopedist of natural history; principal author of *Histoire naturelle* (36 vols., 1749–89), containing the *Époques de la nature* (1777), which foreshadowed later theories of evolution
buffoon Ⓣ *n* clown or fool **buffoonery** *n*
bug Ⓣ *n* **1** small insect **2** *informal* minor illness

THESAURUS

clasp **3 = distort**, collapse, twist, fold, bend, bulge, warp, crumple, contort, cave in
bud *n* **1 = shoot**, embryo, germ, sprout ▶ *v* **2 = develop**, shoot, grow, burgeon, sprout, burst forth
budding *adj* **= developing**, potential, beginning, promising, embryonic, fledgling, nascent, burgeoning, growing, incipient
buddy *n (Informal)* **= chum** *(informal)*, friend, pal *(informal)*, crony *(old-fashioned)* • *We've been buddies since we were kids.*
budge *v* **= move**, push, shift, stir, dislodge
budget *n* **1 = allowance**, cost, means, allocation, finances, funds, resources ▶ *v* **2 = plan**, cost, estimate, allocate, ration, apportion
budgetary *See* **economic**
budgeting *See* **finance**
buff[1] *adj* **1 = yellowish-brown**, tan, straw, sandy, yellowish ▶ *v* **2 = polish**, shine, brush, smooth, rub, burnish
buff[2] *n (Informal)* **= expert**, fan, addict, enthusiast, admirer, devotee, aficionado, connoisseur
buffer *n* **= safeguard**, screen, shield, cushion, bumper, intermediary, fender, bulwark, shock absorber
buffet *v* **= batter**, strike, beat, pound, knock, bump, thump, pummel, wallop *(informal)*
buffoon *n* **= clown**, comedian, comic, fool, harlequin, wag, joker, jester
bug *n* **1 = insect**, creepy-crawly *(informal)*, beastie *(informal)* • *Bugs destroyed my garden last year.* **2** *(Informal)* **= illness**, disease, infection, virus **3 = fault**, error, flaw, defect, glitch,

DICTIONARY

3 small mistake in a computer program **4** concealed microphone ▷ *v* **bugging, bugged 5** *informal* irritate (someone) **6** conceal a microphone in (a room or phone)

bugbear Ⓣ *n* thing that causes obsessive anxiety

bugger *n* **1** *taboo slang* unpleasant or difficult person or thing **2** person who practises buggery ▷ *v* **3** *slang* tire **4** practise buggery

▸**buggery** *n* anal intercourse

buggy[1] *n, pl* **-gies 1** lightweight folding pram **2** light horse-drawn carriage having two or four wheels

buggy[2] *adj informal computers* containing errors or faults

bugle *n* instrument like a small trumpet **bugler** *n*

build Ⓣ *v* **building, built 1** make, construct, or form by joining parts or materials ▷ *n* **2** shape of the body **builder** *n*

▸**building** *n* structure with walls and a roof

▸**build-up** *n* gradual increase

▸**built-up** *adj* having many buildings

bulb *n* **1** glass part of an electric lamp **2** onion-shaped root which grows into a flower or plant

▸**bulbous** *adj* round and fat

bulge Ⓣ *n* **1** swelling on a normally flat surface **2** sudden increase in number ▷ *v* **3** swell outwards **bulging** *adj*

bulimia *n* disorder characterized by compulsive overeating followed by vomiting

bulk Ⓣ *n* **1** great size or volume **2** main part **bulky** *adj*

▸**in bulk** in large quantities

bulkhead *n* partition in a ship or airplane

bull[1] *n* male of some animals, such as cattle, elephants, and whales

▸**bullock** *n* castrated bull

▸**bulldog** *n* sturdy thickset dog with a broad head and a muscular body

▸**bulldozer** *n* powerful tractor for moving earth **bulldoze** *v*

▸**bullfight** *n* public show in which a matador kills a bull

▸**bull's-eye** *n* central disc of a target

bull[2] *n* papal decree

bull[3] Ⓣ *n informal* complete nonsense

Bull *n* **1 John**. 1563–1628, English composer and organist **2** See **John Bull**

bullet Ⓣ *n* small piece of metal fired from a gun

bulletin Ⓣ *n* short official report or announcement

bullion *n* gold or silver in the form of bars

bully Ⓣ *n, pl* **-lies 1** person who hurts, persecutes, or intimidates a weaker person ▷ *v* **-lying, -lied 2** hurt, intimidate, or persecute (a weaker person)

bulrush *n* tall stiff reed

bulwark Ⓣ *n* **1** wall used as a fortification **2** person or thing acting as a defence

bum[1] *n slang* buttocks or anus

bum[2] *n informal* person who avoids work

THESAURUS

gremlin ▸*v* **4** (*Informal*) = **annoy**, disturb, bother, irritate, hassle (*informal*), vex, pester, get on one's nerves (*informal*) **5** = **tap**, spy, wiretap, eavesdrop, listen in

bugbear *n* = **pet hate**, bogey, horror, nightmare, dread, bane, bête noire

build *v* **1** = **construct**, make, form, assemble, erect, fabricate • *The house was built last year.* OPPOSITE: dismantle **2** = **develop**, increase, extend, strengthen, intensify • *I want to build a relationship with them.* ▷ **build up** *See* **reconstruct** ▸*n* **3** = **physique**, body, figure, form, shape, frame • *He is of medium build.*

See also: **base**

building *n* = **structure**, edifice • *a glass building*

See also: **house, making**

build-up *n* = **increase**, gain, growth, development, expansion, escalation, accumulation, enlargement

bulbous *adj* = **bulging**, bloated, rounded, convex, swelling, swollen

bulge *v* **1** = **stick out**, expand, swell, protrude • *He bulges out of his black T-shirt.* ▸*n* **2** = **lump**, bump, hump, protrusion, swelling • *My wallet made a bulge in my pocket.* **3** = **increase**, rise, boost, surge, intensification

bulk *n* **1** = **size**, weight, volume, substance, magnitude, dimensions, immensity, largeness **2** = **main part**, most, body, majority, mass, preponderance, better part, lion's share, nearly all

bulky *adj* = **large**, big, heavy, massive, substantial, cumbersome, weighty, unwieldy, voluminous, hulking

bull *See* **nonsense**

bulldoze *v* = **demolish**, level, flatten, raze

bullet *n* = **projectile**, shot, ball, missile, pellet, slug

bulletin *n* = **announcement**, report, statement, account, message, communication, dispatch, notification, communiqué, news flash

bully *n* **1** = **persecutor**, oppressor • *the class bully* ▸*v* **2** = **persecute**, intimidate, tease, oppress, torment, pick on • *I wasn't going to let him bully me.* **3** = **force**, pressure, intimidate • *bullied into doing his work for him*

bulwark *n* **1** = **fortification**, defence, bastion, buttress, embankment, partition, rampart **2** = **defence**, support, security, guard, safeguard, mainstay, buffer

DICTIONARY

bumble *v* speak, do, or move in a clumsy way **bumbling** *adj, n*
bumblebee *n* large hairy bee
bump Ⓣ *v* **1** knock or strike with a jolt **2** travel in jerks and jolts ▷ *n* **3** (dull thud from) an impact or collision **4** raised uneven part
▸ **bumper** *n* **1** bar on the front and back of a vehicle to protect against damage ▷ *adj* **2** unusually large or abundant
▸ **bump off** *v informal* murder
bumph, bumf *n informal* official documents or forms
bumpkin Ⓣ *n* awkward simple country person
bumptious Ⓣ *adj* offensively self-assertive
bun *n* **1** small round cake **2** hair gathered into a bun shape **buns 3** *slang* the buttocks
bunch Ⓣ *n* **1** number of things growing, fastened, or grouped together **2** group: *a bunch of boys* ▷ *v* **3** group or be grouped together in a bunch
bundle Ⓣ *n* **1** number of things gathered loosely together ▷ *v* **2** cause to go roughly or unceremoniously
▸ **bundle up** *v* make into a bundle
bung *n* **1** stopper for a cask etc. ▷ *v* **2** (foll. by *up*) *informal* close with a bung
bungalow *n* one-storey house
bungee jumping [**bun**-jee] sport of jumping off a high place secured by a rubber cord attached to the ankle
bungle Ⓣ *v* spoil through incompetence
bungler *n* **bungling** *adj, n*
bunion *n* inflamed swelling on the big toe
bunk[1] Ⓣ *n* narrow shelflike bed
▸ **bunk bed** one of a pair of beds constructed one above the other
bunk[2] Ⓣ *n* same as **bunkum**
bunk[3] *n* **do a bunk** *slang* leave a place without telling anyone
bunker *n* **1** sandy hollow on a golf course **2** underground shelter **3** large storage container for coal etc.
bunkum *n* nonsense
bunny *n, pl* **-nies** child's word for a rabbit
Bunsen *n* **Robert Wilhelm**. 1811–99, German chemist who with Kirchhoff developed spectrum analysis and discovered the elements cesium and rubidium. He invented the Bunsen burner and the ice calorimeter
Bunsen burner *n* gas burner used in laboratories
bunt *baseball* ▷ *v* **1** tap the ball with the bat without swinging it ▷ *n* **2** gentle hit made without swinging the bat
bunting *n* decorative flags
Buñuel *n* **Luis**. 1900–83, Spanish director. He collaborated with Salvador Dali on the first surrealist movies, *Un Chien andalou* (1929) and *L'Age d'or* (1930). His later films include *Viridiana* (1961), *Belle de jour* (1966), and *The Discreet Charm of the Bourgeoisie* (1972)
Bunyan *n* **John**. 1628–88, English preacher and writer, noted particularly for his allegory *The Pilgrim's Progress* (1678)
buoy Ⓣ *n* **1** floating marker anchored in the sea ▷ *v* **2** prevent from sinking **3** encourage or hearten

THESAURUS

bumbling *adj* = **clumsy**, awkward, inept, incompetent, inefficient, blundering, bungling, maladroit, muddled
bump *v* **1** = **knock**, hit, strike, collide, bang, jolt • *He bumped his head on the wall.* **2** = **jerk**, shake, bounce, jolt, rattle ▷ **bump into** *See* **meet** ▸ *n* **3** = **knock**, bang, thump, thud • *He heard a bump outside.* **4** = **lump**, bulge, hump, knob, swelling • *a bump in the road*
See also: **crash**
bumper *adj* = **exceptional**, massive, excellent, whopping (*informal*), abundant, jumbo (*informal*), bountiful
bumpkin *n* = **yokel**, rustic, peasant, redneck (*slang*), hick (*informal*), hillbilly, country bumpkin
bumptious *adj* = **cocky**, forward, arrogant, brash, overconfident, conceited, full of oneself, pushy (*informal*), self-assertive
bumpy *adj* = **rough**, jerky, uneven, choppy, bouncy, jarring, jolting, rutted
bunch *n* **1** = **group**, lot, crowd, band, gang, multitude, gaggle • *The players were a great bunch.* **2** = **bouquet**, spray, posy **3** = **cluster**, set, load, pile, batch, bundle, heap • *He took out a bunch of keys.* ▸ *v* **4** = **group**, mass, collect, pack, cluster, assemble, bundle, huddle
bundle *n* **1** = **bunch**, group, mass, collection, pile, stack, batch, heap, assortment ▸ *v* **2** (with *out, off, into, etc.*) = **push**, throw, rush, thrust, shove, hurry, hustle ▷ **bundle up** *v* = **wrap up**, swathe, swaddle
bungle *v* = **mess up**, blow (*slang*), ruin, spoil, blunder, botch, muff, foul up, make a mess of
bungling *adj* = **incompetent**, blundering, clumsy, inept, maladroit
bunk *n* **1** = **cot**, bed, berth **2** (*Informal*) = **nonsense**, garbage (*informal*), BS *or* bull shit, baloney (*informal*), hogwash, balderdash, hot air (*informal*), moonshine, poppycock (*informal*), twaddle
buoy *n* = **marker**, guide, signal, float, beacon ▸ *v* ▷ **buoy up** = **encourage**, support, raise, lift, boost, cheer, sustain, hearten, cheer up, keep afloat
buoyancy *n* **1** = **lightness**, weightlessness **2** = **cheerfulness**, bounce (*informal*), animation, good humour,

DICTIONARY

▶**buoyant** *adj* **1** able to float **2** cheerful or resilient **buoyancy** *n*
bur *n* same as **burr**[1]
burble Ⓣ *v* **1** make a bubbling sound **2** talk quickly and excitedly
burden[1] Ⓣ *n* **1** heavy load **2** something difficult to cope with ▷*v* **3** put a burden on **4** oppress **burdensome** *adj*
burden[2] *n* theme of a speech etc.
bureau Ⓣ *n, pl* **-reaus, -reaux 1** office that provides a service **2** writing desk with shelves and drawers
bureaucracy Ⓣ *n, pl* **-cies 1** administrative system based on complex rules and procedures **2** excessive adherence to complex procedures **bureaucrat** *n* **bureaucratic** *adj*
burgeon *v* develop or grow rapidly
Burgess *n* **Anthony**, real name *John Burgess Wilson*. 1917–93, English novelist and critic: his novels include *A Clockwork Orange* (1962), *Nothing Like the Sun* (1964), *Earthly Powers* (1980), and *A Dead Man in Deptford* (1993)
burgh *n* Scottish borough
burglar Ⓣ *n* person who enters a building to commit a crime, esp. theft **burglary** *n* **burglarize** *v*
burgundy *n* **1** type of French wine ▷*adj* **2** dark purplish-red
burial Ⓣ *n* burying of a dead body
Burke *n* **1 Edmund**. 1729–97, British Whig statesman, conservative political theorist, and orator, born in Ireland: defended parliamentary government and campaigned for a more liberal treatment of the American colonies; denounced the French Revolution **2 William**. 1792–1829, Irish murderer and body snatcher; associate of William Hare
burlesque Ⓣ *n* artistic work which satirizes a subject by caricature
burly Ⓣ *adj* **-lier, -liest** (of a person) broad and strong
burn[1] Ⓣ *v* **burning, burnt** *or* **burned 1** be or set on fire **2** destroy or be destroyed by fire **3** damage, injure, or mark by heat **4** feel strong emotion **5** record data on (a compact disc) ▷*n* **6** injury or mark caused by fire or exposure to heat
burn[2] *n Scot* small stream
Burne-Jones *n* Sir **Edward**. 1833–98, English Pre-Raphaelite painter and designer of stained-glass windows and tapestries
Burnett *n* **Frances Hodgson**. 1849–1924, US novelist, born in England; author of *Little Lord Fauntleroy* (1886) and *The Secret Garden* (1911)
Burney *n* **1 Charles**. 1726–1814, English composer and music historian, whose books include *A General History of Music* (1776–89) **2** his daughter, **Frances**, known as *Fanny*; married name *Madame D'Arblay*. 1752–1840, English novelist and diarist: author of *Evelina*

THESAURUS

high spirits, liveliness
buoyant *adj* **1 = floating**, light, weightless, afloat **2 = cheerful**, happy, upbeat (*informal*), light-hearted, carefree, jaunty, chirpy (*informal*)
burble *See* **babble**
burden *n* **1 = load**, weight • *My wet clothes were an added burden.* **2 = trouble**, care, worry, stress, strain, anxiety • *the burden of looking after a sick parent* ▶*v* **3 = weigh down**, tax, worry, load, bother, oppress, handicap, saddle with RELATED WORD *adj*: onerous
bureau *n* **1 = office**, service, agency, division, department, branch **2 = desk**, writing desk
bureaucracy *n* **1 = red tape**, administration, officialdom, regulations • *Is there too much bureaucracy in government?* **2 = government**, administration, authorities, civil service, corridors of power, officials, the system
bureaucrat *n* **= official**, officer, administrator, mandarin, functionary, civil servant, public servant
burglar *n* **= housebreaker**, thief, robber, cat burglar, filcher, pilferer, sneak thief
burglarize *See* **rob**
burglary *n* **= breaking and entering**, theft, robbery, break-in, larceny, housebreaking, stealing, thieving
burial *n* **= interment**, funeral, entombment, exequies, obsequies
buried *adj* **1 = interred**, entombed, laid to rest **2 = hidden**, private, concealed, sequestered, tucked away
burlesque *n* **1 = parody**, satire, caricature, mockery, send-up (*informal*), takeoff (*informal*), spoof (*informal*), travesty, piss-take (*informal*) **2 = striptease**, strip, lap dance **3 = cabaret**, vaudeville, music-hall ▶*v* **4 = satirize**, mock, caricature, ape, parody, exaggerate, ridicule, imitate, lampoon, make a monkey out of, make fun of, send up (*informal*), spoof (*informal*), travesty
burly *adj* **= brawny**, big, hefty, beefy (*informal*), bulky, sturdy, stocky, stout, hulking, thickset, well-built
burn *v* **1 = be on fire**, flame, blaze, flare, flicker, be ablaze • *a fire burning in the fireplace* **2 = scorch**, char, singe, incinerate, shrivel • *The old house burned down.* **3 = be passionate**, simmer, fume, smoulder, seethe, be angry, be aroused, be inflamed
burning *adj* **1 = intense**, eager, passionate, impassioned, ardent, vehement, fervent **2 = crucial**, important, significant, critical, essential, vital, urgent, acute,

DICTIONARY

(1778). Her *Diaries and Letters* (1768–1840) are of historical interest
burning Ⓣ *adj* **1** intense **2** urgent or crucial
burnish Ⓣ *v* make smooth and shiny by rubbing
Burns *n* **1 Robert**. 1759–96, Scottish lyric poet. His verse, written mostly in dialect, includes love songs, nature poetry, and satires. *Auld Lang Syne* and *Tam o' Shanter* are among his best known poems **2 Tommy**. 1881–1955, Canadian boxer: world heavyweight champion (1906–08)
burp *v, n informal* belch
burr[1] *n* head of a plant with prickles or hooks
burr[2] *n* **1** soft trilling sound given to the letter (r) in some English dialects **2** whirring sound
Burr *n* **Aaron**. 1756–1836, US vice-president (1800–04), who fled after killing a political rival in a duel and plotted to create an independent empire in the western US; acquitted (1807) of treason
Burroughs *n* **1 Edgar Rice**. 1875–1950, US novelist, author of the *Tarzan* stories **2 William S**(**eward**). 1914–97, US novelist, noted for his experimental works exploring themes of drug addiction, violence, and homosexuality. His novels include *Junkie* (1953), *The Naked Lunch* (1959), and *Interzone* (1989)
burrow Ⓣ *n* **1** hole dug in the ground by a rabbit etc. ▷ *v* **2** dig holes in the ground
bursar *n* treasurer of a school, college, or university
▸ **bursary** *n* scholarship
burst Ⓣ *v* **bursting, burst 1** (cause to) break open or apart noisily and suddenly **2** come or go suddenly and forcibly **3** be full to the point of breaking open ▷ *n* **4** instance of breaking open suddenly **5** sudden and violent outbreak or occurrence
▸ **burst into** *v* give vent to (an emotion) suddenly
Burton *n* **1 Richard**, real name *Richard Jenkins*. 1925–84, Welsh stage and movie actor: movies include *Becket* (1964), *Who's Afraid of Virginia Woolf?* (1966), and *Equus* (1977) **2 Tim**. born 1958, US film director whose work includes *Beetlejuice* (1988), *Batman* (1989), *Charlie and the Chocolate Factory* (2005), and *Sweeney Todd: the Demon Barber of Fleet Street* (2007)
bury Ⓣ *v* **burying, buried 1** place in a grave **2** place in the earth and cover with soil **3** conceal or hide
bus *n* **1** large motor vehicle for carrying passengers ▷ *v* **bussing, bussed 2** travel or transport by bus
busby *n, pl* **-bies** tall fur hat worn by certain soldiers
bush Ⓣ *n* **1** dense woody plant, smaller than a tree **2** wild uncultivated part of a country
▸ **bushed** *adj* **1** tired out **2** mentally disturbed from living in isolation
▸ **bushy** *adj* (of hair) thick and shaggy
▸ **bushbaby** *n* small tree-living mammal with large eyes
▸ **bush-league** *adj informal* inferior or lacking sophistication
▸ **bush pilot** pilot who flies in northern or remote areas
Bush *n* **1 George**. born 1924, US Republican politician; vice president of the US (1981–89): 41st president of the US (1989–93) **2** his son, **George W**(**alker**). born 1946, US Republican statesman: 43rd president of the US (2001–09)
bushel *n* unit of measure equal to eight gallons
business Ⓣ *n* **1** purchase and sale of goods and services **2** commercial establishment **3** trade or profession **4** proper concern or responsibility **5** affair: *it's a dreadful*

THESAURUS

pressing, compelling **3 = blazing**, fiery, glowing, flaming, flashing, gleaming, illuminated, scorching, smouldering
burnish *v* **= polish**, shine, smooth, brighten, buff, glaze, furbish, rub up
burrow *n* **1 = hole**, retreat, shelter, tunnel, den, lair ▸ *v* **2 = dig**, tunnel, delve, excavate, hollow out, scoop out
burst *v* **1 = explode**, break, split, crack, rupture, puncture • *The balloon burst.* **2 = rush**, break, erupt, barge, gush • *to burst into flames* ▸ *n* **3 = rush**, outbreak, surge, fit, spate, torrent • *a burst of energy* **4 = explosion**, break, blast, split, crack, bang, discharge, blowout, rupture ▸ *adj* **5 = ruptured**, split, rent, punctured
See also: **broken, flash**
bury *v* **1 = inter**, entomb, consign to the grave, inhume, lay to rest **2 = embed**, engulf, submerge **3 = hide**, cover, conceal, secrete, enshroud, stow away
bush *n* **= shrub**, plant, hedge, shrubbery, thicket ▷ **the bush = the wild**, forest, brush, scrub, woodland, scrubland, backwoods, woods
bushy *adj* **= thick**, rough, fuzzy, unruly, fluffy, shaggy, bristling, luxuriant
busily *adv* **= actively**, briskly, strenuously, diligently, purposefully, assiduously, energetically, industriously, speedily
business *n* **1 = trade**, industry, transaction, commerce, trading, dealings • *a career in business* **2 = establishment**, company, firm, organization, corporation, enterprise • *a family business* **3 = matter**, issue, problem, question, affair, subject • *This business has upset*

DICTIONARY

business **businesslike** *adj* **businessman** (**businesswoman**) *n*
busker *n* street entertainer
▸**busk** *v* act as a busker
bust[1] Ⓣ *n* **1** woman's bosom **2** sculpture of the head and shoulders
bust[2] Ⓣ *informal* ▹ *v* **busting, bust** *or* **busted** **1** break **2** (of the police) raid (a place) or arrest (someone) ▹ *adj* **3** broken
▸**go bust** become bankrupt
bustle[1] Ⓣ *v* **1** hurry with a show of activity or energy ▹ *n* **2** energetic and noisy activity **bustling** *adj*
bustle[2] *n hist* cushion worn by women to hold out their dress below the waist at the back
busy Ⓣ *adj* **busier, busiest 1** actively employed **2** full of activity ▹ *v* **busying, busied 3** keep (someone) busy **busily** *adv*
▸**busybody** *n* meddlesome or nosy person
but Ⓣ *conj* **1** contrary to expectation **2** in contrast **3** other than **4** without it happening ▹ *prep* **5** except ▹ *adv* **6** only
▸**but for** were it not for
butane [**bew**-tane] *n* gas used for fuel
butch *adj slang* markedly or aggressively masculine
butcher Ⓣ *n* **1** person who sells the meat of slaughtered animals **2** brutal murderer ▹ *v* **3** slaughter (animals) for meat **4** kill (people) brutally or indiscriminately **butchery** *n*
butler *n* chief male servant
butt[1] Ⓣ *n* **1** thick end of something **2** unused end of a cigar or cigarette **3** *informal* the buttocks
butt[2] Ⓣ *n* person or thing that is the target of ridicule
butt[3] Ⓣ *v* strike with the head or horns
▸**butt in** *v* interrupt a conversation
butt[4] *n* large cask
butte *n* steep, often flat-topped hill in W Canada
butter *n* **1** edible fatty solid made from cream by churning ▹ *v* **2** put butter on **buttery** *adj*
▸**butter tart** small tart with sugar and butter filling
▸**butter up** *v* flatter
buttercup *n* small yellow flower
Butterfield *n* **William**. 1814–1900, British architect of the Gothic Revival; his buildings include Keble College, Oxford (1870) and All Saints, Margaret Street, London (1849–59)
butterfingers *n informal* person who drops things by mistake
butterfly *n* **1** insect with brightly coloured wings **2** swimming stroke in which both arms move together in a forward circular action
buttermilk *n* sourish milk that remains after the butter has been separated from milk
butterscotch *n* kind of hard brittle toffee
Butterworth *n* **George**. 1885–1916, British composer, noted for his interest in folk song and his settings of Housman's poems
buttock *n* either of the two fleshy masses that form the human rump

THESAURUS

me. **4 = profession**, work, trade, job, line, career, function, employment, occupation, vocation
See also: **concern, event, scene, undertaking**
businesslike *adj* **= efficient**, professional, organized, practical, thorough, systematic, orderly, methodical, well-ordered
businessman *n* **= executive**, employer, merchant, tycoon, entrepreneur, financier, capitalist, industrialist, tradesman
bust[1] *n* **= bosom**, front, breast, chest, torso
bust[2] (*Informal*) ▸ *v* **1 = break**, burst, fracture, rupture **2 = arrest**, search, catch, raid ▹ **go bust = go bankrupt**, fail, become insolvent, be ruined
bustle *v* **1 = hurry**, rush, dash, scuttle, fuss, scurry • *Salespeople bustled about the store.* ▸ *n* **2 = activity**, flurry, excitement, hurry, fuss, commotion • *the bustle of modern life* OPPOSITE: peace
bustling *adj* **= busy**, full, active, crowded, lively, buzzing, humming, swarming, teeming
busy *adj* **1 = occupied**, active, working, employed, engaged (in), engrossed • *What is it? I'm busy.* OPPOSITE: idle **2 = hectic**, full, active, lively, restless • *Halifax is a busy port.* ▸ *v* **3 = occupy**, engage, employ, absorb, immerse • *We busied ourselves in the kitchen.*
See also: **industrious**
busybody *n* **= meddler** • *the neighbourhood busybody*
but *conj* **1 = although**, while, though, yet • *Heat the cider until it is very hot but not boiling.* ▸ *preposition* **2 = except**, save, except for, other than • *The crew gave them nothing but bread to eat.* **3 = only**, just, simply, merely, solely, singly
butcher *n* **1 = murderer**, killer, destroyer, slaughterer, slayer ▸ *v* **2 = slaughter**, cut, prepare, clean, dress, joint, carve, cut up **3 = kill**, destroy, slay, slaughter, massacre, assassinate, liquidate, exterminate, cut down, put to the sword
butt[1] *n* **1 = end**, stock, handle, shaft, shank, haft, hilt **2 = stub**, tip, cigarette (*slang*), leftover, butt end, cigarette end **3** (*Informal*) **= buttocks**, behind (*informal*), bottom, derrière (*euphemistic*), bum (*informal*), rump (*informal*), tush (*slang*), buns (*slang*)
butt[2] *n* **= target**, victim, dupe,

DICTIONARY

button *n* **1** small hard object sewn to clothing to fasten it **2** knob that operates a piece of equipment when pressed ▷ *v* **3** fasten with buttons

▶ **buttonhole** *n* **1** slit in a garment through which a button is passed **2** flower worn on a lapel ▷ *v* **3** detain (someone) in conversation

buttress Ⓣ *n* **1** structure to support a wall ▷ *v* **2** support with a buttress

buxom Ⓣ *adj* (of a woman) healthily plump and full-bosomed

Buxtehude *n* **Dietrich**. 1637–1707, Danish composer and organist, resident in Germany from 1668, who influenced Bach and Handel

buy Ⓣ *v* **buying, bought 1** acquire by paying money for **2** bribe **3** *slang* accept as true ▷ *n* **4** thing acquired through payment

▶ **buyer** *n* **1** customer **2** person employed to buy merchandise

buzz *n* **1** rapidly vibrating humming sound **2** *informal* sense of excitement ▷ *v* **3** make a humming sound **4** be filled with an air of excitement **buzzer** *n*

▶ **buzz around** *v* move around quickly and busily

▶ **buzz word** jargon word which becomes fashionably popular

buzzard *n* bird of prey of the hawk family

by Ⓣ *adv* **1** near **2** past ▷ *prep* **3** used to indicate the person responsible for a creative work: *an opera by Verdi* **4** used to indicate a means used: *I go home by bus* **5** past **6** not later than **7** during **8** near **9** placed between measurements: *a plank fourteen inches by seven*

▶ **by and by** presently

▶ **by and large** in general

Byatt *n* Dame **A(ntonia) S(usan)**. born 1936, British novelist; her books include *The Virgin in the Garden* (1978), *Possession* (1990), *A Whistling Woman* (2002), and *The Children's Book* (2009)

bye, bye-bye *interj informal* goodbye

by-election *n* election held during parliament to fill a vacant seat

bygone Ⓣ *adj* **1** past or former

bylaw, bye-law *n* rule made by a local authority

by-line *n* line under the title of a newspaper or magazine article giving the author's name

Byng *n* **Julian Hedworth George**, 1st Viscount Byng of Vimy. 1862–1935, British general in World War I; governor general of Canada (1921–26)

bypass Ⓣ *n* **1** main road built to avoid a city **2** operation to divert blood flow away from a damaged part of the heart ▷ *v* **3** go round or avoid

by-product *n* secondary or incidental product of a process

Byrd *n* **1 Richard Evelyn**. 1888–1957, US rear admiral, aviator, and polar explorer **2 William**. 1543–1623, English composer and organist, noted for his madrigals, masses, and music for virginals

Byron *n* **George Gordon**, 6th Baron. 1788–1824, British Romantic poet, noted also for his passionate and disastrous love affairs. His major works include *Childe Harold's Pilgrimage* (1812–18), and *Don Juan* (1819–24). He spent much of his life abroad and died while fighting for Greek independence **Byronic** *adj* **Byronically** *adv* **Byronism** *n*

bystander Ⓣ *n* person present but not involved

byte *n computers* group of bits processed as one unit of data

byway *n* side road

byword Ⓣ *n* person or thing regarded as a perfect example of something

THESAURUS

laughing stock, object

butt[3] *v*, *n* (with or of the head or horns) = **knock**, push, bump, poke, thrust, shove, ram, prod, bunt ▶ *v* ▷ **butt in** = **interfere**, interrupt, meddle, intrude, cut in, put one's oar in, stick one's nose in

butt[4] *n* = **cask**, barrel, firkin

buttocks *pl n* = **butt** (*informal*), behind, bottom, bum (*informal*), backside, posterior, rear (end), buns (*slang*) • *exercises for your buttocks*

buttonhole *v* = **detain**, catch, grab, bore, accost, importune, take aside, waylay

buttress *n* **1** = **support**, brace, prop, reinforcement, mainstay, strut, stanchion ▶ *v* **2** = **support**, strengthen, uphold, sustain, bolster, reinforce, back up, prop up, shore up

buxom *adj* = **plump**, healthy, ample, plump, well-rounded, voluptuous, busty, full-bosomed, bosomy, curvaceous

buy *v* = **purchase**, acquire, obtain, procure, invest in, pay for • *I'd like to buy him lunch.* OPPOSITE: sell ▷ **buy off** *See* **corrupt**

buyer *See* **customer**

by *prep* **1** = **via**, over, by way of **2** = **through**, through the agency of **3** = **near**, past, along, beside, close to, next to ▶ *adv* **4** = **near**, close, handy, at hand, in reach **5** = **past**, away, aside, to one side

bygone *adj* = **past**, former, lost, extinct, antiquated, forgotten, of old, olden

bypass *v* = **go around**, avoid, circumvent, depart from, detour around, deviate from, get around, give a wide berth to, pass around

bystander *n* = **onlooker**, witness, viewer, observer, watcher, spectator, eyewitness, passer-by, looker-on

byword *n* = **saying**, slogan, adage, motto, maxim, proverb, precept

DICTIONARY

Cc

C **1** *chem* carbon **2** Celsius **3** centigrade
c. **1** cent **2** century **3** circa **4** copyright
Ca *chem* calcium
CA Chartered Accountant
ca. circa
CAA Canadian Automobile Association
cab Ⓣ *n* **1** taxi **2** enclosed driver's compartment on a train, truck, etc.
▸ **cabbie** *n informal* taxi driver
cabal Ⓣ [kab-**bal**] *n* **1** small group of political plotters **2** secret plot
Caballé *n* **Montserrat**. born 1933, Spanish operatic soprano
cabaret [**kab**-a-ray] *n* dancing and singing show in a nightclub
cabbage *n* vegetable with a large head of green leaves
caber *n* tree trunk tossed in competition at Highland games
cabin Ⓣ *n* **1** compartment in a ship or aircraft **2** small hut
▸ **cabin cruiser** motorboat with a cabin
cabinet Ⓣ *n* **1** piece of furniture with drawers or shelves **2 Cabinet** committee of senior government ministers
▸ **cabinet-maker** *n* person who makes fine furniture
cable *n* **1** strong thick rope **2** bundle of wires that carries electricity or telegraph messages **3** telegram sent abroad ▷ *v* **4** send (a message) to (someone) by cable
▸ **cable car** vehicle pulled up a steep slope by a moving cable
▸ **cable television** television service conveyed by cable to subscribers
caboodle *n* **the whole caboodle** *informal* the whole lot
caboose *n US* crew's van on a train
Cabot *n* **1 John**, Italian name *Giovanni Caboto*. 1450–98, Italian explorer, who landed in North America in 1497, under patent from Henry VII of England, and explored the coast from Nova Scotia to Newfoundland **2** his son, **Sebastian**. ?1476–1557, Italian navigator and cartographer, who served the English and Spanish crowns: explored the La Plata region of Brazil (1526–30)
cacao [kak-**kah**-oh] *n* tropical tree with seed pods from which chocolate and cocoa are made
cache Ⓣ [**kash**] *n* **1** hiding place, esp. for supplies and provisions **2** hidden store of weapons or treasure
cachet [**kash**-shay] *n* **1** prestige, distinction **2** distinctive mark
cackle *v* **1** laugh or chatter shrilly **2** (of a hen) squawk with shrill broken notes ▷ *n* **3** cackling noise
cacophony [kak-**koff**-on-ee] *n* harsh discordant sound **cacophonous** *adj*
cactus *n, pl* **-tuses, -ti** fleshy desert plant with spines but no leaves
cad Ⓣ *n old-fashioned* dishonourable man **caddish** *adj*
cadaver [kad-**dav**-ver] *n* corpse
▸ **cadaverous** *adj* **1** deathly pale **2** gaunt
caddie, caddy *n, pl* **-dies** **1** person who carries a golfer's clubs ▷ *v* **-dying, -died** **2** act as a caddie
caddis fly *n* insect whose larva (**caddis worm**) lives underwater in a protective case of sand and stones
caddy *n, pl* **-dies** small box for tea
cadence Ⓣ [**kade**-enss] *n* **1** rise and fall in the pitch of a voice **2** close of a musical phrase
cadenza *n* complex passage for a soloist in a piece of music
cadet *n* young person training for the armed forces or police

THESAURUS

cab *n* = **taxi**, taxicab, hackney carriage, minicab
cabal *n* **1** = **clique**, set, party, league, caucus, faction, conclave, golden circle **2** = **plot**, scheme, conspiracy, intrigue, machination
cabin *n* **1** = **room**, berth, compartment, quarters **2** = **hut**, shed, cottage, lodge, shack, chalet, shanty
cabinet *n* = **cupboard**, case, locker, closet, dresser, chiffonier, commode, escritoire
Cabinet *n* = **council**, administration, ministry, assembly, counsellors
cache *n* = **store**, fund, reserve, supply, treasury, stockpile, stash (*informal*), hoard, accumulation
cad *n* (*Old-fashioned, informal*) = **scoundrel**, rat (*informal*), heel (*slang*)
caddish *adj* = **ungentlemanly**, low, despicable, lousy (*slang*), ill-bred, scuzzy (*slang*), unmannerly
cadence *See* **beat**

DICTIONARY

cadge ⓣ *v* get (something) from someone by taking advantage of his or her generosity **cadger** *n*
cadmium *n* bluish-white metallic element used in alloys
cadre [**kah**-der] *n* (member of) a group of selected trained people forming the core of a military unit, Communist Party, etc.
caecum [**seek**-um] *n, pl* **-ca** pouch at the beginning of the large intestine
Caerphilly *n* creamy white mild-flavoured cheese
Caesar *n* **1 Gaius Julius**. 100–44 BC, Roman general, statesman, and historian. He formed the first triumvirate with Pompey and Crassus (60), conquered Gaul (58–50), invaded Britain (55–54), mastered Italy (49), and defeated Pompey (46). As dictator of the Roman Empire (49–44) he destroyed the power of the corrupt Roman nobility. He also introduced the Julian calendar and planned further reforms, but fear of his sovereign power led to his assassination (44) by conspirators led by Marcus Brutus and Cassius Longinus **2** any Roman emperor **3** a title of the Roman emperors from Augustus to Hadrian
Caesarean section [sa-**zair**-ee-an] *n* surgical incision into the womb to deliver a baby
caesium *n* same as **cesium**
caesura [siz-**your**-ra] *n, pl* **-s, -rae** [-ree] pause in a line of verse
café ⓣ *n* small or inexpensive restaurant serving light refreshments
▸ **cafeteria** *n* self-service restaurant
caffeine *n* stimulant found in tea and coffee
caftan *n* same as **kaftan**
cage ⓣ *n* **1** enclosure of bars or wires, for keeping animals or birds **2** enclosed platform of a elevator, esp. in a mine
▸ **caged** *adj* kept in a cage
Cage *n* **John**. 1912–92, US composer of experimental music for a variety of conventional, modified, or invented instruments. He evolved a type of music apparently undetermined by the composer, such as in *Imaginary Landscape* (1951) for 12 radio sets. Other works include *Reunion* (1968), *Apartment Building 1776* (1976), and *Europeras 3 and 4* (1990)
cagey ⓣ *adj* **cagier, cagiest 1** not frank **2** wary **caginess** *n*
Cagney *n* **James**. 1899–1986, US movie actor, esp. in gangster roles; his films include *The Public Enemy* (1931), *Angels with Dirty Faces* (1938), *The Roaring Twenties* (1939), and *Yankee Doodle Dandy* (1942) for which he won an Oscar.
cagoule [kag-**gool**] *n* lightweight hooded waterproof jacket
cahoots *pl n* **in cahoots** *informal* conspiring together
Caine *n* Sir **Michael**, real name *Maurice Micklewhite*. born 1933, British movie actor. His films include *The Ipcress File* (1965), *Get Carter* (1971), *Educating Rita* (1983), *Hannah and Her Sisters* (1986), and *The Cider House Rules* (1999)
cairn *n* mound of stones erected as a memorial or marker
▸ **cairn terrier** small rough-haired terrier
cairngorm *n* yellow or brownish quartz gemstone
caisse populaire [**kayss** pop-oo-**layr**] *n Canad* (in Quebec and other French-speaking communities) financial institution run cooperatively, similar to a credit union
caisson [**kay**-son] *n* watertight chamber used to carry out construction work under water
cajole ⓣ *v* persuade by flattery **cajolery** *n*
cake ⓣ *n* **1** sweet food baked from a mixture of flour, eggs, etc. **2** flat compact mass ▸ *v* **3** form into a hardened mass or crust
calabash *n* type of large gourd
calamine *n* pink powder consisting chiefly of zinc oxide, used in skin lotions and ointments
calamity ⓣ *n, pl* **-ties** disaster **calamitous** *adj*
Calamity Jane *n* real name *Martha Canary*. ?1852–1903, US frontierswoman, noted for her skill at shooting and riding
calcify *v* **-fying, -fied** harden by the

THESAURUS

cadge *See* **scrounge**
café *n* = **snack bar**, restaurant, cafeteria, brasserie, coffee bar, coffee shop, lunchroom, tearoom
cage *n* = **enclosure**, pound, pen
cagey *adj* (*Informal*) = **wary**, careful, cautious, wily, shrewd, discreet, guarded, noncommittal, chary
cajole *v* = **persuade**, flatter, coax, seduce, brown-nose (*slang*), sweet-talk (*informal*), wheedle
cake *n* **1** = **block**, bar, mass, lump, cube, slab, loaf ▸ *v* **2** = **encrust**, bake, solidify, coagulate, congeal
cakewalk *n* = **walkover**, pushover (*slang*), breeze (*informal*), child's play (*informal*), picnic (*informal*), piece of cake (*informal*), laugher (*informal*), slam dunk (*informal*), cinch (*slang*), no-brainer (*slang*)
calamitous *adj* = **disastrous**, deadly, fatal, tragic, dire, catastrophic, ruinous, cataclysmic, devastating
calamity *n* = **disaster**, tragedy, ruin, catastrophe, mishap, misadventure,

DICTIONARY

depositing of calcium salts **calcification** *n*
calcium *n* silvery-white metallic element found in bones, teeth, limestone, and chalk
calculate ⓣ *v* **1** solve (a problem) mathematically **2** estimate **3** plan deliberately **calculable** *adj* **calculation** *n*
▸ **calculating** *adj* selfishly scheming
▸ **calculator** *n* small electronic device for making calculations
calculus *n, pl* **-luses 1** branch of mathematics dealing with infinitesimal changes to a variable number or quantity **2** *pathol* stone
Calder *n* **Alexander**. 1898–1976, US sculptor, who originated mobiles and stabiles (moving or static abstract sculptures, generally suspended from wire)
Calderón *n* **Felipe**. born 1962, Mexican politician; President from 2006
Caldwell *n* **Erskine**. 1903–87, US novelist whose works include *Tobacco Road* (1933)
Caledonian *adj* of Scotland
calendar *n* **1** chart showing a year divided into months, weeks, and days **2** system for determining the beginning, length, and division of years **3** schedule of events or appointments
calender *n* machine in which paper or cloth is smoothed by passing it between rollers
calends *pl n* first day of each month in the ancient Roman calendar
calendula *n* marigold
calf[1] *n, pl* **calves 1** young cow, bull, elephant, whale, or seal **2** leather made from calf skin
▸ **calve** *v* give birth to a calf
▸ **calf love** adolescent infatuation
calf[2] *n, pl* **calves** back of the leg between the ankle and knee
calibre ⓣ [**kal**-lib-ber] *n* **1** ability, personal worth **2** diameter of the bore of a gun or of a shell or bullet
▸ **calibrate** *v* **1** mark the scale or check the accuracy of (a measuring instrument) **2** measure the calibre of **calibration** *n*
calico *n, pl* **-coes, -co** plain white cotton cloth
Caligula *n* original name *Gaius Caesar*, son of Germanicus. 12–41 AD, Roman emperor (37–41), noted for his cruelty and tyranny; assassinated
caliph *n hist* Muslim ruler
call ⓣ *v* **1** name **2** shout to attract attention **3** telephone **4** ask to come **5** (often foll. by *on*) visit **6** arrange (a meeting, strike, etc.) ▹ *n* **7** shout **8** animal's or bird's cry **9** telephone communication **10** visit **11** summons or invitation **12** need, demand **caller** *n*
▸ **calling** *n* vocation or profession
▸ **callbox** *Brit* telephone booth
▸ **call for** *v* need, demand
▸ **call off** *v* cancel
▸ **call up** *v* **1** summon to serve in the armed forces **2** evoke
Callaghan *n* **1** (**Leonard**) **James**, Baron Callaghan of Cardiff. 1912–2005, British Labour statesman; prime minister (1976–79) **2 Morley** (**Edward**). 1903–90, Canadian novelist and short-story writer. His novels include *Such Is My Beloved* (1934) and *The Loved and the Lost* (1951)
Callas *n* **Maria**, real name *Maria Anna Cecilia Kalageropoulos*. 1923–77, Greek operatic soprano, born in the US
Callicrates *n* 5th century BC, Greek architect: with Ictinus, designed the Parthenon
calligraphy *n* (art of) beautiful handwriting **calligrapher** *n*
Callimachus *n* late 5th century BC, Greek sculptor, reputed to have invented the Corinthian capital

THESAURUS

misfortune, tribulation, cataclysm
calculate *v* **1 = work out**, count, determine, reckon • *how to calculate the cost of setting up a business* **2 = plan**, aim, design, intend
calculated *adj* **= deliberate**, planned, intended, aimed, designed • *Everything they said was calculated to hurt his feelings*. OPPOSITE: unplanned
calculating *adj* **= scheming**, sharp, crafty, shrewd, manipulative, sly, cunning, devious, Machiavellian
calculation *n* **1 = working out**, result, estimate, answer, forecast, judgment, reckoning, computation **2 = planning**, deliberation, precaution, discretion, foresight, contrivance, forethought
calibre *n* **1 = worth**, standard, quality, ability, capacity, talent, merit, distinction, stature **2 = diameter**, measure, gauge, bore
call *v* **1 = name**, term, label, style, dub, entitle, designate, christen, describe as • *We called our dog Bandit*. **2 = phone**, telephone • *He called me at my office*. **3 = cry**, hail, shout, yell • *Did someone call my name?* **4 = summon**, rally, gather, assemble, convene, muster ▹ **call for = require**, need, suggest, involve, demand, occasion, entail, necessitate ▹ **call off** *See* **cancel** ▹ **call on = visit**, see, drop in on, look in on, look up ▹ **call to mind** *See* **remember** ▹ **call upon** *See* **appeal** ▸ *n* **5 = cry**, hail, shout, scream, yell, whoop • *a call for help* **6 = summons**, order, demand, appeal, request, notice, plea, command, invitation **7 = need**, cause, reason, occasion, excuse, justification, grounds
calling *n* **= profession**, trade, career,

DICTIONARY

calliper *n* **1** *usu pl* metal splint for the leg **2** instrument for measuring diameters
callisthenics *pl n* light keep-fit exercises **callisthenic** *adj*
callous Ⓣ *adj* showing no concern for other people's feelings **callously** *adv* **callousness** *n*
▸ **calloused** *adj* covered in calluses
callow Ⓣ *adj* immature and inexperienced
callus *n, pl* **-luses** area of thick hardened skin
calm Ⓣ *adj* **1** not showing or feeling agitation or excitement **2** not ruffled by the wind **3** windless ▹ *n* **4** peaceful state ▹ *v* **5** make or become calm **calmly** *adv* **calmness** *n*
Calor Gas *n* ® butane gas liquefied under pressure in containers for domestic use
calorie *n* **1** unit of heat **2** unit of measurement for the energy value of food
▸ **calorific** *adj* of calories or heat
calumny *n, pl* **-nies** slander
▸ **calumniate** *v* slander
Calvert *n* **1** Sir **George**, 1st Baron Baltimore. ?1580–1632, English statesman; founder of a settlement in Newfoundland and of the colony of Maryland **2** his son, **Leonard**. 1606–47, English statesman; first colonial governor of Maryland (1634–47)
Calvin *n* **1** **John**, original name *Jean Cauvin, Caulvin*, or *Chauvin*. 1509–64, French theologian: a leader of the Protestant Reformation in France and Switzerland, establishing the first presbyterian government in Geneva. His theological system is described in his *Institutes of the Christian Religion* (1536) **2** **Melvin**. 1911–97, US chemist, noted particularly for his research on photosynthesis: Nobel prize for chemistry 1961
Calvinism *n* theological system of John Calvin, stressing predestination and salvation solely by God's grace **Calvinist** *n, adj* **Calvinistic** *adj*
calypso *n, pl* **-sos** West Indian song with improvised topical lyrics
calyx *n, pl* **calyxes, calyces** outer leaves that protect the bud of a flower
cam *n* device which converts rotary motion to to-and-fro motion
▸ **camshaft** *n* part of an engine consisting of a rod to which cams are fixed
camaraderie Ⓣ *n* comradeship
camber *n* slight upward curve to the centre of a surface
cambric *n* fine white linen fabric
camcorder *n* combined portable video camera and recorder
came *v* past tense of **come**
camel *n* **1** humped mammal of Asia and Africa ▹ *adj* **2** fawn-coloured
camellia [kam-**meal**-ya] *n* evergreen ornamental shrub with roselike white, pink, or red flowers
Camembert [**kam**-mem-bare] *n* soft creamy French cheese
cameo *n, pl* **cameos** **1** brooch or ring with a profile head carved in relief **2** small, brief part in a film or television play performed by a well-known actor or actress
camera *n* apparatus used for taking photographs
▸ **in camera** in private
▸ **cameraman** *n* photographer, esp. for television or cinema
Cameron *n* **1** **David** (**William Donald**). born 1966, British Conservative politician; prime minister from 2010, heading a coalition government with the Liberal Democrats **2** **James**. born 1954, US director, screenwriter, and producer, born in Canada. His movies include *The Terminator* (1984), *Titanic* (1997), and *Avatar* (2009)
camisole *n* woman's bodice-like garment
camomile *n* aromatic plant, used to make herbal tea
camouflage Ⓣ [**kam**-moo-flahzh] *n* **1** use of natural surroundings or artificial aids to conceal or disguise something ▹ *v* **2** conceal or disguise by camouflage

C

THESAURUS

mission, vocation, life's work
callous *adj* = **heartless**, cold, indifferent, insensitive • *his callous disregard for other people's safety* OPPOSITE: caring
See also: **cruel, merciless**
callousness *See* **cruelty**
callow *adj* = **inexperienced**, green, raw, naive, immature, unsophisticated, guileless
calm *adj* **1** = **cool**, collected, composed, impassive, relaxed • *Try to keep calm.* OPPOSITE: worried **2** = **still**, mild, balmy, tranquil • *Tuesday was a clear and calm day.* OPPOSITE: rough ▸ *n* **3** = **peacefulness**, peace, quiet, serenity, calmness, stillness • *He liked the calm of the evening.* ▸ *v* **4** = **soothe**, relax • *We were trying to calm the puppy.*
See also: **ease, pacify, patient, peaceful, silence**
calmness *n* **1** = **coolness**, cool (*slang*), poise, composure, equanimity, impassivity, sang-froid, self-possession **2** = **peacefulness**, quiet, calm, hush, serenity, repose, stillness, tranquillity, restfulness
camaraderie *See* **fellowship**
camouflage *n* **1** = **disguise**, cover, screen, mask, blind, cloak, masquerade, subterfuge, concealment ▸ *v* **2** = **disguise**, cover, screen, hide, mask, cloak, veil,

DICTIONARY

camp[1] Ⓣ *n* **1** (place for) temporary lodgings consisting of tents, huts, or cabins **2** group supporting a particular doctrine ▷ *v* **3** stay in a camp **camper** *n*
camp[2] Ⓣ *adj informal* **1** homosexual **2** consciously artificial or affected
▶ **camp it up** *informal* behave in a camp way
Camp *n* **Walter** (**Chauncey**). 1859–1925, US sportsman and administrator; he introduced new rules to football, which distinguished it from rugby
campaign Ⓣ *n* **1** series of coordinated activities designed to achieve a goal ▷ *v* **2** conduct or take part in a campaign
campanology *n* art of ringing bells
campanologist *n*
campanula *n* plant with blue or white bell-shaped flowers
Campbell *n* **1 Avril Phaedra**, known as *Kim*. born 1947, Canadian Progressive Conservative politician; Prime Minister (1993) **2 Gordon**. born 1948, Canadian politician; Premier of British Columbia (2001–05; 2005–09; 2009–)
Campbell-Bannerman *n* Sir **Henry**. 1836–1908, British statesman and leader of the Liberal Party (1899–1908); prime minister (1905–08), who granted self-government to the Transvaal and the Orange River Colony
camphor *n* aromatic crystalline substance used medicinally and in mothballs
camphorated *adj*
campion *n* white or pink wild flower
Campion *n* **Thomas**. 1567–1620, English poet and musician, noted particularly for his songs for the lute
campus *n, pl* **-puses** grounds of a college or university
Camus *n* **Albert**. 1913–60, French novelist, dramatist, and essayist, noted for his pessimistic portrayal of man's condition of isolation in an absurd world: author of the novels *L'Étranger* (1942) and *La Peste* (1947), the plays *Le Malentendu* (1945) and *Caligula* (1946), and the essays *Le Mythe de Sisyphe* (1942) and *L'Homme révolté* (1951): Nobel prize for literature 1957
can[1] *v, past* **could 1** be able **2** be allowed
can[2] *n* **1** metal container for liquid or foods ▷ *v* **canning, canned 2** put (something) in a can
▶ **canned** *adj* **1** preserved in a can **2** (of music etc.) prerecorded
▶ **cannery** *n* factory where food is canned
Canada Day July 1st, anniversary of establishment of Confederation in 1867
Canada goose large greyish-brown N American goose
Canada jay N American bird with grey, white-tipped feathers
Canadarm *n* extension of spacecraft to fetch and deploy objects
Canadian *n, adj* (native) of Canada
▶ **Canadianize** *v* make or become Canadian
canal Ⓣ *n* **1** artificial watercourse **2** duct in the body
Canaletto *n* original name *Giovanni Antonio Canale*. 1697–1768, Italian painter and etcher, noted particularly for his highly detailed paintings of cities, esp. Venice, which are marked by strong contrasts of light and shade
canapé [**kan**-nap-pay] *n* small piece of bread or toast spread with a savoury topping
canard *n* false report
canary *n, pl* **-ries** small yellow songbird often kept as a pet
canasta *n* card game like rummy, played with two packs
cancan *n* lively high-kicking dance performed by a female group
cancel Ⓣ *v* **-celling, -celled 1** postpone indefinitely **2** cross out **3** mark (a cheque or stamp) to prevent reuse **cancellation** *n*
▶ **cancel out** *v* counterbalance or neutralize
cancer Ⓣ *n* **1** serious disease caused by a malignant growth or tumour **2** malignant growth or tumour **cancerous** *adj*
Cancer *n* **tropic of Cancer** see **tropic**
candela [kan-**dee**-la] *n* unit of luminous intensity
candelabrum *n, pl* **-bra** ornamental candleholder for several candles
candid Ⓣ *adj* frank and outspoken **candidly** *adv*

THESAURUS

conceal, obscure, obfuscate
camp[1] *n* = **camp site**, encampment, bivouac, camping ground, tents
camp[2] *adj* (*Informal*) = **effeminate**, artificial, affected, mannered, ostentatious, posturing
campaign *n* = **operation**, push, movement, crusade, blitz • *a campaign to educate people*
See also: **agitate**
canal *n* = **waterway**, channel, passage, duct, conduit, watercourse
cancel *v* **1** = **call off**, abandon • *We're going to have to cancel our picnic.* **2** = **annul**, quash, revoke, repeal • *They were forced to cancel their contract.* ▷ **cancel out** = **make up for**, offset, neutralize, nullify, counterbalance, balance out, compensate for
See also: **lift**
cancellation *n* = **abandonment**, elimination, repeal, abolition, annulment, revocation, deletion
cancer *n* = **growth**, corruption, tumour, sickness, malignancy, pestilence
candid *adj* = **honest**, open, blunt,

DICTIONARY

candidate Ⓣ *n* **1** person seeking a job or position **2** person taking an examination **candidacy** *or* **candidature** *n*
candle *n* stick of wax enclosing a wick, which is burned to produce light
▸ **candlestick** *n* holder for a candle
▸ **candlewick** *n* cotton fabric with a tufted surface
candour, candor Ⓣ *n* frankness
CANDU *n* ® type of nuclear reactor pioneered in Canada
candy Ⓣ *n, pl* **-dies** shaped piece of food consisting mainly of sugar
▸ **candied** *adj* coated with sugar
▸ **candyfloss** *n* light fluffy mass of spun sugar on a stick
▸ **candy-striped** *adj* having coloured stripes on a white background
Candy *n* **John**. 1950–94, Canadian comedian and film actor. His films include *Splash* (1984), *Planes, Trains, and Automobiles* (1987), and *Cool Runnings* (1993)
cane Ⓣ *n* **1** stem of the bamboo or similar plant **2** slender walking stick **3** flexible rod used to beat someone ▷ *v* **4** beat with a cane
canine Ⓣ [**kay**-nine] *adj* of or like a dog
▸ **canine tooth** sharp pointed tooth between the incisors and the molars
canister *n* metal container
canker Ⓣ *n* **1** ulceration or ulcerous disease **2** something that spreads and corrupts ▷ *v* **3** infect or become infected with canker **cankerous** *adj*
cannabis *n* drug obtained from the hemp plant
cannelloni *pl n* tubular pieces of pasta filled with meat etc.
cannibal *n* **1** person who eats human flesh **2** animal that eats others of its own kind **cannibalism** *n*
▸ **cannibalize** *v* use parts from (one machine) to repair another
Canning *n* **George**. 1770–1827, British Tory statesman; foreign secretary (1822–27) and prime minister (1827)
cannon[1] Ⓣ *n* large gun on wheels
▸ **cannonade** *n* continuous heavy gunfire
▸ **cannonball** *n* heavy metal ball fired from a cannon
cannon[2] *n* **1** billiard stroke in which the cue ball hits two balls successively ▷ *v* **2** make this stroke **3** rebound, collide
cannot can not
canny Ⓣ *adj* **-nier, -niest** shrewd and cautious **cannily** *adv*
canoe *n* **1** light narrow boat propelled by a paddle or paddles **canoeing** *n* **canoeist** *n*
canola *n* rapeseed oil
canon[1] Ⓣ *n* **1** Church law or decree **2** general rule or principle **3** set of writings accepted as genuine **canonical** *adj*
▸ **canonize** *v* declare (a person) officially to be a saint **canonization** *n*
canon[2] *n* priest serving in a cathedral
canoodle *v slang* kiss and cuddle
canopy Ⓣ *n, pl* **-pies 1** covering above a throne, bed, etc. **2** any large or wide covering **canopied** *adj*
Canova *n* **Antonio**. 1757–1822, Italian neoclassical sculptor
cant[1] Ⓣ *n* **1** insincere talk **2** specialized vocabulary of a particular group
cant[2] Ⓣ *v, n* tilt or slope
can't can not
cantaloupe, cantaloup *n* kind of melon with sweet orange flesh
cantankerous Ⓣ *adj* bad-tempered, quarrelsome
cantata [kan-**tah**-ta] *n* musical work consisting of arias, duets, and choruses
canteen *n* **1** restaurant attached to a workplace **2** case of cutlery
Canteloube *n* (**Marie**) **Joseph**. 1879–1957, French composer, best known for his

THESAURUS

straightforward, frank, truthful • *a candid interview*
See also: **direct, natural, straight**
candidate *n* = **contender**, competitor, applicant • *a candidate for the presidency of the debating team*
candour *n* = **honesty**, openness, truthfulness, directness, forthrightness, frankness, outspokenness, straightforwardness
candy *n* = **sweets**, confectionery • *I ate too many candies and I feel sick.*
cane *See* **stick**
canine *See* **dog**
canker *n* = **disease**, cancer, infection, corruption, sore, scourge, ulcer, rot, blight, bane
cannon *n* = **gun**, mortar, big gun, field gun
canny *adj* = **shrewd**, careful, cautious, wise, prudent, clever, astute, judicious
canon *n* **1** = **rule**, regulation, standard, principle, formula, criterion, dictate, statute, yardstick, precept **2** = **list**, roll, catalogue
canopy *n* = **awning**, shade, marquee, covering, sunshade
cant[1] *n* **1** = **hypocrisy**, pretense, humbug, insincerity, lip service, pretentiousness, sanctimoniousness **2** = **jargon**, lingo, slang, vernacular, argot, patter
cant[2] *v* = **tilt**, rise, slope, angle, incline, slant, bevel
cantankerous *adj* = **bad-tempered**, contrary, testy, grumpy, irritable, irascible, choleric, disagreeable, waspish

DICTIONARY

Chants d'Auvergne (1923–30)
canter Ⓣ *n* **1** horse's gait between a trot and a gallop ▷ *v* **2** (cause to) move at a canter
canticle *n* short hymn with words from the Bible
cantilever *n* beam or girder fixed at one end only
canto [**kan**-toe] *n, pl* **-tos** main division of a long poem
canton *n* political division of a country, esp. Switzerland
cantonment [kan-**toon**-ment] *n* military camp
cantor *n* man employed to lead services in a synagogue
Canuck *n, adj informal* Canadian
Canute, Cnut, Knut *n* died 1035, Danish king of England (1016–35), Denmark (1018–35), and Norway (1028–35). He defeated Edmund II of England (1016), but divided the kingdom with him until Edmund's death. An able ruler, he invaded Scotland (1027) and drove Olaf II from Norway (1028)
canvas *n* **1** heavy coarse cloth used for sails and tents, and for painting on **2** a painting on canvas
canvass Ⓣ *v* **1** try to get votes or support (from) **2** determine the opinions of (people) by conducting a survey ▷ *n* **3** canvassing
canyon *n* deep steep-sided valley
cap Ⓣ *n* **1** soft close-fitting covering for the head **2** small lid **3** small explosive device used in a toy gun ▷ *v* **capping, capped 4** cover or top with something **5** select (a player) for a national team **6** impose an upper limit on (a tax) **7** outdo
CAP (in the EU) Common Agricultural Policy
Capa *n* **Robert**, real name *André Friedmann*. 1913–54, Hungarian photographer, who established his reputation as a photojournalist during the Spanish Civil War
capable Ⓣ *adj* **1** (foll. by *of*) having the ability or skill to do something **2** competent and efficient **capably** *adv* **capability** *n*
capacity Ⓣ *n, pl* **-ties 1** ability to contain, absorb, or hold **2** maximum amount that can be contained or produced **3** physical or mental ability **4** position or function
▸ **capacious** *adj* roomy
▸ **capacitance** *n* (measure of) the ability of a system to store electric charge
▸ **capacitor** *n* device for storing electric charge
caparisoned [kap-**par**-riss-sond] *adj* magnificently decorated or dressed
cape[1] *n* short cloak
cape[2] Ⓣ *n* large piece of land jutting into the sea
Čapek *n* **Karel**. 1890–1938, Czech dramatist and novelist; author of *R.U.R.* (1921), which introduced the word "robot," and (with his brother **Josef**) *The Insect Play* (1921).
capelin [**kap**-ill-in] *n* small food fish of the N Atlantic and Pacific
caper[1] Ⓣ *n* **1** high-spirited prank ▷ *v* **2** skip or dance about
caper[2] *n* pickled flower bud of a Mediterranean shrub used in sauces
capercaillie, capercailzie [kap-per-**kale**-yee] *n* large black European grouse
Capet *n* **Hugh** *or* **Hugues**. ?938–996 AD, king of France (987–96); founder of the Capetian dynasty.
capillary [kap-**pill**-a-ree] *n, pl* **-laries** very fine blood vessel
capital Ⓣ *n* **1** chief town of a country **2** accumulated wealth **3** wealth used to produce more wealth **4** large letter, as used at the beginning of a name or sentence

THESAURUS

canter *n* **1** = **jog**, amble, dogtrot, lope ▸ *v* **2** = **jog**, amble, lope
canvass *v* **1** = **campaign**, solicit, electioneer, solicit votes **2** = **poll**, study, investigate, examine, inspect, scrutinize ▸ *n* **3** = **poll**, investigation, survey, tally, scrutiny, examination
cap *v* = **beat**, top, crown, surpass, exceed, eclipse, better, outstrip, outdo, transcend
capability *n* = **ability**, power, potential, capacity, means, qualification *or* qualifications, competence, proficiency, wherewithal
capable *adj* = **able**, efficient, competent, accomplished, adept, proficient, skilful • *a capable leader* OPPOSITE: incompetent
▷ **capable of** *See* **equal to**
capacious *adj* = **spacious**, wide, broad, extensive, substantial, vast, sizable *or* sizeable, expansive, voluminous, roomy, commodious
capacity *n* **1** = **size**, space, room, volume, dimensions • *the vehicle's fuel capacity* **2** = **ability**, power, potential, facility, gift, capability • *Our capacity for giving care, love, and attention is limited.* **3** = **function**, post, province, office, role, position, sphere
See also: **part, talent**
cape *n* = **headland**, point, head, peninsula, promontory
caper *n* **1** = **escapade**, stunt, mischief, prank, antic, lark (*informal*), high jinks, jape, practical joke ▸ *v* **2** = **dance**, jump, trip, spring, skip, bound, frolic, cavort, gambol
capital *n* **1** = **money**, cash, investment *or* investments, principal, wealth, means, wherewithal, assets, funds, resources, finances, venture capital ▸ *adj*

DICTIONARY

5 top part of a pillar ▷ *adj* **6** involving or punishable by death **7** chief or principal **8** *old-fashioned* excellent
▶ **capitalism** *n* economic system based on the private ownership of industry
▶ **capitalist** *adj* **1** based on or supporting capitalism ▷ *n* **2** supporter of capitalism **3** person who owns capital
▶ **capitalize** *v* **1** convert into or provide with capital **2** write or print (text) in capital letters
▶ **capitalize on** *v* take advantage of (a situation)
capitation *n* charge or grant of a fixed amount per person
capitulate Ⓣ *v* surrender on agreed terms **capitulation** *n*
capon [**kay**-pon] *n* castrated cock fowl fattened for eating
Capote *n* **Truman**. 1924–84, US writer; his novels include *Other Voices, Other Rooms* (1948) and *In Cold Blood* (1964), based on an actual multiple murder
Capp *n* **Al**, full name *Alfred Caplin*. 1909–79, US cartoonist, famous for his comic strip *Li'l Abner*
cappuccino [kap-poo-**cheen**-oh] *n, pl* **-nos** coffee with steamed milk
Capra *n* **Frank**. 1896–1992, US film director born in Italy. His films include *It Happened One Night* (1934), *It's a Wonderful Life* (1946), and several propaganda films during World War II.
caprice Ⓣ [kap-**reess**] *n* whim
▶ **capricious** *adj* changeable **capriciously** *adv*
Capricorn *n* **tropic of Capricorn** see **tropic**
capsicum *n* kind of pepper used as a vegetable or as a spice
capsize Ⓣ *v* overturn accidentally
capstan *n* rotating cylinder on which a rope etc. is wound
capsule Ⓣ *n* **1** soluble case containing a dose of medicine **2** seed vessel of a plant **3** detachable crew compartment of a spacecraft
captain Ⓣ *n* **1** leader of a team or group **2** commander of a ship or civil aircraft **3** middle-ranking naval officer **4** junior officer in the armed forces ▷ *v* **5** be captain of **captaincy** *n*
caption *n* **1** title or explanation accompanying an illustration ▷ *v* **2** provide with a caption
captious *adj* tending to make trivial criticisms **captiously** *adv* **captiousness** *n*
captivate Ⓣ *v* fascinate or enchant **captivating** *adj* **captivation** *n*
captive Ⓣ *n* **1** person kept in confinement ▷ *adj* **2** kept in confinement **3** (of an audience) unable to leave **captivity** *n*
captor *n* person who captures a person or animal
capture Ⓣ *v* **1** take prisoner **2** gain control over **3** succeed in representing (something elusive) artistically ▷ *n* **4** capturing
capybara *n* very large S American rodent
car Ⓣ *n* **1** motor vehicle designed to carry a small number of people **2** passenger compartment of a cable car, elevator, etc. **3** railway carriage
▶ **car park** area or building reserved for parking cars
carafe [kar-**raff**] *n* glass bottle for serving water or wine

THESAURUS

2 = principal, major, prime, vital, cardinal **3** (*Old-fashioned*) **= first-rate**, fine, excellent, superb, splendid, sterling
capitalism *n* **= private enterprise**, free enterprise, laissez faire *or* laisser faire, private ownership
capitalize *v* **capitalize on = take advantage of**, exploit, benefit from, cash in on (*informal*), gain from, make the most of, profit from
capitulate *v* **= give in**, submit, surrender, yield, succumb, relent, come to terms, give up
capitulation *See* **surrender**
caprice *n* **= whim**, notion, impulse, fancy, fad, whimsy, fickleness, inconstancy
capricious *adj* **= unpredictable**, inconsistent, variable, erratic, whimsical, wayward, fickle, impulsive, mercurial, changeful, fitful, inconstant
capsize *v* **= overturn**, upset, invert, keel over, tip over, turn over, turn turtle
capsule *n* **1 = pill**, tablet, lozenge **2** (*Botany*) **= pod**, case, vessel, shell, sheath, receptacle, seed case
captain *n* **= leader**, head, chief, commander, boss (*informal*), master, skipper
captivate *v* **= charm**, attract, entrance, fascinate, allure, mesmerize, enchant, enthrall, bewitch, beguile, enrapture, infatuate
captive *n* **1 = prisoner**, convict, hostage, detainee, slave, internee, prisoner of war ▶ *adj* **2 = confined**, restricted, caged, enslaved, ensnared, imprisoned, incarcerated, locked up, penned, subjugated
captivity *n* **= confinement**, custody, detention, imprisonment, slavery, incarceration, internment, bondage
capture *v* **1 = catch**, take, arrest, seize, apprehend • *captured by rebels* OPPOSITE: release ▶ *n* **2 = catching**, arrest, seizure, taking, trapping • *She evaded capture for eight years.*
See also: **kidnap**
car *n* **1 = automobile**, vehicle • *I finally left the car at the garage* **2 = carriage** *or* **railway carriage**, coach, van, buffet car, cable car,

DICTIONARY

caramel *n* **1** chewy candy made from sugar and milk **2** burnt sugar used for colouring and flavouring food

▸ **caramelize** *v* turn into caramel

carapace *n* hard upper shell of tortoises and crustaceans

carat *n* **1** unit of weight of precious stones **2** measure of the purity of gold in an alloy

Caravaggio *n* **Michelangelo Merisi da**. 1571–1610, Italian painter, noted for his realistic depiction of religious subjects and for his dramatic use of chiaroscuro

caravan *n* **1** group travelling together for safety in the East **2** *Brit* large enclosed vehicle for living in, able to be towed by an automobile or horse

caraway *n* plant whose seeds are used as a spice

carb *n informal* short for **carbohydrate**

carbide *n* compound of carbon with a metal

carbine *n* light automatic rifle

carbohydrate *n* any of a large group of energy-producing compounds in food, such as sugars and starches

carbolic, carbolic acid *n* disinfectant derived from coal tar

carbon *n* nonmetallic element occurring as charcoal, graphite, and diamond, found in all organic matter

▸ **carbonate** *n* salt or ester of carbonic acid

▸ **carbonated** *adj* containing carbon dioxide

▸ **carbonize** *v* **1** turn into carbon as a result of heating **2** coat with carbon

▸ **carbon copy 1** copy made with carbon paper **2** very similar person or thing

▸ **carbon dioxide** colourless gas exhaled by people and animals

▸ **carbon footprint** measure of the carbon dioxide produced by an individual or organization

▸ **carbonic acid** weak acid formed from carbon dioxide and water

▸ **carbon-neutral** *adj* not affecting the overall volume of carbon dioxide in the atmosphere

▸ **carbon offset** act which compensates for carbon emissions of an individual or company

▸ **carbon paper** paper covered with a dark waxy pigment, used to make a duplicate of something as it is typed or written

Carborundum *n* ® compound of silicon and carbon, used for grinding and polishing

carboy *n* large bottle with a protective casing

carbuncle *n* **1** inflamed boil **2** rounded garnet cut without facets

carburetor *n* device which mixes gasoline and air in an internal-combustion engine

carcass, carcase Ⓣ *n* dead body or skeleton of an animal

carcinogen *n* substance producing cancer

carcinogenic *adj*

▸ **carcinoma** *n* malignant tumour, cancer

card[1] *n* **1** piece of thick stiff paper or cardboard used for identification, reference, or sending greetings or messages **2** one of a set of cards with a printed pattern, used for playing games **3** small rectangle of stiff plastic for use as a credit card or banker's card **4** *old-fashioned* witty or eccentric person

cards 5 any card game, or card games in general

▸ **cardboard** *n* thin stiff board made from paper pulp

▸ **cardholder** *n* person who owns a credit or debit card

▸ **cardsharp** *or* **cardsharper** *n* professional card player who cheats

card[2] *n* machine or tool for combing wool before spinning **carder** *n*

cardamom, cardamon *n* seeds of a tropical plant, used as a spice

Cardenal *n* **Ernesto**. born 1925, Nicaraguan poet, revolutionary, and Roman Catholic priest; an influential figure in the Sandinista movement.

Cárdenas *n* **Lázaro**. 1895–1970, Mexican statesman and general; president of Mexico (1934–40)

cardiac *adj* of the heart

▸ **cardiograph** *n* instrument which records heart movements

▸ **cardiogram** *n* record of heart movements

▸ **cardiology** *n* study of the heart and its diseases **cardiologist** *n*

▸ **cardiovascular** *adj* of the heart and the blood vessels

cardigan *n* knitted jacket

cardinal Ⓣ *n* **1** one of the high-ranking clergymen of the RC Church who elect the Pope and act as his counsellors ▹ *adj* **2** chief, principal **3** deep red

▸ **cardinal number** number denoting quantity but not order in a group, for example one, two, or three

▸ **cardinal point** one of the four main points of the compass

Cardoso *n* **Fernando Henrique**. born 1931, Brazilian statesman; president (1995–2002)

THESAURUS

dining car, sleeping car

carcass *n* = **body**, shell, skeleton, framework, corpse, hulk, cadaver (*medical*), dead body, remains

cardinal *adj* = **principal**, first, chief, key, capital, main, central, primary, essential, fundamental, paramount, leading

DICTIONARY

care ⓣ *v* **1** be concerned **2** have regard or liking for **3** have a desire for **4** look after ▷ *n* **5** serious attention **6** protection or supervision **7** worry, anxiety **8** caution
careful *adj* **carefully** *adv* **carefulness** *n*
careless *adj* **carelessly** *adv* **carelessness** *n*
▸ **carefree** *adj* without worry or responsibility
▸ **caretaker** *n* person employed to look after a place
▸ **careworn** *adj* showing signs of worry
careen *v* tilt over to one side
career ⓣ *n* **1** profession or occupation **2** course through life ▷ *v* **3** rush in an uncontrolled way
▸ **careerist** *n* person who seeks advancement by any possible means
caress ⓣ *n* **1** gentle affectionate touch or embrace ▷ *v* **2** touch gently and affectionately
caret [**kar**-rett] *n* symbol (‸) showing the place in written or printed matter where something is to be inserted
Carey *n* **Peter**. born 1943, Australian novelist and writer; his novels include *Illywhacker* (1985), *Oscar and Lucinda* (1988), and *True History of the Kelly Gang* (2001)
cargo ⓣ *n, pl* **-goes** goods carried by a ship, aircraft, etc.
▸ **cargo pants** *or* **cargo trousers** loose trousers with a large pocket on each leg
caribou *n* N American reindeer
caricature ⓣ *n* **1** likeness of a person which exaggerates features for comic effect ▷ *v* **2** portray by a caricature
caries [**care**-reez] *n* tooth decay
carillon [kar-**rill**-yon] *n* **1** set of bells played by keyboard or mechanically **2** tune played on this
Carl XVI Gustaf *n* born 1946, king of Sweden from 1973
Carlyle *n* **Thomas**. 1795–1881, Scottish essayist and historian. His works include *Sartor Resartus* (1833–34), *The French Revolution* (1837), lectures *On Heroes, Hero-Worship, and the Heroic in History* (1841), and the *History of Frederick the Great* (1858–65)
Carmichael *n* **Hoaglund Howard**, known as *Hoagy*. 1899–1981, US pianist, singer, and composer of such standards as "Star Dust" (1929)
carmine *adj* vivid red
carnage ⓣ *n* slaughter
carnal ⓣ *adj* of a sexual or sensual nature
▸ **carnal knowledge** sexual intercourse
carnation *n* cultivated plant with sweet-

THESAURUS

care *v* **1** = **be concerned**, mind, be bothered, be interested • *a company that cares about the environment* ▷ **care for** = **look after**, protect, attend, nurse, tend, foster, take care of, minister to, provide for, watch over; = **like**, want, love, enjoy, desire, prize, be fond of, take to ▸ *n* **2** = **worry**, concern, stress, trouble, woe, anxiety • *without a care in the world* **3** = **caution**, attention, pains • *We took great care in choosing a location.* **4** = **protection**, charge, control, management, custody, supervision, guardianship, keeping
See also: **burden**
career *n* **1** = **occupation**, employment, pursuit, calling, livelihood, vocation, life's work ▸ *v* **2** = **rush**, race, barrel *or* barrel along (*informal*), speed, tear, bolt, dash, hurtle
carefree *adj* = **untroubled**, cheerful, easy-going, breezy, light-hearted, happy-go-lucky, blithe, halcyon
careful *adj* **1** = **cautious**, prudent • *Be careful what you say to him.* OPPOSITE: careless **2** = **thorough**, precise, painstaking, meticulous • *It needs careful planning.* OPPOSITE: careless
See also: **deliberate, economical, thrifty**
careless *adj* **1** = **slapdash**, irresponsible, sloppy (*informal*), neglectful • *careless driving* OPPOSITE: careful **2** = **nonchalant**, casual, offhand • *careless laughter* **3** = **negligent**, hasty, thoughtless, remiss, absent-minded, forgetful, unthinking
carelessness *n* = **negligence**, neglect, omission, indiscretion, irresponsibility, laxity, slackness, sloppiness (*informal*), thoughtlessness
caress *v* **1** = **stroke**, pet, embrace, neck (*informal*), kiss, hug, cuddle, fondle, make out (*informal*), nuzzle ▸ *n* **2** = **stroke**, embrace, kiss, hug, pat, cuddle, fondling
caretaker *n* = **warden**, curator, keeper, superintendent, concierge, janitor, custodian, porter, watchman
cargo *n* = **load**, shipment, merchandise, freight, baggage, consignment, contents, goods
caricature *n* **1** = **parody**, cartoon, satire, distortion, farce, lampoon, burlesque, travesty, piss-take (*informal*) ▸ *v* **2** = **parody**, mock, mimic, ridicule, distort, satirize, lampoon, burlesque
caring *adj* = **compassionate**, warm, sensitive, soft, tender, loving, sympathetic, responsive, receptive, kindly, considerate, softhearted, tenderhearted, touchy-feely (*informal*), warmhearted
carnage *n* = **slaughter**, murder, massacre, havoc, bloodshed, holocaust, shambles, blood bath, butchery, mass murder
carnal *adj* = **sexual**, erotic, lewd, sensual, fleshly, lascivious, libidinous, lustful

DICTIONARY

scented white, pink, or red flowers
carnival Ⓣ *n* festive period with processions and entertainment
carnivore *n* flesh-eating animal **carnivorous** *adj*
Carnot *n* **1 Lazare** (**Nicolas Marguerite**), known as *the Organizer of Victory*. 1753–1823, French military engineer and administrator: organized the French Revolutionary army (1793–95) **2 Nicolas Léonard Sadi**. 1796–1832, French physicist, whose work formed the basis for the second law of thermodynamics, enunciated in 1850; author of *Réflexions sur la puissance motrice du feu* (1824).
Caro *n* **Joseph** (**ben Ephraim**). 1488–1575, Jewish legal scholar and mystic, born in Spain; compiler of the *Shulhan Arukh* (1564–65), the most authoritative Jewish legal code.
carob *n* Mediterranean tree with edible pods used as a chocolate substitute
carol Ⓣ *n* **1** joyful religious song sung at Christmas ▷ *v* **-olling, -olled 2** sing carols **3** sing joyfully
carotid [kar-**rot**-id] *adj*, *n* (of) one of the two arteries supplying blood to the head
carouse *v* have a merry drinking party ▶ **carousal** *n* merry drinking party
carousel [kar-roo-**sell**] *n* **1** revolving conveyor **2** merry-go-round
carp[1] *n* freshwater fish
carp[2] Ⓣ *v* complain or find fault
Carpaccio *n* **Vittore**. ?1460–?1525, Italian painter of the Venetian school
carpel *n* female reproductive organ of a flowering plant
carpenter Ⓣ *n* person who makes or repairs wooden structures **carpentry** *n*
Carpenter *n* **John Alden**. 1876–1951, US composer, who used jazz rhythms in orchestral music: his works include the ballet *Skyscrapers* (1926) and the orchestral suite *Adventures in a Perambulator* (1915)
Carpentier *n* **Georges**, known as *Gorgeous Georges*. 1894–1975, French boxer: world light-heavyweight champion (1920–22)
carpet *n* **1** heavy fabric for covering a floor ▷ *v* **carpeting, carpeted 2** cover with a carpet ▶ **on the carpet** *informal* being reprimanded
carpus *n*, *pl* **-pi** set of eight small bones forming the wrist
Carr *n* **Emily**. 1871–1945, Canadian artist and writer whose work was inspired by Canada's indigenous peoples and wilderness
Carrel *n* **Alexis**. 1873–1944, French surgeon and biologist, active in the US (1905–39): developed a method of suturing blood vessels, making the transplantation of arteries and organs possible: Nobel prize for physiology or medicine 1912
Carreras *n* **José**. born 1947, Spanish tenor
carriage Ⓣ *n* **1** one of the sections of a train for passengers **2** person's bearing **3** four-wheeled horse-drawn vehicle **4** moving part of a machine that supports and shifts another part **5** act or cost of conveying goods ▶ **carriageway** *n* part of a road along which traffic passes in one direction
carrier *n* **1** person or thing that carries something **2** person or animal that does not show symptoms of a disease but can transmit it to others ▶ **carrier pigeon** homing pigeon used for carrying messages
carrion *n* dead and rotting flesh
Carroll *n* **Lewis**, real name *Reverend Charles Lutwidge Dodgson*. 1832–98, English writer; an Oxford mathematics don who wrote *Alice's Adventures in Wonderland* (1865) and *Through the Looking-Glass* (1872) and the nonsense poem *The Hunting of the Snark* (1876)
carrot *n* **1** long tapering orange root vegetable **2** incentive ▶ **carroty** *adj* reddish
carry Ⓣ *v* **-rying, -ried 1** take (something) from one place to another, transport **2** have on one's person **3** transmit **4** have as a penalty or result **5** bear (the head, body, etc.) in a specified manner **6** win acceptance for (a bill or motion) **7** (of sound) travel over a distance ▶ **carryall** *n* large strong travelling bag ▶ **carry on** *v* **1** continue or persevere **2** *informal* fuss unnecessarily ▶ **carry-on** *adj* (of luggage) to be taken inside the cabin of an aircraft by a passenger

THESAURUS

carnival *n* = **festival**, holiday, fair, celebration, gala, jamboree, revelry, fête, fiesta, jubilee, merrymaking
carol *n* = **song**, lay, chorus, hymn, ditty
carp *v* = **find fault**, criticize, complain, reproach, quibble, cavil, pick holes
carpenter *n* = **joiner**, cabinet-maker, woodworker
carping *See* **critical**
carriage *n* **1** = **coach**, railway car, cab, conveyance **2** = **bearing**, air, conduct, manner, behaviour, posture, gait, demeanour, comportment, deportment
carry *v* **1** = **transport**, take, bear, convey (*formal*), lug • *She was carrying a briefcase.* **2** = **win**, gain, effect, capture, secure, accomplish ▷ **carry on** = **continue**, last, maintain, endure, persist, perpetuate, persevere, keep going ▷ **carry out** = **perform**, achieve, accomplish, fulfill • *the surgeon who carried out the operation*
See also: **administer, commit, conduct, do, keep**
See also: **bring, hold**

DICTIONARY

▸ **carry out** *v* perform or complete
Carson *n* **1 Christopher**, known as *Kit Carson*. 1809–68, US frontiersman, trapper, scout, and Indian agent **2 Rachel** (**Louise**). 1907–64, US marine biologist and science writer; author of *Silent Spring* (1962)
cart *n* **1** open two-wheeled horse-drawn vehicle for carrying goods or passengers ▹ *v* **2** carry in a cart **3** carry with effort
▸ **carthorse** *n* large heavily built horse
▸ **cartwheel** *n* **1** sideways somersault supported by the arms with the legs outstretched **2** large spoked wheel of a cart
carte blanche *n French* complete authority
cartel *n* association of competing firms formed to fix prices
Carter *n* **1 Elliot** (**Cook**). born 1908, US composer. His works include the *Piano Sonata* (1945–46), four string quartets, and other orchestral pieces: Pulitzer Prize 1960, 1973 **2 Howard**. 1873–1939, English Egyptologist: excavated the tomb of the Pharaoh Tutankhamen **3 James Earl**, known as *Jimmy*. born 1924, US Democratic statesman; 39th president of the US (1977–81)
Cartier *n* **Jacques**. 1491–1557, French navigator and explorer in Canada, who discovered the St Lawrence River (1535)
Cartier-Bresson *n* **Henri**. 1908–2004, French photographer
cartilage [**kar**-till-ij] *n* firm elastic tissue forming part of the skeleton **cartilaginous** *adj*
cartography *n* map making **cartographer** *n* **cartographic** *adj*
carton Ⓣ *n* container made of cardboard or waxed paper
cartoon Ⓣ *n* **1** humorous or satirical drawing **2** sequence of these telling a story **3** film made by photographing a series of drawings which give the illusion of movement when projected **4** preliminary sketch for a painting **cartoonist** *n*
cartridge Ⓣ *n* **1** casing containing an explosive charge for a firearm **2** sealed container of film, tape, etc. **3** unit in the pick-up of a record player holding the stylus
▸ **cartridge paper** strong thick paper
Caruso *n* **Enrico**. 1873–1921, an outstanding Italian operatic tenor; one of the first to make phonograph records
carve Ⓣ *v* **1** cut **2** form (an object or design) by cutting, esp. in stone or wood **3** slice (meat) into pieces **carving** *n*
Carver *n* **George Washington**. ?1864–1943, US agricultural chemist and botanist
caryatid [kar-ree-**at**-id] *n* supporting column in the shape of a female figure
CAS *Canad* Children's Aid Society: organization providing help for abused or homeless children
Casanova *n* **1 Giovanni Jacopo**. 1725–98, Italian adventurer noted for his *Mémoires*, a vivid account of his sexual adventures and of contemporary society **2** any man noted for his amorous adventures; a rake
cascade Ⓣ *n* **1** waterfall **2** something that flows or falls like a waterfall ▹ *v* **3** fall in cascades
case[1] Ⓣ *n* **1** instance or example **2** matter for discussion **3** condition or state of affairs **4** set of arguments for an action or cause **5** person attended to by a doctor, solicitor, or social worker **6** lawsuit **7** grounds for a lawsuit **8** *grammar* form of a noun, pronoun, or adjective showing its relation to other words in the sentence
▸ **in case** so as to allow for eventualities
case[2] Ⓣ *n* **1** container or protective covering **2** container and its contents ▹ *v* **3** *slang* inspect (a building) with the intention of burgling it
▸ **case-harden** *v* harden (an iron alloy) by carbonizing the surface
▸ **case-hardened** *adj* made callous by experience
casement *n* window that is hinged on one side
Casement *n* Sir **Roger** (**David**). 1864–1916, British diplomat and Irish nationalist: hanged by the British for treason in attempting to gain German support for Irish independence

THESAURUS

carton *n* = **box**, case, package, pack, container, packet
cartoon *n* **1** = **drawing**, sketch, satire, caricature, parody, lampoon, comic strip **2** = **animation**, animated cartoon, animated film
cartridge *n* **1** = **shell**, charge, round **2** = **container**, case, magazine, capsule, cylinder, cassette
carve *v* = **cut**, sculpt, engrave, inscribe, chisel • *He carves his figures from pine.*
See also: **model**
cascade *n* **1** = **waterfall**, flood, avalanche, shower, cataract, fountain, outpouring, deluge, downpour, torrent, falls ▸ *v* **2** = **flow**, fall, pitch, surge, flood, tumble, spill, plunge, pour, descend, overflow, teem, gush
case[1] *n* **1** = **instance**, example, occasion, occurrence, illustration • *a case of mistaken identity* **2** = **lawsuit**, trial, action, proceedings • *a libel case*
See also: **argument, patient, situation**
case[2] *n* **1** = **container**, box • *an eyeglass case* **2** = **covering**, jacket, shell, capsule, envelope, casing, wrapper, sheath
See also: **cover**

DICTIONARY

cash Ⓣ *n* **1** banknotes and coins ▷ *v* **2** obtain cash for
▶ **cash in on** *v informal* gain profit or advantage from
▶ **cash register** till that displays and adds the prices of the goods sold
Cash *n* **Johnny**. 1932–2003, US country-and-western singer, guitarist, and songwriter. His recordings include the hits "I Walk the Line" (1956), "Ring of Fire" (1963), "A Boy named Sue" (1969), and the *American Recordings* series of albums (1994–2003)
cashew *n* edible tropical American nut
cashier[1] Ⓣ *n* person responsible for handling cash in a bank or shop
cashier[2] Ⓣ *v* dismiss with dishonour from the armed forces
cashmere *n* **1** fine soft wool **2** fabric made from this
casing *n* protective case or covering
casino *n, pl* **-nos** public building or room where gambling is done
cask *n* barrel for holding alcoholic drink
casket Ⓣ *n* **1** small box for valuables **2** coffin
Cassatt *n* **Mary**. 1845–1926, US impressionist painter, who lived in France
cassava *n* flour obtained from the roots of a tropical American plant, used to make tapioca
casserole *n* **1** covered dish in which food is cooked and served **2** food cooked in this way ▷ *v* **3** cook in a casserole
cassette *n* plastic case containing a reel of film or magnetic tape
Cassini *n* **Giovanni Domenico**. 1625–1712, French astronomer, born in Italy. He discovered (1675)
▶ **Cassini's division**, the gap that divides Saturn's rings into two parts, and four of Saturn's moons
Cassiodorus *n* **Flavius Magnus Aurelius**. ?490–?585 AD, Roman statesman, writer, and monk; author of *Variae*, a collection of official documents written for the Ostrogoths
Cassivelaunus *n* 1st century BC, British chieftain, king of the Catuvellauni tribe, who organized resistance to Caesar's invasion of Britain (54 BC)
cassock *n* long tunic worn by the clergy
Casson *n* Sir **Hugh** (**Maxwell**). 1910–99, British architect; president of the Royal Academy of Arts (1976–84)
cassowary *n, pl* **-waries** large flightless bird of Australia and New Guinea
cast Ⓣ *n* **1** actors in a play or film collectively **2** something shaped by a mould while molten **3** mould used to shape something **4** rigid casing to help set a broken bone **5** quality or nature **6** slight squint in the eye ▷ *v* **casting, cast 7** select (actors) to play parts in a play or film **8** give (a vote) **9** let fall, shed **10** shape (molten material) in a mould **11** throw with force **12** direct (a glance)
▶ **castaway** *n* shipwrecked person
▶ **casting vote** deciding vote used by the chairman when the votes on each side are equal
▶ **cast-iron** *adj* **1** made of a hard but brittle type of iron **2** rigid or unchallengeable
▶ **cast-off** *adj, n* discarded (garment)
castanets *pl n* two small curved pieces of hollow wood clicked together in the hand, used esp. by Spanish dancers
caste Ⓣ *n* **1** one of the hereditary classes into which Hindu society is divided **2** social rank
castellated *adj* having battlements
caster sugar *n Brit* finely ground white sugar
castigate Ⓣ *v* criticize or scold severely
castigation *n*
castle Ⓣ *n* **1** large fortified building **2** rook in chess
Castlereagh *n* **Viscount**, title of *Robert Stewart*, Marquis of Londonderry. 1769–1822, British statesman: as foreign secretary (1812–22) led the Grand Alliance against Napoleon and attended the Congress of Vienna (1815)
castor *n* small swivelled wheel fixed to a

THESAURUS

cash *n* = **money**, silver, currency, dough (*slang*), coinage, funds, notes, ready money
cashier[1] *n* = **teller**, banker, clerk, treasurer, bank clerk, bursar, purser
cashier[2] *v* = **dismiss**, expel, discharge, discard, drum out, give the boot to (*slang*)
casket *n* = **box**, case, chest, coffer, jewel box
cast *n* **1** = **actors**, company, troupe, characters, dramatis personae, players **2** = **type**, style, stamp, manner, complexion ▶ *v* **3** = **choose**, name, pick, select, appoint, assign, allot **4** = **give out**, spread, distribute, shed, deposit, emit, scatter, bestow, radiate, diffuse **5** = **form**, set, model, shape, found, mould **6** = **throw**, launch, pitch, toss, hurl, thrust, fling, sling ▷ **cast aside** *See* **discard** ▷ **cast a vote** *See* **vote**
caste *n* = **class**, order, status, rank, estate, grade, stratum, social order
castigate *v* = **reprimand**, criticize, rebuke, chastise, censure, scold, berate, lambast *or* lambaste
cast-iron *adj* = **certain**, established, definite, copper-bottomed, fixed, guaranteed, settled
castle *n* = **fortress**, keep, tower, palace, stronghold, chateau, citadel

DICTIONARY

piece of furniture to allow it to be moved easily
castor oil *n* oil obtained from an Indian plant, used as a lubricant and purgative
castrate Ⓣ *v* **1** remove the testicles of **2** deprive of vigour or masculinity
castration *n*
Castro *n* **1** **Fidel**, full name *Fidel Castro Ruz*. born 1927, Cuban statesman: prime minister from 1959, when he led the Communist overthrow of Batista and president 1976–2006 **2** **Raúl**. born 1931, Cuban politician; took over the Presidency from his brother Fidel in 2008
casual Ⓣ *adj* **1** appearing unconcerned **2** (of work or workers) occasional **3** shallow or superficial **4** for informal wear **5** happening by chance **casually** *adv*
casualty Ⓣ *n, pl* **-ties 1** person killed or injured in an accident or war **2** anything lost or destroyed
casuistry *n* reasoning that is misleading or oversubtle **casuist** *n*
cat Ⓣ *n* **1** small domesticated furry mammal **2** related wild mammal, such as the lion or tiger **3** *informal* spiteful woman
▸ **catty** *adj informal* spiteful
▸ **catkin** *n* drooping flower spike of certain trees
▸ **catcall** *n* derisive whistle or cry
▸ **catgut** *n* strong cord used to string musical instruments
▸ **catnap** *v, n* doze
▸ **cat's paw** person used as a tool by another
▸ **catwalk** *n* narrow pathway or platform
cataclysm [**kat**-a-kliz-zum] *n* **1** violent upheaval **2** disaster, such as an earthquake
cataclysmic *adj*
catacombs Ⓣ [**kat**-a-kooms] *pl n* underground burial place consisting of tunnels with recesses for tombs
catafalque [**kat**-a-falk] *n* raised platform on which a body lies in state before or during a funeral
catalepsy *n* trancelike state in which the body is rigid **cataleptic** *adj*
catalogue Ⓣ *n* **1** book containing details of items for sale **2** systematic list of items ▹ *v* **3** make such a list **4** enter (an item) in a catalogue
catalyst *n* substance that speeds up a chemical reaction without itself changing
▸ **catalyse** *v* speed up (a chemical reaction) by a catalyst **catalysis** *n* **catalytic** *adj*
catamaran *n* boat with twin parallel hulls
catapult Ⓣ *n* **1** *Brit* slingshot **2** device used to launch aircraft from a warship ▹ *v* **3** launch as if from a catapult
cataract *n* **1** eye disease in which the lens becomes opaque **2** opaque area of an eye **3** waterfall
catarrh [kat-**tar**] *n* inflammation of a mucous membrane causing a flow of mucus
catarrhal *adj*
catastrophe Ⓣ [kat-**ass**-trof-fee] *n* great and sudden disaster **catastrophic** *adj*
catatonia *n* form of schizophrenia characterized by stupor, with outbreaks of excitement **catatonic** *adj, n*
catch Ⓣ *v* **catching, caught 1** seize or capture **2** surprise: *catch someone red-handed*

THESAURUS

cast-off *adj* **1** = **unwanted**, useless, unneeded, discarded, rejected, scrapped, surplus to requirements ▸ *n* **2** = **reject**, second, failure, discard, outcast
castrate *v* = **neuter**, emasculate, geld
casual *adj* **1** = **chance**, accidental, incidental • *a casual remark* OPPOSITE: deliberate **2** = **careless**, cursory, nonchalant, offhand, relaxed • *a casual look over his shoulder* OPPOSITE: concerned **3** = **informal**, sporty, non- dressy
casualty *n* = **victim**, death, loss, wounded, fatality, sufferer
cat *n* = **feline**, kitty, puss *or* pussy (cat) (*informal*) • *sharing his apartment with four cats* RELATED WORDS *adj*: feline *male*: tom *female*: tabby *young*: kitten
catacombs *pl n* = **vault**, tomb, crypt
catalogue *n* **1** = **list**, record, schedule, roll, index, register, inventory, roster, directory, gazetteer ▸ *v* **2** = **list**, file, index, register, inventory, classify, tabulate, accession, alphabetize
catapult *n* **1** = **sling**, slingshot (*US*) ▸ *v* **2** = **shoot**, pitch, plunge, propel, hurl, heave
catastrophe *n* = **disaster**, trouble, tragedy, fiasco, adversity, calamity, misfortune, cataclysm
catastrophic *See* **fatal**
catcall *n* = **jeer**, boo, whistle, raspberry, hiss, gibe
catch *v* **1** = **capture**, arrest, trap, snare, apprehend • *another technique for catching criminals* **2** = **seize**, take, get, grab, grip, clutch, snatch, grasp, lay hold of **3** = **discover**, surprise, expose, detect, unmask, catch in the act, find out, take unawares **4** = **contract**, get, develop, incur, go down with, succumb to, suffer from **5** = **make out**, get, hear, recognize, sense, perceive, grasp, comprehend, discern, take in ▹ **catch on** = **understand**, see, grasp, comprehend, find out, get the picture, see through ▸ *n* **6** = **fastener**, clip, bolt, latch, clasp • *windows fitted with safety catches* **7** = **drawback**, snag, disadvantage • *The catch is that you have to change planes twice.*
See also: **stick, tangle**

DICTIONARY

3 hit unexpectedly **4** be in time for **5** see or hear by chance or with difficulty **6** contract (a disease) **7** understand **8** entangle or become entangled **9** check (one's breath) suddenly **10** begin to burn ▷ *n* **11** catching **12** thing caught **13** device that fastens **14** *informal* concealed or unforeseen difficulty
▸ **catch it** *informal* be punished
▸ **catching** *adj* infectious
▸ **catchy** *adj* (of a tune) pleasant and easily remembered
▸ **catchment area** area served by a particular school or hospital
▸ **catch on** *v informal* **1** become popular **2** understand
▸ **catch out** *v informal* trap (someone) in an error or lie
▸ **catch phrase** *or* **catchword** *n* well-known and frequently used phrase or slogan
▸ **catch 22** inescapable dilemma
catechism [**kat**-ti-kiz-zum] *n* doctrine of a Christian Church in a series of questions and answers
▸ **catechize** *v* **1** instruct by using a catechism **2** question (someone) thoroughly **catechist** *n*
category Ⓣ *n, pl* **-ries** class or group
▸ **categorical** *adj* absolute or unconditional **categorically** *adv*
▸ **categorize** *v* put in a category **categorization** *n*
cater Ⓣ *v* provide what is needed or wanted, esp. food or services **caterer** *n*
caterpillar *n* **1** wormlike larva of a moth or butterfly **2** ® endless track, driven by cogged wheels, used to propel a heavy vehicle.
caterwaul *v* wail, yowl
Catesby *n* **Robert**. 1573–1605, English conspirator, leader of the Gunpowder Plot (1605): killed while resisting arrest
catharsis [kath-**thar**-siss] *n, pl* **-ses** release of strong suppressed emotions **cathartic** *adj*
cathedral *n* principal church of a diocese
Catherine *n* **Saint**. died 307 AD, legendary Christian martyr of Alexandria, who was tortured on a spiked wheel and beheaded
Catherine I *n* ?1684–1727, second wife of Peter the Great, whom she succeeded as empress of Russia (1725–27)
Catherine II *n* known as *Catherine the Great*. 1729–96, empress of Russia (1762–96), during whose reign Russia extended her boundaries at the expense of Turkey, Sweden, and Poland: she was a patron of literature and the arts
Catherine de' Medici, **Catherine de Médicis** *n* 1519–89, queen of Henry II of France; mother of Francis II, Charles IX, and Henry III of France; regent of France (1560–74). She was largely responsible for the massacre of Protestants on Saint Bartholomew's Day (1572)
Catherine wheel *n* rotating firework
catheter [**kath**-it-er] *n* tube inserted into a body cavity to drain fluid
cathode *n* negative electrode, by which electrons leave a circuit
▸ **cathode rays** stream of electrons from a cathode in a vacuum tube
catholic *adj* **1** (of tastes or interests) covering a wide range ▷ *n, adj* **2 Catholic** (member) of the Roman Catholic Church **Catholicism** *n*
Catiline *n* Latin name *Lucius Sergius Catilina*. ?108–62 BC, Roman politician: organized an unsuccessful conspiracy against Cicero (63–62) **Catilinarian** *adj*
Cato *n* **1 Marcus Porcius**, known as *Cato the Elder* or *the Censor*. 234–149 BC, Roman statesman and writer, noted for his relentless opposition to Carthage **2** his great-grandson, **Marcus Porcius**, known as *Cato the Younger* or *Uticensis*. 95–46 BC, Roman statesman, general, and Stoic philosopher; opponent of Catiline and Caesar
cattle Ⓣ *pl n* domesticated cows, bulls, or oxen
Cattrall *n* **Kim**. born 1956, Canadian film and TV actress born in England. Noted for her role as Samantha Jones in the TV series *Sex and the City* (1998–2004) and the subsequent movie version (2008)
Caucasoid *adj* of the light-skinned racial group of mankind
caucus *n, pl* **-cuses 1** local committee or faction of a political party **2** political meeting to decide future plans
caught *v* past of **catch**

THESAURUS

catching *adj* = **infectious**, contagious, communicable, transferable, transmittable
catchword *n* = **slogan**, password, motto, byword, watchword
catchy *adj* = **memorable**, popular, haunting, captivating
categorical *adj* = **absolute**, positive, express, explicit, downright, unconditional, emphatic, unequivocal, unqualified, unambiguous, unreserved
categorize *v* = **classify**, class, sort, peg (*informal*)
category *n* = **class**, group, set, type, sort, genre, classification, subgenre • *The items were organized into six different categories.*
See also: **kind, variety**
cater *v* = **provide**, supply, outfit, furnish, purvey
cattle *pl n* = **cows**, stock, livestock, beasts, bovines
catty *adj* = **spiteful**, malicious, venomous,

DICTIONARY

caul *n anat* membrane sometimes covering a child's head at birth
cauldron *n* large pot used for boiling
Caulfield *n* **Patrick (Joseph)**. 1936–2005, British painter and printmaker
cauliflower *n* type of cabbage with an edible white flower head
caulk *v* stop up (cracks, esp. in a ship) with filler
causal *adj* **1** of or being a cause **2** of cause and effect **causally** *adv*
▸ **causality** *or* **causation** *n* relationship of cause and effect
cause Ⓣ *n* **1** aim or principle supported by a person or group **2** something that produces an effect **3** reason or motive ▹ *v* **4** be the cause of
cause célèbre [**kawz** sill-**leb**-ra] *n*, *pl* **causes célèbres** [**kawz** sill-**leb**-ra] controversial legal case or issue
causerie *n* informal talk or piece of writing
causeway *n* raised road or path across water or marshland
caustic Ⓣ *adj* **1** capable of burning by chemical action **2** sarcastic or cutting ▹ *n* **3** caustic substance **caustically** *adv*
cauterize *v* burn (body tissue) with heat or a chemical to treat a wound **cauterization** *n*
caution Ⓣ *n* **1** care, attention to safety **2** warning ▹ *v* **3** warn or advise
▸ **cautionary** *adj* warning
▸ **cautious** *adj* showing caution **cautiously** *adv*
cavalcade Ⓣ *n* procession of people on horseback or in cars
cavalier Ⓣ *adj* **1** arrogant, offhand ▹ *n* **2 Cavalier** supporter of Charles I in the English Civil War
cavalry Ⓣ *n*, *pl* **-ries** mounted troops
cave Ⓣ *n* large hole in a hill or cliff
▸ **caving** *n* sport of exploring caves
▸ **cave in** *v* **1** collapse inwards **2** give in
▸ **caveman** *n* prehistoric cave dweller
caveat [**kav**-vee-at] *n* warning
Cavendish *n* **Henry**. 1731–1810, British physicist and chemist: recognized hydrogen, determined the composition of water, and calculated the density of the earth by an experiment named after him
cavern Ⓣ *n* large cave **cavernous** *adj*
caviar, caviare *n* salted sturgeon roe
cavil *v* **-illing, -illed 1** make petty objections ▹ *n* **2** petty objection
cavity Ⓣ *n*, *pl* **-ties 1** hole **2** decayed area in a tooth
cavort *v* prance, caper
caw *n* **1** cry of a crow, rook, or raven ▹ *v* **2** make this cry
Cawley *n* **Evonne** (née *Goolagong*). born 1951, Australian tennis player: Wimbledon champion 1971 and 1980; Australian champion 1974–76
Caxton *n* **William**. ?1422–91, English printer and translator: published, in Bruges, the first book printed in English (1475) and established the first printing press in England (1477)
cayenne pepper, cayenne *n* hot red spice made from capsicum seeds
Cayley *n* **Arthur**. 1821–93, British mathematician, who invented matrices
cayman *n*, *pl* **-mans** S American reptile similar to an alligator
CB Citizens' Band
CBC Canadian Broadcasting Corporation
CBE Commander of the Order of the British Empire
cc cubic centimetre(s)

THESAURUS

malevolent, rancorous, snide, backbiting, bitchy (*informal*), shrewish
cause *n* **1 = origin**, source, root • *the most common cause of back pain* **2 = aim**, movement, ideal • *dedication to the cause of peace* **3 = reason**, basis, motivation, motive, justification, grounds • *They gave us no cause to believe that.* ▸ *v* **4 = produce**, create, generate, provoke, bring about • *This may cause delays.*
See also: **bring, factor, lead to, prompt, result in**
caustic *adj* **1 = burning**, vitriolic, corrosive, acrid, astringent, biting, corroding, mordant **2 = sarcastic**, scathing, virulent, cutting, acrimonious, vitriolic, pungent, stinging, trenchant
caution *n* **1 = care**, prudence • *Drivers are urged to exercise extreme caution in icy weather.* **2 = warning**, advice, counsel, injunction, admonition ▸ *v* **3 = warn**, reprimand • *The two men were cautioned, but police say they will not be charged.*
See also: **advise**
cautious *adj* **= careful**, tentative, wary, guarded • *a cautious approach* OPPOSITE: daring
See also: **deliberate**
cavalcade *n* **= parade**, train, array, procession, spectacle, march-past
cavalier *adj* **= haughty**, lofty, arrogant, disdainful, lordly, offhand, scornful, supercilious
cavalry *n* **= horsemen**, horse, mounted troops
cave *n* **= hollow**, cavity, den, grotto, cavern ▸ *v* ▹ **cave in** *See* **give**
cavern *n* **= cave**, hollow, pothole
cavernous *adj* **= deep**, sunken, hollow, yawning
cavity *n* **= hollow**, hole, gap, pit, dent, crater

DICTIONARY

Cd *chem* cadmium
CD compact disc
CD-ROM compact disc read-only memory
CDT Central Daylight Time
cease Ⓣ *v* bring or come to an end **ceaseless** *adj* **ceaselessly** *adv*
▸ **cease-fire** *n* **1** order to stop firing **2** temporary truce
Cecilia *n* **Saint.** died ?230 AD, Roman martyr; patron saint of music. Feast day: Nov 22
cedar *n* **1** large evergreen tree **2** its wood
cede Ⓣ *v* surrender (territory or legal rights)
cedilla *n* hooklike symbol (¸) placed under a letter *c* to show that it is pronounced *s*, not *k*
Ceefax *n* ® BBc teletext service
CEGEP [**see**-jep] *Canad* (in Quebec) Collège d'enseignement général et professionnel: a post-secondary educational institution providing university preparation and training for trades and professions
ceilidh [**kay**-lee] *n* informal social gathering for singing and dancing, esp. in Scotland
ceiling Ⓣ *n* **1** inner upper surface of a room **2** upper limit set on something
celandine *n* wild plant with yellow flowers
celebrate Ⓣ *v* **1** hold festivities to mark (a happy event, anniversary, etc.) **2** perform (a religious ceremony) **celebration** *n*
▸ **celebrated** *adj* famous
▸ **celebrant** *n* person who performs a religious ceremony
▸ **celebrity** *n* **1** famous person **2** fame
celeriac [sill-**ler**-ee-ak] *n* kind of celery with a large turnip-like root
celerity [sill-**ler**-rit-tee] *n* swiftness
celery *n* vegetable with crisp juicy edible stalks
celestial Ⓣ *adj* **1** heavenly, divine **2** of the sky
celibate *adj* **1** unmarried or abstaining from sex, esp. because of a religious vow of chastity ▹ *n* **2** celibate person **celibacy** *n*
Céline *n* **Louis-Ferdinand**, real name *Louis-Ferdinand Destouches.* 1894–1961, French novelist and physician; became famous with his controversial first novel *Journey to the End of the Night* (1932)
cell Ⓣ *n* **1** smallest unit of an organism that is able to function independently **2** small room for a prisoner, monk, or nun **3** small compartment **4** small group operating as the core of a larger organization **5** device which generates electrical energy from a chemical reaction
▸ **cellular** *adj* **1** of or consisting of cells **2** woven with an open texture
▸ **cell phone** *or* **cellular phone** telephone operating by radio communication via a network of transmitters each serving a small area
cellar *n* **1** underground room for storage **2** stock of wine
Cellini *n* **Benvenuto.** 1500–71, Italian sculptor, goldsmith, and engraver, noted also for his autobiography
cello [**chell**-oh] *n, pl* **-los** low-pitched instrument of the violin family **cellist** *n*
Cellophane *n* ® thin transparent cellulose sheeting used as wrapping
cellulite *n* fat deposits under the skin alleged to resist dieting
celluloid *n* **1** plastic formerly used to make photographic film **2** cinema or films generally

THESAURUS

cease *v* **1 = stop**, end, finish, be over, come to an end, die away • *Almost miraculously, the noise ceased.* OPPOSITE: begin **2 = discontinue**, stop, finish, suspend, desist from, give up • *A small number of companies have ceased doing business.* OPPOSITE: start
See also: **disappear, fail, halt, vanish**
ceaseless *adj* **= continual**, constant, endless, eternal, perpetual, nonstop, incessant, interminable, everlasting, never-ending, twenty-four-seven (*slang*), unremitting
cede *v* **= surrender**, resign, transfer, concede, yield, renounce, relinquish, hand over, make over
ceiling *See* **maximum**
celebrate *v* **1 = rejoice**, party, commemorate • *I was in a mood to celebrate.* OPPOSITE: mourn **2 = perform**, bless, honour, solemnize
celebrated *adj* **= well-known**, popular, famous, prominent, acclaimed, renowned, notable, marquee, illustrious, distinguished, eminent
celebration *n* **1 = party**, festival, gala, festivity • *his eightieth birthday celebration* **2 = performance**, anniversary, remembrance, commemoration, observance, honouring, solemnization
celebrity *n* **1 = personality**, name, star, superstar, VIP, big name • *At the age of twelve, he was already a celebrity.* **2 = fame**, reputation, distinction, prominence, stardom, prestige, renown, repute, notability
See also: **success**
celestial *adj* **= heavenly**, spiritual, astral, divine, supernatural, sublime, ethereal, angelic
celibacy *n* **= chastity**, purity, virginity, continence
cell *n* **1 = room**, tank (*slang*), stall, chamber, cavity, compartment, cubicle,

DICTIONARY

cellulose *n* main constituent of plant cell walls, used in making plastics, paper, etc.
Celsius *adj* of the temperature scale in which water freezes at 0° and boils at 100°
Celt [**kelt**] *n* person who speaks a Celtic language
▸ **Celtic** [**kel**-tik, **sel**-tik] *n* **1** group of languages including Gaelic and Welsh ▷ *adj* **2** of the Celts or the Celtic languages
cement Ⓣ *n* **1** fine grey powder mixed with water and sand to make mortar or concrete **2** adhesive **3** material used to fill teeth ▷ *v* **4** join, bind, or cover with cement **5** make (a relationship) stronger
cemetery Ⓣ *n, pl* **-teries** burial ground not attached to a church
cenotaph *n* monument honouring soldiers who died in a war
censer *n* container for burning incense
censor Ⓣ *v* **1** ban or cut parts of (a film, book, etc.) considered obscene or otherwise unacceptable ▷ *n* **2** official employed to examine and censor films, books, etc.
censorship *n* **censorial** *adj*
▸ **censorious** *adj* harshly critical
censure Ⓣ *n* **1** severe disapproval ▷ *v* **2** criticize severely
census *n, pl* **-suses** official count, esp. of population
cent *n* hundredth part of a monetary unit such as the dollar
centaur *n* mythical creature resembling a horse with the head, arms, and torso of a man
centenary [sen-**teen**-a-ree] *n, pl* **-naries** 100th anniversary or its celebration
▸ **centenarian** *n* person at least 100 years old
▸ **centennial** *n* centenary
centigrade *adj* same as **Celsius**
centigram, centigramme *n* hundredth part of a gram
centilitre *n* hundredth part of a litre
centime [**son**-teem] *n* hundredth part of a franc
centimetre *n* hundredth part of a metre
centipede *n* small wormlike creature with many legs
central Ⓣ *adj* **1** of, at, or forming the centre **2** main or principal **centrally** *adv* **centrality** *n*
▸ **centralism** *n* principle of central control of a country or organization
▸ **centralize** *v* bring under central control
centralization *n*
▸ **central heating** system for heating a building from one central source of heat
Central Daylight Time *n* one of the standard times used in North America, five hours behind Greenwich Mean Time Abbreviation: **CDT**
Central Standard Time *n* one of the standard times used in North America, six hours behind Greenwich Mean Time Abbreviation: **CST**
centre, center Ⓣ *n* **1** middle point or part **2** place for a specified activity **3** political party or group favouring moderation **4** *sports* player who plays in the middle of the field **5** *hockey* forward who plays between the two wingers ▷ *v* **6** move towards, put, or be at the centre
▸ **centre field** *baseball* part of the outfield between right field and left field
▸ **centre fielder** *baseball* fielder who covers centre field
▸ **centre on** *v* have as a centre or main theme
▸ **centrist** *n, adj* (person) favouring political moderation
▸ **centrifugal** *adj* moving away from the centre
▸ **centrifuge** *n* machine which separates substances by centrifugal force
▸ **centripetal** *adj* moving towards the centre

THESAURUS

dungeon **2 = unit**, group, core, caucus, nucleus, coterie
cement *n* **1 = mortar**, gum, paste, glue, plaster, adhesive, sealant ▸ *v* **2 = stick together**, join, bond, combine, seal, bind, unite, attach, glue, plaster, weld
cemetery *n* **= graveyard**, necropolis, burial ground, churchyard, God's acre
censor *v* **= cut**, blue-pencil, bowdlerize, expurgate
censorious *adj* **= critical**, severe, scathing, captious, carping, cavilling, condemnatory, disapproving, disparaging, fault-finding, hypercritical
censure *n* **1 = disapproval**, blame, criticism, condemnation, reproach • *a controversial policy that has attracted international censure* ▸ *v* **2 = criticize**, condemn, denounce, pan (*informal*), reproach • *He should not have been censured for his personal opinions.*
See also: **abuse, accuse, attack, fault**
central *adj* **1 = middle**, mean, interior, inner, median, mid **2 = main**, chief, key, primary, principal, essential, fundamental, focal
centralize *v* **= unify**, concentrate, incorporate, streamline, rationalize, condense
centre *n* **1 = middle**, heart, focus, core, hub, pivot, nucleus, kernel, midpoint • *the centre of the room* OPPOSITE: edge ▸ *v* **2 = focus**, concentrate, cluster, revolve, converge • *All his thoughts were centred around himself.*
See also: **base**

DICTIONARY

centurion *n* Roman officer commanding 100 men
century *n, pl* **-ries 1** period of 100 years **2** cricket score of 100
CEO chief executive officer
cephalopod [**seff**-a-loh-pod] *n* sea mollusc with a head and tentacles, such as the octopus
ceramic *n* **1** hard brittle material made by firing clay **2** object made of this **ceramics 3** art of producing ceramic objects ▷ *adj* **4** made of ceramic **5** of ceramics
cereal *n* **1** grass plant with edible grain, such as wheat or rice **2** this grain **3** breakfast food made from this grain
cerebellum [serr-rib-**bell**-lum] *n, pl* **-s, -la** [-la] rear part of the brain
cerebral [**ser**-rib-ral] *adj* **1** of the brain **2** intellectual
▸ **cerebrum** *n* main part of the human brain
ceremony Ⓣ *n, pl* **-nies 1** formal act or ritual **2** formally polite behaviour **ceremonial** *adj, n* **ceremonially** *adv* **ceremonious** *adj* **ceremoniously** *adv*
cerise [ser-**reess**] *adj* cherry-red
cert *n informal* certainty: *a dead cert*
certain Ⓣ *adj* **1** sure, without doubt **2** reliable or unerring **3** some but not much **certainly** *adv*
▸ **certainty** *n* **1** state of being sure **2** thing sure to happen
certificate Ⓣ *n* official document stating the details of a birth, death, etc.
certify Ⓣ *v* **-fying, -fied 1** declare formally or officially **2** declare (someone) legally insane **certifiable** *adj* **certification** *n*
certitude *n* confidence, certainty
cerulean [ser-**rule**-ee-an] *adj* of a deep blue colour
Cervantes *n* **Miguel de**, full surname *Cervantes Saavedra*. 1547–1616, Spanish dramatist, poet, and prose writer, most famous for *Don Quixote* (1605), which satirizes the chivalric romances and greatly influenced the development of the novel
cervix *n, pl* **cervixes, cervices 1** narrow entrance of the womb **2** neck **cervical** [**ser**-vik-kl, ser-**vie**-kl] *adj*
cesium, caesium *n* silvery-white metallic element used in photocells
cessation *n* ceasing
cesspool, cesspit *n* covered tank or pit for sewage
cetacean [sit-**tay**-shun] *n, adj* (member) of the whale family
Cézanne *n* **Paul**. 1839–1906, French postimpressionist painter, who was a major influence on modern art, esp. cubism, in stressing the structural elements latent in nature, such as the sphere and the cone
cf. compare
CFC chlorofluorocarbon
CFL Canadian Football League
CGI computer-generated image(s)
ch. 1 chapter **2** church
Chabrier *n* (**Alexis**) **Emmanuel**. 1841–94, French composer; noted esp. for the orchestral rhapsody *España* (1883)
cha-cha-cha, cha-cha *n* (music for) a modern ballroom dance from Latin America
Chadwick *n* Sir **James**. 1891–1974, British physicist: discovered the neutron (1932): Nobel prize for physics 1935
chafe Ⓣ *v* **1** make or become sore or worn by rubbing **2** make or be impatient or annoyed
chafer *n* large beetle

THESAURUS

ceremonial *adj* **1** = **ritual**, formal, solemn, stately, liturgical, ritualistic ▸ *n* **2** = **ritual**, ceremony, rite, formality, solemnity
ceremonious *adj* = **formal**, civil, stiff, solemn, dignified, stately, courteous, deferential, punctilious
ceremony *n* **1** = **ritual**, service, rite, observance, pomp • *The awards ceremony was followed by a banquet*. **2** = **formality**, protocol, etiquette, decorum, niceties • *He hung up without ceremony*.
certain *adj* **1** = **definite**, inevitable, definitive, established, guaranteed, sure, undeniable, known • *One thing is certain – they respect each other*. OPPOSITE: uncertain **2** = **sure**, clear, positive, confident, convinced, definite, satisfied • *She's absolutely certain she's going to win*. OPPOSITE: uncertain **3** = **known**, true, conclusive, unequivocal, undeniable, irrefutable, incontrovertible **4** = **inevitable**, sure, bound, definite, inescapable, destined, fated
See also: **necessary**
certainly *adv* = **definitely**, undoubtedly, undeniably, unquestionably, without doubt • *I'll certainly do all I can to help*. ▷ **certainly not** See **no**
See also: **really**
certainty *n* **1** = **sureness**, trust, confidence, conviction, faith, assurance, validity, positiveness **2** = **fact**, reality, truth, sure thing (*informal*)
certificate *n* = **document**, warrant, license, authorization, credential *or* credentials, diploma, voucher, testimonial
certified See **official**
certify *v* = **confirm**, declare, testify, guarantee, assure, verify, authenticate, validate, attest
chafe *v* **1** = **rub**, scratch, scrape, rasp, abrade **2** = **be annoyed**, worry, rage,

DICTIONARY

chaff Ⓣ *n* **1** grain husks **2** chopped hay and straw used to feed cattle **3** light-hearted teasing ▷ *v* **4** tease good-naturedly
Chagall *n* **Marc**. 1887–1985, French painter and illustrator, born in Russia, noted for his richly coloured pictures of men, animals, and objects in fantastic combinations and often suspended in space: his work includes 12 stained glass windows for a synagogue in Jerusalem (1961) and the decorations for the ceiling of the Paris Opera House (1964)
chagrin [**shag**-grin] *n* **1** annoyance and embarrassment ▷ *v* **2** annoy and embarrass
chain Ⓣ *n* **1** flexible length of connected metal links **2** connected series of things or events **3** group of shops, hotels, etc. owned by one firm **4** unit of length equal to 22 yards
▶ **pull someone's chain** *informal* tease, mislead, or harass ▷ *v* **5** confine or fasten with or as if with a chain
▶ **chain reaction** series of events, each of which causes the next
▶ **chain-smoke** *v* smoke (cigarettes) continuously **chain-smoker** *n*
chair *n* **1** seat with a back, for one person **2** official position of authority **3** person holding this **4** professorship ▷ *v* **5** preside over (a meeting)
▶ **chair lift** series of chairs on a cable for carrying people, esp. skiers, up a slope
▶ **chairman, chairperson,** *or* **chairwoman** *n* person who presides over a meeting
chaise [**shaze**] *n* light horse-drawn carriage
chaise longue [**long**] *n* sofa with a back and single armrest
chalcedony [kal-**sed**-don-ee] *n, pl* **-nies** variety of quartz
chalet *n* **1** kind of Swiss wooden house **2** house like this, used as a holiday home
chalice [**chal**-liss] *n* large goblet
chalk *n* **1** soft white rock consisting of calcium carbonate **2** piece of this, often coloured, used for drawing and writing on blackboards ▷ *v* **3** draw or mark with chalk
chalky *adj*
challenge Ⓣ *v* **1** invite (someone) to take part in a contest or fight **2** call (something) into question **3** order (someone) to stop and be identified **4** be difficult but stimulating to ▷ *n* **5** act of challenging **challenger** *n*
▶ **challenged** *adj* disabled as specified: *physically challenged; mentally challenged*
chamber Ⓣ *n* **1** hall used for formal meetings **2** legislative or judicial assembly **3** compartment or cavity **4** *obsolete* bedroom **chambers 5** set of rooms used as offices by a barrister
▶ **chamberlain** *n* official who manages the household of a king or nobleman
▶ **chambermaid** *n* woman employed to clean bedrooms in a hotel
▶ **chamber music** classical music to be played by a small group of players
▶ **chamber pot** bowl for urine, formerly used in bedrooms
Chamberlain *n* (**Arthur**) **Neville**. 1869–1940, British Conservative statesman; prime minister (1937–40): pursued a policy of appeasement towards Germany; following the German invasion of Poland, he declared war on Germany on Sept 3, 1939
chameleon [kam-**meal**-ee-yon] *n* small lizard that changes colour according to its surroundings
chamfer [**cham**-fer] *v* bevel the edge of
chamois [**sham**-wah] *n, pl* **-ois 1** small mountain antelope **2** [**sham**-ee] soft leather **3** [**sham**-ee] cloth of this
chamomile [**kam**-mo-mile] *n* same as **camomile**
champ[1] *v* **1** chew noisily **2** be impatient
champ[2] *n* short for **champion**
champagne *n* sparkling white French wine
champion Ⓣ *n* **1** overall winner of a competition **2** someone who defends a person

THESAURUS

fume, fret, be impatient
chaff[1] *n* = **waste**, refuse, garbage, trash, dregs, remains, husks
chaff[2] *v* = **tease**, mock, rib (*informal*), taunt, scoff, ridicule
chain *n* **1** = **link**, bond, shackle, coupling, fetter, manacle **2** = **series**, set, train, string, sequence, progression, succession ▶ *v* **3** = **bind**, handcuff, restrain, confine, tether, shackle, enslave, fetter, manacle
chairman *n* = **director**, president, spokesman, speaker, chairwoman, chairperson, master of ceremonies
challenge *n* **1** = **dare** • *They issued a challenge to their rivals.* **2** = **test**, trial, question, confrontation, provocation, ultimatum, throwdown (*slang*) ▶ *v* **3** = **dare**, defy • *He challenged his rival to a duel.* **4** = **question**, dispute, throw down (*slang*) • *challenging the authority of the government* **5** = **test**, question, dispute, tackle, defy, confront, object to, throw down the gauntlet
See also: **contest, query**
challenger *See* **competitor, rival**
challenging *See* **formidable**
chamber *n* **1** = **room**, apartment, hall, bedroom, compartment, enclosure, cubicle **2** = **council**, legislature, assembly, legislative body
champion *n* **1** = **winner**, hero, victor, title holder • *the world chess champion* **2** = **defender**, advocate, guardian,

DICTIONARY

or cause ▷ *v* **3** support ▷ *adj* **4** excellent
championship *n*
Champlain *n* **Samuel de.** ?1567–1635, French explorer; founder of Quebec (1608) and governor of New France (1633–35)
chance Ⓣ *n* **1** likelihood, probability **2** opportunity **3** risk, gamble **4** unpredictable element that causes things to happen one way rather than another ▷ *v* **5** risk **6** happen by chance ▷ *adj* **7** accidental
▸ **chancy** *adj* risky
chancel *n* part of a church containing the altar and choir
chancellor *n* **1** state or legal officer of high rank **2** head of a university **chancellorship** *n*
Chancery *n* division of the British High Court of Justice
chancre [**shang**-ker] *n* small hard growth which is the first sign of syphilis
chandelier [shan-dill-**eer**] *n* hanging branched holder for lights
chandler *n* dealer, esp. in ships' supplies
Chandler *n* **Raymond** (**Thornton**). 1888–1959, US thriller writer: created Philip Marlowe, one of the first detective heroes in fiction
Chandrasekhar *n* **Subrahmanyan.** 1910–95, US astronomer, born in Lahore, India (now Pakistan). His work on stellar evolution led to an understanding of white dwarfs: shared the Nobel prize for physics 1983
change Ⓣ *n* **1** becoming different **2** variety or novelty **3** different set **4** balance received when the amount paid is more than the cost of a purchase **5** coins of low value ▷ *v* **6** make or become different **7** interchange or exchange **8** exchange (money) for its equivalent in a smaller denomination or different currency **9** put different clothes or coverings on **10** leave one vehicle and board another
▸ **changeable** *adj* changing often
▸ **changeling** *n* child believed to have been exchanged by fairies for another
▸ **change up** *baseball* slow pitch thrown like a fast pitch to deceive the batter
channel Ⓣ *n* **1** band of broadcasting frequencies **2** means of access or communication **3** broad strait connecting two areas of sea **4** course along which a river, shipping, etc. moves **5** groove ▷ *v* **-nelling, -nelled 6** direct or convey through a channel
chant Ⓣ *v* **1** sing or utter (a psalm or slogan) ▷ *n* **2** rhythmic or repetitious slogan **3** psalm with a short simple melody
chanter *n* (on bagpipes) pipe on which the melody is played
chaos Ⓣ *n* complete disorder or confusion
chaotic *adj* **chaotically** *adv*
chap Ⓣ *n informal* man or boy
chapatti, chapati *n* (in Indian cookery) flat thin unleavened bread
chapel *n* **1** place of worship with its own altar, within a church **2** similar place of worship in a large house or institution **3** Nonconformist place of worship **4** section of

THESAURUS

protector • *He received acclaim as a champion of the oppressed.* ▸ *v* **3 = support**, defend, promote, uphold, stick up for (*informal*), fight for • *He passionately championed the poor.* *See also*: **supporter**
championship *See* **competition**
chance *n* **1 = probability**, possibility, prospect, likelihood, odds • *a good chance of success* **2 = opportunity**, time, opening, occasion • *He didn't give me a chance to explain.* **3 = luck**, accident, fortune, coincidence • *events that were merely the result of chance* RELATED WORD *adj*: fortuitous **4 = risk**, speculation, gamble, uncertainty, hazard, jeopardy ▸ *v* **5 = risk**, try, stake, gamble, venture, hazard, endanger, jeopardize, wager *See also*: **accidental, casual, fate, turn, unexpected, unpredictable**
chances *See* **probability**
chancy *adj* (*Slang*) **= dangerous**, difficult, risky, hazardous, perilous
change *n* **1 = alteration**, difference, transformation, modification • *a change in her attitude* **2 = variety**, break (*informal*), departure, variation, diversion, novelty **3 = exchange**, trade, swap, conversion, substitution, interchange ▸ *v* **4 = alter**, reform, convert, moderate, modify, transform • *My views have changed since I began working here.* **5 = exchange**, trade, replace, swap, substitute, interchange, barter • *Can I change this sweater for one a size bigger?* *See also*: **adapt, affect, reverse, turn, vary**
changeable *adj* **= variable**, volatile, unpredictable, unstable, irregular, erratic, fickle • *changeable weather* OPPOSITE: constant
channel *n* **1 = route**, way, medium, course, approach, path, means, artery, avenue **2 = passage**, route, canal, groove, duct, strait, gutter, conduit, furrow ▸ *v* **3 = direct**, conduct, guide, transmit, convey
chant *v* **1 = sing**, chorus, recite, carol, intone, descant, warble ▸ *n* **2 = song**, chorus, melody, carol, psalm
chaos *n* **= disorder**, confusion, mayhem, lawlessness, pandemonium, anarchy, tumult, bedlam, disorganization
chaotic *adj* **= disordered**, confused, tumultuous, lawless, uncontrolled, topsy-turvy, anarchic, deranged, disorganized, riotous
chap *n* (*Informal*) **= fellow**, man, person, guy

DICTIONARY

a trade union in the print industry
chaperone Ⓣ [**shap**-per-rone] *n* **1** older person who accompanies and supervises a young person ▷ *v* **2** act as a chaperone to
chaplain *n* cleric attached to a chapel, military body, or institution **chaplaincy** *n*
chaplet *n* garland for the head
Chaplin *n* Sir **Charles Spencer**, known as *Charlie Chaplin*. 1889–1977, English comedian, film actor, and director. He is renowned for his portrayal of a downtrodden little man with baggy pants, derby, and cane. His films, most of which were made in Hollywood, include *The Gold Rush* (1924), *Modern Times* (1936), and *The Great Dictator* (1940) **Chaplinesque** *adj*
chapped *adj* (of the skin) raw and cracked, through exposure to cold
chaps *pl n* cowboy's leggings of thick leather
chapter Ⓣ *n* **1** division of a book **2** period in a life or history **3** branch of a society or club **4** group of canons of a cathedral
char[1] Ⓣ *v* **charring, charred** blacken by partial burning
char[2] *Brit informal* ▷ *n* **1** charwoman ▷ *v* **charring, charred 2** work as a charwoman
char[3] *n Brit slang* tea
character Ⓣ *n* **1** combination of qualities distinguishing an individual **2** moral strength **3** reputation, esp. good reputation **4** person represented in a play, film, or story **5** notable or eccentric person **6** letter, numeral, or symbol used in writing or printing
▸ **characteristic** *n* **1** distinguishing feature or quality ▷ *adj* **2** distinguishing **characteristically** *adv*
▸ **characterize** *v* **1** be a characteristic of **2** describe the character of **characterization** *n*
charade Ⓣ [shar-**rahd**] *n* **1** absurd pretence **charades 2** game in which one team acts out a word, which the other team has to guess
charcoal *n* black substance formed by partially burning wood
Charcot *n* **Jean Martin**. 1825–93, French neurologist, noted for his attempt using hypnotism to find an organic cause for hysteria, which influenced Freud
Charest *n* **Jean**. born 1958, Canadian politician, Premier of Quebec (2003–07; 2007; 2008–)
charge Ⓣ *v* **1** ask as a price **2** enter a debit against (a person or an account) **3** accuse formally **4** assign a task to **5** make a rush or sudden attack (upon) **6** fill (a battery) with electricity **7** fill or load ▷ *n* **8** price charged **9** formal accusation **10** attack or rush **11** command or exhortation **12** custody **13** person or thing entrusted to someone's care **14** amount of electricity stored in a battery **chargeable** *adj*
▸ **in charge** in command
▸ **charger** *n* **1** device for charging an accumulator **2** horse used in battle
chargé d'affaires [**shar**-zhay daf-**fair**] *n*, *pl* **chargés d'affaires** head of a diplomatic mission in the absence of an ambassador or in a small or unimportant mission
chariot *n* two-wheeled horse-drawn vehicle used in ancient times in wars and races
▸ **charioteer** *n* chariot driver

THESAURUS

(*informal*), individual, character
chaperone *n* **1 = escort**, companion ▸ *v* **2 = escort**, protect, attend, accompany, safeguard, shepherd, watch over
chapter *n* **= section**, part, period, stage, division, phase, episode, topic, clause
char *See* **burn**
character *n* **1 = personality**, makeup, temperament, nature • *He has a dark side to his character.* **2 = integrity**, honour, strength • *She showed real character in her attempt to win over the crowd.* **3 = role**, part, portrayal, persona **4 = eccentric**, card (*informal*), original, oddball (*informal*) **5 = symbol**, sign, mark, figure, letter, device, hieroglyph, rune
See also: **individual, name, reputation**
characteristic *n* **1 = feature**, quality, property, attribute, trait • *His chief characteristic is honesty.* ▸ *adj* **2 = typical**, distinctive, distinguishing • *She responded with characteristic generosity.* OPPOSITE: uncharacteristic
See also: **individual, point, representative, special**
characterize *v* **= identify**, mark, represent, indicate, brand, stamp, distinguish, typify
charade *n* **= pretense**, fake, parody, farce, travesty, pantomime
charge *v* **1 = ask (for)**, bill, levy • *Most electricians charge a fair price.* **2 = rush**, storm, dash, stampede • *He charged into the room.* **3 = accuse**, blame, indict, arraign, incriminate, impeach **4 = fill**, load **5 = command**, order, bid, demand, require, commit, instruct, entrust ▸ *n* **6 = price**, cost, fee, payment • *We can arrange this for a small charge.* **7 = accusation**, allegation, indictment, imputation **8 = rush**, attack, assault, onset, stampede, onslaught, sortie **9 = care**, office, trust, duty, responsibility, custody, safekeeping **10 = ward** **11 = instruction**, order, demand, direction, command, mandate, injunction, precept
See also: **rate, tear**
charges *See* **bill**

DICTIONARY

charisma Ⓣ [kar-**rizz**-ma] *n* person's power to attract or influence people **charismatic** [kar-rizz-**mat**-ik] *adj*
charity Ⓣ *n, pl* **-ties 1** organization that helps those in need **2** giving of help, such as money or food, to those in need **3** help given **4** kindly attitude towards people **charitable** *adj* **charitably** *adv*
charlady *n* same as **charwoman**
charlatan Ⓣ [**shar**-lat-tan] *n* person who claims expertise that he or she does not have
Charlemagne *n* ?742–814 AD, king of the Franks (768–814) and, as Charles I, Holy Roman Emperor (800–814). He conquered the Lombards (774), the Saxons (772–804), and the Avars (791–799). He instituted many judicial and ecclesiastical reforms, and promoted commerce and agriculture throughout his empire, which extended from the Ebro to the Elbe. Under Alcuin his court at Aachen became the centre of a revival of learning
Charles *n* **1 Prince**, Prince of Wales. born 1948, son of Elizabeth II; heir apparent to the throne of Great Britain and Northern Ireland. He married (1981) Lady Diana Spencer; they separated in 1992 and were divorced in 1996; their son, Prince William of Wales, was born in 1982 and their second son, Prince Henry (known as Harry), in 1984. He married Camilla Parker Bowles (now Duchess of Cornwell) in 2005 **2 Ray** real name *Ray Charles Robinson*. 1930–2004, US singer, pianist, and songwriter, whose work spans jazz, blues, gospel, pop, and country music
Charles I *n* **1** title as Holy Roman Emperor of **Charlemagne 2** title as king of France of **Charles II** (Holy Roman Emperor) **3** title as king of Spain of **Charles V** (Holy Roman Emperor) **4** title of *Charles Stuart*. 1600–49, king of England, Scotland, and Ireland (1625–49); son of James I. He ruled for 11 years (1629–40) without parliament, advised by his minister Strafford, until rebellion broke out in Scotland. Conflict with the Long Parliament led to the Civil War and after his defeat at Naseby (1645) he sought refuge with the Scots (1646). He was handed over to the English army under Cromwell (1647) and executed **5** 1887–1922, emperor of Austria, and, as Charles IV, king of Hungary (1916–18). The last ruler of the Austro-Hungarian monarchy, he was forced to abdicate at the end of World War I
Charles II *n* **1** known as *Charles the Bald*. 823–877 AD, Holy Roman Emperor (875–877) and, as Charles I, king of France (843–877) **2** the title as king of France of **Charles III** (Holy Roman Emperor) **3** 1630–85, king of England, Scotland, and Ireland (1660–85) following the Restoration (1660); son of Charles I. He did much to promote commerce, science, and the Navy, but his Roman Catholic sympathies caused widespread distrust **4** 1661–1700, the last Hapsburg king of Spain: his reign saw the end of Spanish power in Europe
Charles III *n* **1** known as *Charles the Fat*. 839–888 AD, Holy Roman Emperor (881–887) and, as Charles II, king of France (884–887). He briefly reunited the empire of Charlemagne **2** 1716–88, king of Spain (1759–88), who curbed the power of the Church and tried to modernize his country
Charles IV *n* **1** known as *Charles the Fair*. 1294–1328, king of France (1322–28): brother of Isabella of France, with whom he intrigued against her husband, Edward II of England **2** 1316–78, king of Bohemia (1346–78) and Holy Roman Emperor (1355–78) **3** 1748–1819, king of Spain (1788–1808), whose reign saw the domination of Spain by Napoleonic France: abdicated **4** title as king of Hungary of **Charles I** (sense 5)
Charles V *n* **1** known as *Charles the Wise*. 1337–80, king of France (1364–80) during the Hundred Years' War **2** 1500–58, Holy Roman Emperor (1519–56), king of Burgundy and the Netherlands (1506–55), and, as Charles I, king of Spain (1516–56): his reign saw the empire threatened by Francis I of France, the Turks, and the spread of Protestantism; abdicated
Charles VI *n* **1** known as *Charles the Mad* or *Charles the Well-Beloved*. 1368–1422, king of France (1380–1422): defeated by Henry V of England at Agincourt (1415), he was forced by the Treaty of Troyes (1420) to recognize Henry as his successor **2** 1685–1740, Holy Roman Emperor (1711–40). His claim to the Spanish throne (1700) led to

THESAURUS

charisma *n* = **charm**, lure, personality, attraction, allure, magnetism, mojo (*slang*)
charismatic *adj* = **charming**, attractive, influential, magnetic, alluring, enticing
charitable *adj* **1** = **tolerant**, understanding, sympathetic, humane, lenient, kindly, considerate, favourable, forgiving, indulgent, magnanimous **2** = **generous**, liberal, kind, lavish, bountiful, philanthropic, benevolent, beneficent
charity *n* **1** = **donations**, help, fund, relief, gift, assistance, endowment, largesse *or* largess, philanthropy, benefaction, contributions, hand-out **2** = **kindness**, humanity, compassion, goodwill, generosity, altruism, indulgence, benevolence, fellow feeling
charlatan *n* = **fraud**, fake, cheat, phony (*informal*), sham, impostor, quack, pretender, con man (*informal*), swindler

DICTIONARY

the War of the Spanish Succession
Charles VII *n* **1** 1403–61, king of France (1422–61), son of Charles VI. He was excluded from the French throne by the Treaty of Troyes, but following Joan of Arc's victory over the English at Orléans (1429), was crowned **2** 1697–1745, Holy Roman Emperor (1742–45) during the War of the Austrian Succession
Charles IX *n* 1550–74, king of France (1560–74), son of Catherine de' Medici and Henry II: his reign was marked by war between Huguenots and Catholics
Charles X *n* **1** title of *Charles Gustavus*. 1622–60, king of Sweden, who warred with Poland and Denmark in an attempt to create a unified Baltic state **2** 1757–1836, king of France (1824–30): his attempt to restore absolutism led to his enforced exile
Charles XI *n* 1655–97, king of Sweden (1660–97), who established an absolute monarchy and defeated Denmark (1678)
Charles XII *n* 1682–1718, king of Sweden (1697–1718), who inflicted defeats on Denmark, Russia, and Poland during the Great Northern War (1700–21)
Charles Martel *n* grandfather of Charlemagne. ?688–741 AD, Frankish ruler of Austrasia (715–41), who checked the Muslim invasion of Europe by defeating the Moors at Poitiers (732)
charleston *n* lively dance of the 1920s
charlotte *n* dessert made with fruit and bread or cake crumbs
charm Ⓣ *n* **1** attractiveness **2** trinket worn on a bracelet **3** magic spell ▷ *v* **4** attract or delight **5** protect or influence as if by magic **6** influence by personal charm **charmer** *n*
▸ **charming** *adj* attractive
charnel house *n* building or vault for the bones of the dead
Charpentier *n* **1 Gustave**. 1860–1956, French composer, whose best-known work is the opera *Louise* (1900) **2 Marc-Antoine**. ?1645–1704, French composer, best known for his sacred music, particularly the *Te Deum*
chart Ⓣ *n* **1** information shown in the form of a diagram, graph, or table **2** map to aid navigation ▷ *v* **3** plot the course of **4** make a chart of
▸ **the charts** *informal* weekly list of best-selling pop records
charter Ⓣ *n* **1** document granting or demanding certain rights **2** constitution of an organization **3** hire of transport for private use ▷ *v* **4** hire by charter **5** grant a charter to
▸ **chartered** *adj* officially qualified to practise a profession: *chartered accountant*
chartreuse [shar-**trerz**] *n* sweet-smelling green or yellow liqueur
charwoman *n* woman who is employed as a cleaner
chary [**chair**-ee] *adj* **-rier, -riest** cautious
charily *adv*
chase[1] Ⓣ *v* **1** run after quickly in order to catch or drive away **2** *informal* hurry **3** *informal* try energetically to obtain ▷ *n* **4** chasing or pursuit
▸ **chaser** *n* drink drunk after another of a different kind
chase[2] *v* engrave or emboss (metal)
chasm Ⓣ [**kaz**-zum] *n* deep crack or ravine in the earth
chassis [**shass**-ee] *n, pl* **-sis** frame, wheels, and mechanical parts of a motor vehicle
chaste Ⓣ *adj* **1** refraining from sex outside marriage or altogether **2** (of style) simple
chastely *adv* **chastity** *n*
chasten Ⓣ [**chase**-en] *v* **1** correct by punishment **2** subdue
chastise Ⓣ *v* **1** scold severely **2** punish

C

THESAURUS

charm *n* **1 = attraction**, appeal, allure, fascination, magnetism, mojo (*slang*) • *a man of great charm* **2 = spell**, magic, sorcery, enchantment **3 = talisman**, trinket, fetish, mojo, amulet ▸ *v* **4 = enchant**, entrance, delight, captivate, bewitch • *He charmed the entire audience.*
See also: **beauty, entertain, please**
charmed *See* **lucky**
charming *adj* **= attractive**, cute, appealing, pleasing, delightful, likable *or* likeable, seductive, captivating, fetching, winsome
chart *n* **1 = table**, plan, map, blueprint, graph, diagram, road map ▸ *v* **2 = plot**, draft, shape, outline, sketch, delineate, map out
charter *n* **1 = document**, contract, permit, license, deed, prerogative
▸ *v* **2 = hire**, commission, employ, rent, lease **3 = authorize**, sanction
chase *v* **1 = pursue**, hunt • *She chased the thief until he surrendered.* **2 = drive**, hound • *Angry protestors chased him away.*
▸ *n* **3 = pursuit**, race, hunt, hunting
chasm *n* **= gulf**, gap, crater, ravine, fissure, abyss, gorge, crevasse
chaste *adj* **= pure**, simple, modest, innocent, unaffected, immaculate, virtuous, undefiled
chasten *v* **= subdue**, correct, humble, discipline, tame, humiliate, chastise, put in one's place
chastise *v* **1 = scold**, correct, discipline, censure, castigate, berate, upbraid **2** (*Old-fashioned*) **= beat**, punish, lash, whip, lick (*informal*), scourge, flog
chastity *n* **= purity**, innocence, virtue,

DICTIONARY

by beating **chastisement** *n*
chasuble [**chazz**-yew-bl] *n* long sleeveless outer vestment worn by a priest while celebrating Mass
chat Ⓣ *v* **chatting, chatted 1** talk in an easy familiar way ▷ *n* **2** easy familiar talk **chatty** *adj* **chattily** *adv*
chateau [**shat**-toe] *n, pl* **-teaux, -teaus** French castle or country house
Chateaubriand *n* **1 François René,** Vicomte de Chateaubriand. 1768–1848, French writer and statesman: a precursor of the romantic movement in France; his works include *Le Génie du Christianisme* (1802) and *Mémoires d'outre-tombe* (1849–50) **2** a thick steak cut from the fillet of beef
chatelaine [**shat**-tell-lane] *n* esp. formerly, mistress of a large house or castle
chattels *pl n* movable possessions
chatter Ⓣ *v* **1** talk about trivial matters rapidly and continuously **2** (of the teeth) rattle with cold or fear ▷ *n* **3** idle talk
▸ **chatterbox** *n* person who chatters incessantly
Chatterton *n* **Thomas**. 1752–70, British poet; author of spurious medieval verse and prose: he committed suicide at the age of 17
Chaucer *n* **Geoffrey**. ?1340–1400, English poet, noted for his narrative skill, humour, and insight, particularly in his most famous work, *The Canterbury Tales.* He was influenced by the continental tradition of rhyming verse. His other works include *Troilus and Criseyde, The Legende of Good Women*, and *The Parlement of Foules*
chauffeur *n* person employed to drive a car **chauffeuse** *n fem*
chauvinism Ⓣ [**show**-vin-iz-zum] *n* **1** irrational belief that one's own race, group, or sex is superior **2** fanatical patriotism **chauvinist** *n, adj* **chauvinistic** *adj*
cheap Ⓣ *adj* **1** low in price **2** of poor quality **3** of little value **4** mean, despicable **cheaply** *adv*
▸ **cheapen** *v* **1** make cheap or cheaper **2** degrade
▸ **cheap shot** *informal* cruel or critical remark directed at a person's known weakness
▸ **cheapskate** *n informal* miserly person
cheat Ⓣ *v* **1** act dishonestly to gain profit or advantage **2** deprive (someone) unfairly ▷ *n* **3** person who cheats **4** fraud or deception
check Ⓣ *v* **1** examine or investigate **2** stop or hinder **3** verify ▷ *n* **4** examination or investigation **5** stoppage or restraint **6** *US* cheque **7** pattern of squares or crossing lines **8** *chess* position of a king under attack
▸ **check in** *v* register one's arrival
▸ **checkmate** *n* **1** *chess* winning position in which an opponent's king is under attack and unable to escape **2** utter defeat ▷ *v* **3** *chess* place (an opponent's king) in checkmate **4** defeat
▸ **check out** *v* **1** pay the bill and leave a hotel **2** examine or investigate **3** *informal* have a look at
▸ **checkout** *n* counter in a supermarket, where customers pay
▸ **checkup** *n* general (medical) examination
checker *n* **1** piece used in Chinese checkers **checkers 2** game played on chessboard with flat, round pieces
▸ **checkered** *adj* **1** marked in squares

THESAURUS

celibacy, virginity, modesty, continence, maidenhood
chat *n* **1 = talk**, conversation • *We sat around and had a chat.* ▸ *v* **2 = talk**, gossip • *He was chatting to his father.*
See also: **word**
chatter *n* **1 = prattle**, chat, gossip, gab (*informal*), babble, blather ▸ *v* **2 = prattle**, chat, gossip, gab (*informal*), babble, blather, chew the fat (*slang*), schmooze (*slang*)
chatty *See* **talkative**
chauvinism *See* **prejudice**
cheap *adj* **1 = inexpensive**, bargain, reasonable, economical • *Cheap flights are available.* OPPOSITE: expensive
2 = inferior, tacky, second-rate • *a suit made of some cheap material*
See also: **petty**
cheapen *v* **= degrade**, lower, discredit, disparage, demean, denigrate, devalue, belittle, depreciate, debase
cheat *v* **1 = deceive**, con (*informal*), rip off (*slang*), defraud, dupe, swindle, fleece • *the people he cheated out of their life savings* **2 = deceiver**, shark, trickster, charlatan, con man (*informal*), double-crosser (*informal*), sharper, swindler **3 = deception**, fraud, scam (*slang*), swindle, deceit, trickery, rip-off (*slang*)
See also: **crook**
cheating *See* **dishonesty**
check *v* **1 = examine**, check out (*informal*), test, inspect, crosscheck • *Check all the details first.* **2 = stop**, control, halt, curb, restrain, inhibit • *a policy to check the inflation rate* ▷ **check out** *See* **check, try** ▸ *n* **3 = examination**, test, inspection • *a thorough check of the equipment* **4 = stoppage**, control, curb, restraint, obstacle, obstruction, limitation, constraint, impediment, damper, hindrance
See also: **block, delay, foil, frustrate, hinder, slow (down)**
checkup *See* **examination**

DICTIONARY

2 marked by varied fortunes: *a checkered career*
Cheddar *n* smooth firm cheese
cheek Ⓣ *n* **1** side of the face below the eye **2** *informal* impudence ▷ *v* **3** *informal* speak impudently to
▸ **cheeky** *adj* impudent **cheekily** *adv* **cheekiness** *n*
cheep *n* **1** young bird's high-pitched cry ▷ *v* **2** utter a cheep
cheer Ⓣ *v* **1** applaud or encourage with shouts **2** (often foll. by *up*) make or become happy or hopeful ▷ *n* **3** shout of applause or encouragement **cheerful** *or* **cheery** *adj* **cheerfully** *or* **cheerily** *adv* **cheerfulness** *n*
▸ **cheerless** *adj* gloomy
cheerio *interj Brit informal* goodbye
cheese *n* **1** food made from coagulated milk curd **2** shaped block of this **cheesy** *adj*
▸ **cheeseburger** *n* hamburger with cheese on it
▸ **cheesecake** *n* **1** dessert with a crumb base and a cream cheese filling **2** *slang* photographs of scantily clad women
▸ **cheesecloth** *n* loosely woven cotton cloth
▸ **cheesed off** bored or annoyed
cheetah *n* swift spotted African animal of the cat family
chef *n* cook in a restaurant
chef-d'oeuvre [shay-**durv**] *n, pl* **chefs-d'oeuvre** masterpiece
Chekhov, Chekov *n* **Anton Pavlovich**. 1860–1904, Russian dramatist and short-story writer. His plays include *The Seagull* (1896), *Uncle Vanya* (1900), *The Three Sisters* (1901), and *The Cherry Orchard* (1904) **Chekhovian** *or* **Chekovian** *adj*
chemical *n* **1** substance used in or resulting from a reaction involving changes to atoms or molecules ▷ *adj* **2** of chemistry or chemicals **chemically** *adv*
chemise [shem-**meez**] *n* woman's loose-fitting slip or dress
chemistry *n* science of the composition, properties, and reactions of substances
▸ **chemist** *n* **1** specialist in chemistry **2** *Brit* pharmacist
chemotherapy *n* treatment of disease by chemical means
Cheney *n* **Richard B**(**ruce**), known as *Dick*. born 1941, US Republican politician; vice-president 2001–2009
Chénier *n* **1** **André** (**Marie de**). 1762–94, French poet; his work was influenced by the ancient Greek elegiac poets. He was guillotined during the French Revolution **2** his brother, **Marie-Joseph** (**Blaise de**). 1764–1811, French dramatist and politician. He wrote patriotic songs and historical plays, such as *Charles IX* (1789)
chenille [shen-**neel**] *n* (fabric of) thick tufty yarn
Cheops *n* original name *Khufu*. Egyptian king of the fourth dynasty (?2613–?2494 BC), who built the largest pyramid at El Gîza
cheque *n* written order to one's bank to pay money from one's account
chequer *n* same as **checker**
cherish Ⓣ *v* **1** care for **2** hold dear **3** cling to (an idea or feeling)
cheroot [sher-**root**] *n* cigar with both ends cut flat
cherry *n, pl* **-ries 1** small red or black fruit with a stone **2** tree bearing this ▷ *adj* **3** deep red
cherub *n* **1** angel, often represented as a winged child **2** sweet child **cherubic** [cher-**rew**-bik] *adj*
Cherubini *n* (**Maria**) **Luigi** (**Carlo Zenobio Salvatore**). 1760–1842, Italian composer, noted particularly for his church music and his operas.
chervil *n* herb with an aniseed flavour
Cherwell *n* **1st Viscount**, title of *Frederick Alexander Lindemann*. 1886–1957, British

THESAURUS

cheek *n* (*Informal*) = **impudence**, audacity, chutzpah (*informal*), nerve, lip (*slang*), disrespect, effrontery, impertinence, insolence, temerity
cheeky *adj* = **impudent**, forward, disrespectful, audacious, saucy, impertinent, insolent, insulting, pert
cheer *v* **1** = **applaud**, hail, acclaim, clap, root for (*sports*) **2** = **cheer up**, encourage, comfort, brighten, uplift, hearten, gladden, buoy up ▷ **cheer up** = **comfort**, encourage, hearten, gladden, enliven; = **take heart**, rally, buck up (*informal*), perk up ▸ *n* **3** = **applause**, ovation, acclamation, plaudits
cheerful *adj* = **happy**, bright, merry, buoyant, jolly, light-hearted, cheery, jaunty • *She was very cheerful despite her illness*. OPPOSITE: miserable
cheerfulness *n* = **happiness**, exuberance, buoyancy, gaiety, geniality, good cheer, good humour, high spirits, jauntiness, light-heartedness
cheerless *adj* = **gloomy**, dismal, bleak, woeful, miserable, dreary, drab, desolate, sombre, forlorn
cheery *adj* = **cheerful**, happy, sunny, upbeat, jolly, chirpy, good-humoured • *He is loved by everyone for his cheery disposition*.
cherish *v* **1** = **cling to**, encourage, sustain, treasure, foster, entertain, nurture, prize, harbour, cleave to, hold dear **2** = **care for**, support, love, nurse, shelter, comfort, hold dear
cherished *See* **beloved, dear**

DICTIONARY

physicist, born in Germany, noted for his research on heat capacity, aeronautics, and atomic physics. He was scientific adviser to Winston Churchill during World War II

chess *n* game of skill for two players with 16 pieces each on a checkered board (**chessboard**) of 64 squares

▸ **chessman** *n* piece used in chess

chest Ⓣ *n* **1** front of the body, from the neck to the belly **2** large strong box

▸ **chest of drawers** piece of furniture consisting of drawers in a frame

chesterfield *n* sofa with high padded sides and back

Chesterton *n* **G(ilbert) K(eith)**. 1874–1936, English essayist, novelist, poet, and critic

chestnut *n* **1** reddish-brown edible nut **2** tree bearing this **3** horse of a reddish-brown colour **4** *informal* old joke ▹ *adj* **5** reddish-brown

cheval glass [shev-**val**] *n* full-length mirror mounted to swivel within a frame

Chevalier *n* **Maurice**. 1888–1972, French singer and film actor

chevron [**shev**-ron] *n* V-shaped pattern, esp. denoting rank

chew Ⓣ *v* grind (food etc.) between the teeth

▸ **chewy** *adj* requiring chewing

▸ **chewing gum** flavoured gum that is chewed but not swallowed

Chiang Ching-kuo, Jiang Jing Guo *n* 1910–88, Chinese statesman; the son of Chiang Kai-shek. He was prime minister of Taiwan (1971–78); president (1978–88)

Chiang Kai-shek, Jiang Jie Shi *n* original name *Chiang Chung-cheng*. 1887–1975, Chinese general: president of China (1928–31; 1943–49) and of the Republic of China (Taiwan) (1950–75). As chairman of the Kuomintang, he allied with the Communists against the Japanese (1937–45), but in the Civil War that followed was forced to withdraw to Taiwan after his defeat by the Communists (1949)

chianti [kee-**ant**-ee] *n* dry red Italian wine

chiaroscuro [kee-ah-roh-**skew**-roh] *n*, *pl* **-ros** distribution of light and shade in a picture

chic Ⓣ [**sheek**] *adj* **1** stylish or elegant ▹ *n* **2** stylishness

chick *n* young bird

▸ **chickadee** *n* small N American bird with a dark crown

▸ **chickpea** *n* edible pealike seed of an Asian plant

▸ **chickweed** *n* weed with small white flowers

chicken Ⓣ *n* **1** domestic fowl **2** flesh of this used as food **3** *slang* coward ▹ *adj* **4** cowardly

▸ **chicken feed** *slang* trifling amount of money

▸ **chicken out** *v informal* fail to do something through cowardice

▸ **chickenpox** *n* infectious disease with an itchy rash

chicory *n*, *pl* **-ries 1** plant whose leaves are used in salads **2** root of this plant, used as a coffee substitute

chide Ⓣ *v* **chiding, chided** *or* **chid, chid** *or* **chidden** rebuke

chief Ⓣ *n* **1** head of a group of people ▹ *adj* **2** principal, foremost

▸ **chiefly** *adv* **1** mainly **2** especially

▸ **chieftain** *n* leader of a tribe

chiffon [**shif**-fon] *n* thin gauzy fabric

chignon [**sheen**-yon] *n* knot of hair worn at the back of the head

chihuahua [chee-**wah**-wah] *n* tiny short-haired dog

chilblain *n* inflammation on the fingers or toes, caused by exposure to cold

child Ⓣ *n*, *pl* **children 1** young human being **2** son or daughter **childhood** *n* **childless** *adj*

THESAURUS

chest *n* = **box**, case, casket, trunk, coffer, crate, strongbox

chew *v* = **munch**, crunch, chomp, gnaw • *Eat slowly and chew your food properly.*
See also: **bite**

chewy *adj* = **tough**, as tough as old boots, leathery

chic *adj* = **stylish**, cool (*informal*), smart, elegant, trendy (*informal*), fashionable, phat (*slang*), designer (*informal*)

chicken *See* **coward, cowardly**

chide *v* (*Old-fashioned*) = **scold**, criticize, rebuke, lecture, reprimand, censure, berate, admonish, reproach, reprove, tell off (*informal*)

chief *n* **1** = **head**, leader, director, manager, boss, warden, chieftain • *the chief of the fire department* ▸ *adj* **2** = **primary**, key, prime, main, principal, foremost, prevailing • *The job went to one of her chief rivals.*
See also: **first, leading, supreme, top**

chiefly *adv* **1** = **especially**, essentially, primarily, principally, above all **2** = **mainly**, usually, mostly, largely, predominantly, in general, in the main, on the whole

chieftain *See* **chief**

child *n* = **youngster**, baby, kid (*informal*), infant, minor, toddler, offspring, juvenile, tot • *I lived in Manitoba as a child.* OPPOSITE: adult RELATED WORDS *adj*: filial *prefix*: pedo-

childbirth *n* = **child-bearing**, delivery, confinement, labour, travail, lying-in, parturition

childhood *n* = **youth**, minority, infancy, boyhood *or* girlhood, immaturity, schooldays

childish *adj* = **immature**, juvenile, infantile, puerile • *I don't have time for this childish*

DICTIONARY

▸ **childish** *adj* **1** immature or silly **2** of or like a child **childishly** *adv*
▸ **childlike** *adj* simple or innocent
▸ **childbirth** *n* giving birth to a child
▸ **child's play** very easy task
chile, chili *n* small hot-tasting red or green pepper used in cooking
chill Ⓣ *n* **1** feverish cold **2** unpleasant coldness ▹ *v* **3** make or become cold ▹ *adj* **4** cold **chilly** *adj* **1** cold **2** unfriendly **chilliness** *n*
▸ **chill out** *v informal* relax, esp. after energetic dancing at a rave
chime Ⓣ *n* **1** bell or set of bells **2** sound of this ▹ *v* **3** ring or be rung **4** produce (sounds) or indicate (the time) by chiming **5** be in agreement
chimera [kime-**meer**-a] *n* **1** illusory hope **2** fabled monster with a lion's head, goat's body, and serpent's tail
chimney *n* hollow vertical structure for carrying away smoke or steam
▸ **chimneypot** *n* short pipe on the top of a chimney
▸ **chimney sweep** person who cleans soot from chimneys
chimp *n informal* short for **chimpanzee**
chimpanzee *n* intelligent ape of central W Africa
chin *n* part of the face below the mouth
china Ⓣ *n* **1** fine earthenware or porcelain **2** cups, saucers, etc.
chinchilla *n* **1** S American rodent with soft grey fur **2** its fur
Chinese *adj* **1** of China or its people ▹ *n* **2** *pl* **-ese** person from China **3** any of the languages of China
chink[1] Ⓣ *n* cleft or crack
chink[2] *n* **1** light ringing sound ▹ *v* **2** make this sound
chinook *n* warm wind during winter in western N America
chintz *n* printed cotton fabric with a glazed finish
chip Ⓣ *n* **1** very thin slice of potato fried till crunchy **2** *Brit* French fried potato **3** tiny wafer of a semiconductor forming an integrated circuit **4** counter used to represent money in gambling **5** small piece broken off **6** mark left where a small piece has broken off ▹ *v* **chipping, chipped 7** break small pieces from
▸ **have a chip on one's shoulder** *informal* bear a grudge
▸ **chip in** *v* **1** *informal* contribute (money) **2** interrupt with a remark
chipboard *n* thin board made of compressed wood particles
chipmunk *n* small striped N American squirrel
chipolata *n Brit* small sausage
Chippendale *n* **1 Thomas**. ?1718–79, English cabinet-maker and furniture designer ▹ *adj* **2** (of furniture) designed by, made by, or in the style of Thomas Chippendale, characterized by the use of Chinese and Gothic motifs, cabriole legs, and massive carving
Chirac *n* **Jacques** (**René**). born 1932, French Gaullist politician: president of France 1995–2007; prime minister (1974–76 and 1986–88); mayor of Paris (1977–95)
chiropodist [kir-**rop**-pod-ist] *n* person who treats minor foot complaints **chiropody** *n*
chiropractic [kire-oh-**prak**-tik] *n* system of treating bodily disorders by manipulation of the spine **chiropractor** *n*
chirp, chirrup Ⓣ *v* **1** (of a bird or insect) make a short high-pitched sound ▹ *n* **2** this sound
▸ **chirpy** *adj informal* cheerful and lively
chisel Ⓣ *n* **1** metal tool with a sharp end for shaping wood or stone ▹ *v* **-elling, -elled 2** carve or form with a chisel
chit *n* note or memorandum
chitchat *n* chat or gossip
chitterlings *pl n* pig's intestines cooked as food

THESAURUS

behaviour. OPPOSITE: mature
childlike *adj* = **innocent**, simple, naive, artless, guileless, ingenuous, trusting
chill *n* **1** = **cold**, bite, nip, sharpness, coolness, crispness, coldness, frigidity, rawness ▸ *v* **2** = **cool**, freeze, refrigerate **3** = **dishearten**, discourage, depress, dampen, dismay, deject ▸ *adj* **4** = **cold**, sharp, raw, bleak, frigid, chilly, wintry, freezing, biting
chilled *See* **cool, frozen**
chilling *See* **scary**
chilly *adj* **1** = **cool**, fresh, sharp, crisp, brisk, drafty, nippy, penetrating **2** = **unfriendly**, hostile, frigid, unresponsive, unsympathetic, unwelcoming
chime *v*, *n* = **ring**, sound, toll, jingle, clang, peal, tinkle
china *n* = **pottery**, service, ware, porcelain, ceramics, crockery, tableware
chink *n* = **opening**, crack, gap, fissure, cleft, cranny, crevice, aperture
chip *n* **1** = **scratch**, notch, fragment, shaving, nick, shard, sliver, wafer ▸ *v* **2** = **nick**, damage, whittle, gash, chisel
chirp *v* = **chirrup**, pipe, peep, twitter, cheep, tweet, warble
chirpy *See* **cheery**
chisel *See* **carve**
chivalrous *adj* = **courteous**, brave, bold, courageous, valiant, gallant, honourable, gentlemanly

DICTIONARY

chivalry Ⓣ *n* **1** courteous and considerate behaviour, esp. towards women **2** medieval system and principles of knighthood
chivalrous *adj*
chive *n* herb with a mild onion flavour
chivvy *v* **-vying, -vied** *informal* urge to do something
chlorine *n* yellowish-green pungent gaseous element
▸ **chlorinate** *v* disinfect or purify (esp. water) with chlorine **chlorination** *n*
▸ **chloride** *n* compound of chlorine
chlorofluorocarbon *n* any of various gaseous compounds of chlorine, fluorine, and carbon, used in refrigerators and aerosol propellants, some of which cause a breakdown of ozone in the earth's atmosphere
chloroform *n* **1** strong-smelling liquid formerly used as an anesthetic ▹ *v* **2** make unconscious with chloroform
chlorophyll *n* green colouring matter in plants, which helps them convert sunlight into energy
chock *n* block or wedge used to prevent a heavy object from moving
▸ **chock-full** *or* **chock-a-block** *adj* completely full
chocolate *n* **1** food made from cacao seeds **2** candy or drink made from this ▹ *adj* **3** dark brown
▸ **chocolate bar** bar of sweetened chocolate, often with a filling such as nuts, raisins, caramel, etc.
choice Ⓣ *n* **1** choosing **2** opportunity or power of choosing **3** thing or person chosen **4** possibilities from which to choose ▹ *adj* **5** of superior quality
choir *n* **1** organized group of singers, esp. in church **2** part of a church occupied by the choir
choke Ⓣ *v* **1** hinder or stop the breathing of (a person) by squeezing or blocking the windpipe **2** have trouble in breathing **3** block or clog up ▹ *n* **4** device controlling the amount of air that is mixed with the fuel in a gasoline engine
▸ **choker** *n* tight-fitting necklace
▸ **choke back** *v* suppress (anger, tears, etc.)
cholera [**kol**-ler-a] *n* dangerous infectious disease characterized by vomiting and diarrhea
choleric *adj* bad-tempered
cholesterol [kol-**lest**-er-oll] *n* fatty substance found in animal tissue
chomp *v* chew noisily
Chomsky *n* (**Avram**) **Noam**. born 1928, US linguist and political critic. His theory of language structure, transformational generative grammar, superseded the behaviourist view of Bloomfield **Chomskyan** *or* **Chomskyite** *n, adj*
choose Ⓣ *v* **choosing, chose, chosen** **1** select from a number of alternatives **2** decide (to do something)
▸ **choosy** *adj informal* fussy, hard to please
chop[1] Ⓣ *v* **chopping, chopped** **1** cut with a blow from an axe or knife **2** cut into pieces **3** hit (an opponent) with a sharp blow ▹ *n* **4** sharp blow **5** slice of meat, usu. with a rib
▸ **chopper** *n* **1** small axe **2** *informal* helicopter
▸ **choppy** *adj* (of the sea) fairly rough
chop[2] *v* **chopping, chopped**
▸ **chop and change** change one's mind repeatedly
Chopin *n* **Frédéric** (**François**). 1810–49, Polish composer and pianist active in France, who wrote chiefly for the piano: noted for his harmonic imagination and his lyrical and melancholy qualities
chops *pl n informal* jaws or cheeks
chopsticks *pl n* pair of thin sticks used to eat with by the Chinese and Japanese
chop suey *n* Chinese-style dish of chopped meat and vegetables fried in soy sauce
choral *adj* of or for a choir
chorale [kor-**rahl**] *n* slow stately hymn tune
chord *n* **1** simultaneous sounding of three or more musical notes **2** *math* straight line joining two points on a curve
chore Ⓣ *n* routine task
chorea [kor-**ree**-a] *n* disorder of the nervous system characterized by uncontrollable brief jerky movements
choreography *n* steps and movements of a ballet or dance **choreographer** *n* **choreographic** *adj*

THESAURUS

chivalry *n* = **courtesy**, courage, knighthood, politeness, gallantry, gentlemanliness, knight-errantry
choice *n* **1** = **range**, variety, selection • *available in a choice of colours* **2** = **option**, say, alternative • *They had little choice in the matter.* ▸ *adj* **3** = **best**, prime, rare, select, excellent, exclusive, elite
See also: **superior, will**
choke *v* **1** = **strangle**, overpower, stifle, suppress, gag, smother, throttle, suffocate, asphyxiate **2** = **block**, stop, bar, clog, bung, obstruct, congest, constrict
choose *v* = **pick**, take, select, opt for • *a number of foods from which to choose*
See also: **decide, determine**
choosy *adj* = **fussy**, particular, selective, picky (*informal*), finicky, discriminating, faddy, fastidious
chop *v* = **cut**, hack, fell, lop • *I heard him chopping wood in the yard.*
chore *n* = **task**, job, duty, burden, errand,

DICTIONARY

chorister *n* singer in a choir
chortle Ⓣ *v* **1** chuckle gleefully ▷ *n* **2** gleeful chuckle
chorus Ⓣ *n, pl* **-ruses 1** large choir **2** group of singers or dancers who perform together **3** part of a song repeated after each verse **4** something expressed by many people at once ▷ *v* **chorusing, chorused 5** sing or say together
▸ **in chorus** in unison
chose *v* past tense of **choose**
▸ **chosen** *v* past participle of **choose**
choux pastry [**shoo**] *n* very light pastry made with eggs
chow[1] *n* thick-coated dog with a curled tail, orig. from China
chow[2] *n informal* food
chowder *n* thick soup containing clams or fish
chow mein *n* Chinese dish consisting of chopped meat or vegetables fried with noodles
Chrétien *n* (**Joseph Jacques**) **Jean**. born 1934, Canadian Liberal politician; prime minister of Canada (1993–2003)
Christ *n* Jesus, regarded by Christians as the Messiah
christen Ⓣ *v* **1** baptize **2** give a name to **3** use for the first time **christening** *n*
Christendom *n* all Christian people or countries
Christian[1] *n* **1** person who believes in and follows Christ ▷ *adj* **2** relating to Christ or Christianity **3** kind or good
▸ **Christianity** *n* religion based on the life and teachings of Christ
▸ **Christian name** person's first name
▸ **Christian Science** religious system which emphasizes spiritual healing
Christian[2] *n* **Charlie**. 1919–42, US jazz guitarist
Christie *n* Dame **Agatha** (**Mary Clarissa**). 1890–1976, British author of detective stories, many featuring Hercule Poirot, and several plays, including *The Mousetrap* (1952)
Christmas Ⓣ *n* **1** annual festival on Dec. 25 commemorating the birth of Christ **2** period around this time **Christmassy** *adj*
▸ **Christmas Day** Dec. 25
▸ **Christmas Eve** Dec. 24
▸ **Christmas tree** evergreen tree or imitation of one, decorated as part of Christmas celebrations
Christo *n* full name **Christo Javacheff**. born 1935, US artist, born in Bulgaria; best known for works in which he wraps buildings, monuments, or natural features in canvas or plastic
Christopher *n* **Saint**. 3rd century AD, Christian martyr; patron saint of travellers
chromatic *adj* **1** of colour or colours **2** *music* (of a scale) proceeding by semitones **chromatically** *adv*
chromatography *n* separation and analysis of the components of a substance by slowly passing it through an adsorbing material
chrome, chromium *n* metallic element used in steel alloys and for electroplating
chromosome *n* microscopic gene-carrying body in the nucleus of a cell
chronic *adj* **1** lasting a long time **2** habitual: *a chronic smoker* **3** *informal* very bad **chronically** *adv*
chronicle Ⓣ *n* **1** record of events in chronological order ▷ *v* **2** record in or as if in a chronicle **chronicler** *n*
chronology *n, pl* **-gies** list or arrangement of events in order of occurrence **chronological** *adj* **chronologically** *adv*
chronometer *n* timepiece designed to be accurate in all conditions
chrysalis [**kriss**-a-liss] *n* insect in the stage between larva and adult, when it is in a cocoon
chrysanthemum *n* garden plant with bright showy flowers
chub *n* freshwater fish of the carp family
chubby Ⓣ *adj* **-bier, -biest** plump **chubbiness** *n*
chuck[1] Ⓣ *v* **1** *informal* throw **2** *informal* give up, reject **3** touch (someone) affectionately under the chin
chuck[2] *n* **1** cut of beef from the neck to the shoulder **2** device that holds a workpiece in a lathe or a tool in a drill
▸ **chuck wagon** wagon carrying cooking supplies for men working in the open
chuckle Ⓣ *v* **1** laugh softly ▷ *n* **2** soft laugh

THESAURUS

joe job (*Canad informal*)
chortle *v*, *n* = **chuckle**, crow, guffaw, cackle
chorus *n* **1** = **choir**, ensemble, choristers, singers, vocalists **2** = **refrain**, response, strain, burden **3** = **unison**, accord, concert, harmony
christen *v* **1** = **baptize** **2** = **name**, call, term, title, style, dub, designate
Christmas *n* = **festive season**, Noel, Xmas, Yule, Yuletide
chronicle *n* **1** = **record**, history, story, account, register, journal, blog (*informal*), diary, narrative, weblog, annals ▸ *v* **2** = **record**, report, tell, enter, relate, register, recount, narrate, put on record, set down
chubby *adj* = **plump**, buxom, flabby, round, portly, stout, rotund, tubby
chuck *v* (*Informal*) = **throw**, pitch, cast, toss, hurl, fling, sling, heave
chuckle *v* = **laugh**, crow, giggle, exult,

DICTIONARY

chug *n* **1** short dull sound, as of an engine ▷ *v* **chugging, chugged 2** operate or move with this sound
chum Ⓣ *informal* ▷ *n* close friend ▷ *v* **chumming, chummed** ▸ **chum up with** form a close friendship with **chummy** *adj*
chump *n informal* stupid person
chunk Ⓣ *n* **1** thick solid piece **2** considerable amount
▸ **chunky** *adj* **1** thick and short **2** with thick pieces
church *n* **1** building for public Christian worship **2 Church** particular Christian denomination **3 Church** Christians collectively **4** clergy
▸ **churchgoer** *n* person who attends church regularly
▸ **churchyard** *n* grounds round a church, used as a graveyard
Churchill *n* Sir **Winston** (**Leonard Spencer**). 1874–1965, British Conservative statesman, orator, and writer, noted for his leadership during World War II. He held various posts under both Conservative and Liberal governments, including 1st Lord of the Admiralty (1911–15), before becoming prime minister (1940–45; 1951–55). His writings include *The World Crisis* (1923–29), *Marlborough* (1933–38), *The Second World War* (1948–54), and *History of the English-Speaking Peoples* (1956–58): Nobel prize for literature 1953
churlish Ⓣ *adj* surly and rude
churn Ⓣ *n* **1** machine in which cream is shaken to make butter **2** large container for milk ▷ *v* **3** stir (cream) vigorously or make butter in a churn **4** move about violently
▸ **churn out** *v informal* produce (things) rapidly in large numbers
chute [**shoot**] *n* **1** steep channel down which things may be slid **2** waterfall or rapids **3** *informal* short for **parachute**
chutney *n* pickle made from fruit, vinegar, and spices
CIA *US* Central Intelligence Agency
cicada [sik-**kah**-da] *n* large insect that makes a high-pitched drone
cicatrix [**sik**-a-trix] *n, pl* **-trices** scar
Cicero *n* **Marcus Tullius**. 106–43 BC, Roman consul, orator, and writer. He foiled Catiline's conspiracy (63) and was killed by Mark Antony's agents after he denounced Antony in the *Philippics*. His writings are regarded as a model of Latin prose. Formerly known in English as **Tully**
CID *Brit* Criminal Investigation Department
cider *n* drink made from apples
cigar *n* roll of cured tobacco leaves for smoking
▸ **cigarette** *n* shredded tobacco in a thin paper cylinder for smoking
cilantro *n* plant widely cultivated for its aromatic seeds and leaves, used in flavouring food etc.
Cimarosa *n* **Domenico**. 1749–1801, Italian composer, chiefly remembered for his opera buffa *The Secret Marriage* (1792)
cinch [**sinch**] *n informal* **1** easy task **2** certainty
cinder *n* piece of incombustible material left after burning coal
cine camera *n* camera for taking moving pictures
cinema Ⓣ *n* **1** place for showing films **2** films collectively **cinematic** *adj*
▸ **cinematography** *n* technique of making films **cinematographer** *n*
cineraria *n* garden plant with daisy-like flowers
cinnamon *n* spice obtained from the bark of an Asian tree
cipher Ⓣ [**sife**-er] *n* **1** system of secret writing **2** unimportant person
circa [**sir**-ka] *prep Latin* about, approximately
circle Ⓣ *n* **1** perfectly round geometric figure, line, or shape **2** group of people sharing an interest or activity **3** *theatre* section of seats above the main level of the auditorium ▷ *v* **4** move in a circle **5** surround
▸ **circlet** *n* circular ornament worn on the head
▸ **circular** *adj* **1** round **2** moving in a circle ▷ *n* **3** letter or notice for general distribution **circularity** *n*
▸ **circulate** *v* send, go, or move around **circulatory** *adj*
▸ **circulation** *n* **1** flow of blood around the

THESAURUS

chortle, snigger, titter
chum *n* (*Informal*) = **friend**, comrade, companion, crony, homeboy (*slang*), homegirl (*slang*), pal (*informal*)
chunk *n* = **piece**, block, mass, portion, lump, slab, nugget, dollop (*informal*), hunk
chunky *See* **stocky**
churlish *adj* = **rude**, harsh, surly, sullen, brusque, ill-tempered, impolite, uncivil
churn *v* = **stir up**, beat, toss, swirl, agitate, convulse
chutzpah *n* (*Informal*) = **impudence**, nerve, lip (*slang*), disrespect, audacity, effrontery, impertinence, insolence, temerity
cinema *n* = **films**, big screen (*informal*), flicks (*slang*), motion pictures, movies, pictures
cipher *n* **1** = **code**, cryptograph **2** = **nobody**, nonentity
circle *n* **1** = **ring**, globe, disc, sphere, orb **2** = **group**, company, set, club, society, clique, coterie ▸ *v* **3** = **go round**, ring, surround, enclose, envelop, encircle,

DICTIONARY

body **2** number of copies of a newspaper or magazine sold **3** sending or moving around
circulatory *adj*
circuit ⓣ *n* **1** complete round or course **2** complete path through which an electric current can flow **3** periodical journey around a district, as made by judges **4** motor-racing track
▸ **circuitous** [sir-**kew**-it-uss] *adj* roundabout, indirect
▸ **circuitry** [**sir**-kit-tree] *n* electrical circuit(s)
circumcise *v* cut off the foreskin of
circumcision *n*
circumference ⓣ *n* **1** boundary of a specified area or shape, esp. of a circle **2** distance round this
circumflex *n* accent (^) over a vowel to show that it is pronounced in a particular way
circumlocution *n* indirect expression
circumlocutory *adj*
circumnavigate *v* sail right round
circumnavigation *n*
circumscribe *v* **1** restrict **2** draw a line round **circumscription** *n*
circumspect *adj* cautious, prudent
circumspectly *adv* **circumspection** *n*
circumstance ⓣ *n usu pl* occurrence or condition that accompanies or influences a person or event
▸ **circumstantial** *adj* **1** (of evidence) strongly suggesting something but not proving it **2** detailed
▸ **circumstantiate** *v* prove by giving details
circumvent *v* avoid or get round (a difficulty etc.) **circumvention** *n*
circus *n, pl* **-cuses** (performance given by) a travelling company of acrobats, clowns, performing animals, etc.
cirrhosis [sir-**roh**-siss] *n* liver disease
cirrus *n, pl* **-ri** high wispy cloud
cisco [**siss**-ko] *n, pl* **-coes** N American whitefish
cistern ⓣ *n* water tank
citadel ⓣ *n* fortress in a city
cite ⓣ *v* **1** quote **2** bring forward as proof
citation *n*
citizen ⓣ *n* **1** native or naturalized member of a state or nation **2** inhabitant of a city or town **citizenship** *n*
▸ **Citizens' Band** range of radio frequencies for private communication by the public
citric acid *n* weak acid found in citrus fruits
citrus fruit *n* juicy, sharp-tasting fruit such as an orange, lemon, or lime
city ⓣ *n, pl* **-ties** large or important town
▸ **the City** area of London as a financial centre
civet [**siv**-vit] *n* **1** spotted catlike African mammal **2** musky fluid from its glands used in perfume
civic ⓣ *adj* of a city or citizens
▸ **civics** *pl n* study of the rights and responsibilities of citizenship
civil ⓣ *adj* **1** relating to the citizens of a state as opposed to the armed forces or the Church **2** polite **civilly** *adv*
▸ **civility** *n* politeness
▸ **civilian** *n, adj* (person) not belonging to the armed forces
▸ **civil service** public service
▸ **civil servant** public servant
▸ **civil war** war between people of the same country

C

THESAURUS

circumnavigate, circumscribe
circuit *n* = **course**, track, tour, route, journey, orbit, revolution, lap
circuitous *adj* = **indirect**, oblique, roundabout, rambling, tortuous, labyrinthine, meandering, winding
circular *adj* **1** = **round**, rotund, ring-shaped, spherical **2** = **orbital**, cyclical, circuitous ▸ *n* **3** = **advertisement**, notice
circulate *v* **1** = **spread**, distribute, propagate • *He circulated rumours about everyone.* **2** = **flow**, revolve, rotate, radiate, gyrate
circulation *n* **1** = **bloodstream** **2** = **flow**, motion, rotation, circling **3** = **distribution**, spread, currency, transmission, dissemination
circumference *n* = **boundary**, border, edge, outline, rim, perimeter, extremity, periphery, limits
circumstance *n* = **event**, condition, situation, incident, accident, respect, particular, contingency, occurrence, happening
circumstances *pl n* = **situation**, state, station, position, status, means, state of affairs
cistern *n* = **tank**, sink, reservoir, basin, vat
citadel *n* = **fortress**, keep, tower, stronghold, bastion, fortification
cite *v* = **quote**, name, advance, mention, extract, specify, adduce, enumerate, allude to
citizen *n* = **inhabitant**, resident, subject, dweller, denizen, townsman
city *n* = **town**, municipality, metropolis • *the city of Regina* RELATED WORD *adj*: civic
civic *adj* = **public**, local, municipal, communal
civil *adj* **1** = **civic**, political, domestic, municipal **2** = **polite**, refined, affable, courteous, obliging, urbane, well-mannered
civility *See* **courtesy, politeness**
civilization *n* **1** = **culture**, development, education, progress, advancement, cultivation, sophistication, refinement, enlightenment **2** = **society**, people, community, nation, polity

DICTIONARY

civilize Ⓣ *v* **1** bring out of barbarism into a state of civilization **2** refine
▸ **civilization** *n* **1** high level of human cultural and social development **2** particular society which has reached this level
civvies *pl n slang* civilian clothes
Cl *chem* chlorine
clack *n* **1** sound made by two hard objects striking together ▹ *v* **2** (cause to) make this sound
clad *v* a past of **clothe**
cladding *n* material used for the outside facing of a building etc.
claim Ⓣ *v* **1** assert **2** demand as a right **3** call for or need ▹ *n* **4** assertion **5** demand for something as due **6** right **7** thing claimed
claimant *n*
clairvoyance *n* power of perceiving things beyond the natural range of the senses
clairvoyant *n, adj*
clam *n* **1.** edible shellfish with a hinged shell ▹ *v* **clamming, clammed 2 clam up** *informal* refuse to talk
clamber Ⓣ *v* climb awkwardly or with difficulty
clammy Ⓣ *adj* **-mier, -miest** unpleasantly moist and sticky **clamminess** *n*
clamour Ⓣ *n* **1** loud protest **2** loud persistent outcry or noise ▹ *v* **3** make a loud outcry or noise **clamorous** *adj*
▸ **clamour for** *v* demand noisily
clamp Ⓣ *n* **1** tool with movable jaws for holding things together tightly ▹ *v* **2** fasten with a clamp
▸ **clamp down on** *v* **1** become stricter about **2** suppress
clan Ⓣ *n* **1** group of families with a common ancestor **2** close group
▸ **clannish** *adj* (of a group) tending to exclude outsiders
Clancy *n* **Tom**. born 1947, US novelist; his thrillers, many of which have been filmed, include *The Hunt for Red October* (1984), *Clear and Present Danger* (1989), *Debt of Honour* (1994) and *Red Rabbit* (2002)
clandestine Ⓣ *adj* secret, furtive
clang Ⓣ *n* **1** loud ringing sound ▹ *v* **2** (cause to) make this sound
▸ **clanger** *n informal* conspicuous mistake
clangour *n* loud continuous clanging sound
clangorous *adj*
clank *n* **1** harsh metallic sound ▹ *v* **2** (cause to) make this sound
clap[1] Ⓣ *v* **clapping, clapped 1** applaud by striking the palms of one's hands sharply together **2** put quickly or forcibly ▹ *n* **3** act or sound of clapping **4** sharp abrupt sound, esp. of thunder
▸ **clapped out** *slang* worn out
▸ **clapper** *n* piece of metal inside a bell, which causes it to sound when struck against the side
▸ **clapperboard** *n* pair of hinged boards clapped together during filming to aid synchronizing sound and picture
▸ **claptrap** *n* empty words
clap[2] *n slang* gonorrhea
Clapton *n* **Eric**. born 1945, British rock guitarist, noted for his virtuoso style, his work with the Yardbirds (1963–65), Cream (1966–68), and, with Derek and the Dominos, the album *Layla* (1970); later solo work includes *Unplugged* (1992)
Clare of Assisi *n* **Saint**. 1194–1253, Italian nun; founder of the Franciscan Order of Poor Clares. Feast day: Aug 11
claret [**klar**-rit] *n* dry red wine from Bordeaux
clarify Ⓣ *v* **-fying, -fied** make or become clear **clarification** *n*

THESAURUS

civilize *v* = **cultivate**, educate, refine, tame, enlighten, sophisticate
civilized *adj* = **cultured**, enlightened • *a highly civilized society*
See also: **refined**
claim *v* **1** = **assert**, hold, allege, maintain, insist, profess • *He claims to have lived here all his life.* **2** = **demand**, need, ask, require, insist, call for ▸ *n* **3** = **assertion**, allegation • *He rejected claims that he had taken bribes.* **4** = **demand**, call, request, application, requirement, petition **5** = **right**, title
See also: **argue**
clairvoyant *n* **1** = **psychic**, visionary, diviner, fortune-teller ▸ *adj* **2** = **psychic**, visionary, extrasensory, second-sighted, telepathic
clamber *v* = **climb**, scale, scramble, claw, shin, scrabble
clammy *adj* = **moist**, close, sticky, damp, sweaty, dank
clamour *n* = **noise**, outcry, uproar, racket, commotion, din, hubbub, shouting
clamp *n* **1** = **vice**, press, grip, bracket, fastener ▸ *v* **2** = **fasten**, fix, secure, brace, make fast
clan *n* = **family**, group, society, faction, tribe, fraternity, brotherhood
clandestine *adj* = **secret**, private, underground, covert, stealthy, surreptitious, cloak-and-dagger, concealed, furtive
clang *See* **ring, sound**
clap *v* = **applaud**, cheer, acclaim
clarification *n* = **explanation**, interpretation, illumination, exposition, elucidation, simplification
clarify *v* = **explain**, interpret, illuminate,

DICTIONARY

clarinet *n* keyed woodwind instrument with a single reed **clarinettist** *n*
clarion *n* **1** obsolete high-pitched trumpet **2** its sound
▸ **clarion call** rousing appeal
clarity Ⓣ *n* clearness
Clark *n* **1 Charles Joseph**, known as *Joe*. born 1939, Canadian Progressive Conservative politician; Prime Minister (1979–80) **2 Helen**. born 1950, New Zealand politician; Labour Prime Minister (1999–2008) **3 William**. 1770–1838, US explorer and frontiersman: best known for his expedition to the Pacific Northwest (1804–06) with Meriwether Lewis
Clarke *n* **1** Sir **Arthur C**(**harles**). 1917–2008, British science-fiction writer, who helped to develop the first communications satellites. He scripted the film *2001, A Space Odyssey* (1968) **2 Jeremiah**. ?1673-1707, English composer and organist, best known for his *Trumpet Voluntary*, formerly attributed to Purcell
Clarkson *n* **1 Adrienne** (**Louise**). born 1939, Canadian public official and television journalist, born in Hong Kong; Governor General (1999–2005) **2 Thomas**. 1760–1846, British campaigner for the abolition of slavery
clash Ⓣ *v* **1** come into conflict **2** (of events) coincide **3** (of colours) look unattractive together **4** (cause to) make a clashing sound ▷ *n* **5** conflict **6** loud harsh noise, esp. of things striking together
clasp Ⓣ *n* **1** device for fastening things **2** firm grasp or embrace ▷ *v* **3** grasp or embrace firmly **4** fasten with a clasp
▸ **clasp knife** knife whose blade folds into the handle
class Ⓣ *n* **1** social group of a particular rank **2** system of dividing society into such groups **3** group of people or things sharing a common characteristic **4** group of pupils or students taught together **5** standard of quality **6** *informal* excellence or elegance ▷ *v* **7** place in a class
▸ **classy** *adj informal* stylish, elegant
▸ **classify** *v* **1** arrange in classes **2** designate (information) as officially secret **classifiable** *adj* **classification** *n*
▸ **classroom** *n* room, esp. in a school, in which classes are conducted
classic Ⓣ *adj* **1** typical **2** of lasting significance because of excellence **3** characterized by simplicity and purity of form ▷ *n* **4** author, artist, or work of art of recognized excellence **classics 5** study of ancient Greek and Roman literature and culture **classicist** *n*
▸ **classical** *adj* **1** traditional and standard **2** *music* denoting serious art music **3** of or influenced by ancient Greek and Roman culture **classically** *adv*
▸ **classicism** *n* artistic style showing regularity of form and emotional restraint
clatter *n* **1** rattling noise ▷ *v* **2** (cause to) make a rattling noise
Claude Lorrain *n* real name *Claude Gelée*.

THESAURUS

simplify, clear up, elucidate, make plain, throw light on *or* shed light on
clarity *n* = **clearness**, definition, transparency, precision, simplicity, lucidity, limpidity
clash *v* **1** = **fight**, battle, wrangle, quarrel • *A group of 400 demonstrators clashed with police.* **2** = **conflict**, contradict, disagree, differ, jar, go against • *Their decisions clashed with company policy.* **3** = **crash**, bang, rattle, jar, clang, clank, clatter, jangle ▸ *n* **4** = **fight**, battle, struggle, conflict, confrontation, skirmish (*informal*), squabble • *a number of clashes between rival parties*
See also: **argument, dispute, game, war**
clasp *v* **1** = **grip**, hold, press, embrace, clutch, hug, squeeze • *I clasped the winning ticket tightly.* **2** = **fasten**, connect ▸ *n* **3** = **fastening**, catch, clip, buckle, fastener • *She undid the clasp of her necklace.* **4** = **grasp**, hold, embrace, grip, hug
class *n* **1** = **group**, set, kind, type, sort, category, grade, genre • *a new class of SUV* ▸ *v* **2** = **classify**, rate, rank, designate, grade, categorize • *He is classed as a comedian.*
See also: **family, form, lesson, polish, range, variety**
classes *See* **course**
classic *adj* **1** = **definitive**, standard, model, ideal, exemplary, quintessential, archetypal **2** = **typical**, standard, regular, usual, characteristic, time-honoured **3** = **best**, world-class, consummate, first-rate, finest, masterly **4** = **lasting**, enduring, immortal, abiding, ageless, deathless, undying **5** (*Informal*) = **hilarious**, comical, ludicrous, hysterical, uproarious ▸ *n* **6** = **standard**, model, masterpiece, prototype, paradigm, exemplar
classical *adj* = **pure**, elegant, refined, restrained, harmonious, symmetrical, understated, well-proportioned
classification *n* = **categorization**, analysis, arrangement, grading, sorting, taxonomy, profiling
classify *v* = **categorize**, rank, sort, arrange, grade • *We can classify frogs according to family.*
See also: **class, group**
classy *adj* (*Informal*) = **high-class**, exclusive,

DICTIONARY

1600–82, French painter, esp. of idealized landscapes, noted for his subtle depiction of light
Claudius *n* full name *Tiberius Claudius Drusus Nero Germanicus*. 10 BC–54 AD, Roman emperor (41–54); invaded Britain (43); poisoned by his fourth wife, Agrippina
clause ⓣ *n* **1** part of a sentence, containing a verb **2** section in a legal document
Clausius *n* **Rudolf Julius**. 1822–88, German physicist and mathematician. He enunciated the second law of thermodynamics (1850) and developed the kinetic theory of gases
claustrophobia *n* abnormal fear of confined spaces **claustrophobic** *adj*
clavichord *n* early keyboard instrument
clavicle *n* collarbone
claw ⓣ *n* **1** sharp hooked nail of a bird or beast **2** similar part, such as a crab's pincer ▷ *v* **3** tear with claws or nails
clay ⓣ *n* fine-grained earth, soft when moist and hardening when baked, used to make bricks and pottery **clayey** *adj*
▸ **clay pigeon** baked clay disc hurled into the air as a target for shooting
Clay *n* **1 Cassius**. See **Muhammad Ali** **2 Henry**. 1777–1852, US statesman and orator; secretary of state (1825–29)
claymore *n* two-edged broadsword formerly used by Scottish Highlanders
CLC Canadian Labour Congress
clean ⓣ *adj* **1** free from dirt or impurities **2** morally sound **3** without obscenity **4** not yet used **5** complete: *a clean break* **6** smooth and regular ▷ *v* **7** free from dirt ▷ *adv* **8** *not standard* completely **cleaner** *n* **cleanly** *adv* **cleanliness** *n*
▸ **come clean** *informal* confess
▸ **cleanse** *v* make clean **cleanser** *n*
clear ⓣ *adj* **1** free from doubt or confusion **2** plain, distinct **3** transparent **4** free from darkness or obscurity, bright **5** free from obstruction **6** (of weather) free from clouds **7** without blemish or defect **8** (of money) net ▷ *adv* **9** clearly **10** completely **11** out of the way: *stand clear of the gates* ▷ *v* **12** make or become clear **13** pass by or over without touching **14** acquit **15** make as profit **clearly** *adv* **clearness** *n*
▸ **clearance** *n* **1** clearing **2** official permission
▸ **clearing** *n* area cleared of trees
▸ **clear off** *v informal* go away
▸ **clear out** *v* **1** empty **2** *informal* go away
▸ **clear-sighted** *adj* perceptive
cleat *n* **1** wedge **2** piece of wood or iron with two projecting ends round which ropes are fastened
cleave[1] *v* **cleaving, cleft, cleaved** *or* **clove,**

THESAURUS

elegant, superior, stylish, swanky, ritzy, up-market, top-drawer
clause *n* = **section**, part, condition, article, passage, chapter, paragraph
claw *n* **1** = **nail**, tentacle, talon, pincer ▸ *v* **2** = **scratch**, tear, rip, dig, maul, scrape, lacerate
clay *See* **earth, soil**
clean *adj* **1** = **spotless**, impeccable, immaculate, laundered, washed • *clean shoes* OPPOSITE: dirty **2** = **hygienic**, antiseptic, uncontaminated, purified, sterilized, unpolluted • *a lack of clean water and sanitation* OPPOSITE: contaminated **3** = **moral**, good, innocent, pure, decent, upright, respectable, honourable, chaste, virtuous **4** = **complete**, final, total, whole, perfect, entire, decisive, thorough, conclusive, unimpaired ▸ *v* **5** = **cleanse**, wash, wipe, dust, scrub, scour, swab, sponge, deep clean • *We cleaned the house from top to bottom*. OPPOSITE: soil
See also: **blank, simple**
cleanliness *See* **hygiene**
cleanse *v* = **clean**, clear, wash, scrub, purge, scour, purify, rinse, absolve
cleanser *n* = **detergent**, soap, solvent, disinfectant, purifier, scourer
clear *adj* **1** = **obvious**, apparent, plain, explicit, evident, blatant, definite, manifest, unequivocal, palpable, conspicuous • *He made it clear that he did not want to talk*. **2** = **transparent**, translucent, crystalline, glassy • *a clear liquid* OPPOSITE: cloudy **3** = **certain**, sure, positive, convinced, definite, satisfied, decided, resolved **4** = **bright**, light, fine, fair, sunny, luminous, cloudless, shining, unclouded **5** = **unobstructed**, open, free, empty, smooth, unimpeded, unhindered **6** = **unblemished**, clean, innocent, pure, immaculate, untarnished ▸ *v* **7** = **absolve**, acquit • *She was cleared of all suspicion*. OPPOSITE: convict **8** = **unblock**, open, free, rid, unload, loosen, extricate, disentangle **9** = **pass over**, miss, jump, leap, vault **10** = **brighten**, lighten, break up **11** = **clean**, wipe, erase, refine, cleanse, tidy *or* tidy up, purify, sweep away **12** = **gain**, make, earn, acquire, secure, reap ▷ **clear up** = **tidy (up)**, order, straighten, rearrange, put in order; = **solve**, explain, resolve, clarify, unravel, elucidate, straighten out
See also: **blank, visible**
clear-cut *adj* = **straightforward**, specific, plain, explicit, precise, definite, black-and-white, unequivocal, unambiguous, cut-and-dried (*informal*)
clearly *adv* = **obviously**, openly,

DICTIONARY

cleft, cleaved, *or* **cloven** split apart
▸ **cleavage** *n* **1** space between a woman's breasts, as revealed by a low-cut dress **2** division, split
▸ **cleaver** *n* heavy butcher's knife
cleave² *v* cling or adhere
clef *n music* symbol at the beginning of a stave to show the pitch
cleft Ⓣ *n* **1** split or indentation ▹ *v* **2** a past of **cleave¹**
▸ **in a cleft stick** in a very difficult position
Cleisthenes *n* 6th century BC, Athenian statesman: democratized the political structure of Athens
clematis *n* climbing plant with showy flowers
Clemenceau *n* **Georges Eugène Benjamin**. 1841–1929, French statesman; prime minister of France (1906–09; 1917–20); negotiated the Treaty of Versailles (1919)
clement *adj* (of weather) mild
▸ **clemency** *n* mercy
clementine *n* small orange citrus fruit
clench *v* **1** close or squeeze (one's teeth or fist) firmly together **2** grasp firmly
Cleopatra *n* ?69–30 BC, queen of Egypt (51–30), renowned for her beauty: the mistress of Julius Caesar and later of Mark Antony. She killed herself with an asp to avoid capture by Octavian (Augustus)
clerestory [**clear**-store-ee] *n, pl* **-ries** row of windows at the top of a wall above an adjoining roof
clergy Ⓣ *n* priests and ministers as a group **clergyman** *n*
cleric *n* member of the clergy
clerical *adj* **1** of clerks or office work **2** of the clergy
clerk *n* employee in an office, bank, or court who keeps records, files, and accounts
Cleveland *n* **Stephen Grover**. 1837–1908, US Democratic politician; the 22nd and 24th president of the US (1885–89; 1893–97)
clever Ⓣ *adj* **1** intelligent, quick at learning **2** showing skill **cleverly** *adv* **cleverness** *n*
cliché Ⓣ [**klee**-shay] *n* hackneyed expression or idea **clichéd** *adj*
click *n* **1** short slight sound ▹ *v* **2** (cause to) make this sound **3** *informal* become suddenly clear **4** *informal* (of two people) get on well **5** *slang* be a success **6** Also **click on** *computers* select a particular function by pressing a button on a mouse
client Ⓣ *n* **1** person who uses the services of a professional **2** customer **3** *computers* program or work station that requests data from a server
▸ **clientele** [klee-on-**tell**] *n* clients collectively
cliff Ⓣ *n* steep rock face, esp. along the sea shore
▸ **cliffhanger** *n* film, game, etc. which is exciting and full of suspense because its outcome is uncertain
climacteric *n* same as **menopause**
climate Ⓣ *n* prevalent weather conditions of an area **climatic** *adj*
climax Ⓣ *n* **1** most intense point of an experience, series of events, or story **2** orgasm ▹ *v* **3** reach a climax **climactic** *adj*
climb Ⓣ *v* **1** go up or ascend **2** rise ▹ *n* **3** place to be climbed **climber** *n*
▸ **climb down** *v* retreat from an opinion or position
clime *n lit* region or its climate
clinch Ⓣ *v* **1** settle (an argument or agreement) decisively ▹ *n* **2** clinching
▸ **clincher** *n informal* something decisive

THESAURUS

undoubtedly, markedly, evidently, distinctly, undeniably, overtly, beyond doubt
cleft *n* = **opening**, break, crack, breach, gap, rent, fracture, fissure, cranny, chink, crevice
clergy *n* = **priesthood**, ministry, churchmen, clergymen, clerics, holy orders, the cloth
clergyman *n* = **minister**, cleric, priest, pastor, chaplain, padre, vicar, man of God, man of the cloth, parson
clever *adj* = **intelligent**, smart, bright, shrewd, brainy (*informal*) • *Today's contestants are all quite clever.*
See also: **astute, brilliant, witty**
cleverness *n* = **intelligence**, ability, ingenuity, brains, quick wits, resourcefulness, shrewdness, smartness
cliché *n* = **platitude**, stereotype, commonplace, truism, banality, hackneyed phrase
clichéd *See* **hackneyed**
client *n* = **customer**, consumer, patient, shopper, buyer, patron, applicant
clientele *n* = **customers**, market, trade, business, following, patronage, clients, regulars
cliff *n* = **rock face**, scar, bluff, overhang, rampart, precipice, escarpment, crag, scarp
climactic *adj* = **crucial**, critical, peak, decisive, paramount
climate *n* = **weather**, temperature
climax *n* = **culmination**, top, summit, highlight, peak, height, zenith, high point
climb *v* = **ascend**, scale, mount, clamber • *Climbing the first hill took half an hour.* ▹ **climb down** = **descend**, dismount; = **back down**, retreat, retract, eat one's words ▹ **climb to** *See* **reach**
See also: **rise**
clinch *v* = **settle**, confirm, decide,

DICTIONARY

Cline *n* **Patsy**, original name *Virginia Patterson Hensley*. 1932–63, US country singer; her bestselling records include "Walking After Midnight," "I Fall to Pieces," and "Leavin' On Your Mind"

cling Ⓣ *v* **clinging, clung** hold fast or stick closely

▸ **clingfilm** *n* thin polythene wrapping

clinic *n* **1** place in which outpatients receive medical advice or treatment **2** private or specialized hospital

▸ **clinical** *adj* **1** of a clinic **2** scientifically detached **clinically** *adv*

clink[1] *n* **1** light sharp metallic sound ▹ *v* **2** (cause to) make such a sound

clink[2] *n slang* prison

clinker *n* fused coal residues from a fire or furnace

clinker-built *adj* (of a boat) made of overlapping planks

Clinton *n* **1 Bill**, full name *William Jefferson Clinton*. born 1946, US Democrat politician; 42nd president of the US (1993–2001) **2** his wife, **Hillary Rodham**. born 1947, US politician and lawyer: first lady (1993–2001); senator (2001–09); first woman US presidential candidate in the 2008 General Election; Secretary of State from 2009

clip[1] Ⓣ *v* **clipping, clipped 1** cut with shears or scissors **2** *informal* hit sharply ▹ *n* **3** short extract of a film **4** *informal* sharp blow

▸ **clippers** *pl n* tool for clipping

▸ **clipping** *n* something cut out, esp. an article from a newspaper

clip[2] Ⓣ *n* **1** device for attaching or holding things together ▹ *v* **clipping, clipped 2** attach or hold together with a clip

clipper *n* fast commercial sailing ship

clique Ⓣ [**kleek**] *n* small exclusive group **cliqueish** *adj*

clitoris [**klit**-or-iss] *n* small sexually sensitive part of the female genitals **clitoral** *adj*

cloak Ⓣ *n* **1** loose sleeveless outer garment ▹ *v* **2** cover or conceal

▸ **cloakroom** *n* room where coats may be left temporarily

clobber *v informal* **1** batter **2** defeat utterly

cloche [**klosh**] *n* **1** cover to protect young plants **2** woman's close-fitting hat

clock *n* **1** instrument for showing the time **2** device with a dial for recording or measuring

▸ **clockwise** *adv, adj* in the direction in which the hands of a clock rotate

▸ **clock in, clock on, clock off,** *or* **clock out** *v* register arrival at *or* departure from work on an automatic time recorder

▸ **clock up** *v* reach (a total)

▸ **clockwork** *n* mechanism similar to that of a clock, as in a wind-up toy

clod *n* **1** lump of earth **2** stupid person **cloddish** *adj*

clog Ⓣ *v* **clogging, clogged 1** block ▹ *n* **2** wooden-soled shoe

cloisonné [klwah-**zon**-nay] *n* design made by filling in a wire outline with coloured enamel

cloister *n* covered pillared arcade, usu. in a monastery

▸ **cloistered** *adj* sheltered

clone *n* **1** group of organisms or cells reproduced asexually from a single plant or animal **2** *informal* person who closely resembles another ▹ *v* **3** produce as a clone

Clooney *n* **George**. born 1961, US film actor; he starred in the television series *ER* (1994–99) and the films *The Perfect Storm* (2000), *Ocean's Eleven* (2001), and *Confessions of a Dangerous Mind* (2002, also directed)

close[1] Ⓣ *v* **1** shut **2** prevent access to **3** finish **4** bring or come nearer together ▹ *n* **5** end

▸ **closed shop** place of work in which all workers must belong to a particular trade union

close[2] Ⓣ *adj* **1** near **2** intimate **3** careful,

THESAURUS

determine, conclude, secure, seal, set the seal on, sew up (*informal*)

cling *v* = **stick**, embrace, grip, clutch, hug, adhere, grasp, clasp

clinical *adj* = **unemotional**, cold, scientific, objective, dispassionate, analytic, detached, impersonal

clip[1] *v* **1** = **trim**, cut, crop, shorten, curtail, pare, prune, shear, snip ▸ *n*, *v* **2** (*Informal*) = **smack**, strike, knock, punch, thump, wallop (*informal*), whack, cuff, clout (*informal*)

clip[2] *v* = **attach**, hold, fix, pin, staple, fasten

clique *n* = **group**, set, gang, circle, faction, cabal, coterie

cloak *n* **1** = **cape**, wrap, coat, mantle ▸ *v* **2** = **cover**, screen, hide, mask, veil, conceal, obscure, disguise, camouflage

clog *v* = **obstruct**, block, jam, hinder, impede, congest

close[1] *v* **1** = **shut**, secure, lock • *Close the gate behind you.* OPPOSITE: open **2** = **block**, bar, seal, plug, obstruct, stop up • *The northbound road is closed due to an accident.* **3** = **end**, finish, complete, conclude, cease, terminate, shut down, wind up **4** = **connect**, join, couple, unite, fuse, come together ▸ *n* **5** = **end**, finish, finale, conclusion, completion, ending, culmination, denouement *See also*: **halt**

close[2] *adj* **1** = **near**, nearby, adjacent, handy, adjoining, nigh, at hand, cheek by jowl, impending, neighbouring • *The*

DICTIONARY

thorough **4** oppressive or stifling **5** secretive **6** compact, dense ▷ *adv* **7** closely or tightly ▷ *n* **8** street closed at one end **9** courtyard or quadrangle **closely** *adv* **closeness** *n*
▶ **close season** period when it is illegal to kill certain kinds of game and fish
▶ **close shave** *informal* narrow escape
▶ **close-up** *n* photograph or film taken at very close range
closer *n* **1** person or thing that closes **2** *baseball* relief pitcher brought in to make the final outs for the team with the lead
closet Ⓣ *n* **1** cupboard **2** small private room ▷ *adj* **3** private or secret ▷ *v* **closeting, closeted 4** shut away in private, esp. for conference
closure *n* **1** closing or being closed **2** a resolution of a significant event or relationship in a person's life
clot Ⓣ *n* **1** soft thick lump formed from liquid **2** *informal* fool ▷ *v* **clotting, clotted 3** form clots
cloth Ⓣ *n* woven fabric
clothe Ⓣ *v* **clothing, clothed** *or* **clad 1** put clothes on **2** provide with clothes
▶ **clothes** *pl n* **1** articles of dress
▶ **clothesline** *n* piece of rope from which clean washing is hung to dry
▶ **clothing** *n* clothes collectively
cloud Ⓣ *n* **1** mass of condensed water vapour floating in the sky **2** floating mass of smoke, dust, etc. ▷ *v* **3** make or become cloudy **4** confuse **5** make gloomy or depressed
cloudless *adj*
▶ **cloudy** *adj* **1** full of clouds **2** (of liquid) opaque
▶ **cloudberry** *n* creeping plant with yellowish fruit
▶ **cloudburst** *n* heavy fall of rain
clout Ⓣ *informal* ▷ *n* **1** blow **2** influence, power ▷ *v* **3** hit
clove[1] *n* **1** dried flower bud of a tropical tree, used as a spice **2** segment of a bulb of garlic
clove[2] *v* a past tense of **cleave**[1]
▶ **clove hitch** knot used to fasten a rope to a spar
cloven *v* a past participle of **cleave**[1]
▶ **cloven hoof** divided hoof of a sheep, goat, etc.
clover *n* plant with three-lobed leaves
▶ **in clover** in luxury
clown Ⓣ *n* **1** comic entertainer in a circus **2** amusing person **3** stupid person ▷ *v* **4** perform as a clown **5** behave foolishly
clownish *adj*
cloy *v* sicken by an excess of something sweet or pleasurable
club Ⓣ *n* **1** association of people with common interests **2** building used by such a group **3** thick stick used as a weapon **4** bat or stick used in some games **5** playing card

THESAURUS

restaurant was close to their home. OPPOSITE: distant **2 = intimate**, confidential, familiar, loving, dear, devoted, inseparable, attached • *We became close friends*. OPPOSITE: distant **3 = careful**, minute, intense, detailed, thorough, rigorous, painstaking **4 = compact**, tight, crowded, packed, dense, jam-packed, impenetrable, congested **5 = stifling**, heavy, oppressive, humid, stuffy, muggy, airless, suffocating, sweltering **6 = secretive**, private, secret, reticent, taciturn, uncommunicative
▷ **close to** *See* **almost**
See also: **alike, beside, friendly, immediate, imminent**
closed *adj* **1 = shut**, sealed, locked, fastened, out of service **2 = exclusive**, restricted **3 = finished**, over, concluded, decided, ended, resolved, settled, terminated
closely *See* **immediately, well**
closeness *See* **friendship**
closest *See* **next**
closet *See* **secret**
closing *See* **final, last**
clot *See* **thicken**
cloth *n* **= fabric**, material, textiles • *a piece of red cloth*
clothe *v* **= dress**, cover, array, equip, drape, robe, attire, garb, swathe, fit out
clothes *pl n* **= clothing**, wear, dress, gear (*informal*), costume, outfit, wardrobe, attire, garments • *They spend too much money on clothes*.
clothing *n* **= clothes**, wear, dress, gear (*informal*), costume, outfit, wardrobe, apparel, attire, garb, garments
clotted *See* **thick**
cloud *n* **1 = mist**, fog, haze, billow, vapour • *The sky was dark with clouds*. ▶ *v* **2 = confuse**, distort, muddle • *Anger has clouded his judgment*. **3 = obscure**, shadow, eclipse, shade, overshadow, darken, dim, obfuscate, becloud, veil
cloudy *adj* **1 = dull**, gloomy, overcast, leaden • *a cloudy sky* OPPOSITE: clear **2 = opaque**, murky, muddy • *a glass of cloudy liquid* OPPOSITE: clear
See also: **dark**
clout (*Informal*) ▶ *n* **1 = influence**, power, authority, pull, weight, prestige ▶ *v* **2 = hit**, strike, punch, thump, wallop (*informal*), clobber (*slang*), sock (*slang*)
clown *n* **1 = comedian**, comic, fool, prankster, harlequin, buffoon, joker, jester ▶ *v* **2 = play the fool**, jest, act the fool, mess around
cloying *See* **sweet**
club *n* **1 = association**, group, union, society, circle, guild • *a swimming club* **2 = stick**, bat

DICTIONARY

of the suit marked with black three-leaved symbols ▷ *v* **clubbing, clubbed 6** strike with a club
▸ **club together** combine resources for a common purpose
club foot *n* congenitally deformed foot
cluck *n* **1** low clicking noise made by a hen ▷ *v* **2** make this noise
clue Ⓣ *n* something that helps to solve a mystery or puzzle
▸ **not have a clue** be completely baffled
▸ **clueless** *adj* stupid
clump[1] Ⓣ *n* **1** cluster or mass ▷ *v* **2** form into a clump
clump[2] *v* **1** walk or tread heavily ▷ *n* **2** dull heavy tread
clumsy Ⓣ *adj* **-sier, -siest 1** lacking skill or physical coordination **2** badly made or done **clumsily** *adv* **clumsiness** *n*
clung *v* past of **cling**
clunk *n* **1** dull metallic sound ▷ *v* **2** make such a sound
cluster Ⓣ *n* **1** small close group ▷ *v* **2** (cause to) form a cluster
clutch[1] Ⓣ *v* **1** grasp tightly **2** try to seize ▷ *n* **3** tight grasp **4** device enabling two revolving shafts to be connected and disconnected
clutch[2] *n* **1** set of eggs laid at the same time **2** brood of chickens
clutter Ⓣ *v* **1** strew objects about (a place) in disorder ▷ *n* **2** disordered heap or mass of objects
cm centimetre(s)
Co *chem* cobalt
CO Commanding Officer
Co. 1 Company **2** County
co- *prefix* **1** together **2** joint or jointly: *coproduction*
c/o 1 care of **2** *book-keeping* carried over
coach Ⓣ *n* **1** long-distance bus **2** railway carriage **3** large four-wheeled horse-drawn carriage **4** trainer, tutor ▷ *v* **5** train or teach
coagulate [koh-**ag**-yew-late] *v* change from a liquid to a semisolid mass **coagulation** *n*
▸ **coagulant** *n* substance causing coagulation
coal *n* black mineral consisting mainly of carbon, used as fuel
▸ **coalfield** *n* area rich in coal
coalesce Ⓣ [koh-a-**less**] *v* come together, merge **coalescence** *n*
coalition Ⓣ [koh-a-**lish**-un] *n* temporary alliance, esp. between political parties
coarse Ⓣ *adj* **1** rough in texture **2** unrefined or indecent **coarsely** *adv* **coarseness** *n* **coarsen** *v*
▸ **coarse fish** *Brit* any freshwater fish not of the salmon family
coast Ⓣ *n* **1** sea shore ▷ *v* **2** move by momentum, without the use of power
coastal *adj*
▸ **coaster** *n* **1** small ship **2** small mat placed under a glass
▸ **coastguard** *n* **1** organization which aids

THESAURUS

• *pictures of cave dwellers armed with clubs* ▸ *v* **3 = beat**, batter, bash, bludgeon • *Two thugs clubbed him with baseball bats.*
See also: **fellowship**
clue *n* = **indication**, lead, sign, evidence, hint, trace, suggestion, suspicion, pointer
clueless *adj* = **stupid**, dim, slow, simple, thick, dull, half-witted, unintelligent, witless
clump *n* **1** = **cluster**, group, mass, bunch, bundle ▸ *v* **2** = **stomp**, lumber, thump, plod, thud, tramp
clumsiness *n* = **awkwardness**, ungainliness • *The accident was entirely the result of his own clumsiness.*
clumsy *adj* = **awkward**, lumbering, ungainly, gauche, unco-ordinated • *He is big and clumsy in his movements.* OPPOSITE: graceful
cluster *n* **1** = **gathering**, group, collection, bunch, knot, batch, clump, assemblage ▸ *v* **2** = **gather**, group, collect, bunch, assemble, flock
clutch *v* = **seize**, catch, grab, embrace, grip, snatch, grasp, clasp, cling to
clutches *pl n* = **power**, control, custody, possession, grip, sway, grasp, claws, hands, keeping
clutter *v* **1** = **litter**, scatter, strew ▸ *n* **2** = **untidiness**, disorder, confusion, disarray, mess, litter, muddle, jumble
cluttered *See* **untidy**
coach *n* **1** = **bus**, car, vehicle, carriage, charabanc **2** = **instructor**, teacher, trainer, handler, tutor ▸ *v* **3** = **instruct**, prepare, train, exercise, drill, tutor
coaching *See* **education, lesson**
coalesce *v* = **blend**, combine, mix, unite, merge, incorporate, integrate, fuse, amalgamate
coalition *n* = **alliance**, union, merger, association, combination, bloc, conjunction, fusion, amalgamation, confederation
coarse *adj* **1** = **rough**, crude, unfinished, homespun, unrefined, unprocessed, impure, unpolished, unpurified **2** = **vulgar**, improper, rude, indecent, earthy, indelicate, ribald, smutty
coarseness *n* **1** = **roughness**, crudity, unevenness **2** = **vulgarity**, bawdiness, crudity, earthiness, indelicacy, ribaldry, smut, uncouthness
coast *n* **1** = **shore**, border, beach, coastline, seaside • *a holiday by the coast* **2** = **cruise**, taxi, sail, drift, glide, freewheel

DICTIONARY

shipping and prevents smuggling **2** member of this

▸ **coastline** *n* outline of a coast

coat Ⓣ *n* **1** long outer garment with sleeves **2** animal's fur or hair **3** covering layer ▹ *v* **4** cover with a layer

▸ **coating** *n* covering layer

▸ **coat of arms** heraldic emblem of a family or institution

coax Ⓣ *v* **1** persuade gently **2** manipulate carefully and patiently

coaxial [koh-**ax**-ee-al] *adj* (of a cable) transmitting by means of two concentric conductors separated by an insulator

cob *n* **1** thickset type of horse **2** male swan **3** stalk of an ear of corn **4** round loaf of bread

cobalt *n* **1** metallic element **2** deep blue pigment made from it

cobber *n Aust informal* (used as a term of address between men) friend, mate

Cobbett *n* **William**. 1763–1835, English journalist and social reformer; founded *The Political Register* (1802); author of *Rural Rides* (1830)

cobble *v* **1** put together roughly ▹ *n* **2** Also **cobblestone** round stone used for paving

▸ **cobbler** *n* shoe mender

cobblers *pl n taboo, slang* nonsense

cobra *n* venomous hooded snake of Asia and Africa

cobweb *n* spider's web

Coca-Cola *n* ® carbonated soft drink

cocaine *n* addictive drug used as a narcotic and local anesthetic

coccyx [**kok**-six] *n, pl* **coccyges** [kok-**sije**-eez] bone at the base of the spinal column

cochineal *n* scarlet dye obtained from a Mexican insect

Cochise *n* died 1874, Apache Indian chief

cock *n* **1** male bird, esp. of the domestic fowl **2** stopcock **3** hammer of a gun ▹ *v* **4** draw back (the hammer of a gun) to firing position **5** lift and turn (part of the body)

▸ **cockerel** *n* young cock

▸ **cock-a-hoop** *adj* in high spirits

▸ **cock-and-bull story** improbable story

▸ **cockeyed** *adj informal* **1** askew **2** absurd

cockade *n* rosette or feather worn on a hat as a badge

cockatoo *n* crested parrot of Australia or the East Indies

cockatrice [**kok**-a-triss] *n* mythical animal like a small dragon

cockchafer *n* large flying beetle

Cockcroft *n* Sir **John Douglas**. 1897–1967, English nuclear physicist. With E. T. S. Walton, he produced the first artificial transmutation of an atomic nucleus (1932) and shared the Nobel prize for physics 1951

cocker spaniel *n* small breed of spaniel

cockle *n* edible bivalve mollusc

Cockney *n* **1** native of the East End of London **2** Cockney dialect

cockpit *n* **1** pilot's compartment in an aircraft **2** driver's compartment in a racing car

cockroach *n* beetle-like insect which is a household pest

cockscomb *n informal* conceited dandy

cocksure *adj* overconfident, arrogant

cocktail Ⓣ *n* **1** mixed alcoholic drink **2** appetizer of seafood or mixed fruits

cocky Ⓣ *adj* **cockier, cockiest** conceited and overconfident **cockily** *adv* **cockiness** *n*

cocoa *n* **1** powder made from the seed of the cacao tree **2** drink made from this powder

coconut *n* **1** large hard fruit of a type of palm tree **2** edible flesh of this fruit

▸ **coconut matting** coarse matting made from the fibrous husk of the coconut

cocoon *n* **1** silky sheath of a chrysalis **2** protective covering ▹ *v* **3** wrap or protect as if in a cocoon

Cocteau *n* **Jean**. 1889–1963, French dramatist, novelist, poet, critic, designer, and film director. His works include the novel *Les Enfants terribles* (1929) and the play *La Machine infernale* (1934)

cod *n* large food fish of the North Atlantic

COD cash on delivery

coda [**kode**-a] *n* final part of a musical composition

coddle *v* overprotect or pamper

code Ⓣ *n* **1** system of letters, symbols, or prearranged signals by which messages can be communicated secretly or briefly **2** set of principles or rules ▹ *v* **3** put into code

▸ **codify** [**kode**-if-fie] *v* organize (rules or

THESAURUS

coastline *See* **coast**

coat *n* **1 = fur**, hide, skin, hair, pelt, wool, fleece • *She gave the dog's coat a brush.* **2 = layer**, coating, covering, overlay ▸ *v* **3 = cover**, spread, apply, smear, plaster

coating *n* **= layer**, coat, covering • *a thin coating of ice*

See also: **cover**

coax *v* **= persuade**, cajole, talk into • *We coaxed her into coming with us.*

See also: **prompt**

cocktail *n* **= mixture**, mix, combination, blend

cocky *adj* **= overconfident**, arrogant, brash, conceited • *He was a bit cocky because he was winning all the time.*

See also: **boastful**

code *n* **1 = cipher**, cryptograph **2 = principles**, system, convention, custom, etiquette, maxim,

DICTIONARY

procedures) systematically **codification** *n*
codeine [**kode**-een] *n* drug used as a painkiller
codex *n, pl* **codices** volume of manuscripts of an ancient text
codger *n informal* old man
codicil [**kode**-iss-ill] *n* addition to a will
codpiece *n hist* bag covering the male genitals, attached to breeches
codswallop *n slang* nonsense
coeducation *n* education of boys and girls together **coeducational** *adj*
coefficient *n math* number or constant placed before and multiplying a quantity
coelacanth [**seel**-a-kanth] *n* primitive marine fish
coeliac disease [**seel**-ee-ak] *n* disease which hampers digestion of food
coerce [koh-**urss**] *v* compel or force **coercion** *n* **coercive** *adj*
Coetzee *n* **J**(**ohn**) **M**(**ichael**). born 1940, South African novelist; his works include *Life and Times of Michael K* (1983), *Age of Iron* (1990), *Disgrace* (1999), and *Elizabeth Costello* (2003): Nobel prize for literature 2003
coeval [koh-**eev**-al] *adj, n* contemporary
coexist *v* exist together, esp. peacefully despite differences **coexistence** *n*
C of E Church of England
coextend *v* (cause to) extend equally in space or time **coextension** *n* **coextensive** *adj*
coffee *n* **1** drink made from the roasted and ground seeds of a tropical shrub **2** beanlike seeds of this shrub ▷ *adj* **3** light brown
▸ **coffee table** small low table
coffer *n* **1** chest for valuables **coffers 2** store of money
cofferdam *n* watertight enclosure pumped dry to enable construction work to be done
coffin *n* box in which a corpse is buried or cremated
cog *n* **1** one of a series of teeth on the rim of a gearwheel **2** unimportant person in a big organization
cogent Ⓣ [**koh**-jent] *adj* forcefully convincing **cogency** *n* **cogently** *adv*
cogitate Ⓣ [**koj**-it-tate] *v* think deeply, ponder **cogitation** *n*
cognac [**kon**-yak] *n* French brandy
cognate *adj* related, akin
cognition *n* act or experience of knowing or acquiring knowledge **cognitive** *adj*
cognizance *n* knowledge, perception **cognizant** *adj*
cognomen [kog-**noh**-men] *n, pl* **-nomens, -nomina** [-**nom**-min-a] **1** nickname **2** surname
cognoscenti [kon-yo-**shen**-tee] *pl n* connoisseurs
cohabit *v* live together as husband and wife without being married **cohabitation** *n*
Cohen *n* **Leonard**. born 1934, Canadian singer, songwriter, and poet; recordings include *Songs of Leonard Cohen* (1968), *Songs of Love and Hate* (1971), *I'm Your Man* (1988), and *Ten New Songs* (2001)
cohere *v* **1** stick together **2** be logically connected and consistent **coherence** *n*
▸ **coherent** *adj* **1** capable of intelligible speech **2** logical and consistent **coherently** *adv*
▸ **cohesion** *n* tendency to unite **cohesive** *adj*
cohort *n* **1** band of associates **2** tenth part of a Roman legion
coif *n* close-fitting cap worn in the Middle Ages
coiffure *n* hairstyle
▸ **coiffeur** (**coiffeuse**) *n* hairdresser
coil Ⓣ *v* **1** wind or be wound in loops **2** move in a winding course ▷ *n* **3** something coiled **4** single loop of this **5** *Brit* contraceptive device inserted in the womb
coin Ⓣ *n* **1** piece of metal money **2** metal currency collectively ▷ *v* **3** invent (a word or phrase)
▸ **coin it in** *informal* make money rapidly
▸ **coinage** *n* **1** coining **2** coins collectively **3** word or phrase coined
coincide Ⓣ *v* **1** happen at the same time **2** agree or correspond exactly
▸ **coincidence** *n* **1** occurrence of simultaneous

THESAURUS

canon, ethics, manners, regulations, rules
cogent *adj* = **convincing**, strong, powerful, effective, potent, influential, forceful, weighty, compelling
cogitate *v* = **think**, consider, reflect, ponder, deliberate, contemplate, muse, meditate, mull over, ruminate
coherent *adj* **1** = **consistent**, organized, meaningful, logical, systematic, rational, orderly, lucid, reasoned **2** = **intelligible**, articulate, comprehensible
coil *v* = **wind**, curl, twist, spiral, loop, twine
• *a coiled spring*
coin *n* **1** = **money**, change, cash, silver, specie, copper ▸ *v* **2** = **invent**, create, originate, forge, mint, fabricate, mould, make up
coincide *v* **1** = **occur simultaneously**, synchronize, coexist, be concurrent **2** = **agree**, accord, match, square, tally, correspond, harmonize, concur
coincidence *n* **1** = **chance**, accident, luck, fluke, happy accident, stroke of luck **2** = **coinciding**, correspondence, conjunction, correlation, concurrence
coincidental *adj* = **chance**, accidental,

DICTIONARY

or apparently connected events **2** coinciding **coincident** *adj* **coincidental** *adj* **coincidentally** *adv*
coir *n* coconut husk fibre
coition [koh-**ish**-un], **coitus** [**koh**-it-uss] *n* sexual intercourse **coital** *adj*
coke[1] *n* solid fuel left after gas has been distilled from coal
coke[2] *n slang* cocaine
Coke *n* ® short for **Coca-Cola**
col *n* high mountain pass
cola *n* soft drink flavoured with an extract from the nuts of a tropical tree
colander *n* perforated bowl for straining or rinsing foods
Colbert *n* **1 Claudette**, real name *Claudette Lily Chauchoin*. 1905–96, French-born Hollywood actress, noted for her sophisticated comedy roles; her films include *It Happened One Night* (1934) and *The Palm Beach Story* (1942) **2 Jean Baptiste**. 1619–83, French statesman; chief minister to Louis XIV: reformed the taille and pursued a mercantilist policy, creating a powerful navy and merchant fleet and building roads and canals
cold Ⓣ *adj* **1** lacking heat **2** lacking affection or enthusiasm **3** (of a colour) giving an impression of coldness **4** *slang* unconscious: *out cold* ▷ *n* **5** lack of heat **6** illness characterized by catarrh and sneezing **coldly** *adv* **coldness** *n*
▸ **cold-blooded** *adj* **1** having a body temperature that varies with that of the surroundings **2** callous or cruel
▸ **cold cream** creamy preparation for softening and cleansing the skin
▸ **cold feet** *slang* fear
▸ **cold-shoulder** *v* treat (someone) with indifference
▸ **cold war** political hostility between countries without actual warfare
Cole *n* **Nat King**, real name *Nathaniel Adams Cole*. 1917–65, US popular singer and jazz pianist
Coleman *n* **Ornette**. born 1930, US avant-garde jazz alto saxophonist and multi-instrumentalist
Coleridge *n* **Samuel Taylor**. 1772–1834, English Romantic poet and critic, noted for poems such as *The Rime of the Ancient Mariner* (1798), *Kubla Khan* (1816), and *Christabel* (1816), and for his critical work *Biographia Literaria* (1817)
Coleridge-Taylor *n* **Samuel**. 1875–1912, British composer, best known for his trilogy of oratorios *Song of Hiawatha* (1898–1900)
coleslaw *n* salad dish of shredded raw cabbage in a dressing
Colette *n* full name *Sidonie Gabrielle Claudine Colette*. 1873–1954, French novelist; her works include *Chéri* (1920), *Gigi* (1944), and the series of *Claudine* books
coley *n* codlike food fish of the N Atlantic
colic *n* severe pains in the stomach and bowels **colicky** *adj*
Coligny, Coligni *n* **Gaspard de**, Seigneur de Châtillon. 1519–72, French Huguenot leader
colitis [koh-**lie**-tiss] *n* inflammation of the colon
collaborate Ⓣ *v* **1** work with another on a project **2** cooperate with an enemy invader **collaboration** *n* **collaborative** *adj* **collaborator** *n*
collage [kol-**lahzh**] *n* **1** art form in which various materials or objects are glued onto a surface **2** picture made in this way
collapse Ⓣ *v* **1** fall down or in suddenly **2** fail completely **3** fold compactly ▷ *n* **4** act of collapsing **5** sudden failure or breakdown **collapsible** *adj*
collar Ⓣ *n* **1** part of a garment round the neck **2** band put round an animal's neck **3** cut of meat from an animal's neck **4** band round a pipe, rod, or shaft ▷ *v informal* **5** seize,

THESAURUS

casual, unintentional, unplanned, fortuitous, fluky (*informal*)
cold *adj* **1 = chilly**, bitter, raw, icy, bleak, arctic, wintry, freezing, biting • *the coldest winter in ten years* OPPOSITE: hot **2 = unfriendly**, distant, frigid, lukewarm, reserved, aloof, stony • *a cold, unfeeling individual* OPPOSITE: warm ▸ *n* **3 = coldness**, chill, frigidity, frostiness, iciness
See also: **callous, cool, impersonal, remote, stiff**
cold-blooded *adj* **= callous**, ruthless, steely, heartless, dispassionate, unemotional, stony-hearted, unfeeling
collaborate *v* **1 = work together**, participate, cooperate, join forces, play ball (*informal*), team up **2 = conspire**, collude, cooperate, fraternize
collaboration *n* **= teamwork**, association, alliance, partnership, cooperation
collaborator *n* **1 = co-worker**, partner, associate, colleague, confederate, team-mate **2 = traitor**, turncoat, fraternizer, quisling
collapse *v* **1 = fall down**, give way • *The whole building is about to collapse.* **2 = fail**, founder, fold • *Thousands of small businesses collapsed last year.* ▸ *n* **3 = failure**, downfall • *the collapse of their marriage* **4 = faint**, breakdown, exhaustion, prostration
See also: **crash, fall, give**
collar *v* (*Informal*) **= seize**, arrest, catch, capture, grab, apprehend, nail (*informal*)

DICTIONARY

arrest **6** catch in order to speak to **7** take for oneself
▸ **collarbone** *n* bone joining the shoulder blade to the breast bone
collate *v* compare carefully **collator** *n*
▸ **collation** *n* **1** collating **2** light meal
collateral *n* security pledged for the repayment of a loan
colleague Ⓣ *n* fellow worker, esp. in a profession
collect[1] Ⓣ *v* **1** gather or be gathered together **2** accumulate (stamps etc.) as a hobby **3** fetch **collector** *n*
▸ **collected** *adj* calm and controlled
▸ **collection** *n* **1** collecting **2** things collected
▸ **collective** *adj* **1** of or done by a group, combined ▷ *n* **2** group of people working together on an enterprise and sharing the benefits from it **collectively** *adv*
collect[2] *n* short prayer
colleen *n Irish* girl
college *n* **1** place of higher education **2** group of people of the same profession or with special duties **collegiate** *adj*
collide Ⓣ *v* **1** crash together violently **2** conflict **collision** *n*
collie *n* silky-coated sheepdog
colliery *n, pl* **-lieries** coal mine
▸ **collier** *n* **1** coal miner **2** coal ship
Collins *n* **1 Michael**. 1890–1922, Irish republican revolutionary: a leader of Sinn Féin; member of the Irish delegation that negotiated the treaty with Great Britain (1921) that established the Irish Free State **2** (**William**) **Wilkie**. 1824–89, British author, noted particularly for his suspense novel *The Moonstone* (1868) **3 William**. 1721–59, British poet, noted for his odes; regarded as a precursor of romanticism
collocate *v* (of words) occur together regularly **collocation** *n*
colloid *n* suspension of particles in a solution
collop *n* small slice of meat
colloquial Ⓣ *adj* suitable for informal speech or writing
▸ **colloquialism** *n* colloquial expression
colloquy *n, pl* **-quies** conversation or conference
collusion *n* secret agreement for a fraudulent purpose
▸ **collude** *v* act in collusion
collywobbles *pl n slang* **1** nervousness **2** upset stomach
cologne *n* perfumed toilet water
colon[1] *n* punctuation mark (:)
colon[2] *n* part of the large intestine connected to the rectum
colonel *n* senior commissioned army or air-force officer
colonnade *n* row of columns
colony Ⓣ *n, pl* **-nies** **1** group of people who settle in a new country but remain subject to their parent state **2** territory occupied by a colony **3** group of people or animals of the same kind living together
▸ **colonial** *adj, n* (inhabitant) of a colony
▸ **colonialism** *n* policy of acquiring and maintaining colonies
▸ **colonist** *n* settler in a colony
▸ **colonize** *v* make into a colony **colonization** *n*
colophon *n* publisher's emblem
Colorado beetle *n* black-and-yellow beetle that is a serious pest of potatoes
coloration *n* colouring
coloratura *n music* complicated vocal passage
colossal Ⓣ *adj* huge

THESAURUS

colleague *n* = **fellow worker**, partner, associate, workmate • *I'll have to consult my colleagues.*
See also: **assistant**
collect *v* **1** = **gather**, raise, assemble, accumulate • *collecting signatures for a petition* OPPOSITE: scatter **2** = **assemble**, rally, cluster, convene, converge, congregate, flock together
See also: **concentrate, stockpile**
collected *adj* = **calm**, cool, serene, composed, poised, self-possessed, unperturbed, unruffled
collection *n* **1** = **accumulation**, group, store, assortment • *my CD collection* **2** = **group**, company, crowd, assembly, cluster, assortment **3** = **contribution**, offering, alms, offertory
See also: **number, variety**
collective *adj* = **combined**, corporate, joint, aggregate, composite, shared, unified, cumulative, united
collectively *See* **together**
collide *v* **1** = **crash**, clash, come into collision, meet head-on **2** = **conflict**, clash ▷ **collide with** *See* **hit**
collision *n* **1** = **crash**, impact, accident, bump, pile-up (*informal*), smash, wreck **2** = **conflict**, opposition, clash, encounter, confrontation, skirmish
colloquial *adj* = **conversational**, everyday, informal • *a colloquial expression*
colony *n* **1** = **dominion**, territory, dependency • *a former British colony* **2** = **community**, settlement, outpost • *an artists' colony*
colossal *adj* = **huge**, massive, vast, enormous, mammoth, immense, gigantic • *a*

DICTIONARY

colossus *n, pl* **-si, -suses 1** huge statue **2** huge or important person or thing
colostomy *n, pl* **-mies** operation to form an opening from the colon onto the surface of the body, for emptying the bowel
colour Ⓣ *n* **1** appearance of things as a result of reflecting light **2** paint or pigment **3** complexion **colours 4** flag **5** *sports* badge or symbol denoting membership of a team ▷ *v* **6** apply or give colour to **7** influence or distort **8** blush **colourless** *adj*
▸ **Coloured** *adj* **1** *offensive* non-White **2** (in S Africa) of mixed race
▸ **colourful** *adj* **1** with bright or varied colours **2** vivid or distinctive **colourfully** *adv*
▸ **colour-blind** *adj* unable to distinguish between certain colours
colt *n* young male horse
Coltrane *n* **John** (**William**). 1926–67, US jazz tenor and soprano saxophonist and composer
Columba *n* **Saint**. ?521–597 AD, Irish missionary: founded the monastery at Iona (563) from which the Picts were converted to Christianity. Feast day: June 9
columbine *n* garden flower with five spurred petals
Columbus *n* **Christopher**, Spanish name *Cristóbal Colón*, Italian name *Cristoforo Colombo*. 1451–1506, Italian navigator and explorer in the service of Spain, who discovered the New World (1492)
column Ⓣ *n* **1** pillar **2** vertical arrangement of numbers **3** long narrow formation of troops **4** vertical division of a newspaper page **5** regular feature in a newspaper
▸ **columnist** *n* journalist writing a regular feature for a newspaper
coma Ⓣ *n* state of deep unconsciousness
▸ **comatose** *adj* **1** in a coma **2** sound asleep
Comaneci *n* **Nadia**. born 1961, Romanian gymnast; gold medal winner in the 1976 Olympic Games: defected to the US in 1989
comb Ⓣ *n* **1** toothed implement for arranging the hair **2** cock's crest **3** honeycomb ▷ *v* **4** use a comb on **5** search with great care
combat Ⓣ *v* **-bating, -bated**, *n* fight, struggle **combatant** *n* **combative** *adj*
combe *n* same as **coomb**
combine Ⓣ *v* **1** join together ▷ *n* **2** association of people or firms for a common purpose
▸ **combination** *n* **1** combining **2** people or things combined **3** set of numbers that opens a special lock **combinations 4** one-piece undergarment with long sleeves and legs
▸ **combine harvester** machine which reaps and threshes grain in one operation
combo *n, pl* **-bos** small group of jazz musicians
combustion Ⓣ *n* process of burning
▸ **combustible** *adj* burning easily
come Ⓣ *v* **coming, came, come 1** move towards a place, arrive **2** occur **3** be available **4** reach a specified point or condition **5** originate (from) **6** become
▸ **come across** *v* **1** meet or find by accident **2** (foll. by *as*) give an impression (of being)

THESAURUS

colossal statue OPPOSITE: tiny
See also: **large, unbelievable**
colour *n* **1 = hue**, shade, tint, pigmentation • *Her favourite colour is blue.* **2 = paint**, dye, pigment • *food colour* ▸ *v* **3 = tint**, paint, dye, stain • *men and women who colour their hair* **4 = bias**, prejudice, distort, slant • *The experience coloured his opinion of lawyers.* **5 = blush**, flush, redden
colourful *adj* **1 = bright**, rich, intense, brilliant, vibrant, vivid, psychedelic, jazzy (*informal*), multicoloured, kaleidoscopic • *colourful clothes* OPPOSITE: dull **2 = interesting**, rich, graphic, vivid, lively • *a colourful character* OPPOSITE: dull
colourless *adj* **1 = drab**, anemic, wan, achromatic, ashen, bleached, faded, washed out **2 = uninteresting**, dull, dreary, lacklustre, characterless, insipid, vapid
column *n* **1 = pillar**, post, support, shaft, upright, obelisk **2 = line**, file, row, rank, procession, cavalcade
coma *n* **= unconsciousness**, oblivion, stupor, trance
comb *v* **1 = untangle**, dress, arrange, groom **2 = search**, hunt, rake, scour, forage, sift, ransack, rummage
combat *n* **1 = fight**, action, war, battle, struggle, contest, conflict, encounter, engagement, skirmish, warfare ▸ *v* **2 = fight**, oppose, resist, defy, withstand, do battle with
combatant *n* **= fighter**, soldier, opponent, enemy, warrior, adversary, antagonist
combination *n* **1 = mixture**, mix, blend, amalgamation • *a combination of charm and skill* **2 = association**, union, coalition, alliance, federation, consortium, syndicate, confederation
See also: **cross**
combine *v* **= mix**, unite, merge, blend, integrate, fuse, amalgamate • *trying to combine business with pleasure* OPPOSITE: separate
combustion *See* **fire**
come *v* **1 = arrive**, appear, enter, materialize, show up (*informal*), turn up (*informal*) • *Two young children came into the room.* **2 = happen**, fall, occur, take place • *It's too bad that birthdays come only once a year.* **3 = move towards**, near, advance, approach, draw near **4 = result**,

DICTIONARY

▶ **comeback** *n informal* **1** return to a former position **2** retort
▶ **comedown** *n* **1** decline in status **2** disappointment
▶ **comeuppance** *n informal* deserved punishment
comedy ⓣ *n, pl* **-dies** humorous play, film, or programme
▶ **comedian** (**comedienne**) *n* entertainer who tells jokes
comely *adj* **-lier, -liest** *old-fashioned* good-looking
comestibles *pl n* food
comet *n* heavenly body with a long luminous tail
comfort ⓣ *n* **1** physical ease or wellbeing **2** relief from suffering **3** person or thing that brings ease ▷ *v* **4** give comfort to **comforter** *n*
▶ **comfortable** *adj* **1** giving comfort **2** free from pain **3** *informal* well-off financially **comfortably** *adv*
comfrey *n* tall plant with bell-shaped flowers
comfy *adj* **-fier, -fiest** *informal* comfortable
comic ⓣ *adj* **1** humorous, funny **2** relating to comedy ▷ *n* **3** comedian **4** magazine consisting of strip cartoons
▶ **comical** *adj* amusing **comically** *adv*
comma *n* punctuation mark (,)
command ⓣ *v* **1** order **2** have authority over **3** deserve and get **4** look down over ▷ *n* **5** authoritative instruction that something must be done **6** authority to command **7** knowledge, mastery **8** military or naval unit with a specific function
▶ **commandant** *n* officer commanding a military group
▶ **commandeer** *v* seize for military use
▶ **commander** *n* **1** military officer in command of a group or operation **2** middle-ranking naval officer
▶ **commander-in-chief** *n* supreme commander
▶ **commandment** *n* divine command
commando *n, pl* **-dos, -does** (member of) a military unit trained for swift

THESAURUS

issue, emerge, flow, arise, originate, emanate **5 = reach**, extend **6 = be available**, be made, be offered, be on offer, be produced ▷ **come about = happen**, result, occur, arise, transpire (*informal*), befall, come to pass, take place ▷ **come across = find**, meet, discover, notice, encounter, unearth, bump into (*informal*), chance upon, stumble upon ▷ **come after** *See* **follow** ▷ **come apart** *See* **split** ▷ **come back = return**, recur, re-enter, reappear ▷ **come between** *See* **divide** ▷ **come first** *See* **win** ▷ **come on** *See* **flourish** ▷ **come out** *See* **appear** ▷ **come to = revive**, rally, recover, come around, regain consciousness; **= amount to**, total, add up to ▷ **come together** *See* **assemble** ▷ **come upon** *See* **meet** ▷ **come up with** *See* **invent** ▷ **come with** *See* **accompany**
comeback *n* **1** (*Informal*) **= return**, rally, rebound, recovery, triumph, revival, resurgence **2 = response**, reply, retaliation, retort, rejoinder, riposte
comedian *n* **= comic**, card (*informal*), clown, wit, wag, joker, humorist, jester, funny man
comedown *n* **1 = decline**, reverse, demotion, deflation **2** (*Informal*) **= disappointment**, blow, humiliation, letdown, anticlimax
comedy *n* **= humour**, fun, farce, hilarity, jesting, joking, light entertainment
comeuppance *n* (*Informal*) **= punishment**, retribution, chastening, deserts, due reward, recompense
comfort *n* **1 = ease**, luxury, well-being • *I settled back in comfort.* **2 = relief**, help, support, satisfaction, consolation • *Her words gave him some comfort.* ▶ *v* **3 = console**, cheer, reassure, soothe • *trying to comfort the upset child*
comfortable *adj* **1 = relaxing**, easy, cozy, restful, homey • *a comfortable chair* OPPOSITE: uncomfortable **2 = at ease**, happy, contented, at home, relaxed • *I don't feel comfortable around him.* OPPOSITE: uneasy **3** (*Informal*) **= well-off**, affluent, prosperous, well-to-do, in clover (*informal*) *See also*: **leisurely, wealthy**
comforting *adj* **= consoling**, soothing, heart-warming, encouraging, cheering, consolatory, reassuring
comic *adj* **1 = funny**, humorous, amusing, witty, comical, farcical, droll, jocular ▶ *n* **2 = comedian**, clown, wit, buffoon, wag, humorist, jester, funny man
comical *adj* **= funny**, comic, hilarious, humorous, amusing, priceless, farcical, droll, side-splitting
coming *adj* **1 = approaching**, near, imminent, forthcoming, nigh, at hand, impending, in store ▶ *n* **2 = arrival**, approach, advent
command *v* **1 = order**, bid (*formal*), demand, direct • *I commanded the dog to lie down.* **2 = control**, lead, head, manage, supervise • *the general who commanded the UN troops* ▶ *n* **3 = order**, instruction, injunction, decree, directive, bidding • *The punishment was carried out at the emperor's command.* **4 = knowledge**, grasp, mastery • *a good command of English* **5 = authority**,

DICTIONARY

raids in enemy territory
commemorate ⊕ *v* honour or keep alive the memory of **commemoration** *n* **commemorative** *adj*
commence ⊕ *v* begin **commencement** *n*
commend ⊕ *v* **1** praise **2** recommend **3** entrust **commendable** *adj* **commendably** *adv* **commendation** *n*
commensurable *adj* measurable by the same standard **commensurability** *n*
commensurate *adj* corresponding in degree, size, or value
comment ⊕ *n* **1** remark **2** gossip **3** explanatory note ▷ *v* **4** make a comment or comments
▶ **commentary** *n* **1** spoken accompaniment to a broadcast or film **2** explanatory notes
▶ **commentate** *v* provide a commentary **commentator** *n*
commerce ⊕ *n* **1** buying and selling, trade **2** dealings
▶ **commercial** *adj* **1** of commerce **2** (of television or radio) paid for by advertisers **3** having profit as the main aim ▷ *n* **4** television or radio advertisement
▶ **commercialize** *v* make commercial **commercialization** *n*
commingle *v* mix or be mixed
commis *n, pl* **-mis** apprentice waiter or chef
commiserate ⊕ *v* (foll. by *with*) express pity or sympathy (for) **commiseration** *n*
commissar *n* official responsible for political education in Communist countries
commissariat *n* military department in charge of food supplies
commissary *n, pl* **-saries 1** *US* shop supplying food or equipment, as in a military camp **2** representative or deputy
commission ⊕ *n* **1** order for a piece of work, esp. a work of art **2** duty or task given to someone **3** percentage paid to a salesperson for each sale made **4** group of people appointed to perform certain duties **5** committing **6** *mil* rank or authority officially given to an officer **7** delegated authority ▷ *v* **8** place an order for **9** *mil* give a commission to **10** grant authority to
▶ **out of commission** not working
▶ **commissioner** *n* **1** appointed official in a government department **2** member of a commission
commissionaire *n* uniformed doorman at a hotel, theatre, etc.
commit ⊕ *v* **-mitting, -mitted 1** perform (a

THESAURUS

government, charge, power, rule, control, management, supervision, mastery
See also: **administer, direction, exact, instruct, tell**
commandeer *v* = **seize**, appropriate, confiscate, sequester, requisition, sequestrate
commander *n* = **officer**, head, leader, chief, captain, boss (*informal*), ruler, alpha male, commanding officer
commanding *adj* = **controlling**, decisive, dominant, superior, advantageous, dominating
commemorate *v* = **celebrate**, honour • *concerts to commemorate the anniversary of his birth*
commemoration *n* = **remembrance**, ceremony, tribute, honouring, memorial service
commence *v* = **begin**, start, open, originate, initiate, embark on, enter upon
commencement *n* = **beginning**, start, launch, birth, opening, origin, dawn, onset, inauguration, outset, inception, initiation, embarkation
commend *v* = **praise**, approve, recommend, applaud, acclaim, compliment, extol, speak highly of
commendable *adj* = **praiseworthy**, worthy, exemplary, deserving, admirable, laudable, meritorious, creditable, estimable
commendation *n* = **praise**, credit, approval, recommendation, acclaim, kudos, encouragement, acclamation, approbation, good opinion, panegyric
comment *v* **1** = **remark**, say, note, mention, observe, point out • *He refused to comment on the rumours.* **2** = **annotate**, explain, interpret, elucidate ▶ *n* **3** = **remark**, statement, observation • *sarcastic comments* **4** = **note**, explanation, commentary, illustration, exposition, annotation
See also: **word**
commentary *n* **1** = **narration**, description, voice-over **2** = **notes**, review, analysis, explanation, critique, treatise
commentator *n* **1** = **reporter**, sportscaster, special correspondent **2** = **critic**, interpreter, annotator
commerce *n* = **trade**, business, traffic, exchange, dealing
commercial *adj* **1** = **mercantile**, trading **2** = **materialistic**, mercenary, profit-making ▶ *n* **3** = **advertisement**, ad (*informal*), announcement, plug (*informal*)
commiserate *v* = **sympathize**, console, pity, feel for
commission *n* **1** = **duty**, mission, task, mandate, errand **2** = **fee**, cut, percentage, rake-off (*slang*), royalties **3** = **committee**, board, delegation, commissioners, deputation, representatives ▶ *v* **4** = **appoint**, order, contract, select, nominate, engage, delegate, authorize, empower, depute
commit *v* **1** = **do**, perform, perpetrate, carry

DICTIONARY

crime or error) **2** pledge to a cause or course of action **3** send (someone) to prison or hospital
▸ **committal** *n* sending of someone for trial, etc.
▸ **commitment** *n* **1** dedication to a cause **2** responsibility or promise that hinders freedom of action
committee Ⓣ *n* group of people appointed to perform a specified service or function
commode Ⓣ *n* **1** seat with a compartment holding a chamber pot **2** chest of drawers
commodious *adj* roomy
commodity Ⓣ *n, pl* **-ities** article of trade
commodore *n* **1** senior naval or air-force officer **2** president of a yacht club
Commodus *n* **Lucius Aelius Aurelius**, son of Marcus Aurelius. 161–192 AD, Roman emperor (180–192), noted for his tyrannical reign
common Ⓣ *adj* **1** occurring often **2** belonging to two or more people **3** public, general **4** low-class ▹ *n* **5** area of grassy land belonging to a community **commons 6** ordinary people **7 Commons** House of Commons **commonly** *adv*
▸ **commoner** *n Brit* person who does not belong to the nobility
▸ **common-law** *adj* (of a relationship) regarded as marriage through being long-standing
▸ **common Market** European Community
▸ **commonplace** *adj* **1** ordinary, everyday ▹ *n* **2** trite remark
▸ **common sense** sound practical understanding
▸ **commonwealth** *n* **1** republic **2 Commonwealth** federation of independent states that used to be ruled by Britain
commotion Ⓣ *n* noisy disturbance
commune[1] Ⓣ *n* group of people living together, sharing property and responsibilities
▸ **communal** *adj* shared **communally** *adv*
commune[2] Ⓣ *v* (foll. by *with*) experience strong emotion (for)
▸ **communion** *n* **1** sharing of thoughts or feelings **2 Communion** Christian ritual of sharing consecrated bread and wine **3** religious group with shared beliefs and practices
communicate Ⓣ *v* **1** make known, reveal (information, thoughts, or feelings) **2** (of rooms) have a connecting door
▸ **communicable** *adj* (of a disease) able to be passed on
▸ **communicant** *n* person who receives Communion
▸ **communication** *n* **1** communicating **2** thing communicated **communications 3** means of travelling or sending messages
▸ **communicative** *adj* willing to talk
communiqué [kom-**mune**-ik-kay] *n* official announcement

THESAURUS

out • *A crime has been committed.* **2 = put in custody**, imprison, confine
commitment *n* **1 = dedication**, involvement, loyalty, devotion **2 = responsibility**, tie, duty, obligation, liability, engagement
committed *See* **fervent**
committee *See* **council**
commode *n* **= washroom**, lavatory, latrine, loo, powder room, convenience *or* public convenience, toilet, water closet, W.C., restroom, bathroom
commodity *See* **product**
common *adj* **1 = general**, popular, widespread, universal, prevalent, prevailing • *a common complaint* OPPOSITE: rare **2 = ordinary**, average, standard, usual, everyday, plain, commonplace • *the common cold* **3 = vulgar**, rude, coarse • *a common, rude guest* OPPOSITE: refined **4 = collective**, public, popular, social, communal, shared • *the common good* ▹ **common sense = good sense**, judgment, prudence, level-headedness • *Use your common sense.*
See also: **head, sense**
See also: **frequent, low, natural**
commonplace *adj* **1 = everyday**, common, obvious, ordinary, mundane, banal, humdrum, widespread ▸ *n* **2 = cliché**, truism, banality, platitude
commotion *n* **= disturbance**, disorder, turmoil, excitement, uproar, fuss, upheaval, furor, tumult, hue and cry, rumpus
communal *adj* **= public**, general, joint, collective, shared
commune *n* **= community**, collective, cooperative, kibbutz ▸ *v* ▹ **commune with = contemplate**, ponder, meditate on, muse on, reflect on
communicate *v* **1 = contact**, correspond, be in contact, be in touch • *We communicate mainly by email.* **2 = pass on**, spread, inform, transmit, convey, impart • *The results will be communicated by mail.* ▹ **communicate with** *See* **contact**
See also: **express**
communication *n* **1 = passing on**, link, contact, transmission, conversation, correspondence, dissemination **2 = message**, report, news, statement, information, word, announcement, disclosure, dispatch
communicative *adj* **= talkative**, open, outgoing, forthcoming, frank, expansive,

DICTIONARY

communism Ⓣ *n* **1** doctrine that all property and means of production should be shared by the people **2 Communism** political and social system of state control of the economy and society in some countries **communist** *n, adj*

community Ⓣ *n, pl* **-ties 1** all the people living in one district **2** group having shared interests or origins **3** society, the public ▸ **community centre** building used by a community for activities

commute *v* **1** travel daily to and from work **2** reduce (a sentence) to a less severe one ▸ **commuter** *n* person who commutes to and from work ▸ **commutator** *n* device used to change alternating electric current into direct current

compact[1] Ⓣ *adj* **1** closely packed **2** neatly arranged **3** concise, brief ▹ *n* **4** small flat case containing a mirror and face powder ▹ *v* **5** pack closely together **compactly** *adv* **compactness** *n* ▸ **compact disc** small digital audio disc on which the sound is read by an optical laser system

compact[2] Ⓣ *n* agreement, contract

companion Ⓣ *n* person who associates with or accompanies another ▸ **companionable** *adj* friendly **companionship** *n*

companionway *n* ladder linking the decks of a ship

company Ⓣ *n, pl* **-nies 1** business firm **2** group of actors **3** small unit of troops **4** crew of a ship **5** companionship **6** gathering of people **7** guest or guests **8** associates

compare Ⓣ *v* **1** examine (things) to find the resemblances or differences **2** declare to be like **3** be worthy of comparison **comparable** *adj* **comparability** *n* ▸ **comparative** *adj* **1** relative **2** involving comparison **3** *grammar* denoting the form of an adjective or adverb indicating *more* ▹ *n* **4** *grammar* comparative form of a word **comparatively** *adv* **comparison** *n*

compartment Ⓣ *n* **1** separate section **2** section of a railway carriage

compass Ⓣ *n* **1** instrument for showing direction, with a needle that points north **2** range **compasses 3** hinged

THESAURUS

informative, chatty, loquacious, voluble

Communism *n* = **socialism**, Bolshevism, collectivism, Marxism, state socialism

Communist *n* = **socialist**, Red (*informal*), Marxist, Bolshevik, collectivist

community *n* = **society**, people, company, public, state, commonwealth, populace, brotherhood, general public, residents

commuter *n* = **daily traveller**, straphanger (*informal*), suburbanite

compact[1] *adj* **1 = closely packed**, solid, thick, dense, condensed, compressed, pressed together **2 = brief**, terse, concise, succinct, compendious, to the point ▸ *v* **3 = pack closely**, stuff, cram, compress, condense, tamp

compact[2] *n* = **agreement**, deal, contract, bond, treaty, bargain, understanding, pact, arrangement, covenant

companion *n* **1 = friend**, partner, comrade, pal (*informal*), crony • *They've been constant companions for the past six years.* **2 = escort**, assistant, aide, attendant, chaperon, squire

companionship *n* = **fellowship**, company, friendship, camaraderie, rapport, togetherness, comradeship, conviviality, esprit de corps

company *n* **1 = business**, house, firm, corporation, establishment, numbered company (*Canad*) • *a publishing company* **2 = group**, party, community, crowd, band, circle, assembly, troupe, ensemble • *the Canadian Opera Company.* **3 = companionship**, presence • *I could do with some company* **4 = guests**, party, callers, visitors

See also: **association, body, enterprise, organization**

comparable *adj* **1 = on a par**, equivalent, equal, tantamount, proportionate, commensurate, a match for, as good as, in a class with, on a level playing field (*informal*) **2 = similar**, related, alike, akin, analogous, cognate, corresponding, cut from the same cloth, of a piece

comparative *adj* = **relative**, qualified, by comparison

compare *v* **1 = contrast**, weigh, juxtapose • *Compare these two illustrations.* **2** (usually with *with*) = **be on a par with**, match, approach, equal, bear comparison, be in the same class as, be the equal of, compete with, hold a candle to ▹ **compare to = liken to**, resemble, parallel, correlate to, equate to, identify with, mention in the same breath as

comparison *n* **1 = contrast**, distinction, juxtaposition **2 = similarity**, likeness, correlation, resemblance, analogy, comparability

compartment *n* **1 = car** • *We shared our compartment with a group of tourists.* **2 = section**, division, chamber, bay • *the freezer compartment of the fridge*

compass *n* = **range**, area, reach, field, limit, extent, scope, boundary, realm, circumference

DICTIONARY

instrument for drawing circles
compassion Ⓣ *n* pity, sympathy
compassionate *adj*
compatible Ⓣ *adj* able to exist, work, or be used together **compatibility** *n*
compatriot *n* fellow countryman or countrywoman
compeer *n* equal, companion
compel Ⓣ *v* **-pelling, -pelled** force (to be or do)
▶ **compelling** *adj* **1** convincing **2** arousing strong interest
compendium *n, pl* **-diums, -dia** selection of different table games in one container
▶ **compendious** *adj* brief but inclusive
compensate Ⓣ *v* **1** make amends to (someone), esp. for injury or loss **2** (foll. by *for*) cancel out a bad effect **compensation** *n*
compensatory *adj*
compère *n Brit* **1** person who presents a stage, radio, or television show ▷ *v* **2** be the compère of
compete Ⓣ *v* **1** take part in (a contest or competition) **2** strive (to achieve something or be successful)
▶ **competition** *n* **1** competing **2** event in which people compete **3** people against whom one competes **competitive** *adj*
competitor *n*
competent Ⓣ *adj* having sufficient skill or knowledge **competently** *adv* **competence** *n*
compile Ⓣ *v* collect and arrange (information), esp. to form a book
compilation *n* **compiler** *n*
complacent Ⓣ *adj* self-satisfied
complacently *adv* **complacency** *n*
complain Ⓣ *v* **1** express resentment or displeasure **2** state that one is suffering from pain or illness
▶ **complaint** *n* **1** complaining **2** mild illness

THESAURUS

compassion *n* = **sympathy**, understanding, humanity, condolence, mercy, sorrow, pity, kindness, tenderness, fellow feeling, tender-heartedness
compassionate *adj* = **sympathetic**, kind, caring, humane, merciful, empathetic, kind-hearted, tender • *My father is a deeply compassionate man*.
See also: **benevolent, understanding**
compassionately *See* **well**
compatibility *n* = **harmony**, agreement, sympathy, empathy, affinity, rapport, concord, like-mindedness
compatible *adj* = **harmonious**, consistent, congenial, in keeping • *Business partners should be compatible*. OPPOSITE: incompatible
compel *v* = **force**, make, pressure, coerce, oblige, railroad (*informal*), obligate, pressurize, constrain, impel, dragoon
compelling *adj* **1** = **fascinating**, irresistible, hypnotic, enchanting, enthralling, gripping, mesmeric, spellbinding **2** = **pressing**, urgent, binding, imperative, unavoidable, coercive, overriding, peremptory **3** = **convincing**, powerful, forceful, conclusive, weighty, irrefutable, cogent, telling
compensate *v* **1** = **repay**, reward, refund, atone • *You will be properly compensated for your loss*. **2** = **cancel out**, balance, offset, counteract, make up for • *His lack of skill was compensated for by his enthusiasm*.
See also: **pay**
compensation *n* = **amends**, payment, atonement, damages • *compensation for his injuries*
compete *v* = **contend**, fight, contest, vie • *companies competing for business*
See also: **play**
competence *n* = **ability**, capacity, skill, fitness, capability, expertise, proficiency, suitability
competent *adj* = **able**, fit, capable, adequate, suitable, qualified, proficient
competently *See* **well**
competition *n* **1** = **rivalry**, opposition, struggle, contest, contention • *There's a lot of competition for this year's Gemini Awards*. **2** = **contest**, event, championship, tournament • *a surfing competition* **3** = **opposition**, field, challengers, rivals
See also: **competitor, match**
competitive *adj* **1** = **cut-throat**, rival, aggressive, antagonistic, at odds, dog-eat-dog, opposing **2** = **ambitious**, combative
competitor *n* = **contestant**, opposition, competition, rival, opponent, challenger, adversary • *one of the youngest competitors in the event*
See also: **candidate**
compilation *n* = **collection**, treasury, accumulation, assortment, anthology, assemblage
compile *v* = **put together**, gather, collect, organize, garner, accumulate, amass, cull, marshal
complacency *n* = **self-satisfaction**, satisfaction, contentment, smugness
complacent *adj* = **self-satisfied**, satisfied, smug, serene, contented, unconcerned, pleased with oneself, resting on one's laurels
complain *v* = **find fault**, whine, carp, grumble, moan, grouse, make a fuss, kick up a fuss (*informal*), kvetch (*informal*) • *They always complain about the noise*.
See also: **protest**
complaint *n* **1** = **grumble**, protest, criticism,

DICTIONARY

▸ **complainant** *n* plaintiff
complaisant [kom-**play**-zant] *adj* obliging, willing to please **complaisance** *n*
complement Ⓣ *n* **1** thing that completes something **2** complete amount or number **3** *grammar* word or words added after a verb to complete the meaning ▷ *v* **4** make complete **complementary** *adj*
complete Ⓣ *adj* **1** thorough **2** perfect in quality or kind **3** finished **4** having all the necessary parts ▷ *v* **5** finish **6** make whole or perfect **completely** *adv*
▸ **completeness** *n* wholeness
▸ **completion** *n* finishing
complex Ⓣ *adj* **1** made up of parts **2** complicated ▷ *n* **3** whole made up of parts **4** group of unconscious feelings that influences behaviour **complexity** *n*
complexion Ⓣ *n* **1** natural appearance of the skin of the face **2** character or nature
complicate Ⓣ *v* make or become complex or difficult to deal with **complication** *n*
complicity *n* fact of being an accomplice, esp. in a crime
compliment Ⓣ *n* **1** expression of praise **compliments 2** formal greetings ▷ *v* **3** praise
▸ **complimentary** *adj* **1** expressing praise **2** free of charge
compline *n* last service of the day in the Roman Catholic Church
comply Ⓣ *v* **-plying, -plied** act in accordance (with a rule, order, or request) **compliance** *n* **compliant** *adj*
component Ⓣ *n* **1** part of a whole ▷ *adj* **2** being a component

THESAURUS

objection, grievance • *There have been a number of complaints about the food.* **2 = illness**, disease, upset, disorder, ailment, sickness, malady, affliction
complement *n* **1 = completion**, supplement, counterpart, companion, consummation, finishing touch, rounding-off **2 = total**, capacity, aggregate, quota, entirety, totality, wholeness ▸ *v* **3 = complete**, cap (*informal*), crown, round off, set off
complementary *adj* **= completing**, companion, reciprocal, corresponding, interdependent, interrelating, matched
complete *adj* **1 = total**, perfect, absolute, outright, utter, thorough, consummate • *a complete transformation* **2 = whole**, full, entire, intact, undivided • *a complete set of tools* OPPOSITE: incomplete **3 = finished**, accomplished, achieved, concluded, ended ▸ *v* **4 = finish**, end, conclude • *He has just completed his first novel.*
See also: **accomplish, achieve, ideal, over, perform, pure, rank, sheer**
completely *adv* **= totally**, fully, absolutely, entirely, perfectly, altogether, thoroughly, wholly, utterly, every inch, hook, line and sinker, in full, lock, stock and barrel, one hundred per cent
completion *n* **= finishing**, end, close, conclusion, culmination, fruition, fulfillment, bitter end
complex *adj* **1 = complicated**, difficult, involved, tangled, intricate • *complex issues* OPPOSITE: simple **2 = compound**, multiple, composite, manifold, heterogeneous, multifarious ▸ *n* **3 = obsession**, problem, thing, preoccupation, phobia, fixation • *I have never had a complex about my height.* **4 = structure**, system, network, organization, scheme, aggregate, composite
See also: **elaborate, hard, sophisticated, tricky**
complexion *n* **1 = skin**, colour, hue, pigmentation, colouring, skin tone **2 = nature**, look, light, appearance, character, aspect, guise, make-up
complexity *n* **= complication**, involvement, ramification, intricacy, entanglement, elaboration
complicate *v* **= make difficult**, involve, confuse, entangle, muddle, ravel
complicated *adj* **1 = complex**, elaborate, involved, intricate, convoluted • *a complicated situation* OPPOSITE: simple **2 = difficult**, problematic, involved, troublesome, perplexing, puzzling
See also: **confusing, hard, sophisticated, tricky**
complication *n* **1 = complexity**, web, confusion, intricacy, entanglement **2 = problem**, difficulty, snag, obstacle, embarrassment, drawback
compliment *n* **1 = praise**, tribute, honour, eulogy, bouquet, commendation, congratulations, flattery ▸ *v* **2 = praise**, congratulate, salute, commend, flatter, extol, brown-nose (*slang*), pay tribute to, speak highly of
complimentary *adj* **1 = flattering**, appreciative, congratulatory, approving, commendatory, laudatory **2 = free**, courtesy, honorary, gratuitous, donated, gratis, on the house
compliments *pl n* **= greetings**, salutation, good wishes, regards, remembrances, respects
comply *v* **= obey**, follow, submit, observe, acquiesce, abide by, adhere to, conform to, toe the line
component *n* **1 = part**, unit, piece, item,

DICTIONARY

comport *v* behave (oneself) in a specified way
compose Ⓣ *v* **1** put together **2** be the component parts of **3** create (music or literature) **4** arrange in order **5** calm (oneself) **composer** *n*
composite *adj* made up of separate parts
composition Ⓣ *n* **1** way that something is put together or arranged **2** musical work **3** essay **4** act of composing
compositor *n* person who arranges type for printing
compos mentis *adj Latin* sane
compost *n* decayed plants used as a fertilizer
composure Ⓣ *n* calmness
compote *n* fruit stewed in syrup
compound[1] Ⓣ *n, adj* **1** (thing, esp. chemical) made up of two or more combined parts or elements ▷ *v* **2** combine or make by combining **3** intensify, make worse
compound[2] *n* fenced enclosure containing buildings
comprehend Ⓣ *v* understand **comprehensible** *adj* **comprehension** *n*
▸ **comprehensive** *adj* of broad scope, fully inclusive
compress Ⓣ *v* **1** squeeze together **2** condense ▷ *n* **3** pad applied to stop bleeding or cool inflammation **compressible** *adj* **compression** *n*
▸ **compressor** *n* device that compresses a gas
comprise Ⓣ *v* be made up of, constitute
compromise Ⓣ [**kom**-prom-mize] *n* **1** settlement reached by concessions on each side ▷ *v* **2** settle a dispute by making concessions **3** put in a dishonourable position
Compton *n* **Arthur Holly**. 1892–1962, US physicist, noted for his research on X-rays, gamma rays, and nuclear energy: Nobel prize for physics 1927
comptroller *n* (in titles) financial controller
compulsion Ⓣ *n* **1** irresistible impulse **2** compelling or being compelled **compulsive** *adj* **compulsively** *adv*
▸ **compulsory** *adj* required by rules or laws, obligatory
compunction *n* feeling of guilt or remorse

THESAURUS

ingredient, element, constituent ▸ *adj* **2** = **constituent**, inherent, intrinsic
compose *v* **1** = **create**, write, produce, invent, devise • *She has composed a symphony.* **2** = **put together**, make, build, form, fashion, construct, constitute, comprise, make up **3** = **calm**, control, collect, quiet, soothe, placate, pacify **4** = **arrange**, adjust
composed *adj* = **calm**, cool, sedate, serene, unflappable, at ease, collected, level-headed, poised, relaxed, self-possessed
composition *n* **1** = **creation**, production, formation, making, compilation, formulation, fashioning, putting together **2** = **design**, organization, structure, arrangement, formation, layout, configuration, make-up **3** = **essay**, work, exercise, piece, opus, treatise, literary work
composure *n* = **calmness**, poise, serenity, aplomb, equanimity, sang-froid, self-assurance, self-possession
compound *n* **1** = **combination**, composite, blend, mixture, alloy, fusion, medley, amalgam, synthesis ▸ *v* **2** = **combine**, mix, unite, blend, amalgamate, synthesize, intermingle **3** = **intensify**, worsen, aggravate, complicate, exacerbate, heighten, magnify, augment, add to ▸ *adj* **4** = **complex**, multiple, composite, intricate
comprehend *v* = **understand**, see, appreciate, grasp, fathom, take in, work out • *I just cannot comprehend your attitude.* *See also*: **know, read, realize**
comprehensible *adj* = **understandable**, clear, plain, explicit, coherent, conceivable, intelligible
comprehension *n* = **understanding**, intelligence, perception, grasp, conception, realization, discernment
comprehensive *adj* = **broad**, complete, full, blanket, thorough, inclusive, exhaustive, all-inclusive, encyclopedic, all-embracing
compress *v* = **squeeze**, contract, press, crush, concentrate, shorten, squash, abbreviate, condense
compressed *See* **firm**
comprise *v* **1** = **be composed of**, include, contain, embrace, encompass, consist of, take in **2** = **make up**, form, compose, constitute
compromise *n* **1** = **give-and-take**, agreement, settlement, concession, adjustment, accommodation, trade-off ▸ *v* **2** = **meet halfway**, agree, settle, adjust, concede, give and take, go fifty-fifty (*informal*), strike a balance **3** = **dishonour**, expose, weaken, embarrass, jeopardize, prejudice, discredit
compulsion *n* **1** = **urge**, need, drive, obsession, necessity, preoccupation **2** = **force**, demand, pressure, obligation, urgency, constraint, coercion, duress
compulsive *adj* = **irresistible**, urgent, obsessive, uncontrollable, neurotic, compelling, driving, overwhelming
compulsory *adj* = **obligatory**, mandatory, required, requisite • *School attendance is*

DICTIONARY

compute ⓣ *v* calculate, esp. using a computer **computation** *n*
▸ **computer** *n* electronic machine that stores and processes data
▸ **computerize** *v* **1** equip with a computer **2** perform or operate by computer **computerization** *n*
comrade ⓣ *n* **1** fellow member of a union or socialist political party **2** companion **comradeship** *n*
Comte *n* (**Isidore**) **Auguste** (**Marie François**). 1798–1857, French mathematician and philosopher; the founder of positivism **Comtism** *n* **Comtist** *or* **Comtian** *adj, n*
con[1] ⓣ *informal* ▹ *v* **conning, conned** **1** deceive or swindle (someone) by gaining his or her trust ▹ *n* **2** such a deception or swindle
con[2] *n* **pros and cons** see **pro**[1]
Conan Doyle *n* Sir **Arthur**. 1859–1930, British author of detective stories and historical romances and the creator of *Sherlock Holmes*
concatenation *n* linked series of events
concave ⓣ *adj* curving inwards **concavity** *n*
conceal ⓣ *v* **1** cover and hide **2** keep secret **concealment** *n*
concede ⓣ *v* **1** admit to be true **2** grant as a right **3** acknowledge defeat in (a contest or argument)
conceit ⓣ *n* **1** too high an opinion of oneself **2** *lit* far-fetched or clever comparison **conceited** *adj*
conceive ⓣ *v* **1** imagine or think **2** form in the mind **3** become pregnant
▸ **conceivable** *adj* imaginable or possible **conceivably** *adv*
concentrate ⓣ *v* **1** fix one's attention or efforts (on) **2** bring or come together in large numbers in one place **3** make (a substance) stronger ▹ *n* **4** concentrated substance
▸ **concentration** *n* **1** concentrating **2** concentrated substance
▸ **concentration camp** prison camp for civilian prisoners, esp. in Nazi Germany
concentric *adj* having the same centre
concept ⓣ *n* abstract or general idea
▸ **conceptual** *adj* of or based on concepts
▸ **conceptualize** *v* form a concept of
conception ⓣ *n* **1** general idea **2** act of conceiving
concern ⓣ *n* **1** anxiety **2** something that concerns a person **3** business or firm ▹ *v*

THESAURUS

compulsory. OPPOSITE: voluntary
compute *v* = **calculate**, total, count, tally, reckon, enumerate, add up, figure out
comrade *n* = **companion**, friend, partner, associate, colleague, fellow, ally, co-worker, homeboy (*slang*), homegirl (*slang*)
con *v* **1** = **swindle**, trick, mislead, cheat, deceive • *He claimed that he'd been conned out of his life savings.* ▸ *n* **2** = **swindle**, fraud, scam, trick, bluff, deception • *Snacks that offer miraculous weight loss are a con.*
See also: **dupe, fool, rob, take in**
concave *adj* = **hollow**, indented
conceal *v* = **hide**, cover, screen, bury, mask, obscure, disguise, camouflage
concealed *See* **invisible**
concede *v* **1** = **admit**, allow, own, accept, grant, acknowledge, confess **2** = **give up**, surrender, yield, relinquish, cede, hand over
conceit *n* = **self-importance**, pride, vanity, egotism • *his insufferable conceit*
conceited *adj* = **self-important**, vain, cocky, bigheaded (*informal*), egotistical • *She's smart and beautiful, but not conceited.* OPPOSITE: modest
See also: **boastful, haughty, pretentious, smug, stuck-up**
conceivable *adj* = **imaginable**, possible, credible, believable, thinkable
conceivably *See* **maybe, perhaps**
conceive *v* **1** = **imagine**, think, believe, understand, suppose, fancy, comprehend, envisage **2** = **think up**, create, design, devise, formulate, contrive **3** = **become pregnant**, become impregnated
▹ **conceive of** *See* **picture**
concentrate *v* **1** = **focus your attention on**, be engrossed in, give your attention to, put your mind to • *Concentrate on your studies.* **2** = **gather**, collect, accumulate • *Condominiums are mostly concentrated in urban areas.* **3** = **focus**, cluster, centre, converge, bring to bear
See also: **essence**
concentrated *adj* **1** = **intense**, hard, deep, intensive, all-out (*informal*) **2** = **condensed**, rich, boiled down, evaporated, reduced, thickened, undiluted
concentration *n* **1** = **single-mindedness**, application, heed, absorption **2** = **focusing**, consolidation, convergence, centring, intensification, bringing to bear, centralization **3** = **convergence**, mass, collection, cluster, accumulation, horde, aggregation
concept *n* = **idea**, view, image, theory, notion, hypothesis, conception, abstraction, conceptualization
conception *n* **1** = **idea**, plan, design, image, concept, notion **2** = **impregnation**, fertilization, insemination, germination
concern *n* **1** = **worry**, anxiety, apprehension, disquiet • *public concern about violence* **2** = **business**, responsibility, affair • *His private life is not my concern.* **3** = **importance**, interest, bearing,

DICTIONARY

4 worry 5 involve or interest 6 be relevant or important to
▸ **concerned** *adj* 1 interested or involved 2 anxious
▸ **concerning** *prep* about, regarding
concert *n* musical entertainment
▸ **in concert** 1 working together 2 (of musicians) performing live
▸ **concerted** *adj* done together
concertina *n* 1 small musical instrument similar to an accordion ▷ *v* **-naing, -naed** 2 collapse or fold up like a concertina
concerto [kon-**chair**-toe] *n, pl* **-tos, -ti** large-scale composition for a solo instrument and orchestra
concession Ⓣ *n* 1 grant 2 reduction in price for a specified category of people 3 conceding 4 thing conceded 5 land division in township survey **concessionary** *adj*
▸ **concession road** one of a series of roads separating concessions in township
conch *n* 1 marine mollusc with a large spiral shell 2 its shell
concierge [kon-see-**airzh**] *n* (in France) caretaker of an apartment block
conciliate Ⓣ *v* overcome the hostility of **conciliation** *n* **conciliator** *n* **conciliatory** *adj*
concise Ⓣ *adj* brief and to the point
concisely *adv* **concision** *or* **conciseness** *n*
conclave *n* 1 secret meeting 2 private meeting of cardinals to elect a new pope
conclude Ⓣ *v* 1 decide by reasoning 2 end, finish 3 arrange or settle finally
▸ **conclusion** *n* 1 decision or opinion 2 ending 3 outcome
▸ **conclusive** *adj* ending doubt, convincing **conclusively** *adv*
concoct Ⓣ *v* 1 make by combining ingredients 2 make up (a story or plan) **concoction** *n*
concomitant *adj* accompanying
concord *n* state of peaceful agreement, harmony
▸ **concordance** *n* 1 similarity or consistency 2 index of words in a book
▸ **concordant** *adj* agreeing
concordat *n* pact or treaty
concourse *n* 1 large open public place where people can gather 2 crowd
concrete Ⓣ *n* 1 mixture of sand, gravel, and cement, used in building ▷ *adj* 2 made of concrete 3 particular, specific 4 real or solid, not abstract
concubine [**kon**-kew-bine] *n* 1 woman living with a man as his wife, but not married to him 2 secondary wife in polygamous societies **concubinage** *n*

THESAURUS

relevance 4 = **company**, business, firm, organization, corporation, establishment, enterprise ▸ *v* 5 = **worry**, trouble, disturb, bother, distress • *It concerns me that he doesn't want to go.* 6 = **involve**, affect, apply to, be relevant to • *This concerns both of us.*
See also: **care, consideration, issue, job**
concerned *adj* 1 = **involved**, active, interested, implicated, mixed up, privy to 2 = **worried**, upset, troubled, anxious, distressed, uneasy, disturbed, bothered
concerning *prep* = **regarding**, about, touching, re, apropos of, as regards, on the subject of, relating to, respecting, with reference to
concession *n* 1 = **grant**, permit, compromise, adjustment, allowance, privilege, boon, indulgence, sop 2 = **conceding**, surrender, confession, admission, acknowledgment, assent, yielding
conciliate *v* = **pacify**, mediate, reconcile, appease, soothe, placate, mollify, clear the air, win over
conciliation *n* = **pacification**, reconciliation, soothing, appeasement, mollification, placation
conciliatory *adj* = **pacifying**, pacific, appeasing, mollifying, peaceable, placatory
concise *adj* = **brief**, short, terse, succinct • *a concise guide* OPPOSITE: long
conclude *v* 1 = **decide**, judge, suppose, reckon (*informal*), infer, surmise, deduce • *He concluded that she had been right.* 2 = **finish**, end, close, round off, wind up • *He concluded the letter with a request.* OPPOSITE: begin 3 = **accomplish**, effect, bring about, carry out, pull off
See also: **complete, gather, stop**
concluding *See* **final, last**
conclusion *n* 1 = **deduction**, verdict, judgment, inference • *I've come to the conclusion that he was telling the truth.* 2 = **end**, close, finish, ending, termination • *the conclusion of the program* OPPOSITE: beginning
See also: **decision**
conclusive *adj* = **decisive**, final, ultimate, definite, irrefutable, clinching, convincing, unanswerable
concoct *v* = **make up**, prepare, invent, brew, hatch, devise, formulate, contrive, think up
concoction *n* = **mixture**, combination, creation, compound, preparation, blend, brew
concrete *adj* 1 = **specific**, explicit, definite 2 = **real**, material, substantial, actual, factual, tangible, sensible

DICTIONARY

concupiscence [kon-**kew**-piss-enss] *n* lust **concupiscent** *adj*
concur Ⓣ *v* **-curring, -curred** agree, be in accord **concurrence** *n* **concurrent** *adj*
▶ **concurrently** *adv* at the same time
concussion *n* brain injury caused by a blow or fall
▶ **concuss** *v* affect with concussion
condemn Ⓣ *v* **1** express disapproval of **2** sentence **3** doom **4** declare unfit for use **condemnation** *n* **condemnatory** *adj*
condense Ⓣ *v* **1** express in fewer words **2** concentrate, make more dense **3** turn from gas into liquid **condensation** *n*
▶ **condenser** *n electricity* capacitor
condescend Ⓣ *v* **1** behave patronizingly towards **2** do something as if it were beneath one's dignity **condescension** *n*
condiment *n* relish or seasoning for food
condition Ⓣ *n* **1** particular state of being **2** necessary requirement for something else to happen **3** restriction or qualification **4** state of health, physical fitness **5** ailment **conditions 6** circumstances ▷ *v* **7** accustom **8** make fit or healthy **9** subject to a condition
▶ **on condition that** only if
▶ **conditional** *adj* dependent on circumstances
▶ **conditioner** *n* thick liquid used when washing to make hair or clothes feel softer
condo *n, pl* **-dos** *informal* condominium building or apartment
condole *v* express sympathy (with someone) **condolence** *n*
condom *n* rubber sheath worn on the penis or in the vagina during sexual intercourse to prevent conception or infection
condominium *n* apartment building in which each apartment is individually owned
condone Ⓣ *v* overlook or forgive (an offence or wrongdoing)
condor *n* large vulture of S America
Condorcet *n* **Marie Jean Antoine Nicolas de Caritat**, Marquis de. 1743–94, French philosopher and politician. His works include *Sketch for a Historical Picture of the Progress of the Human Mind* (1795)
conducive *adj* (foll. by *to*) likely to produce (a result)
conduct Ⓣ *n* **1** behaviour **2** management ▷ *v* **3** carry out **4** behave (oneself) **5** direct (musicians) by moving the hands or a baton **6** lead, guide **7** transmit (heat or electricity)
▶ **conduction** *n* transmission of heat or electricity
▶ **conductive** *adj* able to conduct heat or electricity **conductivity** *n*
▶ **conductor** *n* **1** person who conducts musicians **2** (**conductress**) official on a bus who collects fares **3** official on a passenger train **4** something that conducts electricity or heat

THESAURUS

concur *v* = **agree**, consent, assent, acquiesce
concurrently *See* **together**
condemn *v* **1** = **criticize**, blame, denounce, damn, censure • *He was condemned for his violent actions.* **2** = **sentence**, doom • *condemned to life in prison*
See also: **disapprove**
condemnation *n* **1** = **disapproval**, blame, censure, denunciation, reproach, reproof, stricture **2** = **sentence**, conviction, judgment, doom, damnation
condemned *See* **doomed**
condensation *n* **1** = **distillation**, precipitation, precipitate, liquefaction **2** = **abridgment**, digest, contraction, synopsis, précis **3** = **concentration**, reduction, consolidation, compression, crystallization, curtailment
condense *v* **1** = **abridge**, concentrate, shorten, compress, summarize, epitomize, abbreviate **2** = **concentrate**, reduce, thicken, boil down
condensed *adj* **1** = **abridged**, potted (*informal*), concentrated, summarized, shortened, compressed, shrunken, slimmed-down **2** = **concentrated**, reduced, boiled down, thickened
condescend *v* **1** = **patronize**, talk down to **2** = **lower oneself**, bend, stoop, deign, humble oneself *or* demean oneself, see fit
condescending *adj* = **patronizing**, superior, lofty, disdainful, lordly, snobbish, snooty (*informal*), supercilious
condition *n* **1** = **state**, form, shape • *The house is in good condition.* **2** = **requirement**, provision, qualification, stipulation, requisite, prerequisite, proviso, terms • *terms and conditions of the contract* **3** = **health**, order, shape, trim, fitness, fettle, kilter, state of health **4** = **ailment**, problem, complaint, weakness, malady, infirmity ▶ *v* **5** = **accustom**, prepare, train, ready, adapt, equip, tone up, work out
See also: **disorder**
conditional *adj* = **dependent**, limited, contingent, qualified, provisional, subject to, with reservations
conditions *pl n* = **circumstances**, situation, environment, surroundings, milieu, way of life
condone *v* = **overlook**, excuse, pardon, forgive, let pass, look the other way, make allowance for, turn a blind eye to
conduct *v* **1** = **carry out**, do, run, perform, manage, direct, organize • *to conduct an*

DICTIONARY

conduit [**kon**-dew-it] *n* channel or tube for fluid or cables
cone *n* **1** hollow or solid object with a circular base, tapering to a point **2** scaly fruit of a conifer tree
coney *n* same as **cony**
confabulation, *informal* **confab** *n* conversation
confection *n* **1** any sweet food **2** elaborate article of clothing
▶ **confectioner** *n* maker or seller of confectionery
▶ **confectionery** *n* candies and cakes
confederate *n* **1** member of a confederacy **2** accomplice ▷ *v* **3** unite in a confederacy ▷ *adj* **4** united, allied
▶ **confederacy** *n* union of states or people for a common purpose
▶ **confederation** *n* **1** alliance of political units **2 Confederation** federation of Canada inaugurated in 1867
confer Ⓣ *v* **-ferring, -ferred 1** discuss together **2** give
▶ **conference** *n* meeting for discussion
▶ **conferment** *n* formal giving
confess Ⓣ *v* **1** admit (a fault or crime) **2** admit to be true **3** declare (one's sins) to God or a priest, in hope of forgiveness
▶ **confession** *n* **1** confessing **2** thing confessed
▶ **confessional** *n* small stall in which a priest hears confessions
▶ **confessor** *n* priest who hears confessions
confetti *n* small bits of coloured paper thrown at weddings
confidant Ⓣ *n* person confided in
confidante *n fem*
confide Ⓣ *v* (foll. by *in*) **1** tell (something) in confidence (to) **2** entrust
▶ **confidence** *n* **1** trust **2** self-assurance **3** something confided, secret
▶ **in confidence** as a secret
▶ **confidence game** same as **con**[1]
▶ **confident** *adj* feeling or showing self-assurance **confidently** *adv*
▶ **confidential** *adj* **1** private or secret **2** entrusted with another's secret affairs
confidentially *adv* **confidentiality** *n*
configuration *n* **1** arrangement of parts **2** shape
confine Ⓣ *v* **1** keep within bounds **2** restrict the free movement of
▶ **confines** *pl n* boundaries, limits

THESAURUS

experiment **2 = accompany**, lead, guide, steer, escort, usher, convey ▷ **conduct yourself = behave**, act • *The way she conducts herself reflects on the school.* ▶ *n* **3 = behaviour**, attitude, manners, ways • *Other people judge you by your conduct.* **4 = management**, control, organization, administration, direction, handling, guidance, supervision, running
See also: **handle, manner, take, way**
confectionery *See* **candy**
confederacy *n* **= union**, league, coalition, alliance, federation, confederation
confederation *n* **= union**, body, organization, association
confer *v* **1 = discuss**, talk, consult, deliberate, discourse, converse **2 = grant**, give, accord, award, present, bestow, hand out ▷ **confer with** *See* **consult**
conference *n* **= meeting**, discussion, convention, forum, congress • *a conference on education*
confess *v* **1 = admit**, acknowledge, own up • *He confessed his love.* OPPOSITE: deny **2 = declare**, confirm, reveal, assert, affirm, profess
confession *n* **= admission**, acknowledgment • *a confession of her guilt*
confidant, confidante *n* **= close friend**, familiar, intimate, crony, alter ego, bosom friend
confide *v* **1 = tell**, reveal, admit, disclose, confess, divulge, whisper, impart **2** (*Formal*) **= entrust**, commit, commend, consign
confidence *n* **1 = trust**, faith, belief, reliance • *I have complete confidence in you.* OPPOSITE: distrust **2 = self-assurance**, assurance, aplomb, self-possession • *I've never had much confidence.* OPPOSITE: shyness ▷ **in confidence = in secrecy**, privately, between you and me *or* between you and me and the gatepost, confidentially
confident *adj* **1 = certain**, sure, positive, secure, convinced, satisfied • *confident of success* OPPOSITE: uncertain **2 = self-assured**, assured, self-possessed • *a confident attitude* OPPOSITE: shy
See also: **bold, optimistic**
confidential *adj* **= secret**, private, classified, intimate, privy, hush-hush (*informal*), off the record
confidentially *adv* **= in secret**, personally, privately, behind closed doors, between ourselves, in camera, in confidence, sub rosa
confine *v* **1 = limit**, restrict • *They confined themselves to talking about the weather.* **2 = imprison**, restrict, incarcerate, hem in, shut up, lock down • *confined to bed for two days*
confinement *n* **= imprisonment**, custody, detention, lockdown, incarceration, internment
confines *pl n* **= limits**, edge, circumference, boundaries, bounds, precincts

DICTIONARY

▸ **confinement** *n* **1** being confined **2** period of childbirth
confirm ⓣ *v* **1** prove to be true **2** reaffirm or strengthen **3** administer the rite of confirmation to
▸ **confirmation** *n* **1** confirming **2** something that confirms **3** *Christianity* rite which admits a baptized person to full church membership
▸ **confirmed** *adj* long-established in a habit or condition
confiscate ⓣ *v* seize (property) by authority **confiscation** *n*
conflagration *n* great destructive fire
conflate *v* combine or blend into a whole **conflation** *n*
conflict ⓣ *n* **1** disagreement **2** struggle or fight ▹ *v* **3** be incompatible
confluence *n* place where two rivers join **confluent** *adj*
conform ⓣ *v* **1** comply with accepted standards, rules, or customs **2** be like or in accordance with **conformity** *n*
▸ **conformist** *n* person who conforms, esp. excessively
confound ⓣ *v* **1** astound, bewilder **2** confuse
▸ **confounded** *adj informal* damned
confront ⓣ *v* come or bring face to face with
▸ **confrontation** *n* serious argument
Confucius *n* Chinese name *Kong Zi* or *K'ung Fu-tse*. 551–479 BC, Chinese philosopher and teacher of ethics. His doctrines were compiled after his death under the title *The Analects of Confucius*
confuse ⓣ *v* **1** mix up, mistake (one thing) for another **2** perplex or disconcert **3** make unclear **confusion** *n*
confute *v* prove wrong **confutation** *n*
conga *n* **1** dance performed by a number of people in single file **2** large single-headed drum played with the hands
congeal ⓣ *v* (of a liquid) coagulate, solidify
congenial ⓣ *adj* **1** pleasant, agreeable **2** of

THESAURUS

confirm *v* **1 = prove**, endorse, verify, validate, substantiate, bear out • *Police confirmed that they had received a call.* **2 = fix**, settle • *Can we confirm the arrangements for tomorrow?* **3 = strengthen**, fix, establish, reinforce, fortify, buttress
See also: **determine**
confirmation *n* **1 = proof**, evidence, testimony, verification, validation, authentication, corroboration, substantiation **2 = sanction**, agreement, approval, endorsement, acceptance, ratification, assent
confirmed *adj* **= long-established**, chronic, seasoned, habitual, hardened, ingrained, dyed-in-the-wool, inveterate
confiscate *v* **= seize**, appropriate, commandeer, sequester, impound, sequestrate
confiscation *n* **= seizure**, takeover, forfeiture, appropriation, sequestration, impounding
conflict *n* **1 = disagreement**, opposition, hostility, strife, friction, discord, antagonism • *conflict between workers and management* **2 = battle**, war, combat, strife, fighting • *the conflict in the Middle East* ▸ *v* **3 = be incompatible**, clash, disagree, differ, be at variance • *conflicting ideas*
See also: **dispute, interfere**
conflicting *adj* **= incompatible**, contrary, inconsistent, contradictory, paradoxical, antagonistic, clashing, discordant, opposing
conform *v* **1 = comply**, follow, adjust, adapt, obey, fall in with, toe the line **2 = agree**, accord, match, suit, tally, correspond, harmonize
conformist *n* **= traditionalist**, stick-in-the-mud (*informal*), yes man
conformity *n* **= compliance**, observance, orthodoxy, conventionality, traditionalism
confound *v* **= bewilder**, confuse, baffle, astound, mystify, perplex, flummox, dumbfound, nonplus
confront *v* **= face**, challenge, oppose, tackle, encounter, defy, accost, stand up to
confrontation *n* **= conflict**, fight, contest, encounter, head-to-head, showdown (*informal*)
confuse *v* **1 = mix up**, mistake, muddle up • *confusing fact with fiction* **2 = bewilder**, puzzle, baffle, mystify • *Politics confuse me.* **3 = disconcert**, upset, rattle (*informal*), disorient, unnerve, fluster, discompose, throw off balance ▹ **confuse with** *See* **mistake**
See also: **cloud, muddle**
confused *adj* **1 = bewildered**, baffled, muddled, perplexed, puzzled • *confused about health risks* **2 = disordered**, chaotic, disorganized, untidy • *The clothes lay in a confused heap.* OPPOSITE: tidy
See also: **dazed, garbled, unclear**
confusing *adj* **= bewildering**, complicated, baffling, puzzling • *a confusing situation*
confusion *n* **1 = disorder**, chaos, mess, disarray, disorganization • *My life is in confusion.* OPPOSITE: order **2 = bewilderment**, puzzlement, disorientation, mystification, perplexity
See also: **fuss, muddle**
congeal *See* **thicken**
congealed *See* **firm**
congenial *adj* **1 = pleasant**, friendly, kindly, affable, favourable, agreeable, genial, companionable **2 = compatible**,

DICTIONARY

similar disposition or tastes **congenially** *adv* **congeniality** *n*
congenital Ⓣ *adj* (of a condition) existing from birth **congenitally** *adv*
conger *n* large sea eel
congested Ⓣ *adj* **1** too full **2** clogged or blocked **congestion** *n*
conglomerate *n* **1** large corporation comprising many companies **2** mass composed of several different things ▷ *v* **3** form into a mass ▷ *adj* **4** made up of several different things **conglomeration** *n*
congratulate Ⓣ *v* express one's pleasure to (a person) at his or her good fortune or success **congratulations** *pl n* **congratulatory** *adj*
congregate Ⓣ *v* gather together in or as a crowd
▶ **congregation** *n* assembled group of worshippers **congregational** *adj*
▶ **Congregationalism** *n* Protestant denomination in which each church is self-governing **Congregationalist** *n, adj*
congress Ⓣ *n* **1** formal meeting for discussion **2 Congress** federal parliament of the US **congressional** *adj*
▶ **Congressman** *or* **Congresswoman** *n* member of the US Congress
congruent *adj* **1** agreeing or corresponding **2** *geom* identical in shape and size **congruence** *n*
conic *adj* of a cone
▶ **conical** *adj* cone-shaped
conifer *n* cone-bearing tree, such as the fir or pine **coniferous** *adj*
conjecture Ⓣ *n, v* guess **conjectural** *adj*
conjoined twins *pl n* the technical name for **Siamese twins**
conjugal Ⓣ [kon-jew-gal] *adj* of marriage
conjugate [kon-jew-gate] *v* give the inflections of (a verb)
▶ **conjugation** *n* complete set of inflections of a verb
conjunction *n* **1** combination **2** simultaneous occurrence of events **3** part of speech joining words, phrases, or clauses
conjunctivitis *n* inflammation of the membrane covering the eyeball and inner eyelid
▶ **conjunctiva** *n* this membrane
conjure Ⓣ *v* perform tricks that appear to be magic **conjurer** *or* **conjuror** *n*
▶ **conjure up** *v* produce as if by magic
conk *n slang* head or nose
▶ **conk out** *v informal* (of a machine) break down
conker *n informal* horse chestnut
Conn *n* 2nd century AD, king of Leinster and high king of Ireland
connect Ⓣ *v* **1** join together **2** associate in the mind **connective** *adj* **connectivity** *n*
▶ **connection** *or* **connexion** *n* **1** association **2** link or bond **3** opportunity to transfer from one public vehicle to another **4** influential acquaintance
Connery *n* Sir **Sean**, real name *Thomas Connery*. born 1929, Scottish film actor, who played James Bond in such films as *Goldfinger* (1964). His later films include *The Name of the Rose* (1986), *Indiana Jones and the Last Crusade*

THESAURUS

sympathetic, like-minded, well-suited, kindred
congenital *adj* = **inborn**, natural, inherent, innate, immanent, inbred
congested *adj* **1** = **overcrowded**, crowded, teeming **2** = **clogged**, packed, jammed, blocked-up, crammed, overfilled, overflowing, stuffed
congestion *n* **1** = **overcrowding**, crowding **2** = **clogging**, jam, bottleneck, surfeit
congratulate *v* = **compliment**, pat on the back, wish joy to
congratulation *See* **praise**
congratulations *pl n, interj* = **good wishes**, best wishes, compliments, felicitations, greetings
congregate *v* = **come together**, meet, gather, mass, collect, assemble, convene, flock, converge
congregation *n* = **assembly**, crowd, flock, throng, multitude, fellowship, brethren
congress *n* = **meeting**, conference, parliament, council, legislature, convention, assembly, caucus, conclave
conjecture *n* **1** = **guess**, speculation, theory, hypothesis, surmise, supposition, shot in the dark ▶ *v* **2** = **guess**, suppose, imagine, speculate, theorize, hypothesize, surmise
conjugal *adj* = **marital**, married, bridal, connubial, matrimonial, nuptial, wedded
conjure *v* = **perform tricks**, juggle
▷ **conjure up** = **bring to mind**, create, recall, evoke, contrive, produce as if by magic, recollect
conjurer, conjuror *n* = **magician**, wizard, sorcerer, illusionist
connect *v* **1** = **join**, link, couple, attach, fasten, affix • *Connect the pipe to the tap*. OPPOSITE: separate **2** = **associate**, link, relate, ally • *evidence connecting them with the crime*
connected *adj* = **linked**, combined, related, akin, allied, affiliated, associated, coupled, joined, united
connection *n* **1** = **association**, link, relationship, bond, relation, affiliation, correspondence, correlation • *a connection*

DICTIONARY

(1989), and *Finding Forrester* (2000)
conning tower *n* raised observation tower containing the periscope on a submarine
connive Ⓣ *v* **1** (foll. by *at*) give assent to (wrongdoing) by ignoring it **2** conspire
connivance *n*
connoisseur Ⓣ [kon-noss-**sir**] *n* person with special knowledge of the arts, food, or drink
Connolly *n* **1 Billy**. born 1942, Scottish comedian **2 James**. 1868–1916, Irish labour leader: executed by the British for his part in the Easter Rising (1916)
Connors *n* **Jimmy**. born 1952, US tennis player: Wimbledon champion 1974 and 1982; US champion 1974, 1976, 1978, 1982, and 1983
connote *v* imply in addition to the literal meaning **connotation** *n*
connubial [kon-**new**-bee-al] *adj* of marriage
conquer Ⓣ *v* **1** defeat **2** overcome **3** take (a place) by force **conqueror** *n*
▸ **conquest** *n* **1** conquering **2** person or thing conquered
Conrad *n* **Joseph**, real name *Teodor Josef Konrad Korzeniowski*. 1857–1924, British novelist born in Poland, noted for sea stories such as *The Nigger of the Narcissus* (1897) and *Lord Jim* (1900) and novels of politics and revolution such as *Nostromo* (1904) and *Under Western Eyes* (1911)
consanguineous *adj* related by birth
consanguinity *n*
conscience Ⓣ *n* sense of right or wrong as regards thoughts and actions
▸ **conscientious** *adj* **1** painstaking **2** governed by conscience **conscientiously** *adv*
▸ **conscientious objector** person who refuses to serve in the armed forces on moral or religious grounds
conscious Ⓣ *adj* **1** alert and awake **2** aware **3** deliberate, intentional **consciously** *adv*
consciousness *n*
conscript *v* **1** enrol (someone) for compulsory military service ▹ *n* **2** conscripted person **conscription** *n*
consecrate Ⓣ *v* **1** make sacred **2** dedicate to a specific purpose **consecration** *n*
consecutive Ⓣ *adj* in unbroken succession
consecutively *adv*
consensus Ⓣ *n* general agreement
consent Ⓣ *n* **1** permission, agreement ▹ *v* **2** permit, agree (to)
consequence Ⓣ *n* **1** result, effect **2** importance
▸ **consequent** *adj* resulting
▸ **consequently** *adv* **1** therefore **2** as a result
▸ **consequential** *adj* important

THESAURUS

between good health and lots of exercise **2 = link**, junction, coupling, fastening • *The fault was just a loose connection.* **3 = contact**, friend, associate, ally, sponsor, acquaintance, homeboy (*slang*), homegirl (*slang*)
See also: **tie**
connivance *n* **= collusion**, complicity, abetting, conspiring, tacit consent
connive *v* **= conspire**, plot, scheme, intrigue, collude, cook up (*informal*)
▹ **connive at = turn a blind eye to**, overlook, disregard, abet, let pass, look the other way, wink at
connoisseur *n* **= expert**, judge, authority, buff (*informal*), devotee, aficionado, appreciator
conquer *v* **1 = defeat**, beat, overcome, crush, master, overpower, quell, overthrow, vanquish, subjugate, get the better of **2 = seize**, win, acquire, obtain, occupy, overrun, annex
conqueror *n* **= winner**, master, victor, conquistador, defeater, subjugator, vanquisher
conquest *n* **1 = defeat**, victory, rout, triumph, overthrow, mastery **2 = takeover**, invasion, occupation, coup, annexation, subjugation
conscience *n* **= principles**, scruples, sense of right and wrong • *He had a guilty conscience.*
See also: **principle**
conscientious *adj* **= thorough**, particular, careful, exact, faithful, painstaking, meticulous, diligent, punctilious
conscious *adj* **1 = aware**, alive, alert, awake, responsive, sensible, sentient **2 = deliberate**, intentional, calculated, self-conscious, wilful, knowing, premeditated, studied
consciousness *n* **= awareness**, knowledge, recognition, sensibility, realization, apprehension
consecrate *v* **= sanctify**, devote, dedicate, ordain, venerate, hallow, set apart
consecrated *See* **holy**
consecutive *adj* **= successive**, running, uninterrupted, in sequence, in turn, sequential, succeeding
consensus *n* **= agreement**, unity, harmony, assent, unanimity, common consent, concord, general agreement
consent *n* **1 = agreement**, approval, sanction, permission, go-ahead (*informal*), compliance, assent, acquiescence, O.K. *or* okay (*informal*) ▸ *v* **2 = agree**, allow, approve, permit, concur, assent, acquiesce
consequence *n* **1 = result**, issue, effect, outcome, sequel, repercussion, upshot, end result **2 = importance**, concern, account, value, weight, moment, import, significance
consequent *adj* **= following**, subsequent, successive, resultant, ensuing, resulting

DICTIONARY

conservative ⓣ *adj* **1** opposing change **2** cautious **3** conventional in style **4 Conservative** of or supporting the Progressive Conservative Party, the most conservative of the three main political parties ▷ *n* **5** one who wishes to preserve political institutions against change **6** one opposed to hasty changes or innovations **7 Conservative** supporter or member of the Progressive Conservative Party **conservatism** *n*
conservatoire [kon-**serv**-a-twahr] *n* school of music
conservatory *n, pl* **-ries 1** greenhouse **2** conservatoire
conserve ⓣ *v* **1** protect from harm, decay, or loss **2** preserve (fruit) with sugar ▷ *n* **3** fruit preserved by cooking in sugar
▸ **conservancy** *n* environmental conservation
▸ **conservation** *n* **1** protection of natural resources and the environment **2** conserving **conservationist** *n*
consider ⓣ *v* **1** be of the opinion that **2** think about **3** be considerate of **4** discuss **5** examine
▸ **considerable** *adj* **1** fairly large **2** much **considerably** *adv*
▸ **considerate** *adj* thoughtful towards others **considerately** *adv*
▸ **consideration** *n* **1** careful thought **2** fact that must be considered **3** kindness **4** payment for a service
▸ **considering** *prep* taking (a specified fact) into account
consign *v* **1** deposit **2** entrust **3** address or deliver (goods)
▸ **consignment** *n* shipment of goods
consist ⓣ *v* **consist in** have as its main or only feature
▸ **consist of** be made up of
consistency ⓣ *n, pl* **-cies 1** degree of thickness or smoothness **2** being consistent
▸ **consistent** *adj* **1** unchanging, constant **2** in agreement **consistently** *adv*
console[1] ⓣ *v* comfort in distress
▸ **consolation** *n* **1** consoling **2** person or thing that consoles
console[2] *n* **1** panel of controls for electronic equipment **2** cabinet for a television or audio

THESAURUS

consequently *adv* = **as a result**, therefore, thus, subsequently, accordingly, hence, ergo
conservation *n* = **protection**, saving, maintenance, preservation, safekeeping, upkeep, guardianship, husbandry, safeguarding
Conservative *adj* **1** = **Tory**, right-wing ▸ *n* **2** = **Tory**, right-winger, righty (*informal*)
conservative *adj* **1** = **traditional**, conventional • *People sometimes become more conservative as they grow older.* OPPOSITE: radical **2** = **traditionalist**, reactionary, stick-in-the-mud (*informal*)
See also: **right-wing**
conserve *v* = **protect**, keep, save, husband, nurse, preserve, hoard, store up, take care of, use sparingly
consider *v* **1** = **think**, rate, believe, judge, deem, regard as • *They do not consider him a suitable candidate.* **2** = **think about**, reflect, ponder, deliberate, contemplate, muse, meditate • *I will consider your offer.* **3** = **bear in mind**, respect, make allowances for, take into account, think about • *We should consider her feelings.*
See also: **feel, reckon, regard, view**
considerable *adj* = **large**, great, substantial, marked, sizable *or* sizeable, plentiful, noticeable, appreciable, goodly, supersize
considerably *adv* = **greatly**, significantly, substantially, remarkably, markedly, noticeably, appreciably, very much
considerate *adj* = **thoughtful**, patient, concerned, mindful, kindly, attentive, unselfish, obliging, tactful
considerately *See* **well**
consideration *n* **1** = **thought**, study, attention, deliberation, contemplation • *a decision requiring careful consideration* **2** = **thoughtfulness**, concern, respect, kindness, tact • *Show some consideration for the other passengers.* **3** = **factor**, point, issue • *Safety is a major consideration.* **4** = **payment**, fee, tip, reward, remuneration, recompense
See also: **aspect**
considering *prep* = **taking into account**, in the light of, in view of
consignment *n* = **shipment**, delivery, batch, goods
consist *v* ▷ **consist in** = **lie in**, be expressed by, be found in *or* be contained in, inhere in, reside in ▷ **consist of** = **be made up of**, include, involve, contain, incorporate, comprise, embody, amount to, be composed of
consistency *n* **1** = **texture**, density, thickness, firmness, compactness, viscosity **2** = **constancy**, regularity, uniformity, evenness, steadfastness, steadiness
consistent *adj* **1** = **unchanging**, regular, steady, persistent, constant, dependable, true to type, undeviating **2** = **agreeing**, logical, compatible, coherent, harmonious, congruous, consonant
consolation *n* = **comfort**, help, support, relief, cheer, solace, encouragement, succour
console *v* = **comfort**, encourage, cheer, calm, soothe, express sympathy for

DICTIONARY

equipment **3** ornamental wall bracket **4** part of an organ containing the pedals, stops, and keys
consolidate ⓣ *v* **1** make or become stronger or more stable **2** combine into a whole
consolidation *n*
consommé [kon-**som**-may] *n* thin clear meat soup
consonant *n* **1** speech sound made by partially or completely blocking the breath stream **2** letter representing this ▷ *adj* **3** (foll. by *with*) agreeing (with) **consonance** *n*
consort ⓣ *v* **1** (foll. by *with*) keep company (with) ▷ *n* **2** husband or wife of a monarch
consortium *n, pl* **-tia** association of business firms
conspectus *n* survey or summary
conspicuous ⓣ *adj* **1** clearly visible **2** striking **conspicuously** *adv*
conspire ⓣ *v* **1** plan a crime together in secret **2** act together as if by design
▶ **conspiracy** *n* **1** conspiring **2** plan made by conspiring **conspirator** *n* **conspiratorial** *adj*
constable *n* police officer of the lowest rank
▶ **constabulary** *n* police force of an area
Constable *n* **John**. 1776–1837, English landscape painter, noted particularly for his skill in rendering atmospheric effects of changing light
constant ⓣ *adj* **1** continuous **2** unchanging **3** faithful ▷ *n* **4** unvarying quantity **5** something unchanging **constantly** *adv* **constancy** *n*
Constantine I *n* known as *Constantine the Great*, Latin name *Flavius Valerius Aurelius Constantinus*. ?280–337 AD, first Christian Roman emperor (306–337): moved his capital to Byzantium, which he renamed Constantinople (330)
constellation *n* group of stars
consternation ⓣ *n* anxiety, dismay, or confusion
constipation *n* difficulty in defecating
▶ **constipated** *adj* having constipation
constituent ⓣ *n* **1** member of a constituency **2** component part ▷ *adj* **3** forming part of a whole
▶ **constituency** *n* **1** area represented by a Member of Parliament **2** voters in such an area
constitute ⓣ *v* form, compose
▶ **constitution** *n* **1** principles on which a state is governed **2** physical condition **3** structure
▶ **constitutional** *adj* **1** of a constitution **2** in accordance with a political constitution ▷ *n* **3** walk taken for exercise **constitutionally** *adv*
constrain ⓣ *v* **1** force, compel **2** restrain or confine
▶ **constraint** *n* **1** compulsion or restraint **2** forced unnatural manner

C

THESAURUS

consolidate *v* **1** = **strengthen**, secure, stabilize, reinforce, fortify **2** = **combine**, join, unite, fuse, amalgamate, federate
consort *v* **1** = **associate**, fraternize, go around with, hang out with *or* hang around with, mix, keep company ▶ *n* **2** = **spouse**, wife, partner, husband, companion
conspicuous *adj* **1** = **obvious**, apparent, evident, blatant, noticeable, perceptible • *Her conspicuous lack of warmth confirmed her disapproval.* **2** = **noteworthy**, signal, prominent, remarkable, notable, outstanding, striking, illustrious, salient
See also: **clear, manifest, visible**
conspiracy *n* = **plot**, scheme, intrigue, treason, collusion, machination
conspirator *n* = **plotter**, traitor, conspirer, intriguer, schemer
conspire *v* **1** = **plot**, plan, scheme, intrigue, manoeuvre, contrive, machinate **2** = **work together**, contribute, combine, tend, cooperate, concur
constant *adj* **1** = **continuous**, relentless, eternal, perpetual, continual, nonstop • *a government under constant attack from the media* OPPOSITE: periodic **2** = **unchanging**, even, regular, stable, steady, uniform, fixed • *a constant temperature* OPPOSITE: changeable **3** = **faithful**, true, loyal, stalwart, staunch, devoted, trustworthy, trusty
See also: **permanent, steadfast**
constantly *adv* = **continuously**, always, continually, invariably, perpetually, nonstop, endlessly, incessantly, all the time, interminably, twenty-four-seven (*slang*)
consternation *n* = **dismay**, fear, alarm, anxiety, distress, dread, trepidation
constituent *n* **1** = **voter**, elector **2** = **component**, part, unit, factor, ingredient, element ▶ *adj* **3** = **component**, basic, essential, integral, elemental
constitute *v* = **make up**, form, establish, found, compose, comprise, set up
constitution *n* **1** = **health**, build, character, disposition, physique **2** = **structure**, form, nature, composition, make-up
constitutional *adj* **1** = **statutory**, chartered, vested ▶ *n* **2** = **walk**, turn, stroll, airing
constrain *v* **1** = **force**, bind, compel, coerce, oblige, pressurize, necessitate, impel **2** = **restrict**, check, curb, restrain, confine, constrict, straiten
constraint *n* **1** = **restriction**, check, curb, rein, limitation, deterrent, hindrance **2** = **force**, pressure, restraint,

DICTIONARY

constrict *v* make narrower or tighter, esp. by squeezing **constriction** *n* **constrictive** *adj*

▶ **constrictor** *n* **1** large snake that squeezes its prey to death **2** muscle that constricts

construct ⓣ *v* build or put together

▶ **construction** *n* **1** constructing **2** thing constructed **3** interpretation **4** *grammar* way in which words are arranged in a sentence, clause, or phrase

▶ **constructive** *adj* (of advice, criticism, etc.) useful and helpful **constructively** *adv*

construe *v* **-struing, -strued 1** interpret **2** analyse grammatically

consul *n* **1** official representing a state in a foreign country **2** one of the two chief magistrates in ancient Rome **consular** *adj* **consulship** *n*

▶ **consulate** *n* position or offices of a consul

consult ⓣ *v* go to for information or advice

▶ **consultant** *n Brit* **1** specialist doctor with a senior position in a hospital **2** specialist who gives professional advice

▶ **consultancy** *n* work or position of a consultant

▶ **consultation** *n* (meeting for) consulting

▶ **consultative** *adj* giving advice

consume ⓣ *v* **1** eat or drink **2** use up **3** destroy **4** obsess

▶ **consumer** *n* person who buys goods or uses services

▶ **consumption** *n* **1** consuming **2** amount consumed **3** *old-fashioned* tuberculosis

▶ **consumptive** *adj, n* (person) having tuberculosis

consummate ⓣ *v* [**kon**-sume-mate] **1** make (a marriage) legal by sexual intercourse **2** complete or fulfil ▷ *adj* [kon-**sum**-mit] **3** supremely skilled **4** perfect **consummation** *n*

cont. continued

contact ⓣ *n* **1** communicating **2** touching **3** useful acquaintance **4** connection between two electrical conductors in a circuit ▷ *v* **5** get in touch with

▶ **contact lens** lens fitting over the eyeball to correct defective vision

contagion *n* **1** passing on of disease by contact **2** contagious disease **3** spreading of a harmful influence

▶ **contagious** *adj* spreading by contact, catching

contain ⓣ *v* **1** hold or be capable of holding **2** consist of **3** control, restrain

▶ **container** *n* **1** receptacle used to hold something **2** large standard-sized box for transporting cargo by truck or ship

▶ **containment** *n* prevention of the

THESAURUS

necessity, coercion, compulsion

constricted *See* **tight**

construct *v* = **build**, make, create, assemble, erect, put together, put up • *to construct a model plane*

See also: **fashion, produce**

construction *n* **1** = **building**, creation, composition, edifice **2** = **interpretation**, reading, explanation, rendering, inference

constructive *adj* = **helpful**, positive, valuable, useful, productive, practical

consult *v* = **ask for advice**, confer with, refer to • *Consult your doctor before beginning an exercise program.*

See also: **refer**

consultant *n* = **specialist**, authority, adviser, counsellor, consigliere

consultation *n* = **meeting**, conference, interview, hearing, discussion, council, appointment, dialogue, deliberation, examination, seminar, session

consume *v* **1** = **eat**, swallow, gobble *or* gobble up, devour, chow down (*slang*), eat up, put away **2** = **use up**, spend, waste, absorb, exhaust, squander, dissipate, expend **3** = **destroy**, devastate, ravage, demolish, annihilate, lay waste **4** (*often passive*) = **obsess**, dominate, absorb, preoccupy, monopolize, engross, eat up

consumer *n* = **buyer**, customer, user, shopper, purchaser

consummate *v* **1** = **complete**, end, finish, conclude, crown, accomplish, fulfill ▶ *adj* **2** = **skilled**, perfect, accomplished, supreme, superb, polished, matchless, practised **3** = **complete**, total, extreme, absolute, utter, supreme, conspicuous

consumption *n* **1** = **using up**, loss, waste, expenditure, exhaustion, depletion, diminution, dissipation **2** (*Old-fashioned*) = **tuberculosis**, T.B.

contact *n* **1** = **communication**, touch, contact • *We keep in daily contact.* **2** = **acquaintance**, connection • *a contact in the music business* **3** = **touch**, contiguity ▶ *v* **4** = **get in touch with**, reach, approach, communicate with, get hold of • *We contacted the company to complain.*

contagious *adj* = **infectious**, communicable, transmissible, catching, spreading

contain *v* **1** = **include**, comprise • *My diary contains personal information.* **2** = **restrain**, control, curb, stifle, repress • *efforts to contain the disease* **3** = **hold**, seat, incorporate, accommodate, enclose, have capacity for

See also: **restrict, suppress**

container *n* = **holder**, vessel • *a plastic container for food*

See also: **box, case**

DICTIONARY

spread of something harmful
contaminate Ⓣ *v* **1** pollute, make impure **2** make radioactive **contamination** *n*
▸ **contaminant** *n* contaminating substance
contemplate Ⓣ *v* **1** think deeply (about) **2** consider as a possibility **3** gaze at **contemplation** *n* **contemplative** *adj* **contemplatively** *adv*
contemporary Ⓣ *adj* **1** present-day, modern **2** living or occurring at the same time ▹ *n, pl* **-raries 3** person or thing living at the same time or of approximately the same age as another **contemporaneous** *adj*
contempt Ⓣ *n* **1** attitude of scornful disregard **2** open disrespect for the authority of a court
▸ **contemptible** *adj* deserving contempt
▸ **contemptuous** *adj* showing contempt **contemptuously** *adv*
contend Ⓣ *v* **1** (foll. by *with*) deal with **2** assert **3** compete
▸ **contender** *n* competitor
▸ **contention** *n* **1** disagreement or dispute **2** point asserted in argument
▸ **contentious** *adj* **1** causing dispute **2** quarrelsome
content[1] Ⓣ *n* **1** meaning or substance of a book etc. **2** amount of a substance in a mixture **contents 3** what something contains **4** list of chapters at the front of a book
content[2] Ⓣ *adj* **1** satisfied with things as they are ▹ *v* **2** make (someone) content ▹ *n* **3** peace of mind **contented** *adj* **contentment** *n*
contest Ⓣ *n* **1** competition or struggle ▹ *v* **2** dispute **3** fight or compete for **contestant** *n*
context Ⓣ *n* **1** circumstances of an event or fact **2** words before and after a word or passage that contribute to its meaning **contextual** *adj*
contiguous *adj* very near or touching **contiguity** *n*
continent[1] *n* one of the earth's large masses of land **continental** *adj*
▸ **the Continent** *Brit* mainland of Europe

THESAURUS

contaminate *v* = **pollute**, infect, taint, corrupt, stain, tarnish, defile, adulterate, befoul
contamination *n* = **pollution**, infection, corruption, taint, poisoning, contagion, defilement, impurity
contemplate *v* **1** = **think about**, consider, ponder, examine, muse on, reflect on • *She carefully contemplated her next move.* **2** = **consider**, plan, envisage, think of • *He contemplated a career as a doctor.* **3** = **look at**, study, survey, view, examine, regard, inspect, eye up, gaze at, stare at
See also: **think**
contemplation *See* **consideration, thought**
contemplative *See* **thoughtful**
contemporary *adj* **1** = **coexisting**, concurrent, contemporaneous **2** = **modern**, recent, current, present, up-to-date, present-day, à la mode, newfangled ▸ *n* **3** = **peer**, fellow
contempt *n* = **scorn**, disregard, disrespect, disdain, derision • *I shall treat that remark with the contempt it deserves.* OPPOSITE: respect
contemptible *adj* = **despicable**, shameful, lousy (*slang*), paltry, worthless, pitiful, ignominious, measly, detestable, scuzzy (*slang*)
contemptuous *adj* = **scornful**, arrogant, derisive, condescending, disdainful, haughty, sneering, supercilious, withering
contend *v* **1** = **compete**, fight, struggle, contest, clash, vie, strive, jostle **2** = **argue**, hold, dispute, allege, maintain, assert, affirm
contender *See* **candidate**
content[1] *n* **1** = **meaning**, substance, significance, essence, gist **2** = **amount**, measure, size, capacity, volume, load
content[2] *adj* **1** = **satisfied**, comfortable, agreeable, contented, at ease, fulfilled, willing to accept ▸ *v* **2** = **satisfy**, please, indulge, appease, placate, humour, mollify ▸ *n* **3** = **satisfaction**, ease, comfort, pleasure, gratification, contentment, peace of mind
contented *adj* = **satisfied**, content, happy, comfortable, glad, thankful, pleased, serene, gratified
contention *See* **competition**
contentious *adj* = **argumentative**, bickering, captious, cavilling, disputatious, quarrelsome, querulous, wrangling
contentment *n* = **satisfaction**, content, peace, ease, comfort, happiness, pleasure, serenity, fulfillment, equanimity
contents *pl n* = **constituents**, load, elements, ingredients
contest *n* **1** = **competition**, game, match, tournament • *first prize in the spelling contest* **2** = **struggle**, fight, battle • *a bitter contest over the party's leadership* ▸ *v* **3** = **dispute**, question, challenge, oppose • *Your former employer has 14 days to contest the case.* OPPOSITE: accept **4** = **compete**, fight, vie, contend, strive
See also: **event**
contestant *n* = **competitor**, player, candidate, participant, contender, entrant
context *n* **1** = **circumstances**, situation, ambience, conditions **2** = **frame of**

DICTIONARY

▸ **continental breakfast** light breakfast of rolls, coffee, etc.
continent² *adj* **1** able to control one's urination and defecation **2** sexually chaste **continence** *n*
contingent *adj* **1** (foll. by *on*) dependent on (something uncertain) ▹ *n* **2** group of people, esp. soldiers, that is part of a larger group
▸ **contingency** *n* something that may happen
continue Ⓣ *v* **-tinuing, -tinued 1** (cause to) remain in a condition or place **2** carry on (doing something) **3** resume
▸ **continual** *adj* **1** constant **2** frequently recurring **continually** *adv*
▸ **continuance** *n* continuing
▸ **continuation** *n* **1** continuing **2** part added
▸ **continuity** *n* smooth development or sequence
▸ **continuous** *adj* continuing uninterrupted **continuously** *adv*
continuo *n, pl* **-tinuos** *music* continuous bass part, usually played on a keyboard instrument
continuum *n, pl* **-tinua, -tinuums** continuous series
contort *v* twist out of normal shape **contortion** *n*
▸ **contortionist** *n* performer who contorts his or her body to entertain
contour *n* **1** outline **2** Also **contour line** line on a map joining places of the same height
contra- *prefix* against or contrasting: *contraflow*
contraband Ⓣ *adj, n* smuggled (goods)
contraception *n* prevention of pregnancy by artificial means
▸ **contraceptive** *n* **1** device used or pill taken to prevent pregnancy ▹ *adj* **2** preventing pregnancy
contract Ⓣ *n* **1** formal agreement ▹ *v* **2** make a formal agreement (to do something) **3** make or become smaller or shorter **4** catch (an illness) **contraction** *n*
▸ **contractor** *n* firm that supplies materials or labour, esp. for building **contractual** *adj*
contradict Ⓣ *v* **1** declare the opposite of (a statement) to be true **2** be at variance with **contradiction** *n* **contradictory** *adj*
contralto *n, pl* **-tos** (singer with) lowest female voice
contraption Ⓣ *n* strange-looking device
contrapuntal *adj music* of or in counterpoint

THESAURUS

reference, connection, relation, background, framework
contingency *n* = **possibility**, event, chance, emergency, incident, accident, happening, eventuality
continual *adj* = **frequent**, regular, repeated, recurrent • *the continual ringing of his cellphone* OPPOSITE: occasional
See also: **constant**
continually *adv* = **constantly**, always, repeatedly, forever, nonstop, persistently, incessantly, all the time, interminably, twenty-four-seven (*slang*)
continuation *n* **1** = **continuing**, resumption, perpetuation, prolongation **2** = **addition**, extension, supplement, sequel, postscript, furtherance
continue *v* **1** = **keep on**, persist, carry on, go on • *He continued to work for another year.* **2** = **remain**, last, survive, endure, persist, carry on • *The discussion continued after they'd left.* **3** = **resume**, recommence, carry on • *After a moment, she continued speaking.*
See also: **extend, proceed, stretch**
continued *See* **continuous**
continuing *adj* = **lasting**, ongoing, sustained, enduring, in progress
continuity *n* = **sequence**, connection, flow, progression, succession, cohesion
continuous *adj* = **constant**, continued, extended, prolonged, endless, eternal, perpetual, uninterrupted, nagging • *continuous growth* OPPOSITE: periodic
See also: **continual, gradual, steady**
continuously *See* **always**
contours *pl n* = **outline**, figure, form, relief, shape, profile, curve, silhouette, lines
contraband *n* **1** = **smuggling**, trafficking, black-marketing, bootlegging ▸ *adj* **2** = **smuggled**, hot (*informal*), illegal, illicit, unlawful, bootleg, banned, forbidden, prohibited
contract *n* **1** = **agreement**, settlement, commitment, bargain, pact, arrangement, covenant ▸ *v* **2** = **agree**, pledge, negotiate, bargain, covenant, come to terms, commit oneself **3** = **shorten**, reduce, shrink, narrow, diminish, dwindle, curtail, lessen, abbreviate, shrivel **4** = **catch**, get, develop, acquire, incur, be afflicted with, go down with
contraction *n* = **shortening**, reduction, compression, shrinkage, abbreviation, narrowing, shrivelling, tightening
contradict *v* = **deny**, challenge, negate, belie, rebut, be at variance with, controvert, fly in the face of
contradiction *n* = **denial**, conflict, opposite, inconsistency, contravention, incongruity, negation
contradictory *adj* = **inconsistent**, opposite, contrary, incompatible, conflicting, paradoxical, opposed
contraption *n* (*Informal*) = **device**, gadget,

DICTIONARY

contrary Ⓣ *adj* **1** opposed, completely different **2** perverse, obstinate ▷ *n* **3** complete opposite ▷ *adv* **4** in opposition **contrarily** *adv* **contrariness** *n*
▶ **contrariwise** *adv* conversely
contrast Ⓣ *n* **1** striking difference **2** something showing this ▷ *v* **3** compare or be compared in order to show differences **4** (foll. by *with*) be very different (from) **contrastive** *adj*
contravene Ⓣ *v* break (a rule or law) **contravention** *n*
contretemps [**kon**-tra-tahn] *n, pl* **-temps** embarrassing minor disagreement
contribute Ⓣ *v* **1** give to a common purpose or fund **2** (foll. by *to*) help (something) to occur **contribution** *n* **contributor** *n* **contributory** *adj*
contrite Ⓣ *adj* guilty and regretful **contritely** *adv* **contrition** *n*
contrive Ⓣ *v* **1** make happen **2** invent and construct
▶ **contrivance** *n* **1** device **2** plan **3** contriving
▶ **contrived** *adj* planned, artificial
control Ⓣ *n* **1** power to direct something **2** curb or check **3** standard of comparison in an experiment **controls 4** instruments used to operate a machine ▷ *v* **-trolling, -trolled 5** have power over **6** limit or restrain **7** regulate **controllable** *adj* **controller** *n*
controversy Ⓣ *n, pl* **-sies** fierce argument or debate
▶ **controversial** *adj* causing controversy
contumacy [**kon**-tume-mass-ee] *n* obstinate disobedience **contumacious** [kon-tume-**may**-shuss] *adj*
contumely [**kon**-tume-mill-ee] *n* scornful or insulting treatment
contusion *n* bruise
conundrum Ⓣ *n* riddle
conurbation *n* large urban area formed by the growth and merging of towns
convalesce Ⓣ *v* recover health after an illness or operation **convalescence** *n* **convalescent** *adj, n*
convection *n* transmission of heat in

THESAURUS

instrument, mechanism, apparatus, contrivance
contrary *n* **1 = opposite**, reverse, converse, antithesis ▶ *adj* **2 = opposed**, counter, opposite, hostile, adverse, inconsistent, contradictory, paradoxical, clashing, discordant **3 = perverse**, difficult, awkward, cantankerous, intractable, disobliging, obstinate, unaccommodating
contrast *n* **1 = difference**, opposition, comparison, foil, distinction, disparity, divergence, dissimilarity ▶ *v* **2 = differentiate**, compare, oppose, differ, distinguish, set in opposition, set off
contrasting *See* **different, opposite**
contravene *See* **break**
contribute *v* **= give**, add, provide, supply, donate, subscribe, bestow, chip in (*informal*) ▷ **contribute to = be partly responsible for**, help, be conducive to, be instrumental in, lead to, tend to
contribution *n* **= gift**, grant, addition, offering, donation, input, subscription
contributor *n* **= giver**, supporter, donor, subscriber, patron
contrite *adj* **= sorry**, humble, remorseful, chastened, conscience-stricken, penitent, regretful, repentant, sorrowful
contrivance *n* **1 = device**, machine, implement, gadget, invention, instrument, mechanism, appliance, contraption, apparatus **2 = plan**, plot, trick, scheme, intrigue, ruse, machination, stratagem
contrive *v* **1 = bring about**, plan, effect, plot, manage, scheme, succeed, arrange, manoeuvre **2 = devise**, create, design, manufacture, construct, invent, improvise, fabricate, concoct
contrived *adj* **= forced**, planned, artificial, elaborate, strained, unnatural, laboured, overdone
control *n* **1 = power**, government, rule, authority, management, direction, command, supremacy • *He was forced to give up control of the company.* **2 = restraint**, check, regulation, curb, brake, limitation ▶ *v* **3 = have power over**, rule, manage, direct, govern, command, administer, be in charge of • *trying to control your mind* **4 = restrain**, contain, limit, check, curb, subdue, constrain, repress, hold back
See also: **determine, grip, head, hold, influence, possess, possession, restriction, run**
controls *pl n* **= instruments**, console, dash, dashboard, control panel, dials
controversial *adj* **= disputed**, contentious, debatable, at issue, disputable, open to question, under discussion, third-rail
controversy *n* **= argument**, debate, dispute, row, altercation, squabble, quarrel, wrangling, third rail (*politics chiefly US*), wedge issue
conundrum *See* **mystery, problem**
convalesce *See* **recover**
convalescence *n* **= recovery**, improvement, rehabilitation, recuperation, return to health
convalescent *adj* **= recovering**, getting better, improving, mending, on the mend, recuperating

DICTIONARY

liquids or gases by the circulation of currents
▸ **convector** *n* heater which emits hot air
convene Ⓣ *v* gather or summon for a formal meeting
▸ **convener** *or* **convenor** *n* person who calls a meeting
convenient Ⓣ *adj* **1** suitable or opportune **2** easy to use **3** nearby **conveniently** *adv*
▸ **convenience** *n* **1** quality of being convenient **2** convenient thing **3** *Brit* public lavatory
▸ **convenience store** small shop open long hours
convent *n* **1** building where nuns live **2** school run by nuns
convention Ⓣ *n* **1** widely accepted view of proper behaviour **2** formal agreement **3** assembly or meeting
▸ **conventional** *adj* **1** (slavishly) following the accepted customs **2** customary **3** (of weapons or warfare) not nuclear **conventionally** *adv* **conventionality** *n*
converge Ⓣ *v* move towards the same point **convergence** *n*
conversant *adj* **conversant with** having knowledge or experience of
converse[1] Ⓣ *v* have a conversation
▸ **conversation** *n* informal talk **conversational** *adj*
▸ **conversationalist** *n* person with a specified ability at conversation
converse[2] Ⓣ *adj, n* opposite or contrary **conversely** *adv*
convert Ⓣ *v* **1** change in form, character, or function **2** cause to change in opinion or belief **3** *sports* score (a touchdown, goal, etc.) after receiving a pass ▹ *n* **4** converted person **converter** *or* **convertor** *n*
▸ **conversion** *n* (thing resulting from) a converting or being converted
▸ **convertible** *adj* **1** capable of being converted ▹ *n* **2** automobile with a folding or removable roof
convex Ⓣ *adj* curving outwards **convexity** *n*
convey Ⓣ *v* **1** communicate (information) **2** carry, transport
▸ **conveyance** *n* **1** *old-fashioned* vehicle **2** transfer of the legal title to property
▸ **conveyancing** *n* branch of law dealing with the transfer of ownership of property
▸ **conveyor belt** continuous moving belt for transporting things, esp. in a factory
convict Ⓣ *v* **1** declare guilty ▹ *n* **2** person serving a prison sentence

THESAURUS

convene *v* = **gather**, call, meet, assemble, summon, congregate, bring together, come together, convoke
convenience *n* **1** = **availability**, benefit, advantage, fitness, utility, accessibility, usefulness, suitability, appropriateness **2** = **appliance**, help, facility, comfort, amenity, labour-saving device
convenient *adj* **1** = **useful**, helpful, handy • *a convenient mode of transport* OPPOSITE: inconvenient **2** = **nearby**, available, accessible, handy, at hand, close at hand, just round the corner, within reach
See also: **ready**
convention *n* **1** = **custom**, practice, code, tradition, etiquette • *It's a social convention that men don't wear skirts.* **2** = **assembly**, conference, meeting, congress • *the annual convention of the Canadian Association of Journalists* **3** = **agreement**, contract, treaty, bargain, pact, protocol
See also: **habit**
conventional *adj* **1** = **conservative**, conformist, unadventurous • *His opinions are generally quite conventional.* **2** = **ordinary**, customary, orthodox, standard, regular, traditional • *the conventional treatment for diabetes* **3** = **unoriginal**, routine, banal, hackneyed, prosaic, stereotyped
See also: **formal, normal, popular, proper**
converge *v* = **come together**, meet, join, gather, combine, merge, coincide
conversation *n* = **talk**, conference, discussion, chat, dialogue, gossip, discourse, tête-à-tête
conversational *See* **colloquial**
converse[1] *v* = **talk**, chat, confer, discourse, commune, chew the fat (*slang*), exchange views
converse[2] *n* **1** = **opposite**, reverse, contrary, antithesis, obverse, other side of the coin ▸ *adj* **2** = **opposite**, counter, reverse, contrary, reversed, transposed
conversion *n* **1** = **change**, transformation, metamorphosis **2** = **adaptation**, reconstruction, reorganization, modification, alteration, remodelling
convert *v* **1** = **change**, turn, alter, transform, transpose **2** = **adapt**, apply, modify, revise, reorganize, customize, remodel, restyle **3** = **reform**, convince, proselytize ▸ *n* **4** = **neophyte**, disciple, proselyte
convex *adj* = **rounded**, bulging, gibbous, protuberant
convey *v* **1** = **communicate**, express, impart, get across • *She conveyed her enthusiasm to her friends.* **2** = **carry**, move, bring, send, bear, conduct, guide, transport, fetch
See also: **take**
convict *v* **1** = **find guilty**, sentence, condemn, imprison, pronounce guilty ▸ *n*

DICTIONARY

▸ **conviction** *n* **1** firm belief **2** instance of being convicted
convince Ⓣ *v* persuade by evidence or argument **convincing** *adj* **convincingly** *adv*
convivial *adj* sociable, lively **conviviality** *n*
convoke *v* call together
▸ **convocation** *n* **1** convoking **2** large formal meeting
convoluted Ⓣ *adj* **1** coiled, twisted **2** (of an argument or sentence) complex and hard to understand **convolution** *n*
convolvulus *n* twining plant with funnel-shaped flowers
convoy *n* group of vehicles or ships travelling together
convulse Ⓣ *v* **1** (of muscles) undergo violent spasms **2** *informal* be overcome (with laughter or rage)
▸ **convulsion** *n* **1** violent muscular spasm **convulsions 2** uncontrollable laughter **convulsive** *adj* **convulsively** *adv*
cony *n, pl* **conies 1** rabbit **2** rabbit fur
coo *v* **cooing, cooed 1** (of a dove or pigeon) make a soft murmuring sound ▹ *n* **2** cooing sound
cooee *interj* call to attract attention
cook Ⓣ *v* **1** prepare (food) by heating **2** (of food) be cooked **3** *informal* falsify (accounts etc.) ▹ *n* **4** person who cooks food
▸ **cooker** *n* **1** apparatus for cooking heated by gas or electricity **2** apple suitable for cooking
▸ **cookery** *n* art of cooking
▸ **cook up** *v informal* devise (a story or scheme)
Cook *n* **1** Captain **James**. 1728–79, British navigator and explorer: claimed the E coast of Australia for Britain, circumnavigated New Zealand, and discovered several Pacific and Atlantic islands (1768–79) **2 Peter** (**Edward**). 1937–95, British comedy actor and writer, noted esp. for his partnership (1960–73) with Dudley Moore
cookie *n* **1** small flat or slightly raised cake **2** *computers* piece of data downloaded to a computer by a website, containing the user's preferences for use when revisiting that website
▸ **toss one's cookies** *or* **lose one's cookies** *slang* vomit
Cookson *n* Dame **Catherine**. 1906-98, British novelist, known for her popular novels set in northeast England
cool Ⓣ *adj* **1** moderately cold **2** calm and unemotional **3** indifferent or unfriendly **4** *informal* sophisticated or excellent **5** *informal* (of a large sum of money) without exaggeration: *a cool ten thousand* ▹ *v* **6** make or become cool ▹ *n* **7** coolness **8** *slang* calmness, composure **coolly** *adv* **coolness** *n*
▸ **coolant** *n* fluid used to cool machinery while it is working
▸ **cooler** *n* **1** container for making or keeping things cool **2** *slang* prison
Coolidge *n* (**John**) **Calvin**. 1872–1933, 30th president of the US (1923–29)
coolie *n old-fashioned, offensive* unskilled Oriental labourer
coomb, coombe *n* valley
Coon Come *n* **Matthew**. former National Chief of the Assembly of First Nations (2000–03)
coop *n* cage or pen for poultry
▸ **coop up** *v* confine in a restricted place
co-op *n* **1** cooperative society **2** shop run by one
cooper *n* person who makes or repairs barrels or casks
Cooper *n* **1 Gary**, real name *Frank James Cooper*. 1901–61, US film actor; his many films include *Sergeant York* (1941) and *High Noon* (1952), for both of which he won Oscars

THESAURUS

2 = prisoner, criminal, lag (*slang*), culprit, felon, jailbird, perp (*informal*)
convicted *See* **guilty**
conviction *n* **1 = belief**, view, opinion, principle, faith, tenet, persuasion, creed **2 = confidence**, assurance, certainty, reliance, firmness, certitude
convince *v* **= persuade**, satisfy, assure • *I convinced him of my innocence.*
convinced *adj* **= sure**, positive, certain, confident
convincing *adj* **= persuasive**, powerful, effective, conclusive, plausible, telling • *a convincing argument* OPPOSITE: unconvincing
convoluted *See* **complicated**
convulse *v* **= shake**, work, disorder, twist, disturb, agitate, derange, churn up
convulsion *n* **= spasm**, fit, seizure, cramp, contraction, paroxysm
cook *v* **= heat**, boil, fry, steam, bake, microwave, grill, roast, barbecue, toast, stew, poach, sauté, stir fry • *I enjoy cooking for friends.*
cool *adj* **1 = cold**, chilly, chilled, refreshing • *a gust of cool air* OPPOSITE: warm **2 = calm**, serene, collected, composed, level-headed, relaxed • *He kept cool through the whole thing.* OPPOSITE: nervous **3 = unfriendly**, distant, indifferent, lukewarm, aloof, offhand, standoffish, unenthusiastic, unwelcoming **4** (*Informal*) **= fashionable**, hip, trendy (*informal*), phat (*slang*) ▸ *v* **5 = chill**, freeze, refrigerate, cool off • *Put the cookies on a wire rack to cool.* OPPOSITE: heat ▹ **cool off** *See* **cool** ▸ *n* **6** (*Slang*) **= calmness**, control, poise, temper, composure, self-control, self-discipline, self-possession
See also: **apathetic, patience**

DICTIONARY

2 James Fenimore. 1789–1851, US novelist, noted for his stories of American Indians, esp. *The Last of the Mohicans* (1826)
cooperate ⓣ *v* work or act together
cooperation *n*
▸ **cooperative** *adj* **1** willing to cooperate **2** (of an enterprise) owned and managed collectively ▷ *n* **3** cooperative organization
co-opt *v* add (someone) to a group by the agreement of the existing members **co-option** *n*
coordinate ⓣ *v* **1** bring together and cause to work together efficiently ▷ *n* **2** *math* any of a set of numbers defining the location of a point **coordinates 3** garments designed to be worn together **coordination** *n* **coordinator** *n*
coot *n* small black water bird
cop *slang* ▷ *n* **1** policeman ▷ *v* **copping, copped 2 cop it** get into trouble or be punished
▸ **cop out** *v* avoid taking responsibility or committing oneself
cope[1] ⓣ *v* deal successfully (with)
cope[2] *n* large ceremonial cloak worn by some Christian priests
Copernicus *n* **Nicolaus**, Polish name *Mikolaj Kopernik*. 1473–1543, Polish astronomer, whose theory of the solar system (the **Copernican system**) was published in 1543 **Copernican** *adj*
copilot *n* second pilot of an aircraft
coping *n* sloping top row of a wall **coping stone**
copious ⓣ [**kope**-ee-uss] *adj* abundant, plentiful **copiously** *adv*
Copland *n* **Aaron**. 1900–90, US composer of orchestral and chamber music, ballets, and film music
copper[1] *n* **1** soft reddish-brown metal **2** copper or bronze coin **3** large metal container used to boil water
▸ **copper-bottomed** *adj* financially reliable
▸ **copperplate** *n* fine handwriting style
copper[2] *n slang* policeman
coppice, copse *n* dense growth of small trees and undergrowth
Coppola *n* **Francis Ford**. born 1939, US film director. His films include *The Godfather* (1972), *Apocalypse Now* (1979), *Tucker* (1988), and *The Rainmaker* (1999)
copra *n* dried oil-yielding kernel of the coconut
copulate *v* have sexual intercourse
copulation *n*
copy ⓣ *n, pl* **copies 1** thing made to look exactly like another **2** single specimen of a book etc. **3** material for printing ▷ *v* **copying, copied 4** make a copy of **5** act or try to be like another
▸ **copyright** *n* **1** exclusive legal right to reproduce and control a book, work of art, etc. ▷ *v* **2** take out a copyright on ▷ *adj* **3** protected by copyright
▸ **copywriter** *n* person who writes advertising copy
coquette *n* woman who flirts **coquettish** *adj* **coquetry** *n*
coracle *n* small round boat of wicker covered with skins
coral *n* **1** hard substance formed from the skeletons of very small sea animals ▷ *adj* **2** made of coral **3** orange-pink
corbel *n* stone or timber support projecting from a wall
cord ⓣ *n* **1** thin rope or thick string **2** cordlike structure in the body **3** corduroy **cords 4** corduroy trousers ▷ *adj* **5** (of fabric) ribbed
Corday *n* **Charlotte**, full name *Marie Anne Charlotte Corday d'Armont*. 1768–93, French Girondist revolutionary, who assassinated Marat
cordial ⓣ *adj* **1** warm and friendly **2** strong: *cordial dislike* ▷ *n* **3** drink with a fruit base
cordially *adv* **cordiality** *n*
cordite *n* explosive used in guns and bombs

THESAURUS

cooperate *v* = **work together**, combine, collaborate, conspire, coordinate, join forces, pool resources, pull together • *The family cooperated with the author of the book.*
See also: **team**
cooperation *n* = **teamwork**, unity, collaboration, combined effort, esprit de corps, give-and-take
cooperative *adj* **1** = **helpful**, supportive, responsive, onside (*informal*), accommodating, obliging **2** = **shared**, joint, collective, combined
coordinate *v* = **bring together**, match, organize, integrate, synchronize, harmonize, systematize
cope *v* = **manage**, survive, carry on, get by (*informal*), hold one's own, make the grade, struggle through ▷ **cope with** = **deal with**, weather, handle, contend with, grapple with, struggle with, wrestle with
copious *adj* = **abundant**, full, extensive, lavish, ample, plentiful, bountiful, profuse
copy *n* **1** = **reproduction**, fake, counterfeit, replica, forgery, duplicate, imitation • *He kept a copy of the letter.* ▸ *v* **2** = **imitate**, follow, mimic, ape, emulate • *She tried to copy the author's writing style.* **3** = **reproduce**, counterfeit, duplicate • *documents copied by hand*
See also: **issue**
cord *n* = **rope**, line, string, twine
cordial *adj* = **warm**, friendly, hearty,

DICTIONARY

Córdoba, Córdova *n* **Francisco Fernández de**. died 1518, Spanish soldier and explorer, who discovered Yucatán
cordon Ⓣ *n* **1** chain of police, soldiers, etc. guarding an area **2** fruit tree grown as a single stem
▸ **cordon off** *v* form a cordon round
cordon bleu [**bluh**] *adj* (of cookery or cooks) of the highest standard
corduroy *n* cotton fabric with a velvety ribbed surface
core Ⓣ *n* **1** central part of certain fruits, containing the seeds **2** central or essential part ▹ *v* **3** remove the core from
Corelli *n*, *n* **Arcangelo**. 1653–1713, Italian violinist and composer of sonatas and concerti grossi
co-respondent *n* person with whom someone being sued for divorce is claimed to have committed adultery
corgi *n* short-legged sturdy dog
coriander *n* plant with aromatic seeds and leaves used for flavouring
cork Ⓣ *n* **1** thick light bark of a Mediterranean oak **2** piece of this used as a stopper ▹ *v* **3** stop up with a cork
▸ **corkage** *n* restaurant's charge for serving wine bought elsewhere
▸ **corkscrew** *n* tool for extracting corks from bottles
corm *n* bulblike underground stem of certain plants
cormorant *n* large dark-coloured long-necked sea bird
corn[1] *n* **1** tall plant bearing kernels on cobs enclosed in husks **2** grain of this plant used for food or fodder **3** cereal grass or grain **4** *slang* something unoriginal or oversentimental
▸ **corny** *adj slang* unoriginal or oversentimental
▸ **cornflakes** *pl n* breakfast cereal of toasted corn flakes
▸ **cornflour** *n* finely ground corn
▸ **cornflower** *n* plant with blue flowers
corn[2] *n* painful hard skin on the foot or toe
cornea [**korn**-ee-a] *n*, *pl* **-neas, -neae** transparent membrane covering the eyeball
corneal *adj*
corned beef *n* beef preserved in salt
cornelian *n* reddish semiprecious stone
corner Ⓣ *n* **1** area or angle where two converging lines or surfaces meet **2** place where two streets meet **3** sharp bend in a road **4** remote or inaccessible place **5** *sports* free kick or shot from the corner of the field ▹ *v* **6** (of a vehicle) turn a corner **7** force into a difficult or inescapable position **8** obtain a monopoly of
▸ **cornerstone** *n* indispensable part or basis
cornet *n* **1** brass instrument similar to the trumpet **2** cone-shaped ice-cream wafer
cornice [**korn**-iss] *n* decorative moulding round the top of a wall
Cornish *adj* **1** of Cornwall in SW England ▹ *pl n* **2** people of Cornwall ▹ *n* **3** Celtic language of Cornwall
▸ **Cornish pasty** *n* pastry case with a filling of meat and vegetables
cornucopia [korn-yew-**kope**-ee-a] *n* **1** great abundance **2** symbol of plenty, consisting of a horn overflowing with fruit and flowers
Cornwell *n* **Patricia D(aniels)**. born 1956, US crime novelist; her novels, many of which feature the pathologist Dr. Kay Scarpetta, include *Postmortem* (1990), *The Last Precinct* (2000), and *Isle of Dogs* (2002)
corolla *n* petals of a flower collectively
corollary [kor-**oll**-a-ree] *n*, *pl* **-laries** idea, fact, or proposition which is the natural result of something else
corona [kor-**rone**-a] *n*, *pl* **-nas, -nae** ring of light round the moon or sun
coronary [**kor**-ron-a-ree] *adj* **1** of the arteries surrounding the heart ▹ *n*, *pl* **-naries** **2** coronary thrombosis
▸ **coronary thrombosis** condition in which the flow of blood to the heart is blocked by a blood clot
coronation *n* ceremony of crowning a monarch
coroner *n* official responsible for the investigation of violent, sudden, or suspicious deaths
coronet *n* small crown
corpora *n* plural of **corpus**
corporal[1] *adj* of the body
▸ **corporal punishment** physical punishment, such as caning
corporal[2] *n* non-commissioned officer below sergeant

THESAURUS

cheerful, affable, agreeable, sociable, genial, congenial
cordon *n* = **chain**, line, ring, barrier ▸ *v* ▹ **cordon off** = **surround**, separate, picket, isolate, enclose, encircle, close off, fence off
core *n* = **centre**, heart, essence, nucleus, kernel, crux, gist, nub, pith
cork *See* **plug**
corner *n* **1** = **angle**, joint, bend, crook **2** = **space**, retreat, hideout, nook, hideaway ▸ *v* **3** = **trap**, run to earth **4** (~ *a market*) = **monopolize**, dominate, hog (*slang*), engross
corny *adj* = **unoriginal**, stale, sentimental, banal, trite, hackneyed, maudlin, stereotyped • *corny old love songs*

DICTIONARY

corporation Ⓣ *n* **1** large business or company **2** city or town council **3** *informal* large paunch
▸ **corporate** *adj* **1** relating to business corporations **2** shared by a group
corporeal [kore-**pore**-ee-al] *adj* physical or tangible
corps Ⓣ [**kore**] *n, pl* **corps 1** military unit with a specific function **2** organized body of people
corpse Ⓣ *n* dead body
corpulent *adj* fat or plump **corpulence** *n*
corpus *n, pl* **corpora** collection of writings, esp. by a single author
corpuscle *n* red or white blood cell
corral *n* **1** enclosure for cattle or horses ▹ *v* **-ralling, -ralled 2** put in a corral
correct Ⓣ *adj* **1** free from error, true **2** in accordance with accepted standards ▹ *v* **3** put right **4** indicate the errors in **5** rebuke or punish **correctly** *adv* **correctness** *n*
▸ **correction** *n* **1** correcting **2** alteration correcting something
▸ **corrective** *n, adj* (thing) intended or tending to correct
correlate Ⓣ *v* **1** place or be placed in a mutual relationship ▹ *n* **2** either of two things mutually related **correlation** *n* **correlative** *adj, n*
correspond Ⓣ *v* **1** be consistent or compatible (with) **2** be similar (to) **3** communicate (with) by letter **corresponding** *adj* **correspondingly** *adv*
▸ **correspondence** *n* **1** communication by letters **2** letters so exchanged **3** relationship or similarity
▸ **correspondent** *n* **1** writer of letters **2** person employed by a newspaper etc. to report on a special subject or from a foreign country
corridor Ⓣ *n* **1** passage in a building or train **2** strip of land or air space providing access through foreign territory
corrie *n Scot* circular hollow on a hillside
corrigendum [kor-rij-**end**-um] *n, pl* **-da** thing to be corrected
corroborate Ⓣ *v* support (a fact or opinion) by giving proof **corroboration** *n* **corroborative** *adj*
corrode Ⓣ *v* eat or be eaten away by chemical action **corrosion** *n* **corrosive** *adj*
corrugate *v* fold into alternate grooves and ridges **corrugated** *adj* **corrugation** *n*
corrupt Ⓣ *adj* **1** open to or involving bribery **2** morally wrong **3** (of a text or data) made

THESAURUS

corporation *n* **1 = business**, society, association, corporate body **2 = town council**, council, civic authorities, municipal authorities
corps *n* **= team**, company, troop, unit, division, band, regiment, detachment, squadron
corpse *n* **= body**, stiff (*slang*), carcass, cadaver, remains
correct *adj* **1 = accurate**, right, true, exact, precise, flawless, faultless • *a correct diagnosis* OPPOSITE: wrong **2 = proper**, OK (*informal*), appropriate, acceptable, fitting, seemly • *correct behaviour* OPPOSITE: unacceptable ▸ *v* **3 = rectify**, right, improve, reform, cure, amend, remedy • *trying to correct his faults* **4 = punish**, discipline, rebuke, chastise, reprimand, chide, admonish, chasten, reprove
See also: **fix, formal, revise, standard**
correction *n* **1 = rectification**, amendment, adjustment, righting • *The newspaper printed a correction of the story.* **2 = punishment**, discipline, reformation, admonition, castigation, chastisement, reproof
See also: **reform**
correctly *adv* **= rightly**, right, properly, perfectly, precisely, accurately
correctness *n* **1 = truth**, precision, accuracy, regularity, fidelity, exactitude, exactness, faultlessness, preciseness **2 = decorum**, civility, good breeding, propriety, seemliness
correlate *See* **correspond**
correlation *n* **= correspondence**, link, connection, relation, equivalence, interrelationship
correspond *v* **1 = match**, agree, fit, tally, coincide, correlate, be related • *The two maps correspond closely.* **2 = communicate**, write, exchange letters, keep in touch
See also: **suit**
correspondence *n* **1 = letters**, post, communication, mail, writing **2 = relation**, agreement, match, comparison, similarity, coincidence, harmony, correlation, conformity
correspondent *n* **1 = letter writer**, pen friend *or* pen pal **2 = reporter**, journalist, contributor
corresponding *adj* **= related**, similar, equivalent, complementary, reciprocal, analogous, answering, matching
corridor *n* **= passage**, alley, hallway, aisle, passageway
corroborate *v* **= support**, confirm, endorse, ratify, authenticate, validate, substantiate, back up, bear out
corrode *v* **= eat away**, consume, corrupt, erode, rust, oxidize, gnaw, wear away
corrosion *See* **wear**
corrosive *adj* **= corroding**, virulent, wasting, vitriolic, caustic, consuming, erosive, wearing
corrupt *adj* **1 = dishonest**, unethical,

DICTIONARY

unreliable by errors or alterations ▷ *v* **4** make corrupt **corruptly** *adv* **corruption** *n* **corruptible** *adj*
corsage [kor-**sahzh**] *n* small bouquet worn on the bodice of a dress
corsair *n* **1** pirate **2** pirate ship
corset Ⓣ *n* close-fitting undergarment worn to support or shape the torso
cortege [kor-**tayzh**] *n* funeral procession
cortex *n, pl* **-tices** *anat* outer layer of the brain or other internal organ **cortical** *adj*
cortisone *n* steroid hormone used to treat various diseases
corundum *n* hard mineral used as an abrasive
coruscate *v* sparkle **coruscation** *n*
corvette *n* lightly armed escort warship
cos[1], **cos lettuce** *n* long crisp-leaved lettuce
cos[2] *math* cosine
cosh *n* **1** heavy blunt weapon ▷ *v* **2** hit with a cosh
cosine [**koh**-sine] *n* (in trigonometry) ratio of the length of the adjacent side to that of the hypotenuse in a right-angled triangle
cosmetic Ⓣ *n* **1** preparation used to improve the appearance of a person's skin ▷ *adj* **2** improving the appearance only
cosmic Ⓣ *adj* of the whole universe
▸ **cosmic rays** electromagnetic radiation from outer space
cosmonaut *n* Russian name for **astronaut**
cosmopolitan Ⓣ *adj* **1** composed of people or elements from many countries **2** having lived and travelled in many countries ▷ *n* **3** cosmopolitan person **cosmopolitanism** *n*
cosmos *n* the universe
▸ **cosmology** *n* study of the origin and nature of the universe **cosmological** *adj*
Cossack *n* member of a S Russian people famous as horsemen
cosset Ⓣ *v* **cosseting, cosseted** pamper or pet
cost Ⓣ *n* **1** amount of money, time, labour, etc. required for something **costs 2** expenses of a lawsuit ▷ *v* **costing, cost 3** have as its cost **4** involve the loss or sacrifice of **5** estimate the cost of
▸ **costly** *adj* **1** expensive **2** involving great loss or sacrifice **costliness** *n*
costive *adj* having or causing constipation
Costner *n* **Kevin**. born 1955, US film actor: his films include *Robin Hood: Prince of Thieves* (1990), *Dances with Wolves* (1990; also directed), *JFK* (1991), *Waterworld* (1995), and *Open Range* (2003)
costume Ⓣ *n* **1** style of dress of a particular place or time, or for a particular activity **2** clothes worn by an actor or performer
▸ **costumier** *n* maker or seller of costumes
▸ **costume jewellery** inexpensive artificial jewellery
cosy Ⓣ *adj* **-sier, -siest 1** snug and warm **2** intimate, friendly ▷ *n, pl* **cosies 3** cover to keep a teapot etc. hot **cosily** *adv* **cosiness** *n*
cot *n Brit* **1** child's bed with high sides **2** small portable bed
coterie [**kote**-er-ee] *n* exclusive group, clique
cotoneaster [kot-tone-ee-**ass**-ter] *n* garden shrub with red berries
cottage Ⓣ *n* small house in the country

C

THESAURUS

fraudulent, crooked, shady (*informal*), unscrupulous, unprincipled, venal • *corrupt politicians* OPPOSITE: honest **2** = **depraved**, vicious, degenerate, debased, dissolute, profligate **3** = **distorted**, altered, doctored, falsified ▸ *v* **4** = **bribe**, fix (*informal*), buy off • *Power is said to corrupt some people.* **5** = **deprave**, pervert • *Is TV really corrupting our children?* **6** = **distort**, doctor, tamper with
See also: **criminal, dirty**
corruption *n* **1** = **dishonesty**, fraud, bribery • *charges of corruption* **2** = **depravity**, evil, vice, perversion, immorality, decadence, wickedness **3** = **distortion**, falsification, doctoring
corset *n* = **girdle**, belt, bodice
cosmetic *adj* = **beautifying**, surface, superficial, nonessential
cosmic *adj* = **universal**, stellar
cosmopolitan *adj* **1** = **sophisticated**, universal, open-minded, broad-minded, catholic, urbane, well-travelled, worldly-wise ▸ *n* **2** = **man of the world** *or* **woman of the world**, jet-setter, sophisticate
cosset *See* **spoil**
cost *n* **1** = **price**, charge, rate, payment, expense, outlay • *The cost of fuel has increased.* **2** = **loss**, penalty, expense, detriment • *the total cost in human misery* ▸ *v* **3** = **sell at**, come to, set someone back (*informal*) • *The air fares were going to cost a lot.* **4** = **lose**, injure, hurt, harm, do disservice to
See also: **value**
cost-effective *See* **economical**
costly *adj* **1** = **expensive**, stiff, steep (*informal*), dear, exorbitant, extortionate, highly-priced **2** = **damaging**, harmful, disastrous, catastrophic, ruinous, deleterious, loss-making
costs *pl n* = **expenses**, budget, outgoings, overheads
costume *n* = **outfit**, dress, uniform, ensemble, apparel, attire, garb, clothing, livery
cosy *adj* (*Esp. Brit*) variant of **cozy**
cottage *n* = **cabin**, lodge, hut, shack, chalet

DICTIONARY

▶ **cottage cheese** soft mild white cheese
▶ **cottage industry** craft industry in which employees work at home
▶ **cottage pie** dish of minced meat topped with mashed potato
cotter *n* pin or wedge used to secure machine parts
cotton *n* **1** white downy fibre covering the seeds of a tropical plant **2** thread or cloth made of this **cottony** *adj*
▶ **cotton batting** *or* **cotton wool** fluffy cotton used for surgical dressings etc.
▶ **cotton on (to)** *v informal* understand
cotyledon [kot-ill-**ee**-don] *n* first leaf of a plant embryo
couch Ⓣ *n* **1** piece of upholstered furniture for seating more than one person ▷ *v* **2** express in a particular way
couchette [koo-**shett**] *n* bed converted from seats in a train
couch grass *n* quickly spreading grassy weed
cougar [**koo**-gar] *n* puma
cough Ⓣ *v* **1** expel air from the lungs abruptly and noisily. ▷ *n* **2** act or sound of coughing **3** illness which causes coughing
could *v* past tense of **can**[1]
couldn't could not
coulee [**koo**-lay] *n* ravine cut by water in western N America
coulomb [**koo**-lom] *n* unit of electric charge
Coulomb *n* **Charles Augustin de.** 1736–1806, French physicist: made many discoveries in the field of electricity and magnetism
coulter [**kole**-ter] *n* blade at the front of a plowshare
council Ⓣ *n* **1** group meeting for discussion or consultation **2** local governing body of a town or county
▶ **councillor** *n* member of a council
counsel Ⓣ *n* **1** advice or guidance **2** barrister or barristers ▷ *v* **-selling, -selled 3** give guidance to **4** urge or recommend
counsellor *n*
count[1] Ⓣ *v* **1** say numbers in order **2** find the total of **3** be important **4** regard as **5** take into account ▷ *n* **6** number reached by counting **7** counting **8** *law* one of a number of charges
▶ **countless** *adj* too many to be counted
▶ **count on** *v* **1** expect **2** rely on
count[2] *n* European nobleman **countess** *n fem*
countdown *n* counting backwards to zero of the seconds before an event
countenance Ⓣ *n* **1** (expression of) the face ▷ *v* **2** support or tolerate
counter[1] *n* **1** long flat surface in a bank or shop, on which business is transacted **2** small flat disc used in board games
counter[2] Ⓣ *v* **1** oppose, retaliate against ▷ *adv* **2** in the opposite direction **3** in direct contrast ▷ *n* **4** opposing or retaliatory action
counter- *prefix* **1** against, opposite: *counterbalance* **2** retaliatory, rival: *counter-revolution; counterclaim*
counteract Ⓣ *v* neutralize or act against
counteraction *n*
counterattack *v, n* attack in response to an attack
counterbalance Ⓣ *n* **1** weight or force balancing or neutralizing another ▷ *v* **2** act as a counterbalance to
counterblast *n* aggressive response to a verbal attack
counterespionage *n* activities to counteract enemy espionage
counterfeit Ⓣ *adj* **1** fake, forged ▷ *n* **2** fake,

THESAURUS

couch *See* **express**
cough *n* **1 = frog in one's throat** *or* **tickle in one's throat**, hack, bark ▶ *v* **2 = clear one's throat**, hack, bark
council *n* **= committee**, board, panel, assembly • *the city council*
counsel *n* **1 = advice**, information, warning, recommendation, direction, suggestion, guidance **2 = legal adviser**, lawyer, advocate, attorney, barrister ▶ *v* **3 = advise**, warn, urge, recommend, advocate, instruct, exhort
count *v* **1 = add up**, tally, calculate • *He counted the votes.* **2 = matter**, rate, weigh, signify, carry weight • *Our opinions don't count.* **3 = consider**, think, rate, judge, regard, deem, look upon **4 = take into account** *or* **take into consideration**, include, number among ▷ **count on, count upon = depend on**, trust, bank on, believe in, lean on, pin one's faith on, reckon on, rely on, take for granted, take on trust ▷ **count up = add**, total, tally, sum, reckon up ▶ *n* **5 = calculation**, tally, sum, reckoning • *The count revealed that our party had the majority.* *See also*: **reckon**
countenance *See* **expression, face**
counter *v* **1 = retaliate**, meet, answer, respond, oppose, resist, parry, hit back, ward off ▶ *adv* **2 = opposite to**, against, versus, conversely, at variance with, contrariwise, in defiance of
counteract *v* **= act against**, offset • *pills to counteract high blood pressure*
See also: **compensate**
counterbalance *v* **= offset**, balance, compensate, make up for, set off
counterfeit *adj* **1 = fake**, false, bogus, phony (*informal*), sham, simulated, imitation, forged ▶ *n* **2 = fake**, fraud, copy,

DICTIONARY

forgery ▷ *v* **3** fake, forge
counterfoil *n Brit* part of a cheque or receipt kept as a record
counterintelligence *n* activities designed to frustrate enemy espionage
countermand ⓣ *v* cancel (a previous order)
counterpane *n* bed covering
counterpart ⓣ *n* person or thing complementary to or corresponding to another
counterpoint *n music* technique of combining melodies
counterpoise *n, v* counterbalance
counterproductive *adj* having an effect opposite to the one intended
countersign *v* sign (a document already signed by another) as confirmation
countersink *v* drive (a screw) into a s haped hole so that its head is below the surface
countertenor *n* male alto
counterterrorism *n* activities intended to prevent terrorism **counterterrorist** *adj*
country ⓣ *n, pl* **-tries 1** nation **2** nation's territory **3** nation's people **4** rural areas as opposed to town
▸ **countrified** *adj* rustic in manner or appearance
▸ **country and western** popular music based on N American White folk music
▸ **countryman** (**countrywoman**) *n* **1** compatriot **2** person who lives in the country
▸ **countryside** *n* rural areas
county ⓣ *n, pl* **-ties** division of a country
coup ⓣ [**koo**] *n* **1** successful action **2** coup d'état
coup de grace [**koo** de **grahss**] *n* final or decisive action
coup d'état [**koo** day-**tah**] *n* sudden violent overthrow of a government
coupé [**koo**-pay] *n* sporty automobile with two doors and a sloping fixed roof
Couperin *n* **François**. 1668–1733, French composer, noted for his harpsichord suites and organ music
Coupland *n* **Douglas**. born 1961, Canadian novelist and journalist; novels include *Generation X* (1991), *Girlfriend in a Coma* (1998), and *City of Glass* (2000)
couple ⓣ *n* **1** two people who are married or romantically involved **2** two partners in a dance or game ▷ *v* **3** connect, associate **4** *lit* have sexual intercourse
▸ **a couple 1** a pair **2** *informal* a few
▸ **couplet** *n* two consecutive lines of verse, usu. rhyming and of the same metre
▸ **coupling** *n* device for connecting things, such as railway carriages
coupon ⓣ *n* **1** piece of paper entitling the holder to a discount or gift **2** detachable order form **3** football pools entry form
courage ⓣ *n* ability to face danger or pain without fear **courageous** *adj* **courageously** *adv*
Courbet *n* **Gustave**. 1819–77, French painter, a leader of the realist movement; noted for his depiction of contemporary life
coureur de bois [koo-rir-di-**bwah**] *n, pl* **coureurs de bois** [koo-rir] French Canadian or Métis woodsman
courgette *n Brit* zucchini
courier ⓣ *n* **1** person who looks after and guides travellers **2** person paid to deliver urgent messages

THESAURUS

reproduction, forgery, phony (*informal*), sham, imitation ▸ *v* **3 = fake**, copy, forge, pretend, fabricate, simulate, sham, imitate, impersonate, feign
countermand *v* **= cancel**, reverse, revoke, retract, rescind, repeal, override, annul
counterpart *n* **= equivalent**, match, fellow, supplement, twin, tally, equal, mate, complement
countless *adj* **= innumerable**, myriad, infinite, untold • *the star of countless movies*
See also: **many**
country *n* **1 = nation**, state, land, kingdom • *the boundary between the two countries* **2 = countryside**, outdoors, bush • *He lives right out in the country*. RELATED WORDS *adjs*: pastoral, rural **3 = territory**, region, land, terrain **4 = people**, public, community, nation, society, populace, citizens, inhabitants
countryside *n* **= country**, outdoors, farmland, outback (*Austral & NZ*), green belt, sticks (*informal*)
county *n* **= province**, shire
coup *n* **= masterstroke**, action, stunt, exploit, accomplishment, feat, deed, manoeuvre
couple *n* **1 = pair**, two, brace, duo, twosome ▸ *v* **2 = link**, join, pair, connect, marry, unite, wed, hitch, yoke
coupling *See* **connection**
coupon *n* **= slip**, card, ticket, certificate, token, voucher
courage *n* **= bravery**, nerve, pluck, daring, grit, valour, heroism, guts (*informal*) • *Her courage impressed everyone*. OPPOSITE: fear
courageous *adj* **= brave**, bold, gritty, daring, valiant, fearless, gallant, intrepid, lion-hearted, stouthearted
courier *n* **1 = guide**, representative **2 = messenger**, carrier, envoy, runner, bearer

DICTIONARY

course Ⓣ *n* **1** series of lessons or medical treatment **2** onward movement in space or time **3** direction or route of movement **4** area where golf is played or a race is run **5** any of the successive parts of a meal **6** continuous layer of masonry at one level in a building **7** mode of conduct or action **8** natural development of events ▷ *v* **9** (of liquid) run swiftly **10** hunt with hounds that follow the quarry by sight and not scent
▶ **of course** naturally

court Ⓣ *n* **1** body which decides legal cases **2** place where it meets **3** marked area for playing a racket game **4** courtyard **5** residence, household, or retinue of a sovereign ▷ *v* **6** *old-fashioned* try to win (someone) as a spouse **7** try to win (someone's favour) **8** invite: *court disaster*
▶ **courtier** *n* attendant at a royal court
▶ **courtly** *adj* ceremoniously polite **courtliness** *n*
▶ **courtship** *n* courting of an intended spouse or mate
▶ **court martial** court for trying naval or military offences
▶ **court shoe** woman's low-cut shoe without straps or laces
▶ **courtyard** *n* paved space enclosed by buildings or walls

Court *n* **Margaret** (née *Smith*). born 1942, Australian tennis player: Australian champion 1960–66, 1969–71, and 1973; US champion 1962, 1965, 1969–70, and 1973; Wimbledon champion 1963, 1965, and 1970

courtesan [kor-tiz-**zan**] *n hist* mistress or high-class prostitute

courtesy Ⓣ *n, pl* **-sies 1** politeness, good manners **2** courteous act
▶ **courtesy of** *or* **by courtesy of** by permission of
▶ **courteous** *adj* polite **courteously** *adv*

cousin *n* child of one's uncle or aunt

Cousteau *n* **Jacques Yves**. 1910–97, French underwater explorer

couture [koo-**toor**] *n* high-fashion designing and dressmaking
▶ **couturier** *n* person who designs women's fashion clothes

cove Ⓣ *n* small bay or inlet

coven [**kuv**-ven] *n* meeting of witches

covenant Ⓣ [**kuv**-ven-ant] *n* **1** formal agreement, esp. to make an annual (charitable) payment ▷ *v* **2** agree (to pay) by a covenant

cover Ⓣ *v* **1** place or spread or be placed or spread over **2** screen or conceal **3** travel over **4** protect from loss or risk by insurance **5** keep a gun aimed at **6** include **7** report (an event)

THESAURUS

course *n* **1 = classes**, curriculum • *a course in information technology* **2 = procedure**, plan, policy • *The premier took the only course left open to her.* **3 = route**, way, line, direction, path, trajectory • *She sensed the plane had changed course.* **4 = progression**, order, development, progress, movement, flow, sequence, unfolding **5 = racecourse**, circuit, cinder track **6 = period**, time, term, sweep, passage, passing, lapse, duration
▷ **course of action** *See* **process** ▷ **of course = naturally**, certainly, obviously, definitely, undoubtedly, indubitably, needless to say, without a doubt ▶ *v* **7 = run**, race, speed, surge, flow, stream, gush **8 = hunt**, follow, pursue, chase, stalk
See also: **pour**

court *n* **1 = law court**, bench, tribunal • *He ended up in court for theft.* **2 = courtyard**, yard, square, quad (*informal*), plaza, piazza, cloister, quadrangle **3 = palace**, hall, manor **4 = royal household**, train, suite, entourage, cortege, attendants, retinue ▶ *v* **5** (*Old-fashioned*) **= go steady** • *My grandparents courted for five years before they married.* **6 = cultivate**, seek, solicit, flatter, brown-nose (*slang*), curry favour with, fawn upon, pander to **7 = invite**, seek, prompt, attract, provoke, incite, bring about

courteous *adj* **= polite**, civil, refined, respectful, gracious, gallant, attentive, affable, urbane, well-mannered

courteousness *See* **courtesy**

courtesy *n* **1 = politeness**, grace, civility, courteousness, gallantry, good manners, graciousness • *a lack of courtesy to other drivers* **2 = favour**, kindness, indulgence, benevolence

courtier *n* **= attendant**, follower, squire

courtly *adj* **= ceremonious**, formal, elegant, refined, dignified, polished, gallant, stately, chivalrous, urbane

courtyard *n* **= yard**, quad, enclosure, quadrangle

cove *n* **= bay**, sound, inlet, anchorage

covenant *n* **1 = promise**, contract, agreement, pledge, commitment, pact, arrangement ▶ *v* **2 = promise**, agree, contract, pledge, undertake, stipulate

cover *v* **1 = conceal**, screen, hide, mask, cloak, shade, obscure, cover up • *He covered his face.* OPPOSITE: reveal **2 = overlay**, coat • *Tears covered his face.* **3 = clothe**, dress, wrap, envelop, put on **4 = submerge**, flood, overrun, engulf, wash over **5 = travel over**, cross, traverse, pass through *or* pass over **6 = protect**, defend, guard, shield **7 = report**, investigate, describe, relate, narrate, tell of, write up ▷ **cover up = conceal**, hide, suppress, whitewash

DICTIONARY

for a newspaper **8** be enough to pay for ▷ *n* **9** anything which covers **10** outside of a book or magazine **11** pretext or disguise **12** shelter or protection **13** insurance
▸ **coverage** *n* amount or extent covered
▸ **coverlet** *n* bed cover
Coverdale *n* **Miles**. 1488–1568, the first translator of the complete Bible into English (1535)
covert Ⓣ *adj* **1** secret, concealed ▷ *n* **2** thicket giving shelter to game birds or animals
covertly *adv*
covet Ⓣ *v* **coveting, coveted** long to possess (what belongs to someone else)
covetous *adj* **covetousness** *n*
covey [**kuv**-vee] *n* small flock of grouse or partridge
cow[1] Ⓣ *n* mature female of cattle and of certain other animals, such as the elephant or whale
▸ **cowboy** *n* **1** ranch worker who herds and tends cattle, usu. on horseback **2** *informal* irresponsible or unscrupulous worker
cow[2] *v* intimidate, subdue
coward Ⓣ *n* person who lacks courage
cowardly *adj*
▸ **cowardice** *n* lack of courage
Coward *n* Sir **Noël** (**Pierce**). 1899–1973, English dramatist, actor, and composer, noted for his sophisticated comedies, which include *Hay Fever* (1925), *Private Lives* (1930), and *Blithe Spirit* (1941)
cower Ⓣ *v* cringe or shrink in fear
cowl *n* **1** loose hood **2** monk's hooded robe **3** cover on a chimney to increase ventilation
cowling *n* cover on an engine
cowrie *n* brightly marked sea shell
cowslip *n* fragrant wild primrose
cox *n* **1** coxswain ▷ *v* **2** act as cox of (a boat)
coxswain [**kok**-sn] *n* person who steers a rowing boat
coy Ⓣ *adj* affectedly shy or modest **coyly** *adv*
coyness *n*
coyote [koy-**ote**-ee] *n* prairie wolf of N America
coypu *n* beaver-like aquatic rodent, bred for its fur
cozen *v* cheat or trick
CP Canadian Pacific
CPU *computers* central processing unit
Cr *chem* chromium
crab *n* edible shellfish with ten legs, the first pair modified into pincers
crab apple *n* small sour apple
crabbed *adj* **1** (of handwriting) hard to read **2** Also **crabby** bad-tempered
crack Ⓣ *v* **1** break or split partially **2** break with a sharp noise **3** (cause to) make a sharp noise **4** break down or yield under strain **5** hit suddenly **6** tell (a joke) **7** solve (a code or problem) **8** (of the voice) become harsh or change pitch suddenly ▷ *n* **9** narrow

C

THESAURUS

(*informal*), draw a veil over, hush up, sweep under the carpet ▸ *n* **8 = covering**, case, screen, jacket, mask, coating, wrapper • *quilts, blankets, and other covers* **9 = disguise**, front, screen, mask, veil, pretext, façade, smoke screen **10 = protection**, guard, shelter, shield, defence, camouflage, concealment **11 = insurance**, protection, compensation, reimbursement, indemnity
See also: **defence, include, safeguard, spread, stretch**
covering *adj* **1 = explanatory**, introductory, descriptive, accompanying ▸ *n* **2 = cover**, layer, blanket, casing, coating, wrapping
covert *See* **secret**
cover-up *n* **= concealment**, front, conspiracy, complicity, whitewash (*informal*), smoke screen
covet *v* **= long for**, desire, envy, crave, aspire to, lust after, set one's heart on, yearn for
covetous *adj* **= envious**, greedy, jealous, yearning, acquisitive, avaricious, close-fisted, grasping, rapacious
cow *n* **= bovine**, cattle • *a herd of dairy cows*
coward *n* **= wimp** (*informal*), chicken (*slang*), wuss (*informal*) • *too much of a coward to fight*
cowardice *n* **= faint-heartedness**, weakness, fearfulness, spinelessness
cowardly *adj* **= faint-hearted**, chicken (*slang*), gutless (*informal*) • *too cowardly to tell the truth* OPPOSITE: brave
See also: **timid**
cowboy *n* **= cowhand**, rancher, cattleman, gaucho, herdsman, drover, stockman
cower *v* **= cringe**, shrink, quail • *The hostages cowered in their seats.*
coy *adj* **= shy**, modest, timid, reserved, demure, bashful, retiring, shrinking
cozy *adj* **= snug**, warm, comfortable, intimate, comfy (*informal*), sheltered, homey, homely, tucked up
crack *v* **1 = break**, snap, fracture • *A gas main has cracked.* **2 = solve**, decipher, work out • *We've managed to crack the problem.* **3 = snap**, crash, ring, pop, explode, burst, detonate **4 = give in**, collapse, yield, succumb, break down, give way, go to pieces, lose control **5** (*Informal*) **= hit**, clip (*informal*), slap, smack, whack, cuff, clout (*informal*) ▸ *n* **6 = break**, fracture, cleft, crevice • *a large crack in the wall* **7 = snap**, report, crash, explosion, pop, burst, clap **8** (*Informal*) **= blow**, clip (*informal*), slap, smack, whack, cuff, clout (*informal*) **9** (*Informal*) **= joke**, dig, gag (*informal*), quip, jibe, wisecrack (*informal*), funny remark, witticism

DICTIONARY

gap **10** sudden sharp noise **11** sharp blow **12** *informal* gibe or joke **13** *slang* pure highly addictive form of cocaine ▷ *adj* **14** *informal* excellent, first-rate: *a crack shot*

▸ **cracker** *n* **1** thin dry biscuit **2** decorated cardboard tube, pulled apart with a bang, containing a paper hat and a motto or toy **3** small explosive firework

▸ **crackers** *adj slang* crazy

▸ **cracking** *adj* first-class

▸ **crackdown** *n* severe disciplinary or repressive measure

▸ **crack down on** *v* take severe measures against

▸ **crackpot** *adj, n informal* eccentric (person)

crackle *v* **1** make small sharp popping noises ▷ *n* **2** crackling sound

▸ **crackling** *n* **1** crackle **2** crisp skin of roast pork

cradle 🅣 *n* **1** baby's bed on rockers **2** place where something originated **3** supporting structure ▷ *v* **4** hold gently as if in a cradle

craft[1] 🅣 *n* **1** skilled trade **2** skill or ability **3** cunning

▸ **crafty** *adj* skilled in deception **craftily** *adv* **craftiness** *n*

▸ **craftsman** (**craftswoman**) *n* skilled worker **craftsmanship** *n*

craft[2] 🅣 *n, pl* **craft** boat, ship, aircraft, or spaceship

crag 🅣 *n* steep rugged rock **craggy** *adj*

cram 🅣 *v* **cramming, crammed 1** force into too small a space **2** fill too full **3** study hard just before an examination

cramp 🅣 *n* **1** painful muscular contraction **2** clamp for holding masonry or timber together ▷ *v* **3** confine or restrict

crampon *n* spiked plate strapped to a boot for climbing on ice

Cranach *n* **Lucas**, known as *the Elder*, real name *Lucas Müller*. 1472–1553, German painter, etcher, and designer of woodcuts

cranberry *n* sour edible red berry

crane *n* **1** machine for lifting and moving heavy weights **2** wading bird with long legs, neck, and bill ▷ *v* **3** stretch (one's neck) to see something

crane fly *n* long-legged insect with slender wings

cranium *n, pl* **-niums, -nia** skull **cranial** *adj*

crank 🅣 *n* **1** arm projecting at right angles from a shaft, for transmitting or converting motion **2** *informal* eccentric person ▷ *v* **3** start (an engine) with a crank

▸ **cranky** *adj* **1** eccentric **2** bad-tempered

▸ **crankshaft** *n* shaft driven by a crank

Cranmer *n* **Thomas**. 1489–1556, the first Protestant archbishop of Canterbury (1533–56) and principal author of the Book of Common Prayer. He was burnt as a heretic by Mary I

cranny 🅣 *n, pl* **-nies** small opening, chink

crap *slang* ▷ *n* **1** nonsense **2** *taboo* feces ▷ *v* **crapping, crapped 3** *taboo* defecate

crape *n* same as **crepe**

craps *n* gambling game played with two dice

crash 🅣 *n* **1** collision involving a vehicle or vehicles **2** sudden loud smashing noise

THESAURUS

See also: **attempt, bang, breach, fissure, gap, leak, opening, split**

crackdown *n* = **suppression**, clampdown, repression, crushing

cracked *adj* = **broken**, split, faulty, damaged, flawed, defective, imperfect, chipped

cracking *See* **excellent, splendid**

cradle *n* **1** = **crib**, cot, bassinet **2** = **birthplace**, source, spring, beginning, origin, fount, fountainhead, wellspring ▸ *v* **3** = **hold**, support, rock, nurse, lull, nestle

craft *n* **1** = **occupation**, work, trade, business, employment, pursuit, vocation, handicraft **2** = **skill**, art, ability, technique, expertise, know-how (*informal*), artistry, ingenuity, workmanship, aptitude **3** = **vessel**, plane, ship, aircraft, boat, spacecraft

craftsman *n* = **skilled worker**, maker, master, technician, artisan, smith, wright

craftsmanship *n* = **workmanship**, technique, expertise, mastery, artistry

crafty *adj* = **cunning**, slippery, wily, sly, devious, artful, scheming • *That crafty old devil has taken us for a ride!*
See also: **shrewd, sneaky**

crag *n* = **rock**, peak, bluff, pinnacle, tor

craggy *See* **jagged, rough**

cram *v* **1** = **stuff**, pack, jam, squeeze • *She crammed the towel into her gym bag.* **2** = **overeat**, stuff, glut, gorge, satiate **3** = **study**, bone up (*informal*), review
See also: **fill**

cramp[1] *n* = **spasm**, pain, ache, stitch, contraction, convulsion, pang, twinge

cramp[2] *v* = **restrict**, hamper, hinder, obstruct, impede, inhibit, handicap, constrain

cramped *adj* = **closed in**, crowded, packed, uncomfortable, confined, congested, hemmed in, overcrowded

crank *See* **eccentric**

cranny *n* = **crevice**, opening, hole, crack, gap, fissure, cleft, chink

crash *n* **1** = **collision**, accident, bump, smash, pile-up (*informal*) • *a plane*

DICTIONARY

3 financial collapse ▷ *v* **4** (cause to) collide violently with a vehicle, a stationary object, or the ground **5** (cause to) make a loud smashing noise **6** (cause to) fall with a crash **7** collapse or fail financially ▷ *adj* **8** requiring or using great effort to achieve results quickly: *a crash course*
▸ **crash helmet** protective helmet worn by a motorcyclist
▸ **crash-land** *v* land (an aircraft) in an emergency, causing it damage **crash-landing** *n*
crass Ⓣ *adj* grossly stupid **crassly** *adv* **crassness** *n*
Crassus *n* **Marcus Licinius.** ?115–53 BC, Roman general; member of the first triumvirate with Caesar and Pompey
crate Ⓣ *n* large wooden container for packing goods
crater Ⓣ *n* **1** bowl-shaped cavity made by the impact of a meteorite or an explosion **2** mouth of a volcano
cravat *n* man's scarf worn like a tie
crave Ⓣ *v* **1** desire intensely **2** beg or plead for **craving** *n*
craven *adj* cowardly
craw *n* **1** bird's crop **2** animal's stomach
crawfish *n* same as **crayfish**
Crawford *n* **Joan**, real name *Lucille le Sueur*. 1908–77, US film actress, who portrayed ambitious women in such films as *Mildred Pierce* (1945)
crawl Ⓣ *v* **1** move on one's hands and knees **2** move very slowly **3** act in a servile manner **4** be or feel as if covered with crawling creatures ▷ *n* **5** crawling motion or pace **6** overarm swimming stroke **crawler** *n*
crayfish *n* edible freshwater shellfish like a lobster
crayon *n* **1** stick or pencil of coloured wax or clay ▷ *v* **2** draw or colour with a crayon
craze Ⓣ *n* short-lived fashion or enthusiasm
▸ **crazed** *adj* **1** demented **2** (of porcelain) having fine cracks
▸ **crazy** *adj informal* **1** ridiculous **2** (foll. by *about*) very fond (of) **3** insane **craziness** *n*
▸ **crazy paving** paving made of irregularly shaped slabs of stone
Crazy Horse *n* Indian name *Ta-Sunko-Witko*. ?1849–77, Sioux Indian chief, remembered for his attempts to resist White settlement in Sioux territory
creak Ⓣ *v, n* (make) a harsh squeaking sound **creaky** *adj*
cream Ⓣ *n* **1** fatty part of milk **2** something, esp. a food or cosmetic, resembling cream in consistency **3** best part (of something) ▷ *adj* **4** yellowish-white ▷ *v* **5** beat to a creamy consistency **6** (foll. by *off*) take the best part from **creamy** *adj*
▸ **cream cheese** rich soft white cheese
crease Ⓣ *n* **1** line made by folding or pressing **2** *hockey* small area in front of goal net ▷ *v* **3** make or develop creases

THESAURUS

crash **2 = bang**, clash, smash, din • *There was a sudden crash outside.* **3 = collapse**, failure, depression, bankruptcy, ruin • *a stock-market crash* ▸ *v* **4 = collide**, bump, wreck, drive into, have an accident, hurtle into, plow into • *His car crashed into the rear of a minivan.* **5 = collapse**, fail, fold, be ruined, fold up, go belly up (*informal*), go bust (*informal*), go to the wall, go under **6 = hurtle**, plunge, topple, lurch, fall headlong, give way, overbalance
See also: **dash**
crass *adj* **= insensitive**, gross, stupid, boorish, unrefined, indelicate, oafish, witless
crate *n* **= container**, case, box, packing case, tea chest
crater *n* **= hollow**, depression, dip
crave *v* **1 = long for**, want, desire, hanker for, hope for, lust after, yearn for **2 = beg**, ask, seek, petition, solicit, implore, beseech, entreat, plead for, pray for, supplicate
craving *n* **= longing**, hope, desire, hunger, appetite, yen (*informal*), thirst, yearning, hankering
crawl *v* **1 = be full of**, swarm, teem, be alive with, be overrun (*slang*) • *The place is crawling with tourists.* **2 = creep**, inch, wriggle, writhe, slither, advance slowly, worm one's way **3 = grovel**, creep, fawn, brown-nose (*slang*), humble oneself, kiss ass (*slang*), toady
craze *n* **= fad**, trend, fashion, vogue • *the latest fitness craze*
See also: **whim**
crazy *adj* **1** (*Informal*) **= ridiculous**, wild, mad, foolish, insane, zany • *a crazy idea* OPPOSITE: sensible **2** (*Informal*) **= fanatical**, wild, mad, passionate, obsessed, smitten • *He's crazy about figure skating.* OPPOSITE: uninterested **3 = insane**, mad, unbalanced, crazed, demented, deranged, nuts (*slang*), out of one's mind
See also: **absurd, idiotic, irrational**
creak *v* **= squeak**, grind, scratch, scrape, grate, screech, groan
cream *n* **1 = lotion**, oil, cosmetic, paste, essence, ointment, emulsion, liniment, salve, unguent **2 = best**, pick, prime, flower, elite, *crème de la crème* (*French*) ▸ *adj* **3 = off-white**, yellowish-white
creamy *adj* **= smooth**, rich, soft, buttery, milky, velvety
crease *n* **1 = line**, fold, wrinkle, groove, ridge, corrugation ▸ *v* **2 = wrinkle**, fold, crumple, corrugate, rumple, double up, screw up

DICTIONARY

create Ⓣ *v* **1** bring into being **2** appoint to a new rank or position **3** *slang* make an angry fuss **creation** *n* **creator** *n*
▸ **creative** *adj* imaginative or inventive **creativity** *n*
creature Ⓣ *n* person, animal, or being
crèche *n* day nursery for very young children
credence [**kreed**-enss] *n* belief in the truth or accuracy of a statement
credentials Ⓣ *pl n* document giving evidence of the bearer's identity or qualifications
credible Ⓣ *adj* **1** believable **2** trustworthy **credibly** *adv* **credibility** *n*
credit Ⓣ *n* **1** system of allowing customers to take goods and pay later **2** reputation for trustworthiness in paying debts **3** money at one's disposal in a bank account **4** side of an account book on which such sums are entered **5** (source or cause of) praise or approval **6** influence or reputation based on the good opinion of others **7** belief or trust **credits 8** list of people responsible for the production of a film, programme, or record ▹ *v* **crediting, credited 9** enter as a credit in an account **10** (foll. by *with*) attribute (to) **11** believe
▸ **creditable** *adj* praiseworthy **creditably** *adv*
▸ **creditor** *n* person to whom money is owed
▸ **credit card** card allowing a person to buy on credit
▸ **credit crunch** period during which there is a sudden reduction in the availability of credit (from banks etc.)
credo *n, pl* **-dos** creed
credulous *adj* too willing to believe **credulity** *n*
creed Ⓣ *n* statement or system of (Christian) beliefs or principles
creek Ⓣ *n* **1** narrow inlet or bay **2** small stream
creel *n* wicker basket used by anglers
creep Ⓣ *v* **creeping, crept 1** move with stealthy slow movements **2** crawl with the body near to the ground **3** (of a plant) grow along the ground or over a surface ▹ *n* **4** *slang* obnoxious or servile person **creeps 5** feeling of fear or disgust
▸ **creeper** *n* creeping plant
▸ **creepy** *adj informal* causing a feeling of fear or disgust

THESAURUS

create *v* **1 = cause**, occasion, bring about, lead to • *The new factory created hundreds of jobs.* **2 = invent**, coin, compose, originate, devise, formulate • *creating a new style of painting* **3 = appoint**, make, establish, invest, install, constitute, set up
See also: **bring, construct, fashion, form, produce, start**
creation *n* **1 = making**, generation, formation, conception, genesis, procreation **2 = setting up**, production, development, institution, foundation, formation, establishment, inception **3 = invention**, production, achievement, brainchild (*informal*), concoction, handiwork, magnum opus, *pièce de résistance* (*French*) **4 = universe**, world, nature, cosmos
creative *adj* **= imaginative**, inspired, fertile, inventive • *her creative talents*
creativity *n* **= imagination**, inspiration, ingenuity, originality, inventiveness, cleverness
creator *n* **= maker**, author, father, designer, architect, inventor, originator, prime mover
creature *n* **1 = living thing**, animal, being, beast, brute **2 = person**, man, woman, individual, soul, mortal, human being
credentials *pl n* **= certification**, document, passport, licence, reference *or* references, authorization, testimonial, papers
credibility *n* **= believability**, integrity, reliability, plausibility, trustworthiness
credible *adj* **1 = believable**, likely, possible, reasonable, probable, imaginable, plausible, conceivable, thinkable **2 = reliable**, honest, sincere, dependable, trustworthy, trusty
credit *n* **1 = praise**, recognition, glory, acclaim, kudos, commendation, thanks, Brownie points, full marks (*Brit & Canad*), props (*informal*) • *He took all the credit for my idea.* **2 = source of satisfaction** *or* **source of pride**, honour, feather in one's cap **3 = prestige**, position, status, influence, regard, standing, reputation, esteem, repute, good name **4 = belief**, trust, confidence, faith, reliance, credence ▹ **on credit = on account**, by deferred payment, by instalments, on the card ▸ *v* **5 = believe**, trust, accept, have faith in, rely on ▹ **credit with = attribute to**, ascribe to, assign to, impute to
See also: **loan**
creditable *adj* **= praiseworthy**, worthy, respectable, admirable, reputable, honourable, commendable, laudable
credulity *n* **= gullibility**, blind faith, credulousness, naivety
creed *n* **= belief**, doctrine, dogma, credo, articles of faith, catechism, principles
creek *n* (*US, Canad, Austral, & NZ*) **= stream**, tributary, bayou, brook, rivulet, runnel, watercourse
creep *v* **1 = sneak**, steal, tiptoe, slink, approach unnoticed, skulk **2 = crawl**, glide, wriggle, squirm, writhe, slither ▸ *n* **3** (*Slang*)

DICTIONARY

cremate *v* burn (a corpse) to ash
cremation *n*
▸ **crematorium** *n* building where corpses are cremated
crème de menthe *n* liqueur flavoured with peppermint
crenellated *adj* having battlements
crenellation *n*
creole *n* **1** language developed from a mixture of languages **2 Creole** native-born W Indian or Latin American of mixed European and African descent
creosote *n* **1** dark oily liquid distilled from coal tar and used for preserving wood ▷ *v* **2** treat with creosote
crepe [**krayp**] *n* **1** fabric or rubber with a crinkled texture **2** very thin pancake
▸ **crepe paper** paper with a crinkled texture
crept *v* past of **creep**
crepuscular *adj* of or like twilight
Crerar *n* **Henry** (**Duncan Graham**). 1888–1965, Canadian army officer. He was commander-in-chief (1944–45) of the First Canadian Army during operations in W Europe
crescendo [krish-**end**-oh] *n, pl* **-dos** gradual increase in loudness, esp. in music
crescent Ⓣ *n* **1** (shape of) the moon as seen in its first or last quarter **2** crescent-shaped street
cress *n* plant with strong-tasting leaves, used in salads
crest Ⓣ *n* **1** top of a mountain, hill, or wave **2** tuft or growth on a bird's or animal's head **3** heraldic device used on a coat of arms, notepaper, and elsewhere **crested** *adj*
▸ **crestfallen** *adj* disheartened
cretin *n* **1** person afflicted with physical and mental retardation caused by a thyroid deficiency **2** *informal* stupid person **cretinous** *adj*
cretonne *n* heavy printed cotton fabric used in furnishings
crevasse *n* deep open chasm, esp. in a glacier
crevice Ⓣ *n* narrow fissure or crack
crew Ⓣ *n* **1** people who man a ship or aircraft **2** group of people working together **3** *informal* any group of people ▷ *v* **4** serve as a crew member on
▸ **crew cut** man's closely cropped haircut
crewel *n* fine worsted yarn used in embroidery
crib Ⓣ *n* **1** child's bed usu. with barred sides **2** barred rack used for fodder **3** plagiarism **4** translation or list of answers used by students, often illicitly ▷ *v* **cribbing, cribbed 5** confine in small space **6** copy (someone's work) dishonestly
▸ **crib death** unexplained death of a baby while asleep
cribbage *n* card game for two to four players
Crichton *n* (**John**) **Michael**. 1942–2008, US novelist, screenwriter, and film director; his thrillers, many of which have been filmed, include *The Andromeda Strain* (1969), *Jurassic Park* (1990), and *Disclosure* (1994)
crick *n* **1** muscle spasm or cramp, esp. in the back or neck ▷ *v* **2** cause a crick in
Crick *n* Sir **Francis Harry Compton**. 1916–2004, English molecular biologist: helped to discover the helical structure of DNA; Nobel prize for physiology or medicine shared with James Watson and Maurice Wilkins 1962
cricket[1] *n* outdoor game played with bats, a ball, and wickets by two teams of eleven
cricketer *n*
cricket[2] *n* chirping insect like a grasshopper
crime Ⓣ *n* **1** unlawful act **2** unlawful acts collectively **3** *informal* disgraceful act

THESAURUS

= **toady**, sneak, bootlicker, brown-noser (*slang*), crawler (*slang*), scuzzbucket (*slang*), sycophant **4** (*Slang*) = **jerk** (*slang*), loser, pervert, scumbag (*slang*), lowlife, scuzzbucket (*slang*)
creeper *n* = **climbing plant**, runner, vine, rambler, trailing plant
creeps *pl n* ▷ **give one the creeps** (*Informal*) = **disgust**, scare, frighten, repel, repulse, make one's hair stand on end, make one squirm
creepy *adj* (*Informal*) = **disturbing**, scary (*informal*), eerie, sinister, spooky, macabre, unnatural • *This place is really creepy at night.*
crescent *n* = **meniscus**, sickle, new moon
crest *n* **1** = **top**, summit, crown, peak, ridge, pinnacle, apex, highest point **2** = **tuft**, crown, comb, plume, mane **3** = **emblem**, device, symbol, badge, insignia, bearings
crestfallen *adj* = **disappointed**, depressed, dejected, despondent, discouraged, downcast, disheartened, downhearted
crevice *n* = **gap**, opening, hole, crack, fissure, slit, cleft, cranny, chink
crew *n* **1** = **company** *or* **ship's company**, complement *or* ship's complement, hands **2** = **team**, gang, squad, corps, posse **3** (*Informal*) = **crowd**, set, band, pack, gang, bunch (*informal*), mob, horde
crib *n* **1** = **cradle**, bed, cot, bassinet **2** = **manger**, stall, rack ▸ *v* **3** (*Informal*) = **copy**, steal, pirate, cheat, plagiarize, purloin
crime *n* **1** = **offence**, wrong, violation, misdemeanour • *the problem of organized crime* **2** = **lawbreaking**, corruption, vice, wrongdoing, misconduct, illegality
See also: **pity, sin**

DICTIONARY

▶ **criminal** *n* **1** person guilty of a crime ▷ *adj* **2** of crime **criminally** *adv* **criminality** *n*
▶ **criminology** *n* study of crime **criminologist** *n*
crimp *v* fold or press into ridges
crimson Ⓣ *adj* deep red
cringe Ⓣ *v* **1** flinch or shrink **2** behave in a servile or timid way
crinkle *v, n* wrinkle, twist, or fold
crinoline *n* hooped petticoat
Crippen *n* **Hawley Harvey**, known as *Doctor Crippen*. 1862–1910, US doctor living in England: executed for poisoning his wife; the first criminal to be apprehended by the use of radiotelegraphy
cripple Ⓣ *n* **1** person who is lame or disabled ▷ *v* **2** make a cripple of (someone) **3** damage (something)
crisis Ⓣ *n, pl* **-ses 1** crucial stage, turning point **2** time of acute trouble or danger
crisp Ⓣ *adj* **1** fresh and firm **2** dry and brittle **3** clean and neat **4** (of weather) cold but invigorating **5** brisk and lively ▷ *n* **6** *Brit* potato chip **crisply** *adv* **crispness** *n* **crispy** *adj*
▶ **crispbread** *n* thin dry biscuit
Crispin *n* **Saint**. 3rd century AD, legendary Roman Christian martyr, with his brother **Crispinian**: they are the patron saints of shoemakers. Feast day: Oct 25
crisscross Ⓣ *v* **1** move in, mark with, or consist of a crosswise pattern ▷ *adj* **2** (of lines) crossing in different directions
criterion Ⓣ *n, pl* **-ria** standard of judgment
critic Ⓣ *n* **1** professional judge of any of the arts **2** person who finds fault
▶ **critical** *adj* **1** very important or dangerous **2** seriously ill **3** fault-finding **4** discerning **5** of a critic or criticism **critically** *adv*
▶ **criticism** *n* **1** fault-finding **2** evaluation of a work of art
▶ **criticize** *v* find fault with
▶ **critique** *n* critical essay
croak Ⓣ *v* **1** (of a frog or crow) give a low hoarse cry **2** utter or speak with a croak ▷ *n* **3** low hoarse cry
▶ **croaky** *adj* hoarse
Croatian [kroh-**ay**-shun], **Croat** [**kroh**-at] *adj* **1** of Croatia ▷ *n* **2** person from Croatia **3** dialect of Serbo-Croat spoken in Croatia
Croce *n* **Benedetto**. 1866–1952, Italian philosopher, critic, and statesman: an opponent of Fascism, he helped re-establish liberalism in postwar Italy

THESAURUS

criminal *n* **1** = **lawbreaker**, offender, culprit, villain, crook (*informal*), perp (*informal*), felon, malefactor • *the country's most dangerous criminals* ▶ *adj* **2** = **unlawful**, illegal, illicit, corrupt, crooked • *criminal activities* **3** = **disgraceful**, ridiculous, foolish, senseless, scandalous, deplorable, preposterous
See also: **guilty**
crimson *See* **blush**
cringe *v* = **shrink**, shy, flinch, wince, recoil, cower, draw back
cripple *v* **1** = **disable**, paralyze, maim • *She was crippled in a car accident.* **2** = **impair**, bring to a standstill, put out of action • *The crisis may cripple the provincial economy.*
crippled *adj* = **disabled**, paralyzed, lame, handicapped, challenged, incapacitated, laid up (*informal*)
crisis *n* **1** = **critical point**, crunch (*informal*), height, climax, culmination, crux, moment of truth, turning point **2** = **emergency**, trouble, plight, meltdown (*informal*), predicament, deep water, dire straits, panic stations (*informal*)
crisp *adj* **1** = **crunchy**, firm, fresh, crispy, brittle, crumbly **2** = **clean**, trim, smart, tidy, neat, spruce, well-groomed, well-pressed **3** = **bracing**, fresh, brisk, invigorating, refreshing
crisscross *See* **cross**
criterion *n* = **standard**, test, rule, measure, principle, gauge, touchstone, yardstick, bench mark
critic *n* **1** = **judge**, expert, authority, analyst, commentator, reviewer, pundit, connoisseur **2** = **fault-finder**, attacker, detractor, knocker (*informal*)
critical *adj* **1** = **crucial**, decisive, vital, pivotal, momentous, deciding • *a critical point in history* OPPOSITE: unimportant **2** = **serious**, grave, precarious • *a critical illness* **3** = **disparaging**, scathing, derogatory, carping, disapproving • *critical remarks* OPPOSITE: complimentary **4** = **analytical**, judicious, perceptive, discerning, discriminating, fastidious, penetrating
See also: **acute, major, severe**
criticism *n* **1** = **fault-finding**, censure, flak (*informal*), disapproval • *The finance minister faced criticism over the budget.* OPPOSITE: praise **2** = **analysis**, comment, assessment, judgment, commentary, appreciation, evaluation, critique, appraisal
See also: **complaint, review**
criticize *v* = **find fault with**, knock (*informal*), condemn, censure, disparage, lambaste, put down, excoriate • *The dictatorial regime has been harshly criticized.* OPPOSITE: praise
See also: **attack, fault**
croak *v* = **squawk**, wheeze, caw, grunt, utter huskily *or* speak huskily
croaky *See* **hoarse**

DICTIONARY

crochet [**kroh**-shay] *n* **1** handicraft like knitting, done with a single hooked needle ▷ *v* **2** do or make such work
crock *n* **1** earthenware jar or pot **2** *informal* old or decrepit person or thing
▶ **crockery** *n* earthenware or china dishes
Crockett *n* **David**, known as *Davy Crockett*. 1786–1836, US frontiersman, politician, and soldier
crocodile *n* **1** large amphibious tropical reptile **2** line of children walking two by two
▶ **crocodile tears** insincere grief
crocus *n, pl* **-cuses** small plant with yellow, white, or purple flowers in spring
Croesus *n* **1** died ?546 BC, the last king of Lydia (560–546), noted for his great wealth **2** any very rich man
croft *n* small farm worked by the occupier in Scotland **crofter** *n*
croissant [**krwah**-son] *n* rich flaky crescent-shaped roll
cromlech *n* circle of prehistoric standing stones
Crompton *n* **Richmal**, full name *Richmal Crompton Lamburn*. 1890–1969, British children's author, best known for her *Just William* stories
Cromwell *n* **Oliver**. 1599–1658, English general and statesman. A convinced Puritan, he was an effective leader of the parliamentary army in the Civil War. After the execution of Charles I he quelled the Royalists in Scotland and Ireland, and became Lord Protector of the Commonwealth (1653–58) **Cromwellian** *adj, n*
crone *n* witchlike old woman
Cronenberg *n* **David**. born 1943, Canadian film director; his films include *The Fly* (1986), *Crash* (1996), and *A History of Violence* (2005)
Cronin *n* **A(rchibald) J(oseph)**. 1896–1981, British novelist and physician. His works include *Hatter's Castle* (1931), *The Judas Tree* (1961), and *Dr. Finlay's Casebook*, a TV series based on his medical experiences
crony Ⓣ *n, pl* **-nies** close friend
crook Ⓣ *n* **1** *informal* criminal **2** bent or curved part **3** hooked pole
▶ **crooked** *adj* **1** bent or twisted **2** set at an angle **3** *informal* dishonest
croon Ⓣ *v* hum, sing, or speak in a soft low tone **crooner** *n*
crop Ⓣ *n* **1** cultivated plant **2** season's total yield of produce **3** group of things appearing at one time **4** hunting whip **5** pouch in a bird's gullet **6** short haircut ▷ *v* **cropping, cropped 7** cut short **8** produce or harvest as a crop **9** (of animals) feed on (grass etc.)
cropper *n*
▶ **come a cropper** *informal* have a disastrous failure or heavy fall
▶ **crop-top** *n* short T-shirt or vest that reveals the wearer's midriff
▶ **crop up** *v informal* happen unexpectedly
croquet [**kroh**-kay] *n* game in which balls are hit through hoops
croquette [kroh-**kett**] *n* fried cake of potato, meat, or fish
Crosbie *n* **John**. born 1931, Canadian politician, Lieutenant Governor of Newfoundland and Labrador (2008–)
Crosby *n* **Bing**, real name *Harry Lillis Crosby*. 1904–77, US singer and film actor; famous for his style of crooning: best known for the song "White Christmas" from the film *Holiday Inn* (1942)
crosier *n* same as **crozier**
cross Ⓣ *v* **1** move or go across (something) **2** meet and pass **3** draw a cross or lines through (something) **4** mark with lines across **5** place (one's arms or legs) crosswise **6** make the sign of the cross on (oneself) **7** thwart or oppose **8** interbreed or cross-

THESAURUS

crony *See* **companion, friend**
crook *n* (*Informal*) **= criminal**, thief, shark, cheat, rogue, villain, scoundrel (*old-fashioned*), swindler • *The man is a crook and a liar.*
crooked *adj* **1 = bent**, twisted, irregular, distorted, deformed, out of shape, warped • *a crooked tree* OPPOSITE: straight **2 = dishonest**, criminal, illegal, corrupt, fraudulent, shady (*informal*), nefarious, unprincipled • *crooked business practices* OPPOSITE: honest **3 = at an angle**, lopsided, awry, askew, off-centre, uneven, squint, slanting
See also: **dirty, dubious, wrong**
croon *v* **= sing**, hum, purr, warble
crop *n* **1 = produce**, yield, gathering, harvest, vintage, fruits, reaping ▶ *v* **2 = cut**, clip, trim, pare, prune, shear, lop, snip **3 = graze**, browse, nibble ▷ **crop up = happen**, appear, occur, emerge, arise, spring up, turn up
cross *v* **1 = go across**, span, traverse, ford • *the bridge that crosses the river* **2 = intersect**, crisscross • *the intersection where the roads cross* **3 = oppose**, block, resist, interfere, obstruct, impede **4 = interbreed**, mix, blend, crossbreed, cross-fertilize, cross-pollinate, hybridize, intercross, mongrelize ▷ **cross out, cross off = strike off** *or* **strike out**, cancel, eliminate, delete, blue-pencil, score out *or* score off ▷ **cross your mind** *See* **occur** ▶ *n* **5 = mixture**, combination, hybrid, blend • *a cross between a collie and a retriever* **6 = crucifix**, rood **7 = trouble**, trial, worry, load, burden, woe, grief, misfortune, affliction, tribulation ▶ *adj* **8 = angry**, fractious, grumpy, annoyed, irritable, fretful,

DICTIONARY

fertilize ▷ *n* **9** structure, symbol, or mark of two intersecting lines **10** such a structure of wood as a means of execution **11** representation of the Cross as an emblem of Christianity **12** mixture of two things **13** affliction ▷ *adj* **14** angry, in a bad mood **15** lying or placed across **crossly** *adv* **crossness** *n*

▶ **the Cross** *Christianity* the cross on which Christ was crucified

▶ **crossing** *n* **1** place where a street etc. may be crossed **2** place where things cross **3** journey across water

▶ **crossbar** *n* horizontal bar across goalposts or on a bicycle

▶ **crossbow** *n* bow fixed across a wooden stock

▶ **crossbred** *adj* bred from two different types of animal or plant

▶ **crossbreed** *n* crossbred animal or plant

▶ **crosscheck** *v* **1** check the accuracy of (something) by using a different method **2** *hockey* illegally check an opponent forcefully with the shaft of the stick held between the hands ▷ *n* **3** act of crosschecking

▶ **cross-country** *adj, adv* by way of open country or fields

▶ **cross-examine** *v* question (a witness in court) to check his or her testimony **cross-examination** *n*

▶ **cross-eyed** *adj* with eyes turning inwards

▶ **cross-fertilize** *v* fertilize (an animal or plant) from one of a different kind **cross-fertilization** *n*

▶ **crossfire** *n* gunfire crossing another line of fire

▶ **cross-ply** *adj* (of a tire) having the fabric cords in the outer casing running diagonally

▶ **cross-purposes** *pl n* **at cross-purposes** misunderstanding each other

▶ **cross-reference** *n* reference within a text to another part

▶ **crossroads** *n* place where roads intersect

▶ **cross section** **1** (diagram of) a surface made by cutting across something **2** representative sample

▶ **crosswalk** *n* place marked where pedestrians may cross a road

▶ **crosswise** *adj, adv* **1** transverse(ly) **2** in the shape of a cross

▶ **crossword puzzle** *or* **crossword** *n* puzzle in which words suggested by clues are written into a grid of squares

crotch *n* fork between the legs

crotchet *n Brit* quarter note

crotchety *adj informal* bad-tempered

crouch Ⓣ *v* **1** bend low with the legs and body close ▷ *n* **2** this position

croup[1] [**kroop**] *n* throat disease of children, with a cough

croup[2] [**kroop**] *n* hind quarters of a horse

croupier [**kroop**-ee-ay] *n* person who collects bets and pays out winnings at a gambling table

crouton *n* small piece of fried or toasted bread served in soup

crow[1] *n* large black bird with a harsh call

▶ **as the crow flies** in a straight line

▶ **crow's feet** wrinkles at the corners of the eyes

▶ **crow's nest** lookout platform high on a ship's mast

crow[2] Ⓣ *v* **1** (of a cock) utter a shrill squawking sound **2** boast of one's superiority **3** (of a baby) utter cries of pleasure ▷ *n* **4** cock's cry

crowbar *n* iron bar used as a lever

crowd Ⓣ *n* **1** large group of people or things **2** particular group of people ▷ *v* **3** flock together **4** fill or occupy fully

Crowe *n* **Russell**. born 1964, Australian film actor, born in New Zealand. His films include *LA Confidential* (1997), *Gladiator* (2000), for which he won an Oscar, *A Beautiful Mind* (2001), and *Master and Commander* (2003)

THESAURUS

in a bad mood • *I'm really cross with you.* **9 = transverse**, oblique, diagonal, crosswise, intersecting

cross-examine *v* **= question**, pump, quiz, grill (*informal*), interrogate

crossing *n* **= crossroads**, intersection, junction

crouch *v* **= bend down**, squat • *crouching behind the car*
See also: **bend**

crow *v* **= gloat**, triumph, boast, brag, swagger, strut, exult, blow one's own trumpet

crowd *n* **1 = multitude**, host (*formal*), mass, mob, swarm, throng, horde • *a large crowd at the garage sale* **2 = group**, set, lot, circle, bunch (*informal*), clique **3 = audience**, house, attendance, gate, spectators ▶ *v* **= gather**, swarm, throng, congregate • *Thousands of fans crowded into the stadium.* **4 = squeeze**, pack, pile, bundle, cram, congest
See also: **band, company, jam, number**

crowded *adj* **= packed**, full, congested, overflowing • *a crowded room*

crowing *See* **boastful**

crown *n* **1 = coronet**, tiara, circlet, diadem **2 = laurel wreath**, trophy, wreath, honour, prize, garland, laurels **3 = high point**, top, tip, summit, crest, pinnacle, apex ▶ *v* **4 = honour**, adorn, festoon, dignify **5 = cap**, top, finish, complete, perfect, be the climax of *or* be the culmination of, put the finishing touch to, round off **6** (*Slang*) **= strike**, belt (*informal*),

DICTIONARY

crown Ⓣ *n* **1** monarch's headdress **2** wreath for the head **3** highest point of something arched or curved **4** artificial cover for a broken or decayed tooth **5** former British coin worth twenty-five pence ▷ *v* **6** put a crown on the head of (someone) to proclaim him or her monarch **7** form or put on the top of **8** put the finishing touch to (a series of events) **9** *informal* hit on the head
▸ **the Crown** power of the monarchy
▸ **crown attorney** lawyer who represents a government at a trial
▸ **crown corporation** business owned by a government but run like a private company
▸ **crown prince** (**crown princess**) heir to the throne

crozier *n* bishop's hooked staff

cruces *n* a plural of **crux**

crucial Ⓣ *adj* very important, critical **crucially** *adv*

crucible *n* pot in which metals are melted

crucify Ⓣ *v* **-fying, -fied 1** put to death by fastening to a cross **2** treat cruelly **3** *informal* ridicule publicly
▸ **crucifix** *n* model of Christ on the Cross
▸ **crucifixion** *n* crucifying
▸ **the Crucifixion** *Christianity* **1** crucifying of Christ **2** representation of this
▸ **cruciform** *adj* cross-shaped

crude Ⓣ *adj* **1** rough and simple **2** tasteless or vulgar **3** in a natural or unrefined state **crudely** *adv* **crudity** *n*

cruel Ⓣ *adj* **1** delighting in others' pain **2** causing pain or suffering **cruelly** *adv* **cruelty** *n*

cruet *n* small container for salt, pepper, etc. at table

cruise Ⓣ *n* **1** voyage for pleasure ▷ *v* **2** sail about for pleasure **3** (of a vehicle, aircraft, or ship) travel at a moderate and economical speed
▸ **cruiser** *n* **1** motorboat with a cabin **2** fast warship **3** police patrol car
▸ **cruise missile** low-flying guided missile

crumb Ⓣ *n* **1** small fragment of bread or other dry food **2** small bit

crumble Ⓣ *v* **1** break into fragments **2** fall apart or decay ▷ *n* **3** pudding of stewed fruit with a crumbly topping **crumbly** *adj*

crummy Ⓣ *adj* **-mier, -miest** *slang* **1** inferior **2** squalid

crumpet *n* **1** round soft yeast cake eaten buttered **2** *slang* sexually attractive women collectively

crumple Ⓣ *v* **1** crush and crease **2** collapse **crumpled** *adj*

crunch Ⓣ *v* **1** crush (food) noisily with the teeth **2** (cause to) make a crisp or brittle

THESAURUS

box, punch, hit over the head

Crown *n* **1 = monarchy**, royalty, sovereignty **2 = monarch**, king *or* queen, ruler, sovereign, emperor *or* empress

crucial *adj* **1 = vital**, central, critical, decisive, pivotal, momentous • *a crucial moment in her career* **2 = critical**, central, decisive, pivotal
See also: **essential, major, serious**

crucify *v* **= execute**, torture, persecute, torment

crude *adj* **1 = rough**, simple, primitive, rudimentary • *a crude weapon* **2 = vulgar**, dirty, obscene, indecent, tasteless, coarse • *a crude sense of humour* OPPOSITE: refined **3 = unrefined**, natural, raw, unprocessed

crudely *adv* **= vulgarly**, roughly, bluntly, coarsely, rudely, impolitely, tastelessly

crudity *n* **1 = roughness**, clumsiness, crudeness **2 = vulgarity**, obscenity, indecency, impropriety, coarseness, indelicacy, smuttiness

cruel *adj* **1 = brutal**, vicious, inhumane, sadistic, callous, heartless, cold-blooded, barbarous • *I can't understand why people are cruel to animals.* OPPOSITE: kind **2 = merciless**, ruthless, unrelenting, pitiless
See also: **harsh, malicious, savage, spiteful, unkind, violent**

cruelly *adv* **1 = brutally**, mercilessly, barbarously, callously, heartlessly, in cold blood, pitilessly, sadistically, spitefully **2 = bitterly**, deeply, severely, fearfully, grievously, monstrously

cruelty *n* **= brutality**, savagery, inhumanity, viciousness, barbarity, callousness • *an act of unbelievable cruelty* OPPOSITE: kindness
See also: **violence**

cruise *n* **1 = sail**, voyage, boat trip, sea trip ▸ *v* **2 = sail**, coast, voyage **3 = travel along**, coast, drift, keep a steady pace

crumb *n* **= bit**, grain, scrap, shred, fragment, morsel, soupçon (*French*)

crumble *v* **1 = disintegrate**, collapse, deteriorate, decay, degenerate, fall apart, go to pieces, go to rack and ruin, tumble down **2 = crush**, pound, grind, powder, fragment, granulate, pulverize

crummy *adj* (*Informal*) **1 = despicable**, mean, lousy (*slang*), contemptible, scuzzy (*slang*) **2 = inferior**, poor, inadequate, lousy (*slang*), deficient, substandard, of poor quality **3 = unwell**, below par, off colour, under the weather (*informal*)

crumple *v* **1 = crush**, crease, wrinkle • *She crumpled the paper in her hand.* **2 = collapse**, fall, break down, cave in, give way, go to pieces
See also: **fold**

crunch *v* **1 = chomp**, grind, champ, munch,

DICTIONARY

sound ▷ *n* **3** crunching sound **4** *informal* critical moment **crunchy** *adj*
crupper *n* strap that passes from the back of a saddle under a horse's tail
crusade Ⓣ *n* **1** medieval Christian war to recover the Holy Land from the Muslims **2** vigorous campaign in favour of a cause ▷ *v* **3** take part in a crusade **crusader** *n*
crush Ⓣ *v* **1** compress so as to break, injure, or crumple **2** break into small pieces **3** defeat utterly ▷ *n* **4** dense crowd **5** *informal* infatuation **6** drink made by crushing fruit
crust Ⓣ *n* **1** hard outer part of something, esp. bread ▷ *v* **2** cover with or form a crust
▶ **crusty** *adj* **1** having a crust **2** irritable
crustacean *n* hard-shelled, usu. aquatic animal with several pairs of legs, such as the crab or lobster
crutch *n* **1** staff with a rest for the armpit, used by a lame person **2** support **3** crotch
crux *n, pl* **cruxes, cruces** crucial or decisive point
cry Ⓣ *v* **crying, cried 1** shed tears **2** call or utter loudly **3** appeal urgently (for) ▷ *n, pl* **cries 4** fit of weeping **5** loud utterance **6** urgent appeal
▶ **crybaby** *n* person who cries too readily
cryogenics *n* branch of physics concerned with very low temperatures **cryogenic** *adj*
crypt *n* vault, esp. one under a church
▶ **cryptic** *adj* obscure in meaning **cryptically** *adv*
▶ **cryptogram** *n* message in code
▶ **cryptography** *n* art of writing in and deciphering codes
cryptogam *n* plant that reproduces by spores, not seeds
crystal *n* **1** glasslike mineral **2** very clear and brilliant glass **3** tumblers, vases, etc. made of such glass **4** (single grain of a) symmetrically shaped solid formed naturally by some substances ▷ *adj* **5** bright and clear
▶ **crystalline** *adj* **1** of or like crystal or crystals **2** clear
▶ **crystallize** *v* **1** make or become definite **2** form into crystals **3** preserve (fruit) in sugar **crystallization** *n*
▶ **crystal meth** *informal* highly addictive drug with dangerous side effects
CSE Certificate of Secondary Education
CS gas *n* gas causing tears and painful breathing, used to control civil disturbances
CSIS Canadian Security and Intelligence Service
CST Central Standard Time
CTV Canadian Television (Network Ltd.)
Cu *chem* copper
cu. cubic
cub Ⓣ *n* **1** young of certain mammals, such as the lion **2 Cub** Cub Scout ▷ *v* **cubbing, cubbed 3** give birth to (cubs)
▶ **Cub Scout** member of a junior branch of the Boy Scouts
cubbyhole *n* small enclosed space or room
cube *n* **1** solid with six equal square sides **2** product obtained by multiplying a number by itself twice ▷ *v* **3** find the cube of (a number) **4** cut into cubes
▶ **cubic** *adj* **1** having three dimensions **2** cube-shaped
▶ **cubism** *n* style of art in which objects are represented by geometrical shapes **cubist** *n, adj*
▶ **cube root** number whose cube is a given number
cubicle *n* enclosed part of a large room, screened for privacy
cuckold *n* **1** man whose wife has committed adultery ▷ *v* **2** make a cuckold of
cuckoo Ⓣ *n* **1** migratory bird with a characteristic two-note call, which lays its eggs in the nests of other birds ▷ *adj* **2** *informal* crazy
cucumber *n* long green-skinned fleshy

THESAURUS

chew noisily ▶ *n* **2** (*Informal*) = **critical point**, test, emergency, crisis, crux, moment of truth
crusade *n* = **campaign**, cause, drive, push, movement
crush *v* **1** = **squash**, crumble, mash, crumple • *Their car was crushed, but nobody was seriously hurt.* **2** = **overcome**, quell, vanquish, put down, stamp out • *The Blue Jays crushed the Yankees.* **3** = **humiliate**, shame, quash, mortify, abash, put down (*slang*) ▶ *n* **4** = **crowd**, jam, huddle
See also: **dash, defeat, press, subdue, suppress**
crust *n* = **layer**, skin, surface, shell, coating, covering
crusty *adj* **1** = **crispy**, hard **2** = **irritable**, cross, testy, cantankerous, prickly, gruff, short-tempered
cry *v* **1** = **weep**, sob, blubber, shed tears, snivel • *Stop crying and tell me what's wrong.* **2** = **shout**, call, scream, roar, yell, howl, exclaim, shriek, bellow, bawl, call out • *"See you soon!" they cried.* ▷ **cry off** (*Informal*) = **back out**, quit, withdraw, excuse oneself ▶ *n* **3** = **shout**, call, howl, bellow, exclamation, scream, roar, screech, shriek **4** = **weeping**, weep, sob, blubbering, snivelling, sobbing • *the act of weeping* **5** = **appeal**, plea
See also: **bay**
cryptic *See* **mysterious, obscure**
crystalline *See* **clear, transparent**
cub *n* = **young**, offspring, whelp
cuckoo *adj* (*Slang*) = **insane**, crazy, stupid,

DICTIONARY

fruit used in salads
cud *n* partially digested food which a ruminant brings back into its mouth to chew again
▶ **chew the cud** reflect or ponder
cuddle Ⓣ *v* **1** hug fondly **2** nestle ▷ *n* **3** fond hug **cuddly** *adj*
cudgel Ⓣ *n* short thick stick used as a weapon
cue[1] Ⓣ *n* **1** signal to an actor or musician to begin speaking or playing **2** signal or reminder ▷ *v* **cueing, cued 3** give a cue to (someone)
cue[2] *n* **1** long tapering stick used in billiards, snooker, or pool ▷ *v* **cueing, cued 2** strike (a ball) with a cue
cuff[1] *n* end of a sleeve
▶ **off the cuff** *informal* impromptu
▶ **cuff link** one of a pair of decorative fastenings for shirt cuffs
cuff[2] *v* **1** strike with an open hand ▷ *n* **2** blow with an open hand
cuisine [quiz-**zeen**] *n* style of cooking
Culbertson *n* **Ely**. 1891–1955, US authority on contract bridge
cul-de-sac Ⓣ *n* road with one end blocked off
culinary *adj* of the kitchen or cookery
cull *v* **1** gather, select **2** remove or kill (inferior or surplus animals) from a herd ▷ *n* **3** culling
culminate Ⓣ *v* reach the highest point or climax **culmination** *n*
culottes *pl n* women's flared trousers cut to look like a skirt
culpable Ⓣ *adj* deserving blame **culpability** *n*
culprit Ⓣ *n* person guilty of an offence or misdeed
cult Ⓣ *n* **1** specific system of worship **2** devotion to a person, idea, or activity **3** popular fashion
cultivate Ⓣ *v* **1** prepare (land) to grow crops **2** grow (plants) **3** develop or improve (something) **4** try to develop a friendship with (someone) **cultivation** *n*
▶ **cultivated** *adj* cultured or well-educated
culture Ⓣ *n* **1** ideas, customs, and art of a particular society **2** particular society **3** developed understanding of the arts **4** cultivation of plants or rearing of animals **5** growth of bacteria for study **cultural** *adj*
▶ **cultured** *adj* showing culture
▶ **cultured pearl** pearl artificially grown in an oyster shell
culvert Ⓣ *n* drain under a road or railway
cum *prep* with: *kitchen-cum-dining room*
cumbersome Ⓣ *adj* awkward or unwieldy
cumin, cummin *n* aromatic seeds of a Mediterranean plant, used in cooking
cummerbund *n* broad sash worn round the waist
Cummings *n* **Edward Estlin** (preferred typographical representation of name **e. e. cummings**). 1894–1962, US poet
cumulative [**kew**-myew-la-tiv] *adj* increasing steadily
cumulus [**kew**-myew-luss] *n, pl* **-li** cloud

C

THESAURUS

foolish, idiotic, bonkers (*informal*), daft (*informal*), nuts (*slang*), out of one's mind
cuddle *v* = **hug**, pet, embrace, snuggle, fondle, bill and coo, cosset
cudgel *n* = **club**, nightstick, billy club, stick, truncheon
cue *n* = **signal**, sign, key, hint, suggestion, reminder, catchword, prompting
cul-de-sac *n* = **dead end**, blind alley
culminate *v* = **end up**, close, finish, conclude, climax, come to a climax, come to a head, wind up
culmination *n* = **climax**, peak, conclusion, finale, pinnacle, zenith, acme, consummation
culpable *adj* = **blameworthy**, guilty, wrong, at fault, found wanting, in the wrong, to blame
culprit *n* = **offender**, criminal, wrongdoer, felon, miscreant, evildoer, guilty party, perp (*informal*), transgressor
cult *n* **1** = **sect**, school, religion, faction, clique **2** = **devotion**, worship, idolization
cultivate *v* **1** = **farm**, work, plant, tend, plow, till **2** = **develop**, improve, promote, foster, refine **3** = **court**, dance attendance upon, run after, seek out
cultivated *See* **educated, sophisticated**
cultivation *n* **1** = **farming**, gardening, husbandry, planting, plowing, tillage **2** = **development**, support, promotion, nurture, encouragement, patronage, fostering, furtherance
cultural *adj* = **artistic**, liberal, educational, humane, civilizing, edifying, enlightening, enriching
culture *n* **1** = **civilization**, society, lifestyle, mores, customs, way of life **2** = **refinement**, education, sophistication, enlightenment, good taste, urbanity **3** = **farming**, cultivation, husbandry
cultured *adj* = **refined**, sophisticated, enlightened, well-informed, educated, highbrow, urbane, well-read
culvert *n* = **drain**, channel, gutter, conduit, watercourse
cumbersome *adj* = **awkward**, heavy, bulky, weighty, unwieldy, unmanageable, burdensome

DICTIONARY

shaped in heaped-up rounded masses
cuneiform [**kew**-nif-form] *n* **1** ancient system of writing using wedge-shaped characters ▷ *adj* **2** written in cuneiform
cunning Ⓣ *adj* **1** clever at deceiving **2** ingenious ▷ *n* **3** cleverness at deceiving **4** ingenuity **cunningly** *adv*
Cunobelinus *n* Also **Cymbeline** died ?42 AD, British ruler of the Catuvellauni tribe (?10–?42); founder of Colchester (?10)
cup Ⓣ *n* **1** small bowl-shaped drinking container with a handle **2** contents of a cup **3** cup-shaped trophy given as a prize **4** hollow rounded shape **5** mixed drink with fruit juice or wine as a base ▷ *v* **cupping, cupped 6** form (one's hands) into the shape of a cup **7** hold in cupped hands **cupful** *n*
cupboard *n* piece of furniture or recess with a door, for storage
cupidity [kew-**pid**-it-ee] *n* greed for wealth or possessions
cupola [**kew**-pol-la] *n* domed roof or ceiling
cupreous *adj* of or containing copper
cur *n* **1** mongrel dog **2** contemptible person
curaçao [**kew**-rah-so] *n* orange-flavoured liqueur
curare [kew-**rah**-ree] *n* poisonous resin of a S American tree, used as a muscle relaxant in medicine
curate *n* cleric who assists a parish priest
▸ **curacy** [**kew**-rah-see] *n* work or position of a curate
curative *adj* **1** able to cure ▷ *n* **2** something curative
curator *n* person in charge of a museum or art gallery **curatorship** *n*
curb Ⓣ *n* **1** check or restraint **2** edge of sidewalk ▷ *v* **3** restrain
curd *n* coagulated milk
▸ **curdle** *v* turn into curd, coagulate
cure Ⓣ *v* **1** heal (an ailment or problem) **2** restore to health **3** preserve by salting, smoking, or drying ▷ *n* **4** restoration to health **5** medical treatment **6** remedy or solution **curable** *adj*
curet, curette *n* **1** surgical instrument for scraping tissue from body cavities ▷ *v* **-retting, -retted 2** scrape with a curet
curettage *n*
curfew *n* **1** law ordering people to stay indoors after a specific time at night **2** time set as a deadline by such a law
curie *n* standard unit of radioactivity
Curie *n* **1 Marie**. 1867–1934, French physicist and chemist, born in Poland: discovered with her husband Pierre the radioactivity of thorium, and discovered and isolated radium and polonium. She shared a Nobel prize for physics (1903) with her husband and Henri Becquerel, and was awarded a Nobel prize for chemistry (1911) **2** her husband, **Pierre**. 1859–1906, French physicist and chemist
curio [**kew**-ree-oh] *n, pl* **-rios** strange or rare thing valued as a collector's item
curious Ⓣ *adj* **1** eager to know **2** eager to find out private details **3** unusual or peculiar
curiously *adv*
▸ **curiosity** *n* **1** eagerness to know **2** eagerness to find out private details **3** strange or rare thing
curium [**kew**-ree-um] *n* artificial radioactive element produced from plutonium
curl Ⓣ *v* **1** twist (hair) or (of hair) be twisted into coils **2** twist into a spiral or curve ▷ *n* **3** coil of hair **4** spiral or curved shape **curly** *adj*
▸ **curling** *n* game like bowls, played with heavy stones on ice
curlew *n* long-billed wading bird

THESAURUS

cunning *adj* **1 = crafty**, wily, sly, devious, artful • *a cunning and ruthless plot* OPPOSITE: open **2 = skilful**, imaginative, ingenious ▸ *n* **3 = deviousness**, guile • *the cunning of today's criminals* **4 = skill**, ingenuity, subtlety, artifice, cleverness
cup *n* **1 = mug**, bowl, chalice, beaker, goblet, teacup **2 = trophy**
curb *v* **1 = restrain**, control, contain, limit, check, suppress • *He must learn to curb that temper of his.* ▸ *n* **2 = restraint**, control, limit, brake, limitation • *She called for stricter curbs on government spending.*
See also: **halt, moderate, restriction**
curdled *See* **sour**
cure *v* **1 = remedy**, heal • *Doctors are still seeking a treatment that will cure the common cold.* ▸ *n* **2 = remedy**, treatment, medicine • *a cure for the disease*
See also: **correct**
curiosity *n* **1 = inquisitiveness**, interest, infomania (*informal*) • *a curiosity about the past* **2 = oddity**, freak, marvel, novelty, rarity • *a museum displaying relics and curiosities*
curious *adj* **1 = inquisitive**, interested, nosy (*informal*), inquiring • *He was curious about my family.* **2 = strange**, odd, unusual, extraordinary, bizarre, singular, peculiar • *a curious mixture of the old and the new* OPPOSITE: ordinary
See also: **weird**
curl *v* **1 = twirl**, turn, wind, twist, spiral, bend, curve, loop, coil ▸ *n* **2 = twist**, spiral, coil, kink, ringlet, whorl
curly *adj* **= curling**, fuzzy, wavy, crinkly, curled, frizzy, winding
currency *n* **1 = money**, coinage, coins, notes **2 = acceptance**, exposure, popularity,

DICTIONARY

curlicue *n* ornamental curl or twist
curmudgeon *n* bad-tempered or mean person
currant *n* **1** dried grape **2** small round berry, such as a redcurrant
current Ⓣ *adj* **1** of the immediate present **2** most recent, up-to-date **3** commonly accepted ▷ *n* **4** flow of water or air in one direction **5** flow of electricity **6** general trend
currently *adv*
▶ **currency** *n* **1** money in use in a particular country **2** state of being current
curriculum Ⓣ *n, pl* **-la, -lums** specified course of study
▶ **curriculum vitae** [**vee**-tie] outline of someone's educational and professional history, prepared for job applications
curry[1] *n, pl* **-ries 1** dish of meat or vegetables in a hot or mild spicy sauce ▷ *v* **-rying, -ried 2** prepare (food) with curry powder
▶ **curry powder** mixture of spices for making curry
curry[2] *v* **-rying, -ried** groom (a horse) with a currycomb
▶ **curry favour** ingratiate oneself, esp. with one's superiors
▶ **currycomb** *n* ridged comb for grooming a horse
curse Ⓣ *v* **1** say profane or obscene things (to) **2** utter a curse against ▷ *n* **3** profane or obscene expression, usu. of anger **4** call to a supernatural power for harm to come to a person **5** affliction, misfortune
▶ **cursed** *adj* hateful
cursive *n, adj* (handwriting) done with joined letters
cursor *n* movable point of light that shows a specific position on a visual display unit
cursory Ⓣ *adj* hasty and superficial
cursorily *adv*
curt Ⓣ *adj* (of speech) impolitely brief
curtly *adv* **curtness** *n*
curtail Ⓣ *v* **1** cut short **2** restrict
curtailment *n*
curtain Ⓣ *n* **1** piece of cloth hung at a window or opening as a screen **2** hanging cloth separating the audience and the stage in a theatre **3** end of a scene or act, marked by the fall or closing of the curtain **4** thing(s) forming a barrier or screen ▷ *v* **5** conceal with a curtain **6** provide with curtains
curtsy, curtsey *n, pl* **-sies, -seys 1** woman's gesture of respect made by bending the knees and bowing the head ▷ *v* **-sying, -sied** *or* **-seying, -seyed 2** make a curtsy
curve Ⓣ *n* **1** continuously bending line with no straight parts ▷ *v* **2** bend into or move in a curve **curvy** *adj*
▶ **curvaceous** *adj informal* (of a woman) having a shapely body
▶ **curvature** *n* state or degree of being curved
▶ **curvilinear** *adj* consisting of or bounded by a curve
cushion Ⓣ *n* **1** bag filled with soft material, to make a seat more comfortable **2** something that provides comfort or absorbs shock ▷ *v* **3** protect from injury or shock **4** lessen the effects of
cushy Ⓣ *adj* **cushier, cushiest** *informal* easy: *a cushy job*
cusp *n* **1** pointed end, esp. on a tooth **2** *astrol* division between houses or signs of the zodiac
cuss *informal* ▷ *n* **1** curse, oath **2** annoying person ▷ *v* **3** swear (at)
▶ **cussed** [**kuss**-id] *adj informal* obstinate

C

THESAURUS

circulation, prevalence, vogue
current *n* **1** = **flow**, tide, undertow • *swept away by the strong current* **2** = **mood**, trend, feeling, atmosphere, tendency, undercurrent ▶ *adj* **3** = **present**, ongoing, contemporary, fashionable, present-day, up-to-the-minute, today's • *current trends* OPPOSITE: past **4** = **prevalent**, popular, common, widespread, customary, topical, accepted, in circulation
See also: **modern, recent**
currently *See* **now**
curriculum *See* **course**
curriculum vitae *See* **résumé**
curse *v* **1** = **swear**, blaspheme, cuss (*informal*), take the Lord's name in vain **2** = **damn**, excommunicate, anathematize ▶ *n* **3** = **oath**, obscenity, expletive, blasphemy, swearing, swearword **4** = **denunciation**, ban, jinx, anathema, excommunication, hoodoo (*informal*) **5** = **affliction**, trouble, plague, hardship, scourge, torment, bane
cursed *adj* = **damned**, doomed, ill-fated, accursed, bedevilled
cursory *See* **casual, quick**
curt *adj* = **short**, brief, blunt, abrupt, terse, gruff, succinct, brusque, monosyllabic
curtail *v* = **cut short**, reduce, decrease, dock, diminish, shorten, lessen, cut back, truncate
curtain *n* = **hanging**, drape
curve *n* **1** = **bend**, turn, arc, trajectory, incurve (*baseball*) • *a curve in the road* RELATED WORD *adj*: sinuous ▶ *v* **2** = **bend**, arc, arch, swerve • *The road curved sharply to the left.*
curved *adj* = **bent**, twisted, rounded, arched, serpentine, bowed, sinuous
cushion *n* **1** = **pillow**, pad, bolster, beanbag, hassock, headrest ▶ *v* **2** = **soften**, stifle, suppress, dampen, muffle, deaden
cushy *adj* (*Informal*) = **easy**, comfortable,

DICTIONARY

custard *n* dish or sauce made of sweetened milk thickened with eggs or cornflour

custody Ⓣ *n* **1** guardianship **2** imprisonment prior to being tried **custodial** *adj*

▸ **custodian** *n* person in charge of a public building or museum collection

custom Ⓣ *n* **1** long-established activity or action **2** usual habit **3** regular use of a shop or business **customs 4** duty charged on imports or exports **5** government department which collects these **6** area at a port, airport, or border where baggage and freight are examined for dutiable goods

▸ **customary** *adj* **1** usual **2** established by custom **customarily** *adv*

▸ **customer** *n* person who buys goods or services

▸ **custom-built** *or* **custom-made** *adj* made to the specifications of an individual customer

cut Ⓣ *v* **cutting, cut 1** open up, penetrate, wound, or divide with a sharp instrument **2** divide **3** intersect **4** trim or shape by cutting **5** abridge **6** reduce **7** *informal* snub (a person) **8** *informal* absent oneself from (classes) ▹ *n* **9** stroke or incision made by cutting **10** piece cut off **11** reduction **12** abridgment **13** style in which hair or a garment is cut **14** *informal* share, esp. of profits

▸ **cutter** *n* **1** person or tool that cuts **2** any of various small fast boats

▸ **cutting** *n* **1** piece cut from a plant for rooting or grafting **2** article cut from a newspaper or magazine **3** passage cut through high ground for a road or railway ▹ *adj* **4** keen, piercing **5** (of a remark) hurtful

▸ **cutting edge** leading position in any field

▸ **cut in** *v* **1** interrupt **2** obstruct another vehicle in overtaking it

▸ **cutthroat** *adj* **1** fierce or relentless ▹ *n* **2** murderer

cutaneous [kew-**tane**-ee-uss] *adj* of the skin

cute Ⓣ *adj* **1** appealing or attractive **2** *informal* clever or shrewd **cutely** *adv* **cuteness** *n*

Cuthbert *n* **Saint**. ?635–687 AD, English monk; bishop of Lindisfarne. Feast day: March 20

cuticle [**kew**-tik-kl] *n* skin at the base of a fingernail or toenail

cutlass *n* short curved one-edged sword

cutlery *n* knives, forks, and spoons, used for eating

▸ **cutler** *n* maker or seller of cutlery

cutlet *n* small piece of meat grilled or fried

cuttlefish *n* sea mollusc like a squid

Cuvier *n* **Georges** (**Jean-Leopold-Nicolas-Frédéric**), Baron. 1769–1832, French zoologist and statesman; founder of the sciences of

THESAURUS

soft, undemanding

custody *n* **1 = safekeeping**, charge, care, protection, supervision, keeping **2 = imprisonment**, detention, confinement, incarceration

custom *n* **1 = tradition**, practice, convention, ritual • *a family custom to have a birthday picnic* **2 = habit**, practice, wont (*formal*) • *It was his custom to start work at 8:30.* **3 = customers**, trade, patronage *See also*: **way**

customary *adj* **= usual**, common, traditional, normal, routine, conventional, ordinary, established, accepted, accustomed

customer *n* **= client**, consumer, shopper, buyer, patron, purchaser • *The store was filled with customers.*

customs *pl n* **= duty**, tax, toll, tariff, import charges

cut *v* **1 = penetrate**, score, wound, slash, slice, chop, sever, pierce, slit • *He accidentally cut his chin while he was shaving.* **2 = divide**, split, slice, dissect, bisect **3 = trim**, clip, shave, mow, pare, prune, lop, snip, hew **4 = abridge**, shorten, delete, curtail, abbreviate, condense **5 = reduce**, contract, lower, decrease, slash, slim *or* slim down, diminish, downsize, rationalize, cut back • *The department's first priority is to cut costs.* OPPOSITE: increase **6 = shape**, form, fashion, carve, sculpt, whittle, engrave, chisel **7 = hurt**, wound, insult, sting, snub, put down ▹ **cut back** *See* **cut** ▹ **cut down = fell**, level, lop, hew; **= reduce**, lower, decrease, lessen ▹ **cut in = interrupt**, intervene, intrude, break in, butt in ▹ **cut off = separate**, isolate, sever; **= interrupt**, intercept, disconnect

▹ **cut out = stop**, cease, give up, refrain from ▹ **cut short** *See* **halt** ▹ **cut up** *See* **divide** ▸ *n* **8 = incision**, wound, stroke, slash, gash, nick, slit, laceration • *a cut on his left eyebrow* **9 = reduction**, fall, saving, decrease, cutback, lowering • *another cut in interest rates* OPPOSITE: increase **10** (*Informal*) **= share**, piece, percentage, section, portion, slice **11 = style**, look, fashion, shape

cutback *n* **= reduction**, cut, economy, decrease, lessening, retrenchment

cute *adj* **= appealing**, pretty, attractive, dear, charming, gorgeous, good-looking • *You were such a cute baby!*

cutthroat *adj* **1 = competitive**, fierce, relentless, ruthless, dog-eat-dog, unprincipled ▸ *n* **2 = murderer**, killer, assassin, butcher, executioner, hit man (*slang*)

cutting *adj* **= hurtful**, bitter, scathing, malicious, barbed, acrimonious, vitriolic, sarcastic, caustic, wounding

DICTIONARY

comparative anatomy and paleontology
CV curriculum vitae
cwm [**koom**] *n* (in Wales) valley
cwt. hundredweight
cyanide *n* extremely poisonous chemical compound
cyanosis *n* blueness of the skin, caused by a deficiency of oxygen in the blood
cyber- *combining form* computers: *cyberspace*
cybernetics *n* branch of science in which electronic and mechanical systems are studied and compared to biological systems
cyberspace *n* place said to contain all the data stored in computers
cyclamen [**sik**-la-men] *n* plant with red, pink, or white flowers having turned-back petals
cycle Ⓣ *n* **1** bicycle **2** motorcycle **3** recurrent series of events **4** time taken for one such series ▷ *v* **5** ride a cycle
▸ **cyclic** *or* **cyclical** *adj* occurring in cycles
▸ **cyclist** *n* person who rides a cycle
cyclone *n* violent wind moving clockwise round a central area **cyclonic** *adj*
cyclotron *n* apparatus which accelerates charged particles by means of a strong vertical magnetic field
cygnet *n* young swan
cylinder *n* **1** solid or hollow body with straight sides and circular ends **2** chamber within which the piston moves in an internal-combustion engine **cylindrical** *adj*
cymbal *n* percussion instrument consisting of a brass plate which is struck against another or hit with a stick
cynic Ⓣ [**sin**-ik] *n* person who believes that people always act selfishly **cynical** *adj* **cynically** *adv* **cynicism** *n*
cynosure [**sin**-oh-zyure] *n* centre of attention
cypher *n* same as **cipher**
cypress *n* evergreen tree with very dark foliage
Cypriot *n, adj* (person) from Cyprus
cyst [**sist**] *n* (abnormal) sac in the body containing fluid or soft matter **cystic** *adj*
▸ **cystitis** [siss-**tite**-iss] *n* inflammation of the bladder
cytology [site-**ol**-a-jee] *n* study of plant and animal cells **cytological** *adj* **cytologist** *n*
czar [**zahr**] *n* same as **tsar**
Czech *adj* **1** of the Czech Republic ▷ *n* **2** person from the Czech Republic **3** language of the Czech Republic

THESAURUS

cycle *n* = **era**, period, circle, phase, revolution, rotation
cylindrical *See* **round**
cynic *n* = **skeptic**, doubter, pessimist, misanthrope, misanthropist, scoffer
cynical *adj* = **skeptical**, distrustful • *a cynical attitude*
cynicism *n* = **skepticism**, doubt, disbelief, pessimism, misanthropy

DICTIONARY

Dd

d *physics* density
D *chem* deuterium
d. **1** died **2** *Brit* old penny
dab[1] Ⓣ *v* **dabbing, dabbed 1** pat lightly **2** apply with short tapping strokes ▷ *n* **3** small amount of something soft or moist **4** light tap or stroke
▶ **dab hand** *informal* person who is particularly good at something
dab[2] *n* small flatfish
dabble Ⓣ *v* **1** deal in something superficially **2** splash about **dabbler** *n*
dace *n* small freshwater fish
dacha *n* Russian country cottage
dachshund *n* dog with a long body and short legs
dactyl *n* metrical foot of three syllables, one long followed by two short **dactylic** *adj*
dad *n informal* father
Dada, Dadaism *n* early 20th-century artistic movement, founded on the principles of incongruity, irrationality, and irreverence **Dadaist** *n, adj*
daddy *n, pl* **-dies** *informal* father
daddy-longlegs *n informal* crane fly
dado [**day**-doe] *n, pl* **-does, -dos** lower part of an interior wall that is decorated differently from the upper part
daffodil *n* spring plant with yellow trumpet-shaped flowers
daft Ⓣ *adj informal* foolish or crazy
Dafydd ap Gruffudd *n* died 1283, Welsh leader. Claiming the title Prince of Wales (1282), he led an unsuccessful revolt against Edward I: executed
dagger Ⓣ *n* short stabbing weapon with a pointed blade
dago [**day**-go] *n offensive* Spanish or other Latin person
daguerreotype [dag-**gair**-oh-type] *n* type of early photograph produced on chemically treated silver
Dahl *n* **Roald**. 1916–90, British writer with Norwegian parents, noted for his short stories and such children's books as *Charlie and the Chocolate Factory* (1964)
dahlia [**day**-lya] *n* garden plant with showy flowers
daily Ⓣ *adj* **1** occurring every day or every weekday ▷ *adv* **2** every day ▷ *n, pl* **-lies 3** daily newspaper **4** *Brit informal* charwoman
dainty Ⓣ *adj* **-tier, -tiest** delicate or elegant **daintily** *adv*
daiquiri [**dak**-eer-ee] *n* iced drink containing rum, lime juice, and sugar
dairy *n, pl* **dairies 1** place for the processing or sale of milk and its products **2** food containing milk or milk products: *I can't eat dairy* ▷ *adj* **3** of milk or its products
dais [**day**-iss] *n* raised platform in a hall
daisy *n, pl* **-sies** flower with a yellow centre and white petals
▶ **daisywheel** *n* flat disc in a word processor with radiating spokes for printing letters
Daladier *n* **Édouard**. 1884–1970, French radical socialist statesman; premier of France (1933; 1934; 1938–40) and signatory of the Munich Pact (1938)
Dalai Lama *n* **1** (until 1959) the chief lama and ruler of Tibet **2** born 1935, the 14th holder of this office (1940), who fled to India (1959): Nobel peace prize 1989
dale *n* valley
d'Alembert *n* **Jean Le Rond**. 1717–83, French mathematician, physicist, and rationalist philosopher, noted for his contribution to Newtonian physics in *Traité de dynamique* (1743) and for his collaboration with Diderot in editing the *Encyclopédie*
Dalhousie *n* **9th Earl of**, title of *George Ramsay*. 1770–1838, British general; governor of the British colonies in Canada (1819–28)

THESAURUS

dab *v* **1 = pat**, touch, tap, daub, stipple ▶ *n* **2 = spot**, drop, bit, pat, speck, smudge **3 = pat**, touch, stroke, tap, flick
dabble *v* **1 = play at**, tinker, putter, trifle *or* trifle with, dip into **2 = splash**, dip
daft *adj (Informal)* **1 = foolish**, crazy, stupid, silly, absurd, idiotic, asinine, bonkers (*informal*), crackpot (*informal*), witless **2 = crazy**, bonkers (*slang*), insane, demented, deranged, nuts (*slang*), touched, unhinged
dagger *n* **= knife**, stiletto, bayonet, dirk
daily *adj* **1 = everyday**, diurnal, quotidian ▶ *adv* **2 = every day**, day by day, once a day
dainty *adj* **= delicate**, fine, pretty, elegant, charming, neat, exquisite, graceful, petite

DICTIONARY

Dali *n* **Salvador**. 1904–89, Spanish surrealist painter
Dallapiccola *n* **Luigi**. 1904–75, Italian composer of twelve-tone music. His works include the opera *Il Prigioniero* (1944–48) and the ballet *Marsia* (1948)
dally *v* **-lying, -lied 1** dawdle **2** (foll. by *with*) amuse oneself (with)
▸ **dalliance** *n* flirtation
Dalmatian *n* large dog with a white coat and black spots
Dalton *n* **John**. 1766–1844, English chemist and physicist, who formulated the modern form of the atomic theory and the law of partial pressures for gases. He also gave the first accurate description of colour blindness, from which he suffered
dam[1] Ⓣ *n* **1** barrier built across a river to create a lake **2** lake created by this ▷ *v* **damming, dammed 3** restrict by a dam
dam[2] *n* female parent of an animal
damage Ⓣ *v* **1** harm ▷ *n* **2** injury or harm to a person or thing **3** *informal* cost: *what's the damage?* **damages 4** money to be paid as compensation for injury or loss
damask *n* fabric with a pattern woven into it, used for tablecloths etc.
dame Ⓣ *n* **1** *slang* woman **2 Dame** title of a woman who has been awarded the Order of the British Empire or another order of chivalry
damn Ⓣ *interj* **1** *slang* exclamation of annoyance ▷ *adv, adj* **2** Also **damned** *slang* extreme or extremely ▷ *v* **3** declare to be bad or worthless **4** swear (at) **5** (of God) condemn to hell **6** prove (someone) guilty: *damning evidence* **damnation** *n*
▸ **damnable** *adj* annoying **damnably** *adv*
Damon *n* **Matt**. born 1970, US film actor and screenwriter. His films include *Good Will Hunting* (1997, which he co-wrote), *Saving Private Ryan* (1998), *The Talented Mr. Ripley* (1999), and the 'Bourne' series of films (2002–07)
damp Ⓣ *adj* **1** slightly wet ▷ *n* **2** slight wetness, moisture ▷ *v* **3** make damp **4** (foll. by *down*) reduce the force of (feelings or actions) **damply** *adv* **dampness** *n*
▸ **dampen** *v* damp
▸ **damper** *n* **1** depressing influence **2** movable plate to regulate the draft in a fire or furnace **3** pad in a piano that deadens the vibration of each string
damsel *n obsolete* young woman
damson *n* small blue-black plumlike fruit
dan *n judo, karate* **1** any one of 10 black-belt grades of proficiency **2** competitor entitled to a dan grading
Danby *n* **1st Earl of**, title of *Thomas Osborne*. 1631–1712, English politician; Lord Treasurer (1673–78): regarded as the founder of the Tory party (Also (from 1694) **1st Duke of Leeds**)
dance Ⓣ *v* **1** move the feet and body rhythmically in time to music **2** perform (a particular kind of dance) **3** skip or leap **4** move rhythmically ▷ *n* **5** social meeting arranged for dancing **6** series of steps and movements in time to music **dancer** *n*
D and C *surgery* dilat(at)ion and curettage: an operation in which the neck of the womb is stretched and the lining of the womb is scraped, for example to remove diseased tissue
dandelion *n* yellow-flowered wild plant

THESAURUS

dam *n* **1 = barrier**, wall, obstruction, barrage, embankment ▸ *v* **2 = block up**, restrict, barricade, obstruct, hold back
damage *v* **1 = harm**, injure, hurt • *A fire had severely damaged the school*. ▸ *n* **2 = harm**, injury • *The flood caused extensive damage to the restaurant*. **3** (*Informal*) **= cost**, charge, bill, expense
See also: **ruin, spoil**
damaged *See* **imperfect**
damages *pl n* (*Law*) **= compensation**, fine, satisfaction, reimbursement, reparation
damaging *adj* **= harmful**, detrimental, hurtful, ruinous, deleterious, injurious, disadvantageous
dame *n* **= noblewoman**, lady, baroness, dowager, *grande dame* (*French*), peeress
damn *v* **1 = condemn**, blast, criticize, denounce, censure, put down **2 = sentence**, condemn, doom
damnation *n* **= condemnation**, doom, denunciation, anathema, damning
damned *adj* **1 = doomed**, lost, accursed, condemned **2** (*Slang*) **= detestable**, hateful, confounded, infernal, loathsome
damp *adj* **1 = moist**, wet, soggy, humid, sodden, clammy, dank • *a damp towel* ▸ *n* **2 = moisture**, drizzle, dampness, dankness ▸ *v* **3 = moisten**, wet, dampen ▷ **damp down = reduce**, check, curb, stifle, diminish, inhibit, allay, pour cold water on
dampen *v* **1 = reduce**, check, moderate, stifle, restrain, lessen, dull **2 = moisten**, spray, wet, make damp
damper *n* **= discouragement**, restraint, hindrance, cold water (*informal*), wet blanket (*informal*)
dampness *n* **= moisture**, humidity • *There was dampness all over the walls*.
See also: **wet**
dance *v* **1 = prance**, trip, skip, hop, sway, whirl, jig ▸ *n* **2 = ball**, hop (*informal, dated*), disco, discotheque, social
dancer *n* **= ballerina**, Terpsichorean

DICTIONARY

dander *n* **get one's dander up** *slang* become angry
dandle *v* move (a child) up and down on one's knee
dandruff *n* loose scales of dry dead skin shed from the scalp
dandy *n, pl* **-dies 1** man who is greatly concerned with the elegance of his appearance ▷ *adj* **-dier, -diest 2** *informal* very good or fine **dandified** *adj*
Dane *n* person from Denmark
▸ **Danish** *adj* **1** of Denmark, its people, or their language ▷ *n* **2** language of Denmark
▸ **Danish blue** white cheese with blue veins and a strong flavour
▸ **Danish pastry** cake made from rich puff pastry filled with fruit, almond paste, etc.
danger Ⓣ *n* **1** state of being vulnerable to injury or loss **2** person or thing that may cause injury **3** likelihood that something unpleasant will happen **dangerous** *adj* **dangerously** *adv*
dangle Ⓣ *v* **1** hang freely **2** display as an enticement
dank Ⓣ *adj* unpleasantly damp and chilly
Dankworth *n* **John** (**Philip William**). 1927–2010, British jazz composer, bandleader, and saxophonist: married to Cleo Laine
D'Annunzio *n* **Gabriele**. 1863–1938, Italian poet, dramatist, novelist, national hero, and Fascist. His works include the poems in *Alcione* (1904) and the drama *La Figlia di Iorio* (1904)
Dante *n* full name *Dante Alighieri*. 1265–1321, Italian poet famous for *La Divina Commedia* (?1309–?1320), an allegorical account of his journey through Hell, Purgatory, and Paradise, guided by Virgil and his idealized love Beatrice. His other works include *La Vita Nuova* (?1292), in which he celebrates his love for Beatrice
Danton *n* **Georges Jacques**. 1759–94, French revolutionary leader: a founder member of the Committee of Public Safety (1793) and minister of justice (1792–94). He was overthrown by Robespierre and guillotined
daphne *n* shrub with small bell-shaped flowers
Da Ponte *n* **Lorenzo**, real name *Emmanuele Conegliano*. 1749–1838, Italian writer; Mozart's librettist for *The Marriage of Figaro* (1786), *Don Giovanni* (1787), and *Così fan tutte* (1790)
dapper Ⓣ *adj* (of a man) neat in appearance and slight in build
dappled *adj* marked with spots of a different colour
▸ **dapple-grey** *n* horse having a grey coat with spots of a different colour
Darby and Joan *n* elderly married couple living in domestic harmony
▸ **Darby and Joan Club** club for elderly people
dare Ⓣ *v* **1** be courageous enough to try (to do something) **2** challenge to do something risky ▷ *n* **3** challenge
▸ **daring** *adj* **1** willing to take risks ▷ *n* **2** courage to do dangerous things **daringly** *adv*
▸ **daredevil** *adj, n* reckless (person)
daren't dare not
Darius I *n* known as *Darius the Great*, surname *Hystaspis*. ?550–486 BC, king of Persia (521–486), who extended the Persian empire and crushed the revolt of the Ionian city states (500). He led two expeditions against Greece but was defeated at Marathon (490)
Darius III *n* died 330 BC, last Achaemenid king of Persia (336–330), who was defeated by Alexander the Great
dark Ⓣ *adj* **1** having little or no light **2** (of a colour) reflecting little light **3** (of hair or skin) brown or black **4** gloomy or sinister **5** secret: *keep it dark* ▷ *n* **6** absence of light **7** night **darkly** *adv* **darkness** *n* **darken** *v*

THESAURUS

danger *n* = **peril**, risk, threat, hazard, menace, jeopardy • *Your life is in danger!* OPPOSITE: safety
dangerous *adj* = **perilous**, risky, hazardous, treacherous • *It's dangerous to ride a bike without a helmet*. OPPOSITE: safe
See also: **fierce, serious**
dangerously *adv* = **perilously**, recklessly, alarmingly, precariously, hazardously, riskily, unsafely
dangle *v* **1** = **hang**, trail, swing, sway, flap, hang down **2** = **wave**, flourish, brandish, flaunt
dank *See* **damp**
dapper *adj* = **neat**, trim, smart, spruce, spry, soigné *or* soignée, well-groomed, well turned out
dare *v* **1** = **challenge**, defy • *I dare you to ask him for a date*. **2** = **risk**, venture • *Nobody dared to complain*. ▸ *n* **3** = **challenge**, taunt, provocation
daredevil *n* **1** = **adventurer**, desperado, exhibitionist, show-off (*informal*), stunt man ▸ *adj* **2** = **daring**, bold, audacious, adventurous, death-defying, reckless
daring *adj* **1** = **brave**, bold, audacious, adventurous, fearless • *a daring escape by helicopter* OPPOSITE: cautious ▸ *n* **2** = **bravery**, nerve (*informal*), courage, audacity, boldness, guts (*informal*) • *His daring may have cost him his life*. OPPOSITE: caution
dark *adj* **1** = **dim**, murky, cloudy, shadowy, overcast, dingy • *It was too dark to see what was happening*. OPPOSITE: light **2** = **black**,

DICTIONARY

▸ **dark horse** person who reveals unexpected talents
▸ **darkroom** *n* darkened room for processing film
darling ⓣ *n* **1** much-loved person **2** favourite: *the darling of the gossip columns* ▹ *adj* **3** beloved
darn[1] ⓣ *v* **1** mend (a garment) with a series of interwoven stitches ▹ *n* **2** patch of darned work
darn[2] *interj, adv, adj, v euphemistic* damn
dart ⓣ *n* **1** small narrow pointed missile that is thrown or shot, esp. in the game of darts **2** sudden quick movement **3** tuck made in dressmaking **darts 4** indoor game in which darts are thrown at a circular numbered board (**dartboard**) ▹ *v* **5** move or throw quickly and suddenly
Darwin *n* **1 Charles** (**Robert**). 1809–82, English naturalist who formulated the theory of evolution by natural selection, expounded on in *On the Origin of Species* (1859) and applied to mankind in *The Descent of Man* (1871) **2** his grandfather, **Erasmus**. 1731–1802, English physician and poet; author of *Zoonomia, or the Laws of Organic Life* (1794–96), anticipating Lamarck's views on evolution
Darwinism *n* theory of the origin of animal and plant species by evolution **Darwinian** *or* **Darwinist** *adj, n*
dash ⓣ *v* **1** move hastily **2** throw or strike violently **3** frustrate (someone's hopes) ▹ *n* **4** sudden quick movement **5** small amount **6** mixture of style and courage **7** punctuation mark (–) showing a change of subject **8** longer symbol used in Morse code
▸ **dashing** *adj* **1** lively **2** stylish
▸ **dashboard** *n* instrument panel in an automobile, boat, or aircraft
dastardly *adj* mean and cowardly
data ⓣ *n* **1** series of observations, measurements, or facts **2** numbers, digits, etc. operated on by a computer
▸ **database** *n* store of information that can be easily handled by a computer
▸ **data capture** process for converting information into a form that can be handled by a computer
▸ **data processing** series of operations performed on data, esp. by a computer, to extract or interpret information
date[1] ⓣ *n* **1** specified day of the month **2** particular day or year when an event happened **3** *informal* appointment, esp. with a person of the opposite sex **4** *informal* this person ▹ *v* **5** mark with the date **6** assign a date of occurrence to **7** (foll. by *from*) originate from (a date): *this house dates from the 16th century* **8** make or become old-fashioned
dated *adj*
date[2] *n* dark-brown sweet-tasting fruit of the date palm
▸ **date palm** tall palm grown in tropical regions for its fruit
dative *n* (in certain languages) the form of the noun that expresses the indirect object
daub ⓣ *v* smear or spread quickly or clumsily
daughter *n* **1** female child **2** woman who comes from a certain place or is connected

THESAURUS

swarthy • *a dark suit* **3 = gloomy**, sad, dismal, bleak, grim, mournful, sombre, morose **4 = evil**, foul, wicked, sinister, vile, infernal **5 = secret**, mysterious, hidden, concealed ▸ *n* **6 = darkness**, dusk, gloom, dimness • *I've always been afraid of the dark.* OPPOSITE: light **7 = night**, evening, twilight, nightfall, night-time
darken *v* **= make dark**, overshadow, obscure, dim, blacken
darkness *n* **= dark**, shade, gloom, nightfall, blackness, duskiness, murk, shadows
darling *n* **1 = beloved**, love, dear, sweetheart, dearest, truelove ▸ *adj* **2 = beloved**, precious, dear, cherished, adored, treasured
darn *v* **1 = mend**, repair, patch, stitch, cobble up, sew up ▸ *n* **2 = mend**, patch, reinforcement, invisible repair
dart *v* **= dash**, run, shoot, race, fly, spring, rush, tear, sprint
dash *v* **1 = rush**, run, race, fly, tear, sprint, bolt • *Suddenly, the dog dashed into the street.* **2 = smash**, break, crash, throw, slam, hurl • *The waves dashed against the rocks.* **3 = frustrate**, destroy, disappoint, crush, thwart, foil, shatter • *They had their hopes raised and then dashed.* ▸ *n* **4 = rush**, run, race, sprint, bolt, stampede • *a dash to the hospital* **5 = drop**, splash, pinch, sprinkling • *a dash of vinegar* **6 = style**, spirit, flourish, flair, panache, verve, brio, élan
See also: **bustle, charge, hurry, trace**
dashing *adj* **1 = bold**, spirited, lively, gallant, swashbuckling, debonair **2 = stylish**, smart, elegant, flamboyant, showy, sporty, jaunty
data *n* **= information**, details, facts, figures, statistics
date *n* **1 = time**, period, age, stage, era, epoch **2 = appointment**, meeting, engagement, rendezvous, tryst, assignation **3 = partner**, friend, escort ▸ *v* **4 = put a date on**, assign a date to, fix the period of **5 = become old-fashioned**, be dated, show one's age ▹ **date from, date back to = come from**, bear a date of, belong to, exist from, originate in
dated *adj* **= old-fashioned**, outdated, obsolete, outmoded, old hat, out of date, passé, unfashionable
daub *v* **= smear**, cover, paint, coat,

DICTIONARY

with a certain thing: *daughter of the church*
daughterly *adj*
▸ **daughter-in-law** *n, pl* **daughters-in-law** son's wife
daunt Ⓣ *v* intimidate or dishearten
daunting *adj*
▸ **dauntless** *adj* fearless
dauphin [**daw**-fin] *n* (formerly) eldest son of the king of France
davenport *n* **1** small writing table with drawers **2** large couch
David *n* **1** the second king of the Hebrews (around 1000–962 BC), who united Israel as a kingdom with Jerusalem as its capital **2 Jacques Louis**. 1748–1825, French neoclassical painter of such works as the *Oath of the Horatii* (1784), *Death of Socrates* (1787), and *The Intervention of the Sabine Women* (1799). He actively supported the French Revolution and became court painter to Napoleon Bonaparte in 1804; banished at the Bourbon restoration **3 Saint**. 6th century AD, Welsh bishop; patron saint of Wales. Feast day: March 1
David I *n* 1084–1153, king of Scotland (1124–53) who supported his niece Matilda's claim to the English throne and unsuccessfully invaded England on her behalf
David II *n* 1324–71, king of Scotland (1329–71): he was forced into exile in France (1334–41) by Edward de Baliol; captured following the battle of Neville's Cross (1346), and imprisoned by the English (1346–57)
Davies *n* **1** Sir **Peter Maxwell**. born 1934, British composer whose works include the operas *Taverner* (1967), *The Martyrdom of St Magnus* (1977), and *Resurrection* (1988), six symphonies, and the ten Strathclyde Concertos (1987–95); appointed Master of the Queen's Music in 2004 **2** (**William**) **Robertson**. 1913–95, Canadian novelist and playwright noted for his Deptford trilogy of novels (1970–75)
Davis *n* **1 Bette**, real name *Ruth Elizabeth Davis*. 1908–89, US film actress, whose films include *Of Human Bondage* (1934), *Jezebel* (1938) for which she won an Oscar, *All About Eve* (1950), *Whatever Happened to Baby Jane?* (1962), *The Nanny* (1965), and *The Whales of August* (1987) **2 Jefferson**. 1808–89, president of the Confederate States of America during the Civil War (1861–65)
davit [**dav**-vit] *n* crane, usu. one of a pair, at a ship's side, for lowering and hoisting boats
Davy *n* Sir **Humphry**. 1778–1829, English chemist who isolated sodium, magnesium, chlorine, and other elements and suggested the electrical nature of chemical combination. He invented the Davy lamp
▸ **Davy lamp** *n* miner's lamp designed to prevent it from igniting gas
Davy Jones's locker *n* the sea, considered as a grave for sailors
dawdle Ⓣ *v* **1** be slow or lag behind **2** waste time **dawdler** *n*
Dawes *n* **Charles Gates**. 1865–1951, US financier, diplomat, and statesman, who devised the Dawes Plan for German reparations payments after World War I; vice president of the US (1925–29); Nobel peace prize 1925
Dawkins *n* **Richard**. born 1941, British zoologist, noted for such works as *The Selfish Gene* (1976), *The Blind Watchmaker* (1986), and *The Greatest Show on Earth* (2009)
dawn Ⓣ *n* **1** daybreak **2** beginning (of something) ▹ *v* **3** begin to grow light **4** begin to develop or appear **5** (foll. by *on* or *upon*) become apparent (to)
Dawson *n* Sir **John William**. 1820–99, Canadian geologist and educator; founded the Royal Society of Canada (1882)
day Ⓣ *n* **1** period of 24 hours **2** period of light

THESAURUS

plaster, slap on (*informal*)
daunt *See* **discourage**
daunting *adj* = **intimidating**, alarming, demoralizing, disconcerting, discouraging, disheartening, frightening, unnerving
dauntless *adj* = **fearless**, bold, unflinching, gallant, resolute, intrepid, undaunted, indomitable, doughty, stouthearted
dawdle *v* = **waste time**, delay, trail, idle, loaf, loiter, dally, drag one's feet *or* drag one's heels, hang about
dawn *n* **1** = **daybreak**, morning, daylight, aurora (*poetic*), sunrise, cockcrow, crack of dawn, sunup **2** = **beginning**, start, rise, birth, origin, emergence, advent, genesis ▸ *v* **3** = **grow light**, break, brighten, lighten **4** = **begin**, rise, appear, develop, emerge, originate, unfold ▹ **dawn on, dawn upon** = **hit**, strike, occur, register (*informal*), become apparent, come into one's head, come to mind
day *n* **1** = **twenty-four hours**, daylight, daytime **2** = **point in time**, time, date **3** = **time**, period, age, era, heyday, epoch, zenith ▹ **days gone by** *See* **the past**
daybreak *n* = **dawn**, morning, sunrise, break of day, cockcrow, crack of dawn, first light, sunup
daydream *n* **1** = **fantasy**, dream • *He learned to escape into daydreams.* ▸ *v* **2** = **fantasize**, dream • *She daydreams of being a famous journalist.*
See also: **vision**
daylight *n* = **sunlight**, sunshine, light of day
day-to-day *See* **everyday**

DICTIONARY

between sunrise and sunset **3** part of a day occupied with regular activity, esp. work **4** period or point in time **5** day of special observance **6** time of success
▸ **daybreak** *n* time in the morning when light first appears
▸ **daydream** *n* **1** pleasant fantasy indulged in while awake ▹ *v* **2** indulge in idle fantasy **daydreamer** *n*
▸ **daylight** *n* light from the sun
▸ **day release** system in which workers go to college one day a week
▸ **day-to-day** *adj* routine
Day-Lewis, Day Lewis *n* **C**(**ecil**). 1904–72, British poet, critic, and (under the pen name *Nicholas Blake*) author of detective stories; poet laureate (1968–72)
daze ⓣ *v* **1** stun, esp. by a blow or shock ▹ *n* **2** state of confusion or shock
dazzle ⓣ *v* **1** impress greatly **2** blind temporarily by sudden excessive light ▹ *n* **3** bright light that dazzles **dazzling** *adj* **dazzlingly** *adv*
dB, db decibel(s)
DC direct current
DCM Distinguished Conduct Medal
DD Doctor of Divinity
D-day *n* day selected for the start of some operation, esp. the Allied invasion of Europe in 1944
DDT kind of insecticide
de- *prefix* **1** *indicating* removal: *deforest* **2** *indicating* reversal: *decode* **3** *indicating* departure: *decamp*
deacon *n Christianity* **1** ordained minister ranking immediately below a priest **2** (in some Protestant churches) lay official who assists the minister **deaconess** *n fem*
deactivate *v* make (a bomb etc.) harmless or inoperative
dead ⓣ *adj* **1** no longer alive **2** no longer in use **3** numb: *my leg has gone dead* **4** complete: *a dead stop* **5** *informal* very tired **6** (of a place) lacking activity ▹ *n* **7** period during which coldness or darkness is most intense: *the dead of night* ▹ *adv* **8** extremely **9** suddenly: *stop dead*
▸ **the dead** dead people
▸ **dead beat** *informal* exhausted
▸ **dead set against** completely opposed to
▸ **deaden** *v* **1** make less sensitive or lively **2** make less resonant
▸ **deadly** *adj* **-lier, -liest 1** likely to cause death **2** *informal* extremely boring ▹ *adv* **3** extremely
▸ **deadly nightshade** plant with poisonous black berries
▸ **deadbeat** *n informal* lazy useless person
▸ **dead end 1** road with one end blocked off **2** situation in which further progress is impossible
▸ **deadhead 1** *informal* person who does not pay on a bus, to get into a sports game, etc. **2** *slang* dull, unenterprising person **3** *informal* train, bus, etc. travelling empty **4** log sticking out of water and hindering navigation
▸ **dead heat** tie for first place between two participants in a contest
▸ **dead letter** law or rule that is no longer enforced
▸ **deadline** *n* time limit
▸ **deadlock** *n* **1** point in a dispute at which further progress is impossible ▹ *v* **2** bring to a deadlock
▸ **deadpan** *adj, adv* showing no emotion or expression
▸ **dead reckoning** method of establishing

THESAURUS

daze *v* **1 = stun**, shock, paralyze, numb, benumb, stupefy ▸ *n* **2 = shock**, confusion, distraction, bewilderment, stupor, trance, trancelike state
dazed *adj* **= stunned**, confused, dizzy, bewildered, light-headed, numbed • *At the end of the interview, I was dazed and exhausted.*
dazzle *v* **1 = impress**, overwhelm, overpower, astonish, amaze, bowl over (*informal*), take one's breath away **2 = blind**, confuse, blur, daze, bedazzle ▸ *n* **3 = splendour**, sparkle, glitter, brilliance, magnificence, razzmatazz (*slang*)
dazzling *adj* **= splendid**, brilliant, sensational (*informal*), sparkling, glorious,
dead *adj* **1 = deceased**, late, extinct, departed • *Our cat's been dead a year now.* OPPOSITE: alive **2 = not working**, defunct • *a dead language* **3 = numb**, paralyzed, inert **4 = total**, complete, absolute, outright, utter, thorough, unqualified **5** (*Informal*) **= exhausted**, tired, spent, worn out **6 = boring**, flat, dull, uninteresting
▹ **dead body** *See* **body** ▹ **dead ringer** *See* **look-alike** ▸ *n* **7 = middle**, depth, midst
deaden *v* **= reduce**, weaken, stifle, diminish, cushion, suppress, blunt, alleviate, smother, lessen, dull, muffle
deadline *n* **= time limit**, limit, cutoff point, target date
deadlock *n* **= impasse**, standoff, standstill, gridlock, stalemate
deadlocked *adj* **1 = even**, level, equal, neck and neck, on a level playing field (*informal*) **2 = gridlocked**, at an impasse, at a standstill
deadly *adj* **= lethal**, fatal, destructive, mortal • *a deadly disease*
deadpan *adj* **= expressionless**, blank, impassive, inexpressive, inscrutable, poker-faced, straight-faced

DICTIONARY

one's position using the distance and direction travelled

▶ **dead weight** heavy weight

deaf Ⓣ *adj* unable to hear **deafness** *n*

▶ **deaf to** refusing to listen to or take notice of

▶ **deafen** *v* make deaf, esp. temporarily

deal¹ Ⓣ *n* **1** transaction or agreement **2** treatment: *a fair deal* **3** large amount ▷ *v* **dealing, dealt** [**delt**] **4** distribute **5** inflict (a blow) on **6** *cards* give out (cards) to the players **dealer** *n*

▶ **dealings** *pl n* transactions or business relations

▶ **deal in** *v* engage in commercially

▶ **deal with** *v* **1** take action on **2** be concerned with

deal² *n* plank of fir or pine wood

dean *n* **1** chief administrative official of a college or university faculty **2** chief administrator of a cathedral

▶ **deanery** *n* **1** office or residence of a dean **2** parishes of a dean

Dean *n* **James** (**Byron**). 1931–55, US film actor, who became a cult figure; his films include *East of Eden* and *Rebel Without a Cause* (both 1955). He died in a car wreck

dear Ⓣ *n* **1** someone regarded with affection ▷ *adj* **2** beloved **3** costly **dearly** *adv* **dearness** *n*

dearth Ⓣ [**dirth**] *n* inadequate amount, scarcity

death Ⓣ *n* **1** permanent end of all functions of life in a person or animal **2** instance of this **3** ending, destruction

▶ **deathly** *adj, adv* like death: *deathly quiet; deathly pale*

▶ **death duty** *Brit* tax paid on property left at death

▶ **death's-head** *n* human skull or a representation of one

▶ **deathtrap** *n* place or vehicle considered very unsafe

▶ **deathwatch beetle** beetle that bores into wood and makes a tapping sound

deb *n informal* debutante

debacle Ⓣ [day-**bah**-kl] *n* disastrous collapse or defeat

debar *v* exclude or bar

debase Ⓣ *v* lower in value, quality, or character **debasement** *n*

debate Ⓣ *n* **1** discussion ▷ *v* **2** discuss, esp. in a formal assembly **3** consider (a course of action)

▶ **in debate** in doubt, uncertain

▶ **debatable** *adj* not absolutely certain

debauch [dib-**bawch**] *v* **1** make someone immoral, esp. sexually ▷ *n* **2** bout of extreme dissipation **debauchery** *n*

▶ **debauched** *adj* immoral, sexually corrupt

de Beauvoir *n* **Simone**. 1908–86, French existentialist novelist and feminist, whose works include *Le sang des autres* (1944), *Le*

THESAURUS

deaf *adj* **1 = hard of hearing**, stone deaf, without hearing **2 = oblivious**, indifferent, unmoved, unconcerned, unhearing

deafen *v* **= make deaf**, din, drown out, split the eardrums *or* burst the eardrums

deafening *adj* **= ear-piercing**, thunderous, piercing, ringing, ear-splitting, booming, overpowering, resounding

deal *n* **1 = agreement**, contract, transaction, bargain, understanding, pact, arrangement **2 = amount**, share, degree, portion, extent, quantity ▶ *v* **3 = sell**, trade, stock, traffic, negotiate, bargain, buy and sell, do business ▷ **deal out = distribute**, give, share, assign, dispense, allot, apportion, dole out, mete out ▷ **deal with = cope with**, manage, handle, attend to, see to, take care of; • *He must learn to deal with stress;* **= be concerned with**, consider

See also: **administer**

dealer *n* **= trader**, supplier, merchant, wholesaler, purveyor, tradesman

dealings *See* **business**

dear *n* **1 = darling**, treasure (*informal*), sweetheart • *What's the matter, dear?* ▶ *adj* **2 = beloved**, precious, prized, darling, cherished, esteemed, treasured • *a dear friend of mine* **3 = expensive**, costly, pricey (*informal*), high-priced, overpriced, at a premium

See also: **cute**

dearest *See* **beloved, favourite**

dearly *adv* **1 = very much**, extremely, greatly, profoundly **2 = at great cost**, at a high price

dearth *n* **= scarcity**, want, lack, shortage, poverty, deficiency, inadequacy, insufficiency, paucity

death *n* **1 = dying**, end, exit, departure, passing, demise **2 = destruction**, finish, ruin, extinction, downfall, undoing

deathly *adj* **= deathlike**, grim, pale, ghastly, pallid, wan

debacle *n* **= disaster**, defeat, collapse, rout, catastrophe, reversal, fiasco

debase *v* **= degrade**, reduce, lower, devalue, cheapen

debatable *adj* **= doubtful**, controversial, uncertain, questionable, problematic, dubious, moot, arguable

debate *n* **1 = discussion**, dispute, controversy, argument, contention ▶ *v* **2 = discuss**, question, dispute, argue **3 = consider**, reflect, weigh, ponder, deliberate, ruminate

debauchery *n* **= depravity**, excess, indulgence, overindulgence, dissipation, dissoluteness, intemperance, lewdness

DICTIONARY

deuxième sexe (1949), and *Les mandarins* (1954)
debenture *n* long-term bond, bearing fixed interest, issued by a company or a government agency
debilitate *v* weaken **debilitation** *n*
▸ **debility** *n* weakness, infirmity
debit *n* **1** acknowledgment of a sum owing by entry on the left side of an account ▹ *v* **debiting, debited 2** record as a debit **3** charge with a debt
debonair Ⓣ *adj* **1** suave or refined **2** carefree
debouch *v* move out from a narrow place to a wider one
debrief Ⓣ *v* receive a report from (a soldier, diplomat, etc.) after an event **debriefing** *n*
debris Ⓣ [**deb**-ree] *n* fragments of something destroyed
debt Ⓣ *n* **1** something owed, esp. money **2** state of owing something **debtor** *n*
debug *v informal* **1** find and remove defects in (a device, computer program, etc.) **2** remove concealed microphones from (a room etc.)
debunk Ⓣ *v informal* expose the pretensions or falseness of
Debussy *n* (**Achille**) **Claude**. 1862–1918, French composer and critic, the creator of impressionism in music and a profound influence on contemporary composition. His works include *Prélude à l'après-midi d'un faune* (1894) and *La Mer* (1905) for orchestra, the opera *Pelléas et Mélisande* (1902), and many piano pieces and song settings
debut Ⓣ [**day**-byoo] *n* first public appearance of a performer
▸ **debutante** [**day**-byoo-tont] *n* young upper-class woman making her first formal appearance in society
Dec. December
deca- *combining form* ten
decade *n* period of ten years
decadence Ⓣ [**dek**-a-denss] *n* state of deterioration of morality or culture
decadent *adj*
decaffeinated [dee-**kaf**-fin-ate-id] *adj* (of tea or coffee) with caffeine removed
decagon *n* geometric figure with ten sides
decagonal *adj*
decahedron [dek-a-**hee**-dron] *n* solid figure with ten sides
Decalogue *n* the Ten Commandments
decamp *v* depart secretly or suddenly
decant *v* **1** pour (a liquid) from one container to another **2** rehouse (people) while their homes are being refurbished
▸ **decanter** *n* stoppered bottle for wine or spirits
decapitate Ⓣ *v* behead **decapitation** *n*
decarbonize *v* remove carbon from (an internal-combustion engine)
decarbonization *n*
decathlon *n* athletic contest with ten events
decay Ⓣ *v* **1** rot **2** become weaker or more corrupt ▹ *n* **3** process of decaying **4** state brought about by this process
decease Ⓣ *n formal* death
▸ **deceased** *adj formal* dead
▸ **the deceased** person who has recently died
deceive Ⓣ *v* **1** mislead by lying **2** be unfaithful to (one's sexual partner) **deceiver** *n*

THESAURUS

debonair *adj* = **elegant**, smooth, charming, refined, courteous, suave, dashing, urbane, well-bred
debrief *v* = **interrogate**, question, probe, examine, quiz, cross-examine
debris *n* = **remains**, waste, wreckage, rubble, detritus, bits, fragments, ruins
debt *n* = **debit**, commitment, obligation, liability ▹ **in debt** = **owing**, liable, in arrears, in the red (*informal*)
debtor *n* = **borrower**, mortgagor
debunk *v* = **expose**, mock, deflate, ridicule, disparage, cut down to size, show up
debut *n* = **introduction**, beginning, bow, presentation, entrance, initiation, coming out, first appearance
decadence *n* = **degeneration**, decline, corruption, deterioration, decay, dissolution, dissipation
decadent *adj* = **degenerate**, corrupt, immoral, self-indulgent, decaying, declining, dissolute
decapitate *v* = **behead**, execute, guillotine
decay *v* **1** = **decline**, deteriorate, crumble, dwindle, wane, wither, disintegrate, shrivel, waste away **2** = **rot**, perish, decompose, corrode, putrefy ▸ *n* **3** = **decline**, collapse, degeneration, deterioration, fading, wasting, failing, withering **4** = **rot**, decomposition, caries, gangrene, putrefaction
decayed *See* **rotten**
decease *n* (*Formal*) = **death**, release, departure, demise, dying
deceased *adj* = **dead**, former, late, defunct, departed, lifeless, expired
deceit *n* = **dishonesty**, fraud, deception, pretense, treachery, trickery, back-stabbing (*informal*), cheating, chicanery, lying
deceitful *adj* = **dishonest**, false, fraudulent, treacherous, deceptive, sneaky, untrustworthy, down and dirty (*informal*), two-faced
deceive *v* = **fool**, trick, mislead, con (*informal*), dupe, double-cross, take in • *I was really hurt that he had deceived me.*
See also: **cheat**
deceiver *n* = **liar**, fraud, cheat, impostor, trickster, con man (*informal*),

DICTIONARY

▸ **deceit** *n* behaviour intended to deceive **deceitful** *adj*
decelerate Ⓣ *v* slow down **deceleration** *n*
December *n* twelfth month of the year
decennial *adj* **1** lasting for ten years **2** happening every ten years
decent Ⓣ *adj* **1** of an acceptable standard or quality **2** polite or respectable **3** fitting or proper **4** conforming to conventions of sexual behaviour **5** *informal* kind **decently** *adv* **decency** *n*
decentralize *v* reorganize into smaller local units **decentralization** *n*
deception Ⓣ *n* **1** deceiving **2** something that deceives, trick
▸ **deceptive** *adj* likely or designed to deceive **deceptively** *adv* **deceptiveness** *n*
deci- *combining form* one tenth
decibel *n* unit for measuring the intensity of sound
decide Ⓣ *v* **1** (cause to) reach a decision **2** settle (a contest or question)
▸ **decided** *adj* **1** unmistakable **2** determined **decidedly** *adv*
▸ **decision** *n* **1** judgment, conclusion, or resolution **2** act of making up one's mind **3** firmness of purpose
▸ **decisive** *adj* **1** indisputable: *a decisive win* **2** having the ability to make (quick) decisions **decisively** *adv* **decisiveness** *n*
deciduous *adj* (of a tree) shedding its leaves annually
decimal *n* **1** fraction written in the form of a dot followed by one or more numbers ▷ *adj* **2** relating to or using powers of ten **3** expressed as a decimal
▸ **decimalize** *v* change (a system or number) to the decimal system **decimalization** *n*
▸ **decimal currency** system of currency in which the units are parts or powers of ten
▸ **decimal point** dot between the unit and the fraction of a number in the decimal system
▸ **decimal system** number system with a base of ten, in which numbers are expressed by combinations of the digits 0 to 9
decimate Ⓣ *v* destroy or kill a large proportion of **decimation** *n*
decipher Ⓣ *v* **1** decode **2** make out the meaning of (poor handwriting) **decipherable** *adj*
deck Ⓣ *n* **1** area of a ship that forms a floor **2** similar area in a bus **3** platform that supports the turntable and pick-up of a record player ▷ *v* **4** decorate
▸ **deck chair** folding chair made of canvas over a wooden frame
▸ **decking** *n* wooden platform in a garden
▸ **deck out** *v* dress (oneself) or decorate (a room)
deckle edge *n* rough edge on paper, often left as ornamentation
declaim Ⓣ *v* **1** speak loudly and dramatically **2** protest loudly **declamation** *n* **declamatory** *adj*

THESAURUS

double-dealer, swindler
decelerate *See* **slow (down)**
decency *n* = **respectability**, courtesy, correctness, etiquette, civility, decorum, modesty, propriety
decent *adj* **1** = **adequate**, reasonable, respectable, satisfactory, tolerable, passable • *to earn a decent salary* **2** = **respectable**, proper • *the decent thing to do* OPPOSITE: improper **3** = **proper**, appropriate, suitable, fitting, becoming, befitting, seemly **4** (*Informal*) = **kind**, friendly, helpful, generous, thoughtful, gracious, courteous, accommodating, obliging
deception *n* **1** = **trickery**, fraud, deceit, cunning, treachery, guile, legerdemain **2** = **trick**, lie, hoax, illusion, bluff, ruse, subterfuge, decoy
deceptive *adj* = **misleading**, false, fraudulent, illusory, unreliable • *First impressions can be deceptive.*
decide *v* = **reach a decision**, choose, determine (*formal*), elect (*formal*), resolve (*formal*), come to a decision, make up your mind • *She decided to write her autobiography.*
▷ **decide on** *See* **select, settle**
See also: **conclude, settle**
decided *See* **definite**
decidedly *adv* = **definitely**, clearly, positively, downright, distinctly, unequivocally, unmistakably
deciding *See* **critical**
decimate *v* = **devastate**, ravage, wreak havoc on
decipher *v* = **figure out** (*informal*), read, crack, solve, interpret, decode, deduce, make out
decision *n* **1** = **judgment**, ruling, finding, resolution, verdict, conclusion • *The umpire's decision is final.* **2** = **decisiveness**, resolution, resolve, purpose, determination, firmness, strength of mind *or* strength of will
decisive *adj* **1** = **influential**, significant, critical, crucial, conclusive, momentous, fateful **2** = **resolute**, firm, determined, forceful, incisive, decided, strong-minded, trenchant
deck *v* = **decorate**, dress, clothe, array, adorn, embellish, festoon, beautify
declaim *v* = **orate**, speak, lecture, proclaim, rant, recite, harangue, hold forth ▷ **declaim against** = **protest against**, attack, rail,

DICTIONARY

declare Ⓣ *v* **1** state firmly and forcefully **2** announce officially **3** acknowledge for tax purposes **declaration** *n* **declaratory** *adj*
declassify *v* officially state (information or a document) to be no longer secret **declassification** *n*
decline Ⓣ *v* **1** become smaller, weaker, or less important **2** say that one is unwilling to give, accept, or do (something) **3** *grammar* list the inflections of (a noun, pronoun, or adjective) ▷ *n* **4** gradual deterioration **5** movement downwards **6** diminution
▶ **declension** *n grammar* changes in the form of nouns, pronouns, or adjectives to show case, number, and gender
declivity *n, pl* **-ties** downward slope **declivitous** *adj*
declutch *v* disengage the clutch of a motor vehicle
decoct *v* extract the essence from (a substance) by boiling **decoction** *n*
decode Ⓣ *v* convert from code into ordinary language **decoder** *n*
décolleté [day-**kol**-tay] *adj* (of a woman's garment) having a low neckline
decoke *v* same as **decarbonize**
decompose Ⓣ *v* be broken down through chemical or bacterial action **decomposition** *n*
decompress *v* **1** free from pressure **2** return (a diver) to normal atmospheric pressure **decompression** *n*
decongestant *n* drug that relieves nasal congestion
decontaminate *v* render harmless by the removal of poisons, radioactivity, etc. **decontamination** *n*
decor Ⓣ [**day**-core] *n* decorative scheme of a room or house
decorate Ⓣ *v* **1** ornament **2** paint or wallpaper (a room) **3** award a (military) medal to **decoration** *n* **decorative** *adj* **decorator** *n*
decorous Ⓣ [**dek**-a-russ] *adj* polite, calm, and sensible in behaviour **decorously** *adv* **decorousness** *n*
▶ **decorum** [dik-**core**-um] *n* decorous behaviour
decoy Ⓣ *n* **1** person or thing used to lure someone into danger **2** image of a bird or animal, used to lure game within shooting range ▷ *v* **3** lure into danger by means of a decoy
decrease Ⓣ *v* **1** diminish ▷ *n* **2** lessening **3** amount by which something has been diminished

d

THESAURUS

denounce, decry, inveigh
declaration *n* **1 = statement**, testimony, affirmation, protestation (*formal*) • *a declaration of war* **2 = announcement**, profession, proclamation, pronouncement, notification, edict
declare *v* **1 = state**, announce, pronounce, assert, certify, proclaim, affirm, profess (*formal*) • *He declared that he was going to be famous.* **2 = make known**, show, reveal, disclose, confess
decline *v* **1 = decrease**, fall, drop, plummet, diminish, go down • *a declining birth rate* OPPOSITE: increase **2 = refuse**, abstain, excuse yourself, turn down • *He declined their invitation.* OPPOSITE: accept **3 = deteriorate**, worsen, weaken, pine, decay, languish, degenerate, droop ▶ *n* **4 = decrease**, fall, drop, slump, recession, downturn, shrinkage • *economic decline* **5 = deterioration**, degeneration, decay, failing, weakening, worsening OPPOSITE: increase
See also: **fail, reject, wither**
decode *v* **= decipher**, crack, solve, interpret, unscramble, decrypt, work out
decompose *v* **= rot**, crumble, decay, fester, break up, fall apart, putrefy
decomposed *See* **rotten**
decor *n* **= decoration**, colour scheme, furnishing style, ornamentation
decorate *v* **1 = adorn**, paper, paint, colour, deck, renovate, wallpaper, do up (*informal*), furbish, pimp (up) (*slang*) • *He decorated his room with pictures.* **2 = pin a medal on**, cite, confer an honour on *or* confer an honour upon
See also: **honour**
decorated *See* **fancy**
decoration *n* **1 = adornment**, enrichment, trimming, embellishment, elaboration, beautification, ornamentation **2 = ornament**, garnish, frill, bauble, trimmings **3 = medal**, award, star, ribbon, badge
decorative *adj* **= ornamental**, pretty, fancy, beautifying, nonfunctional
decorous *adj* **= proper**, correct, decent, fitting, polite, dignified, becoming, seemly, well-behaved
decorum *n* **= propriety**, protocol, dignity, decency, etiquette, respectability, politeness, good manners
decoy *n* **1 = lure**, trap, bait, inducement, pretense, enticement ▶ *v* **2 = lure**, entice, deceive, tempt, seduce, ensnare, entrap
decrease *v* **1 = lessen**, drop, reduce, decline, lower, shrink, diminish, dwindle, cut down • *Population growth is decreasing by 1.4 per cent each year.* OPPOSITE: increase ▶ *n* **2 = lessening**, drop, decline, reduction, cutback • *a decrease in the number of unemployed* OPPOSITE: increase
See also: **abate, cut, fall**

DICTIONARY

decree Ⓣ *n* **1** law made by someone in authority **2** court judgment ▷ *v* **3** order by decree

decrepit Ⓣ *adj* weakened or worn out by age or long use **decrepitude** *n*

decriminalize *v* make (a formerly illegal act) no longer a crime **decriminalization** *n*

decry Ⓣ *v* **-crying, -cried** express disapproval of

Dedekind *n* (**Julius Wilhelm**) **Richard**. 1831–1916, German mathematician, who devised a way (the **Dedekind cut**) of according irrational and rational numbers the same status

dedicate Ⓣ *v* **1** commit (oneself or one's time) wholly to a special purpose or cause **2** inscribe or address (a book etc.) to someone as a tribute **dedication** *n*

▶ **dedicated** *adj* devoted to a particular purpose or cause

deduce Ⓣ *v* reach (a conclusion) by reasoning from evidence **deducible** *adj*

deduct Ⓣ *v* subtract

deduction Ⓣ *n* **1** deducting **2** something that is deducted **3** deducing **4** conclusion reached by deducing **deductive** *adj*

Dee *n* **John**. 1527–1608, English mathematician, astrologer, and magician: best known for his preface (1570) to the first edition of Euclid in English

deed Ⓣ *n* **1** something that is done **2** legal document

deejay *n informal* disc jockey

deem Ⓣ *v* have as an opinion

deep Ⓣ *adj* **1** extending or situated far down, inwards, backwards, or sideways **2** of a specified dimension downwards, inwards, or backwards **3** coming from or penetrating to a great depth **4** difficult to understand **5** of great intensity **6** (foll. by *in*) immersed (in) **7** (of a colour) strong or dark **8** low in pitch **deepen** *v*

▶ **the deep** *poetic* the sea

▶ **deeply** *adv* profoundly or intensely

▶ **deepfreeze** *n* same as **freezer**

deer *n, pl* **deer** hoofed mammal with antlers in the male

▶ **deerstalker** *n* cloth hat with peaks back and front and earflaps

deface Ⓣ *v* spoil the surface or appearance of **defacement** *n*

de facto Ⓣ *adv* **1** in fact ▷ *adj* **2** existing in

THESAURUS

decree *n* **1 = law**, order, act, ruling, command, proclamation, statute, edict ▶ *v* **2 = order**, rule, demand, command, prescribe, pronounce, proclaim, ordain

decrepit *adj* **1 = weak**, frail, feeble, infirm, aged, doddering **2 = worn-out**, battered, dilapidated, rickety, ramshackle, run-down, beat-up (*informal*), broken-down, tumbledown, weather-beaten

decry *v* **= condemn**, criticize, denounce, discredit, disparage, denigrate, belittle, put down, run down

dedicate *v* **1 = devote**, commit, pledge, surrender, give over to **2 = inscribe**, address

dedicated *adj* **= devoted**, enthusiastic, committed, zealous, purposeful, single-minded, wholehearted

dedication *n* **1 = devotion**, commitment, loyalty, allegiance, adherence, faithfulness, single-mindedness, wholeheartedness **2 = inscription**, message, address

deduce *v* **= conclude**, draw, reason, understand, gather, glean, infer, take to mean

deduct *v* **= subtract**, remove, decrease by, knock off (*informal*), reduce by, take away, take off

deduction *n* **1 = subtraction**, reduction, withdrawal, decrease, discount, diminution **2 = conclusion**, result, finding, assumption, reasoning, inference

deed *n* **1 = action**, act, fact, performance, achievement, exploit, feat **2** (*Law*) **= document**, contract, title

deem *v* **= consider**, think, hold, believe, judge, account, estimate, regard, suppose, imagine, conceive, reckon, esteem

deep *adj* **1 = bottomless**, yawning • *a deep hole* OPPOSITE: shallow **2 = intense**, great, serious, extreme, grave, profound • *his deep love of his country* **3 = low**, bass • *a deep voice* OPPOSITE: high **4 = mysterious**, secret, abstract, obscure, hidden, arcane, esoteric, abstruse, recondite **5 = absorbed**, lost, engrossed, immersed, preoccupied, rapt **6 = dark**, strong, rich, intense, vivid ▷ **the deep** (*Poetic*) **= ocean**, main, sea, briny (*informal*), high seas

See also: **far, heavy, severe**

deepen *v* **= intensify**, increase, grow, strengthen, reinforce, magnify

deeply *adv* **1 = thoroughly**, completely, seriously, severely, profoundly, gravely, to the core, to the heart, to the quick **2 = intensely**, sadly, passionately, acutely, affectingly, distressingly, feelingly, mournfully, movingly

deface *v* **= vandalize**, damage, spoil, mar, tarnish, disfigure, mutilate, deform virtuoso, glittering, scintillating, stunning

de facto *adv* **1 = in fact**, really, actually, in effect, in reality ▶ *adj* **2 = actual**, real, existing

DICTIONARY

fact, whether legally recognized or not
defame Ⓣ *v* attack the good reputation of **defamation** *n* **defamatory** [dif-**fam**-a-tree] *adj*
default Ⓣ *n* **1** failure to do something **2** *computers* instruction to a computer to select a particular option unless the user specifies otherwise ▷ *v* **3** fail to fulfil an obligation **defaulter** *n*
▸ **in default of** in the absence of
defeat Ⓣ *v* **1** overcome **2** thwart ▷ *n* **3** defeating or being defeated
▸ **defeatism** *n* ready acceptance or expectation of defeat **defeatist** *n, adj*
defecate *v* discharge waste from the body through the anus **defecation** *n*
defect Ⓣ *n* **1** imperfection ▷ *v* **2** desert one's cause or country to join the opposing forces **defection** *n* **defector** *n*
▸ **defective** *adj* having a flaw
defence Ⓣ *esp. US* **defense** *n* **1** resistance to attack **2** plea in support of something **3** a country's military resources **4** defendant's case in a court of law **defenceless** *adj*
defend Ⓣ *v* **1** protect from harm or danger **2** support in the face of criticism, esp. by argument **3** represent (a defendant) in court **4** protect (a title) against a challenge **defender** *n*
▸ **defendant** *n* person accused of a crime
▸ **defensible** *adj* capable of being defended because believed to be right **defensibility** *n*
▸ **defensive** *adj* **1** intended for defence **2** overanxious to protect oneself against (threatened) criticism **defensively** *adv*
defer[1] Ⓣ *v* **-ferring, -ferred** delay (something) until a future time **deferment** *or* **deferral** *n*
defer[2] Ⓣ *v* **-ferring, -ferred** (foll. by *to*) comply with the wishes (of)
▸ **deference** *n* **1** compliance with the wishes of another **2** respect **deferential** *adj* **deferentially** *adv*
defiance Ⓣ *n* see **defy**

THESAURUS

defame *v* = **slander**, knock (*informal*), smear, libel, discredit, disparage, malign, denigrate, bad-mouth (*slang*), cast aspersions on
default *n* **1** = **failure**, neglect, lapse, evasion, deficiency, omission, dereliction, nonpayment ▸ *v* **2** = **fail**, neglect, evade, dodge
defeat *v* **1** = **beat**, crush, rout, trounce, conquer, vanquish (*formal*), whitewash (*informal*), whup (*informal*) • *to defeat the enemy* **2** = **frustrate**, ruin, thwart, foil, baffle, balk, confound, get the better of ▸ *n* **3** = **conquest**, rout, debacle (*formal*), whitewash (*informal*), trouncing • *a 2-1 defeat by Russia* OPPOSITE: victory **4** = **frustration**, failure, reverse, setback, rebuff, thwarting *See also*: **subdue**
defeatist *n* **1** = **pessimist**, quitter, prophet of doom ▸ *adj* **2** = **pessimistic**
defect *n* **1** = **fault**, flaw, weakness, deficiency, shortcoming, failing, imperfection • *A defect in the aircraft caused the crash*. ▸ *v* **2** = **desert**, rebel, abandon, revolt, change sides, go over, walk out on (*informal*) *See also*: **handicap, hole**
defection *n* = **desertion**, rebellion, apostasy
defective *adj* = **faulty**, flawed, deficient, imperfect, broken, not working, on the blink (*slang*), out of order
defector *n* = **deserter**, renegade, apostate, turncoat
defence *n* **1** = **protection**, security, cover, resistance, safeguard • *The high walls around the city made a good defence against attackers*. **2** = **argument**, plea, excuse, explanation, justification • *the mayor's defence of her position* **3** = **shield**, barricade, buttress, fortification, rampart, bulwark **4** (*Law*) = **plea**, testimony, denial, rebuttal, alibi
defenceless *adj* = **helpless**, vulnerable, naked, unarmed, unprotected, powerless, exposed, unguarded, wide open
defend *v* **1** = **protect**, cover, guard, shelter, shield, safeguard • *The wolves defended their cubs*. **2** = **support**, endorse, uphold, justify, stick up for (*informal*) • *I can't defend what he did*. *See also*: **champion**
defendant *n* = **the accused**, defence, offender, respondent, prisoner at the bar
defender *n* **1** = **supporter**, champion, advocate • *a committed defender of human rights* **2** = **protector**, guard, escort, bodyguard
defensive *adj* = **on guard**, protective, watchful, uptight (*informal*), on the defensive
defer[1] *v* = **postpone**, delay, suspend, shelve, procrastinate, hold over, put off, put on ice
defer[2] *v* = **comply**, submit, yield, bow, accede, capitulate, give in, give way to
deference *n* = **respect**, attention, regard, courtesy, consideration, honour, civility, politeness, reverence
deferential *adj* = **respectful**, polite, obedient, submissive, ingratiating, obeisant, obsequious, reverential
defiance *n* = **resistance**, opposition, confrontation, contempt, disregard, disobedience, insubordination, insolence, rebelliousness
defiant *adj* = **resisting**, bold, provocative, daring, audacious, rebellious, disobedient, insolent, insubordinate, mutinous
deficiency *n* **1** = **lack**, deficit, deprivation, inadequacy • *signs of a vitamin*

DICTIONARY

deficient ⓣ *adj* **1** lacking some essential **2** inadequate in quality or quantity
▸ **deficiency** *n* **1** lack **2** state of being deficient
▸ **deficit** *n* amount by which a sum of money is too small
defile[1] *v* desecrate **defilement** *n*
defile[2] *n* narrow pass or valley
define ⓣ *v* **1** describe the nature of **2** state precisely the meaning of **3** show clearly the outline of **definable** *adj*
▸ **definite** *adj* **1** firm, clear, and precise **2** having precise limits **3** known for certain **definitely** *adv*
▸ **definition** *n* **1** statement of the meaning of a word or phrase **2** quality of being clear and distinct
▸ **definitive** *adj* **1** providing an unquestionable conclusion **2** being the best example of something
deflate ⓣ *v* **1** (cause to) collapse through the release of gas **2** take away the self-esteem or conceit from **3** *economics* cause deflation of (an economy)
▸ **deflation** *n* **1** *economics* reduction in economic activity resulting in lower output and investment **2** feeling of sadness following excitement **deflationary** *adj*
deflect ⓣ *v* (cause to) turn aside from a course **deflection** *n* **deflector** *n*
deflower *v lit* deprive (a woman) of her virginity
Defoe *n* **Daniel**. ?1660–1731, English novelist, journalist, spymaster, and pamphleteer, noted particularly for his novel *Robinson Crusoe* (1719). His other novels include *Moll Flanders* (1722) and *A Journal of the Plague Year* (1722)
defoliate *v* deprive (a plant) of its leaves **defoliant** *n* **defoliation** *n*
deforest *v* clear of trees **deforestation** *n*
deform ⓣ *v* **1** cause to be misshapen **2** make ugly **deformation** *n* **deformity** *n*
defraud ⓣ *v* take away or withhold money, rights, etc. from (a person) by fraud
defray *v* provide money for (costs or expenses)
defrock *v* deprive (a priest) of priestly status
defrost *v* **1** make or become free of frost or ice **2** thaw (frozen food) by removing it from a freezer
deft ⓣ *adj* quick and skilful in movement **deftly** *adv* **deftness** *n*
defunct ⓣ *adj* no longer existing or operative
defuse *v* **1** remove the triggering device from (an explosive device) **2** remove the tension from (a situation)
defy ⓣ *v* **-fying, -fied 1** resist openly and boldly **2** elude, esp. in a baffling way: *defy description*

THESAURUS

deficiency OPPOSITE: abundance **2 = failing**, flaw, weakness, defect, fault, shortcoming, frailty, imperfection, demerit
See also: **failure, shortage, want**
deficient *adj* **1 = lacking**, short, poor, inadequate, wanting • *a diet deficient in vitamins* **2 = unsatisfactory**, weak, faulty, incomplete, impaired, flawed, defective, lousy (*slang*), inferior, imperfect
See also: **insufficient**
deficit *n* **= shortfall**, loss, shortage, deficiency, arrears
define *v* **1 = describe**, explain, designate, characterize, specify, interpret, expound, spell out **2 = mark out**, limit, outline, bound, delineate, circumscribe, demarcate
definite *adj* **1 = certain**, assured, decided, fixed, guaranteed, settled • *It's too soon to give a definite answer.* **2 = clear**, positive • *The police had nothing definite against them.*
See also: **final, sure**
definitely *adv* **= certainly**, clearly, absolutely, surely, positively, categorically, undeniably, unquestionably, unmistakably, without doubt ▹ **definitely not** *See* **no**
definition *n* **1 = explanation**, clarification, exposition, elucidation, statement of meaning **2 = sharpness**, focus, contrast, precision, clarity, distinctness
definitive *adj* **1 = final**, complete, decisive, absolute, conclusive **2 = authoritative**, perfect, ultimate, reliable, exhaustive
deflate *v* **1 = collapse**, shrink, empty, exhaust, flatten, puncture **2 = humiliate**, humble, squash, disconcert, mortify, dispirit, chasten, put down (*slang*) **3** (*Economics*) **= reduce**, diminish, depress, devalue
deflect *v* **= turn aside**, bend, veer, swerve, ricochet, deviate, diverge, glance off
deflection *n* **= deviation**, bend, swerve, divergence
deform *v* **1 = distort**, twist, buckle, mangle, warp, contort, gnarl, misshape **2 = disfigure**, ruin, spoil, mar, mutilate, maim, deface
deformed *See* **distorted**
deformity *n* **= abnormality**, defect, malformation, disfigurement
defraud *v* **= cheat**, con (*informal*), trick, swindle, fleece, pilfer, embezzle, rip off (*slang*)
deft *adj* **= skilful**, expert, neat, adept, nimble, agile, proficient, adroit, dexterous
defunct *adj* **1 = dead**, extinct, deceased, departed, gone **2 = obsolete**, invalid, expired, bygone, nonexistent, inoperative, out of commission
defy *v* **= resist**, slight, confront, brave, scorn, disregard, spurn, flout

DICTIONARY

▸ **defiance** *n* open resistance to authority or opposition **defiant** *adj*
Degas *n* **Hilaire Germain Edgar**. 1834–1917, French impressionist painter and sculptor, noted for his brilliant draftsmanship and ability to convey movement, esp. in his studies of horse racing and ballet dancers
De Gasperi *n* **Alcide**. 1881–1954, Italian statesman; prime minister (1945–53). An antifascist, he led the Christian Democratic party during World War II from the Vatican City
de Gaulle *n* **Charles** (**André Joseph Marie**). 1890–1970, French general and statesman. During World War II, he refused to accept Pétain's armistice with Germany and founded the Free French movement in England (1940). He was head of the provisional governments (1944–46) and, as first president of the Fifth Republic (1959–69), he restored political and economic stability to France
degenerate Ⓣ *adj* **1** having deteriorated to a lower mental, moral, or physical level ▹ *n* **2** degenerate person ▹ *v* **3** become degenerate **degeneration** *n*
▸ **degeneracy** *n* degenerate behaviour
degrade Ⓣ *v* **1** reduce to dishonour or disgrace **2** reduce in status or quality **3** *chem* decompose into smaller molecules **degradation** *n*
degree Ⓣ *n* **1** stage in a scale of relative amount or intensity **2** academic award given by a university or college on successful completion of a course **3** unit of measurement for temperature or angles
de Havilland *n* Sir **Geoffrey**. 1882–1965, British aircraft designer. He produced many military aircraft, including the Mosquito and the Tiger Moth, some of the first jet airliners, and the Otter and Beaver light aircraft (built by de Havilland Canada)
dehumanize *v* **1** deprive of human qualities **2** make (an activity) mechanical or routine **dehumanization** *n*
dehydrate Ⓣ *v* **1** cause to lose water **2** deprive the body of (someone) of water **dehydration** *n*
de-ice *v* free of ice **de-icer** *n*
deify [**day**-if-fie] *v* **-fying, -fied** treat or worship as a god **deification** *n*
Deighton *n* **Len**. born 1929, British thriller writer. His books include *The Ipcress File* (1962), *Bomber* (1970), and the trilogy *Berlin Game*, *Mexico Set*, and *London Match* (1983–85)
deign [**dane**] *v* think it worthy of oneself (to do something), condescend
deity Ⓣ [**day**-it-ee] *n, pl* **-ties 1** god or goddess **2** state of being divine
déjà vu [**day**-zhah **voo**] *n* feeling of having experienced before something that is actually happening now
dejected Ⓣ *adj* in low spirits **dejectedly** *adv* **dejection** *n*
de jure Ⓣ *adv, adj* according to law
deke *ice hockey* ▹ *n* **1** feigned move which draws an opponent out of position ▹ *v* **2** feign a move
de Klerk *n* **F**(**rederik**) **W**(**illem**). born 1936, South African statesman; president (1989–94), second executive deputy president (1994–97). In 1990 he legalized the ANC and released Nelson Mandela from prison, and initiated the abolition of apartheid: Nobel peace prize 1993 jointly with Mandela
de Kooning *n* **Willem**. 1904–97, US abstract expressionist painter, born in Holland
Delacroix *n* (**Ferdinand Victor**) **Eugène**. 1798–1863, French romantic painter whose use of colour and free composition influenced impressionism. His paintings of historical and contemporary scenes include *The Massacre at Chios* (1824)
De La Warr *n* **Baron**, title of *Thomas West*, known as *Lord Delaware*. 1577–1618, English administrator in America; first governor of Virginia (1610)
delay Ⓣ *v* **1** put off to a later time **2** slow up or

THESAURUS

degenerate *adj* **1** = **depraved**, low, corrupt, immoral, decadent, perverted, debauched, dissolute ▸ *v* **2** = **worsen**, decline, slip, sink, decrease, deteriorate, lapse, decay, fall off
degradation *n* **1** = **disgrace**, shame, humiliation, discredit, dishonour, ignominy, mortification **2** = **deterioration**, decline, degeneration, demotion, downgrading
degrade *v* **1** = **disgrace**, humble, shame, humiliate, discredit, demean, debase, dishonour **2** = **demote**, lower, downgrade
degrading *adj* = **demeaning**, dishonourable, humiliating, shameful, unworthy, undignified
degree *n* = **stage**, point, step, unit, notch, grade, rung
dehydrate *See* **dry**
deity *n* = **god**, idol, goddess, immortal, divinity, godhead, supreme being
dejected *adj* = **downhearted**, sad, depressed, miserable, despondent, glum, downcast, crestfallen, disconsolate, disheartened
dejection *n* = **low spirits**, depression, sadness, sorrow, despair, gloom, unhappiness, doldrums, melancholy, despondency, downheartedness
de jure *adv* = **legally**, rightfully, by right
delay *v* **1** = **put off**, suspend, postpone, shelve, defer, procrastinate • *the decision to*

DICTIONARY

cause to be late ▷ *n* **3** act of delaying **4** interval of time between events
delectable ⓣ *adj* very attractive
▸ **delectation** *n formal* great pleasure
delegate ⓣ *n* **1** person chosen to act for others, esp. at a meeting ▷ *v* **2** entrust (duties or powers) to another person **3** appoint as a delegate
▸ **delegation** *n* **1** group of people appointed as delegates **2** delegating
de Lesseps *n* Vicomte **Ferdinand Marie**. 1805–94, French diplomat: directed the construction of the Suez Canal (1859–69) and the unsuccessful first attempt to build the Panama Canal (1881–89)
delete ⓣ *v* remove (something written or printed) **deletion** *n*
deleterious [del-lit-**eer**-ee-uss] *adj* harmful, injurious
Delft *n* type of earthenware, orig. from the town of Delft in the Netherlands, usu. with blue decoration on a white background (Also **delftware**)
deli *n* delicatessen
deliberate ⓣ *adj* **1** carefully thought out in advance **2** careful and unhurried ▷ *v* **3** consider (something) deeply **deliberately** *adv* **deliberation** *n*
▸ **deliberative** *adj* for the purpose of deliberating: *a deliberative assembly*
Delibes *n* (**Clément Philibert**) **Léo**. 1836–91, French composer, noted particularly for his ballets *Coppélia* (1870) and *Sylvia* (1876), and the opera *Lakmé* (1883)
delicate ⓣ *adj* **1** fine or subtle in quality or workmanship **2** having a fragile beauty **3** (of a taste etc.) pleasantly subtle **4** easily damaged **5** requiring tact **delicately** *adv*
▸ **delicacy** *n* **1** being delicate **2** something particularly good to eat
delicatessen *n* shop selling imported or unusual foods, already cooked or prepared
delicious ⓣ *adj* very appealing, esp. to taste or smell **deliciously** *adv*
delight ⓣ *n* **1** great pleasure ▷ *v* **2** please greatly **3** (foll. by *in*) take great pleasure (in)
delightful *adj* **delightfully** *adv*
delimit *v* mark or prescribe the limits of
delimitation *n*
delineate [dill-**lin**-ee-ate] *v* **1** show by

THESAURUS

delay the anncement until tomorrow **2** = **hinder**, check, obstruct, impede, set back • *Various setbacks delayed production*. OPPOSITE: hurry ▸ *n* **3** = **hold-up**, setback, obstruction, interruption • *a seven-hour work stoppage that caused delays on most flights* **4** = **putting off**, suspension, postponement, procrastination, deferment
See also: **pause, wait**
delayed *See* **late**
delectable *See* **delicious**
delegate *n* **1** = **representative**, agent, commissioner, ambassador, deputy, envoy, legate ▸ *v* **2** = **entrust**, give, transfer, assign, devolve, consign, hand over, pass on **3** = **appoint**, commission, mandate, designate, authorize, empower, accredit, depute
delegation *n* **1** = **deputation**, mission, commission, embassy, contingent, envoys, legation **2** = **devolution**, commitment, assignment, deputation, transferance
delete *v* = **remove**, erase, cross out, rub out, cancel, blue-pencil, edit out, strike out • *I accidentally deleted the email*.
deliberate *adj* **1** = **intentional**, conscious, calculated, premeditated, studied • *a deliberate act of sabotage* OPPOSITE: accidental **2** = **careful**, cautious, measured, methodical • *His movements were gentle and deliberate*. OPPOSITE: casual ▸ *v* **3** = **ponder**, debate, reflect, meditate, mull over • *The jury deliberated for five days before reaching a verdict*.
See also: **consider, think**
deliberately *adv* = **intentionally**, knowingly, consciously, willfully, by design, calculatingly, in cold blood, on purpose, wittingly
deliberation *n* **1** = **consideration**, thought, reflection, calculation, meditation, circumspection, forethought **2** = **discussion**, conference, debate, consultation
delicacy *n* **1** = **fineness**, precision, accuracy, lightness, elegance, subtlety, daintiness, exquisiteness **2** = **fragility**, weakness, frailty, tenderness, flimsiness, slenderness **3** = **treat**, luxury, tidbit, dainty, savoury **4** = **fastidiousness**, taste, discrimination, sensibility, finesse, purity, refinement **5** = **sensitivity**, tact, sensitiveness
delicate *adj* **1** = **fine**, skilled, subtle, precise, elegant, exquisite, graceful, deft **2** = **subtle**, fine, choice, tender, delicious, yummy (*informal*), dainty, savoury **3** = **fragile**, weak, slight, tender, frail, slender, flimsy **4** = **considerate**, diplomatic, sensitive, discreet, tactful
delicately *adv* **1** = **finely**, precisely, deftly, gracefully, elegantly, subtly, exquisitely, daintily, skillfully **2** = **tactfully**, diplomatically, sensitively
delicious *adj* = **delectable**, tasty, luscious, appetizing • *a wide selection of delicious foods*
delight *n* **1** = **pleasure**, happiness, joy, satisfaction, glee, rapture • *To my great delight, it worked*. ▸ *v* **2** = **please**, thrill, charm,

DICTIONARY

drawing **2** describe in words **delineation** *n*
delinquent Ⓣ *n* **1** someone, esp. a young person, who repeatedly breaks the law ▷ *adj* **2** repeatedly breaking the law **delinquency** *n*
delirium Ⓣ *n* **1** state of excitement and mental confusion, often with hallucinations **2** violent excitement **delirious** *adj* **deliriously** *adv*
Delius *n* **Frederick**. 1862–1934, English composer, who drew inspiration from folk tunes and the sounds of nature. His works include the opera *A Village Romeo and Juliet* (1901), *A Mass of Life* (1905), and the orchestral variations *Brigg Fair* (1907)
deliver Ⓣ *v* **1** carry (goods etc.) to a destination **2** hand over **3** aid in the birth of **4** release or rescue **5** present (a speech etc.) **6** strike (a blow) suddenly
▸ **deliverance** *n* rescue from danger or captivity
▸ **delivery** *n* **1** act of delivering **2** something that is delivered **3** act of giving birth to a child **4** style, esp. in public speaking
dell *n* small wooded hollow
Delphic *adj* ambiguous, like the ancient Greek oracle at Delphi
delphinium *n* plant with spikes of blue flowers
delta *n* **1** fourth letter of the Greek alphabet **2** flat area at the mouth of some rivers where the main stream splits up into several tributaries
delude Ⓣ *v* deceive
▸ **delusion** *n* **1** mistaken idea or belief **2** state of being deluded **delusive** *adj*
deluge Ⓣ [del-lyooj] *n* **1** great flood of water **2** torrential rain **3** overwhelming number ▷ *v* **4** flood **5** overwhelm
deluxe Ⓣ *adj* **1** rich or sumptuous **2** superior in quality
delve Ⓣ *v* research deeply or intensively (for information)
demagogue Ⓣ *n* political agitator who appeals to the prejudice and passions of the mob **demagogic** *adj* **demagogy** *n*
demand Ⓣ *v* **1** ask for forcefully **2** require as just, urgent, etc. **3** claim as a right ▷ *n* **4** forceful request **5** *economics* willingness

d

THESAURUS

amuse, captivate, enchant • *The report has delighted environmentalists.* ▷ **delight in = take pleasure in**, like, love, enjoy, appreciate, relish, feast on, revel in, savour
See also: **ecstasy, entertain, entrance, pride, rejoice**
delighted *adj* = **pleased**, happy, ecstatic, jubilant, joyous, elated, enchanted, overjoyed, thrilled, jazzed (*slang*)
delightful *adj* = **pleasant**, thrilling, charming, enjoyable, delectable, agreeable, pleasurable, enchanting, rapturous
delinquent *n* = **criminal**, offender, culprit, villain, wrongdoer, lawbreaker, miscreant
delirious *adj* **1** = **mad**, crazy, insane, incoherent, demented, raving, deranged, unhinged **2** = **ecstatic**, wild, excited, frantic, frenzied, hysterical, beside oneself, carried away, wired (*slang*)
delirium *n* **1** = **madness**, insanity, hallucination, raving, derangement **2** = **frenzy**, fever, passion, ecstasy, hysteria
deliver *v* **1** = **carry**, bring, bear, distribute, transport, cart, convey **2** = **hand over**, commit, grant, transfer, surrender, yield, relinquish, give up, make over, turn over **3** = **give**, announce, present, read, declare, utter **4** = **release**, save, free, rescue, loose, ransom, liberate, emancipate **5** = **strike**, give, deal, launch, aim, direct, administer, inflict
deliverance *n* = **release**, rescue, escape, ransom, redemption, liberation, salvation, emancipation
delivery *n* **1** = **handing over**, distribution, transfer, transmission, surrender, dispatch, consignment, conveyance **2** = **speech**, utterance, articulation, elocution, enunciation, intonation **3** = **childbirth**, confinement, labour, parturition
delude *v* = **deceive**, kid (*informal*), mislead, fool, dupe, hoodwink, beguile, trick
deluge *n* **1** = **flood**, spate, downpour, torrent, cataclysm, inundation, overflowing **2** = **rush**, flood, avalanche, barrage, spate, torrent ▸ *v* **3** = **flood**, drown, soak, swamp, douse, drench, inundate, submerge **4** = **overwhelm**, swamp, overrun, overload, engulf, inundate
delusion *n* = **misconception**, mistake, error, fancy, illusion, hallucination, fallacy, false impression, misapprehension
deluxe *adj* = **luxurious**, special, select, expensive, grand, costly, exclusive, superior, splendid, opulent
delve *v* = **research**, search, probe, investigate, explore, forage, burrow, rummage, ferret out, look into
demagogue *n* = **agitator**, firebrand, rabble-rouser
demand *v* **1** = **require**, take, want, need, involve • *This situation demands hard work.* **2** = **request**, ask, question, challenge, interrogate, inquire **3** = **claim**, expect, order, exact, insist on ▸ *n* **4** = **request**, order, question, inquiry, requisition **5** = **need**, call, want, market, claim, requirement
See also: **command, insist**
demanding *adj* = **difficult**, hard, tough,

DICTIONARY

and ability to purchase goods and services **demands 6** something that requires special effort or sacrifice
▸ **demanding** *adj* requiring a lot of time or effort
demarcate *v formal* establish limits or boundaries, esp. between the work performed by different trade unions **demarcation** *n*
demean Ⓣ *v* lower (someone) in dignity, character, or status
demeanour Ⓣ *n* way a person behaves
demented Ⓣ *adj* mad **dementedly** *adv*
▸ **dementia** [dim-**men**-sha] *n* state of serious mental deterioration
demerara sugar *n* brown crystallized cane sugar
demerger *n* separation of two or more companies which have previously been merged
demerit *n* flaw, disadvantage
demesne [dim-**mane**] *n* **1** land surrounding a house **2** *law* possession of one's own property or land
demi- *combining form* half
demigod *n* **1** being who is part mortal, part god **2** godlike person
demijohn *n* large bottle with a short neck, often encased in wicker
demilitarize *v* remove the military forces from **demilitarization** *n*
De Mille *n* **Cecil B(lount).** 1881–1959, US film producer and director
demimonde *n* **1** (esp. in the 19th century) class of women considered to be outside respectable society, because of promiscuity **2** group considered not wholly respectable
demise Ⓣ *n* **1** *formal* death **2** eventual failure (of something successful)
demist *v* make or become free of condensation **demister** *n*
demo *n informal* demonstration, organized expression of public opinion
demob *v informal* demobilize
▸ **demobilize** *v* release from the armed forces **demobilization** *n*
democracy Ⓣ *n, pl* **-cies 1** government by the people or their elected representatives **2** state governed in this way **3** social equality
▸ **democrat** *n* **1** advocate of democracy **2 Democrat** member or supporter of the Democratic Party in the US
▸ **democratic** *adj* **1** connected with democracy **2** upholding democracy **3 Democratic** of the Democratic Party, the more liberal of the two main political parties in the US **democratically** *adv*
Democritus *n* ?460–?370 BC, Greek philosopher who developed the atomist theory of matter of his teacher, Leucippus
demography *n* study of human populations **demographer** *n* **demographic** *adj*
demolish Ⓣ *v* **1** tear down or break up (buildings) **2** put an end to (an argument etc.) **demolisher** *n* **demolition** *n*
demon Ⓣ *n* **1** evil spirit **2** person extremely skilful in or devoted to a given activity **demonic** *adj*
▸ **demoniacal** *or* **demoniac** *adj* **1** appearing to be possessed by a devil **2** frenzied **demoniacally** *adv*
▸ **demonology** *n* study of demons
demonstrate Ⓣ *v* **1** show or prove by reasoning or evidence **2** reveal the existence of **3** display and explain the workings of **4** show support or protest by

THESAURUS

exacting, challenging, high-maintenance, taxing, trying, wearing
demarcation *n* = **delimitation**, division, separation, distinction, differentiation
demean *v* = **humiliate** • *I wasn't going to demean myself by becoming possessive.*
See also: **reduce**
demeanour *n* = **behaviour**, air, conduct, manner, carriage, bearing, comportment, deportment
demented *adj* = **mad**, crazy, insane, frenzied, unbalanced, crazed, deranged, maniacal, unhinged
demise *n* **1** = **failure**, end, fall, collapse, ruin, downfall **2** (*Euphemistic*) = **death**, departure, decease
democracy *n* = **self-government**, republic, commonwealth
democratic *adj* = **self-governing**, popular, representative, populist, autonomous, egalitarian
demolish *v* **1** = **knock down**, level, destroy, dismantle, flatten, raze, bulldoze, tear down **2** = **defeat**, destroy, overturn, wreck, overthrow, undo, annihilate
demolished *See* **broken**
demolition *n* = **knocking down**, explosion, destruction, bulldozing, levelling, razing, tearing down, wrecking
demon *n* **1** = **evil spirit**, devil, fiend, goblin, ghoul, malignant spirit **2** = **wizard**, master, ace (*informal*), fiend
demonic, demoniac, demoniacal *adj* **1** = **devilish**, satanic, diabolical, hellish, diabolic, fiendish, infernal **2** = **frenzied**, furious, frantic, hectic, frenetic, manic, crazed, maniacal
demonstrable *adj* = **provable**, obvious, evident, unmistakable, palpable, verifiable, self-evident, irrefutable
demonstrate *v* **1** = **prove**, show, indicate, display, exhibit, manifest, testify

DICTIONARY

public parades or rallies
▸ **demonstrable** *adj* able to be proved **demonstrably** *adv*
▸ **demonstration** *n* **1** organized expression of public opinion **2** explanation or experiment showing how something works **3** proof
▸ **demonstrative** *adj* tending to express one's feelings unreservedly **demonstratively** *adv*
▸ **demonstrator** *n* **1** person who demonstrates machines, products, etc. **2** person who takes part in a public demonstration
demoralize Ⓣ *v* undermine the morale of **demoralization** *n*
Demosthenes *n* 384–322 BC, Athenian statesman, orator, and lifelong opponent of the power of Macedonia over Greece
demote Ⓣ *v* reduce in status or rank **demotion** *n*
demotic *adj* **1** of the common people **2 Demotic** in or denoting the everyday as distinct from literary form of various languages: *Demotic Greek*
Dempsey *n* **Jack**, real name *William Harrison Dempsey*. 1895–1983, US boxer; world heavyweight champion (1919–26)
demur Ⓣ *v* **-murring, -murred** show reluctance
▸ **without demur** without objecting
demure Ⓣ *adj* quiet, reserved, and rather shy **demurely** *adv* **demureness** *n*
demystify *v* remove the mystery from; make clear **demystification** *n*
den Ⓣ *n* **1** home of a wild animal **2** small secluded room in a home **3** place where people indulge in criminal or immoral activities: *den of iniquity*
denationalize *v* transfer (an industry) from public to private ownership **denationalization** *n*
denature *v* **1** change the nature of **2** make (alcohol) unfit to drink
Deneuve *n* **Catherine**, original name *Catherine Dorléac*. born 1943, French film actress: her films include *Les Parapluies de Cherbourg* (1964), *Belle de Jour* (1967), *Indochine* (1992), and *Dancing in the Dark* (2000)
Deng Xiaoping, Teng Hsiao-ping *n* 1904–97, Chinese Communist statesman; deputy prime minister (1973–76; 1977–80) and the dominant figure in the Chinese government from 1977 until his death. He was twice removed from office (1967–73, 1976–77) and rehabilitated. He introduced economic liberalization, but suppressed demands for political reform, most notably in 1989 when over 2500 demonstrators were killed by the military in Tiananmen Square in Beijing
denigrate Ⓣ *v* criticize unfairly **denigration** *n* **denigrator** *n*
denim *n* **1** hard-wearing cotton fabric **denims 2** jeans made of denim
De Niro *n* **Robert**. born 1943, US film actor. His films include *Taxi Driver* (1976), *Raging Bull* (1980), *GoodFellas* (1990), *Casino* (1995), and *Analyze This* (1999)
Denis, Denys *n* **Saint**. 3rd century AD, first bishop of Paris; patron saint of France. Feast day: Oct 9
denizen *n* inhabitant
denominate *v* give a specific name to
▸ **denomination** *n* **1** group having a distinctive interpretation of a religious faith **2** grade or unit of value, measure, etc. **denominational** *adj*
▸ **denominator** *n* divisor of a fraction
denote Ⓣ *v* **1** be a sign of **2** have as a literal meaning **denotation** *n*
denouement [day-**noo**-mon] *n* final outcome or solution, esp. in a play or book
denounce Ⓣ *v* **1** speak violently against

d

THESAURUS

to **2 = show how**, describe, explain, teach, illustrate, make clear **3 = march**, rally, protest, parade, picket
demonstration *n* **1 = march**, rally, protest, parade, picket, sit-in, mass lobby **2 = explanation**, test, trial, presentation, description, exposition **3 = proof**, evidence, display, testimony, exhibition, expression, confirmation, illustration
demoralize *v* **= dishearten**, weaken, undermine, discourage, depress, unnerve, dispirit, deject
demote *v* **= downgrade**, relegate, degrade, kick downstairs (*slang*), lower in rank
demur *v* **1 = object**, protest, refuse, dispute, balk, hesitate, waver, take exception ▸ *n* **2 = objection**, protest, dissent, hesitation, qualm, misgiving, compunction
demure *adj* **= shy**, modest, sedate, reserved, reticent, unassuming, diffident, retiring
den *n* **1 = lair**, hole, shelter, cave, haunt, hideout, cavern **2** (*Chiefly US*) **= study**, retreat, sanctuary, hideaway, sanctum, cubbyhole, living room
denial *n* **1 = negation**, dissent, contradiction, retraction, repudiation, renunciation **2 = refusal**, veto, rejection, rebuff, prohibition, repulse
denigrate *v* **= disparage**, knock (*informal*), malign, belittle, bad-mouth (*slang*), vilify, slander, run down
denomination *n* **1 = religious group**, school, belief, sect, persuasion, creed **2 = unit**, value, size, grade
denote *v* **= indicate**, show, mean, mark, express, designate, imply, signify, betoken
denounce *v* **= condemn**, attack, accuse,

DICTIONARY

2 give information against
▶ **denunciation** *n* open condemnation
dense Ⓣ *adj* 1 closely packed 2 difficult to see through 3 stupid **densely** *adv*
▶ **density** *n* 1 degree to which something is filled or occupied 2 *physics* measure of the compactness of a substance, expressed as its mass per unit volume
dent Ⓣ *n* 1 hollow in a surface, as made by a blow ▷ *v* 2 make a dent in
dental *adj* of or relating to the teeth or dentistry
▶ **dental floss** waxed thread used to remove food particles from between the teeth
▶ **dentifrice** [**den**-tif-riss] *n* paste or powder for cleaning the teeth
▶ **dentine** [**den**-teen] *n* calcified tissue comprising the bulk of a tooth
▶ **denture** *n* 1 artificial tooth **dentures** 2 set of artificial teeth
dentist *n* person qualified to practise dentistry
▶ **dentistry** *n* branch of medicine concerned with the teeth and gums
denude *v* (foll. by *of*) remove the covering or protection from **denudation** *n*
deny Ⓣ *v* **-nying, -nied** 1 declare to be untrue 2 refuse to give or allow 3 refuse to acknowledge **deniable** *adj*
▶ **denial** *n* 1 denying 2 statement that something is not true
deodorize *v* remove or disguise the smell of **deodorization** *n*
▶ **deodorant** *n* substance applied to the body to mask the smell of perspiration
dep. 1 department 2 departure
Depardieu *n* **Gérard**. born 1948, French film actor. His films include *Jean de Florette* (1986), *Cyrano de Bergerac* (1990), *Green Card* (1991), *The Man in the Iron Mask* (1997), and *Tais-toi* (2003)
depart Ⓣ *v* 1 leave 2 differ **departure** *n*
▶ **departed** *adj euphemistic* dead
▶ **the departed** dead people
department Ⓣ *n* 1 specialized division of a large organization 2 major subdivision of the administration of a government **departmental** *adj*
▶ **department store** large shop selling many kinds of goods
depend Ⓣ *v* (foll. by *on* or *upon*) 1 put trust (in) 2 be influenced or determined (by) 3 rely (on) for income or support **dependable** *adj* **dependably** *adv* **dependability** *n*
▶ **dependant** *n* person who depends on another for financial support
▶ **dependence** *n* state of being dependent
▶ **dependency** *n* 1 territory subject to a state on which it does not border 2 overreliance on another person or a drug
▶ **dependent** *adj* depending on a person or thing for support
depict Ⓣ *v* 1 give a picture of 2 describe in words **depiction** *n*
depilate [**dep**-pill-ate] *v* remove hair

THESAURUS

censure, vilify, revile, stigmatize, denunciate
dense *adj* 1 = **thick**, heavy, solid, compact, condensed, close-knit, opaque, impenetrable 2 = **stupid**, thick, dull, obtuse, slow-witted, stolid
density *n* = **tightness**, mass, bulk, consistency, thickness, compactness, denseness, impenetrability, solidity
dent *n* 1 = **hollow**, chip, depression, dip, pit, impression, crater, dimple, indentation ▶ *v* 2 = **make a dent in**, gouge, hollow, press in, push in
deny *v* 1 = **contradict**, refute • *She denied both accusations.* OPPOSITE: admit 2 = **refuse**, reject, withhold • *denied access to the property* 3 = **renounce**, retract, recant, repudiate, disown, disclaim ▷ **deny oneself** *See* **abstain**
See also: **dispute**
depart *v* 1 = **leave**, go, retire, quit, withdraw, exit, disappear, retreat, absent (oneself), go away 2 = **deviate**, vary, differ, veer, stray, swerve, diverge, digress, turn aside
departed *See* **dead, late**
department *n* = **section**, office, unit, division • *the marketing department*
See also: **field**
departure *n* 1 = **leaving**, retirement, exit, withdrawal, exodus, going, moving, going away, leave-taking 2 = **divergence**, variation, deviation, digression 3 = **shift**, change, difference, innovation, novelty, whole new ball game (*informal*)
depend *v* 1 = **rely on**, trust, bank on, count on • *You can depend on me.* 2 = **be determined by**, hinge on • *Success depends on the dedication of the team.* ▷ **depend on** *See* **require, trust**
dependable *adj* = **reliable**, responsible, sure, steady, faithful, staunch, trustworthy, reputable, trusty, unfailing
dependant *n* = **relative**, child, minor, subordinate, protégé
dependence *See* **habit**
dependency *See* **colony**
dependent *adj* = **relying on**, weak, vulnerable, helpless, reliant, defenceless ▷ **dependent on, dependent upon** = **determined by**, conditional on, contingent on, depending on, influenced by, subject to
depict *v* 1 = **draw**, picture, paint, outline, portray, sketch, illustrate, delineate 2 = **describe**, represent, outline, characterize, narrate
depiction *n* = **representation**, picture,

DICTIONARY

from **depilation** *n*
▸ **depilatory** [dip-**pill**-a-tree] *adj, n, pl* **-ries** (substance) designed to remove unwanted hair
deplete Ⓣ *v* **1** use up **2** reduce in number **depletion** *n*
deplore Ⓣ *v* express or feel strong disapproval of
▸ **deplorable** *adj* very bad
deploy Ⓣ *v* organize (troops or resources) into a position ready for immediate action **deployment** *n*
depopulate *v* cause to be reduced in population **depopulation** *n*
deport Ⓣ *v* remove forcibly from a country **deportation** *n* **deportee** *n*
▸ **deport oneself** behave oneself in a specified manner
▸ **deportment** *n* manner in which a person behaves
depose Ⓣ *v* **1** remove from an office or position of power **2** *law* make a statement on oath
deposit Ⓣ *v* **1** put down **2** entrust for safekeeping, esp. to a bank **3** lay down naturally ▷ *n* **4** entrusting of money to a bank **5** money entrusted **6** money given in part payment or as security **7** accumulation of sediments, minerals, etc. **depositor** *n*
▸ **depositary** *n* person to whom something is entrusted for safety
▸ **depository** *n* store for furniture etc.
deposition *n* **1** *law* sworn statement of a witness used in court in his or her absence **2** deposing **3** depositing **4** something deposited
depot Ⓣ [**dee**-poh, **dep**-oh] *n* **1** building used for storage **2** building for the storage and servicing of buses or railway engines **3** bus or railway station
Depp *n* **Johnny**, full name *John Christopher Depp*. born 1963, US actor; his films include *Edward Scissorhands* (1990), *Fear and Loathing in Las Vegas* (1998), and the *Pirates of the Caribbean* series (2003–11)
deprave Ⓣ *v* make morally bad
▸ **depravity** *n* moral corruption
deprecate *v* express disapproval of, protest against **deprecation** *n* **deprecatory** *adj*
depreciate Ⓣ *v* **1** decline in value or price **2** criticize **depreciation** *n* **depreciatory** *adj*
depredation *n* plundering
depress Ⓣ *v* **1** lower the spirits of (someone) **2** lower (prices or wages) **3** push down **depressing** *adj* **depressingly** *adv*
▸ **depressant** *n* drug which reduces nervous activity
▸ **depression** *n* **1** mental state in which a person has feelings of gloom and inadequacy **2** economic condition in which there is a lot of unemployment and low output and investment **3** area of low air

THESAURUS

portrayal, description, sketch, delineation
deplete *v* = **use up**, reduce, consume, empty, drain, exhaust, lessen, expend, impoverish
deplorable *adj* **1** = **regrettable**, sad, unfortunate, grievous, lamentable, wretched, pitiable **2** = **disgraceful**, shameful, scandalous, reprehensible, dishonourable
deplore *v* = **disapprove of**, condemn, denounce, censure, abhor, object to, take a dim view of
deploy *v* = **position**, use, station, arrange, utilize, set out
deployment *n* = **position**, use, organization, spread, arrangement, utilization, stationing
deport *v* = **expel**, oust, exile, extradite, banish, expatriate ▷ **deport oneself** = **behave**, act, acquit oneself, bear oneself, carry oneself, comport oneself, conduct oneself, hold oneself
depose *v* **1** = **remove from office**, dismiss, oust, displace, demote, dethrone **2** (*Law*) = **testify**, declare, avouch, make a deposition
deposit *v* **1** = **put**, leave, place, drop, lay, put down • *The waiter deposited a hamburger in front of him.* **2** = **store**, bank, lodge, entrust, consign ▸ *n* **3** = **down payment**, security, pledge, stake, instalment, retainer, part payment **4** = **sediment**, accumulation, precipitate, silt, dregs, lees
See also: **dump, keep, payment, set**
depot *n* **1** = **storehouse**, warehouse, repository, depository **2** = **bus station**, garage, terminus
deprave *See* **corrupt**
depraved *adj* = **corrupt**, evil, vicious, wicked, immoral, degenerate, vile, sinful, dissolute
depravity *n* = **corruption**, evil, vice, immorality, debauchery, sinfulness, wickedness
depreciate *v* **1** = **devalue**, reduce, lower, decrease, lessen, deflate, lose value **2** = **disparage**, scorn, deride, detract, denigrate, belittle, run down, sneer at
depreciation *n* **1** = **devaluation**, fall, drop, slump, depression, deflation **2** = **disparagement**, denigration, belittlement, deprecation, detraction
depress *v* **1** = **sadden**, discourage, oppress, dishearten, dispirit, deject, make despondent, weigh down, harsh someone's buzz (*slang*) **2** = **lower**, reduce, diminish, downgrade, lessen, devalue, cheapen, depreciate **3** = **press down**, level, lower,

DICTIONARY

pressure **4** sunken place

▸ **depressive** *adj* tending to cause depression

Depretis *n* **Agostino**. 1813–87, Italian statesman; prime minister (1876–78; 1878–79; 1881–87). His policy led to the Triple Alliance (1882) between Italy, Austria-Hungary, and Germany

deprive Ⓣ *v* (foll. by *of*) prevent from (possessing or enjoying) **deprivation** *n*

▸ **deprived** *adj* lacking adequate living conditions, education, etc.

dept department

d

depth Ⓣ *n* **1** distance downwards, backwards, or inwards **2** intensity of emotion **3** profundity of character or thought **4** intensity of colour

▸ **depth charge** bomb used to attack submarines by exploding at a preset depth of water

depute *v* appoint (someone) to act on one's behalf

▸ **deputation** *n* body of people appointed to represent others

▸ **deputize** *v* act as a deputy

▸ **deputy** *n* person appointed to act on behalf of another

De Quincey *n* **Thomas**. 1785–1859, English critic and essayist, noted particularly for his *Confessions of an English Opium Eater* (1821)

derail *v* cause (a train) to go off the rails

derailment *n*

derange *v* **1** make insane **2** throw into disorder **derangement** *n*

derby *n, pl* **-bies** **1** sporting event between teams from the same area **2** bowler hat

▸ **the Derby** annual horse race run at Epsom Downs

Derby *n* **Earl of**, title of *Edward George Geoffrey Smith Stanley*. 1799–1869, British statesman; Conservative prime minister (1852; 1858–59; 1866–68)

deregulate *v* remove regulations or controls from **deregulation** *n*

derelict Ⓣ *adj* **1** deserted or abandoned **2** falling into ruins ▹ *n* **3** social outcast, vagrant

▸ **dereliction** *n* **1** wilful neglect (of duty) **2** state of being abandoned

derestrict *v* make (a road) free from speed limits

deride Ⓣ *v* speak of or treat with contempt or ridicule **derision** *n*

▸ **derisive** *adj* mocking or scornful

▸ **derisory** *adj* so small or inadequate that it is not worth serious consideration

de rigueur [de rig-**gur**] *adj* required by fashion

derive Ⓣ *v* (foll. by *from*) draw or be drawn

THESAURUS

flatten, push down

depressed *adj* **1 = low-spirited**, blue, sad, unhappy, dejected, despondent, discouraged, downcast, dispirited, downhearted, fed up **2 = poverty-stricken**, poor, disadvantaged, needy, run-down, deprived **3 = lowered**, weakened, cheapened, depreciated, devalued **4 = sunken**, hollow, concave, indented, recessed

depressing *adj* **= bleak**, sad, dismal, gloomy, discouraging, disheartening, dispiriting, harrowing, saddening

depression *n* **1 = low spirits**, sadness, despair, melancholy, despondency, dejection, downheartedness, dumps (*informal*), gloominess, the blues **2 = recession**, slump, inactivity, stagnation, economic decline, hard times *or* bad times, credit crunch **3 = hollow**, dip, pit, bowl, dent, valley, cavity, dimple, indentation

deprivation *n* **1 = withholding**, withdrawal, removal, denial, expropriation, dispossession **2 = want**, need, distress, hardship, destitution, privation

deprive *v* **= withhold**, strip, rob, bereave, despoil, dispossess

deprived *adj* **= poor**, disadvantaged, needy, destitute, bereft, down at heel, in need, lacking

depth *n* **1 = deepness**, drop, measure, extent **2 = insight**, wisdom, penetration, discernment, astuteness, profoundness, profundity, sagacity

depths *See* **bottom**

deputation *n* **= delegation**, commission, embassy, envoys, legation

deputize *v* **= stand in for**, understudy, act for, take the place of

deputy *n* **= substitute**, representative, delegate, lieutenant, proxy, surrogate, second-in-command, legate, number two

deranged *adj* **= mad**, crazy, insane, irrational, unbalanced, crazed, demented, distracted, unhinged

derelict *adj* **1 = abandoned**, dilapidated, neglected, ruined • *a derelict warehouse* ▸ *n* **2 = tramp**, outcast, bag lady, down-and-out, vagrant

deride *v* **= mock**, insult, scorn, taunt, scoff, jeer, ridicule, disparage, disdain, sneer

derision *n* **= mockery**, insult, laughter, scorn, contempt, ridicule, disrespect, disdain, denigration, contumely, disparagement, raillery, scoffing, sneering

derisory *adj* **= ridiculous**, outrageous, lousy (*slang*), ludicrous, laughable, preposterous, contemptible, insulting

derivation *n* **= origin**, source, beginning, root, foundation

DICTIONARY

(from) in origin **derivation** *n* **derivative** *adj, n*
dermatitis *n* inflammation of the skin
dermatology *n* branch of medicine concerned with the skin **dermatologist** *n*
Dermot MacMurrough *n* ?1110–71, king of Leinster, who, by enlisting the support of the English to win back his kingdom, was responsible for the English conquest of Ireland
derogatory Ⓣ [dir-**rog**-a-tree] *adj* intentionally offensive
derrick *n* **1** simple crane **2** framework erected over an oil well
Derrida *n* **Jacques**. 1930–2004, French philosopher and literary critic, regarded as the founder of deconstruction: author of *L'Ecriture et la différence* (1967)
derring-do *n old-fashioned or lit* spirited bravery, boldness
derringer *n* small pistol with a large bore
dervish *n* member of a Muslim religious order noted for a frenzied whirling dance
descale *v* remove the hard coating which sometimes forms inside kettles, pipes, etc.
descant *n music* tune played or sung above a basic melody
Descartes *n* **René**. 1596–1650, French philosopher and mathematician. He provided a mechanistic basis for the philosophical theory of dualism and is regarded as the founder of modern philosophy. He also founded analytical geometry and contributed greatly to the science of optics. His works include *Discours de la méthode* (1637), *Meditationes de Prima Philosophia* (1641), and *Principia Philosophiae* (1644)
descend Ⓣ *v* **1** move down (a slope etc.) **2** move to a lower level, pitch, etc. **3** (foll. by *to*) stoop to (unworthy behaviour) **4** (foll. by *on*) visit unexpectedly
▸ **be descended from** be connected by a blood relationship to
▸ **descendant** *n* person or animal descended from an individual, race, or species
▸ **descendent** *adj* descending
▸ **descent** *n* **1** act of descending **2** downward slope **3** derivation from an ancestor
Deschamps *n* **Émile**, full name *Émile Deschamps de Saint-Armand*. 1791–1871, French poet, dramatist, and librettist: a leading figure in the French romantic movement
describe Ⓣ *v* **1** give an account of (something or someone) in words **2** trace the outline of (a circle etc.)
▸ **description** *n* **1** statement that describes something or someone **2** sort: *reptiles of every description* **descriptive** *adj* **descriptively** *adv*
descry *v* **-scrying, -scried 1** catch sight of **2** discover by looking carefully
desecrate *v* violate the sacred character of (an object or place) **desecration** *n*
desegregate *v* end racial segregation in **desegregation** *n*
desensitize *v* make insensitive or less sensitive
desert[1] Ⓣ *n* region that has little or no vegetation because of low rainfall
desert[2] Ⓣ *v* **1** abandon (a person or place) without intending to return **2** *mil* abscond from (a post or duty) with no intention of returning **deserter** *n* **desertion** *n*

THESAURUS

derive *v* **derive from = come from**, arise from, emanate from, flow from, issue from, originate from, proceed from, spring from, stem from
derogatory *adj* = **disparaging**, offensive, unflattering, defamatory, belittling, slighting, uncomplimentary, unfavourable
descend *v* **1 = go down**, fall, sink, dive, dip, plummet • *as we descend to the basement* OPPOSITE: ascend **2 = slope**, dip, incline, slant **3 = lower oneself**, deteriorate, degenerate, stoop ▹ **be descended = originate**, issue, spring, proceed, derive, be handed down, be passed down ▹ **descend on = attack**, arrive, raid, invade, swoop
See also: **drop**
descendants *See* **family**
descent *n* **1 = coming down**, fall, drop, plunge, swoop **2 = slope**, drop, dip, incline, slant, declivity **3 = ancestry**, origin, extraction, genealogy, lineage, parentage, family tree **4 = decline**, degeneration, deterioration
describe *v* **1 = relate**, define, portray, depict • *Describe what you do in your spare time.* **2 = trace**, draw, outline, delineate, mark out
See also: **explain, report, represent**
description *n* **1 = account**, report, explanation, portrayal, representation, sketch, depiction, narrative **2 = kind**, order, type, class, brand, sort, category, variety
descriptive *adj* = **graphic**, detailed, pictorial, vivid, picturesque, expressive, explanatory, illustrative
desert[1] *n* = **wilderness**, waste, solitude, wasteland, wilds
desert[2] *v* = **abandon**, leave, quit, strand, maroon, jilt, forsake, abscond, leave stranded, walk out on (*informal*)
deserted *adj* = **abandoned**, empty, vacant, derelict, desolate, neglected, unoccupied, forsaken
deserter *n* = **defector**, runaway, fugitive, renegade, traitor, escapee, absconder, truant
desertion *n* = **abandonment**, flight, escape,

DICTIONARY

deserts *pl n* **get one's just deserts** get the punishment one deserves
deserve Ⓣ *v* be entitled to or worthy of
▸ **deserved** *adj* rightfully earned **deservedly** *adv*
▸ **deserving** *adj* worthy, esp. of praise or help
Des Groseilliers *n* **Médard Chouart**. 1618–c1696, French explorer and fur trader in Canada. His expedition to Hudson Bay on behalf of English merchants led to the creation of the Hudson's Bay Company
deshabille *n* same as **dishabille**
desiccate *v* remove most of the water from **desiccation** *n*
design Ⓣ *v* **1** work out the structure or form of (something), as by making a sketch or plans **2** plan and make artistically **3** intend for a specific purpose ▹ *n* **4** preliminary drawing **5** arrangement or features of an artistic or decorative work **6** art of designing **7** intention: *by design*
▸ **designedly** *adv* by intention
▸ **designer** *n* **1** person who draws up original sketches or plans from which things are made ▹ *adj* **2** designed by a well-known designer **3** fashionable or trendy: *designer stubble*
▸ **designing** *adj* crafty, cunning
designate Ⓣ [**dez**-zig-nate] *v* **1** give a name to **2** select (someone) for an office or duty ▹ *adj* **3** appointed but not yet in office
▸ **designation** *n* name
desire Ⓣ *v* **1** long for ▹ *n* **2** strong feeling of wanting something **3** sexual appetite **4** person or thing desired
▸ **desirable** *adj* **1** worth having **2** arousing sexual desire **desirability** *n*
▸ **desirous of** [diz-**zire**-uss] having a desire for
desist Ⓣ *v* (foll. by *from*) stop or abstain (from)
desk *n* **1** piece of furniture with a writing surface and usually drawers **2** service counter in a public building **3** section of a newspaper covering a specific subject: *the news desk*
▸ **desktop** *adj* denoting a computer system small enough to use at a desk
Desmoulins *n* (**Lucie Simplice**) **Camille** (**Benoît**). 1760–94, French revolutionary leader, pamphleteer, and orator
desolate Ⓣ *adj* **1** uninhabited and bleak **2** without hope ▹ *v* **3** lay waste **4** make (a person) very sad **desolation** *n*
De Soto *n* **Hernando**. ?1500–42, Spanish explorer, who discovered the Mississippi River (1541) (Also **Fernando De Soto**)
despair Ⓣ *n* **1** total loss of hope ▹ *v* **2** lose hope

THESAURUS

evasion, betrayal, defection, dereliction, absconding, apostasy, relinquishment
deserve *v* = **merit**, earn, warrant, justify, be entitled to, be worthy of • *He deserves a rest.*
deserved *adj* = **well-earned**, due, proper, fitting, justified, rightful, earned, merited, warranted
deserving *adj* = **worthy**, commendable, righteous, laudable, meritorious, estimable, praiseworthy
design *v* **1** = **plan**, draft, outline, draw up • *They wanted to design a new product that was both attractive and practical.* **2** = **create**, fashion, originate, invent, conceive, fabricate, think up **3** = **intend**, plan, mean, aim, propose, purpose ▸ *n* **4** = **plan**, draft, model, outline • *her design for a new office* **5** = **style**, form, shape, pattern • *a new design of clock* **6** = **intention**, end, goal, target, aim, object, purpose, objective
See also: **layout, structure**
designate *v* **1** = **name**, call, term, label, style, dub, entitle **2** = **appoint**, choose, select, nominate, delegate, assign, depute
designation *n* = **name**, mark, title, label, description
designed *See* **calculated**
designer *n* = **creator**, architect, inventor, planner, originator, deviser
desirable *adj* **1** = **worthwhile**, good, profitable, beneficial, preferable, win-win (*informal*), advantageous, advisable **2** = **attractive**, sexy (*informal*), glamorous, alluring, seductive, adorable, fetching
desire *v* **1** = **want**, wish, fancy, crave, yearn, long for • *We can stay longer if you desire.* ▸ *n* **2** = **wish**, appetite, yen (*informal*), longing, craving, yearning, hankering • *a strong desire to help people* **3** = **lust**, passion, appetite, libido
See also: **urge**
desist *v* = **stop**, end, cease, pause, discontinue, break off, forbear, leave off, refrain from
desolate *adj* **1** = **uninhabited**, wild, bare, bleak, solitary, barren, dreary, godforsaken **2** = **miserable**, gloomy, dejected, despondent, downcast, wretched, disconsolate, forlorn ▸ *v* **3** = **lay waste**, destroy, devastate, ruin, ravage, plunder, pillage, depopulate, despoil, lay low **4** = **deject**, discourage, grieve, distress, depress, dismay, dishearten
desolation *n* **1** = **ruin**, destruction, havoc, devastation **2** = **bleakness**, isolation, solitude, barrenness **3** = **misery**, woe, distress, sadness, despair, anguish, gloom, dejection, wretchedness
despair *n* **1** = **hopelessness**, gloom,

DICTIONARY

despatch *v, n* same as **dispatch**
desperado Ⓣ *n, pl* **-does, -dos** reckless person ready to commit any violent illegal act
desperate Ⓣ *adj* **1** careless of danger, as from despair **2** (of an action) undertaken as a last resort **3** having a great need or desire **desperately** *adv* **desperation** *n*
despise Ⓣ *v* look down on with contempt
▸ **despicable** *adj* worthy of being despised **despicably** *adv*
despite Ⓣ *prep* in spite of
despoil *v formal* plunder **despoliation** *n*
despondent Ⓣ *adj* dejected or depressed **despondently** *adv* **despondency** *n*
despot Ⓣ *n* person in power who acts tyrannically **despotic** *adj* **despotically** *adv*
▸ **despotism** *n* tyrannical government or behaviour
des Prés, Desprez *n* **Josquin.** ?1450–1521, Flemish Renaissance composer of masses, motets, and chansons
dessert *n* sweet course served at the end of a meal
▸ **dessertspoon** *n* spoon between a tablespoon and a teaspoon in size
destabilize *v* make (a country or government) politically or economically unstable **destabilization** *n*
destination Ⓣ *n* place to which someone or something is going
destine [dess-tin] *v* set apart (for a certain purpose)
destiny Ⓣ *n, pl* **-nies 1** future destined for a person or thing **2 Destiny** the power that predetermines the course of events
destitute Ⓣ *adj* totally impoverished **destitution** *n*
destroy Ⓣ *v* **1** ruin **2** put an end to **3** kill (an animal) **destructible** *adj*
▸ **destroyer** *n* **1** small heavily armed warship **2** person or thing that destroys
▸ **destruction** *n* **1** destroying or being destroyed **2** cause of ruin
▸ **destructive** *adj* **1** causing destruction **2** intending to discredit someone, without positive suggestions: *destructive criticism* **destructively** *adv*
desuetude [diss-**syoo**-it-tude] *n* condition of not being in use
desultory [**dez**-zl-tree] *adj* **1** changing fitfully from one thing to another **2** random **desultorily** *adv*

d

THESAURUS

despondency, dejection • *feelings of despair* ▸ *v* **2 = lose hope**, feel dejected, feel despondent, lose heart • *Don't despair. I know things will be all right.*
See also: **misery**
despairing *adj* = **hopeless**, desperate, frantic, miserable, dejected, grief-stricken, despondent, inconsolable, wretched, disconsolate
desperado *n* = **criminal**, outlaw, villain, bandit, lawbreaker
desperate *adj* **1 = reckless**, risky, furious, frantic, daring, audacious **2 = grave**, extreme, urgent, drastic
desperately *adv* **1 = gravely**, seriously, badly, severely, perilously, dangerously **2 = hopelessly**, shockingly, appallingly, fearfully, frightfully
desperation *n* **1 = recklessness**, frenzy, madness, foolhardiness, impetuosity, rashness **2 = misery**, worry, trouble, despair, anguish, agony, unhappiness, hopelessness
despicable *adj* = **contemptible**, mean, disgraceful, shameful, lousy (*slang*), worthless, hateful, vile, sordid, detestable, wretched, scuzzy (*slang*)
despise *v* = **look down on**, scorn, loathe, detest, revile, abhor
despite *prep* = **in spite of**, notwithstanding (*formal*), regardless of • *Despite its condition, he bought the car anyway.*
despondency *n* = **dejection**, depression, misery, sadness, despair, desperation, gloom, melancholy, low spirits
despondent *adj* = **dejected**, sad, depressed, glum, disconsolate, disheartened, dispirited, downhearted, in despair, sorrowful
despot *n* = **tyrant**, dictator, autocrat, oppressor
despotic *adj* = **tyrannical**, authoritarian, oppressive, autocratic, dictatorial, imperious, domineering
despotism *n* = **tyranny**, dictatorship, oppression, totalitarianism, autocracy
destination *n* = **journey's end**, stop, station, haven, resting-place, terminus
destined *adj* = **fated**, certain, doomed, bound, intended, meant, predestined
destiny *n* = **fate**, lot, portion, fortune, doom, karma, kismet
destitute *adj* = **penniless**, poor, impoverished, insolvent, poverty-stricken, down and out, down on one's luck (*informal*), indigent, moneyless, penurious
destitution *See* **hardship, poverty**
destroy *v* = **ruin**, devastate, wreck, demolish, annihilate, raze, obliterate • *The building was completely destroyed.*
See also: **bomb, dash, eat away, erode, kill, put down, spoil**
destruction *n* = **ruin**, devastation, demolition, annihilation, obliteration • *the destruction of the ozone layer*
destructive *adj* = **damaging**, deadly, fatal, harmful, lethal, catastrophic, ruinous, calamitous, devastating

DICTIONARY

detach ⓣ *v* disengage and separate
detachable *adj*
▸ **detached** *adj* **1** standing apart **2** showing no emotional involvement
▸ **detachment** *n* **1** aloofness **2** small group of soldiers
detail ⓣ *n* **1** item that is considered separately **2** unimportant item **3** treatment of particulars **4** (*chiefly*) *mil* personnel assigned a specific duty ▹ *v* **5** list fully
detain ⓣ *v* **1** delay (someone) **2** hold (someone) in custody **detainee** *n*
detainment *n*
detect ⓣ *v* **1** notice **2** discover the existence or presence of **detectable** *adj* **detection** *n*
▸ **detective** *n* policeman or private agent who investigates crime
▸ **detector** *n* instrument used to find something: *smoke detector*
detente [day-**tont**] *n* easing of tension between nations
detention ⓣ *n* **1** imprisonment **2** form of punishment in which a pupil is detained after school
deter ⓣ *v* **-terring, -terred** discourage (someone) from doing something by instilling fear or doubt
▸ **deterrent** *n* **1** something that deters **2** weapon, esp. nuclear, to deter attack by another nation ▹ *adj* **3** tending to deter
detergent ⓣ *n* **1** chemical cleansing agent ▹ *adj* **2** having cleansing power
deteriorate ⓣ *v* become worse
deterioration *n*
determine ⓣ *v* **1** settle (an argument or a question) conclusively **2** find out the facts about (something) **3** fix in scope, extent, etc. **4** make a decision to do something
▸ **determinant** *n* factor that determines
▸ **determinate** *adj* definitely limited or fixed
▸ **determination** *n* **1** condition of being determined or resolute **2** act of determining
▸ **determined** *adj* firmly decided, unable to be persuaded **determinedly** *adv*
▸ **determiner** *n grammar* word that determines the object to which a noun phrase refers: *all*
▸ **determinism** *n* theory that human choice is not free, but decided by past events
determinist *n, adj*

THESAURUS

detach *v* = **separate**, remove, divide, sever, disconnect, disengage, cut off, tear off, unfasten
detached *adj* **1** = **separate**, unconnected, disconnected, discrete **2** = **uninvolved**, objective, neutral, impartial, unbiased, reserved, disinterested, hands-off, dispassionate, impersonal
detachment *n* **1** = **indifference**, remoteness, coolness, aloofness, nonchalance, unconcern **2** = **impartiality**, neutrality, fairness, objectivity **3** (*Mil*) = **unit**, force, party, body, patrol, squad, task force
detail *n* **1** = **point**, respect, particular, element, aspect • *We discussed every detail of the performance.* **2** = **fine point**, particular, nicety, triviality **3** (*Mil*) = **party**, force, body, duty, squad, fatigue, assignment, detachment ▸ *v* **4** = **list**, relate, recount, rehearse, recite, catalogue, tabulate, enumerate, itemize **5** = **appoint**, charge, send, commission, delegate, assign, allocate
detailed *adj* = **comprehensive**, minute, full, particular, thorough, exhaustive, intricate, blow-by-blow
detain *v* **1** = **delay**, check, hinder, impede, hold up, keep back, retard, slow up *or* slow down **2** = **hold**, arrest, restrain, confine, intern
detect *v* **1** = **notice**, note, spot, identify, recognize, observe, perceive, ascertain **2** = **discover**, find, uncover, unmask, track down
detective *n* = **investigator**, cop (*slang*), gumshoe (*slang*), sleuth (*informal*), private eye, private investigator, skip tracer, peeper (*slang*)
detention *n* = **imprisonment**, custody, quarantine, confinement, incarceration
deter *v* = **discourage**, stop, prevent, intimidate, frighten, dissuade, inhibit from, put off, talk out of
detergent *n* = **cleaner**, cleanser
deteriorate *v* = **decline**, lower, slump, worsen, degenerate, go downhill (*informal*)
deterioration *See* **rot, wear**
determination *n* = **resolution**, resolve (*formal*), perseverance, persistence, tenacity • *the government's determination to improve health care*
See also: **drive, will**
determine *v* **1** = **affect**, control, decide, shape, govern, dictate • *The size of the chicken pieces will determine the cooking time.* **2** = **decide**, choose, settle, fix, resolve, arrange • *The final wording had not yet been determined.* **3** = **find out**, confirm, discover, establish, verify, ascertain (*formal*) • *The investigation will determine what really happened.*
See also: **calculate, learn, see**
determined *adj* = **resolute**, persistent, dogged, tenacious, purposeful, single-minded, bent on, intent on • *She was determined not to repeat the error.*
See also: **firm, set on**
deterrent *n* = **discouragement**, check, curb, restraint, obstacle, impediment, hindrance, disincentive

DICTIONARY

detest Ⓣ *v* dislike intensely **detestable** *adj* **detestation** *n*
dethrone *v* remove from a throne or deprive of high position
detonate Ⓣ *v* cause (an explosive device) to explode or (of an explosive device) explode **detonation** *n*
▸ **detonator** *n* small amount of explosive, or a device, used to set off an explosion
detour Ⓣ *n* deviation from a direct route or course of action
detox *v, n informal* (undergo) treatment to rid the body of poisonous substances
detoxify *v* **-fying, -fied** remove poison from **detoxification** *n*
detract Ⓣ *v* (foll. by *from*) lessen the value of, diminish **detractor** *n* **detraction** *n*
detriment Ⓣ *n* disadvantage or damage **detrimental** *adj* **detrimentally** *adv*
detritus [dit-**trite**-uss] *n* loose mass of stones or silt worn away from rocks, debris **detrital** *adj*
de trop [de **troh**] *adj* **1** not wanted **2** in the way
deuce [**dyewss**] *n* **1** *tennis* score of forty all **2** playing card or dice with two spots
deuterium *n* isotope of hydrogen twice as heavy as the normal atom
Deutschmark [**doytch**-mark], **Deutsche Mark** [**doytch**-a] *n* former monetary unit of Germany
devalue *v* **-valuing, -valued 1** reduce the exchange value of (a currency) **2** reduce the value of (something or someone) **devaluation** *n*
devastate Ⓣ *v* damage (a place) severely or destroy it **devastation** *n*
▸ **devastated** *adj* shocked and extremely upset
develop Ⓣ *v* **1** grow or bring to a later, more elaborate, or more advanced stage **2** come or bring into existence **3** improve the value or change the use of (land) **4** treat (a photographic plate or film) to produce a visible image **development** *n*
▸ **developer** *n* **1** person who develops property **2** chemical used to develop photographs or films
▸ **developing country** poor or nonindustrial country that is seeking to develop its resources by industrialization
deviate Ⓣ *v* **1** differ from others in belief or thought **2** turn aside from a course of action **deviation** *n* **deviance** *n*
▸ **deviant** *n, adj* (person) deviating from what is considered acceptable behaviour
device Ⓣ *n* **1** machine or tool used for a specific task **2** scheme or trick
devil Ⓣ *n* **1** evil spirit **2** person regarded as wicked **3** person: *poor devil* **4** person regarded as daring **5** *informal* something difficult or annoying ▹ *v* **-illing, -illed 6** prepare (food)

THESAURUS

detest *v* = **hate**, loathe, despise, abhor, abominate, dislike intensely, recoil from
detested *See* **unpopular**
detonate *v* = **explode**, blast, trigger, discharge, blow up, set off
detonation *See* **bang**
detour *n* = **diversion**, bypass, circuitous route *or* indirect route, roundabout way
detract *v* ▹ **detract from** = **lessen**, reduce, lower, diminish, devaluate, take away from
detriment *n* = **damage**, injury, loss, hurt, harm, disadvantage, impairment, disservice
detrimental *adj* = **damaging**, harmful, adverse, destructive, prejudicial, deleterious, disadvantageous, unfavourable
devastate *v* = **destroy**, level, sack, ruin, wreck, ravage, demolish, raze, lay waste
devastating *adj* = **overwhelming**, cutting, savage, vitriolic, overpowering, trenchant, withering
devastation *n* = **destruction**, ruin, havoc, demolition, desolation
develop *v* **1** = **grow**, result, advance, spring, progress, evolve, mature • *to develop at different rates* **2** = **fall ill with**, contract (*formal*), catch, succumb, come down with, pick up • *He developed a bad cold.* **3** = **form**, establish, generate, breed, originate, invent **4** = **expand**, elaborate, broaden, unfold, augment, amplify, enlarge, work out *See also*: **build, enlarge on, expand on, extend**
development *n* **1** = **growth**, increase, advance, spread, progress, expansion, improvement, evolution **2** = **event**, result, incident, occurrence, happening, upshot, turn of events
deviant *adj* **1** = **perverted**, sick (*informal*), twisted, kinky (*slang*), warped ▸ *n* **2** = **pervert**, freak, degenerate, misfit, weirdo *or* weirdie (*informal*), sicko *or* sickie (*informal*)
deviate *v* = **differ**, depart, wander, veer, stray, swerve, diverge
deviation *n* = **departure**, shift, irregularity, variation, discrepancy, disparity, inconsistency, divergence, digression
device *n* **1** = **gadget**, tool, machine, implement, instrument, appliance, contraption, apparatus **2** = **ploy**, plan, trick, scheme, gambit, maneuver, stratagem, wile
devil *n* **1** = **brute**, terror, monster, beast, demon, ogre, fiend **2** = **scamp**, rogue, rascal, scoundrel **3** = **person**, thing, creature, beggar, wretch ▹ **the Devil** = **Satan**, Beelzebub, Evil One, Lucifer, Mephistopheles, Prince of Darkness

DICTIONARY

with a highly flavoured spiced mixture **7** do routine literary work, esp. for a lawyer or author
▸ **the Devil** *Christianity* chief spirit of evil and enemy of God
▸ **devilish** *adj* **1** of or like the devil ▹ *adv* **2** Also **devilishly** *informal* extremely
▸ **devilment** *n* mischievous conduct
▸ **devilry** *n* **1** reckless fun **2** wickedness
▸ **devil-may-care** *adj* happy-go-lucky
▸ **devil's advocate** person who takes an opposing or unpopular point of view for the sake of argument
devious Ⓣ *adj* **1** not sincere or straightforward **2** indirect **deviously** *adv* **deviousness** *n*
devise Ⓣ *v* work out (something) in one's mind
devoid Ⓣ *adj* (foll. by *of*) destitute (of) or free (from)
devolve *v* (foll. by *on* or *upon* or *to*) pass (power or duties) or (of power or duties) be passed to a successor or substitute
▸ **devolution** *n* transfer of authority from a central government to regional governments
devote Ⓣ *v* apply or dedicate to some cause
▸ **devoted** *adj* feeling loyalty or devotion **devotedly** *adv*
▸ **devotee** [dev-vote-**tee**] *n* **1** person ardently enthusiastic about something **2** zealous follower of a religion
▸ **devotion** *n* **1** strong affection for or loyalty to a cause or person **2** religious zeal or piety **devotions 3** prayers **devotional** *adj*
devour Ⓣ *v* **1** eat up greedily **2** engulf and destroy **3** read or look at avidly **devouring** *adj*
devout Ⓣ *adj* deeply religious **devoutly** *adv*
De Vries *n* **Hugo**. 1848–1935, Dutch botanist, who rediscovered Mendel's laws and developed the mutation theory of evolution
dew *n* drops of water condensed on a cool surface at night from vapour in the air **dewy** *adj*
Dewar *n* **1 Donald**. 1937–2000, Scottish Labour politician; secretary of state for Scotland (1997–99); first minister of Scotland (1999–2000) **2** Sir **James**. 1842–1923, Scottish chemist and physicist. He worked on the liquefaction of gases and the properties of matter at low temperature, invented the vacuum flask, and (with Sir Frederick Abel) was the first to prepare cordite
dewclaw *n* nonfunctional claw on a dog's leg
Dewey *n* **John**. 1859–1952, US pragmatist philosopher and educator: an exponent of progressivism in education, he formulated an instrumentalist theory of learning through experience. His works include *The School and Society* (1899), *Democracy and Education* (1916), and *Logic: the Theory of Inquiry* (1938)
dewlap *n* loose fold of skin hanging under the throat in dogs, cattle, etc.
Dexter *n* **Darrell**. born 1957, Canadian politician, Premier of Nova Scotia (2009–)
dexterity Ⓣ *n* **1** skill in using one's hands **2** mental quickness **dexterous** *adj* **dexterously** *adv*
dextrose *n* glucose occurring in fruit, honey, and the blood of animals
dg decigram
dhal, dal *n* **1** nutritious pealike seed of a tropical shrub **2** curry made from lentils or other pulses

THESAURUS

devilish *adj* = **fiendish**, wicked, atrocious, satanic, diabolical, detestable, hellish, damnable, infernal
devious *adj* = **sly**, wily, scheming, calculating, underhand • *devious ways of getting the starring role in the play*
See also: **crafty, cunning, sneaky**
deviousness *See* **cunning**
devise *v* = **work out**, design, construct, invent, conceive, formulate, contrive, dream up, think up
devoid *adj* = **lacking**, without, empty, deficient, destitute, bereft, free from, wanting
devote *v* = **dedicate**, give, reserve, commit, pledge, apply, assign, allot, set apart
devoted *adj* = **dedicated**, true, constant, loyal, faithful, loving, doting • *a devoted parent*
See also: **ardent, enthusiastic, fond**
devotee *n* = **enthusiast**, fan, supporter, follower, buff (*informal*), fanatic, admirer, aficionado, adherent, disciple
devotion *n* **1** = **dedication**, commitment, loyalty, allegiance, adherence, fidelity, constancy, faithfulness **2** = **love**, passion, affection, attachment, fondness **3** = **devoutness**, holiness, spirituality, reverence, piety, godliness
▹ **devotions** = **prayers**, church service, divine office, religious observance
devotional *See* **religious**
devour *v* **1** = **eat**, consume, swallow, wolf, gobble, guzzle, gulp, chow down (*slang*), polish off (*informal*) **2** = **destroy**, waste, consume, ravage, annihilate, wipe out **3** = **enjoy**, read compulsively *or* read voraciously, take in
devout *adj* = **religious**, holy, pure, orthodox, pious, godly, prayerful, reverent, saintly
dexterity *n* **1** = **skill**, touch, expertise, finesse, proficiency, adroitness, deftness, nimbleness **2** = **cleverness**, ability, ingenuity, aptitude

DICTIONARY

dhoti *n, pl* **-tis** long loincloth worn by men in India
dhow *n* type of Arab sailing vessel
DHSS formerly, Department of Health and Social Security
diabetes [die-a-**beet**-eez] *n* disorder in which an abnormal amount of urine containing an excess of sugar is excreted **diabetic** *n, adj*
diabolic *adj* **1** of the devil **2** extremely cruel ▸ **diabolical** *adj informal* extremely bad **diabolically** *adv* ▸ **diabolism** *n* witchcraft, devil worship
diaconate *n* position or period of office of a deacon **diaconal** *adj*
diacritic *n* sign above or below a letter or character to indicate phonetic value or stress
diadem *n old-fashioned* crown
diaeresis *n, pl* **-ses** same as **dieresis**
diagnosis Ⓣ [die-ag-**no**-siss] *n, pl* **-ses** [-seez] discovery and identification of diseases from the examination of symptoms **diagnose** *v* **diagnostic** *adj*
diagonal Ⓣ *adj* **1** from corner to corner **2** slanting ▷ *n* **3** diagonal line **diagonally** *adv*
diagram Ⓣ *n* sketch demonstrating the form or workings of something **diagrammatic** *adj* **diagrammatically** *adv*
dial *n* **1** face of a clock or watch **2** graduated disc on a measuring instrument **3** control on a radio or television used to change the station **4** numbered disc on the front of some telephones ▷ *v* **dialling, dialled 5** try to establish a telephone connection with (someone) by operating the dial or buttons on a telephone
dialect Ⓣ *n* form of a language spoken in a particular area **dialectal** *adj*
dialectic *n* logical debate by question and answer to resolve differences between two views **dialectical** *adj*
dialogue Ⓣ *n* **1** conversation between two people **2** discussion between representatives of two nations or groups ▸ **dialogue box** small window on a computer screen prompting the user to enter information
dialysis [die-**al**-iss-iss] *n med* filtering of blood through a membrane to remove waste products
diamanté [die-a-**man**-tee] *adj* decorated with artificial jewels or sequins
diameter *n* (length of) a straight line through the centre of a circle or sphere ▸ **diametric** *or* **diametrical** *adj* **1** of a diameter **2** completely opposed: *the diametric opposite* **diametrically** *adv*
diamond *n* **1** usually colourless, exceptionally hard precious stone **2** *geom* figure with four sides of equal length forming two acute and two obtuse angles **3** playing card marked with red diamond-shaped symbols ▸ **diamond wedding** sixtieth anniversary of a wedding
Diana *n* **1** the virginal Roman goddess of the hunt and the moon. Greek counterpart **Artemis 2** title *Diana, Princess of Wales*, original name *Lady Diana Frances Spencer*. 1961–97, she married Charles, Prince of Wales, in 1981; they were divorced in 1996: died in a car wreck
diaper *n* piece of absorbent material fastened round a baby's lower torso to absorb urine and feces
diaphanous [die-**af**-fan-ous] *adj* fine and almost transparent
diaphragm [**die**-a-fram] *n* **1** muscular partition that separates the abdominal cavity and chest cavity **2** contraceptive device placed over the neck of the womb
diarrhea, diarrhoea [die-a-**ree**-a] *n* frequent discharge of abnormally liquid feces
diary Ⓣ *n, pl* **-ries** (book for) a record of daily events, appointments, or observations **diarist** *n*
diatribe *n* bitter critical attack
Diaz *n* **Cameron**. born 1972, US film actress; films include *The Mask* (1994), *There's Something About Mary* (1998), and *The Gangs of New York* (2003)
dibble *n* small hand tool used to make holes in the ground for seeds or plants
d'Iberville *n* **Pierre le Moyne, Sieur**. 1661–1706, French-Canadian explorer, who

THESAURUS

diabolical *adj* (*Informal*) = **dreadful**, terrible, shocking, outrageous, appalling, atrocious, abysmal, hellish
diagnose *v* = **identify**, determine, recognize, analyze, pronounce, interpret, pinpoint, distinguish
diagnosis *n* **1** = **examination**, investigation, analysis, scrutiny **2** = **opinion**, conclusion, interpretation, pronouncement
diagonal *adj* = **slanting**, cross, oblique, angled, crossways, crosswise
diagonally *adv* = **aslant**, obliquely, at an angle, cornerwise, crosswise
diagram *n* = **plan**, figure, chart, drawing, representation, sketch, graph
dialect *n* = **language**, speech, jargon, vernacular, brogue, idiom, patois, provincialism
dialogue *n* = **conversation**, conference, discussion, communication, discourse
diary *n* = **journal**, blog (*informal*), chronicle, weblog, appointment book, daily record,

DICTIONARY

founded (1700) the first French colony in Louisiana
DiCaprio *n* **Leonardo**. born 1974, US film actor; his films include *Romeo and Juliet* (1996), *Titanic* (1997), and *The Gangs of New York* (2003)
dice *n, pl* **dice 1** small cube each of whose sides has a different number of spots (1 to 6), used in games of chance ▷ *v* **2** cut (food) into small cubes
▶ **dice with death** take a risk
▶ **dicey** *adj informal* dangerous or risky
dichotomy [die-**kot**-a-mee] *n, pl* **-mies** division into two opposed groups or parts
dick *n taboo, slang* penis
▶ **clever dick** obnoxiously smart or opinionated person
Dickens *n* **Charles** (**John Huffam**), pen name *Boz*. 1812–70, English novelist, famous for the humour and sympathy of his characterization and his criticism of social injustice. His major works include *The Pickwick Papers* (1837), *Oliver Twist* (1839), *Nicholas Nickleby* (1839), *The Old Curiosity Shop* (1840–41), *Martin Chuzzlewit* (1844), *David Copperfield* (1850), *Bleak House* (1853), *Little Dorrit* (1857), and *Great Expectations* (1861) **Dickensian** *adj*
Dickinson *n* **Emily**. 1830–86, US poet, noted for her short mostly unrhymed mystical lyrics
dicky[1] *n, pl* **dickies** false shirt front
▶ **dicky-bird** *n* child's word for a bird
dicky[2] *adj* **dickier, dickiest** *informal* shaky or weak: *a dicky heart*
Dictaphone *n* ® tape recorder for recording dictation for subsequent typing
dictate Ⓣ *v* **1** say aloud for another person to transcribe **2** give (commands) authoritatively ▷ *n* **3** authoritative command **4** guiding principle **dictation** *n*
▶ **dictator** *n* **1** ruler who has complete power **2** tyrannical person **dictatorship** *n*
▶ **dictatorial** *adj* like a dictator, tyrannical **dictatorially** *adv*
diction Ⓣ *n* manner of pronouncing words and sounds
dictionary Ⓣ *n, pl* **-aries 1** book that consists of an alphabetical list of words with their meanings **2** reference book listing terms and giving information about a particular subject
dictum *n, pl* **-tums, -ta 1** formal statement **2** popular saying
did *v* past tense of **do**
didactic *adj* intended to instruct **didactically** *adv*
diddle *v informal* swindle
Diderot *n* **Denis**. 1713–84, French philosopher, noted particularly for his direction (1745–72) of the great French *Encyclopédie*
didgeridoo *n music* Australian Aboriginal deep-toned wind instrument
didn't did not
die[1] Ⓣ *v* **dying, died 1** (of a person, animal, or plant) cease all biological activity permanently **2** (of something inanimate) cease to exist or function
▶ **be dying for** *informal* be eager for
▶ **die-hard** *n* person who resists change
die[2] *n* **1** shaped block used to cut or form metal **2** casting mould
Diefenbaker *n* **John George**. 1895–1979, Canadian Conservative statesman; prime minister of Canada (1957–63)
dieresis [die-**air**-iss-iss] *n, pl* **-ses** [-seez] mark (¨) placed over a vowel to show that it is pronounced separately from the preceding one, as in *Noël*

THESAURUS

engagement book, Filofax (*trademark*)
dictate *v* **1 = speak**, say, utter, read out **2 = order**, demand, direct, impose, command, pronounce, decree, lay down the law ▶ *n* **3 = command**, order, demand, direction, injunction, decree, edict, fiat **4 = principle**, rule, law, code
dictator *n* **= absolute ruler**, tyrant, despot, autocrat, oppressor
dictatorial *adj* **1 = absolute**, unlimited, unrestricted, arbitrary, autocratic, despotic, totalitarian, tyrannical **2 = domineering**, authoritarian, oppressive, imperious, bossy (*informal*), overbearing
dictatorship *n* **= absolute rule**, tyranny, totalitarianism, absolutism, authoritarianism, autocracy, despotism
diction *n* **= pronunciation**, speech, delivery, inflection, fluency, articulation, elocution, enunciation, intonation
dictionary *n* **= wordbook**, vocabulary, glossary, lexicon
die *v* **1 = pass away**, expire (*formal*), depart, perish (*formal*), pass on, bite the big one (*slang*), buy it (*slang*), check out (*slang*), kick it (*slang*), croak (*slang*), give up the ghost, go belly-up (*slang*), snuff it (*slang*), peg out (*informal*), kick the bucket (*slang*), buy the farm (*slang*), peg it (*informal*), pop your clogs (*informal*), breathe your last • *to die in an accident* **2 = fade away**, fade out, peter out • *My love for you will never die.* **3 = stop**, fail, halt, break down, fade out *or* fade away, fizzle out, lose power, peter out, run down ▷ **be dying = long**, desire, hunger, ache, yearn, be eager, pine for ▷ **die away** *See* **cease, fade** ▷ **die out = disappear**, fade, vanish • *That custom has died out now.*
die-hard *n* **= reactionary**, fanatic, old fogey, stick-in-the-mud (*informal*)

DICTIONARY

diesel *n* **1** diesel engine **2** vehicle driven by a diesel engine **3** *informal* diesel oil
▸ **diesel engine** internal-combustion engine in which oil is ignited by compression
▸ **diesel oil** fuel obtained from petroleum distillation
diet[1] Ⓣ *n* **1** food that a person or animal regularly eats **2** specific allowance of food, to control weight or for health reasons ▹ *v* **3** follow a special diet so as to lose weight ▹ *adj* **4** (of food or drink) suitable for eating with a weight-reduction diet **dietary** *adj* **dieter** *n*
▸ **dietary fibre** fibrous substances in fruit and vegetables that aid digestion
▸ **dietetic** *adj* prepared for special dietary requirements
▸ **dietetics** *pl n* study of food intake and preparation
▸ **dietician** *n* person who specializes in dietetics
diet[2] Ⓣ *n* parliament of some countries
Dietrich *n* **Marlene**, real name *Maria Magdalene von Losch*. 1901–92, US film actress and cabaret singer, born in Germany
differ Ⓣ *v* **1** be unlike **2** disagree
▸ **difference** *n* **1** state or quality of being unlike **2** disagreement **3** remainder left after subtraction
▸ **different** *adj* **1** unlike **2** unusual
differently *adv*
differential *adj* **1** of or using a difference **2** *math* involving differentials ▹ *n* **3** factor that differentiates between two comparable things **4** *math* slight difference between values in a scale **5** difference between rates of pay for different types of labour
▸ **differential calculus** branch of calculus concerned with derivatives and differentials
▸ **differential gear** mechanism in a road vehicle that allows one driving wheel to rotate faster than the other when cornering
▸ **differentiate** *v* **1** perceive or show the difference (between) **2** make (one thing) distinct from other such things **3** *math* determine the derivative of (a function or variable) **differentiation** *n*
difficult Ⓣ *adj* **1** requiring effort or skill to do or understand **2** not easily pleased **difficulty** *n*
diffident Ⓣ *adj* lacking self-confidence
diffidence *n* **diffidently** *adv*
diffract *v* cause to undergo diffraction
▸ **diffraction** *n physics* **1** deviation in the direction of a wave at the edge of an obstacle in its path **2** formation of light and dark fringes by the passage of light through a small aperture

d

THESAURUS

diet[1] *n* **1 = food**, fare, nourishment, sustenance, nutriment, provisions, rations, victuals **2 = regime**, fast, regimen, abstinence ▸ *v* **3 = slim**, fast, abstain, eat sparingly, lose weight
diet[2] *n* **= council**, meeting, parliament, legislature, convention, chamber, congress
differ *v* **1 = be dissimilar**, contrast, vary, contradict, diverge, depart from, run counter to, stand apart **2 = disagree**, debate, dispute, oppose, clash, contend, dissent, demur, take exception, take issue
difference *n* **1 = dissimilarity**, contrast, variation, discrepancy, distinction, disparity, divergence • *the vast difference in size* OPPOSITE: similarity **2 = remainder**, balance • *The difference is 853.* **3 = disagreement**, debate, dispute, conflict, clash, argument, quarrel, contretemps ▹ **difference of opinion** *See* **division**
See also: **change, gap**
different *adj* **1 = unlike**, disparate (*formal*), divergent (*formal*), dissimilar, contrasting, opposed • *We have totally different views.* OPPOSITE: similar **2 = unusual**, special, unique • *The result is interesting and different.* **3 = various**, another, individual, separate, distinct, discrete (*formal*) • *to support a different charity each year* ▹ **different from** *See* **unlike**
differentiate *v* **1 = distinguish**, separate, contrast, discriminate, make a distinction, mark off, set off *or* set apart, tell apart **2 = make different**, change, convert, modify, alter, adapt, transform
difficult *adj* **1 = hard**, uphill, arduous, demanding, intractable (*formal*), laborious • *a difficult decision to make* OPPOSITE: easy **2 = troublesome**, demanding, trying • *I hope they're not going to be difficult.* **3 = problematic**, complex, complicated, obscure, involved, intricate, abstruse, baffling, knotty
See also: **formidable, rough, serious, stiff, tough, tricky**
difficulty *n* **1 = problem**, trouble, hurdle, complication, snag, obstacle, pitfall, hassle (*informal*) • *The main difficulty is his inability to get along with others.* **2 = hardship**, strain, tribulation (*formal*) • *a problem of great difficulty* **3 = predicament**, trouble, jam (*informal*), mess, plight, embarrassment, dilemma, quandary, hot water (*informal*)
See also: **bother, distress, drawback, fix**
diffidence *n* **= shyness**, reserve, insecurity, modesty, hesitancy, bashfulness, self-consciousness, timidity
diffident *adj* **= shy**, modest, doubtful, hesitant, timid, insecure, reserved,

DICTIONARY

diffuse Ⓣ *v* **1** spread in all directions ▷ *adj* **2** widely spread **3** lacking conciseness **diffusely** *adv* **diffusion** *n*

dig Ⓣ *v* **digging, dug** (often foll. by *up*) **1** cut into, break up, and turn over or remove (earth etc.), esp. with a spade **2** (foll. by *out* or *up*) find by effort or searching **3** (foll. by *in* or *into*) thrust or jab ▷ *n* **4** act of digging **5** thrust or poke **6** cutting remark **7** archaeological excavation **digs 8** *informal* lodgings **digger** *n*

digest Ⓣ *v* **1** subject to a process of digestion **2** absorb mentally ▷ *n* **3** methodical compilation of information, often a condensed one **digestible** *adj*

▶ **digestion** *n* process of breaking down food into easily absorbed substances **digestive** *adj*

digit Ⓣ [**dij**-it] *n* **1** finger or toe **2** numeral from 0 to 9

▶ **digital** *adj* displaying information as numbers rather than with a dial: *digital clock* **digitally** *adv*

▶ **digital recording** sound-recording process that converts audio or analogue signals into a series of pulses

▶ **digitate** *adj* **1** (of leaves) shaped like a hand **2** (of animals) having digits

▶ **digitized** *adj computers* recorded or stored in digital form

digitalis *n* drug made from foxglove leaves, used as a heart stimulant

dignity Ⓣ *n, pl* **-ties 1** serious, calm, and controlled behaviour or manner **2** quality of being worthy of honour **3** sense of self-importance

▶ **dignify** *v* **-fying, -fied** give dignity to

▶ **dignitary** *n* person of high official position

digress Ⓣ *v* depart from the main subject in speech or writing **digression** *n* **digressive** *adj*

dike *n* same as **dyke**

dilapidated Ⓣ *adj* (of a building) having fallen into ruin **dilapidation** *n*

dilate Ⓣ *v* make or become wider or larger **dilation** *or* **dilatation** *n*

dilatory Ⓣ [**dill**-a-tree] *adj* tending or intended to waste time

dildo *n, pl* **-dos** object used as a substitute for an erect penis

dilemma Ⓣ *n* situation offering a choice between two equally undesirable alternatives

dilettante Ⓣ [dill-it-**tan**-tee] *n* person whose interest in a subject, esp. art, is superficial rather than serious **dilettantism** *n*

diligent Ⓣ *adj* **1** careful and persevering in carrying out duties **2** carried out with care and perseverance **diligently** *adv* **diligence** *n*

dill *n* sweet-smelling herb used for flavouring

dilly-dally *v* **-lying, -lied** *informal* dawdle or waste time

THESAURUS

unassuming, self-conscious, bashful, unassertive

diffuse *See* **distribute**

diffusion *See* **spread**

dig *v* **1** = **excavate**, tunnel, till, gouge, burrow, quarry, hollow out • *to dig a hole in the ground* **2** = **poke**, thrust, jab • *He could feel the coins digging into his palm.* **3** = **investigate**, research, search, probe, delve, dig down, go into **4** (with *out* or *up*) = **find**, discover, expose, uncover, unearth, uproot ▶ *n* **5** = **poke**, thrust, jab, prod • *a dig in the ribs* **6** = **cutting remark**, barb, insult, taunt, jeer, wisecrack (*informal*), sneer, gibe *See also*: **stick**

digest *v* **1** = **ingest**, absorb, incorporate, dissolve, assimilate **2** = **take in**, study, consider, understand, absorb, contemplate, grasp ▶ *n* **3** = **summary**, abstract, synopsis, epitome, abridgment, précis, résumé

digestion *n* = **ingestion**, conversion, transformation, absorption, assimilation, incorporation

digit *See* **figure, number**

dignified *adj* = **distinguished**, formal, grave, solemn, noble, stately, reserved, imposing

dignitary *n* = **public figure**, notable, worthy, high-up (*informal*), personage, pillar of society, V.I.P.

dignity *n* **1** = **decorum**, gravity, loftiness, majesty, grandeur, nobility, courtliness, solemnity, stateliness **2** = **honour**, status, rank, standing, importance, respectability, eminence **3** = **self-importance**, pride, self-esteem, self-respect

digress *v* = **wander**, depart, drift, stray, ramble, deviate, diverge, get off the point *or* get off the subject, go off at a tangent

digression *n* = **departure**, aside, diversion, detour, deviation, divergence, straying, wandering

dilapidated *adj* = **ruined**, rickety, decrepit, ramshackle, run-down, broken-down, crumbling, in ruins, tumbledown, raggedy

dilate *v* = **enlarge**, expand, stretch, widen, swell, broaden, puff out

dilatory *adj* = **time-wasting**, slow, sluggish, delaying, lingering, procrastinating, tardy, tarrying

dilemma *n* = **predicament**, problem, spot (*informal*), difficulty, puzzle, mess, plight, quandary

dilettante *n* = **amateur**, aesthete, dabbler, trifler

diligence *n* = **application**, industry, care, attention, perseverance, laboriousness

diligent *adj* = **hard-working**, careful,

DICTIONARY

dilute Ⓣ *v* **1** make (a liquid) less concentrated, esp. by adding water **2** make (a quality etc.) weaker in force **dilution** *n*
diluvial, diluvian *adj* of a flood, esp. the great Flood described in the Old Testament
dim Ⓣ *adj* **dimmer, dimmest 1** badly illuminated **2** not clearly seen **3** mentally dull ▷ *v* **dimming, dimmed 4** make or become dim **dimly** *adv* **dimness** *n*
▶ **take a dim view of** disapprove of
▶ **dimmer** *n* device for dimming an electric light
DiMaggio *n* **Joe**. 1914–99, US baseball player
dime *n* coin of Canada and the US, worth ten cents
dimension Ⓣ *n* **1** aspect or factor: *a new dimension to politics* **dimensions 2** scope or extent **3** measurement of the size of something in a particular direction
diminish Ⓣ *v* make or become smaller, fewer, or less **diminution** *n*
▶ **diminutive** *adj* **1** very small ▷ *n* **2** word or affix which implies smallness or unimportance **diminutiveness** *n*
diminuendo *n music* gradual decrease in loudness
dimple *n* **1** small natural dent, esp. in the cheeks or chin ▷ *v* **2** produce dimples by smiling
dimwit *n informal* stupid person **dim-witted** *adj*
din Ⓣ *n* **1** loud discordant confused noise ▷ *v* **dinning, dinned 2** instil (something) into someone by constant repetition
dinar [**dee**-nahr] *n* monetary unit of various Balkan, Middle Eastern, and North African countries
d'Indy *n* (**Paul Marie Theodore**) **Vincent**. 1851–1931, French composer. His works include operas, chamber music, and the *Symphony on a French Mountaineer's Song* (1866)
dine Ⓣ *v* eat dinner
▶ **diner** *n* **1** person eating a meal **2** small cheap restaurant
▶ **dining car** railway coach in which meals are served
▶ **dining room** room where meals are eaten
ding-dong *n* **1** sound of a bell **2** *informal* violent exchange of blows or words
dinghy [**ding**-ee] *n, pl* **-ghies** small boat, powered by sails, oars, or an outboard motor
dingle *n* small wooded dell
dingo *n, pl* **-goes** wild dog of Australia
dingy Ⓣ [**din**-jee] *adj* **-gier, -giest** dirty-looking, dull **dinginess** *n*
dinkum *adj Aust & NZ informal* genuine or right
dinky *adj* **-kier, -kiest** *informal* small and neat
dinner Ⓣ *n* **1** main meal of the day, taken either in the evening or at midday **2** official banquet
▶ **dinner jacket** man's semiformal evening jacket, usu. black
dinosaur *n* extinct prehistoric reptile, often of gigantic size
dint *n* **by dint of** by means of
diocese [**die**-a-siss] *n* district under the jurisdiction of a bishop **diocesan** *adj*
Diocletian *n* full name *Gaius Aurelius Valerius Diocletianus*. 245–313 AD, Roman emperor (284–305), who divided the empire into four administrative units (293) and instigated the

THESAURUS

persistent, painstaking, conscientious, tireless, attentive, industrious, assiduous, studious
dilute *v* **1 = water down**, cut, weaken, thin *or* thin out, adulterate, make thinner **2 = reduce**, decrease, weaken, diminish, temper, lessen, mitigate, diffuse, attenuate
diluted *See* **thin**
dim *adj* **1 = dull**, dark, grey, murky, shadowy, poorly lit • *the dim light of the streetlamp* **2 = vague**, faint, obscure, hazy, shadowy, indistinct • *a dim memory* OPPOSITE: clear **3** (*Informal*) **= stupid**, slow, thick (*informal*), dense, obtuse • *He is rather dim.* OPPOSITE: bright ▷ **take a dim view = disapprove**, suspect, reject, be displeased, be skeptical, look askance, take exception, view with disfavour ▶ *v* **4 = dull**, cloud, fade, obscure, darken, blur
See also: **soft**
dimension *n* (*often pl*) **= measurement**, size, capacity, volume, extent, bulk, amplitude, proportions
diminish *v* **1 = reduce**, lower, decrease, weaken, lessen • *This scandal has diminished her credibility.* **2 = dwindle**, contract, decline, shrink, wane, recede, subside, die out
See also: **abate, drop, fall**
diminutive *adj* **= small**, minute, little, tiny, mini, miniature, petite, undersized
dimness *See* **dark**
din *n* **= noise**, crash, row, uproar, clamour, racket, commotion, pandemonium, clatter ▶ *v* ▷ **din (something) into (someone) = instill**, teach, instruct, drum into, go on at, hammer into, inculcate
dine *v* **= eat**, lunch, feast, banquet, chow down (*slang*), sup
dingy *adj* **= dull**, dark, obscure, gloomy, murky, dim, dreary, drab, sombre
dinner *n* **= meal**, spread (*informal*), feast, banquet, main meal, repast

DICTIONARY

last severe persecution of the Christians (303)
diode *n* semiconductor device for converting alternating current to direct current
Diogenes *n* ?412–?323 BC, Greek Cynic philosopher, who rejected social conventions and advocated self-sufficiency and simplicity of life
Dion *n* **Céline**. born 1968, Canadian pop singer. Her recordings include "My Heart Will Go On" (1998)
Dionysius *n* called *the Elder*. ?430–367 BC, tyrant of Syracuse (405–367), noted for his successful campaigns against Carthage and S Italy
Diophantus *n* 3rd century AD, Greek mathematician, noted for his treatise on the theory of numbers, *Arithmetica*
dioptre [die-**op**-ter] *n* unit for measuring the refractive power of a lens
dioxide *n* oxide containing two oxygen atoms per molecule
dip Ⓣ *v* **dipping, dipped 1** plunge quickly or briefly into a liquid **2** slope downwards **3** switch (automobile headlights) from the main to the lower beam **4** lower briefly ▷ *n* **5** act of dipping **6** brief swim **7** liquid chemical in which farm animals are dipped to rid them of insects **8** depression, esp. in a landscape **9** creamy mixture into which pieces of food are dipped before being eaten ▶ **dip into** *v* read passages at random from (a book or journal)
DipEd Diploma in Education
diphtheria [dif-**theer**-ya] *n* contagious disease producing fever and difficulty in breathing and swallowing
diphthong *n* union of two vowel sounds in a single compound sound
diploma *n* document conferring a qualification or recording successful completion of a course of study
diplomacy Ⓣ *n* **1** conduct of the relations between nations by peaceful means **2** tact or skill in dealing with people ▶ **diplomat** *n* official engaged in diplomacy ▶ **diplomatic** *adj* **1** of or relating to diplomacy **2** tactful in dealing with people **diplomatically** *adv*
dipper *n* **1** ladle used for dipping **2** Also **ousel, ouzel** European songbird that lives by a river
dipsomania *n* compulsive craving for alcohol **dipsomaniac** *n, adj*
dipstick *n* notched rod dipped into a container to measure the level of a liquid
dipsy-doodle *Canad informal* ▷ *v* **-dling, -dled 1** *hockey* evade defenders by using swerves, feints, stickhandling, etc. ▷ *n* **2** an evasive movement of this sort
diptych [**dip**-tik] *n* painting on two hinged panels
Dirac *n* **Paul Adrien Maurice**. 1902–84, English physicist, noted for his work on the application of relativity to quantum mechanics and his prediction of electron spin and the positron: shared the Nobel prize for physics 1933
dire Ⓣ *adj* **1** desperate or urgent **2** indicating disaster
direct Ⓣ *adj* **1** (of a route) shortest, straight **2** without anyone or anything intervening **3** honest, frank ▷ *adv* **4** in a direct manner ▷ *v* **5** conduct or control the affairs of **6** give orders with authority to (a person or group) **7** tell (someone) the way to a place **8** address (a letter, package, remarks, etc.) **9** provide guidance to (actors, cameramen, etc.) in (a play or film) **directness** *n*

THESAURUS

dip *v* **1 = plunge**, duck, dunk, douse, immerse, bathe **2 = slope**, fall, drop *or* drop down, decline, lower, sink, descend, subside ▷ **dip into = sample**, browse, skim, peruse, glance at ▶ *n* **3 = plunge**, immersion, douche, drenching, ducking, soaking **4 = bathe**, swim, plunge, dive **5 = hollow**, hole, depression, slope, basin, incline, concavity **6 = drop**, fall, decline, slip, slump, sag, lowering
diplomacy *n* **1 = statesmanship**, international negotiation, statecraft **2 = tact**, skill, craft, discretion, delicacy, finesse, subtlety, artfulness, savoir-faire
diplomat *n* **= negotiator**, politician, mediator, conciliator, moderator, go-between, tactician
diplomatic *adj* **= tactful**, sensitive, subtle, prudent, polite, adept, discreet, politic
dire *adj* **1 = disastrous**, terrible, horrible, awful, catastrophic, woeful, ruinous, calamitous **2 = desperate**, critical, crucial, extreme, urgent, drastic, pressing, now or never **3 = grim**, dismal, gloomy, fearful, ominous, dreadful, portentous
direct *adj* **1 = straight**, personal, immediate, first-hand, uninterrupted • *the direct route* OPPOSITE: indirect **2 = straightforward**, straight, blunt, frank, candid, forthright • *He can sometimes be very direct*. OPPOSITE: devious **3 = immediate**, personal, head-on, face-to-face, first-hand **4 = explicit**, express, absolute, plain, blunt, point-blank, downright, unequivocal, unambiguous, categorical ▶ *v* **5 = control**, lead, run, manage, guide, oversee, supervise • *She will direct day-to-day operations at work*. **6 = order**, charge, bid, demand, command, dictate,

DICTIONARY

▶ **directly** *adv* **1** in a direct manner **2** at once ▷ *conj* **3** as soon as
▶ **direction** *n* **1** course or line along which a person or thing moves, points, or lies **2** management or guidance **directions 3** instructions for doing something or for reaching a place **directional** *adj*
▶ **directive** *n* instruction, order
▶ **director** *n* **1** person or thing that directs or controls **2** member of the governing board of a business etc. **3** person responsible for the artistic and technical aspects of the making of a film etc. **directorial** *adj* **directorship** *n*
▶ **directorate** *n* **1** board of directors **2** position of director
▶ **directory** *n* **1** book listing names, addresses, and telephone numbers of individuals and firms **2** *computers* area of a disk containing the names and locations of the files it currently holds
dirge Ⓣ *n* slow sad song of mourning
dirigible [dir-rij-jib-bl] *adj* **1** able to be steered ▷ *n* **2** airship
dirk *n* dagger, formerly worn by Scottish Highlanders
dirndl *n* (dress with) full gathered skirt
dirt Ⓣ *n* **1** unclean substance, filth **2** loose earth or soil **3** obscene speech or writing **4** *informal* scandal, harmful gossip
▶ **dirt track** racetrack made of packed earth or cinders
dirty Ⓣ *adj* **dirtier, dirtiest 1** covered or marked with dirt **2** unfair or dishonest **3** obscene **4** displaying dislike or anger: *a dirty look* ▷ *v* **dirtying, dirtied 5** make dirty **dirtiness** *n*
dis- *prefix* **1** *indicating* reversal: *disconnect* **2** *indicating* negation or lack: *dissimilar; disgrace* **3** *indicating* removal or release: *disembowel*
disable Ⓣ *v* make ineffective, unfit, or incapable **disablement** *n*
▶ **disabled** *adj* lacking one or more physical powers, such as the ability to walk
▶ **disability** *n* **1** condition of being physically or mentally impaired **2** something that disables someone
disabuse *v* (foll. by *of*) rid (someone) of a mistaken idea
disadvantage Ⓣ *n* unfavourable circumstance, thing, or situation **disadvantageous** *adj*
▶ **disadvantaged** *adj* socially or economically deprived
disaffected *adj* having lost loyalty to or affection for someone or something **disaffection** *n*

THESAURUS

instruct **7 = guide**, lead, show, indicate, point in the direction of, point the way **8 = address**, send, label, route, mail **9 = aim**, point, level, focus, train
See also: **administer, conduct, head, influence, require, tell**
direction *n* **1 = way**, course, route, path • *five kilometres in the opposite direction* **2 = management**, charge, control, leadership, command, guidance • *He was chopping vegetables under the chef's direction.*
directions *pl n* **= instructions**, plan, recommendation, guidance, briefing, guidelines, regulations
directive *n* **= order**, ruling, regulation, command, mandate, instruction, injunction, decree, edict
directly *adv* **1 = straight**, exactly, precisely, by the shortest route, in a beeline, unswervingly, without deviation **2 = honestly**, openly, point-blank, unequivocally, truthfully, plainly, straightforwardly **3 = at once**, immediately, promptly, straightaway, as soon as possible, forthwith, right away
director *n* **= controller**, head, leader, chief, executive, manager, governor, administrator, supervisor
directors *See* **management**
directory *See* **list**
dirge *n* **= lament**, requiem, dead march, elegy, funeral song, threnody
dirt *n* **1 = filth**, dust, mud, muck, grime • *I started to scrub off the dirt.* **2 = soil**, earth • *He drew a circle in the dirt with the stick.* **3 = obscenity**, pornography, indecency, sleaze, smut
See also: **gossip, ground**
dirty *adj* **1 = filthy**, muddy, grimy, unclean, grubby, mucky, soiled • *The kids' clothes are dirty.* OPPOSITE: clean **2 = dishonest**, corrupt, crooked • *a dirty fight* OPPOSITE: honest **3 = obscene**, blue, rude, pornographic, filthy • *a dirty joke* **4** (~ *look*) **= angry**, bitter, annoyed, resentful, choked, indignant, offended, scorching ▶ *v* **5 = soil**, foul, spoil, pollute, stain, muddy, blacken, defile, smirch
See also: **crude, indecent, shabby, vulgar**
disability *n* **1 = handicap**, complaint, disorder, defect, ailment, impairment, malady, affliction, infirmity **2 = incapacity**, inability, unfitness
disable *v* **1 = handicap**, damage, impair, paralyze, cripple, incapacitate, immobilize, enfeeble **2 = disqualify**, invalidate, render incapable *or* declare incapable
disabled *adj* **= handicapped**, paralyzed, weakened, lame, crippled, infirm, challenged (*informal*), incapacitated
disadvantage *n* **1 = drawback**, weakness, minus, handicap • *the advantages and*

d

DICTIONARY

disagree Ⓣ *v* **-greeing, -greed 1** have different opinions **2** fail to correspond **3** (foll. by *with*) cause physical discomfort (to): *curry disagrees with me* **disagreement** *n*
▸ **disagreeable** *adj* **1** (of a person) bad-tempered or disobliging **2** unpleasant **disagreeably** *adv*
disallow Ⓣ *v* reject as untrue or invalid
disappear Ⓣ *v* **1** cease to be visible **2** cease to exist **disappearance** *n*
disappoint Ⓣ *v* fail to meet the expectations or hopes of
▸ **disappointment** *n* **1** feeling of being disappointed **2** person or thing that disappoints
disapprobation *n* disapproval
disapprove Ⓣ *v* (foll. by *of*) consider wrong or bad **disapproval** *n*
disarm Ⓣ *v* **1** deprive of weapons **2** win the confidence or affection of **3** (of a nation) decrease the size of one's armed forces **disarmament** *n*
▸ **disarming** *adj* removing hostility or suspicion **disarmingly** *adv*
disarrange Ⓣ *v* throw into disorder **disarrangement** *n*
disarray Ⓣ *n* **1** confusion and lack of discipline **2** extreme untidiness
disassociate *v* same as **dissociate**
disaster Ⓣ *n* **1** occurrence that causes great distress or destruction **2** project etc. that fails **disastrous** *adj* **disastrously** *adv*

THESAURUS

disadvantages of changing the law OPPOSITE: advantage **2 = harm**, injury, loss, damage, hurt, prejudice, detriment, disservice
See also: **catch, snag**
disagree *v* **1 = differ**, dispute, dissent • *They can communicate even when they disagree.* OPPOSITE: agree **2 = object**, oppose, take issue with • *I disagree with that policy in general.* **3 = conflict**, counter, vary, differ, contradict, diverge, be dissimilar, run counter to **4 = make ill**, hurt, trouble, upset, sicken, bother, distress, discomfort, nauseate
See also: **argue, clash, protest**
disagreeable *adj* **1 = unpleasant**, nasty, horrible, objectionable, horrid, obnoxious • *a disagreeable odour* OPPOSITE: agreeable **2 = rude**, difficult, unpleasant, unfriendly, irritable, surly, bad-tempered, churlish, disobliging
See also: **sour, uncomfortable**
disagreement *n* **1 = argument**, dispute, difference, row, altercation (*formal*), squabble, quarrel, tiff • *My driving instructor and I had a brief disagreement.* OPPOSITE: agreement **2 = objection**, opposition, dissent • *Britain and France have expressed some disagreement with the proposal.* **3 = incompatibility**, difference, discrepancy, disparity, variance, divergence, incongruity, dissimilarity
See also: **conflict**
disallow *v* **= reject**, refuse, dismiss, rebuff, disavow, repudiate, disown
disappear *v* **1 = vanish**, fade, recede, be lost to view, drop out of sight • *The aircraft disappeared off the radar.* OPPOSITE: appear **2 = cease**, pass, vanish, die out, go away, melt away • *The pain has finally disappeared.*
See also: **melt**
disappearance *n* **= vanishing**, departure, eclipse, passing, going, evaporation, evanescence, melting
disappoint *v* **= let down**, fail, dismay, dissatisfy, disillusion, dishearten, disgruntle, disenchant
disappointed *adj* **= let down**, dejected, despondent, disenchanted, downcast, disillusioned, saddened • *I was disappointed that my best friend was not there.* OPPOSITE: satisfied
disappointing *adj* **= unsatisfactory**, sorry, sad, inadequate, insufficient, lousy (*slang*), depressing, disconcerting, discouraging
disappointment *n* **1 = regret**, despondency, dejection • *Book early to avoid disappointment.* **2 = let-down**, blow, setback • *The reunion was a bitter disappointment.*
See also: **failure**
disapproval *n* **= condemnation**, criticism, censure • *their disapproval of his coaching style* OPPOSITE: approval
See also: **opposition**
disapprove *v* **= condemn**, dislike, deplore (*formal*), find unacceptable, take a dim view of • *Everyone disapproved of their marrying so young.* OPPOSITE: approve
See also: **protest**
disapproving *See* **critical, severe**
disarm *v* **1 = render defenceless**, disable **2 = win over**, persuade, set at ease **3 = demilitarize**, disband, deactivate, demobilize
disarmament *n* **= arms reduction**, arms limitation, de-escalation, demilitarization, demobilization
disarming *adj* **= charming**, winning, irresistible, likable *or* likeable, persuasive
disarrange *v* **= disorder**, shake *or* shake up, mess *or* mess up, disturb, confuse, shuffle, scatter, jumble *or* jumble up, disorganize
disarray *n* **1 = confusion**, disorder, disorganization, disunity, indiscipline, unruliness **2 = untidiness**, chaos, clutter, mess, muddle, jumble, shambles
disaster *n* **= catastrophe**, tragedy, calamity

DICTIONARY

disavow *v* deny connection with or responsibility for (something) **disavowal** *n*
disband *v* (cause to) cease to function as a group or unit
disbelieve *v* **1** reject as false **2** (foll. by *in*) have no faith (in) **disbelief** *n*
disburse *v* pay out **disbursement** *n*
disc *n* **1** flat circular object **2** gramophone record **3** *anat* circular flat structure in the body, esp. between the vertebrae **4** *computers* same as **disk**
▸ **disc jockey** person who introduces and plays pop records on a radio programme or at a disco
discard Ⓣ *v* get rid of (something or someone) as useless or undesirable
discern Ⓣ *v* see or be aware of (something) clearly **discernible** *adj* **discernment** *n*
▸ **discerning** *adj* having or showing good judgment
discharge Ⓣ *v* **1** release, allow to go **2** dismiss (someone) from duty or employment **3** fire (a gun) **4** pour forth, emit **5** meet the demands of (an obligation etc.) **6** relieve oneself of (a responsibility or debt) ▹ *n* **7** something that is discharged **8** dismissal from duty or employment **9** pouring forth of a fluid, emission
disciple Ⓣ [diss-**sipe**-pl] *n* follower of the doctrines of a teacher, esp. Jesus Christ
discipline Ⓣ *n* **1** practice of imposing strict rules of behaviour on other people **2** ability to behave and work in a controlled manner **3** branch of learning ▹ *v* **4** (attempt to) improve the behaviour of (oneself or another) by training or rules **5** punish **disciplinary** *adj*
▸ **disciplinarian** *n* person who practises strict discipline
disclaim *v* deny (responsibility for or knowledge of something)
▸ **disclaimer** *n* repudiation, denial
disclose Ⓣ *v* **1** make known **2** allow to be seen **disclosure** *n*
disco *n, pl* **-cos 1** occasion at which people dance to pop records **2** place where such dances are held **3** mobile equipment for providing music for a disco
discolour Ⓣ *v* change in colour, stain **discoloration** *n*
discomfit *v* make uneasy or confused **discomfiture** *n*
discomfort Ⓣ *n* inconvenience, distress, or mild pain

THESAURUS

(*formal*), misfortune, train wreck, car crash, perfect storm • *another air disaster*
disastrous *adj* = **terrible**, fatal, tragic, catastrophic, ruinous, cataclysmic, calamitous, devastating
disbelief *n* = **skepticism**, doubt, distrust, mistrust, dubiety, incredulity, unbelief
discard *v* = **get rid of**, dump (*informal*), shed, jettison, cast aside, dispose of, throw away, throw out • *Read the instructions before discarding the box.*
See also: **banish**
discern *v* (*Formal*) = **see**, spot, notice, detect, observe, perceive, make out • *trying to discern a pattern in his behaviour*
See also: **distinguish, tell**
discernment *See* **wisdom**
discharge *v* **1** = **emit**, release, empty, expel, flush, give off • *The motorboat discharged fuel into the lake.* **2** = **release**, free, liberate, let go, set free • *He has a broken nose, but may be discharged today.* **3** = **dismiss**, fire, remove, oust, sack (*informal*), expel, eject, discard, cashier, give (someone) the boot (*slang*), give (someone) the sack (*informal*) • *discharged when caught stealing a computer* **4** = **fire**, shoot, explode, detonate, let loose (*informal*), let off, set off **5** = **carry out**, do, perform, execute, observe, accomplish, fulfil **6** = **pay**, meet, clear, settle, satisfy, relieve, honor, square up ▸ *n* **7** = **dismissal**, ejection, expulsion, the sack (*informal*) • *a dishonourable discharge from the army* **8** = **release**, pardon, clearance, acquittal, liberation **9** = **firing**, report, shot, blast, explosion, burst, salvo, volley, detonation **10** = **emission**, ooze, secretion, seepage, excretion, pus, suppuration
See also: **drain, dump**
disciple *n* = **follower**, student, supporter, pupil, devotee, apostle, adherent
disciplinarian *n* = **authoritarian**, tyrant, stickler, despot, martinet, taskmaster
discipline *n* **1** = **training**, practice, regulation, exercise, drill, method, regimen **2** = **punishment**, correction, castigation, chastisement **3** = **self-control**, control, conduct, regulation, restraint, orderliness, strictness **4** = **field of study**, area, course, subject, specialty, curriculum, branch of knowledge ▸ *v* **5** = **train**, prepare, exercise, drill, educate, bring up **6** = **punish**, correct, penalize, chastise, reprimand, castigate, chasten, bring to book, reprove
disclose *v* **1** = **make known**, publish, broadcast, reveal, relate, communicate, confess, divulge, let slip **2** = **show**, reveal, unveil, expose, uncover, bring to light, lay bare
disclosure *n* = **revelation**, announcement, leak, publication, declaration, confession, admission, acknowledgment, divulgence
discolour *v* = **stain**, mark, streak, soil, fade, tarnish, tinge
discomfort *n* **1** = **pain**, hurt, ache, malaise,

DICTIONARY

discommode *v* cause inconvenience to **discommodious** *adj*
discompose *v* disturb the composure of, disconcert **discomposure** *n*
disconcert Ⓣ *v* disturb the confidence or self-possession of
disconnect Ⓣ *v* **1** undo or break the connection between (two things) **2** stop the supply of (electricity or gas) of ▷ *n* **3** lack of a connection; disconnection: *a disconnect between political discourse and the public* **disconnection** *n*
▶ **disconnected** *adj* (of speech or ideas) not logically connected
disconsolate Ⓣ *adj* sad beyond comfort **disconsolately** *adv*
discontent Ⓣ *n* lack of contentment, as with one's lot in life **discontented** *adj* **discontentedly** *adv*
discontinue Ⓣ *v* **-uing, -ued** come or bring to an end
▶ **discontinuous** *adj* characterized by interruptions
▶ **discontinuity** *n* lack of smooth or unbroken development
discord Ⓣ *n* **1** lack of agreement or harmony between people **2** harsh confused sounds **discordant** *adj* **discordance** *n*
discotheque *n* full name for **disco**
discount Ⓣ *v* **1** leave (something) out of account as being unreliable, prejudiced, or irrelevant **2** deduct (an amount) from the price of something ▷ *n* **3** deduction from the full price of something
discountenance *v* make (someone) ashamed or confused
discourage Ⓣ *v* **1** deprive of the will to persist in something **2** oppose by expressing disapproval **discouragement** *n*
discourse Ⓣ *n* **1** conversation **2** formal treatment of a subject in speech or writing ▷ *v* **3** (foll. by *on*) speak or write (about) at length
discourteous Ⓣ *adj* showing bad manners **discourteously** *adv* **discourtesy** *n*

THESAURUS

irritation, soreness **2 = uneasiness**, trouble, distress, hardship, nuisance, irritation, annoyance
disconcert *v* **= disturb**, worry, upset, rattle (*informal*), unsettle, faze, fluster, perturb, take aback
disconcerting *adj* **= disturbing**, confusing, awkward, alarming, bewildering, distracting, embarrassing, perplexing, upsetting
disconnect *v* **= cut off**, part, separate, divide, sever, detach, disengage, take apart, uncouple
disconnected *adj* **= illogical**, confused, incoherent, rambling, disjointed, unintelligible, jumbled, mixed-up
disconsolate *adj* **= inconsolable**, miserable, crushed, dejected, heartbroken, desolate, grief-stricken, wretched, forlorn
discontent *n* **= dissatisfaction**, regret, displeasure, envy, unhappiness, restlessness, uneasiness
discontented *adj* **= dissatisfied**, unhappy, disgruntled, disaffected, displeased, exasperated, fed up, vexed
discontinue *v* **= stop**, end, drop, suspend, quit, abandon, cease, terminate, break off, give up
discord *n* **1 = disagreement**, division, conflict, strife, friction, dissension, incompatibility, disunity **2 = disharmony**, racket, cacophony, din, tumult, harshness, dissonance, jarring
discordant *adj* **1 = disagreeing**, different, contrary, contradictory, incompatible, conflicting, at odds, clashing **2 = inharmonious**, harsh, strident, shrill, grating, cacophonous, dissonant, jarring
discount *v* **1 = leave out**, ignore, overlook, disregard, disbelieve, brush off (*slang*), pass over **2 = deduct**, reduce, lower, mark down, take off ▶ *n* **3 = deduction**, cut, reduction, concession, rebate
discourage *v* **1 = put off**, deter, dissuade, daunt • *Don't let these problems discourage you.* **2 = dishearten**, intimidate, depress, dampen, demoralize, dispirit, deject, overawe, put a damper on OPPOSITE: encourage
discouraged *adj* **= put off**, glum, dismayed, downcast, crestfallen, deterred, disheartened, dispirited, down in the mouth
discouragement *n* **1 = loss of confidence**, depression, disappointment, dismay, despair, despondency, dejection, downheartedness **2 = deterrent**, opposition, setback, obstacle, impediment, damper, hindrance, disincentive
discouraging *adj* **= disheartening**, daunting, dampening, depressing, disappointing, dispiriting, unfavourable
discourse *n* **1 = conversation**, talk, speech, discussion, communication, chat, dialogue, seminar **2 = speech**, lecture, essay, sermon, homily, treatise, dissertation, oration ▶ *v* **3 = hold forth**, talk, speak, expatiate
discourteous *adj* **= rude**, disrespectful, boorish, bad-mannered, ill-mannered, impolite, insolent, offhand, ungentlemanly, ungracious
discourtesy *n* **1 = rudeness**,

DICTIONARY

discover Ⓣ *v* **1** be the first to find or to find out about **2** learn about for the first time **3** find after study or search **discoverer** *n*
▸ **discovery** *n* **1** act of discovering **2** person, place, or thing that has been discovered
discredit Ⓣ *v* **1** damage the reputation of (someone) **2** cause (an idea) to be disbelieved or distrusted ▹ *n* **3** (something that causes) damage to someone's reputation
▸ **discreditable** *adj* bringing discredit
discreet Ⓣ *adj* **1** careful to avoid embarrassment, esp. by keeping confidences secret **2** unobtrusive **discreetly** *adv*
discrepancy Ⓣ *n, pl* **-cies** conflict or variation between facts, figures, or claims
discrete Ⓣ *adj* separate or distinct
discretion Ⓣ [diss-**kresh**-on] *n* **1** quality of behaving in a discreet way **2** freedom or authority to make judgments and to act as one sees fit **discretionary** *adj*
discriminate Ⓣ *v* **1** (foll. by *against* or *in favour of*) single out a particular person or group for special disfavour *or* favour **2** (foll. by *between* or *among*) recognize or understand the difference (between) **discrimination** *n*
▸ **discriminating** *adj* showing good taste and judgment
▸ **discriminatory** *adj* based on prejudice
discursive *adj* passing from one topic to another
discus *n* disc-shaped object with a heavy middle, thrown in sports competitions
discuss Ⓣ *v* **1** consider (something) by talking it over **2** treat (a subject) in speech or writing **discussion** *n*
disdain Ⓣ *n* **1** feeling of superiority and dislike ▹ *v* **2** refuse with disdain **disdainful** *adj* **disdainfully** *adv*
disease Ⓣ *n* illness, sickness **diseased** *adj*
disembark Ⓣ *v* (cause to) land from a ship, aircraft, or bus **disembarkation** *n*
disembodied *adj* **1** lacking a body **2** seeming not to be attached to or coming from anyone

THESAURUS

bad manners, disrespectfulness, impertinence, impoliteness, incivility, insolence **2 = insult**, slight, snub, rebuff, affront, cold shoulder, kick in the teeth (*slang*)
discover *v* **1 = find**, unearth, come across, stumble on *or* stumble across • *to discover a new planet* **2 = find out**, learn, recognize, notice, realize, detect, uncover, perceive, ascertain
See also: **determine, hear, observe, see**
discovery *n* **1 = finding**, location, disclosure, exploration, revelation, detection, uncovering **2 = breakthrough**, find, secret, invention, innovation
discredit *v* **1 = disgrace**, smear, defame, disparage, vilify, slander, dishonour, bring into disrepute **2 = doubt**, question, deny, challenge, dispute, discount, distrust, mistrust, disbelieve ▸ *n* **3 = disgrace**, scandal, shame, stigma, disrepute, dishonour, ignominy, ill-repute
discreditable *adj* **= disgraceful**, shameful, scandalous, reprehensible, ignominious, unworthy, dishonourable
discreet *adj* **= tactful**, diplomatic, careful, cautious, wary, prudent, considerate, guarded, judicious, circumspect
discrepancy *n* **= disagreement**, difference, conflict, variation, disparity, inconsistency, contradiction, divergence, incongruity
discrete *adj* **= separate**, individual, distinct, disconnected, detached, discontinuous, unattached
discretion *n* **1 = tact**, caution, consideration, diplomacy, prudence, wariness, carefulness, judiciousness **2 = choice**, will, pleasure, preference, inclination, volition
discretionary *See* **flexible**
discriminate *v* **1 = show prejudice**, favour, victimize, show bias, single out, treat as inferior, treat differently **2 = differentiate**, separate, distinguish, segregate, draw a distinction, tell the difference
discriminating *adj* **= discerning**, particular, refined, selective, tasteful, cultivated, fastidious
discrimination *n* **1 = prejudice**, bias, intolerance, bigotry, unfairness, favouritism **2 = discernment**, taste, judgment, perception, refinement, subtlety
discuss *v* **= talk about**, debate, exchange views on, go into • *I will be discussing the situation with students tomorrow.*
discussion *n* **= talk**, debate, conversation, dialogue, consultation, discourse • *informal discussions*
See also: **conference, word**
disdain *n* **1 = contempt**, scorn, arrogance, derision, haughtiness, superciliousness ▸ *v* **2 = scorn**, reject, slight, disregard, spurn, deride, look down on, sneer at
disdainful *adj* **= contemptuous**, proud, superior, arrogant, aloof, derisive, haughty, scornful, sneering, supercilious
disease *n* **= illness**, condition, infection, complaint, disorder, ailment, sickness, malady, affliction, infirmity
diseased *adj* **= sick**, infected, ailing, unhealthy, rotten, unwell, sickly, unsound, unwholesome
disembark *v* **= land**, arrive, alight, get off, go ashore, step out of

DICTIONARY

disembowel *v* **-elling, -elled** remove the entrails of
disenchanted ⓣ *adj* disappointed and disillusioned (with something) **disenchantment** *n*
disenfranchise *v* deprive (a person) of the right to vote or of other rights of citizenship
disengage ⓣ *v* release from a connection **disengagement** *n*
disentangle ⓣ *v* release from entanglement or confusion **disentanglement** *n*
disequilibrium *n* loss or absence of stability or balance
disfavour ⓣ *n* disapproval or dislike
disfigure ⓣ *v* spoil the appearance or shape of **disfigurement** *n*
disfranchise *v* same as **disenfranchise**
disgorge ⓣ *v* **1** vomit **2** discharge (contents)
disgrace ⓣ *n* **1** condition of shame, loss of reputation, or dishonour **2** shameful person or thing ▷ *v* **3** bring shame upon (oneself or others) **disgraceful** *adj* **disgracefully** *adv*
disgruntled ⓣ *adj* sulky or discontented **disgruntlement** *n*
disguise ⓣ *v* **1** change the appearance or manner in order to conceal the identity of (someone or something) **2** misrepresent (something) in order to obscure its actual nature or meaning ▷ *n* **3** mask, costume, or manner that disguises **4** state of being disguised
disgust ⓣ *n* **1** great loathing or distaste ▷ *v* **2** sicken, fill with loathing
dish ⓣ *n* **1** shallow container used for holding or serving food **2** portion or variety of food **3** short for **4** *informal* attractive person
▸ **dish aerial** aerial consisting of a concave disc-shaped reflector
▸ **dishcloth** *n* cloth for washing dishes
▸ **dish out** *v informal* distribute
▸ **dish up** *v informal* serve (food)
dishabille [diss-a-**beel**] *n* state of being partly dressed
disharmony *n* lack of agreement, discord
dishearten ⓣ *v* weaken or destroy the hope, courage, or enthusiasm of
dishevelled ⓣ *adj* (of a person's hair, clothes, or general appearance) disordered and untidy
dishonest ⓣ *adj* not honest or fair **dishonestly** *adv* **dishonesty** *n*

THESAURUS

disenchanted *adj* = **disillusioned**, disappointed, indifferent, cynical, soured, jaundiced, let down, sick of
disenchantment *n* = **disillusionment**, disappointment, disillusion, rude awakening
disengage *v* = **release**, free, loosen, extricate, untie, disentangle, set free, unloose
disentangle *v* = **untangle**, free, loose, unravel, disconnect, extricate, disengage
disfavour *n* = **disapproval**, dislike, displeasure, disapprobation
disfigure *v* = **damage**, mar, scar, distort, mutilate, blemish, deface, deform
disfigured *See* **distorted**
disgorge *v* = **vomit**, empty, expel, discharge, eject
disgrace *n* **1** = **shame**, scandal • *to bring disgrace upon the whole team* OPPOSITE: credit **2** = **stain**, scandal, stigma, slur, blemish, blot, reproach ▸ *v* **3** = **shame**, discredit • *to disgrace their family's name*
See also: **humble, humiliate**
disgraceful *adj* = **shameful**, shocking, scandalous • *disgraceful behaviour*
disgruntled *adj* = **discontented**, grumpy, annoyed, irritated, dissatisfied, displeased, peeved, put out, vexed
disguise *v* **1** = **hide**, cover, screen, mask, cloak, veil, conceal, shroud, camouflage **2** = **misrepresent**, fake, falsify ▸ *n* **3** = **costume**, cover, screen, mask, veil, camouflage **4** = **façade**, front, deception, pretense, trickery, veneer, semblance, dissimulation
disguised *adj* = **in disguise**, fake, false, undercover, covert, masked, camouflaged, feigned, incognito
disgust *n* **1** = **revulsion**, nausea, repulsion • *his disgust at the incident* ▸ *v* **2** = **sicken**, revolt, repel • *He disgusted many with his behaviour.*
See also: **horrify, horror, shock**
disgusted *adj* = **sickened**, appalled, nauseated, offended, repulsed, scandalized
disgusting *adj* = **sickening**, foul, gross, repellent, vile, obnoxious, revolting • *one of the most disgusting sights I had ever seen*
See also: **nasty**
dish *n* **1** = **bowl**, plate, platter, salver **2** = **food**, fare, recipe
dishearten *v* = **discourage**, deter, depress, dismay, dispirit, cast down, deject, put a damper on
dishevelled *adj* = **untidy**, messy, bedraggled, disordered, ruffled, rumpled, tousled, uncombed, unkempt
dishonest *adj* = **deceitful**, corrupt, fraudulent, crooked, hypocritical, lying • *It would be dishonest to mislead people.* OPPOSITE: honest
See also: **dubious, insincere, sneaky, two-faced**
dishonesty *n* = **deceit**, corruption, trickery, cheating • *She accused the government of dishonesty.* OPPOSITE: honesty
See also: **lying**

DICTIONARY

dishonour Ⓣ *v* **1** treat with disrespect ▷ *n* **2** lack of respect **3** state of shame or disgrace **4** something that causes a loss of honour **dishonourable** *adj* **dishonourably** *adv*
disillusion *v* **1** destroy the illusions or false ideas of ▷ *n* **2** Also **disillusionment** state of being disillusioned
disincentive *n* something that acts as a deterrent
disinclined Ⓣ *adj* unwilling or reluctant **disinclination** *n*
disinfect Ⓣ *v* rid of harmful germs, esp. by chemical means **disinfection** *n* ▸ **disinfectant** *n* substance that destroys harmful germs
disinformation *n* false information intended to mislead
disingenuous *adj* not sincere **disingenuously** *adv*
disinherit Ⓣ *v law* deprive (an heir) of inheritance **disinheritance** *n*
disintegrate Ⓣ *v* break up into fragments **disintegration** *n*
disinter *v* **-terring, -terred 1** dig up **2** reveal, make known
disinterested Ⓣ *adj* free from bias or involvement **disinterest** *n*
disjointed Ⓣ *adj* **1** having no coherence **2** disconnected
disk *n computers* storage device, consisting of a stack of plates coated with a magnetic layer, which rotates rapidly as a single unit
dislike Ⓣ *v* **1** consider unpleasant or disagreeable ▷ *n* **2** feeling of not liking something or someone
dislocate *v* **1** displace (a bone or joint) from its normal position **2** disrupt or shift out of place **dislocation** *n*
dislodge Ⓣ *v* remove (something) from a previously fixed position
disloyal Ⓣ *adj* not loyal, deserting one's allegiance **disloyalty** *n*
dismal Ⓣ *adj* **1** causing gloom or depression **2** *informal* of poor quality **dismally** *adv*
dismantle Ⓣ *v* take apart piece by piece
dismay Ⓣ *v* **1** fill with alarm or depression

THESAURUS

dishonour *v* **1 = shame**, disgrace, defame, discredit, degrade, sully, debase, debauch ▸ *n* **2 = shame**, scandal, disgrace, discredit, disrepute, infamy, reproach, ignominy, obloquy **3 = insult**, abuse, slight, outrage, offence, indignity, affront, discourtesy, sacrilege
dishonourable *adj* **1 = shameful**, infamous, disgraceful, despicable, scandalous, lousy (*slang*), ignominious, contemptible, discreditable, scuzzy (*slang*) **2 = untrustworthy**, corrupt, treacherous, shameless, unscrupulous, disreputable, unprincipled
disillusioned *adj* **= disenchanted**, disappointed, enlightened, disabused, undeceived
disinclination *n* **= reluctance**, opposition, resistance, objection, dislike, unwillingness, aversion, hesitance, repugnance
disinclined *adj* **= reluctant**, resistant, unwilling, loath, averse, hesitating, not in the mood, opposed
disinfect *v* **= sterilize**, clean, sanitize, cleanse, purify, decontaminate, deodorize, fumigate
disinfectant *n* **= antiseptic**, germicide, sterilizer
disinherit *v* (*Law*) **= cut off**, oust, repudiate, disown, dispossess
disintegrate *v* **= break up**, crumble, fragment, fall apart, fall to pieces • *The sculpture fell off the table and disintegrated.*
See also: **erode**
disinterest *n* **= impartiality**, neutrality, fairness, detachment
disinterested *adj* **= impartial**, objective, neutral, unbiased, even-handed, dispassionate, detached, impersonal, unprejudiced
disjointed *adj* **= incoherent**, confused, rambling, disconnected, disordered
dislike *v* **1 = hate**, loathe, detest, abhor (*formal*), be averse to, not be able to abide, not be able to bear, not be able to stand • *We don't serve it often because many people dislike it.* OPPOSITE: like ▸ *n* **2 = hatred**, hostility, animosity, distaste, aversion, loathing, antipathy • *She looked at him with dislike.* OPPOSITE: liking
See also: **disapprove, resent**
disliked *See* **unpopular**
dislodge *v* **= displace**, remove, oust, disturb, uproot, extricate, force out, knock loose
disloyal *adj* **= treacherous**, false, subversive, untrustworthy, unfaithful, faithless, traitorous, two-faced
disloyalty *n* **= treachery**, treason, infidelity, back-stabbing (*informal*), breach of trust, deceitfulness, double-dealing, falseness, inconstancy, unfaithfulness
dismal *adj* **= gloomy**, dark, bleak, dreary, sombre, wretched, cheerless, depressing, discouraging, forlorn
dismantle *v* **= take apart**, strip, demolish, disassemble, take to pieces
dismay *v* **1 = alarm**, scare, paralyze, terrify, frighten, distress, horrify, appall, unnerve **2 = disappoint**, discourage, disillusion, dishearten, daunt, dispirit, put off ▸ *n* **3 = alarm**, fear, horror, anxiety, dread, apprehension, trepidation,

DICTIONARY

▷ *n* **2** alarm mixed with sadness
dismember Ⓣ *v* **1** remove the limbs of **2** cut to pieces **dismemberment** *n*
dismiss Ⓣ *v* **1** remove (an employee) from a job **2** allow (someone) to leave **3** put out of one's mind **4** (of a judge) state that (a case) will not be brought to trial **dismissal** *n*
▸ **dismissive** *adj* scornful, contemptuous
dismount *v* get off a horse or a bicycle
Disney *n* **Walt(er Elias)**. 1901–66, US film producer, who pioneered animated cartoons: noted esp. for his creations *Mickey Mouse* and *Donald Duck* and films such as *Fantasia* (1940)
Disneyesque *adj*
disobey Ⓣ *v* neglect or refuse to obey
disobedient *adj* **disobedience** *n*
disobliging *adj* unwilling to help
disorder Ⓣ *n* **1** state of untidiness and disorganization **2** public violence or rioting **3** an illness
▸ **disordered** *adj* untidy
▸ **disorderly** *adj* **1** very untidy, disorganized **2** uncontrolled, unruly
disorganize *v* disrupt the arrangement or system of **disorganization** *n*
disorientate, disorient *v* cause (someone) to lose his or her bearings **disorientation** *n*
disown Ⓣ *v* deny any connection with (someone)
disparage Ⓣ *v* speak contemptuously of **disparagement** *n*
disparate Ⓣ *adj* utterly different in kind **disparity** *n*
dispassionate Ⓣ *adj* uninfluenced by emotion **dispassionately** *adv*
dispatch Ⓣ *v* **1** send off to a destination or to perform a task **2** carry out (a duty or a task) with speed **3** *old-fashioned* kill ▷ *n* **4** official communication or report, sent in haste **5** report sent to a newspaper by a correspondent
▸ **dispatch rider** motorcyclist who carries dispatches
dispel Ⓣ *v* **-pelling, -pelled** disperse or drive away
dispense Ⓣ *v* **1** distribute in portions **2** prepare and distribute (medicine) **3** administer (the law etc.) **dispenser** *n*

THESAURUS

consternation **4 = disappointment**, disillusionment, chagrin, discouragement
dismember *v* **= cut into pieces**, sever, amputate, mutilate, dissect
dismiss *v* **1 = discharge**, fire (*informal*), remove, sack (*informal*), axe (*informal*), cashier, give notice to, give (someone) their marching orders, lay off **2 = let go**, release, free, dissolve, disperse, send away **3 = put out of one's mind**, reject, banish, dispel, discard, disregard, lay aside, set aside
dismissal *n* **= the sack** (*informal*), notice, removal, expulsion, marching orders (*informal*), the boot (*slang*)
disobedience *n* **= defiance**, revolt, insubordination, mutiny, indiscipline, noncompliance, nonobservance, recalcitrance, unruliness, waywardness
disobedient *adj* **= defiant**, contrary, undisciplined, naughty, disorderly, unruly, wayward, intractable, insubordinate, refractory
disobey *v* **= defy**, break, violate, infringe, flout • *He was forever disobeying the rules*. OPPOSITE: obey
disorder *n* **1 = untidiness**, disarray, clutter, muddle • *Inside, all was disorder*. OPPOSITE: order **2 = confusion**, chaos, turmoil, disarray • *Regular fire drills prevent disorder in a real emergency*. **3 = illness**, disease, condition, complaint, ailment, affliction • *a rare nerve disorder* **4 = disturbance**, riot, turmoil, unrest, uproar, commotion, unruliness
See also: **mess**
disordered *See* **confused**
disorderly *adj* **1 = untidy**, chaotic, confused, disorganized, messy, jumbled **2 = unruly**, turbulent, tumultuous, disruptive, lawless, rowdy, indisciplined, riotous, ungovernable
disorganization *See* **confusion, muddle**
disorganized *adj* **= muddled**, chaotic, confused, haphazard, disordered, jumbled, unsystematic
disown *v* **= deny**, reject, renounce, disavow, repudiate, cast off, disclaim
disparage *v* **= run down**, ridicule, deride, vilify, malign, slander, denigrate, belittle, deprecate, put down
disparagement *See* **criticism**
disparaging *See* **abusive, critical**
disparate *See* **different, various**
disparity *See* **difference, gap**
dispassionate *adj* **1 = unemotional**, cool, calm, serene, collected, composed, imperturbable, unruffled **2 = objective**, fair, neutral, impartial, unbiased, disinterested, detached, impersonal, unprejudiced
dispatch *v* **1 = send**, dismiss, hasten, consign **2 = carry out**, finish, perform, settle, discharge, dispose of **3 = murder**, kill, slay, execute, slaughter, assassinate ▸ *n* **4 = message**, report, news, story, account, communication, bulletin, communiqué
dispel *v* **= drive away**, eliminate, dismiss, expel, banish, disperse, chase away
dispense *v* **1 = distribute**, share, assign, allocate, allot, apportion, deal out, dole out **2 = prepare**, supply, measure, mix **3 = administer**, operate, apply, execute, implement, enforce, discharge, carry out

DICTIONARY

▸ **dispensable** *adj* not essential
▸ **dispensation** *n* **1** act of dispensing **2** exemption from an obligation **3** administrative system
▸ **dispensary** *n* place where medicine is dispensed
▸ **dispense with** *v* **1** do away with **2** manage without
disperse Ⓣ *v* **1** scatter over a wide area **2** (cause to) leave a gathering **dispersal** *or* **dispersion** *n*
dispirit *v* make downhearted
displace Ⓣ *v* **1** move from the usual location **2** remove from office **displacement** *n*
▸ **displaced person** person forced from his or her home or country, esp. by war or revolution
display Ⓣ *v* **1** make visible or noticeable ▹ *n* **2** act of displaying **3** something displayed **4** exhibition
displease Ⓣ *v* annoy **displeasure** *n*
disport *v* **disport oneself** indulge oneself in pleasure
dispose Ⓣ *v* place in a particular way
▸ **disposable** *adj* **1** designed to be thrown away after use **2** available for use if needed: *disposable assets*
▸ **disposal** *n* getting rid of something
▸ **at one's disposal** available for use
▸ **disposed** *adj* **1** willing (to do something) **2** inclined as specified (towards someone or something): *well disposed*
▸ **disposition** *n* **1** person's usual temperament **2** tendency **3** arrangement
▸ **dispose of** *v* **1** throw away **2** give or sell to another **3** deal with (a problem, etc.) **4** kill
dispossess *v* (foll. by *of*) deprive (someone) of (a possession) **dispossession** *n*
disproportion Ⓣ *n* lack of proportion or equality **disproportionate** *adj* **disproportionately** *adv*
disprove Ⓣ *v* show (an assertion or claim) to be incorrect
dispute Ⓣ *n* **1** disagreement between workers and their employers **2** argument ▹ *v* **3** argue about (something) **4** doubt the validity of **5** fight over possession of
▸ **disputation** *n formal* argument

THESAURUS

▹ **dispense with** = **do away with**, cancel, abolish, brush aside, dispose of, get rid of; = **do without**, relinquish, forgo, abstain from, give up
disperse *v* **1** = **scatter**, broadcast, spread, distribute, strew, disseminate, diffuse **2** = **break up**, separate, dissolve, scatter, disband
dispirited *adj* = **disheartened**, sad, depressed, gloomy, dejected, despondent, glum, discouraged, downcast, crestfallen
displace *v* **1** = **move**, shift, disturb, misplace, transpose **2** = **replace**, oust, succeed, supplant, supersede, take the place of
display *v* **1** = **show**, reveal, present, expose, exhibit, disclose, demonstrate, manifest **2** = **show off**, parade, flourish, flaunt, vaunt ▸ *n* **3** = **exhibition**, show, demonstration, presentation, array, revelation **4** = **show**, parade, flourish, spectacle, pageant, pomp, ostentation
displease *v* = **annoy**, upset, anger, offend, irk, pique, irritate, vex, put out
displeasure *n* = **annoyance**, anger, dissatisfaction, resentment, irritation, disapproval, indignation, distaste
disposable *adj* **1** = **throwaway**, biodegradable, nonreturnable **2** = **available**, expendable, consumable
disposal *n* = **throwing away**, removal, ejection, riddance, discarding, dumping (*informal*), jettisoning, scrapping ▹ **at one's disposal** = **available**, expendable, consumable, at one's service, free for use
dispose *v* = **arrange**, group, put, place, order, distribute, array, marshal ▹ **dispose of** = **get rid of**, dump, discard, jettison, dispense with, throw away • *Dispose of your garbage in the proper containers.*
See also: **process, settle**
disposed *See* **prone**
disposition *n* **1** = **character**, nature, spirit, constitution, temper, make-up, temperament **2** = **tendency**, habit, bias, bent, inclination, leaning, propensity, proclivity **3** = **arrangement**, organization, distribution, placement, classification, grouping, ordering
disproportion *n* = **inequality**, imbalance, discrepancy, disparity, asymmetry, lopsidedness, unevenness
disproportionate *adj* = **unequal**, excessive, unreasonable, uneven, unbalanced, inordinate, out of proportion
disprove *v* = **prove false**, refute, discredit, invalidate, give the lie to • *the statistics that will prove or disprove the statement* OPPOSITE: prove
dispute *n* **1** = **argument**, conflict, row, clash, feud, disagreement, wrangle, turf war (*informal*) • *The dispute between them is settled.* **2** = **disagreement**, debate, discussion, controversy, argument, contention, dissension ▸ *v* **3** = **contest**, question, deny, challenge, contradict, query • *He disputed the allegations.* OPPOSITE: accept **4** = **argue**, debate, clash, squabble, quarrel, cross swords
See also: **disagree, fight**
disqualification *n* = **ban**, elimination, rejection, exclusion, ineligibility, DQ

DICTIONARY

disqualify ⓣ *v* **-fying, -fied 1** debar from a contest **2** make ineligible **disqualification** *n*
disquiet ⓣ *n* **1** feeling of anxiety ▷ *v* **2** make (someone) anxious
▶ **disquietude** *n* anxiety, uneasiness
Disraeli *n* **Benjamin**, 1st Earl of Beaconsfield. 1804–81, British Tory statesman and novelist; prime minister (1868; 1874–80). He gave coherence to the Tory principles of protectionism and imperialism, was responsible for the Reform Bill (1867) and, as prime minister, bought a controlling interest in the Suez Canal. His novels include *Coningsby* (1844) and *Sybil* (1845)
disregard ⓣ *v* **1** give little or no attention to ▷ *n* **2** lack of attention or respect
disrepair ⓣ *n* condition of being worn out or in poor working order
disrepute ⓣ *n* loss or lack of good reputation
▶ **disreputable** *adj* having or causing a bad reputation
disrespect ⓣ *n* lack of respect
disrespectful *adj* **disrespectfully** *adv*
disrobe *v* undress
disrupt ⓣ *v* interrupt the progress of
disruption *n* **disruptive** *adj*
dissatisfied ⓣ *adj* not pleased, disappointed
dissatisfaction *n*
dissect ⓣ *v* **1** cut open (a dead body) to examine it **2** examine critically and minutely
dissection *n*
dissemble *v* conceal one's real motives or emotions by pretence
disseminate ⓣ *v* scatter about
dissemination *n*
dissent ⓣ *v* **1** disagree **2** *Christianity* reject the doctrines of an established church ▷ *n* **3** disagreement **4** *Christianity* separation from an established church **dissension** *n*
dissenter *n*
dissertation ⓣ *n* **1** written thesis, usu. required for a higher university degree **2** long formal speech
disservice ⓣ *n* bad turn or wrong
dissident ⓣ *n* **1** person who disagrees, esp. with the government ▷ *adj* **2** disagreeing
dissidence *n*

THESAURUS

disqualified *adj* = **ineligible**, debarred, eliminated, knocked out, out of the running
disqualify *v* = **ban**, prohibit, preclude, debar, declare ineligible, rule out
disquiet *n* **1** = **uneasiness**, concern, worry, alarm, anxiety, disturbance, nervousness, trepidation, foreboding ▶ *v* **2** = **make uneasy**, concern, worry, trouble, upset, disturb, bother, unsettle, perturb
disregard *v* **1** = **ignore**, discount, overlook, neglect, brush aside *or* brush away, make light of, pass over, pay no heed to, turn a blind eye to ▶ *n* **2** = **inattention**, negligence, oversight, neglect, contempt, disrespect, indifference, disdain
disrepair *n* = **dilapidation**, collapse, deterioration, decay, ruination
disreputable *adj* = **discreditable**, notorious, infamous, shameful, scandalous, shady (*informal*), ignominious, dishonourable, louche
disrepute *n* = **discredit**, shame, disgrace, infamy, unpopularity, dishonour, ignominy, ill repute, obloquy
disrespect *n* = **contempt**, sauce, cheek, irreverence, impertinence, impoliteness, impudence, insolence, lack of respect, rudeness
disrespectful *adj* = **rude**, impertinent, impudent, insolent • *They were disrespectful to the older workers.*
disrupt *v* **1** = **disturb**, upset, disorder, spoil, confuse, disorganize **2** = **interrupt**, upset, obstruct, unsettle, intrude, break up *or* break into, interfere with
disruption *n* = **disturbance**, interference, stoppage, interruption
disruptive *adj* = **disturbing**, troublesome, disorderly, unruly, distracting, unsettling, upsetting
dissatisfaction *n* = **discontent**, frustration, disappointment, displeasure, resentment, irritation, unhappiness, annoyance, chagrin
dissatisfied *adj* = **discontented**, frustrated, unhappy, disappointed, disgruntled, displeased, fed up, unsatisfied
dissect *v* **1** = **cut up** *or* **cut apart**, dismember, anatomize, lay open **2** = **analyze**, study, research, investigate, explore, inspect, scrutinize, break down
disseminate *v* = **spread**, broadcast, distribute, circulate, scatter, disperse, publicize
dissension *n* = **disagreement**, dispute, conflict, row, dissent, strife, friction, quarrel, discord
dissent *v* **1** = **disagree**, protest, refuse, object, differ, withhold assent *or* withhold approval ▶ *n* **2** = **disagreement**, opposition, resistance, refusal, objection, discord, dissension
dissenter *n* = **objector**, dissident, nonconformist
dissertation *n* = **thesis**, essay, critique, discourse, exposition, treatise, disquisition
disservice *n* = **bad turn**, injury, wrong, harm, injustice, unkindness
dissident *adj* **1** = **dissenting**, disagreeing, discordant, heterodox, nonconformist ▶ *n*

DICTIONARY

dissimilar Ⓣ *adj* not alike, different
dissimilarity *n*
dissimulate *v* conceal one's real feelings by pretence **dissimulation** *n*
dissipate Ⓣ *v* **1** waste or squander **2** scatter
dissipation *n*
▸ **dissipated** *adj* showing signs of overindulging in alcohol and other pleasures
dissociate Ⓣ *v* regard or treat as separate
dissociation *n*
▸ **dissociate oneself from** deny or break a connection with
dissolute Ⓣ *adj* leading an immoral life
dissolve Ⓣ *v* **1** (cause to) become liquid **2** bring to an end **3** dismiss (a meeting, Parliament, etc.) **4** collapse emotionally
▸ **dissolution** *n* **1** destruction by breaking up and dispersing **2** termination of a meeting, assembly, or legal relationship
dissonance *n* **1** discordant combination of sounds **2** lack of agreement or consistency
dissonant *adj*
dissuade Ⓣ *v* deter (someone) by persuasion from a course of action, policy, etc.
dissuasion *n*
distaff *n* rod on which wool, flax, etc. is wound for spinning
▸ **distaff side** female side of a family
distance Ⓣ *n* **1** space between two points **2** state of being apart **3** distant place **4** remoteness in manner
▸ **distance oneself from** separate oneself mentally from
▸ **distant** *adj* **1** far apart **2** separated by a specified distance **3** remote in manner
distantly *adv*
distaste Ⓣ *n* dislike, aversion
▸ **distasteful** *adj* unpleasant or offensive
distemper[1] *n* highly contagious disease of animals, esp. dogs
distemper[2] *n* paint mixed with water, glue, etc., which is used for painting walls
distend *v* expand by pressure from within
distension *n*
distill Ⓣ *v* **-tilling, -tilled 1** subject to or obtain by distillation **2** give off (a substance) in drops **3** extract the essence of
▸ **distillation** *n* **1** process of evaporating a liquid and condensing its vapour **2** Also **distillate** concentrated essence
▸ **distiller** *n* person or company that makes spirits
▸ **distillery** *n* place where alcoholic drinks are made by distillation
distinct Ⓣ *adj* **1** not the same **2** clearly seen, heard, or recognized **3** clear and definite: *a distinct possibility of rain* **distinctly** *adv*
▸ **distinction** *n* **1** act of distinguishing

THESAURUS

2 = protester, rebel, dissenter, agitator
dissimilar *adj* = **different**, various, unlike, diverse, unrelated, disparate, divergent, heterogeneous
dissipate *v* **1 = squander**, spend, waste, consume, deplete, expend, fritter away, run through **2 = disperse**, disappear, dissolve, vanish, scatter, dispel, evaporate, drive away
dissipation *n* **1 = dispersal**, disappearance, dissolution, disintegration, scattering, vanishing **2 = debauchery**, waste, excess, indulgence, extravagance, dissoluteness, intemperance, prodigality, profligacy, wantonness
dissociate *v* **1 = break away**, quit, break off, part company **2 = separate**, divorce, distance, isolate, disconnect, detach, segregate, set apart
dissolute *adj* = **immoral**, wild, degenerate, wanton, debauched, depraved, dissipated, profligate, rakish
dissolution *n* **1 = breaking up**, division, separation, parting, disintegration **2 = adjournment**, end, finish, suspension, termination, discontinuation
dissolve *v* **1 = melt**, soften, thaw, fuse, liquefy, deliquesce **2 = end**, suspend, terminate, discontinue, break up, wind up
dissuade *v* = **deter**, warn, discourage, advise against, put off, remonstrate, talk out of
distance *n* **1 = space**, range, stretch, gap, length, span, extent, interval **2 = reserve**, restraint, stiffness, remoteness, coolness, aloofness, coldness ▷ **in the distance = far off**, afar, far away, on the horizon, yonder ▸ *v* ▷ **distance oneself = separate oneself**, be distanced from, dissociate oneself
distant *adj* **1 = far**, remote, outlying, out-of-the-way • *a distant land* OPPOSITE: close **2 = reserved**, aloof, detached, withdrawn • *He is polite, but distant.* OPPOSITE: friendly **3 = apart**, separate, distinct, scattered, dispersed
See also: **cold, foreign**
distaste *n* = **dislike**, horror, disgust, revulsion, aversion, loathing, odium, repugnance
distasteful *adj* = **unpleasant**, offensive, objectionable, repulsive, repugnant, unpalatable, disagreeable, scuzzy (*slang*), uninviting, unsavoury
distill *v* = **extract**, refine, purify, condense
distilled *See* **refined**
distinct *adj* **1 = different**, individual, separate, unconnected, discrete, detached **2 = definite**, clear, obvious, evident, marked, noticeable, unmistakable, palpable, well-defined, decided ▷ **distinct from** *See* **unlike**

DICTIONARY

2 distinguishing feature **3** state of being different **4** special honour, recognition, or fame
▸ **distinctive** *adj* easily recognizable **distinctively** *adv* **distinctiveness** *n*
distinguish Ⓣ *v* **1** (foll. by *between* or *among*) make, show, or recognize a difference (between *or* among) **2** be a distinctive feature of **3** perceive **distinguishable** *adj*
▸ **distinguished** *adj* **1** noble or dignified in appearance **2** highly respected
distort Ⓣ *v* **1** alter or misrepresent (facts) **2** twist out of shape **distortion** *n*
distract Ⓣ *v* **1** draw the attention of (a person) away from something **2** confuse, trouble **3** entertain **distraction** *n*
distrait [diss-**tray**] *adj* absent-minded or abstracted
distraught Ⓣ [diss-**trawt**] *adj* extremely anxious or agitated
distress Ⓣ *n* **1** extreme unhappiness or worry **2** great physical pain **3** financial trouble ▷ *v* **4** upset badly **distressing** *adj* **distressingly** *adv*
▸ **distressed** *adj* **1** much troubled **2** in financial difficulties
distribute Ⓣ *v* **1** hand out or deliver (leaflets, etc.) **2** share (something) among the members of a particular group
▸ **distribution** *n* **1** act of distributing **2** arrangement or spread of anything over an area, period of time, etc.

d

THESAURUS

distinction *n* **1** = **differentiation**, discrimination, perception, separation, discernment **2** = **feature**, mark, quality, characteristic, individuality, distinctiveness, particularity, peculiarity **3** = **difference**, division, contrast, separation, differential **4** = **excellence**, fame, importance, merit, honour, prominence, greatness, repute, eminence
distinctive *adj* = **characteristic**, special, individual, original, unique, typical, singular, peculiar, idiosyncratic
distinctly *adv* = **definitely**, obviously, clearly, markedly, noticeably, decidedly, patently, plainly, unmistakably
distinguish *v* **1** = **differentiate**, tell, discriminate, tell apart, tell the difference • *Could he distinguish right from wrong?* **2** = **make out**, recognize, discern, pick out • *I heard shouting, but was unable to distinguish the words.* **3** = **characterize**, mark, separate, classify, categorize, set apart, single out
distinguishable *See* **visible**
distinguished *adj* = **eminent**, famous, acclaimed, famed, renowned, well-known, celebrated, illustrious, noted
distinguishing *See* **characteristic, peculiar**
distort *v* **1** = **misrepresent**, colour, twist, bias, falsify, slant, pervert **2** = **deform**, twist, bend, disfigure, buckle, warp, contort, misshape
distorted *adj* = **deformed**, disfigured • *the distorted image caused by the projector*
See also: **crooked, garbled**
distortion *n* **1** = **misrepresentation**, bias, slant, perversion, falsification **2** = **deformity**, twist, bend, buckle, warp, malformation, contortion, crookedness
distract *v* **1** = **divert**, draw away • *Playing computer games distracts him from his homework.* **2** = **amuse**, occupy, entertain, engross, beguile
distracted *adj* = **agitated**, troubled, at sea, flustered, harassed, in a flap (*informal*), perplexed, puzzled
distraction *n* **1** = **diversion**, interference, disturbance, interruption **2** = **entertainment**, diversion, recreation, amusement, pastime **3** = **agitation**, disorder, confusion, disturbance, commotion, discord, bewilderment
distraught *adj* = **frantic**, desperate, distressed, overwrought, agitated, beside oneself, distracted, out of one's mind, worked-up
distress *n* **1** = **suffering**, pain, sorrow, heartache • *Kindness eased their distress.* **2** = **need**, trouble, difficulty, straits • *The ship might be in distress.* ▷ **distress signal** *See* **alarm** ▸ *v* **3** = **upset**, worry, pain, trouble, disturb, bother, grieve, sadden • *Our fight greatly distressed me.*
See also: **agitate, alarm, concern, grief, hurt, shake, shock**
distressed *adj* **1** = **upset**, troubled, worried, distraught, wretched, agitated, distracted, tormented **2** = **poverty-stricken**, poor, needy, destitute, down at heel, indigent, straitened
distressing *adj* = **upsetting**, sad, painful, heart-breaking, disturbing, harrowing, worrying
distribute *v* **1** = **hand out**, circulate, pass around • *They publish and distribute flyers.* **2** = **spread**, scatter, disperse, diffuse • *Distribute the berries evenly over the cake.* **3** = **share**, divide, allocate, dispense, allot, dole out • *Distribute chores equally among all family members.*
distribution *n* **1** = **delivery**, handling, transportation, dealing, mailing **2** = **sharing**,

DICTIONARY

▶ **distributor** *n* **1** wholesaler who distributes goods to retailers in a specific area **2** device in a gasoline engine that sends the electric current to the spark plugs
district Ⓣ *n* area of land regarded as an administrative or geographical unit
distrust Ⓣ *v* **1** regard as untrustworthy ▷ *n* **2** suspicion or doubt **distrustful** *adj*
disturb Ⓣ *v* **1** intrude on **2** disarrange **3** worry, make anxious **disturbance** *n* **disturbing** *adj* **disturbingly** *adv*
▶ **disturbed** *adj psychiatry* emotionally upset, troubled, or maladjusted
disunite *v* cause disagreement among **disunity** *n*
disuse Ⓣ *n* condition of being unused **disused** *adj*
ditch Ⓣ *n* **1** narrow channel dug in the earth for drainage or irrigation ▷ *v* **2** *slang* abandon
dither Ⓣ *v* **1** be uncertain or indecisive ▷ *n* **2** state of indecision or agitation **ditherer** *n* **dithery** *adj*
ditto *n, pl* **-tos 1** the same ▷ *adv* **2** in the same way
ditty *n, pl* **-ties** short simple poem or song
diuretic [die-yoor-**et**-ik] *n* drug that increases the flow of urine
diurnal [die-**urn**-al] *adj* happening during the day or daily
diva *n* distinguished female singer
divan *n* **1** backless sofa or couch **2** low backless bed
dive Ⓣ *v* **diving, dived 1** plunge headfirst into water **2** (of a submarine or diver) submerge under water **3** fly in a steep nose-down descending path **4** move quickly in a specified direction **5** (foll. by *in* or *into*) start (doing something) enthusiastically ▷ *n* **6** act of diving **7** steep nose-down descent **8** *slang* disreputable bar or club
▶ **diver** *n* **1** person who works or explores underwater **2** person who dives for sport
▶ **dive bomber** military aircraft designed to release bombs during a dive
diverge Ⓣ *v* **1** separate and go in different directions **2** deviate (from a prescribed course) **divergence** *n* **divergent** *adj*
divers *adj old-fashioned* various
diverse Ⓣ *adj* **1** having variety **2** different in kind **diversify** *v* **diversification** *n*
▶ **diversity** *n* **1** quality of being different or varied **2** range of difference

THESAURUS

division, allocation, allotment, apportionment **3 = classification**, organization, arrangement, placement, grouping
district *n* **= area**, quarter, region, sector, neighbourhood, parish, locale, vicinity, locality
distrust *v* **1 = suspect**, question, doubt, mistrust, disbelieve, be suspicious of, be wary of, smell a rat (*informal*) ▶ *n* **2 = suspicion**, question, doubt, skepticism, disbelief, mistrust, misgiving, wariness
distrustful *adj* **= suspicious**, skeptical, wary, doubtful, dubious, cynical, uneasy, leery (*slang*), chary, disbelieving, distrusting, doubting, mistrustful
disturb *v* **1 = interrupt**, disrupt, bother, intrude on • *Don't disturb me while I'm studying.* **2 = upset**, worry, trouble, shake, distress, agitate, unsettle • *Some scenes in the movie may disturb you.* **3 = muddle**, disorder, disarrange
See also: **concern**
disturbance *n* **1 = interruption**, bother, distraction, intrusion, annoyance **2 = disorder**, brawl, fray, commotion, fracas, rumpus
disturbed *adj* **1** (*Psychiatry*) **= unbalanced**, upset, troubled, neurotic, disordered, maladjusted **2 = worried**, upset, troubled, nervous, anxious, concerned, uneasy, apprehensive, bothered, wired (*slang*)
disturbing *adj* **= worrying**, startling, alarming, disconcerting, distressing, frightening, harrowing, unsettling, upsetting
disuse *n* **= neglect**, decay, abandonment, idleness
ditch *n* **1 = channel**, drain, trench, gully, moat, furrow, dyke, watercourse ▶ *v* **2** (*Slang*) **= get rid of**, drop, dump (*informal*), abandon, scrap, discard, jettison, dispose of, throw out *or* throw overboard
dither *v* **1 = vacillate**, hesitate, waver, teeter, hum and haw, shillyshally (*informal*) ▶ *n* **2 = flutter**, flap (*informal*), tizzy (*informal*), fluster
dive *v* **1 = plunge**, jump, leap, submerge • *She was standing by the pool, about to dive in.* ▶ *n* **2 = plunge**, jump, spring, leap, lunge, nose dive
See also: **descend**
diverge *v* **1 = separate**, part, spread, split, divide, branch, fork **2 = deviate**, depart, wander, stray, meander, digress, turn aside
divergence *See* **difference, split**
divergent *See* **different**
divergent from *See* **unlike**
diverse *adj* **1 = various**, several, assorted, varied, miscellaneous, manifold, of every description, sundry **2 = different**, separate, unlike, distinct, disparate, divergent, dissimilar, discrete, varying
diversify *v* **= vary**, change, expand, branch out, have a finger in every pie, spread out
diversion *n* **1 = distraction**, deflection,

DICTIONARY

divert Ⓣ *v* **1** change the direction of (traffic) **2** distract the attention of **3** entertain ▸ **diversion** *n* **1** something that distracts someone's attention **2** an entertainment **diversionary** *adj*

divest *v* **1** strip (of clothes) **2** dispossess or deprive

divide Ⓣ *v* **1** separate into parts **2** share or be shared out in parts **3** (cause to) disagree **4** keep apart, be a boundary between **5** calculate how many times (one number) can be contained in (another) ▹ *n* **6** division, split
▸ **dividend** *n* **1** sum of money representing part of the profit made, paid by a company to its shareholders **2** bonus
▸ **divider** *n* **1** screen used to divide a room into separate areas ▹ *pl n* **2** compasses with two pointed arms, used for measuring or dividing lines

divine Ⓣ *adj* **1** of God or a god **2** godlike **3** *informal* splendid ▹ *v* **4** discover (something) by intuition or guessing **divinely** *adv*
▸ **divination** *n* art of discovering future events, as though by supernatural powers
▸ **divinity** *n* **1** theology **2** state of being divine **3** god
▸ **divining rod** forked twig said to move when held over ground in which water or metal is to be found

division Ⓣ *n* **1** act of dividing or sharing out **2** one of the parts into which something is divided **3** difference of opinion **4** mathematical operation of dividing **divisible** *adj* **divisibility** *n*
▸ **divisional** *adj* of a division in an organization
▸ **divisive** [div-**vice**-iv] *adj* tending to cause disagreement
▸ **divisor** *n* number to be divided into another number

divorce Ⓣ *n* **1** legal ending of a marriage **2** separation, esp. one that is total ▹ *v* **3** separate or be separated by divorce **4** remove or separate
▸ **divorcé** (**divorcée**) *n* person who is divorced

divot *n* small piece of turf

divulge Ⓣ *v* make known, disclose **divulgence** *n*

divvy *informal* ▹ *v* **-vying, -vied 1** (esp. foll. by *up*) divide and share ▹ *n, pl* **-vies 2** dividend

Dixie *n* southern states of the US

Dixon *n* **Willie**, full name *William James Dixon*. 1915–92, US blues musician, songwriter, and record producer, whose songs have been recorded by many other artists

dizzy Ⓣ *adj* **-zier, -ziest 1** having or causing a whirling sensation **2** mentally confused ▹ *v* **-zying, -zied 3** make dizzy **dizzily** *adv* **dizziness** *n*

THESAURUS

deviation, digression **2 = pastime**, game, play, sport (*old-fashioned*), entertainment, delight, distraction, pleasure, recreation, amusement, hobby, relaxation, enjoyment, gratification, divertissement, beguilement

diversity *n* = **difference**, range, variety, distinctiveness, diverseness, heterogeneity, multiplicity

divert *v* **1 = redirect**, switch, avert, deflect, turn aside **2 = distract**, sidetrack, draw away from *or* lead away from, lead astray **3 = entertain**, delight, amuse, gratify, regale, beguile

diverting *adj* = **entertaining**, fun, pleasant, enjoyable, humorous, amusing, beguiling

divide *v* **1 = separate**, split, partition, segregate, cut up, split up • *Divide the pizza into six slices.* OPPOSITE: join **2 = bisect**, separate • *the border dividing the countries* **3 = split**, come between, set against one another • *the enormous differences that still divide them* **4 = share**, distribute, allocate, dispense, allot, deal out
See also: **sort**

dividend *n* = **bonus**, share, cut (*informal*), gain, extra, surplus, plus, portion, divvy (*informal*)

divine *adj* **1 = heavenly**, holy, spiritual, celestial, supernatural, superhuman, angelic, godlike **2 = sacred**, religious, holy, spiritual, consecrated, sanctified **3** (*Informal*) **= wonderful**, perfect, beautiful, excellent, glorious, splendid, marvellous, superlative ▸ *v* **4 = infer**, suppose, guess, perceive, apprehend, discern, surmise, deduce

divinity *n* **1 = theology**, religion, religious studies **2 = god** *or* **goddess**, spirit, deity, guardian spirit **3 = godliness**, holiness, sanctity, deity, divine nature

divisible *adj* = **dividable**, separable, splittable

division *n* **1 = separation**, partition • *equal division of the money* **2 = disagreement**, split, breach, rupture, difference of opinion • *There were divisions in the club over who should be in charge.* **3 = section**, sector, department • *the research division of the toy company* **4 = sharing**, distribution, allotment, apportionment
See also: **compartment**

divorce *n* **1 = separation**, dissolution, annulment, split-up, talaq *or* talak ▸ *v* **2 = separate**, part, divide, dissolve (marriage), sever, disconnect, dissociate, split up

divorced *See* **separate**

divulge *v* = **make known**, tell, reveal, declare, disclose, confess, proclaim, let slip

dizzy *adj* **1 = giddy**, lightheaded • *He kept*

DICTIONARY

DJ **1** disc jockey **2** dinner jacket
djellaba *n* same as **jellaba**
Djilas *n* **Milovan**. 1911–95, Yugoslav politician and writer; vice president (1953–54): imprisoned (1956–61, 1962–66) for his criticism of the communist system
dl decilitre
dm decimetre
DM Deutschmark
DNA *n* deoxyribonucleic acid, the main constituent of the chromosomes of all living things
do Ⓣ *v* **does, doing, did, done 1** perform or complete (a deed or action) **2** be suitable, suffice **3** provide, serve: *this place doesn't do lunch on Sundays* **4** make tidy, elegant, or ready: *do one's hair* **5** improve: *that hat does nothing for you* **6** find the answer to (a problem or puzzle) **7** cause or produce: *complaints do nothing to help* **8** give or render: *do me a favour* **9** work at, esp. as a course of study or a job **10** travel (a distance) **11** *informal* cheat or rob **12** used to form questions: *do you agree?* **13** used to intensify positive statements and commands: *I do like your new house; do hurry!* **14** used to form negative statements and commands: *do not leave me here alone!* **15** used to replace an earlier verb: *he likes you as much as I do* ▷ *n, pl* **dos, do's 16** *informal* festive gathering or party
▸ **do away with** *v* **1** kill **2** get rid of
▸ **do-it-yourself** *n* practice of constructing and repairing things oneself, esp. as a hobby
▸ **do up** *v* **1** fasten **2** renovate
▸ **do with** *v* find useful or benefit from
▸ **do without** *v* manage without
Doberman, Doberman pinscher *n* large slender dog with a glossy black-and-tan coat
docile Ⓣ *adj* (of a person or animal) easily managed **docilely** *adv* **docility** *n*
dock[1] Ⓣ *n* **1** enclosed area of water where ships are loaded, unloaded, or repaired ▷ *v* **2** moor or be moored at dock **3** link (two spacecraft) or (of two spacecraft) be linked together in space
▸ **docker** *n* person employed in the loading or unloading of ships
▸ **dockyard** *n* place with docks and equipment where ships are built or repaired
dock[2] Ⓣ *v* **1** deduct (an amount) from (a person's wages) **2** remove part of (an animal's tail) by cutting through the bone
dock[3] *n* enclosed space in a court of law where the accused person sits or stands
dock[4] *n* weed with broad leaves
docket *n* **1** piece of paper accompanying a package or other delivery, stating contents, delivery instructions, etc. ▷ *v* **2** fix a docket to (a package etc.)
doctor Ⓣ *n* **1** person licensed to practise medicine **2** person who has been awarded a doctorate ▷ *v* **3** make different in order to deceive **4** poison or drug (food or drink) **5** *informal* castrate or sterilize (a cat, dog, etc.)
doctoral *adj*
▸ **doctorate** *n* highest academic degree in any field of knowledge
doctrine Ⓣ [**dock**-trin] *n* **1** body of teachings

THESAURUS

getting dizzy spells. **2 = confused**, bemused, at sea, befuddled, bewildered, dazed, dazzled, muddled
See also: **faint**
do *v* **1 = perform**, execute (*formal*), undertake, carry out • *He just didn't want to do any work.* **2 = be sufficient**, suffice (*formal*), be adequate • *Homemade soup is best, but canned soup will do.* **3 = get on**, manage, fare • *She did well at school.* **4 = get ready**, prepare, fix, arrange, look after, see to **5 = solve**, resolve, decode, decipher, figure out, puzzle out, work out **6 = cause**, create, produce, effect, bring about ▷ **do away with = kill**, murder, slay, exterminate; **= get rid of**, remove, eliminate, abolish, discard, discontinue, put an end to, put paid to ▷ **do business** *See* **trade** ▷ **do up** *See* **decorate, renovate** ▷ **do well = succeed**, thrive, flourish ▷ **do without = manage without**, kick (*informal*), forgo, abstain from, dispense with, get along without, give up ▷ **do wrong** *See* **sin** ▷ **do your best** *See* **strive**
See also: **accomplish, achieve, commit, conduct, practise, suit**
docile *adj* **= submissive**, manageable, compliant, amenable, obedient, biddable, pliant
docility *n* **= submissiveness**, compliance, obedience, manageability, meekness
dock[1] *n* **1 = wharf**, waterfront, pier, harbour, quay ▸ *v* **2 = moor**, land, berth, anchor, drop anchor, put in, tie up **3** (Of a spacecraft) **= link up**, join, couple, unite, rendezvous, hook up
dock[2] *v* **1 = deduct**, reduce, decrease, withhold, diminish, lessen, subtract **2 = cut off**, clip, crop, shorten, curtail, cut short
doctor *n* **1 = G.P.**, physician, medic (*informal*), general practitioner, medical practitioner ▸ *v* **2 = change**, alter, disguise, misrepresent, falsify, pervert, tamper with **3 = add to**, cut, spike, dilute, adulterate, mix with, water down
doctrinaire *adj* **= dogmatic**, rigid, opinionated, fanatical, inflexible, insistent, biased
doctrinal *See* **religious**
doctrine *n* **= teaching**, opinion, conviction, principle, belief, tenet, creed,

DICTIONARY

of a religious, political, or philosophical group **2** principle or body of principles that is taught or advocated
▸ **doctrinal** *adj* of or related to doctrine
▸ **doctrinaire** *adj* stubbornly insistent on the application of a theory without regard to practicality
document ⓣ *n* **1** piece of paper, booklet, etc. providing information, esp. of an official nature ▷ *v* **2** record or report (something) in detail **3** support (a claim) with evidence **documentation** *n*
documentary *n, pl* **-ries 1** film or television programme presenting the facts about a particular subject ▷ *adj* **2** of or based on documents
dodder *v* move unsteadily **dodderer** *n* **doddery** *adj*
doddle *n informal* something easily accomplished
dodecagon [doe-**deck**-a-gon] *n* geometric figure with twelve sides
dodge ⓣ *v* **1** avoid (a blow, being seen, etc.) by moving suddenly **2** evade by cleverness or trickery ▷ *n* **3** plan contrived to deceive **4** sudden evasive movement **dodger** *n*
▸ **dodgy** *adj informal* **1** difficult or dangerous **2** untrustworthy
Dodgem *n* ® electrically propelled vehicle driven and bumped against similar vehicles in a rink at a funfair
dodo *n, pl* **dodos, dodoes** large flightless extinct bird
doe *n* female deer, hare, or rabbit
does *v* third person singular of the present tense of **do**
doesn't does not
doff *v* take off or lift (one's hat) as a mark of respect
dog ⓣ *n* **1** domesticated four-legged meat-eating mammal occurring in many different breeds **2** any other member of the dog family, such as the dingo or coyote **3** male of animals of the dog family **4** *informal* fellow, chap: *you lucky dog!* ▷ *v* **dogging, dogged 5** follow (someone) closely **6** trouble or plague
▸ **go to the dogs** go to ruin physically or morally
▸ **let sleeping dogs lie** leave things undisturbed
▸ **dogged** [**dog**-gid] *adj* obstinately determined **doggedly** *adv* **doggedness** *n*
▸ **doggy** *or* **doggie** *n* child's word for a dog
▸ **dogcart** *n* light horse-drawn two-wheeled vehicle
▸ **dog collar 1** collar for a dog **2** *informal* clerical collar
▸ **dog-eared** *adj* **1** (of a book) having pages folded down at the corner **2** shabby or worn
▸ **dogfight** *n* **1** close-quarters combat between fighter aircraft **2** any rough fight
▸ **dogfish** *n* small shark
▸ **doghouse** *n* kennel
▸ **in the doghouse** *informal* in disfavour
▸ **dogleg** *n* sharp bend
▸ **dog rose** wild rose with pink or white flowers
▸ **dogsbody** *n informal* person who carries out menial tasks for others
▸ **dogsled** *n* sled drawn by dogs
▸ **dog-tired** *adj informal* exhausted
doge [**doje**] *n* (formerly) chief magistrate of Venice or Genoa
dogged ⓣ [**dog**-gid] *adj* obstinately determined **doggedly** *adv* **doggedness** *n*
doggerel *n* poorly written, usually comic verse
doggo *adv* **lie doggo** *informal* hide and keep quiet
dogma ⓣ *n* doctrine or system of doctrines proclaimed by authority as true **dogmatism** *n*
▸ **dogmatic** *adj* (of a statement or opinion) **1** forcibly asserted as if unchallengeable **2** (of a person) prone to making such statements **dogmatically** *adv*
Dohnányi *n* **Ernö** or **Ernst von.** 1877–1960, Hungarian pianist and composer whose works include *Variations on a Nursery Theme* (1913) for piano and orchestra
doily *n, pl* **-lies** decorative mat of lace or lacelike paper, laid on plates

THESAURUS

dogma, article of faith, precept
document *n* **1** = **paper**, report, record, certificate ▸ *v* **2** = **support**, detail, verify, certify, authenticate, validate, substantiate, corroborate
dodge *v* **1** = **duck**, swerve • *We dodged to the side as the joggers approached.* **2** = **avoid**, elude, evade, sidestep, shirk, get out of • *dodging responsibilities by pretending to be ill*
See also: **escape, manoeuvre**
dog *n* **1** = **canine**, pooch, mutt, mongrel • *a children's book about dogs* RELATED WORDS *adj*: canine *female*: bitch *young*: pup, puppy
▷ **go to the dogs** (*Informal*) = **go to ruin**, deteriorate, degenerate, go down the drain, go to pot ▸ *v* **2** = **trouble**, follow, track, trail, pursue, plague, haunt, hound, stalk
dogged *adj* = **determined**, persistent, stubborn, steadfast, resolute, tenacious, unshakable, indefatigable, obstinate, unflagging
dogma *n* = **doctrine**, opinion, belief, creed, credo, teachings
dogmatic *adj* = **opinionated**, arrogant, emphatic, assertive, doctrinaire, obdurate, overbearing

DICTIONARY

Dolby *n* ® system used in tape recorders which reduces noise level on recorded or broadcast sound
doldrums Ⓣ *pl n* **1** depressed state of mind **2** state of inactivity
dole Ⓣ *n* **1** *informal* money received from the state while out of work ▷ *v* **2** (foll. by *out*) distribute (something), esp. in small portions
doleful *adj* dreary or mournful **dolefully** *adv* **dolefulness** *n*
doll *n* **1** small model of a human being, used as a toy **2** *slang* girl or young woman, esp. a pretty one
dollar *n* standard monetary unit of Canada, the US, and various other countries
dollop Ⓣ *n informal* semisolid lump
dolly *n, pl* **-lies 1** child's word for a doll **2** wheeled support on which a camera may be moved
dolman sleeve *n* sleeve that is very wide at the armhole and tapers to a tight wrist
dolmen *n* prehistoric monument consisting of a horizontal stone supported by vertical stones
dolomite *n* mineral consisting of calcium magnesium carbonate
dolorous *adj* causing or involving pain or sorrow
dolphin *n* sea mammal of the whale family, with a beaklike snout
dolt Ⓣ *n* stupid person **doltish** *adj*
domain Ⓣ *n* **1** field of knowledge or activity **2** land under one ruler or government
dome *n* **1** rounded roof built on a circular base **2** something shaped like this **domed** *adj*
domestic Ⓣ *adj* **1** of the home or family **2** home-loving **3** (of an animal) bred or kept as a pet or for the supply of food **4** of one's own country or a specific country: *domestic and foreign affairs* ▷ *n* **5** household servant
domestically *adv* **domesticity** *n*
▸ **domesticate** *v* **1** bring or keep (wild animals or plants) under control or cultivation **2** accustom (someone) to home life **domestication** *n*
▸ **domestic science** study of household skills
domicile [**dom**-miss-ile] *n* person's regular dwelling place **domiciliary** *adj*
dominant Ⓣ *adj* **1** having authority or influence **2** main or chief: *the dominant topic of the day* **dominance** *n*
dominate Ⓣ *v* **1** control or govern **2** tower above (surroundings) **3** be the most important of (a particular set of people or things) **domination** *n*
domineering Ⓣ *adj* acting arrogantly or tyrannically
Domingo *n* **Placido**. born 1941, Spanish operatic tenor
Dominic *n* **Saint**, original name *Domingo de Guzman*. ?1170–1221, Spanish priest. Feast day: Aug 7
▸ **Dominican** *n, adj* (friar or nun) of an order founded by Saint Dominic
dominion Ⓣ *n* **1** rule or authority **2** land governed by one ruler or government **3** formerly, self-governing division of the British Empire
domino *n, pl* **-noes 1** small rectangular block marked with dots, used in dominoes
dominoes 2 game in which dominoes with matching halves are laid together
Domino *n* **Fats**, real name *Antoine Domino*. born 1928, US rhythm-and-blues and rock-and-roll pianist, singer, and songwriter. His singles include "Ain't that a Shame"

THESAURUS

doldrums *n* ▷ **the doldrums = inactivity**, depression, gloom, malaise, dumps (*informal*), listlessness
dole *v* ▷ **dole out = give out**, distribute, assign, allocate, dispense, allot, apportion, hand out
dollop *n* **= lump**, portion, scoop, serving, helping
dolt *n* **= idiot**, ass, chump (*informal*), blockhead, dope (*informal*), fool, dork (*slang*), dunce, oaf, schmuck (*slang*)
domain *See* **field, territory**
domestic *adj* **1 = home**, family, private, household **2 = home-loving**, stay-at-home, homey, domesticated, housewifely **3 = domesticated**, pet, tame, trained, house-trained **4 = native**, internal, indigenous ▸ *n* **5 = servant**, help, daily, maid, charwoman
dominance *See* **advantage, hold**
dominant *adj* **1 = controlling**, ruling, superior, supreme, authoritative, assertive, commanding, governing **2 = main**, chief, primary, prominent, principal, pre-eminent, predominant
dominate *v* **1 = control**, rule, direct, govern, monopolize, have the whip hand over, tyrannize **2 = tower above**, survey, overlook, loom over, stand head and shoulders above, stand over
domination *n* **= control**, power, rule, authority, influence, command, supremacy, superiority, ascendancy
domineering *adj* **= overbearing**, arrogant, authoritarian, oppressive, dictatorial, tyrannical, imperious, high-handed, bossy (*informal*)
dominion *n* **1 = control**, power, rule, authority, command, sovereignty, jurisdiction, supremacy **2 = kingdom**, country, territory, empire, domain, realm

DICTIONARY

(1955) and "Blueberry Hill" (1956)
don[1] Ⓣ *v* **donning, donned** put on (clothing)
don[2] *n* **1** *Brit* member of the teaching staff at a university or college **2** Spanish gentleman or nobleman
▸ **donnish** *adj* resembling a university don
Donald *n* ?1031–1100, king of Scotland (1093–94; 1094–97)
donate Ⓣ *v* give (something), esp. to a charity
▸ **donation** *n* **1** act of donating **2** a contribution
▸ **donor** *n* **1** *med* person who gives blood, organs, etc. for use in the treatment of another person **2** person who makes a donation
Donatello *n* real name *Donato di Betto Bardi*. 1386–1466, Florentine sculptor, regarded as the greatest sculptor of the quattrocento, who was greatly influenced by classical sculpture and contemporary humanist theories. His marble relief of *St George Killing the Dragon* (1416–17) shows his innovative use of perspective. Other outstanding works are the classic bronze *David*, and the bronze equestrian monument to Gattamelatta, which became the model of subsequent equestrian sculpture
done Ⓣ *v* past participle of **do**
doner kebab *n* grilled minced lamb served in a split slice of unleavened bread
Dönitz, Doenitz *n* **Karl**. 1891–1980, German admiral; commander in chief of the German navy (1943–45); as head of state after Hitler's death he surrendered to the Allies (May 7, 1945)
Donizetti *n* **Gaetano**. 1797–1848, Italian operatic composer: his works include *Lucia di Lammermoor* (1835), *La Fille du régiment* (1840), and *Don Pasquale* (1843)
Don Juan *n* successful seducer of women
donkey *n* long-eared member of the horse family
▸ **donkey jacket** man's thick hip-length jacket with a waterproof panel across the shoulders
▸ **donkey's years** *informal* a long time
▸ **donkey-work** *n* **1** groundwork **2** drudgery
don't do not
Donne *n* **John**. 1573–1631, English metaphysical poet and preacher. He wrote love and religious poems, sermons, epigrams, and elegies
doodle *v* **1** scribble or draw aimlessly ▹ *n* **2** shape or picture drawn aimlessly
Doolittle *n* **Hilda**, known as *H.D.* 1886–1961, US imagist poet and novelist, living in Europe
doom Ⓣ *n* **1** death or a terrible fate ▹ *v* **2** destine or condemn to death or a terrible fate
▸ **doomsday** *n* **1** *Christianity* day on which the Last Judgment will occur **2** any dreaded day
door Ⓣ *n* **1** hinged or sliding panel for closing the entrance to a room, cupboard, etc. **2** entrance
▸ **doormat** *n* **1** mat, placed at an entrance, for wiping dirt from shoes **2** *informal* person who offers little resistance to ill-treatment
▸ **doorway** *n* opening into a building or room
dope Ⓣ *n* **1** *slang* illegal drug, usu. cannabis **2** drug, esp. one administered to a racehorse etc. to affect its performance **3** *informal* slow-witted person **4** confidential information ▹ *v* **5** administer a drug to
▸ **dopey** *or* **dopy** *adj* **1** half-asleep **2** *slang* silly
Doppelgänger *n legend* ghostly double of a living person
dormant Ⓣ *adj* temporarily quiet, inactive, or not being used **dormancy** *n*
dormer (window) *n* window that projects from a sloping roof
dormitory *n, pl* **-ries** large room, esp. at a school, containing several beds
dormouse *n* small rodent resembling a mouse with a furry tail
dorsal *adj* of or on the back

THESAURUS

don *v* = **put on**, clothe oneself in, dress in, get into, pull on, slip on *or* slip into
donate *v* = **give**, present, contribute, subscribe, make a gift of
donation *n* = **contribution**, present, grant, gift, offering, subscription, hand-out
done *See* **over, right**
donor *n* = **giver**, contributor, benefactor, philanthropist, donator
doom *n* **1** = **destruction**, lot, fate, ruin, fortune, catastrophe, downfall ▸ *v* **2** = **condemn**, sentence, destine, damn, consign
doomed *adj* = **hopeless**, ill-fated, condemned • *a doomed attempt to rescue the miners*
door *n* = **opening**, exit, entry, entrance, doorway
doorway *See* **entrance, entry**
dope *n* **1** (*Slang*) = **drug**, narcotic, opiate **2** (*Informal*) = **idiot**, fool, dimwit (*informal*), doofus (*slang*), dork (*slang*), dunce, dweeb (*slang*), nitwit (*informal*), schmuck (*slang*) ▸ *v* **3** = **drug**, sedate, anesthetize, knock out, narcotize, stupefy
dork *n* (*Slang*) = **idiot**, dope (*slang*), fool, geek (*slang*), nerd, doofus (*slang*), dunce, dweeb (*slang*)
dormant *adj* = **inactive**, asleep, suspended, sleeping, latent, hibernating, inert, inoperative, slumbering
dose *n* = **quantity**, measure, draft,

DICTIONARY

dory *n, pl* **-ries** spiny-finned sea fish
dose ⓣ *n* **1** specific quantity of a medicine taken at one time **2** *informal* something unpleasant to experience ▷ *v* **3** administer a dose to (someone)
▸ **dosage** *n* size of a dose
dosh *n slang* money, esp. cash
doss *v* **doss down** *Brit slang* sleep, esp. on a makeshift bed
▸ **dosshouse** *n Brit slang* cheap lodging house for homeless people
dossier [**doss**-ee-ay] *n* collection of papers with information about a subject or person
Dostoevsky, Dostoyevsky, Dostoevski, Dostoyevski *n* **Fyodor Mikhailovich**. 1821–81, Russian novelist, the psychological perception of whose works has greatly influenced the subsequent development of the novel. His best-known works are *Crime and Punishment* (1866), *The Idiot* (1868), *The Possessed* (1871), and *The Brothers Karamazov* (1879–80)
dot ⓣ *n* **1** small round mark **2** shorter symbol used in Morse code ▷ *v* **dotting, dotted 3** mark with a dot **4** scatter or intersperse
▸ **on the dot** at exactly the arranged time
▸ **dotty** *adj slang* slightly mad **dottiness** *n*
dote *v* **dote on** love to an excessive or foolish degree
▸ **dotage** [**dote**-ij] *n* feebleness of mind as a result of old age
▸ **dotard** [**dote**-ard] *n* person who is feeble-minded through old age
dotterel *n* plover with white bands around the head and neck
double ⓣ *adj* **1** as much again in size, strength, number, etc. **2** composed of two equal or similar parts **3** designed for two users **4** folded in two ▷ *adv* **5** twice over, twofold ▷ *n* **6** twice the number, amount, size, etc. **7** duplicate or counterpart, esp. a person who closely resembles another **8** *baseball* hit that enables the batter to run to second base **doubles 9** game between two pairs of players ▷ *v* **10** make or become twice as much **11** bend or fold (material etc.) **12** play two parts **13** turn sharply **doubly** *adv*
▸ **at the double** quickly or immediately
▸ **double agent** spy employed simultaneously by two opposing sides
▸ **double bass** stringed instrument, largest and lowest member of the violin family
▸ **double chin** fold of fat under the chin
▸ **double cream** thick cream with a high fat content
▸ **double-cross** *v* **1** cheat or betray ▷ *n* **2** instance of double-crossing
▸ **double-dealing** *n* treacherous or deceitful behaviour
▸ **double-decker** *n* **1** bus with two passenger decks one on top of the other **2** *informal* sandwich made from three slices of bread with two fillings
▸ **double-double** *n Canad* cup of coffee with two helpings of cream and sugar
▸ **double Dutch** *informal* incomprehensible talk, gibberish
▸ **double glazing** two panes of glass in a window, fitted to reduce heat loss
▸ **double-header** *n sports* two games played consecutively on the same day at the same venue
▸ **double take** (esp. in comedy) delayed reaction by a person to a remark or situation
▸ **double talk** deceptive or ambiguous talk
double entendre [**doob**-bl on-**tond**-ra] *n* word or phrase that can be interpreted in two ways, esp. with one meaning that is rude
doublet [**dub**-lit] *n* (formerly) man's close-fitting jacket, with or without sleeves
doubloon *n* former Spanish gold coin
doubt ⓣ *n* **1** uncertainty about the truth, facts, or existence of something **2** unresolved difficulty or point ▷ *v* **3** be inclined to disbelieve (a fact or story) **4** distrust or be

THESAURUS

prescription, portion, dosage, potion
dot *n* **1** = **spot**, point, mark, speck, jot, speckle, fleck ▷ **on the dot** = **on time**, exactly, promptly, precisely, on the button (*informal*), punctually, to the minute ▸ *v* **2** = **spot**, sprinkle, dabble, stud, dab, speckle, fleck, stipple
dotage *n* = **senility**, weakness, decrepitude, feebleness, imbecility, old age, second childhood
dote on, dote upon *v* = **adore**, treasure, admire, prize, idolize, hold dear, lavish affection on
doting *adj* = **adoring**, fond, foolish, devoted, indulgent, lovesick
double *adj* **1** = **twice**, twofold • *a double scoop* **2** = **twofold**, twin, dual • *a double check of her work* ▸ *v* **3** = **multiply**, increase, grow, duplicate, magnify, enlarge ▸ *n* **4** = **twin**, clone, replica, duplicate, lookalike, dead ringer (*slang*), Doppelgänger, spitting image (*informal*) ▷ **on the double** = **quickly**, immediately, briskly, at full speed, posthaste, without delay
double-cross *v* = **betray**, trick, mislead, two-time (*informal*), cheat, defraud, swindle, hoodwink
doubt *n* **1** = **uncertainty**, skepticism, qualm, misgiving • *This raises doubts about the point of advertising.* OPPOSITE: certainty **2** = **suspicion**, skepticism, apprehension, distrust, mistrust, qualm, misgiving ▸ *v* **3** = **be dubious**, question, query, be skeptical • *No one doubted his*

DICTIONARY

suspicious of (a person) **doubter** *n*
▶ **doubtful** *adj* **1** unlikely **2** feeling doubt
doubtfully *adv*
▶ **doubtless** *adv* **1** certainly **2** probably
douche [**doosh**] *n* **1** (instrument for applying) a stream of water directed onto or into the body for cleansing or medical purposes ▷ *v* **2** cleanse or treat by means of a douche
dough Ⓣ *n* **1** thick mixture of flour and water or milk, used for making bread **2** *slang* money
▶ **doughnut** *n* small cake of sweetened dough cooked in hot fat
doughty [**dowt**-ee] *adj* **-tier, -tiest** hardy or resolute
Douglas *n* **1 Michael K**(**irk**). born 1944, US film actor; his films include *Romancing the Stone* (1984), *Wall Street* (1987), *Basic Instinct* (1992), and *Wonder Boys* (2000) **2 Thomas Clement**, known as *Tommy*. 1904–86, Canadian social democratic politician born in Scotland. As Premier of Saskatchewan (1944–61) he introduced socialized medicine; he led the New Democratic Party (1961–71)
dour Ⓣ [**doo**-er] *adj* sullen and unfriendly
dourness *n*
douse [rhymes with **mouse**] *v* **1** drench with water or other liquid **2** put out (a light)
dove *n* **1** bird with a heavy body, small head, and short legs **2** *politics* person opposed to war
▶ **dovecote** *or* **dovecot** *n* structure for housing pigeons
▶ **dovetail** *n* **1** joint containing wedge-shaped tenons ▷ *v* **2** fit together neatly
dowager *n* widow possessing property or a title obtained from her husband
dowdy Ⓣ *adj* **-dier, -diest** shabby or old-fashioned **dowdily** *adv* **dowdiness** *n*
dowel *n* wooden or metal peg that fits into two corresponding holes to join two adjacent parts
dower *n* life interest in a part of her husband's estate allotted to a widow by law
Dowland *n* **John**. ?1563–1626, English lutenist and composer of songs and lute music
down[1] Ⓣ *prep* **1** from a higher to a lower position in or on **2** at a lower or further level or position on, in, or along ▷ *adv* **3** at or to a lower position or level **4** used to indicate lowering or destruction: *knock down* **5** used with several verbs to indicate intensity or completion: *calm down* **6** immediately: *cash down* **7** on paper: *write this down* **8** lower in price **9** from an earlier to a later time ▷ *adj* **10** depressed, sad ▷ *v* **11** *informal* drink, esp. quickly
▶ **have a down on** *informal* bear ill will towards
▶ **download** *v* transfer (data) from the memory of one computer to that of another
▶ **downtown** *n* the central or lower part of a city, especially the main commercial area
▶ **down under** *informal* Australia or New Zealand
▶ **downward** *adj* **1** descending from a higher to a lower level, condition, or position ▷ *adv* **2** downwards
▶ **downwards** *adv* from a higher to a lower place, level, etc.
▶ **down-and-out** *adj* **1** without any means of livelihood ▷ *n* **2** person who is destitute and, often, homeless
▶ **downbeat** *adj informal* **1** gloomy **2** relaxed
▶ **downcast** *adj* **1** dejected **2** directed downwards

THESAURUS

ability. OPPOSITE: believe **4 = suspect**, fear, discredit, distrust, mistrust, lack confidence in
doubtful *adj* **1 = unlikely**, uncertain, questionable, dubious, debatable • *It is doubtful whether she will compete in the next Olympics*. OPPOSITE: certain **2 = unsure**, tentative, suspicious, skeptical, uncertain, unconvinced, distrustful, hesitating, in two minds (*informal*), wavering
See also: **hesitant, improbable, suspect, unpredictable**
doubtless *adv* **1 = certainly**, surely, undoubtedly, unquestionably, assuredly, indisputably, of course, without doubt **2 = probably**, apparently, seemingly, presumably, supposedly, ostensibly, most likely
dough *See* **money**
dour *adj* **= gloomy**, sour, dismal, grim, dreary, unfriendly, sullen, forbidding, morose
dovetail *See* **fit**
dowdy *adj* **= frumpy**, drab, dingy, dumpy (*informal*), frowzy, shabby, homely (*US*), unfashionable
down *adv* **1 = downward**, downstairs • *We went down in the elevator*. OPPOSITE: up ▶ *adj* **2 = depressed**, miserable, dejected, melancholy, despondent, glum, dispirited, fed up (*informal*), morose • *He sounded really down*. ▶ *v* **3** (*Informal*) **= swallow**, drink *or* drink down, drain, gulp, put away, toss off ▶ *n* ▷ **have a down on, be down on** (*Informal*) **= be antagonistic to** *or* **be hostile to**, bear a grudge towards, be prejudiced against, be set against, have it in for (*slang*)
See also: **below, gloomy, pile, sad, unhappy**
down-and-out *adj* **1 = destitute**, impoverished, derelict, down on one's luck (*informal*), short, poor, distressed, needy, insolvent, poverty-stricken, penniless, without two pennies to rub together

DICTIONARY

▶ **downfall** *n* **1** sudden loss of position or reputation **2** cause of this
▶ **downgrade** *v* reduce in importance or value
▶ **downhearted** *adj* sad and discouraged
▶ **downhill** *adj* **1** going or sloping down ▷ *adv* **2** towards the bottom of a hill
▶ **downpour** *n* heavy fall of rain
▶ **downright** *adj, adv* extreme(ly)
▶ **downstairs** *adv* **1** to or on a lower floor ▷ *n* **2** lower or ground floor
▶ **down-to-earth** *adj* sensible or practical
▶ **downtrodden** *adj* oppressed and lacking the will to resist
down² *n* soft fine feathers or hair **downy** *adj*
downs *pl n* rolling upland, esp. in the chalk areas of S England
Down's syndrome *n* genetic disorder characterized by a flat face, slanting eyes, and mental retardation
dowry *n, pl* **-ries** property brought by a woman to her husband at marriage
dowse [rhymes with **cows**] *v* search for underground water or minerals using a divining rod
doxology *n, pl* **-gies** short hymn of praise to God
doyen [**doy**-en] *n* senior member of a group, profession, or society **doyenne** [doy-**en**] *n fem*
doyley *n* same as **doily**
D'Oyly Carte *n* **Richard**. 1844–1901, British impresario noted for his productions of the operettas of Gilbert and Sullivan
doze Ⓣ *v* **1** sleep lightly or intermittently ▷ *n* **2** short sleep
▶ **dozy** *adj* **1** drowsy **2** *informal* stupid
▶ **doze off** *v* fall into a light sleep
dozen *adj, n* twelve **dozenth** *adj, n*
Dr **1** Doctor **2** Drive
drab Ⓣ *adj* **drabber, drabbest 1** dull or dingy **2** cheerless or dreary **drabness** *n*
Drabble *n* **Margaret**. born 1939, British novelist and editor. Her novels include *The Needle's Eye* (1972), *The Radiant Way* (1987), and *The Seven Sisters* (2002). She edited the 1985 edition of the *Oxford Companion to Literature*
drachma *n, pl* **-mas, -mae** former standard monetary unit of Greece
Draco *n* 7th century BC, Athenian statesman and lawmaker, whose code of laws (621) prescribed death for almost every offence
▶ **draconian** *adj* harsh or severe
draft¹ Ⓣ *n* **1** preliminary outline of a book, speech, etc. **2** written order for payment of money by a bank **3** *US* selection for compulsory military service ▷ *v* **4** write a preliminary outline of a book, speech, etc. **5** detach (personnel) from one place to another **6** *US* select for compulsory military service
draft², draught Ⓣ *n* **1** current of air, esp. in an enclosed space **2** act of pulling a load by a vehicle or animal **3** portion of liquid to be drunk, esp. medicine **4** instance of drinking
▶ **drafty** *adj* exposed to drafts of air
▶ **draftsman** *n* person employed to prepare detailed scale drawings of machinery,

d

THESAURUS

(*informal*), ruined, dirt-poor (*informal*), flat broke (*informal*), on the rocks, indigent, impecunious, on the breadline (*informal*), penurious, necessitous, moneyless ▶ *n* **2 = tramp**, derelict, beggar, bag lady, pauper, vagabond, vagrant
downcast *adj* **= dejected**, depressed, disappointed, despondent, dismayed, discouraged, crestfallen, disconsolate, disheartened, dispirited
downer *n* (*Informal*) **= moaner**, pessimist, killjoy, prophet of doom, sourpuss (*informal*), spoilsport, wet blanket (*informal*), buzzkill (*slang*)
downfall *n* **= ruin**, fall, collapse • *Lack of support led to the team's downfall.*
See also: **failure**
downgrade *v* **= demote**, humble, degrade, lower in rank *or* reduce in rank, take down a peg (*informal*)
downhearted *adj* **= dejected**, sad, unhappy, depressed, despondent, discouraged, downcast, crestfallen, disheartened, dispirited
downpour *n* **= rainstorm**, flood, deluge, cloudburst, inundation, torrential rain
downright *adj* **= complete**, total, absolute, plain, outright, utter, unqualified, out-and-out, thoroughgoing, undisguised
downstairs *See* **down**
down-to-earth *adj* **= sensible**, realistic, practical, no-nonsense, sane, unsentimental, matter-of-fact, plain-spoken
downtrodden *adj* **= oppressed**, helpless, subservient, exploited, subjugated, tyrannized
downturn *See* **decline, recession**
downward *adj* **= descending**, declining, earthward, heading down, sliding, slipping
doze *v* **1 = nap**, sleep, snooze (*informal*), slumber, nod off (*informal*) ▶ *n* **2 = nap**, catnap, forty winks (*informal*), snooze (*informal*), siesta, shuteye (*slang*)
drab *adj* **= dull**, grey, dismal, sombre, gloomy, dreary, dingy • *the same drab grey outfit* OPPOSITE: bright
draft¹ *n* **1 = outline**, plan, version, rough, sketch, abstract **2 = order**, check, bill of exchange, money order ▶ *v* **3 = outline**, plan, draw, design, compose, sketch, formulate, draw up
draft² *n* **1 = breeze**, current, movement,

DICTIONARY

buildings, etc. **draftsmanship** *n*
▶ **draft beer** beer stored in a cask
drag ⓣ *v* **dragging, dragged 1** pull with force, esp. along the ground **2** trail on the ground **3** (foll. by *along* or *to*) bring (oneself or someone else) with effort or difficulty **4** (foll. by *on* or *out*) last, prolong, or be prolonged tediously **5** search (a river) with a dragnet or hook ▷ *n* **6** person or thing that slows up progress **7** *informal* tedious person or thing **8** *slang* women's clothes worn by a man
▶ **dragnet** *n* net used to scour the bottom of a pond or river, when searching for something
▶ **drag race** race in which specially built automobiles or motorcycles are timed over a measured course
dragon *n* **1** mythical fire-breathing monster with a scaly body, wings, claws, and a long tail **2** *informal* fierce woman
▶ **dragonfly** *n, pl* **-flies** brightly coloured insect with a long slender body and two pairs of wings
dragoon ⓣ *n* **1** heavily armed cavalryman ▷ *v* **2** coerce or force
drain ⓣ *n* **1** pipe or channel that carries off water or sewage **2** cause of continuous diminution of resources or energy ▷ *v* **3** draw off or remove liquid from **4** flow away or filter off **5** drink the entire contents of (a glass or cup) **6** make constant demands on (resources, energy, etc.) **7** exhaust (someone) physically and emotionally
▶ **drainage** *n* **1** process or method of draining **2** system of drains
drake *n* male duck
dram *n* **1** small amount of spirits, esp. whisky **2** one sixteenth of an ounce

drama ⓣ *n* **1** a work to be performed by actors **2** art of the writing or production of plays **3** situation that is highly emotional, turbulent, or tragic
▶ **dramatic** *adj* **1** of or like drama **2** striking or effective **dramatically** *adv*
▶ **dramatist** *n* playwright
▶ **dramatize** *v* **1** put into dramatic form **2** express (something) in a dramatic or exaggerated way **dramatization** *n*
dramatis personae [**drah**-mat-tiss per-**soh**-nigh] *n* characters in a play
drank *v* past tense of **drink**
drape ⓣ *v* **1** cover with material, usu. in folds **2** place casually and loosely ▷ *n* **3** curtain
▶ **draper** *n Brit* dealer in fabrics and sewing materials
▶ **drapery** *n* **1** fabric or clothing arranged and draped **2** fabrics and cloth collectively **draperies 3** curtains
Drapeau *n* **Jean**. 1916–99, Canadian politician and lawyer. He was twice mayor of Montreal (1954–57), (1960–86) and was responsible for securing the 1967 International and Universal Exposition (Expo 67) and the 1976 summer Olympic Games for his city
drastic ⓣ *adj* sudden and extreme
draught *n* **1** same as **draft**[2] **draughts 2** *Brit* checkers
draw ⓣ *v* **drawing, drew, drawn 1** depict or sketch (a figure, picture, etc.) in lines, with a pencil or pen **2** cause (a person or thing) to move out, as from a drawer, holster, etc. **3** move in a specified direction **4** arouse the interest or attention of **5** formulate or derive: *draw conclusions* **6** take from a source:

THESAURUS

flow, puff **2 = drink**, cup, dose, quantity, potion
drag *v* **1 = pull**, draw, trail, haul, tow, lug • *He dragged his chair toward the table.* ▷ **drag on, drag out = last**, extend, persist, prolong, lengthen, draw out, keep going, protract, spin out, stretch out ▶ *n* **2** (*Informal*) **= nuisance**, pain (*informal*), bother, bore, pest, downer (*informal*), annoyance
See also: **tug**
dragoon *v* **= force**, drive, bully, compel, intimidate, coerce, railroad (*informal*), constrain, browbeat, impel
drain *v* **1 = pump** • *We drained the pipes till the water ran clear.* **2 = flow**, empty, discharge, seep • *rivers that drain into lakes* **3 = exhaust**, tax, consume, sap, use up • *The prolonged feud drained him of energy.* **4 = drink up**, finish, swallow, quaff, gulp down ▶ *n* **5 = pipe**, sink, channel, ditch, trench, sewer, duct, culvert, conduit **6 = reduction**, strain, withdrawal, drag, exhaustion, sap, depletion

See also: **dry, tire**
drained *See* **tired, weary**
drama *n* **1 = play**, show, dramatization, stage show **2 = theatre**, acting, dramaturgy, stagecraft **3 = excitement**, scene, crisis, turmoil, spectacle, histrionics
dramatic *adj* **1 = theatrical**, dramaturgical, Thespian **2 = powerful**, impressive, striking, vivid, expressive, moving **3 = exciting**, thrilling, tense, sensational, breathtaking, climactic, suspenseful, electrifying, melodramatic
dramatist *n* **= playwright**, screenwriter, scriptwriter, dramaturge
dramatize *v* **= exaggerate**, overstate, overdo, lay it on *or* lay it on thick (*slang*), play to the gallery
drape *v* **= cover**, wrap, fold, cloak, swathe
drastic *adj* **= extreme**, severe, harsh, radical • *It's time for drastic action.*
draw *v* **1 = sketch**, paint, trace • *to draw pictures of flowers* **2 = move**, pull • *as the car*

DICTIONARY

draw money from the bank **7** (of two teams or contestants) finish a game with an equal number of points ▷ *n* **8** raffle or lottery **9** contest or game ending in a tie **10** event, act, etc. that attracts a large audience
▸ **drawer** *n* boxlike container in a chest, table, etc. made for sliding in and out
▸ **drawers** *old-fashioned* undergarment worn below the waist
▸ **drawing** *n* **1** picture or plan made by means of lines on a surface **2** art of making drawings
▸ **drawing pin** short tack with a broad smooth head
▸ **drawing room** *old-fashioned* room where visitors are received and entertained
▸ **drawback** *n* disadvantage
▸ **drawbridge** *n* bridge that may be raised to prevent access or to enable vessels to pass
▸ **draw out** *v* **1** extend **2** encourage (a person) to talk freely
▸ **drawstring** *n* cord run through a hem around an opening, so that when it is pulled tighter, the opening closes
▸ **draw up** *v* **1** (of a vehicle) come to a halt **2** formulate and write out (a contract)

drawl *v* **1** speak slowly, esp. prolonging the vowel sounds ▷ *n* **2** drawling manner of speech

drawn Ⓣ *v* **1** past participle of **draw** ▷ *adj* **2** haggard, tired, or tense in appearance

dray *n* low cart used for carrying heavy loads

dread Ⓣ *v* **1** anticipate with apprehension or terror ▷ *n* **2** great fear
▸ **dreadful** *adj* **1** extremely disagreeable, shocking, or bad **2** extreme **dreadfully** *adv*

dreadlocks *pl n* hair worn in the Rastafarian style of tightly curled strands

dream Ⓣ *n* **1** mental activity, usu. an imagined series of events, occurring during sleep **2** cherished hope **3** *informal* something wonderful ▷ *v* **dreaming, dreamt** *or* **dreamed 4** experience (a dream) **5** (foll. by *of* or *about*) have an image (of) or fantasy (about) **6** (foll. by *of*) consider the possibility (of) **dreamer** *n*
▸ **dream catcher** webbed hoop used by some N American native peoples as a charm to catch good dreams and block bad ones
▸ **dreamy** *adj* **1** vague or impractical **2** *informal* wonderful **dreamily** *adv*

dreary Ⓣ *adj* **drearier, dreariest** dull or boring **drearily** *adv* **dreariness** *n*

dredge[1] *v* remove (silt or mud) from (a river bed etc.)
▸ **dredger** *n* boat fitted with machinery for dredging

dredge[2] *v* sprinkle (food) with flour etc.

dregs Ⓣ *pl n* **1** solid particles that settle at

THESAURUS

drew away **3 = pull**, drag, haul • *He drew his chair nearer the fire.* **4 = take out**, extract, pull out **5 = attract**, influence, invite, persuade, induce, entice, allure, evoke, elicit **6 = deduce**, make, take, derive, infer ▷ **draw away** *See* **distract** ▷ **draw back** *See* **retreat** ▷ **draw off** *See* **drain** ▷ **draw on = make use of**, use, employ, extract, exploit, fall back on, have recourse to, rely on, take from ▷ **draw out = extend**, stretch, prolong, lengthen, drag out, make longer, protract, spin out, string out ▷ **draw up = draft**, prepare, frame, compose, formulate, write out; **= halt**, stop, bring to a stop, pull up ▸ *n* **7** (*Informal*) **= attraction**, pull (*informal*), lure, enticement **8 = tie**, deadlock, gridlock, impasse, stalemate, dead heat, saw-off (*Canad*)
See also: **earn, tug**

drawback *n* **= problem**, trouble, difficulty, snag, hitch • *The only drawback was that the apartment was too small.*
See also: **catch, disadvantage, fault, handicap**

drawing *n* **= picture**, study, cartoon, outline, portrayal, representation, sketch, depiction, illustration

drawn *adj* **= tense**, tired, haggard, pinched, stressed, worn

dread *v* **1 = fear**, quail, tremble, shudder, cringe at, have cold feet (*informal*), shrink from ▸ *n* **2 = fear**, terror, alarm, horror, dismay, apprehension, trepidation, fright

dreadful *adj* **= terrible**, awful, horrendous, appalling, atrocious, ghastly, frightful • *He told us the dreadful news* OPPOSITE: wonderful
See also: **horrible**

dream *n* **1 = vision**, hallucination, trance • *He had a dream about horses.* **2 = daydream**, fantasy • *rich beyond her wildest dreams* **3 = ambition**, goal, hope, aim, wish, desire, aspiration **4 = delight**, beauty, treasure, joy, gem, pleasure, marvel ▸ *v* **5 = have dreams**, think, imagine, fancy, envisage, visualize, conjure up, hallucinate **6 = daydream**, fantasize, build castles in the air *or* build castles in Spain, stargaze

dreamer *n* **= idealist**, visionary, utopian, escapist, daydreamer, fantasist, Walter Mitty

dreamy *adj* **1 = vague**, absent, faraway, abstracted, daydreaming, pensive, preoccupied, with one's head in the clouds **2 = impractical**, speculative, imaginary, fanciful, airy-fairy, quixotic

dreary *adj* **= dull**, boring, drab, uneventful, tedious, monotonous, humdrum • *the dreary winter months* OPPOSITE: exciting
See also: **gloomy**

dregs *pl n* **1 = sediment**, waste, deposit,

DICTIONARY

the bottom of some liquids **2** most despised elements: *the dregs of society*
Dreiser *n* **Theodore** (**Herman Albert**). 1871–1945, US novelist; his works include *Sister Carrie* (1900) and *An American Tragedy* (1925)
drench Ⓣ *v* make completely wet **drenching** *n*
Dresden, Dresden china *n* delicate and decorative porcelain ware made near Dresden in Germany
dress Ⓣ *n* **1** one-piece garment for a woman or girl, consisting of a skirt and bodice and sometimes sleeves **2** complete style of clothing ▷ *v* **3** put clothes on **4** put on formal clothes **5** apply protective covering to (a wound) **6** arrange or prepare
▶ **dressing** *n* **1** sauce for salad **2** covering for a wound
▶ **dressing-down** *n informal* severe scolding
▶ **dressing gown** robe worn before dressing
▶ **dressing room** room used for changing clothes, esp. backstage in a theatre
▶ **dressy** *adj* (of clothes) elegant **dressiness** *n*
▶ **dress circle** first gallery in a theatre
▶ **dressmaker** *n* person who makes clothes for women **dressmaking** *n*
▶ **dress rehearsal** last rehearsal of a play, using costumes, lighting, etc., as for the first night
dressage [**dress**-ahzh] *n* training of a horse to perform manoeuvres in response to the rider's body signals
dresser[1] *n* set of shelves, usu. with cupboards, for storing or displaying dishes
dresser[2] *n theatre* person employed to assist actors with their costumes
drew *v* past tense of **draw**
drey *n* squirrel's nest
dribble Ⓣ *v* **1** (allow to) flow in drops **2** allow saliva to trickle from the mouth **3** propel (a ball) by repeatedly tapping it with the foot, hand, or a stick ▷ *n* **4** small quantity of liquid falling in drops **dribbler** *n*
dribs and drabs *pl n informal* small occasional amounts
dried *v* past of **dry**
drier *adj* **1** comparative of **dry** ▷ *n* **2** same as **dryer**
driest *adj* superlative of **dry**
drift Ⓣ *v* **1** be carried along by currents of air or water **2** move aimlessly from one place or activity to another ▷ *n* **3** something piled up by the wind or current, such as a snowdrift **4** general movement or development **5** main point of an argument or speech
▶ **drifter** *n* person who moves aimlessly from place to place or job to job
▶ **driftwood** *n* wood floating on or washed ashore by the sea
drill[1] Ⓣ *n* **1** tool or machine for boring holes **2** strict and often repetitious training **3** *informal* correct procedure ▷ *v* **4** pierce, bore, or cut (a hole) in (material) (as if) with a drill **5** teach by rigorous exercises and training
drill[2] *n* **1** machine for sowing seed in rows **2** small furrow for seed
drill[3] *n* hard-wearing cotton cloth
drily *adv* same as **dryly**
drink Ⓣ *v* **drinking, drank, drunk** **1** swallow (a liquid) **2** consume alcohol, esp. to excess ▷ *n* **3** liquid suitable for drinking

THESAURUS

residue, scum, dross, grounds, lees, residuum **2 = scum**, rabble, good-for-nothings, riffraff
drench *v* = **soak**, flood, wet, drown, steep, saturate, swamp, inundate, souse
drenched *See* **wet**
dress *n* **1 = garment**, gown, robe • *a black dress* **2 = clothing**, clothes, costume, attire (*formal*), garb (*formal*) • *casual dress* ▶ *v* **3 = put on**, clothe, attire, garb (*formal*) • *She often dressed in black.* OPPOSITE: undress **4 = bandage**, treat, wrap, swathe, Band-Aid (*trademark*), bind up **5 = arrange**, prepare, adjust, align, straighten, get ready
dressmaker *n* = **seamstress**, tailor, couturier
dribble *v* **1 = run**, drop, leak, trickle, drip, seep, ooze, fall in drops **2 = drool**, drivel, slaver, slobber
dried-up *See* **dry**
drift *v* **1 = float**, go *or* go aimlessly, coast, wander, stray, meander, waft, be carried along **2 = pile up**, drive, gather, accumulate, amass, bank up ▶ *n* **3 = pile**, bank, mass, mound, heap, accumulation **4 = meaning**, import, direction, intention, significance, thrust, tendency, purport, gist
drifter *n* = **wanderer**, bum (*informal*), beachcomber, hobo, itinerant, rolling stone, vagrant
drill *n* **1 = boring tool**, bit, borer, gimlet **2 = training**, practice, exercise, preparation, discipline, instruction, repetition ▶ *v* **3 = bore**, penetrate, puncture, pierce, perforate, sink in **4 = train**, coach, practise, exercise, teach, discipline, instruct, rehearse
drink *v* **1 = swallow**, sip, guzzle, gulp, imbibe, quaff, sup • *I drank some water.* **2 = booze** (*informal*), tipple • *He drinks little and eats carefully.* ▶ *n* **3 = beverage**, liquid, potion, refreshment **4 = alcohol**, booze (*informal*), hooch *or* hootch (*informal*), liquor, spirits, the bottle (*informal*) **5 = glass**, draft, cup

DICTIONARY

4 portion of liquid for drinking 5 alcohol or its habitual or excessive consumption
drinkable *adj* **drinker** *n*
▸ **drink in** *v* pay close attention to
▸ **drink to** *v* drink a toast to
drip Ⓣ *v* **dripping, dripped** 1 fall or let fall in drops ▹ *n* 2 falling of drops of liquid 3 sound made by falling drops 4 *informal* weak or foolish person 5 *med* apparatus for the administration of a solution drop by drop into a vein
▸ **drip-dry** *adj* denoting clothing that will dry free of creases if hung up when wet
dripping *n* fat that comes from meat while it is being roasted or fried
drive Ⓣ *v* **driving, drove, driven** 1 guide the movement of (a vehicle) 2 transport or be transported in a vehicle 3 goad into a specified state 4 push or propel 5 *sports* hit (a ball) very hard and straight ▹ *n* 6 journey in a driven vehicle 7 road for vehicles, esp. a private road leading to a house 8 united effort towards a common goal: *an investment drive* 9 energy, ambition, or initiative 10 *psychol* motive or interest: *sex drive* 11 means by which force, motion, etc. is transmitted in a mechanism
▸ **driver** *n* 1 person who drives a vehicle 2 *golf* club used for tee shots
▸ **drive at** *v informal* intend or mean: *what are you driving at?*
▸ **drive-in** *adj, n* (denoting) a public facility used by patrons in their automobiles
drivel Ⓣ *n* 1 foolish talk ▹ *v* **-elling, -elled** 2 speak foolishly
drizzle Ⓣ *n* 1 very light rain ▹ *v* 2 rain lightly
drizzly *adj*
Drobny *n* **Jaroslav**. 1921–2001, British tennis and hockey player, born in Czechoslovakia: Wimbledon champion 1954: a member of the Czech hockey team in the 1948 Olympic Games
droll Ⓣ *adj* quaintly amusing **drolly** *adv*
drollery *n*
dromedary [**drom**-mid-er-ee] *n, pl* **-daries** camel with a single hump
drone[1] *n* male bee
drone[2] Ⓣ *v, n* (make) a monotonous low dull sound
▸ **drone on** *v* talk for a long time in a monotonous tone
drool Ⓣ *v* 1 (foll. by *over*) show excessive enthusiasm (for) or pleasure (in) 2 allow saliva to flow from the mouth
droop Ⓣ *v* sag, as from weakness **droopy** *adj*
drop Ⓣ *v* **dropping, dropped** 1 (allow to) fall vertically 2 decrease in amount, strength, or value 3 mention casually 4 discontinue (an activity) ▹ *n* 5 small quantity of liquid forming a round shape 6 very small quantity of liquid 7 act of falling 8 decrease in amount or value 9 vertical distance that anything may fall **drops** 10 liquid medication applied drop by drop **droplet** *n*
▸ **droppings** *pl n* feces of certain animals, such as rabbits or birds

THESAURUS

drip *v* 1 = **drop**, splash, trickle, dribble • *water dripping from the kitchen tap* ▸ *n* 2 = **drop**, bead, droplet • *drips of water* 3 (*Informal*) = **weakling**, mama's boy (*informal*)
drive *v* 1 = **operate**, work, power, pilot, propel, steer • *Don't drive a car after taking this medication.* 2 = **force**, lead, push, prompt, spur, motivate, compel • *Her love of acting drove her into a life in the theatre.* 3 = **thrust**, sink, knock, hammer, ram • *I used the sledgehammer to drive in the pegs.* 4 = **push**, send, urge, propel, herd, hurl, impel ▹ **drive into** *See* **crash** ▹ **drive off** *See* **repel** ▹ **drive someone up the wall** *See* **pester** ▸ *n* 5 = **run**, trip, ride, journey, spin, excursion, jaunt • *We might go for a drive on Sunday.* 6 = **determination**, energy, initiative, motivation, ambition, enterprise, vigour • *We remember her great drive and enthusiasm.* 7 = **campaign**, action, effort, push (*informal*), appeal, crusade
See also: **blow, chase, go, make, reduce**
drivel *n* 1 = **nonsense**, garbage (*informal*), trash, rubbish, hogwash, gibberish, hot air (*informal*), poppycock (*informal*) ▸ *v* 2 = **babble**, prattle, ramble, gab (*informal*), blether, prate
driving *adj* = **forceful**, violent, energetic, dynamic, vigorous, compelling, sweeping
drizzle *n* 1 = **fine rain**, mist ▸ *v* 2 = **rain**, spray, shower, sprinkle, spot with rain *or* spit with rain
droll *adj* = **amusing**, funny, humorous, whimsical, comical, entertaining, jocular, waggish
drone *v* 1 = **hum**, buzz, purr, vibrate, thrum, whirr ▹ **drone on** = **speak monotonously**, chant, spout, intone, be boring, talk interminably ▸ *n* 2 = **hum**, buzz, vibration, purr, murmuring, thrum, whirring
drool *v* = **dribble**, salivate, drivel, slaver, slobber, water at the mouth ▹ **drool over** = **gloat over**, gush, dote on, make much of, rave about (*informal*)
droop *v* = **sag**, drop, sink, hang *or* hang down, bend, dangle, fall down
drooping *See* **limp**
drop *v* 1 = **fall**, sink, tumble, plummet, descend • *She let her head drop.* 2 = **decrease**, fall, decline, sink, slump, tumble, plummet, diminish • *Temperatures can drop to freezing at night.* OPPOSITE: rise 3 = **drip**, trickle,

DICTIONARY

▸ **drop in** *or* **drop by** *v* pay someone a casual visit
▸ **drop off** *v* **1** grow smaller or less **2** *informal* fall asleep
▸ **dropout** *n* **1** person who rejects conventional society **2** person who fails to complete a course of study
▸ **drop out of** *v* abandon or withdraw from (a school, job, etc.)
dropsy *n* illness in which watery fluid collects in the body
dross *n* **1** scum formed on the surfaces of molten metals **2** worthless matter
drought ⓣ *n* prolonged shortage of rainfall
drove[1] *v* past tense of **drive**
drove[2] ⓣ *n* **1** moving herd of livestock **2** moving crowd of people
▸ **drover** *n* person who drives sheep or cattle
drown ⓣ *v* **1** die or kill by immersion in liquid **2** forget (one's sorrows) temporarily by drinking alcohol **3** drench thoroughly **4** render (a sound) inaudible by making a loud noise
drowse *v* be sleepy, dull, or sluggish
drowsy *adj* **drowsily** *adv* **drowsiness** *n*
drubbing *n* utter defeat, as in a contest
drudge ⓣ *n* **1** person who works hard at wearisome menial tasks ▹ *v* **2** toil at such tasks **drudgery** *n*
drug ⓣ *n* **1** substance used in the treatment or prevention of disease **2** chemical substance, esp. a narcotic, taken for the effect it produces ▹ *v* **drugging, drugged** **3** administer a drug to (a person or animal) in order to induce sleepiness or unconsciousness **4** mix a drug with (food or drink)
▸ **drugstore** *n* pharmacy where a wide variety of goods is available
Druid *n* member of an ancient order of Celtic priests **Druidic** *or* **Druidical** *adj*
drum ⓣ *n* **1** percussion instrument sounded by striking a skin stretched across the opening of a hollow cylinder **2** cylindrical object or container ▹ *v* **drumming, drummed** **3** play (music) on a drum **4** tap rhythmically or regularly **drummer** *n*
▸ **drum into** *v* instil into (someone) by constant repetition
▸ **drumstick** *n* **1** stick used for playing a drum **2** lower joint of the leg of a cooked fowl
▸ **drum up** *v* obtain (support) by solicitation or canvassing
drunk ⓣ *v* **1** past participle of **drink** ▹ *adj* **2** intoxicated with alcohol to the extent of losing control over normal functions **3** overwhelmed by a strong influence or emotion ▹ *n* **4** person who is drunk
▸ **drunkard** *n* person who is frequently or habitually drunk
▸ **drunken** *adj* **1** drunk **2** caused by or relating to alcoholic intoxication

THESAURUS

dribble, fall in drops **4 = discontinue**, kick (*informal*), quit, axe (*informal*), relinquish, give up ▹ **drop off = set down**, leave, deliver, let off; (*Informal*) = **fall asleep**, nod *or* nod off, snooze (*informal*), doze *or* doze off, have forty winks (*informal*); = **decrease**, decline, diminish, dwindle, lessen, slacken, fall off ▹ **drop out = leave**, stop, quit, withdraw, abandon, fall by the wayside, give up ▹ **drop out of sight** *See* **disappear** ▸ *n* **5 = droplet**, bead, drip • *a drop of blue ink* **6 = dash**, shot (*informal*), spot, sip, mouthful, swig (*informal*), trace, trickle **7 = decrease**, cut, decline, slump, reduction, downturn, deterioration, fall-off, lowering **8 = fall**, plunge, descent *See also*: **ball, blob, deposit, dump, lose, lower**
droplet *n* = **drop**, drip, blob
drought *n* = **dry spell**, dehydration, dryness, aridity
drove *n* = **herd**, company, crowd, collection, mob, flock, swarm, throng, multitude, horde
drown *v* **1 = drench**, flood, sink, swamp, engulf, inundate, deluge, submerge, immerse, go under **2 = overpower**, overcome, overwhelm, stifle, obliterate, muffle, deaden, swallow up, wipe out
drowsy *adj* = **sleepy**, heavy, tired, lethargic, dopey (*slang*), dozy, half asleep, somnolent, torpid
drudge *n* = **menial**, servant, factotum, worker, slave, toiler
drudgery *n* = **menial labour**, donkey-work, grind (*informal*), labour, hard work, toil, slog
drug *n* **1 = medication**, medicine • *a new drug in the fight against AIDS* RELATED WORD *combining form*: pharmaco- **2 = dope** (*slang*), narcotic, stimulant • *She was sure her cousin was taking drugs.* ▸ *v* **3 = dose**, treat, dope (*slang*), medicate, administer a drug **4 = knock out**, poison, numb, deaden, anesthetize, stupefy
drum *v* = **beat**, tap, tattoo, rap, reverberate, throb, pulsate ▹ **drum into = drive home**, reiterate, din into, hammer away, harp on, instill into
drunk *adj* **1 = intoxicated** (*formal*), tipsy • *He got drunk.* OPPOSITE: sober ▸ *n* **2 = drunkard**, alcoholic, boozer (*informal*) • *A drunk lay in the alley.*
drunkard *n* = **drinker**, drunk, alcoholic, lush (*slang*), wino (*informal*), dipsomaniac, tippler
drunkenness *n* = **intoxication**, alcoholism, bibulousness, dipsomania, inebriation, insobriety, intemperance

DICTIONARY

drunkenly *adv* **drunkenness** *n*
dry Ⓣ *adj* **drier, driest** *or* **dryer, dryest** **1** lacking moisture **2** having little or no rainfall **3** *informal* thirsty **4** (of wine) not sweet **5** uninteresting: *a dry book* **6** (of humour) subtle and sarcastic **7** prohibiting the sale of alcohol: *a dry area* ▷ *v* **drying, dried 8** make or become dry **9** preserve (food) by removing the moisture **dryly** *adv* **dryness** *n*
▸ **dryer** *n* apparatus for removing moisture
▸ **dry-clean** *v* clean (clothes etc.) with a solvent other than water **dry-cleaner** *n* **dry-cleaning** *n*
▸ **dry out** *v* **1** make or become dry **2** (cause to) undergo treatment for alcoholism or drug addiction
▸ **dry rot** crumbling and drying of timber, caused by certain fungi
▸ **dry run** *informal* rehearsal
dryad *n* wood nymph
Dryden *n* **John**. 1631–1700, English poet, dramatist, and critic of the Augustan period, commonly regarded as the chief exponent of heroic tragedy. His major works include the tragedy *All for Love* (1677), the verse satire *Absalom and Achitophel* (1681), and the *Essay of Dramatick Poesie* (1668)
DSc Doctor of Science
DT's *informal* delirium tremens
dual Ⓣ *adj* **1** relating to or denoting two **2** twofold **duality** *n*
▸ **dual carriageway** *Brit* road on which traffic travelling in opposite directions is separated by a central strip of turf or concrete
dub[1] Ⓣ *v* **dubbing, dubbed** give (a person or place) a name or nickname
dub[2] *v* **dubbing, dubbed 1** provide (a film) with a new soundtrack, esp. in a different language **2** provide (a film or tape) with a soundtrack
dubbin *n* greasy preparation applied to leather to soften and waterproof it
dubious Ⓣ [**dew**-bee-uss] *adj* feeling or causing doubt **dubiously** *adv* **dubiety** [dew-**by**-it-ee] *n*
Dubois *n* **W**(**illiam**) **E**(**dward**) **B**(**urghardt**). 1868–1963, US Black sociologist, writer, and political activist; a founder of the National Association for the Advancement of Colored People (NAACP)
ducal [**duke**-al] *adj* of a duke
ducat [**duck**-it] *n* former European gold or silver coin
Duchamp *n* **Marcel**. 1887–1968, US painter and sculptor, born in France; noted as a leading exponent of Dada. His best-known work is *Nude Descending a Staircase* (1912)
Duchesne *n* **Pierre**. born 1940, Canadian politician; Lieutenant Governor of Quebec (2007–)
duchess *n* **1** woman who holds the rank of duke in her own right **2** wife or widow of a duke
duchy *n, pl* **duchies** territory of a duke or duchess
duck[1] *n* **1** water bird with short legs, webbed feet, and a broad blunt bill **2** female of this bird **3** flesh of this bird, used as food **4** *cricket* score of nothing
▸ **duckling** *n* young duck
duck[2] Ⓣ *v* **1** move (the head or body) quickly downwards, to escape observation or to dodge a blow **2** plunge suddenly into water **3** *informal* dodge or escape (a duty etc.)
duct *n* **1** tube, pipe, or canal by means of which a fluid or gas is conveyed **2** bodily passage conveying secretions or excretions
▸ **ductile** *adj* **1** (of metal) able to be shaped into sheets or wires **2** easily influenced **ductility** *n*
dud Ⓣ *informal* ▷ *n* **1** person or thing that proves ineffectual ▷ *adj* **2** bad or useless
dude *n US informal* **1** man, chap **2** *old-fashioned* dandy
dudgeon Ⓣ *n* **in high dudgeon** angry or resentful

d

THESAURUS

dry *adj* **1 = dehydrated**, arid, parched, dried-up • *The path was dry after the sunshine*. OPPOSITE: wet **2 = dull**, plain, boring, dreary, tedious, tiresome, monotonous, uninteresting **3 = sarcastic**, low-key, sly, deadpan, droll ▸ *v* **4 = dehydrate**, drain • *Wash and dry the lettuce*. OPPOSITE: moisten
▷ **dry out, dry up = become dry**, wither, wilt, harden, shrivel up, wizen
See also: **barren**
dual *adj* **= twofold**, double, twin, duplicate, duplex, binary, matched, paired
dub *See* **name**
dubious *adj* **1 = suspect**, suspicious, questionable, unreliable, crooked, dishonest • *a rather dubious claim* **2 = unsure**, nervous, suspicious, skeptical, undecided, doubtful, unconvinced • *My parents were a bit dubious about it all*.
See also: **improbable, uncertain**
duck *v* **1 = bob**, drop, lower, bow, bend, dodge, crouch, stoop **2 = plunge**, dive, dip, wet, dunk, douse, submerge, immerse, souse **3** (*Informal*) **= dodge**, avoid, escape, shun, evade, sidestep, shirk ▷ **duck out of** *See* **avoid**
dud (*Informal*) ▸ *n* **1 = failure**, flop (*informal*), washout (*informal*) ▸ *adj* **2 = useless**, broken, failed, worthless, inoperative
dudgeon *n* ▷ **in high dudgeon = indignant**, angry, resentful, choked, fuming, offended,

DICTIONARY

due Ⓣ *adj* **1** expected or scheduled to be present or arrive **2** owed as a debt **3** fitting, proper ▷ *n* **4** something that is owed, required, or due **dues 5** charges for membership of a club or organization ▷ *adv* **6** directly or exactly: *due north*
▶ **due to** attributable to or caused by

duel Ⓣ *n* **1** formal prearranged combat with deadly weapons between two people, to settle a quarrel ▷ *v* **duelling, duelled 2** fight in a duel **duellist** *n*

duenna *n* (esp. in Spain) elderly woman acting as chaperone to a young woman

duet *n* piece of music for two performers

duffel, duffle *n* short for **duffel coat**
▶ **duffel bag** *or* **duffle bag** cylindrical canvas bag fastened with a drawstring
▶ **duffel coat** *or* **duffle coat** coat made of heavy woollen cloth

duffer *n informal* dull or incompetent person

Du Fu, Tu Fu *n* 712–770 AD, Chinese poet of the Tang dynasty

dug[1] *v* past of **dig**

dug[2] *n* teat or udder

dugong *n* whalelike mammal found in tropical waters

dugout *n* **1** canoe made by hollowing out a log **2** (at a sports ground) covered bench where managers and substitutes sit **3** *mil* covered excavation dug to provide shelter

Dukas *n* **Paul**. 1865–1935, French composer best known for the orchestral scherzo *The Sorcerer's Apprentice* (1897)

duke *n* **1** nobleman of the highest rank **2** prince or ruler of a small principality or duchy **dukedom** *n*

dulcet [**dull**-sit] *adj* (of a sound) soothing or pleasant

dulcimer *n* tuned percussion instrument consisting of a set of strings stretched over a sounding board and struck with hammers

dull Ⓣ *adj* **1** uninteresting **2** stupid **3** (of a pain) not acute or intense **4** (of weather) not bright or clear **5** lacking in spirit **6** (of a blade) lacking sharpness ▷ *v* **7** make or become dull **dullness** *n* **dully** *adv*
▶ **dullard** *n* dull or stupid person

Dulles *n* **John Foster**. 1888–1959, US statesman and lawyer; secretary of state (1953–59)

duly Ⓣ *adv* **1** in a proper manner **2** at the proper time

Dumas *n* **1 Alexandre**, known as *Dumas père*. 1802–70, French novelist and dramatist, noted for his historical romances *The Count of Monte Cristo* (1844) and *The Three Musketeers* (1844) **2** his son, **Alexandre**, known as *Dumas fils*. 1824–95, French novelist and dramatist, noted esp. for the play he adapted from an earlier novel, *La Dame aux camélias* (1852)

Du Maurier *n* **George Louis Palmella Busson**. 1834–96, English novelist, caricaturist, and illustrator; author of *Peter Ibbetson* (1891) and *Trilby* (1894)

dumb Ⓣ *adj* **1** lacking the power to speak **2** silent **3** *informal* stupid **dumbly** *adv* **dumbness** *n*
▶ **dumbbell** *n* exercising weight consisting of a short bar with a heavy ball or disc at either end
▶ **dumbfounded** *adj* speechless with amazement

THESAURUS

ticked off (*informal*), vexed

due *adj* **1 = expected**, scheduled **2 = payable**, outstanding, unpaid, in arrears, owed, owing **3 = fitting**, appropriate, proper, suitable, justified, rightful, deserved, merited, well-earned ▶ *n* **4 = right** *or* **rights**, privilege, deserts, merits ▶ *adv* **5 = directly**, dead, straight, exactly, undeviatingly

duel *n* **1 = single combat**, affair of honour **2 = contest**, fight, competition, clash, encounter, engagement, rivalry, head-to-head ▶ *v* **3 = fight**, struggle, rival, contest, compete, clash, contend, lock horns, vie with

dues *pl n* **= membership fee**, charge, fee, contribution, levy, charges

dull *adj* **1 = boring**, drab, tedious, monotonous, humdrum, uninteresting • *I found the play rather dull.* OPPOSITE: interesting **2 = drab**, sombre, gloomy, muted, subdued • *a dark, dull blue colour* OPPOSITE: bright **3 = cloudy**, murky, overcast, leaden • *It seems as if it's always dull and raining.* **4 = stupid**, dense, dim-witted (*informal*), slow, thick, unintelligent **5 = lifeless**, blank, listless, indifferent, apathetic, unresponsive, passionless **6 = blunt**, blunted, unsharpened ▶ *v* **7 = relieve**, moderate, soften, blunt, alleviate, lessen, allay, take the edge off
See also: **dim, dreary, fade, flat, numb, sleepy, stuffy**

dullness *See* **boredom**

duly *adv* **1 = properly**, correctly, appropriately, accordingly, suitably, rightfully, fittingly, deservedly, befittingly, decorously **2 = on time**, at the proper time, punctually

dumb *adj* **1 = mute**, silent, speechless • *We were all struck dumb for a minute.* **2** (*Informal*) **= stupid**, thick, dense, dull, foolish, asinine, dim-witted (*informal*), unintelligent

dumbfounded *adj* **= amazed**, speechless, staggered, overwhelmed, astonished,

DICTIONARY

▸ **dumb show** meaningful gestures without speech
dumdum *n* soft-nosed bullet that expands on impact and inflicts extensive wounds
dummy Ⓣ *n, pl* **-mies 1** figure representing the human form, used for displaying clothes etc. **2** copy of an object, often lacking some essential feature of the original **3** *slang* stupid person ▷ *adj* **4** imitation or substitute
▸ **dummy run** practice, rehearsal
Du Mont *n* **Allen Balcom**. 1901–65, US inventor and electronics manufacturer. He developed the cathode-ray tube used in television sets and oscilloscopes
dump Ⓣ *v* **1** drop or let fall heavily or in a mass **2** *informal* abandon (something or someone) carelessly **3** dispose of (nuclear waste) **4** market (goods) in bulk and at low prices, esp. abroad ▷ *n* **5** place where waste materials are dumped **6** *informal* dirty unattractive place **7** *mil* place where weapons or supplies are stored
▸ **down in the dumps** in a state of depression
▸ **dumpy** *adj* short and plump
dumpling *n* **1** small ball of dough cooked and served with stew **2** round pastry case filled with fruit
dun *adj* brownish-grey
Dunant *n* **Jean Henri**. 1828–1910, Swiss humanitarian, founder of the International Red Cross (1864): shared the Nobel peace prize 1901
Dunbar *n* **William**. ?1460–?1520, Scottish poet, noted for his satirical, allegorical, and elegiac works
Duncan I *n* died 1040, king of Scotland (1034–40); killed by Macbeth
dunce Ⓣ *n* person who is stupid or slow to learn
dunderhead *n* slow-witted person
dune *n* mound or ridge of drifted sand
dung *n* excrement of animals
dungarees *pl n* trousers with a bib attached
dungeon Ⓣ *n* underground prison cell
dunk *v* **1** dip (a cookie etc.) into liquid before eating it **2** submerge (something) in liquid **3** *basketball* drop (the ball) through the hoop with the hands above the rim ▷ *n* **4** *basketball* scoring shot in which a player drops the ball through the hoop with the hands above the rim **5** see **slam dunk**
dunlin *n* small sandpiper with a brown back
Dunlop *n* **John Boyd**. 1840–1921, Scottish veterinarian, who devised the first successful pneumatic tire, which was manufactured by the company named after him
Duns Scotus *n* **John**. ?1265–1308, Scottish scholastic theologian and Franciscan priest: opposed the theology of St Thomas Aquinas
Dunstable *n* **John**. died 1453, English composer, esp. of motets and mass settings, noted for his innovations in harmony and rhythm
Dunstan *n* **Saint**. ?909–988 AD, English prelate and statesman; archbishop of Canterbury (959–988). He revived monasticism in England on Benedictine lines and promoted education. Feast day: May 19
duo *n, pl* **duos 1** pair of performers **2** *informal* pair of closely connected people
duodecimal *adj* reckoned in twelves or twelfths
duodenum [dew-oh-**deen**-um] *n, pl* **-na, -nums** first part of the small intestine, just below the stomach **duodenal** *adj*
Duparc *n* **Henri**, full name *Marie Eugène Henri Fouques Duparc*. 1848–1933, French composer of songs noted for their sad brooding quality
dupe Ⓣ *v* **1** deceive or cheat ▷ *n* **2** person who is easily deceived
duple *adj music* having two beats in a bar
Duplessis *n* **Maurice Le Noblet**. 1890–1959, Canadian politician. Premier of Quebec (1936–39, 1944–59); founder of the conservative Union Nationale (1935)

THESAURUS

astounded, flabbergasted (*informal*), lost for words, nonplussed, stunned
dumbness *See* **silence**
dummy *n* **1** = **model**, figure, form, mannequin, manikin **2** = **copy**, counterfeit, substitute, duplicate, sham, imitation **3** (*Slang*) = **fool**, idiot, blockhead, dork (*slang*), dunce, nitwit (*informal*), oaf, schmuck (*slang*), simpleton ▸ *adj* **4** = **imitation**, fake, false, artificial, mock, bogus, phony (*informal*), sham, simulated
dump *v* **1** = **get rid of**, discharge, jettison, dispose of, throw away, throw out • *The thieves were arrested when they dumped the stolen car in the police station's parking lot.* **2** = **drop**, deposit • *We dumped our bags at the hotel and went for a walk.* ▸ *n* **3** = **landfill**, transfer station, rubbish heap, junkyard, refuse heap, garbage dump, nuisance grounds (*Canad*), dumping ground, slag pit **4** (*Informal*) = **pigsty**, mess, slum, hovel
See also: **discard**
dumpy *adj* (*Informal*) = **dowdy**, frowzy, frumpy, homely (*US*), unfashionable
dunce *n* = **simpleton**, blockhead, moron, dunderhead, ignoramus, thickhead
dungeon *n* = **prison**, cell, vault, cage, oubliette
dupe *v* = **trick**, fool, con (*informal*), cheat, deceive, delude, play a trick on • *I was duped into believing the autograph was authentic.*
See also: **take in, trap**

DICTIONARY

duplex *adj* **1** twofold ▷ *n* **2** house divided into two separate dwellings **3** either dwelling
duplicate Ⓣ *adj* **1** copied exactly from an original ▷ *n* **2** exact copy ▷ *v* **3** make a replica of **4** do again (something that has already been done) **duplication** *n* **duplicator** *n*
duplicity *n* deception or double-dealing
Dupré *n* **Marcel**. 1886–1971, French organist and composer, noted as an improviser
durable Ⓣ *adj* long-lasting **durability** *n*
▶ **durables** *or* **durable goods** *pl n* goods that require infrequent replacement
Durán *n* **Roberto**. born 1951, Panamanian boxer
duration Ⓣ *n* length of time that something lasts
Dürer *n* **Albrecht**. 1471–1528, German painter and engraver, regarded as the greatest artist of the German Renaissance and noted particularly as a draftsman and for his copper engravings and woodcuts
duress Ⓣ *n* compulsion by use of force or threats
during *prep* throughout or within the limit of (a period of time)
Durrell *n* **Gerald** (**Malcolm**). 1925–95, British zoologist and writer: his books include *The Bafut Beagles* (1954), *My Family and Other Animals* (1956), and *The Aye-aye and I* (1992)
Duruflé *n* **Maurice**. 1902–86, French composer and organist, best known for his *Requiem* (1947)
dusk Ⓣ *n* time just before nightfall, when it is almost dark
▶ **dusky** *adj* **1** dark in colour **2** shadowy **duskiness** *n*
dust Ⓣ *n* **1** dry fine powdery material, such as particles of dirt ▷ *v* **2** remove dust from (furniture) by wiping **3** sprinkle (something) with dust or some other powdery substance
▶ **duster** *n* cloth used for dusting
▶ **dusty** *adj* covered with dust
▶ **dustbin** *n Brit* garbage can
▶ **dustbowl** *n* dry area in which the surface soil is exposed to wind erosion
▶ **dust jacket** *or* **dust cover** removable paper cover used to protect a book
▶ **dustman** *n Brit* garbage collector
▶ **dustpan** *n* short-handled hooded shovel into which dust is swept from floors
Dutch *adj* of the Netherlands, its inhabitants, or their language
▶ **go Dutch** *informal* share the expenses on an outing
▶ **Dutch courage** false courage gained from drinking alcohol
duty Ⓣ *n, pl* **-ties 1** task that a person is bound to perform for moral or legal reasons **2** government tax, esp. on imports
▶ **on duty** at work
▶ **dutiable** *adj* (of goods) requiring payment of duty
▶ **dutiful** *adj* showing or resulting from a sense of duty **dutifully** *adv*
duvet [**doo**-vay] *n* quilt filled with down or artificial fibre
Dvořák *n* **Antonín**, known as *Anton Dvořák*. 1841–1904, Czech composer, much of whose work reflects the influence of folk music. His best-known work is the *Symphony No. 9 From the New World* (1893)
DVT deep-vein thrombosis
dwarf Ⓣ *n, pl* **dwarfs, dwarves 1** undersized person **2** (in folklore) small ugly manlike creature, often possessing magical powers ▷ *adj* **3** denoting an animal or plant much

THESAURUS

duplicate *adj* **1 = identical**, twin, twofold, corresponding, matched, matching ▶ *n* **2 = copy**, double, clone, reproduction, replica, photocopy, facsimile, carbon copy ▶ *v* **3 = copy**, double, repeat, clone, replicate, reproduce
durability *n* = **durableness**, endurance, persistence, constancy, imperishability, permanence
durable *adj* = **long-lasting**, strong, tough, persistent, reliable, resistant, enduring, sturdy, dependable, hard-wearing
duration *n* = **length**, time, term, period, stretch, span, spell, extent
duress *n* = **pressure**, threat, constraint, coercion, compulsion
dusk *n* = **twilight**, evening, dark, sunset, nightfall, sundown, eventide, gloaming (*Scot, poetic*)
dusky *adj* **1 = dark**, dark-complexioned, sable, swarthy **2 = dim**, obscure, gloomy, murky, shady, cloudy, shadowy, tenebrous, twilit
dust *n* **1 = grime**, powder, grit, particles ▶ *v* **2 = sprinkle**, cover, spread, spray, powder, scatter, sift, dredge
dusty *adj* = **dirty**, unclean, grubby, scuzzy (*slang*), sooty, unswept
dutiful *adj* = **conscientious**, respectful, devoted, obedient, submissive, reverential
duty *n* **1 = responsibility**, obligation • *Citizens have a duty to vote.* **2 = job**, role, responsibility, assignment • *He carried out his duties conscientiously.* **3 = tax**, tariff, levy, excise • *customs duties* **4 = loyalty**, respect, allegiance, deference, obedience, reverence ▷ **on duty = at work**, busy, engaged, on active service, on the job (*informal*)
See also: **function, part, task, work**
dwarf *v* **1 = tower above** *or* **tower over**, dominate, diminish, overshadow

DICTIONARY

below the average size for a species ▷ *v* **4** cause (someone or something) to seem small by being much larger
dwell Ⓣ *v* **dwelling, dwelt** *or* **dwelled** live as a permanent resident **dweller** *n*
▸ **dwelling** *n* place of residence
▸ **dwell on** *or* **dwell upon** *v* think, speak, or write at length about
dwindle Ⓣ *v* grow less in size, intensity, or number
dye Ⓣ *n* **1** staining or colouring substance **2** colour produced by dyeing ▷ *v* **dyeing, dyed 3** colour or stain (fabric, hair, etc.) by the application of dye **dyer** *n*
▸ **dyed-in-the-wool** *adj* uncompromising or unchanging in attitude or opinion
dying Ⓣ *v* present participle of **die**[1]
dyke *n* **1** wall built to prevent flooding **2** ditch **3** *slang* lesbian
Dylan *n* **Bob**, real name *Robert Allen Zimmerman*. born 1941, US rock singer and songwriter, also noted for his ac
dynamic Ⓣ *adj* **1** characterized by force of personality, ambition, and energy **2** of or concerned with energy or forces that produce motion **dynamically** *adv*
▸ **dynamism** *n* forcefulness of an energetic personality
dynamics *n* branch of mechanics concerned with the forces that change or produce the motions of bodies
dynamite *n* **1** high-explosive mixture containing nitroglycerin **2** *informal* spectacular or potentially dangerous person or thing ▷ *v* **3** mine or blow (something) up with dynamite
dynamo *n, pl* **-mos** device for converting mechanical energy into electrical energy
dynasty Ⓣ *n, pl* **-ties** sequence of hereditary rulers **dynastic** *adj*
dysentery *n* infection of the intestine causing severe diarrhea
dysfunction *n med* disturbance or abnormality in the function of an organ or part
dyslexia *n* disorder causing impaired ability to read **dyslexic** *adj*
dysmenorrhea, dysmenorrhoea *n* painful menstruation
dyspepsia *n* indigestion **dyspeptic** *adj*
dystrophy [**diss**-trof-fee] *n* wasting of the body tissues, esp. the muscles

d

THESAURUS

▸ *adj* **2 = miniature**, small, baby, tiny, diminutive, undersized, bonsai ▸ *n* **3 = midget**, pygmy *or* pigmy, Lilliputian, Tom Thumb
dweeb *n* (*Slang*) **= idiot**, dope (*slang*), fool, geek, nerd, slang, doofus (*slang*), dunce
dwell *v* **= live**, abide, lodge, reside, inhabit
dwelling *n* **= home**, house, pad (*slang*), residence, lodging, abode, habitation, domicile, quarters
dwindle *v* **= lessen**, decline, decrease, shrink, fade, diminish, wane, subside, die away, peter out, taper off
dye *n* **1 = colouring**, colour, stain, pigment, tint, tinge, colourant ▸ *v* **2 = colour**, stain, pigment, tint, tinge
dying *adj* **= expiring**, failing, moribund, at death's door, *in extremis* (*Latin*), not long for this world ▷ **be dying for = long for**, ache for, hunger for, pine for, yearn for • *I'm dying for a breath of fresh air!*
dynamic *adj* **= energetic**, powerful, vital, go-ahead, lively, high-powered, forceful, go-getting (*informal*)
dynasty *n* **= empire**, government, rule, house, regime, sovereignty

DICTIONARY

Ee

E East(ern)
e- *prefix* electronic: *e-mail*
each Ⓣ *adj, pron* every (one) taken separately
Eadwig, Edwy *n* died 959 AD, king of England (955–57)
eager Ⓣ *adj* showing or feeling great desire, keen **eagerly** *adv* **eagerness** *n*
eagle *n* **1** large bird of prey with keen eyesight **2** *golf* score of two strokes under par for a hole
▶ **eaglet** *n* young eagle
Eakins *n* **Thomas**. 1844–1916, US painter of portraits and sporting life: a noted realist
ear[1] Ⓣ *n* **1** organ of hearing, esp. the external part of it **2** sensitivity to musical or other sounds
▶ **earache** *n* pain in the ear
▶ **eardrum** *n* thin piece of skin inside the ear which enables one to hear sounds
▶ **earmark** *v* **1** set (something) aside for a specific purpose ▷ *n* **2** distinguishing mark
▶ **earphone** *n* receiver for a radio etc. held to or put in the ear
▶ **earring** *n* ornament for the lobe of the ear
▶ **earshot** *n* hearing range
ear[2] *n* head of corn
earl *n* British nobleman ranking next below a marquess **earldom** *n*
early Ⓣ *adj, adv* **-lier**, **-liest** **1** before the expected or usual time **2** in the first part of a period **3** in a period far back in time
earn Ⓣ *v* **1** obtain by work or merit **2** (of investments etc.) gain (interest) **3** *baseball* score (a run) without the fielding side making an error **earner** *n*
▶ **earnings** *pl n* money earned
earnest[1] Ⓣ *adj* serious and sincere **earnestly** *adv*
▶ **in earnest** seriously
earnest[2] *n* part payment given in advance, esp. to confirm a contract
earth Ⓣ *n* **1** planet that we live on **2** land, the ground **3** soil **4** fox's hole **5** wire connecting an electrical apparatus with the earth ▷ *v* **6** connect (a circuit) to earth
▶ **earthen** *adj* made of baked clay or earth
▶ **earthenware** *n* pottery made of baked clay
▶ **earthly** *adj* conceivable or possible: *no earthly reason*
▶ **earthy** *adj* **1** coarse or crude **2** of or like earth
▶ **earthquake** *n* violent vibration of the earth's surface
▶ **earthwork** *n* fortification made of earth
▶ **earthworm** *n* worm which burrows in the soil
earwig *n* small insect with a pincer-like tail

THESAURUS

each *adj* **1 = every** ▶ *pron* **2 = every one**, each and every one, each one, one and all ▶ *adv* **3 = apiece**, respectively, individually, for each, per capita, per head, per person, to each
eager *adj* **= keen**, anxious, enthusiastic, avid, ardent, raring to go (*informal*) • *She is eager to earn some extra money*
See also: **impatient, ready, willing**
eagerness *n* **= keenness**, hunger, enthusiasm, thirst, zeal, impatience, yearning, ardour, fervour
ear *n* **= sensitivity**, taste, discrimination, perception, appreciation
earlier *adv* **1 = before**, previously ▶ *adj* **2 = previous**, former, past, prior, preceding
earliest *See* **first**
early *adj* **1 = premature**, advance, untimely • *You're not late - I'm early!* OPPOSITE: late **2 = primitive**, primeval • *the early 1990s* ▶ *adv* **3 = ahead of time**, prematurely, beforehand, in advance, in good time • *We left early so we wouldn't have to line up*
earmark *v* **= set aside**, reserve, label, flag, designate, allocate, mark out
earn *v* **1 = make**, get, obtain, bring in • *He earns a lot more than I do.* **2 = win**, acquire, attain (*formal*) • *She earned the respect of her team.*
See also: **deserve, gain, merit**
earnest *adj* **= serious**, grave, intent, solemn, sincere, thoughtful, resolute, resolved ▶ *n* ▷ **in earnest = seriously**, sincerely, truthfully
earnings *pl n* **= income**, pay, salary, remuneration, proceeds, profits, receipts, takings, wages
earth *n* **1 = world**, planet, globe • *the tallest mountain on earth* RELATED WORD *adjective*: terrestrial **2 = soil**, ground, dirt, turf, clay, topsoil, loam • *He filled a pot with earth and planted the seeds in it.*
earthenware *n* **= crockery**, pottery, terracotta, ceramics, pots
earthly *adj* **= worldly**, human, material, secular, mortal, temporal
earthy *adj* **= crude**, robust, raunchy (*slang*),

DICTIONARY

ease Ⓣ *n* **1** freedom from difficulty, discomfort, or worry **2** rest or leisure: *at one's ease* ▷ *v* **3** give bodily or mental ease to **4** lessen (severity, tension, pain, etc.) **5** move carefully or gradually
easel *n* frame to support an artist's canvas or a blackboard
east *n* **1** part of the horizon where the sun rises **2** eastern lands or the orient ▷ *adj* **3** on, in, or near the east **4** (of the wind) from the east ▷ *adv* **5** in, to, or towards the east **eastward** *adj, adv* **eastwards** *adv*
▸ **easterly** *adj, adv* **1** to the east **2** (of a wind) from the east
▸ **eastern** *adj* of, in, or from the east
▸ **East Coast** Atlantic Coast of N America
Easter *n* Christian spring festival commemorating the Resurrection of Jesus Christ
▸ **Easter egg** chocolate egg given at Easter
Eastern Daylight Time *n* one of the standard times used in North America, four hours behind Greenwich Mean Time Abbreviation: **EDT**
Eastern Standard Time *n* one of the standard times used in North America, five hours behind Greenwich Mean Time Abbreviation: **EST**
Eastwood *n* **Clint**. born 1930, US film actor and director. His films as an actor include *The Good The Bad and The Ugly* (1966), *Dirty Harry* (1971), and as actor and director *Play Misty for Me* (1971), *Unforgiven* (1993), and *Mystic River* (2003).
easy Ⓣ *adj* **easier, easiest 1** not needing much work or effort **2** free from pain, care, or anxiety **3** easy-going **easily** *adv* **easiness** *n*
▸ **easy chair** comfortable armchair
▸ **easy-going** *adj* relaxed in attitude, tolerant
eat Ⓣ *v* **eating, ate, eaten 1** take (food) into the mouth and swallow it **2** (foll. by *away* or *up*) destroy **3** have a meal
▸ **eatable** *adj* fit or suitable for eating
Eaton *n* **Timothy**. 1834–1907, Canadian businessman born in Ireland. He founded Eaton's department stores (1869) and launched a successful mail-order catalogue
eau de Cologne [**oh** de kol-**lone**] *n French* light perfume
eaves *pl n* overhanging edges of a roof
eavesdrop Ⓣ *v* **-dropping, -dropped** listen secretly to a private conversation **eavesdropper** *n* **eavesdropping** *n*
ebb Ⓣ *v* **1** (of tide water) flow back **2** become weaker ▷ *n* **3** flowing back of the tide
▸ **at a low ebb** in a state of weakness
ebony *n, pl* **-onies 1** hard black wood ▷ *adj* **2** deep black
e-book *n* **1** electronic book ▷ *v* **2** book (airline tickets, appointments, etc.) on the internet
ebullient *adj* overflowing with enthusiasm and excitement **ebullience** *n*
eccentric Ⓣ *adj* **1** odd or unconventional

e

THESAURUS

coarse, bawdy, unsophisticated, ribald, uninhibited
ease *n* **1 = easiness**, facility, simplicity, readiness, effortlessness • *He passed his test with ease.* **2 = content**, peace, quiet, comfort, happiness, leisure, serenity, tranquillity, peace of mind **3 = rest**, leisure, relaxation, repose, restfulness ▸ *v* **4 = relieve**, calm, relax, abate, slacken • *The doctor gave him medication to ease the pain.* **5 = edge**, lower, guide, inch, creep, squeeze, manoeuvre • *He eased the door open and peered outside.*
See also: **moderate**
easily *adv* **= without difficulty**, smoothly, readily, comfortably, effortlessly, with ease, with one hand tied behind one's back ▷ **easily offended** *See* **sensitive, touchy** ▷ **easily upset** *See* **sensitive**
easy *adj* **1 = simple**, light, smooth, straightforward, painless • *The software is very easy to install.* OPPOSITE: hard **2 = carefree**, quiet, comfortable, leisurely, relaxed • *He has not had an easy life.* **3 = tolerant**, mild, lenient, easy-going, indulgent, permissive, unoppressive
See also: **fluent, informal**
easy-going *adj* **= relaxed**, easy, casual, tolerant, laid-back (*informal*), carefree, happy-go-lucky, nonchalant, even-tempered, placid, undemanding
eat *v* **1 = consume**, swallow, ingest, chew, gobble, scoff (*slang*), devour, munch • *For lunch he ate a cheese sandwich.* **2 = have a meal**, feed, dine, picnic, chow down (*slang*), take nourishment • *We like to eat early.* **3 = destroy**, dissolve, erode, decay, rot, corrode, waste away, wear away ▷ **eat away = destroy**, dissolve, erode, rot, corrode, wear away • *The front of the car had been eaten away by rust.*
eavesdrop *v* **= listen in**, monitor, spy, overhear, snoop (*informal*)
eavesdropping *See* **nosy**
ebb *v* **1 = flow back**, retire, withdraw, retreat, wane, recede, subside, go out **2 = decline**, flag, decrease, diminish, dwindle, lessen, fade away, fall away, peter out ▸ *n* **3 = flowing back**, withdrawal, retreat, wane, going out, low tide, low water, subsidence
eccentric *adj* **1 = strange**, bizarre, weird, outrageous, quirky, outlandish, screwball (*slang*), ding-a-ling (*slang*) • *His math teacher was considered a bit eccentric.* ▸ *n* **2 = crank**

DICTIONARY

2 (of circles) not having the same centre ▷ *n* 3 unconventional person **eccentrically** *adv*
▸ **eccentricity** *n* 1 unconventional behaviour 2 odd habit
ecclesiastic Ⓣ *adj* 1 Also **ecclesiastical** of the Christian Church or clergy ▷ *n* 2 clergyman
Ecevit *n* **Bülent**. 1925–2006, Turkish politician and journalist: prime minister of Turkey (1974, 1977, 1978–79, 1998–2002)
ECG 1 electrocardiogram 2 electrocardiograph
echelon Ⓣ [**esh**-a-lon] *n* 1 level of power or responsibility 2 *mil* formation in which units follow one another but are spaced out sideways to allow each a line of fire ahead
echo Ⓣ *n, pl* **-oes** 1 repetition of sounds by reflection of sound waves off a surface 2 close imitation ▷ *v* **-oing**, **-oed** 3 repeat or be repeated as an echo 4 imitate closely
▸ **echo sounder** sonar
▸ **echo sounding** use of sonar to navigate
éclair *n* finger-shaped pastry filled with cream and covered with chocolate
éclat [ake-**lah**] *n* 1 brilliant success 2 splendour
eclectic *adj* selecting from various ideas or sources **eclecticism** *n*
eclipse Ⓣ *n* 1 temporary obscuring of one heavenly body by another ▷ *v* 2 surpass or outclass
▸ **ecliptic** *n* apparent path of the sun
eclogue *n* short poem on a rural theme
Eco *n* **Umberto**. born 1932, Italian semiologist and writer. His novels include *The Name of the Rose* (1981) and *Foucault's Pendulum* (1988)
eco- *combining form* ecology or ecological: *ecosystem*
ecological *adj* 1 of ecology 2 intended to protect the environment **ecologically** *adv*
▸ **ecology** *n* study of the relationships between living things and their environment **ecologist** *n*
e-commerce, ecommerce *n* business transactions done on the internet
economy Ⓣ *n, pl* **-mies** 1 system of interrelationship of money, industry, and employment in a country 2 careful management of resources to avoid waste
▸ **economic** *adj* 1 of economics 2 profitable
▸ **economics** *n* 1 social science concerned with the production and consumption of goods and services ▷ *pl n* 2 financial aspects
▸ **economical** *adj* not wasteful, thrifty **economically** *adv*
▸ **economist** *n* specialist in economics
▸ **economize** *v* limit or reduce waste
ecosystem *n* system involving interactions between a community and its environment
ecru *adj* greyish-yellow
ecstasy Ⓣ *n* 1 state of intense delight 2 *slang* powerful drug that can produce hallucinations **ecstatic** *adj* **ecstatically** *adv*
ECT electroconvulsive therapy
ectoplasm *n spiritualism* substance that supposedly is emitted from the body of a medium during a trance
ECU European Currency Unit
ecumenical *adj* of the Christian Church

THESAURUS

(*informal*), character (*informal*), screwball (*slang*), ding-a-ling (*slang*) • *He's always been regarded as a bit of an eccentric.*
eccentricity *n* = **oddity**, irregularity, abnormality, quirk, foible, caprice, capriciousness, idiosyncrasy, peculiarity
ecclesiastic *n* 1 = **clergyman**, minister, cleric, priest, pastor, churchman, holy man, man of the cloth, parson ▸ *adj* 2 *Also* **ecclesiastical** = **clerical**, religious, holy, spiritual, divine, pastoral, priestly
echelon *See* **rank**
echo *n* 1 = **repetition**, answer, reverberation 2 = **copy**, parallel, reflection, reproduction, imitation, mirror image, reiteration ▸ *v* 3 = **repeat**, resound, reverberate 4 = **copy**, recall, reflect, mirror, resemble, parallel, ape, imitate
eclipse *n* 1 = **obscuring**, extinction, darkening, dimming, shading ▸ *v* 2 = **surpass**, exceed, outshine, excel, outdo, transcend, put in the shade (*informal*)
economic *adj* 1 = **financial**, commercial, budgetary • *the need for economic reform* 2 = **profitable**, productive, viable, money-making, profit-making, remunerative
See also: **economical**
economical *adj* 1 = **economic**, cheap, inexpensive, cost-effective • *Our car may not be fast, but it's very economical.* 2 = **thrifty**, careful, prudent, frugal • *He's never been very economical about shopping for clothes.* 3 = **efficient**, cost-effective, money-saving, sparing, time-saving
economics *See* **finance**
economize *v* = **cut back**, save, be economical, be frugal, draw in one's horns, retrench, scrimp, tighten one's belt, cheap out (*informal*)
economy *n* = **thrift**, restraint, prudence, frugality (*formal*) • *improvements in the fuel economy of new cars*
ecstasy *n* = **rapture**, delight, joy, bliss, euphoria, elation, exaltation • *his feeling of ecstasy after winning the medal*
See also: **happiness, heaven**
ecstatic *adj* = **rapturous**, joyous, euphoric,

DICTIONARY

throughout the world, esp. with regard to its unity

eczema [**ek**-sim-a] *n* skin disease causing intense itching

Edam *n* round Dutch cheese with a red rind

Edberg *n* **Stefan**. born 1966, Swedish tennis player: Wimbledon champion 1988, 1990

eddy Ⓣ *n, pl* **eddies 1** small whirling movement in air, water, etc. ▷ *v* **eddying, eddied 2** move in eddies

Eddy *n* **Mary Baker**. 1821–1910, US religious leader; founder of the Christian Science movement (1866)

edelweiss [**ade**-el-vice] *n* alpine plant with white flowers

Eden[1] *n* **1** *Bible* garden in which Adam and Eve were placed at the Creation **2** place of delight or contentment

Eden[2] *n* Sir (**Robert**) **Anthony**, Earl of Avon. 1897–1977, British Conservative statesman; foreign secretary (1935–38; 1940–45; 1951–55) and prime minister (1955–57). He resigned after the controversy caused by the occupation of the Suez Canal zone by British and French forces (1956)

Edgar *n* **1** 944–975 AD, king of Mercia and Northumbria (957–975) and of England (959–975) **2** ?1074–1107, king of Scotland (1097–1107), fourth son of Malcolm III. He overthrew his uncle Donald to gain the throne

edge Ⓣ *n* **1** border or line where something ends or begins **2** cutting side of a blade **3** sharpness of tone ▷ *v* **4** provide an edge or border for **5** push (one's way) gradually

▸ **have the edge on** have an advantage over

▸ **on edge** nervous or irritable

▸ **edgeways** *adv* with the edge forwards or uppermost

▸ **edging** *n* anything placed along an edge

▸ **edgy** *adj* nervous or irritable

edible Ⓣ *adj* fit to be eaten **edibility** *n*

edict Ⓣ [**ee**-dikt] *n* order issued by an authority

edifice Ⓣ [**ed**-if-iss] *n* large building

edify Ⓣ [**ed**-if-fie] *v* **-fying, -fied** improve morally by instruction **edification** *n*

Edinburgh *n* **Duke of**, title of Prince *Philip Mountbatten*. born 1921, husband of Elizabeth II of Great Britain and Northern Ireland

edit Ⓣ *v* prepare (a book, film, etc.) for publication or broadcast

▸ **edition** *n* **1** form in which something is published **2** number of copies of a new publication printed at one time

▸ **editor** *n* **1** person who edits **2** person in overall charge of a newspaper or magazine

▸ **editorial** *adj* **1** of editing or editors ▷ *n* **2** newspaper article stating the opinion of the editor

Edmund *n* **Saint**, also called *Saint Edmund Rich*. 1175–1240, English churchman: archbishop of Canterbury (1234–40). Feast day: Nov 16

Edmund I *n* ?922–946 AD, king of England (940–946)

Edmund II *n* called *Edmund Ironside*. ?980–1016, king of England in 1016. His succession was contested by Canute and they divided the kingdom between them

EDT Eastern Daylight Time

educate Ⓣ *v* **1** teach **2** provide schooling for **education** *n* **educational** *adj* **educationally** *adv*

▸ **educationalist** *n* expert in the theory of education

▸ **educative** *adj* educating

Edward *n* **1** known as *the Black Prince*. 1330–76, Prince of Wales, the son of Edward III of

THESAURUS

blissful, elated, enraptured, entranced, in seventh heaven, on cloud nine (*informal*), overjoyed

eddy *n* **1 = swirl**, undertow, whirlpool, vortex, counter-current, counterflow ▸ *v* **2 = swirl**, whirl

edge *n* **1 = border**, margin, rim, lip, boundary, fringe, perimeter, brim, periphery • *on the edge of the forest* OPPOSITE: centre **2 = sharpness**, point, force, bite, effectiveness, incisiveness, keenness **3 = advantage**, lead, dominance, superiority, ascendancy, upper hand **on edge = nervous**, tense, impatient, edgy, apprehensive, irritable, ill at ease, keyed up, on tenterhooks, wired (*slang*) ▸ *v* **4 = inch**, creep, sidle • *He edged toward the phone, ready to grab it if it rang.* **5 = border**, fringe, hem

See also: **bank, ease, outskirts, side**

edgy *adj* **= nervous**, anxious, tense, restive, irritable, ill at ease, keyed up, on edge, on tenterhooks, wired (*slang*)

edible *adj* **= eatable**, good, harmless, palatable, wholesome, digestible, fit to eat

edict *n* **= decree**, order, law, act, ruling, command, injunction, proclamation

edifice *n* **= building**, house, construction, structure, erection

edify *v* **= instruct**, school, improve, guide, teach, inform, educate, nurture, enlighten

edit *v* **= revise**, correct, adapt, rewrite, polish, condense, emend

edition *n* **= version**, issue, program (*TV, radio*), number, copy, volume, impression, printing

educate *v* **= teach**, school, develop, improve, train, inform, discipline, instruct, enlighten, tutor, civilize

educated *adj* **1 = cultured**, intellectual, cultivated, learned • *an educated, tolerant,*

DICTIONARY

England. He won victories over the French at Crécy (1346) and Poitiers (1356) in the Hundred Years' War **2 Prince**. born 1964, Earl of Wessex, third son of Elizabeth II of Great Britain and Northern Ireland. In 1999 he married Sophie Rhys-Jones (born 1965); their daughter Louise was born in 2003

Edward I *n* 1239–1307, king of England (1272–1307); son of Henry III. He conquered Wales (1284) but failed to subdue Scotland

Edward II *n* 1284–1327, king of England (1307–27); son of Edward I. He invaded Scotland but was defeated by Robert Bruce at Bannockburn (1314). He was deposed by his wife Isabella and Roger Mortimer; died in prison

Edward III *n* 1312–77, king of England (1327–77); son of Edward II. His claim to the French throne in right of his mother Isabella provoked the Hundred Years' War (1337)

Edward IV *n* 1442–83, king of England (1461–70; 1471–83); son of Richard, duke of York. He defeated Henry VI in the Wars of the Roses and became king (1461). In 1470 Henry was restored to the throne, but Edward recovered the crown by his victory at Tewkesbury

Edward V *n* 1470–?83, king of England in 1483; son of Edward IV. He was deposed by his uncle, Richard, Duke of Gloucester (Richard III), and is thought to have been murdered with his brother in the Tower of London

Edward VI *n* 1537–53, king of England (1547–53), son of Henry VIII and Jane Seymour. His uncle the Duke of Somerset was regent until 1552, when he was executed. Edward then came under the control of Dudley, Duke of Northumberland

Edward VII *n* 1841–1910, king of Great Britain and Ireland (1901–10); son of Queen Victoria

Edward VIII *n* 1894–1972, king of Great Britain and Ireland in 1936; son of George V and brother of George VI. He abdicated in order to marry an American divorcée, Mrs Wallis Simpson (1896–1986); created Duke of Windsor (1937)

Edwardian *adj* of the reign of King Edward VII of Great Britain and Ireland (1901–10)

Edwards *n* **Jonathan**. 1703–58, American Calvinist theologian and metaphysician; author of *The Freedom of the Will* (1754)

Edward the Confessor *n* **Saint**. ?1002–66, king of England (1042–66); son of Ethelred II; founder of Westminster Abbey. Feast day: Oct 13

Edward the Elder *n* died 924 AD, king of England (899–924), son of Alfred the Great

Edward the Martyr *n* **Saint**. ?963–978 AD, king of England (975–78), son of Edgar: murdered. Feast day: March 18

Edwin *n* ?585–633 AD, king of Northumbria (617–633) and overlord of all England except Kent

EEG electroencephalogram

eel *n* snakelike fish

eerie Ⓣ *adj* uncannily frightening or disturbing **eerily** *adv*

efface Ⓣ *v* **1** remove by rubbing **2** make (oneself) inconspicuous **effacement** *n*

effect Ⓣ *n* **1** change or result caused by someone or something **2** overall impression **3** condition of being operative: *the law comes into effect next month*
▶ **effects 4** property **5** lighting, sounds, etc. to accompany a film or a broadcast ▷ *v* **6** cause to happen, accomplish
▶ **effective** *adj* **1** producing a desired result **2** impressive **3** operative **effectively** *adv*
▶ **effectual** *adj* successful in producing a desired result **effectually** *adv*

effeminate Ⓣ *adj* (of a man) displaying

THESAURUS

and reasonable person **2** = **taught**, informed, coached, instructed, nurtured, schooled, tutored

education *n* = **teaching**, training, instruction, schooling, coaching • *the importance of a good education*
See also: **knowledge**

educational *adj* = **instructive**, cultural, informative, edifying, educative, enlightening, improving

eerie *adj* = **frightening**, mysterious, strange, scary (*informal*), weird, spooky (*informal*), creepy (*informal*), ghostly, uncanny, unearthly

efface *v* = **obliterate**, cancel, destroy, erase, delete, eradicate, blot out, expunge, rub out, wipe out

effect *n* **1** = **result**, fruit, consequence, upshot, end result • *the effect that divorce has on children*
See also: **influence** **2** = **operation**, force, action, execution, enforcement, implementation **3** = **impression**, impact, sense, tenor, significance, essence ▶ *v* **4** = **bring about**, complete, produce, perform, achieve, execute, accomplish, fulfill

effective *adj* **1** = **efficient**, active, capable, useful, adequate, productive, competent, serviceable **2** = **in operation**, current, active, operative, in effect, in force **3** = **powerful**, impressive, forceful, persuasive, cogent, compelling, convincing, telling

effectively *See* **well**

effectiveness *See* **value**

effects *pl n* = **belongings**, property, gear, paraphernalia, goods, possessions, things

effeminate *adj* = **womanly**, camp (*informal*), weak, soft, tender, feminine, sissy, unmanly, womanish

DICTIONARY

characteristics thought to be typical of a woman **effeminacy** *n*
effervescent ⓣ *adj* (of a liquid) **1** giving off bubbles **2** (of a person) lively and enthusiastic **effervescence** *n*
effete ⓣ [if-**feet**] *adj* powerless, feeble
efficacious ⓣ *adj* producing the intended result, effective **efficacy** *n*
efficient ⓣ *adj* functioning effectively with little waste of effort **efficiently** *adv* **efficiency** *n*
effigy ⓣ [**ef**-fij-ee] *n, pl* **-gies** image or likeness of a person
efflorescence *n* flowering
effluent ⓣ *n* liquid discharged as waste
▸ **effluence** *n* something that flows out
▸ **effluvium** *n, pl* **-via** unpleasant smell, as decaying matter or gaseous waste
effort ⓣ *n* **1** physical or mental exertion **2** attempt **effortless** *adj*
effrontery ⓣ *n* brazen impudence
effusion *n* unrestrained outburst
▸ **effusive** *adj* openly emotional, demonstrative **effusively** *adv* **effusiveness** *n*
EFTA European Free Trade Association
EFTPOS electronic funds transfer at point of sale
e.g. for example
egalitarian *adj* **1** upholding the equality of all people ▹ *n* **2** person who holds egalitarian beliefs **egalitarianism** *n*
Egbert *n* ?775–839 AD, king of Wessex (802–839); first overlord of all England (829–830)
egg[1] *n* **1** oval or round object laid by the females of birds and other creatures, containing a developing embryo **2** hen's egg used as food **3** Also **egg cell** ovum
▸ **egghead** *n informal* intellectual person
▸ **eggplant** *n* plant bearing egg-shaped purple fruit eaten as a vegetable
egg[2] ⓣ *av* **egg on** encourage or incite, esp. to do wrong
eglantine *n* sweetbrier
ego *n, pl* **egos 1** self-esteem **2** the self of an individual person
▸ **egoism** *or* **egotism** *n* **1** excessive concern for one's own interests **2** excessively high opinion of oneself **egoist** *or* **egotist** *n* **egoistic** *or* **egotistic** *adj*
▸ **egocentric** *adj* self-centred
Egoyan *n* **Atom**. born 1960, Canadian film director, born in Egypt to Armenian parents; his films include *Exotica* (1994) and *The Sweet Hereafter* (1997)
egregious [ig-**greej**-uss] *adj* outstandingly bad
egress ⓣ [**ee**-gress] *n* **1** way out **2** departure
egret [**ee**-grit] *n* lesser white heron
Egyptian *adj* **1** relating to Egypt ▹ *n* **2** person from Egypt

THESAURUS

effervescent *adj* **1 = bubbling**, sparkling, frothy, carbonated, fizzy, foaming **2 = lively**, animated, enthusiastic, bubbly, exuberant, irrepressible, ebullient, vivacious
effete *adj* **= decadent**, weak, feeble, ineffectual, dissipated, enfeebled, spoiled
efficacious *adj* **= effective**, powerful, successful, efficient, potent, useful, adequate, productive, operative
efficiency *n* **= competence**, power, economy, capability, productivity, effectiveness, proficiency, adeptness
efficient *adj* **= competent**, effective, organized, economical, businesslike, productive • *The new hatchback has a much more efficient engine*. OPPOSITE: inefficient
See also: **able, capable, proficient**
efficiently *See* **well**
effigy *n* **= likeness**, figure, guy, picture, image, icon, portrait, statue, representation, idol, dummy
effluent *n* **= waste**, pollutant, sewage, effluvium
effort *n* **1 = exertion**, work, energy, trouble, application • *It took a lot of effort, but we managed in the end*. **2 = attempt**, bid, struggle, stab (*informal*), blitz • *an unsuccessful effort to ban Sunday shopping*
See also: **enterprise, hassle, labour, try**
effortless *adj* **= easy**, simple, smooth, painless, uncomplicated, plain sailing, undemanding
effrontery *n* **= insolence**, nerve, arrogance, cheek (*informal*), presumption, audacity, brazenness, impertinence, impudence, temerity
effusive *adj* **= demonstrative**, lavish, expansive, exuberant, ebullient, unrestrained, gushing, unreserved
egg *v* ▹ **egg on = encourage**, urge, push, prompt, spur, incite, prod, goad, exhort
egocentric *adj* **= self-centred**, selfish, egoistic, egoistical, egotistic, egotistical
egoistic *See* **selfish**
egoistical *See* **selfish**
egotism, egoism *n* **= self-centredness**, self-esteem, vanity, selfishness, self-interest, narcissism, self-importance, conceitedness, self-absorption
egotist, egoist *n* **= egomaniac**, bighead (*informal*), boaster, braggart, narcissist
egotistic, egotistical, egoistic, egoistical *adj* **= self-centred**, vain, self-absorbed, egocentric, narcissistic, boasting, conceited, full of oneself, self-important
egress *n* (*Formal*) **= exit**, withdrawal, departure, exodus, way out

DICTIONARY

Egyptology *n* study of the culture of ancient Egypt
Ehrlich *n* **Paul**. 1854–1915, German bacteriologist, noted for his pioneering work in immunology and chemotherapy and for his discovery of a remedy for syphilis: Nobel prize for physiology or medicine 1908
Eichmann *n* **Karl Adolf**. 1902–62, Austrian Nazi official, who took a leading role in organizing the extermination of the European Jews. He escaped to Argentina after World War II, but was captured and executed in Israel as a war criminal
eider *n* Arctic duck
▸ **eiderdown** *n* quilt (orig. stuffed with eider feathers)
eight *adj, n* **1** one more than seven ▹ *n* **2** eight-oared boat **3** its crew
▸ **eighth** *adj, n* (of) number eight in a series
▸ **eighteen** *adj, n* eight and ten **eighteenth** *adj, n*
▸ **eighty** *adj, n* eight times ten **eightieth** *adj, n*
Einstein *n* **Albert**. 1879–1955, US physicist and mathematician, born in Germany. He formulated the special theory of relativity (1905) and the general theory of relativity (1916), and made major contributions to the quantum theory, for which he was awarded the Nobel prize for physics in 1921. He was noted also for his work for world peace
Einsteinian *adj*
Einthoven *n* **Willem**. 1860–1927, Dutch physiologist. A pioneer of electrocardiography, he was awarded the Nobel prize for physiology or medicine in 1924
Eisenhower *n* **Dwight David**, known as *Ike*. 1890–1969, US general and Republican statesman; Supreme Commander of the Allied Expeditionary Force (1943–45) and 34th president of the US (1953–61). He commanded Allied forces in Europe and North Africa (1942), directed the invasion of Italy (1943), and was Supreme Commander of the combined land forces of NATO (1950–52)
Eisenstaedt *n* **Alfred**. 1898–1995, US photographer, born in Germany
Eisenstein *n* **Sergei Mikhailovich**. 1898–1948, Soviet film director. His films include *Battleship Potemkin* (1925), *Alexander Nevsky* (1938), and *Ivan the Terrible* (1944)
eisteddfod [ice-**sted**-fod] *n* Welsh festival with competitions in music and other performing arts
either *adj, pron* **1** one or the other (of two) **2** each of two ▹ *conj* **3** used preceding two or more possibilities joined by *or* ▹ *adv* **4** likewise: *I don't eat meat and he doesn't either*
ejaculate *v* **1** eject (semen) **2** utter abruptly **ejaculation** *n*
eject Ⓣ *v* force out, expel **ejection** *n* **ejector** *n*
eke Ⓣ *v* **eke out 1** make (a supply) last by frugal use **2** make (a living) with difficulty
Ekman *n* **Vagn Walfrid**. 1874–1954, Swedish oceanographer: discoverer of the **Ekman spiral** (a complex interaction on the surface of the sea between wind, rotation of the earth, and friction forces) and the **Ekman layer** (the thin top layer of the sea that flows at 90° to the wind direction)
elaborate Ⓣ *adj* **1** with a lot of fine detail ▹ *v* **2** expand upon **elaboration** *n*
élan [ale-**an**] *n* style and vigour
eland [**eel**-and] *n* large antelope of southern Africa
elapse Ⓣ *v* (of time) pass by
elastic Ⓣ *adj* **1** resuming normal shape after distortion **2** adapting easily to change ▹ *n* **3** tape or fabric containing interwoven strands of flexible rubber **elasticity** *n*
elate *v* fill with high spirits or pride **elation** *n*
elbow Ⓣ *n* **1** joint between the upper arm and the forearm **2** part of a garment that covers this ▹ *v* **3** shove or strike with the elbow
▸ **elbow grease** vigorous physical labour
▸ **elbowroom** *n* sufficient room to move freely

THESAURUS

eject *v* = **throw out**, remove, oust, expel, banish, evict, drive out, turn out
ejection *n* = **expulsion**, deportation, exile, removal, eviction, banishment
eke *v* ▹ **eke out** = **be sparing with**, husband, economize on, stretch out
elaborate *adj* **1** = **complicated**, complex, detailed, involved, intricate OPPOSITE: simple **2** = **ornate**, fancy, fussy • *elaborate wooden carvings* ▸ *v* **3** = **expand**, develop, enlarge • *He promised to elaborate on what had been said last night.* ▹ **elaborate on** *See* **enlarge on, expand on** *See also*: **sophisticated**
elapse *v* = **pass**, lapse, glide by, go by, roll by, slip away
elastic *adj* **1** = **stretchy**, plastic, resilient, rubbery, supple, pliable, pliant, springy, tensile **2** = **adaptable**, flexible, variable, tolerant, compliant, adjustable, supple, accommodating, yielding
elated *adj* = **joyful**, ecstatic, jubilant, delighted, euphoric, gleeful, exhilarated, overjoyed
elation *n* = **joy**, delight, ecstasy, bliss, euphoria, glee, jubilation, exhilaration, rapture, high spirits
elbow *n* **1** = **joint**, angle ▹ **elbow room** = **scope**, play, space, room, freedom, latitude, leeway ▸ *v* **2** = **push**, knock, nudge, shove, jostle

DICTIONARY

elder[1] ⓣ *adj* **1** older ▷ *n* **2** older person **3** (in certain Protestant Churches) lay officer
▸ **elderly** *adj* (fairly) old
▸ **eldest** *adj* oldest
elder[2] *n* small tree with white flowers and black berries
El Dorado [el dor-**rah**-doe] *n* fictitious country rich in gold
eldritch *adj Scot* weird, uncanny
Eleanor of Aquitaine *n* ?1122–1204, queen of France (1137–52) by her marriage to Louis VII and queen of England (1154–89) by her marriage to Henry II; mother of the English kings Richard I and John
Eleanor of Castile *n* 1246–90, Spanish wife of Edward I of England. **Eleanor Crosses** were erected at each place at which her body rested between Nottingham, where she died, and London, where she is buried
elect ⓣ *v* **1** choose by voting **2** decide (to do something) ▷ *adj* **3** appointed but not yet in office: *president elect*
▸ **election** *n* **1** choosing of representatives by voting **2** act of choosing
▸ **electioneer** *v* be active in a political election
▸ **elective** *adj* **1** chosen by election **2** optional
▸ **elector** *n* someone who has the right to vote in an election **electoral** *adj*
▸ **electorate** *n* people who have the right to vote
electricity *n* **1** form of energy associated with stationary or moving electrons or other charged particles **2** electric current or charge
▸ **electric** *adj* **1** produced by, producing, transmitting, or powered by electricity **2** exciting or tense
▸ **electrics** *pl n* electric appliances
▸ **electric chair** *US* chair in which criminals who have been sentenced to death are electrocuted
▸ **electric cord** flexible insulated cable that conducts electricity
▸ **electrical** *adj* using or concerning electricity
▸ **electrician** *n* person trained to install and repair electrical equipment
▸ **electrify** *v* **-fying**, **-fied 1** adapt for operation by electric power **2** charge with electricity **3** startle or excite intensely **electrification** *n*
electro- *combining form* operated by or caused by electricity
▸ **electrocardiograph** *n* instrument for recording the electrical activity of the heart
▸ **electrocardiogram** *n* tracing produced by this
▸ **electrodynamics** *n* branch of physics concerned with the interactions between electrical and mechanical forces
▸ **electroencephalograph** [ill-lek-tro-en-**sef**-a-loh-graf] *n* instrument for recording the electrical activity of the brain
▸ **electroencephalogram** *n* tracing produced by this
▸ **electromagnet** *n* magnet containing a coil of wire through which an electric current is passed **electromagnetic** *adj* **electromagnetism** *n*
▸ **electroplate** *v* coat with silver etc. by electrolysis
electrocute *v* kill or injure by electricity **electrocution** *n*
electrode *n* conductor through which an electric current enters or leaves a battery, vacuum tube, etc.
electrolysis [ill-lek-**troll**-iss-iss] *n* **1** conduction of electricity by an electrolyte, esp. to induce chemical change **2** destruction of living tissue such as hair roots by an electric current
electrolyte *n* solution or molten substance that conducts electricity **electrolytic** *adj*
electron *n* elementary particle in all atoms that has a negative electrical charge
▸ **electronic** *adj* **1** (of a device) dependent on the action of electrons **2** (of a process) using electronic devices
▸ **electronic mail** see **e-mail**
▸ **electronics** *n* technology concerned with the development of electronic devices and circuits
▸ **electron microscope** microscope that uses electrons, rather than light, to produce a magnified image
▸ **electron volt** unit of energy used in nuclear physics
elegant ⓣ *adj* **1** tasteful in dress, style, or design **2** graceful **elegance** *n*
elegy [**el**-lij-ee] *n, pl* **-egies** mournful poem,

THESAURUS

elder *adj* **1** = **older**, senior, first-born
▸ *n* **2** = **older person**, senior
elect *v* = **choose**, vote, pick, determine, select, appoint, prefer, opt for, settle on
election *n* = **voting**, vote, choice, selection, appointment, judgment, preference
elector *n* = **voter**, constituent, selector
electric *adj* = **charged**, exciting, thrilling, tense, dynamic, rousing, stimulating, stirring
electrify *v* = **startle**, shock, excite, stir, thrill, jolt, astound, invigorate, galvanize
electrifying *See* **exciting**
elegance *n* = **style**, taste, luxury, dignity, grace, grandeur, refinement, exquisiteness, gracefulness
elegant *adj* = **stylish**, fine, delicate, chic, refined, handsome, exquisite, polished, graceful, tasteful

DICTIONARY

esp. a lament for the dead
▸ **elegiac** *adj* mournful or plaintive
element Ⓣ *n* **1** component part **2** substance which cannot be separated into other substances by ordinary chemical techniques **3** distinguishable section of a social group: *liberal elements in Polish society* **4** heating wire in an electric kettle, stove, etc. **elements** **5** basic principles of something **6** weather conditions, esp. wind, rain, and cold
▸ **in one's element** in a situation where one is happiest
▸ **elemental** *adj* **1** fundamental **2** of primitive natural forces or passions
▸ **elementary** *adj* simple and straightforward
elephant *n* huge four-footed thick-skinned animal with ivory tusks and a long trunk
▸ **elephantine** *adj* unwieldy, clumsy
▸ **elephantiasis** [el-lee-fan-**tie**-a-siss] *n* disease with hardening of the skin and enlargement of the legs etc.
elevate Ⓣ *v* **1** raise in rank or status **2** lift up
▸ **elevation** *n* **1** raising **2** scale drawing of one side of a building **3** height above sea level
▸ **elevator** *n* cage raised or lowered in a vertical shaft to transport people or goods
eleven *adj, n* **1** one more than ten ▷ *n* **2** *sports* team of eleven people
▸ **eleventh** *adj, n* (of) number eleven in a series
▸ **elevenses** *n informal* light mid-morning snack
elf *n, pl* **elves** (in folklore) small mischievous fairy
▸ **elfin** *adj* small and delicate
Elgar *n* Sir **Edward** (**William**). 1857–1934, English composer, whose works include the *Enigma Variations* (1899), the oratorio *The Dream of Gerontius* (1900), two symphonies, a cello concerto, and a violin concerto
Elgin *n* **8th Earl of**, title of *James Bruce*. 1811–63, British statesman and diplomat; Governor General of Canada (1847–54); Viceroy of India (1862–63)
El Greco *n* real name *Domenikos Theotocopoulos*. 1541–1614, Spanish painter, born in Crete; noted for his elongated human forms and dramatic use of colour
elicit Ⓣ *v* draw out (information) from someone
elide *v* omit (a vowel or syllable) from a spoken word **elision** *n*
eligible Ⓣ *adj* **1** qualified to be chosen **2** desirable as a spouse **eligibility** *n*
eliminate Ⓣ *v* get rid of **elimination** *n*
Eliot *n* **1 George**, real name *Mary Ann Evans*. 1819–80, English novelist, noted for her analysis of provincial Victorian society. Her best-known novels include *Adam Bede* (1859), *The Mill on the Floss* (1860), *Silas Marner* (1861), and *Middlemarch* (1872) **2 T**(**homas**) **S**(**tearns**). 1888–1965, British poet, dramatist, and critic, born in the US. His poetry includes *Prufrock and Other Observations* (1917), *The Waste Land* (1922), *Ash Wednesday* (1930), and *Four Quartets* (1943). Among his verse plays are *Murder in the Cathedral* (1935), *The Family Reunion* (1939), *The Cocktail Party* (1950), and *The Confidential Clerk* (1954): Nobel prize for literature 1948
elite Ⓣ [ill-**eet**] *n* most powerful, rich, or gifted members of a group
▸ **elitism** *n* belief that society should be governed by a small group of superior people
elitist *n, adj*
elixir Ⓣ [ill-**ix**-er] *n* liquid medicine in syrup

THESAURUS

element *n* = **component**, part, unit, factor, section, ingredient, constituent, subdivision ▷ **be in one's element = be in one's natural environment**, be in one's domain, be in one's field, be in one's habitat, be in one's medium, be in one's milieu, be in one's sphere, feel at home
elementary *adj* = **simple**, clear, easy, plain, straightforward, rudimentary, uncomplicated
elements *pl n* **1** = **basics**, essentials, foundations, fundamentals, nuts and bolts (*informal*), principles, rudiments **2** = **weather conditions**, atmospheric conditions, powers of nature
elevate *v* **1** = **raise**, lift, heighten, hoist, uplift, lift up **2** = **promote**, advance, upgrade, prefer, exalt, aggrandize
elevated *adj* = **high-minded**, grand, inflated, lofty, dignified, noble, sublime, exalted, high-flown
elevation *n* **1** = **promotion**, advancement, aggrandizement, exaltation, preferment, upgrading **2** = **altitude**, pitch, height
elicit *v* **1** = **bring about**, cause, evolve, derive, bring forth, bring out, bring to light, call forth, give rise to **2** = **obtain**, exact, extract, evoke, extort, wrest, draw out
eligible *adj* = **qualified**, fit, appropriate, proper, acceptable, worthy, suitable, desirable, preferable
eliminate *v* **1** = **get rid of**, remove, eradicate, cut out, do away with, stamp out • *We've eliminated two of the four options so far.* **2** = **knock out**, put out • *Our team was eliminated in the first round.*
See also: **banish, exclude**
elite *n* = **best**, pick, cream, flower, nobility, aristocracy, *crème de la crème* (*French*), upper class
elitist *adj* = **snobbish**, exclusive, selective
elixir *n* = **panacea**, nostrum

DICTIONARY

Elizabeth *n* **1 Queen**, title *the Queen Mother*, original name Lady *Elizabeth Bowes-Lyon*. 1900–2002, queen of Great Britain and Northern Ireland (1936–52) as the wife of George VI; mother of Elizabeth II **2 Saint**. Also **Saint Elisabeth** *New Testament* the wife of Zacharias, mother of John the Baptist, and kinswoman of the Virgin Mary. Feast day: Nov 5 or 8
Elizabeth I *n* 1533–1603, queen of England (1558–1603); daughter of Henry VIII and Anne Boleyn. She established the Church of England (1559) and put an end to Catholic plots, notably by executing Mary Queen of Scots (1587) and defeating the Spanish Armada (1588). Her reign was notable for commercial growth, maritime expansion, and the flourishing of literature, music, and architecture
Elizabeth II *n* born 1926, queen of Great Britain and Northern Ireland from 1952; daughter of George VI
Elizabethan *adj* of the reign of Elizabeth I of England (1558–1603)
elk *n* large deer of N Europe and Asia
Ellington *n* **Duke**, nickname of *Edward Kennedy Ellington*. 1899–1974, US jazz composer, pianist, and conductor, famous for such works as "Mood Indigo" and "Creole Love Call"
ellipse *n* oval shape
▸ **elliptical** *adj* **1** oval-shaped **2** (of speech or writing) obscure or ambiguous
ellipsis [ill-**lip**-siss] *n, pl* **-ses** omission of letters or words in a sentence
elm *n* tree with serrated leaves
elocution Ⓣ *n* art of speaking clearly in public
elongate Ⓣ [**eel**-long-gate] *v* make or become longer **elongation** *n*
elope Ⓣ *v* run away secretly to get married
elopement *n*
eloquence Ⓣ *n* fluent powerful use of language **eloquent** *adj* **eloquently** *adv*
else *adv* **1** otherwise **2** besides **3** instead
▸ **elsewhere** *adv* in or to another place
Elton *n* **Charles Sutherland**. 1900–91, British zoologist: initiated the study of animal ecology
elucidate Ⓣ *v* make (something difficult) clear, explain **elucidation** *n*
elude Ⓣ *v* **1** baffle **2** escape from by cleverness or quickness
▸ **elusive** *adj* difficult to catch or remember
elver *n* young eel
elves *n* plural of **elf**
em *n printing* the square of any size of type
emaciated Ⓣ [im-**mace**-ee-ate-id] *adj* abnormally thin **emaciation** *n*
e-mail *n* **1** Also **electronic mail** sending of messages between computer terminals ▹ *v* **2** communicate in this way
emanate Ⓣ [**em**-a-nate] *v* issue, proceed from a source **emanation** *n*
emancipate Ⓣ *v* free from social, political, or legal restraints **emancipation** *n*
emasculate *v* deprive of power
emasculation *n*
embalm Ⓣ *v* preserve (a corpse) from decay by the use of chemicals etc.
embalmment *n*
embankment *n* man-made ridge that carries a road or railway or holds back water
embargo Ⓣ *n, pl* **-goes 1** order stopping the movement of ships **2** legal stoppage of trade **3** ban ▹ *v* **-going, -goed 4** put an embargo on

THESAURUS

elocution *n* = **diction**, speech, delivery, pronunciation, oratory, articulation, declamation, enunciation, speechmaking
elongate *v* = **make longer**, extend, stretch, prolong, lengthen, draw out, protract
elope *v* = **run away**, leave, escape, disappear, bolt, abscond, decamp, run off, slip away, steal away
eloquence *n* = **expressiveness**, expression, rhetoric, oratory, fluency, forcefulness, persuasiveness, way with words
eloquent *adj* **1** = **silver-tongued**, articulate, fluent, forceful, moving, persuasive, stirring, well-expressed **2** = **expressive**, meaningful, vivid, suggestive, telling
elsewhere *adv* = **in another place** *or* **to another place**, away, abroad, hence (*archaic*), not here, somewhere else
elucidate *v* = **clarify**, explain, illustrate, illuminate, expound, clear up, explicate, make plain, shed light on *or* throw light on, spell out
elude *v* **1** = **escape**, duck (*informal*), avoid, flee, evade, dodge, outrun, get away from **2** = **baffle**, escape, frustrate, puzzle, thwart, foil, stump, confound, be beyond (someone)
elusive *adj* **1** = **difficult to catch**, slippery, tricky, shifty **2** = **indefinable**, subtle, intangible, fleeting, transient, transitory
emaciated *adj* = **skeletal**, thin, lean, gaunt, scrawny, cadaverous, haggard, pinched, undernourished, wasted
emanate *v* = **flow**, issue, spring, emerge, stem, proceed, arise, originate, derive, come forth
emancipate *v* = **free**, release, deliver, liberate, set free, unchain, unfetter
emancipation *n* = **freedom**, release, liberty, liberation, deliverance
embalm *v* = **preserve**, mummify
embargo *n* **1** = **ban**, bar, restriction,

DICTIONARY

embark Ⓣ *v* **1** board a ship or aircraft **2** (foll. by *on* or *upon*) begin (a new project) **embarkation** *n*
embarrass Ⓣ *v* cause to feel self-conscious or ashamed **embarrassed** *adj* **embarrassment** *n*
embassy *n, pl* **-sies 1** offices or official residence of an ambassador **2** ambassador and his staff
embattled *adj* having a lot of difficulties
embed *v* **-bedding**, **-bedded** fix firmly in something solid
embellish Ⓣ *v* **1** decorate **2** embroider (a story) **embellishment** *n*
ember *n* glowing piece of wood or coal in a dying fire
embezzle Ⓣ *v* steal money that has been entrusted to one **embezzlement** *n* **embezzler** *n*
embitter *v* make bitter **embitterment** *n*
emblazon [im-**blaze**-on] *v* **1** decorate with bright colours **2** proclaim or publicize
emblem Ⓣ *n* object or representation that symbolizes a quality, type, or group **emblematic** *adj*
embody Ⓣ *v* **-bodying**, **-bodied 1** be an example or expression of **2** comprise, include **embodiment** *n*
embolden Ⓣ *v* encourage (someone)
embolism *n* blocking of a blood vessel by a blood clot or air bubble
emboss *v* mould or carve a raised design on
embrace Ⓣ *v* **1** clasp in the arms, hug **2** accept (an idea) eagerly **3** comprise ▷ *n* **4** act of embracing
embrasure *n* **1** door or window having splayed sides so that the opening is larger on the inside **2** opening like this in a fortified wall, for shooting through
embrocation *n* lotion for rubbing into the skin to relieve pain
embroider *v* **1** decorate with needlework **2** make (a story) more interesting with fictitious detail **embroidery** *n*
embroil Ⓣ *v* involve (a person) in problems **embroilment** *n*
embryo Ⓣ [**em**-bree-oh] *n, pl* **-bryos 1** unborn creature in the early stages of development **2** something at an undeveloped stage **embryology** *n*
▸ **embryonic** *adj* at an early stage

THESAURUS

boycott, restraint, stoppage, prohibition, interdiction ▸ *v* **2 = ban**, stop, block, bar, prohibit, restrict, boycott
embark *v* **= go aboard**, board ship, take ship ▷ **embark on**, **embark upon = begin**, start, launch, enter, commence, plunge into, set about, set out, take up
embarrass *v* **= shame**, humiliate, disconcert, fluster • *You always embarrass me in front of my friends!*
embarrassed *adj* **= ashamed**, awkward, red-faced, self-conscious, sheepish, humiliated • *I was embarrassed about making a fool of myself in public.*
See also: **uncomfortable**
embarrassing *adj* **= humiliating**, sensitive, uncomfortable, awkward, shameful, compromising, discomfiting, disconcerting, mortifying, toe-curling (*informal*)
embarrassment *n* **1 = shame**, humiliation, awkwardness, bashfulness, self-consciousness • *I laughed loudly to cover my embarrassment.* **2 = predicament**, difficulty, bind (*informal*), mess, scrape (*informal*), pickle (*informal*)
embellish *v* **= decorate**, enhance, elaborate, enrich, adorn, ornament, embroider, festoon, beautify
embellishment *n* **= decoration**, enrichment, ornament, enhancement, exaggeration, embroidery, adornment, elaboration, ornamentation
embezzle *v* **= misappropriate**, steal, appropriate, misuse, pilfer, filch, peculate, purloin, rip off (*slang*)
embezzlement *n* **= misappropriation**, fraud, theft, misuse, appropriation, filching, peculation, pilfering, stealing
embittered *adj* **= resentful**, angry, bitter, disaffected, rancorous, soured, disillusioned, with a chip on one's shoulder (*informal*)
emblem *n* **= symbol**, sign, mark, image, crest, badge, token, insignia
embodiment *n* **= personification**, example, symbol, expression, representation, avatar, incarnation, epitome, exemplar
embody *v* **1 = personify**, represent, symbolize, manifest, exemplify, typify, stand for **2 = incorporate**, include, contain, combine, comprise, encompass
embolden *v* **= encourage**, fire, strengthen, stir, stimulate, inflame, invigorate, rouse
embrace *v* **1 = hug**, hold, seize, squeeze, envelop, cuddle, clasp, take in one's arms *or* hold in one's arms **2 = accept**, welcome, seize, adopt, espouse, take on board, take up **3 = include**, involve, contain, cover, comprise, encompass, comprehend, take in ▸ *n* **4 = hug**, clinch (*slang*), squeeze, cuddle, clasp
embroil *v* **= involve**, implicate, incriminate, mire, entangle, ensnare, enmesh, mix up
embryo *n* **= germ**, beginning, root, nucleus, rudiment

DICTIONARY

emend Ⓣ *v* remove errors from **emendation** *n*
emerald *n* **1** bright green precious stone ▷ *adj* **2** bright green
emerge Ⓣ *v* **1** come into view **2** (foll. by *from*) come out of **3** become known **emergence** *n* **emergent** *adj*
emergency Ⓣ *n, pl* **-cies 1** sudden unforeseen occurrence needing immediate action ▷ *adj* **2** for use in an emergency: *emergency exit*
emeritus [im-**mer**-rit-uss] *adj* retired, but retaining an honorary title: *emeritus professor*
Emerson *n* **Ralph Waldo**. 1803–82, US poet, essayist, and transcendentalist
emery *n* hard mineral used for smoothing and polishing
▸ **emery board** cardboard strip coated with crushed emery, for filing the nails
emetic [im-**met**-ik] *n* **1** substance that causes vomiting ▷ *adj* **2** causing vomiting
emigrate Ⓣ *v* go and settle in another country **emigrant** *n* **emigration** *n*
émigré [**em**-mig-gray] *n* someone who has left his native country for political reasons
Eminem *n* real name *Marshall Mathers III*. born 1972, US White rap performer noted for his controversial lyrics; recordings include *The Slim Shady LP* (1999) and *The Eminem Show* (2002); he also starred in the film *8 Mile* (2002)
eminent Ⓣ *adj* distinguished, well-known **eminently** *adv*
▸ **eminence** *n* **1** position of superiority or fame **2 Eminence** title of a cardinal
emir [em-**meer**] *n* Muslim ruler
▸ **emirate** *n* his country
emissary *n, pl* **-saries** agent sent on a mission by a government
emit Ⓣ *v* **emitting, emitted 1** give out (heat, light, or a smell) **2** utter **emission** *n*
emollient *adj* **1** softening, soothing ▷ *n* **2** substance which softens or soothes something
emolument *n formal* payment for work, salary
emoticon [i-**mote**-i-kon] *n computers* symbol depicting a smile or other facial expression, used in e-mail
emotion Ⓣ *n* strong feeling
▸ **emotional** *adj* readily affected by or appealing to the emotions
▸ **emotive** *adj* tending to arouse emotion
empathy Ⓣ *n* power of imaginatively entering into and understanding another's feelings
Empedocles *n* ?490–430 BC, Greek philosopher and scientist, who held that the world is composed of four elements, air, fire, earth, and water, which are governed by the opposing forces of love and discord
emperor *n* ruler of an empire **empress** *n fem*
emphasis Ⓣ *n, pl* **-ses 1** special importance or significance given to something, such as an idea **2** stress on a word or phrase in speech **emphasize** *v*
▸ **emphatic** *adj* showing emphasis **emphatically** *adv*

THESAURUS

emend *v* = **revise**, improve, correct, edit, amend, rectify
emendation *n* = **revision**, improvement, amendment, correction, editing, rectification
emerge *v* **1** = **come into view**, issue, rise, appear, surface, arise, emanate, come forth, spring up **2** = **become apparent**, transpire, become known, come out, come out in the wash, come to light, crop up
emergence *n* = **coming**, rise, development, appearance, arrival, advent, materialization
emergency *n* = **crisis**, pinch • *This is an emergency!*
emergent *See* **in the making**
emigrate *v* = **move abroad**, move, migrate
emigration *n* = **departure**, migration, exodus
eminence *n* = **prominence**, note, fame, importance, distinction, greatness, prestige, esteem, renown, repute
eminent *adj* = **prominent**, famous, renowned, well-known, celebrated, high-ranking, illustrious, distinguished, noted, esteemed
emission *n* = **giving off** *or* **giving out**, transmission, radiation, discharge, ejection, ejaculation, exhalation, shedding
emit *v* = **give out**, release, utter, exude, give off, send out • *She blinked and emitted a long sigh.*
See also: **discharge**
emotion *n* = **feeling**, passion, sentiment, sensation, excitement, warmth, ardour, fervour, vehemence
emotional *adj* **1** = **sensitive**, passionate, sentimental, temperamental, hot-blooded, demonstrative, excitable **2** = **moving**, poignant, sentimental, touching, heart-warming, emotive, affecting, stirring
emotive *adj* = **sensitive**, controversial, delicate, touchy
empathize *v* ▷ **empathize with** *See* **identify with**
empathy *See* **sympathy**
emphasis *n* = **importance**, weight, accent, prominence • *too much emphasis on materialism*
emphasize *v* = **stress**, highlight, underline, accent, accentuate, play up • *He emphasized the need for everyone to remain calm.*
See also: **feature**

DICTIONARY

emphysema [em-fiss-**see**-ma] *n* condition in which the air sacs of the lungs are grossly enlarged, causing breathlessness
empire Ⓣ *n* **1** group of territories under the rule of one state or person **2** large organization that is directed by one person or group
empirical Ⓣ *adj* relying on experiment or experience, not on theory **empirically** *adv* ▸ **empiricism** *n* doctrine that all knowledge derives from experience **empiricist** *n*
emplacement *n* prepared position for a gun
employ Ⓣ *v* **1** hire (a person) **2** provide work or occupation for **3** use ▷ *n* **4** state of being employed: *in someone's employ* **employee** *n* **employer** *n*
▸ **employment** *n* **1** state of being employed **2** work done by a person to earn money
emporium Ⓣ *n old-fashioned* large general shop
empower Ⓣ *v* enable, authorize
empress *n* see **emperor**
empty Ⓣ *adj* **-tier**, **-tiest 1** containing nothing **2** unoccupied **3** without purpose or value **4** (of words) insincere ▷ *v* **-tying**, **-tied 5** make or become empty **emptiness** *n* ▸ **empties** *pl n* empty boxes, bottles, etc.
EMS European Monetary System
emu *n* large Aust. flightless bird with long legs
emulate Ⓣ *v* attempt to equal or surpass by imitating **emulation** *n*
emulsion *n* **1** light-sensitive coating on photographic film **2** type of water-based paint ▷ *v* **3** paint with emulsion paint ▸ **emulsify** *v* **-fying**, **-fied** make into an emulsion **emulsifier** *n*
en *n printing* unit of measurement, half an em
enable Ⓣ *v* provide (a person) with the means, opportunity, or authority (to do something)
enact Ⓣ *v* **1** establish by law **2** represent as in a play **enactment** *n*
enamel *n* **1** glasslike coating applied to metal etc. to preserve the surface **2** hard white coating on a tooth ▷ *v* **-elling**, **-elled 3** cover with enamel
enamoured Ⓣ *adj* inspired with love

THESAURUS

emphatic *adj* = **forceful**, positive, vigorous, pronounced, definite, unmistakable, unequivocal, insistent, categorical, resounding
empire *n* = **kingdom**, domain, realm, commonwealth
empirical *adj* = **first-hand**, experimental, practical, pragmatic, observed, experiential
employ *v* **1** = **hire**, commission, appoint, engage (*formal*), take on • *He was employed by the singer as a bodyguard.* **2** = **use**, utilize, bring to bear, make use of • *the tactics employed by the police* **3** = **keep busy**, fill, engage, occupy, make use of, take up, use up ▸ *n* ▷ **in the employ of** = **in the service of**, employed by, engaged by, hired by
See also: **busy**
employed *adj* = **working**, active, busy, occupied, engaged, in a job, in employment, in work
employee *n* = **worker**, hand • *the way they look after their employees*
employees *See* **labour, staff**
employer *n* = **boss** • *a meeting with her employer to discuss the issue*
employers *See* **management**
employment *n* **1** = **hiring**, engagement, recruitment, enlistment, taking on • *the employment of teenagers to work in restaurants* **2** = **use**, exercise, application, utilization, exertion **3** = **job**, work, trade, line, occupation, profession, vocation
emporium *n* (*Old-fashioned*) = **store**, market, shop, warehouse, bazaar, mart
empower *v* = **enable**, allow, commission, warrant, sanction, qualify, permit, delegate, license, entitle, authorize
emptiness *n* **1** = **bareness**, waste, void, vacuum, vacancy, blankness, desolation **2** = **purposelessness**, futility, vanity, banality, hollowness, inanity, meaninglessness, senselessness, worthlessness **3** = **insincerity**, cheapness, hollowness, idleness
empty *adj* **1** = **bare**, clear, blank, vacant, uninhabited, deserted, unfurnished • *The roads were empty.* OPPOSITE: full **2** = **meaningless**, worthless, inane • *My life is empty without you.* **3** = **insincere**, cheap, hollow, idle ▸ *v* **4** = **evacuate**, clear, drain, unload • *He emptied all the drawers before the guests arrived.* OPPOSITE: fill
See also: **barren, discharge, fond**
empty-headed *adj* = **scatterbrained**, silly, dizzy (*informal*), brainless, featherbrained, harebrained, vacuous
emulate *v* = **imitate**, follow, rival, copy, echo, mimic, compete with
enable *v* = **allow**, warrant, sanction, qualify, permit, license, entitle, authorize, empower
enact *v* **1** = **establish**, order, sanction, command, authorize, proclaim, legislate, decree, ordain **2** = **perform**, play, represent, portray, depict, act out, play the part of
enamoured *adj* = **in love**, fond, captivated, charmed, enraptured, infatuated, smitten, taken

DICTIONARY

en bloc *adv French* as a body or a whole, all together
encamp *v* set up in a camp **encampment** *n*
encapsulate Ⓣ *v* **1** abridge **2** enclose as in a capsule
encase *v* place or enclose as in a case **encased** *adj*
encephalitis [en-sef-a-**lite**-iss] *n* inflammation of the brain
encephalogram *n* short for **electroencephalogram**
enchant Ⓣ *v* bewitch or delight **enchantment** *n* **enchanter** *n* **enchantress** *n fem*
enchilada [en-chill-**lah**-duh] *n* Mexican dish consisting of a tortilla filled with meat, served with chili sauce
▸ **the whole enchilada** *slang* the whole thing; everything
encircle Ⓣ *v* form a circle around **encirclement** *n*
Encke *n* **Johann Franz.** 1791–1865, German astronomer, who discovered **Encke's division** in the outer ring of Saturn
enclave *n* part of a country entirely surrounded by foreign territory
enclose Ⓣ *v* **1** surround completely **2** include along with something else **enclosure** *n*
encomium *n, pl* **-miums, -mia** formal expression of praise
encompass Ⓣ *v* **1** surround **2** include comprehensively
encore *interj* **1** again, once more ▹ *n* **2** extra performance due to enthusiastic demand
encounter Ⓣ *v* **1** meet unexpectedly **2** be faced with ▹ *n* **3** unexpected meeting **4** contest
encourage Ⓣ *v* **1** inspire with confidence **2** spur on **encouragement** *n*
encroach Ⓣ *v* intrude gradually on a person's rights or land **encroachment** *n*
encrust *v* cover with a layer of something
encumber Ⓣ *v* hamper or burden
▸ **encumbrance** *n* impediment
encyclical [en-**sik**-lik-kl] *n* letter sent by the Pope to all bishops
encyclopedia, encyclopaedia *n* book or set of books containing facts about many subjects, usually in alphabetical order
▸ **encyclopedic** *or* **encyclopaedic** *adj* comprehensive
end Ⓣ *n* **1** furthest point or part **2** limit **3** last part of something **4** act of bringing or coming to a finish **5** fragment **6** *lit* death **7** destruction **8** purpose **9** *sports* either of the two defended areas of a playing field ▹ *v* **10** bring or come

THESAURUS

encampment *n* = **camp**, base, campsite, bivouac, camping ground, cantonment, quarters, tents
encapsulate *v* = **sum up**, digest, compress, summarize, epitomize, condense, abridge, précis
enchant *v* = **fascinate**, charm, delight, captivate, enthrall, bewitch, spellbind, beguile, enrapture, ravish
enchanter *n* = **sorcerer**, wizard, witch, magician, conjurer, magus, necromancer, warlock
enchanting *adj* = **fascinating**, attractive, lovely, pleasant, charming, delightful, alluring, bewitching, captivating, entrancing
encircle *See* **enclose, surround**
enclose *v* **1** = **surround**, border, wrap, encircle, fence off, hem in • *The CDs arrived enclosed in a small brown box.* **2** = **send with**, include, insert, put in
encompass *v* **1** = **surround**, ring, circle, enclose, envelop, encircle **2** = **include**, hold, contain, cover, admit, embrace, incorporate, comprise, take in
encounter *v* **1** = **meet**, face, experience, confront, bump into (*informal*), chance upon, come upon, run across ▸ *n* **2** = **meeting**, brush, confrontation, rendezvous **3** = **battle**, contest, conflict, dispute, clash, head-to-head, run-in (*informal*)
encourage *v* **1** = **hearten**, cheer, reassure • *We were very encouraged by the response.* OPPOSITE: discourage **2** = **support**, help, boost, aid, favour, incite • *the need to encourage people to be sensible*
See also: **back, push, strengthen**
encouragement *n* = **inspiration**, support, cheer, promotion, stimulus, stimulation, incitement, reassurance
encouraging *adj* = **promising**, good, bright, hopeful, rosy, cheerful, comforting, heartening, reassuring
encroach *v* = **intrude**, invade, infringe, trespass, overstep, usurp, impinge, make inroads
encumber *v* = **burden**, hamper, hinder, inconvenience, saddle, obstruct, impede, handicap, weigh down
end *n* **1** = **finish**, close, stop, closure, ending, cessation, expiration, termination, expiry • *the end of the 20th century* OPPOSITE: beginning RELATED WORDS *adjectives*: final, terminal, ultimate **2** = **extremity**, point, limit, edge, tip, extreme, extent, boundary, terminus • *the room at the end of the hallway* **3** = **purpose**, point, goal, aim, reason, object, intention, objective • *The army is being used for political ends.* **4** = **conclusion**, resolution, finale, ending, culmination,

DICTIONARY

to a finish **ending** *n* **endless** *adj*
▸ **make ends meet** have just enough money for one's needs
▸ **endways** *adv* having the end forwards or upwards
endanger ⓣ *v* put in danger
endear *v* cause to be liked **endearing** *adj*
▸ **endearment** *n* affectionate word or phrase
endeavour ⓣ *v* **1** try ▹ *n* **2** effort
endemic *adj* present within a localized area or peculiar to a particular group of people
Enders *n* **John Franklin**. 1897–1985, US microbiologist: shared the Nobel prize for physiology or medicine (1954) with Frederick Robbins and Thomas Weller for their work on viruses
endive *n* curly-leaved plant used in salads
endocrine *adj* relating to the glands which secrete hormones directly into the bloodstream
endogenous [en-**dodge**-in-uss] *adj* originating from within
endorse ⓣ *v* **1** give approval to **2** sign the back of (a cheque) **3** record a conviction on (a driving licence) **endorsement** *n*
endow ⓣ *v* provide permanent income for **endowment** *n*
▸ **endowed with** provided with
endure ⓣ *v* **1** bear (hardship) patiently **2** last for a long time **endurable** *adj*
▸ **endurance** *n* act or power of enduring
enema [**en**-im-a] *n* medicine injected into the rectum to empty the bowels
enemy ⓣ *n, pl* **-mies** hostile person or nation, opponent
energy ⓣ *n, pl* **-gies 1** capacity for intense activity **2** capacity to do work and overcome resistance **3** source of power, such as electricity **energetic** *adj* **energetically** *adv*
▸ **energize** *v* give vigour to
▸ **energy drink** soft drink supposed to boost the drinker's energy levels
enervate *v* weaken, deprive of vigour **enervation** *n*
Enesco *n* **Georges**, original name *George Enescu*. 1881–1955, Romanian violinist and composer
enfant terrible [**on**-fon ter-**reeb**-la]

THESAURUS

denouement **5 = remnant**, scrap, butt, remainder, fragment, leftover, stub, oddment **6 = destruction**, death, ruin, extinction, doom, demise, extermination ▹ **end result** *See* **effect**
▸ *v* **7 = finish**, close, stop, conclude, cease, terminate, culminate, bring to an end, put a stop to, lower the boom (*slang*) • *talks being held to end the players' strike* OPPOSITE: begin
See also: **back, complete, halt, lift, use**
endanger *v* **= put at risk**, risk, threaten, compromise, jeopardize • *a dispute that could endanger the peace talks*
endearing *adj* **= attractive**, winning, sweet, cute, charming, engaging, lovable, captivating
endearment *n* **= loving word**, sweet nothing
endeavour *v* **1 = try**, attempt, aim, struggle, strive, aspire, labour, make an effort, take pains ▸ *n* **2 = effort**, try, trial, attempt, venture, enterprise, undertaking *See also*: **attempt, enterprise, seek, strive, try, undertaking**
ending *n* **= finish**, end, close, conclusion, finale, completion, cessation, culmination, denouement
endless *adj* **= eternal**, unlimited, infinite, continual, incessant, boundless, interminable, everlasting
endorse *v* **1 = approve**, back, support, champion, promote, recommend, advocate, authorize, ratify **2 = sign**, countersign
endorsement *n* **1 = approval**, support, recommendation, advocacy, authorization, backing, favour, ratification, approbation, seal of approval **2 = signature**, countersignature
endow *v* **= provide**, give, award, fund, finance, donate, bestow, confer, bequeath
endowment *n* **= provision**, award, grant, gift, donation, legacy, bequest, benefaction
endurable *adj* **= bearable**, acceptable, sustainable, tolerable, sufferable
endurance *n* **1 = staying power**, strength, resolution, patience, stamina, perseverance, persistence, tenacity, fortitude, toleration **2 = permanence**, stability, duration, longevity, continuity, durability
endure *v* **1 = go through**, stand, suffer, experience, cope with • *He had to endure hours of discomfort*. **2 = last**, remain, survive, live on • *Our friendship has endured through everything*.
See also: **bear, continue, have, tolerate, undergo**
enduring *adj* **= long-lasting**, persistent, lasting, perennial, steadfast, abiding, continuing, unfaltering, unwavering
enemy *n* **= foe**, opponent, adversary, antagonist • *She has many enemies in the government*. OPPOSITE: friend
energetic *adj* **= vigorous**, animated, dynamic, spirited, tireless, indefatigable • *She is an able, energetic, and very determined politician*.
See also: **active, alive, lively, vital**
energy *n* **= vigour**, life, drive, strength, spirit, vitality • *I'm saving my energy for tomorrow*.
See also: **activity, effort**

DICTIONARY

n, pl **enfants terribles** *French* clever but unconventional or indiscreet person
enfeeble *v* weaken **enfeeblement** *n*
enfold *v* **1** cover by wrapping something around **2** embrace
enforce Ⓣ *v* **1** impose obedience (to a law etc.) **2** impose (a condition) **enforceable** *adj* **enforcement** *n*
▸ **enforcer** *n* **1** person who enforces something **2** *hockey* tough player meant to intimidate the opposition and protect teammates
enfranchise *v* grant (a person) the right to vote **enfranchisement** *n*
engage Ⓣ *v* **1** take part, participate **2** involve (a person or his or her attention) intensely **3** employ (a person) **4** bring (a mechanism) into operation **5** *mil* begin a battle with
▸ **engaged** *adj* **1** pledged to be married **2** in use **engagement** *n*
▸ **engaging** *adj* charming
Engel *n* **Marian**. 1933–85, Canadian writer. Her novels include *No Clouds of Glory* (1968) and *The Honeyman Festival* (1970)
Engels *n* **Friedrich**. 1820–95, German socialist leader and political philosopher, in England from 1849. He collaborated with Marx on *The Communist Manifesto* (1848) and his own works include *Condition of the Working Classes in England* (1844) and *The Origin of the Family, Private Property and the State* (1884)
engender Ⓣ *v* produce, cause to occur
engine Ⓣ *n* **1** any machine which converts energy into mechanical work **2** railway locomotive
▸ **engineer** *n* **1** person trained in any branch of engineering ▹ *v* **2** plan in a clever manner **3** design or construct as an engineer
▸ **engineering** *n* profession of applying scientific principles to the design and construction of engines, automobiles, buildings, or machines
English *n* **1** language of Britain, the US, Canada, most parts of the Commonwealth, and certain other countries ▹ *adj* **2** relating to England
▸ **the English** the people of England
▸ **English muffin** small, round, flat baked yeast roll, usually served toasted and split
engorge *v* *pathol* clog with blood **engorgement** *n*
engrave Ⓣ *v* **1** carve (a design) onto a hard surface **2** fix deeply in the mind **engraver** *n*
▸ **engraving** *n* print made from an engraved plate
engross Ⓣ [en-**groce**] *v* occupy the attention of (a person) completely
engulf Ⓣ *v* cover or surround completely
enhance Ⓣ *v* increase in quality, value, or attractiveness **enhancement** *n*
enigma Ⓣ *n* puzzling thing or person **enigmatic** *adj* **enigmatically** *adv*
enjoin *v* order (someone) to do something
enjoy Ⓣ *v* **1** receive pleasure from **2** have or

THESAURUS

enforce *v* = **impose**, apply, execute, implement, prosecute, administer, carry out, insist on, put into effect
engage *v* **1** = **participate**, join, undertake, embark on, enter into, set about, take part **2** = **occupy**, involve, grip, absorb, preoccupy, engross **3** = **captivate**, arrest, gain, catch, fix **4** = **employ**, hire, appoint, retain, enlist, enrol, take on **5** (*Mil*) = **begin battle with**, attack, meet, encounter, assail, fall on, join battle with, take on **6** = **set going**, apply, activate, energize, bring into operation, switch on
engaged *adj* **1** = **betrothed** (*archaic*), promised, affianced, pledged, spoken for **2** = **occupied**, busy, unavailable, employed, in use, tied up
engagement *n* **1** = **appointment**, meeting, date, commitment, arrangement **2** = **betrothal**, troth (*archaic*) **3** = **battle**, fight, action, conflict, combat, encounter
engaging *adj* = **charming**, winning, attractive, pleasing, likable *or* likeable, agreeable, fetching (*informal*), winsome
engender *v* = **produce**, cause, create, generate, breed, induce, instigate, give rise to, lead to
engine *n* = **machine**, mechanism, motor
engineer *v* = **bring about**, plan, create, effect, plot, scheme, mastermind, devise, contrive
engrave *v* **1** = **carve**, cut, etch, inscribe, chisel **2** = **fix**, impress, embed, lodge, imprint, ingrain
engraving *n* = **carving**, plate, inscription, etching, woodcut
engross *v* = **absorb**, involve, engage, occupy, immerse, preoccupy
engrossed *adj* = **absorbed**, lost, caught up, enthralled, fascinated, gripped, immersed, preoccupied, rapt, riveted
engulf *v* = **immerse**, overwhelm, swamp, overrun, inundate, envelop, submerge, swallow up
enhance *v* = **improve**, increase, lift, boost, strengthen, swell, reinforce, heighten, add to
enhancement *See* **improvement**
enigma *n* = **mystery**, problem, puzzle, riddle, teaser, conundrum
enigmatic *adj* = **mysterious**, obscure, cryptic, ambiguous, unfathomable, equivocal, inscrutable, puzzling
enjoy *v* **1** = **take pleasure in**, like, love,

DICTIONARY

experience something: *enjoy excellent health*
enjoyable *adj* **enjoyment** *n*
▶ **enjoy oneself** have a good time
enlarge Ⓣ *v* **1** make or grow larger **2** (foll. by *on* or *upon*) speak or write about in greater detail **enlargement** *n*
enlighten Ⓣ *v* give information to **enlightenment** *n*
enlist Ⓣ *v* **1** enter the armed forces **2** obtain the support of **enlistment** *n*
enliven Ⓣ *v* make lively or cheerful
en masse Ⓣ *adv French* in a group, all together
enmesh *v* entangle
enmity Ⓣ *n, pl* **-ties** ill will, hatred
ennoble Ⓣ *v* make noble, elevate **ennoblement** *n*
ennui [on-**nwee**] *n* boredom, dissatisfaction
enormous Ⓣ *adj* very big, vast
▶ **enormity** *n, pl* **-ties 1** great wickedness **2** gross offence **3** *informal* great size
enough Ⓣ *adj* **1** as much or as many as necessary ▷ *n* **2** sufficient quantity ▷ *adv* **3** sufficiently **4** just adequately
en passant [**on pass**-on] *adv French* in passing, by the way
enquire Ⓣ *v* same as **inquire**
▶ **enquiry** *n*
enrapture *v* fill with delight
enrich Ⓣ *v* **1** improve in quality **2** make rich
enrol Ⓣ *v* **-rolling, -rolled** (cause to) become a member **enrolment** *n*
en route Ⓣ *adv French* on the way
ensconce *v* settle firmly or comfortably
ensemble Ⓣ [on-**som**-bl] *n* **1** all the parts of something taken together **2** complete outfit

THESAURUS

appreciate, relish, delight in, revel in, take pleasure from • *I haven't enjoyed a movie as much as that in ages!* **2 = have**, use, own, experience, possess, be blessed with *or* be favoured with, have the benefit of, reap the benefits of
enjoyable *adj* **= pleasurable**, pleasant, delightful, agreeable, entertaining, gratifying, satisfying, to one's liking
enjoyment *n* **= pleasure**, fun, entertainment, delight, happiness, joy, amusement, relish, gratification, delectation
enlarge *v* **= expand**, increase, extend, magnify, add to • *plans to enlarge the stadium* ▷ **enlarge on = expand on**, develop, elaborate on • *I'd like you to enlarge on that last point.*
See also: **elaborate**
enlargement *See* **growth**
enlighten *v* **= inform**, advise, teach, counsel, educate, instruct, cause to understand, edify, make aware
enlightened *adj* **= informed**, aware, reasonable, sophisticated, civilized, knowledgeable, open-minded, cultivated, educated
enlightenment *n* **= understanding**, education, knowledge, awareness, instruction, insight, wisdom, learning, comprehension
enlist *v* **1 = join up**, join, enter *or* enter into, register, volunteer, muster, enrol, sign up **2 = obtain**, engage, recruit, procure
enlistment *See* **employment**
enliven *v* **= cheer up**, spark, inspire, excite, stimulate, animate, invigorate, rouse, pep up, vitalize
en masse *See* **together**
enmity *n* **= hostility**, hatred, animosity, bitterness, acrimony, malice, bad blood, ill will
ennoble *v* **= dignify**, raise, enhance, honour, elevate, glorify, magnify, exalt, aggrandize
enormity *n* **1 = wickedness**, atrocity, depravity, monstrousness, outrageousness, vileness, villainy **2 = atrocity**, crime, outrage, evil, horror, disgrace, abomination, monstrosity **3** (*Informal*) **= hugeness**, magnitude, greatness, vastness, immensity
enormous *adj* **= huge**, massive, vast, tremendous, immense, gigantic, colossal • *an enormous dust cloud* OPPOSITE: tiny
See also: **excessive, large**
enough *adj* **1 = sufficient**, plenty, adequate, ample, abundant ▶ *n* **2 = sufficiency**, plenty, abundance, adequacy, ample supply, right amount ▶ *adv* **3 = sufficiently**, adequately, reasonably, abundantly, satisfactorily, amply, tolerably
enquire see **inquire**
enquiry see **inquiry**
enrage *v* **= anger**, inflame, incense, infuriate, exasperate, madden
enraged *adj* **= furious**, wild, mad (*informal*), angry, irate, raging *or* raging mad, incandescent, irritated, incensed, angered, infuriated, inflamed, fuming, exasperated, aggravated, choked, boiling mad, fit to be tied, on the warpath, very angry
enrich *v* **1 = enhance**, develop, improve, supplement, refine, augment **2 = make rich**, make wealthy
enrol *v* **= enlist**, accept, admit, register, recruit, join up, sign up *or* sign on, take on *See also*: **join, recruit**
enrolment *n* **= enlistment**, admission, registration, engagement, acceptance, recruitment, matriculation
en route *adv* **= on the way** *or* **along the way**, in transit, on the road
ensemble *n* **1 = whole**, set, total, collection, aggregate, sum, entirety, totality **2 = outfit**, suit, costume, get-up (*informal*) **3 = group**,

DICTIONARY

of clothes **3** company of actors or dancers **4** *music* group of musicians playing together
enshrine *v* cherish or treasure
ensign Ⓣ *n* **1** naval flag **2** banner **3** *US* naval officer
ensilage *n* **1** process of storing green fodder in a silo **2** silage
enslave *v* make a slave of (someone) **enslavement** *n*
ensnare *v* catch in or as if in a snare
ensue Ⓣ *v* come next, result
en suite *adv French* as part of a set or single unit
ensure Ⓣ *v* **1** make certain or sure **2** make safe or protect
ENT *med* ear, nose, and throat
entail Ⓣ *v* bring about or impose inevitably
entangle Ⓣ *v* catch or involve in or as if in a tangle **entanglement** *n*
entente [on-**tont**] *n* friendly understanding between nations
enter Ⓣ *v* **1** come or go in **2** join **3** become involved or take part (in) **4** record (an item) in a journal etc. **5** begin: *enter upon a new career*
▸ **entrance** *n* **1** way into a place **2** act of entering **3** right of entering
▸ **entrant** *n* person who enters a university, contest, etc.
▸ **entry** *n, pl* **-tries 1** entrance **2** entering **3** item entered in a journal etc.
enteric [en-**ter**-ik] *adj* intestinal
▸ **enteritis** [en-ter-**rite**-iss] *n* inflammation of the intestine, causing diarrhea
enterprise Ⓣ *n* **1** company or firm **2** bold or difficult undertaking **3** boldness and energy
▸ **enterprising** *adj* full of boldness and initiative
entertain Ⓣ *v* **1** amuse **2** receive as a guest **3** consider (an idea) **entertainer** *n* **entertainment** *n*
enthrall Ⓣ [en-**thrawl**] *v* **-thralling, -thralled** hold the attention of **enthralling** *adj* **enthralment** *n*
enthusiasm Ⓣ *n* ardent interest, eagerness **enthusiastic** *adj* **enthusiastically** *adv*
▸ **enthuse** *v* (cause to) show enthusiasm
▸ **enthusiast** *n* ardent supporter of something

THESAURUS

company, band, cast, troupe, chorus
ensign *n* = **flag**, standard, banner, pennant, jack, streamer, colours, pennon
ensue *v* = **follow**, issue, result, stem, flow, proceed, arise, derive, come next
ensuing *See* **next**
ensure *v* **1** = **make sure**, guarantee, make certain • *We must ensure that this never happens again.* **2** = **protect**, guard, secure, safeguard, make safe
entail *v* = **involve**, demand, require, occasion, necessitate, bring about, call for, give rise to
entangle *v* **1** = **tangle**, catch, trap, snag, implicate, embroil, snare, ensnare, enmesh, entrap **2** = **mix up**, puzzle, confuse, complicate, perplex, muddle, jumble
enter *v* **1** = **come in, come into, go in,** *or* **go into**, arrive, penetrate, pierce, make an entrance, pass into **2** = **join**, start, enlist, enrol, commence, embark upon, set out on, take up **3** = **record**, list, note, register, log, inscribe, set down, take down ▷ **enter into** *See* **participate**
enterprise *n* **1** = **business**, company, concern, operation, firm, establishment • *a small enterprise that grew into a major corporation* **2** = **undertaking**, effort, project, operation, venture, endeavour • *a creative enterprise such as painting or photography* **3** = **initiative**, drive, energy, enthusiasm, daring, boldness, adventurousness, resourcefulness
See also: **racket**
enterprising *adj* = **resourceful**, go-ahead, bold, energetic, enthusiastic, daring, spirited, adventurous, intrepid
entertain *v* **1** = **amuse**, please, charm, delight, enthrall • *things that might entertain children during the spring break* **2** = **show hospitality to**, treat, accommodate, lodge, harbour, be host to, have company, put up **3** = **consider**, imagine, contemplate, conceive, keep in mind, think about
See also: **receive** ▷ **entertain oneself** *See* **play**
entertaining *adj* = **enjoyable**, funny, pleasant, humorous, amusing, interesting, pleasurable, cheering, diverting
entertainment *n* = **enjoyment**, fun, pleasure, recreation, amusement • *Their main form of entertainment is TV.*
See also: **festival**
enthrall *v* = **fascinate**, grip, entrance, charm, captivate, mesmerize, enchant, enrapture *See* **entertain, entrance, fascinate**
enthuse *See* **rave**
enthusiasm *n* = **keenness**, interest, excitement, warmth, eagerness • *We were disappointed by their lack of enthusiasm.*
See also: **spirit**
enthusiast *n* = **fan**, supporter, lover, follower, buff (*informal*), jock (*slang*), fanatic, devotee, aficionado, keener (*Canad informal*), groupie (*slang*)
enthusiastic *adj* = **keen**, eager, passionate, excited, avid, devoted, ardent • *He was very enthusiastic about the new plan.* OPPOSITE: apathetic

DICTIONARY

entice Ⓣ *v* attract by exciting hope or desire, tempt **enticement** *n*
entire Ⓣ *adj* **1** complete **2** unbroken or undivided **entirely** *adv* **entirety** *n*
entitle Ⓣ *v* **1** give a right to **2** give a title to **entitlement** *n*
entity Ⓣ *n, pl* **-ties** separate distinct thing
entomology *n* study of insects **entomological** *adj* **entomologist** *n*
entourage Ⓣ [**on**-toor-ahzh] *n* group of people who assist an important person
entrails Ⓣ *pl n* **1** intestines **2** innermost parts of something
entrance[1] Ⓣ *n* see **enter**
entrance[2] Ⓣ *v* **1** delight **2** put into a trance
entrap *v* **1** catch in a trap, or catch as if in a trap **2** trick into difficulty etc. **entrapment** *n*
entreat *v* ask earnestly
▸ **entreaty** *n, pl* **-ties** earnest request
entrecôte [**on**-tra-coat] *n* beefsteak cut from between the ribs
entrée [**on**-tray] *n* **1** right of admission **2** main course of a meal **3** dish served before a main course
entrench *v* **1** establish firmly **2** establish in a fortified position with trenches **entrenchment** *n*
entrepreneur Ⓣ *n* business person who attempts to make a profit by risk and initiative
entropy [**en**-trop-ee] *n formal* lack of organization
entrust Ⓣ *v* put into the care or protection of
entwine Ⓣ *v* twist together or around
enumerate Ⓣ *v* name one by one **enumeration** *n*
enunciate Ⓣ *v* **1** pronounce clearly **2** proclaim **enunciation** *n*
envelop Ⓣ *v* **enveloping, enveloped** wrap up, enclose **envelopment** *n*
envelope Ⓣ *n* folded gummed paper cover for a letter
environment Ⓣ [en-**vire**-on-ment] *n* external conditions and surroundings

THESAURUS

See also: **active, fervent**
entice *v* = **attract**, lure, persuade, allure, coax, tempt, seduce, cajole, lead on
entire *adj* = **whole**, complete, full, total, gross
entirely *adv* = **completely**, fully, absolutely, totally, altogether, thoroughly, wholly, utterly, in every respect
entitle *v* **1** = **give the right to**, allow, permit, license, enable, authorize, empower **2** = **call**, term, name, title, label, dub, christen
entity *n* = **thing**, individual, object, substance, being, creature, organism
entourage *n* = **retinue**, company, court, train, staff, escort, associates, attendants, followers
entrails *pl n* = **intestines**, bowels, guts, innards (*informal*), insides (*informal*), offal, viscera
entrance[1] *n* **1** = **way in**, door, entry, gate, doorway • *I met my cousin in front of the arena entrance.* **2** = **appearance**, entry, arrival • *The actors made their entrance when the curtain went up.* **3** = **admission**, access, entry • *His happy manner gained him entrance to the group.*
entrance[2] *v* **1** = **charm**, delight, fascinate, captivate, enthrall, bewitch • *The audience was entranced by her voice.* **2** = **mesmerize**, hypnotize, put in a trance
entrant *n* = **competitor**, player, candidate, participant, entry, contestant
entreaty *n* = **plea**, appeal, request, prayer, petition, earnest request, exhortation, supplication
entrenched *adj* = **fixed**, set, deep-rooted, well-established, ingrained, deep-seated, unshakable, ineradicable, rooted
entrepreneur *n* = **businessman** *or* **businesswoman**, tycoon, magnate, impresario, industrialist
entrust *v* = **give custody of**, deliver, commit, delegate, assign, confide, hand over, turn over
entry *n* **1** = **appearance**, arrival, entrance • *her dramatic entry* **2** = **way in**, door, entrance, gate, doorway • *He was hanging around at the entry to the station.* **3** = **record**, note, item • *the final entry in his journal* **4** = **admission**, access, entrance, entrée, permission to enter
entwine *v* = **twist**, wind, weave, knit, interweave, interlace, twine, plait
enumerate *v* = **list**, name, cite, relate, quote, mention, recount, recite, itemize, spell out
enunciate *v* **1** = **pronounce**, say, speak, sound, voice, utter, articulate, enounce, vocalize **2** = **state**, publish, declare, pronounce, proclaim, promulgate, propound
envelop *v* = **enclose**, cover, surround, wrap, cloak, shroud, engulf, encircle, encase
envelope *n* = **wrapping**, case, cover, jacket, casing, wrapper, covering
enviable *adj* = **desirable**, lucky, fortunate, privileged, win-win (*informal*), advantageous, favoured, to die for (*informal*)
envious *adj* = **covetous**, jealous, resentful, green with envy, grudging
environment *n* = **surroundings**, medium, situation, background, atmosphere, setting, habitat, conditions
environmental *adj* = **ecological**, green, conservationist • *Children and adolescents are*

DICTIONARY

in which people, animals, or plants live
environmental *adj*
▸ **environmentalist** *n* person concerned with the protection of the natural environment
environs Ⓣ *pl n* surrounding area, esp. of a town
envisage Ⓣ *v* **1** visualize **2** conceive of as a possibility
envoy Ⓣ *n* **1** messenger **2** diplomatic minister ranking below an ambassador
envy Ⓣ *v* **-vying**, **-vied 1** grudge (another's good fortune, success, or qualities) ▷ *n* **2** bitter contemplation of another's good fortune
▸ **enviable** *adj* arousing envy, fortunate
▸ **envious** *adj* full of envy
enzyme *n* any of a group of complex proteins that act as catalysts in specific biochemical reactions
Eolithic *adj* of the early part of the Stone Age
eon, aeon [**ee**-on] *n* immeasurably long period of time
EPA Environmental Protection Agency
epaulette *n* shoulder ornament on a uniform
ephemeral Ⓣ *adj* short-lived
epic *n* **1** long poem, book, or film about heroic events or actions ▷ *adj* **2** very impressive or ambitious
epicentre *n* point on the earth's surface immediately above the origin of an earthquake
epicure *n* person who enjoys good food and drink **epicurism** *n*
▸ **epicurean** *adj* **1** devoted to sensual pleasures, esp. food and drink ▷ *n* **2** epicure **epicureanism** *n*
Epicurus *n* 341–270 BC, Greek philosopher, who held that the highest good is pleasure and that the world is a series of fortuitous combinations of atoms
epidemic Ⓣ *n* **1** widespread occurrence of a disease **2** rapid spread of something
epidermis *n* outer layer of the skin
epidural [ep-pid-**dure**-al] *adj, n* (of) spinal anesthetic injected to relieve pain during childbirth
epiglottis *n* thin flap that covers the opening of the larynx during swallowing
epigram Ⓣ *n* short witty remark or poem
epigrammatic *adj*
epigraph *n* **1** quotation at the start of a book **2** inscription
epilepsy *n* disorder of the nervous system causing loss of consciousness and sometimes convulsions
▸ **epileptic** *n* **1** person who has epilepsy ▷ *adj* **2** of or having epilepsy
epilogue Ⓣ *n* short speech or poem at the end of a literary work, esp. a play
Epiphany *n* Christian festival held on January 6 commemorating the manifestation of Christ to the Magi
episcopal [ip-**piss**-kop-al] *adj* of or governed by bishops
▸ **episcopalian** *n* **1** member of an episcopal Church ▷ *adj* **2** advocating Church government by bishops
episode Ⓣ *n* **1** incident in a series of incidents **2** section of a serialized book, television programme, etc.
▸ **episodic** *adj* occurring at irregular intervals
epistemology [ip-iss-stem-**ol**-a-jee] *n* study of the source, nature, and limitations of knowledge **epistemological** *adj*
epistemologist *n*
epistle Ⓣ *n* letter, esp. of an apostle
epistolary *adj*
epitaph Ⓣ *n* **1** commemorative inscription on a tomb **2** commemorative speech or passage
epithet Ⓣ *n* descriptive word or name

e

THESAURUS

now aware of environmental issues.
environmentalist *n* = **conservationist**, green, ecologist
environs *pl n* = **surrounding area**, district, neighbourhood, vicinity, locality, outskirts, precincts, suburbs
envisage *v* **1** = **imagine**, picture, contemplate, conceive *or* conceive of, fancy, visualize, conceptualize, think up **2** = **foresee**, see, predict, anticipate, envision
envoy *n* = **messenger**, agent, ambassador, representative, diplomat, delegate, courier, intermediary, emissary
envy *n* **1** = **jealousy**, resentment • *his feelings of envy toward his cousin* ▸ *v* **2** = **be jealous**, covet, resent, be envious, begrudge • *I don't envy you one bit.*
ephemeral *adj* = **brief**, temporary, passing, short-lived, momentary, fleeting, transient, transitory
epidemic *n* = **spread**, growth, outbreak, wave, plague, rash, upsurge, contagion
epigram *n* = **witticism**, quip, aphorism, bon mot
epilogue *n* = **conclusion**, postscript, coda, concluding speech
episode *n* **1** = **event**, experience, matter, incident, affair, adventure, occurrence, happening, escapade **2** = **part**, scene, section, passage, chapter, instalment, webisode
epistle *n* = **letter**, note, message, communication, missive
epitaph *n* = **monument**, inscription
epithet *n* = **name**, title, tag, description,

DICTIONARY

epitome Ⓣ [ip-**pit**-a-mee] *n* typical example ▸ **epitomize** *v* be the epitome of
epoch Ⓣ [**ee**-pok] *n* period of notable events ▸ **epoch-making** *adj* extremely important
eponymous [ip-**pon**-im-uss] *adj* after whom a book, play, etc. is named
equable Ⓣ [**ek**-wab-bl] *adj* even-tempered **equably** *adv*
equal Ⓣ *adj* **1** identical in size, quantity, degree, etc. **2** having identical rights or status **3** evenly balanced **4** (foll. by *to*) having the necessary ability (for) ▹ *n* **5** person or thing equal to another ▹ *v* **equalling**, **equalled** **6** be equal to **equally** *adv*
▸ **equality** *n* state of being equal
▸ **equalize** *v* **1** make or become equal **2** reach the same score as one's opponent **equalization** *n*
▸ **equal opportunity** nondiscrimination as to sex, race, etc. in employment
equanimity *n* calmness of mind
equate Ⓣ *v* make or regard as equivalent ▸ **equation** *n* **1** mathematical statement that two expressions are equal **2** act of equating
equator *n* imaginary circle round the earth, equidistant from the poles **equatorial** *adj*
equerry [**ek**-kwer-ee] *n, pl* **-ries** officer who acts as an attendant to a member of a royal family
equestrian *adj* of horses and riding
equidistant *adj* equally distant
equilateral *adj* having equal sides
equilibrium Ⓣ *n, pl* **-ria** steadiness or stability
equine Ⓣ *adj* of or like a horse
equinox *n* time of year when day and night are of equal length **equinoctial** *adj*
equip Ⓣ *v* **equipping**, **equipped** provide with what is needed
▸ **equipment** *n* **1** set of tools or devices used for a particular purpose **2** equipping
equipoise *n* perfect balance
equity Ⓣ *n, pl* **-ties** **1** fairness **2** legal system, founded on the principles of natural justice, that supplements common law **equities** **3** interest of ordinary shareholders in a company
▸ **equitable** *adj* fair, just **equitably** *adv*
equivalent Ⓣ *n* **1** something having the same function as something else ▹ *adj* **2** equal in value **3** having the same meaning or result **equivalence** *n*

THESAURUS

nickname, designation, moniker *or* monicker (*slang*), appellation, sobriquet
epitome *n* = **personification**, type, representation, essence, embodiment, archetype, quintessence, typical example
epitomize *v* = **typify**, represent, illustrate, symbolize, embody, exemplify, personify
epoch *n* = **era**, time, period, age, date
equable *adj* = **even-tempered**, calm, easy-going, serene, unflappable (*informal*), composed, imperturbable, level-headed, placid
equal *adj* **1** = **identical**, equivalent, the same • *equal numbers of men and women* **2** = **regular**, uniform, symmetrical, unvarying **3** = **even**, balanced, evenly matched, fifty-fifty (*informal*) **4** = **fair**, just, impartial, unbiased, even-handed, egalitarian, on a level playing field (*informal*) ▹ **equal to** = **capable of**, up to • *She was equal to any task they gave her.* ▸ *v* **5** = **match**, be equal to • *the runner's time equalled her previous record* ▸ *n* **6** = **match**, rival, twin, counterpart, equivalent
See also: **same**
equality *n* **1** = **sameness**, balance, identity, similarity, correspondence, likeness, uniformity, equivalence, evenness **2** = **fairness**, parity, egalitarianism, equal opportunity
equalize *v* = **make equal**, level, match, balance, square, equal, smooth, standardize, even up, regularize
equally *See* **alike**
equate *v* = **make equal** *or* **be equal**, compare, parallel, liken, be commensurate, correspond with *or* correspond to, mention in the same breath
equation *n* = **equating**, comparison, parallel, correspondence
equilibrium *n* = **stability**, rest, balance, symmetry, equipoise, evenness, steadiness
equine *See* **horse**
equip *v* = **supply**, provide, arm, endow, fit out • *The boat was equipped with an outboard motor.*
See also: **issue**
equipment *n* = **apparatus**, tackle, stuff, gear, paraphernalia • *a shed full of gardening equipment*
See also: **supplies**
equitable *adj* = **fair**, just, proper, reasonable, honest, impartial, unbiased, even-handed
equity *n* = **fairness**, justice, integrity, honesty, impartiality, reasonableness, equitableness, even-handedness, fair-mindedness, fair play, rectitude, righteousness, uprightness OPPOSITE: unfairness
equivalence *n* = **equality**, parity, similarity, correspondence, likeness, evenness, sameness
equivalent *n* **1** = **equal**, match, twin, counterpart, parallel, opposite number ▸ *adj* **2** = **equal**, same, similar, comparable, alike, tantamount, interchangeable,

DICTIONARY

equivocal Ⓣ *adj* **1** ambiguous **2** deliberately misleading **3** of doubtful character or sincerity **equivocally** *adv*
▸ **equivocate** *v* use equivocal words to mislead people **equivocation** *n*
ER Queen Elizabeth
era Ⓣ *n* period of time considered as distinctive
ERA *baseball* earned run average: rating of a pitcher's performance, equal to the number of earned runs allowed per nine innings pitched
eradicate Ⓣ *v* destroy completely **eradication** *n*
erase Ⓣ *v* **1** rub out **2** remove
▸ **eraser** *n* object for erasing something written
▸ **erasure** *n* **1** erasing **2** place or mark where something has been erased
Erasmus *n* **Desiderius**, real name *Gerhard Gerhards*. ?1466–1536, Dutch humanist, the leading scholar of the Renaissance in northern Europe. He published the first Greek edition of the New Testament in 1516; his other works include the satirical *Encomium Moriae* (1509); *Colloquia* (1519), a series of dialogues; and an attack on the theology of Luther, *De Libero Arbitrio* (1524)
Eratosthenes *n* ?276–?194 BC, Greek mathematician and astronomer, who calculated the circumference of the earth by observing the angle of the sun's rays at different places
ere *prep, conj poetic* before
erect Ⓣ *v* **1** build **2** set up ▹ *adj* **3** upright **4** (of the penis, clitoris, or nipples) rigid as a result of sexual excitement **erection** *n*
▸ **erectile** *adj* capable of becoming erect from sexual excitement
erg *n* unit of work or energy
ergo *adv* therefore
ergonomics *n* study of the relationship between workers and their environment **ergonomic** *adj*
ergot *n* **1** fungal disease of cereal **2** dried fungus used in medicine
Erhard *n* **Ludwig**. 1897–1977, German statesman: chief architect of the *Wirtschaftswunder* ("economic miracle") of West Germany's recovery after World War II; chancellor (1963–66)
Erickson *n* **Arthur Charles**. 1924–2009, Canadian architect. His designs include the Roy Thomson Hall in Toronto (1982) and the Canadian Chancery in Washington DC (1989)
Ericson, Ericsson *n* **Leif**. 10th–11th centuries AD, Norse navigator, who discovered Vinland (?1000), variously identified as the coast of New England, Labrador, or Newfoundland; son of Eric the Red
Erigena *n* **John Scotus**. ?800–?877 AD, Irish Neo-Platonist philosopher
ermine *n* **1** stoat in northern regions **2** its white winter fur
Ernst *n* **Max**. 1891–1976, German painter, resident in France and the US, a prominent exponent of Dada and surrealism: developed the technique of collage
erode Ⓣ *v* wear away **erosion** *n*
erogenous [ir-**roj**-in-uss] *adj* sexually sensitive or arousing
erotic Ⓣ *adj* relating to sexual pleasure or desire **eroticism** *n*
▸ **erotica** *n* sexual literature or art
err Ⓣ *v formal* make a mistake
▸ **erratum** *n, pl* **-ta** error in writing or printing
▸ **erroneous** *adj* incorrect, mistaken
errand Ⓣ *n* short trip to do something for someone
errant *adj* behaving in a manner considered to be unacceptable
erratic Ⓣ *adj* irregular or unpredictable **erratically** *adv*

e

THESAURUS

commensurate, corresponding, of a piece, on a level playing field (*informal*)
equivocal *adj* = **ambiguous**, uncertain, vague, obscure, indefinite, oblique, evasive, indeterminate, misleading
era *n* = **age**, time, day *or* days, period, date, generation, epoch
eradicate *v* = **wipe out**, remove, destroy, eliminate, erase, extinguish, annihilate, obliterate, exterminate, root out
erase *v* = **wipe out**, remove, cancel, delete, blot, obliterate, expunge, rub out
erect *v* **1** = **build**, raise, construct, put up, set up **2** = **found**, create, form, establish, organize, institute, initiate, set up ▸ *adj* **3** = **upright**, straight, stiff, elevated, vertical, perpendicular, pricked-up
erode *v* = **wear away**, destroy, deteriorate, disintegrate, corrode, eat away, wear down • *The cliffs were being eroded by the constant pounding of the waves.*
See also: **wash, wear**
erosion *n* = **deterioration**, destruction, attrition, disintegration, abrasion, eating away, grinding down, wearing down *or* wearing away
erotic *adj* = **sexual**, sexy (*informal*), seductive, sensual, voluptuous, amatory, carnal, lustful
err *v* = **make a mistake**, blunder, miscalculate, go wrong • *The builders had erred in their original estimate.*
errand *n* = **job**, charge, mission, message, commission, task
erratic *adj* = **unpredictable**, inconsistent,

DICTIONARY

error ⓣ *n* something considered to be wrong or incorrect
ersatz [**air**-zats] *adj* made in imitation: *ersatz coffee*
Erse *n* **1** Gaelic ▷ *adj* **2** of or relating to the Gaelic language
Ershad *n* **Hussain Mohammed**. born 1930, Bangladeshi soldier and statesman. He seized power in a coup in 1982, becoming president in 1983. He was deposed in 1990
erstwhile ⓣ *adj* former
erudite ⓣ [**air**-rude-ite] *adj* having great academic knowledge **erudition** *n*
erupt ⓣ *v* **1** eject (steam, water, or volcanic material) violently **2** (of a blemish) appear on the skin **3** burst forth suddenly and violently **eruption** *n*
erysipelas *n* acute skin infection causing purplish patches
erythrocyte [ir-**rith**-roe-site] *n* red blood cell of vertebrates that transports oxygen and carbon dioxide
escalate ⓣ *v* increase in extent or intensity **escalation** *n*
escalator *n* moving staircase
escalope [**ess**-kal-lop] *n* thin slice of meat, esp. veal
escapade ⓣ *n* mischievous adventure
escape ⓣ *v* **1** get free (of) **2** avoid: *escape attention* **3** (of a gas, liquid, etc.) leak gradually **4** be forgotten by: *the figure escapes me* ▷ *n* **5** act of escaping **6** means of relaxation or relief
▶ **escapee** *n* person who has escaped
▶ **escapism** *n* taking refuge in fantasy to avoid unpleasant reality
▶ **escapologist** *n* entertainer who specializes in freeing himself or herself from confinement **escapology** *n*
escarpment *n* steep face of a ridge or mountain
eschew ⓣ [iss-**chew**] *v* abstain from, avoid
escort ⓣ *n* **1** people or vehicles accompanying another person for protection or as an honour **2** person who accompanies a person of the opposite sex to a social event ▷ *v* **3** act as an escort to
escudo [ess-**kyoo**-doe] *n, pl* **-dos** former monetary unit of Portugal
escutcheon *n* shield with a coat of arms
▶ **blot on one's escutcheon** stain on one's honour
Eskimo *n* **1** member of the aboriginal race inhabiting N Canada, Greenland, Alaska, and E Siberia **2** their language
ESN educationally subnormal
esoteric [ee-so-**ter**-rik] *adj* understood by only a small number of people with special knowledge
ESP extrasensory perception
esp. especially
espadrille [**ess**-pad-drill] *n* light canvas shoe with a braided cord sole
espalier [ess-**pal**-yer] *n* **1** shrub or fruit tree trained to grow flat **2** trellis for this
esparto *n, pl* **-tos** grass used for making rope etc.
especial ⓣ *adj formal* special
▶ **especially** *adv* particularly

THESAURUS

unstable, irregular, unreliable, variable, uneven, wayward, changeable
erroneous *adj* = **incorrect**, wrong, false, faulty, mistaken, flawed, invalid, unsound, fallacious
error *n* = **lapse**, slip, mistake, fault, blunder • *a mathematical error*
See also: **hole**
erstwhile *adj* = **former**, late, past, old, once, previous, one-time, sometime, bygone
erudite *adj* = **learned**, knowledgeable, scholarly, cultured, well-educated, cultivated, educated, well-read
erupt *v* **1** = **explode**, gush, spout, belch forth, blow up, burst out, pour forth, spew forth *or* spew out, throw off **2** (*Medical*) = **break out**, appear
eruption *n* **1** = **explosion**, outbreak, discharge, outburst, ejection, flare-up **2** (*Medical*) = **inflammation**, outbreak, rash
escalate *v* = **increase**, rise, grow, extend, expand, mount, intensify, heighten
escapade *n* = **adventure**, stunt, scrape (*informal*), prank, antic, caper
escape *v* **1** = **get away**, break free, break out, make your escape, run away, run off • *Three prisoners who escaped have given themselves up.* **2** = **avoid**, duck, elude, evade, dodge • *He was lucky to escape injury.* **3** = **leak**, issue, flow, seep, gush, exude, emanate, pour forth ▶ *n* **4** = **distraction**, relief, diversion • *Cycling gives her an escape from the routine of work.* **5** = **getaway**, break, flight, break-out **6** = **avoidance**, evasion, circumvention **7** = **leak**, emission, seepage, emanation
See also: **bolt, flee**
eschew *See* **avoid**
escort *n* **1** = **guard**, train, convoy, bodyguard, entourage, cortege, retinue **2** = **companion**, partner, guide, attendant, beau, chaperon ▶ *v* **3** = **accompany**, lead, conduct, partner, guide, usher, shepherd, chaperon
especial *adj* (*Formal*) = **exceptional**, special, unusual, principal, outstanding, uncommon, noteworthy
especially *adv* = **exceptionally**, notably, unusually, remarkably, specially, markedly, strikingly, conspicuously, uncommonly,

DICTIONARY

Esperanto *n* universal artificial language
espionage Ⓣ [**ess**-pyon-ahzh] *n* spying
esplanade *n* wide open road used as a public promenade
espouse Ⓣ *v* adopt or give support to (a cause etc.) **espousal** *n*
espresso *n, pl* **-sos** strong coffee made by forcing steam or boiling water through ground coffee beans
esprit [ess-**pree**] *n* spirit, liveliness
▶ **esprit de corps** [de **core**] pride in and loyalty to a group
espy *v* **espying, espied** catch sight of
Esq. esquire
esquire *n* courtesy title placed after a man's name
essay Ⓣ *n* **1** short literary composition **2** short piece of writing on a subject done as an exercise by a student ▷ *v* **3** attempt **essayist** *n*
essence Ⓣ *n* **1** most important feature of a thing which determines its identity **2** concentrated extract obtained by distillation: *vanilla essence*
▶ **essential** *adj* **1** vitally important **2** fundamental ▷ *n* **3** something essential **essentially** *adv*
EST Eastern Standard Time
establish Ⓣ *v* **1** set up on a permanent basis **2** make secure or permanent in a certain place, job, etc. **3** prove **4** cause to be accepted
▶ **establishment** *n* **1** act of establishing **2** commercial or other institution
▶ **the Establishment** group of people having authority within a society
estate Ⓣ *n* **1** landed property **2** large area of property development, esp. of new houses or factories **3** property of a deceased person
▶ **estate agent** *Brit* real estate agent
▶ **estate car** *Brit* station wagon
esteem Ⓣ *v* **1** think highly of **2** judge or consider ▷ *n* **3** high regard
ester *n chem* compound produced by the reaction between an acid and an alcohol
esthetic *n, adj* same as **aesthetic**
estimate Ⓣ *v* **1** calculate roughly **2** form an opinion about ▷ *n* **3** approximate calculation **4** opinion **5** statement from a workman etc. of the likely charge for a job
▶ **estimable** *adj* worthy of respect
▶ **estimation** *n* judgment, opinion
estranged *adj* **1** no longer living with one's spouse **2** having lost someone's affection and loyalty **estrangement** *n*

THESAURUS

outstandingly, distinctively
espionage *n* = **spying**, intelligence, surveillance, counter-intelligence, undercover work
espousal *n* = **support**, championship, promotion, advocacy, adoption, defence, backing, championing, embracing, taking up
espouse *v* = **support**, back, champion, promote, advocate, adopt, uphold, embrace, stand up for, take up
essay *n* **1** = **composition**, paper, article, piece, tract, discourse, treatise, dissertation ▶ *v* **2** (*Formal*) = **attempt**, try, aim, undertake, endeavour
essence *n* **1** = **nature**, heart, core, spirit, soul • *The essence of good manners is the ability to listen.* **2** = **concentrate**, extract, distillate, spirits, tincture
essential *adj* **1** = **vital**, crucial, indispensable • *Good ventilation is essential in a greenhouse.* **2** = **fundamental**, key, main, basic, principal, cardinal • *an essential part of any child's development*
See also: **necessary, requirement**
essentials *pl n* = **necessities**, basics, fundamentals, prerequisites, rudiments • *We had only enough food money for the essentials.*
establish *v* **1** = **create**, form, ground, settle, found, institute, constitute, inaugurate, set up **2** = **prove**, confirm, demonstrate, verify, certify, authenticate, substantiate, corroborate
established *adj* **1** = **accepted**, traditional, historic, conventional, customary, time-honoured, officially recognized **2** = **famous**, prominent, acclaimed, legendary, remarkable, renowned, well-known, notable, celebrated, glorious, illustrious, distinguished, conspicuous, eminent, noted, much-publicized, honoured, lionized
establishment *n* **1** = **creation**, organization, institution, foundation, formation, installation, inauguration, founding, setting up **2** = **organization**, company, business, concern, firm, institution, corporation, outfit (*informal*), enterprise ▷ **the Establishment** = **the authorities**, ruling class, the powers that be, the system
estate *n* **1** = **lands**, area, property, domain, manor, holdings **2** (*Law*) = **property**, wealth, fortune, assets, belongings, effects, goods, possessions
esteem *n* **1** = **respect**, regard, admiration, estimation, reverence • *held in high esteem by her students* ▶ *v* **2** = **respect**, love, value, treasure, admire, revere, prize, regard highly, think highly of **3** = **consider**, think, believe, judge, view, estimate, regard, deem, reckon
See also: **approval, favour**
esteemed *See* **dear**
estimate *n* **1** = **reckoning**, quote, guess, assessment, valuation, appraisal, estimation • *This figure is five times the*

DICTIONARY

estuary Ⓣ *n, pl* **-aries** mouth of a river
ETA estimated time of arrival
et al. and others
etc. et cetera
et cetera Ⓣ [et **set**-ra] *n, v* **1** and the rest, and others **2** or the like
▸ **etceteras** *pl n* miscellaneous extra things or people
etch Ⓣ *v* **1** wear away or cut the surface of (metal, glass, etc.) with acid **2** imprint vividly (on someone's mind) **etching** *n*
eternal Ⓣ *adj* **1** without beginning or end **2** unchanging **eternally** *adv*
▸ **eternity** *n* **1** infinite time **2** timeless existence after death
▸ **eternity ring** ring given as a token of lasting affection
Ethelbert, Æthelbert *n* **Saint.** ?552–616 AD, king of Kent (560–616): converted to Christianity by St Augustine; issued the earliest known code of English laws. Feast day: Feb 24 or 25
Ethelred I, Æthelred I *n* died 871, king of Wessex (866–71). He led resistance to the Danish invasion of England; died following his victory at Ashdown
Ethelred II, Æthelred II *n* known as *Ethelred the Unready.* ?968–1016 AD, king of England (978–1016). He was temporarily deposed by the Danish king Sweyn (1013) but was recalled on Sweyn's death (1014)
Ethelwulf, Æthelwulf *n* died 858 AD, king of Wessex (839–858)
ether *n* **1** colourless sweet-smelling liquid used as an anesthetic **2** region above the clouds
▸ **ethereal** [eth-**eer**-ee-al] *adj* extremely delicate
ethic *n* **1** moral principle **ethics 2** code of behaviour **3** study of morals **ethical** *adj* **ethically** *adv*
ethnic Ⓣ *adj* **1** relating to a people or group that shares a culture, religion, or language **2** belonging or relating to such a group, esp. one that is a minority group in a particular place
▸ **ethnic cleansing** practice, by the dominant ethnic group in an area, of removing other ethnic groups by expulsion or extermination
▸ **ethnology** *n* study of human races **ethnological** *adj* **ethnologist** *n*
ethos [**eeth**-oss] *n* distinctive spirit and attitudes of a people, culture, etc.
ethyl [**eth**-ill] *adj* of, consisting of, or containing the hydrocarbon group C_2H_5
▸ **ethylene** *n* poisonous gas used as an anesthetic and as fuel
etiolate [**ee**-tee-oh-late] *v* **1** become pale and weak **2** *botany* whiten through lack of sunlight
etiology *n* study of the causes of diseases
etiquette Ⓣ *n* conventional code of conduct
étude [**ay**-tewd] *n* short musical composition for a solo instrument, esp. intended as a technical exercise
etymology *n, pl* **-gies** study of the sources and development of words **etymological** *adj* **etymologist** *n*
EU European Union
eucalyptus, eucalypt *n* tree, mainly grown in Australia, that provides timber and gum
Eucharist [**yew**-kar-ist] *n* **1** Christian sacrament commemorating Christ's Last Supper **2** consecrated elements of bread

THESAURUS

original estimate. **2 = opinion**, assessment, judgment, belief, appraisal, estimation
▸ *v* **3 = calculate roughly**, number, judge, value, guess, assess, evaluate, gauge, reckon **4 = form an opinion**, rate, believe, consider, judge, rank, reckon, conjecture, surmise
See also: **price, tender**
estimated *See* **approximate, rough**
estimation *n* **= opinion**, view, assessment, judgment, belief, consideration, appreciation, appraisal, considered opinion
estuary *n* **= inlet**, mouth, creek, fjord, firth
et cetera *adv* **1 = and so on**, and so forth
▸ *n* **2 = and the rest**, and others, and the like, et al.
etch *v* **= cut**, stamp, impress, carve, engrave, imprint, inscribe, eat into
etching *n* **= print**, impression, imprint, carving, inscription, engraving
eternal *adj* **1 = everlasting**, immortal, unchanging • *the secret of eternal life* **2 = permanent**, lasting, enduring, unchanging, indestructible, deathless, immutable, imperishable
See also: **constant, continual, infinite**
eternity *n* **1 = infinity**, immortality, perpetuity, ages, endlessness, timelessness **2** (*Theology*) **= the afterlife**, heaven, paradise, the hereafter, the next world
ethical *adj* **= moral**, good, just, right, fair, proper, upright, principled, conscientious, honourable, virtuous
ethics *pl n* **= moral code**, conscience, morality, moral philosophy, moral values, principles, rules of conduct, standards
ethnic *adj* **= cultural**, national, native, traditional, folk, racial, indigenous • *They appeared in full ethnic costume.* ▹ **ethnic group** *See* **race**
etiquette *n* **= good behaviour** *or* **proper**

DICTIONARY

and wine **Eucharistic** *adj*
Euclid *n* **1** 3rd century BC, Greek mathematician of Alexandria; author of *Elements*, which sets out the principles of geometry and remained a text until the 19th century at least **2** the works of Euclid, esp. his system of geometry **Euclidean** *or* **Euclidian** *adj*
Eudoxus of Cnidus *n* ?406–?355 BC, Greek astronomer and mathematician; believed to have calculated the length of the solar year
eugenics [yew-**jen**-iks] *n* study of methods of improving the human race
eulogy *n, pl* **-gies** speech or writing in praise of a person
▸ **eulogize** *v* praise (a person or thing) highly in speech or writing **eulogist** *n* **eulogistic** *adj*
eunuch *n* castrated man, esp. (formerly) a guard in a harem
euphemism *n* inoffensive word or phrase substituted for one considered offensive or upsetting **euphemistic** *adj* **euphemistically** *adv*
euphony *n, pl* **-nies** pleasing sound
▸ **euphonious** *adj* pleasing to the ear
▸ **euphonium** *n* brass musical instrument, tenor tuba
euphoria ⓣ *n* sense of elation **euphoric** *adj*
Eurasian *adj* **1** of Europe and Asia **2** of mixed European and Asian parentage ▹ *n* **3** person of Eurasian parentage
eureka [yew-**reek**-a] *interj* exclamation of triumph at finding something
Eurodollar *n* US dollar as part of a European holding
European *n, adj* (person) from Europe
▸ **European Union** association of a number of European nations for trade, etc.
Eustachian tube *n* passage leading from the ear to the throat
euthanasia *n* act of killing someone painlessly, esp. to relieve his or her suffering
evacuate ⓣ *v* **1** send (someone) away from a place of danger **2** empty **evacuation** *n* **evacuee** *n*
evade ⓣ *v* **1** get away from or avoid **2** elude **evasion** *n*
▸ **evasive** *adj* not straightforward: *an evasive answer* **evasively** *adv*
evaluate ⓣ *v* find or judge the value of **evaluation** *n*
evanescent *adj* quickly fading away **evanescence** *n*
evangelical *adj* **1** of or according to gospel teaching **2** of certain Protestant sects which maintain the doctrine of salvation by faith ▹ *n* **3** member of an evangelical sect **evangelicalism** *n*
evangelist *n* **1** writer of one of the four gospels **2** travelling preacher
▸ **evangelism** *n* teaching and spreading of the Christian gospel
▸ **evangelize** *v* preach the gospel **evangelization** *n*
Evans *n* **Gil**, born *Ian Ernest Gilmore Green*. 1912–88, Canadian jazz pianist
evaporate ⓣ *v* **1** change from a liquid or solid to a vapour **2** disappear **evaporation** *n*
▸ **evaporated milk** thick unsweetened canned milk
eve ⓣ *n* **1** evening or day before some special event **2** period immediately before an event
▸ **evensong** *n* evening prayer
even ⓣ *adj* **1** flat or smooth **2** (foll. by *with*) on the same level (as) **3** constant **4** calm **5** equally balanced **6** divisible by two ▹ *adv* **7** equally **8** simply **9** nevertheless ▹ *v* **10** make even

THESAURUS

behaviour, courtesy, protocol, civility, decorum, politeness, formalities, manners, propriety
euphoria *n* = **elation**, joy, ecstasy, intoxication, jubilation, exhilaration, rapture, exaltation
evacuate *v* = **clear**, leave, quit, withdraw, abandon, desert, vacate, forsake, move out, pull out
evacuation *See* **retreat**
evade *v* **1** = **avoid**, duck, escape, elude, dodge, sidestep, get away from, steer clear of **2** = **avoid answering**, hedge, fudge, parry, equivocate, fend off
evaluate *v* = **assess**, rate, judge, estimate, weigh, calculate, gauge, reckon, appraise, size up (*informal*)
evaporate *v* **1** = **dry up**, dry, dehydrate, vaporize, desiccate **2** = **disappear**, dissolve, vanish, dematerialize, fade away, melt away
evasion *n* **1** = **avoidance**, escape, dodging **2** = **deception**, equivocation, evasiveness, prevarication
evasive *adj* = **deceptive**, slippery, indirect, cagey (*informal*), oblique, shifty, equivocating, prevaricating
eve *n* **1** = **night before**, vigil, day before **2** = **brink**, point, edge, verge, threshold
even *adj* **1** = **level**, flat, smooth, horizontal • *I need an even surface to write on.* OPPOSITE: uneven **2** = **regular**, steady, uniform, constant, smooth • *an even flow of liquid* **3** = **equal**, identical, neck and neck • *At half-time, the scores were still even.* **4** = **calm**, cool, well-balanced, composed, even-tempered, imperturbable, placid, unruffled ▹ **even though** *See* **in spite of**
▹ **get even, get even with** = **pay back**, repay, retaliate, reciprocate, give tit for tat, requite
See also: **straight**

DICTIONARY

evening Ⓣ *n* **1** end of the day or early part of the night **2** concluding period
even-strength *adj* *hockey* (of a goal etc.) occurring when both teams have the same number of players on the ice
event Ⓣ *n* **1** anything that takes place **2** actual outcome **3** contest in a sporting programme
▸ **eventful** *adj* full of exciting incidents
▸ **eventing** *n* riding competitions, usually involving cross-country, jumping, and dressage
▸ **eventual** *adj* ultimate **eventually** *adv*
▸ **eventuality** *n* possible event
ever Ⓣ *adv* **1** at any time **2** always
everlasting *adj*
▸ **evergreen** *n, adj* (tree or shrub) having leaves throughout the year
▸ **evermore** *adv* all time to come
every Ⓣ *adj* **1** each without exception **2** all possible **everything** *pron*
▸ **everybody** *pron* every person
▸ **everyday** *adj* usual or ordinary
▸ **everyone** *pron* every person
▸ **everywhere** *adv* in all places
evict Ⓣ *v* legally expel (someone) from his or her home **eviction** *n*
evidence Ⓣ *n* **1** ground for belief or disbelief **2** matter produced before a lawcourt to prove or disprove a point ▹ *v* **3** demonstrate, prove
▸ **in evidence** on display
▸ **evident** *adj* easily noticed or understood **evidently** *adv*
▸ **evidential** *adj* of, serving as, or based on evidence **evidentially** *adv*
evil Ⓣ *n* **1** wickedness **2** wicked deed ▹ *adj* **3** morally bad **4** harmful **5** very unpleasant **evilly** *adv*
▸ **evildoer** *n* wicked person
evince *v* make evident

THESAURUS

evening *n* = **dusk**, twilight, gloaming (*Scot, poetic*)
event *n* **1** = **incident**, business, experience, matter, affair, circumstance, episode • *still amazed at the events of last week* **2** = **competition**, contest, bout • *The next event is the long jump.*
See also: **occasion**
even-tempered *adj* = **calm**, cool, tranquil, composed, imperturbable, level-headed, placid, unexcitable, unruffled
eventful *adj* = **exciting**, full, active, dramatic, busy, remarkable, memorable, lively
eventual *adj* = **final**, overall, ultimate, concluding
eventuality *n* = **possibility**, case, event, chance, likelihood, contingency, probability
eventually *adv* = **in the end**, finally, ultimately, after all, at the end of the day, one day, some time, when all is said and done
ever *adv* **1** = **at any time**, at all, at any period, at any point, by any chance, in any case, on any occasion **2** = **always**, constantly, continually, perpetually, at all times, evermore, for ever, twenty-four-seven (*slang*)
everlasting *adj* = **eternal**, endless, timeless, perpetual, immortal, indestructible, never-ending, undying
evermore *adv* = **for ever**, always, ever, eternally, to the end of time
every *adj* = **each**, all, each one ▹ **every now and then** *See* **sometimes** ▹ **every one** *See* **all** ▹ **every so often** *See* **sometimes** ▹ **every time** *See* **always**
everybody *pron* = **everyone**, all and sundry, each one, each person, every person, one and all, the whole world
everyday *adj* = **ordinary**, common, daily, routine, day-to-day, mundane • *the drudgery of everyday life*
See also: **colloquial, frequent, natural, regular**
everyone *pron* = **everybody**, all and sundry, each one, each person, every person, one and all, the whole world
everything *pron* = **all**, each thing, the lot, the whole lot, the whole schmear (*informal*), the whole enchilada (*slang*)
everywhere *adv* = **to every place** *or* **in every place**, all around, all over, far and wide *or* far and near, high and low, in every nook and cranny, the world over, ubiquitously
evict *v* = **expel**, remove, oust, eject, boot out (*informal*), kick out (*informal*), throw out, turn out
evidence *n* **1** = **proof**, sign, testimony, demonstration, indication, confirmation, corroboration, grounds, substantiation ▸ *v* **2** = **show**, reveal, prove, witness, indicate, display, exhibit, demonstrate, signify
evident *adj* = **obvious**, clear, apparent, visible, plain, noticeable, palpable • *He spoke with evident emotion about his ordeal.*
See also: **conspicuous, naked**
evidently *adv* **1** = **obviously**, clearly, undoubtedly, plainly, manifestly, unmistakably, without question **2** = **apparently**, seemingly, ostensibly, outwardly, to all appearances
evil *n* **1** = **wickedness**, vice, sin, immorality, badness • *the conflict between good and evil* OPPOSITE: good **2** = **harm**, ill, misery, sorrow, affliction • *a lecture on the evils of alcohol* ▸ *adj* **3** = **wicked**, bad, vile, sinful, malevolent, depraved • *an utterly evil person* OPPOSITE: good **4** = **harmful**, disastrous, dire, catastrophic,

DICTIONARY

eviscerate *v* disembowel **evisceration** *n*
evoke Ⓣ *v* call or summon up (a memory, feeling, etc.) **evocation** *n* **evocative** *adj*
evolve Ⓣ *v* **1** develop gradually **2** (of an animal or plant species) undergo evolution
▸ **evolution** *n* gradual change in the characteristics of living things over successive generations, esp. to a more complex form **evolutionary** *adj*
ewe *n* female sheep
ewer *n* large jug with a wide mouth
ex *n informal* former wife or husband
ex- *prefix* **1** out of, outside, from: *exodus* **2** former: *ex-wife*
exacerbate [ig-**zass**-er-bate] *v* make (pain, emotion, or a situation) worse **exacerbation** *n*
exact Ⓣ *adj* **1** correct and complete in every detail **2** precise, as opposed to approximate ▹ *v* **3** demand (payment or obedience) **exactness** *or* **exactitude** *n*
▸ **exactly** *adv* precisely, in every respect
▸ **exacting** *adj* making rigorous or excessive demands
exaggerate Ⓣ *v* **1** regard or represent as greater than is true **2** make greater or more noticeable **exaggeratedly** *adv* **exaggeration** *n*
exalt Ⓣ *v* **1** praise highly **2** elevate in rank
▸ **exaltation** *n* **1** feeling of great joy **2** act of praising highly
exam Ⓣ *n* short for **examination**
examine Ⓣ *v* **1** inspect carefully **2** test the knowledge of **3** formally question someone on oath **examinee** *n* **examiner** *n*
▸ **examination** *n* **1** examining **2** test of a candidate's knowledge or skill
example Ⓣ *n* **1** specimen typical of its group **3** person or thing worthy of imitation **4** punishment regarded as a warning to others

THESAURUS

destructive, ruinous, calamitous, pernicious **5 = offensive**, foul, unpleasant, noxious, vile, pestilential
See also: **sinister, wrong**
evoke *v* **= recall**, call, induce, awaken, rekindle, arouse, give rise to, stir up, summon up
evolution *n* **= development**, increase, growth, progress, expansion, maturation, unfolding, working out
evolve *v* **= develop**, increase, grow, expand, progress, mature, unfold, work out
exact *adj* **1 = accurate**, true, faithful, authentic, precise, faultless • *It's an exact reproduction of the first steam engine.* OPPOSITE: approximate ▸ *v* **2** (*Formal*) **= demand**, command, impose, extract, wring, insist on, insist upon • *They are certain to exact a high price for their co-operation.*
See also: **correct, particular, right, strict**
exacting *adj* **= demanding**, hard, tough, difficult, severe, strict, harsh, rigorous, stringent, taxing
exactly *adv* **1 = precisely**, just, accurately, faithfully, on the dot, quite • *He arrived at exactly five o'clock.* OPPOSITE: approximately **2 = in every respect**, quite, absolutely, indeed, specifically, precisely, to the letter ▸ *interjection* **3 = indeed**, quite, absolutely, precisely • *"We'll never know the answer." – "Exactly. So let's stop speculating."*
See also: **prompt**
exactness *n* **= precision**, accuracy, correctness, veracity, exactitude, rigorousness, scrupulousness, strictness
exaggerate *v* **= overstate**, overestimate, overdo • *He thinks I'm exaggerating, but I'm not!*
exaggerated *See* **excessive**
exaggeration *n* **= overstatement**, embellishment, enlargement, hyperbole, amplification, overemphasis, overestimation
exalt *v* **1 = praise**, acclaim, worship, glorify, idolize, extol, set on a pedestal **2 = raise**, advance, promote, upgrade, honour, elevate, ennoble
exaltation *n* **1 = praise**, tribute, acclaim, worship, glorification, reverence, idolization **2 = rise**, promotion, advancement, elevation, ennoblement, upgrading
exalted *adj* **= high-ranking**, grand, prestigious, lofty, dignified, eminent, honoured
exam *n* **= test**, examination • *a final exam*
examination *n* **1 = inspection**, study, analysis • *a careful examination of all the evidence* **2 = check**, physical, checkup • *The doctor suggested an immediate examination of his ear.* **3 = questioning**, test, probe, inquiry, quiz, inquisition
See also: **exam, research, review**
examine *v* **1 = inspect**, study, analyze, go over, go through, look over • *Police are examining the scene of the crash.* **2 = check**, test, look at • *I was examined by several specialists.* **3 = question**, test, quiz, grill (*informal*), interrogate, inquire, cross-examine
See also: **contemplate, investigate, research, scrutinize**
example *n* **1 = specimen**, sample, illustration • *some examples of well-made horror movies* **2 = ideal**, model, prototype, paragon • *His dedication is an example to us all.* **3 = warning**, caution, lesson
See also: **case**

DICTIONARY

exasperate ⓣ *v* cause great irritation to **exasperation** *n*
excavate ⓣ *v* **1** unearth buried objects from (a piece of land) methodically to learn about the past **2** make (a hole) in solid matter by digging **excavation** *n*
▸ **excavator** *n* large machine used for digging
exceed ⓣ *v* **1** be greater than **2** go beyond (a limit)
▸ **exceedingly** *adv* very
excel ⓣ *v* **-celling**, **-celled 1** be superior to **2** be outstandingly good at something
▸ **excellent** *adj* very good **excellence** *n*
▸ **Excellency** *n* title used to address a high-ranking official, such as an ambassador
except ⓣ *prep* **1** (sometimes foll. by *for*) other than, not including ▹ *v* **2** not include
▸ **except that** with the exception that
▸ **excepting** *prep* except
▸ **exception** *n* thing that is excluded from or does not conform to the general rule
▸ **exceptionable** *adj* causing offence
▸ **exceptional** *adj* **1** not ordinary **2** much above the average
excerpt ⓣ *n* passage taken from a book, speech, etc.
excess ⓣ *n* **1** state or act of exceeding the permitted limits **2** immoderate amount **3** amount by which a thing exceeds the permitted limits **excessive** *adj* **excessively** *adv*
exchange ⓣ *v* **1** give or receive (something) in return for something else ▹ *n* **2** act of exchanging **3** thing given or received in place of another **4** centre in which telephone lines are interconnected **5** *finance* place where securities or commodities are traded **6** *finance* transfer of sums of money of equal value between different currencies **exchangeable** *adj*
Exchequer *n Brit* government department in charge of state money
excise[1] ⓣ *n* tax on goods produced for the home market
excise[2] *v* cut out or away **excision** *n*
excite ⓣ *v* **1** arouse to strong emotion

THESAURUS

exasperate *v* = **irritate**, anger, annoy, inflame, pique, incense, infuriate, enrage, madden
exasperation *n* = **irritation**, anger, rage, wrath, pique, provocation, fury, annoyance
excavate *v* = **dig out**, mine, uncover, tunnel, unearth, delve, burrow, quarry, dig up
exceed *v* **1** = **surpass**, top, beat, pass, cap (*informal*), eclipse, overtake, better, outstrip, outdo **2** = **go over the limit of**, overstep, go over the top
exceeding *See* **above, over**
exceedingly *adv* = **extremely**, very, unusually, hugely, extraordinarily, exceptionally, enormously, superlatively, surpassingly
excel *v* = **be superior**, beat, surpass, eclipse, outshine, outdo, transcend ▹ **excel in, excel at** = **be good at**, be proficient in, be skillful at, be talented at, shine at, show talent in
excellence *n* = **high quality**, merit, distinction, greatness, goodness, supremacy, superiority, eminence, pre-eminence
excellent *adj* = **outstanding**, great, fine, brilliant, superb, first-class, peachy-keen (*slang, now usu. facetious*) • *It's an excellent book, one of my favourites*. OPPOSITE: terrible
See also: **exceptional, first-rate, marvellous, splendid, wonderful**
except *prep* **1** = **apart from**, but, save (*formal*), other than, with the exception of • *I don't eat dessert, except for the occasional slice of pie*. ▹ **except for** *See* **but** ▸ *v* **2** = **exclude**, omit, leave out, pass over
exception *n* **1** = **special case**, irregularity, oddity, freak, inconsistency, anomaly, deviation, peculiarity **2** = **exclusion**, omission, leaving out, passing over
exceptional *adj* **1** = **remarkable**, excellent, extraordinary, talented, outstanding, phenomenal • *Her piano playing is exceptional*. OPPOSITE: mediocre **2** = **unusual**, special, rare, isolated, unheard-of, out of the ordinary • *The traffic is exceptional for this time of day*. OPPOSITE: common
See also: **extreme, first-rate, particular, singular, superior, uncommon**
excerpt *n* = **extract**, part, piece, section, selection, passage, fragment, quotation
excess *n* **1** = **overindulgence**, indulgence, extravagance, debauchery, dissipation, intemperance • *a life of excess* **2** = **surfeit**, surplus, glut, plethora, overabundance, superabundance, superfluity • *An excess of houseplants made the room look like a jungle*. OPPOSITE: shortage ▸ *adj* **3** = **surplus**, extra, superfluous • *travelling with excess baggage*
excessive *adj* = **immoderate**, enormous, exaggerated, unreasonable, needless, undue • *an excessive reliance on government funding*
See also: **extreme, steep**
excessively *See* **too**
exchange *v* **1** = **interchange**, change, trade, switch, swap, barter • *We exchanged phone numbers*. ▹ **exchange views on** *See* **discuss** ▸ *n* **2** = **interchange**, trade, switch, swap • *a ceasefire to allow the exchange of prisoners*
See also: **substitute**
excise *See* **duty, tax**
excitable *adj* = **nervous**, emotional, volatile, mercurial, temperamental, highly

DICTIONARY

2 arouse or evoke (an emotion) **3** arouse sexually **excitement** *n*
▸ **excitable** *adj* easily excited **excitability** *n*
exclaim Ⓣ *v* speak suddenly, cry out **exclamation** *n* **exclamatory** *adj*
▸ **exclamation mark** punctuation mark (!) used after exclamations
exclude Ⓣ *v* **1** leave out of consideration **2** keep out, leave out **exclusion** *n*
▸ **exclusive** *adj* **1** catering for a privileged minority **2** not shared **3** excluding everything else ▷ *n* **4** story reported in only one newspaper **exclusively** *adv* **exclusiveness** *or* **exclusivity** *n*
excommunicate Ⓣ *v* exclude from membership and the sacraments of the Church **excommunication** *n*
excoriate *v* **1** censure severely **2** strip skin from **excoriation** *n*
excrement *n* waste matter discharged from the body
excrescence *n* lump or growth on the surface of an animal or plant
excrete *v* discharge (waste matter) from the body **excretion** *n* **excretory** *adj*
▸ **excreta** [ik-**skree**-ta] *n* excrement
excruciating Ⓣ *adj* **1** agonizing **2** very intense **excruciatingly** *adv*
exculpate Ⓣ *v* free from blame or guilt
excursion Ⓣ *n* short journey, esp. for pleasure
excuse Ⓣ *n* **1** explanation offered to excuse (a fault etc.) ▷ *v* **2** put forward a reason or justification for (a fault etc.) **3** forgive (a person) or overlook (a fault etc.) **4** make allowances for **5** exempt **6** allow to leave **excusable** *adj*
ex-directory *adj* not listed in a telephone directory by request
execrable [**eks**-sik-rab-bl] *adj* of very poor quality
execute Ⓣ *v* **1** put (a condemned person) to death **2** perform (a plan or action) **3** produce (a work of art) **4** render (a legal document) effective, as by signing **execution** *n*
▸ **executioner** *n* person employed to execute criminals
▸ **executor** (**executrix**) *n* person appointed to

THESAURUS

strung, hot-headed, quick-tempered, wired (*slang*)
excite *v* **1** = **thrill**, agitate, animate, titillate • *The idea of travelling across Canada really excited the kids.* **2** = **arouse**, inspire, provoke, incite, evoke, elicit, stir up • *The meeting failed to excite strong feelings in anyone.*
excited *adj* = **thrilled**, enthusiastic, feverish, agitated, jazzed (*slang*) • *We are very excited about getting a new dog.* OPPOSITE: bored
excitement *n* = **thrill**, activity, adventure, enthusiasm, agitation, commotion • *The release of her latest book has caused great excitement.*
See also: **bustle, heat, passion**
exciting *adj* = **thrilling**, dramatic, rousing, electrifying, exhilarating, stimulating, kicky (*slang*) • *the most exciting race I've ever seen* OPPOSITE: boring
See also: **impressive**
exclaim *v* = **cry out**, declare, shout, yell, utter, proclaim, call out
exclamation *n* = **cry**, call, shout, yell, outcry, utterance, interjection
exclude *v* **1** = **leave out**, eliminate, ignore, omit, rule out • *We cannot exclude this possibility altogether.* OPPOSITE: include **2** = **keep out**, ban, bar, forbid • *Nobody is excluded from this club.*
See also: **boycott**
exclusion *n* **1** = **ban**, bar, boycott, veto, embargo, prohibition, disqualification, interdict **2** = **elimination**, rejection, omission
exclusive *adj* **1** = **select**, upscale, chic, posh (*informal*), classy • *one of the city's most exclusive golf clubs* **2** = **sole**, complete, full, total, whole, entire, absolute, undivided **3** = **limited**, unique, restricted, peculiar, confined
See also: **private**
excommunicate *v* = **expel**, ban, exclude, denounce, banish, repudiate, anathematize, cast out
excruciating *adj* = **agonizing**, violent, severe, intense, unbearable, piercing, harrowing, insufferable
exculpate *v* = **absolve**, clear, excuse, acquit, discharge, pardon, exonerate, vindicate
excursion *n* = **trip**, tour, journey, outing, expedition, ramble, jaunt, day trip, pleasure trip
excusable *adj* = **forgivable**, allowable, understandable, justifiable, permissible, defensible, pardonable, warrantable
excuse *n* **1** = **justification**, reason, explanation, pretext • *Stop making excuses and get on with it!* ▸ *v* **2** = **forgive**, overlook, pardon, turn a blind eye to • *Please excuse my late arrival.* **3** = **justify**, defend, explain, mitigate, vindicate, apologize for **4** = **free**, release, relieve, spare, discharge, exempt, absolve, let off ▷ **excuse yourself** *See* **decline**
See also: **defence, grounds**
excused *See* **exempt**
execute *v* **1** = **put to death**, kill, shoot, hang, behead, electrocute, guillotine **2** = **carry out**, effect, perform, implement, accomplish, prosecute, administer, discharge, enact

DICTIONARY

perform the instructions of a will
executive ❶ *n* **1** person or group in an administrative position **2** branch of government responsible for carrying out laws etc. ▷ *adj* **3** having the function of carrying out plans, orders, laws, etc.
exegesis [eks-sij-**jee**-siss] *n, pl* **-ses** explanation of a text, esp. of the Bible
exemplar *n* **1** example **2** person or thing to be copied, model
▸ **exemplary** *adj* **1** being a good example **2** serving as a warning
exemplify ❶ *v* **-fying, -fied 1** be an example of **2** show an example of **exemplification** *n*
exempt ❶ *adj* **1** not subject to an obligation etc. ▷ *v* **2** release from an obligation etc. **exemption** *n*
exequies [**eks**-sik-wiz] *pl n* funeral rites
exercise ❶ *n* **1** activity to train the body or mind **2** set of movements or tasks designed to improve or test a person's ability **3** performance of a function ▷ *v* **4** take exercise or perform exercises **5** make use of: *to exercise one's rights*
exert ❶ *v* use (influence, authority, etc.) forcefully or effectively **exertion** *n*
▸ **exert oneself** make a special effort
exeunt [**eks**-see-unt] *Latin* they go out: used as a stage direction
exfoliate *v* scrub away dead skin cells, esp. by washing with an abrasive lotion
ex gratia [**eks gray**-sha] *adj* given as a favour where no legal obligation exists
exhale *v* breathe out **exhalation** *n*
exhaust ❶ *v* **1** tire out **2** use up **3** discuss (a subject) thoroughly ▷ *n* **4** gases ejected from an engine as waste products **5** pipe through which an engine's exhaust fumes pass **exhaustible** *adj*
▸ **exhaustion** *n* **1** extreme tiredness **2** exhausting
▸ **exhaustive** *adj* comprehensive **exhaustively** *adv*
exhibit ❶ *v* **1** show (a quality) **2** display to the public ▷ *n* **3** object exhibited to the public **4** *law* document or object produced in court as evidence **exhibitor** *n*
▸ **exhibition** *n* **1** public display of art, skills, etc. **2** exhibiting
▸ **exhibitionism** *n* **1** compulsive desire to

THESAURUS

execution *n* **1 = carrying out**, operation, performance, administration, prosecution, enforcement, accomplishment, implementation, enactment **2 = killing**, hanging, capital punishment
executioner *n* **1 = hangman**, headsman **2 = killer**, murderer, assassin, exterminator, hit man (*slang*), liquidator, slayer
executive *n* **1 = administrator**, official, director, manager **2 = administration**, government, leadership, management, hierarchy, directorate, directors ▸ *adj* **3 = administrative**, decision-making, managerial, controlling, directing, governing
exemplary *adj* **1 = ideal**, good, fine, model, excellent, admirable, commendable, praiseworthy **2 = warning**, cautionary
exemplify *v* **= show**, represent, display, exhibit, demonstrate, illustrate, embody, serve as an example of
exempt *adj* **1 = immune**, excused, not liable • *exempt from paying the tax* ▸ *v* **2 = grant immunity**, release, free, excuse, relieve, spare, discharge, absolve, let off
exemption *n* **= immunity**, release, freedom, exception, discharge, exoneration, absolution, dispensation
exercise *n* **1 = exertion**, work, activity, training • *I need to get more exercise.* **2 = task**, problem, practice, drill, lesson **3 = use**, practice, application, discharge, implementation, utilization, fulfillment
▸ *v* **4 = put to use**, use, apply, employ, exert, utilize, bring to bear **5 = train**, practice, work out
exert *v* **= use**, exercise, apply, employ, wield, utilize, bring to bear, make use of ▸ **exert oneself = make an effort**, work, struggle, strain, strive, labour, toil, endeavour, apply oneself, do one's best
exertion *n* **= effort**, industry, struggle, exercise, strain, toil, endeavour, elbow grease (*facetious*)
exhaust *v* **1 = tire out**, drain, fatigue, wear out • *Don't exhaust yourself by taking on too many projects.* **2 = use up**, consume, deplete, run through • *She has exhausted all my patience.*
See also: **tax, tire**
exhausted *adj* **1 = worn out**, debilitated, done in (*informal*), drained, fatigued, beat (*informal*), spent, tired out, whipped (*informal*) **2 = used up**, finished, spent, consumed, depleted, dissipated, expended, squandered, wasted
exhausting *adj* **= tiring**, strenuous, gruelling, backbreaking, debilitating, laborious, punishing, sapping, taxing
exhaustion *n* **1 = tiredness**, fatigue, debilitation, weariness **2 = depletion**, consumption, emptying, using up
exhaustive *adj* **= thorough**, complete, extensive, comprehensive, intensive, full-scale, in-depth, all-embracing
exhibit *v* **= display**, show, reveal, indicate, express, demonstrate, parade, manifest, put on view

DICTIONARY

draw attention to oneself **2** compulsive desire to display one's genitals in public
exhibitionist *n*
exhilarate *v* make lively and cheerful
exhilaration *n*
exhort Ⓣ *v* urge earnestly **exhortation** *n*
exhume Ⓣ [ig-**zyume**] *v* dig up (something buried, esp. a corpse) **exhumation** *n*
exigency Ⓣ *n, pl* **-cies** urgent demand or need **exigent** *adj*
exiguous *adj* scanty, meagre
exile Ⓣ *n* **1** prolonged, usu. enforced, absence from one's country **2** person banished or living away from his or her country ▷ *v* **3** expel from one's country
exist Ⓣ *v* **1** have being or reality **2** eke out a living **3** live **existence** *n* **existent** *adj*
existential *adj* of or relating to existence, esp. human existence
▸ **existentialism** *n* philosophical movement stressing the personal experience and responsibility of the individual, who is seen as a free agent **existentialist** *adj, n*
exit Ⓣ *n* **1** way out **2** going out **3** actor's going off stage ▷ *v* **4** go out **5** go offstage: used as a stage direction
exocrine *adj* relating to a gland, such as the sweat gland, that secretes externally through a duct
exodus Ⓣ [**eks**-so-duss] *n* departure of a large number of people
▸ **the Exodus** departure of the Israelites from Egypt
ex officio [**eks** off-**fish**-ee-oh] *adv, adj Latin* by right of position or office
exonerate Ⓣ *v* free from blame or a criminal charge **exoneration** *n*
exorbitant Ⓣ *adj* (of prices, demands, etc.) excessive, immoderate **exorbitantly** *adv*
exorcise Ⓣ *v* (attempt to) expel (evil spirits) by prayers and religious rites **exorcism** *n* **exorcist** *n*
exotic Ⓣ *adj* **1** having a strange allure or beauty **2** originating in a foreign country ▷ *n* **3** non-native plant **exotically** *adv*
▸ **exotica** *pl n* (collection of) exotic objects
expand Ⓣ *v* **1** make or become larger **2** spread out **3** (foll. by *on*) enlarge (on) **4** become more relaxed, friendly, and talkative
expansion *n*
▸ **expanse** *n* uninterrupted wide area
▸ **expansive** *adj* **1** friendly and talkative **2** wide or extensive
expatiate [iks-**pay**-shee-ate] *v* (foll. by *on*) speak or write at great length (on)
expatiation *n*

THESAURUS

exhibition *n* = **display**, show, performance, demonstration, presentation, representation, spectacle, ex (*Canad*), exposition
exhilarating *adj* = **exciting**, thrilling, breathtaking, enlivening, invigorating, stimulating
exhort *v* = **urge**, press, advise, spur, persuade, beseech, call upon, entreat
exhume *v* = **dig up**, unearth, disentomb, disinter
exigency *n* = **need**, demand, requirement, necessity, constraint
exile *n* **1** = **banishment**, deportation, expulsion, expatriation **2** = **expatriate**, refugee, outcast, deportee, émigré ▸ *v* **3** = **banish**, deport, expel, eject, expatriate, drive out
exist *v* **1** = **be**, live, survive, occur, endure, be present **2** = **survive**, subsist, eke out a living, get along *or* get by, keep one's head above water, stay alive
existence *n* = **being**, life, actuality, subsistence
existent *adj* = **in existence**, present, alive, standing, living, existing, extant, surviving
exit *n* **1** = **way out**, door, outlet, gate **2** = **departure**, withdrawal, retreat, farewell, exodus, going, good-bye, leave-taking ▸ *v* **3** = **depart**, leave, retire, withdraw, retreat, go away, go offstage (*theatre*), go out, make tracks, take one's leave
exodus *n* = **departure**, flight, exit, evacuation, withdrawal, retreat, migration, going out, leaving
exonerate *v* = **clear**, excuse, acquit, justify, discharge, pardon, vindicate, absolve, exculpate
exorbitant *adj* = **excessive**, outrageous, unreasonable, extravagant, inordinate, preposterous, extortionate, immoderate
exorcise *v* = **drive out**, deliver *or* deliver from, expel, purify, cast out
exotic *adj* **1** = **unusual**, mysterious, strange, glamorous, striking, unfamiliar, colourful, fascinating **2** = **foreign**, external, alien, imported, naturalized
expand *v* **1** = **increase**, develop, extend, enlarge OPPOSITE: decrease **2** = **grow**, swell, fill out • *The rails expanded and buckled in the fierce heat.* **3** = **spread** *or* **spread out**, stretch *or* stretch out, unfold, unravel, unfurl, diffuse, unroll
See also: **bulge, elaborate** ▷ **expand on** = **go into detail about**, develop, elaborate on, enlarge on • *an idea that I will expand on later*
expanse *n* = **area**, space, sweep, range, stretch, extent, tract, breadth
expansion *n* = **increase**, growth, development, spread, enlargement, amplification, magnification, opening out
expansive *adj* **1** = **wide**, broad, widespread, extensive, wide-ranging, far-reaching,

DICTIONARY

expatriate ⓣ [eks-**pat**-ree-it] *n* **1** person living outside his or her native country ▷ *adj* **2** living outside one's native country **expatriation** *n*
expect ⓣ *v* **1** regard as probable **2** look forward to, await **3** require as an obligation
▸ **expectation** *n* **1** act or state of expecting **2** something looked forward to **3** attitude of anticipation or hope
▸ **expectancy** *n* **1** something expected on the basis of an average: *life expectancy* **2** feeling of anticipation
▸ **expectant** *adj* **1** expecting or hopeful **2** pregnant **expectantly** *adv*
expectorate *v* spit out (phlegm etc.) **expectoration** *n*
▸ **expectorant** *n* medicine that helps to bring up phlegm from the respiratory passages
expedient ⓣ [iks-**pee**-dee-ent] *n* **1** something that achieves a particular purpose ▷ *adj* **2** suitable to the circumstances, appropriate **expediency** *n*
expedite *v* hasten the progress of
▸ **expedition** *n* **1** organized journey, esp. for exploration **2** people and equipment comprising an expedition **3** pleasure trip or excursion
▸ **expeditionary** *adj* relating to an expedition, esp. a military one
▸ **expeditious** *adj* prompt, speedy
expel ⓣ *v* **-pelling, -pelled 1** dismiss from a school etc. permanently **2** drive out with force **expulsion** *n*
expend ⓣ *v* spend, use up
▸ **expendable** *adj* able to be sacrificed to achieve an objective
▸ **expenditure** *n* **1** something expended, esp. money **2** amount expended
▸ **expense** *n* **1** cost **2** (cause of) spending **expenses 3** charges, outlay incurred
▸ **expensive** *adj* high-priced
experience ⓣ *n* **1** direct personal participation **2** particular incident, feeling, etc. that a person has undergone **3** accumulated knowledge ▷ *v* **4** participate in **5** be affected by (an emotion)
▸ **experienced** *adj* skilful from extensive participation
experiment ⓣ *n* **1** test to provide evidence to prove or disprove a theory **2** attempt at

THESAURUS

voluminous **2 = talkative**, open, friendly, outgoing, affable, effusive, sociable, communicative, loquacious, unreserved
expatriate *adj* **1 = exiled**, banished, emigrant, émigré ▸ *n* **2 = exile**, refugee, emigrant, émigré
expect *v* **1 = think**, believe, assume, anticipate, imagine, presume, reckon • *The trial is expected to last several weeks.* **2 = require**, demand, rely on • *I was expecting to have a bit of time to myself.* **3 = look forward to**, predict, await, anticipate, contemplate, envisage, hope for, watch for
See also: **figure, suppose**
expectant *adj* **1 = expecting**, ready, hopeful, eager, watchful, apprehensive, anticipating, in suspense **2 = pregnant**, expecting (*informal*), gravid
expectation *n* **1 = probability**, forecast, belief, likelihood, assumption, presumption, conjecture, supposition **2 = anticipation**, hope, promise, suspense, expectancy, apprehension
expected *See* **likely, supposed**
expediency *n* **= suitability**, benefit, utility, profitability, convenience, usefulness, prudence, pragmatism, advisability
expedient *n* **1 = means**, measure, device, resort, scheme, method, makeshift, stopgap, contrivance ▸ *adj* **2 = advantageous**, effective, appropriate, useful, helpful, practical, beneficial, suitable, convenient, win-win (*informal*), opportune
expedition *n* **= journey**, mission, tour, quest, trek, voyage, excursion, safari
expel *v* **1 = drive out**, remove, discharge, eject, spew, belch, cast out **2 = dismiss**, ban, exclude, exile, banish, evict, chuck out (*slang*), drum out, throw out
expend *v* **= spend**, use *or* use up, consume, exhaust, dissipate, go through, pay out
expendable *adj* **= dispensable**, unnecessary, unimportant, nonessential, inessential, replaceable
expenditure *n* **= spending**, cost, payment, expense, consumption, output, outlay, expenses, outgoings
expense *n* **= cost**, charge, loss, payment, expenditure, spending, outlay
expensive *adj* **= costly**, pricey, dear • *a very expensive suit* OPPOSITE: inexpensive
See also: **precious, valuable**
experience *n* **1 = knowledge**, training, understanding, expertise, know-how • *They're looking for someone with experience.* **2 = incident**, affair, episode, encounter, adventure, ordeal • *a terrifying experience that they still talk about* ▸ *v* **3 = undergo**, have, meet, encounter • *We are experiencing a few technical problems.*
See also: **endure, event, feel, go through, suffer**
experienced *adj* **= knowledgeable**, expert, seasoned, practised, well versed • *an experienced diver* OPPOSITE: inexperienced
See also: **practical, skilled**
experiment *n* **1 = test**, trial, research, investigation, procedure, proof, examination,

DICTIONARY

something new ▷ *v* **3** make an experiment
experimental *adj* **experimentally** *adv*
experimentation *n*
expert Ⓣ *n* **1** person with extensive skill or knowledge in a particular field ▷ *adj* **2** skilful or knowledgeable
▶ **expertise** [eks-per-**teez**] *n* special skill or knowledge
expiate *v* make amends for **expiation** *n*
expire Ⓣ *v* **1** finish or run out **2** *lit* die **3** breathe out **expiration** *n*
▶ **expiry** *n* end, esp. of a contract period
explain Ⓣ *v* **1** make clear and intelligible **2** account for **explanation** *n* **explanatory** *adj*
expletive [iks-**plee**-tiv] *n* swearword
explicable *adj* able to be explained
▶ **explicate** *v formal* explain **explication** *n*
explicit Ⓣ *adj* **1** precisely and clearly expressed **2** shown in realistic detail
explicitly *adv*
explode Ⓣ *v* **1** burst with great violence, blow up **2** react suddenly with emotion **3** increase rapidly **4** show (a theory etc.) to be baseless **explosion** *n*
▶ **explosive** *adj* **1** tending to explode ▷ *n* **2** substance that causes explosions
exploit Ⓣ *v* **1** take advantage of for one's own purposes **2** make the best use of ▷ *n* **3** notable feat or deed **exploitation** *n* **exploiter** *n*
explore Ⓣ *v* **1** travel into (unfamiliar regions), esp. for scientific purposes **2** investigate **exploration** *n* **exploratory** *adj*
explorer *n*
expo *n informal* exposition, large public exhibition
exponent Ⓣ *n* **1** person who advocates an idea, cause, etc. **2** skilful performer, esp. a musician
▶ **exponential** *adj informal* very rapid
exponentially *adv*

e

THESAURUS

experimentation, trial run ▶ *v* **2 = test**, try, research, investigate, examine, sample, verify, put to the test
experimental *adj* **= test**, trial, pilot, tentative, preliminary, provisional, speculative, exploratory, probationary, trial-and-error
expert *n* **1 = specialist**, authority, professional, ace (*informal*), wizard, buff (*informal*), guru • *A team of experts will be on hand to offer advice.* OPPOSITE: beginner ▶ *adj* **2 = skilful**, able, skilled, experienced, knowledgeable, adept, proficient • *Her expert approach impressed everyone.*
See also: **perfect**
expertise *n* **= skill**, facility, knowledge, command, judgment, mastery, know-how (*informal*), proficiency, adroitness
expertly *See* **well**
expire *v* **1 = finish**, end, close, stop, conclude, cease, terminate, lapse, come to an end, run out **2 = breathe out**, expel, emit, exhale **3 = die**, depart, perish, kick the bucket (*informal*), pass away *or* pass on
explain *v* **1 = make clear**, describe, define, illustrate • *He explained to us how the system worked.* **2 = account for**, excuse, justify, give a reason for
explanation *n* **1 = description**, definition, clarification, exposition • *her clear explanation of the parliamentary system* **2 = reason**, account, answer, excuse, motive, justification, vindication
See also: **defence, statement**
explanatory *adj* **= descriptive**, interpretive, illustrative
explicit *adj* **= clear**, specific, precise, straightforward, frank, definite, unambiguous, categorical
explode *v* **1 = blow up**, burst, detonate, go off, set off • *the sound of fireworks exploding in the air* **2 = go mad**, blow up, go berserk • *I asked him if he'd finished, and he just exploded.* **3 = shoot up**, soar, skyrocket • *Sales of digital cameras have exploded in recent years.* **4 = disprove**, refute, discredit, debunk, invalidate, repudiate, give the lie to
See also: **fire**
exploit *v* **1 = take advantage of**, abuse, milk, manipulate, misuse, play on *or* play upon **2 = make the best use of**, use, utilize, capitalize on, cash in on (*informal*), profit by *or* profit from ▶ *n* **3 = feat**, achievement, adventure, stunt, accomplishment, deed, escapade, attainment
exploitation *n* **= misuse**, abuse, manipulation
exploration *n* **1 = investigation**, research, search, inquiry, analysis, inspection, scrutiny, examination **2 = expedition**, survey, travel, trip, tour, reconnaissance
exploratory *adj* **= investigative**, trial, experimental, fact-finding, probing, searching
explore *v* **1 = investigate**, research, search, probe, examine, inspect, inquire into, look into **2 = travel**, survey, tour, scout, reconnoitre
explosion *n* **1 = bang**, blast • *The explosion shattered windows all along the street.* **2 = outburst**, outbreak, fit, eruption
explosive *adj* **1 = unstable**, volatile **2 = violent**, fiery, stormy, vehement, touchy
exponent *n* **1 = advocate**, champion, supporter, defender, promoter, backer,

DICTIONARY

export *n* **1** selling or shipping of goods to a foreign country **2** product shipped or sold to a foreign country ▷ *v* **3** sell or ship (goods) to a foreign country **exporter** *n*

expose Ⓣ *v* **1** uncover or reveal **2** make vulnerable, leave unprotected **3** subject (a photographic film) to light
▶ **expose oneself** display one's sexual organs in public
▶ **exposure** *n* **1** exposing **2** lack of shelter from the weather, esp. the cold **3** appearance before the public, as on television

exposé [iks-**pose**-ay] *n* bringing of a crime, scandal, etc. to public notice

exposition Ⓣ *n* see **expound**

expostulate *v* (foll. by *with*) reason (with), esp. to dissuade **expostulation** *n*

expound Ⓣ *v* explain in detail
▶ **exposition** *n* **1** explanation **2** large public exhibition

express Ⓣ *v* **1** put into words **2** show (an emotion) **3** indicate by a symbol or formula **4** squeeze out (juice etc.) ▷ *adj* **5** explicitly stated **6** (of a purpose) particular **7** of or for rapid transportation of people, mail, etc. ▷ *n* **8** fast train or bus stopping at only a few stations ▷ *adv* **9** by express delivery
▶ **expression** *n* **1** expressing **2** word or phrase **3** showing or communication of emotion **4** look on the face that indicates mood **5** *math* variable, function, or some combination of these **expressionless** *adj* **expressive** *adj*

expressionism *n* early 20th-century artistic movement which sought to express emotions rather than represent the physical world **expressionist** *n, adj*

expresso *n* same as **espresso**

expropriate *v* deprive an owner of (property) **expropriation** *n*

expulsion Ⓣ *n* see **expel**

expunge [iks-**sponge**] *v* delete, erase, blot out

expurgate [**eks**-per-gate] *v* remove objectionable parts from (a book etc.)

exquisite Ⓣ *adj* **1** of extreme beauty or delicacy **2** intense in feeling **exquisitely** *adv*

extant *adj* still existing

extemporize *v* speak, perform, or compose without preparation

extend Ⓣ *v* **1** increase in size or scope **2** draw out or be drawn out, stretch **3** last for a certain time **4** (foll. by *to*) include **5** offer: *extend one's sympathy* **extendable** *adj*
▶ **extension** *n* **1** continuation or additional part of a building etc. **2** additional telephone connected to the same line as another **3** extending
▶ **extensive** *adj* **1** covering a large area **2** very

THESAURUS

proponent, upholder **2 = performer**, player

expose *v* **1 = uncover**, show, reveal • *The original floor was exposed as we began sanding.* **2 = reveal**, uncover, unearth, bring to light, show up • *He has been exposed as a liar and a cheat.* **3 = make vulnerable**, subject, endanger, jeopardize, imperil, lay open, leave open
See also: **betray**

exposed *adj* **1 = unconcealed**, bare, uncovered, on display, on show, on view, revealed **2 = unsheltered**, open, unprotected **3 = vulnerable**, susceptible, in peril, laid bare, wide open

exposition *See* **explanation**

exposure *n* **= publicity**, display, exhibition, showing, presentation, revelation, unveiling, uncovering

expound *v* **= explain**, describe, unfold, interpret, elucidate, set forth, spell out

express *v* **1 = state**, communicate, couch, put, voice, phrase, put across • *She expressed interest in trying out for the part.* **2 = show**, represent, reveal, indicate, exhibit, intimate, convey, signify, symbolize, make known, stand for ▷ **express regret** *See* **apologize** ▶ *adj* **3 = fast**, direct, high-speed, non-stop • *express delivery service* **4 = explicit**, clear, plain, distinct, definite, unambiguous, categorical **5 = specific**, special, particular, singular, clear-cut, especial
See also: **swift**

expression *n* **1 = look**, face, countenance • *a pleasant expression* **2 = phrase**, term, remark, idiom • *It's my grandmother's favourite expression.* **3 = statement**, announcement, communication, declaration, utterance **4 = indication**, show, sign, demonstration, exhibition, symbol, representation, token, manifestation

expressive *adj* **= vivid**, poignant, striking, eloquent, moving, telling

expressly *adv* **1 = definitely**, clearly, explicitly, categorically, distinctly, plainly, unambiguously, in no uncertain terms **2 = specifically**, especially, particularly, specially

expulsion *n* **= ejection**, removal, dismissal, eviction, exclusion, banishment

exquisite *adj* **1 = beautiful**, attractive, lovely, charming, striking, pleasing, comely **2 = fine**, beautiful, precious, delicate, elegant, lovely, dainty **3 = intense**, sharp, acute, keen

extempore *adv* **1 = impromptu**, freely, spontaneously, ad lib, offhand, off the cuff (*informal*) ▶ *adj* **2 = impromptu**, unprepared, unpremeditated, ad-lib, offhand, off-the-cuff (*informal*)

extend *v* **1 = reach**, continue, hang,

DICTIONARY

great in effect: *extensive damage*
▸ **extensor** *n* muscle that extends a part of the body
▸ **extent** *n* length, area, or size of something
extenuate *v* make (an offence or fault) less blameworthy **extenuation** *n*
exterior Ⓣ *n* **1** part or surface on the outside **2** outward appearance ▷ *adj* **3** of, on, or coming from the outside
exterminate Ⓣ *v* destroy (animals or people) completely **extermination** *n* **exterminator** *n*
external Ⓣ *adj* of, situated on, or coming from the outside **externally** *adv*
extinct Ⓣ *adj* **1** having died out **2** (of a volcano) no longer liable to erupt **extinction** *n*
extinguish Ⓣ *v* **1** put out (a fire or light) **2** remove or destroy entirely **extinguisher** *n*
extirpate [**eks**-ter-pate] *v* destroy utterly
extol Ⓣ *v* **-tolling, -tolled** praise highly
extort Ⓣ *v* get (something) by force or threats **extortion** *n*
▸ **extortionate** *adj* (of prices) excessive
extra Ⓣ *adj* **1** additional **2** more than usual ▷ *n* **3** additional person or thing **4** something for which an additional charge is made **5** *films* actor hired for crowd scenes ▷ *adv* **6** unusually or exceptionally
extra- *prefix* outside or beyond an area or scope: *extrasensory; extraterritorial*
extract Ⓣ *v* **1** pull out by force **2** remove **3** derive **4** copy out (an article, passage, etc.) from a publication ▷ *n* **5** something extracted, such as a passage from a book etc. **6** preparation containing the concentrated essence of a substance: *beef extract* **extraction** *n* **extractor** *n*
extracurricular *adj* **1** taking place outside the normal school timetable **2** beyond regular duties
extradite *v* send (an accused person)

THESAURUS

stretch • *The city will soon extend way beyond its present borders.* **2 = stick out**, project, protrude, jut out • *She extended her hand and shook mine.* **3 = enlarge**, develop, expand, widen, add to • *We'd like to extend the house and build a sunroom.* **4 = make longer**, stretch, prolong, lengthen, drag out, draw out, spin out, spread out **5 = last**, continue, carry on, go on **6 = offer**, present, confer, impart, proffer ▸ **extend to** *See* **reach**
See also: **build, increase, range, spread**
extended *See* **continuous**
extension *n* **1 = annex**, addition, supplement, appendage, appendix **2 = lengthening**, increase, development, spread, expansion, enlargement, broadening, widening
extensive *adj* **1 = large**, wide, broad, vast, spacious, expansive, sweeping • *the mansion's extensive grounds* **2 = widespread**, great, comprehensive, considerable, far-reaching, untold, pervasive • *The blast caused extensive damage.*
See also: **full**
extent *n* **= size**, level, measure, degree, scale • *The full extent of the damage was revealed yesterday.*
See also: **area, length, quantity, range, spread, stretch**
extenuating *adj* **= mitigating**, justifying, moderating, qualifying
exterior *n* **1 = outside**, face, skin, surface, shell, coating, covering, façade ▸ *adj* **2 = outside**, external, surface, outer, outward, outermost
exterminate *v* **= destroy**, eliminate, eradicate, abolish, annihilate
external *adj* **1 = outer**, outside, surface, exterior, outward, outermost **2 = outside**, foreign, alien, extrinsic
extinct *adj* **= dead**, lost, defunct, gone, vanished
extinction *n* **= dying out**, destruction, eradication, abolition, oblivion, extermination, annihilation, obliteration
extinguish *v* **1 = put out**, stifle, douse, smother, quench, blow out, snuff out **2 = destroy**, end, remove, eliminate, eradicate, annihilate, exterminate, wipe out
extol *v* **= praise**, acclaim, commend, glorify, eulogize, exalt, sing the praises of
extort *v* **= force**, bully, squeeze, extract, coerce, blackmail
extortionate *adj* **= exorbitant**, excessive, outrageous, inflated, unreasonable, sky-high, extravagant, preposterous
extra *adj* **1 = additional**, more, new, further, excess, added, supplementary, auxiliary, ancillary • *The company is taking on extra staff for the summer.* **2 = surplus**, excess, spare, unused, leftover, redundant, superfluous ▸ *n* **3 = addition**, bonus, accessory • *The cost of the extras added to the price of the vacation.* ▸ *adv* **4 = exceptionally**, especially, particularly, extremely, unusually, remarkably, extraordinarily, uncommonly
See also: **luxury, supplement**
extract *v* **1 = take out**, draw, remove, mine, obtain, pull out • *Citric acid can be extracted from orange juice.* **2 = elicit**, get, draw, obtain, glean • *She tried to extract further information from the witness.* ▸ *n* **3 = passage**, section, reading, snatch, excerpt, snippet • *an extract from his latest novel* **4 = concentrate** • *vanilla extract*
See also: **exact, quote, withdraw**
extraction *See* **origin, stock**

e

DICTIONARY

back to his or her own country for trial **extradition** *n*
extramural *adj* connected with but outside the normal courses of a university or college
extraneous ⓣ [iks-**train**-ee-uss] *adj* irrelevant
extraordinary ⓣ *adj* **1** very unusual **2** (of a meeting) specially called to deal with a particular subject **extraordinarily** *adv*
extrapolate [iks-**trap**-a-late] *v* **1** infer (something not known) from the known facts **2** *math* estimate (a value of a function or measurement) beyond the known values by the extension of a curve **extrapolation** *n*
extrasensory *adj* **extrasensory perception** supposed ability to obtain information other than through the normal senses
extraterrestrial *adj* of or from outside the earth's atmosphere
extravagant ⓣ *adj* **1** spending money excessively **2** going beyond reasonable limits **extravagance** *n*
▸ **extravaganza** *n* elaborate and lavish entertainment, display, etc.
extreme ⓣ *adj* **1** of a high or the highest degree or intensity **2** immoderate **3** severe **4** farthest or outermost ▹ *n* **5** either of the two limits of a scale or range **extremely** *adv*
▸ **extremist** *n* **1** person who favours immoderate methods ▹ *adj* **2** holding extreme opinions
▸ **extremity** *n, pl* **-ties 1** farthest point **2** extreme condition, as of misfortune **extremities 3** hands and feet
▸ **extreme sport** sport with a high risk of injury or death
extricate ⓣ *v* free from complication or difficulty **extrication** *n*
extrovert ⓣ *adj* **1** lively and outgoing **2** concerned more with external reality than inner feelings ▹ *n* **3** extrovert person
extrude *v* squeeze or force out **extrusion** *n*
exuberant ⓣ *adj* **1** high-spirited **2** growing luxuriantly **exuberance** *n*
exude ⓣ *v* **1** make apparent by mood or behaviour: *exude confidence* **2** ooze out as sweat or sap
exult ⓣ *v* be joyful or jubilant **exultation** *n* **exultant** *adj*
exurb *n* region outside a suburb, where rich commuters live
eye ⓣ *n* **1** organ of sight **2** *often pl* ability to see **3** external part of an eye **4** attention: *his new shirt caught my eye* **5** ability to judge or appreciate: *a good eye for detail* **6** one end of a

THESAURUS

extraneous *adj* = **irrelevant**, inappropriate, unrelated, unconnected, immaterial, beside the point, off the subject
extraordinary *adj* = **unusual**, odd, amazing, strange, bizarre, singular, surprising • *He really is an extraordinary man*. OPPOSITE: ordinary
See also: **curious, exceptional, incredible, uncommon, weird**
extravagance *n* **1** = **waste**, wastefulness, lavishness, overspending, prodigality, profligacy, squandering **2** = **excess**, exaggeration, wildness, outrageousness, preposterousness
extravagant *adj* **1** = **wasteful**, lavish, spendthrift, prodigal, profligate **2** = **excessive**, reckless, outrageous, unreasonable, preposterous, over the top (*slang*)
extreme *adj* **1** = **great**, acute, deep, severe, intense, dire, profound • *living in extreme poverty* **2** = **excessive**, exceptional, drastic, extravagant, radical, unreasonable • *I think that's rather an extreme reaction*. **3** = **maximum**, great, severe, intense, ultimate, acute, supreme, utmost, highest **4** = **farthest**, far-off, most distant, outermost, remotest ▸ *n* **5** = **limit**, end, depth, height, ultimate, boundary • *We're just going from one extreme to the other*.
See also: **serious, uncommon**
extremely *adv* = **very**, severely, unusually, terribly, extraordinarily, exceptionally, awfully (*informal*), exceedingly, uncommonly
extremist *n* = **fanatic**, radical, die-hard, zealot
extremity *n* **1** = **limit**, border, edge, tip, extreme, boundary, frontier, pinnacle **2** = **crisis**, emergency, trouble, disaster, adversity, dire straits, exigency ▹ **extremities** = **hands and feet**, fingers and toes, limbs
extricate *v* = **free**, release, remove, rescue, disengage, disentangle, get out, wriggle out of
extrovert *adj* = **outgoing**, exuberant, gregarious, sociable
exuberance *n* **1** = **high spirits**, spirit, enthusiasm, vitality, zest, cheerfulness, ebullience, liveliness, vivacity **2** = **luxuriance**, abundance, copiousness, lavishness, profusion
exuberant *adj* **1** = **high-spirited**, animated, energetic, enthusiastic, spirited, lively, cheerful, ebullient, vivacious **2** = **luxuriant**, lavish, abundant, plentiful, copious, profuse
exude *See* **emit**
exult *v* = **be joyful**, celebrate, rejoice, be overjoyed, jump for joy
eye *n* **1** = **eyeball**, optic (*informal*), peeper (*informal, often pl*) **2** = **appreciation**, taste, judgment, recognition, discrimination,

DICTIONARY

sewing needle **7** dark spot on a potato from which a stem grows **8** small area of calm at the centre of a hurricane ▷ *v* **eyeing** *or* **eying**, **eyed 9** look at carefully or warily **eyeless** *adj*
▸ **eyelet** *n* **1** small hole for a lace or cord to be passed through **2** ring that strengthens this
▸ **eyeball** *n* ball-shaped part of the eye
▸ **eyebrow** *n* line of hair on the bony ridge above the eye
▸ **eyeglass** *n* lens for aiding defective vision
▸ **eyelash** *n* short hair that grows out from the eyelid
▸ **eyelid** *n* fold of skin that covers the eye when it is closed
▸ **eyeliner** *n* cosmetic used to outline the eyes
▸ **eye-opener** *n informal* something startling or revealing
▸ **eye shadow** coloured cosmetic worn on the upper eyelids
▸ **eyesight** *n* ability to see
▸ **eyesore** *n* ugly object
▸ **eyetooth** *n* canine tooth
▸ **eyewash** *n informal* nonsense
▸ **eyewitness** *n* person who was present at an event and can describe what happened
eyrie *n* **1** nest of an eagle **2** high isolated place

THESAURUS

perception, discernment ▸ *v* **3 = look at**, study, survey, watch, view, inspect, contemplate, check out (*informal*)
eye-catching *See* **prominent**
eyesight *n* = **vision**, sight, perception
eyesore *n* = **mess**, sight (*informal*), horror, blemish, blot, disfigurement, monstrosity
eyewitness *n* = **observer**, witness, viewer, spectator, bystander, onlooker, passer-by

DICTIONARY

Ff

f *music* forte
F **1** Fahrenheit **2** farad **3** *chem* fluorine
Fabergé *n* **Peter Carl**. 1846–1920, Russian goldsmith and jeweller, known for the golden Easter eggs and other ornate and fanciful objects that he created for the Russian and other royal families
Fabius Maximus *n* full name *Quintus Fabius Maximus Verrucosus*, called *Cunctator* (the delayer). died 203 BC, Roman general and statesman. As commander of the Roman army during the Second Punic War, he withstood Hannibal by his strategy of harassing the Carthaginians while avoiding a pitched battle
fable Ⓣ *n* **1** story with a moral **2** legend **3** lie
▸ **fabled** *adj* made famous in legend
fabric Ⓣ *n* **1** knitted or woven cloth **2** framework or structure
▸ **fabricate** *v* **1** make or build **2** make up (a story or lie) **fabrication** *n* **fabricator** *n*
fabulous Ⓣ *adj* **1** *informal* excellent **2** astounding **3** told of in fables **fabulously** *adv*
façade Ⓣ [fas-**sahd**] *n* **1** front of a building **2** (false) outward appearance
face Ⓣ *n* **1** front of the head **2** facial expression **3** distorted expression **4** front or main side **5** dial of a clock **6** exposed area of coal or ore in a mine **7** dignity, self-respect **8** outward appearance ▹ *v* **9** look or turn towards **10** be opposite **11** be confronted by **12** provide with a surface
▸ **faceless** *adj* impersonal, anonymous
▸ **face-lift** *n* operation to tighten facial skin, to remove wrinkles
▸ **face-saving** *adj* maintaining dignity or self-respect
▸ **face up to** *v* accept (an unpleasant fact or reality)
▸ **face value** apparent worth or meaning
facet Ⓣ *n* **1** surface of a cut gem **2** aspect
facetious Ⓣ [fas-**see**-shuss] *adj* funny or trying to be funny, esp. at inappropriate times **facetiousness** *n*
facia *n, pl* **-ciae** same as **fascia**
facial *adj* **1** of the face ▹ *n* **2** beauty treatment for the face

THESAURUS

fable *n* **1 = story**, legend, tale, myth, allegory, parable **2 = fiction**, invention, fantasy, fabrication, yarn (*informal*), fish story (*informal*), tall tale (*informal*), urban legend
fabric *n* **1 = cloth**, material, web, stuff, textile **2 = framework**, organization, construction, structure, constitution, make-up, foundations
fabricate *v* **1 = make up**, fake, forge, invent, devise, falsify, concoct, feign, trump up **2 = build**, make, form, manufacture, shape, assemble, construct, erect
fabrication *n* **1 = forgery**, lie, fake, fiction, invention, myth, concoction, falsehood **2 = construction**, production, building, manufacture, assembly, erection
fabulous *adj* **1** (*Informal*) **= wonderful**, spectacular, brilliant, fantastic (*informal*), sensational (*informal*), superb, marvellous, out-of-this-world (*informal*) **2 = astounding**, amazing, incredible, unbelievable, phenomenal, breathtaking, inconceivable **3 = legendary**, fantastic, fictitious, imaginary, mythical, unreal, made-up, apocryphal, invented
façade *n* **= appearance**, show, face, front, mask, exterior, guise, pretense, semblance
See also: **outside**
face *n* **1 = countenance**, mug (*slang*), features, lineaments, physiognomy • *A strong wind was blowing in my face.* **2 = side**, front, surface, aspect, exterior • *the north face of Everest* **3 = expression**, look, appearance, aspect **4 = scowl**, grimace, frown, pout, smirk **5 = façade**, show, front, appearance, display, mask, exterior **6 = self-respect**, authority, image, status, standing, reputation, dignity, honour, prestige
▹ **face down** *See* **prone** ▸ *v* **7 = look onto**, overlook, be opposite • *a room that faces on to the street* **8 = meet**, experience, oppose, tackle, encounter, confront, brave, come up against, deal with **9 = coat**, finish, cover, dress, clad
See also: **outside** ▹ **face up to = accept**, acknowledge, tackle, confront, come to terms with, cope with, deal with, meet head-on
faceless *adj* **= impersonal**, remote, anonymous
facet *n* **= aspect**, part, face, side, plane, surface, phase, angle, slant
facetious *adj* **= funny**, humorous, amusing, frivolous, playful, comical, droll, flippant,

DICTIONARY

facile Ⓣ [**fas**-sile] *adj* superficial and showing lack of real thought
facilitate Ⓣ *v* make easy **facilitation** *n*
facility Ⓣ *n, pl* **-ties 1** ability to do things easily or well **facilities 2** means or equipment for an activity
facing *n* **1** lining or covering for decoration or reinforcement **facings 2** contrasting collar and cuffs on a jacket
facsimile Ⓣ [fak-**sim**-ill-ee] *n* exact copy
fact Ⓣ *n* **1** event or thing known to have happened or existed **2** provable truth **factual** *adj*
▸ **facts of life** details of sex and reproduction
faction[1] Ⓣ *n* **1** (dissenting) minority group within a larger body **2** dissension
▸ **factious** *adj* of or producing factions
faction[2] Ⓣ *n* dramatized presentation of a factual event
factitious *adj* artificial
factor Ⓣ *n* **1** element contributing to a result **2** *math* one of the integers multiplied together to give a given number **3** level on a scale: *factor 15 suntan cream*
▸ **factorial** *n* product of all the integers from one to a given number
▸ **factorize** *v* calculate the factors of (a number)
factory Ⓣ *n, pl* **-ries** building where goods are manufactured
factotum *n* person employed to do all sorts of work
faculty Ⓣ *n, pl* **-ties 1** physical or mental ability **2** department in a university or college
fad Ⓣ *n* **1** short-lived fashion **2** whim **faddy** *or* **faddish** *adj*
fade Ⓣ *v* **1** (cause to) lose brightness, colour, or strength **2** vanish slowly
▸ **fade-in** *or* **fade-out** *n* gradual increase or decrease, as of vision or sound in a film or broadcast
faeces *pl n* same as **feces**
faff *v* (often foll. by *about*) *Brit informal* dither or fuss
fag[1] *n* **1** *informal* boring task **2** *Brit* young public schoolboy who does menial chores for a senior boy ▹ *v* **3** (often foll. by *out*) *informal* tire **4** do menial chores in a public school
fag[2] *n offensive* male homosexual
faggot *n offensive* male homosexual
Fahd ibn Abdul Aziz *n* 1923–2005, king of Saudi Arabia (1982–2005)
Fahrenheit[1] [**far**-ren-hite] *adj* of a temperature scale with the freezing point of water at 32° and the boiling point at 212°
Fahrenheit[2] *n* **Gabriel Daniel**. 1686–1736, German physicist, who invented the mercury thermometer and devised the temperature scale that bears his name
faïence [**fie**-ence] *n* tin-glazed earthenware
fail Ⓣ *v* **1** be unsuccessful **2** stop operating **3** be or judge to be below the required standard in a test **4** disappoint or be useless to (someone) **5** omit or be unable to do

THESAURUS

jocular, tongue in cheek
facile *adj* = **superficial**, slick, shallow, hasty, cursory, glib
facilitate *v* = **promote**, help, forward, further, expedite, make easy, pave the way for, speed up
facility *n* **1** = **skill**, ability, ease, efficiency, proficiency, dexterity, fluency, adroitness, effortlessness **2** (*often pl*) = **equipment**, aid, opportunity, advantage, resource, means, convenience, appliance, amenity
facsimile *n* = **copy**, print, transcript, reproduction, replica, fax, duplicate, photocopy, carbon copy
fact *n* **1** = **truth**, reality, certainty • *a statement of fact* OPPOSITE: lie **2** = **event**, act, performance, incident, occurrence, deed, happening, *fait accompli* (*French*)
faction *n* **1** = **group**, set, party, gang, bloc, contingent, clique, cabal, coterie, splinter group **2** = **dissension**, division, conflict, rebellion, disagreement, infighting, discord, disunity
factor *n* = **element**, part, cause, influence, aspect, consideration • *Physical activity is an important factor in maintaining fitness.*
factory *n* = **works**, plant, mill • *He owned furniture factories in several locations.*
facts *See* **information**
factual *adj* = **true**, real, correct, exact, genuine, authentic, precise, true-to-life
faculties *pl n* = **powers**, reason, intelligence, capabilities, senses, wits
faculty *n* **1** = **ability**, power, facility, capacity, skill, propensity, aptitude **2** = **department**, school
fad *n* = **craze**, trend, fashion, rage, mania, vogue, whim
fade *v* **1** = **dull**, dim, discolour, wash out • *The fabric had faded in the bright sunlight.* **2** = **dwindle**, decline, disappear, dissolve, vanish, wane, die away, melt away ▹ **fade away** *See* **die, vanish** ▹ **fade out** *See* **die**
See also: **die out, wither**
faded *adj* = **discoloured**, dull, pale, bleached, indistinct, washed out
fading *adj* = **declining**, decreasing, disappearing, dying, on the decline, vanishing
fail *v* **1** = **be unsuccessful**, flunk (*informal*), be defeated, be in vain, come to grief, fall through, go belly up (*informal*) • *He failed in his attempt to fire the coach.* OPPOSITE:

DICTIONARY

(something) **6** go bankrupt ▷ *n* **7** instance of not passing an exam or test
▶ **without fail** **1** definitely **2** regularly
▶ **failing** *n* **1** weak point ▷ *prep* **2** in the absence of
▶ **failure** *n* **1** act or instance of failing **2** unsuccessful person or thing
fain *adv obsolete* gladly
faint Ⓣ *adj* **1** lacking clarity, brightness, or volume **2** lacking conviction or force **3** feeling dizzy or weak ▷ *v* **4** lose consciousness temporarily ▷ *n* **5** temporary loss of consciousness
fair[1] Ⓣ *adj* **1** unbiased and reasonable **2** light in colour **3** beautiful **4** quite good **5** unblemished **6** (of weather) fine ▷ *adv* **7** fairly **8** absolutely **fairness** *n*
▶ **fairly** *adv* **1** as deserved, reasonably **2** moderately **3** to a great degree or extent
▶ **fairway** *n golf* smooth area between the tee and the green
fair[2] Ⓣ *n* **1** travelling entertainment with stalls and machines to ride on, etc. **2** exhibition of commercial or industrial products
▶ **fairground** *n* open space used for a fair
Fairbanks *n* **1** **Douglas** (**Elton**), real name *Julius Ullman*. 1883–1939, US film actor and producer **2** his son, **Douglas, Jnr**. 1909–2000, US film actor
Fair Isle *n* intricate multicoloured knitted pattern
fairy Ⓣ *n, pl* **fairies** **1** imaginary small creature with magic powers **2** *offensive* male homosexual **fairyland** *n*
▶ **fairy godmother** person who helps in time of trouble
▶ **fairy light** small coloured light used as decoration
▶ **fairy tale** *or* **fairy story** **1** story about fairies or magic **2** unbelievable story or explanation
Faisal I, Feisal I *n* 1885–1933, king of Syria (1920) and first king of Iraq (1921–33): a leader of the Arab revolt against the Turks (1916–18)
Faisal II, Feisal II *n* 1935–58, last king of Iraq (1939–58)

THESAURUS

succeed **2 = omit**, neglect • *They failed to email her.* **3 = give out**, decline, sink, cease, wane, stop working • *His eyesight began to fail.* **4 = disappoint**, forget, abandon, desert, neglect, forsake, let down **5 = go bankrupt**, fold (*informal*), become insolvent, close down, go broke (*informal*), go bust (*informal*), go into receivership, go out of business, go to the wall, go under ▷ **fail to notice** *See* **miss** ▷ **fail to remember** *See* **forget** ▶ *n* ▷ **without fail = regularly**, constantly, religiously, conscientiously, dependably, like clockwork, punctually, twenty-four-seven (*slang*), without exception
See also: **collapse, weaken**
failing *n* **1 = weakness**, flaw, defect, fault, deficiency, shortcoming, blemish, drawback, imperfection ▶ *preposition* **2 = in the absence of**, in default of, lacking
failure *n* **1 = defeat**, breakdown, miscarriage, downfall, fiasco, flameout (*informal*) • *to end in failure* OPPOSITE: success **2 = disappointment**, loser, turkey (*slang*), flop (*informal*), incompetent, ne'er-do-well • *The new business was a complete failure.* **3 = shortcoming**, deficiency • *a failure in the insurance system* **4 = bankruptcy**, crash, ruin, downfall, liquidation, insolvency
See also: **collapse**
faint *adj* **1 = dim**, low, vague, muted, faded, indistinct • *a faint smell of perfume* OPPOSITE: strong **2 = dizzy**, giddy, light-headed • *Feeling faint is one of the symptoms of lack of food.* **3 = slight**, weak, remote, feeble, unenthusiastic ▶ *v* **4 = pass out**, collapse, black out • *to faint from shock* ▶ *n* **5 = blackout**, collapse, swoon (*lit*), unconsciousness
See also: **slender, soft**
faint-hearted *See* **cowardly**
faintly *adv* **1 = softly**, weakly, feebly, in a whisper, indistinctly **2 = slightly**, somewhat, dimly, a little
fair[1] *adj* **1 = unbiased**, equal, proper, legitimate, upright, impartial, equitable • *a fair trial* OPPOSITE: unfair **2 = light**, blonde *or* blond • *long, fair hair* OPPOSITE: dark **3 = respectable**, average, moderate, reasonable, decent, adequate, satisfactory, tolerable, passable, O.K. *or* okay (*informal*) **4 = beautiful**, pretty, lovely, handsome, bonny, comely **5 = fine**, clear, dry, bright, sunny, cloudless, unclouded
See also: **acceptable, all right**
fair[2] *n* **= carnival**, show, festival, exhibition, fete, bazaar • *a country fair*
See also: **market**
fairly *adv* **1 = moderately**, rather, quite, somewhat, adequately, reasonably, pretty well, tolerably **2 = deservedly**, properly, honestly, objectively, equitably, impartially, justly, without fear or favour **3 = positively**, really, absolutely
fairness *n* **= impartiality**, justice, equity, legitimacy, decency, disinterestedness, equitableness, rightfulness
fairy *n* **= sprite**, brownie, elf, pixie, imp, leprechaun, peri, Robin Goodfellow
▷ **fairy tale**, **fairy story = folk tale**, romance; **= lie**, fiction, invention, fabrication, cock-and-bull story (*informal*), tall tale (*informal*), untruth

DICTIONARY

Faisal Ibn Abdul Aziz *n* 1905–75, king of Saudi Arabia (1964–75)
fait accompli [**fate** ak-**kom**-plee] *n French* something already done that cannot be altered
faith ⓣ *n* **1** strong belief, esp. without proof **2** religion **3** complete confidence or trust **4** allegiance to a person or cause
▸ **faithful** *adj* **1** loyal **2** firm in support **3** accurate **faithfully** *adv*
▸ **faithless** *adj* disloyal or dishonest
fake ⓣ *v* **1** cause (something) to appear real or more valuable by fraud **2** pretend to have (an illness, emotion, etc.) ▹ *n* **3** person, thing, or act that is not genuine ▹ *adj* **4** not genuine **faker** *n*
fakir [**fay**-keer] *n* **1** member of any Islamic religious order **2** Hindu holy man
falcon *n* small bird of prey
▸ **falconry** *n* **1** art of training falcons **2** sport of hunting with falcons **falconer** *n*
Faldo *n* **Nick**. born 1957, British golfer: winner of the British Open Championship (1987, 1990, 1992) and the US Masters (1989, 1990, 1996)
fall ⓣ *v* **falling, fell, fallen 1** drop from a higher to a lower place through the force of gravity **2** collapse to the ground **3** decrease in number or quality **4** slope downwards **5** die in battle **6** be captured **7** pass into a specified condition **8** (of the face) take on a sad expression **9** yield to temptation **10** occur ▹ *n* **11** falling **12** thing or amount that falls **13** decrease in value or number **14** decline in power or influence **15** season between summer and winter **16** capture or overthrow **falls 17** waterfall
▸ **fall for** *v* **1** fall in love with **2** be taken in by
▸ **fall guy** *informal* **1** victim of a confidence trick **2** scapegoat
▸ **fallout** *n* radioactive particles spread as a result of a nuclear explosion
Falla *n* **Manuel de**. 1876–1946, Spanish composer and pianist, composer of the opera *La Vida Breve* (1905), the ballet *The Three-Cornered Hat* (1919), guitar and piano music, and songs
fallacy ⓣ *n, pl* **-cies 1** false belief **2** unsound reasoning **fallacious** *adj*
fallen *v* past participle of **fall**
▸ **fallen arch** collapse of the arch formed by the instep of the foot, resulting in flat feet
fallible ⓣ *adj* liable to error **fallibility** *n*
Fallopian tube *n* either of a pair of tubes through which egg cells pass from the ovary to the womb
fallow[1] ⓣ *adj* (of land) plowed but left unseeded to regain fertility
fallow[2] *adj* **fallow deer** reddish-brown deer with white spots in summer
false ⓣ *adj* **1** not true or correct **2** not genuine

f

THESAURUS

faith *n* **1 = trust**, confidence • *to have great faith in something* **2 = religion**, belief, persuasion, creed • *the faith of their family* **3 = allegiance**, loyalty, fidelity, constancy, faithfulness
faithful *adj* **1 = loyal**, true, staunch, devoted • *a faithful dog* OPPOSITE: unfaithful **2 = accurate**, true, strict, exact • *The play was faithful to the novel*.
See also: **realistic, reliable, steadfast, trusty**
faithfully *See* **exactly**
faithless *adj* **= disloyal**, false, unreliable, treacherous, fickle, unfaithful, inconstant, traitorous
fake *n* **1 = fraud**, copy, reproduction, forgery, sham, imitation • *These paintings are fakes*. ▸ *adj* **2 = artificial**, false, counterfeit, phony (*informal*), imitation • *fake fur* OPPOSITE: real ▸ *v* **3 = pretend**, simulate, feign • *He faked his own death*.
See also: **mock**
fall *v* **1 = drop**, trip, collapse, plunge, topple • *The tile fell from the roof*. OPPOSITE: rise **2 = decrease**, decline, plummet, diminish, dwindle, subside, abate, ebb, depreciate • *The value of the Canadian dollar fell last week*. OPPOSITE: increase **3 = be overthrown**, surrender, succumb, capitulate, pass into enemy hands **4 = die**, perish, be killed, meet one's end **5 = occur**, happen, chance, befall, come about, come to pass, take place **6 = slope**, incline, fall away **7 = lapse**, offend, sin, err, trespass, go astray, transgress ▹ **fall apart** *See* **disintegrate** ▹ **fall behind** *See* **lag** ▹ **fall down** *See* **collapse** ▹ **fall ill** *See* **develop** ▹ **fall out = argue**, fight, clash, disagree, differ, squabble, quarrel, come to blows, throw down (*slang*) ▹ **fall over** *See* **trip** ▹ **fall to** *See* **reach** ▹ **fall to pieces** *See* **disintegrate** ▸ *n* **8 = decrease**, drop, decline, slump, reduction • *a fall in the exchange rate* OPPOSITE: rise **9 = descent**, drop, slip, tumble, plunge, dive, plummet, nose dive, face-plant (*informal*) **10 = collapse**, defeat, destruction, ruin, overthrow, downfall, capitulation **11 = lapse**, sin, transgression
See also: **descend**
fallacy *n* **= error**, mistake, flaw, misconception, delusion, falsehood, misapprehension, untruth
fallible *adj* **= imperfect**, weak, uncertain, ignorant, frail, erring
fallow *adj* **= uncultivated**, idle, unused, dormant, inactive, resting, unplanted
false *adj* **1 = untrue**, fictitious • *He*

DICTIONARY

but intended to seem so **3** deceptive or misleading **falsely** *adv* **falseness** *or* **falsity** *n*
▸ **falsehood** *n* **1** quality of being untrue **2** lie
▸ **falsify** *v* **-fying**, **-fied** alter fraudulently **falsification** *n*
falsetto *n, pl* **-tos** voice pitched higher than one's natural range
falter Ⓣ *v* **1** lose power momentarily **2** be unsure **3** utter hesitantly **4** move unsteadily
fame Ⓣ *n* state of being widely known or recognized
▸ **famed** *adj* famous
familiar Ⓣ *adj* **1** well-known **3** acquainted **4** too friendly **5** intimate, friendly ▹ *n* **6** friend **7** demon supposed to attend a witch **familiarly** *adv* **familiarity** *n*
▸ **familiarize** *v* acquaint fully with a particular subject **familiarization** *n*
family Ⓣ *n, pl* **-lies** **1** group of parents and their children **2** one's spouse and children **3** one's children **4** group descended from a common ancestor **5** group of related objects or beings ▹ *adj* **6** suitable for parents and children together **familial** *adj*
▸ **family planning** control of the number of children in a family, esp. through contraception
famine Ⓣ *n* severe shortage of food
famished Ⓣ *adj* very hungry
famous Ⓣ *adj* very well-known
▸ **famously** *adv* *informal* excellently
fan[1] Ⓣ *n* **1** hand-held or mechanical object used to create a current of air for ventilation or cooling ▹ *v* **fanning**, **fanned** **2** blow or cool with a fan **3** spread out like a fan
▸ **fan belt** belt that drives a cooling fan in an automobile engine
fan[2] Ⓣ *n* *informal* devotee of a pop star, sport, or hobby
▸ **fanbase** *n* body of admirers of a particular pop singer, sports team, etc.
fanatic Ⓣ *n* person who is excessively enthusiastic about something **fanatical** *adj* **fanatically** *adv* **fanaticism** *n*

THESAURUS

gave a false name and address. OPPOSITE: true **2 = incorrect**, wrong, faulty, inaccurate, mistaken, invalid, erroneous, inexact • *false information* **3 = artificial**, fake, bogus, simulated, forged • *false eyelashes* OPPOSITE: genuine **4 = deceitful**, unfaithful, disloyal, insincere • *They turned out to be false friends.*
See also: **deceptive, lying, mock, phony, two-faced**
falsehood *n* **1 = untruthfulness**, deception, deceit, dishonesty, dissimulation, mendacity **2 = lie**, story, fiction, fabrication, fib, untruth
falsify *v* **= forge**, doctor, fake, counterfeit, alter, misrepresent, distort, tamper with
falter *v* **= hesitate**, stumble, waver, stutter, vacillate, stammer, totter
faltering *adj* **= hesitant**, weak, tentative, uncertain, timid, broken, irresolute, stammering
fame *n* **= prominence**, reputation, glory, renown, eminence • *The movie brought her international fame.*
See also: **success**
familiar *adj* **1 = acquainted with**, aware of, knowledgeable about, versed in • *Most children are familiar with fairy tales.* OPPOSITE: unfamiliar **2 = well-known**, common, routine, frequent, ordinary, recognizable, customary, accustomed **3 = friendly**, close, easy, intimate, amicable, relaxed **4 = disrespectful**, forward, bold, intrusive, presumptuous, impudent
▹ **familiar with** *See* **aware of**
See also: **informal**
familiarity *n* **1 = acquaintance**, experience, understanding, awareness, grasp **2 = friendliness**, ease, openness, intimacy, informality, sociability **3 = disrespect**, presumption, boldness, forwardness
familiarize *v* **= accustom**, season, school, train, instruct, inure, habituate
family *n* **1 = relations**, descendants, relatives • *My family is always supportive of me.* RELATED WORD *adjective*: familial **2 = class**, kind, classification • *Tigers are members of the cat family.* **3 = clan**, house, race, tribe, dynasty
See also: **kin, young**
famine *n* **= hunger**, starvation, scarcity, dearth
famished *adj* **= starving**, voracious, ravenous
famous *adj* **= well-known**, legendary, renowned, celebrated, illustrious, distinguished, noted • *She was undoubtedly the most famous singer of her time.* OPPOSITE: unknown ▹ **famous name** *See* **personality**
See also: **prominent**
fan[1] *n* **1 = blower**, ventilator, air conditioner ▸ *v* **2 = blow**, cool, refresh, ventilate, air-condition ▹ **fan out** *See* **spread**
fan[2] *n* **= enthusiast**, supporter, lover, buff (*informal*), admirer, devotee, aficionado, adherent, zealot, groupie (*slang*) • *a fan of the new band*
See also: **follower**
fanatic *n* **= extremist**, militant, activist, devotee, zealot • *a soccer fanatic*
fanatical *adj* **= obsessive**, wild, passionate, rabid, fervent • *a fanatical supporter of the*

DICTIONARY

fancy Ⓣ *adj* **-cier, -ciest 1** elaborate, not plain **2** (of prices) higher than usual ▷ *n, pl* **-cies 3** sudden irrational liking or desire **4** uncontrolled imagination ▷ *v* **-cying, -cied 5** *informal* have a wish for **6** picture in the imagination **7** suppose **8** *Brit informal* be sexually attracted to
▸ **fancy oneself** *informal* have a high opinion of oneself
▸ **fanciful** *adj* **1** not based on fact **2** excessively elaborate **fancifully** *adv*
▸ **fancy dress** party costume representing a historical figure, animal, etc.
▸ **fancy-free** *adj* not in love
fandango *n, pl* **-gos** lively Spanish dance
fanfare *n* short loud tune played on brass instruments
fang *n* **1** snake's tooth which injects poison **2** long pointed tooth
Fangio *n* **Juan Manuel**. 1911–95, Argentinian racing driver who won the World Championship five times between 1951 and 1957
Fang Lizhi *n* born 1936, Chinese astrophysicist and human-rights campaigner, living in the US from 1990
fantasy Ⓣ *n, pl* **-sies 1** far-fetched idea **2** imagination unrestricted by reality **3** daydream **4** fiction with a large fantasy content
▸ **fantasize** *v* indulge in daydreams
▸ **fantasia** *n* musical composition of an improvised nature
▸ **fantastic** *adj* **1** *informal* very good **2** unrealistic or absurd **3** strange or difficult to believe **fantastically** *adv*
fanzine [fan-zeen] *n* magazine produced for and by devotees of a particular interest, football team, etc.
FAQ *computers* frequently asked question *or* questions
far Ⓣ *adv* **farther** *or* **further, farthest** *or* **furthest 1** at, to, or from a great distance **2** at or to a remote time **3** very much ▷ *adj* **4** remote in space or time
▸ **Far East** East Asia
▸ **far-fetched** *adj* hard to believe
▸ **Far North** the Arctic
farad *n* unit of electrical capacitance
Faraday *n* **Michael**. 1791–1867, English physicist and chemist who discovered electromagnetic induction, leading to the invention of the dynamo. He also carried out research into the principles of electrolysis
farce Ⓣ *n* **1** boisterous comedy **2** ludicrous situation
▸ **farcical** *adj* ludicrous **farcically** *adv*
fare Ⓣ *n* **1** charge for a passenger's journey **2** passenger **3** food provided ▷ *v* **4** get on (as specified): *we fared badly*
farewell Ⓣ *interj* **1** goodbye ▷ *n* **2** act of saying goodbye and leaving
farinaceous *adj* mealy, starchy

THESAURUS

baseball team
See also: **crazy**
fanciful *adj* = **unreal**, wild, romantic, visionary, imaginary, whimsical, mythical
fancy *v* **1** = **want**, be attracted to, hanker after, have a yen for, would like • *He fancied an ice-cream cone.* **2** = **suppose**, think, believe, imagine, reckon, conjecture, think likely ▸ *adj* **3** = **elaborate**, extravagant, intricate, ornate, decorated • *dressed up in fancy clothes* OPPOSITE: plain ▸ *n* **4** = **whim**, urge, idea, thought, desire, notion, impulse, inclination, humour, caprice **5** = **delusion**, dream, vision, fantasy, chimera, daydream
See also: **illusion**
fantasize *v* = **daydream**, dream, imagine, envision
fantastic *adj* **1** (*Informal*) = **excellent**, wonderful, awesome (*slang*), sensational (*informal*), superb, marvellous, first-rate **2** = **strange**, grotesque, outlandish, fanciful **3** = **unrealistic**, wild, ridiculous, ludicrous, extravagant, far-fetched **4** = **implausible**, unlikely, incredible, absurd, preposterous, cock-and-bull (*informal*)
fantasy *n* **1** = **imagination**, invention, fancy, creativity, originality **2** = **daydream**, dream, vision, illusion, mirage, reverie, flight of fancy, pipe dream
far *adv* **1** = **a long way**, deep, afar, a great distance • *The ocean was far below us.* **2** = **much**, considerably, incomparably, very much • *far better than the others* ▷ **far from** *See* **unlike** ▸ *adj* **3** = **remote**, long, distant, outlying • *in the far south of the country* OPPOSITE: near
farce *n* **1** = **comedy**, satire, burlesque, slapstick, buffoonery **2** = **mockery**, joke, nonsense, parody, sham, travesty
farcical *adj* = **ludicrous**, comic, ridiculous, absurd, laughable, preposterous, nonsensical, derisory, risible
fare *n* **1** = **charge**, price, ticket money **2** = **food**, sustenance, provisions, rations, victuals ▸ *v* **3** = **get on**, do, manage, prosper, get along, make out
farewell *n* = **good-bye**, departure, adieu, parting, sendoff (*informal*), leave-taking, valediction
far-fetched *adj* = **unconvincing**, unlikely, incredible, fantastic, unbelievable, unrealistic, preposterous, implausible, cock-and-bull (*informal*)

DICTIONARY

farm Ⓣ *n* **1** area of land for growing crops or rearing livestock ▷ *v* **2** cultivate (land) **3** rear (stock) **farmer** *n* **farmhouse** *n* **farmyard** *n*
▸ **farmers' market** market at which farm produce is sold directly to the public by the producer
▸ **farm out** *v* send (work) to be done by others
▸ **farmstead** *n* farm and its buildings
Farmer *n* **John**. ?1565–1605, English madrigal composer and organist
Farouk I, Faruk I *n* 1920–65, last king of Egypt (1936–52). He was forced to abdicate (1952)
farrago [far-**rah**-go] *n, pl* **-gos, -goes** jumbled mixture of things
farrier *n* person who shoes horses
farrow *n* **1** litter of pigs ▷ *v* **2** (of a sow) give birth
fart *taboo* ▷ *n* **1** emission of gas from the anus ▷ *v* **2** break wind
farther, farthest *adv, adj* see **far**
farthing *n* former British coin equivalent to a quarter of a penny
farthingale *n obsolete* hoop worn under skirts
fascia [**fay**-shya] *n, pl* **-ciae** **1** flat surface above a shop window **2** outer surface of a dashboard
fascinate Ⓣ *v* **1** attract and interest strongly **2** make motionless from fear or awe **fascinating** *adj* **fascination** *n*
fascism [**fash**-iz-zum] *n* right-wing political system characterized by state control and extreme nationalism **fascist** *adj, n*
fashion Ⓣ *n* **1** style in clothes, esp. the latest style **2** manner of doing something ▷ *v* **3** form or make into a particular shape
▸ **fashionable** *adj* currently popular **fashionably** *adv*
Fassbinder *n* **Rainer Werner**. 1946–82, West German film director. His films include *The Bitter Tears of Petra von Kant* (1972), *Fear Eats the Soul* (1974), and *The Marriage of Maria Braun* (1978)
fast[1] Ⓣ *adj* **1** (capable of) acting or moving quickly **2** done in or lasting a short time **3** allowing rapid movement **4** (of a clock) showing a time later than the correct time **5** dissipated **6** firmly fixed **7** steadfast ▷ *adv* **8** quickly **9** tightly, firmly **10** soundly, deeply
▸ **fast food** food, such as hamburgers, prepared and served very quickly
▸ **fast-track** *adj* taking the quickest but most competitive route to success: *fast-track executives*
fast[2] Ⓣ *v* **1** go without food, esp. for religious reasons ▷ *n* **2** period of fasting
fasten Ⓣ *v* **1** make or become firmly fixed or joined **2** close by fixing in place or locking **3** (foll. by *on*) direct (one's attention) towards
▸ **fastener** *or* **fastening** *n* device that fastens
fastidious Ⓣ *adj* **1** very fussy about details **2** easily disgusted **fastidiously** *adv* **fastidiousness** *n*
fastness *n* fortress, safe place

THESAURUS

farm *n* **1** = **smallholding**, ranch, plantation, homestead, farmstead, grange ▸ *v* **2** = **cultivate**, work, plant
fascinate *v* = **entrance**, absorb, intrigue, captivate, bewitch, enthral • *He was fascinated by the new discovery*.
See also: **appeal, interest**
fascinating *adj* = **entrancing**, engaging, irresistible, alluring, captivating, compelling, engrossing, enticing, gripping, intriguing, riveting
fascination *n* = **attraction**, pull, lure, magic, charm, allure, magnetism, enchantment
fashion *n* **1** = **style**, trend, vogue, fad, craze • *changing fashions in clothing* **2** = **manner**, way, method, mode • *It works in a similar fashion*. ▸ *v* **3** = **make**, work, create, shape, construct, mould • *fashioned from rough wood*
See also: **form, model**
fashionable *adj* = **popular**, in (*informal*), current, designer (*informal*), latest, chic, trendsetting, prevailing, in vogue, kicky (*slang*) • *a fashionable restaurant* OPPOSITE: old-fashioned
See also: **trendy**
fast[1] *adj* **1** = **quick**, rapid, speedy, swift, hurried, accelerated • *a fast train* OPPOSITE: slow **2** = **fixed**, close, firm, sound, secure, tight, steadfast, fastened, immovable **3** = **dissipated**, wild, loose, reckless, extravagant, wanton, self-indulgent, dissolute, profligate ▸ *adv* **4** = **quickly**, rapidly, swiftly, hastily, hurriedly • *You'll have to move fast*. OPPOSITE: slowly **5** = **firmly**, tightly, securely • *Hold fast to the rail*.
See also: **express**
fast[2] *v* **1** = **go hungry**, abstain, deny oneself, go without food ▸ *n* **2** = **fasting**, abstinence
fasten *v* = **secure**, join, tie, fix, lock, attach • *Fasten your seatbelts*.
See also: **bond, connect, hang, link, shut**
fastened *See* **secure, shut**
fastener *See* **clasp**
fastening *See* **clasp, connection**
fastidious *adj* = **particular**, difficult, critical, nice, picky (*informal*), meticulous, fussy, squeamish, finicky, choosy, dainty, pernickety, punctilious, hypercritical, nit-picky (*informal*), hard to please, discriminating, overdelicate,

DICTIONARY

fat ⓣ *n* **1** extra flesh on the body **2** oily substance obtained from animals or plants ▷ *adj* **fatter, fattest 3** having excess flesh on the body **4** containing much fat **5** thick **6** profitable **fatness** *n*
▶ **fatten** *v* (cause to) become fat
▶ **fatty** *adj* containing fat
▶ **fathead** *n informal* fool **fat-headed** *adj*
fatal ⓣ *adj* causing death or ruin **fatally** *adv*
▶ **fatality** *n* death caused by an accident or disaster
fatalism *n* belief that all events are predetermined and man is powerless to change his destiny **fatalist** *n* **fatalistic** *adj*
fate ⓣ *n* **1** power supposed to predetermine events **2** inevitable fortune that befalls a person or thing
▶ **fated** *adj* **1** destined **2** doomed to death or destruction
▶ **fateful** *adj* having important, usu. disastrous, consequences
father ⓣ *n* **1** male parent **2** man who originates or founds something **3** title of some priests **4 Father** God **fathers 5** ancestors ▷ *v* **6** be the father of (offspring) **fatherhood** *n* **fatherless** *adj* **fatherly** *adj*
▶ **father-in-law** *n* father of one's husband or wife
▶ **fatherland** *n* one's native country
fathom ⓣ *n* **1** unit of measurement of the depth of water, equal to six feet ▷ *v* **2** understand **fathomable** *adj*
▶ **fathomless** *adj* too difficult to fathom
fatigue ⓣ [fat-**eeg**] *n* **1** physical or mental exhaustion caused by exertion **2** weakening of a material due to stress **3** soldier's nonmilitary duty ▷ *v* **4** tire out
fatuous ⓣ *adj* foolish **fatuously** *adv* **fatuity** *n*
faucet *n* valve with handle, plug, etc. to regulate or stop flow of fluid
Faulkner, Falkner *n* **William**. 1897–1962, US novelist and short-story writer. Most of his works portray the problems of the southern US, esp. the novels set in the imaginary county of Yoknapatawpha in Mississippi. Other novels include *The Sound and the Fury* (1929) and *Light in August* (1932): Nobel prize for literature 1949
fault ⓣ *n* **1** responsibility for something wrong **2** mistake **3** defect or flaw **4** *geology* break in layers of rock **5** *tennis, squash, etc.*

THESAURUS

overnice OPPOSITE: careless
fat *adj* **1 = overweight**, heavy, obese, portly, plump, stout, rotund, pudgy, corpulent, tubby • *a fat cat* OPPOSITE: thin **2 = fatty**, oily, greasy, adipose, oleaginous ▶ *n* **3 = fatness**, obesity, bulk, flesh, lard (*slang*), blubber, corpulence, flab, paunch, spare tire (*informal*), saddlebags (*informal*), muffin top (*informal*)
See also: **thick**
fatal *adj* **1 = lethal**, deadly, terminal, incurable, mortal • *fatal injuries* **2 = disastrous**, catastrophic, calamitous • *The mistake was fatal to my plans*.
fatality *n* **= death**, loss, casualty, mortality
fate *n* **1 = destiny**, chance, fortune, providence • *the fickleness of fate* **2 = fortune**, lot, cup, portion, horoscope, stars
See also: **luck**
fated *adj* **= destined**, sure, inevitable, doomed, inescapable, foreordained, predestined, preordained, written
fateful *adj* **1 = crucial**, important, significant, critical, decisive, portentous **2 = disastrous**, deadly, fatal, lethal, destructive, ominous, ruinous
father *n* **1 = parent**, dad (*informal*), pa (*informal*), daddy (*informal*), papa (*old-fashioned, informal*), old man (*informal*), pop (*informal*), sire, pater (*old-fashioned, informal, chiefly Brit*) **2 = forefather**, predecessor, ancestor, progenitor, forebear **3 = founder**, author, maker, creator, architect, inventor, originator, prime mover **4 = priest**, pastor, padre (*informal*) ▶ *v* **5 = sire**, get, beget, procreate
fatherland *n* **= homeland**, motherland, native land
fatherly *adj* **= paternal**, protective, supportive, benign, kindly, affectionate, benevolent, patriarchal
fathom *v* **= understand**, interpret, grasp, comprehend, get to the bottom of
fatigue *n* **1 = tiredness**, lethargy, heaviness, languor, listlessness ▶ *v* **2 = tire**, drain, exhaust, weaken, weary, take it out of (*informal*), wear out
fatigued *adj* **= tired**, weary, overtired, zonked (*slang*), bushed (*informal*), wasted, tired out, exhausted, (dead) beat (*informal*), all in (*slang*)
fatten *v* **1 = grow fat**, spread, expand, swell, thicken, gain weight, put on weight **2** (*often with up*) **= feed up**, feed, stuff, nourish, build up, overfeed
fatty *adj* **= greasy**, fat, rich, oily, adipose, oleaginous
fatuous *adj* **= foolish**, stupid, silly, ludicrous, mindless, idiotic, inane, moronic, brainless, witless
fault *n* **1 = responsibility**, blame, liability • *It was all my fault!* **2 = flaw**, weakness, defect, deficiency, blemish, drawback, failing, imperfection • *a minor technical fault* OPPOSITE: strength **3 = mistake**, slip, error, oversight, lapse, blunder, indiscretion **at fault**

DICTIONARY

invalid serve ▷ *v* **6** criticize or find mistakes in **faulty** *adj* **faultily** *adv* **faultless** *adj* **faultlessly** *adv*
▸ **at fault** guilty of error
▸ **find fault with** seek out minor imperfections in
▸ **to a fault** excessively
faun *n* (in Roman legend) rural god with goat's horns and legs
fauna *n, pl* **-nas**, **-nae** animals of a given place or time
Fauré *n* **Gabriel** (**Urbain**). 1845–1924, French composer and teacher, noted particularly for his song settings of French poems, esp. those of Verlaine, his piano music, and his *Messe de Requiem* (1887)
faux pas [**foe pah**] *n, pl* **faux pas** social blunder
favour Ⓣ *n* **1** goodwill, approval **2** act of goodwill or generosity **3** partiality ▷ *v* **4** prefer **5** regard or treat with especial kindness **6** support or advocate **7** *informal* resemble
▸ **favourable** *adj* **1** encouraging **2** giving consent **3** useful or beneficial **favourably** *adv*
▸ **favourite** *n* **1** preferred person or thing **2** *sports* competitor expected to win ▷ *adj* **3** most liked
▸ **favouritism** *n* practice of unfairly favouring one person or group
Fawkes *n* **Guy**. 1570–1606, English conspirator, executed for his part in the Gunpowder Plot to blow up King James I and the Houses of Parliament (1605). Effigies of him (guys) are burnt in Britain on Guy Fawkes Day (Nov 5)
fawn[1] Ⓣ *n* **1** young deer ▷ *adj* **2** light yellowish-brown
fawn[2] Ⓣ *v* **1** (foll. by *on*) seek attention from (someone) by being obsequious **2** (of a dog) try to please by a show of extreme affection
fax *n* **1** electronic system for sending facsimiles of documents by telephone **2** document sent by this system ▷ *v* **3** send by this system
faze *v informal* disconcert or fluster
FBI *US* Federal Bureau of Investigation
FC Football Club
Fe *chem* iron
fealty *n obsolete* subordinate's loyalty to his ruler or lord
fear Ⓣ *n* **1** distress or alarm caused by impending danger or pain **2** cause of this ▷ *v* **3** be afraid of (something or someone) **4** feel anxiety about (something) **fearless** *adj* **fearlessly** *adv*

THESAURUS

= **guilty**, responsible, culpable, answerable, blamable, in the wrong, to blame **find fault with** = **criticize**, complain, quibble, carp at, pick holes in, pull to pieces, take to task **to a fault** = **excessively**, unduly, immoderately, in the extreme, overmuch ▸ *v* **4** = **criticize**, blame, censure • *Her conduct cannot be faulted*.
See also: **fissure, hole**
faultfinding *See* **criticism**
faultless *adj* = **flawless**, model, perfect, correct, exemplary, impeccable, foolproof, unblemished
faulty *adj* = **defective**, flawed, invalid, imperfect, buggy (*informal*), unsound, imprecise, fallacious, malfunctioning • *Faulty goods should be sent back*.
See also: **weak, wrong**
favour *n* **1** = **approval**, support, grace, esteem • *The proposals met with favour*. OPPOSITE: disapproval **2** = **good turn**, service, courtesy, kindness • *Can you do me a favour?* OPPOSITE: wrong ▸ *v* **3** = **prefer**, single out • *They favoured the cuter puppy*. **4** = **advocate**, support, approve, champion, encourage, prefer, commend, incline towards
See also: **back, goodwill**
favourable *adj* **1** = **advantageous**, good, beneficial, suitable, opportune • *favourable conditions* OPPOSITE: unfavourable **2** = **positive**, friendly, sympathetic, affirmative, amicable, approving, welcoming • *a positive response* OPPOSITE: unfavourable
favourably *adv* **1** = **advantageously**, well, fortunately, conveniently, profitably, auspiciously, opportunely, to one's advantage **2** = **positively**, enthusiastically, helpfully, approvingly, with approval *See also*: **well**
favoured *See* **favourite**
favourite *adj* **1** = **preferred**, best-loved, dearest, favoured • *my favourite teacher* ▸ *n* **2** = **darling**, pick, pet, idol • *The collie was always her favourite*.
See also: **popular**
favouritism *n* = **bias**, one-sidedness • *There was never a hint of favouritism*. OPPOSITE: impartiality
fawn[1] *adj* = **beige**, neutral, buff, greyish-brown
fawn[2] *v* (often with *on* or *upon*) = **ingratiate oneself**, creep, crawl, flatter, cringe, curry favour, brown-nose (*slang*), dance attendance, grovel, kiss ass (*slang*), kowtow, pander to
fawning *adj* = **obsequious**, deferential, crawling, cringing, flattering, grovelling, servile, sycophantic
fear *n* **1** = **dread**, terror, alarm, panic, awe, trepidation, fright, apprehensiveness, cravenness • *shivering with fear* **2** = **bugbear**, bogey, horror, nightmare, bête noire,

DICTIONARY

▶ **fearful** *adj* **1** feeling fear **2** causing fear **3** *informal* very unpleasant **fearfully** *adv*
▶ **fearsome** *adj* terrifying
feasible Ⓣ *adj* able to be done, possible **feasibly** *adv* **feasibility** *n*
feast Ⓣ *n* **1** lavish meal **2** periodic religious celebration **3** something extremely pleasing ▷ *v* **4** eat a feast **5** (foll. by *on*) enjoy eating (something) **6** give a feast to **7** delight
feat Ⓣ *n* remarkable, skilful, or daring action
feather *n* **1** one of the barbed shafts forming the plumage of birds ▷ *v* **2** fit or cover with feathers **3** turn (an oar) edgeways **feathered** *adj* **feathery** *adj*
▶ **feather in one's cap** achievement one can be pleased with
▶ **feather one's nest** make one's life comfortable
▶ **featherbedding** *n* overprotection
▶ **featherweight** *n* **1** boxer weighing up to 126lb (professional) or 57kg (amateur) **2** insignificant person or thing
feature Ⓣ *n* **1** prominent or distinctive part **2** part of the face, such as the eyes **3** special article in a newspaper or magazine **4** main film in a cinema programme ▷ *v* **5** have as a feature or be a feature in **6** give prominence to **featureless** *adj*
Feb. February
febrile [**fee**-brile] *adj* feverish
February *n* second month
feces, faeces [**fee**-seez] *pl n* waste matter discharged from the anus **fecal** *or* **faecal** *adj*
feckless Ⓣ *adj* ineffectual or irresponsible
feculent *adj* muddy, filthy, or foul
fecund *adj* fertile **fecundity** *n*
fed *v* past of **feed**
▶ **fed up** *informal* bored, dissatisfied
federal *adj* **1** of a system in which power is divided between one central government and several regional governments **2** of the central government of a federation **federalism** *n* **federalist** *n*
▶ **federate** *v* unite in a federation
▶ **federation** *n* **1** union of several states, provinces, etc. **2** association
Federer *n* **Roger**. born 1981, Swiss tennis player: won both the Wimbledon men's singles and the US Open each year 2004–2007. He lost the Wimbledon men's singles final in 2008 but regained the title in 2009, winning his 15th Grand Slam singles title.
fedora [fid-**or**-a] *n* man's soft hat with a brim
fee Ⓣ *n* **1** charge paid to be allowed to do something **2** payment for professional services
feeble Ⓣ *adj* **1** lacking physical or mental power **2** unconvincing **feebleness** *n* **feebly** *adv*

THESAURUS

spectre ▶ *v* **3 = be afraid**, dread, be frightened, be scared, take fright • *There is nothing to fear.* ▷ **fear for = worry about**, be anxious about, feel concern for
See also: **anxiety, worry**
fearful *adj* **1 = scared**, afraid, nervous, frightened, uneasy, timid, alarmed, jumpy, timorous, wired (*slang*) **2 = frightful**, terrible, dire, awful, horrific, gruesome, horrendous, dreadful, hair-raising
fearfully *adv* **1 = nervously**, apprehensively, diffidently, timidly, timorously, uneasily **2 = very**, terribly, excessively, tremendously, awfully, exceedingly, frightfully
fearless *adj* **= brave**, bold, courageous, valiant, plucky, intrepid, undaunted, unafraid, indomitable, dauntless
fearsome *adj* **= terrifying**, daunting, formidable, awe-inspiring, frightening, horrifying, menacing, unnerving
feasible *adj* **= possible**, likely, reasonable, viable, achievable, attainable, workable, practicable
feast *n* **1 = banquet**, treat, spread (*informal*), dinner, repast **2 = festival**, holiday, celebration, fête, holy day, red-letter day, saint's day **3 = treat**, delight, pleasure, enjoyment, gratification ▶ *v* **4 = eat one's fill**, indulge, gorge, overindulge, gormandize, pig out (*slang*), wine and dine
feat *n* **= accomplishment**, act, performance, achievement, exploit, deed, attainment
feathers *pl n* **= plumage**, down, plumes
feature *n* **1 = aspect**, mark, quality, property, attribute, characteristic • *an unusual feature of the room* **2 = article**, report, story, piece, item, blog, column • *a news feature* **3 = highlight**, attraction, specialty, main item ▶ *v* **4 = spotlight**, emphasize, give prominence to, star • *featuring an interview with the premier*
See also: **point**
features *pl n* **= face**, countenance, lineaments, physiognomy
feckless *adj* **= irresponsible**, incompetent, worthless, hopeless, ineffectual, good-for-nothing, shiftless
federation *n* **= union**, league, coalition, association, combination, alliance, syndicate, amalgamation
fed up *adj* **= dissatisfied**, bored, tired, depressed, glum, discontented, down in the mouth, sick and tired (*informal*)
fee *n* **= charge**, bill, payment, toll, remuneration
feeble *adj* **1 = weak**, frail, infirm, sickly, puny, weedy (*informal*), debilitated, doddering, effete **2 = unconvincing**, poor, thin,

f

DICTIONARY

▸ **feeble-minded** *adj* mentally deficient
feed ⓣ *v* **feeding, fed 1** give food to **2** give (something) as food **3** eat **4** supply or prepare food for **5** supply (what is needed) ▹ *n* **6** act of feeding **7** food, esp. for babies or animals **8** *informal* meal
▸ **feeder** *n* **1** baby's bib **2** road or railway line linking outlying areas to the main traffic network
▸ **feedback** *n* **1** information received in response to something done **2** return of part of the output of an electrical circuit or loudspeaker to its source
feel ⓣ *v* **feeling, felt 1** have a physical or emotional sensation of **2** become aware of or examine by touch **3** believe ▹ *n* **4** act of feeling **5** way something feels **6** impression **7** sense of touch **8** instinctive aptitude
▸ **feeler** *n* **1** organ of touch in some animals **2** remark made to test others' opinion
▸ **feeling** *n* **1** emotional reaction **2** intuitive understanding **3** opinion **4** sympathy, understanding **5** ability to experience physical sensations **6** sensation experienced **feelings 7** emotional sensitivities
▸ **feel like** wish for, want
feet *n* plural of **foot**
feign ⓣ [**fane**] *v* pretend
feint[1] [**faint**] *n* **1** sham attack or blow meant to distract an opponent ▹ *v* **2** make a feint
feint[2] [**faint**] *n* narrow lines on ruled paper
feisty *adj informal* lively, resilient, and self-reliant
feldspar *n* hard mineral that is the main constituent of igneous rocks
felicity *n, pl* **-ties 1** happiness **2** appropriate expression or style **felicitous** *adj*
▸ **felicitate** *v* congratulate **felicitation** *n*
feline ⓣ *adj* **1** of cats **2** catlike ▹ *n* **3** animal of the cat family
fell[1] *v* past tense of **fall**
fell[2] ⓣ *v* **1** knock down **2** cut down (a tree)
fell[3] *adj old-fashioned* fierce, terrible
▸ **one fell swoop** single action or occurrence
fell[4] *n* (in N England) a mountain, hill, or moor
Fellini *n* **Federico**. 1920–93, Italian film director. His films include *La Dolce Vita* (1959), *8½* (1963), *Satyricon* (1969), and *Intervista* (1987)
felloe *n* (segment of) the rim of a wheel
fellow ⓣ *n* **1** *informal* man or boy **2** comrade or associate **3** person in the same group or condition **4** member of a learned society or the governing body of a college ▹ *adj* **5** in the same group or condition
▸ **fellowship** *n* **1** sharing of aims or interests **2** group with shared aims or interests **3** feeling of friendliness **4** college research post
felon *n* person guilty of a felony **felonious** *adj*
▸ **felony** *n, pl* **-nies** serious crime
felspar *n* same as **feldspar**

THESAURUS

inadequate, tame, insufficient, pathetic, lousy (*slang*), lame, paltry, flimsy
feebleness *n* = **weakness**, frailty, effeteness, infirmity, languor, lassitude, sickliness
feed *v* **1 = cater for**, supply, sustain, provision, nourish, provide for, victual, wine and dine **2** (sometimes with *on*) **= eat**, devour, chow down (*slang*), exist on, live on, partake of ▸ *n* **3 = food**, fodder, pasturage, provender **4** (*Informal*) **= meal**, feast, spread (*informal*), repast
feedback *See* **reaction**
feel *v* **1 = experience**, suffer, undergo • *I felt enormous happiness.* **2 = believe**, think, consider, judge, deem • *She feels she is in control of her life.* **3 = touch**, stroke, finger, fondle • *Feel this lovely material!* **4 = sense**, be convinced, intuit ▹ **feel dejected** *See* **despair** ▹ **feel despondent** *See* **despair** ▹ **feel for** *See* **identify with, pity** ▹ **feel sorry for** *See* **pity** ▹ **feel uneasy** *See* **worry** ▸ *n* **5 = texture**, finish, touch, surface **6 = impression**, air, quality, sense, feeling, atmosphere, ambience
See also: **handle, have, suspect**
feeler *n* **1 = antenna**, tentacle, whisker **2 = approach**, probe, advance
feeling *n* **1 = emotion**, heat, passion, sentiment, fervour • *feelings of envy* **2 = sensation**, sense • *a feeling of pain* **3 = opinion**, view, perspective, inclination, point of view • *strong feelings on politics* **4 = impression**, idea, sense, suspicion, notion, hunch, inkling, presentiment **5 = sympathy**, concern, understanding, sensitivity, compassion, empathy, pity, sensibility **6 = atmosphere**, feel, air, quality, mood, aura, ambience
See also: **guess, instinct**
feign *See* **fake, pretend**
feigned *See* **mock**
feline *See* **cat**
fell *v* **= cut down**, cut, level, demolish, hew, knock down
fellow *n* **1 = man**, person, guy (*informal*), individual, character, chap (*informal*) **2 = associate**, partner, colleague, peer, comrade, companion ▸ *adj* ▹ **fellow worker** *See* **colleague**
fellowship *n* **1 = camaraderie**, companionship • *a sense of community and fellowship* **2 = society**, order, club, league, association, guild, fraternity, brotherhood

DICTIONARY

felt[1] *v* past of **feel**
felt[2] *n* matted fabric made by bonding fibres by pressure
▸ **felt-tip pen** pen with a writing point made from pressed fibres
fem. feminine
female ⓣ *adj* **1** of the sex which bears offspring **2** (of plants) producing fruits ▷ *n* **3** female person or animal
feminine ⓣ *adj* **1** of women **2** having qualities traditionally regarded as suitable for, or typical of, women **3** belonging to a particular class of grammatical inflection in some languages **femininity** *n*
▸ **feminism** *n* advocacy of equal rights for women **feminist** *n, adj*
femme fatale [**fam** fat-**tahl**] *n, pl* **femmes fatales** alluring woman who causes men distress
femur [**fee**-mer] *n* thighbone
▸ **femoral** *adj* of the thigh
fen ⓣ *n* low-lying flat marshy land
fence ⓣ *n* **1** barrier of posts linked by wire or wood, enclosing an area **2** *slang* dealer in stolen property ▷ *v* **3** enclose with or as if with a fence **4** fight with swords as a sport **5** avoid a question **fencer** *n*
▸ **fencing** *n* **1** sport of fighting with swords **2** material for making fences
fend *v* **fend for oneself** provide for oneself
fend off *v* ward off
fender *n* **1** part of an automobile bodywork surrounding the wheels **2** soft but solid object hung over a ship's side to prevent damage when docking **3** low metal frame in front of a fireplace
feng shui [fung **shway**] *n* Chinese art of deciding the best design of a building, etc., in order to bring good luck
fennel *n* fragrant plant whose seeds, leaves, and root are used in cookery
fenugreek *n* Mediterranean plant grown for its pungent seeds
feral *adj* wild
Ferdinand I *n* **1** known as *Ferdinand the Great*. ?1016–65, king of Castile (1035–65) and León (1037–65): achieved control of the Moorish kings of Saragossa, Seville, and Toledo **2** 1751–1825, king of the Two Sicilies (1816–25); king of Naples (1759–1806; 1815–25), as Ferdinand IV, being dispossessed by Napoleon (1806–15) **3** 1793–1875, king of Hungary (1830–48) and emperor of Austria (1835–48); abdicated after the Revolution of 1848 in favour of his nephew, Franz Josef I
Ferdinand II *n* **1** 1578–1637, Holy Roman Emperor (1619–37); king of Bohemia (1617–19; 1620–37) and of Hungary (1617–37). His anti-Protestant policies led to the Thirty Years' War **2** title as king of Aragon and Sicily of **Ferdinand V**
Ferdinand III *n* **1** 1608–57, Holy Roman Emperor (1637–57) and king of Hungary (1625–57); son of Ferdinand II **2** title as king of Naples of **Ferdinand V**
Ferdinand V *n* known as *Ferdinand the Catholic*. 1452–1516, king of Castile (1474–1504); as Ferdinand II, king of Aragon (1479–1516) and Sicily (1468–1516); as Ferdinand III, king of Naples (1504–16). His marriage to Isabella I of Castile (1469) led to the union of Aragon and Castile and his reconquest of Granada from the Moors (1492) completed the unification of Spain. He introduced the Inquisition (1478), expelled the Jews from Spain (1492), and financed Columbus' voyage to the New World
Ferdinand VII *n* 1784–1833, king of Spain (1808; 1814–33). He precipitated the Carlist Wars by excluding his brother Don Carlos as his successor
Fermat *n* **Pierre de**. 1601–65, French mathematician, regarded as the founder of the modern theory of numbers. He studied the properties of whole numbers and, with Pascal, investigated the theory of probability
ferment ⓣ *n* **1** commotion, unrest ▷ *v* **2** undergo or cause to undergo fermentation
▸ **fermentation** *n* reaction in which an organic molecule splits into simpler substances, esp. conversion of sugar to alcohol
Fermi *n* **Enrico**. 1901–54, Italian nuclear physicist, in the US from 1939. He was awarded a Nobel prize for physics in 1938 for his work on radioactive substances and nuclear bombardment and headed the group that produced the first controlled nuclear reaction (1942)
fern *n* flowerless plant with fine fronds
ferocious ⓣ *adj* fierce, violent **ferocity** *n*
Ferrari *n* **Enzo**. 1898–1988, Italian designer

f

THESAURUS

female *n* **1** = **woman**, girl, lady • *Hay fever affects males more than females.* ▸ *adj* **2** = **feminine** • *the world's greatest female skater*
feminine *adj* = **womanly**, soft, tender, delicate, gentle, ladylike
fen *n* = **marsh**, swamp, bog, quagmire, slough, morass
fence *n* **1** = **barrier**, wall, hedge, defense, barricade, rampart, palisade, railings ▸ *v* **2** (often with *in* or *off*) = **enclose**, protect, surround, pen, confine, bound, encircle **3** = **evade**, dodge, equivocate, parry
ferment *n* = **commotion**, stir, disruption, turmoil, unrest, excitement, frenzy, uproar, furor, tumult
ferocious *adj* **1** = **fierce**, violent,

DICTIONARY

and manufacturer of racing cars
ferret ⓣ *n* **1** tamed polecat used to catch rabbits or rats ▷ *v* **ferreting, ferreted 2** hunt with ferrets **3** search around
▶ **ferret out** *v* find by searching
ferric, ferrous *adj* of or containing iron
ferris wheel *n* large vertical fairground wheel with hanging seats for riding in
ferrule *n* metal cap to strengthen the end of a stick
ferry ⓣ *n, pl* **-ries 1** boat for transporting people and vehicles ▷ *v* **-rying, -ried 2** carry by ferry **3** convey (goods or people) **ferryman** *n*
fertile ⓣ *adj* **1** capable of producing young, crops, or vegetation **2** highly productive **fertility** *n* **fertilizer** *n*
▶ **fertilize** *v* **1** provide (an animal or plant) with sperm or pollen to bring about fertilization **2** supply (soil) with nutrients **fertilization** *n*
fervent, fervid ⓣ *adj* intensely passionate and sincere **fervently** *adv*
▶ **fervour** *n* intensity of feeling
fescue *n* pasture and lawn grass with stiff narrow leaves
Fessenden *n* **Reginald Aubrey**. 1866–1932, US physicist born in Canada. A pioneer of radio transmission, he made the first sound broadcast in N America (1906)
festal *adj* festive
fester ⓣ *v* **1** form or cause to form pus **2** rot, decay **3** become worse
festival ⓣ *n* **1** organized series of special events or performances **2** day or period of celebration
▶ **festive** *adj* of or like a celebration
▶ **festivity** *n, pl* **-ties 1** joyful celebration, merriment **festivities 2** celebrations
festoon ⓣ *v* hang decorations in loops
feta *n* white salty Greek cheese
fetch ⓣ *v* **1** go after and bring back **2** be sold for **3** *informal* deal (a blow)
▶ **fetching** *adj* attractive
▶ **fetch up** *v informal* arrive or end up
fete, fête ⓣ [fate] *n* **1** gala, bazaar, etc., usu. held outdoors ▷ *v* **2** honour or entertain regally
fetid *adj* stinking
fetish ⓣ *n* **1** form of behaviour in which sexual pleasure is derived from looking at or handling an inanimate object **2** thing with which one is excessively concerned **3** object believed to have magical powers **fetishism** *n* **fetishist** *n*
fetlock *n* projection behind and above a horse's hoof
fetter *n* **1** chain or shackle for the foot **fetters 2** restrictions ▷ *v* **3** restrict **4** bind in fetters
fettle *n* state of health or spirits
fetus [fee-tuss] *n, pl* **-tuses** embryo of a mammal in the later stages of development **fetal** *adj*
feud ⓣ *n* **1** long bitter hostility between two people or groups ▷ *v* **2** carry on a feud
feudalism *n* medieval system in which vassals held land from a lord, and in return

THESAURUS

wild, savage, predatory, rapacious, ravening **2 = cruel**, brutal, vicious, barbaric, ruthless, bloodthirsty
ferocity *n* = **savagery**, cruelty, brutality, viciousness, wildness, bloodthirstiness, fierceness
ferret *n* ▶ *v* ▷ **ferret out = track down**, discover, trace, unearth, elicit, dig up, root out, search out
ferry *n* **1 = ferry boat**, packet, packet boat ▶ *v* **2 = carry**, run, ship, shuttle, transport, convey, chauffeur
fertile *adj* = **productive**, rich, prolific, fruitful • *fertile soil* OPPOSITE: barren
See also: **creative**
fertility *n* = **fruitfulness**, abundance, richness, fecundity, luxuriance, productiveness
fertilizer *n* = **compost**, manure, dressing, dung
fervent *adj* = **ardent**, passionate, enthusiastic, committed, devout, zealous, impassioned • *a fervent admirer of her work*
See also: **fanatical, intense**
fervour *n* = **intensity**, passion, excitement, enthusiasm, warmth, zeal, ardour, vehemence
See also: **feeling, heat, violence**
fester *v* **1 = decay**, putrefy, suppurate, ulcerate **2 = intensify**, aggravate, smoulder
festival *n* **1 = fair**, entertainment, gala, fete, carnival • *the Toronto Film Festival* **2 = holiday** • *different religious festivals*
See also: **celebration**
festive *adj* = **celebratory**, happy, jubilant, merry, joyful, joyous, cheery, jovial, convivial
festivity *n* (*often pl*) = **celebration**, party, festival, entertainment
festoon *v* = **decorate**, hang, array, deck, drape, swathe, garland, wreathe
fetch *v* **1 = bring**, get, carry, deliver, obtain, transport, retrieve, convey, go for **2 = sell for**, make, earn, realize, yield, bring in, go for
fetching *adj* = **attractive**, cute, charming, alluring, captivating, enticing, winsome
fete *See* **fair, festival**
fetish *n* **1 = fixation**, thing (*informal*), obsession, mania **2 = talisman**, amulet
feud *n* **1 = hostility**, conflict, row, argument, rivalry, disagreement, quarrel, vendetta,

DICTIONARY

worked and fought for him
▸ **feudal** *adj* of or like feudalism
fever Ⓣ *n* **1** (illness causing) high body temperature **2** nervous excitement **fevered** *adj*
▸ **feverish** *adj* **1** suffering from fever **2** in a state of nervous excitement **feverishly** *adv*
few Ⓣ *adj* not many
▸ **a few** a small number
▸ **a good few** *or* **quite a few** several
fey *adj* **1** whimsically strange **2** clairvoyant
Feynman *n* **Richard**. 1918–88, US physicist, noted for his research on quantum electrodynamics; shared the Nobel prize for physics in 1965
fez *n, pl* **fezzes** brimless tasselled cap, orig. from Turkey
ff *music* fortissimo
fiancé [fee-**on**-say] *n* man engaged to be married **fiancée** *n fem*
fiasco Ⓣ *n, pl* **-cos, -coes** ridiculous or humiliating failure
fiat [**fee**-at] *n* **1** arbitrary order **2** official permission
fib Ⓣ *n* **1** trivial lie ▷ *v* **fibbing, fibbed 2** tell a fib **fibber** *n*
fibre Ⓣ *n* **1** thread that can be spun into yarn **2** threadlike animal or plant tissue **3** fibrous material in food **4** strength of character **5** essential substance or nature **fibrous** *adj*
▸ **fibreboard** *n* board made of compressed plant fibres
▸ **fibreglass** *n* material made of fine glass fibres
▸ **fibre optics** transmission of information by light along very thin flexible fibres of glass
fibroid [**fibe**-royd] *n* benign tumour derived from fibrous connective tissue
▸ **fibrositis** [fibe-roh-**site**-iss] *n* inflammation of muscle tissue, causing pain and stiffness
fibula [**fib**-yew-la] *n, pl* **-lae, -las** slender outer bone of the lower leg **fibular** *adj*
fiche [**feesh**] *n* sheet of film for storing publications in miniaturized form
fickle Ⓣ *adj* changeable, inconstant
fickleness *n*
fiction Ⓣ *n* **1** literary works of the imagination, such as novels **2** invented story
fictional *adj*
▸ **fictionalize** *v* turn into fiction
▸ **fictitious** *adj* **1** not genuine **2** of or in fiction
fiddle Ⓣ *n* **1** violin **2** *informal* dishonest action or scheme ▷ *v* **3** play the violin **4** move or touch something restlessly **5** falsify (accounts)
▸ **fiddling** *adj* trivial
▸ **fiddly** *adj* awkward to do or use
▸ **fiddlehead** *n* edible coiled tip of young fern frond
fidelity Ⓣ *n* **1** faithfulness **2** accuracy in detail **3** quality of sound reproduction
fidget Ⓣ *v* **1** move about restlessly ▷ *n* **2** person who fidgets **fidgets 3** restlessness
fidgety *adj*
fiduciary [fid-**yew**-sheer-ee] *adj* **1** relating to a trust or trustee ▷ *n, pl* **-aries 2** trustee

THESAURUS

enmity ▸ *v* **2** = **quarrel**, war, dispute, row, clash, contend, squabble, bicker, fall out
fever *n* = **excitement**, frenzy, agitation, delirium, ferment, restlessness, fervour
feverish *adj* **1** = **hot**, febrile, fevered, flushed, inflamed, pyretic (*medical*) **2** = **excited**, frantic, frenzied, restless, frenetic, overwrought, agitated, wired (*slang*)
few *adj* = **not many**, scarce, meagre, sparse, infrequent • *a few moments ago* OPPOSITE: many
See also: **rare, uncommon**
fewest *See* **least**
fiasco *n* = **failure**, disaster, mess, catastrophe, debacle, washout (*informal*)
fib *n* = **lie**, story, fiction, untruth, white lie
fibbing *See* **lying**
fibre *n* **1** = **thread**, strand, pile, texture, filament, wisp **2** = **essence**, quality, nature, substance, spirit ▷ **moral fibre** = **strength of character**, strength, resolution, toughness, stamina
fickle *adj* = **changeable**, volatile, variable, temperamental, capricious, unfaithful, faithless, inconstant, irresolute
fiction *n* **1** = **tale**, story, novel, legend, fantasy, romance, myth, yarn (*informal*) **2** = **lie**, invention, fabrication, falsehood, cock and bull story (*informal*), tall tale (*informal*), untruth, urban legend
fictional *adj* = **imaginary**, legendary, unreal, nonexistent, made-up, invented
fictitious *adj* = **false**, bogus, untrue, imaginary, mythical, made-up, make-believe, fabricated, invented
fiddle *v* **1** = **fidget**, play, finger, tinker, interfere with, mess around with, tamper with ▸ *n* **2** = **violin** ▷ **fit as a fiddle** = **healthy**, strong, sound, blooming, hale and hearty, in fine fettle, in good form, in good shape, in rude health, in the pink
fiddling *adj* = **trivial**, petty, insignificant, futile, pettifogging, trifling
fidelity *n* **1** = **loyalty**, devotion, allegiance, dependability, constancy, faithfulness, staunchness, trustworthiness **2** = **accuracy**, precision, correspondence, closeness, exactness, faithfulness, scrupulousness
fidget *v* = **twitch**, fiddle (*informal*), squirm, jiggle • *fidgeting in his seat* ▸ *n* ▷ **the**

DICTIONARY

fief [**feef**] *n hist* land granted by a lord in return for war service
field Ⓣ *n* **1** enclosed piece of agricultural land **2** marked off area for sports **3** area rich in a specified natural resource **4** sphere of knowledge or activity **5** place away from the laboratory or classroom where practical work is done **6** all the competitors in a competition **7** all the competitors except the favourite **8** battlefield **9** area over which electric, gravitational, or magnetic force is exerted **10** background, as of a flag ▷ *v* **11** *sports* catch and return (a ball) **12** *sports* send a (player or team) on to the field **13** *sports* play as a fielder **14** deal with (a question) successfully
▸ **fielder** *n sports* player whose task is to field the ball
▸ **field day** day or time of exciting activity
▸ **field events** throwing and jumping events in athletics
▸ **field glasses** binoculars
▸ **field hockey** game similar to hockey played on a field with a ball and curved sticks
▸ **field marshal** army officer of the highest rank
▸ **field sports** hunting, shooting, and fishing
▸ **fieldwork** *n* investigation made in the field as opposed to the classroom or the laboratory
Field *n* **John**. 1782–1837, Irish composer and pianist, lived in Russia from 1803: invented the nocturne
Fielding *n* **Henry**. 1707–54, English novelist and dramatist, noted particularly for his picaresque novel *Tom Jones* (1749) and for *Joseph Andrews* (1742), which starts as a parody of Richardson's *Pamela*: also noted as an enlightened magistrate and a founder of the Bow Street runners (1749)
Fields *n* **W. C.**, real name *William Claude Dukenfield*. 1880–1946, US film actor, noted for his portrayal of comic roles
fiend Ⓣ [**feend**] *n* **1** evil spirit **2** cruel or wicked person **3** *informal* person devoted to something: *fresh-air fiend*
▸ **fiendish** *adj* **1** cruel **2** *informal* cunning **3** *informal* very difficult **fiendishly** *adv*
Fiennes *n* Sir **Ranulph** (**Twistleton-Wykeham-**). born 1944, British explorer; led the first surface journey around the earth's polar axis (1979–82); unsupported crossing of Antarctica (1992–93)
fierce Ⓣ *adj* **1** wild or aggressive **2** intense **3** turbulent **fiercely** *adv* **fierceness** *n*
fiery Ⓣ [**fire**-ee] *adj* **fierier**, **fieriest** **1** consisting of or like fire **2** easily angered **3** (of food) very spicy
fiesta *n* religious festival, carnival
FIFA [**fee**-fa] Fédération Internationale de Football Association (International Association Football Federation)
fife *n* small high-pitched flute
fifteen *adj, n* **1** five and ten ▷ *n* **2** Rugby Union team **fifteenth** *adj, n*
fifth *adj, n* **1** (of) number five in a series ▷ *n* **2** one of five equal parts of something
▸ **fifth column** group secretly helping the enemy
fifty *adj, n, pl* **-ties** five times ten **fiftieth** *adj, n*
▸ **fifty-fifty** *informal* ▷ *adv* **1** equally divided: *they split the profits fifty-fifty* ▷ *adj* **2** having an equal chance of happening or not happening: *a fifty-fifty chance of success*
fig *n* **1** soft pear-shaped fruit **2** tree bearing it
fight Ⓣ *v* **fighting**, **fought** **1** struggle

THESAURUS

fidgets = **restlessness**, nervousness, unease, uneasiness, fidgetiness, jitters (*informal*)
See also: **fuss**
fidgety *adj* = **restless**, nervous, impatient, uneasy, jittery (*informal*), restive, jumpy, twitchy (*informal*), antsy (*slang*), on edge, wired (*slang*)
field *n* **1** = **meadow**, pasture • *a field full of sheep* **2** = **area**, province, department, territory, specialty, domain • *a breakthrough in the field of physics* **3** = **competitors**, competition, applicants, candidates, contestants, entrants, possibilities, runners ▸ *v* **4** = **retrieve**, return, stop, catch, pick up **5** = **deal with**, handle, deflect, turn aside
See also: **range**
fiend *n* **1** = **demon**, devil, evil spirit **2** = **brute**, monster, beast, savage, barbarian, ogre, ghoul **3** (*Informal*) = **enthusiast**, addict, freak (*informal*), fanatic, maniac
fiendish *adj* = **wicked**, cruel, malignant, satanic, monstrous, unspeakable, diabolical, devilish, hellish, infernal
fierce *adj* **1** = **ferocious**, dangerous, aggressive, murderous • *a fierce lion* OPPOSITE: gentle **2** = **intense**, strong, keen, relentless • *fierce competition* **3** = **stormy**, strong, powerful, violent, furious, raging, inclement, tempestuous, howling
See also: **wild**
fiercely *adv* = **ferociously**, passionately, furiously, viciously, savagely, tempestuously, tigerishly, tooth and nail, with no holds barred
fiery *adj* **1** = **burning**, ablaze, flaming, aflame, afire, blazing, on fire **2** = **excitable**, fierce, passionate, irritable, irascible, hot-headed, impetuous
fight *v* **1** = **battle**, struggle, brawl, grapple,

DICTIONARY

(against) in battle or physical combat **2** struggle to overcome someone or obtain something **3** carry on (a battle or struggle) **4** make (a way) by fighting ▷ *n* **5** aggressive conflict between two (groups of) people **6** quarrel or contest **7** resistance **8** boxing match

▶ **fighter** *n* **1** boxer **2** determined person **3** aircraft designed to destroy other aircraft

▶ **fight off** *v* **1** repulse **2** struggle to avoid

figment *n* **figment of one's imagination** imaginary thing

figure Ⓣ *n* **1** numerical symbol **2** amount expressed in numbers **3** bodily shape **4** well-known person **5** representation in painting or sculpture of a human form **6** diagram or illustration **7** set of movements in dancing or skating **8** *math* any combination of lines, planes, points, or curves ▷ *v* **9** consider, conclude **10** (usu. foll. by *in*) be included (in) **11** calculate

▶ **figure of speech** expression in which words do not have their literal meaning

▶ **figurative** *adj* (of language) abstract, imaginative, or symbolic **figuratively** *adv*

▶ **figurine** *n* statuette

▶ **figurehead** *n* **1** nominal leader **2** carved bust at the bow of a ship

▶ **figure out** *v* solve or understand

filament *n* **1** fine wire in a light bulb that gives out light **2** fine thread

filbert *n* hazelnut

filch Ⓣ *v* steal (small amounts)

file[1] Ⓣ *n* **1** box or folder used to keep documents in order **2** documents in a file **3** information about a person or subject **4** line of people one behind the other **5** *computers* organized collection of related material ▷ *v* **6** place (a document) in a file **7** place (a legal document) on official record **8** bring a lawsuit, esp. for divorce **9** walk or march in a line

▶ **file sharing** sharing computer data on a network, esp. the internet

file[2] Ⓣ *n* **1** tool with a roughened blade for smoothing or shaping ▷ *v* **2** shape or smooth with a file

▶ **filings** *pl n* shavings removed by a file

filial *adj* of or befitting a son or daughter

filibuster *v* **1** obstruct legislation by making long speeches ▷ *n* **2** act of filibustering **3** person who filibusters

filigree *n* **1** delicate ornamental work of gold or silver wire ▷ *adj* **2** made of filigree

Filipino *adj* **1** of the Philippines ▷ *n* **2** (**Filipina**) person from the Philippines

fill Ⓣ *v* **1** make or become full **2** occupy completely **3** plug (a gap) **4** satisfy (a need) **5** hold and perform the duties of (a position) **6** appoint to (a job or position)

▶ **one's fill** sufficient for one's needs or wants

▶ **filler** *n* substance that fills a gap or increases bulk

THESAURUS

throw down (*slang*) • *He fought the world boxing champion.* **2 = oppose**, dispute, contest, resist, defy, withstand, make a stand against, stand up to **3 = engage in**, conduct, wage, prosecute, carry on ▷ **fight against** *See* **oppose** ▷ **fight for** *See* **champion** ▷ **fight off = repel**, resist, repress, repulse, beat off, keep at bay *or* hold at bay, stave off, ward off ▶ *n* **4 = battle**, action, combat, bout, duel, skirmish, slugfest (*informal*), throwdown (*slang*) • *a fight between gladiators* **5 = argument**, dispute, row, squabble • *a fight with my best friend* **6 = resistance**, spirit, pluck, militancy, belligerence

See also: **argue, clash, compete, quarrel, war**

fighter *n* **1 = soldier**, warrior, mercenary • *killing 15 rebel fighters* **2 = boxer**, pugilist, prize fighter

fighting *See* **conflict, war**

figure *n* **1 = number**, total, amount, statistic, digit, numeral • *No one really knows the true figures.* **2 = shape**, body, build, form, silhouette, physique • *A figure appeared in the doorway.* **3 = person**, player, character, personality, dignitary • *international political figures* **4 = amount**, price, cost, total, value, sum **5 = diagram**, design, pattern, drawing, representation, sketch, illustration ▶ *v* **6** (*Informal*) **= suppose**, expect, guess, reckon (*informal*) • *I figure I'll learn from experience* **7 = calculate**, count, tally, compute, reckon, tot up, work out **8** (usually with *in*) **= feature**, appear, act, be featured, contribute to, play a part

▷ **figure out = calculate**, compute, reckon, work out; **= understand**, see, comprehend, decipher, fathom, make out

See also: **outline, symbol**

figurehead *n* **= front man**, puppet, mouthpiece, titular head *or* nominal head

filch *v* **= steal**, take, pinch (*informal*), misappropriate, pilfer, embezzle, thieve, walk off with

file[1] *n* **1 = folder**, case, information, portfolio, data, dossier, documents **2 = line**, row, column, queue ▶ *v* **3 = register**, record, enter, document, pigeonhole, put in place **4 = march**, troop, parade

file[2] *v* **= smooth**, shape, scrape, rub, polish, rasp, abrade

fill *v* **1 = pack**, stock, stuff, cram, gorge • *Fill the bottle with water.* OPPOSITE:

DICTIONARY

▸ **filling** *n* **1** substance that fills a gap or cavity, esp. in a tooth ▷ *adj* **2** (of food) substantial and satisfying
▸ **filling station** garage selling gasoline, oil, etc.
fillet *n* **1** boneless piece of meat or fish ▷ *v* **filleting, filleted 2** remove the bones from
fillip *n* something that adds stimulation or enjoyment
Fillmore *n* **Millard**. 1800–74, 13th president of the US (1850–53); a leader of the Whig Party
filly *n, pl* **-lies** young female horse
film Ⓣ *n* **1** sequence of images projected on a screen, creating the illusion of movement **2** story told in such a sequence of images **3** thin strip of light-sensitive cellulose used to make photographic negatives and transparencies **4** thin sheet or layer ▷ *v* **5** photograph with a movie or video camera **6** make a film of (a scene, story, etc.) **7** cover or become covered with a thin layer ▷ *adj* **8** connected with cinema
▸ **filmy** *adj* very thin, delicate
▸ **film strip** set of pictures on a strip of film, projected separately as slides
filter Ⓣ *n* **1** material or device permitting fluid to pass but retaining solid particles **2** device that blocks certain frequencies of sound or light **3** traffic signal that allows vehicles to turn either left or right while the main signals are at red ▷ *v* **4** pass slowly or faintly **5** remove impurities from (a substance) with a filter
▸ **filtrate** *n* **1** filtered gas or liquid ▷ *v* **2** remove impurities with a filter **filtration** *n*
filth Ⓣ *n* **1** disgusting dirt **2** offensive material or language **filthy** *adj* **filthily** *adv* **filthiness** *n*
fin *n* **1** projection from a fish's body enabling it to balance and swim **2** vertical tailplane of an aircraft
finagle [fin-**nay**-gl] *v* get or achieve by craftiness or trickery
final Ⓣ *adj* **1** at the end **2** having no possibility of further change, action, or discussion ▷ *n* **3** deciding contest in a competition **finals 4** last examinations in an educational course **finally** *adv* **finality** *n*
▸ **finalist** *n* competitor in a final
▸ **finalize** *v* put into final form
▸ **finale** [fin-**nah**-lee] *n* concluding part of a dramatic performance or musical work
finance Ⓣ *v* **1** provide or obtain funds for ▷ *n* **2** management of money **3** (provision of) funds **finances 4** money resources **financial** *adj* **financially** *adv*
▸ **financier** *n* person involved in large-scale financial business
▸ **financial year** twelve-month period used for financial calculations

THESAURUS

empty **2 = saturate**, charge, pervade, imbue, impregnate, suffuse **3 = plug**, close, stop, block, seal, cork, bung **4 = perform**, hold, execute, occupy, fulfill, discharge, carry out ▷ **fill in = complete**, answer, fill out (*US*), fill up; (*Informal*) **= inform**, acquaint, apprise, bring up to date, give the facts *or* give the background; **= replace**, represent, sub, substitute, deputize, stand in, take the place of ▷ **fill out = complete**, answer, fill in, fill up ▸ *n* ▷ **one's fill = sufficient**, enough, plenty, ample, all one wants
See also: **load**
filled *See* **full**
filler *n* **= padding**, stopgap, makeweight
filling *n* **1 = stuffing**, inside, filler, contents, insides, padding, wadding ▸ *adj* **2 = satisfying**, heavy, square, substantial, ample
film *n* **1 = layer**, skin, tissue, coating, membrane, covering, dusting **2 = movie**, flick (*slang*), motion picture ▸ *v* **3 = photograph**, take, shoot, video, videotape
filter *n* **1 = sieve**, mesh, riddle, membrane, gauze, strainer ▸ *v* **2 = purify**, screen, strain, refine, clarify, sift, winnow, sieve, filtrate **3 = trickle**, escape, leak, penetrate, dribble, seep, ooze, exude, percolate
filtered *See* **refined**
filth *n* **1 = dirt**, refuse, sewage, sludge, muck, excrement, grime, squalor, slime **2 = obscenity**, pornography, indecency, vulgarity, impurity, smut
filthy *adj* **1 = dirty**, foul, polluted, slimy, squalid, unclean, putrid **2 = muddy**, grimy, grubby, begrimed, blackened, scuzzy (*slang*) **3 = obscene**, corrupt, pornographic, indecent, lewd, X-rated, depraved, impure, licentious, smutty
final *adj* **1 = last**, ultimate, eventual, closing, concluding • *the fifth and final day* OPPOSITE: first **2 = definitive**, absolute, definite, conclusive • *The judges' decision is final.*
finale *n* **= ending**, close, conclusion, climax, culmination, epilogue, denouement
finalize *v* **= complete**, decide, settle, conclude, clinch, tie up, wind up, work out, wrap up (*informal*)
finally *adv* **1 = eventually**, at last, at the last moment, in the end, in the long run • *It finally arrived.* **2 = in conclusion**, lastly, in summary • *Finally, I'd like to talk about safety measures.*
finance *v* **1 = pay for**, back, support, fund • *financed by the government* ▸ *n* **2 = economics**, investment, banking, commerce, budgeting • *the world of high finance*
finances *pl n* **= resources**, money, capital,

DICTIONARY

finch *n* small songbird with a stout bill
find Ⓣ *v* **finding, found 1** discover by chance **2** discover by search or effort **3** become aware of **4** consider to have a particular quality **5** experience (a particular feeling) **6** *law* pronounce (the defendant) guilty or not guilty **7** provide, esp. with difficulty ▷ *n* **8** person or thing found, esp. when valuable
finder *n*
▸ **finding** *n* conclusion from an investigation
▸ **find out** *v* **1** gain knowledge of **2** detect (a crime, deception, etc.)
fine[1] Ⓣ *adj* **1** very good **2** in good health **3** acceptable **4** thin or slender **5** in small particles **6** subtle or abstruse: *a fine distinction* **7** of delicate workmanship **8** (of weather) clear and dry **finely** *adv* **fineness** *n*
▸ **finery** *n* showy clothing
▸ **fine art** art produced to appeal to the sense of beauty
▸ **fine-tune** *v* make small adjustments to (something) so that it works really well
fine[2] Ⓣ *n* **1** payment imposed as a penalty ▷ *v* **2** impose a fine on
finesse Ⓣ [fin-**ness**] *n* **1** delicate skill **2** subtlety and tact
finger Ⓣ *n* **1** one of the four long jointed parts of the hand **2** part of a glove that covers a finger **3** quantity of liquid in a glass as deep as a finger is wide ▷ *v* **4** touch or handle with the fingers
▸ **fingering** *n* technique of using the fingers in playing a musical instrument
▸ **fingerboard** *n* part of a stringed instrument on which the fingers are placed
▸ **fingerprint** *n* **1** impression of the ridges on the tip of the finger ▷ *v* **2** take the fingerprints of (someone)
finial *n archit* ornament at the apex of a gable or spire
finicky *adj* **1** excessively particular, fussy **2** overelaborate
finis *n Latin* end: used at the end of a book
finish Ⓣ *v* **1** bring to an end, stop **2** use up **3** bring to a desired or completed condition **4** put a surface texture on (wood, cloth, or metal) **5** defeat or destroy ▷ *n* **6** end, last part **7** death or defeat **8** surface texture
finite Ⓣ [**fine**-ite] *adj* having limits in space, time, or size

f

THESAURUS

cash, pocketbook (*informal*), wherewithal, affairs, assets, funds
financial *adj* = **economic**, fiscal, monetary • *financial difficulties*
find *v* **1** = **discover**, locate, unearth, come across, track down, turn up, scare up (*informal*), descry, espy, ferret out • *I can't find that computer file.* OPPOSITE: lose **2** = **realize**, learn, discover, detect, become aware • *We found that we had a lot in common.* ▷ **find a solution to** *See* **resolve** ▷ **find fault** *See* **complain, put down** ▷ **find fault with** *See* **criticize** ▷ **find out** = **learn**, note, discover, realize, detect, observe, perceive; = **detect**, catch, reveal, expose, disclose, uncover, unmask ▷ **find unacceptable** *See* **disapprove** ▸ *n* **3** = **discovery**, catch, acquisition, asset, bargain, good buy
finding *See* **decision, verdict**
fine[1] *adj* **1** = **excellent**, beautiful, outstanding, magnificent, splendid, admirable • *fine clothes* **2** = **delicate**, slender, powdery • *powder with very fine particles* **3** = **thin**, light, sheer, lightweight, flimsy, diaphanous, gauzy, gossamer • *fine fabrics* **4** = **subtle**, sensitive, keen, precise, refined, fastidious • *the fine details* **5** = **sunny**, clear, fair, dry, bright, pleasant, balmy, cloudless, clement **6** = **satisfactory**, good, acceptable, suitable, convenient, all right, O.K. *or* okay (*informal*)
See also: **narrow, sound**
fine[2] *n* **1** = **penalty**, punishment, forfeit, damages ▸ *v* **2** = **penalize**, punish
finery *n* = **splendour**, gear (*informal*), frippery, glad rags (*informal*), ornaments, showiness, Sunday best, trappings, trinkets
finesse *n* = **skill**, craft, diplomacy, discretion, delicacy, sophistication, tact, subtlety, adeptness, adroitness, savoir-faire
finger *v* = **touch**, feel, handle, manipulate, maul, paw (*informal*), fiddle with (*informal*), toy with
finish *v* **1** = **complete**, end, close, conclude, finalize • *I have to finish a report.* OPPOSITE: start **2** = **consume**, eat, empty, exhaust, devour, dispose of, use up **3** = **destroy**, defeat, overcome, rout, ruin, exterminate, bring down, knock down, dispose of, put an end to, put paid to **4** = **perfect**, refine, polish **5** = **coat**, stain, polish, wax, texture, veneer, lacquer, gild ▸ *n* **6** = **end**, close, conclusion, finale, completion, ending • *to see it through to the finish* OPPOSITE: start **7** = **surface**, grain, shine, polish, texture, lustre • *a glossy finish* **8** = **defeat**, end, death, ruin, annihilation, curtains (*informal*), end of the road
See also: **cease, stop**
finished *adj* **1** = **polished**, professional, accomplished, refined, perfected **2** = **over**, through, complete, closed, done, ended, finalized **3** = **spent**, empty, done, drained, exhausted, used up **4** = **ruined**, through, lost, doomed, defeated, done for (*informal*), undone, wiped out
finite *adj* = **limited**, restricted, bounded, circumscribed, delimited, demarcated

DICTIONARY

Finn *n* native of Finland
▸ **Finnish** *adj* **1** of Finland ▹ *n* **2** official language of Finland
Finzi *n* **Gerald**. 1901–56, British composer. His works include the cantata *Dies Natalis* (1940)
fiord *n* same as **fjord**
fir *n* pyramid-shaped tree with needle-like leaves and erect cones
fire Ⓣ *n* **1** state of combustion producing heat, flames, and smoke **2** uncontrolled destructive burning **3** burning coal or wood, or a gas or electric device, used to heat a room **4** shooting of guns **5** intense passion, ardour ▹ *v* **6** operate (a weapon) so that a bullet or missile is released **7** *informal* dismiss from employment **8** excite **9** bake (ceramics etc.) in a kiln
▸ **firearm** *n* rifle, pistol, or shotgun
▸ **firebrand** *n* person who causes unrest
▸ **firebreak** *n* strip of cleared land to stop the advance of a fire
▸ **firebug** *n informal* person who deliberately starts fires
▸ **firedamp** *n* explosive gas, composed mainly of methane, formed in mines
▸ **fire department** organized body of people whose job it is to put out fires
▸ **fire drill** rehearsal of procedures for escape from a fire
▸ **fire engine** vehicle with apparatus for extinguishing fires
▸ **fire escape** metal staircase or ladder down the outside of a building for escape in the event of fire
▸ **firefly** *n* beetle that glows in the dark
▸ **fireguard** *n* protective grating in front of a fire
▸ **fire hall** building housing fire department
▸ **fire irons** tongs, poker, and shovel for tending a domestic fire
▸ **fireman** *n* member of a fire brigade
▸ **fireplace** *n* recess in a room for a fire
▸ **firepower** *n mil* amount a weapon or unit can fire
▸ **fire station** building where fire-fighting vehicles and equipment are stationed
▸ **firewall** *n computers* computer that prevents unauthorized access to a computer network from the internet
▸ **firework** *n* **1** device containing chemicals that is ignited to produce spectacular explosions and coloured sparks **fireworks** **2** show of fireworks **3** *informal* outburst of temper
▸ **firing squad** group of soldiers ordered to execute an offender by shooting
firkin *n* small cask
firm[1] Ⓣ *adj* **1** not soft or yielding **2** securely in position **3** definite **4** determined, resolute ▹ *adv* **5** in an unyielding manner: *hold firm* ▹ *v* **6** make or become firm **firmly** *adv* **firmness** *n*
firm[2] Ⓣ *n* business company
firmament *n lit* sky, heavens
first Ⓣ *adj* **1** earliest in time or order **2** graded or ranked above all others ▹ *n* **3** person or thing coming before all others **4** outset, beginning **5** first-class honours degree at university **6** lowest forward gear in a motor

THESAURUS

fire *n* **1 = flames**, blaze, combustion, inferno • *a ball of fire* **2 = bombardment**, hail, barrage, salvo, volley, flak, cannonade, fusillade, shelling, sniping **3 = passion**, spirit, intensity, excitement, enthusiasm, sparkle, eagerness, vigour, verve, ardour, fervour ▸ *v* **4 = shoot**, launch, explode, detonate, set off • *to fire a starter's pistol* **5** (*Informal*) **= dismiss**, sack (*informal*), discharge, lay off, make redundant • *She was fired yesterday*. **6 = inspire**, excite, stir, inflame, animate, galvanize, rouse, enliven, impassion
firebrand *n* **= rabble-rouser**, instigator, incendiary, agitator, demagogue, tub-thumper
fireworks *pl n* **1 = pyrotechnics**, illuminations **2 = rage**, storm, trouble, row, uproar, hysterics
firm[1] *adj* **1 = hard**, set, solid, stiff, rigid, compressed, congealed • *Freeze the ice cream until it is firm*. OPPOSITE: soft **2 = determined**, staunch, adamant, resolute, inflexible, unshakable • *The debating team needs a firm coach*. **3 = secure**, fast, tight, stable, steady, unshakable, embedded, fixed, immovable, rooted
See also: **positive, steadfast, strict, trusty**
firm[2] *n* **= company**, business, organization, corporation, enterprise • *a firm of builders*
firmly *adv* **1 = securely**, steadily, tightly, immovably, like a rock, unflinchingly, unshakably **2 = resolutely**, steadfastly, staunchly, unchangeably, unwaveringly
firmness *n* **1 = hardness**, resistance, stiffness, rigidity, inelasticity, inflexibility, solidity **2 = resolve**, resolution, constancy, inflexibility, staunchness, steadfastness
first *adj* **1 = earliest**, opening, original, initial, primeval • *the first moon landing* OPPOSITE: last **2 = foremost**, chief, prime, principal, leading • *our first responsibility* **3 = elementary**, key, primary, basic, fundamental, cardinal, rudimentary ▸ *adv* **4 = to begin with**, earlier, initially, beforehand, firstly • *You must do that first*. ▸ *n* ▹ **from the first = from the start**, from the beginning, from the

DICTIONARY

vehicle ▷ *adv* **7** before anything else **8** for the first time **firstly** *adv*
▶ **first aid** immediate medical assistance given in an emergency
▶ **first-class** *adj* **1** of the highest quality **2** excellent
▶ **first-hand** *adj, adv* (obtained) directly from the original source
▶ **first mate** *or* **first officer** officer of a merchant ship second in command to the captain
▶ **First Minister** premier of a Canadian province or territory or the Canadian prime minister
▶ **First Nations** Canadian aboriginal communities
▶ **First Peoples** Indian, Inuit, and Métis in Canada
▶ **first person** *grammar* category of verbs and pronouns used by a speaker to refer to himself or herself
▶ **first-rate** *adj* excellent
▶ **first-strike** *adj* (of a nuclear missile) for use in an opening attack to destroy enemy weapons
firth *n* narrow inlet of the sea
fiscal ⓣ *adj* of government finances, esp. taxes
Fischer *n* **Robert James**, known as *Bobby*. 1943–2008, US chess player; world champion 1972–75
Fischer-Dieskau *n* **Dietrich**. born 1925, German baritone, noted particularly for his interpretation of Schubert's song cycles
fish *n, pl* **fish, fishes 1** cold-blooded vertebrate with gills, that lives in water **2** its flesh as food ▷ *v* **3** try to catch fish **4** try to catch fish in (a specified place) **5** (foll. by *for*) grope for and find with difficulty **6** (foll. by *for*) seek indirectly
▶ **fisherman** *n* person who catches fish for a living or for pleasure
▶ **fishery** *n, pl* **-eries** area of the sea used for fishing
▶ **fishy** *adj* **1** of or like fish **2** *informal* suspicious or questionable
▶ **fish finger** oblong piece of fish covered in breadcrumbs
▶ **fish meal** dried ground fish used as animal feed or fertilizer
▶ **fishmonger** *n Brit* seller of fish
▶ **fishnet** *n* open mesh fabric resembling netting
▶ **fishwife** *n* coarse scolding woman
fishplate *n* metal plate joining one rail to the next on a track
fission *n* **1** splitting **2** *biol* asexual reproduction involving a division into two or more equal parts **3** splitting of an atomic nucleus with the release of a large amount of energy **fissionable** *adj*
▶ **fissile** *adj* **1** capable of undergoing nuclear fission **2** tending to split
fissure ⓣ [**fish**-er] *n* long narrow cleft or crack
fist *n* clenched hand
▶ **fisticuffs** *pl n* fighting with the fists
fistula [**fist**-yew-la] *n* long narrow ulcer
fit[1] ⓣ *v* **fitting, fitted 1** be appropriate or suitable for **2** be of the correct size or shape (for) **3** adjust so as to make appropriate **4** try (clothes) on and note any adjustments needed **5** make competent or ready **6** correspond with the facts or circumstances ▷ *adj* **7** appropriate **8** in good health **9** worthy or deserving ▷ *n* **10** way in which something fits **fitness** *n*
▶ **fitter** *n* **1** person skilled in the installation and adjustment of machinery **2** person who fits garments
▶ **fitting** *adj* **1** appropriate, suitable ▷ *n* **2** accessory or part **3** trying on of clothes for

THESAURUS

commencement, from the inception, from the introduction, from the outset, from the starting point
first-class *adj* = **excellent**, prime, premium, exceptional, world-class, outstanding, superb, exemplary, marvellous, blue-chip, five-star, top-notch (*informal*), superlative, first-rate, A1 *or* A-one (*informal*), tiptop, twenty-four carat *or* 24-carat, tops (*slang*), second to none OPPOSITE: terrible
first-hand *See* **direct**
first-rate *adj* = **excellent**, exceptional, outstanding, superb, marvellous, splendid, first-class • *They were dealing with a first-rate professional.*
See also: **able, prime, prize, select, superior**
fiscal *See* **financial**
fishy *adj* **1** (*Informal*) = **suspicious**, suspect, odd, unlikely, funny (*informal*), questionable, dubious, implausible **2** = **fishlike**, piscatorial, piscatory, piscine
fissure *n* = **crack**, split, fault, rift, pothole, cleft, crevice • *There was a rumbling, and a fissure opened up.*
See also: **abyss, leak**
fit[1] *v* **1** = **match**, go, belong, correspond, dovetail • *made to fit a child* **2** = **position**, place, arrange • *a fitted carpet* **3** = **prepare**, arm, equip, fit out, provide **4** = **adapt**, shape, adjust, modify, alter, arrange, customize ▷ **fit out** *See* **equip** ▶ *adj* **5** = **healthy**, well, trim, robust, buff (*informal*), in good condition • *a reasonably fit person* OPPOSITE: unfit **6** = **appropriate**, right, correct, proper, suitable, fitting, apt, becoming, seemly

DICTIONARY

size **fittings 4** furnishings and accessories in a building
▶ **fitment** *n* detachable part of the furnishings of a room
▶ **fit in** *v* **1** give a place or time to **2** belong or conform
▶ **fit out** *v* provide with the necessary equipment
fit² Ⓣ *n* **1** sudden attack or convulsion, such as an epileptic seizure **2** sudden short burst or spell
fitful Ⓣ *adj* occurring in irregular spells
fitfully *adv*
Fittipaldi *n* **Emerson.** born 1946, Brazilian motor-racing driver: world champion in 1972 and 1974
Fitzgerald *n* **Ella.** 1918–96, US jazz singer, noted esp. for her vocal range and scat singing
Fitzsimmons *n* **Bob.** 1862–1917, New Zealand boxer, born in England: world middleweight (1891–97), heavyweight (1897–99), and light-heavyweight (1903–05) champion
five *adj, n* one more than four
▶ **fives** *n* ball game resembling squash but played with bats or the hands
fix Ⓣ *v* **1** make or become firm, stable, or secure **2** repair **3** place permanently **4** settle definitely **5** direct (the eyes etc.) steadily **6** *informal* unfairly influence the outcome of ▷ *n* **7** *informal* difficult situation **8** ascertaining of the position of a ship by radar etc. **9** *slang* injection of a narcotic drug **fixed** *adj*
▶ **fixedly** [**fix**-id-lee] *adv* steadily
▶ **fixation** *n* preoccupation, obsession
▶ **fixated** *adj* obsessed
▶ **fixative** *n* liquid used to preserve or hold things in place
▶ **fixer** *n* **1** solution used to make a photographic image permanent **2** *slang* person who arranges things
▶ **fixture** *n* **1** permanently fitted piece of household equipment **2** person whose presence seems permanent **3** sports match or the date fixed for it
▶ **fix up** *v* **1** arrange **2** provide (with)
fizz Ⓣ *v* **1** give off small bubbles **2** make a hissing or bubbling noise ▷ *n* **3** hissing or bubbling noise **4** releasing of small bubbles of gas by a liquid **5** effervescent drink **fizzy** *adj* **fizziness** *n*
fizzle *v* make a weak hissing or bubbling sound
▶ **fizzle out** *v informal* come to nothing, fail
fjord [fee-**ord**] *n* long narrow inlet of the sea between cliffs, esp. in Norway
flab *n informal* unsightly body fat
flabbergast *v* amaze utterly
flabby Ⓣ *adj* **-bier**, **-biest 1** loose or limp **2** having flabby flesh **flabbiness** *n*
flaccid [**flas**-sid] *adj* soft and limp
flaccidity *n*
flag¹ Ⓣ *n* **1** piece of cloth attached to a pole as an emblem or signal ▷ *v* **flagging, flagged 2** mark with a flag or sticker **3** (often foll. by

THESAURUS

See also: **burst, sound**
fit² *n* **1 = seizure**, attack, bout, spasm, convulsion, paroxysm **2 = outbreak**, burst, spell, bout, outburst
fitful *adj* **= irregular**, uneven, sporadic, intermittent, disturbed, desultory, broken, inconstant, spasmodic
fitness *n* **1 = appropriateness**, readiness, eligibility, competence, suitability, aptness, propriety **2 = health**, strength, vigour, good condition, good health, robustness
fitting *adj* **1 = appropriate**, right, correct, proper, suitable • *a fitting thank-you speech* ▶ *n* **2 = accessory**, part, unit, component, attachment • *fixtures and fittings*
fix *v* **1 = fasten**, stick, secure, bind, attach • *fixed to the wall* **2 = repair**, correct, mend, patch up • *They fixed the broken window.* **3 = place**, set, plant, position, establish, locate, install, implant, embed **4 = decide**, set, determine, settle, establish, arrange, specify, agree on, arrive at **5 = focus**, direct **6** (*Informal*) **= manipulate**, influence, rig ▷ **fix up = arrange**, plan, settle, fix, organize, agree on, sort out; (often with *with*) **= provide**, arrange for, bring about, lay on ▶ *n* **7** (*informal*) **= difficulty**, mess, predicament, quandary • *in a bit of a fix*
See also: **confirm, corrupt, glue, hang, hole, jam, limit**
fixation *n* **= preoccupation**, thing (*informal*), complex, obsession, mania, hang-up (*informal*), *idée fixe* (*French*), infatuation
fixed *adj* **1 = permanent**, set, secure, established, rigid, immovable, rooted **2 = intent**, steady, resolute, unwavering **3 = agreed**, planned, established, definite, arranged, decided, resolved, settled
fixture *See* **attachment**
fizz *v* **= bubble**, sparkle, fizzle, froth, sputter, hiss, effervesce
fizzy *adj* **= bubbly**, sparkling, effervescent, bubbling, carbonated, gassy
flabbergasted *adj* **= astonished**, speechless, staggered, overwhelmed, dumbfounded, amazed, astounded, lost for words, stunned
flabby *adj* **= limp**, slack, floppy, sagging • *a flabby stomach* OPPOSITE: taut
flag¹ *n* **1 = banner**, standard, pennant,

DICTIONARY

down) signal (a vehicle) to stop by waving the arm
▶ **flagpole** *or* **flagstaff** *n* pole for a flag
▶ **flagship** *n* **1** admiral's ship **2** most important product of an organization
flag² Ⓣ *v* **flagging, flagged** lose enthusiasm or vigour
flag³, flagstone Ⓣ *n* flat paving-stone
▶ **flagged** *adj* paved with flagstones
flagellate [**flaj**-a-late] *v* whip **flagellation** *n*
▶ **flagellant** *n* person who whips himself, esp. in religious penance
flageolet [flaj-a-**let**] *n* small instrument like a recorder
flagon *n* **1** wide bottle for wine or cider **2** narrow-necked jug for liquid
flagrant Ⓣ [**flayg**-rant] *adj* openly outrageous **flagrantly** *adv* **flagrancy** *n*
flail Ⓣ *v* **1** wave about wildly **2** beat or thrash ▷ *n* **3** tool formerly used for threshing grain by hand
flair Ⓣ *n* **1** natural ability **2** stylishness
flak Ⓣ *n* **1** anti-aircraft fire **2** *informal* adverse criticism
flake Ⓣ *n* **1** small thin piece, esp. chipped off something ▷ *v* **2** peel off in flakes **flaky** *adj*
▶ **flake out** *v informal* collapse or fall asleep from exhaustion
flambé [**flahm**-bay] *v* **flambéing, flambéed** cook or serve (food) in flaming brandy
flamboyant Ⓣ *adj* **1** very bright and showy **2** behaving in a very noticeable, extravagant way **flamboyance** *n*
flame Ⓣ *n* **1** luminous burning gas coming from burning material ▷ *v* **2** burn brightly **3** become bright red
▶ **old flame** *informal* former sweetheart
flamenco *n, pl* **-cos 1** rhythmical Spanish dance accompanied by a guitar and vocalist **2** music for this dance
flamingo *n, pl* **-gos, -goes** large pink wading bird with a long neck and legs
flammable *adj* easily set on fire
flammability *n*
Flamsteed *n* **John**. 1646–1719, English astronomer: the first Astronomer Royal and first director of the Royal Observatory, Greenwich (1675). He increased the accuracy of existing stellar catalogues, greatly aiding navigation
flan *n* **1** egg custard with caramelized topping **2** *Brit* open sweet or savoury tart
flange *n* projecting rim or collar **flanged** *adj*
flank Ⓣ *n* **1** part of the side between the hips and ribs **2** side of a body of troops ▷ *v* **3** be at or move along the side of
flannel *n* **1** soft woollen fabric for clothing **2** small piece of cloth for washing the face and hands **3** *informal* evasive talk **flannels** **4** trousers made of flannel ▷ *v* **-nelling, -nelled 5** *informal* talk evasively
▶ **flannelette** *n* cotton imitation of flannel
flap Ⓣ *v* **flapping, flapped 1** move back and forwards or up and down ▷ *n* **2** action or sound of flapping **3** piece of something attached by one edge only **4** *informal* state of excitement or panic
flapjack *n* thin pancake
flare Ⓣ *v* **1** blaze with a sudden unsteady flame **2** *informal* (of temper, violence, or trouble) break out suddenly **3** (of a skirt or trousers) become wider towards the hem ▷ *n* **4** sudden unsteady flame **5** signal light **flares 6** flared trousers

THESAURUS

streamer, colours, ensign, pennon ▶ *v* **2 = mark**, note, indicate, label **3** (sometimes with *down*) **= hail**, warn, wave, signal
flag² *v* **= weaken**, fade, wane, sag, languish, weary, abate, wilt, droop, peter out
flagging *adj* **= fading**, declining, deteriorating, faltering, waning, weakening, wilting
flagrant *adj* **= outrageous**, brazen, scandalous, blatant, shameless, heinous, glaring, barefaced
flagstone *n* **= paving stone**, block, flag, slab
flail *v* **= thrash**, beat, windmill, thresh
flair *n* **1 = ability**, feel, gift, talent, faculty, mastery, genius, knack, aptitude **2 = style**, taste, dash, chic, elegance, panache, discernment, stylishness
flak *See* **criticism**
flake *n* **1 = wafer**, scale, layer, shaving, sliver, peeling ▶ *v* **2 = blister**, chip, peel *or* peel off ▷ **flake out = collapse**, faint, keel over, pass out
flamboyant *adj* **1 = extravagant**, elaborate, theatrical, showy, ornate, swashbuckling, dashing, florid, ostentatious **2 = colourful**, brilliant, glamorous, glitzy (*slang*), dazzling
flame *n* **1 = fire**, light, blaze, brightness **2** (*Informal*) **= sweetheart**, lover, girlfriend, boyfriend, beau, heart-throb (*Brit*) ▶ *v* **3 = burn**, blaze, shine, flash, flare, glow, glare
flames *See* **fire**
flaming *adj* **= burning**, red-hot, fiery, ablaze, glowing, raging, blazing
flank *n* **1 = side**, hip, thigh, loin **2 = wing**, side
flap *v* **1 = flutter**, beat, wave, shake, thrash, vibrate, flail, wag ▶ *n* **2 = flutter**, beating, swish, shaking, swinging, waving
flare *v* **1 = blaze**, glare, flicker, burn up **2 = widen**, broaden, spread out ▷ **flare up = lose one's temper**, explode, blow one's

DICTIONARY

▸ **flared** *adj* (of a skirt or trousers) becoming wider towards the hem

flash Ⓣ *n* **1** sudden burst of light or flame **2** sudden occurrence (of intuition or emotion) **3** very short time **4** brief unscheduled news announcement **5** *photog* small bulb that produces an intense flash of light ▷ *v* **6** (cause to) burst into flame **7** (cause to) emit light suddenly or intermittently **8** move very fast **9** come rapidly (to mind or view) **10** *informal* display ostentatiously **11** *slang* expose oneself indecently ▷ *adj* **12** Also **flashy** vulgarly showy

▸ **flasher** *n slang* man who exposes himself indecently

▸ **flashing** *n* watertight material used to cover joins in a roof

▸ **flashback** *n* scene in a book, play, or film, that shows earlier events

▸ **flash flood** sudden short-lived flood

▸ **flashlight** *n* small portable battery-powered lamp

▸ **flash point 1** critical point beyond which a situation will inevitably erupt into violence **2** lowest temperature at which vapour given off by a liquid can ignite

flask *n* **1** vacuum flask **2** flat bottle for carrying alcoholic drink in the pocket **3** narrow-necked bottle

flat[1] Ⓣ *adj* **flatter, flattest 1** level and horizontal **2** even, smooth **3** (of a tire) deflated **4** outright **5** fixed **6** without variation or emotion **7** (of a battery) with no electrical charge **8** (of a drink) no longer fizzy **9** *music* below the true pitch ▷ *adv* **10** in or into a flat position **11** exactly **12** completely, absolutely **13** *music* too low in pitch ▷ *n* **14** flat surface **15** *music* symbol lowering the pitch of a note by a semitone **16** punctured automobile tire **17** level ground **18** mudbank exposed at low tide **flatly** *adv* **flatness** *n* **flatten** *v*

▸ **flat out** with maximum speed or effort

▸ **flatfish** *n* sea fish, such as the sole, which has a flat body

▸ **flat racing** horse racing over level ground with no jumps

▸ **flatscreen** *n* slim lightweight TV set or computer with a flat screen

flat[2] *n Brit* apartment

flatter Ⓣ *v* **1** praise insincerely **2** show to advantage **3** make (a person) appear more attractive in a picture than in reality **flatterer** *n* **flattery** *n*

flatulent *adj* suffering from, or caused by, excess gas in the intestines **flatulence** *n*

Flaubert *n* **Gustave**. 1821–80, French novelist and short-story writer, regarded as a leader of the 19th-century naturalist school. His most famous novel, *Madame Bovary* (1857), for which he was prosecuted (and acquitted) on charges of immorality, and *L'Éducation sentimentale* (1869) deal with the conflict of romantic attitudes and bourgeois society. His other major works include *Salammbô* (1862), *La Tentation de Saint Antoine* (1874), and *Trois contes* (1877)

flaunt Ⓣ *v* display (oneself or one's possessions) arrogantly

flautist [**flaw**-tist] *n* flute player

THESAURUS

top (*informal*), boil over, fly off the handle (*informal*), throw a tantrum ▸ *n* **3 = flame**, blaze, burst, flash, glare, flicker

flash *n* **1 = flare**, burst, sparkle • *a flash of lightning* **2 = moment**, second, instant, jiffy (*informal*), split second, trice, twinkling of an eye ▸ *v* **3 = flare**, sparkle, glitter, twinkle, glint • *They signalled by flashing a light.* **4 = speed**, shoot, race, fly, streak, whistle, dash, zoom, dart **5 = show**, display, expose, exhibit, flourish, flaunt

See also: **minute**

flashy *adj* **= showy**, flamboyant, tacky (*informal*), garish • *flashy clothes* OPPOSITE: modest

See also: **bold, gaudy, loud, ostentatious, tasteless, vulgar**

flat *adj* **1 = level**, smooth, horizontal, unbroken • *a flat surface* OPPOSITE: uneven **2 = dull**, weak, boring, monotonous, insipid • *a dreadfully flat speech* **3 = absolute**, positive, explicit, downright, unequivocal, unqualified, categorical, out-and-out **4 = punctured**, burst, empty, collapsed, blown out, deflated ▸ *adv* **5 = completely**, exactly, absolutely, precisely, utterly, categorically, point blank ▷ **flat out = at full speed**, all out, at full tilt, for all one is worth

See also: **even, stale**

flatly *adv* **= absolutely**, completely, positively, categorically, unhesitatingly

flatness *n* **1 = evenness**, uniformity, smoothness **2 = dullness**, monotony, tedium

flatten *v* **= level**, squash, trample, compress, raze, even out, iron out, smooth off

flatter *v* **1 = compliment**, fawn • *flattering remarks* **2 = suit**, enhance, set off • *clothes that flatter your figure*

See also: **humour**

flattering *adj* **1 = becoming**, kind, effective, well-chosen, enhancing **2 = ingratiating**, complimentary, fulsome, adulatory, fawning, laudatory

flattery *n* **= fawning**, adulation • *susceptible to flattery*

flaunt *v* **= show off**, sport (*informal*), display,

DICTIONARY

flavour Ⓣ *n* **1** distinctive taste **2** distinctive characteristic or quality ▷ *v* **3** give flavour to **flavourless** *adj*
▸ **flavouring** *n* substance used to flavour food
flaw Ⓣ *n* **1** imperfection or blemish **2** mistake that makes a plan or argument invalid **flawed** *adj* **flawless** *adj*
flax *n* **1** plant grown for its stem fibres and seeds **2** its fibres, spun into linen thread
▸ **flaxen** *adj* (of hair) pale yellow
flay *v* **1** strip the skin off, esp. by whipping **2** criticize severely
flea *n* small wingless jumping bloodsucking insect
▸ **flea market** market for cheap goods
▸ **fleapit** *n informal* shabby cinema or theatre
fleck *n* **1** small mark, streak, or speck ▷ *v* **2** speckle
fled *v* past of **flee**
fledged *adj* **1** (of young birds) able to fly **2** (of people) fully trained
▸ **fledgling** *or* **fledgeling** *n* **1** young bird ▷ *adj* **2** new, inexperienced
flee Ⓣ *v* **fleeing, fled** run away (from)
fleece Ⓣ *n* **1** sheep's coat of wool **2** sheepskin used as a lining for coats etc. ▷ *v* **3** defraud or overcharge
▸ **fleecy** *adj* made of or like fleece
fleet[1] Ⓣ *n* **1** number of warships organized as a unit **2** number of vehicles under the same ownership
fleet[2] *adj* swift in movement
▸ **fleeting** *adj* rapid and soon passing **fleetingly** *adv*
Fleming *n* **1** Sir **Alexander**. 1881–1955, Scottish bacteriologist: discovered lysozyme (1922) and penicillin (1928): shared the Nobel prize for physiology or medicine in 1945 **2 Ian** (**Lancaster**). 1908–64, English author of spy novels; creator of the secret agent James Bond **3** Sir **Sandford**. 1827–1915, Canadian civil engineer, born in Scotland. Chief engineer of the Intercolonial and Canadian Pacific railways; founded the Royal Canadian Institute (1849); advocate of standard time zones; designer of Canada's first stamp (1851)
Flemish *n* **1** one of two official languages of Belgium ▷ *adj* **2** of Flanders, in Belgium
flesh Ⓣ *n* **1** soft part of a human or animal body **2** *informal* excess fat **3** meat of animals as opposed to fish or fowl **4** thick soft part of a fruit or vegetable **5** human body as opposed to the soul ▷ *adj* **6** yellowish-pink
▸ **in the flesh** in person, actually present
▸ **one's own flesh and blood** one's family
▸ **fleshly** *adj* **1** carnal **2** worldly
▸ **fleshy** *adj* **1** plump **2** like flesh
▸ **flesh wound** wound affecting only superficial tissue
fleur-de-lis, fleur-de-lys [flur-de-**lee**] *n, pl* **fleurs-de-lis, fleurs-de-lys** heraldic lily with three petals
Fleury *n* **André Hercule de**. 1653–1743, French cardinal and statesman: Louis XV's chief adviser and virtual ruler of France (1726–43)
flew *v* past tense of **fly**[1]
flex *v* **1** bend ▷ *n* **2** *Brit* electric cord
▸ **flexible** *adj* **1** easily bent **2** adaptable **flexibly** *adv* **flexibility** *n*
▸ **flexitime** *n* system permitting variation in starting and finishing times of work
flibbertigibbet *n* flighty gossiping person
flick Ⓣ *v* **1** touch or strike lightly ▷ *n* **2** tap or quick stroke **flicks 3** *slang* the cinema
▸ **flick knife** knife with a spring-loaded blade which shoots out when a button is pressed
▸ **flick through** *v* look at (a book or magazine) quickly or idly

f

THESAURUS

exhibit, parade, flourish, brandish, flash around
flavour *n* **1 = taste**, smack, aroma, relish, seasoning, zest, flavouring, piquancy, savour, tang **2 = quality**, feel, character, style, feeling, tone, essence, tinge ▸ *v* **3 = season**, spice, infuse, imbue, ginger up, leaven
See also: **taste**
flaw *n* **= imperfection**, defect, fault, blemish • *a flaw in his argument*
See also: **hole, weakness**
flawed *adj* **= damaged**, faulty, defective, erroneous, imperfect, unsound, blemished
flawless *adj* **= perfect**, spotless, impeccable, unblemished, faultless, unsullied
flee *v* **= run away**, leave, fly, escape, bolt, take flight • *to flee the country*
fleece *See* **cheat, coat**
fleet *n* **= navy**, flotilla, armada, task force
fleeting *adj* **= momentary**, brief, temporary, passing, short-lived, transient, ephemeral, transitory
flesh *n* **1 = meat**, weight, fat, tissue, brawn **2 = human nature**, carnality, flesh and blood ▷ **one's own flesh and blood = family**, blood, kin, kinsfolk, kith and kin, relations, relatives
flexibility *n* **= adaptability**, give (*informal*), resilience, elasticity, adjustability, pliability, pliancy, springiness
flexible *adj* **1 = supple**, elastic, lithe, pliable • *flexible wire* **2 = adaptable**, open, discretionary • *flexible working hours*
See also: **soft**
flick *v* **= strike**, hit, touch, tap, flip, dab ▷ **flick through = browse**, skip, thumb, skim, flip through, glance at

DICTIONARY

flicker Ⓣ *v* **1** shine unsteadily or intermittently **2** move quickly to and fro ▷ *n* **3** unsteady brief light **4** brief faint indication
flier *n* see **fly**[1]
flight[1] Ⓣ *n* **1** act or manner of flying through the air **2** journey by air **3** group of birds or aircraft flying together **4** aircraft flying on a scheduled journey **5** set of stairs between two landings **6** stabilizing feathers or plastic fins on an arrow or dart
▶ **flightless** *adj* (of certain birds or insects) unable to fly
▶ **flight deck 1** crew compartment in an airliner **2** runway deck on an aircraft carrier
▶ **flight recorder** electronic device in an aircraft storing information about its flight
flight[2] Ⓣ *n* act of running away
flighty *adj* **flightier**, **flightiest** frivolous and fickle
flimsy Ⓣ *adj* **-sier**, **-siest 1** not strong or substantial **2** thin **3** unconvincing, weak
flimsily *adv* **flimsiness** *n*
flinch Ⓣ *v* draw back or wince, as from pain
▶ **flinch from** *v* shrink from, avoid
fling Ⓣ *v* **flinging**, **flung 1** throw, send, or move forcefully or hurriedly ▷ *n* **2** spell of self-indulgent enjoyment **3** brief romantic or sexual relationship
▶ **fling oneself into** (start to) do with great vigour
flint *n* **1** hard grey stone **2** piece of this **3** small piece of an iron alloy producing a spark when struck, as in a cigarette lighter
▶ **flinty** *adj* **1** cruel **2** of or like flint
flip Ⓣ *v* **flipping**, **flipped 1** flick **2** turn (something) over **3** *slang* fly into an emotional state (Also **flip one's lid**) ▷ *n* **4** snap or tap **5** alcoholic drink containing beaten egg ▷ *adj* **6** *informal* flippant
▶ **flipper** *n* **1** limb of a sea animal adapted for swimming **2** one of a pair of paddle-like rubber devices worn on the feet to help in swimming
▶ **flip-flop** *n* rubber-soled sandal held on by a thong between the big toe and the next toe
▶ **flip side** less important side of a record
▶ **flip through** *v* look at (a book or magazine) quickly or idly
flippant Ⓣ *adj* treating serious things lightly **flippantly** *adv* **flippancy** *n*
flirt Ⓣ *v* **1** behave amorously without emotional commitment **2** consider lightly, toy (with) ▷ *n* **3** person who flirts **flirtation** *n* **flirtatious** *adj*
flit Ⓣ *v* **flitting**, **flitted 1** move lightly and rapidly **2** *informal* depart hurriedly and secretly ▷ *n* **3** act of flitting
flitch *n* side of bacon
flitter *v, n* same as **flutter**
float Ⓣ *v* **1** rest on the surface of liquid **2** move lightly and freely **3** move about aimlessly **4** launch (a company) **5** offer for sale on the stock market **6** allow (a currency) to fluctuate against other currencies ▷ *n* **7** inflatable object used to help people to swim **8** indicator on a fishing line that moves when a fish bites **9** small delivery vehicle **10** motor vehicle carrying a tableau in a parade **11** sum of money used for minor expenses or to provide change
▶ **floating** *adj* **1** moving about, changing: *floating population* **2** (of a voter) not committed to one party
flocculent *adj* like tufts of wool

THESAURUS

flicker *v* **1 = twinkle**, flash, flare, sparkle, shimmer, glimmer, gutter **2 = flutter**, waver, vibrate, quiver ▶ *n* **3 = glimmer**, spark, flash, flare, gleam **4 = trace**, spark, breath, glimmer, iota
flight[1] *n* **1 = journey**, trip, voyage **2 = aviation**, aeronautics, flying **3 = flock**, unit, cloud, formation, swarm, squadron
flight[2] *n* **= escape**, exit, retreat, departure, getaway, exodus, fleeing, running away
flimsy *adj* **1 = fragile**, shaky, delicate, makeshift, frail, rickety, insubstantial **2 = thin**, light, transparent, sheer, gauzy, gossamer **3 = unconvincing**, poor, weak, inadequate, pathetic, lousy (*slang*), unsatisfactory, feeble, implausible
flinch *v* **= wince**, start, shrink, cringe • *The sharp pain made me flinch.*
fling *v* **1 = throw**, cast, toss, propel, hurl, catapult, sling, heave ▶ *n* **2 = binge** (*informal*), party, bash, good time, spree
flip *verb, n* **= toss**, throw, snap, spin, flick
flippancy *n* **= frivolity**, irreverence, impertinence, levity, pertness, sauciness
flippant *adj* **= frivolous**, disrespectful, cheeky, superficial, irreverent, glib, impertinent, offhand
flirt *v* **1 = lead on**, hit on (*slang*), make advances, make eyes at, philander **2** (usually with *with*) **= toy with**, consider, entertain, dabble in, expose oneself to, give a thought to, play with, trifle with ▶ *n* **3 = tease**, coquette, heart-breaker, hussy, philanderer
flirtatious *adj* **= teasing**, provocative, coy, amorous, come-hither, coquettish, enticing, flirty, sportive
flit *See* **fly**
float *v* **1 = stay afloat**, drift, bob, be on the surface, lie on the surface • *leaves floating on the river* OPPOSITE: sink **2 = glide**, hang, hover, drift • *floating on the breeze* **3 = launch**, promote, get going, set up
floating *adj* **1 = buoyant**, afloat, sailing,

DICTIONARY

flock[1] ⊕ *n* **1** number of animals of one kind together **2** large group of people **3** *Christianity* congregation ▷ *v* **4** gather in a crowd
flock[2] *n* **1** very small tufts of wool giving a raised pattern on wallpaper **2** wool or cotton waste used as stuffing
floe *n* sheet of floating ice
flog ⊕ *v* **flogging, flogged 1** beat with a whip, stick, etc. **2** *slang* sell **flogging** *n*
flood ⊕ *n* **1** overflow of water onto a normally dry area **2** large amount of water **3** rising of the tide ▷ *v* **4** cover or become covered with water **5** fill to overflowing **6** come in large numbers or quantities
▸ **floodgate** *n* gate used to control the flow of water
▸ **floodlight** *n* **1** lamp that casts a broad intense beam of light ▷ *v* **-lighting, -lit 2** illuminate by floodlight
floor ⊕ *n* **1** lower surface of a room **2** level of a building **3** flat bottom surface **4** (right to speak in) a legislative hall ▷ *v* **5** *informal* disconcert or defeat **6** knock down
▸ **floored** *adj* covered with a floor
▸ **flooring** *n* material for floors
▸ **floor show** entertainment in a nightclub
floozy *n, pl* **-zies** *slang* disreputable woman
flop ⊕ *v* **flopping, flopped 1** bend, fall, or collapse loosely or carelessly **2** *informal* fail ▷ *n* **3** flopping movement **4** *informal* failure
▸ **floppy** *adj* hanging downwards, loose **floppiness** *n*
▸ **floppy disk** *computers* flexible magnetic disk that stores information
flora *n* plants of a given time or place
▸ **floral** *adj* consisting of or decorated with flowers
floret [**flaw**-ret] *n* small flower forming part of a composite flower head
Florey *n* **Howard Walter**, Baron Florey. 1898–1968, British pathologist: shared the Nobel prize for physiology or medicine (1945) with E. B. Chain and Alexander Fleming for their work on penicillin
floribunda *n* type of rose whose flowers grow in large clusters
florid ⊕ *adj* **1** with a red or flushed complexion **2** ornate
florin *n* former British coin equivalent to ten pence
florist *n* seller of flowers
floss *n* fine silky fibres
flotation *n* launching or financing of a business enterprise
flotilla *n* **1** fleet of small ships **2** small fleet
Flotow *n* **Friedrich von**. 1812–83, German composer of operas, esp. *Martha* (1847)
flotsam ⊕ *n* floating wreckage
▸ **flotsam and jetsam 1** odds and ends **2** homeless or vagrant people
flounce[1] *v* **1** go with emphatic movements ▷ *n* **2** flouncing movement
flounce[2] *n* ornamental ruffle on a garment
flounder[1] ⊕ *v* **1** move with difficulty, as in mud **2** behave or speak in a bungling or hesitating manner
flounder[2] *n* edible flatfish
flour *n* **1** powder made by grinding grain, esp. wheat ▷ *v* **2** sprinkle with flour **floury** *adj* **flouriness** *n*
flourish ⊕ *v* **1** be active, successful, or widespread **2** be at the peak of development **3** wave (something) dramatically ▷ *n* **4** dramatic waving motion **5** ornamental curly line in writing **6** extravagant action or part **flourishing** *adj*

f

THESAURUS

buoyed up, swimming **2 = fluctuating**, free, variable, movable, unattached, wandering
flock *n* **1 = herd**, flight, colony, drove, gaggle, skein **2 = crowd**, company, group, host, mass, collection, gathering, herd, congregation ▸ *v* **3 = gather**, crowd, mass, collect, herd, converge, throng, huddle, congregate
flog *v* **= beat**, lash, whip, trounce, whack, scourge, thrash, flagellate, flay
flood *n* **1 = deluge**, spate, downpour, torrent • *Many people were drowned in the floods.* **2 = rush**, stream, spate, torrent • *a flood of angry letters* ▸ *v* **3 = immerse**, swamp, overflow, deluge, submerge • *The river flooded its banks.* **4 = engulf**, sweep, surge, overwhelm, swarm **5 = oversupply**, fill, choke, saturate, glut
See also: **flow, rash, wave**
floor *n* **1 = tier**, level, stage, story ▸ *v* **2 = knock down**, deck (*slang*), prostrate **3** (*Informal*) **= bewilder**, defeat, throw (*informal*), puzzle, baffle, stump, perplex, disconcert, confound, dumbfound
flop *v* **1 = fall**, drop, collapse, slump, sag, dangle, droop **2** (*Informal*) **= fail**, founder, fold (*informal*), misfire, come unstuck, fall flat, go belly-up (*slang*) ▸ *n* **3** (*Informal*) **= failure**, disaster, debacle, fiasco, washout (*informal*), nonstarter
floppy *adj* **= droopy**, loose, soft, limp, baggy, flaccid, pendulous, sagging
floral *adj* **= flowery**, flower-patterned
florid *adj* **1 = flushed**, blowsy, high-coloured, rubicund, ruddy **2 = flowery**, flamboyant, ornate, baroque, fussy, high-flown, overelaborate
flotsam *n* **= debris**, wreckage, junk, detritus, jetsam, odds and ends
flounder *v* **= fumble**, struggle, toss, stumble, thrash, grope
flourish *v* **1 = thrive**, boom, succeed,

DICTIONARY

flout Ⓣ [rhymes with **out**] *v* deliberately disobey (a rule, law, etc.)
flow Ⓣ *v* (of liquid) **1** move in a stream **2** (of blood or electricity) circulate **3** proceed smoothly **4** hang loosely **5** be abundant ▷ *n* **6** act, rate, or manner of flowing **7** continuous stream or discharge
▸ **flow chart** diagram showing a sequence of operations in a process
flower Ⓣ *n* **1** part of a plant that produces seeds **2** plant grown for its colourful flowers **3** best or finest part ▷ *v* **4** produce flowers, bloom **5** come to prime condition
▸ **in flower** with flowers open
▸ **flowered** *adj* decorated with a floral design
▸ **flowery** *adj* **1** decorated with a floral design **2** (of language or style) elaborate
▸ **flowerbed** *n* piece of ground for growing flowers on
flown *v* past participle of **fly**[1]
fl. oz. fluid ounce(s)
flu *n* short for **influenza**
fluctuate Ⓣ *v* change frequently and erratically **fluctuation** *n*
flue *n* passage or pipe for smoke or hot air
fluent Ⓣ *adj* **1** able to speak or write with ease **2** spoken or written with ease **fluently** *adv* **fluency** *n*
fluff Ⓣ *n* **1** soft fibres **2** down **3** *informal* mistake ▷ *v* **4** make or become soft and light **5** *informal* make a mistake **fluffy** *adj*
fluid Ⓣ *n* **1** liquid ▷ *adj* **2** able to flow or change shape easily **fluidity** *n*
▸ **fluid ounce** one twentieth of a pint
fluke[1] Ⓣ *n* accidental stroke of luck **fluky** *adj*
fluke[2] *n* **1** flat triangular point of an anchor **2** lobe of a whale's tail
fluke[3] *n* parasitic worm
flume *n* narrow sloping channel for water
flummox *v* perplex or bewilder
flung *v* past of **fling**
flunk Ⓣ *v informal* fail
flunky, flunkey *n, pl* **flunkies, flunkeys** **1** manservant who wears a livery **2** servile person
fluorescence *n* emission of light from a substance bombarded by particles, such as electrons, or by radiation **fluorescent** *adj*
▸ **fluoresce** *v* exhibit fluorescence
fluoride *n* compound containing fluorine
▸ **fluoridate** *v* add fluoride to (water) as protection against tooth decay **fluoridation** *n*
fluorine *n* toxic yellow gas, most reactive of all the elements
fluorspar *n* mineral consisting of calcium fluoride
flurry Ⓣ *n, pl* **-ries** **1** sudden commotion **2** squall or gust of rain, wind, or snow ▷ *v* **-rying, -ried** **3** fluster
flush[1] Ⓣ *v* **1** blush **2** send water through (a toilet or pipe) so as to clean it **3** elate ▷ *n* **4** blush **5** rush of water **6** excitement or elation

THESAURUS

bloom, prosper, do well • *Business was flourishing.* OPPOSITE: fail **2 = wave,** display, brandish (*lit*), hold aloft • *She flourished her scarf for dramatic effect.* ▸ *n* **3 = wave,** sweep, flick • *with a flourish of his hand* **4 = ornamentation,** sweep, decoration, plume, embellishment, curlicue
See also: **grow, shake**
flourishing *adj* **= successful,** rampant, blooming, going places, in the pink, luxuriant, prospering, thriving
flout *v* **= defy,** mock, scorn, spurn, laugh in the face of, scoff at, sneer at
flow *v* **1 = run,** roll, slide, circulate, glide • *a river flowing gently down into the valley* **2 = pour,** sweep, surge, flood, rush, stream, cascade, gush **3 = result,** issue, spring, emerge, proceed, arise, emanate ▸ *n* **4 = stream,** current, flood, tide, drift, outrush • *traffic flow*
See also: **drain, movement**
flower *n* **1 = bloom,** blossom, efflorescence **2 = elite,** French, pick, cream, best, crème de la crème ▸ *v* **3 = blossom,** open, mature, flourish, unfold, bloom
flowery *adj* **= ornate,** fancy, baroque, embellished, florid, high-flown
flowing *adj* **1 = streaming,** smooth, falling, gushing, rolling, rushing, sweeping **2 = fluent,** easy, smooth, continuous, uninterrupted, unbroken
fluctuate *v* **= change,** shift, swing, vary, alternate, veer, waver, seesaw, oscillate
fluctuating *See* **uneven**
fluency *n* **= ease,** control, facility, command, assurance, readiness, articulateness, glibness, slickness, smoothness
fluent *adj* **= articulate,** ready, easy, effortless, flowing • *a fluent speaker of Italian* OPPOSITE: hesitant
fluff *n* **= fuzz,** down, pile, nap
fluffy *adj* **= soft,** fuzzy, downy, feathery, fleecy
fluid *n* **1 = liquid,** solution, liquor ▸ *adj* **2 = liquid,** runny, watery, flowing, liquefied, melted, molten
fluke *n* **= lucky break,** chance, accident, coincidence, serendipity, quirk of fate, stroke of luck
flunk *See* **fail**
flurry *n* **1 = commotion,** stir, excitement, disturbance, fuss, bustle, flutter, ado **2 = gust,** squall
flush[1] *v* **1 = blush,** glow, colour, go red, redden **2 = rinse out,** flood, cleanse, hose

DICTIONARY

flush² Ⓣ *adj* **1** level with the surrounding surface **2** *informal* having plenty of money
flush³ *n* (in card games) hand all of one suit
flush⁴ *v* drive out of a hiding place
fluster Ⓣ *v* **1** make nervous or upset ▷ *n* **2** nervous or upset state
flute *n* **1** wind instrument consisting of a tube with sound holes and a mouth hole in the side **2** decorative groove **3** tall thin wineglass
▸ **fluted** *adj* having decorative grooves
fluting *n*
flutter Ⓣ *v* **1** wave rapidly **2** flap the wings **3** move quickly and irregularly **4** (of the heart) beat abnormally quickly ▷ *n* **5** flapping movement **6** nervous agitation **7** *informal* small bet **8** abnormally fast heartbeat
fluvial [**flew**-vee-al] *adj* of rivers
flux *n* **1** constant change or instability **2** flow or discharge **3** substance mixed with metal to assist in fusion
fly¹ Ⓣ *v* **flying**, **flew**, **flown** **1** move through the air on wings or in an aircraft **2** control the flight of **3** float, flutter, display, or be displayed in the air **4** transport or be transported by air **5** move quickly or suddenly **6** (of time) pass rapidly **7** flee ▷ *n, pl* **flies** **8** *often pl* fastening at the front of trousers **9** flap forming the entrance to a tent **flies** **10** space above a stage, used for storage
▸ **flyer** *or* **flier** *n* **1** small advertising leaflet **2** aviator
▸ **fly ball** *baseball* ball that is hit high up into the air
▸ **flyleaf** *n* blank leaf at the beginning or end of a book
▸ **flyover** *n Brit* road passing over another by a bridge
▸ **flywheel** *n* heavy wheel regulating the speed of a machine
fly² *n, pl* **flies** two-winged insect, esp. the housefly
▸ **flyblown** *adj* covered with bluebottle eggs
▸ **flycatcher** *n* small insect-eating songbird
▸ **fly-fishing** *n* fishing with an artificial fly as a lure
▸ **flypaper** *n* paper with a sticky poisonous coating, used to kill flies
▸ **flyweight** *n* boxer weighing up to 112lb (professional) or 51kg (amateur)
flying Ⓣ *adj* hurried, brief
▸ **flying boat** aircraft fitted with floats instead of landing wheels
▸ **flying buttress** *archit* buttress supporting a wall by an arch
▸ **flying colours** conspicuous success: *pass with flying colours*
▸ **flying fish** fish with winglike fins used for gliding above the water
▸ **flying fox** large fruit-eating bat
▸ **flying saucer** unidentified disc-shaped flying object, supposedly from outer space
▸ **flying squad** small group of police, soldiers, etc., ready to act quickly
▸ **flying start** very good start
Flynn *n* **Errol**. 1909–59, Australian-born Hollywood actor, who was noted for his swashbuckling roles; his films included *Captain Blood* (1935), *The Adventures of Robin Hood* (1938), and *Too Much Too Soon* (1958)
FM frequency modulation
Fo *n* **Dario**. born 1926, Italian playwright and actor. His plays include *The Accidental Death of an Anarchist* (1970), *Trumpets and Raspberries* (1984), and *The Tricks of the Trade* (1991): Nobel prize for literature 1997
foal *n* **1** young of a horse or related animal ▷ *v* **2** give birth to a foal
foam Ⓣ *n* **1** mass of small bubbles on a liquid **2** frothy saliva **3** light spongelike solid used for insulation, packing, etc. ▷ *v* **4** produce foam **foamy** *adj*
fob¹ *n* **1** short watch chain **2** small pocket in a waistcoat

THESAURUS

down, wash out ▸ *n* **3** = **blush**, glow, colour, redness, rosiness
flush² *adj* **1** = **level**, even, true, square, flat **2** (*Informal*) = **wealthy**, rich, well-heeled (*informal*), well-off, moneyed, in the money (*informal*)
flushed *adj* = **blushing**, hot, red, rosy, embarrassed, glowing, crimson, ruddy
fluster *v* **1** = **upset**, disturb, confuse, bother, rattle (*informal*), agitate, ruffle, unnerve, perturb ▸ *n* **2** = **turmoil**, flurry, flap (*informal*), disturbance, furor, flutter, dither
flutter *v* **1** = **beat**, flap, ripple, waver, vibrate, tremble, quiver, palpitate ▸ *n* **2** = **vibration**, tremor, shiver, tremble, palpitation, shudder, quiver, twitching **3** = **agitation**, confusion, excitement, commotion, dither, fluster
fly *v* **1** = **soar**, sail, flutter, flit • *to fly to Paris* **2** = **rush**, race, dash, hurry, dart, speed, tear • *She flew down the stairs.* **3** = **pilot**, control, operate, manoeuvre **4** = **display**, show, wave, float, flap, flutter **5** = **pass**, glide, elapse, flit, pass swiftly, roll on, run its course, slip away **6** = **flee**, escape, get away, run for it, skedaddle (*informal*), take to one's heels
See also: **bolt, go**
flying *adj* = **hurried**, brief, short-lived, hasty, fleeting, transitory, rushed
foam *n* **1** = **froth**, head, bubbles, lather • *waves tipped with foam* ▸ *v* **2** = **froth**, bubble, fizz • *a foaming river*
See also: **boil**
focal point *See* **focus**

DICTIONARY

fob² *v* **fobbing, fobbed** (foll. by *off*) **1** pretend to satisfy (a person) with lies or excuses **2** sell or pass off (something inferior) as valuable
fo'c's'le *n* same as **forecastle**
focus Ⓣ *v* **-cusing, -cused** *or* **-cussing, -cussed 1** adjust one's eyes or an instrument so that an image becomes clear **2** concentrate (on) ▷ *n, pl* **-cuses, -ci** [-sye] **3** point at which light or sound waves converge **4** state of an optical image when it is clearly defined **5** state of an instrument producing such an image **6** centre of interest or activity
▸ **focal** *adj* of or at a focus
▸ **focus group** group of people gathered by a market-research company to discuss and assess a product or service
fodder *n* feed for livestock
foe Ⓣ *n* enemy, opponent
foetid *adj* same as **fetid**
foetus *n, pl* **-tuses** same as **fetus**
fog Ⓣ *n* **1** mass of condensed water vapour in the lower air, often greatly reducing visibility ▷ *v* **fogging, fogged 2** cover with steam
foggy *adj*
▸ **foghorn** *n* large horn sounded to warn ships in fog
fogy, fogey *n, pl* **-gies, -geys** old-fashioned person
foible *n* minor weakness, idiosyncrasy
foil¹ Ⓣ *v* ruin (someone's plan)
foil² Ⓣ *n* **1** metal in a thin sheet **2** anything which sets off another thing to advantage
foil³ *n* light slender flexible sword tipped with a button
foist Ⓣ *v* (usu. foll. by *on*) force or impose on
fold¹ Ⓣ *v* **1** bend so that one part covers another **2** interlace (the arms) **3** *lit* clasp (in the arms) **4** *cooking* mix gently **5** *informal* fail ▷ *n* **6** folded piece or part **7** mark, crease, or hollow made by folding
▸ **folder** *n* piece of folded cardboard for loose papers
fold² *n* **1** enclosure for sheep **2** church or its members
foliage *n* leaves
▸ **foliaceous** *adj* of or like leaves
▸ **foliate** *adj* **1** having leaves **2** leaflike
▸ **foliation** *n* process of producing leaves
folio *n, pl* **-lios 1** sheet of paper folded in half to make two leaves of a book **2** book made up of such sheets **3** page number
folk Ⓣ *n* **1** people in general **2** race of people **3** *informal* folk music **folks 4** relatives
▸ **folksy** *adj* simple and unpretentious
▸ **folk dance** traditional country dance
▸ **folklore** *n* traditional beliefs and stories of a people
▸ **folk song 1** song handed down among the common people **2** modern song like this **folk singer**
follicle *n* small cavity in the body, esp. one from which a hair grows
follow Ⓣ *v* **1** go or come after **2** be a logical or natural consequence of **3** keep to the course or track of **4** act in accordance with **5** accept the ideas or beliefs of **6** understand **7** have a keen interest in
▸ **follower** *n* disciple or supporter
▸ **following** *adj* **1** about to be mentioned **2** next in time ▷ *n* **3** group of supporters ▷ *prep* **4** as a result of
▸ **follow up** *v* **1** investigate **2** do a second, often similar, thing after (a first)

THESAURUS

focus *v* **1 = concentrate**, aim, direct, fix • *His eyes began to focus.* ▷ **focus your attention on** *See* **concentrate** ▸ *n* **2 = centre**, target, hub, focal point • *the focus of the conversation*
foe *n* **= enemy**, rival, opponent, adversary, antagonist
fog *n* **= mist**, gloom, miasma, murk, smog
foggy *adj* **= misty**, murky, dim, cloudy, hazy, smoggy, indistinct, vaporous
foil¹ *v* **= thwart**, defeat, check, frustrate, counter • *The police foiled an armed robbery.* *See also*: **dash, prevent**
foil² *n* **= contrast**, background, complement, antithesis • *a perfect foil for his personality*
foist *v* **= impose**, unload, fob off, palm off, pass off, sneak in
fold *v* **1 = bend**, crease, tuck, crumple, turn under • *He folded the paper carefully.* **2** (*Informal*) **= go bankrupt**, crash, fail, collapse, go bust (*informal*), go to the wall, go under, shut down ▸ *n* **3 = crease**, bend, wrinkle, pleat • *hanging in folds*
folder *n* **= file**, portfolio, envelope, binder
folk *n* **= people**, family, race, tribe, clan, kin, kindred
follow *v* **1 = pursue**, track, hound, stalk • *We were being followed.* **2 = come after**, succeed, supersede • *Night follows day.* OPPOSITE: precede **3 = obey**, comply, observe, conform • *Follow the instructions carefully.* **4 = accompany**, attend, escort, tag along **5 = understand**, realize, appreciate, grasp, comprehend, fathom, catch on (*informal*), take in **6 = result**, issue, develop, spring, flow, proceed, arise, ensue **7 = be interested in**, support, cultivate, keep abreast of
See also: **copy, happen, heed, practise, see**
follower *n* **= supporter**, fan, believer, disciple • *a loyal follower of the team* OPPOSITE: leader
following *adj* **1 = next**, later, subsequent, successive, consequent, ensuing, succeeding ▸ *n* **2 = supporters**, train, suite,

DICTIONARY

▶ **follow-up** *n* something done to reinforce an initial action
folly Ⓣ *n, pl* **-lies 1** foolishness **2** foolish action or idea **3** useless extravagant building
foment [foam-**ent**] *v* encourage or stir up (trouble) **fomentation** *n*
fond Ⓣ *adj* **1** tender, loving **2** unlikely to be realized: *a fond hope* **3** indulgent **fondly** *adv* **fondness** *n*
▶ **fond of** having a liking for
Fonda *n* **1 Henry**. 1905–82, US film actor. His many films include *Young Mr Lincoln* (1939), *The Grapes of Wrath* (1940), *Twelve Angry Men* (1957), and *On Golden Pond* (1981) for which he won an Oscar **2** his daughter **Jane**. born 1937, US film actress. Her films include *Klute* (1971) for which she won an Oscar, *Julia* (1977), *The China Syndrome* (1979), *On Golden Pond* (1981), and *The Old Gringo* (1989) **3** her brother, **Peter**. born 1939, US film actor, who made his name in *Easy Rider* (1969); later films include *Ulee's Gold* (1997)
fondant *n* (sweet made from) flavoured paste of sugar and water
fondle Ⓣ *v* caress
fondue *n* Swiss dish typically of a hot melted cheese sauce into which pieces of bread are dipped
font *n* bowl in a church for baptismal water
Fontaine *n* **Larry Philip**, known as *Phil*. born 1944, Native Canadian leader, former National Chief of the Assembly of First Nations (1997–2000; 2003–09)
fontanelle *n* soft membranous gap between the bones of a baby's skull
Fonyo *n* **Stephen Charles**, known as *Steve*. born 1965, Canadian charity fundraiser. After losing a leg to cancer, he undertook a run across Canada (1984–85) to raise money for cancer research; completed a similar charity run in the UK (1986–87)
food Ⓣ *n* what one eats, solid nourishment
▶ **foodie** *n informal* gourmet
▶ **food group** category of food based on its nutritional content
▶ **foodstuff** *n* substance used as food
fool[1] Ⓣ *n* **1** person lacking sense or judgment **2** person made to appear ridiculous **3** *hist* jester, clown ▷ *v* **4** deceive (someone)
▶ **foolish** *adj* unwise, silly, or absurd **foolishly** *adv* **foolishness** *n*
▶ **foolery** *n* foolish behaviour
▶ **fool around** *v* act or play irresponsibly or aimlessly
▶ **foolproof** *adj* unable to fail
fool[2] *n* dessert of puréed fruit mixed with cream
foolhardy Ⓣ *adj* recklessly adventurous **foolhardiness** *n*
foolscap *n* size of paper, 13 or 13.5 by 16 or 17 inches (33 or 44 by 41 or 43 centimetres)
foot Ⓣ *n, pl* **feet 1** part of the leg below the ankle **2** unit of length of twelve inches (0.3048 metre) **3** lowest part of anything **4** unit of poetic rhythm **5** *obsolete* infantry
▶ **foot the bill** pay the entire cost

THESAURUS

clientele, entourage, coterie, fans, retinue
folly *n* = **foolishness**, nonsense, madness, stupidity, indiscretion, lunacy, imprudence, rashness
fond *adj* **1** = **loving**, devoted, affectionate, adoring, doting, having a liking for • *a fond greeting* **2** = **foolish**, empty, naive, vain, deluded, delusive, overoptimistic ▷ **fond of** = **keen on**, into (*informal*), addicted to, attached to, enamoured of, having a soft spot for, hooked on, partial to
fondle *v* = **caress**, pet, stroke, pat, cuddle, dandle
fondly *adv* **1** = **lovingly**, dearly, affectionately, indulgently, possessively, tenderly, with affection **2** = **foolishly**, stupidly, credulously, naively, vainly
fondness *n* **1** = **liking**, love, taste, weakness, fancy, attachment, penchant, partiality, soft spot **2** = **devotion**, love, affection, attachment, kindness, tenderness
food *n* = **nourishment**, diet, fare, grub (*informal*), refreshment, foodstuffs, provisions • *our favourite food* RELATED WORDS *adjective*: alimentary *noun*: gastronomy
foodstuffs *See* **food**
fool *n* **1** = **idiot**, moron, dunce, ignoramus • *I felt like such a fool!* **2** = **dupe**, mug (*Brit slang*), sucker (*slang*), stooge (*slang*), fall guy (*informal*), laughing stock **3** = **clown**, harlequin, buffoon, jester ▶ *v* **4** = **deceive**, trick, mislead, con (*informal*), dupe • *Don't let him fool you.*
See also: **take in**
foolhardy *adj* = **rash**, irresponsible, reckless, imprudent, hot-headed, impetuous
foolish *adj* = **unwise**, silly, senseless, nonsensical, inane, unintelligent, stunned (*Canad informal*) • *feeling foolish* OPPOSITE: wise
See also: **crazy, fond, frivolous, idiotic, mad, stupid**
foolishly *adv* = **unwisely**, mistakenly, stupidly, idiotically, ill-advisedly, imprudently, injudiciously
foolishness *n* = **stupidity**, weakness, folly, indiscretion, absurdity, silliness, irresponsibility, imprudence
foolproof *adj* = **infallible**, safe, certain, unassailable, unbreakable, sure-fire (*informal*), guaranteed
foot *See* **base, bottom**

DICTIONARY

▸ **footage** *n* amount of film used
▸ **foot-and-mouth disease** infectious viral disease of sheep, cattle, etc.
▸ **footbridge** *n* bridge for pedestrians
▸ **footfall** *n* sound of a footstep
▸ **foothills** *pl n* hills at the foot of a mountain
▸ **foothold** *n* **1** small place giving a secure grip for the foot **2** secure position from which progress may be made
▸ **footlights** *pl n* lights across the front of a stage
▸ **footloose** *adj* free from ties
▸ **footman** *n* male servant in livery
▸ **footnote** *n* note printed at the foot of a page
▸ **footprint** *n* mark left by a foot
▸ **footsore** *adj* having sore or tired feet
▸ **footstep** *n* **1** step in walking **2** sound made by walking
▸ **footstool** *n* low stool used to rest the feet on while sitting
▸ **footwear** *n* anything worn to cover the feet
▸ **footwork** *n* skilful use of the feet, as in sport or dancing
football *n* **1** game played by two teams, each side attempting to kick, pass, or carry a ball across a goal line in order to score points **2** rugby **3** *Brit* soccer **footballer** *n*
▸ **football pools** *Brit* form of gambling on the results of football matches
footing ⓣ *n* **1** secure grip by or for the feet **2** basis, foundation **3** relationship between people
footsie *n informal* flirtation involving the touching together of feet
fop *n* man excessively concerned with fashion **foppery** *n* **foppish** *adj*
for *prep* **1** intended to be received or used by **2** in order to help or benefit **3** representing: *speaking for the opposition* **4** because of: *I could not see for the fog* **5** over a span of (time or distance) **6** in the direction of: *heading for the border* **7** at a cost of **8** in favour of: *vote for me* ▹ *conj* **9** because
▸ **for it** *informal* liable for punishment or blame
forage ⓣ [for-ridge] *v* **1** search about (for) ▹ *n* **2** food for cattle or horses
foray ⓣ *n* **1** brief raid or attack **2** first attempt or new undertaking
forbear ⓣ *v* cease or refrain (from doing something)
▸ **forbearance** *n* tolerance, patience
forbearing *adj*
forbid ⓣ *v* prohibit, refuse to allow
forbidden *adj*
▸ **forbidding** *adj* severe, threatening
force ⓣ *n* **1** strength or power **2** compulsion **3** *physics* influence tending to produce a change in a physical system **4** mental or moral strength **5** person or thing with strength or influence **6** vehemence or intensity **7** group of people organized for a particular task or duty **8** body of troops, police, etc. ▹ *v* **9** compel, make (someone) do something **10** acquire or produce through effort, strength, etc. **11** propel or drive **12** break open **13** impose or inflict **14** cause to grow at an increased rate **15** strain to the utmost
▸ **in force 1** having legal validity **2** in great numbers
▸ **forced** *adj* **1** compulsory **2** false or unnatural **3** due to an emergency
▸ **forceful** *adj* **1** emphatic **2** effective
forcefully *adv* **forcefulness** *n*
▸ **forcible** *adj* **1** involving physical force or violence **2** strong and emphatic **forcibly** *adv*

THESAURUS

footing *n* **1 = basis**, foundation, groundwork **2 = relationship**, position, status, rank, standing, grade
footling *adj* (*Informal*) **= trivial**, minor, silly, petty, insignificant, unimportant, fiddling, hairsplitting, trifling
footpath *See* **path**
footstep *n* **= step**, tread, footfall
forage *v* **1 = search**, seek, hunt, explore, scour, rummage, cast about ▸ *n* **2** (Cattle, etc.) **= fodder**, food, feed, provender
foray *n* **= raid**, invasion, incursion, swoop, inroad, sortie, sally
forbear *v* **= refrain**, stop, cease, abstain, desist, hold back, keep from, restrain oneself
forbearance *n* **= patience**, resignation, restraint, tolerance, moderation, long-suffering, self-control, temperance
forbearing *adj* **= patient**, moderate, lenient, merciful, tolerant, long-suffering, forgiving, indulgent
forbid *v* **= prohibit**, ban, exclude, veto, outlaw • *forbidden to go out* OPPOSITE: allow
forbidden *adj* **= prohibited**, taboo, outlawed, banned, out of bounds, proscribed, vetoed
forbidding *adj* **= threatening**, hostile, daunting, ominous, sinister, unfriendly, frightening, menacing
force *v* **1 = compel**, make, drive, pressure, coerce, oblige, obligate • *We were forced to turn right.* **2 = break open**, blast, wrest, pry, wrench **3 = push**, propel, thrust ▸ *n* **4 = compulsion**, pressure, duress • *They made him agree by force.* **5 = power**, might, pressure, impact, strength • *the force of the explosion* **6 = intensity**, emphasis, vigour, fierceness, vehemence **7 = army**, troop, host, unit, patrol, squad, regiment, legion ▹ **in force = valid**, current, effective, working, binding, operative, in operation; **= in great**

DICTIONARY

forceps *pl n* surgical pincers
ford Ⓣ *n* **1** shallow place where a river may be crossed ▷ *v* **2** cross (a river) at a ford **fordable** *adj*
Ford *n* **1 Ford Maddox**, original name *Ford Madox Hueffer*. 1873–1939, English novelist, editor, and critic; works include *The Good Soldier* (1915) and the war tetralogy *Parade's End* (1924–28). **2 Gerald R**(**udolph**). 1913–2006, US politician; 38th president of the US (1974–77) **3 Harrison**. born 1942, US film actor. His films include *Star Wars* (1977) and its sequels, *Raiders of the Lost Ark* (1981) and its sequels, *Bladerunner* (1982), *Clear and Present Danger* (1994), and *What Lies Beneath* (2000) **4 Henry**. 1863–1947, US automaker, who pioneered mass production **5 John**, real name *Sean O'Feeney*. 1895–1973, US film director, esp. of Westerns such as *Stagecoach* (1939) and *She Wore a Yellow Ribbon* (1949)
fore *adj* **1** in, at, or towards the front ▷ *n* **2** front part
▸ **to the fore** in a conspicuous position
fore- *prefix* **1** before in time or rank: *forefather* **2** at the front: *forecourt*
fore-and-aft *adj* located at both ends of a ship
forearm[1] *n* arm from the wrist to the elbow
forearm[2] *v* prepare beforehand
forebear Ⓣ *n* ancestor
foreboding Ⓣ *n* feeling that something bad is about to happen
forecast Ⓣ *v* **-casting**, **-cast** *or* **-casted** **1** predict (weather, events, etc.) ▷ *n* **2** prediction
forecastle [**foke**-sl] *n* raised front part of a ship
foreclose *v* take possession of (property bought with borrowed money which has not been repaid) **foreclosure** *n*
forecourt *n* courtyard or open space in front of a building
forefather Ⓣ *n* ancestor
forefinger *n* finger next to the thumb
forefront Ⓣ *n* **1** most active or conspicuous position **2** very front
foregather *v* same as **forgather**
forego *v* same as **forgo**
foregoing Ⓣ *adj* going before, preceding
▸ **foregone conclusion** inevitable result
foreground *n* part of a view, esp. in a picture, nearest the observer
forehand *adj* **1** (of a stroke in tennis, squash, etc.) made with the palm of the hand forward ▷ *n* **2** such a stroke
forehead *n* part of the face above the eyebrows
foreign Ⓣ *adj* **1** not of, or in, one's own country **2** relating to or connected with other countries **3** unfamiliar, strange **4** in an abnormal place or position: *foreign matter*
foreigner *n*
foreknowledge *n* knowledge of something before it actually happens
foreland *n* headland
foreleg *n* either of the front legs of a horse or other animal
forelock *n* lock of hair over the forehead
foreman *n* **1** person in charge of a group of workers **2** leader of a jury
Foreman *n* **George**. born 1949, US boxer: WBA world heavyweight champion (1973–74); he regained the title in 1994 but refused to fight the WBA's top-ranked challenger and was stripped of the title in 1995; recognized as WBU champion until 1997
foremast *n* mast nearest the bow of a ship
foremost Ⓣ *adj, adv* first in time,

THESAURUS

numbers, all together, in full strength
See also: **bully, jam, reduce, spirit, stuff, violence**
forced *adj* **1 = compulsory**, mandatory, involuntary, obligatory, conscripted, enforced **2 = false**, artificial, stiff, affected, wooden, strained, contrived, unnatural, insincere, laboured
forceful *adj* **1 = assertive**, aggressive, ambitious, bossy, obtrusive, pushy (*informal*) • *She is notorious for her forceful nature.* **2 = powerful**, effective, dynamic, persuasive, cogent, compelling, convincing
forcible *adj* **1 = violent**, aggressive, armed, compulsory, coercive **2 = strong**, powerful, potent, energetic, forceful, weighty, compelling
ford *See* **cross**
forebear *n* **= ancestor**, father, predecessor, forerunner, forefather
foreboding *n* **= dread**, fear, chill, anxiety, apprehension, misgiving, apprehensiveness, premonition, presentiment
forecast *v* **1 = predict**, anticipate, foresee, divine, augur, foretell, prophesy ▸ *n* **2 = prediction**, guess, prognosis, prophecy, conjecture
forefather *n* **= ancestor**, father, predecessor, forerunner, forebear
forefront *n* **= lead**, front, centre, spearhead, prominence, fore, foreground, vanguard
foregoing *adj* **= preceding**, former, previous, above, prior, anterior, antecedent
foreign *adj* **= alien**, overseas, distant, exotic • *foreign travel*
See also: **strange, unfamiliar**
foreigner *n* **= alien**, immigrant, stranger, incomer
foremost *adj* **= leading**, first, top, chief, prime, principal, best, greatest, most

DICTIONARY

place, or importance
forename *n* first name
forenoon *n* morning
forensic ⓣ [for-**ren**-sik] *adj* used in or connected with courts of law
▸ **forensic medicine** use of medical knowledge for the purposes of the law
forepaw *n* either of the front feet of a land mammal that does not have hooves
foreplay *n* sexual stimulation before intercourse
forerunner ⓣ *n* person or thing that goes before, precursor
foresee ⓣ *v* see or know beforehand
foreseeable *adj*
foreshadow ⓣ *v* show or indicate beforehand
foreshore *n* part of the shore between high- and low-tide marks
foreshorten *v* represent (an object) in a picture as shorter than it really is in accordance with perspective
foresight ⓣ *n* ability to anticipate and provide for future needs
foreskin *n* fold of skin covering the tip of the penis
forest *n* large area with a thick growth of trees **forested** *adj*
▸ **forestry** *n* science of planting and caring for trees
▸ **forester** *n* person skilled in forestry
forestall *v* prevent or guard against in advance
Forester *n* **C**(**ecil**) **S**(**cott**). 1899–1966, English novelist; creator of Captain Horatio Hornblower in a series of novels on the Napoleonic Wars
foretaste *n* early limited experience of something to come
foretell ⓣ *v* tell or indicate beforehand
forethought ⓣ *n* thoughtful planning for future events
forever ⓣ *adv* **1** without end **2** at all times **3** *informal* for a long time
forewarn ⓣ *v* warn beforehand
foreword ⓣ *n* preface
forfeit ⓣ [**for**-fit] *n* **1** thing lost or given up as a penalty for a fault or mistake ▷ *v* **2** lose as a forfeit ▷ *adj* **3** lost as a forfeit **forfeiture** *n*
forgather *v* meet together, assemble
forge[1] ⓣ *n* **1** place where metal is worked, smithy **2** furnace for melting metal ▷ *v* **3** make a fraudulent imitation of (something) **4** shape (metal) by heating and hammering it **5** create (an alliance etc.)
forge[2] *v* advance steadily
▸ **forge ahead** *v* increase speed or take the lead
forgery ⓣ *n, pl* **-ries 1** something forged **2** act of making a fraudulent imitation **forger** *n*
forget ⓣ *v* **-getting, -got, -gotten 1** fail to remember **2** neglect **3** leave behind by mistake
▸ **forgetful** *adj* tending to forget
forgetfulness *n*
▸ **forget-me-not** *n* plant with clusters of small blue flowers

THESAURUS

important • *one of the world's foremost scholars*
See also: **important, main, supreme**
forensic *See* **legal**
forerunner *n* = **precursor**, envoy, herald, prototype, harbinger, point-man
foresee *v* = **anticipate**, forecast, predict, envisage, foretell, prophesy
foreshadow *v* = **predict**, promise, indicate, signal, augur, presage, forebode, portend, prefigure
foresight *n* = **anticipation**, precaution, preparedness, prudence, far-sightedness, forethought, prescience
forest *n* = **wood** *or* **woods**, trees, bush (*Canad*), grove, woodland, bushland, rainforest, thicket, copse
foretell *v* = **predict**, forecast, forewarn, presage, prognosticate, prophesy
forethought *n* = **anticipation**, provision, precaution, foresight, prudence, providence, far-sightedness
forever *adv* **1** = **evermore**, always, for all time, for keeps, in perpetuity, till Doomsday, till the cows come home (*informal*) **2** = **constantly**, continually, perpetually, endlessly, eternally, incessantly, all the time, interminably, twenty-four-seven (*slang*), unremittingly
forewarn *v* = **caution**, alert, advise, apprise, give fair warning, put on guard, tip off
foreword *See* **introduction**
forfeit *n* **1** = **penalty**, loss, fine, forfeiture, damages ▸ *v* **2** = **lose**, surrender, renounce, relinquish, be deprived of, be stripped of, give up, say good-bye to
forge *v* **1** = **create**, make, work, form, fashion, shape, frame, construct, devise, mould **2** = **falsify**, copy, fake, counterfeit, imitate, feign
forged *See* **false, phony**
forgery *n* **1** = **fraudulence**, falsification, coining, counterfeiting, fraudulent imitation **2** = **fake**, counterfeit, phony (*informal*), sham, imitation, falsification
forget *v* = **fail to remember**, overlook, omit • *I forgot to lock the door*. OPPOSITE: remember
See also: **neglect**
forgetful *adj* = **absent-minded**, vague, oblivious, careless, inattentive, neglectful, unmindful

DICTIONARY

forgive Ⓣ *v* cease to blame or hold resentment against, pardon **forgiveness** *n*
forgo Ⓣ *v* do without, give up
forgot *v* past tense of **forget**
▸ **forgotten** *v* past participle of **forget**
fork Ⓣ *n* **1** tool for eating food, with prongs and a handle **2** large similarly-shaped tool for digging or lifting **3** point where a road, river, etc. divides into branches **4** one of the branches ▹ *v* **5** branch **6** take one or other branch at a fork in the road **7** pick up, dig, etc. with a fork **forked** *adj*
▸ **fork-lift truck** vehicle with a forklike device at the front which can be raised or lowered to move loads
▸ **fork out** *v informal* pay
forlorn Ⓣ *adj* forsaken and unhappy **forlornly** *adv*
▸ **forlorn hope** hopeless enterprise
form Ⓣ *n* **1** shape or appearance **2** mode in which something appears **3** type or kind **4** printed document with spaces for details **5** physical or mental condition **6** previous record of an athlete, racehorse, etc. **7** class in school **8** procedure or etiquette **9** bench **10** hare's nest ▹ *v* **11** give a (particular) shape to or take a (particular) shape **12** come or bring into existence **13** make or be made **14** train **15** acquire or develop **16** be an element of **formless** *adj*
▸ **formation** *n* **1** forming **2** thing formed **3** structure or shape **4** arrangement of people or things acting as a unit
▸ **formative** *adj* **1** shaping **2** of or relating to development
formal Ⓣ *adj* **1** of or characterized by established conventions of ceremony and behaviour **2** of or for formal occasions **3** stiff in manner **4** organized **5** symmetrical **formally** *adv*
▸ **formality** *n* **1** requirement of custom or etiquette **2** necessary procedure without real importance
▸ **formalize** *v* make official or formal
formaldehyde [for-**mal**-de-hide] *n* colourless pungent gas used to make formalin
▸ **formalin** *n* solution of formaldehyde in water, used as a disinfectant or a preservative for biological specimens
Forman *n* **Milos**. born 1932, Czech film director working in the USA since 1968. His films include *One Flew over the Cuckoo's Nest* (1976), *Amadeus* (1985), and *The People vs Larry Flynt* (1996)
format Ⓣ *n* **1** size and shape of a publication **2** style in which something is arranged ▹ *v* **-matting**, **-matted 3** arrange in a format

THESAURUS

forgive *v* = **pardon**, excuse, condone, absolve • *Can you ever forgive me?* OPPOSITE: blame
forgiveness *n* = **pardon**, mercy, acquittal • *I ask for your forgiveness.*
forgiving *adj* = **merciful**, compassionate, lenient, tolerant, clement, forbearing, magnanimous, soft-hearted
forgo *v* = **give up**, resign, abandon, surrender, yield, renounce, waive, relinquish, do without
forgotten *adj* = **unremembered**, past, lost, bygone, left behind, omitted, past recall
fork *v* = **branch**, part, split, divide, diverge, bifurcate
forked *adj* = **branching**, split, divided, angled, bifurcate *or* bifurcated, branched, pronged, zigzag
forlorn *adj* = **miserable**, unhappy, pathetic, helpless, hopeless, pitiful, wretched, disconsolate, down in the dumps (*informal*), woebegone
form *n* **1** = **kind**, type, class, sort, variety, variant • *a rare form of the illness* **2** = **shape**, structure, outline, layout, contours • *Valleys often take the form of deep canyons.* **3** = **condition**, health, shape, trim, fitness, fettle **4** = **procedure**, convention, protocol, custom, etiquette **5** = **document**, paper, application, sheet **6** = **class**, rank, grade ▸ *v* **7** = **constitute**, compose, make up, serve as • *the ideas that formed the basis of the argument* **8** = **make**, create, develop, establish, fashion, assemble • *The bowl was formed out of clay.* **9** = **arrange**, combine, organize, draw up **10** = **take shape**, rise, grow, appear, materialize, crystallize, become visible, come into being **11** = **develop**, contract, acquire, cultivate, pick up
See also: **body, build, design, figure, model**
formal *adj* **1** = **conventional**, correct, stiff, precise • *a formal dinner* OPPOSITE: informal **2** = **official**, legal, regular, prescribed, approved • *No formal anncement has been made.*
See also: **impersonal, stuffy**
formality *n* **1** = **convention**, procedure, custom, ritual, rite, red tape **2** = **correctness**, protocol, etiquette, decorum
format *n* = **style**, plan, look, form, type, construction, appearance, arrangement, layout, make-up
formation *n* **1** = **establishment**, production, development, manufacture, generation, constitution, genesis, forming **2** = **pattern**, design, structure, arrangement, configuration, grouping
formative *adj* = **developmental**, influential • *her formative years*

DICTIONARY

former Ⓣ *adj* of an earlier time, previous **formerly** *adv*
▸ **the former** first mentioned of two
Formica *n* ® kind of laminated sheet used to make heat-resistant surfaces
formic acid *n* acid derived from ants
formidable Ⓣ *adj* **1** difficult to overcome or manage **2** extremely impressive **formidably** *adv*
formula Ⓣ *n, pl* **-las**, **-lae** **1** group of numbers, letters, or symbols expressing a scientific or mathematical rule **2** set form of words used in religion, law, etc. **3** method or rule for doing or producing something **4** specific category of vehicle in motor racing **formulaic** *adj*
▸ **formulate** *v* plan or describe precisely and clearly **formulation** *n*
fornicate *v* have sexual intercourse without being married **fornication** *n* **fornicator** *n*
forsake Ⓣ *v* **-saking**, **-sook**, **-saken** **1** withdraw support or friendship from **2** give up, renounce
forsooth *adv obsolete* indeed
Forster *n* **E**(**dward**) **M**(**organ**). 1879–1970, English novelist, short-story writer, and essayist. His best-known novels are *A Room with a View* (1908), *Howard's End* (1910), and *A Passage to India* (1924), in all of which he stresses the need for sincerity and sensitivity in human relationships and criticizes English middle-class values
forswear *v* renounce or reject
forsythia [for-**syth**-ee-a] *n* shrub with yellow flowers in spring
fort Ⓣ *n* fortified building or place
▸ **hold the fort** *informal* keep things going during someone's absence
forte[1] Ⓣ [**for**-tay] *n* thing at which a person excels
forte[2] *adv music* loudly
forth Ⓣ *adv* forwards, out, or away
forthcoming Ⓣ *adj* **1** about to appear or happen **2** available **3** (of a person) communicative
forthright Ⓣ *adj* direct and outspoken
forthwith Ⓣ *adv* at once
fortieth *adj, n* see **four**
fortify Ⓣ *v* **-fying**, **-fied** **1** make (a place) defensible, as by building walls **2** strengthen **3** add alcohol to (wine) to make sherry or port **4** add vitamins etc. to (food) **fortification** *n*
fortissimo *adv music* very loudly
fortitude Ⓣ *n* courage in adversity or pain
fortnight *n* two weeks **fortnightly** *adv, adj*
FORTRAN *n computers* programming language for mathematical and scientific purposes
fortress Ⓣ *n* large fort or fortified town

THESAURUS

former *adj* = **previous**, past, old, ancient, bygone • *a former tennis champion* ▷ **former times** *See* **the past**
formerly *adv* = **previously**, before, once, lately, at one time
formidable *adj* **1** = **difficult**, mammoth, daunting, onerous, challenging, intimidating • *They faced formidable obstacles.* **2** = **impressive**, great, powerful, cool (*informal*), tremendous, terrific (*informal*), awesome, mighty, phat (*slang*), redoubtable *See also*: **stiff**
formula *n* = **method**, rule, procedure, principle, recipe, blueprint, precept
formulate *v* **1** = **define**, detail, express, frame, specify, give form to, set down, systematize **2** = **devise**, plan, develop, originate, forge, invent, map out, work out
forsake *v* **1** = **desert**, abandon, strand, disown, leave in the lurch **2** = **give up**, surrender, yield, renounce, relinquish, forgo, set aside
forsaken *adj* = **deserted**, abandoned, outcast, disowned, forlorn, left in the lurch, marooned, stranded
fort *n* = **fortress**, castle, fortification, citadel • *They had to abandon the fort.* ▷ **hold the fort** = **stand in**, carry on, keep things on an even keel, take over the reins
forte *n* = **specialty**, gift, strength, talent, métier, strong point
forth *adv* = **forward**, out, away, ahead, outward, onward
for that reason *See* **therefore**
forthcoming *adj* **1** = **approaching**, future, upcoming, imminent, prospective, coming, expected, impending **2** = **accessible**, available, ready, at hand, in evidence, obtainable, on tap (*informal*) **3** = **communicative**, open, free, expansive, informative, sociable, talkative, chatty, unreserved
forthright *adj* = **outspoken**, open, direct, blunt, straightforward, frank, candid, upfront (*informal*), plain-spoken
forthwith *adv* = **at once**, immediately, quickly, directly, instantly, straightaway, right away, without delay
fortification *n* **1** = **defence**, protection, stronghold, fort, fortress, bastion, fastness **2** = **strengthening**, reinforcement
fortified *See* **secure**
fortify *v* = **strengthen**, support, protect, reinforce, augment, buttress, shore up
fortitude *n* = **courage**, strength, resolution, backbone, grit, bravery, perseverance, fearlessness, valour
fortress *n* = **castle**, stronghold, fort,

DICTIONARY

fortuitous Ⓣ [for-**tyew**-it-uss] *adj* happening by (lucky) chance **fortuitously** *adv* **fortuity** *n*
fortunate Ⓣ *adj* **1** having good luck **2** occurring by good luck **fortunately** *adv*
fortune Ⓣ *n* **1** luck, esp. when favourable **2** power regarded as influencing human destiny **3** wealth, large sum of money **fortunes 4** person's destiny
▸ **fortune-teller** *n* person who claims to predict the future of others
forty *adj, n* see **four**
forty-ninth parallel *n informal* border between Canada and the US
forum Ⓣ *n* meeting or medium for open discussion or debate
forward Ⓣ *adj* **1** directed or moving ahead **2** in, at, or near the front **3** presumptuous **4** well developed or advanced **5** relating to the future ▹ *n* **6** *sports* attacking player in various team games, such as hockey or soccer ▹ *v* **7** send (a letter etc.) on to an ultimate destination **8** advance or promote ▹ *adv* **9** forwards **forwardly** *adv* **forwardness** *n*
▸ **forwards** *adv* **1** towards or at a place further ahead in space or time **2** towards the front
fossil *n* hardened remains of a prehistoric animal or plant preserved in rock
▸ **fossilize** *v* **1** turn into a fossil **2** become out-of-date or inflexible **fossilization** *n*
▸ **fossil fuel** fuel, like coal and oil, found in the remains of prehistoric organisms
foster Ⓣ *v* **1** bring up (a child not one's own) **2** promote the growth or development of ▹ *adj* **3** of or involved in fostering a child
Foster *n* **1 Jodie**. born 1962, US film actress and director: her films include *Taxi Driver* (1976), *The Accused* (1988), *The Silence of the Lambs* (1990), *Little Man Tate* (1991; also directed), *Nell* (1995), and *Panic Room* (2002) **2 Norman**, Baron. born 1935, British architect. His works include the Willis Faber building (1978) in Ipswich, Stansted Airport, Essex (1991), Chek Lap Kok Airport, Hong Kong (1998), the renovation of the Reichstag, Berlin (1999), and City Hall, London (2002) **3 Stephen Collins**. 1826–64, US composer of songs such as *The Old Folks at Home* and *Oh Susanna*
Foucault *n* **1 Jean Bernard Léon**. 1819–68, French physicist. He determined the velocity of light and proved that light travels more slowly in water than in air (1850). He demonstrated by means of the pendulum named after him the rotation of the earth on its axis (1851) and invented the gyroscope (1852) **2 Michel**. 1926–84, French philosopher and historian of ideas. His publications include *Histoire de la folie* (1961) and *Les Mots et les choses* (1966)
fought *v* past of **fight**
foul Ⓣ *adj* **1** loathsome or offensive **2** stinking or dirty **3** (of language) obscene or vulgar **4** unfair ▹ *n* **5** *sports* violation of the rules ▹ *v* **6** make dirty or polluted **7** make or become entangled or clogged **8** *sports* commit a foul against (an opponent) **foully** *adv* **foulness** *n*
▸ **fall foul of** come into conflict with
▸ **foul-mouthed** *adj* (habitually) using foul language
▸ **foul play** unfair conduct, esp. involving violence
found[1] *v* past of **find**
found[2] Ⓣ *v* **1** establish or bring into being **2** lay the foundation of **3** (foll. by *on* or *upon*)

f

THESAURUS

citadel, fastness, redoubt
fortuitous *See* **lucky**
fortunate *adj* **1 = lucky**, favoured, in luck, successful, well-off **2 = favourable**, timely, helpful, convenient, win-win (*informal*), opportune, fortuitous, advantageous, expedient, felicitous, providential
fortunately *adv* **= luckily**, happily, by a happy chance, by good luck, providentially
fortune *n* **1 = wealth**, property, treasure, prosperity, affluence, riches, opulence, possessions **2 = luck**, chance, fate, destiny, providence, kismet ▹ **fortunes = destiny**, lot, history, success, adventures, experiences
forum *See* **conference**
forward *adj* **1 = leading**, first, head, front, advance, foremost **2 = presumptuous**, familiar, bold, brazen, cheeky, brash, impertinent, impudent, pushy (*informal*) **3 = well-developed**, advanced, premature, precocious ▸ *adv* **4 = ahead**, on, forth, onward ▸ *v* **5 = promote**, further, assist, advance, hurry, expedite, hasten **6 = send**, mail, dispatch, send on
foster *v* **1 = promote**, support, feed, encourage, uphold, stimulate, nurture, cultivate **2 = bring up**, raise, mother, nurse, rear, take care of
foul *adj* **1 = dirty**, funky (*slang*), filthy, squalid, repulsive, unclean, putrid, fetid, malodorous, nauseating, scuzzy (*slang*), stinking **2 = obscene**, blue, abusive, indecent, vulgar, lewd, profane, coarse, scurrilous **3 = offensive**, disgraceful, despicable, shameful, wicked, scandalous, lousy (*slang*), abhorrent, detestable, scuzzy (*slang*) **4 = unfair**, fraudulent, crooked, shady (*informal*), dishonest, unscrupulous, underhand ▸ *v* **5 = pollute**, contaminate, taint, dirty, stain, besmirch, defile, sully
found *v* **= establish**, start, create, organize, institute, originate, constitute, inaugurate, set up
foundation *n* **1 = groundwork**,

DICTIONARY

have a basis (in) **founder** *n*
▸ **foundation** *n* **1** basis or base **2** act of founding **3** institution supported by an endowment **4** cosmetic used as a base for make-up **foundations 5** part of a building or wall below the ground
found[3] *v* **1** cast (metal or glass) by melting and setting in a mould **2** make (articles) by this method **founder** *n*
▸ **foundry** *n* place where metal is melted and cast
founder ⓘ *v* **1** break down or fail **2** (of a ship) sink **3** stumble or fall
foundling ⓘ *n* abandoned infant
fount *n* **1** *lit* fountain **2** source **3** set of printing type of one style and size
fountain ⓘ *n* **1** pool or structure from which a jet or water spurts **2** jet of water **3** source
▸ **fountainhead** *n* source
▸ **fountain pen** pen supplied with ink from a container inside it
Fouquier-Tinville *n* **Antoine Quentin**. 1746–95, French revolutionary; as public prosecutor (1793–94) during the Reign of Terror, he sanctioned the guillotining of Desmoulins, Danton, and Robespierre
four *adj, n* **1** one more than three ▷ *n* **2** (crew of) four-oared rowing boat
▸ **on all fours** on hands and knees
▸ **fourth** *adj, n* **1** (of) number four in a series ▷ *n* **2** quarter **fourthly** *adv*
▸ **foursome** *n* group of four people
▸ **fourteen** *adj, n* four and ten **fourteenth** *adj, n*
▸ **forty** *adj, n* four times ten **fortieth** *adj, n*
▸ **fourth dimension** time
▸ **fourth estate** the press
▸ **four-letter word** short obscene word referring to sex or excrement
▸ **four-poster** *n* bed with four posts supporting a canopy
Fourier *n* **Jean Baptiste Joseph**. 1768–1830, French mathematician, Egyptologist, and administrator, noted particularly for his research on the theory of heat and the method of analysis named after him
fowl *n* **1** domestic cock or hen **2** any bird used for food or hunted as game ▷ *v* **3** hunt or snare wild birds **fowler** *n*
fox *n* **1** reddish-brown bushy-tailed animal of the dog family **2** its fur **3** cunning person ▷ *v* **4** *informal* perplex or deceive **foxy** *adj*
▸ **foxglove** *n* tall plant with purple or white flowers
▸ **foxhole** *n mil* small pit dug for protection
▸ **foxhound** *n* dog bred for hunting foxes
▸ **fox terrier** small short-haired terrier
▸ **foxtrot** *n* **1** ballroom dance with slow and quick steps **2** music for this
Fox *n* **1 George**. 1624–91, English religious leader; founder (1647) of the Society of Friends (Quakers) **2 Michael J**. born 1961, Canadian film and TV actor. Noted for his role in the *Back to the Future* series of films (1985–90) **3 Terrance Stanley**, known as *Terry*. 1958–81, Canadian charity fundraiser. After losing a leg to cancer he undertook a "Marathon of Hope" (1980) across Canada to raise money for cancer research. He was forced to abandon the run after the disease spread but raised over $24 million **4 Vicente**. born 1942, Mexican politician; president of Mexico 2000–06
Fox Talbot *n* **William Henry**. 1800–77, English physicist; a pioneer of photography
foyer ⓘ [**foy**-ay] *n* entrance hall in a theatre, cinema, or hotel
fracas ⓘ [**frak**-ah] *n, pl* **-cas** noisy quarrel
fraction ⓘ *n* **1** numerical quantity that is not a whole number **2** fragment, piece **3** *chem* substance separated by distillation
fractional *adj* **fractionally** *adv*
fractious ⓘ *adj* easily upset and angered
fracture ⓘ *n* **1** breaking, esp. of a bone ▷ *v* **2** break
fragile ⓘ *adj* **1** easily broken or damaged **2** in

THESAURUS

base, bottom, basis, footing, bedrock, underpinning, substructure **2 = setting up**, organization, settlement, institution, establishment, inauguration, endowment
founder[1] *n* = **initiator**, author, father, architect, inventor, beginner, originator
founder[2] *v* **1** = **sink**, submerge, be lost, go down, go to the bottom **2** = **fail**, collapse, misfire, miscarry, break down, come to grief, come unstuck, fall through **3** = **stumble**, trip, sprawl, stagger, lurch
foundling *n* = **stray**, orphan, outcast, waif
fountain *n* **1** = **jet**, well, spring, spray, reservoir, spout, font, fount **2** = **source**, cause, origin, derivation, fount, fountainhead, wellspring
foyer *n* = **entrance hall**, lobby, antechamber, anteroom, reception area, vestibule
fracas *n* = **brawl**, riot, scuffle, skirmish, disturbance, melee *or* mêlée, affray (*law*), rumpus
fraction *n* = **piece**, part, share, percentage, section, portion, segment, slice
fractious *adj* = **irritable**, cross, testy, touchy, captious, petulant, querulous, refractory, tetchy
fracture *n* **1** = **break**, opening, split, crack, rift, rupture, fissure, cleft ▸ *v* **2** = **break**, split, crack, rupture, splinter
fractured *See* **broken**
fragile *adj* = **delicate**, frail, flimsy, dainty,

DICTIONARY

a weakened physical state **fragility** *n*
fragment ⓣ *n* **1** piece broken off **2** incomplete piece ▷ *v* **3** break into pieces **fragmentary** *adj* **fragmentation** *n*
fragrant ⓣ *adj* sweet-smelling **fragrantly** *adv*
▸ **fragrance** *n* **1** pleasant smell **2** perfume, scent
frail ⓣ *adj* **1** physically weak **2** easily damaged **frailty** *n*
frame ⓣ *n* **1** structure giving shape or support **2** enclosing case or border, as round a picture **3** person's build **4** individual exposure on a strip of film **5** individual game of snooker in a match ▷ *v* **6** put into a frame **7** put together, construct **8** put into words **9** *slang* incriminate (a person) on a false charge
▸ **frame of mind** mood, attitude
▸ **frame-up** *n slang* false incrimination
▸ **framework** *n* supporting structure
franc *n* monetary unit of Switzerland
franchise *n* **1** right to vote **2** authorization to sell a company's goods
Francis *n* **Mayann**. Canadian politician, Lieutenant Governor of Nova Scotia (2006–)
Francis II *n* **1** 1544–60, king of France (1559–60); son of Henry II and Catherine de' Medici; first husband of Mary, Queen of Scots **2** 1768–1835, last Holy Roman Emperor (1792–1806) and, as Francis I, first emperor of Austria (1804–35). The Holy Roman Empire was dissolved (1806) following his defeat by Napoleon at Austerlitz
Franciscan *n, adj* (friar or nun) of a Christian religious order founded by St Francis of Assisi
Francis of Assisi *n* **Saint**, original name *Giovanni di Bernardone*. ?1181–1226, Italian monk; founder of the Franciscan order of friars. He is remembered for his humility and love for all creation and was the first person to exhibit stigmata (1224). Feast day: Oct 4
francization *n* practice of making French the main language in the workplace, esp. in Quebec
Franck *n* **César** (**Auguste**). 1822–90, French composer, organist, and teacher, born in Belgium. His works, some of which make use of cyclic form, include a violin sonata, a string quartet, the *Symphony in D Minor* (1888), and much organ music
Franco *n* **Francisco**, called *el Caudillo*. 1892–1975, Spanish general and statesman; head of state (1939–1975). He was commander-in-chief of the Falangists in the Spanish Civil War (1936–39), defeating the republican government and establishing a dictatorship (1939). He kept Spain neutral in World War II
Franco- *combining form* of France or the French
Francophone *n* native speaker of French
frangipani [fran-jee-**pah**-nee] *n* fragrant tropical American shrub
frank ⓣ *adj* **1** honest and straightforward **2** outspoken or blunt ▷ *v* **3** put a mark on (a letter) to allow it delivery ▷ *n* **4** official mark on a letter allowing delivery **frankly** *adv* **frankness** *n*
Frank *n* **1** **Anne**. 1929–45, German Jewess, whose *Diary* (1947) recorded the experiences of her family while in hiding from the Nazis in Amsterdam (1942–44). They were betrayed and she died in a concentration camp **2** **Robert**. born 1924, US photographer and film maker, born in Switzerland; best known for his photographic book *The Americans* (1959)
Frankenstein's monster, Frankenstein *n* creation or monster that brings disaster and

f

THESAURUS

breakable • *fragile china* OPPOSITE: tough
fragility *See* **weakness**
fragment *n* **1** = **piece**, bit, chip, portion, scrap, particle, shred, sliver ▸ *v* **2** = **break**, shatter, crumble, splinter, disintegrate, break up, come apart, come to pieces, split up
fragmentary *adj* = **incomplete**, partial, scattered, sketchy, scrappy, piecemeal, incoherent, disconnected, bitty, broken
fragmented *See* **broken**
fragrance *n* = **aroma**, smell, scent, perfume, bouquet • *the fragrance of the roses*
fragrant *adj* = **aromatic**, perfumed, sweet-smelling • *fragrant oils* OPPOSITE: smelly
See also: **sweet**
frail *adj* = **weak**, vulnerable, delicate, fragile, feeble, flimsy, infirm, puny, insubstantial
frailty *n* = **feebleness**, weakness, susceptibility, fallibility, frailness, infirmity
frame *n* **1** = **casing**, construction, structure, shell, framework **2** = **physique**, body, build, anatomy, carcass ▷ **frame of mind** = **mood**, state, outlook, attitude, temper, disposition, humour ▸ *v* **3** = **construct**, make, build, manufacture, assemble, put together **4** = **draft**, compose, sketch, devise, formulate, draw up, map out **5** = **mount**, case, surround, enclose
framework *n* = **structure**, plan, frame, foundation, shell, skeleton, groundwork, the bare bones
frank *adj* = **honest**, open, plain, blunt, straightforward, candid • *a frank discussion*
See also: **direct, natural, straight**
frankly *adv* **1** = **honestly**, candidly, in truth, to be honest **2** = **openly**, directly, freely, bluntly, plainly, without reserve
frankness *n* = **outspokenness**, openness, truthfulness, bluntness, candour, forthrightness, plain speaking

DICTIONARY

is beyond the control of its creator
frankfurter *n* smoked sausage
frankincense *n* aromatic gum resin burned as incense
Franklin *n* **1 Aretha**. born 1942, US soul, pop, and gospel singer **2 Benjamin**. 1706–90, American statesman, scientist, and author. He helped draw up the Declaration of Independence (1776) and, as ambassador to France (1776–85), he negotiated an alliance with France and a peace settlement with Britain. As a scientist, he is noted particularly for his researches in electricity, esp. his invention of the lightning rod **3** Sir **John**. 1786–1847, English explorer of the Arctic: lieutenant-governor of Van Diemen's Land (now Tasmania) (1836–43): died while on a voyage to discover the Northwest Passage
frantic Ⓣ *adj* **1** distracted with rage, grief, joy, etc. **2** hurried and disorganized **frantically** *adv*
Franz Ferdinand *n* English name *Francis Ferdinand*. 1863–1914, archduke of Austria; heir apparent of Franz Josef I. His assassination contributed to the outbreak of World War I
Franz Josef I *n* English name *Francis Joseph I*. 1830–1916, emperor of Austria (1848–1916) and king of Hungary (1867–1916)
frappé *adj* (of drinks) chilled
fraternal *adj* of a brother, brotherly **fraternally** *adv*
▸ **fraternity** *n* **1** group of people with shared interests, aims, etc. **2** brotherhood **3** male social club at college
▸ **fraternize** *v* associate on friendly terms **fraternization** *n*
▸ **fratricide** *n* **1** crime of killing one's brother **2** person who does this
Frau [rhymes with **how**] *n* German title, equivalent to *Mrs*
▸ **Fräulein** [**froy**-line] *n* German title, equivalent to *Miss*
fraud Ⓣ *n* **1** (criminal) deception, swindle **2** person who acts in a deceitful way **fraudulent** *adj* **fraudulence** *n*
fraught [**frawt**] *adj* tense or anxious
▸ **fraught with** involving, filled with
fray[1] Ⓣ *v* **1** make or become ragged at the edge **2** become strained
fray[2] *n* noisy quarrel or conflict
Frazier *n* **Joe**. born 1944, US boxer: won the world heavyweight title in 1970 and was the first to beat Muhammad Ali professionally (1971)
frazzle *n informal* exhausted state
freak Ⓣ *n* **1** abnormal person or thing **2** person who is excessively enthusiastic about something ▷ *adj* **3** abnormal **freakish** *adj*
▸ **freak out** *v slang* (cause to) be in a heightened emotional state
freckle *n* small brown spot on the skin
▸ **freckled** *adj* marked with freckles
Frederick I *n* **1** See **Frederick Barbarossa** **2** 1657–1713, first king of Prussia (1701–13); son of Frederick William
Frederick II *n* **1** 1194–1250, Holy Roman Emperor (1220–50), king of Germany (1212–50), and king of Sicily (1198–1250) **2** See **Frederick the Great**
Frederick III *n* **1** 1415–93, Holy Roman Emperor (1452–93) and, as Frederick IV, king of Germany (1440–93) **2** called *the Wise*. 1463–1525, elector of Saxony (1486–1525). He protected Martin Luther in Wartburg Castle after the Diet of Worms (1521)
Frederick Barbarossa *n* official title *Frederick I*. ?1123–90, Holy Roman Emperor (1155–90), king of Germany (1152–90). His attempt to assert imperial rights in Italy ended in his defeat at Legnano (1176) and the independence of the Lombard cities (1183)
Frederick the Great *n* official title *Frederick II*. 1712–86, king of Prussia (1740–86); son of Frederick William I. He gained Silesia during the War of Austrian Succession (1740–48) and his military genius during the Seven Years' War (1756–63) established Prussia as a European power. He was also a noted patron of the arts

THESAURUS

frantic *adj* **1 = furious**, wild, distraught, berserk, at the end of one's tether, beside oneself, distracted **2 = hectic**, desperate, fraught (*informal*), frenzied, frenetic
fraternity *n* **1 = club**, company, union, league, association, circle, guild, brotherhood **2 = companionship**, fellowship, brotherhood, camaraderie, kinship
fraternize *v* **= associate**, mix, cooperate, mingle, socialize, hobnob, consort, keep company
fraud *n* **1 = deception**, hoax, deceit, trickery, guile • *The votes were recounted because of electoral fraud.* **2 = fake**, forgery, cheater, quack, imposter, charlatan • *Many psychics are frauds.*
See also: **con, corruption, racket**
fraudulent *adj* **= deceitful**, sham, crooked (*informal*), treacherous, dishonest, double-dealing, duplicitous, swindling
fray *v* **= wear thin**, wear, rub, chafe
freak *n* **1 = oddity**, anomaly, aberration, malformation, weirdo *or* weirdie (*informal*), monstrosity **2 = enthusiast**, fan, addict, nut (*slang*), buff (*informal*), fanatic, devotee, aficionado, fiend (*informal*) ▸ *adj* **3 = abnormal**, unusual, exceptional, unparalleled

DICTIONARY

free ⓣ *adj* **freer, freest 1** able to act at will, not compelled or restrained **2** not subject (to) **3** independent **4** provided without charge **5** generous, lavish **6** not in use **7** (of a person) not busy **8** not fixed or joined ▷ *v* **freeing, freed 9** release, liberate **10** remove (obstacles, pain, etc.) from **11** make available or usable **freely** *adv*
▶ **freedom** *n* being free
▶ **freebooter** *n* pirate
▶ **free fall** part of a parachute descent before the parachute opens
▶ **free-for-all** *n informal* brawl
▶ **freehand** *adj* drawn without guiding instruments
▶ **free hand** unrestricted freedom to act
▶ **freehold** *n* tenure of land for life without restrictions **freeholder** *n*
▶ **free house** *Brit* public house not bound to sell only one brewer's products
▶ **freelance** *adj, n* (of) self-employed person doing specific pieces of work for various employers
▶ **freeloader** *n slang* habitual scrounger
▶ **Freemason** *n* member of a secret fraternity pledged to help each other
▶ **free-range** *adj* kept or produced in natural conditions
▶ **freeway** *n* highway
▶ **freewheel** *v* travel downhill on a bicycle without pedalling
-free *adj combining form* without: *a trouble-free journey*
freesia *n* plant with fragrant tubular flowers
freeze ⓣ *v* **freezing, froze, frozen 1** change from a liquid to a solid by the reduction of temperature, as water to ice **2** preserve (food etc.) by extreme cold **3** (cause to) be very cold **4** become motionless with fear, shock, etc. **5** fix (prices or wages) at a particular level **6** ban the exchange or collection of (loans, assets, etc.) ▷ *n* **7** period of very cold weather **8** freezing of prices or wages
▶ **freezer** *n* insulated cabinet for cold-storage of perishable foods
▶ **freeze-dry** *v* preserve (food) by rapid freezing and drying in a vacuum
▶ **freeze-up** *n* freezing of watercourses and wetlands during fall and winter
freight ⓣ [**frate**] *n* **1** commercial transport of goods **2** cargo transported **3** cost of this ▷ *v* **4** send by freight
▶ **freighter** *n* ship or aircraft for transporting goods
French ⓣ *n* **1** language of France ▷ *adj* **2** of France, its people, or their language
▶ **French bread** white bread in a long thin crusty loaf
▶ **French dressing** salad dressing of oil and vinegar
▶ **French fries** thin strips of potato, fried
▶ **French horn** brass wind instrument with a coiled tube
▶ **French polish** shellac varnish for wood
▶ **French window** window extending to floor level, used as a door
Freneau *n* **Philip**. 1752–1832, US poet, journalist, and patriot; editor of the *National Gazette* (1791–93)
frenetic [frin-**net**-ik] *adj* uncontrolled, excited **frenetically** *adv*
frenzy ⓣ *n, pl* **-zies 1** violent mental

f

THESAURUS

free *adj* **1 = at liberty**, loose, liberated, at large, on the street • *a free person* OPPOSITE: captive **2 = without charge**, unpaid, complimentary, gratis • *a free brochure* **3 = allowed**, able, clear, unrestricted, unimpeded, permitted **4 = available**, empty, spare, idle, vacant, unused, unemployed, unoccupied **5 = generous**, liberal, lavish, unsparing, unstinting ▷ **free time** *See* **leisure** ▶ *v* **6 = release**, discharge, liberate, set at liberty, set loose • *to free the caged animals* OPPOSITE: imprison **7 = extricate**, rescue, disengage, cut loose, disentangle *See also*: **immune, independent, wild**
freedom *n* **1 = licence**, scope, discretion, latitude, leeway • *freedom of action* **2 = liberty**, release, emancipation • *gaining their freedom after months of captivity* OPPOSITE: captivity **3 = exemption**, immunity • *freedom from pain*
free-for-all *n* **= fight**, brawl, row, riot, melee *or* mêlée, scrimmage, fracas, throwdown (*slang*)
freely *adv* **1 = willingly**, voluntarily, spontaneously, of one's own accord, of one's own free will, without prompting **2 = openly**, frankly, plainly, candidly, unreservedly, without reserve **3 = abundantly**, liberally, lavishly, amply, copiously, extravagantly, unstintingly
freeze *v* **1 = chill**, stiffen, harden, ice over *or* ice up **2 = suspend**, stop, fix, peg, inhibit, hold up
freezing *adj* **= icy**, bitter, raw, chill, arctic, frosty, glacial, wintry, biting
freight *n* **1 = transportation**, shipment, carriage, conveyance **2 = cargo**, load, burden, merchandise, payload, consignment, goods
French *adj* **= Gallic**
frenzied *adj* **= furious**, wild, frantic, feverish, frenetic, rabid, uncontrolled, distracted
frenzy *n* **= fury**, rage, madness, agitation,

DICTIONARY

derangement **2** wild excitement **frenzied** *adj* **frenziedly** *adv*
frequent Ⓣ *adj* **1** happening often **2** habitual ▷ *v* **3** visit habitually **frequently** *adv*
▸ **frequency** *n* **1** rate of occurrence **2** *physics* number of times a wave repeats itself in a given time
fresco *n, pl* **-coes**, **-cos** watercolour painting done on wet plaster on a wall
Frescobaldi *n* **Girolamo**. 1583–1643, Italian organist and composer, noted esp. for his organ and harpsichord music
fresh Ⓣ *adj* **1** newly made, acquired, etc. **2** novel, original **3** most recent **4** further, additional **5** (of food) not preserved **6** (of water) not salty **7** (of weather) brisk or invigorating **8** not tired **9** *informal* impudent **freshly** *adv* **freshness** *n* **freshen** *v*
▸ **freshman** *or* **fresher** *n* first-year student
Fresnel *n* **Augustin Jean**. 1788–1827, French physicist: worked on the interference of light, contributing to the wave theory of light
fret[1] Ⓣ *v* **fretting**, **fretted** be worried
▸ **fretful** *adj* irritable
fret[2] *n* small bar on the fingerboard of a guitar etc.
▸ **fret saw** fine saw with a narrow blade, used for fretwork
▸ **fretwork** *n* decorative carving in wood
Freud *n* **1 Anna**. 1895–1982, Austrian psychiatrist: daughter of Sigmund Freud and pioneer of child psychoanalysis **2 Sigmund**. 1856–1939, Austrian psychiatrist; originator of psychoanalysis, based on free association of ideas and analysis of dreams. He stressed the importance of infantile sexuality in later development, evolving the concept of the Oedipus complex. His works include *The Interpretation of Dreams* (1900) and *The Ego and the Id* (1923)
Freudian [**froy**-dee-an] *adj* of or relating to the psychoanalyst Sigmund Freud or his theories
friable [**fry**-a-bl] *adj* easily crumbled **friability** *n*
friar *n* member of a male Roman Catholic religious order
▸ **friary** *n* house of friars
fricassee *n* stewed meat served in a thick sauce
friction Ⓣ *n* **1** rubbing **2** resistance met with by a body moving over another **3** clash of wills or personalities **frictional** *adj*
Friday *n* sixth day of the week
▸ **Good Friday** Friday before Easter
fridge *n* short for **refrigerator**
fried *v* past of **fry**[1]
Friedan *n* **Betty**. 1921–2006, US feminist, founder and first president (1966–70) of the National Organization for Women. Her books include *The Feminine Mystique* (1963), *The Second Stage* (1982), and *The Fountain of Life* (1993)
Friedrich *n* **Caspar David**. 1774–1840, German romantic landscape painter, noted for his skill in rendering changing effects of light
friend Ⓣ *n* **1** person whom one knows well and likes **2** supporter **3 Friend** Quaker **friendliness** *n* **friendless** *adj* **friendship** *n*
▸ **friendly** *adj* **1** showing or expressing liking **2** not hostile, on the same side
▸ **-friendly** *combining form* good or easy for the person or thing specified: *user-friendly*
▸ **friendly fire** *military* firing by one's own side, esp when it harms one's own personnel
fries *pl n* see **fry**[1]

THESAURUS

hysteria • *The room was a frenzy of activity.*
frequency *See* **rate**
frequent *adj* **1 = common**, repeated, everyday, habitual, continual, recurrent • *his frequent visits* OPPOSITE: rare ▸ *v* **2 = visit**, attend, haunt, patronize • *a restaurant that we frequent* OPPOSITE: avoid
frequently *adv* **= often**, much, repeatedly, commonly, habitually, many times, not infrequently
fresh *adj* **1 = new**, recent, different, original, novel, modern, up-to-date **2 = additional**, more, other, further, extra, added, supplementary, auxiliary **3 = invigorating**, clean, cool, pure, crisp, brisk, bracing, refreshing, unpolluted **4 = lively**, alert, keen, energetic, vigorous, spry, refreshed, sprightly **5 = natural**, unprocessed **6** (*Informal*) **= cheeky**, forward, familiar, disrespectful, presumptuous, impudent, insolent
freshen *v* **= refresh**, restore, revitalize, enliven, freshen up, liven up
freshness *n* **1 = novelty**, originality, inventiveness, newness **2 = cleanness**, shine, glow, sparkle, vigour, brightness, clearness, wholesomeness
fret *v* **= worry**, grieve, brood, agonize, lose sleep over, upset oneself *or* distress oneself
fretful *adj* **= irritable**, uneasy, edgy, fractious, testy, touchy, crotchety, querulous, short-tempered
friction *n* **1 = rubbing**, resistance, rasping, abrasion, grating, chafing, scraping **2 = hostility**, conflict, disagreement, resentment, animosity, discord, dissension, bad blood
friend *n* **1 = companion**, buddy, pal, confidant *or* confidante, crony • *lifelong friends* OPPOSITE: enemy **2 = supporter**, associate, ally, patron, well-wisher
friendliness *n* **= kindliness**, warmth,

DICTIONARY

Friese-Greene *n* **William**. 1855–1921, British photographer. He invented (with Mortimer Evans) the first practicable motion-picture camera
Friesian [**free**-zhan] *n Brit* Holstein
frieze [**freeze**] *n* ornamental band on a wall
frigate [**frig**-it] *n* medium-sized fast warship
fright Ⓣ *n* **1** sudden fear or alarm **2** sudden alarming shock **3** *informal* grotesque person
▸ **frighten** *v* **1** scare or terrify **2** force (someone) to do something from fear **frightening** *adj*
▸ **frightful** *adj* **1** horrifying **2** *informal* very great **frightfully** *adv*
frigid Ⓣ [**frij**-id] *adj* **1** (of a woman) sexually unresponsive **2** very cold **3** excessively formal **frigidly** *adv* **frigidity** *n*
frill *n* **1** gathered strip of fabric attached at one edge **frills 2** superfluous decorations or details **frilled** *adj* **frilly** *adj*
fringe Ⓣ *n* **1** hair cut short over the forehead **2** ornamental edge of hanging threads, tassels, etc. **3** outer edge **4** less important parts of an activity or group ▹ *v* **5** decorate with a fringe ▹ *adj* **6** (of theatre) unofficial or unconventional **fringed** *adj*
▸ **fringe benefit** benefit given in addition to a regular salary
frippery *n, pl* **-peries 1** useless ornamentation **2** trivia
frisk Ⓣ *v* **1** move or leap playfully **2** *informal* search (a person) for concealed weapons etc.
▸ **frisky** *adj* lively or high-spirited **friskily** *adv*
frisson [**frees**-sonn] *n* shiver of fear or excitement
fritter *n* piece of food fried in batter
fritter away Ⓣ *v* waste
frivolous Ⓣ *adj* **1** not serious or sensible **2** enjoyable but trivial **frivolously** *adv* **frivolity** *n*
frizz *v* form (hair) into stiff wiry curls **frizzy** *adj*
frizzle *v* cook or heat until crisp and shrivelled
Frobisher *n* Sir **Martin**. ?1535–94, English navigator and explorer: made three unsuccessful voyages in search of the Northwest Passage (1576; 1577; 1578), visiting Labrador and Baffin Island
frock *n* dress
▸ **frock coat** man's skirted coat as worn in the 19th century
frog[1] *n* smooth-skinned tailless amphibian with long back legs used for jumping
▸ **frog in one's throat** phlegm on the vocal cords, hindering speech
▸ **frogman** *n* swimmer with a rubber suit and breathing equipment for working underwater
▸ **frogmarch** *v* force (a resisting person) to move by holding his arms
▸ **frogspawn** *n* jelly- like substance containing frog's eggs
frog[2] *n* military-style fastening on a coat

THESAURUS

affability, amiability, congeniality, conviviality, geniality, neighbourliness, sociability
friendly *adj* = **amiable**, close, cordial, affectionate, genial, welcoming • *a very friendly group of people* OPPOSITE: unfriendly
See also: **cozy, favourable, pleasant, sociable, warm**
friendship *n* = **goodwill**, affection, attachment, closeness • *I value our friendship*. OPPOSITE: hostility
fright *n* = **fear**, shock, scare, alarm, panic, horror, dread, trepidation, consternation
frighten *v* = **scare**, alarm, intimidate, terrify, terrorize, startle, unnerve • *trying to frighten us*
frightened *adj* = **afraid**, scared, alarmed, petrified, startled, terrified • *frightened of thunder*
frightening *adj* = **terrifying**, hair-raising, alarming, intimidating, menacing • *a frightening experience*
See also: **scary, spooky**
frightful *adj* = **terrifying**, terrible, horrible, awful, fearful, traumatic, horrendous, dreadful, ghastly, alarming
frigid *adj* **1** = **cold**, icy, arctic, frosty, glacial, wintry, frozen **2** = **forbidding**, formal, austere, aloof, unresponsive, unapproachable, unfeeling
frills *pl n* = **trimmings**, fuss, additions, bells and whistles, embellishments, extras, frippery, ornamentation, ostentation
fringe *n* **1** = **border**, hem, trimming, edging **2** = **edge**, margin, perimeter, borderline, periphery, limits, outskirts ▸ *adj* **3** = **unofficial**, unconventional, unorthodox
frisk *v* **1** = **frolic**, play, jump, trip, skip, caper, prance, cavort, gambol **2** = **search**, check, inspect, run over, shake down (*US slang*)
frisky *adj* = **lively**, playful, coltish, frolicsome, high-spirited, kittenish, sportive
fritter *v* ▹ **fritter away** = **waste**, squander, misspend, dissipate, idle away, run through, spend like water
frivolity *n* = **fun**, silliness, flippancy, frivolousness, gaiety, levity, light-heartedness, superficiality, triviality
frivolous *adj* **1** = **flippant**, silly, juvenile, foolish, puerile • *a frivolous remark* OPPOSITE: serious **2** = **trivial**, minor, shallow, petty, unimportant, trifling

DICTIONARY

consisting of a button and loop
▸ **frogging** *n* set of such fastenings on a coat
frolic Ⓣ *v* **-icking**, **-icked** **1** run and play in a lively way ▷ *n* **2** lively and merry behaviour
▸ **frolicsome** *adj* playful
from *prep* indicating the point of departure, source, distance, cause, change of state, etc.
Fromm *n* **Erich**. 1900–80, US psychologist and philosopher, born in Germany. His works include *The Art of Loving* (1956) and *To Have and To Be* (1976)
frond *n* long leaf or leaflike part of a fern, palm, or seaweed
front Ⓣ *n* **1** fore part **2** position directly before or ahead **3** seaside promenade **4** battle line or area **5** *meteorol* dividing line between two different air masses **6** outward aspect **7** *informal* cover for another, usu. criminal, activity **8** group with a common goal ▷ *v* **9** face (onto) **10** be the presenter of (a television show) ▷ *adj* **11** of or at the front **frontal** *adj*
▸ **frontage** *n* façade of a building
▸ **frontispiece** *n* illustration facing the title page of a book
▸ **front bench** parliamentary leaders of the government or opposition **front-bencher** *n*
▸ **front court** *basketball* **1** half of the court into which a given team is attacking **2** centre and forwards of a team
▸ **frontrunner** *n informal* person regarded as most likely to win a race, election, etc.
Frontenac, Frontenac et Palluau *n* **Comte de**, title of *Louis de Buade*. 1620–98, governor of New France (1672–82; 1689–98)
frontier Ⓣ *n* area of a country bordering on another
frost Ⓣ *n* **1** white frozen dew or mist **2** atmospheric temperature below freezing point ▷ *v* **3** become covered with frost
▸ **frosted** *adj* **1** (of glass) having a rough surface to make it opaque **2** covered with frosting
▸ **frosting** *n* sugar icing
▸ **frosty** *adj* **1** characterized or covered by frost **2** unfriendly **frostily** *adv* **frostiness** *n*
▸ **frostbite** *n* destruction of tissue, esp. of the fingers or ears, by cold **frostbitten** *adj*
▸ **frost boil** bulge in road caused by freezing
Frost *n* **1** Sir **David** (**Paradine**). born 1939, British television host and executive, noted esp. for political interviews **2 Robert** (**Lee**). 1874–1963, US poet, noted for his lyrical verse on country life in New England. His books include *A Boy's Will* (1913), *North of Boston* (1914), and *New Hampshire* (1923)
froth Ⓣ *n* **1** mass of small bubbles ▷ *v* **2** foam **frothy** *adj*
frown Ⓣ *v* **1** wrinkle one's brows in worry, anger, or thought **2** look disapprovingly (on) ▷ *n* **3** frowning expression
frowsy *adj* **-sier**, **-siest** dirty or unkempt
froze *v* past tense of **freeze**
▸ **frozen** *v* past participle of **freeze**
fructify *v* **-fying**, **-fied** (cause to) bear fruit **fructification** *n*
fructose *n* crystalline sugar occurring in many fruits
frugal Ⓣ [**froo**-gl] *adj* **1** thrifty, sparing **2** meagre and inexpensive **frugally** *adv* **frugality** *n*
fruit Ⓣ *n* **1** part of a plant containing seeds, esp. if edible **2** any plant product useful to man **3** *often pl* result of an action or effort ▷ *v* **4** bear fruit
▸ **fruiterer** *n* person who sells fruit

THESAURUS

frolic *v* **1** = **play**, sport, romp, caper, cavort, frisk, lark, gambol, make merry ▸ *n* **2** = **revel**, game, romp, spree, antic, lark
frolicsome *adj* = **playful**, lively, merry, coltish, frisky, kittenish, sportive
from time to time *See* **sometimes**
front *n* **1** = **exterior**, face, frontage • *the front of the house* OPPOSITE: back **2** = **appearance**, show, face, exterior • *She put on a brave front.* **3** = **forefront**, lead, head, vanguard, front line **4** = **disguise**, show, cover, mask, blind, cover-up, pretext, façade ▷ **in front** = **ahead**, before, leading • *too close to the car in front* ▸ *adj* **5** = **first**, lead, head, foremost, cutting edge, leading, topmost ▸ *v* **6** = **face onto**, overlook, look over *or* look into
frontage *See* **front**
frontier *n* = **boundary**, limit, edge, verge, perimeter, borderline
frost *n* = **hoarfrost**, freeze, rime
frosty *adj* **1** = **cold**, icy, chilly, wintry, frozen **2** = **unfriendly**, frigid, discouraging, standoffish, unenthusiastic, unwelcoming
froth *n* **1** = **foam**, head, scum, suds, bubbles, effervescence, lather, spume ▸ *v* **2** = **fizz**, foam, bubble over, come to a head, effervesce, lather
frothy *adj* = **foamy**, foaming, sudsy
frown *v* = **scowl**, glare, glower • *She frowned in displeasure.* ▷ **frown on** = **disapprove of**, discourage, dislike, look askance at, take a dim view of
frozen *adj* = **icy**, arctic, frigid, numb, chilled • *I was frozen in the arena.*
frugal *adj* = **thrifty**, careful, prudent, economical, abstemious, niggardly, parsimonious, sparing
frugality *See* **economy**
fruit *n* **1** = **produce**, product, crop, yield, harvest **2** = **result**, return, profit, effect, benefit, advantage, reward, consequence, outcome, end result

DICTIONARY

▸ **fruitful** *adj* useful or productive **fruitfully** *adv*
▸ **fruition** [froo-**ish**-on] *n* fulfilment of something worked for or desired
▸ **fruitless** *adj* useless or unproductive **fruitlessly** *adv*
▸ **fruity** *adj* **1** of or like fruit **2** (of a voice) mellow **3** *informal* mildly bawdy
▸ **fruit machine** coin-operated gambling machine
frump *n* dowdy woman **frumpy** *adj*
frustrate Ⓣ *v* **1** upset or anger **2** hinder or prevent **frustrated** *adj* **frustrating** *adj* **frustration** *n*
fry[1] Ⓣ *v* **frying**, **fried 1** cook or be cooked in fat or oil ▹ *n, pl* **fries 2** dish of fried food **3** social occasion at which fried food is eaten
fry[2] *pl n* young fishes
▸ **small fry** young or insignificant people
Fry *n* **Elizabeth**. 1780–1845, English prison reformer and Quaker
Frye *n* **(Herman) Northrop**. 1912–91, Canadian literary critic. His works include *Fearful Symmetry* (1947) and *The Anatomy of Criticism* (1957)
ft. 1 foot **2** feet
Fuchs *n* **1 Klaus Emil**. 1911–88, East German physicist. He was born in Germany, became a British citizen (1942), and was imprisoned (1950–59) for giving secret atomic research information to the Soviet Union **2** Sir **Vivian Ernest**. 1908–99, English explorer and geologist: led the Commonwealth Trans-Antarctic Expedition (1955–58)
fuchsia [**fyew**-sha] *n* ornamental shrub with hanging flowers
fuddle *v* cause to be intoxicated or confused **fuddled** *adj*
fuddy-duddy Ⓣ *n, pl* **-dies**, *adj informal* old-fashioned (person)
fudge[1] *n* soft caramel-like candy
fudge[2] Ⓣ *v* avoid making a firm statement or decision
fuel Ⓣ *n* **1** substance burned or treated to produce heat or power **2** something that intensifies (a feeling etc.) ▹ *v* **fuelling**, **fuelled 3** provide with fuel
fug *n* hot stale atmosphere **fuggy** *adj*
fugitive Ⓣ [**fyew**-jit-iv] *n* **1** person who flees, esp. from arrest or pursuit ▹ *adj* **2** fleeing **3** transient
fugue [**fyewg**] *n* musical composition in which a theme is repeated in different parts
Führer *n German* leader; title used by Hitler as Nazi dictator
fulcrum *n, pl* **-crums**, **-cra** pivot about which a lever turns
fulfill *v* **-filling**, **-filled 1** bring about the achievement of (a desire or promise) **2** carry out (a request or order) **3** do what is required **fulfillment** *n*
▸ **fulfill oneself** *v* achieve one's potential
full[1] Ⓣ *adj* **1** containing as much or as many as possible **2** abundant in supply **3** having had enough to eat **4** plump **5** complete, whole **6** (of a garment) of ample cut **7** (of a sound or flavour) rich and strong ▹ *adv* **8** completely **9** directly **10** very **fully** *adv* **fullness** *n*
▸ **in full** without shortening
▸ **full-blooded** *adj* vigorous or enthusiastic

THESAURUS

fruitful *adj* = **useful**, effective, successful, productive, profitable, beneficial, worthwhile, rewarding, win-win (*informal*), advantageous
fruition *n* = **maturity**, completion, realization, perfection, fulfillment, attainment, materialization, ripeness
fruitless *adj* = **useless**, unsuccessful, pointless, vain, futile, unproductive, unprofitable, ineffectual, profitless, unavailing
frustrate *v* = **thwart**, block, check, foil • *His efforts were frustrated.*
See also: **dash, hamper, hinder**
frustrated *adj* = **disappointed**, discouraged, resentful, disheartened, embittered
frustration *n* **1** = **obstruction**, blocking, circumvention, foiling, thwarting **2** = **annoyance**, disappointment, grievance, dissatisfaction, resentment, irritation, vexation
fry *See* **cook**
fuddy-duddy *n* = **conservative**, square (*informal*), fogey *or* old fogey, stick-in-the-mud (*informal*), stuffed shirt (*informal*)
fudge *v* = **misrepresent**, change, fake, cook (*slang*), alter, forge, distort, falsify, misstate, tamper with, tinker with
fuel *n* = **incitement**, ammunition, provocation
fugitive *n* **1** = **runaway**, refugee, runner, deserter, escapee ▸ *adj* **2** = **momentary**, brief, temporary, passing, short-lived, fleeting, transient, ephemeral, transitory
fulfill *v* **1** = **achieve**, perform, realize, satisfy, accomplish, carry out • *He decided to fulfill his dream and become a photographer.* **2** = **comply with**, meet, fill, answer, observe, obey, conform to
See also: **keep**
fulfillment *n* = **achievement**, accomplishment, completion, implementation, realization, attainment, consummation
full *adj* **1** = **filled**, packed, loaded, saturated • *full of books* OPPOSITE: empty **2** = **comprehensive**, maximum,

DICTIONARY

▸ **full-blown** *adj* fully developed
▸ **full moon** phase of the moon when it is visible as a fully illuminated disc
▸ **full-scale** *adj* **1** (of a plan) of actual size **2** using all resources
▸ **full stop** punctuation mark (.) at the end of a sentence and after abbreviations
full[2] *v* clean, shrink, and press cloth **fuller** *n*
▸ **fuller's earth** absorbent clay used for clarifying oils and fats, fulling cloth, etc.
Fuller *n* (**Richard**) **Buckminster**. 1895–1983, US architect and engineer: developed the geodesic dome
fulmar *n* Arctic sea bird
fulminate *v* (foll. by *against*) criticize angrily **fulmination** *n*
fulsome Ⓣ *adj* insincerely excessive
fumble Ⓣ *v* **1** handle awkwardly **2** say awkwardly
fume Ⓣ *v* **1** be very angry **2** give out smoke or vapour **3** treat with fumes ▹ *n* **4** *usu pl* pungent smoke or vapour
fumigate Ⓣ [**fyew**-mig-gate] *v* disinfect with fumes **fumigation** *n*
fun Ⓣ *n* enjoyment or amusement
▸ **make fun of** mock or tease
▸ **funny** *adj* **1** comical, humorous **2** odd **funnily** *adv*
▸ **funny bone** part of the elbow where the nerve is near the surface
function Ⓣ *n* **1** purpose something exists for **2** way something works **3** large or formal social event **4** *math* quantity whose value depends on the varying value of another **5** series of operations done by a computer ▹ *v* **6** operate or work **7** (foll. by *as*) fill the role of
▸ **functional** *adj* **1** of or as a function **2** practical rather than decorative **3** in working order **functionally** *adv*
▸ **functionary** *n* official
fund Ⓣ *n* **1** stock of money for a special purpose **2** supply or store **funds 3** money resources ▹ *v* **4** provide money to **funding** *n*
fundamental Ⓣ *adj* **1** essential or primary **2** basic **fundamentals** *pl n* **3** basic rules or facts **fundamentally** *adv*
▸ **fundamentalism** *n* literal or strict interpretation of a religion **fundamentalist** *n, adj*
funeral Ⓣ *n* ceremony of burying or

THESAURUS

extensive, detailed, thorough, exhaustive • *I want a full account of what happened.* **3 = loose**, baggy, voluminous • *a full skirt* **4 = plentiful**, extensive, comprehensive, adequate, generous, ample, abundant, exhaustive **5 = rich**, clear, deep, loud, distinct, rounded, resonant **6 = plump**, rounded, voluptuous, buxom, curvaceous ▹ **full of life** *See* **alive** ▸ *n* ▹ **in full = completely**, in its entirety, in total, without exception
See also: **busy, complete, crowded, whole**
full-blooded *adj* = **vigorous**, hearty, lusty, red-blooded, virile
full-grown *See* **mature**
fullness *n* **1 = plenty**, fill, abundance, saturation, satiety, sufficiency, copiousness, profusion **2 = richness**, strength, resonance, clearness, loudness
full-scale *adj* = **major**, comprehensive, wide-ranging, thorough, in-depth, all-out, exhaustive, sweeping, thoroughgoing
fully *adv* = **totally**, completely, entirely, perfectly, altogether, thoroughly, wholly, utterly, in all respects, one hundred per cent
fully-fledged *See* **mature**
fulsome *adj* = **insincere**, excessive, extravagant, inordinate, immoderate, sycophantic, unctuous
fumble *v* = **grope**, flounder, scrabble, feel around
fume *v* = **rage**, storm, rant, smoulder, seethe, get hot under the collar (*informal*), see red (*informal*)
fumes *pl n* = **smoke**, gas, pollution, exhaust, smog, vapour
fumigate *v* = **disinfect**, sanitize, cleanse, purify, sterilize, clean out *or* clean up
fuming *adj* = **furious**, angry, enraged, raging, incensed, seething, in a rage, on the warpath (*informal*), up in arms
fun *n* **1 = enjoyment**, entertainment, pleasure, recreation, amusement • *It was great fun.* ▹ **make fun of = mock**, taunt, ridicule, deride, laugh at • *Don't make fun of him.* ▸ *adj* **2 = enjoyable**, lively, amusing, witty, convivial, diverting, entertaining
function *n* **1 = purpose**, job, duty, responsibility, role • *What is the function of this software?* **2 = reception**, party, dinner, gathering • *We were going to a function downtown.* ▸ *v* **3 = work**, go, run, operate, perform • *The furnace was not functioning properly.*
See also: **act, behave, part**
functional *adj* **1 = practical**, useful, utilitarian, serviceable, hard-wearing **2 = working**, operative
fund *n* **1 = reserve**, supply, capital, pool, foundation • *the pension fund* **2 = store**, reserve, mine, reservoir, hoard • *an extraordinary fund of energy* ▸ *v* **3 = finance**, support, subsidize, pay for • *to raise money to fund scientific research*
See also: **bank**
fundamental *adj* **1 = essential**, key, central, primary, basic, principal, cardinal, elementary, rudimentary, underlying

DICTIONARY

cremating a dead person
▸ **funerary** *adj* of or for a funeral
▸ **funereal** [fyew-**neer**-ee-al] *adj* gloomy or sombre
funfair *n* entertainment with machines to ride on and stalls
fungus *n, pl* **-gi**, **-guses** plant without leaves, flowers, or roots, such as a mushroom or mould **fungal** *or* **fungous** *adj*
▸ **fungicide** *n* substance that destroys fungi
funicular [fyew-**nik**-yew-lar] *n* cable railway on a mountainside or cliff
funk[1] *n* style of dance music with a strong beat
▸ **funky** *adj* (of music) passionate or soulful
funk[2] *informal* ▷ *n* **1** nervous or fearful state ▷ *v* **2** avoid (doing something) through fear
Funk *n* **Casimir**. 1884–1967, US biochemist, born in Poland: studied and named vitamins
funnel Ⓣ *n* **1** cone-shaped tube for pouring liquids into a narrow opening **2** chimney of a ship or locomotive ▷ *v* **-nelling**, **-nelled** **3** (cause to) move through or as if through a funnel
funny Ⓣ *adj* **-nier**, **-niest** see **fun**
fur Ⓣ *n* **1** soft hair of a mammal **2** animal skin with the fur left on **3** garment made of this **4** whitish coating on the tongue or inside a kettle ▷ *v* **5** cover or become covered with fur **furry** *adj*
▸ **furrier** *n* dealer in furs
furbelow *n* **1** flounce or ruffle **2** *often pl* showy ornamentation
furbish *v* smarten up
furcate *v* **1** divide into two parts ▷ *adj* **2** forked, branching
furious Ⓣ *adj* **1** very angry **2** violent or unrestrained **furiously** *adv*
furl *v* roll up and fasten (a sail, umbrella, or flag)
furlong *n* eighth of a mile
furlough [**fur**-loh] *n* leave of absence from military duty
furnace *n* enclosed chamber containing a very hot fire
furnish Ⓣ *v* **1** fit up (a house or room) with furniture **2** (foll. by *with*) supply, provide
▸ **furnishings** *pl n* furniture, carpets, and fittings
▸ **furniture** *n* large movable articles such as chairs and wardrobes
furor Ⓣ [fyew-**ror**-ee] *n* very excited or angry reaction
furrow Ⓣ *n* **1** trench made by a plow **2** groove ▷ *v* **3** make or become wrinkled **4** make furrows in
Furtado *n* **Nelly** (**Kim**). born 1978, Canadian pop singer of Portuguese ancestry. Her recordings include "I'm Like a Bird" (2000)
further Ⓣ *adv* **1** in addition **2** to a greater distance or extent ▷ *adj* **3** additional **4** more distant ▷ *v* **5** assist the progress of **furtherance** *n*
▸ **furthest** *adv* **1** to the greatest distance or extent ▷ *adj* **2** most distant
▸ **furthermore** *adv* besides
▸ **furthermost** *adj* most distant
furtive Ⓣ *adj* sly and secretive **furtively** *adv*

f

THESAURUS

▸ *n* **2 = principle**, rule, law, cornerstone, axiom, rudiment
fundamentally *adv* **= essentially**, basically, primarily, radically, intrinsically, at bottom, at heart
fundamentals *See* **essentials**
funds *pl n* **= money**, capital, cash, finance, ready money, resources, savings, the wherewithal
funeral *n* **= burial**, cremation, interment, inhumation, obsequies
funnel *v* **= channel**, move, pass, conduct, direct, pour, filter, convey
funny *adj* **1 = strange**, odd, unusual, mysterious, peculiar, puzzling • *They heard a funny noise.* **2 = amusing**, comic, hilarious, humorous, witty, comical • *a funny story* OPPOSITE: serious ▷ **funny feeling** *See* **premonition**
See also: **suspicious, weird**
fur *See* **coat, pile**
furious *adj* **1 = enraged**, mad, raging, livid, fuming, infuriated • *furious about the poor service they received* **2 = frantic**, intense, fierce, frenzied, breakneck, manic • *a furious battle*
See also: **angry, violent**
furnish *v* **1 = decorate**, stock, equip, fit out **2 = supply**, give, offer, provide, present, grant, hand out
furniture *n* **= household goods**, appliances, fittings, furnishings, goods, possessions, things (*informal*)
furor *n* **= disturbance**, stir, outcry, uproar, commotion, to-do, hullabaloo
furrow *n* **1 = groove**, line, channel, crease, wrinkle, trench, seam, hollow, rut ▸ *v* **2 = wrinkle**, crease, knit, corrugate, draw together
further *adv* **1 = in addition**, also, besides, moreover, furthermore, additionally, into the bargain, to boot ▸ *adj* **2 = additional**, more, new, other, extra, fresh, supplementary ▸ *v* **3 = promote**, help, forward, assist, advance, encourage, lend support to, work for
furthermore *adv* **= besides**, too, further, moreover, additionally, as well, in addition, into the bargain, to boot
furthest *adj* **= most distant**, extreme, ultimate, terminal, farthest, furthermost,

DICTIONARY

Furtwängler *n* **Wilhelm**. 1886–1954, German conductor, noted for his interpretations of Wagner
fury Ⓣ *n, pl* **-ries 1** wild anger **2** uncontrolled violence
furze *n* gorse
fuse[1] *n* cord containing an explosive for detonating a bomb
fuse[2] Ⓣ *v* **1** join or combine **2** melt with heat **3** unite by melting **4** (cause to) fail as a result of a blown fuse ▷ *n* **5** safety device for electric circuits, containing a wire that melts and breaks the connection when the circuit is overloaded **fusible** *adj*
fuselage [fyew-zill-lahzh] *n* body of an aircraft
Fuseli *n* **Henry**, original name *Johann Heinrich Füssli*. 1741–1825, British painter, born in Switzerland. His paintings include *Nightmare* (1782)
fusilier [fyew-zill-**leer**] *n* soldier of certain regiments
▸ **fusillade** [fyew-zill-**lade**] *n* **1** continuous discharge of firearms **2** outburst of criticism, questions, etc.
fusion Ⓣ *n* **1** melting **2** product of fusing **3** Also **nuclear fusion** combination of the nucleus of two atoms with the release of energy **4** something new created by a mixture of qualities, ideas, or things **5** popular music blending styles, esp. jazz and funk ▷ *adj* **6** of a style of cooking that combines traditional Western techniques and ingredients with those used in Eastern cuisine
fuss Ⓣ *n* **1** needless activity or worry **2** complaint or objection **3** great display of attention ▷ *v* **4** make a fuss
▸ **fussy** *adj* **1** inclined to fuss **2** overparticular **3** overelaborate **fussily** *adv* **fussiness** *n*
fustian *n* **1** thick cotton cloth **2** pompous language
fusty Ⓣ *adj* **-tier, -tiest 1** stale-smelling **2** behind the times **fustiness** *n*
futile Ⓣ [**fyew**-tile] *adj* unsuccessful or useless **futility** *n*
futon [**foo**-tonn] *n* Japanese padded quilt, laid on the floor as a bed
future Ⓣ *n* **1** time to come **2** what will happen **3** prospects ▷ *adj* **4** yet to come or be **5** of or relating to time to come **6** (of a verb tense) indicating that the action specified has not yet taken place
▸ **futuristic** *adj* of a design appearing to belong to some future time
fuzz[1] *n* mass of fine or curly hairs or fibres
▸ **fuzzy** *adj* **1** of, like, or covered with fuzz **2** blurred or indistinct **3** (of hair) tightly curled **fuzzily** *adv* **fuzziness** *n*
fuzz[2] *n slang* police(man)

THESAURUS

outmost, remotest
furtive *adj* = **sly**, clandestine, secretive, sneaky, stealthy, surreptitious, conspiratorial, underhand, under-the-table
fury *n* **1** = **anger**, rage, passion, frenzy, wrath, madness, impetuosity **2** = **violence**, force, intensity, severity, ferocity, savagery, fierceness, vehemence
fuse *v* **1** = **join**, combine, unite, merge, dissolve, blend, integrate, amalgamate, meld, coalesce, intermix, intermingle, federate (*politics*), commingle, agglutinate, run together, put together OPPOSITE: separate **2** = **bond**, join, stick, melt, smelt, weld, solder
fusion *n* = **merging**, union, merger, blend, federation (*politics*), integration, mixture, amalgamation, synthesis, blending, coalescence, uniting, commixture, commingling
fuss *n* **1** = **bother**, stir, confusion, agitation, commotion, to-do • *What's all the fuss about?* **2** = **argument**, trouble, complaint, row, objection, squabble, furor ▸ *v* **3** = **fret**, bustle, fidget, carry on (*informal*) • *The servers fussed and hovered around our table.*
fussy *adj* **1** = **particular**, exacting, choosy (*informal*), discriminating, fastidious • *fussy about his food* **2** = **overelaborate**, busy, cluttered, overworked, rococo
See also: **elaborate**
fusty *adj* = **stale**, damp, stuffy, airless, mildewed, mouldering, musty
futile *adj* = **useless**, unsuccessful, vain, abortive, forlorn • *a futile effort to run away* OPPOSITE: successful
See also: **hopeless**
futility *n* = **uselessness**, emptiness, ineffectiveness, hollowness
future *adj* **1** = **forthcoming**, later, forward, prospective, approaching, coming, impending • *to predict future growth* OPPOSITE: past ▸ *n* **2** = **hereafter**, time to come **3** = **outlook**, expectation, prospect
fuzzy *adj* **1** = **fluffy**, woolly, downy, frizzy **2** = **indistinct**, unclear, vague, obscure, distorted, bleary, blurred, ill-defined, out of focus

DICTIONARY

Gg

g **1** gram(s) **2** (acceleration due to) gravity
G *slang* grand (thousand pounds or dollars)
gab *n, v* **gabbing, gabbed** *informal* talk or chatter
▸ **gift of the gab** eloquence
▸ **gabby** *adj informal* talkative
gabardine, gaberdine *n* strong twill cloth used esp. for raincoats
gabble Ⓣ *v* **1** speak rapidly and indistinctly ▷ *n* **2** rapid indistinct speech
gable *n* triangular upper part of a wall between sloping roofs **gabled** *adj*
Gable *n* (**William**) **Clark**. 1901–60, US film actor. His films include *It Happened One Night* (1934), *San Francisco* (1936), *Gone with the Wind* (1939), *Mogambo* (1953), and *The Misfits* (1960)
Gabrieli, Gabrielli *n* **1 Andrea**. 1520–86, Italian organist and composer; chief organist of St Mark's, Venice **2** his nephew, **Giovanni**. 1558–1612, Italian organist and composer
gad *v* **gadding, gadded** ▸ **gad about** *or* **gad around** go around in search of pleasure
▸ **gadabout** *n* pleasure-seeker
Gaddafi, Qaddafi *n* **Mu'ammar Muhammad al-**. born 1942, Libyan army officer and statesman; head of state from 1969
gadfly *n* **1** fly that bites cattle **2** constantly annoying person
gadget Ⓣ *n* small mechanical device or appliance **gadgetry** *n* gadgets
Gael [**gayl**] *n* Gaelic-speaker
▸ **Gaelic** [**gal**-lik] *n* **1** Celtic language of Ireland and the Scottish Highlands ▷ *adj* **2** of the Gaels or their language
gaff[1] *n* **1** stick with an iron hook for landing large fish ▷ *v* **2** hook or land (a fish) with a gaff
gaff[2] *n* **blow the gaff** *slang* divulge a secret
gaffe Ⓣ *n* social blunder
gaffer *n* **1** old man **2** *informal* foreman or boss
gag[1] Ⓣ *v* **gagging, gagged 1** stop up the mouth of (a person) with cloth etc. **2** deprive of free speech **3** retch **4** choke ▷ *n* **5** cloth etc. put into or tied across the mouth
gag[2] Ⓣ *n informal* joke
gaga [**gah**-gah] *adj slang* **1** senile **2** crazy
gage *n* **1** thing given as security **2** formerly, something thrown down as a challenge to combat
Gage *n* **Thomas**. 1721–87, British general and governor in North America; commander in chief of British forces at Bunker Hill (1775)
gaggle Ⓣ *n* **1** flock of geese **2** *informal* disorderly crowd
Gagnon *n* **Marc**. born 1975, Canadian short track speed skater: winner of three Olympic gold medals
gaiety Ⓣ *n* **1** cheerfulness **2** merrymaking
gaily *adv* **1** merrily **2** colourfully
gain Ⓣ *v* **1** acquire or obtain **2** win in competition **3** increase or improve **4** reach **5** (of a watch or clock) be or become too fast ▷ *n* **6** profit **7** increase or improvement
▸ **gainful** *adj* useful or profitable **gainfully** *adv*

g

THESAURUS

gabble *v* **1 = prattle**, gush, spout, babble, blabber, gibber, jabber ▸ *n* **2 = gibberish**, chatter, babble, drivel, blabber, prattle, twaddle
gadabout *n* **= pleasure-seeker**, rover, wanderer, gallivanter, rambler
gadget *n* **= device**, tool, machine, appliance • *kitchen gadgets such as blenders and can openers*
gaffe *n* **= blunder**, bloomer (*informal*), faux pas, slip, mistake, lapse, indiscretion, solecism
gag[1] *v* **1 = suppress**, quiet, silence, curb, stifle, muzzle, muffle, stop up **2 = retch**, vomit, spew, heave, puke (*slang*), barf (*slang*), throw up (*informal*), toss one's cookies (*slang*)
gag[2] *n* **= joke**, crack (*slang*), funny (*informal*), hoax, jest, wisecrack (*informal*), witticism
gaggle *See* **bunch**
gaiety *n* **1 = cheerfulness**, glee, exhilaration, merriment, blitheness, high spirits, jollity, light-heartedness, mirth **2 = merrymaking**, fun, festivity, revelry, conviviality, jollification
gaily *adv* **1 = cheerfully**, happily, gleefully, blithely, joyfully, light-heartedly, merrily **2 = colourfully**, brightly, brilliantly, flamboyantly, flashily, gaudily, showily
gain *v* **1 = acquire**, win, secure, obtain, achieve, earn • *Students can gain valuable experience by working.* **2 = benefit**, profit • *Would any areas of the world gain from global warming?* **3 = reach**, attain, arrive at, come to, get to ▷ **gain on = get nearer**, close, approach, overtake, catch up with, narrow

DICTIONARY

▸ **gain on** *or* **upon** *v* get nearer to or catch up with

gainsay Ⓣ *v* **-saying**, **-said** deny or contradict

Gainsborough *n* **Thomas**. 1727–88, English painter, noted particularly for his informal portraits and for his naturalistic landscapes

gait Ⓣ *n* manner of walking

gaiter *n* cloth or leather covering for the lower leg

gala Ⓣ [**gah**-la] *n* **1** festival **2** competitive sporting event

galantine *n* dish of white meat served in a cold jelly

galaxy *n, pl* **-axies 1** system of stars **2** gathering of famous people **galactic** *adj*

Galbraith *n* **John Kenneth**. 1908–2006, US economist and diplomat born in Canada; author of *The Affluent Society* (1958), *The New Industrial State* (1967), and *The Culture of Contentment* (1992) **Galbraithian** *adj*

gale Ⓣ *n* **1** strong wind **2** *informal* loud outburst

Galen *n* Latin name *Claudius Galenus*. ?130–?200 AD, Greek physician, anatomist, and physiologist. He codified existing medical knowledge and his authority continued until the Renaissance

Galileo *n* full name *Galileo Galilei*. 1564–1642, Italian mathematician, astronomer, and physicist. He discovered the isochronism of the pendulum and demonstrated that falling bodies of different weights descend at the same rate. He perfected the refracting telescope, which led to his discovery of Jupiter's satellites, sunspots, and craters on the moon. He was forced by the Inquisition to recant his support of the Copernican system

gall[1] Ⓣ [**gawl**] *n* **1** *informal* impudence **2** bitter feeling

▸ **gall bladder** sac attached to the liver, storing bile

▸ **gallstone** *n* hard growth in the gall bladder or its ducts

gall[2] Ⓣ [**gawl**] *n* **1** sore caused by chafing ▷ *v* **2** make sore by rubbing **3** annoy

gall[3] [**gawl**] *n* abnormal outgrowth on a tree or plant

gallant Ⓣ *adj* **1** brave and noble **2** (of a man) attentive to women **gallantly** *adv* **gallantry** *n*

Gallant *n* **Mavis Leslie**. born 1922, Canadian short-story writer and novelist living in France. Her short-story collections include *The Other Paris* (1953), *My Heart is Broken* (1964), and *Across the Bridge* (1976); her two novels are *Green Water, Green Sky* (1959) and *A Fairly Good Time* (1970)

galleon *n* large three-masted sailing ship of the 15th–17th centuries

gallery *n, pl* **-ries 1** room or building for displaying works of art **2** balcony in a church, theatre, etc. **3** long narrow room for a specific purpose: *shooting gallery* **4** passage in a mine

galley *n* **1** kitchen of a ship or aircraft **2** *hist* ship propelled by oars, usu. rowed by slaves

▸ **galley proof** printer's proof in long slip form

▸ **galley slave 1** slave forced to row in a galley **2** *informal* drudge

Gallic *adj* **1** French **2** of ancient Gaul

▸ **Gallicism** *n* French word or idiom

gallium *n* soft grey metallic element used in semiconductors

gallivant Ⓣ *v* go about in search of pleasure

gallon *n* liquid measure of eight pints,

THESAURUS

the gap ▸ *n* **4 = increase**, rise, growth, advance, improvement • *Our party has made substantial gains in local elections.* **5 = profit**, return, benefit, advantage, dividend, yield

gainful *adj* **= profitable**, lucrative, useful, productive, beneficial, worthwhile, rewarding, win-win (*informal*), fruitful, advantageous, remunerative

gains *pl n* **= profits**, revenue, prize, earnings, proceeds, takings, winnings

gainsay *v* **= contradict**, deny, dispute, retract, contravene, rebut, controvert, disagree with

gait *n* **= walk**, step, pace, stride, carriage, tread, bearing

gala *n* **= festival**, celebration, festivity, pageant, carnival, jamboree, fête

gale *n* **1 = storm**, blast, hurricane, tornado, cyclone, typhoon, squall, tempest **2 = outburst**, outbreak, explosion, fit, burst, shout, eruption, howl, shriek, peal

gall[1] *n* **1** (*Informal*) **= impudence**, nerve (*informal*), cheek (*informal*), chutzpah (*informal*), brazenness, effrontery, impertinence, insolence **2 = bitterness**, hostility, animosity, acrimony, bile, rancour

gall[2] *v* **1 = scrape**, irritate, chafe, abrade **2 = annoy**, provoke, irk, irritate, vex, exasperate, rankle

gallant *adj* **1 = brave**, bold, heroic, courageous, valiant, noble, honourable, manly, intrepid **2 = chivalrous**, polite, noble, gracious, attentive, courteous, gentlemanly

gallantry *n* **1 = bravery**, spirit, courage, heroism, boldness, intrepidity, manliness, valour **2 = attentiveness**, courtesy, nobility, politeness, chivalry, courteousness, gentlemanliness, graciousness

galling *adj* **= annoying**, bitter, exasperating, irksome, irritating, provoking, vexatious

gallivant *v* **= wander**, roam, rove,

DICTIONARY

equal to 4.55 litres
gallop Ⓣ *n* **1** horse's fastest pace **2** galloping ▷ *v* **galloping, galloped 3** go or ride at a gallop **4** move or progress rapidly
gallows *n* wooden structure used for hanging criminals
Gallup *n* **George Horace.** 1901–84, US statistician: devised the Gallup Poll; founded the American Institute of Public Opinion (1935) and its British counterpart (1936)
▶ **Gallup poll** public opinion poll carried out by questioning a cross section of the population
galore Ⓣ *adv* in plenty: *presents galore*
galoshes *pl n* waterproof overshoes
Galsworthy *n* **John.** 1867–1933, English novelist and dramatist, noted for *The Forsyte Saga* (1906–28): Nobel prize for literature 1932
Galton *n* Sir **Francis.** 1822–1911, English explorer and scientist, a cousin of Charles Darwin, noted for his researches in heredity, meteorology, and statistics. He founded the study of eugenics and the theory of anticyclones
galumph *v informal* leap or move about clumsily
Galvani *n* **Luigi.** 1737–98, Italian physiologist: observed that muscles contracted on contact with dissimilar metals. This led to the galvanic cell and the electrical theory of muscle control by nerves
galvanic *adj* **1** of or producing an electric current generated by chemical means **2** *informal* stimulating or startling
▶ **galvanize** *v* **1** stimulate into action **2** coat (metal) with zinc
gambit *n* **1** opening line or move intended to secure an advantage **2** *chess* opening move involving the sacrifice of a pawn
gamble Ⓣ *v* **1** play games of chance to win money **2** act on the expectation of something ▷ *n* **3** risky undertaking **4** bet or wager
gambler *n* **gambling** *n*
gamboge [gam-**boje**] *n* gum resin used as a yellow pigment and purgative
gambol Ⓣ *v* **-bolling, -bolled 1** jump about playfully, frolic ▷ *n* **2** frolic
game Ⓣ *n* **1** amusement or pastime **2** contest for amusement **3** single period of play in a contest **4** scheme or trick **5** animals or birds hunted for sport or food **6** their flesh ▷ *v* **7** gamble ▷ *adj* **8** brave **9** willing **gamely** *adv*
▶ **gamer** *n* person who plays computer games
▶ **gaming** *n* gambling
▶ **gamekeeper** *n* person employed to breed game and prevent poaching
▶ **gameplan** *n* **1** strategy for playing a particular game **2** any plan or strategy
▶ **gamesmanship** *n* art of winning by cunning practices without actually cheating
gamete [**gam**-eet] *n biol* reproductive cell
gamin *n* street urchin
gamine [**gam**-een] *n* slim boyish young woman
gamma *n* third letter of the Greek alphabet
▶ **gamma ray** electromagnetic ray of shorter wavelength and higher energy than x-rays
gammon *n* cured or smoked ham
gamp *n informal* umbrella
gamut Ⓣ *n* whole range or scale (of music etc.)
gander *n* **1** male goose **2** *informal* quick look
Gandhi *n* **1 Indira** (**Priyadarshini**), daughter of Jawaharlal Nehru. 1917–84, Indian stateswoman; prime minister of India (1966–77; 1980–84); assassinated **2 Mohandas Karamchand**, known as *Mahatma Gandhi.* 1869–1948, Indian political and spiritual leader and social reformer. He played a major part in India's struggle for home rule and was frequently imprisoned by the British for organizing acts of civil disobedience. He advocated passive resistance and hunger strikes as means of achieving reform, campaigned for the untouchables, and attempted to unite Muslims and Hindus. He was assassinated by a Hindu extremist **3 Rajiv**, son of Indira Gandhi. 1944–91, Indian statesman; prime minister of India (1984–89); assassinated

g

THESAURUS

ramble, gad about
gallop *v* = **run**, race, career, speed, rush, sprint, bolt, dash, hurry
galore *adv* = **in abundance**, everywhere, aplenty, all over the place, in great quantity, in great numbers, in profusion, to spare
galvanize *v* = **stimulate**, spur, inspire, provoke, excite, stir, jolt, electrify, invigorate
gamble *v* **1** = **bet** • *He gambled on the horses.* **2** = **risk**, chance, stake • *Few networks seem willing to gamble on new TV series.* ▶ *n* **3** = **risk**, chance, lottery, wager • *We are taking a gamble on a young player.* **4** = **bet**, wager
gambol *v* **1** = **frolic**, jump, skip, hop, caper, prance, cavort, frisk ▶ *n* **2** = **frolic**, jump, skip, hop, caper, prance
game *n* **1** = **pastime**, sport, entertainment, distraction, diversion, recreation, amusement, lark **2** = **match**, contest, clash • *the Blue Jays' first game of the season* **3** = **wild animals**, prey, quarry **4** = **scheme**, plan, design, plot, trick, tactic, ploy, stratagem ▶ *adj* **5** = **brave**, persistent, gritty, spirited, courageous, plucky, gallant, intrepid **6** = **willing**, ready, interested, eager, keen, prepared, desirous
See also: **agreeable**
gamut *n* = **range**, area, series, field, sweep,

DICTIONARY

gang Ⓣ *n* **1** (criminal) group **2** organized group of workmen
▸**gangland** *n* criminal underworld
▸**gang up** *v* form an alliance (against)
gangling Ⓣ *adj* lanky and awkward
ganglion *n* **1** group of nerve cells **2** small harmless tumour
gangplank *n* portable bridge for boarding or leaving a ship
gangrene *n* decay of body tissue as a result of disease or injury interrupting blood supply **gangrenous** *adj*
gangster Ⓣ *n* member of a criminal gang
gangway *n* **1** passage between rows of seats **2** gangplank
gannet *n* **1** large sea bird **2** *slang* greedy person
gantry *n, pl* **-tries** structure supporting something such as a crane or rocket
gaol [**jayl**] *n* same as **jail**
gap Ⓣ *n* **1** break or opening **2** interruption or interval **3** divergence or difference **gappy** *adj*
gape Ⓣ *v* **1** stare in wonder **2** open the mouth wide **3** be or become wide open **gaping** *adj*
garage *n* **1** building used to house automobiles **2** place for the refuelling and repair of automobiles ▷*v* **3** put or keep an automobile in a garage
garb Ⓣ *n* **1** clothes ▷*v* **2** clothe
garbage Ⓣ *n* waste matter
▸**garbage can** large usu. cylindrical container for household rubbish
▸**garbage collector** person whose job is to collect household rubbish
garble *v* jumble or distort (a story etc.)
Garbo *n* **Greta**, real name *Greta Lovisa Gustafson*. 1905–90, US film actress, born in Sweden. Her films include *Grand Hotel* (1932), *Queen Christina* (1933), *Anna Karenina* (1935), *Camille* (1936), and *Ninotchka* (1939)
García Márquez *n* **Gabriel**. born 1928, Colombian novelist and short-story writer. His novels include *One Hundred Years of Solitude* (1967), *The Autumn of the Patriarch* (1977), *Love in the Time of Cholera* (1984), and *News of a Kidnapping* (1996). Nobel prize for literature 1982
garden *n* **1** piece of land for growing flowers, fruit, or vegetables **gardens 2** ornamental park ▷*v* **3** cultivate a garden **gardener** *n* **gardening** *n*
▸**garden centre** place selling plants and gardening equipment
gardenia [gar-**deen**-ya] *n* **1** large fragrant white waxy flower **2** shrub bearing this
Gardner *n* **Ava**. 1922–90, US film actress. Her films include *The Killers* (1946), *The Sun also Rises* (1957), and *The Night of the Iguana* (1964)
Garfield *n* **James Abram**. 1831–81, 20th president of the US (1881); assassinated in office
gargantuan *adj* huge
gargle *v* **1** wash the throat with (a liquid) by breathing out slowly through the liquid ▷*n* **2** act or sound of gargling **3** liquid used for gargling
gargoyle *n* waterspout carved in the form of a grotesque face, esp. on a church
Garibaldi *n* **Giuseppe**. 1807–82, Italian patriot; a leader of the Risorgimento. He fought against the Austrians and French in Italy (1848–49; 1859) and, with 1000 volunteers, conquered Sicily and Naples for the emerging kingdom of Italy (1860)
garish Ⓣ *adj* crudely bright or colourful **garishly** *adv* **garishness** *n*
garland Ⓣ *n* **1** wreath of flowers worn or hung as a decoration ▷*v* **2** decorate with garlands
Garland *n* **Judy**, real name *Frances Gumm*. 1922–69, US singer and film actress. Already a child star, she achieved international fame with *The Wizard of Oz* (1939). Later films included *Meet Me in St Louis*

THESAURUS

scale, scope, compass, catalogue
gang *n* = **group**, company, team, club, crowd, band, pack, squad, mob, clique, coterie
gangling *adj* = **tall**, awkward, lanky, angular, rangy, rawboned, spindly
gangster *n* = **racketeer**, hood (*slang*), mobster (*slang*), crook (*informal*), hoodlum
gap *n* **1** = **opening**, break, space, hole, clearing, chink • *They squeezed through a gap in the fence.* **2** = **interval**, pause, hiatus (*formal*), lull, interlude • *After a gap of nearly a decade, she returned to politics.* **3** = **difference**, disparity (*formal*), inconsistency • *the gap between rich and poor*
See also: **breach**
gape *v* **1** = **stare**, gawk, wonder, goggle **2** = **open**, split, crack, yawn
gaping *adj* = **wide**, open, great, broad, vast, cavernous, wide open, yawning
garb *See* **dress**
garbage *n* **1** = **trash**, refuse, waste, debris, junk (*informal*), litter • *piles of garbage* **2** (*Informal*) = **nonsense**, rubbish, drivel, gibberish • *I personally think this is complete garbage.*
garbled *adj* = **jumbled**, confused, distorted, incomprehensible, unintelligible • *a garbled voice-mail message*
gardens *See* **grounds**
garish *adj* = **gaudy**, loud, tasteless, flashy, showy, tacky (*informal*), vulgar, brash, brassy
garland *n* **1** = **wreath**, crown, honours, festoon, bays, chaplet, laurels ▸*v* **2** = **adorn**, crown, deck, festoon, wreathe

DICTIONARY

(1944) and *A Star is Born* (1954)
garlic *n* pungent bulb of a plant of the onion family, used in cooking
garment *n* article of clothing
Garneau *n* **Mark**. born 1949, Canadian astronaut, first Canadian to go into space (1984); entered politics in 2006
garner Ⓣ *v* collect or store
Garner *n* **Erroll**. 1921–77, US jazz pianist and composer
garnet *n* red semiprecious stone
garnish Ⓣ *v* **1** decorate (food) ▷ *n* **2** decoration for food
garret *n* attic in a house
garrison Ⓣ *n* **1** troops stationed in a town or fort **2** fortified place ▷ *v* **3** station troops in
garrotte *n* **1** Spanish method of execution by strangling **2** cord or wire used for this ▷ *v* **3** kill by this method
garrulous Ⓣ *adj* talkative **garrulously** *adv* **garrulity** *n*
garter *n* band worn round the leg to hold up a sock or stocking
Garvey *n* **Marcus**. 1887–1940, Jamaican Black nationalist leader, active in the US. He founded (1914) the Universal Negro Improvement Association and led the Back-to-Africa movement: jailed for fraud (1925–27)
gas *n, pl* **gases** *or* **gasses 1** airlike substance that is not liquid or solid **2** fossil fuel in the form of a gas, used for heating **3** gaseous anesthetic **4** gasoline **5** *informal* idle talk, boasting ▷ *v* **gassing, gassed 6** poison or render unconscious with gas **7** *informal* talk idly or boastfully
▸ **gassy** *adj* filled with gas
▸ **gaseous** *adj* of or like gas
▸ **gasbag** *n informal* person who talks too much
▸ **gas chamber** airtight room filled with poison gas to kill people or animals
▸ **gasholder** *or* **gasometer** [gas-**som**-it-er] *n* large tank for storing gas
▸ **gas mask** mask with a chemical filter to protect the wearer against poison gas
gash Ⓣ *v* **1** make a long deep cut in, slash ▷ *n* **2** long deep cut
Gaskell *n* **Mrs**, married name of *Elizabeth Cleghorn Stevenson*. 1810–65, English novelist. Her novels include *Mary Barton* (1848), an account of industrial life in Manchester, and *Cranford* (1853), a social study of a country village
gasket *n* piece of rubber etc. placed between two metal surfaces to act as a seal
gasoline *n* inflammable liquid obtained from petroleum, used as fuel in internal-combustion engines
▸ **gasoline bomb** incendiary device consisting of a bottle filled with gasoline
gasp Ⓣ *v* **1** draw in breath sharply or with difficulty **2** utter breathlessly ▷ *n* **3** convulsive intake of breath
Gassendi *n* **Pierre**. 1592–1655, French physicist and philosopher, who promoted an atomic theory of matter
gastric *adj* of the stomach
▸ **gastritis** *n* inflammation of the stomach
gastroenteritis *n* inflammation of the stomach and intestines
gastronomy *n* art of good eating **gastronomic** *adj*
gastropod *n* mollusc, such as a snail, with a single flattened muscular foot
gate Ⓣ *n* **1** movable barrier, usu. hinged, in a wall or fence **2** opening with a gate **3** any entrance or way in **4** (entrance money paid by) those attending a sporting event
▸ **gate-crash** *v* enter (a party) uninvited
▸ **gatehouse** *n* building at or above a gateway
▸ **gateway** *n* **1** entrance with a gate **2** means of access: *Bombay, gateway to India*
gâteau [**gat**-toe] *n, pl* **-teaux** [-toes] *Brit* rich elaborate cake
Gates *n* **1 Henry Louis**. born 1950, US scholar and critic, who pioneered African-American studies in such works as *Figures in Black* (1987) **2 Robert** (**Michael**). born 1943, US government official; Director of the CIA (1991–93); Secretary of Defense from 2006
gather Ⓣ *v* **1** assemble **2** increase gradually **3** collect gradually **4** learn from information

g

THESAURUS

garments *pl n* = **clothes**, dress, gear (*slang*), costume, uniform, outfit, apparel, attire, garb, clothing
garner *v* = **collect**, save, store, gather, stockpile, accumulate, amass, hoard, stow away
garnish *v* **1** = **decorate**, trim, enhance, adorn, ornament, embellish, set off ▸ *n* **2** = **decoration**, enhancement, trimming, embellishment, adornment, ornamentation
garrison *n* **1** = **troops**, unit, command, detachment, armed force **2** = **fort**, post, base, station, camp, stronghold, fortress, fortification, encampment ▸ *v* **3** = **station**, post, position, assign, put on duty
garrulous *adj* = **talkative**, chatty, verbose, gossiping, loquacious, prattling, voluble
gash *v* **1** = **cut**, wound, tear, split, slash, gouge, slit, lacerate ▸ *n* **2** = **cut**, wound, tear, split, slash, gouge, slit, laceration, incision
gasp *v* **1** = **gulp**, pant, puff, choke • *She gasped for air.* ▸ *n* **2** = **gulp**, puff • *An audible gasp went through the theatre.*
gate *n* = **barrier**, opening, door, exit, passage, entrance, portal, gateway
gather *v* **1** = **assemble**, mass, flock,

DICTIONARY

given **5** draw (material) into small tucks or folds **6** pick or harvest
▸ **gathers** *pl n* gathered folds in material
▸ **gathering** *n* assembly
gauche Ⓣ [gohsh] *adj* socially awkward **gaucheness** *n*
▸ **gaucherie** *n* **1** awkwardness **2** gauche act
gaucho [gow-choh] *n, pl* **-chos** S American cowboy
Gaudí *n* **Antonio**. 1852–1926, Spanish architect, regarded as one of the most original exponents of Art Nouveau in Europe and noted esp. for the church of the Sagrada Familia, Barcelona
gaudy Ⓣ *adj* **gaudier, gaudiest** vulgarly bright or colourful **gaudily** *adv* **gaudiness** *n*
gauge Ⓣ [gayj] *v* **1** measure the amount or condition of **2** estimate or judge ▷ *n* **3** scale or standard of measurement **4** measuring instrument **5** distance between the rails of a railway track
Gauguin *n* **Paul**. 1848–1903, French postimpressionist painter, who worked in the South Pacific from 1891. Inspired by primitive art, his work is characterized by flat contrasting areas of pure colours
gaunt Ⓣ *adj* **1** lean and haggard **2** (of a place) desolate or bleak **gauntness** *n*
gauntlet[1] *n* heavy glove with a long cuff
▸ **throw down the gauntlet** offer a challenge
gauntlet[2] *n* **run the gauntlet 1** be forced to run between, and be struck by, two rows of men, as a former military punishment **2** be exposed to criticism or unpleasant treatment
Gauss *n* **Karl Friedrich**. 1777–1855, German mathematician: developed the theory of numbers and applied mathematics to astronomy, electricity and magnetism, and geodesy **Gaussian** *adj*
gauze *n* **1** transparent loosely-woven fabric **2** fine wire mesh **gauzy** *adj*
gave *v* past tense of **give**
gavel [gahv-el] *n* small hammer banged on a table by a judge, auctioneer, or chairman to call for attention
gavotte *n* **1** old formal dance **2** music for this
gawk *v slang* stare stupidly
▸ **gawky** *adj* clumsy or awkward **gawkiness** *n*
gawp *v slang* stare stupidly
gay Ⓣ *adj* **1** homosexual **2** carefree and merry **3** colourful ▷ *n* **4** homosexual
▸ **gayness** *n* homosexuality
Gay *n* **John**. 1685–1732, English poet and dramatist; author of *The Beggar's Opera* (1728)
Gaye *n* **Marvin**. 1939–84, US soul singer and songwriter; recordings include "I Heard It Through the Grapevine" (1969), *What's Going On* (1971), and "Sexual Healing" (1982): shot dead by his father
Gay-Lussac *n* **Joseph Louis**. 1778–1850, French physicist and chemist: discovered the law named after him (1808), investigated the effects of terrestrial magnetism, isolated boron and cyanogen, and discovered methods of manufacturing sulphuric and oxalic acids
gaze Ⓣ *v* **1** look fixedly ▷ *n* **2** fixed look
gazebo [gaz-**zee**-boh] *n, pl* **-bos, -boes** summerhouse with a good view

THESAURUS

congregate, round up, convene, muster, marshal • *We gathered around the fireplace*. OPPOSITE: scatter **2 = collect**, stockpile, accumulate, amass, hoard • *I suggest we gather enough firewood to last the night*. **3 = learn**, hear, understand, conclude, assume • *"He speaks English." "I gathered that."* **4 = pick**, select, harvest, garner, reap, cull, pluck, glean **5 = intensify**, increase, rise, grow, expand, swell, deepen, heighten, thicken **6 = fold**, tuck, pleat
See also: **concentrate, crowd, imagine, meet**
gathering *n* = **assembly**, meeting, rally, congregation, muster, get-together (*informal*), conference, convention, congress • *polite social gatherings*
See also: **function, party**
gauche *adj* = **awkward**, clumsy, unsophisticated, ill-mannered, inelegant, tactless
gaudy *adj* = **garish**, bright, loud, flashy, showy • *gaudy fake jewellery*
See also: **tasteless, vulgar**
gauge *v* **1 = measure**, check, count, determine, weigh, calculate, compute, ascertain **2 = judge**, rate, value, estimate, guess, assess, evaluate, reckon, appraise, adjudge ▸ *n* **3 = indicator**, test, measure, standard, guide, guideline, criterion, meter, touchstone, yardstick
gaunt *adj* = **emaciated**, lean, spare, skinny, anorexic, skeletal, bony, angular, scrawny, cadaverous, pinched
gawky *adj* = **awkward**, clumsy, lumbering, ungainly, gauche, loutish, maladroit
gay *adj* **1 = homosexual**, lesbian, bent (*informal, derogatory*), queer (*informal, derogatory*) **2 = carefree**, sparkling, lively, merry, cheerful, light-hearted, jovial, blithe **3 = colourful**, rich, bright, brilliant, flamboyant, vivid, flashy, showy ▸ *n* **4 = homosexual**, lesbian
gaze *v* **1 = stare**, look, watch, view, wonder, regard, gape ▸ *n* **2 = stare**, look, fixed look

gazelle *n* small graceful antelope
gazette Ⓣ *n* official publication containing announcements
▸ **gazetteer** *n* (part of) a book that lists and describes places
gazump *v* raise the price of a house after verbally agreeing it with (a prospective buyer)
gazunder *v* reduce an offer on a property immediately before exchanging contracts having earlier agreed a higher price with the seller
GB **1** Great Britain **2** Also **Gb** gigabyte
GDP gross domestic product
gear Ⓣ *n* **1** set of toothed wheels connecting with another or with a rack to change the direction or speed of transmitted motion **2** mechanism for transmitting motion by gears **3** setting of a gear to suit engine speed: *first gear* **4** clothing or belongings **5** equipment ▷ *v* **6** adapt (one thing) to fit in with another
▸ **in** *or* **out of gear** with the gear mechanism engaged or disengaged
▸ **gearbox** *n* case enclosing a set of gears in a motor vehicle
▸ **gear up** *v* prepare for an activity
Geber *n* Latinized form of Jabir, assumed in honour of Jabir ibn Hayyan by a 14th-century alchemist, probably Spanish: he described the preparation of nitric and sulphuric acids
Gebrselassie *n* **Haile**. born 1973, Ethiopian athlete; Olympic gold medallist in the 10 000 metres in 1996 and 2000
gecko *n, pl* **geckos**, **geckoes** small tropical lizard
gee *interj US informal* mild exclamation of surprise, admiration, etc.
geese *n* plural of **goose**
geezer *n informal* (old or eccentric) man
Gehry *n* **Frank O**(**wen**). born 1929, US architect and furniture designer, born in Canada; best known for the Guggenheim Museum in Bilbao, Spain (1997)
Geiger *n* **Hans**. 1882–1945, German physicist: developed the Geiger counter
▸ **Geiger counter** [**guy**-ger] instrument for detecting and measuring radiation
geisha [**gay**-sha] *n, pl* **-sha**, **-shas** (in Japan) professional female companion for men
gel [**jell**] *n* **1** jelly-like substance ▷ *v* **gelling**, **gelled** **2** form a gel **3** *informal* take on a definite form
gelatin [**jel**-at-tin], **gelatine** *n* **1** substance made by boiling animal bones **2** edible jelly made of this
▸ **gelatinous** [jel-**at**-in-uss] *adj* of or like jelly
geld *v* castrate
▸ **gelding** *n* castrated horse
Geldof *n* **Bob**, full name *Robert Frederick Zenon Geldof*. born 1954, Irish rock singer and philanthropist: formerly lead vocalist with the Boomtown Rats (1977–86): organizer of the Band Aid charity for famine relief in Africa. He received an honorary knighthood in 1986
gelid Ⓣ [**jel**-lid] *adj* very cold
gelignite *n* type of dynamite used for blasting
gem Ⓣ *n* **1** precious stone or jewel **2** highly valued person or thing
gen *n informal* information
▸ **gen up on** *v* **genning**, **genned** *informal* make or become fully informed about
gendarme [**zhahn**-darm] *n* member of the French police force
gender *n* **1** state of being male or female, sex **2** *grammar* classification of nouns in certain languages as masculine, feminine, or neuter
gene [**jean**] *n* part of a cell which determines inherited characteristics
genealogy [jean-ee-**al**-a-gee] *n, pl* **-gies** (study of) the history and descent of a family or families **genealogical** *adj* **genealogist** *n*
genera [**jen**-er-a] *n* plural of **genus**
general Ⓣ *adj* **1** common or widespread **2** of or affecting all or most **3** not specific

THESAURUS

gazette *n* = **newspaper**, paper, journal, periodical, news-sheet
gear *n* **1** = **cog**, cogwheel, gearwheel **2** = **mechanism**, machinery, cogs, works **3** = **equipment**, tackle, apparatus, paraphernalia, accoutrements, instruments, supplies, tools **4** = **clothing**, wear, dress, clothes, costume, outfit, garments, togs ▸ *v* **5** = **equip**, fit, adjust, adapt
geek *n* (*Slang*) = **nerd**, bore, drip (*informal*), obsessive, wonk (*informal*), anorak (*informal*), dork (*slang*), trainspotter (*informal*)
gelatinous *adj* = **jelly-like**, sticky, gummy, gluey, glutinous, viscous
gelid *adj* = **cold**, icy, arctic, frigid, chilly, frosty, glacial, ice-cold, freezing, frozen
gem *n* **1** = **precious stone**, stone, jewel **2** = **prize**, treasure, jewel, masterpiece, pearl
general *adj* **1** = **overall**, broad, comprehensive • *a general decline in employment* OPPOSITE: specific **2** = **widespread**, common, broad, universal, accepted • *The project should raise general awareness about animal rights*. OPPOSITE: special **3** = **imprecise**, loose, vague, indefinite, approximate, inexact, ill-defined, unspecific
See also: **mass, popular, public**
generally *adv* **1** = **usually**, normally, typically, ordinarily, customarily, as a rule,

DICTIONARY

4 including or dealing with various or miscellaneous items **5** highest in authority or rank: *general manager* **6** true in most cases ▷ *n* **7** very senior army officer **generally** *adv*
▸ **generality** *n* **1** general principle **2** state of being general
▸ **generalize** *v* **1** draw general conclusions **2** speak in generalities **3** make widely known or used **generalization** *n*
▸ **general delivery** post office department where a traveller's letters are kept until called for
▸ **general election** election in which representatives are chosen for every constituency
▸ **general practitioner** nonspecialist doctor serving a local area
generalissimo *n, pl* **-mos** supreme commander of combined armed forces
generate 🅣 *v* produce or bring into being
▸ **generative** *adj* capable of producing
▸ **generator** *n* machine for converting mechanical energy into electrical energy
generation 🅣 *n* **1** all the people born about the same time **2** average time between two generations (about 30 years) **3** generating
generic 🅣 [jin-**ner**-ik] *adj* of a class, group, or genus **generically** *adv*
generous 🅣 *adj* **1** free in giving **2** free from pettiness **3** plentiful **generously** *adv* **generosity** *n*
genesis 🅣 [**jen**-iss-iss] *n, pl* **-eses** [-iss-eez] beginning or origin
genetic [jin-**net**-tik] *adj* of genes or genetics
▸ **genetics** *n* study of heredity and variation in organisms **geneticist** *n*
▸ **genetic engineering** alteration of the genetic structure of an organism for a particular purpose
▸ **genetic fingerprinting** use of a person's unique DNA pattern for identification
Genghis Khan *n* original name *Temuchin* or *Temujin*. ?1162–1227, Mongol ruler, whose empire stretched from the Black Sea to the Pacific (Also **Jinghis Khan**, **Jenghis Khan**)
genial 🅣 [**jean**-ee-al] *adj* cheerful and friendly **genially** *adv* **geniality** *n*
genie [**jean**-ee] *n* (in fairy tales) a servant who appears by magic and grants wishes
genital *adj* of the sexual organs or reproduction
▸ **genitals** *or* **genitalia** [jen-it-**ail**-ya] *pl n* external sexual organs
genitive *adj, n* (of) the grammatical case indicating possession or association
genius 🅣 [**jean**-yuss] *n* (person with) exceptional ability in a particular field
genocide [**jen**-no-side] *n* murder of a race of people
genre 🅣 [**zhahn**-ra] *n* style of literary, musical, or artistic work
Genseric, Gaiseric *n* ?390–477 AD, king of the Vandals (428–77). He seized Roman lands, esp. extensive parts of N Africa, and sacked Rome (455)
gent *n informal* **1** gentleman **gents 2** men's public lavatory
genteel 🅣 *adj* affectedly proper and polite **genteelly** *adv*
gentian [**jen**-shun] *n* mountain plant with deep blue flowers
gentile *adj, n* non-Jewish (person)
Gentile *n* **Giovanni**. 1875–1944, Italian Idealist philosopher and Fascist politician:

THESAURUS

by and large, on the whole **2 = commonly**, publicly, widely, extensively, universally, popularly
generate *v* **= produce**, make, cause, create, breed, engender, propagate, give rise to
generation *n* **1 = production**, creation, formation, reproduction, genesis, propagation **2 = age group**, crop, breed **3 = age**, time, period, era, epoch
generic *adj* **= collective**, general, common, wide, comprehensive, blanket, universal, inclusive
generosity *n* **1 = charity**, kindness, benevolence • *She is well known for her generosity*. OPPOSITE: meanness **2 = unselfishness**, goodness, high-mindedness, magnanimity, nobleness
generous *adj* **1 = charitable**, liberal, kind, lavish, hospitable, munificent, open-handed, prodigal, unstinting • *Not all wealthy people are so generous*. OPPOSITE: stingy **2 = plentiful**, ample, abundant • *a generous portion of spaghetti* OPPOSITE: meagre **3 = unselfish**, good, lofty, noble, big-hearted, high-minded, magnanimous
See also: **handsome**
genesis *n* **= beginning**, start, birth, creation, origin, formation, inception
genial *adj* **= cheerful**, warm, friendly, pleasant, affable, good-natured, agreeable, amiable, jovial, congenial
geniality *n* **= cheerfulness**, warmth, friendliness, affability, agreeableness, amiability, conviviality, cordiality, good cheer, joviality
genius *n* **1 = master**, brain, mastermind, virtuoso • *a mathematical genius* **2 = brilliance**, intellect, brains • *a poet of genius*
See also: **talent**
genre *n* **= type**, group, kind, class, style, sort, category, species
genteel *adj* **= refined**, elegant, polite, respectable, courteous, gentlemanly,

DICTIONARY

minister of education (1922–24)
gentility *n* **1** noble birth or ancestry **2** polite and well-mannered behaviour
gentle ⓣ *adj* **1** mild or kindly **2** not rough or severe **3** gradual **4** easily controlled, tame **5** noble or well-born **gentleness** *n* **gently** *adv*
▸ **gentleman** *n* **1** polite well-bred man **2** man of high social position **3** polite name for a man **gentlemanly** *adj* **gentlewoman** *n fem*
gentry ⓣ *n* people just below the nobility in social rank
▸ **gentrification** *n* taking-over of a traditionally working-class area by middle-class incomers **gentrify** *v*
genuflect *v* bend the knee as a sign of reverence or deference **genuflection** *or* **genuflexion** *n*
genuine ⓣ *adj* **1** not fake, authentic **2** sincere **genuinely** *adv* **genuineness** *n*
genus [**jean**-uss] *n, pl* **genera** **1** group into which a family of animals or plants is divided **2** kind, type
geocentric *adj* **1** having the earth as a centre **2** measured as from the earth's centre
geode *n* cavity lined with crystals within a rock
Geoffrey of Monmouth *n* ?1100–54, Welsh bishop and chronicler; author of *Historia Regum Britanniae,* the chief source of Arthurian legends
geography *n* study of the earth's physical features, climate, population, etc. **geographer** *n* **geographical** *or* **geographic** *adj* **geographically** *adv*
geology *n* study of the earth's origin, structure, and composition **geological** *adj* **geologically** *adv* **geologist** *n*
geometry *n* branch of mathematics dealing with points, lines, curves, and surfaces **geometric** *or* **geometrical** *adj* **geometrically** *adv* **geometrician** *n*
geopolitics *n* **1** study of the effect of the geographical position of a country on its politics **2** global politics **geopolitical** *adj*
George *n* **1 David Lloyd**. See **Lloyd George** **2 Saint**. died ?303 AD, Christian martyr, the patron saint of England; the hero of a legend in which he slew a dragon. Feast day: April 23
George I *n* 1660–1727, first Hanoverian king of Great Britain and Ireland (1714–27) and elector of Hanover (1698–1727). His dependence in domestic affairs on his ministers led to the emergence of Walpole as the first prime minister
George II *n* **1** 1683–1760, king of Great Britain and Ireland and elector of Hanover (1727–60); son of George I. His victory over the French at Dettingen (1743) in the War of the Austrian Succession was the last appearance on a battlefield by a British king **2** 1890–1947, king of Greece (1922–24; 1935–47). He was overthrown by the republicans (1924) and exiled during the German occupation of Greece (1941–45)
George III *n* 1738–1820, king of Great Britain and Ireland (1760–1820) and of Hanover (1814–20). During his reign the American colonies were lost. He became insane in 1811, and his son acted as regent for the rest of the reign
George IV *n* 1762–1830, king of Great Britain and Ireland and also of Hanover (1820–30); regent (1811–20). His father (George III) disapproved of his profligate ways, which undermined the prestige of the crown, and of his association with the Whig opposition
George V *n* 1865–1936, king of Great Britain and Northern Ireland and emperor of India (1910–36)
George VI *n* 1895–1952, king of Great Britain and Northern Ireland (1936–52) and emperor of India (1936–47). The second son of George V, he succeeded to the throne after the

THESAURUS

cultured, ladylike, urbane, well-mannered
gentle *adj* **1 = kind**, soft, tender, benign, kindly, meek, placid • *a quiet and gentle man* OPPOSITE: cruel **2 = moderate**, light, mild, slight, soft, muted, soothing **3 = gradual**, light, slow, easy, moderate, mild, slight, imperceptible **4 = tame**, manageable, docile, biddable, broken, placid, tractable
See also: **leisurely**
gentleman *See* **man**
gentlemanly *adj* **= polite**, civil, refined, gallant, honourable, courteous, genteel, urbane, well-mannered
gentleness *n* **= tenderness**, compassion, kindness, softness, sweetness, mildness
gentry *n* **= nobility**, elite, aristocracy, upper class, upper crust (*informal*)
genuine *adj* **1 = authentic**, real, bona fide • *They're convinced the picture is genuine.* OPPOSITE: fake **2 = sincere**, honest, earnest, heartfelt, frank, candid, unaffected, unfeigned
See also: **actual, natural, right, serious, true**
germ *n* **1 = microbe**, virus, bacterium, bug (*informal*), microorganism **2 = beginning**, source, spark, seed, root, origin, embryo, rudiment
germane *adj* **= relevant**, material, appropriate, related, fitting, pertinent, connected, apposite, apropos, to the point *or* to the purpose
germ-free *See* **pure, sterile**
germinate *v* **= sprout**, shoot, grow, develop, generate, swell, originate, bud, vegetate

DICTIONARY

abdication of his brother, Edward VIII

georgette [jor-**jet**] *n* fine silky fabric

Georgian *adj* **1** of the time of any of the kings of Britain called George, esp. 1714–1830 **2** of or from Georgia

geostationary *adj* (of a satellite) orbiting so as to remain over the same point of the earth's surface

geothermal *adj* of or using the heat in the earth's interior

geranium *n* cultivated plant with red, pink, or white flowers

gerbil [**jer**-bill] *n* burrowing desert rodent of Asia and Africa

geriatrics *n* branch of medicine dealing with old age and its diseases

▸ **geriatric** *adj, n* old (person)

Géricault *n* (**Jean Louis André**) **Théodore**. 1791–1824, French romantic painter, noted for his skill in capturing movement, esp. of horses

g

germ Ⓣ *n* **1** microbe, esp. one causing disease **2** beginning from which something may develop **3** simple structure that can develop into a complete organism

▸ **germicide** *n* substance that kills germs

germicidal *adj*

german *adj* **1** having the same parents: *brother-german* **2** being a first cousin: *cousin-german*

German *adj* **1** of Germany ▹ *n* **2** person from Germany **3** language of Germany, Austria, and parts of Switzerland

▸ **German measles** contagious disease accompanied by a cough, sore throat, and red spots

▸ **German shepherd dog** Alsatian

germane Ⓣ *adj* **germane to** relevant to

germinate Ⓣ *v* (cause to) sprout or begin to grow **germination** *n*

▸ **germinal** *adj* of or in the earliest stage of development

Geronimo *n* 1829–1909, Apache Indian chieftain: led a campaign against the White settlers until his final capture in 1886

gerrymandering *n* division of voting constituencies in order to give an unfair advantage to one party

Gershwin *n* **1 George**, original name *Jacob Gershvin*. 1898–1937, US composer: incorporated jazz into works such as *Rhapsody in Blue* (1924) for piano and jazz band and the opera *Porgy and Bess* (1935) **2** his brother, **Ira**, original name *Israel Gershvin*. 1896–1983, US song lyricist, noted esp. for his collaboration with George Gershwin

gerund [**jer**-rund] *n* noun formed from a verb: *living*

Gestapo *n* secret state police of Nazi Germany

gestation *n* **1** (period of) carrying of babies in the womb during pregnancy **2** developing of a plan or idea in the mind

gesticulate Ⓣ *v* make expressive movements of the hands and arms

gesticulation *n*

gesture Ⓣ *n* **1** movement to convey meaning **2** thing said or done to show one's feelings ▹ *v* **3** gesticulate

Gesualdo *n* **Carlo**, Prince of Venosa. ?1560–1613, Italian composer, esp. of madrigals

get Ⓣ *v* **getting, got 1** obtain or receive **2** bring or fetch **3** contract (an illness) **4** (cause to) become as specified: *get wet* **5** understand **6** (often foll. by *to*) come (to) or arrive (at) **7** go on board (a plane, bus, etc.) **8** persuade **9** *informal* annoy **10** *informal* have the better of **11** be revenged on **12** receive a broadcast signal **13** prepare (a meal)

▸ **get across** *v* (cause to) be understood

THESAURUS

gesticulate *v* = **signal**, sign, indicate, wave, motion, gesture, make a sign

gesture *n* **1** = **signal**, sign, action, motion, indication, gesticulation ▸ *v* **2** = **signal**, sign, indicate, wave, motion, gesticulate

get *v* **1** = **obtain**, receive, acquire, secure (*formal*), fetch, procure (*formal*) • *I'll get us all something to eat*. **2** = **become**, turn, grow • *People draw the curtains once it gets dark*. **3** = **contract**, take, catch, come down with, fall victim to **4** = **capture**, grab, lay hold of, take, seize **5** = **understand**, see, follow, catch, perceive, comprehend, fathom, take in, work out **6** = **persuade**, influence, convince, induce, prevail upon **7** (*Informal*) = **annoy**, upset, bug (*informal*), irritate, gall, vex **get across** = **cross**, negotiate, traverse, ford, pass over; = **communicate**, transmit, convey, impart, bring home to, make clear or make understood, put over ▹ **get along** = **be friendly**, agree, click (*slang*), concur, be compatible, hit it off (*informal*) ▹ **get at** = **gain access to**, reach, acquire, attain, come to grips with, get hold of; = **imply**, suggest, mean, intend, hint, lead up to • *What are you getting at?*; = **criticize**, attack, blame, nag, find fault with, pick on ▹ **get away** *See* **escape** ▹ **get back** *See* **recover** ▹ **get back at** *See* **retaliate** ▹ **get better** *See* **recover** ▹ **get by** = **manage**, survive, exist, fare, cope, get along, keep one's head above water, make both ends meet ▹ **get even** *See* **revenge** ▹ **get even with** *See* **retaliate** ▹ **get going** *See* **start** ▹ **get hold of** *See* **contact, obtain** ▹ **get in the way** *See* **impede** ▹ **get in touch with** *See* **contact** ▹ **get off** = **leave**,

DICTIONARY

▸ **get at** *v* **1** gain access to **2** imply or mean **3** criticize
▸ **getaway** *adj, n* (used in) escape
▸ **get by** *v* manage in spite of difficulties
▸ **get off** *v* (cause to) avoid the consequences of, or punishment for, an action
▸ **get off with** *v informal* start a romantic or sexual relationship with
▸ **get over** *v* recover from
▸ **get through** *v* **1** (cause to) succeed **2** contact by telephone **3** use up (money or supplies)
▸ **get through to** *v* make (a person) understand
▸ **get-up** *n informal* costume
▸ **get up to** *v* be involved in

Getty *n* **J(ean) Paul.** 1892–1976, US oil executive, millionaire, and art collector

Getz *n* **Stanley**, known as *Stan.* 1927–91, US jazz saxophonist: leader of his own group from 1949

geyser [**geez**-er] *n* **1** spring that discharges steam and hot water **2** *Brit* domestic gas water heater

ghastly Ⓣ *adj* **-lier**, **-liest** **1** *informal* very unpleasant **2** deathly pale **3** *informal* horrible **ghastliness** *n*

ghat *n* (in India) **1** steps leading down to a river **2** mountain pass

Ghazali *n* **al-**. 1058–1111, Muslim theologian, philosopher, and mystic

ghee [**gee**] *n* (in Indian cookery) clarified butter

gherkin *n* small pickled cucumber

ghetto *n, pl* **-tos**, **-toes** slum area inhabited by a deprived minority
▸ **ghetto-blaster** *n informal* large portable cassette-recorder

ghillie *n* same as **gillie**

Ghiz *n* **Robert.** born 1974, Canadian politician, Premier of Prince Edward Island (2007–)

ghost Ⓣ *n* **1** disembodied spirit of a dead person **2** faint trace ▹ *v* **3** ghostwrite **ghostly** *adj*
▸ **ghost town** deserted town
▸ **ghostwrite** *v* write (a book or article) on behalf of another person who is credited as the author **ghostwriter** *n*

ghoul [**gool**] *n* **1** person with morbid interests **2** demon that eats corpses **ghoulish** *adj*

GHQ *mil* General Headquarters

GI *n informal* US soldier

Giacometti *n* **Alberto.** 1901–66, Swiss sculptor and painter, noted particularly for his long skeletal statues of isolated figures

giant Ⓣ *n* **1** mythical being of superhuman size **2** very large person or thing ▹ *adj* **3** huge **giantess** *n fem*

Giauque *n* **William Francis.** 1895–1982, US physical chemist born in Canada. Winner of the 1949 Nobel Prize for Chemistry for his work on low-temperature phenomena

gibber [**jib**-ber] *v* speak or utter rapidly and unintelligibly
▸ **gibberish** *n* rapid unintelligible talk

gibbet [**jib**-bit] *n* gallows

gibbon [**gib**-bon] *n* agile tree-dwelling ape of S Asia

Gibbon *n* **Lewis Grassic**, real name *James*

THESAURUS

escape, exit, depart, descend, disembark, dismount, alight ▹ **get off your chest** *See* **reveal** ▹ **get on = board**, climb, mount, embark, ascend, enter • *Hurry up and get on the boat!* ▹ **get on someone's nerves = annoy**, provoke, plague, aggravate (*informal*), bug (*informal*), irk, rile, irritate, ruffle, exasperate, peeve, madden, make someone's blood boil, rub someone up the wrong way (*informal*), get in someone's hair (*informal*), get someone's goat (*slang*), piss off (*taboo slang*), tee off (*slang*) ▹ **get out of** *See* **dodge** ▹ **get over = recover from**, rally, survive, revive, mend, get better, pull through ▹ **get rid of = dispose of**, remove, eliminate, dump, expel, eject, throw away *or* throw out ▹ **get through** *See* **pass** ▹ **get to** *See* **reach** ▹ **get together** *See* **meet** ▹ **get well** *See* **recover**
See also: **develop, do, earn, extract, win**

getaway *n* = **escape**, break, flight, break-out

get-together *n* = **gathering**, party, meeting, social, function, celebration, reception, bash (*informal*), festivity, rave (*slang*), do (*informal*), shindig (*informal*), soirée, social gathering

ghastly *adj* = **horrible**, terrible, shocking, gruesome, horrendous, dreadful, hideous, frightful, loathsome, terrifying

ghost *n* **1** = **spirit**, spectre, phantom, apparition • *the ghost in the haunted house* RELATED WORD *adjective*: spectral **2** = **trace**, possibility, hint, suggestion, shadow, glimmer, semblance

ghostly *adj* = **supernatural**, eerie, spooky (*informal*), phantom, ghostlike, spectral, unearthly, wraithlike

ghoulish *adj* = **macabre**, sick (*informal*), gruesome, grisly, morbid, disgusting, unwholesome

giant *n* **1** = **ogre**, monster, titan, colossus ▸ *adj* **2** = **huge**, vast, enormous, mammoth, immense, titanic, gigantic, colossal, gargantuan

gibberish *n* = **nonsense**, babble, drivel, gobbledygook (*informal*), mumbo jumbo, twaddle

DICTIONARY

Leslie Mitchell. 1901–35, Scottish writer: best known for his trilogy of novels *A Scots Quair* (1932–34)
Gibbons *n* **1 Grinling**. 1648–1721, English sculptor and woodcarver, noted for his delicate carvings of fruit, flowers, birds, etc. **2 Orlando**. 1583–1625, English organist and composer, esp. of anthems, motets, and madrigals
gibbous *adj* (of the moon) more than half but less than fully illuminated
Gibbs *n* **1 James**. 1682–1754, British architect; his buildings include St Martin's-in-the-Fields, London (1722–26), and the Radcliffe Camera, Oxford (1737–49) **2 Josiah Willard**. 1839–1903, US physicist and mathematician: founder of chemical thermodynamics
gibe Ⓣ [**jibe**] *v, n* same as **jibe**[1]

g

giblets [**jib**-lets] *pl n* gizzard, liver, heart, and neck of a fowl
Gibran *n* **Kahlil**. 1883–1931, Syro-Lebanese poet, mystic, and painter, resident in the US after 1910; author of *The Prophet* (1923)
Gibson *n* **Mel**. born 1956, Australian film actor and director: his films include *Mad Max* (1979), *Hamlet* (1990), *Braveheart* (1996; also directed), *What Women Want* (2000), and *The Passion of the Christ* (2004; director only)
GIC *Canad* guaranteed investment certificate: certificate guaranteeing a fixed rate of interest on a sum deposited for a fixed term
giddy Ⓣ *adj* **-dier, -diest 1** feeling unsteady on one's feet, as if about to faint **2** scatter-brained **giddily** *adv* **giddiness** *n*
gift Ⓣ *n* **1** present **2** natural talent ▷ *v* **3** present with
▸ **gifted** *adj* talented
gig[1] *n* **1** single performance by pop or jazz musicians ▷ *v* **gigging, gigged 2** play gigs
gig[2] *n* light two-wheeled horse-drawn carriage
giga- *prefix* **1** denoting 10^9: *gigavolt* **2** *computers* denoting 2^{30}: *gigabyte*
gigantic Ⓣ *adj* enormous
giggle Ⓣ *v* **1** laugh nervously or foolishly ▷ *n* **2** such a laugh **giggly** *adj*
gigolo [**jig**-a-lo] *n, pl* **-los** man paid by an older woman to be her escort or lover
gigot *n* leg of lamb or mutton
Gilbert *n* **1** Sir **Humphrey**. ?1539–83, English navigator: founded the colony at St John's, Newfoundland (1583) **2** Sir **W**(**illiam**) **S**(**chwenck**). 1836–1911, English dramatist, humorist, and librettist. He collaborated (1871–96) with Arthur Sullivan on the famous series of comic operettas, including *The Pirates of Penzance* (1879), *Iolanthe* (1882), and *The Mikado* (1885) **3 William**. 1540–1603, English physician and physicist, noted for his study of terrestrial magnetism in *De Magnete* (1600)
gild Ⓣ *v* **gilding, gilded** *or* **gilt 1** put a thin layer of gold on **2** make falsely attractive
▸ **gilt** *adj* **1** gilded ▷ *n* **2** thin layer of gold used as decoration
▸ **gilt-edged** *adj* denoting government stocks on which interest payments and final repayment are guaranteed
Giles *n* **Saint**. 7th century AD, Greek hermit in France; patron saint of cripples, beggars, and lepers. Feast day: Sept 1
gill [**jill**] *n* liquid measure of quarter of a pint, equal to 0.142 litres
Gillespie *n* **Dizzy**, nickname of *John Birks Gillespie*. 1917–93, US jazz trumpeter
gillie *n* (in Scotland) attendant for hunting or fishing
Gillray *n* **James**. 1757–1815, English caricaturist
gills [**gillz**] *pl n* breathing organs in fish and other water creatures
gimbals *pl n* set of pivoted rings which allow nautical instruments to remain horizontal at sea
gimcrack [**jim**-krak] *adj* **1** showy but cheap **2** shoddy
gimlet [**gim**-let] *n* small tool with a screwlike tip for boring holes in wood
▸ **gimlet-eyed** *adj* having a piercing glance
gimmick Ⓣ *n* something designed to attract attention or publicity **gimmickry** *n* **gimmicky** *adj*

THESAURUS

gibe, jibe *v* **1 = taunt**, mock, scorn, scoff, jeer, ridicule, sneer, make fun of, poke fun at ▸ *n* **2 = taunt**, crack (*slang*), dig, barb, jeer, sarcasm, sneer, scoffing, cheap shot (*informal*)
giddiness *n* **= dizziness**, vertigo, faintness, light-headedness
giddy *adj* **= dizzy**, faint, unsteady, dizzying, light-headed, reeling, vertiginous
gift *n* **1 = donation**, present, contribution, legacy, bequest (*formal*) • *He showered us with gifts.* **2 = talent**, ability, flair, aptitude • *a gift for comedy*
See also: **blessing, capacity**
gifted *adj* **= talented**, expert, able, capable, brilliant, skilled, accomplished, clever, ingenious, masterly
gigantic *adj* **= enormous**, huge, giant, tremendous, mammoth, immense, titanic, colossal, stupendous
giggle *verb, n* **= laugh**, chuckle, chortle, twitter, cackle, snigger, titter
gild *v* **= adorn**, coat, enhance, brighten, ornament, embellish, embroider, beautify, dress up
gimmick *n* **= stunt**, device, scheme, dodge, ploy, contrivance

DICTIONARY

gin[1] *n* alcoholic drink flavoured with juniper berries
gin[2] *n* **1** machine for separating seeds from raw cotton **2** wire noose used to trap small animals
ginger *n* **1** root of a tropical plant, used as a spice **2** light orange-brown colour **gingery** *adj*
▸ **ginger ale** *or* **ginger beer** fizzy ginger-flavoured soft drink
▸ **gingerbread** *n* moist cake flavoured with ginger
▸ **ginger group** group within a larger group that agitates for a more active policy
▸ **ginger snap** hard ginger-flavoured cookie
gingerly Ⓣ *adv* **1** cautiously ▷ *adj* **2** cautious
gingham *n* cotton cloth, usu. checked or striped
gingivitis [jin-jiv-**vite**-iss] *n* inflammation of the gums
ginkgo [**gink**-go] *n, pl* **-goes** ornamental Chinese tree
Ginsberg *n* **Allen**. 1926–97, US poet of the Beat Generation. His poetry includes *Howl* (1956) and *Kaddish* (1960)
ginseng [**jin**-seng] *n* (root of) a plant believed to have tonic and energy-giving properties
Giotto *n* also known as *Giotto di Bondone*. ?1267–1337, Florentine painter, who broke away from the stiff linear design of the Byzantine tradition and developed the more dramatic and naturalistic style characteristic of the Renaissance: his work includes cycles of frescoes in Assisi, the Arena Chapel in Padua, and the Church of Santa Croce, Florence
Gipsy *n, pl* **-sies** same as **Gypsy**
giraffe *n* African ruminant mammal with a spotted yellow skin and long neck and legs
Giraldus Cambrensis *n* literary name of *Gerald de Barri*. ?1146–?1223, Welsh chronicler and churchman, noted for his accounts of his travels in Ireland and Wales
Giraudoux *n* (**Hyppolyte**) **Jean**. 1882–1944, French dramatist. His works include the novel *Suzanne et le Pacifique* (1921) and the plays *Amphitryon 38* (1929) and *La Guerre de Troie n'aura pas lieu* (1935)
gird Ⓣ *v* **girding, girded** *or* **girt 1** put a belt round **2** secure with or as if with a belt **3** surround
▸ **gird (up) one's loins** prepare for action
girder *n* large metal beam
girdle[1] Ⓣ *n* **1** woman's elastic corset **2** belt **3** *anat* encircling structure or part ▷ *v* **4** surround or encircle
girl Ⓣ *n* **1** female child **2** young woman
girlhood *n* **girlish** *adj*
▸ **girlie** *adj informal* featuring photographs of naked or scantily clad women
▸ **girlfriend** *n* **1** girl or woman with whom a person is romantically or sexually involved **2** female friend
giro [**jire**-oh] *n, pl* **-ros** *Brit* **1** system of transferring money within a post office or bank directly from one account to another **2** *informal* social security payment by giro cheque
girt *v* past of **gird**
girth Ⓣ *n* **1** measurement round something **2** band round a horse to hold the saddle in position
gist Ⓣ [**jist**] *n* substance or main point of a matter
give Ⓣ *v* **giving, gave, given 1** present (something) to another person **2** transfer in exchange or payment **3** grant or provide **4** utter or emit **5** perform or do: *give an interview* **6** organize or host **7** sacrifice or devote **8** concede **9** yield or break under pressure ▷ *n* **10** resilience or elasticity
▸ **give away** *v* **1** donate as a gift **2** reveal **3** hand over (a bride) formally to her husband in a marriage ceremony
▸ **giveaway** *n* **1** unintentional disclosure ▷ *adj* **2** very cheap or free
▸ **give in** *v* admit defeat

THESAURUS

gingerly *adv* = **cautiously**, carefully, reluctantly, suspiciously, warily, charily, circumspectly, hesitantly, timidly
gird *v* = **surround**, ring, encompass, enclose, encircle, enfold, hem in
girdle *n* **1** = **belt**, band, waistband, sash, cummerbund ▸ *v* **2** = **surround**, ring, bound, encompass, enclose, encircle, gird
girl *n* = **female child**, schoolgirl • *She was a strong girl, and quite tall.*
See also: **female**
girth *n* = **circumference**, measure, size, bulk
gist *n* = **point**, force, idea, sense, core, substance, meaning, significance, essence
give *v* **1** = **present**, award, provide, supply, deliver, grant, donate, hand • *I gave her a CD.* OPPOSITE: take **2** = **collapse**, yield, buckle, cave in, give way • *My knees gave out under me.* **3** = **announce**, issue, notify, communicate, transmit, pronounce, utter **4** = **concede**, grant, surrender, yield, relinquish, hand over **5** = **produce**, make, cause, occasion, engender ▷ **give a talk** *See* **lecture** ▷ **give away** = **reveal**, expose, leak, disclose, uncover, betray, divulge, let out, let slip ▷ **give back** *See* **return** ▷ **give in** = **surrender**, submit, concede, yield, succumb, capitulate • *Who do you think will give in first?* ▷ **give off** = **emit**, release,

g

DICTIONARY

▶ **give off** *v* emit
▶ **give out** *v* **1** distribute **2** emit **3** come to an end or fail
▶ **give over** *v* **1** set aside for a specific purpose **2** *informal* cease
▶ **give up** *v* **1** acknowledge defeat **2** abandon
gizzard *n* part of a bird's stomach
glacé [**glass**-say] *adj* crystallized or candied
glacier *n* slow-moving mass of ice formed by accumulated snow
▶ **glacial** *adj* **1** of ice or glaciers **2** very cold **3** unfriendly
▶ **glaciated** *adj* covered with or affected by glaciers **glaciation** *n*
glad Ⓣ *adj* **gladder, gladdest 1** pleased and happy **2** causing happiness **gladly** *adv* **gladness** *n*
▶ **glad to** very willing to (do something)
▶ **the glad eye** *informal* an inviting or seductive glance
▶ **gladden** *v* make glad
▶ **glad rags** *informal* best clothes
glade *n* open space in a forest
gladiator *n* (in ancient Rome) man trained to fight in arenas to provide entertainment
gladiolus *n, pl* **-lus, -li, -luses** garden plant with sword-shaped leaves
Gladstone *n* **William Ewart**. 1809–98, British statesman. He became leader of the Liberal Party in 1867 and was four times prime minister (1868–74; 1880–85; 1886; 1892–94). In his first ministry he disestablished the Irish Church (1869) and introduced educational reform (1870) and the secret ballot (1872). He succeeded in carrying the Reform Act of 1884 but failed to gain support for a Home Rule Bill for Ireland, to which he devoted much of the latter part of his career
glamour Ⓣ *n* alluring charm or fascination
glamorize *v*
▶ **glamorous** *adj* alluring
glance Ⓣ *n* **1** quick look ▷ *v* **2** look quickly
▶ **glancing** *adj* hitting at an oblique angle
▶ **glance off** *v* strike and be deflected off (an object) at an oblique angle
gland *n* organ that produces and secretes substances in the body **glandular** *adj*
glanders *n* contagious disease of horses
glare Ⓣ *v* **1** stare angrily **2** be unpleasantly bright ▷ *n* **3** angry stare **4** unpleasant brightness
▶ **glaring** *adj* **1** conspicuous **2** unpleasantly bright **glaringly** *adv*
glasnost *n* policy of openness and accountability, developed in the USSR in the 1980s
glass *n* **1** hard brittle, usu. transparent substance made by melting sand **2** objects made of glass **3** tumbler **4** its contents **5** mirror **6** barometer **glasses 7** spectacles
▶ **glassy** *adj* **1** like glass **2** expressionless **glassiness** *n*
▶ **glasshouse** *n* **1** greenhouse **2** *informal* army prison
▶ **glass wool** fine glass fibres used for insulating
Glass *n* **Philip**. born 1937, US avant-garde composer noted for his minimalist style: his works include *Music in Fifths* (1970), *Akhnaten* (1984), *The Voyage* (1992), and *Monsters of Grace* (1998)
glaucoma *n* eye disease

THESAURUS

produce, discharge, exude, send out, throw out ▷ **give out = emit**, release, produce, discharge, exude, send out, throw out ▷ **give up = abandon**, stop, quit, surrender, cease, renounce, relinquish, desist, call it a day *or* call it a night, leave off ▷ **give way** *See* **collapse, give**
See also: **hand down, spare**
given *See* **prone**
glad *adj* **1 = happy**, pleased, delighted, joyful, overjoyed • *They'll be glad to get away from it all.* OPPOSITE: sorry **2 = pleasing**, pleasant, cheerful, cheering, gratifying
gladden *v* **= please**, cheer, delight, gratify, hearten
gladly *adv* **= happily**, freely, readily, willingly, gleefully, cheerfully, with pleasure
gladness *n* **= happiness**, delight, joy, pleasure, glee, cheerfulness, gaiety, high spirits, mirth
glamorous *adj* **= elegant**, smart, exciting, prestigious, attractive, glossy, dazzling, fascinating, glittering
glamour *n* **= charm**, appeal, beauty, attraction, allure, fascination, prestige, enchantment
glance *n* **1 = peek**, look, glimpse, peep • *The boys exchanged glances.* ▶ *v* **2 = peek**, look, glimpse, peep, scan • *He glanced at his watch.* **3 = bounce**, brush, skim • *The car glanced off the guardrail.* **4 = gleam**, reflect, shine, flash, shimmer, glitter, glimmer, twinkle, glisten, glint ▷ **glance at** *See* **read**
glare *v* **1 = scowl**, frown, glower • *He glared at his brother.* **2 = blaze**, flame, flare, dazzle ▶ *n* **3 = scowl**, frown • *The server lowered his eyes to avoid my furious glare.* **4 = blaze**, flare, glow, dazzle, brilliance • *the glare of the headlights*
See also: **light**
glaring *adj* **1 = conspicuous**, obvious, gross, outrageous, blatant, flagrant, manifest, unconcealed **2 = dazzling**, bright, glowing, garish, blazing
glassy *adj* **1 = transparent**, clear, smooth, slippery, shiny, glossy **2 = expressionless**,

DICTIONARY

glaze Ⓣ *v* **1** fit or cover with glass **2** cover with a glassy substance **3** become glassy ▷ *n* **4** transparent coating **5** substance used for this
▶ **glazier** *n* person who fits windows with glass
Glazunov *n* **Aleksandr Konstantinovich**. 1865–1936, Russian composer, in France from 1928. A pupil of Rimsky-Korsakov, he wrote eight symphonies and concertos for piano and for violin among other works
gleam Ⓣ *n* **1** small beam or glow of reflected light **2** brief or faint indication ▷ *v* **3** shine **gleaming** *adj*
glean Ⓣ *v* **1** gather (facts etc.) bit by bit **2** gather (the useful remnants of a crop) after harvesting **gleaner** *n*
glebe *n* land belonging to a parish church
glee Ⓣ *n* **1** triumph and delight **2** musical composition for three or more unaccompanied voices **gleeful** *adj* **gleefully** *adv*
glen *n* deep narrow valley
Glenn *n* **John**. born 1921, US astronaut and politician. The first American to orbit the earth (Feb. 1962), he later became a senator (1975–99) and in 1998 returned to space at the age of 77
glib Ⓣ *adj* **glibber**, **glibbest** fluent but insincere or superficial **glibly** *adv* **glibness** *n*
glide Ⓣ *v* **1** move easily and smoothly **2** (of an aircraft) move without the use of engines ▷ *n* **3** smooth easy movement
▶ **glider** *n* aircraft without an engine which floats on air currents
▶ **gliding** *n* sport of flying gliders
glimmer Ⓣ *v* **1** shine faintly, flicker ▷ *n* **2** faint gleam **3** faint indication
glimpse Ⓣ *n* **1** brief or incomplete view ▷ *v* **2** catch a glimpse of
Glinka *n* **Mikhail Ivanovich**. 1803–57, Russian composer who pioneered the Russian national school of music. His works include the operas *A Life for the Tsar* (1836) and *Russlan and Ludmilla* (1842)
glint Ⓣ *v* **1** gleam brightly ▷ *n* **2** bright gleam
glissade *n* **1** gliding step in ballet **2** controlled slide down a snow slope ▷ *v* **3** perform a glissade
glissando *n music* slide between two notes in which all intermediate notes are played
glisten Ⓣ *v* gleam by reflecting light
glitch Ⓣ *n* sudden malfunction in an electronic system
glitter Ⓣ *v* **1** shine with bright flashes **2** be showy ▷ *n* **3** sparkle or brilliance **4** shiny powder used as decoration
glitzy *adj* **glitzier**, **glitziest** *slang* showily attractive
gloaming *n* twilight
gloat Ⓣ *v* (often foll. by *over*) look (at) or think (of) with smug or malicious pleasure
glob *n* rounded mass of thick fluid
global Ⓣ *adj* **1** worldwide **2** total or comprehensive **globally** *adv*
▶ **globalization** *n* process by which a company, etc., expands to operate internationally

g

THESAURUS

cold, blank, empty, vacant, dull, lifeless, fixed, glazed
glaze *v* **1** = **coat**, polish, gloss, enamel, varnish, lacquer ▶ *n* **2** = **coat**, finish, shine, polish, gloss, enamel, varnish, lacquer, patina, lustre
gleam *n* **1** = **glow**, flash, ray, beam, sparkle, glimmer **2** = **trace**, hint, suggestion, flicker, glimmer, inkling ▶ *v* **3** = **shine**, flash, glow, sparkle, shimmer, glitter, glimmer, glisten, glint
gleaming *See* **brilliant, shining**
glean *See* **extract**
glee *n* = **delight**, triumph, joy, exuberance, elation, exhilaration, merriment, exultation
gleeful *adj* = **delighted**, triumphant, jubilant, joyful, exuberant, elated, exultant, overjoyed
glib *adj* = **smooth**, ready, easy, quick, slick, fluent, plausible, suave, insincere, voluble
glide *v* = **slide**, run, roll, coast, skate, slip, flow, float, sail, drift
glimmer *v* **1** = **flicker**, shine, glow, sparkle, shimmer, glitter, blink, gleam, twinkle, glisten ▶ *n* **2** = **gleam**, ray, glow, sparkle, shimmer, blink, flicker, twinkle **3** = **trace**, hint, suggestion, gleam, flicker, inkling
glimpse *n* **1** = **look**, sight, glance, peek, sighting, peep ▶ *v* **2** = **catch sight of**, view, spot, spy, sight, espy
glint *v* **1** = **gleam**, shine, flash, sparkle, glitter, glimmer, twinkle ▶ *n* **2** = **gleam**, shine, flash, sparkle, glitter, glimmer, twinkle, twinkling
glisten *v* = **gleam**, shine, flash, glance, sparkle, shimmer, glitter, glare, glimmer, twinkle, glint
glitch *n* = **problem**, difficulty, malfunction, snag, hitch, interruption, blip, gremlin
glitter *v* **1** = **shine**, flash, sparkle, shimmer, glare, gleam, glimmer, twinkle, glisten, glint ▶ *n* **2** = **shine**, flash, sparkle, shimmer, glare, gleam, brightness, sheen, radiance **3** = **glamour**, show, display, tinsel, pageantry, splendour, gaudiness, showiness
gloat *v* = **relish**, triumph, glory, brag, crow, drool, exult, revel in, rub it in (*informal*)
global *adj* **1** = **worldwide**, world, international, universal, planetary **2** = **comprehensive**, general,

DICTIONARY

▸ **global warming** increase in the planet's temperature believed to be caused by the greenhouse effect
globe ⓣ *n* **1** sphere with a map of the earth on it **2** spherical object
▸ **the globe** the earth
▸ **globetrotter** *n* habitual worldwide traveller **globetrotting** *n, adj*
globule ⓣ *n* small round drop **globular** *adj*
globulin *n* simple protein found in living tissue
glockenspiel *n* percussion instrument consisting of small metal bars played with hammers
gloom ⓣ *n* **1** melancholy or depression **2** darkness **gloomy** *adj* **gloomily** *adv*
glory ⓣ *n, pl* **-ries 1** praise or honour **2** splendour **3** praiseworthy thing **4** adoration or worship ▹ *v* **-rying**, **-ried 5** (foll. by *in*) take great pleasure in **6** (foll. by *in*) triumph or exalt
▸ **glorify** *v* **1** make (something) seem more important than it is **2** praise **3** worship (God) **glorification** *n*
▸ **glorious** *adj* **1** brilliantly beautiful **2** delightful **3** having or full of glory **gloriously** *adv*
▸ **glory hole** *informal* untidy cupboard or storeroom
gloss[1] ⓣ *n* **1** surface shine or lustre **2** paint or cosmetic giving a shiny finish
▸ **glossy** *adj* **1** smooth and shiny **2** (of a magazine) printed on shiny paper **glossily** *adv* **glossiness** *n*
▸ **gloss over** *v* (try to) cover up or pass over (a fault or error)
gloss[2] ⓣ *n* **1** explanatory comment added to the text of a book ▹ *v* **2** add glosses to
glossary *n, pl* **-ries** list of special or technical words with definitions
glottis *n, pl* **-tises**, **-tides** vocal cords and the space between them **glottal** *adj*
glove *n* covering for the hand with individual sheaths for each finger and the thumb
▸ **gloved** *adj* covered by a glove
▸ **glove compartment** small storage area in the dashboard of an automobile
glow ⓣ *n* **1** light produced by a great heat **2** brightness of complexion **3** feeling of wellbeing ▹ *v* **4** produce a steady light without flames **5** shine **6** have a feeling of wellbeing or satisfaction **7** (of a colour) look warm
▸ **glow-worm** *n* insect giving out a green light
glower ⓣ [rhymes with **power**] *v, n* scowl
gloxinia *n* tropical plant with large bell-shaped flowers

THESAURUS

total, unlimited, exhaustive, all-inclusive
globe *n* = **sphere**, world, ball, planet, earth, orb
globule *n* = **droplet**, drop, particle, bead, bubble, pellet, pearl
gloom *n* **1** = **darkness**, dark, shadow, shade, dusk, twilight, obscurity, blackness, murk **2** = **depression**, woe, sorrow, unhappiness, melancholy, despondency, dejection, low spirits
gloomy *adj* **1** = **miserable**, down, sad, dejected, glum • *They are gloomy about the team's chances of success.* OPPOSITE: cheerful **2** = **dark**, dismal, dull, dreary • *a gloomy house on the edge of the park* OPPOSITE: sunny **3** = **depressing**, bad, sad, dismal, dreary, sombre, cheerless, disheartening, dispiriting
See also: **cloudy, drab, pessimistic**
glorify *v* **1** = **enhance**, elevate, magnify, aggrandize, dignify, ennoble **2** = **worship**, bless, honour, revere, adore, idolize, venerate, exalt, pay homage to **3** = **praise**, celebrate, extol, eulogize, sing the praises of *or* sound the praises of
glorious *adj* **1** = **famous**, renowned, celebrated, magnificent, illustrious, distinguished, majestic, eminent, honoured **2** = **splendid**, beautiful, brilliant, gorgeous, superb, dazzling, shining **3** = **delightful**, fine, excellent, wonderful, gorgeous, marvellous
glory *n* **1** = **honour**, praise, fame, immortality, prestige • *It was her moment of glory.* OPPOSITE: disgrace **2** = **splendour**, majesty, grandeur, magnificence • *Spring arrived in all its glory.* ▸ *v* **3** = **revel**, relish, gloat • *The curling team was glorying in its unexpected win.*
See also: **credit, rejoice**
gloss[1] *n* = **shine**, polish, brilliance, gleam, sheen • *paper with a high gloss finish*
gloss[2] *n* **1** = **comment**, note, explanation, commentary, translation, interpretation, footnote, annotation, elucidation ▸ *v* **2** = **interpret**, comment, explain, translate, annotate, elucidate
glossy *adj* = **shiny**, bright, brilliant, sleek, polished, lustrous • *glossy paint*
See also: **smooth**
glow *n* **1** = **light**, gleam, glimmer • *the glow of the fire* **2** = **radiance**, brilliance, brightness, splendour, effulgence, vividness ▸ *v* **3** = **shine**, smoulder, gleam, glimmer • *A light glowed behind the curtains.*
See also: **blush, glare**
glower *v* **1** = **scowl**, glare, frown, give a dirty look, look daggers, lour *or* lower ▸ *n* **2** = **scowl**, glare, frown, black look, dirty look, lour *or* lower

DICTIONARY

Gluck *n* **Christoph Willibald von**. 1714–87, German composer, esp. of operas, including *Orfeo ed Euridice* (1762) and *Alceste* (1767)
glucose *n* kind of sugar found in fruit
glue Ⓣ *n* **1** natural or synthetic sticky substance used as an adhesive ▷ *v* **glueing** *or* **gluing, glued 2** fasten with glue **3** (foll. by *to*) pay full attention to: *her eyes were glued to the TV* **gluey** *adj*
▶ **glue-sniffing** *n* inhaling of glue fumes for intoxicating or hallucinatory effects
glum Ⓣ *adj* **glummer, glummest** sullen or gloomy **glumly** *adv*
glut Ⓣ *n* **1** excessive supply ▷ *v* **glutting, glutted 2** feed or fill to excess **3** oversupply
gluten [**gloo**-ten] *n* protein found in cereal grain
glutinous [**gloo**-tin-uss] *adj* sticky or gluey
glutton[1] Ⓣ *n* **1** greedy person **2** person with a great capacity for something **gluttonous** *adj* **gluttony** *n*
glutton[2] *n* wolverine
glycerin, glycerine *n* colourless sweet liquid used widely in chemistry and industry
glycerol *n* technical name for **glycerin(e)**
gm gram
GM genetically modified
G-man *n, pl* **G-men** *US slang* FBI agent
GMT Greenwich Mean Time
gnarled Ⓣ *adj* rough, twisted, and knobbly
gnash *v* grind (the teeth) together in anger or pain
gnat *n* small biting two-winged fly
gnaw Ⓣ *v* **gnawing, gnawed, gnawed** *or* **gnawn 1** bite or chew steadily **2** (foll. by *at*) cause constant distress (to)
gneiss *n* coarse-grained metamorphic rock
gnome *n* imaginary creature like a little old man
gnomic [**no**-mik] *adj* of pithy sayings
Gnosticism *n* religious movement believing in intuitive spiritual knowledge
Gnostic *n, adj*
GNP gross national product
gnu [**noo**] *n* oxlike S African antelope
go Ⓣ *v* **going, went, gone 1** move to or from a place **2** depart **3** make regular journeys **4** function **5** be, do, or become as specified **6** contribute to a result: *it just goes to show* **7** be allotted to a specific purpose or recipient **8** be sold **9** blend or harmonize **10** fail or break down **11** elapse **12** be got rid of **13** attend **14** reach or exceed certain limits: *she's gone too far this time* **15** be acceptable **16** carry authority ▷ *n* **17** attempt **18** verbal attack **19** turn **20** *informal* energy or vigour
▶ **make a go of** be successful at
▶ **go back on** *v* break (a promise etc.)
▶ **go-between** *n* intermediary
▶ **go for** *v* **1** choose **2** attack **3** apply to equally
▶ **go-getter** *n* energetically ambitious person

g

THESAURUS

glowing *adj* **1 = bright**, flaming, luminous, radiant, aglow **2 = complimentary**, enthusiastic, ecstatic, rave (*informal*), adulatory, laudatory, rhapsodic
glue *v* **1 = stick**, fix, seal, paste • *Glue the two halves together.* ▶ *n* **2 = adhesive**, gum, paste, cement
See also: **bond**
glum *adj* **= gloomy**, low, pessimistic, dejected, sullen, crestfallen, doleful, morose
glut *n* **1 = surfeit**, surplus, excess, plethora, oversupply, saturation, superfluity ▶ *v* **2 = saturate**, flood, choke, clog, overload, inundate, deluge, oversupply
glutton *n* **= gourmand**, pig (*informal*)
gluttonous *adj* **= greedy**, voracious, insatiable, ravenous, gormandizing, piggish
gluttony *n* **= greed**, gormandizing, greediness, voracity
gnarled *adj* **= twisted**, rough, rugged, knotted, contorted, knotty, weather-beaten, wrinkled
gnaw *v* **= bite**, chew, nibble, munch
go *v* **1 = move**, drive, travel, advance, fly, proceed (*formal*), journey (*formal*) • *I went home on the weekend.* **2 = function**, work • *stuck on the highway in a car that won't go* **3 = leave**, withdraw, depart, make tracks, move out, set off, slope off **4 = contribute**, serve, tend, lead to, work towards **5 = harmonize**, agree, match, suit, fit, blend, complement, correspond, chime **6 = elapse**, pass, flow, expire, lapse, slip away ▷ **go across** *See* **cross** ▷ **go against** *See* **clash** ▷ **go as far as** *See* **reach** ▷ **go away** *See* **disappear, vanish** ▷ **go back** *See* **return** ▷ **go beyond** *See* **pass, top** ▷ **go down** *See* **decline, descend** ▷ **go for = favour**, like, choose, prefer, admire, be attracted to, be fond of; **= attack**, assault, assail, launch oneself at, rush upon, set about *or* set upon, spring upon ▷ **go into** *See* **discuss** ▷ **go off = explode**, fire, detonate, blow up; **= leave**, part, quit, depart, decamp, go away, move out, slope off ▷ **go on = happen**, occur, take place; **= continue**, last, proceed, keep going, carry on; **= ramble on**, chatter, carry on, prattle ▷ **go on at** *See* **hassle** ▷ **go out = leave**, exit, depart; **= be extinguished**, expire, die out, fade out ▷ **go over = examine**, study, review, revise, reiterate, inspect, rehearse, work over ▷ **go through = suffer**, experience, undergo, endure • *I was going through a very*

DICTIONARY

▸ **go-go dancer** scantily-dressed erotic dancer
▸ **go off** *v* **1** explode **2** ring or sound **3** *informal* stop liking **4** *informal* become stale or rotten
▸ **go out** *v* **1** go to social events **2** be romantically involved (with) **3** be extinguished
▸ **go over** *v* examine or check
▸ **go-slow** *n* deliberate slowing of work-rate as an industrial protest
▸ **go through** *v* **1** suffer or undergo **2** examine or search
goad ⊕ *v* **1** provoke (someone) to take action, usu. in anger ▹ *n* **2** spur or incentive **3** spiked stick for driving cattle
goal ⊕ *n* **1** *sports* posts through which the ball or puck has to be propelled to score **2** *sports* score made in this way **3** aim or purpose
▸ **goalie** *n informal* goalkeeper
▸ **goalkeeper** *n* player whose task is to stop shots entering the goal
▸ **goalpost** *n* one of the two posts supporting the crossbar of a goal
▸ **move the goalposts** change the aims of an activity to ensure the desired result
goat *n* sure-footed ruminant animal
▸ **get someone's goat** *slang* annoy someone
▸ **goatee** *n* small pointed beard
gob *n* **1** lump of a soft substance **2** *slang* mouth
gobbet *n* lump, esp. of food
gobble[1] ⊕ *v* eat hastily and greedily
gobble[2] *n* **1** rapid gurgling cry of the male turkey ▹ *v* **2** make this noise
gobbledygook, gobbledegook ⊕ *n* unintelligible (official) language or jargon
Gobind Singh, Govind Singh *n* 1666–1708, tenth and last guru of the Sikhs (1675–1708): assassinated
goblet *n* drinking cup
goblin *n* (in folklore) small malevolent creature
goby *n, pl* **-by, -bies** small spiny-finned fish
god *n* **1** spirit or being worshipped as having supernatural power **2** object of worship, idol **3 God** (in monotheistic religions) the Supreme Being, creator and ruler of the universe **goddess** *n fem* **godlike** *adj*
▸ **the gods** top balcony in a theatre
▸ **godly** *adj* devout or pious **godliness** *n*
▸ **god-fearing** *adj* pious and devout
▸ **godforsaken** *adj* desolate or dismal
▸ **godsend** *n* something unexpected but welcome
Godard *n* **Jean-Luc.** born 1930, French film director and writer associated with the New Wave of the 1960s. His works include *À bout de souffle* (1960), *Weekend* (1967), *Sauve qui peut* (1980), *Nouvelle Vague* (1990), and *Éloge de l'amour* (2003)
Godefroy de Bouillon *n* ?1060–1100, French leader of the First Crusade (1096–99), becoming first ruler of the Latin kingdom of Jerusalem
godetia *n* garden plant with showy flowers
godparent *n* person who promises at a person's baptism to look after his or her religious upbringing **godmother** *n*
▸ **godchild** *n* child for whom a person stands as godparent **goddaughter** *n* **godson** *n*
▸ **godfather** *n* **1** male godparent **2** head of a criminal, esp. Mafia, organization
Godwin *n* died 1053, Earl of Wessex. He was chief adviser to Canute and Edward the Confessor. His son succeeded Edward to the throne as Harold II
Goebbels *n* **Paul Joseph.** 1897–1945, German Nazi politician; minister of propaganda (1933–45)

THESAURUS

difficult time; = **examine**, look, search, check, hunt, explore, forage ▹ **go together with** *See* **accompany** ▹ **go up** *See* **rise** ▹ **go well** *See* **blend** ▹ **go with** = **match**, suit, fit, blend, complement, harmonize, correspond with, agree with ▹ **go wrong** *See* **err** ▸ *n* **7** = **attempt**, try, shot (*informal*), stab (*informal*) • *I always wanted to have a go at waterskiing.* **8** (*Informal*) = **energy**, force, life, drive, spirit, vitality, vigour, verve, vivacity ▹ **go-ahead** *See* **permission** ▹ **go-between** = **intermediary**, medium, agent, dealer, broker, mediator, middleman
See also: **range, turn, work out**
goad *v* **1** = **provoke**, drive, prompt, spur, incite, prod, exhort, egg on ▸ *n* **2** = **provocation**, urge, spur, incentive, stimulus, incitement, impetus, irritation
goal *n* = **aim**, end, target, object, purpose, intention, objective • *The goal seems to be to make as much money as possible.*
See also: **point**
gobble *v* = **devour**, wolf • *I gobbled all the beef stew.*
gobbledygook, gobbledegook *n* = **nonsense**, cant, jargon, babble, gabble, gibberish, hocus-pocus, mumbo jumbo, twaddle
godforsaken *adj* = **desolate**, remote, dismal, bleak, gloomy, abandoned, lonely, dreary, wretched, deserted, forlorn
godlike *adj* = **divine**, celestial, heavenly, superhuman, transcendent
godly *adj* = **devout**, good, religious, holy, righteous, pious, god-fearing, saintly
godsend *n* = **blessing**, boon, windfall, manna, stroke of luck

DICTIONARY

goer *n* person who attends something regularly: *film-goer*
Goethe *n* **Johann Wolfgang von**. 1749–1832, German poet, novelist, and dramatist, who settled in Weimar in 1775. His early works of the *Sturm und Drang* period include the play *Götz von Berlichingen* (1773) and the novel *The Sorrows of Young Werther* (1774). After a journey to Italy (1786–88) his writings, such as the epic play *Iphigenie auf Tauris* (1787) and the epic idyll *Hermann und Dorothea* (1797), showed the influence of classicism. Other works include the *Wilhelm Meister* novels (1796–1829) and his greatest masterpiece *Faust* (1808; 1832)
goggle *v* stare with wide- open eyes
▸ **goggles** *pl n* protective spectacles
Gogol *n* **Nikolai Vasilievich**. 1809–52, Russian novelist, dramatist, and short-story writer. His best-known works are *The Government Inspector* (1836), a comedy satirizing bureaucracy, and the novel *Dead Souls* (1842)
going *n* **1** departure **2** condition of the ground for walking or riding over **3** rate of travel ▷ *adj* **4** thriving **5** current or accepted **6** available
▸ **going-over** *n, pl* **goings-over** *informal* **1** investigation or examination **2** scolding or thrashing
▸ **goings-on** *pl n* mysterious or unacceptable events
goitre [**goy**-ter] *n* swelling of the thyroid gland in the neck
go-kart *n* small low-powered racing car
gold *n* **1** yellow precious metal **2** jewellery or coins made of this ▷ *adj* **3** made of gold **4** deep yellow
▸ **gold-digger** *n* **2** *informal* woman who uses her sexual attractions to get money from a man
▸ **goldeye** *n* edible N American fish, often smoked
▸ **goldfinch** *n* kind of finch, the male of which has yellow-and-black wings
▸ **goldfish** *n* orange fish kept in ponds or aquariums
▸ **gold leaf** thin gold sheet used for gilding
▸ **gold medal** medal given to the winner of a competition or race
golden ⓣ *adj* **1** made of gold **2** gold-coloured **3** very successful or promising
▸ **golden eagle** large mountain eagle of the N hemisphere
▸ **golden handshake** *informal* payment to a departing employee
▸ **golden mean** middle course between extremes
▸ **golden rule** important principle
▸ **golden wedding** fiftieth wedding anniversary
Golding *n* Sir **William** (**Gerald**). 1911–93, English novelist noted for his allegories of man's proclivity for evil. His novels include *Lord of the Flies* (1954), *Darkness Visible* (1979), *Rites of Passage* (1980), *Close Quarters* (1987), and *Fire Down Below* (1989). Nobel prize for literature 1983
Goldsmith *n* **Oliver**. ?1730–74, Irish poet, dramatist, and novelist. His works include the novel *The Vicar of Wakefield* (1766), the poem *The Deserted Village* (1770), and the comedy *She Stoops to Conquer* (1773)
golf *n* **1** outdoor game in which a ball is struck with clubs into a series of holes ▷ *v* **2** play golf **golfer** *n*
Golgi *n* **Camillo**. 1844–1926, Italian neurologist and histologist, noted for his work on the central nervous system and his discovery in animal cells of the bodies known by his name: shared the Nobel prize for physiology or medicine 1906
golliwog *n* soft black-faced male doll
golly *interj* exclamation of mild surprise
Gompers *n* **Samuel**. 1850–1924, US labour leader, born in England; a founder of the American Federation of Labor and its president (1886–94; 1896–1924)
gonad *n* organ producing reproductive cells, such as a testicle or ovary
Goncharov *n* **Ivan Aleksandrovich**. 1812–91, Russian novelist: his best-known work is *Oblomov* (1859)
gondola *n* **1** long narrow boat used in Venice **2** suspended cabin of a cable car, airship, etc.
▸ **gondolier** *n* person who rows a gondola
gone ⓣ *v* past participle of **go**
▸ **goner** *n informal* person or thing beyond help or recovery
gong *n* **1** rimmed metal disc that produces a note when struck **2** *slang* medal
gonorrhea, gonorrhoea [gon-or-**ree**-a] *n* venereal disease with a discharge from the genitals
good ⓣ *adj* **better**, **best** **1** giving pleasure **2** kindly **3** commendable **4** morally excellent

THESAURUS

golden *adj* **1 = yellow**, blond *or* blonde, flaxen **2 = successful**, happy, rich, glorious, prosperous, flourishing, halcyon **3 = promising**, excellent, opportune, favourable
gone *adj* **1 = finished**, over, past, elapsed, ended **2 = missing**, away, lost, absent, astray, lacking, vanished
good *adj* **1 = excellent**, great, fine, acceptable, superior, satisfactory, splendid, pleasing, first-class, admirable, first-rate • *We had a really good time.* OPPOSITE: bad **2 = praiseworthy**, moral, ethical, honest, worthy, upright, admirable,

DICTIONARY

5 talented **6** well-behaved **7** beneficial **8** valid **9** reliable **10** financially sound **11** complete or full ▷ *n* **12** benefit **13** positive moral qualities **goods 14** merchandise **15** property **goodness** *n*
▶ **as good as** virtually
▶ **for good** permanently
▶ **goodly** *adj* considerable
▶ **goody** *n, pl* **-dies 1** enjoyable thing **2** *informal* hero in a book or film
▶ **goody-goody** *adj, n* smugly virtuous (person)
▶ **good-for-nothing** *adj, n* irresponsible or worthless (person)
▶ **Good Samaritan** person who helps another in distress
▶ **goodwill** *n* **1** kindly feeling **2** popularity and good reputation of a business

g

good-bye Ⓣ *interj, n* expression used on parting

Goodman *n* **Benny**, full name *Benjamin David Goodman*. 1909–86, US jazz clarinetist and bandleader, whose treatment of popular songs created the jazz idiom known as swing

Goodwin *n* **Betty** (**Roodish**). 1923–2008, Canadian artist of Romanian ancestry

gooey *adj* **gooier, gooiest** *informal* sticky and soft

goof *informal* ▷ *n* **1** mistake ▷ *v* **2** make a mistake

Google *n* **1** popular search engine on the internet ▷ *v* **2 google** search for (something on the internet) using a search engine

goon *n informal* **1** stupid person **2** hired thug

goose *n, pl* **geese 1** web-footed bird like a large duck **2** female of this bird
▶ **goose flesh** *or* **goose pimples** bristling of the skin due to cold or fright
▶ **goose-step** *v* march with the legs high and without bending the knees

gooseberry *n* **1** edible yellowy-green berry **2** *informal* unwanted single person accompanying a couple

gopher [**go**-fer] *n* N American burrowing rodent

Gorbachov, Gorbachev *n* **Mikhail Sergeevich**. born 1931, Soviet statesman; general secretary of the Soviet Communist Party (1985–91): president (1988–91). Nobel peace prize 1990. His reforms ended the Communist monopoly of power and led to the break-up of the Soviet Union

Gordon *n* **1 Dexter** (**Keith**). 1923–90, US jazz tenor saxophonist **2** Lord **George**. 1751–93, English religious agitator. He led the Protestant opposition to legislation relieving Roman Catholics of certain disabilities, which culminated in the Gordon riots (1780) **3 George Hamilton**. See (4th Earl of) **Aberdeen**

gore¹ Ⓣ *n* blood from a wound

gore² Ⓣ *v* pierce with horns

THESAURUS

trustworthy, honourable, righteous, virtuous **3 = expert**, able, skilled, talented, competent, accomplished, clever, adept, proficient, adroit • *I'm not very good at waterskiing*. OPPOSITE: incompetent **4 = beneficial**, useful, profitable, helpful, suitable, fitting, convenient, win-win (*informal*), wholesome, favourable, advantageous **5 = kind**, friendly, charitable, humane, merciful, kindly, benevolent, altruistic, kind-hearted, obliging • *You are so good to me*. OPPOSITE: unkind **6 = valid**, real, true, proper, legitimate, genuine, authentic, bona fide **7 = well-behaved**, polite, orderly, obedient, dutiful, well-mannered **8 = full**, large, complete, extensive, substantial, adequate, considerable, sufficient, ample ▶ *n* **9 = benefit**, use, interest, profit, gain, advantage, welfare, usefulness, wellbeing **10 = virtue**, right, worth, excellence, merit, morality, goodness, rectitude, righteousness ▷ **for good = permanently**, finally, for ever, irrevocably, once and for all *See also*: **favourable, respectable, sound**

good-bye *n* = **farewell**, adieu, parting, leave-taking

good-for-nothing *n* **1 = idler**, couch potato (*slang*), slacker (*informal*), waster, wastrel ▶ *adj* **2 = worthless**, idle, irresponsible, useless, feckless

good-looking *See* **cute, handsome**

goodly *adj* = **considerable**, large, significant, substantial, sizable *or* sizeable, ample, tidy (*informal*)

goodness *n* **1 = excellence**, value, worth, quality, merit, superiority **2 = kindness**, mercy, goodwill, generosity, friendliness, benevolence, humaneness, kind-heartedness, kindliness **3 = virtue**, integrity, merit, honesty, honour, morality, probity, rectitude, righteousness, uprightness **4 = benefit**, advantage, salubriousness, wholesomeness

goods *pl n* **1 = property**, gear, paraphernalia, belongings, chattels, effects, possessions, things, trappings **2 = merchandise**, stock, stuff, commodities, wares

goodwill *n* = **friendliness**, favour, benevolence • *They invited us to dinner as a gesture of goodwill*.
See also: **friendship**

gore¹ *n* = **blood**, slaughter, carnage, bloodshed, butchery

gore² *v* = **pierce**, wound, impale, transfix

DICTIONARY

gore[3] *n* tapering piece of material in a garment, sail, or umbrella
Gore *n* **Al(bert) Jr.** born 1948, US Democrat politician; vice president of the US (1993–2001); defeated in the disputed presidential election of 2000; leading environmental campaigner; shared the 2007 Nobel Peace Prize with the Intergovernmental Panel For Climate Change
Górecki *n* **Henryk (Mikołaj)**. born 1933, Polish composer, best known for his sombre third symphony (1979)
gorge ⓣ *n* **1** deep narrow valley ▷ *v* **2** eat greedily
▸ **make one's gorge rise** cause feelings of disgust
gorgeous ⓣ *adj* **1** strikingly beautiful or attractive **2** *informal* very pleasant
gorgeously *adv*
gorgon *n* terrifying or repulsive woman
Gorgonzola *n* sharp-flavoured blue-veined Italian cheese
gorilla *n* largest of the apes, found in Africa
Göring, Goering *n* **Hermann Wilhelm**. 1893–1946, German Nazi leader and field marshal. He commanded Hitler's storm troops (1923) and as Prussian prime minister and German commissioner for aviation (1933–45) he founded the Gestapo and mobilized Germany for war. Sentenced to death at Nuremberg, he committed suicide
Gorki, Gorky *n* **Maxim**, pen name of *Aleksey Maximovich Peshkov*. 1868–1936, Russian novelist, dramatist, and short-story writer, noted for his depiction of the outcasts of society. His works include the play *The Lower Depths* (1902), the novel *Mother* (1907), and an autobiographical trilogy (1913–23)
gormless *adj informal* stupid
gorse *n* prickly yellow-flowered shrub
gory ⓣ *adj* **gorier, goriest 1** horrific or bloodthirsty **2** involving bloodshed
gosh *interj* exclamation of mild surprise or wonder
goshawk *n* large hawk
gosling *n* young goose
gospel ⓣ *n* **1** unquestionable truth **2 Gospel** any of the first four books of the New Testament
gossamer *n* **1** filmy cobweb **2** very fine fabric
gossip ⓣ *n* **1** idle talk, esp. about other people **2** person who engages in gossip ▷ *v* **gossiping, gossiped 3** engage in gossip
gossipy *adj*
got *v* past of **get**
▸ **have got** possess
▸ **have got to** need or be required to
Goth *n* member of an East Germanic people who invaded the Roman Empire
Gothic *adj* **1** (of architecture) of or in the style common in Europe from the 12th–16th centuries, with pointed arches **2** of or in an 18th-century literary style characterized by gloom and the supernatural **3** in a heavy ornate script typeface
gotten *v US* past participle of **get**
gouache *n* (painting using) watercolours mixed with glue
Gouda *n* mild-flavoured Dutch cheese
gouge ⓣ **[gowj]** *v* **1** scoop or force out **2** cut (a hole or groove) in (something) ▷ *n* **3** chisel with a curved cutting edge **4** hole or groove
goulash [**goo**-lash] *n* rich stew seasoned with paprika
Gould *n* **Glenn**. 1932–82, Canadian pianist
Gounod *n* **Charles François**. 1818–93, French composer of the operas *Faust* (1859) and *Romeo and Juliet* (1867)
gourd [**goord**] *n* **1** fleshy fruit of a climbing plant **2** its dried shell, used as a container
gourmand [**goor**-mand] *n* person who is very keen on food and drink
gourmet ⓣ [**goorm**-may] *n* connoisseur of food and drink
gout [**gowt**] *n* disease causing inflammation of the joints **gouty** *adj*
Gouzenko *n* **Igor (Sergeievich)**. 1919–82, Canadian intelligence officer, born in Russia. A cipher clerk working for the Soviet Embassy

THESAURUS

gorge *n* **1** = **ravine**, pass, canyon, fissure, chasm, defile, cleft ▸ *v* **2** = **overeat**, feed, stuff, wolf, gobble, cram, guzzle, devour, glut, gulp
gorgeous *adj* **1** = **beautiful**, elegant, magnificent, superb, splendid, sumptuous, dazzling, ravishing, stunning (*informal*) **2** (*Informal*) = **pleasing**, good, fine, lovely, glorious, enjoyable, exquisite, delightful
gory *adj* = **bloodthirsty**, bloody, murderous, blood-soaked, bloodstained, sanguinary
gospel *n* **1** = **truth**, fact, certainty, the last word **2** = **doctrine**, news, message, revelation, creed, credo, tidings
gossip *n* **1** = **hearsay**, dirt • *Gossip doesn't interest me.* **2** = **busybody**, telltale, chatterbox (*informal*), chatterer, gossipmonger, scandalmonger, tattler ▸ *v* **3** = **chat**, jaw (*slang*), blether, chew the fat (*slang*), gabble, prate, prattle, tattle
See also: **rumour**
gouge *v* **1** = **scoop**, cut, dig *or* dig out, claw, hollow *or* hollow out, chisel ▸ *n* **2** = **gash**, cut, scratch, scoop, groove, trench, hollow, furrow
gourmet *n* = **connoisseur**, foodie (*informal*), *bon vivant* (*French*), epicure, gastronome

DICTIONARY

in Canada, he defected in 1945 and revealed evidence of a Soviet spy ring in N America

govern ⓣ *v* **1** rule, direct, or control **2** exercise restraint over (temper etc.) **governable** *adj*
▸ **governance** *n* governing
▸ **governess** *n* woman teacher in a private household
▸ **government** *n* **1** executive policy-making body of a state **2** the state and its administration **3** system by which a country or state is ruled **governmental** *adj*
▸ **Government House** residence of Canadian governor general or lieutenant governor
▸ **governor** *n* **1** official governing a province or state **2** senior administrator of a society, institution, or prison
▸ **governor general** representative of the Crown in a Commonwealth dominion

gown ⓣ *n* **1** woman's long formal dress **2** surgeon's overall **3** official robe worn by judges, clergymen, etc.

goy *n slang* Jewish word for a non-Jew

Goya *n* **Francisco de**, full name *Francisco José de Goya y Lucientes*. 1746–1828, Spanish painter and etcher; well known for his portraits, he became court painter to Charles IV of Spain (1799). He recorded the French invasion of Spain in a series of etchings *The Disasters of War* (1810–14) and two paintings *2 May 1808* and *3 May 1808* (1814)

GP general practitioner

GPO General Post Office

GPS Global Positioning System: a satellite-based navigation system

grab ⓣ *v* **grabbing, grabbed 1** grasp suddenly, snatch ▷ *n* **2** sudden snatch

grace ⓣ *n* **1** beauty and elegance **2** polite, kind behaviour **3** goodwill or favour **4** delay granted **5** courtesy or decency **6** short prayer of thanks for a meal **7 Grace** title of a duke, duchess, or archbishop ▷ *v* **8** add grace to **9** honour **graceful** *adj* **gracefully** *adv* **graceless** *adj*
▸ **gracious** *adj* **1** kind and courteous **2** condescendingly polite **3** elegant **graciously** *adv*
▸ **grace note** *music* note ornamenting a melody

grade ⓣ *n* **1** place on a scale of quality, rank, or size **2** mark or rating **3** class in school ▷ *v* **4** arrange in grades **5** assign a grade to
▸ **make the grade** succeed
▸ **gradation** *n* **1** (stage in) a series of degrees or steps **2** arrangement in stages

gradient ⓣ *n* (degree of) slope

gradual ⓣ *adj* occurring, developing, or moving in small stages **gradually** *adv*

graduate ⓣ *n* **1** person with a degree or diploma ▷ *v* **2** receive a degree or diploma **3** change by degrees **4** mark (a container etc.) with units of measurement **graduation** *n*

Graf *n* **Steffi**. born 1969, German tennis player: Wimbledon champion 1988, 1989, 1991, 1992, 1993, 1995, and 1996

graffiti [graf-**fee**-tee] *pl n* words or drawings scribbled or sprayed on walls etc.

THESAURUS

govern *v* **1 = rule**, lead, order, control, manage, direct, handle, guide, command, administer **2 = restrain**, control, check, regulate, curb, master, discipline, subdue, tame, hold in check

government *n* **1 = rule**, authority, administration, sovereignty, governance, statecraft **2 = executive**, administration, regime, ministry, powers-that-be

governor *n* **= leader**, head, director, chief, executive, manager, commander, controller, administrator, ruler

gown *n* **= dress**, habit, costume, robe, garment, garb, frock

grab *v* **= snatch**, seize, clutch, grasp • *I grabbed him by the arm*.

grace *n* **1 = elegance**, poise • *the grace of a ballet dancer* OPPOSITE: clumsiness **2 = goodwill**, favour, goodness, kindness, generosity, benefaction, benevolence, kindliness **3 = manners**, consideration, decency, etiquette, decorum, tact, propriety **4 = indulgence**, pardon, reprieve, mercy **5 = prayer**, blessing, benediction, thanks, thanksgiving ▸ *v* **6 = honour**, enhance, enrich, decorate, adorn, favour, ornament, embellish, dignify, set off
See also: **courtesy, favour, polish**

graceful *adj* **= elegant**, easy, beautiful, charming, pleasing, tasteful, comely

gracious *adj* **= kind**, civil, friendly, charitable, polite, cordial, considerate, courteous, well-mannered

graciousness *See* **courtesy**

grade *v* **1 = classify**, group, rate, class, sort • *Eggs are graded according to quality*. **2 = level**, group, stage, class, rank, category, degree, echelon
See also: **kind, quality**

gradient *n* **= slope**, rise, bank, hill, grade, incline, declivity

gradual *adj* **= steady**, slow, continuous, progressive • *the gradual improvement in communications* OPPOSITE: sudden

gradually *adv* **= steadily**, slowly, gently, progressively, by degrees, little by little, step by step, unhurriedly

graduate *v* **1 = mark off**, regulate, grade, proportion, calibrate, measure out **2 = classify**, group, order, rank,

DICTIONARY

graft[1] ➊ *n* **1** shoot of a plant set in the stalk of another **2** surgical transplant of skin or tissue ▷ *v* **3** insert (a plant shoot) in another stalk **4** transplant (living tissue) surgically
graft[2] *informal* ▷ *n* **1** hard work **2** obtaining of money by misusing one's position ▷ *v* **3** work hard **grafter** *n*
Graham *n* **1 Sean.** born 1968, Canadian politician, Premier of New Brunswick (2006–) **2 William Franklin,** known as *Billy Graham.* born 1918, US evangelist
Grahame *n* **Kenneth**. 1859–1932, Scottish author, noted for the children's classic *The Wind in the Willows* (1908)
grail *n* same as **Holy Grail**
grain ➊ *n* **1** seedlike fruit of a cereal plant **2** cereal plants in general **3** small hard particle **4** arrangement of fibres, as in wood **5** texture or pattern resulting from this **6** very small amount **grainy** *adj*
▸ **go against the grain** be contrary to one's natural inclination
Grainger *n* **Percy Aldridge**. 1882–1961, Australian pianist, composer, and collector of folk music on which many of his works are based
gram, gramme *n* metric unit of mass equal to one thousandth of a kilogram
grammar *n* **1** branch of linguistics dealing with the form, function, and order of words **2** book on the rules of grammar **3** use of words **grammarian** *n*
▸ **grammatical** *adj* according to the rules of grammar **grammatically** *adv*
▸ **grammar school** esp. formerly, a secondary school providing an education with a strong academic bias
gramophone *n* record player
grampus *n, pl* **-puses** sea mammal
gran *n informal* grandmother
Granados *n* **Enrique**, full name *Enrique Granados y Campina*. 1867–1916, Spanish composer, noted for the *Goyescas* (1911) for piano, which formed the basis for an opera of the same name
granary *n, pl* **-ries** building for storing threshed grain
grand ➊ *adj* **1** large or impressive, imposing **2** dignified or haughty **3** *informal* excellent **4** (of a total) final **5** chief ▷ *n* **6** grand piano **7** *slang* thousand pounds or dollars
▸ **grandchild** *n* child of one's child
▸ **granddaughter** *n* female grandchild
▸ **grandfather** *n* male grandparent
▸ **grandfather clock** tall standing clock with a pendulum and wooden case
▸ **grandmother** *n* female grandparent
▸ **grandparent** *n* parent of one's parent
▸ **grand piano** large harp-shaped piano with the strings set horizontally
▸ **grand slam** see **slam**
▸ **grandson** *n* male grandchild
▸ **grandstand** *n* terraced block of seats giving the best view at a sports ground
grandee *n* **1** Spanish nobleman of the highest rank **2** person of high station
grandeur ➊ *n* **1** magnificence **2** nobility or dignity
grandiloquent *adj* using pompous language **grandiloquently** *adv* **grandiloquence** *n*
grandiose ➊ *adj* **1** imposing **2** pretentiously grand **grandiosity** *n*
Grand Prix [gron **pree**] *n* international formula motor race
grange *n* country house with farm buildings
granite [**gran**-nit] *n* very hard igneous rock often used in building
granivorous *adj* feeding on grain or seeds
granny, grannie *n informal* grandmother
▸ **granny apartment** apartment in or added to a house, suitable for an elderly parent
grant ➊ *v* **1** give formally **2** consent to fulfil

g

THESAURUS

sort, arrange, grade
graft *n* **1 = shoot**, implant, bud, sprout, splice, scion ▸ *v* **2 = transplant**, join, implant, insert, splice, affix, ingraft
grain *n* **1 = cereals**, crops **2 = seed**, kernel, grist **3 = bit**, piece, trace, scrap, particle, fragment, speck, modicum, granule, morsel **4 = texture**, surface, pattern, weave, nap, fibre **5 = inclination**, character, temper, disposition, make-up, humour
grand *adj* **1 = impressive**, magnificent, splendid, monumental, majestic, imposing • *a grand building in the centre of town* **2** (*Informal*) **= wonderful**, great (*informal*), terrific, marvellous • *It was a grand day.*
grandeur *n* **= splendour**, dignity, majesty, pomp, nobility, magnificence, stateliness, sublimity
grandiose *adj* **1 = pretentious**, affected, flamboyant, showy, extravagant, pompous, bombastic, high-flown, ostentatious **2 = imposing**, grand, impressive, lofty, magnificent, monumental, majestic, stately
grant *n* **1 = award**, subsidy, allocation, bursary • *My application for a grant has been accepted.* ▸ *v* **2 = give**, allow, award, permit, allocate • *France has agreed to grant him political asylum.* OPPOSITE: deny **3 = admit**, allow, accept, acknowledge, concede • *I grant that you had some justification for your actions.* OPPOSITE: deny **4 = consent to**, allow, permit, accede to, agree to
See also: **present**

DICTIONARY

(a request) **3** admit ▷ *n* **4** sum of money provided by a government for a specific purpose, such as education
▶ **take for granted 1** accept as true without proof **2** take advantage of without due appreciation
Grant *n* **1 Cary**, real name *Alexander Archibald Leach*. 1904–86, US film actor, born in England. His many films include *Bringing up Baby* (1938), *The Philadelphia Story* (1940), *Arsenic and Old Lace* (1944), and *Mr. Blandings Builds his Dream House* (1948) **2 George Parkin**. 1918–1988, Canadian social philosopher, espoused nationalism and conservativism. His works include *Lament for a Nation: the Defeat of Canadian Nationalism* (1965) and *Technology and Justice* (1986) **3 Ulysses S(impson)**, real name *Hiram Ulysses Grant*. 1822–85, 18th president of the US (1869–77); commander in chief of Union forces in the American Civil War (1864–65)
granule Ⓣ *n* small grain
▶ **granular** *adj* of or like grains
▶ **granulated** *adj* (of sugar) in coarse grains
grape *n* small juicy green or purple berry, eaten raw or used to produce wine, raisins, currants, or sultanas
▶ **grapevine** *n* **1** grape-bearing vine **2** *informal* unofficial way of spreading news
grapefruit *n* large round yellow citrus fruit
graph *n* drawing showing the relation of different numbers or quantities plotted against a set of axes
graphic Ⓣ *adj* **1** vividly descriptive **2** of or using drawing, painting, etc. **graphically** *adv*
▶ **graphics** *pl n* diagrams, graphs, etc., esp. as used on a television programme or computer screen
graphite *n* soft black form of carbon, used in pencil leads
graphology *n* study of handwriting
graphologist *n*
grapnel *n* tool with several hooks, used to grasp or secure things
Grappelli, Grappelly *n* **Stéphane**. 1908–97, French jazz violinist: with Django Reinhardt, he led the Quintet of the Hot Club of France between 1934 and 1939
grapple Ⓣ *v* **1** come to grips with (a person) **2** try to cope with (something difficult)
▶ **grappling iron** grapnel
grasp Ⓣ *v* **1** grip something firmly **2** understand ▷ *n* **3** grip or clasp **4** understanding **5** total rule or possession
▶ **grasping** *adj* greedy or avaricious
grass *n* **1** common type of plant with jointed stems and long narrow leaves, including cereals and bamboo **2** lawn **3** pasture land **4** *slang* marijuana ▷ *v* **5** cover with grass
grassy *adj*
▶ **grasshopper** *n* jumping insect with long hind legs
▶ **grass roots** ordinary members of a group, as distinct from its leaders **grassroots** *adj*
▶ **grass widow** wife whose husband is absent for a time
Grass *n* **Günter** (**Wilhelm**). born 1927, German novelist, dramatist, and poet. His novels include *The Tin Drum* (1959), *Dog Years* (1963), *The Rat* (1986), *Toad Croaks* (1992), and *Crabwalk* (2002). Nobel prize for literature 1999
grate[1] *n* framework of metal bars for holding fuel in a fireplace
▶ **grating** *n* framework of metal bars covering an opening
grate[2] Ⓣ *v* **1** rub into small bits on a rough surface **2** scrape with a harsh rasping noise **3** annoy **grater** *n*
▶ **grating** *adj* **1** harsh or rasping **2** annoying
grateful Ⓣ *adj* feeling or showing thanks
gratefully *adv* **gratefulness** *n*
gratify Ⓣ *v* **-fying, -fied 1** satisfy or please

THESAURUS

granule *n* = **grain**, scrap, particle, fragment, molecule, atom, crumb, speck
graphic *adj* **1** = **vivid**, clear, detailed, explicit, striking, lively, expressive, lucid **2** = **pictorial**, visual, diagrammatic
grapple *v* **1** = **grip**, grab, seize, clutch, wrestle, grasp **2** = **deal with**, struggle, tackle, confront, address oneself to, get to grips with, take on
grasp *v* **1** = **grip**, hold, grab, seize, clutch, snatch • *He grasped both my hands.* **2** = **understand**, realize, appreciate, absorb, assimilate, take in • *Has anybody grasped the seriousness of the problem?* ▶ *n* **3** = **grip**, hold, embrace, clasp • *She slipped her hand from my grasp.* **4** = **understanding**, knowledge, grip, awareness, comprehension • *They have a good grasp of languages.* **5** = **control**, power, reach, scope
See also: **command, comprehend, handle, learn, master, see**
grasping *adj* = **greedy**, acquisitive, avaricious, covetous, rapacious
grate *v* **1** = **shred**, grind, mince, pulverize, triturate **2** = **scrape**, grind, scratch, rub, creak, rasp **3** = **annoy**, jar, irritate, rankle, exasperate, get on one's nerves (*informal*), set one's teeth on edge
grateful *adj* = **thankful**, appreciative, indebted • *I am grateful to you for your help.* OPPOSITE: ungrateful
gratification *n* = **satisfaction**, reward, thrill, delight, pleasure, relish, enjoyment, indulgence, fulfilment
gratified *See* **proud**
gratify *v* = **please**, satisfy, delight, humour,

DICTIONARY

2 indulge (a desire or whim) **gratification** *n*
gratis ⓣ *adv, adj* free, for nothing
gratitude ⓣ *n* feeling of being thankful for a favour or gift
gratuitous ⓣ [grat-**tyoo**-it-uss] *adj* **1** unjustified: *gratuitous violence* **2** given free **gratuitously** *adv*
gratuity ⓣ [grat-**tyoo**-it-ee] *n, pl* **-ties** money given for services rendered, tip
grave[1] ⓣ *n* hole for burying a corpse
▸ **gravestone** *n* stone marking a grave
▸ **graveyard** *n* cemetery
grave[2] ⓣ *adj* **1** serious and worrying **2** serious and solemn **gravely** *adv*
grave[3] [rhymes with **halve**] *n* accent (`) over a vowel to indicate a special pronunciation
gravel *n* mixture of small stones and coarse sand
▸ **gravelled** *adj* covered with gravel
▸ **gravelly** *adj* **1** covered with gravel **2** rough-sounding
graven [**grave**-en] *adj* carved or engraved
Graves *n* **Robert** (**Ranke**). 1895–1985, English poet, novelist, and critic, whose works include his World War I autobiography, *Goodbye to All That* (1929), and the historical novels *I, Claudius* (1934) and *Claudius the God* (1934)
gravid [**grav**-id] *adj med* pregnant
gravitate *v* **1** be influenced or drawn towards **2** *physics* move by gravity
gravitation *n* **gravitational** *adj*
gravity ⓣ *n, pl* **-ties 1** force of attraction of one object for another, esp. of objects to the earth **2** seriousness or importance **3** solemnity
gravy *n, pl* **-vies 1** juices from meat in cooking **2** sauce made from these
gray *adj US* same as **grey**
grayling *n* fish of the salmon family
graze[1] ⓣ *v* feed on grass
▸ **grazier** *n* person who feeds cattle for market
graze[2] ⓣ *v* **1** touch lightly in passing **2** scratch or scrape the skin ▷ *n* **3** slight scratch or scrape
grease *n* **1** soft melted animal fat **2** any thick oily substance ▷ *v* **3** apply grease to **greasy** *adj* **greasiness** *n*
▸ **grease gun** appliance for injecting oil or grease into machinery
▸ **greasepaint** *n* theatrical make-up
great ⓣ *adj* **1** large in size or number **2** extreme **3** important **4** pre-eminent **5** *informal* excellent **greatly** *adv* **greatness** *n*
▸ **great-** *prefix* one generation older or younger than: *great-grandfather*
▸ **greatcoat** *n* heavy overcoat
▸ **Great Dane** very large graceful dog
greave *n* piece of armour for the shin

THESAURUS

gladden, give pleasure, requite
grating[1] *adj* = **irritating**, offensive, harsh, raucous, strident, unpleasant, annoying, discordant, displeasing, jarring
grating[2] *n* = **grille**, grid, grate, gridiron, lattice, trellis
gratis *See* **free**
gratitude *n* = **thankfulness**, recognition, appreciation, thanks • *We wish to express our gratitude to the coach*. OPPOSITE: ingratitude
gratuitous *adj* **1** = **free**, voluntary, unpaid, spontaneous, complimentary, gratis, unasked-for, unrewarded **2** = **unjustified**, unnecessary, baseless, unwarranted, needless, groundless, wanton, superfluous, causeless, uncalled-for, unmerited
gratuity *n* = **tip**, gift, reward, donation, bonus, largesse *or* largess
grave[1] *n* = **tomb**, pit, mausoleum • *They visited the grave twice a year*. RELATED WORD *adjective*: sepulchral
grave[2] *adj* **1** = **critical**, serious, acute • *The situation in his country is very grave*. **2** = **solemn**, serious, sombre, sober, earnest, dignified, dour, unsmiling
See also: **deep, grim, heavy, severe**
graveyard *n* = **cemetery**, necropolis, burial ground, charnel house, churchyard
gravity *n* **1** = **importance**, severity, significance, urgency, seriousness, acuteness, momentousness, perilousness, weightiness **2** = **solemnity**, dignity, seriousness, sobriety, gravitas, earnestness
graze[1] *v* = **feed**, crop, browse, pasture
graze[2] *v* **1** = **scratch**, skin, scrape • *He fell and grazed his left arm*. **2** = **touch**, brush, scrape, shave, rub, skim, glance off ▸ *n* **3** = **scratch**, abrasion (*formal*), road rash (*informal*) • *He has just a slight graze on his elbow*.
greasy *adj* = **fatty**, slippery, oily, slimy, oleaginous
great *adj* **1** = **large**, big, huge, vast, enormous, immense, gigantic, voluminous, prodigious, supersize • *great columns of ice* OPPOSITE: small **2** = **important**, serious, significant, critical, crucial, momentous • *the great events of the 20th century* **3** = **famous**, prominent, remarkable, renowned, outstanding, illustrious, noteworthy, eminent **4** (*Informal*) = **excellent**, fine, wonderful, tremendous (*informal*), fantastic (*informal*), terrific (*informal*), superb, marvellous • *I thought it was a great idea*. OPPOSITE: terrible ▷ **great deal** *See* **plenty**
See also: **acute, brilliant, deep, extensive, extreme, grand, intense, splendid, uncommon**

DICTIONARY

grebe *n* diving water bird
Grecian [**gree**-shan] *adj* of ancient Greece
greed Ⓣ *n* excessive desire for something, such as food or money **greedy** *adj* **greedily** *adv* **greediness** *n*
Greek *n* **1** language of Greece **2** person from Greece ▷ *adj* **3** of Greece, the Greeks, or the Greek language
Greeley *n* **Horace**. 1811–72, US journalist and political leader: founder (1841) and editor of the *New York Tribune*, which championed the abolition of slavery
green Ⓣ *adj* **1** of a colour between blue and yellow **2** covered with grass or plants **3** unripe **4** of or concerned with environmental issues **5** envious or jealous **6** immature or gullible ▷ *n* **7** colour between blue and yellow **8** area of grass kept for a special purpose **9 Green** person concerned with environmental issues **greens 10** green vegetables **greenness** *n* **greenish** *or* **greeny** *adj*
▸ **greenery** *n* vegetation
▸ **green belt** protected area of open country around a town
▸ **greengage** *n* sweet green plum
▸ **greengrocer** *n Brit* shopkeeper selling vegetables and fruit
▸ **greenhorn** *n* novice
▸ **greenhouse** *n* glass building for rearing plants
▸ **greenhouse effect** rise in the temperature of the earth caused by heat absorbed from the sun being unable to leave the atmosphere
▸ **green light 1** signal to go **2** permission to proceed with something
▸ **greenroom** *n* room for actors when offstage
▸ **greenshank** *n* large European sandpiper
▸ **green thumb** skill in gardening
Greer *n* **Germaine**. born 1939, Australian writer and feminist. Her books include *The Female Eunuch* (1970), *Sex and Destiny* (1984), and *The Whole Woman* (1998)
greet Ⓣ *v* **1** meet with expressions of welcome **2** receive in a specified manner **3** be immediately noticeable to **greeting** *n*
gregarious Ⓣ *adj* **1** fond of company **2** (of animals) living in flocks or herds
Gregorian chant *n* same as **plainsong**
Gregory I *n* **Saint**, known as *Gregory the Great*. ?540–604 AD, pope (590–604), who greatly influenced the medieval Church. He strengthened papal authority by centralizing administration, tightened discipline, and revised the liturgy. He appointed Saint Augustine missionary to England. Feast day: March 12 or Sept 3
gremlin *n* imaginary being blamed for mechanical malfunctions
grenade *n* small bomb thrown by hand or fired from a rifle
▸ **grenadier** *n* soldier of a regiment formerly trained to throw grenades
grenadine [gren-a-**deen**] *n* syrup made from pomegranates, used in cocktails
Grenfell *n* **1 Joyce**, real name *Joyce Irene Phipps*. 1910–79, British comedy actress and writer **2** Sir **Wilfrid Thomason**. 1865–1940, English doctor and missionary working in Canada. He established orphanages, schools, hospitals, and cooperatives in Labrador and Newfoundland, helping both settlers and aboriginal peoples
Grenville *n* **George**. 1712–70, British statesman; prime minister (1763–65). His policy of taxing the American colonies precipitated the War of Independence
Gretzky *n* **Wayne**. born 1961, Canadian hockey player, based in Canada and the US. He is the only NHL player to score over 200 points in a single season; he retired in 1999
grew *v* past tense of **grow**

THESAURUS

greatest *adj* = **supreme**, ultimate, foremost
greatly *adv* = **very much**, considerably, remarkably, hugely, vastly, tremendously, enormously, immensely, exceedingly
greatness *n* **1** = **immensity**, size, magnitude, enormity, vastness, hugeness, prodigiousness **2** = **importance**, weight, gravity, significance, urgency, seriousness, momentousness **3** = **fame**, note, celebrity, glory, distinction, kudos, renown, grandeur, eminence, illustriousness
greed, greediness *n* **1** = **gluttony**, hunger, edacity, esurience, gormandizing, voracity **2** = **avarice**, desire, longing, craving, selfishness, acquisitiveness, avidity, covetousness
greedy *adj* **1** = **grasping**, materialistic
• *greedy people who take more than their fair share* **2** = **gluttonous**, hungry, voracious, insatiable, ravenous, gormandizing, piggish
green *adj* **1** = **leafy**, grassy, verdant **2** = **ecological**, conservationist, environment-friendly, non-polluting, ozone-friendly, green-collar **3** = **immature**, new, raw, naive, inexperienced, gullible, untrained, wet behind the ears (*informal*) **4** = **jealous**, envious, resentful, covetous, grudging ▸ *n* **5** = **lawn**, common, turf, sward
greet *v* = **welcome**, meet, receive (*formal*)
• *The champions were greeted by their fans.*
greeting *n* = **welcome**, address, reception, salute, salutation
gregarious *adj* = **outgoing**, social, friendly, cordial, affable, sociable, companionable, convivial

DICTIONARY

grey Ⓣ *adj* **1** of a colour between black and white **2** (of hair) partly turned white ▷ *n* **3** colour between black and white **4** grey or whitish horse **greyness** *n* **greyish** *adj*
▸ **grey matter** *informal* brains
Grey *n* **1 Charles**, 2nd Earl Grey. 1764–1845, British statesman. As Whig prime minister (1830–34), he carried the Reform Bill of 1832 and the bill for the abolition of slavery throughout the British Empire (1833) **2 Lady Jane**. 1537–54, queen of England (July 9–19, 1553); great-granddaughter of Henry VII. Her father-in-law, the Duke of Northumberland, persuaded Edward VI to alter the succession in her favour, but after ten days as queen she was imprisoned and later executed
greyhound *n* swift slender dog used in racing
Grey Owl *n* original name *Archibald Belaney*. 1888–1938, Canadian writer and conservationist, born in England; adopted Native Canadian identity
grid *n* **1** network of horizontal and vertical lines, bars, etc. **2** national network of electricity supply cables
griddle *n* flat iron plate for cooking
gridiron *n* **1** frame of metal bars for grilling food **2** N American football field
grief Ⓣ *n* deep sadness
▸ **grieve** *v* (cause to) feel grief
▸ **grievance** *n* real or imaginary cause for complaint
▸ **grievous** *adj* **1** very severe or painful **2** very serious
Grieg *n* **Edvard** (**Hagerup**). 1843–1907, Norwegian composer. His works, often inspired by Norwegian folk music, include the incidental music for *Peer Gynt* (1876), a piano concerto, and many songs
Grierson *n* **John**. 1898–1972, Scottish film director, active in Canada, where he founded the National Film Board. He coined the noun *documentary*, of which genre his *Industrial Britain* (1931) and *Song of Ceylon* (1934) are notable examples
griffin *n* mythical monster with an eagle's head and wings and a lion's body
Griffith *n* **D**(**avid Lewelyn**) **W**(**ark**). 1875–1948, US film director and producer. He introduced several cinematic techniques, including the flashback and the fade-out, in his masterpiece *The Birth of a Nation* (1915)
Griffith-Joyner *n* **Florence**, known as *Flojo*. 1959–98, US sprinter, winner of two gold medals at the 1988 Olympic Games
grill Ⓣ *n* **1** device on a cooker that radiates heat downwards **2** grilled food **3** gridiron ▷ *v* **4** cook under a grill **5** question relentlessly
▸ **grilling** *n* relentless questioning
grille, grill *n* grating over an opening
grilse [**grills**] *n* salmon on its first return from the sea to fresh water
grim Ⓣ *adj* **grimmer, grimmest 1** harsh and unpleasant **2** stern **3** disagreeable **grimly** *adv* **grimness** *n*
grimace Ⓣ *n* **1** ugly or distorted facial expression of pain, disgust, etc. ▷ *v* **2** make a grimace
grimalkin *n* old female cat
grime Ⓣ *n* **1** ingrained dirt ▷ *v* **2** make very dirty **grimy** *adj* **griminess** *n*
grin Ⓣ *v* **grinning, grinned 1** smile broadly, showing the teeth ▷ *n* **2** broad smile
grind Ⓣ *v* **grinding, ground 1** crush or rub to a powder **2** smooth or sharpen by friction **3** scrape together with a harsh noise **4** (foll. by *down*) treat harshly so as to prevent resistance ▷ *n* **5** *informal* hard or tedious work

THESAURUS

grey *adj* **1 = pale**, pallid, wan, ashen **2 = dismal**, dark, gloomy, dull, dim, dreary, drab, depressing **3 = characterless**, anonymous, dull, colourless
See also: **dim, drab**
gridlock *n* = **standstill**, deadlock, impasse, stalemate
grief *n* = **sadness**, distress, misery, sorrow, unhappiness, heartache • *a huge outpouring of national grief* OPPOSITE: happiness
See also: **pain, regret**
grief-stricken *See* **sad**
grievance *n* = **complaint**, injury, injustice, gripe (*informal*), axe to grind
grieve *v* **1 = mourn**, lament • *He still grieves for his wife.* **2 = sadden**, pain, upset, distress • *It grieved us to be separated from our loved ones.* OPPOSITE: cheer
See also: **regret**
grievous *adj* **1 = painful**, severe, grave, harmful, dreadful **2 = deplorable**, offensive, shocking, outrageous, shameful, atrocious, dreadful, monstrous
grill *See* **cook, interrogate**
grim *adj* = **stern**, severe, grave, solemn • *Her face was grim.*
See also: **horrible, serious**
grimace *n* **1 = scowl**, face, frown, sneer ▸ *v* **2 = scowl**, frown, sneer, lour *or* lower, make a face *or* make faces
grime *n* = **dirt**, grease, filth, soot, smut
grimy *adj* = **dirty**, foul, filthy, unclean, grubby, scuzzy (*slang*), soiled, sooty
grin *See* **smile**
grind *v* **1 = crush**, pound, mill, powder, grate, granulate, pulverize, abrade, triturate, kibble **2 = smooth**, sand, polish, sharpen, whet **3 = scrape**, grate, gnash ▸ *n* **4** (*Informal*) = **hard work**, sweat (*informal*), chore, labour, toil, drudgery

DICTIONARY

▸ **grind out** *v* produce in a routine or uninspired manner
▸ **grindstone** *n* stone used for grinding
grip Ⓣ *n* **1** firm hold or grasp **2** way in which something is grasped **3** control or understanding **4** travelling bag **5** handle ▷ *v* **gripping**, **gripped 6** grasp or hold tightly **7** hold the interest or attention of **gripping** *adj*
gripe *v* **1** *informal* complain persistently ▷ *n* **2** sudden intense bowel pain **3** *informal* complaint
Gris *n* **Juan**. 1887–1927, Spanish cubist painter, resident in France from 1906
Grisham *n* **John**. born 1955, US novelist and lawyer; his legal thrillers, many of which have been filmed, include *A Time to Kill* (1989), *The Pelican Brief* (1992), and *The Summons* (2002)
grisly Ⓣ *adj* **-lier**, **-liest** horrifying or ghastly
grist *n* grain for grinding
▸ **grist to one's mill** something which can be turned to advantage
gristle *n* cartilage in meat **gristly** *adj*
grit Ⓣ *n* **1** rough particles of sand **2** courage **3 Grit** *informal* member or supporter of Liberal Party **grits 3** meal consisting of coarsely ground grain ▷ *v* **gritting**, **gritted 4** spread grit on (an icy road) **5** clench or grind (the teeth) **gritty** *adj* **grittiness** *n*
grizzle *v informal* whine or complain
grizzled *adj* grey-haired
grizzly *n, pl* **-zlies** Also **grizzly bear** large American bear
groan Ⓣ *n* **1** deep sound of grief or pain **2** *informal* complaint ▷ *v* **3** utter a groan **4** *informal* complain
groat *n hist* fourpenny piece
groats *pl n* hulled and crushed grain of various cereals
grocer *n* shopkeeper selling foodstuffs
▸ **grocery** *n, pl* **-ceries 1** business or premises of a grocer **groceries 2** goods sold by a grocer
Groening *n* **Matt**(**hew**). born 1954, US cartoonist and writer, creator and producer of *The Simpsons* television series from 1989
grog *n* spirit, usu. rum, and water
groggy Ⓣ *adj* **-gier**, **-giest** *informal* faint, shaky, or dizzy
grogram *n* coarse fabric of silk mixed with wool or mohair
groin *n* **1** place where the legs join the abdomen **2** edge made by the intersection of two vaults
grommet *n* **1** ring or eyelet **2** *med* tube inserted in the ear to drain fluid from the middle ear
groom Ⓣ *n* **1** person who looks after horses **2** bridegroom **3** officer in a royal household ▷ *v* **4** make or keep one's clothes and appearance neat and tidy **5** brush or clean a horse **6** train (someone) for a future role
groove Ⓣ *n* **1** long narrow channel in a surface ▷ *v* **2** cut groove(s) in
grope Ⓣ *v* feel about or search uncertainly **groping** *n*
Gropius *n* **Walter**. 1883–1969, US architect, designer, and teacher, born in Germany. He founded (1919) and directed (1919–28) the Bauhaus in Germany. His influence stemmed from his adaptation of architecture to modern social needs and his pioneering use of industrial materials, such as concrete and steel. His buildings include the Fagus factory at Alfeld (1911) and the Bauhaus at Dessau (1926)
grosgrain [**grow**-grain] *n* heavy ribbed silk or rayon fabric
gross Ⓣ *adj* **1** outrageously wrong **2** vulgar **3** repulsively fat **4** total, without deductions

THESAURUS

grip *n* **1 = grasp**, hold, clasp • *He tightened his grip on the wallet.* **2 = control**, power, influence, clutches • *The dictator maintains an iron grip on his country.* **3 = understanding**, command, grasp, mastery, comprehension
▸ *v* **4 = grasp**, hold, clutch **5 = engross**, hold, entrance, absorb, fascinate, mesmerize, rivet, enthrall
See also: **handle**
gripping *adj* = **fascinating**, exciting, thrilling, compelling, engrossing, enthralling, entrancing, riveting, spellbinding
grisly *adj* = **gruesome**, horrible, shocking, awful, appalling, dreadful, macabre, ghastly, terrifying
grit *n* **1 = gravel**, dust, sand, pebbles **2 = courage**, resolution, spirit, determination, backbone, perseverance, tenacity, fortitude, guts (*informal*)
▸ *v* **3 = grind**, grate, clench, gnash
gritty *adj* **1 = rough**, dusty, sandy, rasping, gravelly, granular **2 = courageous**, brave, spirited, plucky, determined, steadfast, resolute, dogged, tenacious
groan *n* **1 = moan**, cry, whine, sigh
▸ *v* **2 = moan**, cry, whine, sigh
groggy *adj* = **dizzy**, weak, shaky, faint, confused, unsteady, wobbly, dazed
groom *n* **1 = stableman**, stableboy
▸ *v* **2 = smarten up**, clean, tidy, preen, primp, spruce up **3 = rub down**, clean, tend, brush, curry **4 = train**, coach, prime, prepare, ready, drill, educate, nurture, make ready
groove *n* = **indentation**, cut, channel, trench, hollow, rut, trough, flute, furrow
grope *v* = **feel**, search, fish, fumble, flounder, forage, scrabble, cast about
gross *adj* **1 = fat**, overweight, obese,

DICTIONARY

▷ *n* **5** twelve dozen ▷ *v* **6** make as total revenue before deductions **grossly** *adv* **grossness** *n*
Grosz *n* **George**. 1893–1959, German painter, in the US from 1932, whose works satirized German militarism and bourgeois society
grotesque ⓣ [grow-**tesk**] *adj* **1** strangely distorted or bizarre **2** ugly ▷ *n* **3** grotesque person or thing **4** artistic style mixing distorted human, animal, and plant forms **grotesquely** *adv*
grotto *n, pl* **-toes, -tos** small picturesque cave
grotty *adj* **-tier, -tiest** *informal* nasty or in bad condition
grouch *informal* ▷ *v* **1** grumble ▷ *n* **2** grumble **3** persistent grumbler **grouchy** *adj*
Groulx *n* **Lionel-Adolphe**. 1878–1967, Canadian Catholic priest, historian, and Quebec nationalist
ground[1] ⓣ *n* **1** surface of the earth **2** soil **3** area used for a specific purpose: *rugby ground* **4** position in an argument or controversy **grounds 5** enclosed land round a house **6** reason or motive **7** coffee dregs **8** *electrical* Also **earth** *US & Canad* connection between an electrical circuit or device and the earth, which is at zero potential ▷ *v* **9** ban an aircraft or pilot from flying **10** forbid (a child) to go out as a punishment **11** run (a ship) aground **12** instruct in the basics **13** base **14** *US & Canad* connect (a circuit or electrical device) to a ground **15** *baseball* hit the ball along the ground
▶ **groundless** *adj* without reason
▶ **grounding** *n* basic knowledge of a subject
▶ **groundhog** *n* marmot with a flat head on a very short neck, and short, rounded ears
▶ **groundnut** *n* peanut
▶ **groundsheet** *n* waterproof sheet put on the ground under a tent
▶ **groundsman** *n* person employed to maintain a sports ground or park
▶ **groundswell** *n* rapidly developing general feeling
▶ **groundwork** *n* preliminary work
ground[2] *v* past of **grind**
group ⓣ *n* **1** number of people or things regarded as a unit **2** small band of musicians or singers ▷ *v* **3** place or form into a group
grouper *n* large edible sea fish
grouse[1] *n* **1** stocky game bird **2** its flesh
grouse[2] ⓣ *v* **1** grumble or complain ▷ *n* **2** complaint
grout *n* **1** thin mortar ▷ *v* **2** fill up with grout
grove ⓣ *n* small group of trees
grovel ⓣ [**grov**-el] *v* **-elling, -elled 1** behave humbly in order to win a superior's favour **2** crawl on the floor
Groves *n* Sir **Charles**. 1915–92, English orchestral conductor
grow ⓣ *v* **growing, grew, grown 1** develop physically **2** (of a plant) exist **3** cultivate (plants) **4** increase in size or degree

g

THESAURUS

corpulent, hulking **2 = total**, whole, entire, aggregate, before deductions, before tax **3 = vulgar**, crude, offensive, obscene, coarse, indelicate **4 = blatant**, rank, utter, sheer, flagrant, heinous, grievous, unmitigated ▶ *v* **5 = earn**, make, take, bring in, rake in (*informal*)
grotesque *adj* = **unnatural**, strange, bizarre, fantastic, distorted, outlandish, preposterous, deformed, freakish
ground *n* **1 = earth**, land, soil, dirt, terrain • *We slid down the roof and dropped to the ground.* **2 = stadium**, field, park, arena **3** (*usually pl*) **= dregs**, deposit, sediment, lees ▶ *v* **4 = base**, set, settle, fix, establish, found **5 = instruct**, train, teach, initiate, tutor, acquaint with, familiarize with
See also: **bottom**
groundless *adj* = **unjustified**, empty, idle, baseless, unwarranted, unfounded, uncalled-for
grounds *pl n* **1 = land**, estate • *the grounds of the university* **2 = basis**, cause, reason, excuse, justification • *I'm against it on the grounds of expense.*
See also: **argument**
groundwork *n* = **preliminaries**, foundation, preparation, fundamentals, spadework, underpinnings
group *n* **1 = set**, party, crowd, band, collection, pack, gang, bunch, platoon, coterie, aggregation, assemblage • *a group of football fans* ▶ *v* **2 = arrange**, class, sort, organize, classify, marshal, assort • *Their responses are grouped into 11 categories.*
See also: **association, category, club, company, grade, lot, mass, movement, organization, society, team, type**
grouping *See* **party**
grouse *v* **1 = complain**, whine, carp, grumble, moan, gripe (*informal*), bellyache (*slang*) ▶ *n* **2 = complaint**, protest, objection, grievance, grumble, moan, gripe (*informal*), grouch (*informal*)
grove *n* = **wood**, covert, plantation, thicket, coppice, copse, spinney
grovel *v* = **humble oneself**, creep, crawl, cringe, fawn, abase oneself, bow and scrape, brown-nose (*slang*), demean oneself, kiss ass (*slang*), kowtow, toady
grow *v* **1 = increase**, develop, expand, multiply • *Bacteria grow more quickly once food is contaminated.* OPPOSITE: shrink **2 = flourish**, sprout, germinate

DICTIONARY

5 originate **6** become gradually: *it was growing dark*
▸ **growth** *n* **1** growing **2** increase **3** something grown or growing **4** tumour
▸ **grown-up** *adj, n* adult
▸ **grow up** *v* mature
growl *v* **1** make a low rumbling sound **2** say in a gruff manner ▷ *n* **3** growling sound
groyne *n* wall built out from the shore to control erosion
grub Ⓣ *n* **1** legless insect larva **2** *slang* food ▷ *v* **grubbing**, **grubbed 3** dig out or uproot **4** dig up the surface of (soil) **5** search
grubby Ⓣ *adj* **-bier**, **-biest** dirty **grubbiness** *n*
grudge Ⓣ *v* **1** be unwilling to give or allow ▷ *n* **2** resentment
gruel *n* thin porridge
gruelling Ⓣ *adj* exhausting or severe
gruesome Ⓣ *adj* causing horror and disgust
gruff Ⓣ *adj* rough or surly in manner or voice **gruffly** *adv* **gruffness** *n*
grumble Ⓣ *v* **1** complain **2** rumble ▷ *n* **3** complaint **4** rumble **grumbler** *n* **grumbling** *adj, n*
grumpy Ⓣ *adj* **grumpier**, **grumpiest** bad-tempered **grumpily** *adv* **grumpiness** *n*
grunge *n* **1** style of rock music with a fuzzy guitar sound **2** deliberately untidy and uncoordinated fashion style
grunt Ⓣ *v* **1** (esp. of pigs) make a low short gruff sound ▷ *n* **2** pig's sound **3** gruff noise
Gruyère [**grew**-yair] *n* hard yellow Swiss cheese with holes
gryphon *n* same as **griffin**
GST goods and services tax
G-string *n* small strip of cloth covering the genitals and attached to a waistband
GT gran turismo, used of a sports automobile
guano [**gwa**-no] *n* dried sea-bird manure
guarantee Ⓣ *n* **1** formal assurance, esp. in writing, that a product will meet certain standards **2** something that makes a specified condition or outcome certain ▷ *v* **-teeing**, **-teed 4** ensure **5** give a guarantee **6** secure against risk etc.
▸ **guarantor** *n* person who gives or is bound by a guarantee
guard Ⓣ *v* **1** watch over to protect or to prevent escape ▷ *n* **2** person or group that guards **3** official in charge of a train **4** protection **5** screen for enclosing anything dangerous **6** posture of defence in sports such as boxing or fencing **7** *basketball* player in the position furthest from the basket **guards 8 Guards** regiment with ceremonial duties

g

THESAURUS

• *Trees and bushes grew down to the water's edge.* **3 = become**, get, turn • *The puppy grew more comfortable with us.* **4 = originate**, issue, spring, stem, arise **5 = improve**, advance, progress, succeed, thrive, flourish, prosper **6 = cultivate**, raise, produce, farm, breed, nurture, propagate ▷ **grow up** *See* **mature**
See also: **rise, spread**
grown *See* **mature**
grown-up *adj* **1 = mature**, adult, fully-grown, of age ▸ *n* **2 = adult**, man, woman
growth *n* **1 = increase**, development, expansion, enlargement • *the growth of the sport-fishing industry* **2 = improvement**, rise, advance, success, progress, expansion, prosperity **3** (*Medical*) **= tumour**, lump
See also: **gain, spread**
grub *n* **1 = larva**, caterpillar, maggot **2** (*Slang*) **= food**, sustenance, rations, victuals ▸ *v* **3 = dig up**, root (*informal*), burrow, pull up **4 = search**, hunt, uncover, unearth, scour, forage, ferret, rummage
grubby *adj* **= dirty**, messy, filthy, grimy, mucky, shabby, sordid, squalid, seedy, unwashed, scuzzy (*slang*)
grudge *v* **1 = resent**, mind, complain, covet, envy, begrudge ▸ *n* **2 = resentment**, grievance, dislike, animosity, bitterness, enmity, antipathy, rancour
grudging *See* **unwilling**
gruelling *adj* **= exhausting**, severe, arduous, strenuous, demanding, backbreaking, laborious, punishing, taxing, tiring
gruesome *adj* **= horrific**, terrible, horrible, shocking, grim, grisly, macabre, ghastly
gruff *adj* **1 = surly**, rough, rude, grumpy, sullen, bad-tempered, brusque, churlish, ungracious **2 = hoarse**, low, rough, harsh, husky, rasping, croaking, guttural, throaty
grumble *v* **1 = complain**, whine, carp, moan, groan, mutter • *"This is very inconvenient," he grumbled.* **2 = rumble**, roar, mutter, growl, murmur, gurgle ▸ *n* **3 = complaint**, protest, objection, murmur • *I didn't hear any grumbles from anyone at the time.* **4 = rumble**, roar, growl, murmur, gurgle, muttering
grumpy *adj* **= irritable**, surly, sullen, sulky
See also: **cross**
grunt *See* **moan**
guarantee *n* **1 = assurance**, promise, word, pledge, undertaking • *a guarantee of job security* ▸ *v* **2 = ensure**, promise, pledge • *Remarks of this kind are guaranteed to cause anxiety*
guaranteed *See* **certain,. definite**
guard *v* **1 = protect**, defend, shelter, shield, safeguard, watch over • *Police were guarding his home yesterday.* **2 = supervise**, police, patrol • *Soldiers were guarding the prisoners.* ▷ **guard against** *See* **beware** ▸ *n* **3 = sentry**, warden, sentinel, watchman, warder • *The prisoners overpowered their guards and locked them*

DICTIONARY

▸**guardsman** *n* member of the Guards
▸**guarded** *adj* cautious or noncommittal
guardedly *adv*
▸**guard against** *v* take precautions against
guardian Ⓣ *n* **1** keeper or protector **2** person legally responsible for a child, mentally ill person, etc. **guardianship** *n*
guava [**gwah**-va] *n* yellow-skinned tropical American fruit
gubernatorial *adj US* of or relating to a governor
gudgeon *n* small European freshwater fish
Guernsey [**gurn**-zee] *n* **1** breed of dairy cattle **2 guernsey** seaman's knitted sweater
guerrilla, guerilla Ⓣ *n* member of an unofficial armed force fighting regular forces
guess Ⓣ *v* **1** estimate or draw a conclusion without proper knowledge **2** estimate correctly by guessing **3** suppose ▷ *n* **4** estimate or conclusion reached by guessing
▸**guesswork** *n* process or results of guessing
guest Ⓣ *n* **1** person entertained at another's house or at another's expense **2** invited performer or speaker **3** customer at a hotel or restaurant
▸**guesthouse** *n* boarding house
Guevara *n* **Ernesto**, known as *Che Guevara*. 1928–67, Latin American politician and soldier, born in Argentina. He developed guerrilla warfare as a tool for revolution and was instrumental in Castro's victory in Cuba (1959), where he held government posts until 1965. He was killed while training guerrillas in Bolivia
guff *n slang* nonsense
guffaw Ⓣ *n* **1** crude noisy laugh ▷ *v* **2** laugh in this way
guide Ⓣ *n* **1** person who shows the way **2** adviser **3** book of instruction or information **4** device for directing motion **5 Guide** member of an organization for girls equivalent to the Scouts ▷ *v* **6** act as a guide for **7** control, supervise, or influence
▸**guidance** *n* leadership, instruction, or advice
▸**guided missile** missile whose flight is controlled electronically
▸**guide dog** dog trained to lead a blind person
▸**guideline** *n* set principle for doing something
Guido d'Arezzo *n* ?995–?1050 AD, Italian Benedictine monk and musical theorist: reputed inventor of solmization
guild Ⓣ *n* **1** organization or club **2** *hist* society of men in the same trade or craft
guilder *n* former monetary unit of the Netherlands
guile Ⓣ [**gile**] *n* cunning or deceit **guileful** *adj* **guileless** *adj*
guillemot [**gil**-lee-mot] *n* black-and-white diving sea bird
guillotine *n* **1** machine for beheading people **2** device for cutting paper or sheet metal **3** method of preventing lengthy debate in parliament by fixing a time for taking the vote ▷ *v* **4** behead by guillotine **5** limit debate by the guillotine

g

THESAURUS

in a cell. **4 = protection**, security, screen, shield, safeguard, defence, buffer ▷ **off guard = unprepared**, unwary, napping, unready ▷ **on guard = prepared**, ready, alert, cautious, wary, vigilant, watchful, circumspect, on the alert, on the lookout
See also: **watch**
guarded *adj* **= cautious**, careful, suspicious, wary, prudent, cagey (*informal*), reserved, reticent, noncommittal, circumspect
guardian *n* **= keeper**, champion, guard, defender, curator, warden, protector, custodian
guerrilla *n* **= freedom fighter**, partisan, underground fighter
guess *v* **1 = estimate**, speculate **2 = suppose**, think, believe, suspect, judge, imagine, fancy, reckon, conjecture ▸ *n* **3 = speculation**, feeling, reckoning • *My guess is that the answer will be no*.
See also: **assume, figure, idea**
guesswork *n* **= speculation**, theory, estimation, conjecture, surmise, supposition
guest *n* **= visitor**, company, caller, boarder, lodger, visitant
guffaw *See* **laugh**
guidance *n* **= advice**, help, leadership, management, direction, instruction, teaching, counselling
guide *v* **1 = lead**, direct, accompany, escort • *He took the child by the arm and guided him to safety*. **2 = influence**, govern, counsel (*formal*) • *He should have let his instinct guide him*. **3 = steer**, control, manage, direct, handle, command, manoeuvre ▸ *n* **4 = escort**, leader, teacher, adviser, conductor, usher, mentor, counsellor **5 = model**, standard, example, ideal, inspiration, paradigm **6 = pointer**, sign, landmark, marker, beacon, signpost, guiding light, lodestar **7 = guidebook**, key, manual, directory, catalogue, handbook, Baedeker, instructions
See also: **ease, take**
guideline *See* **rule, standard**
guild *n* **= society**, company, order, union, club, league, organization, association, corporation, lodge, fellowship, fraternity, brotherhood
guile *n* **= cunning**, craft, deceit, trickery, artifice, cleverness, slyness, wiliness
guileless *See* **innocent**

DICTIONARY

guilt Ⓣ *n* **1** fact or state of having done wrong **2** remorse for wrongdoing
▸ **guiltless** *adj* innocent
▸ **guilty** *adj* **1** responsible for an offence or misdeed **2** feeling or showing guilt **guiltily** *adv*
guinea *n* **1** former British monetary unit worth 21 shillings (1.05 pounds) **2** former gold coin of this value
▸ **guinea fowl** bird related to the pheasant
▸ **guinea pig 1** tailless S American rodent **2** *informal* person used for experimentation
Guinness *n* Sir **Alec**. 1914–2000, British stage and film actor. His films include *Kind Hearts and Coronets* (1949), *The Bridge on the River Kwai* (1957), for which he won an Oscar, and *Star Wars* (1977); TV roles include Le Carré's George Smiley
guipure [geep-**pure**] *n* heavy lace with the pattern connected by threads
guise Ⓣ [rhymes with **size**] *n* false appearance
guitar *n* six-stringed instrument played by plucking or strumming **guitarist** *n*
Gulag *n* department of the Soviet security service in charge of prisons and labour camps
gulch *n* deep narrow valley in western N America
gulf Ⓣ *n* **1** large deep bay **2** chasm **3** large difference in opinion or understanding
gull *n* long-winged sea bird
gullet *n* muscular tube through which food passes from the mouth to the stomach
gullible Ⓣ *adj* easily tricked **gullibility** *n*
gully Ⓣ *n, pl* **-lies** channel cut by running water
gulp Ⓣ *v* **1** swallow hastily **2** gasp ▷ *n* **3** gulping **4** thing gulped
gum[1] *n* firm flesh in which the teeth are set
▸ **gummy** *adj* toothless
gum[2] Ⓣ *n* **1** sticky substance obtained from certain trees **2** adhesive **3** gumdrop **4** chewing gum **5** gumtree ▷ *v* **gumming, gummed 6** stick with gum **gummy** *adj*
▸ **gumboots** *pl n* Wellington boots
▸ **gumdrop** *n* hard jelly-like candy
▸ **gumtree** *n* eucalypt tree
gumption Ⓣ *n informal* **1** resourcefulness **2** courage
gun Ⓣ *n* **1** weapon with a metal tube from which missiles are fired by explosion **2** device from which a substance is ejected under pressure ▷ *v* **gunning, gunned 3** cause (an engine) to run at high speed
▸ **jump the gun** see **jump**
▸ **gunner** *n* artillery soldier
▸ **gunnery** *n* use or science of large guns
▸ **gunboat** *n* small warship
▸ **gun dog** dog used to retrieve game
▸ **gun down** *v* shoot (a person)
▸ **gun for** *v* seek or pursue vigorously
▸ **gunman** *n* armed criminal
▸ **gunmetal** *n* **1** alloy of copper, tin, and zinc ▷ *adj* **2** dark grey
▸ **gunpowder** *n* explosive mixture of potassium nitrate, sulfur, and charcoal
▸ **gunrunning** *n* smuggling of guns and ammunition **gunrunner** *n*
▸ **gunshot** *n* shot or range of a gun
gunge *n informal* sticky unpleasant substance **gungy** *adj*
gunk *n informal* slimy or filthy substance
gunny *n* strong coarse fabric used for sacks
gunwale, gunnel [**gun**-nel] *n* top of a ship's side
guppy *n, pl* **-pies** small colourful aquarium fish
Gurdjieff *n* **Georgei Ivanovitch**. ?1877–1949, Russian mystic: founded a teaching centre in Paris (1922)

THESAURUS

guilt *n* **1 = culpability**, blame, responsibility, wrongdoing, misconduct, guiltiness, sinfulness, wickedness **2 = remorse**, regret, shame, stigma, contrition, guilty conscience, self-reproach
guiltless *adj* **= innocent**, clean (*slang*), pure, spotless, untainted, blameless, irreproachable, sinless, squeaky-clean
guilty *adj* **1 = responsible**, criminal, convicted OPPOSITE: innocent **2 = ashamed**, sorry, remorseful (*formal*), regretful • *When she saw me, she looked guilty.*
guise *n* **= form**, appearance, shape, aspect, mode, disguise, pretense, semblance, demeanour
gulf *n* **1 = bay**, bight, sea inlet **2 = chasm**, opening, split, gap, separation, void, rift, abyss
gullibility *n* **= credulity**, innocence, simplicity, naivety
gullible *adj* **= naive**, trusting • *I'm so gullible I would have believed him.* OPPOSITE: suspicious *See also*: **impressionable**
gully *n* **= channel**, ditch, gutter, watercourse
gulp *v* **1 = swallow**, wolf, gobble, guzzle, devour, swig (*informal*), quaff, swill **2 = gasp**, choke, swallow ▸ *n* **3 = swallow**, draft, mouthful, swig (*informal*)
gum *n* **1 = glue**, paste, cement, resin, adhesive ▸ *v* **2 = stick**, paste, cement, glue, affix
gumption *n* (*Informal*) **= resourcefulness**, initiative, enterprise, savvy (*slang*), wit *or* wits, acumen, astuteness, common sense, mother wit
gun *n* **= firearm**, piece (*slang*), rifle, handgun, pistol, revolver, saturday night special (*slang*)
gunman *n* **= terrorist**, killer, bandit, gunslinger (*slang*)

DICTIONARY

gurgle Ⓣ *v, n* (make) a bubbling noise
Gurkha *n* person, esp. a soldier, belonging to a Hindu people of Nepal
Gurney *n* **Ivor** (**Bertie**). 1890–1937, British composer and poet
guru Ⓣ *n* **1** Indian spiritual teacher **2** leader or adviser
gush Ⓣ *v* **1** flow out suddenly and profusely **2** express admiration effusively ▷ *n* **3** sudden copious flow **4** effusiveness
▶ **gusher** *n* spurting oil well
gusset *n* piece of material sewn into a garment to strengthen it
gust Ⓣ *n* **1** sudden blast of wind ▷ *v* **2** blow in gusts **gusty** *adj*
gustation *n* act of tasting or the faculty of taste **gustatory** *adj*
gusto Ⓣ *n* enjoyment or zest
gut Ⓣ *n* **1** intestine **2** short for **catgut** **3** *informal* fat stomach **guts** **4** internal organs **5** *informal* courage ▷ *v* **gutting, gutted** **6** remove the guts from **7** (of a fire) destroy the inside of (a building) ▷ *adj* **8** basic or instinctive: *gut reaction*
▶ **gutsy** *adj informal* **1** courageous **2** vigorous or robust: *a gutsy performance*
▶ **gutted** *adj informal* disappointed and upset
gutter Ⓣ *n* **1** shallow trough for carrying off water from a roof or roadside ▷ *v* **2** (of a candle) burn unsteadily, with wax running down the sides
▶ **the gutter** degraded or criminal environment
▶ **guttering** *n* material for gutters
▶ **gutter press** newspapers that rely on sensationalism
guttural Ⓣ [**gut**-ter-al] *adj* **1** (of a sound) produced at the back of the throat **2** (of a voice) harsh-sounding
guy[1] Ⓣ *n* **1** *informal* man or boy **2** *Brit* effigy of Guy Fawkes burnt on Nov. 5th (**Guy Fawkes Day**)
guy[2] *n* rope or chain to steady or secure something **guyrope** *n*
guzzle Ⓣ *v* eat or drink greedily
gybe [**jibe**] *v* **1** (of a fore-and-aft sail) swing suddenly from one side to the other **2** (of a boat) change course by gybing
gym *n* short for **gymnasium, gymnastics**
gymkhana [jim-**kah**-na] *n* horse-riding competition
gymnasium *n* large room with equipment for physical training
▶ **gymnast** *n* expert in gymnastics
gymnastic *adj*
▶ **gymnastics** *pl n* exercises to develop strength and agility
gynecology, gynaecology [guy-nee-**kol**-la-jee] *n* branch of medicine dealing with diseases and conditions specific to women **gynecological** *or* **gynaecological** *adj* **gynecologist** *or* **gynaecologist** *n*
gyp *n* **give someone gyp** *slang* cause someone severe pain
gypsophila *n* garden plant with small white flowers
gypsum *n* chalklike mineral used to make plaster of Paris
Gypsy Ⓣ *n, pl* **-sies** member of a travelling people found throughout Europe
gyrate [jire-**rate**] *v* rotate or spiral about a point or axis **gyration** *n* **gyratory** *adj* gyrating
gyrocompass *n* compass using a gyroscope
gyroscope [**jire**-oh-skohp] *n* disc rotating on an axis that can turn in any direction, used to keep navigation instruments steady
gyroscopic *adj*

g

THESAURUS

gurgle *v* **1** = **murmur**, lap, splash, bubble, ripple, babble, plash, purl ▶ *n* **2** = **murmur**, ripple, babble, purl
guru *n* = **teacher**, leader, authority, master, sage, mentor, tutor, Svengali
gush *v* **1** = **flow**, pour, stream, spurt • *Water gushed out of the broken pipe.* **2** = **enthuse**, overstate, chatter, spout, babble, effervesce, effuse ▶ *n* **3** = **stream**, flood, rush, jet, flow, spurt, cascade, torrent, spout
See also: **rave**
gust *n* **1** = **blast**, blow, rush, breeze, puff, squall ▶ *v* **2** = **blow**, blast, squall
gusto *n* = **relish**, delight, pleasure, enthusiasm, enjoyment, zeal, verve, fervour
gut *n* **1** (*Informal*) = **paunch**, belly, potbelly, spare tire (*slang*) ▷ **guts** = **intestines**, stomach, belly, bowels, entrails, innards (*informal*), insides (*informal*), viscera; (*Informal*) = **courage**, backbone, audacity, spirit, nerve, pluck, daring, mettle ▶ *v* **2** = **disembowel**, clean **3** = **ravage**, empty, clean out, despoil ▶ *adj* **4** (~ *reaction*) = **instinctive**, natural, basic, heartfelt, spontaneous, involuntary, visceral, intuitive, unthinking
gutless *See* **cowardly**
gutsy *adj* = **brave**, bold, gritty, spirited, courageous, plucky, determined, resolute, indomitable
gutter *n* = **drain**, channel, ditch, trench, conduit, trough, sluice
guttural *adj* = **throaty**, deep, rough, thick, husky, rasping, gruff, gravelly, hoarse
guy *n* (*Informal*) = **man**, person, fellow, dude (*slang*), lad, chap
guzzle *v* = **devour**, drink, bolt, wolf, gobble, cram, swill, stuff (oneself)
Gypsy, Gipsy *n* = **traveler**, rover, nomad, Bohemian, wanderer, rambler, roamer, Romany

DICTIONARY

Hh

H *chem* hydrogen
Haakon VII *n* 1872–1957, king of Norway (1905–57). During the Nazi occupation of Norway (1940–45) he led Norwegian resistance from England
habeas corpus [**hay**-bee-ass **kor**-puss] *n* writ ordering a prisoner to be brought before a court
haberdasher *n Brit* dealer in small articles used for sewing **haberdashery** *n*
habit Ⓣ *n* **1** established way of behaving **2** addiction to a drug **3** costume of a nun or monk **4** woman's riding costume
▸ **habitual** *adj* done regularly and repeatedly **habitually** *adv*
▸ **habituate** *v* accustom **habituation** *n*
▸ **habitué** [hab-**it**-yew-ay] *n* frequent visitor to a place
habitable *adj* fit to be lived in
▸ **habitant** *n* (descendant of) original French settler
▸ **habitat** *n* natural home of an animal or plant
▸ **habitation** *n* **1** dwelling place **2** occupation of a dwelling place
hacienda [hass-ee-**end**-a] *n* ranch or large estate in Latin America
hack[1] Ⓣ *v* **1** cut or chop (at) violently **2** utter a harsh dry cough
hack[2] Ⓣ *n* **1** horse kept for riding **2** *informal* (inferior) writer or journalist
▸ **hackwork** *n* dull repetitive work
hacker *n slang* computer enthusiast, esp. one who breaks into the computer system of a company or government
hackles *pl n* hairs or feathers on the back of the neck of some animals and birds, which are raised in anger
Hackman *n* **Gene**. born 1930, US film actor; his films include *The French Connection* (1971), *Mississippi Burning* (1988), *Absolute Power* (1997), and *The Royal Tenenbaums* (2001)
hackney carriage *n* **1** taxi **2** coach or carriage for hire
hackneyed Ⓣ [**hak**-need] *adj* (of language) stale or trite because of overuse
hacksaw *n* small saw for cutting metal
had *v* past of **have**
haddock *n* large edible sea fish
Haden *n* **Charles** (**Edward**). born 1937, US jazz bassist
Hades [**hay**-deez] *n Greek myth* underworld home of the dead
Hadfield *n* **Chris**. born 1959, Canadian astronaut, first Canadian to walk in space (2001)
hadj *n* same as **hajj**
Hadrian, Adrian *n* Latin name *Publius Aelius Hadrianus*. 76–138 AD, Roman emperor (117–138); adopted son and successor of Trajan. He travelled throughout the Roman Empire, strengthening its frontiers and encouraging learning and architecture, and in Rome he reorganized the army and codified Roman law
haematic *adj* same as **hematic**
haematology *n* same as **hematology**
haemoglobin *n* same as **hemoglobin**
haemophilia *n* same as **hemophilia**
haemorrhage *n* same as **hemorrhage**
haemorrhoids *pl n* same as **hemorrhoids**
haft *n* **1** handle of an axe, knife, or dagger ▹ *v* **2** provide with a haft
hag Ⓣ *n* **1** ugly old woman **2** witch
▸ **hag-ridden** *adj* distressed or worried
Hagen *n* **Walter**. 1892–1969, US golfer
Hagerman *n* **Barbara**. born 1943, Canadian music teacher, Lieutenant

THESAURUS

habit *n* **1 = custom**, practice, convention, tradition, routine • *his habit of smiling at everyone he sees* **2 = addiction**, dependence • *a drug habit*
habitat *n* **= home**, environment, territory • *the habitat of the spotted owl*
habitation *n* **1 = dwelling**, home, house, residence, lodging, abode, domicile, living quarters, quarters **2 = occupancy**, occupation, inhabitance, tenancy
habitual *adj* **= customary**, standard, regular, traditional, normal, usual, routine, familiar, accustomed
hack[1] *v* **= cut**, slash, chop, mutilate, mangle, lacerate, hew
hack[2] *n* **1 = scribbler**, literary hack, penny-a-liner **2 = horse**, nag, crock
hackneyed *adj* **= clichéd**, tired, stale, banal, trite • *hackneyed phrases like "tried and true"* OPPOSITE: original
See also: **corny, stock**
hag *n* **= witch**, crone, harridan

DICTIONARY

Governor of Prince Edward Island (2006–)
haggard Ⓣ *adj* looking tired and ill
Haggard *n* Sir (**Henry**) **Rider**. 1856–1925, British author of romantic adventure stories, including *King Solomon's Mines* (1885)
haggis *n* Scottish dish made from sheep's offal, oatmeal, suet, and onion
Haggis *n* **Paul**. born 1953, Canadian screenwriter and film director; as a writer his credits include *Million Dollar Baby* (2004), and as a director and writer *Crash* (2004)
haggle Ⓣ *v* bargain or wrangle over a price
hagiology *n, pl* **-gies** literature about the lives of the saints
▶ **hagiography** *n* writing of this
hagiographer *n*
ha-ha[1] *interj* representation of the sound of laughter
ha-ha[2] *n* sunken fence bordering a garden or park, that allows an uninterrupted view from within
hail[1] Ⓣ *n* **1** (shower of) small pellets of ice **2** large amount of words, missiles, blows, etc. ▷ *v* **3** fall as or like hail **hailstone** *n*
hail[2] Ⓣ *v* **1** greet **2** call (out to) **3** acclaim, acknowledge
▶ **hail from** *v* come originally from
Haile Selassie *n* title of *Ras Tafari Makonnen*. 1892–1975, emperor of Ethiopia (1930–36; 1941–74). During the Italian occupation of Ethiopia (1936–41), he lived in exile in England. He was a prominent figure in the Pan-African movement: deposed 1974
hair Ⓣ *n* **1** threadlike growth on the skin **2** such growths collectively, esp. on the head
▶ **hairy** *adj* **1** covered with hair **2** *slang* dangerous or exciting **hairiness** *n*
▶ **hairdo** *n* style in which a person's hair is cut and arranged
▶ **hairdresser** *n* person who cuts and styles hair
▶ **hairline** *n* **1** margin of hair at the top of the forehead ▷ *adj* **2** very fine or narrow
▶ **hairpin** *n* U-shaped wire used to hold the hair in place
▶ **hairpin bend** U-shaped bend in the road
▶ **hair-raising** *adj* terrifying
▶ **hairsplitting** *n* making of petty distinctions
▶ **hairspring** *n* very fine spring in a watch or clock
hajj *n* pilgrimage a Muslim makes to Mecca
▶ **hajji** *n* Muslim who has made a pilgrimage to Mecca
hake *n* edible fish of the cod family
halal *n* meat from animals slaughtered according to Muslim law
halberd *n* spear with an axe blade
halcyon Ⓣ [**hal**-see-on] *adj* peaceful and happy
▶ **halcyon days** time of peace and happiness
hale Ⓣ *adj* robust, healthy: *hale and hearty*
Hale *n* **George Ellery**. 1868–1938, US astronomer: undertook research into sunspots and invented the spectroheliograph
Halévy *n* **1** (**Jacques François**) **Fromental**, original name *Elias Levy*. 1799–1862, French composer, noted for his operas, which include *La Juive* (1835) **2** his nephew, **Ludovic**. 1834–1908, French dramatist and novelist, who collaborated with Meilhac on opera libretti
Haley *n* **Bill**, full name *William John Clifton Haley*. 1925–81, US rock and roll singer, best known for his recording of "Rock Around the Clock" (1955)
half Ⓣ *n, pl* **halves** **1** either of two equal parts **2** *informal* half-pint **3** half-price ticket ▷ *adj* **4** incomplete ▷ *adv* **5** to the extent of half **6** partially
▶ **half-baked** *adj informal* poorly planned
▶ **half-breed** *n* half-caste
▶ **half-brother** *or* **half-sister** *n* brother or sister related through one parent only

h

THESAURUS

haggard *adj* = **gaunt**, thin, wan, careworn, drawn, emaciated, pinched
haggle *v* = **bargain**, barter, beat down
hail[1] *n* **1** = **shower**, storm, barrage, volley, bombardment • *a hail of bullets* ▶ *v* **2** = **rain down on**, rain, batter, shower, pelt, bombard, beat down upon
hail[2] *v* **1** = **call**, flag down, signal to • *He hailed me from across the street.* **2** = **greet**, welcome, acknowledge, cheer, applaud, salute, honour, acclaim ▷ **hail from** = **come from**, be a native of, be born in, originate in
hair *n* = **locks**, shock, mop, mane, head of hair, tresses
hairdresser *n* = **stylist**, barber, coiffeur *or* coiffeuse
hair-raising *adj* = **frightening**, shocking, scary, alarming, bloodcurdling, horrifying, spine-chilling, terrifying
hairstyle *n* = **haircut**, cut, style, hairdo, coiffure
hairy *adj* = **shaggy**, furry, woolly, unshaven, bushy, hirsute, stubbly
halcyon *adj* **1** = **peaceful**, quiet, calm, gentle, tranquil, serene, undisturbed **2** (~ *days*) = **happy**, golden, prosperous, carefree, flourishing, palmy
hale *adj* = **healthy**, well, strong, sound, fit, robust, vigorous, able-bodied, flourishing, in the pink
half *n* **1** = **equal part**, section, portion, hemisphere, fifty per cent ▶ *adj* **2** = **partial**, moderate, limited, halved ▶ *adv* **3** = **partially**, partly, in part

DICTIONARY

▶ **half-caste** *n* person with parents of different races
▶ **half-cocked** *adj* **go off half-cocked** fail because of inadequate preparation
▶ **half-hearted** *adj* unenthusiastic
▶ **half-life** *n* time taken for half the atoms in radioactive material to decay
▶ **half-nelson** *n* hold in wrestling in which one wrestler's arm is pinned behind his back by his opponent
▶ **half note** musical note half the length of a whole note
▶ **halfpenny** [**hayp**-nee] *n* former British coin worth half an old penny
▶ **half-pipe** *n* large U-shaped ramp used for skateboarding, snowboarding, etc.
▶ **half-timbered** *adj* having an exposed wooden frame filled in with plaster
▶ **half-time** *n sports* interval between two halves of a game
▶ **halftone** *n* illustration showing lights and shadows by means of very small dots
▶ **halfway** *adv, adj* at or to half the distance
▶ **halfwit** *n* foolish or feeble-minded person

Haliburton *n* **Thomas Chandler**. 1796–1865, Canadian writer, historian, judge, and politician. Noted esp. for his satire *The Clockmaker; or the Sayings and Doings of Sam Slick of Slickville* (1836)

halibut *n* large edible flatfish

halitosis *n* bad-smelling breath

hall Ⓣ *n* **1** (entrance) passage **2** large room or building belonging to a particular group or used for a particular purpose **3** large country house

Hallé *n* Sir **Charles**, original name *Karl Hallé*. 1819–95, German conductor and pianist, in Britain from 1848. In 1857 he founded the Hallé Orchestra in Manchester

hallelujah [hal-ee-**loo**-ya] *interj* exclamation of praise to God

Halley *n* **Edmund**. 1656–1742, English astronomer and mathematician. He predicted the return of the comet now known as **Halley's comet**, constructed charts of magnetic declination, and produced the first wind maps

hallmark Ⓣ *n* **1** mark indicating the standard of tested gold and silver **2** distinguishing feature ▷ *v* **3** stamp with a hallmark

hallo *interj* same as **hello**

hallowed Ⓣ *adj* regarded as holy

Hallowe'en *n* October 31, the eve of All Saints' Day

hallucinate *v* seem to see something that is not really there
▶ **hallucination** *n* experience of seeming to see something that is not really there
hallucinatory *adj*
▶ **hallucinogen** *n* drug that causes hallucinations

halo Ⓣ [**hay**-loh] *n, pl* **-loes, -los 1** disc of light round the head of a sacred figure **2** ring of light round the sun or moon

halogen [**hal**-oh-jen] *n chem* any of a group of nonmetallic elements including chlorine and iodine

Hals *n* **Frans**. ?1580–1666, Dutch portrait and genre painter: his works include *The Laughing Cavalier* (1624)

halt Ⓣ *v* **1** stop ▷ *n* **2** temporary stop **3** minor railway station without a building
▶ **halting** *adj* hesitant: *halting speech*

halter *n* strap around a horse's head with a rope to lead it with
▶ **halterneck** *n* top or dress with a strap fastened at the back of the neck

THESAURUS

half-baked *adj* = **ill-judged**, impractical, short-sighted, ill-conceived, poorly planned, unformed, unthought out *or* unthought through

half-hearted *adj* = **unenthusiastic**, tame, listless, indifferent, lukewarm, apathetic, lacklustre, perfunctory

halfway *adv* **1** = **midway**, to the middle *or* in the middle ▶ *adj* **2** = **midway**, central, middle, mid, intermediate, equidistant ▷ **halfway point** *See* **middle**

halfwit *n* = **fool**, idiot, moron, imbecile (*informal*), airhead (*slang*), dork (*slang*), dunderhead, schmuck (*slang*), simpleton

hall *n* **1** = **entrance hall**, lobby, entry, passage, corridor, hallway, foyer, passageway, vestibule **2** = **meeting place**, chamber, auditorium, assembly room, concert hall

hallmark *n* **1** = **seal**, sign, mark, device, stamp, symbol, endorsement **2** = **indication**, sure sign, telltale sign

hallow *See* **bless**

hallowed *See* **holy**

hallucination *n* = **illusion**, dream, vision, fantasy, delusion, mirage, apparition, figment of the imagination

halo *n* = **ring of light**, aura, corona, nimbus, radiance

halt *v* **1** = **stop**, draw up, pull up • *She held her hand out to halt him.* **2** = **end**, check, curb, cease, terminate, cut short • *Production was halted on the movie.* OPPOSITE: begin ▶ *n* **3** = **stop**, end, close, pause, standstill, stoppage • *He brought the car to a halt.* *See also*: **block**

halting *adj* = **faltering**, awkward, hesitant, laboured, stammering, stumbling, stuttering

DICTIONARY

halve ⓣ *v* **1** cut in half **2** reduce to half **3** share
halves *n* plural of **half**
halyard *n* rope for raising a ship's sail or flag
ham *n* **1** smoked or salted meat from a pig's thigh **2** *informal* amateur radio operator **3** *informal* actor who overacts ▷ *v* **hamming, hammed 4 ham it up** *informal* overact
▸ **ham-fisted** *or* **ham-handed** *adj* clumsy
hamburger *n* flat round piece of minced beef, often served in a bread roll
Hamilton *n* **Alexander**. ?1757–1804, American statesman. He was a leader of the Federalists and as first secretary of the Treasury (1789–95) established a federal bank
hamlet *n* small village
Hamlisch *n* **Marvin**. born 1944, US composer, best known for the musical *A Chorus Line* (1975)
Hamlyn *n* Baron **Paul**. 1926–2001, British businessman and publisher
hammer ⓣ *n* **1** tool with a heavy head, used to drive in nails, beat metal, etc. **2** part of a gun which causes the bullet to be fired **3** metal ball on a wire, thrown as a sport **4** auctioneer's mallet **5** striking mechanism in a piano ▷ *v* **6** strike (as if) with a hammer **7** *informal* defeat
▸ **hammer and tongs** with great effort or energy
▸ **hammerhead** *n* shark with a wide flattened head
▸ **hammertoe** *n* condition in which the toe is permanently bent at the joint
Hammerstein II *n* **Oscar**. 1895–1960, US librettist and songwriter: collaborated with the composer Richard Rodgers in musicals such as *South Pacific* (1949) and *The Sound of Music* (1959)
Hammett *n* **Dashiell**. 1894–1961, US writer of detective novels. His books include *The Maltese Falcon* (1930) and *The Thin Man* (1932)
hammock *n* hanging bed made of canvas or net
Hammurabi, Hammurapi *n* ?18th century BC, king of Babylonia; promulgator of one of the earliest known codes of law
hamper[1] ⓣ *v* make it difficult for (someone or something) to move or progress
hamper[2] *n* **1** large basket with a lid **2** selection of food and drink packed as a gift
Hampton *n* **Lionel**. 1913–2002, US jazz-band leader and vibraphone player
hamster *n* small rodent with a short tail and cheek pouches
hamstring *n* **1** tendon at the back of the knee ▷ *v* **2** make it difficult for someone to take any action
Hancock *n* **John**. 1737–93, American statesman; first signatory of the Declaration of Independence
hand ⓣ *n* **1** end of the arm beyond the wrist **2** style of writing **3** applause **4** pointer on a dial **5** manual worker **6** cards dealt to a player in a card game **7** unit of four inches used to measure horses ▷ *v* **8** pass or give
▸ **at hand, on hand**, *or* **to hand** nearby
▸ **hand in glove** in close association
▸ **hands down** easily
▸ **have a hand in** be involved in
▸ **lend a hand** help
▸ **out of hand** beyond control
▸ **handful** *n* **1** the amount that can be held in the hand **2** small quantity or number **3** *informal* person or thing that is difficult to control
▸ **handbag** *n* purse
▸ **handbill** *n* small printed notice
▸ **handbook** *n* small reference or instruction book
▸ **handcuff** *n* **1** one of a linked pair of metal rings used for securing a prisoner ▷ *v* **2** put handcuffs on

h

THESAURUS

halve *v* = **bisect**, cut in half, divide equally, share equally, split in two
hammer *v* **1** = **hit**, strike, beat, drive, knock, tap, bang **2** (*Informal*) = **defeat**, beat, trounce, drub, thrash, run rings around (*informal*), wipe the floor with (*informal*)
hamper *v* = **hinder**, restrict, frustrate, obstruct, impede • *I was hampered by a lack of information.*
See also: **handicap, restrain**
hand *n* **1** = **palm**, fist, paw (*informal*), mitt (*slang*) **2** = **hired man**, worker, employee, operative, artisan, craftsman, labourer, workman **3** = **penmanship**, script, handwriting, calligraphy **4** = **ovation**, clap, round of applause ▷ **at hand, on hand** = **nearby**, close, near, available, ready, handy, at one's fingertips, within reach ▷ **hand-out** = **charity**, alms; = **leaflet**, literature (*informal*), bulletin, circular, mailshot, press release ▸ *v* **5** = **pass**, deliver, hand over ▷ **hand down** = **pass on**, will, give, bestow, bequeath, pass down • *stories handed down from parents to children* ▷ **hand in** *See* **submit, tender** ▷ **hand out** *See* **distribute, present** ▷ **hand-pick** *See* **pick**
handbook *n* = **guidebook**, guide, manual, Baedeker, instruction book
handcuff *v* = **shackle**, fetter, manacle
handcuffs *pl n* = **shackles**, cuffs (*informal*), fetters, manacles
handful *n* = **few**, smattering, sprinkling, small number

DICTIONARY

▸ **handheld** *adj* **1** (of a computer) small enough to be held in the hand ▷ *n* **2** computer small enough to be held in the hand
▸ **handicraft** *n* objects made by hand
▸ **handiwork** *n* work of a particular person
▸ **hand-out** *n* **1** thing given free **2** written information given out at a talk etc.
▸ **handprint** *n* mark left by the impression of a hand
▸ **hands-on** *adj* involving practical experience of equipment
▸ **handstand** *n* act of supporting the body on the hands in an upside-down position
▸ **handwriting** *n* (style of) writing by hand

h & c hot and cold (water)

Handel *n* **George Frederick**, German name *Georg Friedrich Händel*. 1685–1759, German composer, resident in England, noted particularly for his oratorios, including the *Messiah* (1741) and *Samson* (1743). Other works include over 40 operas, 12 concerti grossi, organ concertos, chamber and orchestral music, esp. *Water Music* (1717)

handicap Ⓣ *n* **1** any physical or mental disability **2** something that makes progress difficult **3** contest in which the competitors are given advantages or disadvantages in an attempt to equalize their chances **4** disadvantage or advantage given ▷ *v* **5** make it difficult for (someone) to do something

handicraft Ⓣ *n* objects made by hand

handiwork Ⓣ *n* work of a particular person

handkerchief *n* small square of fabric used to wipe the nose

handle Ⓣ *n* **1** small lever used to open and close a door etc. **2** part of an object that is held so that it can be used ▷ *v* **3** hold, feel, or move with the hands **4** control or deal with
▸ **handler** *n* person who controls an animal
▸ **handlebars** *pl n* curved metal bar used to steer a cycle

Handler *n* **Daniel**. born 1970, US writer for older children, best known for the macabre humour of his *A Series of Unfortunate Events*, a sequence of books written in the persona of Lemony Snicket

handsome Ⓣ *adj* **1** attractive in appearance **2** large or generous: *a handsome reward*

handy Ⓣ *adj* **handier**, **handiest** **1** convenient, useful **2** good at manual work **handily** *adv* **handiness** *n*
▸ **handyman** *n* man skilled at odd jobs

Handy *n* **W(illiam) C(hristopher)**. 1873–1958, US blues musician and songwriter, esp. noted for the song "St Louis Blues"

hang Ⓣ *v* **hanging**, **hung 1** attach or be attached at the top with the lower part free **2** *past* **hanged** suspend or be suspended by the neck until dead **3** fasten to a wall **4** droop
▸ **get the hang of** *informal* understand
▸ **hanger** *n* curved piece of wood or hook for hanging clothes on
▸ **hang back** *v* hesitate
▸ **hangdog** *adj* sullen, dejected
▸ **hang-glider** *n* glider with a light framework from which the pilot hangs in a harness **hang-gliding** *n*
▸ **hangman** *n* person who executes people by hanging
▸ **hangover** *n* aftereffects of drinking too much alcohol
▸ **hang-up** *n* *informal* emotional or psychological problem
▸ **hang up** *v* end a telephone call

hangar *n* large shed for storing aircraft

THESAURUS

handicap *n* **1 = disadvantage**, barrier, obstacle, impediment, drawback, hindrance • *Being short was a slight handicap for the basketball player.* **2 = advantage**, head start **3 = disability**, defect, impairment ▸ *v* **4 = hinder**, restrict, burden, hamper, impede • *Greater levels of stress may handicap some students.*

handicraft *n* **= craftsmanship**, art, skill, craft, workmanship, handiwork

handiwork *n* **= creation**, product, production, design, achievement, invention

handle *n* **1 = grip**, knob, hilt • *a broom handle* ▸ *v* **2 = hold**, feel, touch, finger, grasp • *Wear protective gloves when handling chemicals.* **3 = control**, manage, direct, guide, manipulate, manoeuvre • *The truck is difficult to handle on the road.* **4 = deal with**, manage, administer, supervise, cope with, take care of • *Can you handle the situation?*
See also: **deal, process**

handsome *adj* **1 = good-looking**, attractive • *a handsome man* OPPOSITE: ugly **2 = generous**, liberal, considerable, sizable, ample, plentiful • *a handsome profit* OPPOSITE: small

handwriting *n* **= penmanship**, hand, script, scrawl, calligraphy

handy *adj* **1 = convenient**, close, nearby, at hand, at your fingertips, on hand • *Keep a pencil and paper handy.* **2 = useful**, helpful, practical, convenient, neat, easy to use • *handy hints on looking after indoor plants* **3 = skilful**, expert, skilled, adept, deft, proficient, adroit, dexterous
See also: **available, ready**

hang *v* **1 = dangle**, sag, droop • *His jacket hung from a hook behind the door.* **2 = suspend**, fix, attach, drape, fasten • *to hang clothes on a line* **3 = execute**, lynch, string up (*informal*) ▷ **hang around** *See* **stay** ▷ **hang back = hesitate**, recoil, be reluctant, demur, hold back ▷ **hang out** *See*

DICTIONARY

hank Ⓣ *n* coil or skein, esp. of yarn
hanker Ⓣ *v* (foll. by *after*) crave, long for
Hanks *n* **Tom**. born 1956, US film actor: his films include *Splash* (1984), *Philadelphia* (1993), *Forrest Gump* (1994), *Saving Private Ryan* (1998), and *The Terminal* (2004)
hanky, hankie *n, pl* **hankies** *informal* handkerchief
hanky-panky *n informal* illicit sexual relations
Hanna *n* **William**. 1910–2001, US animator and film producer who with **Joseph Barbera** (1911–2006) created the cartoon characters Tom and Jerry in the 1940s; the Hanna-Barbera company later produced numerous cartoon series for television
Hansen *n* **Rick**. born 1957, Canadian charity fundraiser. He travelled in his wheelchair through 34 countries (1985–87) raising money for spinal cord research
hansom *n* formerly, a two-wheeled horse-drawn cab for hire
haphazard Ⓣ *adj* not organized or planned **haphazardly** *adv*
hapless Ⓣ *adj* unlucky
happen Ⓣ *v* **1** occur, take place **2** be or do by chance, turn out
▶ **happening** *n* occurrence, event
happy Ⓣ *adj* **-pier, -piest 1** glad or content **2** lucky or fortunate **3** willing **happily** *adv* **happiness** *n*
▶ **happy-go-lucky** *adj* carefree and cheerful
hara-kiri *n* Japanese ritual suicide by disembowelment
harangue Ⓣ *v* **1** address angrily or forcefully ▷ *n* **2** angry or forceful speech
harass Ⓣ *v* annoy or trouble constantly **harassed** *adj* **harassment** *n*
harbinger [**har**-binge-er] *n* person or thing that announces the approach of something
harbour Ⓣ *n* **1** sheltered port ▷ *v* **2** give shelter or protection to **3** maintain secretly in the mind
hard Ⓣ *adj* **1** firm, solid, or rigid **2** difficult **3** requiring a lot of effort **4** unkind or unfeeling **5** difficult to bear **6** (of water) containing calcium salts which stop soap lathering freely **7** (of a drug) strong and addictive ▷ *adv* **8** with great energy or effort **9** carefully **10** intensely **harden** *v* **hardness** *n*
▶ **hard of hearing** slightly deaf
▶ **hard up** *informal* short of money

THESAURUS

associate ▶ *n* ▷ **get the hang of = grasp**, understand, comprehend ▷ **hang-up = preoccupation**, problem, thing (*informal*), block, difficulty, obsession, inhibition
See also: **extend, float, stretch**
hangdog *adj* = **guilty**, downcast, wretched, cowed, cringing, defeated, furtive, shamefaced
hangover *n* = **aftereffects**, crapulence, morning after (*informal*)
hank *n* = **coil**, roll, piece, length, loop, skein
hanker *v* (with *for* or *after*) = **desire**, long, hunger, pine, thirst, crave, itch, lust, yearn
hankering *n* = **desire**, hope, urge, wish, hunger, ache, longing, craving, thirst, itch, yearning, pining
haphazard *adj* = **disorganized**, random, casual, indiscriminate, aimless, hit or miss (*informal*), slapdash
haphazardly *See* **at random**
hapless *See* **unlucky**
happen *v* **1** = **occur**, follow, result, come about, take place • *The accident happened on Wednesday*. **2** = **chance**, turn out
See also: **come, work out**
happening *n* = **event**, experience, incident, affair, episode, proceeding, occurrence
happily *adv* **1** = **willingly**, freely, gladly, with pleasure **2** = **joyfully**, gleefully, blithely, cheerfully, joyously, gaily, merrily **3** = **luckily**, fortunately, opportunely, providentially
happiness *n* = **joy**, delight, pleasure, satisfaction, ecstasy, elation, contentment • *Money can't buy happiness*. OPPOSITE: sadness
happy *adj* **1** = **joyful**, content, glad, ecstatic, jubilant, merry, pleased, delighted, cheerful, blissful, elated, overjoyed, thrilled • *a happy atmosphere* OPPOSITE: sad **2** = **fortunate**, lucky, timely, win-win (*informal*), favourable, advantageous, auspicious • *a happy coincidence* OPPOSITE: unlucky
See also: **agreeable, bright, cheery, comfortable, ready, satisfied, willing**
happy-go-lucky *adj* = **carefree**, easy-going, light-hearted, unconcerned, nonchalant, blithe, untroubled
harangue *v* **1** = **rant**, address, lecture, spout (*informal*), exhort, declaim, hold forth ▶ *n* **2** = **speech**, address, tirade, diatribe, declamation, exhortation
harass *v* = **annoy**, trouble, plague, bother, hound, hassle (*informal*), persecute, vex, harry, pester
harassed *adj* = **worried**, troubled, strained, distraught, careworn, hassled (*informal*), tormented, under pressure, vexed
harassment *n* = **trouble**, bother, persecution, hassle (*informal*), nuisance, irritation, annoyance, pestering
harbour *n* **1** = **port**, haven, anchorage ▶ *v* **2** = **shelter**, protect, hide, shield, provide refuge **3** = **maintain**, hold, nurse, retain, foster, entertain, nurture, cling to
See also: **bear, refuge**
hard *adj* **1** = **solid**, strong, firm, tough,

DICTIONARY

▶ **hardship** *n* **1** suffering **2** difficult circumstances
▶ **hard-bitten** *adj* tough
▶ **hardboard** *n* thin stiff board made of compressed sawdust and woodchips
▶ **hard-boiled** *adj* **1** (of eggs) boiled until solid **2** *informal* tough, unemotional
▶ **hard copy** computer output printed on paper
▶ **hard-core** *adj* (of pornography) showing sexual acts in explicit detail
▶ **hard drive** *computers* mechanism that handles the reading, writing, and storage of data on the hard disk
▶ **hard-headed** *adj* shrewd, practical
▶ **hard-hearted** *adj* unfeeling, unkind
▶ **hard sell** aggressive sales technique
▶ **hardware** *n* **1** metal tools or implements **2** machinery used in a computer system **3** military weapons
▶ **hardwood** *n* wood of a deciduous tree such as oak or ash

Harding *n* **Warren G(amaliel)**. 1865–1923, 29th president of the US (1921–23)

hardly Ⓣ *adv* **1** scarcely or not at all **2** with great difficulty

hardy Ⓣ *adj* **-dier**, **-diest** able to stand difficult conditions **hardiness** *n*

Hardy *n* **Thomas**. 1840–1928, British novelist and poet. Most of his novels are set in his native Dorset (part of his fictional Wessex) and include *Far from the Madding Crowd* (1874), *The Return of the Native* (1878), *The Mayor of Casterbridge* (1886), *Tess of the d'Urbervilles* (1891), and *Jude the Obscure* (1895), after which his work consisted chiefly of verse

hare *n* **1** animal like a large rabbit, with longer legs and ears ▷ *v* **2** run fast
▶ **harebell** *n* blue bell-shaped flower
▶ **harebrained** *adj* foolish or impractical
▶ **harelip** *n* split in the upper lip

harem *n* (apartments of) a Muslim man's wives and concubines

haricot [**har**-rik-oh] *n* white bean which can be dried

hark Ⓣ *v* *old-fashioned* listen
▶ **hark back** *v* return (to an earlier subject)

harlequin *n* **1** stock comic character, with a diamond-patterned costume and mask ▷ *adj* **2** in varied colours

harlot *n* *obsolete* prostitute

Harlow *n* **Jean**, real name *Harlean Carpentier*. 1911–37, US film actress, whose films include *Hell's Angels* (1930), *Red Dust* (1932), and *Bombshell* (1933)

harm Ⓣ *v* **1** injure physically, mentally, or morally ▷ *n* **2** physical, mental, or moral injury **harmful** *adj* **harmless** *adj*

THESAURUS

stiff, rigid • *a hard piece of cheese* OPPOSITE: soft **2 = strenuous**, rigorous, arduous, exhausting, laborious, tough • *hard work* OPPOSITE: easy **3 = difficult**, complex, complicated, baffling, puzzling • *That's a very hard question*. OPPOSITE: simple **4 = unfeeling**, cold, cruel, stern, callous, unsympathetic, unkind, hardhearted, pitiless **5 = painful**, unpleasant, intolerable, grievous, disagreeable, distressing ▷ **hard up = poor**, short, impoverished, broke (*informal*), penniless, impecunious, on the breadline, out of pocket, strapped for cash (*informal*) ▶ *adv* **6 = energetically**, heavily, sharply, strongly, severely, vigorously, fiercely, violently, intensely, forcibly, forcefully, powerfully, with all one's might, with might and main **7 = diligently**, steadily, persistently, doggedly, industriously, untiringly
See also: **harsh, rough, severe, tricky**

hard-boiled *adj* **= tough**, realistic, practical, cynical, hard-nosed (*informal*), unsentimental, matter-of-fact

harden *v* **1 = solidify**, set, freeze, bake, cake, stiffen • *The cement finally hardened*. OPPOSITE: soften **2 = accustom**, season, train, inure, habituate
See also: **strengthen**

hardened *adj* **1 = habitual**, chronic, shameless, incorrigible, inveterate **2 = accustomed**, seasoned, habituated, inured, toughened

hard-headed *adj* **= sensible**, tough, realistic, practical, pragmatic, shrewd, unsentimental, level-headed

hardhearted *adj* **= unsympathetic**, hard, cold, insensitive, callous, heartless, uncaring, unfeeling

hardiness *n* **= resilience**, resolution, toughness, robustness, ruggedness, sturdiness

hardly *adv* **= barely**, just, scarcely, only just • *I could hardly believe what I was seeing*.

hardship *n* **= suffering**, want, difficulty, adversity, misfortune, destitution • *Many people are suffering economic hardship*.
See also: **ordeal, poverty, sorrow**

hardy *adj* **= strong**, tough, sound, robust, rugged, sturdy, stout

hark See **listen**

harm *v* **1 = injure**, damage, abuse, hurt, wound, ruin, ill-treat • *The robbers seemed anxious not to harm anyone*. ▶ *n* **2 = injury**, damage, abuse, hurt • *Even friendly bears are capable of doing harm to human beings*.
See also: **spoil**

harmful *adj* **= damaging**, destructive, detrimental, hurtful • *Most stress is harmful, but some is beneficial*. OPPOSITE: harmless

DICTIONARY

harmonica *n* mouth organ
harmonium *n* small organ
harmony Ⓣ *n, pl* **-nies 1** peaceful agreement and cooperation **2** combination of notes to make a pleasing sound **harmonious** *adj* **harmoniously** *adv*
▸ **harmonic** *adj* **1** of harmony **2** harmonious
▸ **harmonics** *n* science of musical sounds
▸ **harmonize** *v* fit in or go well with each other **harmonization** *n*
▸ **harmonica** *n* mouth organ
▸ **harmonium** *n* small organ
harness Ⓣ *n* **1** equipment for attaching a horse to a cart or plow **2** set of straps fastened round someone's body to attach something: *a parachute harness* ▷ *v* **3** put a harness on **4** control (something) in order to use its energy
Harold I *n* surname *Harefoot*. died 1040, king of England (1037–40); son of Canute
Harold II *n* ?1022–66, king of England (1066); son of Earl Godwin and successor of Edward the Confessor. His claim to the throne was disputed by William the Conqueror, who defeated him at the Battle of Hastings (1066)
harp *n* large triangular stringed instrument played with the fingers **harpist** *n*
▸ **harp on about** *v* talk about continuously
Harper *n* **Stephen**. born 1959, Canadian politician, leader of the Conservative Party, prime minister of Canada (2006)
harpoon *n* **1** barbed spear attached to a rope used for hunting whales ▷ *v* **2** spear with a harpoon
harpsichord *n* stringed keyboard instrument
harpy *n, pl* **-pies** cruel or grasping woman
harridan *n* shrewish (old) woman
harrier *n* cross-country runner
Harriman *n* **W(illiam) Averell**. 1891–1986, US diplomat: negotiated the Nuclear Test Ban Treaty with the Soviet Union (1963); governor of New York (1955–58)
Harris *n* **1 Lawren Stewart**. 1885–1970, Canadian painter who, with the other members of the Group of Seven, attempted to create a distinctly Canadian style of art **2 Roy**. 1898–1979, US composer, esp. of orchestral and choral music incorporating American folk tunes
Harrison *n* **1 Benjamin**. 1833–1901, 23rd president of the US (1889–93) **2 George**. 1943–2001, British rock singer, guitarist, and songwriter: a member of the Beatles (1962–70). His solo recordings include *All Things Must Pass* (1970) and *Cloud Nine* (1987) **3** grandfather of Benjamin, **William Henry**. 1773–1841, 9th president of the US (1841); first president to die in office; shortest tenure of US presidency in history (32 days)
harrow *n* **1** implement used to break up clods of soil ▷ *v* **2** draw a harrow over
harrowing Ⓣ *adj* very distressing
harry Ⓣ *v* **-rying, -ried** keep asking (someone) to do something, pester
harsh Ⓣ *adj* **1** unpleasant to the senses **2** severe or cruel **harshly** *adv* **harshness** *n*
hart *n* adult male deer
Hart *n* **1 Lorenz**. 1895–1943, US lyricist: collaborated with Richard Rodgers in writing musicals **2 Moss**. 1904–61, US dramatist: collaborated with George Kaufman on Broadway comedies and wrote libretti for musicals
hartebeest *n* large African antelope
Harthacanute, Hardecanute, Hardicanute *n* ?1019–42, king of Denmark (1035–42) and of England (1040–42); son of Canute
Hartley *n* **L(eslie) P(oles)**. 1895–1972, British novelist. His novels include the trilogy *The Shrimp and the Anemone* (1944), *The Sixth Heaven*

h

THESAURUS

See also: **unhealthy**
harmless *adj* = **safe**, innocuous, nontoxic, not dangerous • *This experiment was harmless to the animals*. OPPOSITE: harmful
harmonious *adj* **1** = **melodious**, musical, agreeable, concordant, consonant, dulcet, mellifluous, sweet-sounding, tuneful **2** = **friendly**, sympathetic, compatible, cordial, amicable, agreeable, congenial
harmonize *v* = **match**, tally, blend, correspond, coordinate, chime with, cohere, tone in with
harmony *n* **1** = **agreement**, accord, peace, sympathy, friendship, compatibility, cooperation, rapport, amicability, concord **2** = **tunefulness**, tune, melody, unison, euphony
harness *n* **1** = **equipment**, tackle, gear, tack ▸ *v* **2** = **exploit**, control, channel, employ, mobilize, utilize
harrowing *adj* = **distressing**, painful, traumatic, nerve-racking, agonizing, disturbing, heart-rending, terrifying, tormenting
harry *v* = **pester**, plague, bother, molest, harass, hassle (*informal*), badger, chivvy
harsh *adj* **1** = **severe**, hard, cruel, stern, ruthless, austere • *harsh weather conditions* OPPOSITE: mild **2** = **raucous**, rough, strident, rasping, grating, discordant, dissonant, guttural
See also: **drastic**
harshly *adv* = **severely**, strictly, roughly, brutally, cruelly, sternly
harshness *n* = **severity**, brutality, austerity,

DICTIONARY

(1946), and *Eustace and Hilda* (1947) as well as *The Go-Between* (1953)
harum-scarum *adj* reckless
Harun al-Rashid *n* ?763–809 AD, Abbasid caliph of Islam (786–809), whose court at Baghdad was idealized in the *Arabian Nights*
harvest Ⓣ *n* **1** (season for) the gathering of crops **2** crops gathered ▷ *v* **3** gather (a ripened crop) **harvester** *n*
Harvey *n* **William**. 1578–1657, English physician who discovered the mechanism of blood circulation, expounded in *On the motion of the heart* (1628)
has *v* third person singular of the present tense of **have**
▶ **has-been** *n informal* person who is no longer popular or successful
Hašek *n* **Jaroslav**. 1883–1923, Czech novelist and short-story writer; author of *The Good Soldier Schweik* (1923)
hash Ⓣ *n* **1** dish of diced meat and vegetables **2** *informal* hashish
▶ **make a hash of** *informal* mess up or destroy
hashish [hash-**eesh**] *n* drug made from the hemp plant, taken for its intoxicating effects
hasp *n* clasp which fits over a staple and is secured by a bolt or padlock, used as a fastening
hassle Ⓣ *informal* ▷ *n* **1** trouble or difficulty **2** nuisance ▷ *v* **3** cause annoyance or trouble to
hassock *n* cushion for kneeling on in church
haste Ⓣ *n* speed or hurry
▶ **make haste** hurry or rush
▶ **hasten** *v* (cause to) increase speed
▶ **hasty** *adj* (too) quick **hastily** *adv*
hat *n* covering for the head, often with a brim, usually worn to give protection from the weather
▶ **keep something under one's hat** keep something secret
▶ **hat trick** any three successive achievements, esp. in sport
hatch[1] Ⓣ *v* **1** (cause to) emerge from an egg **2** devise (a plot or plan)
▶ **hatchery** *n* place for hatching eggs
hatch[2] *n* **1** (hinged door covering) an opening in a floor or wall **2** opening in the wall between a kitchen and a dining area **3** door in an aircraft or spacecraft
▶ **hatchback** *n* automobile with a single lifting door in the rear
▶ **hatchway** *n* opening in the deck of a ship
hatchet *n* small axe
▶ **bury the hatchet** make peace
▶ **hatchet job** malicious verbal or written attack
▶ **hatchet man** *informal* person carrying out unpleasant tasks for an employer
hate Ⓣ *v* **1** dislike intensely **2** be unwilling (to do something) ▷ *n* **3** intense dislike **4** person or thing that is hated
▶ **hateful** *adj* causing or deserving hate
▶ **hatred** *n* intense dislike
Hatoyama *n* **Yukio**. born 1947, Japanese politician; Prime Minister from 2009
Hatshepsut, Hatshepset *n* queen of Egypt of the 18th dynasty (?1512–1482 BC). She built a great mortuary temple at Deir

h

THESAURUS

roughness, rigour, asperity, sternness
harvest *n* **1** = **crop**, produce, yield ▶ *v* **2** = **gather**, pick, reap, pluck, mow
hash *n* ▷ **make a hash of** (*Informal*) = **mess up**, mishandle, botch, bungle, muddle, mismanage, make a pig's ear of (*informal*)
hassle *n* **1** (*Informal*) = **trouble**, effort, bother, inconvenience, upheaval • *It's not worth the hassle.* **2** = **argument**, fight, dispute, row, disagreement, squabble, quarrel, bickering ▶ *v* **3** (*Informal*) = **bother**, harass, nag, badger, pester • *The picky customer hassled the server.*
See also: **annoy, difficulty, nuisance, stress, worry**
haste *n* **1** = **speed**, urgency, velocity, quickness, alacrity, rapidity, swiftness **2** = **rush**, hurry, hustle, impetuosity
hasten *v* = **rush**, race, fly, speed, dash, hurry *or* hurry up, scurry, make haste
hastily *adv* **1** = **speedily**, quickly, rapidly, promptly **2** = **hurriedly**, impetuously, precipitately, rashly
hasty *adj* **1** = **speedy**, prompt, rapid, swift, brisk, hurried • *The signs of their hasty departure could be seen everywhere.* **2** = **impetuous**, rash, precipitate, impulsive, thoughtless
See also: **quick, sudden**
hatch *v* **1** = **incubate**, breed, brood, bring forth **2** = **devise**, design, conceive, concoct, contrive, cook up (*informal*), dream up (*informal*), think up
hate *v* **1** = **detest**, dislike, loathe, despise, abhor, be sick of • *Most people hate him, but they don't care to say so.* OPPOSITE: love **2** = **be unwilling**, dislike, be loath, be reluctant, be sorry, feel disinclined, shrink from ▶ *n* **3** = **hatred**, hostility, dislike, animosity, aversion, loathing • *a violent bully, destructive and full of hate* OPPOSITE: love
hateful *adj* = **horrible**, offensive, despicable, abhorrent, obnoxious, loathsome • *It was a hateful thing to say to me.*
hatred *n* = **hate**, dislike, animosity, revulsion, aversion, antipathy • *He has been accused of inciting racial hatred.* OPPOSITE: love
See also: **horror, hostility**

DICTIONARY

el Bahri near Thebes
haughty Ⓣ *adj* **-tier**, **-tiest** proud, arrogant **haughtily** *adv* **haughtiness** *n*
haul Ⓣ *v* **1** pull or drag with effort ▷ *n* **2** amount gained by effort or theft
▸ **long haul** something that takes a lot of time and effort to achieve
▸ **haulage** *n* (charge for) transporting goods
▸ **haulier** *n* firm or person that transports goods by road
haunch *n* human hip or fleshy hindquarter of an animal
haunt Ⓣ *v* **1** visit in the form of a ghost **2** remain in the thoughts or memory of ▷ *n* **3** place visited frequently
▸ **haunted** *adj* **1** visited by ghosts **2** worried
▸ **haunting** *adj* extremely beautiful or sad
haute couture [**oat** koo-**ture**] *n French* high fashion
hauteur [oat-**ur**] *n* haughtiness
have Ⓣ *v* **has, having, had 1** hold, possess **2** experience or be affected with **3** be obliged (to do) **4** *slang* cheat or outwit **5** receive, take, or obtain **6** cause to be done **7** give birth to **8** used to form past tenses (with a past participle): *I have gone; I had gone*
▸ **have it out** *informal* settle by argument
▸ **have-not province** *Canad* province whose own tax revenue entitles it to receive payments from the federal government
▸ **have on** *v informal* trick or tease
▸ **have province** *Canad* province whose own tax revenue does not entitle it to receive payments from the federal government
haven Ⓣ *n* place of safety
haversack *n* canvas bag carried on the back or shoulder
havoc Ⓣ *n* disorder and confusion
haw *n* hawthorn berry
hawk[1] *n* **1** bird of prey with short rounded wings and a long tail **2** supporter or advocate of warlike policies **hawkish** *or* **hawklike** *adj*
▸ **hawk-eyed** *adj* having extremely good eyesight
hawk[2] Ⓣ *v* offer (goods) for sale in the street or door-to-door **hawker** *n*
Hawking *n* **Stephen William**. born 1942, British physicist. Stricken with a progressive nervous disease since the 1960s, he has nevertheless been a leader in cosmological theory. His *A Brief History of Time* (1987) was a bestseller
Hawkins *n* **Coleman**. 1904–69, US pioneer of the tenor saxophone for jazz
Hawks *n* **Howard** (**Winchester**). 1896–1977, US film director. His films include *Sergeant York* (1941) and *The Big Sleep* (1946)
Hawksmoor *n* **Nicholas**. 1661–1736, English architect. His designs include All Souls', Oxford, and a number of London churches, notably St Anne's, Limehouse
hawser *n* large rope used on a ship
hawthorn *n* thorny shrub or tree
hay *n* grass cut and dried as fodder
▸ **hay fever** allergic reaction to pollen or dust
▸ **haystack** *n* large pile of stored hay
▸ **haywire** *adj* **go haywire** *informal* not function properly
Haydn *n* **1** (**Franz**) **Joseph**. 1732–1809, Austrian composer, who played a major part in establishing the classical forms of the symphony and the string quartet. His other works include the oratorios *The Creation* (1796–98) and *The Seasons* (1798–1801) **2** his brother, **Johann Michael**. 1737–1806, Austrian composer, esp. of Church music
Hayek *n* **Friedrich August von**. 1899–1992, British economist and political philosopher, born in Austria: noted for his advocacy of free-market ideas; shared the Nobel prize for economics 1974
Hayes *n* **Rutherford B**(**irchard**). 1822–93,

THESAURUS

haughty *adj* = **proud**, arrogant, conceited, disdainful, snobbish, stuck-up (*informal*) • *He spoke in a haughty tone.* OPPOSITE: humble *See also*: **superior**
haul *v* **1** = **drag**, pull, draw, tug, heave, lug ▸ *n* **2** = **gain**, catch, yield, harvest, loot, booty, spoils, takings
haunt *v* **1** = **plague**, trouble, possess, recur, obsess, torment, prey on, stay with, weigh on ▸ *n* **2** = **meeting place**, hangout (*informal*), rendezvous, stamping ground
haunted *adj* **1** = **possessed**, eerie, spooky (*informal*), ghostly, cursed, jinxed **2** = **preoccupied**, troubled, worried, obsessed, plagued, tormented
haunting *adj* = **poignant**, persistent, nostalgic, unforgettable, evocative
have *v* **1** = **own**, hold, keep, possess • *We have two tickets for the concert.* **2** = **experience**, feel, enjoy, undergo, endure, sustain • *He had a marvellous time.* **3** = **receive**, take, get, gain, accept, acquire, secure, obtain, procure **4** = **give birth to**, bear, deliver, beget, bring forth ▷ **have fun** *See* **play** ▷ **have on** = **wear**, be clothed in, be dressed in; = **tease**, kid (*informal*), deceive, pull someone's leg, trick ▷ **have to** = **be obliged**, should, must, ought, be bound, be compelled, be forced, have got to
haven *n* = **sanctuary**, retreat, shelter, refuge, asylum, sanctum
havoc *n* = **disorder**, chaos, confusion, disruption, mayhem, shambles
hawk *See* **sell**
haywire *adj* = **topsy-turvy**, chaotic, confused, disordered, disorganized, mixed

DICTIONARY

19th president of the US (1877–81)
hazard ⓣ *n* **1** risk, danger ▷ *v* **2** put at danger **3** venture (a guess) **hazardous** *adj*
haze ⓣ *n* mist, often caused by heat
▶ **hazy** *adj* **1** misty **2** vague
hazel *n* **1** bush producing nuts ▷ *adj* **2** (of eyes) greenish-brown **hazelnut** *n*
Hazlitt *n* **William**. 1778–1830, English critic and essayist: works include *Characters of Shakespeare's Plays* (1817), *Table Talk* (1821), and *The Plain Speaker* (1826)
HB (on pencils) hard black
H-bomb *n* hydrogen bomb
he *pron* **1** male person or animal **2** person or animal of unspecified sex
He *chem* helium
head ⓣ *n* **1** upper or front part of the body, containing the sense organs and the brain **2** upper or most forward part of anything **3** aptitude, intelligence **4** chief of a group or organization **5** person or animal considered as a unit **6** white froth on beer **7** headline or title **8** *informal* headache ▷ *adj* **9** chief, principal ▷ *v* **10** be at the top or front of **11** lead, direct **12** move (in a particular direction) **13** provide with a heading **14** hit (a ball) with the head
▶ **go to someone's head** make someone drunk or conceited
▶ **head over heels** very much in love
▶ **not make head nor tail of** not understand
▶ **off one's head** *slang* insane
▶ **header** *n* **1** action of striking a ball with the head **2** headlong dive
▶ **heading** *n* title written or printed at the top of a page
▶ **heads** *adv informal* with the side of a coin which has a portrait of a head on it uppermost
▶ **heady** *adj* intoxicating or exciting
▶ **headache** *n* **1** continuous pain in the head **2** cause of worry or annoyance
▶ **headboard** *n* vertical board at the head of a bed
▶ **head-hunter** *n* person who sets out to recruit someone from another company for a particular job
▶ **headland** *n* area of land jutting out into the sea
▶ **headlight** *n* powerful light on the front of a vehicle
▶ **headline** *n* **1** news summary in large type in a newspaper **headlines 2** main points of a news broadcast
▶ **headlong** *adv* **1** head foremost **2** with haste
▶ **head-on** *adj, adv* **1** front foremost **2** direct(ly) and uncompromising(ly)
▶ **headphones** *pl n* two small loudspeakers held against the ears by a strap
▶ **headquarters** *pl n* centre from which operations are directed
▶ **head start** advantage in a competition
▶ **headstone** *n* gravestone
▶ **headstrong** *adj* **1** self-willed **2** obstinate
▶ **headway** *n* progress
▶ **headwind** *n* wind blowing against the

THESAURUS

up, out of order, shambolic (*informal*)
hazard *n* **1 = danger**, risk, threat, peril, jeopardy, pitfall ▶ *v* **2 = jeopardize**, risk, threaten, expose, endanger, imperil **3** (*~ a guess*) **= conjecture**, offer, advance, volunteer, venture, presume, throw out
hazardous *adj* **= dangerous**, difficult, unsafe, risky, perilous, precarious, insecure
haze *n* **= mist**, cloud, fog, obscurity, vapour
hazy *adj* **1 = misty**, dull, dim, cloudy, foggy, overcast **2 = vague**, unclear, uncertain, indefinite, fuzzy, nebulous, ill-defined, indistinct, muddled
head *n* **1 = mind**, brain, intelligence, aptitude, common sense, wits • *I don't have a head for business.* **2 = top**, start, front, source, beginning • *the head of the line* OPPOSITE: tail **3 = leader**, president, director, chief, manager, boss, principal • *heads of government* **4 = skull**, crown, nut (*slang*), noodle (*slang*), pate ▷ **go to one's head = excite**, intoxicate, make conceited, puff up ▷ **head of state** *See* **ruler** ▷ **head over heels = uncontrollably**, completely, thoroughly, utterly, intensely, wholeheartedly ▶ *v* **5 = be in charge of**, lead, run, control, manage, direct • *She heads the department.* **6 = lead**, top, cap, crown, precede, be first *or* go first, lead the way **7 = make for**, point, turn, aim, steer, go to, make a beeline for, set off for, set out, start towards ▶ *adj* **8 = chief**, first, prime, main, premier, principal, supreme, arch, pre-eminent, leading
See also: **command, foam**
headache *n* **1 = migraine**, neuralgia **2 = problem**, worry, trouble, bother, inconvenience, nuisance, bane, vexation
heading *n* **= title**, name, headline, caption, rubric
headlong *adverb, adj* **1 = headfirst**, head-on ▶ *adv* **2 = hastily**, hurriedly, heedlessly, helter-skelter, pell-mell, precipitately, rashly, thoughtlessly ▶ *adj* **3 = hasty**, dangerous, reckless, precipitate, breakneck, impulsive, thoughtless, impetuous, inconsiderate
headquarters *See* **base**
headstrong *adj* **= obstinate**, stubborn, unruly, perverse, foolhardy, impulsive, wilful, heedless, pig-headed, self-willed
headway *n* **= progress**, way, advance, improvement, progression

DICTIONARY

course of an aircraft or ship

heal ⓣ *v* make or become well **healer** *n*

health ⓣ *n* **1** normal good condition of someone's body **2** toast drunk in a person's honour

▸ **healthy** *adj* **1** having good health **2** of or producing good health **3** functioning well, sound **healthily** *adv*

▸ **health centre** surgery and offices of the doctors in a district

▸ **health food** natural food, organically grown and free from additives

▸ **health visitor** nurse who visits elderly people and mothers of newborn babies in their homes

Heaney *n* **Seamus (Justin)**. born 1939, Irish poet and critic, born in Northern Ireland. His collections include *Death of a Naturalist* (1966), *North* (1975), *The Haw Lantern* (1987), *The Spirit Level* (1996), and *Electric Light* (2001): Nobel prize for literature 1995

heap ⓣ *n* **1** pile of things lying one on top of another **2** large quantity ▷ *v* **3** gather into a pile **4** (foll. by *on*) give abundantly (to)

hear ⓣ *v* **hearing, heard 1** perceive (a sound) by ear **2** listen to **3** learn or be informed **4** *law* try (a case) **hearer** *n*

▸ **hear! hear!** exclamation of approval or agreement

▸ **hearing** *n* **1** ability to hear **2** trial of a case

▸ **within hearing** close enough to be heard

hearken *v obsolete* listen

hearsay ⓣ *n* **1** gossip **2** rumour

hearse *n* funeral vehicle used to carry a casket

Hearst *n* **William Randolph**. 1863–1951, US newspaper publisher, whose newspapers were noted for their sensationalism

heart ⓣ *n* **1** organ which pumps blood round the body **2** centre of emotions and affections **3** tenderness **4** enthusiasm or courage **5** central or most important part **6** figure representing a heart **7** playing card of the suit marked with the figure of a heart

▸ **break someone's heart** cause someone great grief

▸ **by heart** from memory

▸ **set one's heart on something** greatly desire something

▸ **take to heart** get upset about

▸ **hearten** *v* make cheerful, encourage

▸ **heartless** *adj* cruel

▸ **hearty** *adj* **1** friendly, enthusiastic **2** substantial, nourishing **heartily** *adv*

▸ **heartache** *n* intense anguish

▸ **heart attack** sudden severe malfunction of the heart

▸ **heartbeat** *n* one complete pulsation of the heart

▸ **heartbreak** *n* intense grief

▸ **heartburn** *n* pain in the chest caused by indigestion

▸ **heart failure** sudden stopping of the heartbeat

▸ **heartfelt** *adj* felt sincerely or strongly

▸ **heart-rending** *adj* causing great sorrow

h

THESAURUS

heady *adj* **1 = inebriating**, strong, potent, intoxicating **2 = exciting**, thrilling, exhilarating, intoxicating, stimulating

heal *v* **= cure**, treat, restore, remedy, mend, regenerate, make well

healing *See* **recovery**

health *n* **1 = condition**, shape, constitution • *Smoking is bad for your health.* **2 = well-being**, fitness, good condition • *In hospital they nursed me back to health.* OPPOSITE: illness

healthy *adj* **1 = well**, strong, fit, active, robust, in good shape • *a very healthy child* OPPOSITE: ill **2** (*Informal*) **= wholesome**, beneficial, nutritious, bracing, good for you, nourishing • *a healthy diet* OPPOSITE: unhealthy

See also: **sound**

heap *n* **1 = pile**, mass, mound, stack, hoard • *a heap of garbage* **2** (*often pl*) **= a lot**, great deal, mass, pot *or* pots (*informal*), plenty, stack *or* stacks, lots (*informal*), tons ▸ *v* **3 = pile**, stack • *She heaped vegetables onto his plate.* **4 = shower upon**, load, assign, bestow, confer

See also: **bunch**

hear *v* **1 = listen to**, catch, heed, overhear, eavesdrop, listen in • *I heard the sound of a car backfiring.* **2 = learn**, discover, understand, gather, ascertain, find out • *I heard that he was forced to resign.* **3** (*Law*) **= try**, judge, investigate, examine

See also: **listen**

hearing *n* **= inquiry**, trial, review, investigation, industrial tribunal, sentencing circle (*chiefly Canad*)

hearsay *n* **= rumour**, report, talk, gossip, idle talk, tittle-tattle, word of mouth

heart *n* **1 = nature**, character, soul, disposition, temperament **2 = bravery**, will, resolution, purpose, spirit, courage, pluck, fortitude **3 = centre**, middle, core, hub, nucleus, quintessence ▷ **by heart = by memory**, pat, by rote, off pat, parrot-fashion (*informal*), word for word

heartache *n* **= sorrow**, pain, torture, suffering, grief, distress, remorse, despair, anguish, heartbreak, agony, torment

heartbreak *n* **= grief**, pain, suffering, misery, sorrow, despair, anguish, desolation

heartbreaking *adj* **= tragic**, sad, poignant, pitiful, agonizing, distressing, harrowing, heart-rending

DICTIONARY

▸ **heart-throb** *n slang* very attractive person
hearth *n* **1** floor of a fireplace **2** home
heat Ⓣ *n* **1** state of being hot **2** energy transferred as a result of a difference in temperature **3** hot weather **4** intensity of feeling **5** preliminary eliminating contest in a competition **6** readiness to mate in some female animals ▷ *v* **7** make hot **heater** *n*
▸ **heated** *adj* angry **heatedly** *adv*
heath *n* **1** area of open uncultivated land **2** low-growing evergreen shrub
Heath *n* Sir **Edward** (**Richard George**). 1916–2005, British statesman; leader of the Conservative Party (1965–75); prime minister (1970–74)
heathen Ⓣ *n* **1** person not believing in an established religion, pagan ▷ *adj* **2** of or relating to heathen peoples
heather *n* shrub with small bell-shaped flowers growing on heaths and mountains
heave Ⓣ *v* **1** lift with effort **2** throw (something heavy) **3** utter (a sigh) **4** rise and fall **5** vomit ▷ *n* **6** act of heaving
heaven Ⓣ *n* **1** home of God **2** place or state of bliss
▸ **the heavens** sky
▸ **heavenly** *adj* **1** wonderful or divine **2** of or like heaven **3** of or occurring in space
Heaviside *n* **Oliver**. 1850–1925, English physicist. Independently of Kennelly, he predicted (1902) the existence of an ionized gaseous layer in the upper atmosphere (the **Heaviside layer**); he also contributed to telegraphy
heavy Ⓣ *adj* **-vier**, **-viest** **1** of great weight **2** great in degree or amount **3** dense **4** difficult or severe **5** sorrowful **6** (of a situation) serious **heavily** *adv* **heaviness** *n*
▸ **heavy industry** large-scale production of raw material or machinery
▸ **heavy metal** very loud rock music featuring guitar riffs
▸ **heavyweight** *n* boxer weighing over 175lb (professional) or 81kg (amateur)
Hébert *n* **Jacques René**. 1755–94, French journalist and revolutionary: a leader of the sans-culottes during the French Revolution. He was guillotined under Robespierre
Hebrew *n* **1** ancient language of the Hebrews **2** its modern form, used in Israel **3** member of an ancient Semitic people ▷ *adj* **4** of this language or people
heckle Ⓣ *v* interrupt (a public speaker) with questions, taunts, and comments **heckler** *n*

THESAURUS

heartbroken *adj* = **miserable**, crushed, desolate, despondent, brokenhearted, disconsolate, dispirited, heartsick
hearten *See* **encourage**
heartfelt *adj* = **sincere**, deep, honest, profound, genuine, earnest, devout, unfeigned, wholehearted
heartily *adv* = **enthusiastically**, vigorously, eagerly, resolutely, earnestly, zealously
heartless *adj* = **cruel**, hard, cold, callous, merciless, hardhearted, pitiless, uncaring, unfeeling
heart-rending *adj* = **moving**, sad, tragic, poignant, heartbreaking, affecting, distressing, harrowing
hearty *adj* **1** = **friendly**, warm, enthusiastic, effusive, genial, jovial, ebullient, back-slapping **2** = **substantial**, solid, square, filling, sizable *or* sizeable, ample, nourishing
heat *n* **1** = **warmth**, high temperature • *the heat of the sun* OPPOSITE: cold RELATED WORD *adjective*: thermal **2** = **passion**, intensity, excitement, fervour, vehemence • *in the heat of the election campaign* ▸ *v* **3** = **warm up**, reheat • *Heat the oil in a frying pan.* OPPOSITE: cool ▷ **heat up** *See* **warm** *See also*: **feeling, warm**
heated *adj* = **angry**, intense, fierce, passionate, stormy, furious, excited, frenzied, impassioned, vehement
heathen *n* **1** = **unbeliever**, infidel, pagan ▸ *adj* **2** = **pagan**, godless, idolatrous, irreligious
heave *v* **1** = **lift**, raise, pull *or* pull up, drag *or* drag up, haul *or* haul up, hoist, tug **2** = **throw**, send, pitch, cast, toss, hurl, fling, sling **3** = **sigh**, puff, groan **4** = **vomit**, barf (*slang*), gag, spew, retch, throw up (*informal*)
heaven *n* **1** (*Informal*) = **bliss**, paradise, ecstasy, rapture • *I was in cinematic heaven.* **2** = **paradise**, bliss, Zion (*Christianity*), nirvana (*Buddhism, Hinduism*), Elysium *or* Elysian fields (*Greek myth*), hereafter, life everlasting, next world ▷ **the heavens** = **sky**, ether, firmament
heavenly *adj* **1** = **wonderful**, beautiful, lovely, divine (*informal*), exquisite, delightful, sublime, blissful, ravishing **2** = **celestial**, holy, divine, immortal, angelic, blessed
heavily *adv* **1** = **ponderously**, awkwardly, clumsily, weightily **2** = **densely**, closely, thickly, compactly **3** = **considerably**, excessively, a great deal, copiously, to excess, very much
heaviness *n* = **weight**, gravity, heftiness, ponderousness
heavy *adj* **1** = **weighty**, massive, bulky • *a heavy frying pan* OPPOSITE: light **2** = **serious**, deep, grave, profound, solemn, weighty • *a heavy speech* OPPOSITE: trivial **3** = **considerable**, large, excessive, abundant, copious, profuse *See also*: **stuffy**
heckle *v* = **jeer**, disrupt, boo, interrupt,

DICTIONARY

hectare *n* one hundred ares or 10 000 square metres (2.471 acres)
hectic Ⓣ *adj* rushed or busy
hector *v* bully
hedge Ⓣ *n* **1** row of bushes forming a barrier or boundary ▷ *v* **2** be evasive or noncommittal **3** (foll. by *against*) protect oneself from (loss)
▸ **hedgerow** *n* bushes forming a hedge
▸ **hedge sparrow** small brownish songbird
hedgehog *n* small mammal with a protective covering of spines
hedonism *n* doctrine that pleasure is the most important thing in life **hedonist** *n* **hedonistic** *adj*
heed Ⓣ *v* pay close attention to **heedless** *adj*
▸ **heedless of** taking no notice of
heel[1] Ⓣ *n* **1** back part of the foot **2** part of a shoe supporting the heel **3** *slang* contemptible person ▷ *v* **4** make or replace the heel of
heel[2] Ⓣ *v* lean to one side
hefty Ⓣ *adj* **heftier, heftiest** large, heavy, or strong
Hegel *n* **Georg Wilhelm Friedrich.** 1770–1831, German philosopher, who created a fundamentally influential system of thought. His view of man's mind as the highest expression of the Absolute is expounded in *The Phenomenology of Mind* (1807). He developed his concept of dialectic, in which the contradiction between a proposition (thesis) and its antithesis is resolved at a higher level of truth (synthesis), in *Science of Logic* (1812–16) **Hegelian** *adj* **Hegelianism** *n*
hegemony [hig-**em**-on-ee] *n* political domination
Hegira *n* Mohammed's flight from Mecca to Medina in 622 AD
Heidegger *n* **Martin.** 1889–1976, German existentialist philosopher: he expounded his ontological system in *Being and Time* (1927)
heifer [**hef**-fer] *n* young cow
height Ⓣ *n* **1** distance from base to top **2** distance above sea level **3** highest degree or topmost point
▸ **heighten** *v* make or become higher or more intense
Heine *n* **Heinrich.** 1797–1856, German poet and essayist, whose chief poetic work is *Das Buch der Lieder* (1827). Many of his poems have been set to music, notably by Schubert and Schumann
heinous *adj* evil and shocking
heir Ⓣ *n* person entitled to inherit property or rank **heiress** *n fem*
▸ **heirloom** *n* object that has belonged to a family for generations
Heisenberg *n* **Werner Karl.** 1901–76, German physicist. He contributed to quantum mechanics and formulated the uncertainty principle (1927): Nobel prize for physics 1932
held *v* past of **hold**[1]
Helena *n* **Saint.** ?248–?328 AD, Roman empress, mother of Constantine I. After converting to Christianity (313) she made a pilgrimage to the Holy Land (?326) where she supposedly discovered the cross on which Christ died. Feast day: May 21
helicopter *n* aircraft lifted and propelled by rotating overhead blades
▸ **heliport** *n* airport for helicopters
heliotrope *n* **1** plant with purple flowers ▷ *adj* **2** light purple
helium [**heel**-ee-um] *n* very light colourless odourless gas
helix [**heel**-iks] *n, pl* **helices, helixes** spiral **helical** *adj*
hell Ⓣ *n* **1** home of the wicked after death **2** place or state of wickedness, suffering, or punishment **hellish** *adj*

THESAURUS

taunt, shout down
hectic *adj* = **frantic**, animated, heated, turbulent, chaotic, feverish, frenetic
hedge *n* **1** = **barrier**, screen, boundary, windbreak ▸ *v* **2** = **dodge**, duck, evade, equivocate, sidestep, prevaricate, temporize **3** = **insure**, protect, cover, guard, shield, safeguard
heed *v* **1** = **pay attention to**, follow, listen to, take notice of • *Few at the conference heeded his warning.* ▸ *n* **2** = **attention**, notice • *He paid little heed to her warning.*
See also: **hear**
heedless *adj* = **careless**, oblivious, foolhardy, thoughtless, inattentive, unmindful
heel[1] *n* (*Slang*) = **swine**, rat, louse, skunk, scumbag, scuzzbucket (*slang*)
heel[2] *v* ▷ **heel over** = **lean over**, list, tilt, keel over
hefty *adj* = **big**, strong, massive, robust, muscular, burly, hulking, strapping
height *n* **1** = **altitude**, loftiness, stature, elevation, highness, tallness **2** = **peak**, top, summit, crown, crest, pinnacle, apex, zenith **3** = **culmination**, limit, maximum, ultimate, climax
heighten *v* = **intensify**, increase, improve, strengthen, enhance, sharpen, magnify, amplify, add to
heir *n* = **successor**, heiress (*feminine*), beneficiary, inheritor, next in line
heirloom *See* **legacy**
heirlooms *See* **valuables**
hell *n* **1** (*Informal*) = **torment**, anguish, agony, nightmare, ordeal, misery • *Bullies can make*

h

DICTIONARY

▶ **hell for leather** at great speed
▶ **hell-bent** *adj* intent
Hellenic *adj* of the (ancient) Greeks or their language
Heller *n* **Joseph**. 1923–99, US novelist. His works include *Catch 22* (1961), *God Knows* (1984), *Picture This* (1988), and *Closing Time* (1994)
hello Ⓣ *interj* expression of greeting or surprise
helm Ⓣ *n* tiller or wheel for steering a ship
helmet *n* hard hat worn for protection
Helmholtz *n* Baron **Hermann Ludwig Ferdinand von**. 1821–94, German physiologist, physicist, and mathematician: helped to found the theory of the conservation of energy; invented the ophthalmoscope (1850); and investigated the mechanics of sight and sound
help Ⓣ *v* **1** make something easier, better, or quicker for (someone) **2** improve (a situation) **3** refrain from: *I can't help laughing* ▷ *n* **4** assistance or support **helper** *n* **helpful** *adj*
▶ **help oneself** **1** serve oneself **2** *informal* steal something
▶ **helping** *n* single portion of food
▶ **helpless** *adj* weak or incapable **helplessly** *adv*
▶ **helpline** *n* telephone line set aside for callers to contact an organization for help with a problem
▶ **helpmate** *or* **helpmeet** *n* **1** companion and helper **2** husband or wife
helter-skelter Ⓣ *adj* **1** haphazard and careless ▷ *adv* **2** in a haphazard and careless manner ▷ *n* **3** high spiral slide at a fairground
hem Ⓣ *n* **1** border of cloth, folded under and stitched down ▷ *v* **hemming, hemmed** **2** provide with a hem
▶ **hem in** *v* surround and prevent from moving
▶ **hemline** *n* level to which the hem of a skirt hangs
he-man *n informal* strong virile man
hematic, haematic *adj* relating to or containing blood
hematology, haematology *n* study of blood and its diseases **hematologist** *or* **haematologist** *n*
Hemingway *n* **Ernest** 1899–1961, US novelist and short-story writer. His novels include *The Sun Also Rises* (1926), *A Farewell to Arms* (1929), *For Whom the Bell Tolls* (1940), and *The Old Man and the Sea* (1952): Nobel prize for literature 1954
hemisphere *n* half of a sphere, esp. the earth **hemispherical** *adj*
hemlock *n* **1** poison derived from a plant with spotted stems and small white flowers **2** evergreen of pine family
hemoglobin, haemoglobin [hee-moh-**globe**-in] *n* protein found in red blood cells which carries oxygen
Hémon *n* **Louis**. 1880–1913, Canadian novelist, born in France. Noted esp. for his posthumously published novel *Maria Chapdelaine: récit du Canada français* (1914) which depicted peasant life in Quebec
hemophilia, haemophilia *n* hereditary illness in which the blood does not clot **hemophiliac** *n*
hemorrhage, haemorrhage [**hem**-or-ij] *n* **1** heavy bleeding ▷ *v* **2** bleed heavily

THESAURUS

your life hell. **2** = **underworld**, abyss, inferno, hellfire, fire and brimstone, Hades (*Greek myth*), nether world
hellish *adj* = **devilish**, diabolical, damnable, fiendish, infernal
hello *interjection* = **hi** (*informal*), good afternoon, good evening, good morning, greetings, how do you do? (*formal*) • *I dropped by to say hello*. OPPOSITE: goodbye
helm *n* = **tiller**, wheel, rudder ▷ **at the helm** = **in charge**, at the wheel, in command, in control, in the driving seat, in the saddle
help *v* **1** = **assist**, support, aid, lend a hand • *He began to help with the chores*. **2** = **improve**, ease, relieve, facilitate, alleviate, mitigate, ameliorate **3** = **refrain from**, prevent, avoid, resist, keep from ▶ *n* **4** = **assistance**, support, aid, advice, guidance, helping hand • *The books were not much help*.
See also: **benefit, blessing, comfort, encourage**
helper *n* = **assistant**, supporter, deputy, aide • *There is an adult helper for every two children*.
helpful *adj* **1** = **co-operative**, kind, supportive, accommodating • *The staff in the office are very helpful*. OPPOSITE: unhelpful **2** = **beneficial**, useful, profitable, constructive, advantageous • *Having the right equipment will be enormously helpful*.
See also: **convenient, handy, positive, valuable**
helping *n* = **portion**, piece, ration, serving, dollop (*informal*), plateful ▶ *adj* ▷ **helping hand** *See* **help**
helpless *adj* = **powerless**, weak, vulnerable, unprotected, defenceless • *a helpless baby*
helter-skelter *adj* **1** = **haphazard**, confused, disordered, random, topsy-turvy, hit-or-miss, jumbled, muddled ▶ *adv* **2** = **carelessly**, wildly, hastily, anyhow, recklessly, headlong, hurriedly, pell-mell, rashly
hem *n* = **edge**, border, margin, fringe, trimming ▶ *verb* ▷ **hem in** = **surround**, restrict, confine, enclose, beset, circumscribe, shut in

DICTIONARY

hemorrhoids, haemorrhoids [**hem**-or-oydz] *pl n* swollen veins in the anus (Also **piles**)
hemp *n* **1** Asian plant **2** its fibre, used to make canvas and rope **3** narcotic drug obtained from hemp
hen *n* **1** female domestic fowl **2** female of any bird
▸ **henpecked** *adj* (of a man) dominated by his wife
hence ⓣ *adv* **1** for this reason **2** from this time
▸ **henceforward** *or* **henceforth** *adv* from now on
henchman ⓣ *n* attendant or follower
Henday *n* **Anthony**. flourished 1750–62, Canadian explorer, born in England. He led a fur-trading expedition sponsored by the Hudson's Bay Company (1754–55) into Canada's interior, and travelled further west than any previous European explorer
Hendrix *n* **Jimi**, full name *James Marshall Hendrix*. 1942–70, US rock guitarist, singer, and songwriter, noted for his innovative guitar technique. His recordings include "Purple Haze" (1967) and *Are you Experienced?* (1967)
Hengist *n* died ?488 AD, a leader, with his brother Horsa, of the first Jutish settlers in Britain; he is thought to have conquered Kent (?455)
henna *n* **1** reddish dye made from a shrub or tree ▹ *v* **2** dye the hair with henna
henry *n, pl* **-ry, -ries, -rys** unit of electrical inductance
Henry *n* **1 Patrick**. 1736–99, American statesman and orator, a leading opponent of British rule during the War of American Independence **2 Prince**, known as *Harry*. born 1984, second son of Charles, Prince of Wales, and Diana, Princess of Wales
Henry I *n* **1** known as *Henry the Fowler*. ?876–936 AD, duke of Saxony (912–36) and king of Germany (919–36): founder of the Saxon dynasty (918–1024) **2** 1068–1135, king of England (1100–35) and duke of Normandy (1106–35); son of William the Conqueror: crowned in the absence of his elder brother, Robert II, duke of Normandy; conquered Normandy (1106)
Henry II *n* **1** known as *Henry the Saint*. 973–1024, king of Germany and Holy Roman Emperor (1014–24): canonized in 1145 **2** 1133–89, first Plantagenet king of England (1154–89): extended his Anglo-French domains and instituted judicial and financial reforms. His attempts to control the church were opposed by Becket **3** 1519–59, king of France (1547–59); husband of Catherine de' Medici. He recovered Calais from the English (1558) and suppressed the Huguenots
Henry III *n* **1** 1017–56, king of Germany and Holy Roman Emperor (1046–56). He increased the power of the Empire but his religious policy led to rebellions **2** 1207–72, king of England (1216–72); son of John. His incompetent rule provoked the Barons' War (1264–67), during which he was captured by Simon de Montfort **3** 1551–89, king of France (1574–89). He plotted the massacre of Huguenots on St Bartholomew's Day (1572) with his mother Catherine de' Medici, thus exacerbating the religious wars in France
Henry IV *n* **1** 1050–1106, Holy Roman Emperor (1084–1105) and king of Germany (1056–1105). He was excommunicated by Pope Gregory VII, whom he deposed (1084) **2** surnamed *Bolingbroke*. 1367–1413, first Lancastrian king of England (1399–1413); son of John of Gaunt: deposed Richard II (1399) and suppressed rebellions led by Owen Glendower and the Earl of Northumberland **3** known as *Henry of Navarre*. 1553–1610, first Bourbon king of France (1589–1610). He obtained toleration for the Huguenots with the Edict of Nantes (1598) and restored prosperity to France following the religious wars (1562–98)
Henry V *n* **1** 1081–1125, king of Germany (1089–1125) and Holy Roman Emperor (1111–25) **2** 1387–1422, king of England (1413–22); son of Henry IV. He defeated the French at the Battle of Agincourt (1415), conquered Normandy (1419), and was recognized as heir to the French throne (1420)
Henry VI *n* **1** 1165–97, king of Germany (1169–97) and Holy Roman Emperor (1190–97): added Sicily to the Empire **2** 1421–71, last Lancastrian king of England (1422–61; 1470–71); son of Henry V. His weak rule was blamed for the loss by 1453 of all his possessions in France except Calais; from 1454 he suffered periods of insanity which contributed to the outbreak of the Wars of the Roses (1455–85). He was deposed by Edward IV (1461) but was briefly restored to the throne (1470)
Henry VII *n* **1** ?1275–1313, Holy Roman Emperor (1312–13) and, as Henry VI, count of Luxembourg (1288–1313). He became king of

THESAURUS

hence *conj* = **therefore**, thus, ergo, for this reason, on that account
henchman *n* = **attendant**, supporter, associate, follower, bodyguard, subordinate, sidekick (*slang*), minder (*slang*), right-hand man, second, aide
henpecked *adj* = **bullied**, timid, meek, browbeaten, dominated, subjugated, pussy-whipped *or* whipped (*slang*)

DICTIONARY

the Lombards in 1313 **2** 1457–1509, first Tudor king of England (1485–1509). He came to the throne (1485) after defeating Richard III at the Battle of Bosworth Field, ending the Wars of the Roses. Royal power and the prosperity of the country greatly increased during his reign

Henry VIII *n* 1491–1547, king of England (1509–47); second son of Henry VII. The declaration that his marriage to Catherine of Aragon was invalid and his marriage to Anne Boleyn (1533) precipitated the Act of Supremacy, making Henry supreme head of the Church in England. Anne Boleyn was executed (1536) and Henry subsequently married Jane Seymour, Anne of Cleves, Catherine Howard, and Catherine Parr. His reign is also noted for the fame of his succession of advisers, Cardinal Wolsey, Sir Thomas More, and Thomas Cromwell

Henry the Navigator *n* 1394–1460, prince of Portugal, noted for his patronage of Portuguese voyages of exploration of the W coast of Africa

Henze *n* **Hans Werner**. born 1926, German composer, whose works, in many styles, include the operas *The Stag King* (1956), *The Bassarids* (1965), *The English Cat* (1983), and *Das verratene Meer* (1990) and the oratorio *The Raft of the Medusa* (1968)

hepatic *adj* of the liver

▸ **hepatitis** *n* inflammation of the liver

Hepburn *n* **1 Audrey**. 1929–93, US actress, born in Belgium. Her films include *Roman Holiday* (1955), *Funny Face* (1957), and *My Fair Lady* (1964) **2 Katharine**. 1907–2003, US film actress, whose films include *The Philadelphia Story* (1940), *Adam's Rib* (1949), *The African Queen* (1951), *The Lion in Winter* (1968) for which she won an Oscar, and *On Golden Pond* (1981)

heptagon *n* figure with seven sides **heptagonal** *adj*

heptathlon *n* athletic contest involving seven events

Hepworth *n* Dame **Barbara**. 1903–75, British sculptor of abstract works

her *pron* **1** refers to a female person or animal or anything personified as feminine when the object of a sentence or clause ▹ *adj* **2** of, belonging to, or associated with her

▸ **herself** *pron* emphatic or reflexive form of **she, her**

Heracleides, Heraclides of Pontus *n* ?390–?322 BC, Greek astronomer and philosopher: the first to state that the earth rotates on its axis

herald Ⓣ *n* **1** person who announces important news **2** forerunner ▹ *v* **3** announce or signal the approach of

▸ **heraldry** *n* study of coats of arms and the histories of families **heraldic** *adj*

herb *n* plant used for flavouring in cookery, and in medicine **herbal** *adj*

▸ **herbalist** *n* person who grows or specializes in the use of medicinal herbs

▸ **herbaceous** *adj* (of a plant) soft-stemmed

▸ **herbaceous border** flower bed that contains perennials rather than annuals

▸ **herbicide** *n* chemical which destroys plants

▸ **herbivore** *n* animal that feeds on plants **herbivorous** [her-**biv**-or-uss] *adj*

herculean [her-kew-**lee**-an] *adj* requiring great strength or effort

herd Ⓣ *n* **1** group of animals feeding and living together **2** large crowd of people ▹ *v* **3** collect into a herd

▸ **herdsman** *n* man who looks after a herd of animals

Herder *n* **Johann Gottfried von**. 1744–1803, German philosopher, critic, and poet, the leading figure in the *Sturm und Drang* movement in German literature. His chief work is *Outlines of a Philosophy of the History of Man* (1784–91)

here Ⓣ *adv* in, at, or to this place or point

▸ **hereabouts** *adv* near here

▸ **hereafter** *n* **1** life after death ▹ *adv* **2** in the future

▸ **hereby** *adv* by means of or as a result of this

▸ **herein** *adv* in this place, matter, or document

▸ **herewith** *adv* with this

heredity Ⓣ [hir-**red**-it-ee] *n* passing on of characteristics from one generation to another

▸ **hereditary** *adj* **1** passed on genetically from one generation to another **2** passed on by inheritance

THESAURUS

herald *n* **1** = **messenger**, crier **2** = **forerunner**, sign, signal, indication, precursor, token, omen, harbinger ▸ *v* **3** = **indicate**, show, promise, presage, portend, foretoken, usher in

herd *n* **1** = **multitude**, crowd, mass, collection, mob, flock, swarm, throng, drove, horde ▸ *v* **2** = **congregate**, rally, gather, collect, assemble, flock, muster, huddle

here *See* **present**

hereafter *adv* **1** = **in future**, hence, from now on, henceforth, henceforward ▸ *n* **2** = **afterlife**, life after death, next world

hereditary *adj* **1** = **genetic**, transmissible, inborn, inbred, inheritable **2** = **inherited**, traditional, ancestral

heredity *n* = **genetics**, constitution, inheritance, genetic make-up

DICTIONARY

heresy Ⓣ [**herr**-iss-ee] *n, pl* **-sies** opinion contrary to accepted opinion or belief
▸ **heretic** [**herr**-it-ik] *n* person who holds unorthodox opinions **heretical** [hir-**ret**-ik-al] *adj*
Hereward *n* called *Hereward the Wake.* 11th-century Anglo-Saxon rebel, who defended the Isle of Ely against William the Conqueror (1070–71): a subject of many legends
heritage Ⓣ *n* possessions, traditions, or conditions passed from one generation to another
hermaphrodite [her-**maf**-roe-dite] *n* person, animal, or plant that has both male and female reproductive organs
hermetic *adj* sealed so as to be airtight **hermetically** *adv*
hermit Ⓣ *n* person living in solitude, esp. for religious reasons
▸ **hermitage** *n* dwelling of a hermit
hernia *n* protrusion of (part of) an organ through the lining of the surrounding body cavity
hero Ⓣ *n, pl* **heroes 1** principal character in a film, book, play, etc. **2** man greatly admired for exceptional qualities or achievements **heroine** *n fem*
▸ **heroic** *adj* **1** courageous **2** of, like, or befitting a hero **heroically** *adv* **heroism** [**herr**-oh-izz-um] *n*
▸ **heroics** *pl n* extravagant behaviour
Hero, Heron *n* 1st century AD, Greek mathematician and inventor
Herod *n* called *the Great.* ?73–4 BC, king of Judaea (37–4). The latter part of his reign was notable for his cruelty: according to the New Testament he ordered the Massacre of the Innocents
Herod Agrippa I *n* 10 BC–44 AD, king of Judaea (41–44), grandson of Herod (the Great). A friend of Caligula and Claudius, he imprisoned Saint Peter and executed Saint James
Herod Agrippa II *n* died ?93 AD, king of territories in N Palestine (50–?93 AD). He presided (60) at the trial of Saint Paul and sided with the Roman authorities in the Jewish rebellion of 66
Herod Antipas *n* died ?40 AD, tetrarch of Galilee and Peraea (4 BC–40 AD); son of Herod the Great. At the instigation of his wife Herodias, he ordered the execution of John the Baptist
heroin *n* highly addictive drug derived from morphine
heron *n* long-legged wading bird
▸ **heronry** *n* place where herons breed
herpes [**her**-peez] *n* any of several inflammatory skin diseases, including shingles and cold sores
Herr [hair] *n, pl* **Herren** German title of address equivalent to Mr
Herrick *n* **Robert**. 1591–1674, English poet. His chief work is the *Hesperides* (1648), a collection of short, delicate, sacred, and pastoral lyrics
herring *n* important food fish of northern seas
▸ **herringbone** *n* pattern of zigzag lines
▸ **herring choker** *Canad slang* native or inhabitant of the Maritime Provinces
hertz *n, pl* **hertz** *physics* unit of frequency
Herzberg *n* **Gerhard**. 1904–99, Canadian chemist born in Germany. Winner of the 1971 Nobel Prize for chemistry for his work on molecular spectroscopy
Herzl *n* **Theodor**. 1860–1904, Austrian writer, born in Hungary; founder of the Zionist movement. In *The Jewish State* (1896), he advocated resettlement of the Jews in a state of their own
Herzog *n* **Werner**. born 1942, German film director. His films include *Signs of Life* (1967), *Fata Morgana* (1970), *Fitzcarraldo* (1982), and *Little Dieter Needs to Fly* (1997)
Hesiod *n* 8th century BC, Greek poet and the earliest author of didactic verse. His two complete extant works are the *Works and Days*, dealing with the agricultural seasons, and the *Theogony*, concerning the origin of the world and the genealogies of the gods **Hesiodic** *adj*

h

THESAURUS

heresy *n* = **unorthodoxy**, apostasy, dissidence, heterodoxy, iconoclasm
heretic *n* = **nonconformist**, dissident, renegade, dissenter, apostate, revisionist
heretical *adj* = **unorthodox**, heterodox, iconoclastic, idolatrous, impious, revisionist
heritage *n* = **inheritance**, tradition, legacy, bequest, endowment, birthright
hermit *n* = **recluse**, monk, loner (*informal*), anchorite, eremite
hero *n* **1** = **star**, champion, superstar, idol, victor, conqueror **2** = **leading man**, protagonist
heroic *adj* = **courageous**, brave, daring, valiant, fearless, gallant, intrepid, lion-hearted
heroine *n* = **leading lady**, diva, protagonist, prima donna
heroism *n* = **bravery**, spirit, courage, fearlessness, courageousness, gallantry, intrepidity, valour
hesitant *adj* = **uncertain**, reluctant, unsure, doubtful, diffident, wavering • *At*

DICTIONARY

hesitate Ⓣ *v* **1** be slow or uncertain in acting **2** pause during speech **3** be reluctant (to do something) **hesitation** *n*
▸ **hesitant** *adj* undecided or wavering **hesitantly** *adv* **hesitancy** *n*
Hess *n* (**Walther Richard**) **Rudolf**. 1894–1987, German Nazi leader. He made a secret flight to Scotland (1941) to negotiate peace with Britain but was held as a prisoner of war; later sentenced to life imprisonment at the Nuremberg trials (1946); committed suicide
Hesse *n* **Hermann**. 1877–1962, German novelist, short-story writer, and poet. His novels include *Der Steppenwolf* (1927) and *Das Glasperlenspiel* (1943): Nobel prize for literature 1946
hessian *n* coarse jute cloth
heterodox *adj* not orthodox **heterodoxy** *n*
heterogeneous [het-er-oh-**jean**-ee-uss] *adj* composed of diverse elements **heterogeneity** *n*
heterosexual *n, adj* (person) sexually attracted to members of the opposite sex **heterosexuality** *n*
het up *adj informal* agitated or excited
heuristic [**hew**-rist-ik] *adj* involving learning by investigation
hew Ⓣ *v* **hewing, hewed, hewed** *or* **hewn** **1** chop or cut with an axe **2** carve from a substance
Hewitt *n* **Foster William**. 1902–85, Canadian radio and TV hockey commentator. He coined the phrase "He shoots! He scores!"
hexagon *n* figure with six sides **hexagonal** *adj*
hey *interj* **1** expression of surprise or for catching attention **2** exclamation used for emphasis at the end of a statement, or alone to seek repetition or confirmation of another person's statement
heyday Ⓣ *n* time of greatest success, prime
Hg *chem* mercury
HGV formerly, heavy goods vehicle
hi Ⓣ *interj informal* hello
hiatus Ⓣ [hie-**ay**-tuss] *n, pl* **-tuses, -tus** break in continuity
Hiawatha *n* a 16th-century Onondaga Indian chief: credited with the organization of the Five Nations
hibernate Ⓣ *v* (of an animal) pass the winter as if in a deep sleep **hibernation** *n*
Hibernia *n poetic* Ireland **Hibernian** *adj*
hibiscus *n, pl* **-cuses** tropical plant with large brightly coloured flowers
hiccup, hiccough *n* **1** spasm of the breathing organs with a sharp coughlike sound ▷ *v* **2** make a hiccup or hiccups
hick *n informal* unsophisticated country person
Hickok *n* **James Butler**, known as *Wild Bill Hickok*. 1837–76, US frontiersman and marshal
hickory *n, pl* **-ries** **1** N American nut-bearing tree **2** its tough wood
hide[1] Ⓣ *v* **hiding, hid, hidden** **1** conceal or obscure (oneself or an object) **2** keep secret ▷ *n* **3** place of concealment, esp. for a bird-watcher
▸ **hide-out** *n* hiding place
hide[2] Ⓣ *n* skin of an animal
▸ **hiding** *n slang* thrashing
▸ **hidebound** *adj* restricted by petty rules
hideous Ⓣ [**hid**-ee-uss] *adj* ugly, revolting **hideously** *adv*
Hideyoshi Toyotomi *n* 1536–98, Japanese military dictator (1582–98). He unified all Japan (1590)

THESAURUS

first he was hesitant to accept the role.
hesitate *v* **1 = waver**, pause, dither • *She hesitated before replying.* **2 = be reluctant**, balk, be unwilling, demur, hang back, scruple, shrink from, think twice
hesitation *n* **1 = indecision**, delay, doubt, uncertainty, hesitancy, irresolution, vacillation **2 = reluctance**, unwillingness, qualm *or* qualms, misgiving *or* misgivings, scruple *or* scruples
hew *v* **1 = cut**, split, axe, chop, hack, lop **2 = carve**, make, form, model, fashion, shape, sculpture, smooth, sculpt
heyday *n* **= prime**, pink, bloom, prime of life, salad days
hi *See* **hello**
hiatus *n* **= pause**, break, space, gap, interruption, interval, respite, discontinuity
hibernate *See* **sleep**
hibernation *See* **sleep**
hidden *adj* **= concealed**, secret, clandestine, covert, unseen, latent, veiled, under wraps
hide[1] *v* **1 = conceal**, stash (*informal*), secrete • *The pirates hid the gold in a cave.* **2 = go into hiding**, go to ground, go underground, hole up, lie low, take cover **3 = disguise**, cover, mask, cloak, veil, conceal, obscure, shroud, camouflage **4 = suppress**, withhold, draw a veil over, hush up, keep dark, keep secret, keep under one's hat
See also: **cover, obscure, shelter**
hide[2] *n* **= skin**, pelt • *the process of tanning hides*
See also: **coat**
hidebound *adj* **= conventional**, rigid, narrow-minded, ultraconservative, set in one's ways, strait-laced
hideous *adj* **= ugly**, grim, gruesome, grisly, grotesque, monstrous, ghastly, unsightly, repulsive, revolting, scuzzy (*slang*)
hideout *n* **= hiding place**, shelter, den,

DICTIONARY

hierarchy ⊕ [**hire**-ark-ee] *n, pl* **-chies** system of people or things arranged in a graded order **hierarchical** *adj*
hieroglyphic [hire-oh-**gliff**-ik] *adj* **1** of a form of writing using picture symbols, as used in ancient Egypt ▷ *n* **2** Also **hieroglyph** symbol representing an object, idea, or sound **3** symbol that is difficult to decipher
hi-fi *n* **1** set of high-quality sound-reproducing equipment ▷ *adj* **2** short for **high-fidelity**
Higgins *n* **Jack**, real name *Harry Patterson*. born 1929, British novelist; his thrillers include *The Eagle Has Landed* (1975), *Confessional* (1985), and *Midnight Runner* (2002)
higgledy-piggledy *adv, adj* in confusion
high ⊕ *adj* **1** tall, of greater than average height **2** far above ground or sea level **3** being at its peak **4** greater than usual in intensity or amount **5** of great importance, quality, or rank **6** (of a sound) acute in pitch **7** *informal* under the influence of alcohol or drugs **8** (of food) slightly decomposed ▷ *adv* **9** at or to a high level ▷ *n* **10** high level **11** *informal* (in names) high school: *Burlington High* **highly** *adv*
▸ **highly strung** nervous and easily upset
▸ **Highness** *n* title used to address or refer to a royal person
▸ **High Arctic** regions of Canada, esp. northern islands, within the Arctic Circle
▸ **highbrow** *n* **1** intellectual or scholar ▷ *adj* **2** appealing to highbrows
▸ **High Commission** embassy of one Commonwealth country in another
▸ **High Church** belonging to a section within the Anglican church stressing the importance of ceremony and ritual
▸ **higher education** education at colleges, universities, and polytechnics
▸ **high-fidelity** *adj* able to reproduce sound with little or no distortion
▸ **high-flown** *adj* (of ideas or speech) grand and elaborate
▸ **high-handed** *adj* overbearing and dogmatic
▸ **highlands** *pl n* area of relatively high ground
▸ **highlight** *n* **1** outstanding part or feature **2** light-toned area in a painting or photograph **3** lightened streak in the hair ▷ *v* **4** give emphasis to
▸ **high-maintenance** *adj* **1** (of equipment) requiring regular maintenance to keep it in working order **2** *informal* (of a person) requiring a lot of care and attention
▸ **high-rise** *adj* (of a building) having many storeys
▸ **high tea** *Brit* early evening meal consisting of a cooked dish, bread, cakes, and tea
▸ **high-tech** *adj* same as **hi-tech**
▸ **high time** latest possible time
▸ **highway** *n* main road for fast-moving traffic
▸ **highwayman** *n* formerly, robber, usually on horseback, who robbed travellers at gunpoint
Highsmith *n* **Patricia**. 1921–95, US author of crime fiction. Her novels include *Strangers on a Train* (1950) and *Ripley's Game* (1974)
hijack ⊕ *v* seize control of (a vehicle or aircraft) while travelling **hijacker** *n*

THESAURUS

hideaway, lair
hiding *n* (*Informal*) = **beating**, drubbing, thrashing, whipping, spanking, licking (*informal*), walloping (*informal*)
hierarchy *n* = **grading**, ranking, pecking order
high *adj* **1** = **tall**, steep, elevated, lofty, towering, soaring • *a high tower* OPPOSITE: low **2** = **extreme**, great, strong, sharp, excessive, extraordinary, intensified • *There is a high risk of heart disease.* OPPOSITE: low **3** = **important**, chief, powerful, superior, arch, eminent, exalted **4** (*Informal*) = **intoxicated**, stoned (*slang*), tripping (*informal*) **5** = **high-pitched**, sharp, acute, strident, piercing, shrill, piping, penetrating ▷ **high point** *See* **peak, top** ▷ **high temperature** *See* **heat** ▸ *adv* **6** = **aloft**, at great height, far up, way up *See also*: **excited, thrill**
highbrow *n* **1** = **intellectual**, scholar, egghead (*informal*), aesthete ▸ *adj* **2** = **intellectual**, sophisticated, cultured, bookish, cultivated
higher *adj* ▷ **higher than** *See* **above**
highest *See* **supreme, top**
high-flown *adj* = **extravagant**, elaborate, exaggerated, inflated, lofty, overblown, grandiose, pretentious, florid
high-handed *adj* = **dictatorial**, oppressive, despotic, tyrannical, wilful, imperious, domineering, overbearing
highlight *n* **1** = **feature**, focus, peak, climax, focal point, high point, high spot ▸ *v* **2** = **emphasize**, stress, flag, spotlight, underline, accent, accentuate, bring to the fore, show up
highly *adv* = **extremely**, very, greatly, vastly, exceptionally, tremendously, immensely, very much ▷ **highly strung** = **nervous**, sensitive, tense, edgy, temperamental, neurotic, twitchy (*informal*), excitable, stressed, wired (*slang*) • *a highly strung individual*
high-ranking *See* **senior**
high-speed *See* **express**
hijack *v* = **seize**, expropriate, commandeer, take over

DICTIONARY

hike Ⓣ *v* **1** walk a long way (for pleasure) in the country **2** (foll. by *up*) pull (up) or raise
hiker *n*
hilarious Ⓣ *adj* very funny **hilariously** *adv*
hilarity *n*
Hildegard of Bingen *n* **Saint**. 1098–1179, German abbess, poet, composer, and mystic
hill Ⓣ *n* **1** raised part of the earth's surface, less high than a mountain **2** incline or slope
hilly *adj*
▸ **hillock** *n* small hill
▸ **hillbilly** *n US* unsophisticated country person
Hillary *n* Sir **Edmund**. 1919–2008, New Zealand explorer and mountaineer. He and his Sherpa guide, Tenzing Norgay, were the first to reach the summit of Mount Everest (1953); New Zealand ambassador to India (1984–89)
Hillel *n* ?60 BC–?9 AD, rabbi, born in Babylonia; president of the Sanhedrin. He was the first to formulate principles of biblical interpretation
hilt Ⓣ *n* handle of a sword or knife
him *pron* refers to a male person or animal or anything personified as masculine when the object of a sentence or clause
▸ **himself** *pron* emphatic or reflexive form of **he, him**
Himmler *n* **Heinrich**. 1900–45, German Nazi leader, head of the SS and the Gestapo (1936–45); committed suicide
hind[1] *adj* **hinder, hindmost** situated at the back
hind[2] *n* female deer
Hindemith *n* **Paul**. 1895–1963, German composer and musical theorist, who opposed the twelve-tone technique. His works include the song cycle *Das Marienleben* (1923) and the opera *Mathis der Maler* (1938)
Hindenburg *n* **Paul von Beneckendorff und von**. 1847–1934, German field marshal and statesman; president (1925–34). During World War I he directed German strategy together with Ludendorff (1916–18)
hinder Ⓣ *v* obstruct the progress of
hindrance *n*
Hinduism *n* dominant religion of India which involves the worship of many gods and a belief in reincarnation
▸ **Hindu** *n* **1** person who practises Hinduism ▹ *adj* **2** of Hinduism
▸ **Hindi** *n* language of N central India
Hines *n* **Earl**, known as *Earl "Fatha" Hines*. 1905–83, US jazz pianist, conductor, and songwriter
hinge Ⓣ *n* **1** device for holding together two parts so that one can swing freely ▹ *v* **2** fit a hinge to **3** (foll. by *on*) depend (on)
hint Ⓣ *n* **1** indirect suggestion **2** piece of advice **3** small amount ▹ *v* **4** suggest indirectly
hinterland *n* land lying behind a coast or near a city, esp. a port
hip[1] *n* either side of the body below the waist and above the thigh
hip[2] *n* fruit of the rose bush
hip[3] Ⓣ *adj* **hipper, hippest** *slang* aware of or following the latest trends
hip-hop *n* pop-culture movement originating in the 1980s, comprising rap music, graffiti, and break dancing
Hipparchus *n* 2nd century BC, Greek astronomer. He discovered the precession of the equinoxes, calculated the length of the solar year, and developed trigonometry
hippie Ⓣ *n* (esp. in the late 1960s) person whose behaviour and dress imply a rejection of conventional values

THESAURUS

hike *n* **1 = walk**, stroll, excursion, ramble • *They went for a hike through the woods.* ▸ *v* **2 = walk**, wander, stroll, backpack, stray, amble • *We hiked through the ravine.* ▹ **hike up = raise**, lift, hitch up, jack up, pull up
hilarious *adj* **= funny**, humorous, amusing, comical, entertaining, rollicking, side-splitting, uproarious
hilarity *n* **= laughter**, amusement, glee, exhilaration, merriment, high spirits, jollity, mirth
hill *n* **= mount**, height, mound, hilltop, fell, knoll, hillock, tor
hillock *n* **= mound**, knoll, hummock
hilly *adj* **= mountainous**, rolling, undulating
hilt *n* **= handle**, grip, haft, handgrip
hinder *v* **= obstruct**, prevent, delay, block, check, frustrate, hamper, stymie, impede, encumber • *A thigh injury hindered her mobility.*
See also: **handicap, interfere, restrain**
hindmost *adj* **= last**, final, furthest, furthest behind, rearmost, trailing
hindrance *n* **= obstacle**, restriction, difficulty, barrier, snag, obstruction, hitch, deterrent, impediment, handicap, drawback, stumbling block
hinge *v* **= depend**, turn, rest, hang, pivot, be contingent, revolve around
hint *n* **1 = suggestion**, indication, clue, intimation • *He gave a strong hint that I would make the team.* **2 = advice**, tip, suggestion, pointer • *I hope to get some fashion hints.* **3 = trace**, touch, suggestion, suspicion, dash, undertone, tinge ▸ *v* **4 = suggest**, indicate, intimate, imply, insinuate • *Criticism is merely hinted at.* ▹ **hint at** *See* **promise**
See also: **idea, mention, note, sign**
hip *See* **fashionable**
hippie *n* **= bohemian**, dropout, beatnik

DICTIONARY

hippo *n, pl* **-pos** *informal* hippopotamus
Hippocrates *n* ?460–?377 BC, Greek physician, commonly regarded as the father of medicine **Hippocratic** *or* **Hippocratical** *adj*
▸ **Hippocratic oath** oath that may be taken by doctors to observe a code of medical ethics
hippodrome *n* music hall, variety theatre, or circus
hippopotamus *n, pl* **-muses, -mi** large African mammal with thick wrinkled skin, living in rivers
hippy *n, pl* **-pies** same as **hippie**
Hiram *n* 10th century BC, king of Tyre, who supplied Solomon with materials and craftsmen for the building of the Temple (II Samuel 5:11; I Kings 5:1–18)
hire Ⓣ *v* **1** obtain temporary use of by payment **2** employ for wages ▷ *n* **3** act of hiring **4** payment for the use of something
▸ **hireling** *n* person who works only for wages
▸ **hire-purchase** *n Brit* instalment plan
Hirohito *n* 1901–89, emperor of Japan 1926–89. In 1946 he became a constitutional monarch
Hiroshige *n* **Ando**. 1797–1858, Japanese artist, esp. of colour wood-block prints
hirsute [**her**-suit] *adj* hairy
his *pron, adj* (something) belonging to him
Hispanic *adj* of Spain or a Spanish-speaking country
hiss Ⓣ *n* **1** sound like that of a long *s* (as an exclamation of contempt) ▷ *v* **2** utter a hiss **3** show derision or anger towards
Hiss *n* **Alger**. 1904–96, US government official: imprisoned (1950–54) for perjury in connection with alleged espionage activities
histamine [**hiss**-ta-meen] *n* substance released by the body tissues, causing allergic reactions
histogram *n* statistical graph in which the frequency of values is represented by vertical bars of varying heights and widths
histology *n* study of the tissues of an animal or plant
history Ⓣ *n, pl* **-ries** **1** (record or account of) past events and developments **2** study of these **3** record of someone's past **4** play that depicts historical events
▸ **historian** *n* writer of history
▸ **historic** *adj* famous or significant in history
▸ **historical** *adj* **1** based on history **2** occurring in the past **historically** *adv*
histrionic Ⓣ *adj* excessively dramatic
▸ **histrionics** *pl n* melodramatic behaviour
hit Ⓣ *v* **hitting, hit** **1** strike forcefully **2** come into violent contact with **3** affect adversely **4** reach (a point or place) **5** *sports* propel (a ball) by striking ▷ *n* **6** impact or blow **7** success **8** *computers* single visit to a website **9** *sports* act or instance of hitting (a ball) **hitter** *n*
▸ **hit it off** *informal* get on well together
▸ **hit the trail** *or* **hit the road** *informal* set out on a journey
▸ **hit-and-run** *n* **1** motor-vehicle accident in which the driver leaves the scene without stopping to give assistance or call the police **2** *baseball* play in which a base runner begins to run as the pitcher throws the ball to the batter
▸ **hit man** hired assassin
▸ **hit on** *v* **1** think of (an idea) **2** make sexual advances to
▸ **hit-or-miss** *adj* haphazard
hitch Ⓣ *v* **1** fasten with a loop or hook **2** pull up with a jerk **3** *informal* obtain (a lift) by hitchhiking ▷ *n* **4** slight difficulty

h

THESAURUS

hire *v* **1 = employ**, commission, appoint, engage, sign up • *I was hired for a summer job.* **2 = rent**, let, engage, charter, lease
hiring *See* **employment**
hiss *n* **1 = sibilation**, buzz, hissing **2 = catcall**, boo, jeer ▸ *v* **3 = whistle**, wheeze, whiz, sibilate, whirr **4 = jeer**, boo, mock, deride, hoot
historic *adj* **= significant**, famous, remarkable, extraordinary, notable, outstanding, ground-breaking, momentous, epoch-making
historical *adj* **= factual**, real, actual, authentic, attested, documented
history *n* **1 = chronicle**, record, story, account, narrative, recital, annals **2 = the past**, yesterday, antiquity, yesteryear, olden days
histrionic *See* **melodramatic**
hit *v* **1 = strike**, beat, pop (*informal*), knock, slap, bang, thump, smack, wallop (*informal*), whack, clout (*informal*) • *He had been hit with a baseball bat.* **2 = collide with**, bump, bang into, meet head-on, run into, smash into, bang into, clash with, crash against • *The car had apparently hit a traffic sign.* **3 = reach**, gain, achieve, accomplish, attain, arrive at **4 = affect**, damage, touch, influence, overwhelm, devastate, impact on, leave a mark on ▷ **hit it off** (*Informal*) **= get on** *or* **get on well**, click (*slang*), be on good terms, get on like a house on fire (*informal*) ▸ *n* **5 = blow**, stroke, knock, slap, belt (*informal*), rap, smack, wallop (*informal*), clout (*informal*) • *Give the nail a good hard hit with the hammer.* **6 = success**, winner, triumph, smash (*informal*), sensation
hitch *n* **1 = problem**, catch, difficulty, snag, obstacle, impediment, drawback, hindrance,

DICTIONARY

▸ **hitchhike** *v* travel by obtaining free lifts **hitchhiker** *n*
Hitchcock *n* Sir **Alfred** (**Joseph**). 1899–1980, English film director, noted for his mastery in creating suspense. His films include *The Thirty-Nine Steps* (1935), *Rebecca* (1940), *Psycho* (1960), and *The Birds* (1963)
hi-tech *adj* using sophisticated technology
hither *adv* to or towards this place
▸ **hitherto** *adv* until this time
Hitler *n* **1** **Adolf**, grandmother's maiden name and father's original surname *Schicklgrüber*. 1889–1945, German dictator, born in Austria. After becoming president of the National Socialist German Workers' Party (Nazi party), he attempted to overthrow the government of Bavaria (1923). While in prison he wrote *Mein Kampf*, expressing his philosophy of the superiority of the Aryan race and the inferiority of the Jews. He was appointed chancellor of Germany (1933), transforming it from a democratic republic into the totalitarian Third Reich, of which he became Führer in 1934. He established concentration camps to exterminate the Jews, rearmed the Rhineland (1936), annexed Austria (1938) and Czechoslovakia, and invaded Poland (1939), which precipitated World War II. He committed suicide **2** a person who displays dictatorial characteristics
HIV human immunodeficiency virus
hive *n* structure in which bees live
▸ **hive of activity** place where people are very busy
▸ **hive off** *v* separate from a larger group
hives *n* disease causing itchy red or whitish patches on the skin
HM Her (*or* His) Majesty
HMCS Her (*or* His) Majesty's Canadian Ship
HMS Her (*or* His) Majesty's Service *or* Ship
Hnatyshyn *n* **Ramon John**, known as *Ray*. 1934–2002, Canadian lawyer and Conservative politician of Ukrainian ancestry; Governor General (1990–95)
hoard Ⓣ *n* **1** store hidden away for future use ▹ *v* **2** gather or accumulate **hoarder** *n*
hoarding *n* large board for displaying advertisements
hoarfrost *n* white ground frost
hoarse Ⓣ *adj* **1** (of a voice) rough and unclear **2** having a rough and unclear voice **hoarsely** *adv* **hoarseness** *n*
hoary *adj* **hoarier**, **hoariest** **1** grey or white (with age) **2** very old
hoax Ⓣ *n* **1** deception or trick ▹ *v* **2** deceive or play a trick upon **hoaxer** *n*
hob *n* flat top part of a cooker
Hobbes *n* **Thomas**. 1588–1679, English political philosopher. His greatest work is *Leviathan* (1651), which contains his defence of absolute sovereignty **Hobbesian** *n, adj*
hobble *v* **1** walk lamely **2** tie the legs of (a horse) together
hobby Ⓣ *n, pl* **-bies** activity pursued in one's spare time
▸ **hobbyhorse** *n* **1** favourite topic **2** toy horse
hobgoblin *n* mischievous goblin
hobnail *n* large-headed nail for boot soles
hobnob Ⓣ *v* **-nobbing**, **-nobbed** (foll. by *with*) socialize (with)
hobo *n, pl* **-bos** tramp or vagrant
Hobson's choice *n* the choice of taking what is offered or nothing at all
Ho Chi Minh *n* original name *Nguyen That Tan*. 1890–1969, Vietnamese statesman; president of North Vietnam (1954–69). He headed the Vietminh (1941), which won independence for Vietnam from the French (1954)
hock[1] *n* joint in the leg of a horse or similar animal corresponding to the human ankle
hock[2] *n* white German wine
hock[3] *v informal* pawn
▸ **in hock** **1** pawned **2** in debt
hockey *n* **1** team game played on ice with a

THESAURUS

hold-up ▸ *v* **2** = **fasten**, join, couple, tie, connect, attach, harness, tether **3** (*Informal*) = **hitchhike**, thumb a lift ▹ **hitch up** = **pull up**, yank, jerk, tug
hitherto *adv* = **previously**, heretofore, so far, thus far, until now
hit-or-miss *adj* = **haphazard**, random, casual, uneven, indiscriminate, aimless, disorganized, undirected
hoard *v* **1** = **store**, save, stockpile • *People have begun to hoard food and gasoline.* ▸ *n* **2** = **store**, fund, reserve, supply, stockpile, cache • *a hoard of silver and jewels*
See also: **bank, gather, heap, pile**
hoarse *adj* = **husky**, rasping, gruff, croaky • *He became hoarse from shouting.*
OPPOSITE: clear
hoax *n* **1** = **trick**, fraud, con (*informal*), prank, spoof (*informal*), deception, swindle, practical joke ▸ *v* **2** = **deceive**, fool, con (*slang*), dupe, swindle, hoodwink, trick
hobbling *See* **lame**
hobby *n* = **pastime**, diversion, leisure activity, leisure pursuit • *My hobbies are music and photography*.
See also: **activity, interest**
hobnob *v* = **socialize**, associate, mix, mingle, consort, fraternize, hang around, hang out (*informal*), keep company
hodgepodge *n* = **mixture**, mess, medley, jumble, mishmash, farrago, *mélange* (*French*), potpourri

DICTIONARY

puck and long sticks **2** *esp. Brit* field hockey
Hockney *n* **David**. born 1937, English painter, best known for his etchings, such as those to Cavafy's poems (1966), naturalistic portraits such as *Mr. and Mrs. Clark and Percy* (1971), and for paintings of water, swimmers, and swimming pools
hocus-pocus *n* trickery
hod *n* **1** open wooden box attached to a pole, for carrying bricks or mortar **2** type of coal scuttle
hodgepodge Ⓣ *n* jumbled mixture
hoe *n* **1** long-handled tool used to loosen soil or to weed ▷ *v* **2** scrape or weed using a hoe
Hoffman *n* **Dustin** (**Lee**). born 1937, US stage and film actor. His films include *The Graduate* (1967), *Midnight Cowboy* (1969), *All the President's Men* (1976), *Kramer vs Kramer* (1979), *Rain Man* (1989), *Accidental Hero* (1992), and *Moonlight Mile* (2002)
Hofmannsthal *n* **Hugo von**. 1874–1929, Austrian lyric poet and dramatist, noted as the librettist for Richard Strauss' operas, esp. *Der Rosenkavalier* (1911), *Elektra* (1909), and *Ariadne auf Naxos* (1912)
hog Ⓣ *n* **1** castrated male pig **2** *informal* greedy person ▷ *v* **hogging, hogged 3** *informal* take more than one's share of
▸ **hog line** *curling* line marked across the ice which must be passed by a played stone
▸ **hogshead** *n* large cask
▸ **hogwash** *n informal* nonsense
Hogan *n* **Ben**, full name *William Benjamin Hogan*. 1912–97, US golfer
Hogarth *n* **William**. 1697–1764, English engraver and painter. He is noted particularly for his series of engravings satirizing the vices and affectations of his age, such as *A Rake's Progress* (1735) and *Marriage à la Mode* (1745) **Hogarthian** *adj*
Hogg *n* **James**, known as *the Ettrick Shepherd*. 1770–1835, Scottish poet and writer. His works include the volume of poems *The Queen's Wake* (1813) and the novel *The Confessions of a Justified Sinner* (1824)
Hogmanay *n* (in Scotland) New Year's Eve
ho-hum *adj informal* dull or mediocre
hoi polloi *n* the ordinary people
hoist Ⓣ *v* **1** raise or lift up ▷ *n* **2** device for lifting things
hoity-toity *adj informal* arrogant or haughty
hokum *n US slang* **1** rubbish, nonsense **2** stereotyped sentimentality in a film or play
Hokusai *n* **Katsushika**. 1760–1849, Japanese artist, noted for the draftsmanship of his colour wood-block prints, which influenced the Impressionists
Holbein *n* **1 Hans**, known as *Holbein the Elder*. 1465–1524, German painter **2** his son, **Hans**, known as *Holbein the Younger*. 1497–1543, German painter and engraver; court painter to Henry VIII of England (1536–43). He is noted particularly for his portraits, such as those of Erasmus (1524; 1532) and Sir Thomas More (1526)
Holberg *n* **Ludvig**, Baron. 1684–1754, Danish playwright, poet, and historian, born in Norway: considered the founder of modern Danish literature
hold[1] Ⓣ *v* **holding, held 1** keep or support in or using the hands or arms **2** consider to be as specified: *who are you holding responsible?* **3** maintain in a specified position or state **4** have the capacity for **5** *informal* wait, esp. on the telephone **6** own, possess **7** keep possession of **8** reserve (a room etc.) **9** restrain or keep back **10** not use **11** cause to take place: *hold a meeting* **12** (cause to) remain committed to (a promise etc.) **13** believe ▷ *n* **14** act or method of holding **15** influence **16** something held onto for support **holder** *n*
▸ **holding** *n* property, such as land or stocks and shares
▸ **holdall** *n Brit* carryall
▸ **hold-up** *n* **1** armed robbery **2** delay

h

THESAURUS

hog *See* **pig**
hoist *v* **1 = raise**, lift, erect, elevate, heave ▸ *n* **2 = lift**, elevator, crane, winch
hold *v* **1 = grasp**, carry, embrace, grip, clutch, clasp • *Hold the baby while I load the car.* **2 = own**, have, keep, maintain, retain, occupy, possess **3 = restrain**, detain, imprison, confine, impound **4 = consider**, think, believe, judge, regard, assume, deem, presume, reckon **5 = convene**, call, run, conduct, preside over **6 = accommodate**, take, contain, seat, have a capacity for ▷ **hold back** *See* **restrain**
▷ **hold forth = speak**, lecture, preach, discourse, spout (*informal*), declaim, go on, spiel (*informal*)
▷ **hold out** *See* **offer**
▷ **hold up = delay**, stop, detain, hinder, retard, set back, slow down; **= support**, sustain, prop, shore up; **= rob**, mug (*informal*), waylay ▸ *n* **7 = control**, sway, dominance • *The leader has a considerable hold over his people.* **8 = grip**, grasp • *He grabbed the rope and got a hold on it.* **9 = foothold**, support, footing
See also: **claim, handle, influence, reserve**
holder *n* **1 = owner**, keeper, proprietor, bearer, possessor **2 = case**, cover, container
hold-up *n* **1 = delay**, wait, snag, setback, stoppage, hitch, bottleneck, traffic jam **2 = robbery**, theft, mugging (*informal*), stick-up (*slang*)

DICTIONARY

hold² *n* cargo compartment in a ship or aircraft
Hölderlin *n* **Friedrich**. 1770–1843, German lyric poet, whose works include the poems *Menon's Lament for Diotima* and *Bread and Wine* and the novel *Hyperion* (1797–99)
hole Ⓣ *n* **1** area hollowed out in a solid **2** opening or hollow **3** animal's burrow **4** *informal* unattractive place **5** *informal* difficult situation **6** *golf* place into which the ball is to be played ▷ *v* **7** make holes in **8** hit (a golf ball) into a hole **holey** *adj*
holiday Ⓣ *n* **1** time spent away from home for rest or recreation **2** day or other period of rest from work or studies
Holiday *n* **Billie**, real name *Eleanora Fagan;* known as *Lady Day.* 1915–59, US jazz singer
holism *n* consideration of the complete person in the treatment of disease **holistic** *adj*
holler *v, n informal* shout or yell
hollow Ⓣ *adj* **1** having a hole or space inside **2** (of sounds) as if echoing in a hollow place **3** without any real value or worth ▷ *n* **4** cavity or space **5** dip in the land ▷ *v* **6** form a hollow in
holly *n* evergreen tree with prickly leaves and red berries
Holly *n* **Buddy**, real name *Charles Harden Holley.* 1936–59, US rock-and-roll singer, guitarist, and songwriter. His hits (all 1956–59) include "That'll be the Day," "Maybe Baby," "Peggy Sue," "Oh, Boy," "Think it over," and "It doesn't Matter anymore"
hollyhock *n* tall garden plant with spikes of colourful flowers
Holmes *n* **Oliver Wendell**. 1809–94, US author, esp. of humorous essays, such as *The Autocrat of the Breakfast Table* (1858) and its sequels
holocaust Ⓣ *n* destruction or loss of life on a massive scale
hologram *n* three-dimensional photographic image
holograph *n* document handwritten by the author
holography *n* science of using lasers to produce holograms
Holst *n* **Gustav** (**Theodore**). 1874–1934, English composer. His works include operas, choral music, and orchestral music such as the suite *The Planets* (1917)
Holstein *n* breed of black-and-white dairy cattle
holster *n* leather case for a pistol, hung from a belt
holy Ⓣ *adj* **-lier**, **-liest 1** of or associated with God or a deity **2** devout or virtuous **holiness** *n*
▸ **holier-than-thou** *adj* self-righteous
▸ **Holy Communion** *Christianity* service in remembrance of the death and resurrection of Jesus Christ
▸ **Holy Grail** (in medieval legend) the bowl used by Jesus Christ at the Last Supper
▸ **Holy Spirit** *or* **Holy Ghost** *Christianity* one of the three aspects of God
▸ **Holy Week** *Christianity* week before Easter
homage Ⓣ *n* show of respect or honour towards something or someone
homburg *n* man's soft felt hat with a dented crown and a stiff upturned brim
home Ⓣ *n* **1** place where one lives **2** institution to care for the elderly, infirm, etc. ▷ *adj* **3** of one's home, birthplace, or

THESAURUS

hole *n* **1** = **opening**, tear, split, gap • *to punch holes in the paper* **2** = **flaw**, error, defect, fault, loophole • *There are some holes in that theory.* **3** (*Informal*) = **predicament**, fix (*informal*), mess, hot water (*informal*), tight spot • *He admitted that the company was in a financial hole.* **4** = **cavity**, pit, chamber, cave, hollow, cavern **5** = **burrow**, earth, shelter, den, lair **6** (*Informal*) = **hovel**, dump (*informal*), dive (*slang*), slum
See also: **breach, jam, leak**
holiday *n* **1** = **vacation**, leave, break, recess, time off, staycation (*informal*) • *They were in Paris on a holiday.* **2** = **statutory holiday** (*Canad*), anniversary, celebration, gala, festivity, feast, public holiday (*US*), fête, red-letter day, mela, name day, saint's day, stat holiday (*Canad*) **3** = **festival**, celebration • *The Thanksgiving holiday always falls on a Monday.*
See also: **rest**
holiness *n* = **divinity**, purity, spirituality, sanctity, piety, godliness, righteousness, sacredness, saintliness
hollow *adj* **1** = **empty**, void, vacant, unfilled **2** = **deep**, low, dull, muted, reverberant **3** = **worthless**, useless, meaningless, pointless, vain, futile, fruitless ▸ *n* **4** = **cavity**, hole, depression, pit, bowl, crater, basin, trough **5** = **valley**, glen, dell, dale, dingle ▸ *v* **6** = **scoop**, dig, gouge, excavate ▷ **hollow out** *See* **dig**
holocaust *n* = **genocide**, destruction, massacre, devastation, annihilation, conflagration
holy *adj* **1** = **sacred**, hallowed, consecrated, sacrosanct, venerated • *We visited the city's holy places.* **2** = **devout**, religious, pious, saintly • *There are holy people in all religions.*
homage *n* = **respect**, honour, devotion, worship, deference, adoration, adulation, reverence
home *n* **1** = **dwelling**, house, residence, abode • *They stayed home and watched TV.* **2** = **birthplace**, home town ▷ **at**

DICTIONARY

native country ▷ *adv* **4** to or at home ▷ *v* **5** (foll. by *in, in on*) direct or be directed onto (a point or target) **homeward** *adj, adv* **homewards** *adv*
▶ **at home** at ease
▶ **bring home to** make clear to
▶ **home and dry** *informal* safe or successful
▶ **home-brew** *n* beer made at home
▶ **homeless** *adj* **1** having nowhere to live ▷ *pl n* **2** people who have nowhere to live **homelessness** *n*
▶ **homely** *adj* **1** unattractive **2** *Brit* simple, ordinary, and comfortable
▶ **home-made** *adj* made at home or on the premises
▶ **home page** *computers* introductory information about a website with hyperlinks to further pages
▶ **home plate** *baseball* base where hitter bats
▶ **homesick** *adj* depressed by absence from home **homesickness** *n*
▶ **homestead** *n* **1** house with outbuildings, esp. on a farm **2** *hist* land assigned to a N American settler **homesteader** *n*
▶ **home truths** unpleasant facts told to a person about himself or herself
▶ **homework** *n* school work done at home

homeopathy [home-ee-**op**-ath-ee] *n* treatment of disease by small doses of a drug that produces symptoms of the disease in healthy people **homeopathic** [home-ee-oh-**path**-ik] *adj* **homeopathically** *adv*
▶ **homeopath** *n* person who practises homeopathy

Homer *n* c. 800 BC, Greek poet to whom are attributed the *Iliad* and the *Odyssey*. Almost nothing is known of him, but it is thought that he was born on the island of Chios and was blind

homicide Ⓣ *n* **1** killing of a human being **2** person who kills another **homicidal** *adj*

homily Ⓣ *n, pl* **-lies** speech telling people how they should behave

homing pigeon *n* pigeon trained to return home after travelling great distances, kept for racing

hominid *n* man or any extinct forerunner of man

homo- *combining form* same: *homosexual*

homogeneous Ⓣ [home-oh-**jean**-ee-uss] *adj* formed of similar parts **homogeneity** *n*
▶ **homogenize** *v* **1** make homogeneous **2** break up fat globules in (milk or cream) to distribute them evenly

homograph *n* word spelt the same as another

homologous [hom-**ol**-log-uss] *adj* having a related or similar position or structure

homonym *n* word with the same spelling or pronunciation as another, but with a different meaning

homophobia *n* hatred or fear of homosexuals **homophobic** *adj*

homophone *n* word with the same pronunciation as another

Homo sapiens [**hoe**-moh **sap**-ee-enz] *n* human beings as a species

homosexual *n, adj* (person) sexually attracted to members of the same sex **homosexuality** *n*

Hon. Honourable

hone Ⓣ *v* sharpen

Honecker *n* **Erich**. 1912–94, German statesman; head of state of East Germany (1976–89)

Honegger *n* **Arthur**. 1892–1955, French composer, one of Les Six. His works include the oratorios *King David* (1921) and *Joan of Arc*

THESAURUS

home = **in**, available, present; = **at ease**, comfortable, familiar, relaxed ▷ **bring home to** = **make clear**, emphasize, drive home, impress upon, press home ▶ *adj* **3** = **domestic**, national, native, internal • *The home team is in town*. OPPOSITE: foreign

homeboy, home girl *n* (*Slang*) = **friend**, comrade, buddy (*informal*), pal (*informal*), chum (*informal*), crony

homeland *n* = **native land**, motherland, country of origin, fatherland, mother country

homeless *adj* = **destitute**, displaced, dispossessed, down-and-out, down on one's luck (*informal*) ▶ *n* ▷ **the homeless** = **vagrants**, squatters

homely *adj* = **dowdy**, dumpy (*informal*), frowzy, ugly, unattractive, frumpy, unfashionable

homespun *adj* = **unsophisticated**, rough, plain, coarse, home-made, homey (US), dumpy (*informal*)

homey *adj* = **comfortable**, simple, friendly, modest, ordinary, plain, cozy, homespun, welcoming • *The room was small and homey*. OPPOSITE: grand

homicidal *adj* = **murderous**, deadly, lethal, mortal, maniacal

homicide *n* **1** = **murder**, killing, manslaughter, slaying, bloodshed **2** = **murderer**, killer, slayer

homily *n* = **sermon**, address, lecture, discourse, preaching

homogeneity *n* = **uniformity**, similarity, correspondence, consistency, sameness

homogeneous *adj* = **uniform**, similar, consistent, comparable, identical, alike, akin, analogous, unvarying

hone *v* = **sharpen**, point, file, edge, grind, polish, whet

DICTIONARY

at the Stake (1935), and *Pacific 231* (1924) for orchestra

honest Ⓣ *adj* **1** not cheating, lying, or stealing **2** genuine or sincere **3** gained or earned fairly **honestly** *adv*

▸ **honesty** *n* **1** quality of being honest **2** plant with silvery seed pods

honey *n* **1** sweet edible fluid made by bees from nectar **2** term of endearment

▸ **honeycomb** *n* waxy structure of hexagonal cells in which honey is stored

▸ **honeydew melon** melon with yellow skin and sweet pale flesh

▸ **honeymoon** *n* holiday taken by a newly married couple

▸ **honeysuckle** *n* climbing shrub with sweet-smelling flowers

Hong-wu, Hung-wu *n* title of *Chu Yuan-Zhang* (or *Chu Yüan-Chang*). 1328–98, first emperor (1368–98) of the Ming dynasty, uniting China under his rule by 1382

honk *n* **1** sound made by an automobile horn **2** sound made by a goose ▹ *v* **3** (cause to) make this sound

honky-tonk *n US slang* **1** cheap disreputable nightclub **2** style of ragtime piano-playing, esp. on a tinny-sounding piano

honour, honor Ⓣ *n* **1** personal integrity **2** (award given out of) respect **3** pleasure or privilege **honours 4** rank or mark of the highest academic standard in a university degree course ▹ *v* **5** give praise and attention to **6** give an award to (someone) out of respect **7** keep (a promise) **8** accept or pay (a cheque or bill) **honourable** *or* **honorable** *adj*

honourably *or* **honorably** *adv*

▸ **do the honours** act as host or hostess by pouring drinks or giving out food

▸ **honorary** *adj* **1** held or given only as an honour **2** holding a position or giving one's services without pay

▸ **honorific** *adj* showing respect

hooch [rhymes with **smooch**] *n US slang* alcoholic drink, esp. illicitly distilled spirits

hood[1] *n* **1** head covering, often part of a coat etc. **2** folding roof of a convertible automobile or a baby carriage **3** metal cover over a vehicle's engine ▹ *v* **4** cover (as if) with a hood

▸ **hooded** *adj* **1** (of a garment) having a hood **2** (of eyes) having heavy eyelids that appear to be half closed

hood[2] *n slang* hoodlum

Hoodless *n* **Adelaide** (née *Hunter*). 1857–1910, Canadian educator and reformer. After her infant son died from the ill effects of consuming impure milk she campaigned to improve the education of young mothers. She founded the first Women's Institute (1897) and helped to found the National Council of Women and the Victorian Order of Nurses

hoodlum Ⓣ *n slang* gangster, lawless youth

hoodoo *n, pl* **-doos** (person or thing that brings) bad luck

hoodwink Ⓣ *v* trick or deceive

hooey *n slang* nonsense

hoof *n, pl* **hooves, hoofs** horny casing of the foot of a horse, deer, etc.

▸ **hoof it** *informal* walk

hoo-ha *n* fuss or commotion

THESAURUS

honest *adj* **1 = trustworthy**, truthful, law-abiding, reputable, virtuous • *He is a very honest, decent man*. OPPOSITE: dishonest **2 = open**, direct, plain, sincere, frank, candid, upfront (*informal*), forthright *See also*: **real, serious, straight, straightforward**

honestly *adv* **1 = ethically**, legally, lawfully, cleanly, by fair means, honourably **2 = frankly**, straight *or* straight out, truthfully, plainly, candidly, in all sincerity, to one's face

honesty *n* **1 = integrity**, honour, virtue, morality, truthfulness, incorruptibility, probity, rectitude, scrupulousness, trustworthiness, uprightness **2 = frankness**, openness, sincerity, bluntness, candour, outspokenness, straightforwardness

honorary *adj* **= nominal**, unofficial, unpaid, complimentary, titular, in name only *or* in title only

honour *n* **1 = integrity**, honesty, decency, goodness • *I can no longer serve with honour in your government*. OPPOSITE: dishonour **2 = tribute**, praise, recognition, homage, accolade, commendation • *He was showered with honours - among them a Gemini award*. **3 = glory**, credit, reputation, fame, dignity, distinction, kudos, prestige, renown **4 = privilege**, credit, pleasure, compliment ▸ *v* **5 = acclaim**, praise, commemorate, decorate, commend, glorify • *She was honoured by the club with a gold medal*. **6 = respect**, value, appreciate, prize, adore, esteem **7 = fulfill**, keep, observe, discharge, be true to, carry out, live up to **8 = accept**, take, pay, pass, acknowledge *See also*: **character, recognize, right, worship**

honourable *adj* **= respected**, respectable, reputable, virtuous, creditable, estimable *See also*: **noble, respectable**

honoured *See* **proud**

hoodlum *n* **= thug**, tough, vandal, hooligan, lout • *The hoodlums hurled rocks at the building*.

hoodwink *v* **= deceive**, trick, mislead, fool, con (*informal*), dupe, swindle, delude

DICTIONARY

hook Ⓣ *n* **1** curved piece of metal or plastic used to hang, hold, or pull something **2** short swinging punch ▷ *v* **3** fasten or catch (as if) with a hook
▸ **hooked** *adj* **1** shaped like a hook **2** caught **3** (foll. by *on*) *slang* addicted (to)
▸ **hooker** *n slang* prostitute
▸ **hook shot** *basketball* shot made by holding the ball to one's side with one hand and throwing it over one's head
▸ **hook-up** *n* linking of radio or television stations
▸ **hookworm** *n* parasitic worm with hooked mouth parts
hookah *n* oriental pipe in which smoke is drawn through water and a long tube
Hooke *n* **Robert**. 1635–1703, English physicist, chemist, and inventor. He formulated Hooke's law (1678), built the first Gregorian telescope, and invented a balance spring for watches
Hooker *n* **1 John Lee**. 1917–2001, US blues singer and guitarist **2 Richard**. 1554–1600, British theologian, who influenced Anglican theology with *The Laws of Ecclesiastical Polity* (1593–97)
hooligan Ⓣ *n* rowdy young person
hooliganism *n*
hoop Ⓣ *n* rigid circular band, used esp. as a child's toy or for animals to jump through in the circus **hooped** *adj*
▸ **be put through the hoops** go through an ordeal or test
hoopla *n* fairground game in which hoops are thrown over objects in an attempt to win them
hooray *interj* same as **hurrah**
hoot Ⓣ *n* **1** sound of an automobile horn **2** owl's cry or similar sound **3** cry of derision **4** *informal* amusing person or thing ▷ *v* **5** jeer or yell contemptuously at (someone) **6** sound (an automobile horn) **7** *informal* laugh
▸ **hooter** *n* **1** device that hoots **2** *slang* nose
Hoover[1] *n* **1** ® vacuum cleaner ▷ *v* **2 hoover** vacuum
Hoover[2] *n* **1 Herbert** (**Clark**). 1874–1964, US statesman; 31st president of the US (1929–33). He organized relief for Europe during and after World War I, but as president he lost favour after his failure to alleviate the effects of the Depression **2 J**(**ohn**) **Edgar**. 1895–1972, US lawyer: director of the FBI (1924–72). He used new scientific methods to combat crime, including the first fingerprint file
hooves *n* a plural of **hoof**
hop[1] Ⓣ *v* **hopping, hopped 1** jump on one foot **2** move in short jumps **3** *informal* move quickly ▷ *n* **4** instance of hopping **5** short journey, esp. by air **6** *informal* dance
hop[2] *n* **1** climbing plant with green conelike flowers used to give beer a bitter flavour **hops 2** the dried flowers
hope Ⓣ *v* **1** want (something) to happen or be true ▷ *n* **2** expectation of something desired **3** thing that gives cause for hope or is desired
hopeless *adj*
▸ **hopeful** *adj* **1** having, expressing, or inspiring hope ▷ *n* **2** person considered to be on the brink of success
▸ **hopefully** *adv* **1** in a hopeful manner **2** it is hoped
Hope *n* **Anthony**, real name *Sir Anthony Hope Hawkins*. 1863–1933, English novelist; author of *The Prisoner of Zenda* (1894)
Hopkins *n* **1 Gerard Manley**. 1844–89, British poet and Jesuit priest, who experimented with sprung rhythm in his highly original poetry **2 Harry L**(**loyd**). 1890–1946, US administrator. During World War II he was a personal aide to President Roosevelt and administered the lend-lease program
hopper *n* container for storing things

THESAURUS

hook *n* **1** = **fastener**, link, catch, peg, clasp ▸ *v* **2** = **fasten**, fix, secure, clasp **3** = **catch**, trap, snare, ensnare, entrap
hooked *adj* **1** = **bent**, aquiline, curved, hook-shaped **2** = **addicted**, devoted, obsessed, enamoured, taken, turned on (*slang*)
hooligan *n* = **delinquent**, vandal, lager lout, ruffian
hooliganism *n* = **delinquency**, violence, disorder, vandalism, loutishness, rowdiness
hoop *n* = **ring**, band, wheel, loop, girdle, circlet
hoot *n* **1** = **cry**, call, toot **2** = **catcall**, boo, jeer, hiss ▸ *v* **3** = **jeer**, boo, hiss, howl down
hop *v* **1** = **jump**, trip, spring, skip, leap, vault, bound, caper ▸ *n* **2** = **jump**, step, spring, bounce, skip, leap, vault, bound
hope *n* **1** = **ambition**, expectation, dream • *There was little hope of recovery.* ▸ *v* **2** = **desire**, long, aspire, cross one's fingers, look forward to, set one's heart on
See also: **possibility, prospect**
hopeful *adj* **1** = **optimistic**, confident, expectant, buoyant, sanguine, looking forward to **2** = **promising**, bright, rosy, auspicious, encouraging, heartening, reassuring
hopefully *adv* = **optimistically**, confidently, expectantly
hopeless *adj* **1** = **impossible**, useless, pointless, vain, futile, forlorn • *Our situation is hopeless.* **2** = **inadequate**, poor, useless (*informal*), pathetic • *I don't drive, and the buses are hopeless.*
See also: **doomed, pessimistic**
hopelessness *See* **despair**

DICTIONARY

such as grain or sand
hopscotch *n* children's game of hopping in a pattern drawn on the ground
Horace *n* Latin name *Quintus Horatius Flaccus*. 65–8 BC, Roman poet and satirist: his verse includes the lyrics in the *Epodes* and the *Odes*, the *Epistles* and *Satires*, and the *Ars Poetica*
horde Ⓣ *n* large crowd
horizon Ⓣ *n* **1** apparent line that divides the earth and the sky **horizons 2** limits of scope, interest, or knowledge
horizontal Ⓣ *adj* **1** flat and level with the ground or with a line considered as a base ▷ *n* **2** horizontal plane, position, or line
horizontally *adv*
hormone *n* **1** substance secreted by certain glands which stimulates certain organs of the body **2** synthetic substance with the same effect **hormonal** *adj*
horn *n* **1** one of a pair of bony growths on the heads of animals such as cows and antelopes **2** substance of which this is made **3** wind instrument with a tube or pipe of brass fitted with a mouthpiece **4** device on a vehicle sounded as a warning **horned** *adj*
▸ **horny** *adj* **1** of or like horn **2** *slang* sexually aroused
▸ **hornbeam** *n* tree with smooth grey bark
▸ **hornbill** *n* bird with a bony growth on its large beak
▸ **hornpipe** *n* (music for) a lively solo dance, traditionally associated with sailors
hornblende *n* mineral containing aluminum, calcium, sodium, magnesium, and iron
hornet *n* large wasp with a severe sting
horology *n* art or science of clock-making and measuring time
horoscope *n* **1** prediction of a person's future based on the positions of the planets, sun, and moon at his or her birth **2** diagram of the positions of these at a particular time and place
horrendous Ⓣ *adj* horrific
horror Ⓣ *n* (thing or person causing) terror or hatred
▸ **horrible** *adj* **1** disagreeable **2** causing horror **horribly** *adv*
▸ **horrid** *adj* **1** unpleasant or disagreeable **2** *informal* unkind
▸ **horrify** *v* **1** cause feelings of horror in **2** shock
▸ **horrific** *adj* particularly horrible
hors d'oeuvre [or **durv**] *n* appetizer served before a main meal
Horsa *n* died ?455 AD, leader, with his brother Hengist, of the first Jutish settlers in Britain. See also **Hengist**
horse Ⓣ *n* **1** four-footed animal with hooves, a mane, and a tail, used for riding and pulling carts, etc. **2** piece of gymnastic equipment used for vaulting over
▸ **straight from the horse's mouth** from the most reliable source
▸ **horsy** *adj* **1** devoted to horses **2** like a horse
▸ **horse about** *or* **horse around** *v informal* play roughly or boisterously
▸ **horse chestnut** tree with broad leaves, white or pink flowers, and large brown shiny nuts
▸ **horsefly** *n* large bloodsucking fly
▸ **horsehair** *n* hair from the tail or mane of a horse
▸ **horse laugh** harsh boisterous laugh
▸ **horseman** (**horsewoman**) *n* rider on a horse
▸ **horseplay** *n* rough or rowdy behaviour
▸ **horsepower** *n* unit of power (equivalent to 745.7 watts), used to measure the power of an engine

THESAURUS

horde *n* = **crowd**, host, band, pack, gang, mob, swarm, throng, multitude, drove
horizon *n* = **skyline**, vista
horizontal *adj* = **level**, flat, parallel
horrendous *adj* = **horrific**, shocking, awful, grim, appalling, grisly, dreadful, ghastly, frightful, frightening, terrifying, horrifying
horrible *adj* **1** = **unpleasant**, mean, nasty, awful, horrid, disagreeable • *a horrible person to work with* **2** = **appalling**, grim, gruesome, dreadful, terrifying • *horrible crimes*
See also: **hateful, terrible**
horrid *adj* **1** = **unpleasant**, terrible, horrible, awful, dreadful, disagreeable **2** (*Informal*) = **unkind**, mean, nasty, cruel, beastly (*informal*)
horrific *adj* = **horrifying**, shocking, awful, horrendous, appalling, grisly, dreadful, ghastly, frightful, terrifying
horrify *v* **1** = **shock**, outrage, sicken, disgust, dismay, appal • *a crime wave that horrified the city* **2** = **terrify**, scare, alarm, intimidate, frighten, petrify, make one's hair stand on end
horror *n* **1** = **terror**, fear, alarm, panic, dread, fright • *He gazed in horror at the knife.* **2** = **hatred**, disgust, revulsion, aversion, loathing, abhorrence • *his horror of speaking in public*
horse *n* = **equine**, pony, nag (*informal*) • *a fall from a horse* RELATED WORDS *adjectives*: equestrian, equine, horsey *noun*: equitation *male*: stallion *female*: mare *young*: foal, colt, filly
horseman *n* = **rider**, cavalier, equestrian, cavalryman, dragoon
horseplay *n* = **fooling around**, rough-and-tumble, buffoonery, clowning, high jinks,

DICTIONARY

▸ **horseradish** *n* plant with a strong-tasting root, used to make a sauce
▸ **horseshoe** *n* protective U-shaped piece of iron nailed to a horse's hoof, often regarded as a symbol of good luck
Horta *n* **Victor**. 1861–1947, Belgian architect, best known for his early buildings in Art Nouveau style
horticulture *n* art or science of cultivating gardens **horticultural** *adj* **horticulturist** *n*
hosanna *interj* exclamation of praise to God
hose[1] *n* **1** flexible tube for conveying liquid or gas ▹ *v* **2** water with a hose
▸ **hoser** *n slang* beer-drinking country dweller
hose[2] *n* stockings, socks, and tights
▸ **hosiery** *n* stockings, socks, etc. collectively
hospice [**hoss**-piss] *n* nursing home for the terminally ill
hospital *n* institution for the care and treatment of sick or injured people
▸ **hospitalize** *v* send or admit for care in a hospital **hospitalization** *n*
hospitality Ⓣ *n* friendliness in welcoming strangers or guests
▸ **hospitable** *adj* welcoming **hospitably** *adv*
host[1] Ⓣ *n* **1** person who entertains another as a guest **2** place or country providing the facilities for an event **3** compère of a show **4** animal or plant on which a parasite lives ▹ *v* **5** be the host of
▸ **hostess** *n* woman who welcomes guests or visitors
host[2] Ⓣ *n* large number
Host *n Christianity* bread used in Holy Communion
hostage Ⓣ *n* person who is illegally held prisoner until certain demands are met by other people
hostel Ⓣ *n* building providing accommodation at a low cost for particular categories of people, such as homeless people
hostelry *n, pl* **-ries** *obsolete* tavern
hostile Ⓣ *adj* **1** unfriendly **2** of an enemy **3** (foll. by *to*) opposed (to)
▸ **hostility** *n* **1** unfriendly and aggressive feelings or behaviour **hostilities 2** acts of warfare
hot Ⓣ *adj* **hotter, hottest 1** having a high temperature **2** giving or feeling heat **3** (of a temper) quick to flare up **4** (of a competition) intense **5** recent or new **6** liked very much: *a hot favourite* **7** spicy **8** *slang* stolen **hotly** *adv* **hotness** *n*
▸ **in hot water** *informal* in trouble
▸ **hotting** *n informal* practice of stealing fast automobiles and putting on a show of skilful but dangerous driving
▸ **hot air** *informal* empty talk
▸ **hotbed** *n* any place encouraging a particular activity: *a hotbed of vice*
▸ **hot-blooded** *adj* passionate or excitable
▸ **hot dog** hot sausage (esp. a frankfurter) in a bread roll
▸ **hotfoot** *v, adv informal* (go) as fast as possible
▸ **hotheaded** *adj* hasty, having a hot temper
▸ **hothouse** *n* heated greenhouse
▸ **hot line** direct telephone link for emergency use
▸ **hotplate** *n* **1** heated metal surface on an electric cooker **2** portable device for keeping food warm
hotel *n* commercial establishment providing lodging and meals

h

THESAURUS

pranks, romping, skylarking (*informal*)
hospitable *adj* = **welcoming**, liberal, kind, friendly, generous, gracious, cordial, sociable
hospitality *n* = **welcome**, warmth, friendliness, conviviality, cordiality, neighbourliness, sociability
host[1] *n* **1** = **master of ceremonies**, entertainer, landlord *or* landlady, proprietor, innkeeper **2** = **presenter**, anchorman *or* anchorwoman ▸ *v* **3** = **present**, front (*informal*), introduce
host[2] *n* = **multitude**, army, array, swarm, throng, legion, myriad, drove, horde
hostage *n* = **prisoner**, captive, pawn
hostel *See* **shelter**
hostile *adj* **1** = **unfriendly**, belligerent, antagonistic, malevolent, unkind • *The umpire faced a hostile crowd.* OPPOSITE: friendly **2** = **opposed**, against, contrary, antagonistic, ill-disposed
See also: **aggressive**
hostilities *pl n* = **warfare**, war, conflict, fighting
hostility *n* = **ill will**, hatred, resentment, animosity, antagonism, malice • *hostility toward the rival team* OPPOSITE: friendship
See also: **conflict, dislike, hate, opposition**
hot *adj* **1** = **heated**, warm, boiling, scalding, scorching • *a hot climate* OPPOSITE: cold **2** = **spicy**, peppery • *a hot, aromatic curry* OPPOSITE: bland **3** = **fierce**, violent, intense, passionate, fiery, stormy, raging **4** = **recent**, new, fresh, latest, just out, up to the minute **5** = **popular**, sought-after, approved, favoured, in demand, in vogue ▹ **hot air** = **empty talk**, wind, bombast, claptrap (*informal*), guff (*slang*), verbiage ▹ **hot water** (usually preceded by *in*) (*Informal*) = **predicament**, spot (*informal*), fix (*informal*), jam (*informal*), mess, scrape (*informal*), dilemma, tight spot
hot-blooded *adj* = **passionate**, wild, fiery,

DICTIONARY

▸ **hotelier** *n* owner or manager of a hotel
Hottentot *n* member of a race of people of southern Africa, now nearly extinct
hound Ⓣ *n* **1** hunting dog ▹ *v* **2** pursue relentlessly
hour *n* **1** twenty-fourth part of a day **2** sixty minutes **3** time of day **4** appointed time
hours 5 period regularly appointed for work or business
▸ **hourly** *adj, adv* **1** (happening) every hour **2** frequent(ly)
▸ **hourglass** *n* device with two glass compartments, containing a quantity of sand that takes an hour to trickle from the top section to the bottom one
houri *n Islam* any of the beautiful nymphs of paradise
house Ⓣ *n* **1** building used as a dwelling **2** building for some specific purpose: *schoolhouse* **3** law-making body or the hall where it meets **4** family or dynasty **5** business firm **6** theatre audience or performance ▹ *v* **7** give accommodation to **8** cover or contain
▸ **get on like a house on fire** *informal* get on very well together
▸ **on the house** *informal* provided free by the management
▸ **housing** *n* **1** (providing of) houses **2** protective case or covering of a machine
▸ **house arrest** confinement to one's home rather than to prison
▸ **houseboat** *n* stationary boat used as a home
▸ **housebreaker** *n* burglar
▸ **housecoat** *n* woman's long loose robelike garment for casual wear
▸ **household** *n* all the people living in a house
▸ **householder** *n* person who owns or rents a house
▸ **housekeeper** *n* person employed to run someone else's household
▸ **housekeeping** *n* (money for) running a household
▸ **housemaid** *n* female servant who does housework
▸ **house-train** *v* train (a domestic animal) to urinate and defecate outside
▸ **housewares** *pl n US & Canad* kitchenware and other utensils for use in the home
▸ **house-warming** *n* party to celebrate moving into a new home
▸ **housewife** *n* woman who runs her own household
▸ **housework** *n* work of running a house, such as cleaning, cooking, and shopping
House music, House *n* kind of disco music based on funk, with fragments of other recordings edited in electronically
Housman *n* **A(lfred) E(dward)**. 1859–1936, English poet and classical scholar, author of *A Shropshire Lad* (1896) and *Last Poems* (1922)
hovel Ⓣ *n* small dirty dwelling
hover Ⓣ *v* **1** (of a bird etc.) remain suspended in one place in the air **2** loiter **3** be in a state of indecision
▸ **hovercraft** *n* vehicle which can travel over both land and sea on a cushion of air
how *adv* **1** in what way **2** by what means **3** in what condition **4** to what degree
▸ **however** *adv* **1** nevertheless **2** by whatever means **3** no matter how
Howard *n* **Catherine**. ?1521–42, fifth wife of Henry VIII of England; beheaded
howdah *n* canopied seat on an elephant's back
Howe *n* **1 Gordon**, known as *Gordie*. born 1928, Canadian ice-hockey player **2 Joseph**. 1804–73, Nova Scotian journalist and political reformer
howitzer *n* cannon firing shells at a steep angle
howl Ⓣ *v* **1** utter a long loud cry ▹ *n* **2** such a

THESAURUS

spirited, ardent, impulsive, temperamental, excitable
hot-headed *adj* = **rash**, volatile, fiery, reckless, hasty, foolhardy, hot-tempered, impetuous, quick-tempered
hound *v* = **harass**, provoke, persecute, badger, goad, harry, pester, impel
house *n* **1** = **home**, building, residence, dwelling, abode • *They live in a large house with eight rooms.* **2** = **family**, household **3** = **dynasty**, tribe, clan **4** = **firm**, company, business, organization, outfit (*informal*) **5** = **assembly**, Commons, parliament, legislative body **on the house** = **free**, for nothing, gratis ▸ *v* **6** = **accommodate**, quarter, lodge, harbour, billet, put up, take in **7** = **contain**, keep, store, protect, cover, shelter, sheathe
See also: **accommodation**
household *n* = **family**, home, house ▹ **household name** *See* **personality**
householder *n* = **occupant**, resident, homeowner, tenant
housing *n* **1** = **accommodation**, dwellings, homes, houses **2** = **case**, cover, container, enclosure, casing, sheath, covering
hovel *n* = **hut**, hole, shed, cabin, den, shack, shanty
hover *v* **1** = **float**, fly, hang, drift, flutter **2** = **linger**, hang about **3** = **waver**, fluctuate, dither, vacillate, oscillate
how do you do? *See* **hello**
however *adv* = **nevertheless**, but, still, though, yet, notwithstanding, nonetheless, anyhow, after all
howl *n* **1** = **cry**, scream, roar, bay, wail,

DICTIONARY

cry **3** loud burst of laughter
▸ **howler** *n informal* stupid mistake
Howlin' Wolf *n* real name *Chester Burnett*. 1910–76, US blues singer and songwriter
hoyden *n* wild or boisterous girl, tomboy
Hoyle *n* Sir **Fred**. 1915–2001, English astronomer and writer: his books include *The Nature of the Universe* (1950) and *Frontiers of Astronomy* (1955), and science-fiction writings
HP, hp **1** hire-purchase **2** horsepower
HQ headquarters
HRH Her (*or* His) Royal Highness
HST harmonized sales tax
HTML hypertext markup language: text description language used on the internet
hub Ⓣ *n* **1** centre of a wheel, through which the axle passes **2** central point of activity
Hubble *n* **Edwin Powell**. 1889–1953, US astronomer, noted for his investigations of nebulae and the recession of the galaxies
hubble-bubble *n* same as **hookah**
hubbub Ⓣ *n* confused noise of many voices, uproar
hubby *n, pl* **-bies** *informal* husband
hubris [**hew**-briss] *n* pride, arrogance
huckster *n* person using aggressive methods of selling
huddle Ⓣ *n* **1** small group **2** *informal* impromptu conference ▷ *v* **3** heap or crowd closely together **4** hunch (oneself) as through cold
Huddleston *n* **Trevor**. 1913–98, British Anglican prelate; suffragan bishop of Stepney (1968–78) and bishop of Mauritius (1978–83); president of the Anti-Apartheid Movement (1981–94)
Hudson *n* **Henry**. died 1611, English navigator: he explored the Hudson River (1609) and Hudson Bay (1610), where his crew mutinied and cast him adrift to die
hue Ⓣ *n* colour
hue and cry *n* public outcry
huff Ⓣ *n* **1** passing mood of anger or resentment ▷ *v* **2** blow or puff heavily **huffy** *adj* **huffily** *adv*
hug Ⓣ *v* **hugging, hugged** **1** clasp tightly in the arms, usually with affection **2** keep close to ▷ *n* **3** tight or fond embrace
huge Ⓣ *adj* very big
▸ **hugely** *adv* very much
Hugo *n* **Victor** (**Marie**). 1802–85, French poet, novelist, and dramatist; leader of the romantic movement in France. His works include the volumes of verse *Les Feuilles d'automne* (1831) and *Les Contemplations* (1856), the novels *Notre-Dame de Paris* (1831) and *Les Misérables* (1862), and the plays *Hernani* (1830) and *Ruy Blas* (1838)
huh *interj* exclamation of derision, bewilderment, or inquiry
hula *n* native dance of Hawaii
Hula-Hoop *n* ® plastic hoop swung round the body by wriggling the hips
hulk Ⓣ *n* **1** body of an abandoned ship **2** *offensive* large or unwieldy person or thing
▸ **hulking** *adj* bulky or unwieldy
hull Ⓣ *n* **1** main body of a boat **2** leaves round the stem of a strawberry, raspberry, or similar fruit **3** shell or husk of a fruit or seed ▷ *v* **4** remove the hulls from (fruit or seeds)
Hull *n* **1** **Cordell**. 1871–1955, US statesman; secretary of state (1933–44). He helped to found the UN: Nobel peace prize 1945 **2** **Robert Marvin**, known as *Bobby*. born 1939, Canadian ice-hockey player
hullabaloo *n, pl* **-loos** loud confused noise or clamour
hum Ⓣ *v* **humming, hummed** **1** make a low continuous vibrating sound **2** sing with closed lips **3** *slang* be very active ▷ *n* **4** humming sound
▸ **hummingbird** *n* very small N American

h

THESAURUS

clamour, groan, shriek, bawl ▸ *v* **2** = **cry**, scream, roar, yell, weep, wail, shriek, bellow, bawl
howler *n* = **mistake**, blunder, bloomer (*informal*), error, malapropism
howling *See* **wild**
hub *n* = **centre**, heart, focus, middle, core, focal point, nerve centre
hubbub *n* **1** = **noise**, uproar, racket, cacophony, din, ruckus (*informal*), tumult, babel **2** = **confusion**, disorder, riot, disturbance, clamour, brouhaha, pandemonium, bedlam, hullabaloo, rumpus, ruction (*informal*), hurly-burly
huddle *v* **1** = **crowd**, gather, press, cluster, flock, converge, throng **2** = **curl up**, crouch, hunch up ▸ *n* **3** (*Informal*) = **conference**, meeting, discussion, powwow
hue *n* = **colour**, tone, shade, dye, tint, tinge
huff *See* **resentment**
huffy *See* **resentful, sulky**
hug *v* **1** = **embrace**, squeeze, cuddle, clasp • *We hugged each other.* ▸ *n* **2** = **embrace** • *She gave him a hug.*
huge *adj* = **enormous**, giant, massive, vast, immense, colossal • *a huge crowd* OPPOSITE: tiny
See also: **large, spacious**
hulk *n* **1** = **wreck**, frame, shell, hull, shipwreck **2** = **oaf**, lump (*informal*), lout, lubber
hull *n* = **frame**, body, framework, casing, covering
hum *v* **1** = **murmur**, buzz, drone, purr, vibrate, throb, whir, thrum **2** = **be busy**, stir, buzz, pulse, bustle, pulsate

DICTIONARY

bird whose powerful wings make a humming noise as they vibrate
human ⓣ *adj* **1** of, concerning, or typical of people ▷ *n* **2** human being
▸ **humanity** *n* **1** human nature **2** mankind **3** kindness or mercy **humanities 4** study of literature, philosophy, and the arts
▸ **human being** man, woman, or child
▸ **humanly** *adv* by human powers or means
▸ **humanize** *v* make human or humane
▸ **humankind** *n* mankind
humane ⓣ *adj* kind or merciful **humanely** *adv*
humanism *n* belief in human effort rather than religion **humanist** *n*
▸ **humanitarian** *n, adj* (person) with the interest of mankind at heart
humble ⓣ *adj* **1** conscious of one's failings **2** modest, unpretentious **3** unimportant ▷ *v* **4** cause to become humble **5** humiliate **humbly** *adv*
Humboldt *n* Baron (**Friedrich Heinrich**) **Alexander von**. 1769–1859, German scientist, who made important scientific explorations in Central and South America (1799–1804). In *Kosmos* (1845–62), he provided a comprehensive description of the physical universe
humbug ⓣ *n* **1** boiled candy flavoured with peppermint **2** nonsense **3** person or thing that deceives people
humdinger *n slang* excellent person or thing
humdrum ⓣ *adj* commonplace and dull
Hume *n* **David**. 1711–76, Scottish empiricist philosopher, economist, and historian, whose skeptic philosophy restricted human knowledge to that which can be perceived by the senses. His works include *A Treatise of Human Nature* (1740), *An Enquiry concerning the Principles of Morals* (1751), *Political Discourses* (1752), and *History of England* (1754–62)
humerus [**hew**-mer-uss] *n, pl* **-eri** bone from the shoulder to the elbow
humid ⓣ *adj* (of the weather) damp and warm **humidity** *n* **humidify** *v*
▸ **humidifier** *n* device for increasing the amount of water vapour in the air in a room
humiliate ⓣ *v* lower the dignity or hurt the pride of **humiliating** *adj* **humiliation** *n*
humility ⓣ *n* quality of being humble
Hummel *n* **Johann Nepomuk**. 1778–1837, German composer and pianist
hummock *n* hillock

THESAURUS

human *adj* **1 = mortal**, manlike ▸ *n* **2 = human being**, man *or* woman, person, individual, soul, creature, mortal
humane *adj* **= kind**, charitable, thoughtful, compassionate, caring, merciful, benevolent • *a more just and humane society*
humanely *See* **well**
humanitarian *adj* **1 = compassionate**, charitable, humane, philanthropic, benevolent, altruistic, public-spirited ▸ *n* **2 = philanthropist**, benefactor, altruist, Good Samaritan
humanity *n* **1 = human race**, people, man, mankind, humankind, Homo sapiens **2 = human nature**, mortality **3 = sympathy**, charity, mercy, compassion, kindness, philanthropy, fellow feeling, kind-heartedness
humanize *v* **= civilize**, improve, educate, soften, tame, enlighten
humankind *n* **= humanity**, human race • *the evolution of humankind*
See also: **people**
humans *See* **people**
humble *adj* **1 = modest**, unassuming, meek • *He gave a great performance, but he was very humble.* OPPOSITE: haughty **2 = ordinary**, simple, modest • *Some fresh herbs will transform a humble stew.* ▸ *v* **3 = humiliate**, disgrace • *the little car company that humbled the industry giants*
See also: **unknown**
humbug *n* **1 = fraud**, phony (*informal*), impostor, trickster, charlatan, con man (*informal*), faker, swindler **2 = nonsense**, garbage, hypocrisy, cant, baloney (*informal*), quackery, claptrap (*informal*) **3 = killjoy**, scrooge (*informal*), spoilsport, wet blanket (*informal*)
humdrum *adj* **= dull**, ordinary, boring, dreary, mundane, uneventful, tedious, tiresome, banal, monotonous
humid *adj* **= damp**, steamy, sticky, muggy, clammy • *a hot, humid summer*
See also: **wet**
humidity *n* **= damp**, moisture, clamminess, dampness, dankness, moistness, mugginess, wetness
humiliate *v* **= embarrass**, humble, shame, disgrace, put down • *Why do you enjoy humiliating me?*
humiliated *See* **ashamed, embarrassed**
humiliating *adj* **= embarrassing**, degrading, ignominious, crushing, humbling, mortifying, shaming
humiliation *n* **= embarrassment**, shame, disgrace, indignity, degradation, dishonour, humbling, ignominy, loss of face, mortification, put-down
humility *n* **= modesty**, humbleness, lowliness, meekness, submissiveness, unpretentiousness
humorist *n* **= comedian**, card (*informal*), comic, wit, wag, joker, jester, funny man
humorous *adj* **= funny**, comic, amusing,

DICTIONARY

humour Ⓣ *n* **1** ability to say or perceive things that are amusing **2** situations, speech, or writings that are humorous **3** state of mind, mood **4** *obsolete* fluid in the body ▷ *v* **5** be kind and indulgent to **humorous** *adj* **humorously** *adv*
▶ **humorist** *n* person who acts, speaks, or writes in a humorous way
hump Ⓣ *n* **1** normal or deforming lump, esp. on the back **2** hillock **3** *informal* fit of sulking ▷ *v* **4** *slang* carry or heave
▶ **humpback** *n* person with an abnormal curvature of the spine **humpbacked** *adj*
▶ **hump-back bridge** road bridge with a sharp slope on either side
Humperdinck *n* **Engelbert**. 1854–1921, German composer, esp. of operas, including *Hansel and Gretel* (1893)
Humphrey *n* **Hubert Horatio**. 1911–78, US statesman; vice-president of the US under President Johnson (1965–69)
humus [**hew**-muss] *n* decomposing vegetable and animal mould in the soil
Hun *n* **1** member of any of several Asiatic peoples who invaded the Roman Empire in the 4th and 5th centuries AD **2** *informal, offensive* (in World War 1) German
hunch Ⓣ *n* **1** *informal* feeling or suspicion not based on facts ▷ *v* **2** draw (one's shoulders) up or together
▶ **hunchback** *n* humpback
hundred *adj, n* ten times ten **hundredfold** *adj, adv*
▶ **hundredth** *adj, n* (of) number one hundred in a series
▶ **hundredweight** *n* unit of weight of 112 lbs (50.8 kg)
hung *v* **1** past of **hang** ▷ *adj* **2** (of a jury) unable to decide **3** (of a parliament) with no clear majority
▶ **hung over** *informal* suffering the effects of a hangover
Hungarian *n* **1** language of Hungary **2** person from Hungary ▷ *adj* **3** of Hungary or its language
hunger Ⓣ *n* **1** discomfort or weakness from lack of food **2** lack of food that causes suffering or death: *refugees dying of hunger* **3** desire or craving ▷ *v* **4** (foll. by *for*) want very much
▶ **hungry** *adj* desiring food **hungrily** *adv*
▶ **hunger strike** refusal of all food, as a means of protest
hunk Ⓣ *n* **1** large piece **2** *slang* sexually attractive man
hunt Ⓣ *v* **1** seek out (animals) to kill or capture for sport or food **2** search (for) ▷ *n* **3** act or instance of hunting **4** (party organized for) hunting wild animals for sport
▶ **hunter** *n* **1** man or animal that seeks out and kills or captures game **2** horse or dog bred for hunting
▶ **huntress** *n obsolete* woman who seeks out and kills or captures game
▶ **huntsman** *n* **1** man in charge of a pack of hounds **2** man who hunts
Hunter *n* **1 John**. 1728–93, British physician, noted for his investigation of venereal and other diseases **2** his brother, **William**. 1718–83, British anatomist and obstetrician
hurdle Ⓣ *n* **1** light barrier for jumping over **2** problem or difficulty **hurdles** **3** race involving hurdles ▷ *v* **4** jump over (something)
▶ **hurdler** *n* person who races over hurdles
hurdy-gurdy *n, pl* **-dies** mechanical musical instrument, such as a barrel organ
hurl Ⓣ *v* **1** throw or utter violently **2** *slang* vomit
▶ **hurler** *n baseball* pitcher
hurling, hurley *n* Irish game resembling hockey

THESAURUS

playful, witty, comical, droll, entertaining, jocular, waggish
humour *n* **1 = comedy**, wit • *The movie's humour contains a serious message.* **2 = mood**, temper, frame of mind, spirits • *He hasn't been in a good humour lately.* ▶ *v* **3 = indulge**, flatter, mollify • *I nodded, partly to humour him.*
humourless *See* **serious**
hump *n* **= lump**, bump, projection, mound, bulge, protrusion, protuberance, swelling
hunch *n* **1 = feeling**, idea, suspicion, impression, intuition, inkling, premonition, presentiment ▶ *v* **2 = draw in**, bend, curve, arch
hunger *n* **1 = famine**, starvation **2 = appetite**, emptiness, hungriness, ravenousness **3 = desire**, appetite, ache, craving, thirst, itch, lust, yearning ▶ *v* **4 = want**, long, wish, desire, ache, thirst, crave, itch, yearn, hanker
hungry *adj* **1 = starving**, ravenous, famished, peckish (*informal*) • *I didn't have any lunch, so I'm really hungry.* **2 = eager**, keen, avid, greedy, craving, yearning, athirst, covetous, desirous
hunk *n* **= lump**, block, piece, mass, chunk, wedge, slab, nugget
hunt *v* **1 = stalk**, track, trail, pursue, chase, hound **2 = search**, look, seek, scour, forage, ferret about ▶ *n* **3 = search**, investigation, chase, hunting, pursuit, quest
hurdle *n* **1 = fence**, barrier, barricade **2 = obstacle**, difficulty, barrier, hazard, obstruction, impediment, handicap, hindrance, stumbling block
hurl *v* **= throw**, launch, pitch, cast, toss,

DICTIONARY

hurly-burly *n* loud confusion
hurrah, hurray *interj* exclamation of joy or applause
hurricane Ⓣ *n* very strong, often destructive wind or storm
▸ **hurricane lamp** kerosene lamp with a glass covering
hurry Ⓣ *v* **-rying**, **-ried** 1 (cause to) move or act in great haste ▷ *n* 2 haste 3 eagerness **hurriedly** *adv*
hurt Ⓣ *v* **hurting**, **hurt** 1 cause physical or mental pain to 2 wound the feelings of 3 *informal* feel pain ▷ *n* 4 physical or mental pain or suffering **hurtful** *adj*
hurtle Ⓣ *v* move rapidly or violently
Husain *n* 1 ?629–680 AD, Islamic caliph, the son of Ali and Fatima and the grandson of Mohammed 2 a variant of **Hussein**
husband Ⓣ *n* 1 woman's partner in marriage ▷ *v* 2 use economically
▸ **husbandry** *n* 1 farming 2 management of resources
hush Ⓣ *v* 1 make or be silent ▷ *n* 2 stillness or quietness
▸ **hush-hush** *adj informal* secret
▸ **hush up** *v* suppress information about
husk *n* 1 outer covering of certain seeds and fruits ▷ *v* 2 remove the husk from
husky[1] Ⓣ *adj* **huskier, huskiest** 1 hoarse or dry in the throat 2 *informal* big and strong **huskily** *adv*
husky[2] *n, pl* **huskies** Arctic sledge dog with a thick coat and a curled tail
Huss *n* **John**, Czech name *Jan Hus*. ?1372–1415, Bohemian religious reformer. Influenced by Wycliffe, he anticipated the Reformation in denouncing doctrines and abuses of the Church. His death at the stake precipitated the Hussite wars in Bohemia and Moravia
hussar [hoo-**zar**] *n hist* lightly armed cavalry soldier
Hussein *n* 1 Also **Husain** 1935–99, king of Jordan (1952–99) 2 **Saddam**. 1937–2006, Iraqi politician: president (1979–2003) and prime minister (1994–2003) of Iraq. He led Iraq into the Iran-Iraq War (1980–88) and the Gulf War (1991) but was deposed and captured in the US-led invasion of 2003; executed 2006
hussy *n, pl* **-sies** brazen or promiscuous woman
hustings *pl n* proceedings at a parliamentary election
hustle Ⓣ *v* 1 push about, jostle 2 *slang* (of a prostitute) solicit ▷ *n* 3 lively activity or bustle
Huston *n* **John**. 1906–87, US film director. His films include *The Treasure of the Sierra Madre* (1947), for which he won an Oscar, *The African Queen* (1951), *The Man Who Would Be King* (1975), *Prizzi's Honour* (1985), and *The Dead* (1987)
hut Ⓣ *n* small house or shelter
hutch *n* cage for small pet animals
Hutton *n* **James**. 1726–97, Scottish geologist, regarded as the founder of modern geology
Huxley *n* 1 **Aldous** (**Leonard**). 1894–1963, British novelist and essayist, noted particularly for his novel *Brave New World* (1932), depicting a scientifically controlled

THESAURUS

propel, fling, sling, heave, let fly
hurricane *n* = **storm**, tornado, cyclone, twister, tempest, gale, typhoon
hurried *adj* = **hasty**, short, quick, brief, speedy, swift, cursory, perfunctory, rushed
hurriedly *See* **fast, quickly**
hurry *v* 1 = **rush**, fly, dash, scurry, get a move on (*informal*) • *She hurried through the empty streets*. 2 = **speed up**, accelerate, hasten, quicken • *an attempt to hurry the building process* OPPOSITE: slow down ▸ *n* 3 = **rush**, speed, flurry, urgency, haste, quickness
See also: **bustle, race**
hurt *v* 1 = **injure**, wound, harm • *I didn't mean to hurt anyone*. 2 = **upset**, wound, distress, sadden • *What you said really hurt me*. 3 = **ache**, burn, smart, sting, throb, be sore, be tender ▸ *adj* 4 = **upset**, wounded, aggrieved, offended • *He felt hurt by all the lies*. 5 = **injured**, cut, wounded, damaged, bruised, harmed, scarred ▸ *n* 6 = **distress**, pain, suffering, discomfort, soreness, pang
See also: **abuse, damage**
hurtful *adj* = **unkind**, nasty, cruel, destructive, malicious, cutting, damaging, spiteful, upsetting, wounding
hurtle *v* = **rush**, charge, shoot, crash, race, fly, speed, tear, plunge, stampede ▷ **hurtle into** *See* **crash**
husband *n* 1 = **partner**, mate, spouse, better half (*humorous*) ▸ *v* 2 = **economize**, save, store, budget, conserve, hoard
husbandry *n* 1 = **farming**, agriculture, cultivation, tillage 2 = **thrift**, economy, frugality
hush *v* 1 = **quieten**, silence, mute, muzzle, shush ▸ *n* 2 = **quiet**, peace, silence, calm, stillness, tranquillity
hushed *See* **quiet, silent**
hush-hush *adj* = **secret**, confidential, classified, restricted, top-secret, under wraps
husky *adj* 1 = **hoarse**, rough, harsh, raucous, gruff, croaky, guttural, throaty 2 = **muscular**, powerful, hefty, rugged, burly, stocky, strapping, thickset
hustle *v* = **jostle**, force, push, elbow, shove, jog
hut *n* = **shed**, shelter, cabin, tilt (*Canad Nfld*), den, shanty, hovel, lean-to, caboose (*Canad*), fish hut (*Canad*), ice-fishing hut

DICTIONARY

civilization of human robots **2** his half-brother, Sir **Andrew Fielding**. born 1917, English biologist: noted for his research into nerve cells and the mechanism by which nerve impulses are transmitted; Nobel prize for physiology or medicine shared with Alan Hodgkin and John Eccles 1963; president of the Royal Society (1980–85) **3 Thomas Henry**. 1825–95, English biologist, the leading British exponent of Darwin's theory of evolution
hyacinth *n* sweet-smelling spring flower which grows from a bulb
hyaena *n* same as **hyena**
hybrid Ⓣ *n* **1** offspring of two plants or animals of different species **2** anything of mixed ancestry **3** vehicle powered by an internal-combustion engine and another source of power ▷ *adj* **4** of mixed ancestry **5** (of a vehicle) powered by more than one source
hydra *n* **1** mythical many-headed water serpent **2** any persistent problem **3** freshwater polyp
hydrangea *n* ornamental shrub with clusters of pink, blue, or white flowers
hydrant *n* outlet from a water main with a nozzle for a hose
hydrate *n* chemical compound of water with another substance
hydraulic *adj* operated by pressure forced through a pipe by a liquid such as water or oil **hydraulically** *adv*
▸ **hydraulics** *n* study of the mechanical properties of fluids as they apply to practical engineering
hydro *n* **1** hydroelectric power **2** electricity as supplied to residence, business, etc. **3 Hydro** hydroelectric power company
hydro- *combining form* **1** water **2** hydrogen
hydrocarbon *n* compound of hydrogen and carbon
hydrocephalus *n* accumulation of fluid within the cavities of the brain, causing enlargement of the head in children **hydrocephalic** *adj*
hydrochloric acid *n* strong colourless acid used in many industrial and laboratory processes
hydrodynamics *n* science concerned with the mechanical properties of fluids
hydroelectric *adj* of the generation of electricity by the use of water
hydrofoil *n* fast light vessel with its hull raised out of the water on one or more pairs of fins
hydrogen *n* light flammable colourless gaseous element which combines with oxygen to form water
▸ **hydrogen bomb** atom bomb of enormous power in which energy is released by the fusion of hydrogen nuclei to give helium nuclei
▸ **hydrogen peroxide** colourless liquid used as a hair bleach and as an antiseptic
hydrolysis [hie-**drol**-iss-iss] *n* decomposition of a chemical compound reacting with water
hydrometer [hie-**drom**-it-er] *n* device for measuring the relative density of a liquid
hydropathy *n* method of treating disease by the use of large quantities of water both internally and externally
hydrophobia *n* **1** fear of water **2** rabies
hydroplane *n* light motorboat which skims the water
hydroponics *n* science of cultivating plants in water without using soil
hydrotherapy *n med* treatment of certain diseases by exercise in water
hydrous *adj* containing water
hyena, hyaena *n* scavenging doglike mammal of Africa and S Asia
hygiene Ⓣ *n* **1** principles and practice of health and cleanliness **2** study of these principles **hygienic** *adj* **hygienically** *adv*
hymen *n* membrane covering the opening of a girl's vagina, which breaks before puberty or at the first occurrence of sexual intercourse
hymn Ⓣ *n* Christian song of praise sung to God or a saint
▸ **hymnal** *adj* **1** of hymns ▷ *n* **2** Also **hymn book** book of hymns
hype Ⓣ *n* **1** intensive or exaggerated publicity or sales promotion ▷ *v* **2** promote (a product) using intensive or exaggerated publicity
hyper *adj informal* overactive or overexcited
hyper- *prefix* over, above, excessively: *hyperactive; hypercritical*
hyperbola [hie-**per**-bol-a] *n* curve produced when a cone is cut by a plane at a steeper angle to its base than its side
hyperbole [hie-**per**-bol-ee] *n* deliberate exaggeration for effect **hyperbolic** *adj*
hyperlink *n computers* link from a hypertext file giving users instant access

THESAURUS

(*Canad*), ice hut (*Canad*)
hybrid *n* = **crossbreed**, cross, compound, composite, mixture, amalgam, half-breed, mongrel
hygiene *n* = **cleanliness**, sanitation • *Be extra careful about personal hygiene.*
hygienic *adj* = **clean**, healthy, pure, sterile, sanitary, aseptic, disinfected, germ-free
hymn *n* = **anthem**, chant, carol, psalm, paean
hype *n* = **publicity**, promotion, brouhaha,

DICTIONARY

to related material in another file
hypermarket *n* huge self-service store
hypersensitive *adj* unduly vulnerable emotionally or physically
hypersonic *adj* having a speed of at least five times the speed of sound
hypertension *n* abnormally high blood pressure
hyperventilation *n* increase in the rate of breathing, sometimes resulting in cramp and dizziness **hyperventilate** *v*
hyphen *n* punctuation mark (-) indicating that two words or syllables are connected
▸ **hyphenate** *v* join with a hyphen **hyphenation** *n*
▸ **hyphenated** *adj* having two words or syllables joined by a hyphen
hypnosis *n* artificially induced state of relaxation in which the mind is more than usually receptive to suggestion **hypnotism** *n* **hypnotist** *n*
▸ **hypnotic** *adj* of or (as if) producing hypnosis
▸ **hypnotize** *v* induce hypnosis in (someone)
hypo- *prefix* below, less than: *hypocrite; hypodermic*
hypoallergenic *adj* (of cosmetics) not likely to cause an allergic reaction
hypochondria *n* undue preoccupation with one's health **hypochondriac** *n*
hypocrisy Ⓣ [hip-**ok**-rass-ee] *n, pl* **-sies** (instance of) pretence of having standards or beliefs that are contrary to one's real character or actual behaviour
▸ **hypocrite** [**hip**-oh-krit] *n* person who pretends to be what he or she is not **hypocritical** *adj* **hypocritically** *adv*
hypodermic *adj, n* (denoting) a syringe or needle used to inject a drug beneath the skin
hypotension *n* abnormally low blood pressure
hypotenuse [hie-**pot**-a-news] *n* side of a right-angled triangle opposite the right angle
hypothermia *n* condition in which a person's body temperature is reduced to a dangerously low level
hypothesis Ⓣ [hie-**poth**-iss-iss] *n, pl* **-ses** [-seez] suggested but unproved explanation of something
▸ **hypothetical** *adj* based on assumption rather than fact or reality **hypothetically** *adv*
hysterectomy *n, pl* **-mies** surgical removal of the womb
hysteria Ⓣ *n* state of uncontrolled excitement, anger, or panic **hysterical** *adj* **hysterically** *adv*
▸ **hysterics** *pl n* attack of hysteria
Hz hertz

THESAURUS

ballyhoo (*informal*), plugging (*informal*), razzmatazz (*slang*)
hypnotic *adj* = **mesmerizing**, soothing, mesmeric, sleep-inducing, soporific, spellbinding
hypnotize *v* = **put in a trance**, put to sleep • *She said he would be hypnotized at the count of three.*
hypocrisy *n* = **insincerity**, cant, deception, pretense, deceitfulness, duplicity
hypocrite *n* = **fraud**, phony (*informal*), impostor, pretender, deceiver, charlatan
hypocritical *adj* = **insincere**, false, fraudulent, phony (*informal*), deceitful, canting, duplicitous, sanctimonious, two-faced
hypothesis *n* = **theory**, assumption, premise, proposition, thesis, postulate, supposition
hypothetical *adj* = **theoretical**, academic, speculative, imaginary, assumed, supposed, conjectural, putative
hysteria *n* = **frenzy**, panic, madness, agitation, delirium, hysterics
hysterical *adj* **1** = **frenzied**, frantic, raving, overwrought • *Calm down! Don't become hysterical.* **2** (*Informal*) = **hilarious**, comical • *His stand-up routine was hysterical.*

I *pron* used by a speaker or writer to refer to himself or herself as the subject of a verb
iambic *adj* (of poetry) written in metrical units formed of one long and one short syllable
IBA Independent Broadcasting Authority
Iberian *adj* of Iberia, the peninsula of Spain and Portugal
Ibert *n* **Jacques** (**François Antoine**). 1890–1962, French composer; his works include the humorous orchestral *Divertissement* (1930)
ibex [**ibe**-eks] *n* wild goat with large backward-curving horns
ibid. (referring to a book, passage, etc. previously cited) in the same place
ibis [**ibe**-iss] *n* wading bird with long legs
ibn-al-Arabi *n* **Muhyi-l-din.** 1165–1240, Muslim mystic and poet, born in Spain, noted for his influence on Sufism
ibn-Saud *n* **Abdul-Aziz.** 1880–1953, first king of Saudi Arabia (1932–53)
Ibsen *n* **Henrik.** 1828–1906, Norwegian dramatist and poet. After his early verse plays *Brand* (1866) and *Peer Gynt* (1867), he began the series of social dramas in prose, including *A Doll's House* (1879), *Ghosts* (1881), and *The Wild Duck* (1886), which have had a profound influence on modern drama. His later plays, such as *Hedda Gabler* (1890) and *The Master Builder* (1892), are more symbolic
ICBM intercontinental ballistic missile
ice *n* **1** frozen water **2** *Brit* portion of ice cream ▷ *v* **3** become covered with ice **4** cover with icing **5** cool with ice
▸ **break the ice** create a relaxed atmosphere, esp. between people meeting for the first time
▸ **iced** *adj* **1** served very cold **2** covered with icing
▸ **icy** *adj* **1** very cold **2** covered with ice **3** aloof and unfriendly **icily** *adv* **iciness** *n*
▸ **ice age** period when much of the earth's surface was covered in glaciers
▸ **iceberg** *n* large floating mass of ice
▸ **ice bridge** road of ice across a frozen watercourse or harbour
▸ **ice cap** mass of ice permanently covering an area
▸ **ice cream** sweet creamy frozen food
▸ **ice cube** small square block of ice added to a drink to cool it
▸ **ice floe** sheet of floating ice
▸ **ice hockey** *esp. Brit* hockey
▸ **ice lolly** flavoured ice on a stick
▸ **ice pick** axe-like tool for breaking ice
▸ **ice skate** boot with a steel blade fixed to the sole, to enable the wearer to glide over ice
ice-skate *v* **ice-skater** *n*
Icelandic *adj* **1** of Iceland, its people, or their language ▷ *n* **2** official language of Iceland
ichthyology [ik-thi-**ol**-a-jee] *n* scientific study of fish
ICI Imperial Chemical Industries
icicle *n* tapering spike of ice hanging where water has dripped
icing *n* mixture of sugar and water etc. used to cover and decorate cakes
▸ **icing sugar** finely ground sugar for making icing
icon *n* **1** picture of Christ or another religious figure, venerated in the Orthodox Church **2** picture on a computer screen representing a computer function that can be activated by moving the cursor over it
iconoclast *n* person who attacks established principles or ideas **iconoclastic** *adj*
Ictinus *n* 5th century BC, Greek architect, who designed the Parthenon with Callicrates
id *n psychoanalysis* the mind's instinctive unconscious energies
ID identification
idea Ⓣ *n* **1** plan or thought formed in the mind **2** thought of something: *the idea horrified her* **3** belief or opinion
ideal Ⓣ *n* **1** conception of something that is

i

THESAURUS

icy *adj* **1 = cold**, bitter, raw, chill, chilly, frosty, ice-cold, freezing, biting **2 = slippery**, glassy, slippy (*informal dialect*) **3 = unfriendly**, cold, distant, frigid, frosty, aloof, unwelcoming
idea *n* **1 = plan**, recommendation, solution, scheme, suggestion • *She said she'd had a brilliant idea.* **2 = opinion**, view, conviction, belief, impression, notion • *old-fashioned ideas about health care* **3 = impression**, hint, guess, suspicion, clue, inkling • *They had no idea where they were.*
See also: **intention, object, thought**
ideal *n* **1 = principle**, value, standard • *Live up*

DICTIONARY

perfect **2** perfect person or thing ▷ *adj* **3** most suitable **4** perfect **ideally** *adv*
▶ **idealism** *n* tendency to seek perfection in everything **idealist** *n* **idealistic** *adj*
▶ **idealize** *v* regard or portray as perfect **idealization** *n*
idem *pron, adj Latin* the same: used to refer to a book, article, etc. already quoted
identical Ⓣ *adj* exactly the same **identically** *adv*
identify Ⓣ *v* **-fying, -fied 1** prove or recognize as being a certain person or thing **2** understand and sympathize with a person or group because one regards oneself as being similar or similarly situated **3** treat as being the same **identifiable** *adj* **identification** *n*
Identikit *n* ® set of pictures of parts of faces that can be built up to form a likeness of a person wanted by the police
identity Ⓣ *n, pl* **-ties 1** state of being a specified person or thing **2** individuality or personality **3** state of being the same
▶ **identity theft** crime of fraudulently setting up and using bank accounts and credit facilities in another person's name
ideogram, ideograph *n* picture, symbol, etc. representing an object rather than the sounds of its name
ideology Ⓣ *n, pl* **-gies** body of ideas and beliefs of a group, nation, etc. **ideological** *adj* **ideologist** *n*
ides *n* the 15th of March, May, July and Oct. and the 13th of other months of the Ancient Roman calendar
idiocy Ⓣ *n, pl* **-cies** utter stupidity
idiom Ⓣ *n* **1** group of words which when used together have a different meaning from the component words: *raining cats and dogs* **2** way of expression natural or peculiar to a language or group **idiomatic** *adj* **idiomatically** *adv*
idiosyncrasy Ⓣ *n, pl* **-sies** personal peculiarity of mind, habit, or behaviour
idiot Ⓣ *n* **1** foolish person **2** mentally retarded person
▶ **idiotic** *adj* utterly stupid **idiotically** *adv*
idle Ⓣ *adj* **1** not doing anything **2** not being used **3** lazy **4** useless: *idle thoughts* ▷ *v* **5** (esp. foll. by *away*) waste (time) **6** (of an engine) run slowly with the gears disengaged **idleness** *n* **idler** *n* **idly** *adv*

THESAURUS

to your ideals. **2 = model**, standard, example, epitome, paragon • *That rose is the ideal of beauty.* ▶ *adj* **3 = perfect**, complete, model, classic, supreme, consummate • *the ideal person for the job*
See also: **cause, vision**
idealist *n* = **romantic**, visionary, dreamer, Utopian
idealistic *adj* = **perfectionist**, optimistic, romantic, visionary, impracticable, starry-eyed, Utopian
idealize *v* = **romanticize**, worship, glorify, magnify, exalt, apotheosize, ennoble, put on a pedestal
ideally *adv* = **in a perfect world**, all things being equal, if one had one's way
ideals *See* **standards**
identical *adj* = **alike**, twin, duplicate, interchangeable, indistinguishable, matching
identification *n* **1 = recognition**, naming, pinpointing **2 = understanding**, connection, relationship, association, involvement, sympathy, empathy, rapport, fellow feeling
identify *v* = **recognize**, name, place, label, diagnose, pinpoint • *I tried to identify the perfume.* ▷ **identify with = relate to**, associate with, empathize with, feel for, respond to • *I can't identify with the characters in the play.*
See also: **associate**
identity *n* **1 = existence**, personality, self, individuality **2 = sameness**, unity, correspondence
ideology *See* **belief**
idiocy *n* = **foolishness**, insanity, lunacy, asininity, fatuousness, imbecility, inanity, senselessness
idiom *n* **1 = phrase**, expression, turn of phrase **2 = language**, style, jargon, parlance, vernacular
idiosyncrasy *n* = **peculiarity**, trick, oddity, characteristic, quirk, mannerism, eccentricity
idiosyncratic *See* **individual**
idiot *n* = **fool**, moron, imbecile, oaf, twit (*informal*), mouth-breather (*slang*), ding-a-ling (*slang*) • *You're an idiot!*
idiotic *adj* = **foolish**, crazy, stupid, senseless • *an idiotic thing to do*
See also: **silly, unwise**
idle *adj* **1 = inactive**, jobless, unemployed • *idle, wealthy people* OPPOSITE: busy **2 = lazy**, sluggish, lackadaisical, good-for-nothing, indolent, shiftless, slothful **3 = useless**, ineffective, unsuccessful, pointless, vain, worthless, futile, fruitless, groundless, unavailing ▶ *v* **4** (often with *away*) **= laze**, lounge, putter, dawdle, loaf, loiter, dally, kill time
See also: **rest**
idleness *n* **1 = inactivity**, unemployment, leisure, inaction, time on one's hands **2 = laziness**, sluggishness, sloth, inertia, shiftlessness, torpor

DICTIONARY

idol Ⓣ [**ide**-ol] *n* **1** image of a god as an object of worship **2** object of excessive devotion
▸ **idolatry** [ide-**ol**-a-tree] *n* **1** worship of idols **2** excessive devotion or reverence **idolater** *n* **idolatrous** *adj*
▸ **idolize** *v* love or admire excessively
idyll [**id**-ill] *n* **1** scene or time of peace and happiness **2** description in literature of a picturesque or charming scene or episode, esp. of country life **idyllic** *adj* **idyllically** *adv*
i.e. that is to say
if Ⓣ *conj* **1** on the condition or supposition that **2** whether **3** even though ▷ *n* **4** uncertainty or doubt: *I won't have any ifs or buts*
▸ **iffy** *adj informal* doubtful, uncertain
igloo *n, pl* **-loos** dome-shaped Inuit house of snow and ice
Ignatieff *n* **Michael** (**Grant**). born 1947, Canadian writer, academic, broadcaster, and Liberal politician. Leader of the Canadian Liberal Party from 2008
Ignatius Loyola *n* **Saint**. 1491–1556, Spanish ecclesiastic. He founded the Society of Jesus (1534) and was its first general (1541–56). His *Spiritual Exercises* (1548) remains the basic manual for the training of Jesuits. Feast day: July 31
igneous [**ig**-nee-uss] *adj* (of rocks) formed as molten rock cools and hardens
ignite Ⓣ *v* catch fire or set fire to
▸ **ignition** *n* **1** system that ignites the fuel-air mixture to start an engine **2** igniting
ignoble *adj* dishonourable **ignobly** *adv*
ignominy Ⓣ [**ig**-nom-in-ee] *n* humiliating disgrace **ignominious** *adj* **ignominiously** *adv*
ignoramus Ⓣ *n, pl* **-muses** ignorant person
ignorance Ⓣ *n* lack of knowledge
▸ **ignorant** *adj* **1** lacking knowledge **2** rude through lack of knowledge of good manners **ignorantly** *adv*
ignore Ⓣ *v* refuse to notice, disregard deliberately
iguana *n* large tropical American lizard
ileum *n* lower part of the small intestine **ileac** *adj*
ilium *n, pl* **-ia** uppermost and widest of the three sections of the hipbone **iliac** *adj*
ilk *n* **of that ilk** of the same type
ill Ⓣ *adj* **1** not in good health **2** bad, evil **3** unfavourable: *an ill omen* ▷ *n* **4** evil, harm ▷ *adv* **5** badly **6** hardly, with difficulty: *I can ill afford the expense* **illness** *n*
▸ **ill at ease** uncomfortable, unable to relax
▸ **ill-advised** *adj* **1** badly thought out **2** unwise
▸ **ill-disposed** *adj* (often foll. by *towards*) unfriendly or unsympathetic
▸ **ill-fated** *adj* doomed or unlucky
▸ **ill-gotten** *adj* obtained dishonestly
▸ **ill-health** *n* condition of being unwell
▸ **ill-mannered** *adj* rude
▸ **ill-treat** *v* treat cruelly
▸ **ill will** unkind feeling, hostility

i

THESAURUS

idol *n* **1 = graven image**, god, deity **2 = hero**, pet, beloved, favorite, darling, pin-up (*slang*)
idolatry *n* **= adoration**, glorification, adulation, exaltation
idolize *v* **= worship**, love, revere, glorify, adore, venerate, exalt, dote upon, hero-worship, look up to
idyllic *adj* **= idealized**, ideal, charming, picturesque, heavenly, unspoiled, halcyon
if *conj* **= provided**, providing, assuming, on condition that, supposing
ignite *v* **1 = catch fire**, burn, inflame, burst into flames, flare up, take fire **2 = set fire to**, light, torch, kindle, set alight
ignominious *adj* **= humiliating**, sorry, disgraceful, shameful, undignified, discreditable, dishonourable, indecorous, inglorious
ignominy *n* **= disgrace**, shame, stigma, humiliation, discredit, disrepute, infamy, dishonour, obloquy
ignoramus *See* **fool**
ignorance *n* **= unawareness**, innocence, inexperience, unconsciousness, unfamiliarity
ignorant *adj* **1 = unaware**, innocent, unconscious, inexperienced, oblivious • *He was completely ignorant of the rules.* **2 = naive**, green, unaware • *People are afraid to appear ignorant.* **3 = uneducated**, illiterate **4 = insensitive**, rude, crass, half-baked (*informal*)
ignore *v* **= disregard**, discount, overlook, neglect • *Her cousin ignored her.*
See also: **exclude**
ill *adj* **1 = unwell**, sick, ailing, unhealthy, queasy • *She was seriously ill with pneumonia.* OPPOSITE: healthy **2 = harmful**, bad, foul, evil, unfortunate, detrimental, deleterious, injurious, damaging ▷ **ill at ease** *See* **uncomfortable** ▷ **ill will = hostility**, hatred, venom, dislike, resentment, animosity, enmity, malice, bad blood, rancour ▸ *n* **3 = harm**, injury, hurt, trouble, woe, misery, hardship, misfortune, affliction, unpleasantness ▸ *adv* **4 = badly**, unfortunately, poorly, inauspiciously, unfavourably, unluckily **5 = hardly**, barely, scantily, by no means
ill-advised *adj* **= misguided**, reckless, rash, foolhardy, unwise, imprudent, thoughtless, ill-considered, ill-judged, incautious,

DICTIONARY

illegal Ⓣ *adj* against the law **illegally** *adv* **illegality** *n*
illegible Ⓣ *adj* unable to be read or deciphered
illegitimate Ⓣ *adj* **1** born to parents not married to each other **2** unlawful **illegitimacy** *n*
illiberal *adj* **1** narrow-minded or intolerant **2** not generous, mean **illiberality** *n*
illicit Ⓣ *adj* **1** illegal **2** forbidden or disapproved of by society
illiterate Ⓣ *adj* **1** unable to read or write **2** uneducated, ignorant **illiteracy** *n*
illogical Ⓣ *adj* **1** unreasonable **2** not logical **illogicality** *n*
illuminate Ⓣ *v* **1** light up **2** make clear, explain **3** decorate with lights **4** *hist* decorate (a manuscript) with designs of gold and bright colours. **illumination** *n*
▸ **illuminating** *adj* helping to explain
illusion Ⓣ *n* deceptive appearance or belief
▸ **illusionist** *n* conjurer
▸ **illusory** *adj* false
illustrate Ⓣ *v* **1** explain by use of examples **2** provide (a book or text) with pictures **3** be an example of **illustrative** *adj* **illustrator** *n*
▸ **illustration** *n* **1** picture or diagram **2** example
illustrious Ⓣ *adj* famous and distinguished
IM instant messaging: communication between two or more people in real time through the transmission of electronic messages over a computer network
image Ⓣ *n* **1** mental picture of someone or something **2** impression people have of a politician, organization, etc. **3** simile or metaphor **4** representation of a person or thing in art or literature **5** optical counterpart, as in a mirror **6** double, copy ▹ *v* **7** make an image of **8** reflect
▸ **imagery** *n* images collectively, esp. in literature

THESAURUS

injudicious, misguided
ill-disposed *adj* = **unfriendly**, hostile, antagonistic, disobliging, inimical, uncooperative, unwelcoming
illegal *adj* = **unlawful**, criminal, illicit, outlawed, banned, prohibited • *an illegal organization* OPPOSITE: legal
See also: **crooked, wrong**
illegality *n* = **crime**, wrong, felony, lawlessness, illegitimacy
illegible *adj* = **indecipherable**, obscure, scrawled, unreadable
illegitimate *adj* **1** = **unlawful**, illegal, unauthorized, illicit, improper **2** = **born out of wedlock**, bastard
ill-fated *adj* = **doomed**, unfortunate, hapless, unhappy, unlucky, ill-omened, ill-starred, luckless, star-crossed
ill-fitting *See* **uncomfortable**
illicit *adj* **1** = **illegal**, criminal, unauthorized, unlawful, unlicensed, illegitimate, felonious, prohibited **2** = **forbidden**, guilty, improper, clandestine, immoral, furtive
illiterate *adj* = **uneducated**, ignorant, uncultured, untaught, untutored
ill-mannered *adj* = **rude**, boorish, badly behaved, churlish, discourteous, impolite, insolent, loutish, uncouth
illness *n* = **sickness**, disease, complaint, disorder, ailment • *a mystery illness*
illogical *adj* = **irrational**, inconsistent, unreasonable, absurd, meaningless, senseless, invalid, unscientific, unsound
ill-treat *v* = **abuse**, damage, injure, harm, misuse, mishandle, oppress, maltreat
ill-treatment *See* **abuse**
illuminate *v* **1** = **light up**, brighten **2** = **explain**, clarify, interpret, enlighten, clear up, elucidate, make clear, shed light on
illuminating *adj* = **informative**, helpful, revealing, instructive, explanatory, enlightening
illumination *n* **1** = **light**, brightness, lighting, radiance **2** = **enlightenment**, revelation, insight, clarification
illusion *n* **1** = **hallucination**, semblance, mirage • *Artists create the illusion of space.* **2** = **delusion**, fancy, misconception, fallacy • *Their hopes proved to be an illusion.*
See also: **vision**
illusory *adj* = **unreal**, false, mistaken, sham, deceptive, chimerical, delusive, fallacious, hallucinatory
illustrate *v* = **demonstrate**, show, explain, emphasize, bring home, elucidate, point up
illustrated *adj* = **pictorial**, graphic, decorated
illustration *n* **1** = **example**, case, instance, specimen **2** = **picture**, figure, plate, sketch, decoration
illustrative *See* **representative**
illustrious *adj* = **famous**, great, prominent, renowned, notable, celebrated, glorious, distinguished, eminent
image *n* **1** = **representation**, figure, picture, icon, portrait, statue, idol, likeness, avatar, effigy **2** = **replica**, double, counterpart, ringer *or* dead ringer (*slang*), facsimile, Doppelgänger, spitting image (*informal*) **3** = **concept**, idea, perception, impression, mental picture
imaginable *adj* = **possible**, likely, credible, plausible, conceivable, believable,

DICTIONARY

imagine Ⓣ *v* **1** form a mental image of **2** think, believe, or guess **imaginable** *adj*
▸ **imaginary** *adj* existing only in the imagination
▸ **imagination** *n* **1** ability to make mental images of things not present **2** creative mental ability **imaginative** *adj* **imaginatively** *adv*
imago [im-**may**-go] *n, pl* **imagoes, imagines** [im-**maj**-in-ees] sexually mature adult insect
imam *n* **1** leader of prayers in a mosque **2** title of some Islamic leaders
IMAX ® [**eye**-max] *n* film projection process which produces an image ten times larger than standard
imbalance *n* lack of proportion
imbecile Ⓣ [**imb**-ess-eel] *n* **1** idiot ▹ *adj* **2** idiotic **imbecility** *n*
imbibe Ⓣ *v* **1** drink (esp. alcohol) **2** *lit* absorb (ideas etc.)
imbroglio Ⓣ [imb-**role**-ee-oh] *n, pl* **-ios** confusing and complicated situation
imbue *v* **-buing, -bued** (usu. foll. by *with*) fill or inspire with (ideals or principles)
IMF International Monetary Fund
Imhotep *n* c. 2600 BC, Egyptian physician and architect. After his death he was worshipped as a god; the Greeks identified him with Asclepius
imitate Ⓣ *v* **1** take as a model **2** mimic or copy **imitator** *n*
▸ **imitation** *n* **1** copy of an original **2** imitating **imitative** *adj*
immaculate Ⓣ *adj* **1** completely clean or tidy **2** completely flawless **immaculately** *adv*
immanent *adj* present within and throughout something **immanence** *n*
immaterial Ⓣ *adj* not important, not relevant
immature Ⓣ *adj* **1** not fully developed **2** lacking wisdom or stability because of youth **immaturity** *n*
immeasurable *adj* incapable of being measured, limitless **immeasurably** *adv*
immediate Ⓣ *adj* **1** occurring at once **2** next or nearest in time, space, or relationship **immediately** *adv* **immediacy** *n*

THESAURUS

comprehensible, tenable
imaginary *adj* = **fictional**, ideal, hypothetical, fictitious, mythological, illusory, invented • *an imaginary friend* OPPOSITE: real
imagination *n* **1** = **creativity**, vision, ingenuity, originality, inventiveness • *a student who lacks imagination* **2** = **unreality**, illusion, supposition
See also: **mind**
imaginative *adj* = **creative**, original, inspired, clever, ingenious, inventive, enterprising
imagine *v* **1** = **envisage**, picture, conceive, visualize, fantasize, ideate • *He could not imagine a more peaceful scene.* **2** = **believe**, suspect, gather, suppose, guess (*informal*), assume • *I imagine you're talking about my brother.*
See also: **expect, think**
imbecile *n* **1** = **idiot**, fool, moron, chump, cretin (*offensive*), dork (*slang*), halfwit, schmuck (*slang*), thickhead ▸ *adj* **2** = **stupid**, thick, foolish, idiotic, moronic, asinine, fatuous, feeble-minded, witless
imbibe *v* **1** = **drink**, sink (*informal*), consume, swallow, swig (*informal*), quaff, knock back (*informal*) **2** (*Lit*) = **absorb**, receive, gain, acquire, gather, ingest, assimilate, take in
imbroglio *n* = **complication**, involvement, embarrassment, misunderstanding, quandary, entanglement
imitate *v* = **copy**, mimic, ape, simulate, emulate, impersonate • *She imitated her parents.*
imitation *n* **1** = **mimicry**, simulation, duplication, likeness, resemblance, counterfeiting **2** = **replica**, fake, impression, reproduction, forgery, sham, substitution, impersonation ▸ *adj* **3** = **artificial**, synthetic, mock, reproduction, phony (*informal*), dummy, sham, man-made, simulated, ersatz
imitative *adj* = **derivative**, second-hand, copycat (*informal*), simulated, mimetic, parrot-like, unoriginal
imitator *n* = **impersonator**, mimic, impressionist, parrot, copycat (*informal*), copier
immaculate *adj* **1** = **clean**, neat, spruce, spotless, spick-and-span, squeaky-clean **2** = **flawless**, perfect, impeccable, unblemished, above reproach, faultless, unexceptionable, untarnished
immaterial *adj* = **irrelevant**, insignificant, trivial, unimportant, inconsequential, extraneous, inessential, of no importance
immature *adj* **1** = **young**, adolescent, undeveloped, unripe, unformed **2** = **childish**, juvenile, inexperienced, callow, infantile, puerile
immaturity *n* **1** = **unripeness**, imperfection, greenness, rawness, unpreparedness **2** = **childishness**, inexperience, callowness, puerility
immediate *adj* **1** = **instant**, instantaneous • *My immediate reaction was fear.* **2** = **nearest**, close, near, direct • *my immediate family*
See also: **prompt, urgent**
immediately *adv* **1** = **at once**, now, directly, promptly, instantly, straightaway, right away • *She answered my email immediately.* **2** = **right**,

DICTIONARY

immemorial *adj* having existed or happened for longer than anyone can remember **immemorially** *adv*
immense Ⓣ *adj* huge or vast **immensely** *adv* **immensity** *n*
immerse Ⓣ *v* **1** plunge (something) into liquid **2** involve deeply: *I immersed myself in my work*
▸ **immersion** *n* immersing
▸ **immersion heater** *or* **immerser** *n* electric heater contained in a domestic hot-water tank
immigrant Ⓣ *n* person who comes to a foreign country in order to settle there
immigrate *v* come to a foreign country in order to settle there **immigration** *n*
imminent Ⓣ *adj* about to happen **imminently** *adv* **imminence** *n*
immobile Ⓣ *adj* **1** unable to move **2** not moving **immobility** *n*
▸ **immobilize** *v* make unable to move or work
immoderate Ⓣ *adj* excessive or unreasonable
immodest *adj* **1** behaving in an indecent or improper manner **2** behaving in a boastful or conceited manner **immodesty** *n*
immolate *v* kill as a sacrifice **immolation** *n*
immoral Ⓣ *adj* **1** morally wrong, corrupt **2** sexually depraved or promiscuous **immorality** *n*
immortal Ⓣ *adj* **1** living forever **2** famed for all time ▹ *n* **3** immortal being **4** person whose fame will last for all time **immortality** *n* **immortalize** *v*
immovable, immoveable Ⓣ *adj* **1** unable to be moved **2** unwilling to change one's opinions or beliefs **3** not affected by feeling, emotionless **immovability** *or* **immoveability** *n*
immune Ⓣ *adj* **1** protected against a specific disease **2** secure (against) **3** exempt (from)
▸ **immunity** *n* **1** ability to resist disease **2** freedom from prosecution, tax, etc.
▸ **immunize** *v* make immune to a disease **immunization** *n*
immunodeficiency *n* deficiency in or breakdown of a person's immune system
immunology *n* study of immunity **immunological** *adj* **immunologist** *n*
immure *v lit* imprison
immutable [im-**mute**-a-bl] *adj* unchangeable **immutability** *n*
imp Ⓣ *n* **1** demon **2** mischievous child
impact Ⓣ *n* **1** strong effect **2** collision ▹ *v*

THESAURUS

directly, closely • *immediately behind the house*
immense *adj* = **huge**, giant, massive, vast, enormous, gigantic, colossal • *an immense cloud of smoke* OPPOSITE: tiny
See also: **large**
immensity *n* = **size**, extent, bulk, magnitude, greatness, expanse, enormity, vastness, hugeness
immerse *v* **1** = **plunge**, duck, sink, dip, dunk, douse, submerge, bathe **2** = **engross**, involve, busy, engage, occupy, absorb, take up
immersed *See* **preoccupied**
immersion *n* **1** = **dipping**, dousing, ducking, dunking, plunging, submerging **2** = **involvement**, concentration, preoccupation, absorption
immigrant *n* = **settler**, newcomer, incomer
imminent *adj* = **coming**, close, near, forthcoming, impending, looming • *my sister's imminent arrival*
immobile *adj* = **stationary**, still, static, rigid, motionless, at a standstill, at rest, fixed, immovable, rooted, stock-still, unmoving
immobility *n* = **stillness**, stability, fixity, inertness, motionlessness, steadiness
immobilize *v* = **paralyze**, stop, halt, freeze, cripple, disable, transfix, bring to a standstill
immoderate *adj* = **excessive**, extreme, exaggerated, unreasonable, unjustified, undue, extravagant, exorbitant, inordinate, over the top (*slang*)
immoral *adj* = **wicked**, bad, wrong, corrupt, unethical, indecent, sinful, debauched, depraved, dissolute, unprincipled
immorality *n* = **wickedness**, wrong, corruption, vice, sin, depravity, debauchery, dissoluteness
immortal *adj* **1** = **eternal**, lasting, perennial, enduring, everlasting, deathless, imperishable, undying ▸ *n* **2** = **god**, goddess (*feminine*) **3** = **hero**, great, genius
immortality *n* **1** = **eternity**, perpetuity, everlasting life **2** = **fame**, celebrity, glory, greatness, renown
immortalize *v* = **commemorate**, celebrate, glorify, exalt
immovable *adj* **1** = **fixed**, set, firm, secure, stable, stationary, stuck, jammed, immutable **2** = **inflexible**, adamant, steadfast, resolute, unyielding, unshakable, obdurate, unwavering
immune *adj* = **unaffected**, free, safe, resistant, exempt, protected • *She seems immune to pressure.*
immunity *n* **1** = **exemption**, release, freedom, licence, amnesty, indemnity, invulnerability **2** = **resistance**, protection, immunization
immunize *v* = **vaccinate**, protect, safeguard, inoculate
imp *n* **1** = **demon**, devil, sprite **2** = **rascal**, rogue, brat, scamp, minx
impact *n* **1** = **collision**, crash, blow,

DICTIONARY

3 press firmly against or into **impaction** *n*
impair Ⓣ *v* weaken or damage **impairment** *n*
▸ **impaired** *adj law* influenced by alcohol while driving a motor vehicle
impala [imp-**ah**-la] *n* southern African antelope
impale *v* pierce with a sharp object **impalement** *n*
impalpable *adj* **1** imperceptible to the touch **2** difficult to understand
impart Ⓣ *v* **1** communicate (information) **2** give: *impart flavour*
impartial Ⓣ *adj* not favouring one side or the other **impartially** *adv* **impartiality** *n*
impassable Ⓣ *adj* (of a road etc.) impossible to travel over or through
impasse Ⓣ [**am**-pass] *n* situation in which progress is impossible
impassible *adj* impassive or unmoved **impassibility** *n*
impassioned Ⓣ *adj* full of emotion
impassive Ⓣ *adj* showing no emotion, calm **impassivity** *n*
impatient Ⓣ *adj* **1** irritable at any delay or difficulty **2** restless to have or do something **impatiently** *adv* **impatience** *n*
impeach Ⓣ *v* charge with a serious crime against the state **impeachment** *n*
impeccable Ⓣ *adj* without fault, excellent **impeccably** *adv*
impecunious Ⓣ *adj* penniless
impedance [imp-**eed**-anss] *n electricity* measure of the opposition to the flow of an alternating current
impede Ⓣ *v* hinder in action or progress
▸ **impediment** *n* something that makes action, speech, or progress difficult
▸ **impedimenta** *pl n* objects impeding progress, esp. baggage or equipment
impel Ⓣ *v* **-pelling**, **-pelled** drive (a person) to do something
impending Ⓣ *adj* (esp. of something bad) about to happen
impenetrable Ⓣ *adj* **1** impossible to get through **2** impossible to understand

THESAURUS

contact, stroke, knock, bump, smash, thump, jolt **2 = effect**, influence, impression, significance, consequences, repercussions ▸ *v* **3 = hit**, strike, crash, clash, crush, collide
impair *v* = **worsen**, reduce, damage, injure, harm, decrease, weaken, undermine, diminish, hinder, blunt, lessen
impaired *adj* = **damaged**, faulty, flawed, defective, imperfect, unsound
impart *v* **1 = communicate**, tell, reveal, relate, disclose, convey, divulge, make known, pass on **2 = give**, accord, grant, afford, lend, yield, bestow, confer
impartial *adj* = **neutral**, just, fair, objective, equitable, unbiased, open-minded, disinterested, even-handed, detached, unprejudiced
impartiality *n* = **neutrality**, equity, fairness, detachment, objectivity, disinterestedness, dispassion, even-handedness, open-mindedness
impassable *adj* = **blocked**, closed, impenetrable, obstructed
impasse *n* = **deadlock**, standoff, standstill, gridlock, stalemate, dead end
impassioned *adj* = **intense**, animated, heated, passionate, fiery, inspired, rousing, fervent, stirring
impassive *adj* = **unemotional**, indifferent, unfazed (*informal*), callous, unmoved, reserved, serene, apathetic, aloof, stoic, unconcerned, dispassionate, stolid, unruffled, emotionless, poker-faced (*informal*), phlegmatic, imperturbable, impassible (*rare*), composed, unexcitable
impatience *n* **1 = haste**, intolerance, impetuosity, rashness **2 = restlessness**, anxiety, agitation, nervousness, eagerness, uneasiness, edginess, fretfulness
impatient *adj* **1 = irritable**, brusque, curt • *You are too impatient with others.* OPPOSITE: patient **2 = eager**, restless • *He was impatient for the play to end.* **3 = hasty**, demanding, hot-tempered, impetuous
impeach *v* = **charge**, accuse, indict, arraign
impeccable *adj* = **faultless**, perfect, flawless, immaculate, unblemished, blameless, irreproachable, unimpeachable
impecunious *adj* = **poor**, broke (*informal*), insolvent, poverty-stricken, destitute, penniless, down and out, down on one's luck (*informal*), indigent
impede *v* = **hinder**, delay, block, disrupt, hamper, obstruct, get in the way • *Fallen rocks are impeding the progress of rescue workers.* *See also*: **handicap, interfere, prevent, restrict**
impediment *n* = **obstacle**, difficulty, barrier, snag, obstruction, hindrance, encumbrance, stumbling block
impel *v* = **force**, drive, push, require, compel, induce, oblige, constrain
impending *adj* = **imminent**, near, upcoming, gathering, forthcoming, looming, approaching, coming, in the pipeline
impenetrable *adj* **1 = solid**, thick, dense, impassable, impervious, impermeable, inviolable **2 = incomprehensible**, mysterious, obscure, enigmatic, arcane,

DICTIONARY

imperative Ⓣ *adj* **1** extremely urgent, vital **2** *grammar* denoting a mood of verbs used in commands ▷ *n* **3** *grammar* imperative mood

imperceptible Ⓣ *adj* too slight or gradual to be noticed **imperceptibly** *adv*

imperfect Ⓣ *adj* **1** having faults or mistakes **2** not complete **3** *grammar* denoting a tense of verbs describing continuous, incomplete, or repeated past actions ▷ *n* **4** *grammar* imperfect tense **imperfection** *n*

imperial Ⓣ *adj* **1** of an empire or emperor **2** majestic **3** denoting weights and measures formerly official in Britain, Canada, and other countries of the Commonwealth ▶ **imperialism** *n* rule by one country over many others **imperialist** *n, adj*

imperil Ⓣ *v* **-illing, -illed** endanger

imperious Ⓣ *adj* used to being obeyed, domineering

impersonal Ⓣ *adj* **1** not influenced by emotion **2** lacking human warmth or personality **3** *grammar* (of a verb) without a personal subject: *it is snowing* **impersonality** *n*

impersonate Ⓣ *v* **1** pretend to be (another person) **2** imitate the mannerisms of (someone) **impersonation** *n* **impersonator** *n*

impertinent Ⓣ *adj* disrespectful or rude **impertinently** *adv* **impertinence** *n*

imperturbable Ⓣ *adj* calm, not excitable **imperturbability** *n*

impervious Ⓣ *adj* **1** not letting (water etc.) through **2** not influenced by (a feeling, argument, etc.)

impetigo [imp-it-**tie**-go] *n* contagious skin disease

impetuous Ⓣ *adj* done or acting without thought, rash. **impetuously** *adv* **impetuosity** *n*

impetus Ⓣ [**imp**-it-uss] *n, pl* **-tuses** **1** impulse **2** force with which a body moves

impinge Ⓣ *v* encroach (upon), affect or restrict

impious Ⓣ [**imp**-ee-uss] *adj* showing a lack of respect or reverence

impish Ⓣ *adj* mischievous

implacable Ⓣ *adj* **1** not to be appeased **2** unyielding **implacably** *adv* **implacability** *n*

implant Ⓣ *v* **1** fix firmly in the mind **2** insert or embed ▷ *n* **3** *med* anything implanted in the body, such as a tissue graft **implantation** *n*

implement Ⓣ *n* **1** tool or instrument

THESAURUS

unfathomable, unintelligible, inscrutable

imperative *adj* = **urgent**, crucial, essential, vital, pressing

imperceptible *adj* = **undetectable**, minute, small, tiny, slight, subtle, faint, microscopic, indiscernible

imperfect *adj* = **flawed**, faulty, damaged, defective, broken • *We live in an imperfect world*. OPPOSITE: perfect

imperfection *n* = **flaw**, weakness, defect, fault, taint, deficiency, shortcoming, blemish, failing, frailty

imperial *adj* = **royal**, sovereign, majestic, regal, princely, kingly, queenly

imperil *v* = **endanger**, risk, expose, jeopardize

imperious *See* **bossy**

impersonal *adj* = **detached**, cold, remote, formal, neutral, aloof • *I found him strangely distant and impersonal*.

impersonate *v* = **imitate**, do (*informal*), mimic, ape, masquerade as, pass oneself off as, pose as (*informal*)

impersonation *n* = **imitation**, impression, caricature, parody, mimicry

impertinence *n* = **rudeness**, front, nerve (*informal*), cheek (*informal*), disrespect, presumption, brazenness, effrontery, impudence, insolence

impertinent *adj* = **rude**, brazen, disrespectful, cheeky (*informal*), presumptuous, impolite, impudent, insolent

imperturbable *adj* = **calm**, cool, serene, unflappable (*informal*), collected, composed, nerveless, self-possessed, unexcitable, unruffled

impervious *adj* **1** = **resistant**, sealed, impassable, impenetrable, impermeable **2** = **unaffected**, immune, untouched, unmoved, invulnerable, proof against

impetuosity *n* = **haste**, impulsiveness, precipitateness, rashness

impetuous *adj* = **rash**, precipitate, hasty, impulsive, unthinking

impetus *n* **1** = **incentive**, push, spur, motivation, stimulus, impulse, catalyst, goad **2** = **force**, power, energy, momentum

impinge *v* **1** = **encroach**, violate, invade, infringe, trespass, obtrude **2** = **affect**, impact, touch, influence, bear upon, have a bearing on, relate to

impious *adj* = **sacrilegious**, wicked, profane, irreverent, blasphemous, sinful, godless, irreligious, ungodly, unholy

impish *adj* = **mischievous**, devilish, puckish, rascally, roguish, sportive, waggish

implacable *adj* = **unyielding**, uncompromising, merciless, inflexible, intractable, pitiless, unbending, unforgiving

implant *v* **1** = **instill**, infuse, inculcate **2** = **insert**, fix, graft

implausible *adj* = **improbable**, suspect, unlikely, incredible, unbelievable, dubious,

DICTIONARY

▷ *v* **2** carry out (instructions etc.)
implementation *n*
implicate ⓣ *v* show to be involved, esp. in a crime
▶ **implication** *n* something implied
implicit ⓣ *adj* **1** expressed indirectly **2** absolute: *implicit belief* **implicitly** *adv*
implode *v* collapse inwards **implosion** *n*
implore ⓣ *v* beg desperately
imply ⓣ *v* **-plying, -plied 1** indicate by hinting, suggest **2** mean
impolite ⓣ *adj* rude, discourteous
impolitic *adj* unwise, ill-advised
imponderable *n, adj* (something) impossible to assess
import ⓣ *v* **1** bring in (goods) from another country ▷ *n* **2** something imported **3** meaning **4** importance **importation** *n*
importer *n*
important ⓣ *adj* **1** of great significance or value **2** famous, powerful **importance** *n*
importunate ⓣ *adj* persistent in making demands
▶ **importune** *v* persist in demands
importunity *n*
impose ⓣ *v* **1** force the acceptance of **2** take unfair advantage of
▶ **imposing** *adj* impressive
▶ **imposition** *n* unreasonable demand, burden
impossible ⓣ *adj* **1** incapable of being done or experienced **2** absurd or unreasonable
impossibly *adv* **impossibility** *n*
impostor ⓣ *n* person who cheats or swindles by pretending to be someone else
impotent ⓣ [**imp**-a-tent] *adj* **1** powerless **2** (of a man) incapable of sexual intercourse
impotence *n* **impotently** *adv*

THESAURUS

far-fetched, flimsy, unconvincing, cock-and-bull (*informal*)
implement *v* **1 = carry out**, complete, effect, perform, realize, execute, enforce, fulfill, bring about ▶ *n* **2 = tool**, device, gadget, instrument, appliance, apparatus, utensil
implicate *v* **= incriminate**, include, involve, associate, embroil, entangle, inculpate
implication *n* **= suggestion**, meaning, significance, presumption, inference, overtone, innuendo
implicit *adj* **1 = implied**, undeclared, tacit, latent, unspoken, inferred, taken for granted, understood **2 = absolute**, firm, full, constant, steadfast, unqualified, fixed, unreserved, wholehearted
implied *adj* **= unspoken**, indirect, undeclared, implicit, suggested, tacit, hinted at, unexpressed, unstated
implore *v* **= beg**, beseech (*lit*), plead with • *"Tell me what to do!" he implored us.*
See also: **ask, plead, press, urge**
imply *v* **1 = hint**, suggest, intimate, signify, insinuate **2 = involve**, mean, indicate, entail, point to, presuppose
impolite *adj* **= bad-mannered**, rude, disrespectful, discourteous, ill-mannered, insolent, loutish, uncouth
impoliteness *n* **= bad manners**, disrespect, boorishness, churlishness, discourtesy, insolence, rudeness
import *v* **1 = bring in**, introduce ▶ *n* **2 = meaning**, sense, intention, implication, drift, significance, thrust, gist **3 = importance**, weight, moment, substance, consequence, magnitude, significance
importance *n* **1 = significance**, concern, interest, value, weight, moment, import, substance, consequence, usefulness **2 = prestige**, status, influence, standing, distinction, prominence, esteem, eminence
important *adj* **1 = significant**, serious, momentous, weighty • *Their puppies are the most important thing to them.* OPPOSITE: unimportant **2 = powerful**, influential, notable, foremost, eminent, leading • *the most important person in the country*
See also: **prominent, special, valuable, vital**
importunate *adj* **= persistent**, urgent, pressing, dogged, demanding, insistent
impose *v* **1 = enforce**, dictate, inflict • *Fines were imposed on the culprits.* **2 = establish**, introduce, fix, institute, levy, decree, ordain ▷ **impose on = take advantage of**, use, abuse • *I should stop imposing on your hospitality.*
See also: **administer, exact**
imposing *adj* **= impressive**, grand, striking, dignified, majestic, stately, commanding
imposition *n* **1 = application**, introduction, levying **2 = intrusion**, liberty, presumption
impossibility *n* **= hopelessness**, inability, impracticability
impossible *adj* **1 = unthinkable**, inconceivable, hopeless, out of the question • *You shouldn't promise impossible things.* OPPOSITE: possible **2 = absurd**, outrageous, unreasonable, ludicrous, preposterous • *We are in an impossible situation.*
impostor, imposter *n* **= impersonator**, fraud, fake, phony (*informal*), sham, trickster, pretender, deceiver, charlatan
impotence *n* **= powerlessness**, weakness, inability, paralysis, incompetence, frailty, helplessness, incapacity, ineffectiveness, feebleness, uselessness
impotent *adj* **= powerless**, weak, ineffective, paralyzed, helpless, frail,

DICTIONARY

impound Ⓣ *v* take legal possession of, confiscate
impoverish Ⓣ *v* make poor or weak **impoverishment** *n*
impracticable Ⓣ *adj* incapable of being put into practice
impractical Ⓣ *adj* not sensible
imprecation *n* curse
impregnable Ⓣ *adj* impossible to break into **impregnability** *n*
impregnate Ⓣ *v* **1** saturate, spread all through **2** make pregnant **impregnation** *n*
impresario *n, pl* **-ios** person who runs theatre performances, concerts, etc.
impress Ⓣ *v* **1** affect strongly, usu. favourably **2** stress or emphasize **3** imprint or stamp
▶ **impression** *n* **1** (strong or favourable) effect **2** vague idea **3** impersonation for entertainment **4** mark made by pressing
▶ **impressionable** *adj* easily influenced
impressionism *n* art style that gives a general effect or mood rather than form or structure **impressionist** *n* **impressionistic** *adj*
impressive Ⓣ *adj* making a strong impression, esp. through size, importance, or quality
imprimatur [imp-rim-**ah**-ter] *n* official approval to print a book
imprint Ⓣ *n* **1** mark made by printing or stamping **2** publisher's name and address on a book ▷ *v* **3** produce (a mark) by printing or stamping
imprison Ⓣ *v* put in prison **imprisonment** *n*
improbable Ⓣ *adj* unlikely **improbability** *n*
improbity *n* dishonesty or wickedness
impromptu Ⓣ *adv, adj* without preparation, improvised
improper Ⓣ *adj* **1** indecent **2** incorrect or irregular **3** (of a fraction) with a numerator larger than the denominator, as in 5/3
impropriety Ⓣ [imp-roe-**pry**-a-tee] *n, pl*

THESAURUS

incompetent, incapable, feeble, incapacitated
impound *See* **seize**
impoverish *v* **1 = bankrupt**, break, ruin, beggar **2 = deplete**, reduce, drain, diminish, exhaust, sap, use up, wear out
impoverished *adj* **= poor**, needy, bankrupt, destitute, impecunious, poverty-stricken, penurious
impracticable *adj* **= unfeasible**, impossible, unworkable, unattainable, out of the question, unachievable
impractical *adj* **1 = unworkable**, wild, impossible, inoperable, unrealistic, impracticable, nonviable **2 = idealistic**, romantic, unrealistic, starry-eyed
imprecise *adj* **= indefinite**, loose, rough, vague, inexact, woolly, hazy, indeterminate, equivocal, ill-defined, inexplicit
impregnable *adj* **= invulnerable**, secure, unbeatable, invincible, unassailable, impenetrable, indestructible, unconquerable
impregnate *v* **1 = saturate**, soak, steep, infuse, permeate, suffuse **2 = make pregnant**, inseminate, fertilize
impress *v* **1 = excite**, move, strike, affect, touch, inspire, stir, make an impression **2 = stress**, fix, emphasize, bring home to, inculcate, instill into **3 = imprint**, mark, print, stamp, engrave, emboss, indent
impression *n* **1 = feeling**, idea, sense, notion, hunch • *your first impressions of high school* **2 = effect**, impact, reaction, influence, feeling **3 = mark**, stamp, outline, dent, hollow, imprint, indentation **4 = imitation**, parody, impersonation ▷ **make an impression = make an impact**, influence, cause a stir • *He certainly made an impression on his teachers.*
impressionable *adj* **= susceptible**, open, vulnerable, sensitive, receptive, gullible • *impressionable minds of children*
impressive *adj* **= grand**, powerful, exciting, awesome, striking, stirring • *an impressive achievement*
See also: **significant, splendid**
imprint *n* **1 = mark**, sign, stamp, impression, indentation ▶ *v* **2 = fix**, print, stamp, impress, engrave, etch
imprison *v* **= jail**, detain, confine, incarcerate, lock up, send to prison • *imprisoned for murder* OPPOSITE: free
imprisoned *adj* **= jailed**, inside (*slang*), captive, behind bars, confined, incarcerated, in jail, locked up, under lock and key
imprisonment *n* **= confinement**, custody, detention, incarceration
improbability *n* **= unlikelihood**, doubt, uncertainty, dubiety
improbable *adj* **= unlikely**, unbelievable, doubtful, dubious, far-fetched, implausible • *improbable stories* OPPOSITE: probable
See also: **incredible**
impromptu *adj* **= spontaneous**, unprepared, unscripted, ad-lib, extemporaneous, improvised, offhand, off the cuff (*informal*), unrehearsed
improper *adj* **1 = indecent**, vulgar, suggestive, unbecoming, untoward, unseemly, risqué, smutty **2 = inappropriate**, unfit, unwarranted, unsuitable, out of place, uncalled-for
impropriety *n* **= indecency**, vulgarity,

DICTIONARY

-**ties** improper behaviour
improve Ⓣ *v* make or become better
improvement *n*
improvident Ⓣ *adj* not planning for future needs **improvidence** *n*
improvise Ⓣ *v* **1** make use of materials at hand **2** make up (a piece of music, speech, etc.) as one goes along **improvisation** *n*
imprudent Ⓣ *adj* rash, heedless, or indiscreet **imprudently** *adv* **imprudence** *n*
impudent Ⓣ *adj* cheeky **impudently** *adv* **impudence** *n*
impugn [imp-**yoon**] *v* call in question, cast doubt on
impulse Ⓣ *n* **1** sudden urge to do something **2** short electrical signal passing along a wire or nerve or through the air
▸ **on impulse** suddenly and without planning
▸ **impulsive** *adj* tending to act without thinking first **impulsively** *adv*
impunity Ⓣ [imp-**yoon**-it-ee] *n* **with impunity** without punishment or unpleasant consequences
impure Ⓣ *adj* **1** having unwanted substances mixed in **2** immoral or obscene **impurity** *n*
impute *v* attribute responsibility to
imputation *n*
in Ⓣ *prep* **1** inside, within **2** during **3** at the end of (a period of time) **4** indicating a state, situation, or manner **5** into ▷ *adv* **6** in or into a particular place **7** at one's home or place of work **8** in office or power **9** in fashion ▷ *adj* **10** fashionable
in. inch(es)
inability Ⓣ *n* lack of means or skill to do something
inaccessible Ⓣ *adj* **1** impossible or very difficult to reach **2** (of a person) unapproachable **inaccessibility** *n*
inaccurate Ⓣ *adj* not correct **inaccuracy** *n*
inaction *n* lack of action, inertia

i

THESAURUS

incongruity, bad taste
improve *v* **1** = **get better**, develop, advance, progress, look up (*informal*) • *The situation has improved since then.* OPPOSITE: worsen **2** = **enhance**, reform, upgrade, upscale, better, ameliorate • *They improved their house over the years.* ▷ **improve on** *See* **top**
See also: **correct, perfect, polish, recover**
improvement *n* = **advance**, development, progress, enhancement, upturn • *dramatic improvements in conditions*
See also: **gain, recovery, reform, rise**
improvident *adj* = **imprudent**, reckless, negligent, careless, spendthrift, wasteful, short-sighted, thoughtless, prodigal, profligate
improvisation *n* **1** = **spontaneity**, invention, ad-libbing, extemporizing **2** = **makeshift**, expedient, ad-lib
improvise *v* **1** = **extemporize**, invent, ad-lib, busk, play it by ear (*informal*), speak off the cuff (*informal*), wing it (*informal*) **2** = **devise**, concoct, contrive, throw together
imprudent *adj* = **unwise**, irresponsible, reckless, rash, careless, ill-advised, foolhardy, ill-considered, ill-judged, injudicious
impudence *n* = **impertinence**, nerve, gall, audacity, chutzpah (*informal*), boldness, insolence • *Have you ever heard such impudence?*
impudent *adj* = **rude**, bold, brazen, audacious, shameless, cheeky (*informal*), presumptuous, impertinent, insolent, pert
impulse *n* = **urge**, wish, feeling, notion, whim, inclination, caprice
impulsive *adj* = **instinctive**, passionate, rash, spontaneous, precipitate, hasty, intuitive, devil-may-care, impetuous
impunity *n* = **immunity**, security, freedom, licence, permission, exemption, liberty, dispensation
impure *adj* **1** = **unrefined**, mixed, adulterated, debased **2** = **contaminated**, tainted, infected, dirty, polluted, defiled **3** = **immoral**, corrupt, obscene, indecent, lewd, lascivious, licentious, unchaste
impurity *n* = **contamination**, infection, pollution, taint, defilement, dirtiness
imputation *n* = **blame**, accusation, slur, censure, slander, reproach, insinuation, aspersion
in *See* **fashionable, trendy** ▷ **in addition** *See* **too** ▷ **in advance** *See* **before, early** ▷ **in charge** *See* **responsible** ▷ **in fact** *See* **really** ▷ **in favour** *See* **popular** ▷ **in keeping** *See* **compatible** ▷ **in part** *See* **partly** ▷ **in sight** *See* **visible** ▷ **in spite of** *See* **despite** ▷ **in the end** *See* **finally** ▷ **in the long run** *See* **finally** ▷ **in the middle of** *See* **among**
inability *n* = **ineptitude**, impotence, incompetence, inadequacy • *an inability to concentrate* OPPOSITE: ability
inaccessible *adj* = **out of reach**, remote, impassable, unattainable, out of the way, unapproachable, unreachable
inaccuracy *n* = **error**, mistake, defect, fault, lapse, erratum
inaccurate *adj* = **incorrect**, out, wrong, faulty, mistaken, unreliable, defective, erroneous, imprecise, unsound
inactive *adj* = **unused**, idle, dormant, unemployed, unoccupied, inoperative
inactivity *n* = **immobility**, unemployment, inaction, hibernation, passivity, dormancy

DICTIONARY

inadequate Ⓣ *adj* **1** not enough **2** not good enough **inadequacy** *n*
inadmissible Ⓣ *adj* not allowable or acceptable
inadvertent Ⓣ *adj* unintentional **inadvertently** *adv*
inalienable *adj* not able to be taken away: *an inalienable right*
inamorata, *masc.* **inamorato** *n, pl* **-s** person with whom one is in love, lover
inane Ⓣ *adj* senseless or silly **inanity** *n*
inanimate Ⓣ *adj* not living
inanition *n* exhaustion or weakness, as from lack of food
inapplicable Ⓣ *adj* not suitable or relevant
inappropriate Ⓣ *adj* not suitable
inapt *adj* **1** not apt or fitting **2** lacking skill **inaptitude** *n*
inarticulate Ⓣ *adj* unable to express oneself clearly or well
inasmuch as *conj* seeing that, because
inattentive Ⓣ *adj* not paying attention
inaudible Ⓣ *adj* not loud enough to be heard **inaudibly** *adv*
inaugurate Ⓣ *v* **1** open or begin the use of, esp. with ceremony **2** formally establish (a new leader) in office **inaugural** *adj* **inauguration** *n*
inauspicious Ⓣ *adj* unlucky, suggesting an unfavourable outcome
inboard *adj* (of a boat's engine) inside the hull
inborn Ⓣ *adj* existing from birth, natural
inbred Ⓣ *adj* **1** produced as a result of inbreeding **2** inborn or ingrained
inbreeding *n* breeding from closely related individuals
inbuilt *adj* present from the start
Inc. (of a company) incorporated
incalculable Ⓣ *adj* impossible to estimate, very great
in camera *adv* in private session
incandescent *adj* **1** glowing with heat **2** (of artificial light) produced by a glowing filament **incandescence** *n*
incantation Ⓣ *n* ritual chanting of magic words or sounds **incantatory** *adj*
incapable Ⓣ *adj* **1** (foll. by *of*) lacking the

THESAURUS

inadequacy *n* **1 = shortage**, poverty, dearth, insufficiency, meagreness, paucity, scantiness **2 = incompetence**, inability, deficiency, incapacity, ineffectiveness **3 = shortcoming**, weakness, defect, failing, imperfection
inadequate *adj* **1 = insufficient**, short, poor, scarce, lacking • *Supplies of medicine are inadequate.* **2 = incompetent**, useless, pathetic, inept, incapable, deficient • *We felt painfully inadequate in the crisis.* OPPOSITE: adequate
See also: **hopeless, meagre, unsatisfactory, weak**
inadmissible *adj* **= unacceptable**, inappropriate, irrelevant, unallowable
inadvertent *See* **accidental**
inadvertently *adv* **= unintentionally**, accidentally, mistakenly, unwittingly, involuntarily, by accident, by mistake
inadvisable *adj* **= unwise**, ill-advised, imprudent, impolitic, inexpedient, injudicious
inane *adj* **= senseless**, empty, stupid, silly, frivolous, futile, mindless, idiotic, fatuous, vacuous
inanimate *adj* **= lifeless**, dead, cold, extinct, defunct, inert
inanity *See* **nonsense, stupidity**
inapplicable *adj* **= irrelevant**, inappropriate, unsuitable
inappropriate *n* **= unsuitable**, unfit, untimely, unseemly, incongruous, improper • *This behaviour is inappropriate.* OPPOSITE: appropriate
inarticulate *adj* **= poorly spoken**, hesitant, faltering, halting
inattention *n* **= neglect**, preoccupation, carelessness, absent-mindedness, daydreaming, inattentiveness, thoughtlessness
inattentive *adj* **= preoccupied**, vague, negligent, careless, dreamy, distracted, unobservant
inaudible *adj* **= indistinct**, low, unheard, mumbling, out of earshot, stifled
inaugural *adj* **= first**, opening, initial, maiden, introductory
inaugurate *v* **1 = launch**, begin, introduce, institute, initiate, commence, get under way, set in motion **2 = invest**, install, induct
inauguration *n* **1 = launch**, opening, institution, initiation, setting up **2 = investiture**, installation, induction
inauspicious *adj* **= unpromising**, bad, unfortunate, ominous, unlucky, discouraging, ill-omened, unfavourable, unpropitious
inborn *adj* **= natural**, native, congenital, inherent, innate, intuitive, ingrained, hereditary, inbred, instinctive
inbred *adj* **= innate**, natural, native, constitutional, inherent, ingrained, deep-seated
incalculable *adj* **= countless**, vast, infinite, untold, limitless, innumerable, boundless, numberless
incantation *n* **= chant**, formula, spell, charm, invocation
incapable *adj* **1 = incompetent**, weak,

DICTIONARY

ability to **2** helpless
incapacitate ⓣ *v* deprive of strength or ability, disable **incapacity** *n*
incarcerate ⓣ *v* imprison **incarceration** *n*
incarnate ⓣ *adj* **1** possessing human form **2** typified: *stupidity incarnate* **incarnation** *n*
▸ **Incarnation** *n Christianity* God's coming to earth in human form as Jesus Christ
incendiary [in-**send**-ee-ya-ree] *adj* **1** (of bombs etc.) designed to cause fires ▹ *n, pl* **-aries 2** bomb designed to cause fires **3** fire raiser or arsonist
incense[1] ⓣ *v* make very angry
incense[2] *n* **1** substance that gives off a sweet perfume when burned **2** its smoke
incentive ⓣ *n* something that encourages effort or action
inception ⓣ *n* beginning
incessant ⓣ *adj* never stopping
incessantly *adv*
incest *n* sexual intercourse between two people too closely related to marry
incestuous *adj*
inch ⓣ *n* **1** unit of length equal to one twelfth of a foot or 2.54 centimetres ▹ *v* **2** move very slowly
inchoate [in-**koe**-ate] *adj* just begun and not yet properly developed
incidence *n* extent or frequency of occurrence
incident ⓣ *n* **1** (memorable) event **2** public disturbance
incidental ⓣ *adj* **1** occurring as a minor part of or accompaniment to something else **2** happening by chance **incidentally** *adv*
▸ **incidental music** background music for a film or play
incinerate ⓣ *v* burn to ashes **incineration** *n*
▸ **incinerator** *n* furnace for burning rubbish
incipient ⓣ *adj* just starting to appear or happen
incise *v* cut into with a sharp tool **incision** *n*
▸ **incisive** *adj* direct and forceful
▸ **incisor** *n* cutting tooth
incite ⓣ *v* stir up or provoke **incitement** *n*

THESAURUS

inadequate, ineffective, unfit, insufficient, lousy (*slang*), inept, feeble, unqualified, inexpert **2 = unable**, helpless, powerless, impotent
incapacitate *v* = **disable**, paralyze, cripple, immobilize, lay up (*informal*), put out of action (*informal*)
incapacitated *adj* = **indisposed**, unfit, *hors de combat* (*French*), immobilized, laid up (*informal*), out of action (*informal*)
incapacity *n* = **inability**, weakness, impotence, inadequacy, ineffectiveness, powerlessness, incapability, incompetency, unfitness
incarcerate *v* = **imprison**, jail, detain, confine, intern, impound, lock up, throw in jail
incarceration *n* = **imprisonment**, detention, confinement, captivity, internment
incarnate *adj* = **personified**, embodied, typified
incarnation *n* = **embodiment**, type, personification, epitome, manifestation
incense *v* = **anger**, rile (*informal*), inflame, irritate, infuriate, enrage, madden, make one's hackles rise
incensed *adj* = **angry**, furious, enraged, irate, fuming, indignant, infuriated, maddened, steamed up (*slang*), up in arms
incentive *n* = **inducement**, motivation, stimulus, encouragement • *the incentive to work*
See also: **reason**
inception *n* = **beginning**, start, birth, origin, opening, dawn, outset, initiation, commencement
incessant *adj* = **constant**, endless, eternal, perpetual, continual, nonstop, unending, interminable, ceaseless, never-ending, twenty-four-seven (*slang*), unceasing
incessantly *adv* = **constantly**, continually, perpetually, nonstop, endlessly, persistently, eternally, ceaselessly, interminably, twenty-four-seven (*slang*)
inch *See* **ease, edge**
incident *n* **1 = event**, circumstance, episode, occasion, occurrence, happening • *Little incidents can shape our lives.* **2 = disturbance**, scene, clash, confrontation, commotion, contretemps
See also: **experience**
incidental *adj* = **secondary**, minor, subsidiary, occasional, subordinate, nonessential, ancillary
incidentally *adv* = **by the way**, by the bye, in passing, parenthetically
incinerate *v* = **burn up**, char, cremate, carbonize, reduce to ashes
incipient *adj* = **beginning**, embryonic, nascent, commencing, developing, inchoate, starting
incision *n* = **cut**, opening, slash, notch, gash, slit
incisive *adj* = **penetrating**, acute, keen, piercing, perspicacious, trenchant
incite *v* = **provoke**, instigate, goad, agitate for, stir up • *Protestors tried to incite a riot.*
See also: **encourage, excite**
incitement *n* = **provocation**, spur, stimulus, encouragement, agitation, impetus, instigation, prompting

DICTIONARY

incivility Ⓣ *n, pl* **-ties** rudeness
inclement Ⓣ *adj* (of weather) bad **inclemency** *n*
incline Ⓣ *v* **1** lean, slope **2** (cause to) have a certain disposition or tendency ▷ *n* **3** slope ▸ **inclination** *n* **1** liking, tendency, or preference **2** slope **3** degree of deviation from the horizontal or vertical
include Ⓣ *v* **1** have as (part of) the contents **2** put in as part of a set or group **inclusion** *n* ▸ **inclusive** *adj* including everything **inclusively** *adv*
incognito Ⓣ [in-kog-**nee**-toe] *adv, adj* **1** under an assumed identity ▷ *n, pl* **-tos 2** false identity
incoherent Ⓣ *adj* (of speech) unclear and impossible to understand **incoherence** *n* **incoherently** *adv*
income Ⓣ *n* amount of money earned from work, investments, etc. ▸ **income tax** personal tax levied on annual income
incoming Ⓣ *adj* **1** about to arrive **2** about to come into office
incommode *v* inconvenience
incommodious *adj* cramped
incommunicado *adj, adv* deprived of communication with other people
incomparable Ⓣ *adj* beyond comparison **incomparably** *adv*
incompatible Ⓣ *adj* inconsistent or conflicting **incompatibility** *n*
incompetent Ⓣ *adj* lacking the necessary ability to do something **incompetence** *n*
inconceivable Ⓣ *adj* impossible to imagine
inconclusive Ⓣ *adj* not giving a final decision or result
incongruous Ⓣ *adj* inappropriate or out of place **incongruously** *adv* **incongruity** *n*

THESAURUS

incivility *n* = **rudeness**, disrespect, bad manners, boorishness, discourteousness, discourtesy, ill-breeding, impoliteness
inclement *adj* = **stormy**, severe, foul, rough, harsh, tempestuous, intemperate
inclination *n* **1** = **tendency**, penchant, disposition, liking, propensity, predisposition, predilection, partiality, proclivity, proneness **2** = **slope**, pitch, grade, angle, tilt, incline, slant, gradient
incline *v* **1** = **predispose**, influence, persuade, sway, prejudice **2** = **slope**, tip, lean, tilt, veer, slant ▷ **incline toward** *See* **prefer** ▸ *n* **3** = **slope**, rise, dip, grade, descent, ascent, gradient
inclined *adj* = **disposed**, likely, willing, prone, liable, apt, given, minded, predisposed
include *v* **1** = **contain**, involve, cover, embrace, incorporate, encompass • *Breakfast always includes pancakes with maple syrup.* OPPOSITE: exclude **2** = **introduce**, add, enter, insert
inclusion *n* = **addition**, insertion, incorporation
inclusive *adj* = **comprehensive**, general, global, blanket, umbrella, across-the-board, all-embracing, sweeping
incognito *adj* = **in disguise**, unknown, unrecognized, disguised, under an assumed name
incoherence *n* = **unintelligibility**, disjointedness, inarticulateness
incoherent *adj* = **unintelligible**, inconsistent, confused, rambling, disjointed, disordered, inarticulate, jumbled, muddled, stammering, stuttering
income *n* = **earnings**, pay, salary, profits, wages • *a two-income family*
incoming *adj* = **arriving**, new, landing, approaching, entering, homeward, returning
incomparable *adj* = **unequalled**, supreme, unparalleled, superlative, unrivalled, inimitable, peerless • *an area of incomparable beauty*
incomparably *See* **far**
incompatible *adj* = **inconsistent**, contradictory, conflicting, incongruous, mismatched, unsuited
incompetence *n* = **ineptitude**, inability, inadequacy, incapacity, ineffectiveness, incapability, unfitness, uselessness
incompetent *adj* = **inept**, unable, useless, incapable, bungling • *You are incompetent, and you know it.* OPPOSITE: competent *See also*: **inadequate, inefficient**
incomplete *adj* = **unfinished**, partial, insufficient, deficient • *an incomplete book* OPPOSITE: complete
incomprehensible *adj* = **unintelligible**, obscure, opaque, unfathomable, impenetrable, baffling, beyond one's grasp, perplexing, puzzling
inconceivable *adj* = **unimaginable**, incredible, unbelievable, unthinkable, incomprehensible, mind-boggling (*informal*), unheard-of, beyond belief, out of the question
inconclusive *adj* = **indecisive**, open, vague, undecided, ambiguous, indeterminate, unconvincing, up in the air (*informal*)
incongruity *n* = **inappropriateness**, conflict, discrepancy, disparity, inconsistency, incompatibility, unsuitability
incongruous *adj* = **inappropriate**, improper, incompatible, unsuitable, unbecoming, discordant, out of keeping, out of place

DICTIONARY

inconsequential *adj* unimportant or irrelevant
inconsiderable Ⓣ *adj* **1** relatively small **2** insignificant
inconsiderate Ⓣ *adj* lacking in care or thought for others, thoughtless
inconsistent Ⓣ *adj* **1** changeable in behaviour or mood **2** containing contradictory elements: *her account of the robbery was inconsistent* **3** not in accordance (with): *actions inconsistent with high office*
inconsistency *n*
inconsolable Ⓣ *adj* impossible to comfort, broken-hearted **inconsolably** *adv*
inconspicuous Ⓣ *adj* not easily noticed or seen **inconspicuously** *adv*
inconstant *adj* liable to change one's loyalties or opinions
incontestable *adj* impossible to deny or argue with
incontinent *adj* not able to control one's bladder or bowels **incontinence** *n*
incontrovertible Ⓣ *adj* impossible to deny or disprove
inconvenience Ⓣ *n* **1** trouble or difficulty ▷ *v* **2** cause trouble or difficulty to
inconvenient *adj*
incorporate Ⓣ *v* include or be included as part of a larger unit **incorporation** *n*
incorporeal *adj* without bodily existence
incorrigible Ⓣ *adj* beyond reform
incorrigibility *n*
incorruptible Ⓣ *adj* **1** impossible to bribe or corrupt, honest **2** not subject to decay
increase Ⓣ *v* **1** make or become greater in size, number, etc. ▷ *n* **2** rise in number, size, etc. **3** amount by which something increases
▸ **increasingly** *adv* more and more
incredible Ⓣ *adj* **1** unbelievable **2** *informal* marvellous, amazing **incredibly** *adv*
incredulous Ⓣ *adj* not willing or able to believe something **incredulity** *n*
increment Ⓣ *n* increase in money or value, esp. a regular salary increase **incremental** *adj*
incriminate Ⓣ *v* make (someone) seem

THESAURUS

inconsiderable *adj* = **insignificant**, small, minor, slight, negligible, trivial, unimportant, inconsequential, trifling
inconsiderate *adj* = **selfish**, rude, insensitive, thoughtless, unkind, indelicate, tactless, unthinking
inconsistency *n* **1** = **incompatibility**, disagreement, discrepancy, disparity, variance, divergence, incongruity **2** = **unreliability**, instability, unsteadiness, unpredictability, fickleness
inconsistent *adj* **1** = **incompatible**, contradictory, irreconcilable, conflicting, incongruous, at odds, discordant, out of step **2** = **changeable**, unpredictable, unstable, variable, erratic, unsteady, fickle, capricious
inconsolable *adj* = **heartbroken**, desolate, brokenhearted, despairing
inconspicuous *adj* = **unobtrusive**, ordinary, plain, insignificant, hidden, unassuming, camouflaged, unnoticeable, unostentatious
incontrovertible *adj* = **indisputable**, sure, positive, certain, established, undeniable, irrefutable, incontestable, indubitable, unquestionable
inconvenience *n* **1** = **trouble**, difficulty, disruption, bother, disturbance, fuss, disadvantage, nuisance, hindrance, awkwardness ▸ *v* **2** = **trouble**, upset, disrupt, disturb, bother, discommode, put out
inconvenient *adj* = **troublesome**, awkward, untimely, unsuitable, bothersome, inopportune, disadvantageous, disturbing
incorporate *v* = **include**, combine, merge, absorb, blend, integrate, assimilate, subsume
incorrect *adj* = **false**, wrong, faulty, inaccurate, mistaken, flawed, untrue, erroneous
incorrigible *adj* = **incurable**, hardened, hopeless, intractable, inveterate, irredeemable, unreformed
incorruptible *adj* **1** = **honest**, straight, upright, trustworthy, above suspicion **2** = **imperishable**, everlasting, undecaying
increase *v* **1** = **grow**, extend, expand, swell, escalate, multiply, augment, enlarge, supersize, step up, turn up • *The population continues to increase.* OPPOSITE: decrease ▸ *n* **2** = **growth**, rise, gain, upsurge, increment • *a pay increase* OPPOSITE: decrease
See also: **addition, build, jump, spread**
increasingly *adv* = **progressively**, more and more
incredible *adj* **1** = **amazing**, extraordinary, sensational, marvellous, astonishing, astounding • *a champion with incredible skill* **2** = **unbelievable**, improbable, absurd, unthinkable, unimaginable, far-fetched • *the incredible stories of some children*
See also: **unlikely, wonderful**
incredulity *n* = **disbelief**, doubt, skepticism, distrust
incredulous *adj* = **disbelieving**, suspicious, skeptical, doubtful, dubious, unconvinced, distrustful, unbelieving
increment *n* = **increase**, gain, addition, supplement, advancement, accrual, enlargement, augmentation, step up
incriminate *v* = **implicate**, charge, accuse,

DICTIONARY

guilty of a crime **incriminating** *adj* **incrimination** *n*

incubate [in-cube-ate] *v* **1** (of birds) hatch eggs by sitting on them **2** grow (bacteria) **3** (of bacteria) remain inactive in an animal or person before causing disease **incubation** *n* ▸**incubator** *n* **1** heated enclosed apparatus for rearing premature babies **2** apparatus for artificially hatching eggs

incubus [in-cube-uss] *n, pl* **-bi, -buses** **1** demon believed to have sex with sleeping women **2** nightmare

inculcate *v* fix in someone's mind by constant repetition **inculcation** *n*

inculpate *v* cause blame to be laid on, incriminate **inculpation** *n*

incumbent Ⓣ *adj* **1 it is incumbent on** it is the duty of ▷ *n* **2** person holding a particular office or position **incumbency** *n*

incur Ⓣ *v* **-curring, -curred** bring (something unpleasant) upon oneself

incurable Ⓣ *adj* not able to be cured **incurably** *adv*

incurious *adj* showing no curiosity or interest

incursion *n* **1** sudden brief invasion **2** inroad

indebted Ⓣ *adj* **1** owing gratitude for help or favours **2** owing money **indebtedness** *n*

indecent Ⓣ *adj* **1** morally or sexually offensive **2** unsuitable or unseemly: *indecent haste* **indecently** *adv* **indecency** *n* ▸**indecent assault** sexual attack which does not include rape ▸**indecent exposure** showing of one's genitals in public

indecipherable Ⓣ *adj* impossible to read

indecisive Ⓣ *adj* unable to make decisions, wavering **indecision** *n*

indeed Ⓣ *adv* **1** really, certainly ▷ *interj* **2** showing surprise, doubt, etc.

indefatigable Ⓣ *adj* never getting tired **indefatigably** *adv*

indefensible Ⓣ *adj* **1** not justifiable **2** unable to be defended **indefensibly** *adv*

indefinable Ⓣ *adj* impossible to be fully described or explained

indefinite Ⓣ *adj* **1** without exact limits: *an indefinite period* **2** vague **indefinitely** *adv* ▸**indefinite article** *grammar* the word *a* or *an*

indelible Ⓣ *adj* **1** impossible to erase or remove **2** producing indelible marks **indelibly** *adv*

indelicate Ⓣ *adj* embarrassing, tasteless **indelicacy** *n*

indemnify Ⓣ *v* **-ifying, -ified** **1** give indemnity to **2** compensate **indemnification** *n*

indemnity Ⓣ *n, pl* **-ties** **1** insurance against loss or damage **2** compensation for loss or damage suffered

indent *v* **1** start (a line of writing) further from the margin than the other lines **2** order (goods) using a special order form ▸**indentation** *n* dent in a surface or edge

indenture *n* contract, esp. one binding an apprentice to his employer

THESAURUS

involve, blame, impeach, inculpate

incumbent *adj* = **obligatory**, necessary, mandatory, binding, compulsory

incur *v* = **earn**, bring *or* bring upon oneself, gain, draw, provoke, arouse, expose oneself to, meet with

incurable *adj* = **fatal**, terminal, inoperable, irremediable

indebted *adj* = **grateful**, beholden, in debt, obligated, obliged, under an obligation

indecency *n* = **obscenity**, pornography, impropriety, vulgarity, immodesty, impurity, indelicacy, lewdness, licentiousness

indecent *adj* **1** = **obscene**, crude, dirty, improper, rude, vulgar, lewd • *indecent lyrics* **2** = **unbecoming**, vulgar, unseemly, in bad taste, indecorous

indecipherable *adj* = **illegible**, indistinguishable, unintelligible, unreadable

indecision *n* = **hesitation**, doubt, dithering, indecisiveness, uncertainty, vacillation, wavering

indecisive *adj* = **hesitating**, tentative, uncertain, undecided, dithering, faltering, in two minds (*informal*), vacillating, wavering

indeed *adv* = **really**, actually, certainly, truly, undoubtedly, in truth

indefatigable *See* **energetic**

indefensible *adj* = **unforgivable**, wrong, inexcusable, untenable, unjustifiable, unpardonable, unwarrantable

indefinable *adj* = **inexpressible**, indescribable, impalpable

indefinite *adj* = **unclear**, uncertain, vague, doubtful, inexact, indeterminate, equivocal, imprecise, ill-defined, unfixed

indefinitely *adv* = **endlessly**, continually, ad infinitum, for ever

indelible *adj* = **permanent**, lasting, enduring, ingrained, indestructible, ineradicable

indelicate *adj* = **offensive**, crude, rude, tasteless, vulgar, coarse, suggestive, embarrassing, immodest, off-colour, risqué

indemnify *v* **1** = **insure**, protect, secure, guarantee, underwrite **2** = **compensate**, repair, reimburse, repay, remunerate

indemnity *n* **1** = **insurance**, security, protection, guarantee **2** = **compensation**, redress, restitution, reimbursement, reparation, remuneration

DICTIONARY

independent ⓣ *adj* **1** free from the control or influence of others **2** separate **3** financially self-reliant **4** capable of acting for oneself or on one's own ▷ *n* **5** politician who does not belong to any party **independently** *adv* **independence** *n*
in-depth *adj* detailed or thorough
indescribable ⓣ *adj* too intense or extreme for words **indescribably** *adv*
indestructible ⓣ *adj* not able to be destroyed
indeterminate ⓣ *adj* uncertain in extent, amount, or nature **indeterminacy** *n*
index ⓣ *n, pl* **indexes**, *math* **indices** [**in**-diss-eez] **1** alphabetical list of names or subjects dealt with in a book **2** file or catalogue used to find things **3** pointer or indicator **4** *math* exponent ▷ *v* **5** provide (a book) with an index **6** enter in an index **7** make index-linked
▸ **index finger** finger next to the thumb
▸ **index-linked** *adj* (of pensions, wages, etc.) rising or falling in line with the cost of living
Indian *n, adj* **1** (person) from India **2** (person) descended from the original inhabitants of the American continents
▸ **Indian summer** period of warm sunny weather in fall
India rubber *n* eraser
indicate ⓣ *v* **1** be a sign or symptom of **2** point out **3** state briefly **4** (of a measuring instrument) show a reading of **indication** *n*
▸ **indicative** [in-**dik**-a-tiv] *adj* **1** suggesting: *clouds indicative of rain* **2** *grammar* denoting a mood of verbs used to make a statement
▸ **indicator** *n* **1** something acting as a sign or indication **2** flashing light on a vehicle showing the driver's intention to turn **3** dial or gauge
indices *n* a plural of **index**
indict ⓣ [in-**dite**] *v* formally accuse of a crime **indictable** *adj* **indictment** *n*
indifferent ⓣ *adj* **1** showing no interest or concern **2** of poor quality or low standard **indifference** *n* **indifferently** *adv*
indigenous [in-**dij**-in-uss] *adj* born in or natural to a country
indigent *adj* so poor as to lack necessities **indigence** *n*
indigestion ⓣ *n* (discomfort or pain caused by) difficulty in digesting food **indigestible** *adj*
indignation ⓣ *n* anger caused by something unfair or wrong
▸ **indignant** *adj* feeling or showing indignation **indignantly** *adv*
indignity ⓣ *n, pl* **-ties** embarrassing or humiliating treatment

THESAURUS

independence *n* = **freedom**, sovereignty, liberty, autonomy, self-sufficiency, self-rule, self-reliance
independent *adj* **1** = **separate**, free, unrelated, liberated • *an independent politician* **2** = **self-sufficient**, liberated, individualistic, unaided • *a fiercely independent woman* **3** = **self-governing**, sovereign, autonomous, nonaligned, self-determining
See also: **individual**
independently *adv* = **separately**, alone, solo, individually, autonomously, by oneself, on one's own, unaided
indescribable *adj* = **beyond description**, beyond words, indefinable, inexpressible, unutterable
indestructible *adj* = **permanent**, lasting, enduring, indelible, immortal, unbreakable, everlasting, imperishable, incorruptible, indissoluble
indeterminate *adj* = **uncertain**, unspecified, vague, indefinite, inexact, undefined, imprecise, unfixed, unstipulated
index *See* **list**
indicate *v* **1** = **show**, reveal, signal, signify, denote • *a gesture that indicates his relief* **2** = **point out**, designate, specify **3** = **register**, show, record, read, express, display
See also: **hint, mean, promise, suggest**
indication *n* = **sign**, warning, signal, hint, suggestion, clue • *She gave no indication that she had heard me.*
See also: **lead, trace**
indicative *adj* = **suggestive**, significant, symptomatic, pointing to
indicator *n* = **sign**, mark, guide, signal, symbol, marker, gauge, meter, pointer
indict *v* = **charge**, accuse, prosecute, arraign, summon, impeach
indictment *n* = **charge**, allegation, prosecution, accusation, summons, impeachment
indifference *n* = **disregard**, negligence, detachment, apathy, inattention, coolness, aloofness, coldness, nonchalance, unconcern
indifferent *adj* **1** = **unconcerned**, cold, cool, callous, unmoved, aloof, impervious, unsympathetic, uninterested, detached, inattentive **2** = **mediocre**, moderate, so-so (*informal*), ordinary, passable, undistinguished
indigestion *n* = **heartburn**, dyspepsia, upset stomach, acid reflux
indignant *adj* = **resentful**, angry, disgruntled, irate, incensed, exasperated, peeved (*informal*), riled, scornful, ticked off (*informal*), up in arms (*informal*)
indignation *n* = **resentment**, anger, rage, scorn, pique, exasperation, umbrage
indignity *n* = **humiliation**, injury, insult,

i

DICTIONARY

indigo *n* **1** deep violet-blue **2** dye of this colour
indirect ⓘ *adj* **1** done or caused by someone or something else **2** not by a straight route
▶ **indirect object** *grammar* person or thing indirectly affected by an action, such as *Sue* in *I bought Sue a book*
▶ **indirect speech** report that gives the content of what someone said but not the actual words
indiscernible *adj* not able or scarcely able to be seen
indiscreet ⓘ *adj* incautious or tactless in revealing secrets **indiscreetly** *adv*
indiscretion *n*
indiscriminate ⓘ *adj* chosen or choosing without thought or care
indispensable ⓘ *adj* impossible to do without
indisposed ⓘ *adj* **1** unwell or ill **2** unwilling
indisposition *n*
indisputable ⓘ *adj* without doubt
indisputably *adv*
indissoluble *adj* permanent
indistinct ⓘ *adj* impossible to be seen or heard clearly
indium *n* soft silver-white metallic element
individual ⓘ *adj* **1** characteristic of or meant for a single person or thing **2** separate or distinct **3** distinctive, unusual ▷ *n* **4** single person or thing
▶ **individually** *adv* singly
▶ **individualism** *n* principle of living one's life in one's own way **individualist** *n*
individualistic *adj*
▶ **individuality** *n* distinctive character or personality
indoctrinate ⓘ *v* teach (someone) to accept a doctrine or belief uncritically
indoctrination *n*
Indo-European *adj, n* (of) a family of languages spoken in most of Europe and much of Asia, including English, Russian, and Hindi
indolent ⓘ *adj* lazy **indolence** *n*
indomitable ⓘ *adj* too strong to be defeated or discouraged **indomitably** *adv*
indoor *adj* inside a building **indoors** *adv*
indubitable ⓘ [in-**dew**-bit-a-bl] *adj* beyond doubt, certain **indubitably** *adv*
induce ⓘ *v* **1** persuade **2** cause **3** *med* bring on (labour) by the use of drugs etc.

THESAURUS

slight, snub, disrespect, affront, dishonour, opprobrium
indirect *adj* **1** = **roundabout**, oblique, rambling, tortuous, meandering, wandering • *an indirect route to school* OPPOSITE: direct **2** = **incidental**, subsidiary, secondary, unintended
indiscreet *adj* = **tactless**, reckless, rash, naive, unwise, imprudent, impolitic, incautious, injudicious
indiscretion *n* = **mistake**, slip, error, gaffe, lapse, folly, foolishness, faux pas
indiscriminate *adj* = **random**, general, wholesale, careless, desultory, uncritical, undiscriminating, unsystematic
indiscriminately *See* **at random**
indispensable *adj* = **essential**, key, necessary, crucial, vital, needed, imperative, requisite
indisposed *adj* = **ill**, ailing, sick, unwell, under the weather
indisposition *n* = **illness**, ailment, sickness, ill health
indisputable *adj* = **undeniable**, certain, irrefutable, incontrovertible, beyond doubt, incontestable, indubitable, unquestionable
indistinct *adj* = **unclear**, vague, faint, fuzzy, hazy, shadowy, indeterminate, undefined, blurred, ill-defined
indistinguishable *See* **same**
individual *adj* **1** = **separate**, single, independent, discrete (*formal*) • *individual servings of pie* **2** = **special**, personal, original, unique, characteristic, distinctive, idiosyncratic • *Develop your own individual writing style.* ▶ *n* **3** = **person**, party, character, soul, human being • *the rights of the individual*
See also: **different, peculiar, private**
individualist *n* = **nonconformist**, independent, original, maverick, loner, freethinker, lone wolf
individualistic *See* **independent**
individuality *n* = **distinctiveness**, character, personality, originality, uniqueness, separateness, singularity
individually *adv* = **separately**, apart, independently, one at a time, one by one, singly
indoctrinate *v* = **train**, school, ground, teach, drill, instruct, initiate, brainwash, imbue
indoctrination *n* = **training**, instruction, schooling, drilling, grounding, brainwashing, inculcation
indolent *adj* = **lazy**, sluggish, idle, listless, inactive, lethargic, inert, languid, slothful, workshy
indomitable *adj* = **invincible**, bold, staunch, unbeatable, unflinching, steadfast, resolute, unyielding, unconquerable
indubitable *adj* = **certain**, sure, obvious, undeniable, indisputable, irrefutable, incontrovertible, incontestable, unquestionable
induce *v* **1** = **persuade**, prompt, encourage, influence, convince, incite, instigate, prevail

DICTIONARY

▸ **inducement** *n* something that encourages someone to do something
induct *v* formally install someone, esp. a cleric, in office
induction *n* **1** reasoning process by which general conclusions are drawn from particular instances **2** process by which electrical or magnetic properties are produced by the proximity of an electrified or magnetic object **3** formal installing of a person into office **inductance** *n* **inductive** *adj*
▸ **induction coil** transformer for producing high voltage from a low voltage
▸ **induction course** training course to help familiarize someone with a new job
indulge Ⓣ *v* **1** allow oneself pleasure: *indulge in daydreaming* **2** allow (someone) to have or do everything he or she wants
▸ **indulgence** *n* **1** something allowed because it gives pleasure **2** act of indulging oneself or someone else **3** favourable or tolerant treatment **indulgent** *adj* **indulgently** *adv*
industrial *adj* of, used in, or employed in industry
▸ **industrialize** *v* develop large-scale industry in (a country or region)
▸ **industrial action** action such as a strike or work-to-rule, by which workers can protest about their conditions
▸ **industrial estate** *Brit* industrial park
▸ **industrial park** area of land set aside for factories and warehouses
▸ **industrial relations** relations between management and workers
industry Ⓣ *n, pl* **-tries 1** manufacture of goods **2** branch of this: *the publishing industry* **3** quality of working hard
▸ **industrious** *adj* hard-working
inebriate *adj, n* habitually drunk (person)
▸ **inebriated** *adj* drunk
▸ **inebriation** *n* drunkenness
inedible *adj* not fit to be eaten
ineffable *adj* too great for words **ineffably** *adv*
ineffectual Ⓣ *adj* having no effect or an inadequate effect
inefficient Ⓣ *adj* unable to perform a task or function to the best advantage **inefficiency** *n*
inelegant *adj* lacking elegance or refinement **inelegance** *n* **inelegantly** *adv*
ineligible Ⓣ *adj* not qualified for or entitled to something
ineluctable *adj* impossible to avoid
inept Ⓣ *adj* clumsy, lacking skill **ineptitude** *n*
inequality Ⓣ *n, pl* **-ties 1** state or quality of being unequal **2** lack of smoothness or regularity of a surface
inequitable Ⓣ *adj* unfair
ineradicable *adj* impossible to remove

THESAURUS

upon, talk into **2 = cause**, produce, effect, generate, occasion, engender, bring about, give rise to, lead to
inducement *n* **= incentive**, reward, lure, carrot (*informal*), attraction, bait, encouragement, incitement
indulge *v* **1 = gratify**, feed, satisfy, give way to, pander to, yield to **2 = spoil**, humour, cosset, give in to, go along with, pamper
indulgence *n* **1 = gratification**, satisfaction, fulfillment, appeasement, satiation **2 = luxury**, treat, privilege, favour, extravagance **3 = tolerance**, understanding, patience, forbearance
indulgent *adj* **= lenient**, liberal, understanding, tolerant, easy-going, kindly, compliant, permissive, forbearing
industrialist *n* **= capitalist**, manufacturer, tycoon, magnate, big businessman, captain of industry
industrious *adj* **= hard-working**, busy, conscientious, diligent, tireless • *industrious students* OPPOSITE: lazy
See also: **active**
industry *n* **1 = business**, trade, production, commerce, manufacturing **2 = effort**, activity, application, labour, diligence, toil, zeal, tirelessness
inebriated *adj* **= drunk**, crocked (*slang*), intoxicated, paralytic (*informal*), plastered (*slang*), three sheets to the wind (*slang*), tipsy, under the influence (*informal*)
ineffective *adj* **= useless**, idle, vain, worthless, inefficient, futile, impotent, fruitless, unproductive, unavailing
ineffectual *adj* **= weak**, inadequate, ineffective, lousy (*slang*), inept, incompetent, feeble, impotent
inefficiency *n* **= incompetence**, muddle, carelessness, disorganization, slackness, sloppiness
inefficient *adj* **= incompetent**, sloppy, inept, incapable, disorganized • *an inefficient retrieval system* OPPOSITE: efficient
ineligible *adj* **= unqualified**, unacceptable, unfit, unsuitable, disqualified, ruled out
inept *adj* **= incompetent**, clumsy, bumbling, bungling, inexpert, maladroit
ineptitude *n* **= incompetence**, clumsiness, inexpertness, unfitness
inequality *n* **= disparity**, difference, irregularity, bias, diversity, prejudice, disproportion, unevenness
inequitable *adj* **= unfair**, partial, partisan, discriminatory, unjust, one-sided, preferential, biased, prejudiced

DICTIONARY

inert ⓣ *adj* **1** without the power of motion or resistance **2** chemically unreactive **inertly** *adv* **inertness** *n*
inertia ⓣ *n* **1** feeling of unwillingness to do anything **2** *physics* property by which a body remains still or continues to move unless a force is applied to it **inertial** *adj*
inescapable ⓣ *adj* unavoidable
inestimable ⓣ *adj* too great to be estimated **inestimably** *adv*
inevitable ⓣ *adj* **1** unavoidable, sure to happen ▷ *n* **2** something inevitable **inevitably** *adv* **inevitability** *n*
inexorable ⓣ *adj* **1** relentless **2** unavoidable **inexorably** *adv*
inexperienced ⓣ *adj* having no knowledge or experience of a particular situation, activity, etc. **inexperience** *n*
inexpert ⓣ *adj* lacking skill
inexplicable ⓣ *adj* impossible to explain **inexplicably** *adv*
in extremis *adv Latin* **1** in great difficulty **2** at the point of death
inextricable *adj* **1** impossible to escape from **2** impossible to disentangle or separate
infallible ⓣ *adj* **1** never wrong **2** always successful **infallibly** *adv* **infallibility** *n*
infamous ⓣ [**in**-fam-uss] *adj* well-known for something bad **infamously** *adv* **infamy** *n*
infant ⓣ *n* very young child
▸ **infancy** *n* **1** early childhood **2** early stage of development
▸ **infantile** *adj* childish
infante [in-**fan**-tee] *n* formerly, son of a king of Spain or Portugal, esp. one who is not heir to the throne
▸ **infanta** *n* **1** formerly, daughter of a king of Spain or Portugal **2** wife of an infante
infanticide *n* **1** murder of an infant **2** person guilty of this
infantry *n* foot soldiers
infatuate ⓣ *v* inspire with intense unreasonable passion **infatuated** *adj* **infatuation** *n*
infect ⓣ *v* **1** affect with a disease **2** affect with a feeling **infection** *n*
▸ **infectious** *adj* **1** (of a disease) spreading without actual contact **2** spreading from

THESAURUS

inert *adj* = **inactive**, still, dead, dormant, static, lifeless, motionless, unresponsive, immobile, unreactive
inertia *n* = **inactivity**, apathy, sloth, lethargy, passivity, immobility, listlessness, unresponsiveness
inescapable *adj* = **unavoidable**, sure, certain, inevitable, inexorable, destined, fated, ineluctable
inestimable *adj* = **incalculable**, precious, invaluable, priceless, immeasurable, prodigious
inevitable *adj* = **unavoidable**, sure, certain, assured, inescapable, inexorable, destined, fixed, ineluctable
inevitably *adv* = **unavoidably**, certainly, necessarily, automatically, surely, as a result, of necessity, perforce, willy-nilly
inexact *See* **approximate**
inexcusable *adj* = **unforgivable**, outrageous, indefensible, unjustifiable, unpardonable, unwarrantable
inexhaustible *See* **infinite**
inexorable *adj* = **unrelenting**, relentless, inescapable, unyielding, remorseless, unbending
inexpensive *adj* = **cheap**, budget, modest, bargain, reasonable, economical
inexperience *n* = **unfamiliarity**, ignorance, newness, callowness, greenness, rawness
inexperienced *adj* = **new**, green (*informal*), raw, novice, unaccustomed, raggedy ass (*offensive slang*) • *inexperienced drivers* OPPOSITE: experienced
See also: **ignorant**
inexpert *adj* = **amateurish**, bungling, inept, unprofessional, clumsy, unskilled, maladroit, unpracticed
inexplicable *adj* = **unaccountable**, mysterious, strange, enigmatic, incomprehensible, unfathomable, unintelligible, baffling, insoluble, mystifying
inextricably *adv* = **inseparably**, totally, irretrievably, intricately, indissolubly, indistinguishably
infallibility *n* = **perfection**, supremacy, impeccability, omniscience, unerringness
infallible *adj* = **foolproof**, sure, certain, reliable, unbeatable, dependable, trustworthy, sure-fire (*informal*), unfailing
infamous *adj* = **notorious**, ignominious, disreputable, ill-famed
infancy *n* = **beginnings**, start, dawn, outset, inception, cradle, origins
infant *n* = **baby**, babe, child, minor, toddler, tot
infantile *adj* = **childish**, immature, babyish, puerile
infatuate *v* = **obsess**, fascinate, captivate, enchant, bewitch, besot, enrapture
infatuated *adj* = **obsessed**, besotted, bewitched, captivated, carried away, enamoured, enraptured, fascinated, possessed, smitten (*informal*), spellbound
infatuation *n* = **obsession**, thing (*informal*), crush (*informal*), passion, madness, fixation
infect *v* = **contaminate**, affect, taint, blight • *One mosquito can infect many people.*

DICTIONARY

person to person: *infectious laughter*
infer Ⓣ *v* **-ferring, -ferred** work out from evidence **inference** *n*
inferior Ⓣ *adj* **1** lower in position, status, or quality ▷ *n* **2** person of lower position or status **inferiority** *n*
infernal Ⓣ *adj* **1** of hell **2** *informal* irritating **infernally** *adv*
inferno Ⓣ *n, pl* **-nos** intense raging fire
infertile Ⓣ *adj* **1** unable to produce offspring **2** (of soil) barren, not productive **infertility** *n*
infest Ⓣ *v* inhabit or overrun in unpleasantly large numbers **infestation** *n*
infidel *n* **1** person with no religion **2** person who rejects a particular religion, esp. Christianity or Islam
infidelity *n, pl* **-ties** sexual unfaithfulness to one's husband, wife, or lover
infield *n baseball* area covered by the home plate and three bases
infighting *n* quarrelling within a group
infiltrate Ⓣ *v* enter gradually and secretly **infiltration** *n* **infiltrator** *n*
infinite Ⓣ [**in**-fin-it] *adj* without any limit or end **infinitely** *adv*
infinitesimal Ⓣ *adj* extremely small
infinitive [in-**fin**-it-iv] *n grammar* form of a verb not showing tense, person, or number, such as *to sleep*
infinity Ⓣ *n* endless space, time, or number
infirm Ⓣ *adj* physically or mentally weak **infirmity** *n*
infirmary *n, pl* **-ries** hospital
in flagrante delicto [in flag-**grant**-ee dee-**lick**-toe] *adv* while committing the offence
inflame Ⓣ *v* make angry or excited
▸ **inflamed** *adj* (of part of the body) red and swollen because of infection
▸ **inflammation** *n* inflamed part of the body
▸ **inflammatory** *adj* likely to provoke anger
inflammable Ⓣ *adj* easily set on fire **inflammability** *n*
inflate Ⓣ *v* **1** expand by filling with air or gas **2** cause economic inflation in
▸ **inflatable** *adj* **1** able to be inflated ▷ *n* **2** plastic or rubber object which can be inflated

THESAURUS

See also: **pollute**
infection *n* = **contamination**, virus, poison, pollution, corruption, contagion, defilement
infectious *adj* = **catching**, contagious • *infectious diseases*
infer *v* = **deduce**, understand, gather, conclude, derive, presume, surmise
inference *n* = **deduction**, reading, conclusion, assumption, presumption, surmise
inferior *adj* **1** = **lower**, minor, secondary, lesser, subordinate, second-class, bush league (*informal*) • *Young people are considered to have inferior status*. OPPOSITE: superior **2** = **second-rate**, poor, hack, mediocre, shoddy, second-class • *inferior-quality DVDs* OPPOSITE: superior ▸ *n* **3** = **subordinate,** junior, underling • *Don't treat me like an inferior*. OPPOSITE: superior
See also: **cheap, rotten**
inferiority *n* **1** = **inadequacy**, deficiency, mediocrity, imperfection, insignificance, shoddiness, worthlessness **2** = **subservience**, subordination, abasement, lowliness
infernal *adj* = **devilish**, damned, satanic, diabolical, hellish, accursed, damnable, fiendish
inferno *See* **fire, hell**
infertile *adj* = **barren**, sterile, unproductive, unfruitful
infertility *n* = **sterility**, barrenness, infecundity, unproductiveness
infest *v* = **overrun**, invade, ravage, swarm, penetrate, throng, beset, permeate
infested *adj* = **overrun**, alive, crawling, ravaged, ridden, swarming, teeming
infiltrate *v* = **penetrate**, permeate, pervade, percolate, filter through, insinuate oneself, make inroads *or* make inroads into, sneak in (*informal*)
infinite *adj* = **limitless**, eternal, untold, perpetual, inexhaustible, boundless, everlasting • *an infinite number of possibilities*
See also: **countless, plentiful**
infinitesimal *adj* = **microscopic**, minute, tiny, insignificant, negligible, minuscule, teeny, unnoticeable
infinity *n* = **eternity**, vastness, boundlessness, endlessness, immensity
infirm *adj* = **frail**, weak, ailing, failing, feeble, decrepit, debilitated, doddering, enfeebled
infirmity *n* = **frailty**, vulnerability, decrepitude, ill health, sickliness
inflame *v* = **enrage**, anger, provoke, excite, stimulate, incense, infuriate, arouse, rouse, madden
inflamed *adj* = **sore**, hot, red, infected, fevered, swollen
inflammable *adj* = **flammable**, incendiary, combustible
inflammation *n* = **soreness**, rash, redness, tenderness, painfulness
inflammatory *adj* = **provocative**, explosive, fiery, intemperate, like a red rag to a bull, rabble-rousing
inflate *v* = **expand**, increase, swell, enlarge, bloat, dilate, blow up, distend, puff up *or* puff out, pump up

DICTIONARY

inflation ⓣ *n* **1** increase in prices and fall in the value of money **2** inflating **inflationary** *adj*
inflection, inflexion *n* **1** change in the pitch of the voice **2** *grammar* change in the form of a word to show grammatical use
inflexible ⓣ *adj* **1** obstinate or unyielding **2** fixed and unalterable **inflexibly** *adv* **inflexibility** *n*
inflict ⓣ *v* impose (something unpleasant) on **infliction** *n*
inflorescence *n botany* arrangement of flowers on a stem
inflow *n* **1** something, such as liquid or gas, that flows in **2** act of flowing in, influx
influence ⓣ *n* **1** effect of one person or thing on another **2** (person with) the power to have such an effect ▷ *v* **3** have an effect on **influential** *adj* **influentially** *adv*
influenza *n* viral disease causing muscle pains, fever, and catarrh
influx ⓣ *n* **1** arrival or entry of many people or things **2** a flowing in
info *n informal* information
inform ⓣ *v* **1** tell **2** give incriminating information to the police
▸ **informant** *n* person who gives information
▸ **information** *n* what is told, knowledge
▸ **information technology** use of computers and electronic technology to store and communicate information
▸ **informative** *adj* giving useful information
▸ **informer** *n* person who informs to the police
informal ⓣ *adj* **1** relaxed and friendly **2** appropriate for everyday life or use **informally** *adv* **informality** *n*
infra dig *adj informal* beneath one's dignity
infrared *adj* of or using rays below the red end of the visible spectrum
infrastructure *n* basic facilities, services, and equipment needed for a country or organization to function properly
infrequent ⓣ *adj* not happening often **infrequently** *adv*
infringe ⓣ *v* break (a law or agreement) **infringement** *n*
infuriate ⓣ *v* make very angry

THESAURUS

inflated *adj* = **exaggerated**, overblown, ostentatious, swollen
inflation *n* = **expansion**, increase, rise, spread, extension, escalation, enlargement, swelling
inflexibility *n* = **obstinacy**, intransigence, obduracy
inflexible *adj* **1** = **obstinate**, stubborn, steadfast, resolute, uncompromising, intractable, implacable, obdurate, set in one's ways, unbending **2** = **inelastic**, hard, stiff, rigid, taut
inflict *v* = **impose**, visit, deliver, apply, administer, levy, wreak, mete out *or* deal out
infliction *n* = **imposition**, administration, perpetration, wreaking
influence *n* **1** = **power**, control, authority, importance, sway, domination, ascendancy, peer pressure • *They have quite a lot of influence.* **2** = **effect**, hold, weight, spell, magnetism • *under the influence of alcohol* ▸ *v* **3** = **affect**, control, direct, guide, sway, manipulate • *His parents never try to influence him.*
See also: **factor, grip**
influential *adj* = **important**, significant, powerful, potent, instrumental, authoritative, weighty, leading, telling
influx *n* = **arrival**, rush, invasion, incursion, inrush, inundation
inform *v* = **tell**, advise (*formal*), notify, enlighten • *Please inform me of your progress.* ▷ **inform of** *See* **report** ▷ **inform on** = **betray**, denounce, tell on (*informal*) • *Somebody must have informed on the thieves.*
See also: **alert, brief, communicate**
informal *adj* = **casual**, easy, natural, familiar, colloquial, relaxed • *His manner was informal and relaxed.* OPPOSITE: formal
See also: **cozy**
informality *n* = **familiarity**, ease, simplicity, relaxation, casualness, naturalness
information *n* = **facts**, news, word, material, notice, data • *I would never give any information about you.*
informative *adj* = **instructive**, educational, forthcoming, revealing, chatty, communicative, edifying, enlightening, illuminating
informed *adj* = **knowledgeable**, expert, familiar, enlightened, erudite, in the picture, learned, up to date, versed, well-read
informer *n* = **betrayer**, sneak, accuser, Judas, stool pigeon, finger man (*slang*)
infrequent *adj* = **occasional**, rare, unusual, uncommon, sporadic, few and far between, once in a blue moon
infringe *v* = **break**, violate, contravene, disobey, transgress
infringed *See* **broken**
infringement *n* = **contravention**, breach, violation, infraction, trespass, transgression
infuriate *v* = **enrage**, anger, provoke, rile, irritate, incense, exasperate, madden
infuriated *See* **furious, mad**
infuriating *adj* = **annoying**, galling, maddening, exasperating, irritating,

DICTIONARY

infuse *v* **1** fill with (an emotion or quality) **2** soak to extract flavour
▶ **infusion** *n* **1** infusing **2** liquid obtained by infusing
ingenious Ⓣ [in-**jean**-ee-uss] *adj* **1** clever at contriving **2** cleverly contrived **ingeniously** *adv* **ingenuity** [in-jen-**new**-it-ee] *n*
ingénue [**an**-jay-new] *n* naive or inexperienced young woman, esp. as a role played by an actress
ingenuous Ⓣ [in-**jen**-new-uss] *adj* unsophisticated and trusting **ingenuously** *adv*
ingest *v* take (food or drink) into the body **ingestion** *n*
inglenook *n* warm seat in a large open fireplace
inglorious Ⓣ *adj* dishonourable or shameful
ingot *n* oblong block of cast metal
ingrained *adj* (of a habit etc.) **1** deep-rooted **2** (of dirt) deeply fixed
ingratiate Ⓣ *v* bring (oneself) into favour (with) **ingratiating** *adj* **ingratiatingly** *adv*
ingratitude Ⓣ *n* lack of gratitude or thanks
ingredient Ⓣ *n* component of a mixture or compound
Ingres *n* **Jean Auguste Dominique**. 1780–1867, French classical painter, noted for his draftsmanship
ingress *n* act or right of entering
ingrowing *adj* (of a toenail) growing abnormally into the flesh
inhabit Ⓣ *v* **-habiting**, **-habited** live in **inhabitable** *adj* **inhabitant** *n*
inhale Ⓣ *v* breathe in (air, smoke, etc.) **inhalation** *n*
▶ **inhalant** [in-**hale**-ant] *n* medical preparation inhaled to help breathing problems
▶ **inhaler** *n* container for an inhalant
inherent Ⓣ *adj* existing as an inseparable part **inherently** *adv*
inherit Ⓣ *v* **-heriting**, **-herited** **1** receive (money etc.) from someone who has died **2** receive (a characteristic) from parents etc. **3** receive from predecessors **inheritance** *n* **inheritor** *n*
inhibit Ⓣ *v* **-hibiting**, **-hibited** **1** restrain (an impulse or desire) **2** hinder or prevent (action)
▶ **inhibition** *n* feeling of fear or embarrassment that stops one from behaving naturally **inhibited** *adj*
inhospitable Ⓣ *adj* **1** not hospitable, unfriendly **2** difficult to live in, harsh
inhuman Ⓣ *adj* **1** cruel or brutal **2** not human
inhumane Ⓣ *adj* cruel or brutal **inhumanity** *n*

THESAURUS

mortifying, provoking, vexatious
ingenious *adj* = **creative**, original, bright, brilliant, clever, crafty, shrewd, inventive, resourceful
ingenuity *n* = **originality**, gift, genius, flair, inventiveness, sharpness, cleverness, resourcefulness, shrewdness
ingenuous *adj* = **naive**, open, simple, innocent, honest, plain, sincere, unsophisticated, artless, guileless, trusting
inglorious *adj* = **dishonourable**, infamous, disgraceful, shameful, ignominious, discreditable, disreputable, ignoble, unheroic
ingratiate *v* = **pander to**, crawl, flatter, fawn, brown-nose (*slang*), curry favour, grovel, insinuate oneself, kiss ass (*slang*), toady
ingratiating *adj* = **sycophantic**, humble, crawling, fawning, flattering, obsequious, servile, toadying, unctuous
ingratitude *n* = **ungratefulness**, thanklessness
ingredient *n* = **component**, element, constituent • *Place all the ingredients in a pan.*
inhabit *v* = **live**, occupy, lodge, populate, reside (*formal*), dwell • *the people who inhabit these islands*
inhabitant *n* = **resident**, native, citizen, inmate, occupant • *an inhabitant of Norway*
inhabitants *See* **people**
inhabited *adj* = **populated**, developed, occupied, colonized, peopled, settled, tenanted
inhale *v* = **breathe in**, gasp, draw in, respire, suck in
inherent *adj* = **innate**, natural, native, essential, built-in, ingrained, hereditary, intrinsic, inborn, inbred, inherited
inherit *v* = **be left**, come into, fall heir to, succeed to
inheritance *n* = **legacy**, heritage, bequest • *This gold watch is my inheritance from my grandfather.*
inhibit *v* = **restrain**, check, frustrate, curb, discourage, hinder, obstruct, impede, constrain, hold back *or* hold in
inhibited *adj* = **shy**, subdued, reserved, guarded, reticent, self-conscious, repressed, constrained
inhibition *n* = **shyness**, reserve, block, restraint, reticence, hang-up (*informal*), self-consciousness
inhospitable *adj* **1** = **unfriendly**, cool, xenophobic, uncongenial, unreceptive, unsociable, unwelcoming **2** = **bleak**, hostile, barren, desolate, forbidding, godforsaken
inhuman *adj* = **cruel**, brutal, savage, barbaric, ruthless, heartless, cold-blooded, merciless, pitiless, unfeeling
inhumane *adj* = **cruel**, brutal, heartless,

DICTIONARY

inimical Ⓣ *adj* unfavourable or hostile **inimically** *adv*
inimitable Ⓣ *adj* impossible to imitate, unique **inimitably** *adv*
iniquity Ⓣ *n, pl* **-ties 1** great injustice **2** wickedness **3** sin **iniquitous** *adj*
initial Ⓣ *adj* **1** first, at the beginning ▷ *n* **2** first letter, esp. of someone's name ▷ *v* **-tialling, -tialled 3** sign with one's initials ▸ **initially** *adv* first, originally
initiate Ⓣ *v* **1** begin or set going **2** admit (someone) into a closed group **3** instruct in the basics of something ▷ *n* **4** initiated person **initiation** *n* **initiator** *n* **initiatory** *adj*
initiative Ⓣ *n* **1** first step, commencing move **2** ability to act independently
inject Ⓣ *v* **1** put (a fluid) into the body with a syringe **2** introduce (a new element): *he injected some humour into the scene* **injection** *n*
injudicious Ⓣ *adj* showing poor judgment, unwise
injunction Ⓣ *n* court order not to do something
injure Ⓣ *v* **1** hurt physically or mentally **2** damage ▸ **injury** *n* **1** physical hurt **2** damage or harm **injurious** *adj* ▸ **injury time** *sports* time added at the end of a match to compensate for time spent treating injured players
injustice Ⓣ *n* **1** unfairness **2** unfair treatment or action
ink *n* **1** coloured liquid used for writing or printing ▷ *v* **2** mark or cover with ink ▸ **inky** *adj* **1** dark or black **2** stained with ink
inkling Ⓣ *n* slight idea or suspicion
inlaid *adj* **1** set in another material so that the surface is smooth **2** made like this: *an inlaid table*
inland Ⓣ *adj, adv* in or towards the interior of a country, away from the sea
in-laws *pl n* relatives by marriage
inlay *n* inlaid substance or pattern
inlet Ⓣ *n* **1** narrow piece of water extending from the sea into the land **2** valve etc. through which liquid or gas enters
in loco parentis [par-**rent**-iss] *Latin* in place of a parent
inmate Ⓣ *n* person living in an institution such as a prison
inmost Ⓣ *adj* furthest inside, most secret
inn *n* **1** hotel **2** *Brit* pub or small hotel, esp. in the country **innkeeper** *n*

THESAURUS

unsympathetic, unkind, pitiless, unfeeling
inhumanity *n* = **cruelty**, atrocity, brutality, barbarism, heartlessness, pitilessness, ruthlessness, unkindness
inimical *adj* = **hostile**, adverse, unfriendly, antagonistic, ill-disposed, opposed, unfavourable, unwelcoming
inimitable *adj* = **unique**, unparalleled, consummate, incomparable, unrivalled, matchless, peerless
iniquitous *adj* = **wicked**, criminal, evil, immoral, unjust, reprehensible, sinful
iniquity *n* = **wickedness**, wrong, evil, sin, injustice, abomination
initial *adj* = **first**, opening, beginning, primary, introductory, incipient
initially *adv* = **at first**, first, originally, primarily, firstly, at the beginning *or* in the beginning
initiate *v* **1** = **begin**, start, open, launch, originate, commence, get under way, kick off (*informal*), set in motion **2** = **induct**, introduce, invest, indoctrinate **3** = **instruct**, coach, train, teach, acquaint with, familiarize with ▸ *n* **4** = **novice**, member, convert, entrant, beginner, learner, probationer
initiation *n* = **introduction**, debut, entrance, installation, inauguration, induction, enrolment, investiture
initiative *n* **1** = **first step**, lead, advantage, first move **2** = **resourcefulness**, drive, leadership, ambition, enterprise, dynamism, get-up-and-go (*informal*)
inject *v* **1** = **vaccinate**, inoculate **2** = **introduce**, insert, infuse, instill, bring in
injection *n* **1** = **vaccination**, inoculation, shot (*informal*) **2** = **introduction**, dose, infusion, insertion
injudicious *adj* = **unwise**, rash, foolish, ill-advised, imprudent, ill-judged, impolitic, incautious, inexpedient, unthinking
injunction *n* = **order**, ruling, command, mandate, instruction, exhortation, precept
injure *v* = **hurt**, wound, harm, maim • *Five people were injured in the ferry accident.* *See also*: **damage**
injured *adj* = **hurt**, disabled, wounded, damaged, weakened, broken, challenged, undermined
injury *n* = **wound**, damage, harm • *He sustained serious injuries in the accident.*
injustice *n* = **unfairness**, wrong, discrimination, bias, prejudice, inequality • *the injustice of the system* OPPOSITE: justice
inkling *n* = **suspicion**, idea, hint, suggestion, indication, clue, notion, conception, whisper, intimation
inland *adj* = **interior**, domestic, internal, upcountry
inlet *n* = **bay**, passage, creek, fjord, bight, firth *or* frith (*Scot*)
inmate *See* **inhabitant**
inmost, innermost *adj* = **deepest**, private,

DICTIONARY

innards Ⓣ *pl n informal* **1** internal organs **2** working parts
innate Ⓣ *adj* being part of someone's nature, inborn
inner Ⓣ *adj* **1** happening or located within **2** of the mind or spirit: *inner peace* **innermost** *adj*
▸ **inner city** parts of a city near the centre, esp. when seen as poor or violent
innings *n* **1** *sports* player's or side's turn of batting **2** spell or turn
innocent Ⓣ *adj* **1** not guilty of a crime **2** without experience of evil **3** harmless ▷ *n* **4** innocent person, esp. a child **innocently** *adv* **innocence** *n*
innocuous Ⓣ *adj* harmless **innocuously** *adv*
innovate *v* introduce new ideas or methods **innovation** *n* **innovative** *adj* **innovator** *n*
innuendo Ⓣ *n, pl* **-does** indirect accusation
innumerable Ⓣ *adj* too many to be counted **innumerably** *adv*
innumerate *adj* having no understanding of mathematics or science **innumeracy** *n*
inoculate *v* protect against disease by injecting with a vaccine **inoculation** *n*
inoffensive Ⓣ *adj* causing no harm or annoyance
inoperable *adj med* unable to be operated on without risk
inoperative Ⓣ *adj* not in force, effect, or operation
inopportune Ⓣ *adj* badly timed
inordinate Ⓣ *adj* excessive
inorganic Ⓣ *adj* **1** not having the characteristics of living organisms **2** of or denoting chemical substances that do not contain carbon **inorganically** *adv*
inpatient *n* patient who stays in a hospital for treatment
input *n* **1** resources put into a project etc. **2** data fed into a computer ▷ *v* **-putting, -put** **3** enter (data) in a computer
inquest Ⓣ *n* official inquiry, esp. into a sudden death
inquietude *n* restlessness, uneasiness, or anxiety
inquire Ⓣ *v* seek information or ask about **inquirer** *n*
▸ **inquiry** *n* **1** question **2** investigation
inquisition Ⓣ *n* **1** thorough investigation

THESAURUS

personal, central, secret, basic, essential, intimate
innards *See* **insides**
innate *adj* = **inborn**, natural, native, constitutional, essential, congenital, inherent, intuitive, ingrained, inbred, instinctive
inner *adj* **1** = **inside**, central, middle, internal, interior, inward **2** = **private**, personal, secret, intimate, hidden, repressed, unrevealed
innermost *See* **inside**
innkeeper *n* = **publican**, host *or* hostess, landlord *or* landlady, hotelier, mine host
innocence *n* **1** = **inexperience**, simplicity, gullibility, naivety • *the innocence of babies* **2** = **guiltlessness**, virtue, purity, blamelessness, clean hands, incorruptibility, probity, uprightness **3** = **harmlessness**, innocuousness, inoffensiveness
innocent *adj* **1** = **not guilty**, clear, spotless, blameless • *the arrest of innocent suspects* OPPOSITE: guilty **2** = **naive**, pure, childlike, guileless • *They seem so young and innocent.* **3** = **harmless**, innocuous, well-intentioned, inoffensive, unobjectionable, well-meant
See also: **ignorant**
innocuous *See* **harmless, safe**
innovation *n* = **modernization**, change, departure, introduction, variation, novelty, alteration, newness
innuendo *n* = **insinuation**, hint, suggestion, implication, whisper, overtone, aspersion, imputation, intimation
innumerable *adj* = **countless**, numerous, myriad, infinite, untold, incalculable, beyond number, multitudinous, numberless, unnumbered
inoffensive *adj* = **harmless**, quiet, innocent, mild, innocuous, retiring, unobjectionable, unobtrusive
inoperative *adj* = **out of action**, ineffective, useless, defective, invalid, broken, null and void, out of order, out of service
inopportune *adj* = **inconvenient**, inappropriate, unfortunate, untimely, unsuitable, unseasonable, ill-chosen, ill-timed, unfavourable, unpropitious
inordinate *adj* = **excessive**, unreasonable, unwarranted, disproportionate, undue, extravagant, unconscionable, preposterous, immoderate, intemperate
inorganic *adj* = **artificial**, chemical, man-made
inquest *n* = **inquiry**, investigation, probe, inquisition
inquire *v* **1** = **investigate**, research, probe, explore, examine, look into, make inquiries **2** *Also* **enquire** = **ask**, question, query
inquiring *See* **curious**
inquiry *n* **1** = **investigation**, study, research, survey, probe, inquest, exploration, interrogation, examination **2** *Also* **enquiry** = **question**, query
inquisition *n* = **investigation**, inquiry, inquest, examination, cross-examination,

DICTIONARY

2 *hist* **Inquisition** organization within the Catholic Church for suppressing heresy
inquisitor *n* **inquisitorial** *adj*
inquisitive Ⓣ *adj* too curious about other people's business **inquisitively** *adv*
inquorate *adj* without enough people present to make a quorum
inroads *pl n* **make inroads into** start affecting or reducing: *my gambling has made inroads into my savings*
insalubrious *adj* likely to cause ill-health
insane Ⓣ *adj* **1** mentally ill **2** stupidly irresponsible **insanely** *adv* **insanity** *n*
insanitary Ⓣ *adj* dirty or unhealthy
insatiable Ⓣ [in-**saysh**-a-bl] *adj* impossible to satisfy
inscribe Ⓣ *v* write or carve words on
▶ **inscription** *n* words inscribed
inscrutable Ⓣ *adj* **1** mysterious or enigmatic **2** incomprehensible **inscrutably** *adv*
inscrutability *n*
insect *n* small invertebrate animal with six legs, a segmented body, and usu. two or four wings
▶ **insecticide** *n* substance for killing insects
▶ **insectivorous** *adj* insect-eating
insecure Ⓣ *adj* **1** anxious or uncertain **2** not safe or firm
inseminate *v* implant semen into
insemination *n*
insensate *adj* **1** without sensation, unconscious **2** unfeeling
insensible Ⓣ *adj* **1** unconscious **2** without feeling **3** not aware **4** imperceptible
insensibility *n*
insensitive Ⓣ *adj* unaware of or ignoring other people's feelings **insensitivity** *n*
inseparable Ⓣ *adj* impossible to separate or divide
insert Ⓣ *v* **1** put inside or between ▷ *n* **2** something inserted **insertion** *n*
inset *adj* **1** decorated with something inserted ▷ *n* **2** small map or diagram within a larger one
inshore *adj* **1** close to the shore ▷ *adj, adv* **2** towards the shore
inside Ⓣ *prep* **1** in or to the interior of ▷ *adj* **2** of or on the inside **3** by or from someone within an organization: *inside information* ▷ *adv* **4** in or into the inside **5** *slang* in prison ▷ *n* **6** inner side, surface, or part **insides** **7** *informal* stomach and bowels
▶ **inside out 1** with the interior facing outwards **2** thoroughly
▶ **insider** *n* member of a group who has exclusive knowledge about it
insidious Ⓣ *adj* subtle or unseen but dangerous **insidiously** *adv*

THESAURUS

grilling (*informal*), questioning, third degree (*informal*)
inquisitive *adj* = **curious**, inquiring, nosy (*informal*), probing, prying, questioning
inquisitiveness *See* **curiosity**
insane *adj* **1** = **mad**, crazy, crazed, demented, deranged, mentally ill, out of one's mind, unhinged **2** = **stupid**, irresponsible, foolish, senseless, irrational, impractical, idiotic, preposterous, bonkers (*informal*), daft (*informal*)
insanitary *adj* = **unhealthy**, dirty, polluted, filthy, unclean, disease-ridden, infested, insalubrious, scuzzy (*slang*), unhygienic
insanity *n* **1** = **madness**, dementia, delirium, mental disorder, mental illness **2** = **stupidity**, folly, lunacy, irresponsibility, senselessness
insatiable *adj* = **unquenchable**, greedy, voracious, ravenous, intemperate, rapacious
inscribe *v* = **carve**, cut, impress, engrave, imprint, etch
inscription *n* = **engraving**, legend, dedication, words
inscrutable *adj* **1** = **enigmatic**, blank, impenetrable, deadpan, poker-faced (*informal*) **2** = **mysterious**, hidden, incomprehensible, inexplicable, unfathomable, unintelligible, unexplainable
insecure *adj* **1** = **anxious**, afraid, uncertain, unsure **2** = **unsafe**, vulnerable, unprotected, wide-open, exposed, unguarded, defenseless
insecurity *n* = **anxiety**, fear, worry, uncertainty
insensible *adj* = **unaware**, unconscious, oblivious, unaffected, impervious, unmindful
insensitive *adj* = **unfeeling**, tough, indifferent, callous, hardened, unconcerned, thick-skinned, uncaring
inseparable *adj* **1** = **indivisible**, indissoluble **2** = **devoted**, close, intimate, bosom
insert *v* = **put**, set, place, enter, introduce, implant • *He inserted the key into the lock.*
See also: **stick**
insertion *n* = **inclusion**, addition, supplement, introduction, implant, interpolation
inside *adj* **1** = **inner**, internal, interior, innermost • *We booked an inside cabin.* OPPOSITE: outside **2** = **confidential**, private, secret, internal, exclusive, classified, restricted ▶ *adv* **3** = **indoors**, within, under cover ▶ *n* **4** = **interior**, contents
insides *pl n* (*Informal*) = **guts**, entrails, innards, internal organs • *My insides ached from eating too much.*
insidious *adj* = **stealthy**, smooth, subtle, deceptive, sly, surreptitious, sneaking

DICTIONARY

insight Ⓣ *n* clear understanding
insignia Ⓣ [in-**sig**-nee-a] *n, pl* **-nias, -nia** badge or emblem of honour or office
insignificant Ⓣ *adj* not important **insignificance** *n*
insincere Ⓣ *adj* pretending what one does not feel **insincerely** *adv* **insincerity** *n*
insinuate Ⓣ *v* **1** suggest indirectly **2** work oneself into a position by gradual manoeuvres **insinuation** *n*
insipid Ⓣ *adj* lacking interest, spirit, or flavour **insipidity** *n*
insist Ⓣ *v* demand or state firmly
▸ **insistent** *adj* **1** making persistent demands **2** demanding attention **insistently** *adv* **insistence** *n*
in situ *adv, adj Latin* in its original position
insofar as *adv* to the extent that
insole *n* inner sole of a shoe or boot
insolent Ⓣ *adj* arrogantly rude **insolence** *n* **insolently** *adv*
insoluble Ⓣ *adj* **1** incapable of being solved **2** incapable of being dissolved
insolvent Ⓣ *adj* unable to pay one's debts **insolvency** *n*
insomnia Ⓣ *n* sleeplessness **insomniac** *n*
insomuch *adv* to such an extent
insouciant *adj* carefree and unconcerned **insouciance** *n*
inspect Ⓣ *v* check closely or officially **inspection** *n*
▸ **inspector** *n* **1** person who inspects **2** high-ranking police officer
inspire Ⓣ *v* **1** fill with enthusiasm, stimulate **2** arouse (an emotion)
▸ **inspiration** *n* **1** good idea **2** creative influence or stimulus **inspirational** *adj*
inst. instant (this month)

THESAURUS

insight *n* = **understanding**, vision, judgment, perception, awareness, observation, penetration, comprehension, discernment, perspicacity
insignia *n* = **badge**, symbol, crest, emblem
insignificance *n* = **unimportance**, irrelevance, inconsequence, meaninglessness, pettiness, triviality, worthlessness
insignificant *adj* = **unimportant**, little, minor, petty, irrelevant, trivial, trifling • *a small, insignificant flaw in the sweater* OPPOSITE: significant
See also: **slight**
insincere *adj* = **deceitful**, false, dishonest, two-faced • *insincere flattery* OPPOSITE: sincere
insincerity *n* = **deceitfulness**, hypocrisy, pretense, dishonesty, dissimulation, duplicity, untruthfulness
insinuate *v* **1** = **imply**, suggest, indicate, hint, intimate, allude **2** = **ingratiate**, curry favour, get in with, worm one's way in *or* work one's way in
insinuation *n* = **implication**, hint, suggestion, slur, innuendo, allusion, aspersion
insipid *adj* **1** = **bland**, anemic, characterless, colourless, prosaic, uninteresting, vapid, wishy-washy (*informal*) **2** = **tasteless**, bland, watery, flavourless, unappetizing
insist *v* **1** = **demand**, urge, press • *My family insisted I should not give in.* **2** = **assert**, claim, maintain, vow, repeat, swear, reiterate, aver
insistence *n* = **persistence**, stress, emphasis, importunity
insistent *adj* = **persistent**, urgent, emphatic, unrelenting, incessant, dogged, importunate, persevering
insist on, insist upon *See* **exact**
insolence *n* = **rudeness**, cheek (*informal*), disrespect, boldness, effrontery, impertinence, impudence
insolent *adj* = **rude**, bold, contemptuous, impertinent, impudent, insubordinate, insulting
insoluble *adj* = **inexplicable**, mysterious, unfathomable, unaccountable, impenetrable, baffling, indecipherable, unsolvable
insolvency *n* = **bankruptcy**, failure, ruin, liquidation
insolvent *adj* = **bankrupt**, failed, broke (*informal*), gone bust (*informal*), gone to the wall, in receivership, ruined
insomnia *n* = **sleeplessness**, wakefulness
inspect *v* = **examine**, survey, investigate, eye, check, scan • *the right to inspect company files*
See also: **scrutinize**
inspection *n* = **examination**, review, investigation, search, survey, check, scrutiny, checkup, once-over (*informal*)
inspector *n* = **examiner**, investigator, censor, supervisor, superintendent, overseer, scrutinizer
inspiration *n* **1** = **influence**, spur, stimulus, muse **2** = **revelation**, insight, creativity, illumination
inspire *v* **1** = **stimulate**, encourage, influence, spur, animate, galvanize, enliven **2** = **arouse**, produce, excite, enkindle, give rise to
inspired *adj* **1** = **brilliant**, cool (*informal*), impressive, wonderful, thrilling, memorable, outstanding, superlative, dazzling, phat (*slang*) **2** = **uplifted**, elated, enthused, exhilarated, stimulated
inspiring *adj* = **uplifting**, exciting, rousing, moving, exhilarating, heartening, stimulating, stirring

DICTIONARY

instability Ⓣ *n* lack of steadiness or reliability
install Ⓣ *v* **1** put in and prepare (equipment) for use **2** formally place (a person) in a position or rank
▶ **installation** *n* **1** installing **2** equipment installed **3** place containing equipment for a particular purpose: *radar installation*
instalment Ⓣ *n* any of the portions of a thing presented or a debt paid in successive parts
▶ **instalment plan** system of purchase by which the buyer pays for goods by instalments
instance Ⓣ *n* **1** particular example ▷ *v* **2** mention as an example
▶ **for instance** for example
instant Ⓣ *n* **1** very brief time **2** particular moment ▷ *adj* **3** immediate **4** (of foods) requiring little preparation
▶ **instantly** *adv* at once
instantaneous Ⓣ *adj* happening at once **instantaneously** *adv*
instead Ⓣ *adv* as a replacement or substitute
instep *n* **1** part of the foot forming the arch between the ankle and toes **2** part of a shoe etc. covering this
instigate Ⓣ *v* cause to happen, bring about **instigation** *n* **instigator** *n*
instill Ⓣ *v* **-stilling, -stilled** introduce (an idea etc.) gradually in someone's mind **instillment** *n*
instinct Ⓣ *n* inborn tendency to behave in a certain way **instinctive** *adj* **instinctively** *adv*
institute Ⓣ *n* **1** organization set up for a specific purpose, esp. teaching or research ▷ *v* **2** start or establish
▶ **institution** *n* **1** large important organization such as a university or bank **2** hospital etc. for people with special needs **3** long-established custom **institutional** *adj*
▶ **institutionalize** *v* make unable to cope with life outside an institution
instruct Ⓣ *v* **1** order to do something **2** teach (someone) how to do something **3** brief (a solicitor or barrister) **instructor** *n*

i

THESAURUS

instability *n* = **unpredictability**, volatility, fluctuation, insecurity, unsteadiness, variability, changeableness, fickleness, impermanence, inconstancy, wavering
install *v* **1** = **set up**, place, station, position, lay, fix, lodge, put in **2** = **institute**, introduce, establish, invest, induct, inaugurate **3** = **settle**, position, ensconce
installation *n* **1** = **setting up**, establishment, fitting, instalment, placing, positioning **2** = **inauguration**, induction, investiture **3** = **equipment**, system, plant, machinery
instalment *n* **1** = **repayment**, part payment *See also*: **payment** **2** = **part**, division, section, episode, chapter
See also: **issue**
instance *n* **1** = **example**, case, situation, occasion, occurrence, illustration ▶ *v* **2** = **quote**, name, cite, mention, specify, adduce
instant *n* **1** = **moment**, second, minute, flash, split second, trice • *The pain disappeared in an instant.* **2** = **point**, time, moment, occasion, juncture ▶ *adj* **3** = **immediate**, prompt, instantaneous • *He had taken an instant dislike to me.* **4** = **precooked**, fast, convenience, ready-mixed
instantaneous *adj* = **immediate**, direct, prompt, instant, on-the-spot
instantaneously *adv* = **immediately**, promptly, instantly, at once, in the twinkling of an eye (*informal*), on the spot, straight away
instantly *adv* = **immediately**, now, directly, at once, instantaneously, right away, straight away, this minute
instead *adv* = **rather**, preferably, alternatively, in lieu, in preference, on second thoughts ▷ **instead of** = **in place of**, in lieu of, rather than
instigate *v* = **provoke**, start, prompt, trigger, influence, stimulate, initiate, incite, bring about, set off
instigation *n* = **prompting**, incentive, encouragement, incitement, bidding, urging, behest
instigator *n* = **ringleader**, leader, agitator, troublemaker, motivator, prime mover
instill *v* = **introduce**, implant, infuse, imbue, engender, insinuate, inculcate
instinct *n* = **intuition**, urge, feeling, impulse, sixth sense • *My first instinct was to protect myself.*
instinctive *adj* = **inborn**, natural, automatic, inherent, spontaneous, reflex, innate, involuntary, visceral, intuitive, unpremeditated
instinctively *adv* = **intuitively**, automatically, naturally, involuntarily, by instinct, without thinking
institute *n* **1** = **society**, school, college, institution, association, foundation, academy, guild ▶ *v* **2** = **establish**, start, launch, introduce, fix, organize, found, pioneer, originate, initiate, set up
institution *n* **1** = **establishment**, school, society, college, foundation, institute, academy **2** = **custom**, rule, law, practice, convention, tradition, ritual
institutional *adj* = **conventional**, formal, established, orthodox, accepted
instruct *v* **1** = **order**, tell, direct, command

DICTIONARY

▸ **instruction** *n* **1** order **2** teaching **instructions 3** information on how to do or use something
▸ **instructive** *adj* informative or helpful
instrument Ⓣ *n* **1** tool used for particular work **2** object played to produce a musical sound **3** measuring device to show height, speed, etc. **4** *informal* person used by another
▸ **instrumental** *adj* **1** helping to cause **2** played by or composed for musical instruments
▸ **instrumentalist** *n* player of a musical instrument
▸ **instrumentation** *n* **1** set of instruments in an automobile etc. **2** arrangement of music for instruments
insubordinate Ⓣ *adj* not submissive to authority **insubordination** *n*
insubstantial Ⓣ *adj* **1** flimsy, fine, or slight **2** imaginary or unreal
insufferable Ⓣ *adj* unbearable
insular Ⓣ *adj* **1** not open to new ideas, narrow-minded **2** of or like an island **insularity** *n*
insulate Ⓣ *v* **1** prevent or reduce the transfer of electricity, heat, sound, etc. by surrounding or lining with nonconductive material **2** isolate or set apart **insulation** *n* **insulator** *n*
insulin [**in**-syoo-lin] *n* hormone produced by the pancreas which controls the amount of sugar in the blood
insult Ⓣ *v* **1** behave rudely to, offend ▹ *n* **2** insulting remark or action **insulting** *adj*
insuperable Ⓣ *adj* impossible to overcome **insuperability** *n* **insuperably** *adv*
insupportable Ⓣ *adj* **1** incapable of being tolerated **2** indefensible
insurance Ⓣ *n* **1** agreement by which one makes regular payments to a company who pay an agreed sum if damage, loss, or death occurs **2** money paid by or for insurance **3** means of protection
▸ **insure** *v* protect by insurance
▸ **insurance policy** contract of insurance
insurgent Ⓣ *adj* **1** in revolt ▹ *n* **2** rebel
▸ **insurgence** *n* revolt
insurmountable Ⓣ *adj* impossible to

THESAURUS

• *They have instructed their lawyers to sue.* **2 = teach**, school, coach, train, educate, tutor • *He instructs people in computer technology.* *See also*: **brief, require, show**
instruction *n* **1 = teaching**, training, education, lesson *or* lessons, tuition, guidance, schooling, grounding, coaching **2 = order**, demand, ruling, command, mandate, injunction, directive
instructions *pl n* = **orders**, information, key, advice, guidance, directions, recommendations, rules
instructive *adj* = **informative**, useful, educational, helpful, revealing, edifying, enlightening, illuminating
instructor *n* = **teacher**, coach, guide, adviser, demonstrator, trainer, mentor, tutor
instrument *n* **1 = tool**, device, implement, gadget, mechanism, appliance, contraption (*informal*), apparatus **2 = means**, medium, agency, vehicle, agent, organ, mechanism
instrumental *adj* = **active**, influential, useful, helpful, involved, contributory
insubordinate *adj* = **disobedient**, defiant, undisciplined, disorderly, unruly, rebellious, recalcitrant, mutinous, refractory, ungovernable
insubordination *n* = **disobedience**, rebellion, revolt, defiance, insurrection, mutiny, indiscipline, recalcitrance
insubstantial *adj* = **flimsy**, poor, weak, thin, slight, frail, tenuous, feeble
insufferable *adj* = **unbearable**, impossible, dreadful, intolerable, detestable, insupportable, unendurable
insufficient *adj* = **inadequate**, short, scant, deficient, lacking • *insufficient information* OPPOSITE: sufficient
See also: **incomplete**
insular *adj* = **narrow-minded**, provincial, limited, narrow, petty, parochial, blinkered, circumscribed, inward-looking
insulate *v* = **isolate**, protect, shield, cushion, cocoon, sequester, close off, cut off
insult *v* **1 = offend**, abuse, slight, snub, affront, put down, rip on (*slang*), bag on (*slang*) • *I did not mean to insult you.* OPPOSITE: compliment ▸ *n* **2 = offence**, abuse, slight, snub, affront • *The two men exchanged insults.*
See also: **provoke**
insulting *adj* = **offensive**, rude, abusive, degrading, contemptuous, disparaging, insolent, scurrilous
insults *See* **abuse**
insuperable *adj* = **insurmountable**, invincible, impassable, unconquerable
insupportable *adj* **1 = intolerable**, unbearable, insufferable, unendurable **2 = unjustifiable**, untenable, indefensible
insurance *n* = **protection**, security, cover, guarantee, safeguard, warranty, assurance, indemnity
insure *v* = **protect**, cover, guarantee, warrant, assure, underwrite, indemnify
insurgent *n* **1 = rebel**, revolutionary, rioter, insurrectionist, mutineer ▸ *adj* **2 = rebellious**, revolutionary, revolting, disobedient, insubordinate, mutinous, riotous, seditious
insurmountable *adj* = **insuperable**,

DICTIONARY

overcome: *insurmountable problems*
insurrection Ⓣ *n* rebellion
intact Ⓣ *adj* not changed or damaged in any way
intaglio [in-**tah**-lee-oh] *n, pl* **-lios**, **-li** (gem carved with) an engraved design
intake *n* **1** thing or quantity taken in **2** opening through which fluid or gas enters an engine, pipe, etc.
intangible *adj* **1** difficult for the mind to grasp: *intangible ideas* **2** incapable of being felt by touch
integer *n* positive or negative whole number or zero
integral Ⓣ *adj* **1** being an essential part of a whole ▷ *n* **2** *math* sum of a large number of very small quantities
integrate Ⓣ *v* **1** combine into a whole **2** amalgamate (a religious or racial group) into a community **integration** *n*
▶ **integrated circuit** tiny electronic circuit on a silicon chip
integrity Ⓣ *n* **1** honesty **2** quality of being sound or whole
integument *n* natural covering such as skin or rind
intellect Ⓣ *n* **1** power of thinking and reasoning [illegible]
▶ **intelle**[illegible]
the intell[illegible]
3 intellec[illegible]
intellige[illegible]
learn, an[illegible]
a computerized device) able to initiate or modify action in the light of ongoing events **intelligently** *adv*
▶ **intelligence** *n* **1** quality of being intelligent **2** collection of secret information **3** people or department collecting military information
▶ **intelligent design** theory that a sentient being designed and created the universe and all life
intelligentsia Ⓣ *n* intellectual or cultured classes
intelligible Ⓣ *adj* understandable **intelligibility** *n*
intemperate Ⓣ *adj* **1** uncontrolled **2** drinking alcohol to excess **3** extreme **intemperance** *n*
intend Ⓣ *v* **1** propose or plan (something or to do something) **2** have as one's purpose
intense Ⓣ *adj* **1** of great strength or degree **2** deeply emotional **intensity** *n*
intensify Ⓣ *v* **-fying**, **-fied** make or become

THESAURUS

impossible, invincible, hopeless, impassable, overwhelming, unconquerable
insurrection *n* = **rebellion**, riot, insurgency, revolution, coup, uprising, revolt, mutiny
intact *adj* = **undamaged**, complete, sound, whole, perfect, entire, unharmed, unscathed, unbroken, unimpaired
integral *adj* = **essential**, necessary, basic, component, fundamental, constituent, indispensable, intrinsic
integrate *v* = **combine**, join, unite, merge, incorporate, blend, fuse, amalgamate, assimilate
integration *n* = **assimilation**, unification, combining, amalgamation, incorporation, blending, fusing, mixing
integrity *n* **1** = **honesty**, principle, honour, virtue, goodness, purity, incorruptibility, probity, rectitude, uprightness **2** = **unity**, cohesion, soundness, coherence, completeness, wholeness
intellect *n* = **intelligence**, reason, sense, mind, judgment, understanding, brains (*informal*)
intellectual *adj* **1** = **scholarly**, intelligent, cerebral, thoughtful, bookish, highbrow, studious, pointy-headed (*informal*) ▶ *n* **2** = **thinker**, academic, egghead (*informal*), highbrow, pointy-head (*informal*)
intelligence *n* **1** = **intellect**, sense, understanding, perception, wit, comprehension, cleverness • *students of high intelligence* **2** = **information**, report, news, knowledge, data, notification, facts, findings
See also: **head, word**
intelligent *adj* = **clever**, quick, sharp, smart, bright, acute, brainy (*informal*) • *Dolphins are intelligent animals.* OPPOSITE: stupid
See also: **brilliant**
intelligentsia *n* = **intellectuals**, highbrows, literati
intelligible *adj* = **understandable**, open, clear, plain, distinct, lucid, comprehensible
intemperate *adj* = **excessive**, wild, extreme, self-indulgent, unrestrained, unbridled, immoderate, profligate
intend *v* **1** = **plan**, mean, aim, propose, resolve, be determined • *She intended to move back to Saskatoon.* **2** = **mean**, aim, design, earmark • *a book intended for serious students*
intended *See* **calculated**
intense *adj* **1** = **extreme**, great, deep, powerful, severe, fierce, acute, profound • *intense heat* **2** = **passionate**, fierce, earnest, impassioned, ardent, vehement, fervent • *She was very intense before the important game.*
See also: **colourful, furious, serious, uncommon, violent**
intensify *v* = **increase**, strengthen, aggravate, escalate, deepen, reinforce, heighten, sharpen, magnify, redouble, add to
intensity *n* = **force**, strength, emotion, passion, vigour, fanaticism, ardour, fervour,

DICTIONARY

more intense **intensification** *n*
intensive Ⓣ *adj* using or needing concentrated effort or resources **intensively** *adv*
intent Ⓣ *n* **1** intention ▷ *adj* **2** paying close attention **intently** *adv* **intentness** *n*
▸ **intent on** determined to
intention Ⓣ *n* something intended
▸ **intentional** *adj* deliberate **intentionally** *adv*
inter Ⓣ [in-**ter**] *v* **-terring, -terred** bury (a corpse)
▸ **interment** *n* burial (of a corpse)
inter- *prefix* between or among: *intercontinental*
interact *v* act on or in close relation with each other **interaction** *n* **interactive** *adj*
interbreed *v* breed within a related group
intercede Ⓣ *v* **1** plead in favour of **2** mediate
intercession *n* **intercessor** *n*
intercept Ⓣ *v* seize or stop in transit
interception *n*
interchange Ⓣ *v* **1** (cause to) exchange places ▷ *n* **2** highway junction
interchangeable *adj*
inter-city *adj* (of a passenger service) travelling fast between cities
intercom *n* internal communication system with loudspeakers
intercontinental *adj* travelling between or linking continents
intercourse Ⓣ *n* **1** act of having sex **2** communication or dealings between people or groups
interdenominational *adj* among or involving more than one denomination of the Christian Church
interdict, interdiction *n* formal order forbidding something
interdisciplinary *adj* involving more than one academic discipline
interest Ⓣ *n* **1** desire to know or hear more about something **2** hobby or subject that one enjoys **3** *often pl* advantage: *in one's own interests* **4** sum paid for use of borrowed money **5** right or share ▷ *v* **6** arouse the interest of
interesting *adj* **interestingly** *adv*
▸ **interested** *adj* **1** feeling or showing interest **2** involved in or affected by
interface Ⓣ *n* **1** area where two things interact or link **2** circuit linking a computer and another device
interfaith *adj* relating to or involving different religions
interfere Ⓣ *v* **1** try to influence other people's affairs where one is not involved or wanted **2** clash (with) **3** *euphemistic* abuse sexually **interfering** *adj*

THESAURUS

fierceness, vehemence
intensive *adj* = **concentrated,** comprehensive, thorough, in-depth, exhaustive, demanding, thoroughgoing
intent *n* **1** = **intention**, plan, end, goal, aim, design, object, purpose, objective, meaning ▸ *adj* **2** = **absorbed**, eager, watchful, determined, steadfast, attentive, engrossed, preoccupied, rapt, resolved
intention *n* = **aim**, goal, idea, object, purpose, objective • *He annced his intention of retiring.*
See also: **point**
intentional *adj* = **deliberate**, planned, intended, calculated, wilful, meant, premeditated
intentionally *adv* = **deliberately**, wilfully, designedly, on purpose
inter *v* = **bury**, entomb, lay to rest
intercede *v* = **mediate**, plead, intervene, arbitrate
intercept *v* = **catch**, stop, block, seize, interrupt, obstruct, cut off, head off
interchange *v* **1** = **switch**, trade, exchange, swap, alternate, reciprocate ▸ *n* **2** = **junction**, crossing, intersection, crossroads
interchangeable *adj* = **identical**, equivalent, synonymous, reciprocal, exchangeable
intercourse *n* **1** = **communication**, contact, commerce, dealings **2** = **sexual intercourse**, sex, carnal knowledge, coitus, copulation
interest *n* **1** = **curiosity**, concern, attention, fascination • *I have a great interest in that period of history.* **2** = **hobby**, activity, pursuit, pastime • *He has a wide range of interests.* **3** = **advantage**, good, profit, benefit **4** = **stake**, right, share, claim, investment ▸ *v* **5** = **intrigue**, appeal, stimulate, fascinate, captivate • *This part of the book interests me most.* OPPOSITE: bore
See also: **enthusiasm**
interested *adj* **1** = **curious**, keen, excited, attracted, drawn, fascinated **2** = **involved**, concerned, implicated
interesting *adj* = **intriguing**, absorbing, compelling, entertaining, gripping, stimulating • *an interesting hobby* OPPOSITE: boring
See also: **colourful**
interface *n* = **connection**, link, border, boundary, frontier
interfere *v* **1** = **meddle**, intervene, tamper, intrude, butt in • *Stop interfering and leave me alone.* **2** = **conflict**, disrupt, hinder, obstruct, impede, inhibit • *His problems interfered with his work.*
See also: **pry**

DICTIONARY

▸ **interference** *n* **1** interfering **2** *radio* interruption of reception by atmospherics or unwanted signals
interferon *n* protein that stops the development of an invading virus
interim Ⓣ *adj* temporary or provisional
interior Ⓣ *n* **1** inside **2** inland region ▷ *adj* **3** inside, inner **4** mental or spiritual
interject *v* make (a remark) suddenly or as an interruption **interjection** *n*
interlace *v* join by lacing or weaving together
interlay *v* insert (layers) between
interlink *v* connect together
interlock *v* **1** join firmly together ▷ *adj* **2** closely knitted
interlocutor [in-ter-**lok**-yew-ter] *n* person who takes part in a conversation
interloper Ⓣ [**in**-ter-lope-er] *n* person in a place or situation where he or she has no right to be
interlude Ⓣ *n* short rest or break in an activity or event
intermarry *v* (of families, races, or religions) become linked by marriage
intermarriage *n*
intermediate Ⓣ *adj* coming between two points or extremes
▸ **intermediary** *n* **1** person trying to create agreement between others **2** messenger
intermezzo [in-ter-**met**-so] *n, pl* **-zos**, **-zi** short piece of music, esp. one performed between the acts of an opera
interminable Ⓣ *adj* seemingly endless because boring **interminably** *adv*
intermingle Ⓣ *v* mix together
intermission Ⓣ *n* interval between parts of a play, film, etc.
intermittent Ⓣ *adj* occurring at intervals
intermittently *adv*
intern Ⓣ *v* **1** imprison, esp. during a war ▷ *n* **2** trainee doctor in a hospital **internment** *n*
▸ **internee** *n* person who has been interned
internal Ⓣ *adj* **1** of or on the inside **2** within a country or organization **3** spiritual or mental
internally *adv*
▸ **internal-combustion engine** engine powered by the explosion of a fuel-and-air mixture within the cylinders
international Ⓣ *adj* **1** of or involving two or more countries ▷ *n* **2** game or match between teams of different countries **3** player in such a match **internationally** *adv*
internecine *adj* mutually destructive
internet Ⓣ *n* large international computer network
interplanetary *adj* of or linking planets
interplay *n* action and reaction of two things upon each other
Interpol International Criminal Police Organization
interpolate [in-**ter**-pole-ate] *v* insert (a comment or passage) in (a conversation or text) **interpolation** *n*
interpose Ⓣ *v* **1** insert between or among things **2** say as an interruption
interposition *n*
interpret Ⓣ *v* **1** explain the meaning of

THESAURUS

interference *n* **1** = **meddling**, intervention, intrusion, prying **2** = **conflict**, opposition, collision, obstruction, clashing
interim *adj* = **temporary**, acting, makeshift, provisional, caretaker, stopgap, improvised
interior *n* **1** = **inside**, heart, core, centre ▸ *adj* **2** = **inside**, internal, inner, inward **3** = **mental**, private, personal, secret, spiritual, intimate, inner, hidden
interloper *n* = **trespasser**, intruder, gate-crasher (*informal*), meddler
interlude *n* = **interval**, break, delay, rest, spell, pause, stoppage, intermission, hiatus, respite, breathing space
intermediary *n* = **mediator**, agent, broker, middleman, go-between
intermediate *adj* = **middle**, midway, halfway, mid, transitional, in-between (*informal*), intervening
interment *n* = **burial**, funeral
interminable *adj* = **endless**, protracted, infinite, perpetual, everlasting, long-winded, ceaseless, long-drawn-out, never-ending
intermingle *v* = **mix**, combine, merge, blend, fuse, interweave, intermix, interlace
intermission *n* = **interval**, break, rest, pause, stoppage, recess, respite, interlude
intermittent *adj* = **periodic**, occasional, irregular, sporadic, broken, fitful, spasmodic
intern *v* = **imprison**, hold, detain, confine, hold in custody
internal *adj* **1** = **inner**, inside, interior **2** = **domestic**, home, civic, in-house, intramural • *the new head of internal affairs* ▷ **internal organs** *See* **insides**
international *adj* = **global**, worldwide, universal, cosmopolitan, intercontinental
internet *n* = **information superhighway**, cyberspace, the net (*informal*), the web (*informal*), World Wide Web, interweb (*humorous*)
interpose *v* = **interrupt**, insert, interject, put one's oar in
interpret *v* = **explain**, translate, render, decode, decipher, construe, elucidate, make sense of
interpretation *n* = **explanation**, version, analysis, portrayal, translation, rendition, clarification, exposition, elucidation
interpreter *n* = **translator**, commentator

DICTIONARY

2 convey the meaning of (a poem, song, etc.) in performance **3** translate orally from one language into another **interpretation** *n* **interpreter** *n*
interprovincial *adj* between or involving two or more provinces
interregnum *n, pl* **-nums, -na** interval between reigns
interrelate *v* (of two or more things) connect or be connected with each other **interrelation** *n* **interrogator** *n*
interrogate Ⓣ *v* question closely **interrogation** *n*
▸ **interrogative** *adj* **1** questioning ▹ *n* **2** word used in asking a question, such as *how* or *why*
interrupt Ⓣ *v* **1** break into (a conversation etc.) **2** temporarily stop (a process or activity) **interruption** *n*
intersect Ⓣ *v* **1** (of roads or lines) meet and cross **2** divide by passing across or through **intersection** *n*
interspersed *adj* scattered among, between, or on
interstate *adj* *US* between or involving two or more states
interstellar *adj* between or among stars
interstice [in-**ter**-stiss] *n* small crack or gap between things
intertwine *v* twist together or entwine
interval Ⓣ *n* **1** time between two particular moments or events **2** break between parts of a play, concert, etc. **3** difference in pitch between notes
▸ **at intervals 1** repeatedly **2** with spaces left between
intervene Ⓣ *v* **1** involve oneself in a situation, esp. to prevent conflict **2** happen so as to stop something **intervention** *n*
interview Ⓣ *n* **1** formal discussion, esp. between a job-seeker and employer **2** questioning of a well-known person about his or her career, views, etc., by a reporter ▹ *v* **3** have an interview with **interviewee** *n* **interviewer** *n*
interwar *adj* of or during the period 1919–39
interweave *v* weave together
intestate *adj* not having made a will **intestacy** *n*
intestine Ⓣ *n usu pl* lower part of the alimentary canal between the stomach and the anus **intestinal** *adj*
intimate[1] Ⓣ *adj* **1** having a close personal relationship **2** private **3** (of knowledge) extensive and detailed **4** *euphemistic* having sexual relations **5** having a friendly quiet atmosphere ▹ *n* **6** intimate friend **intimately** *adv* **intimacy** *n*
intimate[2] Ⓣ *v* **1** hint or suggest **2** announce **intimation** *n*

THESAURUS

interrogate *v* = **question**, examine, quiz, grill • *I interrogated everyone even slightly involved.*
See also: **ask**
interrogation *n* = **questioning**, inquiry, examination, cross-examination, inquisition, grilling (*informal*), third degree (*informal*)
interrupt *v* **1** = **butt in**, heckle • *He tried to speak, but she interrupted him.* **2** = **suspend**, break, discontinue • *The game was interrupted by rain.*
See also: **intrude**
interruption *n* = **stoppage**, break, suspension, disruption, pause, disturbance, hitch, intrusion
intersect *See* **cross**
intersection *n* = **junction**, crossing, interchange, crossroads
interval *n* = **break**, gap, pause, hiatus, interlude • *There was a long interval of silence.*
See also: **period, space, time, wait**
intervene *v* **1** = **mediate**, arbitrate • *I relied on them to intervene if anything happened.* **2** = **happen**, occur, ensue, befall, come to pass, take place
See also: **interfere**
intervention *n* = **mediation**, agency, interference, intrusion
interview *n* **1** = **meeting**, talk, conference, audience, dialogue, consultation, press conference ▸ *v* **2** = **question**, examine, interrogate, talk to
interviewer *n* = **questioner**, reporter, investigator, interrogator, examiner
intestines *pl n* = **guts**, bowels, entrails, innards (*informal*), insides (*informal*), viscera
intimacy *n* = **familiarity**, confidentiality, closeness
intimate[1] *adj* **1** = **close**, near, confidential, thick (*informal*), dear, bosom, buddy-buddy (*informal*) **2** = **personal**, private, secret, confidential **3** = **detailed**, deep, immediate, profound, thorough, first-hand, in-depth, exhaustive **4** = **snug**, warm, friendly, cozy, comfy (*informal*), homey ▸ *n* **5** = **friend**, companion *or* constant companion, confidant *or* confidante (*feminine*), crony, close friend, homeboy (*slang*), homegirl (*slang*), soul mate
intimate[2] *v* **1** = **suggest**, indicate, hint, imply, insinuate **2** = **announce**, state, declare, communicate, make known
intimately *adv* **1** = **confidingly**, personally, warmly, affectionately, confidentially, familiarly, tenderly **2** = **in detail**, fully, thoroughly, inside out, very well
intimation *n* **1** = **hint**, warning, suggestion, indication, reminder, inkling, allusion,

DICTIONARY

intimidate Ⓣ *v* subdue or influence by frightening **intimidation** *n* **intimidating** *adj*
into Ⓣ *prep* **1** to the inner part of **2** to the middle of **3** (up) against **4** used to indicate the result of a change: *he turned into a monster* **5** *math* used to indicate division: *three into six is two* **6** *informal* interested in
intolerable Ⓣ *adj* more than can be endured **intolerably** *adv*
intolerant Ⓣ *adj* narrow-minded or bigoted **intolerance** *n*
intonation *n* sound pattern produced by variations in the voice
intone Ⓣ *v* speak or recite in an unvarying tone of voice
in toto *adv Latin* totally, entirely
intoxicate *v* **1** make drunk **2** excite to excess **intoxication** *n*
▸ **intoxicant** *n, adj* (drink) capable of intoxicating
intractable Ⓣ *adj* (of a person) **1** difficult to influence **2** (of a problem or illness) hard to solve or cure
intranet *n computers* internal network that makes use of internet technology
intransigent Ⓣ *adj* refusing to change one's attitude **intransigence** *n*
intransitive *adj* (of a verb) not taking a direct object
intrauterine *adj* within the womb
intravenous [in-tra-**vee**-nuss] *adj* into a vein **intravenously** *adv*
intrepid Ⓣ *adj* fearless or bold **intrepidity** *n*
intricate Ⓣ *adj* **1** involved or complicated **2** full of fine detail **intricately** *adv* **intricacy** *n*
intrigue Ⓣ *v* **1** make interested or curious **2** plot secretly ▷ *n* **3** secret plotting **4** secret love affair **intriguing** *adj*
intrinsic Ⓣ *adj* part of the basic nature of **intrinsically** *adv*
introduce Ⓣ *v* **1** present (someone) by name (to another person) **2** present (a radio or television programme) **3** bring forward for

THESAURUS

insinuation **2 = announcement**, communication, notice, declaration
intimidate *v* **= frighten**, threaten, scare, bully, subdue, coerce, terrorize, daunt, browbeat, overawe
intimidating *See* **formidable, frightening**
intimidation *n* **= bullying**, pressure, threat *or* threats, coercion, arm-twisting (*informal*), browbeating, menaces, terrorization
into *See* **keen**
intolerable *adj* **= unbearable**, impossible, painful, excruciating, insufferable, insupportable, unendurable
intolerance *n* **= narrow-mindedness**, discrimination, prejudice, bigotry, fanaticism, chauvinism, dogmatism, illiberality
intolerant *adj* **= narrow-minded**, dictatorial, chauvinistic, fanatical, dogmatic, bigoted, illiberal, prejudiced, small-minded
intone *v* **= chant**, recite
intoxicated *adj* **1 = drunk**, drunken, inebriated, paralytic (*informal*), plastered (*slang*), tipsy, under the influence (*informal*) **2 = euphoric**, high (*informal*), excited, dizzy, elated, enraptured, exhilarated, wired (*slang*)
intoxicating *adj* **1 = alcoholic**, strong **2 = exciting**, thrilling, heady, exhilarating
intoxication *n* **1 = drunkenness**, inebriation, insobriety, tipsiness **2 = excitement**, delirium, euphoria, elation, exhilaration
intractable *See* **difficult, obstinate**
intransigent *adj* **= uncompromising**, hardline, stubborn, intractable, unyielding, obdurate, obstinate, stiff-necked, unbending
intrepid *adj* **= fearless**, brave, bold, daring, courageous, audacious, valiant, plucky, gallant, stouthearted
intricacy *n* **= complexity**, complication, convolutions, elaborateness
intricate *adj* **= complicated**, complex, elaborate, fancy, involved, tangled, tortuous, convoluted, labyrinthine
intrigue *v* **1 = interest**, attract, fascinate, rivet, titillate **2 = plot**, scheme, conspire, manoeuvre, connive, machinate ▸ *n* **3 = plot**, scheme, conspiracy, collusion, machination, manoeuvre, chicanery, stratagem, wile **4 = affair**, romance, liaison, intimacy, amour
intriguing *adj* **= interesting**, exciting, beguiling, compelling, diverting, fascinating, tantalizing, titillating
intrinsic *adj* **= inborn**, natural, native, basic, constitutional, essential, fundamental, built-in, congenital, inherent, inbred
introduce *v* **1 = present**, acquaint, familiarize, make known **2 = bring in**, start, launch, establish, found, pioneer, institute, initiate, set up **3 = bring up**, air, advance, submit, moot, broach, put forward **4 = insert**, add, inject, put in, throw in (*informal*)
introduction *n* **1 = launch**, institution, establishment, inauguration, initiation • *the introduction of the loonie in 1987* **2 = foreword**, preface, prologue • *The book contains a new introduction by the author.*
See also: **appearance**
introductory *adj* **= preliminary**, first, opening, initial, inaugural, preparatory

DICTIONARY

discussion **4** bring into use **5** insert
▸ **introduction** *n* **1** introducing **2** preliminary part or treatment **3** presentation of one person to another
▸ **introductory** *adj* preliminary
introspection *n* examination of one's own thoughts and feelings **introspective** *adj*
introvert *n* person concerned more with his or her thoughts and feelings than with external reality **introverted** *adj* **introversion** *n*
intrude Ⓣ *v* come in or join in without being invited **intruder** *n* **intrusion** *n* **intrusive** *adj*
intuition Ⓣ *n* instinctive knowledge or insight without conscious reasoning **intuitive** *adj* **intuitively** *adv*
Inuit *n* Eskimo of North America or Greenland
Inuk *n* a member of any Inuit people
Inuktitut [in-**nook**-ti-toot] *n* language of Inuit, Eskimo
inundate Ⓣ *v* **1** flood **2** overwhelm **inundation** *n*
inure *v* accustom, esp. to hardship or danger
invade Ⓣ *v* **1** enter (a country) by military force **2** enter in large numbers **3** disturb (privacy etc.) **invader** *n*
invalid[1] Ⓣ *n* **1** disabled or chronically ill person ▹ *v* **2** dismiss from active service because of illness etc. **invalidity** *n*
invalid[2] Ⓣ *adj* **1** having no legal force **2** (of an argument etc.) not valid because based on a mistake
▸ **invalidate** *v* make or show to be invalid
invaluable Ⓣ *adj* priceless
invasion Ⓣ *n* **1** act of invading **2** intrusion
invective Ⓣ *n* abusive speech or writing
inveigh [in-**vay**] *v* (foll. by *against*) criticize (something) harshly
inveigle *v* coax or entice **inveiglement** *n*
invent Ⓣ *v* **1** think up or create (something new) **2** make up (a story, excuse, etc.) **inventor** *n*
▸ **invention** *n* **1** something invented **2** ability to invent
▸ **inventive** *adj* **1** resourceful **2** creative **inventiveness** *n*

THESAURUS

introspective *adj* = **inward-looking**, meditative, contemplative, brooding, introverted, pensive
introverted *adj* = **introspective**, self-contained, inner-directed, inward-looking, withdrawn
intrude *v* = **butt in**, violate, interrupt, infringe, trespass, encroach • *I don't want to intrude on your parents.* ▹ **intrude on** *See* **disturb**
See also: **interfere, pry**
intruder *n* = **trespasser**, invader, interloper, gate-crasher (*informal*), infiltrator, prowler
intrusion *n* = **invasion**, violation, infringement, interference, interruption, trespass, encroachment
intrusive *adj* = **interfering**, unwanted, presumptuous, impertinent, importunate, meddlesome, nosy (*informal*), pushy (*informal*), uncalled-for
intuition *n* = **instinct**, perception, insight, hunch, presentiment, sixth sense
intuitive *adj* = **instinctive**, spontaneous, innate, untaught
inundate *v* = **flood**, overwhelm, drown, swamp, overflow, overrun, engulf, submerge, immerse
invade *v* **1** = **attack**, enter, violate, occupy • *The allies invaded the mainland.* **2** = **infest**, overrun, permeate, pervade, swarm over
See also: **raid**
invader *n* = **attacker**, raider, aggressor, plunderer, trespasser
invalid[1] *adj* **1** = **disabled**, ill, sick, ailing, frail, bedridden, infirm, challenged ▸ *n* **2** = **patient**, convalescent, valetudinarian, sickie (*informal*)
invalid[2] *adj* = **null and void**, false, void, unfounded, irrational, worthless, illogical, unsound, fallacious, inoperative
invalidate *v* = **nullify**, cancel, undermine, overthrow, undo, annul
invaluable *adj* = **precious**, valuable, priceless, inestimable, worth one's weight in gold *or* worth its weight in gold
invariably *adv* = **always**, regularly, consistently, perpetually, customarily, day in, day out, habitually, unfailingly, without exception
invasion *n* **1** = **attack**, campaign, assault, offensive, raid, foray, incursion, onslaught, inroad **2** = **intrusion**, breach, violation, infringement, infraction, encroachment, usurpation
invective *n* = **abuse**, tirade, censure, diatribe, denunciation, tongue-lashing, vilification, vituperation
invent *v* **1** = **create**, coin, originate, conceive, formulate, come up with (*informal*) • *He invented the first electric clock.* **2** = **make up**, manufacture, fabricate, concoct • *I tried to invent a plausible excuse.*
See also: **compose, produce**
invented *See* **imaginary**
invention *n* **1** = **creation**, design, device, discovery, gadget, instrument, contraption, brainchild (*informal*), contrivance **2** = **creativity**, imagination, genius, ingenuity, originality, inventiveness, resourcefulness **3** = **fiction**, lie, fantasy,

DICTIONARY

inventory ⓣ [**in**-ven-tree] *n, pl* **-tories** detailed list of goods or furnishings
inverse ⓣ *adj* **1** opposite, inverted **2** *math* linking two variables in such a way that one increases as the other decreases **inversely** *adv*
invert ⓣ *v* turn upside down or inside out **inversion** *n*
▸ **inverted commas** raised commas in writing to show where speech begins and ends
invertebrate *n* animal with no backbone
invest ⓣ *v* spend (money, time, etc.) on something with the expectation of profit **investor** *n*
▸ **investment** *n* **1** money invested **2** something invested in
▸ **invest in** *v* buy
▸ **invest with** *v* give (power or rights) to
investigate ⓣ *v* **1** inquire into **2** examine **investigation** *n* **investigative** *adj* **investigator** *n*
investiture ⓣ *n* formal installation of a person in an office or rank
inveterate ⓣ *adj* **1** deep-rooted **2** confirmed in a habit or practice **inveteracy** *n*
invidious ⓣ *adj* likely to cause resentment **invidiously** *adv*
invigilate ⓣ [in-**vij**-il-late] *v* supervise examination candidates **invigilator** *n*
invigorate ⓣ *v* give energy to or refresh
invincible ⓣ *adj* unconquerable **invincibly** *adv* **invincibility** *n*
inviolable ⓣ *adj* that must not be broken or violated
inviolate ⓣ *adj* unharmed, unaffected
invisible ⓣ *adj* not able to be seen **invisibly** *adv* **invisibility** *n*
invite ⓣ *v* **1** request the company of **2** ask politely for **3** attract: *the plan invited criticism* ▹ *n* **4** *informal* invitation **inviting** *adj* **invitation** *n*
in vitro *adj* (of a biological process) happening outside the body in an artificial environment
invoice ⓣ *v, n* (send) a bill for goods or services supplied
invoke ⓣ *v* **1** put (a law or penalty) into

THESAURUS

forgery, fabrication, yarn, falsehood, untruth
inventive *adj* = **creative**, original, innovative, inspired, fertile, imaginative, ingenious, resourceful
inventiveness *See* **imagination**
inventor *n* = **creator**, author, maker, designer, architect, originator, coiner
inventory *n* = **list**, record, file, account, roll, register, roster, catalogue
inverse *adj* = **opposite**, reverse, contrary, reversed, converse, transposed
invert *v* = **overturn**, upset, reverse, upturn, transpose
invest *v* **1** = **spend**, advance, sink, devote, lay out, put in **2** = **empower**, charge, sanction, license, authorize, vest in ▹ **invest in** *See* **buy**
investigate *v* = **examine**, study, research, probe, explore, sift • *Police are still investigating the incidents.*
See also: **inspect**
investigation *n* = **examination**, study, review, search, survey, probe, inquiry, inspection, inquest, exploration
investigator *n* = **examiner**, researcher, detective *or* private detective, gumshoe (*slang*), sleuth, inquirer, private eye (*informal*)
investiture *n* = **installation**, inauguration, induction, ordination, enthronement
investment *n* **1** = **transaction**, speculation, venture **2** = **stake**, contribution, ante (*informal*)
investments *See* **stock**
inveterate *adj* = **long-standing**, chronic, incurable, habitual, entrenched, hardened, deep-seated, confirmed, dyed-in-the-wool, incorrigible
invidious *adj* = **undesirable**, hateful
invigilate *v* = **watch over**, run, conduct, oversee, supervise, keep an eye on, preside over, superintend
invigorate *v* = **refresh**, stimulate, fortify, energize, revitalize, exhilarate, galvanize, enliven, liven up
invincible *adj* = **unbeatable**, indomitable, impregnable • *When the skating pair is at their best, they're invincible.*
inviolable *adj* = **sacrosanct**, holy, sacred, hallowed, inalienable, unalterable
inviolate *adj* = **intact**, whole, entire, pure, untouched, unhurt, unbroken, undefiled, unpolluted, unsullied
invisible *adj* = **unseen**, hidden, concealed, disguised, inconspicuous • *His face was invisible beneath his hat.* OPPOSITE: visible
invitation *n* = **request**, call, invite (*informal*), summons
invite *v* **1** = **request**, ask, bid, beg, summon **2** = **encourage**, court, welcome, attract, provoke, entice, tempt, ask for (*informal*)
inviting *adj* = **tempting**, attractive, appealing, alluring, seductive, enticing, mouthwatering, welcoming
invocation *n* = **appeal**, prayer, petition, entreaty, supplication
invoice *See* **bill**
invoke *v* **1** = **call upon**, pray, petition, beg, implore, beseech, appeal to, entreat, supplicate **2** = **apply**, use, implement,

DICTIONARY

operation **2** prompt or cause (a certain feeling) **3** call on (a god) for help, inspiration, etc. **invocation** *n*
involuntary Ⓣ *adj* **1** not done consciously **2** unintentional **involuntarily** *adv*
involve Ⓣ *v* **1** include as a necessary part **2** affect **3** implicate (a person) **4** make complicated **involvement** *n*
▸ **involved** *adj* **1** complicated **2** concerned in
invulnerable Ⓣ *adj* not able to be wounded or harmed
inward Ⓣ *adj* **1** internal **2** situated within **3** spiritual or mental ▷ *adv* **4** Also **inwards** towards the inside or middle **inwardly** *adv*
iodine *n* bluish-black element used in medicine, photography, and dyeing
▸ **iodize** *v* treat with iodine
ion *n* electrically charged atom **ionic** *adj*
▸ **ionize** *v* change into ions **ionization** *n*
▸ **ionosphere** *n* region of ionized air in the upper atmosphere which reflects radio waves
iota [eye-**oh**-ta] *n* **1** ninth letter in the Greek alphabet **2** very small amount
IOU *n* signed paper acknowledging debt
IPA International Phonetic Alphabet
iPod *n* ® pocket-sized device used to play digital music files
ipso facto *adv Latin* by that very fact
IQ intelligence quotient
Iqbal *n* Sir **Muhammad**. 1875–1938, Indian Muslim poet, philosopher, and political leader, who advocated the establishment of separate nations for Indian Hindus and Muslims and is generally regarded as the originator of Pakistan
IRA Irish Republican Army
Iranian *n* **1** person from Iran ▷ *adj* **2** of Iran, its people, or their language
Iraqi *n* **1** person from Iraq ▷ *adj* **2** of Iraq or its people
irascible *adj* easily angered **irascibly** *adv* **irascibility** *n*
irate Ⓣ *adj* very angry
ire *n lit* anger
Ireland *n* **John** (**Nicholson**). 1879–1962, English composer, esp. of songs
iridescent *adj* having shimmering changing colours like a rainbow **iridescence** *n*
iris *n* **1** circular membrane of the eye containing the pupil **2** plant with sword-shaped leaves and showy flowers
Irish *adj* of Ireland
▸ **Irish coffee** hot coffee mixed with whiskey and topped with cream
irk *v* irritate or annoy
▸ **irksome** *adj* tiresome
iron Ⓣ *n* **1** metallic element widely used for structural and engineering purposes **2** tool made of iron **3** appliance used, when heated, to press clothes or fabric **4** metal-headed golf club **irons 5** fetters or chains ▷ *adj* **6** made of iron **7** inflexible: *an iron will* ▷ *v* **8** smooth (clothes or fabric) with an iron
▸ **iron out** *v* settle (a problem) through discussion
▸ **Iron Age** era when iron tools were used
▸ **ironing** *n* clothes to be ironed
▸ **ironing board** long cloth-covered board, usu. with folding legs, on which to iron clothes
ironic, ironical Ⓣ *adj* using irony
ironically *adv*
ironmonger *n Brit* shopkeeper or shop

THESAURUS

initiate, put into effect, resort to
involuntary *adj* = **unintentional**, automatic, unconscious, spontaneous, reflex, uncontrolled, instinctive, unthinking
involve *v* **1** = **require**, incorporate, take in • *Running a kitchen involves a great deal of organization.* **2** = **concern**, affect, touch, implicate, draw in
See also: **demand, include**
involved *adj* **1** = **complicated**, complex, elaborate, confusing, tangled, intricate, tortuous, convoluted, labyrinthine **2** = **concerned**, caught *or* caught up, implicated, mixed up in *or* mixed up with, participating, taking part
involvement *n* = **connection**, interest, commitment, association, participation
invulnerable *adj* = **safe**, secure, invincible, unassailable, impenetrable, indestructible, insusceptible, proof against
inward *adj* **1** = **incoming**, inbound, entering, ingoing **2** = **internal**, inside, interior, inner **3** = **private**, personal, secret, confidential, hidden, innermost, inmost
inwardly *adv* = **privately**, inside, secretly, at heart, deep down
irate *adj* = **angry**, cross, furious, enraged, annoyed, livid, incensed, indignant, infuriated
irksome *adj* = **irritating**, troublesome, tiresome, bothersome, annoying, disagreeable, exasperating, trying, vexing, wearisome
iron *adj* **1** = **ferrous**, chalybeate, ferric **2** = **inflexible**, strong, hard, tough, adamant, rigid, steely, unyielding, implacable, indomitable, unbending ▸ *v* ▷ **iron out** = **settle**, resolve, reconcile, clear up, get rid of, put right, smooth over, sort out, straighten out
ironic *adj* **1** = **sarcastic**, satirical, wry, double-edged, sardonic, mocking, with tongue in cheek **2** = **paradoxical**, incongruous

DICTIONARY

dealing in hardware **ironmongery** *n*
Irons *n* **Jeremy**. born 1948, British film and stage actor. His films include *The French Lieutenant's Woman* (1981), *The Mission* (1986), *Reversal of Fortune* (1990), and *Lolita* (1997)
ironstone *n* **1** rock consisting mainly of iron ore **2** tough durable earthenware
irony ⓣ *n, pl* **-nies 1** mildly sarcastic use of words to imply the opposite of what is said **2** event or situation that is the opposite of what is expected
irradiate *v* subject to or treat with radiation **irradiation** *n*
irrational ⓣ *adj* not based on logical reasoning
irreconcilable *adj* not able to be resolved or settled: *irreconcilable disagreement*
irrecoverable *adj* not able to be recovered, remedied, or rectified
irredeemable *adj* **1** not able to be reformed, improved, or corrected **2** not able to be recovered, bought back, or converted into coin
irreducible *adj* impossible to put in a reduced or simpler form
irrefutable ⓣ *adj* impossible to deny or disprove
irregular ⓣ *adj* **1** not regular or even **2** unconventional **3** (of a word) not following the typical pattern of formation in a language **irregularly** *adv* **irregularity** *n*
irrelevant ⓣ *adj* not connected with the matter in hand **irrelevantly** *adv* **irrelevance** *n*
irreparable ⓣ *adj* not able to be put right or repaired **irreparably** *adv*
irreplaceable *adj* impossible to replace
irrepressible ⓣ *adj* not capable of being repressed, controlled, or restrained **irrepressibly** *adv*
irreproachable ⓣ *adj* blameless, faultless **irreproachably** *adv*
irresistible ⓣ *adj* too attractive or strong to resist **irresistibly** *adv*
irresolute *adj* unable to make decisions, hesitating **irresolutely** *adv*
irrespective of *prep* without taking account of
irresponsible ⓣ *adj* not showing or done with due care for the consequences of one's actions or attitudes **irresponsibly** *adv*
irretrievable *adj* impossible to put right or make good **irretrievably** *adv*
irreverence *n* **1** lack of due respect **2** disrespectful remark or act **irreverent** *adj*
irreversible ⓣ *adj* not able to be reversed or put right again: *the damage may be irreversible* **irreversibly** *adv*
irrevocable ⓣ *adj* not possible to change or undo **irrevocably** *adv*
irrigate ⓣ *v* water by artificial channels or pipes **irrigation** *n*

THESAURUS

irony *n* **1 = sarcasm**, satire, mockery **2 = paradox**, incongruity
irrational *adj* **= illogical**, crazy, absurd, nonsensical, unsound • *irrational fears*
irrefutable *adj* **= undeniable**, sure, certain, indisputable, incontrovertible, incontestable, indubitable, unquestionable
irregular *adj* **1 = uneven**, lopsided, bumpy, jagged, ragged, asymmetrical • *an irregular surface* OPPOSITE: regular **2 = variable**, random, occasional, erratic, patchy, haphazard • *She worked irregular hours.* OPPOSITE: regular **3 = unconventional**, unusual, extraordinary, unofficial, exceptional, abnormal, peculiar, unorthodox *See also*: **changeable, crooked**
irregularity *n* **1 = inconsistency**, desultoriness, disorganization, haphazardness **2 = abnormality**, oddity, anomaly, peculiarity, unorthodoxy **3 = unevenness**, roughness, asymmetry, bumpiness, jaggedness, lopsidedness, raggedness
irrelevant *adj* **= unconnected**, inappropriate, unrelated, immaterial, extraneous, beside the point, impertinent, inapplicable, neither here nor there
irreparable *adj* **= beyond repair**, incurable, irreversible, irremediable, irretrievable
irrepressible *adj* **= unstoppable**, boisterous, buoyant, ebullient, effervescent
irreproachable *adj* **= blameless**, perfect, innocent, pure, impeccable, beyond reproach, faultless, unimpeachable
irresistible *adj* **= overwhelming**, urgent, compulsive, compelling, overpowering
irresponsible *adj* **= thoughtless**, wild, reckless, careless • *an irresponsible attitude* OPPOSITE: responsible *See also*: **unwise**
irreverent *adj* **= disrespectful**, cheeky (*informal*), tongue-in-cheek, flippant, iconoclastic, impertinent, impudent, mocking
irreversible *adj* **= irrevocable**, final, incurable, irreparable, unalterable
irrevocable *adj* **= fixed**, irreversible, fated, immutable, predestined, predetermined, settled, unalterable
irrigate *v* **= water**, flood, wet, inundate, moisten
irritability *n* **= bad temper**, impatience, ill humour, irascibility, prickliness, testiness, tetchiness, touchiness
irritable *adj* **= bad-tempered**,

DICTIONARY

irritate Ⓣ *v* **1** annoy or anger **2** cause (a body part) to itch or become inflamed **irritation** *n* ▸ **irritable** *adj* easily annoyed **irritably** *adv* ▸ **irritant** *n, adj* (person or thing) causing irritation
irrupt *v* enter forcibly or suddenly **irruption** *n*
Irving *n* **1 Kenneth Colin**. 1899–1992, Canadian industrialist. His commercial empire included interests in oil, broadcasting, newspapers, paper, and forestry **2 Washington**. 1783–1859, US essayist and short-story writer, noted for *The Sketch Book of Geoffrey Crayon* (1820), which contains the stories *Rip Van Winkle* and *The Legend of Sleepy Hollow*
is *v* third person singular present tense of **be**
Isabella of France *n* 1292–1358, wife (1308–27) of Edward II of England, whom, aided by her lover, Roger de Mortimer, she deposed; mother of Edward III
Isherwood *n* **Christopher**, full name *Christopher William Bradshaw-Isherwood*. 1904–86, US novelist and dramatist, born in England. His works include the novel *Goodbye to Berlin* (1939) and three verse plays written in collaboration with W.H. Auden
Ishiguro *n* **Kazuo**. born 1954, British novelist born in Japan. His novels include *An Artist of the Floating World* (1986), the Booker-prizewinning *The Remains of the Day* (1989), and *Never Let Me Go* (2005).
isinglass [ize-ing-glass] *n* kind of gelatine obtained from some freshwater fish
Islam *n* **1** Muslim religion teaching that there is one God and that Mohammed is his prophet **2** Muslim countries and civilization **Islamic** *adj*
island Ⓣ *n* piece of land surrounded by water ▸ **islander** *n* person who lives on an island
isle *n* island
▸ **islet** *n* little island
-ism *n suffix* **1** *indicating* political or religious belief: *socialism; Judaism* **2** *indicating* characteristic quality: *heroism* **3** *indicating* an action: *exorcism* **4** *indicating* prejudice on the basis specified: *sexism*
isobar [**ice**-oh-bar] *n* line on a map connecting places of equal barometric pressure **isobaric** *adj*
isolate Ⓣ *v* **1** place apart or alone **2** *chem* obtain (a substance) in uncombined form **isolation** *n*
▸ **isolationism** *n* policy of not participating in international affairs **isolationist** *n, adj*
isomer [**ice**-oh-mer] *n* substance whose molecules contain the same atoms as another but in a different arrangement **isomeric** *adj* **isomerism** *n*
isometric *adj* **1** having equal dimensions **2** relating to muscular contraction without movement **3** (of a three-dimensional drawing) having three equally inclined axes and drawn to scale in every direction
▸ **isometrics** *pl n* system of isometric exercises
isosceles triangle [ice-**soss**-ill-eez] *n* triangle with two sides of equal length
isotherm [**ice**-oh-therm] *n* line on a map connecting points of equal mean temperature
isotope [**ice**-oh-tope] *n* one of two or more atoms with the same number of protons in the nucleus but a different number of neutrons
Israeli *n* **1** person from Israel ▹ *adj* **2** of Israel or its people
issue Ⓣ *n* **1** topic of interest or discussion **2** question requiring a decision **3** particular edition of a magazine or newspaper **4** outcome or result **5** *law* children ▹ *v* **6** make (a statement etc.) publicly **7** officially supply

THESAURUS

cantankerous, crabby, petulant • *He's unusually tense and irritable.*
See also: **grumpy, impatient, moody**
irritate *v* **1 = annoy**, anger, needle (*informal*), bother, ruffle, exasperate, piss off (*taboo slang*), tee off (*slang*) • *Their attitude irritates me.* **2 = inflame**, pain, rub, chafe
See also: **provoke**
irritated *adj* **= annoyed**, cross, angry, bothered, exasperated, nettled, piqued, put out, vexed
irritating *adj* **= annoying**, troublesome, maddening, disturbing, infuriating, irksome, nagging, trying
irritation *n* **1 = annoyance**, anger, displeasure, resentment, indignation, exasperation, testiness, vexation **2 = nuisance**, drag (*informal*), irritant, pain in the neck (*informal*), thorn in one's flesh
island *n* **= isle**, islet, atoll, cay *or* key
isolate *v* **= separate**, disconnect, detach, insulate, segregate, cut off, set apart
isolated *adj* **= remote**, lonely, outlying, hidden, secluded, off the beaten track, out-of-the-way
isolation *n* **= separation**, detachment, segregation, solitude, seclusion, remoteness
issue *n* **1 = topic**, problem, question, concern, matter, subject • *important issues of the day* **2 = edition**, copy, instalment • *the latest issue of* Maclean's *magazine* **3 = outcome**, result, effect, consequence, upshot, end result **4 = children**, offspring, progeny, descendants, heirs ▹ **take issue = disagree**, challenge, dispute, oppose, object,

DICTIONARY

(with) **8** send out or distribute **9** publish
▶ **take issue** disagree
-ist *n suffix* **1** *indicating* person who performs a particular action: *exorcist* **2** *indicating* person who does a particular type of work: *physicist* ▷ *n suffix, adj suffix* **3** *indicative of* a person who holds a particular political or religious belief: *socialist; Buddhist* **4** *indicative of* a person who is prejudiced on the basis specified: *sexist*
isthmus Ⓣ [**iss**-muss] *n, pl* **-muses** narrow strip of land connecting two areas of land
it *pron* **1** refers to a nonhuman, animal, plant, or inanimate object **2** refers to the thing mentioned or being discussed **3** used as the subject of impersonal verbs: *it is snowing* **4** *informal* crucial or ultimate point
▶ **its** *adj* belonging to it
▶ **it's** **1** it is **2** it has
▶ **itself** *pron* emphatic form of **it**
IT information technology
Italian *n* **1** official language of Italy and one of the official languages of Switzerland **2** person from Italy ▷ *adj* **3** of Italy, its people, or their language
italic *adj* (of printing type) sloping to the right
▶ **italics** *pl n* this type, now used for emphasis etc.
▶ **italicize** *v* put in italics
itch Ⓣ *n* **1** skin irritation causing a desire to scratch **2** restless desire ▷ *v* **3** have an itch
itchy *adj*
item Ⓣ *n* **1** single thing in a list or collection **2** piece of information
▶ **itemize** *v* **1** put on a list **2** make a list of
iterate *v* repeat **iteration** *n*
itinerant Ⓣ *adj* travelling from place to place
itinerary Ⓣ *n, pl* **-aries** **1** detailed plan of a journey **2** route
IUD intrauterine device: coil-shaped contraceptive fitted into the womb
IVF in vitro fertilization
ivory *n, pl* **-ries** **1** hard white bony substance forming the tusks of elephants ▷ *adj* **2** yellowish-white
▶ **ivory tower** remoteness from the realities of everyday life
ivy *n, pl* **ivies** climbing evergreen plant

THESAURUS

raise an objection, take exception ▶ *v* **5 = pronounce**, make, give, release, deliver, read out • *They have issued a statement denying the allegations.* OPPOSITE: withdraw **6 = provide**, supply, equip, furnish, give out • *Staff will be issued with badges.*
See also: **affair, business, consideration**
isthmus *n* = **strip**, spit
itch *n* **1 = irritation**, itchiness, prickling, tingling **2 = desire**, passion, hunger, yen (*informal*), longing, craving, lust, yearning, hankering ▶ *v* **3 = prickle**, irritate, tickle, tingle **4 = long**, hunger, pine, ache, crave, lust, yearn, hanker
itching *adj* = **longing**, eager, avid, impatient, raring, spoiling for
itchy *adj* = **impatient**, eager, edgy, restive, restless, unsettled, fidgety
it could be *See* **maybe, perhaps**
item *n* **1 = article**, point, matter • *an item on the agenda* **2 = report**, feature, article, piece, notice • *There was an item in the paper about them.*
See also: **entry**
itinerant *adj* = **wandering**, migratory, nomadic, peripatetic, roaming, roving, travelling, vagrant
itinerary *n* = **schedule**, program, route, timetable

jab Ⓣ *v* **jabbing, jabbed 1** poke roughly ▷ *n* **2** quick short punch **3** *informal* injection
jabber Ⓣ *v* talk rapidly or incoherently
Jabir ibn Hayyan *n* ?721–?815. Arab alchemist, whose many works enjoyed enormous esteem among later alchemists, such as Geber
jabot [**zhab**-oh] *n* frill or ruffle on the front of a blouse or shirt
jacaranda *n* tropical tree with sweet-smelling wood
jacinth *n* reddish-orange precious stone
jack Ⓣ *n* **1** device for raising an automobile or other heavy object **2** playing card with a picture of a pageboy **3** *bowls* small white ball aimed at by the players **4** socket in electrical equipment into which a plug fits **5** flag flown at the bow of a ship, showing nationality
▸ **jack up** *v* lift with a jack
jackal *n* doglike wild animal of Asia and Africa
jackanapes *n* impertinent person
jackass *n* **1** male of the ass **2** fool
▸ **laughing jackass** same as **kookaburra**
jackboot *n* high military boot
jackdaw *n* black-and-grey bird of the crow family
jacket Ⓣ *n* **1** short coat **2** outer paper cover on a hardback book **3** skin of a baked potato
jackknife *n* **1** large clasp knife **2** dive with a sharp bend at the waist in mid-air ▷ *v* **3** (of a tractor-trailer) go out of control so that the trailer swings round at a sharp angle to the cab
jackpot Ⓣ *n* large prize or accumulated stake that may be won in a game
▸ **hit the jackpot** be very successful through luck
jack rabbit *n* American hare with long ears
Jackson *n* **1 Andrew**. 1767–1845, US statesman, general, and lawyer; seventh president of the US (1829–37). He became a national hero after successfully defending New Orleans from the British (1815). During his administration the spoils system was introduced and the national debt was fully paid off **2 Jesse** (**Louis**). born 1941, US Democrat politician and clergyman; Black campaigner for minority rights **3 Michael** (**Joe**). 1958–2009, US pop singer, lead vocalist with the Jacksons (originally the Jackson 5) (1969–86). His solo albums include *Thriller* (1982), *Bad* (1989), and *Invincible* (2001). He died of cardiac arrest while in preparation for a series of concerts in London **Jacksonian** *adj, n*
Jacobean [jak-a-**bee**-an] *adj* of the reign of James I of England
Jacobite *n* supporter of the exiled Stuarts after the overthrow of James II of England
Jacobs *n* **Jane**. 1916–2006, Canadian urban theorist, born in the US. Noted esp. for her book *The Death and Life of Great American Cities* (1961), a critique of US urban renewal policies
Jacobsen *n* **Arne**. 1902–71, Danish architect and designer. His buildings include the Town Hall at Rodovre (1955)
Jacquard [**jak**-ard] *n* fabric in which the design is incorporated into the weave
Jacuzzi [jak-**oo**-zee] *n* ® circular bath with a device that swirls the water
jade *n* **1** ornamental semiprecious stone, usu. dark green ▷ *adj* **2** bluish-green
jaded Ⓣ *adj* tired and unenthusiastic
Jaffa *n* large orange with a thick skin
jag[1] *n* **1** sharp or ragged projection **2** *informal* injection **jagged** [**jag**-gid] *adj*
jag[2] *n* spree or drinking bout
Jagger *n* Sir **Mick**, full name *Michael Philip Jagger*. born 1943, English rock singer and songwriter: lead vocalist with the Rolling Stones
jaguar *n* large S American spotted cat
jail Ⓣ *n* **1** building for confinement of criminals or suspects ▷ *v* **2** send to jail **jailer** *n*
▸ **jailbird** *n informal* person who is or has

THESAURUS

jab *verb, n* = **poke**, tap, stab, punch, dig, nudge, thrust, prod, lunge
jabber *v* = **chatter**, mumble, babble, blether, gabble, ramble, yap (*informal*)
jack *v* ▷ **jack up** = **raise**, lift, hoist, elevate, lift up
jacket *n* = **covering**, case, skin, coat, casing, wrapper, sheath, wrapping
jackpot *n* = **prize**, award, reward, bonanza, winnings
jaded *adj* = **tired**, weary, spent, exhausted, fatigued
jagged *adj* = **uneven**, rough, barbed, craggy, serrated • *jagged cliffs* OPPOSITE: smooth
See also: **irregular, sharp**
jail *n* **1** = **prison** • *sentenced to six months in*

DICTIONARY

often been in jail

jalopy [jal-**lop**-ee] *n, pl* **-lopies** *informal* old automobile

jam[1] *n* spread made from fruit boiled with sugar

jam[2] ⓣ *v* **jamming, jammed 1** pack tightly into a place **2** crowd or congest **3** make or become stuck **4** *radio* block (another station) with impulses of equal wavelength ▷ *n* **5** hold-up of traffic **6** *informal* awkward situation

▸ **jam on** *v* apply (brakes) fiercely

▸ **jam-packed** *adj* filled to capacity

▸ **jam session** informal rock or jazz performance

jamb *n* side post of a door or window frame

jamboree ⓣ *n* **1** large rally of Scouts **2** large celebration

James *n* **1** *New Testament* **a** known as *James the Great.* one of the twelve apostles, a son of Zebedee and brother to John the apostle (Matthew 4:21). Feast day: July 25 or April 30 **b** known as *James the Less.* one of the twelve apostles, son of Alphaeus (Matthew 10:3). Feast day: May 3 or Oct 9 **c** known as *James the brother of the Lord.* a brother or close relative of Jesus (Mark 6:3; Galatians 1:19). Feast day: Oct 23 **d** the book ascribed to his authorship (in full *The Epistle of James*) **2 Henry**. 1843–1916, British novelist, short-story writer, and critic, born in the US. Among his novels are *Washington Square* (1880), *The Portrait of a Lady* (1881), *The Bostonians* (1886), *The Wings of the Dove* (1902), *The Ambassadors* (1903), and *The Golden Bowl* (1904) **3 P(hyllis) D(orothy)**, Baroness James of Holland Park. born 1920, British detective novelist. Her books include *Cover Her Face* (1962), *Death of an Expert Witness* (1977), and *The Private Patient* (2008) **4 William**, brother of Henry James. 1842–1910, US philosopher and psychologist, whose theory of pragmatism is expounded in *Essays in Radical Empiricism* (1912). His other works include *The Will to Believe* (1897), *The Principles of Psychology* (1890), and *The Varieties of Religious Experience* (1902)

James I *n* **1** 1394–1437, king of Scotland (1406–37), second son of Robert III **2** 1566–1625, king of England and Ireland (1603–25) and, as James VI, king of Scotland (1567–1625), in succession to Elizabeth I of England and his mother, Mary Queen of Scots, respectively. He alienated Parliament by his assertion of the divine right of kings, his favourites, esp. the Duke of Buckingham, and his subservience to Spain

James II *n* **1** 1430–60, king of Scotland (1437–60), son of James I **2** 1633–1701, king of England, Ireland, and, as James VII, of Scotland (1685–88); son of Charles I. His pro-Catholic sympathies and arbitrary rule caused the Whigs and Tories to unite in inviting his eldest surviving daughter, Mary, and her husband, William of Orange, to take the throne as joint monarchs. James was defeated at the Boyne (1690) when he attempted to regain the throne

James III *n* 1451–88, king of Scotland (1460–88), son of James II

James IV *n* 1473–1513, king of Scotland (1488–1513), son of James III; he invaded England (1496) in support of Perkin Warbeck; he was killed at Flodden

James V *n* 1512–42, king of Scotland (1513–42), son of James IV

jammy *adj* **-mier, -miest** *slang* lucky

Jan. January

Janáček *n* **Leos**. 1854–1928, Czech composer. His music is influenced by Czech folksong and speech rhythms and is remarkable for its integration of melody and language. His works include the operas *Jenufa* (1904) and *The Cunning Little Vixen* (1924), the *Glagolitic Mass* (1927), as well as orchestral and chamber music and songs

jangle ⓣ *v* **1** (cause to) make a harsh ringing noise **2** (of nerves) be upset or irritated

janitor ⓣ *n* caretaker of a school or other building

January *n* first month of the year

japan *n* **1** very hard varnish, usu. black ▷ *v* **-panning, -panned 2** cover with this varnish

Japanese *adj* **1** of Japan or its people ▷ *n* **2** *pl* **-ese** person from Japan **3** language of Japan

jape *n old-fashioned* joke or prank

japonica *n* shrub with red flowers

Jaques-Dalcroze *n* **Émile**. 1865–1950, Swiss composer and teacher: invented eurythmics

jar[1] ⓣ *n* wide-mouthed container, usu.

THESAURUS

jail ▸ *v* **2 = imprison**, detain, incarcerate • *He was jailed for 20 years.*

jailer *n* = **guard**, keeper, warden

jam *n* **1 = mass**, crowd, crush, mob, throng, multitude • *There was quite a traffic jam on the highway.* **2 = predicament**, hole (*slang*), fix (*informal*), trouble, plight, dilemma, quandary • *We're in a real jam now.* ▸ *v* **3 = cram**, force, stuff, ram • *She jammed on the brakes.* **4 = stick**, stall • *The paper has jammed in the photocopier again.* **5 = crowd**, crush, throng

See also: **mess**

jamboree *n* = **festival**, celebration, festivity, spree, carnival, revelry, fête

jangle *v* = **rattle**, clash, chime, vibrate, jingle, clank, clatter

janitor *n* = **caretaker**, concierge, custodian, porter, doorkeeper

jar[1] *n* = **pot**, pitcher, container, vase, jug, urn, crock

DICTIONARY

cylindrical and made of glass
jar² Ⓣ *v* **jarring, jarred 1** have a disturbing or unpleasant effect on **2** (cause to) vibrate suddenly or violently ▷ *n* **3** jolt or shock
jardinière *n* ornamental plant pot
jargon Ⓣ *n* specialized technical language of a particular subject
Jarman *n* **Derek**. 1942–94, British film director and writer; his films include *Jubilee* (1977), *Caravaggio* (1986), and *Wittgenstein* (1993)
Jarrett *n* **Keith**. born 1945, US jazz pianist and composer
jasmine *n* shrub with sweet-smelling yellow or white flowers
jasper *n* red, yellow, dark green, or brown variety of quartz
jaundice *n* disease marked by yellowness of the skin
▸ **jaundiced** *adj* **1** (of an attitude or opinion) bitter or cynical **2** having jaundice
jaunt Ⓣ *n* **1** short journey for pleasure ▷ *v* **2** make such a journey
jaunty Ⓣ *adj* **-tier, -tiest 1** sprightly and cheerful **2** smart **jauntily** *adv*
javelin *n* light spear thrown in sports competitions
Javex *n* ® chlorine bleach
jaw Ⓣ *n* **1** one of the bones in which the teeth are set **2** lower part of the face below the mouth **3** *slang* long chat ▷ *v* **4** *slang* have a long chat
jay *n* bird of crow family in Europe and N America
Jay *n* **John**. 1745–1829, American statesman, jurist, and diplomat; first chief justice of the Supreme Court (1789–95). He negotiated the treaty with Great Britain (**Jay's treaty**, 1794), that settled outstanding disputes
jaywalking *n* crossing the road in a careless or dangerous manner **jaywalker** *n*
jazz Ⓣ *n* rhythmic music of African-American origin
▸ **jazzy** *adj* flashy or showy
▸ **jazz up** *v* make more lively
jealous Ⓣ *adj* **1** fearful of losing a partner or possession to a rival **2** envious **3** resulting from jealousy: *jealous rage* **jealously** *adv*
jealousy *n*
Jean *n* **Michaëlle**. born 1957, Haitian-born Canadian journalist and broadcaster, Governor General (2005–)
Jean Paul *n* real name *Johann Paul Friedrich Richter*. 1763–1825, German novelist
jeans Ⓣ *pl n* casual denim trousers
Jeep *n* ® four-wheel-drive motor vehicle
jeer Ⓣ *v* **1** scoff or deride ▷ *n* **2** cry of derision
jeezly *adj Canad slang* (intensifier): *a jeezly idiot*
Jefferson *n* **Thomas**. 1743–1826, US statesman: secretary of state (1790–93); third president (1801–09). He was the chief drafter of the Declaration of Independence (1776), the chief opponent of the centralizing policies of the Federalists under Hamilton, and effected the Louisiana Purchase (1803) **Jeffersonian** *adj, n*
Jehovah *n* God
jejune *adj* **1** simple or naive **2** dull or boring
jell Ⓣ *v* **1** take on a definite form **2** form a gel
jellaba, jellabah *n* loose cloak with a hood, worn by Arab men
jelly *n, pl* **-lies 1** fruit-flavoured dessert set with gelatine **2** jam made from fruit juice and sugar
▸ **jellied** *adj* prepared in a jelly
jellyfish *n* small jelly-like sea animal
jemmy *n, pl* **-mies** short steel crowbar used by burglars
Jenner *n* **1 Edward**. 1749–1823, English physician, who discovered vaccination by showing that injections of cowpox virus produce immunity against smallpox (1796) **2** Sir **William**. 1815–98, English physician and pathologist, who differentiated between

THESAURUS

jar² *v* **1** = **jolt**, rock, shake, bump, rattle, vibrate, convulse **2** = **irritate**, offend, irk, annoy, grate, get on one's nerves (*informal*), nettle ▸ *n* **3** = **jolt**, shock, bump, vibration, convulsion
jargon *n* = **parlance**, usage, argot, idiom
jaundiced *adj* **1** = **cynical**, skeptical **2** = **bitter**, suspicious, hostile, jealous, envious, resentful, spiteful
jaunt *n* = **outing**, trip, tour, expedition, stroll, airing, excursion, ramble
jaunty *adj* = **sprightly**, lively, buoyant, carefree, perky, high-spirited, self-confident, sparky
jaw *v* = **talk**, chat, gossip, chatter, spout, chew the fat (*slang*)
jaws *pl n* = **opening**, mouth, entrance
jazz *n* ▸ *v* ▷ **jazz up** = **enliven**, improve, enhance, animate
jazzy *adj* = **flashy**, fancy, gaudy, snazzy (*informal*)
jealous *adj* **1** = **envious**, resentful • *He was jealous of my success.* **2** = **wary**, suspicious, protective, vigilant, watchful, mistrustful
jealousy *n* = **envy**, suspicion, spite, resentment, mistrust, covetousness, possessiveness
jeans *pl n* = **denims**, Levis (*trademark*)
jeer *v* **1** = **scoff**, mock, taunt, barrack, heckle, ridicule, deride, gibe ▸ *n* **2** = **taunt**, abuse, boo, ridicule, derision, catcall, gibe
jeering *See* **mockery**
jell *v* **1** = **solidify**, set, thicken, harden, congeal **2** = **take shape**, materialize,

DICTIONARY

typhus and typhoid fevers (1849)
jenny *n, pl* **-nies 1** female ass **2** female wren
jeopardy ⓣ *n* danger
▶ **jeopardize** *v* place in danger
jerboa *n* small mouselike African rodent with long hind legs
jeremiad *n* long lamenting complaint
jerk ⓣ *n* **1** sharp or abruptly stopped movement **2** sharp pull **3** *slang* contemptible person ▷ *v* **4** move or throw with a jerk
▶ **jerky** *adj* sudden or abrupt **jerkily** *adv* **jerkiness** *n*
jerkin *n* sleeveless jacket
Jerome *n* **1 Jerome K(lapka)**. 1859–1927, English humorous writer; author of *Three Men in a Boat* (1889) **2 Saint**, Latin name *Eusebius Hieronymus*. ?347–?420 AD, Christian monk and scholar, whose outstanding work was the production of the Vulgate. Feast day: Sept 30
Jerry *n Brit slang* German or Germans collectively
jerry-built ⓣ *adj* built badly using flimsy materials
jerry can *n* flat-sided can for carrying gasoline etc.
jersey *n* **1** knitted jumper **2** machine-knitted fabric **3 Jersey** breed of cow
Jerusalem artichoke *n* small yellowish-white root vegetable
jest ⓣ *n, v* joke
▶ **jester** *n* **1** joker **2** *hist* professional clown at court
Jesuit [**jezz**-yoo-it] *n* member of the Society of Jesus, a Roman Catholic order
▶ **jesuitical** *adj* crafty through using oversubtle reasoning
Jesus *n* **1** Also **Jesus Christ, Jesus of Nazareth** ?4 BC–?29 AD, founder of Christianity, believed by Christians to be the Son of God ▷ *interj* **2** *taboo, slang* used to express intense surprise, dismay, etc.
jet[1] ⓣ *n* **1** aircraft driven by jet propulsion **2** stream of liquid or gas, esp. one forced from a small hole **3** nozzle from which gas or liquid is forced **4** burner on a gas fire ▷ *v* **jetting, jetted 5** travel by jet aircraft
▶ **jet lag** fatigue caused by crossing time zones in an aircraft
▶ **jet propulsion** propulsion by thrust provided by a jet of gas or liquid **jet-propelled** *adj*
▶ **jet set** rich and fashionable people who travel the world for pleasure
jet[2] ⓣ *n* hard black mineral
▶ **jet-black** *adj* glossy black
jetsam *n* goods thrown overboard to lighten a ship and later washed ashore
jettison ⓣ *v* **-soning, -soned 1** abandon **2** throw overboard
jetty ⓣ *n, pl* **-ties** small pier
Jew *n* **1** person whose religion is Judaism **2** descendant of the ancient Hebrews **Jewish** *adj*
▶ **Jewry** *n* Jews collectively
▶ **jew's-harp** *n* musical instrument held between the teeth and played by plucking a metal strip with one's finger
jewel ⓣ *n* **1** precious stone **2** special person or thing **jewellery** *n*
▶ **jeweller** *n* dealer in jewels
Jewison *n* **Norman**. born 1926, Canadian film director; his films include *In the Heat of the Night* (1967), *Fiddler on the Roof* (1971), and *Moonstruck* (1987). He founded the Canadian Film Centre (1988)
Jezebel *n* shameless or scheming woman
Jhabvala *n* **Ruth Prawer**, original name *Ruth Prawer*. born 1927, British writer living in India and the US, born in Germany to Polish parents: author of the Booker-prizewinning novel *Heat and Dust* (1975) and scripts for films by James Ivory
Jiang Qing, Chiang Ch'ing *n* 1913–91, Chinese Communist actress and politician; widow of Mao Tse-tung. She was a leading member of the Gang of Four
Jiang Zemin *n* born 1926, Chinese Communist politician: president (1993–2003)

THESAURUS

crystallize, come together
jeopardize *v* = **endanger**, risk, chance, stake, expose, gamble, venture, imperil
jeopardy *n* = **danger**, risk, peril, vulnerability, insecurity
jerk *verb, n* = **tug**, pull, jolt, yank, thrust, wrench, lurch, twitch
jerky *adj* = **bumpy**, shaky, jumpy, twitchy, convulsive, jolting, spasmodic
jerry-built *adj* = **ramshackle**, cheap, defective, shabby, flimsy, rickety, slipshod, thrown together
jest *n* **1** = **joke**, crack (*slang*), prank, quip, wisecrack (*informal*), bon mot, jape, pleasantry, witticism ▶ *v* **2** = **joke**, kid (*informal*), mock, quip, tease
jester *n* = **clown**, fool, harlequin, buffoon
jet[1] *n* **1** = **stream**, spring, flow, spray, fountain, gush, spout **2** = **sprayer**, sprinkler, nozzle, atomizer ▶ *v* **3** = **fly**, soar, zoom
jet[2] *adj* = **black**, raven, inky, coal-black, ebony, pitch-black, sable
jettison *v* = **discard**, dump, abandon, scrap, expel, eject, unload, throw overboard
jetty *n* = **pier**, dock, mole, wharf, breakwater, groyne, quay
jewel *n* **1** = **gemstone**, rock (*slang*), ornament, sparkler (*informal*) **2** = **treasure**, find, gem, collector's item, wonder, pearl, rarity

DICTIONARY

jib[1] Ⓣ *v* **jibbing, jibbed** (of a horse, person, etc.) stop and refuse to go on
▸ **jib at** *v* object to (a proposal etc.)
jib[2] *n* **1** projecting arm of a crane or derrick **2** triangular sail set in front of a mast
jibe[1] Ⓣ *n* **1** insulting remark ▹ *v* **2** make insulting remarks
jibe[2] *v informal* be consistent
jiffy Ⓣ *n, pl* **-fies** *informal* very short period of time
jig Ⓣ *n* **1** type of lively dance **2** music for it **3** device that holds a component in place for cutting etc. ▹ *v* **jigging, jigged 4** make jerky up-and-down movements
jigger *n* small glass for spirits
jiggery-pokery *n informal* trickery or mischief
jiggle Ⓣ *v* move up and down with short jerky movements
jigsaw *n* **1** machine fret saw **2** Also **jigsaw puzzle** picture cut into interlocking pieces, which the user tries to fit together again
jihad *n* Islamic holy war against unbelievers
jilt Ⓣ *v* leave or reject (one's lover)
jingle Ⓣ *n* **1** short catchy song used to advertise a product **2** gentle ringing sound ▹ *v* **3** make a jingling sound
jingoism *n* aggressive nationalism **jingoist** *n* **jingoistic** *adj*
jinks *pl n* **high jinks** boisterous merrymaking
jinni *n, pl* **jinn** spirit in Muslim mythology
jinx Ⓣ *n* **1** person or thing bringing bad luck ▹ *v* **2** be or put a jinx on
jitters Ⓣ *pl n* worried nervousness
▸ **jittery** *adj* nervous
jiujitsu *n* same as **jujitsu**
jive *n* **1** lively dance of the 1940s and '50s ▹ *v* **2** dance the jive
Joachim *n* **1 Joseph.** 1831–1907, Hungarian violinist and composer **2 Saint.** 1st century BC, traditionally the father of the Virgin Mary; feast day: July 25 or Sept 9
Joan *n* **1** known as *the Fair Maid of Kent.* 1328–85, wife of Edward the Black Prince; mother of Richard II **2 Pope** legendary female pope, first mentioned in the 13th century: said to have been elected while disguised as a man and to have died in childbirth
Joan of Arc *n* **Saint**, known as *the Maid of Orléans;* French name *Jeanne d'Arc.* ?1412–31, French national heroine, who led the army that relieved Orléans in the Hundred Years' War, enabling Charles VII to be crowned at Reims (1429). After being captured (1430), she was burnt at the stake as a heretic. She was canonized in 1920. Feast day: May 30
job Ⓣ *n* **1** task to be done **2** occupation or paid employment **3** *informal* difficult task **4** *informal* crime, esp. robbery
▸ **jobbing** *adj* doing individual jobs for payment
▸ **jobless** *adj, pl n* unemployed (people)
▸ **job lot** assortment sold together
▸ **job sharing** splitting of one post between two people working part-time
Job's comforter *n* person who adds to distress while pretending to give sympathy
jock *n* **1** same as **jockstrap 2** *informal* male athlete **3** *informal* an enthusiast
jockey *n* **1** (professional) rider of racehorses ▹ *v* **2 jockey for position** manoeuvre to obtain an advantage
jockstrap *n* belt with a pouch to support the genitals, worn by male athletes
jocose [joke-**kohss**] *adj* playful or humorous **jocosely** *adv*
jocular Ⓣ *adj* **1** joking **2** fond of joking **jocularly** *adv* **jocularity** *n*
jocund [**jok**-kund] *adj lit* merry or cheerful
jodhpurs *pl n* riding breeches, stretchy or loose-fitting above the knee but tight below

j

THESAURUS

jewellery *n* = **jewels**, treasure, regalia, finery, gems, ornaments, trinkets
jib *v* = **refuse**, retreat, shrink, balk, recoil, stop short
jibe see **gibe**
jiffy *n (Slang)* = **instant**, second, flash, heartbeat (*informal*), blink of an eye (*informal*), two shakes of a lamb's tail (*slang*)
jig *v* = **skip**, bounce, bob, caper, wiggle, prance
jiggle *See* **fidget**
jilt *See* **abandon**
jingle *n* **1** = **rattle**, clang, ringing, clink, reverberation, tinkle **2** = **song**, tune, chorus, melody, ditty ▸ *v* **3** = **ring**, rattle, chime, clatter, clink, jangle, tinkle
jinx *n* **1** = **curse**, nemesis, hex (*informal*), evil eye (*informal*), hoodoo (*informal*) ▸ *v* **2** = **curse**, hex (*informal*), bewitch
jitters *pl n* = **nerves**, anxiety, nervousness, butterflies *or* butterflies in one's stomach (*informal*), cold feet (*informal*), fidgets, the shakes (*informal*)
jittery *adj* = **nervous**, shaky, anxious, fidgety, jumpy, twitchy (*informal*), agitated, trembling, wired (*slang*)
job *n* **1** = **occupation**, post, trade, position, employment, profession • *I'm still looking for a job.* **2** = **duty**, concern, role, responsibility, function, task • *It's your job to find out what's going on.*
See also: **appointment, undertaking, work**
jobless *adj* = **unemployed**, idle, inactive, unoccupied, out of work
jocular *adj* = **humorous**, funny, amusing, playful, jovial, droll, facetious, joking,

DICTIONARY

Joe Blow, Joe Six-Pack *n sometimes not capitals, slang* an average or typical man
jog Ⓣ *v* **jogging, jogged 1** run at a gentle pace, esp. for exercise **2** nudge slightly ▷ *n* **3** jogging **jogger** *n* **jogging** *n*
joggle *v* **1** move to and fro in jerks **2** shake
john *n US slang* toilet
John *n* **1** See **John the Baptist 2** *New Testament* **a** the apostle John, the son of Zebedee, identified with the author of the fourth Gospel, three epistles, and the book of Revelation. Feast day: Dec 27 or Sept 26 **b** the fourth Gospel **c** any of three epistles (in full *The First*, *Second*, and *Third Epistles of John*) **3** known as *John Lackland*. 1167–1216, king of England (1199–1216); son of Henry II. He succeeded to the throne on the death of his brother Richard I, having previously tried to usurp the throne. War with France led to the loss of most of his French possessions. After his refusal to recognize Stephen Langton as archbishop of Canterbury an interdict was imposed on England (1208–14). In 1215 he was compelled by the barons to grant the Magna Carta **4** Sir **Elton** (**Hercules**), original name *Reginald Dwight*. born 1947, British rock pianist, composer, and singer; his hits include "Goodbye Yellow Brick Road" (1973) and "Candle in the Wind 1997" (1997), a tribute to Diana, Princess of Wales
John II *n* called *the Good*. 1319–64, king of France (1350–64): captured by the English at Poitiers (1356) and forced to sign treaties (1360) surrendering SW France to England
Johnny Canuck *n informal* **1** a Canadian **2** Canada
John of the Cross *n* **Saint**, original name *Juan de Yepis y Alvarez*. 1542–91, Spanish Carmelite monk, poet, and mystic. He founded the Discalced Carmelites with Saint Teresa (1568). Feast day: Dec 14
Johns *n* **Jasper**. born 1930, US artist, noted for his collages and constructions
Johnson *n* **1 Andrew** 1808–75, US Democrat statesman who was elected vice president under the Republican Abraham Lincoln; 17th president of the US (1865–69), became president after Lincoln's assassination. His lenience towards the South after the American Civil War led to strong opposition from radical Republicans, who tried to impeach him **2 Lyndon Baines**, known as *LBJ*. 1908–73, US Democrat statesman; 36th president of the US (1963–69). His administration carried the Civil Rights Acts of 1964 and 1965, but he lost popularity by increasing US involvement in the Vietnam war **3 Robert**. ?1898–1937, US blues singer and guitarist
John the Baptist *n* **Saint**. *New Testament* the son of Zacharias and Elizabeth and the cousin and forerunner of Jesus, whom he baptized. He was beheaded by Herod (Matthew 14:1–2). Feast day: June 24
joie de vivre Ⓣ [jwah de **veev**-ra] *n French* enjoyment of life
join Ⓣ *v* **1** come or bring together **2** become a member (of) **3** come into someone's company **4** take part (in) ▷ *n* **5** place of joining
▸ **join up** *v* enlist in the armed services
▸ **joined-up** *adj* integrated by an overall strategy: *joined-up government*
joiner *n* maker of finished woodwork
▸ **joinery** *n* joiner's work
joint Ⓣ *adj* **1** shared by two or more ▷ *n* **2** place where bones meet but can move **3** junction of two or more parts or objects **4** piece of meat for roasting **5** *slang* house or place, esp. a disreputable bar or nightclub **6** *slang* cannabis cigarette ▷ *v* **7** divide meat into joints **jointed** *adj* **jointly** *adv*
▸ **out of joint 1** dislocated **2** disorganized
▸ **joint-stock company** firm whose capital is jointly owned by shareholders
jointure *n* property settled on a wife for her use after her husband's death
joist *n* horizontal beam that helps support a floor or ceiling
jojoba [hoe-**hoe**-ba] *n* shrub whose seeds yield oil used in cosmetics
joke Ⓣ *n* **1** thing said or done to cause laughter **2** amusing or ridiculous person or

THESAURUS

sportive, teasing, waggish
jog *v* **1** = **nudge**, push, shake, stir, prod **2** = **run**, trot, canter, lope ▷ **jog someone's memory** *See* **remind**
John Doe *n* (*Informal*) = **man in the street**, average guy, average person, know-nothing (*slang*)
joie de vivre *n* = **enthusiasm**, relish, enjoyment, zest, gusto, ebullience
join *v* **1** = **enrol**, enlist, sign up • *He joined the team last year.* OPPOSITE: resign **2** = **connect**, link, couple, tie, attach, fasten • *two sticks joined together by a chain* OPPOSITE: separate ▷ **join forces** = **co-operate**, unite, team up ▷ **join in** *See* **participate, take part in** *See also*: **piece together, unite**
joint *adj* **1** = **shared**, collective, combined, mutual, communal, cooperative, joined, united ▸ *n* **2** = **junction**, connection, intersection, hinge, node, nexus ▸ *v* **3** = **divide**, segment, carve, sever, dissect, cut up
jointly *adv* = **collectively**, together, mutually, as one, in common, in conjunction, in league, in partnership
joke *n* **1** = **jest**, gag (*informal*), prank, quip,

j

DICTIONARY

thing ▷ *v* **3** make jokes **jokey** *adj* **jokingly** *adv*
▸ **joker** *n* **1** person who jokes **2** *slang* fellow **3** extra card in a pack, counted as any other in some games
Jolliet *n* **Louis**. 1645–1700, French-Canadian explorer, with Jaques Marquette, of the Mississippi river
jolly Ⓣ *adj* **-lier**, **-liest** **1** full of good humour **2** involving a lot of fun ▷ *v* **-lying**, **-lied** **3 jolly along** try to keep (someone) cheerful by flattery or coaxing **jolliness** *n* **jollity** *n*
▸ **jollification** *n* merrymaking
Jolson *n* **Al**, real name *Asa Yoelson*. 1886–1950, US singer and film actor, born in Russia; star of the first talking picture *The Jazz Singer* (1927)
jolt Ⓣ *n* **1** sudden jerk or bump **2** unpleasant surprise or shock ▷ *v* **3** move or shake with jolts **4** surprise or shock
Jonah *n* person believed to bring bad luck to those around him or her
Jones *n* **1 Inigo**. 1573–1652, English architect and theatrical designer, who introduced Palladianism to England. His buildings include the Banqueting Hall of Whitehall. He also designed the settings for court masques, being the first to use the proscenium arch and movable scenery in England **2 (Everett) Le Roi**, Muslim name *Imanu Amir i Baraka*. born 1934, US Black poet, dramatist, and political figure **3 Robert Tyre**, known as *Bobby Jones*. 1902–71, US golfer
jonquil *n* fragrant narcissus
Jonson *n* **Ben**. 1572–1637, English dramatist and poet, who developed the "comedy of humours," in which each character is used to satirize one particular humour or temperament. His plays include *Volpone* (1606), *The Alchemist* (1610), and *Bartholomew Fair* (1614), and he also wrote court masques
Joplin *n* **1 Janis**. 1943–70, US rock singer, noted for her hoarse and passionate style. Her albums include *Cheap Thrills* (1968) and *Pearl* (1971) **2 Scott**. 1868–1917, US pianist and composer: creator of ragtime
Jordan *n* **1 Michael (Jeffrey)**. born 1963, US basketball player **2 Neil**. born 1950, Irish film director and writer; his films include *The Company of Wolves* (1984), *Mona Lisa* (1986), *The Crying Game* (1992), *Michael Collins* (1996), and *The End of the Affair* (2000)
josh *v slang* joke or tease
Jospin *n* **Lionel (Robert)**. born 1937, French politician; prime minister (1997–2002)
joss stick *n* stick of incense giving off a sweet smell when burnt
jostle Ⓣ *v* **1** knock or push against **2** compete
jot Ⓣ *n* **1** very small amount ▷ *v* **jotting**, **jotted** **2** write briefly **3** make a note of
▸ **jotter** *n* notebook
▸ **jottings** *pl n* notes jotted down
joual *n* French Quebec working-class dialect
joule [**jool**] *n physics* unit of work or energy
Joule *n* **James Prescott**. 1818–89, English physicist, who evaluated the mechanical equivalent of heat and contributed to the study of heat and electricity
journal Ⓣ *n* **1** daily newspaper or other periodical **2** daily record of events
▸ **journalese** *n* superficial and clichéd writing, as found in newspapers
▸ **journalism** *n* writing in or editing of periodicals **journalist** *n* **journalistic** *adj*
journey Ⓣ *n* **1** act or process of travelling from one place to another ▷ *v* **3** travel
journeyman *n* qualified craftsman employed by another
joust *hist* ▷ *n* **1** combat with lances between two mounted knights ▷ *v* **2** fight on horseback using lances
jovial Ⓣ *adj* happy and cheerful **jovially** *adv* **joviality** *n*
jowl *n* **1** lower jaw **2** fatty flesh hanging from

THESAURUS

wisecrack, lark, witticism • *I heard a great joke today.* **2 = laughing stock**, clown, buffoon
▸ *v* **3 = jest**, kid (*informal*), quip, tease, banter, chaff • *She was always joking about her friends.*
joker *n* = **comedian**, comic, clown, wit, prankster, buffoon, wag, trickster, humorist, jester
jolly *adj* = **happy**, upbeat (*informal*), merry, playful, cheerful, genial, jovial, chirpy (*informal*), sprightly
jolt *n* **1 = jerk**, start, jump, shake, bump, jar, jog, lurch **2 = surprise**, blow, shock, setback, bombshell, bolt from the blue ▸ *v* **3 = jerk**, push, knock, shake, shove, jar, jog, jostle **4 = surprise**, stun, disturb, stagger, startle, discompose, perturb
jostle *v* = **push**, shake, bump, elbow, jolt, shove, jog, hustle
jot *v* **1 = note down**, record, list, scribble
▸ *n* **2 = bit**, grain, scrap, fraction, speck, morsel
jotting *See* **note**
journal *n* **1 = newspaper**, magazine, daily, weekly, monthly, periodical, gazette **2 = diary**, record, blog (*informal*), log, chronicle, weblog
journalist *n* = **reporter**, broadcaster, columnist, commentator, correspondent, hack, newsman *or* newswoman, pressman
journey *n* **1 = trip**, tour, expedition, trek, voyage, excursion • *the journey across the continent* ▸ *v* **2 = travel**, go, tour, proceed, trek, voyage • *Last year, she journeyed through South America.*
See also: **drive**
jovial *adj* = **cheerful**, happy, animated,

DICTIONARY

the lower jaw **jowls 3** cheeks
joy Ⓣ *n* **1** feeling of great delight or pleasure **2** cause of this feeling **joyful** *adj* **joyless** *adj*
▸ **joyous** *adj* extremely happy and enthusiastic
▸ **joyriding** *n* driving for pleasure, esp. in a stolen vehicle **joyride** *n*
▸ **joystick** *n informal* control device for an aircraft or computer
Joyce *n* **James** (**Augustine Aloysius**). 1882–1941, Irish novelist and short-story writer. He profoundly influenced the development of the modern novel by his use of complex narrative techniques, esp. stream of consciousness and parody, and of compound and coined words. His works include the novels *Ulysses* (1922) and *Finnegans Wake* (1939) and the short stories *Dubliners* (1914)
JP Justice of the Peace
JPEG [**jay**-peg] *computers* **1** standard compressed file format used for pictures **2** picture held in this file format
Jr Junior
Juan Carlos *n* born 1938, king of Spain from 1975: nominated by Franco as the first king of the restored Spanish monarchy that was to follow his death
Juantorena *n* **Alberto**. born 1951, Cuban runner: won the 400 metres and the 800 metres in the 1976 Olympic Games
jubilant Ⓣ *adj* feeling or expressing great joy **jubilantly** *adv* **jubilation** *n*
jubilee Ⓣ *n* special anniversary, esp. 25th (**silver jubilee**) or 50th (**golden jubilee**)
Judaism *n* religion of the Jews, having only one God and based on the teachings of the Old Testament and the Talmud **Judaic** *adj*
Judas *n* person who betrays a friend
judder *v* **1** vibrate violently ▷ *n* **2** violent vibration
judge Ⓣ *n* **1** public official who hears cases and passes sentence in a court of law **2** person who decides the result of a competition ▷ *v* **3** act as a judge **4** decide the result of (a competition) **5** appraise critically **6** consider something to be the case
▸ **judgment** *or* **judgement** *n* **1** opinion reached after careful thought **2** sentence of a court **3** faculty of judging **judgmental** *or* **judgemental** *adj*
judicature *n* **1** administration of justice **2** body of judges
judicial Ⓣ *adj* **1** of or by a court or judge **2** showing or using judgment **judicially** *adv*
judiciary Ⓣ *n* system of courts and judges
judicious Ⓣ *adj* well-judged, sensible **judiciously** *adv*
judo *n* modern sport derived from jujitsu, where the opponent must be defeated using the minimum physical effort
jug Ⓣ *n* **1** container for liquids, with a handle and small spout **2** its contents **3** *slang* prison
▸ **jugged hare** *Brit* hare stewed in an earthenware pot
juggernaut *n* **1** large heavy truck **2** any irresistible destructive force
juggle Ⓣ *v* **1** throw and catch (several objects) so that most are in the air at the same time **2** manipulate (figures, situations, etc.) to suit one's purposes **juggler** *n*

THESAURUS

merry, jolly, cheery, convivial, mirthful
joy *n* = **delight**, ecstasy, bliss, elation, rapture • *Her face shone with joy.* OPPOSITE: misery
See also: **happiness, pleasure**
joyful *adj* = **delighted**, jubilant, elated, over the moon (*informal*) • *a joyful smile*
See also: **glad**
joyless *adj* = **unhappy**, sad, dismal, depressed, gloomy, miserable, dreary, cheerless
joyous *adj* = **joyful**, merry, festive, rapturous
jubilant *adj* = **overjoyed**, triumphant, exuberant, euphoric, elated, enraptured, exultant, thrilled
jubilation *n* = **joy**, celebration, triumph, excitement, festivity, ecstasy, elation, exultation
jubilee *n* = **celebration**, holiday, festival, festivity
judge *n* **1** = **justice** • *The judge sentenced her to three years in prison.* RELATED WORD *adjective*: judicial **2** = **referee**, umpire • *A panel of judges are selecting the finalists.* **3** = **critic**, expert, authority, arbiter, connoisseur, assessor ▸ *v* **4** = **consider**, rate, estimate, assess, evaluate, appraise • *Don't judge people by their looks.* **5** = **referee**, umpire • *Entrants will be judged in two categories.*
See also: **conclude, feel, reckon, regard, think, view**
judgment *n* **1** = **opinion**, view, ruling, verdict, assessment, conclusion, appraisal • *It's hard to form a judgment without all the facts.* **2** = **sense**, understanding, discrimination, wisdom, prudence, acumen, discernment, shrewdness **3** = **verdict**, decision, sentence, ruling, finding, arbitration, decree
See also: **belief, common sense, reason**
judicial *adj* = **legal**, official
judiciary *See* **legal**
judicious *adj* = **sensible**, careful, wise, prudent, thoughtful, shrewd, enlightened, astute, discriminating, well-judged
jug *n* = **container**, pitcher, vessel, jar, urn, crock, carafe, ewer
juggle *v* = **manipulate**, change, modify,

DICTIONARY

jugular vein *n* one of three large veins of the neck returning blood from the head
juice Ⓣ *n* **1** liquid part of vegetables, fruit, or meat **2** fluid secreted by an organ of the body **3** *informal* gasoline
▸ **juicy** *adj* **1** succulent **2** interesting
jujitsu *n* Japanese art of wrestling and self-defence
juju *n* W African magic charm or fetish
jujube *n* chewy candy of flavoured gelatine
jukebox *n* automatic coin-operated record player
Jul. July
julep *n* sweet alcoholic drink
Julian calendar *n* calendar introduced by Julius Caesar, in which leap years occurred every fourth year
julienne *n* clear soup containing thinly shredded vegetables
July *n* seventh month of the year
jumble Ⓣ *v* **1** mix in a disordered way ▷ *n* **2** confused heap or state **3** articles for a jumble sale
▸ **jumble sale** sale of miscellaneous second-hand items
jumbo Ⓣ *adj informal* very large
▸ **jumbo jet** large jet airliner
jump Ⓣ *v* **1** leap or spring into the air using the leg muscles **2** leap over (an obstacle) **3** move quickly and suddenly **4** jerk with surprise **5** increase suddenly **6** pass over or miss out (intervening material) **7** change the subject abruptly **8** come off (tracks, rails, etc.) **9** *informal* attack without warning **10** *informal* pass through (a red traffic light) ▷ *n* **11** jumping **12** obstacle to be jumped **13** sudden nervous jerk **14** sudden rise in prices **15** break in continuity
▸ **jump the gun** act prematurely
▸ **jump the queue** not wait one's turn
▸ **jumpy** *adj* nervous
▸ **jump at** *v* accept (a chance etc.) gladly
▸ **jumper cables** electric cables to connect a discharged automobile battery to an external battery to aid starting an engine
▸ **jump jet** fixed-wing jet that can take off and land vertically
▸ **jump on** *v* criticize suddenly and forcefully
▸ **jump shot** *basketball* shot made as a player jumps
▸ **jump suit** one-piece garment of trousers and top
jumper[1] *n* **1** person or animal that jumps **2** *basketball* a jump shot
jumper[2] *n* sleeveless dress worn over a blouse etc.
Jun. Junior
junction Ⓣ *n* **1** place where routes, railway lines, or roads meet **2** point where traffic can leave or enter a highway **3** join
juncture Ⓣ *n* point in time, esp. a critical one
June *n* sixth month of the year
jungle *n* **1** tropical forest of dense tangled vegetation **2** tangled mass **3** place of intense struggle for survival
junior Ⓣ *adj* **1** of lower standing **2** younger ▷ *n* **3** junior person
juniper *n* evergreen shrub with berries yielding oil
junk[1] Ⓣ *n* **1** discarded or useless objects **2** *informal* rubbish **3** *slang* narcotic drug, esp. heroin
▸ **junkie** *n slang* drug addict
▸ **junk food** snack food of low nutritional value

THESAURUS

alter, manoeuvre
juice *n* = **liquid**, liquor, extract, fluid, sap, nectar
juicy *adj* **1** = **moist**, lush, succulent **2** = **interesting**, sensational, provocative, vivid, colourful, spicy (*informal*), racy, suggestive, risqué
jumble *n* **1** = **muddle**, disorder, mess, confusion, mixture, disarray, clutter, mishmash ▸ *v* **2** = **mix**, mistake, disorder, confuse, shuffle, muddle, disorganize
jumbled *See* **garbled, untidy**
jumbo *adj* = **giant**, large, huge, immense, gigantic, oversized, supersize
jump *v* **1** = **leap**, clear, spring, hurdle, vault, bound • *I jumped over the fence.* **2** = **increase**, rise, surge, escalate • *Sales jumped by 25 per cent last year.* **3** = **recoil**, start, jerk, flinch, wince **4** = **miss**, avoid, skip, evade, omit ▸ *n* **5** = **leap**, vault, bound • *the longest-ever jump by a human being* **6** = **interruption**, break, space, gap, hiatus, lacuna **7** = **rise**, increase, advance, upsurge, increment, upturn
See also: **bounce, dive**
jumped-up *adj* = **conceited**, arrogant, pompous, presumptuous, insolent, overbearing
jumpy *adj* = **nervous**, anxious, tense, jittery (*informal*), restless, apprehensive, fidgety, agitated, on edge, wired (*slang*)
junction *n* **1** = **connection**, union, coupling, linking **2** = **intersection**, crossing, underpass, crossroads, overpass
juncture *n* = **moment**, time, point, occasion
junior *adj* = **inferior**, lower, lesser, subordinate • *a junior counsellor* OPPOSITE: senior
See also: **young**
junk *n* = **garbage**, refuse, scrap, trash, clutter, rubbish, odds and ends • *What are you going to do with all that junk?*

DICTIONARY

▸ **junk mail** unsolicited mail advertising goods and services
junk² *n* flat-bottomed Chinese sailing vessel
junket *n* **1** excursion by public officials paid for from public funds **2** dessert made of milk set with rennet **junketing** *n*
junta *n* group of military officers holding power in a country after a revolution
Jupiter *n* **1** Roman chief of the gods **2** largest of the planets
juridical *adj* of law or the administration of justice
jurisdiction Ⓣ *n* **1** right or power to administer justice and apply laws **2** extent of this right or power
jurisprudence *n* science or philosophy of law
jurist *n* expert in law
jury *n, pl* **-ries** group of people sworn to deliver a verdict in a court of law **juror**, **juryman**, *or* **jurywoman** *n*
just Ⓣ *adv* **1** very recently **2** exactly **3** barely **4** at this instant **5** merely, only **6** really ▹ *adj* **7** fair or impartial in action or judgment **8** proper or right **9** well-founded **justly** *adv* **justness** *n*
justice Ⓣ *n* **1** quality of being just **2** fairness **3** judicial proceedings **4** judge or magistrate
▸ **justice of the peace** person who is authorized to act as a judge in a local court of law
justify Ⓣ *v* **-fying**, **-fied** **1** prove right or reasonable **2** show to be free from blame or guilt **3** align (text) so the margins are straight **justifiable** *adj* **justifiably** *adv* **justification** *n*
jut Ⓣ *v* **jutting, jutted** project or stick out
jute *n* fibre of certain plants, used for rope, canvas, etc.
juvenile Ⓣ *adj* **1** young **2** suitable for young people **3** immature and rather silly ▹ *n* **4** young person or child
▸ **juvenilia** *pl n* works produced in an author's youth
▸ **juvenile delinquent** young person guilty of a crime
juxtapose Ⓣ *v* put side by side **juxtaposition** *n*

THESAURUS

jurisdiction *n* **1 = authority**, power, rule, control, influence, command **2 = range**, province, area, field, scope, compass, sphere, bounds
just *adv* **1 = exactly**, completely, absolutely, entirely, perfectly, precisely **2 = recently**, hardly, lately, scarcely, only now **3 = merely**, only, simply, solely, by the skin of one's teeth ▹ **just about** *See* **nearly** ▸ *adj* **4 = fair**, good, honest, upright, equitable, conscientious, fair-minded, virtuous **5 = proper**, due, appropriate, fitting, apt, justified, rightful, deserved, merited
justice *n* **1 = fairness**, equity, impartiality • *We want freedom, justice, and equality.* OPPOSITE: injustice **2 = judge** • *his appointment as a justice of the Supreme Court* *See also*: **right**
justifiable *adj* **= reasonable**, legitimate, acceptable, valid, sensible, understandable, defensible, excusable, warrantable
justification *n* **1 = explanation**, excuse, defence, vindication, rationalization **2 = reason**, basis, warrant, grounds, reasonable cause *or* probable cause
justify *v* **= defend**, explain, warrant, excuse, vindicate • *How can you justify what you've done?* *See also*: **deserve**
justly *adv* **= properly**, fairly, correctly, lawfully, equitably
jut *v* **= stick out**, project, extend, poke, bulge, protrude, overhang
jutting *See* **prominent**
juvenile *adj* **1 = young**, youthful, inexperienced, childish, immature, babyish, callow, infantile, puerile ▸ *n* **2 = child**, girl, boy, youth, infant, minor, adolescent
juxtapose *See* **compare**
juxtaposition *n* **= proximity**, contact, vicinity, closeness, adjacency, nearness, propinquity

j

Kk

K 1 kelvin **2** *chem* potassium **3** *informal* thousand(s)
Kabir *n* 1440–1518, Indian religious leader who pioneered a religious movement that combined elements of Islam and Hinduism and is considered the precursor of Sikhism
Kabloona *n* person who is not of Inuit ancestry, esp. a White person
Kaffir [**kaf**-fer] *n S Afr offensive, obsolete* a Black African
Kafka *n* **Franz**. 1883–1924, Czech novelist writing in German. In his two main novels *The Trial* (1925) and *The Castle* (1926), published posthumously against his wishes, he portrays man's fear, isolation, and bewilderment in a nightmarish dehumanized world **Kafkaesque** *adj*
kaftan *n* **1** long loose Eastern garment **2** woman's dress resembling this
kail *n* same as **kale**
kaiser [**kize**-er] *n hist* German or Austro-Hungarian emperor
Kalashnikov *n* Russian-made automatic rifle
kale *n* cabbage with crinkled leaves
kaleidoscope *n* tube-shaped toy containing loose pieces of coloured glass reflected by mirrors so that various symmetrical patterns form when the tube is twisted **kaleidoscopic** *adj*
kalends *pl n* same as **calends**
kamik *n* traditional Inuit boot made of caribou hide or sealskin
kamikaze ⓘ [kam-mee-**kah**-zee] *n* **1** (in World War II) Japanese pilot who performed a suicide mission ▷ *adj* **2** (of an action) undertaken in the knowledge that it will kill or injure the person performing it
Kandinsky *n* **Vasili**. 1866–1944, Russian expressionist painter and theorist, regarded as the first to develop an entirely abstract style: a founder of *der Blaue Reiter*
Kane *n* **Paul**. 1810–1871, Canadian artist, born in Ireland. Noted esp. for his many paintings and sketches of Aboriginal peoples in the Canadian west
kangaroo *n, pl* **-roos** Aust. marsupial which moves by jumping with its powerful hind legs
▸ **kangaroo court** unofficial court set up by a group to discipline its members
Kant *n* **Immanuel**. 1724–1804, German idealist philosopher. He sought to determine the limits of man's knowledge in *Critique of Pure Reason* (1781) and propounded his system of ethics as guided by the categorical imperative in *Critique of Practical Reason* (1788)
kaolin *n* fine white clay used to make porcelain and in some medicines
kapok *n* fluffy fibre from a tropical tree, used to stuff cushions etc.
kaput [kap-**poot**] *adj informal* ruined or broken
Karadžić *n* **Radovan**. born 1945, Bosnian Serb political leader and psychiatrist; charged with genocide by the International War Crimes Tribunal for his role in the Bosnian civil war of 1992–95
Karajan *n* **Herbert von**. 1908–89, Austrian conductor
karaoke [kar-a-**oh**-kee] *n* kind of entertainment in which members of the public sing well-known songs over a prerecorded backing tape
karate *n* Japanese system of unarmed combat using blows with feet, hands, elbows, and legs
Karloff *n* **Boris**, real name *William Pratt*. 1887–1969, English film actor, famous for his roles in horror films, esp. *Frankenstein* (1931)
karma *n Buddhism, Hinduism* person's actions affecting his or her fate for his or her next reincarnation
karoo *n S Afr* high arid plateau
Karpov *n* **Anatoly**. born 1951, Russian chess player: world champion (1975–85); FIDE world champion (1993–99)
Karsh *n* **Yousuf**. 1908–2002, became official portrait photographer to Canadian government (1935)
Karzai *n* **Hamid**. born 1957, Afghan military and political leader: president from 2002
kasbah *n* citadel of N African town
Kasparov *n* **Garry**, real name *Garik Weinstein*. born 1963, Armenian-Jewish chess player, born in Azerbaijan: world champion (1985–

THESAURUS

kamikaze *adj* = **self-destructive**, suicidal, foolhardy

DICTIONARY

93); PCA world champion (1993–2000)

kayak *n* **1** Inuit canoe made of sealskins stretched over a frame **2** fibreglass or canvas-covered canoe of this design

Kazan *n* **Elia**, real name *Elia Kazanjoglous*. 1909–2003, US stage and film director and writer, born in Turkey. His films include *Gentleman's Agreement* (1947) and *On the Waterfront* (1954) for both of which he won Oscars, and *East of Eden* (1955).

Kazantzakis *n* **Nikos**. 1885–1957, Greek novelist, poet, and dramatist, noted esp. for his novels *Zorba the Greek* (1946) and *Christ Recrucified* (1954) and his epic poem *The Odyssey* (1938).

kazoo *n, pl* **-zoos** cigar-shaped metal musical instrument that produces a buzzing sound when the player hums into it

kbyte *computers* kilobyte

kcal kilocalorie

Keaton *n* **Buster**, real name *Joseph Francis Keaton*. 1895–1966, US film comedian who starred in silent films such as *The Navigator* (1924), *The General* (1926), and *Steamboat Bill Junior* (1927)

Keats *n* **John**. 1795–1821, English poet. His finest poetry is contained in *Lamia and other Poems* (1820), which includes *The Eve of St Agnes*, *Hyperion*, and the odes *On a Grecian Urn*, *To a Nightingale*, *To Autumn*, and *To Psyche*

kebab *n* dish of small pieces of meat grilled on skewers

kedge *n* **1** small anchor ▷ *v* **2** move (a ship) by hauling on a cable attached to a kedge

kedgeree *n* dish of fish with rice and eggs

keel Ⓣ *n* main lengthways timber or steel support along the base of a ship

▸ **keel over** *v* **1** turn upside down **2** *informal* collapse suddenly

keen¹ Ⓣ *adj* **1** eager or enthusiastic **2** intense or strong **3** intellectually acute **4** (of the senses) capable of recognizing small distinctions **5** sharp **6** cold and penetrating **7** competitive **keenly** *adv* **keenness** *n*

keen² *v* **1** wail over the dead ▷ *n* **2** funeral lament

keep Ⓣ *v* **keeping, kept 1** have or retain possession of **2** take temporary charge of **3** store **4** look after or maintain **5** stay (in, on, or at a place or position) **6** detain (someone) **7** support financially **8** continue or persist **9** remain good ▷ *n* **10** cost of food and everyday expenses **11** central tower of a castle

▸ **keeper** *n* **1** person who looks after animals in a zoo **2** person in charge of a museum or collection **3** short for **goalkeeper**

▸ **keeping** *n* care or charge

▸ **in** *or* **out of keeping with** appropriate or inappropriate for

▸ **keep fit** exercises designed to promote physical fitness

▸ **keepsake** *n* gift treasured for the sake of the giver

▸ **keep up** *v* maintain at the current level

▸ **keep up with** maintain a pace set by (someone)

keg Ⓣ *n* small metal beer barrel

Kelly *n* **1 Gene**, full name *Eugene Curran Kelly*. 1912–96, US dancer, choreographer, film actor, and director. His many films include *An American in Paris* (1951) and *Singin' in the Rain* (1952) **2 Grace**. 1929–82, US film actress. Her films included *High Noon* (1952) and *High Society* (1956). She married Prince Rainier III of Monaco in 1956 and died following a car wreck **3 Ned**. 1855–80, Australian horse and

THESAURUS

keel *v* ▷ **keel over = collapse**, faint, black out (*informal*), pass out

keen *adj* **1 = eager**, into (*informal*), enthusiastic, avid, ardent, fond of • *a keen amateur photographer* **2 = perceptive**, quick, brilliant, shrewd, astute • *a keen intellect* **3 = sharp**, cutting, incisive, razor-like

See also: **acute, fierce, fine, ready**

keenness *n* **= eagerness**, passion, intensity, enthusiasm, zest, zeal, ardour, fervour

keep *v* **1 = care for**, maintain, preserve • *I'd like to keep horses.* **2 = store**, hold, deposit • *He keeps his money under the mattress.* **3 = carry out**, honour, fulfil • *I always keep my promises.* **4 = retain**, hold, control, maintain, preserve, possess, conserve **5 = support**, maintain, feed, sustain, subsidize, provide for **6 = detain**, prevent, delay, hinder, restrain, obstruct, hold back, keep back ▷ **keep an eye on** *See* **mind, supervise** ▷ **keep on** *See* **continue** ▷ **keep out** *See* **exclude** ▷ **keep safe** *See* **save** ▷ **keep up = maintain**, continue, preserve, sustain, keep pace ▷ **keep your eyes open** *See* **watch out** ▶ *n* **7 = board**, food, living, maintenance **8 = tower**, castle

See also: **breed, have, own, reserve, save, upkeep**

keeper *n* **= guardian**, guard, curator, attendant, caretaker, warden, preserver, steward, janitor, custodian, groundskeeper

keeping *n* **= care**, charge, protection, custody, possession, safekeeping, guardianship ▷ **in keeping with = in agreement with**, in accord with, in balance with, in compliance with, in conformity with, in correspondence with, in harmony with, in observance with

keepsake *n* **= souvenir**, symbol, reminder, relic, token, memento

keg *n* **= barrel**, drum, cask, vat

DICTIONARY

cattle thief and bushranger: captured by the police and hanged
kelp *n* large brown seaweed
kelvin *n* SI unit of temperature
▶ **Kelvin scale** temperature scale starting at absolute zero (–273.15° Celsius)
Kelvin *n* **William Thomson,** 1st Baron Kelvin. 1824–1907, British physicist, noted for his work in thermodynamics, inventing the Kelvin scale, and in electricity, pioneering undersea telegraphy
Kempis *n* **Thomas à**. ?1380–1471, German Augustinian monk, generally regarded as the author of the devotional work *The Imitation of Christ*
ken *n* **1** range of knowledge ▷ *v* **kenning, kenned** *or* **kent 2** *Scot* know
kendo *n* Japanese sport of fencing using wooden staves
Keneally *n* **Thomas (Michael)**. born 1935, Australian writer. His novels include the Booker prizewinner *Schindler's Ark* (1982); other works are *The Playmaker* (1987), *The Great Shame* (1998), and *The Office of Innocence* (2002)
Kennedy *n* **1 Edward (Moore)**, known as *Ted*. 1932–2009, US Democrat politician; senator 1962–2009 **2** his brother, **John (Fitzgerald)**, known as *JFK*. 1917–63, US Democrat statesman; 35th president of the US (1961–63), the first Roman Catholic and the youngest man ever to be president. He demanded the withdrawal of Soviet missiles from Cuba (1962) and prepared civil rights reforms; assassinated 1963 **3 Robert (Francis)**, known as *Bobby*, brother of John Kennedy. 1925–68, US Democrat statesman; attorney general (1961–64) and senator for New York (1965–68); assassinated
kennel *n* **1** hutlike shelter for a dog
kennels 2 place for breeding, boarding, or training dogs
Kenneth I *n* surnamed *MacAlpine*. died 858, king of the Scots of Dalriada and of the Picts (?844–858): considered the first Scottish king
Kent *n* **William**. ?1685–1748, English architect, landscape gardener, and interior designer
kepi *n* French military cap with a flat top and horizontal peak
Kepler *n* **Johannes**. 1571–1630, German astronomer. As discoverer of Kepler's laws of planetary motion he is regarded as one of the founders of modern astronomy
kept *v* past of **keep**
keratin *n* fibrous protein found in the hair and nails
kerb *n Brit* curb
kerchief *n* piece of cloth worn over the head or round the neck
Kerenski, Kerensky *n* **Aleksandr Fyodorovich**. 1881–1970, Russian liberal revolutionary leader; prime minister (July–October 1917): overthrown by the Bolsheviks
kerfuffle *n informal* commotion or disorder
kermes [**kur**-meez] *n* red dyestuff obtained from dried insects
Kern *n* **Jerome (David)**. 1885–1945, US composer of musical comedies, esp. *Show Boat* (1927)
kernel Ⓣ *n* **1** inner seed of a nut or fruit stone **2** central and essential part of something
kerosene *n* paraffin oil distilled from petroleum or coal and shale and used as fuel, solvent, etc.
Kerouac *n* **Jack**, real name *Jean-Louis Lebris de Kérouac*. 1922–69, US novelist and poet of the Beat Generation. His works include *On the Road* (1957) and *Big Sur* (1962)
Kerry *n* **John Forbes**. born 1943, US politician; Democratic Party candidate in the presidential election of 2004
Kesey *n* **Ken**. 1935–2001, US novelist, best-known for *One Flew Over the Cuckoo's Nest* (1962)
kestrel *n* small falcon
ketch *n* two-masted sailing ship
ketchup *n* thick cold sauce, usu. of tomatoes
kettle *n* container with a spout and handle used for boiling water
▶ **a different kettle of fish** a different matter entirely
kettledrum *n* large metal drum with a brass bottom
key Ⓣ *n* **1** device for operating a lock by moving a bolt **2** device turned to wind a clock, operate a machine, etc. **3** any of a set of levers or buttons pressed to operate a piano, typewriter, etc. **4** *music* set of related notes **5** list of explanations of codes, symbols, etc. **6** something crucial in providing an explanation or interpretation **7** means of achieving a desired end **8** *basketball* area of the court under the basket from the end line to the circle around the free throw line ▷ *adj* **9** of great importance ▷ *v* **10** (foll. by *to*) adjust to
▶ **keyed up** very excited or nervous
▶ **key in** *v* keyboard
keyboard *n* **1** set of keys on a piano, typewriter, etc. **2** musical instrument played using a keyboard ▷ *v* **3** enter (text) using a keyboard
keyhole *n* opening for inserting a key into a lock

THESAURUS

kernel *n* = **essence**, core, substance, germ, gist, nub, pith

key *n* **1** = **opener**, latchkey **2** = **answer**, solution, explanation ▶ *adj* **3** = **essential**,

DICTIONARY

keynote Ⓣ *n* **1** dominant idea of a speech etc. **2** basic note of a musical key
key ring *n* decorative metal ring for keeping keys on
keystone *n* central stone of an arch which locks others in position
kg kilogram(s)
KGB *n* formerly, the Soviet secret police
Khachaturian *n* **Aram Ilich**. 1903–78, Russian composer. His works, which often incorporate Armenian folk tunes, include a piano concerto and the ballets *Gayaneh* (1942) and *Spartacus* (1954)
Khafre *n* Greek name *Chephren*. king of Egypt (*c*. 2550 BC) of the 4th dynasty. He built the second pyramid and is thought to have built the Sphinx at Giza
khaki *adj* **1** dull yellowish-brown ▷ *n* **2** hard-wearing fabric of this colour used for military uniforms
Khamenei *n* Ayatollah **Seyed Ali**. born 1940, Iranian political and religious leader: president of Iran (1981–89); leader of the Islamic Republic from 1989
khan *n* title of respect in Afghanistan and central Asia
Khatami *n* **Seyed Mohammad**. born 1943, Iranian politician: president of Iran 1997–2005
Khomeini *n* **Ruholla**, known as *Ayatollah Khomeini*. 1900–89, Iranian Shiite Muslim religious and political leader. Following the overthrow of the shah of Iran (1979) he returned from exile and instituted an Islamic republic. His rule saw deteriorating relations with the West and war (1980–88) with Iraq
Khrushchev *n* **Nikita Sergeyevich**. 1894–1971, Soviet statesman; premier of the Soviet Union (1958–64). After Stalin's death he became first secretary of the Soviet Communist Party (1953–64) and initiated a policy to remove the influence of Stalin (1956). As premier, he pursued a policy of peaceful coexistence with the West, but alienated Communist China
kHz kilohertz
kibbutz *n, pl* **kibbutzim** communal farm or factory in Israel
kibosh *n* **put the kibosh on** *slang* put a stop to
kick Ⓣ *v* **1** drive, push, or strike with the foot **2** score with a kick **3** (of a gun) recoil when fired **4** *informal* object or resist **5** *informal* free oneself of (an addiction) ▷ *n* **6** thrust or blow with the foot **7** recoil **8** *informal* excitement or thrill
▸ **kickback** *n* money paid illegally for favours done
▸ **kick off** *v* **1** start a game of football **2** *informal* begin
▸ **kick out** *v* dismiss or expel forcibly
▸ **kick-start** *v* start a motorcycle engine by kicking a pedal
▸ **kick up** *v informal* create (a fuss)
kid[1] Ⓣ *n* **1** *informal* child **2** young goat **3** leather made from the skin of a kid
kid[2] Ⓣ *v* **kidding, kidded** *informal* tease or deceive (someone)
Kidman *n* **Nicole**. born 1967, Australian film actress, born in Hawaii. Her films include *Far and Away* (1992), *To Die For* (1995), *Eyes Wide Shut* (1999), and *The Hours* (2002): formerly married to Tom Cruise
kidnap Ⓣ *v* **-napping, -napped** seize and hold (a person) to ransom **kidnapper** *n*
kidney *n* **1** either of the pair of organs which filter waste products from the blood to produce urine **2** animal kidney used as food
▸ **kidney bean** reddish-brown kidney-shaped bean, edible when cooked
Kierkegaard *n* **Søren Aabye**. 1813–55, Danish philosopher and theologian. He rejected organized Christianity and anticipated the existentialists in emphasizing man's moral responsibility and freedom of choice. His works include *Either/Or* (1843), *The Concept of Dread* (1844), and *The Sickness unto Death* (1849) **Kierkegaardian** *adj*
Kieślowski *n* **Krzysztof**. 1941–96, Polish film director, whose later films were made in France; his work includes the television series *Decalogue* (1988–89) and the film trilogy *Three Colours* (1993–94)
kill Ⓣ *v* **1** cause the death of **2** *informal* cause

THESAURUS

major, important, main, crucial, principal, decisive, fundamental, pivotal, cutting-edge, leading ▸ *v* ▷ **key in = type**, enter, input, keyboard
keynote *n* = **heart**, core, substance, theme, centre, essence, gist
kick *v* **1 = boot**, punt **2** (*Informal*) = **give up**, stop, quit, abandon, desist from, leave off ▷ **kick off = begin**, start, open, initiate, commence, get the show on the road ▷ **kick out = dismiss**, remove, sack (*informal*), axe, expel, eject, evict, get rid of ▷ **kick up a fuss** *See* **complain** ▸ *n* **3** (*Informal*) = **thrill**, buzz (*slang*), pleasure, stimulation
kid[1] *n* (*Informal*) = **child**, baby, youth, infant, teenager, minor, youngster, tot
kid[2] *v* = **tease**, joke, trick, fool, pretend, hoax, jest, delude
kidnap *v* = **abduct**, capture, seize • *Four tourists have been kidnapped by rebels.*
kill *v* **1 = slay**, murder, destroy, execute, slaughter, massacre, assassinate, butcher, exterminate • *The earthquake killed 62 people.* **2 = suppress**, stop, halt, quash, stifle,

DICTIONARY

(someone) pain or discomfort **3** put an end to **4** pass (time) ▷ *n* **5** act of killing **6** animals or birds killed in a hunt **killer** *n*
▶ **killing** *informal* ▷ *adj* **1** very tiring **2** very funny ▷ *n* **3** sudden financial success
▶ **killjoy** *n* person who spoils others' pleasure
kiln *n* oven for baking, drying, or processing pottery, bricks, etc.
kilo *n* short for **kilogram(me)**
kilo- *combining form* one thousand: *kilolitre*
kilobyte *n computers* 1000 or 1024 units of information
kilocalorie *n* one thousand calories
kilogram, kilogramme *n* one thousand grams
kilohertz *n* one thousand hertz
kilometre, kilometer *n* one thousand metres
kilowatt *n electricity* one thousand watts
kilt *n* knee-length pleated tartan skirt worn orig. by Scottish Highlanders **kilted** *adj*
Kim Il Sung *n* 1912–94, North Korean statesman and marshal; prime minister (1948–72) and president (1972–94) of North Korea
Kim Jong Il *n* born 1942, Korean politician; ruler of North Korea from 1994, official head of state from 1998: son of Kim Il Sung
kimono [kim-**moan**-no] *n, pl* **-nos 1** loose wide-sleeved Japanese robe, fastened with a sash **2** European dressing gown like this
kin Ⓣ *n* Also **kinsfolk** person's relatives collectively **kinship** *n*
kind[1] Ⓣ *adj* considerate, friendly, and helpful **kindness** *n* **kind-hearted** *adj*
▶ **kindly** *adj* **-lier, -liest 1** having a warm-hearted nature **2** pleasant or agreeable ▷ *adv* **3** in a considerate way **4** please: *will you kindly be quiet!* **kindliness** *n*
kind[2] Ⓣ *n* **1** class or group having common characteristics **2** essential nature or character
▶ **in kind 1** (of payment) in goods rather than money **2** with something similar
▶ **kind of** to a certain extent
kindergarten *n* class or school for children of about four to six years old
kindle Ⓣ *v* **1** set (a fire) alight **2** (of a fire) start to burn **3** arouse or be aroused
▶ **kindling** *n* dry wood or straw for starting fires
kindred Ⓣ *adj* **1** having similar qualities **2** related ▷ *n* **3** person's relatives collectively
kine *pl n obsolete* cows or cattle
kinetic [kin-**net**-ik] *adj* relating to or caused by motion
king Ⓣ *n* **1** male ruler of a monarchy **2** ruler or chief **3** best or most important of its kind **4** most important piece in chess **5** playing card with a picture of a king on it **kingly** *adj* **kingship** *n*
▶ **kingdom** *n* **1** state ruled by a king or queen **2** division of the natural world

THESAURUS

quell, smother, scotch, extinguish
See also: **put down**
killer *n* = **murderer**, gunman, assassin, butcher, executioner, exterminator, cut-throat, hit man (*slang*), slayer
killing *n* **1** = **murder**, homicide, slaughter, massacre, manslaughter, slaying, carnage, bloodshed, extermination **2** (*Informal*) = **profit**, gain, success, cleanup (*informal*), coup, windfall, bonanza
killjoy *n* = **spoilsport**, grinch (*informal*), dampener, wet blanket (*informal*), buzzkill (*slang*)
kin *n* = **family**, people, relations, relatives • *"Next of kin" means the person most closely related to you.*
See also: **relation**
kind[1] *adj* = **considerate**, good, charitable, benign, thoughtful, compassionate, humane, kindly, unselfish, benevolent, kind-hearted • *Thank you for being so kind to me.* OPPOSITE: cruel
See also: **accommodating, generous, gentle, helpful, merciful, tender**
kind[2] *n* = **type**, class, brand, sort, category, variety, species, grade, breed, genre, classification • *I don't like that kind of movie.*
See also: **breed, class, family, form, sort, type, variety**
kind-hearted *adj* = **sympathetic**, kind, helpful, generous, compassionate, humane, considerate, good-natured, altruistic, tender-hearted
kindle *v* **1** = **set fire to**, light, ignite, inflame **2** = **arouse**, inspire, provoke, stir, stimulate, induce, awaken, rouse
kindliness *n* = **kindness**, charity, humanity, compassion, friendliness, amiability, benevolence, gentleness, kind-heartedness
kindly *adj* **1** = **benevolent**, kind, warm, helpful, benign, pleasant, sympathetic, compassionate, good-natured ▶ *adv* **2** = **benevolently**, politely, graciously, thoughtfully, cordially, agreeably, tenderly
kindness *n* = **benevolence**, charity, humanity, compassion, gentleness • *Everyone has treated me with great kindness.* OPPOSITE: cruelty
See also: **consideration, favour, generosity, mercy, pity**
kindred *adj* **1** = **similar**, like, related, akin, corresponding, matching ▶ *n* **2** = **family**, kin, kinsfolk, relations, relatives
king *n* = **monarch**, sovereign • *the next king of England* RELATED WORDS *adjectives*: royal, regal, monarchical

DICTIONARY

▸ **king-size** or **king-sized** *adj informal* larger than standard size
King *n* **1 B.B.**, real name *Riley B. King.* born 1925, US blues singer and guitarist **2 Billie Jean** (née *Moffitt*). born 1943, US tennis player: Wimbledon champion 1966–68, 1972–73, and 1975; US champion 1967, 1971–72, and 1974 **3 Martin Luther**. 1929–68, US Baptist minister and civil-rights leader. He advocated nonviolence in his campaigns against the segregation of Black people in the South: assassinated: Nobel Peace Prize 1964 **4 Stephen** (**Edwin**). born 1947, US writer esp. of horror novels; his books, many of which have been filmed, include *Carrie* (1974), *The Shining* (1977), *Misery* (1988), and *Everything's Eventual* (2002) **5 William Lyon Mackenzie**. 1874–1950, Canadian Liberal statesman; prime minister (1921–26; 1926–30; 1935–48)
kingfisher *n* small bird with a bright plumage that dives for fish
kingpin *n* most important person in an organization
Kingsley *n* **Charles**. 1819–75, British clergyman and author. His works include the historical romances *Westward Ho!* (1855) and *Hereward the Wake* (1866) and the children's story *The Water Babies* (1863)
King-Smith *n* **Ronald Gordon**, known as *Dick*. (1922–2011), British writer for children; his numerous books include *The Sheep Pig* (1984) and the *Sophie* series
kink Ⓣ *n* **1** twist or bend in rope, wire, hair, etc. **2** *informal* quirk in personality
▸ **kinky** *adj* **1** full of kinks **2** *slang* given to deviant or unusual sexual practices
Kinsey *n* **Alfred Charles**. 1894–1956, US zoologist, who directed a survey of human sexual behaviour
kinsfolk *pl n* same as **kin**
kinship Ⓣ *n* **1** blood relationship **2** state of having common characteristics
kinsman, kinswoman Ⓣ *n* relative
kiosk Ⓣ *n* **1** small booth selling drinks, cigarettes, newspapers, etc. **2** public telephone box
kip *n, v* **kipping**, **kipped** *informal* sleep
Kipling *n* (**Joseph**) **Rudyard**. 1865–1936, English poet, short-story writer, and novelist, born in India. His works include *Barrack-Room Ballads* (1892), the two *Jungle Books* (1894, 1895), *Stalky and Co* (1899), *Kim* (1901), and the *Just So Stories* (1902): Nobel prize for literature 1907
kipper *n* cleaned, salted, and smoked herring
kirk *n Scot* church
Kirke *n* Sir **David**. c.1597–1654, English colonizer and adventurer. He took Quebec in 1629 but was forced to return it to French control in 1632; became first governor of Newfoundland in 1632 but was recalled on grounds of withholding tax revenue
Kirsch *n* brandy made from cherries
kismet *n* fate or destiny
kiss Ⓣ *v* **1** touch with the lips in affection or greeting **2** join lips with a person in love or desire ▹ *n* **3** touch with the lips
▸ **kisser** *n slang* mouth or face
▸ **kiss of life** mouth-to-mouth resuscitation
Kissinger *n* **Henry** (**Alfred**). born 1923, US academic and diplomat, born in Germany; assistant to President Nixon for national security affairs (1969–75); Secretary of State (1973–77): shared the Nobel peace prize 1973
kit Ⓣ *n* **1** outfit or equipment for a specific purpose **2** set of pieces of equipment sold ready to be assembled
▸ **kitbag** *n* bag for a soldier's or traveller's belongings
▸ **kit out** *v* **kitting**, **kitted** provide with clothes or equipment needed for a particular activity
kitchen *n* room used for cooking
▸ **kitchenette** *n* small kitchen
▸ **kitchen garden** garden for growing vegetables, herbs, etc.
kite *n* **1** light frame covered with a thin material flown on a string in the wind **2** large hawk with a forked tail
kith *n* **kith and kin** friends and relatives
kitsch *n* vulgarized or pretentious art or literature with popular sentimental appeal
kitten *n* young cat
▸ **kittenish** *adj* lively and flirtatious
kittiwake *n* type of seagull

THESAURUS

kingdom *n* = **country**, state, nation, territory, realm
kink *n* **1** = **twist**, bend, wrinkle, coil **2** = **quirk**, whim, foible, fetish, vagary, eccentricity, idiosyncrasy
kinky *adj* **1** (*Slang*) = **weird**, odd, strange, quirky, eccentric, peculiar, outlandish, queer **2** = **twisted**, tangled, coiled, curled
kinship *n* **1** = **relationship**, kin, consanguinity, ties of blood **2** = **similarity**, connection, relationship, association, correspondence, affinity
kinsman *See* **relation**
kinswoman *See* **relation**
kiosk *n* = **booth**, stand, stall, counter, newsstand, bookstall
kiss *v* **1** = **osculate**, neck (*informal*), peck (*informal*) **2** = **brush**, touch, glance, scrape, graze ▸ *n* **3** = **osculation**, peck (*informal*), smooch (*slang*), smacker (*slang*)
kit *n* = **equipment**, tackle, gear, apparatus, paraphernalia, tools, fit-out (*Canad Nfld*)

DICTIONARY

kitty *n, pl* **-ties 1** communal fund for buying drinks etc. **2** pool in certain gambling games
kiwi *n* **1** NZ flightless bird with a stout beak and no tail **2** *informal* a New Zealander
▶ **kiwi fruit** edible fruit with a fuzzy brown skin and green flesh
klaxon *n* loud horn used on emergency vehicles as a warning signal
Klee *n* **Paul**. 1879–1940, Swiss painter and etcher. A founder member of *der Blaue Reiter*, he subsequently evolved an intensely personal style of unusual fantasy and wit
Klein *n* **Melanie**. 1882–1960, Austrian psychoanalyst resident in England (from 1926), noted for her work on child behaviour
Klemperer *n* **Otto**. 1885–1973, orchestral conductor, born in Germany. He was best known for his interpretations of Beethoven
kleptomania *n* compulsive tendency to steal **kleptomaniac** *n*
klick *n informal* kilometre
Klimt *n* **Gustav**. 1862–1918, Austrian painter. He founded the Vienna Sezession (1897), a group of painters influenced by Art Nouveau
km kilometre(s)
knack Ⓣ *n* **1** skilful way of doing something **2** innate ability
knacker *n* buyer of old horses for killing
knapsack *n* soldier's or traveller's bag worn strapped on the back
knave Ⓣ *n* **1** jack at cards **2** *obsolete* rogue **knavish** *adj*
▶ **knavery** *n* dishonest behaviour
knead Ⓣ *v* **1** work (flour) into dough using the hands **2** squeeze or press with the hands
knee *n* **1** joint between thigh and lower leg **2** part of a garment covering the knee **3** lap ▷ *v* **kneeing, kneed 4** strike or push with the knee
▶ **kneecap** *n* **1** bone in front of the knee ▷ *v* **2** shoot in the kneecap
▶ **kneejerk** *adj* (of a reply or reaction) automatic and predictable
kneel Ⓣ *v* **kneeling, kneeled** *or* **knelt** fall or rest on one's knees
knell Ⓣ *n* **1** sound of a bell, esp. at a funeral or death **2** portent of doom
knew *v* past tense of **know**
knickerbockers *pl n* loose-fitting short trousers gathered in at the knee
knickers *pl n* woman's or girl's undergarment covering the lower trunk and having legs or leg holes
knick-knack Ⓣ *n* trifle or trinket
knife Ⓣ *n, pl* **knives 1** cutting tool or weapon consisting of a sharp-edged blade with a handle ▷ *v* **2** cut or stab with a knife
knight *n* **1** honorary title given to a man by the British sovereign **2** *hist* man who served his lord as a mounted armoured soldier **3** chess piece shaped like a horse's head ▷ *v* **4** award a knighthood to **knighthood** *n* **knightly** *adj*
knit Ⓣ *v* **knitting, knitted** *or* **knit 1** make (a garment) by interlocking a series of loops in wool or other yarn **2** draw (one's eyebrows) together **3** join closely together **knitter** *n* **knitting** *n*
▶ **knitwear** *n* knitted clothes, such as sweaters
knob Ⓣ *n* **1** rounded projection, such as a switch on a radio **2** rounded handle on a door or drawer **3** small amount of butter
▶ **knobbly** *adj* covered with small bumps
knock Ⓣ *v* **1** give a blow or push to **2** rap sharply with the knuckles **3** make or drive by striking **4** *informal* criticize adversely **5** (of an engine) make a regular banging noise as a result of a fault ▷ *n* **6** blow or rap **7** knocking sound

THESAURUS

kitty *See* **cat**
knack *n* = **skill**, facility, ability, gift, capacity, trick, talent, expertise, propensity, aptitude
knave *n* = **rogue**, rascal, villain, scoundrel
knead *v* = **squeeze**, work, form, press, shape, manipulate, massage, rub, mould
kneel *v* = **genuflect**, stoop, get on one's knees *or* get down on one's knees
knell *n* = **ringing**, sound, toll, chime, peal
knick-knack *n* = **trinket**, plaything, trifle, bauble, bagatelle, bric-a-brac
knife *n* **1** = **blade**, cutter ▶ *v* **2** = **cut**, wound, stab, slash, pierce, lacerate
knit *v* **1** = **join**, link, tie, bind, unite, weave, intertwine, fasten **2** = **wrinkle**, knot, crease, pucker, furrow ▷ **knit your brows** *See* **frown**
knob *n* = **lump**, bump, knot, projection, stud, hump, protrusion
knock *v* **1** = **hit**, strike, punch, belt (*informal*), rap, thump, smack, cuff **2** (*Informal*) = **criticize**, abuse, condemn, censure, disparage, denigrate, belittle, deprecate, find fault, run down ▷ **knock around** = **hit**, strike, abuse, batter, maul, mistreat, manhandle, maltreat, beat up (*informal*) ▷ **knock down** = **demolish**, level, destroy, raze, fell ▷ **knock out** *See* **eliminate** ▷ **knock over** *See* **overturn, upset** ▶ *n* **3** = **blow**, clip, slap, rap, thump, smack, cuff, clout (*informal*) **4** = **setback**, defeat, failure, rejection, rebuff, reversal
knockabout *adj* = **boisterous**, farcical, slapstick, riotous, rollicking
knockout *n* **1** = **killer blow**, KO *or* K.O. (*slang*), *coup de grâce* (*French*) **2** = **success**, hit, winner, triumph, smash, sensation, smash hit

k

DICTIONARY

▸ **knocker** *n* metal fitting for knocking on a door
▸ **knock about** *or* **knock around** *v* **1** travel or wander **2** hit or kick brutally
▸ **knockabout** *adj* (of comedy) boisterous
▸ **knock back** *v informal* **1** drink quickly **2** cost **3** reject or refuse
▸ **knock down** *v* reduce the price of
▸ **knockdown** *adj* (of a price) very low
▸ **knock-knees** *pl n* legs that curve in at the knees
▸ **knock off** *v* **1** take (a specified amount) off a price **2** *informal* make or do (something) hurriedly or easily **3** *informal* cease work **4** *informal* steal
▸ **knock out** *v* **1** render (someone) unconscious **2** *informal* overwhelm or amaze **3** defeat in a knockout competition
▸ **knockout** *n* **1** blow that renders an opponent unconscious **2** competition from which competitors are progressively eliminated **3** *informal* overwhelmingly attractive person or thing
▸ **knock up** *v* **1** *slang* make pregnant **2** *Brit informal* waken
knoll *n* small rounded hill
knot Ⓣ *n* **1** fastening made by looping and pulling tight strands of string, cord, or rope **2** tangle, as of hair **3** small cluster or huddled group **4** round lump or spot in timber **5** unit of speed used by ships, equal to one nautical mile per hour ▷ *v* **knotting, knotted 6** tie with or into a knot
▸ **knotty** *adj* **1** full of knots **2** puzzling or difficult
know Ⓣ *v* **knowing, knew, known 1** be aware of **2** be or feel certain of the truth of (information etc.) **3** be acquainted with **4** have a grasp of or understand (a skill or language) **knowable** *adj*
▸ **in the know** *informal* informed or aware
▸ **knowing** *adj* cunning or shrewd
▸ **knowingly** *adv* **1** shrewdly **2** deliberately
▸ **know-all** *n offensive* person who acts as if knowing more than other people
▸ **know-how** *n informal* ingenuity, aptitude, or skill
knowledge Ⓣ *n* **1** facts or experiences known by a person **2** state of knowing **3** specific information on a subject
▸ **knowledgeable** *or* **knowledgable** *adj* intelligent or well-informed
Knowles *n* **Beyoncé**. born 1981, US singer, songwriter, and actress. A member of the successful Destiny's Child, she later found solo success with *Dangerously in Love* (2003) and the single "Crazy in Love" (2003)
knuckle Ⓣ *n* **1** bone at the finger joint **2** knee joint of a calf or pig
▸ **near the knuckle** *informal* approaching indecency
▸ **knuckle ball** Also **knuckler** *baseball* pitch that moves slowly and erratically, delivered by gripping the ball with the knuckles
▸ **knuckle-duster** *n* metal appliance worn on the knuckles to add force to a blow
▸ **knuckle under** *v* yield or submit
KO knockout
koala *n* tree-dwelling Aust. marsupial with dense grey fur
Kodály *n* **Zoltán**. 1882–1967, Hungarian composer. His works were often inspired by native folk songs and include the comic opera *Háry János* (1926) and *Psalmus Hungaricus* (1923) for chorus and orchestra
Koestler *n* **Arthur**. 1905–83, British writer, born in Hungary. Of his early antitotalitarian novels *Darkness at Noon* (1940) is outstanding. His later works, *The Sleepwalkers* (1959), *The Act of Creation* (1964), and *The Ghost in the Machine* (1967), reflect his interest in science, philosophy, and psychology. He committed suicide
kohl *n* cosmetic powder used to darken the

THESAURUS

knot *n* **1 = connection**, tie, bond, joint, loop, ligature **2 = cluster**, collection, bunch, clump ▸ *v* **3 = tie**, secure, bind, loop, tether
know *v* **1 = understand**, see, perceive, apprehend, comprehend, be aware of • *I don't know a lot about cars.* **2 = be acquainted with**, recognize, be familiar with • *I believe you know my brother.*
know-how *n* **= capability**, ability, knowledge, skill, talent, expertise, knack, ingenuity, aptitude, savoir-faire
knowing *adj* **= meaningful**, significant, expressive
knowingly *adv* **= deliberately**, intentionally, purposely, consciously, wilfully, on purpose, wittingly
knowledge *n* **1 = learning**, education, wisdom, scholarship • *She had no knowledge of world history.* **2 = acquaintance**, familiarity, intimacy, cognizance
See also: **command, experience, grasp, understanding**
knowledgeable *adj* **1 = well-informed**, aware, familiar, experienced, cognizant, *au fait* (*French*), clued-up (*informal*), conversant, in the know (*informal*) **2 = intelligent**, scholarly, educated, erudite, learned
known *adj* **= famous**, well-known, celebrated, noted, acknowledged, avowed, recognized
knuckle *n* ▸ *v* ▷ **knuckle under = give in**, submit, surrender, yield, succumb, acquiesce, accede, capitulate, cave in (*informal*), give way

DICTIONARY

edges of the eyelids
Kohl *n* **Helmut**. born 1930, German statesman: chancellor of West Germany (1982–90) and of Germany (1990–98)
kohlrabi [kole-**rah**-bee] *n, pl* **-bies** type of cabbage with an edible stem
Koizumi *n* **Junichiro**. born 1941, Japanese politician; prime minister (2001–06)
kokanee [koh-**kah**-nee] *n* salmon of N American lakes
kook *n US informal* eccentric person **kooky** *adj*
kookaburra *n* large Aust. kingfisher with a cackling cry
kopeck *n* monetary unit of the former Soviet republics, one hundredth of a rouble
kopje, koppie *n S Afr* small hill
Koran *n* sacred book of Islam
Korbut *n* **Olga**. born 1955, Soviet gymnast: noted for her highly individualistic style, which greatly increased the popularity of the sport, esp. following her performance in the 1972 Olympic Games
Korchnoi *n* **Victor**. born 1931, Soviet-born chess player: Soviet champion 1960, 1962, and 1964: defected to the West in 1976
Korda *n* Sir **Alexander**, real name *Sandor Kellner*. 1893–1956, British film producer and director, born in Hungary: his films include *The Scarlet Pimpernel* (1934), *Anna Karenina* (1948), and *The Third Man* (1949)
Korean *n* **1** language of North and South Korea **2** person from North or South Korea ▷ *adj* **3** of North or South Korea or their language
kosher [**koh**-sher] *adj* **1** conforming to Jewish religious law, esp. (of food) to Jewish dietary law **2** *informal* legitimate or authentic ▷ *n* **3** kosher food
Kostunica *n* **Vojislav**. born 1944, Serbian politician; president of the Federal Republic of Yugoslavia (2000–03); prime minister of Serbia and Montenegro (2004–08)
kowtow *v* **1** touch one's forehead to the ground in deference **2** be humble and servile (towards)
kph kilometres per hour
kraal *n* S African village surrounded by a strong fence
Krafft-Ebing *n* **Richard**, Baron von Krafft-Ebing. 1840–1902, German neurologist and psychiatrist who pioneered the systematic study of sexual behaviour in *Psychopathia Sexualis* (1886)
kraken *n* mythical Norwegian sea monster
Krall *n* **Diana**. born 1964, Canadian jazz singer and pianist. Her recordings include *Love Scenes* (1997)
Krebs *n* Sir **Hans Adolf**. 1900–81, British biochemist, born in Germany, who shared a Nobel prize for physiology or medicine (1953) for the discovery of the **Krebs cycle**
Kremlin *n* central government of Russia and, formerly, of the Soviet Union
Krieghoff *n* **Cornelius David**. 1815–1872, Canadian painter, born in the Netherlands. Noted esp. for his landscapes, paintings of French-Canadian life, and Aboriginal peoples
krill *n, pl* **krill** small shrimplike sea creature
kris *n* Malayan or Indonesian knife with a scalloped edge
Kristiansen *n* **Ingrid**. born 1956, Norwegian long-distance runner: former London marathon winner: world 10 000 metres record holder (1986–93)
krona *n, pl* **krona** standard monetary unit of Sweden
krone [**kroh**-na] *n, pl* **-ner** [-ner] standard monetary unit of Norway and Denmark
krypton *n* colourless gas present in the atmosphere and used in fluorescent lights and lasers
Kublai Khan *n* ?1216–94, Mongol emperor of China: grandson of Genghis Khan. He completed his grandfather's conquest of China by overthrowing the Sung dynasty (1279) and founded the Yuan dynasty (1279–1368)
Kubrick *n* **Stanley**. 1928–99, US film writer, director, and producer. He directed *Lolita* (1962), *Dr. Strangelove* (1963), *2001: A Space Odyssey* (1968), *A Clockwork Orange* (1971), *The Shining* (1980), *Full Metal Jacket* (1987), and *Eyes Wide Shut* (1999)
kudos Ⓣ [**kyoo**-doss] *n* fame or credit
Ku Klux Klan *n* secret organization of White Protestant Americans who use violence against African Americans and Jews
kulak *n hist* independent well-to-do Russian peasant
Kumaratunge *n* **Chandrika Bandaranaike**. born 1945, Sri Lankan politician: prime minister (1994); Sri Lanka's first female president 1994–2005
kümmel *n* German liqueur flavoured with caraway seeds
kumquat *n* citrus fruit resembling a tiny orange
Kundera *n* **Milan**. born 1929, Czech novelist living in France. His novels include *The Book of Laughter and Forgetting* (1979), *The Unbearable Lightness of Being* (1984), and *Ignorance* (2002)
Küng *n* **Hans**. born 1928, Swiss Roman

THESAURUS

kudos *n* = **credit**, praise, recognition, applause, acclaim, laudation, plaudits, props (*informal*)

k

DICTIONARY

Catholic theologian, who questioned the doctrine of infallibility: his licence to teach was withdrawn in 1979. His books include *Global Responsibility* (1991)

kung fu *n* Chinese martial art combining hand, foot, and weapon techniques

Kurosawa *n* **Akira**. 1910–99, Japanese film director. His works include *Rashomon* (1950), *The Seven Samurai* (1954), *The Throne of Blood* (1957), *Kagemusha* (1980), *Ran* (1985), and *Madadayo* (1993)

kW kilowatt

kWh kilowatt-hour

Ll

l litre
L 1 large **2** Latin **3** learner (driver)
laager *n S Afr* camp defended by a circle of wagons
lab *n informal* short for **laboratory**
label Ⓣ *n* **1** piece of card or other material fixed to an object to show its ownership, destination, etc. ▷ *v* **-elling, -elled 2** give a label to
labia *pl n, sing.* **labium** four liplike folds of skin forming part of the female genitals
▸ **labial** [**lay**-bee-al] *adj* **1** of the lips **2** pronounced with the lips
laboratory *n, pl* **-ries** building or room designed for scientific research or for the teaching of practical science
laborious Ⓣ *adj* involving great prolonged effort **laboriously** *adv*
labour Ⓣ *n* **1** physical work or exertion **2** workers in industry **3** final stage of pregnancy, leading to childbirth ▷ *v* **4** work hard **5** stress to excess or too persistently **6** be at a disadvantage because of a mistake or false belief
▸ **laboured** *adj* uttered or done with difficulty
▸ **labourer** *n* person who labours, esp. someone doing manual work for wages
labrador *n* large retriever dog with a yellow or black coat
laburnum *n* ornamental tree with yellow hanging flowers
labyrinth Ⓣ [**lab**-er-inth] *n* **1** network of tortuous passages, maze **2** interconnecting cavities in the internal ear **labyrinthine** *adj*
Lacan *n* **Jacques**. 1901–81, French psychoanalyst, who reinterpreted Freud in terms of structural linguistics: an important influence on poststructuralist thought
lace Ⓣ *n* **1** delicate decorative fabric made from threads woven into an open weblike pattern **2** cord drawn through eyelets and tied ▷ *v* **3** fasten with laces **4** thread a cord or string through holes in something **5** add a small amount of alcohol or drug to (food or drink)
▸ **lacy** *adj* fine, like lace
▸ **lace-ups** *pl n* shoes which fasten with laces
lacerate Ⓣ [**lass**-er-rate] *v* **1** tear (flesh) jaggedly **2** wound (feelings) **laceration** *n*
lachrymal *adj* same as **lacrimal**
lachrymose *adj* **1** tearful **2** sad
lack Ⓣ *n* **1** shortage or absence of something needed or wanted ▷ *v* **2** need or be short of (something)
lackadaisical Ⓣ *adj* **1** lacking vitality and purpose **2** lazy and careless in a dreamy way

THESAURUS

label *n* **1 = tag**, ticket, sticker • *He checked the label on the bottle.* ▸ *v* **2 = tag**, flag, sticker • *The shirt was labelled "Made in Canada."*
See also: **identify**
laborious *adj* **= hard**, tough, arduous, strenuous, onerous, backbreaking, exhausting, tiring, wearisome
labour *n* **1 = work**, effort, toil, exertion, industry • *the labour involved in weeding and digging* **2 = workers**, workforce, employees • *unskilled labour* **3 = childbirth**, delivery, parturition ▸ *v* **4 = work**, slave, toil • *harvesters labouring in the fields* **5** (usually with *under*) **= be disadvantaged**, suffer, be a victim of, be burdened by **6 = overemphasize**, strain, elaborate, overdo, dwell on OPPOSITE: relax
See also: **struggle**
laboured *adj* **= forced**, difficult, heavy, stiff, strained, awkward
labourer *n* **= worker**, hand, blue-collar worker, drudge, manual worker, roustabout
See also: **worker**
labyrinth *n* **= maze**, jungle, tangle, intricacy
lace *n* **1 = netting**, filigree, openwork **2 = cord**, tie, string, shoelace, bootlace ▸ *v* **3 = fasten**, tie, bind, thread, do up **4 = mix in**, spike, fortify, add to
lacerate *v* **= tear**, cut, wound, slash, rip, claw, mangle, gash
laceration *n* **= cut**, wound, tear, slash, rent, rip, gash
lack *n* **1 = shortage**, want (*formal*), absence, deficiency, scarcity • *a lack of funds* OPPOSITE: abundance ▸ *v* **2 = be short of**, miss, be deficient in • *She lacks confidence.*
lackadaisical *adj* **1 = lethargic**, listless, dull, indifferent, apathetic, half-hearted, languid **2 = lazy**, idle, dreamy, abstracted, indolent, inert

DICTIONARY

lackey ⓣ *n* **1** servile follower **2** uniformed male servant
lacklustre ⓣ *adj* lacking brilliance or vitality
laconic ⓣ *adj* using only a few words, terse
laconically *adv*
lacquer *n* **1** hard varnish for wood or metal **2** clear sticky substance sprayed onto the hair to hold it in place ▷ *v* **3** apply lacquer to
lacrimal, lachrymal *adj* of tears or the glands which produce them
lacrosse *n* sport in which teams catch and throw a ball using long sticks with a pouched net at the end, in an attempt to score goals
lactation *n* secretion of milk by female mammals to feed young
▸ **lactic** *adj* of or derived from milk
▸ **lactose** *n* white crystalline sugar found in milk
lacuna [lak-**kew**-na] *n, pl* **-nae**, **-nas** gap or missing part, esp. in a document or series
lad ⓣ *n* boy or young fellow
ladder *n* **1** frame of two poles connected by horizontal steps used for climbing **2** line of stitches that have come undone in a stocking or tights ▷ *v* **3** have or cause to have such a line of undone stitches
laden ⓣ *adj* **1** loaded **2** burdened
la-di-da, lah-di-dah *adj informal* affected or pretentious
ladle *n* **1** spoon with a long handle and a large bowl, used for serving soup etc. ▷ *v* **2** serve out liquid with a ladle
lady ⓣ *n, pl* **-dies** **1** polite term of address for a woman **2** woman regarded as having characteristics of good breeding or high rank **3 Lady** title of some women of rank
▸ **Our Lady** the Virgin Mary
▸ **lady-in-waiting** *n, pl* **ladies-in-waiting** female servant of a queen or princess
▸ **ladykiller** *n informal* man who is or thinks he is irresistible to women
▸ **ladylike** *adj* polite, well-mannered
ladybug *n* small red beetle with black spots
Laënnec *n* **René Théophile Hyacinthe**. 1781–1826, French physician, who invented the stethoscope
Lafayette, La Fayette *n* **Marie Joseph Paul Yves Roch Gilbert du Motier**, Marquis de Lafayette. 1757–1834, French general and statesman. He fought on the side of the colonists in the War of American Independence and, as commander of the National Guard (1789–91; 1830), he played a leading part in the French Revolution and the revolution of 1830
Lafontaine *n* Sir **Louis-Hippolyte**. 1807–64, Canadian politician and lawyer. As first Premier (1848–51) of the United Province of Canada he led the country's first responsible government
La Fontaine *n* **Jean de**. 1621–95, French poet, famous for his *Fables* (1668–94)
lag[1] ⓣ *v* **lagging, lagged** **1** go too slowly, fall behind ▷ *n* **2** delay between events
▸ **laggard** *n* person who lags behind
lag[2] *v* **lagging, lagged** wrap (a boiler, pipes, etc.) with insulating material
▸ **lagging** *n* insulating material
lager *n* light-bodied type of beer
lagoon *n* saltwater lake enclosed by an atoll or separated by a sandbank from the sea
Lagrange *n* Comte **Joseph Louis**. 1736–1813, French mathematician and astronomer, noted particularly for his work on harmonics, mechanics, and the calculus of variations
Lagrangian *adj*
La Guardia *n* **Fiorello H**(**enry**). 1882–1947, US politician. As mayor of New York (1933–45), he organized slum-clearance and labour safeguard schemes and suppressed racketeering
laid *v* past of **lay**[1]
▸ **laid-back** *adj informal* relaxed
lain *v* past participle of **lie**[2]

THESAURUS

lackey *n* **1** = **hanger-on**, minion, brown-noser (*slang*), flatterer, sycophant, toady, yes man **2** = **manservant**, attendant, valet, flunky, footman
lacking *adj* = **deficient**, missing, inadequate, minus (*informal*), impaired, flawed, wanting, needing, sans (*archaic*)
lacklustre *adj* = **dull**, flat, muted, lifeless, drab, uninspired, leaden, prosaic, vapid
laconic *adj* = **terse**, short, brief, concise, succinct, curt, monosyllabic, pithy
lad *n* = **boy**, kid (*informal*), guy (*informal*), youth, fellow, youngster, juvenile
laden *adj* = **loaded**, full, charged, burdened, encumbered, weighed down
lady *n* **1** = **gentlewoman**, dame **2** = **woman**, female
lady-killer *n* (*Informal*) = **womanizer**, rake, libertine, Casanova, heartbreaker, Don Juan, ladies' man, philanderer, roué
ladylike *adj* = **refined**, modest, proper, sophisticated, elegant, polite, respectable, genteel, well-bred
lag *v* = **fall behind**, trail • *He is now lagging a metre behind the champion.*
laggard *n* = **straggler**, dawdler, idler, loiterer, snail, slowpoke (*informal*), sluggard
laid-back *adj* = **relaxed**, casual, easy-going, unflappable (*informal*), unhurried, free and easy

DICTIONARY

Laine *n* **Cleo**, full name *Clementina Dinah Laine*. born 1927, British jazz singer, noted esp. for her recordings with her husband John Dankworth
Laing *n* **R(onald) D(avid)**. 1927–89, Scottish psychiatrist; his best known books include *The Divided Self* (1960), *The Politics of Experience and the Bird of Paradise* (1967), and *Knots* (1970)
lair Ⓣ *n* resting place of an animal
laird *n* Scottish landowner
laissez faire Ⓣ [less-ay-**fair**] *n* principle of nonintervention, esp. by a government in commercial affairs
laity [lay-it-ee] *n* people who are not members of the clergy
lake[1] Ⓣ *n* expanse of water entirely surrounded by land **lakeside** *n*
lake[2] *n* red pigment
Lalo *n* **(Victor-Antoine-)Édouard**. 1823–92, French composer of Spanish descent. His works include the *Symphonie espagnole* (1873) and the ballet *Namouna* (1882)
lam *v* **lamming, lammed** *slang* beat or hit
lama *n* Buddhist priest in Tibet or Mongolia
▸ **lamasery** *n* monastery of lamas
Lamarck *n* **Jean Baptiste Pierre Antoine de Monet**, Chevalier de Lamarck. 1744–1829, French naturalist. He outlined his theory of organic evolution (Lamarckism) in *Philosophie zoologique* (1809)
lamb *n* **1** young of sheep **2** its meat **3** innocent or helpless creature ▷ *v* **4** (of sheep) give birth to a lamb or lambs
lambskin *n* **lambswool** *n*
Lamb *n* **Charles**, pen name *Elia*. 1775–1834, English essayist and critic. He collaborated with his sister Mary on *Tales from Shakespeare* (1807). His other works include *Specimens of English Dramatic Poets* (1808) and the largely autobiographical essays collected in *Essays of Elia* (1823; 1833)
lambaste, lambast *v* **1** beat or thrash **2** reprimand severely
lambent *adj lit* (of a flame) flickering softly
Lambton *n* **John George**, Earl of Durham. 1792–1840, British Whig statesman and colonial administrator. Governor General and high commissioner of British North America (1838). His *Report on the Affairs of British North America* (1839) looked into the causes of two rebellions (1837–38) and recommended responsible government for the colonies
lame Ⓣ *adj* **1** having an injured or disabled leg or foot **2** (of an excuse) unconvincing ▷ *v* **3** make lame **lamely** *adv* **lameness** *n*
▸ **lame duck** person or thing unable to cope without help
lamé [**lah**-may] *n, adj* (fabric) interwoven with gold or silver thread
lament Ⓣ *v* **1** feel or express sorrow (for) ▷ *n* **2** passionate expression of grief **3** song of grief **lamentation** *n*
▸ **lamentable** *adj* deplorable
▸ **lamented** *adj* grieved for
laminate *v* **1** make (a sheet of material) by bonding together two or more thin sheets **2** cover with a thin sheet of material ▷ *n* **3** laminated sheet **laminated** *adj* **lamination** *n*
lamp *n* device which produces light from electricity, oil, or gas **lampshade** *n*
▸ **lampblack** *n* pigment made from soot
▸ **lamppost** *n* post supporting a lamp in the street
lampoon Ⓣ *n* **1** humorous satire ridiculing someone ▷ *v* **2** satirize or ridicule
lamprey *n* eel-like fish with a round sucking mouth
lance Ⓣ *n* **1** long spear used by a mounted soldier ▷ *v* **2** pierce (a boil or abscess) with a lancet
▸ **lancer** *n* formerly, cavalry soldier armed with a lance
▸ **lance corporal** lowest non-commissioned rank in the army
lanceolate *adj* narrow and tapering to a point at each end
lancet *n* **1** pointed two-edged surgical knife **2** narrow window in the shape of a pointed arch
land Ⓣ *n* **1** solid part of the earth's surface **2** ground, esp. with reference to its type or use **3** rural or agricultural area **4** property

THESAURUS

lair *n* = **nest**, hole, earth, den, burrow
laissez faire *n* = **nonintervention**, free enterprise, free trade
lake *n* = **pond**, basin, lagoon, pool, mere, reservoir, tarn
lame *adj* **1** = **limping** • *lame in one leg* **2** = **unconvincing**, poor, weak, pathetic, feeble, flimsy • *a lame excuse*
lament *v* **1** = **grieve**, mourn, weep, wail • *She lamented the death of her friend.* ▸ *n* **2** = **moan**, wail • *a lament for his vanished youth* **3** = **dirge**, requiem, elegy, threnody
See also: **regret**
lamentable *adj* = **regrettable**, tragic, unfortunate, woeful, deplorable, mournful, grievous, distressing
lampoon *n* **1** = **satire**, caricature, parody, burlesque, takeoff (*informal*), spoof (*informal*), piss-take (*informal*) ▸ *v* **2** = **ridicule**, mock, caricature, parody, satirize, make fun of
lance *See* **pierce**
land *n* **1** = **property**, estate, grounds • *a*

DICTIONARY

consisting of land **5** country or region ▷ *v* **6** come or bring to earth after a flight, jump, or fall **7** go or take from a ship at the end of a voyage **8** come to or touch shore **9** come or bring to some point or condition **10** *informal* obtain **11** take (a hooked fish) from the water **12** *informal* deliver (a punch)
landless *adj*
▸ **landed** *adj* possessing or consisting of lands
▸ **landed immigrant** former name for Canadian permanent resident
▸ **landward** *adj* nearest to or facing the land
▸ **land up** *v* arrive at a final point or condition
landau [**lan**-daw] *n* four-wheeled carriage with a folding hood
landfall *n* ship's first landing after a voyage
landing *n* **1** floor area at the top of a flight of stairs **2** bringing or coming to land **3** Also
▸ **landing stage** place where people or goods go onto or come off a boat
landlocked *adj* completely surrounded by land
landlord, landlady Ⓣ *n* **1** person who rents out land, houses, etc. **2** owner or manager of a pub or boarding house
landlubber *n* person who is not experienced at sea
landmark Ⓣ *n* **1** prominent object in or feature of a landscape **2** event, decision, etc. considered as an important development
landscape Ⓣ *n* **1** extensive piece of inland scenery seen from one place **2** picture of it ▷ *v* **3** improve natural features of (a piece of land)
Landseer *n* Sir **Edwin Henry**. 1802–73, English painter, noted for his studies of animals
landslide Ⓣ *n* **1** Also **landslip** falling of soil, rock, etc. down the side of a mountain **2** overwhelming electoral victory
lane Ⓣ *n* **1** narrow road **2** area of road for one stream of traffic **3** specified route followed by ships or aircraft **4** strip of a running track or swimming pool for use by one competitor
Lang *n* **1 Fritz**. 1890–1976, Austrian film director, later in the US, most notable for his silent films, such as *Metropolis* (1926), *M* (1931), and *The Testament of Dr. Mabuse* (1932) **2 k.d.**, full name *Kathryn Dawn Lang*. born 1961, Canadian singer-songwriter. Her recordings include "Constant Craving" (1992)
language Ⓣ *n* **1** system of sounds, symbols, etc. for communicating thought **2** particular system used by a nation or people **3** system of words and symbols for computer programming
languid Ⓣ *adj* lacking energy or enthusiasm
languidly *adv*
languish Ⓣ *v* **1** suffer neglect or hardship **2** lose or diminish in strength or vigour **3** pine (for) **languishing** *adj*
languor [**lang**-ger] *n* **1** laziness or weariness **2** dreamy relaxation **3** oppressive stillness
languorous *adj*
lank Ⓣ *adj* **1** (of hair) greasy and limp **2** lean and tall
▸ **lanky** *adj* ungracefully tall and thin
lankiness *n*
lanolin *n* grease from sheep's wool used in ointments etc.
lantern *n* light in a transparent protective case

THESAURUS

dispute over land **2 = country**, province, region, nation, territory • *the land of opportunity* **3 = ground**, earth, dry land, terra firma **4 = soil**, ground, dirt, loam **5 = countryside**, farmland ▸ *v* **6 = arrive**, dock, alight, touch down • *We landed in New York at noon*. **7 = end up**, turn up, wind up **8** (*Informal*) **= obtain**, win, get, gain, acquire, secure
See also: **state**
landlord *n* **1 = innkeeper**, host, hotelier **2 = owner**, proprietor, freeholder, lessor
landmark *n* **1 = feature**, monument **2 = milestone**, watershed, turning point
landscape *n* **= scenery**, view, scene, prospect, outlook, countryside, vista, panorama
landslide *n* **1 = rockfall**, avalanche, mudslide, landslip ▸ *adj* **2 = overwhelming**, decisive, runaway, conclusive
lane *n* **= road**, way, street, path, alley, pathway, passageway, footpath
language *n* **1 = tongue**, dialect, vocabulary, lingo (*informal*), jargon, vernacular, idiom • *She speaks four languages*. **2 = style**, wording, phrasing • *He explained the process in plain language*.
languid *adj* **1 = lazy**, listless, indifferent, lackadaisical, languorous, unenthusiastic **2 = lethargic**, heavy, sluggish, dull, torpid
languish *v* **1 = decline**, fail, flag, weaken, fade, faint, wither, wilt, droop **2** (often with *for*) **= pine**, long, desire, hunger, yearn, hanker **3 = waste away**, suffer, rot, be abandoned, be neglected
lank *adj* **1 = limp**, lifeless, straggling **2 = thin**, lean, slim, spare, skinny, slender, gaunt, scrawny, emaciated
lanky *adj* **= gangling**, tall, spare, gaunt, bony, angular, rangy

DICTIONARY

▸ **lantern jaw** long thin jaw **lantern-jawed** *adj*
lanthanum *n* silvery-white metallic element
▸ **lanthanide series** class of 15 elements chemically related to lanthanum
lanyard *n* **1** short cord worn round the neck to hold a knife or whistle **2** *naut* short rope
Lao Zi, Lao-tzu *n* ?604–?531 BC, Chinese philosopher, traditionally regarded as the founder of Taoism and the author of the *Tao-te Ching*
lap[1] Ⓣ *n* **1** single circuit of a racecourse or track **2** stage of a journey **3** overlap ▹ *v* **lapping, lapped 4** overtake an opponent so as to be one or more circuits ahead **5** enfold or wrap around
lap[2] Ⓣ *v* **lapping, lapped** (of waves) beat softly against (a shore etc.)
▸ **lap up** *v* **1** drink by scooping up with the tongue **2** accept (information or attention) eagerly
lap[3] *n* part between the waist and knees of a person when sitting
▸ **lapdog** *n* small pet dog
▸ **laptop** *adj* (of a computer) small enough to fit on a user's lap
lapel [lap-**pel**] *n* part of the front of a coat or jacket folded back towards the shoulders
lapidary *adj* of stones, esp. gemstones
lapis lazuli [**lap**-iss **lazz**-yoo-lie] *n* bright blue gemstone
Laplace *n* **Pierre Simon**, Marquis de Laplace. 1749–1827, French mathematician, physicist, and astronomer. He formulated the nebular hypothesis (1796). He also developed the theory of probability
Lapp *n, adj* (member or language) of a people living chiefly in N Scandinavia
lapse Ⓣ *n* **1** temporary drop in a standard, esp. through forgetfulness or carelessness **2** instance of bad behaviour by someone usually well-behaved **3** break in occurrence or usage ▹ *v* **4** drop in standard **5** end or become invalid, esp. through disuse **6** (of time) slip away **7** abandon religious faith **lapsed** *adj*
lapwing *n* plover with a tuft of feathers on the head
larboard *adj, n old-fashioned* port (side of a ship)
larceny *n, pl* **-nies** theft
larch *n* deciduous coniferous tree
lard *n* **1** soft white fat obtained from a pig ▹ *v* **2** insert strips of bacon in (meat) before cooking **3** decorate (speech or writing) with strange words unnecessarily
larder *n* storeroom for food
large Ⓣ *adj* great in size, number, or extent **largely** *adv* **largish** *adj*
▸ **at large 1** in general **2** free, not confined
▸ **large-scale** *adj* wide-ranging or extensive
largesse, largess [lar-**jess**] *n* generous giving, esp. of money
largo *adv music* in a slow and dignified manner
lariat *n* **1** lasso
lark[1] *n* small brown songbird, skylark
lark[2] Ⓣ *n informal* **1** harmless piece of mischief **2** unnecessary activity or job
▸ **lark about** *v* play pranks
Larkin *n* **Philip**. 1922–85, English poet: his verse collections include *The Less Deceived* (1955) and *The Whitsun Weddings* (1964)
larkspur *n* plant with spikes of blue, pink, or white flowers with spurs
La Rochefoucauld *n* **François**, Duc de La Rochefoucauld. 1613–80, French writer. His best-known work is *Réflexions ou sentences et maximes morales* (1665), a collection of epigrammatic and cynical observations on human nature
Larousse *n* **Pierre Athanase**. 1817–75, French grammarian, lexicographer, and encyclopedist. He edited and helped to compile the *Grand Dictionnaire universel du XIX siècle* (1866–76)

THESAURUS

lap[1] *n* = **circuit**, tour, circle, orbit, loop
lap[2] *v* **1** = **ripple**, wash, splash, swish, gurgle, plash, purl **2** = **drink**, lick, sip, sup
lapse *n* **1** = **mistake**, slip, error, fault, negligence, oversight, omission, failing, indiscretion **2** = **interval**, break, gap, pause, intermission, interruption, lull, breathing space **3** = **decline**, fall, drop, deterioration ▸ *v* **4** = **decline**, fall, drop, slip, sink, slide, deteriorate, degenerate **5** = **end**, stop, expire, terminate, run out
lapsed *adj* = **expired**, finished, invalid, discontinued, ended, out of date, run out
large *adj* = **big**, great, huge, giant, massive, vast, enormous, immense, gigantic, colossal • *a large room* OPPOSITE: small ▹ **at large** = **free**, at liberty, on the loose, on the run, unconfined; = **in general**, generally, mainly, chiefly, as a whole, in the main; = **at length**, greatly, exhaustively, in full detail ▹ **large numbers** *See* **many**
See also: **broad, extensive, spacious**
largely *adv* = **mainly**, mostly, generally, primarily, predominantly, principally, chiefly, as a rule, by and large, to a great extent
large-scale *adj* = **wide-ranging**, global, wide, broad, extensive, vast, wholesale, far-reaching, sweeping
lark *n* = **prank**, game, fun, mischief, escapade, caper, jape ▸ *verb* ▹ **lark about** = **play**, caper, cavort, have fun, make mischief

DICTIONARY

larva *n, pl* **-vae** insect in an immature stage, often resembling a worm **larval** *adj*
larynx *n, pl* **larynges** part of the throat containing the vocal cords **laryngeal** *adj*
▶ **laryngitis** *n* inflammation of the larynx
lasagne, lasagna [laz-**zan**-ya] *n* **1** pasta in wide flat sheets **2** dish made from layers of lasagne, meat, vegetables, etc.
La Salle *n* Sieur **Robert Cavelier de.** 1643–87, French explorer and fur trader in North America; founder of Louisiana (1682)
lascar *n* E Indian seaman
lascivious [lass-**iv**-ee-uss] *adj* lustful **lasciviously** *adv*
laser [**lay**-zer] *n* device that produces a very narrow intense beam of light, used for cutting very hard materials and in surgery etc.
lash[1] Ⓣ *n* **1** eyelash **2** sharp blow with a whip ▷ *v* **3** hit with a whip **4** (of rain or waves) beat forcefully against **5** attack verbally, scold **6** flick or wave sharply to and fro
▶ **lash out** *v* **1** make a sudden physical or verbal attack **2** *informal* spend (money) extravagantly
lash[2] Ⓣ *v* fasten or bind tightly with cord etc.
lashings *pl n Brit informal* large amount
lass, lassie Ⓣ *n* girl
Lassa fever *n* serious African disease with high fever and muscular pains
lassitude *n* physical or mental weariness
lasso [lass-**oo**] *n, pl* **-sos, -soes 1** rope with a noose for catching cattle and horses ▷ *v* **-soing, -soed 2** catch with a lasso
Lassus *n* **Roland de**, Italian name *Orlando di Lasso.* ?1532–94, Flemish composer, noted for his mastery in both sacred and secular music
last[1] Ⓣ *adj, adv* **1** coming at the end or after all others **2** most recent(ly) ▷ *adj* **3** only remaining ▷ *n* **4** last person or thing
▶ **lastly** *adv* finally
▶ **last-ditch** *adj* done as a final resort
▶ **last post** army bugle-call played at sunset or funerals
▶ **last straw** small irritation or setback that, coming after others, is too much to bear
▶ **last word 1** final comment in an argument **2** most recent or best example of something
last[2] Ⓣ *v* **1** continue **2** be sufficient for (a specified amount of time) **3** remain fresh, uninjured, or unaltered **lasting** *adj*
last[3] *n* model of a foot on which shoes and boots are made or repaired
latch Ⓣ *n* **1** fastening for a door with a bar and lever **2** lock which can only be opened from the outside with a key ▷ *v* **3** fasten with a latch
▶ **latchkey** *n* key for a latch
▶ **latch onto** *v* become attached to (a person or idea)
late Ⓣ *adj* **1** arriving or occurring after the normal or expected time **2** towards the end of (a period of time) **3** being at an advanced time **4** recently dead **5** recent **6** former ▷ *adv* **7** after the normal or expected time **8** at a relatively advanced age **9** recently **lateness** *n* **latish** *adj, adv* **latecomer** *n*
▶ **lately** *adv* not long since
lateen sail *n* triangular sail on a long yard hoisted to the head of a mast
latent Ⓣ *adj* hidden and not yet developed **latency** *n*
lateral Ⓣ [**lat**-ter-al] *adj* **1** of, at, to, or from

THESAURUS

lash[1] *n* **1 = blow**, hit, stroke, swipe (*informal*), stripe ▶ *v* **2 = whip**, beat, scourge, thrash, flog, birch **3 = pound**, strike, beat, hammer, smack, dash, drum, buffet **4 = criticize**, attack, blast, censure, scold, put down, upbraid
lash[2] *v* **= fasten**, tie, secure, bind, strap, make fast
lass *n* **= girl**, damsel, maiden, maid, young woman
last[1] *adj* **1 = most recent**, previous, latest, preceding • *last year* OPPOSITE: first **2 = final**, ultimate, closing, concluding • *the last three chapters of the book* OPPOSITE: first **3 = hindmost**, at the end, rearmost
See also: **remainder**
last[2] *v* **= continue**, remain, survive, endure, persist • *The movie lasted for two and a half hours.*
See also: **stretch, ultimate**
lasting *adj* **= continuing**, long-term, permanent, long-standing, perennial, durable, enduring, abiding
lastly *See* **finally**
last-minute *See* **late**
latch *n* **1 = fastening**, catch, bar, lock, hook, bolt, hasp ▶ *v* **2 = fasten**, bar, secure, bolt, make fast
late *adj* **1 = overdue**, behind, last-minute, delayed, belated, behind schedule • *The train was late.* OPPOSITE: early **2 = dead**, deceased, departed • *my late husband* **3 = recent**, new, fresh, modern, advanced ▶ *adv* **4 = belatedly**, at the last minute, behindhand, behind time, dilatorily, tardily
lately *adv* **= recently**, in recent times, just now, latterly, not long ago, of late
lateness *n* **= delay**, tardiness, belatedness
latent *adj* **= hidden**, potential, invisible, dormant, undeveloped, unrealized, concealed
later *adv* **= afterwards**, after, subsequently, thereafter, by and by, in a while, in time, later on
lateral *adj* **= sideways**, edgeways, flanking
latest *adj* **= up-to-date**, current, cool

DICTIONARY

the side ▷ *n* **2** *football* pass thrown sideways
laterally *adv*
latex *n* milky sap found in some plants, esp. the rubber tree, used in making rubber and glue
lath *n* thin strip of wood used to support plaster, tiles, etc.
lathe *n* machine for turning wood or metal while it is being shaped
lather ⓣ *n* **1** froth of soap and water **2** frothy sweat **3** *informal* state of agitation ▷ *v* **4** make frothy **5** rub with soap until lather appears
Latimer *n* **Hugh**. ?1485–1555, English Protestant bishop: burnt at the stake for refusing to disavow his Protestant beliefs when Mary I assumed the throne
Latin *n* **1** language of the ancient Romans ▷ *adj* **2** of or in Latin **3** of a people whose language derives from Latin
▸ **Latin America** parts of South and Central America whose official language is Spanish or Portuguese **Latin American** *n, adj*
latitude ⓣ *n* **1** angular distance measured in degrees N or S of the equator **2** scope for freedom of action or thought **latitudes** **3** regions considered in relation to their distance from the equator **latitudinal** *adj*
latitudinarian *adj* liberal, esp. in religious matters
latrine *n* toilet in a barracks or camp
latter ⓣ *adj* **1** second of two **2** near or nearer the end **3** more recent **latterly** *adv*
▸ **latter-day** *adj* modern
lattice ⓣ [**lat**-iss] *n* **1** framework of intersecting strips of wood, metal, etc. **2** gate, screen, etc. formed of such a framework
latticed *adj*
laud *v* praise or glorify
▸ **laudable** *adj* praiseworthy **laudably** *adv*
▸ **laudatory** *adj* praising or glorifying
Lauda *n* **Niki**. born 1949, Austrian motor-racing driver: world champion 1975, 1977, 1984
laudanum [**lawd**-a-num] *n* opium-based sedative
Lauder *n* Sir **Harry**, real name *Hugh MacLennan*. 1870–1950, Scottish ballad singer and music-hall comedian
laugh ⓣ *v* **1** make inarticulate sounds with the voice expressing amusement, merriment, or scorn **2** utter or express with laughter ▷ *n* **3** laughing **4** manner of laughing **5** *informal* person or thing causing amusement
▸ **laughable** *adj* ludicrous
▸ **laughter** *n* sound or action of laughing
▸ **laughing gas** nitrous oxide as an anesthetic
▸ **laughing stock** object of general derision
▸ **laugh off** *v* treat (something serious or difficult) lightly
launch[1] ⓣ *v* **1** put (a ship or boat) into the water, esp. for the first time **2** begin (a campaign, project, etc.) **3** put a new product on the market **4** send (a missile or spacecraft) into space or the air ▷ *n* **5** launching
launcher *n*
▸ **launch into** *v* start doing something enthusiastically
▸ **launch out** *v* start doing something new
launch[2] *n* large open motorboat
launder ⓣ *v* **1** wash and iron (clothes and linen) **2** make (illegally obtained money) seem legal by passing it through foreign banks or legitimate businesses
▸ **laundry** *n, pl* **-dries** **1** place for washing clothes and linen, esp. as a business **2** clothes etc. for washing or which have recently been washed
▸ **Laundromat** *n* ® shop with coin-operated washing and drying machines
▸ **laundry list** *US & Canad* long list of things to be done

THESAURUS

(*informal*), modern, fashionable, up-to-the-minute, most recent, newest, phat (*slang*)
lather *n* **1** = **froth**, foam, suds, bubbles, soapsuds ▸ *v* **2** = **froth**, foam, soap
latitude *n* = **scope**, play, freedom, license, liberty, leeway, elbowroom, laxity
latter *adj* = **last-mentioned**, last, second, closing, concluding
latterly *adv* = **recently**, lately, of late
lattice *n* = **grid**, grating, grille, trellis
laudable *adj* = **praiseworthy**, excellent, worthy, admirable, commendable, meritorious, creditable, of note
laugh *v* **1** = **chuckle**, guffaw, giggle, chortle, snigger, titter, be in stitches, split one's sides • *You never laugh at my jokes.* ▷ **laugh at** *See* **make fun of, mock** ▷ **laugh off** = **disregard**, dismiss, ignore, minimize, pooh-pooh, brush aside, shrug off ▸ *n* **2** = **chuckle**, guffaw, giggle, chortle, snigger, titter • *She has a very infectious laugh.* **3** (*Informal*) = **joke**, scream (*informal*), hoot (*informal*), lark
laughable *adj* = **ridiculous**, absurd, ludicrous, preposterous, farcical, nonsensical, derisory, risible
laughing stock *n* = **figure of fun**, target, victim, butt
laughter *n* = **amusement**, glee, merriment, hilarity, mirth
launch *v* **1** = **propel**, fire, project, dispatch, discharge, send off, set in motion **2** = **begin**, start, open, introduce, initiate, commence, inaugurate, instigate, embark upon
launder *See* **wash**
laundered *See* **clean**

DICTIONARY

laureate [lor-ee-at] *adj* **poet laureate** poet appointed by the British sovereign to write poems on important occasions
laurel *n* **1** glossy-leaved shrub, bay tree **laurels 2** wreath of laurel, an emblem of victory or merit
Laurence *n* **Margaret** (née *Jean Margaret Wemyss*). 1926–87, Canadian novelist and short-story writer. Her novels include *The Stone Angel* (1964) and *A Jest of God* (1966); *A Bird in the House* (1970) is a collection of her short stories
Laurier *n* Sir **Wilfrid**. 1841–1919, Canadian Liberal politician; the first French-Canadian prime minister (1896–1911)
lava *n* molten rock thrown out by volcanoes, which hardens as it cools
Laval *n* **Pierre**. 1883–1945, French statesman. He was premier of France (1931–32; 1935–36) and premier of the Vichy government (1942–44). He was executed for collaboration with Germany
lavatory ⓣ *n, pl* **-ries** toilet
lavender *n* **1** shrub with fragrant flowers ▷ *adj* **2** bluish-purple
▶ **lavender water** light perfume made from lavender
Laver *n* **Rod**(**ney**) (**George**). born 1938, Australian tennis player: Wimbledon champion 1961, 1962, 1968, 1969; US champion 1962, 1969
Lavigne *n* **Avril Ramona**. born 1984, Canadian pop singer and songwriter. Her recordings include "Complicated" (2002) and "Girlfriend" (2005)
lavish ⓣ *adj* **1** great in quantity or richness **2** giving or spending generously **3** extravagant ▷ *v* **4** give or spend generously **lavishly** *adv*
Lavoisier *n* **Antoine Laurent**. 1743–94, French chemist; one of the founders of modern chemistry. He disproved the phlogiston theory, named oxygen, and discovered its importance in respiration and combustion
law ⓣ *n* **1** rule binding on a community **2** system of such rules **3** *informal* police **4** general principle deduced from facts **law-breaker** *n*
▶ **lawful** *adj* allowed by law **lawfully** *adv*
▶ **lawless** *adj* breaking the law, esp. in a violent way **lawlessly** *adv* **lawlessness** *n*
▶ **law-abiding** *adj* adhering to the laws
▶ **lawsuit** *n* court case brought by one person or group against another
Law *n* **Andrew Bonar**. 1858–1923, British Conservative statesman, born in Canada; prime minister (1922–23)
Lawes *n* **1 Henry**. 1596–1662, English composer, noted for his music for Milton's masque *Comus* (1634) and for his settings of some of Robert Herrick's poems **2** his brother, **William**. 1602–45, English composer, noted for his harmonically experimental instrumental music
lawn[1] *n* area of tended and mown grass
▶ **lawn mower** machine for cutting grass
▶ **lawn tennis** tennis, esp. when played on a grass court
lawn[2] *n* fine linen or cotton fabric
Lawrence *n* **1 D**(**avid**) **H**(**erbert**). 1885–1930, British novelist, poet, and short-story writer. Many of his works deal with the destructiveness of modern industrial society, contrasted with the beauty of nature and instinct, esp. the sexual impulse. His novels include *Sons and Lovers* (1913), *The Rainbow* (1915), *Women in Love* (1920), and *Lady Chatterley's*

THESAURUS

laurels *pl n* = **glory**, credit, praise, recognition, fame, honour, distinction, kudos, prestige, renown
lavatory *n* = **washroom**, bathroom, loo, latrine, toilet, convenience *or* public convenience, restroom, powder room, water closet, W.C., commode
lavish *adj* **1** = **plentiful**, prolific, abundant, copious, profuse **2** = **generous**, liberal, free, bountiful, munificent, open-handed, unstinting **3** = **extravagant**, wild, excessive, exaggerated, wasteful, unrestrained, immoderate, prodigal ▶ *v* **4** = **spend**, waste, pour, shower, squander, heap, deluge, dissipate, expend
law *n* **1** = **constitution**, code, charter • *The sale of lottery tickets to minors is against the law.* RELATED WORDS *adjectives*: legal, judicial **2** = **rule**, act, regulation, code, bylaw, decree, statute • *He was charged under the anti-stalking law.* **3** = **principle**, canon, axiom, precept
law-abiding *adj* = **obedient**, good, honest, lawful, orderly, compliant, honourable, dutiful, peaceable
law-breaker *n* = **criminal**, convict, offender, culprit, villain, crook (*informal*), delinquent, wrongdoer, felon, miscreant, perp (*informal*)
law court *See* **court**
lawful *adj* = **legal**, constitutional, legitimate, valid, authorized, rightful, permissible, legalized, licit, warranted
lawless *adj* = **disorderly**, wild, chaotic, unruly, rebellious, anarchic, riotous
lawlessness *n* = **disorder**, chaos, anarchy, mob rule
lawsuit *n* = **case**, trial, action, dispute, suit, prosecution, litigation, industrial tribunal, proceedings

DICTIONARY

Lover (1928) **2 Saint**. died 258 AD, Roman martyr: according to tradition he was roasted to death on a gridiron. Feast day: Aug 10
3 T(homas) E(dward), known as *Lawrence of Arabia*. 1888–1935, British soldier and writer. He took a major part in the Arab revolt against the Turks (1916–18), proving himself an outstanding guerrilla leader. He described his experiences in *The Seven Pillars of Wisdom* (1926)

lawyer Ⓣ *n* professionally qualified legal expert

lax Ⓣ *adj* not strict **laxity** *n* **laxly** *adv*

laxative *n, adj* (medicine) having a loosening effect on the bowels

lay[1] Ⓣ *v* **laying, laid 1** cause to lie **2** set in a particular place or position **3** arrange (a table) for a meal **4** put forward (a plan, argument, etc.) **5** attribute (blame) **6** (of a bird or reptile) produce eggs **7** devise or prepare **8** place (a bet)
▸ **lay waste** devastate
▸ **lay-by** *n Brit* stopping place for traffic beside a road
▸ **lay off** *v* dismiss staff during a slack period **lay-off** *n*
▸ **lay on** *v* provide or supply
▸ **lay out** *v* **1** arrange or spread out **2** prepare (a corpse) for burial **3** *informal* spend money, esp. lavishly **4** *slang* knock unconscious
▸ **layout** *n* arrangement, esp. of matter for printing or of a building

lay[2] Ⓣ *adj* **1** of or involving people who are not clergy **2** nonspecialist
▸ **layman** *n* ordinary person

lay[3] *v* past tense of **lie**[2]
▸ **layabout** *n* lazy person, loafer

lay[4] *n* short narrative poem designed to be sung

layer Ⓣ *n* **1** single thickness of some substance, as a stratum or coating on a surface **2** laying hen ▹ *v* **3** form a layer **layered** *adj*

layette *n* clothes for a newborn baby

lay figure *n* **1** jointed figure of the body used by artists **2** nonentity

Layton *n* **Irving**, born *Israel Lazarovitch*. 1912–2006, Canadian poet and writer, born in Romania. His works include *A Red Carpet for the Sun* (1959)

laze Ⓣ *v* **1** be idle or lazy ▹ *n* **2** lazing

lazy Ⓣ *adj* **lazier, laziest 1** not inclined to work or exert oneself **2** done in a relaxed manner with little effort **3** (of a movement) slow and gentle **lazily** *adv* **laziness** *n*
▸ **lazybones** *n informal* lazy person

lb pound (weight)

lea *n poetic* meadow

leach Ⓣ *v* remove or be removed from a substance by a liquid passing through it

Leacock *n* **Stephen Butler**. 1869–1944, Canadian humorist and economist: his comic works include *Literary Lapses* (1910) and *Frenzied Fiction* (1917)

lead[1] Ⓣ *v* **leading, led 1** guide or conduct **2** cause to feel, think, or behave in a certain

THESAURUS

lawyer *n* = **legal adviser**, advocate, attorney, counsel, solicitor, barrister and solicitor (*Canad*) • *I'm discussing the matter with my lawyer.*

lax *adj* = **slack**, casual, negligent, careless, lenient, remiss, overindulgent, slapdash, slipshod

lay[1] *v* **1** = **place**, set, put, spread, set down • *Lay a sheet of newspaper on the floor.* **2** = **arrange**, set out • *to lay the carpet* **3** = **produce**, bear, deposit **4** = **put forward**, offer, advance, present, submit, lodge, bring forward **5** = **attribute**, assign, allocate, allot, ascribe, impute **6** = **devise**, plan, prepare, design, plot, hatch, concoct, contrive, work out **7** = **bet**, risk, stake, gamble, hazard, give odds, wager ▹ **lay off** = **dismiss**, discharge, let go, pay off ▹ **lay on** = **provide**, give, supply, cater *or* cater for, furnish, purvey ▹ **lay out** = **arrange**, plan, design, display, exhibit, spread out; (*informal*) = **spend**, pay, invest, expend, disburse, fork out (*slang*), shell out (*informal*); (*informal*) = **knock out**, KO *or* K.O. (*slang*), knock for six (*informal*), knock unconscious

lay[2] *adj* **1** = **nonclerical**, secular **2** = **nonspecialist**, amateur, inexpert, nonprofessional

layabout *n* = **idler**, loafer, couch potato (*slang*), good-for-nothing, lounger, wastrel

layer *n* **1** = **covering**, film, sheet, coat, blanket, coating • *A fresh layer of snow covered the street.* **2** = **tier**, row, seam, thickness, stratum • *the layers of rock on the canyon wall*

layman *n* = **amateur**, outsider, lay person, nonprofessional

layoff *n* = **unemployment**, discharge, dismissal

layout *n* = **arrangement**, plan, design, format • *the layout of the pages*
See also: **form**

laze *v* = **idle**, lounge, loaf • *We spent a few days lazing around by the pool.* OPPOSITE: work
See also: **relax, rest**

laziness *n* = **idleness**, inactivity, sluggishness, sloth, indolence, slackness

lazy *adj* **1** = **idle**, slack • *a lazy and incompetent employee* **2** = **lethargic**, sluggish, drowsy, sleepy, slow-moving, languid, languorous, somnolent, torpid OPPOSITE: industrious

leach *v* = **extract**, strain, drain, filter, seep, percolate

lead *v* **1** = **guide**, conduct, steer, escort, usher

DICTIONARY

way **3** control or direct **4** be the most important person or thing in **5** be, go, or play first **6** (of a road, path, etc.) go towards **7** pass or spend (one's life) **8** result in ▷ *n* **9** first or most prominent place **10** example or leadership **11** amount by which a person or group is ahead of another **12** clue **13** length of leather or chain attached to a dog's collar to control it **14** principal role or actor in a film, play, etc. **15** cable bringing current to an electrical device ▷ *adj* **16** acting as a leader or lead **leading** *adj*

▸ **leading question** question worded to prompt the answer desired

▸ **lead-in** *n* introduction to a subject

lead² *n* **1** soft heavy grey metal **2** (in a pencil) graphite **3** lead weight on a line, used for sounding depths of water

▸ **leaded** *adj* (of windows) made from many small panes of glass held together by lead strips

▸ **leaden** *adj* **1** heavy or sluggish **2** dull grey **3** made from lead

Leadbelly *n* real name *Huddie Ledbetter*. 1888–1949, US blues singer and guitarist

leader Ⓣ *n* **1** person who leads or guides others **2** Also **leading article** article in a newspaper expressing editorial views **leadership** *n*

leaf Ⓣ *n, pl* **leaves 1** flat usu. green blade attached to the stem of a plant **2** single sheet of paper in a book **3** very thin sheet of metal **4** extending flap on a table **leafy** *adj* **leafless** *adj*

▸ **leaf mould** rich soil composed of decayed leaves

▸ **leaf through** *v* turn pages without reading them

leaflet Ⓣ *n* **1** sheet of printed matter for distribution **2** small leaf

league¹ Ⓣ *n* **1** association promoting the interests of its members **2** association of sports clubs organizing competitions between its members **3** *informal* class or level

league² *n obsolete* measure of distance, about three miles

leak Ⓣ *n* **1** hole or defect that allows the escape or entrance of liquid, gas, radiation, etc. **2** liquid etc. that escapes or enters **3** disclosure of secrets ▷ *v* **4** let fluid etc. in or out **5** (of fluid etc.) find its way through a leak **6** disclose secret information **leaky** *adj*

▸ **leakage** *n* **1** leaking **2** gradual escape or loss

THESAURUS

• *She led him into the house.* **2 = command**, head, manage, direct, govern, supervise • *Lester B. Pearson led the country between 1963 and 1968.* **3 = persuade**, cause, draw, prompt, influence, prevail, dispose, induce, incline **4 = come first**, surpass, exceed, excel, outstrip, outdo, transcend, be ahead *or* be ahead of, blaze a trail **5 = live**, have, spend, pass, experience, undergo ▷ **lead on = entice**, lure, deceive, tempt, seduce, beguile, draw on, string along (*informal*) ▷ **lead to = cause**, produce, contribute to • *A proper diet can lead to better health.*
See also: **create, result in** ▷ **lead up to = introduce**, pave the way, prepare for ▸ *n* **6 = clue**, trace, indication • *The police are following up several leads.* **7 = first place**, priority, supremacy, precedence, vanguard, primacy **8 = advantage**, start, edge, margin **9 = example**, leadership, model, direction, guidance **10 = leading role**, principal, protagonist, title role ▸ *adj* **11 = main**, first, head, chief, prime, premier, primary, principal, foremost, cutting-edge, leading
See also: **bring, drive, motivate, rule, take, top**

leaden *See* **cloudy, dull**

leader *n* **= head**, director, chief, captain, commander, boss (*informal*), principal, ringleader, point-man • *the leader of the New Democratic Party* OPPOSITE: follower
See also: **ruler**

leadership *n* **1 = guidance**, management, direction, domination, running, superintendency **2 = authority**, control, influence, initiative, command, supremacy, pre-eminence

leading *adj* **= main**, top, major, chief, key, prominent, principal, eminent • *a leading industrial nation*
See also: **first, foremost, important, in front, prime, supreme**

leaf *n* **1 = frond**, blade **2 = page**, sheet, folio ▸ *verb* ▷ **leaf through = browse**, flip, thumb *or* thumb through, glance, skim, riffle

leaflet *n* **= booklet**, flyer, brochure, circular, pamphlet • *Protesters were handing out leaflets in the street.*

leafy *adj* **= green**, shady, shaded, verdant, bosky (*lit*)

league *n* **1 = association**, group, union, coalition, alliance, partnership, federation, consortium, guild, fraternity, confederation **2 = class**, level, category

leak *v* **1 = escape**, spill, seep, ooze • *The gas had leaked.* **2 = disclose**, tell, reveal, divulge, give away, let slip, make known, make public, pass on ▸ *n* **3 = hole**, crack, puncture, fissure • *Have you plugged the leaks?* **4 = drip**, leakage, seepage, percolation **5 = disclosure**, divulgence

leaky *adj* **= leaking**, split, porous, perforated, cracked, holey, punctured

DICTIONARY

lean[1] Ⓣ *v* **leaning, leant** *or* **leaned 1** rest against **2** bend or slope from an upright position **3** tend (towards)
▸ **leaning** *n* tendency
▸ **lean on** *v* **1** *informal* threaten or intimidate **2** depend on for help or advice
▸ **lean-to** *n* shed built against an existing wall
lean[2] Ⓣ *adj* **1** thin but healthy-looking **2** (of meat) lacking fat **3** unproductive ▷ *n* **4** lean part of meat **leanness** *n*
Lean *n* Sir **David**. 1908–91, English film director. His films include *In Which We Serve* (1942), *Blithe Spirit* (1945), *Brief Encounter* (1946), *Great Expectations* (1946), *Oliver Twist* (1948), *The Bridge on the River Kwai* (1957), *Lawrence of Arabia* (1962), *Dr Zhivago* (1965), and *A Passage to India* (1984)
leap Ⓣ *v* **leaping, leapt** *or* **leaped 1** make a sudden powerful jump ▷ *n* **2** sudden powerful jump **3** abrupt increase, as in costs or prices
▸ **leapfrog** *n* game in which a player vaults over another bending down
▸ **leap year** year with February 29th as an extra day
Lear *n* **Edward**. 1812–88, English humorist and painter, noted for his illustrated nonsense poems and limericks
learn Ⓣ *v* **learning, learnt** *or* **learned 1** gain skill or knowledge by study, practice, or teaching **2** memorize (something) **3** find out or discover **learner** *n*
▸ **learned** *adj* **1** erudite, deeply read **2** showing much learning
▸ **learning** *n* knowledge got by study
lease Ⓣ *n* **1** contract by which land or property is rented for a stated time by the owner to a tenant ▷ *v* **2** let or rent on lease
▸ **leasehold** *adj* held on lease **leaseholder** *n*
leash Ⓣ *n* lead for a dog
least Ⓣ *adj* **1** smallest **2** superlative of **little** ▷ *n* **3** smallest one ▷ *adv* **4** in the smallest degree
leather *n* **1** material made from specially treated animal skins ▷ *adj* **2** made of leather ▷ *v* **3** beat or thrash
▸ **leathery** *adj* like leather, tough
leave[1] Ⓣ *v* **leaving, left 1** go away from **2** discontinue membership of **3** allow to remain, accidentally or deliberately **4** cause to be or remain in a specified state **5** permit **6** deposit **7** entrust **8** bequeath
▸ **leave out** *v* exclude or omit
leave[2] Ⓣ *n* **1** permission to be absent from work or duty **2** period of such absence **3** permission to do something **4** formal parting
leaven [**lev**-ven] *n* **1** yeast **2** influence that produces a gradual change ▷ *v* **3** raise with

THESAURUS

lean[1] *v* **1 = rest**, prop, recline, repose, be supported **2 = bend**, tip, heel, slope, tilt, incline, slant **3 = tend**, prefer, favor, be disposed to, be prone to ▷ **lean on = depend on**, trust, count on, have faith in, rely on
lean[2] *adj* **1 = thin**, slim, spare, skinny, slender, gaunt, bony, angular, rangy, wiry **2 = unproductive**, poor, barren, meager, scanty, unfruitful
leaning *n* **= tendency**, bias, bent, penchant, disposition, inclination, propensity, predilection, partiality, proclivity
leap *v* **1 = jump**, spring, bounce, vault, bound • *The deer leaped into the air.* ▸ *n* **2 = jump**, spring, bound • *a leap of 2.37 m.* **3 = increase**, rise, surge, escalation, upswing, upsurge
See also: **dive**
learn *v* **1 = master**, grasp, pick up • *I am trying to learn Spanish.* **2 = discover**, hear, determine, understand, gather, ascertain, find out • *On learning who she was, I asked to meet her.*
See also: **find, study**
learned *adj* **= scholarly**, academic, intellectual, literate, erudite • *a very learned person*
See also: **educated**
learner *n* **= beginner**, apprentice, novice, neophyte, tyro
learning *n* **= knowledge**, study, information, culture, education, wisdom, scholarship, lore, erudition
lease *v* **= rent** • *She leases her house for the summer.*
leash *n* **= lead**, rein, tether
least *adj* **= smallest**, minimum, fewest, lowest, slightest • *Stick to foods with the least fat.* OPPOSITE: most ▷ **least possible** *See* **minimum**
leathery *adj* **= tough**, hard, rough
leave[1] *v* **1 = depart**, go, quit, withdraw, abandon, desert, forsake, bail on (*slang*) • *He is not allowed to leave the country.* **2 = forget**, leave behind, mislay **3 = cause**, produce, generate, deposit, result in **4 = give up**, drop, abandon, surrender, renounce, relinquish **5 = entrust**, commit, refer, assign, cede, allot, consign, give over **6 = bequeath**, will, hand down ▷ **leave behind** *See* **abandon** ▷ **leave out = omit**, reject, ignore, exclude, overlook, neglect, disregard, blow off (*slang*), cast aside
See also: **flee, resign**
leave[2] *n* **1 = vacation**, holiday, sabbatical, furlough, time off • *Why don't you take a few days' leave?* **2 = permission**, freedom, sanction, concession, consent,

DICTIONARY

leaven **4** spread through and influence (something)

Leavis *n* **F(rank) R(aymond)**. 1895–1978, English literary critic. He edited *Scrutiny* (1932–53) and his books include *The Great Tradition* (1948) and *The Common Pursuit* (1952)
Leavisite *adj, n*

LeBlanc *n* **Roméo**. 1927–2009, Canadian journalist and politician; Governor General (1995–99)

Lebrun *n* **1 Albert**. 1871–1950, French statesman; president (1932–40) **2** Also **Le Brun Charles** 1619–90, French historical painter. He was court painter to Louis XIV and executed much of the decoration of the palace of Versailles

lecher *n* lecherous man **lechery** *n*

lecherous **T** [**letch**-er-uss] *adj* (of a man) having or showing excessive sexual desire
lecherously *adv* **lecherousness** *n*

Le Corbusier *n* real name *Charles Édouard Jeanneret*. 1887–1965, French architect and town planner, born in Switzerland. He is noted for his use of reinforced concrete and for his modular system, which used units of a standard size. His works include Unité d'Habitation at Marseilles (1946–52) and the city of Chandigarh, India (1954)

lectern *n* sloping reading desk, esp. in a church

lecture **T** *n* **1** informative talk to an audience on a subject **2** lengthy rebuke or scolding ▷ *v* **3** give a talk **4** reprove **lecturer** *n*
▸ **lectureship** *n* appointment as a lecturer

led *v* past of **lead**[1]

LED light-emitting diode

ledge **T** *n* **1** narrow shelf sticking out from a wall **2** shelflike projection from a cliff etc.

ledger *n* book of debit and credit accounts of a firm

lee *n* **1** sheltered part or side **2** side away from the wind
▸ **leeward** *adj, n* **1** (on) the lee side ▷ *adv* **2** towards this side
▸ **leeway** *n* room for free movement within certain limits

Lee *n* **1 Ang**. born 1954, Taiwanese film director; his films include *Sense and Sensibility* (1995), *The Ice Storm* (1997), *Crouching Tiger, Hidden Dragon* (2000), and *Brokeback Mountain* (2005) **2 Bruce**, original name *Lee Yuen Kam*. 1940–73, US film actor and kung fu expert who starred in such films as *Enter the Dragon* (1973) **3 Gypsy Rose**, original name *Rose Louise Hovick*. 1914–70, US striptease and burlesque artiste, who appeared in the Ziegfeld Follies (1936) and in films **4 Laurie**. 1914–97, British poet and writer, best known for the autobiographical *Cider with Rosie* (1959) **5 Philip**. born 1944, Lieutenant Governor of Manitoba (2009–) **6 Richard Henry**. 1732–94, American Revolutionary statesman, who moved the resolution in favour of American independence (1776) **7 Robert E(dward)**. 1807–70, American general; commander-in-chief of the Confederate armies in the Civil War **8 Spike**, real name *Shelton Jackson Lee*. born 1957, US film director: his films include *She's Gotta Have It* (1985), *Malcolm X* (1992), and *25th Hour* (2002)

leech *n* **1** species of bloodsucking worm **2** person who lives off others

leek *n* vegetable of the onion family with a long bulb and thick stem

leer **T** *v* **1** look or grin at in a sneering or suggestive manner ▷ *n* **2** sneering or suggestive look or grin

leery *adj informal* suspicious or wary (of)

lees **T** *pl n* sediment of wine

Leeuwenhoek *n* **Anton van**. 1632–1723, Dutch microscopist, whose microscopes enabled him to give the first accurate description of blood corpuscles, spermatozoa, and microbes

Le Fanu *n* **(Joseph) Sheridan**. 1814–73, Irish writer, best known for his stories of mystery and the supernatural, esp. *Uncle Silas* (1864) and the collection *In a Glass Darkly* (1872)

left[1] **T** *adj* **1** denotes the side that faces west

THESAURUS

allowance, authorization, liberty, dispensation **3 = parting**, retirement, withdrawal, departure, farewell, adieu, good-bye, leave-taking
See also: **blessing**

lecherous *adj* = **lustful**, lewd, lascivious, libidinous, licentious, prurient, salacious

lecture *n* **1 = talk**, speech, address, presentation, sermon, discourse • *In his lecture, he covered several topics.* **2 = scolding**, warning, reprimand • *The police gave us a stern lecture on safety.* ▸ *v* **3 = talk**, speak, teach, give a talk • *She has lectured all over the world.* **4 = scold**, reprimand, censure, castigate, berate, admonish, reprove, tell off (*informal*)
See also: **lesson**

lecturer *See* **teacher**

ledge *n* = **shelf**, step, projection, ridge, mantle, sill

leer *n, v* = **grin**, stare, goggle, ogle, gloat, smirk, squint

lees *pl n* = **sediment**, deposit, dregs, grounds

leeway *n* = **room**, play, space, margin, scope, latitude, elbowroom

left *adj* **1 = left-hand**, port, larboard (*naut*), sinistral **2** (Of politics) = **socialist**, radical, leftist, left-wing

DICTIONARY

when the front faces north **2** opposite to right ▷ *n* **3** left hand or part **4** *politics* people supporting socialism rather than capitalism ▷ *adv* **5** on or towards the left
▸ **leftist** *n, adj* (person) of the political left
▸ **left-handed** *adj* more adept with the left hand than with the right
▸ **left-wing** *adj* **1** socialist **2** belonging to the more radical part of a political party
▸ **lefty** *n informal* **1** left-handed person **2** *baseball* left-handed pitcher **3** a leftist
left[2] *v* past of **leave**[1]
left field *n baseball* area of the outfield to the batter's left
▸ **out of left field** unexpected or surprising: *their proposal came out of left field*
▸ **left fielder** *baseball* fielder who covers left field
leftover Ⓣ *n* unused portion of food or material
leg Ⓣ *n* **1** one of the limbs on which a person or animal walks, runs, or stands **2** part of a garment covering the leg **3** structure that supports, such as one of the legs of a table **4** stage of a journey **5** *sports* (part of) one game or race in a series
▸ **pull someone's leg** tease someone
▸ **leggy** *adj* long-legged
▸ **legless** *adj* **1** without legs **2** *slang* very drunk
▸ **leggings** *pl n* **1** covering of leather or other material for the legs **2** close-fitting trousers for women or children
legacy Ⓣ *n, pl* **-cies 1** thing left in a will **2** thing handed down to a successor
legal Ⓣ *adj* **1** established or permitted by law **2** relating to law or lawyers **legality** *n* **legally** *adv*
▸ **legalize** *v* make legal **legalization** *n*
legate *n* messenger or representative, esp. from the Pope
▸ **legation** *n* **1** diplomatic minister and his staff **2** official residence of a diplomatic minister
legatee *n* recipient of a legacy
legato [leg-**ah**-toe] *adv music* smoothly
legend Ⓣ *n* **1** traditional story or myth **2** traditional literature **3** famous person or event **4** stories about such a person or event **5** inscription
▸ **legendary** *adj* **1** famous **2** of or in legend
Léger *n* **Jules**. 1913–80, Canadian academic and diplomat: Governor General (1974–79)
legerdemain [lej-er-de-**main**] *n* **1** sleight of hand **2** cunning deception
leger line *n* same as **ledger line**
Leghorn *n* breed of domestic fowl
legible Ⓣ *adj* easily read **legibility** *n* **legibly** *adv*
legion Ⓣ *n* **1** large military force **2** large number **3** association of veterans **4** infantry unit in the Roman army **legionary** *adj, n*
▸ **legionnaire** *n* member of a legion
▸ **legionnaire's disease** serious bacterial disease similar to pneumonia
legislate *v* make laws
▸ **legislation** *n* **1** legislating **2** laws made
legislative *adj*
▸ **legislator** *n* maker of laws
▸ **legislature** *n* body of persons that makes, amends, or repeals the laws of a state

THESAURUS

leftist *See* **left-wing**
leftover *n* = **remnant**, scrap, oddment
leftovers *See* **remains**
left-wing *adj* = **socialist**, liberal, radical, leftist • *a left-wing demonstration*
leg *n* **1** = **limb**, member, pin (*informal*), stump (*informal*), lower limb **2** = **support**, brace, prop, upright **3** = **stage**, part, stretch, section, portion, segment, lap ▷ **pull someone's leg** (*Informal*) = **tease**, kid (*informal*), trick, fool, make fun of
legacy *n* = **bequest**, estate, inheritance, heirloom • *He left his children a generous legacy.* *See also*: **gift**
legal *adj* **1** = **judicial**, forensic, judiciary • *the Dutch legal system* **2** = **lawful**, legitimate, valid, authorized, rightful, permissible • *The strike was perfectly legal.* OPPOSITE: illegal *See also*: **formal**
legality *n* = **lawfulness**, legitimacy, validity, rightfulness
legalize *v* = **allow**, approve, sanction, permit, license, authorize, legitimate, validate, legitimize, decriminalize
legation *n* = **delegation**, embassy, representation, consulate
legend *n* **1** = **myth**, story, tale, fiction, saga, fable, folk tale **2** = **celebrity**, phenomenon, luminary, prodigy, megastar (*informal*) **3** = **inscription**, motto, caption
legendary *adj* **1** = **mythical**, traditional, romantic, fabulous, fictitious, fabled, apocryphal **2** = **famous**, famed, renowned, well-known, celebrated, illustrious, immortal
legibility *n* = **readability**, clarity, neatness
legible *adj* = **readable**, clear, distinct, neat, decipherable, easy to read
legion *n* **1** = **army**, company, force, troop, division, brigade **2** = **multitude**, number, host, mass, throng, myriad, drove, horde
legislation *n* **1** = **lawmaking**, regulation, prescription, enactment **2** = **law**, bill, act, measure, ruling, regulation, charter, statute
legislative *adj* = **law-making**, judicial, law-giving
legislator *n* = **lawmaker**, lawgiver
legislature *n* = **parliament**, assembly,

DICTIONARY

legitimate ⓣ *adj* **1** authorized by or in accordance with law **2** fairly deduced **3** born to parents married to each other ▷ *v* **4** make legitimate **legitimately** *adv* **legitimacy** *n*

▶ **legitimize** *v* make legitimate, legalize **legitimization** *n*

Lego *n* ® construction toy of plastic bricks fitted together by studs

legume *n* **1** pod of a plant of the pea or bean family **legumes 2** peas or beans

▶ **leguminous** *adj* (of plants) pod-bearing

Lehár *n* **Franz**. 1870–1948, Hungarian composer of operettas, esp. *The Merry Widow* (1905)

lei *n* (in Hawaii) garland of flowers

Leibnitz, Leibniz *n* Baron **Gottfried Wilhelm von**. 1646–1716, German rationalist philosopher and mathematician. He conceived of the universe as a hierarchy of independent units or monads, synchronized by pre-established harmony. His works include *Théodicée* (1710) and *Monadologia* (1714). He also devised a system of calculus, independently of Newton **Leibnitzian** *adj*

Leibovitz *n* **Annie**. born 1949, US photographer, known for her portraits of celebrities

Leigh *n* **1 Mike**. born 1943, British dramatist and theatre, film, and television director, noted for his use of improvisation. His plays include *Abigail's Party* (1977), and his films include *All or Nothing* (2002), *Secrets and Lies* (1996), *Vera Drake* (2004), and *Another Year* (2010) **2 Vivien**, real name *Vivian Hartley*. 1913–67, English stage and film actress. Her films include *Gone with the Wind* (1939) and *A Streetcar Named Desire* (1951), for both of which she won Oscars

leisure ⓣ *n* time for relaxation or hobbies

▶ **at one's leisure** when one has time

▶ **leisurely** *adj* **1** deliberate, unhurried ▷ *adv* **2** slowly

▶ **leisured** *adj* with plenty of spare time

▶ **leisure centre** building with facilities such as a swimming pool, gymnasium, and café

leitmotif [**lite**-mote-eef] *n music* recurring theme associated with a person, situation, or thought

Lemaître *n* Abbé **Georges** (**Édouard**). 1894–1966, Belgian astronomer and priest, who first proposed the big-bang theory of the universe (1927)

lemming *n* rodent of Arctic regions, reputed to run into the sea and drown during mass migrations

lemon *n* **1** yellow acid fruit that grows on trees **2** *slang* useless or defective person or thing ▷ *adj* **3** pale-yellow

▶ **lemonade** *n* lemon-flavoured soft drink, often fizzy

▶ **lemon curd** creamy spread made of lemons, butter, etc.

▶ **lemon sole** edible flatfish

Lemper *n* **Ute**. born 1963, German singer and actress, noted esp. for her performances of songs by Kurt Weill

lemur *n* nocturnal animal like a small monkey, found on Madagascar

lend ⓣ *v* **lending, lent 1** give the temporary use of **2** provide (money) temporarily, often for interest **3** add (a quality or effect): *her presence lent beauty to the scene* **lender** *n*

▶ **lend itself to** be suitable for

Lendl *n* **Ivan**. born 1960, Czech tennis player; US Open champion (1985–87)

Lenglen *n* **Suzanne**. 1899–1938, French tennis player: Wimbledon champion (1919–25)

length ⓣ *n* **1** extent or measurement from end to end **2** duration **3** quality of being long **4** piece of something narrow and long **lengthways** *or* **lengthwise** *adj, adv*

▶ **at length 1** in full detail **2** at last

▶ **lengthy** *adj* very long or tiresome **lengthily** *adv*

▶ **lengthen** *v* make or become longer

THESAURUS

chamber, congress, senate

legitimate *adj* **1 = lawful**, legal, genuine, authentic, authorized, kosher (*informal*), rightful, licit **2 = reasonable**, correct, valid, logical, sensible, justifiable, admissible, well-founded, warranted ▶ *v* **3 = legalize**, sanction, permit, authorize, legitimize, pronounce lawful

legitimize *v* **= legalize**, sanction, permit, authorize

leisure *n* **= free time**, recreation, relaxation, time off • *There wasn't a lot of time for leisure.* OPPOSITE: work
See also: **ease, rest**

leisurely *adj* **= unhurried**, easy, comfortable, gentle, relaxed • *a leisurely walk along the beach*
See also: **slow**

lend *v* **1 = loan**, advance **2 = add**, give, provide, supply, grant, bestow, confer, impart ▷ **lend a hand** *See* **help** ▷ **lend itself to = suit**, be appropriate, be serviceable

length *n* **1 = distance**, span, extent • *The length of the box is 45 cm.* **2 = duration**, term, period, space, span • *The movie is over two hours in length.* **3 = piece**, measure, section, portion, segment ▷ **at length = in detail**, completely, fully, thoroughly, in depth, to the full; **= for a long time**, for ages, for hours,

DICTIONARY

lenient Ⓣ [**lee**-nee-ent] *adj* tolerant, not strict or severe **leniency** *n* **leniently** *adv*
Lenin *n* **Vladimir Ilyich**, original surname *Ulyanov*. 1870–1924, Russian statesman and Marxist theoretician; first premier of the Soviet Union. He formed the Bolsheviks (1903) and led them in the October Revolution (1917), which established the Soviet Government. He adopted the New Economic Policy (1921) after the Civil War had led to the virtual collapse of the Russian economy, formed the Comintern (1919), and was the originator of the guiding doctrine of the Soviet Union, Marxism-Leninism. After the Soviet Union broke up in 1991, many statues of Lenin were demolished
lenity *n, pl* **-ties** mercy or clemency
Lennon *n* **John** (**Ono**), original name *John Winston Lennon*. 1940–80, English rock guitarist, singer, and songwriter: member of the Beatles (1962–70). His subsequent recordings, many in collaboration with his wife Yoko Ono, include "Instant Karma" (1970), *Imagine* (1971), and *Double Fantasy* (1980). He was shot dead by a demented fan
lens *n, pl* **lenses 1** piece of glass or similar material with one or both sides curved, used to converge or diverge light rays in cameras, spectacles, telescopes, etc. **2** transparent structure in the eye that focuses light
lent *v* past of **lend**
Lent *n* period from Ash Wednesday to Easter Eve
▸ **Lenten** *adj* of, in, or suitable to Lent
lentil *n* edible seed of a leguminous Asian plant
lento *adv music* slowly
Lenya *n* **Lotte**, original name *Caroline Blamauer*. 1900–81, Austrian singer and actress, associated esp. with the songs of her husband Kurt Weill
Leo III *n* **1** called *the Isaurian*. ?675–741 AD, Byzantine emperor (717–41): he checked Arab expansionism and began the policy of iconoclasm, which divided the empire for the next century **2 Saint**. ?750–816 AD, pope (795–816). He crowned Charlemagne emperor of the Romans (800). Feast day: June 12
Leo X *n* original name *Giovanni de' Medici*. 1475–1521, pope (1513–21): noted for his patronage of Renaissance art and learning; excommunicated Luther (1521)
Leonard *n* **Sugar Ray**, real name *Ray Charles Leonard*. born 1956, US boxer: the first man to have won world titles at five officially recognized weights
Leonardo da Vinci *n* 1452–1519, Italian painter, sculptor, architect, and engineer: the most versatile talent of the Italian Renaissance. His most famous paintings include *The Virgin of the Rocks* (1483–85), the *Mona Lisa* (or *La Gioconda*, 1503), and the *Last Supper* (?1495–97). His numerous drawings, combining scientific precision in observation with intense imaginative power, reflect the breadth of his interests, which ranged over biology, physiology, hydraulics, and aeronautics. He invented the first armoured tank and foresaw the invention of aircraft and submarines **Leonardesque** *adj*
Leoncavallo *n* **Ruggiero**. 1858–1919, Italian composer of operas, notably *I Pagliacci* (1892)
Leonidas *n* died 480 BC, king of Sparta (?490–480), hero of the Battle of Thermopylae, in which he was killed by the Persians under Xerxes
leonine *adj* like a lion
leopard *n* large spotted carnivorous animal of the cat family **leopardess** *n fem*
Leopold I *n* **1** 1640–1705, Holy Roman Emperor (1658–1705). His reign was marked by wars with Louis XIV of France and with the Turks **2** 1790–1865, first king of the Belgians (1831–65)
Leopold II *n* **1** 1747–92, Holy Roman Emperor (1790–92). He formed an alliance with Prussia against France (1792) after the downfall of his brother-in-law Louis XVI **2** 1835–1909, king of the Belgians (1865–1909); son of Leopold I. He financed Stanley's explorations in Africa, becoming first sovereign of the Congo Free State (1885)
Leopold III *n* 1901–83, king of the Belgians (1934–51); son of Albert I. His surrender to the Nazis (1940) forced his eventual abdication in favour of his son, Baudouin
leotard *n* tight-fitting garment covering most of the body, worn by acrobats, dancers, etc.
Lepage *n* **Robert**. born 1957, Canadian writer, director, and actor in film and theatre. His films include *Le Confessionnal* (1995) which he wrote and directed
Le Pen *n* **Jean-Marie**. born 1928, French

THESAURUS

interminably; = **at last**, finally, eventually, at long last, in the end
lengthen *v* = **extend**, stretch, prolong, make longer • *The airport runway had to be lengthened*. OPPOSITE: shorten
lengthy *adj* = **long**, extended, prolonged, protracted, drawn-out, tedious, interminable, long-winded, long-drawn-out
leniency *n* = **mercy**, quarter, tolerance, compassion, clemency, pity, moderation, indulgence, forbearance
lenient *adj* = **merciful**, kind, compassionate, tolerant, forgiving, indulgent, forbearing, sparing

DICTIONARY

politician; leader of the extreme right-wing Front National from 1972; runner-up in the presidential election of 2002
leper *n* **1** person suffering from leprosy **2** ignored or despised person
lepidoptera *pl n* order of insects with four wings covered with fine gossamer scales, as moths and butterflies **lepidopterous** *ad* ▸ **lepidopterist** *n* person who studies or collects butterflies or mothsj
Lepidus *n* **Marcus Aemilius**. died ?13 BC, Roman statesman: formed the Second Triumvirate with Octavian (later Augustus) and Mark Antony
leprechaun *n* mischievous elf of Irish folklore
leprosy *n* disease attacking the nerves and skin, resulting in loss of feeling in the affected parts **leprous** *adj*
Lermontov *n* **Mikhail Yurievich**. 1814–41, Russian novelist and poet: noted esp. for the novel *A Hero of Our Time* (1840)
Lerner *n* **Alan Jay**. 1914–86, US songwriter and librettist. With Frederick Loewe he wrote *My Fair Lady* (1956) and *Camelot* (1960) as well as a number of film scripts, including *Gigi* (1958)
Lesage *n* **Jean**. 1912–80, Canadian lawyer and Liberal politician. Leader of the Liberal Party of Quebec (1958–70); Premier of Quebec 1960–66. His reforms led to a secularization of Quebec society known as the Quiet Revolution
lesbian Ⓣ *n* **1** homosexual woman ▹ *adj* **2** of homosexual women **lesbianism** *n*
lese-majesty [lezz-**maj**-est-ee] *n* **1** treason **2** taking of liberties against people in authority
lesion *n* **1** structural change in an organ of the body caused by illness or injury **2** injury or wound
less Ⓣ *adj* **1** smaller in extent, degree, or duration **2** not so much **3** comparative of **little** ▹ *n* **4** smaller part or quantity **5** lesser amount ▹ *adv* **6** to a smaller extent or degree ▹ *prep* **7** after deducting, minus
▸ **lessen** *v* make or become smaller or not as much
▸ **lesser** *adj* not as great in quantity, size, or worth
lessee *n* person to whom a lease is granted
lesson Ⓣ *n* **1** single period of instruction in a subject **2** content of this **3** experience that teaches **4** portion of Scripture read in church
lessor *n* person who grants a lease
lest *conj* **1** so as to prevent any possibility that **2** for fear that
let[1] Ⓣ *v* **letting, let 1** allow, enable, or cause **2** allow to escape **3** grant use of for rent, lease **4** used as an auxiliary to express a proposal, command, threat, or assumption
▸ **let alone** not to mention
▸ **let down** *v* **1** disappoint **2** lower **3** deflate
▸ **letdown** *n* disappointment
▸ **let off** *v* **1** excuse from (a duty or punishment) **2** fire or explode (a weapon) **3** emit (gas, steam, etc.)
▸ **let on** *v informal* reveal (a secret)
▸ **let out** *v* **1** emit **2** release
▸ **let up** *v* diminish or stop
▸ **let-up** *n* lessening
let[2] *n* **1** hindrance **2** *tennis* minor infringement or obstruction of the ball requiring a replay of the point
lethal Ⓣ *adj* deadly

THESAURUS

lesbian *adj* = **homosexual**, gay, sapphic
less *adj* **1** = **smaller**, shorter ▸ *preposition* **2** = **minus**, without, excepting, lacking, subtracting
lessen *v* = **decrease**, reduce, lower, shrink, diminish, minimize, dwindle, abate • *changes to their diet that would lessen the risk of disease* OPPOSITE: increase
See also: **weaken**
lessening *See* **decrease**
lesser *adj* = **minor**, lower, secondary, inferior, less important
lesson *n* **1** = **class**, period, lecture, coaching, tutoring • *I'm taking piano lessons.* **2** = **example**, message, moral, deterrent
lessons *See* **study**
let[1] *v* = **allow**, sanction, permit, give permission • *Don't let the cat out of the house.* OPPOSITE: forbid ▹ **let down** = **disappoint**, fail, dissatisfy, disillusion, disenchant, fall short, leave in the lurch, leave stranded ▹ **let go** *See* **discharge** ▹ **let in** *See* **admit** ▹ **let off** = **fire**, explode, detonate, discharge; = **emit**, release, leak, exude, give off; = **excuse**, release, spare, discharge, pardon, forgive, exempt, exonerate, absolve ▹ **let on** = **reveal**, say, admit, disclose, divulge, give away, let the cat out of the bag (*informal*), make known ▹ **let out** = **emit**, produce, give vent to; = **release**, free, discharge, liberate, let go ▹ **let up** = **stop**, ease *or* ease up, decrease, moderate, relax, diminish, subside, abate, slacken
let[2] *n* (*Archaic*) = **hindrance**, restriction, interference, obstacle, obstruction, prohibition, constraint, impediment
letdown *n* = **disappointment**, blow, setback, washout (*informal*), anticlimax, comedown (*informal*)
lethal *adj* = **deadly**, dangerous, fatal, destructive, murderous, virulent, mortal, devastating
lethargic *adj* = **sluggish**, listless, dull,

DICTIONARY

lethargy Ⓣ *n* **1** sluggishness or dullness **2** abnormal lack of energy **lethargic** *adj* **lethargically** *adv*
letter Ⓣ *n* **1** alphabetical symbol **2** written message, usu. sent by post **3** strict meaning (of a law etc.) ▷ *pl n* **4** literary knowledge or ability **lettering** *n*
▸ **lettered** *adj* learned
▸ **letter bomb** explosive device in a parcel or letter that explodes when it is opened
▸ **letter box 1** slot in a door through which letters are delivered **2** box in a street or post office where letters are posted
▸ **letterhead** *n* printed heading on stationery giving the sender's name and address
lettuce *n* plant with large green leaves used in salads
leucocyte [**loo**-koh-site] *n* white blood corpuscle
leukemia, leukaemia [loo-**kee**-mee-a] *n* disease caused by uncontrolled overproduction of white blood corpuscles
levee[1] *n* **1** natural or artificial river embankment **2** landing-place
levee[2] *n* formal reception for visitors, orig. held by a sovereign on rising
level Ⓣ *adj* **1** horizontal **2** having an even surface **3** of the same height as something else **4** equal to or even with (someone or something else) **5** not going above the top edge of (a spoon etc.) ▷ *v* **-elling, -elled** **6** make even or horizontal **7** make equal in position or status **8** direct (a gun, accusation, etc.) at **9** raze to the ground ▷ *n* **10** horizontal line or surface **11** device for showing or testing if something is horizontal **12** position on a scale **13** standard or grade **14** flat area of land
▸ **on the level** *informal* honest or trustworthy
▸ **level crossing** point where a railway line and road cross
▸ **level-headed** *adj* not apt to be carried away by emotion
lever Ⓣ *n* **1** rigid bar pivoted about a fulcrum to transfer a force with mechanical advantage **2** bar used to move a heavy object or to open something **3** handle pressed, pulled, etc. to operate machinery **4** means of exerting pressure to achieve an aim ▷ *v* **5** prise or move with a lever
▸ **leverage** *n* **1** action or power of a lever **2** influence or strategic advantage
Lévesque *n* **René**. 1922–87, Canadian journalist, broadcaster, and politician. One of the founders of the Parti Québécois and its leader (1968–85). During his Premiership of Quebec (1976–85) the first referendum (1980) on sovereignty-association was held
leviathan [lev-**vie**-ath-an] *n* **1** sea monster **2** anything huge or formidable
Levis *pl n* ® denim jeans
Lévi-Strauss *n* **Claude**. 1908–2009, French anthropologist, leading exponent of structuralism. His books include *The Elementary Structures of Kinship* (1969), *Totemism* (1962), *The Savage Mind* (1966), *Mythologies* (1964–71), and *Saudades do Brazil* (Memories of Brazil; 1994)
levitation *n* raising of a solid body into the air supernaturally
▸ **levitate** *v* rise or cause to rise into the air
levity Ⓣ *n, pl* **-ties** inclination to make a joke of serious matters
levy Ⓣ [**lev**-vee] *v* **levying, levied 1** impose and collect (a tax) **2** raise (troops) ▷ *n, pl* **levies 3** imposition or collection of taxes **4** enrolling of troops **5** amount or number levied

THESAURUS

drowsy, sleepy, apathetic, languid, slothful
lethargy *n* = **sluggishness**, sleepiness, apathy, drowsiness, sloth, inertia, languor, lassitude, listlessness
letter *n* **1** = **character**, sign, symbol **2** = **message**, note, line, communication, dispatch, missive, epistle
let-up *n* = **lessening**, break, pause, lull, interval, respite, remission, breathing space, slackening
level *adj* **1** = **flat**, horizontal • *a plateau of level ground* OPPOSITE: uneven **2** = **even**, uniform, consistent, smooth, plain **3** = **equal**, even, equivalent, balanced, comparable, proportionate, commensurate, neck and neck, on a level playing field (*informal*), on a par ▸ *v* **4** = **flatten**, plane, smooth • *We levelled the ground.* **5** = **equalize**, balance, even up **6** = **raze**, destroy, devastate, demolish, flatten, bulldoze, knock down, pull down, tear down **7** = **direct**, point, aim, focus, train ▸ *n* **8** = **grade**, stage, standard, status, rank • *Crime levels have started to decline.* ▷ **on the level** (*Informal*) = **honest**, straight, fair, square, genuine, above board
See also: **extent**
level-headed *adj* = **steady**, cool, calm, balanced, sensible, unflappable (*informal*), collected, composed
level-headedness *See* **common sense**
levelled *See* **flat**
lever *n* **1** = **handle**, bar ▸ *v* **2** = **pry**, force
leverage *n* = **influence**, authority, pull (*informal*), weight, clout (*informal*)
levity *n* = **light-heartedness**, silliness, facetiousness, flippancy, frivolity, skittishness, triviality
levy *v* **1** = **impose**, charge, demand, collect, exact **2** = **conscript**, raise, muster, mobilize, call up ▸ *n* **3** = **imposition**, collection,

DICTIONARY

lewd Ⓣ *adj* lustful or indecent **lewdly** *adv* **lewdness** *n*
Lewis *n* **1** See (Cecil) **Day-Lewis** **2** **C(live) S(taples)**. 1898–1963, English novelist, critic, and Christian apologist, noted for his critical work, *Allegory of Love* (1936), his theological study, *The Screwtape Letters* (1942), and for his children's books chronicling the land of Narnia **3** **Meriwether**. 1774–1807, American explorer who, with William Clark, led an overland expedition from St Louis to the Pacific Ocean (1804–06)
lexicon *n* **1** dictionary **2** vocabulary of a language
▶ **lexical** *adj* relating to the vocabulary of a language
▶ **lexicographer** *n* writer of dictionaries **lexicography** *n*
ley *n* land temporarily under grass
LGV large goods vehicle
liable Ⓣ *adj* **1** legally obliged or responsible **2** given to or at risk from a condition
▶ **liability** *n* **1** state of being liable **2** financial obligation **3** hindrance or disadvantage
liaise Ⓣ *v* establish and maintain communication (with)
▶ **liaison** *n* **1** communication and cooperation between groups **2** secret or adulterous relationship
liana *n* climbing plant in tropical forests
liar Ⓣ *n* person who tells lies
lib *n informal* short for **liberation**
libation [lie-**bay**-shun] *n* drink poured as an offering to the gods
libel Ⓣ *n* **1** published statement falsely damaging a person's reputation ▷ *v* **-belling, -belled** **2** defame falsely
▶ **libellous** *adj* defamatory
liberal Ⓣ *adj* **1** having political views that favour progress and reform **2** generous in behaviour or temperament **3** tolerant **4** abundant **5** (of education) designed to develop general cultural interests ▷ *n* **6** person who has liberal ideas or opinions **liberally** *adv*
▶ **liberalism** *n* belief in democratic reforms and individual freedom
▶ **liberality** *n* generosity
▶ **liberalize** *v* make (laws, a country, etc.) less restrictive **liberalization** *n*
▶ **Liberal Party** major political party with viewpoints between those of the Progressive Conservative Party and the New Democratic Party
liberate Ⓣ *v* set free **liberation** *n* **liberator** *n*
libertarian *n* **1** believer in freedom of thought and action ▷ *adj* **2** having such a belief
libertine Ⓣ [**lib**-er-teen] *n* morally dissolute person

THESAURUS

assessment, gathering, exaction **4** = **tax**, fee, duty, toll, tariff, excise
lewd *adj* = **indecent**, obscene, pornographic, bawdy, wanton, X-rated, lascivious, libidinous, licentious, lustful, smutty
lewdness *n* = **indecency**, pornography, obscenity, depravity, debauchery, bawdiness, carnality, lasciviousness, lechery, licentiousness, wantonness
liability *n* **1** = **responsibility**, accountability, culpability, answerability **2** = **debt**, obligation, debit **3** = **disadvantage**, burden, inconvenience, nuisance, handicap, drawback, hindrance, encumbrance, millstone
liable *adj* **1** = **responsible**, accountable, answerable, obligated **2** = **vulnerable**, open, subject, susceptible, exposed **3** = **likely**, prone, apt, inclined, disposed, tending
liaise *v* = **communicate**, link, mediate, keep contact
liaison *n* **1** = **communication**, connection, contact, interchange, hook-up **2** = **affair**, romance, intrigue, entanglement, amour, love affair
liar *n* = **falsifier**, fabricator, fibber, perjurer
libel *n* **1** = **defamation**, smear, denigration, aspersion, calumny ▶ *v* **2** = **defame**, smear, slur, blacken, vilify, malign, revile
libellous *adj* = **defamatory**, false, malicious, untrue, derogatory, injurious, scurrilous
liberal *adj* **1** = **progressive**, radical, reformist, libertarian **2** = **generous**, kind, charitable, bountiful, beneficent, open-handed, open-hearted, unstinting **3** = **tolerant**, indulgent, permissive, broad-minded **4** = **abundant**, rich, lavish, handsome, ample, plentiful, bountiful, copious, munificent, profuse
liberality *n* **1** = **generosity**, charity, bounty, kindness, largesse *or* largess, philanthropy, beneficence, benevolence, munificence **2** = **tolerance**, latitude, liberalism, broad-mindedness, libertarianism, permissiveness
liberalize *v* = **relax**, ease, moderate, modify, soften, loosen, slacken
liberate *v* = **free**, release, deliver, rescue, emancipate, let loose, let out, set free
liberated *See* **free, independent**
liberation *n* = **deliverance**, release, freedom, liberty, emancipation, freeing
liberator *n* = **deliverer**, rescuer, emancipator, freer, redeemer, savior
libertine *n* = **reprobate**, rake, womanizer, debauchee, lecher, profligate, roué, sensualist, voluptuary

DICTIONARY

liberty Ⓣ *n, pl* **-ties 1** freedom **2** act or comment regarded as forward or socially unacceptable
▸ **at liberty 1** free **2** having the right
▸ **take liberties** be presumptuous
Libeskind *n* **Daniel**. born 1946, US architect, born in Poland. Based in Berlin, he designed the Jewish Museum there (1999), the Imperial War Museum in Manchester (2000), the proposed spiral extension to London's Victoria and Albert Museum, and the "Freedom Tower" that will replace the World Trade Center in New York
libido [lib-**ee**-doe] *n, pl* **-dos 1** life force **2** emotional drive, esp. of sexual origin
▸ **libidinous** *adj* lustful
library *n, pl* **-braries 1** room or building where books are kept **2** collection of books, records, etc. for consultation or borrowing
▸ **librarian** *n* keeper of or worker in a library
librarianship *n*
libretto *n, pl* **-tos, -ti** words of an opera
librettist *n*
Librium *n* ® drug used as a tranquillizer
lice *n* a plural of **louse**
licence Ⓣ *n* **1** document giving official permission to do something **2** formal permission **3** excessive liberty **4** disregard of conventions for effect: *poetic licence*
▸ **licence number** numbers and letters displayed on a vehicle to identify it
▸ **licence plate** plate mounted on front and back of motor vehicle showing the licence number
▸ **license** *v* grant a licence to **licensed** *adj*
▸ **licensee** *n* holder of a licence, esp. to sell alcohol
licentiate *n* person licensed as competent to practise a profession
licentious Ⓣ *adj* sexually immoral, dissolute
licentiously *adv*
lichee *n* same as **lychee**
lichen *n* small flowerless plant forming a crust on rocks, trees, etc.
Lichtenstein *n* **Roy**. 1923–97, US pop artist
licit *adj* lawful, permitted
lick Ⓣ *v* **1** pass the tongue over **2** touch lightly or flicker round **3** *slang* defeat ▷ *n* **4** licking **5** small amount (of paint etc.) **6** *informal* fast pace
licorice *n* same as **liquorice**
lid Ⓣ *n* **1** movable cover **2** short for **eyelid**
lie[1] Ⓣ *v* **lying, lied 1** make a deliberately false statement ▷ *n* **2** deliberate falsehood
▸ **white lie** untruth said without evil intent
lie[2] Ⓣ *v* **lying, lay, lain 1** place oneself or be in a horizontal position **2** be situated **3** be or remain in a certain state or position **4** exist or be found ▷ *n* **5** way something lies
▸ **lie-down** *n* rest
▸ **lie in** *v* remain in bed late into the morning
▸ **lie-in** *n* long stay in bed in the morning
Lie *n* **Trygve Halvdan**. 1896–1968, Norwegian statesman; first secretary-general of the United Nations (1946–52)
lied [**leed**] *n, pl* **lieder** *music* setting for voice and piano of a romantic poem
lief *adv obsolete* gladly, willingly
liege [**leej**] *n* **1** lord **2** vassal or subject ▷ *adj* **3** bound to give or receive feudal service **4** faithful
lien *n* right to hold another's property until a debt is paid
lieu [**lyew**] *n* **in lieu of** instead of
lieutenant [lef-**ten**-ant] *n* **1** junior officer in the army or navy **2** main assistant
▸ **lieutenant governor** representative of the Crown in a province

THESAURUS

liberty *n* **1** = **freedom**, release, independence, sovereignty, immunity, autonomy, liberation, self-determination, emancipation **2** = **impertinence**, impropriety, presumption, impudence, insolence ▷ **at liberty** = **free**, unrestricted, on the loose
libidinous *adj* = **lustful**, carnal, debauched, lascivious, lecherous, sensual, wanton
licence *n* **1** = **certificate**, warrant, permit, charter **2** = **permission**, right, leave, authority, exemption, immunity, authorization, liberty, entitlement, dispensation, blank check, carte blanche **3** = **freedom**, independence, liberty, latitude, leeway **4** = **excess**, indulgence, irresponsibility, immoderation, laxity
license *v* = **permit**, allow, warrant, sanction, authorize, certify, empower, accredit
licensed *See* **official**
licentious *adj* = **promiscuous**, abandoned, immoral, sensual, wanton, debauched, dissolute, lascivious, lustful
lick *v* **1** = **taste**, lap, tongue **2** (Of a flame) = **flicker**, touch, flick, ripple, dart, play over **3** (*Slang*) = **beat**, defeat, overcome, master, rout, trounce, outstrip, outdo, vanquish ▸ *n* **4** = **dab**, bit, touch, stroke **5** (*Informal*) = **pace**, rate, speed, clip (*informal*)
lid *See* **top**
lie[1] *v* **1** = **fib**, perjure oneself, tell a lie • *He always lies about his age.* ▸ *n* **2** = **falsehood**, fabrication, deceit, fiction, fib • *His whole story was a lie.*
lie[2] *v* **1** = **recline**, sprawl, lounge, loll • *I like to lie on my back when I sleep.* **2** = **be situated**, be, remain, exist, be placed

DICTIONARY

life Ⓣ *n, pl* **lives 1** state of living beings, characterized by growth, reproduction, and response to stimuli **2** period between birth and death or between birth and the present time **3** amount of time something is active or functions **4** way of living **5** biography **6** liveliness or high spirits **7** living beings collectively **lifelike** *adj*
▶ **lifeless** *adj* **1** dead **2** inert **3** dull
▶ **lifelong** *adj* lasting all of a person's life
▶ **life belt** *or* **life jacket** buoyant device to keep afloat a person in danger of drowning
▶ **life cycle** series of changes undergone by each generation of an animal or plant
▶ **lifeline** *n* **1** means of contact or support **2** rope used in rescuing a person in danger
▶ **life science** any science concerned with living organisms, such as biology, botany, or zoology
▶ **lifestyle** *n* particular attitudes, habits, etc.
▶ **life-support** *adj* (of equipment or treatment) necessary to keep a person alive
▶ **lifetime** *n* length of time a person is alive
lift Ⓣ *v* **1** move upwards in position, status, volume, etc. **2** revoke or cancel **3** take (plants) out of the ground for harvesting **4** disappear **5** make or become more cheerful ▷ *n* **6** lifting **7** *Brit* elevator **8** ride in an automobile etc. as a passenger **9** *informal* feeling of cheerfulness
▶ **liftoff** *n* moment a rocket leaves the ground
ligament *n* band of tissue joining bones
ligature *n* **1** link, bond, or tie **2** *printing* two or more joined letters
Ligeti *n* **György**. 1923–2006, Hungarian composer, resident in Vienna. His works, noted for their experimentalism, include *Atmospheres* (1961) for orchestra, *Volumina* (1962) for organ, and a requiem mass (1965)
light[1] Ⓣ *n* **1** electromagnetic radiation by which things are visible **2** source of this, lamp **3** anything that lets in light, such as a window **4** mental vision **5** light part of a photograph etc. **6** means of setting fire to **7** understanding **lights 8** traffic lights ▷ *adj* **9** bright **10** (of a colour) pale ▷ *v* **lighting, lighted** *or* **lit 11** ignite **12** illuminate or cause to illuminate
▶ **lighten** *v* make less dark
▶ **lighting** *n* **1** apparatus for supplying artificial light **2** use of artificial light in theatres, films, etc.
▶ **light bulb** glass part of an electric lamp
▶ **lighthouse** *n* tower with a light to guide ships
▶ **light year** *astronomy* distance light travels in one year, about six million million miles
light[2] Ⓣ *adj* **1** not heavy, weighing relatively little **2** relatively low in strength, amount, density, etc. **3** not serious or profound **4** not

THESAURUS

life *n* **1 = existence**, lifetime, lifespan • *a long and active life* RELATED WORDS *adjectives:* animate, vital **2 = being**, vitality, sentience **3 = biography**, history, story, autobiography, confessions, life story, memoirs **4 = behaviour**, conduct, life style, way of life **5 = liveliness**, energy, spirit, animation, vitality, zest, vigor, verve, high spirits, vivacity ▷ **life force** *See* **spirit**
lifeless *adj* **1 = dead**, extinct, deceased, defunct, inanimate **2 = dull**, flat, sluggish, wooden, lacklustre, listless, lethargic, colourless **3 = unconscious**, comatose, dead to the world (*informal*), insensible
lifelike *adj* **= realistic**, natural, exact, faithful, authentic, vivid, true-to-life
lifelong *adj* **= long-standing**, persistent, lasting, long-lasting, perennial, enduring
lifespan *See* **life**
lifetime *n* **= existence**, time, day *or* days, career, span
lift *v* **1 = raise**, hoist, elevate, pick up • *straining to lift heavy weights* OPPOSITE: lower **2 = revoke**, end, remove, cancel, relax, rescind • *the decision to lift sanctions against the country* **3 = disappear**, vanish, disperse, dissipate, be dispelled ▶ *n* **4 = ride**, run, drive **5 = boost**, encouragement, pick-me-up, shot in the arm (*informal*)
light[1] *n* **1 = brightness**, glow, glare, brilliance, illumination, radiance, incandescence, luminescence, luminosity, phosphorescence • *Cracks of light filtered through the shutters.* OPPOSITE: dark RELATED WORD *prefix*: photo- **2 = lamp**, torch, flare, candle, flashlight, beacon, lantern, taper **3 = aspect**, viewpoint, context, angle, interpretation, slant, point of view, vantage point **4 = match**, flame, lighter ▶ *adj* **5 = pale**, fair, pastel, bleached, blonde *or* blond • *a light blue shirt* OPPOSITE: dark **6 = bright**, brilliant, luminous, illuminated, lustrous, shining, well-lit OPPOSITE: dark ▶ *v* **7 = illuminate**, brighten, light up • *The room was lit by many candles.* OPPOSITE: darken **8 = ignite**, kindle • *It's time to light the bonfire.* OPPOSITE: extinguish
light[2] *adj* **1 = insubstantial**, slight, portable, lightweight, flimsy • *working out with light weights* OPPOSITE: heavy **2 = weak**, moderate, mild, slight, soft, faint, gentle, indistinct **3 = insignificant**, small, slight, trivial, inconsequential, inconsiderable, scanty, trifling **4 = nimble**, graceful, agile, lithe, sprightly, sylphlike **5 = light-hearted**, funny, humorous, amusing, frivolous,

DICTIONARY

clumsy **5** easily digested **6** carrying light arms or equipment **7** (of industry) producing small goods, using light machinery ▷ *adv* **8** with little equipment or luggage ▷ *v* **lighting, lighted** *or* **lit 9** (esp. of birds) settle after flight **10** come (upon) by chance **lightly** *adv* **lightness** *n*
▶ **lighten** *v* **1** make less heavy or burdensome **2** make more cheerful or lively
▶ **light-fingered** *adj* liable to steal
▶ **light-headed** *adj* **1** feeling faint, dizzy **2** frivolous
▶ **light-hearted** *adj* carefree
▶ **lightweight** *n, adj* **1** (person) of little importance ▷ *n* **2** boxer weighing up to 135lb (professional) or 60kg (amateur)
lighter[1] *n* device for lighting cigarettes etc.
lighter[2] *n* flat-bottomed boat for unloading ships
Lightfoot *n* **Gordon (Meredith)**. born 1938, Canadian singer-songwriter. His albums include *Sundown* (1974)
lightning *n* **1** visible discharge of electricity in the atmosphere ▷ *adj* **2** fast and sudden
lights *pl n* lungs of animals as animal food
ligneous *adj* of or like wood
lignite [**lig**-nite] *n* woody textured rock used as fuel
like[1] Ⓣ *adj* **1** resembling **2** similar **3** characteristic of ▷ *prep* **4** in the manner of **5** such as ▷ *adv* **6** in the manner of ▷ *pron* **7** similar thing
▶ **liken** *v* compare
▶ **likeness** *n* **1** resemblance **2** portrait
▶ **likewise** *adv* in a similar manner
like[2] Ⓣ *v* **1** find enjoyable **2** be fond of **3** prefer, choose, or wish **likeable** *or* **likable** *adj*
▶ **liking** *n* **1** fondness **2** preference
likely Ⓣ *adj* **1** probable **2** tending or inclined **3** hopeful, promising ▷ *adv* **4** probably
▶ **not likely** *informal* definitely not
▶ **likelihood** *n* probability
lilac *n* **1** shrub bearing pale mauve or white flowers ▷ *adj* **2** light purple
Liliuokalani *n* **Lydia Kamekeha**. 1838–1917, queen and last sovereign of the Hawaiian Islands (1891–95)
Lilliputian [lil-lip-**pew**-shun] *adj* tiny
lilt *n* **1** pleasing musical quality in speaking **2** jaunty rhythm **3** graceful rhythmic motion **lilting** *adj*
lily *n, pl* **lilies** plant which grows from a

THESAURUS

witty, entertaining **6 = digestible**, modest, frugal ▶ *v* **7 = settle**, land, perch, alight ▷ **light on, light upon = come across**, find, discover, encounter, chance upon, happen upon, hit upon, stumble on ▷ **light up** *See* **light**
See also: **easy**
lighten[1] *v* = **brighten**, illuminate, irradiate, become light, light up
lighten[2] *v* **1 = ease**, reduce, relieve, alleviate, lessen, mitigate, allay, assuage, ameliorate **2 = cheer**, lift, revive, brighten, buoy up, perk up
light-headed *adj* = **faint**, dizzy, hazy, giddy, woozy (*informal*), vertiginous
light-hearted *adj* = **carefree**, upbeat (*informal*), playful, jolly, cheerful, jovial, happy-go-lucky, blithe
lightly *adv* **1 = gently**, slightly, softly, delicately, faintly **2 = moderately**, thinly, sparsely, sparingly **3 = easily**, simply, readily, effortlessly **4 = carelessly**, breezily, flippantly, frivolously, heedlessly, thoughtlessly
lightweight *adj* = **unimportant**, slight, petty, insignificant, paltry, worthless, trivial, inconsequential, trifling
like[1] *adj* = **similar**, same, parallel, identical, alike, akin, analogous • *He looks just like his father*. OPPOSITE: unlike
like[2] *v* **1 = enjoy**, love, appreciate, relish, adore (*informal*), be fond of, be keen on, be partial to, go for (*informal*), have a soft spot for, have a weakness for, revel in • *I really like this music*. OPPOSITE: dislike **2 = admire**, approve, appreciate, cherish, prize, esteem, hold dear, take to **3 = wish**, want, choose, prefer, desire, fancy, care to, feel inclined **4** (*Informal*) **= be attracted to**, be captivated by, be turned on by (*informal*), lust after, take a liking to, take to ▷ **like better** *See* **prefer**
likeable *adj* = **pleasant**, nice, attractive, charming, sympathetic, engaging, appealing, agreeable, amiable *See* **pleasant**
likelihood *n* = **probability**, chance, possibility, prospect
likely *adj* **1 = probable**, possible, anticipated, liable, expected • *It seems likely that he will come back*. OPPOSITE: unlikely **2 = inclined**, prone, liable, apt, disposed, tending **3 = plausible**, possible, reasonable, credible, feasible, believable **4 = promising**, hopeful, up-and-coming
See also: **potential, probably**
liken *v* = **compare**, match, relate, parallel, equate, set beside
likeness *n* **1 = resemblance**, similarity, correspondence, affinity **2 = portrait**, picture, image, representation, depiction, effigy
likewise *adv* = **similarly**, in like manner, in the same way
liking *n* = **fondness**, love, taste, weakness,

DICTIONARY

bulb and has large, often white, flowers
limb Ⓣ *n* **1** arm or leg **2** wing **3** main branch of a tree
limber *adj* pliant or supple
▶ **limber up** *v* loosen stiff muscles by exercising
limbo[1] *n, pl* **-bos 1** supposed region intermediate between Heaven and Hell for the unbaptized **2** unknown intermediate place or state
limbo[2] *n, pl* **-bos** West Indian dance in which dancers lean backwards to pass under a bar
lime[1] calcium compound used as a fertilizer or in making cement
▶ **limelight** *n* glare of publicity
▶ **limestone** *n* sedimentary rock used in building
lime[2] *n* small green citrus fruit
▶ **lime-green** *adj* greenish-yellow
lime[3] *n* linden tree
limerick [**lim**-mer-ik] *n* nonsensical humorous verse of five lines
limey *n slang* British person
limit Ⓣ *n* **1** ultimate extent, degree, or amount of something **2** boundary or edge ▷ *v* **-iting, -ited 3** restrict or confine
limitation *n* **limitless** *adj*
▶ **limited company** company whose shareholders' liability is restricted
limn *v* represent in drawing or painting
limousine *n* large luxurious automobile
limp[1] Ⓣ *adj* without firmness or stiffness
limply *adv*
limp[2] Ⓣ *v* **1** walk lamely ▷ *n* **2** limping gait
limpet *n* shellfish which sticks tightly to rocks
limpid *adj* **1** clear or transparent **2** easy to understand **limpidity** *n*
linchpin *n* **1** pin to hold a wheel on its axle **2** essential person or thing
Lincoln *n* **Abraham**. 1809–65, US Republican statesman; 16th president of the US. His fame rests on his success in saving the Union in the Civil War (1861–65) and on his emancipation of slaves (1863); assassinated by Booth
linctus *n, pl* **-tuses** syrupy cough medicine
Lind *n* **1 James**. 1716–94, British physician. He demonstrated (1754) that citrus fruits can cure and prevent scurvy, a remedy adopted by the British navy in 1796 **2 Jenny**, original name *Johanna Maria Lind Goldschmidt*. 1820–87, Swedish coloratura soprano
linden *n* large deciduous tree with heart-shaped leaves and fragrant yellowish flowers, the lime
line Ⓣ *n* **1** long narrow mark **2** indented mark or wrinkle **3** continuous length without breadth **4** row of words **5** queue of people **6** boundary or limit **7** mark on a sports ground showing divisions of a field or track **8** string or wire for a particular use **9** telephone connection **10** wire or cable for transmitting electricity **11** shipping company **12** railway track **13** course or direction of movement **14** class of goods **15** prescribed way of thinking **16** field of interest or activity **17** ancestors collectively **lines 18** words of a theatrical part **19** school punishment of writing out a sentence a specified number of times **20** protected boundary of an area occupied by an army ▷ *v* **21** mark with lines **22** bring into line **23** be or form a border or edge **24** give a lining to **25** cover the inside of
▶ **in line for** candidate for

THESAURUS

affection, preference, penchant, inclination, partiality, soft spot
limb *n* **1 = part**, member, arm, leg, wing, extremity, appendage **2 = branch**, spur, projection, offshoot, bough
limelight *n* **= publicity**, attention, celebrity, recognition, fame, prominence, stardom, public eye, the spotlight
limit *n* **1 = bounds**, deadline, maximum, ultimate, utmost • *the speed limit* **2 = boundary**, border, edge, frontier, perimeter ▶ *v* **3 = restrict**, fix, curb, confine, ration • *Limit yourself to one evening out a week.*
See also: **extreme**
limitation *n* **= restriction**, control, condition, check, curb, restraint, reservation, qualification, constraint
limited *adj* **= restricted**, controlled, finite, bounded, checked, circumscribed, confined, constrained, curbed
limitless *adj* **= infinite**, vast, unlimited, countless, endless, untold, inexhaustible, boundless, unbounded
limits *See* **border, range**
limp[1] *adj* **= floppy**, drooping, flabby, soft • *a limp lettuce leaf* OPPOSITE: stiff
limp[2] *v* **1 = hobble**, falter, hop, shuffle, shamble ▶ *n* **2 = lameness**, hobble
limping *See* **lame**
line *n* **1 = rule**, streak, stripe • *Draw a line down the centre of the page.* **2 = row**, file, rank, column, queue • *a long line at the box office* **3 = course**, track, route, path, trajectory • *the line of flight* **4 = wrinkle**, mark, crease, furrow, crow's foot **5 = boundary**, border, limit, edge, frontier, borderline **6 = string**, cable, wire, cord, rope, thread **7 = job**, trade, business, area, field, employment, occupation, profession, calling, specialization ▷ **in line for = due for**, in the running for ▶ *v* **8 = mark**, score, rule, crease, furrow **9 = border**, edge, fringe, bound

DICTIONARY

▶ **in line with** in accordance with
▶ **line dancing** form of dancing performed by rows of people to country and western music
▶ **line drive** *baseball* ball hit hard and travelling low above the ground
▶ **line-up** *n* people or things assembled for a particular purpose
lineage Ⓣ [**lin**-ee-ij] *n* descent from or descendants of an ancestor
▶ **lineal** *adj* in direct line of descent
lineament *n* facial feature
linear [**lin**-ee-er] *adj* of or in lines
lineman *n, pl* **-men 1** *football* player who lines up in the row closest to the line of scrimmage **2** person who maintains railway, electricity, or telephone lines
linen *n* **1** cloth or thread made from flax **2** sheets, tablecloths, etc.
liner *n* **1** large passenger ship **2** something used as a lining
linesman *n* **1** (in some sports) official who helps the referee or umpire **2** *hockey* official who makes offside decisions, breaks up fights, etc.
ling *n* slender food fish
linger Ⓣ *v* **1** delay or prolong departure **2** continue in a weakened state for a long time before dying or disappearing **3** spend a long time doing something **lingering** *adj*
lingerie [**lan**-zher-ee] *n* women's underwear or nightwear
lingo Ⓣ *n, pl* **-goes** *informal* foreign or unfamiliar language or jargon
lingua franca *n, pl* **lingua francas, linguae francae** language used for communication between people of different mother tongues
lingual *adj* **1** of the tongue **2** made by the tongue
linguist *n* **1** person skilled in foreign languages **2** person who studies linguistics
▶ **linguistic** *adj* **1** of languages **2** of linguistics
▶ **linguistics** *pl n* scientific study of language
liniment *n* medicated liquid rubbed on the skin to relieve pain or stiffness
lining *n* **1** layer of cloth attached to the inside of a garment etc. **2** inner covering of anything
link Ⓣ *n* **1** any of the rings forming a chain **2** person or thing forming a connection ▷ *v* **3** connect with or as if with links **4** connect by association **linkage** *n*
▶ **link-up** *n* joining together of two systems or groups
links *pl n* golf course, esp. one by the sea
Linnaeus *n* **Carolus**, original name *Carl von Linné*. 1707–78, Swedish botanist, who established the binomial system of biological nomenclature that forms the basis of modern classification
linnet *n* songbird of the finch family
lino *n* short for **linoleum**
linocut *n* **1** design cut in relief on a block of linoleum **2** print from such a block
linoleum *n* floor covering of hessian or jute with a smooth decorative coating of powdered cork
Linotype *n* ® typesetting machine which casts lines of words in one piece
linseed *n* seed of the flax plant
lint *n* soft material for dressing a wound
lintel *n* horizontal beam at the top of a door or window
lion *n* large animal of the cat family, the male of which has a shaggy mane **lioness** *n fem*
▶ **the lion's share** the biggest part
▶ **lionize** *v* treat as a celebrity
▶ **lion-hearted** *adj* brave
lip Ⓣ *n* **1** either of the fleshy edges of the mouth **2** rim of a jug etc. **3** *slang* impudence
▶ **lip-reading** *n* method of understanding speech by interpreting lip movements
▶ **lip service** insincere tribute or respect
▶ **lipstick** *n* cosmetic in stick form, for colouring the lips
Li Po, Li T'ai-po *n* ?700–762 AD, Chinese poet. His lyrics deal mostly with wine, nature, and women and are remarkable for their imagery
Lippershey, Lippersheim *n* **Hans**. died

THESAURUS

lineage *See* **origin, stock**
lineaments *pl n* = **features**, face, countenance, physiognomy
lined *adj* **1** = **ruled**, feint **2** = **wrinkled**, furrowed, wizened, worn
lines *pl n* = **words**, part, script
line-up *n* = **arrangement**, team, row, selection, array
linger *v* **1** = **stay**, remain, stop, wait, loiter, hang around, tarry **2** = **delay**, idle, dawdle, dally, drag one's feet *or* drag one's heels, take one's time
lingering *See* **slow**
lingo *See* **language**
link *n* **1** = **connection**, tie, relationship, bond, association, affiliation, attachment • *the link between diet and health* **2** = **component**, part, member, piece, element, constituent ▶ *v* **3** = **connect**, join, couple, tie, attach, fasten • *He was linked to the crime.* OPPOSITE: separate **4** = **associate**, identify, relate, connect, bracket ▷ **link up** *See* **team, unite**
See also: **relation**
lip *n* **1** = **edge**, margin, rim, brink, brim **2** (*Slang*) = **impudence**, cheek (*informal*), backchat (*informal*), effrontery, impertinence, insolence

DICTIONARY

?1619, Dutch lens grinder, who built the first telescope
liquefy *v* **-fying, -fied** make or become liquid **liquefaction** *n*
liqueur [lik-**cure**] *n* flavoured and sweetened alcoholic spirit
liquid Ⓣ *n* **1** substance in a physical state which can change shape but not size ▷ *adj* **2** of or being a liquid **3** flowing smoothly **4** (of assets) in the form of money or easily converted into money
▸ **liquidize** *v* make or become liquid
▸ **liquidity** *n* state of being able to meet financial obligations
liquidate Ⓣ *v* **1** pay (a debt) **2** dissolve a company and share its assets between creditors **3** wipe out or kill **liquidation** *n*
▸ **liquidator** *n* official appointed to liquidate a business
liquor Ⓣ *n* **1** alcoholic drink, esp. spirits **2** liquid in which food has been cooked
liquorice [**lik**-ker-iss] *n* black substance used in medicine and as candy
lira *n, pl* **-re, -ras** monetary unit of Turkey
lisle [rhymes with **mile**] *n* strong fine cotton thread or fabric
Lismer *n* **Arthur**. 1885–1969, Canadian painter born in England; a member of the Group of Seven and noted for his landscape paintings
lisp *n* **1** speech defect in which 's' and 'z' are pronounced 'th' ▷ *v* **2** speak or utter with a lisp
lissom, lissome *adj* supple, agile
list[1] Ⓣ *n* **1** item-by-item record of names or things, usu. written one below another ▷ *v* **2** make a list of **3** include in a list
list[2] Ⓣ *v* **1** (of a ship) lean to one side ▷ *n* **2** leaning to one side
listen Ⓣ *v* **1** concentrate on hearing something **2** heed or pay attention to
listener *n*
▸ **listen in** *v* listen secretly, eavesdrop
Lister *n* **Joseph**, 1st Baron Lister. 1827–1912, British surgeon, who introduced the use of antiseptics
listeriosis *n* dangerous form of food poisoning
listless Ⓣ *adj* lacking interest or energy
listlessly *adv*
Liston *n* **Sonny**, real name *Charles*. 1922–70, US boxer: former world heavyweight champion
Liszt *n* **Franz**. 1811–86, Hungarian composer and pianist. The greatest piano virtuoso of the 19th century, he originated the symphonic poem, pioneered the one-movement sonata form, and developed new harmonic combinations. His works include the symphonies *Faust* (1861) and *Dante* (1867), piano compositions and transcriptions, songs, and church music
lit *v* a past of **light**[1], **light**[2]
litany *n, pl* **-nies 1** prayer with responses from the congregation **2** any tedious recital
litchi *n* same as **lychee**
literacy Ⓣ *n* ability to read and write
literal Ⓣ *adj* **1** according to the explicit meaning of a word or text, not figurative **2** (of a translation) word for word **3** actual, true
literally *adv*
literary Ⓣ *adj* **1** of or learned in literature **2** (of a word) formal, not colloquial
literariness *n*
literate Ⓣ *adj* **1** able to read and write **2** educated
▸ **literati** *pl n* literary people
literature Ⓣ *n* **1** written works such as novels, plays, and poetry **2** books and writings of a country, period, or subject

THESAURUS

liquid *n* **1 = fluid**, solution • *a clear liquid* ▸ *adj* **2 = fluid**, runny, molten • *wash in warm water with liquid detergent* **3** (~ assets) **= convertible**, negotiable
liquidate *v* **1 = pay**, clear, settle, square, discharge, honour, pay off **2 = annul**, cancel, dissolve, terminate, abolish **3 = kill**, murder, destroy, eliminate, dispatch, exterminate, get rid of, wipe out (*informal*)
liquor *n* **1 = alcohol**, drink, booze (*informal*), hard stuff (*informal*), spirits, strong drink **2 = juice**, stock, liquid, extract, broth
list[1] *n* **1 = record**, index, register, inventory, catalogue, listing, directory, laundry list • *There were six names on the list.* ▸ *v* **2 = record**, index, register, catalogue • *All the ingredients are listed on the label.*
list[2] *v* **1 = lean**, tip, tilt, incline, careen, heel over ▸ *n* **2 = tilt**, cant, slant, leaning
listen *v* **1 = hear** • *She was listening to the radio.* **2 = pay attention** • *Nobody listens to a word I say.* ▷ **listen in** *See* **hear**
listing *See* **list**
listless *adj* **= languid**, sluggish, indifferent, lethargic, apathetic, indolent
literacy *n* **= education**, knowledge, learning
literal *adj* **1 = exact**, close, strict, accurate, faithful, verbatim, word for word **2 = actual**, real, true, simple, plain, genuine, bona fide, unvarnished
literally *adv* **= exactly**, really, actually, strictly, truly, precisely, faithfully, verbatim, to the letter, word for word
literary *adj* **= well-read**, formal, scholarly, bookish, erudite, learned
literate *adj* **= educated**, informed, knowledgeable
literature *n* **= writings**, lore, letters

DICTIONARY

lithe Ⓣ *adj* flexible or supple, pliant
lithium *n* chemical element, the lightest known metal
litho *n, pl* **-thos 1** short for **lithograph** ▷ *adj* **2** short for **lithographic**
lithography [lith-**og**-ra-fee] *n* method of printing from a metal or stone surface in which the printing areas are made receptive to ink
▸ **lithograph** *n* **1** print made by lithography ▷ *v* **2** reproduce by lithography **lithographer** *n* **lithographic** *adj*
litigate Ⓣ *v* **1** bring or contest a law suit **2** engage in legal action
▸ **litigant** *n* person involved in a lawsuit
▸ **litigation** *n* lawsuit
▸ **litigious** [lit-**ij**-uss] *adj* **1** frequently going to law **2** argumentative
litmus *n* blue dye turned red by acids and restored to blue by alkali
▸ **litmus paper** paper impregnated with litmus
▸ **litmus test** something which is regarded as a simple and accurate test of a particular thing
litotes *n* ironical understatement for rhetorical effect
litre *n* unit of liquid measure equal to 1.76 pints
litter Ⓣ *n* **1** untidy rubbish dropped in public places **2** group of young animals produced at one birth **3** straw etc. as bedding for an animal **4** dry material to absorb a cat's excrement ▷ *v* **5** strew with litter **6** scatter or be scattered about untidily **7** give birth to young
little Ⓣ *adj* **1** small or smaller than average **2** young ▷ *n* **3** small amount, extent, or duration ▷ *adv* **4** not a lot **5** hardly **6** not much or often
▸ **Little League** baseball league for children
littoral *adj* **1** of or by the seashore ▷ *n* **2** coastal district
liturgy *n, pl* **-gies** prescribed form of public worship **liturgical** *adj*
Liu Shao Qi, Liu Shao-ch'i *n* 1898–1974, Chinese Communist statesman; chairman of the People's Republic of China (1959–68); deposed during the Cultural Revolution
live[1] Ⓣ *v* **1** be alive **2** remain in life or existence **3** exist in a specified way: *we live well* **4** reside **5** continue or last **6** subsist **7** enjoy life to the full
▸ **live down** *v* wait till people forget a past mistake or misdeed
▸ **live-in** *adj* sharing a house with one's sexual partner
▸ **live together** *v* (of an unmarried couple) share a house and have a sexual relationship
▸ **live up to** *v* meet (expectations)
▸ **live with** *v* tolerate
live[2] Ⓣ *adj* **1** living, alive **2** (of a broadcast) transmitted during the actual performance **3** (of a performance) done in front of an audience **4** (of a wire, circuit, etc.) carrying an electric current **5** current **6** glowing or burning **7** capable of exploding ▷ *adv* **8** in the form of a live performance
▸ **lively** *adj* **1** full of life or vigour **2** animated **3** vivid **liveliness** *n*
▸ **liven up** *v* make (more) lively
livelihood Ⓣ *n* occupation or employment
livelong [**liv**-long] *adj lit* long
liver *n* **1** organ secreting bile **2** animal liver as food **liverish** *adj* **1** unwell **2** touchy or irritable
Liverpool *n* **Robert Banks Jenkinson, 2nd Earl of Liverpool.** 1770–1828, British Tory statesman; prime minister (1812–27). His government was noted for its repressive

THESAURUS

lithe *adj* = **supple**, flexible, limber, lissom *or* lissome, loose-limbed, pliable
litigant *n* = **claimant**, party, plaintiff
litigate *v* = **go to court**, sue, prosecute, press charges
litigation *n* = **lawsuit**, case, action, prosecution
litter *n* **1** = **trash**, garbage, debris, detritus, refuse, rubbish, muck **2** = **brood**, young, offspring, progeny ▸ *v* **3** = **clutter**, disorder, derange, disarrange, mess up **4** = **scatter**, strew
little *adj* **1** = **small**, minute, short, tiny, miniature, wee, diminutive, petite • *a little kitten* OPPOSITE: large **2** = **young**, junior, infant, immature, undeveloped, babyish ▷ **little ones** *See* **young** ▸ *adv* **3** = **hardly**, barely **4** = **rarely**, seldom, scarcely, hardly ever, not often ▸ *n* **5** = **bit**, spot, touch, hint, trace, particle, fragment, speck • *Would you like a little juice?*
See also: **insignificant, low**
live[1] *v* **1** = **dwell**, reside, inhabit • *She has lived here for 20 years.* **2** = **be alive**, exist • *She has lived a happy life.* **3** = **persist**, last, prevail **4** = **survive**, endure, subsist, get along, make ends meet, support oneself **5** = **thrive**, flourish, prosper ▷ **live on** *See* **endure**
live[2] *adj* **1** = **living**, alive, animate • *a live spider* **2** = **topical**, current, controversial, hot, burning, prevalent, pressing, pertinent **3** = **burning**, hot, active, glowing, alight, blazing, ignited, smouldering
livelihood *n* = **occupation**, work, job, living, employment, bread and butter (*informal*)
liveliness *n* = **energy**, spirit, animation, vitality, dynamism, boisterousness,

DICTIONARY

policies until around 1822, when more liberal measures were introduced by such men as Peel and Canning

liverwort *n* plant resembling seaweed or leafy moss

livery Ⓣ *n, pl* **-eries** distinctive dress, esp. of a servant or servants **liveried** *adj*

▸ **livery stable** stable where horses are kept at a charge or hired out

lives *n* plural of **life**

livestock *n* farm animals

Livia Drusilla *n* 58 BC–29 AD, Roman noblewoman: wife (from 39 BC) of Emperor Augustus and mother of Emperor Tiberius

livid Ⓣ *adj* **1** *informal* angry or furious **2** bluish-grey

living Ⓣ *adj* **1** possessing life, not dead or inanimate **2** currently in use or existing **3** of everyday life: *living conditions* ▹ *n* **4** condition of being alive **5** manner of life **6** financial means **7** church benefice

▸ **living room** room in a house used for relaxation and entertainment

Livingstone *n* **David**. 1813–73, Scottish missionary and explorer in Africa. After working as a missionary in Botswana, he led a series of expeditions and was the first European to discover Lake Ngami (1849), the Zambezi River (1851), the Victoria Falls (1855), and Lake Malawi (1859). In 1866 he set out to search for the source of the Nile and was found in dire straits and rescued (1871) by the journalist H. M. Stanley

lizard *n* four-footed reptile with a long body and tail

llama *n* woolly animal of the camel family used as a beast of burden in S America

LLB Bachelor of Laws

Lloyd George *n* **David**, 1st Earl Lloyd George of Dwyfor. 1863–1945, British Liberal statesman: prime minister (1916–22). As chancellor of the exchequer (1908–15) he introduced old age pensions (1908), a radical budget (1909), and an insurance scheme (1911)

Llywelyn ap Gruffudd *n* died 1282, prince of Wales (1258–82): the only Welsh ruler to be recognized as such by the English

Llywelyn ap Iorwerth *n* called *Llywelyn the Great*. died 1240, prince of Gwynedd, N Wales (1194–1238), who extended his rule over most of Wales

loach *n* carplike freshwater fish

Loach *n* **Ken(neth)**. born 1936, British television and film director; his works for television include *Cathy Come Home* (1966) and his films include *Kes* (1970), *Riff-Raff* (1991), *Bread and Roses* (2000), *Ae Fond Kiss* (2004), and *Looking for Eric* (2009)

load Ⓣ *n* **1** burden or weight **2** amount carried **3** amount of electrical energy drawn from a source **4** source of worry **loads** **5** *informal* lots ▹ *v* **6** put a load on or into **7** burden or oppress **8** cause to be biased **9** put ammunition into a weapon **10** put film into a camera **11** transfer (a program) into computer memory

▸ **loaded** *adj* **1** (of a question) containing a hidden trap or implication **2** *slang* wealthy **3** (of dice) dishonestly weighted

loadstar *n* same as **lodestar**

loadstone *n* same as **lodestone**

loaf[1] Ⓣ *n, pl* **loaves** **1** shaped mass of baked bread **2** shaped mass of food **3** *slang*

THESAURUS

sprightliness, vivacity

lively *adj* **1 = energetic**, active, animated, sparkling, perky, vivacious, sprightly • *a lively personality* OPPOSITE: dull **2 = vivid**, bright, exciting, colourful, forceful, invigorating, refreshing, stimulating
See also: **alive, busy, colourful, vital**

liven up *v* **= stir**, brighten, animate, rouse, enliven, buck up (*informal*), perk up

liverish *adj* **1 = sick**, bilious, queasy **2 = irritable**, grumpy, crusty, irascible, crotchety, disagreeable, ill-humored, splenetic, tetchy

livery *n* **= costume**, suit, dress, uniform, attire, garb, regalia, clothing

livid *adj* **1** (*Informal*) **= angry**, furious, outraged, enraged, incensed, beside oneself, fuming, indignant, infuriated **2 = discoloured**, purple, black-and-blue, bruised, contused

living *adj* **1 = alive**, active, breathing, existing **2 = current**, active, contemporary, extant, in use ▸ *n* **3 = existence**, life, being, existing, subsistence **4 = life style**, way of life ▹ **living soul** *See* **person**

load *n* **1 = cargo**, shipment, freight, consignment • *This truck can carry a large load.* **2 = burden**, worry, weight, trouble, onus, albatross, encumbrance, millstone ▸ *v* **3 = fill**, pack, pile, stack • *The trucks were loaded with blankets and supplies.* **4 = burden**, worry, oppress, encumber, saddle with, weigh down **5** (*~a firearm*) **= make ready**, charge, prime
See also: **bunch, mass, stuff**

loaded *adj* **1 = biased**, distorted, weighted **2 = tricky**, manipulative, insidious, prejudicial, artful **3** (*Slang*) **= rich**, wealthy, affluent, flush (*informal*), well-heeled (*informal*), well-to-do, moneyed, well off

loads *pl n* (*Informal*) **= plenty**, heaps, lots, stacks, tons (*informal*), scads • *I've got loads of money.*

loaf[1] *n* **= lump**, block, cake, cube, slab

DICTIONARY

common sense: *use your loaf*
loaf² Ⓣ *v* idle, loiter **loafer** *n*
loam *n* fertile soil
loan Ⓣ *n* **1** money borrowed at interest **2** lending **3** thing lent ▷ *v* **4** lend, grant a loan of
▸ **loan shark** person who lends money at an extremely high interest rate
loath, loth Ⓣ [rhymes with **both**] *adj* unwilling or reluctant (to)
loathe Ⓣ *v* hate, be disgusted by **loathing** *n* **loathsome** *adj*
loaves *n* plural of **loaf¹**
lob Ⓣ *sports* ▷ *n* **1** ball struck or thrown high in the air ▷ *v* **lobbing, lobbed 2** strike or throw (a ball) high in the air
lobby Ⓣ *n, pl* **-bies 1** corridor into which rooms open **2** group which tries to influence legislators **3** hall in a legislative building to which the public has access ▷ *v* **-bying, -bied 4** try to influence (legislators) in the formulation of policy **lobbyist** *n*
lobe *n* **1** rounded projection **2** soft hanging part of the ear **3** subdivision of a body organ **lobed** *adj*
▸ **lobar** [**loh**-ber] *adj* of or affecting a lobe
lobelia *n* garden plant with blue, red, or white lobed flowers
lobotomy *n, pl* **-mies** surgical incision into a lobe of the brain
lobster *n* shellfish with a long tail and claws, which turns red when boiled
▸ **lobster pot** basket-like trap for catching lobsters
local Ⓣ *adj* **1** of or existing in a particular place **2** confined to a particular place ▷ *n* **3** person belonging to a particular district **4** *Brit informal* nearby pub **locally** *adv*
▸ **locality** *n* neighbourhood or area
▸ **localize** *v* restrict to a definite place
▸ **locale** [loh-**kahl**] *n* scene of an event
▸ **local anesthetic** anesthetic which produces insensibility in one part of the body
▸ **local authority** governing body of a county or district
▸ **local government** government of towns, counties, and districts by locally elected political bodies
locate Ⓣ *v* **1** discover the whereabouts of **2** situate or place
▸ **location** *n* **1** site or position **2** site of a film production away from the studio
loch *n Scot* **1** lake **2** long narrow bay
loci *n* plural of **locus**
lock¹ Ⓣ *n* **1** appliance for fastening a door, case, etc. **2** section of a canal shut off by gates between which the water level can be altered to aid boats moving from one level to another **3** extent to which a vehicle's front wheels will turn **4** interlocking of parts **5** mechanism for firing a gun **6** wrestling hold ▷ *v* **7** fasten or become fastened securely **8** become or cause to become immovable **9** become or cause to become

THESAURUS

loaf² *v* = **idle**, loiter, laze, lie around, lounge around, take it easy
loan *n* **1** = **advance**, credit, mortgage • *a small business loan* ▸ *v* **2** = **lend**, advance • *He loaned us the painting for our exhibition.*
loath, loth *adj* = **unwilling**, reluctant, averse, disinclined, opposed
loathe *v* = **hate**, dislike, detest, despise, abhor, abominate
loathing *n* = **hatred**, disgust, revulsion, aversion, antipathy, abhorrence, detestation, repugnance, repulsion
loathsome *adj* = **hateful**, offensive, abhorrent, vile, obnoxious, repulsive, repugnant, disgusting, odious, detestable, revolting, nauseating, scuzzy (*slang*)
lob *See* **throw**
lobby *n* **1** = **corridor**, passage, hallway, porch, foyer, entrance hall, vestibule **2** = **pressure group**, committee, organization, activist, coalition, movement, advocate, association, initiative, agenda, demonstrator, faction, lobbyist, campaigner, special interest group, public interest group ▸ *v* **3** = **campaign**, urge, push, pressure, press, promote, influence, persuade
local *adj* **1** = **neighbourhood**, community, district, regional • *We shop at our local stores.* **2** = **confined**, limited, restricted (*chiefly US*) ▸ *n* **3** = **resident**, inhabitant • *That's what the locals call the place.*
locality *n* **1** = **neighbourhood**, area, region, district, vicinity, neck of the woods (*informal*) **2** = **site**, place, position, spot, scene, location, setting, locale
localize *v* = **restrict**, contain, limit, confine, circumscribe, delimit
locate *v* **1** = **find**, pinpoint, track down • *We have been unable to locate him.* **2** = **place**, set, put, seat, settle, fix, establish, situate
See also: **position, trace**
located *adj* = **situated**, placed • *The restaurant is located near the park.*
location *n* = **place**, point, site, position, situation, spot, whereabouts • *a house in a beautiful location*
See also: **scene, surroundings**
lock¹ *v* **1** = **fasten**, latch, padlock • *Are you sure you locked the door?* OPPOSITE: unlock **2** = **unite**, link, join, engage, entangle, clench, entwine **3** = **embrace**, press, clutch, hug, grasp, enclose, encircle, clasp ▷ **lock up** = **imprison**, jail, detain, confine, cage, incarcerate, put behind bars,

DICTIONARY

fixed or united **10** embrace closely
▸ **lockdown** *n US & Canad* security measure in which people are temporarily confined to a building
▸ **lockout** *n* exclusion of workers by an employer as a means of coercion
▸ **locksmith** *n* person who makes and mends locks
▸ **lockstep** *n* standard procedure that is closely, often mindlessly, followed
▸ **lockup** *n* **1** prison **2** garage or storage place away from the main premises
lock² Ⓣ *n* tress of hair
Locke *n* **1 John**. 1632–1704, English philosopher, who discussed the concept of empiricism in his *Essay Concerning Human Understanding* (1690). He influenced political thought, esp. in France and America, with his *Two Treatises on Government* (1690), in which he sanctioned the right to revolt **2 Matthew**. ?1630–77, English composer, esp. of works for the stage
locker *n* small cupboard with a lock
locket *n* small hinged pendant for a portrait etc.
lockjaw *n* tetanus
locomotive *n* **1** self-propelled engine for pulling trains ▹ *adj* **2** of locomotion
▸ **locomotion** *n* action or power of moving
locum *n* temporary stand-in for a doctor or clergyman
locus *n, pl* **loci** **1** area or place where something happens **2** *math* set of points or lines satisfying one or more specified conditions
locust *n* destructive African insect that flies in swarms and eats crops
locution *n* word or phrase
lode *n* vein of ore
▸ **lodestar** *n* Pole Star
▸ **lodestone** *n* magnetic iron ore
lodge Ⓣ *n* **1** house or cabin used occasionally by hunters, skiers, etc. **2** gatekeeper's house **3** porters' room in a university or college **4** local branch of some societies ▹ *v* **5** live in another's house at a fixed charge **6** stick or become stuck (in a place) **7** deposit for safety or storage **8** make (a complaint etc.) formally
lodger *n*
▸ **lodgings** *pl n* rented room or rooms in another person's house
Loewe *n* **1 Frederick**. 1904–88, US composer of such musical comedies as *Brigadoon* (1947), *My Fair Lady* (1956), and *Camelot* (1960), all with librettos by Alan Jay Lerner **2** (**Johann**) **Karl** (**Gottfried**). 1796–1869, German composer, esp. of songs, such as *Der Erlkönig* (1818)
loft *n* **1** space between the top storey and roof of a building **2** gallery in a church etc. ▹ *v* **3** *sports* strike, throw, or kick (a ball) high into the air
lofty Ⓣ *adj* **loftier**, **loftiest** **1** of great height **2** exalted or noble **3** haughty
▸ **loftily** *adv* haughtily **loftiness** *n*
log¹ Ⓣ *n* **1** portion of a felled tree stripped of branches **2** detailed record of a journey of a ship, aircraft, etc. ▹ *v* **logging**, **logged** **3** record in a log **4** saw logs from a tree
logbook *n*
▸ **logging** *n* work of cutting and transporting logs
▸ **log in** *or* **log out** *v* gain entrance to *or* leave a computer system by keying in a special command
log² *n* short for **logarithm**
loganberry *n* purplish-red fruit, a cross between a raspberry and a blackberry
logarithm *n* one of a series of arithmetical functions used to make certain calculations easier **logarithmic** *adj*
loggerheads Ⓣ *pl n* **at loggerheads** quarrelling, disputing
loggia [**loj**-ya] *n* covered gallery at the side of a building
logic Ⓣ *n* **1** philosophy of reasoning **2** reasoned thought or argument **logician** *n*

THESAURUS

shut up ▸ *n* **4** = **fastening**, latch, padlock
• *The lock had been forced open*.
See also: **secure**
lock² *n* = **strand**, curl, tress, tuft, ringlet
locked *See* **secure**
lockup *n* = **prison**, jail, cell
lodge *n* **1** = **cabin**, shelter, shed, cottage, hut, chalet, gatehouse **2** = **society**, group, club, branch, chapter ▸ *v* **3** = **stay**, board, room **4** = **stick**, implant, come to rest, imbed **5** = **register**, file, submit, put on record
lodger *n* = **tenant**, resident, boarder, paying guest
lodging *n (often pl)* = **accommodation**, abode, apartments, shelter, residence, quarters, rooms
lofty *adj* **1** = **high**, elevated, towering, raised, soaring **2** = **noble**, grand, renowned, elevated, illustrious, distinguished, dignified, exalted **3** = **haughty**, proud, arrogant, condescending, disdainful, patronizing, supercilious
log *n* **1** = **stump**, block, chunk, trunk **2** = **record**, account, journal, logbook ▸ *v* **3** = **chop**, cut, fell, hew **4** = **record**, note, register, chart, set down
loggerheads *pl n* ▹ **at loggerheads** = **quarrelling**, at daggers drawn, at each other's throats, at odds, feuding, in dispute, opposed
logic *n* = **reason**, sense, good sense

DICTIONARY

▸ **logical** *adj* **1** of logic **2** reasonable **3** capable of or using clear valid reasoning **logically** *adv*
logistics *pl n* detailed planning and organization of a large, esp. military, operation **logistical** *adj*
logo Ⓣ [**loh**-go] *n, pl* **-os** company emblem or similar device
loin *n* **1** part of the body between the ribs and the hips **2** cut of meat from this part of an animal **loins 3** hips and inner thighs
▸ **loincloth** *n* piece of cloth covering the loins only
loiter Ⓣ *v* stand or wait aimlessly or idly **loiterer** *n*
loll Ⓣ *v* **1** lounge lazily **2** (esp. of the tongue) hang out
lollipop *n* boiled candy on a small wooden stick
lollop *v* run clumsily
lolly *n, pl* **-ies 1** *Brit informal* lollipop or ice lolly **2** *Brit slang* money
Lombardi *n* **Vincent Thomas**. 1913–70, American football coach, whose team won the first two Superbowls, and after whom the Superbowl trophy is named
Lombardo *n* **Gaetano Alberto**, known as *Guy*. 1902–77, Canadian bandleader, noted esp. for his orchestra's New Year's Eve concerts (1929–62) from New York that were broadcast across N America
London *n* **Jack**, full name *John Griffith London*. 1876–1916, US novelist, short-story writer, and adventurer. His works include *Call of the Wild* (1903), *The Sea Wolf* (1904), *The Iron Heel* (1907), and the semiautobiographical *John Barleycorn* (1913)
lone Ⓣ *adj* solitary
▸ **lonely** *adj* **1** sad because alone **2** unfrequented **3** resulting from being alone **loneliness** *n*
▸ **loner** *n informal* person who prefers to be alone
▸ **lonesome** *adj* lonely
long[1] Ⓣ *adj* **1** having length, esp. great length, in space or time ▹ *adv* **2** for a long time
▸ **long-distance** *adj* going between places far apart
▸ **long-drawn-out** *adj* lasting too long
▸ **long face** glum expression
▸ **longhand** *n* ordinary writing, not shorthand or typing
▸ **long johns** *informal* long underpants
▸ **long-life** *adj* (of milk, batteries, etc.) lasting longer than the regular kind
▸ **long-lived** *adj* living or lasting for a long time
▸ **long-range** *adj* **1** (of weapons) designed to hit a distant target **2** into the future
▸ **long shot** competitor, undertaking, or bet with little chance of success
▸ **long-standing** *adj* existing for a long time
▸ **long-suffering** *adj* enduring trouble or unhappiness without complaint
▸ **long-term** *adj* lasting or effective for a long time
▸ **long wave** radio wave with a wavelength of over 1000 metres
▸ **long-winded** *adj* speaking or writing at tedious length
long[2] Ⓣ *v* (foll. by *for*) have a strong desire for
▸ **longing** *n* yearning **longingly** *adv*
longevity [lon-**jev**-it-ee] *n* long existence or life
Longfellow *n* **Henry Wadsworth**. 1807–82,

THESAURUS

logical *adj* **1 = rational**, sound, consistent, valid, reasoned • *a logical theory* **2 = reasonable**, obvious, wise, sensible, plausible, judicious • *a logical deduction* OPPOSITE: illogical
logo *See* **sign, symbol**
loiter *v* **= linger**, idle, dawdle, loaf, dally, dilly-dally (*informal*), hang about *or* hang around, skulk
loll *v* **1 = lounge**, slump, relax, sprawl, recline, loaf, slouch **2 = droop**, drop, hang, flap, sag, dangle, flop
lone *adj* **= solitary**, one, only, single, sole, unaccompanied
loneliness *n* **= solitude**, isolation, seclusion, desolation
lonely *adj* **1 = lonesome**, alone, forlorn, forsaken • *He's lonely and just wants to talk.* **2 = desolate**, remote, isolated, secluded, uninhabited, deserted • *a lonely hillside* **3 = solitary**, single, alone, apart, lone, isolated, companionless, withdrawn
loner *n* **= individualist**, maverick, outsider, recluse, lone wolf
lonesome *adj* **= lonely**, gloomy, dreary, desolate, companionless, forlorn, friendless
long[1] *adj* **1 = prolonged**, lengthy, sustained, protracted, interminable, lingering, long-drawn-out • *a long interval when nobody spoke* OPPOSITE: short **2 = elongated**, extensive, lengthy, extended, expanded, far-reaching, stretched, spread out • *a long line of people* OPPOSITE: short ▹ **long ago** *See* **past, the past** ▹ **long shot = outsider**, dark horse
See also: **far**
long[2] *v* **= desire**, want, wish, hunger, pine, ache, covet, crave, itch, lust, yearn, hanker • *He longed for peace and quiet.*
longing *n* **= desire**, hunger, craving, thirst, yearning, hankering • *her longing to return home*
See also: **urge, wish**
long-lived *adj* **= long-lasting**, enduring

DICTIONARY

US poet, noted particularly for his long narrative poems *Evangeline* (1847) and *The Song of Hiawatha* (1855)
longitude *n* distance east or west from a standard meridian
▸ **longitudinal** *adj* **1** of length or longitude **2** lengthwise
longshoreman *n* docker
loo *n Brit informal* lavatory
loofah *n* dried pod of a gourd, used as a sponge
look Ⓣ *v* **1** direct the eyes or attention (towards) **2** seem **3** face in a particular direction **4** search (for) **5** hope (for) ▹ *n* **6** looking **7** search **8** *often pl* appearance
▸ **look after** *v* take care of
▸ **lookalike** *n* person who is the double of another
▸ **look down on** *v* treat as inferior or unimportant
▸ **look forward to** *v* anticipate with pleasure
▸ **look on** *v* **1** be an onlooker **2** consider or regard
▸ **lookout** *n* **1** guard **2** place for watching **3** chances or prospect **4** *informal* worry or concern
▸ **look out** *v* be careful
▸ **look up** *v* **1** discover or confirm by checking in a book **2** visit **3** improve
▸ **look up to** *v* respect
loom[1] *n* machine for weaving cloth
loom[2] Ⓣ *v* **1** appear dimly **2** seem ominously close **3** assume great importance
loon *n* N American diving bird
▸ **loonie** *or* **loony** *n informal* Canadian dollar coin
loony Ⓣ *slang* ▹ *n, pl* **loonies 1** foolish or insane person ▹ *adj* **loonier, looniest 2** foolish or insane
▸ **loony bin** *slang* mental hospital
loop Ⓣ *n* **1** rounded shape made by a curved line or rope crossing itself ▹ *v* **2** form a loop
▸ **loop the loop** fly or be flown in a complete vertical circle
▸ **loophole** *n* means of evading a rule without breaking it
loose Ⓣ *adj* **1** not tight, fastened, fixed, or tense **2** slack **3** vague **4** dissolute or promiscuous ▹ *adv* **5** in a loose manner ▹ *v* **6** free **7** unfasten **8** slacken **9** let fly (an arrow, bullet, etc.) **loosely** *adv* **looseness** *n*
▸ **at a loose end** bored, with nothing to do
▸ **loosen** *v* make loose
▸ **loosen up** *v* relax, stop worrying

THESAURUS

long-standing *adj* = **established**, long-lasting, enduring, long-established, abiding, fixed, time-honoured, timeless
long-suffering *adj* = **uncomplaining**, patient, tolerant, easy-going, forgiving, forbearing, resigned, stoical
long-winded *adj* = **rambling**, lengthy, prolonged, tedious, tiresome, verbose, long-drawn-out, prolix, repetitious, wordy
look *v* **1** = **see**, study, survey, watch, view, eye, read, examine, scan, observe, contemplate, glance, gaze • *She looked at me with affection*. **2** = **seem**, appear, look like, seem to be, strike one as • *the desire to look older* **3** = **face**, front, overlook **4** = **hope**, expect, await, anticipate, reckon on **5** = **search**, seek, hunt, forage ▹ **look after** = **take care of**, watch, mind, nurse, tend, care for • *Will you look after my cats this weekend?*
See also: **run, safeguard** ▹ **look down on** = **disdain**, scorn, spurn, despise, sneer, contemn ▹ **look for** = **search**, seek, hunt, forage • *I'm looking for my winter boots*. ▹ **look forward to** = **anticipate**, expect, await, hope for, long for, look for, wait for ▹ **look like** = **resemble**, echo, take after, be the image of, remind one of, make one think of, put one in mind of ▹ **look on** *See* **regard** ▹ **look out** = **be careful**, beware, keep an eye out, pay attention, watch out ▹ **look up** = **research**, find, hunt for, search for, seek out, track down; = **improve**, progress, get better, perk up, pick up, shape up (*informal*); = **visit**, call on, drop in on (*informal*), look in on ▹ **look up to** = **respect**, admire, honour, revere, esteem, defer to ▸ *n* **6** = **gaze**, view, inspection, sight, examination, glimpse, observation, glance, peek • *He took a last look in the mirror*. **7** = **appearance**, face, air, aspect, manner, expression, bearing, demeanour, semblance, countenance • *He had the look of a confident man*.
See also: **regard, stare**
look-alike *n* = **double**, spitting image (*informal*), dead ringer (*informal*) • *an Elvis look-alike*
lookout *n* **1** = **watch**, guard, vigil, readiness **2** = **watchman**, guard, sentry, sentinel **3** = **watchtower**, post, observatory, observation post
looks *See* **appearance**
loom *v* = **appear**, threaten, emerge, bulk, hover, menace, impend, take shape
looming *See* **imminent, near**
loony *See* **mad**
loop *n* **1** = **curve**, ring, curl, circle, twist, spiral, coil, twirl, whorl ▸ *v* **2** = **twist**, turn, roll, curl, knot, spiral, coil, wind round
loophole *n* = **let-out**, escape, excuse
loose *adj* **1** = **unsecured**, free, wobbly • *a loose tooth* OPPOSITE: secure **2** = **slack**, baggy • *Wear loose clothes for comfort*. OPPOSITE: tight **3** = **vague**, random, inaccurate,

DICTIONARY

▶ **loose-leaf** *adj* allowing the addition or removal of pages
loot Ⓣ *n, v* plunder **looter** *n* **looting** *n*
lop Ⓣ *v* **lopping, lopped 1** cut away twigs and branches **2** chop off
lope *v* run with long easy strides
lop-eared *adj* having drooping ears
Lopez *n* **Jennifer**. born 1970, Puerto Rican singer and film actress, known as *J-Lo*; her films include *Selena* (1997) and *The Wedding Planner* (2001) and her records include *On the 6* (1999) and *This is Me...Then* (2002)
lopsided Ⓣ *adj* greater in height, weight, or size on one side
loquacious *adj* talkative **loquacity** *n*
Lorca *n* **Federico García**. 1898–1936, Spanish poet and dramatist. His poetry, such as *Romancero gitano* (1928), shows his debt to Andalusian folk poetry. His plays include the trilogy *Bodas de sangre* (1933), *Yerma* (1934), and *La Casa de Bernarda Alba* (1936)
lord Ⓣ *n* **1** person with power over others, such as a monarch or master **2** male member of the nobility **3** *hist* feudal superior **4 Lord** God **5 Lord** title given to certain male officials and peers
▶ **House of Lords** unelected upper chamber of the British parliament
▶ **lord it over** act in a superior manner towards
▶ **the Lord's Prayer** prayer taught by Christ to his disciples
▶ **lordly** *adj* imperious, proud
▶ **Lordship** *n* title of some male officials and peers
lore Ⓣ *n* body of traditions on a subject
Loren *n* **Sophia**, real name *Sophia Scicolone*. born 1934, Italian film actress. Her films include *Two Women* (1961) for which she won an Oscar, *The Millionairess* (1961), *Man of La Mancha* (1972), *The Cassandra Crossing* (1977), and *Prêt à Porter* (1994)
Lorenz *n* **Konrad Zacharias**. 1903–89, Austrian zoologist, who founded ethology. His works include *On Aggression* (1966): shared the Nobel prize for physiology or medicine 1973
lorgnette [lor-**nyet**] *n* pair of spectacles mounted on a long handle
Lorne *n* **Marquess of**, title of *John Douglas Sutherland Campbell*. 1845–1914, British Liberal politician. Governor General of Canada (1978–83); founded the Canadian Academy of Arts (1880) and the Royal Society of Canada (1882)
lorry *n Brit* truck
lose Ⓣ *v* **losing, lost 1** come to be without, as by accident or carelessness **2** fail to keep or maintain **3** be deprived of **4** fail to get or make use of **5** have an income less than one's expenditure **6** fail to perceive or understand **7** be defeated in a competition etc. **8** be or become engrossed: *lost in thought* **9** go astray or allow to go astray **10** die or be destroyed **11** (of a clock etc.) run slow (by a specified amount)
loser *n*
loss Ⓣ *n* **1** losing **2** that which is lost **3** damage resulting from losing
▶ **at a loss 1** confused or bewildered **2** not earning enough to cover costs
▶ **loss leader** item sold at a loss to attract customers

THESAURUS

inexact, rambling, imprecise, ill-defined, indistinct **4 = promiscuous**, fast, abandoned, immoral, debauched, dissipated, dissolute, profligate ▶ *v* **5 = free**, release, unleash, disconnect, detach, liberate, untie, set free, unfasten
See also: **approximate, full**
loosen *v* **1 = untie**, undo, slacken • *He loosened his tie.* **2 = free**, release, liberate, set free ▷ **loosen up = relax**, soften, de-stress, ease up *or* ease off, go easy (*informal*), let up OPPOSITE: tighten
loot *v* **1 = plunder**, raid, ransack, pillage • *Gangs began breaking windows and looting stores.* ▶ *n* **2 = plunder**, haul, booty, spoils • *The loot was never recovered.*
See also: **rob**
lop *See* **chop**
lopsided *adj* **= crooked**, disproportionate, awry, asymmetrical, askew, cockeyed, uneven, unbalanced, squint, warped
lord *n* **1 = master**, leader, commander, governor, superior, ruler, overlord, liege **2 = nobleman**, peer, noble, earl, viscount ▷ **Our Lord = Jesus**, Jesus Christ, the Lord God, Christ, Jehovah, the Almighty ▶ *verb* ▷ **lord it over = order around**, swagger, boss around (*informal*), domineer, pull rank, put on airs
lordly *adj* **= proud**, lofty, arrogant, imperious, high-handed, condescending, disdainful, domineering, haughty, overbearing
lore *n* **= traditions**, teaching, wisdom, doctrine, beliefs, sayings
lose *v* **1 = mislay**, drop, misplace • *I've lost my keys.* OPPOSITE: find **2 = be beaten**, be defeated • *We lost the game.* OPPOSITE: win **3 = forfeit**, miss, yield, pass up (*informal*) ▷ **lose hope** *See* **despair** ▷ **lose your nerve** *See* **panic** ▷ **lose your temper** *See* **rage**
loser *n* **1 = failure**, flop (*informal*), dud (*informal*), also- ran **2 = nerd**, drip (*informal*), geek (*slang*), dork (*slang*), dweeb (*slang*)
loss *n* **1 = defeat**, failure, waste, forfeiture,

DICTIONARY

lost Ⓣ *v* **1** past of **lose** ▷ *adj* **2** unable to find one's way **3** unable to be found **4** bewildered or confused **5** no longer possessed or existing **6** (foll. by *on*) not used, noticed, or understood by

lot Ⓣ *pron* **1** great number ▷ *n* **2** collection of people or things **3** large quantity **4** fate or destiny **5** item at auction **6** one of a set of objects drawn at random to make a selection or choice **lots 7** *informal* great numbers or quantities
▸ **a lot** *adv informal* a great deal

loth Ⓣ *adj* same as **loath**

lotion Ⓣ *n* medical or cosmetic liquid for use on the skin

lottery Ⓣ *n, pl* **-teries 1** method of raising funds by selling tickets that win prizes by chance **2** gamble

lotto *n* game of chance like bingo

lotus *n* **1** legendary plant whose fruit induces forgetfulness **2** Egyptian water lily

loud Ⓣ *adj* **1** relatively great in volume **2** capable of making much noise **3** insistent and emphatic **4** unpleasantly patterned or colourful **loudly** *adv* **loudness** *n*
▸ **loudspeaker** *n* instrument for converting electrical signals into sound

lough *n Irish* loch

Louis *n* **Joe**, real name *Joseph Luis Barrow*, nicknamed *the Brown Bomber*. 1914–81, US boxer; world heavyweight champion (1937–49)

Louis I *n* known as *Louis the Pious* or *Louis the Debonair*. 778–840 AD, king of France and Holy Roman Emperor (814–23, 830–33, 834–40): he was twice deposed by his sons

Louis II *n* **1** known as *Louis the German*. ?804–876 AD, king of Germany (843–76); son of Louis I **2** 1845–86, king of Bavaria (1864–86): noted for his extravagant castles and his patronage of Wagner. Declared insane (1886), he drowned himself

Louis IV *n* known as *Louis the Bavarian*. ?1287–1347, king of Germany (1314–47) and Holy Roman Emperor (1328–47)

Louis V *n* known as *Louis le Fainéant*. ?967–987 AD, last Carolingian king of France (986–87)

Louis VII *n* known as *Louis le Jeune*. *c*. 1120–80, king of France (1137–80). He engaged in frequent hostilities (1152–74) with Henry II of England

Louis VIII *n* known as *Coeur-de-Lion*. 1187–1226, king of France (1223–26). He was offered the English throne by opponents of King John but his invasion failed (1216)

Louis IX *n* known as *Saint Louis*. 1214–70, king of France (1226–70): led the Sixth Crusade (1248–54) and was held to ransom (1250); died at Tunis while on another crusade

Louis XI *n* 1423–83, king of France (1461–83); involved in a struggle with his vassals, esp. the duke of Burgundy, in his attempt to unite France under an absolute monarchy

Louis XII *n* 1462–1515, king of France (1498–1515), who fought a series of unsuccessful wars in Italy

Louis XIII *n* 1601–43, king of France (1610–43). His mother (Marie de Médicis) was regent until 1617; after 1624 he was influenced by his chief minister Richelieu

Louis XIV *n* known as *le roi soleil* (the Sun King). 1638–1715, king of France (1643–1715); son of Louis XIII and Anne of Austria. Effective ruler from 1661, he established an absolute monarchy. His attempt to establish French supremacy in Europe, waging almost continual wars from 1667 to 1714, ultimately failed. But his reign is regarded as a golden age of French literature and art

Louis XV *n* 1710–74, king of France (1715–74); great-grandson of Louis XIV. He engaged France in a series of wars, esp. the disastrous Seven Years' War (1756–63), which undermined the solvency and authority of the crown

Louis XVI *n* 1754–93, king of France (1774–92);

THESAURUS

mislaying, squandering **2 = damage**, injury, cost, hurt, harm, destruction, ruin **3** (*sometimes pl*) **= deficit**, debt, debit, deficiency, depletion ▷ **at a loss = confused**, helpless, at one's wits' end, baffled, perplexed, bewildered, nonplussed, puzzled, stumped

lost *adj* **1 = off course**, adrift, astray • *I think we're lost.* **2 = missing**, mislaid, misplaced • *I wonder if my lost keys will ever turn up.*

lot *n* **1 = group**, set, crowd, bunch (*informal*), quantity, batch • *We've just sacked one lot of builders.* **2 = destiny**, chance, accident, fate, fortune, doom ▷ **a lot, lots = plenty**, abundance, piles (*informal*), a great deal, masses (*informal*), quantities, scores • *Remember to drink lots of water.*
See also: **loads, many, numerous, whole**

loth *See* **loath**

lotion *n* **= cream**, solution, balm, embrocation, liniment, salve

lottery *n* **1 = raffle**, drawing, sweepstakes **2 = gamble**, risk, chance, hazard, toss-up (*informal*)

loud *adj* **1 = noisy**, strident, thunderous, blaring, deafening, resounding • *a loud explosion* OPPOSITE: quiet **2 = garish**, flamboyant, flashy, lurid, gaudy • *a loud tie* OPPOSITE: dull
See also: **bold**

loudly *adv* **= noisily**, vigorously, vehemently, lustily, deafeningly, fortissimo (*music*), shrilly, uproariously, vociferously

DICTIONARY

grandson of Louis XV. He married Marie Antoinette in 1770 and they were guillotined during the French Revolution
Louis XVII *n* 1785–95, titular king of France (1793–95) during the Revolution, after the execution of his father Louis XVI; he died in prison
Louis XVIII *n* 1755–1824, king of France (1814–24); younger brother of Louis XVI. He became titular king after the death of Louis XVII (1795) and ascended the throne at the Bourbon restoration in 1814. He was forced to flee during the Hundred Days
Louis Philippe *n* known as the *Citizen King*. 1773–1850, king of the French (1830–48). His régime became excessively identified with the bourgeoisie and he was forced to abdicate by the revolution of 1848
lounge ⊕ *n* **1** living room in a private house **2** area for waiting in an airport **3** more comfortable bar in a pub ▷ *v* **4** sit, lie, or stand in a relaxed manner **5** pass time idly
▸ **lounge suit** man's suit for daytime wear
lour *v* same as **lower**[2]
louse *n* **1** *pl* **lice** wingless parasitic insect **2** *pl* **louses** unpleasant person
▸ **lousy** *adj slang* **1** very bad or unpleasant **2** bad, inferior **3** unwell
lout ⊕ *n* crude, oafish, or aggressive person **loutish** *adj*
louvre [**loo**-ver] *n* one of a set of parallel slats slanted to admit air but not rain **louvred** *adj*
lovage *n* European plant used for flavouring food
love ⊕ *n* **1** warm affection **2** sexual passion **3** wholehearted liking for something **4** beloved person **5** *tennis, squash, etc.* score of nothing ▷ *v* **6** have a great affection for **7** feel sexual passion for **8** enjoy (something) very much **lovable** *adj* **loveless** *adj* **lover** *n* **lovemaking** *n*
▸ **fall in love** become in love
▸ **in love (with)** feeling a strong emotional (and sexual) attraction (for)
▸ **make love (to)** have sexual intercourse (with)
▸ **lovely** *adj* **1** very attractive **2** highly enjoyable
▸ **loving** *adj* affectionate, tender **lovingly** *adv*
▸ **love affair** romantic or sexual relationship between two people who are not married to each other
▸ **lovebird** *n* small parrot
▸ **love life** person's romantic or sexual relationships
▸ **lovelorn** *adj* forsaken by or pining for a lover
Lovelace *n* **Countess of**, title of *Ada Augusta King*. 1815–52, English mathematician and personal assistant to Charles Babbage: daughter of Lord Byron. She wrote the first computer program
Lovell *n* Sir **Bernard**. born 1913, English radio astronomer; founder (1951) and director of Jodrell Bank
low[1] ⊕ *adj* **1** not tall, high, or elevated **2** of little or less than the usual amount, degree, quality, or cost **3** coarse or vulgar **4** dejected **5** ill **6** not loud **7** deep in pitch **8** (of a gear) providing a relatively low speed ▷ *n* **9** low position, level, or degree **10** area of low atmospheric pressure, depression ▷ *adv* **11** in or to a low position, level, or degree

THESAURUS

lounge *v* = **relax**, sprawl, loaf, loiter, laze, lie around, loll, take it easy
lousy *adj* (*Informal*) = **awful**, terrible, inadequate, shoddy, inferior, crappy (*slang*), shabby, crummy
lout *n* = **oaf**, boor, dolt, lummox (*informal*), schlub (*slang*)
lovable *adj* = **adorable**, sweet, charming, enchanting, endearing • *His vulnerability makes him very lovable*. OPPOSITE: hateful
love *v* **1** = **adore**, worship, cherish • *They loved each other very much*. OPPOSITE: hate **2** = **enjoy**, like, appreciate, relish • *We both love fishing*. OPPOSITE: hate ▸ *n* **3** = **adoration**, passion, affection, devotion, ardour, infatuation • *their love for their children* OPPOSITE: hatred **4** = **liking**, weakness, devotion, fondness • *her love of animals* OPPOSITE: hatred **5** = **beloved**, lover, dear, sweetheart, darling, dearest, truelove ▷ **in love** = **enamoured**, besotted, charmed, enraptured, infatuated, smitten
▷ **love affair** = **romance**, relationship, affair, intrigue, liaison, amour
See also: **attachment**
loveliness *See* **beauty**
lovely *adj* **1** = **attractive**, pretty, beautiful, pleasant, enjoyable, delightful • *You look lovely*. OPPOSITE: horrible **2** = **enjoyable**, nice, pleasant, engaging, pleasing, delightful, agreeable
lover *n* = **sweetheart**, flame (*informal*), beloved, boyfriend *or* girlfriend, suitor, admirer, mistress, main squeeze (*slang*)
loving *adj* = **affectionate**, warm, tender, fond, devoted, doting • *their loving parents* OPPOSITE: cold
See also: **romantic**
low *adj* = **small**, little, short, sunken, squat, stunted • *a low bench* OPPOSITE: high **1** = **meagre**, small, poor, modest, minimal, scant, reduced • *low prices* OPPOSITE: high **2** = **inferior**, poor, inadequate, shoddy, lousy (*slang*), deficient,

L

DICTIONARY

▶ **lowly** *adj* modest, humble **lowliness** *n*
▶ **lowbrow** *n, adj* (person) with nonintellectual tastes and interests
▶ **Low Church** section of the Anglican Church stressing evangelical beliefs and practices
▶ **lowdown** *n informal* inside information
▶ **low-down** *adj informal* mean, shabby, or dishonest
▶ **low-key** *adj* subdued, restrained, not intense
▶ **lowland** *n* **1** low-lying country **lowlands** **2 Lowlands** less mountainous parts of Scotland
▶ **low post** *basketball* area of the court beneath the opposing team's basket
▶ **low profile** position or attitude avoiding prominence or publicity
▶ **low-spirited** *adj* depressed
low² *n* **1** cry of cattle, moo ▷ *v* **2** moo
lower¹ Ⓣ *v* **1** cause or allow to move down **2** diminish or degrade **3** lessen ▷ *adj* **4** below one or more other things **5** smaller or reduced in amount or value
▶ **lower case** small, as distinct from capital, letters
lower², lour *v* (of the sky or weather) look gloomy or threatening **lowering** *adj*
Lowry *n* **1 L(awrence) S(tephen)**. 1887–1976, English painter, noted for his bleak northern industrial scenes, often containing primitive or stylized figures **2 (Clarence) Malcolm**. 1909–57, British novelist and writer, best known for his semiautobiographical novel *Under the Volcano* (1947)
loyal Ⓣ *adj* faithful to one's friends, country, or government **loyally** *adv* **loyalty** *n* **loyalist** *n*
▶ **loyalty card** swipe card issued by a supermarket or chain store to a customer, used to record credit points awarded for money spent in the store
lozenge *n* **1** medicated tablet held in the mouth until it dissolves **2** four-sided diamond-shaped figure
LP *n* record playing approximately 20–25 minutes each side
LSD lysergic acid diethylamide, a hallucinogenic drug
Lt Lieutenant
Ltd Limited (Liability)
lubber *n* clumsy person
lubricate Ⓣ [**loo**-brik-ate] *v* oil or grease to lessen friction **lubrication** *n*
▶ **lubricant** *n* lubricating substance such as oil
lubricious [loo-**brish**-uss] *adj lit* lewd
Lucas *n* **George**. born 1944, US film director, producer, and writer of screenplays. Films include *American Graffiti* (1973) and *Star Wars* (1977) and its prequels *The Phantom Menace* (1999) and *Attack of the Clones* (2002)
lucerne *n* fodder plant like clover, alfalfa
lucid Ⓣ *adj* **1** clear and easily understood **2** able to think clearly **3** bright and clear **lucidly** *adv* **lucidity** *n*
Lucifer *n* Satan
luck Ⓣ *n* **1** fortune, good or bad **2** good fortune **3** chance
▶ **lucky** *adj* having good luck

THESAURUS

second-rate **3 = coarse**, common, crude, rough, rude, vulgar, undignified, disreputable **4 = dejected**, depressed, gloomy, miserable, despondent, glum, downcast, disheartened, down in the dumps (*informal*), fed up **5 = ill**, weak, frail, stricken, debilitated **6 = quiet**, soft, gentle, muted, subdued, hushed, muffled, whispered
See also: **deep, faint, reasonable, sad**
lowdown *n* (*Informal*) **= information**, intelligence, info (*informal*), inside story
lower *v* **1 = drop**, let down, take down • *They lowered the coffin into the grave.* OPPOSITE: raise **2 = lessen**, cut, reduce, decrease, slash, diminish, minimize • *a commitment to lower taxes* OPPOSITE: increase ▶ *adj* **3 = minor**, junior, secondary, lesser, inferior, subordinate, second-class, smaller **4 = reduced**, diminished, curtailed, decreased, lessened
See also: **below, ease**
lowering *See* **cut**
lowest *See* **bottom, least**
low-key *adj* **= subdued**, quiet, muted, restrained, toned down, understated
lowly *adj* **1 = disreputable**, despicable, vulgar, contemptible • *his lowly status* **2 = humble**, modest, mild, unassuming, meek
low-spirited *adj* **= depressed**, down, low, sad, dismal, miserable, dejected, despondent, down-hearted, fed up
loyal *adj* **= faithful**, true, constant, staunch, dependable, trusty • *a loyal friend* OPPOSITE: treacherous
See also: **devoted**
loyalty *n* **= faithfulness**, devotion, allegiance, fidelity, dependability, constancy, staunchness, steadfastness, trustworthiness
lubricate *v* **= oil**, smear, grease
lucid *adj* **1 = clear**, explicit, transparent, comprehensible, intelligible **2 = translucent**, clear, transparent, crystalline, glassy, diaphanous, limpid, pellucid **3 = clear-headed**, rational, sane, all there, *compos mentis* (*Latin*), in one's right mind
luck *n* **1 = fortune**, chance, accident, fate,

DICTIONARY

▸ **luckily** *adv* fortunately
▸ **luckless** *adj* having bad luck
lucrative Ⓣ *adj* very profitable
lucre Ⓣ [**loo**-ker] *n* **filthy lucre** *informal*, (*usu.*) *facetious* money
Lucretius *n* full name *Titus Lucretius Carus*. ?96–55 BC, Roman poet and philosopher. In his didactic poem *De rerum natura*, he expounds Epicurus' atomist theory of the universe **Lucretian** *adj*
Lucy *n* **Saint**. died ?303 AD, a virgin martyred by Diocletian in Syracuse. Feast day: Dec 13
Luddite *n* person opposed to change in industrial methods
ludicrous Ⓣ *adj* absurd or ridiculous
ludicrously *adv*
luff *v* sail (a ship) towards the wind
lug[1] Ⓣ *v* **lugging, lugged** carry or drag with great effort
lug[2] *n* **1** projection serving as a handle **2** *informal* ear
luggage Ⓣ *n* traveller's cases, bags, etc.
lugger *n* working boat rigged with an oblong sail
lugubrious Ⓣ [loo-**goo**-bree-uss] *adj* mournful, gloomy **lugubriously** *adv*
lugworm *n* large worm used as bait
lukewarm Ⓣ *adj* **1** moderately warm, tepid **2** indifferent or half-hearted
lull Ⓣ *n* **1** brief time of quiet in a storm etc. ▷ *v* **2** soothe (someone) by soft sounds or motions **3** calm (fears or suspicions) by deception
lullaby *n, pl* **-bies** quiet song to send a child to sleep
Lully *n* **Jean Baptiste**, Italian name *Giovanni Battista Lulli*. 1632–87, French composer, born in Italy; founder of French opera. With Philippe Quinault as librettist, he wrote operas such as *Alceste* (1674) and *Armide* (1686); as superintendent of music at the court of Louis XIV, he wrote incidental music to comedies by Molière
lumbago [lum-**bay**-go] *n* pain in the lower back
▸ **lumbar** *adj* relating to the lower back
lumber[1] Ⓣ *n* **1** useless disused articles, such as old furniture **2** sawn timber ▷ *v* **3** *informal* burden with something unpleasant
▸ **lumberjack** *n* man who fells trees and prepares logs for transport
lumber[2] Ⓣ *v* move heavily and awkwardly
lumbering *adj*
Lumière *n* **Auguste Marie Louis Nicolas**. 1862–1954, and his brother, **Louis Jean**, 1864–1948, French chemists and cinema pioneers, who invented a cinematograph and a process of colour photography
luminous Ⓣ *adj* reflecting or giving off light
luminosity *n*
▸ **luminary** *n* **1** famous person **2** *lit* heavenly body giving off light
▸ **luminescence** *n* emission of light at low temperatures by any process other than burning **luminescent** *adj*
lump[1] Ⓣ *n* **1** shapeless piece or mass **2** swelling **3** *informal* awkward or stupid

THESAURUS

destiny • *It was just luck that we happened to meet.* **2 = good fortune**, advantage, success, blessing, prosperity, windfall, serendipity, godsend
luckily *adv* **= fortunately**, happily, favourably, opportunely, propitiously, providentially
luckless *adj* **= unlucky**, unfortunate, hapless, doomed, ill-fated, hopeless, cursed, jinxed
lucky *adj* **1 = fortunate**, blessed, charmed • *He had always been lucky at cards.* OPPOSITE: unlucky **2 = opportune**, fortunate, timely, fortuitous • *a lucky break* OPPOSITE: unlucky
lucrative *adj* **= profitable**, productive, fruitful, advantageous, well-paid, remunerative
lucre *n* **= money**, profit, gain, wealth, riches, mammon, pelf, spoils
ludicrous *adj* **= ridiculous**, crazy, silly, absurd, laughable, outlandish, preposterous, farcical, nonsensical
lug *See* **carry, drag**
luggage *n* **= baggage**, gear, paraphernalia, bags, cases, impedimenta, suitcases, things
lugubrious *adj* **= gloomy**, serious, sad, mournful, melancholy, somber, doleful, sorrowful, woebegone
lukewarm *adj* **1 = tepid**, warm **2 = half-hearted**, cool, indifferent, apathetic, unresponsive, unenthusiastic
lull *v* **1 = calm**, subdue, quell, allay, soothe, pacify, tranquilize ▸ *n* **2 = respite**, quiet, silence, calm, pause, hush, let-up (*informal*)
lumber[1] *n*, *v* **1 = trundle**, career, barrel, shuffle, rumble, bound, thunder, stagger, barge, lunge, meander, lurch, chug, amble, waddle, totter, canter **2 = timber**, wood, planks, boards
lumber[2] *v* **= plod**, shuffle, stump, clump, trudge, trundle, waddle, shamble
lumbering *adj* **= awkward**, heavy, clumsy, ungainly, hulking, ponderous
luminary *See* **star**
luminous *adj* **= bright**, glowing, luminescent, radiant, illuminated, lustrous, shining
lump *n* **1 = piece**, ball, chunk, cake, wedge, hunk • *a big lump of clay* **2 = bump**, bulge, hump, swelling • *I've got a big lump on my*

DICTIONARY

person ▷ *v* **4** consider as a single group
lumpy *adj*
▶ **lump in one's throat** tight dry feeling in one's throat, usu. caused by great emotion
▶ **lump sum** relatively large sum of money paid at one time
lump² *v* **lump it** *informal* tolerate or put up with it
lunar *adj* relating to the moon
▶ **lunar month** *or* **lunation** *n* time taken for the moon to go once round the earth, approx. 29½ days
lunatic Ⓣ *adj* **1** foolish and irresponsible ▷ *n* **2** foolish or annoying person **3** *old-fashioned* insane person **lunacy** *n*
lunch Ⓣ *n* **1** meal taken in the middle of the day ▷ *v* **2** eat lunch
▶ **luncheon** *n* formal lunch
▶ **luncheon meat** canned ground mixture of meat and cereal
▶ **luncheon voucher** voucher for a certain amount, given to an employee and accepted by some restaurants as payment for a meal
lung *n* organ that allows an animal or bird to breathe air: humans have two lungs in the chest
lunge Ⓣ *n* **1** sudden forward motion **2** thrust with a sword ▷ *v* **3** move with or make a lunge
lupin *n* garden plant with tall spikes of flowers
lupine *adj* like a wolf
lupus *n* ulcerous skin disease
lurch¹ Ⓣ *v* **1** tilt or lean suddenly to one side **2** stagger ▷ *n* **3** lurching movement
lurch² *n* **leave someone in the lurch** abandon someone in difficulties
lurcher *n* crossbred dog trained to hunt silently
lure Ⓣ *v* **1** tempt or attract by the promise of reward ▷ *n* **2** person or thing that lures **3** brightly coloured artificial angling bait
lurid Ⓣ *adj* **1** vivid in shocking detail, sensational **2** glaring in colour **luridly** *adv*
lurk Ⓣ *v* **1** lie hidden or move stealthily, esp. for sinister purposes **2** be latent
luscious Ⓣ [**lush**-uss] *adj* **1** extremely pleasurable to taste or smell **2** very attractive
lush¹ Ⓣ *adj* **1** (of grass etc.) growing abundantly **2** opulent **lushly** *adv* **lushness** *n*
lush² *n slang* alcoholic
lust Ⓣ *n* **1** strong sexual desire **2** any strong desire ▷ *v* **3** have passionate desire (for)
lustful *adj*
▶ **lusty** *adj* vigorous, healthy **lustily** *adv*
lustre Ⓣ *n* **1** gloss, sheen **2** splendour or glory **3** metallic pottery glaze
▶ **lustrous** *adj* shining, luminous
lute *n* ancient guitar-like musical instrument with a body shaped like a half pear
▶ **lutenist** *n* person who plays a lute
Luther *n* **Martin**. 1483–1546, German leader of the Protestant Reformation. As professor of biblical theology at Wittenberg University from 1511, he began preaching the crucial

THESAURUS

head. ▶ *v* **3 = group**, mass, collect, combine, pool, consolidate, conglomerate
See also: **block**
lumpy *adj* **= bumpy**, uneven, knobbly
lunacy *n* **1 = insanity**, dementia, madness, mania, psychosis, derangement **2 = foolishness**, madness, stupidity, folly, craziness, absurdity, foolhardiness
lunatic *adj* **1 = mad**, crazy, insane, irrational, bonkers (*informal*), crackbrained (*informal*), crackpot (*informal*), daft, deranged ▶ *n* **2 = madman**, psychopath, maniac, nutcase (*slang*), sicko (*informal*), sickie (*informal*), ding-a-ling (*slang*)
lunch *See* **eat**
lunge *n* **1 = thrust**, charge, spring, swing, pounce, jab ▶ *v* **2 = pounce**, charge, plunge, dive, leap, thrust
lurch *v* **1 = tilt**, list, rock, pitch, roll, lean, heel, heave **2 = stagger**, stumble, reel, sway, weave, totter
lure *v* **1 = tempt**, draw, attract, entice, beckon • *We are being lured into a trap.* ▶ *n* **2 = temptation**, pull, attraction, magnet, bait • *the lure of rural life*
lurid *adj* **1 = sensational**, shocking, graphic, vivid, melodramatic **2 = glaring**, intense
lurk *v* **= hide**, sneak, prowl, slink, conceal oneself, lie in wait, skulk
luscious *adj* **= delicious**, sweet, juicy, palatable, yummy (*informal*), succulent, appetizing, mouth-watering, toothsome
lush *adj* **1 = abundant**, green, rank, dense, verdant, flourishing **2 = luxurious**, grand, elaborate, lavish, plush (*informal*), extravagant, ornate, sumptuous, opulent, palatial
lust *n* **1 = lechery**, lasciviousness, lewdness, sensuality **2 = appetite**, desire, passion, greed, longing, craving, thirst ▶ *v* **3 = desire**, want, covet, crave, yearn, hunger for *or* hunger after
lustful *adj* **= lascivious**, lewd, carnal, lecherous • *lustful thoughts*
lustre *n* **1 = sparkle**, shine, glow, shimmer, glitter, gloss, gleam, sheen, glint **2 = glory**, fame, honour, distinction, kudos, prestige, renown *See also*: **finish**
lusty *adj* **= vigorous**, strong, healthy, powerful, robust, energetic, hearty, sturdy, virile

DICTIONARY

doctrine of justification by faith rather than by works, and in 1517 he nailed 95 theses to the church door at Wittenberg, attacking Tetzel's sale of indulgences. He was excommunicated and outlawed by the Diet of Worms (1521) as a result of his refusal to recant, but he was protected in Wartburg Castle by Frederick III of Saxony (1521–22). He translated the Bible into German (1521–34) and approved Melanchthon's Augsburg Confession (1530), defining the basic tenets of Lutheranism **Lutheran** *adj* **Lutherism** *n*

Lutosławski *n* **Witold**. 1913–94, Polish composer, whose works frequently juxtapose aleatoric and notated writing

Lutyens *n* Sir **Edwin**. 1869–1944, British architect, noted for his neoclassical country houses and his planning of New Delhi, India

lux *n, pl* **lux** unit of illumination

luxuriant Ⓣ *adj* **1** rich and abundant **2** very elaborate **luxuriantly** *adv* **luxuriance** *n*

luxuriate *v* **1** take self-indulgent pleasure (in) **2** flourish

luxury Ⓣ *n, pl* **-ries 1** enjoyment of rich, very comfortable living **2** enjoyable but not essential thing ▷ *adj* **3** of or providing luxury

▸ **luxurious** *adj* full of luxury, sumptuous **luxuriously** *adv*

LV luncheon voucher

lychee [lie-**chee**] *n* Chinese fruit with a whitish juicy pulp

Lycra *n* ® elastic fabric used for tight-fitting garments, such as swimming costumes

lye *n* water made alkaline with wood ashes etc., esp. as formerly used for washing

lying Ⓣ *v* present participle of **lie**[1] and **lie**[2]

▸ **lying-in** *n old-fashioned* period of confinement during childbirth

lymph *n* colourless bodily fluid consisting mainly of white blood cells **lymphatic** *adj*

lymphocyte *n* type of white blood cell

lynch *v* put to death without a trial

lynx *n* animal of the cat family with tufted ears and a short tail

lyre *n* ancient musical instrument like a U-shaped harp

lyric *n* **1** short poem expressing personal emotion in a songlike style **lyrics 2** words of a popular song ▷ *adj* **3** of such poems **4** in the style of a song

▸ **lyrical** *adj* **1** lyric **2** enthusiastic

▸ **lyricist** *n* person who writes the words of songs or musicals

THESAURUS

luxuriant *See* **thick**

luxurious *adj* = **sumptuous**, lavish, posh, plush (*informal*), deluxe, opulent • *a luxurious lifestyle* OPPOSITE: plain

luxury *n* **1** = **opulence**, affluence, sumptuousness • *a life of luxury* **2** = **extravagance**, treat, extra, indulgence • *Telephones are still a luxury in some countries.* *See also*: **comfort**

lying *n* **1** = **dishonesty**, perjury, fabrication, deceit, fibbing • *I've had enough of your lying.* ▸ *adj* **2** = **deceitful**, false, dishonest, untruthful • *The man is just a lying cheat.* OPPOSITE: honest

lyrical *adj* = **enthusiastic**, inspired, impassioned, poetic, effusive, rhapsodic

Mm

m 1 metre(s) 2 mile(s) 3 minute(s)
M 1 Monsieur 2 Motorway
m. 1 male 2 married 3 masculine 4 meridian 5 month
ma *n informal* mother
MA Master of Arts
ma'am *n* madam
mac *n informal* mackintosh
macabre [mak-**kahb**-ra] *adj* strange and horrible, gruesome
macadam *n* road surface of pressed layers of small broken stones
▸ **macadamize** *v* pave a road with macadam
macaque [mac-**kahk**] *n* monkey of Asia and Africa with cheek pouches and either a short tail or no tail
macaroni *n* pasta in short tubes
macaroon *n* small cookie or cake made with ground almonds
macaw *n* large tropical American parrot
Macbeth *n* died 1057, king of Scotland (1040–57): succeeded Duncan, whom he killed in battle; defeated and killed by Duncan's son Malcolm III
Macdonald *n* Sir **John Alexander**. 1815–91, Canadian statesman, born in Scotland, who was the first prime minister of the Dominion of Canada (1867–73; 1878–91)
MacDonald *n* (**James**) **Ramsay**. 1866–1937, British statesman, who led the first and second Labour Governments (1924 and 1929–31). He also led a coalition (1931–35), which the majority of the Labour Party refused to support
mace¹ *n* 1 ceremonial staff of office 2 medieval weapon with a spiked metal head
mace² *n* spice made from the dried husk of the nutmeg
macerate [**mass**-a-rate] *v* soften by soaking
maceration *n*
Mach¹ [**mak**] *n* short for **Mach number**
Mach² *n* **Ernst**. 1838–1916, Austrian physicist and philosopher. He devised the system of speed measurement using the Mach number. He also founded logical positivism, asserting that the validity of a scientific law is proved only after empirical testing
Machaut *n* **Guillaume de**. c. 1300–77, French composer and poet; a leading exponent of ars nova
machete [mash-**ett**-ee] *n* broad heavy knife used for cutting or as a weapon
Machiavelli *n* **Niccolò**. 1469–1527, Florentine statesman and political philosopher; secretary to the war council of the Florentine republic (1498–1512). His most famous work is *Il Principe* (*The Prince*, 1532)
machiavellian [mak-ya-**vel**-ee-yan] *adj* unprincipled, crafty, and opportunist
machinations [mak-in-**nay**-shunz] *pl n* cunning plots and ploys
machine *n* 1 apparatus, usu. powered by electricity, designed to perform a particular task 2 vehicle, such as an automobile or aircraft 3 controlling system of an organization ▷ *v* 4 make or produce by machine
▸ **machinery** *n* machines or machine parts collectively
▸ **machinist** *n* person who operates a machine
▸ **machine gun** automatic gun that fires rapidly and continuously
▸ **machine-gun** *v* fire at with such a gun
▸ **machine-readable** *adj* (of data) in a form suitable for processing by a computer
machismo [mak-**izz**-mow] *n* strong or exaggerated masculinity
Mach number [**mak**] *n* ratio of the speed of a body in a particular medium to the speed of sound in that medium
macho [**match**-oh] *adj* strongly or

THESAURUS

macabre *adj* = **gruesome**, grim, eerie, grisly, dreadful, morbid, ghostly, ghoulish, ghastly, frightening
mace *See* **stick**
machiavellian *adj* = **scheming**, cynical, crafty, unscrupulous, opportunist, sly, cunning, astute, double-dealing, underhand
machine *n* 1 = **appliance**, device, instrument, mechanism, contraption, apparatus • *a washing machine* 2 = **system**, organization, structure, setup (*informal*), machinery
See also: **gadget**
machinery *n* = **equipment**, tackle, gear, apparatus, instruments, tools
macho *adj* = **manly**, masculine, chauvinist, virile

DICTIONARY

exaggeratedly masculine
Mackenzie *n* **1** Sir **Alexander**. ?1755–1820, Scottish explorer and fur trader in Canada. He explored the Mackenzie River (1789) and was the first European to cross America north of Mexico (1793) **2** **Alexander**. 1822–92, Canadian politician; first Liberal prime minister (1873–78) **3** Sir **Compton**. 1883–1972, English author. His works include *Sinister Street* (1913–14) and the comic novel *Whisky Galore* (1947) **4** **William Lyon**. 1795–1861, Canadian journalist and politician, born in Scotland. He led an unsuccessful rebellion against the oligarchic Family Compact (1837)
mackerel *n* edible sea fish with blue and silver stripes
mackinaw coat *n* thick, short plaid coat
mackintosh *n* **1** waterproof raincoat of rubberized cloth **2** any raincoat
Mackintosh *n* **1** Sir **Cameron** (**Anthony**). born 1946, British producer of musicals and theatre owner; his productions include *Cats* (1981), *Les Misérables* (1985), *Miss Saigon* (1987), and *My Fair Lady* (2001) **2** **Charles Rennie**. 1868–1928, Scottish architect and artist, exponent of the Art Nouveau style; designer of the Glasgow School of Art (1896)
Macleish *n* **Archibald**. 1892–1982, US poet and public official; his works include *Collected Poems* (1952) and *J.B.* (1958)
MacLennan *n* (**John**) **Hugh**. 1907–90, Canadian novelist, writer, and academic. His novels include *Two Solitudes* (1945)
Macmahon *n* **Marie Edme Patrice Maurice**, Comte de Macmahon. 1808–93, French military commander. He commanded the troops that suppressed the Paris Commune (1871) and was elected president of the Third Republic (1873–79)
Macmillan *n* (**Maurice**) **Harold**, 1st Earl of Stockton. 1894–1986, British statesman; Conservative prime minister (1957–63)
MacMillan *n* **1** Sir **Ernest Alexander Campbell**. 1893–1973, Canadian conductor and educator: conductor of the Toronto Symphony (1931–56) **2** **Margaret** (**Olwen**). born 1943, Canadian historian. Her most noted work is *Peacemakers: The Paris Peace Conference of 1919 and Its Attempt to End War*
Maconchy *n* Dame **Elizabeth**, married name *Elizabeth LeFanu*. 1907–94, British composer of Irish parentage; noted esp. for her chamber music, which includes 13 string quartets and *Romanza* (1980) for viola and ensemble
Macpherson *n* **James**. 1736–96, Scottish poet and translator. He published supposed translations of the legendary Gaelic poet Ossian, in reality largely his own work
macramé [mak-**rah**-mee] *n* ornamental work of knotted cord
macrobiotics *n* dietary system advocating whole grains and vegetables grown without chemical additives **macrobiotic** *adj*
macrocosm *n* **1** the universe **2** any large complete system
mad Ⓣ *adj* **madder, maddest** **1** mentally deranged, insane **2** very foolish **3** (foll. by *about* or *on*) very enthusiastic (about) **4** frantic **5** *informal* angry **madly** *adv* **madness** *n* **madman** (**madwoman**) *n*
▸ **like mad** *informal* with great energy, enthusiasm, or haste
▸ **madden** *v* infuriate or irritate **maddening** *adj*
madam *n* **1** polite form of address to a woman **2** *informal* spoilt or conceited girl
madame [mad-**dam**] *n, pl* **mesdames** [may-**dam**] French title equivalent to *Mrs*
madcap Ⓣ *adj, n* reckless (person)
madder *n* **1** climbing plant **2** red dye made from its root
made *v* past of **make**
Madeira [mad-**deer**-a] *n* fortified white wine
▸ **Madeira cake** rich sponge cake
mademoiselle [mad-mwah-**zel**] *n, pl* **mesdemoiselles** [maid-mwah-**zel**] French title equivalent to *Miss*
madhouse *n* **1** *informal* place filled with

m

THESAURUS

mad *adj* **1 = insane**, crazy (*informal*), unstable, psychotic, demented, raving, deranged, *non compos mentis* (*Latin*), nuts (*slang*), of unsound mind, out of one's mind, unhinged **2 = foolish**, crazy (*informal*), stupid, foolhardy • *He'd be mad to refuse.* **3 = angry**, crazy, furious, enraged, irate, livid, incensed, fuming, infuriated • *They both got mad at me for interfering.* **4 = enthusiastic**, wild, crazy (*informal*), avid, impassioned, ardent, fanatical, infatuated **5 = frenzied**, wild, excited, frenetic, uncontrolled, unrestrained, wired (*slang*) ▹ **like mad** (*Informal*) **= energetically**, rapidly, wildly, violently, enthusiastically, furiously, excitedly, speedily
madcap *adj* **= reckless**, crazy, rash, foolhardy, impulsive, imprudent, thoughtless, hare-brained
madden *v* **= infuriate**, upset, annoy, inflame, irritate, incense, enrage, derange, drive one crazy
madly *adv* **1 = insanely**, frantically, hysterically, crazily, deliriously, distractedly, frenziedly **2 = foolishly**, wildly, absurdly, irrationally, ludicrously, senselessly **3 = energetically**, wildly, recklessly, furiously, excitedly, like

DICTIONARY

uproar or confusion **2** *old-fashioned* mental hospital
Madison *n* **James**. 1751–1836, US statesman; 4th president of the US (1809–17). He helped to draft the US Constitution and Bill of Rights. His presidency was dominated by the War of 1812
Madonna[1] *n* **1** the Virgin Mary **2** picture or statue of her
Madonna[2] *n* full name *Madonna Louise Veronica Ciccone*. born 1958, US rock singer and film actress. Her records include "Like a Virgin" (1985), "Like a Prayer" (1989), *Ray of Light* (1998), and *Music* (2000). Her films include *Desperately Seeking Susan* (1985), and *Evita* (1996)
madrigal *n* 16th–17th century part song for unaccompanied voices
maelstrom Ⓣ [**male**-strom] *n* **1** great whirlpool **2** turmoil
maestro Ⓣ [**my**-stroh] *n, pl* **-tri, -tros** **1** outstanding musician or conductor **2** any master of an art
Maeterlinck *n* Comte **Maurice**. 1862–1949, Belgian poet and dramatist, noted particularly for his symbolist plays, such as *Pelléas et Mélisande* (1892), which served as the basis for an opera by Debussy, and *L'Oiseau bleu* (1909). Nobel prize for literature 1911
mae west *n* inflatable life jacket
Mafia *n* international secret criminal organization founded in Sicily
▸ **mafioso** *n* member of the Mafia
magazine Ⓣ *n* **1** periodical publication with articles by different writers **2** television or radio programme made up of short nonfictional items **3** appliance for automatically supplying cartridges to a gun or slides to a projector **4** storehouse for explosives or arms
magenta [maj-**jen**-ta] *adj* deep purplish-red
maggot *n* larva of an insect, esp. the blowfly **maggoty** *adj*
Magi [**maje**-eye] *pl n* wise men from the East at the Nativity
magic Ⓣ *n* **1** supposed art of invoking supernatural powers to influence events **2** mysterious quality or power ▷ *adj* **3** Also **magical** of, using, or like magic **magically** *adv*
▸ **magician** *n* **1** conjurer **2** person with magic powers
magistrate Ⓣ *n* **1** public officer administering the law **2** justice of the peace
▸ **magisterial** *adj* **1** commanding or authoritative **2** of a magistrate
magma *n* molten rock inside the earth's crust
magnanimous Ⓣ *adj* noble and generous **magnanimously** *adv* **magnanimity** *n*
magnate Ⓣ *n* influential or wealthy person, esp. in industry
magnesium *n* silvery-white metallic element
▸ **magnesia** *n* compound of magnesium used in medicine
magnet Ⓣ *n* piece of iron or steel capable

m

THESAURUS

mad (*informal*), speedily **4** (*Informal*) **= passionately**, desperately, intensely, devotedly, to distraction
madman madwoman ▸ *n* **= lunatic**, psychopath, psycho (*slang*), maniac, nutcase (*slang*)
madness *n* **1 = insanity**, dementia, distraction, mania, delusion, craziness, aberration, lunacy, psychosis, derangement, mental illness, psychopathy **2 = foolishness**, nonsense, folly, idiocy, absurdity, wildness, daftness (*informal*), foolhardiness, preposterousness
maelstrom *n* **1 = whirlpool**, vortex **2 = turmoil**, disorder, chaos, confusion, upheaval, tumult
maestro *n* **= master**, expert, genius, virtuoso
magazine *n* **1 = journal**, pamphlet, periodical **2 = storehouse**, store, warehouse, arsenal, depot
magic *n* **1 = sorcery**, witchcraft • *They believe in magic.* **2 = conjuring**, illusion, trickery, legerdemain, prestidigitation, sleight of hand **3 = charm**, power, glamour, fascination, magnetism, mojo (*slang*), enchantment, allurement ▸ *adj* **4 = enchanting**, charming, miraculous, marvellous, bewitching, entrancing, fascinating, spellbinding
magical *adj* **= enchanting**, bewitching • *Paris is a magical city.*
magician *n* **= sorcerer**, wizard, witch, illusionist, conjurer, enchanter *or* enchantress, necromancer, warlock
magisterial *adj* **= authoritative**, masterful, commanding, lordly
magistrate *n* **= judge**, justice, J.P., justice of the peace
magnanimity *n* **= generosity**, largesse *or* largess, nobility, selflessness, benevolence, big-heartedness, unselfishness
magnanimous *adj* **= generous**, kind, charitable, noble, selfless, bountiful, unselfish, big-hearted
magnate *n* **= tycoon**, mogul, baron, captain of industry, plutocrat
magnet *See* **lure**
magnetic *adj* **= attractive**, charismatic, charming, irresistible, seductive, hypnotic,

DICTIONARY

of attracting iron and pointing north when suspended
▸ **magnetic** *adj* **1** having the properties of a magnet **2** powerfully attractive **magnetically** *adv*
▸ **magnetic tape** plastic strip coated with a magnetic substance for recording sound or video signals
▸ **magnetism** *n* **1** magnetic property **2** science of this **3** powerful personal charm
▸ **magnetize** *v* **1** make into a magnet **2** attract strongly **magnetization** *n*
magneto [mag-**nee**-toe] *n, pl* **-tos** apparatus for ignition in an internal-combustion engine
magnificent Ⓣ *adj* **1** splendid or impressive **2** excellent **magnificently** *adv* **magnificence** *n*
magnify Ⓣ *v* **-fying, -fied 1** increase in apparent size, as with a lens **2** exaggerate **magnification** *n*
magniloquent *adj* speaking pompously **magniloquence** *n*
magnitude Ⓣ *n* **1** relative importance **2** relative size or extent
magnolia *n* shrub or tree with showy white or pink flowers
magnum *n* large wine bottle holding about 1.5 litres
magnum opus *n* greatest single work of art or literature of a particular artist
magpie *n* black-and-white bird
Magritte *n* **René**. 1898–1967, Belgian surrealist painter. By juxtaposing incongruous objects, depicted with meticulous realism, his works create a bizarre and disturbing impression
Magyar *n* **1** member of the main ethnic group in Hungary **2** Hungarian language ▹ *adj* **3** of the Magyars or their language
maharajah *n* former title of some Indian princes **maharanee** *n fem*
maharishi *n* Hindu religious teacher or mystic
mahatma *n Hinduism* person revered for holiness and wisdom
Mahavira *n* the title of *Vardhamana*. 599–527 BC, Indian ascetic and religious teacher, regarded as the founder of Jainism
mahjong, mahjongg *n* Chinese table game for four, played with tiles bearing different designs
Mahler *n* **Gustav**. 1860–1911, Austrian composer and conductor, whose music links the romantic tradition of the 19th century with the music of the 20th century. His works include nine complete symphonies for large orchestras, the symphonic song cycle *Das Lied von der Erde* (1908), and the song cycle *Kindertotenlieder* (1902)
mahogany *n, pl* **-nies** hard reddish-brown wood of several tropical trees
mahout [ma-**howt**] *n* elephant driver or keeper
maid Ⓣ *n* **1** Also **maidservant** female servant **2** *lit* young unmarried woman
maiden Ⓣ *n* **1** *lit* young unmarried woman ▹ *adj* **2** unmarried **3** first: *maiden voyage* **maidenhood** *n*
▸ **maidenly** *adj* modest
▸ **maidenhair** *n* fern with delicate fronds
▸ **maidenhead** *n* virginity
▸ **maiden name** woman's surname before marriage
mail[1] Ⓣ *n* **1** letters and packages transported and delivered by the post office **2** postal system **3** single collection or delivery of mail **4** train, ship, or aircraft carrying mail ▹ *v* **5** send by post
▸ **mailbox** *n* **1** public box into which letters are put for collection and delivery **2** private box outside house where

THESAURUS

captivating, fascinating, mesmerizing
magnetism *n* = **attraction**, pull, appeal, magic, charm, allure, charisma, mojo (*slang*), seductiveness, drawing power
magnification *n* = **increase**, expansion, enhancement, enlargement, amplification, intensification, heightening
magnificence *n* = **splendour**, glory, brilliance, majesty, grandeur, nobility, opulence, stateliness, sumptuousness
magnificent *adj* **1** = **splendid**, cool (*informal*), impressive, glorious, gorgeous, sublime, majestic, sumptuous, regal, imposing **2** = **excellent**, fine, brilliant, outstanding, superb, splendid, phat (*slang*)
magnify *v* **1** = **enlarge**, increase, boost, expand, intensify, heighten, amplify, dilate, blow up (*informal*) **2** = **exaggerate**, inflate, overstate, overplay, overemphasize
magnitude *n* **1** = **importance**, note, weight, moment, consequence, significance, greatness **2** = **size**, amount, mass, volume, extent, quantity, amplitude
maid *n* **1** = **girl**, damsel, lass, maiden, wench **2** = **servant**, housemaid, maidservant, serving-maid
maiden *n* **1** = **girl**, damsel, lass, virgin, maid, wench ▸ *adj* **2** = **unmarried**, unwed **3** = **first**, initial, inaugural, introductory
maidenly *adj* = **modest**, pure, decent, demure, chaste, decorous, virginal
mail *n* **1** = **letters**, post, correspondence, junk mail **2** = **postal service**, collection, delivery, post office ▸ *v* **3** = **send**, post, forward, transmit, dispatch

DICTIONARY

occupant's mail is delivered
▸ **mail drop** receptacle or chute for mail
▸ **mailman** *n* person who collects or delivers mail
▸ **mail order** system of buying goods by post
mail[2] *n* flexible armour of interlaced rings or links **mailed** *adj*
Mailer *n* **Norman**. 1923–2007, US author. His works, which are frequently critical of modern American society, include the war novel *The Naked and the Dead* (1948), *An American Dream* (1965), his account of the 1967 peace march on Washington *The Armies of the Night* (1968), *The Executioner's Song* (1979), and *Barbary Shore* (1998)
Maillet *n* **Antonine**. born 1929, Canadian novelist and playwright. An important figure in Acadian literature, her works include *Pélagie-la-charrette* (1979)
maim Ⓣ *v* cripple or mutilate
main Ⓣ *adj* **1** chief or principal ▷ *n* **2** principal pipe or line carrying water, gas, or electricity
▸ **in the main** on the whole
▸ **mainly** *adv* for the most part, chiefly
▸ **mainframe** *n, adj computers* (denoting) a high-speed general-purpose computer
▸ **mainland** *n* stretch of land which forms the main part of a country
▸ **mainmast** *n* chief mast in a ship
▸ **mainsail** *n* largest sail on a mainmast
▸ **mainspring** *n* **1** chief spring of a watch or clock **2** chief cause or motive
▸ **mainstay** *n* **1** chief support **2** rope securing a mainmast
▸ **mainstream** *n* prevailing cultural trend
maintain Ⓣ *v* **1** continue or keep in existence **2** keep up or preserve **3** support financially **4** assert
▸ **maintenance** *n* **1** maintaining **2** upkeep of a building, automobile, etc. **3** provision of money for a separated or divorced spouse
maître d'hôtel [met-ra dote-**tell**] *n French* head waiter
maize *n* type of corn with spikes of yellow grains
majesty Ⓣ *n, pl* **-ties 1** stateliness or grandeur **2** supreme power **majestic** *adj* **majestically** *adv*
major Ⓣ *adj* **1** greater in number, quality, or extent **2** significant or serious ▷ *n* **3** middle-ranking army officer **4** scale in music **5** principal field of study at a university etc. ▷ *v* **6** (foll. by *in*) do one's principal study in (a particular subject)
▸ **major-domo** *n* chief steward of a great household
▸ **major junior** *hockey* highest level in junior amateur competition
▸ **major penalty** *hockey* penalty in which a player is sent off for five minutes
Major *n* Sir **John**. born 1943, British Conservative politician: Chancellor of the Exchequer (1989–90); prime minister (1990–97)
majority Ⓣ *n, pl* **-ties 1** greater number **2** largest party voting together **3** number by which the votes on one side exceed those on the other **4** full legal age
Makarios III *n* original name *Mikhail Christodoulou Mouskos*. 1913–77, Cypriot archbishop, patriarch, and statesman; first president of the republic of Cyprus (1960–74; 1974–77)

THESAURUS

maim *v* = **cripple**, injure, hurt, wound, disable, mutilate
main *adj* **1** = **chief**, major, prime, primary, principal, cardinal, foremost, predominant, leading • *the main reason* ▸ *n* **2** = **conduit**, line, cable, channel, pipe, duct ▷ **in the main** = **on the whole**, mostly, generally, mainly, for the most part, in general
See also: **essential**
mainly *adv* = **chiefly**, mostly, largely, generally, primarily, predominantly, principally • *The staff members were mainly young.*
See also: **as a rule**
mainstay *n* = **pillar**, anchor, prop, backbone, buttress, bulwark, lynchpin
mainstream *adj* = **conventional**, general, current, established, orthodox, accepted, prevailing, received, lamestream (*informal*)
maintain *v* **1** = **continue**, preserve, retain, sustain, prolong, perpetuate, carry on, keep up **2** = **support**, supply, care for, look after, provide for, take care of **3** = **assert**, claim, state, declare, insist, contend, profess, avow
maintenance *n* **1** = **continuation**, carrying-on, perpetuation, prolongation **2** = **upkeep**, care, conservation, nurture, preservation, repairs, keeping **3** = **allowance**, keep, support, alimony
majestic *adj* = **grand**, impressive, magnificent, superb, splendid, monumental, sublime, stately, grandiose, regal
majesty *n* = **grandeur**, glory, pomp, nobility, splendour, magnificence, stateliness
major *adj* **1** = **important**, significant, critical, crucial, outstanding, leading • *a major problem* OPPOSITE: minor **2** = **main**, chief, senior, higher, supreme, bigger, greater, leading
See also: **principal**
majority *n* **1** = **most**, bulk, best part, better part • *The majority of our cheeses are made with cow's milk.* **2** = **adulthood**, maturity, manhood *or* womanhood, seniority

DICTIONARY

make ⓣ *v* **making, made 1** create, construct, or establish **2** cause to do or be **3** bring about or produce **4** perform (an action) **5** amount to **6** earn **7** serve as or become ▷ *n* **8** brand, type, or style **maker** *n*
▸ **make do** manage with an inferior alternative
▸ **make it** *informal* be successful
▸ **on the make** *informal* intent on gain
▸ **making** *n* **1** creation or production **makings 2** necessary requirements or qualities
▸ **make-believe** *n* fantasy or pretence
▸ **make for** *v* head towards
▸ **make off with** *v* steal or abduct
▸ **makeshift** *adj* serving as a temporary substitute
▸ **make up** *v* **1** form or constitute **2** prepare **3** invent **4** supply what is lacking, complete **5** (foll. by *for*) compensate (for) **6** settle a quarrel **7** apply cosmetics
▸ **make-up** *n* **1** cosmetics **2** mental or physical constitution **3** way something is made
▸ **makeweight** *n* something unimportant added to make up a lack

Makeba *n* **Miriam**. 1932–2008, South African singer and political activist; banned from South Africa from 1960 to 1990

mako *n, pl* **makos** powerful shark of the Atlantic and Pacific Oceans

mal- *combining form* bad or badly: *malformation; malfunction*

malachite [**mal**-a-kite] *n* green mineral

maladjusted ⓣ *adj psychol* unable to meet the demands of society **maladjustment** *n*

maladministration ⓣ *n* inefficient or dishonest administration

maladroit ⓣ [mal-a-**droyt**] *adj* clumsy or awkward

malady ⓣ [**mal**-a-dee] *n, pl* **-dies** disease or illness

malaise ⓣ [mal-**laze**] *n* vague feeling of illness or unease

Malamud *n* **Bernard**. 1914–86, US novelist

THESAURUS

make *v* **1 = create**, build, produce, form, manufacture, fashion, assemble, construct, fabricate • *She makes all her own clothes.* **2 = force**, drive, compel, coerce, oblige, impel • *He tried to make me lie for him.* **3 = produce**, cause, create, effect, generate, accomplish, bring about, give rise to, lead to **4 = amount to**, form, compose, constitute, add up to **5 = perform**, do, effect, execute, carry out **6 = earn**, win, get, gain, clear, net, obtain ▷ **make a difference** *See* **matter** ▷ **make a mistake** *See* **err** ▷ **make an attempt** *See* **try** ▷ **make an effort** *See* **strive, try** ▷ **make certain** *See* **ensure** ▷ **make for = head for**, aim for, be bound for, head towards ▷ **make fun of** *See* **mock, tease** ▷ **make it** (*Informal*) **= succeed**, arrive (*informal*), prosper, get on ▷ **make known** *See* **advise, announce** ▷ **make off = flee**, bolt, clear out (*informal*), run away *or* run off, take to one's heels ▷ **make off with = steal**, kidnap, abduct, carry off, filch, pinch (*informal*), run away with *or* run off with ▷ **make out = see**, discover, recognize, detect, perceive, distinguish, discern; **= understand**, follow, grasp, comprehend, decipher, fathom, work out; **= write out**, complete, draw up, fill in *or* fill out; **= pretend**, claim, assert, let on, make as if *or* make as though; **= fare**, manage, get on ▷ **make sure** *See* **ensure** ▷ **make up = form**, compose, constitute, comprise • *Westerners make up the majority of the team*; **= invent**, manufacture, fabricate, formulate, concoct • *It's very unkind of you to make up stories about him*; **= complete**, supply, fill; **= settle**, reconcile, bury the hatchet, call it quits ▷ **make up for = compensate for**, balance, offset, atone for, make amends for, recompense ▷ **make up your mind** *See* **decide, resolve** ▷ **make use of** *See* **employ** ▸ *n* **7 = brand**, model
See also: **issue, reach, shape, sort, type**

make-believe *n* **= fantasy**, imagination, pretense, play-acting, unreality

maker *n* **= manufacturer**, producer, builder, constructor

makeshift *adj* **= temporary**, substitute, provisional, expedient, stopgap

make-up *n* **1 = cosmetics**, face (*informal*), paint (*informal*), powder, greasepaint (*theatre*) **2 = structure**, organization, construction, constitution, assembly, format, arrangement, composition, configuration **3 = nature**, character, constitution, disposition, temperament

making *n* **= creation**, production, building, construction, manufacture, assembly, fabrication • *the making of this movie* ▷ **in the making = budding**, potential, up-and-coming, emergent • *a captain in the making* ▷ **makings = beginnings**, potential, capacity, ingredients

maladjusted *adj* **= disturbed**, unstable, neurotic, alienated

maladministration *n* **= mismanagement**, corruption, inefficiency, incompetence, malpractice, dishonesty, misrule

maladroit *adj* **= clumsy**, awkward, inept, inexpert, unskilful

malady *n* **= disease**, complaint, illness, disorder, ailment, sickness, affliction, infirmity

malaise *n* **= unease**, depression, anxiety, melancholy, disquiet

DICTIONARY

and short-story writer. His works include *The Fixer* (1966) and *Dubin's Lives* (1979)

malapropism *n* comical misuse of a word by confusion with one which sounds similar

malaria *n* infectious disease caused by the bite of some mosquitoes **malarial** *adj*

Malay *n* **1** member of a people of Malaysia or Indonesia **2** their language **Malayan** *adj, n*

Malcolm III *n* died 1093, king of Scotland (1057–93). He became king after Macbeth

Malcolm X *n* original name *Malcolm Little*. 1925–65, US Black civil-rights leader: assassinated

malcontent Ⓣ *n* discontented person

male Ⓣ *adj* **1** of the sex which can fertilize female reproductive cells ▷ *n* **2** male person or animal

malediction [mal-lid-**dik**-shun] *n* curse

malefactor Ⓣ [**mal**-if-act-or] *n* criminal or wrongdoer

Malevich *n* **Kasimir**. 1878–1935, Russian painter. He founded the abstract art movement known as Suprematism

malevolent Ⓣ [mal-**lev**-a-lent] *adj* wishing evil to others **malevolently** *adv* **malevolence** *n*

malfeasance [mal-**fee**-zanss] *n* misconduct, esp. by a public official

malformed Ⓣ *adj* misshapen or deformed **malformation** *n*

malfunction Ⓣ *v* **1** function imperfectly or fail to function ▷ *n* **2** defective functioning or failure to function

malice Ⓣ [**mal**-iss] *n* desire to cause harm to others **malicious** *adj* **maliciously** *adv*

malign Ⓣ [mal-**line**] *v* **1** slander or defame ▷ *adj* **2** evil in influence or effect ▶ **malignity** *n* evil disposition

malignant Ⓣ [mal-**lig**-nant] *adj* **1** seeking to harm others **2** (of a tumour) harmful and uncontrollable **malignancy** *n*

malinger [mal-**ling**-ger] *v* feign illness to avoid work **malingerer** *n*

mall *n* street or shopping centre closed to vehicles

mallard *n* wild duck

Mallarmé *n* **Stéphane**. 1842–98, French symbolist poet, noted for his free verse, in which he chooses words for their evocative qualities; his works include *L'Après-midi d'un Faune* (1876), *Vers et Prose* (1893), and *Divagations* (1897)

Malle *n* **Louis**. 1932–95, French film director: his films include *Le Feu follet* (1963), *Au revoir les enfants* (1987), and *Vanya on 42nd Street* (1994)

malleable Ⓣ [**mal**-lee-a-bl] *adj* **1** capable of being hammered or pressed into shape **2** easily influenced **malleability** *n*

mallet *n* **1** (wooden) hammer **2** stick with a head like a hammer, used in croquet or polo

mallow *n* plant with pink or purple flowers

malmsey *n* kind of strong sweet wine

malnutrition *n* inadequate nutrition

malodorous Ⓣ [mal-**lode**-or-uss] *adj* bad-smelling

Malory *n* Sir **Thomas**. 15th-century English author of *Le Morte d'Arthur* (?1470), a prose collection of Arthurian legends, translated from the French

Malpighi *n* **Marcello**. 1628–94, Italian

THESAURUS

malcontent *n* = **troublemaker**, rebel, agitator, mischief-maker, stirrer (*informal*)

male *n* **1** = **man**, boy, gentleman • *a pride of lions with three males, ten females, and six cubs* ▶ *adj* **2** = **masculine** • *the finest male actor in movies today*

malefactor *n* = **wrongdoer**, criminal, offender, villain, delinquent, miscreant, evildoer

malevolence *n* = **malice**, hate, hatred, spite, ill will, rancour, vindictiveness

malevolent *adj* (*Formal*) = **malicious**, hostile, malign, vengeful, vindictive, ill-natured, spiteful

malformation *n* = **deformity**, distortion, misshapenness

malformed *adj* = **misshapen**, twisted, abnormal, irregular, crooked, distorted, deformed

malfunction *v* **1** = **break down**, fail, go wrong ▶ *n* **2** = **fault**, failure, flaw, defect, glitch, breakdown

malice *n* = **ill will**, hate, hatred, spite, animosity, enmity, evil intent, malevolence, vindictiveness, ill will

malicious *adj* = **spiteful**, mean, vicious, cruel, malevolent (*formal*) • *She described the charges as malicious.*
See also: **unkind**

malign *v* **1** = **disparage**, abuse, smear, libel, defame, vilify, slander, denigrate, run down ▶ *adj* **2** = **evil**, bad, harmful, hostile, destructive, wicked, malignant, injurious, malevolent, pernicious

malignant *adj* **1** = **harmful**, hostile, destructive, hurtful, malign, malevolent, pernicious, spiteful **2** (*Medical*) = **uncontrollable**, deadly, dangerous, fatal, cancerous, irremediable

malleable *adj* **1** = **workable**, plastic, soft, ductile, tensile **2** = **manageable**, compliant, impressionable, adaptable, biddable, pliable, tractable

malodorous *adj* = **smelly**, offensive, funky (*slang*), putrid, fetid, mephitic, nauseating, noisome, reeking, stinking

malpractice *n* = **misconduct**, abuse, negligence, mismanagement, dereliction

DICTIONARY

physiologist. A pioneer in microscopic anatomy, he identified the capillary system (1661) **Malpighian** *adj*
malpractice ❶ *n* immoral, illegal, or unethical professional conduct
Malraux *n* **André**. 1901–76, French writer and statesman. His novels include *La Condition humaine* (1933) on the Kuomintang revolution (1927–28) and *L'Espoir* (1937) on the Spanish Civil War, in both of which events he took part. He also wrote on art, notably in *Les Voix du silence* (1951)
malt *n* **1** grain, such as barley, prepared for use in making beer or whisky
maltreat ❶ *v* treat badly **maltreatment** *n*
malware *n computers* program designed specifically to damage or disrupt a system, such as a virus
mama, mamma [mam-**ma**] *n old-fashioned* mother
mamba *n* deadly S African snake
Mamet *n* **David**. born 1947, US dramatist and film director. His plays include *Sexual Perversity in Chicago* (1974), *American Buffalo* (1976), *Glengarry Glen Ross* (1983), and *Oleanna* (1992); films include *House of Games* (1987) and *Spartan* (2004)
mammal *n* animal of the type that suckles its young **mammalian** *adj*
mammary *adj* of the breasts or milk-producing glands
mammon *n* **1** wealth regarded as a source of evil **2 Mammon** wealth personified in the New Testament as a false god
mammoth ❶ *n* **1** extinct animal like an elephant ▷ *adj* **2** colossal
man ❶ *n, pl* **men 1** adult male **2** human being or person **3** mankind **4** manservant **5** piece used in chess etc. ▷ *v* **manning, manned 6** supply with sufficient people for operation or defence **manhood** *n*
▸ **manful** *adj* determined and brave **manfully** *adv*
▸ **mankind** *n* human beings collectively
▸ **manly** *adj* (possessing qualities) appropriate to a man **manliness** *n*
▸ **mannish** *adj* like a man
▸ **manhandle** *v* treat roughly
▸ **manhole** *n* hole with a cover, through which a person can enter a drain or sewer
▸ **man-hour** *n* work done by one person in one hour
▸ **man-made** *adj* synthetic
▸ **manpower** *n* available number of workers
▸ **manservant** *n* male servant, esp. a valet
▸ **manslaughter** *n* unlawful but unintentional killing of a person
Man. Manitoba
manacle ❶ [**man**-a-kl] *n, v* handcuff or fetter
manage ❶ *v* **1** succeed in doing **2** be in charge of, administer **3** handle or control **4** cope with (financial) difficulties **manageable** *adj*
▸ **management** *n* **1** managers collectively **2** administration or organization
▸ **manager** (**manageress**) *n* person in charge of a business, institution, actor, sports team, etc. **managerial** *adj*
manatee *n* large tropical plant-eating aquatic mammal
mandarin *n* **1** high-ranking government official **2** kind of small orange
mandate ❶ *n* **1** official or authoritative command **2** authorization or instruction from an electorate to its representative or

m

THESAURUS

maltreat *v* = **abuse**, injure, hurt, harm, bully, mistreat, ill-treat
mammoth *adj* = **gigantic**, huge, giant, massive, enormous, mountainous, immense, monumental, colossal, prodigious
man *n* **1** = **male**, guy (*informal*), gentleman • *a young man* **2** = **human**, person, individual, soul, human being **3** = **mankind**, people, humanity, humankind, Homo sapiens, human race **4** = **manservant**, servant, attendant, retainer, valet ▸ *adj* ▷ **man-made** = **artificial**, synthetic, mock, ersatz, manufactured ▸ *v* **5** = **staff**, people, crew, occupy, garrison
manacle *n* **1** = **handcuff**, bond, chain, iron, shackle, fetter ▸ *v* **2** = **handcuff**, chain, bind, shackle, fetter, put in chains
manage *v* **1** = **succeed in**, effect, engineer, accomplish, arrange, contrive • *We managed to find somewhere to sit.* **2** = **be in charge of**, run, control, direct, command • *Within two years, he was managing the store.* **3** = **handle**, use, control, operate, manipulate **4** = **cope**, survive, carry on, get by (*informal*), make do, muddle through
See also: **administer, conduct, deal, do, head, lead, oversee, supervise, take care of**
manageable *adj* = **docile**, easy, compliant, amenable, submissive
management *n* **1** = **running**, control, direction • *The zoo needed better management.* **2** = **directors**, board, administration, bosses (*informal*), employers • *The management is doing its best.*
manager *n* = **supervisor**, director, executive, boss (*informal*) • *the manager of the company's Atlantic division*
See also: **chief, head, superior**
mandate *n* = **command**, order, commission, instruction, decree, directive, edict
mandatory *adj* = **compulsory**, binding,

DICTIONARY

government ▷ *v* **3** give authority to
▸ **mandatory** *adj* compulsory
Mandela *n* **1 Nelson** (**Rolihlahla**). born 1918, Black South African statesman: president of South Africa (1994–99). Jailed in 1962 for 5 years and, in 1964, for life, he was released in 1990 after a long international campaign; deputy president of the African National Congress (1990–91) and president (1991–97); president of South Africa (1994–99); Nobel peace prize jointly with F. W. de Klerk 1993 **2** (**Numzano**) **Winnie**. born 1934, Black South African political activist: campaigned for the release of her husband Nelson Mandela; they divorced in 1996
mandible *n* lower jawbone or jawlike part
mandolin *n* musical instrument with four pairs of strings
mandrake *n* plant with a forked root, formerly used as a narcotic
mandrel *n* shaft on which work is held in a lathe
mandrill *n* large blue-faced baboon
mane *n* long hair on the neck of a horse, lion, etc.
Manet *n* **Édouard**. 1832–83, French painter. His painting *Le Déjeuner sur l'herbe* (1863), which was condemned by the Parisian establishment, was acclaimed by the Impressionists, whom he decisively influenced
manful *adj* determined and brave **manfully** *adv*
manganese *n* brittle greyish-white metallic element
mange *n* skin disease of domestic animals
▸ **mangy** *adj* **1** having mange **2** scruffy or shabby
mangelwurzel *n Brit* variety of beet used as cattle food
manger *n* eating trough in a stable or barn
mangetout [**mawnzh**-too] *n Brit* snow pea
mangle[1] **T** *v* **1** destroy by crushing and twisting **2** spoil
mangle[2] *n* **1** machine with rollers for squeezing water from washed clothes ▷ *v* **2** put through a mangle
mango *n, pl* **-goes, -gos** tropical fruit with sweet juicy yellow flesh
mangrove *n* tropical tree with exposed roots, which grows beside water
Mani *n* ?216–?276 AD, Persian prophet who founded Manichaeism (Also **Manes, Manichaeus**)
mania **T** *n* **1** madness **2** extreme enthusiasm
▸ **maniac** *n* **1** mad person **2** *informal* person with an extreme enthusiasm for something
▸ **maniacal** [man-**eye**-a-kl], **manic** *adj* affected by mania
manicure *n* **1** cosmetic care of the fingernails and hands ▷ *v* **2** care for (the hands and fingernails) in this way
manicurist *n*
manifest **T** *adj* **1** easily noticed, obvious ▷ *v* **2** show plainly **3** be evidence of ▷ *n* **4** list of cargo or passengers for customs
manifestation *n*
manifesto *n, pl* **-toes, -tos** declaration of policy as issued by a political party
manifold **T** *adj* **1** numerous and varied ▷ *n* **2** pipe with several outlets, esp. in an internal-combustion engine
manikin *n* **1** little man or dwarf **2** model of the human body
manila, manilla *n* strong brown paper used for envelopes
manipulate **T** *v* **1** handle skilfully **2** control

THESAURUS

required, requisite, obligatory
manfully *adv* = **bravely**, hard, boldly, valiantly, resolutely, courageously, determinedly, gallantly, stoutly
mangle *v* = **crush**, destroy, tear, ruin, spoil, wreck, distort, disfigure, mutilate, deform
mangy *adj* = **scruffy**, dirty, shoddy, shabby, squalid, seedy, moth-eaten, scuzzy (*slang*)
manhandle *v* = **rough up**, maul, paw (*informal*), knock about *or* knock around
manhood *n* = **manliness**, masculinity, virility
mania *n* **1** = **madness**, dementia, insanity, delirium, lunacy, derangement **2** = **obsession**, thing (*informal*), passion, preoccupation, fad (*informal*), craze, fixation, fetish
maniac *n* **1** = **madman** *or* **madwoman**, lunatic, psychopath, psycho (*slang*) **2** = **fanatic**, fan, enthusiast, freak (*informal*), fiend (*informal*)
manic *See* **furious**
manifest *adj* **1** (*Formal*) = **obvious**, clear, patent, plain, blatant, glaring, conspicuous
• *the manifest failure of the policy* ▸ *v* **2** = **display**, show, reveal, express, expose, exhibit, demonstrate
See also: **betray, visible**
manifestation *n* = **display**, show, sign, mark, symptom, demonstration, exhibition, indication, expression
manifold *adj* = **numerous**, many, various, multiple, diverse, assorted, varied, copious, multifarious
manipulate *v* **1** = **operate**, use, work, handle **2** = **influence**, control, direct, engineer, maneuver
mankind *n* = **people**, man, humanity, humankind, Homo sapiens, human race
manliness *n* = **virility**, courage, bravery,

DICTIONARY

cleverly or deviously **manipulation** *n* **manipulative** *adj* **manipulator** *n*
manitou, manito *n* spirit of good or evil among N American Indians
Mann *n* **1 Heinrich**. 1871–1950, German novelist: works include *Professor Unrat* (1905), which was filmed as *The Blue Angel* (1928), and *Man of Straw* (1918) **2** his brother, **Thomas**. 1875–1955, German novelist, in the US after 1937. His works deal mainly with the problem of the artist in bourgeois society and include the short story *Death in Venice* (1913) and the novels *Buddenbrooks* (1900), *The Magic Mountain* (1924), and *Doctor Faustus* (1947): Nobel prize for literature 1929
manna *n* **1** *Bible* miraculous food which sustained the Israelites in the wilderness **2** windfall
mannequin *n* **1** woman who models clothes at a fashion show **2** life-size dummy of the human body used to fit or display clothes
manner Ⓣ *n* **1** way a thing happens or is done **2** person's bearing or behaviour **3** type or kind **4** custom or style **manners 5** (polite) social behaviour
▶ **mannered** *adj* affected
▶ **mannerism** *n* person's distinctive habit or trait
mannikin *n* same as **manikin**
manoeuvre Ⓣ [man-**noo**-ver] *v* **1** move or do something with skill **2** manipulate a situation to gain some advantage **3** perform manoeuvres ▷ *n* **4** skilful movement **5** contrived, complicated, and possibly deceptive plan or action **manoeuvres 6** military or naval exercises **manoeuvrable** *adj*
manor *n* large country house and its lands **manorial** *adj*
manqué [**mong**-kay] *adj* would-be: *an actor manqué*
mansard roof *n* roof with a break in its slope, the lower part being steeper than the upper
manse *n* minister's house in some religious denominations
Mansfield *n* **Katherine**, real name *Kathleen Mansfield Beauchamp*. 1888–1923, British writer, born in New Zealand, noted for her short stories, such as those in *Bliss* (1920) and *The Garden Party* (1922)
mansion Ⓣ *n* large house
Manson *n* Sir **Patrick**. 1844–1922, British physician, who established that mosquitoes transmit certain parasites responsible for human diseases
mantel *n* structure round a fireplace
▶ **mantelpiece** *or* **mantel shelf** *n* shelf above a fireplace
mantilla *n* (in Spain) lace scarf covering a woman's head and shoulders
mantis *n, pl* **-tises, -tes** carnivorous insect like a grasshopper
mantle Ⓣ *n* **1** loose cloak **2** covering **3** responsibilities and duties that go with a particular job or position **4** incandescent gauze round a gas jet
mantra *n Hinduism, Buddhism* any sacred word or syllable used as an object of concentration
manual Ⓣ *adj* **1** of or done with the hands **2** by human labour rather than automatic means ▷ *n* **3** handbook **4** organ keyboard **manually** *adv*
manufacture Ⓣ *v* **1** process or make (goods) on a large scale using machinery **2** invent or concoct (an excuse etc.) ▷ *n* **3** process of manufacturing goods **manufacturer** *n*

m

THESAURUS

masculinity, vigour, boldness, fearlessness, valour
manly *adj* = **virile**, strong, brave, bold, vigorous, courageous, fearless, masculine, manful, strapping
manner *n* **1** = **way**, fashion, style, mode • *She smiled again in a friendly manner.* **2** = **behaviour**, conduct, bearing, demeanour • *her kind manner* **3** = **type**, form, kind, brand, sort, category, variety
mannered *adj* = **affected**, artificial, pretentious, stilted
mannerism *n* = **habit**, trick, characteristic, trait, quirk, foible, idiosyncrasy, peculiarity
manners *pl n* **1** = **behaviour**, conduct, demeanour **2** = **politeness**, courtesy, etiquette, decorum, refinement, p's and q's
manoeuvre *v* **1** = **steer**, negotiate, guide, navigate • *It took expertise to manoeuvre the boat so close to the shore.* **2** = **manipulate**, engineer, scheme, contrive, machinate, pull strings, wangle (*informal*) ▶ *n* **3** = **tactic**, dodge, ploy, ruse • *manoeuvres to block the changes on the team* **4** = **movement**, operation, exercise
See also: **ease, measure**
mansion *n* = **residence**, seat, hall, villa, manor
manslaughter *See* **murder**
mantle *n* **1** = **cloak**, wrap, hood, cape, shawl **2** = **covering**, screen, blanket, veil, curtain, shroud, pall, canopy
manual *adj* **1** = **hand-operated**, human, physical ▶ *n* **2** = **handbook**, bible, instructions
manufacture *v* **1** = **make**, process, produce, assemble, fabricate, mass-produce • *Several models are being manufactured here.* **2** = **concoct**, invent, devise, fabricate, cook up (*informal*), make up, think up, trump

DICTIONARY

manure Ⓣ *n* **1** animal excrement used as a fertilizer ▷ *v* **2** fertilize (land) with this
manuscript *n* **1** book or document, orig. one written by hand **2** copy for printing
Manx *adj* **1** of the Isle of Man or its inhabitants ▷ *n* **2** Manx language
▶ **Manx cat** tailless breed of cat
many Ⓣ *adj* **more, most 1** numerous ▷ *n* **2** large number
Maoism *n* form of Marxism advanced by Mao Tse-tung in China **Maoist** *n, adj*
Maori *n* **1** member of the indigenous race of New Zealand **2** Maori language ▷ *adj* **3** of the Maoris or their language
Mao Tse-tung, Mao Ze Dong *n* 1893–1976, Chinese Marxist theoretician and statesman. The son of a peasant farmer, he helped to found the Chinese Communist Party (1921) and established a soviet republic in SE China (1931–34). He led the retreat of Communist forces to NW China known as the Long March (1935–36), emerging as leader of the party. In opposing the Japanese in World War II, he united with the Kuomintang regime, which he then defeated in the ensuing civil war. He founded the People's Republic of China (1949) of which he was chairman until 1959. As party chairman until his death, he instigated the Cultural Revolution in 1966
map *n* **1** representation of the earth's surface or some part of it, showing geographical features ▷ *v* **mapping, mapped 2** make a map of
▶ **map out** *v* plan
maple *n* tree with broad leaves, a variety of which yields sugar
▶ **maple syrup** syrup made from the sap of the sugar maple
mar Ⓣ *v* **marring, marred** spoil or impair
Mar. March
marabou *n* **1** kind of African stork **2** its soft white down, used to trim hats etc.
maraca [mar-**rak**-a] *n* shaken percussion instrument made from a gourd containing dried seeds etc.
Maradona *n* **Diego Armando**. born 1960, Argentinian soccer player
maraschino cherry [mar-rass-**kee**-no] *n* cherry preserved in a cherry liqueur with a taste like bitter almonds
Marat *n* **Jean Paul**. 1743–93, French revolutionary leader and journalist. He founded the radical newspaper *L'Ami du peuple* and was elected to the National Convention (1792). He was instrumental in overthrowing the Girondists (1793); he was stabbed to death in his bathtub by Charlotte Corday
marathon *n* **1** long-distance race of just over 26 miles **2** long or arduous task
marauding *adj* **1** hunting for plunder **2** pillaging **marauder** *n*
marble *n* **1** kind of limestone with a mottled appearance, which can be highly polished **2** slab of or sculpture in this **3** small glass ball used in playing marbles **marbles 4** game of rolling these
▶ **marbled** *adj* having a mottled appearance like marble
Marceau *n* **Marcel**. 1923–2007, French mime artist
Marcellus *n* **Marcus Claudius**. ?268–208 BC, Roman general and consul, who captured Syracuse (212 BC) in the Second Punic War
march[1] Ⓣ *v* **1** walk with a military step **2** make (a person or group) proceed **3** progress steadily ▷ *n* **4** action of marching **5** distance covered by marching **6** steady progress **7** piece of music, as for a march **marcher** *n*
march[2] *n* border or frontier
March *n* third month of the year
marchioness [marsh-on-**ness**] *n* **1** woman holding the rank of marquis **2** wife or widow of a marquis
Marciano *n* **Rocky**, original name *Rocco Francis Marchegiano*. 1923–69, US heavyweight boxer; world heavyweight champion, 1952–56
Marconi *n* **Guglielmo**. 1874–1937, Italian physicist, who developed radiotelegraphy and succeeded in transmitting signals across the Atlantic (1901): Nobel prize for physics 1909
Marcus Aurelius Antoninus *n* original

THESAURUS

up ▶ *n* **3 = making**, production, assembly, fabrication, mass production • *the manufacture of cardboard boxes*
manufacturer *n* = **maker**, producer, creator, builder, industrialist, constructor
manure *n* = **compost**, fertilizer, droppings, dung, muck, excrement, ordure, road apple (*slang*)
many *adj* **1 = numerous**, countless, myriad, innumerable, umpteen (*informal*) • *Cooking is one of his many hobbies.* OPPOSITE: few ▶ *n* **2 = a lot**, plenty, a mass, a multitude, large numbers, lots (*informal*), scores, millions (*informal*) • *in many of these neighbourhoods* OPPOSITE: few
mar *v* = **spoil**, damage, hurt, ruin, taint, impair, stain, scar, tarnish, disfigure, blemish, detract from
maraud *v* = **raid**, loot, ravage, forage, ransack, plunder, pillage
marauder *n* = **raider**, bandit, outlaw, buccaneer, plunderer
march *v* **1 = walk**, file, pace, parade, stride, strut ▶ *n* **2 = walk**, trek, routemarch **3 = progress**, advance, development, evolution, progression

DICTIONARY

name *Marcus Annius Verus*. 121–180 AD, Roman emperor (161–180) noted particularly for his *Meditations*, propounding his stoic view of life
Mardi Gras [**mar**-dee **grah**] *n* festival of Shrove Tuesday, celebrated in some cities with great revelry
mare *n* female horse
▸ **mare's nest 1** discovery which proves worthless **2** disordered situation or thing
Marenzio *n* **Luca**. 1553–99, Italian composer of madrigals
Margaret *n* **1** called the *Maid of Norway*. ?1282–90, queen of Scotland (1286–90); daughter of Eric II of Norway. Her death while sailing to England to marry the future Edward II led Edward I to declare dominion over Scotland **2** 1353–1412, queen of Sweden (1388–1412) and regent of Norway and Denmark (1380–1412), who united the three countries under her rule **3 Princess**. 1930–2002, younger sister of Queen Elizabeth II of Great Britain and Northern Ireland
Margaret of Anjou *n* 1430–82, queen of England. She married the mentally unstable Henry VI of England in 1445 to confirm the truce with France during the Hundred Years' War. She became a leader of the Lancastrians in the Wars of the Roses and was defeated at Tewkesbury (1471) by Edward IV
Margaret of Navarre *n* Also **Margaret of Angoulême** 1492–1549, queen of Navarre (1544–49) by marriage to Henry II of Navarre; sister of Francis I of France. She was a poet, a patron of humanism, and author of the *Heptaméron* (1558)
Margaret of Scotland *n* **Saint**. 1045–93, queen consort of Malcolm III of Scotland. Her piety and benefactions to the church led to her canonization (1250). Feast days: June 10, Nov 16
Margaret of Valois *n* 1553–1615, daughter of Henry II of France and Catherine de' Medici; queen of Navarre (1572) by marriage to Henry of Navarre. The marriage was dissolved (1599) after his accession as Henry IV of France: noted for her *Mémoires*
margarine *n* butter substitute made from animal or vegetable fats
marge *n informal* margarine
margin Ⓣ *n* **1** edge or border **2** blank space round a printed page **3** additional amount or one greater than necessary **4** limit
▸ **marginal** *adj* **1** insignificant, unimportant **2** near a limit **3** (of a constituency) won by only a small margin ▷ *n* **4** marginal constituency **marginally** *adv*
marguerite *n* large daisy
Maria de' Medici *n* French name *Marie de Médicis*. 1573–1642, queen of France (1600–10) by marriage to Henry IV of France; daughter of Francesco, grand duke of Tuscany. She became regent for her son (later Louis XIII) but continued to wield power after he came of age (1614). She was finally exiled from France in 1631 after plotting to undermine Richelieu's influence at court
Marie Antoinette *n* 1755–93, queen of France (1774–93) by marriage to Louis XVI of France. Her opposition to reform during the Revolution contributed to the overthrow of the monarchy; guillotined
marigold *n* plant with yellow flowers
marijuana Ⓣ [mar-ree-**wah**-na] *n* dried flowers and leaves of the hemp plant, used as a drug, esp. in cigarettes
marimba *n* Latin American percussion instrument resembling a xylophone
marina *n* harbour for yachts and other pleasure boats
marinade *n* **1** seasoned liquid in which fish or meat is soaked before cooking ▷ *v* **2** Also **marinate** soak in marinade
marine Ⓣ *adj* **1** of the sea or shipping **2** used at or found in the sea ▷ *n* **3** soldier trained for land or sea combat **4** country's shipping or fleet
▸ **mariner** *n* sailor
Marinetti *n* **Filippo Tommaso**. 1876–1944, Italian poet; founder of futurism (1909)
marionette *n* puppet worked with strings
marital Ⓣ *adj* relating to marriage
maritime Ⓣ *adj* **1** relating to shipping **2** of, near, or living in the sea
Marius *n* **Gaius**. ?155–86 BC, Roman general and consul. He defeated Jugurtha, the Cimbri, and the Teutons (107–101 BC), but his rivalry with Sulla caused civil war (88 BC). He was exiled but returned (87 BC) and took Rome
marjoram *n* aromatic herb

THESAURUS

margin *n* = **edge**, border, side, rim, brink, boundary, verge, perimeter, periphery
marginal *adj* **1** = **borderline**, peripheral, bordering, on the edge **2** = **insignificant**, small, minor, slight, minimal, negligible
marijuana *n* = **cannabis**, pot (*slang*), dope (*slang*), grass (*slang*), hemp
marinate *See* **steep**
marine *adj* = **nautical**, naval, maritime, seagoing, seafaring
mariner *n* = **sailor**, salt, seaman, seafarer, sea dog
marital *adj* = **matrimonial**, conjugal, connubial, nuptial
maritime *adj* **1** = **nautical**, marine, naval, oceanic, seafaring **2** = **coastal**, seaside, littoral

m

DICTIONARY

mark¹ Ⓣ *n* **1** line, dot, scar, etc. visible on a surface **2** distinguishing sign or symbol **3** written or printed symbol **4** letter or number used to grade academic work **5** indication of position **6** indication of some quality **7** target or goal ▷ *v* **8** make a mark on **9** be a distinguishing mark of **10** indicate **11** pay attention to **12** notice or watch **13** grade (academic work) **14** stay close to (a sporting opponent) to hamper his play **marker** *n*
▸ **marked** *adj* noticeable **markedly** [**mark**-id-lee] *adv*
mark² *n* same as **Deutschmark**
market Ⓣ *n* **1** assembly or place for buying and selling **2** demand for goods ▷ *v* **-keting, -keted 3** offer or produce for sale **marketable** *adj*
▸ **on the market** for sale
▸ **marketing** *n* part of a business that controls the way that goods or services are sold
▸ **market garden** place where fruit and vegetables are grown for sale
▸ **marketing board** board that regulates the price of agricultural commodities
▸ **market maker** *Stock Exchange* person who uses a firm's money to create a market for a stock
▸ **marketplace** *n* **1** market **2** commercial world
▸ **market research** research into consumers' needs and purchases
marksman Ⓣ *n* person skilled at shooting **marksmanship** *n*
marl *n* soil formed of clay and lime, used as fertilizer
Marley *n* **Bob**, full name *Robert Nesta Marley.* 1945–81, Jamaican reggae singer, guitarist, and songwriter. With his group, the Wailers, his albums included *Burnin'* (1973), *Natty Dread* (1975), *Rastaman Vibration* (1976), and *Exodus* (1977)
marlinespike, marlinspike *n* pointed hook used to separate strands of rope
Marlowe *n* **Christopher**. 1564–93, English dramatist and poet, who established blank verse as a creative form of dramatic expression. His plays include *Tamburlaine the Great* (1590), *Edward II* (?1592), and *Dr. Faustus* (1604). He was stabbed to death in a tavern brawl
marmalade *n* jam made from citrus fruits
marmoreal [mar-**more**-ee-al] *adj* of or like marble
marmoset *n* small bushy-tailed monkey
marmot *n* burrowing rodent
maroon¹ *adj* reddish-purple
maroon² Ⓣ *v* **1** abandon ashore, esp. on an island **2** isolate without resources
marquee *n* large tent used for a party or exhibition
marquess [**mar**-kwiss] *n* nobleman of the rank below a duke
marquetry *n, pl* **-quetries** ornamental inlaid work of wood
Marquette *n* **Jacques**, known as *Père Marquette.* 1637–75, French Jesuit missionary and explorer, with Louis Jolliet, of the Mississippi river
marquis *n, pl* **-quises, -quis** (in various countries) nobleman of the rank above a count
marquise [mar-**keez**] *n* same as **marchioness**
marram grass *n* grass that grows on sandy shores
marrow *n* **1** fatty substance inside bones **2** oblong green striped vegetable
marry Ⓣ *v* **-rying, -ried 1** take as a husband

THESAURUS

mark *n* **1 = stain**, line, spot, streak, scratch, fingerprint, scar, blemish, blot, smudge, handprint • *I can't get this mark off the curtain.* **2 = sign**, device, label, flag, symbol, hallmark, badge, token, emblem **3 = criterion**, measure, standard, norm, yardstick **4 = target**, goal, aim, object, purpose, objective ▸ *v* **5 = stain**, streak, scratch, scar, blemish, blot, smudge • *to stop the shoes from marking the floor* **6 = characterize**, identify, label, brand, flag, stamp **7 = distinguish**, show, illustrate, exemplify, denote **8 = observe**, note, watch, attend, mind, notice, pay attention, pay heed **9 = grade**, assess, correct, evaluate, appraise
See also: **feature, quality**
marked *adj* **= noticeable**, clear, patent, prominent, obvious, distinct, striking, pronounced, blatant, conspicuous, decided
markedly *adv* **= noticeably**, obviously, clearly, considerably, decidedly, distinctly, strikingly, conspicuously
market *n* **1 = fair**, bazaar, farmers' market • *the local market* ▷ **market price** *See* **value** ▸ *v* **2 = sell**, retail, vend
See also: **shop** **marketable** *adj* **= in demand**, wanted, salable, sought after
marksman, markswoman *n* **= sharpshooter**, crack shot (*informal*), good shot
maroon *v* **= abandon**, leave, strand, desert, leave high and dry (*informal*)
marriage *n* **= matrimony** (*formal*), wedlock (*formal*) • *six years of marriage* RELATED WORDS *adjs*: conjugal, connubial, marital, nuptial
marry *v* **1 = wed**, get hitched (*slang*), tie the

DICTIONARY

or wife **2** join or give in marriage **3** unite closely
▶ **marriage** *n* **1** state of being married **2** wedding **marriageable** *adj*
Mars *n* **1** Roman god of war **2** fourth planet from the sun
▶ **Martian** *adj* **1** of Mars ▷ *n* **2** supposed inhabitant of Mars
Marsala [mar-**sah**-la] *n* dark sweet wine
Marsalis *n* **Wynton**. born 1962, US jazz and classical trumpeter
marsh Ⓣ *n* low-lying wet land **marshy** *adj*
marshal Ⓣ *n* **1** officer of the highest rank **2** official who organizes ceremonies or events **3** *US* law officer ▷ *v* **-shalling, -shalled** **4** arrange in order **5** assemble **6** conduct with ceremony
▶ **marshalling yard** railway depot for goods trains
Marshall *n* **1 George Catlett**. 1880–1959, US general and statesman. He was chief of staff of the US army (1939–45) and, as secretary of state (1947–49), he proposed the Marshall Plan (1947), later called the European Recovery Programme: Nobel peace prize 1953 **2 John**. 1755–1835, US jurist and statesman. As chief justice of the Supreme Court (1801–35), he established the principles of US constitutional law
marshmallow *n* spongy pink or white candy
marsupial [mar-**soop**-ee-yal] *n* animal that carries its young in a pouch, such as a kangaroo
mart *n* market
Martello tower *n* round tower for coastal defence
marten *n* **1** weasel-like animal **2** its fur
Martha *n* **Saint**. *New Testament* a sister of Mary and Lazarus, who lived at Bethany and ministered to Jesus (Luke 10:38–42). Feast day: July 29 or June 4
martial Ⓣ *adj* of war, warlike
▶ **martial art** any of various philosophies and techniques of self-defence, orig. Eastern, such as karate
▶ **martial law** law enforced by military authorities in times of danger or emergency
Martial *n* full name *Marcus Valerius Martialis*. ?40–?104 AD, Latin epigrammatist and poet, born in Spain
Martian *adj* **1** of Mars ▷ *n* **2** supposed inhabitant of Mars
martin *n* bird with a slightly forked tail
Martin *n* **1 Chris**. born 1977, British rock musician, lead singer of Coldplay. He is married to the US actress Gwyneth Paltrow **2 Frank**. 1890–1974, Swiss composer. He used a modified form of the twelve-note technique in some of his works, which include *Petite Symphonie Concertante* (1946) and the oratorio *Golgotha* (1949) **3** Sir **George** (**Henry**). born 1926, British record producer and arranger, noted for his work with the Beatles **4 Paul Edgar Philippe**. born 1938, Canadian Liberal politician; Minister of Finance (1996–2002); Prime Minister (2003–06) **5 Saint**, called *Saint Martin of Tours*. ?316–?397 AD, bishop of Tours (?371–?397); a patron saint of France. He furthered monasticism in Gaul. Feast day: Nov 11 or 12 **6 Steve**(**n**). born 1945, US film actor and comedian; his films include *The Jerk* (1979), *Roxanne* (1987), and *Shopgirl* (2005), which he also wrote
Martinu *n* **Bohuslav**. 1890–1959, Czech composer
martinet Ⓣ *n* strict disciplinarian
martini *n* cocktail of vermouth and gin
martyr *n* **1** person who dies or suffers for his or her beliefs ▷ *v* **2** make a martyr of **martyrdom** *n*
▶ **be a martyr to** be constantly suffering from
marvel Ⓣ *v* **-velling, -velled** **1** be filled with wonder ▷ *n* **2** wonderful thing
▶ **marvellous** *adj* **1** excellent **2** causing great surprise
Marx *n* **Karl**. 1818–83, German founder of modern communism, in England from 1849. With Engels, he wrote *The Communist Manifesto* (1848). He developed his theories of the class struggle and the economics of capitalism in *Das Kapital* (1867; 1885; 1895). He was one of the founders of the International Workingmen's

m

THESAURUS

knot (*informal*) **2 = unite**, link, join, bond, ally, merge, unify, knit, yoke
marsh *n* **= swamp**, bog, quagmire, slough, morass, fen
marshal *v* **1 = arrange**, group, order, organize, deploy, array, align, draw up, line up **2 = conduct**, lead, guide, escort, usher, shepherd
marshy *adj* **= swampy**, wet, waterlogged, boggy, quaggy
martial *adj* **= military**, belligerent, bellicose, warlike
martinet *n* **= disciplinarian**, stickler
martyrdom *n* **= persecution**, suffering, ordeal
marvel *v* **1 = wonder**, gape, be amazed, be awed ▶ *n* **2 = wonder**, phenomenon, miracle, prodigy, portent
marvellous *adj* **= excellent**, wonderful, remarkable, brilliant, magnificent, superb, splendid, first-rate
• *a marvellous actor* OPPOSITE: terrible
See also: **grand, incredible**

DICTIONARY

Association (First International) (1864)
Marxism *n* socialism as conceived by Karl Marx **Marxist** *n, adj*
Mary I *n* family name *Tudor,* known as *Bloody Mary.* 1516–58, queen of England (1553–58). The daughter of Henry VIII and Catherine of Aragon, she married Philip II of Spain in 1554. She restored Roman Catholicism to England and around 300 Protestants were burnt at the stake as heretics
Mary II *n* 1662–94, queen of England, Scotland, and Ireland (1689–94), ruling jointly with her husband William III. They were offered the crown by parliament, which objected to the arbitrary rule of her father James II
Mary, Queen of Scots *n* family name *Stuart.* 1542–87, queen of Scotland (1542–67); daughter of James V of Scotland and Mary of Guise. She was married to Francis II of France (1558–60), her cousin Lord Darnley (1565–67), and the Earl of Bothwell (1567–71), who was commonly regarded as Darnley's murderer. She was forced to abdicate in favour of her son (later James VI of Scotland) and fled to England. Imprisoned by Elizabeth I until 1587, she was beheaded for plotting against the English crown
marzipan *n* paste of ground almonds, sugar, and egg whites
masc. masculine
Mascagni *n* **Pietro.** 1863–1945, Italian composer of operas, including *Cavalleria rusticana* (1890)
mascara *n* cosmetic for darkening the eyelashes
mascot *n* thing supposed to bring good luck
masculine Ⓣ *adj* **1** relating to males **2** manly **3** *grammar* of the gender of nouns that includes some male animate things
masculinity *n*
Masefield *n* **John.** 1878–1967, English poet, novelist, and critic; poet laureate (1930–67)
mash Ⓣ *n* **1** bran or meal mixed with warm water as food for horses etc. **2** *informal* mashed potatoes ▷ *v* **3** crush into a soft mass
mask Ⓣ *n* **1** covering for the face, as a disguise or protection **2** behaviour that hides one's true feelings ▷ *v* **3** cover with a mask **4** hide or disguise
masochism [**mass**-oh-kiz-zum] *n* form of (sexual) perversion marked by love of pain or of being humiliated **masochist** *n* **masochistic** *adj*
mason *n* **1** person who works with stone **2 Mason** Freemason
▸ **Masonic** *adj* of Freemasonry
▸ **masonry** *n* **1** stonework **2 Masonry** Freemasonry
masque [**mask**] *n hist* 16th–17th-century form of dramatic entertainment
masquerade Ⓣ [mask-a-**raid**] *n* **1** deceptive show or pretence **2** party at which masks and costumes are worn ▷ *v* **3** pretend to be someone or something else
mass Ⓣ *n* **1** coherent body of matter **2** large quantity or number **3** *physics* amount of matter in a body ▷ *adj* **4** large-scale **5** involving many people ▷ *v* **6** form into a mass
▸ **the masses** ordinary people
▸ **massive** *adj* large and heavy
▸ **mass-market** *adj* for or appealing to a large number of people
▸ **mass media** means of communication to many people, such as television and newspapers
▸ **mass-produce** *v* manufacture standardized goods in large quantities
Mass *n* service of the Eucharist, esp. in the RC Church
massacre Ⓣ [**mass**-a-ker] *n* **1** indiscriminate killing of large numbers of people ▷ *v* **2** kill in large numbers
massage Ⓣ [**mass**-ahzh] *n* **1** rubbing and kneading of parts of the body to reduce pain or stiffness ▷ *v* **2** give a massage to
▸ **masseur** [mass-**ur**], **masseuse** [mass-**urz**]

THESAURUS

masculine *adj* = **male**, manly, manlike, mannish, virile
mash *See* **crush, press**
mask *n* **1** = **disguise**, front, cover, screen, veil, camouflage, guise, façade ▸ *v* **2** = **disguise**, cover, screen, hide, cloak, veil, conceal, obscure, camouflage
masquerade *n* **1** = **masked ball**, revel, fancy dress party **2** = **pretense**, screen, pose, mask, cloak, disguise, deception, cover-up, subterfuge ▸ *v* **3** = **pose**, pretend *or* pretend to be, disguise, impersonate, dissemble, dissimulate, pass oneself off
mass *n* **1** = **lot**, crowd, load, pile, mob, lump, throng, heap • *a mass of papers* **2** = **piece**, block, chunk, lump, hunk **3** = **size**, bulk, magnitude, greatness ▸ *adj* **4** = **widespread**, general, popular, universal • *mass unemployment* ▷ **mass production** *See* **manufacture** ▸ *v* **5** = **gather**, group, assemble, congregate • *The crowd began to mass in the square.*
See also: **jam, majority, tangle**
massacre *n* **1** = **slaughter**, murder, carnage, holocaust, extermination, annihilation, blood bath, butchery ▸ *v* **2** = **slaughter**, kill, murder, butcher, exterminate, cut to pieces, mow down, wipe out
massage *n* **1** = **rub-down**, manipulation ▸ *v* **2** = **rub down**,

m

DICTIONARY

n person who gives massages
Massasoit *n* died 1661, Wampanoag Indian chief, who negotiated peace with the Pilgrim Fathers (1621)
Massenet *n* **Jules Émile Frédéric**. 1842–1912, French composer of operas, including *Manon* (1884), *Werther* (1892), and *Thaïs* (1894)
Massey *n* **Vincent**. 1887–1967, Canadian diplomat: first Canadian governor general of Canada (1952–59)
massif [**mass**-seef] *n* connected group of mountains
mast[1] *n* tall pole for supporting something, esp. a ship's sails
mast[2] *n* fruit of the beech, oak, etc., used as pig fodder
mastectomy [mass-**tek**-tom-ee] *n, pl* **-mies** surgical removal of a breast
master Ⓣ *n* **1** person in control, such as an employer or an owner of slaves or animals **2** expert **3** great artist **4** original thing from which copies are made **5** male teacher ▷ *adj* **6** overall or controlling **7** main or principal ▷ *v* **8** overcome **9** acquire knowledge of or skill in
▶ **masterful** *adj* **1** domineering **2** showing great skill
▶ **masterly** *adj* showing great skill
▶ **mastery** *n* **1** expertise **2** control or command
▶ **master key** key that opens all the locks of a set
▶ **mastermind** *v* **1** plan and direct (a complex task) ▷ *n* **2** person who plans and directs a complex task
▶ **masterpiece** *n* outstanding work of art
mastic *n* **1** gum obtained from certain trees **2** putty-like substance used as a filler, adhesive, or seal
masticate *v* chew **mastication** *n*
mastiff *n* large dog
mastitis *n* inflammation of a breast or udder
mastodon *n* extinct elephant-like mammal
mastoid *n* projection of the bone behind the ear
▶ **mastoiditis** *n* inflammation of this area
Mastroianni *n* **Marcello**. 1924–96, Italian film actor; his films include *Le notti bianche* (1957), *La dolce vita* (1960), *Ginger and Fred* (1985), and *Prêt à Porter* (1995)
masturbate *v* caress the genitals (of)
masturbation *n*
mat Ⓣ *n* **1** piece of fabric used as a floor covering or to protect a surface ▷ *v* **matting, matted 2** become tangled
▶ **on the mat** *informal* summoned for a reprimand
matador *n* man who kills the bull in bullfights
match[1] Ⓣ *n* **1** contest in a game or sport **2** person or thing exactly like, equal to, or in harmony with another **3** marriage ▷ *v* **4** be exactly like, equal to, or in harmony with **5** put in competition (with) **6** find a match for **7** join (in marriage)
▶ **matchless** *adj* unequalled
▶ **matchmaker** *n* person who schemes to bring about a marriage **matchmaking** *n*
match[2] *n* small stick with a tip which ignites when scraped on a rough surface **matchbox** *n*
▶ **matchstick** *n* **1** wooden part of a match

m

THESAURUS

manipulate, knead
masses *See* **lot, public**
massive *adj* = **huge**, big, enormous, hefty, mammoth, whopping (*informal*), immense, monumental, gigantic, colossal
mass-produce *See* **manufacture**
master *v* **1** = **learn**, grasp, become proficient in, get the hang of (*informal*) • *She found it easy to master the latest technology.* **2** = **overcome**, defeat, tame, conquer, vanquish, triumph over **3** = **ruler**, director, chief, manager, commander, governor, boss (*informal*), controller, lord **4** = **expert**, ace (*informal*), wizard, genius, maestro, virtuoso, doyen, past master **5** = **teacher**, guide, instructor, guru, tutor ▶ *adj* **6** = **main**, chief, prime, principal, foremost, predominant, leading
masterful *adj* **1** = **skilful**, expert, fine, world-class, supreme, consummate, superlative, first-rate, adroit, masterly **2** = **domineering**, arrogant, imperious, high-handed, bossy (*informal*), overbearing, overweening
masterly *adj* = **skilful**, expert, crack (*slang*), world-class, supreme, masterful, consummate, first-rate, adroit
mastermind *v* **1** = **plan**, manage, direct, organize, conceive, devise ▶ *n* **2** = **organizer**, director, manager, brain *or* brains (*informal*), engineer, architect, planner
masterpiece *n* = **classic**, jewel, magnum opus, *pièce de résistance* (*French*), *tour de force* (*French*)
mastery *n* **1** = **expertise**, skill, prowess, know-how (*informal*), finesse, proficiency, virtuosity **2** = **control**, command, domination, supremacy, superiority, ascendancy, upper hand, whip hand
mat *See* **tangle**
match *n* **1** = **game**, competition, contest • *a tennis match* **2** = **equal**, rival, counterpart, peer **3** = **marriage**, alliance, partnership, pairing ▶ *v* **4** = **correspond**, agree, suit, fit, tally, go with • *The shoes matched her dress.* **5** = **rival**, compare, compete, equal, emulate, measure up to

DICTIONARY

▷ *adj* **2** (of drawn figures) thin and straight
▶ **matchwood** *n* small splinters
mate[1] ⓣ *n* **1** sexual partner of an animal **2** officer in a merchant ship **3** tradesman's assistant **4** *Brit informal* friend or associate **5** *informal* common Brit. and Aust. term of address between males ▷ *v* **6** pair (animals) or (of animals) be paired for reproduction
▶ **matey** *adj informal* friendly or intimate
mate[2] *n, v chess* checkmate
material ⓣ *n* **1** substance of which a thing is made **2** cloth **3** information on which a piece of work may be based **materials 4** things needed for an activity ▷ *adj* **5** of matter or substance **6** affecting physical wellbeing **7** unspiritual **8** relevant
▶ **materially** *adv* considerably
▶ **materialism** *n* **1** excessive interest in or desire for money and possessions **2** belief that only the material world exists **materialist** *adj, n* **materialistic** *adj*
▶ **materialize** *v* **1** come into existence or view **2** actually happen **materialization** *n*
maternal ⓣ *adj* **1** of a mother **2** related through one's mother
▶ **maternity** *n* **1** motherhood ▷ *adj* **2** of or for pregnant women
math *n informal* mathematics
mathematics *n* science of number, quantity, shape, and space **mathematical** *adj* **mathematically** *adv* **mathematician** *n*
maths *n Brit informal* mathematics
Matilda *n* known as *the Empress Maud*. 1102–67, only daughter of Henry I of England and wife of Geoffrey of Anjou. After her father's death (1135) she unsuccessfully waged a civil war with Stephen for the English throne; her son succeeded as Henry II
matinée [**mat**-in-nay] *n* afternoon performance in a theatre
matins *pl n* early morning service in various Christian churches
Matisse *n* **Henri**. 1869–1954, French painter and sculptor; leader of Fauvism
matriarch [**mate**-ree-ark] *n* female head of a tribe or family **matriarchal** *adj*
▶ **matriarchy** *n* society with matriarchal government and descent traced through the female line
matricide *n* **1** crime of killing one's mother **2** person who commits this crime
matriculate *v* enrol or be enrolled in a college or university **matriculation** *n*
matrimony ⓣ *n* marriage **matrimonial** *adj*
matrix [**may**-trix] *n, pl* **matrices** [**may**-triss-eez] **1** substance or situation in which something originates, takes form, or is enclosed **2** mould for casting **3** *math* rectangular array of numbers or elements
matron *n* **1** staid or dignified married woman **2** woman who supervises the domestic or medical arrangements of an institution **matronly** *adj*
matt *adj* dull, not shiny
matter ⓣ *n* **1** substance of which something is made **2** physical substance **3** event, situation, or subject **4** written material in general **5** pus ▷ *v* **6** be of importance
▶ **what's the matter?** what is wrong?
Matthias *n* **Saint**. *New Testament* the disciple chosen by lot to replace Judas as one of the 12 apostles (Acts 1:15–26). Feast day: May 14 or Aug 9
matting *n* coarsely woven fabric used as a floor-covering and packing material
mattock *n* large pick with one of its blade

THESAURUS

See also: **blend**
matching *adj* = **identical**, like, twin, equivalent, coordinating, corresponding
matchless *adj* = **unequalled**, supreme, unparalleled, unmatched, superlative, incomparable, unsurpassed, unrivalled, inimitable
mate *n* **1** = **partner**, husband *or* wife, spouse **2** = **colleague**, associate, companion **3** = **assistant**, helper, subordinate ▶ *v* **4** = **couple**, pair, breed
material *n* **1** = **cloth**, fabric • *the thick material of her skirt* **2** = **substance**, matter, stuff • *the materials needed to build the shed* **3** = **information**, evidence, data, facts, notes ▶ *adj* **4** = **physical**, substantial, concrete, bodily, tangible, palpable, corporeal **5** = **important**, serious, significant, essential, vital, meaningful, momentous, weighty **6** = **relevant**, applicable, pertinent, apposite, apropos, germane
materialistic *See* **greedy**
materialize *v* = **occur**, appear, happen, come about, come to pass, take shape, turn up
materially *adv* = **significantly**, much, seriously, essentially, greatly, substantially, gravely
maternal *adj* = **motherly**
maternity *n* = **motherhood**, motherliness (*informal*)
matrimonial *adj* = **marital**, conjugal, connubial, nuptial
matrimony *n* = **marriage**, nuptials, wedlock, wedding ceremony
matted *adj* = **tangled**, knotted, tousled, uncombed
matter *n* **1** = **situation**, issue, business, question, affair, subject • *business matters* **2** = **substance**, material, stuff • *The atom is the smallest divisible particle of matter.* **3** = **problem**, worry, trouble,

DICTIONARY

ends flattened for loosening soil
mattress *n* large stuffed flat case, often with springs, used on or as a bed
mature Ⓣ *adj* **1** fully developed or grown-up **2** ripe ▷ *v* **3** make or become mature **4** (of a bill or bond) become due for payment
maturity *n* **maturation** *n*
maudlin Ⓣ *adj* foolishly or tearfully sentimental
Maugham *n* **W**(**illiam**) **Somerset**. 1874–1965, English writer. His works include the novels *Of Human Bondage* (1915) and *Cakes and Ale* (1930), short stories, and comedies
maul Ⓣ *v* **1** handle roughly **2** beat or tear
maunder *v* talk or act aimlessly or idly
Maupassant *n* (**Henri René Albert**) **Guy de**. 1850–93, French writer, noted esp. for his short stories, such as *Boule de suif* (1880), *La Maison Tellier* (1881), and *Mademoiselle Fifi* (1883). His novels include *Bel Ami* (1885) and *Pierre et Jean* (1888)
mausoleum Ⓣ [maw-so-**lee**-um] *n* stately tomb
mauve *adj* pale purple
maverick Ⓣ *n* independent unorthodox person
maw *n* animal's mouth, throat, or stomach
mawkish Ⓣ *adj* foolishly sentimental
max. maximum
maxim Ⓣ *n* general truth or principle
Maximilian I *n* 1459–1519, king of Germany (1486–1519) and Holy Roman Emperor (1493–1519)
maximum Ⓣ *n, pl* **-mums, -ma 1** greatest possible amount or number ▷ *adj* **2** greatest
maximal *adj*
▸ **maximize** *v* increase to a maximum
Maxwell *n* **1 James Clerk**. 1831–79, Scottish physicist. He made major contributions to the electromagnetic theory, developing the equations (**Maxwell equations**) upon which classical theory is based. He also contributed to the kinetic theory of gases, and colour vision **2 Lois**. 1927–2007, Canadian film and TV actress, best known for her role as Miss Moneypenny (1962–85) in the *James Bond* series of films
may *v, past tense* **might** used as an auxiliary to express possibility, permicssion, opportunity, etc.
May *n* **1** fifth month of the year **2 may** same as **hawthorn**
▸ **mayfly** *n* short-lived aquatic insect
▸ **maypole** *n* pole set up for dancing round on the first day of May (**May Day**)
maybe Ⓣ *adv* **1** perhaps **2** possibly
Mayday *n* international radiotelephone distress signal
Mayer *n* **Louis B**(**urt**). 1885–1957, US film producer, born in Russia; founder and first head (1924–48) of the Metro-Goldwyn-Mayer (MGM) film company
mayhem Ⓣ *n* violent destruction or confusion
mayonnaise *n* creamy sauce of egg yolks, oil, and vinegar
mayor *n* head of a municipality **mayoral** *adj*
▸ **mayoress** *n* **1** mayor's wife **2** lady mayor
▸ **mayoralty** *n* (term of) office of a mayor
maze Ⓣ *n* **1** complex network of paths or lines designed to puzzle **2** confusing

THESAURUS

difficulty, complication, distress ▸ *v* **4 = be important**, count, be of consequence, make a difference • *It doesn't matter what you wear to the party.*
See also: **event, item**
matter-of-fact *adj* **= unsentimental**, plain, sober, mundane, down-to-earth, deadpan, unimaginative, emotionless, prosaic
mature *v* **1 = grow up**, come of age, reach adulthood • *Some children mature earlier than others.* ▸ *adj* **2 = grown-up**, adult, full-fledged, full-grown, grown • *He's very mature for his age.*
See also: **develop**
maturity *n* **= adulthood**, experience, wisdom, manhood *or* womanhood, ripeness
maudlin *adj* **= sentimental**, slushy (*informal*), mawkish, overemotional, tearful, weepy (*informal*)
maul *v* **1 = ill-treat**, abuse, molest, paw, manhandle **2 = tear**, batter, claw, mangle, lacerate
mausoleum *See* **grave, tomb**
maverick *n* **1 = rebel**, protester, radical, eccentric, dissenter, heretic, iconoclast, individualist, nonconformist ▸ *adj* **2 = rebel**, radical, eccentric, heretical, dissenting, iconoclastic, individualistic, nonconformist
mawkish *adj* **= sentimental**, emotional, slushy (*informal*), maudlin, schmaltzy (*slang*)
maxim *n* **= saying**, rule, adage, motto, dictum, proverb, aphorism, axiom
maximum *n* **1 = most**, height, ceiling, utmost, upper limit • *The restaurant can seat a maximum of 30 people.* OPPOSITE: minimum ▸ *adj* **2 = top**, utmost • *the maximum recommended dosage* OPPOSITE: minimum
See also: **full, limit**
maybe *adv* **= perhaps**, possibly, conceivably, it could be • *Maybe I should have done a bit more.*
mayhem *n* **= chaos**, violence, trouble, disorder, destruction, confusion, havoc, commotion, fracas
maze *n* **1 = labyrinth** **2 = web**, confusion,

m

DICTIONARY

network or system
mazurka *n* **1** lively Polish dance **2** music for this
MB **1** Bachelor of Medicine **2** Manitoba
MBE Member of the Order of the British Empire
Mbeki *n* **Thabo** (**Mvuyelwa**). born 1942, South African politician: a member of the African National Congress (ANC); deputy president of South Africa (1994–99); president of South Africa (1999–2008)
McCain *n* **John** (**Sidney**) **III**. born 1936, US politician; he served in the US Navy as a pilot in the Vietnam war and was a prisoner of war between 1967 and 1973; Republican Congressman from 1982 and unsuccessful Presidential candidate in 2008
McCarthy *n* **Joseph R**(**aymond**). 1908–57, US Republican senator, who led (1950–54) the notorious investigations of alleged Communist infiltration into the US government
McCartney *n* Sir **Paul**. born 1942, English rock musician and songwriter; member of the Beatles (1961–70); leader of Wings (1971–81). His recordings include *Band on the Run* (1973), "Mull of Kintyre" (1977), *Flowers in the Dirt* (1989), and *Driving Rain* (2001)
McConnell *n* **Jack**. born 1960, Scottish Labour politician; first minister of the Scottish Parliament (2001–07)
McEnroe *n* **John** (**Patrick Jr**.). born 1959, US tennis player: US singles champion (1979–81; 1984) and doubles champion (1979; 1981; 1989): Wimbledon singles champion (1981; 1983; 1984) and doubles champion (1979; 1981; 1983; 1984; 1992)
McGarrigle *n* **Kate**. 1946–2010, Canadian folk music singer-songwriter and instrumentalist noted for performing and writing with her sister **Anna**, born 1944. Kate's children, Rufus and Martha Wainwright, are also noted musicians
McGee *n* **Thomas D'Arcy**. 1825–68, Canadian politician, born in Ireland. One of the Fathers of Confederation; assassinated by an Irish nationalist
McGonagall *n* **William**. 1830–?1902, Scottish writer of doggerel, noted for its bathos, repetitive rhymes, poor scansion, and ludicrous effect
McGuinty *n* **Dalton**. born 1955, Canadian politician, Premier of Ontario (2003–07; 2007–)
McGwire *n* **Mark** (**David**). born 1963, US baseball player
McIndoe *n* Sir **Archibald Hector**. 1900–60, New Zealand plastic surgeon; noted for his pioneering work with wounded World War II airmen
McKenzie *n* **Robert**. 1867–1938, Canadian physician and sculptor: during his service in WWI he made contributions to rehabilitation medicine; also noted for his sculptures and reliefs of athletes
McKinley *n* **William**. 1843–1901, 25th president of the US (1897–1901). His administration was marked by high tariffs and by expansionist policies. He was assassinated
McLachlan *n* **Sarah**. born 1968, Canadian singer-songwriter. Her recordings include *Fumbling Towards Ecstasy* (1993) and *Surfacing* (1997)
McLuhan *n* (**Herbert**) **Marshall**. 1911–80, Canadian author of works analysing the mass media, including *Understanding Media* (1964) and *The Medium is the Message* (1967)
McPherson *n* **Aimee Semple** (neé *Kennedy*). 1890–1944, US evangelist, born in Canada. Used mass media to create a revivalist movement and founded the Angelus Temple of the Foursquare Gospel in Los Angeles (1923); her later career was blighted by scandal
McQueen *n* **Steve**. 1930–80, US film actor, noted for his portrayal of tough characters. His films include *The Thomas Crown Affair* (1968) and *Papillon* (1973)
McTavish *n* **Simon**. *c*. 1750–1804, Canadian fur trader and businessman, born in Scotland. He played an important role in the founding of the North West Company (1779)
MC Master of Ceremonies
MCC Marylebone Cricket Club
MD Doctor of Medicine
MDMA *n* same as **ecstasy 2**
MDT Mountain Daylight Time
me *pron* the objective form of **I**
ME myalgic encephalomyelitis, postviral syndrome
mead *n* alcoholic drink made from honey
meadow Ⓣ *n* piece of grassland
▸ **meadowsweet** *n* plant with dense heads of small fragrant flowers
meagre Ⓣ *adj* scanty or insufficient
meal[1] Ⓣ *n* **1** occasion when food is served and eaten **2** the food itself
meal[2] *n* grain ground to powder **mealy** *adj*
▸ **mealy-mouthed** *adj* not outspoken enough

m

THESAURUS

tangle, imbroglio
meadow *n* = **field**, pasture, grassland, lea (*poetic*)
meagre *adj* = **inadequate**, sparse, paltry, scant, measly (*informal*) • *a meagre pension*
See also: **few**
meal *n* = **repast**, dinner, feast, banquet • *She sat next to me throughout the meal*.

DICTIONARY

mean[1] Ⓣ *v* **meaning, meant 1** intend to convey or express **2** signify, denote, or portend **3** intend **4** have importance as specified
▸ **meaning** *n* **1** sense, significance ▷ *adj* **2** expressive **meaningful** *adj* **meaningless** *adj*
mean[2] Ⓣ *adj* **1** miserly, ungenerous, or petty **2** despicable or callous **3** *informal* bad-tempered **meanly** *adv* **meanness** *n*
▸ **meanie** *or* **meany** *n* miserly person
mean[3] Ⓣ *n* **1** middle point between two extremes **2** average **means 3** that by which something is done **4** money ▷ *adj* **5** intermediate in size or quantity **6** average
▸ **by all means** certainly
▸ **by no means** not at all
▸ **means test** enquiry into a person's means to decide eligibility for financial aid
▸ **meantime** *n* **1** intervening period ▷ *adv* **2** meanwhile
▸ **meanwhile** *adv* **1** during the intervening period **2** at the same time
meander Ⓣ [mee-**and**-er] *v* **1** follow a winding course **2** wander aimlessly ▷ *n* **3** winding course
measles *n* infectious disease producing red spots
▸ **measly** *adj informal* meagre
measure Ⓣ *n* **1** size or quantity **2** graduated scale etc. for measuring size or quantity **3** unit of size or quantity **4** extent **5** action taken **6** law **7** poetical rhythm ▷ *v* **8** determine the size or quantity of **9** be (a specified amount) in size or quantity
measurable *adj*
▸ **measured** *adj* **1** slow and steady **2** carefully considered
▸ **measurement** *n* **1** measuring **2** size
▸ **measure up to** *v* fulfil (expectations or requirements)
meat Ⓣ *n* animal flesh as food
▸ **meaty** *adj* **1** (tasting) of or like meat **2** brawny **3** full of significance or interest

THESAURUS

mean[1] *v* **1 = signify**, indicate, denote • *The flashing signal means stop*. **2 = intend**, plan, aim • *I meant to phone you, but didn't have time*.
See also: **represent**
mean[2] *adj* **1 = spiteful**, nasty, malicious, hurtful • *Why are you being so mean to me?* **2 = miserly**, tight (*informal*), stingy, parsimonious, penny-pinching, tight-fisted • *Don't be mean with the tip*. **3 = despicable**, petty, shameful, lousy (*slang*), callous, shabby, vile, sordid, contemptible, hard-hearted, scuzzy (*slang*)
See also: **horrible, sneaky, unkind**
mean[3] *n* **1 = average**, middle, balance, compromise, norm, midpoint, happy medium ▸ *adj* **2 = average**, standard, middle
meander *v* **1 = wind**, turn, snake, zigzag **2 = wander**, stroll, ramble ▸ *n* **3 = curve**, turn, twist, bend, loop, coil, zigzag
meandering *See* **indirect**
meaning *n* **= significance**, message, sense, drift, gist • *the meaning of this dream*
meaningful *adj* **= significant**, important, material, useful, relevant, valid, worthwhile, purposeful
meaningless *adj* **= pointless**, empty, useless, senseless, vain, insignificant, worthless, futile, inconsequential, inane
meanness *n* **1 = miserliness**, selfishness, niggardliness, parsimony, stinginess **2 = pettiness**, disgracefulness, ignobility, narrow-mindedness, shabbiness, shamefulness
means *pl n* **1 = method**, way, medium, agency, process, instrument, mode **2 = money**, income, capital, wealth, fortune, affluence, wherewithal, funds, resources ▷ **by all means = certainly**, definitely, surely, doubtlessly, of course ▷ **by no means = in no way**, definitely not, not in the least, on no account
meant *See* **supposed**
meantime, meanwhile *adv* **= at the same time**, simultaneously, concurrently, in the interim
measly *adj* **= meagre**, poor, pathetic, miserable, paltry, pitiful, skimpy, puny, scanty
measurable *adj* **= quantifiable**, significant, assessable, perceptible
measure *v* **1 = gauge**, survey • *We measured the size of the room*. ▷ **measure up to = achieve**, be equal to, be suitable, come up to scratch (*informal*), fit the bill *or* fill the bill, make the grade (*informal*) ▸ *n* **2 = amount**, degree, portion, proportion • *There has been a measure of agreement*. **3 = action**, step, procedure, means, manoeuvre, expedient • *Tough measures are needed to maintain safety*. **4 = gauge**, rule, scale, metre, yardstick **5 = law**, bill, act, resolution, statute **6 = rhythm**, beat, meter, verse, cadence
See also: **extent, quantity**
measured *adj* **1 = steady**, even, slow, regular, solemn, dignified, sedate, leisurely, stately, unhurried **2 = considered**, deliberate, sober, calculated, reasoned, studied, well-thought-out
measurement *n* **= calculation**, assessment, evaluation, valuation, calibration, computation, mensuration
meat *n* **= flesh**
meaty *adj* **1 = brawny**, heavy, solid,

DICTIONARY

Mecca *n* **1** holy city of Islam **2** place that attracts visitors
mechanic *n* person skilled in repairing or operating machinery
▸ **mechanics** scientific study of motion and force
▸ **mechanical** *adj* **1** of or done by machines **2** (of an action) without thought or feeling **mechanically** *adv*
mechanism Ⓣ *n* **1** way a machine works **2** piece of machinery **3** process or technique: *defence mechanism*
▸ **mechanize** *v* **1** equip with machinery **2** make mechanical or automatic **3** *mil* equip (an army) with armoured vehicles **mechanization** *n*
med. **1** medical **2** medicine **3** medieval **4** medium
medal *n* piece of metal with an inscription etc., given as a reward or memento
▸ **medallion** *n* **1** disc-shaped ornament worn on a chain round the neck **2** large medal **3** circular decorative device in architecture
▸ **medallist** *n* winner of a medal
meddle Ⓣ *v* interfere annoyingly **meddler** *n* **meddlesome** *adj*
media *n* **1** a plural of **medium** **2** the mass media collectively
mediaeval [med-**eve**-al] *adj* same as **medieval**
medial [**mee**-dee-al] *adj* of or in the middle
▸ **median** *adj, n* middle (point or line)
mediate Ⓣ [**mee**-dee-ate] *v* **1** intervene to bring about agreement **2** resolve (a dispute) by mediation **mediation** *n* **mediator** *n*
medic *n informal* doctor or medical student
medical Ⓣ *adj* **1** of the science of medicine ▷ *n* **2** *informal* medical examination **medically** *adv*
▸ **medicament** [mid-**dik**-a-ment] *n* a medicine
▸ **medicate** *v* treat with a medicinal substance
▸ **medication** *n* (treatment with) a medicinal substance
Medicare *n* system of national medical services financed mainly by taxation
Medici *n* **1** an Italian family of bankers, merchants, and rulers of Florence and Tuscany, prominent in Italian political and cultural history in the 15th, 16th, and 17th centuries, including: **2 Catherine de'**. See **Catherine de' Medici** **3 Cosimo de'**, known as *Cosimo the Elder*. 1389–1464, Italian banker, statesman, and patron of arts, who established the political power of the family in Florence (1434) **4 Giovanni de'**. See **Leo X** **5 Giulio de'**. See **Clement VII** **6 Lorenzo de'**, known as *Lorenzo the Magnificent*. 1449–92, Italian statesman, poet, and scholar; ruler of Florence (1469–92) and first patron of Michelangelo **7 Maria de'**. See **Maria de' Medici** **8 Cosimo I**, known as *Cosimo the Great*. 1519–74, duke of Florence and first grand duke of Tuscany (1569–74) (Also **Médicis**) **Medicean** *adj*
medicine Ⓣ *n* **1** substance used to treat disease **2** science of preventing, diagnosing, or curing disease
▸ **medicinal** [med-**diss**-in-al] *adj* having therapeutic properties
▸ **medicine man** witch doctor
medieval, mediaeval [med-**eve**-al] *adj* of the Middle Ages
mediocre Ⓣ [mee-dee-**oak**-er] *adj* **1** average

THESAURUS

beefy (*informal*), muscular, sturdy, burly, heavily built, strapping **2** = **interesting**, significant, rich, substantial, meaningful, profound
mechanical *adj* **1** = **automatic**, automated **2** = **unthinking**, routine, automatic, involuntary, cursory, perfunctory, impersonal, instinctive, unfeeling
mechanism *n* **1** = **machine**, device, tool, instrument, appliance, apparatus, contrivance **2** = **process**, system, agency, operation, procedure, method, technique, means
meddle *v* = **interfere**, intervene, tamper, pry, intrude, butt in
meddler *n* = **busybody**, snooper • *a meddler in everyone's personal affairs*
meddlesome *adj* = **interfering**, intrusive, mischievous, meddling, officious, prying
mediate *v* = **intervene**, referee, umpire, reconcile, arbitrate, conciliate, intercede, step in (*informal*)
mediation *n* = **intervention**, arbitration, reconciliation, conciliation, intercession
mediator *n* = **negotiator**, referee, arbitrator, umpire, middleman, peacemaker, intermediary, arbiter, go-between, honest broker
medical *See* **examination**
medication *See* **drug, medicine**
medicinal *adj* = **therapeutic**, medical, healing, remedial, restorative, curative
medicine *n* = **remedy**, drug, medication
• *Don't forget to take your medicine.*
See also: **cure**
mediocre *adj* = **second-rate**, average, ordinary, pedestrian, indifferent, inferior, passable, middling, so-so (*informal*), undistinguished, meh (*slang*)
mediocrity *n* = **insignificance**, indifference, inferiority, ordinariness, unimportance

DICTIONARY

in quality **2** second-rate **mediocrity** [mee-dee-**ok**-rit-ee] *n*
meditate Ⓣ *v* **1** reflect deeply, esp. on spiritual matters **2** think about or plan
meditator *n*
▸ **meditation** *n* meditating **meditative** *adj*
meditatively *adv*
medium Ⓣ *adj* **1** midway between extremes, average ▷ *n, pl* **-dia, -diums 2** middle state, degree, or condition **3** intervening substance producing an effect **4** means of communicating news or information to the public, such as radio or newspapers **5** person who can supposedly communicate with the dead **6** surroundings or environment **7** category of art according to the material used
▸ **medium wave** radio wave with a wavelength between 100 and 1000 metres
medlar *n* apple-like fruit of a small tree, eaten when it begins to decay
medley Ⓣ *n* **1** miscellaneous mixture **2** musical sequence of different tunes
meds [medz] *pl n informal* medicinal substances
medulla [mid-**dull**-la] *n, pl* **-las, -lae** marrow, pith, or inner tissue **medullary** *adj*
meek Ⓣ *adj* submissive or humble **meekly** *adv* **meekness** *n*
meerschaum [**meer**-shum] *n* **1** white substance like clay **2** tobacco pipe with a bowl made of this
meet[1] Ⓣ *v* **meeting, met 1** come together (with) **2** come into contact (with) **3** be at the place of arrival of **4** make the acquaintance of **5** satisfy (a need etc.) **6** experience ▷ *n* **7** sports meeting **8** assembly of a hunt
▸ **meeting** *n* **1** coming together **2** assembly
meet[2] Ⓣ *adj obsolete* fit or suitable
mega *adj slang* extremely good, great, or successful
mega- *combining form* **1** denoting one million: *megawatt* **2** very great: *megastar*
megabyte *n computers* 2^{20} or 1 048 576 bytes
megahertz *n, pl* **-hertz** one million hertz
megalith *n* great stone, esp. as part of a prehistoric monument **megalithic** *adj*
megalomania *n* craving for or mental delusions of power **megalomaniac** *adj, n*
megaphone *n* cone-shaped instrument used to amplify the voice
megaton *n* explosive power equal to that of one million tons of TNT
Meighen *n* **Arthur**. 1874–1960, Canadian lawyer and Conservative politician; Prime Minister (1920–21, 1926)
Meilhac *n* **Henri**. 1831–97, French dramatist, who collaborated with Halévy on opera libretti, esp. Offenbach's *La Belle Hélène* (1865) and *La Vie parisienne* (1867)
meiosis [my-**oh**-siss] *n* type of cell division in which reproductive cells are produced, each containing half the chromosome number of the parent nucleus
melamine *n* colourless crystalline compound used in making synthetic resins
▸ **melamine resin** resilient kind of plastic
melancholy Ⓣ [**mel**-an-kol-lee] *n* **1** sadness

THESAURUS

meditate *v* **1 = reflect**, think, consider, ponder, deliberate, contemplate, muse, cogitate, ruminate **2 = plan**, intend, purpose, scheme, have in mind
meditation *n* **= reflection**, study, thought, musing, contemplation, cogitation, pondering, rumination
medium *adj* **1 = average**, medium-sized, middling • *He was of medium height.* ▸ *n* **2 = means**, vehicle, channel • *the medium of television* **3 = middle**, mean, average, compromise, centre, midpoint **4 = environment**, atmosphere, setting, surroundings, milieu, conditions **5 = spiritualist**
See also: **moderate**
medium-sized *See* **medium**
medley *n* **= mixture**, assortment, jumble, mishmash, hodgepodge, farrago, *mélange* (*French*), miscellany, mixed bag (*informal*), potpourri
meek *adj* **= submissive**, timid, unassuming, docile, deferential • *a meek, mild-mannered young man* OPPOSITE: bold
See also: **gentle, humble, mild**
meekness *n* **= submissiveness**, compliance, humility, deference, modesty, acquiescence, docility, gentleness, mildness, timidity
meet *v* **1 = encounter**, bump into (*informal*), come upon, run across, run into • *I met him at the mall yesterday.* **2 = gather**, assemble, convene, congregate, get together • *We meet for lunch once a week.* **3 = fulfill**, answer, satisfy • *services intended to meet the needs of the elderly* **4 = converge**, join, cross, touch, connect, intersect, come together, link up **5 = experience**, face, bear, suffer, undergo, endure, encounter, go through
See also: **greet, receive** ▷ **meet head-on** *See* **hit**
meeting *n* **1 = gathering**, conference, convention, reunion, congress, get-together (*informal*) • *a business meeting* **2 = encounter**, rendezvous, tryst • *a chance meeting*
See also: **appointment**
melancholy *n* **1 = sadness**, depression, misery, sorrow, gloom, unhappiness, despondency, dejection, low spirits ▸ *adj* **2 = sad**, depressed, gloomy, miserable,

DICTIONARY

or gloom ▷ *adj* **2** sad or gloomy
▸ **melancholia** [mel-an-**kole**-ya] *n* old name for depression **melancholic** *adj, n*
melange [**may**-lahnzh] *n* mixture
melanin *n* dark pigment found in the hair, skin, and eyes of man and animals
Melba *n* Dame **Nellie**, stage name of *Helen Porter Mitchell*. 1861–1931, Australian operatic soprano
▸ **do a Melba** *Austral slang* to make repeated farewell appearances
Melbourne *n* **William Lamb**, 2nd Viscount. 1779–1848; Whig prime minister (1834; 1835–41). He was the chief political adviser to the young Queen Victoria
melee, mêlée Ⓣ [**mel**-lay] *n* noisy confused fight or crowd
Méliès *n* **Georges**. 1861–1938, French pioneer film director
mellifluous Ⓣ [mel-**lif**-flew-uss] *adj* (of sound) smooth and sweet
mellow Ⓣ *adj* **1** soft, not harsh **2** kind-hearted, esp. through maturity **3** (of fruit) ripe ▷ *v* **4** make or become mellow
melodrama *n* **1** play full of extravagant action and emotion **2** overdramatic behaviour or emotion **melodramatic** *adj*
melody Ⓣ *n, pl* **-dies 1** series of musical notes which make a tune **2** sweet sound
▸ **melodic** [mel-**lod**-ik] *adj* **1** of melody **2** melodious
▸ **melodious** [mel-**lode**-ee-uss] *adj* **1** pleasing to the ear **2** tuneful
melon *n* large round juicy fruit with a hard rind
melt Ⓣ *v* **1** (cause to) become liquid by heat **2** dissolve **3** soften through emotion **4** blend (into) **5** disappear
▸ **meltdown** *n* (in a nuclear reactor) melting of the fuel rods, with the possible release of radiation
Melville *n* **Herman**. 1819–91, US novelist and short-story writer. Among his works, *Moby Dick* (1851) and *Billy Budd* (written 1891, published 1924) are outstanding
member Ⓣ *n* **1** individual making up a body or society **2** limb **membership** *n*
▸ **Member of Parliament** person elected to parliament
membrane *n* thin flexible tissue in a plant or animal body **membranous** *adj*
memento Ⓣ *n, pl* **-tos, -toes** thing serving to remind, souvenir
memo Ⓣ *n, pl* **memos** short for **memorandum**
memoir Ⓣ [**mem**-wahr] *n* **1** biography or historical account based on personal knowledge **memoirs 2** collection of these **3** autobiography
memory Ⓣ *n, pl* **-ries 1** ability to remember **2** sum of things remembered **3** particular recollection **4** length of time one can remember **5** commemoration **6** part of a computer which stores information

m

THESAURUS

mournful, despondent, glum, dispirited, downhearted, sorrowful
melee, mêlée *n* = **fight**, brawl, scuffle, scrimmage, fracas, free-for-all (*informal*), rumpus, skirmish, tussle
mellifluous *adj* = **sweet**, soft, smooth, soothing, silvery, dulcet, euphonious, honeyed, sweet-sounding
mellow *adj* **1** = **soft**, rich, sweet, mature, delicate, ripe, full-flavoured ▸ *v* **2** = **mature**, season, develop, improve, soften, sweeten, ripen
melodious *adj* = **tuneful**, musical, melodic, harmonious, dulcet, euphonious, sweet-sounding
melodramatic *adj* = **theatrical**, sensational, histrionic • *Don't you think you're being rather melodramatic?*
melody *n* **1** = **tune**, music, air, song, strain, theme **2** = **tunefulness**, harmony, euphony, melodiousness, musicality
melt *v* **1** = **dissolve**, thaw • *The snow had melted.* **2** = **disappear**, dissolve, vanish, disperse, evaporate • *My inhibitions melted.* **3** = **soften**, relax, disarm, mollify
See also: **warm**
member *n* **1** = **representative**, associate, fellow **2** = **limb**, part, arm, leg, extremity, appendage
membership *n* **1** = **members**, body, associates, fellows **2** = **participation**, belonging, fellowship, enrolment
memento *n* = **souvenir**, memorial, trophy, reminder, remembrance, relic, token, keepsake
memo *See* **message, note**
memoir *n* = **account**, record, life, journal, biography, essay, narrative, monograph
memoirs *pl n* = **autobiography**, diary, experiences, journals, life story, memories, recollections, reminiscences
memorable *adj* = **notable**, historic, striking, catchy, unforgettable • *a memorable victory*
memorandum *n* = **note**, minute, message, communication, memo, reminder, jotting
memorial *n* **1** = **monument**, record, plaque, souvenir, remembrance, memento ▸ *adj* **2** = **commemorative**, monumental
memorize *v* = **remember**, learn, commit to memory, learn by heart, learn by rote
memory *n* **1** = **recall**, remembrance (*formal*) • *Every detail is fresh in my*

DICTIONARY

▸ **memorial** *n* **1** something serving to commemorate a person or thing ▹ *adj* **2** serving as a memorial
▸ **memorable** *adj* worth remembering, noteworthy **memorably** *adv*
▸ **memorandum** *n* **1** written record or communication within a business **2** note of things to be remembered
▸ **memorize** *v* commit to memory
▸ **memory card** small removable data storage device
memsahib *n* (formerly, in India) term of respect used for a European married woman
men *n* plural of **man**
menace Ⓣ *n* **1** threat **2** *informal* nuisance ▹ *v* **3** threaten, endanger **menacing** *adj*
ménage [**may**-nahzh] *n* household
menagerie [min-**naj**-er-ee] *n* collection of wild animals for exhibition
Mencius *n* Chinese name *Mengzi* or *Meng-tze*. ?372–?289 BC, Chinese philosopher, who propounded the ethical system of Confucius
Mencken *n* **H(enry) L(ouis)**. 1880–1956, US journalist and literary critic, noted for *The American Language* (1919): editor of the *Smart Set* and the *American Mercury*, which he founded (1924)
mend Ⓣ *v* **1** repair or patch **2** make or become better **3** recover or heal ▹ *n* **4** mended area
▸ **on the mend** regaining health
mendacity *n* (tendency to) untruthfulness **mendacious** *adj*
Mendel *n* **Gregor Johann**. 1822–84, Austrian monk and botanist; founder of the science of genetics. He developed his theory of organic inheritance from his experiments on the hybridization of green peas. His findings were published (1865) but remained unrecognized until 1900
Mendeleyev, Mendeleev *n* **Dmitri Ivanovich**. 1834–1907, Russian chemist. He devised the original periodic table of the elements (1869)
Mendelssohn *n* **Felix**, full name *Jacob Ludwig Felix Mendelssohn-Bartholdy*. 1809–47, German romantic composer. His works include the overtures *A Midsummer Night's Dream* (1826) and *Fingal's Cave* (1832), five symphonies, the oratorio *Elijah* (1846), piano pieces, and songs. He was instrumental in the revival of the music of J. S. Bach in the 19th century
Mendes *n* **Sam(uel) (Alexander)**. born 1965, British theatre and film director, who made his name as artistic director of the Donmar Warehouse, London (1992–2002) before directing the films *American Beauty* (1999), *The Road to Perdition* (2002), and *Revolutionary Road* (2008).
mendicant *adj* **1** begging ▹ *n* **2** beggar
Mendoza *n* **Pedro de**. died 1537, Spanish soldier and explorer; founder of Buenos Aires (1536)
Menes *n* the first king of the first dynasty of Egypt (?3100 BC). He is said to have united Upper and Lower Egypt and founded Memphis
menfolk *pl n* men collectively, esp. the men of a particular family
menhir [**men**-hear] *n* single upright prehistoric stone
menial Ⓣ [**mean**-ee-yal] *adj* **1** involving boring work of low status ▹ *n* **2** domestic servant
meningitis [men-in-**jite**-iss] *n* inflammation of the membranes of the brain
meniscus *n, pl* **-nisci, -niscuses 1** curved surface of a liquid **2** crescent-shaped lens
menopause *n* time when a woman's menstrual cycle ceases **menopausal** *adj*
Menotti *n* **Gian Carlo**. 1911–2007, Italian composer, in the US from 1928. His works include the operas *The Medium* (1946), *The Consul* (1950), *Amahl and the Night Visitors* (1951), and *Giorno di Nozze* (1988)
menstruation *n* approximately monthly discharge of blood and cellular debris from the womb of a nonpregnant woman **menstruate** *v* **menstrual** *adj*
mensuration *n* measuring, esp. in geometry
mental Ⓣ *adj* **1** of, in, or done by the mind

THESAURUS

memory. **2 = commemoration**, honor, remembrance
menace *n* **1 = threat**, warning, intimidation **2** (*Informal*) **= nuisance**, plague, pest, troublemaker, annoyance ▸ *v* **3 = threaten**, loom, bully, intimidate, frighten, terrorize, lour *or* lower
menacing *adj* **= threatening**, ominous, forbidding, frightening, intimidating, looming, louring *or* lowering
mend *v* **1 = repair**, fix, restore, patch, renovate • *to mend a broken chain* **2 = improve**, reform, correct, amend, rectify, ameliorate, emend **3 = heal**, recover, recuperate, convalesce, get better ▸ *n* **4 = repair**, patch, stitch, darn ▹ **on the mend = convalescent**, getting better, improving, recovering, recuperating
See also: **piece together**
mendacious *adj* **= lying**, false, fraudulent, deceptive, dishonest, deceitful, duplicitous, fallacious, insincere, untruthful
menial *adj* **1 = unskilled**, routine, boring, dull, humdrum, low-status ▸ *n* **2 = servant**, attendant, lackey, drudge, flunky, underling
mental *adj* **1 = intellectual**,

m

DICTIONARY

2 of or for mental illness 3 *informal* insane
mentally *adv*
▸ **mentality** *n* way of thinking
menthol *n* organic compound found in peppermint, used medicinally
mention Ⓣ *v* 1 refer to briefly 2 acknowledge ▹ *n* 3 acknowledgment 4 brief reference to a person or thing
mentor Ⓣ *n* adviser or guide
menu Ⓣ *n* 1 list of dishes to be served, or from which to order 2 *computers* list of options displayed on a screen
Menuhin *n* **Yehudi**, Baron. 1916–99, British violinist, born in the US
mercantile Ⓣ *adj* of trade or traders
Mercator *n* **Gerardus**, Latinized name of *Gerhard Kremer.* 1512–94, Flemish cartographer and mathematician
▸ **Mercator projection** [mer-**kate**-er] method of map-making in which latitude and longitude form a rectangular grid
mercenary Ⓣ *adj* 1 influenced by greed 2 working merely for reward ▹ *n, pl* **-aries** 3 hired soldier
Mercer *n* **Johnny**, full name *John Herndon Mercer.* 1909–76, US popular songwriter and singer. His most popular songs include "Blues in the Night" (1941) and "Moon River" (1961)
mercerized *adj* (of cotton) given lustre by treating with chemicals
merchandise Ⓣ *n* commodities
merchant Ⓣ *n* person engaged in trade, wholesale trader
▸ **merchant bank** bank dealing mainly with businesses and investment
▸ **merchantman** *n* trading ship
▸ **merchant navy** ships or crew engaged in a nation's commercial shipping
Merchant *n* **Ismail**. 1936–2005, Indian film producer, noted for his collaboration with James Ivory on such films as *Shakespeare Wallah* (1965), *The Europeans* (1979), *A Room with a View* (1986), *The Remains of the Day* (1993), and *The Golden Bowl* (2000)
Merckx *n* **Eddy**. born 1945, Belgian professional biker: five times winner of the Tour de France, including four consecutive victories (1969–72)
mercury *n* 1 silvery liquid metal 2 **Mercury** *Roman myth* messenger of the gods 3 **Mercury** planet nearest the sun
▸ **mercurial** [mer-**cure**-ee-al] *adj* lively, changeable
mercy Ⓣ *n, pl* **-cies** 1 compassionate treatment of an offender or enemy who is in one's power 2 merciful act **merciless** *adj*
▸ **merciful** *adj* 1 compassionate 2 giving relief
mere[1] Ⓣ *adj* nothing more than: *mere chance*
merely *adv*
mere[2] *n obsolete* lake
meretricious Ⓣ *adj* superficially or garishly attractive but of no real value
merganser [mer-**gan**-ser] *n* large crested diving duck

THESAURUS

cerebral 2 (*Informal*) = **insane**, mad, unstable, psychotic, disturbed, unbalanced, deranged, mentally ill
mentality *n* = **attitude**, character, outlook, personality, psychology, disposition, make-up, cast of mind
mentally *adv* = **in the mind**, psychologically, intellectually, in one's head, inwardly
mention *v* 1 = **refer to**, hint, intimate, broach, allude to, bring up, touch on, touch upon • *I may not have mentioned it to her.* ▸ *n* 2 = **reference**, allusion • *There was no mention of elections.* 3 = **acknowledgment**, tribute, recognition, citation
See also: **comment, note, observe, refer, remark**
mentor *n* = **guide**, coach, teacher, adviser, instructor, guru, tutor, counselor
menu *n* = **bill of fare**, *carte du jour* (*French*)
mercantile *adj* = **commercial**, trading
mercenary *adj* 1 = **greedy**, sordid, acquisitive, avaricious, grasping, money-grubbing (*informal*), venal ▸ *n* 2 = **hireling**, soldier of fortune
merchandise *n* = **goods**, stock, produce, commodities, products, wares
merchant *n* = **tradesman**, retailer, dealer, supplier, trader, seller, broker, vendor, trafficker, salesman, wholesaler, shopkeeper, purveyor
merciful *adj* 1 = **compassionate**, kind, humane • *merciful and sympathetic to others* OPPOSITE: merciless 2 = **forgiving**, lenient • *We can only hope the court is merciful.* OPPOSITE: merciless
merciless *adj* = **cruel**, ruthless, callous, heartless, implacable • *a merciless dictator* OPPOSITE: merciful
mercurial *adj* = **changeable**, mobile, active, volatile, unpredictable, spirited, lively, impulsive, irrepressible, capricious, quicksilver, sprightly
mercy *n* 1 = **compassion**, quarter, pity, kindness • *She showed no mercy.* 2 = **forgiveness**, leniency • *He threw himself upon the mercy of the court.* 3 = **blessing**, boon, godsend
mere *adj* = **simple**, common, pure, plain, bare, sheer, nothing more than
merely *See* **only**
meretricious *adj* = **trashy**, flashy, showy,

DICTIONARY

merge Ⓣ *v* (cause to) combine or blend
▸ **merger** *n* combination of business firms into one
meridian *n* **1** imaginary circle of the earth passing through both poles **2** peak or zenith
meringue [mer-**rang**] *n* **1** baked mixture of egg whites and sugar **2** small cake of this
merino *n, pl* **-nos 1** breed of sheep with fine soft wool **2** this wool
merit Ⓣ *n* **1** excellence or worth **merits 2** admirable qualities ▹ *v* **-iting, -ited 3** deserve
▸ **meritorious** *adj* deserving praise
▸ **meritocracy** [mer-it-**tok**-rass-ee] *n* rule by people of superior talent or intellect
merlin *n* small falcon
mermaid *n* imaginary sea creature with the upper part of a woman and the lower part of a fish
merry Ⓣ *adj* **-rier, -riest 1** cheerful or jolly **2** *informal* slightly drunk **merrily** *adv* **merriment** *n*
▸ **merry-go-round** *n* revolving circular platform on which people ride for amusement
▸ **merrymaking** *n* revelry
Merton *n* **Thomas** (**Feverel**). 1915–68, US writer, monk, and mystic; noted esp. for his autobiography *The Seven Storey Mountain* (1948)
mescaline *n* hallucinogenic drug obtained from the tops of mescals
▸ **mescal** [mess-**kal**] *n* spineless globe-shaped cactus of Mexico and the SW of the USA
mesdames *n* plural of **madame**
mesdemoiselles *n* plural of **mademoiselle**
mesh Ⓣ *n* **1** network or net **2** (open space between) strands forming a network ▹ *v* **3** (of gear teeth) engage
mesmerize Ⓣ *v* **1** hold spellbound **2** *obsolete* hypnotize
meson [**mee**-zon] *n* elementary atomic particle
mess Ⓣ *n* **1** untidy or dirty confusion **2** trouble or difficulty **3** group of servicemen who regularly eat together **4** place where they eat ▹ *v* **5** muddle or dirty **6** (foll. by *about*) potter about **7** (foll. by *with*) interfere with **8** (of servicemen) eat in a group
message Ⓣ *n* **1** communication sent **2** meaning or moral
▸ **messenger** *n* bearer of a message
▸ **message board** internet discussion forum
Messager *n* **André** (**Charles Prosper**). 1853–1929, French composer and conductor
Messiaen *n* **Olivier**. 1908–92, French composer and organist. His music is distinguished by its rhythmic intricacy; he was influenced by Hindu and Greek rhythms and bird song
Messiah *n* **1** Jews' promised deliverer **2** Christ **Messianic** *adj*
messieurs *n* plural of **monsieur**
Messrs [**mess**-erz] *n* plural of **Mr**
messy Ⓣ *adj* **messier, messiest** dirty, confused, or untidy **messily** *adv* **messiness** *n*
met *v* past of **meet**[1]

THESAURUS

gaudy, garish, tinsel, gimcrack, tawdry
merge *v* = **combine**, meet, join, mix, unite, blend, converge, fuse, mingle, amalgamate, coalesce
merger *n* = **union**, coalition, combination, consolidation, fusion, amalgamation, incorporation
merit *n* **1** = **worth**, value, excellence, virtue • *Box-office success mattered more than artistic merit.* **2** = **advantage**, asset, strength, virtue, strong point • *Despite its merits, the work would never be used.* ▸ *v* **3** = **deserve**, earn, warrant, be entitled to, be worthy of • *Such ideas merit careful consideration.*
See also: **quality**
meritorious *adj* = **praiseworthy**, good, excellent, worthy, deserving, admirable, commendable, laudable, virtuous, creditable
merriment *n* = **fun**, laughter, festivity, amusement, glee, revelry, hilarity, jollity, joviality, mirth
merry *adj* = **cheerful**, happy, festive, jolly, joyous, carefree, blithe, convivial
mesh *n* **1** = **net**, network, web, netting, tracery ▸ *v* **2** = **engage**, connect, combine, knit, coordinate, harmonize, interlock, dovetail, link
mesmerize *v* = **entrance**, grip, fascinate, captivate, enthrall, hypnotize, hold spellbound
mess *n* **1** = **disorder**, chaos, disarray • *I'll clear up the mess later.* **2** = **difficulty**, fix (*informal*), jam (*informal*), turmoil, muddle • *the reasons why the economy is in such a mess* ▸ *v* **3** (often with *up*) = **bungle**, botch up (*informal*), make a hash of (*informal*), muck up (*slang*) • *He had messed up his career.* **4** (often with *up*) = **dirty**, clutter, dishevel, disarrange, scramble, pollute, muddle **5** (often with *with*) = **interfere**, play, tamper, meddle, tinker
▹ **mess around** = **putter**, fool, dabble, amuse oneself *or* fool around, play around, trifle, toy with
See also: **confusion, hole**
message *n* **1** = **communication**, note, word, dispatch, memo, bulletin, memorandum • *He left a voice-mail message.* **2** = **point**, moral, meaning, theme • *the story's anti-violence message*
messenger *n* = **courier**, envoy • *A messenger will deliver the documents.*
messy *adj* = **untidy**, dirty, sloppy (*informal*),

DICTIONARY

Met *adj, n informal* Meteorological (Office)
metabolism [met-**tab**-oh-liz-zum] *n* chemical processes of a living body **metabolic** *adj*
▸ **metabolic syndrome** condition associated with obesity, which increases the risk of cardiovascular disease and diabetes
▸ **metabolize** *v* produce or be produced by metabolism
metal *n* **1** mineral substance, such as iron or copper, that is malleable and capable of conducting heat and electricity **2** short for **road metal** ▸ **metallic** *adj*
▸ **metallurgy** *n* scientific study of the structure, properties, extraction, and refining of metals **metallurgical** *adj* **metallurgist** *n*
metamorphosis Ⓣ [met-a-**more**-foss-is] *n, pl* **-phoses** [-foss-eez] change of form or character
▸ **metamorphic** *adj* (of rocks) changed in texture or structure by heat and pressure
▸ **metamorphose** *v* transform
metaphor Ⓣ *n* figure of speech in which a term is applied to something it does not literally denote in order to imply a resemblance, such as *he is a lion in battle* **metaphorical** *adj* **metaphorically** *adv*
metaphysics *n* branch of philosophy concerned with being and knowing **metaphysical** *adj*
Metastasio *n* **Pietro**, original name *Pietro Antonio Domenico Trapassi*. 1698–1782, Italian poet and librettist; Viennese court poet (from 1730). His works include *La clemenza di Tito* (1732)
mete Ⓣ *v* (usu. foll. by *out*) deal out as punishment
meteor *n* small fast-moving heavenly body, visible as a streak of incandescence if it enters the earth's atmosphere
▸ **meteoric** [meet-ee-**or**-rik] *adj* **1** of a meteor **2** brilliant but short-lived
▸ **meteorite** *n* meteor that has fallen to earth
meteorology *n* study of the earth's atmosphere, esp. for weather forecasting **meteorological** *adj* **meteorologist** *n*
meter *n* **1** instrument for measuring and recording something, such as the consumption of gas or electricity ▹ *v* **2** measure by meter
methamphetamine *n* variety of amphetamine used for its stimulant action
methane *n* colourless inflammable gas
methanol *n* colourless poisonous liquid used as a solvent and fuel (Also **methyl alcohol**)
methinks *v, past tense* **methought** *obsolete* it seems to me
method Ⓣ *n* **1** way or manner **2** technique **3** orderliness
▸ **methodical** *adj* orderly **methodically** *adv*
▸ **methodology** *n* particular method or procedure
Methodist *n* **1** member of any of the Protestant churches originated by Wesley and his followers ▹ *adj* **2** of Methodists or their Church **Methodism** *n*
Methodius *n* **Saint**, with his younger brother Saint Cyril called *the Apostles of the Slavs*. 815–885 AD, Greek Christian theologian sent as a missionary to the Moravians. Feast day: Feb 14 or May 11
methyl *n* (compound containing) a saturated hydrocarbon group of atoms
▸ **methylated spirits** alcohol with methanol added, used as a solvent and for heating
meticulous Ⓣ *adj* very careful about details **meticulously** *adv*
métier [**met**-ee-ay] *n* **1** profession or trade **2** one's strong point
metonymy [mit-**on**-im-ee] *n* figure of speech in which one thing is replaced by another associated with it, such as 'the Crown' for 'the king'
metre Ⓣ *n* **1** basic unit of length equal to

THESAURUS

chaotic, confused, cluttered, dishevelled, disordered, disorganized, muddled, scuzzy (*slang*), shambolic
metamorphosis *n* = **transformation**, change, conversion, mutation, alteration, transmutation
metaphor *n* = **figure of speech**, image, symbol, analogy, allegory, trope
metaphorical *adj* = **figurative**, symbolic, emblematic, allegorical
mete *v* = **distribute**, deal, assign, administer, dispense, apportion, portion
meteoric *adj* = **spectacular**, fast, overnight, sudden, rapid, brilliant, speedy, swift, dazzling
method *n* **1** = **way**, approach, procedure, technique, mode • *her favourite method of making popcorn* **2** = **orderliness**, system, order, organization, purpose, pattern, regularity, planning
See also: **fashion, plan, practice, process, style**
methodical *adj* = **orderly**, regular, organized, deliberate, precise, systematic, structured, disciplined, meticulous, businesslike
meticulous *adj* = **thorough**, particular, strict, exact, precise, painstaking, fussy, scrupulous, fastidious, punctilious
meticulously *See* **well**
metre *See* **beat**

m

DICTIONARY

about 1.094 yards **2** rhythm of poetry
▸ **metric** *adj* of the decimal system of weights and measures based on the metre
▸ **metrical** *adj* **1** of measurement **2** of poetic metre
▸ **metrication** *n* conversion to the metric system
metro *n, pl* **metros** underground railway system, esp. in Paris
Metro *n* metropolitan city administration
metronome *n* instrument which marks musical time by means of a ticking pendulum
metropolis Ⓣ [mit-**trop**-oh-liss] *n* chief city of a country or region
▸ **metropolitan** *adj* of a metropolis
mettle Ⓣ *n* courage or spirit
mew *n* **1** cry of a cat ▹ *v* **2** utter this cry
mews *n Brit* yard or street orig. of stables, now often converted to houses
Mexican *adj* **1** of Mexico ▹ *n* **2** person from Mexico
Meyerbeer *n* **Giacomo**, real name *Jakob Liebmann Beer.* 1791–1864, German composer, esp. of operas, such as *Robert le diable* (1831) and *Les Huguenots* (1836)
mezzanine [**mez**-zan-een] *n* intermediate storey, esp. between the ground and first floor
mezzo-soprano [**met**-so-] *n* voice or singer between a soprano and contralto
mezzotint [**met**-so-tint] *n* **1** method of engraving by scraping the roughened surface of a metal plate **2** print so made
mg milligram(s)
Mg *chem* magnesium
Mgr manager
MHz megahertz
miaow [mee-**ow**] *n, v* same as **mew**
miasma [mee-**azz**-ma] *n* unwholesome or foreboding atmosphere
mica [**my**-ka] *n* glasslike mineral used as an electrical insulator
mice *n* plural of **mouse**
Michael *n* **Saint**. *Bible* one of the archangels. Feast day: Sept 29 or Nov 8
Michaelmas [**mik**-kl-mass] *n* Sept. 29th, feast of St Michael the archangel
Michelangelo *n* full name *Michelangelo Buonarroti.* 1475–1564, Florentine sculptor, painter, architect, and poet; one of the outstanding figures of the Renaissance. Among his creations are the sculptures of *David* (1504) and of *Moses* which was commissioned for the tomb of Julius II, for whom he also painted the ceiling of the Sistine Chapel (1508–12). *The Last Judgment* (1533–41), also in the Sistine, includes a torturous vision of Hell and a disguised self-portrait. His other works include the design of the Laurentian Library (1523–29) and of the dome of St Peter's, Rome
Michelozzo *n* full name *Michelozzo di Bartolommeo.* 1396–1472, Italian architect and sculptor. His most important design was the Palazzo Riccardo for the Medici family in Florence (1444–59)
Michener *n* **(Daniel) Roland**. 1900–91, Canadian lawyer and politician; Speaker of the House of Commons (1957–62) and Governor General (1967–74)
mickey[1] *n* half bottle of alcoholic liquor
mickey[2] *n* **take the mickey (out of)** *informal* tease
micro *n, pl* **-cros** short for **microcomputer, microprocessor**
micro- *combining form* **1** small or minute: *microcopy* **2** denoting a millionth part: *microsecond*
microbe Ⓣ *n* minute organism, esp. one causing disease **microbial** *adj*
microbiology *n* branch of biology involving the study of microorganisms
microbiologist *n*
microblog *n* **1** social networking site consisting only of updates ▹ *v* **2** participate in microblogging **microblogging** *n, adj*
microchip *n* small wafer of silicon containing electronic circuits
microcomputer *n* computer having a central processing unit contained in one or more silicon chips
microcosm *n* **1** miniature representation of something **2** man regarded as epitomizing the universe
microdot *n* photographic copy of a document reduced to pinhead size
microfiche [**my**-crow-feesh] *n* microfilm in sheet form
microfilm *n* miniaturized recording of books or documents on a roll of film
microlight *n* very small light private aircraft with large wings
micrometer [my-**krom**-it-er] *n* instrument for measuring very small distances or angles
micron [**my**-kron] *n* one millionth of a metre
microorganism *n* organism of microscopic size
microphone *n* instrument for amplifying or transmitting sounds
microprocessor *n* integrated circuit acting

THESAURUS

metropolis *See* **city**
mettle *n* = **courage**, life, resolution, spirit, nerve, pluck, bravery, fortitude, vigour, gallantry, valour
microbe *n* = **microorganism**, virus, bacterium, bug (*informal*), germ, bacillus

m

DICTIONARY

as the central processing unit in a small computer
microscope *n* instrument with lens(es) which produces a magnified image of a very small body
▶ **microscopic** *adj* **1** too small to be seen except with a microscope **2** very small **3** of a microscope **microscopically** *adv*
▶ **microscopy** *n* use of a microscope
microsurgery *n* intricate surgery using a special microscope and miniature precision instruments
microwave Ⓣ *n* **1** electromagnetic wave with a wavelength of a few centimetres, used in radar and cooking **2** microwave oven ▷ *v* **3** cook in a microwave oven
▶ **microwave oven** oven using microwaves to cook food quickly
micturate *v* urinate **micturition** *n*
mid *adj* intermediate, middle
▶ **midday** *n* noon
▶ **midland** *n* middle part of a country
▶ **midnight** *n* twelve o'clock at night
▶ **midshipman** *n* naval officer of the lowest commissioned rank
▶ **midsummer** *n* **1** middle of summer **2** summer solstice
▶ **Midsummer Day** June 24th
▶ **midtown** *n* the centre of a town
▶ **midway** *adj, adv* **1** halfway ▷ *n* **2** place for games, rides, etc. at a fair
▶ **midwinter** *n* **1** middle or depth of winter **2** winter solstice
midden *n* dunghill or rubbish heap
middle Ⓣ *n* **1** point or part equidistant from two extremes ▷ *adj* **2** equidistant from two extremes **3** medium, intermediate
▶ **middle age** period of life between youth and old age **middle-aged** *adj*
▶ **Middle Ages** period from about 1000 AD to the 15th century
▶ **middle class** social class of businessmen and professional people **middle-class** *adj*
▶ **Middle East** area around the eastern Mediterranean up to and including Iran
▶ **middleman** *n* trader who buys from the producer and sells to the consumer
▶ **middle-of-the-road** *adj* **1** politically moderate **2** (of music) generally popular
▶ **middleweight** *n* boxer weighing up to 160lb (professional) or 75kg (amateur)
middling Ⓣ *adj* **1** mediocre **2** moderate ▷ *adv* **3** moderately
midge *n* small mosquito-like insect
midget Ⓣ *n* very small person or thing
MIDI [**mid**-ee] *adj* denoting a specification for the external control of electronic musical instruments: *a MIDI system*
midriff *n* middle part of the body
midst Ⓣ *n* **in the midst of 1** surrounded by **2** at a point during
midwife *n* trained person who assists at childbirth **midwifery** *n*
mien [**mean**] *n lit* person's bearing, demeanour, or appearance
Mies van der Rohe *n* **Ludwig**. 1886–1969, US architect, born in Germany. He directed the Bauhaus (1929–33) and developed a functional style, characterized by geometrical design. His works include the Seagram building, New York (1958)
miffed *adj informal* offended or upset
might[1] *v* past tense of **may**
might[2] Ⓣ *n* power or strength
▶ **with might and main** energetically or forcefully
▶ **mighty** *adj* **1** powerful **2** important ▷ *adv* **3** *informal* very **mightily** *adv*
mignonette [min-yon-**net**] *n* grey-green plant with sweet-smelling flowers
migraine [**mee**-grain] *n* severe headache, often with nausea and other symptoms

THESAURUS

microscopic *adj* = **tiny**, minute, invisible, negligible, minuscule, imperceptible, infinitesimal
microwave *See* **cook**
midday *n* = **noon**, noonday, twelve o'clock
middle *n* **1** = **centre**, midst, halfway point • *in the middle of the room* ▶ *adj* **2** = **central**, halfway • *the middle house*
middle-class *adj* = **bourgeois**, traditional, conventional
middling *adj* **1** = **mediocre**, indifferent, so-so (*informal*), tolerable, unremarkable, unexceptional **2** = **moderate**, medium, average, fair, modest, ordinary, adequate, passable, serviceable, all right, O.K. *or* okay (*informal*)
midget *n* = **dwarf**, shrimp (*informal*), pygmy *or* pigmy, Tom Thumb
midnight *n* = **twelve o'clock**, dead of night, middle of the night, the witching hour
midst *n* ▷ **in the midst of** = **among**, during, amidst, in the middle of, in the thick of, surrounded by
midway *adj, adv* = **halfway**, betwixt and between, in the middle
might *n* = **power**, force, energy, strength, vigor ▷ **with might and main** = **forcefully**, vigorously, mightily, lustily, manfully
mightily *adv* **1** = **very**, much, highly, extremely, greatly, hugely, intensely, decidedly, exceedingly **2** = **powerfully**, strongly, vigorously, forcefully, lustily, energetically, manfully
mighty *adj* = **powerful**, strong, robust, vigorous, forceful, sturdy, lusty, strapping
migrant *n* **1** = **wanderer**, immigrant,

DICTIONARY

migrate ❶ *v* **1** move from one place to settle in another **2** (of animals) journey between different habitats at specific seasons **migration** *n*
▸ **migrant** *n, adj* (person or animal) that migrates **migratory** *adj*
mike *n informal* microphone
milch [**miltch**] *adj* (of a cow) giving milk
mild ❶ *adj* **1** not strongly flavoured **2** gentle **3** calm or temperate **mildly** *adv* **mildness** *n*
mildew *n* destructive fungus on plants or things exposed to damp **mildewed** *adj*
mile *n* unit of length equal to 1760 yards or 1.609 km
▸ **mileage** *n* **1** distance travelled in miles **2** miles travelled by a motor vehicle per gallon of gasoline **3** *informal* usefulness of something
▸ **milestone** *n* **1** stone marker showing the distance to a certain place **2** significant event
Milhaud *n* **Darius**. 1892–1974, French composer; member of Les Six. A notable exponent of polytonality, his large output includes operas, symphonies, ballets, string quartets, and songs
milieu ❶ [**meal**-yoo] *n, pl* **milieus, milieux** [**meal**-yooz] environment or surroundings
militant ❶ *adj* aggressive or vigorous in support of a cause **militancy** *n*
military ❶ *adj* **1** of or for soldiers, armies, or war ▹ *n* **2** armed services **militarized** *adj*
▸ **militarism** *n* belief in the use of military force and methods **militarist** *n*
militate ❶ *v* (usu. foll. by *against* or *for*) have a strong influence or effect
militia [mill-**ish**-a] *n* military force of trained citizens for use in emergency only **militiaman** *n*
milk ❶ *n* **1** white fluid produced by female mammals to feed their young **2** milk of cows, goats, etc. used by man as food **3** fluid in some plants. ▹ *v* **4** draw milk from **5** exploit (a person or situation) **milky** *adj*
▸ **Milky Way** luminous band of stars stretching across the night sky
▸ **milkmaid** *n* (esp. formerly) woman who milks cows
▸ **milkman** *n* man who delivers milk to people's houses
▸ **milkshake** *n* frothy flavoured cold milk drink
▸ **milksop** *n* feeble man
▸ **milk teeth** first set of teeth in young mammals
mill[1] ❶ *n* **1** factory **2** machine for grinding, processing, or rolling ▹ *v* **3** put through a mill **4** move in a confused manner **5** cut fine grooves across the edges of (coins)
▸ **miller** *n* person who works in a mill
▸ **millstone** *n* flat circular stone for grinding corn
▸ **mill wheel** water wheel that drives a mill
mill[2] *n* one thousandth of a dollar
Mill *n* **1 James**. 1773–1836, Scottish philosopher, historian, and economist. He expounded Bentham's utilitarian philosophy in *Elements of Political Economy* (1821) and *Analysis of the Phenomena of the Human Mind* (1829) and also wrote a *History of British India* (1817–18) **2** his son, **John Stuart**. 1806–73, English philosopher and economist. He modified Bentham's utilitarian philosophy in *Utilitarianism* (1861) and in his treatise *On Liberty* (1859) he defended the rights and freedom of the individual. Other works include *A System of Logic* (1843) and *Principles of Political Economy* (1848)
Millais *n* Sir **John Everett**. 1829–96, English painter, who was a founder of the Pre-

THESAURUS

rover, traveller, nomad, itinerant, drifter, emigrant ▸ *adj* **2** = **travelling**, immigrant, migratory, nomadic, transient, itinerant, drifting, roving, shifting, vagrant, wandering
migrate *v* = **move**, travel, journey, wander, roam, trek, voyage, emigrate, rove
migration *n* = **wandering**, travel, movement, journey, trek, voyage, emigration, roving
migratory *adj* = **nomadic**, migrant, transient, itinerant, peripatetic, roving
mild *adj* **1** = **weak**, insipid • *a mild shampoo* OPPOSITE: strong **2** = **gentle**, meek, placid • *a mild approach* **3** = **temperate**, balmy • *The area is famous for its mild winter climate.*
See also: **calm, quiet**
mildness *n* = **gentleness**, clemency, warmth, moderation, calmness, tranquillity, docility, placidity
miles *See* **far**
milieu *n* = **surroundings**, environment, scene, location, element, background, setting, locale
militant *adj* = **aggressive**, active, vigorous, combative, assertive
military *adj* **1** = **warlike**, armed, martial, soldierly ▸ *n* **2** = **armed forces**, army, forces, services
militate *v* ▹ **militate against** = **counteract**, oppose, counter, resist, be detrimental to, conflict with, tell against, weigh against
milk *v* = **exploit**, pump, extract, take advantage of
mill *n* **1** = **factory**, plant, foundry, works **2** = **grinder**, crusher ▸ *v* **3** = **grind**, pound, crush, powder, grate **4** = **swarm**, crowd, throng
millstone *n* **1** = **grindstone**, quernstone **2** = **burden**, weight, load, affliction,

DICTIONARY

Raphaelite Brotherhood. His works include *The Order of Release* (1853) and *The Blind Girl* (1856)
millennium [mill-**en**-ee-yum] *n, pl* **-niums, -nia** **1** period of a thousand years **2** future period of peace and happiness
millepede [**mill**-lip-peed] *n* same as **millipede**
Miller *n* **1** (**Alton**) **Glenn**. 1904–44, US composer, trombonist, and band leader. His popular compositions include "Moonlight Serenade." During World War II he was leader of the US Air Force band in Europe. He disappeared without trace on a flight between England and France **2** Sir **Jonathan** (**Wolfe**). born 1934, British doctor, actor, and theatre director. His productions include Shakespeare, Ibsen, and Chekhov as well as numerous operas. He has also presented many television medical programs
millet *n* a cereal grass
Millet *n* **Jean François**. 1814–75, French painter of the Barbizon school, noted for his studies of peasants at work
milli- *combining form* denoting a thousandth part: *millisecond*
millibar *n* unit of atmospheric pressure
Milligan *n* **Spike**, real name *Terence Alan Milligan*. 1918–2002, Irish radio, stage, and film comedian and author, born in India. He appeared in *The Goon Show* (with Peter Sellers and Harry Secombe; BBc Radio, 1952–60) and his films include *Postman's Knock* (1962), *Adolf Hitler, My Part in his Downfall* (1972), *The Three Musketeers* (1974), *The Last Remake of Beau Geste* (1977), and *Yellowbeard* (1982). He was awarded an honorary knighthood in 2000
milligram *n* thousandth part of a gram
Millikan *n* **Robert Andrews**. 1868–1953, US physicist. He measured the charge of an electron (1910), verified Einstein's equation for the photoelectric effect (1916), and studied cosmic rays; Nobel prize for physics 1923
millilitre *n* thousandth part of a litre
millimetre *n* thousandth part of a metre
milliner *n* maker or seller of women's hats
millinery *n*
million *n* one thousand thousands
millionth *adj, n*
▸ **millionaire** *n* person who owns at least a million pounds, dollars, etc.
millipede, millepede [**mill**-lip-peed] *n* small animal with a jointed body and many pairs of legs
Milne *n* **A**(**lan**) **A**(**lexander**). 1882–1956, English writer, noted for his books and verse for children, including *When We Were Very Young* (1924) and *Winnie the Pooh* (1926)
Milošević *n* **Slobodan**. 1941–2006, Serbian politician, president of Serbia (1989–97) and of the Federal Republic of Yugoslavia (1997–2000). He supported ethnic cleansing in Bosnia-Herzegovina (1992–95) and Kosovo (1998–99). He was ousted in 2000 and brought to trial (2001) for war crimes
milt *n* sperm of fish
Milton *n* **John**. 1608–74, English poet. His early works, notably *L'Allegro* and *Il Penseroso* (1632), the masque *Comus* (1634), and the elegy *Lycidas* (1637), show the influence of his Christian humanist education and his love of Italian Renaissance poetry. A staunch Parliamentarian and opponent of episcopacy, he published many pamphlets during the Civil War period, including *Areopagitica* (1644), which advocated freedom of the press. His greatest works were the epic poems *Paradise Lost* (1667; 1674), and *Paradise Regained* (1671) and the verse drama *Samson Agonistes* (1671)
mime Ⓣ *n* **1** acting without the use of words **2** performer who does this ▹ *v* **3** act in mime
mimic Ⓣ *v* **-icking, -icked** **1** imitate (a person or manner), esp. for satirical effect ▹ *n* **2** person or animal clever at mimicking
mimicry *n*
mimosa *n* shrub with fluffy yellow flowers and sensitive leaves
min. **1** minimum **2** minute(s)
mina *n* same as **myna**
Minamoto Yoritomo *n* 1147–99, Japanese nobleman; the first shogun (1192–99) of the feudal era
minaret *n* tall slender tower of a mosque
minatory *adj* threatening or menacing
mince Ⓣ *Brit* ▹ *v* **1** cut or grind into very small pieces **2** soften or moderate (one's words) **3** walk or speak in an affected manner ▹ *n* **4** minced meat
▸ **mincer** *n* machine for mincing meat
▸ **mincing** *adj* affected in manner
▸ **mincemeat** *n* sweet mixture of dried fruit and spices
▸ **mince pie** pie containing mincemeat

THESAURUS

albatross, encumbrance
mime *v* = **act out**, represent, gesture, simulate
mimic *v* **1** = **imitate**, do (*informal*), caricature, ape, parody, impersonate ▸ *n* **2** = **imitator**, impressionist, copycat (*informal*), impersonator, caricaturist
mimicry *n* = **imitation**, caricature, parody, mockery, impersonation, burlesque, mimicking
mince *v* **1** = **cut**, grind, chop, crumble, hash **2** (~ *words*) = **tone down**, moderate, weaken, spare, soften
mincing *adj* = **affected**, camp (*informal*), precious, pretentious, dainty, effeminate, foppish, sissy

DICTIONARY

mind Ⓣ *n* **1** thinking faculties **2** memory or attention **3** intention **4** sanity ▷ *v* **5** take offence at **6** take care of **7** pay attention to **8** be cautious or careful about (something)
▸ **minded** *adj* having an inclination as specified: *politically minded*
▸ **minder** *n Brit slang* aide or bodyguard
▸ **mindful** *adj* **1** keeping aware **2** heedful
▸ **mindless** *adj* **1** stupid **2** requiring no thought **3** careless
mine[1] *pron* belonging to me
mine[2] Ⓣ *n* **1** deep hole for digging out coal, ores, etc. **2** bomb placed under the ground or in water **3** profitable source ▷ *v* **4** dig for minerals **5** dig (minerals) from a mine **6** place explosive mines in or on
▸ **miner** *n* person who works in a mine
▸ **minefield** *n* area of land or water containing mines
▸ **minesweeper** *n* ship for clearing away mines
mineral *n* **1** naturally occurring inorganic substance, such as metal or coal ▷ *adj* **2** of, containing, or like minerals
▸ **mineralogy** [min-er-**al**-a-jee] *n* study of minerals **mineralogist** *n*
▸ **mineral water** water containing dissolved mineral salts or gases
minestrone [min-ness-**strone**-ee] *n* soup containing vegetables and pasta
mingle Ⓣ *v* **1** mix or blend **2** come into association (with)
Mingus *n* **Charles**, known as *Charlie Mingus*. 1922–79, US jazz double bassist, composer, and band leader
mingy *adj* **-gier, -giest** *informal* miserly
mini *n, adj* **1** (something) small or miniature **2** short (skirt)
mini- *combining form* smaller or shorter than usual: *mini-budget; minidress*
miniature Ⓣ *n* **1** small portrait, model, or copy ▷ *adj* **2** small-scale **miniaturist** *n*
▸ **miniaturize** *v* make to a very small scale
minibus *n* small bus
minicab *n Brit* ordinary automobile used as a taxi
minicomputer *n* computer smaller than a mainframe but more powerful than a microcomputer
minidisc *n* small recordable compact disc
minim *n Brit* half note
minimum Ⓣ *adj, n* least possible (amount or quantity)
▸ **minimal** *adj* minimum
▸ **minimize** *v* **1** reduce to a minimum **2** belittle
minion Ⓣ *n* servile assistant
miniseries *n* TV programme shown in several parts, often on consecutive days
miniskirt *n* very short skirt
minister Ⓣ *n* **1** head of a government department **2** diplomatic representative **3** member of the clergy ▷ *v* **4** (foll. by *to*) attend to the needs of **ministerial** *adj*

m

THESAURUS

mind *n* **1** = **brain**, head, imagination, psyche, intellect • *You have a very suspicious mind.* RELATED WORD *adj*: mental **2** = **memory**, remembrance, recollection **3** = **intention**, urge, wish, desire, notion, fancy, disposition, inclination, leaning **4** = **sanity**, reason, judgment, marbles (*informal*), mental balance, rationality, senses, wits ▷ **make up one's mind** = **decide**, choose, determine, resolve ▸ *v* **5** = **be bothered**, care, object • *I don't mind what you do.* **6** = **look after**, watch, keep an eye on, take care of • *My mother is minding the store.* **7** = **pay attention**, note, mark, observe, heed, obey, listen to, pay heed to, take heed **8** = **be careful**, watch, be cautious, be on guard *or* be on one's guard, be wary, take care
See also: **will**
mindful *adj* = **aware**, alert, careful, wary, conscious, watchful, alive to, heedful
mindless *adj* = **stupid**, foolish, idiotic, thoughtless, inane, moronic, unthinking, witless
mine *n* **1** = **pit**, deposit, shaft, excavation, colliery **2** = **source**, fund, stock, store, reserve, supply, wealth, treasury, abundance, hoard ▸ *v* **3** = **dig up**, extract, unearth, quarry, excavate, dig for, hew
miner *n* = **coalminer**
mingle *v* **1** = **mix**, join, combine, unite, merge, blend, interweave, intermingle **2** = **associate**, socialize, hobnob, consort, fraternize, hang about *or* hang around, rub shoulders (*informal*)
miniature *adj* = **small**, minute, little, toy, tiny, diminutive, minuscule, scaled-down
minimal *adj* = **minimum**, least, token, nominal, least possible, slightest, smallest
minimize *v* **1** = **reduce**, decrease, shrink, diminish, curtail, prune, miniaturize **2** = **play down**, discount, decry, disparage, underrate, belittle, deprecate, make light of *or* make little of
minimum *adj* **1** = **least possible**, minimal • *the minimum requirements for the job* OPPOSITE: maximum ▸ *n* **2** = **least**, lowest, nadir
minion *n* = **follower**, henchman, underling, lackey, flunky, hanger-on, hireling, yes man
minister *n* **1** = **clergyman**, cleric, priest, pastor, preacher, vicar, rector, parson ▸ *v* **2** = **attend**, serve, tend, administer, cater to, pander to, take care of
ministry *n* **1** = **department**, office, council,

DICTIONARY

▸ **ministration** *n* giving of help
▸ **ministry** *n* **1** profession or duties of a cleric **2** ministers collectively **3** government department
mink *n* **1** stoatlike animal **2** its highly valued fur
Minnelli *n* **Liza.** born 1946, US actress and singer, daughter of Judy Garland. Her films include *Charlie Bubbles* (1968), *Cabaret* (1972), *Arthur* (1981), and *Stepping Out* (1991)
minnow *n* small freshwater fish
minor Ⓣ *adj* **1** lesser **2** under age **3** *music* (of a scale) having a semitone above the second note ▹ *n* **4** person below the age of legal majority **5** *music* minor scale
▸ **minority** *n* **1** lesser number **2** smaller party voting together **3** group in a minority in any state **4** state of being a minor
▸ **minority government** (in parliamentary democracies) government that has fewer elected representatives than the combined total of the other parties
▸ **minor penalty** *hockey* penalty in which a player is sent off for two minutes
minster *n* cathedral or large church
minstrel Ⓣ *n* medieval singer or musician
mint[1] Ⓣ *n* **1** place where money is coined ▹ *v* **2** make (coins)
mint[2] *n* **1** aromatic herb **2** peppermint **3** candy flavoured with this
Minto *n* **4th Earl of**, title of *Gilbert John Murray Kynynmond Eliot*. 1845–1914, British soldier and statesman; Governor General of Canada (1898–1904)
minuet [min-new-**wet**] *n* **1** stately dance **2** music for this
minus Ⓣ *prep, adj* **1** reduced by the subtraction of **2** *informal* without **3** less than zero ▹ *n* **4** sign (–) denoting subtraction or a number less than zero
minuscule Ⓣ [**min**-niss-skyool] *adj* very small
minute[1] Ⓣ [**min**-it] *n* **1** 60th part of an hour or degree **2** moment **minutes 3** record of the proceedings of a meeting ▹ *v* **4** record in the minutes
minute[2] Ⓣ [my-**newt**] *adj* **1** very small **2** precise **minutely** *adv*
▸ **minutiae** [my-**new**-shee-eye] *pl n* trifling or precise details
minx Ⓣ *n* bold or flirtatious girl
Mirabeau *n* **Comte de**, title of *Honoré-Gabriel Riqueti*. 1749–91, French Revolutionary politician
miracle Ⓣ *n* **1** wonderful supernatural event **2** marvel **miraculous** *adj* **miraculously** *adv*
▸ **miracle play** medieval play based on a sacred subject
mirage Ⓣ [mir-**rahzh**] *n* optical illusion, esp. one caused by hot air
mire Ⓣ *n* **1** swampy ground **2** mud
Miró *n* **Joan.** 1893–1983, Spanish surrealist painter
mirror Ⓣ *n* **1** coated glass surface for reflecting images ▹ *v* **2** reflect in or as if in a mirror
mirth Ⓣ *n* laughter, merriment, or gaiety
mirthful *adj* **mirthless** *adj*
mis- *prefix* wrong(ly), bad(ly)
misadventure Ⓣ *n* unlucky chance

THESAURUS

bureau, quango **2** = **holy orders**, the church, the priesthood
minor *adj* = **lesser**, slight, secondary, petty, trivial, trifling • *a minor injury* OPPOSITE: major
See also: **child, inferior, insignificant, unimportant**
minstrel *n* = **musician**, singer, bard, songstress, troubadour
mint *v* = **make**, strike, produce, cast, stamp, punch, coin
minus *See* **disadvantage**
minuscule *adj* = **tiny**, minute, little, miniature, diminutive, microscopic, infinitesimal
minute[1] *n* = **moment**, second, flash, instant • *I'll be with you in just a minute.*
minute[2] *adj* **1** = **tiny**, small, negligible, microscopic, slender • *Only a minute amount is needed.* OPPOSITE: vast **2** = **precise**, close, critical, detailed, exact, exhaustive, painstaking, meticulous, punctilious
minutes *pl n* = **record**, transcript, memorandum, notes, proceedings, transactions
minutiae *pl n* = **details**, finer points, ins and outs, niceties, particulars, subtleties, trifles, trivia
minx *n* = **flirt**, coquette, hussy
miracle *n* = **wonder**, marvel • *It was a miracle that nobody was seriously hurt in the crash.*
miraculous *adj* = **wonderful**, amazing, extraordinary, incredible, unbelievable, phenomenal, unaccountable, prodigious, astonishing, astounding
mirage *n* = **illusion**, hallucination, optical illusion
mire *n* **1** = **swamp**, bog, quagmire, marsh, morass **2** = **mud**, dirt, ooze, muck, slime
mirror *n* **1** = **looking-glass**, glass, reflector ▸ *v* **2** = **reflect**, follow, copy, echo, emulate
mirth *n* = **merriment**, fun, laughter, amusement, glee, revelry, cheerfulness, gaiety, hilarity, jollity, joviality
mirthful *adj* = **merry**, happy, festive, playful, jolly, cheerful, light-hearted, cheery, jovial, blithe, sportive
misadventure *n* = **misfortune**, accident,

m

DICTIONARY

misanthrope [**miz**-zan-thrope], **misanthropist** [miz-**zan**-thrope-ist] *n* person who dislikes people in general **misanthropic** [miz-zan-**throp**-ik] *adj* **misanthropy** [miz-**zan**-throp-ee] *n*
misapprehend Ⓣ *v* misunderstand **misapprehension** *n*
misappropriate Ⓣ *v* take and use (money) dishonestly **misappropriation** *n*
misbehave Ⓣ *v* behave badly **misbehaviour** *n*
miscalculate Ⓣ *v* calculate or judge wrongly **miscalculation** *n*
miscarriage Ⓣ *n* **1** spontaneous premature expulsion of a fetus from the womb **2** failure: *a miscarriage of justice*
▸ **miscarry** *v* **1** have a miscarriage **2** fail
miscast *v* **-casting, -cast** cast (a role or actor) in (a play or film) inappropriately
miscegenation [miss-ij-in-**nay**-shun] *n* interbreeding of races
miscellaneous Ⓣ [miss-sell-**lane**-ee-uss] *adj* mixed or assorted
▸ **miscellany** [miss-**sell**-a-nee] *n* mixed assortment
mischance Ⓣ *n* unlucky event
mischief Ⓣ *n* **1** annoying but not malicious behaviour **2** inclination to tease **3** harm
▸ **mischievous** [**miss**-chiv-uss] *adj* **1** full of mischief **2** intended to cause harm **mischievously** *adv*
miscible [**miss**-sib-bl] *adj* able to be mixed
misconception Ⓣ *n* wrong idea or belief
misconduct Ⓣ *n* **1** immoral or unethical behaviour **2** *hockey* penalty in which a player is usually sent off for 10 minutes
misconstrue *v* interpret wrongly **misconstruction** *n*
miscreant Ⓣ [**miss**-kree-ant] *n* wrongdoer
misdeed Ⓣ *n* wrongful act
misdemeanour Ⓣ *n* minor wrongdoing
misdirect *v* give (someone) wrong directions or instructions **misdirection** *n*
miser Ⓣ *n* person who hoards money and hates spending it **miserly** *adj*
miserable Ⓣ *adj* **1** very unhappy, wretched **2** causing misery **3** squalid **4** mean
▸ **misery** *n* **1** great unhappiness **2** *informal* complaining person

THESAURUS

disaster, reverse, setback, catastrophe, debacle, mishap, calamity, bad luck
misanthropic *adj* = **antisocial**, cynical, unfriendly, malevolent
misapprehend *v* = **misunderstand**, mistake, misinterpret, misread, misconstrue
misapprehension *n* = **misunderstanding**, mistake, error, misconception, delusion, fallacy, misinterpretation
misappropriate *v* = **steal**, pocket, misuse, misspend, embezzle, peculate
misbehave *v* = **act up**, be disobedient, make a fuss, make trouble, make waves
miscalculate *v* = **misjudge**, underestimate, err, blunder, overrate, overestimate, underrate, slip up
miscarriage *n* = **failure**, error, breakdown, mishap, perversion
miscarry *v* = **fail**, misfire, come to grief, fall through, go awry, go wrong
miscellaneous *adj* = **assorted**, various, mixed, diverse, varied, jumbled, motley, sundry
miscellany *n* = **assortment**, collection, variety, mixture, medley, jumble, anthology, hodgepodge, *mélange* (*French*), mixed bag, potpourri
mischance *n* = **misfortune**, accident, disaster, mishap, misadventure, calamity
mischief *n* **1** = **misbehavior**, trouble, impishness, monkey business (*informal*), naughtiness, shenanigans (*informal*), waywardness **2** = **harm**, injury, damage, hurt, trouble, evil, misfortune
mischievous *adj* **1** = **naughty**, troublesome, playful, wayward, impish, puckish, rascally, roguish, sportive **2** = **malicious**, harmful, evil, vicious, destructive, wicked, hurtful, damaging, spiteful
misconception *n* = **delusion**, error, misunderstanding, fallacy, misapprehension
misconduct *n* = **immorality**, wrongdoing, mismanagement, impropriety, malpractice
miscreant *n* = **wrongdoer**, criminal, rogue, villain, rascal, sinner, reprobate, scoundrel, vagabond
misdeed *n* = **offence**, crime, wrong, fault, misconduct, sin, misdemeanor, transgression
misdemeanour *n* = **offence**, fault, infringement, misdeed, transgression, peccadillo
See also: **crime**
miser *n* = **skinflint**, cheapskate (*informal*), niggard, penny-pincher (*informal*), Scrooge
miserable *adj* **1** = **unhappy**, down, low, sad, depressed, mournful, dejected, melancholy, downcast, wretched • *a job that made me miserable* OPPOSITE: cheerful **2** = **gloomy**, sorry, pathetic, wretched • *It's a miserable job, but someone has to do it.*
miserly *adj* = **mean**, stingy, avaricious, grasping, niggardly, parsimonious, penny-pinching (*informal*), tightfisted, ungenerous
misery *n* = **unhappiness**, depression, woe, grief, sadness, sorrow, despair, melancholy • *All that money brought nothing but misery.* OPPOSITE: joy

m

DICTIONARY

misfire ⓣ *v* **1** (of a firearm or engine) fail to fire correctly **2** (of a plan) fail to turn out as intended
misfit ⓣ *n* person not suited to his or her environment
misfortune ⓣ *n* (piece of) bad luck
misgiving ⓣ *n* feeling of fear or doubt
misguided ⓣ *adj* mistaken or unwise
mishandle ⓣ *v* handle or treat badly or inefficiently
mishap ⓣ *n* minor accident
mishear *v* hear (what someone says) wrongly
Mishima *n* **Yukio**. 1925–70, Japanese novelist and short-story writer, whose works reflect a preoccupation with homosexuality and death. He committed harakiri in protest at the decline of traditional Japanese values
mishmash *n* confused collection or mixture
misinform ⓣ *v* give incorrect information to **misinformation** *n*
misinterpret ⓣ *v* understand or represent (something) wrongly **misinterpretation** *n*
misjudge ⓣ *v* judge wrongly or unfairly **misjudgment** *or* **misjudgement** *n*
mislay ⓣ *v* lose (something) temporarily
mislead ⓣ *v* give false or confusing information to **misleading** *adj*
mismanage ⓣ *v* organize or run (something) badly **mismanagement** *n*
misnomer [miss-**no**-mer] *n* **1** wrongly applied name **2** use of this
misogyny [miss-**oj**-in-ee] *n* hatred of women **misogynist** *n*
misplace ⓣ *v* **1** put in the wrong place **2** mislay **3** give (trust or affection) inappropriately
misprint ⓣ *n* printing error
mispronounce *v* pronounce (a word) wrongly **mispronunciation** *n*
misquote ⓣ *v* quote inaccurately **misquotation** *n*
misrepresent ⓣ *v* represent wrongly or inaccurately
misrule ⓣ *v* **1** govern inefficiently or unjustly ▷ *n* **2** inefficient or unjust government
miss ⓣ *v* **1** fail to hit, reach, find, catch, or notice **2** not be in time for **3** notice or regret the absence of **4** avoid **5** fail to take advantage of ▷ *n* **6** fact or instance of missing
▶ **missing** *adj* lost or absent
Miss *n* title of a girl or unmarried woman
missal *n* book containing the prayers and rites of the Mass
misshapen ⓣ *adj* badly shaped, deformed
missile ⓣ *n* object or weapon thrown, shot, or launched at a target

m

THESAURUS

See also: **evil, hell, pain**
misfire *v* = **fail**, miscarry, fall through, go wrong
misfit *n* = **nonconformist**, eccentric, oddball (*informal*), fish out of water (*informal*), square peg *or* square peg in a round hole (*informal*)
misfortune *n* **1** = **mishap**, disaster, tragedy, reverse, setback, calamity, affliction • *I had the misfortune of seeing that movie.* **2** = **bad luck**, trouble, adversity, tribulation
See also: **blow, hardship, sorrow**
misgiving *n* = **unease**, worry, doubt, suspicion, uncertainty, anxiety, reservation, apprehension, distrust, qualm, trepidation
misguided *adj* = **unwise**, mistaken, unwarranted, erroneous, ill-advised, imprudent, deluded, injudicious, misplaced
mishandle *v* = **mismanage**, botch, bungle, muff, make a mess of, mess up (*informal*)
mishap *n* = **accident**, misadventure, calamity, misfortune, mischance
misinform *v* = **mislead**, deceive, misdirect, misguide
misinterpret *v* = **misunderstand**, mistake, misrepresent, distort, misread, misconstrue, misjudge, misapprehend, misconceive
misjudge *v* = **miscalculate**, underestimate, overrate, overestimate, underrate
mislaid *See* **lost**
mislay *v* = **lose**, misplace, lose track of
mislead *v* = **deceive**, fool, misinform, misdirect, delude, hoodwink, misguide
misleading *adj* = **confusing**, false, deceptive, ambiguous, disingenuous, evasive
mismanage *v* = **mishandle**, misconduct, botch, misdirect, bungle, make a mess of, mess up, misgovern
misplace *v* = **lose**, lose track of, mislay
misplaced *See* **lost**
misprint *n* = **mistake**, literal, typo (*informal*), corrigendum, erratum
misquote *v* = **misrepresent**, twist, falsify
misrepresent *v* = **distort**, twist, falsify • *The salesperson deliberately misrepresented the condition of the used printer.*
misrule *n* = **disorder**, chaos, confusion, turmoil, lawlessness, anarchy
miss *v* **1** = **fail to notice**, mistake, overlook • *It's on the second floor. You can't miss it.* **2** = **long for**, pine for, yearn for • *We missed our friends when we moved.* **3** = **avoid**, escape, evade **4** = **mistake**, failure, error, oversight, blunder, omission
See also: **lack**
misshapen *adj* = **deformed**, twisted, grotesque, crooked, distorted, contorted, malformed, warped
missile *n* = **rocket**, weapon, projectile
missing *adj* = **absent**, lost, astray, lacking,

DICTIONARY

mission Ⓣ *n* **1** specific task or duty **2** group of people sent on a mission **3** building in which missionaries work **4** military expedition or operation for a specific purpose
▸ **missionary** *n, pl* **-aries** person sent abroad to spread religion
missive Ⓣ *n* letter
misspell *v* spell (a word) wrongly
misspent Ⓣ *adj* wasted or misused
missus, missis *n informal* one's wife or the wife of the person addressed or referred to
mist Ⓣ *n* **1** thin fog **2** fine spray of liquid
▸ **misty** *adj* **1** full of mist **2** dim or obscure
mistiness *n*
mistake Ⓣ *n* **1** error or blunder ▹ *v* **-taking, -took, -taken 2** misunderstand **3** confuse (a person or thing) with another
Mister *n* polite form of address to a man
mistime *v* do (something) at the wrong time
Mistinguett *n* original name *Jeanne-Marie Bourgeois*. 1875–1956, French dancer, chanteuse, and entertainer
mistletoe *n* evergreen plant with white berries growing as a parasite on trees
mistral *n* strong dry northerly wind of S France
mistreat Ⓣ *v* treat (a person or animal) badly
mistress Ⓣ *n* **1** woman who is the illicit lover of a married man **2** woman in control of people or things **3** female teacher
mistrial *n law* trial which is invalid because of some error
mistrust Ⓣ *v* **1** not trust ▹ *n* **2** lack of trust
mistrustful *adj*
misunderstand Ⓣ *v* fail to understand properly **misunderstanding** *n*
misuse Ⓣ *n* **1** incorrect, improper, or careless use ▹ *v* **2** use wrongly **3** treat badly
Mitchell *n* **1 Joni**, original name *Roberta Joan Anderson*. born 1943, Canadian folk-rock singer and songwriter. Her albums include *Blue* (1971), *Court and Spark* (1974), *Mingus* (1979), *Turbulent Indigo* (1994), and *Travelogue* (2002) **2 Margaret**. 1900–49, US novelist; author of *Gone with the Wind* (1936)
Mitchum *n* **Robert**. 1917–97, US film actor. His many films include *Night of the Hunter* (1955) and *Farewell my Lovely* (1975)
mite *n* **1** very small spider-like animal **2** very small thing or amount
mitigate Ⓣ *v* make less severe **mitigation** *n*
mitre [**my**-ter] *n* **1** bishop's pointed headdress **2** joint between two pieces of wood bevelled to meet at right angles ▹ *v* **3** join with a mitre joint
mitt *n* **1** short for **mitten 2** baseball catcher's glove
mitten *n* glove with one section for the thumb and one for the four fingers together
Mitterrand *n* **François Maurice Marie**.

THESAURUS

left out, mislaid, misplaced, unaccounted-for
mission *n* = **task**, job, commission, duty, quest, assignment, undertaking, errand, vocation
missionary *n* = **evangelist**, preacher, apostle
missive *n* = **letter**, report, note, message, communication, dispatch, memorandum, epistle
misspent *adj* = **wasted**, imprudent, dissipated, profitless, squandered
mist *n* = **fog**, film, spray, cloud, steam, smog, haze, vapour
mistake *n* **1** = **error**, oversight, gaffe, blunder, blooper (*informal*), slip-up • *spelling mistakes* ▸ *v* **2** = **confuse with**, misinterpret as, mix up with, take for • *I mistook her for the owner of the house.* **3** = **misunderstand**, misinterpret, misread, misconstrue, misjudge, misapprehend
See also: **confuse, miss, mix-up**
mistaken *adj* = **wrong**, false, faulty, incorrect, inaccurate, misguided, erroneous, unsound, wide of the mark
mistakenly *adv* = **incorrectly**, wrongly, falsely, erroneously, inaccurately, by mistake, fallaciously, misguidedly
mistimed *adj* = **inopportune**, untimely, badly timed, ill-timed
mistreat *v* = **ill-treat**, abuse • *The dog had been mistreated by its former owner*
mistress *n* = **lover**, girlfriend, concubine, kept woman, paramour
mistrust *v* **1** = **doubt**, suspect, fear, distrust, be wary of ▸ *n* **2** = **suspicion**, doubt, uncertainty, skepticism, distrust, misgiving, wariness
mistrustful *adj* = **suspicious**, skeptical, wary, uncertain, fearful, doubtful, cynical, hesitant, chary, distrustful
misty *adj* = **foggy**, obscure, murky, dim, cloudy, hazy, overcast, opaque, blurred, indistinct
misunderstand *v* = **misinterpret**, mistake, misread, misconstrue, misjudge, be at cross-purposes, get the wrong end of the stick, misapprehend
misunderstanding *n* = **mistake**, error, mix-up, misconception, misjudgment, misinterpretation
misuse *n* **1** = **waste**, abuse, desecration, misapplication, squandering ▸ *v* **2** = **waste**, abuse, prostitute, squander, desecrate, misapply
mitigate *v* = **ease**, moderate, soften, subdue, temper, lessen, lighten, extenuate
mitigation *n* = **alleviation**, relief, moderation, remission, diminution, extenuation

DICTIONARY

1916–96, French statesman; first secretary of the socialist party (1971–95); president (1981–95)
mix Ⓣ *v* **1** combine or blend into one mass **2** form (something) by mixing **3** be sociable ▷ *n* **4** mixture **mixed** *adj* **mixer** *n*
▶ **mixture** *n* **1** something mixed **2** combination
▶ **mix up** *v* **1** confuse **2** make into a mixture
▶ **mix-up** *n* confused situation
▶ **mixed-up** *adj informal* confused
mizzenmast *n* mast nearest the stern of a full-rigged ship
mks units *pl n* metric system of units based on the metre, kilogram, and second
ml millilitre(s)
MLA Member of the Legislative Assembly
Mlle *pl* **Mlles** Mademoiselle
mm millimetre(s)
MM plural of **M 1**
Mme *pl* **Mmes** Madame
Mn *chem* manganese
MNA Member of the National Assembly (of Quebec)
mnemonic [nim-**on**-ik] *n, adj* (rhyme etc.) intended to help the memory
mo *n Brit informal* short for **moment**
MO Medical Officer
moan Ⓣ *n* **1** low cry of pain **2** *informal* grumble ▷ *v* **3** make or utter with a moan **4** *informal* grumble
moat *n* deep wide ditch, esp. round a castle
mob Ⓣ *n* **1** disorderly crowd **2** *slang* gang ▷ *v* **mobbing, mobbed 3** surround in a mob to acclaim or attack
mobile Ⓣ *adj* **1** able to move ▷ *n* **2** hanging structure designed to move in air currents **mobility** *n*
▶ **mobile phone** cordless phone powered by batteries
mobilize Ⓣ *v* **1** (of the armed services) prepare for active service **2** organize for a purpose **mobilization** *n*
moccasin *n* soft leather shoe
mocha [**mock**-a] *n* **1** kind of strong dark coffee **2** flavouring made from coffee and chocolate
mock Ⓣ *v* **1** make fun of **2** mimic ▷ *n* **3** imitation **mocks 4** *informal* practice exams taken before public exams ▷ *adj* **5** sham or imitation
▶ **put the mockers on** *informal* ruin the chances of success of
▶ **mockery** *n* **1** derision **2** inadequate attempt
▶ **mocking bird** N American bird which imitates other birds' songs
▶ **mock orange** shrub with white fragrant flowers

m

THESAURUS

mix *v* **1 = combine**, merge, blend, mingle, amalgamate • *Mix the ingredients together slowly.* **2 = socialize**, associate, mingle, hobnob, consort, fraternize, hang out (*informal*) ▷ **mix up = confuse**, muddle • *People often mix us up*; **= combine**, mix, blend ▷ **mix up with** *See* **mistake** ▶ *n* **3 = mixture**, combination, compound, blend, alloy, fusion, medley, assortment, amalgam
mixed *adj* **1 = combined**, joint, compound, composite, amalgamated, blended, mingled, united **2 = varied**, diverse, assorted, cosmopolitan, miscellaneous, heterogeneous, motley
mixed-up *adj* **= confused**, upset, distraught, disturbed, at sea, bewildered, maladjusted, muddled, perplexed, puzzled
mixture *n* **= combination**, compound, hybrid, blend, alloy, fusion, medley, amalgamation • *a sticky mixture of flour and water*
See also: **cross, union, variety**
mix-up *n* **= mistake**, misunderstanding, muddle • *a mix-up in the hotel reservations*
moan *v* **1 = groan**, grunt • *He moaned in his sleep.* **2 = complain**, whine, grumble, groan • *He's always moaning about how much homework he has.* ▶ *n* **3 = groan**, grunt • *He let out a moan when he heard the sad news.* **4 = complaint**, protest, whine, grumble, gripe (*informal*), grouse, grouch (*informal*)
See also: **lament**
mob *n* **1 = crowd**, host, mass, pack, flock, swarm, throng, multitude, drove, horde **2** (*Slang*) **= gang**, group, set, lot, crew (*informal*) ▷ **mob violence** *See* **riot** ▶ *v* **3 = surround**, jostle, crowd around, set upon, swarm around
mobile *adj* **= movable**, portable, moving, itinerant, peripatetic, travelling, wandering
mobilize *v* **= prepare**, rally, ready, organize, activate, marshal, call to arms, call up, get ready *or* make ready
mock *v* **1 = make fun of**, ridicule, deride (*formal*), laugh at, poke fun at, scoff at • *Don't mock me when I'm only trying to help.* **2 = mimic**, caricature, ape, parody, satirize, imitate, lampoon ▶ *adj* **3 = imitation**, fake, false, counterfeit, artificial, bogus, phony (*informal*), dummy, sham, feigned, pretended • *mock laughter*
See also: **tease**
mockery *n* **1 = derision**, ridicule, jeering • *Was there a hint of mockery in his eyes?* **2 = farce**, apology (*informal*), joke, disappointment, letdown
See also: **scorn**
mocking *adj* **= derisive**, satirical, disrespectful, sarcastic, sardonic, contemptuous, disdainful, scoffing, scornful

DICTIONARY

▸ **mock-up** *n* full-scale model for test or study
mod[1] *n* member of a group of young people, orig. in the mid-1960s, who are very clothes-conscious, ride motor scooters, and like a particular kind of pop music
mod[2] *n* annual Highland Gaelic meeting with musical and literary competitions
MOD Ministry of Defence
mod. **1** moderate **2** modern
mod cons *pl n informal* modern conveniences, such as heating and hot water
mode Ⓣ *n* **1** method or manner **2** particular fashion
▸ **modish** [**mow**-dish] *adj* in fashion
model Ⓣ *n* **1** (miniature) representation **2** pattern **3** person or thing worthy of imitation **4** person who poses for an artist or photographer **5** person who wears clothes to display them to prospective buyers ▹ *v* -**elling, -elled 7** make a model of **8** mould **9** display (clothing) as a model
modem [**mow**-dem] *n* device for connecting two computers by a telephone line
moderate Ⓣ *adj* **1** not extreme **2** temperate **3** average ▹ *n* **4** person of moderate views ▹ *v* **5** make or become less violent or extreme **6** preside over a meeting etc. **moderately** *adv* **moderation** *n*
▸ **moderator** *n* **1** president of a Presbyterian body **2** arbitrator
modern Ⓣ *adj* **1** of present or recent times **2** in current fashion **modernity** *n*
▸ **modernism** *n* (support of) modern tendencies, thoughts, or styles **modernist** *n*
▸ **modernize** *v* bring up to date **modernization** *n*
modest Ⓣ *adj* **1** not vain or boastful **2** shy **3** not excessive **4** not showy or pretentious **modestly** *adv* **modesty** *n*
modicum Ⓣ *n* small quantity
modify Ⓣ *v* **-fying, -fied 1** change slightly **2** tone down **3** (of a word) qualify (another word) **modification** *n*
▸ **modifier** *n* word that qualifies another
modulate Ⓣ *v* **1** vary in tone **2** adjust **3** change the key of (music) **modulator** *n*
▸ **modulation** *n* **1** modulating **2** *electronics* superimposing of a wave or signal on to another wave or signal
module *n* self-contained unit, section, or component with a specific function
modus operandi [**mow**-duss op-er-**an**-die] *n Latin* method of operating
moggy *n, pl* **-gies** *slang* cat
mogul Ⓣ [**mow**-gl] *n* important or powerful person

THESAURUS

mode *n* **1 = method**, way, system, process, form, style, procedure, technique, manner **2 = fashion**, look, trend, style, rage, vogue, craze
model *n* **1 = representation**, replica, dummy • *an architect's model of the new art gallery* **2 = paragon**, example, ideal, epitome • *The essay is a model of clarity.* **3 = sitter**, subject, poser ▸ *v* **4 = shape**, form, fashion, carve, mould, sculpt • *clay modelled into the shape of a bear* **5 = show off**, sport (*informal*), wear, display
See also: **design, make**
moderate *adj* **1 = average**, medium, fair, reasonable, middling • *moderate exercise* **2 = mild**, steady, limited, modest, reasonable, gentle, controlled, restrained, middle-of-the-road ▸ *v* **3 = tone down**, ease, curb, relax, soften, temper, abate • *They are hoping he will moderate his views.*
See also: **change**
moderately *adv* **= reasonably**, rather, quite, slightly, somewhat, fairly, passably, tolerably
moderation *n* **= restraint**, fairness, reasonableness, temperance
modern *adj* **1 = current**, recent, present, contemporary, present-day • *modern society* **2 = up-to-date**, new, latest, up-to-the-minute • *modern technology* OPPOSITE: old-fashioned
modernity *n* **= newness**, currency, innovation, novelty, freshness
modernize *v* **= update**, renew, revamp, renovate, remake, rejuvenate, remodel, make over
modest *adj* **1 = small**, moderate, limited, middling • *a modest improvement* **2 = humble**, unassuming • *Although an award-winning writer, she is modest about her achievements.* OPPOSITE: conceited
See also: **low, reasonable**
modesty *n* **= reserve**, humility, reticence, bashfulness, coyness, demureness, diffidence, shyness, timidity
modicum *n* **= little**, drop, bit, touch, scrap, shred, fragment, crumb
modification *n* **= change**, variation, adjustment, revision, qualification, alteration, refinement
modify *v* **1 = change**, reform, convert, adjust, revise, alter, adapt, rework, remodel **2 = tone down**, lower, ease, qualify, moderate, soften, temper, restrain, lessen
modish *adj* **= fashionable**, in, current, cool (*informal*), smart, contemporary, stylish, chic, chic, trendy (*informal*), up-to-the-minute, phat (*slang*), voguish
modulate *v* **= adjust**, balance, regulate, tune, vary, attune
mogul *n* **= tycoon**, baron, big cheese (*informal*), magnate, big shot (*informal*), V.I.P.

DICTIONARY

mohair *n* **1** fine hair of the Angora goat **2** yarn or fabric made from this
Mohammed II *n* ?1430–81, Ottoman sultan of Turkey (1451–81). He captured Constantinople (1453) and conquered large areas of the Balkans
Mohammedan *adj, n* (not in Muslim use) same as **Muslim**
mohawk *n* punk hairstyle with shaved sides and a stiff central strip of hair, often brightly coloured
mohican *n esp. Brit* mohawk
moiety [**moy**-it-ee] *n, pl* **-ties** half
moiré [**mwahr**-ray] *adj* **1** having a watered or wavelike pattern ▷ *n* **2** any fabric that has such a pattern
moist Ⓣ *adj* slightly wet
▸ **moisten** *v* make or become moist
▸ **moisture** *n* liquid diffused as vapour or condensed in drops
▸ **moisturize** *v* add moisture to (the skin etc.)
molar *n* large back tooth used for grinding
molasses *n* dark syrup, a by-product of sugar refining
mold *n* same as **mould**
mole[1] *n* small dark raised spot on the skin
mole[2] *n* **1** small burrowing mammal **2** *informal* spy who has infiltrated and become a trusted member of an organization
mole[3] *n* **1** breakwater **2** harbour protected by this
mole[4] *n* unit of amount of substance
molecule Ⓣ [**mol**-lik-kyool] *n* **1** simplest freely existing chemical unit, composed of two or more atoms **2** very small particle
molecular [mol-**lek**-yew-lar] *adj*
molest Ⓣ *v* **1** interfere with sexually **2** annoy or injure **molester** *n* **molestation** *n*
moll *n slang* **1** gangster's female accomplice **2** prostitute
mollify Ⓣ *v* **-fying, -fied** pacify or soothe
mollification *n*
mollusc *n* soft-bodied, usu. hard-shelled animal such as a snail or oyster
mollycoddle Ⓣ *v* pamper
Molotov *n* **Vyacheslav Mikhailovich,** original surname *Skriabin.* 1890–1986, Soviet statesman. As commissar and later minister for foreign affairs (1939–49; 1953–56) he negotiated the nonaggression pact with Nazi Germany and attended the founding conference of the United Nations and the Potsdam conference (1945)
Molotov cocktail *n* gasoline bomb
molten Ⓣ *adj* liquefied or melted
molybdenum [mol-**lib**-din-um] *n* silver-white metallic element
mom *n* an informal word for **mother**
moment Ⓣ *n* **1** short space of time **2** (present) point in time
▸ **momentary** *adj* lasting only a moment
momentarily *adv*
momentous Ⓣ [mow-**men**-tuss] *adj* of great significance
momentum Ⓣ [mow-**men**-tum] *n, pl* **-ta, -tums 1** product of a body's mass and velocity **2** impetus of a moving body
monarch Ⓣ *n* sovereign ruler of a state
monarchical *adj*
▸ **monarchist** *n* supporter of monarchy
▸ **monarchy** *n* government by or a state ruled by a sovereign
monastery Ⓣ *n, pl* **-teries** residence of a religious order
▸ **monastic** *adj* **1** of monks, nuns, or monasteries **2** ascetic **monasticism** *n*

THESAURUS

moist *adj* = **damp**, wet, soggy, humid, clammy, dewy
moisten *v* = **dampen**, water, wet, soak, damp, moisturize
moisture *n* = **dampness**, water, liquid, dew, wetness
molecule *n* = **particle**, speck, jot
molest *v* **1** = **annoy**, worry, disturb, plague, bother, harass, persecute, beset, torment, badger, pester **2** = **abuse**, attack, hurt, harm, maltreat, ill-treat, interfere with
mollify *v* = **pacify**, quiet, calm, sweeten, appease, soothe, placate, conciliate, de-stress
mollycoddle *v* = **pamper**, baby, spoil, indulge, cosset
molten *See* **liquid**
moment *n* **1** = **instant**, second, minute, split second • *He paused for a moment.* **2** = **point**, time, instant • *At that moment, the doorbell rang.*
momentarily *adv* = **briefly**, temporarily, for a moment
momentary *adj* = **brief**, short, temporary, passing, short-lived, fleeting, transitory
momentous *adj* = **significant**, important, critical, historic, crucial, vital, pivotal, fateful, weighty
momentum *n* = **impetus**, force, power, drive, energy, push, strength, thrust, propulsion
monarch *n* = **ruler**, king, queen, prince *or* princess, sovereign, emperor *or* empress, potentate
monarchy *n* **1** = **sovereignty**, autocracy, kingship, monocracy, royalism **2** = **kingdom**, empire, realm, principality
monastery *n* = **abbey**, convent, cloister, friary, nunnery, priory
monastic *adj* = **monkish**, reclusive, secluded, contemplative, ascetic, cloistered, hermit-like, sequestered, withdrawn

DICTIONARY

Monck *n* **Charles Stanley**, 4th Viscount. 1819–1894, British statesman, born in Ireland. Governor General of British North America (1861–67); first Governor General of Canada (1867–68)
Mondale *n* **Walter** (**Frederick**). born 1928, US Democratic politician; vice president of the US (1977–81)
Monday *n* second day of the week
Mondrian *n* **Piet**. 1872–1944, Dutch painter, noted esp. as an exponent of the abstract art movement De Stijl
Monet *n* **Claude**. 1840–1926, French landscape painter; the leading exponent of impressionism. His interest in the effect of light on colour led him to paint series of pictures of the same subject at different times of day. These include *Haystacks* (1889–93), *Rouen Cathedral* (1892–94), the *Thames* (1899–1904), and *Water Lilies* (1899–1906)
monetary Ⓣ *adj* of money or currency
▸ **monetarism** *n* theory that inflation is caused by an increase in the money supply
monetarist *n, adj*
money Ⓣ *n* medium of exchange, coins or banknotes
▸ **moneyed** *or* **monied** *adj* rich
Mongolian *n* **1** person from Mongolia **2** language of Mongolia ▹ *adj* **3** of Mongolia or its language
mongolism *n offensive* Down's syndrome
▸ **mongol** *n, adj offensive* (person) affected by this
mongoose *n, pl* **-gooses** stoatlike mammal of Asia and Africa that kills snakes
mongrel Ⓣ *n* **1** animal, esp. a dog, of mixed breed **2** hybrid ▹ *adj* **3** of mixed breed
monitor Ⓣ *n* **1** person or device that checks, controls, warns, or keeps a record of something **2** pupil assisting a teacher with duties **3** television set used in a studio to check what is being transmitted **4** type of large lizard ▹ *v* **5** watch and check on
monk Ⓣ *n* member of an all-male religious community bound by vows **monkish** *adj*
▸ **monkshood** *n* poisonous plant with hooded flowers
Monk *n* **Thelonious** (**Sphere**). 1920–82, US jazz pianist and composer
monkey Ⓣ *n* **1** long-tailed primate **2** mischievous child ▹ *v* **3** (usu. foll. by *about* or *around*) meddle or fool
▸ **monkey puzzle** coniferous tree with sharp stiff leaves
▸ **monkey wrench** wrench with adjustable jaws
Monmouth *n* **James Scott**, Duke of Monmouth. 1649–85, the illegitimate son of Charles II of England, he led a rebellion against James II in support of his own claim to the Crown; captured and beheaded
mono- *combining form* single: *monolingual*
monochrome *adj* **1** in only one colour **2** black-and-white
monocle [**mon**-a-kl] *n* eyeglass for one eye only
monocular *adj* having or for one eye only
monogamy *n* custom of being married to one person at a time
monogram *n* design of combined letters, esp. a person's initials
monograph *n* book or paper on a single subject
monolith *n* large upright block of stone
monolithic *adj*
monologue Ⓣ *n* **1** dramatic piece for one performer **2** long speech by one person
monomania *n* obsession with one thing
monomaniac *n, adj*
monoplane *n* airplane with one pair of wings
monopoly *n* **1** *pl* **-lies** exclusive possession of or right to do something **monopolist** *n*
▸ **monopolize** *v* have or take exclusive possession of
monorail *n* single-rail railway
monosodium glutamate *n* white crystalline substance used as a food additive to enhance protein flavours
monosyllable *n* word of one syllable
monosyllabic *adj*
monotheism *n* belief in only one God

m

THESAURUS

monetary *adj* = **financial**, capital, cash, fiscal, budgetary, pecuniary
money *n* = **cash**, capital, dough (*informal*), funds • *I needed to earn some money*. RELATED WORD *adj*: pecuniary
See also: **financial, wealth**
mongrel *n* **1** = **hybrid**, cross, crossbreed, half-breed ▸ *adj* **2** = **hybrid**, crossbred
monitor *n* **1** = **watchdog**, guide, invigilator, supervisor ▸ *v* **2** = **check**, follow, survey, watch, observe, stalk, keep an eye on, keep tabs on, keep track of, bird dog (*informal*)
monk *n* = **friar**, brother
monkey *n* **1** = **simian**, primate **2** = **rascal**, devil, rogue, scamp, imp ▸ *v* **3** = **tinker**, play, mess, fool, meddle
monolithic *adj* = **huge**, massive, solid, monumental, colossal, impenetrable, intractable
monologue *n* = **speech**, lecture, sermon, harangue, soliloquy
monopolize *v* = **control**, dominate, hog (*slang*), corner the market in, keep to oneself, take over

DICTIONARY

monotheist *n* **monotheistic** *adj*
monotone *n* unvaried pitch in speech or sound **monotony** *n*
▸ **monotonous** *adj* tedious due to lack of variety **monotonously** *adv*
monoxide *n* oxide that contains one oxygen atom per molecule
Monroe *n* **1 James.** 1758–1831, US statesman; fifth president of the US (1817–25). He promulgated the Monroe Doctrine (1823) **2 Marilyn**, real name *Norma Jean Baker* or *Mortenson.* 1926–62, US film actress. Her films include *Niagara* (1952), *Gentlemen Prefer Blondes* (1953), and *Some Like It Hot* (1959)
Monseigneur [mon-sen-**nyur**] *n, pl* **Messeigneurs** [may-sen-**nyur**] title of French prelates
monsieur [muss-**syur**] *n, pl* **messieurs** [may-**syur**] French title of address equivalent to *sir* or *Mr*
Monsignor *n RC Church* title attached to certain offices
monsoon *n* **1** seasonal wind of SE Asia **2** rainy season accompanying this
monster Ⓣ *n* **1** imaginary, usu. frightening beast **2** very wicked person **3** huge person, animal, or thing ▷ *adj* **4** huge
▸ **monstrosity** *n* large ugly thing
▸ **monstrous** *adj* **1** unnatural or ugly **2** shocking or unjust **3** huge **monstrously** *adv*
monstrance *n RC Church* container in which the consecrated Host is exposed for adoration
montage [mon-tahzh] *n* **1** (making of) a picture composed from pieces of others **2** method of film editing incorporating several shots to form a single image
Montaigne *n* **Michel Eyquem de.** 1533–92, French writer. His life's work, the *Essays* (begun in 1571), established the essay as a literary genre and record the evolution of his moral ideas
Montana *n* **Joe.** born 1958, American football quarterback
Montcalm *n* **Louis Joseph**, Marquis de Montcalm de Saint-Véran. 1712–59, French general in Canada (1756); killed in Quebec by British forces under General Wolfe
Montespan *n* **Marquise de**, title of *Françoise Athénaïs de Rochechouart.* 1641–1707, French noblewoman; mistress of Louis XIV of France
Montesquieu *n* **Baron de la Brède et de**, title of *Charles Louis de Secondat.* 1689–1755, French political philosopher. His chief works are the satirical *Lettres persanes* (1721) and *L'Esprit des lois* (1748), a comparative analysis of various forms of government, which had a profound influence on political thought in Europe and the US
Monteverdi *n* **Claudio.** ?1567–1643, Italian composer, noted esp. for his innovations in opera and for his expressive use of dissonance. His operas include *Orfeo* (1607) and *L'Incoronazione di Poppea* (1642) and he also wrote many motets and madrigals
Montezuma II *n* 1466–1520, Aztec emperor of Mexico (?1502–20). He was overthrown and killed by the Spanish conquistador Cortés
Montgomery *n* **1 Bernard Law**, 1st Viscount Montgomery of Alamein, nicknamed *Monty*. 1887–1976, British field marshal. As commander of the 8th Army in North Africa, he launched the offensive, beginning with the victory at El Alamein (1942), that drove Rommel's forces back to Tunis **2 L(ucy) M(aud)**. 1874–1942, Canadian writer; author of *Anne of Green Gables* (1908)
month *n* **1** one of the twelve divisions of the calendar year **2** period of four weeks
▸ **monthly** *adj* **1** happening or payable once a month ▷ *adv* **2** once a month ▷ *n* **3** monthly periodical
monument Ⓣ *n* something that commemorates, esp. a building or statue
▸ **monumental** *adj* **1** large, impressive, or lasting **2** of or being a monument **3** *informal* extreme **monumentally** *adv*
moo *n* **1** long deep cry of a cow ▷ *v* **2** make this noise
mooch *v slang* loiter about aimlessly

THESAURUS

monotonous *adj* = **tedious**, boring, dull, repetitive, tiresome, unchanging, mind-numbing, humdrum, wearisome
monotony *n* = **tedium**, routine, boredom, monotonousness, repetitiveness, sameness, tediousness
monster *n* **1** = **brute**, devil, beast, villain, demon, fiend **2** = **freak**, mutant, monstrosity **3** = **giant**, mammoth, titan, colossus ▸ *adj* **4** = **huge**, massive, tremendous, enormous, mammoth, immense, gigantic, colossal, stupendous
monstrosity *n* = **eyesore**, horror, monster, freak
monstrous *adj* **1** = **unnatural**, horrible, gruesome, grotesque, hideous, frightful, fiendish, freakish **2** = **outrageous**, foul, shocking, disgraceful, scandalous, inhuman, intolerable, diabolical **3** = **huge**, massive, tremendous, enormous, mammoth, immense, colossal, prodigious, stupendous
monument *n* = **memorial**, marker, shrine, commemoration, tombstone, mausoleum, cenotaph, headstone, gravestone, cairn
monumental *adj* **1** = **important**, significant, historic, enormous, memorable, awesome, unforgettable, majestic, epoch-making **2** (*Informal*) = **immense**, great,

DICTIONARY

mood[1] Ⓣ *n* temporary (gloomy) state of mind ▸ **moody** *adj* **1** gloomy or sullen **2** changeable in mood **moodily** *adv*

mood[2] *n grammar* form of a *v* indicating whether it expresses a fact, wish, supposition, or command

Moodie *n* **Susanna** (née *Strickland*). 1803–85, Canadian writer, born in England. Her book *Roughing It in the Bush* (1852) describes her life as a settler in Upper Canada

moon Ⓣ *n* **1** natural satellite of the earth **2** natural satellite of any planet ▷ *v* **3** (foll. by *about* or *around*) be idle in a listless or dreamy way

▸ **moonlight** *n* **1** light from the moon ▷ *v* **2** *informal* work at a secondary job, esp. illegally

▸ **moonshine** *n* **1** illicitly distilled whisky **2** nonsense

▸ **moonstone** *n* translucent semiprecious stone

▸ **moonstruck** *adj* deranged

moor[1] Ⓣ *n* tract of open uncultivated ground covered with grass and heather

▸ **moorhen** *n* small black water bird

moor[2] Ⓣ *v* secure (a ship) with ropes etc.

▸ **mooring** *n* **1** place for mooring a ship

▸ **moorings 2** ropes etc. used to moor a ship

Moor *n* member of a Muslim people of NW Africa who ruled Spain between the 8th and 15th centuries **Moorish** *adj*

Moore *n* **1 Brian**. 1921–91, Canadian writer, born in Belfast. His novels include *The Luck of Ginger Coffey* (1960) and *The Great Victorian Collection* (1975) **2 Henry**. 1898–1986, British sculptor. His works are characterized by monumental organic forms and include the *Madonna and Child* (1943) at St Matthew's Church, Northampton

moose *n* large N American deer

▸ **moose pasture** *slang* worthless mining claim

moot Ⓣ *adj* **1** debatable: *a moot point* ▷ *v* **2** bring up for discussion

mop Ⓣ *n* **1** long stick with twists of cotton or a sponge on the end, used for cleaning **2** thick mass of hair ▷ *v* **mopping, mopped 3** clean or soak up with or as if with a mop

mope Ⓣ *v* be gloomy and apathetic

moped [**mow**-ped] *n* light motorcycle not over 50cc

moraine *n* accumulated mass of debris deposited by a glacier

moral Ⓣ *adj* **1** concerned with right and wrong conduct **2** based on a sense of right and wrong **3** (of support or a victory) psychological rather than practical ▷ *n* **4** lesson to be obtained from a story or event **morals 5** behaviour with respect to right and wrong **morally** *adv*

▸ **moralist** *n* person who lives by or expresses moral principles

▸ **morality** *n* **1** good moral conduct **2** moral goodness or badness

▸ **morality play** medieval play with a moral lesson

▸ **morality squad** *Canad* police unit enforcing laws concerning drugs, gambling, prostitution, pornography, etc.

▸ **moralize** *v* make moral pronouncements

morale Ⓣ [mor-**rahl**] *n* degree of confidence or hope of a person or group

Moranis *n* **Rick**. born 1953, Canadian comedian and actor. With Dave Thomas, he created the characters Bob and Doug Mackenzie, who humorously embody Canadian sterotypes. His films include the Ghostbusters series of films (1984–89) and *Honey, I Shrunk the Kids* (1989)

THESAURUS

massive, colossal, staggering

mood *n* = **state of mind**, humour, frame of mind, spirits, temper • *She was in a really cheerful mood.*

moody *adj* **1** = **sulky**, irritable, sullen, morose • *Despite his charm, he could sulk and be moody.* **2** = **temperamental**, volatile • *What a moody person - cheerful one moment and miserable the next.*

moon *n* **1** = **satellite** ▸ *v* **2** = **idle**, languish, daydream, mope, waste time

moor[1] *n* = **moorland**, heath

moor[2] *v* = **tie up**, secure, berth, anchor, dock, lash, make fast

moot *adj* **1** = **debatable**, controversial, undecided, doubtful, unresolved, unsettled, arguable, contestable, disputable ▸ *v* **2** = **bring up**, suggest, propose, broach, put forward

mop *n* **1** = **squeegee**, swab, sponge **2** = **mane**, shock, tangle, thatch ▸ *v* ▷ **mop up** = **clean up**, wash, wipe, swab, sponge, soak up

mope *v* = **brood**, moon, pine, languish, fret, pout, sulk

moral *adj* **1** = **good**, just, right, ethical, decent, noble, principled, honorable, virtuous, high-minded ▸ *n* **2** = **lesson**, point, message, meaning, significance

morale *n* = **confidence**, heart, spirit, self-esteem, esprit de corps

morality *n* **1** = **integrity**, justice, honesty, virtue, decency, goodness, righteousness **2** = **standards**, conduct, philosophy, mores, ethics, manners, morals, principles

morals *pl n* = **morality**, conduct, integrity, behaviour, mores, ethics, habits, manners,

DICTIONARY

morass Ⓣ *n* **1** marsh **2** mess
moratorium Ⓣ *n, pl* **-ria, -riums** legally authorized ban or delay
moray *n* large voracious eel
Moray, Murray *n* **1st Earl of**, title of *James Stuart*. ?1531–70, regent of Scotland (1567–70) following the abdication of Mary, Queen of Scots, his half-sister. He defeated Mary and Bothwell at Langside (1568); assassinated by a follower of Mary
morbid Ⓣ *adj* **1** unduly interested in death or unpleasant events **2** gruesome
mordant Ⓣ *adj* **1** sarcastic or scathing ▷ *n* **2** substance used to fix dyes
more Ⓣ *adj* **1** greater in amount or degree **2** comparative of **much, many 3** additional or further ▷ *adv* **4** to a greater extent **5** in addition ▷ *pron* **6** greater or additional amount or number
▸ **moreover** *adv* besides
More *n* Sir **Thomas**. 1478–1535, English statesman, humanist, and Roman Catholic Saint; Lord Chancellor to Henry VIII (1529–32). His opposition to the annulment of Henry's marriage to Catherine of Aragon and his refusal to recognize the Act of Supremacy resulted in his execution on a charge of treason. In *Utopia* (1516) he set forth his concept of the ideal state. Feast day: June 22 or July 6
Moreau *n* **Jeanne**. born 1928, French stage and film actress. Her films include *Jules et Jim* (1961), *Diary of a Chambermaid* (1964), and *The Proprietor* (1996)
mores [**more**-rayz] *pl n* customs and conventions embodying the fundamental values of a community
Morgan *n* **John Pierpont**. 1837–1913, US financier, philanthropist, and art collector
morganatic marriage *n* marriage of a person of high rank to a lower-ranking person whose status remains unchanged
Morgentaler *n* **Henry**. born 1923, Canadian physician, born in Poland. Campaigner for the legalization of abortion
morgue Ⓣ *n* mortuary
moribund Ⓣ *adj* without force or vitality
Morissette *n* **Alanis**. born 1974, Canadian singer-songwriter. Her albums include *Jagged Little Pill* (1995), *Under Rug Swept* (2004), and *Flavors of Entanglement* (2008)
Morley *n* **Thomas**. ?1557–?1603, English composer and organist, noted for his madrigals and his textbook on music, *A Plaine and Easie Introduction to Practicall Musicke* (1597)
Mormon *n* member of a religious sect founded in the USA **Mormonism** *n*
morn *n poetic* morning
mornay *adj* served with a cheese sauce: *sole mornay*
morning Ⓣ *n* part of the day before noon
▸ **morning-glory** *n* plant with trumpet-shaped flowers which close in the late afternoon
Moroccan *adj* **1** of Morocco ▷ *n* **2** person from Morocco
morocco *n* goatskin leather
moron Ⓣ *n* **1** mentally deficient person **2** *informal* fool **moronic** *adj*
morose Ⓣ [mor-**rohss**] *adj* sullen or moody
morphine, morphia *n* drug extracted from opium, used as an anesthetic and sedative
morphology *n* science of forms and structures of organisms or words **morphological** *adj*
Morphy *n* **Paul**. 1837–84, US chess player, widely considered to have been the world's greatest player
Morris *n* **William**. 1834–96, English poet, designer, craftsman, and socialist writer. He founded the Kelmscott Press (1890)
morris dance *n* traditional English folk

THESAURUS

principles, scruples, standards
morass *n* **1 = marsh**, swamp, bog, quagmire, slough, fen **2 = mess**, confusion, mix-up, tangle, muddle
moratorium *n* **= postponement**, halt, freeze, suspension, standstill
morbid *adj* **1 = unwholesome**, sick, unhealthy, gloomy, melancholy, sombre, ghoulish **2 = gruesome**, grisly, dreadful, macabre, horrid, hideous, ghastly
mordant *adj* **= sarcastic**, scathing, cutting, caustic, pungent, incisive, biting, stinging, trenchant
more *adj* **1 = extra**, further, additional, added • *I have more fries than you*. OPPOSITE: less ▸ *adv* **2 = to a greater extent**, further, longer, better ▷ **more than** *See* **over**
moreover *adv* **= furthermore**, also, too, further, besides, additionally, as well, in addition
morgue *n* **= mortuary**
moribund *adj* **= declining**, weak, stagnant, on its last legs, waning
morning *n* **1 = dawn**, sunrise, daybreak, morn (*poetic*), break of day **2 = forenoon**, a.m.
moron *n* **= fool**, idiot, imbecile, blockhead, cretin (*offensive*), dork (*slang*), dunce, dunderhead, halfwit, oaf, schmuck (*slang*)
moronic *adj* **= idiotic**, stupid, foolish, mindless, cretinous (*offensive*), halfwitted, imbecilic, unintelligent
morose *adj* **= sullen**, sour, depressed, gloomy, moody, surly, dour, glum, ill-tempered, sulky, taciturn

DICTIONARY

dance performed by men

Morrison *n* **1 Jim**, full name *James Douglas Morrison*. 1943–71, US rock singer and songwriter, lead vocalist with the Doors **2 Toni**, full name *Chloe Anthony Morrison*. born 1931, US novelist, whose works include *Sula* (1974), *Song of Solomon* (1977), *Beloved* (1987), *Jazz* (1992), and *Paradise* (1998): awarded the Nobel Prize for literature in 1993 **3 Van**, full name *George Ivan Morrison*. born 1945, Northern Irish rock singer and songwriter. His albums include *Astral Weeks* (1968), *Moondance* (1970), *Avalon Sunset* (1989), and *Days Like These* (1995)

Morrisseau *n* **Norval**, also known as *Copper Thunderbird*. 1932–2007, self-taught Canadian artist of Ojibwa ancestry

morrow *n poetic* next day

Morse *n* system of signalling in which letters of the alphabet are represented by combinations of short and long signals

morsel Ⓣ *n* small piece, esp. of food

mortal Ⓣ *adj* **1** subject to death **2** causing death ▷ *n* **3** mortal creature **mortally** *adv* ▶ **mortality** *n* **1** state of being mortal **2** great loss of life **3** death rate ▶ **mortal sin** *RC Church* sin meriting damnation

mortar *n* **1** mixture of lime, sand, and water for holding bricks and stones together **2** small cannon with a short range **3** bowl in which substances are pounded ▶ **mortarboard** *n* square academic cap

mortgage Ⓣ *n* **1** conditional pledging of property, esp. a house, as security for the repayment of a loan **2** the loan itself ▷ *v* **3** pledge (property) as security thus ▶ **mortgagee** *n* creditor in a mortgage ▶ **mortgagor** *or* **mortgager** *n* debtor in a mortgage

mortify Ⓣ *v* **-fying, -fied 1** humiliate **2** subdue by self-denial **3** (of flesh) become gangrenous **mortification** *n*

Mortimer *n* **1** Sir **John** (**Clifford**). 1923–2009, British barrister, playwright, and novelist, best known for the television series featuring the barrister Horace Rumpole. His novels include *Paradise Postponed* (1985) and *The Sound of Trumpets* (1998) **2 Roger de**, 8th Baron of Wigmore and 1st Earl of March. 1287–1330, lover of Isabella, the wife of Edward II of England: they invaded England in 1326 and compelled the king to abdicate in favour of his son, Edward III; executed

mortise, mortice [**more**-tiss] *n* hole in a piece of wood or stone shaped to receive a matching projection on another piece **mortise lock** lock set into a door

Morton *n* **Jelly Roll**, real name *Ferdinand Joseph La Menthe Morton*. 1885–1941, US jazz pianist, singer, and songwriter; one of the creators of New Orleans jazz

mortuary Ⓣ *n, pl* **-aries** building where corpses are kept before burial or cremation

mosaic [mow-**zay**-ik] *n* design or decoration using small bits of coloured stone or glass

Mosaic *adj* of Moses

Moselle *n* light white wine

Moses *n* **1** *Old Testament* the Hebrew prophet who led the Israelites out of Egypt to the Promised Land and gave them divinely revealed laws **2 Ed**. born 1956, US hurdler; winner of the 400 m hurdles in the 1976 and 1984 Olympic Games **3 Grandma**, real name *Anna Mary Robertson Moses*. 1860–1961, US painter of primitives, who began to paint at the age of 75

Moslem *n, adj* same as **Muslim**

Mosley *n* Sir **Oswald Ernald**. 1896–1980, British politician; founder of the British Union of Fascists (1932)

mosque *n* Muslim temple

mosquito *n, pl* **-toes, -tos** blood-sucking flying insect

moss *n* small flowerless plant growing in masses on moist surfaces **mossy** *adj*

Moss *n* **Carrie-Anne**. born 1967, Canadian film actress. Noted for her role in the *The Matrix* series of films (1999–2003)

m

THESAURUS

morsel *n* = **piece**, part, bit, taste, bite, scrap, crumb, tidbit, mouthful, *soupçon* (*French*)

mortal *adj* **1** = **human**, passing, transient, temporal, ephemeral, worldly, impermanent **2** = **fatal**, deadly, killing, terminal, lethal, destructive, murderous, death-dealing ▶ *n* **3** = **human being**, man, woman, human, person, individual, being, earthling

mortality *n* **1** = **humanity**, impermanence, transience **2** = **death**, killing, destruction, fatality, carnage, bloodshed

mortgage *See* **loan**

mortification *n* **1** = **humiliation**, shame, embarrassment, annoyance, chagrin, discomfiture, vexation **2** = **discipline**, control, denial, abasement, chastening, subjugation **3** (*Medical*) = **gangrene**, corruption, festering

mortified *adj* = **humiliated**, ashamed, crushed, embarrassed, chagrined, chastened, deflated, humbled, shamed

mortify *v* **1** = **humiliate**, crush, humble, embarrass, shame, deflate, chagrin, chasten **2** = **discipline**, control, deny, subdue, chasten, abase **3** (Of flesh) = **putrefy**, die, fester, deaden

mortuary *n* = **morgue**, funeral parlour

DICTIONARY

most Ⓣ *adj* **1** greatest in number or degree **2** superlative of **much, many** ▷ *n* **3** greatest number or degree ▷ *adv* **4** in the greatest degree
▶ **mostly** *adv* for the most part, generally
motel *n* roadside hotel for motorists
motet [mow-**tet**] *n* short sacred choral song
moth *n* nocturnal insect like a butterfly
▶ **mothball** *n* **1** small ball of camphor or naphthalene used to repel moths from stored clothes ▷ *v* **2** store (something operational) for future use **3** postpone (a project etc.)
▶ **moth-eaten** *adj* **1** eaten or damaged by moth larvae **2** decayed or scruffy
mother Ⓣ *n* **1** femalpe parent **2** head of a female religious community ▷ *adj* **3** native or inborn: *mother wit* ▷ *v* **4** look after as a mother **motherhood** *n* **motherly** *adj* **motherless** *adj*
▶ **mother-in-law** *n* mother of one's husband or wife
▶ **mother of pearl** iridescent lining of certain shells
▶ **mother tongue** one's native language
motif Ⓣ [mow-**teef**] *n* (recurring) theme or design
motion Ⓣ *n* **1** process, action, or way of moving **2** proposal in a meeting **3** *Brit* evacuation of the bowels ▷ *v* **4** direct (someone) by gesture
▶ **motionless** *adj* not moving
▶ **motion picture** film
Motion *n* Sir **Andrew**. born 1952, British poet and biographer; his collections include *Pleasure Steamers* (1978) and *Public Property* (2002): poet laureate 1999–2009
motive Ⓣ *n* **1** reason for a course of action ▷ *adj* **2** causing motion
▶ **motivate** *v* give incentive to **motivation** *n*
motley Ⓣ *adj* **1** miscellaneous **2** multicoloured ▷ *n* **3** *hist* jester's costume
motocross *n* motorcycle race over a rough course
motor *n* **1** engine, esp. of a vehicle **2** machine that converts electrical energy into mechanical energy **3** automobile ▷ *v* **4** travel by automobile **motorbike** *n* **motorboat** *n* **motorcar** *n* **motorcycle** *n* **motorcyclist** *n*
▶ **motorist** *n* driver of an automobile
▶ **motorize** *v* equip with a motor or motor transport
▶ **motorhome** *n* large motor vehicle designed for living in while travelling
▶ **motor scooter** a light motorcycle with small wheels and an enclosed engine
▶ **motorway** *n Brit* highway
mottled Ⓣ *adj* marked with blotches
motto Ⓣ *n, pl* **-toes, -tos** **1** saying expressing an ideal or rule of conduct **2** verse or maxim in a paper cracker
mould[1], mold Ⓣ *n* **1** hollow container in which metal etc. is cast **2** shape, form, or pattern **3** nature or character ▷ *v* **4** shape **5** influence or direct

THESAURUS

most *See* **majority, maximum** ▷ **most important** *See* **foremost** ▷ **most recent** *See* **last**
mostly *adv* = **generally**, usually, largely, mainly, primarily, predominantly, principally, chiefly, as a rule, on the whole
moth-eaten *adj* = **decayed**, dilapidated, shabby, ragged, decrepit, worn-out, tattered, threadbare
mother *n* **1** = **parent**, mom (*informal*), dam, mater (*old-fashioned, informal, chiefly Brit*), ma (*informal*), mommy (*informal*), mama *or* momma (*old-fashioned, informal*), old lady (*informal*) ▶ *adj* **2** = **native**, natural, innate, inborn ▶ *v* **3** = **nurture**, raise, protect, nurse, tend, rear, cherish, care for
motherly *adj* = **maternal**, protective, loving, caring, affectionate, comforting, sheltering
motif *n* **1** = **theme**, idea, subject, concept, leitmotif **2** = **design**, shape, decoration, ornament
motion *n* **1** = **movement**, move, travel, progress, flow, mobility, locomotion **2** = **proposal**, recommendation, suggestion, submission, proposition ▶ *v* **3** = **gesture**, direct, wave, signal, nod, beckon, gesticulate
motionless *adj* = **still**, standing, paralyzed, stationary, static, immobile, frozen, fixed, stock-still, transfixed, unmoving
motivate *v* = **drive**, lead, move, prompt, inspire, provoke • *What motivates athletes to excel?*
motivation *n* = **incentive**, reason, spur, inspiration, motive, stimulus, incitement, inducement
motive *n* = **reason**, ground *or* grounds, object, purpose, incentive, inspiration, stimulus, rationale, inducement
motley *adj* **1** = **miscellaneous**, mixed, disparate, assorted, varied, heterogeneous **2** = **multicolored**, checkered, variegated
mottled *adj* = **blotchy**, spotted, dappled, flecked, piebald, speckled, stippled, streaked
motto *n* = **saying**, rule, slogan, adage, maxim, dictum, proverb, precept, watchword
mould[1], mold *n* **1** = **cast**, shape, pattern **2** = **design**, build, form, kind, construction, fashion, style, shape, pattern, format **3** = **nature**, kind, type, quality, character, sort, stamp, calibre ▶ *v* **4** = **shape**, make, work, create, form, model, fashion,

DICTIONARY

▶ **moulding** *n* moulded ornamental edging
mould², mold Ⓣ *n* fungal growth caused by dampness
▶ **mouldy** *adj* **1** stale or musty **2** dull or boring
mould³, mold *n* loose soil
▶ **moulder** *v* decay into dust
Moulin *n* **Jean**. 1899–1943, French lawyer and Resistance hero; Chairman of the National Council of the Resistance (1943): tortured to death by the Nazis
moult *v* **1** shed feathers, hair, or skin to make way for new growth ▷ *n* **2** process of moulting
mound Ⓣ *n* **1** heap, esp. of earth or stones **2** small hill
mount Ⓣ *v* **1** climb or ascend **2** get up on (a horse etc.) **3** organize: *mount a campaign* **4** increase **5** fix on a support or backing ▷ *n* **6** backing or support on which something is fixed **7** horse for riding **8** hill
mountain Ⓣ *n* **1** hill of great size **2** large heap
▶ **mountainous** *adj* **1** full of mountains **2** huge
▶ **mountaineer** *n* person who climbs mountains **mountaineering** *n*
▶ **mountain bike** bicycle with straight handlebars and heavy-duty tires
Mountain Daylight Time *n* one of the standard times used in North America, six hours behind Greenwich Mean Time Abbreviation: **MDT**
Mountain Standard Time *n* one of the standard times used in North America, seven hours behind Greenwich Mean Time Abbreviation: **MST**
mountebank *n* charlatan or fake
Mountie *n informal* member of the Royal Canadian Mounted Police
mourn Ⓣ *v* feel or express sorrow for (a dead person or lost thing) **mourner** *n*
▶ **mournful** *adj* sad or dismal **mournfully** *adv*
▶ **mourning** *n* **1** grieving **2** conventional symbols of grief for death, such as the wearing of black
Mousavi *n* **Mir-Hossein**. born 1941, Iranian politician; Prime Minister (1981–89); opposition candidate in the disputed Presidential election of 2009
mouse *n, pl* **mice** **1** small long-tailed rodent **2** timid person **3** *computers* hand-held device for moving the cursor without keying
▶ **mouser** *n* cat used to catch mice
▶ **mousy** *adj* **1** like a mouse, esp. in hair colour **2** meek and shy
moussaka *n* dish made with meat, eggplant, and tomatoes, topped with cheese sauce
mousse *n* **1** dish of flavoured cream whipped and set
moustache *n* hair on the upper lip
mouth Ⓣ *n* **1** opening in the head for eating and issuing sounds **2** opening **3** entrance **4** point where a river enters the sea ▷ *v* **5** speak or utter insincerely, esp. in public **6** form (words) with the lips without speaking
▶ **mouth organ** small musical instrument played by sucking and blowing
▶ **mouthpiece** *n* **1** part of a telephone into which a person speaks **2** part of a wind instrument into which the player blows **3** spokesman

THESAURUS

forge, construct, sculpt **5 = influence**, make, control, form, affect, direct, shape
mould², mold *n* **= fungus**, blight, mildew, mustiness
See also: **rot**
mouldy *adj* **= stale**, bad, rotten, blighted, decaying, fusty, mildewed, musty *See* **rotten**
mound *n* **1 = heap**, pile, drift, stack, rick **2 = hill**, rise, bank, dune, embankment, knoll, hillock
mount *v* **1 = climb**, scale, ascend, clamber up, go up **2 = climb onto**, bestride, jump on **3 = increase**, grow, build, swell, escalate, intensify, accumulate, multiply, pile up ▶ *n* **4 = backing**, support, base, stand, frame, setting **5 = horse**, steed (*archaic or lit*)
mountain *n* **1 = peak**, mount, fell (*Brit*), alp **2 = heap**, mass, pile, mound, ton, stack, abundance
mountainous *adj* **1 = high**, steep, alpine, rocky, towering, highland, soaring, upland **2 = huge**, great, enormous, mammoth, mighty, immense, daunting, monumental, gigantic
mourn *v* **= grieve**, lament, weep, bemoan, deplore, wail, rue, bewail
mournful *adj* **1 = sad**, tragic, unhappy, woeful, melancholy, piteous, plaintive, sorrowful **2 = dismal**, gloomy, miserable, somber, downcast, disconsolate, grieving, heavy-hearted, lugubrious, rueful
mourning *n* **1 = grieving**, woe, grief, bereavement, lamentation, weeping **2 = black**, sackcloth and ashes, widow's weeds
mouth *n* **1 = lips**, jaws, maw **2 = opening**, door, entrance, gateway, inlet, aperture, orifice
mouthful *n* **= taste**, little, bit, sample, bite, swallow, spoonful, morsel
mouthpiece *n* **= spokesperson**, spokesman *or* spokeswoman, agent, representative, delegate
movable *adj* **= portable**, mobile,

DICTIONARY

move Ⓣ *v* **1** change in place or position **2** change (one's house etc.) **3** take action **4** stir the emotions of **5** incite **6** suggest (a proposal) formally ▷ *n* **7** moving **8** action towards some goal **movable** *or* **moveable** *adj, n* ▶ **movement** *n* **1** action or process of moving **2** moving parts of a machine **3** group with a common aim **4** division of a piece of music
movie Ⓣ *n informal* film
mow Ⓣ *v* **mowing, mowed, mowed** *or* **mown** cut (grass or crops) **mower** *n* ▶ **mow down** *v* kill in large numbers
Mowat *n* **Farley**. born 1921, Canadian writer and conservationist. Many of his books, including *People of the Deer* (1952) and *Sea of Slaughter* (1984), are concerned with the welfare of indigenous peoples, animals, and the environment
Mowlam *n* **Mo**, full name *Marjorie Mowlam*. 1949–2005, British Labour politician; secretary of state for Northern Ireland (1997–99) and minister for the cabinet office (1999–2001)
Mozart *n* **Wolfgang Amadeus**. 1756–91, Austrian composer. A child prodigy and prolific genius, his works include operas, such as *The Marriage of Figaro* (1786), *Don Giovanni* (1787), and *The Magic Flute* (1791), symphonies, concertos for piano, violin, clarinet, and French horn, string quartets and quintets, sonatas, songs, and Masses, such as the unfinished *Requiem* (1791) **Mozartean** *or* **Mozartian** *adj*
mozzarella [mot-sa-**rel**-la] *n* moist white cheese originally made in Italy from buffalo milk
MP **1** Member of Parliament **2** Military Police
MP3 *computing* Motion Picture Expert Group-1, Audio Layer-3: a digital compression format used to compress audio files to a fraction of their original size without loss of sound quality
MPEG [**em**-peg] *computing* Motion Picture Expert Group: standard compressed file format used for audio and video files
mpg miles per gallon
mph miles per hour
MPP Member of the Provincial Parliament
Mr Mister
Mrs *n* title of a married woman
Ms [**mizz**] *n* title used instead of Miss or Mrs
MS **1** manuscript **2** multiple sclerosis
MSc Master of Science
MSS manuscripts
MST Mountain Standard Time
Mt Mount
Mubarak *n* (**Muhammad**) **Hosni**. born 1928, Egyptian statesman; president of Egypt from 1981
much Ⓣ *adj* **more, most 1** existing in quantity ▷ *n* **2** large amount or degree ▷ *adv* **more, most 3** to a great degree **4** nearly
mucilage [**mew**-sill-ij] *n* gum or glue
muck Ⓣ *n* **1** dirt, filth **2** manure ▷ *v* **3** *hockey* play tenaciously in attempting to win the puck **mucky** *adj* ▶ **mucker** *n hockey* player who is physically

m

THESAURUS

transferable, detachable, transportable
move *v* **1 = go**, advance, progress, shift, proceed, stir, budge • *The train began to move.* **2 = change**, transfer, shift, switch, transpose **3 = relocate**, leave, remove, quit, migrate, pack one's bags (*informal*) • *She had often considered moving to the Maritimes.* **4 = drive**, start, turn, operate, shift, propel, activate **5 = touch**, affect, excite, impress • *The story moved us to tears.* **6 = incite**, cause, prompt, influence, inspire, persuade, motivate, induce, rouse **7 = propose**, suggest, urge, recommend, advocate, put forward ▷ **move to** *See* **settle** ▷ **move up** *See* **rise** ▶ *n* **8 = action**, turn, step, measure, stroke, ploy, manoeuvre, stratagem **9 = transfer**, shift, removal, relocation
See also: **draw**
moved *See* **sorry**
movement *n* **1 = motion**, flow • *They monitor the movement of the fish swimming upstream.* **2 = group**, campaign, organization, faction • *the peace movement* **3 = workings**, action, mechanism, machinery, works **4** (*Music*) **= section**, part, division, passage
See also: **cause, wave**
movie *n* **= film**, feature, picture, flick (*slang*)
moving *adj* **1 = emotional**, poignant, touching, affecting, stirring • *It was a moving moment.* **2 = mobile**, portable, running, movable, unfixed
See also: **sad**
mow *v* **= cut**, crop, trim, shear, scythe ▷ **mow down = massacre**, slaughter, butcher, cut down, cut to pieces, shoot down
much *adj* **1 = a lot of**, great, substantial, considerable, sizable *or* sizeable, ample, abundant, copious, plenty of ▶ *n* **2 = a lot**, a good deal, a great deal, heaps (*informal*), scads (*informal*), tons (*informal*), plenty, lots (*informal*) ▶ *adv* **3 = greatly**, considerably, decidedly, exceedingly, a great deal, a lot
muck *n* **1 = manure**, dung, ordure **2 = dirt**, filth, mud, mire, sludge, ooze, slime ▶ *v* ▷ **muck up = ruin**, blow (*slang*), spoil, botch, bungle, muff, make a mess of, make a pig's ear of (*informal*), mess up
mucky *adj* **= dirty**, messy, muddy, filthy,

DICTIONARY

aggressive and tenacious rather than highly talented
muckamuck *n* **high muckamuck** *informal* important person
mucus [**mew**-kuss] *n* slimy secretion of the mucous membranes
▸ **mucous membrane** membrane lining body cavities or passages
mud Ⓣ *n* wet soft earth **muddy** *adj*
▸ **mudguard** *n* cover over a wheel to prevent mud or water being thrown up by it
▸ **mudpack** *n* cosmetic paste to improve the complexion
muddle Ⓣ *n* **1** state of confusion ▷ *v* (often foll. by *up*) **2** confuse **3** mix up
muesli [**mewz**-lee] *n* mixture of grain, nuts, and dried fruit eaten with milk
muezzin [moo-**ezz**-in] *n* official who summons Muslims to prayer
muff[1] *n* tube-shaped covering to keep the hands warm
muff[2] *v* bungle (an action)
muffin *n* **1** small cup-shaped sweet bread roll **2** see **English muffin**
muffle Ⓣ *v* wrap up for warmth or to deaden sound
▸ **muffler** *n* scarf
mufti *n* civilian clothes worn by a person who usually wears a uniform
mug[1] Ⓣ *n* large drinking cup
mug[2] Ⓣ *n* **1** *slang* face **2** *Brit slang* person who is easily swindled ▷ *v* **mugging, mugged** **3** *informal* rob violently **mugger** *n*
mug[3] Ⓣ *v* **mugging, mugged** (esp. foll. by *up*) *Brit informal* study hard
Mugabe *n* **Robert**. born 1925, Zimbabwean politician; leader of one wing of the Patriotic Front against the government of Ian Smith of Rhodesia, and of the Zanu party; prime minister (1980–87); president from 1988
muggy Ⓣ *adj* **-gier, -giest** (of weather) damp and stifling
Muhammad *n* ?570–632 AD, the prophet believed by Muslims to be the channel for the final unfolding of God's revelation to mankind: popularly regarded as the founder of Islam. He began to teach in Mecca in 610 but persecution forced him to flee with his followers to Medina in 622. After several battles, he conquered Mecca (630), establishing the principles of Islam (embodied in the Koran) over all Arabia
Muhammad Ali, Muhammed Ali, Mohammed Ali *n* original name *Cassius (Marcellus) Clay.* born 1942, US boxer, who was world heavyweight champion three times (1964–67; 1974–78; 1978)
Muir *n* **Edwin**. 1887–1959, Scottish poet, novelist, and critic
mujaheddin, mujahedeen [moo-ja-hed-**deen**] *pl n* fundamentalist Muslim guerrillas
mukluk *n* Inuit's soft (sealskin) boot
mulatto [mew-**lat**-toe] *n, pl* **-tos, -toes** child of one Black and one White parent
mulberry *n* **1** tree whose leaves are used to feed silkworms **2** purple fruit of this tree
mulch *n* **1** mixture of wet straw, leaves, etc., used to protect the roots of plants ▷ *v* **2** cover (land) with mulch
mulct *v* fine (a person)
mule[1] *n* offspring of a horse and a donkey
▸ **mulish** *adj* obstinate
▸ **muleteer** *n* mule driver
mule[2] *n* backless shoe or slipper
mull Ⓣ *v* **1** heat (wine) with sugar and spices **2** think (over) or ponder
mullah *n* Muslim theologian
mullet *n* edible sea fish
Mulligan *n* **Gerry**, full name *Gerald Joseph Mulligan*. 1927–96, US jazz saxophonist, who

THESAURUS

grimy, begrimed, scuzzy (*slang*)
mud *n* = **dirt**, clay, mire, sludge, ooze, silt, slime
muddle *n* **1** = **disorder**, chaos, mess, confusion, tangle, disarray, jumble, disorganization • *Our finances are in a muddle*. ▸ *v* **2** = **mix up**, confuse, jumble • *Their names are so similar, they often get muddled*. **3** = **jumble**, disorder, scramble, mess, spoil, tangle, disorganize, disarrange **4** = **confuse**, daze, bewilder, perplex, disorient, confound, befuddle, stupefy ▷ **muddle up** *See* **confuse**
See also: **cloud, mix-up**
muddled *See* **confused**
muddy *adj* **1** = **dirty**, grimy, bespattered, mucky, mud-caked, scuzzy (*slang*), soiled **2** = **boggy**, swampy, marshy, quaggy
muffle *v* **1** = **wrap up**, cover, cloak, shroud, envelop, swathe, swaddle **2** = **deaden**, silence, stifle, soften, suppress, muzzle, quieten
muffled *adj* = **indistinct**, faint, muted, subdued, stifled, strangled, suppressed
mug[1] *n* = **cup**, pot, beaker, flagon, tankard
mug[2] *n* **1** = **face**, visage, countenance, features **2** = **fool**, dork (*slang*), schmuck (*slang*), sucker (*slang*) ▸ *v* **3** = **attack**, assault, rob, beat up, set about *or* set upon
mug[3] *v* ▷ **mug up** (*Brit slang*) = **study**, review, cram (*informal*), bone up on (*informal*), burn the midnight oil (*informal*)
mugger *See* **thief**
muggy *adj* = **humid**, close, sticky, oppressive, moist, sultry, stuffy, clammy
mull *v* = **ponder**, consider, weigh, deliberate, contemplate, meditate, reflect on, ruminate, think over

m

DICTIONARY

pioneered the cool jazz style of the 1950s
mulligatawny *n* soup made with curry powder
mullion *n* upright dividing bar in a window **mullioned** *adj*
Mulroney *n* (**Martin**) **Brian**. born 1939, Canadian politician; Conservative prime minister (1984–93)
multi- *combining form* many: *multicultural*
multicoloured *adj* having many different colours
multifarious Ⓣ [mull-tiff-**fare**-ee-uss] *adj* having many various parts
multilateral *adj* of or involving more than two nations or parties
multilingual *adj* speaking or written in more than two languages
multimillionaire *n* person who owns several million pounds, dollars, etc.
multinational *adj, n* (large business company) operating in several countries
multiple Ⓣ *adj* **1** having many parts ▷ *n* **2** quantity which contains another an exact number of times
multiplex *adj* **2** having many elements, complex
multiplicity *n, pl* **-ties** large number or great variety
multiply Ⓣ *v* **-plying, -plied 1** (cause to) increase in number, quantity, or degree **2** add (a number or quantity) to itself a given number of times **3** increase in number by reproduction **multiplication** *n*
▸ **multiplicand** *n math* number to be multiplied
multipurpose *adj* having many uses: *a multipurpose vehicle*
multiracial *adj* made up of people from many races: *a multiracial society*
multitude Ⓣ *n* **1** great number **2** great crowd
▸ **multitudinous** *adj* very numerous
mum[1] *n informal* mother
mum[2] *adj* silent: *keep mum*
mumble Ⓣ *v* speak indistinctly, mutter
mumbo jumbo *n* **1** meaningless religious ritual **2** deliberately complicated language
mummer *n* actor in a folk play or mime
mummy[1] *n, pl* **-mies** body embalmed and wrapped for burial in ancient Egypt
▸ **mummify** *v* **-fying, -fied** preserve (a body) as a mummy
mummy[2] *n, pl* **-mies** child's word for **mother**
mumps *n* infectious disease with swelling in the glands of the neck
munch Ⓣ *v* chew noisily and steadily
Munch *n* **Edvard**. 1863–1944, Norwegian painter and engraver, whose works, often on the theme of death, include *The Scream* (1893); a major influence on the expressionists, esp. on *die Brücke*
mundane Ⓣ *adj* **1** everyday **2** earthly
Mundell *n* **Robert Alexander**. born 1932, Canadian economist; won the Nobel prize for economics (1999)
municipal Ⓣ *adj* relating to a city or town
▸ **municipality** *n* **1** city or town with local self-government **2** governing body of this
munificent Ⓣ [mew-**niff**-fiss-sent] *adj* very generous **munificence** *n*
muniments [**mew**-nim-ments] *pl n* title deeds or similar documents
munitions [mew-**nish**-unz] *pl n* military stores
Munro *n* **1 Alice**, original name *Alice Laidlaw*. born 1931, Canadian short-story writer; her books include *Lives of Girls and Women* (1971), *The Moons of Jupiter* (1982), and *The Love of a Good Woman* (1999) **2 H**(**ector**) **H**(**ugh**), pen name *Saki*. 1870–1916, Scottish author, born in Burma (now Myanmar), noted for his collections of satirical short stories, such as *Reginald* (1904) and *Beasts and Superbeasts* (1914)
mural [**myoor**-al] *n* **1** painting on a wall ▷ *adj* **2** of or on a wall
Murat *n* **Joachim**. 1767–1815, French marshal during the Napoleonic Wars; king of Naples (1808–15)

THESAURUS

multifarious *adj* = **diverse**, many, different, multiple, numerous, legion, varied, miscellaneous, manifold, sundry
multiple *adj* = **many**, several, various, numerous, manifold, multitudinous, sundry
multiply *v* **1** = **increase**, spread, proliferate • *The problems with my old computer just seem to multiply*. **2** = **reproduce**, breed, propagate
See also: **grow**
multitude *n* = **mass**, host, crowd, army, mob, swarm, throng, myriad, horde
mumble *v* = **murmur**, mutter • *He mumbled a few words*.
munch *v* = **chew**, crunch, champ, chomp
mundane *adj* **1** = **ordinary**, routine, everyday, day-to-day, commonplace, banal, humdrum, prosaic, workaday **2** = **earthly**, secular, mortal, terrestrial, temporal, worldly
municipal *adj* = **civic**, public, urban
municipality *n* = **town**, city, district, borough, township
munificence *n* = **generosity**, bounty, largesse *or* largess, philanthropy, beneficence, benevolence, liberality, magnanimousness
munificent *adj* = **generous**, liberal, lavish, bountiful, philanthropic, benevolent, beneficent, magnanimous, open-handed, unstinting

DICTIONARY

Murchison *n* Sir **Roderick Impey**. 1792–1871, Scottish geologist: played a major role in establishing parts of the geological time scale, esp. the Silurian, Permian, and Devonian periods
murder ⓣ *n* **1** unlawful intentional killing of a human being ▷ *v* **2** kill thus **murderer** (**murderess**) *n* **murderous** *adj*
Murdoch *n* **1** Dame (**Jean**) **Iris**. 1919–99, British writer. Her books include *The Bell* (1958), *A Severed Head* (1961), *The Sea, The Sea* (1978), which won the Booker Prize, *The Philosopher's Pupil* (1983), and *Existentialists and Mystics* (1997) **2** (**Keith**) **Rupert**. born 1931, US publisher and media entrepreneur, born in Australia; chairman of News International Ltd (including Times Newspapers Ltd), 20th Century-Fox, and HarperCollins
murk *n* thick darkness
▶ **murky** *adj* dark or gloomy
murmur ⓣ *v* **-muring, -mured 1** speak in a quiet indistinct way **2** complain ▷ *n* **3** continuous low indistinct sound
Murphy *n* **Eddie**, full name *Edward Regan Murphy*. born 1951, US film actor and comedian. His films include *48 Hours* (1982), *Beverly Hills Cop* (1984), *Coming to America* (1988), and *Dr. Dolittle* (1998)
murrain [**murr**-rin] *n* cattle plague
Murray *n* **1** (**Morna**) **Anne**. born 1945, Canadian singer-songwriter. Her recordings include "Snowbird" (1970) and "You Needed Me" (1978) **2** Sir **James Augustus Henry**. 1837–1915, Scottish lexicographer; one of the original editors (1879–1915) of what became the *Oxford English Dictionary*
muscat *n* sweet white grape
▶ **muscatel** [musk-a-**tell**] *n* **1** wine from muscat grapes **2** muscat grape or raisin
muscle ⓣ *n* **1** tissue in the body which produces movement by contracting **2** strength or power
▶ **muscular** *adj* **1** with well-developed muscles **2** of muscles
▶ **muscular dystrophy** disease with wasting of the muscles
▶ **muscle in** *v informal* force one's way in
muse ⓣ *v* ponder
Muse *n* **1** *Greek myth* one of nine goddesses, each of whom inspired an art or science **2 muse** force that inspires a creative artist
museum *n* building where natural, artistic, historical, or scientific objects are exhibited and preserved
Museveni *n* **Yoweri**. born 1944, Ugandan politician; president of Uganda from 1986
mush[1] *n* **1** soft pulpy mass **2** *informal* cloying sentimentality **mushy** *adj*
mush[2] *interj* **1** order to dogs in sled team to advance ▷ *v* **2** travel by or drive dogsled ▷ *n* **3** journey with dogsled
Musharraf *n* **Pervez**. born 1943, Pakistani general and politician; president of Pakistan (2001–08)
mushroom *n* **1** edible fungus with a stem and cap ▷ *v* **2** grow rapidly
music *n* **1** art form using a melodious and harmonious combination of notes **2** written or printed form of this **musician** *n*
▶ **musical** *adj* **1** of or like music **2** talented in or fond of music **3** pleasant-sounding ▷ *n* **4** play or film with songs and dancing **musically** *adv*
▶ **musicology** *n* scientific study of music **musicologist** *n*
▶ **music hall** variety theatre
musk *n* scent obtained from a gland of the musk deer or produced synthetically **musky** *adj*
▶ **muskrat** *n* **1** N American beaver-like rodent **2** its fur
muskeg *n* bog or swamp
muskellunge *n* N American freshwater game fish

THESAURUS

murder *n* **1 = killing**, assassination, homicide, slaughter, manslaughter, slaying (*lit*) • *after being found guilty of murder* ▶ *v* **2 = kill**, slay (*lit*), slaughter, assassinate, take the life of • *a book about two men who murder a third*
murderer *n* = **killer**, homicide, assassin, butcher, cut-throat, hit man (*slang*), slaughterer, slayer
murderous *adj* = **deadly**, brutal, lethal, cruel, ferocious, savage, bloodthirsty, cut-throat
murky *adj* = **dark**, misty, gloomy, dull, dim, gray, cloudy, overcast
murmur *v* **1 = mumble**, whisper, mutter **2 = grumble**, complain, moan (*informal*) ▶ *n* **3 = drone**, rumble, whisper, purr, buzzing, humming
muscle *n* **1 = tendon**, sinew **2 = strength**, power, might, weight, clout (*informal*), stamina, brawn, forcefulness
muscular *adj* = **strong**, powerful, robust, athletic, vigorous, sturdy, sinewy, strapping
muse *v* = **ponder**, consider, reflect, deliberate, contemplate, brood, meditate, cogitate, mull over, ruminate
mushy *adj* **1 = soft**, slushy, pulpy, semi-solid, squashy, squelchy **2** (*Informal*) = **sentimental**, sloppy (*informal*), slushy (*informal*), maudlin, mawkish, saccharine, schmaltzy (*slang*)
musical *adj* = **melodious**, lyrical, melodic, harmonious, dulcet, euphonious, sweet-sounding, tuneful

m

DICTIONARY

musket *n hist* long-barrelled gun
musketeer *n*
▸ **musketry** *n* (use of) muskets
Muslim *n* **1** follower of the religion of Islam ▹ *adj* **2** of or relating to Islam
muslin *n* fine cotton fabric
muss *v informal* make untidy
mussel *n* kind of bivalve mollusc
must[1] **T** *v* **1** used as an auxiliary to express obligation, certainty, or resolution ▹ *n* **2** something one must do
must[2] *n* newly pressed grape juice
mustang *n* wild horse of SW America
mustard *n* **1** paste made from the powdered seeds of a plant, used as a condiment **2** the plant
▸ **mustard gas** poisonous gas causing blistering
muster **T** *v* **1** assemble ▹ *n* **2** assembly
musty **T** *adj* **-tier, -tiest** smelling mouldy and stale **mustiness** *n*
mutable **T** [**mew**-tab-bl] *adj* liable to change **mutability** *n*
mutation **T** [mew-**tay**-shun] *n* (genetic) change
▸ **mutate** [mew-**tate**] *v* (cause to) undergo mutation
▸ **mutant** [**mew**-tant] *n* mutated animal, plant, etc.
mute **T** *adj* **1** unable to speak **2** silent ▹ *n* **3** person unable to speak **4** *music* device to soften the tone of an instrument **mutely** *adv*
▸ **muted** *adj* **1** (of a reaction) subdued **2** (of sound or colour) softened
mutilate **T** [**mew**-till-ate] *v* **1** deprive of a limb or other part **2** damage (a book or text)
mutilation *n*
mutiny **T** [**mew**-tin-ee] *n, pl* **-nies** **1** rebellion against authority, esp. by soldiers or sailors ▹ *v* **-nying, -nied** **2** commit mutiny
mutineer *n* **mutinous** *adj*
mutt **T** *n slang* **1** stupid person **2** mongrel dog
mutter **T** *v* **1** utter or speak indistinctly **2** grumble ▹ *n* **3** muttered sound or grumble
mutton *n* flesh of sheep, used as food
mutual **T** [**mew**-chew-al] *adj* **1** felt or expressed by each of two people about the other **2** *informal* common to both or all
mutually *adv*
Muzak *n* ® recorded light music played in shops etc.
muzzle **T** *n* **1** animal's mouth and nose **2** cover for these to prevent biting **3** open end of a gun ▹ *v* **4** put a muzzle on **5** force to keep silent
muzzy *adj* **-zier, -ziest** **1** confused or muddled **2** blurred or hazy **muzziness** *n*
mW milliwatt(s)
MW megawatt(s)
my *adj* belonging to me
mycology *n* study of fungi
myna, mynah *n* Indian bird which can mimic human speech
myocardium *n, pl* **-dia** the muscular tissue of the heart **myocardial** *adj*
myopia [my-**oh**-pee-a] *n* short-sightedness
myopic [my-**op**-ic] *adj*
myriad **T** [**mir**-ree-ad] *adj* **1** innumerable

THESAURUS

must *n* = **necessity**, requirement, essential, fundamental, imperative, requisite, prerequisite, *sine qua non* (*Latin*)
muster *v* **1** = **assemble**, rally, gather, convene, marshal, summon, mobilize, call together ▸ *n* **2** = **assembly**, meeting, rally, collection, convention, gathering, roundup, congregation
musty *adj* = **stale**, old, funky (*slang*), smelly, stuffy, airless, dank, fusty, mildewed, moldy
mutability *n* = **change**, transition, variation, evolution, alteration, metamorphosis, vicissitude
mutable *adj* = **changeable**, volatile, inconsistent, unstable, variable, fickle, unsettled, adaptable, alterable, inconstant
mutate *See* **turn**
mutation *n* = **change**, variation, evolution, transformation, modification, alteration, metamorphosis, transfiguration
mute *adj* = **silent**, dumb, mum, speechless, unspoken, voiceless, wordless
muted *adj* = **subdued**, delicate, subtle, low-key, discreet, restrained, pastel, understated, toned down, faded
muteness *See* **silence**
mutilate *v* **1** = **maim**, damage, injure, amputate, disfigure, dismember, mangle, lacerate, cut up **2** = **distort**, cut, damage, censor, adulterate, bowdlerize, expurgate
mutinous *adj* = **rebellious**, insurgent, subversive, unruly, unmanageable, disobedient, insubordinate, refractory, riotous
mutiny *n* **1** = **rebellion**, riot, revolution, uprising, revolt, disobedience, insurrection, insubordination ▸ *v* **2** = **rebel**, resist, revolt, disobey, rise up
mutt *See* **dog**
mutter *v* = **grumble**, complain, rumble, mumble, murmur, grouse
mutual *adj* = **shared**, common, joint, interchangeable, reciprocal, requited, returned
muzzle *n* **1** = **jaws**, mouth, nose, snout ▸ *v* **2** = **suppress**, silence, curb, censor, stifle, restrain, gag
myopic *adj* = **short-sighted**, near-sighted
myriad *adj* (*Formal*) **1** = **innumerable**, countless, untold, immeasurable,

DICTIONARY

▷ *n* **2** large indefinite number
myriapod *n* invertebrate with a long segmented body and many legs, such as a centipede
myrrh [**mur**] *n* aromatic gum, formerly used in incense
myrtle [**mur**-tl] *n* flowering evergreen shrub
myself *pron* emphatic or reflexive form of **I, me**
mystery Ⓣ *n, pl* **-teries 1** strange or inexplicable event or phenomenon **2** obscure or secret thing **3** story or film that arouses suspense **mysterious** *adj* **mysteriously** *adv*
mystic Ⓣ *n* **1** person who seeks spiritual knowledge ▷ *adj* **2** having a spiritual or religious significance beyond human understanding **mysticism** *n*
▶ **mystical** *adj* mystic
mystify Ⓣ *v* **-fying, -fied** bewilder or puzzle **mystification** *n*
mystique Ⓣ [miss-**steek**] *n* aura of mystery or power
myth Ⓣ *n* **1** tale with supernatural characters, usu. of how the world and mankind began **2** untrue idea or explanation **3** imaginary person or object **mythical** *adj*
▶ **mythology** *n* **1** myths collectively **2** study of myths **mythological** *adj*
myxomatosis [mix-a-mat-**oh**-siss] *n* contagious fatal viral disease of rabbits

THESAURUS

incalculable, multitudinous ▶ *n* **2 = multitude**, host, army, swarm, horde
mysterious *adj* **1 = mystifying**, cryptic, enigmatic, arcane (*formal*), baffling • *He died in mysterious circumstances.* **2 = secretive**, furtive • *Stop being so mysterious.*
See also: **funny**
mystery *n* **= puzzle**, riddle, conundrum, enigma • *the mystery surrounding her fortune*
mystic, mystical *adj* **= supernatural**, mysterious, paranormal, occult, otherworldly, inscrutable, metaphysical, preternatural, transcendental
mystify *v* **= puzzle**, confuse, baffle, stump, bewilder, perplex, confound, flummox, nonplus
mystifying *See* **mysterious**
mystique *n* **= fascination**, magic, spell, charm, awe, glamour, charisma, mojo (*slang*)
myth *n* **1 = legend**, story, fiction, saga, allegory, fable, fairy story, folk tale, urban legend *or* urban myth **2 = imagination**, fantasy, fancy, illusion, delusion, superstition, figment, tall tale (*informal*)
mythical *adj* **1 = legendary**, fabulous, fabled, fairy-tale, mythological **2 = imaginary**, fantasy, untrue, fictitious, unreal, nonexistent, made-up, make-believe, fabricated, invented, pretended
mythological *adj* **= legendary**, traditional, fabulous, mythical, mythic
mythology *n* **= legend**, tradition, lore, folklore

DICTIONARY

Nn

n *adj* indefinite number (of) **nth** *adj*
N **1** *chess* knight **2** *chem* nitrogen **3** *physics* newton(s) **4** north(ern)
n. **1** neuter **2** noun **3** number
Na *chem* sodium
naan *n* same as **nan bread**
nab Ⓣ *v* **nabbing, nabbed** *informal* **1** arrest (someone) **2** catch (someone) in wrongdoing
Nabokov *n* **Vladimir Vladimirovich**. 1899–1977, US novelist, born in Russia. His works include *Lolita* (1955), *Pnin* (1957), *Pale Fire* (1962), and *Ada* (1969) **Nabokovian** *adj*
Nader *n* **Ralph**. born 1934, US lawyer and campaigner for consumer rights and the environment: a candidate for president in 1996, 2000, and 2004
nadir Ⓣ *n* **1** point in the sky opposite the zenith **2** lowest point
naevus Ⓣ [**nee**-vuss] *n, pl* **-vi** birthmark or mole
naff Ⓣ *adj slang* inferior or useless
NAFTA North American Free Trade Agreement
nag[1] Ⓣ *v* **nagging, nagged** **1** scold or find fault (with) constantly **2** be a constant source of discomfort, pain, or worry (to) ▷ *n* **3** person who nags **nagging** *adj, n*
nag[2] Ⓣ *n informal* (old) horse
Nagarjuna *n c.* 150–*c.* 250 AD, Indian Buddhist monk, founder of the Madhyamika (Middle Path) school of Mahayana Buddhism: noted for his philosophical writings
Nagy *n* **Imre**. 1896–1958, Hungarian statesman; prime minister (1953–55; 1956). He was removed from office and later executed when Soviet forces suppressed the revolution of 1956; reburied with honours in 1989
naiad [**nye**-ad] *n Greek myth* water nymph
nail Ⓣ *n* **1** hard covering of the upper tips of the fingers and toes **2** pointed piece of metal with a head, hit with a hammer to join two objects together ▷ *v* **3** attach (something) with nails **4** *informal* catch or arrest
▶ **hit the nail on the head** say something exactly correct
▶ **nailfile** *n* small metal file used to smooth or shape the finger or toe nails
▶ **nail polish** *or* **nail varnish** cosmetic lacquer applied to the finger or toe nails
Naipaul *n* Sir **V**(**idiadhar**) **S**(**urajprasad**). born 1932, Trinidadian novelist of Indian descent, living in Britain. His works include *A House for Mr. Biswas* (1961), *In a Free State* (1971), which won the Booker Prize, *A Bend in the River* (1979), *The Enigma of Arrival* (1987), and *Beyond Belief* (1998): Nobel prize for literature 2001
naive Ⓣ [nye-**eev**] *adj* **1** innocent and credulous **2** lacking developed powers of reasoning and criticism **naively** *adv* **naivety** *or* **naïveté** [nye-**eev**-tee] *n*
naked Ⓣ *adj* without clothes or covering **nakedness** *n*
▶ **the naked eye** the eye unassisted by any optical instrument
namby-pamby Ⓣ *adj* sentimental or insipid

THESAURUS

nab *v* = **catch**, arrest, capture, grab, seize, snatch, collar (*informal*), apprehend
nadir *n* = **bottom**, minimum, depths, lowest point, rock bottom
naevus *n* = **birthmark**, mole
naff *adj* = **bad**, poor, shoddy, low-grade, inferior, worthless, shabby, second-rate, rubbishy
nag[1] *v* **1** = **scold**, worry, plague, harass, annoy, irritate, hassle (*informal*), badger, pester, upbraid, henpeck ▶ *n* **2** = **scold**, shrew, harpy, tartar, virago
nag[2] *n* = **horse**, hack
nagging *adj* **1** = **persistent**, irritating, worrying **2** = **scolding**, shrewish
nail *v* = **fasten**, join, fix, secure, hammer, attach, pin, tack
naive *adj* **1** = **gullible**, green, callow, credulous, unsuspicious, wet behind the ears (*informal*) **2** = **innocent**, open, simple, unsophisticated, artless, guileless, ingenuous, trusting, unworldly
naivety, naïveté *n* **1** = **gullibility**, callowness, credulity **2** = **innocence**, simplicity, openness, inexperience, artlessness, guilelessness, ingenuousness, naturalness
naked *adj* **1** = **nude**, bare, unclothed • *a naked body* OPPOSITE: clothed **2** = **open**, evident, blatant, manifest, unmistakable • *naked aggression* OPPOSITE: secret
nakedness *n* = **nudity**, undress, bareness
namby-pamby *adj* = **feeble**, weak, sentimental, spineless, weedy (*informal*), insipid, vapid, wimpish *or* wimpy (*informal*), wishy-washy (*informal*)

DICTIONARY

name Ⓣ *n* **1** word by which a person or thing is known **2** reputation, esp. a good one **3** abusive word or description ▷ *v* **4** give a name to **5** refer to by name **6** specify
▸ **nameless** *adj* **1** without a name **2** unspecified **3** too horrible to be mentioned
▸ **namely** *adv* that is to say
▸ **namesake** *n* person with the same name as another
nan bread *n* slightly leavened Indian bread in a large flat leaf shape
Nanak *n* 1469–1538, Indian religious leader; founder and first guru of Sikhism
Nana Sahib *n* real name *Dandhu Panth*. ?1825–?1860, Indian nationalist, who led the uprising at Cawnpore during the Indian Mutiny
nanny *n, pl* **-nies** woman whose job is looking after young children
▸ **nanny goat** female goat
Nansen *n* **Fridtjof**. 1861–1930, Norwegian arctic explorer, statesman, and scientist. He crossed Greenland (1888–89) and attempted to reach the North Pole (1893–96), attaining a record 86°14′ N (1895). He was the League of Nations' high commissioner for refugees (1920–22): Nobel peace prize 1922
nap[1] Ⓣ *n* **1** short sleep ▷ *v* **napping, napped** **2** have a short sleep
nap[2] Ⓣ *n* raised fibres of velvet or similar cloth
nap[3] *n* card game similar to whist
napalm *n* highly inflammable gasoline, used in bombs
nape *n* back of the neck
naphtha *n* liquid mixture distilled from coal tar or petroleum, used as a solvent and in petrol
▸ **naphthalene** *n* white crystalline product distilled from coal tar or petroleum, used in disinfectants, mothballs, and explosives
Napier *n* **1** Sir **Charles James**. 1782–1853, British general and colonial administrator: conquered Sind (1843): governor of Sind (1843–47) **2 John**. 1550–1617, Scottish mathematician: invented logarithms and pioneered the decimal notation used today **3 Robert** (**Cornelis**), 1st Baron Napier of Magdala. 1810–90, British field marshal, who commanded in India during the Sikh Wars (1845, 1848–49) and the Indian Mutiny (1857–59). He captured Magdala (1868) while rescuing British diplomats from Ethiopia
napkin Ⓣ *n* piece of cloth or paper for wiping the mouth or protecting the clothes while eating
Napoleon I *n* full name *Napoleon Bonaparte*. 1769–1821, Emperor of the French (1804–15). He came to power as the result of a coup in 1799 and established an extensive European empire. A brilliant general, he defeated every European coalition against him until, irreparably weakened by the Peninsular War and the Russian campaign (1812), his armies were defeated at Leipzig (1813). He went into exile but escaped and ruled as emperor during the Hundred Days. He was finally defeated at Waterloo (1815). As an administrator, his achievements were of lasting significance and include the *Code Napoléon*, which remains the basis of French law
Napoleon II *n* Duke of Reichstadt. 1811–32, son of Napoleon Bonaparte and Marie Louise. He was known as the *King of Rome* during the first French empire and was entitled Napoleon II by Bonapartists after Napoleon I's death (1821)
Napoleon III *n* full name *Charles Louis Napoleon Bonaparte*, known as *Louis-Napoleon*. 1808–73, Emperor of the French (1852–70); nephew of Napoleon I. He led two abortive Bonapartist risings (1836; 1840) and was elected president of the Second Republic (1848), establishing the Second Empire in 1852. Originally successful in foreign affairs, he was deposed after the disastrous Franco-Prussian War
nappy *n, pl* **-pies** *Brit* diaper
narc, nark Ⓣ *Brit slang* ▷ *v* **1** annoy ▷ *n*

n

THESAURUS

name *n* **1** = **title**, term, nickname, designation, epithet • *My name is Joe.* RELATED WORD *adj*: nominal **2** = **reputation**, character • *to protect his good name* ▸ *v* **3** = **call**, term, dub • *a little girl named Anna* **4** = **nominate**, choose, select, appoint, designate, specify
See also: **celebrity, identify**
named *adj* **1** = **called**, baptized, christened, dubbed, entitled, known as, labelled, styled, termed **2** = **nominated**, selected, specified, appointed, chosen, designated, mentioned, picked, singled out
nameless *adj* **1** = **anonymous**, unnamed, untitled **2** = **unknown**, obscure, unsung, unheard-of, incognito, undistinguished **3** = **horrible**, unspeakable, indescribable, abominable, unmentionable, unutterable
namely *adv* = **specifically**, to wit, viz.
naming *See* **appointment**
nap[1] *n* **1** = **sleep**, catnap, forty winks (*informal*), rest, siesta ▸ *v* **2** = **sleep**, doze, catnap, drop off (*informal*), rest, snooze (*informal*), nod off (*informal*)
nap[2] *n* = **pile**, down, grain, weave, fibre
napkin *n* = **cloth**, linen, wipe
narc, nark *n* (*Slang*) = **informer**, sneak,

DICTIONARY

2 someone who complains in an irritating manner **3** informer
▸ **narky** *adj slang* irritable or complaining
narcissism Ⓣ *n* abnormal love and admiration for oneself **narcissistic** *adj*
narcissus *n, pl* **-cissi** yellow, orange, or white flower related to the daffodil
narcotic Ⓣ *n, adj* (of) a drug, such as morphine or opium, which produces numbness and drowsiness, used medicinally but addictive
▸ **narcosis** *n* effect of a narcotic
narrate Ⓣ *v* **1** tell (a story) **2** speak the words accompanying and telling what is happening in a film or TV programme **narration** *n* **narrator** *n*
▸ **narrative** *n* account, story
narrow Ⓣ *adj* **1** of little breadth in comparison to length **2** limited in range, extent, or outlook **3** with little margin: *a narrow escape* ▹ *v* **4** make or become narrow **5** (often foll. by *down*) limit or restrict **narrowly** *adv* **narrowness** *n*
▸ **narrows** *pl n* narrow part of a strait, river, or current
▸ **narrow-minded** *adj* intolerant or bigoted
narwhal *n* arctic porpoise with a long spiral tusk
NASA *US* National Aeronautics and Space Administration
nasal *adj* **1** of the nose **2** pronounced with air passing through the nose **nasally** *adv*
nascent *adj* starting to grow or develop
Nash *n* **1 John**. 1752–1835, English town planner and architect. He designed Regent's Park, Regent Street, and the Marble Arch in London **2 Ogden**. 1902–71, US humorous poet **3 Paul**. 1889–1946, English painter, noted esp. as a war artist in both World Wars and for his landscapes **4 Richard**, known as *Beau Nash*. 1674–1762, English dandy **5** See (Thomas) **Nashe 6** Sir **Walter**. 1882–1968, New Zealand Labour statesman, born in England: prime minister of New Zealand (1957–60)
Nashe, Nash *n* **Thomas**. 1567–1601, English pamphleteer, satirist, and novelist, author of the first picaresque novel in English, *The Unfortunate Traveller, or the Life of Jack Wilton* (1594)
Nasser *n* **Gamal Abdel**. 1918–70, Egyptian soldier and statesman; president of Egypt (1956–70). He was one of the leaders of the coup that deposed King Farouk (1952) and became premier (1954). His nationalization of the Suez Canal (1956) led to an international crisis, and during his presidency Egypt was twice defeated by Israel (1956; 1967)
nasturtium *n* plant with yellow, red, or orange trumpet-shaped flowers
nasty Ⓣ *adj* **-tier, -tiest 1** unpleasant **2** (of an injury) dangerous or painful **3** spiteful or unkind **nastily** *adv* **nastiness** *n*
natal [**nay**-tal] *adj* of or relating to birth
nation Ⓣ *n* people of one or more cultures or races organized as a single state
▸ **national** *adj* **1** of or characteristic of a nation ▹ *n* **2** citizen of a nation **nationally** *adv*
▸ **nationalism** *n* **1** policy of national

n

THESAURUS

accuser, traitor, Judas, betrayer, double-crosser, quisling, stool pigeon, snake in the grass, two-timer, squealer (*slang*)
narcissism *n* = **egotism**, vanity, self-love
narcotic *n* **1** = **drug**, painkiller, anesthetic, sedative, opiate, tranquilizer, analgesic, anodyne ▸ *adj* **2** = **sedative**, analgesic, hypnotic, calming, painkilling, soporific
narrate *v* = **tell**, report, detail, describe, relate, recount, chronicle, recite
narration *n* = **telling**, account, relation, reading, explanation, description, recital
narrative *n* = **story**, report, statement, history, account, blog (*informal*), tale, chronicle, weblog
narrator *n* = **storyteller**, reporter, author, writer, commentator, chronicler
narrow *adj* **1** = **thin**, fine, slim, slender • *a narrow stream* OPPOSITE: wide **2** = **limited**, close, tight, restricted, meagre, confined, constricted, contracted **3** = **insular**, partial, intolerant, narrow-minded, dogmatic, illiberal, prejudiced, small-minded ▸ *v* **4** = **restrict**, reduce, limit, tighten, constrict
See also: **shrink**
narrowly *adv* = **just**, barely, scarcely, by the skin of one's teeth, only just
narrow-minded *adj* = **intolerant**, insular, opinionated, biased, bigoted, prejudiced • *their own narrow-minded view of the world* OPPOSITE: tolerant
nastiness *n* = **spitefulness**, malice, meanness
nasty *adj* **1** = **unpleasant**, foul, horrible, repellent, vile, disgusting, disagreeable • *a nasty taste* OPPOSITE: pleasant **2** = **spiteful**, mean, vicious, malicious, despicable, lousy (*slang*), unpleasant, vile, distasteful, disagreeable, scuzzy (*slang*) **3** = **serious**, bad, dangerous, critical, severe
See also: **unkind**
nation *n* = **country**, people, state, race, society, tribe, realm
national *adj* **1** = **nationwide**, public, widespread, countrywide ▸ *n* **2** = **citizen**, resident, native, subject, inhabitant
nationalism *n* = **patriotism**, loyalty, allegiance, chauvinism, jingoism
nationality *n* = **race**, nation, birth
nationwide *adj* = **national**, general,

DICTIONARY

independence **2** patriotism **nationalist** *n, adj*
▶ **nationality** *n* **1** fact of being a citizen of a particular nation **2** nation
▶ **nationalize** *v* put (an industry or a company) under state control **nationalization** *n*
▶ **national insurance** state insurance scheme providing payments to the unemployed, sick, and retired
▶ **national park** area of countryside protected by a government for its natural or environmental importance
native Ⓣ *adj* **1** relating to a place where a person was born **2** born in a specified place **3** (foll. by *to*) originating (in) **4** inborn ▷ *n* **5** person born in a specified place **6** member of the original race of a country **7** indigenous animal or plant
▶ **Native Canadian** Canadian Inuit, Indian, or Metis
Nativity *n Christianity* birth of Jesus Christ
NATO North Atlantic Treaty Organization
natter Ⓣ *informal* ▷ *v* **1** talk idly or chatter ▷ *n* **2** long idle chat
natty Ⓣ *adj* **-tier, -tiest** *informal* smart and spruce
natural Ⓣ *adj* **1** normal **2** genuine, not affected **3** of, according to, existing in, or produced by nature **4** not created by human beings **5** not synthetic **6** (of a parent) not adoptive **7** (of a child) illegitimate **8** *music* not sharp or flat ▷ *n* **9** person with an inborn talent or skill
▶ **naturally** *adv* **1** of course **2** in a natural or normal way **3** instinctively
▶ **naturalist** *n* student of natural history
▶ **naturalism** *n* movement in art and literature advocating detailed realism **naturalistic** *adj*
▶ **naturalize** *v* give citizenship to (a person born in another country) **naturalization** *n*
▶ **natural gas** gas found below the ground, used mainly as a fuel
▶ **natural history** study of animals and plants
▶ **natural selection** process by which only creatures and plants well adapted to their environment survive
nature Ⓣ *n* **1** whole system of the existence, forces, and events of the physical world that are not controlled by human beings **2** fundamental or essential qualities of a person or thing **3** kind or sort
naturism *n* nudism **naturist** *n*
naught Ⓣ *n* **1** *obsolete* nothing **2** figure 0
naughty Ⓣ *adj* **-tier, -tiest 1** disobedient or mischievous **2** mildly indecent **naughtily** *adv* **naughtiness** *n*
nausea Ⓣ [**naw**-zee-a] *n* feeling of being about to vomit
▶ **nauseate** *v* **1** make (someone) feel sick **2** disgust
▶ **nauseous** *adj* **1** as if about to vomit **2** sickening

THESAURUS

widespread, countrywide
native *adj* **1 = local**, home, domestic, indigenous **2 = inborn**, natural, congenital, innate, ingrained, hereditary, intrinsic, inbred, instinctive ▶ *n* **3 = inhabitant**, national, resident, citizen, dweller, countryman, aborigine
natter *See* **chat**
natty *adj* **= smart**, trim, elegant, stylish, fashionable, neat, spruce, dapper, snazzy (*informal*), phat (*slang*)
natural *adj* **1 = normal**, common, usual, typical, ordinary, everyday • *the natural reaction to such sad news* OPPOSITE: unnatural **2 = unaffected**, real, genuine, frank, candid • *He was so natural with the children.* OPPOSITE: false **3 = innate**, inherent, intuitive, inborn, instinctive • *He's a natural comedian.* **4 = pure**, whole, organic, plain, unrefined
See also: **automatic, informal, wild**
naturalist *n* **= biologist**, ecologist, zoologist, botanist
naturalistic *adj* **= realistic**, lifelike, true-to-life
naturally *adv* **1 = of course**, certainly **2 = genuinely**, simply, normally, typically, spontaneously, unaffectedly, unpretentiously
nature *n* **1 = personality**, character, makeup • *It's not in my nature to sit still.* **2 = creation**, world, environment, earth, universe, cosmos **3 = kind**, type, style, sort, category, variety, species, description **4 = character**, constitution, makeup, essence, complexion
naught *n* (*archaic*) **= nothing**, nothing, zero, zip (*informal*), nil, zilch (*informal*), nada (*slang*), diddley-squat (*slang*)
naughty *adj* **1 = disobedient**, bad, wayward, mischievous, impish • *a naughty child* OPPOSITE: well-behaved **2 = obscene**, vulgar, lewd, bawdy • *naughty song lyrics*
See also: **wicked**
nausea *n* **= sickness**, biliousness, queasiness, retching, squeamishness, vomiting
nauseate *v* **= sicken**, offend, disgust, revolt, repel, repulse, turn one's stomach
nauseous *adj* **= sickening**, offensive, abhorrent, distasteful, repulsive, repugnant, disgusting, revolting, nauseating, scuzzy (*slang*)

DICTIONARY

nautical Ⓣ *adj* of the sea or ships
▸ **nautical mile** 1852 metres
nautilus *n, pl* **-luses, -li** shellfish with many tentacles
naval Ⓣ *adj* see **navy**
nave *n* main part of a church
navel *n* hollow in the middle of the abdomen where the umbilical cord was attached
navigate Ⓣ *v* **1** direct or plot the path or position of a ship, aircraft, or automobile **2** travel over or through **navigation** *n* **navigator** *n*
▸ **navigable** *adj* **1** wide, deep, or safe enough to be sailed through **2** able to be steered
Navratilova *n* **Martina**. born 1956, Czech-born US tennis player: Wimbledon champion 1978, 1979, 1982–87, 1990; world champion 1980 and 1984
navvy Ⓣ *n, pl* **-vies** *Brit* labourer employed on a road or a building site
navy Ⓣ *n, pl* **-vies 1** branch of a country's armed services comprising warships with their crews and organization **2** warships of a nation ▹ *adj* **3** navy-blue
▸ **naval** *adj* of or relating to a navy or ships
▸ **navy-blue** *adj* very dark blue
nay *interj obsolete* no
Nazi *n* **1** member of the National Socialist Party, which seized political control in Germany in 1933 under Adolf Hitler ▹ *adj* **2** of or relating to the Nazis **Nazism** *n*
NB **1** note well **2** Also **N.B.** New Brunswick
NCO non-commissioned officer
N'Dour *n* **Youssou**. born 1959, Senegalese singer and musician, whose work has popularized African music in the West; recordings include *Nelson Mandela* (1986), *Eyes Open* (1992), and *Nothing's in Vain* (2002)
NDP New Democratic Party
NDT Newfoundland Daylight Time
Ne *chem* neon
NE northeast(ern)
Neanderthal [nee-**ann**-der-tahl] *adj* of a type of primitive man that lived in Europe before 12 000 BC
neap tide *n* tide at the first and last quarters of the moon when there is the smallest rise and fall in tidal level
near Ⓣ *prep* **1** close to, not far from ▹ *adv* **2** at or to a place or time not far away ▹ *adj* **3** (situated) at or in a place or time not far away **4** (of people) closely related **5** almost being the thing specified: *a near tragedy* ▹ *v* **6** approach and be about to reach **nearness** *n*
▸ **nearly** *adv* almost
▸ **nearby** *adj* not far away
▸ **nearside** *n* side of a vehicle that is nearer the curb
neat Ⓣ *adj* **1** tidy and clean **2** smoothly or competently done **3** undiluted **neatly** *adv* **neatness** *n*
nebula [**neb**-yew-la] *n astronomy* hazy cloud of particles and gases

n

THESAURUS

nautical *adj* = **maritime**, marine, naval
naval *adj* = **nautical**, marine, maritime
navigable *adj* **1** = **passable**, clear, unobstructed, negotiable **2** = **sailable**, controllable, dirigible
navigate *v* = **steer**, drive, pilot, handle, guide, sail, voyage, manoeuvre
navigation *n* = **sailing**, helmsmanship, seamanship, voyaging
navigator *n* = **pilot**, mariner, seaman
navvy *n* (*Informal*) = **labourer**, worker, workman
navy *n* = **fleet**, flotilla, armada
near *adj* **1** = **close**, nearby, adjacent, adjoining • *The Rockies are near.* OPPOSITE: far **2** = **imminent**, upcoming, forthcoming, approaching, looming • *The time of birth is near.* ▸ *preposition* **3** = **close to**, alongside, adjacent to, next to, not far from • *Take a chair near the*
See also: **beside, immediate**
nearby *adj* = **neighbouring**, adjacent, convenient, handy, adjoining
nearest *See* **next**
nearly *adv* = **almost**, virtually, practically, as good as, just about • *The beach was nearly empty.*
See also: **about**
nearness *n* = **closeness**, proximity, availability, accessibility, vicinity, handiness
near-sighted *adj* = **short-sighted**, myopic
neat *adj* **1** = **tidy**, trim, smart, orderly • *The house was clean and neat.* OPPOSITE: untidy **2** = **graceful**, efficient, elegant, stylish, adept, deft, nimble, skilful, adroit, dexterous **3** (~ *alcoholic drinks*) = **undiluted**, straight, pure, unmixed
See also: **handy**
neatly *adv* **1** = **tidily**, systematically, methodically, smartly, daintily, fastidiously, sprucely **2** = **gracefully**, efficiently, deftly, expertly, elegantly, adeptly, adroitly, dexterously, nimbly, skillfully
neatness *n* **1** = **tidiness**, daintiness, orderliness, smartness, spruceness, trimness **2** = **grace**, skill, style, efficiency, elegance, dexterity, adroitness, deftness, nimbleness
nebulous *adj* = **vague**, unclear, uncertain, indefinite, confused, dim, hazy, shadowy, imprecise, indistinct
necessarily *adv* = **inevitably**, certainly, automatically, naturally, undoubtedly, compulsorily, incontrovertibly, inexorably, of necessity

DICTIONARY

▶ **nebulous** *adj* vague, indistinct
necessary ⓘ *adj* **1** indispensable or required: *the necessary skills* **2** certain or unavoidable: *the necessary consequences* **necessarily** *adv*
▶ **necessitate** *v* compel or require
▶ **necessitous** *adj* very needy
▶ **necessity** *n* **1** something needed **2** compulsion
neck *n* **1** part of the body joining the head to the shoulders **2** part of a garment round the neck **3** narrow part of a bottle or violin ▷ *v* **4** *slang* kiss and cuddle
▶ **neck and neck** absolutely level in a race or competition
▶ **neckerchief** *n* piece of cloth worn tied round the neck
▶ **necklace** *n* decorative piece of jewellery worn around the neck
Necker *n* **Jacques**. 1732–1804, French financier and statesman, born in Switzerland; finance minister of France (1777–81; 1788–90). He attempted to reform the fiscal system and in 1789 he recommended summoning the States General. His subsequent dismissal was one of the causes of the storming of the Bastille (1789)
necromancy ⓘ [**neck**-rome-man-see] *n* **1** communication with the dead **2** sorcery
necropolis ⓘ [neck-**rop**-pol-liss] *n* cemetery
nectar *n* **1** sweet liquid collected from flowers by bees **2** drink of the gods
nectarine *n* smooth-skinned peach
née [**nay**] *prep* indicating the maiden name of a married woman
need ⓘ *v* **1** want or require **2** be obliged (to do something) ▷ *n* **3** condition of lacking something **4** requirement, necessity **5** poverty
▶ **needs** *adv* (foll. by *must*) necessarily
▶ **needy** *adj* poor, in need of financial support
▶ **needful** *adj* necessary or required
▶ **needless** *adj* unnecessary
needle ⓘ *n* **1** thin pointed piece of metal with an eye through which thread is passed for sewing **2** long pointed rod used in knitting **3** pointed part of a hypodermic syringe **4** small pointed part in a record player that touches the record and picks up the sound signals **5** pointer on a measuring instrument or compass **6** long narrow stiff leaf ▷ *v* **7** *informal* goad or provoke
▶ **needlework** *n* sewing and embroidery
ne'er *adv lit* never
▶ **ne'er-do-well** *n* useless or lazy person
nefarious ⓘ [nif-**fair**-ee-uss] *adj* wicked
Nefertiti, Nofretete *n* 14th century BC, Egyptian queen; wife of Akhenaton
negate ⓘ *v* **1** invalidate **2** deny **negation** *n*

THESAURUS

necessary *adj* **1 = needed**, essential, vital, required, imperative, indispensable • *Make the necessary arrangements.* OPPOSITE: unnecessary **2 = certain**, inevitable, unavoidable, inexorable • *a necessary consequence of overindulgence*
See also: **basic**
necessitate *v* = **compel**, force, demand, require, coerce, oblige, constrain, call for, impel
necessities *pl n* = **essentials**, exigencies, fundamentals, needs, requirements
necessity *n* **1 = inevitability**, obligation, compulsion, inexorableness **2 = need**, requirement, essential, fundamental, requisite, prerequisite, desideratum, *sine qua non* (*Latin*)
neck and neck *See* **even**
necromancy *n* = **magic**, sorcery, witchcraft, wizardry, black magic, divination, enchantment
necropolis *n* = **cemetery**, graveyard, burial ground, churchyard
need *v* **1 = require**, want, demand • *You need some fresh air.* ▶ *n* **2 = poverty**, lack, shortage, deprivation, inadequacy, insufficiency, destitution, paucity, penury **3 = requirement**, demand, essential, requisite, desideratum **4 = emergency**, want, obligation, urgency, necessity, exigency
See also: **distress**
needed *adj* = **necessary**, wanted, required, called for, desired, lacked
needful *adj* = **necessary**, essential, vital, needed, required, indispensable, requisite, stipulated
needle *v* = **irritate**, provoke, harass, taunt, rile, annoy, nag, goad, pester, get on one's nerves (*informal*)
needless *adj* = **unnecessary**, unwanted, useless, pointless, redundant, groundless, gratuitous, superfluous, uncalled-for
needlework *n* = **embroidery**, needlecraft, sewing, stitching, tailoring
needy *adj* = **poor**, impoverished, disadvantaged, poverty-stricken, underprivileged, destitute, penniless, deprived
ne'er-do-well *n* = **good-for-nothing**, black sheep, couch potato (*slang*), idler, loser, loafer, wastrel
nefarious *adj* = **wicked**, criminal, foul, evil, heinous, villainous, depraved, infernal
negate *v* **1 = invalidate**, cancel, reverse, neutralize, annul, nullify, countermand, obviate, wipe out **2 = deny**, oppose, contradict, refute, disallow, disprove, rebut, gainsay (*archaic or lit*)
negation *n* **1 = cancellation**, neutralization,

DICTIONARY

negative Ⓣ *adj* **1** expressing a denial or refusal **2** lacking positive qualities **3** (of an electrical charge) having the same electrical charge as an electron ▷ *n* **4** negative word or statement **5** *photog* image with a reversal of tones or colours from which positive prints are made

neglect Ⓣ *v* **1** take no care of **2** disregard **3** fail (to do something) through carelessness ▷ *n* **4** neglecting or being neglected **neglectful** *adj*

negligee [**neg**-lee-zhay] *n* woman's lightweight usu. lace-trimmed dressing gown

negligence Ⓣ *n* neglect or carelessness **negligent** *adj* **negligently** *adv*

negligible Ⓣ *adj* so small or unimportant as to be not worth considering

negotiate Ⓣ *v* **1** discuss in order to reach (an agreement) **2** succeed in passing round or over (a place or problem) **negotiation** *n* **negotiator** *n* **negotiable** *adj*

Negro *n, pl* **-groes** *now considered offensive* member of any of the Black peoples originating in Africa

▶ **Negroid** *adj* of or relating to a Black people

Nehru *n* **1 Jawaharlal**. 1889–1964, Indian statesman and nationalist leader. He spent several periods in prison for his nationalist activities and practiced a policy of noncooperation with Britain during World War II. He was the first prime minister of the republic of India (1947–64) **2** his father, **Motilal**, known as *Pandit Nehru*. 1861–1931, Indian nationalist, lawyer, and journalist; first president of the reconstructed Indian National Congress

neigh *n* **1** loud high-pitched sound made by a horse ▷ *v* **2** make this sound

neighbour, neighbor *n* one who lives or is situated near another

▶ **neighbouring** *or* **neighboring** *adj* situated nearby

▶ **neighbourhood** *or* **neighborhood** *n* **1** district where people live **2** surroundings

▶ **neighbourly** *or* **neighborly** *adj* kind, friendly, and helpful

neither *adj, pron* **1** not one nor the other ▷ *conj* **2** not

nelson *n* wrestling hold in which a wrestler places his arm(s) under his opponent's arm(s) from behind and exerts pressure with his palms on the back of his opponent's neck

Nelson *n* **1 Horatio**, Viscount Nelson. 1758–1805, British naval commander during the Revolutionary and Napoleonic Wars. He became rear admiral in 1797 after the battle of Cape St Vincent and in 1798 almost destroyed the French fleet at the battle of the Nile. He was killed at Trafalgar (1805) after defeating Villeneuve's fleet **2 Willie**. born 1933, US country singer and songwriter

nemesis Ⓣ [**nem**-miss-iss] *n, pl* **-ses**

n

THESAURUS

nullification **2** = **denial**, reverse, opposite, rejection, contradiction, converse, inverse, renunciation, disavowal

negative *adj* **1** = **contradictory**, contrary, denying, dissenting, opposing, refusing, rejecting, resisting **2** = **pessimistic**, unwilling, gloomy, cynical, jaundiced, uncooperative, unenthusiastic ▶ *n* **3** = **contradiction**, refusal, denial

neglect *v* **1** = **disregard**, ignore, overlook, turn your back on • *unhappy and neglected children* **2** = **fail**, forget, omit • *He had neglected to give her his address.* ▶ *n* **3** = **disregard**, indifference, unconcern • *Most of her plants died from neglect.* **4** = **negligence**, failure, oversight, dereliction, carelessness, laxity, slackness

neglected *adj* **1** = **abandoned**, derelict, overgrown **2** = **disregarded**, unappreciated, undervalued, underestimated

neglectful *adj* = **careless**, lax, negligent, indifferent, thoughtless, remiss, heedless, inattentive, uncaring

negligence *n* = **carelessness**, neglect, disregard, indifference, dereliction, inattention, laxity, slackness, thoughtlessness

negligent *adj* = **careless**, slack, thoughtless, remiss, forgetful, heedless, inattentive, neglectful, slapdash, unthinking

negligible *adj* = **insignificant**, minute, small, minor, trivial, unimportant, inconsequential, imperceptible, trifling

negotiable *adj* = **debatable**, variable

negotiate *v* **1** = **bargain**, deal, debate, discuss, arrange, mediate, haggle, conciliate, transact, work out **2** = **get round**, pass, clear, cross, surmount, get over, get past

negotiation *n* = **bargaining**, transaction, debate, discussion, arbitration, diplomacy, mediation, haggling, wheeling and dealing (*informal*)

negotiator *n* = **mediator**, ambassador, diplomat, delegate, moderator, intermediary, honest broker

neighbourhood *n* = **district**, quarter, community, region, locale, vicinity, locality, environs

neighbouring *adj* = **nearby**, near, adjacent, adjoining, connecting, next to, surrounding, bordering

neighbourly *adj* = **helpful**, kind, friendly, considerate, sociable, harmonious, hospitable, obliging

nemesis *n* = **retribution**, fate, destruction, destiny, vengeance

retribution or vengeance
neo- *combining form* new, recent, or a modern form of: *neoclassicism*
neolithic *adj* of the later Stone Age
neologism [nee-**ol**-a-jiz-zum] *n* new-coined word or an established word used in a new sense
neon *n* colourless odourless gaseous element used in illuminated signs and lights
neonatal *adj* relating to the first few weeks of a baby's life
neophyte *n* **1** beginner or novice **2** new convert
nephew *n* son of one's sister or brother
nephritis [nif-**frite**-tiss] *n* inflammation of a kidney
nepotism ⓣ [**nep**-a-tiz-zum] *n* favouritism in business shown to relatives and friends
Neptune *n* **1** Roman god of the sea **2** eighth planet from the sun
neptunium *n* synthetic metallic element
nerd, nurd ⓣ *n slang* **1** boring person obsessed with a particular subject **2** stupid and feeble person
Nero *n* full name *Nero Claudius Caesar Drusus Germanicus*, original name *Lucius Domitius Ahenobarbus*. 37–68 AD, Roman emperor (54–68). He became notorious for his despotism and cruelty, and was alleged to have started the fire (64) that destroyed a large part of Rome
Neruda *n* **Pablo**, real name *Neftali Ricardo Reyes*. 1904–73, Chilean poet. His works include *Veinte poemas de amor y una canción desesperada* (1924) and *Canto general* (1950), an epic history of the Americas: Nobel prize for literature 1971
Nerva *n* full name *Marcus Cocceius Nerva*. ?30–98 AD, Roman emperor (96–98), who introduced some degree of freedom after the repressive reign of Domitian. He adopted Trajan as his son and successor
nerve ⓣ *n* **1** cordlike bundle of fibres that conducts impulses between the brain and other parts of the body **2** bravery and determination **3** impudence **nerves** **4** anxiety or tension **5** ability or inability to remain calm in a difficult situation
▸ **get on someone's nerves** irritate someone
▸ **nerve oneself** prepare oneself (to do something difficult or unpleasant)
▸ **nerveless** *adj* **1** fearless **2** numb, without feeling
▸ **nervy** *adj informal* brash or cheeky
▸ **nerve centre** place from which a system or organization is controlled
▸ **nerve-racking** *adj* very distressing or harrowing
Nervi *n* **Pier Luigi**. 1891–1979, Italian engineer and architect; noted for his pioneering use of reinforced concrete as a decorative material. He codesigned the UNESCO building in Paris (1953)
nervous ⓣ *adj* **1** apprehensive or worried **2** of or relating to the nerves **nervously** *adv* **nervousness** *n*
▸ **nervous breakdown** mental illness in which the sufferer ceases to function properly
Nesbit *n* **E(dith)**. 1858–1924, British writer of children's books, including *The Phoenix and the Carpet* (1904) and *The Railway Children* (1906)
Nesselrode *n* Count **Karl Robert**. 1780–1862, Russian diplomat: as foreign minister (1822–56), he negotiated the Treaty of Paris after the Crimean War (1856)
nest ⓣ *n* **1** place or structure in which birds or certain animals lay eggs or give birth to young **2** snug retreat **3** set of things of graduated sizes designed to fit together

THESAURUS

nepotism *n* = **favoritism**, bias, patronage, partiality, preferential treatment
nerd, nurd *n* = **bore**, drip (*informal*), geek (*slang*), egghead (*informal*), doofus (*slang*), dork (*slang*), dweeb (*slang*), goober (*informal*)
nerve *n* **1** = **impudence**, gall, audacity, insolence, rudeness • *I'm amazed they had the nerve to ask in the first place.* **2** = **bravery**, will, resolution, courage, pluck, daring, grit, fearlessness, guts (*informal*) ▸ *v* ▹ **nerve oneself** = **brace oneself**, fortify oneself, steel oneself
nerveless *adj* = **calm**, cool, controlled, unemotional, composed, impassive, imperturbable, self-possessed
nerve-racking *adj* = **tense**, difficult, stressful, white-knuckle (*informal*), distressing, frightening, harrowing, trying, worrying
nerves *pl n* = **tension**, worry, stress, strain, anxiety, nervousness, butterflies *or* butterflies in one's stomach (*informal*), cold feet (*informal*), fretfulness
nervous *adj* = **apprehensive**, anxious, tense, worried, edgy, jittery, uptight, jumpy • *She had been nervous before the finals.* OPPOSITE: calm
See also: **afraid, dubious, timid, uneasy**
nervousness *n* = **anxiety**, worry, tension, agitation, fluster, excitability, disquiet, touchiness
nervy *adj* = **anxious**, nervous, tense, jittery (*informal*), fidgety, jumpy, twitchy (*informal*), agitated, on edge, wired (*slang*)
nest *n* = **refuge**, retreat, haunt, den, hideaway ▹ **nest egg** *n* = **savings**, fund *or* funds, store, reserve, deposit, cache, fall-back

DICTIONARY

▷ *v* **4** make or inhabit a nest
▸ **nest egg** fund of money kept in reserve
nestle Ⓣ *v* **1** snuggle **2** be in a sheltered position
nestling Ⓣ *n* bird too young to leave the nest
net[1] Ⓣ *n* **1** openwork fabric of meshes of string, thread, or wire **2** piece of net used to protect or hold things or to trap animals ▷ *v* **netting, netted 3** cover with or catch in a net
▸ **netting** *n* material made of net
net[2]**, nett** Ⓣ *adj* **1** left after all deductions **2** (of weight) excluding the wrapping or container ▷ *v* **netting, netted 3** yield or earn as a clear profit
Netanyahu *n* **Benjamin**. born 1949, Israeli politician: leader of the Likud party (1993–99); prime minister (1996–99; 2009–)
nether Ⓣ *adj* lower
nettle *n* **1** plant with stinging hairs on the leaves ▷ *v* **2** irritate
network Ⓣ *n* **1** system of intersecting lines, roads, etc. **2** interconnecting group or system **3** (in broadcasting) group of stations that all transmit the same programmes simultaneously
neural *adj* of a nerve or the nervous system
neuralgia *n* severe pain along a nerve
neuritis [nyoor-**rite**-tiss] *n* inflammation of a nerve or nerves
neurology *n* scientific study of the nervous system **neurologist** *n*
neurosis Ⓣ *n, pl* **-ses** mental disorder producing hysteria, anxiety, depression, or obsessive behaviour
▸ **neurotic** *adj* **1** abnormally sensitive **2** suffering from neurosis ▷ *n* **3** neurotic person
neurosurgery *n* branch of surgery concerned with the nervous system
neurosurgical *adj* **neurosurgeon** *n*
neuter Ⓣ *adj* **1** belonging to a particular class of grammatical inflections in some languages ▷ *v* **2** castrate (an animal)
neutral Ⓣ *adj* **1** taking neither side in a war or dispute **2** of or belonging to a neutral party or country **3** (of a colour) not definite or striking **4** of no distinctive quality or type ▷ *n* **5** neutral person or nation **6** neutral gear
neutrality *n*
▸ **neutralize** *v* **1** make ineffective or neutral **2** *mil euphemistic* kill or render harmless
neutralization *n*
▸ **neutral gear** position of the controls of a gearbox that leaves the gears unconnected to the engine
▸ **neutral zone** *hockey* area between the two blue lines
neutrino [new-**tree**-no] *n, pl* **-nos** elementary particle with no mass or electrical charge
neutron *n* electrically neutral elementary particle of about the same mass as a proton
▸ **neutron bomb** nuclear bomb designed to kill people and animals while leaving buildings virtually undamaged
never Ⓣ *adv* at no time
▸ **nevertheless** *adv* in spite of that
new Ⓣ *adj* **1** not existing before **2** having lately come into some state **3** additional

THESAURUS

nestle *v* = **snuggle**, huddle, cuddle, curl up, nuzzle
nestling *n* = **chick**, fledgling
net[1] *n* **1** = **mesh**, network, web, lattice, netting, openwork, tracery ▸ *v* **2** = **catch**, capture, bag, trap, entangle, ensnare, enmesh
net[2] *adj* **1** = **after taxes**, final, clear, take-home ▸ *v* **2** = **earn**, make, gain, clear, realize, reap, accumulate, bring in
nether *adj* = **lower**, under, below, bottom, underground, beneath, inferior
nettled *adj* = **irritated**, annoyed, incensed, exasperated, galled, harassed, peeved, put out, riled, vexed
network *n* **1** = **web**, grid, maze, labyrinth, lattice **2** = **system**, organization, complex, structure, arrangement
neurosis *n* = **obsession**, abnormality, instability, phobia, affliction, derangement, maladjustment, mental illness
neurotic *adj* = **unstable**, nervous, unhealthy, abnormal, compulsive, obsessive, disturbed, manic, maladjusted
neuter *v* = **castrate**, doctor (*informal*), fix (*informal*), spay, emasculate, geld
neutral *adj* **1** = **impartial**, disinterested, dispassionate, nonaligned • *We stayed neutral during their dispute*. OPPOSITE: biased **2** = **indeterminate**, dull, intermediate, undefined, indistinct
See also: **impersonal**
neutrality *n* = **impartiality**, detachment, nonalignment, noninterference, noninvolvement, nonpartisanship
neutralize *v* = **counteract**, cancel, frustrate, offset, undo, negate, nullify, counterbalance, compensate for
never *adv* = **at no time**, not ever • *I never said I was leaving*.
nevertheless *adv* = **even so**, but, still, however, though *or* even though, yet, regardless, notwithstanding, nonetheless
new *adj* **1** = **modern**, recent, current, original, novel, fresh, contemporary, latest, state-of-the-art, unfamiliar, up-to-date, ground-breaking • *a new invention* OPPOSITE: old **2** = **changed**,

DICTIONARY

4 (foll. by *to*) unfamiliar ▷ *adv* 5 recently
newness *n*
▸ **New Age** philosophy characterized by a belief in alternative medicine and spiritualism
▸ **newbie** *n informal* person new to a job, club, etc.
▸ **newborn** *adj* recently or just born
▸ **newcomer** *n* recent arrival or participant
▸ **New Democrat** *Canad* member of the New Democratic Party
▸ **New Democratic Party** major political party with policies to the left of Liberal and Progressive Conservative Parties
▸ **new-fangled** *adj* objectionably or unnecessarily modern
▸ **new moon** moon when it appears as a narrow crescent at the beginning of its cycle
Newcastle *n* **Duke of**, the title of *Thomas Pelham Holles*. 1693–1768, English Whig prime minister (1754–56; 1757–62): brother of Henry Pelham
Newcombe *n* **John** (**David**). born 1944, Australian tennis player; winner of seven Grand Slam singles titles (1967–74)
newel *n* post at the top or bottom of a flight of stairs that supports the handrail
Newfie *n informal* person from Newfoundland
Newfoundland Daylight Time *n* standard time used only in Newfoundland and Labrador, 2½ hours behind Greenwich Mean Time Abbreviation: **NDT**
Newfoundland Time *n* standard time used only in Newfoundland and Labrador, 3½ hours behind Greenwich Mean Time Abbreviation: **NT**
Ne Win *n* **U**. 1911–2002, Burmese statesman and general; prime minister (1958–60), head of the military government (1962–74), and president (1974–81)
Newman *n* **1 John Henry**. 1801–90, British theologian and writer. Originally an Anglican minister, he was a prominent figure in the Oxford Movement. He became a Roman Catholic (1845) and a priest (1847) and was made a cardinal (1879). His writings include the spiritual autobiography, *Apologia pro vita sua* (1864), a treatise on the nature of belief, *The Grammar of Assent* (1870), and hymns **2 Paul**. 1925–2008, US film actor and director, who appeared in such films as *Hud* (1963), *Butch Cassidy and the Sundance Kid* (1969), *The Sting* (1973), *The Verdict* (1982), *The Colour of Money* (1986), *Nobody's Fool* (1994), and *Road to Perdition* (2002)
news 🅣 *n* **1** important or interesting recent happenings **2** information about such events reported in the mass media
▸ **newsy** *adj* full of news
▸ **newsagent** *n* shopkeeper who sells newspapers and magazines
▸ **newscaster** *n* person who reads the news on the television or radio
▸ **newsflash** *n* brief important news item, which interrupts a radio or television programme
▸ **newsgroup** *n* electronic discussion group on the internet that is devoted to a specific topic
▸ **newsletter** *n* bulletin issued periodically to members of a group
▸ **newspaper** *n* weekly or daily publication containing news
▸ **newsprint** *n* inexpensive paper used for newspapers
▸ **newsroom** *n* room where news is received and prepared for publication or broadcasting
▸ **newsworthy** *adj* sufficiently interesting to be reported as news
newt *n* small amphibious creature with a long slender body and tail
newton *n* unit of force
Newton *n* Sir **Isaac**. 1642–1727, English mathematician, physicist, astronomer, and philosopher, noted particularly for his law of gravitation, his three laws of motion, his theory that light is composed of corpuscles, and his development of calculus independently of Leibnitz. His works include *Principia Mathematica* (1687) and *Opticks* (1704)
Newtonian *adj*
next 🅣 *adj, adv* **1** immediately following **2** nearest

THESAURUS

renewed, altered, modernized, improved, redesigned, restored **3 = extra**, more, added, supplementary
See also: **inexperienced, strange**
newcomer *n* = **beginner**, arrival, Johnny-come-lately (*informal*), new kid in town (*informal*), novice, parvenu, cheechako (*Canad*)
newfangled *adj* = **new**, recent, novel, cool (*informal*), modern, contemporary, state-of-the-art, fashionable, gimmicky, phat (*slang*)
newly *adv* = **recently**, just, lately, freshly, anew, latterly
newness *n* = **novelty**, innovation, oddity, freshness, originality, uniqueness, unfamiliarity, strangeness
news *n* = **information**, word, intelligence, disclosure, dispatch, latest (*informal*), bulletin, tidings (*formal*) • *news about the trial*
newsworthy *adj* = **interesting**, important, significant, remarkable, notable, noteworthy, stimulating
next *adj* **1 = following**, subsequent, ensuing, succeeding • *Their next car will be a convertible.* **2 = nearest**, adjacent,

DICTIONARY

▶ **next-of-kin** *n* closest relative
nexus *n, pl* **nexus** connection or link
NF, N.F. Newfoundland
Nfld. Newfoundland
Ni *chem* nickel
NI National Insurance
nib Ⓣ *n* writing point of a pen
nibble Ⓣ *v* **1** take little bites (of) ▷ *n* **2** little bite **3** light meal
nibs *n* **his** *or* **her nibs** *slang* mock title of respect
nice Ⓣ *adj* **1** pleasant **2** kind: *a nice gesture* **3** good or satisfactory: *they made a nice job of it* **4** subtle: *a nice distinction* **nicely** *adv* **niceness** *n*
▶ **nicety** *n* **1** subtle point **2** refinement or delicacy
niche Ⓣ [**neesh**] *n* **1** hollow area in a wall **2** exactly suitable position for a particular person
Nicholas *n* **1 Graydon.** Lieutenant Governor of New Brunswick (2009–) **2 Saint.** 4th-century AD bishop of Myra, in Asia Minor; patron saint of Russia and of children, sailors, merchants, and pawnbrokers. Feast day: Dec 6 See also **Santa Claus**
Nicholas I *n* **1** 1796–1855, tsar of Russia (1825–55). He gained notoriety for his autocracy and his emphasis on military discipline and bureaucracy **2 Saint**, called *the Great*. died 867 AD, Italian ecclesiastic; pope (858–867). He championed papal supremacy. Feast day: Nov 13
Nicholas II *n* 1868–1918, tsar of Russia (1894–1917). After the disastrous Russo-Japanese War (1904–05), he was forced to summon a representative assembly, but his continued autocracy and incompetence precipitated the Russian Revolution (1917): he abdicated and was shot
Nicholas of Cusa *n* 1401–64, German cardinal, philosopher, and mathematician: anticipated Copernicus in asserting that the earth revolves around the sun
Nicholson *n* **1 Ben.** 1894–1982, English painter, noted esp. for his abstract geometrical works **2 Jack.** born 1937, US film actor. His films include *Easy Rider* (1969), *One Flew Over the Cuckoo's Nest* (1974), *Terms of Endearment* (1983), *Batman* (1989), *As Good As It Gets* (1998), and *About Schmidt* (2002) **3 John.** 1821–57, British general and administrator, born in Ireland: deputy commissioner in the Punjab (1851–56), where he became the object of hero-worship among the natives and kept the Punjab loyal during the Indian Mutiny: played a major role in the capture of Delhi
Nicias *n* died 414 BC, Athenian statesman and general. He ended the first part of the Peloponnesian War by making peace with Sparta (421)
nick Ⓣ *v* **1** make a small cut in **2** *slang* steal **3** *Brit slang* arrest ▷ *n* **4** small cut **5** *Brit slang* prison or police station
▶ **in good nick** *informal* in good condition
▶ **in the nick of time** just in time
nickel *n* **1** silvery-white metal often used in alloys **2** Canadian and US coin worth five cents
nickelodeon *n US* early type of jukebox
Nicklaus *n* **Jack.** born 1940, US professional golfer: won the British Open Championship (1966; 1970; 1978) and the US Open Championship (1962; 1967; 1972; 1980)
nickname Ⓣ *n* **1** familiar name given to a person or place ▷ *v* **2** call by a nickname
Nicolai *n* **Carl Otto Ehrenfried.** 1810–49, German composer: noted for his opera *The Merry Wives of Windsor* (1849)
Nicolson *n* Sir **Harold** (**George**). 1886–1968, British diplomat, politician, and author: married to Vita Sackville-West

THESAURUS

adjoining, closest, neighbouring • *in the next room* ▷ **next world** *See* **heaven**
▶ *adv* **3 = afterwards**, subsequently • *My brother arrived next.* ▷ **next to** *See* **beside, near**
nib *See* **point**
nibble *v* **1 = bite**, eat, nip, peck, munch, gnaw, pick at ▶ *n* **2 = snack**, taste, bite, peck, crumb, tidbit, morsel, *soupçon* (*French*)
nice *adj* **1 = pleasant**, good, attractive, charming, delightful, agreeable, pleasurable • *We had a nice vacation.* **2 = kind**, friendly, polite, likable *or* likeable, courteous, well-mannered **3 = neat**, fine, trim, tidy, dainty **4 = subtle**, fine, strict, careful, delicate, precise, meticulous, fastidious
nicely *adv* **1 = pleasantly**, well, attractively, charmingly, delightfully, acceptably, agreeably, pleasurably **2 = kindly**, politely, amiably, commendably, courteously **3 = neatly**, finely, daintily, tidily, trimly
niceties *See* **ceremony**
nicety *n* **= subtlety**, discrimination, distinction, delicacy, nuance, refinement, daintiness
niche *n* **1 = alcove**, opening, corner, recess, hollow, nook **2 = position**, place, slot (*informal*), calling, vocation, pigeonhole (*informal*)
nick *v* **1 = cut**, score, mark, chip, notch, scratch, dent, scar, snick ▶ *n* **2 = cut**, mark, chip, notch, scratch, dent, scar
nickname *n* **= pet name**, label, moniker *or* monicker (*slang*), diminutive, epithet, sobriquet

DICTIONARY

nicotine *n* poisonous substance found in tobacco
Niebuhr *n* **Reinhold.** 1892–1971, US Protestant theologian. His works include *Moral Man and Immoral Society* (1932) and *The Nature and Destiny of Man* (1941–43)
niece *n* daughter of one's sister or brother
Nielsen *n* **1 Carl (August).** 1865–1931, Danish composer. His works include six symphonies and the opera *Masquerade* (1906) **2 Leslie.** born 1926, Canadian film and TV actor. Noted for his role in the *The Naked Gun* series of films (1988–94)
Niemeyer *n* **Oscar.** born 1907, Brazilian architect. His work includes many buildings in Brasília, esp. the president's palace (1959) and the cathedral (1964)
Nietzsche *n* **Friedrich Wilhelm.** 1844–1900, German philosopher, poet, and critic, noted esp. for his concept of the superman and his rejection of traditional Christian values. His chief works are *The Birth of Tragedy* (1872), *Thus Spake Zarathustra* (1883–91), and *Beyond Good and Evil* (1886) **Nietzschean** *n, adj* **Nietzscheism** *or* **Nietzscheanism** *n*
nifty Ⓣ *adj* **-tier, -tiest** *informal* neat or smart
niggard Ⓣ *n* stingy person **niggardly** *adj*
nigger *n offensive* Black person
niggle Ⓣ *v* **1** worry slightly **2** continually find fault (with) ▷ *n* **3** small worry or doubt
nigh Ⓣ *adv, prep lit* near
night Ⓣ *n* time of darkness between sunset and sunrise
▸ **nightly** *adj, adv* (happening) each night
▸ **nightcap** *n* **1** drink taken just before bedtime **2** soft cap formerly worn in bed **3** *baseball* second game in a double-header, played in the evening
▸ **nightclub** *n* establishment for dancing, music, etc., open late at night
▸ **nightdress** *n* woman's loose dress worn in bed
▸ **nightfall** *n* approach of darkness
▸ **nightie** *n informal* nightdress
▸ **nightingale** *n* small bird with a musical song usually heard at night
▸ **nightjar** *n* nocturnal bird with a harsh cry
▸ **nightlife** *n* entertainment and social activities available at night in a town or city
▸ **nightmare** *n* **1** very bad dream **2** very unpleasant experience
▸ **night school** place where adults can attend educational courses in the evenings
▸ **nightshade** *n* plant with bell-shaped flowers which are often poisonous
▸ **nightshirt** *n* man's long loose shirt worn in bed
▸ **night-time** *n* time from sunset to sunrise
Nightingale *n* **Florence**, known as *the Lady with the Lamp.* 1820–1910, English nurse, famous for her work during the Crimean War. She helped to raise the status and quality of the nursing profession and founded a training school for nurses in London (1860)
nihilism [nye-ill-liz-zum] *n* rejection of all established authority and institutions **nihilist** *n* **nihilistic** *adj*
nil Ⓣ *n* nothing, zero
nimble Ⓣ *adj* **1** agile and quick **2** mentally alert or acute **nimbly** *adv*
nimbus *n, pl* **-bi, -buses 1** dark grey rain cloud **2** halo
nimrod *n* **1** *slang* boring social misfit **2 Nimrod** person who is dedicated to or skilled in hunting
nincompoop Ⓣ *n informal* stupid person
nine *adj, n* one more than eight
▸ **ninth** *adj, n* (of) number nine in a series
▸ **nineteen** *adj, n* ten and nine **nineteenth** *adj, n*
▸ **ninety** *adj, n* ten times nine **ninetieth** *adj, n*
▸ **ninepins** *n* game of skittles
Ninian *n* **Saint.** ?360–?432 AD, the first known apostle of Scotland; built a stone church (*candida casa*) at Whithorn on his

THESAURUS

nifty *adj* = **neat**, smart, attractive, stylish, chic, pleasing, deft
niggard *n* = **miser**, cheapskate (*informal*), Scrooge, skinflint
niggardly *adj* = **stingy**, mean, frugal, miserly, avaricious, grudging, parsimonious, tightfisted, ungenerous
niggle *v* **1** = **worry**, annoy, irritate, rankle **2** = **criticize**, fuss, carp, cavil, find fault
niggling *adj* **1** = **persistent**, gnawing, irritating, troubling, worrying **2** = **petty**, picky (*informal*), fussy, finicky, nit-picking (*informal*), pettifogging, quibbling
nigh *See* **near**
night *n* = **darkness**, dark, night-time
nightfall *n* = **evening**, sunset, dusk, twilight, sundown
nightly *adj* **1** = **nocturnal**, night-time ▸ *adv* **2** = **every night**, each night, night after night, nights (*informal*)
nightmare *n* **1** = **bad dream**, hallucination **2** = **ordeal**, trial, horror, torment, tribulation
nil *n* = **nothing**, love, none, zero, naught
nimble *adj* = **agile**, quick, swift, brisk, lively, deft, spry, dexterous, sprightly
nimbly *adv* = **agilely**, quickly, easily, readily, swiftly, briskly, deftly, smartly, dexterously, spryly
nincompoop *n* = **idiot**, fool, chump, blockhead, dork (*slang*), nitwit (*informal*), schmuck (*slang*)

DICTIONARY

native Solway; preached to the Picts. Feast day: Sept 16

Ninus *n* a king of Assyria and the legendary founder of Nineveh, husband of Semiramis

nip Ⓣ *v* **nipping, nipped 1** *informal* hurry **2** pinch or squeeze **3** bite lightly ▷ *n* **4** pinch **5** light bite **6** small alcoholic drink **7** sharp coldness: *a nip in the air*

▸ **nippy** *adj* **1** frosty or chilly **2** *Brit informal* quick or nimble

▸ **nipper** *n informal* small child

nipple *n* projection in the centre of a breast

nirvana Ⓣ [near-**vah**-na] *n Buddhism, Hinduism* absolute spiritual enlightenment and bliss

nisi [**nye**-sigh] *adj* see **decree nisi**

nit *n* **1** egg or larva of a louse **2** *informal* short for **nitwit**

▸ **nit-picking** *adj informal* overconcerned with insignificant detail, esp. to find fault

▸ **nitwit** *n informal* stupid person

nitrogen [**nite**-roj-jen] *n* colourless odourless gas that forms four fifths of the air

▸ **nitric, nitrous,** *or* **nitrogenous** *adj* of or containing nitrogen

▸ **nitrate** *n* compound of nitric acid, used as a fertilizer

▸ **nitroglycerin** *or* **nitroglycerine** *n* explosive liquid

nitty-gritty Ⓣ *n informal* basic facts

Niven *n* **David**. 1909–83, British film actor and author. His films include *The Prisoner of Zenda* (1937), *Around the World in 80 Days* (1956), *Casino Royale* (1967), and *Paper Tiger* (1975). He wrote the autobiographical *The Moon's a Balloon* (1972) and *Bring on the Empty Horses* (1975)

Nixon *n* **Richard M(ilhous)**. 1913–94, US Republican politician; 37th president from 1969 until he resigned over the Watergate scandal in 1974

Nizam al-Mulk *n* title of *Abu Ali Hasan Ibn Ali*. ?1018–92, Persian statesman; vizier of Persia (1063–92) for the Seljuk sultans: assassinated

Nkomo *n* **Joshua**. 1917–99, Zimbabwean politician; coleader, with Robert Mugabe, of the Patriotic Front (1976–80) against the government of Ian Smith in Rhodesia; minister (1980–82; 1988–99) and vice-president (1990–96).

Nkrumah *n* **Kwame**. 1909–72, Ghanaian statesman, prime minister (1957–60) and president (1960–66). He led demands for self-government in the 1950s, achieving Ghanaian independence in 1957. He was overthrown by a military coup (1966)

NL Newfoundland and Labrador

no Ⓣ *interj* **1** expresses denial, disagreement, or refusal ▷ *adj* **2** not any, not a ▷ *adv* **3** not at all ▷ *n, pl* **noes, nos 4** answer or vote of 'no' **5** person who answers or votes 'no'

▸ **no-go area** district barricaded off so that the police or army can enter only by force

▸ **no-hitter** *n baseball* game in which a team's pitchers allow no base hits

▸ **no-man's-land** *n* land between boundaries, esp. contested land between two opposing forces

▸ **no-one** *or* **no one** *pron* nobody

no. number

nob Ⓣ *n slang* person of wealth or social distinction

nobble Ⓣ *v slang* **1** attract the attention of (someone) in order to talk to him or her **2** bribe or threaten

Nobel *n* **Alfred Bernhard**. 1833–96, Swedish chemist and philanthropist, noted for his invention of dynamite (1866) and his bequest founding the Nobel prizes

▸ **Nobel prize** [no-**bell**] prize awarded annually for outstanding achievement in various fields

noble Ⓣ *adj* **1** showing or having high moral qualities **2** of the nobility **3** impressive and magnificent ▷ *n* **4** member of the nobility **nobly** *adv* **nobleman** (**noblewoman**) *n*

THESAURUS

nip[1] *v* = **pinch**, bite, squeeze, tweak

nip[2] *n* = **dram**, drop, shot (*informal*), draft, sip, mouthful, snifter (*informal*)

nipper *n* (*Informal*) = **child**, girl, baby, boy, kid (*informal*), infant, tot

nippy *adj* = **chilly**, sharp, biting, stinging

nirvana *n* = **paradise**, peace, joy, bliss, serenity, tranquillity

nit-picking *adj* = **fussy**, finicky, captious, carping, hairsplitting, pedantic, pettifogging, quibbling

nitty-gritty *n* = **basics**, core, substance, crux, gist, brass tacks (*informal*), essentials, fundamentals

nitwit *n* (*Informal*) = **fool**, dummy (*slang*), dimwit (*informal*), doofus (*slang*), dork (*slang*), halfwit, oaf, schmuck (*slang*), simpleton

no *interj* **1** = **not at all**, absolutely not, certainly not, definitely not, of course not, in a pig's eye (*informal*) • *"Any problems?" "No, everything's fine."* OPPOSITE: yes **2** = **refusal**, denial, negation ▷ **no go** = **impossible**, futile, hopeless, vain

nob *n* = **aristocrat**, toff (*Brit, slang*), V.I.P.

nobble *v* = **bribe**, influence, intimidate, get at, win over

nobility *n* **1** = **integrity**, honour, virtue, incorruptibility, uprightness **2** = **aristocracy**, elite, lords, nobles, patricians, peerage, upper class

noble *adj* **1** = **worthy**, generous, upright, honourable, virtuous, magnanimous • *a good and noble thing to do* OPPOSITE: ignoble **2** = **aristocratic**, blue-blooded,

DICTIONARY

▸ **nobility** *n* **1** quality of being noble **2** class of people holding titles and high social rank
noblesse oblige [no-**bless** oh-**bleezh**] *n* (*oft.*) *ironic* supposed obligation of the nobility to be honourable and generous
nobody Ⓣ *pron* **1** no person ▹ *n, pl* **-bodies** **2** person of no importance
nocturnal Ⓣ *adj* **1** of the night **2** active at night
nocturne *n* short dreamy piece of music
nod Ⓣ *v* **nodding, nodded 1** lower and raise (one's head) briefly in agreement or greeting **2** let one's head fall forward with sleep ▹ *n* **3** act of nodding
▸ **nod off** *v informal* fall asleep
node *n* **1** point on a plant stem from which leaves grow **2** point at which a curve crosses itself
nodule *n* **1** small knot or lump **2** rounded mineral growth on the root of a plant
Noel *n* Christmas
noggin Ⓣ *n* **1** small quantity of an alcoholic drink **2** *informal* head
noise Ⓣ *n* sound, usually a loud or disturbing one **noiseless** *adj*
▸ **be noised abroad** be rumoured
▸ **noisy** *adj* **1** making a lot of noise **2** full of noise **noisily** *adv*
noisome Ⓣ *adj* **1** (of smells) offensive **2** harmful or poisonous
Nolde *n* **Emil.** 1867–1956, German painter and engraver, noted particularly for his violent use of colour and the primitive masklike quality of his figures
nomad Ⓣ *n* member of a tribe with no fixed dwelling place, wanderer **nomadic** *adj*
nom de plume Ⓣ *n, pl* **noms de plume** pen name
nomenclature Ⓣ [no-**men**-klatch-er] *n* system of names used in a particular subject
nominal Ⓣ *adj* **1** in name only **2** very small in comparison with real worth **nominally** *adv*
nominate Ⓣ *v* **1** suggest as a candidate **2** appoint to an office or position
nomination *n*
▸ **nominee** *n* candidate
▸ **nominative** *n* form of a *n* indicating subject of a verb
non- *prefix* **1** *indicating* negation: *nonexistent* **2** *indicating* refusal or failure: *noncooperation* **3** *indicating* exclusion from a specified class: *nonfiction* **4** *indicating* lack or absence: *nonevent*
nonagenarian *n* person aged between ninety and ninety-nine
non-aggression *n* (of countries) not attacking
nonagon *n* geometric figure with nine sides **nonagonal** *adj*
non-alcoholic *adj* containing no alcohol
nonaligned *adj* (of a country) not part of a major alliance or power bloc
nonce *n* **for the nonce** for the present

THESAURUS

highborn, lordly, patrician, titled **3 = great**, grand, impressive, lofty, distinguished, dignified, splendid, stately, imposing ▸ *n* **4 = aristocrat**, nobleman • *He claims to come from a family of British nobles.*
nobleman *See* **noble**
nobody *pron* **1 = no-one** ▸ *n* **2 = nonentity**, lightweight (*informal*), cipher, menial
nocturnal *adj* **= nightly**, night-time
nod *v* **1 = gesture**, indicate, acknowledge, signal, bow **2 = sleep**, nap, doze, drowse ▸ *n* **3 = gesture**, sign, signal, indication, greeting, acknowledgment
noggin *n* **1 = cup**, nip, mug, tot, dram **2** (*Informal*) **= head**, block (*informal*), nut (*slang*), noodle (*slang*)
noise *n* **= din**, uproar, racket, commotion, pandemonium, hubbub • *He is making an awful noise.* OPPOSITE: silence
See also: **sound**
noiseless *adj* **= silent**, still, quiet, mute, inaudible, hushed, soundless
noisome *adj* **1 = poisonous**, bad, harmful, unhealthy, pernicious, pestilential, unwholesome **2 = disgusting**, offensive, foul, funky (*slang*), noxious, smelly, putrid, fetid, malodorous, stinking
noisy *adj* **= loud**, tumultuous, strident, piercing, vociferous, deafening • *a noisy audience of schoolchildren* OPPOSITE: quiet
See also: **rowdy**
nomad *n* **= wanderer**, rover, migrant, itinerant, drifter, rambler, vagabond
nomadic *adj* **= wandering**, migrant, itinerant, peripatetic, roaming, roving, traveling, vagrant
nom de plume *n* **= pseudonym**, alias, assumed name, nom de guerre, pen name
nomenclature *n* **= terminology**, classification, vocabulary, codification, phraseology, taxonomy
nominal *adj* **1 = so-called**, formal, purported, puppet, theoretical, titular, supposed, ostensible, professed **2 = small**, symbolic, minimal, insignificant, token, trivial, inconsiderable, trifling
nominate *v* **= propose**, name, suggest, recommend, select, submit • *The partyrefused to nominate him as its candidate.*
nomination *n* **= choice**, election, proposal, recommendation, selection, appointment, suggestion, designation
nominee *n* **= candidate**, runner, contestant, entrant, aspirant, protégé
nonaligned *adj* **= neutral**, undecided, impartial, uncommitted

DICTIONARY

nonchalant Ⓣ [**non**-shall-ant] *adj* casually unconcerned or indifferent **nonchalantly** *adv* **nonchalance** *n*
noncombatant Ⓣ *n* member of the armed forces whose duties do not include fighting
non-commissioned officer *n* (in the armed forces) a subordinate officer, risen from the ranks
noncommittal Ⓣ *adj* not committing oneself to any particular opinion
non compos mentis *adj* of unsound mind
non-conductor *n* substance that is a poor conductor of heat, electricity, or sound
non-confidence *Canad* ▷ *n* **1** absence of majority support in a legislature for a government ▷ *adj* **2** indicating or arising from an absence of majority support for a government: *a non-confidence motion*
nonconformist Ⓣ *n* **1** person who does not conform to generally accepted patterns of behaviour or thought **2 Nonconformist** member of a Protestant group separated from the Church of England ▷ *adj* **3** (of behaviour or ideas) not conforming to accepted patterns **nonconformity** *n*
non-contributory *adj* denoting a pension scheme for employees, the premiums of which are paid entirely by the employer
nondescript Ⓣ *adj* lacking outstanding features
none Ⓣ *pron* **1** not any **2** no-one
▸ **nonetheless** *adv* despite that, however
nonentity Ⓣ [non-**enn**-tit-tee] *n, pl* **-ties** insignificant person or thing
nonessential Ⓣ *adj* not absolutely necessary
nonevent Ⓣ *n* disappointing or insignificant occurrence
nonexistent Ⓣ *adj* not existing, imaginary **nonexistence** *n*
non-flammable *adj* not easily set on fire
non-intervention *n* refusal to intervene in the affairs of others
non-nuclear *adj* not involving or using nuclear power or weapons
Nono *n* **Luigi**. 1924–90, Italian composer of 12-tone music
nonpareil [non-par-**rail**] *n* person or thing that is unsurpassed
nonpartisan *adj* not supporting any single political party
nonpayment *n* failure to pay money owed
nonplussed *adj* perplexed
nonsectarian *adj* not confined to any specific religion
nonsense Ⓣ *n* **1** something that has or makes no sense **2** absurd language **3** foolish behaviour **nonsensical** *adj*
non sequitur [**sek**-wit-tur] *n* statement with little or no relation to what preceded it
nonsmoker *n* **1** person who does not smoke **2** train carriage or compartment in which smoking is forbidden
▸ **nonsmoking** *or* **no-smoking** *adj* denoting an area in which smoking is forbidden
non-standard *adj* denoting language that is not regarded as correct by educated native speakers
nonstarter Ⓣ *n* person or idea that has little chance of success
non-status *adj Canad* of or relating to any person of Indian ancestry who is not registered as such under the Indian Act
non-stick *adj* coated with a substance that food will not stick to when cooked

THESAURUS

nonchalance *n* = **indifference**, calm, composure, equanimity, imperturbability, sang-froid, self-possession, unconcern
nonchalant *adj* = **indifferent**, calm, casual, careless, laid-back (*informal*), unconcerned, blasé, insouciant, offhand, unperturbed
noncombatant *n* = **civilian**, neutral, nonbelligerent
noncommittal *adj* = **evasive**, tentative, cautious, wary, neutral, vague, guarded, politic, equivocal, circumspect, temporizing
nonconformist *n* = **dissenter**, protester, rebel, radical, maverick, eccentric, heretic, iconoclast, individualist
nonconformity *n* = **dissent**, heresy, eccentricity, heterodoxy
nondescript *adj* = **ordinary**, dull, commonplace, featureless, unremarkable, undistinguished, unexceptional
none *pron* = **not any**, nothing, nobody, zero, nil, no-one, not one
nonentity *n* = **nobody**, lightweight (*informal*), mediocrity, cipher, small fry
nonessential *adj* = **unnecessary**, peripheral, expendable, unimportant, extraneous, superfluous, dispensable, inessential
nonetheless *adv* = **nevertheless**, however, yet, despite that, even so, in spite of that
nonevent *n* = **failure**, disappointment, flop (*informal*), fiasco, dud (*informal*), washout
nonexistent *adj* = **imaginary**, legendary, fictional, hypothetical, mythical, unreal, illusory, chimerical
nonsense *n* = **garbage** (*informal*), garbage (*informal*), rubbish, drivel, inanity • *I say the accusation is complete nonsense.*
nonsensical *adj* = **senseless**, crazy, ridiculous, silly, absurd, foolish, meaningless, irrational, incomprehensible, inane
non-specific *See* **broad**
nonstarter *n* = **dead loss**, loser, lemon (*informal*), turkey (*informal*), dud (*informal*),

DICTIONARY

nonstop Ⓣ *adj, adv* without a stop
non-toxic *adj* not poisonous
noodle Ⓣ *n* strip of pasta
nook Ⓣ *n* sheltered place
noon Ⓣ *n* twelve o'clock midday
▶ **noonday** *n lit* noon
noose *n* loop in the end of a rope, tied with a slipknot
nor *conj* and not
Nordau *n* **Max Simon**, original name *Max Simon Südfeld*. 1849–1923, German author, born in Hungary; a leader of the Zionist movement
Nordenskjöld *n* Baron **Nils Adolf Erik**. 1832–1901, Swedish Arctic explorer and geologist, born in Finland. He was the first to navigate the Northeast Passage (1878–79)
Nordic *adj* of Scandinavia
▶ **Nordic skiing** cross-country skiing
▶ **Nordic walking** recreational walking using poles to aid movement
norm Ⓣ *n* standard that is regarded as normal
normal Ⓣ *adj* **1** usual, regular, or typical **2** free from mental or physical disorder
normally *adv* **normality** *n* **normalize** *v*
Norman *n* **Greg**. born 1955, Australian golfer
Norse *n, adj* (language) of ancient and medieval Norway
north Ⓣ *n* **1** direction towards the North Pole, opposite south **2** area lying in or towards the north ▷ *adv* **3** in, to, or towards the north ▷ *adj* **4** to or in the north **5** (of a wind) from the north **northerly** *adj* **northern** *adj* **northwards** *adv*
▶ **northerner** *n* person from the north of a country or area
▶ **northeast** *n, adj, adv* (in or to) direction between north and east
▶ **northwest** *n, adj, adv* (in or to) direction between north and west
▶ **North Pole** northernmost point on the earth's axis
North *n* **1 Frederick**, 2nd Earl of Guildford, called *Lord North*. 1732–92, British statesman; prime minister (1770–82), dominated by George III. He was held responsible for the loss of the American colonies **2** Sir **Thomas**. ?1535–?1601, English translator of Plutarch's *Lives* (1579), which was the chief source of Shakespeare's Roman plays
Northumberland *n* **1st Duke of**, title of *John Dudley*. 1502–53, English statesman and soldier, who governed England (1549–53) during the minority of Edward VI. His attempt (1553) to gain the throne for his daughter-in-law, Lady Jane Grey, led to his execution
nos. numbers
nose Ⓣ *n* **1** organ of smell, used also in breathing **2** front part of a vehicle ▷ *v* **3** move forward slowly and carefully **4** pry or snoop
▶ **nosy** *or* **nosey** *adj informal* prying or inquisitive **nosiness** *n*
▶ **nose dive** (of an aircraft) sudden drop
▶ **nosegay** *n* small bunch of flowers
nosh *slang* ▷ *n* **1** food ▷ *v* **2** eat
nostalgia Ⓣ *n* sentimental longing for the past **nostalgic** *adj*
Nostradamus *n* Latinized name of *Michel de Notredame*. 1503–66, French physician and astrologer; author of a book of prophecies in rhymed quatrains, *Centuries* (1555)
nostril *n* one of the two openings at the end of the nose
nostrum Ⓣ *n* **1** quack medicine **2** favourite remedy

THESAURUS

washout (*informal*), no-hoper (*informal*)
nonstop *adj* **1** = **continuous**, constant, endless, relentless, uninterrupted, incessant, unbroken, interminable, twenty-four-seven (*slang*) ▶ *adv* **2** = **continuously**, constantly, relentlessly, perpetually, endlessly, incessantly, ceaselessly, interminably, twenty-four-seven (*slang*), unremittingly
noodle *n* (*Slang*) = **head**, common sense, sense, intuition, gut feeling (*informal*)
nook *n* = **niche**, opening, corner, retreat, recess, hideout, alcove, cubbyhole
noon *n* = **midday**, high noon, noonday, noontide, twelve noon
norm *n* = **standard**, rule, average, par, pattern, benchmark, criterion, yardstick
normal *adj* **1** = **usual**, average, standard, regular, routine, conventional, typical, ordinary, habitual • *my normal routine* OPPOSITE: unusual **2** = **sane**, reasonable, rational, well-adjusted
See also: **natural**
normality *n* **1** = **regularity**, conventionality, naturalness **2** = **sanity**, reason, balance, rationality
normally *adv* = **usually**, generally, regularly, typically, commonly, ordinarily, as a rule, habitually
north *adj* **1** = **northern**, Arctic, polar, boreal, northerly ▶ *adv* **2** = **northward** *or* **northwards**, northerly
nose *n* **1** = **snout**, bill, beak, honker (*slang*), proboscis ▶ *v* **2** = **ease forward**, push, nudge, shove, nuzzle **3** = **pry**, meddle, snoop (*informal*)
nosegay *n* = **posy**, bouquet
nostalgia *n* = **reminiscence**, remembrance, longing, yearning, homesickness, pining, regretfulness, wistfulness
nostalgic *adj* = **sentimental**, emotional, homesick, longing, wistful, maudlin, regretful
nostrum *n* = **medicine**, drug, treatment, cure, remedy, elixir, potion, panacea

DICTIONARY

not *adv* expressing negation, refusal, or denial
notable Ⓣ [**note**-a-bl] *adj* **1** worthy of being noted, remarkable ▷ *n* **2** person of distinction
notably *adv* **notability** [note-a-**bill**-lit-tee] *n*
notary [**note**-a-ree] *n, pl* **-ries** person authorized to witness the signing of legal documents
notation Ⓣ [no-**tay**-shun] *n* **1** representation of numbers or quantities in a system by a series of symbols **2** set of such symbols
notch Ⓣ *n* **1** V-shaped cut **2** *informal* step or level ▷ *v* **3** make a notch in
note Ⓣ *n* **1** short letter **2** brief comment or record **3** banknote **4** (symbol for) a musical sound **5** hint or mood ▷ *v* **6** notice, pay attention to **7** record in writing **8** remark upon
▸ **noted** *adj* well-known
▸ **notebook** *n* book for writing in
▸ **noteworthy** *adj* worth noting, remarkable
nothing Ⓣ *pron* **1** not anything **2** matter of no importance **3** figure 0 ▷ *adv* **4** not at all
▸ **nothingness** *n* **1** nonexistence **2** insignificance
notice Ⓣ *n* **1** observation or attention **2** sign giving warning or an announcement **3** advance notification of intention to end a contract of employment ▷ *v* **4** observe, become aware of **5** point out or remark upon
▸ **noticeable** *adj* easily seen or detected, appreciable
notify Ⓣ *v* **-fying, -fied** inform
notification *n*
▸ **notifiable** *adj* having to be reported to the authorities
notion Ⓣ *n* **1** idea or opinion **2** whim
▸ **notional** *adj* speculative, imaginary, or unreal

THESAURUS

nosy *adj* = **inquisitive**, curious, eavesdropping, prying • *nosy neighbours watching us through the curtains*
notability *n* = **fame**, celebrity, distinction, esteem, renown, eminence
notable *adj* **1** = **remarkable**, rare, unusual, extraordinary, memorable, outstanding, uncommon, striking, noteworthy, conspicuous ▸ *n* **2** = **celebrity**, dignitary, big name, personage, V.I.P.
notably *adv* = **particularly**, especially, strikingly, outstandingly
not at all *See* **no**
notation *n* = **symbols**, system, code, script, characters, signs
not be able to abide *See* **dislike**
not be able to bear *See* **dislike**
not be able to stand *See* **dislike**
notch *n* **1** = **cut**, score, mark, nick, incision, cleft, indentation **2** (*Informal*) = **grade**, level, step, degree ▸ *v* **3** = **cut**, score, mark, scratch, nick, indent ▷ **notch up** = **achieve**, make, score, gain, register
not dangerous *See* **harmless**
note *n* **1** = **message**, email, letter, communication (*formal*), memo, reminder, memorandum • *I wrote him a note asking him to visit.* **2** = **record**, account, jotting • *I made a note of his address.* **3** = **tone**, touch, hint, trace • *I detected a note of bitterness in his voice.* **4** = **symbol**, sign, mark, indication, token ▸ *v* **5** = **notice**, see, register, observe, perceive • *I noted that the rain had stopped.* **6** = **mention**, remark **7** = **indicate**, record, mark, register, designate, denote
See also: **comment, entry**
notebook *n* = **notepad**, journal, diary, exercise book, jotter
noted *adj* = **famous**, prominent, acclaimed, renowned, well-known, notable, celebrated, illustrious, distinguished, eminent
not ever *See* **never**
noteworthy *adj* = **remarkable**, important, significant, unusual, extraordinary, notable, exceptional, outstanding
not far from *See* **near**
not guilty *See* **innocent**
nothing *n* = **naught**, zero, void, nil, nada (*informal*), emptiness, nothingness, nullity
nothingness *n* **1** = **oblivion**, nonbeing, nonexistence, nullity **2** = **insignificance**, unimportance, worthlessness
notice *v* **1** = **observe**, see, note, spot, detect, perceive, discern • *Then I noticed he wasn't laughing.* ▸ *n* **2** = **sign**, bill, poster, advertisement • *a handwritten notice posted on the wall* **3** = **advance warning**, warning, notification, intimation • *She was transferred without notice.* **4** = **observation**, note, interest, regard, consideration, heed, cognizance **5** = **attention**, respect, civility
See also: **information, item, review**
noticeable *adj* = **obvious**, evident, unmistakable, conspicuous, perceptible • *a noticeable improvement*
See also: **prominent, visible**
notification *n* = **announcement**, statement, information, warning, message, notice, intelligence, advice, declaration, heads-up
notify *v* = **inform**, tell, warn, advise (*formal*)
See also: **alert, report**
notion *n* **1** = **idea**, view, opinion, belief, concept, sentiment, impression, inkling **2** = **whim**, wish, desire, impulse, fancy, inclination, caprice
notional *adj* = **hypothetical**, abstract, speculative, imaginary, theoretical, unreal, conceptual
not level *See* **uneven**

n

DICTIONARY

notorious Ⓣ *adj* well known for something bad **notoriously** *adv* **notoriety** *n*
notwithstanding Ⓣ *prep* in spite of
▸ **notwithstanding clause** clause in the Canadian Charter of Rights and Freedoms allowing provincial legislatures and the federal Parliament to override Charter clauses pertaining to equality and legal rights
nougat *n* chewy candy containing nuts and fruit
nought Ⓣ *n* **1** nothing **2** figure 0
▸ **noughties** *pl n informal* decade from 2000 to 2009
noun *n* word that refers to a person, place, or thing
nourish Ⓣ *v* **1** feed **2** encourage or foster (an idea or feeling) **nourishment** *n*
▸ **nourishing** *adj* providing the food necessary for life and growth
nouveau riche [**noo**-voh **reesh**] *n, pl* **nouveaux riches** [**noo**-voh **reesh**] person who has recently become rich and is regarded as vulgar
nouvelle cuisine [**noo**-vell kwee-**zeen**] *n* style of preparing and presenting food with light sauces and unusual combinations of flavours
Nov. November
nova *n, pl* **-vae, -vas** star that suddenly becomes brighter and then gradually decreases to its original brightness
novel[1] Ⓣ *n* long fictitious story in book form
▸ **novelist** *n* writer of novels
▸ **novella** *n, pl* **-las, -lae** short novel
novel[2] Ⓣ *adj* fresh, new, or original
▸ **novelty** *n* **1** newness **2** something new or unusual **3** cheap toy or trinket
Novello *n* **Ivor**, real name *Ivor Novello Davies*. 1893–1951, Welsh actor, composer, songwriter, and dramatist
November *n* eleventh month of the year
novena [no-**vee**-na] *n, pl* **-nae** *RC Church* set of prayers or services on nine consecutive days
novice Ⓣ [**nov**-viss] *n* **1** beginner **2** person who has entered a religious order but has not yet taken vows
now Ⓣ *adv* **1** at or for the present time **2** immediately ▹ *conj* **3** seeing that, since
▸ **just now** very recently
▸ **now and again** *or* **now and then** occasionally
▸ **nowadays** *adv* in these times
nowhere *adv* not anywhere
noxious Ⓣ *adj* **1** poisonous or harmful **2** extremely unpleasant
nozzle *n* projecting spout through which fluid is discharged
NS, N.S. Nova Scotia
NST Newfoundland Standard Time
NT **1** New Testament **2** Newfoundland Time
Nu *n* **U**, original name *Thakin Nu*. 1907–95, Burmese statesman and writer; prime minister (1948–56, 1957–58, 1960–62). He attempted to establish parliamentary democracy, but was ousted (1962) by Ne Win
NU Nunavut
nuance Ⓣ [**new**-ahnss] *n* subtle difference in colour, meaning, or tone

THESAURUS

not liable *See* **exempt**
not many *See* **few**
notoriety *n* = **infamy**, scandal, disrepute, dishonour, obloquy, opprobrium
notorious *adj* = **infamous**, scandalous, disreputable • *The district was notorious for violent crime.*
notoriously *adv* = **infamously**, dishonorably, disreputably, opprobriously, scandalously
not quite *See* **almost**
not smooth *See* **uneven**
not well *See* **unhealthy**
notwithstanding *prep* = **despite**, in spite of
nought *n* (*archaic*) = **naught**, nothing, zero, zip (*informal*), nil, zilch (*informal*), nada (*slang*)
nourish *v* **1** = **feed**, supply, nurse, tend, sustain, nurture **2** = **encourage**, support, maintain, promote, comfort, foster, cultivate
nourishing *adj* = **nutritious**, beneficial, wholesome, nutritive
nourishment *n* = **food**, nutrition, sustenance, nutriment
novel[1] *n* = **story**, tale, fiction, romance, narrative
novel[2] *adj* = **new**, different, original, fresh, unusual, strange, innovative, uncommon, unfamiliar
novelty *n* **1** = **newness**, surprise, innovation, oddity, freshness, originality, uniqueness, unfamiliarity, strangeness **2** = **gimmick**, gadget, curiosity **3** = **knick-knack**, souvenir, memento, trinket, trifle, bauble
novice *n* = **beginner**, amateur, newcomer, pupil, apprentice, trainee, learner, probationer
now *adv* **1** = **at the moment**, currently, nowadays • *I'm feeling much better now.* **2** = **immediately**, straightaway, at once, right now, without delay • *Tell her I need to see her now.* ▹ **now and then, now and again** = **occasionally**, sometimes, sporadically, infrequently, intermittently, from time to time, on and off
nowadays *adv* = **now**, today, anymore, at the moment, in this day and age
noxious *adj* = **harmful**, deadly, foul, unhealthy, destructive, poisonous, hurtful, injurious, unwholesome
nuance *n* = **subtlety**, degree, shade,

DICTIONARY

nub *n* point or gist (of a story etc.)
nubile Ⓣ [**new**-bile] *adj* **1** (of a young woman) sexually attractive **2** old enough to get married
nuclear *adj* **1** of nuclear weapons or energy **2** of a nucleus, esp. the nucleus of an atom
▸ **nuclear bomb** bomb whose force is due to uncontrolled nuclear fusion or fission
▸ **nuclear energy** energy released as a result of nuclear fission or fusion
▸ **nuclear fission** splitting of an atomic nucleus
▸ **nuclear fusion** combination of two nuclei to form a heavier nucleus with the release of energy
▸ **nuclear power** power produced by a nuclear reactor
▸ **nuclear reaction** change in structure and energy content of an atomic nucleus by interaction with another nucleus or particle
▸ **nuclear reactor** device in which a nuclear reaction is maintained and controlled to produce nuclear energy
▸ **nuclear winter** theoretical period of low temperatures and little light after a nuclear war
nucleic acid *n* complex compound, such as DNA or RNA, found in all living cells
nucleonics *n* branch of physics dealing with the applications of nuclear energy
nucleus Ⓣ *n, pl* **-clei 1** centre, esp. of an atom or cell **2** central thing around which others are grouped
nude Ⓣ *adj* **1** naked ▹ *n* **2** naked figure in painting, sculpture, or photography **nudity** *n*
▸ **nudism** *n* practice of not wearing clothes **nudist** *n*
nudge Ⓣ *v* **1** push gently, esp. with the elbow ▹ *n* **2** gentle push or touch
nugatory [**new**-gat-tree] *adj* **1** trifling **2** not valid
nugget Ⓣ *n* **1** small lump of gold in its natural state **2** something small but valuable
nuisance Ⓣ *n* something or someone that causes annoyance or bother
nuke *slang* ▹ *v* **1** attack with nuclear weapons ▹ *n* **2** nuclear bomb
null Ⓣ *adj* **null and void** not legally valid **nullity** *n*
▸ **nullify** *v* **1** make ineffective **2** cancel
Numa Pompilius *n* the legendary second king of Rome (?715–?673 BC), said to have instituted religious rites
numb Ⓣ *adj* **1** without feeling, as through cold, shock, or fear ▹ *v* **2** make numb **numbly** *adv* **numbness** *n*
▸ **numbskull** *n* same as **numskull**
number Ⓣ *n* **1** sum or quantity **2** word or symbol used to express a sum or quantity, numeral **3** one of a series, such as a copy of a magazine **4** *grammar* classification of words depending on how many persons or things are referred to **5** song or piece of music **6** group of people **7** numeral or string of numerals used to identify a person or thing ▹ *v* **8** count **9** give a number to **10** amount to **11** include in a group
▸ **numberless** *adj* too many to be counted
▸ **number crunching** *computers* large-scale processing of numerical data
▸ **number one 1** *informal* oneself **2** first in

THESAURUS

distinction, refinement, nicety, tinge, gradation
nubile *adj* = **marriageable**, ripe (*informal*)
nucleus *n* = **centre**, heart, focus, basis, core, pivot, kernel, nub
nude *adj* = **naked**, bare, disrobed, in one's birthday suit, stark-naked, stripped, unclad, unclothed, undressed, without a stitch on (*informal*)
nudge *v* = **push**, touch, bump, elbow, dig, poke, shove, jog, prod
nudity *n* = **nakedness**, undress, bareness, deshabille, nudism
nugget *n* = **lump**, piece, mass, chunk, clump, hunk
nuisance *n* = **bother**, pain (*informal*), inconvenience, pest, hassle, irritation, annoyance • *Sorry to be a nuisance.*
null *adj* ▹ **null and void** = **invalid**, void, useless, worthless, inoperative, valueless
nullify *v* = **cancel**, veto, neutralize, negate, counteract, invalidate, obviate, render null and void
nullity *n* = **nonexistence**, powerlessness, invalidity, uselessness, worthlessness
numb *adj* **1** = **frozen**, paralyzed, insensitive • *Your right arm goes numb.* ▸ *v* **2** = **deaden**, freeze, stun, paralyze, dull • *The cold numbed my fingers.*
See also: **shock**
numbed *See* **dazed**
number *n* **1** = **numeral**, figure, digit • *Pick a number between one and ten.* **2** = **collection**, crowd, multitude, horde • *She has introduced me to a large number of people.* **3** = **issue**, copy, edition, printing, imprint ▸ *v* **4** = **count**, include, add, total, account, calculate, compute, reckon, enumerate
See also: **quantity**
numberless *adj* = **infinite**, countless, endless, myriad, untold, innumerable, multitudinous, unnumbered
numbness *n* = **deadness**, paralysis, insensitivity, dullness, torpor
numbskull, numskull *n* = **fool**, blockhead, dummy (*slang*), dolt, dork (*slang*),

DICTIONARY

importance or quality
numeral ⓣ *n* word or symbol used to express a sum or quantity
numerate *adj* able to do basic arithmetic **numeracy** *n*
numeration *n* act or process of numbering or counting
numerator *n math* number above the line in a fraction
numerical *adj* measured or expressed in numbers **numerically** *adv*
numerous ⓣ *adj* existing or happening in large numbers
numismatist *n* coin collector
numskull *n* stupid person
nun *n* female member of a religious order
▸ **nunnery** *n* convent
nuncio ⓣ *n RC Church* pope's ambassador
nuptial ⓣ *adj* relating to marriage
▸ **nuptials** *pl n* wedding
Nurhachi *n* 1559–1626, Manchurian leader, who unified the Manchurian state and began (1618) the Manchurian conquest of China
Nuri as-Said *n* 1888–1958, Iraqi soldier and statesman: prime minister of Iraq 14 times between 1930 and 1958: he died during a military coup
nurse ⓣ *n* **1** person employed to look after sick people, usu. in hospital **2** woman employed to look after children ▹ *v* **3** look after (a sick person) **4** breast-feed (a baby) **5** try to cure (an ailment) **6** harbour or foster (a feeling)
▸ **nursery** *n* **1** room where children sleep or play **2** place where children are taken care of while their parents are at work **3** place where plants are grown for sale
▸ **nurseryman** *n* person who raises plants for sale
▸ **nursery school** school for children from 3 to 5 years old
▸ **nursery slope** gentle ski slope for beginners
▸ **nursing home** private hospital or home for old people
nurture ⓣ *n* **1** act or process of promoting the development of a child or young plant ▹ *v* **2** promote or encourage the development of
nut ⓣ *n* **1** fruit consisting of a hard shell and a kernel **2** small piece of metal that screws onto a bolt **3** *slang* head **4** *slang* eccentric person
▸ **nutty** *adj* **1** containing or resembling nuts **2** *slang* insane or eccentric
▸ **nutter** *n slang* insane or violent person
▸ **nutcracker** *n* device for cracking the shells of nuts
▸ **nuthatch** *n* small songbird
▸ **nutmeg** *n* spice made from the seed of a tropical tree
nutria [**new**-tree-a] *n* fur of the coypu
nutrient [**new**-tree-ent] *n* substance that provides nourishment
nutriment [**new**-tree-ment] *n* food or nourishment required by all living things to grow and stay healthy
nutrition ⓣ [new-**trish**-shun] *n* **1** process of taking in and absorbing nutrients **2** process of being nourished
▸ **nutritious** *or* **nutritive** *adj* nourishing
nuzzle ⓣ *v* push or rub gently with the nose or snout
NW northwest(ern)
NWT, N.W.T. Northwest Territories
nylon *n* **1** synthetic material used for clothing etc. **nylons 2** stockings made of nylon
nymph ⓣ *n* mythical spirit of nature, represented as a beautiful young woman
nymphet *n* sexually precocious young girl
nymphomaniac *n* woman with an abnormally intense sexual desire
NZ New Zealand

THESAURUS

dunce, oaf, schmuck (*slang*)
numeral *n* = **number**, figure, digit, integer
numerous *adj* = **many**, several, lots • *on numerous occasions*
nuncio *n* = **ambassador**, envoy, messenger, legate
nunnery *n* = **convent**, house, abbey, cloister
nuptial *adj* = **marital**, bridal, conjugal, connubial, matrimonial
nuptials *pl n* = **wedding**, marriage, matrimony
nurse *v* **1** = **look after**, treat, tend, care for, minister to **2** = **breast-feed**, feed, nurture, nourish, suckle, wet-nurse **3** = **foster**, support, promote, encourage, preserve, cultivate, cherish, harbour, succour
nursery *n* = **nursery school**, daycare, kindergarten, playroom
nurture *n* **1** = **upbringing**, development, training, education, discipline, instruction, rearing ▸ *v* **2** = **bring up**, school, develop, train, discipline, educate, instruct, rear
nut *n* (*Slang*) = **lunatic**, crank (*informal*), madman, psycho (*slang*), maniac, nutcase (*slang*)
nutrition *n* = **food**, nourishment, sustenance, nutriment
nutritious *adj* = **nourishing**, beneficial, wholesome, health-giving, invigorating, nutritive, strengthening
nuts *adj* (*Informal*) = **insane**, mad, unstable, psychotic, disturbed, unbalanced, deranged, mentally ill
nuzzle *v* = **snuggle**, pet, burrow, nestle, cuddle, fondle
nymph *n* = **sylph**, girl, maiden, dryad, naiad

DICTIONARY

Oo

oaf Ⓣ *n* stupid or clumsy person **oafish** *adj*
oak *n* **1** deciduous forest tree **2** its wood, used for furniture **oaken** *adj*
▸ **oak apple** brownish lump found on oak trees
oakum *n* fibre obtained by unravelling old rope
oar *n* pole with a broad blade, used for rowing a boat
oasis *n, pl* **-ses** fertile area in a desert
oast *n* kiln for drying hops
Oates *n* **1** Captain **Lawrence Edward Grace.** 1880–1912, English explorer. He died on Scott's second Antarctic expedition **2 Titus.** 1649–1705, English conspirator. He fabricated the Popish Plot (1678), a supposed Catholic conspiracy to kill Charles II, burn London, and massacre Protestants. His perjury caused the execution of many innocent Catholics
oath Ⓣ *n* **1** solemn promise, esp. to be truthful in court **2** swearword
oats *pl n* grain of a cereal plant, used for food
▸ **sow one's wild oats** have many sexual relationships when young **oaten** *adj*
▸ **oatmeal** *adj* pale brownish-cream
Obama *n* **Barack (Hussein).** born 1961, US Democrat politician: 44th president of the US from 2009
Obasanjo *n* **Olusegun.** born 1937, Nigerian politician and general; head of the military government (1976–79); president (1999–2007)
obbligato [ob-lig-**gah**-toe] *n music* essential part or accompaniment
obdurate Ⓣ *adj* **1** hardhearted **2** stubborn **obduracy** *n*
OBE Officer of the Order of the British Empire
obedient Ⓣ *adj* obeying or willing to obey **obediently** *adv* **obedience** *n*
obeisance [oh-**bay**-sanss] *n* **1** attitude of respect **2** bow or curtsy
obelisk Ⓣ [**ob**-bill-isk] *n* four-sided stone column tapering to a pyramid at the top
obese Ⓣ [oh-**beess**] *adj* very fat **obesity** *n*
obey Ⓣ *v* **1** carry out the instructions of (someone) **2** comply with (instructions)
obfuscate Ⓣ *v* **1** darken **2** make (something) confusing
obituary *n, pl* **-aries** announcement of someone's death, esp. in a newspaper **obituarist** *n*
object[1] Ⓣ *n* **1** physical thing **2** focus of thoughts or action **3** aim or purpose **4** *grammar* word that a verb or preposition affects
▸ **no object** not a hindrance
object[2] Ⓣ *v* (foll. by *to*) oppose **objection** *n* **objector** *n*
▸ **objectionable** *adj* unpleasant

THESAURUS

oaf *n* = **lout**, brute • *You stupid oaf!*
See also: **idiot**
oafish *adj* = **loutish**, stupid, thick, dense, dumb (*informal*), moronic, dim-witted (*informal*), doltish
oath *n* **1** = **promise**, pledge, vow • *an oath of loyalty to the government* **2** = **swearword**, curse, profanity, expletive, blasphemy
See also: **word**
obdurate *adj* = **stubborn**, dogged, inflexible, unyielding, implacable, hard-hearted, immovable, obstinate, pig-headed
obedience *n* = **submissiveness**, respect, compliance, observance, reverence, acquiescence, docility, subservience
obedient *adj* = **submissive**, law-abiding, subservient • *He was always very obedient to his parents.* OPPOSITE: disobedient
obelisk *n* = **column**, needle, monument, shaft, pillar, monolith
obese *adj* = **fat**, heavy, overweight, gross, portly, plump, stout, rotund, corpulent, paunchy, tubby
obesity *n* = **fatness**, bulk, corpulence, grossness, portliness, stoutness, tubbiness
obey *v* = **abide by**, follow, observe, adhere to, comply with • *Most people obey the law.* OPPOSITE: disobey
obfuscate *v* = **confuse**, cloud, obscure, darken, perplex, befog, muddy the waters
object[1] *n* **1** = **thing**, article • *everyday objects such as wooden spoons* **2** = **purpose**, goal, aim, idea, intention, objective • *The object of the exercise is to raise money for the charity.* **3** = **target**, victim, focus, recipient
See also: **point, subject, use**
object[2] *v* = **protest against**, oppose • *A lot of people will object to the book.* OPPOSITE: approve ▷ **object to** *See* **query, resent**
See also: **disagree, mind, protest**
objection *n* = **protest**, opposition • *despite objections by the committee* OPPOSITE: support
See also: **complaint, disagreement, grumble**
objectionable *adj* = **unpleasant**, offensive,

DICTIONARY

objective ⓣ *adj* **1** existing in the real world outside the human mind **2** not biased ▷ *n* **3** aim or purpose **objectively** *adv* **objectivity** *n*
objet d'art [**ob**-zhay **dahr**] *n, pl* **objets d'art** small object of artistic value
oblate *adj* (of a sphere) flattened at the poles
oblation *n* religious offering
oblige ⓣ *v* **1** compel (someone) morally or by law to do (something) **2** do a favour for (someone)
▸ **obliging** *adj* ready to help other people **obligingly** *adv*
▸ **obligate** *v* cause (someone) to be obliged to do (something)
▸ **obligation** *n* duty
▸ **obligatory** *adj* required by a rule or law
oblique ⓣ [oh-**bleak**] *adj* **1** slanting **2** indirect ▷ *n* **3** the symbol (/) **obliquely** *adv* **obliqueness** *n*
▸ **oblique angle** angle that is not a right angle
obliterate ⓣ *v* wipe out, destroy **obliteration** *n*
oblivious ⓣ *adj* (foll. by *to* or *of*) unaware (of)
▸ **oblivion** *n* **1** state of being forgotten **2** state of being unaware or unconscious
oblong *adj* **1** having two long sides, two short sides, and four right angles ▷ *n* **2** oblong figure
obloquy ⓣ [**ob**-lock-wee] *n, pl* **-quies 1** verbal abuse **2** discredit
obnoxious ⓣ *adj* offensive **obnoxiousness** *n*
oboe *n* double-reeded woodwind instrument **oboist** *n*
Obote *n* **(Apollo) Milton.** 1924–2005, Ugandan politician; prime minister of Uganda (1962–66) and president (1966–71; 1980–85). He was deposed by Amin in 1971 and remained in exile until 1980; deposed again in 1985 by the Acholi army
O'Brien *n* **1 Conor Cruise.** 1917–2008, Irish diplomat and writer. As an Irish Labour MP he served in the coalition government of 1973–77, becoming a senator (1977–79). He edited the *Observer* (1978–81) **2 Edna.** born 1936, Irish novelist. Her books include *The Country Girls* (1960), *Johnny I Hardly Knew You* (1977), and *In the forest* (2002) **3 Flann,** real name *Brian O'Nolan.* 1911–66, Irish novelist and journalist. His novels include *At Swim-Two-Birds* (1939) and the posthumously published *The Third Policeman* (1967). As Myles na Gopaleen he wrote a satirical column for the *Irish Times*
obscene ⓣ *adj* **1** portraying sex offensively **2** disgusting **obscenity** *n*

THESAURUS

regrettable, deplorable, intolerable, obnoxious, unseemly, repugnant, disagreeable
objective *n* **1** = **purpose**, end, goal, target, mark, aim, object, intention, ambition ▸ *adj* **2** = **unbiased**, fair, impartial, open-minded, disinterested, even-handed, dispassionate, detached, unprejudiced
objectively *adv* = **impartially**, disinterestedly, dispassionately, even-handedly, with an open mind
objectivity *n* = **impartiality**, detachment, disinterestedness, dispassion
obligation *n* = **duty**, charge, responsibility, requirement, burden, accountability, liability, compulsion
obligatory *adj* = **compulsory**, necessary, mandatory, essential, binding, required, imperative, unavoidable, requisite, *de rigueur* (*French*)
oblige *v* **1** = **compel**, make, force, require, bind, constrain, necessitate, impel **2** = **indulge**, benefit, please, accommodate, gratify
obliged *adj* **1** = **grateful**, thankful, appreciative, indebted, beholden, in (someone's) debt **2** = **forced**, bound, required, compelled
obliging *adj* = **cooperative**, kind, willing, helpful, polite, considerate, good-natured, agreeable, accommodating
oblique *adj* **1** = **slanting**, tilted, angled, aslant, sloping **2** = **indirect**, implied, backhanded, roundabout, circuitous, sidelong
obliterate *v* = **destroy**, erase, eradicate, annihilate, blot out, efface, expunge, extirpate, root out, wipe out
obliteration *n* = **annihilation**, elimination, eradication, extirpation, wiping out
oblivion *n* **1** = **neglect**, disregard, forgetfulness, abeyance **2** = **unconsciousness**, insensibility, obliviousness, unawareness
oblivious *adj* = **unaware**, regardless, unconscious, ignorant, negligent, unconcerned, forgetful, heedless, insensible, neglectful, unmindful
obloquy *n* **1** = **abuse**, attack, blame, criticism, censure, slander, reproach, vilification, aspersion, invective **2** = **disgrace**, shame, stigma, humiliation, discredit, infamy, dishonour, ignominy
obnoxious *adj* = **objectionable**, offensive, nasty, unpleasant, repulsive, odious, revolting, disagreeable, insufferable, loathsome, nauseating, scuzzy (*slang*)
obscene *adj* **1** = **indecent**, blue, dirty, pornographic, lewd, filthy, bawdy • *obscene*

O

DICTIONARY

obscure Ⓣ *adj* **1** not well known **2** hard to understand **3** indistinct ▷ *v* **4** make (something) obscure **obscurity** *n*
obsequies [**ob**-sick-weez] *pl n* funeral rites
obsequious Ⓣ [ob-**seek**-wee-uss] *adj* too eager to please in order to be liked **obsequiousness** *n*
observe Ⓣ *v* **1** watch (someone or something) carefully **2** perceive visually **3** remark **4** act according to (a law or custom) **observer** *n* **observable** *adj* **observably** *adv*
▶ **observation** *n* **1** action or habit of observing **2** something observed **3** remark
▶ **observance** *n* observing of a custom
▶ **observant** *adj* quick to notice things
▶ **observatory** *n* building equipped for astronomical or meteorological observations
obsess *v* preoccupy (someone) compulsively **obsessed** *adj* **obsessive** *adj* **obsession** *n*
obsidian *n* dark glassy volcanic rock
obsolete Ⓣ *adj* no longer in use
▶ **obsolescent** *adj* becoming obsolete **obsolescence** *n*
obstacle Ⓣ *n* something that makes progress difficult
obstetrics *n* branch of medicine concerned with pregnancy and childbirth **obstetric** *adj* **obstetrician** *n*
obstinate Ⓣ *adj* **1** stubborn **2** (of a stain) difficult to remove **obstinately** *adv* **obstinacy** *n*
obstreperous Ⓣ *adj* unruly, noisy
obstruct Ⓣ *v* block with an obstacle **obstruction** *n* **obstructive** *adj*

THESAURUS

pictures **2 = disgusting**, evil, shocking, outrageous, wicked, atrocious, heinous, sickening, vile, loathsome
See also: **crude, naughty**
obscenity *n* **1 = indecency**, pornography, impropriety, coarseness, dirtiness, lewdness, licentiousness, smut **2 = swearword**, profanity, four-letter word, vulgarism **3 = outrage**, wrong, evil, atrocity, offense, blight, affront, abomination
obscure *adj* **1 = little-known**, unknown • *an obscure Canadian law* OPPOSITE: famous **2 = arcane**, cryptic, opaque • *The news was shrouded in obscure language.* OPPOSITE: simple **3 = indistinct**, faint, gloomy, murky, dim, cloudy, shadowy, blurred ▶ *v* **4 = hide**, screen, cloud, mask, cloak, conceal, shroud • *His view was obscured by trees.* OPPOSITE: expose
See also: **blot out, cover**
obscurity *n* **1 = darkness**, dusk, haze, gloom, dimness, shadows **2 = insignificance**, lowliness, unimportance
obsequious *adj* **= sycophantic**, deferential, submissive, cringing, fawning, flattering, grovelling, ingratiating, servile, unctuous
observable *adj* **= noticeable**, apparent, obvious, visible, evident, recognizable, detectable, discernible, perceptible
observance *n* **= carrying out**, performance, compliance, fulfillment, honouring
observant *adj* **= alert**, vigilant, watchful, attentive, perceptive • *Painting makes you really observant of things.*
See also: **sharp**
observation *n* **1 = study**, review, inspection, surveillance, scrutiny, examination, monitoring, watching **2 = remark**, note, comment, opinion, thought, reflection, pronouncement, utterance
observe *v* **1 = watch**, study, survey, view, monitor, scrutinize, bird dog (*informal*) • *He has spent years observing the habits of frogs.* **2 = notice**, see, note, spot, discover, witness • *I observed a number of strange phenomena.* **3 = remark**, say, state, comment, mention • *"You've had your hair cut," he observed.* **4 = abide by**, keep, follow, respect, comply, heed, honour, obey, adhere to, conform to
See also: **discern, practise**
observer *n* **= spectator**, witness, viewer, watcher, bystander, eyewitness, onlooker, beholder, fly on the wall, looker-on
obsessed *adj* **= preoccupied**, troubled, haunted, dominated, gripped, hung up on (*slang*), infatuated
obsession *n* **= preoccupation**, thing (*informal*), complex, fixation • *Chess is an obsession of mine.*
obsessive *adj* **= compulsive**, haunting, besetting, consuming, gripping
obsolescent *adj* **= outdated**, ageing, declining, dying out, on the wane, on the way out, past its prime, waning
obsolete *adj* **= outdated**, old, old-fashioned, extinct, antiquated, archaic, outmoded, discarded, disused, out of date, passé
obstacle *n* **= difficulty**, hurdle, barrier, obstruction, impediment, hindrance • *a large obstacle to improving the team's standing*
See also: **handicap**
obstinacy *n* **= stubbornness**, persistence, tenacity, intransigence, doggedness, inflexibility, obduracy, pig-headedness, wilfulness
obstinate *adj* **= stubborn**, wilful, dogged, inflexible, intractable, headstrong • *He is obstinate and will not give up.* OPPOSITE: flexible
obstreperous *adj* **= unruly**, wild, loud, turbulent, noisy, disorderly, rowdy, unmanageable, riotous
obstruct *v* **= block**, bar, choke, clog • *Trucks*

O

DICTIONARY

▸ **obstructionist** *n* person who deliberately obstructs formal proceedings
obtain Ⓣ *v* **1** acquire intentionally **2** be customary **obtainable** *adj*
obtrude *v* push oneself or one's ideas on others **obtrusion** *n* **obtrusive** *adj* **obtrusively** *adv*
obtuse Ⓣ *adj* **1** mentally slow **2** *math* (of an angle) between 90° and 180° **3** not pointed **obtusely** *adv* **obtuseness** *n*
obverse *n* **1** opposite way of looking at an idea **2** main side of a coin or medal
obviate Ⓣ *v* make unnecessary
obvious Ⓣ *adj* easy to see or understand, evident **obviously** *adv*
ocarina *n* small oval wind instrument made of clay
occasion Ⓣ *n* **1** time at which a particular thing happens **2** special event **3** reason: *no occasion for complaint* ▷ *v* **4** cause
▸ **occasional** *adj* **1** happening sometimes **2** for a special event **occasionally** *adv*
Occident *n lit* the West **Occidental** *adj*
occiput [**ox**-sip-put] *n* back of the head
occlude *v* **1** obstruct **2** close off **occlusion** *n* **occlusive** *adj*
▸ **occluded front** *meteorol* front formed when a cold front overtakes a warm front and warm air rises
occult Ⓣ *n* **1 the occult** knowledge or study of the supernatural ▷ *adj* **2** relating to the supernatural
occupant Ⓣ *n* person occupying a specified place
▸ **occupancy** *n* (length of a) person's stay in a specified place
occupation Ⓣ *n* **1** profession **2** activity that occupies one's time **3** control of a country by a foreign military power **4** being occupied **occupational** *adj*
▸ **occupational therapy** treatment of physical, emotional, or social problems by means of purposeful activity
occupy Ⓣ *v* **-pying, -pied 1** live or work in (a building) **2** take up the attention of (someone) **3** take up (space or time) **4** take

THESAURUS

obstructed the road.
See also: **close, delay, hamper, impede, interfere**
obstruction *n* = **obstacle**, bar, difficulty, barrier, barricade, impediment, blockage, hindrance
obstructive *adj* = **uncooperative**, awkward, restrictive, unhelpful, blocking, delaying, hindering, stalling
obtain *v* **1** = **get**, acquire, secure (*formal*), procure (*formal*), get hold of, get your hands on (*informal*) • *to obtain a false passport* **2** = **exist**, hold, prevail, be in force, be prevalent, be the case
See also: **buy, earn, extract, gain**
obtainable *adj* = **available**, achievable, attainable, on tap (*informal*), to be had
obtrusive *adj* = **noticeable**, prominent, obvious, blatant, protruding, protuberant, sticking out
obtuse *adj* = **stupid**, slow, thick, dense, dull, stolid, uncomprehending
obviate *v* = **prevent**, remove, avert, preclude
obvious *adj* = **clear**, apparent, plain, evident, blatant, overt, palpable, self-evident • *an obvious injustice*
See also: **conspicuous, logical, manifest, noticeable, prominent, visible**
obviously *adv* = **clearly**, undeniably, patently, plainly, unquestionably, manifestly, of course, palpably, unmistakably, without doubt
occasion *n* **1** = **event**, affair • *The launch of a ship was a big occasion.* **2** = **opportunity**, time, chance • *an important occasion for celebrating our friendship* **3** = **reason**, call, cause, ground *or* grounds, excuse, motive, justification, provocation, prompting ▸ *v* **4** (*Formal*) = **cause**, produce, prompt, provoke, induce, bring about, give rise to • *damage occasioned by fire*
See also: **case, create, incident**
occasional *adj* = **infrequent**, odd, sporadic, periodic, intermittent • *an occasional fumble of the ball* OPPOSITE: frequent
See also: **irregular**
occasionally *adv* = **sometimes**, periodically, irregularly, at times, from time to time, now and again, once in a while
occult *adj* = **supernatural**, mysterious, magical, mystical, arcane, esoteric
occupancy *n* = **tenancy**, use, possession, residence, tenure
occupant *n* = **resident**, inmate, incumbent, tenant, inhabitant, occupier, indweller, lessee
occupation *n* **1** = **job**, trade, business, line *or* line of work, employment, pursuit, profession, calling, vocation, walk of life **2** = **occupancy**, control, possession, holding, residence, tenure, tenancy **3** = **invasion**, seizure, conquest, subjugation
occupied *adj* **1** = **busy**, working, engaged, employed **2** = **in use**, full, unavailable, engaged, taken **3** = **inhabited**, lived-in, peopled, settled, tenanted
occupy *v* **1** (*often passive*) = **take up**, involve, engage, employ, divert, preoccupy, monopolize, engross, tie up **2** = **live in**, own, possess, inhabit, dwell in, reside in **3** = **fill**, cover, permeate, pervade, take

DICTIONARY

possession of (a place) by force **occupier** *n*
occur Ⓣ *v* **-curring, -curred 1** take place **2** exist **3** (foll. by *to*) come to the mind (of)
▶ **occurrence** *n* **1** something that occurs **2** occurring
ocean *n* vast area of sea between continents **oceanic** *adj*
▶ **oceanography** *n* scientific study of the oceans
▶ **ocean-going** *adj* able to sail on the open sea
ocelot [oss-ill-lot] *n* American wild cat with a spotted coat
oche [ok-kee] *n darts* mark on the floor behind which a player must stand
ochre [oak-er] *adj* brownish-yellow
Ockeghem, Okeghem *n* **Johannes, Jean d', or Jan van.** ?1430–?95, Flemish composer (Also **Ockenheim**)
Ockham, Occam *n* **William of.** died ?1349, English nominalist philosopher, who contested the temporal power of the papacy and ended the conflict between nominalism and realism
o'clock *adv* used after a number to specify an hour
O'Connell *n* **Daniel.** 1775–1847, Irish nationalist leader and orator, whose election to the British House of Commons (1828) forced the acceptance of Catholic emancipation (1829)
O'Connor *n* **1 Feargus.** 1794–1855, Irish politician and journalist, a leader of the Chartist movement **2 (Mary) Flannery.** 1925–64, US novelist and short-story writer, author of *Wise Blood* (1952) and *The Violent Bear it Away* (1960) **3 Frank,** real name *Michael O'Donovan.* 1903–66, Irish short-story writer and critic **4 Thomas Power,** known as *Tay Pay.* 1848–1929, Irish journalist and nationalist leader
Oct. October
octagon *n* geometric figure with eight sides **octagonal** *adj*
octahedron [ok-ta-**heed**-ron] *n, pl* **-drons, -dra** three-dimensional geometric figure with eight faces
octane *n* hydrocarbon found in gasoline
▶ **octane rating** measure of gasoline quality
octave *n music* (interval between the first and) eighth note of a scale
octet *n* **1** group of eight performers **2** music for such a group
October *n* tenth month of the year
octogenarian *n* person aged between eighty and eighty-nine
octopus *n, pl* **-puses** sea creature with a soft body and eight tentacles
ocular *adj* relating to the eyes or sight
oculist *n old-fashioned* ophthalmologist
OD *n* **1** *med* overdose ▷ *v* **OD'ing, OD'd 2** *informal* take an overdose
Oda Nobunaga *n* 1534–82, Japanese general and feudal leader, who unified much of Japan under his control: assassinated
odd Ⓣ *adj* **1** unusual **2** occasional **3** not divisible by two **4** not part of a set
▶ **odds** *pl n* (ratio showing) the probability of something happening
▶ **at odds** in conflict
▶ **odds and ends** small miscellaneous items
▶ **oddness** *n* quality of being odd
▶ **oddity** *n* odd person or thing
▶ **oddments** *pl n* things left over
ode *n* lyric poem, usu. addressed to a particular subject
odium [oh-dee-um] *n* widespread dislike
▶ **odious** *adj* offensive
Odoacer, Odovacar *n* ?434–493 AD, barbarian ruler of Italy (476–493); assassinated by Theodoric
odometer *n* device that records the distance a vehicle has travelled

THESAURUS

up **4 = invade**, capture, seize, overrun, take over
occur *v* **1 = happen**, appear, arise, take place • *The changes occurred over a long period.* **2 = exist**, be present • *The disease occurs more commonly among the over-50s.* ▷ **occur to = cross your mind**, strike, dawn on • *It didn't occur to me to check.*
See also: **come**
occurrence *n* **1 = incident**, event, affair, circumstance, episode, instance, adventure, happening **2 = existence**, development, appearance, manifestation, materialization
odd *adj* **1 = strange**, funny, bizarre, weird, curious, singular (*formal*), peculiar • *an odd coincidence* OPPOSITE: frequent **2 = occasional**, various, random, casual, irregular, periodic, incidental, sundry **3 = spare**, surplus, leftover, solitary, unmatched, remaining, unpaired
See also: **extraordinary**
oddity *n* **1 = irregularity**, freak, abnormality, quirk, anomaly, eccentricity, idiosyncrasy, peculiarity **2 = misfit**, maverick, crank (*informal*), oddball (*informal*)
oddment *n* **= leftover**, bit, scrap, remnant, fragment, snippet, fag end, off cut
odds *pl n* **= probability**, likelihood, chances ▷ **at odds = in conflict**, at daggers drawn, at loggerheads, at sixes and sevens, at variance, out of line
odds and ends *pl n* **= scraps**, debris, bits, bits and pieces, oddments, remnants
odious *adj* **= offensive**, unpleasant, horrid, obnoxious, repulsive, detestable, revolting, loathsome, scuzzy (*slang*)

DICTIONARY

odour, odor Ⓣ *n* particular smell **odorous** *adj* **odourless** *or* **odorless** *adj*
▸ **odoriferous** *adj* giving off a pleasant smell
▸ **odorize** *v* fill (something) with scent
odyssey Ⓣ [**odd**-iss-ee] *n* long eventful journey
OECD Organization for Economic Cooperation and Development
oedema [id-**deem**-a] *n, pl* **-mata** abnormal swelling
o'er *prep, adv lit* over
oesophagus [ee-**soff**-a-guss] *n, pl* **-gi** passage between the mouth and stomach
oestrogen [**ee**-stra-jen] *n* female hormone that controls the reproductive cycle
of *prep* **1** belonging to **2** consisting of **3** connected with **4** characteristic of
off Ⓣ *prep* **1** away from ▹ *adv* **2** away ▹ *adj* **3** not operating **4** cancelled or postponed **5** (of food) gone bad **6** not up to the usual standard: *an off day*
▸ **off colour** slightly ill
▸ **off-line** *adj* (of a computer) not directly controlled by a central processor
▸ **off-message** *adj* (esp. of a politician) not following the official party line
Offa *n* died 796 AD, king of Mercia (757–796), who constructed an earthwork (**Offa's Dyke**) between Wales and Mercia
offal *n* edible organs of an animal, such as liver or kidneys
offcut *n* piece remaining after the required parts have been cut out
Offenbach *n* **Jacques**. 1819–80, German-born French composer of many operettas, including *Orpheus in the Underworld* (1858), and of the opera *The Tales of Hoffmann* (1881)
offend Ⓣ *v* **1** hurt the feelings of, insult **2** commit a crime **offender** *n*
▸ **offence** *n* **1** (cause of) hurt feelings or annoyance **2** illegal act
▸ **offensive** *adj* **1** insulting **2** aggressive **3** disagreeable ▹ *n* **4** position or action of attack
offer Ⓣ *v* **1** present (something) for acceptance or rejection **2** provide **3** be willing (to do something) **4** propose (a sum of money) as payment ▹ *n* **5** instance of offering something
▸ **offering** *n* thing offered
▸ **offertory** *n Christianity* offering of the bread and wine for Communion
offhand Ⓣ *adj* **1** Also **offhanded** casual, curt ▹ *adv* **2** without preparation
office Ⓣ *n* **1** room or building where people work at desks **2** department of a commercial organization **3** formal position of responsibility **4** duty, function **5** *usu pl*

THESAURUS

odour, odor *n* = **smell**, stink, scent, perfume, essence, aroma, fragrance, bouquet, stench, redolence
See also: **smell**
odyssey *n* = **journey**, quest, trek, voyage, pilgrimage, crusade
of course not *See* **no**
off *adv* **1** = **away**, out, aside, apart, elsewhere ▸ *adj* **2** = **unavailable**, finished, gone, canceled, postponed **3** = **bad**, sour, rotten, rancid, moldy, turned ▹ **off colour** = **ill**, sick, poorly (*informal*), unwell, out of sorts, peaky, queasy, run down, under the weather (*informal*)
offbeat *adj* = **unusual**, novel, strange, eccentric, left-field (*informal*), unconventional, unorthodox, outré, way-out (*informal*)
offence *n* **1** = **crime**, fault, wrongdoing, sin, trespass, misdemeanour, misdeed, transgression **2** = **insult**, hurt, slight, outrage, snub, injustice, indignity, affront **3** = **annoyance**, anger, wrath, pique, displeasure, resentment, indignation, umbrage
offend *v* = **upset**, insult, outrage, affront • *He says he had no intention of offending the community.* OPPOSITE: please
See also: **repel, shock**
offended *adj* = **upset**, disgruntled, outraged, resentful, affronted, displeased, piqued, put out (*informal*), smarting, stung
offender *n* = **criminal**, culprit, villain, crook, delinquent, wrongdoer, lawbreaker, miscreant, sinner, perp (*informal*), transgressor
offensive *adj* **1** = **insulting**, abusive, objectionable • *offensive behaviour* **2** = **disagreeable**, repellent, unpleasant, vile, obnoxious, disgusting, odious, revolting, nauseating **3** = **aggressive**, attacking, invading ▸ *n* **4** = **attack**, drive, campaign, push (*informal*), onslaught
See also: **hateful**
offer *v* **1** = **bid**, tender, hold out • *I offered him an apple.* **2** = **provide**, present, afford, furnish **3** = **propose**, suggest, advance, submit **4** = **volunteer**, come forward, offer one's services ▸ *n* **5** = **bid**, tender, proposition • *She had refused several excellent job offers.*
offering *n* = **donation**, present, gift, contribution, sacrifice, subscription, hand-out
offhand *adj* **1** = **casual**, careless, aloof, glib, brusque, curt ▸ *adv* **2** = **impromptu**, ad lib, extempore, off the cuff (*informal*)
office *n* = **post**, place, role, situation, responsibility, function, occupation

DICTIONARY

something done for another
▸ **officer** *n* **1** person in authority in the armed services **2** member of the police force **3** person with special responsibility in an organization
official ⓣ *adj* **1** approved or arranged by someone in authority **2** of a position of authority ▹ *n* **3** person who holds a position of authority
▸ **officialdom** *n offensive* officials collectively
officiate ⓣ *v* conduct a ceremony in an official role
officious ⓣ *adj* **1** giving unnecessary instructions **2** interfering
offing ⓣ *n* area of the sea visible from the shore
▸ **in the offing** likely to happen soon
off-licence *n* shop licensed to sell alcohol
offset ⓣ *v* cancel out, compensate for
offshoot ⓣ *n* **1** something developed from something else **2** shoot growing on the main stem of a plant
offside *adj, adv sports* (positioned) illegally ahead of the ball or puck
offspring ⓣ *n, pl* **offspring** one's child
often ⓣ *adv* frequently, much of the time
▸ **oft** *adv poetic* often
ogee arch [**oh**-jee] *n* pointed arch with an S-shaped curve on both sides
ogle ⓣ *v* stare at (someone) lustfully
Oglethorpe *n* **James Edward**. 1696–1785, English general and colonial administrator; founder of the colony of Georgia (1733)
ogre ⓣ *n* giant that eats human flesh
oh *interj* exclamation of surprise, pain, etc.
Oh *n* **Sandra**. born 1971, Canadian film and TV actress, noted for her role in the US TV medical drama *Grey's Anatomy* (from 2005)
O. Henry *n* pen name of *William Sidney Porter*. 1862–1910, US short-story writer. His collections of stories, characterized by his use of caricature and surprising endings, include *Cabbages and Kings* (1904) and *The Four Million* (1906)
O'Higgins *n* **1 Ambrosio**. ?1720–1801, Irish soldier, who became viceroy of Chile (1789–96) and of Peru (1796–1801) **2** his son, **Bernardo**. 1778–1842, Chilean revolutionary. He was one of the leaders in the struggle for independence from Spain and was Chile's first president (1817–23)
ohm *n* unit of electrical resistance
Ohm *n* **Georg Simon**. 1787–1854, German physicist, who formulated the law named after him
oil ⓣ *n* **1** viscous liquid, insoluble in water and usu. flammable **2** same as **petroleum** **3** petroleum derivative, used as a fuel or lubricant **oils 4** oil-based paints used in art ▹ *v* **5** lubricate (a machine) with oil **oily** *adj*
▸ **oilfield** *n* area containing oil reserves
▸ **oil rig** platform constructed for boring oil wells
▸ **oilskins** *pl n* waterproof clothing
ointment ⓣ *n* greasy substance used for healing skin or as a cosmetic
OK, okay ⓣ *informal* ▹ *interj* **1** all right ▹ *n* **2** approval ▹ *v* **3** approve (something)
okapi [ok-**kah**-pee] *n* African animal related to the giraffe but with a shorter neck
O'Keeffe *n* **Georgia**. 1887–1986, US painter, best known for her semiabstract still lifes, esp. of flowers: married the photographer Alfred Stieglitz

THESAURUS

officer *n* = **official**, executive, agent, representative, appointee, functionary, office-holder
official *adj* **1** = **authorized**, formal, licensed, certified • *the official figures* OPPOSITE: unofficial ▸ *n* **2** = **officer**, executive, representative • *a senior UN official*
officialdom *See* **bureaucracy**
officiate *v* = **preside**, serve, conduct, manage, chair, oversee, superintend
officious *adj* = **interfering**, intrusive, overzealous, dictatorial, meddlesome, obtrusive, pushy (*informal*), self-important
offing *n* ▹ **in the offing** = **imminent**, upcoming, in prospect, on the horizon
off-putting *adj* = **discouraging**, daunting, formidable, disconcerting, dispiriting, disturbing, intimidating, unnerving, unsettling
offset *v* = **cancel out**, neutralize, counteract, counterbalance, balance out, compensate for, make up for
offshoot *n* = **by-product**, development, spin-off, adjunct, appendage
offspring *n* **1** = **child**, successor, heir, descendant, scion **2** = **children**, family, issue, young, brood, progeny, descendants, heirs
often *adv* = **frequently**, repeatedly • *They often spent their summers at the lake.*
ogle *v* = **leer**, eye up (*informal*)
ogre *n* = **monster**, giant, devil, demon, bogeyman, bugbear, spectre
oil *v* = **lubricate**, grease
oily *adj* = **greasy**, fatty, oleaginous
ointment *n* = **lotion**, cream, balm, embrocation, emollient, liniment, salve, unguent
OK *adj* **1** = **all right**, acceptable • *Is it OK if I show up early?* ▸ *interjection* **2** = **all right**, right, yes, roger, agreed, very good, very well ▸ *v* **3** = **approve**, endorse, sanction, authorize, rubber-stamp (*informal*), agree to, give the green light ▸ *n* **4** = **approval**,

DICTIONARY

okra *n* tropical plant with edible green pods
Olaf I, Olav I *n* known as *Olaf Tryggvesson.* ?965–?1000 AD, king of Norway (995–?1000). He began the conversion of Norway to Christianity
Olaf II, Olav II *n* **Saint**. 995–1030 AD, king of Norway (1015–28), who worked to complete the conversion of Norway to Christianity; deposed by Canute; patron saint of Norway. Feast day: July 29
Olaf V, Olav V *n* 1903–91, king of Norway 1957–91; son of Haakon VII
old Ⓣ *adj* **1** having lived or existed for a long time **2** of a specified age: *two years old* **3** former
▸ **olden** *adj* old: *in the olden days*
▸ **oldie** *n informal* old but popular song or film
▸ **old-fashioned** *adj* no longer commonly used or valued
▸ **old guard** group of people in an organization who have traditional values
▸ **old hat** boring because so familiar
▸ **old maid** elderly unmarried woman
▸ **old master** European painter or painting from the period 1500–1800
▸ **Old Nick** *informal* the Devil
▸ **old school tie** system of mutual help between former pupils of a British public school
▸ **Old Testament** part of the Bible recording Hebrew history
▸ **Old World** world as it was known before the discovery of the Americas
Oldcastle *n* Sir **John**, Baron Cobham. ?1378–1417, Lollard leader. In 1411 he led an English army in France but in 1413 he was condemned as a heretic and later hanged and burnt. He is thought to have been a model for Shakespeare's character Falstaff in *Henry IV*
oleaginous [ol-lee-**aj**-in-uss] *adj* oily, producing oil
oleander [ol-lee-**ann**-der] *n* Mediterranean flowering evergreen shrub
O level *n* former basic level of the General Certificate of Education
olfactory *adj* relating to the sense of smell
oligarchy [**ol**-lee-gark-ee] *n, pl* **-chies** **1** government by a small group of people **2** state governed this way **oligarchic** *or* **oligarchical** *adj*
▸ **oligarch** *n* member of an oligarchy
olive *n* **1** small green or black fruit used as food or pressed for its oil **2** tree on which this fruit grows ▷ *adj* **3** greyish-green
▸ **olive branch** conciliatory gesture
Oliver *n* **1** one of Charlemagne's 12 paladins See also **Roland 2 Joseph**, known as *King Oliver.* 1885–1938, US pioneer jazz cornetist
Olivier *n* **Laurence** (**Kerr**), Baron Olivier of Brighton. 1907–89, English stage, film, and television actor and director: director of the National Theatre Company (1961–73): films include the Shakespeare adaptations *Henry V* (1944), *Hamlet* (1948), and *Richard III* (1956)
Olympiad *n* staging of the Olympic Games
Olympian *adj* **1** of Mount Olympus or the classical Greek gods **2** majestic or godlike
Olympic Games *pl n* four-yearly international sports competition
Omar, Umar *n* died 644 AD, the second caliph of Islam (634–44). During his reign Islamic armies conquered Syria and Mesopotamia: murdered
Omar Khayyám *n* ?1050–?1123, Persian poet, mathematician, and astronomer, noted for the *Rubáiyát*, a collection of quatrains, popularized in the West by Edward Fitzgerald's version (1859)
ombudsman *n* official who investigates complaints against government organizations
omega *n* last letter in the Greek alphabet
▸ **alpha and omega** see **alpha**
omelet *n* dish of eggs beaten and fried
omen Ⓣ *n* happening or object thought to foretell success or misfortune
▸ **ominous** *adj* worrying, seeming to foretell of misfortune
omit Ⓣ *v* **omitting, omitted 1** leave out **2** neglect (to do something) **omission** *n*

O

THESAURUS

agreement, sanction, permission, go-ahead (*informal*), consent, authorization, assent, green light, say-so (*informal*), seal of approval
See also: **all right, correct, right, safe, tolerable, yes**
old *adj* **1 = aged**, elderly, ancient, mature, venerable, decrepit, senile • *an old turtle* OPPOSITE: young **2 = dated**, antique, obsolete, antiquated, antediluvian, timeworn OPPOSITE: new **3 = former**, previous, earlier, one-time, erstwhile • *my old art teacher* OPPOSITE: new
See also: **stale**
olden *See* **past**
old-fashioned *adj* **= out of date**, outdated, obsolete, antiquated, archaic, dated, outmoded, passé • *old-fashioned shoes* OPPOSITE: fashionable
See also: **stuffy**
omen *n* **= sign**, warning • *Her showing up at this moment is an omen of disaster.*
See also: **premonition**
ominous *adj* **= sinister**, threatening • *an ominous silence*
omission *n* **1 = exclusion** **2 = failure**, lack, oversight, neglect
omit *v* **= leave out**, skip, exclude • *Omit the salt in thisrecipe.*

DICTIONARY

omni- *combining form* all, everywhere: *omnidirectional*
omnibus *n* **1** *old-fashioned* bus **2** several books or TV or radio programmes made into one
omnipotent Ⓣ [om-**nip**-a-tent] *adj* having unlimited power **omnipotence** *n*
omnipresent *adj* present everywhere **omnipresence** *n*
omniscient Ⓣ [om-**nish**-yent] *adj* knowing everything **omniscience** *n*
omnivorous [om-**niv**-vor-uss] *adj* eating food obtained from both animals and plants **omnivore** *n* omnivorous animal
on Ⓣ *prep* **1** above and touching **2** attached to **3** concerning: *an article on slimming* **4** during: *on Monday* **5** through the medium of: *on television* ▷ *adv* **6** in operation **7** forwards **8** continuing ▷ *adj* **9** operating **10** taking place: *the party's on*
▸ **on-message** *adj* (esp. of a politician) following the official party line
ON, O.N. Ontario
onanism *n* masturbation
ONC Ordinary National Certificate
once Ⓣ *adv* **1** on one occasion **2** formerly ▷ *conj* **3** as soon as
▸ **at once 1** immediately **2** simultaneously
▸ **once-over** *n informal* quick examination
oncogene [**on**-koh-jean] *n* gene that can cause cancer when abnormally activated
oncoming Ⓣ *adj* approaching from the front
OND Ordinary National Diploma
Ondaatje *n* **Michael**. born 1943, Sri Lankan-born Canadian writer: his works include the poetry collection *There's a Trick with a Knife I'm Learning to Do* (1979), the Booker-prizewinning novel *The English Patient* (1992, filmed 1997), and *Anil's Ghost* (2000)
one Ⓣ *adj* **1** single, lone ▷ *n* **2** number or figure 1 **3** single unit ▷ *pron* **4** any person
▸ **oneness** *n* unity
▸ **oneself** *pron* reflexive form of **one**
▸ **one-armed bandit** fruit machine operated by a lever on one side
▸ **one-liner** *n* witty remark
▸ **one-night stand** sexual encounter lasting one night
▸ **one-sided** *adj* considering only one point of view
▸ **one-way** *adj* allowing movement in one direction only
O'Neill *n* **James Edward**, known as *Tip*. 1858–1915, Canadian baseball player
onerous Ⓣ [**own**-er-uss] *adj* (of a task) difficult to carry out
ongoing Ⓣ *adj* in progress, continuing
onion *n* strongly flavoured edible bulb
Onley *n* **David**. born 1950, Lieutenant Governor of Ontario (2007–)
on-line *adj computers* (of equipment) directly connected to and controlled by the computer
onlooker Ⓣ *n* person who watches something happening without taking part
only Ⓣ *adj* **1** alone of its kind ▷ *adv* **2** exclusively **3** merely **4** no more than ▷ *conj* **5** but
o.n.o. or near(est) offer
onomatopoeia [on-a-mat-a-**pee**-a] *n* formation of a word which imitates the sound it represents, such as *hiss*
onomatopoeic *adj*
onset Ⓣ *n* beginning
onslaught Ⓣ *n* violent attack
Ont. Ontario
onto *prep* **1** to a position on: *we got onto the bus*

O

THESAURUS

See also: **fail, forget, neglect**
omnipotence *n* = **supremacy**, mastery, invincibility
omnipotent *adj* = **all-powerful**, supreme, almighty
omniscient *adj* = **all-knowing**, all-wise
on *preposition* ▷ **on account of** *See* **by virtue of** ▷ **on edge** *See* **restless** ▷ **on guard** *See* **alert** ▷ **on hand** *See* **handy** ▷ **on the dot** *See* **exactly, prompt** ▷ **on the whole** *See* **as a rule** ▷ **on time** *See* **punctual**
once *adv* = **at one time**, previously, formerly, long ago, once upon a time ▷ **at once** = **immediately**, now, directly, instantly, forthwith, right away, straight away, this minute *or* this very minute; = **at the same time**, together, simultaneously ▷ **once in a while** *See* **sometimes** ▷ **once more** *See* **again**
oncoming *adj* = **approaching**, forthcoming, onrushing, advancing, looming
one *See* **only, single**
onerous *adj* = **difficult**, hard, heavy, oppressive, demanding, exacting, burdensome, laborious, taxing
one-sided *adj* = **biased**, unfair, partial, partisan, lopsided, unjust, prejudiced
one-sidedness *See* **favouritism**
one-time *See* **previous**
ongoing *adj* = **in progress**, continuous, unfinished, developing, evolving, progressing, unfolding
onlooker *n* = **observer**, witness, viewer, watcher, spectator, bystander, eyewitness, looker-on
only *adv* **1** = **solely**, just, simply, merely, purely • *Only the singer herself knows whether she will make a comeback.* ▷ **only just** *See* **hardly** ▸ *adj* **2** = **sole**, one • *their only hit single*
See also: **single**
onset *n* = **beginning**, start, outbreak, inception
onslaught *n* = **attack**, charge, assault, offensive, blitz, onset, onrush

DICTIONARY

2 aware of: *she's onto us*
ontology *n philosophy* study of existence **ontological** *adj*
onus [**own**-uss] *n, pl* **onuses** responsibility or burden
onward *adj* **1** directed or moving forward ▷ *adv* **2** Also **onwards** ahead, forward
onyx *n* type of quartz with coloured layers
oodles *pl n informal* great quantities
Oort *n* **Jan Hendrick**. 1900–92, Dutch astronomer, who confirmed (1927) and developed the theory of galactic rotation. He was the first to propose (1950) the existence of a mass of comets orbiting the sun far beyond the orbit of Pluto (the **Oort cloud**)
ooze *v* **1** flow slowly ▷ *n* **2** sluggish flow **3** soft mud at the bottom of a lake or river **oozy** *adj*
op *n informal* operation
opacity [oh-**pass**-it-tee] *n* state of being opaque
opal *n* iridescent precious stone
▸ **opalescent** *adj* iridescent like an opal
opaque *adj* not able to be seen through, not transparent
op. cit. [**op sit**] in the work cited
OPEC Organization of Petroleum Exporting Countries
open *adj* **1** not closed **2** uncovered **3** unfolded **4** ready for business **5** free from obstruction, accessible **6** unrestricted **7** not finalized **8** frank ▷ *v* **9** (cause to) become open **10** begin ▷ *n* **11** *sports* competition open to everyone
▸ **in the open** outdoors
▸ **openly** *adv* without concealment
▸ **opening** *n* **1** hole **2** opportunity ▷ *adj* **3** first
▸ **open-and-shut case** problem that is easily solved
▸ **open day** day on which a school or college is open to the public
▸ **open-handed** *adj* generous
▸ **open-hearted** *adj* **1** generous **2** frank
▸ **open-heart surgery** surgery on the heart during which the blood circulation is maintained by machine
▸ **open house** hospitality to visitors at any time
▸ **open letter** letter to an individual that the writer makes public in a newspaper or magazine
▸ **open-minded** *adj* receptive to new ideas
▸ **open-pit mining** mining at the surface and not underground
▸ **open-plan** *adj* (of a house or office) having few interior walls
▸ **open source** intellectual property, esp. computer source code, that is made freely available to the general public
▸ **openwork** *n* patterns made by leaving spaces in a design
opera[1] *n* drama in which the text is sung to an orchestral accompaniment **operatic** *adj*
▸ **operetta** *n* light-hearted comic opera
opera[2] *n* a plural of **opus**
operate *v* **1** (cause to) function **2** direct **3** perform an operation **operator** *n*
▸ **operation** *n* **1** method or procedure of working **2** medical procedure in which the body is worked on to repair a damaged part

O

THESAURUS

onus *n* = **burden**, responsibility, task, load, obligation, liability
onward, onwards *adv* = **forward**, on, ahead, beyond, forth, in front
ooze[1] *v* = **seep**, escape, leak, drain, filter, drip, dribble
ooze[2] *n* = **mud**, mire, sludge, silt, slime, alluvium
opaque *adj* = **cloudy**, dull, murky, dim, muddy, hazy, impenetrable, filmy
open *v* **1** = **unfasten**, uncover, unlock, undo • *She opened the door.* OPPOSITE: shut **2** = **start**, begin, launch, initiate, commence, inaugurate, kick off (*informal*), set in motion **3** = **unfold**, spread *or* spread out, expand, unfurl, unroll ▸ *adj* **4** = **unfastened**, uncovered, ajar, undone, unlocked • *an open box of chocolates* OPPOSITE: shut **5** = **frank**, honest, candid • *He had always been open with her.* **6** = **accessible**, public, free, available, vacant, unrestricted, unoccupied **7** = **unresolved**, undecided, moot, debatable, unsettled, arguable
See also: **bare, flexible, impressionable, straightforward**
open-air *adj* = **outdoor**, alfresco
open-handed *adj* = **generous**, liberal, free, lavish, bountiful, munificent, unstinting
opening *adj* **1** = **first**, initial, inaugural, introductory • *the opening day of the fishing season* OPPOSITE: closing ▸ *n* **2** = **beginning**, start, commencement (*formal*) • *The opening was the best part of the movie.* OPPOSITE: conclusion **3** = **hole**, space, crack, gap, slot, vent, cleft, chink • *a narrow opening in the fence* **4** = **opportunity**, chance, occasion, vacancy
See also: **breach**
openly *adv* = **frankly**, overtly, plainly, candidly, unreservedly, forthrightly, unhesitatingly
open-minded *adj* = **broad-minded**, liberal, reasonable, receptive, impartial, tolerant, unbiased, undogmatic, unprejudiced
operate *v* **1** = **work**, go, run, act, perform, function **2** = **handle**, use, work, manage, maneuver, be in charge of
operation *n* = **procedure**, action, process,

DICTIONARY

▸ **operational** *adj* **1** in working order **2** relating to a working procedure: *operational difficulties*
▸ **operative** [**op**-rat-tiv] *adj* **1** working ▹ *n* **2** worker with a special skill
ophidian *adj, n* (reptile) of the snake family
ophthalmic *adj* relating to the eyes
▸ **ophthalmic optician** see **optician**
▸ **ophthalmology** *n* study of the eye and its diseases **ophthalmologist** *n*
opiate [**oh**-pee-ate] *n* narcotic drug containing opium
opinion Ⓣ *n* personal belief or judgment
▸ **opinion poll** see **poll**
▸ **opinionated** *adj* having strong opinions
▸ **opine** *v old-fashioned* express an opinion
opium [**oh**-pee-um] *n* addictive narcotic drug made from poppy seeds
opossum *n* small marsupial of N America or Australia
Oppenheimer *n* **J**(**ulius**) **Robert**. 1904–67, US nuclear physicist. He was director of the Los Alamos laboratory (1943–45), which produced the first atomic bomb. He opposed the development of the hydrogen bomb (1949) and in 1953 was alleged to be a security risk. He was later exonerated
opponent Ⓣ *n* person one is working against in a contest, battle, or argument
opportunity Ⓣ *n, pl* **-ties** **1** favourable time or condition **2** good chance
▸ **opportune** *adj* happening at a suitable time **opportunism** *n*
▸ **opportunist** *n* person who does whatever is advantageous without regard for principles
oppose Ⓣ *v* work against
▸ **be opposed to** disagree with or disapprove of
▸ **opposition** *n* **1** obstruction or hostility **2** largest political party not in power **3** group opposing another
opposite Ⓣ *adj* **1** situated on the other side **2** facing **3** diametrically different ▹ *n* **4** person or thing that is opposite ▹ *prep, adv* **5** facing **6** on the other side (from)
oppress Ⓣ *v* **1** subjugate by cruelty or force **2** depress **oppression** *n* **oppressor** *n*
▸ **oppressive** *adj* **1** tyrannical **2** (of weather) hot and humid **oppressively** *adv*
opprobrium [op-**probe**-ree-um] *n* state of being criticized severely for wrong one has done **opprobrious** *adj*

THESAURUS

performance, course, exercise, motion, movement
operational *adj* = **working**, ready, viable, operative, prepared, functional, going, workable, usable, up and running
operative *adj* **1** = **in operation**, effective, active, operational, functioning, in force ▸ *n* **2** = **worker**, employee, artisan, laborer
operator *n* = **worker**, driver, conductor, mechanic, technician, operative, handler, practitioner
opinion *n* = **belief**, view, assessment, judgment, viewpoint, estimation, point of view • *I wasn't asking for your opinion.*
See also: **advice, feeling, idea, thought, verdict**
opinionated *adj* = **dogmatic**, single-minded, bigoted, cocksure, doctrinaire, overbearing, pig-headed, prejudiced
opponent *n* = **adversary**, rival, competitor, enemy, contestant, challenger, foe, antagonist
opportune *adj* = **timely**, appropriate, suitable, fitting, convenient, apt, favourable, advantageous, auspicious, well-timed
opportunism *n* = **expediency**, exploitation, pragmatism, unscrupulousness
opportunity *n* = **chance**, time, moment, opening, occasion, scope
oppose *v* = **be against**, resist, fight against, speak out against • *students opposing the new rules* OPPOSITE: support
See also: **contest, disagree, object, protest**
opposed *adj* = **contrary**, hostile, conflicting, averse, antagonistic, clashing, dissentient
opposing *adj* = **conflicting**, rival, enemy, opposite, contrary, hostile, incompatible
opposite *adj* **1** = **reverse**, contrary, conflicting, contrasting, opposed • *I take a completely opposite view.* **2** = **facing**, fronting ▸ *n* **3** = **reverse**, contrary, converse, antithesis • *He was the complete opposite of his cousin.*
opposition *n* **1** = **hostility**, resistance, disapproval • *Much of the opposition to this plan has come from the media.* OPPOSITE: support **2** = **opponent**, competition, rival, foe, antagonist, other side
See also: **competitor, conflict, disagreement, objection**
oppress *v* **1** = **depress**, burden, sadden, harass, afflict, torment, vex, dispirit **2** = **persecute**, abuse, wrong, subdue, suppress, maltreat, subjugate
oppressed *adj* = **downtrodden**, abused • *a member of an oppressed minority*
oppression *n* = **persecution**, tyranny • *the oppression of slaves*
See also: **abuse**
oppressive *adj* **1** = **tyrannical**, severe, harsh, brutal, cruel, unjust, inhuman, repressive, despotic **2** = **stifling**, close, sultry, stuffy, muggy, airless

DICTIONARY

oppugn [op-**pewn**] *v* **1** dispute **2** question
opt Ⓣ *v* (foll. by *for*) show a preference (for), choose
optic *adj* relating to the eyes or sight **optical** *adj*
▸ **optics** *n* science of sight and light
▸ **optical character reader** device that electronically reads and stores text
▸ **optical fibre** fine glass-fibre tube used to transmit information
optician *n* person who makes or sells glasses
▸ **dispensing optician** person who supplies and fits glasses
▸ **ophthalmic optician** person qualified to prescribe glasses
optimism *n* tendency to always take the most hopeful view **optimist** *n* **optimistic** *adj* **optimistically** *adv*
optimum Ⓣ *n, pl* **-ma, -mums 1** best possible conditions ▹ *adj* **2** most favourable **optimal** *adj*
▸ **optimize** *v* make the most of
option Ⓣ *n* **1** choice **2** thing chosen **3** right to buy or sell something at a specified price within a given time
▸ **optional** *adj* possible but not compulsory
optometrist [op-**tom**-met-trist] *n* person qualified to prescribe glasses **optometry** *n*
opulent Ⓣ [**op**-pew-lent] *adj* having or indicating wealth **opulence** *n*
opus Ⓣ [**oh**-puss] *n, pl* **opuses, opera** artistic creation, esp. a musical work
or *conj* used to join alternatives: *tea or coffee*
oracle Ⓣ *n* **1** shrine of an ancient god **2** prophecy, often obscure, revealed at a shrine **3** person believed to make infallible predictions **oracular** *adj*
oral Ⓣ *adj* **1** spoken **2** (of a drug) to be taken by mouth ▹ *n* **3** spoken examination **orally** *adv*
orange *adj* **1** reddish-yellow ▹ *n* **2** reddish-yellow citrus fruit
▸ **orangeade** *n* orange-flavoured, usu. fizzy drink
▸ **orangery** *n* greenhouse for growing orange trees
Orangeman *n* member of a society, formed in Ireland, for the upholding of Protestantism
orang-utan, orang-outang *n* large reddish-brown ape with long arms
orator Ⓣ [**or**-rat-tor] *n* skilful public speaker
▸ **oration** *n* formal speech
▸ **oratory** [**or**-rat-tree] *n* **1** art of making speeches **2** small private chapel **oratorical** *adj*
oratorio [or-rat-**tor**-ee-oh] *n, pl* **-rios** musical composition for choir and orchestra, usu. with a religious theme
orb Ⓣ *n* ceremonial decorated sphere with a cross on top, carried by a monarch
Orbison *n* **Roy** (**Kelton**). 1936–89, US pop singer and songwriter. His records include the singles "Only the Lonely" (1960) and "Oh Pretty Woman" (1964) and the album *Mystery Girl* (1989)
orbit Ⓣ *n* **1** curved path of a planet, satellite, or spacecraft around another heavenly body **2** sphere of influence ▹ *v* **orbiting, orbited 3** move in an orbit around **4** put (a satellite or spacecraft) into orbit **orbital** *adj*

O

THESAURUS

oppressor *n* = **persecutor**, bully, scourge, tyrant, despot, autocrat, slave-driver, tormentor
opt *v* (often with *for*) = **choose**, decide *or* decide on, elect, prefer, go for, plump for
optimistic *adj* = **hopeful**, positive, confident, buoyant, sanguine • *He is in an optimistic mood*. OPPOSITE: pessimistic
optimum *adj* = **ideal**, perfect, peak, best, optimal, superlative, highest
option *n* = **choice**, alternative, selection, preference
optional *adj* = **voluntary**, open, possible, extra, discretionary, elective
opulence *n* **1** = **wealth**, plenty, luxury, prosperity, affluence, riches, luxuriance **2** = **abundance**, richness, fullness, cornucopia, copiousness, profusion, superabundance
opulent *adj* **1** = **wealthy**, rich, affluent, lavish, prosperous, luxurious, sumptuous, well-off, well-to-do, moneyed **2** = **abundant**, prolific, lavish, plentiful, copious, luxuriant, profuse
opus *n* = **work**, production, piece, creation, composition, brainchild, *oeuvre* (*French*)
oracle *n* **1** = **prophecy**, prediction, revelation, prognostication, divination **2** = **authority**, adviser, mastermind, wizard, guru, mentor, pundit
oral *adj* = **spoken**, verbal • *oral history*
See also: **exam**
oration *n* = **speech**, address, lecture, discourse, homily, harangue
orator *n* = **public speaker**, speaker, lecturer, declaimer, rhetorician
oratorical *adj* = **rhetorical**, eloquent, bombastic, declamatory, grandiloquent, high-flown, magniloquent, sonorous
oratory *n* = **rhetoric**, eloquence, declamation, elocution, grandiloquence, public speaking, speech-making
orb *n* = **sphere**, ball, ring, circle, globe
orbit *n* **1** = **path**, course, cycle, circle, revolution, rotation, trajectory **2** = **sphere of influence**, reach, sweep, range, influence,

DICTIONARY

Orcagna *n* **Andrea**, original name *Andrea di Cione*. ?1308–68, Florentine painter, sculptor, and architect
orchard *n* area where fruit trees are grown
orchestra Ⓣ *n* large group of musicians, esp. playing a variety of instruments **orchestral** *adj*
▸ **orchestrate** *v* **1** arrange (music) for orchestra **2** organize (something) to particular effect **orchestration** *n*
▸ **orchestra pit** area of a theatre in front of the stage, for the orchestra
orchid *n* plant with flowers that have unusual lip-shaped petals
ordain Ⓣ *v* **1** make (someone) a member of the clergy **2** order or establish with authority
ordeal Ⓣ *n* painful or difficult experience
order Ⓣ *n* **1** instruction to be carried out **2** request for goods to be supplied **3** methodical arrangement or sequence **4** established social system **5** condition of a law-abiding society **6** social class **7** group of similar plants or animals **8** kind, sort **9** religious society, usu. of monks or nuns ▹ *v* **10** give an instruction to **11** request (something) to be supplied **12** arrange methodically
▸ **in order** so that it is possible
▸ **orderly** *adj* **1** well organized **2** well behaved ▹ *n, pl* **-lies 3** male hospital attendant **orderliness** *n*
▸ **Order of Canada** order awarded to Canadians for outstanding achievement
ordinal number *n* number showing a position in a series: *first; second*
ordinance *n* official rule or order
ordinary Ⓣ *adj* **1** usual or normal **2** dull or commonplace **ordinarily** *adv*
ordination *n* ordaining
ordnance *n* weapons and military supplies
ordure *n* excrement
ore *n* (rock containing) a mineral which yields metal
oregano [or-rig-**gah**-no] *n* aromatic herb used in cooking
Oresme *n* **Nicole d'**. ?1320–82, French economist, mathematician, and cleric: bishop of Lisieux (1378–82)
Orff *n* **Carl**. 1895–1982, German composer. His works include the secular oratorio *Carmina Burana* (1937) and the opera *Antigone* (1949)
organ Ⓣ *n* **1** part of an animal or plant that has a particular function, such as the heart or lungs **2** musical keyboard instrument in which notes are produced by forcing air through pipes **3** means of conveying information, esp. a newspaper
▸ **organist** *n* organ player
organdie *n* fine cotton fabric
organic Ⓣ *adj* **1** of or produced from animals or plants **2** *chem* relating to compounds of carbon **3** grown without artificial fertilizers

THESAURUS

domain, scope, compass, ambit ▸ *v* **3 = circle**, encircle, circumnavigate, revolve around
orchestra *See* **band**
orchestrate *v* **1 = score**, arrange **2 = organize**, arrange, coordinate, put together, set up, stage-manage
ordain *v* **1 = appoint**, invest, nominate, anoint, consecrate **2 = order**, will, rule, demand, fix, prescribe, dictate, legislate, decree, lay down
ordeal *n* **= hardship**, trial, torture, nightmare, tribulation • *the ordeal of being arrested*
See also: **experience, hell**
order *n* **1 = command**, instruction, dictate, decree, directive • *I don't take orders from them any more.* **2 = harmony**, regularity, symmetry • *the wish to impose order upon confusion* OPPOSITE: disorder **3 = sequence**, series, structure, arrangement, array, progression, layout, line-up, grouping **4 = discipline**, law, control, peace, quiet, calm, tranquillity, law and order **5 = request**, commission, application, reservation, booking, requisition **6 = class**, position, status, rank, grade, caste **7 = kind**, family, type, class, sort, genre, ilk **8 = society**, company, community, organization, association, guild, fraternity, brotherhood ▸ *v* **9 = command**, direct, instruct, decree, ordain • *The troops were ordered to withdraw.* OPPOSITE: forbid **10 = request**, book, reserve, apply for, send away for **11 = arrange**, group, organize, classify, marshal, catalog, sort out, systematize
See also: **require, routine, rule, tell**
orderly *adj* **1 = neat**, regular, tidy • *Their bicycles were parked in orderly rows.* OPPOSITE: disorderly **2 = well-behaved**, quiet, controlled, disciplined, restrained, law-abiding, peaceable
ordinarily *adv* **= usually**, generally, normally, commonly, customarily, as a rule, habitually, in general
ordinary *adj* **1 = usual**, standard, regular, normal, routine, conventional • *an ordinary day* OPPOSITE: special **2 = commonplace**, modest, humble, plain, mundane, banal, humdrum, unremarkable, workaday
See also: **common, everyday, natural**
organ *n* **1 = part**, unit, structure, element **2 = mouthpiece**, medium, vehicle, voice, forum
organic *adj* **1 = natural**, live, living, biological, animate **2 = systematic**,

DICTIONARY

or pesticides **4** organized systematically **organically** *adv*
organism ⓣ *n* any living animal or plant
organize ⓣ *v* **1** make arrangements for **2** arrange systematically **3** unite (people) for a shared purpose **organizer** *n*
▸ **organization** *n* **1** group of people working together **2** act of organizing **organizational** *adj*
orgasm *n* most intense point of sexual pleasure **orgasmic** *adj*
orgy ⓣ *n, pl* **-gies 1** party involving promiscuous sexual activity **2** unrestrained indulgence: *an orgy of destruction*
oriel *n* upper window built out from a wall
Orient *n* **the Orient** *lit* East Asia **Oriental** *adj*
▸ **Orientalist** *n* specialist in the languages and history of the Far East
▸ **orient** *or* **orientate** *v* **1** position (oneself) according to one's surroundings **2** position (a map) in relation to the points of the compass **orientation** *n*
▸ **orienteering** *n* sport in which competitors hike over a course using a compass and map
orifice ⓣ [**or**-rif-fiss] *n* opening or hole
origami [or-rig-**gah**-mee] *n* Japanese decorative art of paper folding
origin ⓣ *n* **1** point from which something develops, derivation **2** beginning
▸ **original** *adj* **1** earliest **2** new, not copied or based on something else **3** able to think up new ideas ▹ *n* **4** first version, from which others are copied **originally** *adv* **originality** *n*
▸ **original sin** human imperfection and mortality as a result of Adam's disobedience
▸ **originate** *v* come or bring into existence **origination** *n* **originator** *n*
oriole *n* tropical or N American songbird
Orléans[2] *n* **1 Charles**, Duc d'Orléans. 1394–1465, French poet; noted for the poems written during his imprisonment in England; father of Louis XII **2 Louis Philippe Joseph**, Duc d'Orléans, known as *Philippe Égalité* (after 1792). 1747–93, French nobleman, who supported the French Revolution and voted for the death of his cousin, Louis XVI, but was executed after his son, the future king Louis-Philippe, defected to the Austrians
Orlov *n* Count **Grigori Grigorievich**. 1734–83, Russian soldier and a lover of Catherine II. He led (with his brother, Count **Aleksey Grigorievich Orlov**, 1737–1808) the coup that brought Catherine to power
ormolu *n* gold-coloured alloy used for decoration
ornament ⓣ *n* **1** decorative object ▹ *v*

THESAURUS

organized, integrated, structured, methodical, ordered
organism *n* = **creature**, body, animal, structure, being, entity
organization *n* **1** = **group**, company, body, institution, association, outfit, confederation • *charitable organizations* **2** = **organizing**, planning, structuring • *We were involved in the organization of the picnic.* **3** = **structure**, pattern, format, unity, arrangement, chemistry, composition, make-up
See also: **business, firm, movement, society**
organize *v* = **arrange**, plan, establish, set up • *Organizing a wedding takes time.*
See also: **book, conduct, group, stage**
organized *See* **efficient, ready**
organizing *See* **organization**
orgy *n* **1** = **revel**, revelry, bacchanalia, carousal, debauch, Saturnalia **2** = **spree**, excess, binge (*informal*), bout, splurge, indulgence, overindulgence, surfeit
orient *v* = **familiarize**, adjust, adapt, align, acclimatize, get one's bearings, orientate
orientation *n* **1** = **position**, location, direction, bearings **2** = **familiarization**, introduction, adjustment, adaptation, assimilation, acclimatization, settling in
orifice *n* = **opening**, hole, rent, mouth, vent, pore, cleft, aperture
origin *n* **1** = **root**, source, derivation • *the origins of the custom* **2** = **ancestry**, stock, descent, extraction, lineage • *She was of Swedish origin.* **3** = **beginning**, start, launch, birth, foundation, creation, emergence, inception, genesis
See also: **cause**
original *adj* **1** = **first**, initial • *the original owner of the cottage* **2** = **new**, novel, fresh • *a stunningly original idea* OPPOSITE: unoriginal **3** = **creative**, fertile, imaginative, ingenious, inventive, resourceful ▸ *n* **4** = **prototype**, standard, model, pattern, master, precedent, paradigm, archetype
See also: **individual**
originality *n* = **novelty**, innovation, imagination, creativity, ingenuity, freshness, inventiveness, newness, unorthodoxy
originally *adv* = **at first**, first, initially, in the beginning, to begin with
originate *v* **1** = **begin**, come, start, rise, result, spring, emerge, stem, arise, derive **2** = **invent**, launch, create, introduce, generate, pioneer, institute, formulate, bring about
originator *n* = **creator**, author, father *or* mother, maker, founder, pioneer, architect, inventor
ornament *n* **1** = **decoration**, trinket, adornment, bauble, knick-knack • *a shelf*

DICTIONARY

2 decorate **ornamental** *adj* **ornamentation** *n*
ornate ⓣ *adj* highly decorated, elaborate
ornithology *n* study of birds **ornithological** *adj* **ornithologist** *n*
orotund *adj* **1** (of a voice) resonant **2** (of language) pompous
orphan *n* child whose parents are dead
▸ **orphanage** *n* children's home for orphans
▸ **orphaned** *adj* having no living parents
Orr *n* **Robert Gordon**, known as *Bobby*. born 1948, Canadian ice-hockey player
orrery *n, pl* **-ries** mechanical model of the solar system
orris *n* **1** kind of iris **2** Also **orrisroot** fragrant root used for perfume
Ortega *n* **Daniel**, full surname *Ortega Saavedra*. born 1945, Nicaraguan politician and former resistance leader; president of Nicaragua (1985–90)
Ortega y Gasset *n* **José**. 1883–1955, Spanish essayist and philosopher. His best-known work is *The Revolt of the Masses* (1930)
orthodontics *n* branch of dentistry concerned with correcting irregular teeth **orthodontist** *n*
orthodox ⓣ *adj* conforming to established views **orthodoxy** *n*
▸ **Orthodox Church** dominant Christian Church in Eastern Europe
orthography *n* correct spelling
orthopedics, orthopaedics *n* branch of medicine concerned with disorders of the muscles or joints **orthopedic** *or* **orthopaedic** *adj* **orthopedist** *or* **orthopaedist** *n*
ortolan *n* small European bird eaten as a delicacy
Orwell *n* **George**, real name *Eric Arthur Blair*. 1903–50, English novelist and essayist, born in India. He is notable for his social criticism, as in *The Road to Wigan Pier* (1932); his account of his experiences of the Spanish Civil War *Homage to Catalonia* (1938); and his satirical novels *Animal Farm* (1945), an allegory on the Russian Revolution, and *1984* (1949), in which he depicts an authoritarian state of the future **Orwellian** *adj*
oryx *n* large African antelope
OS **1** outsize(d) **2** Ordnance Survey
Oscar *n* award in the form of a statuette given for achievements in films
oscillate ⓣ [**oss**-ill-late] *v* swing back and forth **oscillation** *n* **oscillator** *n* **oscillatory** *adj*
▸ **oscilloscope** [oss-**sill**-oh-scope] *n* instrument that shows the shape of a wave on a cathode-ray tube
osculate *v jocular* kiss **osculation** *n*
osier [**oh**-zee-er] *n* **1** willow tree **2** willow branch used in basketwork
Osler *n* Sir **William**. 1849–1919, Canadian physician; his *Principles and Practice of Medicine* (1892) was the standard text for medical students for many years
Osman I, Othman I *n* 1259–1326, Turkish sultan; founder of the Ottoman Empire
osmium *n* heaviest known metallic element
osmosis *n* **1** movement of a liquid through a membrane from a lower to a higher concentration **2** process of subtle influence **osmotic** *adj*
osprey *n* large fish-eating bird of prey
osseous *adj* made of or like bone
Ossian *n* a legendary Irish hero and bard of the 3rd century AD See also (James) **Macpherson**
ossify ⓣ *v* **-fying, -fied** **1** (cause to) become bone, harden **2** become inflexible **ossification** *n*
ostensible ⓣ *adj* apparent, seeming **ostensibly** *adv*
ostentation ⓣ *n* pretentious display **ostentatious** *adj* **ostentatiously** *adv*
osteopathy *n* medical treatment involving manipulation of the joints **osteopath** *n*
osteoporosis *n* brittleness of the bones,

O

THESAURUS

containing ornaments ▸ *v* **2** = **decorate**, grace, adorn, embellish, festoon, beautify, prettify
ornamental *adj* = **decorative**, attractive, showy, beautifying, embellishing, for show
ornamentation *n* = **decoration**, embellishment, embroidery, adornment, elaboration, frills, ornateness
ornate *adj* = **elaborate**, busy, fancy, baroque, fussy, decorated, florid, ornamented, overelaborate, rococo
orthodox *adj* = **established**, official, traditional, conventional, customary, accepted, well-established, approved, received
orthodoxy *n* = **conformity**, authority, conventionality, received wisdom, traditionalism, compliance
oscillate *v* = **fluctuate**, swing, vary, sway, waver, seesaw, vibrate, vacillate
oscillation *n* = **fluctuation**, swing, variation, instability, vacillation, wavering
ossify *v* = **harden**, solidify, stiffen, fossilize
ostensible *adj* = **apparent**, so-called, purported, superficial, seeming, outward, supposed, pretended, professed
ostensibly *adv* = **apparently**, seemingly, supposedly, on the face of it, professedly
ostentation *n* = **display**, show, parade, pomp, affectation, exhibitionism, flamboyance, flashiness, flaunting, pretentiousness, showing off (*informal*)
ostentatious *adj* = **showy**, flamboyant,

DICTIONARY

caused by lack of calcium
ostler *n hist* stableman at an inn
ostracize Ⓣ *v* exclude (a person) from a group **ostracism** *n*
ostrich *n* large African bird that runs fast but cannot fly
OT Old Testament
OTC Officers' Training Corps
other Ⓣ *adj* **1** remaining in a group of which one or some have been specified **2** different from the ones specified or understood **3** additional ▷ *n* **4** other person or thing
▸ **otherwise** *adv* **1** differently, in another way ▷ *conj* **2** or else, if not
▸ **otherworldly** *adj* concerned with spiritual rather than practical matters
otiose [**oh**-tee-oze] *adj* not useful: *otiose language*
otter *n* small brown freshwater mammal that eats fish
ottoman *n, pl* **-mans** storage chest with a padded lid for use as a seat
▸ **Ottoman** *n, adj hist* (member) of the former Turkish empire
ouananiche [wah-ni-**neesh**] *n* variety of Atlantic salmon found only in lakes
oubliette [oo-blee-**ett**] *n* dungeon entered only by a trapdoor
ouch *interj* exclamation of sudden pain
ought *v* (foll. by *to*) **1** *used to express* obligation: *you ought to pay* **2** *used to express* advisability: *you ought to diet* **3** *used to express* probability: *you ought to know by then*
Ouija *n* ® lettered board on which supposed messages from the dead are spelt out
ounce Ⓣ *n* unit of weight equal to one sixteenth of a pound (28.4 grams)
our *adj* belonging to us
▸ **ours** *pron* thing(s) belonging to us
▸ **ourselves** *pron* emphatic and reflexive form of **we, us**
oust Ⓣ *v* force (someone) out, expel
out Ⓣ *adv, adj* **1** away from inside **2** not at home **3** revealed or made public **4** used up **5** no longer burning or shining **6** not correct: *the calculations were out* **7** not fashionable **8** on strike **9** openly homosexual **10** *sports* dismissed ▷ *v* **11** *informal* name (a public figure) as being homosexual
▸ **out of** at or to a point outside
▸ **outer** *adj* on the outside
▸ **outermost** *adj* furthest out
▸ **outing** *n* leisure trip
▸ **outward** *adj* **1** apparent ▷ *adv* **2** Also **outwards** away from somewhere **outwardly** *adv*
out- *prefix* surpassing: *outlive; outdistance*
outback Ⓣ *n* remote bush country of Australia
outbid *v* offer a higher price than
outboard motor *n* engine externally attached to the stern of a boat
outbreak Ⓣ *n* sudden occurrence (of something unpleasant)
outbuilding *n* outhouse
outburst Ⓣ *n* sudden expression of emotion
outcast Ⓣ *n* person rejected by a particular group
outclass Ⓣ *v* surpass in quality
outcome Ⓣ *n* result
outcrop *n geology* area where bedrock is covered by little or no soil

O

THESAURUS

flashy, extravagant, grandiose, pretentious • *an ostentatious lifestyle*
See also: **pompous, vain**
ostracism *n* = **exclusion**, exile, rejection, isolation, banishment
ostracize *v* = **exclude**, reject, exile, banish, cast out, cold-shoulder, give (someone) the cold shoulder, shun
other *adj* **1** = **additional**, more, further, extra, alternative, spare, added, supplementary, auxiliary **2** = **different**, separate, distinct, diverse, unrelated, variant, dissimilar, contrasting
others *See* **remainder, rest**
otherwise *conj* **1** = **or else**, if not, or then ▸ *adv* **2** = **differently**, any other way, contrarily
ounce *n* = **shred**, drop, grain, trace, scrap, atom, crumb, speck
oust *v* = **expel**, topple, displace, depose, eject, unseat, dislodge, dispossess, throw out, turn out
out *adj* **1** = **away**, outside, elsewhere, abroad, absent, gone, not at home **2** = **extinguished**, dead, finished, expired, at an end, ended, exhausted, used up ▷ **out loud** *See* **aloud** ▷ **out of danger** *See* **safe** ▷ **out of shape** *See* **crooked** ▷ **out of the ordinary** *See* **exceptional, uncommon** ▷ **out of the question** *See* **impossible**
out-and-out *See* **total, utter**
outback *See* **country**
outbreak *n* = **eruption**, explosion • *the outbreak of war*
See also: **burst, rash**
outburst *n* = **eruption**, outbreak, surge, explosion, outpouring, flare-up, spasm, paroxysm
outcast *n* = **pariah**, refugee, exile, Latin, castaway, leper, persona non grata, vagabond, wretch
outclass *v* = **surpass**, eclipse, overshadow, outshine, excel, outstrip, outdo, leave standing (*informal*), run rings around (*informal*)
outcome *n* = **result**, end, issue, consequence, conclusion, payoff (*informal*), upshot

DICTIONARY

outcry Ⓣ *n, pl* **-cries** expression of vehement or widespread protest
outdated Ⓣ *adj* out of date, old-fashioned
outdo Ⓣ *v* surpass in performance
outdoors Ⓣ *adv* **1** in(to) the open air ▷ *n* **2** the open air **outdoor** *adj*
outface *v* subdue or disconcert (someone) by staring
outfall *n* mouth of a river or pipe
outfield *n baseball* area beyond home plate and the three bases
outfit Ⓣ *n* **1** matching set of clothes **2** *informal* group of people working together
▸ **outfitter** *n old-fashioned* supplier of men's clothes
outflank *v* **1** get round the side of (an enemy army) **2** outdo (someone)
outgoing Ⓣ *adj* **1** leaving **2** sociable
▸ **outgoings** *pl n* expenses
outgrow *v* become too large or too old for
▸ **outgrowth** *n* **1** thing growing out from a main body **2** natural development
outhouse *n* building near a main building
outlandish Ⓣ *adj* extravagantly eccentric
outlast *v* last longer than
outlaw Ⓣ *n* **1** *hist* criminal deprived of legal protection, bandit ▷ *v* **2** make illegal **3** *hist* make (someone) an outlaw
outlay Ⓣ *n* expenditure
outlet Ⓣ *n* **1** means of expressing emotion **2** market for a product **3** place where a product is sold **4** opening or way out
outline Ⓣ *n* **1** line defining the shape of something **2** short general explanation ▷ *v* **3** draw the outline of **4** summarize
outlive Ⓣ *v* **1** live longer than **2** live through (an unpleasant experience)
outlook Ⓣ *n* **1** attitude **2** probable outcome
outlying Ⓣ *adj* distant from the main area
outmanoeuvre *v* get an advantage over
outmatch *v* surpass
outmoded Ⓣ *adj* no longer fashionable or accepted
outnumber *v* exceed in number
outpatient *n* patient who does not stay in hospital overnight
outport *n* isolated fishing village, esp. in Newfoundland
outpost Ⓣ *n* outlying settlement
outpourings *pl n* passionate outburst

THESAURUS

outcry *n* = **protest**, complaint, outburst, uproar, clamour, commotion, hue and cry, hullaballoo
outdated *adj* = **old-fashioned**, obsolete, antiquated, archaic, outmoded, out of date, passé, unfashionable
outdo *v* = **surpass**, top, outshine, go one better than • *She would love to outdo the previous champion.*
See also: **beat, pass**
outdoor *adj* = **open-air**, outside, alfresco, out-of-door *or* out-of-doors
outdoors *See* **country**
outer *adj* = **external**, outside, surface, exterior, exposed, outlying, peripheral, outward
outfit *n* **1** = **costume**, clothes, ensemble, garb, get-up (*informal*), suit **2** = **group**, company, team, organization, unit, crew, squad, setup (*informal*)
outgoing *adj* **1** = **leaving**, former, departing, retiring, withdrawing **2** = **sociable**, open, warm, friendly, expansive, gregarious, approachable, extrovert, communicative
outing *n* = **trip**, spin (*informal*), expedition, excursion, jaunt
outlandish *adj* = **strange**, bizarre, fantastic, weird, exotic, preposterous, unheard-of, far-out (*slang*), freakish, outré
outlaw *n* **1** = **bandit**, fugitive, robber, outcast, desperado, highwayman, marauder ▸ *v* **2** = **forbid**, ban, bar, prohibit, exclude, disallow, proscribe
outlawed *See* **illegal**
outlay *n* = **expenditure**, investment, spending, cost(s), expenses, outgoings, overhead(s)
outlet *n* **1** = **release**, opening, exit, channel, vent, avenue, duct **2** = **store**, market, shop
outline *v* **1** = **summarize**, sketch • *The mayor outlined his plan to clean up the town.* ▸ *n* **2** = **summary**, rundown, synopsis • *an outline of the archaeologist's findings* **3** = **shape**, figure, form, silhouette, contours • *the hazy outline of the buildings*
outlive *v* = **outlast**, survive
outlook *n* **1** = **attitude**, view, perspective • *I adopted a positive outlook on life.* **2** = **prospects**, future • *The economic outlook is one of rising unemployment.*
See also: **prospect**
outlying *adj* = **remote**, provincial, distant, peripheral, far-flung, out-of-the-way
outmoded *adj* = **old-fashioned**, obsolete, antiquated, archaic, out-of-date, anachronistic, outworn, passé, unfashionable • *Fax machines are an outmoded technology.*
out-of-date *adj* = **outdated**, old-fashioned, invalid, obsolete, antiquated, expired, archaic, dated, outmoded, lapsed, outworn, passé OPPOSITE: modern
out-of-the-way *See* **distant**
outpost *See* **colony**
outpouring *n* = **stream**, flow, spate, spurt, cascade, torrent, effusion

DICTIONARY

output Ⓣ *n* **1** amount produced **2** power, voltage, or current delivered by an electrical circuit **3** *computers* data produced ▷ *v* **4** *computers* produce (data) at the end of a process
outrage Ⓣ *n* **1** great moral indignation **2** gross violation of morality ▷ *v* **3** offend morally
▶ **outrageous** *adj* **1** shocking **2** offensive
outrageously *adv*
outré Ⓣ [**oo**-tray] *adj* shockingly eccentric
outrider *n* motorcyclist acting as an escort
outrigger *n* stabilizing frame projecting from a boat
outright Ⓣ *adj, adv* **1** absolute(ly) **2** open(ly) and direct(ly)
outrun *v* **1** run faster than **2** exceed
outsell *v* be sold in greater quantities than
outset Ⓣ *n* beginning
outshine Ⓣ *v* surpass (someone) in excellence
outside Ⓣ *prep* **1** to the exterior of **2** beyond the limits of ▷ *adj* **3** exterior **4** unlikely: *an outside chance* **5** coming from outside ▷ *adv* **6** on or to the exterior **7** in(to) the open air ▷ *n* **8** external area or surface
▶ **outsider** *n* **1** person outside a specific group **2** contestant thought unlikely to win
outsize, outsized Ⓣ *adj* larger than normal
outskirts Ⓣ *pl n* outer areas, esp. of a town
outsmart *v informal* outwit
outspoken Ⓣ *adj* **1** tending to say what one thinks **2** said openly
outstanding Ⓣ *adj* **1** excellent **2** still to be dealt with or paid
outstay *v* overstay
outstretched *adj* stretched out as far as possible
outstrip Ⓣ *v* **1** go faster than **2** surpass
outtake *n* unreleased take from a recording session, film, or TV programme
outvote *v* defeat by a majority of votes
outweigh Ⓣ *v* be more important, significant or influential than
outwit Ⓣ *v* get the better of (someone) by cunning

THESAURUS

output *n* = **production**, manufacture, yield, achievement, productivity
outrage *n* **1** = **violation**, violence, abuse, insult, offense, desecration, indignity, affront, sacrilege **2** = **indignation**, hurt, shock, anger, wrath, resentment, fury ▶ *v* **3** = **offend**, shock, incense, infuriate, affront, scandalize, madden
outrageous *adj* **1** = **atrocious**, offensive, disgraceful, wicked, flagrant, heinous, unspeakable, nefarious, villainous, iniquitous **2** = **unreasonable**, steep (*informal*), shocking, scandalous, extravagant, exorbitant, preposterous, immoderate
outré *adj* = **eccentric**, odd, bizarre, fantastic, weird, unconventional, outlandish, off-the-wall (*slang*), freakish
outright *adj* **1** = **absolute**, complete, total, perfect, thorough, unconditional, unqualified, unmitigated, out-and-out, thoroughgoing **2** = **direct**, flat, straightforward, definite, unequivocal, unqualified ▶ *adv* **3** = **absolutely**, completely, openly, thoroughly, overtly, straightforwardly, to the full
outset *n* = **beginning**, start, opening, onset, kickoff (*informal*), inauguration, inception, commencement
outshine *v* = **outclass**, surpass, eclipse, overshadow, upstage, outstrip, outdo, transcend, leave in the shade *or* put in the shade
outside *n* **1** = **exterior**, face, surface, facade • *The moth was on the outside of the glass.* OPPOSITE: inside ▶ *adj* **2** = **exterior**, external, surface, outdoor, outer, outward • *an outside water tap* OPPOSITE: inside **3** (~ *chance*) = **unlikely**, small, remote, slight, slim, distant, faint, marginal
outsider *n* = **interloper**, stranger, newcomer, intruder, incomer, odd man out
outsize *adj* = **extra-large**, huge, giant, monster, mammoth, gigantic, oversized, jumbo (*informal*), supersize
outskirts *pl n* = **edge**, perimeter, periphery • *the outskirts of Toronto*
outspoken *adj* = **forthright**, open, explicit, blunt, abrupt, frank, unequivocal, plain-spoken, unceremonious
outstanding *adj* **1** = **excellent**, great, brilliant, exceptional, superb, first-class, first-rate • *an outstanding tennis player* **2** = **unpaid**, due, overdue, payable, owing • *The total debt outstanding is $2 billion.*
See also: **fine, major, prize**
outstrip *v* = **surpass**, exceed, eclipse, overtake, better, excel, outdo, transcend, outdistance
outward *adj* = **apparent**, surface, obvious, visible, noticeable, observable, ostensible, perceptible
outwardly *adv* = **apparently**, seemingly, ostensibly, externally, on the face of it, on the surface, superficially, to all intents and purposes
outweigh *v* = **override**, cancel *or* cancel out, eclipse, compensate for, prevail over, take precedence over, tip the scales
outwit *v* = **outthink**, fool, cheat, dupe, outsmart (*informal*), get the better of, outfox, outmanoeuvre, swindle

O

DICTIONARY

outworks *pl n* secondary external defences of a fort
outworn Ⓣ *adj* no longer in use
ouzel, ousel [**ooze**-el] *n* see **dipper**
ouzo [**ooze**-oh] *n* strong aniseed-flavoured spirit from Greece
ova *n* plural of **ovum**
oval Ⓣ *adj* **1** egg-shaped ▷ *n* **2** anything that is oval in shape
ovary *n, pl* **-ries** female egg-producing organ **ovarian** *adj*
ovation Ⓣ *n* enthusiastic round of applause
oven *n* heated compartment or container for cooking or for drying or firing ceramics
over Ⓣ *prep* **1** higher than **2** on or across the top of **3** on or to the other side of **4** during **5** more than **6** recovered from ▷ *adv* **7** above or across something **8** onto its side: *the jug toppled over* **9** in excess ▷ *adj* **10** finished ▷ *n* **11** *cricket* series of six balls bowled from one end
▸ **overly** *adv* excessively
over- Ⓣ *prefix* **1** too much: *overeat* **2** above: *overlord* **3** on top: *overshoe*
overact Ⓣ *v* act in an exaggerated way
overall Ⓣ *n* **1** coat-shaped protective garment **overalls 2** protective garment consisting of trousers with a jacket or bib and braces attached ▷ *adj, adv* **3** in total
overarm *adv, adj* (thrown) with the arm above the shoulder
overawe Ⓣ *v* affect (someone) with an overpowering sense of awe
overbalance Ⓣ *v* lose balance
overbearing Ⓣ *adj* domineering
overblown Ⓣ *adj* inflated or excessive: *ovlown pride*
overboard *adv* from a boat into the water
▸ **go overboard** go to extremes, esp. in enthusiasm
overcast Ⓣ *adj* (of the sky) covered by clouds
overcharge Ⓣ *v* charge too much
overcoat *n* heavy coat
overcome Ⓣ *v* **1** gain control over after an effort **2** (of an emotion) affect strongly
overcrowd *v* cause to be too crowded
overdo Ⓣ *v* **1** do to excess **2** exaggerate (something)
▸ **overdo it** do something to a greater degree than is advisable
overdose Ⓣ *n* **1** excessive dose of a drug ▷ *v* **2** take an overdose

THESAURUS

outworn *adj* = **outdated**, discredited, obsolete, antiquated, out-of-date, worn-out, outmoded, disused, hackneyed, threadbare
oval *adj* = **elliptical**, egg-shaped, ovoid
ovation *n* = **applause**, tribute, acclaim, acclamation, big hand, cheers, clapping, plaudits
over *prep* **1** = **more than**, above, exceeding, in excess of • *It cost over a million dollars.* **2** = **on top of**, on, above, upon ▷ **over the moon** *See* **joyful** RELATED WORDS *prefixes*: hyper-, super-, supra-, sur- ▸ *adj* **3** = **finished**, up, past, complete, gone, at an end, done • *I am glad it's all over.* ▸ *adv* **4** = **above**, overhead, aloft, on high **5** = **extra**, beyond, in addition, in excess, left over
over- *See* **too**
overact *v* = **exaggerate**, ham *or* ham up (*informal*), overdo, overplay
overall *adj* **1** = **total**, general, global, complete, comprehensive, blanket, inclusive, all-embracing ▸ *adv* **2** = **in general**, on the whole
overawe *v* = **intimidate**, scare, alarm, terrify, frighten, daunt, abash
overbalance *v* = **overturn**, slip, tumble, capsize, keel over, tip over, topple over, turn turtle
overbearing *adj* = **domineering**, superior, arrogant, dictatorial, imperious, high-handed, bossy (*informal*), haughty, supercilious
overblown *adj* = **excessive**, inflated, disproportionate, undue, immoderate, overdone, over the top
overcast *adj* = **cloudy**, dismal, dull, murky, gray, dreary, leaden, louring *or* lowering
overcharge *v* = **cheat**, sting (*informal*), surcharge, fleece, short-change, rip off (*slang*)
overcome *v* **1** = **conquer**, master, vanquish (*formal*), surmount, get the better of, triumph over • *I had overcome my fear of flying.* ▸ *adj* **2** = **overwhelmed**, affected, speechless, at a loss for words, bowled over (*informal*), swept off one's feet
See also: **beat, crush, resolve, subdue**
overconfident *adj* = **cocky**, brash, foolhardy, presumptuous, cocksure, overweening
overcrowded *adj* = **packed**, jam-packed, bursting at the seams, choked, congested, overloaded, overpopulated, packed out, swarming
overdo *v* = **exaggerate**, overstate, overindulge, overreach, belabour, gild the lily, go overboard (*informal*) ▷ **overdo it** = **overwork**, overload, bite off more than one can chew, burn the candle at both ends (*informal*), strain oneself *or* overstrain oneself, wear oneself out
overdone *adj* **1** = **excessive**, unnecessary, exaggerated, undue, inordinate, fulsome, immoderate, overelaborate, too much **2** = **overcooked**, burnt, charred, dried up, spoiled
overdose *See* **excess**

DICTIONARY

overdraft *n* **1** overdrawing **2** amount overdrawn
overdraw *v* withdraw more money than is in (one's bank account)
▸ **overdrawn** *adj* **1** having overdrawn one's account **2** (of an account) in debit
overdress *v* dress too elaborately or formally
overdrive *n* very high gear in a motor vehicle
overdue Ⓣ *adj* still due after the time allowed
overestimate Ⓣ *v* estimate too highly
overflow Ⓣ *v* **1** flood **2** be filled beyond capacity ▹ *n* **3** outlet for excess liquid **4** excess amount
overgrown *adj* thickly covered with plants and weeds
overhang Ⓣ *v* **1** project beyond something ▹ *n* **2** overhanging part
overhaul Ⓣ *v* **1** examine and repair ▹ *n* **2** examination and repair
overhead Ⓣ *adv* **1** in the sky ▹ *adj* **2** over one's head
▸ **overheads** *pl n* general cost of maintaining a business
overhear Ⓣ *v* hear (a speaker or remark) unintentionally or without the speaker's knowledge
overjoyed Ⓣ *adj* very pleased
overkill *n* treatment that is greater than required
overland *adj, adv* by land
overlap *v* **1** share part of the same space or period of time (as) ▹ *n* **2** area overlapping
overlay Ⓣ *v* cover with a thin layer
overleaf *adv* on the back of the current page
overload Ⓣ *v* **1** put too large a load on or in ▹ *n* **2** excessive load
overlook Ⓣ *v* **1** fail to notice **2** ignore **3** look at from above
overmuch *adv, adj* too much
overnight *adj, adv* **1** (taking place) during one night **2** (happening) very quickly
overpower Ⓣ *v* subdue or overcome (someone)
overrate Ⓣ *v* have too high an opinion of
overreach *v* **overreach oneself** fail by trying to be too clever
override Ⓣ *v* **1** overrule **2** replace
overrule Ⓣ *v* **1** reverse the decision of (a person with less power) **2** reverse (someone else's decision)
overrun Ⓣ *v* **1** spread over (a place) rapidly **2** extend beyond a set limit

THESAURUS

overdue *adj* = **late**, belated, behindhand, behind schedule, owing, tardy, unpunctual
overeat *v* = **gorge**, binge (*informal*), guzzle, overindulge, gormandize, pig out (*slang*), stuff oneself
overemphasize *v* = **exaggerate**, belabour, blow up out of all proportion, make a mountain out of a molehill (*informal*), overdramatize, overstress
overestimate *See* **exaggerate**
overflow *v* **1** = **spill**, brim over, bubble over, pour over, run over, well over ▸ *n* **2** = **surplus**, overabundance, spilling over
overflowing *See* **crowded**
overhang *v* = **stick out**, project, extend, loom, protrude, jut
overhaul *v* **1** = **check**, service, repair, restore, examine, inspect, refurbish, do up (*informal*), recondition **2** = **overtake**, pass, catch up with, get ahead of ▸ *n* **3** = **checkup**, check, examination, service, inspection, reconditioning
overhead *adv* **1** = **above**, upward, aloft, skyward, in the sky, on high, up above ▸ *adj* **2** = **raised**, upper, aerial, overhanging
overheads *pl n* = **running costs**, operating costs
overhear *See* **hear**
overindulgence *n* = **excess**, immoderation, intemperance, overeating, surfeit
overjoyed *adj* = **delighted**, jubilant, euphoric, elated, on cloud nine (*informal*), over the moon (*informal*), thrilled
overlay *See* **cover, spread**
overload *v* = **weigh down**, strain, burden, saddle *or* saddle with, oppress, overburden, overtax, encumber
overlook *v* **1** = **ignore**, neglect, disregard, turn a blind eye to • *We tend to overlook warning signals about our health.* **2** = **miss**, forget • *One crucial detail was overlooked.* **3** = **have a view of**, look over *or* look out on
See also: **excuse, face**
overly *See* **too**
overpower *v* = **overwhelm**, defeat, overcome, crush, master, subdue, quell, overthrow, conquer, vanquish, subjugate
overpowering *adj* = **overwhelming**, strong, powerful, forceful, irresistible, invincible, irrefutable
overrate *v* = **overestimate**, exaggerate, overvalue
override *v* = **overrule**, cancel, outweigh, annul, nullify, supersede, countermand
overriding *adj* = **major**, primary, dominant, ultimate, supreme, paramount, predominant
overrule *v* = **overturn**, reverse • *The Court of Appeal overruled this decision.*
overrun *v* **1** = **invade**, overwhelm, rout, occupy **2** = **infest**, choke, ravage, inundate, permeate, spread over, swarm over **3** = **exceed**, overshoot, go beyond,

DICTIONARY

overseas Ⓣ *adj, adv* to, of, or from a distant country
oversee Ⓣ *v* watch over from a position of authority **overseer** *n*
overshadow Ⓣ *v* **1** reduce the significance of (a person or thing) by comparison **2** sadden the atmosphere of
overshoe *n* protective shoe worn over an ordinary shoe
overshoot *v* go beyond (a mark or target)
oversight Ⓣ *n* mistake caused by not noticing something
overskate *v* **-skating, -skated** *hockey* inadvertently skate past (the puck)
oversleep *v* sleep beyond the intended time
overspill *n* rehousing of people from crowded cities to smaller towns
overstate Ⓣ *v* state too strongly **overstatement** *n*
overstay *v* **overstay one's welcome** stay longer than one's host or hostess would like
overstep *v* go beyond (a certain limit)
overt Ⓣ *adj* open, not hidden **overtly** *adv*
overtake Ⓣ *v* move past (a vehicle or person) while travelling in the same direction
overtax *v* **1** put too great a strain on **2** tax too heavily
overthrow Ⓣ *v* **1** defeat and replace ▷ *n* **2** downfall, destruction
overtime *n, adv* (paid work done) in addition to one's normal working hours
overtone Ⓣ *n* additional meaning
overture Ⓣ *n* **1** *music* orchestral introduction **overtures 2** opening moves in a new relationship
overturn Ⓣ *v* **1** turn upside down **2** overrule (a legal decision) **3** overthrow (a government)
overview *n* general survey
overweening *adj* excessive or immoderate
overweight Ⓣ *adj* weighing more than is healthy
overwhelm Ⓣ *v* **1** overpower, esp. emotionally **2** defeat by force **overwhelming** *adj* **overwhelmingly** *adv*
overwork Ⓣ *v* **1** work too much **2** use too much ▷ *n* **3** excessive work
overwrought Ⓣ *adj* nervous and agitated
oviparous [oh-**vip**-par-uss] *adj* producing young by laying eggs
ovoid [**oh**-void] *adj* egg-shaped
ovulate [**ov**-yew-late] *v* release an egg cell from an ovary **ovulation** *n*
ovum [**oh**-vum] *n, pl* **ova** unfertilized egg cell
owe Ⓣ *v* be obliged to pay (a sum of money) to (a person)

THESAURUS

run over *or* run on
overseas *See* **foreign**
oversee *v* = **supervise**, manage, direct, co-ordinate, preside, be in charge of • *Get a supervisor to oversee the work.*
overseer *n* = **supervisor**, chief, boss (*informal*), master, superintendent, foreman
overshadow *v* **1** = **outshine**, dominate, surpass, eclipse, dwarf, leave in the shade *or* put in the shade, tower above **2** = **spoil**, ruin, temper, mar, blight, put a damper on
oversight *n* = **mistake**, slip, error, fault, neglect, lapse, blunder, omission, carelessness
overstate *See* **exaggerate**
overt *adj* = **open**, public, obvious, plain, blatant, manifest, observable, unconcealed, undisguised
overtake *v* **1** = **pass**, overhaul, outstrip, outdo, outdistance, catch up with, get past, leave behind **2** = **befall**, hit, strike, happen, overwhelm, engulf
overthrow *v* **1** = **depose**, oust, topple, bring down • *The government was overthrown in a military coup.* ▶ *n* **2** = **downfall**, fall, defeat, destruction, undoing, dethronement, ousting, unseating
overtone *n* = **connotation**, sense, hint, suggestion, implication, nuance, innuendo, undercurrent, intimation
overture *n* (*Music*) = **introduction**, opening, prelude ▷ **overtures** = **approach**, offer, advance, proposal, invitation, proposition
overturn *v* **1** = **tip over**, upset, topple, capsize, knock over • *to overturn a can of paint* **2** = **overrule**, reverse • *The referee's decision was overturned.*
See also: **abolish**
overused *See* **stock**
overweight *adj* = **fat**, obese, hefty, stout • *Being overweight increases your risk of heart problems.*
overwhelm *v* **1** = **overcome**, devastate, stagger, bowl over (*informal*), knock (someone) for six (*informal*), sweep (someone) off his feet *or* sweep (someone) off her feet, take (someone's) breath away **2** = **destroy**, crush, rout, overpower, massacre, overrun, cut to pieces
overwhelming *adj* = **overpowering**, towering, breathtaking, irresistible, crushing, devastating, shattering, stunning
overwork *v* **1** = **wear oneself out**, strain, sweat (*informal*), burn the midnight oil, work one's fingers to the bone **2** = **exploit**, fatigue, exhaust, weary, oppress, overuse, wear out
overwrought *adj* = **agitated**, tense, excited, frantic, uptight (*informal*), overexcited, distracted, keyed up, on edge, wired (*slang*)
owe *v* = **be in debt**, be in arrears, be obligated *or* be indebted

DICTIONARY

▸ **owing to** as result of
owl *n* night bird of prey **owlish** *adj*
▸ **owlet** *n* young owl
own Ⓣ *adj* **1** used to emphasize possession: *my own idea* ▷ *v* **2** possess **owner** *n* **ownership** *n*
▸ **own up** *v* confess
ox *n, pl* **oxen** castrated bull
Oxbridge *n* British universities of Oxford and Cambridge
oxeye *n* plant with daisy-like flowers
oxide *n* compound of oxygen and one other element
▸ **oxidize** *v* combine chemically with oxygen, as in burning or rusting
oxygen *n* gaseous element essential to life and combustion
▸ **oxygenate** *v* add oxygen to
▸ **oxyacetylene** *n* mixture of oxygen and acetylene used in high-temperature welding
oxymoron [ox-see-**more**-on] *n* figure of speech that combines two apparently contradictory ideas, such as *cruel kindness*
oyez *interj hist* (shouted three times by a public crier) listen
oyster *n* edible shellfish
▸ **oystercatcher** *n* wading bird with black-and-white feathers
oz. ounce
ozone *n* highly reactive strong-smelling form of oxygen
▸ **ozone layer** layer of ozone in the upper atmosphere that filters out ultraviolet radiation

THESAURUS

owing *adj* = **unpaid**, due, overdue, outstanding, payable, unsettled, owed
owing to *prep* = **because of**, as a result of, on account of
own *adj* **1** = **personal**, private • *I have my own website.* ▸ *v* **2** = **possess**, have • *His parents own a hardware store.* **3** = **acknowledge**, allow, admit, recognize, grant, concede, confess ▷ **hold one's own** = **keep going**, compete, keep one's end up, keep one's head above water ▷ **on one's own** = **alone**, independently, by oneself, unaided • *I work best on my own.* ▷ **own up** = **confess**, admit, come clean, make a clean breast, tell the truth
owner *n* = **possessor**, proprietor • *the owner of thestore*
ownership *n* = **possession**, title, dominion

O

DICTIONARY

Pp

p **1** page **2** *music* piano
P *chem* phosphorus
PA **1** personal assistant **2** public-address system
p.a. per annum
Pabst *n* **G(eorge) W(ilhelm)**. 1885–1967, German film director, whose films include *Joyless Street* (1925), *Pandora's Box* (1929), and *The Last Act* (1954)
pace ⊕ *n* **1** single step in walking **2** length of a step **3** rate of progress ▷ *v* **4** walk with regular steps **5** set the speed for (competitors in a race) **6** cross or measure with steps
▶ **put someone through his** *or* **her paces** test someone's ability
▶ **pacemaker** *n* **1** person who sets the speed of a race **2** electronic device surgically implanted in a person with heart disease to regulate the heartbeat
Pachelbel *n* **Johann**. 1653–1706, German organist and composer, noted esp. for his popular *Canon in D Major*
pachyderm [**pak**-ee-durm] *n* thick-skinned animal such as an elephant
Pacific Daylight Time *n* one of the standard times used in North America, seven hours behind Greenwich Mean Time Abbreviation: **PDT**
Pacific Standard Time *n* one of the standard times used in North America, eight hours behind Greenwich Mean Time Abbreviation: **PST**
pacifist ⊕ *n* person who refuses on principle to take part in war **pacifism** *n*
pacify ⊕ *v* **-fying, -fied** **1** soothe, calm **2** establish peace in **pacification** *n*
▶ **pacifier** *n* rubber or plastic teat for a baby to suck
Pacino *n* **Al**, full name *Alfredo James Pacino*. born 1940, US film actor; his films include *The Godfather* (1972), *Dog Day Afternoon* (1975), *Scent of a Woman* (1992), for which he won an Oscar, and *Insomnia* (2002)
pack ⊕ *n* **1** load carried on the back **2** set of things sold together **3** container for things sold **4** same as **packet** **5** set of playing cards **6** group of hunting animals ▷ *v* **7** put (clothes etc.) together in a suitcase or bag **8** put (goods) into containers or parcels **9** press tightly together, cram **10** fill with things
▶ **packhorse** *n* horse for carrying goods
▶ **pack ice** mass of floating ice in the sea
▶ **pack in** *v* *informal* stop doing
▶ **pack off** *v* send away
package ⊕ *n* **1** parcel **2** set of things offered together ▷ *v* **3** put into packages **packaging** *n*
▶ **package holiday** holiday in which everything is arranged by one company for a fixed price
packet ⊕ *n* **1** small parcel **2** small container (and contents) **3** *Brit slang* large sum of money
▶ **packet boat** *hist* boat that carried mail, goods, or passengers on a fixed short route
packsack *n* canvas bag carried on the back or shoulder
pact ⊕ *n* formal agreement

THESAURUS

pace *n* **1 = step**, walk, stride, gait **2 = speed**, rate, velocity, tempo ▶ *v* **3 = stride**, pound, march, patrol, tread ▷ **pace out = measure**, step, count, mark out
pacifist *n* **= peace lover**, dove, conscientious objector
pacify *v* **= calm**, appease, soothe, placate, mollify • *They tried to pacify the upset fans.*
pack *v* **1 = package**, store, load, bundle, stow **2 = cram**, crowd, fill, press, stuff, jam, ram, compress ▷ **pack off = send away**, dismiss, send packing (*informal*) ▷ **pack up = put away**, store; (*Informal*) **= stop**, finish, give up, pack it in (*informal*); **= break down**, fail, conk out (*informal*) ▶ *n* **3 = bundle**, load, burden, backpack, knapsack, back pack, kitbag, nunny-bag (*Canad Nfld*), rucksack **4 = package**, package, parcel, packet **5 = group**, company, troop, crowd, band, gang, bunch, herd, mob, flock
package *n* **1 = parcel**, box, container, carton, packet **2 = collection**, unit, whole, combination ▶ *v* **3 = pack**, box, wrap, parcel *or* parcel up
packed *adj* **= full**, crowded, jam-packed, jammed, chock-a-block, chock-full, crammed, filled
packet *n* **= package**, bag, container, carton, parcel
pact *n* **= agreement**, deal, alliance, treaty,

DICTIONARY

pad Ⓣ *n* **1** piece of soft material used for protection, support, absorption of liquid, etc. **2** block of sheets of paper fastened at the edge **3** fleshy underpart of an animal's paw **4** place for launching rockets **5** *slang* home ▷ *v* **padding, padded 6** protect or fill in with soft material **7** walk with soft or muffled steps
▶ **padding** *n* **1** material used to pad **2** words put in simply to increase length
paddle[1] Ⓣ *n* **1** short oar with a broad blade at one or each end ▷ *v* **2** move (a canoe etc.) with a paddle
▶ **paddle steamer** ship propelled by paddle wheels
▶ **paddle wheel** wheel with crosswise blades that strike the water successively to propel a ship
paddle[2] Ⓣ *v* walk with bare feet in shallow water
paddock *n* small field or enclosure for horses
paddy field *n* field where rice is grown
Paderewski *n* **Ignace Jan**. 1860–1941, Polish pianist, composer, and statesman; prime minister (1919)
padlock Ⓣ *n* detachable lock with a hinged hoop fastened over a ring on the object to be secured
padre [**pah**-dray] *n* chaplain in the armed forces
paean [**pee**-an] *n* song of triumph or thanksgiving
paediatrics *n* same as **pediatrics**
paedophilia *n* same as **pedophilia**
paella [pie-**ell**-a] *n* Spanish dish made of rice, chicken, shellfish, and vegetables
Páez *n* **José Antonio**. 1790–1873, Venezuelan revolutionary leader; first president (1831–46) of independent Venezuela
pagan Ⓣ *adj* **1** not belonging to one of the world's main religions ▷ *n* **2** pagan person
Paganini *n* **Niccolò**. 1782–1840, Italian violinist and composer
page[1] Ⓣ *n* (one side of) a sheet of paper forming a book etc.
page[2] Ⓣ *n* **1** *hist* boy in training for knighthood **2** attendant ▷ *v* **3** summon (a person whose whereabouts are unknown), for example by electronic bleeper or loudspeaker announcement
pageant Ⓣ *n* parade or display of people in costume, usu. illustrating a scene from history **pageantry** *n*
paginate *v* number the pages of (a book etc.) **pagination** *n*
Paglia *n* **Camille**. born 1947, US writer and academic, noted for provocative cultural studies such as *Sexual Personae* (1990) and *Vamps and Tramps* (1995)
pagoda *n* pyramid-shaped Asian temple or tower
Pahlavi *n* **1 Mohammed Reza**. 1919–80, shah of Iran (1941–79); forced into exile (1979) during civil unrest following which an Islamic republic was established led by the Ayatollah Khomeini **2** his father, **Reza**. 1877–1944, shah of Iran (1925–41). Originally an army officer, he gained power by a coup d'état (1921) and was chosen shah by the National Assembly. He reorganized the army and did much to modernize Iran
paid *v* past of **pay**
▶ **put paid to** *informal* end, destroy
pail *n* bucket **pailful** *n*
pain Ⓣ *n* **1** bodily or mental suffering **pains 2** trouble, effort **painful** *adj* **painfully** *adv* **painless** *adj* **painlessly** *adv*
▶ **on pain of** subject to the penalty of
▶ **painkiller** *n* drug that reduces pain
Paine *n* **Thomas**. 1737–1809, American political pamphleteer, born in England. His works include the pamphlets *Common Sense* (1776) and *Crisis* (1776–83), supporting the American colonists' fight for independence; *The Rights of Man* (1791–92), a justification of the French Revolution; and *The Age of Reason*

THESAURUS

bargain, understanding, covenant
pad[1] *n* **1 = cushion**, protection, buffer, stuffing, wad **2 = notepad**, block, jotter, writing pad **3 = paw**, foot, sole **4** (*Slang, dated*) **= home**, place, apartment, flat ▶ *v* **5 = pack**, protect, fill, stuff, cushion ▷ **pad out = lengthen**, stretch, elaborate, fill out, flesh out, protract, spin out
pad[2] *v* **= sneak**, steal, creep, go barefoot
padding *n* **1 = filling**, packing, stuffing, wadding **2 = wordiness**, hot air (*informal*), verbiage, verbosity
paddle[1] *n* **1 = oar**, scull ▶ *v* **2 = row**, pull, propel, scull
paddle[2] *v* **1 = wade**, splash *or* splash about, slop **2 = dabble**, stir
padlock *See* **lock**
pagan *adj* **1 = heathen**, infidel, idolatrous, polytheistic, pre-Christian ▶ *n* **2 = heathen**, infidel, idolater, polytheist
page[1] *n* **= folio**, side, leaf, sheet
page[2] *n* **1 = attendant**, servant, pageboy, squire ▶ *v* **2 = call**, summon, send for
pageant *n* **= show**, display, parade, procession, spectacle, tableau
pageantry *n* **= spectacle**, show, display, parade, grandeur, pomp, splendour, theatricality
pain *n* **1 = soreness**, trouble, ache, discomfort, irritation, twinge • *I felt a sharp pain in my lower back.* **2 = distress**, grief, misery, anguish, agony • *the pain of rejection*

P

DICTIONARY

(1794–96), a defence of deism

painstaking Ⓣ *adj* thorough and careful

paint Ⓣ *n* **1** colouring spread on a surface with a brush or roller ▷ *v* **2** colour or coat with paint **3** make a picture of **painter** *n* **painting** *n*

painter *n* rope at the bow of a boat for tying it up

pair Ⓣ *n* **1** set of two things ▷ *v* **2** group or be grouped in twos

paisley pattern *n* pattern of small curving shapes

Paisley *n* Rev. **Ian** (**Richard Kyle**). born 1926, Northern Ireland politician and Presbyterian minister; cofounder (1971) and leader of the Ulster Democratic Unionist Party; First Minister of Northern Ireland (2007–08)

pajamas *pl n* same as **pyjamas**

Pakistani *adj* **1** of or relating to Pakistan ▷ *n* **2** person from Pakistan

pal Ⓣ *n informal* friend

palace *n* **1** residence of a king, bishop, etc. **2** large grand building

palatable Ⓣ *adj* pleasant to eat

palate Ⓣ *n* **1** roof of the mouth **2** sense of taste

palatial Ⓣ *adj* **1** like a palace **2** magnificent

palaver Ⓣ [pal-**lah**-ver] *n* time-wasting fuss

pale[1] Ⓣ *adj* **1** light, whitish **2** having less colour than normal ▷ *v* **3** become pale

pale[2] *n* **1** *hist* fence **2** boundary

▶ **beyond the pale** outside the limits of social convention

paleography, palaeography [pal-ee-**og**-ra-fee] *n* study of ancient writings

paleolithic, palaeolithic [pal-ee-oh-**lith**-ik] *adj* of the Old Stone Age

paleontology, palaeontology [pal-ee-on-**tol**-a-jee] *n* study of past geological periods and fossils **paleontological** *or* **palaeontological** *adj*

Palestrina *n* **Giovanni Pierluigi da**. ?1525–94, Italian composer and master of counterpoint. His works, nearly all for unaccompanied choir and religious in nature, include the *Missa Papae Marcelli* (1555)

palette *n* artist's flat board for mixing colours on

Palin *n* **Sarah** (**Louise**) (neé *Heath*). born 1964, US politician; Governor of Alaska (2006–09); first woman to run as the Republican Party's vice-presidential candidate (2008)

palindrome *n* word, phrase, or sentence that reads the same backwards as forwards

paling *n* any of the upright planks in a fence

palisade *n* fence made of stakes

pall[1] Ⓣ *n* **1** cloth spread over a coffin **2** depressing oppressive atmosphere **3** dark cloud (of smoke)

▶ **pallbearer** *n* person carrying a coffin at a funeral

pall[2] Ⓣ *v* become boring

Palladio *n* **Andrea**. 1508–80, Italian architect who revived and developed classical architecture, esp. the ancient Roman ideals of symmetrical planning and harmonic

THESAURUS

▷ **pain in the neck** *See* **annoyance, pest** ▶ *v* **3 = hurt**, smart, sting, throb **4 = distress**, hurt, torture, grieve, sadden, agonize, torment, cut to the quick

See also: **annoyance, nuisance, pest, sorrow**

pained *adj* **= distressed**, hurt, upset, injured, wounded, aggrieved, offended

painful *adj* **1 = distressing**, unpleasant, grievous, saddening • *painful memories* **2 = sore**, tender, aching, excruciating • *a painful cramp in the stomach*

See also: **uncomfortable**

painfully *adv* **= distressingly**, clearly, unfortunately, sadly, dreadfully

painkiller *n* **= analgesic**, drug, anesthetic, anodyne

painless *adj* **= simple**, easy, fast, quick, effortless

pains *pl n* **= trouble**, effort, care, bother, diligence

painstaking *adj* **= thorough**, careful, conscientious, meticulous, diligent, scrupulous, assiduous

paint *n* **1 = colouring**, dye, stain, colour, pigment, tint ▶ *v* **2 = depict**, draw, represent, picture, portray, sketch **3 = coat**, cover, apply, colour, daub

painting *See* **picture**

pair *n* **1 = couple**, brace, duo, twins ▶ *v* **2 = couple**, team, join, match *or* match up, twin, bracket ▷ **pair up** *See* **team**

pal *n* (*Informal*) **= friend**, comrade, companion, buddy (*informal*), chum (*informal*), crony, homeboy (*slang*), homegirl (*slang*)

palatable *adj* **= delicious**, tasty, yummy (*informal*), luscious, appetizing, mouthwatering

palate *n* **= taste**, stomach, appetite

palatial *adj* **= magnificent**, grand, splendid, majestic, stately, regal, opulent, imposing

palaver *n* **= fuss**, big deal (*informal*), performance (*informal*), to-do, rigmarole, song and dance (*informal*)

pale *adj* **1 = light**, colourless, wan, ashen, faded, sallow • *Migrating birds filled the pale sky.* ▶ *v* **2 = become pale**, whiten, blanch, go white, lose colour

See also: **soft**

pall[1] *n* **1 = cloud**, shadow, veil, shroud, mantle **2 = gloom**, check, damper, damp

pall[2] *v* **= become boring**, tire, sicken, weary, become dull, become tedious, cloy, jade

DICTIONARY

proportions. His treatise *Four Books on Architecture* (1570) and his designs for villas and palaces profoundly influenced 18th-century domestic architecture in England and the US
pallet[1] *n* portable platform for storing and moving goods
pallet[2] *n* **1** straw mattress **2** small bed
palliasse *n* straw mattress
palliate *v* lessen the severity of (something) without curing it
▸ **palliative** *adj* **1** giving temporary or partial relief ▹ *n* **2** something, for example a drug, that palliates
pallid Ⓣ *adj* pale, esp. because ill or weak
pallor *n*
Palliser *n* **John**. 1817–1887, Irish explorer. Undertook expeditions for the Royal Geographical Society and the British Colonial Office to explore western British North America
pally *adj* **-lier, -liest** *informal* on friendly terms
palm *n* **1** inner surface of the hand **2** tropical tree with a straight trunk crowned with long pointed leaves
▸ **palm off** *v* get rid of (an unwanted thing or person), esp. by deceit
▸ **Palm Sunday** the Sunday before Easter
▸ **palmtop** *n* computer small enough to be held in the hand
Palmer *n* **Arnold**. born 1929, US professional golfer: won the US Open Championship (1960) and the British Open Championship (1961; 1962)
Palmerston *n* **Henry John Temple**, 3rd Viscount Palmerston. 1784–1865, British statesman; foreign secretary (1830–34; 1835–41; 1846–51); prime minister (1855–58; 1859–65). His talent was for foreign affairs, in which he earned a reputation as a British nationalist and for high-handedness and gunboat diplomacy
palmistry *n* fortune-telling from lines on the palm of the hand **palmist** *n*
palomino *n, pl* **-nos** gold-coloured horse with a white mane and tail
palpable Ⓣ *adj* **1** obvious **2** able to be touched or felt **palpably** *adv*
palpate *v med* examine (an area of the body) by touching
palpitate Ⓣ *v* **1** (of the heart) beat rapidly **2** flutter or tremble **palpitation** *n*
palsy [**pawl**-zee] *n* paralysis
▸ **palsied** *adj* affected with palsy
Paltrow *n* **Gwyneth** (**Kate**). born 1973, US film actress; her films include *Emma* (1996), *Sliding Doors* (1998), *Shakespeare in Love* (1998), and *Sylvia* (2003)
paltry Ⓣ *adj* **-trier, -triest** worthless, insignificant
pampas *pl n* vast grassy treeless plains in S America
▸ **pampas grass** tall grass with feathery ornamental flower branches
pamper Ⓣ *v* treat (someone) with great indulgence, spoil
pamphlet Ⓣ *n* thin paper-covered booklet
▸ **pamphleteer** *n* writer of pamphlets
pan[1] Ⓣ *n* **1** wide long-handled metal container used in cooking **2** *Brit* bowl of a lavatory ▹ *v* **panning, panned 3** sift gravel from (a riverbed) in a pan to search for gold **4** *informal* criticize harshly
▸ **pan out** *v* result
pan[2] Ⓣ *v* **panning, panned** move a film camera slowly so as to cover a whole scene or follow a moving object
pan- *combining form* all: *pan-African*
panacea Ⓣ [pan-a-**see**-a] *n* remedy for all diseases or problems
panache Ⓣ [pan-**ash**] *n* confident elegant style
panama *n* straw hat
panatella *n* long slender cigar
pancake *n* thin flat circle of fried batter
panchromatic *adj photog* sensitive to light of all colours
pancreas [pang-kree-ass] *n* large gland behind the stomach that produces insulin

THESAURUS

pallid *adj* = **pale**, anemic, pasty, wan, ashen, colourless
pallor *n* = **paleness**, lack of colour, pallidness, wanness, whiteness
palm off *v* = **fob off**, foist off, pass off
palpable *adj* = **obvious**, clear, visible, plain, evident, manifest, unmistakable, conspicuous
palpitate *v* = **beat**, pound, flutter, tremble, throb, pulsate
paltry *adj* = **insignificant**, despicable, lousy (*slang*), meagre, contemptible, inconsiderable, small, poor, minor, slight, petty, miserable, worthless, trivial, unimportant, measly, puny, scuzzy (*slang*), trifling
pamper *v* = **spoil**, indulge, coddle, cater to, cosset, pet, overindulge
pamphlet *n* = **booklet**, tract, brochure, circular, leaflet
pan[1] *n* **1** = **pot**, container, saucepan ▸ *v* **2** = **sift out**, look for, search for **3** (*Informal*) = **criticize**, slam (*slang*), knock (*informal*), censure
pan[2] *v* = **move**, follow, track, sweep
panacea *n* = **cure-all**, nostrum, universal cure
panache *n* = **style**, dash, élan, flamboyance

DICTIONARY

and helps digestion **pancreatic** *adj*
panda *n* large black-and-white bearlike mammal from China
pandemic *adj* (of a disease) occurring over a wide area
pandemonium Ⓣ *n* **1** wild confusion **2** uproar
pander Ⓣ *n* person who procures a sexual partner for someone
▸ **pander to** *v* indulge (a person or his or her desires)
pane *n* single piece of glass in a window or door
panegyric [pan-ee-**jire**-ik] *n* formal speech or piece of writing in praise of someone or something
panel Ⓣ *n* **1** flat distinct section of a larger surface, such as that in a door **2** group of people as a team in a quiz etc. **3** list of jurors, doctors, etc. ▹ *v* **-elling, -elled 4** decorate or cover with panels
▸ **panelling** *n* panels collectively, such as those on a wall
▸ **panellist** *n* member of a panel
▸ **panel beater** person who repairs damage to car bodies
pang Ⓣ *n* sudden sharp feeling of pain or sadness
pangolin *n* scaly anteater
panic Ⓣ *n* **1** sudden overwhelming fear, often infectious ▹ *v* **-icking, -icked 2** feel or cause to feel panic **panicky** *adj* **panic-stricken** *or* **panic-struck** *adj*
panicle *n* loose, irregularly branched cluster of flowers
panini *n, pl* **-ni, -nis** Italian bread usu. served grilled with a variety of fillings
pannier *n* **1** bag fixed on the back of a bike or motorbike **2** basket carried by a beast of burden
panoply Ⓣ [pan-a-plee] *n* magnificent array
panorama Ⓣ *n* wide or complete view **panoramic** *adj*
pansy *n, pl* **-sies 1** garden flower with velvety petals **2** *offensive* effeminate or homosexual man
pant Ⓣ *v* breathe quickly and noisily after exertion
pantaloons *pl n* baggy trousers gathered at the ankles
pantechnicon *n* large van for furniture removals
pantheism *n* belief that God is present in everything **pantheist** *n* **pantheistic** *adj*
pantheon *n* (in ancient Greece and Rome) temple to all the gods
panther *n* leopard, esp. a black one
panties *pl n* women's underpants
pantile *n* roofing tile with an S-shaped cross section
pantograph *n* **1** instrument for copying maps etc. to any scale **2** device on the roof of an electric train for picking up the electric current
pantomime Ⓣ *n* play based on a fairy tale, performed in Britain at Christmas time
pantry *n, pl* **-tries** room or cupboard for storing food or cooking utensils
pants Ⓣ *pl n* **1** undergarment for the lower part of the body **2** trousers
Panufnik *n* Sir **Andrzej**. 1914–91, British composer and conductor, born in Poland. His works include nine symphonies, the cantata *Winter Solstice* (1972), Polish folk-song settings, and ballet music
Paolozzi *n* Sir **Eduardo** (**Luigi**). 1924–2005, British sculptor and designer, noted esp. for his semiabstract metal figures
pap[1] *n* **1** soft food for babies or invalids **2** worthless or oversimplified ideas
pap[2] *n obsolete* nipple
papacy [**pay**-pa-see] *n, pl* **-cies** the position or term of office of a pope
▸ **papal** *adj* of the pope or papacy
Papandreou *n* **Andreas** (**George**). 1919–96, Greek economist and socialist politician; prime minister (1981–89; 1993–96)
paparazzo [pap-a-**rat**-so] *n, pl* **-razzi**

THESAURUS

pandemonium *n* = **uproar**, chaos, confusion, turmoil, racket, din, bedlam, hullabaloo, rumpus
pander *v* ▹ **pander to** = **indulge**, please, satisfy, gratify, cater to, play up to (*informal*)
panel *See* **council**
pang *n* = **twinge**, pain, stab, sting, ache, spasm, prick ▹ **pang of conscience** *See* **regret**
panic *n* **1** = **terror**, fear, alarm, dismay, hysteria, fright • *The earthquake caused panic among the population.* ▸ *v* **2** = **go to pieces**, become hysterical, lose your nerve • *I panicked when the elevator came to a sudden stop between floors and didn't move.* **3** = **alarm**, scare, unnerve
See also: **horror**
panic-stricken *adj* = **terrified**, frightened, scared, hysterical, panicky, frightened out of one's wits, in a cold sweat (*informal*), scared stiff
panoply *n* = **array**, dress, attire, garb, regalia, trappings
panorama *n* = **view**, prospect, vista
panoramic *adj* = **wide**, overall, extensive, comprehensive, sweeping
pant *v* = **puff**, blow, breathe, wheeze, gasp, heave
pantomime *See* **play**
pants *pl n* = **trousers**, slacks

DICTIONARY

photographer specializing in unposed shots of famous people
papaya [pa-**pie**-ya], **papaw** [pa-**paw**] *n* large sweet West Indian fruit
paper Ⓣ *n* **1** material made in sheets from wood pulp or other fibres **2** printed sheet of this **3** newspaper **4** set of examination questions **5** article or essay **papers** **6** personal documents ▷ *v* **7** cover (walls) with wallpaper
▶ **paperback** *n* book with flexible paper covers
▶ **paperweight** *n* heavy decorative object placed on top of loose papers
▶ **paperwork** *n* the part of a job that consists of dealing with routine letters, forms, etc.
papier-mâché [**pay**-per mash-**ay** *or* **pap**-yay **mash**-ay] *n* material made from paper mixed with paste, shaped by moulding and dried hard
Papineau *n* **Louis-Joseph**. 1786–1871, Canadian lawyer and politician, leader of the Patriote movement prior to the Lower Canada Rebellion; escaped to the US and then France but was pardoned by the British in 1844 and returned to Canada in 1845
papist *n, adj offensive* Roman Catholic
papoose *n* N American Indian baby or toddler
paprika *n* (powdered seasoning made from) a type of red pepper
Pap test *n med* examination of stained cells in a specimen taken from the neck or lining of the womb for detection of cancer (Also **smear**)
papyrus [pap-**ire**-uss] *n, pl* **-ri, -ruses** **1** tall water plant **2** (manuscript written on) a kind of paper made from this plant
par Ⓣ *n* **1** usual or average condition **2** face value of stocks and shares **3** *golf* expected standard score
▶ **on a par with** equal to
parable Ⓣ *n* story that illustrates a religious teaching
parabola [par-**ab**-bol-a] *n* regular curve resembling the course of an object thrown forward and up **parabolic** *adj*
paracetamol *n* mild pain-relieving drug
parachute *n* **1** large fabric canopy that slows the descent of a person or object from an aircraft ▷ *v* **2** land or drop by parachute
parachutist *n*
parade Ⓣ *n* **1** ordered march or procession **2** public promenade or street of shops **3** blatant display: *parade of one's grief* ▷ *v* **4** display or flaunt **5** march in procession
paradigm Ⓣ [**par**-a-dime] *n* example or model
paradise Ⓣ *n* **1** heaven **2** state of bliss **3** Garden of Eden
paradox Ⓣ *n* statement that seems self-contradictory but may be true **paradoxical** *adj* **paradoxically** *adv*
paraffin *n* waxy substance derived from petroleum and used as a solvent, etc.
paragliding *n* cross-country gliding using a parachute
paragon Ⓣ *n* model of perfection
paragraph Ⓣ *n* section of a piece of writing starting on a new line
parakeet *n* small long-tailed parrot
parallax *n* apparent difference in an object's position or direction as viewed from different points
parallel Ⓣ *adj* **1** separated by equal distance at every point **2** precisely corresponding

P

THESAURUS

paper *n* **1** = **newspaper**, daily, journal, gazette **2** = **essay**, report, article, treatise, dissertation ▷ **papers** = **documents**, certificates, deeds, records; = **letters**, file, archive, dossier, diaries, documents, records ▶ *v* **3** = **wallpaper**, hang
par *n* ▷ **above par** = **excellent**, superior, exceptional, outstanding, first-rate (*informal*) ▷ **below** *or* **under par** = **inferior**, poor, substandard, imperfect, second-rate, lacking, wanting, below average, two-bit (*slang*), not up to scratch (*informal*), dime-a-dozen (*informal*), bush-league (*informal*), not up to snuff (*informal*), tinhorn (*US slang*) ▷ **on a par with** = **equal to**, the same as, much the same as, well-matched with ▷ **par for the course** = **usual**, average, standard, typical, ordinary, predictable, expected ▷ **up to par** = **satisfactory**, acceptable, adequate, passable, good enough, up to scratch (*informal*), up to the mark
parable *n* = **lesson**, story, allegory, fable, moral tale
parade *n* **1** = **procession**, march, motorcade, pageant • *the Grey Cup parade* **2** = **show**, display, spectacle ▶ *v* **3** = **flaunt**, display, exhibit, show off (*informal*) **4** = **march**, process
paradigm *n* = **model**, example, pattern, ideal
paradise *n* **1** = **heaven**, Elysian fields, Happy Valley, Promised Land **2** = **bliss**, delight, heaven, utopia, felicity
paradox *n* = **contradiction**, puzzle, oddity, anomaly, enigma
paradoxical *adj* = **contradictory**, enigmatic, baffling, confounding, puzzling
paragon *n* = **model**, pattern, ideal, epitome, exemplar, nonpareil, quintessence
paragraph *n* = **section**, part, item, passage, clause, subdivision
parallel *adj* **1** = **equidistant**, alongside,

DICTIONARY

▷ *n* **3** line equidistant from another at all points **4** thing with similar features to another **5** line of latitude ▷ *v* **6** be parallel to **7** correspond to **parallelism** *n*
parallelogram *n* four-sided geometric figure with opposite sides parallel
paralysis Ⓣ *n* inability to move or feel, because of damage to the nervous system
▸ **paralyze** *v* **1** affect with paralysis **2** make immobile
▸ **paralytic** *n, adj* (person) affected with paralysis
paramedic *n* person working in support of the medical profession **paramedical** *adj*
parameter Ⓣ [par-**am**-it-er] *n* limiting factor, boundary
paramilitary *adj* organized on military lines
paramount Ⓣ *adj* of the greatest importance or significance
paramour *n obsolete* illicit lover, mistress
paranoia *n* **1** mental illness causing delusions of fame or persecution **2** *informal* intense fear or suspicion **paranoiac** *or* **paranoid** *adj, n*
paranormal *adj* beyond scientific explanation
parapet *n* low wall or railing along the edge of a balcony, bridge, etc.
paraphernalia Ⓣ *n* personal belongings or bits of equipment
paraphrase Ⓣ *v* express (meaning) in different words
paraplegia [par-a-**pleej**-ya] *n* paralysis of the lower half of the body **paraplegic** *n, adj*
parapsychology *n* study of phenomena outside normal human ability, such as telepathy
parasite Ⓣ *n* **1** animal or plant living in or on another **2** person who lives at the expense of others, sponger **parasitic** *adj*
parasol *n* umbrella-like sunshade
paratroops, -troopers *pl n* troops trained to attack by descending by parachute
parboil *v* boil until partly cooked
parcel Ⓣ *n* **1** something wrapped up, a package ▷ *v* **-celling, -celled 2** wrap up
▸ **parcel out** *v* divide into parts
parch Ⓣ *v* **1** make very hot and dry **2** make thirsty
parchment *n* thick smooth writing material made from animal skin
pardon Ⓣ *v* **1** forgive or excuse ▷ *n* **2** forgiveness **3** official release from punishment **pardonable** *adj* **pardonably** *adv*
pare Ⓣ *v* trim or cut the edge of
▸ **paring** *n* piece pared off
Paré *n* **Ambroise**. 1510–90, French surgeon. He reintroduced ligature of arteries following amputation instead of cauterization
parent Ⓣ *n* father or mother **parental** *adj* **parenthood** *n*

THESAURUS

side by side **2 = matching**, like, similar, analogous, corresponding, resembling ▸ *n* **3 = equivalent**, match, twin, counterpart, equal, analogue **4 = similarity**, comparison, likeness, resemblance, analogy
paralysis *n* **1 = immobility**, palsy **2 = standstill**, halt, breakdown, stoppage
paralytic *adj* **= paralyzed**, disabled, lame, crippled, challenged, incapacitated, palsied
paralyze *v* **1 = disable**, cripple, lame, incapacitate **2 = immobilize**, halt, freeze, stun, numb, petrify
paralyzed *See* **numb**
parameter *n* **= limit**, restriction, framework, limitation, specification
paramount *adj* **= principal**, first, chief, prime, main, primary, cardinal, foremost, supreme
paranoid *adj* **1 = mentally ill**, psychotic, disturbed, neurotic, manic, deluded, paranoiac **2** (*Informal*) **= suspicious**, nervous, fearful, worried, wired (*slang*)
paraphernalia *n* **= equipment**, tackle, stuff, gear, baggage, apparatus, belongings, effects, things, trappings
paraphrase *n* **1 = rewording**, restatement, rephrasing ▸ *v* **2 = reword**, restate, express in other words *or* express in one's own words, rephrase
parasite *n* **= sponger** (*informal*), leech, bloodsucker (*informal*), hanger-on, scrounger (*informal*)
parasitic, parasitical *adj* **= sponging** (*informal*), bloodsucking (*informal*), scrounging (*informal*)
parcel *n* **1 = package**, pack, bundle ▸ *v* **2** (often with *up*) **= wrap**, package, pack, do up, tie up
parch *v* **= dry up**, evaporate, wither, dehydrate, shrivel, desiccate
parched *adj* **= dried out** *or* **dried up**, dry, thirsty, arid, dehydrated
pardon *v* **1 = forgive**, excuse, acquit, overlook, exonerate, absolve, let off (*informal*) ▸ *n* **2 = forgiveness**, amnesty, acquittal, exoneration, absolution
pardonable *adj* **= forgivable**, minor, understandable, excusable, venial
pare *v* **1 = peel**, cut, skin, clip, trim, shave **2 = cut back**, cut, reduce, decrease, crop, dock
parent *n* **= father** *or* **mother**, progenitor, sire, procreator
parentage *n* **= family**, stock, birth, descent, pedigree, ancestry, lineage

DICTIONARY

▸ **parentage** *n* ancestry or family
▸ **parenting** *n* activity of bringing up children
parenthesis [par-**en**-thiss-iss] *n, pl* **-ses** **1** word or sentence inserted in a passage, usu. marked off by brackets, dashes, or commas **parentheses 2** round brackets, ( ) **parenthetical** *adj*
par excellence *adv* beyond comparison: *she is a hostess par excellence*
pargeting *n* ornamental plasterwork on the outside of a house
pariah Ⓣ [par-**rye**-a] *n* social outcast
parietal [par-**rye**-it-al] *adj* of the walls of body cavities such as the skull
parish Ⓣ *n* area that has its own church and cleric
▸ **parishioner** *n* inhabitant of a parish
parity Ⓣ *n* equality or equivalence
park Ⓣ *n* **1** area of open land for recreational use by the public **2** area containing a number of related businesses **3** large enclosed piece of ground attached to a country house ▷ *v* **4** stop and leave (a vehicle) temporarily
▸ **parking lot** area or building where vehicles may be left for a time
Park *n* **1** **Mungo**. 1771–1806, Scottish explorer. He led two expeditions (1795–97; 1805–06) to trace the course of the Niger in Africa. He was drowned during the second expedition **2 Nick**, full name *Nicholas Wulstan Park*. born 1958, British animator and film director; his films include *A Grand Day Out* (1992), which introduced the characters Wallace and Gromit, and the feature-length *Chicken Run* (2000)
parka *n* warm waterproof hooded jacket
parkade *n* a building used as a car park
Parker *n* **1** Sir **Alan** (**William**). born 1944, British film director and screenwriter; his films include *Midnight Express* (1978), *Mississippi Burning* (1988), *The Commitments* (1991), and *Angela's Ashes* (2000); chairman of the British Film Institute (1998–99) **2 Charlie**, nickname *Bird* or *Yardbird*. 1920–55, US jazz alto saxophonist and composer; the leading exponent of early bop **3 Dorothy** (**Rothschild**). 1893–1967, US writer, noted esp. for the ironical humour of her short stories
parkette *n* a small public park
Parkinson's disease *n* progressive disorder of the central nervous system which causes impaired muscular coordination and tremor (Also **Parkinsonism**)
parlance Ⓣ *n* particular way of speaking, idiom
parley *n* **1** meeting between leaders or representatives of opposing forces to discuss terms ▷ *v* **2** have a parley
parliament Ⓣ *n* law-making assembly of a country **parliamentary** *adj*
parlor, parlour Ⓣ *n old-fashioned* living room for receiving visitors
parlous Ⓣ *adj obsolete* dangerous
Parmesan *n* hard strong-flavoured Italian cheese
Parnell *n* **Charles Stewart**. 1846–91, Irish nationalist, who led the Irish Home Rule movement in Parliament (1880–90) with a calculated policy of obstruction. Although Gladstone was converted to Home Rule (1886), Parnell's career was ruined by the scandal over his adultery with Mrs. O'Shea **Parnellism** *n* **Parnellite** *n, adj*
parochial Ⓣ *adj* **1** narrow in outlook, provincial **2** of a parish **parochialism** *n*
parody Ⓣ *n, pl* **-dies 1** exaggerated and amusing imitation of someone else's style ▷ *v* **-dying, -died 2** make a parody of
parole *n* **1** early freeing of a prisoner on condition that he or she behaves well ▷ *v* **2** place on parole
▸ **on parole** (of a prisoner) released on condition that he or she behaves well
parotid gland *n* large salivary gland in front of and below each ear
paroxysm Ⓣ *n* **1** uncontrollable outburst, as of laughter **2** spasm or convulsion, as of pain
parquet [**par**-kay] *n* wooden blocks

P

THESAURUS

pariah *n* = **outcast**, exile, undesirable, untouchable
parish *n* = **community**, church, flock, congregation
parity *n* = **equality**, unity, consistency, uniformity, equivalence
park *n* = **parkland**, estate, garden, woodland, grounds, parkette (*Canad*)
parlance *n* = **language**, talk, speech, tongue, jargon, idiom, phraseology
parliament *n* = **assembly**, council, legislature, convention, congress, senate
parliamentary *adj* = **governmental**, legislative, law-making
parlor, parlour *n* (*Old-fashioned*) = **sitting room**, lounge, drawing room, front room, living room
parlous *adj* (*Archaic or humorous*) = **dangerous**, risky, hazardous
parochial *adj* = **provincial**, limited, narrow, petty, insular, narrow-minded, small-minded
parody *n* **1** = **takeoff** (*informal*), satire, skit, spoof (*informal*), imitation, lampoon, piss-take (*informal*) • *a parody of the newscast* ▸ *v* **2** = **take off** (*informal*), satirize (*informal*), caricature, burlesque
paroxysm *n* = **outburst**, attack, fit, seizure, spasm, convulsion

DICTIONARY

arranged in a pattern and forming a floor
parquetry *n*

parricide *n* **1** person who kills one of his or her parents **2** act of killing either of one's parents

parrot Ⓣ *n* **1** tropical bird with a short hooked beak, some varieties of which can imitate speaking ▷ *v* **-roting, -roted 2** repeat (words) without thinking

parry Ⓣ *v* **-rying, -ried 1** ward off (an attack) **2** cleverly avoid (an awkward question)

Parry *n* **1** Sir (**Charles**) **Hubert** (**Hastings**). 1848–1918, English composer, noted esp. for his choral works **2** Sir **William Edward**. 1790–1855, English arctic explorer, who searched for the Northwest Passage (1819–25) and attempted to reach the North Pole (1827)

parse [parz] *v* analyse (a sentence) in terms of grammar

parsec *n* unit of length used in expressing the distance of stars

parsimony *n* stinginess **parsimonious** *adj*

parsley *n* herb used for seasoning and decorating food

parsnip *n* long tapering cream-coloured root vegetable

parson Ⓣ *n* parish priest in the Anglican Church
▸ **parsonage** *n* parson's house
▸ **parson's nose** rump of a cooked fowl

Parsons *n* **Gram**, real name *Cecil Connor*. 1946–73, US country-rock singer and songwriter; founder of the Flying Burrito Brothers (1968–70), he later released the solo albums *G.P.* (1973) and *Grievous Angel* (1974)

part Ⓣ *n* **1** piece or portion **2** one of several equal divisions **3** actor's role **4** region, area **5** component of a vehicle or machine **6** division between sections of hair on the head ▷ *v* **7** divide **8** (of people) leave each other
▸ **take someone's part** support someone in an argument etc.
▸ **take something in good part** respond (to criticism etc.) with good humour
▸ **parting** *n* **1** separation **2** leave-taking
▸ **parting shot** hostile remark or gesture delivered while departing
▸ **partly** *adv* not completely
▸ **part of speech** particular grammatical class of words, such as *n* or *v*
▸ **part song** song for several voices singing in harmony
▸ **part-time** *adj* occupying or working less than the full working week
▸ **part with** *v* give up ownership of

partake Ⓣ *v* **-taking, -took, -taken 1** (foll. by *of*) take food or drink **2** (foll. by *in*) take part in

parterre *n* formally patterned flower garden

partial Ⓣ *adj* **1** not general or complete **2** prejudiced **partially** *adv*
▸ **partial to** very fond of
▸ **partiality** *n* **1** favouritism **2** fondness for

participate Ⓣ *v* become actively involved in **participant** *n* **participation** *n* **participator** *n*

THESAURUS

parrot *v* = **repeat**, copy, echo, mimic, imitate

parry *v* **1** = **ward off**, block, deflect, rebuff, repel, repulse **2** = **evade**, avoid, dodge, sidestep

parsimonious *adj* = **mean**, close, stingy, frugal, miserly, niggardly, penny-pinching (*informal*), tightfisted

parson *n* = **clergyman**, minister, cleric, priest, pastor, preacher, vicar, churchman

part *n* **1** = **piece**, bit, section, portion, fraction, fragment • *I like that part of Hamilton.* **2** = **involvement**, role, duty, capacity, function • *He tried to conceal his part in the accident.* **3** = **component**, member, unit, division, branch, constituent **4** (*Theatre*) = **role**, character, lines **5** = **side**, cause, concern, interest, behalf **6** (*often pl*) = **region**, area, quarter, district, neighbourhood, vicinity ▷ **in good part** = **good-naturedly**, well, cheerfully, without offence ▷ **in part** = **partly**, somewhat, partially, a little, in some measure ▷ **take part in** = **participate in**, be instrumental in, be involved in, have a hand in, join in, play a part in • *Thousands took part in the celebrations.* ▸ *v* **7** = **divide**, break, separate, tear, split, sever, detach, come apart, rend **8** = **separate**, go, leave, withdraw, depart, go away, split up
See also: **aspect, attachment, factor, fitting, quantity**

partake *v* ▷ **partake of** = **consume**, take, eat, chow down (*slang*) ▷ **partake in** = **participate in**, engage in, share in, take part in

partial *adj* **1** = **incomplete**, unfinished, imperfect, uncompleted **2** = **biased**, unfair, partisan, discriminatory, unjust, one-sided, prejudiced

partiality *n* **1** = **bias**, preference, prejudice, favouritism **2** = **liking**, love, taste, weakness, penchant, fondness, inclination, predilection

partially *adv* = **partly**, somewhat, fractionally, incompletely, in part, not wholly

participant *n* = **participator**, player, member, stakeholder, contributor

participate *v* = **take part**, be involved in, engage in, enter into, join in • *More than half the class participated in the event.*

DICTIONARY

participle *n* form of a *v* used in compound tenses or as an adjective: *worried; worrying* **participial** *adj*

particle Ⓣ *n* **1** extremely small piece or amount **2** *physics* minute piece of matter, such as a proton or electron

parti-coloured *adj* differently coloured in different parts

particular Ⓣ *adj* **1** relating to one person or thing, not general **2** exceptional or special **3** very exact **4** not easily satisfied, fastidious ▷ *n* **5** detail **6** item of information **particularly** *adv* **particularity** *n* ▸ **particularize** *v* give details about

Parti Québécois [par-**tee** kay-beck-**wah**] *n* political party in Quebec originally advocating separation of Quebec from rest of country

partisan Ⓣ *n* **1** strong supporter of a party or group **2** guerrilla, member of a resistance movement ▷ *adj* **3** prejudiced or one-sided

partition Ⓣ *n* **1** screen or thin wall that divides a room **2** division of a country into independent parts ▷ *v* **3** divide with a partition

partner Ⓣ *n* **1** either member of a couple in a relationship or activity **2** member of a business partnership ▷ *v* **3** be the partner of (someone)

▸ **partnership** *n* joint business venture between two or more people

Parton *n* **Dolly**. born 1946, US country and pop singer and songwriter

partridge *n* game bird of the grouse family

parturition *n* act of giving birth

party Ⓣ *n, pl* **-ties 1** social gathering for pleasure **2** group of people travelling or working together **3** group of people with a common political aim **4** person or people forming one side in a lawsuit etc.

▸ **party line** official view of a political party

▸ **party wall** common wall separating adjoining buildings

parvenu [**par**-ven-new] *n* person newly risen to a position of power or wealth, upstart

pascal *n* unit of pressure

Pascal *n* **Blaise**. 1623–62, French philosopher, mathematician, and physicist. As a scientist, he made important contributions to hydraulics and the study of atmospheric pressure and, with Fermat, developed the theory of probability. His chief philosophical works are *Lettres provinciales* (1656–57), written in defence of Jansenism and against the Jesuits, and *Pensées* (1670), fragments of a Christian apologia

paschal [**pass**-kal] *adj* of the Passover or Easter

Pasionaria *n* **La**, real name *Dolores Ibarruri*. 1895–1989, Spanish Communist leader, who lived in exile in the Soviet Union (1939–75)

Pasolini *n* **Pier Paolo**. 1922–75, Italian film director. His films include *The Gospel according to St Matthew* (1964), *Oedipus Rex* (1967), *Theorem*

THESAURUS

See also: **play** ▷ **participate in** *See* **take part in**

participation *n* = **taking part**, contribution, involvement, joining in, partaking, sharing in

particle *n* = **bit**, piece, grain, scrap, shred, mite, speck, iota, jot

particular *adj* **1** = **specific**, express, exact, distinct, precise, peculiar, discrete • *That particular place is dangerous.* **2** = **special**, notable, exceptional, marked, uncommon, singular • *Pay particular attention to the instructions.* **3** = **fussy**, meticulous, exacting, choosy (*informal*), fastidious • *He was very particular about the colours he used.* ▸ *n* **4** (*usually pl*) = **detail**, fact, feature, item, circumstance, specification ▷ **in particular** = **especially**, particularly, exactly, specifically, distinctly

See also: **personal, strict**

particularly *adv* **1** = **especially**, notably, unusually, exceptionally, uncommonly, singularly **2** = **specifically**, especially, explicitly, distinctly, expressly, in particular

parting *n* **1** = **farewell**, going, good-bye **2** = **division**, split, separation, rift, rupture, breaking

partisan *n* **1** = **supporter**, devotee, adherent, upholder **2** = **underground fighter**, guerrilla, resistance fighter ▸ *adj* **3** = **prejudiced**, interested, sectarian, partial, one-sided, biased

partition *n* **1** = **screen**, wall, barrier **2** = **division**, separation, segregation **3** = **allotment**, distribution, apportionment ▸ *v* **4** = **separate**, screen, divide

partly *adv* = **partially**, half-, in part, to some degree, to some extent • *This is partly my fault.*

partner *n* **1** = **spouse**, wife, husband, mate • *My partner moved in with me last year.* **2** = **companion**, teammate • *my tennis partner*

See also: **colleague**

partnership *n* = **company**, house, firm, union, society, alliance, cooperative

party *n* **1** = **get-together**, function, celebration, reception, gathering, afterparty • *Most teenagers like to go to parties.* **2** = **faction**, coalition, alliance • *his resignation as chairman of the party* **3** = **team**, unit, crew, band, gang, squad • *a search party looking for the lost child* **4** = **person**, someone, individual

See also: **celebrate, company, group, side**

P

DICTIONARY

(1968), *Pigsty* (1969), and *Decameron* (1970)
pass Ⓣ *v* **1** go by, beyond, through, etc. **2** be successful in a test etc. **3** spend (time) or (of time) elapse **4** exchange **5** be inherited by **6** bring (a law) into force **7** move onwards or over **8** exceed **9** choose not to take one's turn in a game or quiz **10** discharge (urine etc.) from the body **11** come to an end **12** *sports* transfer (the ball) to another player ▷ *n* **13** successful result in a test **14** *sports* transfer of a ball **15** permit or licence **16** narrow gap through mountains
▶ **make a pass at** *informal* try to start a sexual relationship
▶ **passable** *adj* **1** (just) acceptable **2** (of a road) capable of being travelled along
▶ **passing** *adj* **1** brief or transitory **2** cursory or casual
▶ **pass away** *v* die
▶ **pass out** *v informal* faint
▶ **pass up** *v informal* ignore or reject
passage Ⓣ *n* **1** channel or opening providing a way through **2** hall or corridor **3** section of a book etc. **4** journey by sea **5** right or freedom to pass
▶ **passageway** *n* passage or corridor
passé [**pas**-say] *adj* out-of-date
passbook *n* book issued by a building society or bank for keeping a record of deposits and withdrawals
passenger Ⓣ *n* **1** person travelling in a vehicle driven by someone else **2** one of a team who does not pull his or her weight
passer-by Ⓣ *n, pl* **passers-by** person who is walking past something or someone
passerine *adj* belonging to the order of perching birds
passim *adv Latin* everywhere, throughout
passion Ⓣ *n* **1** intense sexual love **2** any strong emotion **3** great enthusiasm **4 Passion** *Christianity* the suffering of Christ
passionate *adj*
▶ **passionflower** *n* tropical American plant
▶ **passion fruit** edible fruit of the passionflower
▶ **Passion play** play about Christ's suffering
passive Ⓣ *adj* **1** not playing an active part **2** submissive and receptive to outside forces **3** *grammar* denoting a form of verbs indicating that the subject receives the action, such as

THESAURUS

pass *v* **1 = exceed**, surpass, overtake, outstrip, outdo, go beyond • *She gave a triumphant wave as she passed the finish line.* **2 = qualify**, succeed, graduate, get through • *I just passed my driving test.* OPPOSITE: fail **3 = go by** *or* **go past**, go, run, move, proceed, lapse, elapse **4 = spend**, fill, occupy, while away **5 = give**, send, hand, deliver, transfer, convey **6 = approve**, accept, ratify, enact, legislate, decree, ordain **7 = end**, go, cease, blow over ▷ **pass around** *See* **distribute** ▷ **pass away, pass on** (*Euphemistic*) **= die**, expire, kick the bucket (*slang*), pass over, shuffle off this mortal coil, snuff it (*informal*) ▷ **pass down** *See* **hand down** ▷ **pass off = fake**, counterfeit, make a pretense of, palm off ▷ **pass on = hand down**, will; **= communicate** ▷ **pass out = faint**, become unconscious, black out (*informal*), lose consciousness ▷ **pass over = disregard**, ignore, overlook, take no notice of ▷ **pass round** *See* **distribute** ▷ **pass up = miss**, decline, abstain, forgo, neglect, let slip ▶ *n* **8 = licence**, ticket, passport, identification • *a free pass to the movies* **9 = gap**, route, ravine, canyon, gorge
See also: **disappear, permit, vanish**
passable *adj* **= adequate**, average, fair, acceptable, mediocre, so-so (*informal*), tolerable, all right
passage *n* **1 = way**, road, course, route, channel, path • *He cleared a passage through the crowd.* **2 = corridor**, hall, aisle • *up some stairs and along a narrow passage toward a door* **3 = extract**, section, excerpt, quotation • *a passage from Shakespeare* **4 = journey**, trip, crossing, trek, voyage **5 = safe-conduct**, right, freedom, permission
passageway *n* **= corridor**, hall, passage, lane, alley, hallway, aisle
passé *adj* **= out-of-date**, old-fashioned, outdated, obsolete, dated, outmoded, old hat, unfashionable
passenger *n* **= traveller**, fare, rider
passer-by *n* **= bystander**, witness, onlooker
passing *adj* **1 = momentary**, brief, temporary, short-lived, fleeting, transient, ephemeral, transitory **2 = superficial**, short, quick, casual, cursory, glancing
passion *n* **1 = emotion**, fire, intensity, excitement, warmth, zeal • *She spoke with great passion.* **2 = love**, desire, lust, ardour, infatuation **3 = rage**, storm, fit, anger, outburst, frenzy, fury, paroxysm **4 = mania**, bug (*informal*), enthusiasm, obsession, craving, fascination, craze
See also: **feeling, heat, weakness**
passionate *adj* **1 = emotional**, strong, intense, heartfelt, impassioned, ardent • *I'm a passionate believer in equal rights.* **2 = loving**, hot, erotic, ardent, amorous, lustful
See also: **crazy, enthusiastic, fanatical, fervent, romantic**
passive *adj* **= submissive**, receptive, docile, resigned • *His passive attitude made things easier for me.*
See also: **apathetic, uninterested**

P

DICTIONARY

was jeered in *He was jeered by the crowd*
▸ **passive resistance** resistance to a government, law, etc. by nonviolent acts
▸ **passive smoking** inhalation of smoke from others' cigarettes by a nonsmoker
Passover *n* Jewish festival commemorating the sparing of the Jews in Egypt
passport Ⓣ *n* official document granting permission to travel abroad
pass-rush *n football* **1** same as **blitz 2 pass-rusher** *n*
▸ **pass-rushing** *n* tactic of trying to tackle the opposing quarterback before he can pass the ball
password Ⓣ *n* secret word or phrase that ensures admission
past Ⓣ *adj* **1** of the time before the present **2** ended, gone by **3** (of a *v* tense) indicating that the action specified took place earlier ▹ *n* **4** bygone times **5** person's past life, esp. an earlier, disreputable period **6** past tense ▹ *adv* **7** by **8** along ▹ *prep* **9** beyond
▸ **past it** *informal* unable to do the things one could do when younger
▸ **past master** person with great talent or experience in a particular subject
pasta *n* type of food, such as spaghetti, that is made in different shapes from flour and water
paste Ⓣ *n* **1** moist soft mixture, such as toothpaste **2** adhesive, esp. for paper **3** pastry dough **4** shiny glass used to make imitation jewellery ▹ *v* **5** fasten with paste
▸ **pasting** *n slang* **1** defeat **2** strong criticism
▸ **pasteboard** *n* stiff thick paper
pastel Ⓣ *n* **1** coloured chalk crayon for drawing **2** picture drawn in pastels **3** pale delicate colour ▹ *adj* **4** pale and delicate in colour
Pasternak *n* **Boris Leonidovich**. 1890–1960, Russian lyric poet, novelist, and translator, noted particularly for his novel of the Russian Revolution, *Dr. Zhivago* (1957). He was awarded the Nobel prize for literature in 1958, but was forced to decline it
Pasteur *n* **Louis**. 1822–95, French chemist and bacteriologist. His discovery that the fermentation of milk and alcohol was caused by microorganisms resulted in the process of pasteurization. He also devised methods of immunization against anthrax and rabies and pioneered stereochemistry
pasteurize *v* sterilize by heat
pasteurization *n*
pastiche Ⓣ [pass-**teesh**] *n* work of art that mixes styles or copies the style of another artist
pastille *n* small fruit-flavoured and sometimes medicated candy
pastime Ⓣ *n* activity that makes time pass pleasantly
pastor Ⓣ *n* clergyman in charge of a congregation
▸ **pastoral** *adj* **1** of or depicting country life **2** of a clergyman or his duties
pastrami *n* highly seasoned smoked beef
pastry *n, pl* **-ries 1** baking dough made of flour, fat, and water **2** cake or pie
pasture Ⓣ *n* grassy land for farm animals to graze on
▸ **pasturage** *n* (right to) pasture
pasty[1] Ⓣ [**pay**-stee] *adj* **pastier, pastiest** (of a complexion) pale and unhealthy
pasty[2] [**pass**-tee] *n, pl* **pasties** round of pastry folded over a savoury filling
pat Ⓣ *v* **patting, patted 1** tap lightly ▹ *n* **2** gentle tap or stroke **3** small shaped mass of butter etc. ▹ *adj* **4** quick, ready, or glib
▸ **off pat** learned thoroughly
patch Ⓣ *n* **1** piece of material sewn on a garment **2** small contrasting section **3** plot of ground **4** protecting pad for the eye

P

THESAURUS

passport *See* **pass, permit**
password *n* = **watchword**, signal, key word
past *adj* **1** = **former**, previous, ancient, bygone, olden • *details of his past activities* OPPOSITE: future **2** = **over**, finished, gone, done, ended ▸ *n* **3** = **background**, life, history, past life ▹ **the past** = **former times**, antiquity, days gone by, long ago • *We would like to put the past behind us.* ▸ *preposition* **4** = **beyond**, by, over • *It's just past the station.* **5** = **after**, beyond, later than
paste *n* **1** = **adhesive**, gum, cement, glue ▸ *v* **2** = **stick**, gum, cement, glue
pastel *adj* = **pale**, light, soft, delicate, muted
pasteurized *See* **pure**
pastiche *n* = **medley**, blend, mixture, hodgepodge, *mélange* (*French*), miscellany
pastime *n* = **activity**, diversion, recreation, hobby • *Her favourite pastime is curling.*
See also: **interest**
pastor *n* = **clergyman**, minister, priest, vicar, rector, churchman, ecclesiastic, parson
pastoral *adj* **1** = **rustic**, country, rural, bucolic **2** = **ecclesiastical**, ministerial, clerical, priestly
pasture *n* = **grassland**, grass, grazing, meadow
pasty *adj* = **pale**, anemic, sickly, pallid, wan
pat *v* **1** = **stroke**, pet, touch, tap, fondle, caress ▸ *n* **2** = **stroke**, tap, clap
patch *n* **1** = **reinforcement** **2** = **spot**, bit, scrap, shred, small piece **3** = **plot**, area, land, ground, tract ▸ *v* **4** = **mend**, cover, repair, reinforce, sew up ▹ **patch together** *See* **piece together** ▹ **patch up** *See* **fix, repair**

DICTIONARY

▷ *v* **5** mend with a patch **6** repair clumsily
▶ **patchy** *adj* of uneven quality or intensity
▶ **patch up** *v* make up (a quarrel)
▶ **patchwork** *n* needlework made of pieces of different materials sewn together
pate *n old-fashioned* head
pâté [**pat**-ay] *n* spread of finely minced liver etc.
patella *n, pl* **-lae** kneecap
paten [**pat**-in] *n* plate for bread in Communion
patent Ⓣ *n* **1** document giving the exclusive right to make or sell an invention ▷ *adj* **2** open to public inspection: *letters patent* **3** obvious **4** protected by a patent ▷ *v* **5** obtain a patent for
▶ **patently** *adv* obviously
▶ **patent leather** leather processed to give a hard glossy surface
paternal Ⓣ *adj* **1** fatherly **2** related through one's father
▶ **paternity** *n* **1** relation of a father to his offspring **2** fatherhood
▶ **paternalism** *n* authority exercised in a way that limits individual responsibility **paternalistic** *adj*
Paternoster *n RC Church* the Lord's Prayer
path Ⓣ *n* **1** surfaced walk or track **2** course of action
pathetic Ⓣ *adj* **1** causing feelings of pity or sadness **2** distressingly inadequate **pathetically** *adv*
pathogen *n* thing that causes disease **pathogenic** *adj*
pathology *n* scientific study of diseases **pathologist** *n*
▶ **pathological** *adj* **1** of pathology **2** *informal* compulsively motivated
pathos Ⓣ *n* power of arousing pity or sadness
patient Ⓣ *adj* **1** enduring difficulties calmly ▷ *n* **2** person receiving medical treatment
▶ **patience** *n* **1** quality of being patient **2** card game for one
patina *n* **1** fine layer on a surface **2** sheen of age on woodwork
patio *n, pl* **-tios** paved area adjoining a house
patois [**pat**-wah] *n, pl* **patois** [**pat**-wahz] regional dialect
patriarch Ⓣ *n* **1** male head of a family or tribe **2** highest-ranking bishop in Orthodox Churches **patriarchal** *adj*
▶ **patriarchy** *n* society in which men have most of the power
patriate *v* pass (powers) from the control of a colonial government to that of the region to which they apply
patrician *n* **1** member of the nobility, esp. of ancient Rome ▷ *adj* **2** of noble birth
patricide *n* **1** crime of killing one's father **2** person who does this
Patrick *n* **Saint**. 5th century AD, Christian missionary in Ireland, probably born in Britain; patron saint of Ireland. Feast day: March 17
patrimony *n, pl* **-nies** property inherited from ancestors
patriot Ⓣ *n* person who loves his or her country and supports its interests **patriotic** *adj* **patriotism** *n*
patrol Ⓣ *n* **1** regular circuit by a guard

P

THESAURUS

patchwork *n* = **mixture**, medley, jumble, hodgepodge, pastiche
patchy *adj* = **uneven**, irregular, variable, erratic, spotty, sketchy, fitful
patent *n* **1** = **copyright**, licence ▶ *adj* **2** = **obvious**, clear, apparent, evident, manifest, glaring
paternal *adj* = **fatherly**, protective, concerned, solicitous
paternity *n* **1** = **fatherhood** **2** = **parentage**, family, descent, extraction, lineage
path *n* **1** = **pathway**, track, trail, footpath • *We followed the paths alongside the river.* **2** = **route**, way, course, direction, passage • *A group of reporters stood in his path.* *See also*: **line**
pathetic *adj* **1** = **sad**, heartbreaking • *small, shrunken, and looking pathetic* **2** = **poor**, sorry, feeble, pitiful, lamentable • *pathetic excuses* *See also*: **hopeless, inadequate, lame, miserable**
pathos *n* = **sadness**, poignancy, pitifulness, plaintiveness
pathway *See* **path**
patience *n* **1** = **forbearance**, cool (*informal*), restraint, tolerance, composure, calmness • *It was exacting work and required all her patience.* **2** = **endurance**, resignation, submission, perseverance, long-suffering, fortitude, constancy, stoicism
patient *adj* **1** = **long-suffering**, calm, philosophical, serene, composed • *Please be patient - your cheque will arrive.* OPPOSITE: impatient **2** = **forbearing**, understanding, mild, lenient, tolerant, forgiving, indulgent, even-tempered ▶ *n* **3** = **sick person**, case, sufferer, invalid, sickie (*informal*) • *patients who wish to change their doctor*
patriarch *See* **parent**
patriot *n* = **nationalist**, loyalist, chauvinist
patriotic *adj* = **nationalistic**, loyal, chauvinistic, jingoistic
patriotism *n* = **nationalism**, jingoism
patrol *n* **1** = **policing**, vigilance, protecting, guarding, watching **2** = **guard**, watch, sentinel, watchman, patrolman ▶ *v*

DICTIONARY

2 person or small group patrolling **3** unit of Scouts or Guides ▷ *v* **-trolling, -trolled 4** go round on guard, or reconnoitring
patron Ⓣ *n* **1** person who gives (financial) support to charities, artists, etc. **2** regular customer of a shop, pub, etc.
▶ **patronage** *n* support given by a patron
▶ **patronize** *v* **1** treat in a condescending way **2** be a patron of
▶ **patron saint** saint regarded as the guardian of a country or group
patronymic *n* name derived from one's father or a male ancestor
patten *n hist* type of clog
patter Ⓣ *v* **1** make repeated soft tapping sounds ▷ *n* **2** quick succession of taps **3** glib rapid speech
pattern Ⓣ *n* **1** arrangement of repeated parts or decorative designs **2** regular way something is done **3** diagram or shape used as a guide to make something ▷ *v* **4** (foll. by *on*) make or do on the model of
▶ **patterned** *adj* decorated with a pattern
patty *n, pl* **-ties 1** small pie **2** minced meat formed into a small disc
paucity Ⓣ *n* **1** scarcity **2** smallness of amount or number
Paul *n* **1 Jean**. See **Jean Paul 2 Les**, real name *Lester Polfuss*. 1915–2009, US guitarist: creator of the solid-body electric guitar and pioneer in multitrack recording **3 Saint**. Also **Paul the Apostle, Saul of Tarsus**, original name *Saul*. died ?67 AD, one of the first Christian missionaries to the Gentiles, who died a martyr in Rome. Until his revelatory conversion he had assisted in persecuting the Christians. He wrote many of the Epistles in the New Testament. Feast day: June 29
Pauling *n* **Linus Carl**. 1901–94, US chemist, noted particularly for his work on the nature of the chemical bond and his opposition to nuclear tests: Nobel prize for chemistry 1954; Nobel peace prize 1962
Paulinus *n* **Saint**. died 644 AD, Roman missionary to England; first bishop of York and archbishop of Rochester. Feast day: Oct 10
paunch Ⓣ *n* belly
pauper Ⓣ *n* very poor person
pause Ⓣ *v* **1** stop for a time ▷ *n* **2** stop or rest
Pavarotti *n* **Luciano**. 1935–2007, Italian operatic tenor, specializing in works by Verdi and Puccini
pave Ⓣ *v* form (a surface) with stone or brick
▶ **pavement** *n* **1** paved surface of road or street **2** *Brit* sidewalk
pavilion *n* **1** clubhouse on a playing field etc. **2** building for housing an exhibition etc.
Pavlov *n* **Ivan Petrovich**. 1849–1936, Russian physiologist. His study of conditioned reflexes in dogs influenced behaviourism. He also made important contributions to the study of digestion: Nobel prize for physiology or medicine 1904
pavlova *n* meringue cake topped with whipped cream and fruit
paw Ⓣ *n* **1** animal's foot with claws and pads ▷ *v* **2** scrape with the paw or hoof **3** handle

THESAURUS

3 = police, guard, safeguard, inspect, keep guard, keep watch
patron *n* **1 = supporter**, friend, champion, sponsor, backer, benefactor, philanthropist, helper **2 = customer**, shopper, client, buyer, frequenter, habitué
patronage *n* **1 = support**, help, aid, sponsorship, assistance, promotion, backing **2 = custom**, trade, business, traffic, commerce, trading, clientele
patronize *v* **1 = talk down to**, look down on **2 = be a customer of** *or* **be a client of**, frequent, do business with, shop at **3 = support**, help, back, fund, maintain, promote, sponsor
patronizing *adj* **= condescending**, superior, gracious, disdainful, haughty, snobbish, supercilious
patter[1] *v* **1 = tap**, beat, pat, pitter-patter **2 = walk lightly**, trip, skip, scuttle, scurry ▶ *n* **3 = tapping**, pattering, pitter-patter
patter[2] *n* **1 = spiel** (*informal*), line, pitch **2 = chatter**, gabble, jabber, nattering, prattle **3 = jargon**, cant, lingo (*informal*), slang, vernacular, argot, patois ▶ *v* **4 = chatter**, spout (*informal*), jabber, prate, rattle on
pattern *n* **1 = design**, motif • *red and purple thread stitched into a pattern of flames* **2 = plan**, design, blueprint, template, stencil, diagram • *sewing patterns* **3 = order**, plan, system, method, sequence ▶ *v* **4 = model**, follow, form, copy, style, imitate, mold
See also: **routine**
paucity *n* (*Formal*) **= scarcity**, lack, shortage, deficiency, rarity, dearth, scantiness, sparseness
paunch *n* **= belly**, pot, potbelly, spare tire (*slang*), muffin top (*informal*)
pauper *n* **= down-and-out**, bankrupt, mendicant, poor person
pause *v* **1 = stop**, break, wait, delay, rest, halt, take a break • *On leaving, she paused for a moment at the door.* ▶ *n* **2 = stop**, break, rest, halt, stoppage, intermission, interruption, interval • *There was a pause between the first and second acts.*
See also: **gap, hesitate**
pave *v* **= cover**, floor, surface, concrete, tile
paw *v* **= manhandle**, grab, molest, maul, handle roughly

DICTIONARY

roughly **4** stroke in an overfamiliar way

pawn[1] Ⓣ *v* deposit (an article) as security for money borrowed
▶ **in pawn** deposited as security with a pawnbroker
▶ **pawnbroker** *n* lender of money on goods deposited

pawn[2] Ⓣ *n* **1** chessman of the lowest value **2** person manipulated by someone else

pawpaw *n* same as **papaya**

Paxton *n* Sir **Joseph**. 1801–65, English architect, who designed Crystal Palace (1851), the first large structure of prefabricated glass and iron parts

pay Ⓣ *v* **paying, paid 1** give (money) in return for goods or services **2** settle (a debt or obligation) **3** compensate (for) **4** give, bestow **5** be profitable to ▷ *n* **6** wages or salary
▶ **payment** *n* **1** act of paying **2** money paid
▶ **payable** *adj* due to be paid
▶ **payee** *n* person to whom money is paid or due
▶ **paying guest** lodger
▶ **pay off** *v* **1** pay (debt) in full **2** turn out successfully
▶ **pay out** *v* **1** spend **2** release (a rope) bit by bit
▶ **payroll** *n* list of employees who receive regular pay

payload *n* **1** passengers or cargo of an aircraft **2** explosive power of a missile etc.

payola *n informal* bribe to get special treatment, esp. to promote a commercial product

Payton *n* **Walter**. 1954–99, American footballer and sports administrator

Pb *chem* lead

pc **1** per cent **2** postcard

PC **1** personal computer **2** Police Constable **3** politically correct **4** Privy Councillor

PDA personal digital assistant

PDF Portable Document Format: format in which electronic documents may be viewed

PDT Pacific Daylight Time

PE **1** physical education **2** Prince Edward Island

pea *n* **1** climbing plant with seeds growing in pods **2** its seed, eaten as a vegetable
▶ **pea-green** *adj* yellowish-green
▶ **peasouper** *n informal* thick fog

peace Ⓣ *n* **1** stillness or silence **2** absence of anxiety **3** freedom from war **4** harmony between people **peaceful** *adj* **peacefully** *adv*
▶ **peaceable** *adj* inclined towards peace **peaceably** *adv*

peach *n* **1** soft juicy fruit with a stone and a downy skin **2** *informal* very pleasing person or thing ▷ *adj* **3** pinkish-orange
▶ **peachy** *or* **peachy-keen** *adj slang, now usually facetious* very good, excellent

peacock *n* large male bird with a brilliantly coloured fanlike tail **peahen** *n fem*
▶ **peafowl** *n* peacock or peahen

THESAURUS

pawn[1] *v* = **hock** (*informal*), pledge, mortgage, deposit

pawn[2] *n* = **tool**, instrument, puppet, plaything, stooge (*slang*), cat's-paw

pay *v* **1** = **settle**, honour, compensate, reimburse, remunerate, recompense, pony up (*informal*) • *You can pay by credit card.* **2** = **be advantageous**, be worthwhile • *It pays to be honest.* **3** = **give**, extend, present, grant, bestow, hand out **4** = **be profitable**, make a return, make money **5** = **yield**, return, produce, bring in ▷ **pay attention** *See* **listen, watch** ▷ **pay attention to** *See* **heed** ▷ **pay back** = **repay**, square, refund, reimburse, settle up; = **get even with** (*informal*), retaliate, hit back ▷ **pay for** = **buy**, fund, finance; = **suffer for**, answer for, atone for, be punished for, compensate for, get one's just deserts, make amends for, suffer the consequences of ▷ **pay off** = **settle**, clear, square, discharge, pay in full; = **succeed**, work, be effective ▷ **pay out** = **spend**, expend, disburse, fork out, fork over, *or* fork up (*slang*), shell out (*informal*) ▷ **pay tribute to** *See* **praise** ▶ *n* **6** = **wages**, income, fee, payment, salary, earnings • *their complaints about pay and conditions*

payable *adj* = **due**, outstanding, owed, owing

payment *n* **1** = **remittance**, advance, premium, deposit, instalment • *mortgage payments* **2** = **paying**, settlement, discharge, remittance **3** = **wage**, fee, salary, reward, remuneration
See also: **charge, compensation, cost, pay**

peace *n* **1** = **stillness**, quiet, silence, calm, tranquility • *They left me in peace to recover from my exhaustion.* **2** = **truce**, armistice, cessation of hostilities • *The people do not believe that the leaders want peace.* OPPOSITE: war **3** = **serenity**, calm, composure, repose, contentment **4** = **harmony**, accord, agreement, concord

peaceable *adj* = **peace-loving**, friendly, peaceful, mild, gentle, conciliatory, unwarlike

peaceful *adj* **1** = **calm**, still, quiet, tranquil, serene, placid • *a peaceful house in the heart of the countryside* **2** = **at peace**, friendly, amicable, harmonious, nonviolent **3** = **peace-loving**, conciliatory, peaceable, unwarlike
See also: **relaxed**

peacefulness *See* **calm**

peacemaker *n* = **mediator**, arbitrator, conciliator, pacifier

DICTIONARY

peak Ⓣ *n* **1** pointed top, esp. of a mountain **2** point of greatest development etc. **3** projecting piece on the front of a cap ▷ *adj* **4** of or at the point of greatest demand ▷ *v* **5** (cause to) form or reach peaks **peaked** *adj*
▶ **peaky** *adj informal* looking pale and sickly
Peake *n* **Mervyn**. 1911–68, English novelist, poet, and illustrator. In his trilogy *Gormenghast* (1946–59), he creates, with vivid imagination, a grotesque Gothic world
peal Ⓣ *n* **1** long loud echoing sound, esp. of bells or thunder ▷ *v* **2** sound with a peal or peals
peanut *n* **1** pea-shaped nut that ripens underground **peanuts 2** *informal* trifling amount of money
pear *n* sweet juicy fruit with a narrow top and rounded base
pearl *n* hard round lustrous object found inside some oyster shells and used as a jewel **pearly** *adj*
Pears *n* Sir **Peter**. 1910–86, British tenor, associated esp. with the works of Benjamin Britten
Pearse *n* **Patrick** (**Henry**), Irish name *Pádraic*. 1879–1916, Irish nationalist, who planned and led the Easter Rising (1916): executed by the British
Pearson *n* **Lester B**(**owles**). 1897–1972, Canadian Liberal statesman; prime minister (1963–68): Nobel peace prize (1957) for helping to resolve the Suez crisis (1956)
Peary *n* **Robert Edwin**. 1856–1920, US arctic explorer, generally regarded as the first man to reach the North Pole (1909)
peasant Ⓣ *n* (in some countries) farmer or farmworker of a low social class
▶ **peasantry** *n* peasants collectively
pease pudding *n* dish of boiled split peas
peat *n* decayed vegetable material found in bogs, used as fertilizer or fuel
pebble *n* small roundish stone **pebbly** *adj*
pecan [pee-kan] *n* edible nut of a N American tree
peccadillo Ⓣ *n, pl* **-los, -loes** trivial misdeed
peccary *n, pl* **-ries** wild pig of American forests
peck Ⓣ *v* **1** strike or pick up with the beak **2** *informal* kiss quickly ▷ *n* **3** pecking movement
▶ **peckish** *adj informal* hungry
▶ **peck at** *v* nibble, eat reluctantly
Peck *n* **Gregory**. 1916–2003, US film actor; his films include *Keys of the Kingdom* (1944), *The Gunfighter* (1950), *The Big Country* (1958), *To Kill a Mockingbird* (1963), *The Omen* (1976), and *Other People's Money* (1991)
Peckinpah *n* **Sam**(**uel David**). 1926–84, US film director, esp. of Westerns, such as *The Wild Bunch* (1969). Among his other films are *Straw Dogs* (1971), *Bring me the Head of Alfredo Garcia* (1974), and *Cross of Iron* (1977)
pectin *n* substance in fruit that makes jam set
pectoral *adj* **1** of the chest or thorax ▷ *n* **2** pectoral muscle or fin
peculation *n* embezzlement, theft
peculiar Ⓣ *adj* **1** strange **2** distinct, special **3** belonging exclusively to
▶ **peculiarity** *n* **1** oddity, eccentricity **2** characteristic
pecuniary *adj* relating to, or consisting of, money
pedagogue Ⓣ *n* schoolteacher, esp. a pedantic one
pedal *n* **1** foot-operated lever used to control a vehicle or machine, or to modify the tone of a musical instrument ▷ *v* **-alling, -alled 2** propel (a bicycle) by using its pedals
pedant Ⓣ *n* person who is overconcerned with details and rules, esp. in academic work
pedantic *adj* **pedantry** *n*

THESAURUS

peak *n* **1 = high point**, climax, culmination, zenith • *the peak of the morning rush hour* **2 = summit**, top, crest, brow, pinnacle • *snow-covered peaks* ▶ *v* **3 = culminate**, climax, be at its height, come to a head, reach its highest point • *Her career peaked when she was in her 40s.*
See also: **ultimate**
peal *n* **1 = ring**, crash, blast, roar, rumble, clap, chime, clang, reverberation ▶ *v* **2 = ring**, crash, roar, rumble, resound, chime
peasant *n* **= rustic**, countryman
peccadillo *n* **= misdeed**, slip, error, lapse, misdemeanour, indiscretion
peck *v*, *n* **= pick**, hit, strike, tap, dig, poke, jab, prick
peculiar *adj* **1 = strange**, odd, funny, bizarre, weird, curious • *a very peculiar sense of humour* **2 = special**, personal, individual, unique, distinctive, distinguishing • *He has his own peculiar way of doing things.*
See also: **particular**
peculiarity *n* **1 = eccentricity**, oddity, abnormality, quirk, foible, mannerism, idiosyncrasy **2 = characteristic**, mark, feature, quality, property, attribute, trait, particularity
pedagogue *n* **= teacher**, master *or* mistress, instructor, schoolmaster *or* schoolmistress
pedant *n* **= hairsplitter**, nit-picker (*informal*), quibbler
pedantic *adj* **= hairsplitting**, particular, formal, academic, precise, fussy, bookish, donnish, nit-picking (*informal*), punctilious
pedantry *n* **= hairsplitting**, punctiliousness, quibbling

P

DICTIONARY

peddle ⓣ *v* sell (goods) from door to door ▸ **peddler** *n* person who sells illegal drugs
pederast *n* man who has homosexual relations with boys **pederasty** *n*
pedestal ⓣ *n* base supporting a column, statue, etc.
pedestrian ⓣ *n* **1** person who is walking, esp. in a street ▹ *adj* **2** dull, uninspiring ▸ **pedestrian crossing** crosswalk ▸ **pedestrian precinct** (shopping) area for pedestrians only
pediatrics, paediatrics *n* branch of medicine concerned with diseases of children **pediatrician** *or* **paediatrician** *n*
pedicel *n* small short stalk of a leaf, flower, or fruit
pedicure *n* medical or cosmetic treatment of the feet
pedigree ⓣ *n* register of ancestors, esp. of a purebred animal
pediment *n* triangular part over a door etc.
pedlar *n* person who sells goods from door to door
pedometer [pid-**dom**-it-er] *n* instrument which measures the distance walked
pedophilia, paedophilia *n* condition of being sexually attracted to children ▸ **pedophile** *or* **paedophile** *n* person who is sexually attracted to children
peduncle *n* **1** flower stalk **2** *anat* stalklike structure
pee *informal* ▹ *v* **peeing, peed 1** urinate ▹ *n* **2** urinating
Peebles *n* **James**. born 1935, Canadian astronomer; noted for his work on cosmology and background radiation
peek ⓣ *v, n* peep or glance
peel ⓣ *v* **1** remove the skin or rind of (a vegetable or fruit) **2** (of skin or a surface) come off in flakes **3** *curling* use a stone to remove another, with both stones going out of play ▹ *n* **4** rind or skin **peelings** *pl n*
Peel *n* Sir **Robert**. 1788–1850, British statesman; Conservative prime minister (1834–35; 1841–46). As Home Secretary (1828–30) he founded the Metropolitan Police and in his second ministry carried through a series of free-trade budgets culminating in the repeal of the Corn Laws (1846), which split the Tory party **Peelite** *n*
peep[1] ⓣ *v* **1** look slyly or quickly ▹ *n* **2** peeping look ▸ **Peeping Tom** man who furtively watches women undressing
peep[2] ⓣ *v* **1** make a small shrill noise ▹ *n* **2** small shrill noise
peer[1] ⓣ *n* **1** (**peeress**) member of nobility **2** person of the same status, age, etc. ▸ **peerage** *n* **1** whole body of peers **2** rank of a peer ▸ **peerless** *adj* unequalled, unsurpassed ▸ **peer group** group of people of similar age, status, etc. ▸ **peer pressure** influence from one's peer group
peer[2] ⓣ *v* look closely and intently
peeved *adj informal* annoyed
peevish ⓣ *adj* **1** fretful **2** irritable **peevishly** *adv* **peevishness** *n*
peewee *Canad* ▹ *n* **1** age level of 12 to 13 in amateur sports, esp. hockey ▹ *adj* **2** (of amateur sports) comprised of players aged 12 to 13 years: *peewee hockey*
peewit *n* same as **lapwing**
peg ⓣ *n* **1** pin or clip for joining, fastening, marking, etc. **2** hook or knob for hanging

THESAURUS

peddle *v* = **sell**, market, trade, push (*informal*), hawk
peddler *n* = **seller**, vendor, door-to-door salesman, hawker, huckster
pedestal *n* = **support**, base, stand, foot, mounting, plinth
pedestrian *n* **1** = **walker**, foot-traveller ▸ *adj* **2** = **dull**, ordinary, mediocre, boring, commonplace, mundane, banal, humdrum, prosaic, uninspired
pedigree *n* **1** = **lineage**, family, line, stock, race, blood, breed, descent, extraction, genealogy, ancestry, family tree ▸ *adj* **2** = **purebred**, thoroughbred, full-blooded
peek *v* **1** = **glance**, peep, catch a glimpse, sneak a look • *She peeked at him through a crack in the wall.* ▸ *n* **2** = **glance**, look, glimpse, peep • *He took his first peek at the new stadium.*
peel *v* **1** = **skin**, scale, pare, flake off, strip off ▸ *n* **2** = **skin**, rind, peeling
peep[1] *v* **1** = **peek**, look, sneak a look, steal a look ▸ *n* **2** = **peek**, look, glimpse, look-see (*slang*)
peep[2] *v, n* = **squeak**, chirp, cheep, tweet
peephole *n* = **spyhole**, opening, hole, crack, chink, aperture
peer[1] *n* **1** = **aristocrat**, lord, noble, nobleman **2** = **equal**, like, fellow, compeer
peer[2] *v* = **squint**, spy, scan, inspect, gaze, snoop, peep
peerage *n* = **aristocracy**, nobility, lords and ladies, peers
peerless *adj* = **unequalled**, excellent, outstanding, unparalleled, unmatched, incomparable, unrivalled, beyond compare, matchless
peevish *adj* = **irritable**, cross, fractious, childish, grumpy, cantankerous, surly, snappy, sullen, churlish, crotchety, fretful, petulant, querulous, sulky
peg *v* = **fasten**, join, fix, secure, attach

DICTIONARY

things on ▷ *v* **pegging, pegged 3** fasten with pegs **4** stabilize (prices) **5** *informal* categorize: *they think they've got you pegged*
▶ **off the peg** (of clothes) ready-to-wear, not tailor-made
Pei *n* **I(eoh) M(ing)**. born 1917, US architect, born in China. His buildings include the E wing of the National Museum of Art, Washington DC (1978), a glass and steel pyramid at the Louvre, Paris (1989), and the Rock and Roll Hall of Fame, Cleveland, USA (1995)
P.E.I. Prince Edward Island
peignoir [**pay**-nwahr] *n* woman's light dressing gown
pejorative Ⓣ [pij-**jor**-a-tiv] *adj* (of words etc.) with an insulting or critical connotation
Pekingese, Pekinese *n, pl* **-ese** small dog with a short wrinkled muzzle
pelargonium *n* plant with red, white, or pink flowers
Pelé *n* real name *Edson Arantes do Nascimento*. born 1940, Brazilian soccer player. He was awarded an honorary knighthood in 1997
Pelham *n* **Henry**. 1696–1754, British statesman: prime minister (1743–54); brother of Thomas Pelham Holles, 1st Duke of Newcastle
pelican *n* large water bird with a pouch beneath its bill for storing fish
pellagra *n* disease caused by lack of vitamin B
pellet Ⓣ *n* small ball of something
pell-mell *adv* in utter confusion, headlong
pellucid *adj* very clear
pelmet *n* ornamental drapery or board, concealing a curtain rail
pelt[1] Ⓣ *v* **1** throw missiles at **2** run fast, rush **3** rain heavily
▶ **at full pelt** at top speed
pelt[2] Ⓣ *n* skin of a fur-bearing animal
pelvis *n* framework of bones at the base of the spine, to which the hips are attached
pelvic *adj*
pemmican *n* dried lean meat and melted fat pounded into paste and used as food for a long journey
pen[1] Ⓣ *n* **1** instrument for writing in ink ▷ *v* **penning, penned 2** write or compose
▶ **pen friend** friend with whom a person corresponds without meeting
▶ **penknife** *n* small knife with blade(s) that fold into the handle
▶ **pen name** name used by an author instead of his or her real name
pen[2] Ⓣ *n* **1** small enclosure for domestic animals ▷ *v* **penning, penned 2** put or keep in a pen
pen[3] *n* female swan
penal Ⓣ [**pee**-nal] *adj* of or used in punishment
▶ **penalize** *v* **1** impose a penalty on **2** handicap, hinder
▶ **penalty** *n* **1** punishment for a crime or offence **2** *sports* handicap or disadvantage imposed for an infringement of a rule
penance Ⓣ *n* voluntary self-punishment to make amends for wrongdoing
pence *n* a plural of **penny**
penchant Ⓣ [**pon**-shon] *n* inclination or liking
pencil *n* **1** thin cylindrical instrument containing graphite, for writing or drawing ▷ *v* **-cilling, -cilled 2** draw, write, or mark with a pencil
Penda *n* died 655 AD, king of Mercia (?634–55)
pendant *n* ornament worn on a chain round the neck
pendent *adj* hanging
Penderecki *n* **Krzystof**. born 1933, Polish composer, noted for his highly individual orchestration. His works include *Threnody for the Victims of Hiroshima* for strings (1960), *Stabat Mater* (1962), *Polish Requiem* (1983–84), and the opera *Ubu Rex* (1991)
pending Ⓣ *prep* **1** while waiting for ▷ *adj* **2** not yet decided or settled

THESAURUS

pejorative *adj* = **derogatory**, negative, unpleasant, deprecatory, depreciatory, disparaging, uncomplimentary
pellet *See* **ball**
pelt[1] *v* **1** = **throw**, strike, cast, batter, pepper, shower, hurl, bombard, sling **2** = **rush**, charge, shoot, speed, tear, belt (*slang*), dash, hurry, run fast **3** = **pour**, teem, bucket down (*informal*), rain cats and dogs (*informal*), rain hard
pelt[2] *n* = **coat**, hide, skin, fell
pen[1] *v* = **write**, draft, compose, draw up, jot down ▶ *n* ▷ **pen name** *n* = **pseudonym**, nom de plume
pen[2] *n* **1** = **enclosure**, pound, fold, cage, coop, hutch, sty ▶ *v* **2** = **enclose**, hedge, confine, cage, coop up, fence in, shut up *or* shut in
penal *adj* = **disciplinary**, punitive, corrective
penal institution *See* **prison**
penalize *v* = **punish**, discipline, handicap, impose a penalty on
penalties *See* **sanctions**
penalty *n* = **punishment**, price, fine, forfeit, handicap
penance *n* = **atonement**, penalty, reparation, sackcloth and ashes
penchant *n* = **liking**, taste, bias, tendency, bent, fondness, inclination, leaning, propensity, predilection, partiality, proclivity
pending *adj* = **undecided**, imminent,

DICTIONARY

pendulous *adj* hanging, swinging
pendulum *n* suspended weight swinging to and fro, esp. as a regulator for a clock
penetrate Ⓣ *v* **1** find or force a way into or through **2** arrive at the meaning of **penetration** *n*
▸ **penetrable** *adj* capable of being penetrated
▸ **penetrating** *adj* **1** quick to understand **2** (of a sound) loud and unpleasant
Penfield *n* **Wilder** (**Graves**). 1891–1976, Canadian scientist, neurosurgeon, and writer born in the US; he developed a surgical treatment for epilepsy
penguin *n* flightless black-and-white Antarctic sea bird
penicillin *n* antibiotic drug effective against a wide range of diseases and infections
peninsula *n* strip of land nearly surrounded by water **peninsular** *adj*
penis *n* organ of copulation and urination in male mammals
penitent Ⓣ *adj* **1** feeling sorry for having done wrong ▹ *n* **2** someone who is penitent **penitence** *n*
▸ **penitentiary** *n* **1** prison ▹ *adj* **2** Also **penitential** relating to penance
Penn *n* **William**. 1644–1718, English Quaker and founder of Pennsylvania
pennant Ⓣ *n* long narrow flag
pennon *n* small triangular or swallow-tailed flag
penny *n, pl* **pence, pennies 1** one cent **2** *Brit* bronze coin now worth one hundredth of a pound
▸ **penniless** *adj* **1** having no money **2** poor
penology [pee-**nol**-a-jee] *n* study of punishment and prison management
Penrose *n* Sir **Roger**. born 1931, British mathematician and theoretical physicist, noted for his investigation of black holes
pension[1] Ⓣ *n* regular payment to people above a certain age, retired employees, widows, etc. **pensionable** *adj*
▸ **pensioner** *n* person receiving a pension
▸ **pension off** *v* force (someone) to retire from a job and pay him or her a pension
pension[2] [**pon**-syon] *n* boarding house in Europe
pensive Ⓣ *adj* deeply thoughtful, often with a tinge of sadness
pentacle, pentagram *n* five-pointed star
pentagon *n* **1** geometric figure with five sides **2 Pentagon** headquarters of the US military **pentagonal** *adj*
pentameter [pen-**tam**-it-er] *n* line of poetry with five metrical feet
Pentateuch [**pent**-a-tyuke] *n* first five books of the Old Testament
pentathlon *n* athletic event consisting of five sports
Pentecost *n* **1** Christian festival celebrating the descent of the Holy Spirit to the apostles, Whitsuntide **2** Jewish harvest festival fifty days after Passover
penthouse *n* apartment built on the roof or top floor of a building
pent-up Ⓣ *adj* (of an emotion) not released, repressed
penultimate *adj* second last
penumbra *n, pl* **-brae, -bras 1** partial shadow **2** (in an eclipse) the partially shadowed region which surrounds the full shadow **penumbral** *adj*
penury Ⓣ *n* extreme poverty **penurious** *adj*
peony *n, pl* **-nies** garden plant with showy red, pink, or white flowers

THESAURUS

undetermined, unsettled, awaiting, impending, in the balance, tba *or* to be announced
penetrate *v* **1 = pierce**, enter, stab, bore, prick, go through **2 = work out**, grasp, comprehend, decipher, fathom, figure out (*informal*), get to the bottom of
penetrating *adj* **1 = piercing**, sharp, harsh, shrill, carrying **2 = perceptive**, quick, sharp, acute, keen, intelligent, shrewd, astute, incisive, perspicacious, sharp-witted
penetration *n* **1 = piercing**, entry, entrance, incision, puncturing **2 = perception**, insight, sharpness, acuteness, astuteness, keenness, shrewdness
penitence *n* **= repentance**, regret, shame, sorrow, remorse, contrition, compunction
penitent *adj* **= repentant**, sorry, remorseful, apologetic, abject, contrite, conscience-stricken, regretful
pennant *n* **= flag**, banner, streamer, ensign, pennon
penniless *adj* **= poor**, impoverished, broke (*informal*), poverty-stricken, destitute, dirt-poor (*informal*), down and out, down on one's luck (*informal*), flat broke (*informal*), impecunious, indigent, penurious
pension *n* **= allowance**, benefit, annuity, superannuation, old age security (*Canad*), social security (*US*)
pensioner *n* **= senior citizen**, O.A.P., retired person
pensive *adj* **= thoughtful**, serious, sad, solemn, musing, reflective, dreamy, meditative, contemplative, wistful, preoccupied
pent-up *adj* **= suppressed**, repressed, inhibited • *a lot of pent-up anger to release*
penury *n* **= poverty**, want, need, beggary, destitution, indigence, privation

DICTIONARY

people Ⓣ *pl n* **1** persons generally **2** the community **3** one's family or ancestors ▷ *n* **4** race or nation ▷ *v* **5** stock with inhabitants **6** populate

pep *n informal* high spirits, energy or enthusiasm

▸ **pep talk** *informal* talk designed to increase confidence, enthusiasm, etc.

▸ **pep up** *v* stimulate, invigorate

Pepin the Short *n* died 768 AD, king of the Franks (751–768); son of Charles Martel and father of Charlemagne. He deposed the Merovingian king (751) and founded the Carolingian dynasty

pepper Ⓣ *n* **1** sharp hot condiment made from the fruit of an East Indian climbing plant **2** colourful tropical fruit used as a vegetable, capsicum ▷ *v* **3** season with pepper **4** sprinkle, dot **5** pelt with missiles

▸ **peppery** *adj* **1** tasting of pepper **2** irritable

▸ **peppercorn** *n* dried berry of the pepper plant

▸ **peppercorn rent** low or nominal rent

▸ **pepper spray** aerosol spray causing temporary blindness and breathing difficulty, used esp. for self-defence

peppermint *n* **1** plant that yields an oil with a strong sharp flavour **2** candy flavoured with this

peptic *adj* relating to digestion or the digestive juices

Péquiste [pay-**keest**] *n* member or supporter of Parti Québécois

Pepys *n* **Samuel**. 1633–1703, English diarist and naval administrator. His diary, which covers the period 1660–69, is a vivid account of London life through such disasters as the Great Plague, the Fire of London, and the intrusion of the Dutch fleet up the Thames

per *prep* **1** for each **2** in the manner of

perambulate *v* walk through or about (a place) **perambulation** *n*

▸ **perambulator** *n Brit* baby carriage

per annum *adv Latin* in each year

percale *n* woven cotton used esp. for sheets

per capita *adj, adv Latin* of or for each person

perceive Ⓣ *v* **1** become aware of (something) through the senses **2** understand

percentage Ⓣ *n* proportion or rate per hundred

▸ **per cent** in each hundred

perceptible Ⓣ *adj* discernible, recognizable

perception Ⓣ *n* **1** act of perceiving **2** intuitive judgment **perceptive** *adj*

Perceval *n* **Spencer**. 1762–1812, British statesman; prime minister (1809–12); assassinated

perch[1] Ⓣ *n* **1** resting place for a bird ▷ *v* **2** alight, rest, or place on or as if on a perch

perch[2] *n* edible freshwater fish

perchance *adv old-fashioned* perhaps

percipient *adj* quick to notice things, observant **percipience** *n*

percolate *v* **1** pass or filter through small holes **2** permeate **3** make (coffee) or (of coffee) be made in a percolator **percolation** *n*

▸ **percolator** *n* coffeepot in which boiling water is forced through a tube and filters down through coffee

percussion Ⓣ *n* striking of one thing against another

▸ **percussion instrument** musical instrument played by being struck, such as drums or cymbals

perdition *n* spiritual ruin

peregrination *n* travels, roaming

peregrine *n* falcon with dark upper parts and a light underside

Perelman *n* **S(idney) J(oseph)**. 1904–79, US humorous writer. After scriptwriting for the Marx Brothers, he published many collections of articles, including *Crazy Like a Fox* (1944) and *Eastward, Hi!* (1977)

peremptory Ⓣ *adj* authoritative, imperious

THESAURUS

people *pl n* **1 = human beings**, humanity, humankind, humans • *Hundreds of people lost their homes in the earthquake.* **2 = inhabitants**, public, population, citizens • *It's a triumph for the Canadian people.* **3 = family**, race, tribe, clan ▸ *v* **4 = inhabit**, settle, occupy, populate, colonize

See also: **kin**

pepper *n* **1 = seasoning**, spice, flavour ▸ *v* **2 = sprinkle**, dot, speck, spatter, fleck **3 = pelt**, shower, bombard

peppery *See* **hot**

perceive *v* **1 = see**, note, spot, discover, recognize, notice, observe, behold, discern, espy, make out **2 = understand**, see, learn, gather, realize, grasp, comprehend

percentage *See* **proportion**

perceptible *adj* **= visible**, clear, apparent, obvious, evident, recognizable, tangible, noticeable, detectable, discernible, appreciable, observable

perception *n* **= understanding**, idea, sense, feeling, awareness, impression, notion, sensation, consciousness, grasp, conception

perceptive *adj* **= astute**, sharp, aware, acute, penetrating • *a perceptive account of the poet's life*

See also: **brilliant, keen, observant, shrewd, wise**

perch *n* **1 = resting place**, post, branch, pole ▸ *v* **2 = sit**, land, rest, settle, balance, roost, alight

percussion *n* **= impact**, crash, blow, knock, clash, bump, smash, collision, thump

DICTIONARY

perennial Ⓣ *adj* **1** lasting through the years **2** recurring perpetually ▷ *n* **3** plant lasting more than two years **perennially** *adv*
Peres *n* **Shimon**. born 1923, Israeli statesman, born in Poland: prime minister (1984–86; 1995–96); Nobel peace prize 1994 jointly with Yasser Arafat and Yitzhak Rabin
perestroika *n* formerly, policy of restructuring the Soviet economy and political system
perfect Ⓣ *adj* **1** having all the essential elements, complete **2** unspoilt **3** faultless **4** correct, precise **5** excellent ▷ *n* **6** *grammar* tense of *v* describing an action that has been completed ▷ *v* **7** improve **8** make fully correct **perfectly** *adv*
▶ **perfection** *n* state of being perfect
▶ **perfectionist** *n* person who demands the highest standards of excellence **perfectionism** *n*
perfidy *n, pl* **-dies** treachery, disloyalty **perfidious** *adj*
perforate Ⓣ *v* make holes in **perforation** *n*
perforce *adv* of necessity
perform Ⓣ *v* **1** carry out (an action) **2** fulfil (a request etc.) **3** act, sing, or present a play before an audience **4** work or function **performance** *n* **performer** *n*
perfume Ⓣ *n* **1** liquid cosmetic worn for its pleasant smell **2** fragrance ▷ *v* **3** give a pleasant smell to
▶ **perfumery** *n* perfumes in general
perfunctory Ⓣ *adj* done only as a matter of routine, superficial **perfunctorily** *adv*
pergola *n* arch or framework of trellis supporting climbing plants
Pergolesi *n* **Giovanni Battista**. 1710–36, Italian composer: his works include the operetta *La Serva padrona* (1733) and the *Stabat Mater* (1736) for women's voices
perhaps Ⓣ *adv* it may be (so), possibly
pericardium *n, pl* **-dia** membrane enclosing the heart
Pericles *n* ?495–429 BC, Athenian statesman and leader of the popular party, who contributed greatly to Athens' political and cultural supremacy in Greece. In power from around 460 BC, he was responsible for the construction of the Parthenon. He conducted the Peloponnesian War (431–404 BC) successfully until his death
perihelion *n, pl* **-lia** point in the orbit of a planet or comet nearest to the sun
peril Ⓣ *n* great danger **perilous** *adj* **perilously** *adv*

THESAURUS

peremptory *adj* **1 = imperative**, final, decisive, absolute, binding, obligatory, compelling **2 = imperious**, authoritative, dictatorial, dogmatic, bossy (*informal*), domineering, overbearing
perennial *adj* **= continual**, persistent, constant, lasting, enduring, incessant, recurrent, abiding, twenty-four-seven (*slang*)
perfect *adj* **1 = faultless**, expert, skilled, flawless, polished, masterly • *His English was perfect.* OPPOSITE: imperfect **2 = complete**, absolute, utter, sheer, consummate, unmitigated • *They have a perfect right to say so.* **3 = excellent**, ideal, supreme, superb, splendid, sublime, superlative **4 = exact**, true, correct, accurate, faithful, precise, unerring ▶ *v* **5 = improve**, refine, polish, hone • *The technique was perfected last year.* **6 = accomplish**, finish, complete, perform, achieve, fulfill, carry out
perfection *n* **1 = completeness**, maturity **2 = purity**, integrity, perfectness, wholeness **3 = excellence**, superiority, exquisiteness, sublimity **4 = exactness**, precision, faultlessness
perfectionist *n* **= stickler**, purist, precisionist
perfectly *adv* **1 = completely**, quite, fully, absolutely, totally, altogether, thoroughly, wholly, utterly **2 = flawlessly**, ideally, wonderfully, superbly, impeccably, supremely, faultlessly
perfidious *adj* (*Lit*) **= treacherous**, unfaithful, disloyal, double-dealing, traitorous, two-faced
perforate *v* **= pierce**, drill, punch, penetrate, bore, puncture
perform *v* **1 = carry out**, do, complete, execute, fulfill • *people who have performed acts of bravery* **2 = present**, do, play, act, stage, put on • *students performing Shakespeare's* Macbeth *See also*: **achieve, administer, appear, commit, conduct, function**
performance *n* **1 = carrying out**, work, act, execution, achievement, accomplishment, completion, fulfillment **2 = presentation**, play, show, production, appearance, exhibition, portrayal, gig (*informal*), acting
performer *n* **= artiste**, player, actor *or* actress, Thespian, trouper
perfume *n* **= fragrance**, smell, scent, aroma, bouquet, odor
perfumed *See* **fragrant, sweet**
perfunctory *adj* **= offhand**, routine, mechanical, indifferent, superficial, sketchy, cursory, heedless
perhaps *adv* **= maybe**, possibly, conceivably, it could be • *Perhaps you're right.*
peril *n* **= danger**, risk, uncertainty, hazard, menace, jeopardy
perilous *adj* **= dangerous**, unsafe, risky, hazardous, precarious, threatening

DICTIONARY

perimeter Ⓣ [per-**rim**-it-er] *n* (length of) the outer edge of an area
perinatal *adj* of or in the weeks shortly before or after birth
period Ⓣ *n* **1** particular portion of time **2** series of years **3** single occurrence of menstruation **4** division of time at school etc. when a particular subject is taught **5** same as **full stop** ▷ *adj* **6** (of furniture, dress, a play, etc.) dating from or in the style of an earlier time in history
▸ **periodic** *adj* recurring at intervals
▸ **periodic table** chart of the elements, arranged to show their relationship to each other
▸ **periodical** *n* **1** magazine issued at regular intervals ▷ *adj* **2** periodic
peripatetic [per-rip-a-**tet**-ik] *adj* travelling about from place to place
periphery Ⓣ [per-**if**-er-ee] *n, pl* **-eries** **1** circumference **2** fringes of a field of activity
▸ **peripheral** [per-**if**-er-al] *adj* **1** unimportant, not central **2** of or on the periphery
periphrasis [per-**if**-ra-siss] *n, pl* **-rases** [-ra-seez] roundabout speech or expression
periphrastic *adj*
periscope *n* instrument used, esp. in submarines, for giving a view of objects on a different level
perish Ⓣ *v* **1** be destroyed or die **2** decay, rot
▸ **perishable** *adj* liable to rot quickly
▸ **perishing** *adj informal* very cold
peritoneum [per-rit-toe-**nee**-um] *n, pl* **-nea, -neums** membrane lining the internal surface of the abdomen
▸ **peritonitis** [per-rit-tone-**ite**-iss] *n* inflammation of the peritoneum
periwig *n hist* wig
periwinkle[1] *n* small edible shellfish, the winkle
periwinkle[2] *n* plant with trailing stems and blue flowers
perjury Ⓣ [**per**-jer-ee] *n, pl* **-juries** act or crime of lying while under oath in a court
perjure *v*
▸ **perjure oneself** commit perjury
perk Ⓣ *n informal* incidental benefit gained from a job, such as a company car
perk up *v* cheer up
▸ **perky** *adj* lively or cheerful
perm *n* **1** long-lasting curly hairstyle produced by treating the hair with chemicals ▷ *v* **2** give (hair) a perm
permafrost *n* permanently frozen ground
permanent Ⓣ *adj* lasting forever
permanently *adv* **permanence** *n*
▸ **permanent resident** immigrant allowed to live and work in Canada but who is not yet a citizen
permanganate *n* a salt of an acid of manganese
permeate Ⓣ *v* pervade or pass through the whole of (something)
▸ **permeable** *adj* able to be permeated, esp. by liquid

THESAURUS

perimeter *n* = **boundary**, border, limit, edge, margin, circumference, periphery, ambit, bounds, confines
period *n* = **time**, while, term, stretch, spell, interval • *a period of a few months*
See also: **length, lesson, round, space, stage**
periodic *adj* = **recurrent**, regular, repeated, occasional, cyclical, sporadic, intermittent
periodical *n* = **publication**, paper, magazine, journal, quarterly, weekly, monthly
peripheral *adj* **1** = **secondary**, minor, marginal, irrelevant, unimportant, incidental, inessential **2** = **outermost**, outside, external, outer, exterior
periphery *See* **outskirts**
perish *v* **1** = **die**, expire, be killed, lose one's life, pass away **2** = **be destroyed**, fall, decline, collapse, disappear, vanish **3** = **rot**, waste, decay, disintegrate, decompose, moulder
perishable *adj* = **short-lived**, decaying, decomposable
perjure *v* ▷ **perjure oneself** (*Criminal law*) = **commit perjury**, bear false witness, forswear, give false testimony, lie under oath, swear falsely
perjury *n* = **lying under oath**, bearing false witness, false statement, forswearing, giving false testimony
perk *n* (*Informal*) = **bonus**, benefit, extra, plus, fringe benefit, perquisite
perky *See* **lively**
permanence *n* = **continuity**, stability, endurance, durability, perpetuity, finality, continuance, constancy, indestructibility
permanent *adj* = **lasting**, constant, enduring, eternal, perpetual, abiding • *a permanent end to the hostilities* OPPOSITE: temporary
permeate *v* = **pervade**, charge, fill, saturate, penetrate, infiltrate, imbue, impregnate, spread through
permissible *adj* = **permitted**, legal, legitimate, acceptable, authorized, lawful, allowable, all right, O.K. *or* okay (*informal*)
permission *n* = **authorization**, approval, licence, go-ahead, consent, assent • *He asked permission to leave the room.* OPPOSITE: ban
See also: **blessing, permit, sanction**
permissive *adj* = **tolerant**, liberal, free, lax, lenient, easy-going, indulgent, forbearing

DICTIONARY

permit ⓣ *v* **-mitting, -mitted 1** give permission **2** allow, agree to ▷ *n* **3** document giving permission to do something
▸ **permission** *n* authorization to do something **permissible** *adj*
▸ **permissive** *adj* (excessively) tolerant, esp. in sexual matters
permutation ⓣ *n* any of the ways a number of things can be arranged or combined
pernicious ⓣ *adj* **1** wicked **2** extremely harmful, deadly
pernickety ⓣ *adj informal* (excessively) fussy about details
Perón *n* **1 Juan Domingo.** 1895–1974, Argentine soldier and statesman; dictator (1946–55). He was deposed in 1955, remaining in exile until 1973, when he was elected president (1973–74) **2** his second wife, (**María**) **Eva** (**Duarte**) **de Perón**, known as *Evita.* 1919–52, Argentine film actress: active in politics and social welfare (1946–52) **3** his third wife, **María Estella**, known as *Isabel.* born 1931, president of Argentina (1974–76); deposed **Peronist** *n, adj*
peroration *n* concluding part of a speech, usu. summing up the main points
peroxide *n* **1** oxide of a given base containing a high proportion of oxygen **2** short for **hydrogen peroxide**
perpendicular ⓣ *adj* **1** at right angles to a line or surface **2** upright or vertical ▷ *n* **3** line at right angles to another line or plane
perpetrate ⓣ *v* commit or be responsible for (a wrongdoing) **perpetration** *n* **perpetrator** *n*
perpetual ⓣ *adj* **1** lasting forever **2** continually repeated **perpetually** *adv*
▸ **perpetuate** *v* cause to continue or be remembered **perpetuation** *n*
▸ **in perpetuity** forever
perplex ⓣ *v* puzzle, bewilder **perplexity** *n*
perquisite ⓣ *n* same as **perk**
Perrault *n* **Charles.** 1628–1703, French author, noted for his *Contes de ma mère l'oye* (1697), which contains the fairy tales *Little Red Riding Hood, Cinderella,* and *The Sleeping Beauty*
perry *n, pl* **-ries** alcoholic drink made from fermented pears
per se [per **say**] *adv Latin* in itself
Perry *n* **Fred**(**erick John**). 1909–95, English tennis and table-tennis player; world singles table-tennis champion (1929); Wimbledon singles champion (1934–36)
persecute ⓣ *v* **1** treat cruelly because of race, religion, etc. **2** subject to persistent harassment **persecution** *n* **persecutor** *n*
persevere ⓣ *v* keep making an effort despite difficulties **perseverance** *n*
Persian *adj* **1** of ancient Persia or modern Iran, their people, or their languages ▷ *n* **2** person from Iran, Iranian
▸ **Persian carpet** *or* **rug** hand-made carpet or rug with flowing or geometric designs in rich colours

THESAURUS

permit *v* **1 = allow**, grant, sanction, enable, authorize, give the green light to • *We aren't permitted to bring our own food to the movies.* OPPOSITE: ban ▸ *n* **2 = licence**, pass, passport, warrant, permission, authorization • *a work permit*
See also: **approve, let**
permutation *n* **= transformation**, change, alteration, transposition
pernicious *adj* **= harmful**, bad, deadly, dangerous, fatal, evil, destructive, poisonous, detrimental, wicked, hurtful, malign, damaging
pernickety *adj* (*Old-fashioned, informal*) **= fussy**, particular, picky (*informal*), exacting, finicky, fastidious, overprecise
perpendicular *adj* **= upright**, straight, vertical, plumb, at right angles to, on end
perpetrate *v* **= commit**, do, perform, execute, enact, wreak, carry out
perpetual *adj* **1 = everlasting**, permanent, lasting, endless, perennial, eternal, infinite, unchanging, unending, never-ending **2 = continual**, persistent, constant, repeated, continuous, endless, incessant, recurrent, interminable, never-ending, twenty-four-seven (*slang*)
perpetually *See* **always**
perpetuate *v* **= maintain**, preserve, immortalize, keep going
perplex *v* **= puzzle**, confuse, baffle, stump, mystify, bewilder, confound
perplexed *See* **confused**
perplexing *adj* **= puzzling**, hard, difficult, complex, complicated, confusing, enigmatic, inexplicable, baffling, bewildering, mystifying
perplexity *n* **1 = puzzlement**, confusion, bewilderment, bafflement, incomprehension, mystification **2 = puzzle**, fix (*informal*), difficulty, mystery, paradox
perquisite *n* (*Formal*) **= bonus**, benefit, extra, plus, dividend, perk (*informal*)
persecute *v* **1 = victimize**, torture, hound, oppress, torment, ill-treat, pick on • *persecuted for religious beliefs* **2 = harass**, bother, annoy, hassle (*informal*), tease, badger, pester
See also: **bully**
persecution *See* **oppression**
persecutor *See* **bully**
perseverance *n* **= persistence**, resolution, determination, endurance, diligence, tenacity, doggedness, pertinacity
persevere *v* **= keep going**, continue,

DICTIONARY

▶ **Persian cat** long-haired domestic cat
persiflage [**per**-sif-flahzh] *n* light frivolous talk or writing
persimmon *n* sweet red tropical fruit
persist Ⓣ *v* **1** continue without interruption **2** continue obstinately despite opposition **persistent** *adj* **persistently** *adv* **persistence** *n*
person Ⓣ *n* **1** human being **2** body of a human being **3** *grammar* form of pronouns and verbs that shows if a person is speaking, spoken to, or spoken of
▶ **in person** actually present
persona [per-**soh**-na] *n, pl* **-nae** someone's personality as presented to others
personable Ⓣ *adj* pleasant in appearance and personality
personage Ⓣ *n* important person
personal Ⓣ *adj* **1** individual or private **2** of the body: *personal hygiene* **3** (of a remark etc.) offensive
▶ **personally** *adv* **1** in one's own opinion **2** directly, not by delegation to others
▶ **personal computer** small computer used for word processing or computer games
▶ **personal foul** *basketball* foul awarded against a player who makes bodily contact with an opponent
▶ **personal pronoun** pronoun like *I* or *she* that stands for a definite person
▶ **personal stereo** very small portable cassette player with headphones
personality Ⓣ *n, pl* **-ties 1** person's whole character **2** celebrity **personalities 3** personal remarks
personify Ⓣ *v* **-fying, -fied 1** give human characteristics to **2** be an example of, typify **personification** *n*
personnel Ⓣ *n* people employed in an organization
perspective Ⓣ *n* **1** mental view **2** method of drawing that gives the effect of solidity and relative distances and sizes
perspicacious Ⓣ *adj* having quick mental insight **perspicacity** *n*
perspire Ⓣ *v* sweat
▶ **perspiration** *n* sweat
persuade Ⓣ *v* **1** make (someone) do something by argument, charm, etc. **2** convince
▶ **persuasion** *n* **1** act of persuading **2** way of thinking or belief **persuasive** *adj*

THESAURUS

remain, persist, carry on, go on, hang on, stick at *or* stick to
persist *v* **1 = continue**, last, remain, linger, carry on, keep up **2 = persevere**, continue, insist, stand firm
persistence *n* **= determination**, resolution, endurance, grit, perseverance, tenacity, doggedness, pertinacity, tirelessness
persistent *adj* **1 = continuous**, constant, repeated, endless, perpetual, continual, incessant, never-ending, twenty-four-seven (*slang*) **2 = determined**, steady, stubborn, steadfast, tireless, dogged, tenacious, obdurate, obstinate, persevering, pertinacious, unflagging
person *n* **= individual**, human, soul, human being, living soul • *The amount of sleep we need varies from person to person.* ▷ **in person = personally**, bodily, oneself, in the flesh
See also: **figure**
personable *adj* **= pleasant**, nice, attractive, charming, handsome, good-looking, likable *or* likeable, agreeable, amiable
personage *n* **= personality**, celebrity, somebody, notable, dignitary, luminary, big shot (*informal*), megastar (*informal*), public figure, V.I.P.
personal *adj* **1 = individual**, own, special, private, particular, unique, peculiar • *personal belongings* **2 = offensive**, nasty, derogatory, disparaging, insulting
See also: **direct**
personality *n* **1 = nature**, character, identity, makeup, individuality, psyche • *She has such a kind, friendly personality.* **2 = celebrity**, star, big name, famous name, household name • *television personalities*
See also: **figure**
personally *adv* **1 = by oneself**, alone, solely, independently, on one's own **2 = in one's opinion**, for one's part, from one's own viewpoint, in one's books, in one's own view **3 = individually**, privately, specially, individualistically, subjectively
personification *n* **= embodiment**, image, portrayal, representation, incarnation, epitome
personify *v* **= embody**, represent, symbolize, exemplify, epitomize, typify
personnel *n* **= employees**, people, staff, workforce, helpers, human resources, workers
perspective *n* **1 = outlook**, attitude, context, angle, frame of reference **2 = objectivity**, relation, proportion, relativity, relative importance
perspicacious *adj* **= perceptive**, alert, sharp, acute, keen, shrewd, astute, discerning, percipient
perspiration *n* **= sweat**, moisture, wetness
perspire *v* **= sweat**, glow, swelter, exude, secrete, pour with sweat
persuade *v* **1 = talk into**, bring around (*informal*), sway, induce, coax, win over • *He persuaded the company to sign her*

P

DICTIONARY

pert Ⓣ *adj* bright and cheeky
pertain Ⓣ *v* belong or be relevant (to)
pertinacious *adj* very persistent and determined **pertinacity** *n*
pertinent Ⓣ *adj* relevant **pertinence** *n*
perturb Ⓣ *v* **1** disturb greatly **2** alarm **perturbation** *n*
peruke *n hist* wig
peruse Ⓣ *v* read in a careful or leisurely manner **perusal** *n*
pervade Ⓣ *v* spread right through (something) **pervasive** *adj*
perverse Ⓣ *adj* deliberately doing something different from what is thought normal or proper **perversely** *adv* **perversity** *n*
pervert Ⓣ *v* **1** use or alter for a wrong purpose **2** lead into abnormal (sexual) behaviour ▷ *n* **3** person who practises sexual perversion
▶ **perversion** *n* **1** sexual act or desire considered abnormal **2** act of perverting
pervious *adj* able to be penetrated, permeable
peseta [pa-**say**-ta] *n* former monetary unit of Spain
peso [**pay**-so] *n, pl* **pesos** standard monetary unit of Argentina, Mexico, etc.
pessary *n, pl* **-ries 1** appliance worn in the vagina, either to prevent conception or to support the womb **2** medicated suppository
pessimism Ⓣ *n* tendency to expect the worst in all things. **pessimist** *n* **pessimistic** *adj* **pessimistically** *adv*
Pessoa *n* **Fernando**. 1888–1935, Portuguese poet, who ascribed much of his work to three imaginary poets, Alvaro de Campos, Alberto Caeiro, and Ricardo Reis
pest Ⓣ *n* **1** annoying person **2** insect or animal that damages crops
▶ **pesticide** *n* chemical for killing insect pests

THESAURUS

up. **2 = convince**, satisfy, cause to believe
See also: **push, reason**
persuasion *n* **1 = urging**, inducement, cajolery, enticement, wheedling **2 = persuasiveness**, force, power, potency, cogency **3 = belief**, opinion, conviction, faith, tenet, creed, credo, views **4 = faction**, party, school, side, camp, denomination, school of thought
persuasive *adj* **= convincing**, sound, effective, influential, valid, credible, forceful, plausible, eloquent, weighty, cogent, compelling, telling
pert *adj* **= impudent**, forward, bold, cheeky, saucy, sassy (*informal*), impertinent, insolent
pertain *v* **= relate**, concern, apply, refer, regard, belong, befit, be relevant
pertinent *adj* **= relevant**, material, fit, appropriate, proper, fitting, applicable, apt, apposite, germane, to the point
pertness *n* **= impudence**, front, cheek (*informal*), audacity, cheekiness, effrontery, forwardness, impertinence, insolence, sauciness
perturb *v* **= disturb**, worry, trouble, bother, agitate, ruffle, unsettle, faze, disconcert, vex, fluster
perturbed *adj* **= disturbed**, troubled, anxious, worried, uncomfortable, uneasy, shaken, agitated, disconcerted, flustered
peruse *v* **= read**, study, check, examine, scan, browse, inspect, scrutinize
pervade *v* **= spread through**, charge, fill, penetrate, infuse, permeate, imbue, suffuse
pervasive *adj* **= widespread**, general, common, extensive, universal, prevalent, ubiquitous, rife, omnipresent
perverse *adj* **1 = abnormal**, contrary, unhealthy, improper, troublesome, rebellious, deviant, disobedient, refractory **2 = wilful**, contrary, dogged, intractable, intransigent, wrong-headed, headstrong, obdurate **3 = stubborn**, contrary, wayward, mulish, obstinate, pig-headed, stiff-necked **4 = ill-natured**, cross, fractious, churlish, ill-tempered, peevish, surly
perversion *n* **1 = deviation**, vice, abnormality, kink (*informal*), aberration, immorality, depravity, debauchery, kinkiness (*slang*), unnaturalness **2 = distortion**, corruption, misrepresentation, falsification, misinterpretation, twisting
perversity *n* **= contrariness**, intransigence, contradictoriness, obduracy, refractoriness, waywardness, wrong-headedness
pervert *n* **1 = deviant**, degenerate, weirdo or weirdie (*informal*), sicko (*informal*), sickie (*informal*) ▶ *v* **2 = distort**, abuse, twist, misrepresent, misuse, falsify, warp, garble **3 = corrupt**, degrade, debase, debauch, deprave, lead astray
perverted *adj* **= deviant**, unhealthy, immoral, depraved • *perverted phone calls and letters*
pessimism *n* **= gloominess**, depression, despair, distrust, gloom, melancholy, hopelessness, despondency, dejection
pessimist *n* **= prophet of doom**, cynic, defeatist, killjoy, wet blanket (*informal*), worrier
pessimistic *adj* **= gloomy**, hopeless, despondent, glum • *a pessimistic view of life* OPPOSITE: optimistic
pest *n* **1 = blight**, scourge, bane • *Aphids and other pests destroyed much of the*

DICTIONARY

pester Ⓣ *v* annoy or nag continually
pestilence Ⓣ *n* deadly epidemic disease ▸ **pestilential** *adj* **1** annoying, troublesome **2** deadly
pestle *n* club-shaped implement for grinding things to powder in a mortar
pet Ⓣ *n* **1** animal kept for pleasure and companionship **2** person favoured or indulged ▹ *adj* **3** kept as a pet **4** particularly cherished ▹ *v* **petting, petted 5** treat as a pet **6** pat or stroke affectionately **7** *informal* kiss and caress erotically
Pétain *n* **Henri Philippe Omer**. 1856–1951, French marshal, noted for his victory at Verdun (1916) in World War I and his leadership of the pro-Nazi government of unoccupied France at Vichy (1940–44); imprisoned for treason (1945)
petal *n* one of the white or coloured outer parts of a flower **petalled** *adj*
petard *n hist* explosive device ▸ **hoist with one's own petard** being the victim of one's own schemes
peter out *v* gradually come to an end
Peter *n New Testament* **1 Saint**. Also **Simon Peter** died ?67 AD, a fisherman of Bethsaida, who became leader of the apostles and is regarded by Roman Catholics as the first pope; probably martyred at Rome. Feast day: June 29 or Jan 18 **2** either of two epistles traditionally ascribed to Peter (in full *The First Epistle* and *The Second Epistle of Peter*)
Peter I *n* known as *Peter the Great*. 1672–1725, tsar of Russia (1682–1725), who assumed sole power in 1689. He introduced many reforms in government and technology, as well as bringing in western European ideas. He also acquired new territories for Russia in the Baltic and founded the new capital of St Petersburg (1703)
Peter III *n* 1728–62, grandson of Peter I and tsar of Russia (1762): deposed in a coup d'état led by his wife (later Catherine II); assassinated
petersham *n* thick corded ribbon used to stiffen belts, etc.
Peterson *n* **Oscar** (**Emmanuel**). 1925–2007, Canadian jazz pianist and singer, who led his own trio from the early 1950s
petite Ⓣ *adj* (of a woman) small and dainty
petition Ⓣ *n* **1** formal request, esp. one signed by many people and presented to parliament ▹ *v* **2** present a petition to **petitioner** *n*
Petrarch *n* Italian name *Francesco Petrarca*. 1304–74, Italian lyric poet and scholar, who greatly influenced the values of the Renaissance. His collection of poems *Canzoniere*, inspired by his ideal love for Laura, was written in the Tuscan dialect. He also wrote much in Latin, esp. the epic poem *Africa* (1341) and the *Secretum* (1342), a spiritual self-analysis **Petrarchan** *adj*
petrel *n* long-winged dark-coloured sea bird
petrify Ⓣ *v* **-fying, -fied 1** frighten severely **2** turn to stone **petrification** *n*
petrochemical *n* a substance, such as acetone, obtained from petroleum
petrodollar *n* money earned by a country by exporting petroleum
petrol *n Brit* gasoline
petroleum *n* thick dark crude oil found underground
Petronius *n* **Gaius**, known as *Petronius Arbiter*. died 66 AD, Roman satirist, supposed author of the *Satyricon*, a picaresque account of the licentiousness of contemporary society
petticoat *n* woman's skirt-shaped undergarment

P

THESAURUS

crop. **2 = nuisance**, pain (*informal*), bore, bane, pain in the neck (*informal*) • *I didn't want to be a cry baby or a pest.*
See also: **annoyance**
pester *v* **= annoy**, bother, bug (*informal*), badger, drive someone up the wall (*informal*), get on someone's nerves (*informal*) • *He gets fed up with people pestering him for money.*
See also: **hassle, worry**
pestilence *n* **= plague**, epidemic, visitation
pestilent *adj* **1 = annoying**, tiresome, bothersome, irksome, irritating, vexing **2 = harmful**, evil, detrimental, injurious, pernicious **3 = contaminated**, infected, infectious, contagious, diseased, catching, disease-ridden
pestilential *adj* **= deadly**, dangerous, harmful, hazardous, destructive, detrimental, injurious, pernicious
pet *n* **1 = favourite**, treasure, jewel, idol, darling ▸ *adj* **2 = favourite**, cherished, dearest, dear to one's heart ▸ *v* **3 = pamper**, baby, coddle, cosset, spoil **4 = fondle**, stroke, pat, caress **5 = cuddle**, neck (*informal*), kiss, smooch (*informal*), make out
peter *v* **peter out = die out**, stop, fail, fade, dwindle, wane, ebb, run out, taper off
petite *adj* **= small**, little, slight, delicate, dainty, elfin
petition *n* **1 = appeal**, request, suit, plea, prayer, solicitation, entreaty, supplication ▸ *v* **2 = appeal**, ask, plead, pray, beg, solicit, beseech, adjure, entreat, supplicate
petrified *See* **frightened**
petrify *v* **1 = terrify**, stun, paralyze, horrify, immobilize, transfix, stupefy **2 = fossilize**, harden, calcify, turn to stone

DICTIONARY

pettifogging *adj* overconcerned with unimportant detail
pettish *adj* fretful, irritable
petty Ⓣ *adj* **-tier, -tiest 1** unimportant, trivial **2** small-minded **3** on a small scale: *petty crime* **pettiness** *n*
▸ **petty cash** cash kept by a firm to pay minor expenses
▸ **petty officer** non-commissioned officer in the navy
petulant Ⓣ *adj* childishly irritable or peevish **petulantly** *adv* **petulance** *n*
petunia *n* garden plant with funnel-shaped flowers
Pevsner *n* **Antoine**. 1886–1962, French constructivist sculptor and painter, born in Russia; brother of Naum Gabo
pew *n* **1** fixed benchlike seat in a church **2** *Brit informal* chair, seat
pewter *n* greyish metal made of tin and lead
pH *chem* measure of the acidity of a solution
Phaedrus *n* ?15 BC–?50 AD, Roman author of five books of Latin verse fables, based chiefly on Aesop
phalanger *n* long-tailed Aust. tree-dwelling marsupial
phalanx *n, pl* **phalanxes, phalanges** closely grouped mass of people
phalarope *n* small wading bird
phallus *n, pl* **-li, -luses** penis, esp. as a symbol of reproductive power in primitive rites **phallic** *adj*
phantasm *n* unreal vision, illusion **phantasmal** *adj*
phantasmagoria *n* shifting medley of dreamlike figures
phantasy *n, pl* **-sies** same as **fantasy**
phantom Ⓣ *n* **1** ghost **2** unreal vision
Pharaoh [**fare**-oh] *n* title of the ancient Egyptian kings
pharisee *n* self-righteous hypocrite **pharisaic** *or* **pharisaical** *adj*
pharmaceutical *adj* of pharmacy
pharmacology *n* study of drugs **pharmacological** *adj* **pharmacologist** *n*
pharmacopoeia [far-ma-koh-**pee**-a] *n* book with a list of and directions for the use of drugs
pharmacy *n, pl* **-cies 1** preparation and dispensing of drugs and medicines **2** pharmacist's shop
▸ **pharmacist** *n* person qualified to prepare and sell drugs and medicines
pharynx [**far**-rinks] *n, pl* **pharynges, pharynxes** cavity forming the back part of the mouth **pharyngeal** *adj*
▸ **pharyngitis** [far-rin-**jite**-iss] *n* inflammation of the pharynx
phase Ⓣ *n* **1** any distinct or characteristic stage in a development or chain of events ▷ *v* **2** arrange or carry out in stages or to coincide with something else
▸ **phase in** *or* **phase out** *v* introduce *or* discontinue gradually
PhD Doctor of Philosophy
pheasant *n* game bird with bright plumage
Pheidippides, Phidippides *n* 5th century BC, Athenian athlete, who ran to Sparta to seek help against the Persians before the Battle of Marathon (490 BC)
phenobarbitone *n* drug inducing sleep or relaxation
phenol *n* chemical used in disinfectants and antiseptics
phenomenon Ⓣ *n, pl* **-ena 1** anything appearing or observed **2** remarkable person or thing
▸ **phenomenal** *adj* extraordinary, outstanding **phenomenally** *adv*
phew *interj* exclamation of relief, surprise, etc.
phial *n* small bottle for medicine etc.
Phidias *n* 5th century BC, Greek sculptor, regarded as one of the greatest of sculptors. He executed the sculptures of the Parthenon and the colossal statue of Zeus at Olympia, one of the Seven Wonders of the World: neither survives in the original **Phidian** *adj*
philadelphus *n* shrub with sweet-scented flowers

THESAURUS

petty *adj* **1 = trivial**, insignificant, unimportant, measly (*informal*), trifling • *endless rules and petty regulations* **2 = small-minded**, mean, cheap, childish • *I think that attitude is a bit petty.*
See also: **minor**
petulance *n* **= sulkiness**, pique, irritability, bad temper, ill humour, peevishness, sullenness
petulant *adj* **= sulky**, moody, sullen, bad-tempered, huffy, ill-humoured, peevish
phantom *n* **1 = specter**, spirit, shade (*lit*), ghost, spook (*informal*), apparition, phantasm, wraith **2 = illusion**, vision, hallucination, figment of the imagination
phase *n* **= stage**, time, point, period, step, position, development, chapter, juncture ▸ *v* ▷ **phase out = eliminate**, close, remove, withdraw, terminate, ease off, pull out, run down, wind down, wind up
phenomenal *adj* **= extraordinary**, unusual, remarkable, fantastic, exceptional, outstanding, miraculous, marvellous, prodigious
phenomenon *n* **1 = occurrence**, event, fact, incident, circumstance, episode, happening **2 = wonder**, exception,

DICTIONARY

philanderer Ⓣ *n* man who flirts or has many casual love affairs **philandering** *n*
philanthropy Ⓣ *n* practice of helping people less well-off than oneself **philanthropic** *adj* **philanthropist** *n*
philately [fill-**lat**-a-lee] *n* stamp collecting **philatelic** *adj* **philatelist** *n*
philharmonic *adj* (in names of orchestras etc.) music-loving
Philip *n* **1** *New Testament* **a** Also **Philip the Evangelist** one of the seven deacons appointed by the early Church **b** Also **Philip the Tetrarch** one of the sons of Herod the Great, who was ruler of part of former Judaea (4 BC–34 AD) (Luke 3:1) **2 King**, American Indian name *Metacomet.* died 1676, American Indian chief, the son of Massasoit. He waged King Philip's War against the colonists of New England (1675–76) and was killed in battle **3 Prince.** See (Duke of) **Edinburgh**
Philip I *n* **1** known as *Philip the Handsome.* 1478–1506, king of Castile (1506); father of Emperor Charles V and founder of the Hapsburg dynasty in Spain **2** title of Philip II of Spain as king of Portugal
Philip II *n* **1** 382–336 BC, king of Macedonia (359–336 BC); the father of Alexander the Great **2** known as *Philip Augustus.* 1165–1223, Capetian king of France (1180–1223); set out on the Third Crusade with Richard I of England (1190) **3** 1527–98, king of Spain (1556–98) and, as Philip I, king of Portugal (1580–98); the husband of Mary I of England (1554–58). He championed the Counter-Reformation, sending the Armada against England (1588)
Philip IV *n* known as *Philip the Fair.* 1268–1314, king of France (1285–1314): he challenged the power of the papacy, obtaining the elevation of Clement V as pope residing at Avignon (the beginning of the Babylonian captivity of the papacy)
Philip V *n* 1683–1746, king of Spain (1700–46) and founder of the Bourbon dynasty in Spain. His accession began the War of Spanish Succession (1701–13)
Philip VI *n* 1293–1350, first Valois king of France (1328–50). Edward III of England claimed his throne, which with other disputes led to the beginning of the Hundred Years' War (1337)
philippic *n* bitter or impassioned speech of denunciation, invective
philistine Ⓣ *adj, n* boorishly uncultivated (person) **philistinism** *n*
philology *n* science of the structure and development of languages **philological** *adj* **philologist** *n*
philosophy Ⓣ *n, pl* **-phies** **1** study of the meaning of life, knowledge, thought, etc. **2** theory or set of ideas held by a particular philosopher **3** person's outlook on life
▸ **philosopher** *n* person who studies philosophy
▸ **philosophical** *adj* **1** of philosophy **2** calm in the face of difficulties or disappointments **philosophically** *adv*
▸ **philosophize** *v* talk in a boring and pretentious manner about basic things
philtre *n* magic drink supposed to arouse love in the person who drinks it
Phiz *n* real name *Hablot Knight Browne.* 1815–82, English painter, noted for his illustrations for Dickens' novels
phlebitis [fleb-**bite**-iss] *n* inflammation of a vein
phlegm [**flem**] *n* thick yellowish substance formed in the nose and throat during a cold
phlegmatic Ⓣ [fleg-**mat**-ik] *adj* not easily excited, unemotional **phlegmatically** *adv*
phlox *n, pl* **phlox, phloxes** flowering garden plant

THESAURUS

sensation, miracle, marvel, rarity, prodigy, black swan
philanderer *n* = **womanizer** (*informal*), flirt, Casanova, Don Juan, gigolo, ladies' man, wolf (*informal*), stud (*slang*), playboy
philanthropic *adj* = **humanitarian**, kind, charitable, humane, benevolent, kind-hearted, beneficent, munificent, public-spirited
philanthropist *n* = **humanitarian**, donor, patron, contributor, benefactor, giver
philanthropy *n* = **humanitarianism**, charity, generosity, almsgiving, beneficence, benevolence, brotherly love, charitableness, kind-heartedness
philistine *n* **1** = **boor**, yahoo, barbarian, ignoramus, lout, lowbrow, vulgarian ▸ *adj* **2** = **uncultured**, ignorant, tasteless, boorish, uneducated, unrefined, lowbrow, uncultivated
philosopher *n* = **thinker**, sage, theorist, logician, metaphysician, wise man
philosophical *adj* **1** = **wise**, abstract, logical, rational, thoughtful, theoretical, sagacious **2** = **stoical**, cool, calm, tranquil, serene, collected, composed, unruffled
philosophy *n* **1** = **thought**, knowledge, wisdom, logic, reasoning, thinking, metaphysics, rationalism **2** = **outlook**, viewpoint, ideology, doctrine, thinking, beliefs, convictions, principles, tenets, values, world view **3** = **stoicism**, composure, serenity, calmness, equanimity, self-possession
phlegmatic *adj* = **unemotional**, indifferent, apathetic, impassive, placid,

DICTIONARY

phobia Ⓣ *n* intense and unreasoning fear or dislike
phoenix *n* legendary bird said to set fire to itself and rise anew from its ashes
phone Ⓣ *n, v informal* telephone
▸ **phonecard** *n* card used to operate certain public telephones
▸ **phone-in** *n* broadcast in which telephone comments or questions from the public are transmitted live
phonetic *adj* **1** of speech sounds **2** (of spelling) written as sounded **phonetically** *adv*
▸ **phonetics** *pl n* science of speech sounds
phonic *adj* of speech sounds
phonograph *n old-fashioned* record player
phonology *n, pl* **-gies** study of the speech sounds in a language **phonological** *adj*
phony, phoney Ⓣ *informal* ▹ *adj* **phonier, phoniest 1** not genuine **2** false **3** insincere ▹ *n, pl* **phonies 4** phony person or thing
phosgene [**foz**-jean] *n* poisonous gas used in warfare
phosphorescence *n* faint glow in the dark **phosphorescent** *adj*
phosphorus *n* toxic flammable nonmetallic element which appears luminous in the dark
▸ **phosphate** *n* **1** compound of phosphorus **2** fertilizer containing phosphorus
photo *n, pl* **photos** short for **photograph**
▸ **photo finish** finish of a race in which the contestants are so close that a photo is needed to decide the result
▸ **Photoshop** *n* **1** ® software application for managing and editing digital images ▹ *v* **2** *informal* alter (a digital image) using Photoshop or a similar application
photocopy *n, pl* **-copies 1** photographic reproduction ▹ *v* **2** make a photocopy of
photoelectric *adj* using or worked by electricity produced by the action of light
photogenic *adj* always looking attractive in photographs
photograph Ⓣ *n* **1** picture made by the chemical action of light on sensitive film ▹ *v* **2** take a photograph of **photographer** *n* **photographic** *adj*
▸ **photography** *n* art of taking photographs
photogravure *n* process in which an etched metal plate for printing is produced by photography
photolithography *n* lithographic printing process using photographically made plates
photometer [foe-**tom**-it-er] *n* instrument for measuring the intensity of light
Photostat *n* **1** ® type of photocopying machine **2** copy made by it
photosynthesis *n* process by which a green plant uses sunlight to build up carbohydrate reserves
phrase Ⓣ *n* **1** group of words forming a unit of meaning, esp. within a sentence **2** short effective expression ▹ *v* **3** express in words
▸ **phrasal** *v* phrase consisting of a *v* and an *adv* or preposition, with a meaning different from the parts, such as *take in* meaning *deceive*
phraseology Ⓣ *n, pl* **-gies** way in which words are used
phrenology *n* formerly, the study of the shape and size of the skull as a means of finding out a person's character and mental ability **phrenologist** *n*
phut *adv* **go phut** *informal* (of a machine) break down
Phyfe, Fife *n* **Duncan**. ?1768–1854, US cabinet-maker, born in Scotland
phylactery *n, pl* **-teries** leather case containing religious texts, worn by Jewish men
phylum *n, pl* **-la** major taxonomic division

THESAURUS

stoical, stolid, undemonstrative, unfeeling
phobia *n* = **terror**, thing (*informal*), fear, horror, hatred, dread, revulsion, aversion, loathing, detestation, repulsion
phone *n* **1** = **telephone**, cell, horn (*informal*), iPhone (*trademark*), blower (*informal*), cell phone, camera phone, smart phone, video phone, carphone, internet phone **2** = **call**, phone, message, phone-call ▸ *v* **3** = **call**, get on the blower (*informal*), get on the horn (*informal*), give someone a call, make a call, telephone
phony, phoney *adj* **1** = **fake**, false, counterfeit, bogus, sham, forged • *a phony accent* OPPOSITE: genuine ▸ *n* **2** = **fake**, fraud, counterfeit, forgery, sham, impostor, pseud (*informal*)
See also: **mock**
photograph *n* **1** = **picture**, shot, photo (*informal*), snap (*informal*), print, transparency, snapshot ▸ *v* **2** = **take a picture of**, record, film, shoot, snap (*informal*), take (someone's) picture
photographic *adj* **1** = **lifelike**, natural, visual, realistic, graphic, pictorial, vivid **2** (~ *memory*) = **accurate**, exact, faithful, precise, retentive
phrase *n* **1** = **expression**, remark, saying, group of words, idiom ▸ *v* **2** = **express**, say, put, word, voice, put into words
phraseology *n* = **wording**, speech, language, style, expression, phrase, phrasing, parlance, choice of words, idiom, syntax
phrasing *See* **language**

DICTIONARY

of animals and plants that contain one or more classes
physical Ⓣ *adj* **1** of the body, as contrasted with the mind or spirit **2** of material things or nature **3** of physics **physically** *adv*
▸ **physical geography** branch of geography dealing with the features of the earth's surface
▸ **physical education** training and practice in sports and gymnastics
physician Ⓣ *n* doctor of medicine
physics *n* science of the properties of matter and energy
▸ **physicist** *n* person skilled in, or studying, physics
physiognomy [fiz-ee-**on**-om-ee] *n, pl* **-mies** face
physiology *n* science of the normal function of living things **physiological** *adj* **physiologist** *n*
physiotherapy *n* treatment of disease or injury by physical means such as massage, rather than by drugs **physiotherapist** *n*
physique Ⓣ *n* person's bodily build and muscular development
pi *n, pl* **pis** *math* ratio of the circumference of a circle to its diameter
Piaf *n* **Edith**, real name *Edith Giovanna Gassion*, known as *the Little Sparrow*. 1915–63, French singer
Piaget *n* **Jean**. 1896–1980, Swiss psychologist, noted for his work on the development of the cognitive functions in children
pianissimo *adv music* very quietly
piano[1] *n, pl* **pianos** Also **pianoforte** musical instrument with strings which are struck by hammers worked by a keyboard **pianist** *n*
▸ **Pianola** *n* ® mechanically played piano
piano[2] *adv music* quietly
Piano *n* **Renzo**. born 1937, Italian architect; buildings include the Pompidou Centre, Paris (1977; with Richard Rogers) and the Potsdamer Platz redevelopment, Berlin (1998)
piazza *n* large open square or marketplace, esp. in Italy
pibroch [**pee**-brok] *n* form of bagpipe music
pic *n, pl* **pics, pix** *informal* photograph or illustration
pica [**pie**-ka] *n* **1** printing type of 6 lines to the inch **2** typewriter typesize of 10 letters to the inch
picador *n* mounted bullfighter with a lance
Picard *n* **Jean**. 1620–82, French astronomer. He was the first to make a precise measurement of a longitude line, enabling him to estimate the earth's radius
picaresque *adj* denoting a type of fiction in which the hero, a rogue, has a series of adventures
Picasso *n* **Pablo**. 1881–1973, Spanish painter and sculptor, resident in France: a highly influential figure in 20th-century art and a founder, with Braque, of cubism. A prolific artist, his works include *The Dwarf Dancer* (1901), belonging to his blue period; the first cubist painting *Les Demoiselles d'Avignon* (1907); *Three Dancers* (1925), which appeared in the first surrealist exhibition; and *Guernica* (1937), inspired by an event in the Spanish Civil War
piccalilli *n* pickle of vegetables in mustard sauce
piccaninny *n, pl* **-nies** *offensive* Black child
piccolo *n, pl* **-los** small flute
pick[1] Ⓣ *v* **1** choose **2** remove (flowers or fruit) from a plant **3** remove loose particles from **4** (foll. by *at*) nibble (at) without appetite **5** provoke (a fight etc.) deliberately **6** open (a lock) by means other than a key ▹ *n* **7** choice: *take your pick* **8** best part
▸ **pick-me-up** *n informal* **1** tonic **2** stimulating drink
▸ **pick on** *v* find fault with
▸ **pick out** *v* recognize, distinguish
▸ **pickpocket** *n* thief who steals from someone's pocket

P

THESAURUS

physical *adj* **1 = bodily**, corporal, mortal, earthly, corporeal, fleshly, incarnate **2 = material**, real, natural, solid, substantial, tangible, palpable
physician *n* = **doctor**, medic (*informal*), doc (*informal*), doctor of medicine, general practitioner, G.P., M.D., medical practitioner
physique *n* = **build**, body, figure, form, shape, frame, structure, constitution
pick *v* **1 = choose**, select, decide upon, hand-pick, opt for, settle on • *She picked ten people to interview for six sales jobs.* **2 = gather**, harvest, pluck • *I picked the most beautiful rose.* **3 = nibble**, have no appetite, peck at, play with *or* toy with, push the food round the plate **4 = provoke**, start, incite, instigate **5 = open**, force, crack, break into, break open ▹ **pick on = torment**, bait, tease • *Bullies pick on weaker children.* *See also*: **bully, persecute** ▹ **pick out = identify**, recognize, perceive, discriminate, distinguish, make out, tell apart ▹ **pick up = lift**, raise, gather, grasp, uplift, take up; **= obtain**, find, buy, purchase, come across; **= recover**, improve, rally, mend, be on the mend, get better, take a turn for the better, turn the corner; **= learn**, acquire, master, get the hang of (*informal*) ▸ *n* **6 = the best**, elite, pride • *the pick of the country's young athletes* **7 = choice**, decision, option, selection, preference
See also: **favourite**

DICTIONARY

▶ **pick up** *v* **1** raise, lift **2** obtain or purchase **3** improve, get better **4** collect **5** *informal* become acquainted with for a sexual purpose **6** accelerate
▶ **pick-up** *n* **1** small truck **2** *informal* casual acquaintance made for a sexual purpose **3** device for conversion of mechanical energy into electric signals, as in a record player
pick² *n* tool with a curved iron crossbar and wooden shaft, for breaking up hard ground or masonry
pickaback *n* same as **piggyback**
pickaxe *n* large pick
picket ⓣ *n* **1** person or group standing outside a workplace to deter would-be workers during a strike **2** sentry or sentries posted to give warning of an attack **3** pointed stick used as part of a fence ▷ *v* **4** form a picket outside (a workplace)
▶ **picket line** line of people acting as pickets
Pickford *n* **Mary**. 1893–1979, US actress born in Canada. She was a film star of the silent era and co-founded United Artists (1919)
pickings *pl n* money easily acquired
pickle ⓣ *n* **1** food preserved in vinegar or salt water **2** *informal* awkward situation ▷ *v* **3** preserve in vinegar or salt water
▶ **pickled** *adj informal* drunk
picnic ⓣ *n* **1** informal meal out of doors ▷ *v* **-nicking, -nicked 2** have a picnic
Pict *n* member of an ancient race of N Britain **Pictish** *adj*
pictorial ⓣ *adj* **1** of or in painting or pictures **2** illustrated ▷ *n* **3** newspaper etc. with many pictures **pictorially** *adv*
picture ⓣ *n* **1** drawing or painting **2** photograph **3** mental image **4** beautiful or picturesque object **5** image on a TV screen **pictures 6** cinema ▷ *v* **7** visualize, imagine **8** represent in a picture
▶ **picturesque** *adj* **1** (of a place or view) pleasant to look at **2** (of language) forceful, vivid
▶ **picture window** large window made of a single sheet of glass
piddle *v informal* urinate
piddling *adj informal* small or unimportant
pidgin *n* language, not a mother tongue, made up of elements of two or more other languages
pie *n* dish of meat, fruit, etc. baked in pastry
▶ **pie chart** circular diagram with sectors representing quantities
piebald ⓣ *n, adj* (horse) with irregular black-and-white markings
piece ⓣ *n* **1** separate bit or part **2** instance: *a piece of luck* **3** example, specimen **4** literary or musical composition **5** coin **6** small object used in checkers, chess, etc.
▶ **piece together** *v* make or assemble bit by bit
pièce de résistance [**pyess** de ray-**ziss**-tonss] *n French* most impressive item
piecemeal ⓣ *adv* a bit at a time
piecework *n* work paid for according to the quantity produced

THESAURUS

P

picket *n* **1 = protester**, demonstrator, picketer **2 = stake**, post, upright, pale, paling, stanchion ▶ *v* **3 = blockade**, demonstrate, boycott
pickle *n* **1** (*Informal*) **= predicament**, fix (*informal*), difficulty, bind (*informal*), jam (*informal*), scrape (*informal*), dilemma, quandary, hot water (*informal*), tight spot ▶ *v* **2 = preserve**, steep, marinade
pick-me-up *n* (*Informal*) **= tonic**, stimulant, restorative, refreshment, bracer (*informal*), shot in the arm (*informal*)
pickpocket *See* **thief**
picnic *n* **= outdoor meal**, outing, excursion
pictorial *adj* **= graphic**, picturesque, scenic, illustrated, representational
pick-up *n* **= improvement**, rise, rally, recovery, revival, upswing, upturn, change for the better, strengthening
picture *n* **1 = representation**, painting, photograph, portrait, drawing, sketch, illustration • *I have a picture of you as my screen saver.* RELATED WORD *adj*: pictorial **2 = description**, report, account, image, impression, depiction **3 = double**, image, copy, twin, replica, duplicate, likeness, lookalike, carbon copy, dead ringer (*slang*), spitting image (*informal*) **4 = personification**, essence, epitome, embodiment **5 = film**, movie, flick (*slang*), motion picture ▶ *v* **6 = imagine**, see, visualize, conceive of • *He pictured her with long black hair.* **7 = represent**, show, draw, paint, photograph, depict, sketch, illustrate
picturesque *adj* **1 = pretty**, beautiful, attractive, charming, striking, scenic, quaint **2 = vivid**, graphic, colorful
piebald *adj* **= dappled**, spotted, black and white, brindled, flecked, mottled, pied, speckled
piece *n* **1 = bit**, part, portion, slice, chunk, fragment • *a piece of cheese* **2 = work**, study, article, creation, composition • *I read his piece on hockey parents.*
See also: **block, feature, item, lump, section** ▶ *v* ▷ **piece together = assemble**, join, repair, restore, mend, patch together • *Doctors painstakingly pieced together the broken bones.*
See also: **reconstruct**
piecemeal *adv* **= bit by bit**, gradually, by degrees, little by little

DICTIONARY

pied *adj* having markings of two or more colours
pied-à-terre [**pyay** da **tair**] *n, pl* **pieds-à-terre** [**pyay** da **tair**] small apartment or house for occasional use
pie-eyed *adj slang* drunk
pier Ⓣ *n* **1** platform on stilts sticking out into the sea **2** pillar, esp. one supporting a bridge
pierce Ⓣ *v* **1** make a hole in or through with a sharp instrument **2** make a way through
▸ **piercing** *adj* **1** (of a sound) shrill and high-pitched **2** (of wind or cold) fierce, penetrating
Pierce *n* **Franklin.** 1804–69, US statesman; 14th president of the US (1853–57)
Piero della Francesca *n* ?1420–92, Italian painter, noted particularly for his frescoes of the *Legend of the True Cross* in San Francesco, Arezzo
pierrot [**pier**-roe] *n* pantomime character, clown
piety Ⓣ *n, pl* **-ties** deep devotion to God and religion
piffle *n informal* nonsense
pig Ⓣ *n* **1** animal kept and killed for pork, ham, and bacon **2** *informal* greedy, dirty, or rude person
▸ **piggish** *or* **piggy** *adj informal* **1** dirty **2** greedy **3** stubborn
▸ **piggery** *n* place for keeping and breeding pigs
▸ **pig-headed** *adj* obstinate
▸ **pig iron** crude iron produced in a blast furnace
pigeon *n* **1** bird with a heavy body and short legs, sometimes trained to carry messages **2** *informal* concern or responsibility
▸ **pigeonhole** *n* **1** compartment for papers in a desk etc. ▹ *v* **2** classify **3** put aside and do nothing about
▸ **pigeon-toed** *adj* with the feet or toes turned inwards
piggyback *n* **1** ride on someone's shoulders ▹ *adv* **2** carried on someone's shoulders ▹ *v* **3** exploit an existing resource, system, or product **4** attach to or mount on an existing piece of equipment or system
pigment Ⓣ *n* colouring matter, paint or dye
pigmentation *n*
Pigmy *adj, n, pl* **-mies** same as **Pygmy**
pigtail *n* plait of hair hanging from the back or either side of the head
pike[1] *n* large predatory freshwater fish
pike[2] *n hist* long-handled spear
pilaster *n* square column, usu. set in a wall
Pilate *n* **Pontius.** Roman procurator of Judaea (?26–?36 AD), who ordered the crucifixion of Jesus, allegedly against his better judgment
pilau, pilaf, pilaff *n* Middle Eastern dish of meat or poultry boiled with rice, spices, etc.
pilchard *n* small edible sea fish of the herring family
pile[1] Ⓣ *n* **1** number of things lying on top of each other **2** *informal* large amount **3** large building ▹ *v* **4** collect into a pile **5** (foll. by *in* or *out* or *off*) (etc.) move in a group
▸ **pile-up** *n informal* traffic accident involving several vehicles
pile[2] Ⓣ *n* beam driven into the ground, esp. as a foundation for building in water or wet ground
pile[3] Ⓣ *n* fibres of a carpet or a fabric, esp.

P

THESAURUS

pier *n* **1 = jetty**, wharf, promenade, landing place, quay **2 = pillar**, post, support, column, pile, upright, buttress
pierce *v* **= penetrate**, drill, bore, puncture, lance • *Pierce the potato with a fork.*
piercing *adj* **1** (*~ sound*) **= penetrating**, sharp, loud, high-pitched, shrill, ear-splitting **2 = perceptive**, alert, sharp, keen, shrewd, penetrating, perspicacious, quick-witted **3** (*~ wind, etc.*) **= cold**, bitter, arctic, wintry, freezing, biting, nippy **4 = sharp**, severe, intense, painful, acute, stabbing, agonizing, excruciating
piety *n* **= holiness**, faith, religion, reverence, godliness, piousness
pig *n* **1 = hog**, swine, piggy (*informal*) • *the number of pigs at the trough* RELATED WORDS *adj*: porcine *male*: boar *female*: sow *young*: piglet *collective n*: litter *habitation*: sty **2** (*Informal*) **= brute**, hog (*informal*), swine, boor, glutton, slob (*slang*)
pigeonhole *n* **1 = compartment**, place, section, locker, niche, cubbyhole ▸ *v* **2 = classify**, label, slot (*informal*), characterize, categorize, compartmentalize, ghettoize **3 = postpone**, shelve, defer, put off
pig-headed *adj* **= stubborn**, contrary, inflexible, unyielding, mulish, obstinate, self-willed, stiff-necked
pigment *n* **= colour**, paint, dye, stain, tint, colouring, tincture
pigmentation *See* **colour**
pile[1] *n* **1 = heap**, mountain, mound, stack, hoard • *a pile of books* **2** (*Informal, often pl*) **= a lot**, ocean, quantity, great deal, stacks **3 = building**, structure, erection, edifice ▸ *v* **4 = heap**, stack • *A few newspapers were piled on the table.* **5 = collect**, gather, assemble, accumulate, amass, hoard **6 = crowd**, flood, rush, pack, crush, stream, jam, flock
See also: **bunch, load, mass**
pile[2] *n* **= foundation**, post, support, column, beam, upright, pillar
pile[3] *n* **= nap**, down, hair, fur • *the carpet's thick pile*

DICTIONARY

velvet, that stand up from the weave
piles *pl n* swollen veins in the rectum, hemorrhoids
pilfer Ⓣ *v* steal in small quantities
pilgrim Ⓣ *n* person who journeys to a holy place. **pilgrimage** *n*
pill Ⓣ *n* small ball of medicine swallowed whole
▸ **the pill** pill taken by a woman to prevent pregnancy
▸ **pillbox** *n* **1** small box for pills **2** small concrete fort
pillage Ⓣ *v* **1** steal property by violence in war ▷ *n* **2** violent seizure of goods, esp. in war
pillar Ⓣ *n* **1** slender upright post, usu. supporting a roof **2** strong supporter
▸ **pillar box** red pillar-shaped letter box in the street
pillion *n* seat for a passenger behind the rider of a motorcycle
pillory Ⓣ *n, pl* **-ries 1** *hist* frame with holes for the head and hands in which an offender was locked and exposed to public abuse ▷ *v* **-rying, -ried 2** ridicule publicly
pillow *n* **1** stuffed cloth bag for supporting the head in bed ▷ *v* **2** rest as if on a pillow
▸ **pillowcase** *n* removable cover for a pillow
pilot Ⓣ *n* **1** person qualified to fly an aircraft or spacecraft **2** person employed to steer a ship entering or leaving a harbour ▷ *adj* **3** experimental and preliminary ▷ *v* **4** act as the pilot of **5** guide, steer
▸ **pilot light** small flame lighting the main one in a gas appliance
pimento *n, pl* **-tos** mild-tasting red pepper
pimp *n* **1** man who gets customers for a prostitute in return for a share of his or her earnings ▷ *v* **2** act as a pimp
pimpernel *n* wild plant with small flowers that close in dull weather
pimple Ⓣ *n* small pus-filled spot on the skin
pimply *adj*
pin Ⓣ *n* **1** short thin piece of stiff wire with a point and head, for fastening things **2** wooden or metal peg or stake ▷ *v* **pinning, pinned 3** fasten with a pin **4** seize and hold fast
▸ **pin down** *v* **1** force (someone) to make a decision, take action, etc. **2** define clearly
▸ **pinball** *n* electrically operated table game, in which a small ball is shot through various hazards
▸ **pin money** small amount earned to buy small luxuries
▸ **pinpoint** *v* locate or identify exactly
▸ **pinstripe** *n* **1** very narrow stripe in fabric **2** the fabric itself
▸ **pin-up** *n* picture of a sexually attractive person, esp. (partly) naked
pinafore *n* **1** apron **2** dress with a bib top
pince-nez [panss-**nay**] *n, pl* **pince-nez** glasses kept in place only by a clip on the bridge of the nose
pincers *pl n* **1** tool consisting of two hinged arms, for gripping **2** claws of a lobster etc.
pinch Ⓣ *v* **1** squeeze between finger and thumb **2** cause pain by being too tight **3** *informal* steal **4** *informal* arrest ▷ *n* **5** squeeze or sustained nip **6** as much as can be taken up between the finger and thumb
▸ **at a pinch** if absolutely necessary
▸ **feel the pinch** have to economize
pinch- *prefix baseball* substitute: *pinch-hitter; pinch-runner*
pinchbeck *n* alloy of zinc and copper, used as imitation gold

P

THESAURUS

pile-up *n (Informal)* = **collision**, crash, accident, smash, multiple collision, smash-up *(informal)*
pilfer *v* = **steal**, appropriate, embezzle, filch, lift *(informal)*, pinch *(informal)*, purloin, take, swipe *(slang)*
pilgrim *n* = **traveller**, wanderer, wayfarer
pilgrimage *n* = **journey**, mission, trip, tour, expedition, excursion
pill *n* = **tablet**, capsule, pellet ▷ **the pill** = **oral contraceptive**
pillage *v* **1** = **plunder**, raid, sack, loot, ravage, ransack, maraud, despoil ▸ *n* **2** = **plunder**, robbery, sack, marauding, spoliation
pillar *n* **1** = **support**, post, column, prop, shaft, upright, pier, stanchion **2** = **supporter**, follower, mainstay, upholder
pillory *v* = **ridicule**, brand, denounce, stigmatize
pilot *n* **1** = **airman**, flyer, aviator **2** = **helmsman**, navigator, steersman ▸ *adj* **3** = **trial**, test, model, experimental ▸ *v* **4** = **fly**, drive, operate, conduct, direct, handle, guide, steer, navigate
pimple *n* = **spot**, boil, pustule, zit *(slang)*
pin *v* **1** = **fasten**, join, fix, secure, attach, affix **2** = **hold fast**, fix, immobilize, hold down, pinion ▷ **pin down** = **force**, make, press, compel, pressurize, constrain; = **determine**, name, identify, locate, specify, pinpoint
pinch *v* **1** = **squeeze**, press, nip, grasp, compress **2** = **hurt**, pain, crush, cramp **3** *(Informal)* = **steal**, filch, lift *(informal)*, pilfer, purloin, swipe *(slang)* ▸ *n* **4** = **squeeze**, nip **5** = **dash**, bit, mite, speck, jot, *soupçon (French)* **6** = **hardship**, emergency, crisis, difficulty, plight, necessity, strait, predicament
pinched *adj* = **thin**, gaunt, drawn, haggard, peaky, worn

DICTIONARY

Pinckney *n* **1 Charles.** 1757–1824, US statesman, who was a leading member of the convention that framed the US Constitution (1787) **2** his cousin, **Charles Cotesworth.** 1746–1825, US soldier, statesman, and diplomat, who also served at the Constitutional Convention **3** his brother, **Thomas.** 1750–1828, US soldier and politician. He was US minister to Britain (1792–96) and special envoy to Spain (1795–96)
Pindar *n* ?518–?438 BC, Greek lyric poet, noted for his *Epinikia*, odes commemorating victories in the Greek games
pine[1] *n* **1** evergreen coniferous tree **2** its wood ▶ **pine cone** woody cone-shaped fruit of the pine tree
pine[2] Ⓣ *v* **1** (foll. by *for*) feel great longing (for) **2** become thin and ill through grief etc.
pineal gland [**pin**-ee-al] *n* small cone-shaped gland at the base of the brain
pineapple *n* large tropical fruit with juicy yellow flesh and a hard skin
ping *v, n* (make) a short high-pitched sound ▶ **pinger** *n* device, esp. a timer, that makes a pinging sound
Ping-Pong *n* ® table tennis
pinion[1] Ⓣ *n* **1** bird's wing ▷ *v* **2** immobilize (someone) by tying or holding his or her arms
pinion[2] *n* small cogwheel
pink Ⓣ *n* **1** pale reddish colour **2** fragrant garden plant ▷ *adj* **3** of the colour pink ▷ *v* **4** (of an engine) make a metallic noise because not working properly, knock ▶ **in the pink** in good health
pinking shears *pl n* scissors with a serrated edge that give a wavy edge to material to prevent fraying
pinnacle Ⓣ *n* **1** highest point of success etc. **2** mountain peak **3** small slender spire
Pinochet, Pinochet Ugarte *n* **Augusto.** 1915–2006, Chilean general and statesman; president of Chile (1974–90) following his overthrow of Allende (1973): charged (2001) with murder and kidnapping but found unfit to stand trial
pint *n* liquid measure, half a quart, ⅛ gallon (.568 litre)
Pinyin *n* system for representing Chinese in Roman letters
pioneer Ⓣ *n* **1** explorer or early settler of a new country **2** originator or developer of something new ▷ *v* **3** be the pioneer or leader of
pious Ⓣ *adj* deeply religious, devout
pip[1] *n* small seed in a fruit
pip[2] *n* **1** high-pitched sound used as a time signal on radio **2** *informal* star on a junior army officer's shoulder showing rank
pip[3] *n* **give someone the pip** *slang* annoy someone
pipe Ⓣ *n* **1** tube for conveying liquid or gas **2** tube with a small bowl at the end for smoking tobacco **3** tubular musical instrument **pipes 4** bagpipes ▷ *v* **5** play on a pipe **6** utter in a shrill tone **7** convey by pipe **8** decorate with piping
▶ **piper** *n* player on a pipe or bagpipes
▶ **piping** *n* **1** system of pipes **2** decoration of icing on a cake etc. **3** fancy edging on clothes
▶ **piped music** recorded music played as background music in public places
▶ **pipe down** *v informal* stop talking
▶ **pipe dream** fanciful impossible plan etc.
▶ **pipeline** *n* **1** long pipe for transporting oil, water, etc. **2** means of communication
▶ **in the pipeline** in preparation
▶ **pipe up** *v* speak suddenly or shrilly
pipette *n* slender glass tube used to transfer or measure fluids
pipit *n* small brownish bird
pippin *n* type of eating apple
piquant Ⓣ [**pee**-kant] *adj* **1** having a pleasant spicy taste **2** mentally stimulating **piquancy** *n*

P

THESAURUS

pine *v* **1** (often with *for*) = **long**, desire, ache, crave, hanker, eat one's heart out over, hunger for, thirst for, wish for, yearn for **2** = **waste**, decline, sicken, fade, languish
pinion *v* = **immobilize**, tie, chain, bind, shackle, fasten, fetter, manacle
pink *adj* = **rosy**, salmon, rose, flushed, reddish, roseate
pinnacle *n* = **peak**, top, summit, crown, height, crest, apex, zenith, vertex
pinpoint *v* = **identify**, locate, define, distinguish
pioneer *n* **1** = **settler**, explorer, colonist **2** = **founder**, leader, developer, innovator, trailblazer ▶ *v* **3** = **develop**, start, create, discover, establish, institute, originate, invent, initiate, instigate, show the way
pious *adj* = **religious**, holy, devout, righteous, God-fearing, godly, reverent, saintly
pipe *n* **1** = **tube**, line, main, pipeline, passage, hose, duct, conduit ▶ *v* **2** = **whistle**, play, sound, sing, peep, cheep, warble **3** = **convey**, conduct, channel
▷ **pipe down** (*Informal*) = **be quiet**, hush, hold one's tongue, quieten down, shush, shut one's mouth, shut up (*informal*)
pipeline *n* = **tube**, pipe, passage, duct, conduit
piquant *adj* **1** = **spicy**, sharp, tart, tangy, pungent, zesty, biting, savory **2** = **interesting**, provocative,

DICTIONARY

pique Ⓣ [**peek**] *n* **1** feeling of hurt pride, baffled curiosity, or resentment ▷ *v* **2** hurt the pride of **3** arouse (curiosity)
piqué [**pee**-kay] *n* stiff ribbed cotton fabric
piquet [pik-**ket**] *n* card game for two
Piranesi *n* **Giambattista**. 1720–78, Italian etcher and architect: etchings include *Imaginary Prisons* and *Views of Rome*
piranha *n* small fierce freshwater fish of tropical America
pirate Ⓣ *n* **1** sea robber **2** person who illegally publishes or sells work owned by someone else **3** person or company that broadcasts illegally ▷ *v* **4** sell or reproduce (artistic work etc.) illegally **piracy** *n* **piratical** *adj*
pirouette Ⓣ *v*, *n* (make) a spinning turn balanced on the toes of one foot
Pisano *n* **Andrea**, real name *Andrea de Pontedera*. ?1290–1348, Italian sculptor and architect, noted for his bronze reliefs on the door of the baptistry in Florence
piscatorial *adj* of fishing or fishes
Pisistratus *n* ?600–527 BC, tyrant of Athens: he established himself in firm control of the city following his defeat of his aristocratic rivals at Pallene (546)
piss *taboo* ▷ *v* **1** urinate ▷ *n* **2** act of urinating **3** urine
Pissarro *n* **Camille**. 1830–1903, French impressionist painter, esp. of landscapes
pistachio *n*, *pl* **-os** edible nut of a Mediterranean tree
piste [**peest**] *n* ski slope
pistil *n* seed-bearing part of a flower
pistol *n* short-barrelled handgun
piston *n* cylindrical part in an engine that slides to and fro in a cylinder
pit Ⓣ *n* **1** deep hole in the ground **2** coal mine **3** dent or depression **4** servicing and refuelling area on a motor-racing track **5** same as **orchestra pit** ▷ *v* **6 pitting, pitted** mark with small dents or scars
▶ **pit one's wits against** compete against in a test or contest
▶ **pit bull terrier** strong muscular terrier with a short coat
pitapat *adv* **1** with quick light taps ▷ *n* **2** such taps
pitch[1] Ⓣ *v* **1** throw, hurl **2** set up (a tent) **3** fall headlong **4** (of a ship or plane) move with the front and back going up and down alternately **5** set the level or tone of **6** *baseball* attempt to throw the ball toward home plate so that it passes through the strike zone without being hit by the batter ▷ *n* **7** degree or angle of slope **8** degree of highness or lowness of a (musical) sound **9** place where a street or market trader regularly sells **10** *baseball* instance of pitching **11** *informal* persuasive sales talk
▶ **pitcher** *n* *baseball* player who pitches the ball to the batter
▶ **pitch in** *v* join in enthusiastically
▶ **pitch into** *v* *informal* attack
pitch[2] *n* dark sticky substance obtained from tar
▶ **pitch-black** *or* **pitch-dark** *adj* very dark
pitchblende *n* mineral composed largely of uranium oxide, yielding radium
pitcher *n* large jug with a narrow neck
pitchfork *n* **1** large long-handled fork for lifting hay ▷ *v* **2** thrust abruptly or violently
pitfall Ⓣ *n* hidden difficulty or danger
pith Ⓣ *n* **1** soft white lining of the rind of

P

THESAURUS

sparkling, lively, scintillating, stimulating
pique *n* **1 = resentment**, offence, displeasure, huff, irritation, annoyance, hurt feelings, umbrage, wounded pride ▶ *v* **2 = displease**, get (*informal*), sting, offend, irk, rile, annoy, irritate, affront, nettle **3 = arouse**, spur, excite, stir, stimulate, rouse, whet
piracy *n* **= robbery**, theft, buccaneering, freebooting, stealing
pirate *n* **1 = buccaneer**, rover, raider, corsair, freebooter, marauder **2 = plagiarist**, infringer, plagiarizer ▶ *v* **3 = copy**, appropriate, steal, reproduce, poach, plagiarize
pirouette *See* **spin**
pit *n* **1 = hole**, pothole, chasm • *He lost his footing and began to slide into the pit.* ▶ *v* **2 = scar**, mark, dent, pockmark, indent
See also: **abyss, grave**
pitch *v* **1 = throw**, cast, toss, hurl, lob (*informal*), fling, sling, heave, chuck (*informal*) **2 = set up**, raise, settle, erect, put up **3 = fall**, drop, tumble, dive, topple **4 = toss**, roll, plunge, lurch ▷ **pitch in = help**, contribute, participate, cooperate, chip in (*informal*), do one's bit, join in, lend a hand ▷ **pitch into** (*Informal*) **= attack**, assault, assail, get stuck into (*informal*), tear into (*informal*) ▶ *n* **5 = sports field**, ground, park, field of play **6 = level**, point, summit, degree, height, highest point **7 = slope**, grade, angle, tilt, incline, gradient **8 = tone**, sound, timbre, modulation **9 = sales talk**, patter, spiel (*informal*)
pitch-black *adj* **= dark**, unlit, inky, jet-black, pitch-dark
piteous *adj* **= pathetic**, sad, poignant, heartbreaking, pitiful, moving, affecting, distressing, harrowing, heart-rending, pitiable, plaintive
pitfall *n* **= danger**, catch, trap, difficulty, hazard, snag, peril, drawback
pith *n* **= essence**, point, heart, core, kernel,

DICTIONARY

oranges etc. **2** soft tissue in the stems of certain plants **3** essential part
▸ **pithy** *adj* short and full of meaning
piton [**peet**-on] *n* metal spike used in climbing to secure a rope
Pitt *n* **1 William**, known as *Pitt the Elder*, 1st Earl of Chatham. 1708–78, British statesman. He was first minister (1756–57; 1757–61; 1766–68) and achieved British victory in the Seven Years' War (1756–63) **2** his son **William**, known as *Pitt the Younger*. 1759–1806, British statesman. As prime minister (1783–1801; 1804–06), he carried through important fiscal and tariff reforms. From 1793, his attention was focused on the wars with revolutionary and Napoleonic France
pitta bread *n* flat, slightly leavened bread orig. from the Middle East
pittance Ⓣ *n* very small allowance of money
pitter-patter *n* **1** sound of light rapid taps or pats, as of raindrops ▹ *v* **2** make a such sound
pituitary *n, pl* **-taries** gland at the base of the brain, that helps to control growth (Also **pituitary gland**)
pity *n, pl* **-ties 1** sympathy or sorrow for others' suffering **2** regrettable fact ▹ *v* **pitying, pitied 3** feel pity for
▸ **piteous** *or* **pitiable** *adj* arousing pity
▸ **pitiful** *adj* **1** arousing pity **2** woeful, contemptible **pitifully** *adv*
▸ **pitiless** *adj* feeling no pity, hard, merciless
Pius II *n* pen name *Aeneas Silvius*, original name *Enea Silvio de' Piccolomini*. 1405–64, Italian ecclesiastic, humanist, poet, and historian; pope (1458–64)
pivot Ⓣ *n* **1** central shaft on which something turns ▹ *v* **2** provide with or turn on a pivot
▸ **pivotal** *adj* of crucial importance
pix *n informal* a plural of **pic**
pixel *n* smallest constituent element of an image, as on a visual display unit
pixie Ⓣ *n* (in folklore) fairy
pizza *n* flat disc of dough covered with a wide variety of savoury toppings and baked
pizzazz *n informal* attractive combination of energy and style
pizzicato [pit-see-**kah**-toe] *adv music* played by plucking the string of a violin etc. with the finger
pl plural
placard Ⓣ *n* large board with a slogan on it that is carried or displayed in public
placate Ⓣ *v* make (someone) stop feeling angry or upset **placatory** *adj*
place Ⓣ *n* **1** particular part of an area or space **2** particular town, building, etc. **3** position or point reached **4** usual position **5** duty or right **6** position of employment **7** seat or space ▹ *v* **8** put in a particular place **9** identify, put in context **10** make (an order, bet, etc.)
▸ **be placed** (of a competitor in a race) be among the first three
▸ **take place** happen, occur
▸ **place-kick** *n football* kick in which the ball is held in place on the field before it is kicked
▸ **place-kicker** *n football* player who specializes in place-kicks
placebo [plas-**see**-bo] *n, pl* **-bos, -boes**

P

THESAURUS

crux, gist, nub, quintessence, salient point
pithy *adj* = **succinct**, short, brief, pointed, terse, concise, cogent, epigrammatic, laconic, to the point, trenchant
pitiful *adj* **1** = **pathetic**, sad, heartbreaking, grievous, wretched, distressing, harrowing, heart-rending, piteous, pitiable **2** = **contemptible**, low, base, mean, sorry, miserable, lousy (*slang*), paltry, shabby, abject
pitiless *adj* = **merciless**, cruel, relentless, ruthless, callous, heartless, cold-blooded, implacable, cold-hearted, hardhearted, unmerciful
pittance *n* = **slave wages**, drop, mite, trifle, chicken feed (*slang*), peanuts (*slang*)
pity *v* **1** = **feel sorry for**, feel for, sympathize with • *I don't know whether to hate or pity him.* ▸ *n* **2** = **compassion**, charity, understanding, sympathy, mercy, kindness • *She saw no pity in their faces.* **3** = **shame**, crime, crying shame • *It's a pity they can't all have the same opportunities.*
pivot *n* **1** = **axis**, swivel, spindle, axle, fulcrum **2** = **centre**, heart, hub, hinge, kingpin ▸ *v* **3** = **turn**, spin, revolve, rotate, twirl, swivel **4** = **rely**, hang, depend, hinge, be contingent
pivotal *adj* = **crucial**, central, critical, decisive, vital
pixie *n* = **elf**, brownie, fairy, sprite
placard *n* = **notice**, bill, poster, advertisement
placate *v* = **calm**, appease, soothe, pacify, assuage, humour, mollify, conciliate, de-stress, propitiate
place *n* **1** = **spot**, point, site, area, position, location • *The pain is always in the same place.* **2** = **region**, quarter, district, neighbourhood, locale, vicinity, locality **3** = **rank**, station, position, status, grade **4** = **space**, room, accommodation **5** = **home**, house, property, pad (*slang, dated*), residence, dwelling, abode, domicile **6** = **duty**, charge, right, concern, role, responsibility, affair, function, prerogative **7** = **job**, post, position, appointment, employment ▹ **take place**

DICTIONARY

sugar pill etc. given to an unsuspecting patient as an active drug
placenta [plass-**ent**-a] *n, pl* **-tas, -tae** organ formed in the womb during pregnancy, providing nutrients for the fetus **placental** *adj*
placid Ⓣ *adj* calm, not easily excited or upset **placidity** *n*
placket *n* opening at the top of a skirt etc. fastened with buttons or a zip
plagiarize Ⓣ [**play**-jer-ize] *v* steal ideas, passages, etc. from (someone else's work) and present them as one's own **plagiarism** *n*
plague Ⓣ *n* **1** fast-spreading fatal disease **2** *hist* bubonic plague **3** widespread infestation ▷ *v* **plaguing, plagued 4** trouble or annoy continually
plaice *n* edible European flatfish
plaid *n* **1** long piece of tartan cloth worn as part of Highland dress **2** tartan cloth or pattern
plain Ⓣ *adj* **1** easy to see or understand **2** expressed honestly and clearly **3** without decoration or pattern **4** simple, ordinary ▷ *n* **5** large stretch of level country **plainly** *adv* **plainness** *n*
▸ **plain clothes** ordinary clothes, as opposed to uniform
▸ **plain sailing** easy progress
▸ **plain speaking** saying exactly what one thinks
plainsong *n* unaccompanied singing, esp. in a medieval church
plaintiff *n* person who sues in a court of law
plaintive Ⓣ *adj* sad, mournful **plaintively** *adv*
plait [**platt**] *v* **1** intertwine separate strands to form one ropelike length ▷ *n* **2** length of hair that has been plaited
plan Ⓣ *n* **1** way thought out to do or achieve something **2** diagram showing the layout or design of something ▷ *v* **planning, planned 3** arrange beforehand **4** make a diagram of
▸ **Plan B** second tactic to be used when the first fails
Planck *n* **Max** (**Karl Ernst Ludwig**). 1858–1947, German physicist who first formulated the quantum theory (1900): Nobel prize for physics 1918
plane[1] Ⓣ *n* **1** an aircraft ▷ *v* **2** (of a boat) rise and partly skim over water
plane[2] Ⓣ *n* **1** *math* flat surface **2** level of attainment etc. **3** tool for smoothing wood ▷ *v* **4** smooth (wood) with a plane ▷ *adj* **5** perfectly flat or level
plane[3] *n* tree with broad leaves

THESAURUS

= **happen**, occur, come about, go on • *The meeting took place on Thursday.* ▸ *v* **8 = put**, plant, position, locate, deposit, situate • *Chairs were placed in rows for the parents.* **9 = classify**, group, order, class, rank, sort, arrange, grade **10 = identify**, know, remember, recognize, put one's finger on **11 = assign**, give, charge, appoint, allocate, entrust
See also: **fit, insert, lay, scene, set**
placed *See* **located**
placid *adj* = **calm**, tranquil, serene, collected, composed, equable, even-tempered, imperturbable, unexcitable, unruffled, untroubled
plagiarism *n* = **copying**, borrowing, theft, infringement, piracy
plagiarize *v* = **copy**, borrow, lift (*informal*), steal, pirate
plague *n* **1 = disease**, infection, epidemic, pestilence **2 = affliction**, evil, curse, scourge, blight, torment, bane ▸ *v* **3 = pester**, trouble, torture, bother, harass, annoy, hassle (*informal*), tease, torment, vex, badger, harry
plain *adj* **1 = simple**, bare, stark, austere, bare-bones, spartan • *It was a plain, grey stone house.* OPPOSITE: fancy **2 = obvious**, clear, evident, distinct, unmistakable, comprehensible • *It was plain to him that I was bored.* **3 = honest**, open, direct, outspoken, blunt, straightforward, frank, candid, upfront (*informal*), downright, forthright **4 = ugly**, unattractive, dumpy (*informal*), frowzy, homely, ill-favoured, no oil painting (*informal*), not beautiful, unlovely, unprepossessing **5 = ordinary**, common, simple, everyday, commonplace, unaffected, unpretentious ▸ *n* **6 = flatland**, prairie, plateau, grassland, steppe, veld
See also: **blank, manifest, straight, visible**
plain-spoken *adj* = **blunt**, direct, outspoken, frank, candid, downright, forthright
plaintive *adj* = **sorrowful**, sad, pathetic, mournful, pitiful, heart-rending, piteous
plan *n* **1 = scheme**, system, proposal, strategy, method, gameplan • *a plan to merge the two teams* **2 = diagram**, blueprint, layout, scale drawing • *a detailed plan of the science project* ▸ *v* **3 = devise**, design, draft, arrange, formulate • *when we plan road construction* **4 = intend**, mean, aim, propose, purpose
See also: **contemplate, course, idea, organize, pattern, plot, suggestion**
plane *n* **1 = airplane**, jet, aircraft **2 = flat surface**, level surface **3 = level**, condition, position, degree ▸ *adj* **4 = level**, even, regular, flat, smooth, horizontal ▸ *v* **5 = skim**, skate, sail, glide

DICTIONARY

planet ⓣ *n* large body in space that revolves round the sun or another star **planetary** *adj*
planetarium *n, pl* **-iums, -ia** building where the movements of the stars, planets, etc. are shown by projecting lights on the inside of a dome
plangent [**plan**-jent] *adj* (of sounds) mournful and resounding
plank *n* long flat piece of sawn timber
plankton *n* minute animals and plants floating in the surface water of a sea or lake
plant ⓣ *n* **1** living organism that grows in the ground and has no power to move **2** equipment or machinery used in industrial processes **3** factory or other industrial premises ▷ *v* **4** put in the ground to grow **5** place firmly in position **6** *informal* hide (stolen goods etc.) on a person to make him or her seem guilty **7** *informal* put (a person) secretly in an organization to spy
▸ **planter** *n* **1** ornamental pot for house plants **2** owner of a plantation
plantain[1] *n* low-growing wild plant with broad leaves
plantain[2] *n* tropical fruit like a green banana
plantation *n* **1** estate for the cultivation of tea, tobacco, etc. **2** wood of cultivated trees
Plante *n* **Jacques**. 1929–1986, Canadian hockey player. A goaltender, he won five consecutive Stanley Cups with the Montreal Canadiens in the 1950s; he pioneered the use of the goaltender mask
plaque *n* **1** inscribed commemorative stone or metal plate fixed to a wall **2** filmy deposit on teeth that causes decay
plasma *n* clear liquid part of blood
▸ **plasma screen** type of high-resolution flat screen on a television or visual display unit
plaster ⓣ *n* **1** mixture of lime, sand, etc. for coating walls **2** adhesive strip of material for dressing cuts etc. ▷ *v* **3** cover with plaster **4** coat thickly
▸ **plastered** *adj slang* drunk
▸ **plaster of Paris** white powder which dries to form a hard solid when mixed with water, used for sculptures and casts for broken limbs
plastic ⓣ *n* **1** synthetic material that can be moulded when soft but sets in a hard long-lasting shape ▷ *adj* **2** made of plastic **3** easily moulded, pliant
▸ **plasticity** *n* ability to be moulded
▸ **plastic bullet** solid PVC cylinder fired by police in riot control
▸ **plastic surgery** repair or reconstruction of missing or malformed parts of the body for medical or cosmetic reasons
Plasticine *n* ® soft coloured modelling material used esp. by children
plate ⓣ *n* **1** shallow round dish for holding food **2** flat thin sheet of metal, glass, etc. **3** thin coating of metal on another metal **4** dishes or cutlery made of gold or silver **5** illustration, usu. on fine quality paper, in a book **6** *baseball* same as **home plate** ▷ *v* **7** cover with a thin coating of gold, silver, or other metal **plateful** *n*
▸ **plate glass** kind of thick glass used for mirrors and windows
▸ **plate tectonics** study of the structure of the earth's crust, esp. the movement of layers of rocks
plateau ⓣ *n, pl* **-teaus, -teaux 1** area of level high land **2** stage when there is no change or development
platelet *n* minute particle occurring in blood of vertebrates and involved in clotting of blood
platen *n* **1** roller of a typewriter, against which the paper is held **2** plate in a printing press by which the paper is pressed against the type
platform ⓣ *n* **1** raised floor for speakers **2** raised area in a station from which passengers board trains **3** programme of a political party **4** structure in the sea which

THESAURUS

planet *See* **earth**
planned *See* **calculated**
planning *See* **organization**
plant *n* **1 = flower**, vegetable, weed, bush, herb, shrub **2 = factory**, yard, shop, mill, foundry, works **3 = machinery**, equipment, gear, apparatus ▸ *v* **4 = sow**, seed, transplant, scatter, put in the ground **5 = place**, set, put, fix, establish, found, insert
plaster *n* **1 = mortar**, stucco, gypsum, plaster of Paris **2** (*Brit*) **= bandage**, dressing, adhesive plaster, Band-Aid (*trademark*), sticking plaster ▸ *v* **3 = cover**, spread, coat, smear, overlay, daub
plastic *adj* **1 = manageable**, responsive, receptive, docile, malleable, pliable, tractable **2 = pliant**, soft, flexible, supple, ductile, mouldable, pliable
plate *n* **1 = platter**, dish, trencher (*archaic*) **2 = helping**, course, portion, dish, serving **3 = layer**, panel, sheet, slab **4 = illustration**, print, lithograph ▸ *v* **5 = coat**, cover, laminate, overlay, gild
plateau *n* **1 = upland**, table, highland, tableland **2 = levelling off**, level, stage, stability
platform *n* **1 = stage**, stand, podium, dais, rostrum **2 = policy**, program, principle, objective *or* objectives, manifesto, party line

DICTIONARY

holds machinery, stores, etc. for drilling an oil well

Plath *n* **Sylvia**. 1932–63, US poet living in England. She wrote two volumes of verse, *The Colossus* (1960) and *Ariel* (1965), and a novel, *The Bell Jar* (1963): she was married to Ted Hughes

platinum *n* very valuable silvery-white metal

▶ **platinum blonde** woman with silvery-blonde hair

platitude Ⓣ *n* remark that is true but not interesting or original. **platitudinous** *adj*

Plato *n* ?427–?347 BC, Greek philosopher: with his teacher Socrates and his pupil Aristotle, he is regarded as the initiator of western philosophy. His influential theory of ideas, which makes a distinction between objects of sense perception and the universal ideas or forms of which they are an expression, is formulated in such dialogues as *Phaedo*, *Symposium*, and *The Republic*. Other works include *The Apology* and *Laws*

platonic *adj* friendly or affectionate but not sexual

platoon Ⓣ *n* **1** subunit of a company of soldiers **2** *sports* pair of players on a team who take turns playing in the same position ▷ *v* **3** be part of a platoon on a sports team

platteland *n S Afr* rural district

platter Ⓣ *n* large dish

platypus *n* Aust. egg-laying amphibious mammal, with dense fur, webbed feet, and a ducklike bill (Also **duck-billed platypus**)

plaudits Ⓣ *pl n* expressions of approval

plausible Ⓣ *adj* **1** apparently true or reasonable **2** persuasive but insincere **plausibly** *adv* **plausibility** *n*

play Ⓣ *v* **1** occupy oneself in (a game or recreation) **2** compete against in a game or sport **3** fulfil (a particular role) in a team game: *he plays in the defence* **4** behave carelessly **5** act (a part) on the stage **6** perform (music) on an instrument **7** cause (a radio, record player, etc.) to give out sound **8** move lightly or irregularly, flicker ▷ *n* **9** story performed on stage or broadcast **10** activities children take part in for amusement **11** playing of a game **12** conduct: *fair play* **13** (scope for) freedom of movement **player** *n*

▶ **playful** *adj* lively

▶ **play back** *v* listen to or watch (something recorded)

▶ **playboy** *n* rich man who lives only for pleasure

▶ **play down** *v* minimize the importance of

▶ **playgroup** *n* regular meeting of very young children for supervised play

▶ **playhouse** *n* theatre

▶ **playing card** one of a set of 52 cards used in card games

▶ **playing fields** extensive piece of ground for open-air games

▶ **play off** *v* set (two people) against each other for one's own ends

▶ **play on** *v* exploit or encourage (someone's sympathy or weakness)

▶ **playschool** *n* nursery group for young children

▶ **PlayStation** *n* ® type of video games console

THESAURUS

platitude *n* = **cliché**, commonplace, truism, banality

platoon *n* = **squad**, company, team, group, patrol, outfit (*informal*), squadron

platter *n* = **plate**, dish, tray, salver, trencher (*archaic*)

plaudits *pl n* = **praise**, approval, applause, acclaim, acclamation, approbation

plausible *adj* **1** = **believable**, likely, possible, reasonable, credible, probable, conceivable, persuasive, tenable **2** = **glib**, smooth, smooth-talking, smooth-tongued, specious

play *v* **1** = **amuse oneself**, frolic, entertain oneself, have fun • *The child was playing with her teddy bear.* **2** = **take part**, compete, participate, take on, vie with • *I was playing cards with my friends.* **3** = **act**, represent, perform, portray, act the part of ▷ **play a part** *See* **appear** ▷ **play a part in** *See* **take part in** ▷ **play a trick on** *See* **dupe** ▷ **play down** = **minimize**, gloss over, make light of, make little of, underrate, underplay ▷ **play on** = **take advantage of**, abuse, exploit, capitalize on, impose on, trade on ▷ **play the part of** *See* **act** ▷ **play up** = **emphasize**, stress, highlight, underline, accentuate ▶ *n* **4** = **drama**, show, comedy, tragedy • *Shakespeare's most popular play* **5** = **amusement**, game, sport, fun, entertainment, diversion, recreation, pastime **6** = **fun**, sport, prank, jest, humour, lark (*informal*), joking **7** = **space**, room, margin, scope, latitude, leeway, elbowroom *See also*: **appear**

playboy *n* = **womanizer**, ladies' man, rake, philanderer, roué

player *n* **1** = **sportsman** *or* **sportswoman**, participant, competitor, contestant **2** = **musician**, artist, performer, virtuoso, instrumentalist **3** = **performer**, actor *or* actress, entertainer, Thespian, trouper

playful *adj* = **lively**, spirited, merry, mischievous, impish, vivacious, frisky, sportive, sprightly

playmate *n* = **friend**, comrade, companion, pal (*informal*), chum (*informal*), playfellow

plaything *n* = **toy**, game, amusement, pastime, trifle

DICTIONARY

▶ **plaything** *n* toy
▶ **play up** *v* **1** cause trouble **2** give prominence to
▶ **playwright** *n* author of plays
Player *n* **Gary**. born 1935, South African professional golfer: won the British Open Championship (1959; 1968; 1974) and the US Open Championship (1965)
plaza *n* **1** modern shopping complex **2** open space or square
PLC, plc Public Limited Company
plea Ⓣ *n* **1** serious or urgent request, entreaty **2** statement of a prisoner or defendant **3** excuse
plead Ⓣ *v* **1** ask urgently or with deep feeling **2** give as an excuse **3** *law* declare oneself to be guilty or innocent of a charge made against one
pleasant Ⓣ *adj* pleasing, enjoyable **pleasantly** *adv*
▶ **pleasantry** *n* polite or joking remark
please Ⓣ *adv* **1** polite word of request ▷ *v* **2** give pleasure or satisfaction to **pleased** *adj*
▶ **please oneself** do as one likes
▶ **pleasing** *adj* giving pleasure or satisfaction
pleasure Ⓣ *n* **1** feeling of happiness and satisfaction **2** something that causes this
▶ **pleasurable** *adj* giving pleasure **pleasurably** *adv*
pleat Ⓣ *n* **1** fold made by doubling material back on itself ▷ *v* **2** arrange (material) in pleats
plebeian Ⓣ [pleb-**ee**-an] *adj* **1** of the lower social classes **2** vulgar or rough ▷ *n* **3** Also **pleb** member of the lower social classes
plebiscite Ⓣ [**pleb**-iss-ite] *n* decision by direct voting of the people of a country
plectrum *n, pl* **-trums, -tra** small implement for plucking the strings of a guitar etc.
pledge Ⓣ *n* **1** solemn promise **2** something valuable given as a guarantee that a promise will be kept or a debt paid ▷ *v* **3** promise solemnly **4** bind by or as if by a pledge: *pledge to secrecy*
plenary *adj* (of a meeting) attended by all members
plenipotentiary *n, pl* **-aries 1** diplomat or representative having full powers ▷ *adj* **2** having full powers
plenitude *n* completeness, abundance
plenteous *adj* plentiful
plentiful Ⓣ *adj* existing in large amounts or numbers **plentifully** *adv*
plenty Ⓣ *n* **1** large amount or number **2** quite enough
pleonasm *n* use of more words than necessary **pleonastic** *adj*
plethora Ⓣ *n* oversupply
pleurisy *n* inflammation of the membrane

THESAURUS

plea *n* **1 = appeal**, request, suit, prayer, petition, entreaty, intercession, supplication **2 = excuse**, explanation, defence, justification
plead *v* **= beg**, ask, appeal, implore, beseech (*formal*) • *I pleaded with them to come home.* ▷ **plead with** *See* **implore**
See also: **press, urge**
pleasant *adj* **1 = enjoyable**, nice, lovely, delightful, agreeable, pleasurable • *a pleasant little apartment* OPPOSITE: unpleasant **2 = friendly**, nice, charming, likable, affable, amiable • *an extremely pleasant and obliging person* OPPOSITE: unpleasant
See also: **warm**
pleasantry *n* **= joke**, quip, jest, banter, badinage, witticism
please *v* **= delight**, charm, entertain, amuse • *I was tidying my bedroom to please my parents.*
See also: **appeal, satisfy, suit**
pleased *adj* **= happy**, glad, delighted, satisfied, contented • *I'm pleased with the way things have been going.*
See also: **proud**
pleasing *adj* **= enjoyable**, charming, engaging, delightful, likable *or* likeable, agreeable, pleasurable, gratifying, satisfying
pleasurable *adj* **= enjoyable**, good, fun, nice, lovely, pleasant, delightful, agreeable
pleasure *n* **= enjoyment**, happiness, joy, satisfaction, amusement • *Almost everybody takes pleasure in eating.*
See also: **delight, entertainment, fun, pride**
pleat *See* **fold**
plebeian *adj* **1 = common**, low, base, working-class, vulgar, coarse, unrefined, lower-class, proletarian, uncultivated ▶ *n* **2 = commoner**, common man, man in the street, pleb, proletarian
plebiscite *See* **vote**
pledge *n* **1 = promise**, word, vow, warrant, assurance, oath, undertaking, covenant **2 = guarantee**, security, bail, deposit, collateral, pawn, surety ▶ *v* **3 = promise**, contract, vow, engage, swear, give one's oath, give one's word
plentiful *adj* **= abundant**, ample, infinite, bountiful, copious • *a plentiful supply* OPPOSITE: scarce
See also: **generous, handsome, rich**
plenty *n* **1 = lots**, enough, great deal, loads (*informal*), plethora • *There's plenty to go around.* **2 = abundance**, wealth, prosperity, fertility, affluence, copiousness, fruitfulness, plenitude, profusion ▷ **plenty of** *See* **ample**
See also: **many**
plethora *n* **= excess**, surplus, glut, profusion, overabundance, superabundance, surfeit

DICTIONARY

lining the chest and covering the lungs

pliable ⓣ *adj* **1** easily bent **2** easily influenced **pliability** *n*

pliant ⓣ *adj* pliable **pliancy** *n*

pliers *pl n* tool with hinged arms and jaws for gripping

plight[1] ⓣ *n* difficult or dangerous situation

plight[2] *v* **plight one's troth** *old-fashioned* promise to marry

Plimsoll line *n* mark on a ship showing the level water should reach when the ship is fully loaded

plinth *n* slab forming the base of a column etc.

Pliny *n* **1** known as *Pliny the Elder*, Latin name *Gaius Plinius Secundus*. 23–79 AD, Roman writer, the author of the encyclopedic *Natural History* (77) **2** his nephew, known as *Pliny the Younger*, Latin name *Gaius Plinius Caecilius Secundus*. ?62–?113 AD, Roman writer and administrator, noted for his letters

PLO Palestine Liberation Organization

plod ⓣ *v* **plodding, plodded 1** walk with slow heavy steps **2** work slowly but determinedly **plodder** *n*

plonk[1] *v* put (something) down heavily and carelessly

plonk[2] *n informal* cheap inferior wine

plop *n* **1** sound of an object falling into water without a splash ▷ *v* **plopping, plopped 2** make this sound

plot[1] ⓣ *n* **1** secret plan to do something illegal or wrong **2** sequence of events on which a film, novel, etc. is based ▷ *v* **plotting, plotted 3** plan secretly, conspire **4** mark the position or course of (a ship or aircraft) on a map **5** mark and join up (points on a graph)

plot[2] ⓣ *n* small piece of land

Plotinus *n* ?205–?270 AD, Roman Neo-Platonist philosopher, born in Egypt

plover *n* shore bird with a straight bill and long pointed wings

plow, plough ⓣ *n* **1** agricultural tool for turning over soil ▷ *v* **2** turn over (earth) with a plow **3** move or work through slowly and laboriously **plowman** *or* **ploughman** *n*

▸ **plowshare** *or* **ploughshare** *n* blade of a plow

▸ **plow back** reinvest (money)

ploy ⓣ *n* manoeuvre designed to gain an advantage

pluck ⓣ *v* **1** pull or pick off **2** pull out the feathers of (a bird for cooking) **3** sound the strings of (a guitar etc.) with the fingers or a plectrum ▷ *n* **4** courage

▸ **plucky** *adj* brave **pluckily** *adv*

▸ **pluck up** *v* summon up (courage)

plug ⓣ *n* **1** thing fitting into and filling a hole **2** device connecting an appliance to an electricity supply **3** *informal* favourable mention of a product etc., designed to encourage people to buy it ▷ *v* **plugging, plugged 4** block or seal (a hole or gap) with a plug **5** *informal* advertise (a product etc.) by constant repetition

▸ **plug away** *v informal* work steadily

▸ **plugger** *n* **1** person or thing that plugs **2** *slang* person who works hard in an unspectacular way

▸ **plug in** *v* connect (an electrical appliance) to a power source by pushing a plug into a socket

P

THESAURUS

pliable *adj* **1 = flexible**, plastic, supple, bendable, bendy, malleable, pliant **2 = easily led**, susceptible, responsive, receptive, compliant, impressionable, docile, adaptable, pliant, tractable

pliant *adj* **1 = flexible**, plastic, supple, bendable, bendy, pliable **2 = easily led**, susceptible, compliant, impressionable, biddable, pliable, tractable

plight *n* **= difficulty**, state, condition, situation, spot (*informal*), trouble, jam (*informal*), scrape (*informal*), predicament

plod *v* **1 = trudge**, lumber, drag, clump, slog, tramp **2 = slog**, grind (*informal*), labour, persevere, plow through, toil, soldier on

plot[1] *n* **1 = scheme**, plan, conspiracy, intrigue • *the plot to assassinate the dictator* **2 = story**, scenario, narrative, storyline • *This book has a ludicrously complicated plot.* ▸ *v* **3 = scheme**, plan, conspire, hatch • *Prosecutors allege that the defendants plotted to overthrow the government.* **4 = devise**, design, lay, conceive, hatch, concoct, contrive, cook up (*informal*) **5 = chart**, mark, locate, map, outline, calculate

plot[2] *n* **= patch**, area, lot, ground, tract, parcel, allotment

plow, plough *v* **1 = turn over**, dig, till, cultivate **2** (usually with *through*) **= push**, cut, drive, press, plunge, forge, wade

ploy *n* **= tactic**, move, device, trick, scheme, dodge, ruse, maneuver, stratagem, wile

pluck *v* **1 = pull out** *or* **pull off**, pick, gather, harvest **2 = tug**, catch, clutch, yank, snatch, tweak, jerk, pull at **3 = strum**, pick, finger, twang ▸ *n* **4 = courage**, backbone, boldness, nerve, grit, bravery, guts (*informal*)

plucky *adj* **= courageous**, game, brave, bold, daring, gutsy (*slang*), intrepid

plug *n* **1 = stopper**, cork • *She put the plug in the sink.* **2** (*Informal*) **= mention**, push, publicity, advertisement, hype ▸ *v* **3 = seal**, block, fill, stop (up) • *working to plug a major oil leak* **4** (*Informal*) **= mention**, push, promote, advertise, hype, publicize, build up

DICTIONARY

plum Ⓣ *n* **1** oval usu. dark red fruit with a stone in the middle ▷ *adj* **2** dark purplish-red **3** very desirable
plumage *n* bird's feathers
plumb Ⓣ *v* **1** understand (something obscure) **2** test with a plumb line ▷ *adv* **3** exactly
▶ **plumb the depths of** experience the worst extremes of (an unpleasant quality or emotion)
▶ **plumber** *n* person who fits and repairs pipes and fixtures for water and drainage systems
▶ **plumbing** *n* pipes and fixtures used in water and drainage systems
▶ **plumb in** *v* connect (an appliance such as a washing machine) to a water supply
▶ **plumb line** string with a weight at the end, used to test the depth of water or to test whether something is vertical
plume Ⓣ *n* feather, esp. one worn as an ornament
▶ **plume oneself on** be proud of oneself because of
Plummer *n* **Christopher.** born 1929, Canadian film, TV, and stage actor. His films include *The Sound of Music* (1965), *Waterloo* (1970), and *The Insider* (1999)
plummet Ⓣ *v* **-meting, -meted** plunge downward
plump[1] Ⓣ *adj* moderately or attractively fat
plumpness *n*
▶ **plump up** *v* make (a pillow) fuller or rounded
plump[2] *v* **1** sit or fall heavily and suddenly ▷ *adv* **2** suddenly and heavily **3** directly
▶ **plump for** *v* choose, vote only for
plunder Ⓣ *v* **1** take by force, esp. in time of war ▷ *n* **2** things plundered, spoils
plunge Ⓣ *v* **1** put or throw forcibly or suddenly (into) ▷ *n* **2** plunging, dive
▶ **take the plunge** *informal* **1** embark on a risky enterprise **2** get married
▶ **plunger** *n* rubber suction cup used to clear blocked pipes
▶ **plunging** *adj* (of the neckline of a dress) cut low so as to show the top of the breasts
▶ **plunge into** *v* become deeply involved in
plunk *v* pluck the strings of (a banjo etc.) to produce a twanging sound
pluperfect *adj, n grammar* (tense) expressing action completed before a past time, such as *had gone* in *his wife had gone already*
plural *adj* **1** of or consisting of more than one ▷ *n* **2** a word in its plural form
pluralism *n* existence and toleration of a variety of peoples, opinions, etc. in a society
pluralist *n* **pluralistic** *adj*
plus Ⓣ *prep* **1** with the addition of: usu. indicated by the sign (+) ▷ *adj* **2** more than zero or the number already mentioned **3** positive **4** advantageous ▷ *n* **5** plus sign **6** advantage
▶ **plus-minus** *n hockey* statistic calculated by adding or subtracting one point for every even-strength goal scored respectively by or against a given player's team while that player is on the ice
plus fours *pl n* trousers gathered in at the knee
plush Ⓣ *n* **1** fabric with long velvety pile ▷ *adj* **2** Also **plushy** luxurious
Plutarch *n* ?46–?120 AD, Greek biographer and philosopher, noted for his *Parallel Lives* of distinguished Greeks and Romans
Pluto *n* **1** Greek god of the underworld **2** farthest planet from the sun
plutocrat *n* person who is powerful because of being very rich **plutocratic** *adj*
plutonium *n* radioactive metallic element used esp. in nuclear reactors and weapons
pluvial *adj* of or caused by the action of rain
ply[1] Ⓣ *v* **plying, plied** **1** work at (a job or trade) **2** use (a tool) **3** (of a ship) travel regularly along or between
▶ **ply with** *v* supply with or subject to persistently
ply[2] *n* thickness of wool, fabric, etc.
plywood *n* board made of thin layers of wood glued together

P

THESAURUS

plum *adj* = **choice**, best, prize, first-class
plumb *v* **1** = **delve**, probe, explore, gauge, unravel, penetrate, fathom, go into ▶ *n* **2** = **weight**, lead, plummet, plumb bob ▶ *adv* **3** = **exactly**, slap, bang, precisely
plume *n* = **feather**, crest, pinion, quill
plummet *v* = **plunge**, fall, crash, tumble, dive, descend, drop down, nose-dive
plump *adj* = **chubby**, fat, beefy, burly, stout • *a plump chicken*
plunder *v* **1** = **loot**, raid, strip, sack, rifle, rob, ransack, pillage ▶ *n* **2** = **loot**, swag (*slang*), prize, booty, pillage, ill-gotten gains, spoils
plunge *v* **1** = **throw**, pitch, cast **2** = **hurtle**, charge, career, jump, rush, tear, dash **3** = **descend**, fall, drop, sink, tumble, dive, dip, plummet, nose-dive ▶ *n* **4** = **dive**, fall, drop, jump, descent
plus *prep* **1** = **and**, with, added to, coupled with ▶ *adj* **2** = **additional**, extra, added, supplementary, add-on ▶ *n* **3** = **advantage**, gain, benefit, extra, asset, bonus, good point
plush *adj* = **luxurious**, rich, luxury, lavish, deluxe, sumptuous, opulent
ply *v* **1** = **work at**, follow, practice, exercise, pursue, carry on **2** = **use**, handle, employ, manipulate, wield

DICTIONARY

pm, PM **1** after noon **2** postmortem
PM prime minister
PMS premenstrual syndrome
PMT premenstrual tension
pneumatic *adj* worked by or inflated with wind or air
pneumonia *n* inflammation of the lungs
PO **1** postal order **2** Post Office
poach[1] Ⓣ *v* **1** catch (animals) illegally on someone else's land **2** encroach on or steal something belonging to someone else
poacher *n*
poach[2] *v* simmer (food) gently in liquid
pocket Ⓣ *n* **1** small bag sewn into clothing for carrying things **2** pouchlike container, esp. for catching balls at the edge of a snooker table **3** isolated or distinct group or area **4** *football* area guarded by blockers from which the quarterback attempts to throw a pass ▷*v* **pocketing, pocketed** **5** put into one's pocket **6** take secretly or dishonestly ▷*adj* **7** small
▶ **in** *or* **out of pocket** having made a profit *or* loss
▶ **pocket money** **1** small regular allowance given to children by parents **2** allowance for small personal expenses
pockmarked *adj* (of the skin) marked with hollow scars where diseased spots have been
pod Ⓣ *n* long narrow seed case of peas, beans, etc.
POD print on demand
podcast *n* **1** audio file similar to a radio broadcast which can be downloaded to a computer, iPod®, etc. ▷*v* **2** create such files and make them available for downloading
podgy *adj* **podgier, podgiest** short and fat
podium Ⓣ *n, pl* **-diums, -dia** small raised platform for a conductor or speaker
Poe *n* **Edgar Allan**. 1809–49, US short-story writer, poet, and critic. Most of his short stories, such as *The Fall of the House of Usher* (1839) and the *Tales of the Grotesque and Arabesque* (1840), are about death, decay, and madness. *The Murders in the Rue Morgue* (1841) is regarded as the first modern detective story
poem Ⓣ *n* imaginative piece of writing in rhythmic lines
poesy *n obsolete* poetry
poet Ⓣ *n* writer of poems
▶ **poet laureate** see **laureate**
▶ **poetaster** *n* would-be or inferior poet
▶ **poetry** *n* **1** poems **2** art of writing poems **3** beautiful or pleasing quality
▶ **poetic** *adj* Also **poetical** of or like poetry
poetically *adv*
▶ **poetic justice** suitable reward or punishment for someone's past actions
po-faced *adj* wearing a disapproving stern expression
pogey *n slang* **1** unemployment insurance **2** dole
pogo stick *n* pole with steps for the feet and a spring at the bottom, so that the user can bounce up, down, and along on it
pogrom *n* organized persecution and massacre
poignant Ⓣ *adj* sharply painful to the feelings **poignancy** *n*
Poincaré *n* **Jules Henri**. 1854–1912, French mathematician, physicist, and philosopher. He made important contributions to the theory of functions and to astronomy and electromagnetic theory
poinsettia *n* Central American shrub widely cultivated for its clusters of scarlet leaves, which resemble petals
point Ⓣ *n* **1** single idea in a discussion, argument, etc. **2** aim or purpose **3** detail or item **4** main or essential aspect

THESAURUS

poach *v* = **infringe**, trespass, encroach, intrude
pocket *n* **1** = **pouch**, bag, sack, compartment, receptacle ▶*v* **2** = **steal**, take, lift (*informal*), appropriate, pilfer, filch, purloin ▶*adj* **3** = **small**, little, portable, compact, miniature, concise, abridged
pod *n*, *v* = **shell**, hull, shuck, husk
podium *n* = **platform**, stage, dais, rostrum
poem *n* = **verse**, song, lyric, ode, rhyme, sonnet
poet *n* = **bard**, lyricist, rhymer, versifier
poetic *adj* = **lyrical**, lyric, elegiac, metrical
poetry *n* = **verse**, rhyme, poems, rhyming
poignancy *n* **1** = **sadness**, feeling, emotion, sentiment, tenderness, pathos **2** = **sharpness**, intensity, bitterness, keenness
poignant *adj* = **moving**, intense, sad, bitter, painful, pathetic, touching, distressing, heart-rending
point *n* **1** = **purpose**, goal, aim, object, intention • *Cutting costs is not the point of the exercise.* **2** = **feature**, attribute, characteristic, side, quality, trait • *Tact was never her strong point.* **3** = **tip**, nib, prong • *the point of a needle* **4** = **essence**, question, heart, import, subject, drift, meaning, thrust, crux, gist, nub, pith **5** = **item**, feature, detail, particular, aspect **6** = **place**, site, stage, position, spot, location **7** = **headland**, head, cape, promontory **8** = **stage**, condition, position, degree, circumstance, extent **9** = **moment**, time, instant, juncture, very minute **10** = **score**, unit, tally ▷ **point of view** = **opinion**, view, idea, approach, thought, feeling, judgment, belief, attitude, viewpoint, sentiment, way of thinking,

DICTIONARY

5 characteristic **6** particular position, stage, or time **7** dot indicating decimals **8** full stop **9** sharp end **10** headland **11** unit for recording a value or score **12** one of the direction marks of a compass **13** electrical socket **points 14** electrical contacts in the distributor of an engine ▷ *v* **15** show the direction or position of something or draw attention to it by extending a finger or other pointed object towards it **16** direct (a gun etc.) towards **17** finish or repair the joints in brickwork with mortar **18** (of a gun dog) show where game is by standing rigidly with the muzzle towards it
▸ **on the point of** very shortly going to
▸ **pointed** *adj* **1** having a sharp end **2** (of a remark) obviously directed at a particular person **pointedly** *adv*
▸ **pointer** *n* **1** helpful hint **2** indicator on a measuring instrument **3** breed of gun dog
▸ **pointless** *adj* meaningless, irrelevant
▸ **point-blank** *adj, adv* **1** fired at a very close target **2** (of a remark or question) direct, blunt
▸ **point duty** policeman's position at a road junction to control traffic
▸ **point guard** *basketball* guard who initiates most of a team's offensive moves
▸ **point of view** way of considering something
▸ **point-to-point** *n* horse race across open country
Point *n* **Steven**. born 1951, Lieutenant Governor of British Columbia (2007–)
poise ⓣ *n* calm dignified manner
▸ **poised** *adj* **1** absolutely ready **2** behaving with or showing poise
poison ⓣ *n* **1** substance that kills or injures when swallowed or absorbed ▷ *v* **2** give poison to **3** have a harmful or evil effect on, spoil **poisoner** *n* **poisonous** *adj*
▸ **poison-pen letter** malicious anonymous letter
Poisson *n* **Siméon Denis**. 1781–1840, French mathematician, noted for his application of mathematical theory to physics, esp. electricity and magnetism
poke ⓣ *v* **1** jab or prod with one's finger, a stick, etc. **2** thrust forward or out ▷ *n* **3** poking
▸ **poke-check** *v hockey* steal the puck from an opponent by holding the stick low and poking with it
▸ **poky** *adj informal* small and cramped
poker[1] *n* metal rod for stirring a fire to make it burn more brightly
poker[2] *n* card game involving bluff
▸ **poker-faced** *adj* expressionless
Polanski *n* **Roman**. born 1933, Polish film director with a taste for the macabre, as in *Repulsion* (1965) and *Rosemary's Baby* (1968): later films include *Tess* (1980), *Death and the Maiden* (1995), and *The Pianist* (2002)
Polanyi *n* **John Charles**. born 1929, Canadian chemist, born in Germany. Noted for his work on infrared radiation; joint winner of the 1986 Nobel Prize for chemistry
polar *adj* of or near either of the earth's poles

THESAURUS

way of looking at it; = **perspective**, position, outlook, viewpoint, stance, angle, orientation, standpoint, slant, frame of reference ▸ *v* **11** = **indicate**, show, direct, designate, signify, denote, call attention to **12** = **aim**, level, train, direct ▷ **point out** = **mention**, show, identify, indicate, specify, allude to, bring up
See also: **consideration, message, use**
point-blank *adj* **1** = **direct**, express, plain, explicit, blunt, downright ▸ *adv* **2** = **directly**, straight, frankly, openly, explicitly, bluntly, plainly, candidly, forthrightly
pointed *adj* **1** = **sharp**, acute, barbed, edged **2** = **cutting**, sharp, acute, keen, pertinent, incisive, biting, penetrating, telling
pointer *n* **1** = **hint**, information, tip, recommendation, advice, caution, suggestion **2** = **indicator**, hand, guide, needle
pointless *adj* = **senseless**, stupid, silly, useless, irrelevant, absurd, meaningless, futile, fruitless, aimless, inane
poise *n* = **composure**, cool (*slang*), presence, assurance, dignity, calmness, aplomb, sang-froid, self-possession
poised *adj* **1** = **ready**, prepared, waiting, all set, standing by **2** = **composed**, together (*informal*), calm, dignified, collected, self-confident, self-possessed
poison *n* **1** = **toxin**, venom • *Mercury is a known poison.* RELATED WORD *adj*: toxic ▸ *v* **2** = **murder**, kill, give (someone) poison **3** = **contaminate**, infect, pollute **4** = **corrupt**, undermine, taint, warp, pervert, subvert, defile, deprave
poisonous *adj* **1** = **toxic**, venomous, noxious • *a large cloud of poisonous gas* **2** = **evil**, malicious, noxious, baleful, corrupting, pernicious
poke *v* **1** = **jab**, stab, elbow, dig, nudge, prod • *She poked a fork into the turkey skin* ▷ **poke fun at** *See* **mock** ▷ **poke your nose in** *See* **pry** ▸ *n* **2** = **jab**, dig, nudge, prod • *She gave him a playful poke.*
See also: **stick**
poky *adj* = **small**, tiny, narrow, cramped, confined

P

DICTIONARY

▶ **polar bear** white bear that lives in the regions around the North Pole
polarize *v* **1** form or cause to form into groups with directly opposite views **2** *physics* restrict (light waves) to certain directions of vibration **polarization** *n*
Polaroid *n* ® **1** plastic which polarizes light and so reduces glare **2** camera that develops a print very quickly inside itself
polder *n* land reclaimed from the sea
pole[1] Ⓣ *n* long rounded piece of wood, metal, or other material
pole[2] *n* **1** point furthest north (**North Pole**) or furthest south (**South Pole**) on the earth's axis of rotation **2** either of the opposite ends of a magnet or electric cell
▶ **Pole Star** star nearest to the North Pole in the northern hemisphere
poleaxe *v* hit or stun with a heavy blow
polecat *n* small animal of the weasel family
polemic [pol-**em**-ik] *n* fierce attack on or defence of a particular opinion, belief, etc. **polemical** *adj*
Poliakoff *n* **Stephen**. born 1952, British playwright and film director; work includes the stage plays *Breaking the Silence* (1984) and *Blinded by the Sun* (1996) and the television serial *The Lost Prince* (2003)
police Ⓣ *n* **1** organized force in a state which keeps law and order ▷ *v* **2** control or watch over with police or a similar body
▶ **policeman** (**policewoman**) *n* member of a police force
policy[1] Ⓣ *n, pl* **-cies** plan of action adopted by a person, group, or state
policy[2] *n, pl* **-cies** document containing an insurance contract
polio *n* disease affecting the spinal cord, which often causes paralysis (Also **poliomyelitis**)
polish Ⓣ *v* **1** make smooth and shiny by rubbing **2** make more nearly perfect ▷ *n* **3** liquid, aerosol, etc. for polishing **4** pleasing elegant style
▶ **polished** *adj* **1** (of a person) socially sophisticated in manner **2** done or performed well or professionally
▶ **polish off** *v* finish completely, dispose of
Polish *adj* **1** of Poland, its people, or their language ▷ *n* **2** official language of Poland
Politburo *n* decision-making committee in a Communist country
polite Ⓣ *adj* **1** showing consideration for others in one's manners, speech, etc. **2** socially correct or refined **politely** *adv* **politeness** *n*
politic Ⓣ *adj* wise and likely to prove advantageous
politics Ⓣ *n* **1** (study of) the art of government **2** person's beliefs about how a country should be governed **3** winning and using of power to govern society
▶ **political** *adj* of the state, government, or public administration **politically** *adv*
▶ **politically correct** (of language) intended to avoid any implied prejudice
▶ **political prisoner** person imprisoned because of his or her political beliefs
▶ **politician** *n* person actively engaged in politics, esp. a Member of Parliament
Polk *n* **James Knox**. 1795–1849, US statesman;

P

THESAURUS

pole *n* = **rod**, post, staff, bar, stick, shaft, spar, mast
police *n* **1** = **cops** (*slang*), boys in blue (*informal*), constabulary, fuzz (*slang*), police force, the law (*informal*) ▶ *v* **2** = **control**, watch, protect, guard, patrol, regulate
policeman *n* = **cop** (*slang*), officer, captain, copper (*slang*), detective, constable, policewoman (*feminine*), fuzz (*slang*), police officer, patrol man, traffic cop
policy *n* = **procedure**, plan, rule, action, course, approach, practice, code, scheme, custom
polish *v* **1** = **shine**, buff, wax • *polishing the furniture* **2** = **improve**, perfect, refine, brush up • *Polish your writing skills.* ▶ *n* **3** = **style**, class (*informal*), grace, elegance, finesse, refinement • *The early stories lacked the polish of his later work.* **4** = **varnish**, wax **5** = **sheen**, finish, gloss, glaze, brightness, lustre
See also: **practise**
polished *adj* **1** = **accomplished**, expert, fine, professional, adept, superlative, skilful, masterly **2** = **shining**, bright, smooth, glossy, burnished, gleaming **3** = **elegant**, sophisticated, refined, polite, cultivated, well-bred
polite *adj* **1** = **well-mannered**, civil, respectful, courteous, well-behaved • *It's not polite to point at people.* OPPOSITE: rude **2** = **refined**, sophisticated, cultured, genteel, urbane • *Certain words are not acceptable in polite society.*
politeness *n* = **courtesy**, decency, etiquette, civility • *She listened to him, but only out of politeness.*
politic *adj* = **wise**, diplomatic, prudent, sensible, advisable, judicious, expedient
political *adj* = **governmental**, parliamentary, policy-making
politician *n* = **statesman**, legislator, bureaucrat, congressman, minister (*Canad, Brit*), representative, office bearer, public servant, junior minister (*Canad, Brit*)
politics *n* = **statesmanship**, government, affairs of state, civics, political science

DICTIONARY

11th president of the US (1845–49). During his administration, Texas and territory now included in New Mexico, Colorado, Utah, Nevada, Arizona, Oregon, and California were added to the Union

polka *n* **1** lively 19th-century dance **2** music for this

▸ **polka dots** pattern of bold spots on fabric

poll Ⓣ *n* **1** Also **opinion poll** questioning of a random sample of people to find out general opinion **2** voting **3** number of votes recorded ▹ *v* **4** receive (votes) **5** question as part of an opinion poll

▸ **pollster** *n* person who conducts opinion polls

▸ **polling station** building where people vote in an election

Pollack *n* **Sydney**. 1934–2008, US film director. His films include *Tootsie* (1982), *Out of Africa* (1986), and *The Firm* (1993)

pollarded *adj* (of a tree) growing very bushy because its top branches have been cut short

pollen *n* fine dust produced by flowers that fertilizes other flowers

▸ **pollinate** *v* fertilize with pollen

▸ **pollen count** measure of the amount of pollen in the air, esp. as a warning to people with hay fever

Pollock *n* **Jackson**. 1912–56, US abstract expressionist painter; chief exponent of action painting in the US

pollute Ⓣ *v* contaminate with something poisonous or harmful **pollution** *n*

▸ **pollutant** *n* something that pollutes

polo *n* game like hockey played by teams of players on horseback

▸ **polo neck** sweater with tight turned-over collar

polonaise *n* **1** old stately dance **2** music for this

Pol Pot *n* original name *Kompong Thom*. 1925–98, Cambodian Communist statesman; prime minister of Kampuchea (1976; 1977–79); his policies led to the deaths of thousands in labour camps before he was overthrown by Vietnamese forces; in 1997 his former supporters in the Khmer Rouge captured him and claimed to have tried and sentenced him to life imprisonment

poltergeist *n* spirit believed to move furniture and throw objects around

poltroon *n obsolete* utter coward

poly- *combining form* many, much

polyandry *n* practice of having more than one husband at the same time

polyanthus *n* garden primrose

polychromatic *adj* many-coloured

Polyclitus, Polycleitus, Polycletus *n* 5th-century BC, Greek sculptor, noted particularly for his idealized bronze sculptures of the male nude, such as the *Doryphoros*

polyester *n* synthetic material used to make plastics and textile fibres

polygamy [pol-**ig**-a-mee] *n* practice of having more than one husband or wife at the same time **polygamous** *adj* **polygamist** *n*

polyglot *adj, n* (person) able to speak or write several languages

Polygnotus *n* 5th century BC, Greek painter: associated with Cimon in rebuilding Athens

polygon *n* geometrical figure with three or more angles and sides **polygonal** *adj*

polygraph *n* instrument for recording pulse rate and perspiration, used esp. as a lie detector

polygyny *n* practice of having more than one wife at the same time

polyhedron *n, pl* **-drons, -dra** solid figure with four or more sides

polymath *n* person of great and varied learning

polymer *n* chemical compound with large molecules made of simple molecules of the same kind

▸ **polymerize** *v* form into polymers **polymerization** *n*

polyp *n* **1** small simple sea creature with a hollow cylindrical body **2** small growth on a mucous membrane

polyphonic *adj music* consisting of several melodies played simultaneously

polystyrene *n* synthetic material used esp. as white rigid foam for packing and insulation

polytheism *n* belief in many gods **polytheist** *n* **polytheistic** *adj*

polythene *n* light plastic used for many everyday articles

polyunsaturated *adj* of a group of fats that do not form cholesterol in the blood

THESAURUS

poll *n* **1 = canvass**, survey, count, ballot, census, sampling **2 = vote**, tally, voting, figures, returns ▸ *v* **3 = tally**, register **4 = question**, survey, interview, ballot, sample, canvass

polls *See* **vote**

pollute *v* **1 = contaminate**, infect, poison, taint • *Heavy industry pollutes our rivers with noxious chemicals.* **2 = defile**, corrupt, desecrate, profane, sully, debase, dishonour, debauch, deprave

See also: **soil**

pollution *n* **= contamination**, corruption, taint, defilement, dirtying, foulness, impurity, uncleanness, carbon footprint

DICTIONARY

polyurethane *n* synthetic material used esp. in paints
polyvinyl chloride *n* see **PVC**
pomade *n* perfumed oil or ointment applied to the hair to make it smooth and shiny
pomander *n* (container for) a mixture of sweet-smelling petals, herbs, etc.
pomegranate *n* round tropical fruit with a thick rind containing many seeds in a red pulp
Pomeranian *n* small dog with long straight hair
pommel *n* **1** raised part on the front of a saddle **2** knob at the top of a sword hilt
pommy *n, pl* **-ies** *Aust & NZ slang* person from Britain (Also **pom**)
pomp Ⓣ *n* stately display or ceremony
Pompey *n* called *Pompey the Great*, Latin name *Gnaeus Pompeius Magnus*. 106–48 BC, Roman general and statesman; a member with Caesar and Crassus of the first triumvirate (60BC). He later quarrelled with Caesar, who defeated him at Pharsalus (48BC). He fled to Egypt and was murdered
pompom *n* decorative ball of tufted wool, silk, etc.
pompous Ⓣ *adj* foolishly serious and grand, self-important **pompously** *adv* **pomposity** *n*
ponce *n offensive* **1** effeminate man **2** pimp
▸ **ponce around** *v offensive* act stupidly, waste time
Ponce de León *n* **Juan**. ?1460–1521, Spanish explorer. He settled (1509) and governed (1510–12) Puerto Rico and discovered (1513) Florida
poncho *n, pl* **-chos** loose circular cloak with a hole for the head
pond Ⓣ *n* small area of still water
▸ **pondweed** *n* plant that grows in ponds
ponder Ⓣ *v* think thoroughly or deeply (about)
ponderous Ⓣ *adj* **1** serious and dull **2** heavy or huge **3** (of movement) slow and clumsy
ponderously *adv*
pong *n, v informal* (give off a) strong unpleasant smell
Pontiac *n* died 1769, chief of the Ottawa Indians, who led a rebellion against the British (1763–66)
pontiff *n* the pope
▸ **pontifical** *adj* pompous and dogmatic
▸ **pontificate** *v* **1** state one's opinions as if they were the only possible correct ones ▹ *n* **2** period of office of a pope
pontoon[1] *n* floating platform supporting a temporary bridge
pontoon[2] *n* gambling card game
pony Ⓣ *n* small horse
▸ **ponytail** *n* long hair tied in one bunch at the back of the head
poodle *n* dog with curly hair often clipped fancifully
poof *n offensive* homosexual man
pooh *interj* exclamation of disdain, contempt, or disgust
▸ **pooh-pooh** *v* express disdain or scorn for
pool[1] Ⓣ *n* **1** small body of still water **2** puddle of spilt liquid **3** swimming pool
pool[2] Ⓣ *n* **1** shared fund or group of workers or resources **2** game like snooker **pools 3** see **football pools** ▹ *v* **4** put in a common fund
poop *n* raised part at the back of a sailing ship
poor Ⓣ *adj* **1** having little money and few possessions **2** less, smaller, or weaker than is needed or expected **3** unproductive

THESAURUS

pomp *n* **1 = ceremony**, state, flourish, pageant, grandeur, pageantry, splendour, magnificence **2 = show**, display, grandiosity, ostentation
pomposity *n* **= self-importance**, pretension, affectation, airs, grandiosity, pompousness, portentousness, pretentiousness
pompous *adj* **1 = self-important**, arrogant, grandiose, pretentious, ostentatious, puffed up • *a pompous man with a high opinion of his own capabilities* **2 = grandiloquent**, inflated, bombastic, boastful, high-flown
pond *n* **= pool**, duck pond, fish pond, millpond, small lake, tarn
ponder *v* **= think**, consider, reflect, contemplate, brood, mull over • *I'm continually pondering how to improve the team.*
See also: **deliberate, wonder**
ponderous *adj* **1 = dull**, heavy, tedious, long-winded, pedantic **2 = unwieldy**, huge, heavy, massive, bulky, cumbersome, weighty **3 = clumsy**, awkward, lumbering, heavy-footed
pontificate *v* **= hold forth**, pronounce, preach, expound, lay down the law, sound off
pony *See* **horse**
pooch *See* **dog**
pool[1] *n* **1 = pond**, lake, mere, puddle, tarn **2 = swimming pool**, swimming bath
pool[2] *n* **1 = syndicate**, team, group, trust, collective, consortium **2 = kitty**, bank, pot, jackpot, funds ▸ *v* **3 = combine**, share, league, merge, amalgamate, join forces, put together
poor *adj* **1 = impoverished**, broke (*informal*), poverty-stricken, destitute, penniless, hard up (*informal*) • *a poor family* OPPOSITE: rich **2 = inferior**, mediocre, shoddy, unsatisfactory, feeble, second-rate • *He was a poor actor.* **3 = inadequate**, incomplete, insufficient, lousy (*slang*),

P

DICTIONARY

4 unlucky, pitiable **poorness** *n*
▶ **poorly** *adv* **1** in a poor manner ▷ *adj* **2** not in good health
pop¹ Ⓣ *v* **popping, popped 1** make or cause to make a small explosive sound **2** *informal* go, put, or come unexpectedly or suddenly ▷ *n* **3** small explosive sound **4** non-alcoholic fizzy drink
▶ **popcorn** *n* corn kernels heated until they puff up and burst
▶ **pop fly** *baseball* ball hit high in the air and not very far, thus easily caught
▶ **pop-up** *n* **1** *computers* image that appears above the open window on a computer screen **2** same as **pop fly**
pop² *n* **1** music of general appeal, esp. to young people ▷ *adj* **2** popular
pop³ *n informal* father
POP 1 point of presence: device that enables access to the internet **2** post office protocol: protocol which brings e-mail to and from a mail server **3** persistent organic pollutant
pope Ⓣ *n* head of the Roman Catholic Church
▶ **popish** *adj offensive* Roman Catholic
Pope *n* **Alexander**. 1688–1744, English poet, regarded as the most brilliant satirist of the Augustan period, esp. with his *Imitations of Horace* (1733–38). His technical virtuosity is most evident in *The Rape of the Lock* (1712–14). Other works include *The Dunciad* (1728; 1742), the *Moral Essays* (1731–35), and *An Essay on Man* (1733–34)
popinjay *n* conceited or talkative person
poplar *n* tall slender tree
poplin *n* ribbed cotton material
poppadom *n* thin round crisp Indian bread
Popper *n* Sir **Karl**. 1902–94, British philosopher, born in Vienna. In *The Logic of Scientific Discovery* (1934), he proposes that knowledge cannot be absolutely confirmed, but rather that science progresses by the experimental refutation of the current theory and its consequent replacement by a new theory, equally provisional but covering more of the known data. *The Open Society and its Enemies* (1945) is a critique of dogmatic political philosophies, such as Marxism. Other works are *The Poverty of Historicism* (1957), *Conjectures and Refutations* (1963), and *Objective Knowledge* (1972)
poppet *n* term of affection for a small child or sweetheart
poppy *n, pl* **-ies** plant with a large delicate red flower
poppycock *n informal* nonsense
Popsicle *n* flavoured ice on a stick
populace Ⓣ *n* **1** the ordinary people **2** the masses
popular Ⓣ *adj* **1** widely liked and admired **2** of or for the public in general **popularly** *adv* **popularity** *n*
▶ **popularize** *v* **1** make popular **2** make (something technical or specialist) easily understood
populate Ⓣ *v* **1** live in, inhabit **2** fill with inhabitants
▶ **population** *n* **1** all the people who live in a particular place **2** the number of people living in a particular place
▶ **populous** *adj* thickly populated
populist *n, adj* (person) appealing to the interests or prejudices of ordinary people
populism *n*
porbeagle *n* kind of shark
porcelain *n* **1** fine china **2** objects made of it
porch *n* covered approach to the entrance of a building
porcine *adj* of or like a pig
porcupine *n* animal covered with long pointed quills

P

THESAURUS

scant, deficient, skimpy, meagre, measly, lacking, scanty
See also: **hopeless, lame, low, pathetic, remote, rotten, sorry, worthless**
poorly *adv* = **badly**, unsuccessfully, inadequately, incompetently, inexpertly, insufficiently, unsatisfactorily
pop *v* **1** = **burst**, snap, crack, explode, bang, go off **2** = **put**, push, stick, slip, insert, tuck, thrust, shove ▶ *n* **3** = **bang**, report, explosion, crack, burst, noise
pope *n* = **Holy Father**, pontiff, Bishop of Rome, Vicar of Christ
populace *n* = **people**, mob, multitude, general public, hoi polloi, masses
popular *adj* **1** = **well-liked**, favourite, fashionable, sought-after, in demand, in favour • *These delicious pastries will be very popular.* OPPOSITE: unpopular **2** = **common**, general, conventional, universal, prevalent • *the popular press*
See also: **mass, public**
popularity *n* = **favour**, approval, currency, regard, acceptance, acclaim, vogue, esteem
popularize *v* = **make popular**, spread, disseminate, give currency to, give mass appeal, make available to all, universalize
popularly *adv* = **generally**, usually, widely, commonly, traditionally, universally, ordinarily, customarily, conventionally
populate *v* = **inhabit**, settle, occupy, colonize, live in
population *n* = **inhabitants**, people, community, society, folk, denizens, natives, residents
populous *adj* = **heavily populated**, crowded, packed, populated, overpopulated, swarming, teeming

DICTIONARY

pore[1] ❶ *n* tiny opening in the skin or in the surface of a plant
pore[2] ❶ *v* (foll. by *over*) make a careful study or examination of (a book, map, etc.)
pork *n* pig meat
▸ **porker** *n* pig raised for food
porn, porno *n, adj informal* short for **pornography, pornographic**
pornography ❶ *n* writing, films, or pictures designed to be sexually exciting **pornographic** *adj*
▸ **pornographer** *n* producer of pornography
porous ❶ *adj* allowing liquid to pass through gradually **porosity** *n*
porphyry [**por**-fir-ee] *n* reddish rock with large crystals in it
porpoise *n* fishlike sea mammal
porridge *n* **1** breakfast food made of oatmeal cooked in water or milk **2** *Brit slang* prison term
porringer *n* small dish for soup or porridge
port[1] ❶ *n* **1** harbour **2** town with a harbour
port[2] *n* left side of a ship or aircraft when facing the front of it
port[3] *n* strong sweet wine, usu. red
port[4] *n* **1** opening in the side of a ship **2** porthole
portable ❶ *adj* easily carried **portability** *n*
portage *n* (place for) transporting boats and supplies overland between navigable waterways
portal *n* large imposing doorway or gate
portcullis *n* grating suspended above a castle gateway, that can be lowered to block the entrance
portend ❶ *v* be a sign of
portent ❶ *n* sign of a future event
▸ **portentous** *adj* **1** of great or ominous significance **2** pompous, self-important
porter ❶ *n* **1** man on duty at the entrance to a hotel etc. **2** man who carries luggage **3** hospital worker who transfers patients between rooms etc.
Porter *n* **1 Cole**. 1893–1964, US composer and lyricist of musical comedies. His most popular songs include *Night and Day* and *Let's do It* **2 William Sidney**. original name of **O. Henry**
portfolio *n, pl* **-os 1** (flat case for carrying) examples of an artist's work **2** area of responsibility of a minister of state **3** list of investments held by an investor
porthole *n* small round window in a ship or aircraft
portico *n, pl* **-cos, -coes** porch or covered walkway with columns supporting the roof
portion ❶ *n* **1** part or share **2** helping of food for one person **3** destiny or fate
▸ **portion out** *v* divide into shares
Portland *n* **3rd Duke of**, title of *William Henry Cavendish Bentinck*. 1738–1809, British statesman; prime minister (1783; 1807–09); father of Lord William Cavendish Bentinck
portly ❶ *adj* **-lier, -liest** rather fat
portmanteau *n, pl* **-teaus, -teaux 1** *old-fashioned* large suitcase that opens into two compartments ▷ *adj* **2** combining aspects of different things
portrait ❶ *n* **1** picture of a person **2** lifelike description
portray ❶ *v* describe or represent by artistic means, as in writing or film **portrayal** *n*

P

THESAURUS

pore[1] *n* = **opening**, hole, outlet, orifice
pore[2] *v* ▷ **pore over** = **study**, read, examine, ponder, scrutinize, peruse
pornographic *adj* = **obscene**, blue, dirty, indecent, lewd, filthy, X-rated, salacious, scuzzy (*slang*), smutty
pornography *n* = **obscenity**, porn (*informal*), dirt, indecency, filth, smut
porous *adj* = **permeable**, spongy, absorbent, absorptive, penetrable
port *n* = **harbour**, haven, seaport, anchorage
portable *adj* = **light**, compact, convenient, manageable, handy, movable, easily carried
portend *v* = **foretell**, promise, indicate, predict, herald, bode, foreshadow, augur, betoken, prognosticate, warn of
portent *n* = **omen**, sign, warning, indication, prognostication, augury, forewarning
portentous *adj* **1** = **significant**, important, crucial, ominous, momentous, fateful, menacing **2** = **pompous**, solemn, ponderous, self-important
porter[1] *n* = **baggage attendant**, carrier, bearer
porter[2] *n* = **doorman**, caretaker, concierge, janitor, gatekeeper
portion *n* **1** = **part**, bit, piece, segment, chunk, serving, helping • *I have spent a considerable portion of my life here.* **2** = **share**, lot, measure, quota, quantity, allowance, ration, allocation, allotment **3** = **helping**, piece, serving **4** = **destiny**, lot, fate, luck, fortune ▸ *v* ▷ **portion out** = **divide**, deal, distribute, allocate, allot, apportion, dole out, share out
See also: **section**
portly *adj* = **stout**, large, heavy, fat, plump, burly, fleshy, corpulent
portrait *n* **1** = **picture**, image, painting, photograph, representation, likeness **2** = **description**, profile, portrayal, depiction, characterization, thumbnail sketch
portray *v* **1** = **represent**, figure, draw, picture, paint, depict, sketch,

DICTIONARY

Portuguese *adj* **1** of Portugal or its inhabitants ▷ *n* **2** person from Portugal **3** language of Portugal and Brazil
▸ **Portuguese man-of-war** sea creature resembling a jellyfish, with stinging tentacles
pose ⓣ *v* **1** place in or take up a particular position to be photographed or drawn **2** behave in an affected way in order to impress others **3** ask (a question) **4** raise (a problem) ▷ *n* **5** position while posing **6** behaviour adopted for effect
▸ **pose as** pretend to be
▸ **poser** *n* **1** *informal* person who wears trendy clothes and frequents fashionable places **2** person who poses **3** puzzling question
▸ **poseur** *n* person who behaves in an affected way to impress others
posh ⓣ *adj informal* **1** smart, luxurious **2** affectedly upper-class
posit ⓣ [**pozz**-it] *v* lay down as a basis for argument
position ⓣ *n* **1** place **2** usual or expected place **3** way in which something is placed or arranged **4** attitude, point of view **5** social standing **6** state of affairs **7** job ▷ *v* **8** place
positive ⓣ *adj* **1** feeling no doubts, certain **2** helpful, providing encouragement **3** confident, hopeful **4** absolute, downright **5** *math* greater than zero **6** *electricity* having a deficiency of electrons **positively** *adv*
▸ **positive discrimination** provision of special opportunities for a disadvantaged group
positron *n* positive electron
posse [**poss**-ee] *n* **1** *US* group of men organized to maintain law and order **2** *informal* group or gang
possess ⓣ *v* **1** have as one's property **2** (of a feeling, belief, etc.) have complete control of, dominate **possessor** *n*
▸ **possession** *n* **1** state of possessing, ownership **possessions 2** things a person possesses
▸ **possessive** *adj* **1** wanting all the attention or love of another person **2** (of a word) indicating the person or thing that something belongs to **possessiveness** *n*

THESAURUS

illustrate **2 = describe**, depict, characterize, put in words **3 = play**, represent, act the part of
portrayal *n* **= representation**, performance, picture, interpretation, depiction, characterization
pose *v* **1 = ask**, put, submit • *When I finally posed the question "Why?" he merely shrugged.* **2 = impersonate**, masquerade as, pass oneself off as, pretend to be • *The police officers posed as gamblers.* **3 = position oneself**, sit, model **4 = put on airs**, posture, show off (*informal*) ▸ *n* **5 = posture**, position, attitude, stance, bearing **6 = act**, air, front, pretense, mannerism, affectation, façade, posturing
See also: **show**
poser *n* **= puzzle**, problem, question, riddle, enigma
posh *adj* (*informal*) **= smart**, exclusive, upscale, elegant, stylish, fashionable, classy (*informal*) • *a posh hotel*
posit *v* **= put forward**, state, advance, assume, presume, postulate, propound
position *n* **1 = location**, point, place, whereabouts • *The ship's name and position were reported to the coastguard.* **2 = posture**, pose, attitude, arrangement, stance **3 = attitude**, view, opinion, outlook, belief, viewpoint, stance, slant, point of view **4 = status**, place, station, rank, standing, reputation, importance, stature, prestige **5 = job**, post, place, office, role, situation, duty, employment, occupation ▸ *v* **6 = put**, place, locate, arrange, lay out • *Position the plants near the edge of the garden.*
See also: **appointment, fit, set, spot, state**
positive *adj* **1 = certain**, sure, confident, convinced • *I was positive he'd known about that money.* **2 = definite**, clear, firm, concrete, conclusive, clear-cut • *positive evidence* **3 = helpful**, constructive • *I anticipate a positive response.*
See also: **favourable, optimistic**
positively *adv* **= definitely**, certainly, absolutely, firmly, surely, categorically, emphatically, unequivocally, unquestionably, assuredly
possess *v* **1 = be endowed with**, have, enjoy, be blessed with, be born with • *He possesses both stamina and creativity.* **2 = own**, hold, acquire • *He was said to possess a huge fortune.* **3 = control**, seize, occupy, take over • *They thought he was possessed by a demon.*
possessed *adj* **= crazed**, frenzied, obsessed, demented, raving, berserk
possession *n* **= ownership**, control, custody, tenure • *How did this picture come into your possession?*
possessions *pl n* **= belongings**, property, estate, assets, effects, things • *People had lost all their possessions.*
possessive *adj* **= jealous**, selfish, controlling, covetous, dominating, domineering, overprotective
possessor *See* **owner**
possibility *n* **1 = likelihood**, risk, hope, chance, prospect, odds • *the possibility of a*

DICTIONARY

possible Ⓣ *adj* **1** able to exist, happen, or be done **2** worthy of consideration ▷ *n* **3** person or thing that might be suitable or chosen **possibility** *n*
▸ **possibly** *adv* perhaps, not necessarily
possum *n* same as **opossum**
▸ **play possum** pretend to be dead or asleep to deceive an opponent
post[1] Ⓣ *n* **1** official system of carrying and delivering letters and parcels **2** (single collection or delivery of) letters and parcels sent by this system ▷ *v* **3** send by post **postal** *adj*
▸ **keep someone posted** inform someone regularly of the latest news
▸ **postage** *n* charge for sending a letter or parcel by post
▸ **postal code** *n* system of letters and numbers used to aid the sorting of mail
▸ **postal order** written money order sent by post and cashed at a post office by the person who receives it
▸ **postcard** *n* card for sending a message by post without an envelope
▸ **postman** *n* man who collects and delivers post
▸ **postmark** *n* official mark stamped on letters showing place and date of posting
▸ **postmaster** (**postmistress**) *n* official in charge of a post office
▸ **post office** place where postal business is conducted
post[2] Ⓣ *n* **1** length of wood, concrete, etc. fixed upright to support or mark something **2** goalpost **3** *basketball* area near the opposing team's basket ▷ *v* **4** put up (a notice) in a public place
post[3] Ⓣ *n* **1** job **2** position to which someone, esp. a soldier, is assigned for duty **3** military establishment ▷ *v* **4** send (a person) to a new place to work **5** put (a guard etc.) on duty
post- *prefix* after, later than: *postwar*
postdate *v* write a date on (a cheque) that is later than the actual date
poster Ⓣ *n* large picture or notice stuck on a wall
poste restante *n Brit* general delivery
posterior Ⓣ *n* **1** buttocks ▷ *adj* **2** behind, at the back of
posterity Ⓣ *n* future generations, descendants
postern *n* small back door or gate
postgraduate *n* person with a degree who is studying for a more advanced qualification
posthaste *adv* with great speed
posthumous [**poss**-tume-uss] *adj* **1** occurring after one's death **2** born after one's father's death **3** published after the author's death **posthumously** *adv*
postilion, postillion *n hist* person riding one of a pair of horses drawing a carriage
postmortem *n* medical examination of a body to establish the cause of death
postnatal *adj* occurring after childbirth
postpone Ⓣ *v* put off to a later time
postponement *n*
postprandial *adj* after dinner
postscript Ⓣ *n* passage added at the end of a letter
postulant *n* candidate for admission to a religious order
postulate Ⓣ *v* assume to be true as the basis of an argument or theory **postulation** *n*
posture Ⓣ *n* **1** position or way in which

P

THESAURUS

strike **2 = feasibility**, likelihood, potentiality, practicability, workableness **3** (*often pl*) **= potential**, promise, talent, prospects, capabilities, potentiality
possible *adj* **1 = feasible**, viable, attainable, workable, practicable • *I am grateful to my teachers for making this project possible.* **2 = conceivable**, potential, imaginable • *It's just possible that he did it deliberately.* **3 = likely**, potential, hopeful, promising, probable
See also: **believable**
possibly *adv* **= perhaps**, maybe, perchance (*archaic*)
post[1] *n* **1 = mail**, collection, delivery, postal service ▸ *v* **2 = send**, mail, transmit, dispatch ▷ **keep someone posted = notify**, advise, brief, inform, fill in on (*informal*), report to
post[2] *n* **1 = support**, stake, pole, column, picket, shaft, upright, pillar ▸ *v* **2 = put up**, display, affix, pin up
post[3] *n* **1 = job**, place, office, position, situation, appointment, employment, assignment **2 = station**, place, beat, position ▸ *v* **3 = station**, put, place, position, assign, situate
poster *n* **= notice**, bill, announcement, sticker, advertisement, placard, public notice
posterior *See* **bottom**
posterity *n* **1 = future**, succeeding generations **2 = descendants**, family, issue, offspring, progeny, children, heirs
postpone *v* **= put off**, delay, shelve, adjourn, defer, put back • *The visit has been postponed until tomorrow.*
postponement *n* **= delay**, stay, suspension, adjournment, deferral, deferment
postscript *n* **= P.S.**, addition, supplement, afterthought
postulate *v* **= presuppose**, propose, suppose, assume, theorize, hypothesize, posit, take for granted
posture *n* **1 = bearing**, set, attitude, stance,

DICTIONARY

someone stands, walks, etc. ▷ *v* **2** behave in an exaggerated way to get attention
posy *n, pl* **-sies** small bunch of flowers
pot Ⓣ *n* **1** round deep container **2** teapot **3** *slang* cannabis **pots 4** *informal* a lot ▷ *v* **potting, potted 5** plant in a pot **6** *snooker* hit (a ball) into a pocket
▸ **potted** *adj* **1** grown in a pot **2** (of meat or fish) preserved in a pot **3** *informal* abridged
▸ **potluck** *n* whatever is available
▸ **potsherd** *n* broken fragment of pottery
▸ **pot shot** shot taken without aiming carefully
▸ **potting shed** shed where plants are potted
potable [**pote**-a-bl] *adj* drinkable
potash *n* white powdery substance obtained from ashes and used as fertilizer
potassium *n* white metallic element
potato *n, pl* **-toes** roundish starchy vegetable that grows underground
▸ **potato chip** very thin slice of potato fried till crunchy
poteen *n* (in Ireland) illicitly distilled alcoholic drink
Potemkin, Potyomkin *n* **Grigori Aleksandrovich**. 1739–91, Russian soldier and statesman; lover of Catherine II, whose favourite he remained until his death
potent Ⓣ *adj* **1** having great power or influence **2** (of a male) capable of having sexual intercourse **potency** *n*
potentate *n* ruler or monarch
potential Ⓣ *adj* **1** possible but not yet actual ▷ *n* **2** ability or talent not yet fully used **3** *electricity* level of electric pressure
potentially *adv* **potentiality** *n*
pothole Ⓣ *n* **1** hole in the surface of a road **2** deep hole in a limestone area
▸ **potholing** *n* sport of exploring underground caves **potholer** *n*
potion Ⓣ *n* dose of medicine or poison
potpourri [po-**poor**-ee] *n* **1** fragrant mixture of dried flower petals **2** musical or literary medley
pottage *n* thick soup or stew
potter[1] *n* person who makes pottery
potter[2]**, putter** *v* be busy in a pleasant but aimless way **potterer** *or* **putterer** *n*
pottery Ⓣ *n, pl* **-ries 1** articles made from baked clay **2** place where they are made
potty[1] *n, pl* **-ties** bowl used by a small child as a toilet
potty[2] *adj* **-tier, -tiest** *Brit informal* crazy or silly
pouch Ⓣ *n* **1** small bag **2** baglike pocket of skin on an animal
pouf, pouffe [**poof**] *n* large solid cushion used as a seat
Poulenc *n* **Francis**. 1899–1963, French composer; a member of Les Six. His works include the operas *Les Mamelles de Tirésias* (1947) and *Dialogues des Carmélites* (1957), and the ballet *Les Biches* (1924)
poulterer *n* person who sells poultry
poultice [**pole**-tiss] *n* moist dressing, often heated, applied to inflamed skin
poultry *n* domestic fowls
pounce Ⓣ *v* **1** spring upon suddenly to attack or capture ▷ *n* **2** pouncing
pound[1] *n* **1** monetary unit of Britain and some other countries **2** unit of weight equal to 0.454 kg
pound[2] Ⓣ *v* **1** hit heavily and repeatedly **2** crush to pieces or powder **3** (of the heart) throb heavily **4** run with heavy steps
pound[3] Ⓣ *n* enclosure for stray animals or officially removed vehicles
Pound *n* **Ezra** (**Loomis**). 1885–1972, US poet, translator, and critic, living in Europe. Indicted for treason by the US government (1945) for pro-Fascist broadcasts during World War II, he was committed to a mental hospital until 1958. He was a founder of imagism and championed the early work of such writers as T. S. Eliot, Joyce, and Hemingway. His life work, the *Cantos* (1925–70), is an unfinished sequence of poems, which incorporates mythological

P

THESAURUS

carriage, disposition ▸ *v* **2 = show off** (*informal*), affect, pose, put on airs
pot *n* **= container**, vessel, bowl, pan
potency *n* **= power**, force, might, strength, influence, effectiveness
potent *adj* **1 = powerful**, dominant, influential, dynamic, authoritative, commanding **2 = strong**, powerful, mighty, vigorous, forceful
potential *adj* **1 = possible**, likely, probable • *potential sources of funding* ▸ *n* **2 = ability**, power, capacity, capability, wherewithal, aptitude • *recognizing the potential of solar energy*
See also: **in the making**
pothole *See* **pit**
potion *n* **= concoction**, draft, dose, mixture, brew, elixir, philtre
pottery *n* **= ceramics**, terracotta, earthenware, stoneware
pouch *n* **= bag**, pocket, sack, container, purse
pounce *v* **1 = spring**, attack, strike, jump, swoop, fall upon, leap at ▸ *n* **2 = spring**, attack, jump, assault, leap, bound, swoop
pound[1] *v* **1 = beat**, strike, batter, hammer, thump, pummel, clobber (*slang*), thrash, belabour **2 = crush**, powder, pulverize **3 = pulsate**, beat, pulse, throb, palpitate **4 = stomp** (*informal*), march, thunder, tramp
pound[2] *n* **= enclosure**, yard, compound, pen

DICTIONARY

and historical materials in several languages as well as political, economic, and autobiographical elements

pour Ⓣ *v* **1** flow or cause to flow out in a stream **2** rain heavily **3** come or go in large numbers

Poussin *n* **Nicolas.** 1594–1665, French painter, regarded as a leader of French classical painting. He is best known for the austere historical and biblical paintings and landscapes of his later years

pout Ⓣ *v* **1** thrust out one's lips, look sulky ▷ *n* **2** pouting look

pouter *n* pigeon that can puff out its crop

poutine [poo-**teen**] *n* dish of French fries with gravy or sauce and cheese curds

poverty Ⓣ *n* **1** state of being without enough food or money **2** lack of, scarcity

POW prisoner of war

powder Ⓣ *n* **1** substance in the form of tiny loose particles **2** medicine or cosmetic in this form ▷ *v* **3** apply powder to **powdery** *adj*

▸ **powdered** *adj* in the form of a powder: *powdered milk*

▸ **powder room** ladies' lavatory

Powell *n* **1 Anthony (Dymoke).** 1905–2000, British novelist, best known for his sequence of novels under the general title *A Dance to the Music of Time* (1951–75) **2 Earl**, known as *Bud Powell.* 1924–66, US modern-jazz pianist **3 Michael.** 1905–90, British film writer, producer, and director, best known for his collaboration (1942–57) with Emeric Pressburger. Films include *The Life and Death of Colonel Blimp* (1943), *A Matter of Life and Death* (1946), *The Red Shoes* (1948), and *Peeping Tom* (1960)

power Ⓣ *n* **1** ability to do or act **2** strength **3** position of authority or control **4** person or thing having authority **5** particular form of energy: *nuclear power* **6** electricity supply **7** *physics* rate at which work is done **8** *math* product from continuous multiplication of a number by itself **powerful** *adj* **powerless** *adj*

▸ **powered** *adj* having or operated by mechanical or electrical power

▸ **power failure** *or* **power cut** temporary interruption in the supply of electricity

▸ **power play** *hockey* situation in which a team has more players on the ice than its opponent because of penalties

▸ **power station** installation for generating and distributing electric power

Powhatan *n* American Indian name *Wahunsonacock.* died 1618, American Indian chief of a confederacy of tribes; father of Pocahontas

powwow *n* talk, conference

pox *n* **1** disease in which skin pustules form **2** *informal* syphilis

pp **1** pages

PQ Parti Québécois

PR **1** proportional representation **2** public relations

practicable Ⓣ *adj* capable of being carried out successfully **practicability** *n*

P

THESAURUS

pour *v* **1 = flow**, run, course, stream, gush, spout • *Blood was pouring from his broken nose.* **2 = let flow**, spill, splash, decant **3 = rain**, pelt *or* pelt down, teem, bucket down (*informal*) **4 = stream**, crowd, swarm, throng, teem

pout *v* **1 = sulk**, glower, look petulant, pull a long face ▸ *n* **2 = sullen look**, glower, long face

poverty *n* **1 = destitution**, want, hardship, insolvency • *The artist died in loneliness and poverty.* **2 = scarcity**, lack, shortage, deficiency, dearth, insufficiency, paucity

poverty-stricken *adj* **= penniless**, poor, impoverished, broke (*informal*), destitute, down and out, down on one's luck (*informal*), flat broke (*informal*), impecunious, indigent

powder *n* **1 = dust**, fine grains, loose particles, talc ▸ *v* **2 = dust**, cover, scatter, sprinkle, strew, dredge

powdery *adj* **= fine**, dry, dusty, grainy, granular, crumbly

power *n* **1 = control**, sovereignty, supremacy, dominion, ascendancy • *a position of great power and influence* **2 = authority**, right, licence, authorization, privilege • *the power to change the rules* **3 = strength**, might, vigour, brawn • *Power and speed are vital to success in hockey.* **4 = ability**, potential, capacity, capability, faculty, competence, competency

See also: **drive, force, grip, influence**

powerful *adj* **1 = influential**, dominant, commanding • *a large, powerful country* **2 = strong**, mighty, vigorous, sturdy, strapping • *It's such a powerful dog.* OPPOSITE: weak **3 = effective**, forceful, persuasive, compelling, convincing, telling • *a powerful argument*

See also: **important, impressive, intense, violent**

powerless *adj* **1 = helpless**, incapable, impotent • *I was powerless to do anything.* **2 = defenceless**, subject, vulnerable, ineffective, unarmed, dependent, tied

See also: **weak**

practicability *n* **= feasibility**, use, advantage, possibility, viability, usefulness, practicality

practicable *adj* **= feasible**, possible, viable, achievable, attainable, doable

DICTIONARY

practical ⓣ *adj* **1** involving experience or actual use rather than theory **2** sensible **3** adapted for use **4** good at making or doing things **5** in effect though not in name ▷ *n* **6** examination in which something has to be done or made **practically** *adv*
▸ **practical joke** trick intended to make someone look foolish

practice ⓣ *n* **1** something done regularly or habitually **2** repetition of something so as to gain skill **3** doctor's or lawyer's place of work
▸ **in practice** what actually happens as distinct from what is supposed to happen
▸ **put into practice** carry out, do

practise ⓣ *v* **1** do repeatedly so as to gain skill **2** take part in, follow (a religion etc.) **3** work at: *practise medicine* **4** do habitually

practitioner *n* person who practises a profession

Praetorius *n* **Michael**. 1571–1621, German composer and musicologist, noted esp. for his description of contemporary musical practices and instruments, *Syntagma musicum* (1615–19)

pragmatic ⓣ *adj* concerned with practical consequences rather than theory **pragmatism** *n* **pragmatist** *n*

prairie *n* large treeless area of grassland, esp. in N America
▸ **Prairies** *pl n* this grassland in Manitoba, Saskatchewan, and Alberta
▸ **prairie dog** rodent that lives in burrows in the N American prairies

praise ⓣ *v* **1** express approval or admiration of (someone or something) **2** express honour and thanks to (one's God) ▷ *n* **3** something said or written to show approval or admiration **praiseworthy** *adj*
▸ **sing someone's praises** praise someone highly

praline [**prah**-leen] *n* candy made of nuts and caramelized sugar

pram *n Brit* baby carriage

prance ⓣ *v* walk with exaggerated bouncing steps

prank ⓣ *n* mischievous trick or escapade, frolic

Prasad *n* **Rajendra**. 1884–1963, Indian statesman and journalist; first president of India (1950–62)

Pratchett *n* Sir **Terence** (**David John**), known as *Terry*. born 1948, British writer, noted for his comic fantasy novels in the *Discworld* series

prattle ⓣ *v* **1** chatter in a childish or foolish way ▷ *n* **2** childish or foolish talk **prattler** *n*

prawn *n* edible shellfish like a large shrimp

praxis *n* practice as opposed to theory

Praxiteles *n* 4th century BC, Greek sculptor: his works include statues of Hermes at Olympia, which survives, and of Aphrodite at Cnidus

pray ⓣ *v* **1** say prayers **2** ask earnestly, entreat
▸ **prayer** *n* **1** thanks or appeal addressed to

THESAURUS

practical *adj* **1 = pragmatic**, applied • *practical suggestions for a nutritious diet* **2 = useful**, functional, sensible • *The clothes are lightweight and practical for camping*. OPPOSITE: impractical **3 = feasible**, useful, doable, workable, serviceable, practicable **4 = skilled**, efficient, experienced, accomplished, proficient
See also: **handy, realistic**

practically *adv* **1 = almost**, nearly, basically, virtually, essentially, fundamentally, all but, in effect, just about, very nearly, well-nigh **2 = sensibly**, clearly, reasonably, realistically, rationally, matter-of-factly

practice *n* **1 = custom**, way, method, routine, habit • *My usual practice is to wake up early*. **2 = training**, exercise, drill, preparation, rehearsal • *I need more practice in this area*. **3 = profession**, work, business, career, vocation **4 = use**, action, operation, experience, exercise, application
See also: **convention, procedure**

practise *v* **1 = rehearse**, train, polish • *She practises the piano every day*. **2 = work at**, pursue, carry on, engage in

practised *adj* **= skilled**, expert, able, experienced, trained, accomplished, seasoned, proficient, versed
See also: **experienced**

pragmatic *adj* **= practical**, realistic, sensible, down-to-earth, utilitarian, businesslike, hard-headed

praise *v* **1 = approve**, applaud, congratulate, pay tribute to • *Many others praised her for taking a strong stand*. OPPOSITE: criticize **2 = give thanks to**, bless, worship, glorify, adore, exalt ▸ *n* **3 = approval**, tribute, accolade, congratulation, commendation • *She is full of praise for her co-workers*. OPPOSITE: criticism **4 = thanks**, glory, homage, worship, kudos, adoration
See also: **credit, honour**

praiseworthy *adj* **= creditable**, worthy, admirable, commendable, laudable, meritorious

prance *v* **1 = dance**, skip, romp, caper, cavort, frisk, gambol **2 = strut**, parade, stalk, swagger, show off (*informal*)

prank *n* **= trick**, antic, escapade, lark (*informal*), jape, practical joke

prattle *v* **= chatter**, babble, blather, blether, gabble, jabber

pray *v* **1 = say one's prayers**, offer a prayer,

P

DICTIONARY

one's God **2** set form of words used in praying **3** earnest request
pre- *prefix* before, beforehand: *prenatal; prerecord; preshrunk*
preach ⓣ *v* **1** give a talk on a religious theme as part of a church service **2** speak in support of (an idea, principle, etc.) **preacher** *n*
preamble ⓣ *n* introductory part to something said or written
prearranged *adj* arranged beforehand
prebendary *n, pl* **-daries** clergyman who is a member of the chapter of a cathedral
precarious ⓣ *adj* insecure, unsafe, likely to fall or collapse. **precariously** *adv*
precaution ⓣ *n* action taken in advance to prevent something bad happening
precautionary *adj*
precede ⓣ *v* go or be before
▸ **precedence** [**press**-ee-denss] *n* formal order of rank or position
▸ **take precedence over** be more important than
▸ **precedent** *n* previous case or occurrence regarded as an example to be followed
precentor *n* person who leads the singing in a church
precept ⓣ *n* rule of behaviour
precession *n* **precession of the equinoxes** slightly earlier occurrence of the equinoxes each year
precinct ⓣ *n* **1** area in a town closed to traffic **2** enclosed area round a building: *cathedral precinct* **3** *US* administrative area of a city **precincts 4** surrounding region
precious ⓣ *adj* **1** of great value and importance **2** loved and treasured **3** (of behaviour) affected, unnatural
▸ **precious metal** gold, silver, or platinum
▸ **precious stone** rare mineral, such as a ruby, valued as a gem
precipice ⓣ *n* very steep cliff or rockface
▸ **precipitous** *adj* sheer
precipitant *adj* hasty or rash
precipitate ⓣ *v* **1** cause to happen suddenly **2** throw headlong **3** *chem* cause to be deposited in solid form from a solution ▷ *adj* **4** done rashly or hastily ▷ *n* **5** *chem* substance precipitated from a solution **precipitately** *adv*
▸ **precipitation** *n* **1** precipitating **2** rain, snow, etc.
précis ⓣ [**pray**-see] *n, pl* **précis 1** short written summary of the main points of a longer piece ▷ *v* **2** make a précis of
precise ⓣ *adj* **1** exact, accurate in every detail **2** strict in observing rules or

THESAURUS

recite the rosary **2 = beg**, ask, plead, request, petition, solicit, implore, beseech, adjure, entreat ▷ **pray to** *See* **worship**
prayer *n* **1 = orison**, devotion, litany, invocation, supplication **2 = plea**, appeal, request, petition, entreaty, supplication
preach *v* **1 = deliver a sermon**, address, evangelize **2 = lecture**, advocate, exhort, moralize, sermonize
preacher *n* **= clergyman**, minister, missionary, evangelist, parson
preamble *n* **= introduction**, prelude, preface, foreword, opening statement *or* opening remarks
precarious *adj* **= dangerous**, unsafe, shaky, risky, hazardous, unsure, tricky, unreliable, perilous, insecure
precaution *n* **1 = safeguard**, insurance, protection, provision, preventive measure • *taking precautions against accidents* **2 = forethought**, care, caution, prudence, wariness, providence
precede *v* **= go before**, lead, head, introduce, preface, antedate, come first
precedence *n* **= priority**, rank, seniority, supremacy, superiority, primacy, antecedence, pre-eminence
precedent *n* **= instance**, standard, model, example, pattern, prototype, paradigm, antecedent
preceding *adj* **= previous**, former, past, above, earlier, prior, aforementioned, aforesaid, foregoing
precept *n* **= rule**, order, law, regulation, principle, command, instruction, decree, statute, commandment, canon
precinct *n* **1 = limits**, confines **2 = area**, quarter, sector, zone, district, section
precious *adj* **1 = valuable**, expensive, prized, invaluable, priceless • *precious jewels* OPPOSITE: worthless **2 = loved**, beloved, dear, prized, darling, cherished, adored, treasured **3 = affected**, artificial, overnice, overrefined
precipice *n* **= cliff**, height, bluff, crag, rock face
precipitate *v* **1 = quicken**, advance, trigger, accelerate, hurry, expedite, hasten, bring on, speed up **2 = throw**, launch, cast, hurl, fling, let fly ▸ *adj* **3 = hasty**, reckless, rash, impulsive, precipitous, heedless, impetuous **4 = swift**, rapid, breakneck, headlong, rushing **5 = sudden**, quick, brief, unexpected, abrupt, without warning
precipitous *adj* **1 = sheer**, high, steep, abrupt, dizzy, perpendicular **2 = hasty**, reckless, rash, hurried, precipitate, heedless
précis *n* **1 = summary**, outline, synopsis, abridgment, résumé ▸ *v* **2 = summarize**, outline, shorten, abridge, sum up
precise *adj* **1 = exact**, very, specific, particular, correct, actual, accurate • *We*

DICTIONARY

standards **precisely** *adv* **precision** *n*
preclude Ⓣ *v* make impossible to happen
precocious Ⓣ *adj* having developed or matured early or too soon **precocity** *or* **precociousness** *n*
precognition *n* alleged ability to foretell the future
preconceived Ⓣ *adj* (of an idea) formed without real experience or reliable information **preconception** *n*
precondition *n* something that must happen or exist before something else can
precursor Ⓣ *n* something that precedes and is a signal of something else, forerunner
predate *v* **1** occur at an earlier date than **2** write a date on (a document) that is earlier than the actual date
predatory Ⓣ [**pred**-a-tree] *adj* habitually hunting and killing other animals for food ▸ **predator** *n* predatory animal
predecease *v* die before (someone else)
predecessor Ⓣ *n* **1** person who precedes another in an office or position **2** ancestor
predestination Ⓣ *n* belief that future events have already been decided by God **predestined** *adj*
predetermined Ⓣ *adj* decided in advance
predicament Ⓣ *n* embarrassing or difficult situation
predicate *n* **1** part of a sentence in which something is said about the subject, eg *went home* in *I went home* ▷ *v* **2** declare or assert ▸ **predicative** *adj* of or in the predicate of a sentence
predict Ⓣ *v* tell about in advance, prophesy **predictable** *adj* **prediction** *n* ▸ **predictive** *adj* (of a word processer or cell phone) able to complete words after only part of a word has been keyed
predilection Ⓣ *n* preference or liking
predispose Ⓣ *v* **1** influence (someone) in favour of something **2** make (someone) susceptible to something **predisposition** *n*
predominate Ⓣ *v* be the main or controlling element. **predominance** *n* **predominant** *adj* **predominantly** *adv*
pre-eminent Ⓣ *adj* excelling all others, outstanding **pre-eminently** *adv* **pre-eminence** *n*

THESAURUS

may never know the precise details. OPPOSITE: vague **2** = **strict**, particular, formal, careful, exact, stiff, rigid, meticulous, scrupulous, finicky, fastidious, punctilious
See also: **fine, right**
precisely *adv* = **exactly**, square, absolutely, strictly, smack (*informal*), correctly, accurately, squarely, plumb (*informal*), just so
precision *n* = **exactness**, care, accuracy, meticulousness, particularity, preciseness
preclude *v* = **prevent**, stop, check, prohibit, exclude, inhibit, forestall, debar, obviate, rule out
precocious *adj* = **advanced**, forward, ahead, quick, smart, bright, developed
preconceived *adj* = **presumed**, forejudged, prejudged, presupposed
preconception *n* = **preconceived idea** *or* **preconceived notion**, bias, notion, prejudice, predisposition, presupposition
precursor *n* **1** = **herald**, forerunner, harbinger, vanguard **2** = **forerunner**, predecessor, antecedent, forebear
predatory *adj* = **hunting**, carnivorous, predacious, raptorial
predecessor *n* **1** = **previous job holder**, precursor, forerunner, antecedent **2** = **ancestor**, forefather, antecedent, forebear
predestination *n* = **fate**, destiny, foreordainment, foreordination, predetermination
predestined *adj* = **fated**, doomed, meant, preordained
predetermined *adj* = **prearranged**, set, agreed, fixed, preplanned
predicament *n* = **fix** (*informal*), jam (*informal*), scrape, hot water (*informal*), tight spot • *He found himself in a peculiar predicament.*
See also: **hole, problem, state**
predict *v* = **foretell**, forecast, foresee, prophesy • *The opinion polls are predicting a very close vote.*
predictable *adj* = **likely**, sure, certain, reliable, anticipated, foreseeable, expected
prediction *n* = **prophecy**, forecast • *He was unwilling to make a prediction for the coming year.*
predilection *n* = **liking**, love, taste, weakness, bias, preference, penchant, fondness, inclination, leaning, propensity, partiality
predispose *v* = **incline**, lead, affect, prompt, influence, bias, dispose, prejudice
predisposed *adj* = **inclined**, ready, subject, willing, liable, susceptible, given, minded
predominant *adj* = **main**, chief, prime, principal, dominant, prevalent, paramount, ascendant, leading, prevailing
predominantly *adv* = **mainly**, mostly, largely, generally, primarily, principally, chiefly, for the most part
predominate *v* = **prevail**, outweigh, overshadow, overrule, be most noticeable, carry weight, hold sway
pre-eminence *n* = **superiority**, excellence, distinction, prominence, prestige, supremacy, renown, predominance
pre-eminent *adj* = **outstanding**, chief,

P

DICTIONARY

pre-empt Ⓣ *v* get or do in advance of or to the exclusion of others. **pre-emption** *n* **pre-emptive** *adj*
preen Ⓣ *v* (of a bird) clean or trim (its feathers) with its beak
▶ **preen oneself 1** smarten oneself **2** show self-satisfaction
prefab *n* prefabricated house
prefabricated *adj* (of a building) manufactured in shaped sections for rapid assembly on site
preface Ⓣ [**pref**-iss] *n* **1** introduction to a book ▷ *v* **2** serve as an introduction to (a book, speech, etc.) **prefatory** *adj*
prefect *n* **1** senior pupil in a school, with limited power over others **2** senior administrative officer in some countries
▶ **prefecture** *n* office or area of authority of a prefect
prefer Ⓣ *v* **-ferring, -ferred 1** like better **2** *law* bring (charges) before a court
preference *n*
▶ **preferable** *adj* more desirable **preferably** *adv*
▶ **preferential** *adj* showing preference
▶ **preferment** *n* promotion or advancement
prefigure *v* represent or suggest in advance
prefix *n* **1** letter or group of letters put at the beginning of a word to make a new word, such as *un* in *unhappy* **2** title before a name ▷ *v* **3** put as an introduction or prefix (to)
pregnant Ⓣ *adj* **1** carrying a fetus in the womb **2** full of meaning or significance
pregnancy *n*
prehensile *adj* capable of grasping
prehensility *n*
prehistoric Ⓣ *adj* of the period before written history begins **prehistory** *n*
prejudge Ⓣ *v* judge beforehand without sufficient evidence
prejudice Ⓣ *n* **1** unreasonable or unfair dislike of someone or something ▷ *v* **2** cause (someone) to have a prejudice **3** harm, cause disadvantage to
▶ **prejudicial** *adj* harmful, disadvantageous
prelate [**prel**-it] *n* bishop or other churchman of high rank **prelacy** *n*
preliminary Ⓣ *adj* **1** happening before and in preparation, introductory ▷ *n, pl* **-naries** **2** something that happens before something else
prelude Ⓣ [**pray**-lood] *n* **1** introductory movement in music **2** event preceding and introducing something else
premarital *adj* occurring before marriage
premature Ⓣ *adj* **1** happening or done before

THESAURUS

excellent, renowned, superior, foremost, supreme, distinguished, predominant, incomparable, matchless
pre-empt *v* = **forestall**, assume, anticipate, appropriate, usurp
preen *v* **1** (Of a bird) = **clean**, plume **2** = **smarten**, dress up, spruce up, titivate ▷ **preen oneself, preen oneself on** = **pride oneself**, congratulate oneself
preface *n* **1** = **introduction**, preliminary, prelude, preamble, prologue, foreword ▶ *v* **2** = **introduce**, open, begin, prefix
prefer *v* = **like better**, favour, be partial to, go for, incline toward • *Does she prefer a particular type of music?*
preferable *adj* = **better**, superior, best, chosen, favoured, more desirable
preferably *adv* = **rather**, first, sooner, by choice, in preference *or* for preference
preference *n* **1** = **first choice**, pick, option, choice, selection, desire, favorite, predilection, partiality **2** = **priority**, precedence, favoured treatment, favouritism, first place
preferential *adj* = **privileged**, special, better, advantageous, favoured
preferment *n* = **promotion**, rise, elevation, advancement, exaltation, upgrading
preferred *See* **favourite**
pregnant *adj* **1** = **expectant**, big with child *or* heavy with child, expecting (*informal*), with child **2** = **meaningful**, significant, loaded, pointed, charged, expressive, eloquent, weighty, telling
prehistoric *adj* = **earliest**, early, primitive, primordial, primeval
prejudge *v* = **jump to conclusions**, anticipate, presume, presuppose
prejudice *n* **1** = **bias**, preconception • *prejudice against workers over 55* **2** = **discrimination**, racism, sexism, bigotry, chauvinism • *racial prejudice* ▶ *v* **3** = **bias**, influence, poison, colour, predispose, distort, slant **4** = **harm**, damage, injure, hurt, undermine, spoil, impair, mar, hinder
See also: **colour, injustice**
prejudiced *adj* = **biased**, unfair, one-sided, intolerant, opinionated, narrow-minded, bigoted, influenced
prejudicial *adj* = **harmful**, detrimental, hurtful, deleterious, injurious, damaging, disadvantageous, unfavourable
preliminary *adj* **1** = **first**, test, trial, opening, pilot, initial, prior, preparatory, introductory, prefatory ▶ *n* **2** = **introduction**, start, opening, beginning, prelude, overture, preamble, preface
prelude *n* = **introduction**, start, beginning, overture, preamble, preface, prologue, foreword
premature *adj* **1** = **early**, forward, untimely, unseasonable **2** = **hasty**, ill-timed,

DICTIONARY

the normal or expected time **2** (of a baby) born before the end of the normal period of pregnancy **prematurely** *adv*
premedication *n* drugs given to prepare a patient for a general anesthetic
premeditated Ⓣ *adj* planned in advance **premeditation** *n*
premenstrual *adj* occurring or experienced before a menstrual period: *premenstrual tension*
premier Ⓣ *n* **1** prime minister ▷ *adj* **2** chief, leading **premiership** *n*
premiere Ⓣ *n* first performance of a play, film, etc.
Preminger *n* **Otto** (**Ludwig**). 1906–86, US film director, born in Austria. His films include *Carmen Jones* (1954) and *Anatomy of a Murder* (1959)
premise, premiss Ⓣ *n* statement assumed to be true and used as the basis of reasoning
premises Ⓣ *pl n* house or other building and its land
premium Ⓣ *n* **1** additional sum of money, as on a wage or charge **2** (regular) sum paid for insurance
▸ **at a premium** in great demand because scarce
premonition Ⓣ *n* feeling that something unpleasant is going to happen **premonitory** *adj*
prenatal *adj* **1** before birth **2** during pregnancy
preoccupy *v* **-pying, -pied** fill the thoughts or attention of (someone) to the exclusion of other things **preoccupation** *n*
preordained *adj* decreed or determined in advance
prep *n informal* preparation for schoolwork
▸ **prep school** short for **preparatory school**
prep. **1** preparatory **2** preposition
prepacked *adj* sold already wrapped
prepaid *adj* paid for in advance
prepare Ⓣ *v* make or get ready
▸ **prepared** *adj* **1** willing **2** ready
▸ **preparation** *n* **1** preparing **2** something done in readiness for something else **3** mixture prepared for use as a cosmetic, medicine, etc.
▸ **preparatory** [prip-**par**-a-tree] *adj* preparing for
▸ **preparatory school** private school for children going on to public school
preponderant *adj* greater in amount, force, or influence. **preponderantly** *adv* **preponderance** *n*
preposition *n* word used before a *n* or pronoun to show its relationship with other words, such as *by* in *go by bus* **prepositional** *adj*
prepossessing Ⓣ *adj* making a favourable impression, attractive
preposterous Ⓣ *adj* utterly absurd
prepuce [**pree**-pyewss] *n* retractable fold of

THESAURUS

overhasty, rash, untimely, too soon
prematurely *See* **early**
premeditated *adj* = **planned**, deliberate, conscious, intentional, calculated, considered, wilful
premeditation *n* = **planning**, design, purpose, intention, forethought, plotting, prearrangement, predetermination
premier *n* **1** = **head of government**, chancellor, chief minister, chief officer, prime minister ▸ *adj* **2** = **chief**, first, head, prime, main, primary, principal, foremost, alpha male, highest, leading
premiere *n* = **first night**, debut, opening
premise, premiss *n* = **assumption**, argument, assertion, hypothesis, proposition, supposition, postulation, presupposition
premises *pl n* = **building**, place, site, property, establishment
premium *n* = **bonus**, fee, reward, perk (*informal*), bounty, prize, perquisite ▷ **at a premium** = **in great demand**, rare, scarce, hard to come by, in short supply
premonition *n* = **foreboding**, funny feeling (*informal*), omen • *He had a premonition that he would die.*
See also: **warning**
preoccupation *n* **1** = **obsession**, fixation, bee in one's bonnet **2** = **absorption**, immersion, abstraction, reverie, absent-mindedness, daydreaming, engrossment, woolgathering
preoccupied *adj* = **absorbed**, oblivious, engrossed, immersed, wrapped up • *I am preoccupied with my tennis career.*
preparation *n* **1** = **groundwork**, preparing, getting ready **2** (*often pl*) = **arrangement**, plan, measure, provision **3** = **mixture**, medicine, compound, concoction
preparatory *adj* = **introductory**, opening, primary, preliminary, prefatory
prepare *v* = **make ready** *or* **get ready**, prime, train, practise, adjust, arrange, adapt, warm up
prepared *adj* **1** = **ready**, set, arranged, in order, in readiness, primed **2** = **willing**, inclined, disposed
preponderance *n* = **predominance**, mass, dominance, domination, prevalence, supremacy, extensiveness, greater numbers, greater part, lion's share
prepossessing *adj* = **attractive**, charming, handsome, good-looking, engaging, pleasing, appealing, likable *or* likeable, fetching
preposterous *adj* = **ridiculous**, crazy,

DICTIONARY

skin covering the tip of the penis, foreskin
prerecorded *adj* recorded in advance to be played or broadcast later
prerequisite Ⓣ *n, adj* (something) that must happen or exist before something else is possible
prerogative Ⓣ *n* special power or privilege
presage Ⓣ [**press**-ij] *v* be a sign or warning of
presbyopia *n* inability of the eye to focus on nearby objects
Presbyterian *adj, n* (member) of a Protestant church governed by lay elders
Presbyterianism *n*
presbytery *n, pl* **-teries 1** *Presbyterian Church* local church court **2** *RC Church* priest's house
prescience Ⓣ [**press**-ee-enss] *n* knowledge of events before they happen **prescient** *adj*
prescribe Ⓣ *v* **1** recommend the use of (a medicine) **2** lay down as a rule
▶ **prescription** *n* written instructions from a doctor for the making up and use of a medicine
▶ **prescriptive** *adj* laying down rules
presence Ⓣ *n* **1** fact of being in a specified place **2** impressive dignified appearance
▶ **presence of mind** ability to act sensibly in a crisis
present[1] Ⓣ *adj* **1** being in a specified place **2** existing or happening now **3** (of a *v* tense) indicating that the action specified is taking place now ▷ *n* **4** present time or tense
▶ **presently** *adv* **1** soon **2** now
present[2] Ⓣ *n* **1** something given to bring pleasure to another person ▷ *v* **2** introduce formally or publicly **3** introduce and compère (a TV or radio show) **4** cause: *present a difficulty* **5** give, award **presentation** *n*
▶ **presentable** *adj* attractive, neat, fit for people to see
▶ **presenter** *n* person introducing a TV or radio show
presentiment [pree-**zen**-tim-ent] *n* sense of something usu. unpleasant about to happen
preserve Ⓣ *v* **1** keep from being damaged, changed, or ended **2** treat (food) to prevent it decaying ▷ *n* **3** area of interest restricted to a particular person or group **4** fruit preserved by cooking in sugar **5** area where game is

THESAURUS

incredible, outrageous, absurd, insane, ludicrous, laughable, unthinkable, nonsensical, out of the question
prerequisite *n* **1 = requirement**, must, condition, essential, necessity, qualification, precondition, requisite, *sine qua non (Latin)* ▶ *adj* **2 = required**, necessary, mandatory, essential, vital, indispensable, requisite, obligatory
prerogative *n* **= right**, due, advantage, exemption, immunity, privilege, liberty
presage *v* **= portend**, signify, bode, foreshadow, augur, betoken, foretoken
prescience *n* **= foresight**, clairvoyance, foreknowledge, precognition, second sight
prescribe *v* **= order**, set, rule, direct, recommend, dictate, specify, decree, stipulate, ordain, lay down
prescribed *See* **formal**
prescription *n* **1 = instruction**, direction, formula, recipe **2 = medicine**, drug, preparation, remedy, mixture
presence *n* **1 = being**, residence, attendance, existence, occupancy, inhabitance **2 = personality**, air, appearance, poise, aspect, aura, carriage, bearing, demeanour, self-assurance ▷ **presence of mind = level-headedness**, cool (*slang*), composure, calmness, coolness, self-possession, wits
present[1] *adj* **1 = there**, here, at hand, in attendance • *He had been present at the meeting.* OPPOSITE: absent **2 = current**, immediate, contemporary, existing, present-day, existent ▶ *n* ▷ **the present = now**, today, here and now, the present moment, the time being ▷ **at present = just now**, now, at the moment, right now ▷ **for the present = for now**, temporarily, for the moment, for the time being, in the meantime
See also: **modern**
present[2] *n* **1 = gift**, offering, donation • *a birthday present* ▶ *v* **2 = give**, award, grant, donate, bestow, hand out • *The mayor presented the prizes.* **3 = introduce**, acquaint with, make known **4 = put on**, show, give, stage, display, exhibit
See also: **perform, submit**
presentable *adj* **= satisfactory**, acceptable, decent, suitable, respectable, passable, becoming, fit to be seen, O.K. *or* okay (*informal*)
presentation *n* **1 = giving**, award, offering, donation, bestowal, conferral **2 = performance**, show, production, display, demonstration, exhibition
present-day *adj* **= current**, recent, present, modern, contemporary, up-to-date, latter-day, newfangled
presently *adv* **= soon**, shortly, anon (*archaic*), before long, by and by
preservation *n* **= protection**, support, safety, conservation, maintenance, salvation, safekeeping, safeguarding
preserve *v* **1 = protect**, keep, save, defend, shelter, shield, safeguard, conserve, care for **2 = maintain**, continue, keep, uphold,

DICTIONARY

kept for private fishing or shooting
preservation *n*
▸ **preservative** *n* chemical that prevents decay
preshrunk *adj* (of fabric or a garment) having been shrunk during manufacture so that further shrinkage will not occur when washed
preside Ⓣ *v* be in charge, esp. of a meeting
president Ⓣ *n* **1** head of state in countries without a king or queen **2** head of a society, institution, etc. **presidential** *adj* **presidency** *n*
Presley *n* **Elvis** (**Aaron** *or* **Aron**). 1935–77, US rock and roll singer. His recordings include "That's all Right (Mama)" (1954), "Heartbreak Hotel" (1956), "Hound Dog" (1956), numbers from the films *Loving You* and *Jailhouse Rock* (both 1957), and "Suspicious Minds" (1970)
press[1] Ⓣ *v* **1** apply force or weight to **2** squeeze **3** smooth by applying pressure or heat **4** crowd, push **5** urge insistently **6** *basketball* guard opponents closely as a defensive tactic ▹ *n* **7** printing machine
▸ **pressed for** short of
▸ **pressing** *adj* urgent
▸ **press box** room at a sports ground reserved for reporters
▸ **press conference** interview for reporters given by a celebrity
press[2] *v* **press into service** force to be involved or used
▸ **press gang** *hist* group of men who captured men and boys and forced them to join the navy
Pressburger *n* **Emeric**. 1902–88, Hungarian film writer and producer, living in Britain: best known for his collaboration (1942–57) with Michael Powell. Films include *The Life and Death of Colonel Blimp* (1943), *I Know Where I'm Going* (1945), and *A Matter of Life and Death* (1946)
pressure Ⓣ *n* **1** force produced by pressing **2** urgent claims or demands: *working under pressure* **3** *physics* force applied to a surface per unit of area
▸ **bring pressure to bear on** use influence or authority to persuade
▸ **pressure cooker** airtight pot which cooks food quickly by steam under pressure
▸ **pressure group** group that tries to influence policies, public opinion, etc.
prestidigitation *n* skilful quickness with the hands, conjuring
prestige Ⓣ *n* high status or respect resulting from success or achievements **prestigious** *adj*
presto *adv music* very quickly
prestressed *adj* (of concrete) containing stretched steel wires to strengthen it
presume Ⓣ *v* **1** suppose to be the case **2** (foll. by *to*) dare (to), take the liberty (of)
▸ **presumably** *adv* one supposes (that)
▸ **presumption** *n* **1** strong probability **2** bold insolent behaviour
▸ **presumptuous** *adj* doing things one has no right or authority to do **presumptuously** *adv*
▸ **presumptive** *adj* assumed to be true or valid until the contrary is proved
▸ **heir presumptive** heir whose right may be defeated by the birth of a closer relative

P

THESAURUS

sustain, perpetuate, keep up ▸ *n* **3** = **area**, field, domain, realm, sphere
preside *v* = **run**, lead, head, control, conduct, manage, direct, chair, govern, administer, officiate
president *See* **head**
press *v* **1** = **compress**, push, crush, squeeze, mash • *Press the blue button.* **2** = **urge**, pressure, plead, petition, beg, implore • *The journalist was pressed to reveal her sources.* **3** = **hug**, crush, embrace, squeeze, clasp, fold in one's arms, hold close **4** = **smooth**, iron, flatten **5** = **crowd**, push, gather, surge, herd, flock, swarm, throng, seethe ▹ **press on** *See* **advance** ▸ *n* ▹ **the press** = **newspapers**, Fleet Street, fourth estate, news media, the papers; = **journalists**, columnists, correspondents, newsmen, pressmen, reporters
See also: **insist, rush**
pressing *adj* = **urgent**, important, serious, crucial, vital, imperative, high-priority, importunate
pressure *n* **1** = **force**, weight, compression, compressing, crushing, squeezing **2** = **power**, force, influence, sway, constraint, coercion, compulsion **3** = **stress**, heat, strain, load, burden, urgency, hassle (*informal*), demands
prestige *n* = **status**, credit, standing, reputation, fame, importance, honour, distinction, kudos, renown, eminence
prestigious *adj* = **celebrated**, great, important, prominent, renowned, notable, respected, illustrious, eminent, esteemed
presumably *adv* = **apparently**, probably, seemingly, in all likelihood, in all probability, it would seem, on the face of it
presume *v* **1** = **believe**, think, suppose, guess (*informal*), assume, infer, conjecture, surmise, postulate, take for granted **2** = **dare**, venture, go so far, make so bold, take the liberty
presumed *See* **supposed**
presumption *n* **1** = **cheek** (*informal*), nerve (*informal*), gall (*informal*), audacity, boldness, effrontery, impudence, insolence **2** = **probability**, chance, basis, likelihood

DICTIONARY

presuppose ⓣ *v* need as a previous condition in order to be true **presupposition** *n*
pretend ⓣ *v* claim or give the appearance of (something untrue) to deceive or in play
▸ **pretender** *n* person who makes a false or disputed claim to a position of power
▸ **pretence** *n* behaviour intended to deceive, pretending
▸ **pretentious** *adj* making (unjustified) claims to special merit or importance
pretension *n*
preterite [**pret**-er-it] *adj, n grammar* (expressing) a past tense, such as *jumped, swam*
preternatural *adj* beyond what is natural, supernatural
pretext ⓣ *n* false reason given to hide the real one
Pretorius *n* **1 Andries Wilhelmus Jacobus.** 1799–1853, a Boer leader in the Great Trek (1838) to escape British sovereignty; he also led an expedition to the Transvaal (1848). The town Pretoria was named after him **2** his son, **Marthinus Wessels**. 1819–1901, first president of the South African Republic (1857–71) and of the Orange Free State (1859–63)
pretty ⓣ *adj* **-tier, -tiest 1** pleasing to look at ▷ *adv* **2** fairly, moderately **prettily** *adv* **prettiness** *n*
pretzel *n* brittle salted biscuit
prevail ⓣ *v* **1** gain mastery **2** be generally established
▸ **prevailing** *adj* **1** widespread **2** predominant
▸ **prevalent** *adj* widespread, common
prevalence *n*
prevaricate ⓣ *v* be evasive, avoid giving a direct or truthful answer **prevarication** *n*
prevent ⓣ *v* keep from happening or doing **preventable** *adj* **prevention** *n* **preventive** *adj, n*
Prévert *n* **Jacques**. 1900–77, Parisian poet, satirist, and writer of film scripts, noted esp. for his song poems. He was a member of the surrealist group from 1925 to 1929
preview ⓣ *n* advance showing of a film or exhibition before it is shown to the public
Previn *n* **André**. born 1929, US orchestral conductor, born in Germany; living in Britain

THESAURUS

presumptuous *adj* = **pushy** (*informal*), forward, bold, audacious, overconfident, insolent, too big for one's boots
presuppose *v* = **presume**, assume, imply, postulate, posit, take as read, take for granted
presupposition *n* = **assumption**, belief, premise, presumption, preconception, supposition
pretend *v* **1** = **feign**, fake, counterfeit, falsify, pass oneself off as • *Sometimes the boy pretended to be asleep.* **2** = **make believe**, act, suppose, imagine, make up ▷ **pretend to be** *See* **pose**
pretended *adj* = **feigned**, fake, false, so-called, counterfeit, pretend (*informal*), bogus, phony (*informal*), sham, pseudo (*informal*)
pretender *n* = **claimant**, aspirant
pretense *n* **1** = **deception**, acting, simulation, sham, deceit, charade, trickery, falsehood, feigning **2** = **show**, display, veneer, affectation, artifice, façade
pretension *n* **1** = **claim**, demand, assumption, profession, aspiration, pretense **2** = **affectation**, show, vanity, snobbery, self-importance, airs, conceit, ostentation, pretentiousness
pretentious *adj* = **affected**, pompous, conceited, ostentatious, snobbish • *Many critics thought his work and ideas pretentious and empty.*
pretext *n* = **guise**, show, cover, excuse, cloak, ploy, ruse, pretense
pretty *adj* **1** beautiful, attractive, cute, lovely • *a very charming and very pretty girl*
▸ *adv* **2** = **fairly**, rather, quite, kind of (*informal*) • *He's a pretty good card player.*
prevail *v* **1** = **win**, overcome, succeed, triumph, overrule, be victorious **2** = **be widespread**, abound, be current, be prevalent, exist generally, predominate
prevailing *adj* **1** = **widespread**, general, current, popular, common, cool (*informal*), usual, ordinary, prevalent, established, fashionable, customary, in vogue, phat (*slang*) **2** = **predominating**, main, ruling, principal, dominant
prevalence *n* = **commonness**, currency, popularity, frequency, universality
prevalent *adj* = **common**, general, current, popular, usual, widespread, frequent, universal, established, customary
prevaricate *v* = **evade**, dodge, deceive, cavil, beat about the bush, equivocate, hedge
prevent *v* = **stop**, thwart, foil, avert, hinder, impede • *the most practical way of preventing crime*
See also: **bar, prohibit**
prevention *n* = **elimination**, precaution, safeguard, avoidance, deterrence, thwarting
preventive *adj* **1** = **hindering**, obstructive, hampering, impeding **2** = **protective**, precautionary, deterrent, counteractive ▷ **preventive measure** *See* **precaution** ▸ *n* **3** = **hindrance**, block, obstacle, obstruction, impediment **4** = **protection**, prevention, shield, safeguard, remedy, deterrent
preview *n* = **advance showing**, trailer, foretaste, sneak preview, taster

P

DICTIONARY

previous Ⓣ *adj* coming or happening before **previously** *adv*
prey Ⓣ *n* **1** animal hunted and killed for food by another animal **2** victim
▸ **bird of prey** bird that kills and eats other birds or animals
▸ **prey on** *v* **1** hunt and kill for food **2** worry, obsess
price Ⓣ *n* **1** amount of money for which a thing is bought or sold **2** unpleasant thing that must be endured to get something desirable ▹ *v* **3** fix or ask the price of
▸ **priceless** *adj* **1** very valuable **2** *informal* very funny
▸ **pricey** *or* **pricy** *adj informal* expensive
prick Ⓣ *v* **1** pierce slightly with a sharp point **2** cause to feel mental pain **3** (of an animal) make (the ears) stand erect ▹ *n* **4** sudden sharp pain caused by pricking **5** mark made by pricking **6** remorse
▸ **prick up one's ears** listen intently
prickle Ⓣ *n* **1** thorn or spike on a plant ▹ *v* **2** have a tingling or pricking sensation **prickly** *adj*
▸ **prickly heat** itchy rash occurring in hot moist weather
pride Ⓣ *n* **1** feeling of pleasure and satisfaction when one has done well **2** too high an opinion of oneself **3** sense of dignity and self-respect **4** something that causes one to feel pride **5** group of lions
▸ **pride of place** most important position
▸ **pride oneself on** feel pride about
prie-dieu [pree-**dyur**] *n* upright frame with a ledge for kneeling upon, for use when praying
priest Ⓣ *n* **1** (in the Christian Church) a person who can administer the sacraments and preach **2** (in some other religions) an official who performs religious ceremonies **priesthood** *n* **priestly** *adj*
▸ **priestess** *n* woman priest
Priestley *n* **1 J(ohn) B(oynton)**. 1894–1984, English author. His works include the novels *The Good Companions* (1929) and *Angel Pavement* (1930) and the play *An Inspector Calls* (1946) **2 Joseph**. 1733–1804, English chemist, political theorist, and clergyman, in the US from 1794. He discovered oxygen (1774) independently of Scheele and isolated and described many other gases
prig Ⓣ *n* self-righteous person who acts as if superior to others **priggish** *adj* **priggishness** *n*
prim Ⓣ *adj* **primmer, primmest** formal, proper, and rather prudish **primly** *adv* **primness** *n*
prima ballerina *n* leading female ballet dancer
primacy *n, pl* **-cies 1** state of being first in rank, grade, etc. **2** office of an archbishop
prima donna Ⓣ *n* **1** leading female opera singer **2** *informal* temperamental person
primaeval *adj* same as **primeval**
prima facie [**prime**-a **fay**-shee] *Latin* as it seems at first

THESAURUS

previous *adj* = **earlier**, former, past, prior, one-time, preceding • *the previous year*
See also: **last**
previously *adv* = **before**, once, earlier, formerly, beforehand, hitherto, in the past
prey *n* **1** = **quarry**, game, kill **2** = **victim**, target, mug (*Brit slang*), dupe, fall guy (*informal*)
price *n* **1** = **cost**, charge, figure, value, amount, fee • *a sharp increase in the price of gasoline* **2** = **consequences**, cost, penalty, toll ▸ *v* **3** = **value**, cost, estimate, appraise, put a price on • *I just can't imagine why it has been priced at this level.*
See also: **rate**
priceless *adj* **1** = **valuable**, expensive, costly, precious, dear, invaluable **2** (*Informal*) = **hilarious**, comic, funny, amusing, droll, rib-tickling, side-splitting
pricey *adj* = **expensive**, costly, steep (*informal*), dear, high-priced
prick *v* **1** = **pierce**, stab, punch, jab, puncture, lance, perforate **2** = **sting**, bite, smart, itch, tingle, prickle ▸ *n* **3** = **puncture**, wound, hole, perforation, pinhole
prickle *n* **1** = **spike**, point, spur, needle, spine, barb, thorn ▸ *v* **2** = **tingle**, smart, sting, itch **3** = **prick**, stick, jab
prickly *adj* **1** = **spiny**, barbed, thorny, bristly **2** = **itchy**, sharp, scratchy, crawling, smarting, stinging, tingling
pride *n* **1** = **satisfaction**, delight, pleasure • *We take pride in offering you the highest standards in the industry.* **2** = **conceit**, arrogance, vanity, snobbery, egotism, smugness • *His pride may still be his downfall.* OPPOSITE: humility **3** = **self-respect**, dignity, honour, self-esteem, self-worth **4** = **gem**, treasure, jewel, pride and joy
See also: **pick**
priest *n* = **clergyman**, minister, father, cleric, pastor, divine, curate, vicar, ecclesiastic
prig *n* = **goody-goody** (*informal*), prude, puritan, stuffed shirt (*informal*)
priggish *adj* = **self-righteous**, prim, puritanical, goody-goody (*informal*), holier-than-thou, prudish
prim *adj* = **prudish**, proper, puritanical, straitlaced • *We tend to assume our great-grandparents were very prim and proper.*
prima donna *n* = **diva**, star, leading lady

DICTIONARY

primal *adj* of basic causes or origins
primary Ⓣ *adj* **1** chief, most important **2** being the first stage, elementary
primarily *adv*
▸ **primary colours** (in physics) red, green, and blue or (in art) red, yellow, and blue, from which all other colours can be produced by mixing
▸ **primary school** school for children from five to eleven years
primate[1] *n* archbishop
primate[2] *n* member of an order of mammals including monkeys and humans
prime Ⓣ *adj* **1** main, most important **2** of the highest quality ▹ *n* **3** time when someone is at his or her best or most vigorous ▹ *v* **4** give (someone) information in advance to prepare them for something **5** prepare (a surface) for painting **6** prepare (a gun, pump, etc.) for use
▸ **Prime Minister** leader of a government
▸ **prime number** number that can be divided exactly only by itself and one
primer *n* **1** special paint applied to bare wood etc. before the main paint **2** beginners' school book or manual
primeval, primaeval Ⓣ [prime-**ee**-val] *adj* of the earliest age of the world
primitive Ⓣ *adj* **1** of an early simple stage of development **2** basic, crude: *a primitive hut*
primogeniture *n* system under which the eldest son inherits all his parents' property
primordial *adj* existing at or from the beginning
primrose *n* pale yellow spring flower
primula *n* type of primrose with brightly coloured flowers
Primus *n* ® portable cooking stove used esp. by campers
prince Ⓣ *n* **1** male member of a royal family, esp. the son of the king or queen **2** male ruler of a small country
▸ **princely** *adj* **1** of or like a prince **2** generous, lavish, or magnificent
▸ **prince consort** husband of a reigning queen
▸ **Prince of Wales** eldest son of the British sovereign
▸ **princess** *n* female member of a royal family, esp. the daughter of the king or queen
▸ **Princess Royal** title sometimes given to the eldest daughter of the British sovereign
Prince *n* full name *Prince Rogers Nelson.* born 1958, US rock singer, songwriter, record producer, and multi-instrumentalist. His albums include *Dirty Mind* (1981), *Purple Rain* (1984), *Parade* (1986), and *Emancipation* (1996)
principal Ⓣ *adj* **1** main, most important ▹ *n* **2** head of a school or college **3** person taking a leading part in something **4** sum of money lent on which interest is paid **principally** *adv*
▸ **principal boy** leading male role in pantomime, played by a woman
principality *n, pl* **-ties** territory ruled by a prince
principle Ⓣ *n* **1** moral rule guiding behaviour **2** general or basic truth: *the principle of equality* **3** scientific law concerning the working of something

P

THESAURUS

primarily *adv* **1 = chiefly**, mostly, largely, generally, mainly, essentially, fundamentally, principally, above all **2 = at first**, initially, originally, at the start *or* from the start, first and foremost, in the beginning, in the first place
primary *adj* **1 = chief**, first, prime, main, principal, cardinal, paramount, cutting-edge, greatest, highest **2 = elementary**, simple, introductory, rudimentary
prime *adj* **1 = main**, chief, principal, leading • *a prime cause of traffic accidents* **2 = best**, choice, select, superior, first-rate • *prime beef* ▸ *n* **3 = peak**, height, flower, bloom, heyday, zenith ▸ *v* **4 = inform**, tell, brief, notify, clue in (*informal*), fill in (*informal*) **5 = prepare**, coach, train, get ready, make ready
See also: **first, foremost, top**
primed *See* **ready**
primeval, primaeval *adj* = **earliest**, first, early, old, ancient, prehistoric, primitive, primal, primordial
primitive *adj* = **crude**, simple, rough, rude, rudimentary • *a primitive shack*
See also: **early**
prince *n* = **ruler**, monarch, lord, sovereign
princely *adj* **1 = regal**, royal, sovereign, noble, majestic, imperial **2 = generous**, liberal, rich, lavish, gracious, bounteous, munificent, open-handed
principal *adj* **1 = main**, first, major, chief, prime, primary, foremost • *His principal concern is that of winning the school election.* ▸ *n* **2 = head teacher**, head (*informal*), dean, superintendent, headmaster *or* headmistress **3 = leader**, lead, star, alpha male **4 = capital**, money, assets
See also: **essential, leading, supreme, top**
principally *adv* = **mainly**, especially, mostly, largely, primarily, predominantly, chiefly, above all
principle *n* **1 = morals**, integrity, conscience, scruples, sense of duty • *a person of principle* **2 = rule**, law, fundamental, doctrine, canon, axiom • *the basic principles of capitalism* ▹ **in principle = in theory**, ideally, theoretically

DICTIONARY

▸ **in principle** in theory but not always in practice
▸ **on principle** because of one's beliefs
print Ⓣ *v* **1** reproduce (a newspaper, book, etc.) in large quantities by mechanical or electronic means **2** reproduce (text or pictures) by pressing ink onto paper etc. **3** write in letters that are not joined up **4** stamp (fabric) with a design **5** *photog* produce (pictures) from negatives ▹ *n* **6** printed words etc. **7** printed lettering **8** photograph **9** printed copy of a painting **10** mark left on a surface by something that has pressed against it **11** printed fabric
▸ **out of print** no longer available from a publisher
▸ **printer** *n* **1** person or company engaged in printing **2** machine that prints
▸ **printed circuit** electronic circuit with wiring printed on an insulating base
▸ **print-out** *n* printed information from a computer
prior[1] Ⓣ *adj* earlier
▸ **prior to** before
prior[2] *n* head monk in a priory
▸ **prioress** *n* deputy head nun in a convent
▸ **priory** *n* place where certain orders of monks or nuns live
priority Ⓣ *n, pl* **-ties 1** most important thing that must be dealt with first **2** right to be or go before others
prise *v* force open by levering
prism *n* transparent block usu. with triangular ends and rectangular sides, used to disperse light into a spectrum or refract it in optical instruments
▸ **prismatic** *adj* **1** of or shaped like a prism **2** (of colour) as if produced by refraction through a prism, rainbow-like
prison Ⓣ *n* building where criminals and accused people are held
▸ **prisoner** *n* person held captive
▸ **prisoner of war** serviceman captured by an enemy in wartime
prissy Ⓣ *adj* **-sier, -siest** prim, correct, and easily shocked **prissily** *adv*
pristine Ⓣ *adj* completely new, clean, and pure
Pritchett *n* Sir **V(ictor) S(awdon)**. 1900–97, British short-story writer, novelist, essayist, and autobiographer; his works include *Mr. Beluncle* (1951) and *A Careless Widow* (1989)
private Ⓣ *adj* **1** for the use of one person or group only **2** secret **3** owned or paid for by individuals rather than by the government **4** quiet, not likely to be disturbed **5** personal, unconnected with one's work ▹ *n* **6** soldier of the lowest rank **privately** *adv* **privacy** *n*
privateer *n hist* **1** privately owned armed vessel authorized by the government to take part in a war **2** captain of such a ship
privation *n* loss or lack of the necessities of life
privatize *v* sell (a publicly owned company) to individuals or a private company
privatization *n*
privet *n* bushy evergreen shrub used for hedges
privilege Ⓣ *n* advantage or favour that only some people have
▸ **privileged** *adj* enjoying a special right or immunity
privy Ⓣ *adj* **1** sharing knowledge of something secret ▹ *n, pl* **privies 2** *obsolete*

THESAURUS

See also: **basis, belief, ideal**
principles *See* **conscience, standards**
print *v* **1 = publish**, issue, mark, stamp, impress, engrave, imprint ▸ *n* **2 = publication**, book, newspaper, magazine, newsprint, periodical, printed matter **3 = reproduction**, photo (*informal*), picture, copy, photograph, engraving
prior *adj* **= earlier**, former, previous, preceding, foregoing, pre-existent, pre-existing ▹ **prior to = before**, preceding, earlier than, previous to
priority *n* **= precedence**, rank, preference, seniority, pre-eminence, right of way
priory *n* **= monastery**, convent, abbey, nunnery, religious house
prison *n* **= jail**, penitentiary, dungeon, penal institution • *a high-security prison*
prisoner *n* **1 = convict** • *top-security prisoners* **2 = captive**, hostage • *concentration-camp prisoners*
prissy *adj* **= prim**, old-maidish (*informal*), prim and proper, prudish, strait-laced
pristine *adj* **= new**, pure, untouched, unspoiled, immaculate, uncorrupted, undefiled, unsullied, virginal
privacy *n* **= seclusion**, retirement, retreat, isolation, solitude
private *adj* **1 = exclusive**, special, personal, individual • *a private bathroom* **2 = secret**, confidential, clandestine • *a private wedding* OPPOSITE: public **3 = secluded**, separate, secret, isolated, solitary, concealed, sequestered
See also: **own**
privilege *n* **= right**, claim, due, advantage, freedom, concession, liberty, entitlement, prerogative
privileged *adj* **= special**, elite, advantaged, entitled, favoured, honoured
privy *adj* ▹ **privy to = informed of**, apprised of, aware of, cognizant of, in on, in the know about (*informal*), wise to (*slang*) ▸ *n* **= lavatory**, bathroom, washroom,

DICTIONARY

lavatory, esp. an outside one
▶ **privy council** council of state of a monarch
prize¹ Ⓣ *n* **1** reward given for success in a competition etc. ▷ *adj* **2** winning or likely to win a prize ▷ *v* **3** value highly
▶ **prizefighter** *n* boxer who fights for money **prizefight** *n*
prize² *v* same as **prise**
pro¹ *adj, adv* in favour of
▶ **pros and cons** arguments for and against
pro² *n* **1** professional **2** prostitute
pro- *prefix* **1** in favour of: *pro-Russian* **2** instead of: *pron*
proactive *adj* tending to initiate change rather than reacting to events
probable Ⓣ *adj* likely to happen or be true **probably** *adv* **probability** *n*
probate *n* **1** process of proving the authenticity of a will **2** certificate of this
probation Ⓣ *n* **1** system of dealing with law-breakers, esp. juvenile ones, by placing them under supervision **2** period when a person is assessed for suitability for a job etc.
▶ **probationer** *n* person on probation
probe Ⓣ *v* **1** search into or examine closely ▷ *n* **2** surgical instrument used to examine a wound, cavity, etc.
probiotic *n* **1** bacterium that protects the body from harmful bacteria ▷ *adj* **2** relating to probiotics: *probiotic yoghurts*
probity *n* honesty, integrity
problem Ⓣ *n* **1** something difficult to deal with or solve **2** question or puzzle set for solution **problematical** *adj*
proboscis [pro-**boss**-iss] *n* **1** elephant's trunk **2** long snout **3** elongated mouthpart of some insects
procedure Ⓣ *n* way of doing something, esp. the correct or usual one
proceed Ⓣ *v* **1** start or continue doing **2** *formal* walk, go **3** start a legal action **4** arise from
▶ **proceeds** *pl n* money obtained from an event or activity
▶ **proceedings** *pl n* **1** organized or related series of events **2** minutes of a meeting **3** legal action
process Ⓣ *n* **1** series of actions or changes **2** method of doing or producing something ▷ *v* **3** handle or prepare by a special method

THESAURUS

latrine, outhouse, outside toilet
prize¹ *n* **1** = **award**, honour, trophy, accolade • *first prize at the piano competition* **2** = **winnings**, haul, jackpot, purse, stakes ▶ *adj* **3** = **champion**, top, award-winning, outstanding, first-rate • *a prize bull*
See also: **reward**
prize² *v* = **value**, treasure, cherish, esteem • *These ornaments are prized by collectors.*
See also: **appreciate**
prized *adj* = **treasured**, beloved, precious, cherished, valued, much loved
probability *n* = **likelihood**, prospect, chances, odds • *the probability of a serious earthquake*
See also: **chance**
probable *adj* = **likely**, apparent, feasible, plausible, in the cards • *a misunderstanding about the probable cost* OPPOSITE: improbable
See also: **believable, potential**
probably *adv* = **likely**, presumably, doubtless, in all probability • *The wedding is probably going to be in late August.*
probation *n* = **trial period**, trial, apprenticeship
probe *v* **1** = **examine**, search, investigate, explore, scrutinize, go into, look into **2** = **explore**, poke, prod, feel around ▶ *n* **3** = **examination**, study, investigation, inquiry, exploration, scrutiny, detection
problem *n* **1** = **difficulty**, trouble, bitch (*informal*), predicament, quandary • *the economic problems of the city* **2** = **puzzle**, riddle, conundrum • *a mathematical problem*
See also: **business, complex, drawback, issue, snag**
problematic *adj* = **tricky**, doubtful, dubious, debatable, problematical, puzzling
procedure *n* = **method**, policy, system, process, practice, strategy • *He did not follow the correct procedure in applying for a permit.*
See also: **course, measure, routine, way**
proceed *v* **1** = **begin**, start, get under way • *I had no idea how to proceed.* OPPOSITE: cease **2** = **continue**, carry on, go on • *They proceeded with the trial.* OPPOSITE: cease **3** = **go on**, continue, travel, advance, progress, make your way • *She proceeded along the hallway.* **4** = **arise**, come, issue, result, spring, stem, flow, originate, derive, emanate
See also: **go, journey**
proceeding *n* = **action**, move, step, process, act, measure, procedure, deed ▷ **proceedings** = **business**, report, account, archives, doings, affairs, minutes, records, transactions
See also: **case**
proceeds *pl n* = **income**, profit, gain, revenue, yield, earnings, products, returns, takings
process *n* **1** = **procedure**, system, method, means, course of action • *The building process was spread over three years.* **2** = **development**, growth, advance, progress, movement, evolution, progression ▶ *v* **3** = **deal with**, handle, dispose of, take care of • *Your*

DICTIONARY

of manufacture **4** treat (food) to prevent it decaying **processor** *n*
procession ⓣ *n* line of people or vehicles moving forward together in order
proclaim ⓣ *v* declare publicly **proclamation** *n*
proclivity *n, pl* **-ties** inclination, tendency
proconsul *n hist* governor of a province, esp. of the Roman Empire
procrastinate ⓣ *v* put off taking action, delay **procrastination** *n* **procrastinator** *n*
procreate *v formal* produce offspring **procreation** *n*
Procrustean *adj* ruthlessly enforcing uniformity
procure ⓣ *v* **1** get, provide **2** obtain (people) to act as prostitutes **procurement** *n*
▸ **procurer** (**procuress**) *n* person who obtains people to act as prostitutes
prod ⓣ *v* **prodding, prodded 1** poke with something pointed **2** goad (someone) to take action ▷ *n* **3** prodding
Prodi *n* **Romano**. born 1939, Italian politician; prime minister (1996–98; 2006–08); president of the European Commission from 1999–2004
prodigal ⓣ *adj* recklessly extravagant, wasteful **prodigality** *n*
prodigy ⓣ *n, pl* **-gies 1** person with some marvellous talent **2** wonderful thing
▸ **prodigious** *adj* **1** very large, immense **2** wonderful **prodigiously** *adv*
produce ⓣ *v* **1** bring into existence **2** present to view, show **3** make, manufacture **4** present on stage, film, or television ▷ *n* **5** food grown for sale
▸ **producer** *n* **1** person with financial and administrative control of a film etc. **2** *Brit* person responsible for the artistic direction of a play **3** person or company that produces something
product ⓣ *n* **1** something produced **2** number resulting from multiplication
▸ **production** *n* **1** producing **2** things produced **3** presentation of a play, opera, etc.
▸ **productive** *adj* **1** producing large quantities **2** useful, profitable **productivity** *n*
profane ⓣ *adj* **1** showing disrespect for

THESAURUS

application is being processed.
See also: **action, manufacture**
processed *See* **refined**
procession *n* = **parade**, file, train, march, cortege, cavalcade
proclaim *v* = **declare**, announce, publish, indicate, advertise, circulate, herald, profess, make known
proclamation *n* = **declaration**, announcement, notice, publication, decree, pronouncement, notification, edict
procrastinate *v* = **delay**, postpone, stall, dally, drag one's feet (*informal*), gain time, play for time, put off, temporize
procure *v* = **obtain**, win, get, find, score (*slang*), buy, gain, purchase, acquire, secure, come by, pick up
prod *v* **1** = **poke**, drive, push, dig, nudge, shove, jab **2** = **prompt**, move, urge, spur, motivate, stimulate, incite, rouse, goad, egg on, impel ▸ *n* **3** = **poke**, push, dig, nudge, shove, jab **4** = **prompt**, signal, reminder, stimulus, cue
prodigal *adj* = **extravagant**, excessive, reckless, spendthrift, wasteful, immoderate, improvident, profligate
prodigious *adj* **1** = **huge**, giant, massive, vast, enormous, immense, gigantic, colossal, monstrous **2** = **wonderful**, amazing, remarkable, extraordinary, fantastic (*informal*), exceptional, fabulous, phenomenal, marvelous, staggering
prodigy *n* **1** = **genius**, talent, mastermind, wizard, whizz (*informal*) **2** = **wonder**, phenomenon, sensation, miracle, marvel
produce *v* **1** = **make**, create, manufacture, construct, invent, scare up (*informal*) • *clothing produced from the finest materials* **2** = **show**, advance, bring forward, bring to light, put forward • *To rent a car, you must produce a driver's licence.* **3** = **cause**, effect, generate, bring about, give rise to **4** = **bring forth**, bear, deliver, breed, beget **5** = **present**, do, show, stage, direct, exhibit, mount, put on ▸ *n* **6** = **fruit and vegetables**, product, crop, yield, harvest, greengrocery
See also: **bring, compose, lead to, occasion, provoke**
producer *n* **1** = **director**, impresario **2** = **maker**, farmer, manufacturer, grower
product *n* **1** = **goods**, produce, commodity, merchandise • *Many household products give off noxious fumes.* **2** = **result**, effect, consequence, outcome, upshot
production *n* **1** = **producing**, construction, manufacture, creation, formation, making, fabrication, manufacturing **2** = **presentation**, management, direction, staging
productive *adj* **1** = **fertile**, prolific, fruitful • *Training makes workers highly productive.* OPPOSITE: unproductive **2** = **useful**, valuable, constructive, worthwhile • *I'm hopeful the talks will be productive.* OPPOSITE: unproductive
See also: **economic, efficient**
productivity *n* = **output**, production, yield, work rate
profane *adj* **1** = **sacrilegious**, wicked,

DICTIONARY

religion or holy things **2** (of language) coarse, blasphemous ▷ *v* **3** treat (something sacred) irreverently, desecrate

▶ **profanation** *n* act of profaning

▶ **profanity** *n* profane talk or behaviour, blasphemy

profess Ⓣ *v* **1** state or claim (something as true), sometimes falsely **2** have as one's belief or religion

▶ **professed** *adj* supposed

profession Ⓣ *n* **1** type of work, such as being a doctor, that needs special training **2** all the people employed in a profession: *the legal profession* **3** declaration of a belief or feeling

▶ **professional** *adj* **1** working in a profession **2** taking part in an activity, such as sport or music, for money **3** very competent ▷ *n* **4** person who works in a profession **5** person paid to take part in sport, music, etc. **professionally** *adv* **professionalism** *n*

professor Ⓣ *n* teacher in a university **professorial** *adj* **professorship** *n*

proffer *v* offer

proficient Ⓣ *adj* skilled, expert **proficiency** *n*

profile Ⓣ *n* **1** outline, esp. of the face, as seen from the side **2** brief biographical sketch

▶ **profiling** *n* practice of categorizing and predicting the behaviour of people according to certain characteristics: *racial profiling*

profit Ⓣ *n* **1** money gained **2** benefit obtained ▷ *v* **3** gain or benefit

▶ **profitable** *adj* making profit **profitably** *adv* **profitability** *n*

▶ **profiteer** *n* person who makes excessive profits at the expense of the public **profiteering** *n*

profligate Ⓣ *adj* **1** recklessly extravagant **2** shamelessly immoral ▷ *n* **3** dissolute person **profligacy** *n*

pro forma *Latin* prescribing a set form

profound Ⓣ *adj* **1** showing or needing great knowledge **2** strongly felt, intense **profundity** *n*

THESAURUS

disrespectful, irreverent, sinful, godless, impious, impure, irreligious, ungodly **2 = crude**, foul, obscene, vulgar, coarse, blasphemous, filthy ▶ *v* **3 = desecrate**, violate, defile, debase, commit sacrilege

profanity *n* **1 = sacrilege**, blasphemy, impiety, profaneness **2 = swearing**, curse, obscenity, irreverence, cursing

profess *v* **1 = claim**, allege, fake, pretend, purport, feign, make out **2 = state**, announce, admit, declare, confess, assert, proclaim, affirm, vouch, avow

professed *adj* **1 = supposed**, alleged, so-called, would-be, purported, self-styled, ostensible, pretended **2 = declared**, proclaimed, self-confessed, avowed, confessed, confirmed, self-acknowledged

profession *n* **1 = occupation**, business, career • *a teacher by profession* **2 = declared**, proclaimed, self-confessed, avowed, confessed, confirmed, self-acknowledged
See also: **job, trade, work**

professional *adj* **1 = expert**, efficient, skilled, experienced, competent, qualified, adept, proficient, masterly ▶ *n* **2 = expert**, specialist, master, pro (*slang*), maestro, adept, virtuoso, past master

professionally *See* **well**

professor *n* **= teacher**, fellow (*Brit*), don (*Brit*), prof (*informal*)

proficiency *n* **= skill**, ability, expertise, mastery, knack, competence, know-how (*informal*), dexterity, aptitude

proficient *adj* **= skilled**, able, capable, efficient, competent, accomplished, adept, skilful • *They tend to be proficient in foreign languages.* OPPOSITE: incompetent
See also: **expert, practical**

profile *n* **1 = outline**, figure, form, drawing, sketch, silhouette, contour, side view **2 = biography**, sketch, characterization, vignette, thumbnail sketch

profit *n* **1 = earnings**, revenue, surplus, proceeds, takings • *The bank made pre-tax profits of $3.5 million.* OPPOSITE: loss **2 = benefit**, good, use, gain, value, advantage, advancement ▶ *v* **3 = take advantage of**, exploit, capitalize on, make the most of • *He profited shamefully at the expense of my family.* **4 = benefit**, help, serve, gain, improve, promote, be of advantage to

profitable *adj* **1 = moneymaking**, productive, viable, economical • *Our new venture has proved highly profitable.* **2 = beneficial**, valuable, useful, productive, worthwhile, rewarding, win-win (*informal*), fruitful, advantageous
See also: **helpful, successful**

profiteer *n* **1 = racketeer**, exploiter ▶ *v* **2 = exploit**, racketeer, make a quick buck (*slang*)

profits *See* **income**

profligate *adj* **1 = extravagant**, reckless, spendthrift, wasteful, immoderate, improvident, prodigal **2 = depraved**, wild, wicked, immoral, shameless, degenerate, wanton, debauched, dissolute, licentious ▶ *n* **3 = spendthrift**, squanderer, waster, wastrel **4 = degenerate**, rake, libertine, debauchee, reprobate, roué

profound *adj* **1 = wise**, deep, sage, philosophical, abstruse, learned, penetrating, sagacious **2 = intense**, great,

DICTIONARY

profuse Ⓣ *adj* plentiful **profusion** *n*
progeny Ⓣ [**proj**-in-ee] *n, pl* **-nies** children
▸ **progenitor** [pro-**jen**-it-er] *n* ancestor
progesterone *n* hormone which prepares the womb for pregnancy and prevents further ovulation
prognathous *adj* having a projecting lower jaw
prognosis Ⓣ *n, pl* **-noses** **1** doctor's forecast about the progress of an illness **2** any forecast
prognostication *n* forecast or prediction
program Ⓣ *n* **1** sequence of coded instructions for a computer ▷ *v* **-gramming, -grammed** **2** arrange (data) so that it can be processed by a computer **3** feed a program into (a computer) **programmer** *n* **programmable** *adj*
programme *n* **1** planned series of events **2** broadcast on radio or television **3** list of items or performers in an entertainment
progress Ⓣ *n* **1** improvement, development **2** movement forward ▷ *v* **3** become more advanced or skilful **4** move forward
▸ **in progress** taking place
▸ **progression** *n* **1** act of progressing, advance **2** sequence of numbers in which each differs from the next by a fixed ratio
▸ **progressive** *adj* **1** favouring political or social reform **2** happening gradually **progressively** *adv*
prohibit Ⓣ *v* forbid or prevent from happening
▸ **prohibition** *n* **1** act of forbidding **2** ban on the sale or drinking of alcohol
▸ **prohibitive** *adj* (of prices) too high to be affordable **prohibitively** *adv*
project Ⓣ *n* **1** planned scheme to do or examine something over a period ▷ *v* **2** make a forecast based on known data **3** make (a film or slide) appear on a screen **4** communicate (an impression) **5** stick out beyond a surface or edge **projection** *n*
▸ **projector** *n* apparatus for projecting photographic images, films, or slides on a screen
▸ **projectionist** *n* person who operates a projector
projectile Ⓣ *n* object thrown as a weapon or fired from a gun
Prokofiev *n* **Sergei Sergeyevich**. 1891–1953, Soviet composer. His compositions include the orchestral fairy tale *Peter and the Wolf* (1936), the opera *The Love for Three Oranges* (1921), and seven symphonies
prolapse *n* slipping down of an internal organ of the body from its normal position

THESAURUS

extreme, acute, keen, heartfelt, deeply felt
profuse *adj* = **plentiful**, prolific, ample, abundant, bountiful, copious, luxuriant, overflowing
profusion *n* = **abundance**, surplus, excess, wealth, quantity, bounty, glut, plethora, extravagance
progeny *n* = **children**, family, issue, young, stock, race, offspring, lineage, descendants, posterity
prognosis *n* = **forecast**, prediction, diagnosis, projection, prognostication
program *n* **1** = **schedule**, agenda, timetable • *We attended several training programs.* **2** = **broadcast**, show • *local news programs*
See also: **routine**
progress *n* **1** = **advance**, improvement, breakthrough, headway • *progress in the fight against cancer* **2** = **movement**, way, advance, course, passage ▷ **in progress** = **going on**, proceeding, happening, being done, occurring, taking place, under way ▸ *v* **3** = **advance**, develop, improve, blossom • *His piano playing is progressing well.* **4** = **move on**, continue, travel, advance, proceed, go forward, make headway
progression *n* **1** = **progress**, gain, advance, advancement, headway, furtherance, movement forward **2** = **sequence**, series, course, chain, string, cycle, succession
progressive *adj* **1** = **enlightened**, liberal, modern, advanced, radical, revolutionary, reformist, avant-garde, forward-looking **2** = **growing**, ongoing, advancing, continuing, developing, increasing
prohibit *v* **1** = **forbid**, ban, prevent, outlaw, interdict • *a law that prohibits parking during certain hours* OPPOSITE: allow **2** = **prevent**, stop, restrict, hamper, hinder, impede
See also: **veto**
prohibited *See* **illegal**
prohibition *n* **1** = **prevention**, restriction, obstruction, exclusion, constraint **2** = **ban**, bar, boycott, injunction, veto, embargo, interdict, proscription, interdict
prohibitive *adj* = **exorbitant**, excessive, steep (*informal*), extortionate
project *n* **1** = **scheme**, work, plan, job, activity, task, venture, occupation, assignment, enterprise, undertaking ▸ *v* **2** = **forecast**, estimate, predict, calculate, gauge, reckon, extrapolate **3** = **stick out**, extend, bulge, protrude, jut, overhang, stand out
projectile *n* = **missile**, rocket, bullet, shell
projection *n* **1** = **protrusion**, shelf, bulge, ridge, ledge, overhang, protuberance **2** = **forecast**, estimate, calculation, estimation, reckoning, computation, extrapolation
proletarian *adj* **1** = **working-class**,

DICTIONARY

prole *adj, n informal* proletarian
proletariat ⓣ [pro-lit-**air**-ee-at] *n* working class **proletarian** *adj, n*
proliferate ⓣ *v* **1** increase rapidly in numbers **2** grow or reproduce (new parts, such as cells) rapidly **proliferation** *n*
prolific ⓣ *adj* very productive **prolifically** *adv*
prolix *adj* (of speech or a piece of writing) overlong and boring **prolixity** *n*
prologue ⓣ *n* introduction to a play or book
prolong ⓣ *v* make (something) last longer **prolongation** *n*
prom *n* **1** formal dance at a school **2** short for **promenade, promenade concert**
promenade ⓣ *n* **1** paved walkway along the seafront at a holiday resort ▷ *v, n* **2** *old-fashioned* (take) a leisurely walk
▶ **promenade concert** concert at which part of the audience stands rather than sits
prominent ⓣ *adj* **1** famous, widely known **2** very noticeable **prominently** *adv* **prominence** *n*
promiscuous ⓣ *adj* having many casual sexual relationships **promiscuity** *n*
promise ⓣ *v* **1** say that one will definitely do or not do something **2** show signs of, seem likely ▷ *n* **3** undertaking to do or not to do something **4** indication of future success
▶ **show promise** seem likely to succeed
▶ **promising** *adj* likely to succeed or turn out well
promo *n informal* short video film made to promote a pop record
promontory ⓣ *n, pl* **-ries** point of high land jutting out into the sea
promote ⓣ *v* **1** help to make (something) happen or increase **2** raise to a higher rank or position **3** encourage the sale of by advertising **promotion** *n* **promotional** *adj*
▶ **promoter** *n* person who organizes or finances an event etc.
prompt ⓣ *v* **1** cause (an action) **2** remind (an actor or speaker) of words that he or she has forgotten ▷ *adj* **3** done without delay ▷ *adv* **4** exactly: *six o'clock prompt* **promptness** *n*

THESAURUS

common, plebeian ▶ *n* **2 = worker**, commoner, man of the people, pleb, plebeian
proletariat *n* = **working class**, commoners, hoi polloi, labouring classes, lower classes, plebs, the common people, the masses
proliferate *v* = **increase**, expand, breed, multiply, grow rapidly
proliferation *n* = **increase**, spread, expansion, multiplication
prolific *adj* = **productive**, abundant, fertile, fruitful, copious, fecund, luxuriant, profuse
prologue *n* = **introduction**, preliminary, prelude, preamble, preface, foreword
prolong *v* = **lengthen**, continue, delay, extend, stretch, perpetuate, drag out, draw out, protract, spin out
prolonged *See* **continuous**
promenade *n* **1** = **walkway**, parade, prom, esplanade **2** = **stroll**, turn, walk, constitutional, saunter ▶ *v* **3** = **stroll**, walk, saunter, perambulate, take a walk
prominence *n* **1** = **conspicuousness**, markedness **2** = **fame**, name, celebrity, reputation, importance, distinction, prestige, eminence
prominent *adj* **1** = **famous**, important, renowned, well-known, notable, eminent, noted • *a prominent journalist* **2** = **noticeable**, obvious, striking, pronounced, conspicuous, eye-catching, jutting • *a prominent feature of the landscape*
See also: **leading**
promiscuity *n* = **licentiousness**, immorality, debauchery, looseness, permissiveness, promiscuousness, wantonness
promiscuous *adj* = **licentious**, fast, wild, loose, abandoned, immoral, libertine, wanton, debauched
promise *v* **1** = **guarantee**, pledge, vow, assure, give your word • *I promise not to be back too late.* **2** = **show signs of**, indicate, hint at • *This promised to be a very long night.* ▶ *n* **3** = **guarantee**, pledge, vow, assurance, undertaking • *If you make a promise, you should keep it.* **4** = **potential**, ability, capacity, talent, capability, flair, aptitude
See also: **bond, oath, prospect, word**
promising *adj* **1** = **encouraging**, likely, bright, hopeful, rosy, favourable, auspicious, propitious, reassuring **2** = **talented**, able, gifted, rising
promontory *n* = **point**, head, cape, headland, foreland
promote *v* **1** = **support**, back • *All attempts to promote interest in putting on a school musical have failed.* **2** = **advertise**, plug (*informal*), publicize • *She's in Europe promoting her new movie.* **3** = **elevate**, upgrade • *He has been promoted twice in two years.*
See also: **advocate, champion**
promotion *n* **1** = **rise**, honor, advancement, elevation, exaltation, move up, preferment, upgrading **2** = **publicity**, advertising, plugging (*informal*) **3** = **encouragement**, support, advancement, boosting, furtherance
prompt *v* **1** = **cause**, spur, inspire, motivate, induce • *The uncertain economy has prompted consumers to stop buying new cars.* **2** = **remind**, coax • *"What was that you were saying about a guided tour?" he prompted her.* ▶ *adj* **3** = **immediate**, quick, rapid, instant, swift,

P

DICTIONARY

▸ **promptly** *adv* immediately, without delay
▸ **prompter** *n* person offstage who prompts actors
promulgate Ⓣ *v* **1** put (a law etc.) into effect by announcing it officially **2** make widely known **promulgation** *n* **promulgator** *n*
prone Ⓣ *adj* **1** (foll. by *to*) likely to do or be affected by (something) **2** lying face downwards
prong Ⓣ *n* one spike of a fork or similar instrument **pronged** *adj*
pronoun *n* word, such as *she, it,* used to replace a *n* **pronominal** *adj*
pronounce Ⓣ *v* **1** form the sounds of (words or letters), esp. clearly or in a particular way **2** declare formally or officially **pronounceable** *adj*
▸ **pronounced** *adj* very noticeable
▸ **pronouncement** *n* formal announcement
▸ **pronunciation** *n* way in which a word or language is pronounced
pronto *adv informal* at once
proof Ⓣ *n* **1** evidence that shows that something is true or has happened **2** copy of something printed, such as the pages of a book, for checking before final production ▹ *adj* **3** able to withstand: *proof against criticism* **4** denoting the strength of an alcoholic drink: *seventy proof*
▸ **proofread** *v* read and correct (printer's proofs) **proofreader** *n*
prop[1] Ⓣ *v* **propping, propped 1** support (something) so that it stays upright or in place ▹ *n* **2** pole, beam, etc. used as a support
prop[2] *n* movable object used on the set of a film or play
prop[3] *n informal* propeller
propaganda Ⓣ *n* (organized promotion of) information to assist or damage the cause of a government or movement **propagandist** *n*
propagate Ⓣ *v* **1** spread (information and ideas) **2** reproduce, breed, or grow **propagation** *n*
propane *n* flammable gas found in petroleum and used as a fuel
propel Ⓣ *v* **-pelling, -pelled** cause to move forward
▸ **propellant** *n* **1** something that provides or causes propulsion **2** gas used in an aerosol spray
▸ **propeller** *n* revolving shaft with blades for driving a ship or aircraft
▸ **propulsion** *n* **1** propelling or being propelled **2** method by which something is propelled
propensity Ⓣ *n, pl* **-ties** natural tendency
proper Ⓣ *adj* **1** real or genuine **2** appropriate **3** suited to a particular purpose **4** correct in behaviour **5** excessively moral **6** *informal* complete **properly** *adv*

THESAURUS

instantaneous • *a serious condition that needs prompt treatment* ▸ *adv* **4** (*Informal*) = **exactly**, sharp, promptly, on the dot, punctually
See also: **drive, hasty, occasion, provoke, punctual**
promptly *adv* = **exactly**, sharp, precisely, on the dot • *He showed up for the interview promptly at ten.*
See also: **immediately**
promptness *n* = **swiftness**, speed, willingness, haste, quickness, eagerness, briskness, punctuality
promulgate *v* = **make known**, publish, broadcast, spread, promote, communicate, circulate, proclaim, disseminate, make public
prone *adj* **1** = **liable**, susceptible, given, inclined, disposed • *He is prone to depression.* **2** = **face down**, prostrate • *We were lying prone on the grass.*
prong *n* = **point**, spike, tine
pronounce *v* **1** = **say**, speak, sound, accent, articulate, enunciate **2** = **declare**, announce, deliver, proclaim, affirm, decree
pronounced *adj* = **noticeable**, obvious, evident, distinct, marked, striking, definite, conspicuous, decided
pronouncement *n* = **announcement**, statement, judgment, declaration, decree, proclamation, edict, dictum
pronunciation *n* = **intonation**, speech, stress, accent, inflection, articulation, diction, enunciation
proof *n* **1** = **evidence**, testimony, confirmation, verification • *We were asked for proof of our age.* ▸ *adj* **2** = **impervious**, strong, resistant, repellent, impenetrable
prop *v* **1** = **support**, stay, uphold, brace, sustain, bolster, buttress, hold up ▸ *n* **2** = **support**, stay, brace, mainstay, buttress, stanchion
propaganda *n* = **information**, promotion, publicity, hype, advertising, disinformation
propagate *v* **1** = **spread**, publish, broadcast, promote, transmit, circulate, disseminate, promulgate **2** = **reproduce**, increase, produce, generate, breed, multiply, engender, beget, procreate
propel *v* = **drive**, force, launch, shoot, send, push, thrust, shove, impel
propensity *n* = **tendency**, liability, bent, penchant, disposition, inclination, predisposition, proclivity
proper *adj* **1** = **suitable**, appropriate, apt, right, fitting • *the proper course of action* OPPOSITE: improper **2** = **correct**, conventional, orthodox, accepted • *It seemed the proper thing to do.* **3** = **polite**, decent,

DICTIONARY

property Ⓣ *n, pl* **-ties 1** something owned **2** possessions collectively **3** land or buildings owned by somebody **4** quality or attribute

prophet Ⓣ *n* **1** person supposedly chosen by God to spread His word **2** person who predicts the future **prophetic** *adj* **prophetically** *adv*

▸ **prophecy** *n* **1** prediction **2** message revealing God's will

▸ **prophesy** *v* foretell

prophylactic *n, adj* (drug) used to prevent disease

propinquity *n* nearness in time, place, or relationship

propitiate *v* appease, win the favour of **propitiation** *n*

▸ **propitiatory** *adj* intended to appease someone

▸ **propitious** *adj* favourable or auspicious

proponent *n* person who argues in favour of something

proportion Ⓣ *n* **1** relative size or extent **2** correct relation between connected parts **3** part considered with respect to the whole **proportions 4** dimensions or size ▹ *v* **5** adjust in relative amount or size

▸ **in proportion 1** comparable in size, rate of increase, etc. **2** without exaggerating

▸ **proportional** *or* **proportionate** *adj* being in proportion **proportionally** *adv*

propose Ⓣ *v* **1** put forward for consideration **2** nominate **3** intend or plan (to do) **4** make an offer of marriage **proposal** *n*

▸ **proposition** *n* **1** offer **2** statement or assertion **3** theorem **4** *informal* thing to be dealt with ▹ *v* **5** *informal* ask (someone) to have sexual intercourse with one

propound Ⓣ *v* put forward for consideration

proprietor Ⓣ *n* owner of a business establishment **proprietress** *n fem*

▸ **proprietary** *adj* **1** made and distributed under a trade name **2** denoting or suggesting ownership

propriety Ⓣ *n, pl* **-ties** correct conduct

propulsion Ⓣ *n* see **propel**

pro rata *Latin* in proportion

prorogue *v* suspend (parliament) without dissolving it **prorogation** *n*

prosaic Ⓣ [pro-**zay**-ik] *adj* lacking imagination, dull **prosaically** *adv*

proscenium *n, pl* **-niums, -nia** arch in a theatre separating the stage from the auditorium

THESAURUS

respectable, gentlemanly, genteel, ladylike, decorous, mannerly, seemly
See also: **fair, prim**

properly *adv* **1 = suitably**, appropriately, rightly, fittingly, aptly **2 = correctly**, accurately **3 = politely**, decently, respectably

P

property *n* **1 = possessions**, estate, assets, belongings, effects • *her personal property* **2 = quality**, feature, attribute, characteristic, trait, hallmark • *Mint is said to have powerful healing properties.* **3 = land**, estate, holding, freehold, real estate

prophecy *n* **= prediction**, forecast, prognostication, augury, divination, second sight, soothsaying

prophesy *v* **= predict**, forecast, foresee, divine, augur, foretell, prognosticate

prophet *n* **= soothsayer**, forecaster, diviner, oracle, prophesier, seer, sibyl

prophetic *adj* **= predictive**, prescient, oracular, prognostic, sibylline

propitious *adj* **= favourable**, happy, bright, lucky, promising, fortunate, auspicious, encouraging

proportion *n* **1 = part**, share, percentage, segment, quota • *a tiny proportion of the population* **2 = relative amount**, relationship, ratio **3 = balance**, correspondence, harmony, symmetry, congruity ▹ **proportions = dimensions**, size, capacity, volume, extent, expanse
See also: **measure**

proportional, proportionate *adj* **= corresponding**, even, consistent, balanced, compatible, equitable, commensurate, in proportion

proposal *n* **= suggestion**, plan, offer, program, bid, project, recommendation, scheme, presentation

propose *v* **1 = put forward**, suggest, advance, present, submit **2 = nominate**, name, present, recommend **3 = intend**, plan, mean, aim, design, scheme, have in mind **4 = offer marriage**, ask for someone's hand *or* ask for someone's hand in marriage, pop the question (*informal*)

proposition *n* **1 = proposal**, plan, recommendation, scheme, suggestion ▸ *v* **2 = make a pass at**, solicit, accost, make an improper suggestion

propound *v* **= put forward**, suggest, propose, advance, present, submit, postulate

proprietor, proprietress *n* **= owner**, landlord *or* landlady, titleholder

propriety *n* **1 = correctness**, fitness, aptness, rightness, seemliness **2 = decorum**, courtesy, decency, etiquette, respectability, politeness, manners, seemliness

propulsion *n* **= propelling force**, drive, push, thrust, impulse, impetus

prosaic *adj* **= dull**, routine, ordinary, everyday, pedestrian, boring, mundane, matter-of-fact, trite, unimaginative, humdrum

DICTIONARY

proscribe ❶ *v* prohibit, outlaw **proscription** *n* **proscriptive** *adj*
prose *n* ordinary speech or writing in contrast to poetry
prosecute ❶ *v* **1** bring a criminal charge against **2** continue to do **prosecution** *n* **prosecutor** *n*
proselyte [**pross**-ill-ite] *n* recent convert ▸ **proselytize** [**pross**-ill-it-ize] *v* attempt to convert
prosody [**pross**-a-dee] *n* study of poetic metre and techniques **prosodic** *adj* **prosodist** *n*
prospect ❶ *n* **1** something anticipated: *the prospect of defeat* **2** *old-fashioned* view from a place **prospects 3** probability of future success ▷ *v* **4** explore, esp. for gold ▸ **prospective** *adj* **1** expected **2** future ▸ **prospector** *n* person who searches, esp. for gold ▸ **prospectus** *n* booklet giving details of a university, company, etc.
prosper ❶ *v* be successful ▸ **prosperity** *n* success and wealth **prosperous** *adj*
Prost *n* **Alain**. born 1955, French motor-racing driver: world champion 1985, 1986, 1989, and 1993
prostate *n* gland in male mammals that surrounds the neck of the bladder
prosthesis [pross-**theess**-iss] *n, pl* **-ses** [-seez] artificial body part, such as a limb or breast **prosthetic** *adj*
prostitute ❶ *n* **1** person who offers sexual intercourse in return for payment ▷ *v* **2** make a prostitute of **3** offer (oneself or one's talents) for unworthy purposes **prostitution** *n*
prostrate ❶ *adj* **1** lying face downwards **2** physically or emotionally exhausted ▷ *v* **3** lie face downwards **4** exhaust physically or emotionally **prostration** *n*
protagonist ❶ *n* **1** leading character in a play or a story **2** supporter of a cause
Protagoras *n* ?485–?411 BC, Greek philosopher and sophist, famous for his dictum "Man is the measure of all things."
protea [**pro**-tee-a] *n* African shrub with showy flowers
protean [pro-**tee**-an] *adj* constantly changing
protect ❶ *v* defend from trouble, harm, or loss **protection** *n* ▸ **protectionism** *n* policy of protecting industries by taxing competing imports **protectionist** *n* ▸ **protective** *adj* **1** giving protection: *protective*

THESAURUS

proscribe *v* **1** = **prohibit**, ban, forbid, embargo, interdict **2** = **outlaw**, deport, exclude, exile, expel, banish, expatriate, ostracize
prosecute *v* (*Law*) = **take to court**, try, sue, indict, arraign, litigate, bring to trial, put on trial
prospect *n* **1** = **expectation**, hope, promise, outlook • *There was no prospect of going home.* **2** (*sometimes pl*) = **likelihood**, chance, possibility **3** = **view**, scene, outlook, sight, landscape, spectacle, vista ▸ *v* **4** = **look for**, seek, search for
See also: **probability**
prospective *adj* = **future**, likely, possible, potential, anticipated, imminent, forthcoming, intended, coming, destined, expected
prospects *See* **outlook**
prospectus *n* = **catalogue**, program, list, outline, synopsis, syllabus
prosper *v* = **succeed**, advance, progress, thrive, flourish, do well, get on
prosperity *n* = **success**, plenty, luxury, wealth, fortune, affluence, riches, good fortune, prosperousness
prosperous *adj* **1** = **wealthy**, rich, affluent, well-heeled (*informal*), well-off, well-to-do, moneyed **2** = **successful**, lucky, fortunate, booming, doing well, flourishing, thriving
prostitute *n* **1** = **whore**, ho (*slang*), hooker (*slang*), call girl, fallen woman, harlot, loose woman, tart (*informal*), streetwalker, strumpet, trollop ▸ *v* **2** = **cheapen**, degrade, demean, profane, devalue, pervert, debase, misapply
prostrate *adj* **1** = **prone**, flat, horizontal **2** = **exhausted**, overcome, depressed, dejected, desolate, spent, inconsolable, drained, worn out ▸ *v* **3** = **exhaust**, tire, drain, fatigue, weary, sap, wear out ▷ **prostrate oneself** = **bow down to**, kneel, abase oneself, fall at (someone's) feet, grovel, kiss ass (*slang*), kowtow
protagonist *n* **1** = **supporter**, champion, advocate, exponent **2** = **leading character**, hero *or* heroine, principal, central character
protect *v* = **keep safe**, defend, guard, shelter, shield, safeguard • *Bank tellers are protected by security barrier shields.*
See also: **save, take care of**
protected *adj* = **safe**, secure, immune
protection *n* **1** = **safeguard**, cover, shelter, barrier, buffer • *a diet believed to offer protection against some diseases* **2** = **safety**, security, care, custody, safeguard, defense, safekeeping, protecting, aegis
See also: **defence, precaution**
protective *adj* = **protecting**, defensive, vigilant, watchful, guarding, maternal,

DICTIONARY

clothing **2** tending or wishing to protect someone
▸ **protector** *n* **1** person or thing that protects **2** regent
▸ **protectorate** *n* **1** territory largely controlled by a stronger state **2** (period of) rule of a regent
protégé [**pro**-ti-zhay] *n* person who is protected and helped by another **protégée** *n fem*
protein *n* any of a group of complex organic compounds that are essential for life
pro tempore *adv, adj* Also **pro tem** for the time being
protest Ⓣ *n* **1** declaration or demonstration of objection ▹ *v* **2** object, disagree **3** assert formally
▸ **protestation** *n* strong declaration
Protestant *adj* **1** of or relating to any of the Christian churches that split from the Roman Catholic Church in the sixteenth century ▹ *n* **2** member of a Protestant church **Protestantism** *n*
proto-, prot- *combining form* first: *protohuman*
protocol Ⓣ *n* **1** rules of behaviour for formal occasions **2** *computers* set of rules for transfer of data, esp. between different systems
proton *n* positively charged particle in the nucleus of an atom
protoplasm *n* substance forming the living contents of a cell
prototype Ⓣ *n* original or model after which something is copied
protozoan [pro-toe-**zoe**-an] *n, pl* **-zoa** microscopic one-celled creature
protract *v* lengthen or extend **protracted** *adj* **protraction** *n*
▸ **protractor** *n* instrument for measuring angles
protrude Ⓣ *v* stick out, project **protrusion** *n*
protuberant *adj* swelling out, bulging **protuberance** *n*
proud Ⓣ *adj* **1** feeling pleasure and satisfaction **2** feeling honoured **3** thinking oneself superior to other people **4** dignified **proudly** *adv*
▸ **proud flesh** flesh growing around a healing wound
Proust *n* **Marcel**. 1871–1922, French novelist whose long novel *À la recherche du temps perdu* (1913–27) deals with the relationship of the narrator to themes such as art, time, memory, and society
Prout *n* **Ebenezer**. 1835–1909, English musicologist and composer, noted for his editions of works by Handel and J. S. Bach
prove Ⓣ *v* **proving, proved, proved** *or* **proven** **1** establish the validity of **2** demonstrate, test **3** be found to be
▸ **proven** *adj* known from experience to work
provenance [**prov**-in-anss] *n* place of origin
provender *n old-fashioned* fodder
proverb Ⓣ *n* short saying that expresses a truth or gives a warning **proverbial** *adj*

THESAURUS

paternal, motherly, fatherly
protector *n* = **defender**, champion, guard, patron, bodyguard, guardian
protest *v* **1** = **object**, complain, disagree, disapprove, oppose • *She protested that the new hours of work were unfair.* **2** = **assert**, declare, maintain, insist, affirm, profess, attest, avow ▸ *n* **3** = **objection**, complaint, outcry • *The council has ignored their protests by granting a building permit.*
See also: **agitate, grumble**
protestation *n* = **declaration**, vow, profession, affirmation, avowal
protester *n* = **demonstrator**, rebel, agitator
protocol *n* = **code of behaviour**, etiquette, decorum, conventions, customs, manners, propriety
prototype *n* = **original**, first, type, standard, model, example, pattern
protracted *adj* = **extended**, prolonged, drawn-out, dragged out, long-drawn-out, spun out
protrude *v* = **stick out**, project, extend, bulge, jut, come through, obtrude, stand out
protrusion *n* = **protuberance**, bump, projection, lump, bulge, outgrowth
protuberance *n* = **bulge**, process, bump, lump, prominence, hump, knob, excrescence, outgrowth, protrusion, swelling
proud *adj* **1** = **satisfied**, pleased, gratified, honoured • *I was proud of our players today.* **2** = **conceited**, arrogant, boastful, imperious, disdainful, haughty, lordly, overbearing, self-satisfied, snobbish, supercilious
See also: **stuck-up, vain**
prove *v* **1** = **verify**, confirm, establish, demonstrate, ascertain • *History will prove him to have been right all along.* OPPOSITE: disprove **2** = **test**, try, check, examine, analyze, assay **3** = **turn out**, result, come out, end up ▹ **prove false** *See* **disprove**
See also: **show**
proven *adj* = **verified**, reliable, established, definite, proved, attested, confirmed, tested
proverb *n* = **saying**, saw, adage, maxim, dictum
proverbial *adj* = **conventional**, current, traditional, famous, famed, legendary, typical, notorious, well-known, acknowledged, axiomatic

DICTIONARY

provide Ⓣ *v* **1** make available **2** (foll. by *for*) take precautions (against) **3** support financially **provider** *n*
▶ **provided that** on condition that
providence Ⓣ *n* God or nature seen as a protective force that arranges people's lives
▶ **provident** *adj* **1** thrifty **2** showing foresight
▶ **providential** *adj* lucky **providentially** *adv*
province Ⓣ *n* **1** territory governed as a unit of a country or empire **2** area of learning, activity, etc. **provinces 3** any part of a country outside the capital
▶ **provincial** *adj* **1** of a province or the provinces **2** unsophisticated or narrow-minded ▷ *n* **3** unsophisticated person **4** person from a province or the provinces
▶ **provincialism** *n* narrow-mindedness and lack of sophistication
provision Ⓣ *n* **1** act of supplying something **2** something supplied **provisions 3** food **4** *law* condition incorporated in a document ▷ *v* **5** supply with food
▶ **provisional** *adj* **1** temporary **2** conditional **provisionally** *adv*
proviso Ⓣ [pro-**vize**-oh] *n, pl* **-sos, -soes** condition, stipulation
provoke Ⓣ *v* **1** deliberately anger **2** cause (an adverse reaction) **provocation** *n* **provocative** *adj*
provost *n* **1** head of certain university colleges **2** chief councillor of a Scottish town
▶ **provost marshal** head of military police
prow *n* bow of a vessel
prowess Ⓣ *n* **1** superior skill or ability **2** bravery, fearlessness
prowl Ⓣ *v* **1** move stealthily around a place as if in search of prey or plunder ▷ *n* **2** prowling **prowler** *n*
proximity Ⓣ *n* **1** nearness in space or time **2** nearness or closeness in a series **proximate** *adj*
proxy Ⓣ *n, pl* **proxies 1** person authorized to act on behalf of someone else **2** authority to act on behalf of someone else
prude *n* person who is excessively modest,

THESAURUS

provide *v* **1 = supply**, contribute, equip, outfit, furnish • *I'll be glad to provide a copy of this.* **2 = give**, add, bring, serve, produce, present, afford, lend, yield, render, impart ▷ **provide for, provide against = take precautions against**, anticipate, forearm, plan ahead, plan for, prepare for ▷ **provide for = support**, keep, maintain, sustain, care for, take care of
See also: **issue**
providence *n* **= fate**, fortune, destiny
provident *adj* **1 = thrifty**, prudent, economical, frugal **2 = foresighted**, careful, cautious, vigilant, wise, shrewd, discreet, well-prepared, far-seeing, forearmed
providential *adj* **= lucky**, happy, fortunate, timely, opportune, fortuitous, heaven-sent
provider *n* **1 = supplier**, source, donor, giver **2 = breadwinner**, supporter, earner, wage earner
providing, provided *conj* **= on condition that**, given, as long as
province *n* **1 = region**, division, department, zone, district, section, patch, domain, colony **2 = area**, business, concern, line, role, field, duty, responsibility, capacity, function, sphere
provincial *adj* **1 = rural**, country, local, rustic, homespun, hick (*informal*) **2 = narrow-minded**, limited, narrow, small-town, insular, parochial, inward-looking, small-minded, unsophisticated ▶ *n* **3 = yokel**, country cousin, hayseed, rustic, hick (*informal*)
provision *n* **1 = supplying**, furnishing, catering, providing, equipping **2 = condition**, term, demand, requirement, rider, clause, stipulation, proviso
provisional *adj* **1 = temporary**, interim **2 = conditional**, tentative, limited, contingent, qualified
provisions *pl n* **= food**, fare, edibles, foodstuff, comestibles, eatables, rations, stores, supplies, victuals
proviso *n* **= condition**, requirement, rider, clause, qualification, stipulation
provocation *n* **1 = cause**, reason, motivation, stimulus, incitement, grounds **2 = offence**, injury, challenge, insult, dare, taunt, grievance, indignity, affront, annoyance
provocative *adj* **= offensive**, galling, annoying, goading, insulting, provoking, stimulating
provoke *v* **1 = anger**, insult, annoy, irritate, tease, enrage, goad • *I didn't want to do anything to provoke him.* **2 = cause**, produce, prompt, evoke, spark, rouse, set off • *His comments have provoked an unexpected response.*
See also: **bring about, excite, incite, motivate, occasion**
prowess *n* **1 = skill**, talent, excellence, accomplishment, expertise, mastery, genius, adeptness, aptitude **2 = bravery**, courage, daring, heroism, mettle, fearlessness, valiance, valor
prowl *v* **= move stealthily**, steal, sneak, stalk, slink, skulk
proximity *n* **= nearness**, closeness
proxy *n* **= representative**, agent, factor, deputy, delegate, substitute

P

DICTIONARY

prim, or proper **prudish** *adj* **prudery** *n*
prudent Ⓣ *adj* cautious, discreet, and sensible **prudence** *n*
▸ **prudential** *adj old-fashioned* prudent
prune[1] *n* dried plum
prune[2] Ⓣ *v* **1** cut out dead parts or excessive branches from (a tree or plant) **2** shorten, reduce
prurient *adj* excessively interested in sexual matters **prurience** *n*
pry Ⓣ *v* **prying, pried** make an impertinent or uninvited inquiry into a private matter
PS postscript
psalm Ⓣ *n* sacred song
▸ **psalmist** *n* writer of psalms
▸ **psalmody** *n* singing of sacred music
Psalter *n* book containing (a version of) psalms from the Bible
▸ **psaltery** *n* ancient instrument played by plucking strings
psephology [sef-**fol**-a-jee] *n* statistical study of elections
pseud *n informal* pretentious person
pseudo-, pseud- Ⓣ *combining form* false, pretending, or unauthentic: *pseudo-intellectual*
pseudonym Ⓣ *n* fictitious name adopted, esp. by an author **pseudonymous** *adj*
psittacosis *n* disease of parrots that can be transmitted to humans
psoriasis [so-**rye**-a-siss] *n* skin disease with reddish spots and patches covered with silvery scales
PST Pacific Standard Time
psyche Ⓣ *n* human mind or soul
psychedelic *adj* **1** denoting a drug that causes hallucinations **2** having vivid colours and complex patterns similar to those experienced during hallucinations
psychiatry *n* branch of medicine concerned with mental disorders **psychiatric** *adj* **psychiatrist** *n*
psychic Ⓣ *adj* Also **psychical 1** having mental powers which cannot be explained by natural laws **2** relating to the mind ▷ *n* **3** person with psychic powers
psycho *n informal* short for **psychopath**
psychoanalysis *n* method of treating mental and emotional disorders by discussion and analysis of one's thoughts and feelings **psychoanalyse** *v* **psychoanalyst** *n*
psychology Ⓣ *n, pl* **-gies 1** study of human and animal behaviour **2** *informal* person's mental make-up **psychologist** *n*
▸ **psychological** *adj* **1** of or affecting the mind **2** of psychology
psychopath Ⓣ *n* person afflicted with a personality disorder causing him or her to commit antisocial or violent acts **psychopathic** *adj*
psychosis *n, pl* **-choses** severe mental disorder in which the sufferer's contact with reality becomes distorted **psychotic** *adj, n*
psychosomatic *adj* (of a physical disorder) thought to have psychological causes
psychotherapy *n* treatment of nervous disorders by psychological methods **psychotherapeutic** *adj* **psychotherapist** *n*
psych up *v* prepare (oneself) mentally for a contest or task

P

THESAURUS

prudence *n* = **common sense**, care, caution, judgment, wisdom, discretion, vigilance, wariness, good sense
prudent *adj* **1** = **sensible**, careful, cautious, wary, vigilant, wise, shrewd, discreet, politic, judicious, discerning **2** = **thrifty**, careful, economical, frugal, canny, far-sighted, provident, sparing
prudish *adj* = **prim**, proper, Victorian, stuffy, starchy (*informal*), puritanical, old-maidish (*informal*), overmodest, priggish, prissy (*informal*), strait-laced
prune *v* = **cut**, reduce, shape, clip, trim, dock, shorten, snip
pry *v* = **be inquisitive**, interfere, snoop (*informal*), intrude, poke your nose in (*informal*) • *We do not want people prying into our business.*
prying *adj* = **inquisitive**, curious, interfering, meddlesome, meddling, nosy (*informal*), snooping (*informal*), spying
psalm *n* = **hymn**, chant
pseudo-, pseud- *adj* = **false**, fake, artificial, mock, phony (*informal*), sham, imitation, spurious, pretended
pseudonym *n* = **false name**, alias, assumed name, incognito, nom de plume, pen name
psyche *n* = **soul**, mind, spirit, personality, self, individuality, anima
psychiatrist *n* = **psychotherapist**, analyst, shrink (*slang*), psychologist, therapist, psychoanalyst, headshrinker (*slang*)
psychic *adj* **1** = **supernatural**, occult, mystic **2** = **mental**, psychological, spiritual
psychological *adj* **1** = **mental**, intellectual, cerebral **2** = **imaginary**, irrational, unreal, all in the mind, psychosomatic
psychology *n* **1** = **behaviourism**, science of mind, study of personality **2** = **way of thinking**, attitude, mental make-up, mental processes, thought processes, what makes one tick
psychopath *n* = **madman**, lunatic, maniac, headcase (*informal*), nutcase (*slang*), psychotic, sociopath, sickie (*informal*), sicko (*informal*)
psychotic *adj* = **mad**, insane, loony (*informal*), lunatic, demented, certifiable, deranged, unbalanced, *non compos mentis* (*Latin*)

DICTIONARY

pt 1 part 2 point 3 port
Pt *chem* platinum
PT *old-fashioned* physical training
pt. pint
PTA Parent-Teacher Association
ptarmigan [**tar**-mig-an] *n* bird of the grouse family which turns white in winter
pterodactyl [terr-roe-**dak**-til] *n* extinct flying reptile with batlike wings
Ptolemy *n* Latin name *Claudius Ptolemaeus*. 2nd century AD, Greek astronomer, mathematician, and geographer. His *Geography* was the standard geographical textbook until the discoveries of the 15th century. His system of astronomy, as expounded in the *Almagest*, remained undisputed until the Copernican system was evolved
Ptolemy I *n* called *Ptolemy Soter*. ?367–283 BC, king of Egypt (323–285 BC), a general of Alexander the Great, who obtained Egypt on Alexander's death and founded the Ptolemaic dynasty: his capital Alexandria became the centre of Greek culture
Ptolemy II *n* called *Philadelphus*. 309–246 BC, the son of Ptolemy I; king of Egypt (285–246). Under his rule the power, prosperity, and culture of Egypt was at its height
ptomaine [**toe**-main] *n* any of a group of poisonous alkaloids found in decaying matter
Pu *chem* plutonium
pub Ⓣ *n* building with a bar licensed to sell alcoholic drinks
puberty Ⓣ [**pew**-ber-tee] *n* sexual maturity **pubertal** *adj*
▸ **pubescent** *adj* 1 reaching or having reached puberty 2 covered with fine short hairs or down, as some plants and animals
pubic [**pew**-bik] *adj* of the lower abdomen
▸ **pubis** *n* [**pew**-biss] *pl* **-bes** [-beez] one of the three sections of the hipbone that forms part of the pelvis
public Ⓣ *adj* 1 of or concerning the people as a whole 2 for use by everyone 3 well-known 4 performed or made openly ▹ *n* 5 the community, people in general **publicly** *adv*
▸ **publican** *n Brit* person who owns or runs a pub
▸ **public house** pub
▸ **public relations** promotion of a favourable opinion towards an organization among the public
▸ **public school** private fee-paying school in Britain
▸ **public servant** member of the public service
▸ **public service** service responsible for the administration of the government
▸ **public-spirited** *adj* having or showing an active interest in the good of the community
publicity Ⓣ *n* 1 process or information used to arouse public attention 2 public interest aroused
▸ **publicize** *v* advertise
▸ **publicist** *n* person who publicizes something, such as a press agent or journalist
publish Ⓣ *v* 1 produce and issue (printed matter) for sale 2 announce formally or in public **publication** *n* **publisher** *n*
Puccini *n* **Giacomo**. 1858–1924, Italian operatic composer, noted for the dramatic realism of his operas, which include *Manon Lescaut* (1893), *La Bohème* (1896), *Tosca* (1900), and *Madame Butterfly* (1904)
puce *adj* purplish-brown
puck[1] *n* small rubber disc used in ice hockey
▸ **puckster** *n hockey slang* hockey player
puck[2] *n* mischievous or evil spirit **puckish** *adj*
pucker Ⓣ *v* 1 gather into wrinkles ▹ *n* 2 wrinkle or crease

P

THESAURUS

pub *n* (*Informal*) = **tavern**, bar, inn, brasserie (*Canad Queb*), public house
puberty *n* = **adolescence**, pubescence, teens
public *n* 1 = **people**, nation, society, populace, masses • *the public's confidence in health care* ▸ *adj* 2 = **general**, popular, civic, universal • *public support for the idea* 3 = **communal**, community, universal, open to the public • *public transit* OPPOSITE: private 4 = **well-known**, important, prominent, respected 5 = **plain**, open, patent, obvious, overt, acknowledged, known
publication *n* 1 = **pamphlet**, issue, title, newspaper, magazine, brochure, leaflet, periodical 2 = **announcement**, disclosure, declaration, proclamation, notification, broadcasting, publishing, reporting
publicity *n* = **advertising**, promotion, plug (*informal*) • *The book's publicity campaign included television and newspaper interviews.*
publicize *v* = **advertise**, promote, plug (*informal*) • *The author appeared on TV to publicize her book.*
public-spirited *adj* = **altruistic**, humanitarian, charitable, philanthropic, unselfish
publish *v* 1 = **bring out**, print • *We publish a range of titles.* 2 = **announce**, broadcast, reveal, spread, advertise, disclose, circulate, proclaim, publicize, divulge
See also: **release**
pucker *v* 1 = **wrinkle**, contract, gather, tighten, crease, purse, knit, draw together, screw up ▸ *n* 2 = **wrinkle**, fold, crease
pudgy *adj* = **tubby**, fat, plump, chubby, stout, rotund, dumpy, roly-poly

DICTIONARY

pudding *n* **1** dessert, esp. a cooked one served hot **2** savoury dish with pastry or batter: *steak-and-kidney pudding* **3** sausage-like mass of meat: *black pudding*
puddle *n* small pool of water, esp. of rain
pudenda [pew-**den**-da] *pl n* human external genital organs, esp. of a female
puerile Ⓣ *adj* silly and childish
puerperium [pure-**peer**-ee-um] *n* period following childbirth **puerperal** [**pure**-per-al] *adj*
puff Ⓣ *n* **1** (sound of) a short blast of breath, wind, etc. **2** instance of breathing in and out **3** act of inhaling cigarette smoke ▷ *v* **4** blow or breathe in short quick drafts **5** take draws at (a cigarette) **6** send out in small clouds **7** swell **puffy** *adj*
▸ **out of puff** out of breath
▸ **puffball** *n* ball-shaped fungus
▸ **puff pastry** light flaky pastry
puffin *n* black-and-white sea bird with a large brightly-coloured beak
pug *n* small snub-nosed dog
▸ **pug nose** short stubby upturned nose
pugilism [**pew**-jil-iz-zum] *n* boxing
pugilist *n* **pugilistic** *adj*
Pugin *n* **Augustus** (**Welby Northmore**). 1812–52, British architect; a leader of the Gothic Revival. He collaborated with Sir Charles Barry on the Palace of Westminster (begun 1836)
pugnacious Ⓣ *adj* ready and eager to fight **pugnacity** *n*
puissant [**pew**-iss-sant] *adj poetic* powerful
▸ **puissance** *n* showjumping competition that tests a horse's ability to jump large obstacles
puke *slang* ▷ *v* **1** vomit ▷ *n* **2** act of vomiting **3** vomited matter
pukka, pucka *adj Indian & Brit* **1** properly done, constructed, etc. **2** genuine, real
pulchritude *n lit* beauty
pule *v* **1** whine **2** whimper
Pulitzer *n* **Joseph**. 1847–1911, US newspaper publisher, born in Hungary. He established the Pulitzer prizes
pull Ⓣ *v* **1** exert force on (an object) to move it towards the source of the force **2** strain or stretch **3** remove or extract **4** attract **5** *informal* act in a way considered characteristic of a particular person: *pull a Greta Garbo* ▷ *n* **6** pulling **7** force used in pulling **8** act of taking in drink or smoke **9** *informal* power, influence
▸ **pull in** *v* **1** (of a vehicle or driver) draw in to the side of the road or stop **2** reach a destination **3** attract in large numbers **4** *slang* arrest
▸ **pull off** *v* **1** *informal* succeed in performing **2** (of a vehicle or driver) move to the side of the road and stop **3** (of a vehicle or driver) start to move
▸ **pull out** *v* **1** (of a vehicle or driver) move away from the side of the road or move out to overtake **2** (of a train) depart **3** withdraw **4** remove by pulling
▸ **pull up** *v* **1** (of a vehicle or driver) stop **2** remove by the roots **3** reprimand
pullet *n* young hen
pulley *n* wheel with a grooved rim in which a belt, chain, or piece of rope runs in order to lift weights by a downward pull
Pullman[1] *n, pl* **-mans** luxurious railway coach
Pullman[2] *n* **Philip.** born 1946, British author. Writing primarily for older children, he is best known for the fantasy trilogy *His Dark Materials* (1997–2000)
pullover *n* sweater that is pulled on over the head
pulmonary *adj* of the lungs
pulp Ⓣ *n* **1** soft moist plant tissue, such as the

THESAURUS

puerile *adj* = **childish**, silly, juvenile, foolish, immature, trivial, babyish
puff *n* **1** = **blast**, draft, breath, gust, whiff **2** = **smoke**, pull, drag (*slang*) ▸ *v* **3** = **blow**, breathe, pant, wheeze, gasp, exhale, gulp **4** = **smoke**, draw, drag (*slang*), suck, inhale, pull at *or* pull on **5** (usually with *up*) = **swell**, expand, inflate, bloat, dilate, distend
puffed up *See* **pompous**
puffy *adj* = **swollen**, enlarged, bloated, distended, puffed up
pugilist *n* = **boxer**, fighter, prizefighter
pugnacious *adj* = **aggressive**, combative, belligerent, hot-tempered, quarrelsome
pull *v* **1** = **draw**, drag, haul, yank, tow, tug • *a wooden plough pulled by oxen* OPPOSITE: push **2** = **strain**, tear, stretch, rip, sprain, dislocate, wrench **3** = **extract**, pick, remove, gather, pluck, uproot, draw out, take out ▷ **pull back** *See* **retreat** ▷ **pull down** = **demolish**, remove, destroy, raze, bulldoze ▷ **pull off** = **succeed**, manage, accomplish, carry out, do the trick ▷ **pull out** = **withdraw**, leave, quit, evacuate, retreat, depart ▷ **pull through** = **survive**, rally, recover, get better ▷ **pull together** *See* **co-operate, unite** ▷ **pull up** = **stop**, halt, brake ▸ *n* **4** = **attraction**, lure, magnetism • *The pull of Mexico was too strong to resist.* **5** = **tug**, yank, jerk, twitch **6** = **puff**, drag (*slang*), inhalation **7** (*Informal*) = **influence**, power, weight, muscle, clout (*informal*)
See also: **attract**
pulp *n* **1** = **paste**, mash, mush **2** = **flesh**, soft part ▸ *v* **3** = **crush**, squash, mash,

DICTIONARY

material used to make paper **2** flesh of a fruit or vegetable **3** any soft soggy mass **4** poor-quality books and magazines ▷ *v* **5** reduce to pulp
pulpit *n* raised platform for a preacher
pulsar *n* small dense star which emits regular bursts of radio waves
pulse[1] ⓣ *n* **1** regular beating of blood through the arteries at each heartbeat which can be felt at the wrists and elsewhere **2** any regular beat or vibration
▸ **pulsate** *v* throb, quiver **pulsation** *n*
pulse[2] *n* edible seed of a pod-bearing plant such as a bean or pea
pulverize ⓣ *v* **1** reduce to fine pieces **2** destroy completely **pulverization** *n*
puma *n* large American cat with a greyish-brown coat
pumice [**pumm**-iss] *n* light porous stone used for scouring
pummel ⓣ *v* **-melling, -melled** strike repeatedly with or as if with the fists
pump[1] ⓣ *n* **1** machine used to force a liquid or gas to move in a particular direction ▷ *v* **2** raise or drive with a pump **3** supply in large amounts **4** extract information from **5** operate or work in the manner of a pump
pump[2] *n* light flat-soled shoe
pumpernickel *n* sour black bread made of coarse rye flour
pumpkin *n* large round fruit with an orange rind, soft flesh, and many seeds
pun ⓣ *n* **1** use of words to exploit double meanings for humorous effect ▷ *v* **punning, punned 2** make puns
▸ **punster** *n* person fond of making puns
punch[1] ⓣ *v* **1** strike at with a clenched fist ▷ *n* **2** blow with a clenched fist **3** *informal* effectiveness or vigour
▸ **punchy** *adj* forceful
▸ **punch-drunk** *adj* dazed by or as if by repeated blows to the head
punch[2] ⓣ *n* **1** tool or machine for shaping, piercing, or engraving ▷ *v* **2** pierce, cut, stamp, shape, or drive with a punch
punch[3] *n* drink made from a mixture of wine, spirits, fruit, sugar, and spices
punctilious ⓣ *adj* **1** paying great attention to correctness in etiquette **2** careful about small details
punctual ⓣ *adj* arriving or taking place at the correct time **punctuality** *n* **punctually** *adv*
punctuate ⓣ *v* **1** put punctuation marks in **2** interrupt at frequent intervals
▸ **punctuation** *n* (use of) marks such as commas, colons, etc. in writing, to assist in making the sense clear
puncture ⓣ *n* **1** small hole made by a sharp object, esp. in a tire ▷ *v* **2** pierce a hole in
pundit *n* expert who speaks publicly on a subject
pungent ⓣ *adj* having a strong sharp bitter flavour **pungency** *n*
punish ⓣ *v* cause (someone) to suffer or undergo a penalty for some wrongdoing **punishment** *n*
▸ **punishing** *adj* harsh or difficult

P

THESAURUS

pulverize ▸ *adj* **4 = cheap**, lurid, trashy, rubbishy
pulsate *v* **= throb**, beat, pound, thump, pulse, quiver, palpitate
pulse *n* **1 = beat**, beating, rhythm, vibration, throb, pulsation, throbbing ▸ *v* **2 = beat**, vibrate, throb, pulsate
pulverize *v* **1 = crush**, pound, mill, grind, granulate **2 = defeat**, destroy, crush, smash, wreck, demolish, flatten, annihilate
pummel *v* **= beat**, strike, pound, batter, hammer, punch, thump
pump *v* **1** (often with *into*) **= drive**, force, send, push, supply, pour, inject **2 = interrogate**, probe, quiz, cross-examine
pun *n* **= play on words**, quip, double entendre, witticism
punch[1] *v* **1 = hit**, strike, box, smash, belt (*informal*), pummel, sock (*slang*), bop (*informal*) ▸ *n* **2 = blow**, hit, wallop (*informal*), sock (*slang*), jab, bop (*informal*) **3** (*Informal*) **= effectiveness**, drive, impact, bite, vigour, verve, forcefulness
punch[2] *v* **= pierce**, cut, drill, stamp, bore, puncture, prick, perforate
punctilious *adj* **= particular**, nice, formal, strict, proper, exact, precise, meticulous, fussy, finicky
punctual *adj* **= on time**, prompt, in good time • *The most punctual airline last year was Swissair.*
punctuality *n* **= promptness**, readiness, promptitude
punctuate *v* **1 = interrupt**, break, pepper, sprinkle, intersperse **2 = emphasize**, stress, underline, accentuate
puncture *n* **1 = hole**, break, cut, damage, opening, leak, nick, slit **2 = flat tire**, flat ▸ *v* **3 = pierce**, cut, penetrate, bore, rupture, nick, prick, perforate
pungent *adj* **= strong**, hot, sharp, bitter, sour, spicy, tart, acrid, peppery, piquant
punish *v* **= discipline**, sentence, penalize, grounded, rap someone's knuckles, throw the book at, lower the boom (*slang*) • *The child was punished for teasing the puppy.*
punishable *adj* **= culpable**, criminal, indictable, blameworthy
punishing *adj* **= hard**, arduous, strenuous,

DICTIONARY

▸ **punitive** [**pew**-nit-tiv] *adj* relating to punishment

punk *n* **1** worthless person **2** anti-Establishment youth movement and style of rock music of the late 1970s **3** follower of this music

punkah *n* fan made of palm leaves

punnet *n* small basket for fruit

punt[1] *n* **1** open flat-bottomed boat propelled by a pole ▷ *v* **2** travel in a punt

punt[2] *sports* ▷ *v* **1** kick (a ball) before it touches the ground when dropped from the hands ▷ *n* **2** such a kick **punter** *n*

punt[3] *n* former monetary unit of the Irish Republic

punter Ⓣ *n* **1** person who bets **2** any member of the public

puny Ⓣ *adj* **-nier, -niest** small and feeble

pup *n* young of certain animals, such as dogs and seals

▸ **pup tent** small triangular tent for one or two people

pupa [**pew**-pa] *n, pl* **-pae, -pas** insect at the stage of development between a larva and an adult **pupal** *adj*

pupil[1] Ⓣ *n* person who is taught by a teacher

pupil[2] *n* round dark opening in the centre of the eye

puppet Ⓣ *n* **1** small doll or figure moved by strings or by the operator's hand **2** person or country controlled by another **puppeteer** *n*

puppy *n, pl* **-pies** young dog

purblind *adj* partly or nearly blind

Purcell *n* **Henry**. ?1659–95, English composer, noted chiefly for his rhythmic and harmonic subtlety in setting words. His works include the opera *Dido and Aeneas* (1689), music for the theatrical pieces *King Arthur* (1691) and *The Fairy Queen* (1692), several choral odes, fantasias, sonatas, and church music

purchase Ⓣ *v* **1** obtain by payment ▷ *n* **2** buying **3** what is bought **4** leverage, grip **purchaser** *n*

purdah *n* Muslim and Hindu custom of keeping women in seclusion, with clothing that conceals them completely when they go out

Purdy *n* **Alfred Wellington**, known as *Al*. 1918–2000, Canadian poet

pure Ⓣ *adj* **1** unmixed, untainted **2** faultless **3** innocent **4** complete: *pure delight* **5** concerned with theory only: *pure mathematics* **purely** *adv* **purity** *n*

▸ **purify** *v* make or become pure **purification** *n*

▸ **purist** *n* person obsessed with strict obedience to the traditions of a subject

purée [**pure**-ray] *n* **1** pulp of cooked food ▷ *v* **-réeing, -réed 2** make into a purée

purgatory *n* **1** place or state of temporary suffering **2 Purgatory** *RC Church* place where souls of the dead undergo punishment for their sins before being admitted to Heaven **purgatorial** *adj*

purge Ⓣ *v* **1** rid (a thing or place) of (unwanted things or people) ▷ *n* **2** purging **purgation** *n*

▸ **purgative** *adj, n* (medicine) designed to cause defecation

Puritan *n* **1** *hist* member of the English Protestant group who wanted simpler church ceremonies **2 puritan** person with strict moral and religious principles **puritanical** *adj* **puritanism** *n*

purl *n* **1** stitch made by knitting a plain stitch backwards ▷ *v* **2** knit in purl

P

THESAURUS

gruelling, backbreaking, exhausting, taxing, tiring, wearing

punishment *n* = **penalty**, retribution • *a punishment that fits the crime*

punitive *adj* = **retaliatory**, in reprisal, retaliative

punt *v* **1** = **bet**, back, lay, stake, gamble, wager ▸ *n* **2** = **bet**, stake, gamble, wager

punter *n* **1** = **gambler**, backer, better **2** (*Informal*) = **person**, man in the street

puny *adj* = **feeble**, weak, skinny, frail, sickly • *It's hard to believe he was a puny child.*

pupil *n* = **learner**, student, novice, beginner, schoolboy *or* schoolgirl, disciple

puppet *n* **1** = **marionette**, doll, ventriloquist's dummy **2** = **pawn**, tool, instrument, mouthpiece, stooge, cat's-paw

purchase *v* **1** = **buy**, get, score (*slang*), gain, acquire, obtain, come by, pay for, pick up ▸ *n* **2** = **buy**, gain, investment, property, acquisition, asset, possession **3** = **grip**, hold, support, leverage, foothold

purchaser *See* **customer**

pure *adj* **1** = **clean**, spotless, germ-free, pasteurized, sterilized • *The water is pure enough to drink.* OPPOSITE: impure **2** = **complete**, absolute, outright, utter, sheer, unmitigated • *a matter of pure luck* **3** = **unmixed**, real, straight, natural, simple, genuine, authentic, neat, flawless, unalloyed **4** = **innocent**, modest, impeccable, chaste, virtuous, blameless, uncorrupted, unsullied, virginal *See also*: **refined**

purely *adv* = **absolutely**, just, only, simply, completely, entirely, merely, exclusively, solely, wholly

purge *v* **1** = **get rid of**, remove, expel, eradicate, exterminate, do away with, wipe out ▸ *n* **2** = **removal**, elimination, eradication, ejection, expulsion

purified *See* **clean, refined**

DICTIONARY

purlieus [**per**-lyooz] *pl n lit* outskirts
purloin Ⓣ *v* steal
purple *adj* of a colour between red and blue
purport Ⓣ *v* **1** claim (to be or do something) ▷ *n* **2** apparent meaning, significance
purpose Ⓣ *n* **1** reason for which something is done or exists **2** determination **3** practical advantage or use: *use the time to good purpose* ▷ *v* **4** *old-fashioned* intend
▶ **purposely** *adv* Also **on purpose** intentionally
purr *n* **1** low vibrant sound that a cat makes when pleased ▷ *v* **2** make this sound
purse Ⓣ *n* **1** small bag for money **2** small bag carried to contain personal articles **3** financial resources **4** prize money ▷ *v* **5** draw (one's lips) together into a small round shape
▶ **purser** *n* ship's officer who keeps the accounts
pursue Ⓣ *v* **1** chase **2** follow (a goal) **3** engage in **4** continue to discuss or ask about (something) **pursuer** *n*
▶ **pursuit** *n* **1** pursuing **2** occupation
▶ **pursuance** *n* carrying out
purulent [**pure**-yoo-lent] *adj* of or containing pus **purulence** *n*
purvey Ⓣ *v* supply (provisions) **purveyance** *n* **purveyor** *n*
purview *n* scope or range of activity or outlook
pus *n* yellowish matter produced by infected tissue
push Ⓣ *v* **1** move or try to move by steady force **2** drive or spur (oneself or another person) to do something **3** *informal* sell (drugs) illegally ▷ *n* **4** pushing **5** special effort
▶ **the push** *slang* **1** dismissal from a job **2** ending of a relationship
▶ **pusher** *n* person who sells illegal drugs
▶ **pushy** *adj* too assertive or ambitious
▶ **pushover** *n informal* **1** something easily

THESAURUS

purify *v* **1 = clean**, wash, refine, clarify, sanitize, cleanse, disinfect, decontaminate, detoxify **2 = absolve**, redeem, cleanse, sanctify
purist *n* **= stickler**, formalist, pedant
puritan *n* **1 = moralist**, fanatic, zealot, prude, rigorist ▶ *adj* **2 = strict**, severe, austere, narrow-minded, ascetic, moralistic, prudish, strait-laced
puritanical *adj* **= strict**, severe, proper, austere, narrow-minded, ascetic, prudish, puritan, strait-laced
purity *n* **1 = cleanness**, cleanliness, faultlessness, immaculateness, pureness, wholesomeness **2 = innocence**, integrity, honesty, virtue, decency, virginity, chastity, chasteness, virtuousness
purloin *v* **= steal**, appropriate, filch, pinch (*informal*), swipe (*slang*), pilfer, thieve
purport *v* **1 = claim**, allege, assert, profess ▶ *n* **2 = significance**, idea, import, implication, drift, meaning, gist
purpose *n* **1 = reason**, point, aim, function, object, intention • *What is the purpose of thismeeting?* **2 = aim**, plan, end, goal, hope, wish, object, intention, desire, ambition **3 = determination**, will, resolution, resolve, persistence, tenacity, firmness, single-mindedness ▷ **on purpose = deliberately**, knowingly, intentionally, purposely, by design • *Did you do that on purpose?*
See also: **use**
purposeful *See* **determined**
purposeless *adj* **= pointless**, empty, unnecessary, senseless, needless, aimless, motiveless, uncalled-for
purposely *adv* **= deliberately**, knowingly, intentionally, consciously, expressly, on purpose, with intent
purse *n* **1 = pouch**, wallet, money-bag **2 = funds**, money, wealth, means, treasury, exchequer, resources ▶ *v* **3 = pucker**, contract, tighten, pout, press together
pursue *v* **1 = follow**, track, dog, hunt, chase, shadow, tail (*informal*), hound, stalk, hunt down, run after **2 = try for**, seek, desire, aim for, strive for, work towards **3 = engage in**, perform, conduct, practise, carry on **4 = continue**, maintain, proceed, carry on, keep on, persevere in, persist in
pursuit *n* **1 = pursuing**, search, hunt, chase, quest, seeking, trailing **2 = occupation**, interest, line, activity, pleasure, hobby, pastime
purvey *v* **= supply**, sell, provide, cater, furnish, deal in, trade in
push *v* **1 = shove**, press, thrust, ram • *She pushed the door open.* OPPOSITE: pull **2 = urge**, press, encourage, persuade • *They tried to push me into playing street hockey.* **3 = make one's way** *or* **force one's way**, move, shoulder, elbow, squeeze, thrust, shove, jostle ▶ *n* **4 = shove**, butt, nudge, thrust **5 = drive**, go (*informal*), energy, initiative, ambition, enterprise, vitality, dynamism, vigour
See also: **advertise, agitate, campaign, rush, stick, stuff**
pushed *adj* (often with *for*) **= short of**, hurried, pressed, rushed, under pressure
pushover *n* **1 = child's play** (*informal*), breeze (*informal*), cinch (*slang*), picnic (*informal*), piece of cake (*informal*), plain sailing, walkover (*informal*) • *Last night's playoff certainly was no pushover.* **2 = sucker** (*slang*), mug (*Brit slang*),

P

DICTIONARY

achieved **2** person or team easily taken advantage of or defeated
pusillanimous *adj* cowardly
pusillanimity *n*
puss, pussy Ⓣ *n, pl* **pusses, pussies** cat
pussyfoot Ⓣ *v informal* behave too cautiously
pustule *n* pimple containing pus **pustular** *adj*
put Ⓣ *v* **putting, put 1** cause to be (in a position, state, or place) **2** express **3** throw (the shot) in the shot put ▷ *n* **4** throw in putting the shot
▶ **put across** *v* express successfully
▶ **put off** *v* **1** postpone **2** disconcert **3** repel
▶ **put up** *v* **1** erect **2** accommodate **3** nominate
▶ **put-upon** *adj* taken advantage of
putative [**pew**-tat-iv] *adj* reputed, supposed
putrid Ⓣ *adj* rotten and foul-smelling
▶ **putrefy** *v* rot and produce an offensive smell **putrefaction** *n*
▶ **putrescent** *adj* **1** becoming putrid **2** rotting
putsch *n* sudden violent attempt to remove a government from power
putt *golf* ▷ *n* **1** stroke on the green with a putter to roll the ball into or near the hole ▷ *v* **2** strike (the ball) in this way
▶ **putter** *n* golf club with a short shaft for putting
puttee *n* strip of cloth worn wound around the leg from the ankle to the knee
putter Ⓣ *v* same as **potter**[2]
putty *n* paste used to fix glass into frames and fill cracks in woodwork
putz [rhymes with **huts**] *n US slang* despicable or stupid person
puzzle Ⓣ *v* **1** perplex and confuse or be perplexed or confused ▷ *n* **2** problem that cannot be easily solved **3** toy, game, or question that requires skill or ingenuity to solve **puzzlement** *n* **puzzling** *adj*
PVC polyvinyl chloride: synthetic thermoplastic material

THESAURUS

easy game (*informal*), easy mark *or* soft mark (*informal*), walkover (*informal*)
pushy *adj* (*informal*) = **forceful**, forward, aggressive, ambitious, assertive, bossy, obtrusive • *a pushy salesperson*
puss *See* **cat**
pussy *See* **cat**
pussycat *See* **cat**
pussyfoot *v* = **hedge**, beat about the bush, be noncommittal, equivocate, hum and haw, prevaricate, sit on the fence
put *v* **1** = **place**, position, rest, lay, deposit • *She put the photograph on the desk.* **2** = **express**, word, phrase • *I think you put that very well.*
See also: **insert, pose, set, stick** ▷ **put across** = **communicate**, explain, convey, get across, make clear, make oneself understood ▷ **put aside, put by** = **save**, store, deposit, stockpile, lay by ▷ **put away** = **save**, keep, deposit, put by; = **lock up**, commit, certify, institutionalize; = **consume**, gobble, devour, eat up, wolf down; = **put back**, replace, tidy away • *Now it's time to put your toys away.* ▷ **put back** *See* **postpone, put off** ▷ **put by** *See* **reserve, save** ▷ **put down** = **humiliate**, criticize, belittle, find fault • *Racist jokes come from wanting to put down other people*; = **put to sleep**, kill, destroy, put out of its misery • *The judge ordered the dog to be put down immediately*; = **record**, enter, set down, take down, write down; = **stamp out**, crush, quash, quell, suppress, repress; (usually with *to*) = **attribute**, ascribe, impute, set down
See also: **attack, insult** ▷ **put forward** = **recommend**, suggest, propose, advance, nominate, submit, tender ▷ **put off** = **postpone**, delay, defer, reschedule, put back, put on ice • *The House of Commons has put off the vote until next month*; = **disconcert**, throw (*informal*), confuse, dismay, unsettle, faze, discomfit, nonplus, perturb; = **discourage**, dishearten, dissuade ▷ **put on** = **don**, dress, change into, get dressed in, slip into; = **fake**, affect, assume, pretend, simulate, sham, feign; = **present**, do, show, stage, produce, mount; = **add**, gain, increase by ▷ **put out** = **annoy**, anger, irk, irritate, vex, exasperate, nettle; = **extinguish**, douse, quench, blow out; = **inconvenience**, trouble, bother, discomfit, discommode, impose upon, incommode ▷ **put through** *See* **subject** ▷ **put to sleep** *See* **hypnotize, put down** ▷ **put together** *See* **assemble, construct** ▷ **put up** = **build**, raise, construct, erect, fabricate; = **accommodate**, board, house, lodge, take in; = **nominate**, offer, propose, present, recommend, submit, put forward ▷ **put up with** = **stand**, bear, stomach, tolerate, abide, brook, countenance, stand for • *They won't put up with a return to the bad old days.*
putrid *adj* = **rotten**, bad, decayed, decomposed, rancid, putrefied, rotting, spoiled
putter *v* = **mess around**, dabble, dawdle, tinker, monkey around (*informal*)
puzzle *v* **1** = **perplex**, confuse, baffle, stump, mystify, bewilder • *There was something about her that puzzled me.* ▶ *n* **2** = **problem**, riddle, brainteaser • *a crossword puzzle*
See also: **mystery, wonder**
puzzled *adj* = **perplexed**, lost, confused, at a loss, at sea, baffled, bewildered, mystified

DICTIONARY

pyemia, pyaemia *n* blood poisoning
Pygmy *n, pl* **-mies 1** member of one of the dwarf peoples of Equatorial Africa ▷ *adj* **2 pygmy** very small
pyjamas, pajamas *pl n* loose-fitting trousers and top worn in bed
pylon *n* **1** plastic orange cone used to mark areas on the ground **2** *Brit* steel tower-like structure supporting electrical cables
pyorrhea, pyorrhoea [pire-**ree**-a] *n* disease of the gums and tooth sockets which causes bleeding of the gums and the formation of pus
pyramid *n* **1** solid figure with a flat base and triangular sides sloping upwards to a point **2** structure of this shape, esp. an ancient Egyptian one **pyramidal** *adj*
pyre *n* pile of wood for burning a dead body on
Pyrex *n* ® heat-resistant glassware
pyrites [pie-**rite**-eez] *n* sulfide of a metal, esp. iron pyrites
pyromania *n* uncontrollable urge to set things on fire **pyromaniac** *n*
pyrotechnics *n* **1** art of making fireworks **2** firework display **pyrotechnic** *adj*
Pyrrhic victory [**pir**-ik] *n* victory in which the victor's losses are as great as those of the defeated
python *n* large nonpoisonous snake that crushes its prey

THESAURUS

puzzlement *n* = **perplexity**, doubt, confusion, bewilderment, bafflement, mystification
puzzling *adj* = **perplexing**, involved, enigmatic, incomprehensible, abstruse, baffling, bewildering, mystifying

DICTIONARY

Qq

QB quarterback
QC 1 Quebec 2 Queen's Counsel
QED which was to be shown or proved
QM Quartermaster
qr. 1 quarter 2 quire
qt. quart
q.t. *n* **on the q.t.** *informal* secretly
qua [**kwah**] *prep* in the capacity of
quack[1] *v* 1 (of a duck) utter a harsh guttural sound ▷ *n* 2 sound made by a duck
quack[2] Ⓣ *n* 1 unqualified person who claims medical knowledge 2 *informal* doctor
quad *n* 1 short for **quadrangle** 2 *informal* quadruplet ▷ *adj* 3 short for **quadraphonic**
▸ **quad bike** vehicle like a small motorcycle with four large wheels, designed for agricultural and sporting uses
quadrangle *n* 1 rectangular courtyard with buildings on all four sides 2 geometric figure consisting of four points connected by four lines **quadrangular** *adj*
quadrant *n* 1 quarter of a circle 2 quarter of a circle's circumference 3 instrument for measuring the altitude of the stars
quadraphonic *adj* using four independent channels to reproduce or record sound
quadratic *math* ▷ *n* 1 equation in which the variable is raised to the power of two, but nowhere raised to a higher power ▷ *adj* 2 of the second power
quadrennial *adj* 1 occurring every four years 2 lasting four years
quadri- *combining form* four: *quadrilateral*
quadrilateral *adj* 1 having four sides ▷ *n* 2 polygon with four sides
quadrille *n* square dance for four couples
quadriplegia *n* paralysis of all four limbs
quadriplegic *adj*
quadruped [**kwod**-roo-ped] *n* any animal with four legs
quadruple *v* 1 multiply by four ▷ *adj* 2 four times as much or as many 3 consisting of four parts
quadruplet *n* one of four offspring born at one birth
quaff Ⓣ [**kwoff**] *v* drink heartily or in one draft
quagmire Ⓣ [**kwog**-mire] *n* soft wet area of land
quail[1] *n* small game bird of the partridge family
quail[2] Ⓣ *v* shrink back with fear
quaint Ⓣ *adj* attractively unusual, esp. in an old-fashioned style **quaintly** *adv*
quaintness *n*
quake Ⓣ *v* 1 shake or tremble with or as if with fear ▷ *n* 2 *informal* earthquake
Quaker *n* member of a Christian sect, the Society of Friends **Quakerism** *n*
qualify Ⓣ *v* **-fying, -fied** 1 provide or be provided with the abilities necessary for a task, office, or duty 2 moderate or restrict (something, esp. a statement) **qualified** *adj*
▸ **qualification** *n* 1 quality or skill needed for a particular activity 2 condition that modifies or limits 3 act of qualifying

THESAURUS

quack *n* = **charlatan**, fraud, fake, phony (*informal*), impostor, pretender, humbug, mountebank
quaff *v* = **drink**, down, swallow, gulp, imbibe, swig (*informal*)
quagmire *n* = **bog**, swamp, mire, marsh, slough, morass, fen, quicksand
quail *v* = **cringe**, shrink, falter, flinch, shudder, recoil, blanch, cower, blench, have cold feet (*informal*)
quaint *adj* 1 = **unusual**, odd, bizarre, curious, old-fashioned, eccentric, peculiar, fanciful, queer, droll, strange, singular 2 = **old-fashioned**, picturesque, antiquated, old-world
quake *v* = **shake**, move, rock, shiver, vibrate, tremble, shudder, quiver
qualification *n* 1 = **capability**, quality, ability, skill, achievement, accomplishment • *Her qualifications are impressive.* 2 = **condition**, exception, reservation, modification • *The argument is not true without qualification.*
qualified *adj* 1 = **capable**, expert, able, fit, efficient, experienced, competent, trained, adept, proficient, skilful, practised 2 = **restricted**, limited, contingent, conditional, provisional, modified, reserved, bounded, confined
qualify *v* 1 = **be certified**, graduate, become licensed • *She qualified as a doctor 20 years ago.* 2 = **restrict**, reduce, limit, ease, regulate, moderate, soften, diminish, temper, restrain, lessen
See also: **pass**

DICTIONARY

quality Ⓣ *n, pl* **-ties 1** degree or standard of excellence **2** distinguishing characteristic or attribute **3** basic character or nature of something
▸ **qualitative** *adj* of or relating to quality
qualm Ⓣ [**kwahm**] *n* **1** pang of conscience **2** sudden sensation of misgiving
quandary Ⓣ *n, pl* **-ries** difficult situation or dilemma
quango *n, pl* **-gos** partly independent official body, set up by a government
quanta *n* plural of **quantum**
quantify *v* **-fying, -fied** discover or express the quantity of **quantifiable** *adj* **quantification** *n*
quantity Ⓣ *n, pl* **-ties 1** specified or definite amount or number **2** aspect of anything that can be measured, weighed, or counted
▸ **quantitative** *adj* of or relating to quantity
quantum *n, pl* **-ta 1** desired or required amount ▷ *adj* **2** designating a major breakthrough or sudden advance: *quantum leap*
▸ **quantum theory** physics theory based on the idea that energy of electrons is discharged in discrete quanta
quarantine *n* **1** period of isolation of people or animals to prevent the spread of disease ▷ *v* **2** isolate in or as if in quarantine
quark[1] *n physics* particle thought to be the fundamental unit of matter
quark[2] *n* low-fat soft cheese
quarrel Ⓣ *n* **1** angry disagreement **2** cause of dispute ▷ *v* **-relling, -relled 3** have a disagreement or dispute **quarrelsome** *adj*
quarry[1] *n, pl* **-ries 1** place where stone is dug from the surface of the earth ▷ *v* **-rying, -ried 2** extract (stone) from a quarry
quarry[2] Ⓣ *n, pl* **-ries** person or animal that is being hunted
quart *n* unit of liquid measure equal to two pints
quarter Ⓣ *n* **1** one of four equal parts of something **2** fourth part of a year **3** region or district of a town or city **4** coin worth 25 cents **6** mercy or pity, as shown towards a defeated opponent **quarters 7** lodgings ▷ *v* **8** divide into four equal parts **9** billet or be billeted in lodgings
▸ **quarterly** *adj* **1** occurring, due, or issued every three months ▷ *adv* **2** once every three months
▸ **quarterback** *n* player in football who directs attacking play
▸ **quarterdeck** *n naut* rear part of the upper deck of a ship
▸ **quarterfinal** *n* round before the semifinal in a competition
▸ **quarter horse** small powerful breed of horse
▸ **quartermaster** *n* military officer responsible for accommodation, food, and equipment
▸ **quarter note** musical note half the length of a half note
quartet *n* **1** group of four performers **2** music for a quartet
quarto *n, pl* **-tos** book size in which the sheets are folded into four leaves
quartz *n* hard glossy mineral, used in making very accurate clocks and watches
quasar [**kway**-zar] *n* extremely distant starlike object that emits powerful radio waves
quash Ⓣ *v* **1** annul or make void **2** subdue forcefully and completely

THESAURUS

quality *n* **1 = standard**, value, worth, grade, merit, distinction, calibre • *The quality of food is very poor.* **2 = characteristic**, mark, feature, property, aspect, trait • *These qualities are essential for success.* **3 = nature**, make, kind, character, sort
See also: **attribute, point, qualification**
qualm *n* **= misgiving**, doubt, anxiety, apprehension, hesitation, uneasiness, compunction, disquiet, scruple, twinge of conscience *or* pang of conscience
quandary *n* **= difficulty**, Catch-22, puzzle, plight, impasse, dilemma, strait, predicament
quantities *See* **lot**
quantity *n* **1 = amount**, part, number, sum • *a large quantity of candy* **2 = size**, measure, volume, extent • *emphasis on quality rather than quantity*
See also: **lot**
quarrel *n* **1 = argument**, fight, dispute, row, feud, disagreement, squabble • *I had a terrible quarrel with my brother.* ▸ *v* **2 = argue**, fight, clash, squabble, bicker • *My brother quarrelled with my cousin.*
quarrelsome *adj* **= argumentative**, contentious, combative, belligerent, pugnacious, disputatious
quarry *n* **= prey**, game, goal, victim, aim, objective, prize
quarter *n* **1 = district**, part, place, province, area, side, region, zone, neighbourhood, locality **2 = mercy**, compassion, clemency, forgiveness, pity, leniency ▸ *v* **3 = accommodate**, post, place, board, house, station, lodge, billet
quarters *pl n* **= lodgings**, residence, dwelling, abode, habitation, barracks, billet, chambers, rooms
quash *v* **1 = annul**, cancel, reverse, revoke, overthrow, rescind, overrule, invalidate **2 = suppress**, beat, crush,

q

DICTIONARY

quasi- ⓣ [**kway**-zie] *combining form* almost but not really: *quasi-religious; quasi-scholar*
quatrain *n* stanza or poem of four lines
quaver ⓣ *v* (of a voice) **1** quiver or tremble ▷ *n* **2** *music* note half the length of a crotchet **3** tremulous sound or note
quay [**kee**] *n* wharf built parallel to the shore
Que. Quebec
queasy ⓣ *adj* **-sier, -siest 1** having the feeling that one is about to vomit **2** feeling or causing uneasiness **queasily** *adv* **queasiness** *n*
queen ⓣ *n* **1** female sovereign who is the official ruler or head of state **2** wife of a king **3** woman, place, or thing considered to be the best of her or its kind **4** *slang* effeminate male homosexual **5** only fertile female in a colony of bees, wasps, or ants **6** the most powerful piece in chess **queenly** *adj*
▶ **queen it** *informal* behave in an overbearing manner
▶ **Queen's Counsel** barrister or advocate appointed Counsel to the Crown
Queensberry rules *pl n* **1** code of rules followed in modern boxing **2** *informal* gentlemanly conduct, esp. in a dispute
queer ⓣ *adj* **1** not normal or usual **2** faint, giddy, or queasy **3** *offensive* homosexual ▷ *n* **4** *offensive* homosexual
▶ **queer someone's pitch** *informal* spoil someone's chances of something
quell ⓣ *v* **1** suppress **2** overcome
quench ⓣ *v* **1** satisfy (one's thirst) **2** put out or extinguish
quern *n* stone hand mill for grinding corn
querulous ⓣ [**kwer**-yoo-luss] *adj* complaining or peevish **querulously** *adv*
query ⓣ *n, pl* **-ries 1** question, esp. one raising doubt **2** question mark ▷ *v* **-rying, -ried 3** express uncertainty, doubt, or an objection concerning (something)
quest ⓣ *n* **1** long and difficult search ▷ *v* **2** (foll. by *for* or *after*) go in search of
question ⓣ *n* **1** form of words addressed to a person in order to obtain an answer **2** point at issue **3** difficulty or uncertainty ▷ *v* **4** put a question or questions to (a person) **5** express uncertainty about
▶ **in question** under discussion
▶ **out of the question** impossible
▶ **questionable** *adj* of disputable value or authority **questionably** *adv*
▶ **questionnaire** *n* set of questions on a form, used to collect information from people
▶ **question mark** punctuation mark (?) written at the end of questions
queue ⓣ *n* **1** line of people or vehicles waiting for something ▷ *v* **queueing** *or* **queuing, queued 2** (often foll. by *up*) form or

THESAURUS

subdue, quell, overthrow, squash, repress, put down
quasi- *adj* = **pseudo-**, so-called, would-be, apparent, seeming, semi-
quaver *v* **1** = **tremble**, shake, quake, waver, flutter, flicker, vibrate, quiver ▶ *n* **2** = **trembling**, shake, vibration, tremor, tremble, quiver
queasy *adj* **1** = **sick**, ill, nauseous, unwell • *He already felt queasy.* **2** = **uneasy**, troubled, anxious, uncertain, worried, restless, fidgety, ill at ease
queen *n* **1** = **sovereign**, monarch, ruler, consort **2** = **star**, model, ideal, mistress
queer *adj* **1** = **strange**, odd, unusual, funny, extraordinary, weird, curious, abnormal, uncommon, peculiar, droll **2** = **faint**, dizzy, giddy, light-headed, queasy
quell *v* **1** = **suppress**, defeat, overcome, crush, overpower, quash, subdue, conquer, vanquish, put down **2** = **calm**, quiet, appease, allay, soothe, pacify, assuage, mollify
quench *v* **1** = **satisfy**, appease, allay, sate, satiate, slake **2** = **put out**, crush, stifle, suppress, douse, smother, extinguish
querulous *adj* = **complaining**, critical, dissatisfied, captious, carping, discontented, fault-finding, grumbling, peevish, whining
query *n* **1** = **question**, problem, inquiry, doubt, suspicion, objection ▶ *v* **2** = **doubt**, suspect, challenge, dispute, distrust, mistrust, disbelieve **3** = **ask**, question, inquire *or* enquire
quest *n* = **search**, mission, hunt, journey, adventure, expedition, enterprise, crusade
question *n* **1** = **inquiry**, query • *If you have any questions, please contact us.* OPPOSITE: response **2** = **issue**, point, motion, subject, topic • *Can we get back to the question of the car?* **3** = **difficulty**, problem, dispute, doubt, controversy, argument, contention, query ▷ **in question** = **under discussion**, at issue, in doubt, open to debate ▷ **out of the question** = **impossible**, unthinkable, inconceivable ▶ *v* **4** = **dispute**, challenge, query, object to • *No one questioned my decision.* **5** = **interrogate**, probe, examine, quiz • *A man is being questioned by police.* OPPOSITE: answer **6** = **doubt**, suspect, dispute, distrust • *She questioned his ability to do his job.*
See also: **affair, ask, business, contest, matter**
questionable *adj* = **dubious**, controversial, debatable, suspect, suspicious, doubtful, moot, iffy (*informal*), sketchy (*informal*)
queue *n* = **line**, file, series, train, chain, string, sequence

DICTIONARY

remain in a line while waiting
quibble Ⓣ *v* **1** make trivial objections ▷ *n* **2** trivial objection
quiche [**keesh**] *n* savoury flan with an egg custard filling to which vegetables etc. are added
quick Ⓣ *adj* **1** speedy, fast **2** lasting or taking a short time **3** alert and responsive **4** easily excited or aroused ▷ *n* **5** area of sensitive flesh under a nail ▷ *adv* **6** *informal* in a rapid manner **quickly** *adv*
▸ **cut someone to the quick** hurt someone's feelings deeply
▸ **quicken** *v* make or become faster or more lively
▸ **quicklime** *n* white solid used in the manufacture of glass and steel
▸ **quicksand** *n* deep mass of loose wet sand that sucks anything on top of it into it
▸ **quicksilver** *n* mercury
▸ **quickstep** *n* fast modern ballroom dance
quid *n* piece of tobacco for chewing
quid pro quo *n* one thing, esp. an advantage or object, given in exchange for another
quiescent [kwee-**ess**-ent] *adj* quiet, inactive, or dormant **quiescence** *n*
quiet Ⓣ *adj* **1** with little noise **2** calm or tranquil **3** untroubled ▷ *n* **4** quietness ▷ *v* **5** make or become quiet **quietly** *adv* **quietness** *n*
▸ **on the quiet** without other people knowing, secretly
▸ **quieten** *v* (often foll. by *down*) make or become quiet
▸ **quietude** *n* quietness, peace, or tranquillity
quietism *n* passivity and calmness of mind towards external events **quietist** *n, adj*
quietus *n* **1** release from life; death **2** discharge or settlement of debts or duties
quiff *n* tuft of hair brushed up above the forehead
quill *n* **1** pen made from the feather of a bird's wing or tail **2** stiff hollow spine of a hedgehog or porcupine
quilt Ⓣ *n* padded covering for a bed
▸ **quilted** *adj* consisting of two layers of fabric with a layer of soft material between them
quince *n* acid-tasting pear-shaped fruit
quinine *n* bitter drug used as a tonic and formerly to treat malaria
Quinn *n* **Anthony**. 1915–2001, US film actor, born in Mexico: noted esp. for his performances in *La Strada* (1954) and *Zorba the Greek* (1964)
quinquennial *adj* **1** occurring every five years **2** lasting five years
quinsy *n* inflammation of the throat or tonsils
quint *n informal* quintuplet
quintessence Ⓣ *n* most perfect

THESAURUS

quibble *v* **1** = **split hairs**, carp, cavil ▸ *n* **2** = **objection**, complaint, criticism, cavil, nicety, niggle
quick *adj* **1** = **fast**, rapid, speedy, swift, brisk, hasty • *You'll have to be quick to catch the flight*. OPPOSITE: slow **2** = **brief**, fast, hurried, cursory, perfunctory • *a quick chat* OPPOSITE: long **3** = **immediate**, prompt, sudden, hasty • *a quick response* **4** = **intelligent**, alert, sharp, smart, bright (*informal*), acute, clever, shrewd, astute, perceptive, quick-witted **5** = **deft**, adept, skilful, adroit, dexterous **6** = **excitable**, passionate, testy, irritable, touchy, irascible
See also: **keen**
quicken *v* **1** = **speed up**, accelerate, hurry, expedite, hasten, precipitate, impel **2** = **stimulate**, inspire, revive, excite, incite, energize, arouse, invigorate, vitalize
quickly *adv* = **swiftly**, fast, rapidly, hastily, hurriedly, speedily • *Stop me if I'm speaking too quickly*. OPPOSITE: slowly
quick-tempered *adj* = **hot-tempered**, fiery, irritable, irascible, choleric, quarrelsome, testy
quick-witted *adj* = **clever**, alert, sharp, smart, bright (*informal*), keen, shrewd, astute, perceptive
quiet *adj* **1** = **silent**, low, soft, inaudible, hushed • *The children were quiet for a change*. OPPOSITE: noisy **2** = **calm**, peaceful, mild, tranquil, serene, restful • *a quiet evening at home* **3** = **undisturbed**, private, isolated, secluded, sequestered, unfrequented **4** = **reserved**, mild, shy, gentle, sedate, meek, retiring ▸ *n* **5** = **peace**, silence, serenity, tranquility, calmness, stillness • *The teacher called for quiet*. OPPOSITE: noise
See also: **easy, sleepy**
quieten *v* **1** = **silence**, still, stop, quiet, stifle, compose, subdue, quell, mute, hush, muffle **2** = **soothe**, calm, blunt, dull, appease, allay, deaden
quietly *adv* **1** = **silently**, softly, in an undertone, inaudibly, in silence, mutely, noiselessly **2** = **calmly**, patiently, mildly, serenely, placidly
quietness *n* = **peace**, quiet, silence, calm, hush, stillness, tranquillity
quilt *n* = **bedspread**, comforter, duvet, continental quilt, counterpane, coverlet, eiderdown
quintessence *n* = **essence**, spirit, soul, distillation
quintessential *adj* = **ultimate**, typical,

DICTIONARY

representation of a quality or state
quintessential *adj*
quintet *n* **1** group of five performers **2** music for such a group
quintuplet *n* one of five offspring born at one birth
quip Ⓣ *n* **1** witty saying ▷ *v* **quipping, quipped 2** make a quip
quire *n* set of 24 or 25 sheets of paper
quirk Ⓣ *n* **1** peculiarity of character **2** unexpected twist or turn: *a quirk of fate*
quirky *adj*
quisling *n* traitor who aids an occupying enemy force
quit Ⓣ *v* **quitting, quit 1** depart from **2** give up (a job) **3** stop (doing something)
▸ **quitter** *n* person who lacks perseverance
▸ **quits** *adj informal* on an equal footing
quitch grass *n* same as **couch grass**
quite Ⓣ *adv* **1** to a greater than average extent: *she's quite pretty* **2** absolutely: *you're quite right* **3** in actuality, truly ▷ *interj* **4** expression of agreement
quiver[1] Ⓣ *v* **1** shake with a tremulous movement ▷ *n* **2** shaking or trembling
quiver[2] *n* case for arrows
quixotic Ⓣ [kwik-**sot**-ik] *adj* romantic and unrealistic **quixotically** *adv*
quiz Ⓣ *n, pl* **quizzes 1** entertainment in which the knowledge of the players is tested by a series of questions ▷ *v* **quizzing, quizzed 2** investigate by close questioning
▸ **quizzical** *adj* questioning and mocking: *a quizzical look* **quizzically** *adv*
quoit *n* **1** large ring used in the game of quoits **quoits 2** game in which quoits are tossed at a stake in the ground in attempts to encircle it
quondam *adj* of an earlier time, former
quorum *n* minimum number of people required to be present at a meeting before any transactions can take place
▸ **quorate** *adj* having or being a quorum
quota Ⓣ *n* **1** share that is due from, due to, or allocated to a group or person **2** prescribed number or quantity allowed, required, or admitted
quote Ⓣ *v* **1** repeat (words) exactly from (an earlier work, speech, or conversation) **2** state (a price) for goods or a job of work ▷ *n* **3** *informal* quotation **quotable** *adj*
▸ **quotation** *n* **1** written or spoken passage repeated exactly in a later work, speech, or conversation **2** act of quoting **3** estimate of costs submitted by a contractor to a prospective client
quoth *v obsolete* said
quotidian *adj* **1** daily **2** commonplace
quotient *n* result of the division of one number or quantity by another
q.v. which see: used to refer a reader to another item in the same book
qwerty *n* standard English language typewriter or computer keyboard

THESAURUS

definitive, prototypical, archetypal
quip *n* = **joke**, jest, retort, wisecrack (*informal*), gibe, pleasantry, riposte, sally, witticism
quirk *n* = **peculiarity**, habit, oddity, characteristic, trait, kink, aberration, foible, mannerism, eccentricity, idiosyncrasy
quirky *adj* = **odd**, unusual, eccentric, peculiar, offbeat, idiosyncratic
quit *v* **1** = **resign**, leave, retire • *He quit his job at the pizza place.* **2** = **stop**, discontinue, give up • *Let's just quit talking about it.*
quite *adv* **1** = **somewhat**, rather, fairly, reasonably, moderately • *He is quite old.* **2** = **absolutely**, completely, fully, totally, entirely, perfectly • *The dog lay quite still.* **3** = **truly**, really, in fact, in reality, in truth
See also: **exactly, pretty**
quiver *v* **1** = **shake**, quake, shiver, vibrate, tremble, shudder, oscillate, quaver ▸ *n* **2** = **shake**, vibration, tremor, shiver, tremble, shudder, oscillation
quixotic *adj* = **unrealistic**, romantic, impractical, fanciful, dreamy, idealistic
quiz *n* **1** = **examination**, test, investigation, questioning ▸ *v* **2** = **question**, ask, investigate, examine, interrogate
quizzical *adj* = **mocking**, arch, sardonic, questioning, teasing
quota *n* = **share**, part, portion, slice, assignment, allowance, ration
quotation *n* **1** = **passage**, quote (*informal*), reference, extract, excerpt, citation **2** (*Commerce*) = **estimate**, charge, price, rate, figure, quote (*informal*), tender, costing
quote *v* = **repeat**, cite, extract, recite • *She quoted a great line from Shakespeare.*
See also: **estimate**

DICTIONARY

r **1** radius **2** ratio **3** right
R **1** Queen **2** King **3** River **4** *chess* rook
Ra *chem* radium
RA **1** Royal Academy **2** Royal Artillery
rabbi [**rab**-bye] *n, pl* **-bis** Jewish spiritual leader **rabbinical** *adj*
rabbit *n* small burrowing mammal with long ears
▸ **rabbit on** *v informal* talk too much
rabble Ⓣ *n* disorderly crowd of noisy people
Rabelais *n* **François**. ?1494–1553, French writer. His written works, esp. *Gargantua and Pantagruel* (1534), contain a lively mixture of earthy wit, common sense, and satire **Rabelaisian** *adj*
rabid Ⓣ *adj* **1** fanatical **2** having rabies **rabidly** *adv*
rabies [**ray**-beez] *n* acute infectious viral disease transmitted by dogs and certain other animals
Rabin *n* **Yitzhak**. 1922–95, Israeli statesman; prime minister of Israel (1974–77; 1992–95); assassinated
raccoon *n* small N American mammal with a long striped tail
race[1] Ⓣ *n* **1** contest of speed **races** **2** meeting for horse racing ▹ *v* **3** compete with in a race **4** run swiftly **5** (of an engine) run faster than normal **racer** *n* **racecourse** *n* **racehorse** *n* **racetrack** *n*
race[2] Ⓣ *n* group of people of common ancestry with distinguishing physical features, such as skin colour **racial** *adj*
▸ **racism** *or* **racialism** *n* hostile attitude or behaviour to members of other races, based on a belief in the innate superiority of one's own race **racist** *or* **racialist** *adj, n*
raceme [rass-**eem**] *n* cluster of flowers along a central stem, as in the foxglove
Rachmaninoff, Rachmaninov *n* **Sergei Vassilievich**. 1873–1943, Russian piano virtuoso and composer
Racine *n* **Jean Baptiste**. 1639–99, French tragic poet and dramatist. His plays include *Andromaque* (1667), *Bérénice* (1670), and *Phèdre* (1677)
rack[1] Ⓣ *n* **1** framework for holding particular articles, such as coats or luggage **2** straight bar with teeth on its edge, to work with a cogwheel **3** *hist* instrument of torture that stretched the victim's body ▹ *v* **4** cause great suffering to
▸ **rack one's brains** try very hard to remember
rack[2] *n* **go to rack and ruin** be destroyed
racket[1] Ⓣ *n* **1** noisy disturbance, din **2** occupation by which money is made illegally
▸ **racketeer** *n* person making illegal profits
racket[2], **racquet** *n* bat with strings stretched in an oval frame, used in tennis etc.
▸ **rackets** *n* ball game played in a paved walled court
raconteur [rak-on-**tur**] *n* skilled storyteller
racoon *n* same as **raccoon**
racy Ⓣ *adj* **racier, raciest** **1** slightly shocking **2** spirited or lively **racily** *adv* **raciness** *n*
radar *n* device for tracking distant objects by bouncing high-frequency radio pulses off them
radial *adj* **1** emanating from a common central point **2** of a radius **3** Also **radial-ply** (of a tire) having flexible sidewalls strengthened with radial cords

r

THESAURUS

rabble *n* = **mob**, crowd, herd, swarm, throng, horde, canaille
rabid *adj* **1** = **fanatical**, extreme, irrational, zealous, fervent, narrow-minded **2** = **mad**, hydrophobic
race[1] *n* **1** = **contest**, competition, chase, pursuit, rivalry, dash ▸ *v* **2** = **run**, fly, speed, tear, dash, hurry • *She raced out of the house.*
See also: **rush**
race[2] *n* = **people**, nation, ethnic group • *Discrimination on the grounds of race is illegal.*
racial *adj* = **ethnic**, national, genetic, folk, tribal, ethnological, genealogical
racism *See* **prejudice**
rack *n* **1** = **frame**, stand, structure, framework ▸ *v* **2** = **torture**, pain, afflict, harrow, oppress, agonize, torment, crucify
racket *n* **1** = **noise**, clamour, commotion, din, hubbub, rumpus • *The racket went on past midnight.* **2** = **fraud**, scam, scheme, con (*informal*), enterprise • *an investment racket*
See also: **sound**
racy *adj* **1** = **risqué**, blue, naughty, bawdy, suggestive, smutty **2** = **lively**, exciting, animated, energetic, sparkling, spirited, entertaining
radiance *n* **1** = **happiness**, delight, joy, pleasure, warmth, rapture,

DICTIONARY

radiate Ⓣ *v* **1** emit or be emitted as radiation **2** spread out from a centre
▶ **radiant** *adj* **1** looking happy **2** shining **3** emitting radiation **radiance** *n*
▶ **radiation** *n* **1** transmission of heat or light from one body to another **2** particles or rays emitted in nuclear decay **3** process of radiating
▶ **radiator** *n* **1** arrangement of pipes containing hot water or steam to heat a room **2** tubes containing water as cooling apparatus for an automobile engine
radical Ⓣ *adj* **1** advocating fundamental change **2** fundamental **3** thorough ▷ *n* **4** person advocating fundamental (political) change **5** number expressed as the root of another **radically** *adv* **radicalism** *n*
radicle *n* small or developing root
radii *n* a plural of **radius**
radio *n, pl* **-dios** **1** use of electromagnetic waves for broadcasting, communication, etc. **2** device for receiving and amplifying radio signals **3** sound broadcasting ▷ *v* **4** transmit (a message) by radio
radio- *combining form* of rays, radiation, or radium
radioactive *adj* emitting radiation as a result of nuclear decay **radioactivity** *n*
radiocarbon *n* radioactive form of carbon used in calculating the age of very old objects
radiography [ray-dee-**og**-ra-fee] *n* production of an image on a film or plate by radiation **radiographer** *n*
radioisotope *n* radioactive isotope
radiology [ray-dee-**ol**-a-jee] *n* science of using x-rays in medicine **radiologist** *n*
radiotherapy *n* treatment of disease, esp. cancer, by radiation **radiotherapist** *n*
radish *n* small hot-flavoured root vegetable eaten raw in salads
Radisson *n* **Pierre-Esprit**. 1636–1710, French explorer and fur trader in Canada. An expedition with his brother-in-law Médard Chouart Des Groseilliers to Hudson Bay on behalf of English Merchants led to the creation of the Hudson's Bay Company
radium *n* radioactive metallic element
radius *n, pl* **radii, radiuses** **1** (length of) a straight line from the centre to the circumference of a circle **2** outer of two bones in the forearm
radon [**ray**-don] *n* radioactive gaseous element
Raeburn *n* Sir **Henry**. 1756–1823, Scottish portrait painter
raffia *n* prepared palm fibre for weaving mats etc.
raffish *adj* disreputable
raffle Ⓣ *n* **1** lottery with an article as a prize ▷ *v* **2** offer as a prize in a raffle
raft *n* floating platform of logs, planks, etc.
rafter *n* one of the main beams of a roof
rag[1] *n* **1** fragment of cloth **2** torn piece **3** *informal* newspaper **rags** **4** tattered clothing
▶ **ragged** [**rag**-gid] *adj* **1** dressed in shabby or torn clothes **2** torn **3** lacking smoothness
▶ **ragtime** *n* style of jazz piano music
rag[2] *v* **ragging, ragged** **1** tease **2** play practical jokes on ▷ *n* **3** carnival with processions etc., organized by students to raise money for charities
▶ **rag the puck** *hockey* deliberately use up time by carefully keeping possession of the puck
ragamuffin Ⓣ *n* ragged dirty child
rage Ⓣ *n* **1** violent anger or passion ▷ *v* **2** speak or act with fury **3** proceed violently and without check: *a storm was raging*
▶ **all the rage** very popular
raglan *adj* (of a sleeve) joined to a garment by diagonal seams from the neck to the underarm
ragout [rag-**goo**] *n* richly seasoned stew

THESAURUS

gaiety **2 = brightness**, light, shine, glow, glare, brilliance, gleam, lustre
radiant *adj* **1 = happy**, ecstatic, delighted, glowing, joyful, joyous, blissful, on cloud nine (*informal*), rapturous **2 = bright**, brilliant, glowing, luminous, gleaming, glittering, lustrous, shining
radiate *v* **1 = spread out**, issue, diverge, branch out **2 = emit**, spread, pour, shed, scatter, diffuse, give off *or* give out, send out
radical *adj* **1 = fundamental**, natural, basic, profound, innate, deep-seated **2 = extreme**, complete, entire, severe, extremist, thorough, drastic, fanatical, sweeping ▶ *n* **3 = extremist**, militant, revolutionary, fanatic
raffle *n* **= draw**, sweep, lottery, sweepstake
ragamuffin *n* **= urchin**, guttersnipe
rage *n* **1 = fury**, anger, frenzy, wrath • *trembling with rage* ▶ *v* **2 = be furious**, storm, fume, rave, lose your temper • *He was raging at their lack of response.* **3 = be at its height**, storm, surge, rampage • *The fire raged out of control.* ▷ **all the rage = in fashion**, trendy, fashionable, *du jour* (*French*), the latest thing, voguish, culty
ragged *adj* **1 = tattered**, shabby, in rags, in tatters, tatty, threadbare, torn, unkempt **2 = rough**, rugged, uneven, unfinished, jagged, serrated
raging *adj* **= furious**, mad, enraged, incensed, seething, raving, beside oneself, fuming, infuriated
rags *pl n* **= tatters**, castoffs, old clothes, tattered clothing

DICTIONARY

of meat and vegetables
raid Ⓣ *n* **1** sudden surprise attack or search ▷ *v* **2** make a raid on **raider** *n*
rail[1] Ⓣ *n* **1** horizontal bar, esp. as part of a fence or track **2** railway
▸ **railing** *n* fence made of rails supported by posts
▸ **railway** *or* **railroad** *n* **1** track of iron rails on which trains run **2** company operating a railway
rail[2] *v* (foll. by *at* or *against*) complain bitterly or loudly
▸ **raillery** *n* teasing or joking
rail[3] *n* small marsh bird
raiment *n obsolete* clothing
rain Ⓣ *n* **1** water falling in drops from the clouds ▷ *v* **2** fall or pour down as rain **rainy** *adj*
▸ **rainbow** *n* arch of colours in the sky
▸ **raincoat** *n* water-resistant overcoat
▸ **rainfall** *n* amount of rain
▸ **rainforest** *n* dense forest in the tropics
Rainier III *n* full name *Rainier Louis Henri Maxence Bertrand de Grimaldi*. 1923–2005, ruling prince of Monaco from 1949. He married (1956) the US actress Grace Kelly (1929–82)
Rais, Retz *n* **Gilles de**. 1404–40, French nobleman who fought with Joan of Arc: marshal of France (1429–40). He was executed for the torture and murder of more than 140 children
raise Ⓣ *v* **1** lift up **2** set upright **3** increase in amount or intensity **4** bring up (a family) **5** put forward for consideration **6** collect or levy **7** build **8** end: *raise a siege* ▷ *n* **9** increase, esp. of wages
raisin *n* dried grape
raison d'être [**ray**-zon **det**-ra] *n French* reason or justification for existence
raita [**rye**-ta] *n* Indian dish of chopped cucumber, mint, etc., in yoghurt, served with curries
Raj *n* **the Raj** former British rule in India
rajah *n* Indian prince or ruler
Rajapaksa *n* **Mahinda**. born 1945, Sri Lankan politician; President from 2005
rake[1] Ⓣ *n* **1** tool with a long handle and a crosspiece with teeth, used for smoothing earth or gathering leaves, hay, etc. ▷ *v* **2** gather or smooth with a rake **3** search (through) **4** sweep (with gunfire)
▸ **rake it in** *informal* make a large amount of money
▸ **rake-off** *n slang* share of profits, esp. illegal
▸ **rake up** *v* revive memories of (a forgotten unpleasant event)
rake[2] Ⓣ *n* dissolute or immoral man
rakish Ⓣ [**ray**-kish] *ad* **1** dashing or jaunty **2** dissolute
Raleigh[2], **Ralegh** *n* Sir **Walter**. ?1552–1618, English courtier, explorer, and writer; favourite of Elizabeth I. After unsuccessful attempts to colonize Virginia (1584–89), he led two expeditions to the Orinoco to search for gold (1595; 1616). He introduced tobacco and potatoes into England, and was imprisoned (1603–16) for conspiracy under James I. He was beheaded in 1618
rally Ⓣ *n, pl* **-lies 1** large gathering of people for a (political) meeting **2** marked recovery of strength **3** *tennis* lively exchange of strokes **4** automobile driving competition on public roads ▷ *v* **rallying, rallied 5** bring or come together after dispersal or for a common

THESAURUS

raid *v* **1** = **attack**, assault, invade, plunder, break into • *Soldiers raided the capital.* ▸ *n* **2** = **attack**, break-in, foray • *Our raid on the kitchen provided enough food for the hike.*
See also: **loot**
raider *n* = **attacker**, thief, robber, invader, marauder, plunderer
rail *See* **bar**
railing *n* = **fence**, barrier, balustrade, paling, rails
rain *n* **1** = **rainfall**, deluge, downpour, drizzle, showers • *A few drops of rain fell on her hand.* ▸ *v* **2** = **pour**, drizzle, teem • *It rained the whole weekend.* **3** = **fall**, drop, deposit, shower, sprinkle
rainfall *See* **rain**
rainy *adj* = **wet**, damp, drizzly, showery
raise *v* **1** = **lift**, hoist, elevate, heave • *a drive to raise standards of literacy* OPPOSITE: lower **2** = **bring up**, rear, nurture • *the house where she was raised* **3** = **mention**, advance, bring up, suggest, introduce, broach • *He had raised no objections at the time.* **4** = **increase**, boost, advance, strengthen, intensify, enhance, heighten, inflate, magnify, amplify, enlarge **5** = **collect**, rally, form, gather, mass, obtain, recruit, assemble • *They raised money for their work in Afghanistan.* **6** = **cause**, start, create, produce, occasion, provoke, originate, engender
See also: **breed**
rake[1] *v* **1** = **gather**, remove, collect **2** = **search**, scrutinize, comb, scour
rake[2] *n* = **libertine**, playboy, debauchee, lecher, roué
rakish *adj* = **dashing**, dapper, jaunty, debonair, devil-may-care, raffish
rally *n* **1** = **gathering**, meeting, convention, assembly, congress **2** = **recovery**, improvement, revival, recuperation ▸ *v* **3** = **reassemble**, unite, regroup, reorganize **4** = **gather**, collect, unite, assemble, convene, muster, marshal,

DICTIONARY

cause **6** regain health or strength, revive
ram ❶ *n* **1** male sheep **2** hydraulic machine ▷ *v* **ramming, rammed 3** strike against with force **4** force or drive **5** cram or stuff **6** *government* (usually foll. by *through*) aggressively force the passage of an act, bill, etc.
▸ **ram raid** *informal* raid on a shop in which a stolen automobile is driven into the window
▸ **ram raider** person who carries out a ram raid
RAM *computers* random access memory
Ramadan *n* **1** 9th Muslim month **2** strict fasting observed during this time
ramble ❶ *v* **1** walk without a definite route **2** talk incoherently ▷ *n* **3** walk, esp. in the country
▸ **rambler** *n* **1** climbing rose **2** person who rambles
Rameau *n* **Jean Philippe**. 1683–1764, French composer. His works include the opera *Castor et Pollux* (1737), chamber music, harpsichord pieces, church music, and cantatas. His *Traité de l'harmonie* (1722) was of fundamental importance in the development of modern harmony
ramekin [**ram**-ik-in] *n* small ovenproof dish for a single serving of food
ramify *v* **-ifying, -ified 1** become complex **2** spread in branches, subdivide
▸ **ramification** *n* consequence
ramp ❶ *n* **1** slope joining two level surfaces **2** small hump on a road to make traffic slow down
rampage ❶ *v* dash about violently
▸ **on the rampage** behaving violently or destructively
rampant ❶ *adj* **1** unrestrained in growth or spread, rife **2** (of a heraldic beast) on its hind legs
rampart ❶ *n* mound or wall for defence
ramrod *n* **1** long thin rod used for cleaning the barrel of a gun or forcing gunpowder into an old-fashioned gun ▷ *adj* **2** (of someone's posture) very straight and upright
Ramsay *n* **1 Allan**. 1713–84, Scottish portrait painter **2 James Andrew Broun**. See (1st Marquis and 10th Earl of) **Dalhousie**
Ramses II, Rameses II *n* died ?1225 BC, king of ancient Egypt (?1292–?25). His reign was marked by war with the Hittites and the construction of many colossal monuments, esp. the rock temple at Abu Simbel
Ramses III, Rameses III *n* died ?1167 BC, king of ancient Egypt (?1198–?67). His reign was marked by wars in Libya and Syria
ramshackle ❶ *adj* tumbledown, rickety, or makeshift
Ram Singh *n* 1816–85, Indian leader of a puritanical Sikh sect, the Kukas, who tried to remove the British from India through a policy of noncooperation
ran *v* past tense of **run**
ranch *n* large cattle farm in the N American West **rancher** *n*
rancid ❶ *adj* (of butter, bacon, etc.) stale and having an offensive smell **rancidity** *n*
rancour ❶ *n* deep bitter hate **rancorous** *adj*
rand *n* monetary unit of S Africa
R & B rhythm and blues
R & D research and development
Randolph *n* **1 Edmund Jennings**. 1753–1813, US politician. He was a member of the convention that framed the US constitution (1787), attorney general (1789–94), and secretary of state (1794–95) **2 John**, called *Randolph of Roanoke*. 1773–1833, US politician, noted for his eloquence: in 1820 he opposed the Missouri Compromise that outlawed slavery **3** Sir **Thomas**, 1st Earl of Moray. died 1332, Scottish soldier: regent after the death of Robert the Bruce (1329)

THESAURUS

round up **5 = recover**, improve, revive, recuperate, get better
ram *v* **1 = hit**, force, drive, crash, impact, smash, butt, dash **2 = cram**, force, crowd, stuff, jam, thrust
ramble *v* **1 = walk**, range, wander, roam, stroll, stray, rove, saunter **2 = babble** ▸ *n* **3 = walk**, tour, hike, stroll, saunter, roaming, roving
rambler *n* **= walker**, rover, hiker, wanderer, wayfarer
rambling *adj* **= long-winded**, incoherent, disjointed, disconnected, circuitous, digressive, discursive, wordy
ramification *n* ▷ **ramifications = consequences**, sequel, upshot, developments, results
ramp *n* **= slope**, rise, grade, incline, gradient
rampage *v* **= go berserk**, rage, run amok, run riot • *children rampaging around the garden* ▸ *n* ▷ **on the rampage = berserk**, wild, amok • *a wild animal on the rampage*
See also: **riot**
rampant *adj* **1 = widespread**, prevalent, unchecked, rife, uncontrolled, unrestrained, profuse, spreading like wildfire **2** (*Heraldry*) **= upright**, standing, erect, rearing
rampart *n* **= defence**, wall, fence, bastion, fortification, bulwark
ramshackle *adj* **= rickety**, unsafe, shaky, unsteady, derelict, flimsy, decrepit, crumbling, tumbledown
rancid *adj* **= rotten**, bad, foul, fetid, rank, tainted, sour, stale, putrid, strong-smelling
rancorous *See* **bitter**
rancour *n* **= hatred**, hate, animosity,

DICTIONARY

random ⓣ *adj* made or done by chance or without plan
▶ **at random** haphazard(ly)
randy ⓣ *adj* **randier, randiest** *slang* sexually aroused
ranee *n* same as **rani**
rang *v* past tense of **ring**[1]
range ⓣ *n* **1** limits of effectiveness or variation **2** distance that a missile or plane can travel **3** distance of a mark shot at **4** whole set of related things **5** place for shooting practice or rocket testing **6** chain of mountains **7** kitchen stove ▷ *v* **8** vary between one point and another **9** cover or extend over **10** roam
▶ **ranger** *n* **1** official in charge of a nature reserve etc. **2 Ranger** member of the senior branch of Guides
▶ **rangefinder** *n* instrument for finding how far away an object is
rangy ⓣ [**rain**-jee] *adj* **rangier, rangiest** having long slender limbs
rani *n* wife or widow of a rajah
Ranjit Singh *n* called *the Lion of the Punjab.* 1780–1839; founder of the Sikh kingdom in the Punjab
rank[1] ⓣ *n* **1** status **2** relative place or position **3** social class **4** order **5** row or line ▷ *v* **6** have a specific rank or position **7** arrange in rows or lines
▶ **rank and file** ordinary people or members
▶ **the ranks** common soldiers
▶ **rise through the ranks** *or* **rise from the ranks 1** *mil* obtain a promotion into the officer class **2** become a success through one's own efforts
rank[2] ⓣ *adj* **1** complete or absolute: *rank favouritism* **2** smelling offensively strong **3** growing too thickly **rankly** *adv*
Rank *n* **J(oseph) Arthur**, 1st Baron. 1888–1972, British industrialist and film executive, whose companies dominated the British film industry in the 1940s and 1950s
rankle ⓣ *v* continue to cause resentment or bitterness
ransack ⓣ *v* **1** search thoroughly **2** pillage, plunder
ransom ⓣ *n* money demanded in return for the release of someone who has been kidnapped
Ransome *n* **Arthur**. 1884–1967, English writer, best known for his books for children, including *Swallows and Amazons* (1930) and *Great Northern?* (1947)
rant ⓣ *v* talk in a loud and excited way
ranter *n*
ranunculus *n, pl* **-luses, -li** genus of plants including the buttercup
rap ⓣ *v* **rapping, rapped 1** hit with a sharp quick blow **2** utter (a command) abruptly **3** perform a rhythmic monologue with musical backing ▷ *n* **4** sharp quick blow **5** rhythmic monologue performed to music
rapper *n*
▶ **take the rap** *slang* suffer punishment for something whether guilty or not
▶ **rap sheet** *chiefly US & Canad informal* police record of an individual's criminal history

THESAURUS

bitterness, bad blood, ill feeling, ill will
random *adj* = **chance**, spot, arbitrary, indiscriminate, haphazard, aimless • *random acts of kindness* ▷ **at random** = **haphazardly**, randomly, indiscriminately, arbitrarily, aimlessly • *chosen at random*
See also: **absent-minded, accidental, irregular**
randomly *See* **at random**
randy *adj* (*Informal*) = **lustful**, hot, amorous, horny (*slang*), aroused, lascivious, turned-on (*slang*)
range *n* **1** = **limits**, province, field, extent, scope, bounds • *What is the range of your cellphone?* **2** = **series**, class, variety, selection, assortment, gamut • *a wide range of colours* ▶ *v* **3** = **vary**, go, run, extend, stretch • *items ranging between the everyday and the exotic* **4** = **roam**, wander, rove, ramble, traverse
See also: **area, choice**
rangy *adj* = **long-limbed**, lanky, leggy, gangling, long-legged
rank[1] *n* **1** = **status**, level, station, class, standing, grade, echelon • *She rose to the rank of captain.* **2** = **row**, file, line, column • *ranks of police* ▷ **rank and file** = **general public**, majority, mass, masses ▶ *v* **3** = **arrange**, order, sort, array, dispose, align, line up
See also: **classify, rate**
rank[2] *adj* **1** = **absolute**, complete, utter, sheer, downright, unmitigated • *It was rank stupidity to go there alone.* **2** = **foul**, bad, offensive, funky (*slang*), noxious, smelly, rancid, disgusting, revolting, noisome, stinking **3** = **abundant**, dense, lush, luxuriant, profuse
rankle *v* = **annoy**, anger, irk, rile, irritate, gall, get on one's nerves (*informal*)
ransack *v* **1** = **search**, explore, comb, scour, rummage, go through, turn inside out **2** = **plunder**, raid, strip, loot, pillage
ransom *n* = **payment**, price, money, payoff
rant *v* = **shout**, cry, roar, yell, rave, declaim
rap *v* **1** = **hit**, strike, knock, crack, tap ▷ **rap someone's knuckles** *See* **punish** ▶ *n* **2** = **blow**, knock, crack, tap, clout (*informal*) **3** (*Slang*) = **punishment**, blame, responsibility

DICTIONARY

rapacious Ⓣ *adj* greedy or grasping
rapacity *n*
rape[1] Ⓣ *v* **1** force to submit to sexual intercourse ▷ *n* **2** act of raping **3** any violation or abuse **rapist** *n*
rape[2] *n* plant with oil-yielding seeds, also used as fodder
Raphael *n* **1** *Bible* one of the archangels; the angel of healing and the guardian of Tobias (Tobit 3:17; 5–12). Feast day: Sept 29 **2** original name *Raffaello Santi* or *Sanzio*. 1483–1520, Italian painter and architect, regarded as one of the greatest artists of the High Renaissance. His many paintings include the *Sistine Madonna* (?1513) and the *Transfiguration* (unfinished, 1520)
rapid Ⓣ *adj* quick, swift **rapidly** *adv*
rapidity *n*
▸ **rapid eye movement** movement of the eyeballs while a person is dreaming
▸ **rapids** *pl n* stretch of a river with a fast turbulent current
rapier [**ray**-pyer] *n* fine-bladed sword
rapine [**rap**-pine] *n* pillage or plundering
rappel [ra-**pell**] *v* descend a vertical cliff by using a rope fixed at a higher point
rapport Ⓣ [rap-**pore**] *n* harmony or agreement
rapprochement Ⓣ [rap-**prosh**-mong] *n* re-establishment of friendly relations, esp. between nations
rapscallion *n old-fashioned* rascal or rogue
rapt Ⓣ *adj* engrossed or spellbound
▸ **rapture** *n* ecstasy **rapturous** *adj*
raptorial *adj* **1** predatory **2** of birds of prey
rare[1] Ⓣ *adj* **1** uncommon **2** infrequent **3** of uncommonly high quality **4** (of air at high altitudes) having low density, thin **rarity** *n*
▸ **rarely** *adv* seldom
rare[2] *adj* (of meat) lightly cooked
rarebit *n* savoury cheese dish
rarefied Ⓣ [**rare**-if-ide] *adj* **1** highly specialized, exalted **2** (of air) thin
raring Ⓣ *adj* **raring to go** enthusiastic, willing, or ready
rascal Ⓣ *n* **1** rogue **2** naughty (young) person
rascally *adj*
rase *v* same as **raze**
rash[1] Ⓣ *adj* hasty, reckless, or incautious
rashly *adv*
rash[2] Ⓣ *n* **1** skin eruption **2** outbreak of (unpleasant) occurrences
rasher *n* thin slice of bacon
Rasmussen *n* **Knud Johan Victor**. 1879–1933, Danish arctic explorer and ethnologist. He led several expeditions through the Arctic in support of his theory that the North American Indians were originally migrants from Asia
rasp Ⓣ *n* **1** harsh grating noise **2** coarse

THESAURUS

rapacious *adj* = **greedy**, predatory, voracious, insatiable, avaricious, grasping, preying
rape *v* **1** = **sexually assault**, force, abuse, violate, outrage, ravish ▸ *n* **2** = **sexual assault**, violation, outrage, ravishment **3** = **desecration**, abuse, violation, defilement
rapid *adj* = **quick**, fast, prompt, express, speedy, swift, brisk, hurried, hasty
rapidity *n* = **speed**, rush, hurry, velocity, haste, quickness, alacrity, briskness, fleetness, promptness, swiftness
rapidly *adv* = **quickly**, fast, promptly, swiftly, briskly, hastily, hurriedly, in haste, pronto (*informal*), speedily
rapport *n* = **bond**, link, tie, relationship, understanding, sympathy, empathy, harmony, affinity
rapprochement *n* = **reconciliation**, reunion, detente
rapt *adj* = **spellbound**, absorbed, engrossed, enthralled, entranced, fascinated, gripped
rapture *n* = **ecstasy**, transport, delight, joy, bliss, euphoria, rhapsody, seventh heaven
rapturous *adj* = **ecstatic**, joyful, euphoric, blissful, in seventh heaven, overjoyed, over the moon (*informal*), transported
rare *adj* **1** = **uncommon**, few, unusual, exceptional, scarce, sparse, sporadic • *a rare species of bird* OPPOSITE: common **2** = **superb**, great, fine, choice, excellent, superlative, peerless
See also: **singular**
rarefied *adj* = **exalted**, high, spiritual, elevated, lofty, noble, sublime
rarely *adv* = **seldom**, hardly, infrequently, hardly ever
raring *adj* ▷ **raring to** = **eager to**, desperate to, enthusiastic to, impatient to, keen to, longing to, ready to ▷ **raring to go** *See* **eager**
rarity *n* **1** = **curio**, find, treasure, gem, collector's item **2** = **uncommonness**, shortage, scarcity, infrequency, sparseness, strangeness, unusualness
rascal *n* = **rogue**, devil, good-for-nothing, imp, villain, scamp, scoundrel
rash[1] *adj* = **reckless**, hasty, foolhardy, impulsive, impetuous • *It would be rash to act on such flimsy evidence.*
See also: **unwise**
rash[2] *n* **1** = **outbreak**, eruption • *I noticed a rash on my leg.* **2** = **spate**, flood, wave, epidemic, plague • *a rash of computer viruses*
rashness *n* = **recklessness**, indiscretion, carelessness, foolhardiness, hastiness, heedlessness, thoughtlessness
rasp *See* **scrape**

r

DICTIONARY

file ▷ *v* **3** speak in a grating voice **4** make a scraping noise
raspberry *n* **1** red juicy edible berry **2** plant which bears it **3** *informal* spluttering noise made with the tongue and lips, to show contempt
Rasputin *n* **Grigori Efimovich**. ?1871–1916, Siberian peasant monk, notorious for his debauchery, who wielded great influence over Tsarina Alexandra. He was assassinated by a group of Russian noblemen
Rastafarian *n, adj* (member) of a cult originating in Jamaica and regarding Haile Selassie as God (Also **Rasta**)
raster *v* use web-based technology to turn a digital image into a picture composed of black and white dots
rat *n* **1** small rodent **2** *informal* contemptible person, esp. a deserter or informer ▷ *v* **ratting, ratted 3** *informal* inform (on) **4** hunt rats
▸ **ratty** *adj slang* bad-tempered, irritable
▸ **rat race** continual hectic competitive activity
ratafia [rat-a-**fee**-a] *n* **1** liqueur made from fruit **2** almond-flavoured biscuit
ratatouille [rat-a-**twee**] *n* vegetable casserole of tomatoes, eggplants, etc.
ratchet *n* set of teeth on a bar or wheel allowing motion in one direction only
rate 🅣 *n* **1** degree of speed or progress **2** proportion between two things **3** charge **rates 4** local tax on property ▷ *v* **5** consider or value **6** estimate the value of **ratepayer** *n*
▸ **at any rate** in any case
▸ **rateable** *or* **ratable** *adj* **1** able to be rated **2** (of property) liable to payment of rates
rather 🅣 *adv* **1** to some extent **2** preferably **3** more willingly
ratify 🅣 *v* **-ifying, -ified** give formal approval to **ratification** *n*
rating 🅣 *n* **1** valuation or assessment **2** classification **3** non-commissioned sailor **ratings 4** size of the audience for a TV programme
ratio 🅣 *n, pl* **-tios** relationship between two numbers or amounts expressed as a proportion
ratiocinate [rat-ee-**oss**-in-nate] *v* reason or think out **ratiocination** *n*
ration 🅣 *n* **1** fixed allowance of food etc. ▷ *v* **2** limit to a certain amount per person
rational 🅣 *adj* **1** reasonable, sensible **2** capable of reasoning **rationally** *adv* **rationality** *n*
▸ **rationale** [rash-a-**nahl**] *n* reason for an action or decision
▸ **rationalism** *n* philosophy that regards reason as the only basis for beliefs or actions **rationalist** *n*
▸ **rationalize** *v* **1** justify by plausible reasoning **2** reorganize to improve efficiency or profitability **rationalization** *n*
rattan *n* **1** climbing palm with jointed stems **2** cane from this
Rattigan *n* Sir **Terence Mervyn**. 1911–77, English playwright. His plays include *The Winslow Boy* (1946), *Separate Tables* (1954), and *Ross* (1960)
rattle 🅣 *v* **1** give out a succession of short sharp sounds **2** clatter **3** shake briskly causing sharp sounds **4** *informal* confuse or fluster ▷ *n* **5** short sharp sound **6** instrument for making it
▸ **rattlesnake** *n* poisonous snake with loose

THESAURUS

rasping *See* **hoarse**
rate *n* **1 = speed**, pace, frequency, velocity, tempo • *appearing at the rate of one a week* **2 = charge**, price, cost, fee, tariff • *cheap telephone rates* **3 = degree**, standard, scale, proportion, ratio ▷ **at any rate = in any case**, anyway, anyhow, at all events ▶ *v* **4 = evaluate**, consider, count, class, regard, rank, appraise • *He was rated as one of the best.* **5 = deserve**, merit, be entitled to, be worthy of ▷ **rate highly** *See* **appreciate, value**
See also: **grade, judge**
rather *adv* **1 = quite**, pretty, slightly, relatively, somewhat, fairly • *We got along rather well.* **2 = preferably**, sooner, more readily, more willingly
ratify *v* **= approve**, confirm, endorse, establish, sanction, uphold, authorize, affirm
rating *n* **= position**, rate, order, class, status, rank, degree, grade, placing
ratio *n* **= proportion**, rate, percentage, relation, fraction
ration *n* **1 = allowance**, part, share, measure, portion, quota, allotment, helping ▶ *v* **2 = limit**, control, budget, restrict
rational *adj* **= logical**, reasonable, sensible, enlightened • *to arrive at a rational conclusion*
See also: **sane, wise**
rationale *n* **= reason**, principle, theory, motivation, philosophy, logic, grounds, *raison d'être (French)*
rationality *See* **reason**
rationalize *v* **= justify**, excuse, vindicate, account for
rations *See* **supplies**
rattle *v* **1 = clatter**, bang, jangle **2 = shake**, bounce, jolt, jar, vibrate **3** *(Informal)* **= fluster**, upset, shake, disturb, faze, disconcert, perturb

r

DICTIONARY

horny segments on the tail that make a rattling sound

Rattle *n* Sir **Simon**. born 1955, British conductor; principal conductor (1980–91) and music director (1991–98) of the City of Birmingham Symphony Orchestra; chief conductor of the Berlin Philharmonic Orchestra from 2002

raucous Ⓣ *adj* hoarse or harsh

raunchy Ⓣ *adj* **raunchier, raunchiest** *slang* earthy, sexy

Rauschenberg *n* **Robert**. 1925–2008, US artist; one of the foremost exponents of pop art

ravage Ⓣ *v lit* lay waste or plunder ▸ **ravages** *pl n* destruction

rave Ⓣ *v* **1** talk wildly in delirium or with enthusiasm ▹ *n* **2** *informal* enthusiastically good review ▸ **raving** *adj* **1** delirious **2** *informal* exceptional: *a raving beauty*

ravel *v* **-elling, -elled** tangle or become entangled

Ravel *n* **Maurice** (**Joseph**). 1875–1937, French composer, noted for his use of unresolved dissonances and mastery of tone colour. His works include *Gaspard de la Nuit* (1908) and *Le Tombeau de Couperin* (1917) for piano, *Boléro* (1928) for orchestra, and the ballet *Daphnis et Chloé* (1912)

raven *n* **1** black bird like a crow ▹ *adj* **2** (of hair) shiny black

ravening *adj* (of animals) hungrily searching for prey

ravenous Ⓣ *adj* very hungry

ravine Ⓣ [rav-**veen**] *n* narrow steep-sided valley worn by a stream

ravioli *pl n* small squares of pasta with a savoury filling

ravish Ⓣ *v* **1** enrapture **2** *lit* rape ▸ **ravishing** *adj* lovely or entrancing

raw Ⓣ *adj* **1** uncooked **2** not manufactured or refined **3** inexperienced: *raw recruits* **4** chilly ▸ **raw deal** unfair or dishonest treatment ▸ **rawhide** *n* untanned hide

ray[1] Ⓣ *n* **1** single line or narrow beam of light **2** any of a set of radiating lines

ray[2] *n* large sea fish with a whiplike tail

Ray *n* **1 Man**, real name *Emmanuel Rudnitsky*. 1890–1976, US surrealist photographer **2 Satyajit**. 1921–92, Indian film director, noted for his *Apu* trilogy (1955–59)

rayon *n* (fabric made of) a synthetic fibre

raze Ⓣ *v* destroy (buildings or a town) completely

razor *n* sharp instrument for shaving ▸ **razorbill** *n* N Atlantic auk

razzle-dazzle, razzmatazz *n slang* **1** showy activity **2** spree

RBI *baseball* runs batted in: runs scored during a player's at-bat

RC **1** Red Cross **2** Roman Catholic

RCAF Royal Canadian Air Force

RCMP Royal Canadian Mounted Police

RCN Royal Canadian Navy

Rd Road

re Ⓣ *prep* with reference to, concerning

re- *prefix* again: *re-enter; retrial*

reach Ⓣ *v* **1** arrive at **2** make a movement in order to grasp or touch **3** succeed in touching **4** make contact or communication with **5** extend to ▹ *n* **6** distance that one can reach **7** range of influence **8** stretch of a river between two bends **reachable** *adj*

THESAURUS

raucous *adj* = **harsh**, rough, loud, noisy, strident, hoarse, grating

raunchy *adj* (*Slang*) = **sexy**, sexual, steamy (*informal*), coarse, earthy, lusty

ravage *v* = **destroy**, devastate, ruin, spoil, demolish, ransack, despoil, lay waste ▸ *n* ▹ **ravages** = **damage**, destruction, ruin, havoc, devastation, ruination, spoliation

rave *v* **1** = **rant**, rage, babble • *He started raving about being treated badly.* **2** (*informal*) = **enthuse**, gush, be wild about (*informal*) • *She raved about the facilities there.*

ravenous *adj* = **starving**, famished, starved

ravine *n* = **canyon**, gorge, defile, gulch, pass, gully

raving *adj* = **mad**, wild, crazy, insane, irrational, delirious, hysterical, crazed

ravish *v* **1** = **enchant**, entrance, charm, delight, fascinate, captivate, spellbind, enrapture **2** = **rape**, force, abuse, violate, sexually assault

ravishing *adj* = **enchanting**, beautiful, lovely, charming, gorgeous, bewitching, entrancing

raw *adj* **1** = **uncooked**, natural, fresh **2** = **unrefined**, natural, crude, basic, rough, unfinished, coarse, unprocessed **3** = **inexperienced**, new, green, immature, callow **4** = **chilly**, cold, bitter, freezing, biting, piercing

ray *n* = **beam**, bar, flash, shaft, gleam

raze *v* = **destroy**, level, ruin, demolish, flatten, knock down, pull down

razor-sharp *See* **sharp**

re *prep* = **concerning**, about, regarding, apropos, with reference to, with regard to

reach *v* **1** = **arrive at**, get as far as, get to, make it to • *He did not stop until he reached the door.* **2** = **extend to**, touch • *Her coat nearly reached to the ground.* **3** = **attain**, climb to, fall to, rise to • *Unemployment has reached record levels.* **4** = **contact**, communicate with, get hold of, get in touch with, get through to ▸ *n*

DICTIONARY

react ⓣ *v* act in response or opposition (to)
▸ **reaction** *n* **1** physical or emotional response to a stimulus **2** any action resisting another **3** opposition to change **4** chemical or nuclear change, combination, or decomposition
▸ **reactionary** *n, adj* (person) opposed to change, esp. in politics
▸ **reactance** *n electricity* resistance in a coil due to the current reacting on itself
▸ **reactive** *adj* chemically active
▸ **reactor** *n* apparatus in which a nuclear reaction is maintained and controlled to produce nuclear energy
read ⓣ *v* **reading, read 1** look at and understand or take in (written or printed matter) **2** look at and say aloud **3** understand (an indicating instrument) **4** (of an instrument) register **5** study **6** matter suitable for reading: *a good read* **reading** *n*
▸ **reader** *n* **1** person who reads **2** senior university lecturer **3** textbook
▸ **readership** *n* readers of a publication collectively
▸ **readable** *adj* **1** enjoyable to read **2** legible **readability** *n*
readjust *v* adapt to a new situation **readjustment** *n*
readmit *v* let (a person, country, etc.) back in to a place or organization
ready ⓣ *adj* **readier, readiest 1** prepared for use or action **2** willing, prompt **readily** *adv* **readiness** *n*
▸ **ready-made** *adj* for immediate use by any customer
▸ **ready cash** *or* **ready money** cash for immediate use
reaffirm *v* state again, confirm
reaffirmation *n*
reafforest *v* plant new trees in (an area that was formerly forested) **reafforestation** *n*
Reagan *n* **Ronald.** 1911–2004, US film actor and Republican statesman: Governor of California (1966–74): 40th president of the US (1981–89)
reagent [ree-**age**-ent] *n* chemical substance that reacts with another, used to detect the presence of the other
real ⓣ *adj* **1** existing in fact **2** happening **3** actual **4** genuine **5** (of property) consisting of land and houses
▸ **really** *adv* **1** very **2** truly ▹ *interj* **3** indeed!
▸ **reality** *n* real existence
▸ **reality TV** television programmes focusing on members of the public living in conditions created especially by the programme makers
▸ **realtor** *n* agent, esp. accredited one who sells houses etc. for others
▸ **realty** *n* real estate
▸ **real ale** *Brit* beer allowed to ferment in the barrel
▸ **real estate** landed property
realistic ⓣ *adj* seeing and accepting things as they really are, practical

THESAURUS

5 = range, power, extension, stretch, scope, influence, capacity, distance, extent, grasp
See also: **extend**
react *v* **1 = respond**, answer, reply **2 = act**, work, operate, proceed, function, behave
reaction *n* **1 = response**, answer, feedback, acknowledgment • *Reaction to the visit was mixed.* **2 = backlash**, counterbalance • *a reaction against rising prices* **3 = conservatism**, the right
reactionary *adj* **1 = conservative**, right-wing ▸ *n* **2 = conservative**, right-winger, die-hard
read *v* **1 = look at**, study, scan, peruse, glance at, pore over • *I love to read in bed.* **2 = interpret**, comprehend, decipher • *as if he could read my thoughts* **3 = register**, show, record, indicate, display ▹ **read out** *See* **issue** ▹ **read up** *See* **study**
readable *adj* **1 = enjoyable**, interesting, entertaining, enthralling, gripping **2 = legible**, clear, comprehensible, decipherable
readily *adv* **1 = willingly**, quickly, promptly, freely, eagerly, gladly **2 = easily**, quickly, smoothly, effortlessly, speedily, unhesitatingly
readiness *n* **1 = willingness**, eagerness, keenness **2 = ease**, facility, dexterity, adroitness, promptness
reading *n* **1 = perusal**, study, inspection, scrutiny, examination **2 = recital**, performance, lesson, sermon **3 = interpretation**, version, impression, grasp **4 = learning**, education, knowledge, scholarship, erudition
ready *adj* **1 = prepared**, set, organized, ripe, primed • *The plums are ready to eat now.* **2 = willing**, happy, eager, keen, agreeable • *She was always ready to give interviews.* **3 = available**, accessible, convenient, handy • *ready cash* **4 = prompt**, quick, alert, sharp, smart, bright, keen, intelligent, clever, perceptive
See also: **fluent**
real *adj* **1 = actual**, true, legitimate, concrete, genuine, authentic, factual, tangible • *You're dealing with real life now.* OPPOSITE: imaginary **2 = genuine**, true, honest, authentic, sincere, unaffected, rightful, bona fide • *Is that a real diamond?* OPPOSITE: fake
See also: **natural**
realism *See* **reality**
realistic *adj* **1 = practical**, sober, sensible,

DICTIONARY

realistically *adv* **realism** *n* **realist** *n*
realize Ⓣ *v* **1** become aware or grasp the significance of **2** achieve (a plan, hopes, etc.) **3** convert into money **realization** *n*
realm Ⓣ *n* **1** kingdom **2** sphere of interest
ream *n* **1** twenty quires of paper, generally 500 sheets **reams 2** *informal* large quantity (of written matter)
reap Ⓣ *v* **1** cut and gather (harvest) **2** receive as the result of a previous activity **reaper** *n*
reappear Ⓣ *v* appear again **reappearance** *n*
reappraise *v* consider or review to see if changes are needed **reappraisal** *n*
rear[1] Ⓣ *n* **1** back part **2** part of an army, procession, etc. behind the others **rearmost** *adj*
▸**bring up the rear** come last
▸ **rear admiral** high-ranking naval officer
rear[2] Ⓣ *v* **1** care for and educate (children) **2** breed (animals) **3** (of a horse) rise on its hind feet
rearguard *n* **1** troops protecting the rear of an army **2** *hockey slang* defensive player
▸ **rearguard action** effort to prevent something unavoidable
rearm *v* **1** arm again **2** equip with better weapons **rearmament** *n*
rearrange *v* organize differently, alter **rearrangement** *n*
reason Ⓣ *n* **1** ground or motive **2** faculty of rational thought **3** sanity ▹ *v* **4** think logically in forming conclusions **5** (usu. foll. by *with*) persuade by logical argument into doing something
▸ **reasonable** *adj* **1** sensible **2** not excessive **3** suitable **4** logical **reasonably** *adv*
reassess *v* reconsider the value or importance of
reassure Ⓣ *v* restore confidence to **reassurance** *n*
rebate Ⓣ *n* discount or refund
rebel Ⓣ *v* **-belling, -belled 1** revolt against the ruling power **2** reject accepted conventions ▹ *n* **3** person who rebels
▸ **rebellion** *n* **1** organized open resistance to authority **2** rejection of conventions **rebellious** *adj*

THESAURUS

down-to-earth, matter-of-fact, level-headed • *It's only realistic to admit that things will go wrong.* **2 = lifelike**, true, faithful, authentic • *His novels are more realistic than his short stories.*
See also: **actual**
reality *n* = **truth**, fact, authenticity, realism • *Fiction and reality were increasingly blurred.*
realization *n* **1 = awareness**, understanding, recognition, perception, grasp, conception, comprehension, cognizance **2 = achievement**, accomplishment, fulfillment
realize *v* **1 = become aware of**, understand, recognize, appreciate, grasp, comprehend • *People don't realize how serious it is.* **2 = achieve**, do, complete, effect, perform, accomplish, fulfill, carry out *or* carry through
See also: **discover, find, see, sense**
really *adv* **1 = very**, extremely, absolutely, truly, remarkably, terribly • *I've had a really good time.* **2 = in fact**, actually, truly, in reality • *He didn't really understand the question.*
realm *n* **1 = kingdom**, country, land, empire, domain, dominion **2 = sphere**, world, province, area, field, department, territory, branch
reap *v* **1 = collect**, cut, gather, harvest, garner, bring in **2 = get**, gain, acquire, derive, obtain
reappear *See* **return**
rear[1] *n* **1 = back**, end, tail, stern, rearguard, tail end ▸ *adj* **2 = back**, last, following, hind
rear[2] *v* **1 = bring up**, raise, train, breed, foster, educate, nurture **2 = rise**, soar, tower, loom
reason *n* **1 = cause**, purpose, incentive, motive, grounds • *for a multitude of reasons* **2 = sense**, judgment, reasoning, intellect, rationality • *a conflict between emotion and reason* ▸ *v* **3 = persuade**, bring around, win over • *It's better to reason with them than to use force.* **4 = deduce**, think, conclude, infer, make out, work out
See also: **argue, excuse, wisdom**
reasonable *adj* **1 = sensible**, fair, moderate, wise, sober, rational, sane • *a reasonable sort of person* **2 = logical**, sound, legitimate, sensible, understandable, justifiable • *It seems reasonable to expect rapid urban growth.* **3 = inexpensive**, low, fair, cheap, competitive, modest • *His fees were quite reasonable.*
See also: **decent, respectable, tolerable**
reasonably *See* **quite**
reasoned *adj* = **sensible**, clear, logical, well-thought-out
reasoning *n* = **thinking**, thought, analysis, logic
reassure *v* = **encourage**, bolster, comfort, cheer up • *She reassured me that everything was fine.*
See also: **satisfy**
reassured *See* **secure**
rebate *n* = **refund**, reduction, discount, bonus, allowance, deduction, tax credit
rebel *v* **1 = revolt**, resist, mutiny • *I rebelled against everything when I was younger.* **2 = defy**, dissent, disobey ▸ *n* **3 = revolutionary**, insurgent, secessionist, revolutionist **4 = nonconformist**, dissenter, apostate, heretic, schismatic ▸ *adj*

r

DICTIONARY

rebirth *n* revival or renaissance
▸ **reborn** *adj* active again after a period of inactivity
rebore, reboring *n* boring of a cylinder to restore its true shape
rebound Ⓣ *v* **1** spring back **2** misfire so as to hurt the perpetrator of a plan or deed **3** (of a ball, puck, etc.) bounce back after a missed or blocked shot **4** *basketball* recover possession of a rebound ▹ *n* **5** a ball or puck that has rebounded **6** *basketball* recovery of a rebound
▸ **on the rebound** *informal* while recovering from rejection
rebuff Ⓣ *v* **1** reject or snub ▹ *n* **2** blunt refusal, snub
rebuke Ⓣ *v* **1** scold sternly ▹ *n* **2** stern scolding
rebus [ree-buss] *n, pl* **-buses** puzzle consisting of pictures and symbols representing words or syllables
rebut Ⓣ *v* **-butting, -butted** refute or disprove **rebuttal** *n*
recalcitrant Ⓣ *adj* wilfully disobedient **recalcitrance** *n*
recall Ⓣ *v* **1** recollect or remember **2** order to return **3** annul or cancel ▹ *n* **4** order to return **5** ability to remember
recant Ⓣ *v* withdraw (a statement or belief) publicly **recantation** *n*
recap *informal* ▹ *v* **-capping, -capped** **1** recapitulate ▹ *n* **2** recapitulation
recapitulate Ⓣ *v* state again briefly, repeat **recapitulation** *n*
recapture Ⓣ *v* **1** experience again **2** capture again
recce *slang* ▹ *v* **-ceing, -ced** *or* **-ceed** **1** reconnoitre ▹ *n* **2** reconnaissance
recede Ⓣ *v* **1** become distant **2** (of the hair) stop growing at the front
receipt Ⓣ *n* **1** written acknowledgment of money or goods received **2** receiving or being received
receive Ⓣ *v* **1** take, accept, or get **2** experience **3** greet (guests)
▸ **received** *adj* generally accepted
▸ **receiver** *n* **1** detachable part of a telephone that is held to the ear **2** equipment in a telephone, radio, or television that converts electrical signals into sound **3** person appointed by court to manage property of a bankrupt **4** person who handles stolen goods knowing they have been stolen **5** *football* player seeking to catch passes from the quarterback
▸ **receivership** *n* **1** state of being or having been received **2** (esp. of a business, company, etc.) state of being administered by a receiver due to bankruptcy
recent Ⓣ *adj* **1** having happened lately **2** new **recently** *adv*

THESAURUS

5 = rebellious, insurgent, revolutionary, insurrectionary
rebellion *n* **1 = revolt**, revolution, uprising, insurrection, mutiny • *the ruthless suppression of the rebellion* **2 = nonconformity**, defiance, heresy, schism
rebellious *adj* **1 = revolutionary**, rebel, insurgent, disorderly, unruly, disloyal, disobedient, mutinous, seditious **2 = defiant**, difficult, resistant, unmanageable, refractory
rebound *v* **1 = bounce**, ricochet, recoil **2 = misfire**, backfire, recoil, boomerang
rebuff *v* **1 = reject**, cut, refuse, slight, snub, spurn, repulse, cold-shoulder, knock back (*slang*), turn down ▸ *n* **2 = rejection**, slight, refusal, snub, repulse, cold shoulder, kick in the teeth (*slang*), knock-back (*slang*), slap in the face (*informal*)
rebuild *See* **reconstruct, restore**
rebuke *v* **1 = scold**, censure, castigate, chide, admonish, reprimand, reprove, tell off (*informal*) ▸ *n* **2 = scolding**, censure, admonition, row, reprimand, telling-off (*informal*)
rebut *v* **= disprove**, overturn, refute, negate, invalidate, confute, prove wrong
rebuttal *n* **= disproof**, confutation, invalidation, negation, refutation
recalcitrant *adj* **= disobedient**, defiant, unruly, wayward, unmanageable, wilful, insubordinate, refractory
recall *v* **1 = recollect**, remember, evoke, bring to mind *or* call to mind **2 = annul**, cancel, withdraw, revoke, retract, repeal, countermand ▸ *n* **3 = recollection**, memory, remembrance **4 = annulment**, withdrawal, cancellation, repeal, retraction, rescindment
recant *v* **= withdraw**, revoke, retract, renege, repudiate, disclaim, forswear, take back
recapitulate *v* **= repeat**, outline, recount, restate, recap (*informal*), summarize
recapture *See* **recover, recovery**
recede *v* **= fall back**, return, retire, withdraw, retreat, subside, abate, ebb, regress
receipt *n* **1 = sales slip**, stub, proof of purchase **2 = receiving**, delivery, reception, acceptance
receive *v* **1 = get**, take, accept, be given, pick up • *Did they receive my letter?* **2 = experience**, suffer, undergo, sustain, encounter • *We received a very warm welcome.* **3 = greet**, meet, welcome, entertain, take in • *She was officially received by the prime minister.*
See also: **admit**
recent *adj* **= new**, current, fresh, up-to-date,

r

DICTIONARY

receptacle Ⓣ *n* object used to contain something
reception Ⓣ *n* **1** area for receiving guests, clients, etc. **2** formal party **3** manner of receiving **4** welcome **5** (in broadcasting) quality of signals received **6** *football* catching of a pass from the quarterback
▸ **receptionist** *n* person who receives guests, clients, etc.
receptive Ⓣ *adj* willing to receive new ideas, suggestions, etc. **receptivity** *n*
recess Ⓣ *n* **1** niche or alcove **2** holiday between sessions of work **3** secret hidden place
▸ **recessed** *adj* hidden or placed in a recess
recession Ⓣ *n* period of reduction in trade
▸ **recessive** *adj* receding
recharge *v* cause (a battery etc.) to take in and store electricity again **rechargeable** *adj*
recherché [rish-**air**-shay] *adj* **1** of studied elegance **2** choice or rare
recidivist *n* person who relapses into crime
recipe Ⓣ *n* **1** directions for cooking a dish **2** method for achieving something
recipient *n* person who receives something
reciprocal Ⓣ [ris-**sip**-pro-kal] *adj* **1** mutual **2** given or done in return **reciprocally** *adv* **reciprocity** *n*
reciprocate Ⓣ *v* **1** give or feel in return **2** (of a machine part) move backwards and forwards **reciprocation** *n*
recite Ⓣ *v* repeat aloud, esp. to an audience
▸ **recital** [ris-**site**-al] *n* **1** musical performance **2** act of reciting
▸ **recitation** *n* recital, usu. from memory, of poetry or prose
▸ **recitative** [ress-it-a-**teev**] *n* musical narration
reckless Ⓣ *adj* heedless of danger **recklessly** *adv* **recklessness** *n*
reckon Ⓣ *v* **1** expect **2** consider or think **3** make calculations, count **reckoner** *n* **reckoning** *n*
reclaim Ⓣ *v* **1** regain possession of **2** make fit for cultivation **reclamation** *n*
recline Ⓣ *v* rest in a leaning position **reclining** *adj*
recluse Ⓣ *n* **1** person avoiding society **2** hermit **reclusive** *adj*
recognize Ⓣ *v* **1** identify as (a person or thing) already known **2** accept as true or existing **3** treat as valid **4** notice, show

THESAURUS

present-day • *his most recent acquisition*
See also: **modern**
recently *adv* = **newly**, currently, lately, freshly, latterly, not long ago, of late
receptacle *n* = **container**, holder, repository
reception *n* **1** = **party**, function, levee, soirée **2** = **response**, treatment, welcome, reaction, greeting, acknowledgment
receptive *adj* = **open**, interested, susceptible, sympathetic, open-minded, amenable, open to suggestions
recess *n* **1** = **alcove**, corner, bay, niche, hollow, nook **2** = **break**, rest, holiday, vacation, intermission, interval, respite
recession *n* = **depression**, decline, slump, downturn • *companies that survived the recession*
recipe *n* **1** = **directions**, ingredients, instructions **2** = **method**, process, procedure, prescription, formula, technique
reciprocal *adj* = **mutual**, equivalent, alternate, complementary, interchangeable, correlative, corresponding, exchanged
reciprocate *v* = **return**, trade, respond, exchange, reply, swap, requite
recital *n* **1** = **performance**, rehearsal, rendering **2** = **account**, statement, relation, narrative, telling **3** = **recitation**, reading
recitation *n* = **recital**, performance, piece, reading, passage, lecture
recite *v* = **repeat**, speak, perform, deliver, narrate, declaim
reckless *adj* = **careless**, wild, rash, precipitate, mindless, hasty, headlong, imprudent, thoughtless, heedless
recklessness *See* **abandon**
reckon *v* **1** (*informal*) = **think**, believe, suppose, assume • *I reckon they're still fond of each other.* **2** = **consider**, rate, judge, account, count, regard, deem, esteem **3** = **count**, estimate, calculate, figure out, work out • *The figure is now reckoned to be 20 per cent.*
See also: **conclude, expect, figure, guess**
reckoning *n* **1** = **count**, estimate, addition, calculation **2** = **bill**, charge, score, due, account
reclaim *v* = **regain**, recover, reform, salvage, retrieve, redeem, recapture
reclamation *See* **recovery**
recline *v* = **lean**, rest, lie *or* lie down, sprawl, lounge, repose, loll
recluse *n* = **hermit**, monk, solitary, anchoress, anchorite
reclusive *adj* = **solitary**, isolated, hermit-like, retiring, withdrawn
recognition *n* **1** = **identification**, discovery, remembrance, recollection **2** = **acceptance**, confession, admission, realization **3** = **appreciation**, respect, notice, props (*informal*)
recognize *v* **1** = **identify**, know, place, spot • *I recognized him at once.* **2** = **acknowledge**, honour, appreciate, salute • *She was recognized as an outstanding pilot.* **3** = **appreciate**, respect, notice
See also: **distinguish, realize, remember**

DICTIONARY

appreciation of **recognition** *n* **recognizable** *adj*
▸ **recognizance** [rik-**og**-nizz-anss] *n* undertaking before a court to observe some condition
recoil Ⓣ *v* **1** jerk or spring back **2** draw back in horror **3** (of an action) go wrong so as to hurt the perpetrator ▷ *n* **4** backward jerk **5** recoiling
recollect Ⓣ *v* call back to mind, remember **recollection** *n*
recommend Ⓣ *v* **1** advise or counsel **2** praise or commend **3** make acceptable **recommendation** *n*
recompense Ⓣ *v* **1** pay or reward **2** compensate or make up for ▷ *n* **3** compensation **4** reward or remuneration
reconcile Ⓣ *v* **1** harmonize (conflicting beliefs etc.) **2** bring back into friendship **3** accept or cause to accept (an unpleasant situation) **reconcilable** *adj* **reconciliation** *n*
recondite Ⓣ *adj* difficult to understand, abstruse
recondition Ⓣ *v* restore to good condition or working order
reconnaissance Ⓣ [rik-**kon**-iss-anss] *n* survey for military or engineering purposes
reconnoitre Ⓣ [rek-a-**noy**-ter] *v* make a reconnaissance of
reconsider Ⓣ *v* think about again, consider changing
reconstitute *v* **1** reorganize in a slightly different form **2** restore (food) to its former state, esp. by the addition of water to a concentrate **reconstitution** *n*
reconstruct Ⓣ *v* **1** use evidence to re-create **2** rebuild **reconstruction** *n*
record Ⓣ *n* **1** document or other thing that preserves information **2** disc with indentations which a record player transforms into sound **3** best recorded achievement **4** known facts about a person's past ▷ *v* **5** put in writing **6** preserve (sound, TV programmes, etc.) on plastic disc, magnetic tape, etc., for reproduction on a playback device **7** show or register **recording** *n*
▸ **off the record** not for publication
▸ **recorder** *n* **1** person or machine that records, esp. a video, cassette, or tape recorder **2** type of flute, blown at one end **3** judge in certain courts
▸ **record player** instrument for reproducing sound on records

THESAURUS

recoil *v* **1 = jerk back**, rebound, kick, react, spring back **2 = draw back**, shrink, falter, quail **3 = backfire**, rebound, misfire, boomerang ▸ *n* **4 = reaction**, rebound, kick, backlash, repercussion
recollect *v* **= remember**, place, recall, summon up
recollection *n* **= memory**, recall, impression, remembrance, reminiscence
recommence *See* **continue, renew**
recommend *v* **1 = advise**, suggest, propose, advance, advocate, counsel, prescribe, put forward **2 = commend**, approve, endorse, praise
recommendation *n* **1 = advice**, proposal, counsel, suggestion **2 = commendation**, approval, praise, sanction, reference, advocacy, endorsement, testimonial
recompense *v* **1 = reward**, pay, remunerate **2 = compensate**, reimburse, repay, redress, make up for, pay for, requite ▸ *n* **3 = compensation**, payment, repayment, amends, restitution, reparation, remuneration, damages, requital **4 = reward**, return, payment, wages
reconcile *v* **1 = resolve**, settle, square, adjust, compose, rectify, put to rights **2 = reunite**, appease, conciliate, make peace between, propitiate **3 = accept**, submit, yield, put up with (*informal*), resign oneself
reconciliation *n* **= reunion**, conciliation, pacification, reconcilement
recondite *adj* **= obscure**, difficult, deep, secret, dark, mysterious, profound, hidden, arcane, occult, concealed
recondition *v* **= restore**, repair, renew, revamp, overhaul, renovate, remodel, do up (*informal*)
reconnaissance *n* **= inspection**, investigation, exploration, observation, survey, scan
reconnoitre *v* **= inspect**, case (*slang*), survey, investigate, explore, scan, observe, spy out
reconsider *v* **= rethink**, review, revise, reassess, think again
reconstruct *v* **1 = rebuild**, restore, renovate, recreate, regenerate • *The old bridge has been completely reconstructed.* **2 = deduce**, piece together • *The police reconstructed the scene of the crime.*
record *n* **1 = document**, file, account, register, journal, archives, minutes, blotter (*US*) • *medical records* **2 = background**, career, curriculum vitae, résumé, track record (*informal*) • *You will be rejected if you have a criminal record.* **3 = evidence**, witness, testimony, trace, documentation **4 = disc**, single, album, vinyl, LP ▷ **off the record = confidential**, private, unofficial, not for publication ▸ *v* **5 = document**, enter, register, log, make a note of, write down • *Her diary records her daily life in detail.* **6 = tape**,

r

DICTIONARY

recount ⓣ *v* tell in detail
re-count *v* **1** count again ▷ *n* **2** second or subsequent count, esp. of votes
recoup ⓣ [rik-**koop**] *v* **1** regain or make good (a loss) **2** recompense or compensate
recourse ⓣ *n* **1** (resorting to) a source of help **2** *law* right of action or appeal
recover ⓣ *v* **1** become healthy again **2** get back (a loss or expense) **recovery** *n* **recoverable** *adj*
recreant *n old-fashioned* cowardly or disloyal person
recreate ⓣ *v* make happen or exist again
recreation ⓣ *n* agreeable or refreshing occupation, relaxation or amusement **recreational** *adj*
▶ **recreational vehicle** *or* **RV** large vanlike vehicle equipped to be lived in
recrimination ⓣ *n* mutual blame **recriminatory** *adj*
recruit ⓣ *n* **1** newly enlisted soldier **2** new member or supporter ▷ *v* **3** enlist (new soldiers, members, etc.) **recruitment** *n*
rectal *adj* see **rectum**
rectangle *n* oblong four-sided figure with four right angles **rectangular** *adj*
rectify ⓣ *v* **-fying, -fied 1** put right, correct **2** purify by distillation **3** *electricity* convert (alternating current) into direct current **rectification** *n* **rectifier** *n*
rectilinear [rek-ti-**lin**-ee-er] *adj* **1** in a straight line **2** characterized by straight lines
rectitude ⓣ *n* moral correctness
recto *n, pl* **-tos 1** right-hand page of a book **2** front of a sheet of paper
rector *n* **1** member of the clergy in charge of a parish **2** head of certain academic institutions
▶ **rectory** *n* rector's house
rectum *n, pl* **-ta** final section of the large intestine **rectal** *adj*
recumbent *adj* lying down
recuperate ⓣ *v* recover from illness **recuperation** *n* **recuperative** *adj*
recur ⓣ *v* **-curring, -curred** happen again
▶ **recurrence** *n* repetition **recurrent** *adj*
recusant [**rek**-yew-zant] *n* **1** *hist* person who refused to obey the Church of England **2** person refusing to obey authority
recycle ⓣ *v* reprocess (used materials) for further use
red ⓣ *adj* **redder, reddest 1** of a colour varying from crimson to orange and seen in blood, fire, etc. **2** flushed in the face from

THESAURUS

video, tape-record, make a recording of, video-tape **7 = register**, say, show, indicate, give evidence of
See also: **entry, list, note, write**
recorder *n* = **chronicler**, clerk, historian, scribe, archivist, diarist
recording *n* = **record**, video, tape, disc
recount *v* = **tell**, report, describe, relate, repeat, depict, narrate, recite
recoup *v* **1** = **regain**, recover, retrieve, win back **2** = **compensate**, refund, reimburse, repay, remunerate, make up for, requite
recourse *n* = **option**, choice, resource, alternative, resort, remedy, expedient, way out
recover *v* **1** = **get better**, improve, revive, recuperate, convalesce, get well • *He has still not fully recovered.* **2** = **regain**, retrieve, recoup, recapture, get back • *They took legal action to recover the money.*
recovery *n* **1** = **improvement**, healing, revival, recuperation • *He made a remarkable recovery after his illness.* **2** = **retrieval**, restoration, recapture, reclamation • *a reward for the recovery of the painting*
recreate *See* **reconstruct**
recreation *n* = **pastime**, play, sport, fun, entertainment, diversion, amusement, hobby, relaxation, enjoyment, leisure activity
recrimination *n* = **bickering**, quarrel, counterattack, mutual accusation, squabbling
recruit *v* **1** = **enlist**, draft, muster, enrol • *He helped to recruit volunteers.* **2** = **win** *or* **win over**, obtain, engage, procure ▶ *n* **3** = **beginner**, convert, novice, trainee • *the latest batch of recruits*
recruitment *See* **employment**
rectify *v* = **correct**, right, improve, fix, repair, adjust, remedy, redress, emend
rectitude *n* = **morality**, principle, integrity, honesty, honor, virtue, decency, goodness, probity
recuperate *v* = **recover**, improve, mend, convalesce, get better
recuperation *See* **recovery**
recur *v* = **happen again**, return, repeat, persist, revert, reappear, come again
recurrent *adj* = **periodic**, continued, frequent, habitual, recurring
recycle *v* = **reprocess**, save, salvage, reclaim, reuse
red *adj* **1** = **crimson**, coral, cherry, ruby, scarlet, carmine, vermilion **2** (~ *hair*) = **chestnut**, sandy, carroty, flame-coloured, reddish, titian **3** = **flushed**, embarrassed, blushing, florid, shamefaced ▷ **red tape** *See* **bureaucracy** ▶ *n* ▷ **in the red** (*Informal*) = **in debt**, insolvent, in arrears, overdrawn ▷ **see red** (*Informal*) = **lose one's temper**, blow one's top, crack up (*informal*), fly off the handle (*informal*), go ballistic (*slang*), go mad (*informal*)
red-blooded *adj* (*Informal*) = **vigorous**, strong, robust, lusty, virile

DICTIONARY

anger, shame, etc. ▷ *n* **3** red colour **4 Red** *informal* communist **redness** *n* **reddish** *adj*
▸ **in the red** *informal* in debt
▸ **see red** *informal* be angry
▸ **redden** *v* make or become red
▸ **red-blooded** *adj informal* **1** vigorous **2** virile
▸ **redbrick** *adj* (of a British university) founded in the late 19th or early 20th century
▸ **red carpet** very special welcome for an important guest
▸ **Red Chamber** the Canadian Senate
▸ **redcoat** *n hist* British soldier
▸ **Red Cross** international organization providing help for victims of war or natural disasters
▸ **Red Ensign** red flag having the Union Jack at the upper corner along the hoist, esp. one used as Canada's national flag until 1965 or those currently used as the provincial flags of Ontario and Manitoba
▸ **red-handed** *adj informal* (caught) in the act of doing something wrong or illegal
▸ **red herring** something which diverts attention from the main issue
▸ **red-hot** *adj* **1** glowing red **2** extremely hot **3** very keen
▸ **red light 1** traffic signal to stop **2** danger signal
▸ **red meat** dark meat, esp. beef or lamb
▸ **red tape** excessive adherence to official rules
▸ **red zone** *football* area of the field within 20 yards of the opposing goal line

Redding *n* **Otis**. 1941–67, US soul singer and songwriter. His recordings include "Respect" (1965), *Dictionary of Soul* (1966), and "(Sittin' on) The Dock of the Bay" (1968)

redeem Ⓣ *v* **1** make up for **2** reinstate (oneself) in someone's good opinion **3** free from sin **4** buy back **5** pay off (a loan or debt) **redeemable** *adj* **redemption** *n* **redemptive** *adj*
▸ **the Redeemer** Jesus Christ

redeploy *v* assign to a new position or task

redevelop *v* rebuild or renovate (an area or building) **redevelopment** *n*

Redford *n* **Robert**. born 1937, US film actor and director. His films include (as actor) *Barefoot in the Park* (1966), *Butch Cassidy and the Sundance Kid* (1969), *The Sting* (1973), *All the President's Men* (1976), *Up Close and Personal* (1996) and (as director) *Ordinary People* (1980), *A River Runs Through It* (1992), and *The Horse Whisperer* (1998)

Redgrave *n* **1 Lynn**. born 1944, British stage and film actress. Her films include *Georgy Girl* (1966), *The Happy Hooker* (1975), and *Gods and Monsters* (1999) **2** her father, Sir **Michael**. 1908–85, British stage and film actor. Among his films are *The Lady Vanishes* (1938), *The Dam Busters* (1955), *The Loneliness of the Long Distance Runner* (1963), and *The Go-Between* (1971) **3** his elder daughter, **Vanessa**. born 1937, British stage and film actress, whose roles include performances in the films *Isadora* (1968), *Julia* (1977), *Howards End* (1992), *Mrs. Dalloway* (1998), and *A Rumour of Angels* (2000): noted also for her active commitment to left-wing politics

redolent Ⓣ *adj* **1** smelling strongly (of) **2** reminiscent (of) **redolence** *n*

Redon *n* **Odilon**. 1840–1916, French symbolist painter and etcher. He foreshadowed the surrealists in his paintings of fantastic dream images

redouble *v* increase, multiply, or intensify

redoubt *n* small fort defending a hilltop or pass

redoubtable Ⓣ *adj* formidable

redound *v* cause advantage or disadvantage (to)

redox *n* chemical reaction in which one substance is reduced and the other is oxidized

redress Ⓣ *v* **1** make amends for ▷ *n* **2** compensation or amends

reduce Ⓣ *v* **1** bring down, lower **2** lessen, weaken **3** bring by force or necessity to some state or action **4** slim **5** simplify **6** make (sauce) more concentrated **7** *chem* separate

THESAURUS

redden *v* = **go red**, flush, colour *or* colour up, crimson, blush

redeem *v* **1** = **make up for**, atone for, compensate for, make amends for **2** = **reinstate**, absolve, restore to favour **3** = **save**, free, deliver, ransom, liberate, emancipate **4** = **buy back**, recover, regain, retrieve, reclaim, repurchase

redemption *n* **1** = **compensation**, amends, reparation, atonement **2** = **salvation**, release, rescue, liberation, emancipation, deliverance **3** = **trade-in**, recovery, repurchase, reclamation, retrieval, repossession

red-faced *See* **embarrassed**

red-handed *adj* = **in the act**, flagrante delicto *or* in flagrante delicto

redolent *adj* **1** = **reminiscent**, suggestive, evocative **2** = **scented**, aromatic, fragrant, odorous, perfumed, sweet-smelling

redoubtable *adj* = **formidable**, strong, powerful, mighty, fearful, fearsome

redress *v* **1** = **make amends for**, compensate for, make up for **2** = **put right**, balance, regulate, correct, adjust, rectify, even up ▸ *n* **3** = **amends**, payment, compensation, reparation, atonement, recompense

reduce *v* **1** = **lessen**, cut, lower, decrease, diminish, shorten, curtail, cut down • *Gradually reduce the dosage.* OPPOSITE:

DICTIONARY

(a substance) from others with which it is combined **reducible** *adj* **reduction** *n*
redundant ⓣ *adj* **1** (of a worker) no longer needed **2** superfluous **redundancy** *n*
reduplicate *v* make double, repeat
re-echo *v* echo over and over again, resound
reed *n* **1** tall grass that grows in swamps and shallow water **2** tall straight stem of this plant **3** *music* vibrating cane or metal strip in certain wind instruments
▸ **reedy** *adj* **1** full of reeds **2** harsh and thin in tone
Reed *n* **1** Sir **Carol**. 1906–76, English film director. His films include *The Third Man* (1949), *An Outcast of the Islands* (1951), and *Oliver!* (1968), for which he won an Oscar **2 Lou**. born 1942, US rock singer, songwriter, and guitarist: member of the Velvet Underground (1965–70). His albums include *Transformer* (1972), *Berlin* (1973), *Street Hassle* (1978), *New York* (1989), *Set the Twilight Reeling* (1996), and *The Raven* (2003) **3 Walter**. 1851–1902, US physician, who proved that yellow fever is transmitted by mosquitoes (1900)
reef[1] *n* **1** ridge of rock or coral near the surface of the sea **2** vein of ore
reef[2] *n* **1** part of a sail which can be rolled up to reduce its area ▷ *v* **2** take in a reef of
▸ **reefer** *n* **1** short thick jacket worn esp. by sailors **2** *old-fashioned, slang* hand-rolled cigarette containing cannabis
▸ **reef knot** two overhand knots turned opposite ways
reek ⓣ *n* **1** strong (unpleasant) smell ▷ *v* **2** smell strongly **3** (foll. by *of*) be full (of)
reel[1] *n* **1** cylindrical object on which film, tape, thread, or wire is wound **2** winding apparatus, as of a fishing rod ▷ *v* **3** wind on a reel **4** draw in by means of a reel
▸ **reel off** *v* recite or write fluently or quickly
reel[2] ⓣ *v* stagger, sway, or whirl
reel[3] *n* lively Scottish dance
re-enter *v* **1** come back into a place, esp. a country **2** (of a spacecraft) return into the earth's atmosphere **re-entry** *n*
reeve *n* **1** president of local (esp. rural) council **2** *hist* manorial steward or official
Reeves *n* **Keanu**. born 1964, Canadian film actor, born in Lebanon. His films include *Bill and Ted's Excellent Adventure* (1989), *Speed* (1994), and the *The Matrix* series of films (1999–2003)
ref *n informal* referee in sport
refectory *n, pl* **-tories** room for meals in a college etc.
refer ⓣ *v* **-ferring, -ferred** (foll. by *to*) **1** mention or allude (to) **2** be relevant (to) **3** send (to) for information **4** submit (to) for decision **referral** *n*
▸ **reference** *n* **1** act of referring **2** citation or direction in a book **3** appeal to the judgment of another **4** testimonial **5** person to whom inquiries as to character etc. may be made
▸ **with reference to** concerning
referee ⓣ *n* **1** umpire in sports, esp. football or boxing **2** person willing to testify to someone's character etc. **3** arbitrator ▷ *v* **-eeing, -eed 4** act as referee of
referendum ⓣ *n, pl* **-dums, -da** submitting of a question to the electorate
refill *v* **1** fill again ▷ *n* **2** subsequent filling **3** replacement supply of something in a permanent container
refine ⓣ *v* **1** purify **2** improve **refiner** *n*
▸ **refined** *adj* **1** cultured or polite **2** purified

THESAURUS

increase **2 = degrade**, force, drive, demote, downgrade • *The village was reduced to rubble.*
See also: **decline, weaken**
reduced *See* **low**
reduction *n* **1 = decrease**, diminution, minimizing, lowering, lessening **2 = cut**, cutback, cutting, depletion, trimming, pruning, scaling down **3 = discount**, slash (*informal*), concession, markdown, price cut
redundancy *n* **1 = superfluity**, surplus, excess, surfeit, uselessness, superabundance, expendability **2 = unemployment**, layoff, joblessness, the axe (*informal*), the sack (*informal*)
redundant *adj* **= superfluous**, extra, surplus, unnecessary, unwanted, inessential, supernumerary
reek *v* **1 = stink**, smell ▸ *n* **2 = stink**, odor, fetor, smell, stench
reeking *See* **smelly**
reel *v* **1 = stagger**, rock, pitch, roll, sway, lurch **2 = whirl**, spin, swirl, revolve
re-establish *See* **renew, restore**
refer *v* **1 = mention**, cite, allude, bring up • *In his speech, he referred to a recent trip to the Maritimes.* **2 = consult**, look up • *I had to refer to the manual.* **3 = relate**, concern, apply, belong, pertain, be relevant to **4 = direct**, point, send, guide
referee *n* **1 = umpire**, judge, arbitrator, ref (*informal*), adjudicator, arbiter ▸ *v* **2 = umpire**, judge, mediate, adjudicate, arbitrate
reference *n* **1 = citation**, note, mention, quotation, allusion **2 = testimonial**, character, recommendation, endorsement, credentials **3 = relevance**, connection, relation, bearing, applicability
referendum *n* **= public vote**, plebiscite, popular vote
refine *v* **1 = purify**, process, clarify, filter, cleanse, distill **2 = improve**, perfect, polish, hone
refined *adj* **1 = cultured**, polite, civilized,

DICTIONARY

▸ **refinement** *n* **1** improvement or elaboration **2** fineness of taste or manners **3** subtle point or distinction
▸ **refinery** *n* place where sugar, oil, etc. is refined
refit *v* **1** make ready for use again by repairing or re-equipping ▹ *n* **2** repair or re-equipping for further use
reflation *n* (steps taken to produce) an increase in the economic activity of a country etc. **reflate** *v* **reflationary** *adj*
reflect Ⓣ *v* **1** throw back, esp. rays of light, heat, etc. **2** form an image of **3** show **4** bring credit or discredit upon **5** consider at length
▸ **reflection** *n* **1** act of reflecting **2** return of rays of heat, light, etc. from a surface **3** image of an object given back by a mirror etc. **4** conscious thought or meditation **5** attribution of discredit or blame
▸ **reflective** *adj* **1** quiet, contemplative **2** capable of reflecting images
▸ **reflector** *n* polished surface for reflecting light etc.
reflex Ⓣ *n* **1** involuntary response to a stimulus or situation ▹ *adj* **2** (of a muscular action) involuntary **3** reflected **4** (of an angle) more than 180°
▸ **reflexive** *adj grammar* denoting a *v* whose subject is the same as its object: *to dress oneself*
reflexology *n* foot massage as a therapy in alternative medicine
reform Ⓣ *v* **1** improve **2** abandon evil practices ▹ *n* **3** improvement **reformer** *n*
▸ **reformation** [ref-fer-**may**-shun] *n* **1** a reforming **2 Reformation** religious movement in 16th-century Europe that resulted in the establishment of the Protestant Churches
▸ **reformatory** *n* (formerly) institution for reforming juvenile offenders
▸ **Reform Party** major political party with policy of low taxation
refract *v* change the course of (light etc.) passing from one medium to another
refraction *n* **refractive** *adj* **refractor** *n*
refractory Ⓣ *adj* **1** unmanageable or rebellious **2** *med* resistant to treatment **3** resistant to heat
refrain[1] Ⓣ *v* (foll. by *from*) keep oneself from doing
refrain[2] Ⓣ *n* frequently repeated part of a song
refrangible *adj* that can be refracted
refrangibility *n*
refresh Ⓣ *v* **1** revive or reinvigorate, as through food, drink, or rest **2** stimulate (the memory) **refresher** *n*
▸ **refreshing** *adj* **1** having a reviving effect **2** pleasantly different or new
▸ **refreshment** *n* something that refreshes, esp. food or drink
refrigerate Ⓣ *v* **1** freeze **2** cool **refrigeration** *n*
▸ **refrigerator** *n* apparatus in which food and drinks are kept cool
refuge Ⓣ *n* (source of) shelter or protection
▸ **refugee** *n* person who seeks refuge, esp. in a foreign country

THESAURUS

genteel • *His speech and manner are very refined.* OPPOSITE: common **2 = purified**, pure, distilled, filtered • *refined oil* **3 = discerning**, fine, sensitive, delicate, precise, discriminating, fastidious
See also: **sophisticated**
refinement *n* **1 = sophistication**, culture, taste, courtesy, discrimination, polish, cultivation, civility, breeding, gentility, good breeding **2 = subtlety**, nuance, nicety, fine point **3 = purification**, clarification, distillation, cleansing, filtering, processing
reflect *v* **1 = return**, mirror, echo, reproduce, throw back **2 = show**, reveal, indicate, display, demonstrate, manifest **3 = think**, consider, wonder, ponder, muse, meditate, cogitate, ruminate
reflection *n* **1 = image**, echo, mirror image **2 = thought**, idea, opinion, consideration, observation, meditation, musing, thinking, contemplation, cogitation
reflective *adj* **= thoughtful**, meditative, contemplative, pensive
reflex *See* **automatic**
reform *n* **1 = improvement**, amendment, correction, rehabilitation • *radical economic reforms* ▸ *v* **2 = improve**, correct, amend, better, rehabilitate, rectify • *their plans to reform the economy* **3 = mend one's ways**, clean up one's act (*informal*), go straight (*informal*), shape up (*informal*), turn over a new leaf
See also: **change, transform**
refractory *adj* **= unmanageable**, difficult, uncontrollable, unruly, intractable, wilful, disobedient, headstrong, high-maintenance
refrain[1] *v* **= stop**, avoid, cease, renounce, abstain, desist, forbear, leave off
refrain[2] *n* **= chorus**, tune, melody
refresh *v* **1 = revive**, brace, rejuvenate, enliven, stimulate • *A glass of juice will refresh you.* **2 = stimulate**, prompt, renew, jog
refreshing *adj* **1 = invigorating**, fresh, bracing, stimulating **2 = new**, original, novel
refreshment *n* ▹ **refreshments = food and drink**, drinks, snacks, tidbits
refrigerate *v* **= cool**, freeze, chill, keep cold
refuge *n* **= shelter**, harbour, haven, asylum, sanctuary • *During the storm, we*

DICTIONARY

refulgent *adj* shining, radiant **refulgence** *n*
refund Ⓣ *v* **1** pay back ▷ *n* **2** return of money **3** amount returned
refurbish Ⓣ *v* renovate and brighten up
refuse[1] Ⓣ *v* decline, deny, or reject
▸ **refusal** *n* denial of anything demanded or offered
refuse[2] Ⓣ *n* garbage or useless matter
refute Ⓣ *v* disprove **refutable** *adj* **refutation** *n*
regain Ⓣ *v* **1** get back or recover **2** reach again
regal Ⓣ *adj* of or like a king or queen **regally** *adv* **regality** *n*
▸ **regalia** *pl n* ceremonial emblems of royalty, an order, etc.
regale Ⓣ *v* (foll. by *with*) attempt to entertain (someone) with (stories)
regard Ⓣ *v* **1** look at **2** relate to **3** consider **4** heed ▷ *n* **5** particular respect **6** attention **7** look **8** esteem **regards 9** expression of goodwill
▸ **as regards** *or* **regarding** in respect of, concerning
▸ **regardless** *adj* **1** heedless ▷ *adv* **2** in spite of everything
regatta *n* meeting for yacht or boat races
regenerate Ⓣ *v* **1** (cause to) undergo spiritual, moral, or physical renewal **2** reproduce or re-create **regeneration** *n* **regenerative** *adj*
regent *n* **1** ruler of a kingdom during the absence, childhood, or illness of its monarch ▷ *adj* **2** ruling as a regent: *prince regent*
▸ **regency** *n* status or period of office of a regent
Reger *n* **Max.** 1873–1916, German composer, noted esp. for his organ works
reggae *n* style of Jamaican popular music with a strong beat
regicide *n* **1** person who kills a king **2** killing of a king
regime Ⓣ [ray-**zheem**] *n* **1** system of government **2** particular administration
regimen *n* **1** prescribed system of diet etc. **2** rule
regiment *n* **1** organized body of troops as a unit of the army ▷ *v* **2** discipline, organize (too) rigidly **regimental** *adj* **regimentation** *n*
▸ **regimentals** *pl n* military uniform
Regiomontanus *n* original name *Johann Müller*. 1436–76, German mathematician and astronomer, who furthered the development of trigonometry
region Ⓣ *n* **1** administrative division of a country **2** area considered as a unit but with no definite boundaries **3** part of the body **regional** *adj*

THESAURUS

took refuge in the abandoned cabin.
See also: **retreat**
refugee *n* = **exile**, escapee, displaced person, émigré
refund *v* **1** = **repay**, return, restore, reimburse, pay back ▸ *n* **2** = **repayment**, return, reimbursement
refurbish *v* = **renovate**, repair, restore, revamp, overhaul, mend, clean up, do up (*informal*)
refusal *n* = **rejection**, denial, rebuff, knock-back (*slang*)
refuse[1] *v* **1** = **deny**, decline, withhold, abstain • *He refused to divulge the contents of the letter.* **2** = **decline**, reject, spurn, turn down • *He offered me a sandwich, which I refused.* OPPOSITE: accept
See also: **resist**
refuse[2] *n* = **garbage**, waste, junk (*informal*), trash, litter, rubbish • *a weekly collection of refuse*
refute *v* = **disprove**, overthrow, discredit, negate, rebut, prove false
regain *v* **1** = **recover**, retrieve, recoup, recapture, get back, take back, win back **2** = **get back to**, reach again, return to
regal *adj* = **royal**, magnificent, noble, majestic, princely, kingly *or* queenly
regale *v* = **entertain**, delight, divert, amuse
regalia *pl n* = **trappings**, paraphernalia, accoutrements, decorations, emblems, finery
regard *v* **1** = **consider**, see, judge, view, look on, think of • *I regard creativity as a gift.* **2** = **look at**, watch, eye, contemplate, scrutinize, gaze • *She regarded him curiously for a moment.* ▷ **as regards** = **concerning**, regarding, pertaining to, relating to ▸ *n* **3** = **respect**, concern, care, thought, consideration, esteem **4** = **look**, scrutiny, glance, stare, gaze
See also: **admiration, rate**
regarding *prep* = **concerning**, about, re, as regards, in regard to *or* with regard to, on the subject of, respecting, with reference to
regardless *adj* **1** = **heedless**, reckless, rash, negligent, indifferent, inconsiderate, neglectful, unmindful ▸ *adv* **2** = **anyway**, nevertheless, in any case, in spite of everything ▷ **regardless of** *See* **despite, in spite of**
regards *pl n* = **good wishes**, best wishes, compliments, greetings, respects
regenerate *v* = **renew**, restore, revive, rejuvenate, invigorate, reinvigorate, reawaken, breathe new life into
regime *n* = **government**, system, rule, leadership, management, reign
regimented *adj* = **controlled**, organized, regulated, disciplined, ordered, systematized
region *n* = **area**, quarter, land, sector, zone,

DICTIONARY

register ⓣ *n* **1** (book containing) an official list or record of things **2** range of a voice or instrument ▷ *v* **3** enter in a register, record, or set down in writing **4** show or be shown on a scale or other measuring instrument **registration** *n*
▸ **registrar** *n* keeper of official records
▸ **register office** *or* **registry office** place where births, marriages, and deaths are recorded
regress ⓣ *v* revert to a former worse condition
▸ **regression** *n* **1** act of regressing **2** *psychol* using an earlier (inappropriate) mode of behaviour **regressive** *adj*
regret ⓣ *v* **-gretting, -gretted 1** feel sorry about **2** express apology or distress ▷ *n* **3** feeling of repentance, guilt, or sorrow **regretful** *adj* **regrettable** *adj*
regular ⓣ *adj* **1** normal **2** symmetrical or even **3** habitual **4** done or occurring according to a rule **5** periodical **6** employed continuously in the armed forces **7** straight or level ▷ *n* **8** regular soldier **9** *informal* regular customer **regularity** *n* **regularize** *v*
regulate ⓣ *v* **1** control, esp. by rules **2** adjust slightly
▸ **regulation** *n* **1** rule **2** regulating
▸ **regulator** *n* device that automatically controls pressure, temperature, etc.
Regulus *n* **Marcus Atilius.** died ?250 BC, Roman general; consul (267; 256). Captured by the Carthaginians in the First Punic War, he was sent to Rome on parole to deliver the enemy's peace terms, advised the Senate to refuse them, and was tortured to death on his return to Carthage
regurgitate ⓣ *v* **1** vomit **2** (of some birds and animals) bring back (partly digested food) into the mouth **3** reproduce (ideas, facts, etc.) without understanding them **regurgitation** *n*
rehabilitate ⓣ *v* **1** help (a person) to readjust to society after illness, imprisonment, etc. **2** restore to a former position or rank **3** restore the good reputation of **rehabilitation** *n*
rehash ⓣ *v* **1** rework or reuse ▷ *n* **2** old materials presented in a new form
rehearse ⓣ *v* **1** practise (a play, concert, etc.) **2** repeat aloud **rehearsal** *n*
rehouse *v* provide with a new (and better) home
Reich[1] [ryke] *n German* kingdom or regime
▸**Third Reich** Nazi dictatorship in Germany from 1933–45
Reich[2] *n* **1** **Steve.** born 1936, US composer, whose works are characterized by the repetition and modification of small

THESAURUS

territory, district, tract, locality • *a remote mountainous region*
regional *adj* = **local**, provincial, district, parochial, zonal
register *n* **1** = **list**, record, file, roll, roster, log, chronicle, diary, archives, catalogue ▸ *v* **2** = **record**, list, note, enter, chronicle, enlist, enrol, catalogue **3** = **show**, mark, reveal, indicate, express, display, exhibit, manifest
regress *v* = **revert**, return, deteriorate, lapse, degenerate, relapse, backslide, fall away *or* fall off, go back
regret *v* **1** = **be sorry**, mourn, grieve, lament, repent • *I gave in to him, and I have regretted it ever since.* ▸ *n* **2** = **sorrow**, grief, remorse, repentance, penitence, pang of conscience • *He expressed regret that he had caused any offence.*
See also: **disappointment**
regretful *adj* = **sorry**, sad, remorseful, apologetic, contrite, penitent, repentant, rueful, sorrowful
regrettable *adj* = **unfortunate**, sad, shameful, lamentable, disappointing, distressing
regular *adj* **1** = **even**, steady, uniform, consistent, constant, periodic, rhythmic • *soft music with a regular beat* OPPOSITE: irregular **2** = **normal**, usual, routine, typical, ordinary, everyday, customary, habitual • *I was filling in for the regular server.* **3** = **systematic**, set, even, steady, uniform, consistent, constant, stated, fixed, ordered
See also: **average, continual, conventional, formal, orderly, standard**
regularity *See* **order**
regulate *v* **1** = **control**, run, rule, manage, direct, handle, guide, govern, supervise **2** = **adjust**, fit, balance, moderate, tune, modulate
regulation *n* **1** = **rule**, order, law, dictate, decree, statute, edict, precept **2** = **control**, government, management, direction, supervision **3** = **adjustment**, modulation, tuning
regulations *See* **bureaucracy**
regurgitate *v* = **vomit**, spew (*slang*), slang, puke (*slang*), disgorge, barf (*slang*), throw up (*informal*), spew out *or* spew up
rehabilitate *v* **1** = **reintegrate**, adjust **2** = **restore**, save, clear, reform, redeem
rehabilitation *See* **reform**
rehash *v* **1** = **rework**, rewrite, reuse, rejig (*informal*), refashion ▸ *n* **2** = **reworking**, rewrite, new version, rearrangement
rehearsal *n* = **practice**, drill, preparation, rehearsing, run-through
rehearse *v* = **practise**, prepare, train, repeat, drill, recite, go over, run through

r

DICTIONARY

rhythmic motifs. His works include *Drumming* (1971), *The Desert Music* (1984), and *City Life* (1995) **2 Wilhelm**. 1897–1957, Austrian psychologist, living in the US. An ardent socialist and advocate of sexual freedom, he proclaimed a cosmic unity of all energy and built a machine (the orgone accumulator) to concentrate this energy on human beings. His books include *The Function of the Orgasm* (1927)

Reid n **William Ronald**, known as *Bill*. 1920–1998, Canadian sculptor and jewellery designer, of Scottish-US and First Nations parentage. His designs explored the Haida side of his heritage and include *The Spirit of Haida Gwaii, the Black Canoe* (exhibited outside the Canadian Embassy in Washington DC) and *The Spirit of Haida Gwaii, the Jade Canoe* (exhibited at Vancouver Airport)

reign Ⓣ *n* **1** period of a sovereign's rule ▷ *v* **2** rule (a country) **3** be supreme

reimburse Ⓣ *v* refund, pay back **reimbursement** *n*

rein Ⓣ *n usu pl* **1** narrow strap attached to a bit to guide a horse **2** means of control ▷ *v* **3** check or manage with reins **4** control

reincarnation Ⓣ *n* **1** rebirth of a soul in successive bodies **2** one of a series of such transmigrations **reincarnate** *v*

reindeer *n* deer of arctic regions with large branched antlers

reinforce Ⓣ *v* **1** strengthen with new support, material, or force **2** strengthen with additional troops, ships, etc. **reinforcement** *n*

Reinhardt *n* **Django**, real name *Jean Baptiste Reinhardt*. 1910–53, French jazz guitarist, whose work was greatly influenced by Gypsy music. With Stéphane Grappelli, he led the Quintet of the Hot Club of France between 1934 and 1939

reinstate Ⓣ *v* restore or re-establish **reinstatement** *n*

reiterate Ⓣ *v* repeat again and again **reiteration** *n*

reject Ⓣ *v* **1** refuse to accept or believe **2** discard as useless **3** rebuff (a person) ▷ *n* **4** person or thing rejected as not up to standard **rejection** *n*

rejig Ⓣ *v* **-jigging, -jigged 1** re-equip (a factory or plant) **2** rearrange

rejoice Ⓣ *v* feel or express great happiness

rejoin Ⓣ *v* **1** reply **2** join again

rejoinder Ⓣ *n* answer, retort

rejuvenate Ⓣ *v* restore youth or vitality to **rejuvenation** *n*

rekindle *v* arouse former emotions or interests

relapse Ⓣ *v* **1** fall back into bad habits,

THESAURUS

reheat *See* **heat**

reign *n* **1 = rule**, power, control, command, monarchy, dominion ▶ *v* **2 = rule**, influence, govern, command, be in power **3 = be supreme**, prevail, hold sway, predominate

reimburse *v* **= pay back**, return, refund, compensate, repay, remunerate, recompense

rein *v* **1 = control**, limit, check, halt, restrict, curb, restrain, hold back ▶ *n* **2 = control**, hold, check, curb, brake, restraint, harness, bridle

reincarnation *n* **= rebirth**, transmigration of souls

reinforce *v* **= support**, stress, supplement, strengthen, bolster, emphasize, prop, toughen, fortify

reinforcement *n* **1 = strengthening**, increase, fortification, augmentation **2 = support**, stay, brace, prop, buttress ▷ **reinforcements = reserves**, support, additional troops *or* fresh troops, auxiliaries

reinstate *v* **= restore**, return, recall, replace, re-establish

reintroduce *See* **restore**

reiterate *v* **= repeat**, restate, do again, say again

reject *v* **1 = refuse**, decline **2 = deny**, renounce, rebuff, spurn, say no to, turn down • *All my suggestions were rejected.* OPPOSITE: accept **3 = rebuff**, refuse, spurn, jilt, repulse, say no to, turn down **4 = discard**, eliminate, scrap, jettison, throw away *or* throw out ▶ *n* **5 = castoff**, second, discard
See also: **boycott**

rejection *n* **1 = refusal**, veto, denial, dismissal, exclusion, repudiation, renunciation, thumbs down **2 = rebuff**, refusal, brushoff (*slang*), kick in the teeth (*slang*), knock-back (*slang*)

rejig *v* **= rearrange**, alter, manipulate, tweak, reorganize, juggle

rejoice *v* **= be overjoyed**, celebrate, delight, glory • *Today we can rejoice in our success.*

rejoicing *n* **= happiness**, celebration, joy, jubilation, elation, exultation, gladness, merrymaking

rejoin *v* **= reply**, answer, respond, retort, riposte

rejoinder *n* **= reply**, response, answer, comeback (*informal*), retort, riposte

rejuvenate *v* **= revitalize**, restore, renew, refresh, reinvigorate, regenerate, breathe new life into

relapse *v* **1 = lapse**, fail, revert, degenerate, backslide, regress, slip back **2 = worsen**, fail, sink, weaken, sicken, fade, deteriorate ▶ *n*

DICTIONARY

illness, etc. ▷ *n* **2** return of bad habits, illness, etc.
relate Ⓣ *v* **1** establish a relation between **2** have reference or relation to **3** (foll. by *to*) have an understanding (of people or ideas): *inability to relate to others* **4** tell (a story) or describe (an event) **related** *adj*
relation Ⓣ *n* **1** connection between things **2** relative **3** connection by blood or marriage **4** act of relating (a story) **relations 5** social or political dealings **6** family **7** *euphemistic* sexual intercourse
▸ **relationship** *n* **1** dealings and feelings between people or countries **2** emotional or sexual affair **3** connection between two things **4** association by blood or marriage, kinship
relative Ⓣ *adj* **1** dependent on relation to something else, not absolute **2** having reference or relation (to) **3** *grammar* referring to a word or clause earlier in the sentence ▷ *n* **4** person connected by blood or marriage **5** *grammar* relative pronoun or clause **relatively** *adv*
▸ **relativity** *n* **1** state of being relative **2** subject of two theories of Albert Einstein, dealing with relationships of space, time, and motion, and acceleration and gravity
relax Ⓣ *v* **1** make or become looser, less tense, or less rigid **2** ease up from effort or attention, rest **3** become more friendly **4** be less strict about **relaxing** *adj* **relaxation** *n*
relay Ⓣ *n* **1** fresh set of people or animals relieving others **2** *electricity* device for making or breaking a local circuit **3** broadcasting station receiving and retransmitting programmes ▷ *v* **-laying, -layed 4** pass on (a message)
▸ **relay race** race between teams of which each runner races part of the distance
release Ⓣ *v* **1** set free **2** let go or fall **3** permit public showing of (a film etc.) **4** emit heat, energy, etc. ▷ *n* **5** setting free **6** written discharge **7** statement to the press **8** act of issuing for sale or publication **9** catch or handle **10** newly issued film, record, etc.
relegate Ⓣ *v* put in a less important position, demote **relegation** *n*

THESAURUS

3 = lapse, backsliding, regression, retrogression **4 = worsening**, deterioration, turn for the worse, weakening
relate *v* **1 = connect**, link, join, couple, associate, correlate **2 = concern**, apply, refer, pertain, be relevant to, have to do with **3 = tell**, report, detail, describe, recount, narrate, recite
related *adj* **1 = akin**, kindred **2 = associated**, joint, akin, connected, affiliated, interconnected, linked
relating to *See* **about**
relation *n* **1 = connection**, link, relationship, bond, bearing, correlation • *This theory bears no relation to reality.* **2 = relative**, kin • *I was staying with relations in Edmonton.* **3 = kinship**, affinity, kindred
relations *pl n* **1 = dealings**, contact, relationship, interaction, intercourse, affairs, connections **2 = family**, tribe, clan, kin, kindred, kinsfolk, kinsmen, relatives
relationship *n* **1 = association**, connection, bond, affinity, rapport • *He has a friendly relationship with his customers.* **2 = connection**, link, parallel, correlation • *the relationship between humans and their environment* **3 = affair**, liaison
See also: **relation, tie**
relative *adj* **1 = dependent**, related, contingent, comparative, allied, associated, proportionate, corresponding **2 = relevant**, appropriate, applicable, pertinent, apposite, apropos, germane ▸ *n* **3 = relation**, kinsman *or* kinswoman, member of one's family *or* member of the family
relatively *adv* **= comparatively**, rather, somewhat
relax *v* **1 = take it easy**, rest, unwind, laze, veg out (*slang*) • *I never have any time to relax.* **2 = lessen**, reduce, lower, ease, moderate, weaken, relieve, loosen, abate, ebb, slacken, let up
See also: **calm, lift**
relaxation *n* **= leisure**, rest, fun, pleasure, recreation, enjoyment
relaxed *adj* **1 = at ease**, easy, cool, calm, comfortable, serene, unflustered • *As soon as I made the decision, I felt more relaxed.* OPPOSITE: tense **2 = comfortable**, calm, peaceful, casual, informal • *The atmosphere at lunch was relaxed.* OPPOSITE: tense
See also: **cozy, leisurely, secure**
relaxing *See* **comfortable**
relay *n* **1 = shift**, turn, relief **2 = message**, transmission, dispatch ▸ *v* **3 = pass on**, send, carry, broadcast, spread, communicate, transmit
release *v* **1 = set free**, free, deliver, discharge, liberate, extricate, let go • *negotiations to release the hostages* **2 = issue**, launch, publish, put out • *The DVD will be released next week.* **3 = acquit**, exonerate, absolve, let go, let off ▸ *n* **4 = liberation**, freedom, discharge, liberty, emancipation • *his release from prison* **5 = acquittal**, exemption, exoneration, absolution **6 = issue**, publication, proclamation
See also: **emit**
relegate *v* **= demote**, downgrade

DICTIONARY

relent Ⓣ *v* give up a harsh intention, become less severe
▸ **relentless** *adj* **1** merciless **2** unremitting
relevant Ⓣ *adj* to do with the matter in hand **relevance** *n*
reliable Ⓣ *adj* see **rely**
reliance Ⓣ *n* see **rely**
relic Ⓣ *n* **1** something that has survived from the past **2** body or possession of a saint, regarded as holy **relics 3** remains or traces
▸ **relict** *n obsolete* widow
relief Ⓣ *n* **1** gladness at the end or removal of pain, distress, etc. **2** money or food given to victims of disaster, poverty, etc. **3** release from monotony or duty **4** person who replaces another at a duty etc. **5** freeing of a besieged city etc. **6** projection of a carved design from the surface **7** distinctness or prominence: *stand out in bold relief*
▸ **relieve** *v* bring relief to
▸ **relieve oneself** urinate or defecate
▸ **relief map** map showing the shape and height of land by shading
▸ **relief pitcher** *baseball* pitcher who replaces another during a game
religion *n* system of belief in and worship of a supernatural power or god
▸ **religious** *adj* **1** of religion **2** pious or devout **3** scrupulous or conscientious **religiously** *adv*
relinquish Ⓣ *v* give up or abandon **relinquishment** *n*
reliquary [rel-lik-wer-ee] *n, pl* **-ries** case or shrine for holy relics
relish Ⓣ *v* **1** enjoy, like very much ▹ *n* **2** liking or gusto **3** appetizing savoury food, such as pickle **4** zestful quality or flavour
relive *v* experience (a sensation or occasion) again, esp. in the imagination
relocate Ⓣ *v* move to a new place to live or work **relocation** *n*
reluctant Ⓣ *adj* unwilling or disinclined **reluctantly** *adv* **reluctance** *n*
rely Ⓣ *v* **-lying, -lied 1** depend (on) **2** trust
▸ **reliable** *adj* able to be trusted, dependable **reliably** *adv* **reliability** *n*
▸ **reliance** *n* dependence, confidence, or trust **reliant** *adj*
REM rapid eye movement
remain Ⓣ *v* **1** continue to be **2** stay, be left behind **3** be left (over) **4** be left to be done, said, etc.
▸ **remains** *pl n* **1** relics, esp. of ancient buildings **2** dead body
▸ **remainder** *n* **1** part which is left **2** amount left over after subtraction or division ▹ *v* **3** offer (copies of a poorly selling book) at reduced prices
remand *v* send back into custody
▸ **on remand** in custody

THESAURUS

relent *v* = **be merciful**, yield, soften, capitulate, change one's mind, come around, have pity, show mercy
relentless *adj* **1** = **unremitting**, persistent, sustained, non-stop, unrelenting, incessant **2** = **merciless**, fierce, cruel, ruthless, unrelenting, implacable, pitiless, remorseless • *The pressure was relentless.*
See also: **constant**
relevant *adj* = **pertinent**, appropriate, applicable, apt • *We have passed along all relevant information.* OPPOSITE: irrelevant
reliable *adj* = **dependable**, safe, sure, sound, true, faithful, staunch, trustworthy • *You have to demonstrate that you are reliable.* OPPOSITE: unreliable
See also: **responsible, trusty**
reliance *n* = **trust**, confidence, faith, belief, dependence
relic *n* = **remnant**, trace, souvenir, fragment, memento, vestige, keepsake ▹ **relics** *See* **remains**
relief *n* **1** = **ease**, release, cure, comfort, remedy, solace, mitigation, deliverance **2** = **rest**, break, breather (*informal*), relaxation, respite **3** = **aid**, help, support, assistance, succour
relieve *v* **1** = **ease**, console, calm, cure, relax, comfort, soften, alleviate, mitigate, soothe, assuage **2** = **help**, support, assist, aid, sustain, succour ▹ **relieve from** *See* **spare**
religious *adj* **1** = **spiritual**, holy, sacred, theological, doctrinal, devotional • *religious worship* **2** = **devout**, righteous, pious, godly • *They are both very religious.* **3** = **conscientious**, faithful, rigid, meticulous, scrupulous, punctilious
relinquish *v* = **give up**, leave, drop, abandon, surrender, renounce, cede, abdicate, forsake, let go
relish *v* **1** = **enjoy**, like, fancy, delight in, revel in, savour ▸ *n* **2** = **enjoyment**, love, taste, fancy, penchant, fondness, liking, gusto, predilection, partiality **3** = **condiment**, sauce, seasoning **4** = **flavour**, taste, trace, smack, spice, piquancy, tang
relocate *See* **move**
reluctance *n* = **unwillingness**, dislike, distaste, aversion, loathing, disinclination, repugnance
reluctant *adj* = **unwilling**, slow, hesitant, loath, averse to, disinclined • *He was reluctant to ask for help.* OPPOSITE: eager
rely *v* = **depend**, bank, trust, count, bet
remain *v* **1** = **stay behind**, wait, linger, be left • *You'll have to remain in hospital for the time being.* **2** = **continue**, last, stay, survive, endure, go on • *The men remained silent.*

DICTIONARY

▸ **remand centre** place where accused people are detained awaiting trial
remark Ⓣ *v* **1** make casual comment (on) **2** say **3** observe or notice ▹ *n* **4** observation or comment
▸ **remarkable** *adj* **1** worthy of note or attention **2** striking or unusual **remarkably** *adv*
Remarque *n* **Erich Maria**. 1898–1970, US novelist, born in Germany, noted for his novel of World War I, *All Quiet on the Western Front* (1929)
remarry *v* marry again following a divorce or the death of one's previous husband or wife
rematch *n sports* second or return game or contest between two players
Rembrandt *n* full name *Rembrandt Harmensz* (or *Harmenszoon*) *van Rijn* (or *van Ryn*). 1606–69, Dutch painter, noted for his handling of shade and light, esp. in his portraits
remedy Ⓣ *n, pl* **-dies 1** means of curing pain or disease **2** means of solving a problem ▹ *v* **-edying, -edied 3** put right
▸ **remedial** *adj* intended to correct a specific disability, handicap, etc.
remember Ⓣ *v* **1** retain in or recall to one's memory **2** have in mind
▸ **remembrance** *n* **1** memory **2** token or souvenir **3** honouring of the memory of a person or event
remind Ⓣ *v* **1** cause to remember **2** put in mind (of)
▸ **reminder** *n* **1** something that recalls the past **2** note to remind a person of something not done
reminisce Ⓣ *v* talk or write of past times, experiences, etc.
▸ **reminiscence** *n* **1** remembering **2** thing recollected **reminiscences 3** memoirs
▸ **reminiscent** *adj* reminding or suggestive (of)
remiss Ⓣ *adj* negligent or careless
remission Ⓣ *n* **1** reduction in the length of a prison term **2** pardon or forgiveness **3** easing of intensity, as of an illness
remit Ⓣ *v* **-mitting, -mitted 1** send (money) for goods, services, etc., esp. by post **2** cancel (a punishment or debt) **3** refer (a decision) to a higher authority or later date ▹ *n* **4** area of competence or authority
▸ **remittance** *n* **1** sending of money **2** money sent
remix *v* **1** change the relative prominence of each performer's part of (a recording) ▹ *n* **2** remixed version of a recording
remnant Ⓣ *n* **1** small piece, esp. of fabric, left over **2** surviving trace

THESAURUS

remainder *n* = **rest**, last, balance, others, remnants, remains • *He gulped down the remainder of his milk.*
See also: **difference**
remaining *adj* = **left-over**, outstanding, unfinished, lingering, persisting, surviving
remains *pl n* **1** = **remnants**, debris, residue, dregs, leftovers, relics, scraps, vestiges • *the remains of an ancient dwelling* **2** = **body**, carcass, corpse, cadaver
See also: **remainder, ruin**
remark *v* **1** = **comment**, say, state, mention, observe • *She had remarked on the boy's improvement.* **2** = **notice**, see, note, mark, observe, perceive, espy, make out ▸ *n* **3** = **comment**, statement, word, observation, utterance • *a funny remark*
See also: **expression**
remarkable *adj* = **extraordinary**, rare, unusual, wonderful, notable, outstanding, uncommon, striking, singular, surprising
remarkably *See* **really**
remedy *n* **1** = **cure**, treatment, medicine, nostrum ▸ *v* **2** = **put right**, fix, correct, rectify, set to rights
remember *v* **1** = **recall**, recognize, retain, call to mind • *I do not remember the exact words.* **2** = **bear in mind**, keep in mind OPPOSITE: forget
remembrance *n* **1** = **memory**, recall, thought, recollection, reminiscence **2** = **souvenir**, reminder, token, memento, keepsake **3** = **commemoration**, memorial, monument
remind *v* = **make someone remember**, bring back to = **jog someone's memory**, put in mind, refresh someone's memory • *He reminds me of myself at that age.*
See also: **prompt**
reminder *See* **note, souvenir**
reminisce *v* = **recall**, remember, hark back, look back, recollect, think back
reminiscence *n* = **recollection**, recall, memory, memoir, remembrance, anecdote
reminiscent *adj* = **suggestive**, similar, evocative
remiss *adj* = **careless**, lax, negligent, thoughtless, forgetful, heedless, neglectful
remission *n* **1** = **pardon**, release, exemption, discharge, amnesty, reprieve, absolution **2** = **lessening**, lull, relaxation, respite, ebb, abatement, alleviation
remit *v* **1** = **send**, forward, mail, dispatch, transmit **2** = **cancel**, stop, halt, rescind, repeal **3** = **postpone**, delay, suspend, shelve, defer, put off ▸ *n* **4** = **instructions**, brief, guidelines, orders
remittance *n* = **payment**, fee, allowance
remnant *n* = **remainder**, end, rest, trace,

DICTIONARY

remonstrate ⓣ *v* argue in protest **remonstrance** *n*
remorse ⓣ *n* feeling of sorrow and regret for something one did **remorseful** *adj* **remorsefully** *adv*
▸ **remorseless** *adj* **1** pitiless **2** persistent **remorselessly** *adv*
remote ⓣ *adj* **1** far away, distant **2** aloof **3** slight or faint **remotely** *adv*
▸ **remote control** control of an apparatus from a distance by an electrical device
remould *v* **1** renovate (a worn tire) ▹ *n* **2** renovated tire
remove ⓣ *v* **1** take away or off **2** dismiss from office **3** get rid of ▹ *n* **4** degree of difference **removable** *adj*
▸ **removal** *n* removing, esp. changing residence
remunerate ⓣ *v* reward or pay **remuneration** *n* **remunerative** *adj*
renaissance ⓣ *n* revival or rebirth, esp.
▸ **Renaissance** the revival of learning in the 14th–16th centuries
renal [**ree**-nal] *adj* of the kidneys
renascent *adj* becoming active or vigorous again **renascence** *n*
rend ⓣ *v* **rending, rent 1** tear or wrench apart **2** (of a sound) break (the silence) violently
Rendell *n* **Ruth** (**Barbara**), Baroness. born 1930, British crime writer: author of detective novels, such as *Wolf to the Slaughter* (1967), and psychological thrillers, such as *The Lake of Darkness* (1980) and (under the name Barbara Vine) *A Fatal Inversion* (1987) and *The Chimney Sweeper's Boy* (1998)
render ⓣ *v* **1** cause to become **2** give or provide (aid, a service, etc.) **3** submit or present (a bill) **4** portray or represent **5** cover with plaster **6** melt down (fat)
rendezvous ⓣ [**ron**-day-voo] *n, pl* **-vous** **1** appointment **2** meeting place ▹ *v* **3** meet as arranged
rendition ⓣ *n* **1** performance **2** translation
renegade ⓣ *n* person who deserts a cause
renege ⓣ [rin-**nayg**] *v* (usu. foll. by *on*) go back on (a promise etc.)
renew ⓣ *v* **1** begin again **2** reaffirm **3** make

THESAURUS

fragment, residue, vestige, leftovers, remains
remonstrate *v* = **argue**, protest, dispute, object, dissent, take issue
remorse *n* = **regret**, shame, grief, guilt, sorrow, anguish, contrition, repentance, penitence, compunction
remorseful *adj* = **regretful**, guilty, sorry, ashamed, apologetic, contrite, conscience-stricken, penitent, repentant
remorseless *adj* **1** = **pitiless**, cruel, inhumane, ruthless, callous, merciless **2** = **relentless**, inexorable
remote *adj* **1** = **distant**, isolated, lonely, outlying, inaccessible, far-off • *a remote cabin in the mountains* **2** = **aloof**, cold, distant, reserved, detached, withdrawn • *She appeared remote and not interested in meeting anyone.* **3** = **slight**, small, poor, slim, slender • *The chances of his making the team are pretty remote.*
See also: **far, impersonal**
removal *n* **1** = **taking away, taking off**, *or* **taking out**, withdrawal, elimination, eradication, ejection, extraction, dislodgment, uprooting, clear-out (*informal*) **2** = **dismissal**, expulsion **3** = **move**, departure, transfer, relocation
remove *v* **1** = **take away**, eliminate, withdraw, erase, extract, eject, delete, detach, excise, get rid of, take off, take out, clear out (*informal*), efface, expunge • *I removed the splinter from my finger.* **2** = **dismiss**, oust, expel, depose, discharge, dethrone, throw out **3** = **move**, depart, relocate, flit (*Scot & Northern English dialect*)
See also: **banish, lift**
remunerate *v* = **pay**, reward, compensate, reimburse, repay, recompense, requite
remuneration *n* = **payment**, return, pay, income, fee, salary, reward, stipend, earnings, wages
remunerative *adj* = **profitable**, economic, lucrative, worthwhile, rewarding, moneymaking, paying
renaissance, renascence *n* = **rebirth**, revival, renewal, restoration, resurgence, reappearance, reawakening
rend *v* = **tear**, separate, rip, rupture, wrench
render *v* **1** = **make**, leave, cause to become **2** = **provide**, give, pay, supply, present, submit, tender, furnish, hand out **3** = **represent**, do, play, give, act, perform, portray, depict
rendezvous *n* **1** = **appointment**, meeting, date, engagement, tryst, assignation **2** = **meeting place**, venue, gathering point ▸ *v* **3** = **meet**, gather, assemble, come together, join up
rendition *n* **1** = **performance**, version, reading, arrangement, presentation, portrayal, interpretation, rendering **2** = **translation**, version, reading, interpretation, transcription
renegade *n* **1** = **deserter**, defector, traitor, apostate, turncoat ▸ *adj* **2** = **traitorous**, rebellious, apostate, unfaithful, disloyal
renege *v* = **break one's word**, default, back out, break a promise, go back
renew *v* **1** = **recommence**, resume, reopen,

DICTIONARY

valid again **4** grow again **5** restore to a former state **6** replace (a worn part) **renewal** *n*
▸ **renewable** *adj* **1** able to be renewed **2** (of energy or an energy source) inexhaustible or capable of being perpetually replenished
▸ **renewables** *pl n* renewable energy sources
Reni *n* **Guido**. 1575–1642, Italian baroque painter and engraver
rennet *n* substance for curdling milk to make cheese
Renoir *n* **1 Jean**. 1894–1979, French film director: his films include *La grande illusion* (1937), *La règle du jeu* (1939), and *Diary of a Chambermaid* (1945) **2** his father, **Pierre Auguste**. 1841–1919, French painter. One of the initiators of impressionism, he broke away from the movement with his later paintings, esp. his many nude studies, which are more formal compositions
renounce Ⓣ *v* **1** give up (a belief, habit, etc.) voluntarily **2** give up (a title or claim) formally **renunciation** *n*
renovate Ⓣ *v* restore to good condition **renovation** *n*
renown Ⓣ *n* widespread good reputation
▸ **renowned** *adj* famous
rent[1] Ⓣ *n* **1** regular payment for use of land, a building, machine, etc. ▹ *v* **2** give or have use of in return for rent
▸ **rental** *n* sum payable as rent
rent[2] Ⓣ *n* **1** tear or fissure ▹ *v* **2** past of **rend**
renunciation Ⓣ *n* see **renounce**
reorganize Ⓣ *v* organize in a new and more efficient way **reorganization** *n*
rep[1] *n* short for **repertory company**
rep[2] *n* short for **representative**
repair[1] Ⓣ *v* **1** restore to good condition, mend ▹ *n* **2** act of repairing **3** repaired part **4** state or condition: *in good repair* **repairable** *adj*
▸ **reparation** *n* something done or given as compensation
repair[2] *v* go (to)
repartee Ⓣ *n* **1** interchange of witty retorts **2** witty retort
repast Ⓣ *n* meal
repatriate *v* send (someone) back to his or her own country **repatriation** *n*
repay Ⓣ *v* **1** pay back, refund **2** make a return for **repayable** *adj* **repayment** *n*
repeal Ⓣ *v* **1** cancel (a law) officially ▹ *n* **2** act of repealing
repeat Ⓣ *v* **1** say, write, or do again **2** disclose **3** happen again, recur ▹ *n* **4** act or instance of repeating **5** programme broadcast again **repeatedly** *adv*
▸ **repeater** *n* firearm that may be discharged many times without reloading
repel Ⓣ *v* **-pelling, -pelled 1** be disgusting to

THESAURUS

re-establish, begin again • *The two countries renewed diplomatic relations.* **2 = restore**, repair, overhaul, mend, renovate, refurbish, modernize, refit **3 = replace**, refresh, replenish, restock
renounce *v* (*Formal*) **= give up**, reject, relinquish, disown • *She renced her claim to the inheritance.*
See also: **deny, surrender**
renovate *v* **= restore**, repair, revamp, refurbish, modernize, make over, recondition • *They spent thousands renovating the house.*
See also: **decorate, mend, reconstruct**
renown *n* **= fame**, note, reputation, distinction, repute, eminence
renowned *adj* **= famous**, well-known, notable, celebrated, distinguished, eminent, noted, esteemed
rent[1] *v* **1 = lease**, hire, charter • *They rented an apartment downtown.* ▸ *n* **2 = lease**, fee, payment, hire, rental
rent[2] *n* **= tear**, opening, hole, split, slash, rip, gash, slit
renunciation *n* **= giving up**, rejection, denial, abandonment, abdication, repudiation, abjuration, disavowal, forswearing, relinquishment
reopen *See* **renew**
reorganize *v* **= rearrange**, restructure, reshuffle
repair *n* **1 = mend**, patch, restoration • *She did the house repairs herself.* ▸ *v* **2 = mend**, fix, restore, patch, renovate, patch up • *The money will be used to repair faulty equipment.*
See also: **piece together**
reparation *n* **= compensation**, satisfaction, restitution, atonement, damages, recompense
repartee *n* **= wit**, banter, wordplay, badinage, riposte, wittiness
repast *n* **= meal**, food
repay *v* **1 = pay back**, refund, settle up • *It will take me years to repay the loan.* **2 = get even with** (*informal*), avenge, revenge, retaliate, reciprocate, hit back
See also: **compensate, return**
repeal *v* **1 = abolish**, recall, cancel, reverse, revoke, annul, nullify, invalidate ▸ *n* **2 = abolition**, cancellation, annulment, invalidation, rescindment
repeat *v* **1 = reiterate**, echo, say again • *Since you didn't listen, I'll repeat that.* **2 = repetition**, echo, replay, rerun, reiteration, reshowing
See also: **quote, stress**
repeated *See* **continual, frequent**
repeatedly *adv* **= over and over**, often, frequently, many times
repel *v* **1 = disgust**, sicken, offend, revolt • *The thought of spiders repels me.* OPPOSITE: attract **2 = drive off**, resist, repulse • *troops*

r

DICTIONARY

2 drive back, ward off **3** resist
▸ **repellent** *adj* **1** distasteful **2** resisting water etc. ▹ *n* **3** something that repels, esp. a chemical to repel insects
repent ⓣ *v* feel regret for (a deed or omission) **repentance** *n* **repentant** *adj*
repercussion ⓣ *n* indirect effect, often unpleasant
repertoire ⓣ *n* stock of plays, songs, etc. that a player or company can give
repertory *n, pl* **-ries** repertoire
▸ **repertory company** permanent theatre company producing a succession of plays
repetition ⓣ *n* **1** act of repeating **2** thing repeated
▸ **repetitive** *or* **repetitious** *adj* full of repetition
rephrase ⓣ *v* express in different words
repine ⓣ *v* fret or complain
replace ⓣ *v* **1** substitute for **2** put back
replacement *n*
replay *n* **1** Also **action replay** immediate reshowing on TV of an incident in sport, esp. in slow motion **2** second sports match, esp. one following an earlier draw ▹ *v* **3** play (a match, recording, etc.) again
replenish ⓣ *v* fill up again, resupply
replenishment *n*
replete ⓣ *adj* filled or gorged
replica ⓣ *n* exact copy
▸ **replicate** *v* make or be a copy of
reply ⓣ *v* **-plying, -plied 1** answer or respond ▹ *n, pl* **-plies 2** answer or response
report ⓣ *v* **1** give an account of **2** make a report (on) **3** announce or relate **4** make a formal complaint about **5** present oneself (to) **6** be responsible (to) ▹ *n* **7** account or statement **8** rumour **9** written statement of a child's progress at school **10** bang
▸ **reportedly** *adv* according to rumour
▸ **reporter** *n* person who gathers news for a newspaper, TV, etc.
repose ⓣ *n* **1** peace **2** composure **3** sleep ▹ *v* **4** lie or lay at rest
repository ⓣ *n, pl* **-ries** place where valuables are deposited for safekeeping, store
repossess *v* (of a lender) take back property from a customer who is behind with payments **repossession** *n*
reprehend *v* find fault with

THESAURUS

along the border ready to repel an enemy attack
repellent *adj* **1 = disgusting**, offensive, sickening, hateful, abhorrent, noxious, horrid, repulsive, repugnant, revolting, loathsome, nauseating, scuzzy (*slang*) **2 = proof**, resistant, impermeable, repelling
repent *v* **= regret**, rue, be sorry, feel remorse
repentance *n* **= regret**, grief, guilt, remorse, contrition, penitence, compunction
repentant *adj* **= regretful**, sorry, remorseful, contrite, penitent, rueful
repercussion *n* ▹ **repercussions = consequences**, result, sequel, backlash, side effects
repertoire *n* **= range**, list, stock, store, supply, collection, repertory
repetition *n* **= repeating**, echo, renewal, recurrence, restatement, reiteration, replication, tautology
repetitious *adj* **= long-winded**, tedious, verbose, prolix, tautological, wordy
repetitive *adj* **= monotonous**, mechanical, boring, dull, tedious, recurrent, unchanging, unvaried
rephrase *v* **= reword**, paraphrase, put differently
repine *v* **= complain**, fret, grumble, moan
replace *v* **= take the place of**, succeed, supplant, supersede, take over from • *She replaced the singer at the last minute.*
See also: **change, substitute**
replacement *n* **= successor**, relief, substitute, proxy, surrogate, stand-in • *He has nominated his assistant as his replacement.*
replenish *v* **= refill**, provide, replace, fill, restore, reload, top up
replete *adj* **= full**, crammed, filled, full up, glutted, gorged, stuffed
replica *n* **= duplicate**, model, copy, reproduction, imitation, facsimile, carbon copy (*informal*)
replicate *v* **= copy**, mimic, recreate, duplicate, reproduce, reduplicate
reply *v* **1 = answer**, return, respond, counter, retort • *He did not even have the courtesy to reply to my email.* ▸ *n* **2 = answer**, response, retort • *There was a trace of irony in his reply.*
report *v* **1 = communicate**, state, cover, describe, notify, inform of • *He reported the theft to the police.* **2 = present oneself**, come, appear, arrive, turn up ▸ *n* **3 = account**, statement, description • *reports of a tornado touching down* **4 = article**, story, piece, write-up **5 = rumor**, talk, buzz, gossip, hearsay **6 = bang**, blast, sound, explosion, boom, crack, noise, discharge, detonation
See also: **announcement, feature, item, review**
reporter *n* **= journalist**, correspondent, hack (*derogatory*), writer, pressman
repose *n* **1 = peace**, rest, ease, relaxation, respite, stillness, tranquillity, quietness **2 = composure**, poise, calmness, self-possession **3 = sleep**, slumber ▸ *v* **4 = rest**, lie, recline, lie down, rest upon
repository *n* **= store**, vault, treasury, storehouse, depository

DICTIONARY

▸ **reprehensible** *adj* open to criticism, unworthy
represent ⊕ *v* **1** stand for **2** act as a delegate for **3** symbolize **4** make out to be **5** portray, as in art **representation** *n*
▸ **representative** *n* **1** person chosen to act for or represent a group **2** (travelling) salesperson ▹ *adj* **3** typical of a class or kind
repress ⊕ *v* **1** keep (feelings) under control **2** subjugate **repression** *n* **repressive** *adj*
reprieve ⊕ *v* **1** postpone the execution of (a condemned person) **2** give temporary relief to ▹ *n* **3** postponement or cancellation of a punishment **4** temporary relief
reprimand ⊕ *v* **1** blame (someone) officially for a fault ▹ *n* **2** official blame
reprint *v* **1** print further copies of (a book) ▹ *n* **2** reprinted copy
reprisal ⊕ *n* retaliation
reproach ⊕ *v* **1** blame or rebuke ▹ *n* **2** scolding or blame **reproachful** *adj* **reproachfully** *adv*
reprobate ⊕ [**rep**-roh-bate] *adj, n* depraved or disreputable (person)
▸ **reprobation** *n* disapproval or blame
reproduce ⊕ *v* **1** produce a copy of **2** bring new individuals into existence **3** re-create **reproducible** *adj*
▸ **reproduction** *n* **1** process of reproducing **2** thing that is reproduced **3** facsimile, as of a painting etc. **4** quality of sound from an audio system **reproductive** *adj*
reprove ⊕ *v* speak severely to (someone) about a fault
▸ **reproof** *n* severe blaming of someone for a fault
reptile *n* cold-blooded air-breathing vertebrate with horny scales or plates, such as a snake or tortoise **reptilian** *adj*
republic ⊕ *n* **1** form of government in which the people or their elected representatives possess the supreme power **2** country in which a president is the head of state
▸ **Republican** *n, adj* **1** (member or supporter) of the Republican Party, the more conservative of the two main political parties in the US **Republicanism** *n*

THESAURUS

reprehensible *adj* = **blameworthy**, bad, disgraceful, shameful, culpable, unworthy
represent *v* **1** = **stand for**, mean, symbolize • *Locate the icon on the desktop that represents your connection.* **2** = **portray**, show, picture, describe, depict • *The media tends to represent him as a hero.* **3** = **symbolize**, embody, exemplify, epitomize, typify, personify
representation *n* = **portrayal**, picture, account, image, model, portrait, description, depiction, illustration, likeness
representative *n* **1** = **delegate**, agent, deputy, spokesperson, proxy • *Employees from each department elect a representative.* **2** = **salesman**, agent, rep, commercial traveller ▸ *adj* **3** = **typical**, characteristic, illustrative • *fairly representative groups ofadults*
See also: **official, substitute**
repress *v* **1** = **inhibit**, control, check, curb, stifle, restrain, suppress, bottle up, hold back **2** = **subdue**, quell, subjugate
repressed *See* **pent-up**
repression *n* = **subjugation**, control, restraint, domination, constraint, tyranny, suppression, despotism
repressive *adj* = **oppressive**, absolute, authoritarian, despotic, dictatorial, tyrannical
reprieve *v* **1** = **grant a stay of execution to**, pardon, let off the hook (*slang*) **2** = **relieve**, alleviate, mitigate, allay, abate, palliate ▸ *n* **3** = **stay of execution**, amnesty, pardon, postponement, remission, deferment **4** = **relief**, respite, mitigation, alleviation, palliation
reprimand *v* **1** = **blame**, censure, rebuke, scold, rap over the knuckles, lower the boom (*slang*) ▸ *n* **2** = **blame**, censure, rebuke, reproach, reproof, talking-to (*informal*)
reprisal *n* = **retaliation**, revenge, vengeance, retribution
reproach *n* **1** = **blame**, rebuke, condemnation, censure, disapproval, opprobrium ▸ *v* **2** = **blame**, criticize, condemn, censure, lambast *or* lambaste, rebuke, reprimand, scold, upbraid
reproachful *adj* = **critical**, censorious, condemnatory, disapproving, fault-finding, reproving
reprobate *n* **1** = **scoundrel**, bad egg (*old-fashioned, informal*), degenerate, miscreant, evildoer, rake, villain, rascal, profligate ▸ *adj* **2** = **depraved**, base, bad, corrupt, abandoned, wicked, immoral, degenerate, sinful, dissolute
reproduce *v* **1** = **copy**, match, repeat, mirror, echo, recreate, replicate, duplicate, imitate **2** = **breed**, spawn, multiply, procreate, propagate
reproduction *n* **1** = **breeding**, increase, generation, multiplication **2** = **copy**, picture, print, replica, duplicate, imitation, facsimile
reproof *n* = **rebuke**, blame, criticism, reprimand, condemnation, censure, scolding
reprove *v* = **rebuke**, blame, condemn, censure, berate, reprimand, scold, tell off (*informal*)
republic *See* **state**

DICTIONARY

repudiate ⓣ [rip-**pew**-dee-ate] *v* **1** reject the authority or validity of **2** disown
repudiation *n*
repugnant ⓣ *adj* offensive or distasteful
repugnance *n*
repulse ⓣ *v* **1** be disgusting to **2** drive (an army) back **3** rebuff or reject ▷ *n* **4** driving back **5** rejection **6** rebuff
▸ **repulsion** *n* **1** distaste or aversion **2** *physics* force separating two objects
▸ **repulsive** *adj* loathsome, disgusting
reputation ⓣ *n* estimation in which a person or thing is held
▸ **reputable** [**rep**-yoo-tab-bl] *adj* of good reputation, respectable
▸ **repute** *n* reputation
▸ **reputed** *adj* supposed **reputedly** *adv*
request ⓣ *n* **1** asking **2** thing asked for ▷ *v* **3** ask or politely demand
Requiem [**rek**-wee-em] *n* **1** Mass for the dead **2** music for this
require ⓣ *v* **1** want or need **2** demand
▸ **requirement** *n* **1** essential condition **2** specific need or want
requisite ⓣ [**rek**-wizz-it] *adj* **1** necessary, essential ▷ *n* **2** an essential
requisition ⓣ *n* **1** formal demand, such as for materials or supplies ▷ *v* **2** demand (supplies)
requite ⓣ *v* return to someone (the same treatment or feeling as received) **requital** *n*
reredos [**rear**-doss] *n* ornamental screen behind an altar
rerun *n* **1** film or programme that is broadcast again, repeat **2** race that is run again ▷ *v* **3** put on (a film or programme) again **4** run (a race) again
resale *n* selling of something purchased earlier
rescind ⓣ *v* annul or repeal
rescue ⓣ *v* **-cuing, -cued 1** deliver from danger or trouble, save ▷ *n* **2** rescuing
rescuer *n*
research ⓣ *n* **1** systematic investigation to discover facts or collect information ▷ *v* **2** carry out investigations **researcher** *n*

THESAURUS

repudiate *v* = **reject**, deny, renounce, disavow, disown, disclaim
repugnance *n* = **distaste**, hatred, disgust, dislike, aversion, loathing, abhorrence
repugnant *adj* = **distasteful**, offensive, repellent, sickening, abhorrent, vile, disgusting, revolting, loathsome, nauseating
repulse *v* **1** = **drive back**, rebuff, repel, beat off, fight off, ward off **2** = **reject**, refuse, snub, rebuff, spurn, turn down
repulsion *n* = **distaste**, hatred, disgust, revulsion, aversion, loathing, abhorrence, detestation, repugnance
repulsive *adj* = **disgusting**, foul, repellent, sickening, abhorrent, vile, revolting, loathsome, nauseating, scuzzy (*slang*)
reputable *adj* = **respectable**, good, excellent, reliable, worthy, trustworthy, honorable, creditable, well-thought-of
reputation *n* = **name**, character, standing, stature, renown, repute • *The college has a good reputation.*
See also: **fame**
repute *n* = **reputation**, name, celebrity, standing, fame, distinction, stature, renown, eminence
reputed *adj* = **supposed**, alleged, estimated, held, considered, believed, deemed, reckoned, regarded
reputedly *adv* = **supposedly**, allegedly, apparently, seemingly
request *v* **1** = **ask for**, seek, beg • *She requested that the door be left open.* ▸ *n* **2** = **appeal**, call, application, plea • *The principal agreed to our request.*
require *v* **1** = **need**, want, demand, be in need of, depend on • *A baby requires warmth and security.* **2** = **demand**, order, direct, compel, instruct, oblige • *The rules require employers to provide safety training.*
See also: **expect, involve, take**
required *adj* = **needed**, necessary, essential, requisite, obligatory, called for
requirement *n* = **necessity**, need, demand, essential, specification • *The products met all safety requirements.*
See also: **condition, standard**
requisite *adj* **1** = **necessary**, essential, needed, required, indispensable, obligatory, called for, needful ▸ *n* **2** = **necessity**, need, must, condition, requirement, essential, prerequisite
requisition *v* **1** = **demand**, request, call for ▸ *n* **2** = **demand**, call, request, summons
requital *n* = **return**, repayment
requite *v* = **return**, respond, repay, retaliate, reciprocate, get even, give in return, pay (someone) back in his own coin *or* pay (someone) back in her own coin
reschedule *See* **put off**
rescind *v* = **annul**, cancel, repeal, invalidate, countermand, declare null and void, set aside
rescue *v* **1** = **save**, release, recover, deliver, salvage, redeem, liberate, get out ▸ *n* **2** = **saving**, release, recovery, salvage, redemption, liberation, salvation, deliverance, search and rescue
research *n* **1** = **investigation**, study, analysis, exploration, examination • *funds for AIDS research* ▸ *v* **2** = **investigate**, study, explore, examine, analyze • *I'm researching the history of the fisheries.*

DICTIONARY

resemble ⓣ *v* be or look like **resemblance** *n*
resent ⓣ *v* feel indignant or bitter about **resentful** *adj* **resentment** *n*
reservation ⓣ *n* **1** doubt **2** exception or limitation **3** seat etc. that has been reserved **4** area of land reserved for use by a particular group, esp. as a home for Native Americans
reserve ⓣ *v* **1** set aside, keep for future use **2** obtain by arranging beforehand, book **3** retain ▷ *n* **4** something, esp. money or troops, kept for emergencies **5** *sports* substitute **6** area of land reserved for a particular purpose, esp. as a home for Canadian Indians **7** concealment of feelings or friendliness
▶ **reserved** *adj* **1** not showing one's feelings, lacking friendliness **2** set aside for use by a particular person
▶ **reservist** *n* member of a military reserve
reservoir ⓣ *n* **1** natural or artificial lake storing water for community supplies **2** store or supply of something
reshuffle ⓣ *n* **1** reorganization ▷ *v* **2** reorganize
reside ⓣ *v* dwell permanently
▶ **residence** *n* home or house **resident** *adj, n*
▶ **residential** *adj* **1** (of part of a town) consisting mainly of houses **2** providing living accommodation
residue ⓣ *n* what is left, remainder **residual** *adj*
resign ⓣ *v* **1** give up office, a job, etc. **2** reconcile (oneself) to
▶ **resigned** *adj* content to endure
▶ **resignation** *n* **1** resigning **2** passive endurance of difficulties
resilient ⓣ *adj* **1** (of a person) recovering quickly from a shock etc. **2** (of an object) able

THESAURUS

resemblance *n* = **similarity**, parallel, correspondence, likeness, analogy • *I can see a resemblance between you.*
resemble *v* = **be like**, parallel, bear a resemblance to, be similar to, look like, take after • *He resembles his grandfather when he was a young man.*
resent *v* = **be bitter about**, dislike, be angry about, be offended by, object to, take offence at • *I resent the slur on my character.*
See also: **envy**
resentful *adj* = **bitter**, angry, aggrieved, embittered, huffy, indignant, offended • *an unhappy and resentful team*
See also: **jealous, sulky**
resentment *n* = **bitterness**, anger, grudge, animosity, huff, indignation, rancour • *There is growing resentment against the new owners.*
See also: **envy, hostility**
reservation *n* **1** = **doubt**, hesitancy, scruple **2** = **condition**, rider, qualification, stipulation, proviso **3** = **reserve**, territory, preserve, sanctuary
reserve *v* **1** = **keep**, hold, save, store, stockpile, hoard, put away, set aside • *Hotel rooms have been reserved for us.* **2** = **book**, secure, engage, prearrange ▶ *n* **3** = **store**, fund, stock, supply, stockpile, cache, hoard • *a drain on the cash reserves* **4** = **reservation**, park, preserve, tract, sanctuary **5** = **shyness**, silence, restraint, reservation, constraint, secretiveness, reticence, taciturnity ▶ *adj* **6** = **substitute**, extra, spare, secondary, auxiliary, fall-back
See also: **bank**
reserved *adj* **1** = **uncommunicative**, shy, silent, secretive, restrained, reticent, retiring, standoffish, taciturn, undemonstrative **2** = **set aside**, restricted, held, engaged, retained, booked, kept, spoken for, taken
reservoir *n* **1** = **lake**, tank, pond, basin **2** = **store**, stock, supply, source, pool, reserves
reshuffle *n* (*Politics*) **1** = **reorganization**, change, revision, redistribution, restructuring, rearrangement, regrouping ▶ *v* **2** = **reorganize**, restructure, revise, regroup, redistribute, rearrange, change around
reside *v* = **live**, stay, abide, lodge, inhabit, dwell
residence *n* = **home**, place, house, apartment, flat, lodging, dwelling, abode, habitation, domicile, bachelorette (*Canad*)
resident *n* = **inhabitant**, local, citizen, tenant, occupant, occupier, lodger, landed immigrant (*Canad*), livyer *or* liveyer (*Canad Nfld*), permanent resident (*Canad*)
residual *adj* = **remaining**, unused, leftover, unconsumed, vestigial
residue *n* = **remainder**, rest, extra, surplus, excess, remnant, dregs, leftovers, remains
resign *v* **1** = **quit**, leave, abdicate, hand in your notice, step down • *I resigned from the company.* **2** = **give up**, abandon, surrender, yield, renounce, relinquish, forgo, forsake ▷ **resign oneself** = **accept**, bow, reconcile oneself • *She had resigned herself to losing her job.*
resignation *n* **1** = **leaving**, departure, abandonment, abdication **2** = **acceptance**, submission, compliance, patience, endurance, passivity, acquiescence, nonresistance, sufferance
resigned *adj* = **stoical**, patient, subdued, compliant, long-suffering, unresisting
resilient *adj* **1** = **tough**, strong, buoyant,

DICTIONARY

to return to normal shape after stretching etc. **resilience** *n*

resin [rezz-in] *n* **1** sticky substance from plants, esp. pines **2** similar synthetic substance **resinous** *adj*

resist ➊ *v* **1** withstand or oppose **2** refrain from despite temptation **3** be proof against **resistible** *adj*

▸ **resistance** *n* **1** act of resisting **2** opposition **3** *electricity* opposition offered by a circuit to the passage of a current through it **resistant** *adj*

▸ **resistivity** *n* measure of electrical resistance

▸ **resistor** *n* component of an electrical circuit producing resistance

resit *v* **1** retake (an exam) ▹ *n* **2** exam that has to be retaken

Resnais *n* **Alain**. born 1922, French film director, whose films include *Hiroshima mon amour* (1959), *L'Année dernière à Marienbad* (1961), *La Vie est un roman* (1983), and *On Connaît la Chanson* (1998)

resolute ➊ *adj* firm in purpose **resolutely** *adv*

▸ **resolution** *n* **1** resolving **2** firmness **3** thing resolved upon **4** decision of a court or vote of an assembly

resolve ➊ *v* **1** make up one's mind **2** decide with an effort of will **3** form (a resolution) by a vote **4** separate the component parts of **5** make clear, settle

▸ **resolved** *adj* determined

resonance *n* **1** echoing, esp. with a deep sound **2** sound produced in one object by sound waves coming from another object **resonant** *adj* **resonate** *v* **resonator** *n*

resort ➊ *v* **1** have recourse (to) for help etc. ▹ *n* **2** place for holidays **3** recourse

resound ➊ [riz-**zownd**] *v* echo or ring with sound

▸ **resounding** *adj* **1** echoing **2** clear and emphatic

resource ➊ *n* **1** thing resorted to for support **2** expedient **3** ingenuity **resources 4** sources of economic wealth **5** stock that can be drawn on, funds **resourceful** *adj* **resourcefully** *adv* **resourcefulness** *n*

respect ➊ *n* **1** consideration **2** deference or esteem **3** point or aspect **4** reference

THESAURUS

hardy, irrepressible **2 = flexible**, plastic, elastic, rubbery, supple, pliable, springy

resist *v* **1 = oppose**, fight, refuse, defy, struggle against • *They resisted our attempts to change the yearbook's format.* OPPOSITE: accept **2 = refrain from**, avoid, forgo, abstain from, forbear, keep from **3 = withstand**, be proof against
See also: **rebel, repel**

resistance *n* **= opposition**, fight, battle, struggle, obstruction, fighting, defiance, impediment, hindrance

resistant *adj* **1 = impervious**, strong, hard, tough, proof against, unaffected by **2 = opposed**, hostile, unwilling, intractable, intransigent, antagonistic

resolute *adj* **= determined**, set, firm, steadfast, dogged, tenacious, inflexible, strong-willed, unshakable, fixed, immovable, unwavering

resolution *n* **1 = determination**, resolve, purpose, perseverance, tenacity, willpower, firmness, doggedness, resoluteness, steadfastness **2 = decision**, aim, resolve, purpose, intention, declaration, intent, determination

resolve *v* **1 = decide**, determine, intend, make up your mind • *She resolved to report the matter.* **2 = work out**, solve, overcome, clear up, find a solution to, sort out • *We must find a way to resolve these problems.* **3 = break down**, reduce, separate, analyze ▸ *n* **4 = determination**, resolution, tenacity • *He didn't weaken in his resolve.* **5 = decision**, resolution, purpose, intention, objective
See also: **settle, will**

resolved *See* **serious**

resonant *adj* **= echoing**, ringing, booming, resounding, reverberating, sonorous

resonate *See* **ring**

resort *n* **1 = holiday centre**, spot, retreat, haunt, tourist centre **2 = recourse**, reference ▸ *v* ▹ **resort to = use**, employ, utilize, fall back on, have recourse to, turn to

resound *v* **= echo**, ring, resonate, reverberate, re-echo

resounding *adj* **= echoing**, full, powerful, ringing, booming, resonant, reverberating, sonorous

resource *n* **1 = ingenuity**, ability, initiative, capability, inventiveness, cleverness **2 = means**, course, device, resort, expedient

resourceful *adj* **= ingenious**, able, bright, capable, creative, clever, inventive

resources *pl n* **= reserves**, money, capital, wealth, riches, assets, funds, holdings, supplies

respect *v* **1 = think highly of**, honour, admire, venerate, have a good opinion of, have a high opinion of, look up to • *I want her to respect me as a dedicated student.* OPPOSITE: disrespect **2 = show consideration for**, follow, observe, heed, honour, obey, abide by, adhere to, comply with ▸ *n* **3 = regard**, admiration, esteem, reverence • *We have no respect for him at all.* OPPOSITE: disrespect **4 = point**, way, feature,

DICTIONARY

or relation: *with respect to* ▷ *v* **5** treat with esteem **6** show consideration for **respecter** *n* **respectful** *adj*
▸ **respecting** *prep* concerning
respectable Ⓣ *adj* **1** worthy of respect **2** fairly good **respectably** *adv* **respectability** *n*
respective Ⓣ *adj* relating separately to each of those in question **respectively** *adv*
Respighi *n* **Ottorino**. 1879–1936, Italian composer, noted esp. for his suites *The Fountains of Rome* (1917) and *The Pines of Rome* (1924)
respiration [ress-per-**ray**-shun] *n* breathing **respiratory** *adj*
▸ **respirator** *n* apparatus worn over the mouth and breathed through as protection against dust, poison gas, etc., or to provide artificial respiration
▸ **respire** *v* breathe
respite Ⓣ *n* **1** pause, interval of rest **2** delay
resplendent Ⓣ *adj* **1** brilliant or splendid **2** shining **resplendence** *n*
respond Ⓣ *v* **1** answer **2** act in answer to any stimulus **3** react favourably
▸ **respondent** *n law* defendant
▸ **response** *n* **1** answer **2** reaction to a stimulus
▸ **responsive** *adj* readily reacting to some influence **responsiveness** *n*
responsible Ⓣ *adj* **1** having control and authority **2** reporting or accountable (to) **3** sensible and dependable **4** involving responsibility **responsibly** *adv*
▸ **responsibility** *n, pl* **-ties 1** state of being responsible **2** person or thing for which one is responsible
respray *n* new coat of paint applied to a vehicle
rest[1] Ⓣ *n* **1** repose **2** freedom from exertion etc. **3** an object used for support **4** pause, esp. in music ▷ *v* **5** take a rest **6** give a rest (to) **7** be supported **8** place on a support **restful** *adj* **restless** *adj*
rest[2] Ⓣ *n* **1** what is left **2** others ▷ *v* **3** remain, continue to be
restaurant Ⓣ *n* commercial establishment serving meals
▸ **restaurateur** [rest-er-a-**tur**] *n* person who owns or runs a restaurant
restitution Ⓣ *n* **1** giving back **2** reparation or compensation
restive Ⓣ *adj* restless or impatient

THESAURUS

matter, detail, sense, particular, aspect, characteristic **5 = relation**, connection, regard, reference, bearing
See also: **appreciate, approval, approve, consider, consideration, value**
respectable *adj* **1 = honourable**, good, proper, decent, worthy, upright, reputable • *respectable families* **2 = reasonable**, fair, decent, considerable, appreciable • *a respectable rate of economic growth*
respectful *adj* **= polite**, civil, courteous, deferential, mannerly, reverent, well-mannered
respective *adj* **= specific**, own, individual, particular, relevant
respite *n* **= pause**, break, rest, halt, relief, recess, cessation, lull, interval
resplendent *adj* **= brilliant**, bright, glorious, splendid, radiant, dazzling, shining
respond *v* **= answer**, return, counter, react, reply, rejoin, retort, reciprocate ▷ **respond to** *See* **identify with**
response *n* **= answer**, return, reaction, reply, feedback, counterattack, retort, rejoinder
responsibility *n* **1 = duty**, obligation, onus • *The garden is your responsibility.* **2 = fault**, blame, liability, guilt • *We must all accept responsibility for our mistakes.* **3 = authority**, power, importance **4 = level-headedness**, dependability, conscientiousness, rationality, sensibleness, trustworthiness
See also: **concern, function, job**
responsible *adj* **1 = in charge**, in control • *The music teacher is responsible for the band.* **2 = to blame**, guilty, at fault • *I hold you responsible for this mess.* **3 = sensible**, sound, reliable, dependable, trustworthy, level-headed • *He had to show that he would be a responsible pet owner.* OPPOSITE: irresponsible **4 = accountable**, liable, answerable
responsive *adj* **= sensitive**, open, alive, susceptible, receptive, reactive, impressionable
rest[1] *n* **1 = break**, holiday, vacation, leisure, relaxation, respite, staycation (*informal*) • *I'll start again after a rest.* **2 = relaxation**, relief, calm, leisure, inactivity, repose, stillness, tranquillity **3 = support**, base, stand, holder, prop ▸ *v* **4 = relax**, idle, have a break, laze, put your feet up, sit down, take it easy • *She rested briefly before going on.* **5 = be supported**, sit, lie, lean, prop, recline, repose
See also: **pause, put, set**
rest[2] *n* **= remainder**, surplus, balance, others • *Take what you want and leave the rest.*
restaurant *n* **= bistro**, cafeteria, diner, café, eatery, tearoom
restful *adj* **= relaxing**, quiet, calm, peaceful, soothing, tranquil, serene, calming, relaxed
restitution *n* **= compensation**, amends, reparation, recompense, requital
restive *adj* **= restless**, nervous, impatient, edgy, fidgety, jumpy, on edge, wired (*slang*)
restless *adj* **1 = unsettled**, edgy, fidgety,

r

DICTIONARY

restore Ⓣ *v* **1** return (a building, painting, etc.) to its original condition **2** re-establish **3** give back, return **4** cause to recover health or spirits **restoration** *n* **restorer** *n*
▸ **restorative** [rest-**or**-a-tiv] *adj* **1** restoring ▹ *n* **2** food or medicine to strengthen etc.
restrain Ⓣ *v* **1** hold (someone) back from action **2** control or restrict
▸ **restraint** *n* **1** restraining **2** control, esp. self-control
▸ **restrained** *adj* not displaying emotion
restrict Ⓣ *v* confine to certain limits **restriction** *n* **restrictive** *adj*
restructure *v* reorganize
result Ⓣ *n* **1** outcome or consequence **2** number obtained from a calculation **3** score **4** exam mark or grade ▹ *v* **5** (foll. by *from*) be the outcome or consequence (of) **6** (foll. by *in*) end (in)
▸ **resultant** *adj* arising as a result
resume Ⓣ *v* **1** begin again **2** occupy or take again **resumption** *n*
résumé Ⓣ [**rez**-yoo-may] *n* summary
resurgence Ⓣ *n* rising again to vigour **resurgent** *adj*
resurrect Ⓣ *v* **1** restore to life **2** use once more (something discarded etc.), revive
▸ **resurrection** *n* **1** rising again (esp. from the dead) **2** revival
resuscitate Ⓣ [ris-**suss**-it-tate] *v* restore to consciousness **resuscitation** *n*
retail *n* **1** selling of goods to the public ▹ *adv* **2** by retail ▹ *v* **3** sell or be sold retail **4** recount in detail **retailer** *n*
retain Ⓣ *v* **1** keep **2** engage the services of
▸ **retainer** *n* **1** fee to retain someone's services **2** old-established servant of a family
retake *v* **1** take something, such as an examination, again **2** recapture ▹ *n* **3** *films* rephotographed scene
retaliate Ⓣ *v* repay (an injury or wrong) in

THESAURUS

jumpy, fretful, on edge • *She had been restless and irritable all day* **2 = moving**, unstable, nomadic, transient, unsettled, roving, wandering
See also: **active, busy, impatient**
restlessness *n* **1 = movement**, activity, unrest, bustle **2 = restiveness**, nervousness, edginess, jitters (*informal*), jumpiness, unsettledness
restoration *n* **1 = repair**, reconstruction, renovation, revival, renewal, revitalization **2 = reinstatement**, return, replacement, restitution, re-establishment
restore *v* **1 = reinstate**, return, reintroduce, re-establish • *He was anxious to restore his reputation.* **2 = repair**, rebuild, mend, renovate, refurbish, reconstruct, fix up • *experts who specialize in restoring old paintings* **3 = revive**, strengthen, refresh, revitalize, build up **4 = return**, recover, replace, reinstate, bring back, give back, hand back, send back
See also: **piece together**
restrain *v* **= hold back**, control, contain, curb, hamper, hinder, inhibit • *He had to be restrained by his friends.*
See also: **check, restrict, suppress**
restrained *adj* **= controlled**, calm, moderate, mild, self-controlled, undemonstrative
restraint *n* **1 = self-control**, control, moderation, inhibition, self-restraint, self-discipline, self-possession **2 = limitation**, ban, limit, check, curb, rein, embargo, interdict
restrict *v* **= limit**, contain, hamper, restrain, confine, impede, inhibit, handicap • *laws to restrict foreign imports*
restriction *n* **= limitation**, control, limit, regulation, curb, restraint, constraint, stipulation • *travel restrictions*
result *n* **1 = consequence**, product, effect, outcome, upshot ▸ *v* **2 = arise**, follow, happen, develop, stem, ensue, derive • *The crash resulted from a defect in the aircraft.* ▹ **result in = cause**, bring about, lead to • *Fifty per cent of road accidents result in head injuries.*
See also: **bring**
resume *v* **= begin again**, continue, proceed, reopen, restart, carry on, go on
résumé *n* **= CV** *or* **curriculum vitae**, summary, rundown (*informal*), synopsis, recapitulation, précis
resumption *n* **= continuation**, restart, renewal, resurgence, carrying on, re-establishment, reopening
resurgence *n* **= revival**, return, resumption, renaissance, rebirth, resurrection, re-emergence
resurrect *v* **= revive**, renew, reintroduce, bring back
resurrection *n* **= revival**, return, renewal, restoration, resurgence, renaissance, reappearance, rebirth
resuscitate *v* **= revive**, save, resurrect, revitalize, bring round
retain *v* **1 = keep**, hold, save, reserve, maintain, preserve, hold back **2 = hire**, pay, reserve, commission, engage, employ
retainer *n* **1 = fee**, advance, deposit **2 = servant**, domestic, attendant
retaliate *v* **= pay someone back**, get back at, get even with, get your own back, hit back, take revenge • *The army will retaliate against any attacks.*
See also: **revenge**

r

DICTIONARY

kind **retaliation** *n* **retaliatory** *adj*
retard Ⓣ *v* delay or slow (progress or development) **retardation** *n*
▸ **retarded** *adj* underdeveloped, esp. mentally
retch Ⓣ *v* try to vomit
retention *n* **1** retaining **2** ability to remember **3** abnormal holding of something, esp. fluid, in the body
▸ **retentive** *adj* capable of retaining or remembering
rethink *v* consider again, esp. with a view to changing one's tactics
reticent Ⓣ *adj* uncommunicative, reserved **reticence** *n*
reticulate *adj* made or arranged like a net **reticulation** *n*
retina *n, pl* **-nas, -nae** light-sensitive membrane at the back of the eye
▸ **retinopathy** *n* any of various noninflammatory diseases of the retina
retinue Ⓣ *n* band of attendants
retire Ⓣ *v* **1** (cause to) give up office or work, esp. through age **2** go away or withdraw **3** go to bed **retirement** *n*
▸ **retired** *adj* having given up work etc.
▸ **retiring** *adj* shy
retort[1] Ⓣ *v* **1** reply quickly, wittily, or angrily ▹ *n* **2** quick, witty, or angry reply
retort[2] *n* glass container with a bent neck used for distilling
retouch *v* restore or improve by new touches, esp. of paint
retrace *v* go back over (a route etc.) again
retract Ⓣ *v* **1** withdraw (a statement etc.) **2** draw in or back **retraction** *n*
▸ **retractable** *or* **retractile** *adj* able to be retracted
retread *v, n* same as **remould**
retreat Ⓣ *v* **1** move back from a position, withdraw ▹ *n* **2** act of or military signal for retiring or withdrawal **3** place to which anyone retires, refuge
retrench Ⓣ *v* reduce expenditure, cut back **retrenchment** *n*
retrial *n* second trial of a case or defendant in a court of law
retribution Ⓣ *n* punishment or vengeance for evil deeds **retributive** *adj*
retrieve Ⓣ *v* **1** fetch back again **2** restore to a better state **3** recover (information) from a computer **retrievable** *adj* **retrieval** *n*
▸ **retriever** *n* dog trained to retrieve shot game
retro *adj* associated with or revived from the past: *retro fashion*
retroactive *adj* effective from a date in the past
retroflex *adj* bent or curved backwards
retrograde Ⓣ *adj* tending towards an earlier worse condition
retrogress Ⓣ *v* go back to an earlier worse condition **retrogression** *n* **retrogressive** *adj*

THESAURUS

retaliation *n* = **revenge**, repayment, reprisal, vengeance, an eye for an eye, counterblow, reciprocation, requital
retard *v* = **slow down**, arrest, delay, check, hinder, impede, handicap, hold back *or* hold up, set back
retch *v* = **gag**, barf (*slang*), vomit, spew, heave, puke (*slang*), regurgitate, throw up (*informal*)
reticence *n* = **silence**, reserve, quietness, taciturnity
reticent *adj* = **uncommunicative**, quiet, silent, tight-lipped, reserved, close-lipped, taciturn, unforthcoming
retinue *n* = **attendants**, escort, entourage, aides, followers, servants
retire *v* **1** = **stop working**, give up work **2** = **withdraw**, leave, exit, depart, go away **3** = **go to bed**, hit the hay (*slang*), hit the sack (*slang*), turn in (*informal*)
retirement *n* = **withdrawal**, privacy, retreat, solitude, seclusion
retiring *adj* = **shy**, quiet, timid, reserved, unassuming, self-effacing, bashful, unassertive
retort *v* **1** = **reply**, return, answer, respond, counter, come back with, riposte ▸ *n* **2** = **reply**, response, answer, comeback (*informal*), rejoinder, riposte
retract *v* **1** = **withdraw**, deny, renounce, revoke, renege, recant, disavow, disclaim, eat one's words, take back **2** = **draw in**, pull back, pull in, sheathe
retreat *v* **1** = **withdraw**, back away, back off, draw back, pull back • *The rebels retreated from the town.* OPPOSITE: advance ▸ *n* **2** = **withdrawal**, flight, evacuation, departure • *the long retreat from the capital* OPPOSITE: advance **3** = **refuge**, haven, sanctuary • *He spent the day hidden away in his country retreat.*
retrench *v* = **economize**, save, cut back, make economies, tighten one's belt
retrenchment *n* = **cutback**, cut, economy, cost-cutting, tightening one's belt
retribution *n* = **punishment**, justice, revenge, retaliation, reprisal, vengeance, reckoning, Nemesis
retrieval *See* **recovery**
retrieve *v* = **get back**, save, recover, restore, regain, recoup, redeem, recapture, win back
retrograde *adj* = **deteriorating**, downward, backward, degenerative, regressive, declining, retrogressive, worsening
retrogress *v* = **deteriorate**, decline, worsen, relapse, backslide, regress, go back, go downhill (*informal*)

DICTIONARY

retrorocket *n* small rocket engine used to slow a spacecraft
retrospect Ⓣ *n* **in retrospect** when looking back on the past
▸ **retrospective** *adj* **1** looking back in time **2** applying from a date in the past ▹ *n* **3** exhibition of an artist's life's work
retroussé [rit-**troo**-say] *adj* (of a nose) turned upwards
retsina *n* resinous Greek wine
return Ⓣ *v* **1** go or come back **2** give, put, or send back **3** reply **4** elect **5** *football* catch (a kicked ball) and run forward with it ▹ *n* **6** returning **7** being returned **8** profit **9** official report, as of taxable income **10** *Brit* return ticket **returnable** *adj*
▸ **returning officer** person in charge of an election
▸ **return ticket** ticket allowing a passenger to travel to a place and back
reunify *v* bring or come together again after separation or division **reunification** *n*
reunion Ⓣ *n* gathering of people who have been apart
▸ **reunite** *v* bring or come together again after a separation
reuse *v* use again **reusable** *adj*
Reuter *n* Baron **Paul Julius von**, original name *Israel Beer Josaphat*. 1816–99, German telegrapher, who founded a news agency in London (1851)
rev *informal* ▹ *n* **1** revolution (of an engine) ▹ *v* **revving, revved 2** (foll. by *up*) increase the speed of revolution of (an engine)
Rev., Revd. Reverend
revalue *v* adjust the exchange value of (a currency) upwards **revaluation** *n*
revamp Ⓣ *v* renovate or restore
reveal Ⓣ *v* **1** make known **2** expose or show
revelation *n*
reveille [riv-**val**-ee] *n* morning bugle call to waken soldiers
revel Ⓣ *v* **-elling, -elled 1** take pleasure (in) **2** make merry ▹ *n* **3** *usu pl* merrymaking
reveller *n*
▸ **revelry** *n* festivity
revenge Ⓣ *n* **1** retaliation for wrong done ▹ *v* **2** avenge (oneself or another) **3** make retaliation for **revengeful** *adj*
revenue Ⓣ *n* income, esp. of a state, as taxes
reverberate Ⓣ *v* echo or resound
reverberation *n*
revere Ⓣ *v* be in awe of and respect greatly
▸ **reverence** *n* awe mingled with respect and esteem
▸ **Reverend** *adj* (as a prefix to a clergyman's name) worthy of reverence
▸ **reverent** *adj* showing reverence
reverently *adv*
▸ **reverential** *adj* marked by reverence
Revere *n* **Paul**. 1735–1818, American patriot and silversmith, best known for

THESAURUS

retrospect *n* = **hindsight**, review, re-examination
return *v* **1** = **go back**, reappear, come back, turn back • *The plane failed to return at the scheduled time.* **2** = **give back**, refund, reimburse, repay, pay back, recompense • *You can return the coat if it doesn't fit.* **3** = **put back**, replace, restore, reinstate, re-establish **4** = **reply**, answer, respond, retort **5** = **elect**, choose, vote in ▸ *n* **6** = **restoration**, reinstatement, re-establishment **7** = **reappearance**, recurrence **8** = **retreat**, rebound, recoil **9** = **profit**, interest, gain, income, revenue, yield, proceeds, takings **10** = **report**, list, statement, form, account, summary **11** = **reply**, response, answer, comeback (*informal*), retort, rejoinder
See also: **vote**
reunion *See* **meeting**
revamp *v* = **renovate**, restore, overhaul, refurbish, do up (*informal*), recondition
reveal *v* **1** = **make known**, announce, disclose, divulge, get off your chest (*informal*) • *They were not ready to reveal any of the details.* **2** = **uncover**, unveil, unearth, bring to light, lay bare • *The carpet was removed to reveal the original pine floor.*
See also: **betray, expose, indicate, show**
revel *v* **1** = **celebrate**, carouse, live it up (*informal*), make merry ▹ **revel in** = **enjoy**, relish, delight in, indulge in, lap up, luxuriate in, take pleasure in, thrive on ▸ *n* **2** (*often pl*) = **merrymaking**, party, celebration, festivity, spree, carousal
revelation *n* = **disclosure**, news, exposure, exhibition, publication, proclamation, unveiling, exposé, uncovering, unearthing
reveller *n* = **merrymaker**, partygoer, carouser
revelry *n* = **festivity**, party, fun, celebration, spree, carousal, jollity, merrymaking
revenge *n* **1** = **retaliation**, reprisal, vengeance, retribution • *acts of revenge* ▸ *v* **2** = **avenge**, retaliate, get even, get your own back, hit back, pay someone back • *He vowed to revenge himself on his enemies.*
revenue *n* = **income**, gain, yield, proceeds, profits, receipts, returns, takings
reverberate *v* = **echo**, ring, resound, vibrate, re-echo
revere *v* = **be in awe of**, respect, honor, worship, reverence, venerate, exalt, look up to
reverence *n* = **awe**, respect, honor, worship, admiration, high esteem, veneration
reverent *adj* = **respectful**, humble,

DICTIONARY

his night ride on April 18, 1775, to warn the Massachusetts colonists of the coming of the British troops
reverie Ⓣ *n* absent-minded daydream
reverse Ⓣ *v* **1** turn upside down or the other way round **2** change completely **3** move (a vehicle) backwards ▹ *n* **4** opposite or contrary **5** back side, obverse **6** defeat **7** reverse gear **8** *football* play in which a player gives the ball to a teammate running in the opposite direction ▹ *adj* **9** opposite or contrary **reversal** *n* **reversible** *adj*
▸ **reverse gear** mechanism enabling a vehicle to move backwards
revert Ⓣ *v* **1** return to a former state **2** come back to a subject **3** (of property) return to its former owner
▸ **reversion** *n* (of property) rightful passing to the owner, designated heir, etc.
revetment *n* facing of stone, sandbags, etc. for a wall
review Ⓣ *v* **1** hold or write a review of **2** examine, reconsider, or look back on **3** inspect formally ▹ *n* **4** critical assessment of a book, concert, etc. **5** periodical with critical articles **6** general survey **7** inspection of troops
▸ **reviewer** *n* writer of reviews
revile Ⓣ *v* be abusively scornful of
revise Ⓣ *v* **1** change or alter **2** look over and correct **3** restudy (work) in preparation for an examination **revision** *n*
revive Ⓣ *v* bring or come back to life, vigour, use, etc.
▸ **revival** *n* **1** reviving or renewal **2** movement seeking to restore religious faith **revivalism** *n* **revivalist** *n*
revoke Ⓣ *v* cancel (a will, agreement, etc.) **revocation** *n*
revolt Ⓣ *n* **1** uprising against authority ▹ *v* **2** rise in rebellion **3** cause to feel disgust
▸ **revolting** *adj* disgusting, horrible
revolution Ⓣ *n* **1** overthrow of a government by the governed **2** great change **3** complete rotation **4** spinning round **revolutionary** *adj, n*

THESAURUS

deferential, awed, reverential
reverie *n* = **daydream**, abstraction, brown study, woolgathering
reverse *v* **1** = **change**, overturn, retract, overrule, invalidate • *They won't reverse the decision to increase prices.* **2** = **turn around**, upend, invert, transpose, turn back, turn over, turn upside down **3** = **go backwards**, back, retreat, back up, move backwards ▸ *n* **4** = **opposite**, contrary, converse • *The reverse seldom applies.* **5** = **back**, rear, underside, other side, wrong side **6** = **misfortune**, blow, failure, setback, disappointment, reversal, mishap, hardship, adversity, misadventure, affliction ▸ *adj* **7** = **opposite**, contrary, converse
revert *v* = **return**, resume, come back, go back
review *n* **1** = **critique**, notice, criticism, commentary • *The school play received excellent reviews.* **2** = **survey**, report, study, analysis, examination • *a review of safety procedures* **3** = **magazine**, journal, periodical **4** (*Mil*) = **inspection**, parade, march past ▸ *v* **5** = **assess**, study, judge, criticize, evaluate **6** = **reconsider**, revise, rethink, reassess, re-examine, re-evaluate, think over **7** = **look back on**, recall, remember, recollect, reflect on **8** = **inspect**, examine
See also: **summary**
reviewer *n* = **critic**, judge, commentator
revile *v* = **malign**, abuse, knock (*informal*), denigrate, reproach, bad-mouth (*slang*), run down, vilify
revise *v* = **change**, update, correct, edit, revamp, amend • *The second edition was completely revised.*
revision *n* = **change**, amendment, correction, emendation, updating
revival *n* = **renewal**, resurgence, renaissance, rebirth, revitalization, resurrection, reawakening
revive *v* = **revitalize**, rally, resuscitate • *an attempt to revive the stagnant economy*
See also: **recover, refresh**
revoke *v* = **cancel**, withdraw, reverse, quash, retract, rescind, repeal, negate, annul, nullify, invalidate, countermand, disclaim, obviate, set aside
revolt *n* **1** = **uprising**, insurgency, revolution, rebellion, rising, insurrection, mutiny ▸ *v* **2** = **rebel**, rise, resist, mutiny **3** = **disgust**, sicken, repel, nauseate, repulse, gross out (*slang*), make one's flesh creep, turn one's stomach
revolting *adj* = **disgusting**, foul, horrible, repellent, sickening, horrid, repulsive, repugnant, nauseating, scuzzy (*slang*), yucky *or* yukky (*slang*)
revolution *n* **1** = **revolt**, insurgency, coup, rebellion, uprising, rising, mutiny **2** = **transformation**, shift, innovation, upheaval, reformation, sea change **3** = **rotation**, turn, cycle, circle, spin, orbit, lap, circuit
revolutionary *adj* **1** = **rebel**, insurgent, extremist, radical, subversive **2** = **innovative**, new, different, novel, radical, progressive, drastic, ground-breaking ▸ *n* **3** = **rebel**, insurgent, revolutionist

DICTIONARY

▶ **revolutionize** *v* change considerably
revolve Ⓣ *v* **1** turn round, rotate **2** (foll. by *around*) be centred (on)
▶ **revolver** *n* repeating pistol
revue *n* theatrical entertainment with topical sketches and songs
revulsion Ⓣ *n* strong disgust
reward Ⓣ *n* **1** something given in return for a service **2** sum of money offered for finding a criminal or missing property ▷ *v* **3** pay or give something to (someone) for a service, information, etc.
▶ **rewarding** *adj* giving personal satisfaction, worthwhile
rewind *v* run (a tape or film) back to an earlier point in order to replay
rewire *v* provide (a house, engine, etc.) with new wiring
rewrite *v* **1** write again in a different way ▷ *n* **2** something rewritten
Reynolds *n* Sir **Joshua**. 1723–92, English portrait painter. He was the first president of the Royal Academy (1768): the annual lectures he gave there, published as *Discourses*, are important contributions to art theory and criticism
Rh rhesus
rhapsody *n, pl* **-dies 1** freely structured emotional piece of music **2** expression of ecstatic enthusiasm **rhapsodic** *adj*
▶ **rhapsodize** *v* speak or write with extravagant enthusiasm
rhea [**ree**-a] *n* S American three-toed ostrich
rheostat *n* instrument for varying the resistance of an electric circuit
rhesus [**ree**-suss] *n* small long-tailed monkey of S Asia
▶ **rhesus factor** *or* **Rh factor** feature distinguishing different types of human blood
rhetoric Ⓣ [**ret**-a-rik] *n* **1** art of effective speaking or writing **2** artificial or exaggerated language
▶ **rhetorical** [rit-**tor**-ik-kal] *adj* (of a question) not requiring an answer **rhetorically** *adv*
rheum [**room**] *n* watery discharge from the eyes or nose **rheumy** *adj*
rheumatism *n* painful inflammation of joints or muscles
▶ **rheumatic** *n, adj* (person) affected by rheumatism
▶ **rheumatoid** *adj* of or like rheumatism
Rh factor *n* see **rhesus**
rhinestone *n* imitation diamond
rhino *n* short for **rhinoceros**
rhinoceros *n, pl* **-oses, -os** large thick-skinned animal with one or two horns on its nose
rhizome *n* thick underground stem producing new plants
Rhodes *n* **Cecil John**. 1853–1902, British colonial financier and statesman in South Africa. He made a fortune in diamond and gold mining and, as prime minister of the Cape Colony (1890–96), he helped to extend British territory. He established the annual Rhodes scholarships to Oxford
rhodium *n* hard metal like platinum
rhododendron *n* evergreen flowering shrub
rhombus *n, pl* **-buses, -bi** parallelogram with sides of equal length but no right angles, diamond-shaped figure
▶ **rhomboid** *n* parallelogram with adjacent sides of unequal length
rhubarb *n* garden plant of which the fleshy stalks are cooked as fruit
rhumba *n* same as **rumba**
rhyme Ⓣ *n* **1** sameness of the final sounds at the ends of lines of verse, or in words **2** word or syllable identical in sound to another **3** verse marked by rhyme ▷ *v* **4** make a rhyme
rhythm Ⓣ *n* measured beat esp. of words, music, etc. **rhythmic** *or* **rhythmical** *adj* **rhythmically** *adv*
▶ **rhythm and blues** popular music, orig. Black American, influenced by the blues
rib[1] *n* **1** one of the curved bones forming

THESAURUS

revolutionize *v* = **transform**, reform, modernize
revolve *v* = **rotate**, turn, circle, spin, orbit, twist, wheel, whirl, go round
revulsion *n* = **disgust**, loathing, abhorrence, detestation, repugnance, repulsion
reward *n* **1** = **payment**, bonus, bounty, prize • *As a reward for good behaviour, praise your child.* **2** = **punishment**, retribution, just deserts ▶ *v* **3** = **pay**, compensate, repay, remunerate, recompense
rewarding *adj* = **worthwhile**, valuable, productive, profitable, beneficial, fruitful, enriching, fulfilling, satisfying
rhapsodize *v* = **enthuse**, rave (*informal*), gush, go into ecstasies
rhetoric *n* **1** = **oratory**, eloquence **2** = **hyperbole**, bombast, grandiloquence, magniloquence, verbosity, wordiness
rhetorical *adj* = **oratorical**, bombastic, verbose, declamatory, grandiloquent, high-flown, magniloquent
rhyme *n* **1** = **poetry**, song, poem, verse, ode ▶ *v* **2** = **sound like**, harmonize
rhythm *n* = **beat**, time, pulse, tempo • *His body twists and sways to the rhythm.*
rhythmic, rhythmical *adj* = **cadenced**, musical, periodic, lilting, metrical,

DICTIONARY

the framework of the upper part of the body **2** cut of meat including the rib(s) **3** curved supporting part, as in the hull of a boat **4** raised series of rows in knitting ▷ *v* **ribbing, ribbed 5** provide or mark with ribs **6** knit to form a rib pattern **ribbed** *adj* **ribbing** *n*
▸ **ribcage** *n* bony structure of ribs enclosing the lungs
rib² *v* **ribbing, ribbed** *informal* tease or ridicule **ribbing** *n*
ribald Ⓣ *adj* humorously or mockingly rude or obscene **ribaldry** *n*
ribbon *n* **1** narrow band of fabric used for trimming, tying, etc. **2** any long strip, for example of inked tape in a typewriter
Ribera *n* **José** (*or* **Jusepe**) **de**, Italian nickname *Lo Spagnoletto* (The Little Spaniard). 1591–1652, Spanish artist, living in Italy. His religious pictures often dwell on horrible suffering, presented in realistic detail
riboflavin [rye-boe-**flay**-vin] *n* form of vitamin B
rice *n* **1** cereal plant grown on wet ground in warm countries **2** its seeds as food
rich Ⓣ *adj* **1** owning a lot of money or property, wealthy **2** fertile **3** abounding **4** valuable **5** (of food) containing much fat or sugar **6** mellow **7** amusing **richness** *n*
▸ **riches** *pl n* wealth
▸ **richly** *adv* **1** elaborately **2** fully
Rich *n* **Buddy**, real name *Bernard Rich*. 1917–87, US jazz drummer and band leader
Richard *n* **Maurice**, full name *Joseph-Henri-Maurice Richard*, known as *The Rocket*. 1921–2000, Canadian ice-hockey player and holder of many scoring records
Richard I *n* nicknamed *Coeur de Lion* or *the Lion-Heart*. 1157–99, king of England (1189–99); a leader of the third crusade (joining it in 1191). On his way home, he was captured in Austria (1192) and held to ransom. After a brief return to England, where he was crowned again (1194), he spent the rest of his life in France
Richard II *n* 1367–1400, king of England (1377–99), whose reign was troubled by popular discontent and baronial opposition. He was forced to abdicate in favour of Henry Bolingbroke, who became Henry IV
Richard III *n* 1452–85, king of England (1483–85), notorious as the suspected murderer of his two young nephews in the Tower of London. He proved an able administrator until his brief reign was ended by his death at the hands of Henry Tudor (later Henry VII) at the battle of Bosworth Field
Richardson *n* Sir **Ralph** (**David**). 1902–83, British stage and screen actor
Richelieu *n* **Armand Jean du Plessis.** 1585–1642, French statesman and cardinal, principal minister to Louis XIII and virtual ruler of France (1624–42). He destroyed the power of the Huguenots and strengthened the crown in France and the role of France in Europe
Richler *n* **Mordecai**. 1931–2001, Canadian novelist. His novels include *St Urbain's Horseman* (1971), *Solomon Gursky Was Here* (1990), and *Barney's Version* (1997)
Richter scale *n* scale for measuring the intensity of earthquakes
rick¹ *n* stack of hay etc.
rick² *v, n* sprain or wrench
rickets *n* disease of children marked by softening of the bones, bow legs, etc., caused by vitamin D deficiency
rickety Ⓣ *adj* shaky or unstable
rickshaw *n* light two-wheeled man-drawn Asian vehicle
ricochet Ⓣ [**rik**-osh-ay] *v* **1** (of a bullet) rebound from a solid surface ▷ *n* **2** such a rebound
rid Ⓣ *v* **ridding, rid** clear or relieve (of)
▸ **get rid of** free oneself of (something undesirable)
▸ **good riddance** relief at getting rid of something or someone
ridden *v* **1** past participle of **ride** ▷ *adj*

THESAURUS

pulsating, throbbing
ribald *adj* = **rude**, blue, broad, naughty, coarse, bawdy, earthy, obscene, racy, vulgar, smutty
rich *adj* **1** = **wealthy**, affluent, prosperous, loaded (*slang*), opulent, well off • *You're going to be a very rich person.* OPPOSITE: poor **2** = **abundant**, plentiful, fertile • *Bananas are rich in vitamin A.* **3** = **well-stocked**, full, productive, well-supplied **4** = **full-bodied**, sweet, fatty, tasty, creamy, luscious, succulent
See also: **colourful**
riches *pl n* = **wealth**, substance, plenty, fortune, treasure, affluence, assets, resources
richly *adv* **1** = **elaborately**, elegantly, exquisitely, lavishly, luxuriously, sumptuously, expensively, gorgeously, opulently, splendidly **2** = **fully**, well, properly, thoroughly, appropriately, suitably, amply
rickety *adj* = **shaky**, precarious, insecure, unsteady, wobbly, ramshackle, unsound, tottering
ricochet *See* **bounce**
rid *v* = **free**, clear, deliver, relieve, purge, disburden, disencumber, make free, unburden ▷ **get rid of** = **dispose of**, remove,

DICTIONARY

2 afflicted or affected by the thing specified: *disease-ridden*

riddle[1] Ⓣ *n* **1** question made puzzling to test one's ingenuity **2** puzzling person or thing

riddle[2] Ⓣ *v* **1** pierce with many holes ▷ *n* **2** coarse sieve for gravel etc.

▸ **riddled with** full of

ride Ⓣ *v* **riding, rode, ridden 1** sit on and control or propel (a horse, bicycle, etc.) **2** go on horseback or in a vehicle **3** be carried on or across **4** travel over **5** lie at anchor ▷ *n* **6** journey on a horse etc., or in a vehicle **7** type of movement experienced in a vehicle

▸ **rider** *n* **1** person who rides **2** supplementary clause added to a document

▸ **ride up** *v* (of a garment) move up from the proper position

RIDE (in Ontario) Reduce Impaired Driving Everywhere: program of police spot checks of drivers

ridge Ⓣ *n* **1** long narrow hill **2** long narrow raised part on a surface **3** line where two sloping surfaces meet **4** elongated area of high pressure **ridged** *adj*

ridiculous Ⓣ *adj* deserving to be laughed at, absurd

▸ **ridicule** *n* **1** treatment of a person or thing as ridiculous ▷ *v* **2** laugh at, make fun of

riding *n* electoral constituency

▸ **riding association** branch of a political party at the riding level

Ridley *n* **Nicholas**. ?1500–55, English bishop, who helped to revise the liturgy under Edward VI. He was burnt at the stake for refusing to disavow his Protestant beliefs when Mary I assumed the throne

Rie *n* Dame **Lucie**, original name *Lucie Gomperz*. 1902–95, British potter, born in Austria

Riefenstahl *n* **Leni**. 1902–2003, German photographer and film director, best known for her Nazi propaganda films, such as *Triumph of the Will* (1934)

riesling *n* type of white wine

rife Ⓣ *adj* widespread or common

▸ **rife with** full of

riff *n jazz, rock* short repeated melodic figure

riffle *v* flick through (pages etc.) quickly

riffraff Ⓣ *n* rabble, disreputable people

rifle[1] *n* firearm with a long barrel

rifle[2] Ⓣ *v* **1** search and rob **2** ransack

rift Ⓣ *n* **1** break in friendly relations **2** crack, split, or cleft

▸ **rift valley** long narrow valley resulting from subsidence between faults

rig Ⓣ *v* **rigging, rigged 1** arrange in a dishonest way **2** (often foll. by *up*) set up, esp. as a makeshift **3** equip **4** provide (a ship) with spars, ropes, etc. ▷ *n* **5** apparatus for drilling for oil and gas **6** way a ship's masts and sails are arranged **7** Also **rigout** *informal* outfit of clothes

▸ **rigging** *n* ship's spars and ropes

right Ⓣ *adj* **1** just **2** in accordance with truth and duty **3** true **4** correct **5** proper **6** of the side that faces east when the front is turned to the north **7** Also **right-wing** *politics* conservative or reactionary **8** straight **9** upright **10** of the outer side of a fabric ▷ *v* **11** bring or come back to a vertical position **12** do justice to ▷ *n* **13** claim, title, etc. allowed or due **14** what is just or due **15** conservative political party ▷ *adv* **16** straight **17** properly **18** very **19** on or to the

THESAURUS

dump, eject, jettison, weed out • *a coach who wanted to get rid of me*

riddle *n* = **puzzle**, problem, mystery, conundrum, enigma, poser

riddled *adj* = **filled**, damaged, infested, permeated, pervaded, spoilt

ride *v* **1** = **control**, manage, handle **2** = **travel**, go, move, be carried ▸ *n* **3** = **trip**, drive, lift, journey, outing, jaunt

ridge *See* **top**

ridicule *n* **1** = **mockery**, laughter, scorn, jeer, derision, chaff, gibe, raillery ▸ *v* **2** = **laugh at**, mock, jeer, deride, sneer, chaff, make fun of, poke fun at

ridiculous *adj* = **laughable**, absurd, ludicrous, preposterous • *It is ridiculous to suggest we are having secret meetings.*
See also: **crazy, silly**

rife *adj* = **widespread**, general, common, frequent, universal, rampant, prevalent, ubiquitous

riffraff *n* = **rabble**, dregs of society (*slang*), hoi polloi, scum of the earth (*slang*)

rifle *v* = **ransack**, strip, sack, rob, loot, plunder, pillage, burglarize, go through

rift *n* **1** = **breach**, division, split, separation, disagreement, quarrel, falling out (*informal*) **2** = **split**, break, opening, crack, gap, flaw, fault, fissure, cleft, crevice

rig *v* **1** = **fix** (*informal*), engineer, arrange, manipulate, gerrymander, tamper with **2** = **equip**, furnish, fit out, supply, outfit ▷ **rig out** = **dress**, clothe, costume, array, attire; = **equip**, fit, furnish, outfit ▷ **rig up** = **set up**, build, arrange, assemble, construct, erect, improvize, fix up, put together, put up ▸ *n* **3** = **apparatus**, equipment, tackle, gear, fittings, fixtures

right *adj* **1** = **correct**, true, strict, accurate, exact, valid, genuine, precise, factual • *That clock never tells the right time.* OPPOSITE: wrong **2** = **proper**, fit, OK (*informal*), appropriate, acceptable, suitable, fitting, desirable, done, seemly • *The time is right for*

DICTIONARY

right side **rightly** *adv* **rightful** *adj*
▸ **in the right** morally or legally correct
▸ **right away** immediately
▸ **rightist** *n, adj* (person) on the political right
▸ **right angle** angle of 90°
▸ **right field** *baseball* area of the outfield to the batter's right
▸ **right fielder** *baseball* fielder who covers right field
▸ **right-handed** *adj* using or for the right hand
▸ **right-hand man** person's most valuable assistant
▸ **Right Honourable** (in Canada) title of respect given for life to the Prime Minister, the Governor General, and the Chief Justice of the Supreme Court
▸ **right of way** *law* **1** right of one vehicle to go before another **2** legal right to pass over someone's land
▸ **righty** *n informal* **1** right-handed person **2** *baseball* right-handed pitcher
righteous Ⓣ [**rye**-chuss] *adj* **1** upright, godly, or virtuous **2** morally justified **righteousness** *n*
rigid Ⓣ *adj* **1** inflexible or strict **2** unyielding or stiff **rigidly** *adv* **rigidity** *n*
rigmarole Ⓣ *n* **1** meaningless string of words **2** long complicated procedure
rigor mortis *n* stiffening of the body after death
rigour, rigor Ⓣ *n* **1** harshness, severity, or strictness **2** hardship
▸ **rigorous** *adj* harsh, severe, or stern
rile Ⓣ *v* anger or annoy
Riley *n* **Bridget** (**Louise**). born 1931, British painter, best known for her black-and-white op art paintings of the 1960s
Rilke *n* **Rainer Maria**. 1875–1926, Austro-German poet, born in Prague. Author of intense visionary lyrics, notably in the *Duino Elegies* (1922) and *Sonnets to Orpheus* (1923)
rill *n* small stream
rim Ⓣ *n* **1** edge or border **2** outer ring of a wheel **rimmed** *adj*
Rimbaud *n* **Arthur**. 1854–91, French poet, whose work, culminating in the prose poetry of *Illuminations* (published 1884), greatly influenced the symbolists. *A Season in Hell* (1873) draws on his tempestuous homosexual affair with Verlaine, after which he abandoned writing (aged around 20) and spent the rest of his life travelling
rime *n lit* hoarfrost
Rimsky-Korsakov *n* **Nikolai Andreyevich**. 1844–1908, Russian composer; noted for such works as the orchestral suite *Scheherazade* (1888) and the opera *Le Coq d'or* (first performed in 1910)
rind Ⓣ *n* outer coating of fruits, cheese, or bacon
ring[1] Ⓣ *v* **ringing, rang, rung 1** give out a clear resonant sound, as a bell **2** resound **3** cause (a bell) to sound **4** Also **ring up**

THESAURUS

our escape. **3 = just**, good, fair, proper, moral, ethical, honest, lawful, equitable
▸ *n* **4 = justice**, honour, equity, integrity, fairness, virtue, morality, legality • *At least he knew right from wrong.* **5 = prerogative**, business, claim, power, authority, due, freedom, licence, permission, privilege, liberty ▸ *adv* **6 = correctly**, exactly, truly, precisely, accurately, genuinely **7 = properly**, appropriately, suitably, fittingly, aptly **8 = straight**, quickly, directly, promptly, straightaway **9 = exactly**, precisely, squarely ▹ **right away** *adv* **= immediately**, now, directly, instantly, straightaway, at once, forthwith, pronto (*informal*) ▹ **right now** *See* **now** ▸ *v* **10 = rectify**, settle, fix, correct, redress, straighten, put right, sort out
See also: **immediately**
righteous *adj* **= virtuous**, good, just, fair, moral, ethical, honest, pure, upright, honorable
righteousness *n* **= virtue**, justice, integrity, honesty, honour, morality, goodness, purity, probity, rectitude, uprightness
rightful *adj* **= lawful**, just, real, legal, due, true, proper, legitimate, valid
right-hand man *See* **assistant, helper**
righting *See* **correction**
right-wing *adj* **= conservative**, reactionary • *some right-wing groups*
rigid *adj* **1 = strict**, set, stringent, inflexible, fixed • *Hospital routines for nurses are sometimes very rigid.* **2 = stiff**, hard, firm, solid • *rigid plastic containers* OPPOSITE: flexible
See also: **tense, tight**
rigmarole *n* **= procedure**, bother, nonsense, fuss, hassle (*informal*), palaver
rigorous *adj* **= strict**, hard, tough, severe, harsh, stringent, stern, demanding, exacting, inflexible
rigorously *See* **well**
rigour, rigor *n* **1 = strictness**, rigidity, harshness, inflexibility, sternness, stringency **2 = hardship**, trial, suffering, ordeal, privation
rig-out *n* **= outfit**, dress, gear (*informal*), costume, garb, get-up (*informal*), togs
rile *v* **= anger**, aggravate (*informal*), irk, annoy, irritate, get one's back up *or* put one's back up
rim *n* **= edge**, border, margin, brink, lip, verge, brim
rind *n* **= skin**, peel, crust, husk, outer layer
ring[1] *v* **1 = chime**, toll, resonate, clang, peal

r

DICTIONARY

telephone ▷ *n* **5** ringing **6** telephone call
ring² 🅣 *n* **1** circle of gold etc., esp. for a finger **2** any circular band, coil, or rim **3** circle of people **4** enclosed area, esp. a circle for a circus or a roped-in square for boxing **5** group operating (illegal) control of a market ▷ *v* **6** put a ring round **7** mark (a bird) with a ring **8** kill (a tree) by cutting the bark round the trunk
▸ **ringer** *n slang* person or thing apparently identical to another (Also **dead ringer)**
▸ **ringlet** *n* curly lock of hair
▸ **ringleader** *n* instigator of a mutiny, riot, etc.
▸ **ring road** *Brit* main road that bypasses a town (centre)
▸ **ringtone** *n* tune played by a cell phone when it receives a call
▸ **ringside** *n* row of seats nearest a boxing or circus ring
▸ **ringworm** *n* fungal skin disease in circular patches
ringette *n sports* game similar to hockey, with a rubber ring used instead of a puck
rink *n* **1** sheet of ice for skating or ice hockey **2** floor for roller skating
▸ **rink rat** *slang* youth who helps with chores at an ice-hockey rink in return for free admission to games
rinse 🅣 *v* **1** remove soap from (washed clothes, hair, etc.) by applying clean water **2** wash lightly ▷ *n* **3** rinsing **4** liquid to tint hair
Riopelle *n* **Jean-Paul**. 1923–2002, Canadian painter, sculptor, and engraver
riot 🅣 *n* **1** disorderly unruly disturbance **2** loud revelry **3** *slang* very amusing person or thing **4** profusion ▷ *v* **5** take part in a riot
▸ **read the riot act** reprimand severely
▸ **run riot 1** behave without restraint **2** grow profusely
▸ **riotous** *adj* **1** unrestrained **2** unruly or rebellious
rip 🅣 *v* **ripping, ripped 1** tear violently **2** tear away **3** *informal* rush ▷ *n* **4** split or tear
▸ **let rip** act or speak without restraint
▸ **ripcord** *n* cord pulled to open a parachute
▸ **rip off** *v slang* cheat by overcharging
▸ **rip-off** *n slang* cheat or swindle
▸ **rip-roaring** *adj informal* boisterous and exciting
RIP rest in peace
riparian [rip-**pair**-ee-an] *adj* of or on the banks of a river
ripe 🅣 *adj* **1** mature enough to be eaten or used **2** fully developed in mind or body **3** suitable: *wait until the time is ripe*
▸ **ripen** *v* **1** grow ripe **2** mature
riposte 🅣 [rip-**posst**] *n* **1** verbal retort **2** counterattack ▷ *v* **3** make a riposte
ripple 🅣 *n* **1** slight wave, ruffling of a surface **2** sound like ripples of water ▷ *v* **3** flow or form into little waves (on) **4** (of sounds) rise and fall gently
rise 🅣 *v* **rising, rose, risen 1** get up **2** move upwards **3** (of the sun or moon) appear above the horizon **4** reach a higher level **5** (of an amount or price) increase **6** rebel **7** (of a court) adjourn **8** have its source ▷ *n* **9** rising **10** upward slope **11** *Brit* raise
▸ **get a rise out of** *slang* provoke an angry reaction from

THESAURUS

• *He heard the school bell ring.* ▸ *n* **2 = chime**, knell, peal
See also: **sound**
ring² *n* **1 = circle**, round, band, hoop, loop • *a ring of blue smoke* **2 = gang**, cell, band, syndicate • *a drug-trafficking ring* **3 = arena**, rink, circus, enclosure ▸ *v* **4 = encircle**, surround, enclose, gird, girdle
ringleader *See* **leader**
rinse *v* **= wash**, clean, dip, splash, cleanse, bathe
riot *n* **1 = disturbance**, disorder, strife, anarchy, mob violence • *a prison riot* **2 = revelry**, festivity, frolic, carousal, high jinks, merrymaking **3 = profusion**, show, display, splash, extravaganza ▷ **run riot = rampage**, be out of control, go wild; **= grow profusely**, spread like wildfire ▸ *v* **4 = rampage**, go on the rampage, run riot, take to the streets • *They rioted in protest against the government.*
riotous *adj* **1 = unrestrained**, wild, loud, noisy, boisterous, uproarious **2 = unruly**, violent, disorderly, lawless, rowdy, rebellious, anarchic, ungovernable
rip *v* **1 = tear**, cut, split, slash, burst, claw, gash, slit, lacerate, rend ▷ **rip off** (*Slang*) **= swindle**, rob, con (*informal*), cheat, defraud, fleece ▸ *n* **2 = tear**, cut, hole, split, slash, rent, gash, slit, laceration
ripe *adj* **1 = mature**, ready, seasoned, mellow, ripened **2 = suitable**, right, ideal, timely, opportune, favourable, auspicious
ripen *v* **= mature**, season, develop, burgeon, grow ripe
rip-off *n* **= swindle**, fraud, theft, scam (*slang*), con (*informal*), cheat, con trick (*informal*)
riposte *n* **1 = retort**, response, answer, comeback (*informal*), reply, rejoinder, sally ▸ *v* **2 = retort**, answer, respond, reply, come back
ripple *See* **wave**
rise *v* **1 = go up**, climb, ascend, move up • *smoke rising from the volcano* **2 = increase**, grow, mount, intensify, go up • *House prices are expected to rise this year.* OPPOSITE:

DICTIONARY

▸ **give rise to** cause
▸ **riser** *n* **1** person who rises, esp. from bed **2** vertical part of a step
▸ **rising** *n* **1** revolt ▹ *adj* **2** increasing in rank or maturity
risible [**riz**-zib-bl] *adj* causing laughter, ridiculous
risk Ⓣ *n* **1** chance of disaster or loss **2** person or thing considered as a potential hazard ▹ *v* **3** act in spite of the possibility of (injury or loss) **4** expose to danger or loss
▸ **risky** *adj* full of risk, dangerous **riskily** *adv*
risotto *n, pl* **-tos** dish of rice cooked in stock with vegetables, meat, etc.
risqué Ⓣ [**risk**-ay] *adj* making slightly rude references to sex
rissole *n* cake of minced meat, coated with breadcrumbs and fried
rite Ⓣ *n* formal practice or custom, esp. religious
▸ **ritual** *n* **1** prescribed order of rites **2** regular repeated action or behaviour ▹ *adj* **3** concerning rites **ritually** *adv*
▸ **ritualistic** *adj* like a ritual
ritzy Ⓣ *adj* **ritzier, ritziest** *slang* luxurious or elegant
rival Ⓣ *n* **1** person or thing that competes with or equals another for favour, success, etc. ▹ *adj* **2** in the position of a rival ▹ *v* **-valling, -valled 3** (try to) equal
▸ **rivalry** *n* keen competition
riven *adj* split
river Ⓣ *n* **1** large natural stream of water **2** copious flow
Rivera *n* **Diego**. 1886–1957, Mexican painter, noted for his monumental murals in public buildings, which are influenced by Aztec art and depict revolutionary themes
rivet [**riv**-vit] *n* **1** bolt for fastening metal plates, the end being put through holes and then beaten flat ▹ *v* **riveting, riveted 2** cause to be fixed, as in fascination **3** fasten with rivets **riveter** *n*
▸ **riveting** *adj* very interesting and exciting
rivulet *n* small stream
Rizzio, Riccio *n* **David**. ?1533–66, Italian musician and courtier who became the secretary and favourite of Mary, Queen of Scots. He was murdered at the instigation of a group of nobles, including Mary's husband, Darnley
RN Royal Navy
RNA ribonucleic acid: substance in living cells essential for the synthesis of protein
roach[1] *n* freshwater fish
roach[2] *n US* cockroach
Roach *n* **Hal**, full name *Harald Eugene Roach*. 1892–1992, US film producer, whose company produced numerous comedy films in the 1920s and 1930s, including those featuring Harold Lloyd and Laurel and Hardy
road Ⓣ *n* **1** way prepared for passengers, vehicles, etc. **2** way or course: *the road to fame* **3** street **roadside** *n, adj*
▸ **on the road** travelling

THESAURUS

fall **3 = get up**, arise, get to one's feet, stand up **4 = get steeper**, ascend, go uphill, slope upwards **5 = rebel**, revolt, mutiny **6 = originate**, issue, happen, spring, occur ▹ **rise to** *See* **reach** ▸ *n* **7 = increase**, improvement, upsurge • *a rise in prices* OPPOSITE: fall **8 = advancement**, progress, climb, promotion **9 = upward slope**, ascent, incline, elevation ▹ **give rise to = cause**, produce, effect, bring about, result in
See also: **gain, jump, slope**
risk *n* **1 = danger**, gamble, peril, pitfall • *That's a risk I'm happy to take.* ▸ *v* **2 = dare**, chance, gamble, jeopardize, put in jeopardy • *If he doesn't play, he risks losing his place in the team.*
See also: **endanger, possibility, threat**
risky *adj* **= dangerous**, chancy (*informal*), unsafe, uncertain, hazardous, perilous
risqué *adj* **= suggestive**, blue, improper, naughty, bawdy, indelicate, racy, ribald
rite *n* **= ceremony**, practice, procedure, custom, ritual, observance
ritual *n* **1 = ceremony**, rite, observance **2 = custom**, practice, procedure, convention, tradition, routine, habit, protocol ▸ *adj* **3 = ceremonial**, routine, conventional, customary, habitual
ritzy *adj* (*Slang*) **= luxurious**, grand, luxury, posh (*informal, chiefly Brit*), plush (*informal*), deluxe, sumptuous, swanky *or* swank (*informal*), high-class
rival *n* **1 = opponent**, challenger, adversary, antagonist • *She is well ahead of her nearest rival.* ▸ *v* **2 = equal**, match, be a match for • *For beauty, few beaches rival those of Prince Edward Island.* ▸ *adj* **3 = competing**, conflicting, opposing
See also: **competitor**
rivalry *n* **= competition**, opposition, contest, conflict, contention
river *n* **1 = stream**, brook, waterway, creek, tributary **2 = flow**, flood, rush, spate, torrent
riveting *adj* **= enthralling**, hypnotic, absorbing, captivating, engrossing, fascinating, gripping, spellbinding
road *n* **= street**, track, route, highway, roadway, grid road (*Canad*), direction, path, lane, artery, avenue, pathway, course, bypass, alley, freeway, interstate (*US*), expressway, boulevard, thoroughfare, parkway, turnpike,

DICTIONARY

▶ **roadie** *n informal* person who transports and sets up equipment for a band
▶ **road apple** *slang* lump of horse manure
▶ **roadblock** *n* barricade across a road to stop traffic for inspection etc.
▶ **road hog** *informal* selfish aggressive driver
▶ **roadhouse** *n* pub or restaurant on a country road
▶ **road metal** broken stones used in building roads
▶ **road test** test of a vehicle etc. in actual use
▶ **roadway** *n* the part of a road used by vehicles
▶ **roadworks** *pl n* repairs to a road, esp. blocking part of the road
▶ **roadworthy** *adj* (of a vehicle) mechanically sound
roam Ⓣ *v* wander about
roan *adj* **1** (of a horse) having a brown or black coat sprinkled with white hairs ▷ *n* **2** roan horse
roar Ⓣ *v* **1** make or utter a loud deep hoarse sound like that of a lion **2** shout (something) as in anger **3** laugh loudly ▷ *n* **4** such a sound
▶ **roaring** *adj* **1** noisy, boisterous **2** *informal* brisk and profitable ▷ *adv* **3** noisily
roast Ⓣ *v* **1** cook by dry heat, as in an oven **2** make or be very hot ▷ *n* **3** roasted joint of meat ▷ *adj* **4** roasted
▶ **roasting** *informal* ▷ *adj* **1** extremely hot ▷ *n* **2** severe criticism or scolding
▶ **roaster** *n* **1** roasting tin **2** piece of food that is suitable for roasting
rob Ⓣ *v* **robbing, robbed 1** steal from **2** deprive **robber** *n* **robbery** *n*
Robbia *n* **1 Andrea della**. 1435–1525, Florentine sculptor, best known for his polychrome reliefs and his statues of infants in swaddling clothes **2** his uncle, **Luca della**. ?1400–82, Florentine sculptor, who perfected a technique of enamelling terra cotta for reliefs
robe Ⓣ *n* **1** long loose outer garment ▷ *v* **2** put a robe on
Robert I *n* known as *Robert the Bruce*. 1274–1329, king of Scotland (1306–29): he defeated the English army of Edward II at Bannockburn (1314) and gained recognition of Scotland's independence (1328)
Robert II *n* 1316–90, king of Scotland (1371–90)
Robert III *n* ?1337–1406, king of Scotland (1390–1406), son of Robert II
Roberts *n* **Julia**. born 1967, US film actress; her films include *Pretty Woman* (1990), *Notting Hill* (1999), *Erin Brockovich* (2000), which earned her an Academy Award, and *Mona Lisa Smile* (2003)
Robertson *n* **George** (**Islay Macneill**), Baron. born 1946, Scottish Labour politician; secretary-general of NATO (1999–2003)
Robeson *n* **Paul**. 1898–1976, US bass singer, actor, and leader in the Black civil rights movement
Robespierre *n* **Maximilien François Marie Isidore de**. 1758–94, French revolutionary and Jacobin leader: established the Reign of Terror as a member of the Committee of Public Safety (1793–94): executed in the coup d'état of Thermidor (1794)
robin *n* large thrush with a red breast
Robinson *n* **1 Edward G.**, real name *Emanuel Goldenberg*. 1893–1973, US film actor, born in Romania, famous esp. for gangster roles. His films include *Little Caesar* (1930), *Brother Orchid* (1940), *Double Indemnity* (1944), and *All My Sons* (1948) **2** (**William**) **Heath**. 1872–1944, British cartoonist and book illustrator, best known for his comic drawings of fantastic machines **3 Smokey**, real name *William Robinson*. born 1940, US Motown singer, songwriter, and producer. His hits include "The Tears of a Clown" (1970) (with the Miracles) and "Being with you" (1981) **4 Sugar Ray**, real name *Walker Smith*. 1921–89, US boxer, winner of the world middleweight championship on five separate occasions
robot Ⓣ *n* **1** automated machine, esp. one performing functions in a human manner **2** person of machine-like efficiency **robotic** *adj*
▶ **robotics** *n* science of designing and using robots

THESAURUS

winter road (*Canad*), ice road (*Canad*) • *There was very little traffic on the mining road*.
See also: **way**
roam *v* = **wander**, travel, walk, range, stray, rove, ramble, prowl
roar *v* **1** = **cry**, shout, yell, bay, howl, bellow, bawl **2** = **guffaw**, hoot, laugh heartily, split one's sides (*informal*) ▶ *n* **3** = **cry**, shout, yell, outcry, howl, bellow **4** = **guffaw**, hoot
roast *See* **cook**
rob *v* = **steal from**, con (*informal*), loot, defraud, swindle, burgle, burglarize • *He was robbed of all his money*.
robber *n* = **thief**, bandit, fraud, cheat, burglar, raider, looter, stealer, con man (*informal*), mugger (*informal*), plunderer
robbery *n* = **theft**, raid, burglary, larceny, swindle, plunder, pillage, mugging (*informal*), rip-off (*slang*), hold-up, stealing, stick-up (*slang*)
robe *n* **1** = **gown**, habit, costume ▶ *v* **2** = **clothe**, dress, garb
robot *n* = **machine**, android, automaton, mechanical man

DICTIONARY

Robson *n* Dame **Flora**. 1902–84, English stage and film actress
robust ⓣ *adj* very strong and healthy
robustly *adv* **robustness** *n*
roc *n* monstrous bird of Arabian mythology
ROC rest of Canada: the areas outside Quebec
rock[1] ⓣ *n* **1** hard mineral substance that makes up part of the earth's crust, stone **2** large rugged mass of stone **3** hard candy in sticks **4** *curling* curling stone
▸ **on the rocks 1** (of a marriage) about to end **2** (of an alcoholic drink) served with ice
▸ **rocky** *adj* having many rocks
▸ **rockery** *n* mound of stones in a garden for (alpine) plants
▸ **rock bottom** lowest possible level
▸ **rock tripe** any of various edible lichens that grow on rocks
rock[2] ⓣ *v* **1** (cause to) sway to and fro ▷ *n* **2** style of pop music with a heavy beat
▸ **rocky** *adj* shaky or unstable
▸ **rock and roll** style of pop music blending rhythm and blues and country music
▸ **rocking chair** chair allowing the sitter to rock backwards and forwards
Rockefeller *n* **1 John D(avison)**. 1839–1937, US industrialist and philanthropist **2** his son, **John D(avison)**. 1874–1960, US capitalist and philanthropist **3** his son, **Nelson (Aldrich)**. 1908–79, US politician; governor of New York State (1958–74); vice president (1974–76)
rocker *n* **1** curved piece of wood etc. on which something may rock **2** rocking chair
▸ **off one's rocker** *informal* insane
rocket ⓣ *n* **1** self-propelling device powered by the burning of explosive contents (used as a firework, weapon, etc.) **2** vehicle propelled by a rocket engine, as a weapon or carrying a spacecraft ▷ *v* **rocketing, rocketed 3** move fast, esp. upwards, as a rocket. **rocketry** *n*
Rockingham *n* **Marquess of**, title of *Charles Watson-Wentworth*. 1730–82, British statesman and leader of the Whig opposition, whose members were known as the **Rockingham Whigs**; prime minister (1765–66; 1782). He opposed the war with the American colonists
Rockwell *n* **Norman**. 1894–1978, US illustrator, noted esp. for magazine covers
rococo [rok-**koe**-koe] *adj* (of furniture, architecture, etc.) having much elaborate decoration in an early 18th-century French style
rod ⓣ *n* **1** slender straight bar, stick **2** cane
Rodchenko *n* **Alexander (Mikhailovich)**. 1891–1956, Soviet painter, sculptor, designer, and photographer, noted for his abstract geometrical style: a member of the constructivist movement
rode *v* past tense of **ride**
rodent *n* animal with teeth specialized for gnawing, such as a rat
rodeo *n, pl* **-deos** display of skill by cowboys, such as bareback riding
Rodgers *n* **Richard**. 1902–79, US composer of musical comedies. He collaborated with the librettist Lorenz Hart on such musicals as *A Connecticut Yankee* (1927), *On Your Toes* (1936), and *Pal Joey* (1940). After Hart's death his librettist was Oscar Hammerstein II. Two of their musicals, *Oklahoma!* (1943) and *South Pacific* (1949), received the Pulitzer Prize
Rodin *n* **Auguste**. 1840–1917, French sculptor, noted for his portrayal of the human form. His works include *The Kiss* (1886), *The Burghers of Calais* (1896), and *The Thinker* (1905)
Rodrigo *n* **Joaquín**. 1902–99, Spanish composer. His works include *Concierto de Aranjuez* (1940) for guitar and orchestra and *Concierto Pastorale* (1978)
roe[1] *n* small species of deer
roe[2] *n* mass of eggs in a fish
Roe n Sir **Edwin Alliott Vernon**. 1877–1958, English aircraft designer and manufacturer. One of his companies, Avro (founded in 1910), built the Lancaster and Vulcan bombers. The Canadian arm of his company (founded in 1945) built the Arrow, a Cold War supersonic fighter ordered then cancelled by the Canadian government
Roeg *n* **Nic(olas)**. born 1928, British film director and cinematographer. Films include *Walkabout* (1970), *Don't Look Now* (1972), *Insignificance* (1984), and *The Witches* (1990)
roentgen [**ront**-gan] *n* unit measuring a radiation dose
Roentgen, Röntgen *n* **Wilhelm Konrad**. 1845–1923, German physicist, who in 1895 discovered x-rays: Nobel prize for physics 1901
roger *interj* (used in signalling) message received and understood
Rogers *n* **1 Ginger**, real name *Virginia*

THESAURUS

robust *adj* = **strong**, tough, healthy, powerful, fit, vigorous, muscular, sturdy, hardy, stout, hale, strapping
rock[1] *n* = **stone**, boulder
rock[2] *v* **1** = **sway**, pitch, roll, toss, swing, reel, lurch **2** = **shock**, surprise, shake, stun, astonish, stagger, astound
rocket *See* **bomb, explode**
rocky[1] *adj* = **rough**, rugged, craggy, stony
rocky[2] *adj* = **unstable**, shaky, unsteady, wobbly, rickety
rod *n* = **stick**, staff, bar, pole, shaft, baton, cane, wand

r

DICTIONARY

McMath. 1911–95, US dancer and film actress, who partnered Fred Astaire **2 Richard**, Baron Rogers of Riverside. born 1933, British architect. His works include the Pompidou Centre in Paris (1971–77; with Renzo Piano), the Lloyd's building in London (1986), and the Millennium Dome in Greenwich, London **3 Stan**. 1949–1983, Canadian folk musician and songwriter. His albums include *Fogarty's Cove* (1976) and *Northwest Passage* (1981)

Roget *n* **Peter Mark**. 1779–1869, English physician, who on retirement devised a *Thesaurus of English Words and Phrases* (1852), a classified list of synonyms

rogue Ⓣ *n* **1** dishonest or unprincipled person **2** mischief-loving person ▷ *adj* **3** (of a wild beast) having a savage temper and living apart from the herd **roguery** *n* **roguish** *adj*

roister *v* make merry noisily or boisterously **roisterer** *n*

Roland *n* the greatest of the legendary 12 peers (paladins, of whom Oliver was another) in attendance on Charlemagne; he died in battle at Roncesvalles (778 AD)

role Ⓣ *n* **1** actor's part **2** task or function

roll Ⓣ *v* **1** move by turning over and over **2** wind round **3** smooth out with a roller **4** move or sweep along **5** undulate **6** (of a ship or aircraft) turn from side to side about a line from nose to tail ▷ *n* **7** act of rolling over or from side to side **8** piece of paper etc. rolled up **9** list or register **10** small rounded individually baked piece of bread **11** swaying unsteady movement or gait **12** continuous sound, as of drums, thunder, etc.

▸ **rolling pin** cylindrical roller for pastry

▸ **rolling stock** locomotives, carriages, etc. of a railway

▸ **rolling stone** restless, wandering person

▸ **roll call** calling out of a list of names, as in a school or the army, to check who is present

▸ **rolled gold** metal coated with a thin layer of gold

▸ **roll-on/roll-off** *adj* denoting a ship which vehicles can be driven straight onto or off

▸ **roll-top** *adj* (of a desk) having a flexible lid sliding in grooves

▸ **roll up** *v informal* appear or arrive

roller *n* **1** rotating cylinder used for smoothing or supporting a thing to be moved, spreading paint, etc. **2** long wave of the sea

▸ **Rollerblade** *n* ® roller skate with the wheels set in one straight line

▸ **roller coaster** (at a funfair) narrow railway with steep slopes

▸ **roller skate** skate with wheels

rollicking Ⓣ *adj* boisterously carefree

Rollins *n* **Sonny**, original name *Theodore Walter Rollins*. born 1930, US jazz tenor saxophonist, noted for his improvisation

roly-poly Ⓣ *adj* round or plump

ROM *computers* read only memory

Roman *adj* of Rome or the Church of Rome

▸ **Roman Catholic** member of that section of the Christian Church that acknowledges the supremacy of the Pope

▸ **roman numerals** the letters I, V, X, L, C, D, M, used to represent numbers

▸ **roman type** plain upright letters in printing

romance Ⓣ *n* **1** love affair **2** mysterious or exciting quality **3** novel or film dealing with love, esp. sentimentally **4** story with scenes remote from ordinary life ▷ *v* **5** exaggerate or fantasize **romancer** *n*

Romance *adj* (of a language) developed from Latin, such as French, Spanish, or Italian

Romanesque *adj, n* (in) a style of architecture of 9th–12th centuries characterized by round arches

romantic Ⓣ *adj* **1** of or dealing with love **2** idealistic but impractical **3** (of literature, music, etc.) displaying passion and imagination rather than order and form ▷ *n* **4** romantic person or artist **romantically** *adv* **romanticism** *n* **romanticist** *n* **romanticize** *v*

THESAURUS

rogue *n* = **scoundrel**, fraud, crook (*informal*), rascal, villain, scamp

role *n* **1** = **job**, post, part, position, duty, capacity, function, task **2** = **part**, character, portrayal, representation

roll *v* **1** = **turn**, spin, wheel, revolve, rotate, whirl, twirl, swivel, trundle, go round **2** = **wind**, wrap, bind, envelop, swathe, enfold, furl **3** = **flow**, run, undulate **4** = **flatten**, even, level, press, smooth **5** = **tumble**, rock, toss, reel, sway, lurch ▸ *n* **6** = **turn**, cycle, spin, wheel, revolution, reel, rotation, whirl, twirl **7** = **register**, record, list, index, census **8** = **rumble**, boom, roar, thunder, reverberation

rollicking *adj* = **boisterous**, lively, hearty, playful, exuberant, carefree, jaunty, devil-may-care

roly-poly *adj* = **plump**, fat, rounded, chubby, pudgy, buxom, tubby

romance *n* **1** = **love affair**, relationship, affair, attachment, liaison, amour **2** = **excitement**, mystery, charm, glamour, colour, fascination **3** = **story**, legend, tale, fantasy, melodrama, fairy tale, love story

romantic *adj* **1** = **loving**, tender,

DICTIONARY

Romany *n, pl* **-nies**, *adj* Gypsy
Romberg *n* **Sigmund**. 1887–1951, US composer of operettas, born in Hungary. He wrote *The Student Prince* (1924) and *The Desert Song* (1926)
Romeo *n, pl* **Romeos** ardent male lover
Romney *n* **George**. 1734–1802, English painter, who painted more than 50 portraits of Lady Hamilton in various historical roles
romp Ⓣ *v* **1** play wildly and joyfully ▷ *n* **2** spell of romping
▸ **romp home** win easily
▸ **rompers** *pl n* child's overalls
rondeau *n, pl* **-deaux** short poem with the opening words used as a refrain
rondo *n, pl* **-dos** piece of music with a leading theme continually returned to
roo *n Aust informal* kangaroo
rood *n Christianity* **1** the Cross **2** crucifix
▸ **rood screen** (in a church) screen separating the nave from the choir
roof *n, pl* **roofs 1** outside upper covering of a building, automobile, etc. ▷ *v* **2** put a roof on
rook[1] *n* **1** bird of the crow family ▷ *v* **2** *old-fashioned, slang* swindle
▸ **rookery** *n* colony of rooks
rook[2] *n* piece in chess
rookie *n informal* recruit, esp. in the army
room Ⓣ *n* **1** space **2** space enough **3** division of a house **4** scope or opportunity **rooms 5** lodgings
▸ **roomy** *adj* spacious
Roosevelt *n* **1** (**Anna**) **Eleanor**. 1884–1962, US writer, diplomat, and advocate of liberal causes: delegate to the United Nations (1945–52) **2** her husband, **Franklin Delano**, known as *FDR*. 1882–1945, 32nd president of the US (1933–45); elected four times. He instituted major reforms (the New Deal) to counter the economic crisis of the 1930s and was a forceful leader during World War II **3 Theodore**. 1858–1919, 26th president of the US (1901–09). A proponent of extending military power, he won for the US the right to build the Panama Canal (1903). He won the Nobel peace prize (1906), for mediating in the Russo-Japanese war
roost *n* **1** perch for fowls ▷ *v* **2** perch
▸ **rooster** *n* domestic cock
root Ⓣ *n* **1** part of a plant that grows down into the earth obtaining nourishment **2** plant with an edible root, such as a carrot **3** part of a tooth, hair, etc. below the skin **4** source or origin **5** form of a word from which other words and forms are derived **6** *math* factor of a quantity which, when multiplied by itself the number of times indicated, gives the quantity **roots 7** person's sense of belonging ▷ *v* **8** establish a root and start to grow **9** dig or burrow
▸ **rootless** *adj* having no sense of belonging
▸ **root for** *v informal* cheer on
▸ **root out** *v* get rid of completely
▸ **root up** *v* pull up by the roots
rope Ⓣ *n* thick cord
▸ **know the ropes** be thoroughly familiar with an activity
▸ **rope in** *v* persuade to join in
ropy, ropey Ⓣ *adj* **ropier, ropiest** *informal* **1** inferior or inadequate **2** not well **ropiness** *n*
Roquefort *n* strong blue-veined cheese made from ewes' or goats' milk
rorqual *n* whalebone whale with a dorsal fin
Rory O'Connor *n* Also **Roderic** ?1116–98, king of Connaught and last High King of Ireland

THESAURUS

passionate, amorous • *a romantic relationship* **2 = idealistic**, unrealistic, impractical, dreamy, starry-eyed **3 = exciting**, mysterious, glamorous, colourful, fascinating ▸ *n* **4 = idealist**, dreamer, sentimentalist
romp *v* **1 = frolic**, sport, caper, cavort, frisk, gambol, have fun **2 = win easily**, walk it (*informal*), win by a mile (*informal*), win hands down ▸ *n* **3 = frolic**, caper, lark (*informal*)
room *n* **1 = chamber**, office • *You can stay in my room.* **2 = space**, capacity, elbow room • *There wasn't enough room in the car.* **3 = opportunity**, chance, occasion, scope ▷ **rooms** *See* **apartment**
roomy *adj* **= spacious**, large, wide, broad, extensive, generous, sizable *or* sizeable, ample, capacious, commodious
root[1] *n* **1 = stem**, rhizome, tuber **2 = source**, cause, base, heart, seat, bottom, seed, core, foundation, origin, nucleus ▷ **roots = sense of belonging**, home, family, heritage, birthplace, cradle, origins ▸ *v* **3 = establish**, set, ground, stick, fix, anchor, implant, moor, fasten
root[2] *v* **= dig**, burrow, ferret ▷ **root out = get rid of**, remove, eliminate, eradicate, abolish, exterminate, do away with, extirpate, weed out
rooted *adj* **= deep-seated**, firm, deep, established, entrenched, ingrained, confirmed, deeply felt, fixed
rope *n* **= cord**, line, cable, strand, hawser ▷ **know the ropes = be experienced**, be an old hand, be knowledgeable
rope in *v* **= persuade**, involve, engage, enlist, inveigle, talk into
ropy, ropey *adj* (*Informal*) **1 = inferior**, poor, inadequate, lousy (*slang*), deficient, substandard, of poor quality **2 = unwell**, lousy (*slang*), below par, off colour, under the weather (*informal*)

DICTIONARY

rosaceous *adj* of or belonging to a family of plants typically having five-petalled flowers, including the rose, strawberry, and many fruit trees
rosary *n, pl* **-saries 1** series of prayers **2** string of beads for counting these prayers
rose[1] *n* **1** shrub or climbing plant with prickly stems and fragrant flowers **2** the flower **3** perforated flat nozzle for a hose **4** pink colour ▷ *adj* **5** reddish-pink
▸ **roseate** [**roe**-zee-ate] *adj* rose-coloured
▸ **rosy** *adj* **1** flushed **2** hopeful or promising
▸ **rose-coloured** *adj* unjustifiably optimistic
▸ **rose window** circular window with spokes branching from the centre
▸ **rosewood** *n* fragrant wood
rose[2] *v* past tense of **rise**
rosé [**roe**-zay] *n* pink wine
Rosebery *n* **Earl of**, title of *Archibald Philip Primrose*. 1847–1929, British Liberal statesman; prime minister (1894–95)
rosehip *n* berry-like fruit of a rose plant
rosemary *n* **1** fragrant flowering shrub **2** its leaves as a herb
Rosenberg *n* **1 Alfred**. 1893–1946, German Nazi politician and writer, who devised much of the racial ideology of Nazism: hanged for war crimes **2 Isaac**. 1890–1918, British poet and painter, best known for his poems about life in the trenches during World War I: died in action **3 Julius**. 1918–53, US spy, who, with his wife **Ethel** (1914–53), was executed for passing information about nuclear weapons to the Russians
rosette *n* rose-shaped ornament, esp. a circular bunch of ribbons
Rosewall *n* **Ken**(**neth**). born 1934, Australian tennis player: Australian champion 1953, 1955, and 1971–72; US champion 1956 and 1970
Rosh Hashanah, Rosh Hashana *n* Jewish New Year festival
rosin [**rozz**-in] *n* resin
Ross *n* **1 Diana**. born 1944, US singer: lead vocalist (1961–69) with Motown group the Supremes, whose hits include "Baby Love" (1964). Her subsequent recordings include *Lady Sings the Blues* (film soundtrack, 1972), and *Chain Reaction* (1986) **2** Sir **James Clark**. 1800–62, British naval officer; explorer of the Arctic and Antarctic. He located the north magnetic pole (1831) and discovered the Ross Sea during an Antarctic voyage (1839–43) **3** Sir **Ronald**. 1857–1932, English bacteriologist, who discovered the transmission of malaria by mosquitoes: Nobel prize for physiology or medicine 1902
Rossellini *n* **Roberto**. 1906–77, Italian film director. His films include *Rome, Open City* (1945), *Paisà* (1946), and *L'Amore* (1948)
Rossetti *n* **1 Christina Georgina**. 1830–94, British poet **2** her brother, **Dante Gabriel**. 1828–82, British poet and painter: a leader of the Pre-Raphaelites
Rossini *n* **Gioacchino Antonio**. 1792–1868, Italian composer, esp. of operas, such as *The Barber of Seville* (1816) and *William Tell* (1829)
roster Ⓣ *n* list of people and their turns of duty
rostrum Ⓣ *n, pl* **-trums, -tra** platform or stage
rot Ⓣ *v* **rotting, rotted 1** decompose or decay **2** slowly deteriorate physically or mentally ▷ *n* **3** decay **4** *informal* nonsense
rota *n* list of people who take it in turn to do a particular task
rotary Ⓣ *n* **1** traffic circle ▷ *adj* **2** revolving **3** operated by rotation
rotate Ⓣ *v* **1** (cause to) move round a centre or on a pivot **2** (cause to) follow a set sequence
rotation Ⓣ *n* **1** act of rotating **2** regular cycle of events **3** *baseball* group of pitchers on a team who take turns starting games
rote *n* mechanical repetition
▸ **by rote** by memory
Roth *n* **Philip**. born 1933, US novelist. His works include *Goodbye, Columbus* (1959), *Portnoy's Complaint* (1969), *My Life as a Man* (1974), *Sabbath's Theater* (1995), *The Human Stain* (2000), and *The Plot Against America* (2004)
Rothermere *n* **Viscount**, title of *Harold Sidney Harmsworth*. 1868–1940, British newspaper magnate
Rothko *n* **Mark**. 1903–70, US abstract

THESAURUS

roster *n* = **rota**, list, schedule, roll, table, register, agenda, catalogue
rostrum *n* = **stage**, stand, platform, podium, dais
rosy *adj* **1** = **pink**, red **2** = **glowing**, radiant, blooming, healthy-looking, ruddy **3** = **promising**, bright, optimistic, hopeful, cheerful, favorable, auspicious, encouraging
rot *v* **1** = **decay**, spoil, decompose, fester • *The grain started rotting in the silos.* RELATED WORD *adj*: putrid **2** = **deteriorate**, decline, waste away ▸ *n* **3** = **decay**, deterioration, mould, putrefaction, putrescence • *The wood was not protected against rot.*
See also: **eat away**
rotary *adj* = **revolving**, turning, rotating, spinning
rotate *v* **1** = **revolve**, turn, spin, wheel, reel, pivot, swivel, gyrate, go round **2** = **take turns**, switch, alternate
rotation *n* **1** = **revolution**, turn, spin, orbit, wheel, reel, turning, spinning **2** = **sequence**, cycle, succession, alternation, switching

DICTIONARY

expressionist painter, born in Russia
Rothschild *n* a powerful family of European Jewish bankers, a prominent member of which was **Lionel Nathan**, Baron de Rothschild, 1809–79, British banker and first Jewish member of Parliament
rotisserie *n* **1** (electrically driven) rotating spit for cooking meat ▷ *adj* **2** *baseball* relating to a fantasy baseball league in which participants select real players for an imaginary team, and points are awarded according to the actual performances of the chosen players
rotor *n* **1** revolving portion of a dynamo, motor, or turbine **2** rotating device with long blades that provides thrust to lift a helicopter
rotten Ⓣ *adj* **1** decomposed **2** *informal* very bad **3** corrupt
rotter *n slang* despicable person
Rottweiler [**rawt**-vile-er] *n* large sturdy dog with a smooth black and tan coat and usu. a docked tail
rotund Ⓣ [roe-**tund**] *adj* **1** round and plump **2** sonorous **rotundity** *n*
rotunda *n* circular building or room, esp. with a dome
rouble [**roo**-bl] *n* monetary unit of Russia
roué [**roo**-ay] *n* man given to immoral living
rouge *n* red cosmetic used to colour the cheeks
Rouget de Lisle *n* **Claude Joseph**. 1760–1836, French army officer: composer of the *Marseillaise* (1792), the French national anthem
rough Ⓣ *adj* **1** not smooth, uneven or irregular **2** violent, stormy, or boisterous **3** approximate **4** incomplete or rudimentary **5** lacking refinement ▷ *v* **6** make rough **7** plan out approximately ▷ *n* **8** rough state or area **roughen** *v* **roughly** *adv* **roughness** *n*
▸ **rough it** live without the usual comforts etc.
▸ **roughage** *n* indigestible constituents of food which aid digestion
▸ **rough-and-ready** *adj* hastily prepared but adequate
▸ **rough-and-tumble** *n* playful fight
▸ **rough-hewn** *adj* roughly shaped
roughcast *n* **1** mixture of plaster and small stones for outside walls ▷ *v* **2** coat with this
roughshod *adv* **ride roughshod over** act with total disregard for
roulette *n* gambling game played with a revolving wheel and a ball
round Ⓣ *adj* **1** spherical, cylindrical, circular, or curved **2** complete or whole: *round numbers* **3** plump ▷ *adv* **4** with a circular or circuitous course **5** on all sides: *books scattered round the room* ▷ *n* **6** thing round in shape **7** recurrent duties **8** customary course, as of a milkman **9** stage in a competition **10** game (of golf) **11** one of several periods in a boxing match etc. **12** number of drinks bought at one time **13** bullet or shell for a gun **14** part song in which singers join at equal intervals **15** circular movement **16** set of sandwiches ▷ *prep* **17** surrounding or encircling **18** on or outside the perimeter of **19** on all sides of ▷ *v* **20** make or become round **21** move round
▸ **roundly** *adv* thoroughly
▸ **round robin** petition signed with names in a circle to conceal the order
▸ **round-the-clock** *adj* throughout the day and night
▸ **round trip** journey out and back again, esp. by a different route

THESAURUS

rotten *adj* **1 = decayed**, bad, sour, mouldy, decomposed • *The old wooden window frame is rotten.* **2** (*informal*) **= inferior**, poor, lousy (*slang*), unsatisfactory • *It's a rotten idea.* **3 = corrupt**, immoral, crooked (*informal*), dishonest, dishonourable, perfidious **4** (*Informal*) **= despicable**, base, mean, dirty, nasty, lousy (*slang*), contemptible, scuzzy (*slang*)
See also: **shabby, terrible**
rotund *adj* **1 = round**, rounded, globular, spherical **2 = plump**, fat, portly, chubby, fleshy, stout, pudgy, corpulent, tubby
rough *adj* **1 = uneven**, rocky, rugged, bumpy, craggy • *My bicycle bumped along the rough ground.* OPPOSITE: smooth **2 = unpleasant**, hard, tough, difficult • *He's been through a rough time.* **3 = approximate**, estimated, vague, sketchy • *I can give you a rough idea of the time.* **4 = ungracious**, blunt, rude, coarse, brusque, impolite, unceremonious, uncivil, uncouth, unmannerly **5 = stormy**, wild, turbulent, choppy, squally **6 = nasty**, hard, tough, violent, harsh, cruel, unpleasant, unfeeling **7 = basic**, crude, incomplete, unfinished, sketchy, imperfect, rudimentary, unrefined, unpolished ▸ *v* ▷ **rough out = outline**, plan, draft, sketch ▸ *n* **8 = outline**, draft, mock-up, preliminary sketch
See also: **broad, jagged, primitive**
rough-and-ready *adj* **= makeshift**, crude, provisional, sketchy, unrefined, stopgap, improvised, unpolished
roughly *See* **about**
round *adj* **1 = spherical**, circular, rounded, cylindrical • *a round pizza in a square box* **2 = plump**, full, ample, fleshy, rotund, full-fleshed ▸ *n* **3 = stage**, period, session, lap • *After round three, two contestants shared the lead.* **4 = sphere**, ball, band, ring, circle, globe, disc, orb **5 = series**, session, cycle,

r

DICTIONARY

▸ **round up** *v* gather (people or animals) together **roundup** *n*
roundabout Ⓣ *n Brit* **1** traffic circle **2** merry-go-round ▷ *adj* **3** not straightforward: *a roundabout route*
roundel *n* **1** small disc **2** rondeau
▸ **roundelay** *n* simple song with a refrain
Roundhead *n* supporter of Parliament against Charles I in the English Civil War
rouse Ⓣ *v* **1** wake up **2** provoke or excite
▸ **rousing** *adj* lively, vigorous
Rousseau *n* **Jean Jacques**. 1712–78, French philosopher and writer, born in Switzerland, who strongly influenced the theories of the French Revolution and the romantics. Many of his ideas spring from his belief in the natural goodness of man, whom he felt was warped by society. His works include *Du contrat social* (1762), *Émile* (1762), and his *Confessions* (1782)
roustabout *n* labourer on an oil rig
rout Ⓣ *n* **1** overwhelming defeat **2** disorderly retreat ▷ *v* **3** defeat and put to flight
▸ **rout out** *v* **1** search for **2** drive out
route Ⓣ *n* **1** choice of roads taken to reach a destination **2** fixed path followed by buses, etc. between two places **3** chosen way or method
▸ **routemarch** *n* long training march
routine Ⓣ *n* **1** usual or regular method of procedure **2** boring repetition of tasks: *mindless routine* **3** set sequence ▷ *adj* **4** ordinary **5** regular
roux [**roo**] *n* fat and flour cooked together as a basis for sauces
rove Ⓣ *v* wander
▸ **rover** *n* **1** person who roves **2** pirate **3** small remote-controlled vehicle which roams over rough, esp. extraterrestrial, terrain taking photographs and samples
row[1] Ⓣ *n* straight line of people or things
▸ **in a row** in succession
row[2] *v* **1** propel (a boat) by oars ▷ *n* **2** spell of rowing
row[3] Ⓣ *informal* ▷ *n* **1** dispute **2** disturbance **3** reprimand ▷ *v* **4** quarrel noisily
rowan *n* tree producing bright red berries, mountain ash
rowdy Ⓣ *adj* **-dier, -diest 1** disorderly, noisy, and rough ▷ *n, pl* **-dies 2** person like this
rowel [rhymes with **towel**] *n* small spiked wheel on a spur
Rowling *n* **J**(**oanne**) **K**(**athleen**). born 1965, British novelist; author of the bestselling series of children's books featuring the boy wizard Harry Potter, which began with *Harry Potter and the Philosopher's Stone* (1995)
rowlock *n* device on the gunwale of a boat that holds an oar in place
royal Ⓣ *adj* **1** of, befitting, or supported by a king or queen **2** splendid ▷ *n* **3** *informal* member of a royal family **royally** *adv*
▸ **royalist** *n* supporter of monarchy
▸ **royalty** *n* **1** royal people **2** rank or power **3** payment to author, musician, inventor, etc.
▸ **royal blue** bright blue

THESAURUS

sequence, succession **6 = course**, beat, series, schedule, tour, routine, circuit ▸ *v* **7 = go round**, turn, circle, bypass, skirt, flank, encircle ▷ **round off = complete**, close, conclude, finish off ▷ **round up = gather**, group, drive, rally, collect, herd, muster, marshal
roundabout *adj* = **indirect**, oblique, evasive, devious, tortuous, circuitous, discursive
rounded *See* **blunt, round**
roundup *n* = **gathering**, rally, collection, assembly, muster, herding, marshalling
rouse *v* **1 = wake up**, call, rise, wake, awaken **2 = excite**, move, anger, provoke, stir, stimulate, incite, inflame, agitate, animate
rousing *adj* = **lively**, exciting, spirited, moving, inspiring, stimulating, stirring
rout *n* **1 = defeat**, beating, overthrow, debacle, drubbing, thrashing ▸ *v* **2 = defeat**, beat, destroy, crush, trounce, overthrow, conquer, drub, thrash, wipe the floor with (*informal*)
route *n* = **way**, road, course, channel, path, itinerary • *the direct route to the downtown area*
See also: **direction, line, passage**
routine *adj* **1 = usual**, standard, regular, normal, typical, ordinary, everyday • *a series of routine medical tests* **2 = boring**, predictable, dull, tedious, tiresome, humdrum ▸ *n* **3 = procedure**, program, system, order, schedule, practice, pattern • *The players had to change their daily routine.*
See also: **custom, habit, stock, straightforward**
rove *v* = **wander**, range, drift, roam, stray, ramble, traipse (*informal*)
row[1] *n* = **line**, bank, rank, column, queue • *She was greeted by a row of glum faces.*
row[2] *n* **1 = quarrel**, argument, altercation, squabble • *This could provoke a major diplomatic row with neighbouring countries.* **2 = disturbance**, noise, uproar, racket, commotion, tumult, rumpus ▸ *v* **3 = quarrel**, fight, dispute, argue, squabble, wrangle
See also: **disagreement**
rowdy *adj* = **disorderly**, wild, noisy, boisterous, unruly • *He complained to the police about rowdy neighbours.*
royal *adj* **1 = regal**, sovereign, imperial • *the*

r

DICTIONARY

rpm revolutions per minute
RRSP Registered Retirement Savings Plan
RSI repetitive strain injury
RSS Rich Site Summary *or* Really Simple Syndication: a way of allowing web users to receive updates from selected websites on their browsers
RSVP please reply
Rt Hon. Right Honourable
rub ⓣ *v* **rubbing, rubbed 1** apply pressure and friction to (something) with a circular or backwards-and-forwards movement **2** clean, polish, or dry by rubbing **3** remove by rubbing **4** chafe or fray through rubbing ▷ *n* **5** act of rubbing
▸ **rub it in** emphasize an unpleasant fact
▸ **rub out** *v* remove with a rubber
rubato *adv music* with expressive flexibility of tempo
rubber[1] *n* **1** strong waterproof elastic material, orig. made from the dried sap of a tropical tree, now usually synthetic **2** piece of rubber used for erasing mistakes **3** *slang* condom **rubbers 4** rubberized waterproof raincoat, overshoe, etc. ▷ *adj* **5** made of or producing rubber
▸ **rubberize** *v* coat or treat with rubber
▸ **rubbery** *adj* like rubber, soft or elastic
▸ **rubberneck** *v* stare with unthinking curiosity
▸ **rubber stamp 1** device for imprinting the date, a name, etc. **2** automatic authorization
rubber[2] *n* match consisting of three games of bridge, whist, etc.
rubbish ⓣ *n* **1** waste matter **2** anything worthless **3** nonsense **rubbishy** *adj*
rubble *n* fragments of broken stone, brick, etc.
rubella [roo-**bell**-a] *n* same as **German measles**
Rubens *n* Sir **Peter Paul**. 1577–1640, Flemish painter, regarded as the greatest exponent of the Baroque: appointed (1609) painter to Archduke Albert of Austria, who gave him many commissions, artistic and diplomatic. He was knighted by Charles I of England in 1629. His prolific output includes the triptych in Antwerp Cathedral, *Descent from the Cross* (1611–14), *The Rape of the Sabines* (1635), and his *Self-Portrait* (?1639)
rubicund [**roo**-bik-kund] *adj* ruddy
rubric [**roo**-brik] *n* heading or explanation inserted in a text
ruby *n, pl* **-bies 1** red precious gemstone ▷ *adj* **2** deep red
ruche [**roosh**] *n* pleat or frill of lace etc. as a decoration
ruck[1] *n* rough crowd of common people
ruck[2] *n, v* wrinkle or crease
rucksack *n* large pack carried on the back
ructions ⓣ *pl n informal* noisy uproar
Rudd *n* **Steele**, pen name of *Arthur Hoey Davis*. 1868–1935, Australian author. His works include *On Our Selection* (1899), *Our New Selection* (1902), and *Back at Our Selection* (1906), which featured the characters Dad and Dave
rudder *n* vertical hinged piece at the stern of a boat or at the rear of an aircraft, for steering
ruddy ⓣ *adj* **-dier, -diest** of a fresh healthy red colour
rude ⓣ *adj* **1** impolite or insulting **2** coarse, vulgar, or obscene **3** roughly made **4** robust **5** unexpected and unpleasant **rudely** *adv* **rudeness** *n*
rudiments ⓣ *pl n* simplest and most basic stages of a subject
▸ **rudimentary** *adj* basic, elementary
Rudolf I, Rudolph I *n* 1218–91, king of Germany (1273–91): founder of the Hapsburg

r

THESAURUS

royal yacht **2 = splendid**, grand, impressive, magnificent, majestic, stately
rub *v* **1 = polish**, clean, shine, wipe, scour **2 = chafe**, scrape, fray, grate, abrade ▷ **rub out = erase**, remove, cancel, delete, obliterate, efface, wipe out ▶ *n* **3 = polish**, stroke, shine, wipe **4 = massage**, caress, kneading
rubbish *n* **1 = waste**, refuse, garbage, trash, litter • *tons of rubbish waiting to be dumped* **2 = nonsense**, garbage, drivel, hot air (*informal*) • *Don't talk rubbish!*
See also: **junk**
ruckus *n* (*Informal*) **= uproar**, trouble, disturbance, fuss, commotion, fracas, hoopla
ructions *pl n* (*Informal*) **= uproar**, trouble, row, disturbance, fuss, commotion, fracas, hue and cry
ruddy *adj* **= rosy**, healthy, red, fresh, glowing, radiant, blooming, reddish, rosy-cheeked
rude *adj* **1 = impolite**, disrespectful, impertinent, impudent, insolent • *He is rude to her friends*. OPPOSITE: polite **2 = unpleasant**, violent, abrupt • *a rude awakening* **3 = vulgar**, rough, coarse, boorish, uncivilized, brutish, graceless, loutish, oafish, uncouth, uncultured **4 = roughly-made**, crude, simple, rough, raw, makeshift, primitive, artless, inartistic, inelegant
See also: **abusive, common, dirty, indecent**
rudimentary *adj* **= basic**, early, initial, fundamental, elementary, primitive, undeveloped
rudiments *pl n* **= basics**, foundation, beginnings, elements, essentials, fundamentals

DICTIONARY

dynasty based on the duchies of Styria and Austria

rue[1] ⓣ *v* **ruing, rued** feel regret for

▸ **rueful** *adj* regretful or sorry **ruefully** *adv*

rue[2] *n* plant with evergreen bitter leaves

ruff *n* **1** starched and frilled collar **2** natural collar of feathers, fur, etc. on certain birds and animals

ruffian ⓣ *n* violent lawless person

ruffle ⓣ *v* **1** disturb the calm of **2** annoy, irritate ▷ *n* **3** frill or pleat

rufty-tufty *adj slang* rugged in appearance or manner

rug *n* **1** small carpet **2** thick woollen blanket

rugby *n* form of football played with an oval ball which may be handled by the players

rugged ⓣ [**rug**-gid] *adj* **1** rough **2** uneven and jagged **3** strong-featured **4** tough and sturdy

rugger *n informal* rugby

ruin ⓣ *v* **1** destroy or spoil completely **2** impoverish ▷ *n* **3** destruction or decay **4** loss of wealth, position, etc. **5** broken-down unused building(s)

▸ **ruination** *n* **1** act of ruining **2** state of being ruined **3** cause of ruin

▸ **ruinous** *adj* **1** causing ruin **2** more expensive than is reasonable **ruinously** *adv*

rule ⓣ *n* **1** statement of what is allowed, for example in a game or procedure **2** what is usual **3** government, authority, or control **4** measuring device with a straight edge ▷ *v* **5** govern **6** restrain **7** give a formal decision **8** be pre-eminent **9** mark with straight line(s)

▸ **as a rule** usually

▸ **ruler** *n* **1** person who governs **2** measuring device with a straight edge

▸ **ruling** *n* formal decision

▸ **rule of thumb** practical but imprecise approach

▸ **rule out** *v* exclude

rum[1] *n* alcoholic drink distilled from sugar cane

rum[2] *adj informal* odd, strange

rumba *n* lively ballroom dance of Cuban origin

rumble[1] *v* **1** (of traffic etc.) make a low continuous noise ▷ *n* **2** such a noise

rumble[2] *v informal* discover the (disreputable) truth about

rumbustious *adj* boisterous or unruly

ruminate ⓣ *v* **1** ponder or meditate **2** chew the cud **ruminative** *adj*

THESAURUS

rue *v* = **regret**, mourn, lament, repent, be sorry for, kick oneself for

rueful *adj* = **regretful**, sorry, mournful, remorseful, contrite, penitent, repentant, sorrowful

ruffian *n* = **thug**, bully, brute, hooligan, hoodlum, tough

ruffle *v* **1** = **disarrange**, disorder, dishevel, rumple, tousle, mess up **2** = **annoy**, upset, irritate, agitate, fluster, peeve (*informal*), nettle, tick off

rugged *adj* **1** = **rough**, difficult, rocky, irregular, bumpy, uneven, jagged, ragged, craggy, broken **2** = **strong-featured**, rough-hewn, weather-beaten **3** = **tough**, strong, robust, husky (*informal*), muscular, sturdy, burly, brawny, well-built

ruin *v* **1** = **destroy**, break, damage, devastate, spoil, wreck, impair, mar, undo, mess up (*informal*) • *The crops have been ruined.* **2** = **bankrupt**, impoverish, pauperize **3** = **spoil**, damage, blow (*slang*), botch, make a mess of, mess up, screw up (*informal*) ▸ *n* **4** = **destruction**, fall, devastation, downfall, decay, disrepair • *The old factory was in a state of ruin.* **5** = **wreckage**, shell, wreck, remains • *the burned-out ruins of the building* **6** = **disrepair**, wreckage, decay, disintegration, ruination **7** = **bankruptcy**, insolvency, destitution

See also: **crash, harm**

ruined *See* **derelict**

ruinous *adj* **1** = **devastating**, disastrous, dire, catastrophic, destructive, calamitous, shattering **2** = **extravagant**, crippling, wasteful, immoderate

rule *n* **1** = **regulation**, order, law, guideline, decree • *This was against the rules.* **2** = **custom**, practice, procedure, convention, tradition, routine, habit **3** = **government**, power, control, authority, regime, command, reign, jurisdiction, mastery, dominion ▷ **as a rule** = **usually**, generally, mainly, normally, on the whole • *As a rule, I eat my meals in front of the TV.* ▸ *v* **4** = **govern**, lead, reign, administer, be in power • *He rules the country with a strong hand.* **5** = **be prevalent**, prevail, be customary, predominate, preponderate **6** = **decree**, judge, decide, settle, pronounce

See also: **line** ▷ **rule out** = **exclude**, ban, reject, eliminate, dismiss, prohibit, disqualify, preclude, debar, leave out

ruler *n* **1** = **governor**, leader, premier, commander, monarch, sovereign, head of state, prime minister **2** = **measure**, rule, yardstick • *He was a weak-willed and indecisive ruler.*

rules *See* **standards**

ruling *n* **1** = **decision**, verdict, judgment, decree, pronouncement, adjudication ▸ *adj* **2** = **governing**, commanding, controlling, reigning **3** = **predominant**, chief, main, principal, dominant, pre-eminent, preponderant, prevailing

ruminate *v* = **ponder**, think, consider,

DICTIONARY

▸ **ruminant** *adj, n* cud-chewing (animal, such as a cow, sheep, or deer)
▸ **rumination** *n* quiet meditation and reflection
rummage Ⓣ *v* **1** search untidily and at length ▹ *n* **2** untidy search through a collection of things
rummy *n* card game in which players try to collect sets or sequences
rumour Ⓣ *n* **1** gossip or common talk **2** unproved statement
▸ **be rumoured** be circulated as a rumour
rump Ⓣ *n* **1** buttocks **2** rear of an animal
rumple *v* make untidy, crumpled, or dishevelled
rumpus Ⓣ *n, pl* **-puses** noisy or confused commotion
Rumsfeld *n* **Donald H.** born 1932, US Republican politician and businessman: US Secretary of Defense (1975–77, 2001–06)
run Ⓣ *v* **running, ran, run 1** move with a more rapid gait than walking **2** go quickly (across) **3** flow **4** compete in a race, election, etc. **5** continue (for a specified period) **6** function **7** travel according to schedule **8** melt **9** spread **10** (of stitches) unravel **11** expose oneself to (a risk) **12** (of a newspaper) publish (a story) **13** smuggle (goods, esp. arms) **14** manage or be in charge of ▹ *n* **15** act or spell of running **16** ride in an automobile **17** unrestricted access **18** tendency or trend: *the run of the market* **19** continuous period: *a run of good luck* **20** sequence **21** heavy demand **22** enclosure for domestic fowls **23** series of unravelled stitches, ladder **24** score of one at baseball **25** steep snow-covered course for skiing
▸ **run away** *v* make one's escape, flee
▸ **run down** *v* **1** be rude about **2** stop working **3** reduce in number or size
rundown *n*
▸ **run-down** *adj* exhausted
▸ **run into** *v* meet
▸ **run-of-the-mill** *adj* ordinary
▸ **run out** *v* be completely used up
▸ **run over** *v* knock down (a person) with a moving vehicle
▸ **run up** *v* incur (a debt)
rune *n* any character of the earliest Germanic alphabet **runic** *adj*
rung[1] *n* crossbar on a ladder
rung[2] *v* past participle of **ring**[1]
runnel *n* small brook or rivulet
runner Ⓣ *n* **1** competitor in a race **2** messenger **3** part underneath an ice skate etc., on which it slides **4** slender horizontal stem of a plant, such as a strawberry, running along the ground and forming new roots at intervals **5** long strip of carpet or decorative cloth

THESAURUS

reflect, deliberate, contemplate, muse, cogitate, mull over, turn over in one's mind
rummage *v* = **search**, hunt, root, forage, delve, ransack
rumour *n* = **story**, word, gossip, hearsay, whisper • *persistent rumours of problems within the team*
rumoured *See* **supposed**
rump *n* = **buttocks**, bottom, backside (*informal*), seat, butt (*informal*), rear, posterior, buns (*slang*), derrière (*euphemistic*), hindquarters, rear end
rumpus *n* = **commotion**, row, noise, uproar, disturbance, fuss, furor, hue and cry
run *v* **1** = **race**, sprint, bolt, jog, gallop • *I excused myself and ran back to the telephone.* **2** = **manage**, control, direct, administer, be in charge of, look after • *He ran a small hotel.* **3** = **flee**, bolt, beat a retreat, beat it (*slang*), escape, make a run for it, take flight, take off (*informal*), take to one's heels **4** = **move**, go, pass, course, roll, skim, glide **5** = **work**, go, operate, perform, function **6** = **continue**, go, reach, extend, stretch, proceed **7** = **flow**, go, leak, spill, pour, stream, discharge, gush, spout **8** = **melt**, dissolve, liquefy, go soft **9** = **publish**, feature, display, print **10** = **compete**, stand, contend, be a candidate, put oneself up for, take part, re-offer (*Canad*) **11** = **smuggle**, bootleg, traffic in ▹ **run across** = **meet**, encounter, bump into, come across, run into ▹ **run amok** *See* **rampage** ▹ **run around** *See* **associate** ▹ **run away** = **flee**, bolt, abscond, escape, fly the coop (*informal*), make a run for it, scram (*informal*), take to one's heels ▹ **run down** = **criticize**, bad-mouth (*slang*), knock (*informal*), decry, disparage, denigrate, belittle; = **reduce**, cut, decrease, trim, curtail, downsize, cut back, downscale; = **knock down**, hit, knock over, run into, run over; = **weaken**, exhaust, debilitate ▹ **run into** = **meet**, encounter, bump into, come across *or* come upon, run across; = **hit**, strike, collide with ▹ **run off** = **flee**, bolt, escape, fly the coop (*informal*), make off, run away, take flight, take to one's heels ▹ **run out** = **be used up**, end, finish, fail, be exhausted, dry up, give out ▹ **run over** = **knock down**, hit, knock over, run down; = **go through**, check, rehearse, go over, run through ▹ **run riot** *See* **rampage, riot** ▹ **run through** = **rehearse**, read, practise, go over, run over ▸ *n* **12** = **race**, rush, sprint, dash, jog, spurt, gallop **13** = **ride**, drive, trip, spin (*informal*), outing, excursion, jaunt **14** = **sequence**, season, period, series, course, stretch, string,

r

DICTIONARY

▸ **runner-up** *n* person who comes second in a competition
running Ⓣ *adj* **1** continuous **2** consecutive **3** (of water) flowing ▹ *n* **4** act of moving or flowing quickly **5** management of a business etc.
▸ **in** *or* **out of the running** having *or* not having a good chance in a competition
▸ **running back** *football* offensive player whose job is to run with the ball
runny Ⓣ *adj* **-nier, -niest 1** tending to flow **2** exuding moisture
runt *n* **1** smallest animal in a litter **2** *offensive* undersized person
runway *n* hard level roadway where aircraft take off and land
Runyon *n* (**Alfred**) **Damon**. 1884–1946, US short-story writer, best known for his humorous tales about racy Broadway characters. His story collections include *Guys and Dolls* (1932), which became the basis of a musical (1950)
rupee *n* monetary unit of India and Pakistan
Rupert *n* **Prince**. 1619–82, German-born nephew of Charles I: Royalist general during the Civil War (until 1646) and commander of the Royalist fleet (1648–50). After the Restoration he was an admiral of the English fleet in wars against the Dutch. He was the first governor of Hudson's Bay Company
rupture Ⓣ *n* **1** breaking, breach **2** hernia ▹ *v* **3** break, burst, or sever
rural Ⓣ *adj* in or of the countryside
ruse Ⓣ [**rooz**] *n* stratagem or trick
rush[1] Ⓣ *v* **1** move or do very quickly **2** force (someone) to act hastily **3** make a sudden attack upon (a person or place) **4** *football* run forwards with the ball ▹ *n* **5** sudden quick or violent movement **6** *football* act of rushing **rushes 7** first unedited prints of a scene for a film ▹ *adj* **8** done with speed, hasty **rushing** *n*
▸ **rush hour** period at the beginning and end of the working day, when many people are travelling to or from work
rush[2] *n* marsh plant with a slender pithy stem
▸ **rushy** *adj* full of rushes
Rushdie *n* (**Ahmed**) **Salman**. born 1947, British writer, born in India, whose novels include *Midnight's Children* (1981), which won the Booker prize, *Shame* (1983), and *The Ground Beneath Her Feet* (1998). His novel *The Satanic Verses* (1988) was regarded as blasphemous by many Muslims and he was forced into hiding (1989) when the Ayatollah Khomeini called for his death
rusk *n* hard brown crisp biscuit, used esp. for feeding babies
Rusk *n* (**David**) **Dean**. 1909–94, US statesman: secretary of state (1961–69). He defended US military involvement in Vietnam and opposed recognition of communist China
Ruskin *n* **John**. 1819–1900, English art critic and social reformer. He was a champion of the Gothic Revival and the Pre-Raphaelites and saw a close connection between art and morality. From around 1860 he argued vigorously for social and economic planning. His works include *Modern Painters* (1843–60),

THESAURUS

spell **15 = enclosure**, pen, coop ▹ **in the long run = eventually**, ultimately, in the end
See also: **conduct, head, range, supervise**
runaway *n* **1 = fugitive**, refugee, deserter, escapee, truant ▸ *adj* **2 = escaped**, wild, loose, fugitive, fleeing
rundown *See* **outline, summary**
run-down *adj* **1 = exhausted**, weak, unhealthy, weary, worn-out, below par, debilitated, drained, enervated **2 = dilapidated**, shabby, seedy, decrepit, worn-out, ramshackle, broken-down
runner *n* **1 = athlete**, sprinter, jogger **2 = messenger**, courier, dispatch bearer, errand boy
running *adj* **1 = continuous**, constant, perpetual, uninterrupted, incessant, unbroken, twenty-four-seven (*slang*) **2 = flowing**, moving, streaming ▸ *n* **3 = management**, control, organization, leadership, administration, direction, supervision **4 = working**, operation, performance, maintenance, functioning
runny *adj* **= flowing**, liquid, fluid, watery, liquefied, melted
run-of-the-mill *adj* **= ordinary**, average, mediocre, tolerable, passable, middling, undistinguished, unexceptional
rupture *n* **1 = break**, tear, split, crack, breach, rent, burst, fissure ▸ *v* **2 = break**, separate, tear, split, crack, burst, sever
rural *adj* **= rustic**, country, agricultural, pastoral, sylvan
ruse *n* **= trick**, device, hoax, dodge, ploy, manoeuvre, subterfuge, stratagem
rush *v* **1 = hurry**, run, shoot, race, fly, dash, hasten, hustle, gush, scurry • *Someone rushed out of the building.* **2 = push**, pressure, press, hurry • *Ministers won't be rushed into a response.* **3 = attack**, charge, storm ▸ *n* **4 = hurry**, race, scramble, dash, stampede, bustle, outrush • *the rush not to be late for school* **5 = attack**, charge, assault, onslaught ▸ *adj* **6 = hasty**, fast, quick, rapid, urgent, swift, hurried
See also: **bolt, burst, flood, speed, wave**

r

DICTIONARY

The Stones of Venice (1851–53), *Unto this Last* (1862), *Time and Tide* (1867), and *Fors Clavigera* (1871–84)
Russell *n* **1 Bertrand** (**Arthur William**), 3rd Earl. 1872–1970, British philosopher and mathematician. His books include *Principles of Mathematics* (1903), *Principia Mathematica* (1910–13) with A. N. Whitehead, *Introduction to Mathematical Philosophy* (1919), *The Problems of Philosophy* (1912), *The Analysis of Mind* (1921), and *An Enquiry into Meaning and Truth* (1940): Nobel prize for literature 1950 **2 John**, 1st Earl. 1792–1878, British statesman; prime minister (1846–52; 1865–66). He led the campaign to carry the 1832 Reform Act **3 Ken**. born 1927, British film director. His films include *Women in Love* (1969), *The Music Lovers* (1970), *The Boy Friend* (1971), *Valentino* (1977), *Gothic* (1986), and *The Rainbow* (1989)
russet *adj* **1** reddish-brown ▷ *n* **2** the colour **3** apple with rough reddish-brown skin
Russian *n* **1** official language of Russia and, formerly, of the Soviet Union **2** person from Russia ▷ *adj* **3** of Russia
▸ **Russian roulette** act of bravado in which a person spins the cylinder of a revolver loaded with only one cartridge and presses the trigger with the barrel against his or her own head
rust Ⓣ *n* **1** reddish-brown coating formed on iron etc. that has been exposed to moisture **2** disease of plants with rust-coloured spots ▷ *adj* **3** reddish-brown ▷ *v* **4** become coated with rust **rustproof** *adj*
▸ **rusty** *adj* **1** coated with rust **2** of a rust colour **3** out of practice
rustic Ⓣ *adj* **1** of or resembling country people **2** rural **3** crude, awkward, or uncouth **4** (of furniture) made of untrimmed branches ▷ *n* **5** person from the country **rusticity** *n*
rusticate *v* banish temporarily from university as a punishment **rustication** *n*
rustle[1] Ⓣ *v* **1** make a low whispering sound, as of dry leaves ▷ *n* **2** this sound
rustle[2] *v* steal (cattle)
▸ **rustler** *n* cattle thief
▸ **rustle up** *v* prepare at short notice
rut[1] Ⓣ *n* **1** furrow made by wheels **2** dull settled habits or way of living
rut[2] *n* **1** recurrent period of sexual excitability in male deer ▷ *v* **rutting, rutted** **2** be in a period of sexual excitability
rutabaga *n* kind of turnip
Ruth *n* **1** *Old Testament* **a** a Moabite woman, who left her own people to remain with her mother-in-law Naomi, and became the wife of Boaz; an ancestress of David **b** the book in which these events are recounted **2 George Herman**, nicknamed *Babe*. 1895–1948, US professional baseball player from 1914 to 1935
Rutherford *n* **Ernest**, 1st Baron. 1871–1937, British physicist, born in New Zealand, who discovered the atomic nucleus (1909): Nobel Prize for chemistry 1908
ruthless Ⓣ *adj* pitiless, merciless **ruthlessly** *adv* **ruthlessness** *n*
rye *n* **1** kind of grain used for fodder and bread **2** whiskey made from rye
rye-grass *n* any of several kinds of grass cultivated for fodder

THESAURUS

rust *n* **1 = corrosion**, oxidation **2 = mildew**, must, rot, blight, mould ▸ *v* **3 = corrode**, oxidize
rustic *adj* **1 = rural**, country, pastoral, sylvan **2 = uncouth**, crude, rough, awkward, coarse ▸ *n* **3 = yokel**, peasant, redneck (*slang*), hick (*informal*), hillbilly, boor, bumpkin, clod, clodhopper (*informal*)
rustle *v* **1 = crackle**, whisper, crinkle ▸ *n* **2 = crackle**, whisper, crinkling, rustling
rusty *adj* **1 = corroded**, oxidized, rust-covered, rusted **2 = reddish-brown**, chestnut, coppery, reddish, russet, rust-coloured **3 = out of practice**, weak, stale, unpractised
rut *n* **1 = groove**, track, trough, furrow, indentation, wheel mark **2 = habit**, system, pattern, routine, dead end
ruthless *adj* **= merciless**, harsh, brutal, cruel, relentless, callous, heartless, pitiless, remorseless
rutted *adj* **= grooved**, cut, marked, furrowed, gouged, holed, indented, scored

r

DICTIONARY

Ss

S 1 second(s) 2 singular
S 1 Saint 2 South(ern) 3 *chem* sulfur
SA 1 Salvation Army 2 South Africa
Sabbath *n* day of worship and rest: Saturday for Jews, Sunday for Christians
▸ **sabbatical** *adj*, *n* (denoting) leave for study
sable *n* 1 dark fur from a small weasel-like Arctic animal ▹ *adj* 2 black
sabot [**sab**-oh] *n* wooden shoe, clog
sabotage Ⓣ *n* 1 intentional damage done to machinery, systems, etc. ▹ *v* 2 damage intentionally
▸ **saboteur** *n* person who commits sabotage
sabre *n* curved cavalry sword
sac *n* pouchlike structure in an animal or plant
saccharin, saccharine *n* artificial sweetener
▸ **saccharine** *adj* excessively sweet
sacerdotal *adj* of priests
sachet *n* small envelope or bag containing a single portion
Sachs *n* **Hans**. 1494–1576, German master shoemaker and Meistersinger, portrayed by Wagner in *Die Meistersinger von Nürnberg*
sack Ⓣ *n* 1 large bag made of coarse material 2 plundering of a captured town 3 *informal* dismissal 4 *slang* bed ▹ *v* 5 plunder (a captured town) 6 *informal* dismiss
▸ **hit the sack** *slang* go to bed
▸ **sackcloth** *n* coarse fabric used for sacks, formerly worn as a penance
Sacks *n* **Jonathan** (**Henry**), Baron. born 1948, British rabbi; Commonwealth chief rabbi from 1991
sacrament *n* ceremony of the Christian Church, esp. Communion **sacramental** *adj*
sacred Ⓣ *adj* 1 holy 2 set apart, reserved 3 connected with religion
sacrifice Ⓣ *n* 1 giving something up 2 thing given up 3 making of an offering to a god 4 thing offered ▹ *v* 5 offer as a sacrifice 6 give (something) up **sacrificial** *adj*
sacrilege Ⓣ *n* misuse or desecration of something sacred **sacrilegious** *adj*
sacristan *n* person in charge of the contents of a church
▸ **sacristy** *n* room in a church where sacred objects are kept
sacrosanct Ⓣ *adj* regarded as sacred, inviolable
sacrum [**say**-krum] *n*, *pl* **-cra** compound bone at the base of the spine
sad Ⓣ *adj* **sadder, saddest** 1 sorrowful, unhappy 2 deplorably bad 3 regrettable
sadly *adv* **sadness** *n*

THESAURUS

sabotage *n* 1 = **damage**, destruction, disruption, subversion, wrecking ▸ *v* 2 = **damage**, destroy, disrupt, wreck, vandalize, disable, incapacitate, subvert
saccharine *adj* = **oversweet**, sugary, sickly, cloying, honeyed, nauseating, syrupy
sack[1] *n* 1 = **bag**, pocket, pouch, receptacle ▸ *v* (*Informal*) 2 = **dismiss**, fire, discharge • *sacked for missing work so often*
sack[2] *n* 1 = **plundering**, pillage, looting ▸ *v* 2 = **plunder**, raid, strip, ruin, rob, loot, pillage
sacred *adj* 1 = **holy**, divine, hallowed, blessed, revered, sanctified 2 = **religious**, holy, ecclesiastical 3 = **inviolable**, protected, sacrosanct
sacrifice *v* 1 = **give up**, surrender, forgo, forfeit • *He sacrificed his personal life for his career.* 2 = **offer**, immolate, offer up ▸ *n* 3 = **surrender**, renunciation, self-denial • *He was willing to make any sacrifice for peace.* 4 = **offering**, oblation
sacrilege *n* = **desecration**, violation, blasphemy, heresy, irreverence, impiety, profanation
sacrilegious *adj* = **profane**, irreverent, blasphemous, desecrating, impious, irreligious
sacrosanct *adj* = **inviolable**, sacred, hallowed, untouchable, inviolate, sanctified, set apart
sad *adj* 1 = **unhappy**, down, low, blue, dismal, depressed, gloomy, mournful, dejected, melancholy, grief-stricken, glum, downcast, wistful • *The loss of our friendship makes me sad.* OPPOSITE: happy 2 = **tragic**, dismal, gloomy, pathetic, poignant, mournful, moving, melancholy, depressing, harrowing, heart-rending, upsetting • *a sad song* 3 = **deplorable**, bad, sorry, lamentable, wretched
See also: **miserable**
sadden *v* = **upset**, grieve, distress, depress, deject, make sad
saddened *See* **disappointed**

S

DICTIONARY

▶ **sadden** *v* make (someone) sad

saddle Ⓣ *n* **1** rider's seat on a horse or bicycle **2** joint of meat ▷ *v* **3** put a saddle on (a horse) **4** burden (with a responsibility)

▶ **saddler** *n* maker or seller of saddles

▶ **saddlebag** *n* pouch or small bag attached to the saddle of a horse, bicycle, etc.

Sade *n* Comte **Donatien Alphonse François de**, known as the *Marquis de Sade*. 1740–1814, French soldier and writer, whose exposition of sexual perversion gave rise to the term sadism

sadism [**say**-dizz-um] *n* gaining of (sexual) pleasure from inflicting pain **sadist** *n* **sadistic** *adj* **sadistically** *adv*

sadomasochism *n* combination of sadism and masochism **sadomasochist** *n*

s.a.e. stamped addressed envelope

safari *n, pl* **-ris** expedition to hunt or observe wild animals, esp. in Africa

▶ **safari park** park where lions, elephants, etc. are kept uncaged so that people can see them from automobiles

Safdie *n* **Moshe**. born 1938, Canadian-US-Israeli architect, born in British Mandate of Palestine. His buildings include the National Gallery of Canada in Ottawa and Vancouver Library Square

safe Ⓣ *adj* **1** secure, protected **2** uninjured, out of danger **3** not involving risk **4** *baseball* having successfully reached a base ▷ *n* **5** strong lockable container **6** *esp. Canad slang* condom **safely** *adv*

▶ **safe-conduct** *n* permit allowing travel through a dangerous area

▶ **safe deposit** place where valuables can be stored safely

▶ **safekeeping** *n* protection

safeguard Ⓣ *n* **1** protection ▷ *v* **2** protect

safety Ⓣ *n, pl* **-ties** **1** state of being safe **2** *football* player who defends the area furthest back in the field **3** *football* Also **safety touch** play in which the offensive team causes the ball to cross its own goal line and fails to bring it out, scoring two points for the opposing team

▶ **safety net** net to catch performers on a trapeze or high wire if they fall

▶ **safety pin** pin with a spring fastening and a guard over the point when closed

▶ **safety valve** valve that allows steam etc. to escape if pressure becomes excessive

saffron *n* **1** orange-coloured flavouring obtained from a crocus ▷ *adj* **2** orange

sag Ⓣ *v* **sagging, sagged** **1** sink in the middle **2** tire **3** (of clothes) hang loosely ▷ *n* **4** droop

saga Ⓣ [**sah**-ga] *n* **1** legend of Norse heroes **2** any long story

sagacious *adj* wise **sagaciously** *adv* **sagacity** *n*

Sagan *n* **Carl** (**Edward**). 1934–96, US astronomer and writer on scientific subjects; host of the television series *Cosmos* (1980)

sage[1] Ⓣ *n* aromatic herb with grey-green leaves

sage[2] Ⓣ *n* **1** very wise man ▷ *adj* **2** *lit* wise **sagely** *adv*

sagebrush *n* aromatic plant of West N America

sago *n* starchy cereal from the powdered pith of the sago palm tree

sahib *n* Indian term of address placed after a man's name as a mark of respect

said *v* past of **say**

THESAURUS

saddening *See* **painful**

saddle *v* = **burden**, load, encumber

sadistic *adj* = **cruel**, brutal, vicious, ruthless, barbarous

sadness *n* = **unhappiness**, depression, melancholy, despondency, dejection • *I said goodbye with a mixture of sadness and joy*. OPPOSITE: happiness

See also: **grief, misery, sorrow**

safe *adj* **1** = **harmless**, innocuous, wholesome • *This is not a safe place after dark*. OPPOSITE: dangerous **2** = **secure**, OK (*informal*), protected, all right, in safe hands, out of danger, out of harm's way, safe and sound • *I feel warm and safe with you*. **3** = **unharmed**, intact, unhurt, unscathed, undamaged, all right, O.K. *or* okay (*informal*) **4** = **risk-free**, certain, sound, secure, impregnable ▶ *n* **5** = **strongbox**, vault, coffer, repository, deposit box, safe-deposit box

See also: **immune, reliable**

safe and sound *See* **safe**

safeguard *v* **1** = **protect**, save, defend, guard, preserve, shield, look after • *international action to safeguard the ozone layer* ▶ *n* **2** = **protection**, defence, cover, barrier • *adequate safeguards for civil liberties*

See also: **precaution**

safely *adv* = **in safety**, in one piece, safe and sound, with impunity, without risk

safety *n* **1** = **security**, protection, immunity • *I was very anxious about their safety*. OPPOSITE: danger **2** = **shelter**, cover, refuge, sanctuary

sag *v* **1** = **sink**, fall, bag, slump, dip, droop, give way, hang loosely **2** = **flag**, weaken, tire, wane, wilt, droop

saga *n* = **tale**, story, legend, epic, narrative, yarn

sage *n* **1** = **wise man**, master, elder, guru, philosopher ▶ *adj* **2** = **wise**, sensible, judicious, sagacious, sapient

S

DICTIONARY

sail ⓣ *n* **1** sheet of fabric stretched to catch the wind for propelling a sailing boat **2** journey by boat **3** arm of a windmill ▷ *v* **4** travel by water **5** move smoothly **6** begin a voyage
▶ **sailor** *n* member of a ship's crew
▶ **sailboard** *n* board with a mast and single sail, used for windsurfing
saint *n* **1** *Christianity* person venerated after death as specially holy **2** exceptionally good person **saintly** *adj* **saintliness** *n*
Saint-Exupéry *n* **Antoine de**. 1900–44, French novelist and aviator. His novels of aviation include *Vol de nuit* (1931) and *Terre des hommes* (1939). He also wrote the fairy tale *Le petit prince* (1943)
Saint-Just *n* **Louis Antoine Léon de**. 1767–94, French Revolutionary leader and orator. A member of the Committee of Public Safety (1793–94), he was guillotined with Robespierre
Saint-Saëns *n* (**Charles**) **Camille**. 1835–1921, French composer, pianist, and organist. His works include the symphonic poem *Danse Macabre* (1874), the opera *Samson and Delilah* (1877), the humorous orchestral suite *Carnival of Animals* (1886), five symphonies, and five piano concertos
Saint-Simon *n* **Comte de**, title of *Claude Henri de Rouvroy*. 1760–1825, French social philosopher, generally regarded as the founder of French socialism. He thought society should be reorganized along industrial lines and that scientists should be the new spiritual leaders. His most important work is *Nouveau Christianisme* (1825)
saithe *n* dark-coloured edible sea fish
sake[1] ⓣ *n* **1** benefit **2** purpose
▶ **for the sake of** **1** for the purpose of **2** to please or benefit (someone)
sake[2], **saki** [**sah**-kee] *n* Japanese alcoholic drink made from fermented rice
Sakharov *n* **Andrei**. 1921–89, Soviet physicist and human-rights campaigner: Nobel peace prize 1975
salaam [sal-**ahm**] *n* low bow of greeting among Muslims
salacious ⓣ *adj* excessively concerned with sex
salad *n* dish of raw vegetables, eaten as a meal or part of a meal
Saladin *n* Arabic name *Salah-ed-Din Yusuf ibn-Ayyub*. ?1137–93, sultan of Egypt and Syria and opponent of the Crusaders. He defeated the Christians near Tiberias (1187) and captured Acre, Jerusalem, and Ashkelon. He fought against Richard I of England and Philip II of France during the Third Crusade (1189–92)
salamander *n* **1** type of lizard **2** mythical reptile supposed to live in fire
salami *n* highly spiced sausage
salary ⓣ *n, pl* **-ries** fixed regular payment, usu. monthly, to an employee **salaried** *adj*
Salazar *n* **Antonio de Oliveira**. 1889–1970, Portuguese statesman; dictator (1932–68)
sale ⓣ *n* **1** exchange of goods for money **2** selling of goods at unusually low prices **3** auction
▶ **saleable** *adj* fit or likely to be sold
▶ **salesman** (**saleswoman**) *n* person who sells goods
▶ **salesmanship** *n* skill in selling
salient ⓣ [**say**-lee-ent] *adj* **1** prominent, noticeable ▷ *n* **2** *mil* projecting part of a front line
Salieri *n* **Antonio**. 1750–1825, Italian composer and conductor, who worked in Vienna (from 1766). The suggestion that he poisoned Mozart has no foundation
saline [**say**-line] *adj* containing salt
salinity *n*
Salinger *n* **J**(**erome**) **D**(**avid**). 1919–2010, US writer, noted particularly for his novel of adolescence *The Catcher in the Rye* (1951). His first novel for 34 years, *Hapworth 16, 1924* was published in 1997
Salisbury *n* **Robert Gascoyne Cecil**, 3rd Marquess of Salisbury. 1830–1903, British statesman; Conservative prime minister (1885–86; 1886–92; 1895–1902). His greatest interest was in foreign and imperial affairs
saliva [sal-**lie**-va] *n* liquid that forms in the mouth, spittle **salivary** *adj*
▶ **salivate** *v* produce saliva
Salk *n* **Jonas Edward**. 1914–95, US virologist:

THESAURUS

sagging *See* **flabby**
sail *v* **1** = **set sail**, embark **2** = **glide**, fly, sweep, soar, wing, float, drift, skim **3** = **pilot**, steer
sailor *n* = **mariner**, marine, seaman, seafarer, sea dog
saintly *adj* = **virtuous**, religious, holy, righteous, pious, godly, saintlike
sake *n* **1** = **benefit**, good, interest, account, behalf, welfare **2** = **purpose**, end, aim, reason, objective, motive
salacious *adj* = **lascivious**, erotic, lewd, carnal, lecherous, libidinous, lustful
salary *n* = **pay**, income, wage, earnings, wages
sale *n* = **selling**, deal, transaction, marketing, disposal ▷ **for sale** = **available to buy**, obtainable, on the market
salient *adj* = **prominent**, important, outstanding, striking, pronounced, noticeable, conspicuous

S

DICTIONARY

developed an injected vaccine against poliomyelitis (1954)
sallow[1] ⓣ *adj* of an unhealthy pale or yellowish colour
sallow[2] *n* tree or shrub related to the willow
sally *n, pl* **-lies 1** sudden brief attack by troops **2** witty remark ▷ *v* **-lying, -lied** (foll. by *forth*) **3** rush out **4** go out
salmon *n* **1** large fish with orange-pink flesh valued as food ▷ *adj* **2** orange-pink
Salmond *n* **Alexander Elliot Anderson**, known as *Alex*. born 1954, Scottish politician; leader of the SNP (1990–2000) and again from 2004; First Minister of Scotland from 2007
salmonella *n, pl* **-lae** bacterium causing food poisoning
salon *n* **1** commercial premises of a hairdresser, beautician, etc. **2** elegant reception room for guests
saloon *n* **1** large public room, as on a ship **2** bar serving alcoholic drinks **3** *Brit* sedan
salsify *n* plant with a long white edible root
salt ⓣ *n* **1** white crystalline substance used to season food **2** chemical compound of acid and metal ▷ *v* **3** season with salt **salty** *adj*
▶ **old salt** experienced sailor
▶ **with a pinch of salt** *or* **with a grain of salt** allowing for exaggeration
▶ **worth one's salt** efficient
▶ **saltcellar** *n* small container for salt at table
SALT Strategic Arms Limitation Talks *or* Treaty
saltpetre *n* compound used in gunpowder and as a preservative
salubrious ⓣ *adj* favourable to health **salubrity** *n*
Saluki *n* tall hound with a silky coat
salutary ⓣ *adj* producing a beneficial result
salute ⓣ *n* **1** motion of the arm as a formal military sign of respect **2** firing of guns as a military greeting of honour ▷ *v* **3** greet with a salute **4** make a salute **5** acknowledge with praise
▶ **salutation** *n* greeting by words or actions
salvage ⓣ *n* **1** saving of a ship or other property from destruction **2** property so saved ▷ *v* **3** save from destruction or waste
salvation ⓣ *n* fact or state of being saved from harm or the consequences of sin
salve ⓣ *n* **1** healing or soothing ointment ▷ *v* **2** soothe or appease: *salve one's conscience*
salver *n* (silver) tray on which something is presented
salvia *n* plant with blue or red flowers
salvo *n, pl* **-vos, -voes 1** simultaneous discharge of guns etc. **2** burst of applause or questions
sal volatile [sal vol-**at**-ill-ee] *n* preparation of ammonia, used to revive a person who feels faint
SAM surface-to-air missile
Samaritan *n* person who helps people in distress
samba *n, pl* **-bas** lively Brazilian dance
same ⓣ *adj* **1** identical, not different, unchanged **2** just mentioned **sameness** *n*
samovar *n* Russian tea urn
Samoyed *n* dog with a thick white coat and tightly curled tail
sampan *n* small boat with oars used in China
samphire *n* plant found on rocks by the seashore
sample ⓣ *n* **1** part taken as representative of a whole **2** *music* short extract from an existing recording mixed into a backing track to produce a new recording ▷ *v* **3** take and test a sample of **sampling** *n*
▶ **sampler** *n* piece of embroidery showing the embroiderer's skill
Sampras *n* **Pete**. born 1971, US tennis player: US singles champion (1990, 1993, 1995,

S

THESAURUS

sallow *adj* = **wan**, unhealthy, pale, anemic, yellowish, pasty, sickly, pallid
salt *n* **1** = **seasoning**, taste, relish, flavour, savour ▷ **with a grain of salt, with a pinch of salt** = **skeptically**, suspiciously, cynically, disbelievingly, with reservations ▶ *adj* **2** = **salty**, saline, brackish, briny
salted *See* **salty**
salty *adj* = **salt**, brackish, briny, salted • *salty bacon*
salubrious *adj* = **healthy**, beneficial, wholesome, good for one, health-giving
salutary *adj* = **beneficial**, valuable, useful, profitable, advantageous, good for one
salute *n* **1** = **greeting**, address, recognition, salutation ▶ *v* **2** = **greet**, address, welcome, acknowledge, hail **3** = **honour**, recognize, acknowledge, pay tribute to *or* pay homage to
salvage *v* = **save**, recover, rescue, retrieve, redeem
salvation *n* = **saving**, rescue, escape, redemption, preservation, deliverance
salve *n* = **balm**, cream, lotion, ointment, emollient
same *adj* **1** = **identical**, equivalent, equal, alike, indistinguishable • *The two words have the same sound but different spellings*. OPPOSITE: different **2** = **aforementioned**, aforesaid **3** = **unchanged**, consistent, constant, unaltered, changeless, invariable, unvarying
See also: **like**
sameness *See* **similarity**
sample *n* **1** = **specimen**, model, example, pattern, instance ▶ *v* **2** = **test**, try, experience, taste, inspect ▶ *adj* **3** = **test**, trial,

DICTIONARY

1996); Wimbledon singles champion (1993–95, 1997–2000)
samurai *n, pl* **-rai** member of an ancient Japanese warrior caste
sanatorium *n, pl* **-riums, -ria** **1** institution for invalids or convalescents **2** room for sick pupils at a boarding school
sanctify Ⓣ *v* **-fying, -fied** make holy **sanctification** *n*
sanctimonious Ⓣ *adj* making a show of piety
sanction Ⓣ *n* **1** permission, authorization **2** *usu pl* coercive measure or penalty ▷ *v* **3** allow, authorize
sanctity Ⓣ *n* sacredness, inviolability
sanctuary Ⓣ *n, pl* **-aries** **1** place of safety for a fugitive **2** place where animals or birds can live undisturbed **3** holy place **4** part of a church nearest the altar
sanctum *n, pl* **-tums, -ta** **1** sacred place **2** person's private room
sand *n* **1** substance consisting of small grains of rock, esp. on a beach or in a desert **sands** **2** stretches of sand forming a beach or desert ▷ *v* **3** smooth with sandpaper
▸ **sander** *n* power tool for smoothing surfaces
▸ **sandy** *adj* **1** covered with sand **2** (of hair) reddish-fair
▸ **sandbag** *n* bag filled with sand, used as protection against gunfire, floodwater, etc.
▸ **sandblast** *v, n* (clean with) a jet of sand blown from a nozzle under pressure
▸ **sandpaper** *n* paper coated with sand for smoothing a surface
▸ **sandpiper** *n* shore bird with a long bill and slender legs
▸ **sandstone** *n* rock composed of sand
▸ **sandstorm** *n* desert wind that whips up clouds of sand
Sand *n* **George**, pen name of *Amandine Aurore Lucie Dupin*. 1804–76, French novelist, best known for such pastoral novels as *La Mare au diable* (1846) and *François le Champi* (1847–48) and for her works for women's rights to independence
sandal *n* light shoe consisting of a sole attached by straps
sandalwood *n* sweet-scented wood
sandwich *n* **1** two slices of bread with a layer of food between ▷ *v* **2** insert between two other things
▸ **sandwich board** pair of boards hung over a person's shoulders to display advertisements in front and behind
sane Ⓣ *adj* **1** of sound mind **2** sensible, rational **sanity** *n*
sang *v* past tense of **sing**
Sanger *n* **Margaret** (**Higgins**). 1883–1966, US leader of the birth-control movement
sang-froid [sahng **frwah**] *n* composure, self-possession
sangria *n* Spanish drink of wine and fruit juice
sanguinary *adj* **1** accompanied by bloodshed **2** bloodthirsty
sanguine Ⓣ *adj* cheerful, optimistic
Sanhedrin [**san**-id-rin] *n Judaism* highest court of the ancient Jewish nation
sanitary Ⓣ *adj* promoting health by getting rid of dirt and germs
▸ **sanitation** *n* sanitary measures, esp. drainage or sewerage
sank *v* past tense of **sink**
Sanskrit *n* ancient language of India
Santa Claus *n* legendary patron saint of children, who brings presents at Christmas
Santayana *n* **George**. 1863–1952, US philosopher, poet, and critic, born in Spain. His works include *The Life of Reason* (1905–06) and *The Realms of Being* (1927–40)
Santer *n* **Jacques**. born 1937, Luxembourg

THESAURUS

representative, specimen
sanctify *v* = **consecrate**, cleanse, hallow
sanctimonious *adj* = **holier-than-thou**, hypocritical, smug, pious, self-righteous
sanction *v* **1** = **permit**, back, support, allow, approve, endorse, authorize • *He is ready to sanction the use of force*. OPPOSITE: veto ▸ *n* **2** = **permission**, support, approval, blessing, authorization, backing • *The treaty required the sanction of Parliament*.
See also: **let**
sanctions *n* = **ban**, boycott, embargo, penalties • *Canada is considering imposing sanctions against the regime*.
sanctity *n* **1** = **sacredness**, inviolability **2** = **holiness**, grace, goodness, piety, godliness, righteousness
sanctuary *n* **1** = **shrine**, church, temple, altar **2** = **protection**, retreat, shelter, refuge, haven, asylum **3** = **reserve**, conservation area, national park, nature reserve
sands *See* **beach**
sane *adj* **1** = **rational**, normal, lucid • *This was not the act of a sane person*. OPPOSITE: mad **2** = **sensible**, sound, reasonable, rational, judicious, level-headed • *a sane and practical policy*
sanguine *adj* = **cheerful**, confident, optimistic, hopeful, buoyant
sanitary *adj* = **hygienic**, healthy, clean, wholesome, germ-free
sanitation *See* **hygiene**
sanity *n* **1** = **mental health**, reason, normality, rationality, saneness **2** = **good sense**, sense, common sense, level-headedness, rationality

S

DICTIONARY

politician: prime minister of Luxembourg (1984–95); president of the European Commission (1994–99)
sap[1] ⓣ *n* 1 moisture that circulates in plants 2 energy 3 *informal* gullible person
sap[2] ⓣ *v* **sapping, sapped** 1 undermine 2 weaken ▷ *n* 3 trench dug to undermine an enemy position
▸ **sapper** *n* soldier in an engineering unit
sapient [**say**-pee-ent] *adj lit* wise, shrewd
sapience *n*
Sapir *n* **Edward**. 1884–1939, US anthropologist and linguist, noted for his study of the ethnology and languages of North American Indians
sapling *n* young tree
Sapper *n* real name *Herman Cyril McNeile*. 1888–1937, British novelist, author of the popular thriller *Bull-dog Drummond* (1920) and its sequels
sapphire *n* 1 blue precious stone ▷ *adj* 2 deep blue
Sappho *n* 6th century BC, Greek lyric poetess of Lesbos
saraband, sarabande *n* slow stately Spanish dance
Saracen *n hist* Arab or Muslim who opposed the Crusades
Sarandon *n* **Susan Abigail**. born 1946, US film actress: her films include *Thelma and Louise* (1991), *Lorenzo's Oil* (1992), *The Client* (1994), *Dead Man Walking* (1996), and *Moonlight Mile* (2002)
Sarazen *n* **Gene**, original name *Eugenio Saraceni*. 1902–99, US golfer; won seven major tournaments between 1922 and 1935
sarcasm ⓣ *n* (use of) bitter or wounding ironic language **sarcastic** *adj* **sarcastically** *adv*
sarcoma *n, pl* **-mata, -mas** malignant tumour beginning in connective tissue
sarcophagus ⓣ *n, pl* **-gi, -guses** stone coffin
sardine *n* small fish of the herring family, usu. preserved in tightly packed cans
sardonic ⓣ *adj* mocking or scornful
sardonically *adv*
sargassum, sargasso *n* type of floating seaweed
Sargent *n* **John Singer**. 1856–1925, US painter, esp. of society portraits; in London from 1885
sari, saree *n* long piece of cloth draped around the body and over one shoulder, worn by Hindu women
sarong *n* long piece of cloth tucked around the waist or under the armpits, worn esp. in Malaysia
sarsaparilla *n* soft drink, orig. made from the root of a tropical American plant
sartorial *adj* of men's clothes or tailoring
Sartre *n* **Jean-Paul**. 1905–80, French philosopher, novelist, and dramatist; chief French exponent of atheistic existentialism. His works include the philosophical essay *Being and Nothingness* (1943), the novels *Nausea* (1938) and *Les Chemins de la liberté* (1945–49), a trilogy, and the plays *Les Mouches* (1943), *Huis clos* (1944), and *Les Mains sales* (1948)
sash[1] *n* decorative strip of cloth worn round the waist or over one shoulder
sash[2] *n* wooden frame containing the panes of a window
▸ **sash window** window consisting of two sashes that can be opened by sliding one over the other
Sask. Saskatchewan
saskatoon *n* N American shrub with purplish berries
Sasquatch *n* same as **Bigfoot**
sassafras *n* American tree with aromatic bark used medicinally
Sassenach *n Scot* English person
Sassoon *n* **Siegfried (Lorraine)**. 1886–1967, British poet and novelist, best known for his poems of the horrors of war collected in *Counterattack* (1918) and *Satirical Poems* (1926). He also wrote a semi-fictitious autobiographical trilogy *The Memoirs of George Sherston* (1928–36)
sat *v* past of **sit**
Satan ⓣ *n* the Devil
▸ **satanic** *adj* 1 of Satan 2 supremely evil
▸ **Satanism** *n* worship of Satan
satay, saté [**sat**-ay] *n* Indonesian and Malaysian dish consisting of pieces of chicken, pork, etc. grilled on skewers and served with peanut sauce
satchel *n* bag, usu. with a shoulder strap, for carrying school books

S

THESAURUS

sap[1] *n* 1 = **vital fluid**, essence, lifeblood 2 (*Informal*) = **fool**, idiot, jerk (*slang*), dork (*slang*), ninny, schmuck (*slang*), simpleton
sap[2] *v* = **weaken**, drain, undermine, exhaust, deplete
sarcasm *n* = **irony**, satire, bitterness, mockery, cynicism, derision
sarcastic *adj* = **ironic**, satirical, caustic, sardonic • *A sarcastic remark was on the tip of her tongue.*
sarcophagus *See* **tomb**
sardonic *adj* = **mocking**, dry, ironic, cynical, sarcastic, wry, derisive, sneering
Satan *n* = **The Devil**, Beelzebub, Lord of the Flies, Lucifer, Mephistopheles, Prince of Darkness, The Evil One
satanic *adj* = **evil**, black, wicked, demonic, devilish, hellish, diabolic, fiendish, infernal

DICTIONARY

sate *v* satisfy (a desire or appetite) fully

satellite *n* **1** man-made device orbiting in space **2** heavenly body that orbits another **3** country that is dependent on a more powerful one **4** of or used in the transmission of television signals from a satellite to the home

satiate Ⓣ [**say**-she-ate] *v* **1** satisfy fully **2** surfeit

▸**satiety** [sat-**tie**-a-tee] *n* feeling of having had too much

Satie *n* **Erik** (**Alfred Leslie**). 1866–1925, French composer, noted for his eccentricity, experimentalism, and his direct and economical style. His music, including numerous piano pieces and several ballets, exercised a profound influence upon other composers, such as Debussy and Ravel

satin *n* silky fabric with a glossy surface on one side

▸**satiny** *adj* of or like satin

▸**satinwood** *n* tropical tree yielding hard wood

satire Ⓣ *n* **1** use of ridicule to expose vice or folly **2** poem or other work that does this **satirical** *adj* **satirist** *n*

▸**satirize** *v* ridicule by means of satire

satisfy Ⓣ *v* **-fying, -fied 1** please, content **2** provide amply for (a need or desire) **3** convince, persuade **satisfaction** *n* **satisfactory** *adj*

satnav *n motoring informal* satellite navigation

satsuma *n* kind of small orange

saturate Ⓣ *v* **1** soak thoroughly **2** cause to absorb the maximum amount of something **saturation** *n*

Saturday *n* seventh day of the week

Saturn *n* **1** Roman god **2** one of the planets

▸**saturnine** *adj* gloomy in temperament or appearance

▸**saturnalia** *n* wild revelry

satyr *n* **1** woodland god, part man, part goat **2** lustful man

sauce *n* **1** liquid added to food to enhance flavour **2** *informal* impudence

▸**saucy** *adj* **1** impudent **2** pert, jaunty **saucily** *adv*

▸**saucepan** *n* cooking pot with a long handle

saucer *n* small round dish put under a cup

Saud *n* full name *Saud ibn Abdul-Aziz*. 1902–69, king of Saudi Arabia (1953–64); son of Ibn Saud. He was deposed by his brother Faisal

sauerkraut *n* shredded cabbage fermented in brine

sauna *n* Finnish-style steam bath

Saunders n Sir **Charles Edward**. 1867–1937, Canadian agronomist. From Red Fife wheat he developed Marquis wheat, a strain which matures earlier than Red Fife and which, by 1920, had become by far the most planted wheat in western Canada and much of the US

saunter Ⓣ *v* **1** walk in a leisurely manner, stroll ▹ *n* **2** leisurely walk

saurian *adj* of or like a lizard

sausage *n* minced meat in an edible tube-shaped skin

▸**sausage roll** skinless sausage covered in pastry

Saussure *n* **Ferdinand de**. 1857–1913, Swiss

THESAURUS

satiate *v* **1 = glut**, stuff, gorge, nauseate, cloy, jade, overfill, surfeit **2 = satisfy**, sate, slake

satire *n* = **mockery**, caricature, parody, irony, spoof (*informal*), ridicule, lampoon, burlesque, piss-take (*informal*)

satirical, satiric *adj* = **mocking**, cutting, ironic, caustic, incisive, biting

satirize *v* = **ridicule**, parody, deride, lampoon, burlesque, pillory

satisfaction *n* **1 = contentment**, content, comfort, pride, happiness, pleasure, enjoyment, satiety, repletion **2 = fulfillment**, achievement, gratification, assuaging

satisfactorily *See* **well**

satisfactory *adj* = **adequate**, acceptable, sufficient, passable, all right, good enough • *a satisfactory explanation* OPPOSITE: unsatisfactory

See also: **decent, suitable**

satisfied *adj* = **content**, happy, pleased, contented • *We are not satisfied with these results.* OPPOSITE: disappointed

See also: **certain, confident, sure**

satisfy *v* **1 = gratify**, please, indulge • *a solution that I hope will satisfy everyone* **2 = convince**, persuade, reassure, put someone's mind at rest • *He had to satisfy the doctors that he was fit to play.* **3 = fulfill**, meet • *Applicants must satisfy the conditions for admission.*

See also: **suit**

saturate *v* = **soak**, steep, drench, imbue, souse, suffuse, waterlog, wet through

saturated *adj* = **soaked**, waterlogged, sodden, dripping, drenched, soaking *or* soaking wet, sopping *or* sopping wet, wet through

saturnine *adj* = **gloomy**, grave, sombre, dour, glum, morose

saucy *adj* **1 = impudent**, forward, rude, cheeky (*informal*), presumptuous, impertinent, insolent, pert **2 = jaunty**, gay, dashing, perky

saunter *v* **1 = stroll**, wander, roam, ramble, meander, amble, mosey (*informal*) ▸ *n* **2 = stroll**, turn, walk, airing, ramble, amble

DICTIONARY

linguist. He pioneered structuralism in linguistics and the separation of scientific language description from historical philological studies
sauté [**so**-tay] *v* fry quickly in a little fat
Sauve *n* **Jeanne(-Mathilde)** (neé *Benoît*). 1922–93, Canadian journalist and politician; she was Canada's first female Speaker of the House of Commons (1980–83) and first female Governor General (1984–90)
savage ⓣ *adj* **1** wild, untamed **2** cruel and violent **3** uncivilized, primitive ▷ *n* **4** uncivilized person ▷ *v* **5** attack ferociously
savagely *adv* **savagery** *n*
savanna, savannah *n* extensive open grassy plain in Africa
savant *n* learned person
save ⓣ *v* **1** rescue or preserve from harm, protect **2** keep for the future **3** set aside (money) **4** *sports* prevent the scoring of (a goal) ▷ *n* **5** *sports* act of preventing a goal **6** *baseball* statistical credit awarded to a relief pitcher for keeping his or her team's lead in a winning game **saver** *n*
▸ **saving** *n* economy
▸ **savings** *pl n* money put by for future use
saveloy *n* spicy smoked sausage
saviour ⓣ *n* **1** person who rescues another **2** **Saviour** Christ
Savitskaya *n* **Svetlana**. born 1949, Soviet cosmonaut, the first woman to walk in space (1984). She was elected to the former Soviet parliament (1989)
savoir-faire ⓣ [**sav**-wahr **fair**] *n French* ability to do and say the right thing in any situation
savory *n* aromatic herb used in cooking
savour ⓣ *n* **1** characteristic taste or odour **2** slight but distinctive quality ▷ *v* **3** (foll. by *of*) have a flavour or suggestion of **4** enjoy, relish
▸ **savoury** *adj* **1** salty or spicy **2** not sweet ▷ *n* **3** *Brit* savoury dish served before or after a meal
savoy *n* variety of cabbage
savvy *slang* ▷ *v* **-vying, -vied** **1** understand ▷ *n* **2** understanding, intelligence
saw[1] *n* **1** cutting tool with a toothed metal blade ▷ *v* **sawing, sawed, sawed** *or* **sawn** **2** cut with a saw **3** move (something) back and forth
▸ **sawyer** *n* person who saws timber for a living
▸ **sawdust** *n* fine wood fragments made in sawing
▸ **sawfish** *n* fish with a long toothed snout
▸ **sawmill** *n* mill where timber is sawn into planks
▸ **saw-off** *n slang* compromise or settlement
saw[2] *v* past tense of **see**[1]
saw[3] *n* wise saying, proverb
sax *n informal* short for **saxophone**
saxifrage *n* alpine rock plant with small flowers
Saxon *n* **1** member of the W Germanic people who settled widely in Europe in the early Middle Ages ▷ *adj* **2** of the Saxons
saxophone *n* brass wind instrument with keys and a curved body **saxophonist** *n*
say ⓣ *v* **saying, said** **1** speak or utter **2** express (an idea) in words **3** suppose as an example or possibility **4** give as one's opinion ▷ *n* **5** right or chance to speak **6** share in a decision
▸ **saying** *n* maxim, proverb
SAYE save as you earn: system by which

THESAURUS

savage *adj* **1 = cruel**, violent, brutal, vicious, ferocious, inhuman, barbaric, barbarous • *a savage attack* **2 = wild**, feral, undomesticated, untamed, animalistic **3 = uncultivated**, rough, rugged, uncivilized **4 = primitive**, rude, unspoiled ▸ *n* **5 = lout**, monster, beast, brute, barbarian • *They really are a bunch of savages.* ▸ *v* **6 = attack**, bite, maul • *savaged to death by the animal*
savagery *n* **= cruelty**, brutality, ferocity, viciousness, barbarity, ruthlessness
save *v* **1 = rescue**, deliver, salvage, redeem, come to someone's rescue • *He saved my life.* **2 = protect**, preserve, safeguard, keep safe • *a new surgical technique which could save lives* **3 = keep**, reserve, hoard, set aside • *I'm saving for a new computer.* OPPOSITE: waste
▷ **save from** *See* **spare**
See also: **but, except, stockpile, store**
saving *n* **1 = economy**, reduction, bargain, discount ▷ **savings = nest egg**, fund, store, reserves, resources ▸ *adj* **2 = redeeming**, compensatory, extenuating
saviour *n* **= rescuer**, defender, preserver, protector, liberator, deliverer, redeemer
Saviour *n* **= Christ**, Jesus, Messiah, Redeemer
savoir-faire *n* **= social graces**, poise, diplomacy, discretion, finesse, tact, social know-how (*informal*), urbanity, worldliness
savour *v* **1 = enjoy**, appreciate, relish, delight in, luxuriate in, revel in **2** (often with *of*) **= suggest**, smack, be suggestive, show signs ▸ *n* **3 = flavour**, taste, smell, smack, relish, piquancy, tang
savoury *adj* **= spicy**, rich, tasty, palatable, luscious, appetizing, full-flavoured, mouthwatering, piquant
say *v* **1 = speak**, announce, state, declare, maintain, voice, remark, mention, pronounce, assert, utter, affirm • *She said they were very impressed.* **2 = suppose**,

DICTIONARY

regular payments are made into a savings account from a salary
Sayers *n* **Dorothy L(eigh).** 1893–1957, English detective-story writer
SC Star of Courage
scab *n* **1** crust formed over a wound **2** *offensive* blackleg
▸**scabby** *adj* **1** covered with scabs **2** *informal* despicable
scabbard *n* sheath for a sword or dagger
scabies [**skay**-beez] *n* itchy skin disease
scabious [**skay**-bee-uss] *n* plant with globular blue flower heads
scabrous [**skay**-bruss] *adj* **1** indecent **2** rough and scaly
scaffold *n* **1** temporary platform for workmen **2** gallows
▸**scaffolding** *n* (materials for building) scaffolds
scalar *n, adj* (variable quantity) having magnitude but no direction
scald *v* **1** burn with hot liquid or steam **2** sterilize with boiling water **3** heat (liquid) almost to boiling point ▷ *n* **4** injury by scalding
scale[1] Ⓣ *n* **1** one of the thin overlapping plates covering fishes and reptiles **2** thin flake **3** coating which forms in kettles etc. due to hard water **4** tartar formed on the teeth ▷ *v* **5** remove scales from **6** come off in scales **scaly** *adj*
scale[2] Ⓣ *n* **1** graduated table or sequence of marks at regular intervals, used as a reference in making measurements **2** fixed series of notes in music **3** ratio of size between a thing and a representation of it **4** relative degree or extent ▷ *v* **6** climb
▸**scale up** *or* **scale down** *v* increase *or* decrease proportionately in size
scale[3] *n often pl* weighing instrument
scalene *adj* (of a triangle) with three unequal sides
scallion *n* spring onion
scallop *n* **1** edible shellfish **2** one of a series of small curves along an edge
▸**scalloped** *adj* decorated with small curves along the edge
scallywag *n informal* scamp, rascal
scalp *n* **1** skin and hair on top of the head ▷ *v* **2** cut off the scalp of
scalpel *n* small surgical knife
scamp Ⓣ *n* **1** mischievous child ▷ *v* **2** do carelessly
scamper Ⓣ *v* **1** run about hurriedly or in play ▷ *n* **2** scampering
scampi *pl n* large prawns
scan Ⓣ *v* **scanning, scanned 1** scrutinize carefully **2** glance over quickly **3** examine or search (an area) by passing a radar or sonar beam over it **4** (of verse) conform to metrical rules ▷ *n* **5** scanning
▸**scanner** *n* electronic device used for scanning
▸**scansion** *n* metrical scanning of verse
scandal Ⓣ *n* **1** disgraceful action or event **2** malicious gossip **scandalous** *adj*
▸**scandalize** *v* shock by scandal
Scandinavian *n, adj* (inhabitant or language) of Scandinavia (Norway, Denmark, Sweden, and Iceland)
scant Ⓣ *adj* barely sufficient, meagre

THESAURUS

estimate, guess, assume, imagine, presume, conjecture, surmise **3 = express**, communicate, convey, imply ▷**say again** *See* **repeat** ▷**say no to** *See* **reject** ▷**say sorry** *See* **apologize** ▸*n* **4 = chance to speak**, vote, voice • *voters who want a say in the matter* **5 = influence**, power, authority, weight, clout (*informal*)
See also: **choice, comment, observe**
saying *n* = **proverb**, adage, maxim, axiom • *the saying "charity begins at home"*
scalding *See* **hot**
scale[1] *n* = **flake**, plate, layer, lamina
scale[2] *n* **1 = graduation**, series, ranking, sequence, progression, ladder, hierarchy, gradation, steps **2 = ratio**, proportion **3 = degree**, reach, range, extent, scope ▸*v* **4 = climb**, mount, ascend, clamber, surmount, escalade **5 = adjust**, regulate, proportion
scale drawing *See* **plan**
scam *v* (*Slang*) **1 = swindle**, fix, cheat, cook the books (*informal*), diddle (*informal*), wangle (*informal*) ▸*n* **2** (*Slang*) = **swindle**, fraud, fix, racket (*slang*)
scamp *n* = **rascal**, monkey, devil, rogue, imp, scallywag (*informal*)
scamper *v* = **run**, romp, dash, scuttle, hurry, hasten, dart, scurry, scoot
scan *v* **1 = glance over**, eye, check, examine, skim, check out (*informal*), look through, run one's eye over, run over **2 = scrutinize**, search, survey, investigate, sweep, scour
scandal *n* **1 = crime**, wrongdoing, disgrace, embarrassment, offence, sin **2 = shame**, stigma, disgrace, discredit, defamation, infamy, dishonour, ignominy, opprobrium **3 = gossip**, talk, dirt, slander, aspersion, rumours, tattle
scandalize *v* = **shock**, outrage, offend, horrify, appall, affront
scandalous *adj* **1 = shocking**, infamous, outrageous, disgraceful, shameful, unseemly, disreputable **2 = slanderous**, untrue, defamatory, libelous, scurrilous
scant *adj* = **meagre**, little, minimal,

DICTIONARY

scanty ⓣ *adj* **scantier, scantiest** barely sufficient or not sufficient **scantily** *adv* **scantiness** *n*
scapegoat ⓣ *n* person made to bear the blame for others
scapula *n, pl* **-lae, -las** shoulder blade ▸**scapular** *adj* of the scapula
scar[1] ⓣ *n* **1** mark left by a healed wound **2** permanent emotional damage left by an unpleasant experience ▹ *v* **scarring, scarred 3** mark or become marked with a scar
scar[2] *n* bare craggy rock formation
scarab *n* sacred beetle of ancient Egypt
scarce ⓣ *adj* **1** not common, rarely found **2** insufficient to meet demand **scarcity** *n* ▸**make oneself scarce** *informal* go away ▸**scarcely** *adv* **1** only just **2** not quite **3** definitely or probably not
scare ⓣ *v* **1** frighten or be frightened ▹ *n* **2** fright, sudden panic ▸**scary** *adj informal* frightening ▸**scarecrow** *n* **1** figure dressed in old clothes, set up to scare birds away from crops **2** raggedly dressed person ▸**scaremonger** *n* person who spreads alarming rumours
scarf[1] *n* piece of material worn round the neck, head, or shoulders
scarf[2] *n* **1** joint between two pieces of timber made by notching the ends and fastening them together ▹ *v* **2** join in this way
Scarfe *n* **Gerald.** born 1936, British cartoonist, famous for his scathing caricatures of politicians and celebrities
scarify *v* **-fying, -fied 1** scratch or cut slightly all over **2** break up and loosen (topsoil) **3** criticize mercilessly **scarification** *n*
Scarlatti *n* **1 Alessandro.** ?1659–1725, Italian composer; regarded as the founder of modern opera **2** his son, (**Giuseppe**) **Domenico**. 1685–1757, Italian composer and harpsichordist, in Portugal and Spain from 1720. He wrote over 550 single-movement sonatas for harpsichord, many of them exercises in virtuoso technique
scarlet *adj, n* brilliant red ▸**scarlet fever** infectious fever with a scarlet rash
scarp *n* steep slope
scarper ⓣ *v slang* run away
scat[1] *v* **scatting, scatted** *informal* go away
scat[2] *n* jazz singing using improvised vocal sounds instead of words
scathing ⓣ *adj* harshly critical
scatology *n* preoccupation with obscenity, esp. with references to excrement **scatological** *adj*
scatter ⓣ *v* **1** throw about in various directions **2** put here and there **3** disperse ▸**scatterbrain** *n* empty-headed person
scatty *adj* **-tier, -tiest** *informal* empty-headed
scavenge *v* search for (anything usable) among discarded material ▸**scavenger** *n* **1** person who scavenges **2** animal that feeds on decaying matter
SCE Scottish Certificate of Education
scenario ⓣ *n, pl* **-rios 1** summary of the plot of a play or film **2** imagined sequence of future events

THESAURUS

sparse, barely sufficient
scanty *adj* = **meagre**, short, poor, thin, inadequate, bare, insufficient, lousy (*slang*), sparse, scant, deficient, skimpy
scapegoat *n* = **whipping boy**, fall guy (*informal*)
scar *n* **1** = **mark**, injury, wound, blemish ▸ *v* **2** = **mark**, damage, disfigure
scarce *adj* = **rare**, few, unusual, uncommon • *Jobs are becoming increasingly scarce*. OPPOSITE: common
See also: **inadequate**
scarcely *adv* **1** = **hardly**, barely **2** = **definitely not**, hardly
scarcity *n* = **shortage**, want, lack, deficiency, dearth, insufficiency, paucity, rareness
scare *v* **1** = **frighten**, alarm, intimidate, terrify, terrorize, startle, unnerve, give someone a fright • *You're scaring me!* ▸ *n* **2** = **fright**, start, shock • *We had a bit of a scare.* **3** = **alert**, panic, hysteria • *Despite the health scare, there are no plans to withdraw the drug*.
scared *adj* = **frightened**, fearful, shaken, panicky, panic-stricken, petrified, startled, terrified
scarper *v* (*Slang*) = **run away**, flee, disappear, abscond, beat it (*slang*), clear off (*informal*), run for it, scram (*informal*), take to one's heels
scary *adj* (*Informal*) = **frightening**, eerie, spooky, creepy (*informal*), hair-raising, alarming, chilling, terrifying, unnerving • *Camping can be scary at night.*
scathing *adj* = **critical**, harsh, cutting, sarcastic, caustic, biting, scornful, trenchant, withering
scatter *v* **1** = **throw about**, shower, sprinkle, sow • *She scattered the rose petals*. OPPOSITE: gather **2** = **disperse**, dispel, disband, dissipate
See also: **distribute**
scatterbrain *n* = **featherbrain**, butterfly, flibbertigibbet
scenario *n* = **story line**, outline, summary, synopsis, résumé

DICTIONARY

scene Ⓣ *n* **1** place of action of a real or imaginary event **2** subdivision of a play or film in which the action is continuous **3** view of a place **4** display of emotion **5** *informal* specific activity or interest: *the fashion scene*
▶ **behind the scenes 1** backstage **2** in secret
▶ **scenery** *n* **1** natural features of a landscape **2** painted backcloths or screens used on stage to represent the scene of action
▶ **scenic** *adj* picturesque

scent Ⓣ *n* **1** pleasant smell **2** smell left in passing, by which an animal can be traced **3** series of clues **4** perfume ▷ *v* **5** detect by smell **6** suspect **7** fill with fragrance

sceptre *n* ornamental rod symbolizing royal power

schedule Ⓣ *n* **1** plan of procedure for a project **2** timetable **3** list ▷ *v* **4** plan to occur at a certain time

schema *n, pl* **-mata** overall plan or diagram
▶ **schematic** *adj* presented as a plan or diagram
▶ **schematize** *v* arrange in a scheme

scheme Ⓣ *n* **1** systematic plan **2** secret plot ▷ *v* **3** plan in an underhand manner
scheming *adj, n*

scherzo [**skairt**-so] *n, pl* **-zos, -zi** brisk lively piece of music

Schiller *n* **Johann Christoph Friedrich von**. 1759–1805, German poet, dramatist, historian, and critic. His concern with the ideal freedom of the human spirit to rise above the constraints placed upon it is reflected in his great trilogy *Wallenstein* (1800) and in *Maria Stuart* (1800)

schilling *n* former standard monetary unit of Austria

schism Ⓣ [**skizz**-um] *n* (group resulting from) division in an organization
schismatic *adj, n*

schist [**skist**] *n* crystalline rock which splits into layers

schizo [**skit**-so] *adj, n, pl* **-os** *offensive* schizophrenic (person)

schizoid *adj* **1** abnormally introverted **2** *informal* contradictory ▷ *n* **3** schizoid person

schizophrenia *n* **1** mental disorder involving deterioration of or confusion about the personality **2** *informal* contradictory behaviour or attitudes **schizophrenic** *adj, n*

Schlesinger *n* **John** (**Richard**). 1926–2003, British film and theatre director. Films include *Billy Liar* (1963), *Midnight Cowboy* (1969), *Sunday Bloody Sunday* (1971), and *Eye for an Eye* (1995)

schmaltz *n* excessive sentimentality
schmaltzy *adj*

schnapps *n* strong alcoholic spirit

Schnittke *n* **Alfred**. 1934–98, Russian composer: his works include four symphonies, four violin concertos, choral, chamber, and film music

schnitzel *n* thin slice of meat, esp. veal

Schoenberg, Schönberg *n* **Arnold**. 1874–1951, Austrian composer and musical theorist, in the US after 1933. The harmonic idiom of such early works as the string sextet *Verklärte Nacht* (1899) gave way to his development of atonality, as in the song cycle *Pierrot Lunaire* (1912), and later of the twelve-tone technique. He wrote many choral, orchestral, and chamber works and the unfinished opera *Moses and Aaron*

scholar Ⓣ *n* **1** learned person **2** pupil

THESAURUS

S

scene *n* **1** = **view**, landscape, panorama • *a village scene* **2** = **site**, place, spot, location, setting • *the scene of the crime* **3** = **world**, business, environment, arena • *the music scene* **4** = **setting**, set, location, background, backdrop **5** = **show**, picture, display, drama, exhibition, sight, spectacle, pageant **6** = **act**, part, division, episode **7** = **fuss**, performance, row, exhibition, tantrum, commotion, to-do

scenery *n* **1** = **landscape**, view, terrain, surroundings, panorama • *Drive slowly, and enjoy the scenery.* **2** (*Theatre*) = **set**, setting, backdrop, flats, stage set

scenic *adj* = **picturesque**, beautiful, spectacular, striking, panoramic

scent *n* **1** = **fragrance**, smell, perfume, aroma, bouquet, odour **2** = **trail**, track, spoor ▶ *v* **3** = **detect**, sense, smell, sniff, discern, nose out

scented *adj* = **fragrant**, aromatic, odoriferous, perfumed, sweet-smelling

schedule *n* **1** = **plan**, program, list, inventory, agenda, timetable, calendar, catalogue ▶ *v* **2** = **plan**, program, book, appoint, organize, arrange

scheduled *See* **set**

scheme *n* **1** = **plan**, program, system, project, proposal, strategy, road map, tactics **2** = **diagram**, draft, outline, pattern, chart, blueprint, layout **3** = **plot**, conspiracy, intrigue, ploy, ruse, manoeuvre, subterfuge, stratagem ▶ *v* **4** = **plan**, project, lay plans, work out **5** = **plot**, intrigue, conspire, collude, manoeuvre, machinate

scheming *adj* = **calculating**, tricky, wily, sly, cunning, artful, conniving, underhand

schism *n* = **division**, break, split, breach, separation, rift, rupture

scholar *n* **1** = **intellectual**, academic, savant **2** = **student**, pupil, schoolboy *or* schoolgirl, learner, disciple

DICTIONARY

3 student receiving a scholarship
▶ **scholarly** *adj* learned
▶ **scholarship** *n* **1** learning **2** financial aid given to a student because of academic merit
▶ **scholastic** *adj* of schools or scholars
school[1] Ⓣ *n* **1** place where children are taught or instruction is given in a subject **2** group of artists, thinkers, etc. with shared principles or methods ▷ *v* **3** educate **4** discipline, train
school[2] *n* shoal of fish, whales, etc.
schooner *n* **1** sailing ship rigged fore-and-aft **2** large glass
Schopenhauer *n* **Arthur**. 1788–1860, German pessimist philosopher. In his chief work, *The World as Will and Idea* (1819), he expounded the view that will is the creative primary factor and idea the secondary receptive factor
schottische *n* type of slow polka
Schreyer *n* **Edward** (**Richard**). born 1935, Canadian politician; Governor General (1979–84)
Schröder *n* **Gerhard**. born 1944, German Social Democrat politician; chancellor of Germany (1998–2005)
Schrödinger *n* **Erwin**. 1887–1961, Austrian physicist, who discovered the wave equation: shared the Nobel prize for physics 1933
Schubert *n* **Franz** (**Peter**). 1797–1828, Austrian composer; the originator and supreme exponent of the modern German lied. His many songs include the cycles *Die Schöne Müllerin* (1823) and *Die Winterreise* (1827). His other works include symphonies and piano and chamber music including string quartets and the *Trout* piano quintet (1819)
Schumacher *n* **Michael**. born 1969, German motor racing driver, who has won more Grand Prix races than any other; Formula One world champion (1994–95, 2000–04)
Schuman *n* **William** (**Howard**). 1910–91, US composer
Schumann *n* **Robert Alexander**. 1810–56, German romantic composer, noted esp. for his piano music, songs, and four symphonies
Schütz *n* **Heinrich**. 1585–1672, German composer, esp. of church music and madrigals
Schweitzer *n* **Albert**. 1875–1965, Franco-German medical missionary, philosopher, theologian, and organist, born in Alsace. He took up medicine in 1905 and devoted most of his life after 1913 to a medical mission at Lambaréné, Gabon: Nobel peace prize 1952
sciatica *n* severe pain in the large nerve in the back of the leg
▶ **sciatic** *adj* **1** of the hip **2** of or afflicted with sciatica
science Ⓣ *n* systematic study and knowledge of natural or physical phenomena
▶ **scientific** *adj* **1** of science **2** systematic
scientifically *adv*
▶ **scientist** *n* person who studies or practises a science
▶ **science fiction** stories making imaginative use of scientific knowledge
sci-fi *n* short for **science fiction**
scimitar *n* curved oriental sword
scintillate *v* **1** give off sparks **2** be animated and witty **scintillating** *adj* **scintillation** *n*
scion [**sy**-on] *n* **1** descendant or heir **2** shoot of a plant for grafting
Scipio *n* **1** full name *Publius Cornelius Scipio Africanus Major.* 237–183 BC, Roman general. He commanded the Roman invasion of Carthage in the Second Punic War, defeating Hannibal at Zama (202) **2** full name *Publius Cornelius Scipio Aemilianus Africanus Minor.* ?185–129 BC, Roman statesman and general; the grandson by adoption of Scipio Africanus Major. He commanded an army against Carthage in the last Punic War and razed the city to the ground (146). He became the leader (132) of the opposition in Rome to popular reforms
scissors *pl n* cutting instrument with two crossed pivoted blades
sclerosis *n, pl* **-ses** abnormal hardening of body tissues
scoff[1] Ⓣ *v* express derision

S

THESAURUS

scholarly *adj* = **learned**, academic, intellectual, bookish, scholastic, erudite, lettered
scholarship *n* **1** = **learning**, education, knowledge, book-learning, erudition **2** = **grant**, fellowship, bursary
scholastic *adj* = **learned**, academic, scholarly, lettered
school *n* **1** = **academy**, college, institution, institute, faculty, seminary **2** = **group**, set, circle, faction, denomination, adherents, devotees, disciples, followers ▶ *v* **3** = **train**, coach, drill, discipline, educate, instruct, tutor
schooling *n* **1** = **teaching**, education, tuition **2** = **training**, drill, instruction, coaching
science *n* **1** = **discipline**, body of knowledge, branch of knowledge **2** = **skill**, art, technique
scientific *adj* = **systematic**, accurate, exact, precise, controlled, mathematical
scientist *n* = **inventor**, technophile
scintillating *adj* = **brilliant**, bright, exciting, animated, sparkling, lively, dazzling, glittering, stimulating
scoff[1] *v* = **scorn**, knock (*informal*), mock, jeer, ridicule, deride, despise, belittle, sneer, pooh-pooh, laugh at

DICTIONARY

scoff[2] Ⓣ *v slang* eat rapidly
Scofield *n* (**David**) **Paul**. 1922–2008, English stage and film actor
scold Ⓣ *v* **1** find fault with, reprimand ▷ *n* **2** person who scolds **scolding** *n*
scollop *n* same as **scallop**
sconce *n* bracket on a wall for holding candles or lights
scone *n* small plain cake baked in an oven or on a griddle
scoop Ⓣ *n* **1** shovel-like tool for ladling or hollowing out **2** news story reported in one newspaper before all its rivals ▷ *v* **3** take up or hollow out with or as if with a scoop **4** beat (rival newspapers) in reporting a news item
scoot *v slang* leave or move quickly
▶ **scooter** *n* **1** child's vehicle propelled by pushing on the ground with one foot **2** light motorcycle
Scopas *n* 4th century BC, Greek sculptor and architect
scope Ⓣ *n* **1** range of activity **2** opportunity for using abilities
scorch Ⓣ *v* **1** burn on the surface **2** parch or shrivel from heat ▷ *n* **3** slight burn
▶ **scorcher** *n informal* very hot day
score Ⓣ *n* **1** points gained in a game or competition **2** twenty **3** written version of a piece of music showing parts for each musician **4** mark or cut **5** grievance: *settle old scores* **scores 6** lots ▷ *v* **7** gain points in a game **8** mark or cut **9** (foll. by *out*) cross out **10** arrange music (for) **11** keep a record of points **12** achieve a success
scorn Ⓣ *n* **1** contempt, derision ▷ *v* **2** despise **3** reject with contempt **scornful** *adj* **scornfully** *adv*
scorpion *n* small lobster-shaped animal with a sting at the end of a jointed tail
Scorsese *n* **Martin**. born 1942, US film director, whose films include *Taxi Driver* (1976), *Raging Bull* (1980), the controversial *The Last Temptation of Christ* (1988), *Casino* (1995), and *Gangs of New York* (2002)
Scot *n* person from Scotland **Scotsman** (**Scotswoman**) *n*
▶ **Scottish** *adj* of Scotland, its people, or their languages (Also **Scots**)
▶ **Scotch** *n* whisky distilled in Scotland
▶ **Scotch tape** *n* **1** ® type of adhesive tape ▷ *v* **2** stick with Scotch tape
scotch *v* put an end to
scot-free *adj* without harm or punishment
Scotland Yard *n* headquarters of the police force of metropolitan London
Scott *n* **1 Frederick George**. 1861–1944, Canadian poet, lawyer, and legal educator. Known as the Poet of the Laurentians, and wrote "The Unnamed Lake" and war memoir *The Great War as I Saw It* **2** Sir **George Gilbert**. 1811–78, British architect, prominent in the Gothic revival. He restored many churches and cathedrals and designed the Albert Memorial (1863) and St Pancras Station (1865) **3** his grandson, Sir **Giles Gilbert**. 1880–1960, British architect, whose designs include the Anglican cathedral in Liverpool (1904–78) and the new Waterloo Bridge (1939–45) **4** Sir **Peter** (**Markham**). 1909–89, British naturalist, wildlife artist, and conservationist, noted esp. for his paintings of birds. He founded (1946) the Slimbridge refuge for waterfowl in Gloucestershire **5** his father, **Robert Falcon**. 1868–1912, British naval officer and explorer of the Antarctic. He commanded two Antarctic expeditions (1901–04; 1910–12) and reached the South Pole on Jan 18, 1912, shortly after Amundsen; he and the rest of his party

THESAURUS

S

scoff[2] *v* = **gobble** *or* **gobble up**, bolt, wolf, guzzle, devour, gorge oneself on, gulp down
scold *v* = **reprimand**, rebuke, lecture, chide, tell off (*informal*) • *She scolded the child for being naughty*.
See also: **abuse**
scolding *n* = **rebuke**, row, lecture, telling-off (*informal*)
scoop *n* **1** = **ladle**, spoon, dipper **2** = **exclusive**, revelation, sensation, exposé ▶ *v* **3** (often with *up*) = **gather up**, lift, pick up, take up **4** (often with *out*) = **hollow**, bail, empty, dig, shovel, gouge, excavate
scope *n* **1** = **opportunity**, space, room, freedom, liberty, latitude **2** = **range**, area, reach, capacity, outlook, orbit, span, sphere
scorch *v* = **burn**, roast, wither, sear, singe, shrivel, parch
scorching *adj* = **burning**, red-hot, fiery, flaming, roasting, baking, boiling, searing
score *n* **1** = **points**, record, result, mark, total, outcome, grade **2** = **grounds**, cause, reason, ground, basis **3** = **grievance**, injury, wrong, injustice, grudge ▷ **scores** = **lots**, hundreds, masses, millions, multitudes, myriads, swarms ▶ *v* **4** = **gain**, make, win, post, net, achieve, nail, chalk up (*informal*), sports, notch up (*informal*) **5** = **keep count**, record, count, register, tally **6** = **cut**, mark, slash, scratch, scrape, gouge, graze, deface **7** (with *out* or *through*) = **cross out**, cancel, delete, obliterate, strike out **8** (*Music*) = **arrange**, set, adapt, orchestrate
scorn *n* **1** = **contempt**, disdain, mockery, derision • *The proposal was greeted with scorn*. ▶ *v* **2** = **despise**, slight, disdain, look down on • *He scorns the work of others*.
See also: **belittle**
scornful *adj* = **contemptuous**, scathing, disdainful, sneering, supercilious, withering

DICTIONARY

died on the return journey
scoundrel Ⓣ *n old-fashioned* villainous person
scour[1] Ⓣ *v* **1** clean or polish by rubbing with something rough **2** clear or flush out
▸ **scourer** *n* small rough nylon pad used for cleaning pots and pans
scour[2] Ⓣ *v* search thoroughly and energetically
scourge Ⓣ *n* **1** person or thing causing severe suffering **2** whip ▹ *v* **3** cause severe suffering to **4** whip
Scouse *informal* ▹ *n* **1** Also **Scouser** person from Liverpool **2** dialect of Liverpool ▹ *adj* **3** of Liverpool, its people, or their dialect
scout Ⓣ *n* **1** person sent out to reconnoitre **2 Scout** member of the Scout Association, an organization for boys which aims to develop character and promotes outdoor activities ▹ *v* **3** act as a scout **4** reconnoitre
▸ **Scouter** *n* leader of a troop of Scouts
scow *n* unpowered barge
scowl Ⓣ *v, n* (have) an angry or sullen expression
scrabble Ⓣ *v* scrape at with the hands, feet, or claws
scrag *n* lean end of a neck of mutton
▸ **scraggy** *adj* thin, bony
scram Ⓣ *v* **scramming, scrammed 1** (of a nuclear reactor) shut or be shut down in an emergency **2** *informal* go away hastily ▹ *n* **3** emergency shutdown of a nuclear reactor
scramble Ⓣ *v* **1** climb or crawl hastily or awkwardly **2** struggle with others (for) **3** mix up **4** cook (eggs beaten up with milk) **5** render (transmitted speech) unintelligible by an electronic device **6** (of an aircraft or aircrew) take off hurriedly in an emergency ▹ *n* **7** scrambling **8** rough climb **9** disorderly struggle **10** motorcycle race over rough ground
▸ **scrambler** *n* electronic device that renders transmitted speech unintelligible
scrap Ⓣ *n* **1** small piece **2** waste metal collected for reprocessing **3** *informal* fight or quarrel **scraps 4** leftover food ▹ *v* **scrapping, scrapped 5** discard as useless **6** *informal* fight or quarrel
▸ **scrappy** *adj* badly organized or done
▸ **scrapbook** *n* book with blank pages in which newspaper cuttings or pictures are stuck
scrape Ⓣ *v* **1** rub with something rough or sharp **2** clean or smooth thus **3** rub with a harsh noise **4** economize ▹ *n* **5** act or sound of scraping **6** mark or wound caused by scraping **7** *informal* awkward situation
scraper *n*
▸ **scrape through** *v* succeed in or obtain with difficulty
scratch Ⓣ *v* **1** mark or cut with claws,

THESAURUS

• *He is deeply scornful of his rivals.*
scoundrel *n* = **rogue**, bastard (*offensive*), heel (*slang*), miscreant, good-for-nothing, rascal, reprobate, villain, swine, scamp
scour[1] *v* = **scrub**, clean, wash, buff, rub, polish, abrade
scour[2] *v* = **search**, beat, hunt, comb, ransack
scourge *n* **1** = **affliction**, terror, plague, curse, pest, misfortune, torment, bane, infliction **2** = **whip**, switch, cat, lash, strap, thong ▸ *v* **3** = **afflict**, plague, curse, terrorize, torment **4** = **whip**, beat, lash, thrash, cane, flog, horsewhip
scout *n* **1** = **vanguard**, lookout, precursor, advance guard, outrider, reconnoitrer ▸ *v* **2** = **reconnoitre**, probe, investigate, observe, survey, watch, spy
scowl *v* **1** = **glower**, frown, lour *or* lower ▸ *n* **2** = **glower**, frown, black look, dirty look
scrabble *v* = **scrape**, scramble, scratch, claw
scraggy *adj* = **scrawny**, lean, skinny, bony, angular
scram *v* = **go away**, leave, abscond, beat it (*slang*), clear off (*informal*), get lost (*informal*), make oneself scarce (*informal*), make tracks, vamoose (*slang*)
scramble *v* **1** = **struggle**, climb, swarm, crawl, scrabble **2** = **strive**, run, push, rush, vie, contend, jostle ▸ *n* **3** = **climb**, trek **4** = **struggle**, race, competition, rush, confusion, melee *or* mêlée, commotion, tussle
scrap[1] *n* **1** = **piece**, part, bit, grain, portion, particle, fragment, snippet, crumb, sliver, morsel **2** = **waste**, junk, off cuts ▹ **scraps** = **leftovers**, bits, leavings, remains ▸ *v* **3** = **discard**, drop, abandon, ditch (*slang*), jettison, throw away *or* throw out, write off
scrap[2] (*Informal*) *n* **1** = **fight**, battle, dispute, row, argument, disagreement, squabble, wrangle, quarrel ▸ *v* **2** = **fight**, argue, row, squabble, wrangle
scrape *v* **1** = **graze**, skin, scratch, scour, scuff • *We had to scrape the frost from the windshield.* **2** = **grate**, grind, scratch, rasp • *her shoes scraping across the ground* **3** = **clean**, remove, erase, rub, scour **4** = **scrimp**, save, stint, pinch, skimp ▹ **scrape through** = **get by** (*informal*), struggle, just make it ▸ *n* **5** (*Informal*) = **predicament**, fix (*informal*), difficulty, mess, plight, dilemma, awkward situation, tight spot
scrapheap *n* ▹ **on the scrapheap** = **discarded**, ditched (*slang*), jettisoned, redundant, put out to pasture (*informal*)
scrappy *adj* = **incomplete**, sketchy, piecemeal, disjointed, bitty, fragmentary, thrown together
scratch *v* **1** = **mark**, score, cut,

DICTIONARY

nails, or anything rough or sharp **2** scrape (skin) with nails or claws to relieve itching **3** withdraw from a race or competition ▷ *n* **4** wound, mark, or sound made by scratching ▷ *adj* **5** put together at short notice **scratchy** *adj*

▸ **from scratch** from the very beginning

▸ **up to scratch** up to standard

scrawl Ⓣ *v* **1** write carelessly or hastily ▷ *n* **2** scribbled writing

scrawny Ⓣ *adj* **scrawnier, scrawniest** thin and bony

scream Ⓣ *v* **1** utter a piercing cry, esp. of fear or pain **2** utter with a scream ▷ *n* **3** shrill piercing cry **4** *informal* very funny person or thing

scree *n* slope of loose shifting stones

screech[1] Ⓣ *v, n* (utter) a shrill cry

screech[2] *n slang* (esp. in Newfoundland) a type of cheap dark rum

screed *n* long tedious piece of writing

screen Ⓣ *n* **1** movable structure used to shelter, divide, or conceal something **2** surface of a television set, VDU, etc., on which an image is formed **3** white surface on which photographs are projected ▷ *v* **4** shelter or conceal with or as if with a screen **5** show (a film) **6** examine (a person or group) to determine suitability for a task or to detect the presence of disease or weapons

▸ **the screen** cinema generally

▸ **screen saver** *computers* changing image on a monitor when the computer is operative but idle

screw Ⓣ *n* **1** metal pin with a spiral ridge along its length, twisted into materials to fasten them together **2** *slang* prison guard ▷ *v* **3** turn (a screw) **4** fasten with screw(s) **5** twist **6** *informal* extort

▸ **screwy** *adj informal* crazy or eccentric

▸ **screwball** *slang* ▷ *n* **1** odd person **2** *baseball* pitch that curves towards the side from which it was thrown ▷ *adj* **3** odd

▸ **screwdriver** *n* tool for turning screws

▸ **screw up** *v informal* **1** bungle **2** distort

Scriabin, Skryabin *n* **Aleksandr Nikolayevich**. 1872–1915, Russian composer, whose works came increasingly to express his theosophic beliefs. He wrote many piano works; his orchestral compositions include *Prometheus* (1911)

scribble Ⓣ *v* **1** write hastily or illegibly **2** make meaningless or illegible marks ▷ *n* **3** something scribbled

scribe Ⓣ *n* **1** person who copied manuscripts before the invention of printing **2** *Bible* scholar of the Jewish Law **scribal** *adj*

Scribe *n* **Augustin Eugène**. 1791–1861, French author or coauthor of over 350 vaudevilles, comedies, and libretti for light opera

scrimmage *n* rough or disorderly struggle

scrimp Ⓣ *v* be very economical

scrip *n* certificate representing a claim to stocks or shares

script Ⓣ *n* **1** text of a film, play, or TV programme **2** particular system of writing: *Arabic script* **3** handwriting

scripture *n* sacred writings of a religion **scriptural** *adj*

scrofula *n* tuberculosis of the lymphatic glands **scrofulous** *adj*

scroll *n* **1** roll of parchment or paper **2** ornamental carving shaped like this ▷ *v* **3** move (text) up or down on a VDU screen

Scrooge *n* miserly person

THESAURUS

damage, claw, scrape, grate, graze, etch, lacerate **2 = withdraw**, cancel, eliminate, erase, delete, abolish, call off, pull out ▸ *n* **3 = mark**, scrape, graze, blemish, gash, laceration, claw mark

▷ **up to scratch = adequate**, acceptable, sufficient, satisfactory, up to standard ▸ *adj* **5 = improvised**, impromptu, rough-and-ready

scrawl *v* **= scribble**, writing, doodle, squiggle

scrawny *adj* **= thin**, lean, skinny, gaunt, bony, scraggy, skin-and-bones (*informal*), undernourished

scream *v* **1 = cry**, shout, yell, howl, screech, shriek, squeal • *lots of people screaming on a roller coaster* ▸ *n* **2 = cry**, yell, howl, screech, shriek, squeal • *The child let out a scream.*

screech *n, v* **= cry**, scream, shriek

screen *n* **1 = cover**, guard, shelter, shield, cloak, shade, canopy, partition, awning, room divider **2 = mesh**, net ▸ *v* **3 = cover**, hide, mask, cloak, veil, shade, conceal **4 = protect**, defend, guard, shelter, shield **5 = vet**, examine, sort, scan, evaluate, filter, gauge, sift **6 = broadcast**, show, present, put on

screw *v* **1 = turn**, tighten, twist **2** (*Informal*) (often with *out of*) **= extort**, extract, wrest, wring

screw up *v* **1** (*Informal*) **= bungle**, botch, spoil, mishandle, make a mess of (*slang*), mess up **2 = distort**, wrinkle, pucker, contort

screwy *adj* **= crazy**, odd, eccentric, nutty (*slang*), loopy (*informal*), off-the-wall (*slang*), crackpot (*informal*), out to lunch (*informal*), weird

scribble *v* **= scrawl**, write, jot, dash off

scribe *n* **= copyist**, writer, amanuensis

scrimp *v* **= economize**, save, stint, scrape, skimp, be frugal, tighten one's belt

script *n* **1 = text**, book, copy, dialogue,

DICTIONARY

scrotum *n, pl* **-ta, -tums** pouch of skin containing the testicles
scrounge Ⓣ *v informal* get by cadging or begging **scrounger** *n*
scrub[1] Ⓣ *v* **scrubbing, scrubbed 1** clean by rubbing, often with a hard brush and water **2** *informal* delete or cancel ▷ *n* **3** scrubbing
▸ **scrubs** *pl n med* light, loose clothing worn by hospital staff
scrub[2] *n* **1** stunted trees **2** area of land covered with scrub
▸ **scrubby** *adj* **1** covered with scrub **2** stunted **3** *informal* shabby
scruff *n* nape (of the neck)
scruffy Ⓣ *adj* **scruffier, scruffiest** unkempt or shabby
scrum, scrummage *n* **1** *rugby* restarting of play in which opposing packs of forwards push against each other to gain possession of the ball **2** disorderly struggle
scrump *v Brit dialect* steal (apples) from an orchard or garden
scrumptious Ⓣ *adj informal* delicious
scrumpy *n* rough dry cider
scrunch *v* **1** crumple or crunch or be crumpled or crunched ▷ *n* **2** act or sound of scrunching
scrunchie *n* loop of elastic covered loosely with fabric, used to hold the hair in a ponytail
scruple Ⓣ *n* **1** doubt produced by one's conscience or morals ▷ *v* **2** have doubts on moral grounds
▸ **scrupulous** *adj* **1** very conscientious **2** very careful or precise **scrupulously** *adv*
scrutiny Ⓣ *n, pl* **-nies** close examination
▸ **scrutinize** *v* examine closely
scuba diving *n* sport of swimming under water using cylinders containing compressed air attached to breathing apparatus
scud *v* **scudding, scudded** move along swiftly
scuff Ⓣ *v* **1** drag (the feet) while walking **2** scrape (one's shoes) by doing so ▷ *n* **3** mark caused by scuffing
scuffle Ⓣ *v* **1** fight in a disorderly manner **2** move by shuffling ▷ *n* **3** disorderly struggle **4** scuffling sound
scull *n* **1** small oar ▷ *v* **2** row (a boat) using a scull
scullery *n, pl* **-leries** small room where washing-up and other kitchen work is done
sculpture Ⓣ *n* **1** art of making figures or designs in wood, stone, etc. **2** product of this art ▷ *v* **3** Also **sculpt** represent in sculpture
sculptor (**sculptress**) *n* **sculptural** *adj*
scum Ⓣ *n* **1** impure or waste matter on the surface of a liquid **2** worthless people
scummy *adj*
scupper Ⓣ *v informal* defeat or ruin
scurf *n* flaky skin on the scalp **scurfy** *adj*
scurrilous *adj* untrue and defamatory
scurrility *n*
scurry Ⓣ *v* **-rying, -ried 1** move hastily ▷ *n* **2** act or sound of scurrying
scurvy *n* disease caused by lack of vitamin C

THESAURUS

libretto, lines, words **2 = handwriting**, writing, calligraphy, penmanship
scriptural *See* **religious**
Scripture *n* = **The Bible**, Holy Bible, Holy Scripture, Holy Writ, The Good Book, The Gospels, The Scriptures
scrounge *v* = **mooch**, beg, bum, sponge (*informal*) • *He's always scrounging for money.*
scrounger *adj* = **cadger**, parasite, freeloder (*slang*), sponger (*informal*)
scrub *v* = **scour**, clean, rub, cleanse
scruffy *adj* = **shabby**, ragged, seedy, tatty, unkempt • *four scruffy boys* OPPOSITE: smart
scrumptious *adj* (*Informal*) = **delicious**, yummy (*informal*), delectable, luscious, succulent, appetizing, mouthwatering
scruple *n* **1** = **misgiving**, doubt, reluctance, hesitation, qualm, uneasiness, compunction, second thoughts ▸ *v* **2** = **have misgivings about**, doubt, hesitate, demur, have qualms about, think twice about
scruples *pl n* = **conscience**, principle, standards
scrupulous *adj* **1** = **moral**, upright, principled, conscientious, honorable **2** = **careful**, strict, exact, precise, rigorous, meticulous, fastidious, punctilious
scrutinize *v* = **examine**, study, search, scan, inspect, pore over • *She scrutinized his features.* *See also*: **observe, regard**
scrutiny *n* = **examination**, study, investigation, search, analysis, inspection, exploration, perusal
scuff *See* **scrape**
scuffle *v* **1** = **fight**, struggle, clash, grapple, jostle, tussle ▸ *n* **2** = **fight**, brawl, skirmish, disturbance, fray, scrimmage, commotion, tussle
sculpt *See* **carve, model**
sculpture *v* = **carve**, form, model, fashion, shape, sculpt, mould, chisel, hew
scum *n* **1** = **impurities**, film, froth, dross **2** = **rabble**, trash, dregs of society, riffraff
scupper *v* = **destroy**, defeat, ruin, wreck, demolish, torpedo, put paid to
scurrilous *adj* = **slanderous**, abusive, scandalous, defamatory, insulting, vituperative
scurry *v* **1** = **hurry**, race, sprint, dash, scuttle, scamper, dart, scoot ▸ *n* **2** = **flurry**, whirl, scampering

DICTIONARY

scut *n* short tail of the hare, rabbit, or deer
scuttle[1] *n* fireside container for coal
scuttle[2] ⓘ *v* **1** run with short quick steps ▷ *n* **2** hurried run
scuttle[3] *v* make a hole in (a ship) to sink it
scythe *n* **1** long-handled tool with a curved blade for cutting grass ▷ *v* **2** cut with a scythe
SE southeast(ern)
sea ⓘ *n* **1** mass of salt water covering three quarters of the earth's surface **2** particular area of this **3** turbulence or swell **4** vast expanse
▸ **at sea** **1** in a ship on the ocean **2** confused or bewildered
▸ **sea anemone** sea animal with suckers like petals
▸ **seaboard** *n* coast
▸ **sea dog** experienced sailor
▸ **seafaring** *adj* working or travelling by sea
▸ **seafood** *n* edible saltwater fish or shellfish
▸ **sea gull** gull
▸ **sea horse** small sea fish with a plated body and horselike head
▸ **sea level** average level of the sea's surface in relation to the land
▸ **sea lion** kind of large seal
▸ **seaman** *n* sailor
▸ **seaplane** *n* aircraft designed to take off from and land on water
▸ **seasick** *adj* suffering from nausea caused by the motion of a ship **seasickness** *n*
▸ **seaside** *n* area, esp. a holiday resort, on the coast
▸ **sea urchin** sea animal with a round spiky shell
▸ **seaweed** *n* plant growing in the sea
▸ **seaworthy** *adj* (of a ship) in fit condition for a sea voyage
Seaborg *n* **Glenn Theodore**. 1912–99, US chemist and nuclear physicist. With E.M. McMillan, he discovered several transuranic elements, including plutonium (1940), curium, and americium (1944), and shared a Nobel prize for chemistry (1951)
seal[1] ⓘ *n* **1** piece of wax, lead, etc. with a special design impressed upon it, attached to a letter or document as a mark of authentication **2** device or material used to close an opening tightly ▷ *v* **3** make airtight or watertight **4** close with or as if with a seal **5** affix a seal to or stamp with a seal **6** decide (one's fate) irrevocably
▸ **sealant** *n* any substance used for sealing
▸ **seal off** *v* enclose or isolate (a place) completely
seal[2] *n* amphibious mammal with flippers as limbs **sealskin** *n*
seam ⓘ *n* **1** line where two edges are joined, as by stitching **2** thin layer of coal or ore ▷ *v* **3** mark with furrows or wrinkles **seamless** *adj*
▸ **seamy** *adj* sordid
seamstress *n* woman who sews
seance [**say**-anss] *n* meeting at which spiritualists attempt to communicate with the dead
sear ⓘ *v* **1** scorch, burn the surface of **2** cause to wither
search ⓘ *v* **1** examine closely in order to find something ▷ *n* **2** searching
▸ **searching** *adj* keen or thorough: *a searching look*
▸ **search engine** *computers* internet service enabling users to search for items of interest
▸ **searchlight** *n* powerful light with a beam that can be shone in any direction
season ⓘ *n* **1** one of four divisions of the year, each of which has characteristic weather conditions **2** period during which a thing happens or is plentiful **3** fitting or

S

THESAURUS

scuttle *v* = **run**, rush, hurry, bustle, hasten, scamper, scurry, scoot
sea *n* **1** = **ocean**, main, the deep, the waves **2** = **mass**, abundance, multitude, expanse, plethora, profusion ▷ **at sea** = **bewildered**, lost, confused, baffled, mystified, puzzled
seafaring *adj* = **nautical**, marine, naval, maritime
seal *n* **1** = **authentication**, stamp, confirmation, ratification, insignia, imprimatur ▸ *v* **2** = **close**, stop, shut, plug, enclose, stopper, fasten, bung, stop up **3** = **authenticate**, confirm, stamp, ratify, validate **4** = **settle**, conclude, clinch, finalize, consummate ▷ **seal off** = **isolate**, quarantine, segregate, put out of bounds
sealed *See* **shut**
seam *n* **1** = **joint**, closure **2** = **layer**, vein, stratum, lode **3** = **ridge**, line, wrinkle, furrow
sear *v* = **scorch**, burn, sizzle
search *v* **1** = **hunt**, look, seek, comb, scour, forage, sift • *The RCMP is searching for the missing men.* ▷ **search for** *See* **seek** ▸ *n* **2** = **hunt**, quest • *Police will resume the search today.*
searching *adj* = **keen**, close, sharp, intent, piercing, penetrating, probing, quizzical
seashore *See* **beach**
seaside *See* **beach, coast**
season *n* **1** = **period**, time, term, spell ▸ *v* **2** = **flavour**, salt, spice, enliven, pep up
seasonable *adj* = **appropriate**, fit, timely, suitable, convenient, opportune, well-timed, providential
seasoned *adj* = **experienced**, veteran, hardened, practised, time-served
seasoning *n* = **flavouring**, sauce, spice, relish, dressing, condiment, salt and pepper

DICTIONARY

proper time ▷ *v* **4** flavour with salt, herbs, etc. **5** dry (timber) till ready for use
▸ **seasonable** *adj* **1** appropriate for the season **2** timely or opportune
▸ **seasonal** *adj* depending on or varying with the seasons
▸ **seasoned** *adj* experienced
▸ **seasoning** *n* salt, herbs, etc. added to food to enhance flavour
▸ **season ticket** ticket for a series of journeys or events within a specified period
seat Ⓣ *n* **1** thing designed or used for sitting on **2** place to sit in a theatre, esp. one that requires a ticket **3** buttocks **4** membership of a legislative or administrative body **5** country house ▷ *v* **6** cause to sit **7** provide seating for
▸ **seat belt** belt worn in an automobile or aircraft to prevent a person being thrown forward in a crash
sebaceous *adj* of, like, or secreting fat or oil
Sebastian *n* **Saint**. died ?288 AD, Christian martyr. According to tradition, he was first shot with arrows and then beaten to death. Feast day: Jan 20
sec[1] *adj* (of wines) dry
sec[2] *n informal* second (of time)
secateurs *pl n* small pruning shears
secede Ⓣ *v* withdraw formally from a political alliance or federation **secession** *n*
seclude *v* keep (a person) from contact with others **seclusion** *n*
▸ **secluded** *adj* private, sheltered
second[1] Ⓣ *adj* **1** coming directly after the first **2** alternate, additional **3** inferior ▷ *n* **4** person or thing coming second **5** sixtieth part of a minute **6** moment **7** attendant in a duel or boxing match **seconds 8** inferior goods ▷ *v* **9** express formal support for (a motion proposed in a meeting) **secondly** *adv*
▸ **second-class** *adj* **1** inferior **2** cheaper, slower, or less comfortable than first-class
▸ **second-hand** *adj* bought after use by another
▸ **second nature** something so habitual that it seems part of one's character
▸ **second sight** supposed ability to predict events
▸ **second thoughts** revised opinion on a matter already considered
▸ **second wind** renewed ability to continue effort
second[2] [si-**kawnd**] *v* transfer (a person) temporarily to another job **secondment** *n*
secondary *adj* **1** coming after or derived from what is primary or first **2** of less importance **3** relating to the education of people between the ages of 11 and 18
Secord *n* **Laura** (née *Ingersoll*). 1775–1868, Canadian heroine. In June 1813 she overheard US officers discussing a planned attack on British forces and then walked 30 km from Queenston to Beaver Dams to raise the alarm. Because of her warning the British countered with an ambush and defeated the Americans
secret Ⓣ *adj* **1** kept from the knowledge of others ▷ *n* **2** something kept secret **3** mystery **4** underlying explanation: *the secret of my success* **secretly** *adv* **secrecy** *n*

THESAURUS

seat *n* **1 = chair**, settle, bench, stall, stool, pew **2 = centre**, place, site, heart, source, capital, situation, hub **3 = residence**, house, mansion, abode, ancestral hall **4 = membership**, place, chair, constituency, incumbency ▸ *v* **5 = sit**, set, place, settle, fix, locate, install **6 = hold**, take, contain, sit, accommodate, cater for
seating *n* **= accommodation**, room, chairs, places, seats
secede *v* **= withdraw**, leave, resign, quit, break with, pull out, split from
secluded *adj* **= private**, isolated, lonely, solitary, sheltered, cloistered, cut off, out-of-the-way
seclusion *n* **= privacy**, shelter, isolation, solitude
second[1] *adj* **1 = next**, subsequent, following, succeeding **2 = additional**, other, further, extra, alternative **3 = inferior**, lower, secondary, lesser, subordinate ▷ **second in command = deputy**, number two, right-hand man ▸ *n* **4 = supporter**, assistant, backer, helper ▸ *v* **5 = support**, back, assist, approve, endorse, go along with
second[2] *n* **= moment**, minute, flash, instant, sec (*informal*), jiffy (*informal*), trice
secondary *adj* **1 = subordinate**, lower, minor, lesser, inferior, unimportant **2 = resultant**, contingent, indirect, derived **3 = backup**, reserve, subsidiary, auxiliary, fall-back, supporting
second-class *adj* **= inferior**, mediocre, indifferent, second-best, second-rate, undistinguished, uninspiring
second-hand *adj* **1 = used**, hand-me-down (*informal*), nearly new ▸ *adv* **2 = indirectly**
secondly *adv* **= next**, second, in the second place
second-rate *adj* **= inferior**, poor, mediocre, shoddy, low-grade, tacky (*informal*), substandard, low-quality, rubbishy, tawdry, two-bit (*slang*)
secrecy *n* **1 = mystery**, privacy, silence, confidentiality, concealment **2 = secretiveness**, stealth, clandestineness, covertness, furtiveness
secret *adj* **1 = undisclosed**, underground, confidential, undercover, closet (*informal*), covert, hidden, furtive • *a secret*

S

DICTIONARY

▶ **in secret** without other people knowing
▶ **secretive** *adj* inclined to keep things secret **secretiveness** *n*
secretariat *n* administrative office or staff of a legislative body
secretary *n, pl* **-ries 1** person who deals with correspondence and general clerical work **2** head of a state department: *Home Secretary* **secretarial** *adj*
▶ **Secretary of State** head of a major government department
secrete Ⓣ *v* **1** hide or conceal **2** (of an organ, gland, etc.) produce and release (a substance) **secretion** *n* **secretory** [sek-**reet**-or-ee] *adj*
sect Ⓣ *n* subdivision of a religious or political group, esp. one with extreme beliefs
▶ **sectarian** *adj* **1** of a sect **2** narrow-minded
section Ⓣ *n* **1** part cut off **2** part or subdivision of something **3** distinct part of a country or community **4** cutting **5** drawing of something as if cut through ▷ *v* **6** cut or divide into sections **sectional** *adj*
sector Ⓣ *n* **1** part or subdivision **2** part of a circle enclosed by two radii and the arc which they cut off
secular Ⓣ *adj* **1** worldly, as opposed to sacred **2** not connected with religion or the church
secure Ⓣ *adj* **1** free from danger **2** free from anxiety **3** firmly fixed **4** reliable ▷ *v* **5** obtain **6** make safe **7** make firm **8** guarantee payment of (a loan) by giving something as security **securely** *adv*
▶ **security** *n* **1** state of being secure **2** precautions against theft, espionage, or other danger **3** something given or pledged to guarantee payment of a loan **4** certificate of ownership of a share, stock, or bond
sedan *n* automobile with a fixed roof
▶ **sedan chair** *hist* enclosed chair for one person, carried on poles by two bearers
sedate[1] Ⓣ *adj* **1** calm and dignified **2** sober or decorous **sedately** *adv*
sedate[2] *v* give a sedative drug to **sedation** *n*
▶ **sedative** *adj* **1** having a soothing or calming effect ▷ *n* **2** sedative drug
sedentary Ⓣ [**sed**-en-tree] *adj* done sitting down, involving little exercise
sedge *n* coarse grasslike plant growing on wet ground
sediment Ⓣ *n* **1** matter which settles to the

THESAURUS

location RELATED WORD *adjective*: cryptic **2 = stealthy**, secretive, sly, underhand **3 = mysterious**, clandestine, cryptic, arcane, occult, abstruse ▶ *n* **4 = mystery**, key, code, enigma ▷ **in secret = secretly**, surreptitiously, slyly
See also: **private**
secrete[1] *v* = **give off**, emit, exude, emanate
secrete[2] *v* = **hide**, conceal, cache, stash (*informal*), stow, harbor
secretive *adj* = **reticent**, cagey (*informal*), reserved • *He was very secretive about his family affairs.*
See also: **mysterious**
secretly *adv* = **in secret**, quietly, privately, surreptitiously, covertly, clandestinely, furtively, stealthily
sect *n* = **group**, party, division, camp, faction, denomination, schism
sectarian *adj* **1 = narrow-minded**, limited, partisan, factional, fanatical, parochial, dogmatic, bigoted, doctrinaire ▶ *n* **2 = bigot**, extremist, partisan, fanatic, zealot, dogmatist
section *n* **1 = part**, division, piece, portion, segment, instalment • *this section of the Trans-Canada Highway* **2** (*Chiefly US*) **= district**, area, region, sector, zone
See also: **compartment, department, extract, passage**
sector *n* = **part**, area, quarter, region, division, zone, district
secular *adj* = **worldly**, lay, civil, earthly, temporal, nonspiritual
secure *v* **1** (*Formal*) **= obtain**, get, gain, acquire, procure • *His achievements helped him to secure the job.* **2 = make safe**, strengthen, fortify, make impregnable • *We need to secure the building against attack.* **3 = fasten**, fix, lock, bind, attach, moor, tie up • *to secure the picture to the wall* OPPOSITE: release ▶ *adj* **4 = safe**, protected, fortified, impregnable, shielded • *Make sure your home is as secure as possible.* **5 = fixed**, firm, solid, tight, stable, locked, fastened • *Those bookshelves don't look very secure.* **6 = confident**, safe, protected, reassured, relaxed • *They felt secure when they were with each other.* OPPOSITE: insecure
See also: **close, steady, tie, win**
securely *See* **fast**
security *n* **1 = precautions**, protection, defence, safeguards, safety measures **2 = safety**, care, custody, refuge, sanctuary, safekeeping **3 = sureness**, confidence, conviction, assurance, certainty, reliance, positiveness **4 = pledge**, insurance, hostage, guarantee, collateral, pawn, surety, gage
sedate *adj* = **calm**, cool, dignified, tranquil, serene, collected, composed
sedative *adj* **1 = calming**, soothing, anodyne, relaxing, tranquilizing ▶ *n* **2 = tranquilizer**, downer *or* down (*slang*), anodyne
sedentary *adj* = **inactive**, desk, sitting, desk-bound, seated
sediment *n* = **dregs**, deposit, residue, grounds, lees

DICTIONARY

bottom of a liquid **2** material deposited by water, ice, or wind **sedimentary** *adj*
sedition Ⓣ *n* speech or action encouraging rebellion against the government **seditious** *adj*
seduce Ⓣ *v* **1** persuade into sexual intercourse **2** tempt into wrongdoing **seducer** (**seductress**) *n* **seduction** *n* **seductive** *adj*
sedulous *adj* diligent or persevering **sedulously** *adv*
see[1] Ⓣ *v* **seeing, saw, seen 1** perceive with the eyes or mind **2** watch **3** find out **4** make sure (of something) **5** consider or decide **6** have experience of **7** meet or visit **8** interview **9** frequent the company of **10** accompany
▸ **seeing** *conj* in view of the fact that
see[2] *n* diocese of a bishop
seed Ⓣ *n* **1** mature fertilized grain of a plant **2** such grains used for sowing **3** origin **4** *obsolete* offspring **5** *sports* seeded player ▹ *v* **6** sow with seed **7** remove seeds from **8** arrange (the draw of a sports tournament) so that the outstanding competitors will not meet in the early rounds
▸ **go to seed** *or* **run to seed 1** (of plants) produce or shed seeds after flowering **2** lose vigour or usefulness
▸ **seedling** *n* young plant raised from a seed
▸ **seedy** *adj* **1** shabby **2** *informal* unwell
Seeger *n* **Pete**. born 1919. US folk singer and songwriter, noted for his protest songs, which include "We shall Overcome" (1960), "Where have all the Flowers gone?" (1961), "If I had a Hammer" (1962), and "Little Boxes" (1962)
seek Ⓣ *v* **seeking, sought 1** try to find or obtain **2** try (to do something)
seem Ⓣ *v* appear to be
▸ **seeming** *adj* apparent but not real **seemingly** *adv*
seemly Ⓣ *adj* **-lier, -liest** proper or fitting **seemliness** *n*
seen *v* past participle of **see**
seep Ⓣ *v* trickle through slowly, ooze **seepage** *n*
seer Ⓣ *n* prophet
seersucker *n* light cotton fabric with a slightly crinkled surface
seesaw Ⓣ *n* **1** plank balanced in the middle so that two people seated on either end ride

THESAURUS

sedition *n* = **rabble-rousing**, agitation, subversion, incitement to riot
seditious *adj* = **revolutionary**, dissident, subversive, rebellious, mutinous, refractory
seduce *v* **1** = **corrupt**, dishonour, debauch, deflower, deprave **2** = **tempt**, lure, mislead, entice, deceive, beguile, inveigle, lead astray
seduction *n* **1** = **corruption 2** = **temptation**, lure, snare, enticement
seductive *adj* = **tempting**, attractive, provocative, alluring, bewitching, enticing, inviting
seductress *n* = **temptress**, siren, enchantress, *femme fatale* (*French*), succubus, vamp (*informal*)
see *v* **1** = **perceive**, look, spot, notice, sight, observe, glimpse, behold, discern, catch sight of, descry, espy • *Did you see what happened?* **2** = **understand**, get, follow, realize, appreciate, grasp, comprehend • *I see what you mean.* **3** = **find out**, discover, determine, ascertain • *I'll see what's happening outside.* **4** = **make sure**, ensure, guarantee, make certain, see to it **5** = **consider**, decide, reflect, deliberate, think over **6** = **visit**, receive, interview, consult, confer with, speak to **7** = **go out with**, court, date (*informal*), go steady with (*informal*) **8** = **accompany**, lead, show, walk, escort, usher ▹ **see eye to eye** *See* **agree** ▹ **see through** = **be undeceived by**, penetrate, fathom, be wise to (*informal*), not fall for ▹ **see (someone) through** = **help out**, support, stick by ▹ **see (something) through** = **persevere** *or* **persevere with**, persist, keep at, stick out (*informal*) ▹ **see to** *See* **deal, take care of**
See also: **know, note, picture, regard, tell, watch, witness**
seed *n* **1** = **grain**, egg, embryo, germ, spore, kernel, pip, ovum **2** = **origin**, start, source, beginning, germ, nucleus **3** = **offspring**, issue, progeny, children, descendants ▹ **go to seed, run to seed** = **decline**, deteriorate, decay, degenerate, go downhill (*informal*), go to pot, let oneself go
seedy (*Informal*) *adj* = **shabby**, dirty, dilapidated, run-down, grubby, mangy, sleazy, squalid, scuzzy (*slang*), tatty
seeing *conj* = **since**, as, inasmuch as, in view of the fact that
seek *v* **1** = **look for**, hunt, be after, search for • *The police were still seeking information.* **2** = **try**, attempt, aim, strive, endeavour, aspire to • *She is seeking re-election as class president.*
See also: **ask, request, search**
seem *v* = **appear**, look, give the impression, look like • *He seemed such a quiet man.* ▹ **seem to be** *See* **look**
seemly *adj* = **fitting**, fit, appropriate, correct, proper, decent, suitable, becoming, decorous
seep *v* = **ooze**, well, leak, soak, trickle, exude, permeate
seer *n* = **prophet**, sibyl, soothsayer
seesaw *v* = **alternate**, swing, fluctuate, oscillate

DICTIONARY

up and down alternately ▷ *v* **2** move up and down
seethe Ⓣ *v* **seething, seethed 1** be very agitated **2** (of a liquid) boil or foam
segment Ⓣ *n* **1** one of several sections into which something may be divided ▷ *v* **2** divide into segments **segmentation** *n*
Segovia *n* **Andrés**, Marquis of Salobreña. 1893–1987, Spanish classical guitarist
segregate Ⓣ *v* set apart **segregation** *n*
seine [**sane**] *n* large fishing net that hangs vertically from floats
seismic *adj* relating to earthquakes
▸ **seismology** *n* study of earthquakes **seismologic** *or* **seismological** *adj* **seismologist** *n*
▸ **seismograph** *or* **seismometer** *n* instrument that records the strength of earthquakes
seize Ⓣ *v* **1** take hold of forcibly or quickly **2** take immediate advantage of **3** (usu. foll. by *up*) (of mechanical parts) stick tightly through overheating
▸ **seizure** *n* **1** seizing or being seized **2** sudden violent attack of an illness
seldom Ⓣ *adv* not often, rarely
select Ⓣ *v* **1** pick out or choose ▷ *adj* **2** chosen in preference to others **3** restricted to a particular group, exclusive **selector** *n*
▸ **selection** *n* **1** selecting **2** things that have been selected **3** range from which something may be selected
▸ **selective** *adj* chosen or choosing carefully **selectively** *adv* **selectivity** *n*
selenium *n* nonmetallic element with photoelectric properties
Seles *n* **Monica**. born 1973, US tennis player, born in Yugoslavia: winner of the US Open (1991, 1992); stabbed while on court in an unprovoked attack
self *n, pl* **selves 1** distinct individuality or identity of a person or thing **2** one's basic nature **3** one's own welfare or interests
▸ **selfish** *adj* caring too much about oneself and not enough about others **selfishly** *adv* **selfishness** *n*
▸ **selfless** *adj* unselfish
self- *combining form* **1** *indicating* of oneself or itself **2** *indicating* by, to, in, due to, for, or from the self **3** *indicating* automatic(ally)
▸ **self-assured** *adj* confident
▸ **self-catering** *adj* (of accommodation) for people who provide their own food
▸ **self-coloured** *adj* having only a single colour
▸ **self-conscious** *adj* embarrassed at being the object of others' attention
▸ **self-contained** *adj* **1** containing everything needed, complete **2** (of an apartment) having its own facilities
▸ **self-determination** *n* right of a nation to decide its own form of government
▸ **self-evident** *adj* obvious without proof
▸ **self-help** *n* **1** use of one's own abilities to solve problems **2** practice of solving one's problems within a group of people with similar problems
▸ **self-interest** *n* one's own advantage

THESAURUS

seethe *v* **1 = be furious**, rage, simmer, fume, be livid, go ballistic (*slang*), see red (*informal*) **2 = bubble**, boil, foam, froth, fizz
segment *n* **= section**, part, bit, division, piece, portion, slice, wedge
segregate *v* **= set apart**, separate, isolate, dissociate, discriminate against
segregation *n* **= separation**, discrimination, isolation, apartheid
seize *v* **1 = grab**, snatch, grasp • *He seized the phone.* **2 = take possession of**, appropriate, confiscate, annex, impound • *Rebels have seized the airport.* **3 = capture**, arrest, catch, hijack, apprehend, take captive
See also: **kidnap, possess**
seizure *n* **1 = attack**, fit, spasm, convulsion, paroxysm **2 = capture**, arrest, apprehension **3 = taking**, confiscation, annexation, commandeering, grabbing
seldom *adv* **= rarely**, infrequently, hardly ever, not often
select *v* **1 = choose**, take, pick, decide on, opt for, settle on, single out • *They selected new members for the debating team.* ▸ *adj* **2 = choice**, prime, special, superior, first-class, hand-picked, first-rate • *a select group of top-ranked skiers* **3 = exclusive**, elite, privileged, cliquish
See also: **nominate**
selection *n* **1 = choice**, pick, option, preference, choosing **2 = range**, choice, collection, variety, medley, assortment
selective *adj* **= particular**, careful, discerning, discriminating
self-assurance *n* **= confidence**, self-confidence, assertiveness, positiveness, self-possession
self-assured *See* **confident**
self-centred *adj* **= selfish**, narcissistic, egotistic, self-seeking
self-confidence *n* **= self-assurance**, confidence, poise, nerve, aplomb
self-confident *adj* **= self-assured**, confident, assured, poised, sure of oneself
self-conscious *adj* **= embarrassed**, nervous, uncomfortable, awkward, insecure, bashful, diffident, ill at ease, wired (*slang*)
self-consciousness *See* **embarrassment**
self-control *n* **= willpower**, restraint, self-restraint, self-discipline

S

DICTIONARY

▸ **self-made** *adj* having achieved wealth or status by one's own efforts
▸ **self-possessed** *adj* having control of one's emotions, calm
▸ **self-righteous** *adj* thinking oneself more virtuous than others
▸ **self-rising** *adj* (of flour) containing a raising agent
▸ **selfsame** *adj* the very same
▸ **self-seeking** *adj, n* seeking to promote only one's own interests
▸ **self-service** *adj* denoting a shop, café, or garage where customers serve themselves and then pay a cashier
▸ **self-styled** *adj* using a title or name that one has taken without right
▸ **self-sufficient** *adj* able to provide for oneself without help
▸ **self-willed** *adj* stubbornly determined to get one's own way
Selinger *n* **Greg.** born 1951, Canadian politician, Premier of Manitoba (2009–)
Selkirk n **Thomas Douglas**, 5th Earl of. 1771–1820, Scottish philanthropist. He established a number of settlements in Canada for poor or displaced Scottish farmers, including one on Prince Edward Island (1803) and the Red River Colony (1812)
sell 🅣 *v* **selling, sold 1** exchange (something) for money **2** stock, deal in **3** (of goods) be sold **4** (foll. by *for*) have a specified price **5** *informal* persuade (someone) to accept (something) ▷ *n* **6** manner of selling **seller** *n*
▸ **sell out** *v* **1** dispose of (something) completely by selling **2** *informal* betray
▸ **sellout** *n* **1** performance of a show etc. for which all the tickets are sold **2** *informal* betrayal
Sellers *n* **Peter.** 1925–80, English radio, stage, and film actor and comedian: noted for his gift of precise vocal mimicry, esp. in *The Goon Show* (with Spike Milligan and Harry Secombe; BBC Radio, 1952–60). His films include *I'm All Right, Jack* (1959), *The Millionairess* (1961), *The Pink Panther* (1963), *Dr. Strangelove* (1964), and *Being There* (1979)
selvage, selvedge *n* edge of cloth, woven so as to prevent unravelling
selves *n* plural of **self**
Selznick *n* **David O(liver).** 1902–62, US film producer, who produced such films as *A Star is Born* (1937), *Gone with the Wind* (1939), and *A Farewell to Arms* (1957)
semantic *adj* relating to the meaning of words
▸ **semantics** *pl n* study of linguistic meaning
semaphore *n* system of signalling by holding two flags in different positions to represent letters of the alphabet
semblance 🅣 *n* outward or superficial appearance

THESAURUS

self-denial *See* **sacrifice**
self-esteem *n* = **self-respect**, confidence, pride, faith in oneself, self-assurance, self-regard
self-evident *adj* = **obvious**, clear, undeniable, inescapable, incontrovertible
self-importance *See* **conceit**
self-important *adj* = **conceited**, cocky, pompous, bigheaded, full of oneself, swollen-headed
self-indulgence *n* = **intemperance**, excess, extravagance
selfish *adj* = **self-centred**, greedy, egoistic *or* egoistical, egotistic *or* egotistical • *his greedy and selfish behaviour*
selfless *adj* = **unselfish**, generous, altruistic, self-denying, self-sacrificing
self-possessed *adj* = **self-assured**, cool, confident, collected, poised, unruffled
self-possession *See* **confidence**
self-propelled *See* **automatic**
self-reliant *adj* = **independent**, self-sufficient, self-supporting
self-respect *n* = **pride**, dignity, morale, self-esteem
self-restraint *n* = **self-control**, willpower, self-command, self-discipline
self-righteous *adj* = **sanctimonious**, superior, complacent, smug, holier-than-thou, priggish, self-satisfied
self-sacrifice *n* = **selflessness**, generosity, altruism, self-denial
self-satisfied *adj* = **smug**, complacent, pleased with oneself, self-congratulatory • *a self-satisfied smile*
self-seeking *adj* = **selfish**, self-serving, careerist, looking out for number one (*informal*), out for what one can get, self-interested
self-sufficient *See* **independent**
sell *v* **1** = **deal in**, stock, peddle, hawk, trade in • *a convenience store that sells stamps* OPPOSITE: buy **2** = **trade**, exchange, barter ▷ **sell at** *See* **cost** ▷ **sell out** = **run out of**, be out of stock of, dispose of, get rid of; (*Informal*) = **betray**, double-cross (*informal*), sell down the river (*informal*), stab in the back
seller *n* = **dealer**, retailer, agent, supplier, merchant, vendor, salesman *or* saleswoman, purveyor
selling *n* = **dealing**, business, traffic, trading
selling price *See* **value**
semblance *n* = **appearance**, show, mask, aspect, resemblance, pretense, veneer, façade

S

DICTIONARY

semen *n* sperm-carrying fluid produced by male animals
semester *n* either of two divisions of the academic year
semi *n informal* semidetached house
semi- *prefix* **1** *indicating* half: *semidome* **2** *indicating* partly or almost: *semiprofessional*
semibreve *n Brit* whole note
semicircle *n* half of a circle **semicircular** *adj*
semicolon *n* the punctuation mark (;)
semiconductor *n* substance with an electrical conductivity that increases with temperature
semidetached *adj* (of a house) joined to another on one side
semifinal *n* match or round before the final **semifinalist** *n*
seminal Ⓣ *adj* **1** capable of developing **2** original and influential **3** of semen or seed
seminar *n* meeting of a group of students for discussion
seminary *n, pl* **-ries** college for priests
semiprecious *adj* (of gemstones) having less value than precious stones
semiquaver *n* musical note half the length of a quaver
semiskilled *adj* partly trained but not for specialized work
Semite *n* member of the group of peoples including Jews and Arabs **Semitic** *adj*
semitone *n* smallest interval between two notes in Western music
semolina *n* hard grains of wheat left after the milling of flour, used to make puddings and pasta
Senate *n* **1** upper house of some parliaments **2** governing body of some universities
▸**senator** *n* member of a Senate **senatorial** *adj*
send Ⓣ *v* **sending, sent 1** cause (a person or thing) to go to or be taken or transmitted to a place **2** bring into a specified state or condition
▸**sendoff** *n* demonstration of good wishes at a person's departure
▸**send up** *v informal* make fun of by imitating
▸**send-up** *n informal* imitation
Seneca *n* **1 Lucius Annaeus**, called *the Younger*. ?4 BC–65 AD, Roman philosopher, statesman, and dramatist; tutor and adviser to Nero. He was implicated in a plot to murder Nero and committed suicide. His works include Stoical essays on ethical subjects and tragedies that had a considerable influence on Elizabethan drama **2** his father, **Marcus** (*or* **Lucius**) **Annaeus**, called *the Elder* or *the Rhetorician*. ?55 BC–?39 AD, Roman writer on oratory and history
senescent *adj* growing old **senescence** *n*
senile Ⓣ *adj* mentally or physically weak because of old age **senility** *n*
senior Ⓣ *adj* **1** superior in rank or standing **2** older **3** of or for older pupils ▹ *n* **4** senior person **seniority** *n*
senna *n* **1** tropical plant **2** its dried leaves or pods used as a laxative
Senna *n* **Ayrton**. 1960–94, Brazilian racing driver: world champion (1988, 1990, 1991)
Sennett *n* **Mack**, original name *Michael Sinott*. 1884–1960, US film producer and director, born in Canada, who produced many silent comedy films featuring the Keystone Kops, Charlie Chaplin, and Harold Lloyd, for the Keystone Company
señor [sen-**nyor**] *n, pl* **-ores** Spanish term of address equivalent to *sir* or *Mr*
▸**señora** [sen-**nyor**-a] *n* Spanish term of address equivalent to *madam* or *Mrs*
▸**señorita** [sen-nyor-**ee**-ta] *n* Spanish term of address equivalent to *madam* or *Miss*
sensation Ⓣ *n* **1** ability to feel things physically **2** physical feeling **3** general

S

THESAURUS

seminal *adj* = **influential**, important, original, innovative, ground-breaking, formative
send *v* **1** = **dispatch**, forward, remit • *She sent a basket of fruit and a card*. **2** = **transmit**, broadcast • *The pilot was trying to send a distress signal*. **3** = **propel**, fire, shoot, cast, hurl, fling, let fly ▹ **send for** = **summon**, order, request, call for ▹ **send in** *See* **submit**
▹ **send out** *See* **emit** ▹ **send up** = **parody**, mock, mimic, spoof (*informal*), satirize, imitate, lampoon, burlesque, make fun of, take off (*informal*)
sendoff *n* = **farewell**, start, departure, leave-taking, valediction
send-up *n* = **parody**, satire, imitation, spoof (*informal*), take-off (*informal*), piss-take (*informal*)
senile *adj* = **doddering**, decrepit, doting, in one's dotage
senility *n* = **dotage**, decrepitude, infirmity, loss of one's faculties, senile dementia
senior *adj* **1** = **higher ranking**, superior, better • *senior jobs* **2** = **older**, elder OPPOSITE: junior
senior citizen *n* = **pensioner**, old fogey (*slang*), old person *or* elderly person, retired person
seniority *n* = **superiority**, rank, priority, precedence
sensation *n* **1** = **feeling**, sense, perception, awareness, impression, consciousness **2** = **excitement**, stir,

DICTIONARY

feeling or awareness **4** state of excitement **5** exciting person or thing
▸ **sensational** *adj* **1** causing intense shock, anger, or excitement **2** *informal* very good
▸ **sensationalism** *n* deliberate use of sensational language or subject matter
sensationalist *adj, n*
sense Ⓣ *n* **1** any of the faculties of perception or feeling (sight, hearing, touch, taste, or smell) **2** ability to perceive **3** feeling perceived through one of the senses **4** awareness **5** *sometimes pl* sound practical judgment or intelligence **6** specific meaning ▹ *v* **7** perceive **senseless** *adj*
sensible Ⓣ *adj* **1** having or showing good sense **2** (foll. by *of*) aware **3** practical: *sensible shoes* **sensibly** *adv*
▸ **sensibility** *n* ability to experience deep feelings
sensitive Ⓣ *adj* **1** responsive to external stimuli **2** easily hurt or offended **3** (of an instrument) responsive to slight changes **4** (of a subject) liable to arouse controversy or strong feelings **sensitively** *adv* **sensitivity** *n*
▸ **sensitize** *v* make sensitive
sensor *n* device that detects or measures the presence of something, such as radiation
sensory *adj* of the senses or sensation
sensual Ⓣ *adj* **1** giving pleasure to the body and senses rather than the mind **2** having a strong liking for physical pleasures
sensually *adv* **sensuality** *n* **sensualism** *n*
sensualist *n*
sensuous Ⓣ *adj* pleasing to the senses
sensuously *adv*
sent *v* past of **send**
sentence Ⓣ *n* **1** sequence of words capable of standing alone as a statement, question, or command **2** punishment passed on a criminal ▹ *v* **3** pass sentence on (a convicted person)
sententious Ⓣ *adj* **1** trying to sound wise **2** pompously moralizing **sententiously** *adv*
sententiousness *n*
sentient Ⓣ [sen-tee-ent] *adj* capable of feeling **sentience** *n*
sentiment Ⓣ *n* **1** thought, opinion, or attitude **2** feeling expressed in words

THESAURUS

thrill, furor, commotion
sensational *adj* **1 = dramatic**, amazing, exciting, thrilling, shocking, awesome, astounding, melodramatic, shock-horror (*facetious*) **2 = excellent**, cool (*informal*), impressive, awesome (*informal*), fabulous (*informal*), marvellous, mind-blowing (*informal*), out of this world (*informal*), phat (*slang*), superb
sense *n* **1 = feeling**, impression, consciousness • *an overwhelming sense of guilt* **2 = intelligence**, reason, judgment, wisdom, brains, common sense • *He had the good sense to call me at once.* **3 = faculty**, feeling, sensation **4 = meaning**, import, implication, drift, significance, gist ▹ **sense of duty** *See* **principle** ▹ **sense of right and wrong** *See* **conscience** ▸ *v* **5 = perceive**, feel, realize, be aware of, get the impression, have a hunch • *She sensed he wasn't telling her the whole story.*
senseless *adj* **1 = stupid**, mad, crazy, ridiculous, silly, foolish, pointless, irrational, mindless, illogical, idiotic, nonsensical, inane, asinine, bonkers (*informal*), daft (*informal*) **2 = unconscious**, out, insensible, out cold, stunned
sensibility *n* **1** (*often pl*) **= feelings**, emotions, moral sense, sentiments, susceptibilities **2 = sensitivity**, susceptibility, responsiveness, sensitiveness
sensible *adj* **1 = wise**, sound, practical, prudent, rational, down-to-earth, judicious • *a sensible, level-headed approach* OPPOSITE: foolish **2** (usually with *of*) **= aware**, conscious, mindful, sensitive to
See also: **logical, realistic, reasonable, responsible, sane**
sensitive *adj* **1 = touchy**, easily offended, easily upset, thin-skinned • *He was sensitive about his height.* **2 = delicate**, tender, easily hurt **3 = susceptible**, responsive, impressionable, easily affected, touchy-feely (*informal*) **4 = responsive**, fine, acute, keen, precise
See also: **sore, tactful, tricky, understanding, vulnerable**
sensitivity *n* **= sensitiveness**, delicacy, susceptibility, responsiveness, receptiveness
sensual *adj* **1 = physical**, animal, bodily, luxurious, voluptuous, carnal, fleshly **2 = erotic**, sexual, raunchy (*slang*), lewd, lascivious, lecherous, lustful
sensuality *n* **= eroticism**, carnality, lasciviousness, lecherousness, lewdness, sexiness (*informal*), voluptuousness
sensuous *adj* **1 = pleasurable**, gratifying **2 = pleasure-seeking**, hedonistic, sybaritic
sentence *n* **1 = punishment**, decision, order, ruling, verdict, judgment, condemnation, decree ▸ *v* **2 = condemn**, penalize, doom
sententious *adj* **= pompous**, judgmental, canting, moralistic, preachifying (*informal*), sanctimonious
sentient *adj* **= feeling**, living, sensitive, conscious
sentiment *n* **1 = emotion**, sensibility, tenderness **2** (*often pl*) **= feeling**,

DICTIONARY

3 exaggerated or mawkish emotion
▸ **sentimental** *adj* excessively romantic or nostalgic **sentimentalism** *n* **sentimentality** *n*
▸ **sentimentalize** *v* make sentimental
sentinel Ⓣ *n* sentry
sentry Ⓣ *n, pl* **-tries** soldier on watch
sepal *n* leaflike division of the calyx of a flower
separate Ⓣ *v* **1** act as a barrier between **2** divide up into parts **3** distinguish between **4** (of a married couple) stop living together ▹ *adj* **5** set apart **6** not the same, different **7** not shared, individual **separately** *adv* **separable** *adj*
▸ **separation** *n* **1** separating or being separated **2** *law* living apart of a married couple without divorce
▸ **separatist** *n* person who advocates the separation of a group or province from an organization or country, such as Quebec from Canada **separatism** *n*
▸ **separate school** school for a large religious minority
sepia *adj, n* reddish-brown (pigment)
sepoy *n* (formerly) Indian soldier in the service of the British
sepsis *n* poisoning caused by pus-forming bacteria
Sept. September
September *n* ninth month of the year
septet *n* **1** group of seven performers **2** music for such a group
septic Ⓣ *adj* **1** (of a wound) infected **2** of or caused by harmful bacteria
▸ **septic tank** tank in which sewage is decomposed by the action of bacteria
septicemia, septicaemia [sep-tis-**see**-mee-a] *n* blood poisoning
septuagenarian *n, adj* (person) between seventy and seventy-nine years old
sepulchre Ⓣ [**sep**-pull-ker] *n* tomb or burial vault
▸ **sepulchral** [sip-**pulk**-ral] *adj* gloomy
sequel Ⓣ *n* **1** novel, play, or film that continues the story of an earlier one **2** consequence
sequence Ⓣ *n* **1** arrangement of two or more things in successive order **2** the successive order of two or more things **3** section of a film showing a single uninterrupted episode **sequential** *adj*
sequester *v* **1** separate **2** seclude
sequestrate *v* confiscate (property) until its owner's debts are paid or a court order is complied with **sequestration** *n*
sequin *n* small ornamental metal disc on a garment **sequined** *adj*
sequoia *n* giant Californian coniferous tree
seraglio [sir-**ah**-lee-oh] *n, pl* **-raglios** **1** harem of a Muslim palace **2** Turkish sultan's palace
seraph *n* member of the highest order of angels **seraphic** *adj*
Serbian, Serb *adj* **1** of Serbia ▹ *n* **2** person from Serbia
▸ **Serbo-Croat** *or* **Serbo-Croatian** *adj, n* (of) the chief official language of Serbia and Croatia
serenade *n* **1** music played or sung to

THESAURUS

view, idea, opinion, judgment, belief, attitude **3 = sentimentality**, emotionalism, mawkishness, romanticism
sentimental *adj* **= romantic**, sloppy (*informal*), nostalgic, mushy (*informal*), maudlin • *sentimental love stories*
See also: **corny**
sentimentality *n* **= romanticism**, nostalgia, corniness (*slang*), emotionalism, mawkishness, schmaltz (*slang*)
sentinel *n* **= guard**, watch, lookout, sentry, watchman
sentry *See* **guard**
separable *adj* **= distinguishable**, detachable, divisible
separate *adj* **1 = unconnected**, isolated, disconnected, discrete, detached, divorced • *The question muddles up two separate issues.* **2 = individual**, single, alone, apart, particular, distinct, solitary ▸ *v* **3 = divide**, disconnect, detach • *We were separated from our friends when we changed schools.* OPPOSITE: connect **4 = split up**, part, divorce, break up • *Her parents separated when she was very young.* **5 = isolate**, segregate, single out
See also: **different, independent, sort, split**
separated *adj* **= disconnected**, separate, apart, divided, disassociated, disunited, parted, sundered
separately *adv* **= individually**, alone, apart, severally, singly
separation *n* **1 = division**, break, gap, disconnection, dissociation, disunion **2 = split-up**, split, divorce, rift, break-up, parting
septic *adj* **= infected**, putrid, festering, poisoned, putrefying, suppurating
sepulchre *n* **= tomb**, grave, vault, mausoleum, burial place
sequel *n* **1 = follow-up**, development, continuation **2 = consequence**, end, result, conclusion, outcome, upshot
sequence *n* **1 = succession**, series, course, chain, string, cycle, progression • *an unbroken sequence of victories* **2 = order**, structure, pattern, arrangement, progression • *the colour sequence: yellow, orange, purple, blue*

DICTIONARY

a woman by a lover ▷ *v* **2** sing or play a serenade to (someone)
serendipity *n* gift of making fortunate discoveries by accident
serene Ⓣ *adj* calm, peaceful **serenely** *adv* **serenity** *n*
serf *n* medieval farm labourer who could not leave the land he worked on **serfdom** *n*
serge *n* strong woollen fabric
sergeant *n* **1** non-commissioned officer in the army **2** police officer ranking between constable and inspector
▸ **sergeant at arms** parliamentary or court officer with ceremonial duties
▸ **sergeant major** highest rank of non-commissioned officer in the army
serial *n* **1** story or play produced in successive instalments ▷ *adj* **2** of or forming a series **3** published or presented as a serial
▸ **serialize** *v* publish or present as a serial
▸ **serial killer** person who commits a series of murders
seriatim [seer-ree-**ah**-tim] *adv* one after another
series Ⓣ *n, pl* **-ries 1** group or succession of related things, usu. arranged in order **2** set of radio or TV programmes about the same subject or characters
serious Ⓣ *adj* **1** giving cause for concern **2** concerned with important matters **3** not cheerful, grave **4** sincere, not joking **5** *informal* extreme or remarkable **seriously** *adv* **seriousness** *n*
sermon Ⓣ *n* **1** speech on a religious or moral subject by a member of the clergy in a church service **2** long moralizing speech
▸ **sermonize** *v* make a long moralizing speech
serpent *n* snake
▸ **serpentine** *adj* twisting like a snake
serrated Ⓣ *adj* having a notched or sawlike edge **serration** *n*
serried *adj* in close formation
serum [**seer**-um] *n* **1** yellowish watery fluid left after blood has clotted **2** this fluid from the blood of immunized animals used for inoculation or vaccination
servant Ⓣ *n* person employed to do household work for another
serve Ⓣ *v* **1** work for (a person, community, or cause) **2** perform official duties **3** attend to (customers) **4** provide with food or drink **5** present (food or drink) **6** provide with a service **7** be a member of the armed forces **8** spend (time) in prison **9** be useful or suitable **10** *tennis etc* put (the ball) into play **11** deliver (a legal document) to (a person) ▷ *n* **12** *tennis etc* act of serving the ball
Servetus *n* **Michael**, Spanish name *Miguel Serveto*. 1511–53, Spanish theologian and physician. He was burnt at the stake by order of Calvin for denying the doctrine of the Trinity and the divinity of Christ
service Ⓣ *n* **1** serving **2** system that provides something needed by the public **3** overhaul of a machine or vehicle **4** availability for use **5** department of public employment and its employees **6** set of dishes etc. for serving a meal **7** formal religious ceremony **8** *tennis etc* act, manner, or right of serving the ball **services 9** armed forces ▷ *v* **10** provide a service or services to **11** overhaul

THESAURUS

serene *adj* = **calm**, peaceful, tranquil, composed, unruffled, untroubled
serenity *n* = **calmness**, peace, calm, composure, stillness, tranquillity, peacefulness, quietness
series *n* = **sequence**, run, chain, string, succession • *a series of loud explosions*
See also: **range, set**
serious *adj* **1** = **grave**, bad, dangerous, critical, severe, intense, extreme, acute, grim, precarious, grievous, alarming, worrying • *They survived their serious injuries.* **2** = **important**, difficult, significant, deep, crucial, grave, urgent, profound, far-reaching, pressing, momentous, weighty • *I regard this as a serious matter.* OPPOSITE: funny **3** = **sincere**, honest, genuine, earnest, heartfelt, resolute, in earnest, resolved • *I was not quite sure whether he was serious.* **4** = **solemn**, grave, sober, earnest, stern, staid, humourless, pensive • *She's quite a serious person.*
See also: **heavy**
seriously *adv* **1** = **gravely**, badly, severely, critically, dangerously, acutely **2** = **sincerely**, gravely, in earnest
seriousness *n* **1** = **importance**, gravity, significance, urgency **2** = **solemnity**, gravity, gravitas, earnestness
sermon *n* **1** = **homily**, address **2** = **lecture**, harangue, talking-to (*informal*)
serrated *See* **jagged**
servant *n* = **attendant**, help, domestic, maid, retainer, slave
serve *v* **1** = **work for**, help, assist, aid, attend to, minister to, wait on **2** = **perform**, do, complete, act, fulfill, discharge **3** = **provide**, supply, present, deliver, dish up, set out **4** = **be adequate**, do, suit, satisfy, suffice, answer the purpose, be acceptable, function as ▷ **serve as** *See* **form**
service *n* **1** = **help**, use, benefit, assistance, avail, usefulness **2** = **work**, business, office, duty, employment, labour **3** = **overhaul**, check, maintenance **4** = **ceremony**, rite, worship, observance ▸ *v* **5** = **overhaul**, check,

S

DICTIONARY

(a machine or vehicle)
▸ **serviceable** *adj* **1** useful or helpful **2** able or ready to be used
▸ **service apartment** apartment where domestic services are provided
▸ **serviceberry** *n* same as **saskatoon**
▸ **serviceman** *n* member of the armed forces
▸ **service road** narrow road giving access to houses and shops
▸ **service station** garage selling fuel for motor vehicles
Service *n* **Robert William**. 1874–1958, Scottish-Canadian poet and writer, born in England. Known as "the Bard of the Yukon" for his depictions of life in the Canadian North, his poems include *The Shooting of Dan McGrew* and *The Cremation of Sam McGee*
serviette *n* table napkin
servile Ⓣ *adj* **1** too eager to obey people, fawning **2** suitable for a slave **servility** *n*
servitude *n* bondage or slavery
servomechanism *n* device which converts a small force into a larger force, used esp. in steering mechanisms
sesame [**sess**-am-ee] *n* plant cultivated for its seeds and oil, which are used in cooking
Sesshu *n* original family name *Oda*. 1420–1506, Japanese landscape painter, who introduced the Chinese technique of ink painting on long scrolls to Japan (Also **Toyo**)
session Ⓣ *n* **1** meeting of a court, parliament, or council **2** series or period of such meetings **3** period spent in an activity **4** academic term or year
Sessions *n* **Roger** (**Huntington**). 1896–1985, US composer
set Ⓣ *v* **setting, set 1** put in a specified position or state **2** make ready **3** make or become firm or rigid **4** put (a broken bone) or (of a broken bone) be put into a normal position for healing **5** establish, arrange **6** prescribe, assign **7** put to music **8** arrange (hair) while wet, so that it dries in position **9** (of the sun) go down ▷ *adj* **10** fixed or established beforehand **11** rigid or inflexible **12** conventional or stereotyped **13** determined (to do something) **14** ready ▷ *n* **15** number of things or people grouped or belonging together **16** *math* group of numbers or objects that satisfy a given condition or share a property **17** television or radio receiver **18** scenery used in a play or film **19** *tennis etc* group of games in a match
▸ **setback** *n* anything that delays progress
▸ **set shot** *basketball* shot made using both hands while stationary
▸ **set square** flat right-angled triangular instrument used for drawing angles
▸ **set theory** branch of mathematics concerned with the properties of sets
▸ **set up** *v* arrange or establish
▸ **setup** *n* way in which anything is organized or arranged
Seton *n* **Ernest Thompson**. 1860–1946, US

THESAURUS

maintain, tune *or* tune up, fine tune, go over
serviceable *adj* = **useful**, profitable, helpful, practical, beneficial, operative, functional, usable, utilitarian
servile *adj* = **subservient**, abject, fawning, grovelling, obsequious, sycophantic, toadying
serving *n* = **portion**, helping
session *n* = **meeting**, period, conference, hearing, discussion, assembly, congress, sitting
set[1] *v* **1** = **put**, place, position, rest, lay, stick, locate, deposit • *She set her briefcase down on the floor.* **2** = **prepare**, spread, lay, arrange, make ready **3** = **harden**, cake, solidify, stiffen, thicken, crystallize, congeal **4** = **arrange**, schedule, decide *or* decide upon, determine, settle, fix, establish, appoint, resolve, specify, fix up **5** = **assign**, impose, prescribe, specify, decree, ordain, allot **6** = **go down**, decline, sink, disappear, dip, vanish, subside ▷ **set about** *See* **begin, start** ▷ **set against one another** *See* **divide** ▷ **set aside** = **reserve**, save, separate, select, earmark, keep (back), single out, set apart, put aside; = **reject**, cancel, dismiss, reverse, overturn, quash, overrule, discard, annul, nullify, repudiate, abrogate, render null and void ▷ **set back** = **hold up**, delay, slow, hinder, impede, retard ▷ **set down** *See* **lay** ▷ **set free** *See* **discharge, release** ▷ **set loose** *See* **free** ▷ **set off** = **leave**, depart, embark, start out, ship out; = **detonate**, explode, ignite ▷ **set out** *See* **lay** ▷ **set up** = **arrange**, establish, organize, install, institute • *setting up a system of communication*; = **build**, raise, assemble, construct, erect, put together, put up
See also: **start** ▷ **set upon** *See* **attack** ▸ *adj* **7** = **fixed**, firm, scheduled, established, arranged, predetermined • *a set charge* **8** = **inflexible**, stubborn, rigid, hard and fast, immovable **9** = **conventional**, stock, traditional, stereotyped, unspontaneous ▷ **set on** = **determined**, intent, bent, resolute ▸ *n* **10** = **position**, attitude, posture, carriage, bearing **11** = **scenery**, scene, setting, stage set
See also: **insert, ready, time**
set[2] *n* **1** = **series**, equipment, kit, outfit, ensemble, batch, compendium, assemblage • *a set of tools* **2** = **group**, company, crowd, band, gang, circle, faction, clique, coterie

S

DICTIONARY

author and illustrator of animal books, born in England
sett, set *n* badger's burrow
settee *n* couch
setter *n* long-haired gun dog
setting Ⓣ *n* **1** background or surroundings **2** time and place where a film, book, etc. is supposed to have taken place **3** music written for the words of a text **4** decorative metalwork in which a gem is set **5** plates and cutlery for a single place at table **6** descending below the horizon of the sun **7** position or level to which the controls of a machine can be adjusted
settle[1] Ⓣ *v* **1** arrange or put in order **2** establish or become established as a resident **3** colonize **4** make quiet, calm, or stable **5** come to rest **6** dispose of, conclude **7** end (a dispute) **8** pay (a bill) **9** bestow (property) legally
▸**settlement** *n* **1** act of settling **2** place newly colonized **3** property bestowed legally **4** subsidence (of a building)
▸**settler** *n* colonist
settle[2] *n* long wooden bench with high back and arms
Seurat *n* **Georges**. 1859–91, French neoimpressionist painter. He developed the pointillist technique of painting, characterized by brilliant luminosity, as in *Dimanche à la Grande-Jatte* (1886)
seven *adj, n* one more than six
▸**seventh** *adj, n* (of) number seven in a series
▸**seventeen** *adj, n* ten and seven **seventeenth** *adj, n*
▸**seventy** *adj, n* ten times seven **seventieth** *adj, n*
sever Ⓣ *v* **1** separate, divide **2** cut off **severance** *n*
▸**severance pay** compensation paid by a firm to an employee for loss of employment
several Ⓣ *adj* **1** some, a few **2** various, separate ▷ *pron* **3** indefinite small number
▸**severally** *adv* separately
severe Ⓣ *adj* **1** strict or harsh **2** very intense or unpleasant **3** strictly restrained in appearance **severely** *adv* **severity** *n*
Severus *n* **Lucius Septimius**. 146–211 AD, Roman soldier and emperor (193–211). He waged war successfully against the Parthians (197–202) and spent his last years in Britain (208–11)
sew *v* **sewing, sewed, sewn** *or* **sewed 1** join with thread repeatedly passed through with a needle **2** make or fasten by sewing
sewage *n* waste matter or excrement carried away in sewers
▸**sewer** *n* drain to remove waste water and sewage
▸**sewerage** *n* system of sewers
Seward *n* **William Henry**. 1801–72, US statesman; secretary of state (1861–69). He was a leading opponent of slavery and was responsible for the purchase of Alaska (1867)

THESAURUS

See also: **bunch, category, class, lot**
setback *n* = **hold-up**, defeat, check, blow, reverse, disappointment, hitch, misfortune
setting *n* = **surroundings**, set, site, scene, location, background, context, backdrop, scenery
settle *v* **1** = **resolve**, decide, reconcile, clear up, dispose of, put an end to, straighten out • *The dispute has been settled.* **2** = **decide on**, agree, determine, fix, arrange • *Let's settle where we're going tonight.* **3** = **move to**, make your home, put down roots, take up residence • *My grandparents settled in Manitoba.* **4** = **put in order**, order, regulate, adjust, straighten out, work out **5** = **land**, light (*archaic*), descend, alight, come to rest **6** = **colonize**, people, pioneer, populate **7** = **calm**, quiet, relax, relieve, reassure, quell, lull, soothe, pacify, quieten **8** = **pay**, clear, square *or* square up, discharge, pony up (*informal*)
See also: **confirm, lay** ▷ **settle on** *See* **pick, select** ▷ **settle up** *See* **repay**
settled *See* **definite**
settlement *n* **1** = **agreement**, conclusion, arrangement, confirmation, establishment, working out **2** = **payment**, discharge, clearing **3** = **colony**, community, outpost, encampment
settler *n* = **colonist**, immigrant, pioneer, colonizer, frontiersman
setup *n* = **arrangement**, system, organization, regime, structure, conditions
sever *v* **1** = **cut**, part, separate, split, divide, disconnect, detach, cut in two, disjoin **2** = **break off**, terminate, dissociate, put an end to
several *adj* = **some**, various, assorted, sundry • *several boxes filled with CDs and DVDs*
See also: **numerous**
severe *adj* **1** = **serious**, deep, critical, intense, extreme, grave, terrible, acute, dire • *severe financial problems* OPPOSITE: mild **2** = **strict**, hard, harsh, stern • *a severe sentence appropriate to the crime* **3** = **grim**, serious, grave, stern, tight-lipped, disapproving, forbidding, unsmiling **4** = **plain**, classic, austere, simple, restrained, Spartan, unadorned, unembellished, unfussy
See also: **drastic, violent**
severely *adv* **1** = **strictly**, sharply, harshly, sternly **2** = **seriously**, extremely, badly, gravely, acutely
severity *n* = **strictness**, toughness,

DICTIONARY

sewn *v* a past participle of **sew**
sex Ⓣ *n* **1** state of being male or female **2** male or female category **3** sexual intercourse **4** sexual feelings or behaviour ▷ *v* **5** ascertain the sex of **sexual** *adj* **sexually** *adv* **sexuality** *n*
▸ **sexy** *adj* **1** sexually exciting or attractive **2** *informal* exciting or trendy
▸ **sexism** *n* discrimination on the basis of a person's sex **sexist** *adj, n*
▸ **sexual intercourse** genital sexual activity between two people
▸ **sex up** *v informal* make (something) more exciting
sexagenarian *n, adj* (person) between sixty and sixty-nine years old
sextant *n* navigator's instrument for measuring angles, as between the sun and horizon, to calculate one's position
sextet *n* **1** group of six performers **2** music for such a group
sexton *n* official in charge of a church and churchyard
sextuplet *n* one of six children born at one birth
SF science fiction
SFA Scottish Football Association
Sforza *n* **1** Count **Carlo**. 1873–1952, Italian statesman; leader of the anti-Fascist opposition **2** **Lodovico**, called *the Moor*. 1451–1508, duke of Milan (1494–1500), but effective ruler from 1480; patron of Leonardo da Vinci
Sgt. Sergeant
sh *interj* be quiet!
shabby Ⓣ *adj* **-bier, -biest** **1** worn or dilapidated in appearance **2** mean or unworthy: *shabby treatment* **shabbily** *adv* **shabbiness** *n*
shack Ⓣ *n* rough hut
▸ **shack up with** *v slang* live with (one's lover)
shackle Ⓣ *n* **1** one of a pair of metal rings joined by a chain, for securing a person's wrists or ankles ▷ *v* **2** fasten with shackles **3** hamper
Shackleton *n* Sir **Ernest Henry**. 1874–1922, British explorer. He commanded three expeditions to the Antarctic (1907–09; 1914–17; 1921–22), during which the south magnetic pole was located (1909)
shad *n* herring-like fish
shade Ⓣ *n* **1** relative darkness **2** place sheltered from sun **3** depth of colour **4** slight amount **5** *lit* ghost **6** screen or cover used to protect from a direct source of light **shades** **7** *slang* sunglasses ▷ *v* **8** screen from light **9** darken **10** represent (darker areas) in drawing **11** change slightly or by degrees
▸ **shady** *adj* **1** situated in or giving shade **2** of doubtful honesty or legality
shadow Ⓣ *n* **1** dark shape cast on a surface when something stands between a light and the surface **2** patch of shade **3** slight trace **4** threatening influence **5** inseparable companion ▷ *v* **6** cast a shadow over **7** follow secretly **shadowy** *adj*
▸ **shadow-boxing** *n* boxing against an imaginary opponent for practice
▸ **Shadow Cabinet** members of the main opposition party in Parliament who would be ministers if their party were in power

THESAURUS

harshness, hardness, severeness, sternness
sex *n* **1** = **gender** **2** = **intercourse** *or* **sexual intercourse**, lovemaking, coition, coitus, copulation, fornication, sexual relations
sexism *See* **prejudice**
sexual *adj* **1** = **carnal**, intimate, sexy, erotic, sensual **2** = **reproductive**, sex, genital, procreative
sexual intercourse *n* = **copulation**, union, sex, carnal knowledge, coition, coitus
sexuality *n* = **desire**, lust, carnality, eroticism, sensuality, sexiness (*informal*)
sexy *adj* = **erotic**, seductive, sensual, voluptuous, sensuous • *a sexy voice*
shabby *adj* **1** = **tatty**, scruffy, dilapidated, ragged, seedy, run-down, threadbare, worn, raggedy, down at heel, the worse for wear • *a shabby overcoat* **2** = **contemptible**, mean, dirty, despicable, rotten (*informal*) • *shabby treatment*
shack *n* = **hut**, shed, cabin, shanty
shackle *n* **1** (*often pl*) = **fetter**, bond, chain, iron, leg-iron, manacle ▸ *v* **2** = **fetter**, chain, bind, manacle, put in irons
shade *n* **1** = **shadow**, dusk, gloom, dimness, gloominess, semidarkness **2** = **screen**, cover, shield, blind, veil, curtain, canopy, covering **3** = **hue**, tone, colour, tint, tinge **4** = **dash**, hint, trace, suggestion **5** (*Lit*) = **ghost**, spirit, phantom, apparition, spectre ▷ **put into the shade** = **outshine**, eclipse, overshadow, outclass ▸ *v* **6** = **cover**, protect, screen, hide, shield, veil, conceal, obscure **7** = **darken**, cloud, shadow, dim
shadow *n* **1** = **shade**, cover, darkness, dusk, gloom, dimness **2** = **trace**, hint, suggestion, suspicion **3** = **cloud**, sadness, gloom, blight ▸ *v* **4** = **shade**, screen, shield, darken, overhang **5** = **follow**, trail, tail (*informal*), stalk
shadowy *adj* **1** = **dark**, gloomy, murky, dim, shady, shaded, dusky **2** = **vague**, faint, dim, phantom, ghostly, nebulous, dreamlike, spectral, unsubstantial
shady *adj* **1** = **shaded**, cool, dim **2** (*Informal*) = **crooked**, disreputable, suspect, suspicious, questionable, unethical,

S

DICTIONARY

shaft Ⓣ *n* **1** long narrow straight handle of a tool or weapon **2** ray of light **3** revolving rod that transmits power in a machine **4** vertical passageway, as for an elevator **5** one of the bars between which an animal is harnessed to a vehicle
shag[1] *n* **1** coarse shredded tobacco ▷ *adj* **2** (of a carpet) having a long pile
▸ **shaggy** *adj* **1** covered with rough hair or wool **2** tousled, unkempt **shagginess** *n*
▸ **shaggy-dog story** long anecdote with a humorous twist at the end
shag[2] *n* kind of cormorant
shag[3] *v baseball* catch and throw back (fly balls) as practice
shagreen *n* **1** rough grainy untanned leather **2** sharkskin
shah *n* formerly, ruler of Iran
Shaka, Chaka *n* died 1828, Zulu military leader, who founded the Zulu Empire in southern Africa
shake Ⓣ *v* **shaking, shook, shaken** **1** move quickly up and down or back and forth **2** make unsteady **3** tremble **4** grasp (someone's hand) in greeting or agreement **5** shock or upset ▷ *n* **6** shaking **7** vibration **8** *informal* short period of time
▸ **shaky** *adj* **1** unsteady **2** uncertain or questionable **shakily** *adv*
Shakespeare *n* **William**. 1564–1616, English dramatist and poet. He was born and died at Stratford-upon-Avon but spent most of his life as an actor and playwright in London. His plays with approximate dates of composition are: *Henry VI, Parts I–III* (1590); *Richard III* (1592); *The Comedy of Errors* (1592); *Titus Andronicus* (1593); *The Taming of the Shrew* (1593); *The Two Gentlemen of Verona* (1594); *Love's Labour's Lost* (1594); *Romeo and Juliet* (1594); *Richard II* (1595); *A Midsummer Night's Dream* (1595); *King John* (1596); *The Merchant of Venice* (1596); *Henry IV, Parts I–II* (1597); *Much Ado about Nothing* (1598); *Henry V* (1598); *Julius Caesar* (1599); *As You Like It* (1599); *Twelfth Night* (1599); *Hamlet* (1600); *The Merry Wives of Windsor* (1600); *Troilus and Cressida* (1601); *All's Well that ends Well* (1602); *Measure for Measure* (1604); *Othello* (1604); *King Lear* (1605); *Macbeth* (1605); *Antony and Cleopatra* (1606); *Coriolanus* (1607); *Timon of Athens* (1607); *Pericles* (1608); *Cymbeline* (1609); *The Winter's Tale* (1610); *The Tempest* (1611); and, possibly in collaboration with John Fletcher, *Two Noble Kinsmen* (1612) and *Henry VIII* (1612). His *Sonnets*, variously addressed to a fair young man and a dark lady, were published in 1609
shale *n* flaky sedimentary rock
shall *v, past tense* **should** used as an auxiliary to make the future tense or to indicate intention, obligation, or inevitability
shallot [shal-**lot**] *n* kind of small onion
shallow Ⓣ *adj* **1** not deep **2** lacking depth of character or intellect **shallowness** *n*
▸ **shallows** *pl n* area of shallow water
sham Ⓣ *n* **1** thing or person that is not genuine ▷ *adj* **2** not real or genuine ▷ *v* **shamming, shammed** **3** fake, feign
shamble *v* walk in a shuffling awkward way
shambles Ⓣ *n* disorderly event or place
shame Ⓣ *n* **1** painful emotion caused by awareness of having done something dishonourable or foolish **2** capacity to feel shame **3** cause of shame **4** cause for regret ▷ *v* **5** cause to feel shame **6** disgrace **7** compel by shame: *she was shamed into helping*
▸ **shameful** *adj* causing or deserving shame **shamefully** *adv*

THESAURUS

dubious, sketchy (*informal*), shifty
shaft *n* **1** = **handle**, stem, pole, rod, shank **2** = **ray**, beam, gleam
shaggy *adj* = **unkempt**, rough, hairy, long-haired, hirsute, tousled, unshorn
shake *v* **1** = **wave**, flourish, agitate, brandish • *You have to shake the bottle before use.* **2** = **vibrate**, quake, jolt, shiver, tremble, shudder, quiver • *The whole building shook with the force of the blast.* **3** = **upset**, shock, disturb, rattle, distress, unnerve • *The news shook me quite a bit.* ▸ *n* **4** = **vibration**, jolt, tremor, jerk, agitation, shiver, convulsion, shudder, quaking, trembling
shake up *v* **1** = **stir** *or* **stir up**, mix, churn *or* churn up, agitate **2** = **upset**, shock, disturb, unsettle
shaky *adj* **1** = **unsteady**, unstable, wobbly, rickety, tottering, trembling • *threatening an already shaky economy* **2** = **uncertain**, suspect, questionable, dubious, iffy (*informal*)
shallow *adj* **1** = **superficial**, surface, empty, slight, trivial **2** = **unintelligent**, simple, ignorant, foolish, frivolous, puerile
sham *n* **1** = **phony** (*informal*), fraud, counterfeit, hoax, forgery, impostor, imitation, pretense, humbug ▸ *adj* **2** = **false**, counterfeit, artificial, mock, bogus, phony (*informal*), simulated, imitation, feigned, pretended ▸ *v* **3** = **fake**, affect, assume, pretend, simulate, feign, put on
shambles *n* = **chaos**, disorder, mess, confusion, havoc, disarray, muddle, madhouse
shame *n* **1** = **embarrassment**, humiliation, ignominy • *She felt a deep sense of shame.* **2** = **disgrace**, scandal, discredit, dishonour • *I don't want to bring shame on the family.* ▸ *v* **3** = **embarrass**, disgrace, humiliate • *Her son's behaviour had shamed*

DICTIONARY

▸**shameless** *adj* with no sense of shame
▸**shamefaced** *adj* looking ashamed
Shamir *n* **Yitzhak**. born 1915, Israeli statesman, born in Poland: prime minister (1983–84; 1986–92): foreign minister (1980–83; 1984–86)
shampoo Ⓣ *n* **1** liquid soap for washing hair, carpets, or upholstery **2** process of shampooing ▹ *v* **3** wash with shampoo
shamrock *n* clover leaf, esp. as the Irish emblem
shandy *n, pl* **-dies** drink made of beer and lemonade
shanghai *v* force or trick (someone) into doing something
shank *n* **1** lower leg **2** shaft or stem
shan't shall not
Shankar *n* **Ravi**. born 1920, Indian sitarist
shantung *n* soft Chinese silk with a knobbly surface
shanty[1] Ⓣ *n, pl* **-ties** shack or crude dwelling
▸**shantytown** *n* slum consisting of shanties
shanty[2] *n, pl* **-ties** sailor's traditional song
shape Ⓣ *n* **1** outward form of an object **2** way in which something is organized **3** pattern or mould **4** condition or state ▹ *v* **5** form or mould **6** devise or develop **shapeless** *adj*
▸**shapely** *adj* having an attractive shape
shard *n* broken piece of pottery
share[1] Ⓣ *n* **1** part of something that belongs to or is contributed by a person **2** one of the equal parts into which the capital stock of a public company is divided ▹ *v* **3** give or take a share of (something) **4** join with others in doing or using (something) **shareholder** *n*
share[2] *n* blade of a plough
shark Ⓣ *n* **1** large usu. predatory sea fish **2** person who cheats others
sharkskin *n* stiff glossy fabric
Sharon *n* **Ariel**. born 1928, Israeli soldier and politician; Likud prime minister (2001–06)
sharp Ⓣ *adj* **1** having a keen cutting edge or fine point **2** not gradual **3** clearly defined **4** mentally acute **5** clever but underhand **6** shrill **7** bitter or sour in taste **8** (of a note) being one semitone above natural pitch **9** (of an instrument or voice) out of tune by being too high in pitch ▹ *adv* **10** promptly ▹ *n music* **11** symbol raising a note one semitone above natural pitch **12** note raised in this way **sharply** *adv* **sharpness** *n*
▸**sharpen** *v* make or become sharp or sharper **sharpener** *n*
▸**sharpshooter** *n* marksman
Sharp *n* **Cecil (James)**. 1859–1924, British musician, best known for collecting, editing, and publishing English folk songs
Shatner *n* **William**. born 1931, Canadian film and TV actor. Best known for his portrayal of Captain James T Kirk in the original *Star Trek* series (1966–69) and its motion picture spin-offs, he has also appeared in many TV series including *Boston Legal* (2004–08)
shatter Ⓣ *v* **1** break into pieces **2** destroy completely **3** upset (someone) greatly

THESAURUS

her. **4 = dishonour**, smear, stain, degrade, blot, defile, debase
See also: **pity**
shamefaced *adj* **= embarrassed**, ashamed, red-faced, sheepish, abashed, humiliated, mortified
shameful *adj* **1 = embarrassing**, humiliating, mortifying **2 = disgraceful**, low, base, mean, outrageous, wicked, scandalous, dishonourable
shameless *adj* **= brazen**, flagrant, unabashed, barefaced, unashamed • *shameless dishonesty*
shampoo *See* **wash**
shanty *n* **= shack**, shed, cabin, hut
shape *n* **1 = form**, figure, outline, contours, lines • *a round shape* **2 = pattern**, model, frame, mould **3 = condition**, health, state, trim, fettle ▸ *v* **4 = form**, make, model, fashion, mould • *Shape the dough into a loaf.* **5 = develop**, plan, frame, modify, adapt, devise
See also: **body, build, design, determine**
shapeless *adj* **= formless**, irregular, amorphous, misshapen, unstructured
shapely *adj* **= well-formed**, trim, elegant, neat, graceful, curvaceous, well-proportioned
share *v* **1 = divide**, split • *We shared a pizza.* ▹ **share out** *See* **distribute** ▸ *n* **2 = portion**, quota, ration, allotment • *a share of the profits* ▹ **shares** *See* **stock**
See also: **proportion**
shark *See* **crook**
sharp *adj* **1 = keen**, pointed, jagged, razor-sharp • *a sharp knife* OPPOSITE: blunt **2 = quick-witted**, quick, alert, bright, observant, astute, perceptive • *a sharp intellect* **3 = sudden**, marked, abrupt • *a sharp rise in prices* **4 = clear**, distinct, crisp, well-defined **5 = dishonest**, wily, crafty, unscrupulous, sly, cunning, artful **6 = cutting**, bitter, harsh, barbed, hurtful, caustic, biting **7 = sour**, hot, acid, tart, pungent, acrid, piquant **8 = acute**, severe, intense, shooting, painful, piercing, stabbing ▸ *adv* **9 = promptly**, exactly, precisely, on the dot, on time, punctually
See also: **brilliant, intelligent, prompt, shrewd, shrill**
sharpen *v* **= whet**, edge, grind, hone
shatter *v* **1 = smash**, break, crack, crush, burst, pulverize **2 = destroy**, ruin,

DICTIONARY

▸ **shattered** *adj informal* completely exhausted
shave Ⓣ *v* **shaving, shaved, shaved** *or* **shaven 1** remove (hair) from (the face, head, or body) with a razor or shaver **2** pare away **3** touch lightly in passing **4** reduce ▹ *n* **5** shaving
▸ **close shave** see **close**
▸ **shaver** *n* electric razor
▸ **shavings** *pl n* parings
Shaw *n* **1 Artie**, original name *Arthur Arshawsky*. 1910–2004, US jazz clarinetist, band leader, and composer **3 George Bernard**, often known as *GBS*. 1856–1950, Irish dramatist and critic, in England from 1876. He was an active socialist and became a member of the Fabian Society but his major works are effective as satiric attacks rather than political tracts. These include *Arms and the Man* (1894), *Candida* (1894), *Man and Superman* (1903), *Major Barbara* (1905), *Pygmalion* (1913), *Back to Methuselah* (1921), and *St Joan* (1923): Nobel prize for literature 1925 **3 Thomas Edward**. the name assumed by (T. E.) **Lawrence** after 1927
shawl *n* piece of cloth worn over a woman's head or shoulders or wrapped around a baby
Shays *n* **Daniel**. ?1747–1825, American soldier and revolutionary leader of a rebellion of Massachusetts farmers against the US government (1786–87)
she *pron* **1** female person or animal previously mentioned **2** thing regarded as female, such as an automobile or ship
sheaf *n, pl* **sheaves 1** bundle of papers **2** tied bundle of reaped corn
shear *v* **shearing, sheared, sheared** *or* **shorn 1** clip hair or wool from **2** cut through **shearer** *n*
▸ **shears** *pl n* large scissors or a cutting tool shaped like these
sheath *n* **1** close-fitting cover, esp. for a knife or sword **2** condom
▸ **sheathe** *v* put into a sheath
shed[1] Ⓣ *n* building used for storage or shelter or as a workshop
shed[2] Ⓣ *v* **shedding, shed 1** pour forth (tears) **2** cast off (skin) **3** lose (hair)
sheen Ⓣ *n* glistening brightness on the surface of something
sheep *n, pl* **sheep** ruminant animal bred for wool and meat
▸ **sheep-dip** *n* liquid disinfectant in which sheep are immersed
▸ **sheepdog** *n* dog used for herding sheep
▸ **sheepskin** *n* skin of a sheep with the fleece still on, used for clothing or rugs
sheepish Ⓣ *adj* embarrassed because of feeling foolish **sheepishly** *adv*
sheer[1] Ⓣ *adj* **1** absolute, complete: *sheer folly* **2** (of material) so fine as to be transparent **3** perpendicular, steep
sheer[2] *v* change course suddenly
sheet[1] Ⓣ *n* **1** large piece of cloth used as an inner bedcover **2** broad thin piece of any material **3** large expanse
sheet[2] *n* rope for controlling the position of a sail
▸ **sheet anchor 1** strong anchor for use in an emergency **2** person or thing relied on
sheikh, sheik [**shake**] *n* Arab chief
sheikhdom *or* **sheikdom** *n*
sheila *n Aust slang* girl or woman
shekel *n* **1** monetary unit of Israel **shekels 2** *informal* money
Shelburne *n* **2nd Earl of**, title of *William Petty Fitzmaurice*, also called (from 1784) *1st Marquess of Lansdowne*. 1737–1805, British statesman; prime minister (1782–83)
shelf *n, pl* **shelves 1** board fixed horizontally for holding things **2** ledge
▸ **shelf life** time a packaged product will remain fresh
shell Ⓣ *n* **1** hard outer covering of an egg, nut, or certain animals **2** explosive projectile fired from a large gun **3** external frame of something ▹ *v* **4** take the shell from **5** fire at with artillery shells
▸ **shellfish** *n* aquatic mollusc or crustacean

THESAURUS

wreck, demolish, torpedo
shattered *adj* (*Informal*) = **devastated**, crushed, blown away
shave *v* = **trim**, crop, pare, shear
shed[1] *n* = **hut**, shack, outhouse, woodshed
shed[2] *v* **1** = **give out**, give, drop, cast, spill, shower, emit, scatter, radiate **2** = **cast off**, discard, slough, moult
sheen *n* = **shine**, polish, gloss, gleam, brightness, lustre
sheepish *adj* = **embarrassed**, ashamed, self-conscious, abashed, mortified, shamefaced
sheer *adj* **1** = **total**, complete, pure, absolute, utter, unqualified • *scenes of sheer beauty* **2** = **steep**, vertical, perpendicular • *There was a sheer drop just outside my window.* **3** = **fine**, thin, delicate, lightweight • *sheer curtains* OPPOSITE: thick
See also: **perfect, rank, transparent**
sheet *n* **1** = **coat**, film, surface, layer, overlay, veneer, stratum, lamina **2** = **piece**, panel, plate, slab **3** = **expanse**, area, sweep, stretch, blanket, covering
shell *n* **1** = **case**, pod, husk **2** = **frame**, structure, framework, hull ▸ *v* **3** = **bomb**, attack, blitz, bombard, strafe ▹ **shell out** *v* = **pay out**, give, fork out (*slang*), hand over

S

DICTIONARY

▶ **shell out** *v informal* pay out or hand over (money)
▶ **shell shock** nervous disorder caused by exposure to battle conditions
shellac *n* **1** resin used in varnishes ▷ *v* **-lacking, -lacked 2** coat with shellac
Shelley *n* **1 Mary (Wollstonecraft)**. 1797–1851, British writer; author of *Frankenstein* (1818); the daughter of William Godwin and Mary Wollstonecraft, she eloped with Percy Bysshe Shelley **2 Percy Bysshe**. 1792–1822, British romantic poet. His works include *Queen Mab* (1813), *Prometheus Unbound* (1820), and *The Triumph of Life* (1824). He wrote an elegy on the death of Keats, *Adonais* (1821), and shorter lyrics, including the odes "To the West Wind" and "To a Skylark" (both 1820). He was drowned in the Ligurian Sea while sailing from Leghorn to La Spezia
shelter Ⓣ *n* **1** structure providing protection from danger or the weather **2** protection ▷ *v* **3** give shelter to **4** take shelter
shelve Ⓣ *v* **1** put aside or postpone **2** slope
▶ **shelving** *n* (material for) shelves
shelves *n* plural of **shelf**
shenanigans *pl n informal* **1** mischief or nonsense **2** trickery
Shepard *n* **Sam**, original name *Samuel Shepard Rogers*. born 1943, US dramatist, film actor, and director. His plays include *Chicago* (1966), *The Tooth of Crime* (1972), and *Buried Child* (1978): films as actor include *Days of Heaven* (1978) and *The Right Stuff* (1983); films as director include *Far North* (1989) and *Silent Tongue* (1994)
shepherd Ⓣ *n* **1** person who tends sheep ▷ *v* **2** guide or watch over (people) **shepherdess** *n fem*
▶ **shepherd's pie** baked dish of mince covered with mashed potato
sherbet *n* fruit-flavoured fizzy powder
sherd *n* same as **shard**
Sheridan *n* **1 Philip Henry**. 1831–88, American Union cavalry commander in the Civil War. He forced Lee's surrender to Grant (1865) **2 Richard Brinsley**. 1751–1816, Irish dramatist, noted for his comedies of manners *The Rivals* (1775), *School for Scandal* (1777), and *The Critic* (1779)
sheriff *n* **1** municipal officer who enforces court orders etc. **2** (in the US) law enforcement officer **3** (in England and Wales) chief executive officer of the Crown in a county **4** (in Scotland) chief judge of a district **sheriffdom** *n*
Sherpa *n* member of a people of Tibet and Nepal
sherry *n, pl* **-ries** pale or dark brown fortified wine
Shetland pony *n* very small sturdy breed of pony
Shevardnadze *n* **Eduard (Amvrosiyevich)**. born 1928, Georgian statesman; president of Georgia (1992–2003); Soviet minister of foreign affairs (1985–91), who played an important part in arms negotiations with the US
shibboleth *n* slogan or principle, usu. considered outworn, characteristic of a particular group
shied *v* past of **shy**
shield Ⓣ *n* **1** piece of armour carried on the arm to protect the body from blows or missiles **2** anything that protects **3** sports trophy in the shape of a shield ▷ *v* **4** protect
Shields *n* **Carol (Ann)**. 1935–2003, Canadian novelist and writer, born in the US; her novels include *Happenstance* (1980), *The Stone Diaries* (1995), and *Unless* (2002)
shift Ⓣ *v* **1** move **2** transfer (blame or responsibility) **3** remove or be removed ▷ *n* **4** shifting **5** group of workers who work during a specified period **6** period of time during which they work **7** loose-fitting straight underskirt or dress
▶ **shiftless** *adj* lacking in ambition or initiative
▶ **shifty** *adj* evasive or untrustworthy **shiftiness** *n*

THESAURUS

shelter *n* **1 = refuge**, sanctuary, hostel • *a bus shelter* **2 = protection**, safety, cover, harbour, refuge, haven, asylum, sanctuary • *During the flood, we took shelter in the school gym.* ▶ *v* **3 = take cover**, hide, huddle • *a man sheltering in a doorway* **4 = protect**, hide, shield, harbour • *A neighbour sheltered the boy for seven days.*
See also: **accommodate, defend, guard**
sheltered *adj* **= protected**, quiet, isolated, shaded, secluded, cloistered, screened, shielded
shelve *v* **= postpone**, suspend, freeze, defer, put aside, put on ice, put on the back burner (*informal*), take a rain check on (*informal*)
shepherd *v* **= guide**, conduct, steer, herd, usher
shield *n* **1 = protection**, cover, screen, guard, shelter, safeguard, defence ▶ *v* **2 = protect**, defend, cover, screen, guard, shelter, safeguard
shielded *See* **secure**
shift *v* **1 = move**, displace, relocate, budge, reposition, rearrange, move around ▶ *n* **2 = move**, displacement, rearrangement, shifting
shiftless *adj* **= lazy**, idle, lackadaisical, aimless, good-for-nothing, slothful, unambitious, unenterprising

S

DICTIONARY

shillelagh [shil-**lay**-lee] *n* (in Ireland) a cudgel
shilling *n* former British coin, replaced by the 5p piece
shillyshally *v* **-lying, -lied** *informal* be indecisive
shimmer Ⓣ *v*, *n* (shine with) a faint unsteady light
shin *n* **1** front of the lower leg ▷ *v* **shinning, shinned 2** climb by using the hands or arms and legs
▸ **shinbone** *n* tibia
shindig *n informal* **1** noisy party **2** brawl
shine Ⓣ *v* **shining, shone 1** give out or reflect light **2** aim (a light) **3** polish **4** excel ▷ *n* **5** brightness or lustre **shiny** *adj*
▸ **take a shine to** *informal* take a liking to (someone)
▸ **shiner** *n informal* black eye
shingle[1] *n* **1** wooden roof tile ▷ *v* **2** cover (a roof) with shingles
shingle[2] *n* coarse gravel found on beaches
shingles *n* disease causing a rash of small blisters along a nerve
Shinto *n* Japanese religion in which ancestors and nature spirits are worshipped **Shintoism** *n*
shinty *n* game like hockey
ship Ⓣ *n* **1** large seagoing vessel ▷ *v* **shipping, shipped 2** send or transport by carrier, esp. a ship **3** bring or go aboard a ship
▸ **shipment** *n* **1** act of shipping cargo **2** consignment of goods shipped
▸ **shipping** *n* **1** freight transport business **2** ships collectively
▸ **shipshape** *adj* orderly or neat
▸ **shipwreck** *n* **1** destruction of a ship through storm or collision ▷ *v* **2** cause to undergo shipwreck
▸ **shipyard** *n* place where ships are built
shire *n* county
shire horse *n* large powerful breed of horse
shirk Ⓣ *v* avoid (duty or work) **shirker** *n*
shirt *n* garment for the upper part of the body
shirty *adj* **-tier, -tiest** *slang* annoyed
shish kebab *n* meat and vegetable dish cooked on a skewer
shiver[1] Ⓣ *v* **1** tremble, as from cold or fear ▷ *n* **2** shivering
shiver[2] Ⓣ *v* splinter into pieces
shoal[1] *n* large number of fish swimming together
shoal[2] *n* **1** stretch of shallow water **2** sandbank
shock[1] Ⓣ *v* **1** horrify, disgust, or astonish ▷ *n* **2** sudden violent emotional disturbance **3** sudden violent blow or impact **4** something causing this **5** state of bodily collapse caused by physical or mental shock **6** pain and muscular spasm caused by an electric current passing through the body **shocker** *n*
▸ **shocking** *adj* **1** causing horror, disgust, or astonishment **2** *informal* very bad
shock[2] *n* bushy mass (of hair)
shod *v* past of **shoe**
shoddy Ⓣ *adj* **-dier, -diest** of poor quality
shoe *n* **1** outer covering for the foot, ending below the ankle **2** horseshoe ▷ *v* **shoeing,**

THESAURUS

shifty *adj* = **untrustworthy**, slippery, tricky, sly, deceitful, evasive, devious, furtive, underhand
shimmer *v* **1** = **gleam**, twinkle, glisten, scintillate ▸ *n* **2** = **gleam**, iridescence
shimmering *See* **shining**
shine *v* **1** = **gleam**, beam, glow, sparkle, shimmer, radiate • *The sun is shining.* **2** = **polish**, brush, buff, burnish **3** = **stand out**, excel, be conspicuous ▸ *n* **4** = **brightness**, light, sparkle, shimmer, glare, gleam, radiance **5** = **polish**, gloss, sheen, lustre
See also: **finish**
shining *adj* = **bright**, brilliant, sparkling, luminous, radiant, gleaming, shimmering • *shining stainless steel*
shiny *adj* = **bright**, polished, glossy, gleaming, glistening, lustrous
ship *n* = **vessel**, boat, craft
shipment *See* **load, transport**
shipshape *adj* = **tidy**, trim, neat, orderly, well-organized, spick-and-span, well-ordered
shirk *v* = **dodge**, avoid, evade, get out of, slack
shirker *n* = **slacker**, dodger, clock-watcher, idler
shiver[1] *v* **1** = **tremble**, shake, quake, shudder, quiver ▸ *n* **2** = **trembling**, tremor, flutter, shudder, quiver
shiver[2] *v* = **splinter**, break, crack, smash, shatter, fragment, smash to smithereens
shivery *adj* = **shaking**, cold, shaky, chilly, chilled, quaking, quivery
shock *n* **1** = **upset**, blow, trauma, distress, bombshell • *The extent of the damage came as a shock.* **2** = **impact**, blow, clash, collision, crash ▸ *v* **3** = **upset**, shake, stun, paralyze, stagger, traumatize, numb • *I was shocked by his appearance.* **4** = **offend**, outrage, disgust, appal • *She is very easily shocked.*
See also: **amaze, amazement, horrify, scare, surprise**
shocking *adj* = **dreadful**, outrageous, disgraceful, appalling, scandalous, atrocious, sickening, ghastly, disgusting, revolting, horrifying, nauseating
shoddy *adj* = **inferior**, poor, second-rate, trashy, rubbishy, slipshod, tawdry

S

DICTIONARY

shod 3 fit with a shoe or shoes

▸ **shoehorn** *n* smooth curved implement inserted at the heel of a shoe to ease the foot into it

▸ **shoestring** *n* **on a shoestring** using a very small amount of money

shone *v* past of **shine**

shoo *interj* 1 go away! ▹ *v* 2 drive away as by saying 'shoo'

shook *v* past tense of **shake**

shoot Ⓣ *v* **shooting, shot** 1 hit, wound, or kill with a missile fired from a weapon 2 fire (a missile from) a weapon 3 send out or move rapidly 4 hunt 5 (of a plant) sprout 6 photograph or film 7 *sports* take a shot at goal ▹ *n* 8 new branch or sprout of a plant 9 hunting expedition

▸ **shooting star** meteor

▸ **shooting stick** stick with a spike at one end and a folding seat at the other

shop Ⓣ *n* 1 place for sale of goods and services 2 workshop ▹ *v* **shopping, shopped** 3 visit a shop or shops to buy goods 4 *slang* inform against (someone)

▸ **talk shop** discuss one's work, esp. on a social occasion

▸ **shop around** *v* visit various shops to compare goods and prices

▸ **shop floor** 1 production area of a factory 2 workers in a factory

▸ **shoplifter** *n* person who steals from a shop

▸ **shopsoiled** *adj* soiled or faded from being displayed in a shop

▸ **shop steward** trade-union official elected to represent his or her fellow workers

shore[1] Ⓣ *n* edge of a sea or lake

shore[2] Ⓣ *v* (foll. by *up*) prop or support

shorn *v* a past participle of **shear**

short Ⓣ *adj* 1 not long 2 not tall 3 not lasting long, brief 4 deficient: *short of cash* 5 abrupt, rude 6 (of a drink) consisting chiefly of a spirit 7 (of pastry) crumbly ▹ *adv* 8 abruptly ▹ *n* 9 drink of spirits 10 short film 11 *informal* short circuit **shorts** 12 short trousers

▸ **shortage** *n* deficiency

▸ **shorten** *v* make or become shorter

▸ **shortly** *adv* 1 soon 2 rudely

▸ **shortbread** *or* **shortcake** *n* crumbly cookie made with butter

▸ **short-change** *v* 1 give (someone) less than the correct amount of change 2 *slang* swindle

▸ **short circuit** faulty or accidental connection in a circuit, which deflects current through a path of low resistance

▸ **shortcoming** *n* failing or defect

▸ **short cut** quicker route or method

▸ **shortfall** *n* deficit

▸ **shorthand** *n* system of rapid writing using symbols to represent words

▸ **short-handed** *adj* not having enough workers

▸ **short list** selected list of candidates for a job or prize, from which the final choice will be made

▸ **short-list** *v* put on a short list

▸ **short shrift** brief and unsympathetic treatment

▸ **short-sighted** *adj* 1 unable to see faraway things clearly 2 lacking in foresight

▸ **short wave** radio wave with a wavelength of less than 60 metres

Shostakovich *n* **Dmitri Dmitriyevich**.

THESAURUS

shoot *v* 1 = **hit**, kill, blast (*slang*), plug (*slang*), bring down, open fire 2 = **fire**, launch, project, propel, discharge, emit, hurl, fling 3 = **speed**, charge, race, fly, streak, rush, tear, bolt, dash, dart, hurtle ▹ **shoot up** *See* **explode** ▸ *n* 4 = **sprout**, branch, bud, offshoot, sprig

shop *n* 1 = **store**, supermarket, boutique, emporium, hypermarket 2 = **factory**, plant, shop, mill, works ▸ *v* 3 = **go shopping**, buy, purchase

shoplifter *See* **thief**

shopper *See* **customer**

shore *n* = **beach**, coast, strand (*poetic*), sands, seashore ▸ *verb* ▹ **shore up** = **support**, hold, strengthen, brace, prop, reinforce, underpin, buttress

short *adj* 1 = **brief**, short-lived, momentary, fleeting • *a short break* OPPOSITE: long 2 = **small**, little, squat, diminutive, petite, dumpy • *a short, elderly man* OPPOSITE: tall 3 = **concise**, brief, summary, terse, succinct, compressed, laconic, pithy, abridged • *a short speech* 4 (often with *of*) = **lacking**, low *or* low on, limited, scarce, scant, deficient, wanting 5 = **abrupt**, sharp, terse, brusque, curt, discourteous, impolite, uncivil ▸ *adv* 6 = **abruptly**, suddenly, without warning

See also: **inadequate, insufficient**

shortage *n* = **lack**, want, shortfall, deficiency, scarcity, dearth • *a shortage of funds* OPPOSITE: abundance

shortcoming *n* = **failing**, flaw, weakness, defect, fault, imperfection

shorten *v* = **cut**, trim, abbreviate OPPOSITE: lengthen

See also: **reduce**

shortfall *See* **shortage**

short-lived *See* **short**

shortly *adv* = **soon**, presently, before long, in a little while

short-sighted *adj* 1 = **near-sighted**, myopic 2 = **imprudent**, ill-advised, impractical, ill-considered, impolitic, improvident, injudicious, unthinking

DICTIONARY

1906–75, Soviet composer, noted esp. for his 15 symphonies and his chamber music
shot ⓣ *n* **1** shooting **2** small lead pellets used in a shotgun **3** person with specified skill in shooting **4** *slang* attempt **5** *sports* act or instance of hitting, kicking, or throwing the ball **6** photograph **7** uninterrupted film sequence **8** *informal* injection **9** *informal* drink of spirits ▷ *adj* **10** woven so that the colour varies according to the angle of light ▷ *v* **11** past of **shoot**
▸ **shotgun** *n* gun for firing a charge of shot at short range
shot put *n* athletic event in which contestants hurl a heavy metal ball as far as possible **shot-putter** *n*
should *v* past tense of **shall** used as an auxiliary to make the subjunctive mood or to indicate obligation or possibility
shoulder ⓣ *n* **1** part of the body to which an arm, foreleg, or wing is attached **2** cut of meat including the upper foreleg **3** part of a garment which covers the shoulder **4** side of a road ▷ *v* **5** bear (a burden or responsibility) **6** put on one's shoulder **7** push with one's shoulder
▸ **shoulder blade** large flat triangular bone at the shoulder
shouldn't should not
shout ⓣ *n* **1** loud cry ▷ *v* **2** cry out loudly
▸ **shout down** *v* silence (someone) by shouting
shove ⓣ *v* **1** push roughly **2** *informal* put ▷ *n* **3** rough push
▸ **shove off** *v informal* go away
shovel ⓣ *n* **1** tool for lifting or moving loose material ▷ *v* **-elling, -elled 2** lift or move as with a shovel
show ⓣ *v* **showing, showed, shown** *or* **showed 1** make, be, or become noticeable or visible **2** exhibit or display **3** indicate **4** instruct by demonstration **5** prove **6** guide **7** reveal or display (an emotion) ▷ *n* **8** public exhibition **9** theatrical or other entertainment **10** mere display or pretence
▸ **showy** *adj* **1** gaudy **2** ostentatious **showily** *adv*
▸ **show business** the entertainment industry
▸ **showcase** *n* **1** glass case used to display objects **2** situation in which something is displayed to best advantage
▸ **showdown** *n* confrontation that settles a dispute
▸ **showjumping** *n* competitive sport of riding horses to demonstrate skill in jumping
▸ **showman** *n* man skilled at presenting anything spectacularly **showmanship** *n*
▸ **show off** *v* **1** exhibit to invite admiration **2** *informal* behave flamboyantly in order to attract attention
▸ **show-off** *n informal* person who shows off
▸ **showpiece** *n* excellent specimen shown for display or as an example
▸ **showroom** *n* room in which goods for sale are on display
▸ **show up** *v* **1** reveal or be revealed clearly **2** expose the faults or defects of **3** *informal* embarrass **4** *informal* arrive
shower ⓣ *n* **1** kind of bath in which a person stands while being sprayed with

THESAURUS

short-tempered *adj* = **quick-tempered**, impatient, irascible, hot-tempered, testy
shot *n* **1** = **throw**, discharge, lob, pot shot **2** = **ammunition**, lead, ball, bullet, pellet, slug, projectile **3** = **marksman**, shooter **4** (*Slang*) = **attempt**, go (*informal*), try, turn, effort, stab (*informal*), endeavour
shoulder *v* **1** = **bear**, carry, accept, assume, be responsible for, take on **2** = **push**, press, elbow, shove, jostle ▸ *noun* ▷ **shoulder to shoulder** *See* **together**
shout *n* **1** = **cry**, scream, roar, yell, bellow • *I heard a distant shout.* ▸ *v* **2** = **cry**, call, scream, roar, yell, bellow, bawl • *He shouted something to his brother.* ▷ **shout down** = **drown out**, silence, overwhelm, drown
shove *v* = **push**, drive, press, propel, elbow, thrust, jostle ▷ **shove off** = **go away**, leave, depart, clear off (*informal*), push off (*informal*), scram (*informal*)
shovel *v* = **move**, load, toss, scoop, heap, ladle, dredge
show *v* **1** = **prove**, demonstrate • *Tests show that drinking impairs your ability to drive.* **2** = **demonstrate**, teach, instruct • *I'll show you how to used this digital camera.* **3** = **display**, reveal, indicate, demonstrate, manifest • *Her sketches showed artistic promise.* **4** = **exhibit**, present, display **5** = **guide**, lead, attend, conduct, accompany, escort ▷ **show off** = **exhibit**, display, demonstrate, parade, flaunt, hot dog (*slang*); = **boast**, brag, swagger, blow one's own trumpet ▷ **show signs of** *See* **promise** ▷ **show up** = **stand out**, appear, be conspicuous, be visible; = **reveal**, highlight, expose, lay bare; (*Informal*) = **embarrass**, mortify, let down, put to shame; = **arrive**, come, appear, turn up ▸ *n* **6** = **exhibition**, display, presentation • *a fashion show* **7** = **pretence**, air, display, pose, semblance • *a show of affection* **8** = **entertainment**, production, presentation
See also: **betray, expose, fair, front, play, program, represent**
showdown *n* = **confrontation**, clash, face-off (*slang*)
shower *n* **1** = **deluge**, stream, barrage,

DICTIONARY

water **2** wash in this **3** short period of rain, hail, or snow **4** sudden abundant fall of objects: *shower of sparks* ▷ *v* **5** wash in a shower **6** bestow (things) or present (someone) with things liberally **showery** *adj*
shown *v* a past participle of **show**
shrank *v* a past tense of **shrink**
shrapnel *n* **1** artillery shell filled with pellets which scatter on explosion **2** fragments from this
shred Ⓣ *n* **1** long narrow strip torn from something **2** small amount ▷ *v* **shredding, shredded** *or* **shred 3** tear to shreds
shrew Ⓣ *n* **1** small mouselike animal **2** bad-tempered nagging woman **shrewish** *adj*
shrewd Ⓣ *adj* clever and perceptive **shrewdly** *adv* **shrewdness** *n*
shriek Ⓣ *n* **1** shrill cry ▷ *v* **2** utter (with) a shriek
shrike *n* songbird with a heavy hooked bill
shrill Ⓣ *adj* (of a sound) sharp and high-pitched **shrillness** *n* **shrilly** *adv*
shrimp *n* **1** small edible shellfish **2** *informal* small person
▸**shrimping** *n* fishing for shrimps
shrine *n* place of worship associated with a sacred person or object
shrink Ⓣ *v* **shrinking, shrank** *or* **shrunk, shrunk** *or* **shrunken 1** become or make smaller **2** recoil or withdraw ▷ *n* **3** *slang* psychiatrist
▸**shrinkage** *n* decrease in size, value, or weight
shrive *v* **shriving, shrived** *or* **shrove, shriven** *old-fashioned* give absolution to after hearing confession
shrivel Ⓣ *v* **-elling, -elled** shrink and wither
shroud Ⓣ *n* **1** piece of cloth used to wrap a dead body **2** anything which conceals ▷ *v* **3** conceal
Shrovetide *n* the three days preceding Lent
▸**Shrove Tuesday** day before Ash Wednesday
shrub *n* woody plant smaller than a tree
▸**shrubbery** *n* area planted with shrubs
shrug *v* **shrugging, shrugged 1** raise and then drop (the shoulders) as a sign of indifference, ignorance, or doubt ▷ *n* **2** shrugging
▸**shrug off** *v* dismiss as unimportant
shrunk *v* a past of **shrink**
shrunken *v* a past participle of **shrink**
shudder Ⓣ *v* **1** shake or tremble violently, esp. with horror ▷ *n* **2** shaking or trembling
shuffle Ⓣ *v* **1** walk without lifting the feet **2** rearrange **3** jumble together ▷ *n* **4** shuffling **5** rearrangement
shun Ⓣ *v* **shunning, shunned** avoid
shunt *v* **1** move (objects or people) to a different position **2** move (a train) from one track to another
shush *interj* be quiet!
shut Ⓣ *v* **shutting, shut 1** bring together

THESAURUS

volley, torrent ▸**showers** *See* **rain** ▸*v* **2** = **inundate**, rain, pour, lavish, heap, deluge
showery *See* **wet**
showman *n* = **performer**, entertainer
show-off *n* = **exhibitionist**, boaster, braggart, poseur, hot dog (*slang*)
showy *adj* **1** = **ostentatious**, flash (*informal*), flamboyant, flashy, brash, over the top (*informal*) **2** = **gaudy**, loud, garish
shred *n* **1** = **strip**, bit, piece, scrap, fragment, tatter, sliver **2** = **particle**, grain, trace, scrap, atom, iota, jot
shrew *n* = **nag**, scold, spitfire, vixen, harpy, harridan
shrewd *adj* = **astute**, sharp, smart, crafty, perceptive, canny • *a shrewd manager*
See also: **acute, clever, keen, wise**
shrewdness *n* = **astuteness**, judgment, discernment, sharpness, canniness, perspicacity, quick wits, smartness
shriek *v, n* = **scream**, cry, yell, screech, squeal
shrill *adj* = **piercing**, sharp, penetrating • *the shrill whistle of the engine*
shrink *v* **1** = **get smaller**, contract, narrow, diminish, dwindle • *My sweater shrank in the wash.* OPPOSITE: grow **2** = **recoil**, cringe, quail, flinch, cower, draw back
See also: **decrease, lessen**
shrinkage *See* **decline**
shrivel *v* = **wither**, shrink, wilt, dehydrate, desiccate, wizen
shroud *n* **1** = **winding sheet**, grave clothes **2** = **covering**, screen, veil, pall, mantle ▸*v* **3** = **conceal**, cover, screen, hide, blanket, cloak, veil, envelop
shudder *v* **1** = **shiver**, shake, quake, tremble, quiver, convulse ▸*n* **2** = **shiver**, tremor, spasm, quiver
shuffle *v* **1** = **scuffle**, drag, scrape, shamble **2** = **rearrange**, disorder, mix, jumble, disarrange
shun *v* = **avoid**, keep away from, steer clear of
shunned *See* **unpopular**
shut *v* **1** = **close**, slam, fasten • *Someone had forgotten to shut the door.* OPPOSITE: open ▸*adj* **2** = **closed**, sealed, fastened • *An aroma of baking bread came from behind the shut door.* OPPOSITE: open
shut down *v* **1** = **stop**, halt, switch off **2** = **close**, shut up
shut out *v* = **exclude**, bar, debar, keep out, lock out

DICTIONARY

or fold, close **2** prevent access to **3** (of a shop etc.) stop operating for the day
▸ **shutter** *n* **1** hinged doorlike cover for closing off a window **2** device in a camera letting in the light required to expose a film
▸ **shut down** *v* close or stop (a factory, machine, or business) **shutdown** *n*
▸ **shut out** *v sports* prevent (an opponent) from scoring for an entire game
▸ **shutout** *n sports* game in which the opposing team does not score
Shute *n* **Nevil**, real name *Nevil Shute Norway*. 1899–1960, English novelist, in Australia after World War II: noted for his novels set in Australia, esp. *A Town like Alice* (1950) and *On the Beach* (1957)
shuttle ⊙ *n* **1** vehicle going to and fro over a short distance **2** instrument which passes the weft thread between the warp threads in weaving ▷ *v* **3** travel by or as if by shuttle
shuttlecock *n* small light cone with feathers stuck in one end, struck to and fro in badminton
shy[1] ⊙ *adj* **1** not at ease in company **2** timid **3** (foll. by *of*) cautious or wary ▷ *v* **shying, shied 4** start back in fear **5** (foll. by *away from*) avoid (doing something) through fear or lack of confidence **shyly** *adv* **shyness** *n*
shy[2] ⊙ *v* **shying, shied 1** throw ▷ *n, pl* **shies 2** throw
shyster *n US informal* unscrupulous person, esp. a lawyer
Si *chem* silicon
SI *French* Système International (d'Unités), international metric system of units of measurement
Siamese *adj* of Siam, former name of Thailand
▸ **Siamese cat** breed of cat with cream fur, dark ears and face, and blue eyes
▸ **Siamese twins** twins born joined to each other at some part of the body
Sibelius *n* **Jean**. 1865–1957, Finnish composer, noted for his seven symphonies, his symphonic poems, such as *Finlandia* (1900) and *Tapiola* (1925), and his violin concerto (1905)
sibilant *adj* **1** hissing ▷ *n* **2** consonant pronounced with a hissing sound
sibling *n* brother or sister
sibyl *n* (in ancient Greece and Rome) prophetess **sibylline** *adj*
sic *Latin* thus (used to indicate that an odd spelling or reading is in fact accurate)
sick ⊙ *adj* **1** vomiting or likely to vomit **2** physically or mentally unwell **3** *informal* amused by something sadistic or morbid **4** (foll. by *of*) *informal* disgusted (by) or weary (of) **sickness** *n*
▸ **sicken** *v* **1** make nauseated or disgusted **2** become ill
▸ **sickly** *adj* **1** unhealthy, weak **2** causing revulsion or nausea
▸ **sickbay** *n* place for sick people, such as that on a ship
Sickert *n* **Walter Richard**. 1860–1942, British impressionist painter, esp. of scenes of London music halls
sickle *n* tool with a curved blade for cutting grass or grain
side ⊙ *n* **1** line or surface that borders anything **2** either surface of a flat object **3** either of two halves into which something can be divided **4** area immediately next to a person or thing **5** region **6** aspect or part **7** one of two opposing groups or teams **8** line

THESAURUS

shuttle *v* = **go back and forth**, alternate, commute, go to and fro
shut up *v* **1** (*Informal*) = **be quiet**, silence, gag, hush, fall silent, hold one's tongue **2** = **confine**, imprison, cage, incarcerate, coop up, immure
shy *adj* **1** = **timid**, self-conscious, self-effacing, bashful, retiring, diffident • *a shy, quiet-spoken man* OPPOSITE: bold **2** = **cautious**, suspicious, wary, hesitant, chary, distrustful ▸ *v* **3** (sometimes with *away*) = **recoil**, start, balk, flinch, draw back
shyness *n* = **timidness**, bashfulness, diffidence, lack of confidence, self-consciousness, timidity, timorousness
sick *adj* **1** = **unwell**, ailing, under par, under the weather • *The emergency room was full of very sick people.* OPPOSITE: well **2** = **nauseous**, ill, queasy • *The very thought of food made him sick.* **3** (*Informal*) = **morbid**, black, sadistic, macabre, ghoulish ▷ **sick of** = **tired**, weary, bored, fed up • *I'm sick of your complaints.*
▷ **sick person** *See* **patient**
See also: **unhealthy**
sicken *v* **1** = **disgust**, revolt, repel, nauseate, gross out (*slang*), turn one's stomach **2** = **fall ill**, ail, take sick
sickening *adj* = **disgusting**, offensive, foul, gross (*slang*), vile, distasteful, repulsive, revolting, loathsome, nauseating, noisome, scuzzy (*slang*), stomach-turning (*informal*), yucky *or* yukky (*slang*)
sickly *adj* **1** = **unhealthy**, weak, ailing, delicate, faint, feeble, infirm, pallid, wan, peaky **2** = **nauseating**, cloying, mawkish
sickness *n* **1** = **illness**, disease, complaint, disorder, bug (*informal*), ailment, malady, affliction **2** = **nausea**, queasiness, vomiting
side *n* **1** = **edge**, shoulder • *Her legs hung over the side of the bed.* RELATED WORD *adjective*: lateral **2** = **party**, team, camp, faction • *Both sides began to prepare for the debate.* **3** = **part**,

S

DICTIONARY

of descent through one parent **9** *slang* conceit ▷ *adj* **10** at or on the side **11** subordinate
▸ **on the side 1** as an extra **2** unofficially
▸ **siding** *n* short stretch of railway track on which trains or cars are shunted from the main line
▸ **sideboard** *n* **1** piece of furniture for holding plates, cutlery, etc. in a dining room **sideboards 2** Also **sideburns** man's side whiskers
▸ **side-effect** *n* additional undesirable effect
▸ **sidekick** *n informal* close friend or associate
▸ **sidelight** *n* either of two small lights on the front of a vehicle
▸ **sideline** *n* **1** subsidiary interest or source of income **2** *sports* line marking the boundary of a playing area
▸ **sidelong** *adj* **1** sideways **2** oblique ▷ *adv* **3** obliquely
▸ **side-saddle** *n* saddle designed to allow a woman rider to sit with both legs on the same side of the horse
▸ **sidestep** *v* **1** dodge (an issue) **2** avoid by stepping sideways
▸ **sidetrack** *v* divert from the main topic
▸ **sidewalk** *n* paved path for pedestrians
▸ **sideways** *adv* **1** to or from the side **2** obliquely
▸ **side with** *v* support (one side in a dispute)
sidereal [side-**eer**-ee-al] *adj* of or determined with reference to the stars
sidle Ⓣ *v* move in a furtive manner
Sidney, Sydney *n* Sir **Philip**. 1554–86, English poet, courtier, and soldier. His works include the pastoral romance *Arcadia* (1590), the sonnet sequence *Astrophel and Stella* (1591), and *The Defence of Poesie* (1595), one of the earliest works of literary criticism in English
SIDS sudden infant death syndrome, crib death
siege *n* surrounding and blockading of a place
sienna *n* reddish- or yellowish-brown pigment made from natural earth
sierra *n* range of mountains in Spain or America with jagged peaks
siesta Ⓣ *n* afternoon nap, taken in hot countries
sieve Ⓣ [**siv**] *n* **1** utensil with mesh through which a substance is sifted or strained ▷ *v* **2** sift or strain through a sieve
sift Ⓣ *v* **1** remove the coarser particles from a substance with a sieve **2** examine (information or evidence) to select what is important
sigh *n* **1** long audible breath expressing sadness, tiredness, relief, or longing ▷ *v* **2** utter a sigh
sight Ⓣ *n* **1** ability to see **2** instance of seeing **3** range of vision **4** thing seen **5** thing worth seeing **6** *informal* unsightly thing **7** device for guiding the eye while using a gun or optical instrument **8** *informal* a lot ▷ *v* **9** catch sight of
▸ **sightless** *adj* blind
▸ **sight-read** *v* play or sing printed music without previous preparation
▸ **sightseeing** *n* visiting places of interest **sightseer** *n*
sign Ⓣ *n* **1** indication of something not immediately or outwardly observable **2** notice displayed to advertise, inform, or warn **3** gesture, mark, or symbol conveying a meaning **4** omen ▷ *v* **5** write (one's name) on (a document or letter) to show its authenticity or one's agreement

THESAURUS

S

face, hand, view, surface, aspect, flank, facet **4 = point of view**, stand, position, opinion, viewpoint, angle, standpoint, slant ▷ **side by side** *See* **together** ▸ *adj* **5 = subordinate**, minor, subsidiary, secondary, lesser, marginal, ancillary, incidental
See also: **bank, point** ▸ *verb* ▷ **side with = support**, agree with, stand up for, take the part of • *He always sided with his sister.*
sidelong *adj* = **sideways**, indirect, covert, oblique
sidestep *v* = **avoid**, duck (*informal*), skirt, circumvent, evade, dodge
sidetrack *v* = **distract**, divert, deflect
sideways *adv* **1 = obliquely**, edgeways, laterally, sidelong, to the side ▸ *adj* **2 = oblique**, sidelong
sidle *v* = **edge**, steal, inch, creep, sneak, slink
siesta *n* = **nap**, sleep, snooze (*informal*), doze, catnap, forty winks (*informal*)
sieve *n* **1 = strainer**, colander ▸ *v* **2 = sift**, separate, strain
sift *v* **1 = sieve**, separate, filter **2 = examine**, research, investigate, analyze, scrutinize, go through, work over
sight *n* **1 = vision**, visibility, eyesight • *The singer lost his sight when he was a child*. RELATED WORDS *adjectives*: optical, visual **2 = spectacle**, scene, display • *It was a ghastly sight*. **3 = view**, appearance, perception, visibility, range of vision **4 = eyesore**, mess, monstrosity ▷ **catch sight of = spot**, glimpse, espy ▸ *v* **5 = spot**, see • *He had been sighted in the Maritimes*.
sign *n* **1 = symbol**, mark, character, icon, logo, emblem • *The negative number is preceded by a minus sign*. **2 = notice**, board, placard • *a sign saying that the highway was closed* **3 = indication**, evidence, symptom, hint, trace, clue, token • *the first signs of*

DICTIONARY

6 communicate using sign language **7** make a sign or gesture
▶ **signing** *n* Also **sign language** system of manual signs used to communicate with deaf people
▶ **sign on** *v* **1** register as unemployed **2** sign a document committing oneself to a job, course, etc.
▶ **signpost** *n* post bearing a sign that shows the way
signal Ⓣ *n* **1** sign or gesture to convey information **2** sequence of electrical impulses or radio waves transmitted or received ▷ *adj* **3** remarkable or striking ▷ *v* **-nalling, -nalled 4** make a signal **5** convey (information) by signal **signally** *adv*
▶ **signal box** building from which railway signals are operated
▶ **signalman** *n* railwayman in charge of signals and points
signatory [**sig**-na-tree] *n, pl* **-ries** one of the parties who sign a document
signature *n* **1** person's name written by himself or herself in signing something **2** sign at the start of a piece of music to show the key or tempo
▶ **signature tune** tune used to introduce a particular television or radio programme
signet *n* small seal used to authenticate documents
▶ **signet ring** finger ring bearing a signet
significant Ⓣ *adj* **1** important **2** having or expressing a meaning **significantly** *adv* **significance** *n*
signify Ⓣ *v* **-fying, -fied 1** indicate or suggest **2** be a symbol or sign for **3** be important
▶ **signification** *n* meaning
signor [see-**nyor**] *n* Italian term of address equivalent to *Sir* or *Mr*
▶ **signora** [see-**nyor**-a] *n* Italian term of address equivalent to *madam* or *Mrs*
▶ **signorina** [see-nyor-**ee**-na] *n* Italian term of address equivalent to *madam* or *Miss*
Signoret *n* **Simone**, original name *Simone Kaminker.* 1921–85, French stage and film actress, whose films include *La Ronde* (1950), *Casque d'Or* (1952), *Room at the Top* (1958), and *Ship of Fools* (1965): married the actor and singer Yves Montand (1921–91)
Sihanouk *n* King **Norodom**. born 1922, Cambodian statesman; king of Cambodia (1941–55 and from 1993); prime minister (1955–60), after which he became head of state. He was deposed in 1970 but reinstated (1975–76) following the victory of the Khmer Rouge in the civil war. He was head of state in exile from 1982; returned in 1991 and became monarch in 1993 under a new constitution
Sikh [**seek**] *n* member of an Indian religion having only one God
Sikorski *n* **Władysław**. 1881–1943, Polish general and statesman: prime minister (1922–23) and prime minister of the Polish government in exile during World War II: died in an air wreck
silage [**sile**-ij] *n* fodder crop harvested while green and partially fermented in a silo
silence Ⓣ *n* **1** absence of noise or speech ▷ *v* **2** make silent **3** put a stop to **silent** *adj* **silently** *adv*
▶ **silencer** *n* device to reduce the noise of an engine exhaust or gun
silhouette Ⓣ *n* **1** outline of a dark shape

THESAURUS

recovery **4 = omen**, warning, auspice, augury, foreboding, portent ▶ *v* **5 = autograph**, endorse, initial, inscribe **6 = gesture**, indicate, signal, beckon, gesticulate ▷ **sign up** *See* **hire, join**
See also: **premonition**
signal *n* **1 = sign**, gesture, cue, beacon • *a distress signal* ▶ *v* **2 = gesture**, sign, wave, motion, nod, beckon, gesticulate • *He was frantically signalling me to stop talking.* ▷ **signal to** *See* **hail**
See also: **indicate, indication**
significance *n* **1 = importance**, weight, moment, consequence, relevance **2 = meaning**, point, force, message, import, sense, implication *or* implications, purport
significant *adj* **1 = important**, impressive, considerable, notable, marked, striking, pronounced • *This drug seems to have a significant effect on the disease.* OPPOSITE: insignificant **2 = meaningful**, indicative, suggestive, expressive, eloquent
See also: **major, serious, special**
signify *v* **1 = indicate**, suggest, mean, intimate, imply, denote, portend, be a sign of, betoken, connote **2 = matter**, count, be important, carry weight
silence *n* **1 = quiet**, peace, calm, lull, hush, stillness • *There was a momentary silence.* OPPOSITE: noise **2 = reticence**, muteness, speechlessness • *breaking his silence for the first time about the incident* ▶ *v* **3 = quiet**, still, stifle, suppress, gag, muffle, deaden • *The shock silenced her completely.*
silent *adj* **1 = mute**, dumb, speechless, taciturn, wordless • *The class fell silent as the teacher entered.* **2 = quiet**, still, hushed, soundless • *The room was silent except for the ticking of the clock.* OPPOSITE: noisy
silently *adj* **= quietly**, inaudibly, in silence, mutely, noiselessly, soundlessly, without a sound, wordlessly
silhouette *n* **1 = outline**, form, shape,

S

DICTIONARY

seen against a light background ▷ *v* **2** show in silhouette
silica *n* hard glossy mineral found as quartz and in sandstone
▸ **silicosis** *n* lung disease caused by inhaling silica dust
silicate *n* compound of silicon, oxygen, and a metal
silicon *n* brittle nonmetallic element widely used in chemistry and industry
▸ **silicone** *n* tough synthetic substance made from silicon and used in lubricants, paints, and resins
▸ **silicon chip** tiny wafer of silicon processed to form an integrated circuit
silicosis *n* lung disease caused by inhaling silica dust
silk *n* **1** fibre made by the larva of a moth called the silkworm **2** thread or fabric made from this
▸ **silky** *or* **silken** *adj* of or like silk
sill *n* ledge at the bottom of a window
Sillitoe *n* **Alan**. 1928–2010, British novelist. His best-known works include *Saturday Night and Sunday Morning* (1958) and *The Loneliness of the Long Distance Runner* (1959)
Sills *n* **Beverley**, original name *Belle Silverman*. 1929–2007, US soprano: director of the New York City Opera (1979–89)
silly Ⓣ *adj* **-lier, -liest** foolish **silliness** *n*
silo *n, pl* **-los 1** pit or airtight tower for storing silage **2** underground structure in which nuclear missiles are kept ready for launching
silt Ⓣ *n* **1** mud deposited by moving water ▷ *v* **2** (foll. by *up*) fill or be choked with silt
silvan *adj* same as **sylvan**
silver *n* **1** white precious metal **2** coins or articles made of silver ▷ *adj* **3** made of or of the colour of silver
▸ **silver birch** tree with silvery-white bark
▸ **silverfish** *n* small wingless silver-coloured insect
▸ **silverside** *n Brit* cut of beef from below the rump and above the leg
▸ **silver thaw** quick-freezing rain that encrusts trees, rocks, etc.
▸ **silver wedding** twenty-fifth wedding anniversary
silviculture *n* cultivation of forest trees
sim *n* computer game that simulates an activity such as flying or playing a sport
Simcoe *n* **John Graves**. 1752–1806, British soldier and colonial administrator in Canada, born in England. Appointed first Lieutenant-Governor of Upper Canada in 1791; founded the city of York (now Toronto); abolished slavery in Upper Canada; introduced English common law and trial by jury
Simenon *n* **Georges**. 1903–89, Belgian novelist. He wrote over two hundred novels, including the detective series featuring Maigret
Simeon Stylites *n* **Saint**. ?390–459 AD, Syrian monk, first of the ascetics who lived on pillars. Feast day: Jan 5 or Sept 1
simian *adj, n* (of or like) a monkey or ape
similar Ⓣ *adj* alike but not identical
similarity *n* **similarly** *adv*
simile [**sim**-ill-ee] *n* figure of speech comparing one thing to another, using 'as' or 'like'
similitude *n* similarity, likeness
simmer Ⓣ *v* **1** cook gently at just below boiling point **2** be in a state of suppressed rage
▸ **simmer down** *v* calm down
simnel cake *n* fruit cake covered with marzipan
Simon *n* **1** the original name of (Saint) **Peter 2** (**Marvin**) **Neil**. born 1927, US dramatist and librettist, whose plays include *Barefoot in the Park* (1963), *California Suite* (1976), *Biloxi Blues* (1985), *Lost in Yonkers* (1990), and *London Suite* (1995): many have been made into films **3 Paul**. born 1942, US pop singer and songwriter. His albums include: with Art Garfunkel (born 1941), *The Sounds of Silence* (1966), and *Bridge over Troubled Water* (1970); and, solo, *Graceland* (1986), *The Rhythm of the Saints* (1990), and *You're The One* (2000)
simper Ⓣ *v* **1** smile in a silly or affected way **2** utter (something) with a simper ▷ *n* **3** simpering smile
simple Ⓣ *adj* **1** easy to understand or do

THESAURUS

profile ▸ *v* **2** = **outline**, etch, stand out
silky *adj* = **smooth**, sleek, velvety, silken
silliness *See* **stupidity**
silly *adj* = **foolish**, stupid, ridiculous, absurd, idiotic, inane • *I know it's silly to get so upset*. *See also*: **frivolous, unwise**
silt *n* = **sediment**, deposit, sludge, ooze, alluvium ▸ *verb* ▷ **silt up** = **clog**, choke, congest
similar *adj* = **like**, uniform, comparable, alike, analogous • *a bike similar to mine* OPPOSITE: different
similarity *n* = **resemblance**, likeness, analogy, sameness • *the similarity of our backgrounds* OPPOSITE: difference
similarly *See* **alike**
simmer *v* = **fume**, rage, smoulder, seethe, be angry ▷ **simmer down** *v* = **calm down**, control oneself, cool off *or* cool down, de-stress
simper *v* = **smile coyly**, smirk, smile affectedly
simple *adj* **1** = **easy**, elementary, straightforward, understandable,

DICTIONARY

2 plain or unpretentious **3** not combined or complex **4** sincere or frank **5** feeble-minded **simply** *adv* **simplicity** *n*
▸ **simplify** *v* **-fying, -fied** make less complicated **simplification** *n*
▸ **simplistic** *adj* oversimplified or oversimplifying
▸ **simpleton** *n* foolish or half-witted person
Simpson *n* **1** Sir **George**. 1787–1860, Canadian explorer and administrator, born in Scotland. He was sent to Quebec by the Hudson's Bay Company, where he became Governor-in-Chief of Rupert's Land and administrator of the Northwestern Territory (1821–60) **2** Sir **James Young**. 1811–70, Scottish obstetrician, who pioneered the use of chloroform as an anesthetic **3 Wallis (Warfield)**. See **Edward VIII**
simulate Ⓣ *v* **1** make a pretence of **2** have the appearance of **3** imitate the conditions of (a particular situation) **simulation** *n* **simulator** *n*
simultaneous Ⓣ *adj* occurring at the same time **simultaneity** *n* **simultaneously** *adv*
sin[1] Ⓣ *n* **1** breaking of a religious or moral law **2** offence against a principle or standard ▹ *v* **sinning, sinned 3** commit a sin **sinner** *n*
▸ **sinful** *adj* **1** being a sin **2** guilty of sin **sinfully** *adv*
sin[2] *math* sine
SIN Social Insurance Number
Sinatra *n* **Francis Albert**, known as *Frank*. 1915–98, US popular singer and movie actor. His recordings include "One for My Baby (and One More for the Road)" (1955) and "My Way" (1969)
since *prep* **1** during the period of time after ▹ *conj* **2** from the time when **3** for the reason that ▹ *adv* **4** from that time
sincere Ⓣ *adj* without pretence or deceit **sincerely** *adv* **sincerity** *n*
sine *n* (in trigonometry) ratio of the length of the opposite side to that of the hypotenuse in a right-angled triangle
sinecure Ⓣ [**sin**-ih-cure] *n* paid job with minimal duties
sine die [**sin**-ay **dee**-ay] *adv Latin* with no date fixed for future action
sine qua non [**sin**-ay kwah **non**] *n Latin* essential requirement
sinew *n* **1** tough fibrous tissue joining muscle to bone **2** muscles or strength **sinewy** *adj*
sing Ⓣ *v* **singing, sang, sung 1** make musical sounds with the voice **2** perform (a song) **3** make a humming or whistling sound **singer** *n*
▸ **singsong** *n* **1** informal singing session

THESAURUS

uncomplicated • *a simple task* OPPOSITE: complicated **2 = plain**, clean, severe, classic • *a simple but stylish outfit* OPPOSITE: elaborate **3 = pure**, elementary, unalloyed, uncombined, unmixed **4 = artless**, natural, innocent, sincere, naive, unaffected, childlike, unsophisticated, guileless, ingenuous **5 = honest**, direct, basic, naked, plain, stark, sincere, frank, bald **6 = humble**, modest, unpretentious, homey, dumpy (*informal*) **7 = feeble-minded**, slow, stupid, foolish, moronic, half-witted
See also: **crude, primitive**
simple-minded *adj* **= feeble-minded**, simple, stupid, idiot, backward, foolish, idiotic, retarded, moronic, dim-witted
simpleton *n* **= halfwit**, fool, idiot, moron, imbecile (*informal*), doofus (*slang*), dork (*slang*), dullard, schmuck (*slang*)
simplicity *n* **1 = ease**, clarity, clearness, straightforwardness **2 = plainness**, restraint, purity, lack of adornment **3 = artlessness**, innocence, openness, candour, directness, naivety
simplify *v* **= make simpler**, streamline • *measures intended to simplify the procedure*
simply *adv* **1 = plainly**, easily, clearly, directly, naturally, intelligibly, straightforwardly, unpretentiously **2 = just**, only, merely, solely, purely **3 = totally**, really, completely, absolutely, wholly, utterly
simulate *v* **= pretend**, act, affect, sham, feign, put on
simulated *See* **false**
simultaneous *adj* **= coinciding**, concurrent, coincident, at the same time, contemporaneous, synchronous
simultaneously *adv* **= at the same time**, together, concurrently
sin *n* **1 = crime**, wrong, offence, evil, wickedness • *preaching against sin* ▸ *v* **2 = do wrong** • *I admit that I have sinned.*
since *See* **because**
sincere *adj* **= honest**, real, genuine, heartfelt, wholehearted • *my sincere apologies* OPPOSITE: insincere
See also: **serious**
sincerely *adv* **= honestly**, seriously, truly, genuinely, wholeheartedly, earnestly, in earnest
sincerity *n* **= honesty**, truth, seriousness, candour, frankness, genuineness
sinecure *n* **= soft job** (*informal*), gravy train (*slang*), money for jam *or* money for old rope (*informal*), soft option
sinful *adj* **= wicked**, bad, guilty, criminal, corrupt, immoral, erring, iniquitous
sing *v* **1 = warble**, chant, pipe, carol, chirp, croon, yodel, trill **2 = hum**, buzz, whine, purr

DICTIONARY

▷ *adj* **2** (of the voice) repeatedly rising and falling in pitch
singe Ⓣ *v* **singeing, singed 1** burn the surface of ▷ *n* **2** superficial burn
single Ⓣ *adj* **1** one only **2** distinct from others of the same kind **3** unmarried **4** designed for one user **5** formed of only one part **6** (of a ticket) valid for an outward journey only ▷ *n* **7** single thing **8** thing intended for one person **9** record with one short song or tune on each side **10** *baseball* hit that enables the batter to run to first base **singles 11** game between two players ▷ *v* **12** (foll. by *out*) pick out from others **singly** *adv*
▸ **single file** (of people or things) arranged in one line
▸ **single-handed** *adj* without assistance
▸ **single-minded** *adj* having one aim only
singlet *n* sleeveless vest
singular Ⓣ *adj* **1** (of a word or form) denoting one person or thing **2** remarkable, unusual ▷ *n* **3** singular form of a word **singularity** *n* **singularly** *adv*
sinister Ⓣ *adj* threatening or suggesting evil or harm
sink Ⓣ *v* **sinking, sank** *or* **sunk, sunk** *or* **sunken 1** submerge (in liquid) **2** cause (a ship) to submerge by attacking it with bombs, etc. **3** descend or cause to descend **4** decline in value or amount **5** become weaker in health **6** dig or drill (a hole or shaft) **7** invest (money) **8** *golf, snooker* hit (a ball) into a hole or pocket ▷ *n* **9** fixed basin with a water supply and drainage pipe
▸ **sinker** *n* **1** weight for a fishing line **2** *baseball* ball which dips considerably after being pitched or hit
▸ **sink in** *v* penetrate the mind
▸ **sinking fund** money set aside regularly to repay a long-term debt
Sino- *combining form* Chinese
sinuous *adj* **1** curving **2** lithe **sinuously** *adv*
sinus [**sine**-uss] *n* hollow space in a bone, esp. an air passage opening into the nose
sip Ⓣ *v* **sipping, sipped 1** drink in small mouthfuls ▷ *n* **2** amount sipped
siphon *n* **1** bent tube which uses air pressure to draw liquid from a container ▷ *v* **2** draw off thus **3** redirect (resources)
sir *n* **1** polite term of address for a man **2 Sir** title of a knight or baronet
sire *n* **1** male parent of a horse or other domestic animal **2** respectful term of address to a king ▷ *v* **3** father
siren Ⓣ *n* **1** device making a loud wailing noise as a warning **2** dangerously alluring woman
sirloin *n* prime cut of loin of beef
sirocco *n, pl* **-cos** hot wind blowing from N Africa into S Europe
sisal [**size**-al] *n* (fibre of) plant used in making ropes
siskin *n* yellow-and-black finch
Sisley *n* **Alfred**. 1839–99, French painter, esp. of landscapes; one of the originators of impressionism
sissy Ⓣ *n, pl* **-sies 1** weak or cowardly person **2** effeminate male
sister *n* **1** girl or woman with the same

THESAURUS

singe *v* = **burn**, char, scorch, sear
singer *n* = **vocalist**, crooner, diva, soloist, balladeer, cantor, chorister, minstrel, divo
single *adj* **1** = **one**, only, lone, sole, solitary • *the beauty of a single rose* **2** = **unmarried**, bachelor *or* bachelorette (*feminine*), unattached • *I'm surprised you're still single.* **3** = **individual**, separate • *a single room* **4** = **simple**, unblended, unmixed ▸ *v* **5** (usually with *out*) = **pick**, choose, separate, select, distinguish, fix on, pick on *or* pick out, set apart
See also: **alone**
single-handed *adv* = **unaided**, alone, solo, independently, unassisted, by oneself, on one's own, without help
single-minded *adj* = **determined**, dedicated, dogged, fixed, unswerving
singly *adv* = **one by one**, separately, individually, one at a time
singular *adj* **1** = **remarkable**, rare, unique, exceptional, uncommon • *an artist of singular talent* **2** = **unusual**, extraordinary • *a singular and eccentric character* **3** = **single**, individual, separate, sole
See also: **curious, odd, particular, weird**
singularly *adv* = **remarkably**, especially, particularly, notably, unusually, exceptionally, uncommonly, outstandingly
sinister *adj* = **threatening**, evil, ominous, forbidding, menacing • *There was something cold and sinister about him.*
See also: **creepy**
sink *v* **1** = **descend**, fall, drop, lower, founder, plunge, dip, subside, submerge, go down, go under **2** = **fall**, drop, collapse, slip, lapse, subside, abate **3** = **decline**, fail, flag, worsen, weaken, fade, deteriorate, diminish, dwindle, lessen, decay **4** = **dig**, drive, drill, bore, excavate **5** = **stoop**, be reduced to, lower oneself ▷ **sink in** = **be understood**, register (*informal*), penetrate, get through to
sinner *n* = **wrongdoer**, offender, miscreant, evildoer, malefactor, transgressor
sip *v* **1** = **drink**, sample, taste, sup ▸ *n* **2** = **swallow**, drop, taste, thimbleful
siren *See* **alarm**
sissy *n* **1** = **wimp** (*informal*), coward, mama's

S

DICTIONARY

parents as another person **2** senior nurse **3** nun **4** female fellow-member of a group ▷ *adj* **5** closely related, similar **sisterly** *adj*
▶ **sisterhood** *n* **1** state of being a sister **2** group of women united by common aims or beliefs
▶ **sister-in-law** *n, pl* **sisters-in-law** **1** sister of one's husband or wife **2** one's brother's wife
sit Ⓣ *v* **sitting, sat** **1** rest one's body upright on the buttocks **2** cause to sit **3** perch **4** (of a bird) incubate (eggs) by sitting on them **5** be situated **6** pose for a portrait **7** occupy an official position **8** (of an official body) hold a session **9** take (an examination)
▶ **sitting room** room in a house where people sit and relax
▶ **sit-in** *n* protest in which demonstrators occupy a place and refuse to move
sitar *n* Indian stringed musical instrument
sitcom *n informal* situation comedy
site Ⓣ *n* **1** place where something is, was, or is intended to be located **2** same as **website** ▷ *v* **3** provide with a site
Sithole *n* **Ndabaningi**. 1920–2000, Zimbabwean clergyman and politician; leader of the Zimbabwe African National Union (1963–74). He was one of the negotiators of the internal settlement (1978) to pave the way for Black majority rule in Rhodesia (now Zimbabwe)
Sitting Bull *n* Indian name *Tatanka Yotanka*. ?1831–90, American Indian chief of the Teton Dakota Sioux. Resisting White encroachment on his people's hunting grounds, he led the Sioux tribes against the US Army in the Sioux War (1876–77) in which Custer was killed. The hunger of the Sioux, whose food came from the diminishing buffalo, forced his surrender (1881). He was killed during renewed strife
situate Ⓣ *v* place
▶ **situation** *n* **1** location and surroundings **2** state of affairs **3** position of employment
▶ **situation comedy** radio or television series involving the same characters in various situations
Sivaji *n* 1627–80, Indian king (1674–80), who led an uprising of Hindus against Muslim rule and founded the Masatha kingdom
six *adj, n* one more than five
▶ **sixth** *adj, n* (of) number six in a series
▶ **sixteen** *adj, n* six and ten **sixteenth** *adj, n*
▶ **sixty** *adj, n* six times ten **sixtieth** *adj, n*
size[1] Ⓣ *n* **1** dimensions, bigness **2** one of a series of standard measurements of goods ▷ *v* **3** arrange according to size
▶ **sizeable** *or* **sizable** *adj* quite large
▶ **size up** *v informal* assess
size[2] *n* gluey substance used as a sealer
sizzle Ⓣ *v* make a hissing sound like frying fat
SK Saskatchewan
skanky *adj slang* dirty or unnattractive
skate[1] *n* **1** boot with a steel blade or sets of wheels attached to the sole for gliding over ice or a hard surface ▷ *v* **2** glide on or as if on skates
▶ **skateboard** *n* board mounted on small wheels for riding on while standing up
▶ **skate over** *or* **skate round** *v* avoid discussing or dealing with (a matter) fully
skate[2] *n* large marine flatfish
skean-dhu [skee-an-**doo**] *n* dagger worn in the stocking as part of the Highland dress
skedaddle Ⓣ *v informal* run off
skein *n* **1** yarn wound in a loose coil **2** flock of geese in flight
skeleton Ⓣ *n* **1** framework of bones inside a person's or animal's body **2** essential framework of a structure ▷ *adj* **3** reduced to a minimum **skeletal** *adj*

S

THESAURUS

boy, softie (*informal*), weakling, pantywaist (*informal*) ▶ *adj* **2 = wimpish** *or* **wimpy** (*informal*), cowardly, feeble, effeminate, weak, soft (*informal*), unmanly
sit *v* **1 = rest**, settle, perch **2 = convene**, meet, deliberate, assemble **3 = officiate**, preside
sit down *See* **rest**
site *n* **1 = location**, place, position, spot, plot, setting ▶ *v* **2 = locate**, set, place, position, install, situate
sited *See* **located**
situate *See* **place**
situated *See* **located**
situation *n* **1 = state of affairs**, case, scenario, plight, circumstances • *a serious situation* **2 = location**, place, site, position, spot, setting **3 = status**, station, rank **4 = job**, post, place, office, position, employment
See also: **affair, matter, state**
sixth sense *See* **instinct**
sizable, sizeable *adj* **= large**, substantial, decent, considerable, respectable, goodly, largish, supersize
size *n* **= dimensions**, extent, bulk, immensity, proportions • *the size of the audience*
See also: **area, capacity, quantity** ▶ *verb* ▷ **size up = assess**, evaluate, appraise, take stock of
sizzle *v* **= hiss**, fry, spit, crackle, frizzle
skedaddle *v* (*Slang*) **= run away**, flee, disappear, abscond, beat it (*slang*), clear off (*informal*), run for it, scram (*informal*), take to one's heels
skeleton *n* **= framework**, draft, frame,

DICTIONARY

▸ **skeleton key** key which can open many different locks
skeptic Ⓣ [**skep**-tik] *n* person who habitually doubts generally accepted beliefs **skeptical** *adj* **skeptically** *adv* **skepticism** *n*
skerry *n, pl* **-ries** rocky island or reef
sketch Ⓣ *n* **1** rough drawing **2** brief description **3** short humorous play ▹ *v* **4** make a sketch (of)
▸ **sketchy** *adj* incomplete or inadequate
skew *adj* **1** slanting or crooked ▹ *v* **2** make slanting or crooked
▸ **skewed** *adj* (of an opinion or analysis) distorted or biased because of prejudice or lack of information
skewbald *adj* (of a horse) marked with patches of white and another colour
skewer *n* **1** pin to hold meat together during cooking ▹ *v* **2** fasten with a skewer
ski *n* **1** one of a pair of long runners fastened to boots for gliding over snow or water ▹ *v* **skiing, skied** *or* **ski'd 2** travel on skis **skier** *n*
skid *v* **skidding, skidded 1** (of a moving vehicle) slide sideways uncontrollably ▹ *n* **2** skidding
▸ **skid row** *slang* dilapidated part of a city frequented by vagrants
skidoo *n* snowmobile
skiff *n* small boat
skill Ⓣ *n* **1** special ability or expertise **2** something requiring special training or expertise **skilled** *adj*
▸ **skilful** *adj* having or showing skill **skilfully** *adv*
skillet *n* small frying pan or shallow cooking pot
skim Ⓣ *v* **skimming, skimmed 1** remove floating matter from the surface of (a liquid) **2** glide smoothly over **3** read quickly
▸ **skimmed milk** *or* **skim milk** milk from which the cream has been removed
skimp Ⓣ *v* not invest enough time, money, material, etc.
▸ **skimpy** *adj* scanty or insufficient
skin Ⓣ *n* **1** outer covering of the body **2** complexion **3** outer layer or covering **4** film on a liquid **5** animal skin used as a material or container ▹ *v* **skinning, skinned 6** remove the skin of **skinless** *adj*
▸ **skinny** *adj* thin
▸ **skin-deep** *adj* superficial
▸ **skin diving** underwater swimming using flippers and light breathing apparatus **skin-diver** *n*
▸ **skinflint** *n* miser
▸ **skinhead** *n* youth with very short hair
Skinner *n* **B**(**urrhus**) **F**(**rederic**). 1904–90, US behavioural psychologist. His "laws of learning," derived from experiments with animals, have been widely applied to education and behaviour therapy
skint *adj slang* having no money
skip[1] Ⓣ *v* **skipping, skipped 1** leap lightly from one foot to the other **2** jump over a rope as it is swung under one **3** *informal* pass over, omit ▹ *n* **4** skipping
skip[2] *n* large open container for builders' rubbish

THESAURUS

structure, outline, sketch, bare bones
skeptic *n* = **doubter**, cynic, disbeliever, doubting Thomas
skeptical *adj* = **doubtful**, dubious, cynical, incredulous, unconvinced, mistrustful, disbelieving
skepticism *n* = **doubt**, disbelief, cynicism, incredulity, unbelief
sketch *n* **1** = **drawing**, plan, design, draft, outline, delineation ▸ *v* **2** = **draw**, represent, draft, outline, depict, delineate, rough out
sketchy *adj* = **incomplete**, rough, inadequate, superficial, scrappy, skimpy, cursory, perfunctory
skilful *adj* = **expert**, able, skilled, competent, accomplished, adept, proficient, masterly • *the NHL's most skilful player* OPPOSITE: incompetent
See also: **capable**
skilfully *See* **well**
skill *n* = **expertise**, facility, ability, knack, competence, proficiency, dexterity • *This task requires great skill.*
See also: **qualification**
skilled *adj* = **expert**, able, professional, experienced, competent, trained, accomplished, proficient, skilful, masterly • *skilled workers, such as plumbers* OPPOSITE: incompetent
See also: **perfect, practical**
skim *v* **1** = **separate**, cream **2** = **glide**, fly, coast, soar, float, sail **3** (usually with *through*) = **scan**, glance, run one's eye over
skimp *v* = **stint**, scamp, be mean with, be sparing with, cut corners, scrimp
skin *n* **1** = **hide**, pelt, fell **2** = **coating**, film, outside, peel, crust, casing, rind, husk ▸ *v* **3** = **peel**, scrape, flay ▹ **skin alive** (*Informal*) = **attack**, assault, assail, let have it (*informal*), let loose on (*informal*)
skinflint *n* = **miser**, niggard, penny-pincher (*informal*), Scrooge
skinny *adj* = **thin**, lean, bony, scrawny, emaciated, undernourished • *a skinny little boy* OPPOSITE: plump
See also: **puny**
skip *v* **1** = **hop**, trip, dance, bounce, bob, caper, prance, flit, frisk, gambol **2** = **leave out**, eschew, omit, give (something) a miss, miss out, pass over

DICTIONARY

skipper *n, v* captain
skirl *n* sound of bagpipes
skirmish Ⓣ *n* **1** brief or minor fight or argument ▷ *v* **2** take part in a skirmish
skirt Ⓣ *n* **1** woman's garment hanging from the waist **2** part of a dress or coat below the waist **3** cut of beef from the flank ▷ *v* **4** border **5** go round **6** avoid dealing with (an issue)
▶ **skirting board** narrow board round the bottom of an interior wall
skit Ⓣ *n* brief satirical sketch
skittish Ⓣ *adj* playful or lively
skittle *n* **1** bottle-shaped object used as a target in some games **skittles 2** game in which players try to knock over skittles by rolling a ball at them
skookum *adj* powerful or big
skua *n* large predatory gull
skulduggery Ⓣ *n informal* trickery
skulk Ⓣ *v* **1** move stealthily **2** lurk
skull *n* bony framework of the head
▶ **skullcap** *n* close-fitting brimless cap
skunk *n* **1** small black-and-white N American mammal which emits an evil-smelling fluid when attacked **2** *slang* despicable person
sky Ⓣ *n, pl* **skies** upper atmosphere as seen from the earth
▶ **skydiving** *n* sport of jumping from an aircraft and performing manoeuvres before opening one's parachute
▶ **skylark** *n* lark that sings while soaring at a great height
▶ **skylight** *n* window in a roof or ceiling
▶ **skyscraper** *n* very tall building
slab Ⓣ *n* broad flat piece
slack[1] Ⓣ *adj* **1** not tight **2** negligent **3** not busy ▷ *n* **4** slack part **slacks 5** informal trousers ▷ *v* **6** neglect one's work or duty
slacker *n* **slackness** *n*
▶ **slacken** *v* make or become slack
slack[2] *n* coal dust or small pieces of coal
slag *n* **1** waste left after metal is smelted ▷ *v* **slagging, slagged 2** *slang* criticize
slain *v* past participle of **slay**
slake Ⓣ *v* **1** satisfy (thirst or desire) **2** combine (quicklime) with water
slalom *n* skiing or canoeing race over a winding course
slam Ⓣ *v* **slamming, slammed 1** shut, put down, or hit violently and noisily **2** *informal* criticize harshly ▷ *n* **3** act or sound of slamming
▶ **grand slam** winning of all the games or major tournaments in a sport in one season
▶ **slam dunk 1** *basketball* scoring shot in which a player jumps up and forces the ball down through the basket **2** task that is easy to achieve
slander Ⓣ *n* **1** false and malicious statement about a person **2** crime of making such a statement ▷ *v* **3** utter slander about
slanderous *adj*
slang *n* very informal language **slangy** *adj*
▶ **slanging match** abusive argument
slant Ⓣ *v* **1** lean at an angle, slope **2** present (information) in a biased way ▷ *n* **3** slope **4** point of view, esp. a biased one **slanting** *adj*

THESAURUS

skirmish *n* **1** = **fight**, battle, conflict, clash, scrap (*informal*), encounter, brush, fracas ▶ *v* **2** = **fight**, clash, collide
skirt *v* **1** = **border**, edge, flank **2** (often with *around* or *round*) = **avoid**, circumvent, evade, steer clear of
skit *n* **1** = **parody**, sketch, spoof (*informal*), burlesque **2** = **play**, performance, drama, comedy
skittish *adj* = **nervous**, lively, restive, fidgety, jumpy, excitable, highly strung, wired (*slang*)
skulduggery *n* (*Informal*) = **trickery**, double-dealing, duplicity, machinations, underhandedness
skulk *v* = **lurk**, creep, sneak, prowl, slink
sky *n* = **heavens**, firmament
slab *n* = **piece**, portion, slice, chunk, lump, wedge
slack *adj* **1** = **loose**, lax, limp, baggy, relaxed **2** = **negligent**, idle, lax, lazy, inactive, remiss, neglectful, slapdash, slipshod **3** = **slow**, quiet, sluggish, dull, inactive, slow-moving ▶ *n* **4** = **room**, give (*informal*), excess, leeway ▶ *v* **5** = **shirk**, idle, dodge
slacken, slack off *v* = **lessen**, reduce, decrease, moderate, relax, diminish, abate, drop off
slacker *n* = **layabout**, idler, dodger, loafer, couch potato (*slang*), shirker
slake *v* = **satisfy**, assuage, quench, sate
slam *v* = **bang**, crash, throw, smash, dash, hurl, fling
slander *n* **1** = **defamation**, scandal, smear, libel, slur • *He is now suing the company for slander.* ▶ *v* **2** = **defame**, smear, libel, malign • *He has been charged with slandering the mayor.*
slanderous *adj* = **defamatory**, malicious, damaging, libellous
slant *v* **1** = **slope**, list, lean, heel, bend, tilt, incline, cant, bevel **2** = **bias**, twist, angle, colour, distort ▶ *n* **3** = **slope**, grade, tilt, incline, camber, gradient **4** = **bias**, emphasis, angle, prejudice, one-sidedness, point of view
slanted *See* **biased**
slanting *adj* = **sloping**, bent, oblique,

DICTIONARY

slap Ⓣ *n* **1** blow with the open hand or a flat object ▷ *v* **slapping, slapped 2** strike with the open hand or a flat object **3** *informal* place forcefully or carelessly
▸ **slapdash** *adj* careless and hasty
▸ **slap-happy** *adj informal* cheerfully careless
▸ **slapstick** *n* boisterous knockabout comedy
▸ **slap-up** *adj Brit* (of a meal) large and luxurious
slash Ⓣ *v* **1** gash **2** cut with a sweeping stroke **3** reduce drastically ▷ *n* **4** gash **5** sweeping stroke
slat *n* narrow strip of wood or metal
slate *n* **1** rock which splits easily into thin layers **2** piece of this for covering a roof or, formerly, for writing on ▷ *v* **3** criticize severely
slater *n* woodlouse
slattern *n old-fashioned* slovenly woman **slatternly** *adj*
slaughter Ⓣ *v* **1** kill (animals) for food **2** kill (people) savagely or indiscriminately ▷ *n* **3** slaughtering
▸ **slaughterhouse** *n* place where animals are killed for food
Slav *n* member of any of the peoples of E Europe or the former Soviet Union who speak a Slavonic language
▸ **Slavonic** *n* **1** language group including Russian, Polish, and Czech ▷ *adj* **2** of this language group
slave Ⓣ *n* **1** person owned by another for whom he or she has to work **2** person dominated by another or by a habit **3** drudge ▷ *v* **4** work like a slave
▸ **slaver** *n* person or ship engaged in the slave trade
▸ **slavery** *n* **1** state or condition of being a slave **2** practice of owning slaves
▸ **slavish** *adj* **1** of or like a slave **2** imitative
▸ **slave-driver** *n* person who makes others work very hard
slaver *v* dribble saliva from the mouth
Slavonic *n, adj* (of) a language group including Russian, Polish, and Czech
slay Ⓣ *v* **slaying, slew, slain** kill
sleazy Ⓣ *adj* **-zier, -ziest** sordid **sleaziness** *n*
sled, sledge *n* **1** carriage on runners for sliding on snow **2** light wooden frame for sliding over snow ▷ *v* **3** travel by sled
sledge, sledgehammer *n* heavy hammer with a long handle
sleek Ⓣ *adj* glossy, smooth, and shiny
sleep Ⓣ *n* **1** state of rest characterized by unconsciousness **2** period of this ▷ *v* **sleeping, slept 3** be in or as if in a state of sleep **4** have sleeping accommodation for (a specified number) **sleepy** *adj* **sleepily** *adv* **sleepiness** *n* **sleepless** *adj*
▸ **sleeper** *n* **1** person who sleeps **2** beam supporting the rails of a railway **3** railway car fitted for sleeping in **4** ring worn in a pierced ear to stop the hole from closing up
▸ **sleeping bag** padded bag for sleeping in
▸ **sleeping sickness** African disease spread by the tsetse fly
▸ **sleepover** *n* occasion when a person stays overnight at a friend's house
▸ **sleep with** *or* **sleep together** *v* have sexual intercourse (with)
sleet *n* rain and snow or hail falling together
sleeve *n* **1** part of a garment which covers the arm **2** tubelike cover **3** gramophone record cover **sleeveless** *adj*
▸ **up one's sleeve** secretly ready
sleigh *n* sled

S

THESAURUS

diagonal, inclined, tilted, angled, at an angle, tilting
slap *n* **1** = **smack**, blow, cuff, spank
▸ *v* **2** = **smack**, paddle, cuff, clap, spank
slapdash *adj* = **careless**, sloppy (*informal*), messy, hurried, hasty, clumsy, slipshod
slash *v* **1** = **cut**, score, rip, hack, gash, slit, lacerate, rend **2** = **reduce**, cut, drop, lower ▸ *n* **3** = **cut**, rent, rip, gash, slit, laceration, incision
slaughter *v* **1** = **murder**, kill, slay, massacre, butcher ▸ *n* **2** = **murder**, killing, massacre, slaying, carnage, bloodshed, butchery
slaughterhouse *n* = **abattoir**
slave *n* **1** = **servant**, drudge, serf, vassal
▸ *v* **2** = **toil**, slog, drudge
slavery *n* = **enslavement**, captivity, bondage, servitude, subjugation
slavish *adj* **1** = **servile**, base, abject, submissive, cringing, fawning, grovelling, obsequious, sycophantic **2** = **imitative**, second-hand, unimaginative, unoriginal
slay *v* = **kill**, murder, slaughter, massacre, butcher, mow down
slaying *See* **murder**
sleaze *n* = **corruption**, fraud, bribery, extortion, dishonesty, unscrupulousness, venality
sleazy *adj* = **sordid**, low, squalid, seedy, run-down, disreputable, scuzzy (*slang*)
sleek *adj* = **glossy**, smooth, shiny, lustrous
sleep *n* **1** = **slumber**, nap, snooze (*informal*), hibernation, doze • *They were exhausted from lack of sleep.* ▸ *v* **2** = **slumber**, hibernate, snooze (*informal*), doze, take a nap • *The baby slept during the car ride.*
sleepless *adj* = **wakeful**, restless, insomniac
sleepy *adj* **1** = **drowsy**, sluggish, lethargic • *Do you feel sleepy during the day?* **2** = **quiet**,

DICTIONARY

sleight of hand [**slite**] *n* skilful use of the hands when performing conjuring tricks
slender Ⓣ *adj* **1** slim **2** small in amount
slept *v* past of **sleep**
sleuth Ⓣ [**slooth**] *n* detective
slew[1] *v* past tense of **slay**
slew[2] *v* twist or swing round
slice Ⓣ *n* **1** thin flat piece cut from something **2** share **3** kitchen tool with a broad flat blade **4** *sports* hitting of a ball so that it travels obliquely ▷ *v* **5** cut into slices **6** *sports* hit (a ball) with a slice
slick Ⓣ *adj* **1** persuasive and glib **2** skilfully devised or carried out **3** well-made and attractive, but superficial ▷ *v* **4** make smooth or sleek ▷ *n* **5** patch of oil on water
slide Ⓣ *v* **sliding, slid 1** slip smoothly along (a surface) **2** pass unobtrusively **3** *baseball* dive feet first or headfirst to catch the ball or reach a base ▷ *n* **4** sliding **5** surface or structure for sliding on or down **6** piece of glass holding an object to be viewed under a microscope **7** photographic transparency **8** ornamental hair clip **9** *baseball* instance of sliding to catch the ball or reach a base
▸ **let things slide** allow things to get worse by neglect
▸ **slider** *n baseball* fast pitch that breaks sharply away from the batter
▸ **sliding scale** variable scale according to which things such as wages fluctuate in response to changes in other factors
slight Ⓣ *adj* **1** small in quantity or extent **2** not important **3** slim and delicate ▷ *v, n* **4** snub **slightly** *adv*
slim Ⓣ *adj* **slimmer, slimmest 1** not heavy or stout, thin **2** slight ▷ *v* **slimming, slimmed 3** make or become slim by diet and exercise **slimmer** *n*
slime *n* unpleasant thick slippery substance
▸ **slimy** *adj* **1** of, like, or covered with slime **2** ingratiating
sling[1] Ⓣ *n* **1** bandage hung from the neck to support an injured hand or arm **2** strap with a string at each end for throwing a stone **3** rope or strap for lifting something ▷ *v* **slinging, slung 4** throw **5** carry, hang, or throw with or as if with a sling
sling[2] *n* sweetened drink with a spirit base: *gin sling*
slink Ⓣ *v* **slinking, slunk** move furtively or guiltily
▸ **slinky** *adj* **1** (of clothes) figure-hugging **2** sinuously graceful
slip[1] Ⓣ *v* **slipping, slipped 1** lose balance by sliding **2** move smoothly, easily, or quietly **3** (foll. by *on* or *off*) put on *or* take off easily or quickly **4** pass out of (the mind) ▷ *n* **5** slipping **6** mistake **7** petticoat **8** small piece (of paper)
▸ **give someone the slip** escape from someone

THESAURUS

dull • *a sleepy little village*
See also: **tired**
slender *adj* **1 = slim**, slight, lean • *a tall, slender woman* **2 = faint**, small, remote, slight, slim • *He won, but only by a slender majority.* **3 = meagre**, little, small, scant, scanty
See also: **minute, narrow**
sleuth *n* **= detective**, investigator *or* private investigator, gumshoe (*slang*), private eye (*informal*)
slice *n* **1 = share**, cut, portion, segment, wedge, sliver, helping ▸ *v* **2 = cut**, divide, carve, sever
slick *adj* **1 = glib**, smooth, polished, plausible, specious **2 = skilful**, professional, polished, deft, adroit, dexterous ▸ *v* **3 = smooth**, sleek, plaster down
slide *v* **= slip**, coast, skim, glide, slither
slight *adj* **1 = small**, minor, insignificant, paltry, negligible, trivial, inconsiderable, scanty • *a slight dent* OPPOSITE: large **2 = slim**, small, spare, delicate, fragile, feeble, lightly-built ▸ *v* **3 = snub**, ignore, insult, scorn, disdain, affront, blow off (*slang*) ▸ *n* **4 = snub**, insult, neglect, rebuff, affront, slap in the face (*informal*), cold shoulder *or* the cold shoulder
See also: **light, remote, slender, unimportant**
slightest *See* **least**
slightly *adv* **= a little**, somewhat
slim *adj* **1 = slender**, trim, narrow, thin, slight, lean, svelte **2 = slight**, poor, remote, faint, slender ▸ *v* **3 = lose weight**, reduce, diet
slimy *adj* **1 = viscous**, clammy, glutinous, oozy **2 = obsequious**, oily, creeping, grovelling, servile, smarmy (*Brit informal*), unctuous
sling *v* **1 = throw**, cast, toss, shy, hurl, lob (*informal*), fling, heave, chuck (*informal*) **2 = hang**, suspend, dangle
slink *v* **= creep**, steal, slip, sneak, prowl, skulk
slinky *adj* **= figure-hugging**, clinging, close-fitting, skintight
slip *v* **1 = sneak**, steal, creep • *She slipped downstairs and out of the house.* **2 = fall**, skid **3 = slide**, skate, glide, slither **4** (sometimes with *up*) **= make a mistake**, err, blunder, miscalculate ▷ **let slip = give away**, reveal, leak, disclose, divulge ▸ *n* **5 = mistake**, error, blunder, slip-up • *a slip of the tongue* ▷ **give (someone) the slip = escape from**, elude, evade, dodge, get

S

DICTIONARY

▶ **slippy** *adj informal* slippery
▶ **slipknot** *n* knot tied so that it will slip along the rope round which it is made
▶ **slipped disc** painful condition in which one of the discs connecting the bones of the spine becomes displaced
▶ **slipshod** *adj* (of an action) careless
▶ **slipstream** *n* stream of air forced backwards by a fast-moving object
▶ **slip up** *v* make a mistake
▶ **slipway** *n* launching slope on which ships are built or repaired
slip² *n* clay mixed with water used for decorating pottery
slipper *n* light shoe for indoor wear
slippery Ⓣ *adj* **1** so smooth or wet as to cause slipping or be difficult to hold **2** (of a person) untrustworthy
slit Ⓣ *v* **slitting, slit 1** make a long straight cut in ▷ *n* **2** long narrow cut or opening
slither Ⓣ *v* slide unsteadily
sliver Ⓣ [**sliv**-ver] *n* small thin piece
slob *n informal* lazy and untidy person
slobbish *adj*
slobber Ⓣ *v* dribble or drool **slobbery** *adj*
sloe *n* sour blue-black fruit
slog Ⓣ *v* **slogging, slogged 1** work hard and steadily **2** make one's way with difficulty **3** hit hard ▷ *n* **4** long and exhausting work or walk
slogan Ⓣ *n* catchword or phrase used in politics or advertising
sloop *n* small single-masted ship
slop Ⓣ *v* **slopping, slopped 1** splash or spill ▷ *n* **2** spilt liquid **3** liquid food **slops 4** liquid refuse and waste food used to feed animals
▶ **sloppy** *adj* **1** careless or untidy **2** gushingly sentimental
slope Ⓣ *v* **1** slant ▷ *n* **2** sloping surface **3** degree of inclination **slopes 4** hills
▶ **slope off** *v informal* go furtively
slosh *n* **1** splashing sound ▷ *v* **2** splash carelessly **3** *slang* hit hard
▶ **sloshed** *adj slang* drunk
slot Ⓣ *n* **1** narrow opening for inserting something **2** *informal* place in a series or scheme **3** *hockey* area in the centre of the offensive zone, directly in front of the net ▷ *v* **slotting, slotted 4** make a slot or slots in **5** fit into a slot
▶ **slot machine** automatic machine worked by placing a coin in a slot
sloth Ⓣ [rhymes with **both**] *n* **1** slow-moving animal of tropical America **2** laziness
▶ **slothful** *adj* lazy or idle
slouch Ⓣ *v* **1** sit, stand, or move with a drooping posture ▷ *n* **2** drooping posture **3** *informal* incompetent or lazy person
slough¹ [rhymes with **now**] *n* bog
slough² [**sluff**] *v* (of a snake) shed (its skin) or (of a skin) be shed
▶ **slough off** *v* get rid of (something unwanted or unnecessary)
sloven *n* habitually dirty or untidy person
▶ **slovenly** *adj* **1** dirty or untidy **2** careless
Slovene, Slovenian *adj, n* **1** (person) from

THESAURUS

away from, lose (someone)
slippery *adj* **1** = **smooth**, unsafe, icy, greasy, glassy, slippy (*informal, dialect*) **2** = **devious**, tricky, dishonest, crafty, cunning, evasive, untrustworthy, shifty
slipshod *adj* = **careless**, casual, sloppy (*informal*), slapdash, slovenly, untidy
slit *n* **1** = **cut**, opening, tear, split, rent, gash, incision ▶ *v* **2** = **cut** *or* **cut open**, slash, rip, knife, pierce, gash, lance
slither *v* = **slide**, slip, snake, glide, undulate, slink
sliver *n* = **shred**, fragment, splinter, shaving, paring
slobber *v* = **drool**, dribble, salivate, drivel, slaver
slobbish *adj* = **messy**, unclean, slovenly, unkempt, untidy
slog *v* **1** = **work**, labour, slave, toil, plod, plow through **2** = **trudge**, trek, tramp **3** = **hit**, strike, punch, thump, wallop (*informal*), sock (*slang*), slug ▷ **slog away** *See* **work** ▶ *n* **4** = **work**, effort, struggle, labour, exertion **5** = **trudge**, hike, trek, tramp
slogan *n* = **motto**, jingle • *Alberta's slogan is "Canada's Rocky Mountain Playground."*
slop *v* **1** = **spill**, splash, overflow, slosh (*informal*) ▶ *n* **2** (*Informal*) = **food**, mess (*slang*), grub (*slang*)
slope *n* **1** = **incline**, pitch, grade, ramp, inclination, gradient, declination, declivity • *The street is on a slope.* ▶ *v* **2** = **slant**, fall, rise • *The bank sloped sharply down to the river.*
See also: **tilt**
sloping *adj* = **slanting**, oblique, leaning, inclined
sloppy *adj* **1** = **careless**, messy, slipshod, slovenly, untidy **2** = **sentimental**, slushy (*informal*), gushing, mawkish
slot *n* **1** = **opening**, hole, groove, vent, slit, aperture **2** (*Informal*) = **place**, time, space, position, opening, vacancy ▶ *v* **3** = **fit**, insert, fit in
sloth *n* = **laziness**, inactivity, sluggishness, inertia, idleness, slackness, torpor
slothful *adj* = **lazy**, idle, inactive, indolent, workshy
slouch *v* = **slump**, stoop, droop, loll
slovenly *adj* = **careless**, sloppy (*informal*), slack, negligent, disorderly, slapdash, slipshod, untidy

S

DICTIONARY

Slovenia ▷ *n* **2** language of Slovenia
slow ⓣ *adj* **1** taking a longer time than is usual or expected **2** not fast **3** (of a clock or watch) showing a time earlier than the correct one **4** stupid ▷ *v* **5** reduce the speed (of) **slowly** *adv* **slowness** *n*
▸ **slowcoach** *n informal* person who moves or works slowly
sludge ⓣ *n* **1** thick mud **2** sewage
slug[1] *n* **1** land snail with no shell **2** bullet
▸ **sluggish** *adj* slow-moving, lacking energy **sluggishly** *adv* **sluggishness** *n*
▸ **sluggard** *n* lazy person
slug[2] *v* **slugging, slugged 1** hit hard ▷ *n* **2** heavy blow **3** *informal* mouthful of an alcoholic drink
▸ **slugger** *n* **1** baseball batter noted for powerful hitting **2** boxer noted for heavy punching
sluice *n* **1** channel carrying off water **2** sliding gate used to control the flow of water in this **3** water controlled by a sluice ▷ *v* **4** pour a stream of water over or through
slum ⓣ *n* **1** squalid overcrowded house or area ▷ *v* **slumming, slummed 2** temporarily and deliberately experience poorer places or conditions than usual
slumber ⓣ *v, n lit* sleep
slump ⓣ *v* **1** sink or fall heavily **2** (of prices or demand) decline suddenly ▷ *n* **3** sudden decline in prices or demand **4** time of substantial unemployment
slung *v* past of **sling**[1]
slunk *v* past of **slink**
slur ⓣ *v* **slurring, slurred 1** pronounce or utter (words) indistinctly **2** *music* sing or play (notes) smoothly without a break ▷ *n* **3** slurring of words **4** remark intended to discredit someone **5** *music* slurring of notes **6** curved line indicating notes to be slurred
slurp *informal* ▷ *v* **1** eat or drink noisily ▷ *n* **2** slurping sound
slurry *n, pl* **-ries** muddy liquid mixture
slush *n* **1** watery muddy substance **2** sloppy sentimental talk or writing **slushy** *adj*
▸ **slush fund** fund for financing bribery or corruption
slut ⓣ *n* dirty or immoral woman **sluttish** *adj*
sly ⓣ *adj* **slyer, slyest** *or* **slier, sliest 1** crafty **2** secretive and cunning **3** roguish ▷ *n* **on the sly** secretly **slyly** *adv* **slyness** *n*
smack[1] ⓣ *v* **1** slap sharply **2** open and close (the lips) loudly in enjoyment or anticipation ▷ *n* **3** sharp slap **4** slapping sound **5** loud kiss ▷ *adv* **6** *informal* squarely or directly: *smack in the middle*
▸ **smacker** *n slang* loud kiss
smack[2] *n* **1** slight flavour or trace **2** *slang* heroin ▷ *v* **3** have a slight flavour or trace (of)
smack[3] *n* small single-masted fishing boat
small ⓣ *adj* **1** not large in size, number, or amount **2** unimportant **3** mean or petty ▷ *n* **4** narrow part of the lower back **smalls 5** *informal* underwear **smallness** *n*

THESAURUS

slow *adj* **1 = unhurried**, sluggish, gradual, leisurely, lingering, ponderous • *slow, regular breathing* OPPOSITE: fast **2 = stupid**, thick, dense, dim, obtuse • *I must be pretty slow if I didn't get that joke.* **3 = prolonged**, gradual, protracted, lingering, long-drawn-out **4 = late**, behind, delayed, backward, tardy
See also: **reluctant** ▸ *verb* ▷ **slow (down) = decelerate**, check • *The car slowed and then stopped.*
slowly *adv* **= gradually**, by degrees, unhurriedly • *She turned and began to walk away slowly.* OPPOSITE: quickly
sludge *n* **= sediment**, mud, mire, residue, ooze, muck, silt, slime
sluggish *adj* **= inactive**, slow, heavy, dull, lethargic, indolent, inert, slothful, torpid
slum *n* **= hovel**, ghetto
slumber *v* **= sleep**, nap, snooze (*informal*), doze, drowse
slump *v* **1 = fall**, crash, collapse, slip, sink, plunge **2 = sag**, hunch, slouch, droop, loll ▸ *n* **3 = fall**, drop, crash, decline, collapse, reverse, downturn, trough **4 = recession**, depression
slur *n* **= insult**, smear, stain, affront, innuendo, insinuation, aspersion, calumny
slushy *See* **sentimental**
slut *n* (*Offensive*) **= tart**, ho (*slang*), whore, trollop
sly *adj* **1 = cunning**, wily, crafty, devious, scheming, underhand • *devious, sly, and manipulative* **2 = roguish**, arch, mischievous, impish, knowing ▸ *noun* ▷ **on the sly = secretly**, privately, surreptitiously, covertly, on the quiet
See also: **sneaky**
smack *v* **1 = slap**, hit, paddle, cuff, clap, strike, spank ▸ *n* **2 = slap**, blow ▸ *adv* **3** (*Informal*) **= directly**, right, straight, exactly, slap (*informal*), precisely, squarely
small *adj* **1 = little**, minute, tiny, mini, miniature, wee, diminutive, petite, pygmy *or* pigmy, undersized, teeny, teeny-weeny • *a small child* OPPOSITE: large **2 = unimportant**, minor, petty, insignificant, paltry, negligible, trivial, trifling • *small changes* **3 = petty**, base, mean, narrow **4 = modest**, humble, unpretentious
See also: **fine, low, remote, slender, slight**
smallest *See* **least**

DICTIONARY

▸**smallholding** *n Brit* small area of farming land
▸**small hours** hours just after midnight
▸**small-minded** *adj* intolerant, petty
▸**smallpox** *n* contagious disease with blisters that leave scars
▸**small talk** light social conversation
▸**small-time** *adj* insignificant or minor
Smallwood *n* **Joseph Roberts**, known as *Joey*. 1900–91, Canadian politician. He was an important figure in bringing Newfoundland and Labrador into confederation with Canada and was Premier of that province from 1949 to 1970
smarmy Ⓣ *adj* **smarmier, smarmiest** *informal* unpleasantly suave or flattering
smart Ⓣ *adj* **1** well-kept and neat **2** astute **3** witty **4** impertinent **5** fashionable **6** brisk ▹ *v* **7** feel or cause stinging pain ▹ *n* **8** stinging pain **smartly** *adv* **smartness** *n*
▸**smart aleck** *informal* irritatingly clever person
▸**smarten** *v* make or become smart
Smart *n* **Elizabeth**. 1913–86, Canadian novelist and poet. Her book *By Grand Central Station I Sat Down and Wept* (1945) details her affair with the British poet George Barker.
smash Ⓣ *v* **1** break violently and noisily **2** throw (against) violently **3** collide forcefully **4** destroy ▹ *n* **5** act or sound of smashing **6** violent collision of vehicles **7** *informal* popular success **8** *sports* powerful overhead shot
▸**smasher** *n informal* attractive person or thing
▸**smashing** *adj informal* excellent
smattering Ⓣ *n* slight knowledge
smear Ⓣ *v* **1** spread with a greasy or sticky substance **2** rub so as to produce a dirty mark or smudge **3** slander ▹ *n* **4** dirty mark or smudge **5** slander **6** *med* sample of a secretion smeared on to a slide for examination under a microscope
smell Ⓣ *v* **smelling, smelt** *or* **smelled** **1** perceive (a scent or odour) by means of the nose **2** have or give off a smell **3** have an unpleasant smell **4** detect by instinct ▹ *n* **5** odour or scent **6** smelling **7** ability to perceive odours by the nose
▸**smelly** *adj* having a nasty smell
▸**smelling salts** preparation of ammonia used to revive a person who feels faint
smelt[1] *v* extract (a metal) from (an ore) by heating **smelter** *n*
smelt[2] *n* small fish of the salmon family
smelt[3] *v* a past of **smell**
Smetana *n* **Bedřich**. 1824–84, Czech composer, founder of his country's national school of music. His works include *My Fatherland* (1874–79), a cycle of six symphonic poems, and the opera *The Bartered Bride* (1866)
smile Ⓣ *n* **1** turning up of the corners of the mouth to show pleasure, amusement, or friendliness ▹ *v* **2** give a smile
▸**smile on** *or* **smile upon** *v* regard favourably
Smiles *n* **Samuel**. 1812–1904, British writer: author of the didactic work *Self-Help* (1859)
smirch *v, n* disgrace
smirk Ⓣ *n* **1** smug smile ▹ *v* **2** give a smirk
smite *v* **smiting, smote, smitten** *old-*

THESAURUS

small-minded *adj* = **petty**, mean, intolerant, narrow-minded, bigoted, ungenerous
small-time *adj* = **minor**, petty, insignificant, unimportant, of no account
smarmy *adj* (*Brit informal*) = **obsequious**, smooth, suave, crawling, ingratiating, servile, sycophantic, toadying, unctuous
smart *adj* **1** = **neat**, elegant, stylish, chic, spruce • *a smart navy blue outfit* OPPOSITE: scruffy **2** = **clever**, bright, intelligent, shrewd, ingenious, astute, canny • *a smart idea* OPPOSITE: stupid **3** = **brisk**, quick, vigorous, lively ▸ *v* **4** = **sting**, hurt, burn ▸ *n* **5** = **sting**, pain, soreness
See also: **brilliant, posh**
smart aleck *n* (*Informal*) = **know-it-all** (*informal*), smarty pants (*informal*), wise guy (*informal*)
smarten *v* = **tidy**, groom, put in order, put to rights, spruce up
smarting *See* **sore**
smash *v* **1** = **break**, crush, shatter, demolish, pulverize **2** = **collide**, crash **3** = **destroy**, ruin, trash (*slang*), wreck, lay waste ▸ **smash into** *See* **hit** ▸ *n* **4** = **destruction**, collapse, failure, ruin, downfall **5** = **collision**, crash, accident
smashed *See* **broken**
smattering *n* = **modicum**, bit, rudiments
smear *v* **1** = **spread over**, cover, coat, bedaub, daub, rub on **2** = **smudge**, soil, dirty, stain, sully **3** = **slander**, blacken, besmirch, malign ▸ *n* **4** = **smudge**, streak, blot, splotch, blotch, daub **5** = **slander**, libel, defamation, calumny
smell *n* **1** = **odour**, scent, perfume, aroma, fragrance • *a smell of damp wood* **2** = **stink**, reek, stench • *the nasty smell of ashtrays* ▸ *v* **3** = **stink**, reek • *Do my feet smell?* **4** = **sniff**, scent • *I could smell muffins baking in the oven.*
smelly *adj* = **stinking**, foul, reeking • *smelly socks* OPPOSITE: fragrant
smile *v* **1** = **grin**, beam, smirk • *When he saw me, he smiled and waved.* ▸ *n* **2** = **grin**, beam, smirk • *She gave me a big smile.*
smirk *n* = **smug look**, simper
smitten *adj* **1** = **afflicted**, laid low, plagued,

S

DICTIONARY

fashioned **1** strike hard **2** affect severely
smith *n* worker in metal
▸ **smithy** *n* blacksmith's workshop
Smith *n* **1 Adam**. 1723–90, Scottish economist and philosopher, whose influential book *The Wealth of Nations* (1776) advocated free trade and private enterprise and opposed state interference **2 Bessie**, known as *Empress of the Blues*. 1894–1937, US blues singer and songwriter **3 Donald Alexander**, 1st Baron Strathcona and Mount Royal. 1820–1914, Canadian fur trader, financier, and banker born in Scotland. He rose from lowly beginnings in the Hudson's Bay Company to become its largest shareholder and then its governor. He was a president of the Bank of Montreal and played an important role in the construction of the Canadian Pacific Railway **4 Ian (Douglas)**. 1919–2007, Zimbabwean statesman; prime minister of Rhodesia (1964–79). He declared independence from Britain unilaterally (1965) **5 John**. ?1580–1631, English explorer and writer, who helped found the North American colony of Jamestown, Virginia. He was reputedly saved by the Indian chief's daughter Pocahontas from execution by her tribe. Among his works is a *Description of New England* (1616) **6 Michael**. 1932–2000, Canadian biochemist, born in England. Winner of the 1993 Nobel Prize for chemistry for his work on the editing of genetic DNA sequences **7 Will(ard) Christopher**. born 1968, US film actor and rap singer; star of the television series *The Fresh Prince of Bel Air* (1990–96) and the films *Men In Black* (1997), *Wild Wild West* (1999), and *Ali* (2001)
smithereens *pl n* shattered fragments
Smithson *n* **James**. original name *James Lewes Macie*. 1765–1829, English chemist and mineralogist, who left a bequest to found the Smithsonian Institution
smitten Ⓣ *v* past participle of **smite**
smock *n* **1** loose overall **2** woman's loose blouselike garment ▹ *v* **3** gather (material) by sewing in a honeycomb pattern
smocking *n*
smog *n* mixture of smoke and fog
smoke *n* **1** cloudy mass that rises from something burning **2** spell of smoking tobacco ▹ *v* **3** give off smoke **4** inhale and expel smoke of (a cigar, cigarette, or pipe) **5** do this habitually **6** cure (meat, fish, or cheese) by treating with smoke **smokeless** *adj* **smoker** *n* **smoky** *adj*
▸ **smoke screen** something said or done to hide the truth
Smollett *n* **Tobias George**. 1721–71, Scottish novelist, whose picaresque satires include *Roderick Random* (1748), *Peregrine Pickle* (1751), and *Humphry Clinker* (1771)
smolt *n* young salmon at the stage when it migrates to the sea
smooch *informal* ▹ *v* **1** kiss and cuddle ▹ *n* **2** smooching
smooth Ⓣ *adj* **1** even in surface, texture, or consistency **2** without obstructions or difficulties **3** charming and polite but possibly insincere **4** free from jolts **5** not harsh in taste ▹ *v* **6** make smooth **7** calm
smoothly *adv*
smorgasbord *n* buffet meal of assorted dishes
smote *v* past tense of **smite**
smother Ⓣ *v* **1** suffocate or stifle **2** cover thickly **3** suppress
smoulder Ⓣ *v* **1** burn slowly with smoke but no flame **2** (of feelings) exist in a suppressed state
SMS short message system: used for sending data to mobile phones
smudge Ⓣ *v* **1** make or become smeared or soiled ▹ *n* **2** dirty mark **3** blurred form
smudgy *adj*
smug Ⓣ *adj* **smugger, smuggest** self-satisfied **smugly** *adv* **smugness** *n*
smuggle Ⓣ *v* **1** import or export (goods) secretly and illegally **2** take somewhere secretly **smuggler** *n*
smut *n* **1** speck of soot **2** mark left by this

THESAURUS

struck **2 = infatuated**, beguiled, bewitched, captivated, charmed, enamoured
smooth *adj* **1 = sleek**, polished, glossy, silky, glassy • *a smooth wooden surface* OPPOSITE: rough **2 = even**, level, plane, flat, flush, horizontal **3 = easy**, effortless, well-ordered **4 = flowing**, regular, steady, uniform, rhythmic **5 = suave**, slick, persuasive, glib, facile, smarmy (*Brit informal*), unctuous, urbane **6 = mellow**, mild, pleasant, agreeable ▸ *v* **7 = flatten**, level, plane, press, iron **8 = calm**, ease, soften, mitigate, appease, assuage, mollify
smoothly *See* **well**
smother *v* **1 = suffocate**, choke, stifle, strangle **2 = suppress**, hide, stifle, conceal, muffle, repress
smoulder *v* **= seethe**, boil, rage, simmer, fume
See also: **glow**
smudge *v* **1 = smear**, mark, dirty, daub, smirch ▸ *n* **2 = smear**, blemish, blot
smug *adj* **= self-satisfied**, superior, complacent, conceited • *They looked at each other in smug satisfaction.*
smuggle *See* **sneak**
smuggler *n* **= trafficker**, runner, bootlegger
smugness *See* **pride**

DICTIONARY

3 obscene jokes, pictures, etc. **smutty** *adj*
Smuts *n* **Jan Christiaan**. 1870–1950, South African statesman; prime minister (1919–24; 1939–48). He fought for the Boers during the Boer War, then worked for Anglo-Boer reconciliation and served the Allies during World Wars I and II
Smyth *n* Dame **Ethel** (**Mary**). 1858–1944, British composer, best known for her operas, such as *The Wreckers* (1906). She was imprisoned for supporting the suffragette movement
Sn *chem* tin
snack Ⓣ *n* light quick meal
▸ **snack bar** place where snacks are sold
snaffle *n* **1** jointed bit for a horse ▷ *v* **2** *slang* steal
snag Ⓣ *n* **1** difficulty or disadvantage **2** sharp projecting point **3** hole in fabric caused by a sharp object ▷ *v* **snagging, snagged 4** catch or tear on a point
snail *n* slow-moving mollusc with a spiral shell
▸ **snail mail** *informal* conventional post, as opposed to e-mail
▸ **snail's pace** very slow speed
snake *n* **1** long thin scaly limbless reptile ▷ *v* **2** move in a winding course like a snake
▸ **snake in the grass** treacherous person
▸ **snaky** *adj* twisted or winding
snap Ⓣ *v* **snapping, snapped 1** break suddenly **2** (cause to) make a sharp cracking sound **3** (of animals) bite (at) suddenly **4** move suddenly **5** speak sharply and angrily **6** take a snapshot of ▷ *n* **7** act or sound of snapping **8** fastener that closes with a snapping sound **9** *informal* snapshot **10** sudden brief spell of cold weather **11** card game in which the word 'snap' is called when two similar cards are put down ▷ *adj* **12** made on the spur of the moment
▸ **snapper** *n* fish of the perch family
▸ **snappy** *adj* **1** irritable **2** *slang* quick **3** *slang* smart and fashionable
▸ **snapdragon** *n* plant with flowers that can open and shut like a mouth
▸ **snapshot** *n* informal photograph
▸ **snap up** *v* take eagerly and quickly
snare[1] Ⓣ *n* **1** trap with a noose ▷ *v* **2** catch in or as if in a snare
snare[2] *n music* set of gut strings wound with wire fitted across the bottom of a drum to increase vibration
▸ **snare drum** cylindrical double-headed drum with snares
snarl Ⓣ *v* **1** (of an animal) growl with bared teeth **2** speak or utter fiercely **3** make tangled ▷ *n* **4** act or sound of snarling **5** tangled mass
▸ **snarl-up** *n informal* confused situation such as a traffic jam
snatch Ⓣ *v* **1** seize or try to seize suddenly **2** take (food, rest, etc.) hurriedly ▷ *n* **3** snatching **4** fragment
snazzy *adj* **-zier, -ziest** *informal* stylish and flashy
Snead *n* **Sam**(**uel Jackson**). 1912–2002, US golfer; winner of seven major tournaments between 1938 and 1951
sneak Ⓣ *v* **1** move furtively **2** bring, take, or put furtively **3** *informal* tell tales ▷ *n* **4** cowardly or underhand person **5** *informal* telltale **sneaky** *adj*
▸ **sneaking** *adj* **1** secret **2** slight but persistent
sneakers *pl n* canvas shoes with rubber soles

THESAURUS

S

smutty *adj* = **obscene**, crude, blue, dirty, indecent, vulgar, coarse, suggestive, bawdy, indelicate
snack *n* = **light meal**, bite, refreshment *or* refreshments
snag *n* **1** = **difficulty**, problem, catch, disadvantage, drawback • *The snag was that he had no transportation.* ▸ *v* **2** = **catch**, tear, rip *See also*: **stick**
snap *v* **1** = **break**, separate, crack **2** = **crackle**, pop, click **3** = **bite at**, bite, nip, snatch **4** = **speak sharply**, bark, jump down (someone's) throat (*informal*), lash out at ▷ **snap up** = **seize**, grab, pounce upon, take advantage of ▸ *n* **5** = **crackle**, pop **6** = **bite**, grab, nip ▸ *adj* **7** = **instant**, immediate, sudden, spur-of-the-moment
snappy *adj* **1** = **irritable**, cross, edgy, testy, touchy **2** = **smart**, cool (*informal*), chic, fashionable, dapper, stylish, phat (*slang*)
snare *n* **1** = **trap**, net, wire, gin, noose ▸ *v* **2** = **trap**, net, catch, seize, wire, entrap
snarl *v* (often with *up*) = **tangle**, entangle, muddle, entwine, ravel
snarl-up *n* = **tangle**, confusion, muddle, entanglement
snatch *v* **1** = **seize**, grab, grip, clutch, grasp ▷ **snatch a glimpse** *See* **peek** ▸ *n* **2** = **bit**, part, piece, fragment, snippet
sneak *v* **1** = **slink**, steal, slip, lurk, sidle • *Sometimes she would sneak out to see me.* **2** = **slip**, spirit, smuggle • *He was caught trying to sneak the book out of the library.* ▷ **sneak a look** *See* **peek** ▸ *n* **3** = **informer**, telltale
sneaking *adj* **1** = **nagging**, persistent, uncomfortable, worrying **2** = **secret**, private, hidden, undivulged, unexpressed, unvoiced
sneaky *adj* = **sly**, dishonest, crafty, deceitful, devious, slippery, untrustworthy • *He only won by using sneaky tactics.*

DICTIONARY

sneer Ⓣ *n* **1** contemptuous expression or remark ▷ *v* **2** show contempt by a sneer
sneeze *v* **1** expel air from the nose involuntarily and noisily ▷ *n* **2** act or sound of sneezing
snib *n* catch of a door or window
snick *v, n* (make) a small cut or notch
snicker *n, v* same as **snigger**
snide Ⓣ *adj* maliciously derogatory
sniff Ⓣ *v* **1** inhale through the nose in short audible breaths **2** smell by sniffing ▷ *n* **3** act or sound of sniffing
▶ **sniffle** *v* **1** sniff repeatedly, as when suffering from a cold ▷ *n* **2** slight cold
▶ **sniff at** *v* express contempt for
▶ **sniffer dog** *Brit* police dog trained to detect drugs or explosives by smell
snifter *n informal* small quantity of alcoholic drink
snigger Ⓣ *n* **1** sly disrespectful laugh, esp. one partly stifled ▷ *v* **2** utter a snigger
snip Ⓣ *v* **snipping, snipped 1** cut in small quick strokes with scissors or shears ▷ *n* **2** act or sound of snipping **3** *informal* bargain
▶ **snippet** *n* small piece
snipe Ⓣ *n* **1** wading bird with a long straight bill ▷ *v* (foll. by *at*) **2** shoot at (a person) from cover **3** make critical remarks about **sniper** *n*
snitch Ⓣ *informal* ▷ *v* **1** act as an informer **2** steal ▷ *n* **3** informer
snivel Ⓣ *v* **-elling, -elled** cry in a whining way
snob Ⓣ *n* **1** person who judges others by social rank **2** person who feels smugly superior in his or her tastes or interests
snobbery *n* **snobbish** *adj*
snog *v* **snogging, snogged** *informal* kiss and cuddle
snood *n* pouch, often of net, loosely holding a woman's hair at the back
snook *n* **cock a snook at** show contempt for
snooker *n* **1** game played on a billiard table ▷ *v* **2** leave (a snooker opponent) in a position such that another ball blocks the target ball **3** *informal* put (someone) in a position where he or she can do nothing
snoop Ⓣ *informal* ▷ *v* **1** pry ▷ *n* **2** snooping
snooper *n*
snooty *adj* **snootier, snootiest** *informal* haughty
snooze Ⓣ *informal* ▷ *v* **1** take a brief light sleep ▷ *n* **2** brief light sleep
snore *v* **1** make snorting sounds while sleeping ▷ *n* **2** sound of snoring
snorkel *n* **1** tube allowing a swimmer to breathe while face down on the surface of the water ▷ *v* **-kelling, -kelled 2** swim using a snorkel
snort *v* **1** exhale noisily through the nostrils **2** express contempt or anger by snorting ▷ *n* **3** act or sound of snorting
snot *n taboo* mucus from the nose
snout *n* animal's projecting nose and jaws
snow *n* **1** frozen vapour falling from the sky in flakes **2** *slang* cocaine ▷ *v* **3** fall as or like snow **snowy** *adj*
▶ **be snowed under** be overwhelmed, esp. with paperwork
▶ **snowball** *n* **1** snow pressed into a ball for throwing ▷ *v* **2** increase rapidly
▶ **snowbird** *n* small N American songbird that breeds in the Arctic
▶ **snowblindness** *n* temporary blindness caused by the reflection of sunlight on snow
▶ **snowboard** *n* board on which a person stands to slide across the snow
snowboarding *n*
▶ **snowdrift** *n* bank of deep snow
▶ **snowdrop** *n* small white bell-shaped spring flower
▶ **snow fence** fence erected in winter to prevent snow drifting across a road
▶ **snowflake** *n* single crystal of snow
▶ **snow line** (on a mountain) height above

THESAURUS

sneer *n* **1** = **scorn**, jeer, ridicule, mockery, derision, gibe ▶ *v* **2** = **scorn**, laugh, mock, jeer, ridicule, deride, disdain
sneering *See* **scornful**
snide *adj* = **nasty**, malicious, cynical, hurtful, sarcastic, disparaging, ill-natured, scornful, sneering, spiteful
sniff *v* = **inhale**, breathe, smell
snigger *n, v* = **laugh**, giggle, snicker, titter
snip *v* **1** = **cut**, clip, crop, trim, dock, shave ▶ *n* **2** = **bit**, piece, scrap, shred, fragment, clipping
snipe *v* = **criticize**, knock (*informal*), jeer, carp, disparage, denigrate, put down
snippet *n* = **piece**, part, scrap, shred, fragment
snitch *v* **1** (*Informal*) = **inform on**, grass on (*Brit slang*), tattle on, tell on (*informal*), tell tales ▶ *n* **2** = **informer**, telltale, tattletale
snivel *v* = **whine**, cry, moan, whimper, sniffle
snob *n* = **elitist**, highbrow, prig
snobbery *n* = **arrogance**, pride, pretension, airs, snobbishness
snobbish *adj* = **superior**, arrogant, pretentious, patronizing, snooty (*informal*), stuck-up (*informal*)
snoop *v* = **pry**, spy, interfere, poke one's nose in (*informal*)
snooper *n* = **busybody**, meddler, snoop (*informal*), nosy rosy (*US informal*)
snooze *v* **1** = **doze**, nap, catnap, take forty winks (*informal*) ▶ *n* **2** = **doze**, nap, siesta, catnap, forty winks (*informal*)

DICTIONARY

which there is permanent snow
▶ **snowman** *n* figure shaped out of snow
▶ **snowmobile** *n* motor vehicle with caterpillar tracks and front skis
▶ **snow pea** variety of pea with an edible pod
▶ **snowplow** *or* **snowplough** *n* vehicle for clearing away snow
▶ **snowshoes** *pl n* racket-shaped shoes for travelling on snow
Snow *n* **1 C**(**harles**) **P**(**ercy**), Baron. 1905–80, British novelist and physicist. His novels include the series *Strangers and Brothers* (1949–70) **2 Clarence Eugene**, known as *Hank*. 1914–99, Canadian songwriter and singer of country music. His songs, a number of which topped the US country music chart, include "I'm Moving On" (1949) and "I've Been Everywhere" (1962)
SNP Scottish National Party
snub Ⓣ *v* **snubbing, snubbed 1** insult deliberately ▷ *n* **2** deliberate insult ▷ *adj* **3** (of a nose) short and blunt **snub-nosed** *adj*
snuff[1] *n* powdered tobacco for sniffing up the nostrils
snuff[2] *v* extinguish (a candle)
▶ **snuff it** *informal* die
snuffle *v* breathe noisily or with difficulty
snug Ⓣ *adj* **snugger, snuggest 1** warm and comfortable **2** comfortably close-fitting **snugly** *adv*
snuggle Ⓣ *v* nestle into a person or thing for warmth or from affection
so Ⓣ *adv* **1** to such an extent **2** in such a manner **3** very **4** also **5** thereupon ▷ *conj* **6** in order that **7** with the result that **8** therefore ▷ *interj* **9** exclamation of surprise, triumph, or realization
▶ **so-and-so** *n informal* **1** person whose name is not specified **2** unpleasant person or thing
▶ **so-called** *adj* called (in the speaker's opinion, wrongly) by that name
▶ **so long** goodbye
▶ **so that** in order that
soak Ⓣ *v* **1** make wet **2** put or lie in liquid so as to become thoroughly wet **3** (of liquid) penetrate ▷ *n* **4** soaking **5** *slang* drunkard **soaking** *n, adj*
▶ **soak up** *v* absorb
Soane *n* Sir **John**. 1753–1837, British architect. His work includes Dulwich College Art Gallery (1811–14) and his own house in Lincoln's Inn Fields, London (1812–13), which is now the Sir John Soane's Museum
soap *n* **1** compound of alkali and fat, used with water as a cleaning agent **2** *informal* soap opera ▷ *v* **3** apply soap to **soapy** *adj*
▶ **soap opera** television or radio serial dealing with domestic themes
soapstone *n* soft mineral used for making table tops and ornaments
soar Ⓣ *v* **1** rise or fly upwards **2** increase suddenly
Soares *n* **Mário**. born 1924, Portuguese statesman; prime minister of Portugal (1976–77; 1978–80; 1983–86); president of Portugal (1986–96)
sob Ⓣ *v* **sobbing, sobbed 1** weep with convulsive gasps **2** utter with sobs ▷ *n* **3** act or sound of sobbing
▶ **sob story** tale of personal distress told to arouse sympathy
sober Ⓣ *adj* **1** not drunk **2** serious **3** (of colours) plain and dull ▷ *v* **4** make or become sober **soberly** *adv*
▶ **sobriety** *n* state of being sober
sobriquet [**so**-brik-ay] *n* nickname
soccer *n* football played by two teams of eleven kicking or heading a spherical ball
sociable *adj* **1** friendly or companionable **2** (of an occasion) providing companionship **sociability** *n* **sociably** *adv*
social Ⓣ *adj* **1** living in a community **2** of

S

THESAURUS

snub *v* **1 = insult**, cut (*informal*), avoid, ignore, slight, humiliate, rebuff, blow off (*slang*), cold-shoulder, put down ▶ *n* **2 = insult**, affront, put-down, slap in the face
snug *adj* **= cozy**, warm, comfortable, comfy (*informal*), homey
snuggle *v* **= nestle**, cuddle, nuzzle
so *See* **therefore** ▷ **so-so** *See* **tolerable**
soak *v* **1 = wet**, steep, bathe, permeate • *The water had soaked his jacket.* **2 = penetrate**, seep, permeate ▷ **soak up = absorb**, assimilate
soaked *See* **wet**
soaking *adj* **= wet through**, sodden, dripping, drenched, saturated, soaked, sopping, streaming, wringing wet
soar *v* **1 = ascend**, rise, fly, wing, mount **2 = rise**, rocket, climb, escalate, shoot up
soaring *See* **tall**
sob *v* **= cry**, weep, howl, shed tears
sober *adj* **1 = abstinent**, moderate, temperate, abstemious **2 = serious**, cool, steady, reasonable, grave, solemn, rational, sedate, staid, composed, level-headed **3 = plain**, dark, drab, dumpy (*informal*), frowzy, quiet, subdued, sombre
sobriety *n* **1 = abstinence**, moderation, abstemiousness, nonindulgence, soberness, temperance **2 = seriousness**, gravity, level-headedness, solemnity, staidness, steadiness
so-called *adj* **= alleged**, self-styled, supposed, pretended, professed
sociable *adj* **= friendly**, outgoing, gregarious • *She's usually outgoing and sociable.*
social *adj* **1 = communal**, group,

DICTIONARY

society or its organization **3** sociable ▷ *n* **4** convivial gathering **socially** *adv*
▸ **socialize** *v* meet others socially
▸ **socialite** *n* member of fashionable society
▸ **social networking site** website that allows subscribers to interact
▸ **social science** scientific study of society and its relationships
▸ **social security** state provision for the unemployed, aged, or sick
▸ **social services** welfare services provided by the local authorities
▸ **social work** work which involves helping people with serious financial or family problems
socialism *n* political system which advocates public ownership of industries, resources, and transport **socialist** *n, adj*
socialistic *adj*
society Ⓣ *n, pl* **-ties 1** human beings considered as a group **2** organized community **3** structure and institutions of such a community **4** organized group with common aims and interests **5** upper-class or fashionable people collectively **6** companionship
sociology *n* study of human societies
sociological *adj* **sociologist** *n*
sock[1] *n* cloth covering for the foot
sock[2] *slang* ▷ *v* **1** hit hard ▷ *n* **2** hard blow
socket *n* hole or recess into which something fits
Socrates *n* ?470–399 BC, Athenian philosopher, whose beliefs are known only through the writings of his pupils Plato and Xenophon. He taught that virtue was based on knowledge, which was attained by a dialectical process that took into account many aspects of a stated hypothesis. He was indicted for impiety and corruption of youth (399) and was condemned to death.
He refused to flee and died by drinking hemlock
sod *n* **1** (piece of) turf **2** *slang* obnoxious person
soda *n* **1** compound of sodium **2** soda water
▸ **soda water** fizzy drink made from water charged with carbon dioxide
sodden Ⓣ *adj* soaked
Soddy *n* **Frederick**. 1877–1956, English chemist, whose work on radioactive disintegration led to the discovery of isotopes: Nobel prize for chemistry 1921
sodium *n* silver-white metallic element
▸ **sodium bicarbonate** white soluble compound used in baking powder
sodomy *n* anal intercourse
▸ **sodomite** *n* person who practises sodomy
sofa Ⓣ *n* couch
soft Ⓣ *adj* **1** not hard, rough, or harsh **2** (of a breeze or climate) mild **3** (too) lenient **4** easily influenced or imposed upon **5** feeble or silly **6** not robust **7** *informal* easy **8** (of water) containing few mineral salts **9** (of drugs) not liable to cause addiction **softly** *adv*
▸ **soften** *v* make or become soft or softer
▸ **soft drink** non-alcoholic drink
▸ **soft option** easiest alternative
▸ **soft-pedal** *v* deliberately avoid emphasizing something
▸ **soft-soap** *v informal* flatter
▸ **software** *n* computer programs
▸ **softwood** *n* wood of a coniferous tree
soggy Ⓣ *adj* **-gier, -giest 1** soaked **2** moist and heavy **sogginess** *n*

THESAURUS

public, community, general, common, collective ▸ *n* **2 = get-together** (*informal*), party, gathering
socialist *See* **left-wing**
socialize *v* = **mix**, fraternize, get about *or* get around, go out
society *n* **1 = culture**, civilization • *a major problem in society* **2 = organization**, group, union, club, league, association, circle, institute, guild • *the school debating society* **3 = upper classes**, elite, beau monde, gentry, high society **4 = companionship**, company, friendship, fellowship
See also: **body, public**
sodden *adj* = **soaked**, soggy, waterlogged, drenched, saturated, sopping
sofa *n* = **couch**, chaise longue, divan, settee
soft *adj* **1 = flexible**, supple, pliable • *a soft bed* OPPOSITE: hard **2 = quiet**, low, gentle, muted, subdued, mellow • *a soft tapping at my door* **3 = pale**, light, faint, dim, subdued, mellow, pastel • *The soft lights made the room seem romantic*. OPPOSITE: bright **4 = yielding**, elastic, spongy, gelatinous, pulpy, squashy **5 = velvety**, smooth, silky, downy, feathery, fleecy **6 = dim**, faint, restful, dimmed **7 = mild**, balmy, temperate **8 = lenient**, lax, easy-going, indulgent, spineless, permissive, overindulgent **9 = out of condition**, weak, limp, effeminate, flabby, flaccid **10** (*Informal*) **= easy**, comfortable, undemanding **11 = kind**, sensitive, gentle, sentimental, compassionate, tenderhearted, touchy-feely (*informal*)
soften *v* = **lessen**, still, ease, moderate, subdue, temper, cushion, mitigate, appease, allay, mollify
softhearted *adj* = **kind**, tender, charitable, sympathetic, sentimental, compassionate, tenderhearted, warm-hearted
soggy *adj* = **sodden**, waterlogged, moist,

DICTIONARY

soigné, soignée [**swah**-nyay] *adj* well-groomed, elegant
soil[1] Ⓣ *n* **1** top layer of earth **2** country or territory
soil[2] Ⓣ *v* **1** make or become dirty **2** disgrace
soiree [**swah**-ray] *n* evening party or gathering
sojourn [**soj**-urn] *v* **1** stay temporarily ▷ *n* **2** temporary stay
solace Ⓣ [**sol**-iss] *n, v* comfort in distress
Solana, Solana Madariaga *n* **Javier**. born 1942, Spanish socialist politician; minister for foreign affairs (1992–95), secretary-general of NATO (1995–99), and EU high representative for foreign policy from 1999
solar *adj* **1** of the sun **2** using the energy of the sun
▶ **solar plexus 1** network of nerves at the pit of the stomach **2** this part of the stomach
▶ **solar system** the sun and the heavenly bodies that go round it
solarium *n, pl* **-laria, -lariums** place with beds and ultraviolet lights used for acquiring an artificial suntan
sold *v* past of **sell**
solder *n* **1** soft alloy used to join two metal surfaces ▷ *v* **2** join with solder
▶ **soldering iron** tool for melting and applying solder
soldier Ⓣ *n* **1** member of an army ▷ *v* **2** serve in an army **soldierly** *adj*
▶ **soldier on** *v* persist doggedly
sole[1] Ⓣ *adj* **1** one and only **2** not shared, exclusive
▶ **solely** *adv* **1** only, completely **2** entirely **3** alone
sole[2] *n* **1** underside of the foot **2** underside of a shoe ▷ *v* **3** provide (a shoe) with a sole
sole[3] *n* small edible flatfish
solecism [**sol**-iss-izz-um] *n* **1** minor grammatical mistake **2** breach of etiquette
solemn Ⓣ *adj* **1** serious, deeply sincere **2** formal **solemnly** *adv* **solemnity** *n*
▶ **solemnize** *v* **1** celebrate or perform (a ceremony) **2** make solemn **solemnization** *n*
solenoid [**sole**-in-oid] *n* coil of wire magnetized by passing a current through it
sol-fa *n* system of syllables used as names for the notes of a scale
solicit *v* **-iting, -ited 1** request **2** (of a prostitute) offer (a person) sex for money **solicitation** *n*
solicitor Ⓣ *n* lawyer who advises clients and prepares documents and cases
solicitous Ⓣ *adj* anxious about someone's welfare **solicitude** *n*
solid Ⓣ *adj* **1** (of a substance) keeping its shape **2** strong or substantial **3** not liquid or gas **4** not hollow **5** of the same substance throughout **6** sound or reliable **7** having three dimensions ▷ *n* **8** three-dimensional shape **9** solid substance **solidity** *n* **solidly** *adv*
▶ **solidify** *v* make or become solid or firm
solidarity Ⓣ *n* agreement in aims or interests, total unity
solidus *n, pl* **-di** short oblique stroke (/) used to separate items in text
soliloquy *n, pl* **-quies** speech made by a person while alone, esp. in a play
▶ **soliloquize** *v* utter a soliloquy
solipsism *n* doctrine that the self is the only thing known to exist **solipsist** *n*
solitaire *n* **1** game for one person played with pegs set in a board **2** gem set by itself
solitary Ⓣ *adj* **1** alone, single **2** (of a place) lonely

THESAURUS

dripping, saturated, soaked, sopping
soil[1] *n* **1 = earth**, ground, dirt, clay • *The soil is reasonably moist after the rain.* **2 = land**, country
soil[2] *v* **= dirty**, foul, pollute, smear, stain, spatter • *He soiled his new white shirt.* OPPOSITE: clean
soiled *See* **dirty**
solace *n* **1 = comfort**, relief, consolation ▶ *v* **2 = comfort**, console
soldier *n* **= fighter**, serviceman, man-at-arms, warrior, trooper
sole *adj* **= only**, one, single, individual, alone, exclusive, solitary
solely *adv* **= only**, alone, completely, entirely, merely, exclusively
solemn *adj* **1 = serious**, grave, sober, earnest, staid • *a taciturn man with a solemn expression* **2 = formal**, grand, grave, ceremonial, dignified, momentous, stately
See also: **grim, heavy**
solemnity *n* **1 = seriousness**, gravity, earnestness **2 = formality**, grandeur, impressiveness, momentousness
solicitor *See* **lawyer**
solicitous *adj* **= concerned**, careful, anxious, attentive
solicitude *n* **= concern**, care, regard, consideration, anxiety, attentiveness
solid *adj* **1 = firm**, hard • *a solid block of ice* **2 = strong**, stable, substantial, sturdy • *a solid structure* **3 = sound**, good, real, pure, reliable, genuine **4 = reliable**, worthy, upright, dependable, trusty, upstanding
See also: **rigid, secure, stiff, stocky, tough**
solidarity *n* **= unity**, accord, unification, cohesion, unanimity, concordance, like-mindedness, team spirit
solidify *v* **= harden**, set, cake, jell, coagulate, cohere, congeal
solitary *adj* **1 = unsociable**, isolated, reclusive, cloistered, unsocial **2 = lone**,

DICTIONARY

solitude ⓣ *n* state of being solitary
solo *n, pl* **-los 1** music for one performer **2** any act done without assistance ▷ *adj* **3** done alone ▷ *adv* **4** by oneself, alone **soloist** *n*
Solon *n* ?638–?559 BC, Athenian statesman, who introduced economic, political, and legal reforms **Solonian** *or* **Solonic** *adj*
solstice *n* either the shortest (in winter) or longest (in summer) day of the year
soluble *adj* **1** able to be dissolved **2** able to be solved **solubility** *n*
solution ⓣ *n* **1** answer to a problem **2** act of solving a problem **3** liquid with something dissolved in it **4** process of dissolving
solve ⓣ *v* find the answer to (a problem) **solvable** *adj*
solvent *adj* **1** able to meet financial obligations ▷ *n* **2** liquid capable of dissolving other substances **solvency** *n*
▸ **solvent abuse** deliberate inhaling of intoxicating fumes from certain solvents
Solzhenitsyn *n* **Alexander Isayevich**. 1918–2008, Russian novelist. His books include *One Day in the Life of Ivan Denisovich* (1962), *The First Circle* (1968), *Cancer Ward* (1968), *August 1914* (1971), *The Gulag Archipelago* (1974), and *October 1916* (1985). His works criticize the Soviet regime and he was imprisoned (1945–53) and exiled to Siberia (1953–56). He was deported to the West from the Soviet Union in 1974; all charges against him were dropped in 1991 and he returned to Russia in 1994. Nobel prize for literature 1970
sombre ⓣ *adj* dark, gloomy
sombrero *n, pl* **-ros** wide-brimmed Mexican hat
some ⓣ *adj* **1** unknown or unspecified **2** unknown or unspecified quantity or number of **3** considerable number or amount of **4** *informal* remarkable ▷ *pron* **5** certain unknown or unspecified people or things **6** unknown or unspecified number or quantity
▸ **somebody** *pron* **1** some person ▷ *n* **2** important person
▸ **somehow** *adv* in some unspecified way
▸ **someone** *pron* somebody
▸ **something** *pron* **1** unknown or unspecified thing or amount **2** impressive or important thing
▸ **sometime** *adv* **1** at some unspecified time ▷ *adj* **2** former
▸ **sometimes** *adv* from time to time, now and then
▸ **somewhat** *adv* to some extent, rather
▸ **somewhere** *adv* in, to, or at some unspecified or unknown place
somersault *n* **1** leap or roll in which the trunk and legs are turned over the head ▷ *v* **2** perform a somersault
Somerville *n* **Mary**, original name *Mary Fairfax*. 1780–1872, British scientific writer, author of *Physical Geography* (1848) and other textbooks. Somerville College, Oxford, was named after her
somnambulist *n* person who walks in his or her sleep **somnambulism** *n*
somnolent *adj* drowsy **somnolence** *n*
son *n* male offspring
▸ **son-in-law** *n, pl* **sons-in-law** daughter's husband
sonar *n* device for detecting underwater objects by the reflection of sound waves
sonata *n* piece of music in several movements for one instrument with or without piano
▸ **sonatina** *n* short sonata
son et lumière [**sawn** eh **loo**-mee-er] *n French* night-time entertainment with lighting and sound effects, telling the story of the place where it is staged
Sondheim *n* **Stephen (Joshua)**. born 1930, US songwriter. He wrote the lyrics for *West*

S

THESAURUS

single, alone, sole **3 = lonely**, lonesome, companionless, friendless **4 = isolated**, remote, hidden, out-of-the-way, unfrequented
solitude *n* = **isolation**, privacy, loneliness, seclusion • *She went to the cottage for a few days of solitude.*
solution *n* **1 = answer**, result, key, explanation **2** (*Chem*) **= mixture**, mix, compound, blend, solvent
solve *v* **= resolve**, crack, decipher, clear up, get to the bottom of, work out • *attempts to solve the mystery*
sombre *adj* **1 = dark**, gloomy, sober, dull, dim, drab **2 = gloomy**, sad, grave, dismal, sober, mournful, lugubrious, joyless, doleful
some *See* **several**
somebody *n* **= celebrity**, name, star, notable, dignitary, luminary, household name, megastar (*informal*), personage
someday *adv* **= one day**, eventually, one of these days *or* one of these fine days, sooner or later
somehow *adv* **= one way or another**, by fair means or foul, by hook or crook *or* by hook or by crook, by some means or other, come hell or high water (*informal*), come what may
sometimes *adv* **= occasionally**, at times, every now and then, every so often, from time to time, now and again, now and then, once in a while • *People sometimes think I'm older than I am.*
somewhat *See* **quite, rather**

DICTIONARY

Side Story (1957), the score for *Company* (1971), and both for *A Little Night Music* (1973), *Into the Woods* (1987), and *Passion* (1994)

song Ⓣ *n* **1** music for the voice **2** tuneful sound made by certain birds **3** singing
▶ **for a song** very cheaply
▶ **songster** (**songstress**) *n* singer
▶ **songbird** *n* any bird with a musical call

sonic *adj* of or producing sound
▶ **sonic boom** loud bang caused by an aircraft flying faster than sound

sonnet *n* fourteen-line poem with a fixed rhyme scheme

sonny *n informal* term of address to a boy

sonorous *adj* (of sound) deep or resonant **sonorously** *adv* **sonority** *n*

Sontag *n* **Susan**. 1933–2004, US intellectual and essayist, noted esp. for her writings on modern culture. Her works include "Notes on Camp" (1964), "Against Interpretation" (1968), *On Photography* (1977), *Illness as Metaphor* (1978), and the novel *The Volcano Lover* (1992)

soon Ⓣ *adv* in a short time
▶ **sooner** *adv* rather: *I'd sooner go alone*
▶ **sooner or later** eventually

soot *n* black powder formed by the incomplete burning of an organic substance **sooty** *adj*

soothe Ⓣ *v* **1** make calm **2** relieve (pain etc.)

soothsayer Ⓣ *n* seer or prophet

sop *n* **1** concession to pacify someone ▷ *v* **sopping, sopped 2** mop up or absorb (liquid)
▶ **sopping** *adj* completely soaked
▶ **soppy** *adj informal* oversentimental

Sophia *n* 1630–1714, electress of Hanover (1658–1714), in whom the Act of Settlement (1701) vested the English Crown. She was a granddaughter of James I of England and her son became George I of Great Britain and Ireland

sophist *n* person who uses clever but invalid arguments
▶ **sophism** *or* **sophistry** *n* clever but invalid argument

sophisticate *v* **1** make less natural or innocent **2** make more complex or refined ▷ *n* **3** sophisticated person **sophistication** *n*
▶ **sophisticated** *adj* **1** having or appealing to refined or cultured tastes and habits **2** complex and refined

sophomore *n* student in second year at college

soporific Ⓣ *adj* **1** causing sleep ▷ *n* **2** drug that causes sleep

soprano *n, pl* **-pranos 1** (singer with) the highest female or boy's voice **2** highest pitched of a family of instruments

sorbet *n* flavoured water ice

sorcerer Ⓣ *n* magician **sorceress** *n fem*
▶ **sorcery** *n* witchcraft or magic

Sordello *n* born ?1200, Italian troubadour

sordid Ⓣ *adj* **1** dirty, squalid **2** base, vile **3** selfish and grasping **sordidly** *adv* **sordidness** *n*

sore Ⓣ *adj* **1** painful **2** causing annoyance **3** resentful **4** (of need) urgent ▷ *adv* **5** *obsolete* greatly ▷ *n* **6** painful area on the body **soreness** *n*
▶ **sorely** *adv* **1** greatly **2** grievously

sorghum *n* kind of grass cultivated for grain

THESAURUS

song *n* = **ballad**, number, air, tune, chant, chorus, anthem, hymn, carol, psalm, ditty

soon *adv* = **before long**, shortly, presently, any minute now, in a minute, in the near future • *You'll be hearing from us very soon*. OPPOSITE: later

sooner *See* **before**

soothe *v* **1** = **calm**, still, quiet, lull, appease, allay, hush, pacify, mollify, de-stress **2** = **relieve**, ease, alleviate, assuage

soothing *adj* = **calming**, palliative, restful, emollient, relaxing

soothsayer *n* = **prophet**, diviner, fortune-teller, seer, sibyl

sophisticated *adj* **1** = **cultured**, cosmopolitan, cultivated, refined, urbane • *a charming, sophisticated companion* **2** = **complicated**, complex, advanced, elaborate, refined, intricate • *a sophisticated piece of equipment* OPPOSITE: simple
See also: **polite**

sophistication *n* = **savoir-faire**, poise, finesse, urbanity, worldliness, worldly wisdom

soporific *adj* **1** = **sleep-inducing**, sedative, somnolent, tranquilizing ▶ *n* **2** = **sedative**, narcotic, opiate, tranquilizer

soppy *adj* (*Informal*) = **sentimental**, slushy (*informal*), overemotional, schmaltzy (*slang*), weepy (*informal*)

sorcerer *n* = **magician**, wizard, witch, enchanter, necromancer, warlock

sorcery *n* = **black magic**, magic, witchcraft, wizardry, black art, enchantment, necromancy

sordid *adj* **1** = **dirty**, foul, filthy, sleazy, squalid, seedy, unclean, scuzzy (*slang*) **2** = **base**, low, vicious, shameful, degenerate, shabby, vile, debauched **3** = **mercenary**, selfish, avaricious, covetous, grasping

sore *adj* **1** = **painful**, sensitive, raw, tender, inflamed, smarting • *a sore throat* **2** = **annoying**, severe, sharp, troublesome **3** = **annoyed**, hurt, cross, upset, angry, irritated, pained, resentful, aggrieved, irked, stung **4** = **urgent**, critical, extreme, desperate, acute, dire, pressing

DICTIONARY

sorority *n, pl* **-ties** US female social club at college
sorrel *n* **1** bitter-tasting plant **2** reddish-brown colour **3** horse of this colour
sorrow ⓣ *n* **1** grief or sadness **2** cause of sorrow ▷ *v* **3** grieve **sorrowful** *adj* **sorrowfully** *adv*
sorry ⓣ *adj* **-rier, -riest 1** feeling pity or regret **2** pitiful or wretched
sort ⓣ *n* **1** group all sharing certain qualities or characteristics **2** *informal* type of character ▷ *v* **3** arrange according to kind **4** mend or fix
▸ **out of sorts** slightly unwell or bad-tempered
sortie *n* **1** short return trip **2** operational flight by military aircraft **3** raid into enemy territory
SOS *n* **1** international code signal of distress **2** call for help
so-so *adj informal* mediocre
sot *n* habitual drunkard
sotto voce [**sot**-toe **voe**-chay] *adv* in an undertone
sou *n* **1** former French coin **2** small amount of money
soubriquet *n* same as **sobriquet**
soufflé [**soo**-flay] *n* light fluffy dish made with beaten egg whites and other ingredients
sough [rhymes with **now**] *v* (of the wind) make a sighing sound
sought [**sawt**] *v* past of **seek**
souk [**sook**] *n* open-air marketplace in Muslim countries
soul ⓣ *n* **1** spiritual and immortal part of a human being **2** essential part or fundamental nature **3** deep and sincere feelings **4** person regarded as typifying some quality **5** person **6** Also **soul music** type of Black music combining blues, pop, and gospel
▸ **soulful** *adj* full of emotion
▸ **soulless** *adj* **1** lacking human qualities, mechanical **2** (of a person) lacking sensitivity
sound[1] ⓣ *n* **1** something heard, noise ▷ *v* **2** make or cause to make a sound **3** seem to be as specified **4** pronounce
▸ **sound barrier** *informal* sudden increase in air resistance against an object as it approaches the speed of sound
▸ **soundproof** *adj* **1** not penetrable by sound ▷ *v* **2** make soundproof
▸ **sound track** recorded sound accompaniment to a film
sound[2] ⓣ *adj* **1** in good condition **2** firm, substantial **3** showing good judgment **4** ethically correct **5** financially reliable **6** thorough **7** (of sleep) deep **soundly** *adv*
sound[3] ⓣ *v* **1** find the depth of (water etc.) **2** ascertain the views of **3** examine with a probe
▸ **soundings** *pl n* **1** measurements of depth taken by sounding **2** questions asked of

THESAURUS

soreness *See* **pain**
sorrow *n* **1 = grief**, pain, regret, woe (*formal*), misery, sadness, unhappiness, heartache, melancholy, mourning • *a time of great sorrow* OPPOSITE: joy **2 = trouble**, worry, woe (*formal*), hardship, misfortune, heartache • *the joys and sorrows of family life* OPPOSITE: joy ▸ *v* **3 = grieve**, mourn, lament, bemoan, agonize, be sad, bewail
See also: **distress, evil**
sorrowful *adj* **= sad**, sorry, dismal, unhappy, woeful, miserable, mournful, dejected, wretched, doleful, grieving, woebegone
sorry *adj* **1 = regretful**, remorseful, apologetic, penitent, repentant • *I'm terribly sorry to bother you.* **2 = sympathetic**, moved • *I was sorry to hear about your grandfather's death.* **3 = wretched**, poor, sad, pathetic, miserable, deplorable, pitiful • *He was in a pretty sorry state when we found him.*
See also: **ashamed, guilty**
sort *n* **1 = kind**, make, group, type, class, brand, style, category, variety, species • *a dozen trees of various sorts* ▸ *v* **2 = arrange**, group, separate, divide, grade, classify, categorize • *He sorted the emails into three folders.*
See also: **form**
sort out *v* **1 = resolve**, clarify, clear up **2 = organize**, tidy up
sought-after *See* **popular**
soul *n* **1 = spirit**, life, essence, vital force **2 = personification**, type, essence, epitome, embodiment, quintessence **3 = person**, man *or* woman, body, individual, being, creature
sound[1] *n* **1 = noise**, tone, racket, din, hubbub • *the sounds of happy children* OPPOSITE: silence RELATED WORDS *adjectives*: sonic, acoustic **2 = idea**, look, impression, drift ▸ *v* **3 = resound**, blow, ring, toll, chime, clang, peal, set off • *A young man sounded the bell.* **4 = seem**, look, appear **5 = express**, announce, declare, pronounce, utter, articulate
sound[2] *adj* **1 = in good condition**, fine, healthy, fit, robust, intact, all right • *His mind and body were still sound.* **2 = sensible**, good, solid, reasonable, reliable, valid, down-to-earth • *a sound financial proposition* **3 = deep**, unbroken, undisturbed, untroubled
See also: **logical, responsible, sane, well**
sound[3] *v* **= fathom**, probe, plumb ▷ **sound out = probe**, question, pump, canvass, see how the land lies

DICTIONARY

someone to find out his or her opinion
▸ **sounding board** person or group used to test a new idea
sound[4] *n* channel or strait
soup *n* liquid food made from meat, vegetables, etc. **soupy** *adj*
▸ **soup kitchen** place where food and drink is served to needy people
▸ **soup up** *v* modify (an engine) to increase its power
soupçon [soop-sonn] *n* small amount
Souphanouvong *n* **Prince**. 1902–95, Laotian statesman; president of Laos (1975–86)
sour Ⓣ *adj* **1** sharp-tasting **2** (of milk) gone bad **3** (of a person's temperament) sullen ▹ *v* **4** make or become sour **sourly** *adv* **sourness** *n*
▸ **sourpuss** *n informal* sullen person
source Ⓣ *n* **1** origin or starting point **2** spring where a river or stream begins **3** person, book, etc. providing information
Sousa *n* **John Philip**. 1854–1932, US bandmaster and composer of military marches, such as *The Stars and Stripes Forever* (1897) and *The Liberty Bell* (1893)
souse *v* **1** plunge (something) into liquid **2** drench **3** pickle
soutane [soo-**tan**] *n* Roman Catholic priest's cassock
south *n* **1** direction towards the South Pole, opposite north **2** area lying in or towards the south ▹ *adj* **3** to or in the south **4** (of a wind) from the south ▹ *adv* **5** in, to, or towards the south **southerly** *adj* **southern** *adj* **southward** *adj, adv* **southwards** *adv*
▸ **southerner** *n* person from the south of a country or area
▸ **southeast** *n, adj, adv* (in or to) direction between south and east
▸ **southwest** *n, adj, adv* (in or to) direction between south and west
▸ **southpaw** *n informal* left-handed person, esp. a boxer
▸ **South Pole** southernmost point on the earth's axis
souvenir Ⓣ *n* keepsake, memento
sou'wester *n* seaman's waterproof hat covering the head and back of the neck
sovereign Ⓣ *n* **1** king or queen **2** former British gold coin worth one pound ▹ *adj* **3** supreme in rank or authority **4** excellent **5** (of a state) independent **sovereignty** *n*
▸ **sovereigntist** *n, adj* promoter of, or promoting, sovereignty for Quebec
▸ **sovereignty-association** *n* proposal for political sovereignty for Quebec with economic association with the rest of Canada
soviet *n* **1** formerly, elected council at various levels of government in the USSR ▹ *adj* **2** **Soviet** of the former USSR
sow[1] Ⓣ *v* **sowing, sowed, sown** *or* **sowed** **1** scatter or plant (seed) in or on (the ground) **2** implant or introduce
sow[2] *n* female adult pig
soya *n* plant whose edible bean (**soya bean**) is used for food and as a source of oil
▸ **soy sauce** sauce made from fermented soya beans, used in Chinese and Japanese cookery
sozzled *adj slang* drunk
spa *n* resort with a mineral-water spring
Spaak *n* **Paul Henri**. 1899–1972, Belgian statesman, first socialist premier of Belgium (1937–38); a leading advocate of European unity, he was president of the consultative assembly of the Council of Europe (1949–51) and secretary-general of NATO (1957–61)
space Ⓣ *n* **1** unlimited expanse in which all objects exist and move **2** interval **3** blank portion **4** unoccupied area **5** the universe beyond the earth's atmosphere ▹ *v* **6** place at intervals
▸ **spacious** *adj* having a large capacity or area
▸ **spacecraft** *or* **spaceship** *n* vehicle for travel

S

THESAURUS

soundless See **silent**
sour *adj* **1 = sharp**, bitter, acid, tart, pungent • *That apple is too sour for me.* OPPOSITE: sweet **2 = rancid**, off, curdled • *This cream's gone sour.* **3 = bitter**, tart, disagreeable, embittered, jaundiced • *a sour expression*
See also: **rotten, stale**
source *n* **1 = origin**, cause, beginning, fountain, originator, derivation, fount, fountainhead, wellspring • *the source of his confidence* **2 = informant**, authority
See also: **head**
souvenir *n* **= keepsake**, reminder, relic, memento • *a souvenir of our vacation*
sovereign *n* **1 = monarch**, chief, king *or* queen, prince *or* princess, ruler, emperor *or* empress, potentate ▸ *adj* **2 = supreme**, ruling, principal, royal, absolute, imperial, kingly *or* queenly **3 = excellent**, efficient, effectual, efficacious
sovereignty *n* **= supreme power**, domination, supremacy, primacy, kingship
sow *v* **= scatter**, plant, seed, implant
space *n* **1 = room**, capacity, accommodation • *a car with plenty of interior space* RELATED WORD *adjective*: spatial **2 = gap**, blank, distance, interval • *the space between the two tables* **3 = period**, time, while, span, interval • *two incidents in the space of a week*
See also: **length, opening, stretch**
spacious *adj* **= roomy**, large, huge, broad, extensive, vast, ample, expansive • *a spacious lobby*

DICTIONARY

beyond the earth's atmosphere
▶ **space shuttle** manned reusable vehicle for repeated space flights
▶ **spacesuit** *n* sealed pressurized suit worn by an astronaut
spade[1] *n* tool for digging
▶ **spadework** *n* hard preparatory work
spade[2] *n* playing card of the suit marked with black leaf-shaped symbols
spaghetti *n* pasta in the form of long strings
spam *computers slang* ▷ *v* **spamming, spammed 1** send unsolicited e-mail or text messages to multiple recipients ▷ *n* **2** unsolicited e-mail or text messages sent in this way
span Ⓣ *n* **1** space between two points **2** complete extent **3** distance from thumb to little finger of the expanded hand ▷ *v* **spanning, spanned 4** stretch or extend across
spangle *n* **1** small shiny metallic ornament ▷ *v* **2** decorate with spangles
Spaniard *n* person from Spain
spaniel *n* dog with long ears and silky hair
Spanish *n* **1** official language of Spain and most countries of S and Central America ▷ *adj* **2** of Spain or its language or people
spank Ⓣ *v* **1** slap with the open hand, esp. on the buttocks ▷ *n* **2** such a slap
▶ **spanking** *n* **1** series of spanks ▷ *adj informal* **2** quick **3** outstandingly fine or smart
spanner *n* tool for gripping and turning a nut or bolt
spar[1] *n* pole used as a ship's mast, boom, or yard
spar[2] Ⓣ *v* **sparring, sparred 1** *boxing, martial arts* fight using light blows for practice **2** argue (with someone)
spare Ⓣ *v* **1** refrain from punishing or harming **2** protect (someone) from (something unpleasant) **3** afford to give ▷ *adj* **4** extra **5** in reserve **6** (of a person) thin ▷ *n* **7** duplicate kept in case of damage or loss
▶ **to spare** in addition to what is needed
▶ **sparing** *adj* economical
▶ **spare ribs** pork ribs with most of the meat trimmed off
spark Ⓣ *n* **1** fiery particle thrown out from a fire or caused by friction **2** flash of light produced by an electrical discharge **3** trace or hint (of a particular quality) ▷ *v* **4** give off sparks **5** initiate
▶ **spark plug** *or* **sparking plug** device in an engine that ignites the fuel by producing an electric spark
Spark *n* Dame **Muriel** (**Sarah**). 1918–2006, British novelist and writer; her novels include *Memento Mori* (1959), *The Prime of Miss Jean Brodie* (1961), *A Far Cry from Kensington* (1988), *Symposium* (1990), and *The Finishing School* (2004)
sparkle Ⓣ *v* **1** glitter with many points of light **2** be vivacious or witty ▷ *n* **3** sparkling points of light **4** vivacity or wit
▶ **sparkler** *n* hand-held firework that emits sparks
▶ **sparkling** *adj* (of wine or mineral water) slightly fizzy
sparrow *n* small brownish bird
▶ **sparrowhawk** *n* small hawk
sparse Ⓣ *adj* thinly scattered **sparsely** *adv* **sparseness** *n*
Spartacus *n* died 71 BC, Thracian slave, who led an ultimately unsuccessful revolt of gladiators against Rome (73–71 BC)
spartan Ⓣ *adj* strict and austere

THESAURUS

spadework *n* = **preparation**, labour, groundwork, donkey-work
span *n* **1** = **extent**, reach, spread, amount, stretch, distance, length **2** = **period**, term, spell, duration ▶ *v* **3** = **extend across**, link, cover, cross, bridge, traverse
spank *v* = **smack**, paddle, cuff, slap
spar *v* = **argue**, row, scrap (*informal*), squabble, wrangle, bicker
spare *adj* **1** = **extra**, free, surplus, superfluous • *Luckily I had a spare pair of glasses.* **2** = **thin**, lean, gaunt, meagre, wiry • *He was a small, spare man with an abrupt and caustic wit.* ▷ **spare time** = **leisure**, free time, odd moments ▶ *v* **3** = **afford**, give, let someone have • *Can you spare a loonie?* **4** = **have mercy on**, pardon, let off (*informal*), relieve from, save from • *I wanted to spare them that suffering.*
sparing *adj* = **economical**, saving, careful, prudent, thrifty, frugal
spark *n* **1** = **flicker**, flash, flare, gleam, glint **2** = **trace**, hint, scrap, atom, vestige, jot ▶ *v* **3** (often with *off*) = **start**, trigger *or* trigger off, inspire, provoke, stimulate, precipitate, set off
sparkle *v* **1** = **glitter**, shimmer, gleam, twinkle, glisten • *Stars sparkled like diamonds.* ▶ *n* **2** = **glitter**, flash, brilliance, gleam, flicker, twinkle, glint **3** = **vivacity**, life, spirit, dash, vitality, élan
See also: **shine**
sparkling *adj* **1** = **carbonated**, frothy, bubbly, effervescent, fizzy, foamy, gassy **2** = **vibrant**, bright, brilliant, animated, lively, ebullient, effervescent, vivacious **3** = **glittering**, twinkling, lustrous, flashing, shining, shimmering, scintillating, glistening, glinting, gleaming
sparse *adj* = **scattered**, scarce, meagre, few and far between, scanty
spartan *adj* = **austere**, severe, strict, plain,

DICTIONARY

spasm Ⓣ *n* **1** involuntary muscular contraction **2** sudden burst of activity or feeling
▸**spasmodic** *adj* occurring in spasms **spasmodically** *adv*
Spassky *n* **Boris**. born 1937, Russian chess player; world champion (1969–72)
spastic *med* ▷ *n* **1** person with cerebral palsy ▷ *adj* **2** suffering from cerebral palsy **3** affected by spasms
spat[1] *v* past of **spit**[1]
spat[2] *n* slight quarrel
spat[3] *n* old-fashioned short gaiter
spate Ⓣ *n* **1** large number of things happening within a period of time **2** sudden outpouring or flood
spathe *n* large sheathlike leaf enclosing a flower cluster
spatial *adj* of or in space
spatter Ⓣ *v* **1** scatter or be scattered in drops over (something) ▷ *n* **2** spattering sound **3** something spattered
spatula *n* utensil with a broad flat blade for spreading or stirring
spawn *n* **1** jelly-like mass of eggs of fish, frogs, or molluscs ▷ *v* **2** (of fish, frogs, or molluscs) lay eggs **3** generate
spay *v* remove the ovaries from (a female animal)
speak Ⓣ *v* **speaking, spoke, spoken 1** say words, talk **2** communicate or express in words **3** give a speech or lecture **4** know how to talk in (a specified language)
▸**speaker** *n* **1** person who speaks, esp. at a formal occasion **2** loudspeaker **3 Speaker** official chairman of a body
spear *n* **1** weapon consisting of a long shaft with a sharp point **2** slender shoot **3** single stalk of broccoli or asparagus ▷ *v* **4** pierce with or as if with a spear **5** *hockey* illegally thrust the blade of a stick at (an opponent) **spearing** *n*
▸**spearhead** *n* **1** leading force in an attack or campaign ▷ *v* **2** lead (an attack or campaign)
spearmint *n* type of mint
Spears *n* **Britney**. born 1981, US pop singer; records include the single "Baby One More Time" (1998) and the album *Britney* (2001)
spec *n* **on spec** *informal* as a risk or gamble
special Ⓣ *adj* **1** distinguished from others of its kind **2** for a specific purpose **3** exceptional **4** particular **specially** *adv*
▸**specialist** *n* expert in a particular activity or subject
▸**specialty** *or* **speciality** *n* **1** special interest or skill **2** product specialized in
▸**specialize** *v* be a specialist **specialization** *n*
▸**special interest group** group with a common political goal
specie *n* coins as distinct from paper money
species Ⓣ *n, pl* **-cies** group of plants or animals that are related closely enough to interbreed naturally
specific Ⓣ *adj* **1** particular, definite ▷ *n* **2** drug used to treat a particular disease **specifics 3** particular details **specifically** *adv*
▸**specification** *n* detailed description of something to be made or done
▸**specify** *v* refer to or state specifically
▸**specific gravity** ratio of the density of a substance to that of water
specimen Ⓣ *n* **1** individual or part typifying

THESAURUS

rigorous, disciplined, frugal, ascetic, self-denying
spasm *n* **1 = convulsion**, contraction, twitch, paroxysm **2 = burst**, fit, seizure, outburst, eruption, frenzy
spasmodic *adj* **= sporadic**, irregular, jerky, erratic, intermittent, convulsive, fitful
spate *n* **= flood**, rush, flow, outpouring, deluge, torrent
spatter *See* **soil**[2]
speak *v* **= say**, talk, lecture ▷ **speak out, speak up = speak one's mind**, have one's say, make one's position plain, voice one's opinions ▷ **speak out against** *See* **oppose**
speaker *n* **= orator**, spokesman *or* spokeswoman, spokesperson, lecturer, public speaker
spearhead *v* **= lead**, head, launch, pioneer, initiate, set in motion, set off
special *adj* **1 = exceptional**, important, significant, unique • *You are very special to me*. OPPOSITE: ordinary **2 = particular**, individual, specific, characteristic, distinctive, peculiar • *the special needs of the chronically ill* OPPOSITE: general
See also: **different, personal, private, select**
specialist *n* **= expert**, authority, professional, master, buff (*informal*), virtuoso, connoisseur
specialty *n* **= forte**, bag (*slang, dated*), speciality, métier, *pièce de résistance* (*French*)
species *n* **= kind**, group, type, class, sort, category, variety, breed
specific *adj* **1 = particular**, special, characteristic, distinguishing **2 = definite**, express, exact, explicit, precise, unequivocal, clear-cut
specification *n* **= requirement**, condition, detail, particular, qualification, stipulation
specify *v* **= state**, name, indicate, stipulate, be specific about, spell out • *Specify the size and colour you want*.
specimen *n* **= sample**, type, model,

DICTIONARY

a whole **2** sample of blood etc. taken for analysis

specious [**spee**-shuss] *adj* apparently true, but actually false

speck Ⓣ *n* small spot or particle

▸ **speckle** *n* **1** small spot ▹ *v* **2** mark with speckles

specs *pl n informal* short for **spectacles**

spectacle Ⓣ *n* **1** strange, interesting, or ridiculous sight **2** impressive public show **spectacles 3** pair of glasses for correcting faulty vision

▸ **spectacular** *adj* **1** impressive ▹ *n* **2** spectacular public show **spectacularly** *adv*

spectate *v* watch

▸ **spectator** *n* person viewing anything, onlooker

Spector *n* **Phil.** born 1940, US record producer and songwriter, noted for the densely orchestrated "Wall of Sound" in his work with groups such as the Ronettes and the Crystals; jailed for murder in 2009

spectre Ⓣ *n* **1** ghost **2** menacing mental image **spectral** *adj*

spectrum *n, pl* **-tra 1** range of different colours, radio waves, etc. in order of their wavelengths **2** entire range of anything

▸ **spectroscope** *n* instrument for producing or examining spectra

speculate Ⓣ *v* **1** guess, conjecture **2** buy property, shares, etc. in the hope of selling them at a profit **speculation** *n* **speculative** *adj* **speculator** *n*

speculum *n, pl* **-la, -lums** medical instrument for examining body cavities

sped *v* a past of **speed**

Spedding *n* **Frank Harold.** 1902–84, US chemist born in Canada. Noted for his work on the processing of the uranium needed for the Manhattan Project

speech Ⓣ *n* **1** act, power, or manner of speaking **2** talk given to an audience **3** language or dialect

▸ **speechify** *v* make speeches, esp. boringly

▸ **speechless** *adj* unable to speak because of great emotion

speed Ⓣ *n* **1** swiftness **2** rate at which something moves or acts **3** *slang* amphetamine ▹ *v* **speeding, sped** *or* **speeded 4** go quickly **5** drive faster than the legal limit

▸ **speedy** *adj* **1** rapid **2** prompt **speedily** *adv*

▸ **speedboat** *n* light fast motorboat

▸ **speedometer** *n* instrument to show the speed of a vehicle

▸ **speed up** *v* accelerate

▸ **speedway** *n* track for motorcycle racing

▸ **speedwell** *n* plant with small blue flowers

speleology *n* study and exploration of caves **speleological** *adj* **speleologist** *n*

spell[1] Ⓣ *v* **spelling, spelt** *or* **spelled 1** give in correct order the letters that form (a word)

THESAURUS

example, representative, pattern, instance, exemplification

speck *n* **1 = mark**, spot, stain, dot, blemish, speckle, fleck, mote **2 = particle**, bit, grain, shred, atom, mite, iota, jot

speckled *adj* **= flecked**, spotted, dotted, dappled, mottled, sprinkled

spectacle *n* **1 = sight**, scene, wonder, phenomenon, marvel, curiosity **2 = show**, event, performance, display, exhibition, extravaganza, pageant

spectacular *adj* **1 = impressive**, cool (*informal*), dramatic, grand, sensational, magnificent, striking, splendid, dazzling, phat (*slang*), stunning (*informal*) ▸ *n* **2 = show**, display, spectacle

spectator *n* **= onlooker**, witness, observer, bystander, eyewitness • *Spectators lined the route.*

spectre *n* **= ghost**, vision, spirit, phantom, apparition, wraith

speculate *v* **1 = conjecture**, consider, wonder, suppose, guess, theorize, hypothesize, surmise **2 = gamble**, risk, venture, hazard

speculation *n* **1 = conjecture**, opinion, theory, hypothesis, surmise, guesswork, supposition **2 = gamble**, risk, hazard

speculative *adj* **= hypothetical**, academic, theoretical, conjectural, notional, suppositional

speech *n* **1 = talk**, address, lecture, discourse • *He delivered his speech in French.* **2 = communication**, talk, discussion, conversation, dialogue **3 = language**, tongue, dialect, jargon, parlance, articulation, diction, enunciation, idiom

speechless *adj* **1 = mute**, silent, dumb, inarticulate, wordless **2 = astounded**, shocked, aghast, amazed, dazed

speechlessness *See* **silence**

speed *n* **1 = swiftness**, pace, momentum, hurry, velocity, haste, rapidity • *a speed of 120 km/h* ▸ *v* **2 = race**, career, rush, tear, flash, gallop • *The pair sped off when the police arrived.* **3 = help**, assist, boost, advance, aid, facilitate, expedite ▹ **speed up = accelerate**, gather momentum, increase the tempo *See also*: **fly, rate**

speedily *See* **quickly**

speedy *adj* **= quick**, fast, prompt, express, immediate, rapid, swift, hurried, precipitate, hasty, headlong

spell[1] *v* **= indicate**, mean, imply, signify, augur, portend, point to ▹ **spell out** *See* **specify**

DICTIONARY

2 (of letters) make up (a word) **3** indicate
▸**spelling** *n* **1** way a word is spelt **2** person's ability to spell
▸**spell out** *v* make explicit
spell² Ⓣ *n* **1** formula of words supposed to have magic power **2** effect of a spell **3** fascination
▸**spellbound** *adj* entranced
spell³ Ⓣ *n* period of time of weather or activity
spelt *v* a past of **spell¹**
Spence *n* Sir **Basil** (**Unwin**). 1907–76, Scottish architect, born in India; designed Coventry Cathedral (1951)
Spencer *n* **Herbert**. 1820–1903, English philosopher, who applied evolutionary theory to the study of society, favouring laissez-faire doctrines
spend Ⓣ *v* **spending, spent 1** pay out (money) **2** use or pass (time) **3** use up completely
▸**spendthrift** *n* person who spends money wastefully
Spender *n* Sir **Stephen**. 1909–95, English poet and critic, who played an important part in the left-wing literary movement of the 1930s. His works include *Journals 1939–83* (1985) and *Collected Poems* (1985)
Spengler *n* **Oswald**. 1880–1936, German philosopher of history, noted for *The Decline of the West* (1918–22), which argues that civilizations go through natural cycles of growth and decay
Spenser *n* **Edmund**. ?1552–99, English poet celebrated for *The Faerie Queene* (1590; 1596), an allegorical romance. His other verse includes the collection of eclogues *The Shephearde's Calendar* (1579) and the marriage poem *Epithalamion* (1594)
sperm *n* **1** male reproductive cell **2** semen
▸**spermicide** *n* substance that kills sperm
▸**sperm whale** large toothed whale
spermaceti [sper-ma-**set**-ee] *n* waxy solid obtained from the sperm whale
spermatozoon [sper-ma-toe-**zoe**-on] *n, pl* **-zoa** sperm
spew Ⓣ *v* **1** vomit **2** send out in a stream
sphagnum *n* moss found in bogs
sphere Ⓣ *n* **1** perfectly round solid object **2** field of activity **spherical** *adj*
sphincter *n* ring of muscle which controls the opening and closing of a hollow organ
Sphinx *n* **1** statue in Egypt with a lion's body and human head **2** **sphinx** enigmatic person
spice Ⓣ *n* **1** aromatic substance used as flavouring **2** something that adds zest or interest ▹ *v* **3** flavour with spices
▸**spicy** *adj* **1** flavoured with spices **2** *informal* slightly scandalous
spick-and-span *adj* neat and clean
spider *n* small eight-legged creature which spins a web to catch insects for food **spidery** *adj*
spiel *n* glib plausible talk
Spielberg *n* **Steven**. born 1947, US film director, noted esp. for the commercial success of such films as *Jaws* (1975), *Close Encounters of the Third Kind* (1977), *Raiders of the Lost Ark* (1981) and its sequels, *E.T.* (1982), and *Jurassic Park* (1993). Other films include *The Color Purple* (1986), *Schindler's List* (1993), *Saving Private Ryan* (1998), and *The Terminal* (2004)
spigot *n* stopper for, or tap fitted to, a cask
spike Ⓣ *n* **1** sharp point **2** sharp pointed metal object ▹ *v* **3** put spikes on **4** pierce or fasten with a spike **5** add alcohol to (a drink) **spiky** *adj*
▸**spike someone's guns** thwart someone
spill¹ Ⓣ *v* **spilling, spilt** *or* **spilled 1** pour from or as if from a container ▹ *n* **2** fall **3** amount spilt **spillage** *n*
▸**spill the beans** *informal* give away a secret

S

THESAURUS

spell² *n* **1** = **incantation**, charm **2** = **enchantment**, magic, allure, glamour, fascination, mojo (*slang*), bewitchment
spell³ *n* = **period**, time, season, term, course, stretch, bout, interval
spellbound *adj* = **entranced**, bewitched, captivated, charmed, enthralled, fascinated, gripped, mesmerized, rapt
spend *v* **1** = **pay out**, expend, disburse, fork out (*slang*) **2** = **pass**, fill, occupy, while away **3** = **use up**, waste, consume, empty, drain, exhaust, squander, dissipate, run through
spendthrift *n* **1** = **squanderer**, spender, big spender, profligate, waster ▸*adj* **2** = **wasteful**, extravagant, improvident, prodigal, profligate
spew *v* = **vomit**, puke (*slang*), disgorge, barf (*slang*), regurgitate, throw up (*informal*)
sphere *n* **1** = **ball**, circle, globe, orb, globule **2** = **field**, province, department, territory, capacity, function, patch, turf (*slang*), domain, scope, realm
spherical *adj* = **round**, rotund, globe-shaped, globular
spice *n* **1** = **seasoning**, relish, savour **2** = **excitement**, colour, pep, zest, zing (*informal*), piquancy
spicy *adj* **1** = **hot**, seasoned, aromatic, piquant, savoury **2** (*Informal*) = **risqué**, hot (*informal*), scandalous, racy, suggestive, indelicate, ribald, titillating
spike *n* **1** = **point**, spine, barb, prong ▸*v* **2** = **impale**, stick, spit, spear
spill *v* **1** = **pour**, discharge, overflow,

DICTIONARY

spill[2] *n* thin strip of wood or paper for lighting pipes or fires
Spillane *n* **Mickey**, original name *Frank Morrison Spillane*. 1918–2006, US detective-story writer, best known for his books featuring the detective Mike Hammer, for example *I, the Jury* (1947) and *The Twisted Thing* (1966)
spin ⓣ *v* **spinning, spun 1** revolve or cause to revolve rapidly **2** draw out and twist (fibres) into thread ▷ *n* **3** revolving motion **4** continuous spiral descent of an aircraft **5** *informal* short drive for pleasure **6** *informal* presenting of information in a way that creates a favourable impression **spinner** *n*
▸ **spin doctor** *informal* person who provides a favourable slant to a news item or policy on behalf of a politician or a political party
▸ **spin a yarn** see **yarn**
▸ **spin-dry** *v* dry (clothes) in a spin-dryer
▸ **spin-dryer** *n* machine in which washed clothes are spun in a perforated drum to remove excess water
▸ **spin-off** *n* incidental benefit
▸ **spin out** *v* prolong
spina bifida *n* condition in which part of the spinal cord protrudes through a gap in the backbone, often causing paralysis
spinach *n* dark green leafy vegetable
spindle *n* **1** rotating rod that acts as an axle **2** weighted rod rotated for spinning thread by hand
▸ **spindly** *adj* long, slender, and frail
spindrift *n* spray blown along the surface of the sea
spine ⓣ *n* **1** backbone **2** sharp point on an animal or plant **3** edge of a book, record sleeve, etc. on which the title is printed
▸ **spinal** *adj* of the spine
▸ **spineless** *adj* lacking courage
▸ **spiny** *adj* covered with spines
spinet *n* small harpsichord
spinnaker *n* large sail on a racing yacht
spinneret *n* organ through which silk threads come out of a spider
spinney *n* small wood
Spinoza *n* **Baruch**. 1632–77, Dutch philosopher who constructed a holistic metaphysical system derived from a series of hypotheses that he judged self-evident. His chief work is *Ethics* (1677)
spinster *n* unmarried woman
spiral ⓣ *n* **1** continuous curve formed by a point winding about a central axis at an ever-increasing distance from it **2** steadily accelerating increase or decrease ▷ *v* **-ralling, -ralled 3** move in a spiral **4** increase or decrease with steady acceleration ▷ *adj* **5** having the form of a spiral
spire *n* pointed part of a steeple
spirit ⓣ *n* **1** nonphysical aspect of a person concerned with profound thoughts **2** nonphysical part of a person believed to live on after death **3** prevailing feeling **4** temperament or disposition **5** liveliness **6** courage **7** essential meaning as opposed to literal interpretation **8** ghost **spirits 9** emotional state **10** strong alcoholic drink ▷ *v* **-iting, -ited 11** carry away mysteriously
▸ **spirited** *adj* lively
▸ **spirituous** *adj* alcoholic
▸ **spirit level** glass tube containing a bubble in liquid, used to check whether a surface is level
spiritual ⓣ *adj* **1** relating to the spirit **2** relating to sacred things ▷ *n* **3** type of religious folk song originating among

THESAURUS

disgorge, slop over ▸ *n* **2** = **fall**, tumble
spin *v* **1** = **revolve**, turn, rotate, whirl, pirouette • *as the earth spins on its axis* **2** = **reel**, swim, whirl ▷ **spin out** = **prolong**, delay, extend, lengthen, amplify, drag out, draw out ▸ *n* **3** = **revolution**, roll, whirl, gyration **4** (*Informal*) = **drive**, ride, joy ride (*informal*)
spine *n* **1** = **backbone**, spinal column, vertebrae, vertebral column **2** = **barb**, spur, spike, needle, ray, quill
spine-chilling *adj* = **frightening**, scary (*informal*), eerie, spooky (*informal*), bloodcurdling, horrifying, terrifying
spineless *adj* = **weak**, soft, cowardly, feeble, gutless (*informal*), faint-hearted, lily-livered, weak-kneed (*informal*)
spiral *n* **1** = **coil**, corkscrew, helix, whorl ▸ *adj* **2** = **coiled**, helical, whorled, winding
spirit *n* **1** = **soul**, life force • *They believed his spirit had left his body.* **2** = **ghost**, spectre, phantom, apparition, sprite • *a protection against evil spirits* **3** = **energy**, force, fire, animation, enthusiasm, vigour, mettle, zest, brio • *They played with spirit.* **4** = **feeling**, atmosphere, tone, tenor, gist **5** = **temperament**, character, outlook, attitude, temper, disposition **6** = **courage**, backbone, grit, gameness, guts (*informal*), spunk (*informal*) **7** = **essence**, sense, purpose, substance, intention, meaning, purport ▷ **spirits** = **mood**, humour, morale, feelings, frame of mind ▸ *v* **8** (with *away* or *off*) = **remove**, carry, steal, seize, abduct, abstract, whisk, purloin
See also: **sneak**
spirited *adj* = **lively**, active, animated, energetic, feisty (*informal*), vivacious, mettlesome
spirits *See* **alcohol**
spiritual *adj* = **sacred**, religious, holy, divine, devotional

S

DICTIONARY

Black slaves in N America **spiritually** *adv* **spirituality** *n*
▶**spiritualism** *n* belief that the spirits of the dead can communicate with the living **spiritualist** *n*
spit[1] ⓣ *v* **spitting, spat** 1 eject (saliva or food) from the mouth 2 throw out particles explosively 3 rain slightly 4 utter (words) in a violent manner ▷ *n* 5 saliva
▶**spitting image** *informal* person who looks very like another
▶**spittle** *n* fluid produced in the mouth, saliva
▶**spittoon** *n* bowl to spit into
spit[2] *n* 1 sharp rod on which meat is skewered for roasting 2 long strip of land projecting into the sea
spite ⓣ *n* 1 deliberate nastiness ▷ *v* 2 annoy or hurt from spite **spiteful** *adj* **spitefully** *adv*
▶**in spite of** in defiance of
spitfire *n* person with a fiery temper
Spitz *n* **Mark**. born 1950, US swimmer, who won seven gold medals at the 1972 Olympic Games
splake *n* hybrid trout
splash ⓣ *v* 1 scatter (liquid) or (of liquid) be scattered in drops 2 scatter liquid on (something) 3 print (a story or photograph) prominently in a newspaper ▷ *n* 4 splashing sound 5 patch (of colour or light) 6 extravagant display 7 small amount of liquid added to a drink
▶**splash out** *v informal* spend extravagantly
splatter *v, n* splash
splay *v* 1 spread out 2 slant outwards ▷ *adj* 3 splayed
spleen *n* 1 abdominal organ which filters bacteria from the blood 2 bad temper
▶**splenetic** *adj* spiteful or irritable
splendid ⓣ *adj* 1 excellent 2 brilliant in appearance **splendidly** *adv* **splendour** *n*
splice *v* join by interweaving or overlapping ends
▶**get spliced** *slang* get married
splint *n* rigid support for a broken bone
splinter ⓣ *n* 1 thin sharp piece broken off, esp. from wood ▷ *v* 2 break into fragments
▶**splinter group** group that has broken away from an organization
split ⓣ *v* **splitting, split** 1 break into separate pieces 2 separate 3 share ▷ *n* 4 crack or division caused by splitting **splits** 5 act of sitting with the legs outstretched in opposite directions
▶**split second** very short period of time
▶**split up** *v* 1 separate (something) into parts 2 (of a couple) end a relationship or marriage
splotch, splodge *n, v* splash, daub
splurge *v* 1 spend money extravagantly ▷ *n* 2 bout of extravagance
splutter *v* 1 make hissing spitting sounds 2 utter with spitting sounds ▷ *n* 3 spluttering
Spock *n* **Benjamin**, known as *Dr. Spock*. 1903–98, US pediatrician, noted for his influential work *The Common Sense Book of Baby and Child Care* (1946), which challenged traditional notions of child care, advocating

THESAURUS

spit *v* 1 = **eject**, expectorate, splutter, throw out ▶ *n* 2 = **saliva**, dribble, drool, slaver, spittle
spite *n* 1 = **malice**, venom, ill will, malevolence, spitefulness • *He just did it out of spite.* ▷ **in spite of** = **despite**, though, although, notwithstanding, even though, regardless of • *In spite of all the rain, we drove to the campgrounds.* ▶ *v* 2 = **hurt**, injure, harm, annoy, vex
spiteful *adj* = **malicious**, nasty, cruel, venomous, vindictive, catty (*informal*), malevolent, snide • *a stream of spiteful telephone calls*
See also: **unkind**
spitefulness *See* **spite**
spitting image *See* **look-alike**
splash *v* 1 = **scatter**, spray, wet, shower, sprinkle, spatter, slop 2 = **publicize**, broadcast, trumpet, plaster ▷ **splash out** (*Informal*) = **spend**, be extravagant, splurge, spare no expense ▶ *n* 3 = **dash**, touch, burst, patch, spattering 4 (*Informal*) = **display**, effect, impact, stir, sensation
splendid *adj* 1 = **excellent**, great (*informal*), fine, wonderful, fantastic (*informal*), glorious, marvellous • *I've had a splendid time.* 2 = **magnificent**, grand, impressive, gorgeous, superb, imposing • *a splendid old mansion*
See also: **first-rate**
splendidly *See* **well**
splendour *n* = **magnificence**, show, display, glory, spectacle, brilliance, richness, grandeur, pomp, brightness, sumptuousness
splinter *n* 1 = **sliver**, chip, fragment, flake ▶ *v* 2 = **shatter**, split, fracture, disintegrate
split *v* 1 = **separate**, part, fork, diverge • *The ship split in two.* 2 = **crack**, burst, rip, come apart • *His trousers split.* 3 = **share out**, distribute, divide, halve, allocate, allot, partition, apportion ▷ **split up** = **separate**, part, divorce, break up ▶ *n* 4 = **crack**, tear, rip, fissure • *There's a split in my mattress.* 5 = **division**, breach, breakup, rift, divergence • *the split between the two sides of the family* ▶ *adj* 6 = **divided**, fractured, ruptured, cleft, broken, cracked
See also: **hole, share**

S

DICTIONARY

a more permissive approach
spoil Ⓣ *v* **spoiling, spoilt** *or* **spoiled** **1** damage **2** harm the character of (a child) by giving it all it wants **3** rot, go bad
▸ **spoiling for** eager for
▸ **spoils** *pl n* booty
▸ **spoilsport** *n* person who spoils the enjoyment of others
spoke[1] *v* past tense of **speak**
spoke[2] *n* bar joining the hub of a wheel to the rim
spoken Ⓣ *v* past participle of **speak**
spokesman, spokeswoman, spokesperson Ⓣ *n* person chosen to speak on behalf of a group
spoliation *n* plundering
sponge Ⓣ *n* **1** sea animal with a porous absorbent skeleton **2** skeleton of a sponge, or a substance like it, used for cleaning **3** type of light cake ▷ *v* **4** wipe with a sponge **5** live at the expense of others **spongy** *adj*
▸ **sponger** *n slang* person who sponges on others
sponsor Ⓣ *n* **1** person who promotes something **2** person who agrees to give money to a charity on completion of a specified activity by another **3** godparent ▷ *v* **4** act as a sponsor for **sponsorship** *n*
spontaneous Ⓣ *adj* **1** voluntary and unpremeditated **2** occurring through natural processes without outside influence **spontaneously** *adv* **spontaneity** *n*
spoof Ⓣ *n* mildly satirical parody
spook *n informal* ghost **spooky** *adj*
spool *n* cylinder round which something can be wound
spoon *n* **1** shallow bowl attached to a handle for eating, stirring, or serving food ▷ *v* **2** lift with a spoon **spoonful** *n*
▸ **spoon-feed** *v* **1** feed with a spoon **2** give (someone) too much help
spoonerism *n* accidental changing over of the initial sounds of a pair of words, such as *half-warmed fish* for *half-formed wish*
spoor *n* trail of an animal
sporadic Ⓣ *adj* intermittent, scattered **sporadically** *adv*
spore *n* minute reproductive body of some plants
sporran *n* pouch worn in front of a kilt
sport Ⓣ *n* **1** activity for pleasure, competition, or exercise **2** such activities collectively **3** enjoyment **4** playful joking **5** person who reacts cheerfully ▷ *v* **6** wear proudly **sporty** *adj*
▸ **sporting** *adj* **1** of sport **2** having a sportsmanlike attitude
▸ **sporting chance** reasonable chance of success
▸ **sportive** *adj* playful
▸ **sports car** fast low-built car, usu. open-topped
▸ **sports jacket** man's casual jacket
▸ **sportsman** (**sportswoman**) *n* **1** person who plays sports **2** person who plays fair and is good-humoured when losing **sportsmanlike** *adj* **sportsmanship** *n*
▸ **sport utility vehicle** powerful four-wheel drive vehicle for rough terrain
spot Ⓣ *n* **1** small mark on a surface **2** pimple **3** location **4** *informal* awkward situation **5** *informal* small quantity ▷ *v* **spotting, spotted** **6** notice **7** watch for and take note of **8** mark with spots

THESAURUS

spoil *v* **1 = ruin**, damage, destroy, harm, wreck, impair, mar, mess up • *Don't let it spoil your vacation.* **2 = indulge**, pamper • *Grandparents often spoil their grandchildren.* **3 = go bad**, decay, decompose, addle, curdle, turn, rot ▸ *noun* ▷ **spoils = booty**, treasure, loot, prey, swag (*slang*), plunder
spoilsport *n* **= killjoy**, damper, misery (*informal*), grinch (*informal*), sourpuss, wet blanket (*informal*), buzzkill (*slang*)
spoken *adj* **= said**, oral, verbal, unwritten, expressed, told, uttered, viva voce, voiced
spokesman *See* **representative**
spokesperson *n* **= speaker**, official, spokesman *or* spokeswoman, voice, mouthpiece, spin doctor (*informal*)
spokeswoman *See* **representative**
sponge *See* **clean, scrounge**
spongy *adj* **= porous**, absorbent
sponsor *n* **1 = backer**, patron, promoter ▸ *v* **2 = back**, fund, finance, promote, support, subsidize, patronize
spontaneous *adj* **= unplanned**, natural, willing, voluntary, impromptu, impulsive, instinctive, unprompted
spoof *n* (*Informal*) **= parody**, satire, caricature, mockery, burlesque
spooky *adj* **= eerie**, scary, supernatural, creepy, haunted, ghostly, uncanny, frightening • *The whole place had a slightly spooky atmosphere.*
sporadic *adj* **= intermittent**, occasional, irregular, scattered, spasmodic
sport *n* **1 = game**, play, exercise, diversion, recreation, amusement, pastime **2 = fun**, jest, banter, badinage, joking, teasing ▸ *v* **3** (*Old-fashioned, informal*) **= wear**, display, exhibit, show off
sporting *adj* **= fair**, game (*informal*), sportsmanlike
sporty *adj* **= athletic**, outdoor, energetic
spot *n* **1 = mark**, blemish, blot, speck, smudge, blotch • *a navy blue dress with white*

DICTIONARY

▸**on the spot 1** at the place in question **2** immediately **3** in an awkward predicament
▸**spotless** *adj* absolutely clean **spotlessly** *adv*
▸**spotty** *adj* with spots
▸**spot check** random examination
▸**spotlight** *n* **1** powerful light illuminating a small area **2** centre of attention
▸**spot-on** *adj informal* absolutely accurate
spouse Ⓣ *n* husband or wife
spout Ⓣ *n* **1** projecting tube or lip for pouring liquids **2** stream or jet of liquid ▷ *v* **3** pour out in a stream or jet **4** *slang* utter (a stream of words) lengthily
sprain Ⓣ *v* **1** injure (a joint) by a sudden twist ▷ *n* **2** such an injury
sprang *v* a past tense of **spring**
sprat *n* small sea fish
sprawl Ⓣ *v* **1** lie or sit with the limbs spread out **2** spread out in a straggling manner ▷ *n* **3** anything that spreads out in an untidy and uncontrolled way: *urban sprawl*
spray[1] Ⓣ *n* **1** (device for producing) fine drops of liquid ▷ *v* **2** scatter in fine drops **3** cover with a spray
▸**spray gun** device for spraying paint etc.
spray[2] Ⓣ *n* **1** branch with buds, leaves, flowers, or berries **2** ornament like this
spread Ⓣ *v* **spreading, spread 1** open out or be displayed to the fullest extent **2** extend over a larger expanse **3** apply as a coating **4** send or be sent in all directions **5** distribute or be distributed over a period of time ▷ *n* **6** spreading **7** extent **8** *informal* ample meal **9** soft food which can be spread
▸**spread-eagled** *adj* with arms and legs outstretched
spree Ⓣ *n* session of overindulgence, usu. in drinking or spending money
sprig *n* **1** twig or shoot
sprightly Ⓣ *adj* **-lier, -liest** lively and brisk **sprightliness** *n*
spring Ⓣ *v* **springing, sprang** *or* **sprung, sprung 1** move suddenly upwards or forwards in a single motion, jump **2** develop unexpectedly **3** originate (from) **4** *informal* arrange the escape of (someone) from prison ▷ *n* **5** season between winter and summer **6** coil which can be compressed, stretched, or bent and returns to its original shape when released **7** natural pool forming the source of a stream **8** jump **9** elasticity
▸**springy** *adj* elastic
▸**springboard** *n* flexible board used to gain height or momentum in diving or gymnastics
▸**spring-clean** *v* clean (a house) thoroughly
▸**spring tide** high tide at new or full moon

THESAURUS

spots **2 = place**, point, site, position, scene, location • *an out-of-the-way spot* **3 = pimple**, pustule, zit (*slang*) **4** (*Informal*) **= predicament**, trouble, difficulty, mess, plight, quandary, hot water (*informal*), tight spot ▸*v* **5 = see**, detect, sight, observe, discern, catch sight of • *Her drama teacher spotted her ability.* **6 = mark**, soil, dirty, stain, spatter, speckle, splotch, fleck, mottle, smirch, splodge
See also: **notice, random, recognize**
spotless *adj* **= clean**, pure, flawless, impeccable, immaculate, unblemished, gleaming, shining, unstained, unsullied, untarnished
spotlight *n* **1 = attention**, fame, limelight, public eye ▸*v* **2 = highlight**, accentuate, draw attention to
spotted *adj* **= speckled**, dotted, dappled, flecked, mottled
spouse *n* **= partner**, husband *or* wife, mate, consort, significant other (*informal*)
spout *v* **= stream**, shoot, surge, spray, discharge, spurt, gush
sprain *See* **twist**
sprawl *v* **= loll**, slump, lounge, flop, slouch
spray[1] *n* **1 = droplets**, drizzle, fine mist **2 = aerosol**, sprinkler, atomizer ▸*v* **3 = scatter**, shower, sprinkle, diffuse
spray[2] *n* **= sprig**, branch, corsage, floral arrangement
spread *v* **1 = open**, extend, sprawl, unfold, unfurl, unroll, fan out • *He spread his coat over the bed.* **2 = coat**, cover, apply, smear, smother, overlay, slather • *Spread the bread with the cream cheese.* **3 = circulate**, increase, grow, travel, expand, proliferate • *The sense of fear is spreading in the neighbourhood.* **4 = proliferate**, escalate, multiply ▸*n* **5 = extent** • *The plant grows to 18 inches with a spread of 24 inches.* **6 = growth**, increase, expansion, progression, proliferation, upsurge, diffusion • *the spread of the disease*
See also: **communicate, distribute, lay, stretch**
spreading *See* **infectious**
spree *n* **= binge** (*informal*), bacchanalia, revel, fling, orgy, carousal
sprightly *adj* **= lively**, active, energetic, brisk, spirited, nimble, agile, spry, vivacious
spring *v* **1 = jump**, bounce, leap, vault, bound **2** (often with *from*) **= originate**, come, start, issue, stem, proceed, arise, descend, derive **3** (often with *up*) **= appear**, develop, mushroom, shoot up ▸*n* **4 = jump**, leap, vault, bound **5 = elasticity**, bounce, flexibility, resilience, buoyancy
springy *adj* **= elastic**, flexible, resilient, buoyant, bouncy, rubbery

DICTIONARY

springbok *n* S African antelope
springer *n* small spaniel
Springsteen *n* **Bruce**. born 1949, US rock singer, songwriter, and guitarist. His albums include *Born to Run* (1975), *Darkness on the Edge of Town* (1978), *Born in the USA* (1984), *The Ghost of Tom Joad* (1995), and *The Rising* (2002)
sprinkle Ⓣ *v* scatter (liquid or powder) in tiny drops or particles over (something)
sprinkler *n*
▸ **sprinkling** *n* small quantity or number
sprint Ⓣ *v* **1** run a short distance at top speed ▹ *n* **2** short race run at top speed **3** fast run
sprinter *n*
sprit *n* small spar set diagonally across a sail to extend it
▸ **spritsail** *n* sail extended by a sprit
sprite Ⓣ *n* elf
sprocket *n* wheel with teeth on the rim, that drives or is driven by a chain
sprout Ⓣ *v* **1** put forth shoots **2** begin to grow or develop ▹ *n* **3** shoot **4** short for **Brussels sprout**
spruce[1] *n* kind of fir
spruce[2] Ⓣ *adj* neat and smart
▸ **spruce up** *v* make neat and smart
sprung *v* a past tense of **spring**
spry Ⓣ *adj* **spryer, spryest** *or* **sprier, spriest** active or nimble
spud *n informal* potato
spume *n, v* froth
spun *v* past of **spin**
spunk *n informal* courage, spirit **spunky** *adj*
spur Ⓣ *n* **1** spiked wheel on the heel of a rider's boot used to urge on a horse **2** stimulus or incentive **3** projection ▹ *v* **spurring, spurred 4** urge on, incite (someone)
▸ **on the spur of the moment** on impulse
spurge *n* plant with milky sap
spurious Ⓣ *adj* not genuine
spurn Ⓣ *v* reject with scorn
spurt Ⓣ *v* **1** gush or cause to gush out in a jet ▹ *n* **2** short sudden burst of activity or speed **3** sudden gush
sputnik *n* early Soviet artificial satellite
sputter *v, n* splutter
sputum *n, pl* **-ta** spittle, usu. mixed with mucus
spy Ⓣ *n, pl* **spies 1** person employed to obtain secret information **2** person who secretly watches others ▹ *v* **spying, spied 3** act as a spy **4** catch sight of
▸ **spyware** *n computers* software secretly installed via the internet to gather and transmit information about the user
Sq. Square
squabble Ⓣ *v, n* (engage in) a petty or noisy quarrel
squad Ⓣ *n* small group of people working or training together
squadron *n* division of an air force, fleet, or cavalry regiment
squalid Ⓣ *adj* **1** dirty and unpleasant **2** morally sordid
▸ **squalor** *n* disgusting dirt and filth
squall *n* **1** sudden strong wind **2** harsh cry ▹ *v* **3** cry noisily, yell
squander Ⓣ *v* waste (money or resources)
square Ⓣ *n* **1** geometric figure with four equal sides and four right angles **2** open area in a town in this shape **3** product of a number

THESAURUS

sprinkle *v* = **scatter**, spray, pepper, dust, shower, powder, strew, dredge
sprinkling *n* = **scattering**, few, handful, dash, sprinkle, dusting
sprint *v* = **run**, dash, dart, shoot, race, tear
sprite *n* = **spirit**, brownie, fairy, elf, pixie, goblin, imp
sprout *v* = **grow**, shoot, develop, spring, bud
spruce *adj* = **smart**, dapper, trim, neat, well-groomed, well turned out ▸ *verb* ▹ **spruce up** = **smarten up**, tidy, titivate
spry *adj* = **active**, nimble, agile, supple, sprightly
spur *n* **1** = **stimulus**, incentive, motive, impulse, incitement, impetus, inducement **2** = **goad**, prick ▹ **on the spur of the moment** = **on impulse**, impromptu, impulsively, on the spot, without planning ▸ *v* **3** = **incite**, drive, urge, prompt, stimulate, prod, animate, goad, prick, impel
spurious *adj* = **false**, fake, artificial, bogus, phony (*informal*), sham, pretended, specious, unauthentic
spurn *v* = **reject**, slight, snub, scorn, rebuff, disdain, despise, repulse
spurt *v* **1** = **gush**, shoot, surge, erupt, burst, squirt ▸ *n* **2** = **burst**, surge, rush, fit, spate
spy *n* **1** = **undercover agent**, mole ▸ *v* **2** = **catch sight of**, spot, notice, observe, glimpse, espy
squabble *v* **1** = **quarrel**, fight, argue, feud, wrangle, bicker • *His parents squabble all the time.* ▸ *n* **2** = **quarrel**, fight, dispute, row, argument, disagreement, altercation, tiff • *There have been minor squabbles about phone bills.* *See also*: **clash**
squad *n* = **team**, company, group, force, troop, crew, band, gang
squalid *adj* = **dirty**, filthy, sleazy, sordid, seedy, unclean, scuzzy (*slang*), slummy
squalor *n* = **filth**, foulness, sleaziness, squalidness
squander *v* = **waste**, spend, blow (*slang*), misuse, misspend, expend, fritter away
squandering *See* **waste**
square *adj* **1** = **honest**, fair, ethical,

DICTIONARY

multiplied by itself ▷ *adj* **4** square in shape **5** denoting a measure of area **6** straight or level **7** fair and honest **8** with all accounts or debts settled ▷ *v* **9** make square **10** multiply (a number) by itself **11** be or cause to be consistent ▷ *adv* **12** squarely, directly
▸ **squarely** *adv* **1** in a direct way **2** in an honest and frank manner
▸ **square dance** formation dance in which the couples form squares
▸ **square meal** substantial meal
▸ **square root** number of which a given number is the square
▸ **square up to** *v* prepare to confront (a person or problem)

squash ⓣ *v* **1** crush flat **2** suppress **3** humiliate with a crushing retort **4** push into a confined space ▷ *n* **5** sweet fruit drink diluted with water **6** crowd of people in a confined space **7** Also **squash rackets** game played in an enclosed court with a rubber ball and long-handled rackets **8** marrow-like vegetable **squashy** *adj*

squat ⓣ *v* **squatting, squatted 1** crouch with the knees bent and the weight on the feet **2** occupy unused premises to which one has no legal right ▷ *n* **3** place where squatters live ▷ *adj* **4** short and broad
▸ **squatter** *n* illegal occupier of unused premises

squaw *n offensive* native American or Canadian Indian woman

squawk ⓣ *n* **1** loud harsh cry ▷ *v* **2** utter a squawk

squeak ⓣ *n* **1** short shrill cry or sound ▷ *v* **2** make or utter a squeak **squeaky** *adj*
▸ **narrow squeak** *informal* narrow escape

squeal ⓣ *n* **1** long shrill cry or sound ▷ *v* **2** make or utter a squeal **3** *slang* inform on someone to the police

squeamish ⓣ *adj* easily sickened or shocked

squeegee *n* tool with a rubber blade for clearing water from a surface

squeeze ⓣ *v* **1** grip or press firmly **2** crush or press to extract liquid **3** push into a confined space **4** hug **5** obtain (something) by force or great effort ▷ *n* **6** squeezing **7** amount extracted by squeezing **8** hug **9** crush of people in a confined space **10** restriction on borrowing **11** *baseball* see **squeeze play, suicide squeeze**
▸ **squeeze play** *baseball* play in which the batter bunts to bring home a runner on third base

squelch *v* **1** make a wet sucking sound, as by walking through mud ▷ *n* **2** squelching sound

squib *n* small firework that hisses before exploding

squid *n* sea creature with a torpedo-shaped body and ten tentacles

squiffy *adj informal* slightly drunk

squiggle *n* wavy line **squiggly** *adj*

squint *v* **1** have eyes which face in different directions **2** glance sideways ▷ *n* **3** squinting condition of the eye **4** *informal* glance ▷ *adj* **5** crooked

squire *n* **1** country gentleman, usu. the main landowner in a community **2** *hist* knight's apprentice

squirm ⓣ *v* **1** wriggle, writhe **2** feel embarrassed ▷ *n* **3** wriggling movement

squirrel *n* small bushy-tailed tree-living animal

squirt ⓣ *v* **1** force (a liquid) or (of a liquid) be forced out of a narrow opening **2** squirt liquid at ▷ *n* **3** jet of liquid **4** *informal* small or insignificant person

squish *v, n* (make) a soft squelching sound **squishy** *adj*

Sr *chem* strontium

Sr. **1** Senior **2** Señor

SS **1** Schutzstaffel: Nazi paramilitary security force **2** steamship

st. stone (weight)

St. **1** Saint **2** Street

THESAURUS

genuine, kosher (*informal*), above board, straight **2** (*Informal*) = **uncool**, nerdy, dorky (*slang*), unhip ▸ *v* **3** = **even up**, level, adjust, align **4** (sometimes with *up*) = **pay off**, settle **5** (often with *with*) = **agree**, match, fit, tally, correspond, reconcile

squash *v* **1** = **crush**, press, smash, pulp, flatten, mash, distort, compress **2** = **suppress**, silence, crush, quell, humiliate, annihilate

squashy *adj* = **soft**, mushy, spongy, pulpy, yielding

squat *See* **crouch, low**

squawk *v* = **cry**, screech, hoot

squeak *v* = **peep**, pipe, squeal

squeal *n, v* = **scream**, yell, wail, screech, shriek

squeamish *adj* **1** = **fastidious**, delicate, prudish, strait-laced **2** = **sick**, nauseous, queasy

squeeze *v* **1** = **press**, crush, grip, clutch, pinch, squash, compress, wring **2** = **cram**, force, crowd, press, pack, stuff, jam, ram **3** = **hug**, embrace, cuddle, clasp, enfold **4** = **extort**, milk, wrest, pressurize ▸ *n* **5** = **hug**, embrace, clasp **6** = **crush**, crowd, press, jam, squash, congestion

squirm *v* = **wriggle**, twist, writhe

squirt *n* (*Informal*) = **child**, girl, baby, boy, kid (*informal*), infant, minor, toddler, youngster, tot, whippersnapper (*old-fashioned*)

DICTIONARY

stab Ⓣ *v* **stabbing, stabbed** **1** pierce with something pointed **2** jab (at) ▷ *n* **3** stabbing **4** sudden unpleasant sensation **5** *informal* attempt
stabilize Ⓣ *v* make or become stable **stabilization** *n*
▸ **stabilizer** *n* device for stabilizing a child's bicycle, an aircraft, or a ship
stable[1] *n* **1** building in which horses are kept **2** establishment that breeds and trains racehorses **3** establishment that manages or trains several entertainers or athletes ▷ *v* **4** put or keep (a horse) in a stable
stable[2] Ⓣ *adj* **1** firmly fixed or established **2** firm in character **3** *science* not subject to decay or decomposition **stability** *n*
staccato [stak-**ah**-toe] *adj, adv* **1** *music* with the notes sharply separated ▷ *adj* **2** consisting of short abrupt sounds
stack Ⓣ *n* **1** ordered pile **2** large amount **3** chimney ▷ *v* **4** pile in a stack **5** control (aircraft waiting to land) so that they fly at different altitudes
stadium *n, pl* **-diums, -dia** sports arena with tiered seats for spectators
Staël *n* **Madame de**, full name *Baronne Anne Louise Germaine* (née *Necker*) *de Staël-Holstein*. 1766–1817, French writer, whose works, esp. *De l'Allemagne* (1810), anticipated French romanticism
staff[1] Ⓣ *n* **1** people employed in an organization **2** stick used as a weapon, support, etc. ▷ *v* **3** supply with personnel
staff[2] *n, pl* **staves** set of five horizontal lines on which music is written
stag *n* adult male deer
▸ **stag beetle** beetle with large branched jaws
▸ **stag party** *or* **stag night** party for men only
stage Ⓣ *n* **1** step or period of development **2** platform in a theatre where actors perform **3** portion of a journey **4** separate unit of a rocket that can be jettisoned ▷ *v* **5** put (a play) on stage **6** organize and carry out (an event)
▸ **the stage** theatre as a profession
▸ **stagy** *adj* overtheatrical
▸ **stagecoach** *n* large horse-drawn vehicle formerly used to carry passengers and mail
▸ **stage fright** nervousness felt by a person about to face an audience
▸ **stage whisper** loud whisper intended to be heard by an audience
stagger Ⓣ *v* **1** walk unsteadily **2** astound **3** arrange in alternating positions or periods ▷ *n* **4** staggering **staggering** *adj*
stagnant Ⓣ *adj* **1** (of water or air) stale from not moving **2** not growing or developing
▸ **stagnate** *v* be stagnant **stagnation** *n*
staid Ⓣ *adj* sedate, serious, and rather dull
stain Ⓣ *v* **1** discolour, mark **2** colour with a penetrating pigment ▷ *n* **3** discoloration or mark **4** moral blemish or slur **5** penetrating liquid used to colour things **stainless** *adj*
▸ **stainless steel** steel alloy that does not rust
Stainer *n* Sir **John**. 1840–1901, British composer and organist, noted for his sacred music, esp. the oratorio *The Crucifixion* (1887)
stairs *pl n* flight of steps between floors, usu. indoors
▸ **staircase** *or* **stairway** *n* flight of stairs with a handrail or banisters
stake Ⓣ *n* **1** pointed stick or post driven into

THESAURUS

stab *v* **1** = **pierce**, wound, stick, knife, thrust, jab, impale, spear, transfix ▸ *n* **2** = **wound**, thrust, jab, puncture, gash, incision **3** = **twinge**, ache, prick, pang ▷ **make a stab at, have a stab at** (*Informal*) = **attempt**, try, endeavour, have a go
stability *n* = **firmness**, strength, soundness, solidity, steadiness
stabilize *See* **balance, steady**
stable *adj* **1** = **firm**, strong, sound, fast, secure, permanent, constant, lasting, established, fixed, immovable **2** = **steady**, sure, reliable, staunch, steadfast
stack *n* **1** = **pile**, mass, mountain, load, mound, heap ▸ *v* **2** = **pile**, load, assemble, accumulate, amass, heap up
staff *n* **1** = **workers**, team, personnel, workforce, employees, human resources • *She made little effort to socialize with other staff members.* **2** = **stick**, pole, stave, rod, crook, cane, wand, sceptre
stage *n* **1** = **step**, point, period, phase, lap • *the closing stages of the race* ▸ *v* **2** = **organize**, engineer, mount, arrange, orchestrate • *Workers have staged a number of one-day strikes.*
See also: **level, perform, round**
stagger *v* **1** = **totter**, reel, sway, wobble, lurch **2** = **astound**, shock, shake, stun, overwhelm, astonish, amaze, confound, stupefy **3** = **overlap**, step, alternate
staggering *See* **amazing**
stagnant *adj* = **stale**, still, quiet, sluggish
stagnate *v* = **vegetate**, decline, idle, rust, decay, languish, rot
staid *adj* = **sedate**, serious, steady, calm, grave, solemn, sober, composed
stain *n* **1** = **mark**, spot, blot • *grass stains* **2** = **stigma**, shame, disgrace, slur, dishonor ▸ *v* **3** = **mark**, spot, soil, dirty • *Some foods can stain the teeth.*
See also: **colour**
stake[1] *n* = **pole**, post, stick, picket, pale, paling, palisade
stake[2] *n* **1** = **bet**, pledge, wager,

DICTIONARY

the ground as a support or marker **2** money wagered **3** an interest, usu. financial, held in something ▷ *v* **4** support or mark out with stakes **5** wager, risk
▸ **at stake** being risked
▸ **stake a claim to** claim a right to
▸ **stakeholder** *n* person who has a concern or interest in something, esp. a business
▸ **stake out** *v slang* (of police) keep (a place) under surveillance
stalactite *n* lime deposit hanging from the roof of a cave
stalagmite *n* lime deposit sticking up from the floor of a cave
stale Ⓣ *adj* **1** not fresh **2** uninteresting from overuse **3** lacking energy or ideas through overwork or monotony **staleness** *n*
stalemate *n* **1** *chess* position in which any of a player's moves would put his or her king in check, resulting in a draw **2** deadlock, impasse
Stalin *n* **Joseph**, original name *Iosif Vissarionovich Dzhugashvili*. 1879–1953, Soviet leader; general secretary of the Communist Party of the Soviet Union (1922–53). He succeeded Lenin as head of the party and created a totalitarian state, crushing all opposition, esp. in the great purges of 1934–37. He instigated rapid industrialization and the collectivization of agriculture and established the Soviet Union as a world power
stalk[1] *n* plant's stem
stalk[2] Ⓣ *v* **1** follow or approach stealthily **2** pursue persistently and, sometimes, attack (a person with whom one is obsessed) **3** walk in a stiff or haughty manner
▸ **stalking-horse** *n* pretext
stall Ⓣ *n* **1** small stand for the display and sale of goods **2** ground-floor seat in a theatre or cinema **3** one of a row of seats in a church for the choir or clergy **4** compartment in a stable **5** small room or compartment ▷ *v* **6** stop (a motor vehicle or engine) or (of a motor vehicle or engine) stop accidentally **7** (of an aircraft) begin to drop because the speed is too low **8** employ delaying tactics
stallion *n* uncastrated male horse
stalwart Ⓣ [**stawl**-wart] *adj* **1** strong and sturdy **2** dependable ▷ *n* **3** stalwart person
stamen *n* pollen-producing part of a flower
stamina Ⓣ *n* enduring energy and strength
stammer Ⓣ *v* **1** speak or say with involuntary pauses or repetition of syllables ▷ *n* **2** tendency to stammer
stamp Ⓣ *v* **1** stick a postage stamp on **2** impress (a pattern or mark) on **3** bring (one's foot) down forcefully **4** walk with heavy footsteps **5** characterize ▷ *n* **6** Also **postage stamp** piece of gummed paper stuck to an envelope or parcel to show that the postage has been paid **7** instrument for stamping a pattern or mark **8** pattern or mark stamped **9** act of stamping the foot **10** characteristic feature
▸ **stamping ground** favourite meeting place
▸ **stamp out** *v* suppress by force
stampede Ⓣ *n* **1** sudden rush of frightened animals or of a crowd ▷ *v* **2** (cause to) take part in a stampede
stance Ⓣ *n* **1** manner of standing **2** attitude
stanch [**stahnch**] *v* same as **staunch**[2]
stanchion *n* upright bar used as a support
stand Ⓣ *v* **standing, stood 1** be in, rise to, or place in an upright position **2** be situated **3** be in a specified state or position **4** remain

THESAURUS

ante **2 = interest**, share, concern, investment, involvement ▸ *v* **3 = bet**, risk, chance, gamble, venture, hazard, wager
stale *adj* **1 = old**, flat, sour, stagnant • *a slice of stale bread* OPPOSITE: fresh **2 = unoriginal**, overused, worn-out, banal, trite, hackneyed, stereotyped, threadbare
See also: **corny, stuffy**
stalk *v* **= pursue**, follow, track, hunt, shadow, haunt
stall *v* **= play for time**, hedge, temporize
stalwart *adj* **= strong**, staunch, sturdy, stout, strapping
stamina *n* **= staying power**, force, power, energy, strength, endurance, resilience
stammer *v* **= stutter**, stumble, falter, pause, hesitate
stamp *n* **1 = imprint**, mark, brand, signature, earmark, hallmark ▸ *v* **2 = trample**, crush **3 = identify**, mark, reveal, label, brand, categorize, show to be **4 = imprint**, mark, print, impress
▷ **stamp out = eliminate**, destroy, crush, quell, eradicate, suppress, scotch, put down
stampede *n* **= rush**, charge, flight, rout
stance *n* **1 = attitude**, stand, position, viewpoint, standpoint **2 = posture**, carriage, bearing, deportment
stand *v* **1 = be upright**, rise, be erect, be vertical **2 = put**, set, place, position, mount **3 = exist**, continue, hold, remain, obtain, prevail, be valid **4 = tolerate**, take, allow, bear, handle, endure, stomach, abide, brook, countenance, deal with (*slang*), put up with (*informal*) ▷ **stand by = be prepared**, wait; **= support**, back, champion, be loyal to, take (someone's) part ▷ **stand for = represent**, mean, indicate, signify, symbolize, denote, betoken; (*Informal*) **= tolerate**, bear, endure, brook, put up with ▷ **stand in for = be a substitute for**, represent, cover for, deputize for, take the

DICTIONARY

unchanged or valid **5** tolerate **6** offer oneself as a candidate **7** *informal* treat to ▷ *n* **8** stall for the sale of goods **9** structure for spectators at a sports ground **10** firmly held opinion **11** *US* witness box **12** rack or piece of furniture on which things may be placed
▶ **standing** *n* **1** reputation or status **2** duration ▷ *adj* **3** permanent, lasting
▶ **stand for** *v* **1** represent or mean **2** *informal* tolerate
▶ **stand in** *v* act as a substitute
▶ **stand-in** *n* substitute
▶ **stand-offish** *adj* reserved or haughty
▶ **stand up for** *v* support or defend
standard Ⓣ *n* **1** level of quality **2** example against which others are judged or measured **3** moral principle **4** distinctive flag **5** upright pole ▷ *adj* **6** usual, regular, or average **7** accepted as correct **8** of recognized authority
▶ **standardize** *v* cause to conform to a standard **standardization** *n*
▶ **standard lamp** lamp attached to an upright pole on a base
standpipe *n* tap attached to a water main to provide a public water supply
standpoint Ⓣ *n* point of view
standstill Ⓣ *n* complete halt
Stanford *n* Sir **Charles** (**Villiers**). 1852–1924, Anglo-Irish composer and conductor, who as a teacher at the Royal College of Music had much influence on the succeeding generation of composers: noted esp. for his church music, oratorios, and cantatas
Stanisław II *n* surnamed *Poniatowski*. 1732–98, the last king of Poland (1764–95), during whose reign Poland was repeatedly invaded and partitioned (1772, 1791, 1795) by its neighbours: abdicated
stank *v* a past tense of **stink**
Stanley *n* Sir **Henry Morton**. 1841–1904, British explorer and journalist, who led an expedition to Africa in search of Livingstone, whom he found on Nov 10, 1871. He led three further expeditions in Africa (1874–77; 1879–84; 1887–89) and was instrumental in securing Belgian sovereignty over the Congo Free State
Stanley Cup *n* trophy awarded annually to the National Hockey League champions
stanza *n* verse of a poem
staple[1] *n* **1** U-shaped piece of metal used to fasten papers or secure things ▷ *v* **2** fasten with staples
▶ **stapler** *n* small device for fastening papers together
staple[2] Ⓣ *adj* **1** of prime importance, principal ▷ *n* **2** main constituent of anything
star Ⓣ *n* **1** hot gaseous mass in space, visible in the night sky as a point of light **2** star-shaped mark used to indicate excellence **3** asterisk **4** celebrity in the entertainment or sports world **stars 5** astrological forecast, horoscope ▷ *v* **starring, starred 6** mark with a star or stars **7** feature or be featured as a star ▷ *adj* **8** leading, famous
▶ **stardom** *n* status of a star in the entertainment or sports world
▶ **starry** *adj* full of or like stars
▶ **starry-eyed** *adj* full of naive optimism
▶ **starfish** *n* star-shaped sea creature

THESAURUS

place of ▷ **stand out = be conspicuous**, be distinct, be obvious, be prominent
▷ **stand up for = support**, defend, champion, uphold, stick up for (*informal*) ▷ **stand up to** *See* **brave** ▶ *n* **5 = stall**, table, booth **6 = position**, opinion, attitude, stance, determination **7 = support**, base, stage, platform, rack, bracket, tripod, dais
standard *n* **1 = level**, quality, guideline, requirement, criterion, norm, calibre • *There will be new standards of hospital cleanliness.* **2 = flag**, banner, ensign ▶ *adj* **3 = usual**, regular, normal, correct, customary, orthodox • *It was standard practice for them to consult the parents.* **4 = accepted**, official, definitive, established, authoritative, approved, recognized
See also: **average, common, conventional, ideal, ordinary, routine, stock, typical**
standardize *v* **= bring into line**, regiment, institutionalize
standards *pl n* **= principles**, ethics, ideals, morals, rules, scruple, values • *My father has always had high moral standards.*
stand-in *n* **= substitute**, reserve, deputy, replacement, surrogate, understudy, stopgap, locum
standing *adj* **1 = permanent**, regular, lasting, fixed **2 = upright**, erect, vertical ▶ *n* **3 = status**, position, rank, reputation, footing, repute, eminence **4 = duration**, existence, continuance
standoffish *adj* **= reserved**, cold, remote, distant, aloof, haughty, unapproachable, unsociable
standpoint *n* **= point of view**, position, viewpoint, stance, angle
standstill *See* **halt**
staple *adj* **= principal**, chief, key, main, basic, fundamental, predominant
star *n* **1 = celebrity**, idol, luminary • *a movie star* **2 = heavenly body** **3 = leading**, major, prominent, brilliant, well-known, celebrated
See also: **feature, personality, success**

S

DICTIONARY

starboard *n* **1** right-hand side of a ship, when facing forward ▷ *adj* **2** of or on this side
starch *n* **1** carbohydrate forming the main food element in bread, potatoes, etc., and used mixed with water for stiffening fabric ▷ *v* **2** stiffen (fabric) with starch
▶ **starchy** *adj* **1** containing starch **2** stiff and formal
stare ⓣ *v* **1** look or gaze fixedly (at) ▷ *n* **2** fixed gaze
stark ⓣ *adj* **1** desolate, bare **2** without elaboration **3** absolute ▷ *adv* **4** completely
Stark *n* Dame **Freya** (**Madeline**). 1893–1993, British traveller and writer, whose many books include *The Southern Gates of Arabia* (1936), *Beyond Euphrates* (1951), and *The Journey's Echo* (1963)
starling *n* songbird with glossy black speckled feathers
Starr *n* **Ringo**, original name *Richard Starkey*. born 1940, British rock musician; drummer (1962–70) with the Beatles
start ⓣ *v* **1** take the first step, begin **2** set or be set in motion **3** establish or set up **4** make a sudden involuntary movement from fright ▷ *n* **5** first part of something **6** place or time of starting **7** advantage or lead in a competitive activity **8** starting movement from fright
▶ **starter** *n* **1** device for starting an automobile's engine **2** person who signals the start of a race **3** *baseball* pitcher who plays at the start of a game **4** first course of a meal, appetizer
▶ **start-up** *n* recently launched project or business enterprise
startle ⓣ *v* slightly surprise or frighten
starve *v* **1** die or suffer or cause to die or suffer from hunger **2** deprive of something needed **starvation** *n*
stash ⓣ *v informal* store in a secret place
state ⓣ *n* **1** condition of a person or thing **2** *informal* excited or agitated condition **3** pomp **4 State** sovereign political power or its territory **5 State** the government ▷ *adj* **6** of or concerning the State **7** involving ceremony ▷ *v* **8** express in words
▶ **stately** *adj* dignified or grand
▶ **statement** *n* **1** something stated **2** printed financial account
▶ **stateroom** *n* **1** private cabin on a ship **2** large room in a palace, used for ceremonial occasions
▶ **statesman** (**stateswoman**) *n* experienced and respected political

THESAURUS

stare *v* = **gaze**, look, ogle • *He stared at the floor, lost in meditation.*
stark *adj* **1** = **harsh**, hard, bare, bleak, grim, barren, austere, severe, plain **2** = **absolute**, pure, utter, blunt, sheer, downright, unmitigated, out-and-out ▶ *adv* **3** = **absolutely**, quite, completely, entirely, altogether, wholly, utterly
stark naked *See* **naked**
start *v* **1** arise = **begin**, originate, commence, come into being, come into existence, get under way • *School starts again next week.* OPPOSITE: finish **2** = **set about**, begin, proceed, commence, embark upon • *The child started to cry.* OPPOSITE: stop **3** = **set in motion**, open, trigger, initiate, instigate, get going • *Who started the fight?* OPPOSITE: stop **4** = **establish**, begin, launch, create, introduce, found, pioneer, institute, inaugurate, set up • *I started the company seven years ago.* **5** = **jump**, shy, jerk, flinch, recoil ▶ *n* **6** = **beginning**, birth, opening, foundation, dawn, onset, inauguration, outset, inception (*formal*), initiation, commencement • *His career had an auspicious start.* OPPOSITE: finish **7** = **advantage**, lead, edge, head start **8** = **jump**, spasm, convulsion
See also: **head, scare, surprise**
starter *See* **beginner**
startle *v* = **surprise**, shock, scare, frighten, make (someone) jump
startled *See* **frightened**
startling *See* **amazing**
starving *adj* = **hungry**, ravenous, famished, starved
stash (*Informal*) *v* **1** = **store**, hide, stockpile, cache, hoard, stow, secrete, save up, save for a rainy day, salt away ▶ *n* **2** = **hoard**, store, supply, collection, stockpile, cache • *Police found a huge stash of arms.*
state *n* **1** = **condition**, position, situation, shape, plight, predicament, circumstances • *the pathetic state of the roads* **2** = **country**, land, nation, republic, kingdom • *the state of Denmark* **3** = **frame of mind**, attitude, mood, humour, spirits **4** = **ceremony**, display, style, glory, majesty, grandeur, pomp, splendour ▷ **state of affairs** *See* **situation** ▷ **state of mind** *See* **mood** ▶ *v* **5** = **say**, declare, express, assert, specify, affirm, articulate, expound, aver, propound • *Please state your occupation.*
See also: **observe, remark, report, territory**
stately *adj* = **grand**, royal, lofty, dignified, noble, majestic, regal, august
statement *n* = **account**, report, announcement, testimony, declaration, explanation, bulletin, proclamation • *He was depressed when he made that statement.*
See also: **bill, comment, remark, word**
state-of-the-art *adj* = **latest**, up-to-date,

S

DICTIONARY

leader **statesmanship** *n*
static Ⓣ *adj* **1** stationary or inactive **2** (of a force) acting but producing no movement ▷ *n* **3** crackling sound or speckled picture caused by interference in radio or television reception **4** Also **static electricity** electric sparks produced by friction
▸ **statics** *n* branch of mechanics dealing with the forces producing a state of equilibrium
station Ⓣ *n* **1** place where trains stop for passengers **2** headquarters of the police **3** building with special equipment for a particular purpose: *power station* **4** television or radio channel **5** position in society ▷ *v* **6** assign (someone) to a particular place
▸ **station wagon** automobile with a rear door and luggage space behind the rear seats
stationary Ⓣ *adj* not moving
stationery *n* writing materials such as paper and pens
▸ **stationer** *n* dealer in stationery
statistic Ⓣ *n* numerical fact collected and classified systematically **statistical** *adj* **statistically** *adv*
▸ **statistics** *n* science of classifying and interpreting numerical information
▸ **statistician** *n* person who compiles and studies statistics
Statius *n* **Publius Papinius**. ?45–96 AD, Roman poet; author of the collection *Silvae* and of two epics, *Thebais* and the unfinished *Achilleis*
statue *n* large sculpture of a human or animal figure
▸ **statuary** *n* statues collectively
▸ **statuesque** [stat-yoo-**esk**] *adj* (of a woman) tall and well-proportioned
▸ **statuette** *n* small statue
stature Ⓣ *n* **1** person's height **2** intellectual or moral greatness
status Ⓣ *n* **1** social position **2** prestige **3** person's legal standing
▸ **status quo** existing state of affairs
statute Ⓣ *n* written law
▸ **statutory** *adj* required or authorized by law
Stauffenberg *n* **Claus**, Graf von. 1907–44, German army officer, who tried to assassinate Hitler (1944). He and his fellow conspirators were executed
staunch[1] Ⓣ *adj* loyal, firm
staunch[2]**, stanch** Ⓣ *v* stop (a flow of blood)
stave *n* **1** one of the strips of wood forming a barrel **2** *music* same as **staff** ▷ *v* **staving, staved** *or* **stove** **3** burst a hole in
▸ **stave off** *v* ward off
staves *n* plural of **staff**[2]**, stave**
stay[1] Ⓣ *v* **1** remain in a place or condition **2** reside temporarily **3** endure ▷ *n* **4** period of staying in a place **5** postponement
▸ **staying power** stamina
stay[2] *n* **1** prop or buttress **stays 2** corset
STD sexually transmitted disease
stead *n* **in someone's stead** in someone's place
▸ **stand someone in good stead** be useful to someone
steadfast Ⓣ *adj* firm, determined **steadfastly** *adv*
steady Ⓣ *adj* **steadier, steadiest 1** not shaky or wavering **2** sensible and dependable **3** regular or continuous ▷ *v* **steadying, steadied 4** make steady ▷ *adv* **5** in a steady

THESAURUS

up-to-the-minute, newest
static *adj* = **stationary**, still, motionless, immobile, fixed, unmoving
station *n* **1** = **headquarters**, base, depot **2** = **place**, post, position, situation, seat, location **3** = **position**, post, situation, status, rank, standing ▸ *v* **4** = **assign**, set, post, establish, locate, install
stationary *adj* = **motionless**, standing, static, fixed, parked, stock-still, unmoving
statistic *See* **figure**
statuesque *adj* = **well-proportioned**, imposing, Junoesque
stature *n* = **importance**, rank, standing, prominence, prestige, eminence
status *n* = **position**, rank, standing, prestige • *the status of children in society*
See also: **level**
statute *See* **law**
staunch[1] *adj* = **loyal**, firm, sound, true, faithful, stalwart, steadfast, trusty
staunch[2] *v* = **stop**, stay, check, halt, stem, dam
stay *v* **1** = **remain**, wait, linger, loiter, hang around (*informal*), tarry (*formal*) • *She stayed in bed till noon.* **2** = **visit**, stop, holiday, vacation, stopover, sojourn, stop-off **3** = **postponement**, delay, halt, suspension, stopping, deferment
See also: **live** ▷ **stay afloat** *See* **float** ▷ **stay behind** *See* **remain**
steadfast *adj* = **firm**, steady, constant, faithful, staunch, resolute, unshakable, immovable • *She remained steadfast in her belief.*
steady *adj* **1** = **continuous**, even, regular, consistent, constant, non-stop, uninterrupted • *a steady rise in profits* **2** = **stable**, firm, secure • *She held out a steady hand.* **3** = **sensible**, calm, balanced, reliable, sober, dependable, equable, level-headed ▸ *v* **4** = **stabilize**, support, secure, brace • *Two men were steadying a ladder.*
See also: **balance, gradual, reasonable, steadfast**

DICTIONARY

manner **steadily** *adv* **steadiness** *n*
steak *n* **1** thick slice of meat, esp. beef **2** slice of fish
steal ⓣ *v* **stealing, stole, stolen 1** take unlawfully or without permission **2** move stealthily **3** *baseball* reach (a base) by running to it while the ball is being pitched to the batter ▷ *n* **4** *informal* something acquired at little cost **5** *baseball* act of stealing a base
▸ **steal the show** (of a performer) draw the audience's attention away from the other performers
stealth ⓣ *n* **1** secret or underhand behaviour ▷ *adj* **2** (of technology) able to render an aircraft almost invisible to radar **3** disguised or hidden: *stealth taxes* **stealthy** *adj* **stealthily** *adv*
steam ⓣ *n* **1** vapour into which water changes when boiled **2** power, energy, or speed ▷ *v* **3** give off steam **4** (of a vehicle) move by steam power **5** cook or treat with steam
▸ **steamer** *n* **1** steam-propelled ship **2** container used to cook food in steam
▸ **steam engine** engine worked by steam
▸ **steamroller** *n* **1** steam-powered vehicle with heavy rollers, used to level road surfaces ▷ *v* **2** use overpowering force to make (someone) do what one wants
steatite [**stee**-a-tite] *n* same as **soapstone**
steed *n lit* horse
steel *n* **1** hard malleable alloy of iron and carbon **2** steel rod used for sharpening knives **3** hardness of character or attitude ▷ *v* **4** make (oneself) hard and unfeeling **steely** *adj*
steep[1] ⓣ *adj* **1** sloping sharply **2** *informal* (of a price) unreasonably high **steeply** *adv* **steepness** *n*
steep[2] ⓣ *v* soak or be soaked in liquid
▸ **steeped in** filled with: *Scotland is steeped in history*
steeple *n* church tower with a spire
▸ **steeplejack** *n* person who repairs steeples and chimneys
steeplechase *n* **1** horse race with obstacles to jump **2** track race with hurdles and a water jump
steer[1] ⓣ *v* **1** direct the course of (a vehicle or ship) **2** direct (one's course)
▸ **steerage** *n* cheapest accommodation on a passenger ship
▸ **steering wheel** wheel turned by the driver of a vehicle in order to steer it
steer[2] *n* castrated male ox
Stefansson *n* **Vilhjalmur**. 1879–1962, Canadian explorer, noted for his books on the Inuit
Steffens *n* (**Joseph**) **Lincoln**. 1866–1936, US political analyst, known for his exposure of political corruption
stein [**stine**] *n* earthenware beer mug
Stein *n* **Gertrude**. 1874–1946, US writer, resident in Paris (1903–46). Her works include *Three Lives* (1908) and *The Autobiography of Alice B. Toklas* (1933)
Steinbeck *n* **John** (**Ernst**). 1902–68, US writer, noted for his novels about agricultural workers, esp. *The Grapes of Wrath* (1939): Nobel prize for literature 1962
Steinway *n* **Henry** (**Engelhard**), original name *Heinrich Engelhardt Steinweg*. 1797–1871, US piano maker, born in Germany
stellar *adj* of stars
Stelmach *n* **Ed**(**ward**). born 1951, Canadian politician, Premier of Alberta (2006–)
stem[1] ⓣ *n* **1** long thin central part of a plant **2** long slender part, as of a wineglass **3** part of a word to which inflections are added ▷ *v* **stemming, stemmed 4 stem from** originate from
stem[2] ⓣ *v* **stemming, stemmed** stop (the flow of something)
stench ⓣ *n* foul smell
stencil ⓣ *n* **1** thin sheet with cut-out pattern through which ink or paint passes to form the pattern on the surface below **2** pattern made thus ▷ *v* **-cilling, -cilled 3** make (a pattern) with a stencil
Stendhal *n* original name *Marie Henri Beyle*.

THESAURUS

steal *v* **1 = take**, appropriate, swipe (*slang*), pilfer • *He was accused of stealing a bicycle.* **2 = sneak**, slip, creep, tiptoe • *They can steal out and join us later.* ▷ **steal from** *See* **rob**
stealing *See* **theft**
stealth *n* **= secrecy**, furtiveness, slyness, sneakiness, stealthiness, surreptitiousness, unobtrusiveness
stealthy *adj* **= secret**, secretive, surreptitious, furtive, sneaking
steam *See* **cook**
steamy *See* **humid**
steep[1] *adj* **1 = sheer**, vertical • *a steep hill* OPPOSITE: gradual **2 = excessive**, high, unreasonable, exorbitant • *steep prices*
steep[2] *v* **1 = soak**, immerse, marinate • *tea leaves steeped in hot water* **2 = saturate**, fill, infuse, pervade, permeate, imbue, suffuse
steer *v* **= direct**, control, conduct, pilot, handle, guide ▷ **steer clear of** *See* **avoid**
stem[1] *n* **= stalk**, shoot, branch, trunk, axis ▸ *verb* ▷ **stem from = originate in**, arise from, be caused by, derive from
stem[2] *v* **= stop**, check, curb, dam, staunch, hold back
stench *n* **= stink**, foul smell, whiff, reek
stencil *See* **pattern**

DICTIONARY

1783–1842, French writer, who anticipated later novelists in his psychological analysis of character. His two chief novels are *Le Rouge et le noir* (1830) and *La Chartreuse de Parme* (1839)
stenography *n* shorthand
▶**stenographer** *n* shorthand typist
stentorian *adj* (of a voice) very loud
step Ⓣ *v* **stepping, stepped 1** move and set down the foot, as when walking **2** walk a short distance ▷ *n* **3** stepping **4** distance covered by a step **5** sound made by stepping **6** foot movement in a dance **7** one of a sequence of actions taken in order to achieve a goal **8** degree in a series or scale **9** flat surface for placing the foot on when going up or down **steps 10** stepladder
▶**step in** *v* intervene
▶**stepladder** *n* folding portable ladder with supporting frame
▶**stepping stone 1** one of a series of stones for stepping on in crossing a stream **2** means of progress towards a goal
▶**step up** *v* increase (something) by steps
step- *combining form* denoting a relationship created by the remarriage of a parent: *stepmother*
Stephen *n* **1** ?1097–1154, king of England (1135–54); grandson of William the Conqueror. He seized the throne on the death of Henry I, causing civil war with Henry's daughter Matilda. He eventually recognized her son (later Henry II) as his successor **2 Saint**. died ?35 AD, the first Christian martyr. Feast day: Dec 26 or 27 **3 Saint**, Hungarian name *István*. ?975–1038 AD, first king of Hungary as Stephen I (997–1038). Feast day: Aug 16 or 20
steppe *n* wide grassy treeless plain
stereo *adj* **1** short for **stereophonic** ▷ *n* **2** stereophonic record player **3** stereophonic sound
stereophonic *adj* using two separate loudspeakers to give the effect of naturally distributed sound
stereoscopic *adj* having a three-dimensional effect
stereotype Ⓣ *n* **1** standardized idea of a type of person or thing ▷ *v* **2** form a stereotype of
sterile Ⓣ *adj* **1** free from germs **2** unable to produce offspring **3** lacking inspiration or vitality **sterility** *n*
▶**sterilize** *v* make sterile **sterilization** *n*
sterling Ⓣ *n* **1** British money system ▷ *adj* **2** genuine **3** reliable
stern[1] Ⓣ *adj* severe, strict **sternly** *adv* **sternness** *n*
stern[2] *n* rear part of a ship
Sterne *n* **Laurence**. 1713–68, English novelist, born in Ireland, author of *The Life and Opinions of Tristram Shandy, Gentleman* (1759–67) and *A Sentimental Journey through France and Italy* (1768)
sternum *n, pl* **-na, -nums** breast bone
steroid *n* organic compound containing a carbon ring system, such as many hormones
stertorous *adj* (of breathing) laboured and noisy
stet *v* **stetting, stetted** (used as an instruction) ignore alteration previously made by a proofreader
stethoscope *n* medical instrument for listening to sounds made inside the body
Stetson *n* ® tall broad-brimmed hat, worn mainly by cowboys
stevedore *n* person who loads and unloads ships
Stevens *n* **1 Thaddeus**. 1792–1868, US Radical Republican politician. An opponent of slavery, he supported Reconstruction and entered the resolution calling for the impeachment of President Andrew Johnson **2 Wallace**. 1879–1955, US poet, whose books include the collections *Harmonium* (1923), *The Man with the Blue Guitar* (1937), and *Transport to Summer* (1947)
Stevenson *n* **Adlai Ewing**. 1900–68, US statesman: twice defeated as Democratic presidential candidate (1952; 1956); US delegate at the United Nations (1961–65)
stew Ⓣ *n* **1** food cooked slowly in a closed pot **2** *informal* troubled or worried state ▷ *v* **3** cook slowly in a closed pot
steward *n* **1** person who looks after passengers on a ship or aircraft **2** official who helps at a public event such as a race

S

THESAURUS

step *n* **1** = **footstep**, track, pace, print, stride, footprint, footfall **2** = **stage**, point, move, phase **3** = **action**, move, act, measure, means, deed, expedient **4** = **degree**, level, rank ▶*v* **5** = **walk**, move, pace, tread ▷ **step down** *See* **resign** ▷ **step in** = **intervene**, become involved, take action ▷ **step up** = **increase**, raise, intensify
stereotype *n* **1** = **formula**, pattern ▶*v* **2** = **categorize**, standardize, pigeonhole, typecast
stereotyped *See* **corny, stock**
sterile *adj* **1** = **germ-free**, antiseptic, sterilized • *Protect the cut with a sterile dressing.* **2** = **barren**, unproductive • *He found out he was sterile.* OPPOSITE: fertile
sterilize *v* = **disinfect**, purify, fumigate
sterilized *adj* = **clean**, pure, sterile
sterling *adj* = **excellent**, fine, sound, true, genuine, superlative
stern *adj* = **severe**, hard, serious, strict, harsh, grim, rigid, austere, inflexible, forbidding
stew *See* **cook**

DICTIONARY

3 person who administers another's property
stewardess *n fem*
Stewart *n* **1** Sir **Jackie**, full name *John Young Stewart*. born 1939, Scottish motor-racing driver: world champion 1969, 1971, and 1973 **2 James** (**Maitland**). 1908–97, US film actor, known for his distinctive drawl; appeared in many films including *Destry Rides Again* (1939), *It's a Wonderful Life* (1946), *The Glenn Miller Story* (1953), and *Vertigo* (1958) **3 Rod**. born 1945, British rock singer: vocalist with the Faces (1969–75). His albums include *Gasoline Alley* (1970), *Every Picture Tells a Story* (1971), and *Atlantic Crossing* (1975)
stick[1] Ⓣ *n* **1** long thin piece of wood **2** such a piece of wood shaped for a special purpose: *hockey stick* **3** something like a stick: *stick of celery* **4** *slang* verbal abuse, criticism
▸ **stickhandle** *v* control a puck or ball in hockey, lacrosse, etc.
stick[2] Ⓣ *v* **sticking, stuck 1** push (a pointed object) into (something) **2** fasten or be fastened by or as if by pins or glue **3** (foll. by *out*) extend beyond something else, protrude **4** *informal* put **5** come to a standstill **6** jam **7** remain for a long time **8** *slang* tolerate, abide
▸ **sticker** *n* adhesive label or sign
▸ **sticky** *adj* **1** covered with an adhesive substance **2** (of weather) warm and humid **3** *informal* difficult, unpleasant
▸ **stick-in-the-mud** *n* person who does not like anything new
▸ **stick-up** *n slang* robbery at gunpoint
▸ **stick up for** *v informal* support or defend
stickleback *n* small fish with sharp spines on its back
stickler Ⓣ *n* person who insists on something: *stickler for accuracy*
Stieglitz *n* **Alfred**. 1864–1946, US photographer, whose work helped to develop photography as an art: among his best photographs are those of his wife Georgia O'Keeffe. He was also well known as a promoter of modern art
stiff Ⓣ *adj* **1** not easily bent or moved **2** firm in consistency **3** unrelaxed or awkward **4** severe: *stiff punishment* **5** strong: *a stiff drink* ▹ *n* **6** *slang* corpse **stiffly** *adv* **stiffness** *n*
▸ **stiffen** *v* make or become stiff
▸ **stiff-necked** *adj* haughtily stubborn
stifle Ⓣ *v* **1** suffocate **2** suppress
stigma Ⓣ *n* **1** mark of social disgrace **2** part of a plant that receives pollen
▸ **stigmata** *pl n* marks resembling the wounds of the crucified Christ
▸ **stigmatize** *v* mark as being shameful
stile *n* set of steps allowing people to climb a fence
stiletto *n, pl* **-tos 1** small slender dagger **2** Also **stiletto heel** high narrow heel on a woman's shoe
still[1] Ⓣ *adv* **1** now or in the future as before **2** up to this or that time **3** even or yet: *still more insults* **4** quietly or without movement ▹ *adj* **5** motionless **6** silent and calm, undisturbed **7** (of a drink) not fizzy ▹ *v* **8** make still ▹ *n* **9** photograph from a film scene **stillness** *n*
▸ **stillborn** *adj* born dead

THESAURUS

stick[1] *n* = **cane**, bat, pole, rod, twig, wand, mace, nightstick • *crowds armed with sticks and stones*
See also: **club**
stick[2] *v* **1** = **thrust**, put, push, stuff, dig, insert, poke, shove, ram, jab • *They stuck a needle in my arm*. **2** = **attach**, fix, bond, paste, cling, adhere, glue, fuse • *Stick down the tiles, following the instructions*. **3** = **catch**, jam, snag, lodge • *The paper is stuck in the copier*. **4** (with *out, up etc.*) = **protrude**, show, project, extend, poke, bulge, jut, obtrude **5** (*Informal*) = **put**, set, place, lay, deposit **6** = **stay**, remain, linger, persist **7** (*Slang*) = **tolerate**, take, stand, stomach, abide ▹ **stick up for** = **defend**, support, champion, stand up for
sticker *See* **label**
stickler *n* = **perfectionist**, fanatic, purist, fusspot (*informal*)
sticky *adj* **1** = **tacky**, adhesive • *a sticky smear of peanut butter* **2** (*Informal*) = **difficult**, nasty, delicate, tricky, awkward, unpleasant, embarrassing **3** = **humid**, close, oppressive, sultry, muggy, clammy, sweltering
stiff *adj* **1** = **inflexible**, hard, firm, solid, rigid, taut • *stiff metal wires* OPPOSITE: limp **2** = **unrelaxed**, cold, formal, wooden, forced, unnatural, stilted • *the rather stiff and formal surroundings of the official residence* **3** = **difficult**, hard, tough, rigorous, formidable, arduous, exacting • *a stiff penalty* **4** = **awkward**, jerky (*informal*), clumsy, ungainly, graceless, inelegant, ungraceful **5** = **severe**, hard, heavy, strict, extreme, harsh, drastic
stiffen *v* **1** = **brace**, reinforce, tense, tauten **2** = **set**, solidify, thicken, harden, crystallize, jell, congeal
stifle *v* **1** = **suppress**, stop, check, silence, restrain, smother, hush, repress **2** = **suffocate**, choke, smother, strangle, asphyxiate
stifling *See* **stuffy**
stigma *n* = **disgrace**, shame, stain, slur, dishonour, smirch
still *adj* **1** = **motionless**, calm, stationary, tranquil, inert • *The air was still*. **2** = **silent**, quiet, hushed ▸ *v* **3** = **quieten**, settle, quiet,

S

DICTIONARY

▸ **still life** painting of inanimate objects
still² *n* apparatus for distilling alcoholic drinks
stilted ⓣ *adj* stiff and formal in manner
Stilton *n* ® strong-flavoured cheese
stilts *pl n* **1** pair of poles with footrests for walking raised from the ground **2** long posts supporting a building above ground level
stimulus ⓣ *n, pl* **-li 1** something that acts as an incentive to (someone) **2** something, such as a drug, capable of causing a response in a person or animal
▸ **stimulant** *n* drug, food, etc. that makes the body work faster, increases heart rate, etc.
▸ **stimulate** *v* **1** encourage to start or progress further: *methods to stimulate job creation* **2** fill (a person) with ideas or enthusiasm **3** act as a stimulus on **stimulation** *n*
sting ⓣ *v* **stinging, stung 1** (of certain animals or plants) wound by injecting with poison **2** feel or cause to feel sharp physical or mental pain **3** *slang* cheat (someone) by overcharging ▹ *n* **4** wound or pain caused by or as if by stinging **5** mental pain **6** sharp pointed organ of certain animals or plants by which poison can be injected
stingy ⓣ *adj* **-gier, -giest** mean or miserly **stinginess** *n*
stink ⓣ *v* **stinking, stank** *or* **stunk, stunk 1** give off a strong unpleasant smell **2** *slang* be very unpleasant ▹ *n* **3** strong unpleasant smell **4** *slang* unpleasant fuss
stint ⓣ *v* **1** (foll. by *on*) be miserly with (something) ▹ *n* **2** allotted amount of work
stipend [**sty**-pend] *n* regular allowance or salary, esp. that paid to a clergyman
▸ **stipendiary** *adj* receiving a stipend
stipple *v* paint, draw, or engrave using dots **stippling** *n*
stipulate ⓣ *v* specify as a condition of an agreement **stipulation** *n*
stir ⓣ *v* **stirring, stirred 1** mix up (a liquid) by moving a spoon etc. around in it **2** move **3** excite or stimulate (a person) emotionally ▹ *n* **4** a stirring **5** strong reaction, usu. of excitement
Stirling *n* Sir **James**. 1926–92, British architect; buildings include the Neue Staatsgalerie in Stuttgart (1977–84)
stirrup *n* metal loop attached to a saddle for supporting a rider's foot
stitch *n* **1** link made by drawing thread through material with a needle **2** loop of yarn formed round a needle or hook in knitting or crochet **3** sharp pain in the side ▹ *v* **4** sew
▸ **in stitches** *informal* laughing uncontrollably
▸ **not a stitch** *informal* no clothes at all
St. Laurent *n* **Louis Stephen**. 1882–1973, Canadian lawyer, academic, and Liberal politician; Prime Minister (1948–57)
stoat *n* small mammal of the weasel family, with brown fur that turns white in winter
stock ⓣ *n* **1** total amount of goods available for sale in a shop **2** supply stored for future use **3** financial shares in, or capital of, a company **4** lineage **5** livestock **6** handle of a rifle **7** liquid produced by boiling meat, fish, bones, or vegetables **8** fragrant flowering plant **9** standing or status **stocks 10** *hist* instrument of punishment consisting of a

THESAURUS

silence, calm, lull, allay, soothe, hush, pacify ▸ *conjunction* **4 = however**, but, yet, nevertheless, notwithstanding
See also: **peaceful**
stillness *n* = **calm**, peace, quiet, silence
stilted *adj* = **stiff**, wooden, forced, unnatural, constrained
stimulant *n* = **pick-me-up** (*informal*), upper (*slang*), tonic, restorative
stimulate *v* = **arouse**, fire, prompt, encourage, spur, provoke, incite, rouse, impel
stimulating *adj* = **exciting**, provocative, rousing, exhilarating, inspiring, stirring
stimulus *n* = **incentive**, encouragement, spur, incitement, impetus, inducement, goad
sting *v* **1** = **hurt**, wound, burn, pain, smart, tingle **2** (*Informal*) = **cheat**, defraud, swindle, fleece, overcharge, rip off (*slang*)
stingy *adj* = **mean**, miserly, niggardly, parsimonious, penny-pinching (*informal*), tightfisted, ungenerous
stink *v* **1** = **reek** • *Something in this kitchen stinks.* ▸ *n* **2** = **stench** • *the stink of old fish*
See also: **smell**
stinking *See* **smelly**
stint *v* **1** = **be mean**, be frugal, be sparing, hold back, skimp on ▸ *n* **2** = **time**, share, term, turn, period, shift, stretch, spell, quota
stipulate *v* = **specify**, agree, contract, require, settle, insist upon
stipulation *n* = **condition**, agreement, requirement, clause, qualification, specification, precondition, proviso
stipulations *See* **terms**
stir *v* **1** = **mix**, beat, shake, agitate **2** = **stimulate**, spur, provoke, excite, incite, awaken, arouse, rouse ▹ **stir up** *See* **excite** ▸ *n* **3** = **commotion**, activity, disorder, flurry, excitement, disturbance, fuss, bustle
stirring *See* **impressive, moving**
stock *n* **1** = **shares**, bonds, investments • *the buying of stocks* **2** = **goods**, merchandise (*formal*) • *The shoe store needs to add more stock.* **3** = **supply**, store, reserve, stockpile, reservoir • *a stock of ammunition* **4** = **lineage**, origin,

DICTIONARY

wooden frame with holes into which the hands and feet of the victim were locked ▷ *adj* **11** kept in stock, standard **12** hackneyed ▷ *v* **13** keep for sale or future use **14** supply (a farm) with livestock or (a lake etc.) with fish
▸ **stockist** *n* dealer who stocks a particular product
▸ **stocky** *adj* (of a person) broad and sturdy
▸ **stockbroker** *n* person who buys and sells stocks and shares for customers
▸ **stock car** standard car modified for racing
▸ **stock exchange** *or* **market** institution for the buying and selling of shares
▸ **stockpile** *v* **1** acquire and store a large quantity of (something) for future use ▷ *n* **2** accumulated store
▸ **stock-still** *adj* motionless
▸ **stocktaking** *n* counting and valuing of the goods in a shop
stockade *n* enclosure or barrier made of stakes
Stockhausen *n* **Karlheinz**. 1928–2007, German composer, whose avant-garde music exploits advanced serialization, electronic sounds, group improvization, and vocal and instrumental timbres and techniques. Works include *Gruppen* (1959) for three orchestras, *Stimmung* (1968) for six vocalists, and the operas *Donnerstag* (1980) and *Freitag* (1996)
stockinet *n* machine-knitted elastic fabric
stocking *n* close-fitting covering for the foot and leg
▸ **stocking stitch** alternate rows of plain and purl in knitting
stodgy Ⓣ *adj* **stodgier, stodgiest 1** (of food) heavy and starchy **2** (of a person) serious and boring
▸ **stodge** *n* heavy starchy food
stoic [**stow**-ik] *n* **1** person who suffers hardship without showing his or her feelings ▷ *adj* **2** Also **stoical** suffering hardship without showing one's feelings **stoically** *adv*
stoicism [**stow**-iss-izz-um] *n*
stoke *v* feed and tend a (fire or furnace)
stoker *n*
Stoker *n* **Bram**, original name *Abraham Stoker*. 1847–1912, Irish novelist, author of *Dracula* (1897)
Stokowski *n* **Leopold**. 1887–1977, US conductor, born in Britain. He did much to popularize classical music with orchestral transcriptions and film appearances, esp. in *Fantasia* (1940)
stole[1] *v* past tense of **steal**
stole[2] *n* long scarf or shawl
stolen *v* past participle of **steal**
stolid Ⓣ *adj* showing little emotion or interest **stolidity** *n* **stolidly** *adv*
stomach Ⓣ *n* **1** organ in the body which digests food **2** front of the body around the waist **3** desire or inclination ▷ *v* **4** put up with
stomp *v* tread heavily
stone *n* **1** material of which rocks are made **2** piece of this **3** gem **4** hard central part of a fruit **5** hard deposit formed in the kidney or bladder **6** *Brit* unit of weight equal to 14 pounds ▷ *v* **7** throw stones at **8** remove stones from (a fruit)
▸ **stoned** *adj slang* under the influence of alcohol or drugs
▸ **stony** *adj* **1** of or like stone **2** unfeeling or hard **stonily** *adv*
▸ **stony-broke** *adj slang* completely penniless
▸ **Stone Age** prehistoric period when tools were made of stone
▸ **stone-cold** *adj* completely cold
▸ **stone-deaf** *adj* completely deaf

S

THESAURUS

descent, extraction, ancestry • *He claims to be of Loyalist stock.* **5 = property**, capital, investment, assets, funds **6 = livestock**, cattle, beasts, domestic animals ▸ *v* **7 = sell**, supply, deal in, trade in • *The store stocks a wide range of paint.* **8 = provide with**, supply, equip, furnish, fit out ▷ **stock up = store** *or* **store up**, save, gather, accumulate, amass, hoard, lay in, put away ▸ *adj* **9 = standard**, usual, routine, typical • *They supply stock sizes.* **10 = hackneyed**, overused, stereotyped • *National security is the stock excuse for government secrecy.*
See also: **bank, fill**
stockpile *v* **1 = store up**, save, gather, collect, accumulate, amass, stash, hoard • *People are stockpiling food for the winter.* ▸ *n* **2 = store**, stock, reserve, arsenal, cache, stash (*informal*), hoard • *stockpiles of fuel*
See also: **supply**
stocky *adj* **= thickset**, solid, sturdy • *a stocky, middle-aged man*
stodgy *adj* **1 = heavy**, filling, starchy, leaden **2 = dull**, boring, tedious, stuffy, staid, heavy going, unexciting
stoical *adj* **= resigned**, philosophical, long-suffering, stoic, dispassionate, impassive, phlegmatic, stolid
stoicism *n* **= resignation**, acceptance, patience, long-suffering, fortitude, forbearance, impassivity, stolidity
stolid *adj* **= apathetic**, wooden, dull, unemotional, lumpish
stomach *n* **1 = belly**, tummy (*informal*), paunch • *Breathe in and flatten your stomach.* **2 = inclination**, taste, desire, appetite, relish ▸ *v* **3 = bear**, take, endure, swallow, tolerate, abide
See also: **put up with**
stony *adj* **= cold**, hard, blank, hostile, icy,

DICTIONARY

▶ **stonewall** *v* obstruct or hinder discussion
▶ **stoneware** *n* hard kind of pottery fired at a very high temperature
Stone *n* **1 Oliver**. born 1946, US film director and screenwriter: his films include *Platoon* (1986), *Born on the Fourth of July* (1989), *JFK* (1991), *Nixon* (1995), and *Alexander* (2004) **2 Sharon**. born 1958, US film actress: her films include *Basic Instinct* (1991), *Casino* (1995), and *Cold Creek Manor* (2003)
stood *v* past of **stand**
stooge *n* **1** actor who feeds lines to a comedian or acts as the butt of his jokes **2** *slang* person taken advantage of by a superior
stool *n* **1** chair without arms or back **2** piece of excrement
stool pigeon *n* informer for the police
stoop Ⓣ *v* **1** bend (the body) forward and downward **2** carry oneself habitually in this way **3** degrade oneself ▷ *n* **4** stooping posture
stop Ⓣ *v* **stopping, stopped 1** bring to or come to a halt **2** cease or cause to cease from doing (something) **3** prevent or restrain **4** withhold **5** block or plug **6** stay or rest ▷ *n* **7** place where something stops **8** stopping or being stopped **9** full stop **10** knob on an organ that is pulled out to allow a set of pipes to sound **stoppage** *n*
▶ **stoppage time** same as **injury time**
▶ **stopper** *n* **1** plug for closing a bottle etc. **2** *baseball* relief pitcher
▶ **stopcock** *n* valve to control or stop the flow of fluid in a pipe
▶ **stopgap** *n* temporary substitute
▶ **stopover** *n* short break in a journey
▶ **stop press** news item put into a newspaper after printing has been started
▶ **stopwatch** *n* watch which can be stopped instantly for exact timing of a sporting event
Stopes *n* **Marie Carmichael**. 1880–1958, English pioneer of birth control, who established the first birth-control clinic in Britain (1921)
Stoppard *n* Sir **Tom**, original name *Thomas Straussler*. born 1937, British playwright, born in Czechoslovakia: his works include *Rosencrantz and Guildenstern are Dead* (1967), *Travesties* (1974), *Hapgood* (1988), *The Invention of Love* (1997), and the trilogy *The Coast of Utopia* (2002)
store Ⓣ *n* **1** place for sale of goods and services, shop **2** supply kept for future use **3** storage place, such as a warehouse **stores 4** stock of provisions ▷ *v* **5** collect and keep (things) for future use **6** put (furniture etc.) in a warehouse for safekeeping **7** stock (goods) **8** *computers* enter or retain (data)
▶ **in store** forthcoming or imminent
▶ **set great store by** value greatly
▶ **storage** *n* **1** storing **2** space for storing
▶ **storage heater** electric device that can accumulate and radiate heat generated by off-peak electricity
storey *n* floor or level of a building
Storey *n* **David** (**Malcolm**). born 1933, British novelist and dramatist. His best-known works include the novels *This Sporting Life* (1960) and *A Serious Man* (1998) and the plays *In Celebration* (1969), *Home* (1970), and *Stages* (1992)
stork *n* large wading bird
storm Ⓣ *n* **1** violent weather with wind,

THESAURUS

chilly, expressionless, unresponsive
stoop *v* **1 = bend**, duck, bow, lean, hunch, crouch ▷ **stoop to = sink to**, descend to, lower oneself by, resort to ▶ *n* **2 = slouch**, bad posture, round-shoulderedness
stop *v* **1 = cease**, end, quit, discontinue, desist, cut out (*informal*) • *I stopped writing when the phone rang.* OPPOSITE: start **2 = end**, finish, conclude, halt, cease, come to an end • *They waited for the blizzard to stop.* OPPOSITE: start **3 = prevent**, arrest, check • *measures to stop smuggling* **4 = plug**, block, stem, seal, staunch, obstruct **5 = stay**, rest, lodge ▷ **stop working** *See* **fail** ▶ *n* **6 = halt**, end, finish, standstill, cessation **7 = stay**, break, rest **8 = station**, depot, terminus
See also: **suppress, visit**
stopgap *n* **= makeshift**, resort, substitute, improvization
stoppage *n* **= stopping**, close, arrest, halt, closure, shutdown, standstill, cutoff, hindrance
stopper *See* **plug**
store *n* **1 = supply**, fund, stock, reserve, stockpile, reservoir, cache, hoard • *I have a store of food and water here.* **2 = shop**, market, supermarket, boutique, emporium, dépanneur (*Canad Queb*), hypermarket, mart • *I had to race around the stores in the mall.* **3 = storeroom**, warehouse, depot • *a grain store* ▶ *v* **4 = put by**, keep, save, reserve, stockpile, stash, hoard • *The information is stored in the computer.* ▷ **store up** *See* **stockpile**
See also: **bank, collection, wealth**
storeroom *See* **store**
stores *See* **supplies**
storm *n* **1 = tempest**, hurricane, blizzard, squall, gale **2 = outburst**, outbreak, row, turmoil, outcry, disturbance, strife, furor, agitation, commotion, tumult, rumpus ▶ *v* **3 = attack**, charge, assault, rush, assail **4 = rage**, rant, thunder, rave, bluster **5 = rush**, fly, stamp, flounce

DICTIONARY

rain, or snow **2** strongly expressed reaction ▷ *v* **3** rush violently or angrily **4** rage **5** attack or capture (a place) suddenly
▸ **stormy** *adj* **1** characterized by storms **2** involving violent emotions
▸ **stormstayed** *adj* unable to leave a place because of stormy conditions
story ⓘ *n, pl* **-ries 1** description of a series of events told or written for entertainment **2** plot of a book or film **3** newspaper report **4** *informal* lie
stoup [**stoop**] *n* small basin for holy water
stout ⓘ *adj* **1** fat **2** thick and strong **3** brave and resolute ▷ *n* **4** strong dark beer **stoutly** *adv* **stoutness** *n*
Stout *n* Sir **Robert**. 1844–1930, New Zealand statesman, born in Scotland: prime minister of New Zealand (1884–87)
stove[1] *n* apparatus for cooking or heating
stove[2] *v* a past of **stave**
stow ⓘ *v* pack or store
▸ **stow away** *v* hide as a stowaway
▸ **stowaway** *n* person who hides on a ship or aircraft in order to travel free
Stowe *n* **Harriet Elizabeth Beecher**. 1811–96, US writer, whose bestselling novel *Uncle Tom's Cabin* (1852) contributed to the antislavery cause
Strachey *n* (**Giles**) **Lytton**. 1880–1932, English biographer and critic, best known for *Eminent Victorians* (1918) and *Queen Victoria* (1921)
straddle *v* have one leg or part on each side of (something)
Stradivari *n* **Antonio**. ?1644–1737, Italian violin, viola, and cello maker
strafe *v* attack (an enemy) with machine guns from the air
straggle *v* go or spread in a rambling or irregular way **straggler** *n* **straggly** *adj*
straight ⓘ *adj* **1** not curved or crooked **2** level or upright **3** orderly **4** honest or frank **5** in continuous succession **6** (of spirits) undiluted **7** *theatre* serious **8** *slang* heterosexual **9** *slang* conventional ▷ *n* **10** straight part ▷ *adv* **11** in a straight line **12** immediately **13** in a level or upright position **straighten** *v*
▸ **go straight** *informal* reform after being a criminal
▸ **straightaway** *adv* immediately
▸ **straight face** serious facial expression concealing a desire to laugh
▸ **straightforward** *adj* **1** (of a task) easy **2** honest, frank
strain[1] ⓘ *n* **1** great demand on strength or resources **2** force exerted by straining **3** injury from overexertion **4** tension or tiredness **5** melody or theme ▷ *v* **6** cause

THESAURUS

stormy *adj* = **wild**, rough, turbulent, windy, raging, blustery, inclement, squally
story *n* **1** = **tale**, account, legend, narrative, anecdote, yarn • *a science-fiction story* **2** = **report**, news, feature, article, scoop, news item
See also: **plot**
storyline *See* **plot**
stout *adj* **1** = **fat**, big, heavy, overweight, bulky, portly, plump, burly, fleshy, rotund, corpulent, tubby **2** = **strong**, robust, stalwart, muscular, sturdy, able-bodied, brawny, strapping **3** = **brave**, bold, courageous, valiant, plucky, fearless, gallant, resolute, intrepid
stow *v* = **pack**, store, load, bundle, stash (*informal*), put away
straight *adj* **1** = **upright**, erect, vertical, perpendicular • *Keep your arms straight*. OPPOSITE: crooked **2** = **level**, even, horizontal • *a straight line* **3** = **frank**, honest, plain, outright, blunt, candid, point-blank, forthright • *They wouldn't give me a straight answer*. **4** = **direct**, near, short **5** = **honest**, just, fair, accurate, upright, law-abiding, trustworthy, honourable, above board **6** = **successive**, consecutive, solid, continuous, running, nonstop **7** = **undiluted**, pure, neat, unadulterated, unmixed **8** = **orderly**, organized, tidy, neat, arranged, in order, shipshape **9** (*Slang*) = **conventional**, conservative, bourgeois ▸ *adv* **10** = **directly**, immediately, instantly, at once
See also: **straightforward** ▸ **straight away** *adv* = **immediately**, now, directly, instantly, at once, right away
straighten *v* = **neaten**, order, arrange, tidy *or* tidy up, put in order ▸ **straighten out** *See* **settle**
straightforward *adj* **1** = **easy**, simple, basic, routine, elementary, uncomplicated • *The question seemed straightforward enough*. OPPOSITE: complicated **2** = **honest**, open, straight, direct, plain, frank, candid, upfront, forthright • *I liked her straightforward, intelligent manner*. OPPOSITE: devious
See also: **blunt**
strain[1] *n* **1** = **stress**, pressure, tension, anxiety • *the stresses and strains of a busy career* **2** = **exertion**, force, effort, struggle **3** = **injury**, pull, sprain, wrench ▸ *v* **4** = **overwork**, tax • *You'll strain your eyes reading in this light*. **5** = **stretch**, tighten, distend, draw tight, tauten **6** = **strive**, struggle, labour, endeavour, bend over backwards (*informal*), give it one's best shot (*informal*), go for it (*informal*), knock oneself out (*informal*) **7** = **sieve**, filter, sift, purify

DICTIONARY

(something) to be used or tested beyond its limits **7** make an intense effort **8** injure by overexertion **9** sieve
▶ **strained** *adj* **1** not relaxed, tense **2** not natural, forced
▶ **strainer** *n* sieve
strain[2] Ⓣ *n* **1** breed or race **2** trace or streak
strait Ⓣ *n* **1** narrow channel connecting two areas of sea **straits 2** position of acute difficulty
▶ **straitjacket** *n* strong jacket with long sleeves used to bind the arms of a violent person
▶ **strait-laced** *adj* prudish or puritanical
straitened *adj* **in straitened circumstances** not having much money
strand[1] *v* **1** run aground **2** leave in difficulties ▷ *n* **3** *poetic* shore
strand[2] Ⓣ *n* single thread of string, wire, etc.
strange Ⓣ *adj* **1** odd or unusual **2** not familiar **strangely** *adv* **strangeness** *n*
▶ **strange to** inexperienced (in) or unaccustomed (to)
▶ **stranger** *n* person who is not known or is new to a place or experience
strangle Ⓣ *v* **1** kill by squeezing the throat **2** prevent the development of **strangler** *n*
▶ **strangulation** *n* strangling
▶ **stranglehold** *n* **1** strangling grip in wrestling **2** powerful control
strap Ⓣ *n* **1** strip of flexible material for lifting, fastening, or holding in place ▷ *v* **strapping, strapped 2** fasten with a strap or straps
▶ **strapping** *adj* tall and sturdy
strata *n* plural of **stratum**
stratagem Ⓣ *n* clever plan, trick
strategy Ⓣ *n, pl* **-gies 1** overall plan **2** art of planning in war **strategist** *n*
▶ **strategic** [strat-ee-jik] *adj* **1** advantageous **2** (of weapons) aimed at an enemy's homeland **strategically** *adv*
strathspey *n* Scottish dance with gliding steps
stratosphere *n* atmospheric layer between about 15 and 50 km above the earth
stratum Ⓣ [**strah**-tum] *n, pl* **strata 1** layer, esp. of rock **2** social class
▶ **stratify** *v* divide into strata **stratification** *n*
Straus *n* **Oscar**. 1870–1954, French composer, born in Austria, noted for such operettas as *Waltz Dream* (1907) and *The Chocolate Soldier* (1908)
Strauss *n* **1 Johann**. 1804–49, Austrian composer, noted for his waltzes **2** his son, **Johann**, called the *Waltz King*. 1825–99, Austrian composer, whose works include *The Blue Danube Waltz* (1867) and the operetta *Die Fledermaus* (1874) **3 Richard**. 1864–1949, German composer, noted esp. for his symphonic poems, including *Don Juan* (1889) and *Till Eulenspiegel* (1895), his operas, such as *Elektra* (1909) and *Der Rosenkavalier* (1911), and his *Four Last Songs* (1948)
Stravinsky *n* **Igor Fyodorovich**. 1882–1971, US composer, born in Russia. He created ballet scores, such as *The Firebird* (1910), *Petrushka* (1911), and *The Rite of Spring* (1913), for Diaghilev. These were followed by neoclassical works, including *Oedipus Rex* (1927) and the *Symphony of Psalms* (1930).

THESAURUS

See also: **burden, difficulty**
strain[2] *n* **1 = breed**, family, race, blood, descent, extraction, ancestry, lineage **2 = trace**, streak, suggestion, tendency
See also: **variety**
strained *adj* **1 = forced**, false, artificial, unnatural, put on **2 = tense**, difficult, stiff, awkward, uneasy, embarrassed
strains *See* **tune**
strait *n (often pl)* **= channel**, sound, narrows ▷ **straits = difficulty**, plight, dilemma, hardship, predicament, extremity
strait-laced *adj* **= puritanical**, strict, proper, prim, narrow-minded, moralistic, prudish
strand *n* **= filament**, string, thread, fibre
stranded *adj* **1 = beached**, ashore, aground, grounded, marooned, shipwrecked **2 = helpless**, abandoned, high and dry
strange *adj* **1 = odd**, funny, extraordinary, bizarre, weird, curious, abnormal, uncommon, peculiar, hinky (*slang*), unaccountable, outré • *A strange thing happened.* **2 = unfamiliar**, new, foreign, novel, alien, exotic • *alone in a strange country*
See also: **eccentric**
stranger *n* **= newcomer**, guest, visitor, foreigner, alien, incomer, outlander
strangle *v* **1 = throttle**, choke, asphyxiate, strangulate **2 = suppress**, stifle, inhibit, repress
strap *n* **1 = tie**, belt, thong ▶ *v* **2 = fasten**, tie, secure, bind, lash, buckle
strapping *adj* **= well-built**, big, powerful, robust, husky (*informal*), sturdy, brawny
stratagem *n* **= trick**, plan, device, scheme, dodge, ploy, ruse, manoeuvre, subterfuge
strategic *adj* **1 = tactical**, diplomatic, planned, deliberate, calculated, politic **2 = crucial**, key, important, critical, decisive, vital, cardinal
strategy *n* **= plan**, policy, approach, procedure, scheme, gameplan
stratum *See* **layer**

DICTIONARY

The 1950s saw him reconciled to serial techniques, which he employed in such works as the *Canticum Sacrum* (1955), the ballet *Agon* (1957), and *Requiem Canticles* (1966)

straw *n* **1** dried stalks of grain **2** single stalk of straw **3** long thin tube used to suck up liquid into the mouth

▸ **straw poll** unofficial poll taken to determine general opinion

strawberry *n* sweet fleshy red fruit with small seeds on the outside

▸ **strawberry mark** red birthmark

stray Ⓣ *v* **1** wander **2** digress **3** deviate from certain moral standards ▹ *adj* **4** having strayed **5** scattered, random ▹ *n* **6** stray animal

Strayhorn *n* **Billy**, full name *William Strayhorn*. 1915–67, US jazz composer and pianist, noted esp. for his association (1939–67) with Duke Ellington

streak Ⓣ *n* **1** long band of contrasting colour or substance **2** quality or characteristic **3** short stretch (of good or bad luck) ▹ *v* **4** mark with streaks **5** move rapidly **6** *informal* run naked in public **streaker** *n* **streaky** *adj*

stream Ⓣ *n* **1** small river **2** steady flow, as of liquid, speech, or people **3** schoolchildren grouped together because of similar ability ▹ *v* **4** flow steadily **5** move in unbroken succession **6** float in the air **7** group (pupils) in streams

▸ **streamer** *n* **1** strip of coloured paper that unrolls when tossed **2** long narrow flag

▸ **streaming** *n computers* method of sending video or audio material over the internet so that the receiving system can process and play it almost simultaneously

streamline Ⓣ *v* **1** make more efficient by removing the parts that are least useful or profitable **2** give (an automobile, plane, etc.) a smooth even shape to offer least resistance to the flow of air or water

street Ⓣ *n* public road, usu. lined with buildings

▸ **on the street** Also **on the streets** homeless

▸ **streetcar** *n* public transport vehicle powered by an overhead wire and running on rails laid in the road

▸ **street hockey** *or* **road hockey** *sports* informal hockey played on a public street with a ball and ordinary footwear

▸ **streetwalker** *n* prostitute

▸ **streetwise** *adj* knowing how to survive in big cities

Streisand *n* **Barbra**. born 1942, US singer, actress, and film director: the films she has acted in include *Funny Girl* (1968) and *A Star is Born* (1976); her films as actress and director include *Yentl* (1983), *Prince of Tides* (1990), and *The Mirror has Two Faces* (1996)

strength Ⓣ *n* **1** quality of being strong **2** quality or ability considered an advantage **3** degree of intensity **4** total number of people in a group **strengthen** *v*

▸ **on the strength of** on the basis of

strenuous Ⓣ *adj* requiring great energy or effort **strenuously** *adv*

streptococcus [strep-toe-**kok**-uss] *n, pl* **-cocci** bacterium occurring in chains, many species of which cause disease

streptomycin *n* antibiotic drug

stress Ⓣ *n* **1** emphasis **2** tension or strain **3** stronger sound in saying a word or

THESAURUS

stray *v* **1 = wander**, drift, err, go astray **2 = digress**, deviate, diverge, get off the point ▸ *adj* **3 = lost**, homeless, abandoned, roaming, vagrant **4 = random**, chance, accidental

streak *n* **1 = band**, line, stroke, strip, slash, layer, stripe, vein **2 = trace**, touch, strain, element, dash, vein ▸ *v* **3 = speed**, fly, tear, flash, sprint, zoom, dart, hurtle, whizz (*informal*)

stream *n* **1 = river**, bayou, brook, beck, tributary, rivulet **2 = flow**, run, current, course, surge, rush, tide, drift, torrent ▸ *v* **3 = flow**, run, issue, course, flood, spill, pour, cascade, gush, spout

streamline *See* **simplify**

streamlined *adj* **= efficient**, organized, slick, rationalized, smooth-running

street *n* **= road**, row, lane, avenue, roadway, terrace, boulevard, parkway

strength *n* **1 = might**, muscle, stamina, brawn • *an astonishing display of physical strength* OPPOSITE: weakness **2 = intensity**, force, power, vigour, potency, vehemence • *the strength of his feelings for her* OPPOSITE: weakness **3 = strong point**, advantage, asset

See also: **character, energy, merit, virtue**

strengthen *v* **1 = fortify**, encourage, consolidate, toughen, stiffen, harden • *This move will strengthen his political standing.* OPPOSITE: weaken **2 = reinforce**, support, brace, bolster, fortify • *The builders had to strengthen the joists with timber.* OPPOSITE: weaken

See also: **build, secure**

strenuous *adj* **= demanding**, hard, tough, uphill, arduous, laborious, taxing

stress *n* **1 = worry**, pressure, strain, tension, anxiety, hassle (*informal*) • *the stresses and strains of a busy career* **2 = emphasis**, force, weight, significance **3 = accent**, beat, emphasis, accentuation ▸ *v* **4 = emphasize**, repeat, underline, accentuate • *The leaders have*

S

DICTIONARY

syllable **4** *physics* force producing strain ▷ *v* **5** emphasize **6** subject to stress **7** put stress on (a word or syllable)

stretch Ⓣ *v* **1** extend or be extended **2** be able to be stretched **3** extend the limbs or body **4** strain (resources or abilities) to the utmost ▷ *n* **5** stretching **6** continuous expanse **7** period **8** ability to be stretched **9** *informal* term of imprisonment **stretchy** *adj*

▸ **stretcher** *n* frame covered with canvas, on which an injured person is carried

strew *v* **strewing, strewed, strewed** *or* **strewn** scatter (things) over a surface

striation *n* **1** scratch or groove **2** pattern of scratches or grooves **striated** *adj*

stricken *adj* seriously affected by disease, grief, pain, etc.

strict Ⓣ *adj* **1** stern or severe **2** adhering closely to specified rules **3** complete, absolute **strictly** *adv* **strictness** *n*

stricture *n* severe criticism

stride Ⓣ *v* **striding, strode, stridden** **1** walk with long steps ▷ *n* **2** long step **3** regular pace **strides 4** progress

strident Ⓣ *adj* loud and harsh **stridently** *adv* **stridency** *n*

strife Ⓣ *n* conflict, quarrelling

strike Ⓣ *v* **striking, struck 1** cease work as a protest **2** hit **3** attack suddenly **4** afflict **5** enter the mind of **6** agree (a bargain) **7** ignite (a match) by friction **8** (of a clock) indicate (a time) by sounding a bell **9** discover (gold, oil, etc.) **10** make (a coin) by stamping it **11** take up (a posture) ▷ *n* **12** stoppage of work as a protest **13** striking **14** *baseball* pitched ball at which the batter either swings and misses or which passes through the strike zone without the batter swinging

▸ **strike camp** dismantle and pack up tents

▸ **strike home** have the desired effect

▸ **striker** *n* **1** striking worker **2** attacking footballer

▸ **striking** *adj* **1** noteworthy **2** impressive

▸ **strike off** *or* **strike out** *v* cross out

▸ **strike out** *v baseball* **1** (of a pitcher) put a batter out by means of three strikes **2** (of a batter) be put out by means of three strikes

▸ **strike up** *v* **1** begin (a conversation or friendship) **2** begin to play music

▸ **strike zone** *baseball* area over home plate at which the pitcher aims and through which a ball must normally pass to count as a strike

Strindberg *n* **August**. 1849–1912, Swedish dramatist and novelist, whose plays include *The Father* (1887), *Miss Julie* (1888), and *The Ghost Sonata* (1907)

string Ⓣ *n* **1** thin cord used for tying **2** set of objects threaded on a string **3** series of things or events **4** stretched wire or cord on a musical instrument that produces sound when vibrated **strings 5** restrictions or conditions **6** section of an orchestra consisting of stringed instruments ▷ *v* **stringing, strung 7** provide with a string or strings **8** thread on a string

▸ **pull strings** use one's influence

▸ **stringed** *adj* (of a musical instrument) having strings that are plucked or played with a bow

▸ **stringy** *adj* **1** like string **2** (of meat) fibrous

▸ **string along** *v informal* **1** accompany **2** deceive over a period of time

▸ **string up** *v informal* kill by hanging

stringent Ⓣ [**strin**-jent] *adj* strictly

THESAURUS

stressed their commitment to the talks.
See also: **burden, care**

stressful *See* **tense**

stretch *v* **1** = **extend**, last, continue, reach, cover, spread, hang, go on • *an artificial reef stretching the length of the coast* **2** = **reach**, extend, straighten • *She arched her back and stretched herself*. OPPOSITE: bend **3** = **pull**, expand, strain, tighten, elongate, distend, draw out ▸ *n* **4** = **expanse**, area, sweep, extent, tract • *It's a very dangerous stretch of road*. **5** = **period**, time, run, term, space, spell, stint • *She would study for eight-hour stretches*.
See also: **lengthen, range, tax**

strict *adj* **1** = **stern**, firm, rigorous, stringent, authoritarian, rigid • *His parents are very strict*. **2** = **exact**, true, particular, accurate, precise, meticulous • *He has never been unemployed, in the strict sense of the word*. **3** = **absolute**, total, utter
See also: **faithful, right, severe**

stride *See* **walk**

strident *adj* = **harsh**, raucous, shrill, grating, discordant, jarring, screeching

strife *n* = **conflict**, battle, clash, friction, quarrel, discord, dissension

strike *v* **1** = **walk out**, revolt, mutiny, down tools **2** = **hit**, beat, knock, hammer, punch, slap, thump, smack, wallop (*informal*), clobber (*slang*), cuff, clout (*informal*) **3** = **collide with**, hit, bump into, run into **4** = **attack**, hit, assault, assail **5** = **occur to**, hit, register (*informal*), come to, dawn on *or* dawn upon

striking *adj* = **impressive**, cool (*informal*), dramatic, outstanding, noticeable, conspicuous, phat (*slang*)

string *n* **1** = **cord**, fibre, twine **2** = **series**, file, line, row, chain, sequence, procession, succession

stringent *adj* = **strict**, tough, severe, tight, rigorous, rigid, inflexible

DICTIONARY

controlled or enforced **stringently** *adv*
stringency *n*
strip Ⓣ *v* **stripping, stripped 1** take (the covering or clothes) off **2** take a title or possession away from (someone) **3** dismantle (an engine) ▷ *n* **4** long narrow piece **5** clothes a football team plays in
▶ **stripper** *n* person who performs a striptease
▶ **strip cartoon** sequence of drawings telling a story
▶ **striptease** *n* entertainment in which a performer undresses to music
stripe Ⓣ *n* **1** long narrow band of contrasting colour or substance **2** chevron on a uniform to indicate rank **striped** *or* **stripy** *adj*
stripling *n* youth
strive Ⓣ *v* **striving, strove, striven** make a great effort
strobe *n* short for **stroboscope**
stroboscope *n* instrument producing a very bright flashing light
strode *v* past tense of **stride**
Stroessner *n* **Alfredo.** 1912–2006, Paraguayan soldier and politician; president (1954–89): deposed in a military coup
stroke Ⓣ *v* **1** touch or caress lightly with the hand ▷ *n* **2** light touch or caress with the hand **3** rupture of a blood vessel in the brain **4** mark made by a pen or paintbrush **5** style or method of swimming **6** blow **7** action or occurrence of the kind specified: *a stroke of luck* **8** chime of a clock
stroll Ⓣ *v* **1** walk in a leisurely manner ▷ *n* **2** leisurely walk
▶ **stroller** *n* chair-shaped carriage for a baby
strong Ⓣ *adj* **1** having physical power **2** not easily broken **3** having an extreme or drastic effect: *strong discipline* **4** great in degree or intensity **5** having moral force **6** (of a drink) containing a lot of alcohol **7** having a specified number: *twenty strong* **strongly** *adv*
▶ **stronghold** *n* **1** fortress **2** area of predominance of a particular belief
▶ **strongroom** *n* room designed for the safekeeping of valuables
strontium *n* silvery-white metallic element
▶ **strontium-90** *n* radioactive isotope present in the fallout of nuclear explosions
strop *n* leather strap for sharpening razors
stroppy *adj* **-pier, -piest** *slang* angry or awkward
strove *v* past tense of **strive**
struck *v* past of **strike**
structure Ⓣ *n* **1** complex construction **2** manner or basis of construction or organization ▷ *v* **3** give a structure to **structural** *adj*
▶ **structuralism** *n* approach to literature, social sciences, etc., which sees changes in the subject as caused and organized by a hidden set of universal rules **structuralist** *n, adj*
strudel *n* thin sheet of filled dough rolled up and baked, usu. with an apple filling
struggle Ⓣ *v* **1** work, strive, or make one's way with difficulty **2** move about violently in an attempt to get free **3** fight (with someone) ▷ *n* **4** striving **5** fight
strum *v* **strumming, strummed** play (a

THESAURUS

stringy *adj* = **fibrous**, tough, gristly, sinewy
strip[1] *v* **1** = **undress**, disrobe, unclothe **2** = **plunder**, empty, sack, rob, loot, ransack, divest, pillage, despoil
strip[2] *n* = **piece**, band, belt, shred
stripe *See* **line**
stripped *See* **bare**
strive *v* = **try**, seek, attempt, endeavour (*formal*), do your best, do your utmost, make an effort • *She strives hard to keep herself fit.*
See also: **aim, struggle**
stroke *v* **1** = **caress**, pet, rub, fondle ▶ *n* **2** = **apoplexy**, attack, collapse, fit, seizure **3** = **blow**, hit, knock, rap, thump, pat
stroll *v* **1** = **walk**, ramble, promenade, amble, saunter ▶ *n* **2** = **walk**, turn, constitutional, ramble, promenade, breath of air
strong *adj* **1** = **powerful**, tough, robust, athletic, muscular, sturdy, burly, hardy, brawny, lusty, strapping • *a strong, robust man* OPPOSITE: weak **2** = **durable**, substantial, sturdy, heavy-duty, hard-wearing, well-built • *a strong material, which won't crack or chip* OPPOSITE: fragile **3** = **persuasive**, sound, effective, potent, weighty, well-founded, compelling, convincing, telling **4** = **intense**, firm, deep, violent, fierce, acute, keen, zealous, vehement, fervent, fervid • *Despite strong opposition, she was victorious.* OPPOSITE: faint **5** = **extreme**, severe, drastic, forceful **6** = **bright**, brilliant, bold, dazzling
See also: **hard, healthy, passionate, solid, well** ▷ **strong point** *See* **merit**
stronghold *n* = **fortress**, castle, fort, bastion, citadel, bulwark
structure *n* **1** = **arrangement**, design, organization, construction, makeup • *the structure of this molecule* **2** = **building**, construction, edifice • *The museum is an impressive structure.* ▶ *v* **3** = **arrange**, design, shape, organize, assemble, build up
See also: **form, sequence, system**
structuring *See* **organization**
struggle *v* **1** = **strive**, work, strain, toil • *They had to struggle to make ends meet.* **2** = **fight**, battle, compete, contend, wrestle, grapple ▷ **struggle against** *See* **resist** ▶ *n* **3** = **effort**,

DICTIONARY

guitar or banjo) by sweeping the thumb or a plectrum across the strings
strumpet *n old-fashioned* prostitute
strung *v* past of **string**
strut Ⓣ *v* **strutting, strutted 1** walk pompously, swagger ▷ *n* **2** bar supporting a structure **3** strutting walk
strychnine [**strik**-neen] *n* very poisonous drug used in small quantities as a stimulant
stub Ⓣ *n* **1** short piece left after use **2** counterfoil of a cheque or ticket ▷ *v* **stubbing, stubbed 3** strike (the toe) painfully against an object **4** put out (a cigarette) by pressing the end against a surface
▸ **stubby** *adj* short and broad
stubble *n* **1** short stalks of grain left in a field after reaping **2** short growth of hair on the chin of a man who has not shaved recently **stubbly** *adj*
▸ **stubble-jumper** *n slang* prairie grain farmer
stubborn Ⓣ *adj* **1** refusing to agree or give in **2** difficult to deal with **stubbornly** *adv* **stubbornness** *n*
Stubbs *n* **George**. 1724–1806, English painter, noted esp. for his pictures of horses
stucco *n* plaster used for coating or decorating walls **stuccoed** *adj*
stuck Ⓣ *v* past of **stick**[2]
▸ **stuck-up** *adj informal* conceited or snobbish
stud[1] Ⓣ *n* **1** small piece of metal attached to a surface for decoration **2** disclike removable fastener for clothes **3** one of several small round objects fixed to the sole of a football boot to give better grip ▷ *v* **studding, studded 4** set with studs
stud[2] *n* **1** male animal, esp. a stallion, kept for breeding **2** Also **stud farm** place where horses are bred **3** *slang* virile or sexually active man
student Ⓣ *n* person who studies a subject, esp. at university
studio Ⓣ *n, pl* **-dios 1** workroom of an artist or photographer **2** room or building in which television or radio programmes, records, or films are made
▸ **studio apartment** one-room apartment with a small kitchen and bathroom
study Ⓣ *v* **studying, studied 1** be engaged in learning (a subject) **2** investigate by observation and research **3** scrutinize ▷ *n, pl* **studies 4** act or process of studying **5** room for studying in **6** book or paper produced as a result of study **7** sketch done as practice or preparation **8** musical composition designed to improve playing technique
▸ **studied** *adj* carefully practised or planned
▸ **studious** [**styoo**-dee-uss] *adj* **1** fond of study **2** careful and deliberate **studiously** *adv*
stuff Ⓣ *v* **1** pack, cram, or fill completely **2** fill (food) with a seasoned mixture **3** fill (an animal's skin) with material to restore the shape of the live animal **4** fill with padding ▷ *n* **5** substance or material **6** collection of unnamed things
▸ **stuff oneself** *informal* eat large quantities
▸ **stuffing** *n* **1** seasoned mixture with which food is stuffed **2** padding

THESAURUS

work, labour, toil • *Life became a struggle for survival.* **4 = fight**, battle, contest, conflict, clash, combat, brush, tussle
See also: **competition**
strut *v* = **swagger**, parade, peacock, prance
stub *n* **1 = butt**, end, remainder, tail, remnant, stump, tail end **2 = counterfoil**, receipt, ticket stub
stubborn *adj* = **obstinate**, wilful, dogged, tenacious, inflexible • *a stubborn character who is used to getting her own way*
stubby *adj* = **stocky**, short, squat, chunky, dumpy, thickset
stuck *adj* **1 = fastened**, fast, cemented, fixed, glued, joined **2** (*Informal*) **= baffled**, beaten, stumped
stuck-up *adj* (*informal*) **= snobbish**, proud, arrogant, conceited, disdainful, haughty • *She was famous, but she wasn't a bit stuck-up.*
See also: **superior, vain**
stud *v* = **ornament**, spot, dot, bejewel, spangle
student *n* = **pupil**, schoolchild • *There are 30 students in my class.*
studied *adj* = **planned**, deliberate, conscious, intentional, premeditated
studio *n* = **workshop**, atelier
studious *adj* = **scholarly**, academic, intellectual, hard-working, diligent, bookish, assiduous
study *v* **1 = learn**, read up • *He is studying history and economics.* **2 = contemplate**, examine, pore over • *He studied the map in silence.* **3 = examine**, research, survey, investigate, analyze, scrutinize, look into ▸ *n* **4 = learning**, research, schoolwork, lessons • *the serious study of architecture* **5 = examination**, review, investigation, survey, inquiry, analysis, inspection, consideration, scrutiny, contemplation
See also: **observe, piece, read**
stuff *n* **1 = material**, fabric, textile, cloth **2 = things**, equipment, tackle, gear, apparatus, paraphernalia, belongings, items • *"That's my stuff," he said, pointing to a bag.* **3 = substance**, material • *The car was covered in some sticky stuff.* ▸ *v* **4 = shove**, force,

DICTIONARY

stuffy Ⓣ *adj* **stuffier, stuffiest 1** lacking fresh air **2** *informal* dull or conventional
stultify *v* **-fying, -fied** dull the mind of (someone) by boring routine
stumble Ⓣ *v* **1** trip and nearly fall **2** walk with frequent stumbling **3** make frequent mistakes in speech ▷ *n* **4** stumbling
▶ **stumble across** *v* discover accidentally
▶ **stumbling block** obstacle or difficulty
stump Ⓣ *n* **1** base of a tree left when the main trunk has been cut away **2** part of a thing left after a larger part has been removed ▷ *v* **3** baffle **4** walk with heavy steps
▶ **stumpy** *adj* short and stubby
stun Ⓣ *v* **stunning, stunned 1** knock senseless **2** shock or overwhelm
▶ **stunning** *adj* very attractive or impressive
stung *v* past of **sting**
stunk *v* a past of **stink**
stunt[1] *v* prevent or impede the growth of
stunted *adj*
stunt[2] Ⓣ *n* **1** acrobatic or dangerous action **2** anything spectacular done to gain publicity
stupefy Ⓣ *v* **-fying, -fied 1** make insensitive or lethargic **2** astound **stupefaction** *n*
stupendous Ⓣ *adj* **1** astonishing **2** huge
stupendously *adv*
stupid Ⓣ *adj* **1** lacking intelligence **2** silly **3** in a stupor **stupidity** *n* **stupidly** *adv*
stupor Ⓣ *n* dazed or unconscious state
sturdy Ⓣ *adj* **-dier, -diest 1** healthy and robust **2** strongly built **sturdily** *adv*
sturdiness *n*
sturgeon *n* fish from which caviar is obtained
stutter Ⓣ *v* **1** speak with repetition of initial consonants ▷ *n* **2** tendency to stutter
Stuyvesant *n* **Peter**. ?1610–72, Dutch colonial administrator of New Netherland (later New York) (1646–64)
sty[1] *n, pl* **sties** pen for pigs
sty[2], **stye** *n, pl* **sties, styes** inflammation at the base of an eyelash
style Ⓣ *n* **1** manner of writing, speaking, or doing something **2** shape or design **3** elegance, refinement **4** prevailing fashion ▷ *v* **5** shape or design **6** name or call
▶ **stylish** *adj* smart, elegant, and fashionable
stylishly *adv*
▶ **stylist** *n* **1** hairdresser **2** designer **3** person

THESAURUS

push, jam, squeeze, thrust, ram, cram • *He stuffed all the paper into a recycling box.* **5 = fill**, pack, load, cram • *He stood there, stuffing his mouth with popcorn.*
See also: **matter, stick**
stuffing *n* = **filling**, packing, wadding
stuffy *adj* **1 = staid**, formal, old-fashioned, dull, straitlaced • *his lack of stuffy formality* **2 = stifling**, close, heavy, stale, oppressive, muggy • *It was hot and stuffy in the classroom.*
stumble *v* **1 = trip**, fall, slip, reel, falter, stagger, lurch **2** (with *across* or *on* or *upon*) = **discover**, find, chance upon, come across
stump *v* = **baffle**, puzzle, confuse, mystify, bewilder, perplex, flummox, nonplus
stumpy *adj* = **stocky**, short, squat, dumpy, stubby, thickset
stun *v* = **overcome**, shock, confuse, overpower, astonish, stagger, astound, bewilder, confound, stupefy
stunned *See* **dazed, unconscious**
stunner *See* **beauty**
stunning *adj* = **wonderful**, cool (*informal*), beautiful, impressive, spectacular, sensational (*informal*), lovely, gorgeous, striking, marvelous, dazzling, phat (*slang*)
stunt *n* = **feat**, act, trick, exploit, deed
stunted *adj* = **undersized**, little, small, tiny, diminutive
stupefy *v* = **astound**, shock, stun, amaze, stagger, daze, dumbfound
stupendous *adj* **1 = wonderful**, amazing, sensational (*informal*), superb, breathtaking, marvellous, astounding, overwhelming, staggering **2 = huge**, vast, enormous, gigantic, mega (*slang*), colossal
stupid *adj* **1 = unintelligent**, thick, dim, moronic, obtuse, stunned (*Canad informal*), cretinous, imbecilic • *I'm not stupid, you know.* **2 = foolish**, absurd, crass, idiotic, inane, asinine, fatuous • *a stupid suggestion* OPPOSITE: smart **3 = dazed**, groggy, insensate, semiconscious, stunned, stupefied
See also: **mad, silly, slow, unwise**
stupidity *n* **1 = lack of intelligence**, thickness, slowness, brainlessness, denseness, dimness, dullness, imbecility, obtuseness • *I was astonished by his stupidity.* **2 = foolishness**, folly, absurdity, silliness, inanity • *the stupidity of their decision*
stupor *n* = **daze**, coma, unconsciousness, insensibility, stupefaction
sturdy *adj* **1 = substantial**, strong, solid, durable, stout, well-built • *The camera was mounted on a sturdy tripod.* OPPOSITE: fragile **2 = robust**, powerful, athletic, muscular, hardy, brawny, lusty
See also: **stocky, tough**
stutter *v* = **stammer**, stumble, falter, hesitate
style *n* **1 = manner**, way, approach, method, technique, mode • *a dictatorial management style* **2 = elegance**, taste, chic, flair, sophistication • *She has not lost*

DICTIONARY

who writes with great attention to style
▸ **stylistic** *adj* of literary or artistic style
▸ **stylize** *v* cause to conform to an established stylistic form
▸ **styling mousse** foamy substance applied to hair before styling to hold the style
stylus *n* needle-like device on a record player that rests in the groove of the record and picks up the sound signals
stymie *v* **-mieing, -mied** hinder or thwart
styptic *n, adj* (drug) used to stop bleeding
suave Ⓣ [**swahv**] *adj* smooth and sophisticated in manner **suavely** *adv* **suavity** *n*
sub *n* **1** submarine **2** subscription **3** substitute **4** *informal* advance payment of wages or salary ▷ *v* **subbing, subbed 5** act as a substitute **6** grant advance payment to
sub- *prefix* **1** *indicating* under or beneath: *submarine* **2** *indicating* subordinate: *sublieutenant* **3** *indicating* falling short of: *subnormal* **4** *indicating* forming a subdivision: *subheading*
subaltern *n* army officer below the rank of captain
subatomic *adj* of or being one of the particles which make up an atom
subcommittee *n* small committee formed from some members of a larger committee
subconscious Ⓣ *adj* **1** happening or existing without one's awareness ▷ *n* **2** *psychoanalysis* that part of the mind of which one is not aware but which can influence one's behaviour **subconsciously** *adv*
subcontinent *n* large land mass that is a distinct part of a continent
subcontract *n* **1** secondary contract by which the main contractor for a job puts work out to others ▷ *v* **2** put out (work) on a subcontract **subcontractor** *n*
subcutaneous [sub-cute-**ayn**-ee-uss] *adj* under the skin
subdivide *v* divide (a part of something) into smaller parts **subdivision** *n*
subdue Ⓣ *v* **-duing, -dued 1** overcome **2** make less intense
subeditor *n Brit* person who checks and edits text for a newspaper or magazine
subhuman *adj* less than human
subject Ⓣ *n* **1** person or thing being dealt with or studied **2** *grammar* word or phrase that represents the person or thing performing the action of the verb in a sentence **3** person under the rule of a monarch or government ▷ *adj* **4** being under the rule of a monarch or government ▷ *v* **5** (foll. by *to*) cause to undergo **subjection** *n*
▸ **subject to 1** liable to **2** conditional upon
▸ **subjective** *adj* based on personal feelings or prejudices **subjectively** *adv*
sub judice [sub **joo**-diss-ee] *adj Latin* under judicial consideration
subjugate Ⓣ *v* bring (a group of people) under one's control **subjugation** *n*
subjunctive *grammar* ▷ *n* **1** mood of verbs used when the content of the clause is doubted, supposed, or wished ▷ *adj* **2** in or of that mood
sublet *v* **-letting, -let** rent out (property rented from someone else)
sublieutenant *n* naval officer of the lowest rank
sublimate *v psychol* direct the energy of (a

THESAURUS

her grace and style. **3 = design**, cut, form, manner **4 = type**, kind, sort, category, variety, genre **5 = fashion**, trend, rage, mode, vogue **6 = luxury**, ease, comfort, affluence, elegance, grandeur ▸ *v* **7 = design**, cut, fashion, shape, arrange, adapt, tailor **8 = call**, term, name, label, dub, entitle, designate
See also: **language, polish**
stylish *adj* **= smart**, cool (*informal*), designer (*informal*), chic, trendy (*informal*), fashionable, dressy (*informal*), modish, phat (*slang*), voguish
suave *adj* **= smooth**, sophisticated, charming, polite, courteous, debonair, urbane
subconscious *adj* **= hidden**, inner, subliminal, intuitive, latent, repressed
subdue *v* **1 = overcome**, defeat, crush, overpower, quell, vanquish • *The government has not been able to subdue the rebels.* **2 = moderate**, soften, suppress, mellow, quieten down, tone down
subdued *adj* **1 = quiet**, serious, sad, dejected, downcast, chastened, crestfallen, down in the mouth **2 = soft**, quiet, subtle, muted, dim, hushed, toned down, unobtrusive
subject *n* **1 = topic**, point, issue, question, matter, object, theme • *They exchanged views on a wide range of subjects.* **2 = citizen**, national **3 = subordinate** ▸ *adj* **4 = subordinate**, satellite, dependent, inferior, obedient ▷ **subject to = liable to**, exposed to, in danger of, open to, prone to, susceptible to, vulnerable to; **= conditional on**, contingent on, dependent on ▸ *v* **5 = put through**, expose, submit • *She was subjected to constant interruptions.*
See also: **affair, business**
subjective *adj* **= personal**, biased, nonobjective, prejudiced
subjugate *v* **= conquer**, overcome, master, overpower, subdue, quell, suppress, vanquish, enslave

S

DICTIONARY

primitive impulse) into socially acceptable activities **sublimation** *n*
sublime ⓣ *adj* **1** of high moral, intellectual, or spiritual value **2** unparalleled, supreme ▷ *v* **3** *chem* change from a solid to a vapour without first melting **sublimely** *adv*
subliminal *adj* relating to mental processes of which the individual is not aware
sub-machine-gun *n* portable machine-gun with a short barrel
submarine *n* **1** vessel which can operate below the surface of the sea ▷ *adj* **2** below the surface of the sea
submerge ⓣ *v* put or go below the surface of water or other liquid **submersion** *n*
submit ⓣ *v* **-mitting, -mitted 1** surrender **2** be (voluntarily) subjected to a process or treatment **3** put forward for consideration
▶**submission** *n* **1** submitting **2** something submitted for consideration **3** state of being submissive
▶**submissive** *adj* meek and obedient
subnormal *adj* less than normal, esp. in intelligence
subordinate ⓣ *adj* **1** of lesser rank or importance ▷ *n* **2** subordinate person or thing ▷ *v* **3** make or treat as subordinate **subordination** *n*
suborn *v* bribe or incite (a person) to commit a wrongful act
subpoena [sub-**pee**-na] *n* **1** writ requiring a person to appear before a lawcourt ▷ *v* **2** summon (someone) with a subpoena
sub rosa [sub **rose**-a] *adv Latin* in secret
subscribe ⓣ *v* **1** pay (a subscription) **2** give support or approval (to) **subscriber** *n*
▶**subscription** *n* **1** payment for issues of a publication over a period **2** money contributed to a charity etc. **3** membership fees paid to a society
subscript *n, adj* (character) printed below the line
subsection *n* division of a section
subsequent ⓣ *adj* occurring after, succeeding **subsequently** *adv*
subservient ⓣ *adj* submissive, servile **subservience** *n*
subside ⓣ *v* **1** become less intense **2** sink to a lower level
▶**subsidence** *n* act or process of subsiding
subsidiary ⓣ *adj* **1** of lesser importance **2** subordinate ▷ *n, pl* **-aries 3** subsidiary person or thing
subsidize ⓣ *v* help financially
▶**subsidy** *n* financial aid
subsist *v* manage to live **subsistence** *n*
subsoil *n* earth just below the surface soil
subsonic *adj* moving at a speed less than that of sound
substance ⓣ *n* **1** solid, powder, liquid, or paste **2** physical composition of something **3** essential meaning of something **4** solid or

THESAURUS

sublime *adj* = **noble**, high, great, grand, elevated, lofty, glorious, exalted
submerge *v* = **immerse**, duck, flood, sink, plunge, dip, overwhelm, swamp, overflow, engulf, inundate, deluge
submission *n* **1** = **surrender**, assent, capitulation, giving in, yielding **2** = **presentation**, entry, handing in, tendering **3** = **meekness**, resignation, compliance, deference, obedience, passivity, docility
submissive *adj* = **meek**, passive, compliant, amenable, obedient, docile, accommodating, acquiescent, pliant, tractable, unresisting, yielding
submit *v* **1** = **surrender**, agree, comply, yield, bow, capitulate, give in • *I submitted to their requests*. OPPOSITE: resist **2** = **present**, propose, table, tender, hand in, put forward, send in • *The teachers submitted their reports to the principal*. OPPOSITE: withdraw
See also: **nominate, pose, subject**
subordinate *adj* **1** = **lesser**, lower, junior, subject, minor, secondary, dependent, inferior ▶*n* **2** = **inferior**, second, junior, assistant, aide, attendant
subordination *n* = **inferiority**, servitude, inferior status *or* secondary status, subjection
subscribe *v* **1** = **donate**, give, contribute **2** = **support**, endorse, advocate
subscription *n* **1** = **membership fee**, annual payment, dues **2** = **donation**, gift, contribution
subsequent *adj* = **following**, after, later, successive, ensuing, succeeding
subsequently *adv* = **later**, afterwards
subservient *adj* = **servile**, abject, deferential, submissive, obsequious, slavish, sycophantic
subside *v* **1** = **decrease**, ease, diminish, wane, lessen, abate, ebb, slacken, quieten **2** = **sink**, drop, settle, collapse, lower, cave in
subsidence *n* **1** = **sinking**, settling **2** = **decrease**, abatement, easing off, lessening, slackening
subsidiary *adj* = **lesser**, minor, secondary, subordinate, supplementary, auxiliary, ancillary
subsidize *v* = **fund**, support, finance, promote, sponsor
subsidy *n* = **aid**, help, support, grant, assistance, allowance
substance *n* **1** = **material**, stuff, element, fabric • *Poisonous substances should be labelled as such*. **2** = **meaning**, import, significance,

S

DICTIONARY

meaningful quality **5** wealth
▶ **substantial** *adj* **1** of considerable size or value **2** (of food or a meal) sufficient and nourishing **3** solid or strong **4** real **substantially** *adv*
▶ **substantiate** *v* support (a story) with evidence **substantiation** *n*
▶ **substantive** *adj* **1** of or being the essential element of a thing ▷ *n* **2** noun
substitute Ⓣ *v* **1** take the place of or put in place of another ▷ *n* **2** person or thing taking the place of another **substitution** *n*
subsume *v* incorporate (an idea, case, etc.) under a comprehensive classification
subterfuge Ⓣ *n* trick used to achieve an objective
subterranean *adj* underground
subtitle *n* **1** secondary title of a book **subtitles 2** printed translation at the bottom of the picture in a film with foreign dialogue ▷ *v* **3** provide with a subtitle or subtitles
subtle Ⓣ *adj* **1** not immediately obvious **2** having or requiring ingenuity **subtly** *adv* **subtlety** *n*
subtract Ⓣ *v* take (one number or quantity) from another **subtraction** *n*
subtropical *adj* of the regions bordering on the tropics
suburb *n* residential area on the outskirts of a city
▶ **suburban** *adj* **1** of or inhabiting a suburb **2** narrow or unadventurous in outlook
▶ **suburbia** *n* suburbs and their inhabitants
subvention *n* subsidy
subvert Ⓣ *v* overthrow the authority of **subversion** *n* **subversive** *adj*
subway *n* **1** passage under a road or railway **2** electric passenger railway operated in underground tunnels
succeed Ⓣ *v* **1** accomplish an aim **2** turn out satisfactorily **3** come next in order after (something) **4** take over a position from (someone)
▶ **success** *n* **1** favourable outcome of an attempt **2** attainment of wealth, fame, or position **3** successful person or thing
▶ **successful** *adj* having success **successfully** *adv*
▶ **succession** *n* **1** series of people or things following one another in order **2** act or right by which one person succeeds another in a position
▶ **successive** *adj* consecutive **successively** *adv*
▶ **successor** *n* person who succeeds someone in a position

THESAURUS

essence, gist, main point **3 = reality**, actuality, concreteness **4 = wealth**, property, estate, means, assets, resources
See also: **matter**
substantial *adj* = **big**, large, important, significant, considerable, sizable *or* sizeable, ample, supersize
substantiate *v* = **support**, confirm, prove, establish, verify, authenticate
substitute *v* **1 = replace**, trade, exchange, switch, swap, interchange • *You can substitute honey for the sugar.* ▶ *n* **2 = replacement**, deputy, representative, makeshift, proxy, surrogate, locum, locum tenens • *an artificial substitute for silk* **3 = replacement**, second, reserve, alternative, proxy, surrogate, fall-back
See also: **change**
substitution *n* = **replacement**, change, trade, exchange, switch, swap
subterfuge *n* = **trick**, dodge, ploy, deception, ruse, manoeuvre, stratagem
subtle *adj* **1 = sophisticated**, delicate, refined **2 = faint**, slight, delicate, implied, understated **3 = crafty**, wily, shrewd, ingenious, sly, cunning, devious, artful
subtlety *n* **1 = sophistication**, delicacy, refinement **2 = cunning**, ingenuity, artfulness, cleverness, craftiness, deviousness, slyness, wiliness
subtract *v* = **take away**, deduct, take from • *If you subtract 3 from 5 you get 2.* OPPOSITE: add
subversive *adj* **1 = seditious**, riotous, treasonous ▶ *n* **2 = dissident**, terrorist, traitor, saboteur, fifth columnist
subvert *v* = **overturn**, undermine, sabotage
succeed *v* **1 = be successful**, work, triumph, thrive, flourish, prosper, do well, make it (*informal*) • *To succeed, you must learn to overcome obstacles.* OPPOSITE: fail **2 = take over from**, replace • *She is almost certain to succeed me as president.* **3 = follow**, result, ensue, come next ▷ **succeed in** *See* **manage**
See also: **pass, win**
succeeding *See* **next**
success *n* **1 = prosperity**, victory, celebrity, fame, triumph, wealth, eminence • *Do you believe that work is the key to success?* OPPOSITE: failure **2 = hit**, star, winner, celebrity, triumph, sensation • *Everyone who knows her says she will be a huge success.* OPPOSITE: failure
See also: **win**
successful *adj* = **thriving**, top, lucrative, profitable, rewarding, flourishing • *My mom is a highly successful artist.*
successfully *adv* = **well**, favourably, victoriously, with flying colours
succession *n* **1 = series**, run, order, train, course, chain, cycle, sequence, progression **2 = taking over**, assumption, inheritance, accession

S

DICTIONARY

succinct ⓣ *adj* brief and clear **succinctly** *adv*
succour ⓣ *v, n* help in distress
succulent ⓣ *adj* **1** juicy and delicious **2** (of a plant) having thick fleshy leaves ▷ *n* **3** succulent plant **succulence** *n*
succumb ⓣ *v* (foll. by *to*) **1** give way (to something overpowering) **2** die of (an illness)
such *adj* **1** of the kind specified **2** so great, so much ▷ *pron* **3** such things
▶ **such-and-such** *adj* specific, but not known or named
▶ **suchlike** *adj informal* of the kind specified
suck *v* **1** draw (liquid or air) into the mouth **2** take (something) into the mouth and moisten, dissolve, or roll it around with the tongue **3** (foll. by *in*) draw in by irresistible force ▷ *n* **4** sucking
▶ **suck it up** *informal* face up to something unpleasant
▶ **sucker** *n* **1** *slang* person who is easily deceived or swindled **2** organ or device which adheres by suction **3** shoot coming from a plant's root or the base of its main stem
▶ **suck up to** *v informal* flatter (someone) for one's own profit
suckle *v* feed at the breast
▶ **suckling** *n* unweaned baby or young animal
Sucre *n* **Antonio José de.** 1795–1830, South American liberator, born in Venezuela, who assisted Bolivar in the colonial revolt against Spain; first president of Bolivia (1826–28)
sucrose [**soo**-kroze] *n* chemical name for sugar
suction *n* **1** sucking **2** force produced by drawing air out of a space to make a vacuum that will suck in a substance from another space
sudden ⓣ *adj* **1** done or occurring quickly and unexpectedly ▷ *n* **2 all of a sudden** quickly and unexpectedly **suddenly** *adv* **suddenness** *n*
▶ **sudden death** *sports* period of extra time in which the first competitor to score wins
sudorific [syoo-dor-**if**-ik] *n, adj* (drug) causing sweating
suds *pl n* froth of soap and water, lather
sue ⓣ *v* **suing, sued** start legal proceedings against
suede *n* leather with a velvety finish on one side
suet *n* hard fat obtained from sheep and cattle, used in cooking
suffer ⓣ *v* **1** undergo or be subjected to **2** tolerate **sufferer** *n* **suffering** *n* **sufferance** *n*
▶ **on sufferance** tolerated with reluctance
suffice ⓣ [suf-**fice**] *v* be enough for a purpose
▶ **sufficiency** *n* adequate amount
▶ **sufficient** *adj* enough, adequate **sufficiently** *adv*
suffix *n* letter or letters added to the end of a word to form another word
suffocate ⓣ *v* **1** kill or be killed by deprivation of oxygen **2** feel or cause to feel discomfort from heat and lack of air **suffocation** *n*
suffragan *n* bishop appointed to assist an archbishop or another bishop
suffrage *n* vote or right of voting
▶ **suffragist** (**suffragette**) *n* one claiming a right of voting
suffuse *v* spread through or over (something) **suffusion** *n*
sugar *n* **1** sweet crystalline carbohydrate found in many plants and used to sweeten food and drinks ▷ *v* **2** sweeten or cover with sugar **sugary** *adj*

THESAURUS

successive *adj* = **consecutive**, following, in succession
successor *See* **replacement**
succinct *adj* = **brief**, compact, terse, concise, laconic, pithy
succour *n* **1** = **help**, aid, assistance ▶ *v* **2** = **help**, assist, aid
succulent *adj* = **juicy**, lush, moist, luscious
succumb *v* **1** = **surrender**, submit, yield, capitulate, give in **2** = **die**, fall
sucker *n* (*Slang*) = **fool**, victim, mug (*Brit slang*), dupe, pushover (*slang*), dork (*slang*), schmuck (*slang*)
sudden *adj* = **abrupt**, quick, unexpected, swift, hasty • *a sudden cry* OPPOSITE: gradual
See also: **sharp**
suddenly *adv* = **abruptly**, unexpectedly, all of a sudden
sue *v* (*Law*) = **take (someone) to court**, charge, prosecute, indict, summon
suffer *v* **1** = **undergo**, bear, experience, endure, sustain, go through • *I knew he was suffering some discomfort.* **2** = **tolerate**, put up with (*informal*)
See also: **feel, receive**
sufferer *See* **patient**
suffering *n* = **pain**, ordeal, distress, misery, hardship, discomfort, anguish, agony, torment
suffice *v* = **be enough**, do, serve, be adequate, be sufficient, meet requirements, pass muster
sufficient *adj* = **enough**, adequate, ample • *He had sufficient time to prepare his speech.* OPPOSITE: insufficient
See also: **satisfactory**
suffocate *v* = **choke**, stifle, smother, asphyxiate
sugary *See* **sweet**

DICTIONARY

▶ **sugar beet** beet cultivated for the sugar obtained from its roots
▶ **sugar bush** plantation of sugar maples
▶ **sugar cane** tropical grass cultivated for the sugar obtained from its canes
▶ **sugar daddy** *slang* elderly man who gives a young woman money and gifts in return for sexual favours
▶ **sugar maple** large N American maple tree yielding sweet sap from which sugar and syrup are made
▶ **sugar off** *v* reduce maple sap to syrup by boiling
suggest Ⓣ *v* **1** put forward (an idea) for consideration **2** bring to mind by the association of ideas **3** give a hint of
▶ **suggestible** *adj* easily influenced
▶ **suggestion** *n* **1** suggesting **2** thing suggested **3** hint or indication
▶ **suggestive** *adj* **1** suggesting something indecent **2** conveying a hint (of) **suggestively** *adv*
Suharto *n* **T. N. J.** 1921–2008, Indonesian general and statesman; president (1968–98)
suicide *n* **1** killing oneself intentionally **2** person who kills himself intentionally **3** self-inflicted ruin of one's own prospects or interests
▶ **suicidal** *adj* liable to commit suicide **suicidally** *adv*
▶ **suicide bomber** terrorist who carries out a bomb attack, knowing he or she will be killed in the explosion
▶ **suicide squeeze** *baseball* play in which a runner on third base runs for home as the ball is pitched
suit Ⓣ *n* **1** set of clothes designed to be worn together **2** outfit worn for a specific purpose **3** one of the four sets into which a pack of cards is divided **4** lawsuit ▷ *v* **5** be appropriate for **6** be acceptable to
▶ **suitable** *adj* appropriate or proper **suitably** *adv* **suitability** *n*
▶ **suitcase** *n* portable travelling case for clothing
suite Ⓣ *n* **1** set of connected rooms in a hotel **2** matching set of furniture **3** set of musical pieces in the same key
suitor Ⓣ *n old-fashioned* man who is courting a woman
Sukarno, Soekarno *n* **Achmed.** 1901–70, Indonesian statesman; first president of the Republic of Indonesia (1945–67)
sulfate *n* salt or ester of sulfuric acid
sulfide *n* compound of sulfur with another element
sulfite *n* salt or ester of sulfurous acid
sulfonamide [sulf-**on**-a-mide] *n* any of a class of drugs that prevent the growth of bacteria
sulfur *n* pale yellow nonmetallic element
▶ **sulfuric** *or* **sulfurous** *adj* of or containing sulfur
sulk Ⓣ *v* **1** be silent and sullen because of resentment or bad temper ▷ *n* **2** resentful or sullen mood **sulky** *adj* **sulkily** *adv* **sulkiness** *n*
sullen Ⓣ *adj* **1** unwilling to talk or be sociable **2** dark and dismal **sullenly** *adv* **sullenness** *n*
Sullivan *n* Sir **Arthur** (**Seymour**). 1842–1900, English composer who wrote operettas, such as *H.M.S. Pinafore* (1878) and *The Mikado* (1885), with W. S. Gilbert as librettist
sully Ⓣ *v* **-lying, -lied 1** make dirty **2** ruin (someone's reputation)
sultan *n* sovereign of a Muslim country
▶ **sultana** *n* **1** kind of raisin **2** sultan's wife, mother, or daughter

THESAURUS

suggest *v* **1 = recommend**, propose, advise, advocate • *My cousin suggested going out for dinner.* **2 = hint**, indicate, intimate, imply, insinuate • *Reports suggested the factory would close.* **3 = bring to mind**, evoke
See also: **nominate, raise, vote**
suggestion *n* **1 = recommendation**, plan, proposal, proposition • *practical suggestions* **2 = hint**, trace, indication, insinuation, intimation • *a suggestion of dishonesty*
See also: **advice, idea**
suggestive *adj* **= smutty**, blue, rude, provocative, racy, bawdy, indelicate, ribald, risqué
suit *v* **1 = be acceptable to**, do, please, satisfy • *They will move only if it suits them.* **2 = match**, agree, correspond, conform to, go with • *The battery can be shaped to suit any device.* **3 = outfit**, dress, habit, costume, ensemble, clothing **4 = lawsuit**, case, cause, trial, action, prosecution, proceeding
See also: **blend, flatter**
suitability *n* **= appropriateness**, fitness, aptness, rightness
suitable *adj* **= appropriate**, right, fit, proper, acceptable, fitting, satisfactory, apt • *Conditions were not suitable for the vegetation to flourish.* OPPOSITE: unsuitable
See also: **favourable**
suite *n* **= rooms**, apartment
suitor *n* (*Old-fashioned*) **= admirer**, beau (*old-fashioned*), young man
sulk *v* **= be sullen**, pout, be in a huff
sulky *adj* **= huffy**, moody, sullen, resentful, petulant • *a sulky adolescent*
See also: **grumpy**
sullen *adj* **= morose**, cross, sour, moody, surly, dour, glowering, unsociable
sully *v* **= defile**, disgrace, stain, tarnish,

S

DICTIONARY

▶ **sultanate** *n* territory of a sultan
sultry Ⓣ *adj* **-trier, -triest 1** (of weather or climate) hot and humid **2** passionate, sensual
sum Ⓣ *n* **1** result of addition, total **2** problem in arithmetic **3** quantity of money
▶ **sum total** complete or final total
▶ **sum up** *v* **summing, summed 1** summarize **2** form a quick opinion of
summary Ⓣ *n, pl* **-ries 1** brief account giving the main points of something ▷ *adj* **2** done quickly, without formalities **summarily** *adv*
▶ **summarize** *v* make or be a summary of (something)
▶ **summation** *n* **1** summary **2** adding up
summer *n* warmest season of the year, between spring and fall **summery** *adj*
▶ **summertime** *n* period or season of summer
summit Ⓣ *n* **1** highest point **2** top of a mountain or hill **3** conference between heads of state
summon Ⓣ *v* **1** order (someone) to come **2** send for (someone) to appear in court **3** call upon (someone) to do something **4** gather (one's courage, strength, etc.)
▶ **summons** *n* **1** command summoning someone **2** order requiring someone to appear in court ▷ *v* **3** order (someone) to appear in court
sumo *n* Japanese style of wrestling
sump *n* **1** receptacle in an internal-combustion engine into which oil can drain **2** hollow into which liquid drains
sumptuous Ⓣ *adj* lavish, magnificent **sumptuously** *adv* **sumptuousness** *n*
sun *n* **1** star around which the earth and other planets revolve **2** any star around which planets revolve **3** heat and light from the sun ▷ *v* **sunning, sunned 4** expose (oneself) to the sun's rays **sunless** *adj*
▶ **sunny** *adj* **1** full of or exposed to sunlight **2** cheerful
▶ **sunbathe** *v* lie in the sunshine in order to get a suntan
▶ **sunbeam** *n* ray of sun
▶ **sunburn** *n* painful reddening of the skin caused by overexposure to the sun **sunburnt** *or* **sunburned** *adj*
▶ **sundial** *n* device showing the time by means of a pointer that casts a shadow on a marked dial
▶ **sundown** *n* sunset
▶ **sunflower** *n* tall plant with large golden flowers
▶ **sunrise** *n* **1** daily appearance of the sun above the horizon **2** time of this
▶ **sunset** *n* **1** daily disappearance of the sun below the horizon **2** time of this
▶ **sunshine** *n* light and warmth from the sun
▶ **sunspot** *n* dark patch appearing temporarily on the sun's surface
▶ **sunstroke** *n* illness caused by prolonged exposure to intensely hot sunlight
▶ **suntan** *n* browning of the skin caused by exposure to the sun
▶ **sun-up** *n* sunrise
sundae *n* ice cream topped with fruit etc.
Sunday *n* first day of the week and the Christian day of worship
▶ **Sunday school** school for teaching children about Christianity
sunder *v* break or tear apart
sundry Ⓣ *adj* several, various
▶ **sundries** *pl n* miscellaneous unspecified items
▶ **all and sundry** everybody
sung *v* past participle of **sing**
sunk, sunken *v* past participle of **sink**
Sun Yat-sen *n* 1866–1925, Chinese statesman, who was instrumental in the overthrow of the Manchu dynasty and was the first president of the Republic of China (1911). He reorganized the Kuomintang
sup *v* **supping, supped 1** take (liquid) by

S

THESAURUS

besmirch, dishonour, smirch
sultry *adj* **1 = humid**, close, hot, sticky, oppressive, muggy, stifling **2 = seductive**, sexy (*informal*), provocative, sensual
sum *n* **= total**, amount, whole, tally, aggregate ▶ *adjective* ▷ **sum total** *See* **whole** ▶ *v* ▷ **sum up = summarize**, recapitulate • *He summed up his weekend in one word: "Disastrous."*
summarize *v* **= sum up**, epitomize, encapsulate, condense, abridge, précis
summary *n* **= synopsis**, review, outline, rundown, summation • *a summary of the report*
summit *n* **= peak**, top, head, height, pinnacle, apex, zenith, acme
summon *v* **1 = send for**, call, bid, invite **2** (often with *up*) **= gather**, muster, draw on
sumptuous *adj* **= luxurious**, grand, lavish, gorgeous, superb, splendid, opulent
sumptuousness *See* **luxury**
sunburned *adj* **= tanned**, red, brown, burnt, peeling, bronzed
sundry *adj* **= various**, some, several, different, assorted, miscellaneous
sunken *adj* **1 = hollow**, drawn, haggard **2 = lowered**, submerged, buried, recessed
sunny *adj* **1 = bright**, clear, fine, radiant, sunlit, summery, unclouded **2 = cheerful**, happy, buoyant, joyful, light-hearted, cheery
sunrise *n* **= dawn**, daybreak, break of day, cockcrow

DICTIONARY

sips **2** *obsolete* take supper
super Ⓣ *adj informal* excellent
super- *prefix* **1** *indicating* above or over: *superimpose* **2** *indicating* outstanding: *supergroup* **3** *indicating* of greater size or extent: *supermarket*
superannuation *n* **1** regular payment by an employee into a pension fund **2** pension paid from this
▸ **superannuated** *adj* discharged with a pension, owing to old age or illness
superb Ⓣ *adj* excellent, impressive, or splendid **superbly** *adv*
superbug *n informal* bacterium resistant to antibiotics
supercharged *adj* (of an engine) having a supercharger
▸ **supercharger** *n* device that increases the power of an internal-combustion engine by forcing extra air into it
supercilious Ⓣ *adj* showing arrogant pride or scorn **superciliousness** *n*
superconductor *n* substance which has almost no electrical resistance at very low temperatures **superconductivity** *n*
superficial Ⓣ *adj* **1** of or on the surface **2** not careful or thorough **3** (of a person) without depth of character, shallow **superficially** *adv* **superficiality** *n*
superfluous Ⓣ [soo-**per**-flew-uss] *adj* more than is needed **superfluity** *n*
supergrass *n* person who acts as a police informer on a large scale
superhuman Ⓣ *adj* beyond normal human ability or experience
superimpose *v* place (something) on or over something else
superintend *v* supervise (a person or activity) **superintendence** *n*
▸ **superintendent** *n* **1** senior police officer **2** supervisor
superior Ⓣ *adj* **1** greater in quality, quantity, or merit **2** higher in position or rank **3** believing oneself to be better than others ▷ *n* **4** person of greater rank or status **superiority** *n*
superlative Ⓣ [soo-**per**-lat-iv] *adj* **1** of outstanding quality **2** *grammar* denoting the form of an adjective or adverb indicating *most* ▷ *n* **3** *grammar* superlative form of a word
superman *n* man of apparently superhuman powers
supermarket Ⓣ *n* large self-service store selling food and household goods
supermodel *n* famous and highly-paid fashion model
supernatural Ⓣ *adj* **1** of or relating to things beyond the laws of nature ▷ *n* **2 the supernatural** supernatural forces, occurrences, and beings collectively
supernova *n, pl* **-vae, -vas** star that explodes and briefly becomes exceptionally bright
supernumerary *adj* **1** exceeding the required or regular number ▷ *n, pl* **-ries** **2** supernumerary person or thing

THESAURUS

sunset *n* = **nightfall**, dusk, close of day *or* close of the day, eventide
super *adj* (*Informal*) = **excellent**, sensational (*informal*), outstanding, glorious, magnificent, marvellous, wonderful, terrific (*informal*), superb
superb *adj* = **splendid**, excellent, wonderful, superior, outstanding, magnificent, breathtaking, marvellous, exquisite, unrivalled • *With superb skill, she managed to make a perfect landing.*
See also: **brilliant, first-rate**
supercilious *adj* = **scornful**, lofty, arrogant, contemptuous, disdainful, haughty, snooty (*informal*), stuck-up (*informal*)
superficial *adj* **1** = **hasty**, casual, hurried, sketchy, desultory, cursory, perfunctory, slapdash **2** = **shallow**, silly, frivolous, trivial, empty-headed **3** = **surface**, external, slight, exterior, on the surface
superfluous *adj* = **excess**, extra, surplus, spare, redundant, left over, remaining, supernumerary
superhuman *adj* **1** = **heroic**, phenomenal, prodigious **2** = **supernatural**, paranormal
superintendence *n* = **supervision**, government, charge, control, management, direction
superintendent *n* = **supervisor**, director, chief, manager, governor, inspector, controller, overseer
superior *adj* **1** = **better**, choice, exceptional, deluxe, first-rate, unrivalled, surpassing • *a superior brand of ice cream* OPPOSITE: inferior **2** = **supercilious**, lofty, condescending, disdainful, haughty, patronizing, snobbish, stuck-up (*informal*) • *He stood there looking superior.* **3** = **first-class**, choice, excellent, exclusive, exceptional, deluxe, first-rate ▸ *n* **4** = **boss** (*informal*), senior, manager, supervisor • *his immediate superior* OPPOSITE: inferior
See also: **prime, select, smug, superb**
superiority *n* = **supremacy**, lead, advantage, excellence, ascendancy, predominance
superlative *adj* = **outstanding**, excellent, supreme, unparalleled, unsurpassed, unrivalled
supermarket *See* **store**
supernatural *adj* = **paranormal**, miraculous, hidden, psychic, ghostly,

S

DICTIONARY

superphosphate *n* chemical fertilizer containing phosphates
superpower *n* extremely powerful nation
superscript *adj* **1** (of a character) printed or written above the line ▷ *n* **2** superscript character
supersede Ⓣ *v* replace, supplant
supersonic *adj* of or travelling at a speed greater than the speed of sound
superstar Ⓣ *n* very famous entertainer or sportsperson
superstition *n* **1** belief in omens, ghosts, etc. **2** idea or practice based on this **superstitious** *adj*
superstore *n* large supermarket
superstructure *n* **1** structure erected on something else **2** part of a ship above the main deck
supertanker *n* large fast tanker
supertax *n* extra tax on incomes above a certain level
supervene *v* occur as an unexpected development **supervention** *n*
supervise Ⓣ *v* watch over to direct or check **supervision** *n* **supervisor** *n* **supervisory** *adj*
supine [**soo**-pine] *adj* lying flat on one's back
supper *n* light evening meal
Suppiluliumas I *n* king of the Hittites (?1375–?1335 BC); founder of the Hittite empire
supplant Ⓣ *v* take the place of, oust
supple Ⓣ *adj* **1** (of a person) moving and bending easily and gracefully **2** bending easily without damage **suppleness** *n* **supply** *adv*
supplement Ⓣ *n* **1** thing added to complete something or make up for a lack **2** magazine inserted into a newspaper **3** section added to a publication to supply further information ▷ *v* **4** provide or be a supplement to (something) **supplementary** *adj*
supplication Ⓣ *n* humble request ▶ **supplicant** *n* person who makes a humble request
supply Ⓣ *v* **-plying, -plied 1** provide with something required **2** make available ▷ *n, pl* **-plies 3** supplying **4** amount available **5** *economics* willingness and ability to provide goods and services **supplies 6** food or equipment **supplier** *n*
support Ⓣ *v* **1** bear the weight of **2** provide the necessities of life for **3** give practical or emotional help to **4** take an active interest in (a sports team, political principle, etc.) **5** help to prove (a theory etc.) **6** speak in favour of ▷ *n* **7** supporting **8** means of support **supportive** *adj*
▶ **supporter** *n* person who supports a team, principle, etc.

THESAURUS

uncanny, occult, mystic, spectral, unearthly
supersede *v* = **replace**, oust, displace, supplant, usurp, take the place of
superstar *See* **celebrity**
supervise *v* = **oversee**, run, manage, direct, be in charge of, have charge of, keep an eye on • *He supervised more than 400 volunteers.*
See also: **administer, command, guard, handle, lead**
supervision *n* = **superintendence**, charge, control, care, management, direction, guidance
supervisor *n* = **boss** (*informal*), chief, manager, inspector, administrator, foreman, overseer
supplant *v* = **replace**, oust, displace, supersede, take the place of
supple *adj* = **flexible**, limber, lissom *or* lissome, lithe, pliable, pliant
supplement *v* **1** = **add to**, reinforce, complement, augment, top up • *I suggest supplementing your diet with vitamin A.* ▶ *n* **2** = **addition**, extra, complement, appendix, sidebar • *a supplement to their basic pension*
See also: **add**
supplementary *adj* = **additional**, extra, secondary, add-on, auxiliary, ancillary
supplication *n* = **plea**, appeal, request, prayer, petition, entreaty
supplies *pl n* = **provisions**, equipment, rations, stores • *I had only a litre of water in my emergency supplies.*
supply *v* **1** = **provide**, give, equip, furnish • *an agreement not to supply chemical weapons* ▶ *n* **2** = **store**, fund, stock, reserve, stockpile, cache, hoard • *a plentiful supply of vegetables*
See also: **issue**
support *v* **1** = **back**, second, defend, champion, promote, uphold, side with, make a pitch for (*slang*) • *We supported her political campaign.* OPPOSITE: oppose **2** = **help**, encourage • *Try to support each other when one of you is feeling down.* **3** = **hold up**, brace, bolster, reinforce, buttress, prop up, shore up • *Thick wooden posts support the deck.* **4** = **provide for**, keep, fund, finance, maintain, sustain, look after **5** = **bear out**, confirm, verify, substantiate, corroborate ▶ *n* **6** = **prop**, post, brace, foundation, pillar, abutment, stanchion • *the metal supports that hold up the canvas* **7** = **help**, aid, assistance, backing, loyalty, encouragement, endorsation (*Canad*) **8** = **supporter**, second, prop, backer, mainstay, tower of strength **9** = **upkeep**, keep, maintenance, sustenance, subsistence
See also: **advocate, bear, blessing, comfort, favour, sanction, steady, strengthen**
supporter *n* = **follower**, fan, champion,

S

DICTIONARY

suppose ⓣ *v* **1** presume to be true **2** consider as a proposal for the sake of discussion
▸ **supposed** *adj* **1** presumed to be true without proof **2** doubtful **supposedly** *adv*
▸ **supposed to** **1** expected or required to: *you were supposed to phone me* **2** permitted to: *we're not supposed to swim here*
▸ **supposition** *n* **1** supposing **2** something supposed
suppository *n, pl* **-ries** solid medication inserted into the rectum or vagina and left to melt
suppress ⓣ *v* **1** put an end to **2** restrain (an emotion or response) **3** prevent publication of (information) **suppression** *n*
suppurate *v* (of a wound etc.) produce pus **suppuration** *n*
supreme ⓣ *adj* highest in authority, rank, or degree
▸ **supremely** *adv* extremely
▸ **supremacy** *n* **1** supreme power **2** state of being supreme
▸ **supremo** *n informal* person in overall authority
surcharge *n* additional charge
surd *n math* number that cannot be expressed in whole numbers
sure ⓣ *adj* **1** free from uncertainty or doubt **2** reliable **3** inevitable ▷ *adv, interj* **4** *informal* certainly
▸ **surely** *adv* it must be true that
▸ **sure-footed** *adj* unlikely to slip or stumble
surety *n, pl* **-ties** person who takes responsibility, or thing given as a guarantee, for the fulfilment of another's obligation
surf *n* **1** foam caused by waves breaking on the shore ▷ *v* **2** take part in surfing **3** move quickly through a medium such as the internet
▸ **surfing** *n* sport of riding towards the shore on a surfboard on the crest of a wave **surfer** *n*
▸ **surfboard** *n* board used in surfing
surface ⓣ *n* **1** outside or top of an object **2** material covering the surface of an object **3** superficial appearance ▷ *v* **4** rise to the surface **5** put a surface on
surfeit ⓣ *n* excessive amount
surge ⓣ *n* **1** sudden powerful increase **2** strong rolling movement of the sea ▷ *v* **3** increase suddenly **4** move forward strongly
surgeon *n* doctor who specializes in surgery
▸ **surgery** *n* **1** treatment in which the patient's body is cut open in order to treat the affected part **2** *Brit* place where, or time when, a doctor, dentist, MP, etc. can be consulted **surgical** *adj* **surgically** *adv*

THESAURUS

advocate, ally, sponsor, adherent • *He is a strong supporter of the plan.*
See also: **defender, helper**
supportive *adj* = **helpful**, understanding, sympathetic, encouraging
suppose *v* **1** = **think**, expect, believe, guess, assume, imagine, presume • *Where do you suppose he has gone?* **2** = **imagine**, consider, pretend, hypothesize, conjecture, postulate
See also: **conclude, figure, reckon, suspect**
supposed *adj* **1** = **expected**, required, meant, obliged • *You're not supposed to leave the children on their own.* **2** = **assumed**, alleged, presumed, reputed, believed, meant, rumoured • *What is his son supposed to have said?*
supposedly *adv* = **presumably**, allegedly, theoretically, hypothetically, ostensibly
supposition *n* = **guess**, speculation, theory, hypothesis, presumption, conjecture, surmise
suppress *v* **1** = **stop**, crush, quash, quell, stamp out • *international attempts to suppress drug trafficking* **2** = **restrain**, contain, curb, stifle, conceal, smother, repress • *She barely suppressed a gasp.*
See also: **silence**
suppressed *See* **pent-up**
suppression *n* = **elimination**, check, crushing, quashing, smothering
supremacy *n* = **domination**, sovereignty, sway, mastery, primacy, predominance, supreme power
supreme *adj* = **highest**, top, chief, principal, ultimate, foremost, pre-eminent, paramount, greatest, leading • *They conspired to seize supreme power.*
See also: **absolute, ideal, incomparable**
supremo *n* = **head**, leader, director, commander, governor, boss (*informal*), master, principal, ruler, alpha male
sure *adj* **1** = **certain**, clear, positive, convinced, definite, satisfied • *She was no longer sure how she felt about him.* OPPOSITE: unsure **2** = **reliable**, definite, dependable, trustworthy, undeniable, foolproof, infallible • *a sure sign that something is wrong* **3** = **inevitable**, bound, assured, inescapable, guaranteed
See also: **confident, yes**
surely *adv* = **undoubtedly**, certainly, definitely, unquestionably, doubtlessly, indubitably, without doubt
surface *n* **1** = **outside**, top, face, side, exterior, covering, veneer ▸ *v* **2** = **appear**, emerge, arise, materialize, transpire, come to light, come up, crop up (*informal*)
surfeit *n* = **excess**, glut, plethora, superfluity
surge *n* **1** = **rush**, flood, flow, outpouring, gush **2** = **wave**, swell, roller, billow ▸ *v* **3** = **rush**, rise, roll, gush, heave

DICTIONARY

surly Ⓣ *adj* **-lier, -liest** ill-tempered and rude **surliness** *n*
surmise Ⓣ *v, n* guess, conjecture
surmount Ⓣ *v* **1** overcome (a problem) **2** be on top of (something) **surmountable** *adj*
surname *n* family name
surpass Ⓣ *v* be greater than or superior to
surplice *n* loose white robe worn by clergymen and choristers
surplus Ⓣ *n* amount left over in excess of what is required
surprise Ⓣ *n* **1** unexpected event **2** amazement and wonder ▷ *v* **3** cause to feel amazement or wonder **4** come upon, attack, or catch suddenly and unexpectedly
▸ **take someone by surprise** catch someone unprepared
surrealism *n* movement in art and literature involving the combination of incongruous images, as in a dream **surreal** *adj* **surrealist** *n, adj* **surrealistic** *adj*
surrender Ⓣ *v* **1** give oneself up **2** give (something) up to another **3** yield (to a temptation or influence) ▷ *n* **4** surrendering
surreptitious Ⓣ *adj* done secretly or stealthily **surreptitiously** *adv*
surrogate Ⓣ *n* substitute
▸ **surrogate mother** woman who gives birth to a child on behalf of a couple who cannot have children
surround Ⓣ *v* **1** be, come, or place all around (a person or thing) ▷ *n* **2** border or edging
▸ **surroundings** *pl n* conditions, scenery, etc. around a person, place, or thing
surtax *n* extra tax on incomes above a certain level
Surtees *n* **John**. born 1934, British racing motorcyclist and motor-racing driver. He was motorcycling world champion (1956, 1958–60) and world champion motor-racing driver (1964), the only man to have been world champion in both sports
surveillance Ⓣ *n* close observation
survey Ⓣ *v* **1** view or consider in a general way **2** make a map of (an area) **3** inspect (a building) to assess its condition and value **4** find out the incomes, opinions, etc. of (a group of people) ▷ *n* **5** surveying **6** report produced by a survey **surveyor** *n*
survive Ⓣ *v* **1** continue to live or exist after (a difficult experience) **2** live after the death of (another) **survivor** *n*
▸ **survival** *n* **1** condition of having survived **2** thing that has survived from an earlier time

THESAURUS

surly *adj* = **ill-tempered**, cross, sullen, churlish, grouchy (*informal*), morose, sulky, uncivil, ungracious
surmise *v* **1** = **guess**, suppose, imagine, speculate, presume, conjecture ▸ *n* **2** = **guess**, speculation, assumption, presumption, conjecture, supposition
surmount *See* **overcome**
surpass *v* = **outdo**, beat, exceed, eclipse, outshine, excel, outstrip, transcend
surpassing *adj* = **supreme**, extraordinary, exceptional, outstanding, incomparable, unrivaled, matchless
surplus *n* **1** = **excess**, balance, remainder, residue, surfeit ▸ *adj* **2** = **excess**, extra, odd, spare, superfluous, remaining
surprise *n* **1** = **shock**, start, revelation, jolt, bombshell • *The resignation came as a complete surprise.* **2** = **amazement**, wonder, astonishment, incredulity • *an exclamation of surprise* ▸ *v* **3** = **amaze**, stun, astonish, stagger, astound, take aback • *I was surprised by the vehemence of his criticism.* **4** = **catch unawares** *or* **catch off-guard**, discover, startle, spring upon
surprised *adj* = **amazed**, speechless, astonished, taken by surprise, thunderstruck
surprising *adj* = **amazing**, unusual, remarkable, extraordinary, unexpected, incredible, astonishing, staggering
surrender *v* **1** = **give in**, submit, yield, succumb, capitulate • *We'll never surrender to terrorists.* **2** = **give up**, yield, renounce, relinquish, cede • *We have surrendered our political authority for economic gain.* ▸ *n* **3** = **submission**, capitulation • *unconditional surrender*
See also: **sacrifice**
surreptitious *adj* = **secret**, covert, sly, stealthy, furtive, underhand
surrogate *n* = **substitute**, representative, proxy, stand-in
surround *v* = **enclose**, encompass, envelop, encircle, hem in • *He was surrounded by bodyguards.*
surrounded by *See* **among**
surroundings *pl n* = **environment**, neighbourhood, location, background, setting • *He felt a longing for familiar surroundings.*
See also: **scenery**
surveillance *n* = **observation**, watch, inspection, scrutiny, supervision
survey *v* **1** = **look over**, view, examine, scan, observe, inspect, contemplate, scrutinize **2** = **assess**, plan, measure, estimate, plot, appraise, size up ▸ *n* **3** = **examination**, inspection, scrutiny **4** = **study**, review, inquiry
survive *v* = **endure**, last, live, outlive, pull through • *companies that survived after the recession*
See also: **continue, remain**

S

DICTIONARY

susceptible ❶ *adj* liable to be influenced or affected by **susceptibility** *n*
suspect ❶ *v* **1** believe (someone) to be guilty without having any proof **2** think (something) to be false or questionable **3** believe (something) to be the case ▷ *adj* **4** not to be trusted ▷ *n* **5** person who is suspected
suspend ❶ *v* **1** hang from a high place **2** cause to remain floating or hanging **3** cause to cease temporarily **4** remove (someone) temporarily from a job or team ▸ **suspenders** *pl n* **1** straps worn over the shoulders to hold up trousers **2** *Brit* straps for holding up stockings
suspense ❶ *n* state of uncertainty while awaiting news, an event, etc.
suspension ❶ *n* **1** suspending or being suspended **2** system of springs and shock absorbers supporting the body of a vehicle **3** mixture of fine particles of a solid in a fluid ▸ **suspension bridge** bridge hanging from cables attached to towers at each end
suspicion ❶ *n* **1** feeling of not trusting a person or thing **2** belief that something is true without definite proof **3** slight trace ▸ **suspicious** *adj* feeling or causing suspicion **suspiciously** *adv*
suss out *v slang* work out using one's intuition
sustain ❶ *v* **1** maintain or prolong **2** suffer (an injury or loss) **3** keep up the vitality or strength of **4** support ▸ **sustenance** *n* food
Sutherland *n* **1 Donald**. born 1935, Canadian film and TV actor. His films include *The Dirty Dozen* (1967), *M*A*S*H* (1970), *Don't Look Now* (1973), and *Cold Mountain* (2003) **2** Dame **Joan**, known as *La Stupenda*. 1926–2010, Australian operatic soprano **3 Keifer**, son of Donald Sutherland. born 1966, Canadian film and TV actor born in England, noted for his performance as Jack Bauer in the US TV drama 24 (from 2001)
suture [**soo**-cher] *n* stitch joining the edges of a wound
SUV sport utility vehicle
suzerain *n* state or sovereign with limited authority over another self-governing state **suzerainty** *n*
Suzuki *n* **David Takayoshi**. born 1936, Canadian scientist, environmentalist, and broadcaster, of Japanese ancestry. He has hosted a number of acclaimed television series on science including *A Planet for the Taking* (1985) and *The Secret of Life* (1993)
svelte *adj* attractively or gracefully slim
SW southwest(ern)
swab ❶ *n* **1** small piece of cotton batting used to apply medication, clean a wound, etc. ▷ *v* **swabbing, swabbed 2** clean (a wound) with a swab **3** clean (the deck of a ship) with a mop
swaddle *v* wrap (a baby) in swaddling clothes ▸ **swaddling clothes** long strips of cloth formerly wrapped round a newborn baby
swag *n* **1** *slang* stolen property **2** *Aust informal* bundle of belongings carried by a swagman ▸ **swagman** *n Aust* tramp who carries his belongings in a bundle on his back
swagger ❶ *v* **1** walk or behave arrogantly ▷ *n* **2** arrogant walk or manner
swain *n poetic* **1** suitor **2** country youth

THESAURUS

susceptible *adj* **1** (usually with *to*) = **liable**, subject, vulnerable, prone, given, inclined, disposed **2** = **responsive**, sensitive, receptive, impressionable, suggestible
suspect *v* **1** = **believe**, feel, suppose, guess • *I suspect they are secretly planning to raise taxes.* **2** = **distrust**, doubt, mistrust • *He suspected her motives.* ▸ *adj* **3** = **dubious**, questionable, doubtful, fishy (*informal*), shifty • *a rather suspect character*
See also: **imagine, question, suspicious**
suspend *v* **1** = **hang**, attach, dangle **2** = **postpone**, shelve, cease, interrupt, defer, discontinue, cut short, put off
suspense *n* = **uncertainty**, doubt, expectation, tension, anxiety, insecurity, apprehension, irresolution
suspension *n* = **postponement**, break, interruption, abeyance, breaking off, deferment, discontinuation
suspicion *n* **1** = **distrust**, doubt, skepticism, mistrust, misgiving • *I was regarded with suspicion.* **2** = **idea**, impression, hunch • *I have a strong suspicion they are lying.* **3** = **trace**, streak, touch, hint, suggestion, shade, tinge, soupçon (*French*)
suspicious *adj* **1** = **distrustful**, skeptical, wary, doubtful, apprehensive • *She was rightly suspicious of their motives.* **2** = **suspect**, funny, questionable, doubtful, dubious, shady, sketchy (*informal*), fishy (*informal*), shifty, hinky (*slang*) • *suspicious circumstances*
sustain *v* **1** = **maintain**, continue, prolong, keep up, protract **2** = **keep alive**, help, assist, aid, nourish **3** = **suffer**, feel, bear, experience, undergo, endure, withstand **4** = **support**, bear, uphold
sustained *adj* = **continuous**, steady, constant, prolonged, perpetual, nonstop, twenty-four-seven (*slang*), unremitting
swab *See* **clean**
swagger *v* = **show off** (*informal*), parade, boast, brag

S

DICTIONARY

swallow[1] ⓣ *v* **1** cause to pass down one's throat **2** make a gulping movement in the throat, as when nervous **3** *informal* believe (something) gullibly **4** refrain from showing (a feeling) **5** engulf or absorb ▷ *n* **6** swallowing **7** amount swallowed
swallow[2] *n* small migratory bird with long pointed wings and a forked tail
swam *v* past tense of **swim**
swamp ⓣ *n* **1** watery area of land, bog ▷ *v* **2** cause (a boat) to fill with water and sink **3** overwhelm **swampy** *adj*
swan *n* large usu. white water bird with a long graceful neck
▸ **swan song** person's last performance before retirement or death
Swan *n* Sir **Joseph Wilson**. 1828–1914, English physicist and chemist, who developed the incandescent electric light (1880) independently of Edison
swank *slang* ▷ *v* **1** show off or boast ▷ *n* **2** showing off or boasting
▸ **swanky** *adj slang* expensive and showy, stylish
swap ⓣ *v* **swapping, swapped 1** exchange (something) for something else ▷ *n* **2** exchange
sward *n* stretch of short grass
swarm[1] ⓣ *n* **1** large group of bees or other insects **2** large crowd ▷ *v* **3** move in a swarm **4** (of a place) be crowded or overrun
swarm[2] *v* (foll. by *up*) climb (a ladder or rope) by gripping with the hands and feet
swarthy ⓣ *adj* **-thier, -thiest** dark-complexioned
swashbuckler *n* daredevil adventurer **swashbuckling** *adj*
swastika *n* symbol in the shape of a cross with the arms bent at right angles, used as the emblem of Nazi Germany
swat *v* **swatting, swatted 1** hit sharply ▷ *n* **2** sharp blow
swatch *n* sample of cloth
swath [**swawth**] *n* the width of one sweep of a scythe or mower
swathe ⓣ *v* **1** wrap in bandages or layers of cloth ▷ *n* **2** same as **swath**
sway ⓣ *v* **1** swing to and fro or from side to side **2** waver or cause to waver in opinion ▷ *n* **3** power or influence **4** swaying motion
swear ⓣ *v* **swearing, swore, sworn 1** use obscene or blasphemous language **2** state earnestly **3** state or promise on oath
▸ **swear by** *v* have complete confidence in
▸ **swear in** *v* cause to take an oath
▸ **swearword** *n* word considered obscene or blasphemous
sweat ⓣ *n* **1** salty liquid given off through the pores of the skin **2** *slang* drudgery or hard labour ▷ *v* **3** have sweat coming through the pores **4** be anxious **5** toil **sweaty** *adj*
▸ **sweatband** *n* strip of cloth tied around the forehead or wrist to absorb sweat
▸ **sweatshirt** *n* long-sleeved cotton jersey
▸ **sweatshop** *n* place where employees work long hours in poor conditions for low pay
sweater *n* (woollen) garment for the upper part of the body
swede *n* kind of turnip
Swede *n* person from Sweden
▸ **Swedish** *n, adj* (language) of Sweden
sweep ⓣ *v* **sweeping, swept 1** remove dirt from (a floor) with a broom **2** move smoothly and quickly **3** spread rapidly

THESAURUS

swaggering *See* **boastful**
swallow *v* = **gulp**, eat, drink, consume, devour, swig (*informal*), chow down (*slang*)
swamp *n* **1** = **bog**, mire, quagmire, marsh, slough, morass, fen ▸ *v* **2** = **flood**, sink, capsize, engulf, inundate, submerge **3** = **overwhelm**, flood, overload, inundate
swap *v* = **exchange**, trade, switch, interchange, barter • *I swapped DVDs with my friend.*
See also: **change, substitute**
swarm *n* **1** = **multitude**, host, crowd, army, mass, herd, flock, throng, horde ▸ *v* **2** = **crowd**, mass, stream, flock, throng **3** = **teem**, abound, crawl, bristle
swarthy *adj* = **dark-skinned**, black, dark, brown, dark-complexioned, dusky
swashbuckling *adj* = **dashing**, bold, daredevil, flamboyant
swathe *v* = **wrap**, cloak, drape, shroud, envelop, bundle up
sway *v* **1** = **move from side to side**, rock, roll, swing, lean, bend **2** = **influence**, affect, guide, persuade, induce ▸ *n* **3** = **power**, control, authority, influence, clout (*informal*)
swear *v* **1** = **curse**, be foul-mouthed, blaspheme **2** = **vow**, promise **3** = **declare**, testify, assert, affirm, attest
swearing *n* = **bad language**, profanity, blasphemy, cursing, foul language
swearword *n* = **oath**, curse, profanity, obscenity, expletive, four-letter word
sweat *n* **1** = **perspiration** **2** (*Informal*) = **labour**, chore, toil, drudgery **3** (*Informal*) = **worry**, strain, panic, anxiety, distress, agitation ▸ *v* **4** = **perspire**, glow **5** (*Informal*) = **worry**, suffer, fret, agonize, torture oneself
sweaty *adj* = **perspiring**, sticky, clammy
sweep *v* **1** = **clear**, remove, clean, brush **2** = **sail**, pass, fly, tear, zoom, skim, glide ▷ **sweep away** *See* **wash** ▸ *n* **3** = **arc**, move, stroke, swing, bend, curve **4** = **extent**, range, stretch, scope

DICTIONARY

4 move majestically **5** carry away suddenly or forcefully **6** stretch in a long wide curve ▷ *n* **7** sweeping **8** sweeping motion **9** wide expanse **10** person who cleans chimneys **11** sweepstake
▸ **sweeper** *n* **1** *curling* player who uses a broom to sweep the ice in front of a played stone **2** *soccer* defensive player usually positioned in front of the goalkeeper
▸ **sweeping** *adj* **1** indiscriminate **2** wide-ranging
▸ **sweepstake** *n* lottery in which the stakes of the participants make up the prize
sweet Ⓣ *adj* **1** tasting of or like sugar **2** kind and charming **3** agreeable to the senses or mind **4** (of wine) with a high sugar content ▷ *n Brit* **5** shaped piece of food consisting mainly of sugar **6** dessert **sweetly** *adv* **sweetness** *n* **sweeten** *v*
▸ **sweetener** *n* **1** sweetening agent that does not contain sugar **2** *slang* bribe
▸ **sweetbread** *n* animal's pancreas used as food
▸ **sweetbrier** *n* wild rose
▸ **sweet corn** type of corn with sweet yellow kernels, eaten as a vegetable
▸ **sweetheart** *n* lover
▸ **sweetmeat** *n old-fashioned* a sweet delicacy such as a small cake
▸ **sweet pea** climbing plant with bright fragrant flowers
▸ **sweet potato** tropical root vegetable with yellow flesh
▸ **sweet-talk** *v informal* coax or flatter
▸ **sweet tooth** strong liking for sweet foods
▸ **sweet william** garden plant with flat clusters of scented flowers
swell *v* **swelling, swelled, swollen** *or* **swelled 1** expand or increase **2** be puffed up with pride or other emotion **3** (of a sound) become gradually louder ▷ *n* **4** swelling or being swollen **5** movement of waves in the sea **6** *old-fashioned, slang* fashionable person ▷ *adj* **7** *slang* excellent or fine
▸ **swelling** *n* enlargement of part of the body, caused by injury or infection
swelter *v* be oppressed by heat
swept *v* past of **sweep**
swerve Ⓣ *v* **1** turn aside from a course sharply or suddenly ▷ *n* **2** swerving
swift Ⓣ *adj* **1** moving or able to move quickly ▷ *n* **2** fast-flying bird with pointed wings **swiftly** *adv* **swiftness** *n*
swig Ⓣ *n* **1** large mouthful of drink ▷ *v* **swigging, swigged 2** drink in large mouthfuls
swill *v* **1** drink greedily **2** rinse (something) in large amounts of water ▷ *n* **3** sloppy mixture containing waste food, fed to pigs **4** deep drink **5** rinsing
swim *v* **swimming, swam, swum 1** move along in water by movements of the limbs **2** be covered or flooded with liquid **3** reel: *her head was swimming* ▷ *n* **4** act or period of swimming **swimmer** *n*
▸ **swimmingly** *adv* successfully and effortlessly
▸ **swimming pool** (building containing an) artificial pond for swimming in
swindle Ⓣ *v* **1** cheat (someone) out of money

THESAURUS

sweeping *adj* **1 = wide-ranging**, global, wide, broad, extensive, comprehensive, all-inclusive, all-embracing **2 = indiscriminate**, blanket, wholesale, exaggerated, unqualified, overstated
sweet *adj* **1 = sugary**, sweetened, cloying • *a cup of sweet tea* OPPOSITE: sour **2 = fragrant**, aromatic, perfumed, sweet-smelling • *the sweet smell of roses* **3 = melodious**, musical, mellow, harmonious, tuneful • *the sweet sounds of children's singing* **4 = charming**, kind, winning, cute, engaging, appealing, delightful, lovable, likable *or* likeable, agreeable ▸ *n* **5** (*usually pl*) **= confectionery**, candy, bonbon
sweeten *v* **1 = sugar 2 = mollify**, appease, soothe, pacify
sweetened *See* **sweet**
sweetheart *n* **= lover**, love, beloved, boyfriend *or* girlfriend, dear, darling, main squeeze (*slang*)
sweet-smelling *See* **fragrant, sweet**
swell *v* **1 = expand**, increase, rise, grow, balloon, bulge, enlarge, bloat, dilate, distend ▸ *n* **2 = wave**, surge, billow
swelling *n* **= enlargement**, bump, lump, inflammation, bulge, distension, protuberance
sweltering *adj* **= hot**, burning, oppressive, boiling, scorching, stifling
swerve *v* **= veer**, turn, swing • *He swerved to avoid a truck.*
See also: **curve, dodge**
swift *adj* **= quick**, fast, prompt, express, rapid, speedy, brisk, hurried • *Make a swift decision.* OPPOSITE: slow
See also: **brief, hasty, sudden**
swiftly *adv* **= quickly**, fast, rapidly, promptly, hurriedly, speedily
swiftness *n* **= speed**, velocity, quickness, promptness, rapidity, speediness
swig *See* **drink**
swindle *v* **1 = cheat**, con, defraud, fleece, rip (someone) off (*slang*), trick, sting (*informal*) ▸ *n* **2 = fraud**, deception, con trick (*informal*), scam (*slang*), racket, rip-off (*slang*)
swindler *n* **= cheat**, fraud, shark, rogue,

S

DICTIONARY

▷ *n* **2** instance of swindling **swindler** *n*
swine Ⓣ *n* **1** contemptible person **2** pig **swinish** *adj*
swing Ⓣ *v* **swinging, swung 1** move to and fro, sway **2** move in a curve **3** hit out with a sweeping motion **4** (of an opinion or mood) change sharply **5** *slang* be hanged **6** *baseball* attempt to hit a pitched ball ▷ *n* **7** swinging **8** suspended seat on which a child can swing to and fro **9** style of popular dance music played by big bands in the 1930s **10** *baseball* attempted hit
▸ **swing by** *v informal* go (somewhere) to pay a visit
swipe Ⓣ *v* **1** strike (at) with a sweeping blow **2** *slang* steal **3** pass (a credit card or debit card) through a machine that electronically reads information stored in the card ▷ *n* **4** sweeping blow
swirl Ⓣ *v* **1** turn with a whirling motion ▷ *n* **2** whirling motion **3** twisting shape
swish *v* **1** move with a whistling or hissing sound ▷ *n* **2** whistling or hissing sound ▷ *adj* **3** *informal* fashionable, smart
Swiss *adj* **1** of Switzerland or its people ▷ *n, pl* **Swiss 2** person from Switzerland
▸ **swiss roll** sponge cake spread with jam or cream and rolled up
switch Ⓣ *n* **1** device for opening and closing an electric circuit **2** abrupt change **3** exchange or swap **4** movable rail used to change a train to other rails **5** flexible rod or twig ▷ *v* **6** change abruptly **7** exchange or swap
▸ **switchback** *n* road or railway with many sharp hills or bends
▸ **switchboard** *n* installation in a telephone exchange or office where telephone calls are connected
▸ **switch on** *or* **switch off** *v* turn (a device) on *or* off by means of a switch
swivel Ⓣ *n* **1** coupling device that allows an attached object to turn freely ▷ *v* **-elling, -elled 2** turn on or as if on a swivel
swizz *n informal* swindle or disappointment
swizzle stick *n* small ornamental stick used to stir a cocktail
swollen Ⓣ *v* a past participle of **swell**
swoon Ⓣ *v, n* faint
swoop Ⓣ *v* **1** sweep down or pounce on suddenly ▷ *n* **2** swooping
swop *v* **swopping, swopped 1** same as **swap** ▷ *n* **2** same as **swap**
sword *n* weapon with a long sharp blade
▸ **swordfish** *n* large fish with a very long upper jaw
▸ **swordsman** *n* person skilled in the use of a sword
swore *v* past tense of **swear**
sworn *v* **1** past participle of **swear** ▷ *adj* **2** bound by or as if by an oath: *sworn enemies*
swot *informal* ▷ *v* **swotting, swotted 1** study hard ▷ *n* **2** person who studies hard
swum *v* past participle of **swim**
swung *v* past of **swing**
sybarite [**sib**-bar-ite] *n* lover of luxury **sybaritic** *adj*
sycamore *n* tree with five-pointed leaves and two-winged fruits
sycophant Ⓣ *n* person who uses flattery to win favour from people with power or influence **sycophantic** *adj* **sycophancy** *n*
syllable *n* part of a word pronounced as a unit **syllabic** *adj*
syllabub *n* dessert of beaten cream, sugar, and wine
syllabus Ⓣ *n* list of subjects for a course of study
syllogism *n* form of logical reasoning consisting of two premises and a conclusion **syllogistic** *adj*
sylph *n* **1** imaginary being supposed to inhabit the air **2** slender graceful girl or woman **sylphlike** *adj*

S

THESAURUS

trickster, con man (*informal*)
swine *See* **pig**
swing *v* **1** = **sway**, rock, wave, veer, oscillate **2** (usually with *round*) = **turn**, curve, pivot, rotate, swivel **3** = **hang**, suspend, dangle ▸ *n* **4** = **swaying**, oscillation
swipe *v* **1** = **hit**, strike, slap, wallop (*informal*), lash out at **2** (*Slang*) = **steal**, lift (*informal*), appropriate, filch, pinch (*informal*), purloin ▸ *n* **3** = **blow**, slap, smack, wallop (*informal*), cuff, clout (*informal*)
swirl *v* = **whirl**, spin, twist, churn, eddy
switch *n* **1** = **change**, shift, reversal **2** = **exchange**, swap, substitution ▸ *v* **3** = **change**, shift, divert, deflect, deviate **4** = **exchange**, swap, substitute
swivel *v* = **turn**, spin, revolve, pivot, rotate
swollen *adj* = **enlarged**, bloated, distended, inflamed, puffed up
swoon *See* **faint**
swoop *v* **1** = **pounce**, sweep, rush, dive, descend, stoop ▸ *n* **2** = **pounce**, drop, sweep, rush, plunge, descent, lunge, stoop
sycophant *n* = **crawler**, suck (*chiefly Canad*), brown-noser (*slang*), fawner, flatterer, toady, yes man, apple polisher (*informal*), groupie (*slang*), appeaser, flunky, kiss-ass (*informal*)
sycophantic *adj* = **obsequious**, slimy, crawling, fawning, flattering, grovelling, ingratiating, servile, smarmy (*Brit informal*), toadying, unctuous
syllabus *n* = **course of study**, curriculum

DICTIONARY

sylvan *adj lit* relating to woods and trees
symbiosis *n* close association of two species living together to their mutual benefit **symbiotic** *adj*
symbol Ⓣ *n* sign or thing that stands for something else **symbolic** *adj* **symbolically** *adv*
▸**symbolism** *n* **1** representation of something by symbols **2** movement in art and literature using symbols to express abstract and mystical ideas **symbolist** *n, adj*
▸**symbolize** *v* **1** be a symbol of **2** represent with a symbol
symmetry Ⓣ *n* state of having two halves that are mirror images of each other **symmetrical** *adj* **symmetrically** *adv*
sympathy Ⓣ *n, pl* **-thies** **1** compassion for someone's pain or distress **2** agreement with someone's feelings or interests
▸**sympathetic** *adj* **1** feeling or showing sympathy **2** likeable or appealing **sympathetically** *adv*
▸**sympathize** *v* feel or express sympathy **sympathizer** *n*
symphony *n, pl* **-nies** composition for orchestra, with several movements **symphonic** *adj*
symposium *n, pl* **-siums, -sia** conference for discussion of a particular topic
symptom Ⓣ *n* **1** sign indicating the presence of an illness **2** sign that something is wrong **symptomatic** *adj*
synagogue *n* Jewish place of worship and religious instruction
sync, synch *n informal* synchronization
synchromesh *adj* (of a gearbox) having a device that synchronizes the speeds of gears before they engage
synchronize *v* **1** (of two or more people) perform (an action) at the same time **2** match (the soundtrack and action of a film) precisely **3** set (watches) to show the same time **synchronization** *n*
▸**synchronous** *or* **synchronic** *adj* happening or existing at the same time
syncline *n* downward fold of rock strata in the earth's surface
syncopate *v music* stress the weak beats in (a rhythm) instead of the strong ones **syncopation** *n*
syncope [**sing**-kop-ee] *n med* a faint
syndicate Ⓣ *n* **1** group of people or firms undertaking a joint business project **2** agency that sells material to several newspapers ▹ *v* **3** form a syndicate **4** publish (material) in several newspapers **syndication** *n*
syndrome *n* **1** combination of symptoms indicating a particular disease **2** set of characteristics indicating a particular problem
synod *n* church council
synonym *n* word with the same meaning as another **synonymous** *adj*
synopsis Ⓣ *n, pl* **-ses** summary or outline
syntax *n grammar* way in which words are arranged to form phrases and sentences **syntactic** *adj* **syntactically** *adv*
synthesis *n, pl* **-ses** **1** combination of objects or ideas into a whole **2** artificial production of a substance
▸**synthesize** *v* produce by synthesis
▸**synthesizer** *n* electronic musical instrument producing a range of sounds
▸**synthetic** *adj* **1** (of a substance) made artificially **2** not genuine, insincere **synthetically** *adv*
syphilis *n* serious sexually transmitted disease **syphilitic** *adj*
syphon *n, v* same as **siphon**
Syrian *adj* **1** of Syria, its people, or their dialect of Arabic ▹ *n* **2** person from Syria
syringa *n* same as **mock orange, lilac**
syringe *n* **1** device for withdrawing or injecting fluids, consisting of a hollow cylinder, a piston, and a hollow needle

S

THESAURUS

symbol *n* = **sign**, mark, figure, icon, logo, representation, token, emblem • *Hg is the chemical symbol for mercury.*
symbolic *adj* = **representative**, emblematic, figurative, allegorical
symbolize *v* = **represent**, mean, signify, denote, typify, personify, stand for
symmetrical *adj* = **balanced**, regular, in proportion
symmetry *n* = **balance**, order, proportion, regularity, evenness
sympathetic *adj* **1** = **caring**, kind, warm, interested, understanding, concerned, supportive, compassionate, pitying **2** = **like-minded**, friendly, compatible, agreeable, congenial, companionable
sympathize *v* **1** = **feel for**, pity, commiserate, condole **2** = **agree**, understand, side with
sympathizer *n* = **supporter**, partisan, well-wisher
sympathy *n* **1** = **compassion**, empathy, understanding, pity • *My heartfelt sympathy goes out to all the relatives.* **2** = **agreement**, affinity, rapport, fellow feeling
symptom *n* = **sign**, mark, warning, indication, expression, token
symptomatic *adj* = **indicative**, characteristic, suggestive
syndicate *See* **association, ring**
synopsis *See* **outline, summary**
synthetic *adj* = **artificial**, fake, man-made

DICTIONARY

▷ *v* **2** wash out or inject with a syringe
syrup *n* **1** solution of sugar in water **2** thick sweet liquid **3** excessive sentimentality
syrupy *adj*
system Ⓣ *n* **1** method or set of methods **2** scheme of classification or arrangement **3** network or assembly of parts that form a whole **systematic** *adj* **systematically** *adv*
▸ **systematize** *v* organize using a system
systematization *n*
▸ **systemic** *adj* affecting the entire animal or body
systole [**siss**-tol-ee] *n* regular contraction of the heart as it pumps blood **systolic** *adj*

THESAURUS

system *n* **1** = **method**, procedure, technique, routine • *the advantages of the new system over the old one*
2 = **arrangement**, structure • *the current systems of animal classification*
See also: **plan, process**
systematic *adj* = **methodical**, efficient, organized, orderly

Tt

t tonne
T *n* **to a T 1** in every detail **2** perfectly
t. ton
ta *interj informal* thank you
tab *n* small flap or projecting label
▸ **keep tabs on** *informal* watch closely
tabard *n* short sleeveless tunic
Tabasco *n* ® very hot red pepper sauce
tabby *n, pl* **-bies**, *adj* (cat) with dark stripes on a lighter background
tabernacle *n* **1** portable shrine of the Israelites **2** *RC Church* receptacle for the consecrated Host **3** Christian place of worship not called a church
tabla *n, pl* **-blas, -bla** one of a pair of Indian drums played with the hands
table ⓣ *n* **1** piece of furniture with a flat top supported by legs **2** arrangement of information in columns ▹ *v* **3** submit (a motion) for discussion by a meeting **4** *US* suspend discussion of (a proposal)
▸ **tableland** *n* high plateau
▸ **tablespoon** *n* large spoon for serving food
▸ **table tennis** game like tennis played on a table with small bats and a light ball
tableau ⓣ [**tab**-loh] *n, pl* **-leaux, -leaus** silent motionless group arranged to represent some scene
table d'hôte [tah-bla **dote**] *n, pl* **tables d'hôte**, *adj* (meal) having a set number of dishes at a fixed price
tablet *n* **1** pill of compressed medicinal substance **2** flattish cake of soap etc. **3** inscribed slab of stone etc.
tabloid *n* small-sized newspaper with many photographs and a concise, usu. sensational style
taboo ⓣ *n, pl* **-boos 1** prohibition resulting from religious or social conventions ▹ *adj* **2** forbidden by a taboo
tabular *adj* arranged in a table
▸ **tabulate** *v* arrange (information) in a table
tabulation *n*
tachograph *n* device for recording the speed and distance travelled by a motor vehicle
tachometer *n* device for measuring speed, esp. that of a revolving shaft
tacit ⓣ [**tass**-it] *adj* implied but not spoken
tacitly *adv*
taciturn ⓣ [**tass**-it-turn] *adj* habitually uncommunicative **taciturnity** *n*
Tacitus *n* **Publius Cornelius**. ?55–?120 AD, Roman historian and orator, famous as a prose stylist. His works include the *Histories*, dealing with the period 68–96, and the *Annals*, dealing with the period 14–68
tack[1] ⓣ *n* **1** short nail with a large head **2** long loose stitch ▹ *v* **3** fasten with tacks **4** stitch with tacks **5** append
tack[2] ⓣ *n* **1** course of a ship sailing obliquely into the wind **2** course of action ▹ *v* **3** sail into the wind on a zigzag course
tack[3] *n* riding harness for horses
tackle ⓣ *n* **1** set of ropes and pulleys for lifting heavy weights **2** equipment for a particular activity **3** *sports* act of tackling an opposing player ▹ *v* **4** undertake (a task)

THESAURUS

table *n* **1 = counter**, board, stand, bench **2 = list**, record, schedule, roll, register, chart, catalogue, diagram, tabulation ▸ *v* **3 = submit**, move, suggest, propose, enter, put forward
tableau *n* **= picture**, scene, representation, spectacle
taboo *n* **1 = prohibition**, ban, restriction, anathema, interdict, proscription ▸ *adj* **2 = forbidden**, unacceptable, outlawed, anathema, banned, prohibited, proscribed, unmentionable
tacit *adj* **= implied**, undeclared, implicit, unspoken, inferred, understood, unexpressed, unstated
taciturn *adj* **= uncommunicative**, quiet, silent, tight-lipped, reserved, reticent, unforthcoming, withdrawn
tack[1] *n* **1 = pin**, nail, pushpin, thumbtack ▸ *v* **2 = fasten**, fix, attach, nail, pin, affix **3 = stitch**, baste ▹ **tack on = append**, add, tag, attach
tack[2] *n* **= course**, plan, way, line, approach, direction, procedure, path, method, heading
tackle *v* **1 = deal with**, attempt, come to grips with *or* get to grips with, embark upon, get stuck into (*informal*), undertake, set about **2 = confront**, challenge **3 = intercept**, stop, halt, grab, seize, grasp ▸ *n* **4 = block**, challenge **5 = equipment**, gear, apparatus,

DICTIONARY

5 confront (an opponent) **6** *sports* attempt to get the ball from (an opposing player)
tacky¹ Ⓣ *adj* **tackier, tackiest** slightly sticky **tackiness** *n*
tacky² Ⓣ *adj* **tackier, tackiest** *informal* **1** vulgar and tasteless **2** shabby
taco [**tah**-koh] *n, pl* **tacos** *Mexican cookery* tortilla fried until crisp, served with a filling
tact Ⓣ *n* skill in avoiding giving offence **tactful** *adj* **tactfully** *adv* **tactless** *adj* **tactlessly** *adv*
tactics *pl n* **1** art of directing military forces in battle **2** methods or plans to achieve an end **tactical** *adj* **tactician** *n*
tactile *adj* of or having the sense of touch
tadpole *n* limbless tailed larva of a frog or toad
taffeta *n* shiny silk or rayon fabric
taffrail *n* rail at the stern of a ship
Taft *n* **William Howard**. 1857–1930, US statesman; 27th president of the US (1909–13)
tag¹ Ⓣ *n* **1** label bearing information **2** pointed end of a cord or lace **3** trite quotation ▷ *v* **tagging, tagged 4** attach a tag to
▸ **tag along** *v* accompany someone, esp. if uninvited
tag² *n* **1** children's game where the person being chased becomes the chaser upon being touched ▷ *v* **tagging, tagged 2** touch and catch in this game **3** *baseball* put out (a baserunner) by touching him or her with the ball while he or she is off base
tagliatelle *n* pasta in long narrow strips
tail Ⓣ *n* **1** rear part of an animal's body, usu. forming a flexible appendage **2** rear or last part or parts of something **3** *informal* person employed to follow and spy on another **tails 4** side of a coin without a portrait of a head on it **5** *informal* tail coat ▷ *v* **6** *informal* follow (someone) secretly ▷ *adj* **7** at the rear **tailless** *adj*
▸ **turn tail** run away
▸ **tailback** *n* queue of traffic stretching back from an obstruction
▸ **tailboard** *n* removable or hinged rear board on a truck etc.
▸ **tail coat** man's coat with a long back split into two below the waist
▸ **tail off** *or* **tail away** *v* diminish gradually
▸ **tailspin** *n* uncontrolled spinning dive of an aircraft
▸ **tailwind** *n* wind coming from the rear
tailor Ⓣ *n* **1** person who makes men's clothes ▷ *v* **2** adapt to suit a purpose
▸ **tailor-made** *adj* **1** made by a tailor **2** perfect for a purpose
Taine *n* **Hippolyte Adolphe**. 1828–93, French literary critic and historian. He applied determinist criteria to the study of literature, art, history, and psychology, regarding them as products of environment and race. His works include *Histoire de la littérature anglaise* (1863–64) and *Les Origines de la France contemporaine* (1875–93)
taint Ⓣ *v* **1** spoil with a small amount of decay, contamination, or other bad quality ▷ *n* **2** something that taints
take Ⓣ *v* **taking, took, taken 1** remove from a place **2** get possession of, esp. dishonestly

THESAURUS

paraphernalia, accoutrements, tools, trappings
tacky¹ *adj* = **sticky**, wet, adhesive, gummy, gluey
tacky² *adj* (*Informal*) = **vulgar**, cheap, shoddy, tasteless, sleazy, shabby, seedy, off-color, scuzzy (*slang*), tatty
tact *n* = **diplomacy**, sensitivity, discretion, delicacy • *He has handled the incident with great tact.*
See also: **consideration**
tactful *adj* = **diplomatic**, sensitive, discreet • *Sorry, that wasn't a very tactful question.* OPPOSITE: tactless
tactic *n* = **policy**, move, approach, scheme, method, ploy, manoeuvre, stratagem ▷ **tactics** = **strategy**, playbook (*football*), campaigning, generalship, manoeuvres, plans, power play (*sports*)
tactical *adj* = **strategic**, diplomatic, smart, shrewd, cunning
tactician *n* = **strategist**, general, mastermind, planner
tactless *adj* = **insensitive**, thoughtless, impolite, impolitic, inconsiderate, indelicate, indiscreet, undiplomatic, unsubtle
tag *n* **1** = **label**, note, mark, ticket, slip, marker, identification, tab, flap ▸ *v* **2** = **label**, mark **3** (with *along* or *on*) = **accompany**, follow, attend, trail, shadow, tail (*informal*), stalk
tail *n* **1** = **extremity**, end, appendage, rear end, tailpiece ▷ **turn tail** = **run away**, flee, retreat, cut and run, run off, take to one's heels ▸ *v* **2** (*Informal*) = **follow**, track, trail, shadow, stalk
tailor *n* **1** = **outfitter**, seamstress, clothier, costumier, couturier, dressmaker ▸ *v* **2** = **adapt**, fashion, style, shape, adjust, modify, alter, customize, mould
taint *v* **1** = **spoil**, damage, contaminate, ruin, corrupt, pollute, stain, tarnish, blemish, defile, sully ▸ *n* **2** = **stain**, spot, flaw, defect, fault, blemish, blot, black mark, demerit
take *v* **1** = **require**, demand • *He takes three hours to get ready.* **2** = **carry**, bring, ferry, transport, fetch, convey • *I'll take these papers home and read them.* **3** = **lead**, bring, conduct,

t

DICTIONARY

3 carry or accompany **4** capture **5** require (time, resources, or ability) **6** use **7** assume **8** write down **9** accept **10** subtract or deduct ▷ *n* **11** one of a series of recordings from which the best will be used
▸ **take place** see **place**
▸ **taking** *adj* charming
▸ **takings** *pl n* money received by a shop
▸ **take after** *v* look or behave like (a parent etc.)
▸ **take against** *v* start to dislike
▸ **take away** *v* subtract
▸ **takeaway** *n Brit* **1** shop or restaurant selling meals for eating elsewhere **2** meal bought at a takeaway
▸ **take in** *v* **1** understand **2** make (clothing) smaller **3** deceive or swindle
▸ **take off** *v* **1** (of an aircraft) leave the ground **2** *informal* depart **3** *informal* parody **take-off** *n*
▸ **takeout** *adj* **1** preparing and selling food for consumption away from the premises ▷ *n* **2** shop or restaurant that sells such food **3** meal bought at such a shop or restaurant
▸ **takeover** *n* act of taking control of a company by buying a large number of its shares
▸ **take up** *v* **1** occupy or fill (space or time) **2** adopt the study or activity of **3** accept (an offer) **4** shorten (a garment)
Talbot *n* (**William Henry**) **Fox**. 1800–77, British scientist, a pioneer of photography, who developed the calotype process
talc *n* **1** soft mineral of magnesium silicate **2** talcum powder
▸ **talcum powder** powder, usu. scented, used to dry or perfume the body
tale ⓣ *n* **1** story **2** malicious piece of gossip
talent ⓣ *n* **1** natural ability **2** ancient unit of weight or money **talented** *adj*
talisman ⓣ *n, pl* **-mans** object believed to have magic power **talismanic** *adj*
talk ⓣ *v* **1** express ideas or feelings by means of speech **2** utter **3** discuss: *let's talk business* **4** reveal information **5** (be able to) speak in a specified language ▷ *n* **6** speech or lecture **talker** *n*

THESAURUS

guide, escort, usher • *She took me to a Mexican restaurant.* **4 = capture**, get, catch, acquire, secure, seize, obtain, grip, grasp **5 = steal**, appropriate, pocket, pinch (*informal*), misappropriate, purloin **6 = tolerate**, stand, bear, endure, stomach, withstand, abide, put up with (*informal*) **7 = have room for**, hold, contain, accept, accommodate **8 = subtract**, remove, eliminate, deduct **9 = assume**, believe, consider, understand, regard, perceive, presume
See also: **choose, receive, select** ▷ **take aback** *See* **surprise** ▷ **take advantage of** *See* **impose on, profit** ▷ **take after** *See* **resemble** ▷ **take away** *See* **remove, subtract** ▷ **take care of** = **look after**, watch, protect, mind, nurse, tend, care for • *There was nobody to take care of the children.* OPPOSITE: neglect; = **deal with**, manage, handle, attend to, cope with, see to • *"Do you need clean sheets?" "No, your husband took care of that."*
See also: **deal, process** ▷ **take down** *See* **lower, write** ▷ **take for** *See* **mistake** ▷ **take from** *See* **subtract** ▷ **take in** = **deceive**, trick, mislead, fool, con (*informal*), dupe • *He was a real charmer who totally took me in*; = **understand**, get, appreciate, absorb, grasp, digest, comprehend, assimilate • *She seemed to take in all he said.*
See also: **admit, involve, receive** ▷ **take into account** *See* **consider** ▷ **take off** = **remove**, discard, peel off, strip off; = **lift off**, take to the air; (*Informal*) = **depart**, go, leave, disappear, abscond, decamp, slope off
▷ **take on** = **compete against**, face, fight, oppose, vie with, pit oneself against, contend with; = **hire**, engage, retain, employ, enlist, enrol; = **accept**, shoulder, tackle, undertake, step up to the plate (*informal*), agree to do; = **acquire**, assume, come to have
▷ **take out** = **extract**, remove, pull out, yank out, draw (out) ▷ **take over** *See* **possess**
▷ **take over from** *See* **replace, succeed**
▷ **take part** *See* **participate, play** ▷ **take place** = **happen**, occur, transpire (*informal*), go on, come about ▷ **take up** = **occupy**, cover, fill, consume, absorb, extend over, use up; = **start**, adopt, become involved in, engage in
takeoff *n* = **departure**, launch, liftoff
takeover *n* = **merger**, coup, incorporation
taking *adj* = **charming**, attractive, engaging, likable *or* likeable, beguiling, captivating, enchanting, fetching (*informal*), prepossessing ▸ *noun* ▷ **taking on** *See* **employment** ▷ **takings** = **revenue**, take, income, earnings, proceeds, profits, receipts, returns
tale *n* = **story**, account, legend, saga, narrative, anecdote, yarn (*informal*), fable
talent *n* = **ability**, gift, capacity, genius, knack, flair, aptitude • *Both children have a talent for music.*
talented *adj* = **gifted**, able, brilliant
talisman *n* = **charm**, mascot, fetish, amulet, lucky charm
talk *v* **1** = **speak**, chat, communicate, gossip, chatter, converse, chew the fat (*slang*), utter • *They were talking about environmental hazards.* **2** = **discuss**, negotiate, confer, confabulate, parley **3** = **inform**, blab, give the game away, let the cat out of the bag, tell

DICTIONARY

▸ **talkative** *adj* fond of talking
▸ **talk back** *v* answer impudently
▸ **talking point** something which provokes discussion
▸ **talking-to** *n informal* reproof
tall ⓣ *adj* **1** higher than average **2** of a specified height
▸ **tall order** difficult task
▸ **tall story** unlikely and probably untrue tale
tallboy *n* high chest of drawers
Tallis *n* **Thomas**. ?1505–85, English composer and organist; noted for his music for the Anglican liturgy
tallow *n* hard animal fat used to make candles
tally ⓣ *v* **-lying, -lied 1** (of two things) correspond ▷ *n, pl* **-lies 2** record of a debt or score
tally-ho *interj* huntsman's cry when the quarry is sighted
Talmud *n* body of Jewish law **Talmudic** *adj*
talon *n* bird's hooked claw
tamarind *n* **1** tropical tree **2** its acid fruit
tamarisk *n* evergreen shrub with slender branches and feathery flower clusters
Tambo *n* **Oliver**. 1917–93, South African politician; president (1977–91) of the African National Congress. He was arrested (1956) with Nelson Mandela but released (1957)
tambourine *n* percussion instrument like a small drum with jingling metal discs attached
tame ⓣ *adj* **1** (of animals) brought under human control **2** (of animals) not afraid of people **3** meek or submissive **4** uninteresting ▷ *v* **5** make tame **tamely** *adv* **tamer** *n*
Tamerlane, Tamburlaine *n* Turkic name *Timur*. ?1336–1405, Mongol conqueror of the area from Mongolia to the Mediterranean; ruler of Samarkand (1369–1405). He defeated the Turks at Angora (1402) and died while invading China
Tamil *n* **1** member of a people of Sri Lanka and S India **2** their language
tam-o'-shanter *n* brimless wool cap with a bobble in the centre
tamp *v* pack down by repeated blows
tamper ⓣ *v* (foll. by *with*) interfere
tampon *n* absorbent plug of cotton batting inserted into the vagina during menstruation
tan *v* **tanning, tanned 1** (of skin) go brown from exposure to sunlight **2** convert (a hide) into leather ▷ *n* **3** brown colour of tanned skin ▷ *adj* **4** yellowish-brown **tanner** *n*
▸ **tannery** *n* place where hides are tanned
tandem *n* bicycle for two riders, one behind the other
▸ **in tandem** together
tandoor *n* Indian clay oven
▸ **tandoori** *adj* cooked in a tandoor
tang ⓣ *n* **1** strong taste or smell **2** trace or hint **tangy** *adj*
tangent *n* **1** line that touches a curve without intersecting it **2** (in trigonometry) ratio of the length of the opposite side to that of the adjacent side of a right-angled triangle
▸ **go off at a tangent** suddenly take a completely different line of thought or action
▸ **tangential** *adj* **1** of a tangent **2** of superficial relevance only **tangentially** *adv*
tangerine *n* small orange-like fruit of an Asian citrus tree
tangible ⓣ *adj* **1** able to be touched **2** clear and definite **tangibly** *adv* **tangibility** *n*

THESAURUS

all ▸ *n* **4** = **conversation**, chat, chatter • *We had a long talk about her future.* **5** = **speech**, address, lecture, sermon, discourse • *a talk about career choices*
See also: **discussion, say, word**
talkative *adj* = **communicative**, chatty, long-winded • *His eyes grew bright, and he suddenly became very talkative.*
talker *n* = **speaker**, lecturer, orator, chatterbox, conversationalist
talking-to *n* = **reprimand**, criticism, rebuke, lecture, scolding, reproach, reproof, telling-off (*informal*)
tall *adj* **1** = **high**, lofty, towering, lanky, soaring • *tall buildings* OPPOSITE: short **2** (~ *tale*) = **implausible**, incredible, unbelievable, exaggerated, absurd, far-fetched, preposterous, cock-and-bull (*informal*) **3** (~ *order*) = **difficult**, hard, unreasonable, demanding, well-nigh impossible
tally *v* **1** = **agree**, accord, match, fit, square, coincide, correspond, conform, harmonize, concur ▸ *n* **2** = **record**, score, mark, total, count, reckoning, running total
tame *adj* **1** = **domesticated**, gentle, disciplined, amenable, obedient, docile, broken, tractable **2** = **submissive**, manageable, subdued, compliant, obedient, docile, meek, unresisting **3** = **uninteresting**, boring, dull, bland, humdrum, insipid, unexciting, uninspiring, vapid ▸ *v* **4** = **domesticate**, train, break in, house-train **5** = **discipline**, master, humble, subdue, suppress, conquer, subjugate, bring to heel
tamper *v* = **interfere**, alter, fiddle (*informal*), meddle, tinker, fool around (*informal*), mess around
tang *See* **taste**
tangible *adj* = **definite**, real, positive,

DICTIONARY

tangle ⓣ *n* **1** confused mass or situation ▷ *v* **2** twist together in a tangle **3** (often foll. by *with*) come into conflict
tango *n, pl* **-gos 1** S American dance ▷ *v* **2** dance a tango
tank *n* **1** container for liquids or gases **2** armoured fighting vehicle moving on tracks
▸ **tanker** *n* ship or truck for carrying liquid in bulk
tankard *n* large beer-mug, often with a hinged lid
Tannhäuser *n* 13th-century German minnesinger, commonly identified with a legendary knight who sought papal absolution after years spent in revelry with Venus. The legend forms the basis of an opera by Wagner
tannic acid, tannin *n* vegetable substance used in tanning
tansy *n, pl* **-sies** yellow-flowered plant
tantalize ⓣ *v* torment by showing but withholding something desired **tantalizing** *adj* **tantalizingly** *adv*
tantalus *n* case in which bottles can be locked with their contents visible
tantamount ⓣ *adj* (foll. by *to*) equivalent in effect to
tantrum ⓣ *n* childish outburst of temper
tap[1] ⓣ *v* **tapping, tapped 1** knock lightly and usu. repeatedly ▷ *n* **2** light knock
▸ **tap dance** dance in which the feet beat out an elaborate rhythm
tap[2] ⓣ *n* **1** valve to control the flow of liquid from a pipe or cask ▷ *v* **tapping, tapped 2** listen in on (a telephone) secretly by making an illegal connection **3** fit a tap to (a pipe etc.) **4** draw off with or as if with a tap
▸ **on tap 1** *informal* readily available **2** (of beer etc.) drawn from a cask
tape ⓣ *n* **1** narrow long strip of material **2** string stretched across a race track to mark the finish **3** recording made on magnetized tape ▷ *v* **4** bind or fasten with tape **5** record on magnetized tape
▸ **have a person** *or* **situation taped** *informal* have full understanding and control of a person *or* situation
▸ **tape measure** tape marked off in centimetres or inches for measuring
▸ **tape recorder** device for recording and reproducing sound on magnetized tape
▸ **tapeworm** *n* long flat parasitic worm living in the intestines of vertebrates
taper ⓣ *v* **1** become narrower towards one end ▷ *n* **2** long thin candle **3** narrowing
▸ **taper off** *v* become gradually less
tapestry *n, pl* **-tries** fabric decorated with coloured woven designs
tapioca *n* beadlike starch made from cassava root, used in puddings
tapir [**tape**-er] *n* piglike mammal of tropical America and SE Asia, with a long snout
tappet *n* short steel rod in an engine, transferring motion from one part to another
taproot *n* main root of a plant, growing straight down
tar *n* **1** thick black liquid distilled from coal etc. ▷ *v* **tarring, tarred 2** coat with tar
▸ **tar sands** deposit of bitumen mixed with sand, clay, etc.
taramasalata *n* creamy pink pâté made from fish roe
tarantella *n* **1** lively Italian dance **2** music for this
Tarantino *n* **Quentin**. born 1963, US film director and screenwriter, noted for violent quirky crime dramas including *Reservoir Dogs* (1993), *Pulp Fiction* (1994), *Jackie Brown* (1998), and the two parts of *Kill Bill* (2003, 2004)
tarantula *n, pl* **-las, -lae** large poisonous hairy spider

THESAURUS

material, actual, concrete, palpable, perceptible
tangle *n* **1** = **knot**, mass, web, mat, muddle, jumble • *a tangle of wires* **2** = **confusion**, fix (*informal*), jam, complication, mess, mix-up, entanglement, imbroglio ▸ *v* **3** = **twist**, catch, knot, jumble • *Dolphins can get tangled in fishing nets and drown.* **4** (often with *with*) = **come into conflict**, dispute, contest, contend, come up against, cross swords, lock horns
tangled *adj* **1** = **twisted**, messy, entangled, knotted, jumbled, matted, snarled, tousled **2** = **complicated**, complex, messy, involved, confused, convoluted, knotty, mixed-up
tangy *adj* = **sharp**, spicy, tart, pungent, piquant
tantalize *v* = **torment**, torture, frustrate, taunt, tease, lead on
tantamount *adj* = **equivalent**, equal, synonymous, commensurate
tantrum *n* = **outburst**, fit, temper, flare-up, hysterics
tap[1] *v* **1** = **knock**, strike, beat, touch, rap, pat, drum ▸ *n* **2** = **knock**, touch, rap, pat
tap[2] *n* **1** = **valve**, stopcock ▷ **on tap** = **on draft**; (*Informal*) = **available**, ready, at hand, in reserve, on hand ▸ *v* **2** = **listen in on**, bug (*informal*), eavesdrop on **3** = **draw off**, drain, bleed, siphon off
tape *n* **1** = **strip**, band, ribbon ▸ *v* **2** = **record**, video, tape-record **3** = **bind**, stick, secure, seal, wrap
taper *v* = **narrow**, thin, come to a point ▷ **taper off** = **lessen**, reduce, decrease,

DICTIONARY

tarboosh *n* felt brimless cap, usu. red and often with a silk tassel, formerly worn by Muslim men
tardy *adj* **-dier, -diest** slow or late **tardily** *adv* **tardiness** *n*
tare[1] *n* **1** weight of the wrapping or container of goods **2** unladen weight of a vehicle
tare[2] *n* **1** type of vetch **2** *Bible* weed
target Ⓣ *n* **1** object or person a missile is aimed at **2** goal or objective **3** object of criticism ▷ *v* **-geting, -geted 4** aim or direct
tariff Ⓣ *n* **1** tax levied on imports **2** list of fixed prices
Tarkovsky *n* **Andrei**. 1932–86, Soviet film director, whose films include *Andrei Rublev* (1966), *Solaris* (1971), *Nostalgia* (1983), and *The Sacrifice* (1986)
Tarmac *n* **1** ® mixture of tar, bitumen, and crushed stones used for roads etc. **2 tarmac** airport runway
tarn *n* small mountain lake
tarnish Ⓣ *v* **1** make or become stained or less bright **2** damage or taint ▷ *n* **3** discoloration or blemish
taro *n* tropical plant with edible roots
tarot [**tarr**-oh] *n* special pack of cards used mainly in fortune-telling **tarot card**
tarpaulin *n* (sheet of) heavy waterproof fabric
tarragon *n* aromatic herb
tarry Ⓣ *v* **-rying, -ried** *old-fashioned* **1** linger or delay **2** stay briefly
tarsier *n* monkey-like mammal of the E Indies
tarsus *n, pl* **-si** bones of the heel and ankle collectively
tart[1] Ⓣ *n* pie or flan with a sweet filling
tart[2] Ⓣ *adj* sharp or bitter **tartly** *adv* **tartness** *n*
tart[3] Ⓣ *n informal* sexually provocative or promiscuous woman
▸ **tart up** *v informal* dress or decorate in a smart or flashy way
tartan *n* **1** design of straight lines crossing at right angles, esp. one associated with a Scottish clan **2** cloth with such a pattern
tartar[1] *n* **1** hard deposit on the teeth **2** deposit formed during the fermentation of wine
tartar[2] *n* fearsome or formidable person
tartar sauce *n* mayonnaise sauce mixed with chopped herbs and capers, served with seafood
tartrazine [**tar**-traz-zeen] *n* artificial yellow dye used in food etc.
task Ⓣ *n* (difficult or unpleasant) piece of work to be done
▸ **take to task** criticize or scold
▸ **task force** (military) group formed to carry out a specific task
▸ **taskmaster** *n* person who enforces hard work
Tasmanian devil *n* small carnivorous marsupial found in Tasmania
tassel *n* decorative fringed knot of threads **tasselled** *adj*
taste Ⓣ *n* **1** sense by which the flavour of a substance is distinguished in the mouth **2** distinctive flavour **3** brief experience of something **4** small amount tasted **5** liking **6** ability to appreciate what is beautiful or excellent ▷ *v* **7** distinguish the taste of (a substance) **8** take a small amount of (something) into the mouth **9** have a specific taste **10** experience briefly

THESAURUS

fade, dwindle, wane, subside, die away, wind down
target *n* **1 = goal**, end, mark, aim, object, intention, objective, ambition **2 = victim**, butt, scapegoat
tariff *n* **= tax**, duty, toll, levy, excise
tarnish *v* **1 = stain**, taint, darken, blacken, blemish, blot, sully, discolour ▸ *n* **2 = stain**, spot, taint, blemish, blot, discoloration
tarry *See* **stay**
tart[1] *n* **= pie**, pastry, tartlet
tart[2] *adj* **= sharp**, bitter, acid, sour, tangy, pungent, piquant, vinegary
tart[3] *n* **= slut**, prostitute, ho (*slang*), whore, call girl, floozy (*slang*), trollop
task *n* **= job**, mission, duty, assignment, chore, undertaking • *I had the task of breaking the bad news.* ▷ **take to task = criticize**, blame, reprimand, censure, scold, reproach, upbraid, reprove, tell off (*informal*)
See also: **work**
taste *n* **1 = flavour**, tang • *I like the taste of this juice.* **2 = mouthful**, bite, sip • *I'll have a taste of your dessert.* **3 = liking**, appetite, penchant (*formal*), fondness • *a taste for adventure* **4 = refinement**, style, judgment, discrimination, appreciation, elegance, sophistication, discernment ▸ *v* **5 = distinguish**, perceive, differentiate, discern **6 = sample**, try, test, sip, savour **7 = have a flavour of**, savour of, smack of **8 = experience**, know, undergo, encounter, meet with, partake of
tasteful *adj* **= refined**, artistic, elegant, stylish, exquisite, polished, cultured, cultivated, discriminating, in good taste
tasteless *adj* **1 = bland**, insipid • *The fish was overcooked and tasteless.* OPPOSITE: tasty **2 = vulgar**, flashy, tacky (*informal*), gaudy, garish, tawdry • *a house crammed with tasteless ornaments* OPPOSITE: tasteful
See also: **crude**

DICTIONARY

▸ **tasteful** *adj* having or showing good taste **tastefully** *adv*
▸ **tasteless** *adj* **1** bland or insipid **2** showing bad taste **tastelessly** *adv*
▸ **tasty** *adj* pleasantly flavoured
▸ **taste bud** small organ on the tongue which perceives flavours
tat *n* tatty or tasteless article(s)
Tati *n* **Jacques**, real name *Jacques Tatischeff*. 1908–82, French film director, pantomimist, and comic actor, creator of the character Monsieur Hulot
tattered Ⓣ *adj* ragged or torn
▸ **tatters** *pl n* ragged pieces
tattle *n, v* gossip or chatter
▸ **tattletale** *n* a scandalmonger or gossip
tattoo[1] *v* **-tooing, -tooed 1** make (a pattern) on the skin by pricking and staining it with indelible inks ▹ *n* **2** pattern so made **tattooist** *n*
tattoo[2] Ⓣ *n* **1** military display or pageant **2** drumming or tapping
tatty Ⓣ *adj* **-tier, -tiest** shabby or worn out **tattiness** *n*
Tatum *n* **Art**, full name *Arthur Tatum*. 1910–56, US jazz pianist
Taube *n* **Henry**. 1915–2005, US inorganic chemist born in Canada. Winner of the 1983 Nobel Prize for chemistry for his work on electron-transfer reactions
taught *v* past of **teach**
taunt Ⓣ *v* **1** tease with jeers ▹ *n* **2** jeering remark
taupe *adj* brownish-grey
taut Ⓣ *adj* **1** drawn tight, tense **2** showing nervous strain, stressed
▸ **tauten** *v* make or become taut
tautology *n, pl* **-gies** use of words which merely repeat something already stated **tautological** *adj*
Tavener *n* Sir **John** (**Kenneth**). born 1944, British composer, whose works include the cantata *The Whale* (1966), the opera *Thérèse* (1979), and the choral work *The Last Discourse* (1998); many of his later works are inspired by the liturgy of the Russian Orthodox Church
tavern Ⓣ *n old-fashioned* pub
Taverner *n* **John**. ?1495–1545, English composer, esp. of church music; best known for the mass *Western Wynde*, based on a secular song
tawdry Ⓣ *adj* **-drier, -driest** cheap, showy, and of poor quality **tawdriness** *n*
tawny *adj* yellowish-brown
tax Ⓣ *n* **1** compulsory payment levied by a government on income, property, etc. to raise revenue **2** heavy demand on something ▹ *v* **3** levy a tax on **4** make heavy demands on **taxable** *adj* **taxpayer** *n*
▸ **taxation** *n* levying of taxes
▸ **tax return** statement of personal income for tax purposes
taxi *n* **1** Also **taxicab** automobile with a driver that may be hired to take people to any specified destination ▹ *v* **taxiing, taxied 2** (of an aircraft) run along the ground before taking off or after landing
▸ **taximeter** *n* meter in a taxi that registers the fare
▸ **taxi rank** place where taxis wait to be hired
taxidermy *n* art of stuffing and mounting animal skins to give them a lifelike appearance **taxidermist** *n*
taxonomy *n* classification of plants and animals into groups **taxonomic** *adj* **taxonomist** *n*
Taylor *n* **1** Dame **Elizabeth**. born 1932, US film actress, born in England: films include *National Velvet* (1944), *Cat on a Hot Tin Roof* (1958), *Suddenly Last Summer* (1959), and *Butterfield 8* (1960) and *Who's Afraid of Virginia Woolf?* (1966), for both of which she won Oscars **2 Zachary**. 1784–1850, 12th president of the US (1849–50); hero of the Mexican War
TB tuberculosis
T-ball *n* type of baseball for young children in which the ball is placed on a stand in front of the batter

THESAURUS

tasty *adj* = **delicious**, palatable, luscious, appetizing • *The food was very tasty.* OPPOSITE: tasteless
tattered *See* **worn out**
tatters *n* ▹ **in tatters** = **ragged**, down at heel, in rags, in shreds, ripped, tattered, threadbare, torn
tattoo *See* **parade**
tatty *adj* = **shabby**, dilapidated, ragged, neglected, run-down, bedraggled, down at heel, threadbare, worn
taunt *v* **1** = **jeer**, insult, provoke, mock, ridicule, tease, deride, torment ▸ *n* **2** = **jeer**, insult, dig, provocation, ridicule, sarcasm, derision, gibe, teasing
taut *adj* = **tight**, tense, strained, rigid, stretched, flexed, stressed
tavern *n* = **bar**, pub, inn, alehouse (*archaic*), hostelry, parlour (*Canad*), brasserie (*Canad Queb*), public house, booze can (*Canad*), beer parlour (*Canad*), beverage room (*Canad*)
tawdry *adj* = **vulgar**, cheap, flashy, gaudy, gimcrack, tasteless, tacky (*informal*), tatty, tinselly
tax *n* **1** = **duty**, tariff, levy (*formal*) • *the tax on new cars* ▸ *v* **2** = **strain**, stretch, drain, exhaust, sap • *Those kids tax my patience.* **3** = **charge**, rate, assess
taxing *adj* = **demanding**, tough, stressful,

DICTIONARY

T-bone steak *n* steak cut from the sirloin of beef, containing a T-shaped bone
tbs., tbsp. tablespoon(ful)
Tchaikovsky *n* **Pyotr Ilyich**. 1840–93, Russian composer. His works, which are noted for their expressive melodies, include the *Sixth Symphony* (the *Pathétique*; 1893), ballets, esp. *Swan Lake* (1876) and *The Sleeping Beauty* (1889), and operas, including *Eugene Onegin* (1879) and *The Queen of Spades* (1890), both based on works by Pushkin
tea *n* **1** dried leaves of an Asian bush **2** drink made by infusing these leaves in boiling water **3** drink made like tea from other plants **4** main evening meal **5** light afternoon meal of tea, cakes, etc.
▸ **tea bag** small porous bag of tea leaves
▸ **tea cosy** covering for a teapot to keep the tea warm
▸ **teapot** *n* container with a lid, spout, and handle for making and serving tea
▸ **teaspoon** *n* small spoon for stirring tea
▸ **tea towel** towel for drying dishes
teach Ⓣ *v* **teaching, taught 1** tell or show (someone) how to do something **2** cause to learn or understand **3** give lessons in (a subject) **teacher** *n* **teaching** *n*
teak *n* very hard wood of an E Indian tree
teal *n* kind of small duck
team Ⓣ *n* **1** group of people forming one side in a game **2** group of people or animals working together
▸ **teamster** *n* **1** driver of team of draft animals **2** truck driver
▸ **team up** *v* make or join a team
▸ **teamwork** *n* cooperative work by a team
tear[1], teardrop *n* drop of fluid appearing in and falling from the eye
▸ **in tears** weeping
▸ **tearful** *adj* weeping or about to weep
▸ **tear gas** gas that stings the eyes and causes temporary blindness
▸ **tear-jerker** *n informal* excessively sentimental film or book
tear[2] Ⓣ *v* **tearing, tore, torn 1** rip a hole in **2** rip apart **3** become ripped **4** rush ▹ *n* **5** hole or split
▸ **tearaway** *n* wild or unruly person
▸ **tear down** *v* demolish
tease Ⓣ *v* **1** make fun of (someone) in a provoking or playful way **2** separate the fibres of ▹ *n* **3** person who teases **teasing** *adj, n*
teasel, teazel, teazle *n* plant with prickly leaves and flowers
teat *n* **1** rubber nipple of a feeding bottle **2** nipple of a breast or udder
tech *n informal* technical college
techie *informal* ▹ *n* **1** person who is skilled in the use of technology ▹ *adj* **2** relating to or skilled in the use of technology
technical Ⓣ *adj* **1** of or specializing in industrial, practical, or mechanical arts and applied sciences **2** skilled in technical subjects **3** relating to a particular field **4** according to the letter of the law **5** showing technique: *technical brilliance*
technically *adv*
▸ **technicality** *n* petty point based on a strict application of rules
▸ **technician** *n* person skilled in a particular technical field
▸ **technical college** higher educational institution with courses in art and technical subjects
▸ **technical foul** *basketball* foul for unsportsman-like conduct, resulting in a free throw for the other team
Technicolor *n* ® system of colour photography used for the cinema

THESAURUS

onerous, exacting, exhausting, punishing, sapping, tiring, trying
teach *v* = **instruct**, school, coach, train, drill, educate, tutor • *She taught me to read*.
See also: **lecture, show**
teacher *n* = **instructor**, coach, professor, guru, lecturer, tutor • *a geography teacher*
team *n* **1** = **group**, side, crew, band, gang, squad, troupe • *the football team* ▸ *v* **2** (*often with up*) = **join forces**, unite, co-operate, collaborate, link up, pair up, work together • *A friend suggested that we team up for a working vacation*.
See also: **party, staff**
teammate *See* **partner**
teamwork *n* = **cooperation**, unity, collaboration, harmony, coordination, fellowship, esprit de corps
tear *n* **1** = **rip**, hole, split, scratch, rupture • *a tear in the curtains* ▸ *v* **2** = **rip**, split, scratch, shred, rupture • *She nearly tore my jacket*. **3** = **rush**, charge, shoot, race, fly, speed, dash, zoom, dart • *He tore through busy streets in a high-speed chase*.
tearful *adj* = **weeping**, blubbering, crying, in tears, lachrymose, sobbing, weepy (*informal*), whimpering
tears *pl n* = **crying**, blubbering, sobbing, wailing, weeping ▹ **in tears** = **crying**, distressed, blubbering, sobbing, weeping
tease *v* = **make fun of**, needle (*informal*), mock, taunt, pull someone's chain (*informal*) • *He used to tease me about wanting to act*.
See also: **bully, joke, pick on, provoke**
technical *adj* = **scientific**, specialist, skilled, specialized, technological, hi-tech *or* high-tech

DICTIONARY

technique Ⓣ *n* **1** method or skill used for a particular task **2** technical proficiency
techno *n* type of very fast disco music, using electronic sounds and having a strong technological influence
technocracy *n, pl* **-cies** government by technical experts **technocrat** *n*
technology *n, pl* **-gies 1** application of practical or mechanical sciences to industry or commerce **2** sciences applied thus **technological** *adj* **technologist** *n*
tectonics *pl n* study of the earth's crust and the forces affecting it
Tecumseh *n* ?1768–1813, American Indian chief of the Shawnee tribe. He attempted to unite western Indian tribes against the White people, but was defeated at Tippecanoe (1811). He was killed while fighting for the British in the War of 1812
teddy *n, pl* **-dies 1** teddy bear **2** combined camisole and knickers
▸ **teddy bear** soft toy bear
teddy boy *n* youth who wore mock Edwardian fashions in Britain, esp. in the mid-1950s
Te Deum [tee **dee**-um] *n* ancient Latin hymn of thanksgiving
tedious Ⓣ *adj* causing fatigue or boredom **tediously** *adv*
▸ **tedium** *n* monotony
tee *n* **1** small peg supporting a golf ball when teeing off **2** area of a golf course from which the first stroke of a hole is made
▸ **tee off** *v* **1** make the first stroke of a hole in golf **2** *slang* make angry
teem Ⓣ *v* **1** abound in **2** rain heavily
teenage *adj* of the period of life between the ages of 13 and 19
▸ **teenager** *n* person aged between 13 and 19
teens *pl n* period of being a teenager
teeny *adj* **teenier, teeniest** *informal* extremely small
teepee *n* same as **tepee**
tee-shirt *n* same as **T-shirt**
teeter Ⓣ *v* wobble or move unsteadily
teeth *n* plural of **tooth**
teethe *v* (of a baby) grow his or her first teeth
▸ **teething troubles** problems during the early stages of something
teetotal *adj* drinking no alcohol **teetotaller** *n*
TEFL Teaching of English as a Foreign Language
Teflon *n* ® substance used for nonstick coatings on pans etc.
Te Kanawa *n* Dame **Kiri**. born 1944, New Zealand operatic soprano
tele- *prefix* **1** at or over a distance: *telescope* **2** involving television or telephone: *telesales*
telecommunications *pl n* communications using telephone, radio, television, etc.
telegram *n* (formerly) message sent by telegraph
telegraph *n* **1** (formerly) system for sending messages over a distance along a cable ▷ *v* **2** communicate by telegraph **telegraphic** *adj*
▸ **telegraphist** *n* person who works a telegraph
▸ **telegraphy** *n* science or use of a telegraph
telekinesis *n* movement of objects by thought or willpower
Telemann *n* **Georg Philipp**. 1681–1767, German composer, noted for his prolific output
telemeter *n* device for recording or measuring a distant event and transmitting the data to a receiver **telemetry** *n* **telemetric** *adj*
teleology *n* belief that all things have a predetermined purpose **teleological** *adj*
telepathy Ⓣ *n* direct communication between minds **telepathic** *adj* **telepathically** *adv*
telephone Ⓣ *n* **1** device for transmitting sound over a distance along wires ▷ *v* **2** call or talk to (a person) by telephone

THESAURUS

technique *n* **1** = **method**, way, system, approach, style, procedure, manner, means, mode **2** = **skill**, performance, touch, execution, craft, proficiency, artistry, craftsmanship
tedious *adj* = **boring**, dull, dreary, drab, tiresome, monotonous, mind-numbing, humdrum, irksome, laborious, wearisome
tedium *n* = **boredom**, routine, drabness, dreariness, dullness, monotony, sameness, tediousness
teem *See* **crawl, rain**
teeming[1] *adj* = **full**, alive, thick, abundant, brimming, bristling, bursting, crawling, overflowing, swarming
teeming[2] *adj* = **pouring**, pelting, raining cats and dogs (*informal*)
teenager *n* = **youth**, girl, boy, minor, adolescent, juvenile
teeter *v* = **wobble**, rock, sway, stagger, waver, seesaw, totter
teetotaller, teetotaler *n* = **nondrinker**, abstainer
telepathy *n* = **mind-reading**, E.S.P., sixth sense
telephone *n* **1** = **phone**, line, cell, handset, horn (*informal*), iPhone (*trademark*), blower (*informal*), cell phone, camera phone, smart phone, video phone, carphone, internet phone ▸ *v* **2** = **call**, phone, dial

DICTIONARY

telephony *n* **telephonic** *adj*
▸ **telephonist** *n* person operating a telephone switchboard
▸ **telephone booth** kiosk for a public telephone
telephoto lens *n* camera lens producing a magnified image of a distant object
teleprinter *n* apparatus like a typewriter for sending and receiving typed messages by wire
Teleprompter *n* ® device under a television camera enabling a speaker to read the script while appearing to look at the camera
telesales *pl n* selling of a product or service by telephone
telescope 🅣 *n* **1** optical instrument for magnifying distant objects ▹ *v* **2** shorten by the sliding of each part over the next **3** shorten by crushing **telescopic** *adj*
teletext *n* system which shows information and news on subscribers' television screens
television 🅣 *n* **1** system of producing a moving image and accompanying sound on a distant screen **2** device for receiving broadcast signals and converting them into sound and pictures **3** content of television programmes **televisual** *adj*
▸ **televise** *v* broadcast on television
teleworking *n* use of home computers, telephones, etc., to enable a person to work from home while maintaining contact with colleagues or customers **teleworker** *n*
telex *n* **1** international communication service using teleprinters **2** message sent by telex ▹ *v* **3** transmit by telex
tell 🅣 *v* **telling, told 1** make known in words **2** order or instruct **3** give an account of **4** discern or distinguish **5** have an effect **6** *informal* reveal secrets
▸ **teller** *n* **1** narrator **2** bank cashier **3** person who counts votes
▸ **telling** *adj* having a marked effect
▸ **tell off** *v* reprimand **telling-off** *n*
▸ **telltale** *n* **1** person who reveals secrets ▹ *adj* **2** revealing
Teller *n* **Edward**. 1908–2003, US nuclear physicist, born in Hungary: a major contributor to the development of the hydrogen bomb (1952)
tellurian *adj* of the earth
telly *n, pl* **-lies** *informal* television
temerity 🅣 [tim-**merr**-it-tee] *n* boldness or audacity
temp *informal* ▹ *n* **1** temporary employee, esp. a secretary ▹ *v* **2** work as a temp
temp. 1 temperature **2** temporary
temper 🅣 *n* **1** outburst of anger **2** tendency to become angry **3** calm mental condition: *I lost my temper* **4** frame of mind ▹ *v* **5** make less extreme **6** strengthen or toughen (metal)
tempera *n* painting medium of pigment and egg yolk
temperament 🅣 *n* person's character or disposition
▸ **temperamental** *adj* **1** having changeable

THESAURUS

telescope *n* **1 = spyglass**, glass ▸ *v* **2 = shorten**, contract, shrink, compress, abbreviate, condense, abridge
television *n* **= TV**, small screen (*informal*), the tube (*slang*)
tell *v* **1 = inform**, advise, notify, acquaint, apprise • *They told us the dreadful news.* **2 = order**, direct, command, instruct, call upon, enjoin • *A passerby told the driver to move his car.* **3 = see**, discern • *I could tell he was scared.* **4 = describe**, report, relate, portray, depict, recount, chronicle, narrate **5 = distinguish**, identify, discriminate, differentiate, discern **6 = have effect** *or* **take effect**, count, register, weigh, carry weight, make its presence felt, take its toll
See also: **announce** ▹ **tell a lie** *See* **lie** ▹ **tell apart** *See* **distinguish** ▹ **tell off** **= reprimand**, censure, berate, chide, lecture, rebuke, scold, reproach ▹ **tell on** *See* **inform on** ▹ **tell the difference** *See* **distinguish**
telling *adj* **= effective**, significant, powerful, impressive, decisive, influential, considerable, marked, striking, forceful
telling-off *n* **= reprimand**, criticism, rebuke, lecture, scolding, reproach, reproof, talking-to
temerity *n* **= audacity**, front, nerve (*informal*), recklessness, chutzpah (*informal*), boldness, effrontery, impudence, rashness
temper *n* **1 = rage**, passion, fury, tantrum, bad mood **2 = irritability**, passion, resentment, hot-headedness, irascibility, petulance, surliness **3 = self-control**, cool (*slang*), composure, calmness, equanimity **4 = frame of mind**, mind, nature, constitution, mood, disposition, humor, temperament ▸ *v* **5 = moderate**, soften, restrain, lessen, mitigate, soothe, assuage, mollify, tone down **6 = strengthen**, toughen, harden, anneal
temperament *n* **1 = nature**, character, outlook, constitution, personality, temper, bent, disposition, make-up, humour **2 = moodiness**, anger, volatility, excitability, hot-headedness, petulance
temperamental *adj* **1 = moody**, emotional, sensitive, volatile, irritable, touchy, capricious, excitable, highly strung, hypersensitive **2 = unreliable**,

DICTIONARY

moods **2** of temperament **3** *informal* erratic and unreliable **temperamentally** *adv*
temperate Ⓣ *adj* **1** (of climate) not extreme **2** self-restrained or moderate
▸**temperance** *n* **1** moderation **2** abstinence from alcohol
temperature *n* **1** degree of heat or cold **2** *informal* abnormally high body temperature
tempest Ⓣ *n* violent storm
▸**tempestuous** *adj* violent or stormy **tempestuously** *adv*
template Ⓣ *n* pattern used to cut out shapes accurately
temple[1] Ⓣ *n* building for worship
temple[2] *n* region on either side of the forehead
Temple *n* **Shirley**, married name *Shirley Temple Black*. born 1928, US film actress and politician. Her films as a child star include *Little Miss Marker* (1934), *Wee Willie Winkie* (1937), and *Heidi* (1937). She was US ambassador to Ghana (1974–76) and to Czechoslovakia (1989–92)
tempo Ⓣ *n, pl* **-pos, -pi** **1** speed of a piece of music **2** rate or pace
temporal *adj* **1** of time **2** secular rather than spiritual **3** of the temple(s) of the head
temporary Ⓣ *adj* lasting only for a short time **temporarily** *adv*
temporize *v* **1** gain time by negotiation or evasiveness **2** adapt to circumstances **temporization** *n*
tempt Ⓣ *v* **1** (try to) entice (a person) to do something wrong **2** risk provoking: *you're tempting fate* **tempter** (**temptress**) *n*
▸**temptation** *n* **1** tempting **2** tempting thing
▸**tempting** *adj* attractive or inviting
ten *adj, n* one more than nine
▸**tenth** *adj, n* (of) number ten in a series
tenable Ⓣ *adj* able to be held or maintained
tenacious Ⓣ *adj* **1** holding fast **2** stubborn **tenacity** *n*
tenant Ⓣ *n* person who rents land or a building **tenancy** *n*
tench *n, pl* **tench** freshwater game fish
tend[1] Ⓣ *v* **1** be inclined **2** go in the direction of
▸**tendency** *n* inclination to act in a certain way
▸**tendentious** *adj* biased, not impartial
tend[2] Ⓣ *v* take care of
tender[1] Ⓣ *adj* **1** not tough **2** gentle and affectionate **3** vulnerable or sensitive **tenderly** *adv* **tenderness** *n*

THESAURUS

unpredictable, inconsistent, erratic, inconstant
temperance *n* **1** = **moderation**, restraint, discretion, self-control, self-restraint, continence, forbearance, self-discipline **2** = **teetotalism**, abstinence, sobriety, abstemiousness
temperate *adj* **1** = **mild**, fair, cool, calm, moderate, gentle, pleasant **2** = **self-restrained**, calm, moderate, reasonable, mild, sensible, dispassionate, composed, even-tempered, self-controlled
tempest *n* = **storm**, hurricane, tornado, cyclone, typhoon, squall, gale
tempestuous *adj* **1** = **stormy**, turbulent, windy, gusty, raging, blustery, inclement, squally **2** = **passionate**, violent, wild, emotional, intense, heated, stormy, furious, turbulent, boisterous
template *See* **pattern**
temple *n* = **shrine**, church, sanctuary, place of worship
tempo *See* **rate, rhythm**
temporarily *adv* = **briefly**, momentarily, fleetingly, for the time being, pro tem
temporary *adj* = **impermanent**, interim, passing, provisional, momentary, fleeting, transient, ephemeral, transitory • *a temporary loss of memory* OPPOSITE: permanent
tempt *v* = **entice**, lure, seduce • *Don't tempt me to eat anything else.*
See also: **attract**
temptation *n* = **enticement**, pull, lure, inducement, seduction, allurement, tantalization
tempting *adj* = **inviting**, attractive, alluring, seductive, appetizing, enticing, mouthwatering, tantalizing
tenable *adj* = **sound**, reasonable, viable, rational, plausible, justifiable, believable, arguable, defensible
tenacious *adj* **1** = **firm**, strong, tight, iron, forceful, unshakable, clinging, immovable **2** = **stubborn**, persistent, adamant, determined, steadfast, resolute, dogged, unyielding, obdurate, obstinate, unswerving
tenacity *n* = **perseverance**, application, resolve, determination, persistence, doggedness, obduracy, steadfastness, stubbornness
tenancy *n* = **lease**, possession, residence, occupancy, renting
tenant *n* = **leaseholder**, resident, renter, occupant, inhabitant, occupier, lessee
tend[1] *v* **1** = **be inclined**, be apt, be liable, be prone, have a tendency • *I tend to forget things.* **2** = **go**, point, head, bear, aim, lean (toward), make for
tend[2] *v* = **take care of**, nurse, care for, look after • *the way we tend our cattle*
tendency *n* = **inclination**, leaning, propensity • *a tendency to be critical*
tender[1] *adj* **1** = **gentle**, kind, warm,

DICTIONARY

▶ **tenderize** *v* soften (meat) by pounding or treatment with a special substance
tenderizer *n*
▶ **tenderloin** *n* tender cut of beef or pork from between the sirloin and ribs
tender[2] Ⓣ *v* **1** offer **2** make a tender ▷ *n* **3** formal offer to supply goods or services at a stated cost
▶ **legal tender** currency that must, by law, be accepted as payment
tender[3] *n* **1** small boat that brings supplies to a larger ship in a port **2** carriage for fuel and water attached to a steam locomotive
tendon *n* sinew attaching a muscle to a bone
tendril *n* slender stem by which a climbing plant clings
tenement *n* building divided into several apartments
tenet Ⓣ [**ten**-nit] *n* doctrine or belief
tenner *n informal* ten-pound note
tennis *n* game in which players use rackets to hit a ball back and forth over a net
Tennyson *n* **Alfred**, Lord Tennyson. 1809–92, English poet; poet laureate (1850–92). His poems include *The Lady of Shalott* (1832), *Morte d'Arthur* (1842), the collection *In Memoriam* (1850), *Maud* (1855), and *Idylls of the King* (1859)
Tennysonian *adj, n*
tenon *n* projecting end on a piece of wood fitting into a slot in another
tenor *n* **1** (singer with) the second highest male voice **2** general meaning ▷ *adj* **3** (of a voice or instrument) between alto and baritone
tenpin bowling *n* game in which players try to knock over ten skittles by rolling a ball at them
tense[1] *n* form of a verb showing the time of action
tense[2] Ⓣ *adj* **1** stretched tight **2** emotionally strained ▷ *v* **3** make or become tense
▶ **tensile** *adj* of tension
▶ **tension** *n* **1** degree of stretching **2** emotional strain **3** hostility or suspense **4** *electricity* voltage
tent *n* portable canvas shelter
tentacle *n* flexible organ of many invertebrates, used for grasping, feeding, etc.
tentative Ⓣ *adj* **1** provisional or experimental **2** cautious or hesitant
tentatively *adv*
tenterhooks *pl n* **on tenterhooks** in anxious suspense
tenuous Ⓣ *adj* slight or flimsy **tenuously** *adv* **tenuousness** *n*
tenure Ⓣ *n* (period of) the holding of an office or position
Tenzing Norgay *n* 1914–86, Nepalese mountaineer. With Sir Edmund Hillary, he was the first to reach the summit of Mount Everest (1953)
tepee [**tee**-pee] *n* N American Indian cone-shaped tent
tepid Ⓣ *adj* **1** slightly warm **2** half-hearted
tequila *n* Mexican alcoholic drink
tercentenary *adj, n, pl* **-naries** (of) a three hundredth anniversary
Teresa, Theresa *n* **1 Mother**, original name *Agnes Gonxha Bojaxhiu*. 1910–97, Indian Roman Catholic missionary, born in Skopje, now in the Former Yugoslav Republic of Macedonia,

THESAURUS

sensitive, loving, compassionate, caring, affectionate • *tender loving care* OPPOSITE: tough **2 = sore**, sensitive, raw, painful, aching, bruised, inflamed • *My stomach felt very tender.* **3 = vulnerable**, young, sensitive, raw, youthful, inexperienced, immature, impressionable
See also: **romantic**
tender[2] *v* **1 = offer**, hand in • *She tendered her resignation from the job.* ▶ *n* **2 = estimate**, bid, package, submission • *Builders will be asked to submit a tender for the work.* ▷ **legal tender = currency**, money, cash
See also: **submit**
tenderness *n* **1 = gentleness**, care, love, consideration, sympathy, affection, compassion, warmth, kindness, sentimentality **2 = soreness**, pain, sensitivity, inflammation
tenet *See* **belief**
tense *adj* **1 = nervous**, anxious, edgy, jittery, uptight (*informal*), jumpy • *Never had she seen him so tense.* OPPOSITE: calm **2 = stressful**, anxious, nerve-racking • *the tense atmosphere during the last moments of the game* **3 = tight**, strained, rigid, taut • *jaw muscles tense with anger* OPPOSITE: relaxed ▶ *v* **4 = tighten**, strain, stretch, brace, flex
tension *n* **1 = strain**, pressure, stress, anxiety, suspense, hostility, apprehension, nervousness, unease **2 = tightness**, pressure, stress, stiffness, rigidity, stretching, tautness
tentative *adj* **1 = unconfirmed**, experimental, indefinite, provisional, speculative, unsettled, conjectural **2 = hesitant**, cautious, uncertain, unsure, undecided, doubtful, timid, diffident, faltering
tenuous *adj* **= slight**, weak, shaky, doubtful, dubious, sketchy, flimsy, nebulous, insubstantial
tenure *See* **possession**
tepid *adj* **1 = lukewarm**, warmish **2 = half-hearted**, cool, indifferent, lukewarm, apathetic, unenthusiastic

DICTIONARY

of Albanian parents: noted for her work among the starving in Calcutta; Nobel peace prize 1979 **2 Saint**, known as *Teresa of Avila*. 1515–82, Spanish nun and mystic. She reformed the Carmelite order and founded 17 convents. Her writings include a spiritual autobiography and *The Way to Perfection*. Feast day: Oct 15 See also **Thérèse de Lisieux**

term Ⓣ *n* **1** word or expression **2** fixed period **3** period of the year when a school etc. is open or a lawcourt holds sessions **terms** **4** conditions **5** mutual relationship ▷ *v* **6** name or designate

termagant *n* unpleasant and bad-tempered woman

terminal Ⓣ *adj* **1** at or being an end **2** (of an illness) ending in death ▷ *n* **3** terminating point or place **4** point where current enters or leaves an electrical device **5** keyboard and VDU having input and output links with a computer **6** place where people or vehicles begin or end a journey **terminally** *adv*

terminate Ⓣ *v* **1** bring or come to an end **2** kill (someone) **termination** *n*

terminology Ⓣ *n, pl* **-gies** technical terms relating to a subject **terminological** *adj*

terminus Ⓣ *n, pl* **-ni, -nuses** **1** final point **2** railway or bus station at the end of a line

termite *n* white antlike insect destructive to timber

tern *n* gull-like sea bird

ternary *adj* consisting of three parts

Terpsichorean *adj* of dancing

terrace *n* **1** row of houses built as one block **2** paved area next to a building **3** level tier cut out of a hill **terraces** **4** Also **terracing** tiered area in a stadium where spectators stand ▷ *v* **5** form into or provide with a terrace

terracotta *adj, n* **1** (made of) brownish-red unglazed pottery ▷ *adj* **2** brownish-red

terra firma *n* dry land or solid ground

terrain Ⓣ *n* area of ground, esp. with reference to its physical character

terrapin *n* kind of aquatic tortoise

terrarium *n, pl* **-rariums, -raria** enclosed container for small plants or animals

terrazzo *n, pl* **-zos** floor of marble chips set in mortar and polished

terrestrial Ⓣ *adj* **1** of the earth **2** of or living on land

terrible Ⓣ *adj* **1** very serious **2** *informal* very bad **3** causing fear **terribly** *adv*

terrier *n* any of various breeds of small active dog

terrific Ⓣ *adj* **1** great or intense **2** *informal* excellent

terrify Ⓣ *v* **-fying, -fied** fill with fear **terrifying** *adj*

terrine [terr-**reen**] *n* **1** pâté or similar food **2** earthenware dish with a lid

territory Ⓣ *n, pl* **-ries** **1** district **2** **Territory** *Canad* any of three political divisions of

THESAURUS

term *n* **1** = **period**, time, session, stretch, spell • *Her term as president of the student council was about to end.* **2** = **word**, name, expression, designation • *the medical term for a heart attack* ▶ *v* **3** = **call**, name, label, style, dub, entitle, designate
See also: **length**

terminal *adj* **1** = **fatal**, deadly, killing, lethal, incurable, mortal **2** = **final**, last, extreme, ultimate, utmost, concluding ▶ *n* **3** = **terminus**, station, depot, end of the line

terminate *v* = **end**, close, stop, finish, complete, conclude, cease, discontinue, abort

termination *n* = **ending**, end, finish, abortion, conclusion, completion, cessation, discontinuation ▷ **termination of employment** *See* **fire, sack**

terminology *n* = **language**, vocabulary, jargon, nomenclature, phraseology, terms

terminus *n* = **end of the line**, station, garage, depot, last stop

terms *pl n* **1** = **conditions**, provisions, proviso, stipulations • *the terms of the agreement* **2** = **relationship**, status, standing, footing, relations
See also: **condition**

terrain *n* = **ground**, country, land, landscape, going, topography

terrestrial *adj* = **earthly**, global, worldly

terrible *adj* **1** = **awful**, desperate, horrible, horrendous, appalling, rotten, dreadful, horrid, frightful • *a terrible illness* **2** = **bad**, horrible, dire, awful, appalling, rotten, dreadful, abysmal • *That is a truly terrible haircut.* OPPOSITE: excellent
See also: **severe**

terribly *adv* = **extremely**, very, seriously, desperately, thoroughly, awfully (*informal*), decidedly, exceedingly

terrific *adj* **1** = **great**, huge, intense, tremendous, enormous, fearful, gigantic **2** (*Informal*) = **excellent**, amazing, wonderful, brilliant, fantastic (*informal*), sensational (*informal*), outstanding, magnificent, superb, marvellous, stupendous

terrified *adj* = **frightened**, scared, alarmed, panic-stricken, appalled, horrified, horror-struck, petrified

terrify *v* = **frighten**, shock, scare, alarm, horrify, appall, terrorize, make one's hair stand on end

terrifying *adj* = **frightening**, scary (*informal*), fearful, daunting, appalling, dreadful, fearsome, hair-raising, alarming, intimidating, unnerving, baleful, menacing

territory *n* = **district**, country, province,

DICTIONARY

Canada that are not provinces **3** area under the control of a particular government **4** area inhabited and defended by an animal **5** area of knowledge or experience **territorial** *adj*

terror Ⓣ *n* **1** great fear **2** terrifying person or thing **3** *informal* troublesome person or thing

▸ **terrorism** *n* use of violence and intimidation to achieve political ends **terrorist** *n, adj*

▸ **terrorize** *v* force or oppress by fear or violence

terry *n* fabric with the loops in its pile uncut

terse Ⓣ *adj* **1** concise **2** curt **tersely** *adv*

tertiary [**tur**-shar-ee] *adj* third in degree, order, etc.

Terylene *n* ® synthetic polyester yarn or fabric

tessellated *adj* paved or inlaid with a mosaic of small tiles

▸ **tessera** *n, pl* **-serae** small square tile used in mosaics

test Ⓣ *v* **1** try out to ascertain the worth, capability, or endurance of **2** carry out an examination on ▷ *n* **3** critical examination **4** method or standard of judgment **5** test match **testing** *adj*

▸ **test case** lawsuit that establishes a precedent

▸ **test match** one of a series of international cricket or rugby matches

▸ **test tube** narrow cylindrical glass vessel used in scientific experiments

▸ **test-tube baby** baby conceived outside the mother's body

testament Ⓣ *n* **1** *law* will **2** proof or tribute **3 Testament** one of the two main divisions of the Bible **testamentary** *adj*

testate *adj* having left a valid will **testacy** *n*

▸ **testator** [test-**tay**-tor] (**testatrix** [test-**tay**-triks]) *n* maker of a will

testicle *n* either of the two male reproductive glands

testify Ⓣ *v* **-fying, -fied 1** give evidence under oath **2** (foll. by *to*) be evidence (of)

testimony Ⓣ *n, pl* **-nies 1** declaration of truth or fact **2** evidence given under oath

▸ **testimonial** *n* **1** recommendation of the worth of a person or thing **2** tribute for services or achievement

testis *n, pl* **-tes** testicle

testosterone *n* male sex hormone secreted by the testes

testy *adj* **-tier, -tiest** irritable or touchy **testily** *adv* **testiness** *n*

tetanus *n* acute infectious disease producing muscular spasms and convulsions

tetchy *adj* **tetchier, tetchiest** cross and irritable **tetchiness** *n*

tête-à-tête *n, pl* **-têtes, -tête** private conversation

tether Ⓣ *n* **1** rope or chain for tying an animal to a spot ▷ *v* **2** tie up with rope

▸ **at the end of one's tether** at the limit of one's endurance

tetrahedron [tet-ra-**heed**-ron] *n, pl* **-drons, -dra** *geom* solid figure with four faces

tetralogy *n, pl* **-gies** series of four related works

Tetrazzini *n* **Luisa.** 1871–1940, Italian coloratura soprano

Tetzel, Tezel *n* **Johann.** ?1465–1519, German Dominican monk. His preaching on papal indulgences provoked Luther's 95 theses at Wittenberg (1517)

Teutonic [tew-**tonn**-ik] *adj* of or like the (ancient) Germans

text Ⓣ *n* **1** main body of a book as distinct

THESAURUS

state, area, land, nation, domain, dominion • *disputed territory*

See also: **colony, field, habitat, region**

terror *n* **1** = **fear**, shock, alarm, panic, horror, anxiety, dread, fright **2** = **scourge**, devil, monster, bogeyman, fiend, bugbear

terrorism *See* **violence**

terrorize *v* browbeat = **bully**, threaten, intimidate, menace, coerce, oppress

terse *adj* **1** = **concise**, short, brief, condensed, succinct, laconic, monosyllabic, pithy **2** = **curt**, short, abrupt, snappy, brusque

test *v* **1** = **check**, try, assess, try out, run up the flagpole (*informal*) • *The company is testing a new product.* ▸ *n* **2** = **check**, trial, assessment • *the banning of nuclear tests*

See also: **exam, examine**

testament *n* **1** = **proof**, evidence, witness, tribute, testimony, demonstration **2** = **will**, last wishes

testify *v* = **bear witness**, state, swear, assert, certify, affirm, vouch, corroborate, attest

testimonial *n* = **tribute**, recommendation, reference, endorsement, commendation

testimony *n* **1** = **evidence**, statement, submission, affidavit, deposition **2** = **proof**, support, evidence, demonstration, indication, verification, manifestation, corroboration

testing *adj* = **difficult**, tough, rigorous, arduous, strenuous, demanding, exacting, challenging, searching, taxing

tether *n* **1** = **rope**, lead, chain, leash, halter, fetter ▷ **at the end of one's tether** = **exasperated**, at one's wits' end, exhausted ▸ *v* **2** = **tie**, secure, chain, bind, fasten, fetter

text *n* **1** = **contents**, body **2** = **words**, wording

DICTIONARY

from illustrations etc. **2** passage of the Bible as the subject of a sermon **3** novel or play needed for a course **4** text message ▷ *v* **5** send a text message to (someone) **textual** *adj*

▶ **textbook** *n* **1** standard book on a particular subject ▷ *adj* **2** perfect: *a textbook landing*

▶ **text message** message sent in text form, esp. by means of a cell phone

textile *n* fabric or cloth, esp. woven

texture ⓣ *n* structure, feel, or consistency **textured** *adj* **textural** *adj*

Thackeray *n* **William Makepeace.** 1811–63, English novelist, born in India. His novels, originally serialized, include *Vanity Fair* (1848), *Pendennis* (1850), *Henry Esmond* (1852), and *The Newcomes* (1855)

Thai *adj* **1** of Thailand ▷ *n* **2** *pl* **-s, Thai** person from Thailand **3** language of Thailand

Thales *n* ?624–?546 BC, Greek philosopher, mathematician, and astronomer, born in Miletus. He held that water was the origin of all things and he predicted the solar eclipse of May 28, 585 BC

thalidomide [thal-**lid**-oh-mide] *n* drug formerly used as a sedative, but found to cause abnormalities in developing fetuses

thallium *n* highly toxic metallic element

than *conj* used to introduce the second element of a comparison

thane *n hist* Anglo-Saxon or medieval Scottish nobleman

thank ⓣ *v* **1** express gratitude to **2** hold responsible

▶ **thanks** *pl n* **1** words of gratitude ▷ *interj* **2** Also **thank you** polite expression of gratitude

▶ **thanks to** because of

▶ **thankful** *adj* grateful

▶ **thankless** *adj* unrewarding or unappreciated

▶ **Thanksgiving Day** public holiday on second Monday of October in Canada and fourth Thursday in November in the US

Thant *n* **U.** 1909–74, Burmese diplomat; secretary-general of the United Nations (1962–71)

that *adj, pron* **1** used to refer to something already mentioned or familiar, or further away ▷ *conj* **2** used to introduce a noun clause ▷ *pron* **3** used to introduce a relative clause

thatch *n* **1** roofing material of reeds or straw ▷ *v* **2** roof (a house) with reeds or straw **thatcher** *n*

Thatcher *n* **Margaret** (**Hilda**), Baroness (née *Roberts*). born 1925, British stateswoman; leader of the Conservative Party (1975–90); prime minister (1979–90) **Thatcherite** *n, adj*

thaw ⓣ *v* **1** make or become unfrozen **2** become more relaxed or friendly ▷ *n* **3** thawing **4** weather causing snow or ice to melt

the *adj* the definite article

theatre *n* **1** place where plays etc. are performed **2** drama and acting in general **3** hospital operating room

▶ **theatrical** *adj* **1** of the theatre **2** exaggerated or affected **theatrically** *adv* **theatricality** *n*

▶ **theatricals** *pl n* (amateur) dramatic performances

thee *pron obsolete* objective form of **thou**

theft ⓣ *n* stealing

their *adj* of or associated with them

▶ **theirs** *pron* (thing or person) belonging to them

theism [**thee**-iz-zum] *n* belief in the creation of the universe by one God **theist** *n, adj* **theistic** *adj*

them *pron* refers to people or things other than the speaker or those addressed

▶ **themselves** *pron* emphatic and reflexive form of **they, them**

theme ⓣ *n* **1** main idea or subject being discussed **2** recurring melodic figure in music **thematic** *adj*

t

THESAURUS

textbook *See* **book**

textiles *See* **cloth**

texture *n* = **feel**, consistency • *the bumpy texture of an orange*
See also: **finish**

thank *v* = **say thank you**, show one's appreciation

thankful *adj* = **grateful**, pleased, appreciative, relieved, indebted, beholden, obliged

thankless *adj* = **unrewarding**, fruitless, unprofitable, unappreciated, unrequited

thanks *pl n* = **gratitude**, credit, recognition, appreciation, kudos, acknowledgment, gratefulness ▷ **thanks to = because of**, through, as a result of, due to, owing to

thaw *v* = **melt**, warm, dissolve, soften, liquefy, defrost, unfreeze

theatrical *adj* **1** = **dramatic**, Thespian **2** = **exaggerated**, dramatic, affected, showy, histrionic, mannered, melodramatic, ostentatious, stagy

theft *n* = **stealing**, robbery • *the theft of classified documents*

theme *n* **1** = **subject**, idea, topic, keynote, subject matter **2** = **motif**, leitmotif, through-line

theological *adj* = **religious**, doctrinal, ecclesiastical

DICTIONARY

▸**theme park** leisure area based on a single theme
then *adv* **1** at that time **2** after that **3** that being so
thence *adv* **1** from that place or time **2** therefore
theocracy *n, pl* **-cies** government by a god or priests **theocratic** *adj*
Theocritus *n* ?310–?250 BC, Greek poet, born in Syracuse. He wrote the first pastoral poems in Greek literature and was closely imitated by Virgil
theodolite [thee-**odd**-oh-lite] *n* surveying instrument for measuring angles
Theodora *n* ?500–548 AD, Byzantine empress; wife and counsellor of Justinian I
Theodorakis *n* **Mikis**. born 1925, Greek composer, who wrote the music for the film *Zorba the Greek* (1965): imprisoned (1967–70) for his opposition to the Greek military government
Theodore I *n* called *Lascaris*. ?1175–1222, Byzantine ruler, who founded a Byzantine state in exile at Nicaea after Constantinople fell to the Crusaders (1204)
Theodoric, Theoderic *n* called *the Great*. ?454–526 AD, king of the Ostrogoths and founder of the Ostrogothic kingdom in Italy after his murder of Odoacer (493)
Theodosius I *n* called *the Great*. ?346–395 AD, Roman emperor of the Eastern Roman Empire (379–95) and of the Western Roman Empire (392–95)
theology *n, pl* **-gies** study of religions and religious beliefs **theologian** *n* **theological** *adj* **theologically** *adv*
Theophilus *n* died 842 AD, Byzantine emperor (829–42); a patron of learning and supporter of iconoclasm
theorem *n* proposition that can be proved by reasoning
theory Ⓣ *n, pl* **-ries** **1** set of ideas to explain something **2** abstract knowledge or reasoning **3** idea or opinion **4** ideal or hypothetical situation **theorist** *n*
▸**theoretical** *adj* based on theory rather than practice or fact **theoretically** *adv*
▸**theorize** *v* form theories, speculate
theosophy *n* religious or philosophical system claiming to be based on intuitive insight into the divine nature **theosophical** *adj*
therapy Ⓣ *n, pl* **-pies** curing treatment **therapist** *n*
▸**therapeutic** [ther-rap-**pew**-tik] *adj* curing
▸**therapeutics** *n* art of curing
there Ⓣ *adv* **1** in or to that place **2** in that respect
▸**thereby** *adv* by that means
▸**therefore** *adv* consequently, that being so
▸**thereupon** *adv* immediately after that
Thérèse de Lisieux *n* **Saint**, known as *the Little Flower of Jesus*. 1873–97, French Carmelite nun, noted for her autobiography, *The Story of a Soul* (1897). Feast day: Oct 3
therm *n* unit of heat
▸**thermal** *adj* **1** of heat **2** hot or warm **3** (of clothing) retaining heat ▷ *n* **4** rising current of warm air
thermionic valve *n* electronic valve in which electrons are emitted from a heated rather than a cold cathode
thermocouple *n* device for measuring heat, consisting of two wires of different metals joined at both ends
thermodynamics *pl n* scientific study of the relationship between heat and other forms of energy
thermoelectric, thermoelectrical *adj* of, relating to, or operated by the conversion of heat energy to electrical energy
thermometer *n* instrument for measuring temperature
thermonuclear *adj* involving nuclear fusion
thermoplastic *adj* (of a plastic) softening when heated and resetting on cooling
thermos *n* double-walled flask with a vacuum between the walls that keeps drinks hot or cold
thermosetting *adj* (of a plastic) remaining hard when heated
thermostat *n* device for automatically regulating temperature **thermostatic** *adj* **thermostatically** *adv*
Theroux *n* **Paul** (**Edward**). born 1941, US novelist and travel writer. His novels include *Picture Palace* (1978), *The Mosquito Coast* (1981), and *My Other Life* (1996); travel writings include *The Great Railway Bazaar* (1975)

THESAURUS

theoretical *adj* = **abstract**, academic, speculative, hypothetical, conjectural, notional
theorize *v* = **speculate**, project, suppose, guess, formulate, hypothesize, conjecture, propound
theory *n* = **hypothesis**, conjecture, supposition • *Darwin's theory of evolution*
therapeutic *adj* = **beneficial**, good, healing, corrective, remedial, restorative, curative, salutary
therapist *n* = **healer**, physician
therapy *n* = **remedy**, treatment, cure, healing
there *See* **present**
therefore *adv* = **consequently**, so, thus, hence, as a result, for that reason • *Muscles need lots of fuel and therefore burn lots of calories.*

DICTIONARY

thesaurus [thiss-**sore**-uss] *n, pl* **-ri, -ruses** book containing lists of synonyms and related words
these *adj, pron* plural of **this**
Thesiger *n* **Wilfred (Patrick)**. 1910–2003, British writer, who explored the Empty Quarter of Arabia (1945–50) and lived with the Iraqi marsh Arabs (1950–58). His books include *Arabian Sands* (1958), *The Marsh Arabs* (1964), and *My Kenya Days* (1994)
thesis Ⓣ *n, pl* **theses 1** written work submitted for a degree **2** doctrine maintained in argument
Thespis *n* 6th century BC, Greek poet, regarded as the founder of tragic drama
▸ **Thespian** *adj* **1** of the theatre ▹ *n* **2** actor or actress
they *pron* **1** refers to people or things other than the speaker or people addressed **2** refers to people in general **3** *informal* refers to he or she
thiamine *n* vitamin found in the outer coat of rice and other grains
thick Ⓣ *adj* **1** of great or specified extent from one side to the other **2** having a dense consistency **3** full of **4** *informal* stupid or insensitive **5** (of a voice) throaty **6** *informal* friendly **thickly** *adv*
▸ **a bit thick** *informal* unfair or unreasonable
▸ **the thick** busiest or most intense part
▸ **thickness** *n* **1** state of being thick **2** dimension through an object **3** layer
▸ **thicken** *v* make or become thick or thicker
▸ **thickset** *adj* **1** stocky in build **2** set closely together
thicket Ⓣ *n* dense growth of small trees
thief Ⓣ *n, pl* **thieves** person who steals
▸ **thieve** *v* steal **thieving** *adj, n*
Thiers *n* **Louis Adolphe**. 1797–1877, French statesman and historian. After the Franco-Prussian war, he suppressed the Paris Commune and became first president of the Third Republic (1871–73). His policies made possible the paying off of the war indemnity exacted by Germany
thigh *n* upper part of the human leg
thimble *n* cap protecting the end of the finger when sewing
thin Ⓣ *adj* **thinner, thinnest 1** not thick **2** slim or lean **3** sparse or meagre **4** of low density **5** poor or unconvincing ▹ *v* **thinning, thinned 6** make or become thin **thinly** *adv* **thinness** *n*
thine *pron obsolete* (something) of or associated with you (thou)
thing Ⓣ *n* **1** material object **2** object, fact, or idea considered as a separate entity **3** *informal* obsession **things 4** possessions, clothes, etc.
think Ⓣ *v* **thinking, thought 1** consider, judge, or believe **2** make use of the mind **3** be considerate enough or remember to do something **thinker** *n* **thinking** *adj, n*
▸ **think-tank** *n* group of experts studying specific problems

THESAURUS

thesis *n* **1 = dissertation**, paper, essay, treatise, monograph **2 = proposition**, view, idea, proposal, opinion, theory, contention, hypothesis
thick *adj* **1 = wide**, fat • *a thick stone wall* OPPOSITE: thin **2 = condensed**, concentrated, clotted • *thick soup* OPPOSITE: watery **3 = dense**, lush, bristling, luxuriant • *thick dark hair* OPPOSITE: sparse **4** (*Informal*) **= friendly**, close, familiar, intimate, devoted, inseparable, pally (*informal*) **5 = full**, packed, covered, brimming, bristling, bursting, crawling, swarming, teeming ▹ **a bit thick = unfair**, unreasonable, unjust
See also: **broad, dim, slow, stupid**
thicken *v* **= set**, clot, condense, congeal • *The clouds thickened.* OPPOSITE: thin
thicket *n* **= wood**, brake, covert, grove, coppice, copse
thickset *adj* **= stocky**, strong, heavy, muscular, bulky, sturdy, burly, well-built
thief *n* **= robber**, burglar, crook, shoplifter, mugger, pickpocket, finger man (*slang*), housebreaker, pilferer • *a car thief*
thieve *v* **= steal**, filch, rob, pinch (*informal*), swipe (*slang*), pilfer, purloin
thin *adj* **1 = narrow**, fine, slim, attenuated • *The material was too thin.* OPPOSITE: thick **2 = slim**, slight, lean, spare, skinny, slender, skeletal, bony, scrawny, emaciated, spindly • *a tall, thin man* **3 = meagre**, scarce, scattered, sparse, deficient, skimpy, scanty, wispy **4 = watery**, weak, diluted, runny • *thin soup* **5 = delicate**, fine, sheer, flimsy, diaphanous, filmy, gossamer, unsubstantial **6 = unconvincing**, poor, weak, inadequate, lousy (*slang*), lame, superficial, feeble, flimsy
thing *n* **1 = article**, object • *What's that thing doing here?* **2** (*Informal*) **= obsession**, mania, preoccupation, phobia, fixation, fetish, bee in one's bonnet, hang-up (*informal*) ▹ **things = possessions**, stuff, gear, belongings, effects • *She told him to take all his things with him.*
See also: **complex, item**
think *v* **1 = ponder**, consider, reflect, deliberate, contemplate, muse, meditate, mull over, cogitate, ruminate • *Let's think what we can do next.* **2 = believe**, hold, consider, judge, imagine, deem, reckon • *I think you're the best rower on the team.*
See also: **assume, expect, feel, guess, suppose** ▹ **think about** *See* **consider, contemplate** ▹ **think of** *See* **contemplate,**

t

DICTIONARY

▶ ***think up*** *v* invent or devise
third *adj* **1** of number three in a series **2** rated or graded below the second level ▷ *n* **3** one of three equal parts
▶ ***third degree*** violent interrogation
▶ ***third party*** (applying to) a person involved by chance or only incidentally in legal proceedings, an accident, etc.
▶ ***Third World*** developing countries of Africa, Asia, and Latin America
thirst Ⓣ *n* **1** desire to drink **2** craving or yearning ▷ *v* **3** feel thirst **thirsty** *adj* **thirstily** *adv*
thirteen *adj, n* three plus ten **thirteenth** *adj, n*
thirty *adj, n* three times ten **thirtieth** *adj, n*
this *adj, pron* **1** used to refer to a thing or person nearby or just mentioned ▷ *adj* **2** used to refer to the present time: *this morning*
thistle *n* prickly plant with dense flower heads
thither *adv obsolete* to or towards that place
tho, tho' *conj, adv* short for **though**
thole *n* wooden pin set in the side of a rowing boat to hold the oar in place (Also **tholepin**)
Thomas *n* **1 Ambroise**. 1811–96, French composer of light operas, including *Mignon* (1866) **2 David William**, known as *Dave*. born 1948, Canadian comedian and actor in films and television **3 R**(**onald**) **S**(**tuart**). 1913–2000, Welsh poet and clergyman. His collections include *Song at the Year's Turning* (1955), *Not that He Brought Flowers* (1968), and *Laboratories of the Spirit* (1975) **4 Saint**. Also **doubting Thomas** one of the twelve apostles, who refused to believe in Christ's resurrection until he had seen his wounds (John 20:24–29). Feast day: July 3 or Dec 21 or Oct 6
Thomas of Erceldoune *n* called *Thomas the Rhymer*. ?1220–?97, Scottish seer and poet; reputed author of a poem on the Tristan legend
Thompson *n* **1 David**. 1770–1857, Canadian fur trader, surveyor, and cartographer, born in England to Welsh parents. Charted large areas of western Canada and the US **2 Hunter S**(**tockton**). 1937–2005, US journalist and author, founder of Gonzo journalism, known for championing the drug culture and anti-authoritarian politics. His works include *Hells' Angels* (1966), *Fear and Loathing in Las Vegas* (1971), and *Fear and Loathing: On the Campaign Trail '72* (1973), the latter two of which were made into films **3** Sir **John**. 1845–1894, Canadian lawyer, judge, and Conservative politician; Prime Minister (1892–94)
Thomson *n* **1 Roy**, 1st Baron Thomson of Fleet. 1894–1976. British newspaper proprietor, born in Canada **2 Thomas John**, known as *Tom*. 1877–1917, Canadian painter noted for his landscapes of the Ontario wilderness **3 Virgil**. 1896–1989, US composer, music critic, and conductor, whose works include two operas, *Four Saints in Three Acts* (1928) and *The Mother of Us All* (1947), piano sonatas, a cello concerto, songs, and film music **4** Sir **William**. See (1st Baron) **Kelvin**
thong *n* **1** thin strip of leather etc. **2** skimpy article of underwear or beachwear that leaves the buttocks bare
thorax *n, pl* **thoraxes, thoraces** part of the body between the neck and the abdomen **thoracic** *adj*
Thorburn *n* **Cliff**. born 1948, Canadian snooker player: world champion 1980
Thoreau *n* **Henry David**. 1817–62, US writer, noted esp. for *Walden, or Life in the Woods* (1854), an account of his experiment in living in solitude. A powerful social critic, his essay *Civil Disobedience* (1849) influenced such dissenters as Gandhi
thorium *n* radioactive metallic element
thorn Ⓣ *n* **1** prickle on a plant **2** bush with thorns **thorny** *adj*
▶ ***thorn in one's side*** *or* ***thorn in one's flesh*** source of irritation
thorough Ⓣ *adj* **1** careful or methodical **2** complete **thoroughly** *adv* **thoroughness** *n*

THESAURUS

regard ▷ **think up** = **devise**, create, invent, concoct, visualize, come up with, contrive, dream up
thinker *n* = **philosopher**, brain (*informal*), mastermind, sage, theorist, intellect (*informal*), wise man
thinking *n* **1** = **reasoning**, position, view, idea, opinion, theory, judgment, conjecture ▶ *adj* **2** = **thoughtful**, intelligent, rational, reasoning, philosophical, reflective, meditative, contemplative
thin-skinned *See* **sensitive**
thirst *n* **1** = **thirstiness**, drought, dryness **2** = **craving**, desire, passion, appetite, longing, yearning, hankering, keenness
thirsty *adj* **1** = **parched**, dry, arid, dehydrated **2** = **eager**, hungry, avid, greedy, craving, desirous, longing, yearning
thorn *n* = **prickle**, spike, spine, barb
thorny *adj* = **prickly**, sharp, barbed, pointed, spiky, spiny, bristly
thorough *adj* = **full**, complete, comprehensive, intensive, exhaustive, painstaking, meticulous, scrupulous • *a thorough examination*
See also: **absolute, careful, utter**
thoroughbred *adj* = **purebred**, pedigree

DICTIONARY

▸ **thoroughbred** *n, adj* (animal) of pure breed
▸ **thoroughfare** *n* way through from one place to another
those *adj, pron* plural of **that**
thou *pron obsolete* singular form of **you**
though Ⓣ *conj* **1** despite the fact that ▷ *adv* **2** nevertheless
thought Ⓣ *v* **1** past of **think** ▷ *n* **2** thinking **3** concept or idea **4** ideas typical of a time or place **5** consideration **6** intention or expectation
▸ **thoughtful** *adj* **1** considerate **2** showing careful thought **3** pensive or reflective
▸ **thoughtless** *adj* inconsiderate
thousand *adj, n* **1** ten hundred **2** large but unspecified number
▸ **thousandth** *adj, n* (of) number one thousand in a series
thrall, thraldom *n* state of being in the power of another person
thrash Ⓣ *v* **1** beat, esp. with a stick or whip **2** defeat soundly **3** move about wildly **4** thresh
▸ **thrashing** *n* severe beating
▸ **thrash out** *v* solve by thorough argument
thread Ⓣ *n* **1** fine strand or yarn **2** spiral ridge on a screw, nut, or bolt **3** unifying theme ▷ *v* **4** pass thread through **5** fit (a film, tape, etc.) into a machine **6** pick (one's way etc.)
▸ **threadbare** *adj* **1** (of fabric) with the nap worn off **2** hackneyed **3** shabby
threat Ⓣ *n* **1** declaration of intent to harm **2** dangerous person or thing
▸ **threaten** *v* **1** make or be a threat to **2** be a menacing indication of
three *adj, n* one more than two
▸ **threefold** *adj, adv* (having) three times as many or as much
▸ **threesome** *n* group of three
▸ **three-dimensional** *or* **3-D** *adj* having three dimensions
▸ **three-ply** *adj* **1** (of wood) having three layers **2** (of wool) having three strands
▸ **three-point** *adj basketball* relating to shots scoring three points
▸ **three-pointer** *n basketball* three-point shot
threnody *n, pl* **-dies** lament for the dead

THESAURUS

thoroughfare *n* = **road**, way, street, highway, passage, avenue, passageway
thoroughly *adv* **1** = **carefully**, fully, efficiently, painstakingly, meticulously, intensively, conscientiously, assiduously, exhaustively, from top to bottom, scrupulously **2** = **completely**, quite, absolutely, totally, perfectly, utterly, downright, to the hilt
though *conj* **1** = **although**, while, notwithstanding, even if, even though ▸ *adv* **2** = **nevertheless**, still, however, yet, notwithstanding, nonetheless, for all that
thought *n* **1** = **idea**, view, opinion, notion • *his thoughts on love* **2** = **thinking**, consideration, deliberation, reflection, meditation, contemplation • *After much thought I decided to become a teacher.* **3** = **consideration**, study, attention, regard, scrutiny, heed **4** = **intention**, plan, aim, idea, design, object, purpose, notion **5** = **expectation**, hope, prospect, anticipation, aspiration
thoughtful *adj* **1** = **pensive**, reflective, contemplative • *She was looking very thoughtful.* **2** = **considerate**, kind, caring, attentive • *a thoughtful and caring man* OPPOSITE: thoughtless **3** = **well-thought-out**, prudent, astute, canny
See also: **humane**
thoughtless *adj* = **inconsiderate**, insensitive, tactless • *It was thoughtless of her to mention it.*
See also: **irresponsible, unkind**
thrash *v* **1** = **beat**, belt (*informal*), cane, flog, paddle, whip, scourge, spank **2** = **defeat**, beat, crush, slaughter (*informal*), trounce, run rings around (*informal*), wipe the floor with (*informal*) **3** = **thresh**, jerk, flail, writhe, toss and turn ▷ **thrash out** = **settle**, debate, discuss, resolve, solve, argue out, have out, talk over
thrashing *n* **1** = **beating**, belting (*informal*), flogging, punishment, whipping **2** = **defeat**, beating, hammering (*informal*), trouncing
thread *n* **1** = **strand**, line, string, fibre, yarn, filament **2** = **theme**, plot, direction, drift, story line, train of thought ▸ *v* **3** = **pass**, pick *or* pick one's way, ease, squeeze through
threadbare *adj* **1** = **shabby**, old, ragged, down at heel, frayed, tattered, tatty, worn **2** = **hackneyed**, familiar, conventional, tired, stale, commonplace, overused, well-worn, trite, stereotyped
threat *n* **1** = **threatening remark**, menace • *death threats* **2** = **danger**, risk, hazard, menace • *the threat of tropical storms* **3** = **warning**, omen, presage, foreboding, foreshadowing, portent, writing on the wall
threaten *v* **1** = **menace**, make threats to • *He threatened to reveal the secret.* **2** = **endanger**, jeopardize, put at risk, put in jeopardy • *The new department store is threatening the business of the smaller shops.* **3** = **foreshadow**, impend, presage, forebode, portend
threatening *adj* **1** = **menacing**, bullying, intimidatory **2** = **ominous**, grim, sinister, inauspicious, forbidding
threatening remark *See* **threat**

t

DICTIONARY

thresh *v* **1** beat (wheat etc.) to separate the grain from the husks and straw **2** move about wildly
threshold Ⓣ *n* **1** bar forming the bottom of a doorway **2** entrance **3** starting point **4** point at which a stimulus produces a response
threw *v* past tense of **throw**
thrice *adv lit* three times
thrift Ⓣ *n* **1** wisdom and caution with money **2** low-growing plant with pink flowers **thrifty** *adj* **thriftily** *adv* **thriftiness** *n* **thriftless** *adj*
thrill Ⓣ *n* **1** sudden feeling of excitementon*v* **2** (cause to) feel a thrill **thrilling** *adj*
▸**thriller** *n* book, film, etc. with an atmosphere of mystery or suspense
thrive Ⓣ *v* **thriving, thrived** *or* **throve, thrived** *or* **thriven 1** grow well **2** flourish or prosper
throat *n* **1** front of the neck **2** passage from the mouth and nose to the stomach and lungs
▸**throaty** *adj* (of the voice) hoarse
throb Ⓣ *v* **throbbing, throbbed 1** pulsate repeatedly **2** vibrate rhythmically ▷ *n* **3** throbbing
throes *pl n* violent pangs or pains
▸**in the throes of** *informal* struggling with difficulty with
thrombosis *n, pl* **-ses** forming of a clot in a blood vessel or the heart
throne *n* **1** ceremonial seat of a monarch or bishop **2** sovereign power
throng Ⓣ *n, v* crowd
throstle *n* song-thrush
throttle Ⓣ *n* **1** device controlling the amount of fuel entering an engine ▷ *v* **2** strangle
through Ⓣ *prep* **1** from end to end or side to side of **2** because of **3** during ▷ *adj* **4** finished **5** (of transport) going directly to a place **6** (on a telephone line) connected
▸**through and through** completely
▸**throughout** *adv, prep* in every part (of)
▸**throughput** *n* amount of material processed
throve *v* past tense of **thrive**
throw Ⓣ *v* **throwing, threw, thrown 1** hurl through the air **2** move or put suddenly or carelessly **3** bring into a specified state, esp. suddenly **4** direct (a look, light, etc.) **5** give (a party) **6** project (the voice) so that it seems to come from elsewhere **7** shape (pottery) on a wheel **8** move (a switch, lever, etc.) **9** *informal* baffle or disconcert ▷ *n* **10** throwing **11** distance thrown
▸**throwaway** *adj* **1** designed to be discarded after use **2** done or said casually
▸**throwback** *n* person or thing that reverts to an earlier type
▸**throw up** *v* vomit
thrum *v* **thrumming, thrummed 1** strum rhythmically but without expression on (a musical instrument) **2** drum incessantly

THESAURUS

threshold *n* **1** = **entrance**, door, doorstep, doorway **2** = **start**, opening, beginning, dawn, brink, verge, outset, inception **3** = **lower limit**, minimum
thrift *n* = **economy**, saving, prudence, frugality, carefulness, parsimony, thriftiness
thrifty *adj* = **economical**, careful, prudent, frugal • *thrifty shoppers*
thrill *n* **1** = **excitement**, high (*informal*), kick (*informal*) • *the thrill of the game* ▸*v* **2** = **excite**, give a kick (*informal*) • *It thrilled me to see her looking so happy.*
See also: **delight**
thrilled *See* **excited**
thrilling *adj* = **exciting**, sensational, rousing, electrifying, gripping, riveting, stimulating, stirring
thrive *v* = **flourish**, prosper, do well • *His company continues to thrive.*
See also: **succeed**
thriving *adj* = **flourishing**, well, healthy, successful, prosperous, blooming, booming, burgeoning
throb *v* **1** = **pulsate**, beat, pound, thump, pulse, vibrate, palpitate ▸*n* **2** = **pulse**, beat, thump, vibration, thumping, palpitation, pounding, pulsating
throng *n* **1** = **crowd**, host, mass, pack, crush, mob, swarm, multitude, horde ▸*v* **2** = **crowd**, pack, flock, converge, congregate, mill around, swarm around
throttle *v* = **strangle**, choke, garrotte, strangulate
through *prep* **1** = **between**, by, past **2** = **because of**, via, by means of, by way of, using **3** = **during**, in, throughout ▸*adj* **4** = **finished**, completed, done, ended ▸*adverb* ▷**through and through** = **completely**, fully, totally, entirely, altogether, thoroughly, wholly, utterly
throughout *adv* = **right through**, everywhere, all over, from start to finish
throw *v* **1** = **hurl**, pitch, cast, toss, lob, fling, sling, chuck • *throwing a tennis ball against a wall* **2** (*Informal*) = **confuse**, baffle, astonish, faze, disconcert, confound, dumbfound ▷**throw away** = **discard**, reject, dump (*informal*), scrap, ditch (*slang*), jettison, dispense with, dispose of, get rid of, throw out ▷**throw out** *See* **discard, dump** ▸*n* **3** = **toss**, pitch, lob (*informal*), fling, sling, heave
throwaway *adj* **1** = **disposable**, one-use, nonreturnable **2** = **casual**, passing,

DICTIONARY

thrush[1] *n* brown songbird
thrush[2] *n* fungal disease of the mouth or vagina
thrust Ⓣ *v* **thrusting, thrust 1** push forcefully **2** stab ▷ *n* **3** lunge or stab **4** force or power **5** intellectual or emotional drive
Thucydides *n* ?460–?395 BC, Greek historian and politician, distinguished for his *History of the Peloponnesian War* **Thucydidean** *adj*
thud Ⓣ *n* **1** dull heavy sound ▷ *v* **thudding, thudded 2** make such a sound
thug Ⓣ *n* violent criminal **thuggery** *n* **thuggish** *adj*
thumb *n* **1** short thick finger set apart from the others ▷ *v* **2** touch or handle with the thumb **3** flick through (a book or magazine) **4** signal with the thumb for (a lift in a vehicle)
▶ **thumbtack** *n* short tack with a smooth broad head
thump Ⓣ *n* **1** (sound of) a dull heavy blow ▷ *v* **2** strike heavily
thunder Ⓣ *n* **1** loud noise accompanying lightning ▷ *v* **2** rumble with thunder **3** shout **4** move fast, heavily, and noisily **thunderous** *adj* **thundery** *adj*
▶ **thunderbolt** *n* **1** lightning flash **2** something sudden and unexpected
▶ **thunderclap** *n* peal of thunder
▶ **thunderstruck** *adj* amazed
Thurber *n* **James** (**Grover**). 1894–1961, US humorist and illustrator. He contributed drawings and stories to the *New Yorker* and his books include *Is Sex Necessary?* (1929), written with E. B. White
Thursday *n* fifth day of the week
thus Ⓣ *adv* **1** in this way **2** therefore
thwack *v, n* whack
thwart Ⓣ *v* **1** foil or frustrate ▷ *n* **2** seat across a boat
thy *adj obsolete* of or associated with you (thou)
▶ **thyself** *pron obsolete* emphatic form of **thou**
thyme [**time**] *n* aromatic herb
thymus *n, pl* **-muses, -mi** small gland at the base of the neck
thyroid *adj, n* (of) a gland in the neck controlling body growth
Ti *chem* titanium
tiara *n* semicircular jewelled headdress
Tiberius *n* full name *Tiberius Claudius Nero Caesar Augustus*. 42 BC–37 AD, Roman emperor (14–37 AD). He succeeded his father-in-law Augustus after a brilliant military career. He became increasingly tyrannical
tibia *n, pl* **tibiae, tibias** inner bone of the lower leg **tibial** *adj*
tic *n* spasmodic muscular twitch
tick[1] Ⓣ *n* **1** mark (√) used to check off or indicate the correctness of something **2** recurrent tapping sound, as of a clock **3** *informal* moment ▷ *v* **4** mark with a tick **5** make a ticking sound
▶ **tick off** *v* **1** mark off **2** reprimand
▶ **tick over** *v* **1** (of an engine) idle **2** function smoothly
▶ **ticktack** *n* bookmakers' sign language
tick[2] Ⓣ *n* tiny bloodsucking parasitic animal
tick[3] Ⓣ *n informal* credit or account
ticket Ⓣ *n* **1** card or paper entitling the holder to admission, travel, etc. **2** label **3** official notification of a parking or traffic offence **4** declared policy of a political party ▷ *v* **-eting, -eted 5** attach or issue a ticket to
ticking *n* strong cotton fabric used for mattress covers

THESAURUS

careless, offhand, understated
thrust *v* **1** = **push**, force, drive, plunge, jam, propel, shove, ram ▶ *n* **2** = **push**, drive, stab, poke, shove, prod, lunge **3** = **momentum**, impetus
thud *n, v* = **thump**, crash, knock, smack, clunk
thug *n* = **ruffian**, tough, bandit, hooligan, hoodlum • *a gang of armed thugs*
thump *n* **1** = **thud**, crash, bang, clunk, thwack **2** = **blow**, knock, punch, rap, smack, wallop (*informal*), whack, clout (*informal*) ▶ *v* **3** = **strike**, hit, beat, pound, knock, punch, smack, wallop (*informal*), clobber (*slang*), whack, clout (*informal*)
thunder *n* **1** = **rumble**, crash, explosion, boom ▶ *v* **2** = **rumble**, crash, boom, roar, resound, reverberate, peal **3** = **shout**, roar, yell, bark, bellow
thunderous *adj* = **loud**, noisy, ear-splitting, tumultuous, booming, deafening, resounding, roaring
thunderstruck *adj* = **amazed**, shocked, staggered, dumbfounded, open-mouthed, astonished, astounded, flabbergasted (*informal*), stunned, taken aback
thus *adv* **1** = **therefore**, so, then, accordingly, hence, consequently, ergo, for this reason, on that account **2** = **in this way**, so, as follows, like this
thwart *v* = **frustrate**, prevent, foil, hinder, stymie, obstruct, snooker, outwit
tick[1] *n* **1** = **mark**, stroke, dash **2** = **clicking**, tapping, ticktock ▶ *v* **3** = **mark**, indicate, check off **4** = **click**, tap, ticktock
tick[2] *n* = **mite**, bug, insect
tick[3] *n* = **credit**, account
ticket *n* **1** = **voucher**, pass, card, slip, certificate, token, coupon **2** = **label**, card, slip, tag, marker, sticker, tab, docket
tidbit *n* = **delicacy**, treat, snack, dainty, morsel

DICTIONARY

tickle *v* **1** touch or stroke (a person) to produce laughter **2** please or amuse **3** itch or tingle ▷ *n* **4** tickling
▸ **ticklish** *adj* **1** sensitive to tickling **2** requiring care or tact
tiddler *n informal* very small fish
▸ **tiddly** *adj* **1** tiny **2** *informal* slightly drunk
tiddlywinks *pl n* game in which players try to flip small plastic discs into a cup
tide Ⓣ *n* **1** rise and fall of the sea caused by the gravitational pull of the sun and moon **2** current caused by this **3** widespread feeling or tendency **tidal** *adj*
▸ **tidal wave** huge wave produced by an earthquake
▸ **tide over** *v* help (someone) temporarily
tidings Ⓣ *pl n* news
tidy Ⓣ *adj* **-dier, -diest 1** neat and orderly **2** *informal* considerable ▷ *v* **-dying, -died 3** put in order **tidily** *adv* **tidiness** *n*
tie Ⓣ *v* **tying, tied 1** fasten or be fastened with string, rope, etc. **2** make (a knot or bow) in (something) **3** restrict or limit **4** score the same as another competitor ▷ *n* **5** bond or fastening **6** long narrow piece of material worn knotted round the neck **7** drawn game or contest
tier Ⓣ *n* row, layer, or level
tiff Ⓣ *n* petty quarrel
Tiffany *n* **Louis Comfort**. 1848–1933, US glass-maker and Art-Nouveau craftsman, best known for creating the Favrile style of stained glass
tiger *n* large yellow-and-black striped Asian cat
▸ **tigress** *n* **1** female tiger **2** fierce woman
tight Ⓣ *adj* **1** stretched or drawn taut **2** closely fitting **3** secure or firm **4** cramped **5** *informal* mean **6** *informal* drunk **7** (of a match or game) very close **tightly** *adv*
▸ **tights** *pl n* one-piece clinging garment covering the body from the waist to the feet
▸ **tighten** *v* make or become tight or tighter
▸ **tight end** *football* offensive player who can receive passes or block
▸ **tightrope** *n* rope stretched taut on which acrobats perform
tike *n informal* same as **tyke**
tikka *adj Indian cookery* marinated in spices and dry-roasted: *chicken tikka*
Tilak *n* **Bal Gangadhar**. 1856–1920, Indian nationalist leader, educator, and scholar, who founded (1914) the Indian Home Rule League (Also **Lokamanya**)
tilde *n* accent (~) used in Spanish to indicate that the letter 'n' is to be pronounced in a particular way
Tilden *n* **Bill**, full name *William Tatem Tilden*, known as *Big Bill*. 1893–1953, US tennis player: won the US singles championship (1920–25, 1929) and the British singles championship (1920–21, 1930)
tile *n* **1** flat piece of ceramic, plastic, etc. used to cover a roof, floor, or wall ▷ *v* **2** cover with tiles **tiled** *adj*
▸ **tiling** *n* tiles collectively
till[1] *prep, conj* until
till[2] Ⓣ *v* cultivate (land) **tillage** *n* **tiller** *n*
till[3] Ⓣ *n* drawer for money, usu. in a cash register
tiller *n* lever used to move the a rudder of a boat when steering
tilt Ⓣ *v* **1** slant at an angle **2** compete against in a jousting contest **3** aim or thrust with a lance ▷ *n* **4** slope **5** *hist* jousting contest
▸ **at full tilt** at full speed or force

THESAURUS

tide *n* **1 = current**, flow, stream, ebb, undertow, tideway **2 = trend**, movement, direction, drift, tendency
tidings *See* **news**
tidy *adj* **1 = neat**, orderly • *a tidy desk* OPPOSITE: untidy **2** (*Informal*) **= considerable**, large, healthy, substantial, generous, sizable *or* sizeable, handsome, ample, goodly ▸ *v* **3 = neaten**, straighten, spruce up • *He tidied the garage.* OPPOSITE: mess up
tie *v* **1 = fasten**, secure, bind, lash, knot, rope, tether, truss • *They tied the ends of the bag securely.* OPPOSITE: untie **2 = restrict**, limit, bind, hamper, hinder, restrain, confine **3 = draw**, match, equal ▷ **tie up** *See* **secure** ▸ *n* **4 = draw**, deadlock, dead heat, saw-off (*Canad*) • *The game ended in a tie.* **5 = bond**, connection, relationship, affiliation, affinity • *I have very close ties with their family.* **6 = fastening**, link, bond, cord, knot, fetter, ligature
See also: **association, attach, join**
tier *n* **= row**, level, line, bank, story, rank, layer, stratum
tiff *See* **disagreement, squabble**
tight *adj* **1 = close-fitting**, snug, constricted • *The shoes are too tight.* OPPOSITE: loose **2 = secure**, firm • *a tight knot* **3 = taut**, tense, rigid • *Pull the rope tight to make a knot.* OPPOSITE: slack **4 = limited**, close, narrow, cramped, constricted **5** (*Informal*) **= miserly**, mean, stingy, grasping, niggardly, parsimonious, tightfisted **6 = close**, even, evenly-balanced, well-matched ▷ **tight spot** *See* **hole, predicament**
tighten *v* **= squeeze**, close, narrow, constrict
tightly *See* **fast**
till[1] *v* **= cultivate**, work, dig, plow
till[2] *n* **= cash register**, cash box
tilt *v* **1 = slant**, list, tip, lean, slope, incline, cant • *He tilted his chair back on two legs.*

DICTIONARY

timber Ⓣ *n* **1** wood as a building material **2** trees collectively **3** wooden beam in the frame of a house, boat, etc. **timbered** *adj*
▸ **timber line** geographical limit beyond which trees will not grow
timbre Ⓣ [**tam**-bra] *n* distinctive quality of sound of a voice or instrument
time Ⓣ *n* **1** past, present, and future as a continuous whole **2** specific point in time **3** unspecified interval **4** period with specific features **5** instance **6** occasion **7** tempo **8** *slang* imprisonment ▹ *v* **9** note the time taken by **10** choose a time for
▸ **timeless** *adj* **1** unaffected by time **2** eternal
▸ **timely** *adj* at the appropriate time
▸ **time bomb 1** bomb containing a timing mechanism that determines when it will explode **2** situation which, if allowed to continue, will develop into a serious problem
▸ **time-honoured** *adj* sanctioned by custom
▸ **time-lag** *n* period between cause and effect
▸ **timepiece** *n* watch or clock
▸ **timeserver** *n* person who changes his or her views to gain support or favour
▸ **time sharing 1** system of part ownership of a holiday property for a specified period each year **2** system enabling users at different terminals of a computer to use it at the same time
▸ **timetable** *n* plan showing the times when something takes place, the departure and arrival times of trains or buses, etc.
timid Ⓣ *adj* **1** easily frightened **2** shy, not bold **timidly** *adv* **timidity** *n*
▸ **timorous** [**tim**-mor-uss] *adj* timid
Timothy *n New Testament* **1 Saint**. a disciple of Paul, who became leader of the Christian community at Ephesus. Feast day: Jan 26 or 22 **2** either of the two books addressed to him (in full *The First and Second Epistles of Paul the Apostle to Timothy*), containing advice on pastoral matters
timpani [**tim**-pan-ee] *pl n* set of kettledrums **timpanist** *n*
tin *n* **1** soft metallic element **2** *Brit* airtight metal container
▸ **tinned** *adj Brit* (of food) preserved by being sealed in a tin
▸ **tinny** *adj* (of sound) thin and metallic
▸ **tinpot** *adj informal* worthless or unimportant
Tinbergen *n* **Niko(laas)**. 1907–88, British zoologist, born in the Netherlands; studied animal behaviour, esp. instincts, and was one of the founders of ethology; Nobel prize for physiology or medicine 1973
tincture *n* medicinal extract in a solution of alcohol
tinder *n* dry easily-burning material used to start a fire **tinderbox** *n*
tine *n* prong of a fork or antler
ting *n* high metallic sound, as of a small bell
tinge Ⓣ *n* **1** slight tint **2** trace ▹ *v* **tingeing, tinged 3** give a slight tint or trace to
tingle Ⓣ *v, n* (feel) a prickling or stinging sensation
tinker Ⓣ *n* **1** travelling mender of pots and pans **2** *Scot & Irish* Gypsy **3** tinkering ▹ *v* **4** fiddle with (an engine etc.) in an attempt to repair it
tinkle *v* **1** ring with a high tinny sound like a small bell ▹ *n* **2** tinkling
tinsel *n* **1** decorative metallic strips or threads **2** anything cheap and gaudy
tint Ⓣ *n* **1** (pale) shade of a colour **2** dye for the hair **3** trace ▹ *v* **4** give a tint to

THESAURUS

▸ *n* **2 = slope**, list, grade, angle, incline, slant, gradient, camber • *the tilt of the earth's axis* **3** (*Medieval hist*) **= joust**, fight, tournament, combat, duel, lists ▹ **full tilt, at full tilt = full speed**, headlong, for dear life
timber *n* **= wood**, beams, boards, logs, planks, trees
timbre *n* **= tone**, ring, resonance, colour
time *n* **1 = period**, while, stretch, spell, interval • *I enjoyed my time in New Brunswick.* RELATED WORD *adjective*: temporal **2 = occasion**, point, stage, instance, juncture **3** (*Music*) **= tempo**, beat, measure, rhythm ▹ **time off = vacation**, leave, holiday, leisure ▸ *v* **4 = schedule**, set • *We had timed our visit for the school break.* *See also*: **chance, life, moment, space, term**
timeless *adj* **= eternal**, permanent, lasting, enduring, immortal, ageless, everlasting, changeless
timely *adj* **= opportune**, appropriate, suitable, convenient, judicious, well-timed, propitious, seasonable
timetable *n* **= schedule**, program, list, agenda, calendar, diary, curriculum
timid *adj* **= nervous**, shy, cowardly, bashful, diffident • *a timid kitten* OPPOSITE: bold *See also*: **meek**
timorous *adj* **= timid**, shy, fearful, apprehensive, coy, bashful, diffident, faint-hearted, shrinking
tinge *n* **1 = tint**, shade, colour **2 = trace**, drop, bit, touch, suggestion, dash, smattering, sprinkling ▸ *v* **3 = tint**, colour, imbue, suffuse
tingle *v* **1 = prickle**, sting, itch, tickle, have goose pimples ▸ *n* **2 = prickling**, thrill, shiver, itch, quiver, goose pimples, pins and needles (*informal*)
tinker *v* **= meddle**, play, fiddle (*informal*), dabble, putter, mess around
tint *n* **1 = shade**, tone, colour, hue **2 = dye**,

DICTIONARY

tintinnabulation *n* the ringing or pealing of bells
Tintoretto *n* **Il**, original name *Jacopo Robusti*. 1518–94, Italian painter of the Venetian school. His works include *Susanna bathing* (?1550) and the fresco cycle in the Scuola di San Rocco, Venice (from 1564)
tiny Ⓣ *adj* **tinier, tiniest** very small
tip[1] Ⓣ *n* **1** narrow or pointed end of anything **2** small piece forming an end ▷ *v* **tipping, tipped 3** put a tip on
tip[2] Ⓣ *n* **1** money given in return for service **2** helpful hint or warning **3** piece of inside information ▷ *v* **tipping, tipped 4** give a tip to
▶ **tipster** *n* person who sells tips about races
tip[3] Ⓣ *v* **tipping, tipped 1** tilt or overturn **2** deflect or lightly tap (a ball or puck) ▷ *n* **3** act or instance of tipping
tippet *n* piece of fur worn as a scarf
tipple Ⓣ *v* **1** drink (alcohol) habitually, esp. in small quantities ▷ *n* **2** drink **tippler** *n*
tipsy Ⓣ *adj* **-sier, -siest** slightly drunk
tiptoe Ⓣ *v* **-toeing, -toed** walk quietly with the heels off the ground
tiptop *adj* of the highest quality or condition
tirade Ⓣ *n* long angry speech
tire[1] Ⓣ *v* **1** reduce the energy of, as by exertion **2** weary or bore **tiring** *adj*
▶ **tired** *adj* **1** weary **2** hackneyed or stale
▶ **tireless** *adj* not tiring easily
▶ **tiresome** *adj* boring and irritating
tire[2] *n* rubber ring, usu. inflated, over the rim of a vehicle's wheel to grip the road
tissue *n* **1** substance of an animal body or plant **2** piece of thin soft paper used as a handkerchief etc. **3** interwoven series: *a tissue of lies*
tit[1] *n* any of various small songbirds
tit[2] *n slang* female breast
titanic *adj* huge
titanium *n* strong light metallic element used to make alloys
titbit *n* **1** tasty piece of food **2** pleasing scrap of scandal
tit for tat *n* equivalent given in retaliation
tithe *n* **1** esp. formerly, one tenth of one's income or produce paid to the church as a tax ▷ *v* **2** charge or pay a tithe
Titian *n* original name *Tiziano Vecellio*. ?1490–1576, Italian painter of the Venetian school, noted for his religious and mythological works, such as *Bacchus and Ariadne* (1523), and his portraits
titillate Ⓣ *v* excite or stimulate pleasurably **titillating** *adj* **titillation** *n*
titivate *v* smarten up **titivation** *n*
title Ⓣ *n* **1** name of a book, film, etc. **2** name signifying rank or position **3** formal designation, such as *Mrs* **4** *sports* championship **5** *law* legal right of possession
▶ **titled** *adj* aristocratic
▶ **title deed** legal document of ownership

THESAURUS

wash, rinse, tinge, tincture ▶ *v* **3 = dye**, colour
tiny *adj* **= minute**, miniature, diminutive, negligible, microscopic • *The living room is tiny.* OPPOSITE: huge
tip[1] *n* **1 = end**, point, top, head, summit, peak, pinnacle, extremity ▶ *v* **2 = cap**, top, finish, crown, surmount
tip[2] *n* **1 = gratuity**, gift **2 = hint**, warning, suggestion, clue, pointer, heads-up ▶ *v* **3 = reward**, remunerate **4 = advise**, suggest, warn, caution, forewarn
tip[3] *v* **1 = tilt**, list, lean, incline, slant **2 = dump**, empty, unload, pour out ▷ **tip over** *See* **overturn** ▶ *n* **3 = dump**, refuse heap, rubbish heap
tipple *v* **1 = drink**, indulge (*informal*), imbibe, swig, quaff, tope ▶ *n* **2 = alcohol**, drink, liquor, booze (*informal*)
tipsy *adj* **= drunk**, happy, fuzzy, mellow, three sheets to the wind
tiptoe *See* **steal**
tirade *n* **= outburst**, lecture, diatribe, fulmination, harangue, invective
tire *v* **1 = exhaust**, drain, fatigue • *Early-morning practice sessions often tire me.* **2 = bore**, irk, irritate, weary, exasperate ▷ **tire out** *See* **exhaust**
See also: **wear out**
tired *adj* **1 = exhausted**, weary, drowsy, sleepy, drained, fatigued, tuckered out (*informal*), worn out • *I'm too tired to go out tonight.* **2 = bored**, sick, weary, fed up **3 = hackneyed**, old, stale, well-worn, corny (*slang*), trite, clichéd, outworn, threadbare
See also: **sick of**
tireless *adj* **= energetic**, vigorous, resolute, industrious, indefatigable, unflagging, untiring
tiresome *adj* **= boring**, dull, tedious, irksome, irritating, trying, vexatious, wearing, wearisome
tiring *adj* **= exhausting**, tough, arduous, strenuous, demanding, exacting, laborious, wearing
titillate *v* **= excite**, interest, thrill, stimulate, tease, arouse, tantalize
titillating *adj* **= exciting**, provocative, lurid, suggestive, interesting, arousing, stimulating, teasing
title *n* **1 = name**, term, handle (*slang*), designation, moniker *or* monicker (*slang*) **2 = championship**,

DICTIONARY

Tito *n* **Marshal**, original name *Josip Broz*. 1892–1980, Yugoslav statesman, who led the communist guerrilla resistance to German occupation during World War II; prime minister of Yugoslavia (1945–53) and president (1953–80)
titter ⓣ *v* **1** laugh in a suppressed way ▷ *n* **2** suppressed laugh
tittle-tattle *n, v* gossip
titular *adj* **1** of a title **2** in name only
Titus *n* **1** *New Testament* **a Saint**. Greek disciple and helper of Saint Paul. Feast day: Jan 26 or Aug 25 **b** the book written to him (in full *The Epistle of Paul the Apostle to Titus*), containing advice on pastoral matters **2** full name *Titus Flavius Sabinus Vespasianus*. ?40–81 AD, Roman emperor (78–81 AD)
tizzy ⓣ *n, pl* **-zies** *informal* confused or agitated state
TNT *n* trinitrotoluene, a powerful explosive
to *prep* **1** towards **2** as far as **3** used to mark the indirect object or infinitive of a verb **4** used to indicate equality or comparison **5** before the hour of ▷ *adv* **6** to a closed position: *pull the door to*
▸ **to and fro** back and forth
toad *n* animal like a large frog
toadstool *n* poisonous fungus like a mushroom
toady ⓣ *n, pl* **toadies 1** ingratiating person ▷ *v* **toadying, toadied 2** be ingratiating
toast ⓣ *n* **1** slice of bread browned by heat **2** tribute or proposal of health or success marked by people raising glasses and drinking together **3** person or thing so honoured ▷ *v* **4** brown bread by heat **5** drink a toast to **6** warm or be warmed
▸ **toaster** *n* electrical device for toasting bread
tobacco *n, pl* **-cos, -coes** plant with large leaves dried for smoking
▸ **tobacconist** *n* person or shop selling tobacco, cigarettes, etc.
toboggan *n* **1** narrow sledge for sliding over snow ▷ *v* **-ganing, -ganed 2** ride a toboggan
toby jug *n* mug in the form of a stout seated man
toccata [tok-**kah**-ta] *n* rapid piece of music for a keyboard instrument
tocsin *n* alarm signal or bell
today *n* **1** this day **2** the present age ▷ *adv* **3** on this day **4** nowadays
toddle *v* walk with short unsteady steps
▸ **toddler** *n* child beginning to walk
toddy *n, pl* **-dies** sweetened drink of spirits and hot water
to-do ⓣ *n, pl* **-dos** *informal* fuss or commotion
toe *n* **1** digit of the foot **2** part of a shoe or sock covering the toes ▷ *v* **toeing, toed 3** touch or kick with the toe
▸ **toe the line** conform
▸ **toerag** *n slang* contemptible person
toff *n Brit slang* well-dressed or upper-class person
toffee *n* chewy candy made of boiled sugar
tofu *n* soft food made from soya-bean curd
tog *n* **1** unit for measuring the insulating power of duvets **togs 2** *informal* clothes
toga [**toe**-ga] *n* garment worn by citizens of ancient Rome
together ⓣ *adv* **1** in company **2** simultaneously ▷ *adj* **3** *informal* organized
toggle *n* **1** small bar-shaped button inserted through a loop for fastening **2** switch used to turn a machine or computer function on or off
toil ⓣ *n* **1** hard work ▷ *v* **2** work hard **3** progress with difficulty
▸ **toilsome** *adj* requiring hard work
toilet ⓣ *n* **1** (room with) a bowl connected to a drain for receiving and disposing of urine and feces **2** washing and dressing

THESAURUS

crown **3 = ownership**, right, claim, privilege, entitlement, prerogative ▷ **title holder** *See* **champion**
titter *v* **= laugh**, chuckle, giggle, chortle (*informal*), snigger
tizzy *n* (*Informal*) **= panic**, state (*informal*), sweat (*informal*), agitation, commotion, fluster
toady *n* **1 = sycophant**, brown-noser (*slang*), creep (*slang*), lackey, minion, flatterer, flunkey, hanger-on, scuzzbucket (*slang*), yes man ▸ *v* **2 = fawn on**, brown-nose (*slang*), flatter, grovel, kiss ass (*slang*), kowtow to, pander to, suck up to (*informal*)
toast[1] *v* **= brown**, warm, heat, grill, roast
toast[2] *n* **1 = tribute**, health, pledge, salute, compliment, salutation **2 = favourite**, hero *or* heroine, darling ▸ *v* **3 = drink to**, salute, drink the health of *or* drink to the health of
today's *See* **current**
toddler *See* **child**
to-do *See* **fuss**
together *adv* **1 = collectively**, jointly, en masse, in unison, shoulder to shoulder, side by side • *We went on long bicycle rides together.* **2 = simultaneously**, concurrently, as one, at once, with one accord • *Three horses crossed the finish line together.* ▸ *adj* **3** (*Informal*) **= composed**, well-balanced, well-adjusted
toil *n* **1 = hard work**, effort, application, exertion, drudgery, elbow grease (*informal*), sweat, slog ▸ *v* **2 = work**, drudge, struggle, sweat (*informal*), slave, strive, labour, slog, work one's fingers to the bone
toilet *n* **= lavatory**, can (*slang*), bathroom, washroom, restroom, latrine, commode,

DICTIONARY

▸ **toiletry** *n, pl* **-ries** object or cosmetic used to clean or groom oneself
▸ **toilet water** light perfume
Tojo *n* **Hideki**. 1885–1948, Japanese soldier and statesman; minister of war (1940–41) and premier (1941–44); hanged as a war criminal
token Ⓣ *n* **1** sign or symbol **2** memento **3** disc used as money in a slot machine **4** voucher exchangeable for goods of a specified value ▷ *adj* **5** nominal or slight
▸ **tokenism** *n* policy of making only a token effort, esp. to comply with a law
told *v* past of **tell**
tolerate Ⓣ *v* **1** put up with **2** permit **toleration** *n*
▸ **tolerable** *adj* **1** bearable **2** *informal* quite good **tolerably** *adv*
▸ **tolerance** *n* **1** acceptance of other people's rights to their own opinions or actions **2** ability to endure something **tolerant** *adj* **tolerantly** *adv*
Tolkien *n* **J**(**ohn**) **R**(**onald**) **R**(**euel**). 1892–1973, British philologist and writer, born in South Africa. He is best known for *The Hobbit* (1937), the trilogy *The Lord of the Rings* (1954–55), and the posthumously published *The Silmarillion* (1977)
toll[1] Ⓣ *v* **1** ring (a bell) slowly and regularly, esp. to announce a death ▷ *n* **2** tolling
toll[2] Ⓣ *n* **1** charge for the use of a bridge or road **2** total loss or damage from a disaster
Tolstoy *n* **Leo**, Russian name *Count Lev Nikolayevich Tolstoy*. 1828–1910, Russian novelist, short-story writer, and philosopher; author of the two monumental novels *War and Peace* (1865–69) and *Anna Karenina* (1875–77). Following a spiritual crisis in 1879, he adopted a form of Christianity based on a doctrine of nonresistance to evil
tom *n* male cat
tomahawk *n* fighting axe of the N American Indians
tomato *n, pl* **-toes** red fruit used in salads and as a vegetable
tomb Ⓣ *n* **1** grave **2** monument over a grave
▸ **tombstone** *n* gravestone
Tombaugh *n* **Clyde William**. 1906–97, US astronomer, who discovered (1930) the planet Pluto
tombola *n* lottery with tickets drawn from a revolving drum
tomboy *n* girl who acts or dresses like a boy
tome Ⓣ *n* large heavy book
tomfoolery Ⓣ *n* foolish behaviour
Tommy *n, pl* **-mies** *informal* private soldier in the British army
Tommy gun *n* light sub-machine-gun
tomorrow *adv, n* **1** (on) the day after today **2** (in) the future
tom-tom *n* drum beaten with the hands
ton Ⓣ *n* unit of weight equal to 2000 lbs or 907 kg (**short ton**) or, in Britain, 2240 lbs or 1016 kg (**long ton**)
▸ **metric ton** same as **tonne**
▸ **tonnage** *n* weight capacity of a ship
tone Ⓣ *n* **1** sound with reference to its pitch, volume, etc. **2** *music* Also **whole tone** interval of two semitones **3** quality of a colour **4** general character **5** healthy bodily condition ▷ *v* **6** give tone to

THESAURUS

comfort station, men's room, ladies' room, urinal, privy, water closet, W.C., honey-bucket (*slang*)
token *n* **1** = **symbol**, sign, note, mark, indication, expression, representation, badge ▸ *adj* **2** = **nominal**, symbolic, minimal, hollow, superficial, perfunctory
tolerable *adj* **1** = **bearable**, acceptable • *The pain was tolerable.* OPPOSITE: unbearable **2** = **acceptable**, OK (*informal*), reasonable, adequate, so-so, passable • *a tolerable salary*
See also: **decent**
tolerance *n* **1** = **broad-mindedness**, indulgence, forbearance, open-mindedness, permissiveness **2** = **endurance**, resistance, toughness, resilience, stamina, fortitude, hardiness, staying power
tolerant *adj* = **broad-minded**, liberal, understanding, open-minded • *a tolerant society* OPPOSITE: narrow-minded
tolerate *v* **1** = **put up with**, accept • *We will not tolerate such behaviour in our classroom.* **2** = **endure**, stand, bear • *She can no longer tolerate the position that she's in.*
See also: **allow**
toleration *n* = **acceptance**, sanction, allowance, endurance, indulgence, permissiveness
toll[1] *v* **1** = **ring**, strike, sound, chime, knell, clang, peal ▸ *n* **2** = **ringing**, chime, knell, clang, peal
toll[2] *n* **1** = **charge**, tax, fee, payment, duty, tariff, levy **2** = **damage**, cost, loss, penalty
tomb *n* = **grave**, vault, sarcophagus, mausoleum, sepulchre • *Howard Carter discovered King Tut's tomb.*
tombstone *n* = **gravestone**, memorial, marker, monument, headstone
tome *See* **book**
tomfoolery *n* = **foolishness**, stupidity, silliness, buffoonery, clowning, fooling around (*informal*), horseplay, shenanigans (*informal*), skylarking (*informal*)
ton *n* (*Informal, often pl*) = **a lot**, ocean, quantity, great deal, stacks
tone *n* **1** = **pitch**, inflection, timbre,

DICTIONARY

7 harmonize (with) **toneless** *adj*
▶ **tonal** *adj music* written in a key **tonality** *n*
▶ **tone-deaf** *adj* unable to perceive subtle differences in pitch
▶ **tone down** *v* make or become more moderate
Tone *n* (**Theobald**) **Wolfe**. 1763–98, Irish nationalist, who founded (1791) the Society of United Irishmen and led (1798) French military forces to Ireland. He was captured and sentenced to death but committed suicide
tongs *pl n* large pincers for grasping and lifting
tongue Ⓣ *n* **1** muscular organ in the mouth, used in speaking and tasting **2** animal tongue as food **3** language **4** flap of leather on a shoe **5** thin projecting strip
tonic Ⓣ *n* **1** medicine to improve body tone **2** *music* first note of a scale ▷ *adj* **3** invigorating
▶ **tonic water** mineral water containing quinine
tonight *adv, n* (in or during) the night or evening of this day
tonne [**tunn**] *n* unit of weight equal to 1000 kg
tonsil *n* small gland in the throat
▶ **tonsillectomy** *n* surgical removal of the tonsils
▶ **tonsillitis** *n* inflammation of the tonsils
tonsure *n* **1** shaving of all or the top of the head as a religious or monastic practice **2** part shaved **tonsured** *adj*
too Ⓣ *adv* **1** also, as well **2** to excess **3** extremely
took *v* past tense of **take**
tool Ⓣ *n* **1** implement used by hand **2** person used by another to perform unpleasant or dishonourable tasks ▷ *v* **3** work on with a tool **4** equip with tools
▶ **toolbar** *n computers* row of buttons displayed on a computer screen, allowing the user to select various functions
toonie, twonie *n informal* Canadian two-dollar coin
toot *n* **1** short hooting sound ▷ *v* **2** (cause to) make such a sound
tooth *n, pl* **teeth 1** bonelike projection in the jaws of most vertebrates for biting and chewing **2** toothlike prong or point **toothless** *adj*
▶ **sweet tooth** see **sweet**
▶ **toothpaste** *n* paste used to clean the teeth
▶ **toothpick** *n* small stick for removing scraps of food from between the teeth
top[1] Ⓣ *n* **1** highest point or part **2** lid or cap **3** highest rank **4** garment for the upper part of the body ▷ *adj* **5** at or of the top ▷ *v* **topping, topped 6** form a top on **7** be at the top of **8** exceed or surpass
▶ **topping** *n* sauce or garnish for food
▶ **topless** *adj* (of a costume or woman) with no covering for the breasts
▶ **topmost** *adj* highest or best
▶ **top brass** most important officers or leaders
▶ **top-dress** *v* spread fertilizer on the surface of the land **top-dressing** *n*
▶ **top hat** man's tall cylindrical hat
▶ **top- heavy** *adj* unstable through being overloaded at the top
▶ **top-notch** *adj* excellent, first-class
▶ **topsoil** *n* surface layer of soil
top[2] *n* toy which spins on a pointed base
topaz [**toe**-pazz] *n* semiprecious stone in various colours
tope[1] *v* drink (alcohol) regularly
tope[2] *n* small European shark
topee, topi [**toe**-pee] *n* lightweight pith hat

THESAURUS

intonation, modulation **2 = manner**, feel, air, character, style, spirit, attitude, mood, temper **3 = colour**, shade, hue, tint, tinge ▶ *v* **4 = harmonize**, match, suit, blend, go well with ▷ **tone down = moderate**, reduce, soften, subdue, temper, restrain, play down
tongue *n* = **language**, speech, dialect, parlance
tonic *n* = **stimulant**, boost, restorative, pick-me-up (*informal*), shot in the arm (*informal*)
too *adv* **1 = as well**, besides, moreover, likewise, in addition, into the bargain • *You were there too.* **2 = excessively**, overly, unduly, unreasonably, over- • *You've had too many late nights.*
See also: **also**
tool *n* **1 = implement**, instrument, utensil • *The best tool for the purpose is a pair of shears.* **2 = puppet**, creature, pawn, lackey, minion, stooge (*slang*), cat's-paw, flunkey, hireling
See also: **gadget**
top *n* **1 = peak**, head, summit, crown, height, crest, ridge, culmination, brow, pinnacle, apex, apex, zenith, high point, acme, apogee • *I waited at the top of the stairs.* OPPOSITE: bottom **2 = first place**, lead, head **3 = lid**, cap, stopper • *a bottle top* ▶ *adj* **4 = leading**, lead, head, chief, prime, premier, principal, elite, best, foremost, pre-eminent, highest • *She was the top student in physics.* ▶ *v* **5 = exceed**, cap, surpass, outstrip, go beyond • *The temperature topped 23°C.* **6 = surpass**, beat, eclipse, better, outdo, improve on • *You'll never manage to top that story.* **7 = cover**, finish, cap, crown, garnish **8 = lead**, head, be first

DICTIONARY

topiary [**tope**-ee-yar-ee] *n* art of trimming trees and bushes into decorative shapes **topiarist** *n*
topic Ⓣ *n* subject of a conversation, book, etc. ▶**topical** *adj* relating to current events **topicality** *n*
topography *n, pl* **-phies** (science of describing) the surface features of a place **topographer** *n* **topographic** *adj*
topology *n* geometry of the properties of a shape which are unaffected by continuous distortion **topological** *adj*
topple Ⓣ *v* **1** (cause to) fall over **2** overthrow (a government etc.)
topsy-turvy Ⓣ *adj* **1** upside down **2** in confusion
toque [**toke**] *n* small round hat
tor *n* high rocky hill
Torah *n* body of traditional Jewish teaching
torch *n* **1** burning brand carried as a light **2** *Brit* flashlight ▷ *v* **3** *slang* set fire to deliberately
tore *v* past tense of **tear**[2]
toreador [**torr**-ee-a-dor] *n* bullfighter
torment Ⓣ *v* **1** cause (someone) great suffering **2** tease cruelly ▷ *n* **3** great suffering **4** source of suffering **tormentor** *n*
torn Ⓣ *v* past participle of **tear**[2]
tornado Ⓣ *n, pl* **-does, -dos** violent whirlwind
torpedo Ⓣ *n, pl* **-does 1** self-propelled underwater missile ▷ *v* **-doing, -doed 2** attack or destroy with or as if with torpedoes
torpid *adj* sluggish and inactive **torpidity** *n* ▶**torpor** *n* torpid state
torque [**tork**] *n* **1** force causing rotation **2** Celtic necklace or armband of twisted metal
Torquemada *n* **Tomás de**. 1420–98, Spanish Dominican monk. As first Inquisitor-General of Spain (1483–98), he was responsible for the burning of some 2000 heretics
torrent Ⓣ *n* **1** rushing stream **2** downpour ▶**torrential** *adj* (of rain) very heavy
torrid Ⓣ *adj* **1** very hot and dry **2** highly emotional
torsion *n* twisting
torso *n, pl* **-sos 1** trunk of the human body **2** statue of a nude human trunk
tort *n law* civil wrong or injury for which damages may be claimed
tortilla *n* thin Mexican pancake
tortoise *n* slow-moving land reptile with a dome-shaped shell ▶**tortoiseshell** *n* **1** mottled brown shell of a turtle, used for making ornaments ▷ *adj* **2** having brown, orange, and black markings
tortuous Ⓣ *adj* **1** winding or twisting **2** not straightforward
torture Ⓣ *v* **1** cause (someone) severe pain or mental anguish ▷ *n* **2** severe physical or mental pain **3** torturing **torturer** *n*
Tory *n, pl* **Tories 1** member or supporter of the Progressive Conservative Party ▷ *adj* **2** of Tories **Toryism** *n*
Toscanini *n* **Arturo**. 1867–1957, Italian conductor; musical director of La Scala, Milan, and of the NBC symphony orchestra (1937–57) in New York

THESAURUS

See also: **maximum, prize, successful, supreme**
▷ **top up** *See* **augment, supplement**
topic *n* = **subject**, point, issue, question, matter, theme, subject matter
topical *adj* = **current**, popular, contemporary, up-to-date, newsworthy, up-to-the-minute
topmost *adj* = **highest**, top, principal, dominant, foremost, supreme, paramount, uppermost, leading
topple *v* **1** = **fall over**, fall, collapse, tumble, overturn, keel over, overbalance, totter **2** = **overthrow**, oust, overturn, unseat, bring down, bring low
topsy-turvy *adj* = **confused**, messy, chaotic, disorderly, upside-down, inside-out, disorganized, jumbled, mixed-up
torment *v* **1** = **torture**, rack, distress, crucify **2** = **tease**, bother, harass, annoy, irritate, nag, hassle (*informal*), vex, pester ▶ *n* **3** = **suffering**, pain, torture, hell, distress, misery, anguish, agony
torn *adj* **1** = **cut**, split, rent, slit, ragged, lacerated, ripped **2** = **undecided**, uncertain, unsure, in two minds (*informal*), irresolute, vacillating, wavering
tornado *n* = **whirlwind**, storm, hurricane, cyclone, typhoon, squall, tempest, gale
torpedo *See* **bomb**
torpor *n* = **inactivity**, sluggishness, apathy, drowsiness, laziness, sloth, lethargy, indolence, listlessness
torrent *n* = **stream**, flood, rush, flow, tide, spate, cascade, deluge, downpour
torrid *adj* **1** = **arid**, parched, dried, scorched **2** = **passionate**, intense, steamy (*informal*), ardent, fervent
tortuous *adj* **1** = **winding**, indirect, twisty, convoluted, mazy, serpentine, circuitous, meandering, sinuous, twisting **2** = **complicated**, tricky, indirect, involved, ambiguous, roundabout, devious, convoluted
torture *v* **1** = **torment**, rack, distress, afflict, persecute, crucify, put on the rack ▶ *n* **2** = **torment**, pain, suffering, distress, persecution, anguish, agony

t

DICTIONARY

toss Ⓣ *v* **1** throw lightly **2** fling or be flung about **3** (of a horse) throw (its rider) **4** coat (food) by gentle stirring or mixing **5** throw up (a coin) to decide between alternatives by guessing which side will land uppermost ▷ *n* **6** tossing
▶ **toss up** *v* toss a coin
▶ **toss-up** *n* even chance or risk
Tostig *n* died 1066, earl of Northumbria (1055–65), brother of King Harold II. He joined the Norwegian forces that invaded England in 1066 and died at Stamford Bridge
tot[1] Ⓣ *n* **1** small child **2** small drink of spirits
tot[2] Ⓣ *v* **totting, totted** ▶ **tot up** add (numbers) together
total Ⓣ *n* **1** whole, esp. a sum of parts ▷ *adj* **2** complete **3** of or being a total ▷ *v* **totalling, totalled 4** amount to **5** add up
totally *adv* **totality** *n*
▶ **totalizator** *n* machine operating a betting system in which money is paid out to the winners in proportion to their stakes
totalitarian Ⓣ *adj* of a dictatorial one-party government **totalitarianism** *n*
tote[1] *n* short for **totalizator**
tote[2] *v* haul or carry
totem *n* tribal badge or emblem
▶ **totem pole** post carved or painted with totems by N American Indians on the Pacific coast
totter Ⓣ *v* **1** move unsteadily **2** be about to fall
toucan *n* large-billed tropical American bird
touch Ⓣ *n* **1** sense by which an object's qualities are perceived when they come into contact with part of the body **2** gentle tap, push, or caress **3** small amount **4** characteristic style **5** detail ▷ *v* **6** come into contact with **7** tap, feel, or stroke **8** affect **9** move emotionally **10** eat or drink **11** refer to in passing **12** equal or match **13** *slang* ask for money
▶ **touch and go** risky or critical
▶ **touch base** make contact, renew communication
▶ **touched** *adj* **1** emotionally moved **2** slightly mad
▶ **touching** *adj* emotionally moving
▶ **touchy** *adj* easily offended
▶ **touch down** *v* (of an aircraft) land
▶ **touchdown** *n football* score gained by being in possession of ball behind opponents' goal line
▶ **touchline** *n* side line of the field in some games
▶ **touchstone** *n* criterion
▶ **touch-type** *v* type without looking at the keyboard
touché [**too**-shay] *interj* acknowledgment of the striking home of a remark or witty reply
tough Ⓣ *adj* **1** strong or resilient **2** difficult

THESAURUS

toss *v* **1** = **throw**, launch, pitch, cast, flip, hurl, lob (*informal*), fling, sling **2** = **thrash**, rock, roll, shake, wriggle, writhe ▶ *n* **3** = **throw**, pitch, lob (*informal*)
tot[1] *n* = **infant**, child, baby, toddler, mite
tot[2] *v* = **add up**, total, tally, calculate, reckon, count up
total *n* **1** = **sum**, whole, aggregate, the whole schmear (*informal*), the whole enchilada (*slang*) • *The companies have a total of 550 employees.* ▶ *adj* **2** = **complete**, absolute, outright, utter, unconditional, unqualified, undivided, unmitigated, out-and-out • *a total failure* ▶ *v* **3** = **amount to**, add up to, come to • *Their debts totalled over a thousand dollars.* **4** = **add up**, reckon, tot up
See also: **add, figure, sheer**
totalitarian *adj* = **dictatorial**, authoritarian, oppressive, undemocratic, despotic, tyrannous
totality *n* = **whole**, total, aggregate, sum, entirety
totally *adv* = **completely**, fully, absolutely, entirely, thoroughly, wholly, utterly, comprehensively, one hundred per cent
totter *v* = **stagger**, stumble, reel, falter, sway, lurch
tottering *See* **shaky, unsteady**
touch *v* **1** = **handle**, feel, finger • *Don't touch the screen.* RELATED WORD *adjective*: tactile **2** = **meet**, brush, graze • *I lowered my legs until my feet touched the floor.* **3** = **affect**, move, stir • *I was touched by his kindness.* **4** = **consume**, eat, drink, chow down (*slang*), partake of **5** = **match**, rival, equal, parallel, compare with, hold a candle to (*informal*) ▷ **touch and go** = **risky**, close, near, critical, precarious, nerve-racking ▷ **touch down** *See* **land** ▷ **touch on** = **refer to**, cover, mention, allude to, bring in, deal with, speak of ▷ **touch upon** *See* **mention** ▶ *n* **6** = **feeling**, handling, physical contact **7** = **contact**, stroke, tap, brush, pat **8** = **bit**, drop, spot, trace, dash, smattering, jot, small amount, *soupçon* (*French*) **9** = **style**, way, method, technique, manner, trademark
See also: **note, reach**
touching *adj* = **moving**, poignant, affecting • *a touching tale*
touchstone *n* = **standard**, measure, par, criterion, gauge, norm, yardstick
touchy *adj* = **oversensitive**, sensitive, easily offended • *He's very touchy about that.*
tough *adj* **1** = **strong**, robust, rugged, resilient, hardened, hardy • *She is tough*

t

DICTIONARY

to chew or cut **3** hardy and fit **4** rough and violent **5** difficult **6** firm and determined **7** *informal* unlucky or unfair ▷ *n* **8** *informal* rough violent person **toughness** *n*
▶ **toughen** *v* make or become tough or tougher

Toulouse-Lautrec *n* **Henri (Marie Raymond) de.** 1864–1901, French painter and lithographer, noted for his paintings and posters of the life of Montmartre, Paris

toupee [**too**-pay] *n* wig

tour Ⓣ *n* **1** journey visiting places of interest along the way **2** trip to perform or play in different places ▷ *v* **3** make a tour (of)
▶ **tourism** *n* tourist travel as an industry
▶ **tourist** *n* person travelling for pleasure
▶ **touristy** *adj* full of tourists or tourist attractions

tour de force *n, pl* **tours de force** *French* brilliant stroke or achievement

Touré *n* **(Ahmed) Sékou.** 1922–84, president of the Republic of Guinea (1958–84)

tourmaline *n* crystalline mineral used for optical instruments and as a gem

tournament Ⓣ *n* **1** sporting competition with several stages to decide the overall winner **2** *hist* Also **tourney** contest between knights on horseback

tourniquet [**tour**-nick-kay] *n* something twisted round a limb to stop bleeding

tousled *adj* ruffled and untidy

Toussaint L'Ouverture *n* **Pierre Dominique.** ?1743–1803, Haitian revolutionary leader. He was made governor of the island by the French Revolutionary government (1794) and expelled the Spanish and British but when Napoleon I proclaimed the re-establishment of slavery he was arrested. He died in prison in France

tout [rhymes with **shout**] *v* **1** solicit custom in a persistent manner **2** obtain and sell information about racehorses ▷ *n* **3** person who sells tickets for a popular event at inflated prices

tow[1] Ⓣ *v* **1** drag, esp. by means of a rope ▷ *n* **2** towing
▶ **in tow** following closely behind
▶ **on tow** being towed
▶ **towbar** *n* metal bar on an automobile for towing vehicles
▶ **towpath** *n* path beside a canal or river, originally for horses towing boats

tow[2] *n* fibre of hemp or flax
▶ **tow-headed** *adj* with blond hair

towards, toward Ⓣ *prep* **1** in the direction of **2** with regard to **3** as a contribution to

towel *n* cloth for drying things
▶ **towelling** *n* material used for making towels

tower Ⓣ *n* **1** tall structure, often forming part of a larger building ▷ *v* **2** be very tall **3** loom (over)
▶ **tower of strength** person who supports or comforts

town Ⓣ *n* **1** group of buildings larger than a village **2** central part of this **3** people of a town
▶ **township** *n* small town
▶ **town hall** large building used for council meetings, concerts, etc.

Townshend *n* **Pete.** born 1945, British rock guitarist, singer, and songwriter: member of The Who (1964–83) and composer of much of their material

toxemia, toxaemia [tox-**seem**-ya] *n* **1** blood poisoning **2** high blood pressure in pregnancy

toxic Ⓣ *adj* **1** poisonous **2** caused by poison **toxicity** *n*
▶ **toxicology** *n* study of poisons
▶ **toxin** *n* poison of bacterial origin

THESAURUS

and ambitious. **2 = resilient**, strong, solid, robust, rugged, durable, sturdy, hard-wearing, leathery • *an apple with a rather tough skin* OPPOSITE: fragile **3 = difficult**, hard, arduous, exacting • *a tough childhood* OPPOSITE: easy **4 = rough**, violent, ruthless, pugnacious, hard-boiled **5 = strict**, hard, firm, severe, stern, resolute, merciless, unbending **6** (*Informal*) **= unlucky**, unfortunate, regrettable, lamentable ▶ *n* **7 = ruffian**, bully, thug, roughneck (*slang*), hooligan, bruiser (*informal*)
See also: **stiff**

toughen *See* **strengthen**

tour *n* **1 = journey**, trip, outing, expedition, excursion, jaunt ▶ *v* **2 = visit**, explore, journey, sightsee, go around, travel through

tourist *n* **= traveller**, globetrotter, tripper, excursionist, holiday-maker, sightseer, voyager

tournament *n* **= competition**, series, event, meeting, contest

tow *v* **= pull**, draw, drag, haul, tug, lug

towards *prep* **1 = in the direction of**, to, for, en route for, on the way to **2 = regarding**, for, about, concerning, with regard to, with respect to

tower *n* **= column**, pillar, skyscraper, turret, obelisk, steeple, belfry

towering *adj* **= tall**, high, impressive, elevated, lofty, magnificent, colossal, imposing, soaring

town *See* **city**

toxic *adj* **= poisonous**, deadly, harmful, lethal, septic, noxious, pernicious, pestilential

DICTIONARY

toy Ⓣ *n* **1** something designed to be played with ▷ *adj* **2** (of a dog) of a variety much smaller than is normal for that breed
▸ **toy with** *v* play or fiddle with
trace[1] Ⓣ *n* **1** track left by something **2** indication **3** minute quantity ▷ *v* **4** follow the course of **5** track down and find **6** copy exactly by drawing on a thin sheet of transparent paper set on top of the original
traceable *adj*
▸ **tracer** *n* projectile which leaves a visible trail
▸ **tracing** *n* traced copy
▸ **tracery** *n* pattern of interlacing lines
▸ **trace element** chemical element occurring in very small amounts in soil etc.
trace[2] *n* strap by which a horse pulls a vehicle
▸ **kick over the traces** escape or defy control
trachea [track-**kee**-a] *n, pl* **tracheae** windpipe
▸ **tracheotomy** [track-ee-**ot**-a-mee] *n* surgical incision into the trachea
track Ⓣ *n* **1** mark or trail left by the passage of anything **2** rough road or path **3** railway line **4** course of action or thought **5** endless band round the wheels of a tank, bulldozer, etc. **6** course for racing **7** separate section on a record, tape, or CD ▷ *v* **8** follow the trail or path of
▸ **track down** *v* hunt for and find
▸ **track event** athletic sport held on a track
▸ **track record** past accomplishments of a person or organization
▸ **tracksuit** *n* warm loose-fitting suit worn by athletes etc., esp. during training
tract[1] Ⓣ *n* **1** wide area **2** *anat* system of organs with a particular function
tract[2] Ⓣ *n* pamphlet, esp. a religious one
tractable Ⓣ *adj* easy to manage or control
traction Ⓣ *n* **1** pulling, esp. by engine power **2** *med* application of a steady pull on an injured limb by weights and pulleys **3** grip of the wheels of a vehicle on the ground
tractor *n* motor vehicle with large rear wheels for pulling farm machinery
▸ **tractor-trailer** *n* freight vehicle consisting of a truck with engine and cab pulling an open or closed trailer
Tracy *n* **Spencer**. 1900–67, US film actor. His films include *The Power and the Glory* (1933), *Captains Courageous* (1937) and *Boys' Town* (1938), for both of which he won Oscars, *Adam's Rib* (1949), and *Bad Day at Black Rock* (1955)
trad *n, adj Brit informal* traditional (jazz)
trade Ⓣ *n* **1** buying, selling, or exchange of goods **2** person's job or craft **3** (people engaged in) a particular industry or business ▷ *v* **4** buy and sell **5** exchange **6** engage in trade **trader** *n* **trading** *n*
▸ **trade-in** *n* used article given in part payment for a new one
▸ **trademark** *or* **tradename** *n* (legally registered) name or symbol used by a firm to distinguish its goods
▸ **trade-off** *n* exchange made as a compromise
▸ **tradesman** *n* **1** skilled worker **2** shopkeeper
▸ **trade union** society of workers for the protection of their interests
▸ **trade wind** wind blowing steadily towards the equator
Tradescant *n* **1** **John**. 1570–1638, English botanist and gardener to Charles I. He

THESAURUS

toxin *See* **poison**
toy *n* **1 = plaything**, game, doll ▸ *v* **2 = play**, fool, fiddle (*informal*), amuse oneself, dally *or* fool around, trifle
trace *v* **1 = find**, locate, track down • *Police are trying to trace the owner.* **2 = copy**, draw, outline, sketch ▸ *n* **3 = indication**, record, sign, evidence, remnant, vestige • *No trace of him had been found.* **4 = bit**, drop, touch, hint, suggestion, suspicion, dash, whiff, tinge • *to write without a trace of sensationalism* **5 = track**, trail, path, footprint, footstep, footmark, spoor
See also: **lead, note**
track *n* **1 = path**, way, line, road, course, orbit, pathway, trajectory **2 = trail**, mark, wake, path, trace, footprint, footstep, footmark, spoor **3 = line**, permanent way, rails ▸ *v* **4 = follow**, trail, pursue, chase, trace, shadow, tail (*informal*), stalk, hunt down ▷ **track down = find**, discover, trace, unearth, dig up, hunt down, run to earth *or* run to ground, sniff out
track record *See* **record**
tract[1] *n* **= area**, region, plot, territory, stretch, district, extent, expanse, townsite (*chiefly Canad*)
tract[2] *n* **= treatise**, essay, pamphlet, booklet, homily, dissertation, monograph
tractable *adj* **= manageable**, willing, tame, compliant, amenable, obedient, docile, submissive, biddable, yielding
traction *n* **= grip**, pull, purchase, resistance, friction
trade *n* **1 = commerce**, business • *foreign trade* RELATED WORD *adjective*: mercantile **2 = occupation**, business, line, profession, line of work • *He learned his trade as an apprentice in the plumbing company.* ▸ *v* **3 = deal**, traffic, do business • *They had years of experience of trading with China.* **4 = exchange**, switch, swap, barter ▷ **trade in** *See* **sell, stock**
See also: **change, job**

t

DICTIONARY

introduced many plants from overseas into Britain **2** his son, **John**. 1608–62, English naturalist and gardener, who continued his father's work
tradition Ⓣ *n* **1** unwritten body of beliefs, customs, etc. handed down from generation to generation **2** custom or practice of long standing **traditional** *adj* **traditionally** *adv*
traduce *v* slander
traffic Ⓣ *n* **1** vehicles coming and going on a road **2** (illicit) trade ▷ *v* **-ficking, -ficked** **3** trade, usu. illicitly **trafficker** *n*
▸ **traffic circle** road junction at which traffic passes around a central island
▸ **traffic cop** *informal* police officer who directs the movement of traffic
▸ **traffic lights** set of coloured lights at a junction to control the traffic flow
tragedy Ⓣ *n, pl* **-dies** **1** shocking or sad event **2** serious play, film, etc. in which the hero is destroyed by a personal failing in adverse circumstances
▸ **tragedian** [traj-**jee**-dee-an] *n* actor in or writer of tragedies
▸ **tragedienne** [traj-jee-dee-**enn**] *n* actress in tragedies
▸ **tragic** *adj* of or like a tragedy **tragically** *adv*
▸ **tragicomedy** *n* play with both tragic and comic elements
trail Ⓣ *v* **1** drag along the ground **2** follow the tracks of **3** lag behind **4** (of plants) grow along the ground or hang loosely ▷ *n* **5** track or trace **6** path, track, or road
▸ **trailer** *n* **1** vehicle designed to be towed by another vehicle **2** extract from a film or programme used to advertise it
▸ **trailer park** site for parking mobile homes
train Ⓣ *v* **1** instruct in a skill **2** learn the skills needed to do a particular job or activity **3** cause (an animal) to perform or (a plant) to grow in a particular way **4** aim (a gun etc.) **5** exercise in preparation for a sports event ▷ *n* **6** line of railway coaches or wagons drawn by an engine **7** sequence or series **8** long trailing back section of a dress **9** body of attendants
▸ **trainee** *n* person being trained
▸ **trainer** *n* person who trains an athlete, sportsperson, or racehorse **2** sports shoe
traipse Ⓣ *v informal* walk wearily
trait Ⓣ *n* characteristic feature
traitor Ⓣ *n* person guilty of treason or treachery **traitorous** *adj*
trajectory Ⓣ *n, pl* **-ries** line of flight, esp. of a projectile
tram *n Brit* streetcar
▸ **tramlines** *pl n* track for trams
trammel *v* **-elling, -elled** hinder or restrain
tramp Ⓣ *v* **1** travel on foot, hike **2** walk

THESAURUS

trader *n* = **dealer**, broker, merchant • *a timber trader*
tradesman *n* **1** = **craftsman**, artisan, journeyman, workman **2** = **shopkeeper**, retailer, dealer, supplier, seller, merchant, vendor, purveyor
trading *See* **business**
tradition *n* = **custom**, convention • *the rich traditions of Afro-Cuban music*
See also: **habit**
traditional *adj* = **conventional**, established • *traditional styles of dress* OPPOSITE: unconventional
See also: **conservative**
traffic *n* **1** = **transportation**, transportation, freight, vehicles **2** = **trade**, business, truck, exchange, commerce, dealings, peddling ▸ *v* **3** = **trade**, deal, exchange, bargain, peddle, do business, have dealings
tragedy *n* = **disaster**, catastrophe, adversity, calamity, misfortune
tragic *adj* = **distressing**, heartbreaking, heart-rending • *a tragic accident*
See also: **sad**
trail *n* **1** = **path**, way, road, track, route, footpath **2** = **tracks**, wake, path, trace, scent, footprints, marks, spoor ▸ *v* **3** = **drag**, pull, draw, haul, tow, dangle **4** = **lag**, follow, linger, dawdle, loiter, hang back, straggle, traipse (*informal*) **5** = **follow**, track, hunt, pursue, chase, trace, shadow, tail (*informal*), stalk
train *v* **1** = **instruct**, school, coach, teach, drill, educate, tutor • *We train them in bricklaying.* **2** = **exercise**, prepare, work out **3** = **aim**, point, level, focus, direct ▸ *n* **4** = **sequence**, set, series, chain, string, progression, succession
See also: **practise**
trained *See* **skilled**
trainee *See* **beginner, recruit**
trainer *n* = **coach**, handler
training *n* **1** = **instruction**, education, tuition, discipline, teaching, schooling, grounding, coaching **2** = **practice**, exercise, preparation, working out
traipse *v* = **trudge**, trail, slouch, drag oneself, footslog, tramp
trait *n* = **characteristic**, feature, quality, attribute, quirk, mannerism, idiosyncrasy, peculiarity
traitor *n* = **betrayer**, rebel, deserter, renegade, defector, Judas, apostate, turncoat, back-stabber, quisling
trajectory *n* = **path**, line, track, course, route, flight path
tramp *v* **1** = **hike**, walk, march, roam, trek, rove, ramble, slog, footslog **2** = **trudge**,

t

DICTIONARY

heavily ▷ *n* **3** homeless person who travels on foot **4** hike **5** sound of tramping **6** cargo ship available for hire **7** promiscuous woman
trample Ⓣ *v* tread on and crush
trampoline *n* **1** tough canvas sheet attached to a frame by springs, used by acrobats etc. ▷ *v* **2** bounce on a trampoline
trance Ⓣ *n* **1** unconscious or dazed state **2** state of ecstasy or total absorption
tranche *n* portion of something large, esp. a sum of money
tranquil Ⓣ *adj* calm and quiet **tranquilly** *adv* **tranquillity** *n*
▶ **tranquillize** *v* make calm
▶ **tranquillizer** *n* drug which reduces anxiety or tension
trans- *prefix* across, through, or beyond
transact *v* conduct or negotiate (a business deal)
▶ **transaction** *n* **1** transacting **2** business deal transacted
transatlantic *adj* on, from, or to the other side of the Atlantic
transceiver *n* combined radio transmitter and receiver
transcend Ⓣ *v* **1** rise above **2** be superior to **transcendence** *n* **transcendent** *adj*
▶ **transcendental** *adj* **1** based on intuition rather than experience **2** supernatural or mystical **transcendentalism** *n*
transcribe Ⓣ *v* **1** copy out **2** write down (something said) **3** record for a later broadcast **4** arrange (music) for a different instrument
▶ **transcript** *n* copy
transducer *n* device that converts one form of energy to another
transept *n* either of the two shorter wings of a cross-shaped church
transfer Ⓣ *v* **-ferring, -ferred 1** move or send from one person or place to another ▷ *n* **2** transferring **3** design which can be transferred from one surface to another
transferable *adj*
▶ **transference** *n* transferring
transfigure *v* change in appearance
transfiguration *n*
transfix Ⓣ *v* **1** astound or stun **2** pierce through
transform Ⓣ *v* change the shape or character of **transformation** *n*
▶ **transformer** *n* device for changing the voltage of an alternating current
transfusion *n* injection of blood into the blood vessels of a patient
▶ **transfuse** *v* **1** give a transfusion to **2** permeate or infuse
transgress Ⓣ *v* break (a moral law)
transgression *n* **transgressor** *n*
transient Ⓣ *adj* lasting only for a short time
transience *n*
transistor *n* **1** semiconducting device used

THESAURUS

stump, toil, plod, traipse (*informal*) ▶ *n* **3 = vagrant**, derelict, down-and-out, drifter **4 = hike**, march, trek, ramble, slog **5 = tread**, stamp, footstep, footfall
trample *v* **= crush**, stamp, squash, flatten, tread, run over, walk over
trance *n* **= daze**, dream, unconsciousness, abstraction, rapture, reverie, stupor
tranquil *adj* **= calm**, still, quiet, peaceful, sedate, serene, undisturbed, restful, placid
tranquility *n* **= calm**, rest, peace, quiet, hush, serenity, repose, stillness, placidity
See also: **peace, quiet**
tranquilize *v* **= calm**, quiet, relax, quell, lull, sedate, soothe, pacify, settle one's nerves
tranquilizer *n* **= sedative**, downer (*slang*), opiate, bromide, barbiturate
transaction *n* **= deal**, business, negotiation, bargain, enterprise, undertaking
transcend *v* **= surpass**, exceed, eclipse, excel, outstrip, outdo, go beyond, rise above
transcendent *adj* **= unparalleled**, pre-eminent, sublime, consummate, incomparable, unrivalled, matchless, unequalled
transcribe *v* **= write out**, transfer, reproduce, copy out, take down
transcript *n* **= copy**, record, manuscript, reproduction, duplicate, transcription
transfer *v* **1 = move**, change, shift, transplant, transport, relocate, convey, hand over, pass on, transpose ▶ *n* **2 = move**, change, shift, transmission, translation, handover, relocation, transference, transposition
transfix *v* **1 = stun**, hold, paralyze, fascinate, mesmerize, engross, hypnotize **2 = pierce**, impale, puncture, spear, skewer, run through
transform *v* **= change**, reform, convert, alter, revolutionize, make over • *This technology has transformed our society.*
See also: **turn**
transformation *n* **= change**, conversion, revolution, alteration, metamorphosis, sea change, transmutation
transgress *v* **= break the law**, violate, offend, infringe, sin, contravene, trespass, disobey, encroach
transgression *n* **= crime**, violation, infringement, wrongdoing, offence, sin, infraction, trespass, misdemeanour, misdeed, encroachment, contravention
transgressor *n* **= criminal**, offender, culprit, villain, wrongdoer, lawbreaker, miscreant, sinner, perp (*informal*), trespasser
transient *adj* **= temporary**, brief, passing,

DICTIONARY

to amplify electric currents **2** portable radio using transistors **transistorized** *adj*
transit ⓣ *n* going from one place to another
▸**transition** *n* change from one state to another **transitional** *adj*
▸**transitive** *adj* (of a verb) requiring a direct object
▸**transitory** *adj* not lasting long
translate ⓣ *v* turn from one language into another **translation** *n* **translator** *n*
transliterate *v* convert to the letters of a different alphabet **transliteration** *n*
translucent ⓣ *adj* letting light pass through, but not transparent **translucence** *n*
transmigrate *v* (of a soul) pass into another body **transmigration** *n*
transmit ⓣ *v* **-mitting, -mitted 1** pass (something) from one person or place to another **2** send out (signals) by radio waves **3** broadcast (a radio or television programme) **transmittable** *adj* **transmitter** *n*
▸**transmission** *n* **1** transmitting **2** shafts and gears through which power passes from a vehicle's engine to its wheels
transmogrify *v* **-fying, -fied** *informal* change completely
transmute *v* change the form or nature of **transmutation** *n*
transom *n* **1** horizontal bar across a window **2** bar separating a door from the window over it
transparent ⓣ *adj* **1** able to be seen through, clear **2** easily understood or recognized **transparently** *adv*
▸**transparency** *n* **1** transparent quality **2** colour photograph on transparent film, viewed by means of a projector
transpire ⓣ *v* **1** become known **2** *informal* happen **3** give off water vapour through pores **transpiration** *n*
transplant ⓣ *v* **1** remove and transfer (a plant) to another place **2** transfer (an organ or tissue) surgically from one part or body to another ▷ *n* **3** surgical transplanting **4** thing transplanted **transplantation** *n*
transport ⓣ *v* **1** convey from one place to another **2** *hist* exile (a criminal) to a penal colony **3** enrapture ▷ *n* **4** business or system of transporting **5** vehicle used in transport **6** ecstasy or rapture **transportation** *n*
▸**transporter** *n* large goods vehicle
transpose ⓣ *v* **1** interchange two things **2** put (music) into a different key **transposition** *n*
transsexual *n* **1** person of one sex who believes their true identity is of the opposite sex **2** person who has had a sex-change operation
transubstantiation *n Christianity* doctrine that the bread and wine consecrated in the Eucharist changes into the substance of Christ's body
transuranic [tranz-yoor-**ran**-ik] *adj* (of an

THESAURUS

short-lived, momentary, fleeting, ephemeral, transitory, impermanent
transit *n* = **movement**, transfer, transport, transportation, passage, crossing, carriage, conveyance
transition *n* = **change**, development, shift, conversion, passing, progression, alteration, metamorphosis, transmutation
transitional *adj* **1** = **changing**, fluid, passing, developmental, intermediate, unsettled **2** = **temporary**, provisional
transitory *adj* = **short-lived**, short, brief, temporary, passing, momentary, fleeting, transient, ephemeral, impermanent
translate *v* = **interpret**, convert, render, decode, decipher, construe, paraphrase
translation *n* = **interpretation**, version, rendition, rendering, paraphrase, decoding
translucent *See* **clear, transparent**
transmission *n* **1** = **transfer**, spread, shipment, dissemination, conveyance, sending, transference **2** = **broadcasting**, showing, dissemination, putting out, relaying, sending **3** = **program**, show, broadcast
transmit *v* **1** = **pass on**, send, carry, bear, spread, transfer, convey, disseminate, impart, hand on **2** = **broadcast**, radio, relay, disseminate, send out
transparency *n* **1** = **clarity**, clearness, limpidity, pellucidness, translucence **2** = **photograph**, slide
transparent *adj* **1** = **clear**, sheer, translucent, crystalline • *a sheet of transparent plastic* **2** = **obvious**, patent, plain, explicit, evident, recognizable, manifest, unambiguous, undisguised
transpire *v* **1** = **become known**, emerge, come out, come to light **2** (*Informal*) = **happen**, chance, occur, arise, befall, come about, take place
transplant *v* = **transfer**, remove, shift, displace, relocate, uproot, resettle
transport *v* **1** = **convey**, carry, ship, transfer • *They use tankers to transport the oil.* **2** = **exile**, deport, banish
See also: **bring, take**
transportation *n* **1** = **vehicle**, transportation, conveyance
2 = **transportation**, transit, shipment • *The prices quoted include transport.*
transpose *v* = **interchange**, change, move, exchange, transfer, shift, switch, alter, swap, substitute, reorder

DICTIONARY

element) having an atomic number greater than that of uranium
transverse *adj* crossing from side to side
transvestite *n* person who seeks sexual pleasure by wearing the clothes of the opposite sex **transvestism** *n*
trap ⓣ *n* **1** device for catching animals **2** plan for tricking or catching a person **3** bend in a pipe containing liquid to prevent the escape of gas **4** *hist* two-wheeled carriage **5** *slang* mouth ▷ *v* **trapping, trapped** **6** catch **7** trick
▶ **trapper** *n* person who traps animals for their fur
▶ **trapdoor** *n* door in a floor or roof
trapeze *n* horizontal bar suspended from two ropes, used by circus acrobats
trapezium *n, pl* **-ziums, -zia** **1** quadrilateral with no sides parallel **2** *Brit* trapezoid
▶ **trapezoid** [**trap**-piz-zoid] *n* **1** quadrilateral with two parallel sides of unequal length **2** *Brit* trapezium
trappings ⓣ *pl n* equipment or ornaments
Trappist *n* member of an order of Christian monks who observe strict silence
trash ⓣ *n* **1** garbage **2** anything worthless ▷ *v* **3** throw away **4** attack or destroy **trashy** *adj*
trauma ⓣ [**traw**-ma] *n* **1** emotional shock **2** injury or wound **traumatic** *adj* **traumatize** *v*
travail *v, n lit* labour or toil
travel ⓣ *v* **-elling, -elled** **1** go from one place to another, through an area, or for a specified distance ▷ *n* **2** travelling, esp. as a tourist **travels** **3** (account of) travelling **traveller** *n*
▶ **travelogue** *n* film or talk about someone's travels
traverse ⓣ *v* **1** move over or back and forth over **2** move sideways ▷ *n* **3** traversing **4** path or road across
travesty ⓣ *n, pl* **-ties** **1** grotesque imitation or mockery ▷ *v* **-tying, -tied** **2** make or be a travesty of
trawl *n* **1** net dragged at deep levels behind a fishing boat ▷ *v* **2** fish with such a net
▶ **trawler** *n* trawling boat
tray *n* **1** flat board, usu. with a rim, for carrying things **2** open receptacle for office correspondence
treachery ⓣ *n, pl* **-eries** wilful betrayal
▶ **treacherous** *adj* **1** disloyal **2** unreliable or dangerous **treacherously** *adv*
treacle *n* thick dark syrup produced when sugar is refined **treacly** *adj*
tread ⓣ *v* **treading, trod, trodden** *or* **trod** **1** set one's foot on **2** crush by walking on ▷ *n* **3** way of walking or dancing **4** treading **5** upper surface of a step **6** part of a tire that touches the ground

THESAURUS

trap *n* **1** = **snare**, net • *a bear trap* **2** = **trick**, ambush, deception, ruse, subterfuge, stratagem, wile ▶ *v* **3** = **catch**, corner, snare • *a more humane way to trap the creatures* **4** = **trick**, dupe • *Were you trying to trap her into making a confession?*
trapping *See* **capture**
trappings *pl n* = **accessories**, equipment, gear, paraphernalia, accoutrements, finery, furnishings, panoply, things, trimmings
trash *n* **1** = **garbage**, refuse, waste, rubbish • *They pick up the trash on Mondays.* **2** = **nonsense**, garbage (*informal*), rubbish • *Don't read that awful trash.* ▶ *v* **3** = **destroy**, defeat, ruin, wreck, trounce, demolish, torpedo, put paid to
See also: **junk**
trashy *adj* = **worthless**, cheap, shoddy, inferior, shabby, rubbishy, tawdry
trauma *n* = **shock**, hurt, pain, torture, suffering, ordeal, anguish, agony
traumatic *adj* = **shocking**, painful, hurtful, injurious, agonizing, damaging, disturbing, scarring, upsetting, wounding
traumatize *See* **shock**
travel *v* **1** = **go**, journey, make your way, take a trip • *You had better travel to Ottawa tomorrow.* ▶ *n* **2** (*usually pl*) = **journey**, trip, tour, expedition, voyage, excursion, globetrotting, wandering
See also: **proceed, spread**
traveller *n* = **voyager**, tourist, explorer, gypsy, globetrotter, wanderer, holiday-maker, wayfarer
travelling *adj* = **itinerant**, mobile, migrant, nomadic, peripatetic, roaming, roving, touring, wandering, wayfaring
traverse *v* = **cross**, span, go over, travel over
travesty *n* **1** = **mockery**, caricature, distortion, parody, lampoon, perversion, burlesque ▶ *v* **2** = **mock**, caricature, parody, ridicule, distort, lampoon, burlesque, make a mockery of
treacherous *adj* **1** = **disloyal**, untrustworthy, unfaithful • *He denounced the party's treacherous leaders.* OPPOSITE: loyal **2** = **dangerous**, hazardous, perilous • *treacherous mountain roads*
See also: **two-faced**
treachery *n* = **betrayal**, treason, infidelity, back-stabbing (*informal*), disloyalty, double-dealing, duplicity, faithlessness, perfidy
tread *v* **1** = **step**, walk, pace, hike, march, stamp, stride **2** = **trample**, squash, crush underfoot ▶ *n* **3** = **step**, walk, pace, stride, footstep, gait, footfall

t

DICTIONARY

▸**treadmill** *n* **1** *hist* cylinder turned by treading on steps projecting from it **2** dreary routine
treadle [**tred**-dl] *n* lever worked by the foot to turn a wheel
treason Ⓣ *n* **1** betrayal of one's sovereign or country **2** treachery or disloyalty
treasonable *or* **treasonous** *adj*
treasure Ⓣ *n* **1** collection of wealth, esp. gold or jewels **2** valued person or thing ▷ *v* **3** prize or cherish
▸**treasurer** *n* official in charge of funds
▸**treasury** *n* **1** storage place for treasure **2** government department in charge of finance
▸**treasure-trove** *n* treasure found with no evidence of ownership
treat Ⓣ *n* **1** pleasure, entertainment, etc. given or paid for by someone else ▷ *v* **2** deal with or regard in a certain manner **3** give medical treatment to **4** subject to a chemical or industrial process **5** provide (someone) with (something) as a treat
▸**treatment** *n* **1** way of treating a person or thing **2** medical care
treatise Ⓣ [**treat**-izz] *n* formal piece of writing on a particular subject
treaty Ⓣ *n, pl* **-ties** signed contract between states
treble *adj* **1** threefold, triple **2** *music* high-pitched ▷ *n* **3** (singer with or part for) a soprano voice ▷ *v* **4** increase threefold **trebly** *adv*
tree *n* large perennial plant with a woody trunk **treeless** *adj*
▸**tree surgery** repair of damaged trees **tree surgeon**
trefoil [**tref**-foil] *n* **1** plant, such as clover, with a three-lobed leaf **2** carved ornament like this
trek Ⓣ *n* **1** long difficult journey, esp. on foot ▷ *v* **trekking, trekked 2** make such a journey
trellis *n* framework of horizontal and vertical strips of wood
Tremblay *n* **Michel**. born 1942, Canadian novelist and playwright. His works include *Les Belles-Sœurs* (1968), noted for its use of working-class Quebec French dialect
tremble Ⓣ *v* **1** shake or quiver **2** feel fear or anxiety ▷ *n* **3** trembling **trembling** *adj*
tremendous Ⓣ *adj* **1** huge **2** *informal* great in quality or amount **tremendously** *adv*
tremolo *n, pl* **-los** *music* quivering effect in singing or playing
tremor Ⓣ *n* **1** involuntary shaking **2** minor earthquake
tremulous *adj* trembling, as from fear or excitement
trench Ⓣ *n* long narrow ditch, esp. one used as a shelter in war

THESAURUS

treason *n* = **disloyalty**, treachery, mutiny, back-stabbing (*informal*), duplicity, lese-majesty, perfidy, sedition, traitorousness
treasonable *adj* = **disloyal**, treacherous, subversive, mutinous, perfidious, seditious, traitorous
treasure *v* **1** = **prize**, value, cherish, hold dear • *We treasure our friendship.* **2** = **riches**, money, gold, cash, wealth, fortune, jewels, valuables **3** = **darling**, jewel, gem, apple of one's eye, nonpareil, paragon, pride and joy
See also: **appreciate, dear**
treasured *See* **beloved, dear**
treasures *See* **valuables**
treasury *n* = **storehouse**, store, bank, vault, cache, hoard, repository
treat *v* **1** = **behave toward**, act toward, deal with • *She treated most of us with indifference.* **2** = **attend to**, nurse, care for • *the doctor who treated me* **3** = **entertain**, provide, stand (*informal*), regale, lay on ▸*n* **4** = **entertainment**, party, gift, celebration, feast, banquet, refreshment **5** = **pleasure**, surprise, fun, thrill, delight, joy, satisfaction, enjoyment
See also: **luxury**
treatise *n* = **essay**, study, work, paper, tract, pamphlet, thesis, dissertation, monograph
treatment *n* **1** = **care**, surgery, medication, therapy, medicine, cure, healing, remedy **2** = **handling**, action, conduct, management, dealing, behaviour, manipulation
treaty *n* = **agreement**, contract, alliance, convention, pact, compact, covenant, concordat, entente
trek *n* **1** = **journey**, hike, march, expedition, odyssey, safari **2** = **slog**, tramp ▸*v* **3** = **journey**, hike, march, rove **4** = **slog**, trudge, footslog, traipse (*informal*), tramp
tremble *v* **1** = **shake**, quake, wobble, shiver, vibrate, shudder, quiver, totter ▸*n* **2** = **shake**, quake, vibration, tremor, wobble, shiver, shudder, quiver
trembling *See* **shaky**
tremendous *adj* **1** = **huge**, great, enormous, terrific, immense, formidable, gigantic, colossal, stupendous **2** (*Informal*) = **excellent**, great, amazing, wonderful, brilliant, extraordinary, fantastic (*informal*), exceptional, sensational (*informal*), marvelous
tremor *n* **1** = **shake**, wobble, shiver, quiver, quaking, quaver, trembling **2** = **earthquake**, shock, quake (*informal*)
trench *n* = **ditch**, channel, drain, excavation, gutter, trough, furrow

DICTIONARY

▸ **trench coat** double-breasted waterproof coat
trenchant Ⓣ *adj* **1** incisive **2** effective
trencher *n hist* wooden plate for serving food
▸ **trencherman** *n* hearty eater
trend Ⓣ *n* **1** general tendency or direction **2** fashion
▸ **trendy** *adj, n informal* consciously fashionable (person) **trendiness** *n*
trepidation Ⓣ *n* fear or anxiety
trespass Ⓣ *v* **1** go onto another's property without permission ▷ *n* **2** trespassing **3** *old-fashioned* sin or wrongdoing **trespasser** *n*
▸ **trespass on** *v* take unfair advantage of (someone's friendship, patience, etc.)
tress *n* long lock of hair
trestle *n* board fixed on pairs of spreading legs, used as a support
Trevino *n* **Lee**. born 1939, US professional golfer: winner of the US Open Championship (1968; 1971) and the British Open Championship (1971; 1972)
trews *pl n* close-fitting tartan trousers
tri- *prefix* three
triad *n* **1** group of three **2 Triad** Chinese criminal secret society
trial Ⓣ *n* **1** trying or testing **2** *law* investigation of a case before a judge **3** thing or person straining endurance or patience **trials 4** sporting competition for individuals
triangle *n* **1** geometric figure with three sides **2** triangular percussion instrument **3** situation involving three people
triangular *adj*
tribe Ⓣ *n* group of clans or families believed to have a common ancestor **tribal** *adj*
▸ **tribalism** *n* loyalty to a tribe
tribulation Ⓣ *n* great distress
tribunal Ⓣ *n* **1** lawcourt **2** board appointed to inquire into a specific matter
tribune *n* **1** person who upholds public rights **2** people's representative in ancient Rome
tributary *n, pl* **-taries 1** stream or river flowing into a larger one ▷ *adj* **2** (of a stream or river) flowing into a larger one
tribute Ⓣ *n* **1** sign of respect or admiration **2** tax paid by one state to another
trice Ⓣ *n* **in a trice** instantly
triceps *n* muscle at the back of the upper arm
trichology [trick-**ol**-a-jee] *n* study and treatment of hair and its diseases
trichologist *n*
trick Ⓣ *n* **1** deceitful or cunning action or plan **2** joke or prank **3** feat of skill or cunning **4** knack **5** mannerism **6** cards played in one round ▷ *v* **7** cheat or deceive **trickery** *n*
trickster *n*
▸ **tricky** *adj* **1** difficult, needing careful handling **2** crafty
trickle Ⓣ *v* **1** (cause to) flow in a thin stream or drops **2** move gradually ▷ *n* **3** gradual flow
tricolour [**trick**-kol-lor] *n* three-coloured striped flag
tricycle *n* three-wheeled cycle

THESAURUS

trenchant *adj* **1** = **scathing**, cutting, pointed, caustic, acerbic, pungent, incisive, penetrating **2** = **effective**, strong, powerful, potent, energetic, vigorous, forceful
trend *n* **1** = **tendency**, current, direction, flow, bias, drift, inclination, leaning **2** = **fashion**, thing, style, rage, mode, vogue, fad (*informal*), craze
trendy *adj* = **fashionable**, in, latest, stylish, chic, in fashion, in vogue • *a trendy night club*
trepidation *n* = **anxiety**, fear, worry, alarm, dread, apprehension, nervousness, consternation, uneasiness, disquiet
trespass *v* **1** = **intrude**, invade, infringe, encroach, obtrude ▸ *n* **2** = **intrusion**, invasion, infringement, encroachment, unlawful entry
trespasser *n* = **intruder**, invader, poacher, interloper
trial *n* **1** = **hearing**, tribunal, litigation **2** = **test**, experiment, probation, audition, dry run (*informal*), test-run **3** = **hardship**, trouble, suffering, ordeal, distress, adversity, affliction, tribulation
tribe *n* = **race**, people, family, clan
tribulation *See* **difficulty, ordeal**
tribunal *n* = **hearing**, court, trial
tribute *n* **1** = **accolade**, honour, testimony, praise, compliment • *Police paid tribute to her courage.* **2** = **payment**, charge, tax, ransom, homage
trice *See* **instant, minute**
trick *n* **1** = **deception**, con (*informal*), hoax, ploy, ruse • *We are playing a trick on my little brother.* **2** = **joke**, antic, jape, stunt, prank, practical joke **3** = **secret**, hang (*informal*), skill, technique, knack, know-how (*informal*) **4** = **mannerism**, practice, habit, characteristic, trait, quirk, foible, idiosyncrasy, peculiarity ▸ *v* **5** = **deceive**, fool, con (*informal*), dupe, take in • *They tricked me into giving them all my money.*
See also: **trap**
trickery *n* = **deception**, deceit, dishonesty, cheating, chicanery, guile, monkey business (*informal*)
trickle *v* **1** = **dribble**, run, drop, stream, drip, seep, ooze, exude ▸ *n* **2** = **dribble**, drip, seepage
tricky *adj* **1** = **difficult**, hard, complex, sensitive, complicated, delicate, problematic, puzzling • *This could be a very tricky problem.* **2** = **crafty**, slippery, wily, sly, cunning, deceitful, devious, artful, scheming

t

DICTIONARY

trident *n* three-pronged spear
triennial *adj* happening every three years
trifle ⓣ *n* **1** insignificant thing **2** small amount **3** dessert of sponge cake, custard, etc. ▷ *v* **4** (usu. foll. by *with*) toy with
▶ **trifling** *adj* insignificant
trigger ⓣ *n* **1** small lever releasing a catch on a gun or machine **2** action that sets off a course of events ▷ *v* **3** (usu. foll. by *off*) set (an action or process) in motion
▶ **trigger-happy** *adj* too quick to use guns
trigonometry *n* branch of mathematics dealing with relations of the sides and angles of triangles **trigonometrical** *adj*
trike *n informal* tricycle
trilateral *adj* having three sides
trilby *n, pl* **-bies** man's soft felt hat
trill *n* **1** rapid alternation between two notes **2** shrill warbling sound made by some birds ▷ *v* **3** play or sing a trill
trillion *n* **1** *US & Canad* one million million, 10^{12} **2** *Brit* one million million million, 10^{18}
trilobite [**trile**-oh-bite] *n* small prehistoric sea animal
trilogy [**trill**-a-jee] *n, pl* **-gies** series of three related books, plays, etc.
trim ⓣ *adj* **trimmer, trimmest 1** neat and smart **2** slender **3** in good condition ▷ *v* **trimming, trimmed 4** cut or prune into good shape **5** decorate with lace, ribbons, etc. **6** adjust the balance of (a ship or aircraft) by shifting the cargo etc. ▷ *n* **7** decoration **8** upholstery and decorative facings in an automobile **9** trim state **10** haircut that neatens the existing style
▶ **trimming** *n* **1** decoration **trimmings 2** usual accompaniments: *turkey with all the trimmings*
trimaran [**trime**-a-ran] *n* three-hulled boat
trinitrotoluene *n* full name of TNT
trinity ⓣ *n, pl* **-ties 1** group of three **2 Trinity** *Christianity* union of three persons, Father, Son, and Holy Spirit, in one God
trinket ⓣ *n* small or worthless ornament or piece of jewellery
trio ⓣ *n, pl* **trios 1** group of three **2** piece of music for three performers
trip ⓣ *n* **1** journey to a place and back, esp. for pleasure **2** stumble **3** switch on a mechanism **4** *informal* hallucinogenic drug experience ▷ *v* **tripping, tripped 5** (cause to) stumble **6** (often foll. by *up*) catch (someone) in a mistake **7** move or tread lightly **8** operate (a switch) **9** *informal* take a hallucinogenic drug
▶ **tripper** *n* tourist
tripartite *adj* involving or composed of three people or parts
tripe *n* **1** stomach of a cow used as food **2** *informal* nonsense
triple ⓣ *adj* **1** having three parts **2** three times as great or as many ▷ *v* **3** increase threefold ▷ *n* **4** *baseball* hit that enables the batter to run to third base
▶ **triplet** *n* one of three babies born at one birth
▶ **triple jump** athletics event in which competitors make a hop, a step, and a jump as a continuous movement
triplicate *adj* **1** triple ▷ *n* **2** one of three copies
▶ **in triplicate** in three copies
tripod [**tripe**-pod] *n* three-legged stand, stool, etc.
tripos [**tripe**-poss] *n* final examinations for the degree of BA at Cambridge University
triptych [**trip**-tick] *n* painting or carving

THESAURUS

trifle *n* **1** = **knick-knack**, toy, plaything, bauble, bagatelle ▶ *v* **2** = **toy**, play, dally, mess around
trifling *adj* = **insignificant**, paltry, worthless, negligible, trivial, unimportant, measly
trigger *v* = **set off**, start, cause, produce, prompt, generate, provoke, activate, set in motion, spark off
trim *adj* **1** = **neat**, dapper, smart, tidy, spruce, shipshape, well-groomed **2** = **slender**, fit, slim, sleek, streamlined, shapely, svelte, willowy ▶ *v* **3** = **cut**, clip, crop, shave, tidy, pare, prune, even up **4** = **decorate**, dress, array, adorn, ornament, embellish, beautify, deck out ▶ *n* **5** = **decoration**, border, trimming, embellishment, frill, piping, adornment, edging, ornamentation **6** = **condition**, health, state, shape (*informal*), fitness, fettle **7** = **cut**, crop, shave, clipping, pruning, shearing, tidying up
trimming *n* = **decoration**, border, embellishment, frill, piping, adornment, edging, ornamentation ▶ **trimmings** = **extras**, paraphernalia, accessories, accompaniments, frills, ornaments, trappings
trinity *n* = **threesome**, trio, triumvirate, triad
trinket *n* = **ornament**, toy, trifle, bauble, bagatelle, knick-knack
trio *n* = **threesome**, trilogy, triumvirate, triad, trinity
trip *n* **1** = **journey**, outing, voyage, excursion, jaunt • *a business trip* **2** = **stumble**, fall, slip, misstep ▶ *v* **3** = **stumble**, fall over, lose your footing • *I tripped on the stairs.* **4** = **catch out**, trap **5** = **skip**, dance, hop, gambol
See also: **drive**
triple *adj* **1** = **threefold**, three-way, tripartite ▶ *v* **2** = **treble**, increase threefold

DICTIONARY

on three hinged panels, often forming an altarpiece
trite Ⓣ *adj* hackneyed or banal
tritium *n* radioactive isotope of hydrogen
triumph Ⓣ *n* **1** (happiness caused by) victory or success ▷ *v* **2** be victorious or successful **3** rejoice over a victory
▶ **triumphal** *adj* celebrating a triumph
▶ **triumphant** *adj* feeling or showing triumph
triumvirate [try-**umm**-vir-rit] *n* group of three people in joint control
trivet [**triv**-vit] *n* metal stand for a pot or kettle
trivial Ⓣ *adj* **1** of little importance **2** everyday, trite **trivially** *adv* **triviality** *n*
▶ **trivia** *pl n* trivial things or details
▶ **trivialize** *v* make (something) seem less important or complex than it is
trod *v* past tense and a past participle of **tread**
trodden *v* a past participle of **tread**
troglodyte *n* cave dweller
troika *n* **1** Russian vehicle drawn by three horses abreast **2** group of three people in authority
Trojan *n* **1** person from ancient Troy **2** hard-working person
▶ **Trojan Horse** trap intended to undermine an enemy
troll *n* giant or dwarf in Scandinavian folklore
trolley *n* **1** small wheeled table for food and drink **2** wheeled cart for moving goods
▶ **trolley car** bus powered by electricity from an overhead wire but not running on rails
trollop *n* promiscuous or slovenly woman
Trollope *n* **1 Anthony**. 1815–82, English novelist. His most successful novels, such as *The Warden* (1855), *Barchester Towers* (1857), and *Dr. Thorne* (1858), are those in the Barsetshire series of studies of English provincial life. The Palliser series of political novels includes *Phineas Redux* (1874) and *The Prime Minister* (1876) **2 Joanna**. born 1943, British novelist: her works include *The Choir* (1988), *A Village Affair* (1989), *The Rector's Wife* (1991), *The Best of Friends* (1995), and *The Girl From the South* (2002)
trombone *n* brass musical instrument with a sliding tube **trombonist** *n*
troop Ⓣ *n* **1** large group **2** artillery or cavalry unit **3** Scout company **troops 4** soldiers ▷ *v* **5** move in a crowd
▶ **trooper** *n* cavalry soldier
trope *n* figure of speech
trophy Ⓣ *n, pl* **-phies 1** cup, shield, etc. given as a prize **2** memento of success
tropic *n* **1** either of two lines of latitude at 23½° N (**tropic of Cancer**) or 23½° S (**tropic of Capricorn**) **tropics 2** part of the earth's surface between these lines
▶ **tropical** *adj* **1** of or in the tropics **2** (of climate) very hot
trot Ⓣ *v* **trotting, trotted 1** move or cause (a horse) to move at a medium pace, lifting the feet in diagonal pairs **2** (of a person) move at a steady brisk pace ▷ *n* **3** trotting
▶ **trotter** *n* pig's foot
▶ **trot out** *v* repeat (old ideas etc.) without fresh thought
troth [rhymes with **growth**] *n* pledge of fidelity, esp. a betrothal
Trotsky, Trotski *n* **Leon**, original name *Lev Davidovich Bronstein*. 1879–1940, Russian revolutionary and Communist theorist. He was a leader of the November Revolution (1917) and, as commissar of foreign affairs and war (1917–24), largely created the Red

THESAURUS

trite *adj* = **unoriginal**, tired, stale, commonplace, banal, clichéd, hackneyed, stereotyped, threadbare
triumph *n* **1** = **success**, victory • *The championships proved to be a personal triumph for the coach.* OPPOSITE: failure **2** = **joy**, pride, happiness, jubilation, elation, exultation, rejoicing ▶ *v* **3** (often with *over*) = **succeed**, win, prevail, come out on top (*informal*) • *a symbol of good triumphing over evil* OPPOSITE: fail **4** = **rejoice**, celebrate, glory, revel, crow, exult, gloat
triumphant *adj* **1** = **victorious**, successful, winning, conquering **2** = **celebratory**, proud, jubilant, elated, exultant
trivia *pl n* = **minutiae**, details, trifles, trivialities
trivial *adj* = **unimportant**, minor, slight, petty, insignificant, paltry, negligible, trifling • *She doesn't concern herself with such trivial details.* OPPOSITE: important
See also: **worthless**
triviality *n* = **insignificance**, meaninglessness, pettiness, unimportance, worthlessness
trivialize *v* = **undervalue**, minimize, underestimate, belittle, laugh off, make light of, play down, scoff at, underplay
troop *n* **1** = **group**, company, team, body, unit, crowd, band, squad, multitude, horde ▷ **troops** = **soldiers**, army, men, armed forces, servicemen, soldiery ▶ *v* **2** = **flock**, march, stream, swarm, throng, traipse (*informal*)
trophy *n* = **prize**, award, cup, souvenir, memento, booty, laurels, spoils
tropical *adj* = **hot**, torrid, steamy, sultry, stifling, sweltering
trot *v* **1** = **run**, jog, scamper, canter, lope ▶ *n* **2** = **run**, jog, canter, lope

DICTIONARY

Army. He was ousted by Stalin after Lenin's death and deported from Russia (1929); assassinated by a Stalinist agent **Trotskyite, Trotskyist** *n, adj*

troubadour [**troo**-bad-oor] *n* medieval travelling poet and singer

trouble Ⓣ *n* **1** (cause of) distress or anxiety **2** disease or malfunctioning **3** state of disorder or unrest **4** care or effort ▷ *v* **5** (cause to) worry **6** cause inconvenience to **7** exert oneself **troubled** *adj* **troublesome** *adj*

▸ **troubleshooter** *n* person employed to locate and deal with faults or problems

trough Ⓣ [**troff**] *n* **1** long open container, esp. for animals' food or water **2** narrow channel between two waves or ridges **3** *meteorol* area of low pressure

trounce Ⓣ *v* defeat utterly

troupe Ⓣ [**troop**] *n* company of performers **trouper** *n*

trousers *pl n* two-legged outer garment with legs reaching usu. to the ankles

▸ **trouser** *adj* of trousers

trousseau [**troo**-so] *n, pl* **-seaux, -seaus** bride's collection of clothing etc. for her marriage

trout *n* game fish related to the salmon

trowel *n* hand tool with a flat wide blade for spreading mortar, lifting plants, etc.

troy weight, troy *n* system of weights used for gold, silver, and jewels

truant Ⓣ *n* pupil who stays away from school without permission **truancy** *n*

▸ **play truant** stay away from school without permission

truce Ⓣ *n* temporary agreement to stop fighting

truck[1] *n* large vehicle for transporting loads by road

▸ **trucker** *n* truck driver

truck[2] *n* **have no truck with** refuse to be involved with

truckle *v* (usu. foll. by *to*) yield weakly

truckle bed *n* low bed on wheels, stored under a larger bed

truculent Ⓣ [**truck**-yew-lent] *adj* aggressively defiant **truculence** *n*

Trudeau *n* **Pierre Elliott.** 1919–2000, Canadian politician; Liberal prime minister (1968–79; 1980–84)

trudge Ⓣ *v* **1** walk heavily or wearily ▷ *n* **2** long tiring walk

true Ⓣ *adj* **truer, truest 1** in accordance with facts **2** faithful **3** exact **4** genuine **truly** *adv*

▸ **truism** *n* self-evident truth

▸ **truth** *n* **1** state of being true **2** something true

▸ **truthful** *adj* **1** honest **2** exact **truthfully** *adv*

Truffaut *n* **François.** 1932–84, French film

THESAURUS

trouble *n* **1 = problem**, difficulty, bother, hassle (*informal*) • *financial troubles* **2 = distress**, worry, pain, woe, anxiety, grief, sorrow, misfortune, torment, disquiet **3 = ailment**, disease, complaint, failure, illness, disorder, defect, malfunction **4 = disorder**, bother (*informal*), unrest, disturbance, strife, agitation, commotion, discord, tumult **5 = effort**, work, care, thought, inconvenience, labour, exertion, pains ▸ *v* **6 = worry**, disturb, bother, agitate • *He was troubled by his brother's decision.* **7 = inconvenience**, disturb, bother, impose upon, put out • *May I trouble you for some milk?* **8 = take pains**, exert oneself, make an effort, take the time

See also: **burden, concern, drawback, jam**

troubled *adj* **1 = anxious**, upset, concerned, distressed, worried, uneasy, disturbed, apprehensive, unsettled, dismayed, disconcerted, perturbed, ill at ease, discomposed, bothered, agitated **2 = difficult**, hard, tough, dark, stressful, problematic, unsettled

troublesome *adj* **1 = worrying**, difficult, tricky, inconvenient, demanding, annoying, irksome, high-maintenance, taxing, trying, vexatious **2 = disorderly**, violent, turbulent, undisciplined, unruly, rowdy, rebellious, uncooperative

trough *n* **1 = manger**, water trough **2 = channel**, depression, ditch, canal, trench, duct, gutter, gully, furrow

trounce *v* **= thrash**, beat, crush, drub, hammer (*informal*), rout, slaughter (*informal*), wipe the floor with (*informal*)

trouncing *See* **defeat**

troupe *n* **= company**, band, cast

truancy *n* **= absence**, absence without leave, malingering, shirking

truant *n* **= absentee**, runaway, malingerer, shirker

truce *n* **= ceasefire**, peace, moratorium, cessation, lull, respite, let-up (*informal*), armistice

truculent *adj* **= hostile**, aggressive, defiant, belligerent, pugnacious, bellicose, ill-tempered, obstreperous

trudge *v* **1 = plod**, lumber, trek, stump, slog, footslog, traipse (*informal*), tramp ▸ *n* **2 = tramp**, hike, march, trek, slog, footslog, traipse (*informal*)

true *adj* **1 = correct**, accurate, factual • *The movie is based on a true story.* OPPOSITE: inaccurate **2 = genuine**, real, authentic, bona fide • *He disguised his true*

t

DICTIONARY

director of the New Wave. His films include *Les Quatre cents coups* (1959), *Jules et Jim* (1961), *Baisers volés* (1968), and *Le Dernier Métro* (1980)
truffle *n* **1** edible underground fungus **2** candy flavoured with chocolate
trug *n* long shallow basket used by gardeners
Trujillo *n* **Rafael** (**Léonidas**), original name *Rafael Léonidas Trujillo Molina*. 1891–1961, Dominican dictator, who governed the Dominican Republic (1930–61) with the help of a powerful police force: assassinated
Truman *n* **Harry S.** 1884–1972, US Democratic statesman; 33rd president of the US (1945–53). He approved the dropping of the two atomic bombs on Japan (1945), advocated the postwar loan to Britain, and involved the US in the Korean War
trump[1] *n, adj* **1** (card) of the suit temporarily outranking the others ▷ *v* **2** play a trump card on (another card) ▷ *pl n* **3** trump suit
▸ **turn up trumps** end unexpectedly well
▸ **trump up** *v* invent or concoct
trump[2] *n lit* (sound of) a trumpet
trumpery *n* foolish talk or actions
trumpet Ⓣ *n* **1** valved brass instrument with a flared tube ▷ *v* **-peting, -peted 2** (of an elephant) cry loudly **3** proclaim loudly
trumpeter *n*
truncate Ⓣ *v* cut short
truncheon Ⓣ *n* small club carried by a policeman
trundle *v* move heavily on wheels
trunk Ⓣ *n* **1** main stem of a tree **2** person's body excluding the head and limbs **3** large case or box for clothes etc. **4** elephant's long nose **5** space in an automobile for luggage
trunks 6 man's swimming shorts
▸ **trunk call** long-distance telephone call
▸ **trunk road** main road
truss Ⓣ *v* **1** tie or bind up ▷ *n* **2** device for holding a hernia in place **3** framework supporting a roof, bridge, etc.
trust Ⓣ *n* **1** confidence in the truth, reliability, etc. of a person or thing **2** obligation arising from responsibility **3** charge or care **4** arrangement in which one person administers property, money, etc. on another's behalf **5** property held for another **6** group of companies joined to control a market ▷ *v* **7** believe in and rely on **8** expect or hope **9** consign to someone's care
▸ **trustee** *n* person holding property on another's behalf **trusteeship** *n*
▸ **trustful** *or* **trusting** *adj* inclined to trust
▸ **trustworthy** *adj* reliable or honest
▸ **trusty** *adj* faithful or reliable
truth Ⓣ *n* see **true**
try Ⓣ *v* **trying, tried 1** make an effort or attempt **2** test or sample **3** put strain on:

THESAURUS

feelings. **3 = faithful**, steady, reliable, loyal, dedicated, staunch, devoted, trustworthy, dutiful **4 = exact**, perfect, accurate, precise, on target, unerring OPPOSITE: false
See also: **actual, realistic, right, strict, trusty**
truism *n* = **cliché**, commonplace, bromide, axiom, platitude
truly *adv* **1 = correctly**, exactly, precisely, genuinely, rightly, legitimately, truthfully, factually, authentically **2 = faithfully**, steadily, sincerely, staunchly, dutifully, devotedly, loyally **3 = really**, very, extremely, indeed, greatly
trumpet *n* **1 = horn**, bugle, clarion ▸ *v* **2 = proclaim**, announce, broadcast, advertise, tout (*informal*), shout from the rooftops
trump up *v* = **invent**, create, fake, fabricate, concoct, contrive, cook up (*informal*), make up
truncate *v* = **shorten**, trim, dock, curtail, pare, prune, abbreviate, lop, cut short
truncheon *n* = **club**, staff, baton, blackjack, cudgel, nightstick, billy club
trunk *n* **1 = stem**, stalk, bole **2 = chest**, case, box, casket, coffer, crate **3 = body**, torso **4 = snout**, proboscis
truss *v* **1 = tie**, secure, bind, strap, tether, fasten, make fast ▸ *n* **2** (*Medical*) **= support**, bandage **3 = joist**, support, stay, brace, prop, beam, buttress, strut, stanchion
trust *v* **1 = believe in**, count on, depend on, have confidence in, have faith in, place your trust in, rely upon • *He can be trusted to honour his promise*. **2 = entrust**, give, commit, delegate, assign, confide, consign **3 = expect**, hope, suppose, assume, presume, surmise ▸ *n* **4 = confidence**, credit, expectation, conviction, faith, belief, assurance, certainty, reliance, credence
See also: **believe, depend, gullible**
trustful, trusting *adj* = **unsuspecting**, naive, gullible, unwary, credulous, unsuspicious
See also: **gullible**
trustworthy *adj* = **dependable**, responsible, honest, reliable, staunch, principled, steadfast, reputable, honourable, trusty
trusty *adj* = **reliable**, firm, true, solid, faithful, staunch, dependable, trustworthy • *a trusty member of the crew*
See also: **loyal**
truth *n* = **fact**, reality • *I'm keen to get to the truth of what happened*. RELATED WORDS *adjectives*: veritable, veracious
truthful *adj* = **honest**, straight, true, precise, sincere, frank, candid, trustworthy
try *v* **1 = attempt**, seek, strive, endeavour

DICTIONARY

he tries my patience **4** investigate (a case) **5** examine (a person) in a lawcourt ▷ *n, pl* **tries 6** attempt or effort **7** *rugby* score gained by touching the ball down over the opponent's goal line
▸ **try it on** *informal* try to deceive or fool someone
▸ **trying** *adj* difficult or annoying
tryst Ⓣ *n old-fashioned* arrangement to meet
tsar [**zahr**] *n hist* Russian emperor
tsetse [**tset**-see] *n* bloodsucking African fly whose bite transmits disease
T-shirt *n* short-sleeved casual shirt or top
tsp. teaspoon
T-square *n* T-shaped ruler
tsunami *n, pl* **-mis, -mi** tidal wave
Tsvangirai *n* **Morgan**. born 1952, Zimbabwean trade unionist and politician; leader of the Movement for Democratic Change, the main opposition party to President Mugabe's Zanu-PF since 1999; prime minister from 2009
tub *n* **1** open, usu. round container **2** bath
▸ **tubby** *adj* (of a person) short and fat
tuba [**tube**-a] *n* valved low-pitched brass instrument
tube *n* **1** hollow cylinder **2** flexible cylinder with a cap to hold pastes
▸ **the tube** underground railway, esp. the one in London
▸ **tubing** [**tube**-ing] *n* **1** length of tube **2** system of tubes
▸ **tubular** [**tube**-yew-lar] *adj* of or like a tube
tuber [**tube**-er] *n* fleshy underground root of a plant such as a potato **tuberous** [**tube**-er-uss] *adj*
tubercle [**tube**-er-kl] *n* small rounded swelling
tuberculosis [tube-berk-yew-**lohss**-iss] *n* infectious disease causing tubercles, esp. in the lungs
▸ **tubercular** [tube-**berk**-yew-lar] *adj* of tuberculosis
▸ **tuberculin** *n* extract from a bacillus used to test for tuberculosis
Tubman *n* **William Vacanarat Shadrach**. 1895–1971, Liberian statesman; president of Liberia (1944–71)
tuck Ⓣ *v* **1** push or fold into a small space **2** stitch in folds ▷ *n* **3** stitched fold **4** *informal* food
▸ **tuck away** *v* store in a safe place
tuckamore *n Canad, esp. Newfoundland* small stunted evergreen tree or scrub
Tudor *adj* **1** of the English royal house ruling from 1485–1603 **2** in an architectural style characterized by half-timbered buildings
Tuesday *n* third day of the week
tufa [**tew**-fa] *n* porous rock formed as a deposit from springs
tuffet *n* small mound or seat
tuft Ⓣ *n* bunch of feathers, grass, hair, etc. held or growing together at the base
tug Ⓣ *v* **tugging, tugged 1** pull hard ▷ *n* **2** hard pull **3** small ship used to tow other vessels
▸ **tug of war** contest in which two teams pull against one another on a rope
tuition Ⓣ *n* instruction, esp. received individually or in a small group
tulip *n* plant with bright cup-shaped flowers
tulle [**tewl**] *n* fine net fabric of silk etc.
tumble Ⓣ *v* **1** (cause to) fall, esp. awkwardly or violently **2** roll or twist, esp. in play **3** rumple ▷ *n* **4** fall **5** somersault
▸ **tumbler** *n* **1** stemless drinking glass **2** acrobat **3** spring catch in a lock
▸ **tumbledown** *adj* dilapidated
▸ **tumble dryer** *or* **tumbler dryer** machine that dries laundry by rotating it in warm air
▸ **tumble to** *v informal* realize, understand
tumbrel, tumbril *n* farm cart used during

THESAURUS

(*formal*), make an attempt, make an effort • *I tried hard to persuade him to stay.* **2 = test**, sample, check out (*informal*), try out • *He wanted me to try the cake.* ▷ **try out** *See* **test, try** ▷ **try your hand at** *See* **attempt** ▸ *n* **3 = attempt**, go (*informal*), shot, effort, endeavour • *After a few tries he pressed the right button.*
trying *adj* **= annoying**, hard, tough, difficult, stressful, tiresome, bothersome, exasperating, high-maintenance, taxing, wearisome
tryst *See* **meeting**
tubby *adj* **= fat**, overweight, obese, portly, plump, chubby, stout, corpulent
tuck *v* **1 = push**, gather, fold, insert ▸ *n* **2 = fold**, gather, pinch, pleat
tuckered out *See* **tired, weary**
tuft *n* **= clump**, collection, bunch, cluster, knot, tussock
tug *v* **1 = pull**, draw, drag, haul, yank, pluck, jerk, wrench, heave • *The puppy tugged at its leash.* ▸ *n* **2 = pull**, yank, jerk, wrench, heave • *He felt a tug at his arm.*
tuition *n* **1 = fees**, price, cost, bill, charges, enrolment fees, maintenance fees **2 = training**, education, instruction, teaching, schooling, tutelage, lessons, tutoring
tumble *v* **1 = fall**, drop, topple, stumble, plummet, flop ▸ *n* **2 = fall**, drop, trip, spill, plunge, stumble
tumbledown *adj* **= dilapidated**, rickety, decrepit, ramshackle, crumbling, ruined

DICTIONARY

the French Revolution to take prisoners to the guillotine
tumescent [tew-**mess**-ent] *adj* swollen or becoming swollen **tumescence** *n*
tummy Ⓣ *n, pl* **-mies** *informal* stomach
tumour Ⓣ [**tew**-mer] *n* abnormal growth in or on the body
tumult Ⓣ [**tew**-mult] *n* uproar or commotion **tumultuous** [tew-**mull**-tew-uss] *adj*
tumulus [**tew**-mew-luss] *n, pl* **-li** burial mound
tun *n* large beer cask
tuna [**tune**-a] *n* large marine food fish
tundra *n* vast treeless Arctic region with permanently frozen subsoil
tune Ⓣ *n* **1** (pleasing) sequence of musical notes **2** correct musical pitch: *she sang out of tune* ▷ *v* **3** adjust (a musical instrument) so that it is in tune **4** adjust (a machine) to obtain the desired performance **tuneful** *adj* **tunefully** *adv* **tuneless** *adj* **tuner** *n*
▸ **tune in** *v* adjust (a radio or television) to receive (a station or programme)
tungsten *n* greyish-white metal
tunic *n* **1** close-fitting jacket forming part of some uniforms **2** loose knee-length garment
tunnel Ⓣ *n* **1** underground passage ▷ *v* **-nelling, -nelled 2** make a tunnel (through)
Tunney *n* **Gene**, original name *James Joseph Tunney*. 1897–1978, US boxer; world heavyweight champion (1926–28)
tunny *n, pl* **-nies, -ny** same as **tuna**
tup *n* male sheep
tupik, tupek *n* traditional type of Inuit dwelling made of animal skins
Tupper *n* Sir **Charles**. 1821–1915, Canadian Conservative politician; Prime Minister (1896)
tuque [**took**] *n* knitted cap with tapering end
turban *n* Muslim or Sikh man's headcovering made by winding cloth round the head
turbid *adj* muddy, not clear **turbidity** *n*
turbine *n* machine or generator driven by gas, water, etc. turning blades
turbo- *combining form* of or powered by a turbine
turbocharger *n* device that increases the power of an internal-combustion engine by using the exhaust gases to drive a turbine
turbofan *n* engine in which a large fan driven by a turbine forces air rearwards around the exhaust gases to increase the thrust
turboprop *n* gas turbine for driving an aircraft propeller
turbot *n* large European flatfish
turbulence Ⓣ *n* **1** confusion, movement, or agitation **2** atmospheric instability causing gusty air currents **turbulent** *adj*
tureen *n* serving dish for soup
turf Ⓣ *n, pl* **turfs, turves 1** short thick even grass **2** square of this with roots and soil attached ▷ *v* **3** cover with turf
▸ **the turf 1** horse racing **2** racecourse
▸ **turf accountant** bookmaker
▸ **turf out** *v informal* throw out
Turgenev *n* **Ivan Sergeyevich**. 1818–83, Russian novelist and dramatist. In *A Sportsman's Sketches* (1852) he pleaded for the abolition of serfdom. His novels, such as *Rudin* (1856) and *Fathers and Sons* (1862), are noted for their portrayal of country life and of the Russian intelligentsia. His plays include *A Month in the Country* (1850)
turgid [**tur**-jid] *adj* **1** swollen and thick **2** (of language) pompous **turgidity** *n*
Turing *n* **Alan Mathison**. 1912–54, English mathematician, who was responsible for formal description of abstract automata, and speculation on computer imitation of humans: a leader of the Allied codebreakers at Bletchley Park during World War II
Turishcheva *n* **Ludmilla**. born 1952, Soviet gymnast: world champion 1970, 1972 (at the

THESAURUS

tummy *See* **stomach**
tumour *n* = **growth**, cancer, lump, sarcoma (*medical*), carcinoma (*pathol*), swelling
See also: **boil**
tumult *n* = **commotion**, row, riot, turmoil, uproar, upheaval, clamor, pandemonium, din, hubbub
tumultuous *adj* = **wild**, excited, turbulent, noisy, boisterous, unruly, rowdy, riotous, uproarious, wired (*slang*)
tune *n* **1** = **melody**, strains • *She was humming a merry little tune.* **2** = **harmony**, pitch, concord, consonance, euphony
▸ *v* **3** = **adjust**, pitch, regulate, adapt, harmonize, attune
tuneful *adj* = **melodious**, musical, pleasant, catchy, melodic, harmonious, euphonious, mellifluous
tuneless *adj* = **discordant**, harsh, atonal, cacophonous, dissonant, unmusical
tunnel *n* **1** = **passage**, hole, channel, subway, shaft, burrow, underpass, passageway
▸ *v* **2** = **dig**, mine, burrow, excavate, scoop out
turbulence *n* = **confusion**, disorder, turmoil, unrest, instability, upheaval, agitation, commotion, tumult
turbulent *adj* = **stormy**, rough, furious, tumultuous, raging, choppy, blustery, tempestuous, agitated, foaming
turf *n* = **grass**, sod, sward ▷ **the turf** = **horse-racing**, racing, the flat

DICTIONARY

Olympic Games), and 1974
turkey *n* large bird bred for food
Turkish *adj* **1** of Turkey, its people, or their language ▷ *n* **2** Turkish language
▸ **Turkish bath** steam bath
▸ **Turkish delight** jelly-like candy coated with icing sugar
turmeric *n* yellow spice obtained from the root of an Asian plant
turmoil Ⓣ *n* agitation or confusion
turn Ⓣ *v* **1** move around an axis, rotate **2** change the position or direction (of) **3** (usu. foll. by *into*) change in nature or character **4** become sour **5** shape on a lathe **6** go round (a corner) **7** reach or pass in age, time, etc.: *she has just turned twenty* ▷ *n* **8** turning **9** direction or drift **10** opportunity to do something as part of an agreed succession **11** period or spell **12** short theatrical performance **turner** *n*
▸ **good** *or* **bad turn** helpful *or* unhelpful act
▸ **turning** *n* road or path leading off a main route
▸ **turning point** moment when a decisive change occurs
▸ **turncoat** *n* person who deserts one party or cause to join another
▸ **turn down** *v* **1** refuse or reject **2** reduce the volume or brightness (of)
▸ **turn in** *v* **1** go to bed **2** hand in
▸ **turn off** *v* stop (something) working by using a knob etc.
▸ **turn on** *v* **1** start (something) working by using a knob etc. **2** become aggressive towards **3** *informal* excite, esp. sexually
▸ **turnout** *n* **1** number of people appearing at a gathering **2** outfit
▸ **turnover** *n* **1** total sales made by a business over a certain period **2** rate at which staff leave and are replaced **3** small pastry
▸ **turnpike** *n* road where a toll is collected at barriers
▸ **turnstile** *n* revolving gate for admitting one person at a time
▸ **turntable** *n* revolving platform
▸ **turn up** *v* **1** arrive or appear **2** find or be found **3** increase the volume or brightness (of)
▸ **turn-up** *n* **1** turned-up fold at the bottom of a trouser leg **2** *informal* unexpected event
Turner *n* **1 J(oseph) M(allord) W(illiam).** 1775–1851, British landscape painter; a master of watercolours. He sought to convey atmosphere by means of an innovative use of colour and gradations of light **2 John (Napier Wyndham)**. born 1929, Canadian Liberal politician, born in England; Prime Minister (1984) **3 Nat**. 1800–31, US rebel slave, who led (1831) Turner's Insurrection, the only major slave revolt in US history: executed **4 Robert Edward III**, known as *Ted*. born 1938, US broadcasting executive and yachtsman; chairman of Turner Broadcasting (1970–96), founder of Cable News Network (1980), and vice-chairman of Time Warner from 1996 **5 Tina**, real name *Annie Mae Bullock*. born 1940,

THESAURUS

turmoil *n* = **confusion**, disorder, chaos, uproar, upheaval, disarray, agitation, commotion, tumult
turn *v* **1** = **rotate**, spin, twist, pivot, rotate, whirl, twirl, swivel • *She had turned the chair to face the door.* **2** = **change**, convert, transform, mutate, metamorphose, transmute, transfigure • *A hobby can be turned into a career.* **3** = **change course**, move, shift, switch, wheel, veer, swerve **4** = **shape**, make, fashion, frame, mould **5** = **go bad**, curdle, spoil, taint, sour ▷ **turn back** *See* **return** ▷ **turn down** = **lower**, soften, lessen, mute, muffle, quieten; = **refuse**, decline, reject, rebuff, spurn, repudiate ▷ **turn in** = **be disloyal to**, double-cross (*informal*), stab in the back, be unfaithful to, sell down the river (*informal*), inform on, sell out (*informal*), be treacherous to; = **go to bed**, go to sleep, hit the sack (*slang*); = **hand in**, return, deliver, submit, surrender, tender, give up, hand over ▷ **turn off** = **switch off**, stop, unplug, cut out, put out, shut down, turn out ▷ **turn on** = **switch on**, start, activate, ignite, kick-start, start up; = **attack**, assault, assail, fall on, round on; (*Informal*) = **arouse**, attract, please, excite, thrill, stimulate, titillate ▷ **turn out** *See* **work out** ▷ **turn red** *See* **blush** ▷ **turn under** *See* **fold** ▷ **turn up** = **arrive**, come, appear, attend, put in an appearance, show one's face, show up (*informal*); = **find**, reveal, discover, expose, disclose, unearth, dig up; = **come to light**, crop up (*informal*), pop up; = **increase**, raise, boost, intensify, enhance, amplify ▸ *n* **6** = **chance**, go (*informal*), opportunity • *Tonight it's my turn to cook.* **7** = **rotation**, cycle, circle, spin, twist, revolution, whirl, gyration **8** = **change of direction**, shift, departure, deviation **9** = **direction**, trend, drift, tendency, heading **10** = **deed**, service, action, act, gesture, favour
See also: **bend, curve, get, grow**
turncoat *n* = **traitor**, deserter, renegade, defector, apostate, backslider
turning *n* = **junction**, turn, bend, curve, turn-off, crossroads, side road ▷ **turning point** = **crossroads**, change, crisis, crux, moment of truth
turnout *n* = **attendance**, number, crowd, audience, assembly, gate, congregation, throng

t

DICTIONARY

US rock singer who performed (1958–75) with her then husband Ike Turner (1931-2007) and later as a solo act. Her recordings include "River Deep, Mountain High" (1966) and "Simply the Best" (1991)
turnip *n* root vegetable with orange or white flesh
turpentine *n* (oil made from) the resin of certain trees
▸ **turps** *n* turpentine oil
turpitude *n* depravity
turquoise *n* **1** blue-green precious stone ▹ *adj* **2** blue-green
turret *n* **1** small tower **2** revolving gun tower on a warship or tank
turtle *n* sea tortoise
▸ **turn turtle** capsize
▸ **turtledove** *n* small wild dove
▸ **turtleneck** *n* (sweater with) a round high close-fitting neck
tusk *n* long pointed tooth of an elephant, walrus, etc.
Tussaud *n* **Marie**. 1760–1850, Swiss modeller in wax, who founded a permanent exhibition in London of historical and contemporary figures
tussle Ⓣ *n, v* fight or scuffle
tussock *n* tuft of grass
Tutankhamen, Tutankhamun *n* king (1361–1352 BC) of the 18th dynasty of Egypt. His tomb near Luxor, discovered in 1922, contained many material objects
tutelage [**tew**-till-lij] *n* **1** tuition **2** guardianship **tutelary** [**tew**-till-lar-ee] *adj*
tutor Ⓣ *n* **1** person teaching individuals or small groups ▹ *v* **2** act as a tutor to
▸ **tutorial** *n* period of instruction with a tutor
tutti-frutti *n* ice cream or other sweet food containing small pieces of candied or fresh fruits
tutu *n* short stiff skirt worn by ballerinas
Tutu *n* **Desmond**. born 1931, South African clergyman, noted for his opposition to apartheid: Anglican Bishop of Johannesburg (1984–86) and Archbishop of Cape Town (1986–96); in 1995 he became leader of the Truth and Reconciliation Commission, established to investigate human rights violations during the apartheid era. Nobel peace prize 1984
tuxedo *n, pl* **-dos** dinner jacket
TV television
twaddle Ⓣ *n* nonsense
twain *n obsolete* two
Twain *n* **1 Mark**, pen name of *Samuel Langhorne Clemens*. 1835–1910, US novelist and humorist, famous for his classics *The Adventures of Tom Sawyer* (1876) and *The Adventures of Huckleberry Finn* (1885) **2 Shania**, real name *Eilleen Regina Edwards*. born 1965, Canadian country-rock singer; her bestselling recordings include *The Woman In Me* (1995), *Come On Over* (1997), and *UP!* (2002)
twang *n* **1** sharp ringing sound **2** nasal speech ▹ *v* **3** (cause to) make a twang
tweak Ⓣ *v* **1** pinch or twist sharply ▹ *n* **2** tweaking
twee *adj informal* too sentimental, sweet, or pretty
tweed *n* **1** thick woollen cloth **tweeds 2** suit of tweed **tweedy** *adj*
tween *n* **1** person from about 9 to 13 years old ▹ *adj* **2** intended for tweens: *the tween market*
tweet *v* **1** chirp **2** post short messages on the Twitter website ▹ *n* **3** short message posted on the Twitter website
▸ **tweeter** *n* **1** loudspeaker reproducing high-frequency sounds **2** person who uses the Twitter website
tweezers *pl n* small pincer-like tool
twelve *adj, n* two more than ten
▸ **twelfth** *adj, n* (of) number twelve in a series
twenty *adj, n* two times ten **twentieth** *adj, n*
▸ **twenty-four-seven** *or* **24/7** *adv informal* all the time
24 Sussex Drive *n* official Ottawa residence of the Prime Minister
twerp *n informal* silly person
twice Ⓣ *adv* two times
twiddle *v* (foll. by *with*) fiddle (with), twirl
▸ **twiddle one's thumbs** be bored, have nothing to do
twig[1] Ⓣ *n* small branch or shoot
twig[2] *v* **twigging, twigged** *informal* realize or understand
twilight Ⓣ *n* soft dim light just after sunset

t

THESAURUS

turnover *n* **1 = output**, business, productivity **2 = movement**, change, coming and going
tussle *n* **1 = fight**, battle, struggle, contest, conflict, scrap (*informal*), brawl, scuffle ▸ *v* **2 = fight**, battle, struggle, scrap (*informal*), vie, wrestle, grapple, scuffle
tutor *n* **1 = teacher**, coach, guide, instructor, guru, mentor, lecturer, educator, guardian ▸ *v* **2 = teach**, school, coach, train, guide, drill, educate, instruct
tutoring *See* **lesson**
twaddle *n* **= nonsense**, garbage (*informal*), rubbish, drivel, claptrap (*informal*), gobbledegook (*informal*), poppycock (*informal*)
tweak *v, n* **= twist**, pull, squeeze, pinch, jerk
twice *See* **double**
twig *n* **= branch**, shoot, stick, spray, sprig
twilight *n* **= dusk**, evening, sunset, gloom, sundown, dimness, gloaming (*poetic*), half-light

DICTIONARY

twill *n* fabric woven to produce parallel ridges
twin Ⓣ *n* **1** one of a pair, esp. of two children born at one birth ▷ *v* **twinning, twinned** **2** pair or be paired
▸ **twin bill** *baseball* same as **double-header**
twine Ⓣ *v* **1** twist or coil round ▷ *n* **2** string or cord
twinge Ⓣ *n* sudden sharp pain or pang
twi-night *adj baseball* designating a double-header that lasts from the afternoon into the evening
twinkle Ⓣ *v* **1** shine brightly but intermittently ▷ *n* **2** flickering brightness
▸ **in the twinkling of an eye** in a very short time
twirl Ⓣ *v* **1** turn or twist around quickly **2** twiddle, esp. idly
twirp *n informal* same as **twerp**
twist Ⓣ *v* **1** turn out of the natural position **2** wind or twine **3** distort or pervert ▷ *n* **4** twisting **5** twisted thing **6** unexpected development in the plot of a film, book, etc. **7** bend or curve **8** distortion **twisty** *adj*
▸ **twisted** *adj* (of a person) cruel or perverted
▸ **twister** *n informal* swindler
twit[1] *v* **twitting, twitted** taunt, esp. in jest
twit[2] *n informal* foolish person
twitch Ⓣ *v* **1** move spasmodically **2** pull sharply ▷ *n* **3** nervous muscular spasm **4** sharp pull
twitter *v* **1** (of birds) utter chirping sounds **2** **Twitter** same as **tweet 2** ▷ *n* **3** chirping **4** **Twitter** popular microblogging website
two *adj, n* one more than one
▸ **two-edged** *adj* (of a remark) having both a favourable and an unfavourable interpretation
▸ **two-faced** *adj* deceitful, hypocritical
▸ **twonie** *n* same as **toonie**
▸ **two-time** *v informal* deceive (a lover) by having an affair with someone else
tycoon Ⓣ *n* powerful wealthy businessman
tyke *n* **1** *informal* small cheeky child **2** small mongrel dog
Tyler *n* **John**. 1790–1862, US statesman; tenth president of the US (1841–45)
tympani *pl n* same as **timpani**
tympanum *n, pl* **-s, -na** **1** cavity of the middle ear **2** tympanic membrane **3** *music* drum or drumhead **tympanic** *adj*
▸ **tympanic membrane** thin membrane separating the external ear from the middle ear
Tyndale, Tindal, Tindale *n* **William**. ?1492–1536, English Protestant and humanist, who translated the New Testament (1525), the Pentateuch (1530), and the Book of Jonah (1531) into English. He was burnt at the stake as a heretic
Tyndall *n* **John**. 1820–93, Irish physicist, noted for his work on the radiation of heat by gases, the transmission of sound through the atmosphere, and the scattering of light
type Ⓣ *n* **1** class or category **2** *informal* person, esp. of a specified kind **3** block with a raised character used for printing **4** printed text ▷ *v* **5** print with a typewriter **6** typify **7** classify
▸ **typist** *n* person who types with a typewriter
▸ **typecast** *v* continually cast (an actor or actress) in similar roles

THESAURUS

twin *n* **1** = **double**, match, fellow, counterpart, mate, clone, duplicate, likeness, look-alike ▸ *v* **2** = **pair**, link, join, couple, match, yoke
twine *n* **1** = **string**, cord, yarn ▸ *v* **2** = **coil**, wind, curl, twist, spiral, bend, loop, encircle
twinge *n* = **pain**, stab, stitch, spasm, prick, pang
twinkle *v* **1** = **sparkle**, shine, flash, shimmer, glitter, blink, gleam, flicker, glisten, glint ▸ *n* **2** = **sparkle**, spark, flash, shimmer, gleam, flicker, glimmer
twirl *v* **1** = **turn**, wind, spin, twist, wheel, revolve, pivot, rotate, whirl, pirouette ▸ *n* **2** = **turn**, spin, twist, wheel, revolution, rotation, whirl, pirouette
twist *v* **1** = **turn around**, curl • *I twisted the light bulb into the socket.* **2** = **wind**, twine • *The fibres are twisted together during spinning.* **3** = **distort**, bend, mangle, screw up • *The truck sat in the intersection with a broken headlight and a twisted fender.* **4** = **sprain**, wrench • *I've twisted my ankle.* ▸ *n* **5** = **wind**, curl, spin, coil, swivel **6** = **development**, change, turn, surprise, revelation, variation, slant **7** = **curve**, turn, bend, arc, meander, undulation, zigzag **8** = **distortion**, flaw, defect, warp, kink, deformation, imperfection
See also: **misrepresent, tangle**
twisted *See* **crooked**
twitch *v* **1** = **jerk**, jump, flutter, squirm ▸ *n* **2** = **jerk**, jump, flutter, spasm, tic
two-faced *adj* = **hypocritical**, false, treacherous, dishonest, deceitful, disloyal, insincere • *a two-faced, manipulative person*
twofold *See* **double**
two-timing *See* **unfaithful**
tycoon *n* = **magnate**, mogul, baron, financier, capitalist, industrialist, fat cat (*slang*), plutocrat
type *n* = **kind**, make, group, class, brand, style, sort, variety, species, breed • *There are various types of dogs suitable as pets.*
See also: **category, form**

DICTIONARY

▸**typewriter** *n* machine which prints a character when the appropriate key is pressed
typhoid fever *n* acute infectious feverish disease
typhoon Ⓣ *n* violent tropical storm
typhus *n* infectious feverish disease
typical Ⓣ *adj* true to type, characteristic **typically** *adv*
typify Ⓣ *v* **-fying, -fied** be typical of
typography *n* art or style of printing **typographical** *adj* **typographer** *n*
tyrant Ⓣ *n* **1** oppressive or cruel ruler **2** person who exercises authority tyrannically **tyrannous** *adj*
▸**tyrannical** *adj* like a tyrant, oppressive **tyrannically** *adv*
▸**tyrannize** *v* exert power (over) oppressively or cruelly
▸**tyranny** *n* tyrannical rule
tyre *n Brit* tire
tyro *n, pl* **-ros** novice or beginner
tzar *n* same as **tsar**
tzetze *n* same as **tsetse**

THESAURUS

typhoon *n* = **storm**, tornado, cyclone, squall, tempest
typical *adj* = **characteristic**, stock, average, standard, regular, normal, representative, usual • *a typical Winnipeg winter* OPPOSITE: uncharacteristic
See also: **natural, routine**
typically *See* **on average**
typify *v* = **symbolize**, represent, characterize, illustrate, embody, exemplify, epitomize, personify, sum up
tyrannical *adj* = **oppressive**, cruel, authoritarian, autocratic, despotic, dictatorial, imperious, high-handed, domineering, overbearing, tyrannous
tyranny *n* = **oppression**, dictatorship, cruelty, absolutism, authoritarianism, autocracy, despotism, high-handedness, imperiousness
tyrant *n* = **dictator**, bully, authoritarian, despot, absolutist, autocrat, martinet, oppressor, slave-driver

DICTIONARY

Uu

UB40 *n Brit* registration card issued to an unemployed person
ubiquitous Ⓣ [yew-**bik**-wit-uss] *adj* being or seeming to be everywhere at once **ubiquity** *n*
U-boat *n* German submarine
udder *n* large baglike milk-producing gland of cows, sheep, or goats
UDI Unilateral Declaration of Independence
UEFA Union of European Football Associations
UFO unidentified flying object
ugh [uhh] *interj* exclamation of disgust
ugly Ⓣ *adj* **uglier, ugliest 1** of unpleasant appearance **2** ominous or menacing
ugliness *n*
UHF ultrahigh frequency
UK United Kingdom
ukulele, ukelele [yew-kal-**lay**-lee] *n* small guitar with four strings
ulcer Ⓣ *n* open sore on the surface of the skin or mucous membrane
▸ **ulcerate** *v* make or become ulcerous
ulceration *n*
▸ **ulcerous** *adj* of, like, or characterized by ulcers
ulna *n, pl* **-nae, -nas** inner and longer of the two bones of the human forearm
ult. ultimo
ulterior Ⓣ [ult-**ear**-ee-or] *adj* lying beyond what is revealed or seen: *ulterior motives*
ultimate Ⓣ *adj* **1** final in a series or process **2** highest or most significant **ultimately** *adv*
ultimatum [ult-im-**may**-tum] *n* final communication stating that action will be taken unless certain conditions are met
ultimo *adv* (in formal correspondence) of the previous month: *the 7th ultimo*
ultra- *prefix* **1** beyond a specified extent, range, or limit: *ultrasonic* **2** extremely: *ultramodern*
ultrahigh frequency *n* radio frequency between 3000 and 300 megahertz
ultramarine *adj* vivid blue
ultrasonic *adj* of or producing sound waves with a higher frequency than the human ear can hear
ultrasound *n* ultrasonic waves used in medical diagnosis and therapy and in echo sounding
ultraviolet *adj, n* (of) light beyond the limit of visibility at the violet end of the spectrum
ulu [**oo**-loo] *n* Inuit domestic knife
ululate [**yewl**-yew-late] *v* howl or wail
ululation *n*
Umar Tal *n* ?1797–1864, African religious and military leader, who created a Muslim empire in W Africa
umber *adj* dark brown to greenish-brown
Umberto I *n* 1844–1900, king of Italy (1878–1900); son of Victor Emmanuel II: assassinated at Monza
Umberto II *n* 1904–83, the last king of Italy (1946), following the abdication of his father Victor Emmanuel III: abdicated when a referendum supported the abolition of the monarchy
umbilical [um-**bill**-ik-al] *adj* of the navel
▸ **umbilical cord** long flexible tube of blood vessels that connects a fetus with the placenta
umbrage *n* displeasure or resentment
▸ **take umbrage** feel offended or upset
umbrella *n* **1** portable device used for protection against rain, consisting of a folding frame covered in material attached to a central rod **2** single organization, idea, etc. that contains or covers many different organizations
umlaut [**oom**-lowt] *n* mark (¨) placed over a vowel, esp. in German, to indicate

THESAURUS

ubiquitous *adj* = **ever-present**, everywhere, universal, pervasive, omnipresent
ugly *adj* **1** = **unattractive**, unsightly • *an ugly expression on his face* **2** = **unpleasant**, terrible, shocking, objectionable, horrid, distasteful, disagreeable **3** = **ominous**, dangerous, sinister, baleful, menacing OPPOSITE: beautiful
ulcer *n* = **sore**, boil, abscess, gumboil, peptic ulcer, pustule
ulterior *adj* = **hidden**, secret, undisclosed, unrevealed, covert, concealed
ultimate *adj* **1** = **final**, last, eventual • *It is not possible to predict the ultimate results.* **2** = **supreme**, utmost, paramount, greatest • *the ultimate goal of any player* ▸ *n* **3** = **epitome**, peak, extreme, height • *This hotel is the ultimate in luxury.*
See also: **limit**
ultimately *adv* = **finally**, eventually, after all, at last, in due time, in the end, sooner or later

DICTIONARY

a change in its sound
ump *informal* ▷ *n* **1** umpire ▷ *v* **2** act as umpire
umpire Ⓣ *n* **1** official who rules on the playing of a game ▷ *v* **2** act as umpire in (a game)
umpteen Ⓣ *adj informal* very many
umpteenth *n, adj*
UN United Nations
un- *prefix* **1** not **2** denoting reversal of an action: *untie* **3** denoting removal from: *unthrone*
unabated *adv* without any reduction in force: *the storm continued unabated*
unable Ⓣ *adj* (foll. by *to*) lacking the necessary power, ability, or authority to (do something)
unaccountable Ⓣ *adj* **1** that cannot be explained **2** (foll. by *to*) not answerable to
unaccountably *adv*
unadulterated *adj* with nothing added, pure
unaffected Ⓣ *adj* **1** unpretentious, natural, sincere **2** not influenced or moved by something
unanimous Ⓣ [yew-**nan**-im-uss] *adj* **1** in complete agreement **2** agreed by all
unanimity *n*
unannounced *adj* **1** not declared or arranged in advance: *an unannounced visit* ▷ *adv* **2** without warning
unapproachable Ⓣ *adj* discouraging friendliness, aloof
unarmed Ⓣ *adj* without weapons
unassailable Ⓣ *adj* unable to be attacked or disputed
unassuming Ⓣ *adj* modest or unpretentious
unattached Ⓣ *adj* **1** not connected with any specific group or organization **2** not married or involved in a steady relationship
unavailing *adj* useless or futile
unavoidable Ⓣ *adj* unable to be avoided or prevented **unavoidably** *adv*
unaware Ⓣ *adj* not aware or conscious

THESAURUS

umpire *n* **1** = **referee**, judge, arbitrator, arbiter, ump (*informal*) ▶ *v* **2** = **referee**, judge, adjudicate, arbitrate
umpteen *See* **many**
unabashed *adj* = **unembarrassed**, bold, brazen, blatant
unable *adj* = **incapable**, unfit, powerless, impotent, unqualified, ineffectual
unabridged *adj* = **uncut**, complete, whole, full-length, unexpurgated
unacceptable *adj* = **unsatisfactory**, objectionable, displeasing
unaccompanied *adj* **1** = **alone**, solo, lone, unescorted, by oneself, on one's own **2** (*Music*) = **a cappella**
unaccountable *adj* **1** = **inexplicable**, odd, mysterious, unfathomable, baffling, puzzling, unexplainable **2** = **not answerable**, exempt, not responsible
unaccustomed *adj* = **unfamiliar**, new, strange, unwonted ▷ **unaccustomed to** = **not used to**, inexperienced at, unfamiliar with, unused to
unadventurous *See* **conventional**
unaffected[1] *adj* = **natural**, simple, plain, genuine, sincere, unpretentious, artless
unaffected[2] *adj* = **impervious**, proof, untouched, unmoved, unresponsive
unafraid *adj* = **fearless**, daring, intrepid, dauntless
unaided *See* **independent, on one's own**
unalterable *adj* = **unchangeable**, permanent, fixed, immutable
unanimity *n* = **agreement**, accord, consensus, harmony, assent, unison, concord, concurrence, like-mindedness
unanimous *adj* = **agreed**, common, concerted, like-minded, harmonious, in agreement, united
unanimously *adv* = **without exception**, as one, in concert, of one mind, with one accord
unanswerable *adj* = **indisputable**, absolute, conclusive, incontrovertible, incontestable
unanswered *adj* = **unresolved**, open, disputed, undecided
unappetizing *adj* = **unpleasant**, distasteful, unattractive, repulsive, unpalatable, unappealing, scuzzy (*slang*)
unappreciative *See* **ungrateful**
unapproachable *adj* **1** = **unfriendly**, cool, remote, distant, chilly, reserved, aloof, standoffish **2** = **inaccessible**, remote, out of reach
unarmed *adj* = **defenceless**, open, weak, unprotected, helpless, exposed
unashamed *See* **shameless**
unassailable *adj* = **impregnable**, secure, invincible, invulnerable
unassuming *adj* = **modest**, quiet, humble, reserved, unpretentious, self-effacing, retiring, unassertive, unobtrusive
unattached *adj* **1** = **free**, independent **2** = **single**, available, unmarried, not spoken for, unengaged
unattended *adj* **1** = **abandoned**, unguarded, unwatched **2** = **alone**, unaccompanied, on one's own
unattractive *See* **ugly**
unauthorized *adj* = **illegal**, unofficial, unlawful, unsanctioned
unavoidable *adj* = **inevitable**, certain, inescapable, fated
unaware *adj* = **ignorant**, unconscious, unsuspecting, oblivious • *Many people are*

u

DICTIONARY

▸**unawares** *adv* **1** by surprise **2** without knowing
unbalanced Ⓣ *adj* **1** mentally deranged **2** biased or one-sided
unbearable Ⓣ *adj* not able to be endured **unbearably** *adv*
unbecoming Ⓣ *adj* unattractive or unsuitable
unbeknown *adv* (foll. by *to*) without the knowledge of (a person)
unbelievable Ⓣ *adj* **1** too unlikely to be believed **2** *informal* marvellous, amazing **3** *informal* terrible, shocking **unbelievably** *adv*
unbend *v informal* become less strict or more informal in one's attitudes or behaviour **unbending** *adj*
unbidden *adj* not ordered or asked
unborn Ⓣ *adj* not yet born
unbosom *v* relieve (oneself) of (secrets or feelings) by telling someone
unbridled Ⓣ *adj* (of feelings or behaviour) not controlled in any way
unburden Ⓣ *v* relieve (one's mind or oneself) of a worry by confiding in someone
uncalled-for Ⓣ *adj* not fair or justified
uncanny Ⓣ *adj* weird or mysterious **uncannily** *adv* **uncanniness** *n*
unceremonious *adj* **1** without ceremony **2** abrupt or rude **unceremoniously** *adv*
uncertain Ⓣ *adj* **1** not able to be accurately known or predicted **2** not able to be depended upon **3** changeable **uncertainty** *n*
uncharacteristic *adj* not typical **uncharacteristically** *adv*
uncharitable Ⓣ *adj* unkind or harsh **uncharitably** *adv*

THESAURUS

unaware of how much they eat. OPPOSITE: aware
unawares *adv* **1 = by surprise**, suddenly, unexpectedly, off guard **2 = unknowingly**, accidentally, inadvertently, unwittingly, by accident
unbalanced *adj* **1 = biased**, unfair, partial, partisan, one-sided, prejudiced **2 = shaky**, unstable, lopsided, uneven, wobbly **3 = deranged**, mad, crazy, unstable, eccentric, insane, irrational, disturbed, demented, *non compos mentis* (*Latin*), not all there, unhinged
unbearable *adj* **= intolerable**, unacceptable, oppressive • *Life was unbearable for the victims of the earthquake.* OPPOSITE: tolerable
unbeatable *adj* **= invincible**, indomitable
unbeaten *adj* **= undefeated**, victorious, triumphant
unbecoming *adj* **1 = unattractive**, unflattering, unsuitable, unsightly, unbefitting **2 = unseemly**, offensive, improper, discreditable
unbelievable *adj* **1 = wonderful**, incredible, colossal, stupendous • *He showed unbelievable courage.* **2 = incredible**, improbable, inconceivable, preposterous, implausible, unconvincing • *He came up with some unbelievable story.* OPPOSITE: believable
See also: **unlikely**
unbending *adj* **= inflexible**, firm, tough, severe, strict, stubborn, rigid, resolute, uncompromising, intractable
unbiased *adj* **= fair**, just, objective, neutral, impartial, equitable, disinterested, unprejudiced
unblemished *adj* **= spotless**, perfect, pure, flawless, impeccable, immaculate, untarnished
unborn *adj* **= expected**, embryonic, fetal, awaited
unbreakable *adj* **= indestructible**, strong, lasting, rugged, durable
unbridled *adj* **= unrestrained**, excessive, unchecked, unruly, wanton, intemperate, licentious, riotous
unbroken *adj* **1 = intact**, complete, whole, entire **2 = continuous**, constant, uninterrupted, incessant, twenty-four-seven (*slang*)
unburden *v* **= confess**, reveal, disclose, confide, get (something) off one's chest (*informal*)
uncalled-for *adj* **= unnecessary**, unwarranted, unjustified, needless, gratuitous, undeserved
uncanny *adj* **1 = weird**, mysterious, strange, supernatural, unnatural, unearthly **2 = extraordinary**, unusual, remarkable, incredible, exceptional, miraculous, astounding
unceasing *adj* **= continual**, constant, continuous, endless, perpetual, nonstop, incessant, twenty-four-seven (*slang*)
uncertain *adj* **1 = unsure**, unclear, undecided, doubtful, dubious • *For a moment he looked uncertain as to how to respond.* OPPOSITE: certain **2 = doubtful**, indefinite, ambiguous, indeterminate • *facing an uncertain future* OPPOSITE: certain
See also: **vague**
uncertainty *n* **= doubt**, confusion, ambiguity, indecision, unpredictability, hesitancy, dubiety, reasonable doubt (*law*)
unchangeable *adj* **= unalterable**, permanent, stable, constant, irreversible, fixed, immutable, invariable
unchanging *adj* **= constant**, permanent, lasting, enduring, eternal, perpetual, continuing, immutable, twenty-four-seven (*slang*), unvarying
uncharitable *adj* **= unkind**, cruel,

DICTIONARY

un-Christian *adj* not in accordance with Christian principles
uncivilized ⓣ *adj* **1** (of a tribe or people) not yet civilized **2** lacking culture or sophistication
uncle *n* **1** brother of one's father or mother **2** husband of one's aunt
unclean ⓣ *adj* lacking moral, spiritual, or physical cleanliness
uncomfortable ⓣ *adj* **1** not physically relaxed **2** anxious or uneasy
uncommon ⓣ *adj* **1** not happening often **2** in excess of what is normal **uncommonly** *adv*
uncompromising ⓣ *adj* not prepared to compromise
unconcerned ⓣ *adj* lacking in concern or involvement **unconcernedly** *adv*
unconditional ⓣ *adj* without conditions or limitations
unconscionable *adj* **1** having no principles, unscrupulous **2** excessive in amount or degree
unconscious ⓣ *adj* **1** lacking normal awareness through the senses **2** not aware of one's actions or behaviour ▷ *n* **3** part of the mind containing instincts and ideas that exist without one's awareness **unconsciously** *adv* **unconsciousness** *n*
unconventional ⓣ *adj* not conforming to accepted rules or standards
uncooperative ⓣ *adj* not willing to cooperate, unhelpful

THESAURUS

hardhearted, unfeeling, ungenerous
uncharted *adj* = **unexplored**, unknown, strange, unfamiliar, undiscovered
uncivil *adj* = **impolite**, rude, bad-mannered, discourteous, ill-mannered, unmannerly
uncivilized *adj* **1** = **primitive**, wild, savage, barbarian **2** = **uncouth**, coarse, boorish, uneducated, philistine, uncultivated
unclean *adj* = **dirty**, foul, evil, corrupt, polluted, filthy, defiled, impure, scuzzy (*slang*), soiled, stained
unclear *adj* **1** = **uncertain**, confused, ambiguous, vague • *It is unclear how much support they have.* OPPOSITE: clear **2** = **indistinct**, vague, faint, obscure, dim, fuzzy, hazy, shadowy, undefined, blurred
unclothed *See* **naked**
uncomfortable *adj* **1** = **painful**, awkward, cramped, ill-fitting, disagreeable • *an uncomfortable bed* OPPOSITE: comfortable **2** = **uneasy**, awkward, embarrassed, self-conscious, ill at ease • *Talking about money made her uncomfortable.* OPPOSITE: comfortable
uncommitted *adj* = **uninvolved**, free, neutral, floating, nonaligned, not involved, unattached
uncommon *adj* **1** = **rare**, few, unusual, extraordinary, exceptional, scarce, sparse, infrequent, out of the ordinary • *This type of weather is uncommon.* OPPOSITE: common **2** = **extraordinary**, great, intense, extreme, remarkable, acute, exceptional • *She had read his last email with uncommon interest.*
See also: **particular, singular, strange**
uncommonly *adv* **1** = **rarely**, occasionally, seldom, infrequently, hardly ever **2** = **exceptionally**, very, particularly
uncommunicative *adj* = **reticent**, close, silent, secretive, tight-lipped, reserved, taciturn, unforthcoming
uncomplicated *See* **simple, straightforward**
uncompromising *adj* = **inflexible**, firm, tough, strict, rigid, intransigent, inexorable, unbending
unconcern *n* = **indifference**, detachment, apathy, aloofness, lack of interest, nonchalance
unconcerned *adj* = **indifferent**, cool, distant, unmoved, apathetic, aloof, dispassionate, uninterested, detached
unconditional *adj* = **absolute**, complete, full, total, positive, entire, outright, unlimited, unqualified, unreserved
unconnected *adj* **1** = **separate**, divided, detached **2** = **incoherent**, irrelevant, meaningless, illogical, disjointed
unconscious *adj* **1** = **senseless**, asleep, stunned • *By the time the ambulance arrived, he was unconscious.* OPPOSITE: conscious **2** = **unaware**, unsuspecting, oblivious, unknowing • *quite unconscious of their presence* OPPOSITE: aware **3** = **unintentional**, accidental, inadvertent, unwitting
See also: **ignorant**
uncontaminated *See* **clean**
uncontrollable *adj* = **wild**, strong, violent, mad, furious, frantic, unruly
uncontrolled *adj* = **unrestrained**, rampant, undisciplined, unchecked, unbridled, riotous
unconventional *adj* = **unusual**, individual, original, odd, irregular, eccentric, left-field (*informal*), unorthodox, offbeat, nonconformist, outré
unconvinced *See* **dubious**
unconvincing *adj* = **implausible**, suspect, weak, unlikely, thin, questionable, improbable, dubious, lame, feeble, flimsy
uncooperative *adj* = **unhelpful**, difficult, obstructive, awkward, disobliging, high-maintenance

DICTIONARY

uncouth Ⓣ *adj* lacking in good manners, refinement, or grace
uncover Ⓣ *v* **1** remove the cap, top, etc. from **2** reveal or disclose
unction *n* act of anointing with oil in sacramental ceremonies
▶ **unctuous** *adj* pretending to be kind and concerned
undeceive *v* reveal the truth to (someone previously misled or deceived)
undecided Ⓣ *adj* **1** not having made up one's mind **2** (of an issue or problem) not agreed or decided upon
undeniable Ⓣ *adj* indisputably true
undeniably *adv*
under Ⓣ *prep* **1** on, to, or beneath the underside or base of **2** less than **3** subject to the supervision, control, or influence of **4** subject to (conditions) ▷ *adv* **5** to a position underneath
under- *prefix* **1** below: *underground* **2** insufficient or insufficiently: *underrate*
underachieve *v* fail to achieve a performance appropriate to one's age or talents **underachiever** *n*
underage *adj* below the required or standard age
underarm *sports* ▷ *adj* **1** denoting a style of throwing, bowling, or serving in which the hand is swung below shoulder level ▷ *adv* **2** in an underarm style
undercarriage *n* **1** landing gear of an aircraft **2** framework supporting the body of a vehicle
underclass *n* class consisting of the most disadvantaged people, such as the long-term unemployed
undercoat *n* coat of paint applied before the final coat
undercover Ⓣ *adj* done or acting in secret
undercurrent Ⓣ *n* **1** current that is not apparent at the surface **2** underlying opinion or emotion
undercut *v* charge less than (a competitor) to obtain trade
underdeveloped *adj* **1** immature or undersized **2** (of a country) lacking the finance, industries, and organization necessary to advance
underdog Ⓣ *n* person or team unlikely to win in a competition
underdone *adj* not cooked enough
underestimate Ⓣ *v* **1** make too low an estimate of **2** not think highly enough of
underfelt *n* thick felt laid under a carpet to increase insulation
underfoot *adv* under the feet
undergarment *n* any piece of underwear
undergo Ⓣ *v* experience, endure, or sustain
undergraduate *n* person studying in a university for a first degree
underground Ⓣ *adj* **1** occurring, situated,

THESAURUS

uncoordinated *adj* = **clumsy**, awkward, lumbering, ungainly, bungling, graceless, maladroit, ungraceful
See also: **clumsy**
uncouth *adj* = **coarse**, crude, rough, rude, vulgar, boorish, graceless, ill-mannered, loutish, oafish
uncover *v* **1** = **reveal**, expose, unearth, bring to light, show up • *Teachers had uncovered evidence of cheating.* **2** = **open**, reveal, unveil, expose, unearth, unwrap, lay bare • *Uncover the pot and drain the vegetables.*
uncovered *See* **bare, open**
uncritical *adj* = **undiscriminating**, indiscriminate, undiscerning
uncultivated *See* **wild**
uncut *See* **whole**
undecided *adj* **1** = **unsure**, uncertain, hesitant, dithering, in two minds, irresolute, torn **2** = **unsettled**, open, indefinite, moot, undetermined, iffy (*informal*), debatable, unconcluded
undefined *adj* **1** = **unspecified**, unclear, inexact, imprecise **2** = **indistinct**, vague, indefinite, formless
undeniable *adj* = **certain**, clear, sure, obvious, indisputable, incontrovertible, unquestionable
undeniably *See* **certainly**
under *prep* **1** = **below**, beneath, underneath • *a labyrinth of tunnels under the ground* OPPOSITE: above **2** = **subject to**, governed by, secondary to, subordinate to ▷ **under the weather** *See* **sick** ▷ **under way** = **in progress**, begun, going on, started ▶ *adv* **3** = **below**, down, lower, beneath
underclothes *pl n* = **underwear**, lingerie, undies (*informal*), undergarments
undercover *adj* = **secret**, private, covert, hidden, concealed
undercurrent *n* **1** = **undertow**, riptide **2** = **undertone**, sense, feeling, hint, suggestion, atmosphere, tendency, overtone, vibes (*slang*), tinge
underdog *n* = **weaker party**, outsider, little fellow (*informal*)
underestimate *v* = **underrate**, minimize, undervalue, belittle, miscalculate
underfed *See* **skinny**
undergo *v* = **experience**, suffer, endure, be subjected to, go through • *He had to undergo major surgery.*
See also: **feel, have, receive**
underground *adj* **1** = **subterranean**, covered, buried **2** = **secret**, clandestine, covert, hidden ▶ *noun* ▷ **the underground**

DICTIONARY

used, or going below ground level **2** secret ▷ *n* **3** movement dedicated to overthrowing a government or occupation forces **4** *Brit* subway
undergrowth Ⓣ *n* small trees and bushes growing beneath taller trees in a wood or forest
underhand Ⓣ *adj* sly, deceitful, and secretive
underlay *n* felt or rubber laid beneath a carpet to increase insulation and resilience
underlie *v* **1** lie or be placed under **2** be the foundation, cause, or basis of
▸ **underlying** *adj* fundamental or basic
underline Ⓣ *v* **1** draw a line under **2** state forcibly, emphasize
underling Ⓣ *n* subordinate
undermine Ⓣ *v* **1** weaken gradually **2** (of the sea or wind) wear away the base of (cliffs)
underneath Ⓣ *prep, adv* **1** under or beneath ▷ *adj, n* **2** lower (part or surface)
underpants *pl n* man's undergarment for the lower part of the body
underpass *n* section of a road that passes under another road or a railway line
underpin *v* give strength or support to
underprivileged Ⓣ *adj* lacking the rights and advantages of other members of society
underrate Ⓣ *v* underestimate **underrated** *adj*
underseal *n* coating of tar etc. applied to the underside of a motor vehicle to retard corrosion
undersecretary *n* senior civil servant or junior minister in a government department
underside *n* bottom or lower surface
undersized Ⓣ *adj* of less than usual size
underskirt *n* skirtlike garment worn under a skirt or dress, petticoat
understand Ⓣ *v* **1** know and comprehend the nature or meaning of **2** realize or grasp (something) **3** assume, infer, or believe
understandable *adj* **understandably** *adv*
▸ **understanding** *n* **1** ability to learn, judge, or make decisions **2** personal interpretation of a subject **3** mutual agreement, usu. an informal or private one ▷ *adj* **4** kind and sympathetic
understate *v* **1** describe or represent (something) in restrained terms **2** state that (something, such as a number) is less than it is **understatement** *n*
understudy Ⓣ *n* **1** actor who studies a part in order to be able to replace the usual actor if necessary ▷ *v* **2** act as an understudy for
undertake Ⓣ *v* **1** agree or commit oneself to (something) or (to do something) **2** promise

THESAURUS

= **the Resistance**, partisans
undergrowth *n* = **scrub**, brush, bracken, briars, underbrush
underhand, underhanded *adj* = **sly**, secret, dishonest, crafty, sneaky, deceitful, devious, stealthy, down and dirty (*informal*), furtive
underline *v* **1** = **underscore**, mark **2** = **emphasize**, stress, highlight, accentuate
underling *See* **inferior**
underlying *adj* = **fundamental**, prime, primary, basic, elementary, intrinsic
undermine *v* = **weaken**, impair, sap, subvert • *You're trying to undermine my confidence again.* OPPOSITE: strengthen
underneath *See* **below, under**
undernourished *See* **skinny**
underprivileged *adj* = **disadvantaged**, poor, impoverished, needy, destitute, deprived
underrate *v* = **underestimate**, discount, undervalue, belittle
undersized *adj* = **stunted**, small, miniature, pygmy *or* pigmy, dwarfish
understand *v* **1** = **comprehend**, get, see, follow, grasp, catch on, take in • *Do you understand what I'm saying?* **2** = **realize**, appreciate, grasp, comprehend, fathom • *too young to understand what was going on* **3** = **hear**, believe, learn, gather • *I understand she hasn't been well.*
See also: **know**
understandable *adj* = **reasonable**, natural, legitimate, justifiable, to be expected
understanding *n* **1** = **perception**, knowledge, appreciation, grasp, comprehension • *a basic understanding of computers* **2** = **agreement**, accord, pact • *There was an understanding among the players.* **3** = **interpretation**, view, idea, opinion, judgment, belief, perception, notion ▸ *adj* **4** = **sympathetic**, sensitive, compassionate, considerate • *Fortunately, he had an understanding family.*
See also: **experience, intelligence, pity, sympathy, tolerant**
understood *adj* **1** = **implied**, implicit, tacit, unspoken, inferred, unstated **2** = **assumed**, accepted, taken for granted
understudy *n* = **stand-in**, reserve, replacement, substitute
undertake *v* = **agree**, contract, promise, pledge, guarantee, engage, bargain
undertaking *n* **1** = **task**, job, business, project, operation, affair, venture, enterprise, endeavour • *Organizing the talent show has been a massive undertaking.* **2** = **promise**, word, pledge, vow, commitment, assurance
See also: **act, guarantee**

DICTIONARY

▸**undertaking** *n* **1** task or enterprise **2** agreement to do something

undertaker *n* person whose profession is to prepare corpses for burial and organize funerals

undertone Ⓣ *n* **1** quiet tone of voice **2** underlying quality or feeling

undertow Ⓣ *n* strong undercurrent flowing in a different direction from the surface current

underwater Ⓣ *adj, adv* (situated, occurring, or for use) below the surface of the sea, a lake, or a river

underwear Ⓣ *n* clothing worn under the outer garments and next to the skin

underworld Ⓣ *n* **1** criminals and their associates **2** *classical myth* regions below the earth's surface regarded as the abode of the dead

underwrite Ⓣ *v* **1** accept financial responsibility for (a commercial project) **2** sign and issue (an insurance policy), thus accepting liability **underwriter** *n*

undesirable Ⓣ *adj* **1** not desirable or pleasant, objectionable ▹ *n* **2** objectionable person **undesirably** *adv*

undies *pl n informal* underwear, esp. women's

undistinguished Ⓣ *adj* not particularly good or bad, mediocre

undo Ⓣ *v* **1** open, unwrap **2** reverse the effects of **3** cause the downfall of **undone** *adj*
▸**undoing** *n* cause of someone's downfall

undoubted Ⓣ *adj* certain or indisputable **undoubtedly** *adv*

undress Ⓣ *v* **1** take off the clothes of (oneself or another person) ▹ *n* **2 in a state of undress** naked or nearly naked

undue Ⓣ *adj* greater than is reasonable, excessive **unduly** *adv*

undulate *v* move in waves **undulation** *n*

undying Ⓣ *adj* never ending, eternal

unearned income *n* income from property

THESAURUS

undertone *n* **1 = murmur**, whisper **2 = undercurrent**, touch, hint, trace, suggestion, tinge

undertow *See* **current**

undervalue *v* **= underrate**, minimize, underestimate, misjudge, depreciate, hold cheap

underwater *adj* **= submerged**, submarine, sunken

underwear *n* **= underclothes**, lingerie, undies (*informal*), undergarments, underthings

underweight *adj* **= skinny**, undersized, puny, emaciated, half-starved, skin and bone (*informal*), undernourished

underworld *n* **1 = criminals**, gangland (*informal*), gangsters, organized crime **2 = nether world**, Hades, nether regions

underwrite *v* **1 = finance**, back, fund, guarantee, sponsor, subsidize, insure **2 = sign**, endorse, initial

undesirable *adj* **= unwanted**, unacceptable, unwelcome, unattractive, unsuitable, objectionable, distasteful, disagreeable

undeveloped *adj* **= potential**, immature, latent

undignified *adj* **= unseemly**, improper, unsuitable, unbecoming, indecorous, inelegant

undisciplined *adj* **= uncontrolled**, wild, unruly, wayward, wilful, unrestrained, obstreperous

undisguised *adj* **= obvious**, open, patent, explicit, evident, blatant, overt, unconcealed

undisputed *adj* **= acknowledged**, certain, unchallenged, accepted, undeniable, indisputable, recognized, undoubted

undistinguished *adj* **= ordinary**, everyday, mediocre, unremarkable, unimpressive, unexceptional

undisturbed *adj* **1 = quiet**, tranquil **2 = calm**, unfazed (*informal*), sedate, tranquil, serene, collected, composed, placid, unperturbed, untroubled

undivided *adj* **= complete**, full, whole, entire, solid, exclusive, thorough, undistracted, united

undo *v* **1 = open**, loose, untie, disentangle, unbutton, unfasten **2 = reverse**, cancel, offset, neutralize, annul, invalidate **3 = ruin**, defeat, destroy, upset, overturn, undermine, quash, shatter, wreck, subvert

undoing *n* **= downfall**, defeat, collapse, ruin, shame, disgrace, overthrow, reversal

undomesticated *See* **wild**

undone *adj* **= unfinished**, left, unfulfilled, neglected, omitted, unperformed

undoubted *adj* **= certain**, sure, definite, undisputed, acknowledged, indisputable, unquestioned, indubitable

undoubtedly *adv* **= certainly**, definitely, surely, doubtless, assuredly, without doubt

undress *v* **1 = strip**, shed, disrobe, take off one's clothes ▸ *n* **2 = nakedness**, nudity

undressed *See* **bare, naked**

undue *adj* **= excessive**, extreme, unnecessary, improper, unwarranted, needless, uncalled-for

unduly *adv* **= excessively**, unnecessarily, overly, unreasonably

undying *adj* **= eternal**, permanent, constant, infinite, perpetual, unending, everlasting, deathless, twenty-four-seven (*slang*)

DICTIONARY

or investments rather than work
unearth Ⓣ *v* **1** dig up out of the earth **2** reveal or discover
unearthly Ⓣ *adj* **1** ghostly or eerie **2** ridiculous or unreasonable: *an unearthly hour* **unearthliness** *n*
uneasy Ⓣ *adj* **1** (of a person) anxious or apprehensive **2** (of a condition) precarious or uncomfortable **uneasily** *adv* **uneasiness** *n* **unease** *n*
unemployed Ⓣ *adj* out of work **unemployment** *n*
unequivocal Ⓣ *adj* completely clear in meaning **unequivocally** *adv*
unerring Ⓣ *adj* never mistaken, consistently accurate
UNESCO United Nations Educational, Scientific, and Cultural Organization
uneven Ⓣ *adj* **1** not level or flat **2** not consistent in quality: *an uneven performance* **3** not fairly matched: *an uneven race*
unexceptionable *adj* beyond criticism or objection
unexceptional Ⓣ *adj* ordinary or normal
unexpected Ⓣ *adj* surprising or unforeseen **unexpectedly** *adv*
unfailing Ⓣ *adj* continuous or reliable **unfailingly** *adv*
unfair Ⓣ *adj* not right, fair, or just **unfairly** *adv* **unfairness** *n*
unfaithful Ⓣ *adj* **1** guilty of adultery **2** not true to a promise or vow **unfaithfulness** *n*

THESAURUS

unearth *v* **1 = discover**, find, reveal, expose, uncover **2 = dig up**, exhume, excavate, dredge up
unearthly *adj* **= eerie**, strange, weird, spooky (*informal*), supernatural, phantom, ghostly, uncanny, spectral
unease *See* **anxiety, worry**
uneasiness *n* **= anxiety**, worry, doubt, trepidation, misgiving, disquiet, qualms
uneasy *adj* **1 = anxious**, nervous, worried, agitated, perturbed • *I was very uneasy about these developments.* OPPOSITE: comfortable **2 = awkward**, shaky, tense, strained, uncomfortable, precarious, insecure
uneconomic *adj* **= unprofitable**, loss-making, nonpaying
uneconomical *See* **wasteful**
uneducated *adj* **1 = ignorant**, illiterate, unlettered, unschooled, untaught **2 = uncultured**, lowbrow, uncultivated
unemotional *adj* **= impassive**, cold, cool, reserved, apathetic, phlegmatic, undemonstrative, unexcitable
unemployed *adj* **= out of work**, jobless, idle, laid off • *an unemployed mechanic* OPPOSITE: employed
unending *adj* **= perpetual**, endless, eternal, continual, interminable, everlasting, unceasing
unendurable *adj* **= unbearable**, intolerable, insufferable, insupportable
unenthusiastic *adj* **= indifferent**, apathetic, half-hearted, nonchalant
unenviable *adj* **= unpleasant**, uncomfortable, undesirable, disagreeable
unequal *adj* **1 = different**, unlike, disparate, unmatched, dissimilar, differing, varying **2 = disproportionate**, irregular, uneven, unbalanced, asymmetrical, ill-matched
unequalled *adj* **= incomparable**, supreme, paramount, unparalleled, unrivalled, matchless, peerless
unequivocal *adj* **= clear**, certain, absolute, plain, explicit, definite, manifest, unambiguous, incontrovertible, indubitable
unerring *adj* **= accurate**, sure, perfect, exact, infallible, unfailing
unethical *adj* **= immoral**, wrong, illegal, improper, shady (*informal*), dishonest, unscrupulous, disreputable, unprincipled
uneven *adj* **1 = rough**, bumpy, not level, not smooth • *I tripped and fell on the uneven pavement.* OPPOSITE: level **2 = irregular**, inconsistent, variable, patchy, fluctuating • *six posts of uneven height* OPPOSITE: even **3 = lopsided**, odd, unbalanced **4 = unequal**, unfair, ill-matched
uneventful *adj* **= humdrum**, routine, boring, dull, ho-hum (*informal*), tedious, monotonous, unexciting
unexceptional *adj* **= ordinary**, normal, conventional, pedestrian, mediocre, commonplace, unremarkable, undistinguished
unexpected *adj* **= unforeseen**, chance, astonishing, surprising • *Their move was completely unexpected.*
See also: **abrupt, sudden**
unfailing *adj* **1 = continuous**, persistent, endless, boundless, unflagging **2 = reliable**, sure, certain, true, loyal, faithful, staunch, dependable
unfair *adj* **1 = unjust**, wrong, wrongful • *It's unfair that she had to miss the final game.* **2 = biased**, partial, partisan, unjust, one-sided, bigoted, prejudiced **3 = unscrupulous**, wrongful, unethical, dishonest, unsporting OPPOSITE: fair
unfairness *See* **injustice**
unfaithful *adj* **1 = adulterous**, two-timing (*informal*) • *an unfaithful husband* OPPOSITE:

u

DICTIONARY

unfathomable Ⓣ *adj* too strange or too complicated to be understood
unfavourable Ⓣ *adj* **1** adverse or inauspicious: *unfavourable weather conditions* **2** disapproving: *an unfavourable opinion*
unfavourably *adv*
unfeeling Ⓣ *adj* without sympathy
unfit Ⓣ *adj* **1** (foll. by *for*) unqualified or unsuitable **2** in poor physical condition
unflappable Ⓣ *adj informal* not easily upset
unflappability *n*
unfold Ⓣ *v* **1** open or spread out from a folded state **2** reveal or be revealed
unforeseen Ⓣ *adj* surprising because not expected
unforgettable Ⓣ *adj* impossible to forget, memorable
unfortunate Ⓣ *adj* **1** unlucky, unsuccessful, or unhappy **2** regrettable or unsuitable
unfortunately *adv*
unfounded Ⓣ *adj* not based on facts or evidence
unfrock *v* deprive (a priest in holy orders) of his priesthood
unfurl Ⓣ *v* unroll or unfold
ungainly Ⓣ *adj* **-lier, -liest** lacking grace when moving **ungainliness** *n*
ungodly Ⓣ *adj* **1** wicked or sinful **2** *informal* unreasonable or outrageous **ungodliness** *n*
ungovernable *adj* not able to be disciplined or restrained
ungrateful Ⓣ *adj* not grateful or thankful
ungratefully *adv* **ungratefulness** *n*

THESAURUS

faithful **2 = disloyal**, false, treacherous, deceitful, untrustworthy, faithless, traitorous
unfamiliar *adj* **= strange**, new, foreign, novel, unknown, alien, exotic • *She grew many plants that were unfamiliar to me.*
unfashionable *adj* **= passé**, old-fashioned, obsolete, antiquated, dated, dumpy (*informal*), frowzy, homely (*US*), old hat
unfasten *v* **= undo**, open, separate, detach, loosen, untie, let go, unlace
unfathomable *adj* **1 = baffling**, deep, profound, incomprehensible, inexplicable, impenetrable, indecipherable **2 = immeasurable**, bottomless, unmeasured
unfavourable *adj* **1 = adverse**, unfortunate, contrary, unlucky, inauspicious, unpropitious **2 = hostile**, negative, unfriendly, inimical
unfeeling *adj* **1 = hardhearted**, cold, cruel, insensitive, callous, apathetic, heartless, pitiless, uncaring **2 = numb**, insensate, insensible
unfinished *adj* **1 = incomplete**, half-done, uncompleted, undone **2 = rough**, natural, crude, raw, bare, unrefined
unfit *adj* **1 = incapable**, inadequate, useless, lousy (*slang*), incompetent, unqualified, no good **2 = unsuitable**, inadequate, ineffective, useless, unsuited **3 = out of shape**, unhealthy, feeble, flabby, in poor condition
unflappable *adj* **= imperturbable**, cool, calm, collected, composed, impassive, level-headed, self-possessed
unflattering *adj* **1 = blunt**, critical, honest, candid **2 = unattractive**, plain, unbecoming, dumpy (*informal*), frowzy, homely (*US*)
unflinching *adj* **= determined**, firm, steady, staunch, steadfast, resolute, immovable, unfaltering
unflustered *See* **relaxed**
unfold *v* **1 = open**, expand, unravel, undo, unfurl, unwrap, unroll, spread out **2 = reveal**, show, present, disclose, uncover, divulge, make known
unforeseeable *See* **unpredictable**
unforeseen *adj* **= unexpected**, sudden, accidental, unanticipated, surprising, unpredicted
unforgettable *adj* **= memorable**, impressive, notable, exceptional
unforgivable *adj* **= inexcusable**, disgraceful, shameful, deplorable, unpardonable
unfortunate *adj* **1 = disastrous**, adverse, ill-fated, calamitous **2 = unlucky**, hapless, unhappy, unsuccessful, doomed, wretched, cursed **3 = regrettable**, deplorable, unsuitable, lamentable
unfounded *adj* **= groundless**, false, idle, baseless, unjustified, spurious
unfriendly *adj* **1 = hostile**, cold, aloof, antagonistic, unkind, disagreeable • *He can expect an unfriendly welcome.* OPPOSITE: friendly **2 = unfavourable**, hostile, alien, inhospitable
See also: **unpleasant**
unfurl *See* **spread**
unfurnished *See* **empty**
ungainliness *See* **clumsiness**
ungainly *adj* **= awkward**, clumsy, lumbering, inelegant, ungraceful
ungodly *adj* **1 = unreasonable**, outrageous, dreadful, intolerable, unearthly **2 = wicked**, corrupt, immoral, profane, sinful, depraved, godless, impious, irreligious
ungracious *adj* **= bad-mannered**, rude, churlish, discourteous, impolite, uncivil, unmannerly
ungrateful *adj* **= unappreciative**, unthankful • *the most miserable and ungrateful*

DICTIONARY

unguarded Ⓣ *adj* **1** not protected **2** incautious or careless
unguent [ung-gwent] *n* ointment
unhand *v old-fashioned, lit* release from one's grasp
unhappy Ⓣ *adj* **1** sad or depressed **2** unfortunate or wretched **unhappily** *adv* **unhappiness** *n*
unhealthy Ⓣ *adj* **1** likely to cause poor health **2** not fit or well **3** morbid, unnatural
unheard-of Ⓣ *adj* **1** without precedent **2** highly offensive or shocking
unhinge *v* derange or unbalance (a person or his or her mind)
unholy Ⓣ *adj* **1** immoral or wicked **2** *informal* unreasonable or outrageous: *an unholy hour*
uni- *combining form* of, consisting of, or having only one: *unicellular*
UNICEF United Nations International Children's Emergency Fund
unicorn *n* imaginary horselike creature with one horn growing from its forehead
uniform Ⓣ *n* **1** special identifying set of clothes for the members of an organization, such as soldiers ▷ *adj* **2** unvarying **3** alike or like **uniformly** *adv* **uniformity** *n*
unify Ⓣ *v* **-fying, -fied** make or become one **unification** *n*
unilateral *adj* made or done by only one person or group **unilaterally** *adv*
unilingual *adj* **1** knowing only one language ▷ *n* **2** person who knows only one language
unimpeachable *adj* completely honest and reliable

THESAURUS

people on earth OPPOSITE: grateful
unguarded *adj* **1 = unprotected**, vulnerable, defenceless, undefended **2 = careless**, rash, imprudent, thoughtless, unwary, heedless, ill-considered, incautious, unthinking
unhappiness *n* **= sadness**, depression, misery, sorrow, gloom, heartache, melancholy, despondency, blues, dejection, low spirits, wretchedness
unhappy *adj* **1 = sad**, down, depressed, miserable, despondent • *He was a shy, sometimes unhappy man.* OPPOSITE: happy **2 = unlucky**, unfortunate, hapless, ill-fated, wretched, cursed
See also: **upset**
unharmed *adj* **= unhurt**, safe, sound, whole, intact, unscathed, undamaged
unhealthy *adj* **1 = harmful**, unsanitary, noxious, bad for you, unwholesome • *an unhealthy lifestyle* OPPOSITE: healthy **2 = sick**, ill, ailing, not well, unwell • *an unhealthy-looking man* OPPOSITE: healthy
See also: **perverted**
unheard-of *adj* **1 = unprecedented**, new, novel, unique, singular, inconceivable **2 = shocking**, outrageous, disgraceful, preposterous **3 = obscure**, unknown, unfamiliar
unhesitating *adj* **1 = instant**, ready, prompt, immediate **2 = wholehearted**, resolute, unfaltering, unquestioning, unreserved
unholy *adj* **= evil**, corrupt, wicked, profane, sinful, ungodly
unhurried *adj* **= leisurely**, slow, easy, sedate
unhurriedly *See* **slowly**
unidentified *adj* **= unnamed**, anonymous, unfamiliar, unrecognized, nameless
unification *n* **= union**, coalition, alliance, federation, amalgamation, confederation, coalescence, uniting
uniform *n* **1 = outfit**, suit, dress, habit, costume, garb, regalia, livery ▸ *adj* **2 = unvarying**, even, regular, consistent, constant, smooth, unchanging **3 = alike**, like, same, similar, equal, on a level playing field (*informal*)
uniformity *n* **1 = regularity**, similarity, constancy, evenness, invariability, sameness **2 = monotony**, dullness, flatness, sameness, tedium
uniformly *See* **alike**
unify *v* **= unite**, join, combine, merge, consolidate, amalgamate, confederate
unimaginable *adj* **= inconceivable**, impossible, incredible, fantastic, unbelievable
unimaginative *adj* **= unoriginal**, ordinary, hack, pedestrian, predictable, derivative, dull, uninspired, banal, hackneyed, prosaic, uncreative
unimportant *adj* **= insignificant**, minor, slight, paltry, trivial • *The difference in their ages seemed unimportant at the time.* OPPOSITE: important
See also: **petty**
uninhabited *adj* **= deserted**, empty, vacant, barren, desolate, unpopulated
uninhibited *adj* **1 = unselfconscious**, open, free, natural, spontaneous, liberated, relaxed, unrepressed, unreserved **2 = unrestrained**, free, unrestricted, unchecked, uncontrolled, unbridled, unconstrained
uninspired *adj* **= unimaginative**, ordinary, dull, banal, humdrum, prosaic, unexciting, unoriginal
unintelligent *adj* **= stupid**, dense, dull, foolish, braindead (*informal*), brainless, slow, thick, obtuse
unintelligible *adj* **= incomprehensible**, meaningless, incoherent, inarticulate, indistinct, jumbled, muddled

DICTIONARY

uninterested Ⓣ *adj* having or showing no interest in someone or something
union Ⓣ *n* **1** uniting or being united **2** short for **trade union** **3** association of individuals or groups for a common purpose
▸ **unionist** *n* member or supporter of a trade union
▸ **unionize** *v* organize (workers) into a trade union **unionization** *n*
▸ **Union Flag** *or* **Union Jack** national flag of the United Kingdom
unique Ⓣ [yoo-**neek**] *adj* **1** being the only one of a particular type **2** without equal or like **uniquely** *adv*
unisex *adj* designed for use by both sexes
unison Ⓣ *n* **1** complete agreement **2** *music* singing or playing the same notes at the same time
unit Ⓣ *n* **1** single undivided entity or whole **2** group or individual regarded as a basic element of a larger whole **3** fixed quantity etc., used as a standard of measurement
Unitarian *n* person who believes that God is one being and rejects the Trinity **Unitarianism** *n*
unitary *adj* **1** of a unit or units **2** based on or marked by unity
unite Ⓣ *v* **1** make or become an integrated whole **2** form an association or alliance
▸ **unity** *n* **1** state of being one **2** mutual agreement
▸ **United Church** Canadian church formed by union of some Presbyterians and Methodists
▸ **United Empire Loyalist** American colonist who settled in Canada in the War of American Independence through loyalty to Britain
universe Ⓣ *n* **1** whole of all existing matter, energy, and space **2** the world
▸ **universal** *adj* **1** of or typical of the whole of mankind or of nature **2** existing everywhere **universally** *adv* **universality** *n*
university *n, pl* **-ties** institution of higher education having the authority to award degrees
unkempt Ⓣ *adj* **1** (of the hair) not combed **2** slovenly or untidy
unkind Ⓣ *adj* unsympathetic or cruel **unkindly** *adv* **unkindness** *n*

THESAURUS

unintentional *adj* = **accidental**, casual, unconscious, unintended, inadvertent, involuntary
uninterested *adj* = **indifferent**, passive, bored, apathetic, unconcerned, nonchalant, impassive • *I'm completely uninterested in anything you have to say.* OPPOSITE: interested
uninteresting *adj* = **boring**, dry, flat, dull, dreary, drab, tedious, monotonous, humdrum, unexciting
uninterrupted *adj* = **continuous**, steady, constant, sustained, nonstop, unbroken
union *n* **1** = **alliance**, league, coalition, association, federation, confederation • *the Canadian Union of Public Employees* **2** = **amalgamation**, combination, blend, mixture, conjunction, fusion, unification, amalgam, synthesis • *The majority voted for union with the larger organization.* **3** = **agreement**, accord, unity, harmony, unison, unanimity, concord
See also: **bond, club, society**
unique *adj* **1** = **distinct**, only, single, lone, solitary **2** = **unparalleled**, unmatched, incomparable, unrivalled, inimitable, matchless, unequalled
unison *n* = **agreement**, accord, concert, unity, accordance, harmony, concord
unit *n* **1** = **item**, whole, entity **2** = **part**, member, section, element, component, segment, constituent **3** = **section**, group, detachment, platoon **4** = **measure**, quantity, measurement
unite *v* **1** = **cooperate**, join, combine, merge, collaborate, join forces, link up, pull together, work together • *We must unite to fight our common enemy.* OPPOSITE: divide **2** = **join**, link, couple, combine, merge, blend, unify, fuse, amalgamate
See also: **team**
united *adj* **1** = **combined**, collective, unified, concerted, allied, affiliated, pooled, banded together **2** = **in agreement**, unanimous, agreed, of one mind, of the same opinion
unity *n* **1** = **wholeness**, union, integrity, entity, oneness, singleness **2** = **agreement**, accord, consensus, solidarity, harmony, assent, unison, concord
universal *adj* = **widespread**, general, common, worldwide, unlimited, multicultural *or* mulitculti, catholic, overarching • *These programs have a universal appeal.*
See also: **broad, mass, popular, public**
universally *adv* = **everywhere**, always, invariably, without exception
universe *n* = **cosmos**, nature, creation, macrocosm
unjust *adj* = **unfair**, wrong, partial, partisan, wrongful, one-sided, biased, prejudiced
unjustifiable *adj* = **inexcusable**, wrong, unacceptable, outrageous, indefensible, unforgivable, unpardonable
unkempt *adj* **1** = **uncombed**, shaggy, tousled **2** = **untidy**, messy, dishevelled, disordered, slovenly, ungroomed
unkind *adj* = **cruel**, mean, nasty, malicious,

DICTIONARY

unknown Ⓣ *adj* **1** not known **2** not famous ▷ *n* **3** unknown person, quantity, or thing
unleaded *adj* (of gasoline) containing less tetraethyl lead, to reduce environmental pollution
unleash Ⓣ *v* set loose or cause (something bad)
unleavened [un-**lev**-vend] *adj* (of bread) made without yeast
unless *conj* except under the circumstances that
unlike Ⓣ *adj* **1** dissimilar or different ▷ *prep* **2** not like or typical of
▸ **unlikely** *adj* improbable
unload Ⓣ *v* **1** remove (cargo) from (a ship, truck, or plane) **2** get rid of **3** remove the ammunition from (a firearm)
unlooked-for Ⓣ *adj* unexpected or unforeseen
unlucky Ⓣ *adj* **1** having bad luck, unfortunate **2** ill-omened or inauspicious
unman *v* cause to lose courage or nerve
unmanned *adj* having no personnel or crew
unmask Ⓣ *v* **1** remove the mask or disguise from **2** (cause to) appear in true character
unmentionable Ⓣ *adj* unsuitable as a topic of conversation
unmistakable, unmistakeable Ⓣ *adj* not ambiguous, clear **unmistakably** *or* **unmistakeably** *adv*
unmitigated Ⓣ *adj* **1** not reduced or lessened in severity, intensity, etc. **2** total and complete
unmoved Ⓣ *adj* not affected by emotion, indifferent
unnatural Ⓣ *adj* **1** strange and frightening because not usual: *an unnatural silence* **2** not in accordance with accepted standards of behaviour
unnecessary Ⓣ *adj* not essential, or more than is essential **unnecessarily** *adv*

THESAURUS

thoughtless, spiteful • *It's very unkind to describe her in those terms.* OPPOSITE: kind
See also: **hostile, unfriendly**
unknowing *See* **unconscious**
unknown *adj* **1 = obscure**, humble, unfamiliar, unsung • *She was an unknown at that time.* OPPOSITE: famous **2 = unrevealed**, secret, dark, mysterious, hidden, concealed **3 = strange**, new, alien **4 = unidentified**, anonymous, unnamed, uncharted, undiscovered, nameless, unexplored
unlawful *adj* **= illegal**, criminal, illicit, outlawed, banned, forbidden, prohibited
unleash *v* **= release**, free, let go, let loose
unlike *adj* **= different from**, dissimilar to, distinct from, divergent from, far from • *She was unlike her sister.* OPPOSITE: like
See also: **different**
unlikely *adj* **1 = unbelievable**, incredible, implausible, unconvincing • *an unlikely story* OPPOSITE: likely **2 = improbable**, remote, slight, faint, doubtful • *It seems unlikely that there will be a sequel to the film.*
unlimited *adj* **1 = infinite**, great, extensive, vast, countless, endless, immense, limitless, boundless, unbounded **2 = total**, complete, full, absolute, unrestricted, unqualified
unload *v* **= empty**, dump, relieve, discharge, unpack, lighten
unlock *v* **= open**, release, undo, unfasten, unlatch
unlocked *See* **open**
unlooked-for *adj* **= unexpected**, chance, unforeseen, fortuitous, unanticipated, surprising, unpredicted
unloved *adj* **= neglected**, unwanted, unpopular, forsaken, loveless, rejected, spurned
unlucky *adj* **1 = unfortunate**, hapless, wretched, cursed, luckless • *He was unlucky not to score during the first period.* OPPOSITE: lucky **2 = ill-fated**, doomed, ominous, inauspicious, unfavourable
unmarked *See* **blank**
unmarried *adj* **= single**, bachelor, maiden, unattached, unwed
unmask *v* **= reveal**, discover, expose, disclose, uncover, lay bare
unmentionable *adj* **= taboo**, shocking, obscene, shameful, indecent, scandalous, unspeakable, forbidden, unsayable
unmerciful *adj* **= merciless**, hard, brutal, cruel, ruthless, implacable, pitiless, remorseless
unmistakable *adj* **= clear**, sure, certain, obvious, plain, evident, distinct, manifest, unambiguous
unmitigated *adj* **1 = unrelieved**, intense, persistent, unbroken, unalleviated, undiminished **2 = complete**, absolute, outright, utter, thorough, sheer, downright, arrant
unmoved *adj* **= unaffected**, cold, untouched, indifferent, unimpressed, unresponsive, impassive
unnatural *adj* **1 = strange**, extraordinary, outlandish, queer, freakish **2 = abnormal**, odd, unusual, irregular, perverse, perverted, anomalous **3 = false**, artificial, stiff, affected, phony (*informal*), forced, stilted, feigned, insincere
unnecessary *adj* **= needless**, pointless, uncalled-for • *He frowns upon unnecessary expense.* OPPOSITE: necessary

DICTIONARY

unnerve Ⓣ *v* cause to lose courage, confidence, or self-control
unnumbered *adj* **1** countless **2** not counted or given a number
UNO United Nations Organization
unobtrusive Ⓣ *adj* not drawing attention to oneself, inconspicuous **unobtrusively** *adv*
unorthodox Ⓣ *adj* **1** (of ideas, methods, etc.) not conventional and not generally accepted **2** (of a person) having unusual opinions or methods
unpack *v* **1** remove the contents of (a suitcase, trunk, etc.) **2** take (something) out of a packed container
unpalatable Ⓣ *adj* **1** (of food) unpleasant to taste **2** (of a fact, idea, etc.) unpleasant and hard to accept
unparalleled Ⓣ *adj* not equalled, supreme
unpick *v* undo (the stitches) of (a piece of sewing)
unpleasant Ⓣ *adj* not pleasant or agreeable **unpleasantly** *adv* **unpleasantness** *n*
unpopular Ⓣ *adj* generally disliked or disapproved of **unpopularity** *n*
unprecedented Ⓣ *adj* never having happened before, unparalleled
unprepossessing *adj* unattractive in appearance
unpretentious Ⓣ *adj* without ostentation
unprincipled Ⓣ *adj* lacking moral principles, unscrupulous
unprintable *adj* unsuitable for printing for reasons of obscenity or libel
unprofessional Ⓣ *adj* **1** contrary to the accepted code of a profession **2** not belonging to a profession **unprofessionally** *adv*
unprofitable *adj* **1** not making a profit **2** not helpful or beneficial
unqualified Ⓣ *adj* **1** lacking the necessary qualifications **2** not modified

THESAURUS

unnerve *v* = **shake**, upset, discourage, rattle (*informal*), intimidate, frighten, dismay, dishearten, demoralize, faze, fluster, psych out (*informal*)
unnerving *See* **scary**
unnoticed *adj* = **unobserved**, unheeded, unseen, unrecognized, neglected, disregarded, ignored, overlooked, unperceived
unobtrusive *adj* = **inconspicuous**, quiet, modest, low-key, restrained, unassuming, self-effacing, retiring
unoccupied *adj* = **empty**, vacant, uninhabited
unofficial *adj* = **unauthorized**, private, informal, unconfirmed
unorthodox *adj* = **unconventional**, unusual, abnormal, irregular, off-the-wall (*slang*)
unpaid *adj* **1** = **voluntary**, honorary, unsalaried **2** = **owing**, due, overdue, outstanding, payable, unsettled
unpalatable *adj* = **unpleasant**, offensive, horrid, distasteful, repugnant, disagreeable, unappetizing, unsavoury
unparalleled *adj* = **unequalled**, unique, unprecedented, unmatched, superlative, incomparable, unsurpassed, matchless
unpardonable *adj* = **unforgivable**, disgraceful, inexcusable, deplorable, indefensible
unperturbed *adj* = **calm**, cool, unfazed (*informal*), as cool as a cucumber, composed, placid, unruffled, untroubled, unworried
unpleasant *adj* **1** = **nasty**, bad, distasteful, repulsive, unpalatable, disagreeable • *It has a very unpleasant smell.* OPPOSITE: pleasant **2** = **obnoxious**, rude, objectionable, unfriendly, horrid, disagreeable • *a thoroughly unpleasant person* OPPOSITE: pleasant
See also: **horrible, painful, rough**
unpolluted *See* **clean**
unpopular *adj* = **disliked**, undesirable, detested, shunned • *an unpopular idea* OPPOSITE: popular
unprecedented *adj* = **extraordinary**, new, original, novel, remarkable, abnormal, singular, unheard-of
unpredictable *adj* = **inconstant**, chance, doubtful, unforeseeable, hit or miss (*informal*) • *England's notoriously unpredictable weather* OPPOSITE: predictable
See also: **changeable**
unprejudiced *adj* = **impartial**, just, fair, objective, balanced, unbiased, open-minded
unprepared *adj* **1** = **taken off guard**, unaware, surprised, unready **2** = **improvised**, spontaneous, ad-lib, off the cuff (*informal*)
unpretentious *adj* = **modest**, simple, humble, plain, straightforward, unaffected, unassuming, homey, dumpy (*informal*), unostentatious
unprincipled *adj* = **dishonest**, unethical, immoral, crooked, unscrupulous, devious, amoral, underhand
unproductive *adj* **1** = **useless**, ineffective, idle, vain, futile, fruitless, unprofitable, unrewarding **2** = **barren**, sterile, fruitless
unprofessional *adj* **1** = **unethical**, lax, improper, negligent, unprincipled **2** = **amateurish**, incompetent, inefficient, inexpert
unprotected *adj* = **vulnerable**, open, helpless, defenceless, undefended
unqualified *adj* **1** = **unfit**, unprepared, incompetent, incapable, ineligible, ill-

DICTIONARY

unquestionable Ⓣ *adj* not to be doubted, indisputable **unquestionably** *adv*
unquote *interj* expression used to indicate the end of a quotation that was introduced with the word 'quote'
unravel Ⓣ *v* **-elling, -elled 1** reduce (something knitted or woven) to separate strands **2** become unravelled **3** explain or solve
unreadable *adj* **1** unable to be read or deciphered **2** too difficult or dull to read
unreal Ⓣ *adj* **1** (as if) existing only in the imagination **2** insincere or artificial **unreality** *n*
unreasonable Ⓣ *adj* **1** immoderate or excessive **2** refusing to listen to reason **unreasonably** *adv*
unremitting Ⓣ *adj* never slackening or stopping
unrequited *adj* not returned: *unrequited love*
unreserved Ⓣ *adj* completely, without reservation **unreservedly** [un-re-**zerv**-id-lee] *adv*
unrest Ⓣ *n* rebellious state of discontent
unrivalled Ⓣ *adj* having no equal
unroll Ⓣ *v* open out or unwind (something rolled or coiled) or (of something rolled or coiled) become opened out or unwound
unruffled *adj* **1** calm and unperturbed **2** smooth and still
unruly Ⓣ *adj* **-lier, -liest** given to disobedience or indiscipline
unsaturated *adj* **1** (of an organic compound) containing a double or triple bond and therefore capable of combining with other substances **2** (of a fat, esp. a vegetable fat) containing a high proportion of fatty acids with double bonds
unsavoury Ⓣ *adj* distasteful or objectionable
unscathed Ⓣ *adj* not harmed or injured
unscrupulous Ⓣ *adj* unprincipled or without scruples

THESAURUS

equipped **2 = total**, complete, absolute, outright, utter, thorough, downright
unquestionable *adj* **= certain**, clear, sure, absolute, definite, conclusive, unmistakable, unequivocal, undeniable, indisputable, incontrovertible
unquestionably *See* **certainly**
unravel *v* **1 = undo**, free, separate, unwind, untangle, disentangle **2 = solve**, explain, resolve, figure out (*informal*), work out
unreal *adj* **1 = imaginary**, fabulous, visionary, fanciful, make-believe, illusory, dreamlike **2 = insubstantial**, intangible, immaterial, nebulous **3 = fake**, false, artificial, mock, sham, insincere, pretended
unrealistic *adj* **= impractical**, romantic, improbable, unworkable, impracticable
unreasonable *adj* **1 = excessive**, unfair, unwarranted, unjust, undue, extortionate, immoderate **2 = biased**, opinionated, blinkered
unreasonably *See* **too**
unrelated *adj* **1 = unconnected**, different, unlike **2 = irrelevant**, inappropriate, unconnected, extraneous, inapplicable
unrelenting *See* **relentless**
unreliable *adj* **1 = undependable**, irresponsible, treacherous, untrustworthy **2 = inaccurate**, false, uncertain, deceptive, implausible, unsound, fallible
unremitting *See* **relentless**
unrepentant *adj* **= impenitent**, abandoned, shameless, callous, hardened, incorrigible, unremorseful
unreserved *adj* **1 = total**, complete, full, entire, absolute, unlimited, wholehearted **2 = open**, free, outgoing, unrestrained, demonstrative, extroverted, uninhibited
unresolved *adj* **= undecided**, unanswered, vague, doubtful, moot, unsolved, undetermined, unsettled
unrest *n* **= discontent**, protest, rebellion, strife, agitation, discord, dissension, sedition
unrestrained *adj* **= uncontrolled**, free, abandoned, unchecked, unbridled, immoderate, intemperate, unbounded, uninhibited
unrestricted *adj* **1 = unlimited**, open, free, absolute, unregulated, unbounded **2 = open**, public
unrivalled *adj* **= unparalleled**, superior, supreme, superb, unmatched, incomparable, unsurpassed, matchless, unequalled, beyond compare
unroll *See* **spread**
unruly *adj* **= uncontrollable**, wild, wayward, rebellious, wilful, disobedient, mutinous
unsafe *adj* **= dangerous**, risky, hazardous, unreliable, perilous, sketchy (*informal*), insecure
unsatisfactory *adj* **= unacceptable**, poor, inadequate, mediocre, disappointing • *His work was judged unsatisfactory.* OPPOSITE: satisfactory
See also: **rotten**
unsavoury *adj* **1 = unpleasant**, offensive, nasty, repellent, distasteful, obnoxious, repulsive, revolting, scuzzy (*slang*) **2 = unappetizing**, sickening, unpalatable, nauseating
unscathed *adj* **= unharmed**, safe, whole, unhurt, unmarked, uninjured
unscrupulous *adj* **= unprincipled**, corrupt,

DICTIONARY

unseasonable *adj* inappropriate or unusual for the time of year **unseasonably** *adv*
unseat ⓣ *v* **1** throw or displace from a seat or saddle **2** depose from an office or position
unseemly ⓣ *adj* not polite, indecorous
unsettled ⓣ *adj* **1** lacking order or stability **2** disturbed and restless **3** constantly changing or moving from place to place
unshakable, unshakeable ⓣ *adj* (of beliefs) completely firm, not wavering **unshakably** *or* **unshakeably** *adv*
unsightly ⓣ *adj* unpleasant to look at
unsocial *adj* **1** avoiding the company of other people **2** falling outside the normal working day: *unsocial hours*
unsound ⓣ *adj* **1** unhealthy or unstable **2** not based on truth or fact
unspeakable ⓣ *adj* indescribably bad or evil **unspeakably** *adv*
unstable ⓣ *adj* **1** lacking stability or firmness **2** having abrupt changes of mood or behaviour
unsteady ⓣ *adj* **1** not securely fixed **2** shaky or staggering **unsteadily** *adv*
unstinting *adj* generous, gladly given: *unstinting praise*
unstructured *adj* without formal or systematic organization
unstuck *adj* **come unstuck** *informal* fail badly
unstudied *adj* natural or spontaneous
unsuccessful ⓣ *adj* not achieving success **unsuccessfully** *adv*
unsuitable ⓣ *adj* not right or appropriate for a particular purpose **unsuitably** *adv*
unsuited *adj* not appropriate for a

THESAURUS

improper, unethical, immoral, dishonest, dishonourable
unseat *v* **1 = throw**, unhorse, unsaddle **2 = depose**, remove, oust, displace, overthrow, dethrone
unsecured *See* **loose**
unseemly *adj* **= improper**, inappropriate, unsuitable, unbecoming, undignified, indecorous
unseen *adj* **1 = unobserved**, unnoticed, undetected **2 = hidden**, invisible, obscure, concealed
unselfish *adj* **= generous**, kind, noble, selfless, altruistic, magnanimous, self-sacrificing
unsettle *v* **= disturb**, trouble, upset, confuse, bother, agitate, ruffle, faze, disconcert, fluster, perturb
unsettled *adj* **1 = unstable**, shaky, disorderly, insecure, unsteady **2 = restless**, anxious, tense, confused, restive, shaken, disturbed, agitated, flustered, wired (*slang*) **3 = changing**, uncertain, variable, inconstant
unshakable *adj* **= firm**, sure, absolute, staunch, steadfast, fixed, immovable, unswerving, unwavering
unsharpened *See* **blunt**
unsightly *adj* **= ugly**, unattractive, horrid, hideous, repulsive, disagreeable, dumpy (*informal*), homely (*US*), scuzzy (*slang*)
unskilled *adj* **= unprofessional**, amateurish, inexperienced, unqualified, untrained
unsociable *adj* **= unfriendly**, cold, distant, hostile, chilly, retiring, unforthcoming, withdrawn
unsolicited *adj* **= unrequested**, gratuitous, uninvited, unasked for, uncalled-for, unsought
unsophisticated *adj* **1 = natural**, unaffected, childlike, artless, guileless, ingenuous **2 = simple**, plain, unrefined, homey, uncomplicated, dumpy (*informal*), frowzy, unspecialized
unsound *adj* **1 = unhealthy**, weak, ill, ailing, unstable, defective, diseased, unbalanced, unwell **2 = unreliable**, weak, false, shaky, flawed, defective, illogical, fallacious, specious
unspeakable *adj* **1 = indescribable**, unbelievable, unimaginable, inconceivable **2 = dreadful**, horrible, shocking, awful, appalling, heinous, monstrous, abominable
unspoiled *adj* **1 = unchanged**, intact, perfect, untouched, undamaged, preserved **2 = natural**, innocent, unaffected, artless
unspoken *adj* **= tacit**, implicit, implied, understood, unexpressed, unstated
unstable *adj* **1 = insecure**, shaky, precarious, unsteady, wobbly, unsettled, tottering **2 = changeable**, volatile, unpredictable, variable, fitful, fluctuating, inconstant **3 = unpredictable**, inconsistent, erratic, irrational, temperamental, capricious, changeable
unsteady *adj* **1 = unstable**, unsafe, shaky, precarious, wobbly, rickety, tottering • *a slightly unsteady item of furniture* OPPOSITE: steady **2 = changeable**, volatile, erratic, temperamental, unsettled, inconstant
unsuccessful *adj* **1 = useless**, failed, vain, futile, fruitless, unproductive, unavailing **2 = unlucky**, unfortunate, hapless, luckless
unsuitable *adj* **= inappropriate**, unacceptable, unfit, improper • *Her shoes were unsuitable for walking any distance.* OPPOSITE: suitable
See also: **useless**

DICTIONARY

particular task or situation
unsung Ⓣ *adj* not acclaimed or honoured: *unsung heroes*
unswerving Ⓣ *adj* firm, constant, not changing
unsympathetic Ⓣ *adj* **1** not feeling or showing sympathy **2** unpleasant, not likeable **3** (foll. by *to*) opposed to
untapped *adj* not yet used: *untapped reserves*
untenable Ⓣ *adj* (of a theory, idea, etc.) incapable of being defended
unthinkable Ⓣ *adj* out of the question, inconceivable
untidy Ⓣ *adj* not neat, slovenly **untidily** *adv* **untidiness** *n*
untie Ⓣ *v* **1** open or free (something that is tied) **2** free from constraint
until *conj* **1** up to the time that ▷ *prep* **2** in or throughout the period before
▸ **not until** not before (a time or event)
untimely Ⓣ *adj* **1** occurring before the expected or normal time **2** inappropriate to the occasion or time **untimeliness** *n*
unto *prep old-fashioned* to
untold Ⓣ *adj* **1** incapable of description **2** incalculably great in number or quantity
untouchable *adj* **1** above reproach or suspicion **2** unable to be touched ▷ *n* **3** member of the lowest Hindu caste in India
untoward Ⓣ *adj* causing misfortune or annoyance
untrue Ⓣ *adj* **1** incorrect or false **2** disloyal or unfaithful
▸ **untruth** *n* statement that is not true, lie
untruthful *adj* **untruthfully** *adv*
unusual Ⓣ *adj* uncommon or extraordinary **unusually** *adv*
unutterable *adj* incapable of being expressed in words **unutterably** *adv*
unvarnished *adj* not elaborated upon
unveil Ⓣ *v* **1** ceremonially remove the cover from (a new picture, plaque, etc.) **2** make

THESAURUS

unsung *See* **unknown**
unsure *adj* **1 = unconfident**, insecure, unassured **2 = doubtful**, suspicious, skeptical, dubious, hesitant, unconvinced, distrustful, mistrustful
unsuspecting *adj* **= trusting**, gullible, unwary, credulous, trustful
unswerving *adj* **= constant**, firm, true, steady, staunch, steadfast, resolute, single-minded, unwavering
unsympathetic *adj* **= insensitive**, hard, cold, harsh, cruel, callous, unmoved, heartless, unkind, unfeeling
untamed *See* **wild**
untangle *v* **= disentangle**, unravel, extricate, unsnarl
untenable *adj* **= unsustainable**, weak, shaky, groundless, illogical, indefensible, unsound, insupportable
unthankful *See* **ungrateful**
unthinkable *adj* **1 = impossible**, unreasonable, absurd, out of the question **2 = inconceivable**, incredible, unimaginable, implausible
untidy *adj* **= messy**, chaotic, cluttered, bedraggled, jumbled, unkempt • *The place quickly became untidy.* OPPOSITE: tidy
See also: **confused**
untie *v* **= undo**, release, free, loosen, unbind, unfasten, unknot, unlace
untimely *adj* **1 = early**, premature **2 = ill-timed**, inappropriate, inconvenient, awkward, inopportune, mistimed
untiring *adj* **= tireless**, steady, constant, determined, dogged, persevering, unflagging, unremitting
untold *adj* **1 = indescribable**, unthinkable, unimaginable, inexpressible, undreamed of, unutterable **2 = countless**, myriad, innumerable, incalculable, numberless, uncountable
untouched *adj* **= unharmed**, intact, unhurt, unscathed, uninjured, undamaged
untoward *adj* **1 = troublesome**, unfortunate, inconvenient, awkward, annoying, irritating **2 = unfavourable**, adverse, unlucky, inauspicious, inopportune
untrained *adj* **= amateur**, green, raw, inexperienced, unqualified, uneducated, unskilled, unschooled, untaught
untroubled *adj* **= undisturbed**, cool, calm, peaceful, unfazed (*informal*), tranquil, placid, unperturbed, unworried
untrue *adj* **1 = false**, incorrect, inaccurate, mistaken, erroneous, fictitious, misleading • *The allegations were completely untrue.* OPPOSITE: true **2 = unfaithful**, false, treacherous, deceitful, untrustworthy, disloyal, faithless, inconstant
See also: **wrong**
untrustworthy *adj* **= unreliable**, false, slippery, tricky, treacherous, dishonest, deceitful, devious, disloyal
untruth *n* **= lie**, deceit, fib, falsehood, story, white lie
untruthful *adj* **= dishonest**, false, deceptive, deceitful, lying, mendacious
unused *See* **waste**
unusual *adj* **1 = rare**, uncommon • *many rare and unusual plants* OPPOSITE: common **2 = extraordinary**, curious, exceptional, unconventional
See also: **funny, scarce, singular**
unveil *v* **= reveal**, expose, disclose, uncover, divulge, make known
unwanted *adj* **= undesired**, unsolicited,

DICTIONARY

public (a secret) **unveiling** *n*

unwarranted Ⓣ *adj* not justified, not necessary

unwell Ⓣ *adj* not healthy, ill

unwieldy Ⓣ *adj* too heavy, large, or awkward to be easily handled

unwind Ⓣ *v* **1** (cause to) slacken, undo, or unravel **2** make or become relaxed

unwitting Ⓣ *adj* **1** not knowing or conscious **2** not intentional **unwittingly** *adv*

unwonted *adj* out of the ordinary

unworthy Ⓣ *adj* **1** not deserving or worthy **2** (foll. by *of*) beneath the level considered befitting (to) **3** lacking merit or value

unwrap Ⓣ *v* remove the wrapping from (something) or (of something wrapped) have the covering removed

unwritten Ⓣ *adj* **1** not printed or in writing **2** operating only through custom

up Ⓣ *prep* **1** indicating movement to a higher position **2** at a higher or further level or position in or on ▷ *adv* **3** to an upward, higher, or erect position **4** indicating readiness for an activity: *up and about* **5** indicating intensity or completion of an action **6** to the place referred to or where the speaker is ▷ *adj* **7** of a high or higher position **8** out of bed **9** *baseball* currently batting ▷ *v* **upping, upped 10** increase or raise **11** *informal* do something suddenly: *he upped and left* ▷ *n* **12** *baseball* turn at bat

▶ **up against** having to cope with

▶ **ups and downs** alternating periods of good and bad luck

▶ **uptown** *n* the part of a city that is away from the centre

▶ **what's up?** *informal* what is wrong?

▶ **upward** *adj* **1** directed or moving towards a higher place or level ▷ *adv* **2** Also **upwards** from a lower to a higher place, level, or condition

up-and-coming Ⓣ *adj* likely to be successful in the future

upbeat Ⓣ *n* **1** *music* unaccented beat ▷ *adj* **2** *informal* cheerful and optimistic

upbraid Ⓣ *v* scold or reproach

upbringing Ⓣ *n* education of a person during the formative years

update Ⓣ *v* **1** bring up to date ▷ *n* **2** act

THESAURUS

unwelcome, outcast, unneeded, uninvited, rejected

unwarranted *adj* = **unnecessary**, unjustified, inexcusable, groundless, unprovoked, gratuitous, indefensible, uncalled-for

unwavering *adj* = **steady**, consistent, staunch, determined, steadfast, resolute, unshakable, immovable, unswerving

unwelcome *adj* **1** = **unwanted**, unacceptable, undesirable, excluded, rejected **2** = **disagreeable**, unpleasant, undesirable, distasteful, displeasing

unwell *adj* = **ill**, sick, ailing, queasy • *He felt unwell and had to go home early*. OPPOSITE: well
See also: **unhealthy**

unwholesome *adj* **1** = **harmful**, unhealthy, poisonous, noxious, deleterious **2** = **wicked**, bad, evil, immoral, degrading, corrupting, demoralizing

unwieldy *adj* **1** = **awkward**, inconvenient, cumbersome, unmanageable **2** = **bulky**, massive, hefty, clumsy, ponderous

unwilling *adj* = **reluctant**, loath, averse to, grudging • *an unwilling participant in school sports* OPPOSITE: willing

unwind *v* **1** = **unravel**, undo, slacken, unroll, uncoil, untwine, untwist **2** = **relax**, de-stress, loosen up, take it easy, wind down

unwise *adj* = **foolish**, stupid, silly, irresponsible, rash, senseless, idiotic • *It would be unwise to expect too much of him*. OPPOSITE: wise

unwitting *adj* **1** = **unintentional**, chance, accidental, unplanned, inadvertent, involuntary **2** = **unknowing**, innocent, unaware, unconscious, unsuspecting, ignorant

unworldly *adj* **1** = **spiritual**, metaphysical, nonmaterialistic **2** = **naive**, innocent, idealistic, unsophisticated

unworthy *adj* **1** = **undeserving**, not fit for, not good enough **2** = **dishonourable**, base, disgraceful, shameful, degrading, lousy (*slang*), contemptible, discreditable, disreputable, ignoble ▷ **unworthy of** = **unbefitting**, inappropriate, beneath, unsuitable, unbecoming, unseemly, unfitting

unwrap *See* **uncover**

unwritten *adj* **1** = **oral**, vocal **2** = **customary**, accepted, tacit, understood

unyielding *adj* = **firm**, tough, stubborn, adamant, rigid, resolute, uncompromising, inflexible, immovable, obdurate, obstinate, stiff-necked

up *See* **over**

up-and-coming *See* **in the making**

upbeat *adj* = **cheerful**, positive, optimistic, hopeful, cheery, encouraging

upbraid *v* = **scold**, rebuke, reprimand, berate, admonish, reproach, reprove

upbringing *n* = **education**, training, raising, breeding, rearing

upcoming *See* **near**

update *v* = **bring up to date**, upgrade, renew, amend, modernize

DICTIONARY

of updating **3** Also **status update** short message on a social networking site with information about the user's current activities or mood
Updike *n* **John** (**Hoyer**). 1932–2009, US writer. His novels include *Rabbit, Run* (1960), *Couples* (1968), *The Coup* (1979), *Brazil* (1993), *Seek My Face* (2003), and *Rabbit is Rich* (1982) and *Rabbit at Rest* (1990), both of which won Pulitzer prizes
upend *v* turn or set or be turned or set on end
upfront *adj* **1** open and frank ▷ *adv, adj* **2** (of money) paid out at the beginning of a business arrangement
upgrade Ⓣ *v* promote (a person or job) to a higher rank
upheaval Ⓣ *n* strong, sudden, or violent disturbance
uphill Ⓣ *adj* **1** sloping or leading upwards **2** requiring a great deal of effort ▷ *adv* **3** up a slope
uphold Ⓣ *v* **1** maintain or defend against opposition **2** give moral support to **upholder** *n*
upholster *v* fit (a chair or sofa) with padding, springs, and covering **upholsterer** *n*
▸ **upholstery** *n* **1** act of upholstering **2** soft covering on a chair or sofa
upkeep Ⓣ *n* act, process, or cost of keeping something in good repair
upland *n* **1** area of high or relatively high ground ▷ *adj* **2** of or in an upland
uplift Ⓣ *v* **1** raise or lift up **2** raise morally or spiritually ▷ *n* **3** act, process, or result of lifting up **uplifting** *adj*
upmarket Ⓣ *adj* expensive and of superior quality
upon *prep* **1** on **2** up and on
upper Ⓣ *adj* **1** higher or highest in physical position, wealth, rank, or status ▷ *n* **2** part of a shoe above the sole
▸ **uppermost** *adj* **1** highest in position, power, or importance ▷ *adv* **2** in or into the highest place or position
▸ **upper-case** *adj* denoting capital letters as used in printed or typed matter
▸ **upper class** highest social class **upper-class** *adj*
▸ **upper crust** *informal* upper class
▸ **upper hand** position of control
uppish, uppity *adj informal* snobbish, arrogant, or presumptuous
upright Ⓣ *adj* **1** vertical or erect **2** honest or just ▷ *adv* **3** vertically ▷ *n* **4** vertical support, such as a post **uprightness** *n*
uprising Ⓣ *n* rebellion or revolt
uproar Ⓣ *n* disturbance characterized by loud noise and confusion
▸ **uproarious** *adj* **1** very funny **2** (of laughter) loud and boisterous **uproariously** *adv*
uproot Ⓣ *v* **1** pull up by or as if by the roots **2** displace (a person or people) from their

THESAURUS

upgrade *v* **1 = improve**, enhance, better **2 = promote**, raise, advance, elevate
upheaval *n* **= disturbance**, disorder, revolution, disruption, turmoil
uphill *adj* **1 = ascending**, rising, mounting, climbing **2 = arduous**, hard, tough, difficult, strenuous, gruelling, exhausting, laborious, taxing
uphold *v* **= support**, back, defend, aid, endorse, champion, maintain, promote, advocate, sustain
upkeep *n* **1 = maintenance**, keep, preservation, running, overheads • *The money will be used for the upkeep of the grounds.* **2 = overheads**, expenditure, expenses, running costs
uplift *v* **1 = raise**, hoist, elevate, lift up **2 = improve**, raise, advance, inspire, refine, better, edify ▸ *n* **3 = improvement**, enrichment, advancement, enhancement, refinement, enlightenment, edification
upmarket *adj* (*Informal*) **= high-class**, grand, luxurious, classy (*informal*), smart, stylish, swanky *or* swank (*informal*), upscale, upper-class
upper *adj* **1 = higher**, high, top, loftier, topmost **2 = superior**, important, eminent, greater ▷ **upper hand = control**, edge, advantage, mastery, supremacy, ascendancy ▷ **upper limit** *See* **maximum**
upper-class *adj* **= aristocratic**, noble, blue-blooded, highborn, high-class, patrician
uppermost *adj* **1 = top**, highest, loftiest, topmost **2 = supreme**, chief, main, principal, dominant, foremost, greatest, leading
uppity *adj* (*Informal*) **= conceited**, cocky, bumptious, full of oneself, impertinent, self-important
upright *adj* **1 = vertical**, straight, erect, perpendicular **2 = honest**, good, just, ethical, principled, conscientious, honourable, righteous, virtuous
uprising *n* **= rebellion**, revolution, disturbance, revolt, rising, insurrection, mutiny, insurgence
uproar *n* **= commotion**, riot, turmoil, noise, outcry, furor, mayhem, racket, pandemonium, din
uproarious *adj* **1 = hilarious**, hysterical, rib-tickling, rip-roaring (*informal*), side-splitting, very funny **2 = boisterous**, loud, unrestrained, rollicking
uproot *v* **1 = pull up**, dig up, rip up, root out,

DICTIONARY

native or usual surroundings
upset Ⓣ *adj* **1** emotionally or physically disturbed or distressed ▷ *v* **2** tip over **3** disturb the normal state or stability of **4** disturb mentally or emotionally **5** make physically ill ▷ *n* **6** unexpected defeat or reversal **7** disturbance or disorder of the emotions, mind, or body **upsetting** *adj*
upshot Ⓣ *n* final result or conclusion
upside down Ⓣ *adj* **1** turned over completely **2** *informal* confused or jumbled ▷ *adv* **3** in an inverted fashion **4** in a chaotic manner
upstage *adj* **1** at the back half of the stage ▷ *v* **2** *informal* draw attention to oneself from (someone else)
upstairs *adv* **1** up the stairs ▷ *n* **2** upper floor ▷ *adj* **3** situated on an upper floor
upstanding Ⓣ *adj* of good character
upstart Ⓣ *n* person who has risen suddenly to a position of power and behaves arrogantly
upstream *adv, adj* in or towards the higher part of a stream
upsurge Ⓣ *n* rapid rise or swell
uptake *n* **quick** *or* **slow on the uptake** *informal* quick *or* slow to understand or learn
uptight Ⓣ *adj informal* nervously tense, irritable, or angry
up-to-date Ⓣ *adj* modern or fashionable
upturn *n* **1** upward trend or improvement **2** upheaval
uranium [yew-**rain**-ee-um] *n* radioactive silvery-white metallic element, used chiefly as a source of nuclear energy
Uranus *n* **1** Greek god of the sky **2** seventh planet from the sun
urban Ⓣ *adj* **1** of or living in a city or town **2** denoting modern pop music of African-American origin, such as hip-hop
▶ **urbanize** *v* make (a rural area) more industrialized and urban **urbanization** *n*
urbane Ⓣ *adj* characterized by courtesy, elegance, and sophistication **urbanity** *n*
urchin Ⓣ *n* mischievous child
Urdu [**oor**-doo] *n* language of Pakistan
urethra [yew-**reeth**-ra] *n, pl* **-thrae, -thras** canal that carries urine from the bladder out of the body
urge Ⓣ *n* **1** strong impulse, inner drive, or yearning ▷ *v* **2** plead with or press (a person to do something) **3** advocate earnestly **4** force or drive onwards
▶ **urgent** *adj* requiring speedy action or attention **urgency** *n* **urgently** *adv*
uric acid *n* white odourless crystalline acid present in the blood and urine
urine *n* pale yellow fluid excreted by the kidneys to the bladder and passed as waste

THESAURUS

weed out **2 = displace**, exile
upscale *See* **exclusive, posh**
upset *adj* **1 = distressed**, hurt, troubled, unhappy, frantic, agitated • *She was very upset when she heard the news.* **2 = sick**, ill, queasy **3 = disordered**, chaotic, confused, disarrayed, in disarray, muddled **4 = overturned**, capsized, spilled, upside down ▶ *v* **5 = distress**, disturb, bother, grieve, agitate, ruffle • *The whole incident upset me terribly.* **6 = overturn**, spill, capsize, knock over • *Don't upset that pile of papers.* **7 = mess up**, change, disorder, disturb, spoil, disorganize **8 = distress**, trouble, disturb, bother, grieve, agitate, ruffle, faze, disconcert, fluster, perturb ▶ *n* **9 = reversal**, defeat, shake-up (*informal*) **10 = illness**, complaint, disorder, bug (*informal*), sickness, malady **11 = distress**, worry, trouble, shock, bother, disturbance, agitation
See also: **blow, shake**
upsetting *See* **sad**
upshot *n* **= result**, end, outcome, finale, sequel, culmination, end result
upside down *adj* **1 = inverted**, backward, overturned, upturned **2 = confused**, chaotic, disordered, topsy-turvy, muddled
upstanding *adj* **= honest**, good, moral, ethical, upright, principled, honourable, incorruptible
upstart *n* **= social climber**, arriviste, *nouveau riche* (*French*), parvenu
upsurge *n* **= increase**, rise, growth, boost, escalation, upturn
uptight *adj* (*Informal*) **= tense**, anxious, uneasy, edgy, on edge, wired (*slang*)
up to *See* **equal to**
up-to-date *adj* **= modern**, current, cool (*informal*), stylish, trendy (*informal*), fashionable, up-to-the-minute, in vogue, phat (*slang*)
up-to-the-minute *See* **current, modern**
upturn *n* **= rise**, increase, improvement, recovery, revival, advancement, upswing, upsurge
urban *adj* **= civic**, city, town, municipal, metropolitan
urbane *adj* **= sophisticated**, smooth, refined, polished, courteous, suave, cultured, cultivated, debonair, well-bred
urchin *n* **= ragamuffin**, brat, gamin, waif
urge *n* **1 = impulse**, drive, wish, desire, longing, compulsion • *stifling the urge to scream* ▶ *v* **2 = beg**, plead, press, implore, beseech (*formal*) • *He urged the referee to change her ruling.* **3 = advocate**, support, recommend, advise, counsel **4 = drive**, force, push, press, spur, compel, induce, incite, goad, impel

DICTIONARY

from the body **uric** *adj* **urinary** *adj*
▶ **urinal** *n* (place with) sanitary fitting(s) used by men for urination
▶ **urinate** *v* discharge urine **urination** *n*
URL uniform resource locator: the address of a location on the internet
urn *n* **1** vase used as a container for the ashes of the dead **2** large metal container with a tap, used for making and holding tea or coffee
Urquhart *n* **Jane**. born 1949, Canadian novelist, poet, and short-story writer. Her novels include *Away* (1993) and *The Stone Carvers* (2001)
ursine *adj* of or like a bear
Ursula *n* **Saint**. legendary British princess of the fourth or fifth century AD, said to have been martyred together with 11 000 virgins by the Huns at Cologne. Feast day: Oct 21
us *pron* objective case of **we**
US, USA United States (of America)
use ⓘ *v* **1** put into service or action **2** take advantage of **3** consume or expend ▷ *n* **4** using or being used **5** ability or permission to use **6** usefulness or advantage **7** purpose for which something is used **user** *n* **useful** *adj* **usefully** *adv* **usefulness** *n* **useless** *adj* **uselessly** *adv* **uselessness** *n*
▶ **user-friendly** *adj* easy to familiarize oneself with, understand, and use
▶ **usable** *adj* able to be used **usability** *n*
▶ **usage** *n* **1** regular or constant use **2** way in which a word is used in a language
▶ **used** *adj* second-hand
▶ **used to** *adj* **1** accustomed to ▷ *v* **2** used as an auxiliary to express past habitual or accustomed actions: *I used to live there*
usher ⓘ *n* **1** official who shows people to their seats, as in a church ▷ *v* **2** conduct or escort
▶ **usherette** *n* female assistant in a cinema who shows people to their seats
Usman dan Fodio *n* 1754–1817, African mystic and revolutionary leader, who created a Muslim state in Nigeria
Ussher, Usher *n* **James**. 1581–1656, Irish prelate and scholar. His system of biblical chronology, which dated the creation at 4004 BC, was for long accepted
USSR formerly, Union of Soviet Socialist Republics
Ustinov *n* Sir **Peter** (**Alexander**). 1921–2004, British stage and film actor, director, dramatist, and raconteur
usual ⓘ *adj* of the most normal, frequent, or regular type
▶ **usually** *adv* most often, in most cases
usurp ⓘ [yewz-**zurp**] *v* seize (a position or power) without authority **usurpation** *n* **usurper** *n*

THESAURUS

See also: **insist, instinct, whim**
urgency *n* = **importance**, need, pressure, gravity, hurry, necessity, seriousness, extremity
urgent *adj* = **crucial**, immediate, pressing, imperative, compelling • *an urgent need for food and water*
See also: **serious**
usable *adj* = **serviceable**, current, available, working, practical, valid, functional, utilizable
usage *n* **1** = **use**, control, operation, management, employment, handling, running **2** = **practice**, procedure, regime, convention, method, routine, habit, custom, mode
use *v* **1** = **employ**, operate, apply, utilize, ply, call into play, avail oneself of • *Use a sharp knife to trim the edges.* **2** = **take advantage of**, exploit, manipulate **3** = **consume**, spend, exhaust, expend, run through
▷ **use up** = **consume**, finish, drain, absorb, exhaust, run through ▶ *n* **4** = **usage**, operation, application, employment • *the use of force* **5** = **purpose**, point, end, object • *of no practical use whatsoever* **6** = **good**, help, point, service, profit, benefit, value, advantage, avail, usefulness
See also: **impose on, wear**
used *adj* = **second-hand**, cast-off, nearly new, shopworn ▷ **used to** = **accustomed to**, familiar with
useful *adj* = **helpful**, effective, valuable, practical, beneficial, worthwhile • *a great deal of useful information* OPPOSITE: useless
See also: **convenient, handy, productive**
usefulness *n* = **helpfulness**, use, benefit, value, worth, utility, effectiveness, convenience, efficacy, practicality
useless *adj* **1** = **worthless**, futile, unproductive, impractical, unsuitable • *We realized that our money was useless here.* OPPOSITE: useful **2** (*Informal*) = **inept**, incompetent, hopeless, ineffectual, no good
See also: **inadequate, vain**
usher *n* **1** = **attendant**, guide, escort, doorkeeper, doorman ▶ *v* **2** = **escort**, lead, conduct, direct, guide
usual *adj* = **normal**, common, standard, regular, customary, habitual, accustomed • *sitting at his usual table*
See also: **average, natural, ordinary, routine, stock, typical**
usually *adv* = **normally**, mostly, generally, mainly, commonly, as a rule, habitually, on the whole
usurp *v* = **seize**, take, assume, appropriate, wrest, commandeer, take over

DICTIONARY

usury *n, pl* **-ries** practice of lending money at an extremely high rate of interest **usurer** [**yewz**-yoor-er] *n*
Utamaro *n* **Kitagawa**, original name *Kitagawa Nebsuyoshi*. 1753–1806, Japanese master of wood-block prints, of the ukiyo-e school; noted esp. for his portraits of women
utensil Ⓣ *n* tool or container for practical use
uterus [**yew**-ter-russ] *n* womb **uterine** *adj*
Uthman *n* died 656 AD, third caliph of Islam, who established an authoritative version of the Koran
utilitarian *adj* **1** of utilitarianism **2** useful rather than beautiful
▸ **utilitarianism** *n* doctrine that the right action is that which brings about the greatest good for the greatest number of people
utility Ⓣ *n, pl* **-ties 1** usefulness **2** public service, such as gas ▷ *adj* **3** designed for use rather than beauty **4** *baseball* designating a substitute who can play in a number of positions
▸ **utilize** *v* make practical use of **utilization** *n*
utmost Ⓣ *adj, n* (of the) greatest possible degree or amount
Utopia Ⓣ [yew-**tope**-ee-a] *n* any real or imaginary society, place, or state considered to be ideal **Utopian** *adj*
utter[1] Ⓣ *v* express (something) audibly
▸ **utterance** *n* **1** something uttered **2** act or power of uttering
utter[2] Ⓣ *adj* total or absolute **utterly** *adv*
uttermost *adj, n* same as **utmost**
U-turn *n* **1** turn, made by a vehicle, in the shape of a U, resulting in a reversal of direction **2** complete change in policy
UV ultraviolet
uvula [**yew**-view-la] *n, pl* **-las, -lae** small fleshy part of the soft palate that hangs in the back of the throat **uvular** *adj*
uxorious [ux-**or**-ee-uss] *adj* excessively fond of or dependent on one's wife

THESAURUS

utensil *See* **tool**
utility *n* = **usefulness**, benefit, convenience, efficacy, practicality, serviceableness
utilize *v* = **use**, employ, avail oneself of, make use of, put to use, take advantage of, turn to account, call into play
utmost *adj* **1** = **greatest**, chief, maximum, supreme, pre-eminent, paramount, highest **2** = **farthest**, last, final, extreme ▸ *n* **3** = **best**, greatest, hardest, highest
Utopia *n* = **paradise**, heaven, Eden, bliss, Garden of Eden, Shangri-la
Utopian *adj* = **perfect**, dream, ideal, fantasy, romantic, visionary, imaginary, idealistic
utter[1] *v* = **say**, speak, express, voice, pronounce, articulate
See also: **emit**
utter[2] *adj* = **absolute**, complete, total, perfect, pure, outright, thorough, sheer, consummate, out-and-out • *scenes of utter chaos*
See also: **rank**
utterance *n* = **speech**, statement, announcement, remark, expression, declaration, words
utterly *adv* = **totally**, completely, fully, extremely, absolutely, entirely, perfectly, thoroughly

u

Vv

V volt
v. **1** versus **2** very
vacant Ⓣ *adj* **1** (of a lavatory, room, etc.) unoccupied **2** without interest or understanding **vacantly** *adv*
▶ **vacancy** *n, pl* **-cies 1** unfilled job **2** unoccupied room in a guesthouse **3** state of being unoccupied
vacate Ⓣ *v* leave (a place or job)
▶ **vacation** *n* **1** time when universities and law courts are closed **2** holiday
vaccinate *v* inoculate with a vaccine **vaccination** *n*
▶ **vaccine** *n* substance designed to cause a mild form of a disease to make a person immune to the disease itself
vacillate [**vass**-ill-late] *v* waver in one's opinions **vacillation** *n*
vacuous Ⓣ *adj* not expressing intelligent thought **vacuity** *n*
vacuum Ⓣ *n, pl* **vacuums, vacua 1** empty space from which all or most air or gas has been removed ▷ *v* **2** clean with a vacuum cleaner
▶ **vacuum cleaner** electrical appliance for removing dust by suction
▶ **vacuum-packed** *adj* contained in packaging from which the air has been removed
vagabond Ⓣ *n* person with no fixed home, esp. a beggar
vagaries [**vaig**-a-reez] *pl n* unpredictable changes
vagina [vaj-**jine**-a] *n, pl* **-nas, -nae** (in female mammals) passage from the womb to the external genitals **vaginal** *adj*
vagrant Ⓣ [**vaig**-rant] *n* **1** person with no settled home ▷ *adj* **2** wandering **vagrancy** *n*
vague Ⓣ *adj* **1** not clearly explained **2** unable to be seen or heard clearly **3** absent-minded **vaguely** *adv*
vain Ⓣ *adj* **1** excessively proud, esp. of one's appearance **2** bound to fail, futile
▶ **in vain** unsuccessfully
vainglorious *adj lit* boastful **vainglory** *n*
valance [**val**-lenss] *n* piece of drapery round the edge of a bed
vale *n lit* valley
valediction [val-lid-**dik**-shun] *n* farewell speech **valedictory** *adj*
valence [**vale**-ence] *n* molecular bonding between atoms
valency *n, pl* **-cies** power of an atom to make molecular bonds
valentine *n* (person to whom one sends) a romantic card on Saint Valentine's Day, 14th February
Valentine *n* **Saint**. 3rd century AD, Christian martyr, associated by historical accident with the custom of sending valentines; bishop of Terni. Feast day: Feb 14
Valentino *n* **Rudolph**, original name *Rodolpho Guglielmi di Valentina d'Antonguolla*. 1895–1926, US silent-film actor, born in Italy. He is famous for his romantic roles in such films as *The Sheik* (1921)
valerian *n* herb used as a sedative
Valerian *n* Latin name *Publius Licinius*

THESAURUS

vacancy *n* = **job**, post, position, situation, opportunity, opening
vacant *adj* **1** = **unoccupied**, free, available, empty, void, idle, unfilled, untenanted **2** = **vague**, blank, idle, dreamy, inane, absent-minded, abstracted, vacuous
vacate *v* = **leave**, quit, evacuate
vacation *n* = **holiday**, leave, break, trip, rest, tour, recess, furlough, time off, staycation (*informal*), leave of absence, mini-break, awayday • *I'm exhausted! I really need a vacation.*
vacuous *adj* = **unintelligent**, blank, stupid, vacant, inane, uncomprehending
vacuum *n* = **emptiness**, space, gap, void, nothingness, vacuity
vagabond *n* = **tramp**, rover, panhandler, beggar, itinerant, vagrant, down-and-out
vagrant *n* **1** = **tramp**, hobo, drifter, itinerant, wanderer, rolling stone ▶ *adj* **2** = **vagabond**, nomadic, unsettled, itinerant, roaming, rootless, roving
vague *adj* = **unclear**, loose, uncertain, indefinite, hazy, indistinct • *vague promises about a raise* OPPOSITE: clear
See also: **broad, dim, faint, rough**
vain *adj* **1** = **conceited**, proud, egotistical, ostentatious, stuck-up (*informal*) • *I think he is shallow and vain.* **2** = **futile**, useless, fruitless, unproductive, abortive • *He made a vain effort to cheer her up.* OPPOSITE: successful ▶ *noun* ▷ **in vain** = **unsuccessful**, fruitless, to no avail, wasted • *Her complaints were in vain.*
See also: **fond, hopeless**

DICTIONARY

Valerianus. died 260 AD, Roman emperor (253–260): renewed persecution of the Christians; defeated by the Persians

valet *n* man's personal male servant

valetudinarian [val-lit-yew-din-**air**-ee-an] *n* **1** person with a long-term illness **2** hypochondriac

valiant Ⓣ *adj* brave or courageous

valid Ⓣ *adj* **1** soundly reasoned **2** having legal force **validity** *n*
▸ **validate** *v* make valid **validation** *n*

valise [val-**leez**] *n old-fashioned* travelling bag

Valium *n* ® drug used as a tranquillizer

valley Ⓣ *n* low area between hills, usu. with a river running through it

valour Ⓣ *n lit* bravery **valorous** *adj*

value Ⓣ *n* **1** importance, usefulness **2** monetary worth **values 3** moral principles ▷ *v* **valuing, valued 4** assess the value of **5** have a high regard for **valueless** *adj* **valuer** *n*
▸ **valuable** *adj* having great worth
▸ **valuables** *pl n* valuable personal property
▸ **valuation** *n* assessment of worth
▸ **value-added tax** *Brit* see **VAT**
▸ **value judgment** opinion based on personal belief

valve *n* **1** device to control the movement of fluid through a pipe **2** *anat* flap in a part of the body allowing blood to flow in one direction only **3** *physics* tube containing a vacuum, allowing current to flow from a cathode to an anode **valvular** *adj*

vamoose *v slang* go away

vamp[1] *n informal* woman who seduces men to her own advantage

vamp[2] *v* **1** (foll. by *up*) renovate **2** improvise an accompaniment to (a tune)

vampire *n* (in folklore) a corpse that rises at night to drink the blood of the living
▸ **vampire bat** tropical bat that feeds on blood

van[1] *n* **1** motor vehicle for transporting goods **2** *Brit* railway carriage for goods in which the guard travels

van[2] *n* short for **vanguard**

vanadium *n* metallic element, used in steel

Van Allen *n* **James Alfred**. 1914–2006, US physicist, noted for his use of satellites to investigate cosmic radiation in the upper atmosphere

Vanbrugh *n* Sir **John**. 1664–1726, English dramatist and baroque architect. His best-known plays are the Restoration comedies *The Relapse* (1697) and *The Provok'd Wife* (1697). As an architect, he is noted esp. for Blenheim Palace

Van Buren *n* **Martin**. 1782–1862, US Democratic statesman; 8th president of the US (1837–41)

Vancouver *n* Captain **George**. 1757–1798, English navigator, noted for his exploration of the Pacific coast of North America (1792–94)

vandal Ⓣ *n* person who deliberately damages property **vandalism** *n* **vandalize** *v*

van der Waals *n* **Johannes Diderik**. 1837–1923, Dutch physicist, noted for his research on the equations of state of gases and liquids: Nobel prize for physics in 1910

van de Velde *n* **Henry**. 1863–1957, Belgian architect and designer, who introduced the British Arts and Crafts movement to the Continent and helped to develop the Art Nouveau style

Van Dyck, Vandyke *n* Sir **Anthony**. 1599–1641, Flemish painter; court painter to Charles I of England (1632–41). He is best

THESAURUS

valiant *adj* = **brave**, bold, heroic, courageous, fearless, gallant, intrepid, lion-hearted

valid *adj* **1** = **sound**, good, logical, well-founded, cogent, convincing, telling, well-grounded **2** = **legal**, official, legitimate, genuine, authentic, lawful, bona fide

validate *v* = **confirm**, endorse, authorize, ratify, certify, authenticate, substantiate, corroborate

validity *n* **1** = **soundness**, force, power, weight, strength, cogency **2** = **legality**, right, authority, legitimacy, lawfulness

valley *n* = **hollow**, depression, glen, dell, dale, vale

valour *n* = **bravery**, spirit, courage, heroism, boldness, fearlessness, gallantry, intrepidity

valuable *adj* **1** = **useful**, important, helpful, beneficial, worthwhile, prized • *The experience was very valuable.* OPPOSITE: useless **2** = **precious**, expensive, costly • *valuable old baseball cards* OPPOSITE: worthless
See also: **productive** ▸ *noun* ▷ **valuables** = **treasures**, heirlooms • *Leave your valuables at home.*

valuation *See* **estimate**

value *n* **1** = **importance**, use, benefit, worth, advantage, merit, effectiveness, virtue, usefulness • *the value of a balanced diet* **2** = **cost**, price, worth, market price, selling price • *The value of their house has doubled.* ▷ **values** = **principles**, ethics, standards *or* moral standards ▸ *v* **3** = **appreciate**, respect, treasure, cherish, prize, have a high opinion of, rate highly • *Do you value your friends?* **4** = **evaluate**, price, cost, estimate, assess, appraise • *I have had my jewellery valued for insurance purposes.*
See also: **admire, ideal, quality**

valueless *See* **worthless**

vandal *n* = **hooligan**, rowdy, delinquent

V

DICTIONARY

known for his portraits of the aristocracy
Vandyke beard *n* short pointed beard (Also **Vandyke**)
vane *n* flat blade on a rotary device such as a weathercock or propeller
Vane *n* Sir **Henry**, known as *Sir Harry Vane*. 1613–62, English Puritan statesman and colonial administrator; governor of Massachusetts (1636–37). He was executed for high treason after the Restoration
van Eyck *n* **Jan**. died 1441, Flemish painter; founder of the Flemish school of painting. His most famous work is the altarpiece *The Adoration of the Lamb*, in Ghent, in which he may have been assisted by his brother **Hubert**, died ?1426
Van Gogh *n* **Vincent**. 1853–90, Dutch postimpressionist painter, noted for his landscapes and portraits, in which colour is used essentially for its expressive and emotive value
vanguard Ⓣ *n* **1** unit of soldiers leading an army **2** most advanced group or position in a movement or activity
Van Horne *n* **William Cornelius**. 1843–1915, Canadian railway executive, born in the US. An important figure in the Canadian Pacific Railway, he oversaw the completion of the line from Port Moody to Montreal and the company's diversification into sea transport, hotels, and telegraphy
Vanier *n* **1 Georges(-Philéas)**. 1888–1967, Canadian lawyer, decorated soldier, and diplomat; Governor General (1959–67) **2** his son, **Jean**. born 1928, Canadian philanthropist and religious leader. He established (1964) a home in France called L'Arche (the Ark) for people with developmental disabilities, then opened similar homes in Canada and many other countries
Vanier Cup *n* trophy awarded to the Canadian university football champions
vanilla *n* seed pod of a tropical climbing orchid, used for flavouring
vanish Ⓣ *v* **1** disappear suddenly or mysteriously **2** cease to exist
vanity Ⓣ *n, pl* **-ties** (display of) excessive pride
vanquish Ⓣ *v lit* defeat (someone) utterly **vanquishable** *adj* **vanquisher** *n*
vantage *n* advantage
▸ **vantage point** position that gives one an overall view
vapid Ⓣ *adj* lacking character, dull **vapidity** *n*
vapour Ⓣ *n* **1** moisture suspended in air as steam or mist **2** gaseous form of something that is liquid or solid at room temperature **vaporize** *v* **vaporizer** *n* **vaporous** *adj*
Varah *n* (**Edward**) **Chad**. 1911–2007, British Anglican clergyman, who founded (1953) the Samaritans counselling service
Vardon *n* **Harry**. 1870–1937, British golfer
Varèse *n* **Edgar(d)**. 1883–1965, US composer, born in France. His works, which combine extreme dissonance with complex rhythms and the use of electronic techniques, include *Ionisation* (1931) and *Poème électronique* (1958)
Vargas *n* **Getúlio Dornelles**. 1883–1954, Brazilian statesman; president (1930–45; 1951–54)
Vargas Llosa *n* (**Jorge**) **Mario** (**Pedro**). born 1936, Peruvian novelist, writer, and political figure. His novels include *The City and the Dogs* (1963), *Conversation in the Cathedral* (1969), *The Storyteller* (1990), and *The Notebooks of Don Rigoberto* (1998). In 1990 he stood unsuccessfully for the presidency of Peru
variable Ⓣ *adj* **1** not always the same ▹ *n* **2** *math* expression with a range of values **variability** *n*
variant Ⓣ *adj* **1** different or alternative ▹ *n* **2** alternative form
▸ **at variance** in disagreement
variation Ⓣ *n* **1** extent to which something

THESAURUS

vanguard *n* = **forefront**, van, spearhead, cutting edge, forerunners, front line, leaders, trailblazers, trendsetters, point-man
vanish *v* **1** = **disappear**, fade, recede, become invisible, be lost to view OPPOSITE: appear **2** = **die out**, pass, cease, dissolve, evaporate, become extinct, cease to exist, fade away, go away, melt away • *Dinosaurs vanished from the earth millions of years ago.*
See also: **melt**
vanished *See* **lost**
vanity *n* = **pride**, arrogance, narcissism, conceit, conceitedness, egotism
vanquish *v* = **defeat**, beat, overcome, crush, rout, trounce, conquer • *a happy ending in which the hero vanquishes the villains*
See also: **subdue**
vapid *adj* = **dull**, weak, flat, tame, boring, bland, insipid, uninspiring, uninteresting, wishy-washy (*informal*)
vapour *n* = **mist**, steam, fog, haze, exhalation
See also: **cloud**
variable *adj* = **changeable**, flexible, unstable, uneven, unsteady, temperamental, fluctuating, inconstant, mutable, shifting
variance *n* ▹ **at variance** = **in disagreement**, at loggerheads, at odds, conflicting, out of line
variant *adj* **1** = **different**, alternative, modified, divergent ▸ *n* **2** = **variation**, development, alternative, modification
variation *n* = **change**, difference, departure, diversification, alteration, deviation • *a*

DICTIONARY

varies **2** *music* repetition in different forms of a basic theme **variational** *adj*
varicose veins *pl n* knotted and swollen veins, esp. in the legs
variegated *adj* having patches or streaks of different colours **variegation** *n*
variety Ⓣ *n, pl* **-ties 1** state of being various **2** different things of the same kind **3** sort or kind **4** light entertainment composed of unrelated acts
various Ⓣ *adj* of several kinds **variously** *adv*
varlet *n obsolete* rascal
Varley *n* **Frederick** (**Horsman**). 1881–1969, Canadian artist born in England; a member of the Group of Seven and noted for his paintings that commemorated Canada's participation in WWI
varnish Ⓣ *n* **1** solution of oil and resin, put on a surface to make it hard and glossy ▷ *v* **2** apply varnish to
varsity *adj informal* relating to a sports team or athlete that represents a university, college, or high school
vary Ⓣ *v* **varying, varied 1** change **2** cause differences in **varied** *adj*
Vasari *n* **Giorgio**. 1511–74, Italian architect, painter, and art historian, noted for his *Lives of the Most Excellent Italian Architects, Painters, and Sculptors* (1550; 1568), a principal source for the history of Italian Renaissance art
vascular *adj biol* relating to vessels
vas deferens *n, pl* **vasa deferentia** *anat* sperm-carrying duct in each testicle
vase *n* ornamental jar, esp. for flowers
vasectomy *n, pl* **-mies** (operation for) the removal of part of the vas deferens, as a contraceptive method
Vaseline *n* ® thick oily cream made from petroleum, used in skin care
vassal *n hist* man given land in return for allegiance to his lord **vassalage** *n*
vast Ⓣ *adj* extremely large **vastly** *adv* **vastness** *n*
vat *n* large container for liquids
VAT *Brit* value-added tax: tax on the difference between the cost of materials and the selling price
Vatican *n* the Pope's palace
vaudeville *n US* variety entertainment in a theatre
Vaudreuil *n* **1 Philippe de Rigaud de,** Marquis de. *c.* 1643–1725, French military commander a nd colonial administrator; Governor of Montreal (1698–1703); Governor of New France (1703–25) **2** his son, **Pierre de Rigaud de Vaudreuil de Cavagnial**, Marquis de. 1698–1778, French-Canadian military commander and colonial administrator; Governor General of New France (1755–60) but surrendered the colony to the British during the French and Indian War
Vaughan *n* **Sarah** (**Lois**). 1924–90, US jazz vocalist and pianist, noted esp. for her skill in vocal improvisation
Vaughan Williams *n* **Ralph**. 1872–1958, English composer, inspired by British folk songs and music of the Tudor period. He wrote operas, symphonies, hymns, and choral music
vault[1] Ⓣ *n* **1** secure room for storing valuables **2** underground burial chamber ▶ **vaulted** *adj* having an arched roof
vault[2] Ⓣ *v* **1** jump over (something) by resting one's hand(s) on it. ▷ *n* **2** such a jump
vaunt *v* describe or display (success or possessions) boastfully **vaunted** *adj*
Vavilov *n* **Nikolai Ivanovich**. 1887–?1943, Soviet plant geneticist, noted for his research into the origins of cultivated plants. His findings were regarded as contrary to official ideology and he was arrested (1940), dying in a labour camp
VC 1 Vice Chancellor **2** Victoria Cross
VCR video cassette recorder
VD venereal disease

THESAURUS

variation of the usual route
varied *adj* = **different**, various, mixed, diverse, assorted, miscellaneous, heterogeneous, motley, sundry
variety *n* **1** = **range**, collection, array, mixture, medley, assortment • *a wide variety of readers* **2** = **type**, kind, class, strain, sort, category • *a new variety of celery* **3** = **diversity**, change, difference, variation, discrepancy, diversification, multifariousness
See also: **breed, choice, form**
various *adj* = **different**, diverse, disparate, assorted, miscellaneous, sundry • *trees of various sorts*
See also: **several**
varnish *n, v* = **lacquer**, polish, gloss, glaze
vary *v* **1** = **change**, alter, alternate, fluctuate • *weather patterns vary greatly* **2** = **alternate**, modify, diversify • *Vary your routes as much as possible.*
See also: **range**
vast *adj* = **huge**, great, giant, massive, enormous, immense, gigantic, colossal • *vast stretches of farmland* OPPOSITE: tiny
See also: **broad, extensive, large, spacious**
vault[1] *n* **1** = **strongroom**, repository, depository **2** = **crypt**, tomb, cellar, mausoleum, catacomb, charnel house, undercroft
vault[2] *v* = **jump**, clear, spring, hurdle, leap, bound
vaulted *adj* = **arched**, cavernous, domed

DICTIONARY

VDU visual display unit
veal *n* calf meat
vector *n* **1** *math* quantity that has size and direction, such as force **2** animal, usu. an insect, that carries disease
veer Ⓣ *v* change direction suddenly
vegan [**vee**-gan] *n* **1** person who eats no meat, fish, eggs, or dairy products ▷ *adj* **2** suitable for a vegan **veganism** *n*
vegetable *n* **1** edible plant **2** *informal* severely brain-damaged person ▷ *adj* **3** of or like plants or vegetables
vegetarian *n* **1** person who eats no meat or fish ▷ *adj* **2** suitable for a vegetarian **vegetarianism** *n*
vegetate Ⓣ *v* live a dull uncreative life
vegetation *n* plant life of a given place
vehement Ⓣ *adj* expressing strong feelings **vehemence** *n* **vehemently** *adv*
vehicle Ⓣ *n* **1** machine, esp. with an engine and wheels, for carrying people or objects **2** means of communicating something **vehicular** *adj*
veil Ⓣ *n* **1** piece of thin cloth covering the head or face **2** something that conceals the truth: *a veil of secrecy* ▷ *v* **3** cover with a veil
▸ **take the veil** become a nun
▸ **veiled** *adj* disguised
Veil *n* **Simone** (**Annie**). born 1927, French stateswoman; president of the European Parliament (1979–82): a survivor of Nazi concentration camps
vein Ⓣ *n* **1** tube that takes blood to the heart **2** line in a leaf or an insect's wing **3** layer of ore or mineral in rock **4** streak in marble **5** feature of someone's writing or speech: *a vein of humour* **6** mood: *in a lighter vein* **veined** *adj*
Velázquez, Velásquez *n* **Diego Rodríguez de Silva y.** 1599–1660, Spanish painter, remarkable for the realism of his portraits, esp. those of Philip IV of Spain and the royal household
Velcro *n* ® fastening consisting of one piece of fabric with tiny hooked threads and another with a coarse surface that adheres to it
veld, veldt *n* high grassland in Southern Africa
vellum *n* **1** fine calfskin parchment **2** type of smooth paper
velocity Ⓣ [vel-**loss**-it-ee] *n, pl* **-ties** speed of movement in a given direction
velours, velour [vel-**loor**] *n* velvety fabric
velvet *n* fabric with a thick pile
▸ **velvety** *adj* soft and smooth
▸ **velveteen** *n* cotton velvet
venal [**vee**-nal] *adj* **1** easily bribed **2** characterized by bribery **venally** *adv* **venality** *n*
vend *v* sell **vendor** *n*
▸ **vending machine** machine that dispenses goods when coins are inserted
vendetta Ⓣ *n* prolonged quarrel between families, esp. one involving revenge killings
veneer Ⓣ *n* **1** thin layer of wood etc. covering a cheaper material **2** superficial appearance: *a veneer of sophistication*
venerable Ⓣ *adj* worthy of deep respect
▸ **venerate** *v* hold (a person) in deep respect **veneration** *n*
venereal disease [ven-**ear**-ee-al] *n* disease transmitted sexually
Venetian *adj* of Venice, port in NE Italy
▸ **Venetian blind** window blind made of horizontal slats that turn to let in more or less light
vengeance Ⓣ *n* revenge
▸ **vengeful** *adj* wanting revenge **vengefully** *adv*

THESAURUS

veer *v* = **change course**, turn, shift, sheer, swerve, change direction
vegetate *v* = **stagnate**, deteriorate, idle, languish, loaf, go to seed
vehemence *n* = **forcefulness**, force, energy, passion, intensity, emphasis, vigour, ardour, fervour
vehement *adj* = **strong**, powerful, intense, fierce, passionate, forceful, impassioned, emphatic, ardent, fervent
vehicle *n* **1** = **conveyance**, transport, transportation **2** = **medium**, channel, organ, means, mechanism, apparatus
veil *n* **1** = **cover**, film, screen, mask, blind, cloak, curtain, disguise, shroud ▸ *v* **2** = **cover**, screen, hide, mask, shield, cloak, conceal, obscure, disguise
veiled *adj* = **disguised**, covert, implied, masked, concealed, hinted at, suppressed
vein *n* **1** = **blood vessel** **2** = **seam**, current, course, streak, stripe, stratum, lode **3** = **mood**, note, style, tone, tenor, mode, temper
velocity *n* = **speed**, pace, quickness, rapidity, swiftness
velvety *adj* = **soft**, smooth, delicate, downy
vendetta *n* = **feud**, quarrel, bad blood
veneer *n* = **mask**, show, front, appearance, guise, pretense, semblance, façade
venerable *adj* = **respected**, wise, sage, august, esteemed, honoured, revered, worshipped
venerate *v* = **respect**, honour, revere, worship, adore, esteem, reverence, look up to
venerated *See* **holy**
vengeance *n* = **revenge**, reprisal, retaliation, retribution

DICTIONARY

venial [**veen**-ee-al] *adj* (of a sin or fault) easily forgiven **veniality** *n*
venison *n* deer meat
Venizélos *n* **Eleuthérios**. 1864–1936, Greek statesman, who greatly extended Greek territory: prime minister (1910–15; 1917–20; 1924; 1928–32; 1933)
venom Ⓣ *n* **1** poison produced by snakes etc. **2** malice or spite **venomous** *adj*
venous [**vee**-nuss] *adj anat* of veins
vent[1] Ⓣ *n* **1** outlet releasing fumes or fluid ▷ *v* **2** express (an emotion) freely
vent[2] *n* vertical slit in a jacket
ventilate *v* **1** let fresh air into **2** discuss (a complaint) openly **ventilation** *n* **ventilator** *n*
ventral *adj* relating to the front of the body
ventricle *n anat* one of the four cavities of the heart or brain
ventriloquist *n* entertainer who can speak without moving his or her lips, so that a voice seems to come from elsewhere **ventriloquism** *n*
venture Ⓣ *n* **1** risky undertaking, esp. in business ▷ *v* **2** do something risky **3** dare to express (an opinion) **4** go to an unknown place **venturesome** *adj*
▸ **venture capitalist** provider of capital for new commercial enterprises **venture capital**
Venturi *n* **Robert**. born 1925, US architect, a pioneer of the postmodernist style. His writings include *Complexity and Contradiction in Architecture* (1966)
venue *n* place where an organized gathering is held
Venus *n* **1** planet second nearest to the sun **2** Roman goddess of love
▸ **Venus's flytrap** *or* **Venus flytrap** plant that traps and digests insects between hinged leaves
veracious *adj* habitually truthful **veracity** *n*
veranda, verandah *n* open porch attached to a house
verb *n* word that expresses the idea of action, happening, or being
▸ **verbal** *adj* **1** spoken **2** of a verb **verbally** *adv*
▸ **verbalize** *v* express (something) in words
verbatim Ⓣ [verb-**bait**-im] *adv, adj* word for word
verbena *n* plant with sweet-smelling flowers
verbiage *n* excessive use of words
verbose Ⓣ [verb-**bohss**] *adj* long-winded **verbosity** *n*
Vercingetorix *n* died ?45 BC, Gallic chieftain and hero, executed for leading a revolt against the Romans under Julius Caesar (52 BC)
verdant Ⓣ *adj lit* covered in green vegetation
Verdi *n* **Giuseppe**. 1813–1901, Italian composer of operas, esp. *Rigoletto* (1851), *Il Trovatore* (1853), *La Traviata* (1853), and *Aïda* (1871)
verdict Ⓣ *n* **1** decision of a jury **2** opinion formed after examining the facts
verdigris [**ver**-dig-riss] *n* green film on copper, brass, or bronze
verdure *n lit* flourishing green vegetation
verge Ⓣ *n Brit* grass border along a road
▸ **on the verge of** having almost reached (a point or condition)
▸ **verge on** *v* be near to (a condition)
verger *n Anglican church* church caretaker
verify Ⓣ *v* **-ifying, -ified** check the truth or accuracy of **verifiable** *adj* **verification** *n*

THESAURUS

venom *n* **1 = malice**, hate, spite, bitterness, virulence, spleen, acrimony, rancour **2 = poison**, toxin, bane
venomous *adj* **1 = malicious**, hostile, vicious, savage, malignant, vindictive, rancorous, spiteful **2 = poisonous**, toxic, virulent, noxious, mephitic
vent *n* **1 = outlet**, opening, duct, aperture, orifice ▸ *v* **2 = express**, release, air, voice, discharge, emit, utter, give vent to, pour out
venture *n* **1 = undertaking**, risk, project, gamble, hazard, adventure, enterprise, endeavour ▸ *v* **2 = risk**, chance, stake, speculate, hazard, wager **3 = dare**, volunteer, hazard, presume, make bold, take the liberty **4 = go**, embark on, plunge into, set out
verbal *adj* **= spoken**, oral, word-of-mouth, unwritten
verbatim *adv* **= exactly**, precisely, to the letter, word for word
verbose *adj* **= long-winded**, windy, diffuse, circumlocutory, periphrastic, prolix, tautological, wordy
verbosity *n* **= long-windedness**, loquaciousness, prolixity, verboseness, wordiness
verdant *adj* **= green**, fresh, leafy, lush, grassy, flourishing
verdict *n* **= decision**, finding, opinion, conclusion, judgment • *The doctor's verdict is that I am fine.*
verge *n* **= border**, limit, edge, margin, brink, boundary, threshold, brim ▸ *verb* ▷ **verge on = come close to**, border, approach
verification *n* **= proof**, confirmation, validation, authentication, corroboration, substantiation
verified *See* **actual**
verify *v* **= confirm**, support, check, prove, authenticate, validate, substantiate, corroborate, bear out

V

DICTIONARY

Verigin *n* **Peter Vasilevich**. 1859–1924, Russian religious leader. After exile to Siberia he followed other members of the Doukhobor Christian sect to Canada and established a community in British Columbia
verily *adv obsolete* in truth
verisimilitude *n* appearance of being real
veritable *adj* rightly called, without exaggeration: *a veritable feast* **veritably** *adv*
verity *n, pl* **-ties** true statement or principle
Verlaine *n* **Paul**. 1844–96, French poet. His verse includes *Poèmes saturniens* (1866), *Fêtes galantes* (1869) and *Romances sans paroles* (1874). He was closely associated with Rimbaud and was a precursor of the symbolists
Vermeer *n* **Jan**, full name *Jan van der Meer van Delft*. 1632–75, Dutch genre painter, noted esp. for his masterly treatment of light
vermicelli [ver-me-**chell**-ee] *n* **1** fine strands of pasta **2** tiny strands of chocolate
vermicide *n* substance for killing worms
vermiform *adj* shaped like a worm
▸ **vermiform appendix** *anat* same as **appendix**
vermilion *adj* orange-red
vermin *pl n* animals, esp. insects and rodents, that spread disease or cause damage **verminous** *adj*
vermouth [**ver**-muth] *n* wine flavoured with herbs
vernacular Ⓣ [ver-**nak**-yew-lar] *n* most widely spoken language of a particular people or place
vernal *adj* occurring in spring
Verne *n* **Jules**. 1828–1905, French writer, esp. of science fiction, such as *Twenty Thousand Leagues under the Sea* (1870) and *Around the World in Eighty Days* (1873)
vernier [**ver**-nee-er] *n* movable scale on a graduated measuring instrument for taking readings in fractions
veronica *n* plant with small flowers
verruca [ver-**roo**-ka] *n, pl* **-cae, -cas** wart, usu. on the foot
versatile Ⓣ *adj* having many skills or uses **versatility** *n*
verse *n* **1** group of lines in a song or poem **2** poetry as distinct from prose **3** subdivision of a book of the Bible
▸ **versed in** knowledgeable about
▸ **versify** *v* write in verse **versification** *n*
version Ⓣ *n* **1** form of something, such as a piece of writing, with some differences from other forms **2** account of an incident from a particular point of view
verso *n, pl* **-sos** **1** left-hand page of a book **2** back of a sheet of paper
versus Ⓣ *prep* **1** *sports, law* against **2** in contrast with
vertebra [**ver**-tib-ra] *n, pl* **vertebrae** [**ver**-tib-ree] one of the bones that form the spine **vertebral** *adj*
▸ **vertebrate** *n, adj* (animal) having a spine
vertex *n math* **1** point on a geometric figure where the sides form an angle **2** highest point of a triangle
vertical Ⓣ *adj* **1** straight up and down ▹ *n* **2** vertical direction
vertigo Ⓣ *n* dizziness when looking down from a high place **vertiginous** *adj*
vervain *n* plant with spikes of blue, purple, or white flowers
verve Ⓣ *n* enthusiasm or liveliness
Verwoerd *n* **Hendrik Frensch**. 1901–66, South African statesman, born in the Netherlands: prime minister of South Africa (1958–66) and the principal architect of the apartheid system: assassinated
very Ⓣ *adv* **1** more than usually, extremely ▹ *adj* **2** absolute, exact: *the very top; the very man*
Vesalius *n* **Andreas**. 1514–64, Flemish anatomist, whose *De Humani Corporis fabrica* (1543) formed the basis of modern anatomical research and medicine
vesicle *n biol* sac or small cavity, esp. one containing fluid
Vespasian *n* Latin name *Titus Flavius Sabinus Vespasianus*. 9–79 AD, Roman emperor (69–79), who consolidated Roman rule, esp. in Britain and Germany. He began the building of the Colosseum
vespers *pl n RC Church* (service of) evening prayer
vessel Ⓣ *n* **1** ship **2** *lit* container for

THESAURUS

vernacular *n* = **speech**, dialect, parlance, idiom, patois
versatile *adj* = **adaptable**, flexible, all-purpose, all-around, variable, adjustable, multifaceted, resourceful
versed *adj* = **knowledgeable**, familiar, experienced, seasoned, proficient, acquainted, conversant, practised, well informed
version *n* **1** = **form**, design, model, style, variant **2** = **account**, portrayal, adaptation, interpretation, rendering
versus *See* **against**
vertical *adj* = **upright**, erect, on end, perpendicular
vertigo *n* = **dizziness**, giddiness, light-headedness
verve *n* = **enthusiasm**, energy, spirit, animation, sparkle, vitality, gusto, liveliness
very *adv* **1** = **extremely**, really, highly, deeply, greatly, terribly • *very bad dreams*
▹ **very much** *See* **far** ▸ *adj* **2** = **exact**, precise, selfsame
vessel *n* **1** = **ship**, boat, craft **2** = **container**,

DICTIONARY

liquid **3** *biol* tubular structure in animals and plants that carries body fluids, such as blood or sap
vest Ⓣ *n* **1** sleeveless garment worn under a jacket or coat **2** *Brit* undershirt ▷ *v* **3** (foll. by *in* or *with*) give (authority) to (someone)
▸ **vested interest** interest someone has in a matter because he or she might benefit from it
▸ **vest-pocket** *adj* small enough to fit into a vest pocket
vestal *adj* pure, chaste
▸ **vestal virgin** (in ancient Rome) one of the virgin priestesses whose lives were dedicated to Vesta and to maintaining the sacred fire in her temple
vestibule Ⓣ *n* entrance hall
vestige Ⓣ [**vest**-ij] *n* small amount or trace
vestigial [vest-**ij**-ee-al] *adj*
vestments *pl n* priest's robes
vestry *n, pl* **-tries** room in a church used as an office by the priest or minister
vet[1] Ⓣ *n* **1** short for **veterinarian** ▷ *v* **vetting, vetted 2** check the suitability of (a candidate)
vet[2] *n* military veteran
vetch *n* climbing plant with a beanlike fruit used as fodder
veteran Ⓣ *n* **1** person with long experience in a particular activity, esp. military service ▷ *adj* **2** long-serving
veterinarian *n* medical specialist who treats sick animals
▸ **veterinary** *adj* concerning animal health
veterinary surgeon *n Brit* **veterinarian**
veto Ⓣ [**vee**-toe] *n, pl* **-toes 1** official power to cancel a proposal ▷ *v* **-toing, -toed 2** enforce a veto against
vex Ⓣ *v* frustrate, annoy **vexatious** *adj*
▸ **vexation** *n* **1** something annoying **2** being annoyed
▸ **vexed question** much debated subject
VHF *radio* very high frequency
VHS ® Video Home System: format for recording on video
via *prep* by way of
viable Ⓣ *adj* **1** able to be put into practice **2** *biol* able to live and grow independently
viability *n*
viaduct *n* bridge over a valley
Viagra [vie-**ag**-ra] *n* ® drug used to treat impotence in men
vial *n* same as **phial**
viands *pl n obsolete* food
vibes *pl n informal* **1** emotional reactions between people, atmosphere of a place **2** short for **vibraphone**
vibrant Ⓣ [**vibe**-rant] *adj* **1** vigorous in appearance, energetic **2** (of a voice) resonant **3** (of a colour) strong and bright
vibraphone *n* musical instrument with metal bars that resonate electronically when hit
vibrate Ⓣ *v* **1** move back and forth rapidly **2** (cause to) resonate **vibration** *n*
▸ **vibrator** *n* device that produces vibratory motion, used for massage or as a sex aid
vibratory *adj*
vibrato *n music* rapid fluctuation in the pitch of a note
vicar *n Anglican church* member of the clergy in charge of a parish
▸ **vicarage** *n* vicar's house
vicarious Ⓣ [vick-**air**-ee-uss] *adj* **1** felt indirectly by imagining what another person experiences **2** delegated **vicariously** *adv*
Vicar of Bray *n* **1** a vicar (Simon Aleyn) appointed to the parish of Bray in Berkshire during Henry VIII's reign who changed his faith to Catholic when Mary I was on the throne and back to Protestant when

THESAURUS

pot, utensil, receptacle
vest *v* (with *in* or *with*) = **place**, settle, invest, bestow, confer, entrust, endow, consign
vestibule *n* = **hall**, lobby, porch, foyer, anteroom, portico
vestige *n* = **trace**, suspicion, scrap, indication, remnant, glimmer
vestiges *See* **remains**
vet *v* = **check**, review, investigate, examine, scrutinize, appraise
veteran *n* **1** = **old hand**, old stager, past master, warhorse (*informal*) ▸ *adj* **2** = **long-serving**, old, seasoned, battle-scarred
veto *v* **1** = **ban**, prohibit, forbid • *They vetoed our plans for a party.* ▸ *n* **2** = **ban**, prohibition • *The five permanent members of the UN Security Council have the power of veto.*
vex *v* = **annoy**, worry, trouble, upset, plague, bother, distress, irritate, exasperate
vexation *n* **1** = **annoyance**, frustration, pique, displeasure, dissatisfaction, irritation, chagrin, exasperation **2** = **problem**, worry, trouble, difficulty, bother, headache (*informal*), hassle (*informal*), nuisance
viable *adj* = **workable**, feasible, applicable, usable, operable, practicable
vibrant *adj* = **energetic**, alive, animated, dynamic, sparkling, vigorous, spirited, vivid, vivacious
vibrate *v* = **shake**, fluctuate, sway, reverberate, tremble, shudder, throb, quiver, pulsate, oscillate
vibration *n* = **shaking**, shake, tremor, shudder, quiver, oscillation, pulsation, reverberation, throbbing, trembling
vicarious *adj* = **indirect**, surrogate, delegated, substituted

V

DICTIONARY

Elizabeth I succeeded and so retained his living **2** a person who changes his or her views or allegiances in accordance with what is suitable at the time
vice[1] Ⓣ *n* **1** immoral personal quality **2** minor imperfection in someone's character **3** criminal activities, esp. involving sex
vice[2] *n* tool with a screw mechanism for holding an object while working on it
vice[3] *adj* serving in place of
vice chancellor *n* chief executive of a university
vicegerent *n* **1** person appointed to exercise all or some of the authority of another ▷ *adj* **2** invested with or characterized by delegated authority **vicegerency** *n*
vice president *n* officer ranking immediately below the president and serving as his deputy **vice-presidency** *n*
viceroy *n* governor of a colony who represents the monarch **viceregal** *adj*
vice versa Ⓣ [**vie**-see **ver**-sa] *adv Latin* conversely, the other way round
Vichy water [**vee**-shee] *n* mineral water from Vichy in France, reputed to be beneficial to health
vicinity Ⓣ [viss-**in**-it-ee] *n* surrounding area
vicious Ⓣ *adj* cruel and violent **viciously** *adv*
▸ **vicious circle** sequence of problems and solutions which always leads back to the original problem
vicissitudes [viss-**iss**-it-yewds] *pl n* changes in fortune
Vickers *n* **Jon(athan Stewart)**. born 1926, Canadian tenor; noted for his interpretations of Wagner, Verdi, and Britten
victim Ⓣ *n* **1** person or thing harmed or killed **2** person or animal killed as a sacrifice
▸ **victimize** *v* **1** punish unfairly **2** discriminate against **victimization** *n*
victor Ⓣ *n* person who has defeated an opponent, esp. in war or in sport **victorious** *adj*
▸ **victory** *n* winning of a battle or contest
Victor Emmanuel II *n* 1820–78, king of Sardinia-Piedmont (1849–78) and first king of Italy from 1861
Victor Emmanuel III *n* 1869–1947, last king of Italy (1900–46): dominated after 1922 by Mussolini, whom he appointed as premier; abdicated
victoria *n* large sweet plum, red and yellow in colour
Victoria *n* **1** 1819–1901, queen of the United Kingdom (1837–1901) and empress of India (1876–1901). She married Prince Albert of Saxe-Coburg-Gotha (1840). Her sense of vocation did much to restore the prestige of the British monarchy **2 Tomás Luis de**. ?1548–1611, Spanish composer of motets and masses in the polyphonic style
Victoria Cross *n Brit* highest award for bravery
Victorian *adj* **1** of or in the reign of Queen Victoria **2** characterized by prudery or hypocrisy ▷ *n* **3** person who lived during Victoria's reign
victuals [**vit**-als] *pl n old-fashioned* food
victualler *n*
▸ **victual** *v* **victualling, victualled** supply with or obtain victuals
vicuña [vik-**koo**-nya] *n* **1** S American animal like the llama **2** fine cloth made from its wool
Vidal *n* **Gore**. born 1925, US novelist and essayist. His novels include *Julian* (1964), *Myra Breckinridge* (1968), *Burr* (1974), *Lincoln* (1984), and *The Season of Conflict* (1996)
vide [**vie**-dee] *Latin* see
videlicet [vid-**deal**-ee-set] *adv Latin* namely
video *n* **1** short for **video cassette (recorder)** ▷ *v* **videoing, videoed 2** record (a TV programme or event) on video ▷ *adj* **3** relating to or used in producing television images
▸ **video cassette** cassette containing video tape
▸ **video cassette recorder** tape recorder for recording and playing back TV programmes and films
▸ **video tape 1** magnetic tape used to record video-frequency signals in TV production

THESAURUS

vice *n* **1 = wickedness**, corruption, evil, sin, immorality, depravity, iniquity, turpitude **2 = fault**, weakness, defect, shortcoming, blemish, failing, imperfection
vice versa *adv* **= the other way round**, conversely, contrariwise, in reverse
vicinity *n* **= neighbourhood**, area, district, proximity, locality, environs, neck of the woods (*informal*)
vicious *adj* **1 = savage**, violent, cruel, ferocious, wicked, barbarous **2 = malicious**, mean, cruel, venomous, vindictive, spiteful
viciousness *See* **cruelty**
victim *n* **= casualty**, sacrifice, fatality, sufferer, martyr, scapegoat
victimize *v* **= persecute**, discriminate against, pick on
victor *n* **= winner**, champion, conqueror, prizewinner, vanquisher
victorious *adj* **= winning**, first, champion, successful, triumphant, conquering, prizewinning, vanquishing
victory *n* **= win**, success, triumph, superiority, laurels • *the Canadiens' fourth consecutive victory* OPPOSITE: defeat

DICTIONARY

2 magnetic tape used to record programmes when they are broadcast
▸ **videotape** *v* record (a TV programme) on video tape
▸ **video tape recorder** tape recorder for vision signals, used in TV production
▸ **videotext** *n* means of representing on a TV screen information that is held in a computer
vie Ⓣ *v* **vying, vied** compete (with someone)
Vietnamese *adj* **1** of Vietnam ▷ *n* **2** *pl* **-ese** native of Vietnam **3** language of Vietnam
view Ⓣ *n* **1** opinion **2** everything that can be seen from a given place **3** picture of this ▷ *v* **4** think of (something) in a particular way
▸ **in view of** taking into consideration
▸ **on view** exhibited to the public
▸ **viewer** *n* **1** person who watches television **2** hand-held device for looking at photographic slides
▸ **viewfinder** *n* window on a camera showing what will appear in a photograph
vigil [**vij**-ill] *n* night-time period of staying awake to look after a sick person, pray, etc.
▸ **vigilant** *adj* watchful in case of danger **vigilance** *n*
vigilante [vij-ill-**ant**-ee] *n* person, esp. as one of a group, who takes it upon himself or herself to enforce the law
Vigneault *n* **Gilles**. born 1928, Canadian songwriter, singer, and poet. A Quebec nationalist, his song "Mon Pays" ("My Country") (1964) is an unofficial Québécois anthem
vignette [vin-**yet**] *n* **1** concise description of the typical features of something **2** small decorative illustration in a book
Vignola *n* **Giacomo Barozzi da**. 1507–73, Italian architect, whose cruciform design for Il Gesù, Rome, greatly influenced later Church architecture
vigour Ⓣ *n* physical or mental energy **vigorous** *adj* **vigorously** *adv*
Viking *n hist* seafaring raider and settler from Scandinavia
vile Ⓣ *adj* **1** very wicked **2** disgusting **vilely** *adv* **vileness** *n*
vilify Ⓣ [**vill**-if-fie] *v* **-ifying, -ified** unjustly attack the character of **vilification** *n*
villa *n* **1** large house with gardens **2** house rented to holiday-makers
Villa *n* **Francisco**, called *Pancho Villa*, original name *Doroteo Arango*. ?1877–1923, Mexican revolutionary leader
village *n* **1** small group of houses in a country area **2** rural community **villager** *n*
villain Ⓣ *n* **1** wicked person **2** main wicked character in a play **villainous** *adj* **villainy** *n*
Villa-Lobos *n* **Heitor**. 1887–1959, Brazilian composer, much of whose work is based on Brazilian folk tunes
villein [**vill**-an] *n hist* peasant bound in service to his lord
Villeneuve *n* **1** **Gilles**. 1950–82, Canadian racing driver **2** his son, **Jacques**. born 1971, Canadian racing driver: Formula One World Champion 1997
vim *n informal* force, energy
vinaigrette *n* salad dressing of oil and vinegar
Vincent de Paul *n* **Saint**. ?1581–1660, French Roman Catholic priest, who founded two charitable orders, the Lazarists (1625)

THESAURUS

vie *v* = **compete**, struggle, contend, strive
view *n* **1** = **opinion**, conviction, feeling, belief, attitude, point of view • *his political views* **2** = **scene**, perspective, aspect, landscape, spectacle, panorama • *There was a beautiful view from the window.* **3** = **vision**, sight ▸ *v* **4** = **regard**, consider, judge, deem • *They viewed me with contempt.*
See also: **idea, judgment, observe, outlook, scenery, thought, watch**
viewer *n* = **watcher**, observer, spectator, onlooker
viewpoint *n* = **point of view**, opinion, conviction, feeling, belief, attitude • *We all have our own personal viewpoints.*
vigilance *n* = **watchfulness**, caution, observance, alertness, attentiveness, carefulness, circumspection
vigilant *adj* = **watchful**, alert, careful, cautious, attentive, circumspect, on one's guard, on the lookout, wakeful
vigorous *adj* = **energetic**, strong, powerful, active, dynamic, spirited, lively, forceful, strenuous, lusty
vigorously *adv* = **energetically**, hard, strongly, forcefully, strenuously, lustily
vigour *n* = **energy**, power, strength, spirit, animation, vitality, dynamism, gusto, verve, liveliness, forcefulness
See also: **drive**
vile *adj* **1** = **wicked**, evil, corrupt, degenerate, nefarious, perverted, depraved **2** = **disgusting**, offensive, foul, nasty, sickening, horrid, repulsive, repugnant, revolting, nauseating, scuzzy (*slang*)
vilify *v* = **malign**, abuse, smear, berate, disparage, slander, denigrate, revile
villain *n* **1** = **evildoer**, criminal, rogue, miscreant, reprobate, scoundrel, wretch **2** = **bad guy** (*informal*), antihero
villainous *adj* = **wicked**, bad, evil, vicious, cruel, degenerate, vile, nefarious, depraved, fiendish
villainy *n* = **wickedness**, vice, delinquency, depravity, devilry, iniquity, turpitude

DICTIONARY

and the Sisters of Charity (1634). Feast day: Sept 27
vindicate Ⓣ *v* **1** clear (someone) of guilt **2** justify (someone) whose behaviour has been challenged **vindication** *n*
vindictive Ⓣ *adj* maliciously seeking revenge **vindictiveness** *n* **vindictively** *adv*
vine *n* climbing plant, esp. one producing grapes
▸ **vineyard** [**vinn**-yard] *n* plantation of grape vines, esp. for making wine
vinegar *n* acid liquid made from wine, beer, or cider **vinegary** *adj*
viniculture *n* process or business of growing grapes and making wine
vino [**vee**-noh] *n informal* wine
vintage Ⓣ *n* **1** wine from a particular harvest of grapes ▹ *adj* **2** best and most typical
▸ **vintage car** high-quality antique car
vintner *n* dealer in wine
vinyl [**vine**-ill] *n* type of plastic used in mock leather and records
viol [**vie**-oll] *n* early stringed instrument preceding the violin
viola[1] [vee-**oh**-la] *n* stringed instrument lower in pitch than a violin
viola[2] [**vie**-ol-la] *n* variety of pansy
violate Ⓣ *v* **1** break (a law or agreement) **2** disturb (someone's privacy) **3** treat (a sacred place) disrespectfully **4** rape
violation *n* **violator** *n*
violent Ⓣ *adj* **1** using or marked by physical strength that is harmful or destructive **2** aggressively intense **3** using excessive force
violence *n* **violently** *adv*
violet *n* **1** plant with bluish-purple flowers ▹ *adj* **2** bluish-purple
violin *n* small four-stringed musical instrument played with a bow **violinist** *n*
violoncello [vie-oll-on-**chell**-oh] *n, pl* **-los** same as **cello**
V.I.P Ⓣ very important person
viper *n* poisonous snake
virago [vir-**rah**-go] *n, pl* **-goes, -gos** aggressive woman
viral [**vie**-ral] *adj* of or caused by a virus
Virchow *n* **Rudolf Ludwig Karl**. 1821–1902, German pathologist, who is considered the founder of modern (cellular) pathology
Viren *n* **Lasse**. born 1949, Finnish distance runner: winner of the 5000 metres and the 10 000 metres in the 1972 and 1976 Olympic Games
Virgil, Vergil *n* Latin name *Publius Vergilius Maro*. 70–19 BC, Roman poet, patronized by Maecenas. The *Eclogues* (42–37), ten pastoral poems, and the *Georgics* (37–30), four books on the art of farming, established Virgil as the foremost poet of his age. His masterpiece is the *Aeneid* (30–19)
virgin Ⓣ *n* **1** person, esp. a woman, who has not had sexual intercourse ▹ *adj* **2** not having had sexual intercourse **3** not yet exploited or explored **virginity** *n*
▸ **virginal** *adj* **1** like a virgin ▹ *n* **2** rectangular keyboard instrument like a small harpsichord
virile Ⓣ *adj* having the traditional male characteristics of physical strength and a high sex drive **virility** *n*
virology *n* study of viruses

THESAURUS

vindicate *v* **1 = clear**, acquit, exonerate, rehabilitate, absolve, exculpate **2 = justify**, defend, excuse
vindication *n*
1 = exoneration, rehabilitation, exculpation **2 = justification**, excuse, defence
vindictive *adj* **= vengeful**, malicious, unrelenting, resentful, implacable, revengeful, spiteful, unforgiving
vintage *adj* **= high-quality**, prime, choice, select, classic, superior, best
violate *v* **1 = break**, infringe, disregard, contravene, disobey, encroach upon, transgress **2 = desecrate**, abuse, pollute, profane, defile, dishonour, befoul **3 = rape**, abuse, assault, debauch, ravish
violated *See* **broken**
violation *n* **1 = breach**, abuse, infringement, infraction, trespass, transgression, encroachment, contravention **2 = desecration**, defilement, profanation, sacrilege, spoliation
violence *n* **1 = brutality**, force, terrorism, bloodshed, cruelty, savagery • *Twenty people were injured in the violence.* **2 = intensity**, force, severity, fervour, harshness, vehemence • *She gestured with sudden violence.*
violent *adj* **1 = brutal**, vicious, cruel, murderous, savage, bloodthirsty • *violent criminals* OPPOSITE: gentle **2 = powerful**, strong, wild, rough, turbulent, raging • *violent storms* **3 = intense**, strong, powerful, severe, acute, furious • *the violent reaction to his plans*
See also: **rude**
V.I.P. *n* **= celebrity**, star, somebody, luminary, big name, muckymuck
virgin *n* **1 = maiden**, girl ▸ *adj* **2 = pure**, immaculate, chaste, uncorrupted, undefiled, vestal, virginal
virginal *See* **innocent**
virginity *n* **= chastity**, maidenhood
virile *adj* **= manly**, strong, vigorous, macho, masculine, lusty, manlike, red-blooded
virility *n* **= masculinity**, manhood, vigour, machismo

DICTIONARY

virtual ⓣ *adj* **1** having the effect but not the form of **2** of or relating to virtual reality
▸ **virtual reality** computer-generated environment that seems real to the user
▸ **virtually** *adv* practically, almost
virtue ⓣ *n* **1** moral goodness **2** positive moral quality **3** merit
▸ **by virtue of** by reason of
▸ **virtuous** *adj* morally good **virtuously** *adv*
virtuoso ⓣ *n, pl* **-sos, -si** person with impressive musical skill **virtuosity** *n*
virulent ⓣ [**vir**-yew-lent] *adj* **1** extremely hostile **2** very infectious **3** violently harmful
virus *n* **1** microorganism that causes disease in animals and plants **2** *computers* program that propagates itself, via disks and electronic networks, to cause disruption
visa *n* permission to enter a country, granted by its government and shown by a stamp on one's passport
visage [**viz**-zij] *n lit* face
vis-à-vis [veez-ah-**vee**] *prep* in relation to, regarding
viscera [**viss**-er-a] *pl n* large abdominal organs
▸ **visceral** *adj* **1** instinctive **2** of or relating to the viscera
viscid [**viss**-id] *adj* sticky **viscidity** *n*
Visconti *n* **1** the ruling family of Milan from 1277 to 1447 **2 Luchino**, real name *Luchino Visconti de Modrone*. 1906–76, Italian stage and film director, whose neorealist films include *Ossessione* (1942). His other films include *The Leopard* (1963), *Death in Venice* (1970), and *The Innocents* (1976)
viscose *n* synthetic fabric made from cellulose
viscount [**vie**-count] *n* British nobleman ranking between an earl and a baron
viscountcy *n*
viscountess [**vie**-count-iss] *n* **1** wife or widow of a viscount **2** woman holding the rank of viscount in her own right
viscous ⓣ *adj* thick and sticky **viscosity** *n*
visible ⓣ *adj* **1** able to be seen **2** able to be perceived by the mind. **visibly** *adv*
▸ **visibility** *n* range or clarity of vision
vision ⓣ *n* **1** ability to see **2** mental image of something **3** hallucination **4** foresight
▸ **visionary** *adj* **1** showing foresight **2** idealistic but impractical ▹ *n, pl* **-aries** **3** visionary person
visit ⓣ *v* **-iting, -ited** **1** go or come to see **2** stay temporarily with **3** (foll. by *upon*) *lit* afflict ▹ *n* **4** instance of visiting **5** official call **visitor** *n*
▸ **visitation** *n* **1** formal visit or inspection **2** catastrophe seen as divine punishment
visor [**vize**-or] *n* **1** part of a helmet that moves up and down over the face **2** eyeshade, esp. in an automobile **3** peak on a cap
vista ⓣ *n* (beautiful) extensive view

THESAURUS

virtual *adj* = **practical**, essential, in all but name
virtually *adv* = **practically**, nearly, almost, as good as, in all but name, in effect, in essence
virtue *n* **1** = **goodness**, integrity, morality • *a paragon of virtue* **2** = **merit**, advantage, asset, strength, plus, attribute • *the virtue of neatness* ▹ **by virtue of** = **because of**, as a result of, by dint of, on account of, thanks to • *The article stuck in my mind by virtue of one detail.*
See also: **right, value**
virtuosity *n* = **mastery**, skill, craft, expertise, polish, flair, brilliance, panache
virtuoso *n* = **master**, artist, genius, maestro, magician
virtuous *adj* = **good**, moral, ethical, worthy, upright, honourable, righteous, incorruptible, praiseworthy
virulent *adj* = **deadly**, toxic, lethal, poisonous, venomous, pernicious
viscous *adj* = **thick**, sticky, gelatinous, syrupy
visibility *See* **sight**
visible *adj* **1** = **perceptible**, clear, conspicuous, distinguishable, in sight, observable • *The warning lights were clearly visible.* OPPOSITE: invisible **2** = **obvious**, apparent, plain, evident, noticeable, manifest • *There was little visible excitement.*
vision *n* **1** = **image**, dream, ideal, fantasy, conception, daydream • *my vision of the future* **2** = **foresight**, insight, imagination, intuition • *a total lack of vision and imagination* **3** = **hallucination**, illusion, spectre, phantom, mirage, apparition • *She was convinced her visions were real.* **4** = **sight**, view, perception, eyesight, seeing
visionary *adj* **1** = **prophetic**, mystical **2** = **idealistic**, romantic, speculative, unrealistic, impractical, unworkable, utopian, quixotic, starry-eyed ▸ *n* **3** = **prophet**, mystic, seer
visit *v* **1** = **call on**, go to see, look up, swing by (*informal*) • *He wanted to visit his brother in California.* ▸ *n* **2** = **call**, stop, stay • *They had recently paid him a visit.*
See also: **frequent**
visitation *n* **1** = **inspection**, visit, examination **2** = **catastrophe**, disaster, punishment, ordeal, scourge, calamity, blight, cataclysm
visitor *n* = **guest**, company, caller
vista *n* = **view**, prospect, perspective, panorama

DICTIONARY

visual Ⓣ *adj* **1** done by or used in seeing **2** designed to be looked at
▸ **visualize** *v* form a mental image of **visualization** *n*
▸ **visual display unit** device with a screen for displaying data held in a computer
vital Ⓣ *adj* **1** essential or highly important **2** lively **3** necessary to maintain life **vitally** *adv*
▸ **vitals** *pl n* body organs
▸ **vitality** *n* physical or mental energy
▸ **vital statistics 1** statistics of births, deaths, and marriages **2** *informal* woman's bust, waist, and hip measurements
vitamin *n* one of a group of substances that are essential in the diet for specific body processes
vitiate [**vish**-ee-ate] *v* spoil the effectiveness of **vitiation** *n*
viticulture *n* cultivation of grape vines
vitreous *adj* like or made from glass
▸ **vitreous humour** gelatinous substance that fills the eyeball
vitrify *v* **-ifying, -ified** change or be changed into glass or a glassy substance **vitrification** *n*
vitriol *n* **1** language expressing bitterness and hatred **2** sulfuric acid **vitriolic** *adj*
Vitruvius Pollio *n* **Marcus**. 1st century BC, Roman architect, noted for his treatise *De architectura*, the only surviving Roman work on architectural theory and a major influence on Renaissance architects
vituperative [vite-**tyew**-pra-tiv] *adj* bitterly abusive **vituperation** *n*
viva[1] *interj* long live (a person or thing)
viva[2] *n* examination in the form of an interview
vivace [viv-**vah**-chee] *adv music* in a lively manner
vivacious Ⓣ *adj* full of energy and enthusiasm **vivacity** *n*
Vivaldi *n* **Antonio**. ?1675–1741, Italian composer and violinist, noted esp. for his development of the solo concerto. His best-known work is *The Four Seasons* (1725)
vivarium *n, pl* **-iums, -ia** place where animals are kept in natural conditions
viva voce [**vive**-a **voh**-chee] *adv* **1** in spoken words ▹ *n* **2** same as **viva**[2]
vivid Ⓣ *adj* **1** very bright **2** conveying images that are true to life **vividly** *adv* **vividness** *n*
viviparous [viv-**vip**-a-russ] *adj* producing live offspring
vivisection *n* performing surgical experiments on living animals **vivisectionist** *n*
vixen *n* **1** female fox **2** *informal* spiteful woman **vixenish** *adj*
viz. (introducing specified items) namely
vizier [viz-**zeer**] *n* (formerly) Muslim high official
vizor *n* same as **visor**
Vladimir *n* **Saint**, called *the Great*. ?956–1015, grand prince of Kiev (980–1015); first Christian ruler of Russia. Feast day: July 15
VLF *radio* very low frequency
V neck *n* neck on a garment shaped like the letter 'V' **V-neck** *or* **V-necked** *adj*
vocabulary Ⓣ *n, pl* **-aries 1** all the words that a person knows **2** all the words in a language **3** specialist terms used in a given subject **4** list of words in another language with their translation
vocal Ⓣ *adj* **1** relating to the voice **2** outspoken **vocally** *adv*
▸ **vocals** *pl n* singing part of a piece of pop music
▸ **vocalist** *n* singer
▸ **vocalize** *v* express with or use the voice **vocalization** *n*
▸ **vocal cords** membranes in the larynx

THESAURUS

visual *adj* **1 = optical**, optic, ocular **2 = observable**, visible, discernible, perceptible
visualize *v* **= picture**, imagine, envisage, conceive of
vital *adj* **1 = important**, central, critical, necessary, crucial, essential, pivotal, indispensable • *a blockade that cut off vital fuel supplies* **2 = lively**, active, energetic, dynamic, spirited, vivacious, sprightly • *My grandparents remained active and vital.* **3 = essential**, necessary, basic, fundamental, imperative, indispensable, requisite
vitality *n* **= energy**, life, strength, animation, exuberance, vigour, liveliness, vivacity
vitriolic *adj* **= bitter**, scathing, virulent, venomous, caustic, acerbic, sardonic, envenomed, withering
vivacious *adj* **= lively**, vital, upbeat (*informal*), sparkling, spirited, ebullient, bubbling, high-spirited, sprightly
vivacity *n* **= liveliness**, energy, spirit, animation, sparkle, ebullience, gaiety, high spirits, sprightliness
vivid *adj* **1 = bright**, clear, rich, intense, brilliant, colourful, glowing **2 = lifelike**, powerful, dramatic, realistic, graphic, memorable, stirring, telling, true to life
vocabulary *n* **1 = language**, words **2 = wordbook**, dictionary, glossary, lexicon
vocal *adj* **1 = spoken**, oral, said, uttered, voiced **2 = outspoken**, frank, articulate, strident, expressive, eloquent, vociferous, forthright, plain-spoken

DICTIONARY

that vibrate to produce sound
vocalic *adj* of a vowel or vowels
vocation ⓣ *n* **1** occupation that someone feels called to **2** profession or trade
▸ **vocational** *adj* directed towards a particular profession or trade
vocative *n* (in some languages) case of nouns used in addressing a person
vociferate *v* exclaim, cry out **vociferation** *n*
vociferous ⓣ *adj* characterized by noisy shouting
vodka *n* (Russian) spirit distilled from potatoes or grain
vogue ⓣ *n* **1** popular style **2** period of popularity
voice ⓣ *n* **1** (quality of) sound made when speaking or singing **2** expression of opinion by a person or group **3** property of verbs that makes them active or passive ▷ *v* **4** express verbally **voiceless** *adj*
▸ **voice mail** electronic system for the storage of telephone messages
▸ **voice-over** *n* film commentary spoken by someone off-camera
void ⓣ *n* **1** lonely feeling **2** empty space ▷ *adj* **3** not legally binding **4** empty ▷ *v* **5** make invalid **6** empty
voile [**voyl**] *n* light semitransparent fabric
vol. volume
volatile ⓣ [**voll**-a-tile] *adj* **1** liable to sudden change, esp. in behaviour **2** evaporating quickly **volatility** *n*
vol-au-vent [**voll**-oh-von] *n* small puff-pastry case with a savoury filling
volcano *n, pl* **-noes, -nos** mountain with a vent through which lava is ejected **volcanic** *adj*
vole *n* small rodent
volition ⓣ *n* faculty of exercising the will
▸ **of one's own volition** through one's own choice
volley ⓣ *n* **1** simultaneous discharge of ammunition **2** burst of questions or critical comments **3** *sports* stroke or kick at a moving ball before it hits the ground ▷ *v* **4** discharge (ammunition) in a volley **5** *sports* hit or kick (a ball) in a volley
▸ **volleyball** *n* team game where a ball is hit with the hands over a high net
volt *n* unit of electric potential
▸ **voltaic** *adj* same as **galvanic**
▸ **voltage** *n* electric potential difference expressed in volts
▸ **voltmeter** *n* instrument for measuring voltage
Volta *n* Count **Alessandro**. 1745–1827, Italian physicist after whom the volt is named. He made important contributions to the theory of current electricity and invented the voltaic pile (1800), the electrophorus (1775), and an electroscope
Voltaire *n* pseudonym of *François Marie Arouet*. 1694–1778, French writer, whose outspoken belief in religious, political, and social liberty made him the embodiment of the 18th-century Enlightenment. His major works include *Lettres philosophiques* (1734) and the satire *Candide* (1759). He also wrote plays, such as *Zaïre* (1732), poems, and scientific studies. He suffered several periods of banishment for his radical views **Voltairean** *or* **Voltairian** *adj, n*
volte-face [volt-**fass**] *n* reversal of opinion
voluble ⓣ *adj* talking easily and at length **volubility** *n* **volubly** *adv*
volume ⓣ *n* **1** size of the space occupied by something **2** amount **3** loudness of sound **4** control on a radio or TV for adjusting this **5** book, esp. one of a series
▸ **voluminous** *adj* **1** (of clothes) large and roomy **2** (of writings) extensive

THESAURUS

vocation *n* = **profession**, trade, job, career, mission, pursuit, calling
vociferous *adj* = **outspoken**, vocal, loud, noisy, strident, vehement, clamorous, uproarious
vogue *n* = **fashion**, way, trend, style, custom, mode, craze ▷ **in vogue** = **popular**, current, prevalent, chic, trendy, accepted, in favor, in use
voice *n* **1** = **sound**, tone, utterance, articulation **2** = **say**, will, vote, view, wish ▸ *v* **3** = **express**, air, declare, utter, articulate, enunciate
void *n* **1** = **emptiness**, space, lack, gap, vacuum, blankness, vacuity ▸ *adj* **2** = **invalid**, ineffective, useless, vain, worthless, inoperative, null and void **3** = **empty**, free, bare, vacant, unfilled, unoccupied, tenantless ▸ *v* **4** = **invalidate**, cancel, rescind, nullify **5** = **empty**, evacuate, drain
volatile *adj* **1** = **changeable**, explosive, unstable, variable, unsteady, unsettled, inconstant **2** = **temperamental**, erratic, fickle, mercurial, up and down (*informal*)
volition *n* = **free will**, will, choice, preference, discretion, choosing
volley *n* = **barrage**, blast, hail, burst, shower, salvo, bombardment, cannonade, fusillade
voluble *adj* = **talkative**, forthcoming, articulate, fluent, glib, loquacious
volume *n* **1** = **capacity**, compass, dimensions **2** = **amount**, body, total, mass, aggregate, bulk, quantity **3** = **book**, title, publication, tome, treatise
voluminous *adj* = **large**, vast, ample,

DICTIONARY

▸ **volumetric** *adj* relating to measurement by volume
voluntary Ⓣ *adj* **1** done by choice **2** done or maintained without payment **3** controlled by the will ▷ *n, pl* **-taries 4** organ solo in a church service **voluntarily** *adv*
volunteer Ⓣ *n* **1** person who offers voluntarily to do something, esp. military service ▷ *v* **2** offer one's services **3** offer the services of (another person) **4** give (information) willingly
voluptuous Ⓣ *adj* **1** (of a woman) sexually alluring through fullness of figure **2** sensually pleasurable
▸ **voluptuary** *n, pl* **-aries** person devoted to sensual pleasures
volute *n* spiral or twisting turn, form, or object
vomit Ⓣ *v* **-iting, -ited 1** eject (the contents of the stomach) through the mouth ▷ *n* **2** matter vomited
Vonnegut *n* **Kurt**. 1922–2007, US novelist. His works include *Cat's Cradle* (1963), *Slaughterhouse Five* (1969), *Galapagos* (1985), and *Hocus Pocus* (1990)
voodoo *n* religion involving ancestor worship and witchcraft
voracious Ⓣ *adj* **1** craving great quantities of food **2** insatiably eager **voraciously** *adv* **voracity** *n*
vortex Ⓣ *n, pl* **-texes, -tices 1** whirlpool **2** whirling motion
votary *n, pl* **-ries** person dedicated to religion or cause
vote Ⓣ *n* **1** choice made by a participant in a shared decision, esp. in electing a candidate **2** right to this choice **3** total number of votes cast **4** collective voting power of a given group: *the Black vote* ▷ *v* **5** make a choice by a vote **6** authorize (something) by vote **voter** *n*
votive *adj* done or given to fulfil a vow
vouch *v* **1** (foll. by *for*) give one's personal assurance about **2** (foll. by *for*) be proof of
▸ **voucher** *n* **1** ticket used instead of money to buy specified goods **2** record of a financial transaction, receipt
vouchsafe *v old-fashioned* **1** give, entrust **2** agree graciously
vow Ⓣ *n* **1** solemn promise, esp. to a god or saint ▷ *v* **2** promise solemnly
vowel *n* **1** speech sound made without obstructing the flow of breath **2** letter representing this
vox pop *n* interviews with members of the public on TV or radio
vox populi *n* public opinion
voyage Ⓣ *n* **1** long journey by sea or in space ▷ *v* **2** make a voyage **voyager** *n*
▸ **voyageur** [vwah-yah-**zher**] *n* guide or trapper in N regions
voyeur *n* person who derives pleasure from watching people undressing or having sex
VPL *jocular* visible panty line
VQA Vintners Quality Alliance: used of Canadian wines that meet certain strict requirements
vs versus
V-sign *n* **1** offensive gesture made by sticking up the index and middle fingers with the palm inwards **2** similar gesture, with the palm outwards, meaning victory or peace
VSOP very superior old pale
VTOL vertical takeoff and landing
VTR video tape recorder
vulcanize *v* strengthen (rubber) by treating it with sulfur **vulcanization** *n*
▸ **vulcanite** *n* vulcanized rubber
vulgar Ⓣ *adj* showing lack of good taste,

THESAURUS

cavernous, roomy, capacious
voluntarily *adv* = **willingly**, freely, by choice, off one's own bat, of one's own accord
voluntary *adj* = **unforced**, free, willing, optional, spontaneous, discretionary
volunteer *v* = **offer**, step forward
voluptuous *adj* **1** = **buxom**, ample, seductive, curvaceous (*informal*), enticing, shapely **2** = **sensual**, luxurious, hedonistic, self-indulgent, epicurean, licentious, sybaritic
vomit *v* = **be sick**, heave, puke (*informal*), bring up, regurgitate • *Any product made from milk made him vomit.*
voracious *adj* **1** = **gluttonous**, hungry, greedy, insatiable, ravenous, omnivorous **2** = **avid**, hungry, insatiable, uncontrolled, rapacious, unquenchable
vortex *n* = **whirlpool**, maelstrom, eddy
vote *n* **1** = **poll**, ballot, referendum, plebiscite • *Do you think we should have a vote on that?* ▸ *v* **2** = **cast a vote**, return, opt, go to the polls • *Many people will vote for the opposition.* **3** = **suggest**, propose, recommend • *I vote that we all go to the mall.*
See also: **say**
vouch *v* ▷ **vouch for** = **guarantee**, certify, answer for, give assurance of, stand witness, swear to; = **confirm**, support, uphold, assert, affirm, attest to
voucher *n* = **ticket**, token, coupon
vow *n* **1** = **promise**, pledge, oath ▸ *v* **2** = **promise**, pledge, swear, affirm
voyage *n* = **journey**, trip, cruise, passage, crossing
vulgar *adj* **1** = **crude**, dirty, rude, indecent, coarse, uncouth • *vulgar language* OPPOSITE: refined **2** = **tasteless**, common, flashy,

DICTIONARY

decency, or refinement **vulgarly** *adv*
vulgarity *n*
▸ **vulgarian** *n* vulgar (rich) person
▸ **vulgarism** *n* coarse word or phrase
▸ **vulgar fraction** simple fraction
Vulgate *n* fourth-century Latin version of the Bible
vulnerable Ⓣ *adj* **1** able to be physically or emotionally hurt **2** exposed to attack
vulnerability *n*
vulpine *adj* of or like a fox
vulture *n* large bird that feeds on the flesh of dead animals
vulva *n* woman's external genitals
vying present participle of **vie**

THESAURUS

gaudy, garish, tawdry • *I think it's a very vulgar building*. OPPOSITE: sophisticated
See also: **low, naughty**
vulgarity *n* **1 = crudeness**, coarseness, indelicacy, ribaldry, rudeness **2 = tastelessness**, bad taste
vulnerability *See* **weakness**
vulnerable *adj* **1 = weak**, sensitive, susceptible, exposed • *vulnerable old people* **2 = exposed**, accessible, unprotected, assailable, defenceless, wide open
See also: **helpless, impressionable**

Ww

W 1 *chem* tungsten 2 watt 3 Wednesday 4 west(ern)
wacky Ⓣ *adj* **wackier, wackiest** *informal* eccentric or funny **wackiness** *n*
wad Ⓣ *n* 1 small mass of soft material 2 roll or bundle ▷ *v* **wadding, wadded** 3 make into a wad 4 pad or stuff with wadding
▸ **wadding** *n* soft material used for padding or stuffing
waddle Ⓣ *v* 1 walk with short swaying steps ▷ *n* 2 swaying walk
wade Ⓣ *v* 1 walk with difficulty through water or mud 2 proceed with difficulty
▸ **wader** *n* 1 long-legged water bird **waders** 2 angler's long waterproof boots
wadi [**wod**-dee] *n, pl* **-dies** (in N Africa and Arabia) watercourse which is dry except in the wet season
wafer *n* 1 thin crisp biscuit 2 thin disc of unleavened bread used at Communion 3 thin slice
waffle[1] Ⓣ *informal* ▷ *v* 1 speak or write in a vague wordy way ▷ *n* 2 vague wordy talk or writing
waffle[2] *n* square crisp pancake with a grid-like pattern
waft Ⓣ *v* 1 drift or carry gently through air or water ▷ *n* 2 something wafted
wag Ⓣ *v* **wagging, wagged** 1 move rapidly from side to side ▷ *n* 2 wagging 3 *informal* humorous witty person **waggish** *adj*
▸ **wagtail** *n* small long-tailed bird
wage Ⓣ *n* 1 *often pl* payment for work done, esp. when paid weekly ▷ *v* 2 engage in (an activity)
wager Ⓣ *n, v* bet on the outcome of something
waggle Ⓣ *v* wag **waggly** *adj*
Wagner *n* (**Wilhelm**) **Richard**. 1813–83, German romantic composer noted chiefly for his invention of the music drama. His cycle of four such dramas *The Ring of the Nibelung* was produced at his own theatre in Bayreuth in 1876. His other operas include *Tannhäuser* (1845; revised 1861), *Tristan and Isolde* (1865), and *Parsifal* (1882)
wagon, waggon *n* 1 four-wheeled vehicle for heavy loads 2 railway freight truck
wagoner *or* **waggoner** *n*
waif Ⓣ *n* homeless child
wail Ⓣ *v* 1 cry out in pain or misery ▷ *n* 2 mournful cry
wain *n poetic* farm wagon
wainscot, wainscoting, wainscotting *n* wooden lining of the lower part of the walls of a room
Wainwright *n* 1 **Martha**. born 1976, Canadian-US singer-songwriter. Her recordings include *I Know You're Married But I've Got Feelings Too* 2 her brother **Rufus**. born 1973, Canadian-US singer-songwriter. His recordings include *Release the Stars* (2007)

THESAURUS

wacky *adj* (*Informal*) = **crazy**, stupid, silly, absurd, foolish, idiotic, asinine, crackpot (*informal*), witless
wad *n* = **mass**, roll, bundle, hunk
waddle *v* = **shuffle**, sway, wobble, toddle, totter
wade *v* = **walk through**, splash, paddle, ford ▷ **wade through** = **work one's way through**, drudge at, labour at, peg away at, plow through, toil at
waffle *v* 1 = **waver**, falter, sway, hesitate, seesaw, teeter, fluctuate, be doubtful, be uncertain, be unsure, oscillate, be undecided, blow hot and cold (*informal*), temporize, be unable to decide, keep changing your mind, swither, be unable to make up your mind, dillydally 2 = **prattle**, blather, jabber, prate ▸ *n* 3 = **verbosity**, padding, prolixity, verbiage, wordiness, yadda yadda yadda (*slang*)
waft *v* = **carry**, bear, transport, float, drift, convey
wag *v* 1 = **wave**, shake, stir, nod, bob, vibrate, quiver, wiggle ▸ *n* 2 = **wave**, shake, nod, vibration, bob, quiver, wiggle
wage *n* 1 *Also* **wages** = **payment**, pay, income, fee, salary, reward, allowance, stipend, remuneration, recompense, emolument ▸ *v* 2 = **engage in**, conduct, pursue, practise, prosecute, undertake, proceed with, carry on
wager *n* 1 = **bet**, gamble ▸ *v* 2 = **bet**, risk, chance, lay, pledge, stake, gamble, venture, speculate
waggle *v* = **wag**, wave, shake, wobble, flutter, wiggle, oscillate
waif *n* = **stray**, orphan, foundling
wail *v* 1 = **cry**, grieve, lament, weep, howl, bawl, yowl ▸ *n* 2 = **cry**, complaint, lament, howl, moan, weeping, yowl

DICTIONARY

waist *n* **1** part of the body between the ribs and hips **2** narrow middle part
▸ **waistband** *n* band of material sewn on to the waist of a garment to strengthen it
▸ **waistcoat** *n Brit* vest
▸ **waistline** *n* (size of) the waist of a person or garment
wait Ⓣ *v* **1** remain inactive in expectation (of something) **2** be ready (for something) **3** delay or be delayed **4** serve in a restaurant etc. ▹ *n* **5** waiting
▸ **waiter** *n* man who serves in a restaurant etc. **waitress** *n fem*
Waite *n* **Terry**, full name *Terence Hardy Waite.* born 1939, British special envoy to the Archbishop of Canterbury, who negotiated the release of Western hostages held in the Middle East before being taken hostage himself (1987–91) in Lebanon
Waitz *n* **Grete**. born 1953, Norwegian long-distance runner and former marathon world champion
waive Ⓣ *v* refrain from enforcing (a law, right, etc.)
▸ **waiver** *n* **1** (written statement of) this act **2** *US & Canad sports* team's waiving of its right to sign a player that another team wants to trade, demote, or release
Wajda *n* **Andrei** *or* **Andrzej**. born 1926, Polish film director. His films include *Ashes and Diamonds* (1958), *The Wedding* (1972), *Man of Iron* (1980), *Danton* (1982), and *Miss Nobody* (1997)
wake[1] Ⓣ *v* **waking, woke, woken 1** rouse from sleep or inactivity ▹ *n* **2** vigil beside a corpse the night before burial **wakeful** *adj*
▸ **waken** *v* wake
wake[2] Ⓣ *n* track left by a moving ship
▸ **in the wake of** following close behind
Walcott *n* **Jersey Joe**, real name *Arnold Raymond Cream.* 1914–94, US boxer: world heavyweight champion 1951–52
Waldemar I, Valdemar I *n* known as *Waldemar the Great.* 1131–82, king of Denmark (1157–82). He conquered the Wends (1169), increased the territory of Denmark, and established the hereditary rule of his line
Waldemar II, Valdemar II *n* known as *Waldemar the Victorious.* 1170–1241, king of Denmark (1202–41); son of Waldemar I. He extended the Danish empire, conquering much of Estonia (1219)
Waldemar IV, Valdemar IV *n* surnamed *Atterdag.* ?1320–75, king of Denmark (1340–75), who reunited the Danish territories but was defeated (1368) by a coalition of his Baltic neighbours
Waldheim *n* **Kurt**. 1918–2007, Austrian diplomat; secretary-general of the United Nations (1972–81); president of Austria (1986–92)
Wałęsa *n* **Lech**. born 1943, Polish statesman: president of Poland (1990–95); leader of the independent trade union Solidarity (1980–90); Nobel peace prize 1983
walk Ⓣ *v* **1** move on foot with at least one foot always on the ground **2** pass through or over on foot **3** escort or accompany on foot **4** *baseball* reach first base by receiving four balls from the pitcher **5** *baseball* allow (a batter) to reach first base by throwing four balls ▹ *n* **6** walking **7** distance walked **8** manner of walking **9** place or route for walking **10** *baseball* free pass to first base given to a batter who has received four balls
▸ **walk of life** occupation or career
▸ **walker** *n* **1** person or thing that walks **2** device consisting of a light metal frame, used by infirm or disabled people for support for walking
▸ **walkabout** *n* informal walk among the public by royalty etc.

THESAURUS

wait *v* **1** = **stay**, remain, linger, pause, stand by • *Wait until we get there.* ▹ **wait on, wait upon** = **serve**, attend, tend, minister to ▸ *n* **2** = **delay**, pause, interval • *They faced a long wait for the ferry to Victoria.*
waiter, waitress *n* = **attendant**, server, steward *or* stewardess
waive *v* = **give up**, abandon, renounce, relinquish, forgo, remit, dispense with, set aside
wake[1] *v* **1** = **awake**, stir, awaken, rouse, come to, waken • *It was still dark when he woke.* **2** = **activate**, fire, provoke, excite, stimulate, arouse, animate, galvanize, kindle, stir up ▸ *n* **3** = **vigil**, watch, funeral, deathwatch
wake[2] *n* = **slipstream**, track, train, trail, path, wash, aftermath, backwash, waves
wakeful *adj* **1** = **sleepless**, restless, insomniac **2** = **watchful**, alive, alert, wary, vigilant, attentive, observant, on guard
waken *v* = **awaken**, stir, activate, awake, arouse, rouse
walk *v* **1** = **go**, move, step, pace, hike, march, stride, stroll, amble • *I walked slowly along the road.* **2** = **escort**, take, convoy, accompany ▸ *n* **3** = **stroll**, hike, march, constitutional, trek, ramble, promenade, saunter, perambulation • *We'll have a quick walk before it gets dark.* **4** = **gait**, step, pace, stride, carriage • *Despite his gangling walk, he is a good dancer.* **5** = **path**, trail, lane, alley, avenue, promenade, esplanade, footpath ▹ **walk of life** = **profession**, trade, line, career, field, calling, vocation

DICTIONARY

▸**walkie-talkie** *n* portable radio transmitter and receiver
▸**walking stick** stick used as a support when walking
▸**walk into** *v* meet with unwittingly
▸**Walkman** *n* ® small portable cassette player with headphones
▸**walkout** *n* **1** strike **2** act of leaving as a protest
▸**walkover** *n informal* easy victory
Walker *n* **1 Alice (Malsenior)**. born 1944, US writer: her works include *In Love and Trouble: Stories of Black Women* (1973) and the novels *Meridian* (1976), *The Color Purple* (1982), and *Possessing the Secret of Joy* (1992) **2 Larry**. born 1966, Canadian baseball player
wall ⓣ *n* **1** structure of brick, stone, etc. used to enclose, divide, or support **2** something having the function or effect of a wall ▹ *v* **3** enclose or seal with a wall or walls
▸**wallflower** *n* **1** fragrant garden plant **2** at a dance, a woman who remains seated for lack of a partner
▸**wallpaper** *n* decorative paper to cover interior walls
Wall *n* **Brad**. born 1965, Canadian politician, Premier of Saskatchewan (2007–)
wallaby *n, pl* **-bies** marsupial like a small kangaroo
Wallace *n* **1 Alfred Russel**. 1823–1913, British naturalist, whose work on the theory of natural selection influenced Charles Darwin **2 Edgar**. 1875–1932, English crime novelist **3** Sir **William**. ?1272–1305, Scottish patriot, who defeated the army of Edward I of England at Stirling (1297) but was routed at Falkirk (1298) and later executed
Waller *n* **Fats**, real name *Thomas Waller*. 1904–43, US jazz pianist and singer
wallet ⓣ *n* small folding case for paper money, documents, etc.
walleyed *adj* having eyes with an abnormal amount of white showing
wallop ⓣ *informal* ▹ *v* **-loping, -loped 1** hit hard ▹ *n* **2** hard blow
▸**walloping** *informal* ▹ *n* **1** thrashing ▹ *adj* **2** large or great
wallow ⓣ *v* **1** roll in liquid or mud **2** revel in an emotion ▹ *n* **3** wallowing
wally *n, pl* **-lies** *slang* stupid person
walnut *n* **1** edible nut with a wrinkled shell **2** tree it grows on **3** its wood
Walpole *n* Sir **Robert**, 1st Earl of Orford. 1676–1745, English Whig statesman. As first lord of the Treasury and Chancellor of the Exchequer (1721–42) he was effectively Britain's first prime minister
walrus *n, pl* **-ruses, -rus** large sea mammal with long tusks
Walter *n* **Bruno**, real name *Bruno Walter Schlesinger*. 1876–1962, US conductor, born in Germany: famous for his performances of Haydn, Mozart, and Mahler
Walther von der Vogelweide *n* ?1170–?1230, German minnesinger, noted for his lyric verse on political and moral themes
Walton *n* **1 Ernest Thomas Sinton**. 1903–95, Irish physicist. He succeeded in producing the first artificial transmutation of an atomic nucleus (1932) with Sir John Cockcroft, with whom he shared the Nobel prize for physics 1951 **2 Izaak**. 1593–1683, English writer, best known for *The Compleat Angler* (1653; enlarged 1676) **3** Sir **William (Turner)**. 1902–83, English composer. His works include *Façade* (1923), a setting of satirical verses by Edith Sitwell, the *Viola Concerto* (1929), and the oratorio *Belshazzar's Feast* (1931)
waltz *n* **1** ballroom dance **2** music for this ▹ *v* **3** dance a waltz **4** move in a relaxed confident way
wampum [**wom**-pum] *n* shells woven together, formerly used by N American Indians for money and ornament
wan ⓣ [rhymes with **swan**] *adj* **wanner, wannest** pale and sickly looking
wand ⓣ *n* thin rod, esp. one used in doing magic
wander ⓣ *v* **1** move about without a definite destination or aim **2** go astray, deviate ▹ *n*

THESAURUS

walker *n* = **pedestrian**, hiker, rambler, wayfarer
walkout *n* = **strike**, protest, stoppage, industrial action
walkover *n* = **pushover** (*slang*), breeze (*informal*), cakewalk (*informal*), child's play (*informal*), picnic (*informal*), laugher (*informal*), no-brainer (*slang*), cinch (*slang*), piece of cake (*informal*), slam dunk (*informal*)
wall *n* **1** = **partition**, screen, enclosure **2** = **barrier**, fence, hedge, obstacle, obstruction, impediment
wallet *n* = **holder**, case, purse, pocketbook, pouch
wallop *v* **1** = **hit**, strike, beat, pound, batter, thump, pummel, clobber (*slang*), whack, thrash ▸ *n* **2** = **blow**, punch, thump, bash, smack, whack, slug, thwack
wallow *v* **1** = **revel**, delight, glory, bask, relish, luxuriate, take pleasure **2** = **roll about**, splash around
wan *adj* = **pale**, white, anemic, pasty, sickly, pallid, ashen, washed out
wand *n* = **stick**, baton, rod
wander *v* **1** = **roam**, range, cruise, drift, stroll, ramble • *They wandered aimlessly around the village.* **2** = **stray**, depart, veer, err, swerve, deviate, diverge, digress, go

DICTIONARY

3 wandering **wanderer** *n*
▶**wanderlust** *n* great desire to travel
wane Ⓣ *v* 1 decrease gradually in size or strength 2 (of the moon) decrease in size
▶**on the wane** in decline
wangle Ⓣ *v informal* get by devious methods
want Ⓣ *v* 1 desire 2 lack ▷ *n* 3 wanting 4 thing wanted 5 lack 6 poverty
▶**wanted** *adj* sought by the police
▶**wanting** *adj* 1 lacking 2 not good enough
wanton Ⓣ *adj* 1 dissolute or immoral 2 without motive 3 unrestrained
wapiti [**wop**-pit-tee] *n, pl* **-tis** large N American and NZ deer
war Ⓣ *n* 1 fighting between nations 2 conflict or contest ▷ *adj* 3 of, like, or caused by war ▷ *v* **warring, warred** 4 make war **warring** *adj*
▶**warlike** *adj* of, for, or fond of war
▶**war crime** crime, such as killing, committed during a war in violation of accepted conventions
▶**war criminal** person who has committed war crimes
▶**warfare** *n* fighting or hostilities
▶**warhead** *n* explosive front part of a missile
▶**warmonger** *n* person who encourages war
▶**warship** *n* ship designed and equipped for naval combat
warble Ⓣ *v* sing with trills
▶**warbler** *n* any of various small songbirds
ward Ⓣ *n* 1 room in a hospital for patients needing a similar kind of care 2 electoral division of a town 3 child under the care of a guardian or court
▶**ward off** *v* avert or repel (something unpleasant)
▶**wardroom** *n* officers' quarters on a warship
warden Ⓣ *n* 1 person in charge of a building, institution, college, etc. 2 official responsible for the enforcement of regulations
wardenship *n*
warder *n* prison officer **wardress** *n fem*
wardrobe Ⓣ *n* 1 cupboard for hanging clothes in 2 person's collection of clothes 3 costumes of a theatrical company
ware *n* 1 articles of a specified type or material: *silverware* **wares** 2 goods for sale
▶**warehouse** *n* building for storing goods prior to sale or distribution
Warhol *n* **Andy**, real name *Andrew Warhola*. ?1926–87, US artist and film maker; one of the

THESAURUS

astray ▶ *n* 3 = **excursion**, cruise, ramble, meander
wanderer *n* = **traveller**, rover, gypsy, nomad, drifter, rambler, vagabond, voyager
wandering *adj* = **nomadic**, migratory, itinerant, peripatetic, rootless, roving, travelling, vagrant, wayfaring
wane *v* = **decline**, fail, decrease, weaken, fade, diminish, dwindle, lessen, subside, ebb, taper off ▶ *noun* ▷ **on the wane** = **declining**, fading, dwindling, ebbing, obsolescent, on the decline, tapering off, weakening
wangle *v* = **contrive**, engineer, arrange, fix (*informal*), manipulate, manoeuvre, pull off
want *v* 1 = **desire**, wish, covet, crave • *I want black running shoes for a change.* 2 = **need**, demand, require, lack, be deficient in • *My hair wants cutting.* ▶ *n* 3 = **lack**, shortage, absence, deficiency, scarcity • *becoming weak from want of rest* OPPOSITE: abundance 4 = **wish**, need, requirement, desire, appetite, longing, craving, yearning 5 = **poverty**, destitution, neediness, penury, privation
See also: **hardship**
wanting *adj* 1 = **lacking**, short, missing, shy, incomplete, absent 2 = **inadequate**, poor, faulty, defective, lousy (*slang*), deficient, substandard, imperfect, unsound
wanton *adj* 1 = **gratuitous**, senseless, arbitrary, needless, groundless, unprovoked, unjustifiable, wilful, motiveless, uncalled-for 2 = **promiscuous**, loose, immoral, shameless, dissipated, dissolute, lecherous, libidinous, lustful, unchaste
war *n* 1 = **fighting**, conflict, combat, warfare, strife, hostilities • *The war dragged on for five years.* OPPOSITE: peace RELATED WORDS *adjectives*: belligerent, martial ▶ *v* 2 = **fight**, battle, clash, combat • *The two countries had been warring with each other for years.*
warble *v* = **sing**, chirp, twitter, trill
ward *n* 1 = **room**, area, department, wing 2 = **district**, area, quarter, division, zone, precinct 3 = **dependant**, charge, minor, pupil, protégé ▶ *verb* ▷ **ward off** = **avert**, avoid, deflect, repel, parry, fend off, stave off
warden *n* 1 = **jailer**, guard, custodian, prison officer 2 = **keeper**, curator, ranger, administrator, superintendent, caretaker, guardian, custodian
wardrobe *n* 1 = **clothes cupboard**, closet 2 = **clothes**, apparel, attire
warehouse *n* = **store**, depot, storehouse, depository, stockroom
wares *pl n* = **goods**, stock, produce, stuff, merchandise, commodities, products
warfare *n* = **war**, battle, conflict, combat, fighting, arms, hostilities
warily *adv* = **cautiously**, carefully, gingerly, suspiciously, charily, circumspectly, distrustfully, vigilantly, watchfully, with care
warlike *adj* = **belligerent**, aggressive, hostile, martial, hawkish, bloodthirsty, bellicose, warmongering

DICTIONARY

foremost exponents of pop art
warlock Ⓣ *n* sorcerer
Warlock *n* **Peter**, real name *Philip Arnold Heseltine*. 1894–1930, British composer and scholar of early English music. His works include song cycles, such as *The Curlew* (1920–22), and the *Capriol Suite* (1926) for strings
warm Ⓣ *adj* **1** moderately hot **2** providing warmth **3** affectionate **4** enthusiastic **5** (of a colour) predominantly yellow or red ▷ *v* **6** make or become warm **warmly** *adv*
▶ **warmth** *n* **1** mild heat **2** cordiality **3** intensity of emotion
▶ **warm up** *v* **1** make or become warmer **2** do preliminary exercises before a race or more strenuous exercise **3** make or become more lively **warm-up** *n*
warn Ⓣ *v* **1** make aware of possible danger or harm **2** caution or scold **3** inform (someone) in advance
▶ **warning** *n* **1** something that warns **2** scolding or caution
▶ **warn off** *v* advise (someone) not to become involved with
warp Ⓣ *v* **1** twist out of shape **2** pervert ▷ *n* **3** state of being warped **4** lengthwise threads on a loom
warrant Ⓣ *n* **1** (document giving) official authorization ▷ *v* **2** guarantee **3** give authority or power to
▶ **warranty** *n* (document giving) a guarantee
▶ **warrant officer** officer in certain armed services with a rank between a commissioned and non-commissioned officer
warren *n* **1** series of burrows in which rabbits live **2** overcrowded building or part of a town with many narrow passages
warrior Ⓣ *n* person who fights in a war
wart *n* small hard growth on the skin
▶ **wart hog** kind of African wild pig
wary Ⓣ [**ware**-ree] *adj* **warier, wariest** watchful or cautious **warily** *adv* **wariness** *n*
was *v* first and third person singular past tense of **be**
wash Ⓣ *v* **1** clean (oneself, clothes, etc.) with water and usu. soap **2** be washable **3** flow or sweep over or against **4** *informal* be believable or acceptable: *that excuse won't wash* ▷ *n* **5** washing **6** clothes washed at one time **7** thin coat of paint **8** trail of water left by a moving ship **washable** *adj*
▶ **washer** *n* **1** ring put under a nut or bolt or in a tap as a seal **2** *informal* washing machine
▶ **washing** *n* clothes to be washed
▶ **wash away** *v* carry or be carried off by moving water
▶ **washout** *n informal* complete failure
▶ **washroom** *n* lavatory
▶ **wash up** *v* wash one's face and hands

THESAURUS

warlock *n* = **magician**, wizard, sorcerer, conjurer, enchanter
warm *adj* **1** = **heated**, pleasant, balmy, lukewarm, tepid • *a warm spring day* OPPOSITE: cold **2** = **friendly**, loving, cordial, affectionate, amiable, genial • *a warm and likable personality* OPPOSITE: unfriendly ▶ *v* **3** = **heat**, melt, thaw, heat up, warm up • *The sun came out and warmed the garden*. OPPOSITE: cool ▷ **warm up** *See* **heat, warm**
See also: **cozy, hot, tender**
warmonger *n* = **belligerent**, hawk, militarist, sabre-rattler
warmth *n* **1** = **heat**, hotness, warmness **2** = **affection**, love, tenderness, amorousness, cordiality, heartiness, kindliness
warn *v* = **caution**, alert, notify, forewarn • *I warned her about the tires on her bike*.
warning *n* = **caution**, alert, notice, alarm, premonition • *advance warning of the attack*
See also: **indication, lecture, omen**
warp *v* **1** = **twist**, bend, distort, deform, contort ▶ *n* **2** = **twist**, bend, distortion, kink, contortion
warped *See* **crooked**
warrant *n* **1** = **authorization**, authority, sanction, permit, licence, permission ▶ *v* **2** = **call for**, demand, require, sanction, permit, deserve, license, excuse, justify, necessitate **3** = **guarantee**, declare, pledge, certify, affirm, attest, vouch for
warranty *n* = **guarantee**, contract, pledge, bond, certificate, assurance, covenant
warrior *n* = **soldier**, fighter, combatant, gladiator, man-at-arms
wary *adj* = **cautious**, suspicious, vigilant, guarded, distrustful • *She was wary of making a commitment*.
See also: **alert**
wash *v* **1** = **clean**, launder, scrub, cleanse, shampoo, rinse, bathe • *He got a job washing dishes*. **2** = **sweep away**, erode, carry off • *washed ashore by the waves* **3** (*Informal*) = **be plausible**, stick, bear scrutiny, be convincing, carry weight, hold up, hold water, stand up ▷ **wash out** *See* **fade** ▶ *n* **4** = **cleaning**, scrub, rinse, cleansing, laundering **5** = **coat**, film, layer, coating, overlay **6** = **surge**, wave, swell
washed *See* **clean**
washout *n* = **failure**, disaster, disappointment, flop (*informal*), fiasco, dud (*informal*)
washroom *n* = **lavatory**, privy, loo, latrine, toilet, bathroom, convenience *or* public convenience, restroom, outhouse, powder room, water closet, W.C.

DICTIONARY

Washington *n* **1 Booker T(aliaferro).** 1856–1915, US Black educator and writer **2 Denzil.** US film actor; his films include *Glory* (1990), *Malcolm X* (1992), *The Hurricane* (1999), and *John Q.* (2002) **3 George.** 1732–99, US general and statesman; first president of the US (1789–97). He was appointed commander in chief of the Continental Army (1775) at the outbreak of the War of American Independence, which ended with his defeat of Cornwallis at Yorktown (1781). He presided over the convention at Philadelphia (1787) that formulated the constitution of the US and elected him president

wasp *n* stinging insect with a black-and-yellow body

▸ **waspish** *adj* bad-tempered

Wasp, WASP *n US offensive* person descended from N European Protestant stock

wassail *n* **1** formerly, festivity when much drinking took place ▹ *v* **2** drink the health of (a person) at a wassail

waste Ⓣ *v* **1** use pointlessly or thoughtlessly **2** fail to take advantage of **3** (foll. by *away*) lose one's health or strength ▹ *n* **4** wasting **5** something left over because in excess of requirements **wastes 6** desert ▹ *adj* **7** rejected as worthless or surplus to requirements **8** not cultivated or inhabited

▸ **wastage** *n* **1** loss by wear or waste **2** reduction in size of a workforce by not filling vacancies

▸ **wasteful** *adj* extravagant **wastefully** *adv*

▸ **waster** *or* **wastrel** *n* layabout

▸ **wastepaper basket** container for discarded paper

watch Ⓣ *v* **1** look at closely **2** wait expectantly (for) **3** guard or supervise ▹ *n* **4** portable timepiece for the wrist or pocket **5** (period of) watching **6** sailor's spell of duty **watchable** *adj* **watcher** *n*

▸ **watchful** *adj* carefully observing everything that happens **watchfully** *adv*

▸ **watchdog** *n* **1** dog kept to guard property **2** person or group guarding against inefficiency or illegality

▸ **watchman** *n* man employed to guard a building or property

▸ **watchword** *n* slogan or motto

water Ⓣ *n* **1** clear colourless tasteless liquid that falls as rain and forms rivers etc. **2** body of water, such as a sea or lake **3** level of the tide **4** urine ▹ *v* **5** put water on or into **6** (of the eyes) fill with tears **7** salivate **watery** *adj*

▸ **water bed** waterproof mattress filled with water

▸ **water buffalo** oxlike Asian animal

▸ **water closet** *old-fashioned* lavatory

▸ **watercolour** *n* **1** paint thinned with water **2** painting done in this

▸ **watercourse** *n* stream or river

▸ **watercress** *n* edible plant growing in clear ponds and streams

▸ **water down** *v* dilute, make less strong

THESAURUS

waste *v* **1 = squander**, fritter away, throw away • *I wouldn't waste my money on something like that.* OPPOSITE: save ▹ **waste away = decline**, fade, crumble, dwindle, wane, decay, wither, atrophy, wear out ▸ *n* **2 = squandering**, misuse, extravagance, dissipation, misapplication, prodigality • *What a complete waste of money!* **3 = garbage**, refuse, scrap, debris, trash, litter, rubbish, dross, leftovers ▹ **wastes = desert**, wilderness, wasteland ▸ *adj* **4 = unwanted**, unused, leftover, superfluous • *waste paper* **5 = uncultivated**, wild, empty, bare, barren, unproductive, uninhabited, desolate

wasted *See* **in vain, weak**

wasteful *adj* **= extravagant**, uneconomical • *wasteful duplication of effort* OPPOSITE: thrifty

waster *n* **= layabout**, idler, loafer, couch potato (*slang*), good-for-nothing, shirker, wastrel

watch *n* **1 = guard**, surveillance, observation, supervision • *Keep a close watch on the swimmers.* **2 = wristwatch**, chronometer, timepiece ▸ *v* **3 = look at**, see, view, observe, gaze at, pay attention • *I don't watch television very often.* **4 = guard**, mind, look after, take care of • *Please watch the baby carefully.* *See also*: **regard, witness** ▹ **watch out = be careful**, be alert, be watchful, keep your eyes open, look out • *You have to watch out for snakes in the swamp.* *See also*: **beware** ▹ **watch over** *See* **guard**

watchdog *n* **1 = guard dog 2 = guardian**, monitor, protector, custodian, scrutineer

watchful *adj* **= alert**, suspicious, wary, vigilant, attentive, observant, on the lookout, wide awake

watchman *n* **= guard**, warden, custodian, sentry, sentinel, security guard

watchword *n* **= motto**, slogan, maxim, catchword, battle cry, byword, catch phrase, rallying cry

water *n* **1 = liquid**, H_2O ▸ *v* **2 = moisten**, spray, soak, douse, dampen, drench, hose, irrigate ▹ **water down = dilute**, water, weaken, thin

waterfall *n* **= cascade**, fall, cataract

waterlogged *See* **wet**

watertight *adj* **1 = waterproof 2 = foolproof**, sound, flawless, airtight, unassailable, impregnable, hermetic

watery *adj* **1 = wet**, liquid, fluid, soggy, damp, moist, aqueous **2 = diluted**, weak,

W

DICTIONARY

▶ **waterfall** *n* place where the waters of a river drop vertically
▶ **waterfront** *n* part of a town alongside a body of water
▶ **water lily** water plant with large floating leaves
▶ **watermark** *n* faint translucent design in a sheet of paper
▶ **watermelon** *n* melon with green skin and red flesh
▶ **water polo** team game played by swimmers with a ball
▶ **waterproof** *adj* **1** not letting water through ▷ *v* **2** make waterproof ▷ *n* **3** waterproof garment
▶ **watershed** *n* **1** line separating two river systems **2** dividing line
▶ **water-skiing** *n* sport of riding over water on skis towed by a speedboat
▶ **watertight** *adj* **1** not letting water through **2** with no loopholes or weak points
▶ **water wheel** large wheel which is turned by flowing water to drive machinery

Waterhouse *n* **Alfred**. 1830–1905, British architect; a leader of the Gothic Revival. His buildings include Manchester Town Hall (1868) and the Natural History Museum, London (1881)

Waters *n* **Muddy**, real name *McKinley Morganfield*. 1915–83, US blues guitarist, singer, and songwriter. His songs include "Rollin' Stone" (1948) and "Got my Mojo Working" (1954)

Watson *n* **1 James Dewey**. born 1928, US biologist, whose contribution to the discovery of the helical structure of DNA won him a Nobel prize for physiology or medicine shared with Francis Crick and Maurice Wilkins in 1962 **2 John B**(**roadus**). 1878–1958, US psychologist; a leading exponent of behaviourism **3 Tom**, full name *Thomas Sturges Watson*. born 1949, US golfer: won the US Open Championship (1982), the British Open Championship (1975, 1977, 1980, 1982, 1983), and the World Series (1975, 1977, 1980)

Watson-Watt *n* Sir **Robert Alexander**. 1892–1973, Scottish physicist, who played a leading role in the development of radar

watt [**wott**] *n* unit of power
▶ **wattage** *n* electrical power expressed in watts

Watteau *n* **Jean-Antoine**. 1684–1721, French painter, esp. of *fêtes champêtres*

wattle [**wott**-tl] *n* **1** branches woven over sticks to make a fence **2** fold of skin hanging from the neck of certain birds

Waugh *n* **Evelyn** (**Arthur St John**). 1903–66, English novelist. His early satirical novels include *Decline and Fall* (1928), *Vile Bodies* (1930), *A Handful of Dust* (1934), and *Scoop* (1938). His later novels include the more sombre *Brideshead Revisited* (1945) and the trilogy of World War II *Men at Arms* (1952), *Officers and Gentlemen* (1955), and *Unconditional Surrender* (1961)

wave ⓣ *v* **1** move the hand to and fro as a greeting or signal **2** move or flap to and fro ▷ *n* **3** moving ridge on water **4** curve(s) in the hair **5** gesture of waving **6** vibration carrying energy through a medium **7** prolonged spell of something **wavy** *adj*
▶ **wavelength** *n* distance between the same points of two successive waves

waver ⓣ *v* **1** hesitate or be irresolute **2** be or become unsteady **waverer** *n*

wax[1] *n* **1** solid shiny fatty or oily substance used for sealing, making candles, etc. **2** similar substance made by bees **3** waxy secretion of the ear ▷ *v* **4** coat or polish with wax **waxy** *adj*
▶ **waxen** *adj* made of or like wax
▶ **waxwing** *n* small songbird
▶ **waxwork** *n* **1** lifelike wax model of a (famous) person **waxworks 2** place exhibiting these

wax[2] ⓣ *v* **1** increase in size or strength **2** (of the moon) get gradually larger

way ⓣ *n* **1** manner or method **2** route or direction **3** track or path **4** room for movement or activity: *you're in the way* **5** distance **6** passage or journey

THESAURUS

thin, runny, watered-down, washy

wave *v* **1 = flap**, shake, flourish, flutter, brandish, undulate, oscillate • *The doctor waved a piece of paper at me.* **2 = signal**, sign, direct, indicate, gesture, beckon, gesticulate ▷ **wave down** *See* **hail** ▶ *n* **3 = ripple**, surge, swell, roller, bore, breaker, tidal bore • *the sound of the waves breaking on the shore* **4 = outbreak**, surge, flood, rush, movement, trend, upsurge • *the heat wave*
See also: **rash**

waver *v* **1 = hesitate**, falter, seesaw, fluctuate, dither, vacillate, hum and haw **2 = tremble**, shake, wobble, flicker, quiver, totter

wavering *See* **hesitant**

wax *v* **= increase**, grow, develop, expand, swell, magnify, enlarge

way *n* **1 = method**, approach, procedure, technique, manner, means • *an excellent way of cooking meat* **2 = custom**, conduct, practice, style, manner • *Our neighbours' ways are certainly different from our own.* **3 = route**, road, course, path, lane • *I can't remember the way.* **4 = journey**, approach, march, passage **5 = distance**, stretch, length

DICTIONARY

7 characteristic manner **8** *informal* state or condition
▶ **wayfarer** *n* traveller
▶ **waylay** *v* lie in wait for and accost or attack
▶ **waypoint** *n* specific location as defined by a GPS
▶ **wayside** *adj, n* (situated by) the side of a road
Wayne *n* **John**, real name *Marion Michael Morrison*. 1907–79, US film actor, noted esp. for his many Westerns, which include *Stagecoach* (1939), *The Alamo* (1960), and *True Grit* (1969), for which he won an Oscar
Wayne and Shuster *n* a team of Canadian radio and television comedians, comprising Johnny Wayne (1918–90) and Frank Shuster (1916–2002)
wayward ⓣ *adj* erratic, selfish, or stubborn **waywardness** *n*
WC water closet
we *pron used as the subject of a verb* **1** the speaker or writer and one or more others **2** people in general **3** formal word for 'I' used by editors and monarchs
weak ⓣ *adj* **1** lacking strength **2** liable to give way **3** lacking flavour **4** unconvincing **weakness** *n*
▶ **weaken** *v* make or become weak
▶ **weakling** *n* feeble person or animal
▶ **weakly** *adj* **1** weak or sickly ▷ *adv* **2** feebly
weal *n* raised mark left on the skin by a blow
wealth ⓣ *n* **1** riches **2** abundance **wealthy** *adj* **wealthiness** *n*
wean *v* **1** accustom to food other than mother's milk **2** (often foll. by *from*) coax away (from)
weapon *n* **1** object used in fighting **2** anything used to get the better of an opponent
▶ **weaponry** *n* weapons collectively
wear ⓣ *v* **wearing, wore, worn 1** have on the body as clothing or ornament **2** show as one's expression **3** (cause to) deteriorate by constant use or action **4** endure constant use **5** *informal* tolerate ▷ *n* **6** wearing **7** things to wear: *leisure wear* **8** damage caused by use **9** ability to endure constant use **wearer** *n*
▶ **wear off** *v* have a gradual decrease in intensity

THESAURUS

See also: **direction, fashion** ▷ **way in** *See* **entrance, entry**
wayfarer *n* = **traveller**, rover, gypsy, nomad, itinerant, wanderer, voyager
ways *See* **conduct**
wayward *adj* = **erratic**, unpredictable, unruly, unmanageable, capricious, inconstant, ungovernable
weak *adj* **1** = **feeble**, delicate, faint, frail, sickly, puny, wasted • *a weak heart* OPPOSITE: strong **2** = **deficient**, faulty, inadequate • *a weak economy* **3** = **spineless**, powerless • *He was a weak man who wouldn't stand up for himself*. OPPOSITE: resolute **4** = **unsafe**, vulnerable, unprotected, helpless, exposed, unguarded, defenceless **5** = **unconvincing**, pathetic, lame, hollow, unsatisfactory, feeble, flimsy **6** = **tasteless**, thin, diluted, runny, watery, insipid
See also: **flat, mild**
weaken *v* **1** = **lessen**, fail, reduce, flag, undermine, diminish, wane, sap • *Her authority was weakened by their actions*. OPPOSITE: strengthen **2** = **dilute**, thin out, water down
weakling *n* = **sissy**, baby (*informal*), drip (*informal*), wimp (*informal*), pantywaist (*informal*)
weakness *n* **1** = **frailty**, vulnerability, fragility • *Extreme weakness caused him to collapse*. OPPOSITE: strength **2** = **liking**, passion, penchant, fondness • *a weakness for chocolate* OPPOSITE: dislike **3** = **failing**, lack, flaw, defect, fault, deficiency, shortcoming, blemish, imperfection
See also: **disadvantage, love**
wealth *n* **1** = **riches**, money, substance, fortune, means, prosperity, affluence • *Wealth cannot buy happiness*. **2** = **abundance**, store, plenty, bounty • *a wealth of information* OPPOSITE: shortage
See also: **success**
wealthy *adj* = **rich**, comfortable, affluent, prosperous, opulent, well-to-do • *She came from a very wealthy background*. OPPOSITE: poor
wear *v* **1** = **be dressed in**, sport, don, be clothed in, have on, put on • *He was wearing a brown suit*. **2** = **deteriorate**, erode, rub, fray, corrode, wash away • *The carpet is badly worn*. **3** = **show**, display, exhibit
▷ **wear away** *See* **eat away, erode** ▷ **wear down** *See* **erode** ▷ **wear off** = **subside**, disappear, decrease, fade, diminish, dwindle, wane, peter out ▷ **wear out** = **exhaust**, tire, weary • *The past few days have really worn me out*. ▶ *n* **4** = **damage**, use, erosion, deterioration, corrosion • *The tires showed signs of wear*. **5** = **clothes**, dress, gear (*informal*), costume, apparel, attire, garb, garments, things
wearied *See* **bored**
weariness *n* = **tiredness**, fatigue, exhaustion, drowsiness, lethargy, languor, lassitude, listlessness
wearing *adj* = **tiresome**, oppressive, exasperating, fatiguing, irksome, trying, wearisome
wearisome *adj* = **tedious**, boring, troublesome, oppressive, tiresome, annoying, exhausting, fatiguing, irksome, trying, wearing

DICTIONARY

▸ **wear on** *v* (of time) pass slowly
weary Ⓣ *adj* **-rier, -riest 1** tired or exhausted **2** tiring ▹ *v* **-rying, -ried 3** make or become weary **wearily** *adv* **weariness** *n*
▸ **wearisome** *adj* tedious
weasel *n* small carnivorous mammal with a long body and short legs
weather Ⓣ *n* **1** day-to-day meteorological conditions of a place ▹ *v* **2** (cause to) be affected by the weather **3** come safely through
▸ **under the weather** *informal* slightly ill
▸ **weather-beaten** *adj* worn, damaged, or (of skin) tanned by exposure to the weather
▸ **weathercock** *or* **weathervane** *n* metal object on a roof showing which way the wind is blowing
weave Ⓣ *v* **weaving, wove** *or* **weaved,**
▸ **woven** *or* **weaved 1** make (fabric) by interlacing (yarn) on a loom **2** compose (a story) **3** move from side to side while going forwards **weaver** *n*
web Ⓣ *n* **1** net spun by a spider **2** anything intricate or complex: *web of deceit* **3** skin between the toes of a duck, frog, etc. **webbed** *adj*
▸ **the Web** short for **World Wide Web**
▸ **Web 2.0** internet viewed as a medium in which interactive experience is more important than accessing information
▸ **web address** same as **URL**
▸ **webbing** *n* strong fabric woven in strips
▸ **weblog** *n* person's online journal (Also **blog**)
▸ **webmail** *n* system of electronic mail that allows account holders to access their mail via an internet site
▸ **website** *n* group of connected pages on the World Wide Web
Weber *n* Baron **Carl Maria Friedrich Ernst von**. 1786–1826, German composer, conductor, pianist, and critic. His three romantic operas are *Der Freischütz* (1821), *Euryanthe* (1823), and *Oberon* (1826)
Webern *n* **Anton von**. 1883–1945, Austrian composer; pupil of Schoenberg, whose twelve-tone technique he adopted. His works include those for chamber ensemble, such as *Five Pieces for Orchestra* (1911–13)
Webster *n* **1 Daniel**. 1782–1852, US politician and orator **2 Noah**. 1758–1843, US lexicographer, famous for his *American Dictionary of the English Language* (1828)
wed Ⓣ *v* **wedding, wedded** *or* **wed 1** marry **2** unite closely
▸ **wedding** *n* act or ceremony of marriage
▸ **wedlock** *n* marriage
wedge Ⓣ *n* **1** piece of material thick at one end and thin at the other ▹ *v* **2** fasten or split with a wedge **3** squeeze into a narrow space
Wedgwood *n* **Josiah**. 1730–95, British potter and industrialist, who founded several pottery works near Stoke-on-Trent in Staffordshire
Wednesday *n* fourth day of the week
wee Ⓣ *adj* small
weed *n* **1** plant growing where undesired **2** *informal* thin ineffectual person ▹ *v* **3** clear of weeds
▸ **weedy** *adj* **1** *informal* thin or weak **2** full of weeds
▸ **weed out** *v* remove or eliminate (what is unwanted)
weeds *pl n obsolete* widow's mourning clothes
week *n* **1** period of seven days, esp. one beginning on a Sunday **2** hours or days of work in a week
▸ **weekly** *adj, adv* **1** happening, done, etc. once a week ▹ *n, pl* **-lies 2** periodical published once a week
▸ **weekday** *n* any day of the week except Saturday or Sunday
▸ **weekend** *n* Saturday and Sunday
Weelkes *n* **Thomas**. ?1575–1623, English composer of madrigals

THESAURUS

weary *adj* **1 = tired**, drained, exhausted, fatigued, tuckered out (*informal*), worn out • *I'm just too weary to walk another step.* **2 = tiring**, arduous, tiresome, laborious, wearisome ▸ *v* **3 = tire**, tax, drain, fatigue, sap, enervate, take it out of (*informal*), tire out, wear out
See also: **sick of**
weather *n* **1 = climate**, conditions ▸ *v* **2 = withstand**, stand, survive, overcome, endure, resist, brave, come through, ride out
weave *v* **1 = knit**, intertwine, braid, entwine, interlace, plait **2 = create**, build, spin, construct, fabricate, contrive, make up, put together **3 = zigzag**, wind, crisscross
web *n* **1 = spider's web**, cobweb **2 = network**, tangle, lattice
wed *v* **1 = marry**, get married, take the plunge (*informal*), tie the knot (*informal*) **2 = unite**, link, join, combine, ally, merge, blend, interweave
wedding *n* **= marriage**, nuptials, wedlock
wedge *n* **1 = block**, chunk, lump ▸ *v* **2 = squeeze**, force, crowd, pack, stuff, jam, lodge, thrust, ram, cram
wedlock *n* **= marriage**, matrimony
wee *See* **tiny**
weed out *v* **= eliminate**, remove, eradicate, uproot, dispense with, get rid of, root out
weedy *adj* **= weak**, frail, feeble, ineffectual, thin, skinny, puny

DICTIONARY

weep Ⓣ *v* **weeping, wept 1** shed tears **2** grieve or lament **3** ooze liquid **weepy** *adj*
▸ **weeping willow** willow with drooping branches

weevil *n* small beetle which eats grain etc.

weft *n* cross threads in weaving

weigh Ⓣ *v* **1** measure the weight of **2** have a specified weight **3** consider carefully **4** be influential **5** be burdensome
▸ **weigh anchor** raise a ship's anchor or (of a ship) have its anchor raised

weight Ⓣ *n* **1** heaviness of an object **2** object of known mass used for weighing **3** unit of measurement of weight **4** heavy object **5** importance or influence ▷ *v* **6** add weight to **7** slant (a system) to favour one group **weightless** *adj* **weightlessness** *n*
▸ **weighting** *n* extra allowance paid in special circumstances
▸ **weighty** *adj* **1** heavy **2** important **3** causing worry **weightily** *adv*

Weill *n* **Kurt**. 1900–50, German composer, in the US from 1935. He wrote the music for Brecht's *The Rise and Fall of the City of Mahagonny* (1927) and *The Threepenny Opera* (1928)

weir *n* river dam

Weir *n* **1 Mike**. born 1970, Canadian golfer: winner of the US Masters (2003) **2 Peter**. born 1944, Australian film director; his films include *Dead Poets Society* (1989), *The Truman Show* (1998), and *Master and Commander* (2003)

weird Ⓣ *adj* **1** unearthly or eerie **2** strange or bizarre
▸ **weirdo** *n informal* peculiar person

Weissmuller *n* **John Peter**, known as *Johnny*. 1904–84, US swimmer and film actor, who won Olympic gold medals in 1924 and 1928 and played the title role in the early Tarzan films

Weizmann *n* **Chaim**. 1874–1952, Israeli statesman, born in Russia. As a leading Zionist, he was largely responsible for securing the Balfour Declaration (1917); first president of Israel (1949–52)

welch *v* same as **welsh**

welcome Ⓣ *adj* **1** received gladly **2** freely permitted ▷ *n* **3** kindly greeting ▷ *v* **-coming, -comed 4** greet with pleasure **5** receive gladly

weld Ⓣ *v* **1** join (pieces of metal or plastic) by softening with heat **2** unite closely ▷ *n* **3** welded joint **welder** *n*

Weldon *n* **Fay**. born 1931, British novelist and writer. Her novels include *Praxis* (1978), *Life and Loves of a She-Devil* (1984), *Big Women* (1998), and *Rhode Island Blues* (2003)

welfare Ⓣ *n* **1** wellbeing **2** help given to people in need
▸ **welfare state** system in which the government takes responsibility for the wellbeing of its citizens

well[1] Ⓣ *adv* **better, best 1** satisfactorily **2** skilfully **3** completely **4** prosperously **5** suitably **6** intimately **7** favourably **8** considerably ▷ *adj* **10** in good health **11** satisfactory ▷ *interj* **12** exclamation of

THESAURUS

weep *v* = **cry**, mourn, lament, sob, whimper, blubber, shed tears, snivel

weepy *adj* (*Informal*) = **sentimental**, slushy (*informal*), overemotional, schmaltzy (*slang*)

weigh *v* **1** = **have a weight of**, tip the scales at (*informal*) **2** = **consider**, examine, evaluate, ponder, contemplate, deliberate upon, meditate upon, reflect upon, think over **3** = **matter**, count, carry weight

weight *n* **1** = **heaviness**, mass, load, tonnage, poundage **2** = **importance**, power, authority, value, impact, import, influence, consequence ▸ *v* **3** = **load**, freight **4** = **bias**, load, slant, unbalance

weighted *See* **biased**

weighty *adj* **1** = **important**, serious, significant, crucial, grave, solemn, momentous, consequential, portentous **2** = **heavy**, massive, hefty (*informal*), cumbersome, burdensome, ponderous

weird *adj* = **strange**, odd, funny, extraordinary, bizarre, curious, singular (*formal*), peculiar • *I had such a weird dream last night.* OPPOSITE: ordinary
See also: **eccentric**

welcome *v* **1** = **greet**, meet, receive, hail, embrace ▸ *n* **2** = **greeting**, reception, acceptance, hospitality, salutation ▸ *adj* **3** = **pleasing**, acceptable, pleasant, desirable, delightful, agreeable, appreciated, gratifying, refreshing **4** = **free**, under no obligation

welcoming *See* **favourable, friendly**

weld *v* = **join**, link, bond, connect, bind, unite, fuse, solder

welfare *n* **1** = **wellbeing**, good, health, interest, benefit, advantage, happiness, prosperity **2** = **benefit**, grant, gift, assistance, handout

well[1] *adv* **1** = **satisfactorily**, successfully, smoothly, splendidly • *The interview went well.* **2** = **skilfully**, effectively, adequately, efficiently, professionally, expertly, admirably, ably, competently • *He draws well.* OPPOSITE: badly **3** = **thoroughly**, completely, highly, fully, closely, rigorously, meticulously, amply • *The dishes should be well washed and well dried.* **4** = **kindly**, favourably, humanely, compassionately, considerately, with consideration • *She treats her employees well.* **5** = **prosperously**,

DICTIONARY

surprise, interrogation, etc.
▸ **wellbeing** *n* state of being well, happy, or prosperous
▸ **well-disposed** *adj* inclined to be friendly or sympathetic
▸ **well-heeled** *adj informal* wealthy
▸ **well-meaning** *adj* having good intentions
▸ **well-spoken** *adj* speaking in a polite or articulate way
▸ **well-worn** *adj* **1** (of a word or phrase) having lost its meaning through overuse **2** so much used as to show signs of wear
well² Ⓣ *n* **1** hole sunk into the earth to reach water, oil, or gas **2** deep open shaft ▷ *v* **3** flow upwards or outwards
Welles *n* (**George**) **Orson**. 1915–85, US film director, actor, producer, and screenwriter. His *Citizen Kane* (1941) and *The Magnificent Ambersons* (1942) are regarded as film classics
Wellesz *n* **Egon**. 1885–1974, British composer, born in Austria
Wellington *n* **1st Duke of**, title of *Arthur Wellesley*. 1769–1852, British soldier and statesman; prime minister (1828–30). He was given command of the British forces against the French in the Peninsular War (1808–14) and routed Napoleon at Waterloo (1815)
wellingtons *pl n* high waterproof rubber boots
Wells *n* **H**(**erbert**) **G**(**eorge**). 1866–1946, British writer. His science-fiction stories include *The Time Machine* (1895), *War of the Worlds* (1898), and *The Shape of Things to Come* (1933). His novels on contemporary social questions, such as *Kipps* (1905), *Tono-Bungay* (1909), and *Ann Veronica* (1909), affected the opinions of his day. His nonfiction works include *The Outline of History* (1920)
welsh *v* fail to pay a debt or fulfil an obligation
Welsh *adj* **1** of Wales ▷ *n* **2** language or people of Wales
▸ **Welsh rabbit** *or* **Welsh rarebit** dish of melted cheese on toast
welt Ⓣ *n* **1** raised or strengthened seam **2** weal ▷ *v* **3** provide with a welt
welter Ⓣ *n* jumbled mass
welterweight *n* boxer weighing up to 147lb (professional) or 67kg (amateur)
wen *n* cyst on the scalp
Wenceslaus, Wenceslas *n* **1** 1361–1419, Holy Roman Emperor (1378–1400) and, as **Wenceslaus IV**, king of Bohemia (1378–1419) **2 Saint**, known as *Good King Wenceslaus*. ?907–929, duke of Bohemia (?925–29); patron saint of Bohemia. Feast day: Sept 28
wench *n facetious* young woman
wend *v* go or travel
wensleydale *n* type of white cheese of flaky texture
went *v* past tense of **go**
wept *v* past of **weep**
were *v* **1** form of the past tense of **be** used after *we, you, they*, or a plural noun **2** subjunctive of **be**
we're we are
weren't were not
werewolf *n* (in folklore) person who can turn into a wolf
Wesley *n* **1 Charles**. 1707–88, English Methodist preacher and writer of hymns **2** his brother, **John**. 1703–91, English preacher, who founded Methodism **3 Mary**, pseudonym of *Mary Aline Siepmann*. 1912–2003, British writer: her novels include *The Camomile Lawn* (1984) and *An Imaginative Experience* (1994)
west *n* **1** (direction towards) the point on the horizon where the sun sets **2** region lying in this direction **3 West** N America and western Europe ▷ *adj* **4** in, going towards, facing, or (of the wind) blowing from the west ▷ *adv* **5** in or to the west

THESAURUS

comfortably **6 = intimately**, fully, deeply, thoroughly, profoundly **7 = suitably**, properly, fairly, rightly, fittingly, justly **8 = considerably**, highly, fully, greatly, substantially, thoroughly, heartily, abundantly, amply, very much ▷ **well off** *See* **rich** ▸ *adj* **9 = healthy**, strong, sound, fit, robust, in good condition, in good health • *I'm not very well today.* OPPOSITE: sick **10 = satisfactory**, right, fine, proper, pleasing, agreeable, thriving
well² *n* **1 = hole**, oiler, pit, shaft, bore ▸ *v* **2 = flow**, spring, surge, jet, pour, spurt, gush, spout
well-behaved *See* **polite**
well-being *See* **comfort, health**
well-built *See* **sturdy**
well-known *adj* **= famous**, popular, familiar, renowned, celebrated, noted
well-liked *See* **popular**
well-mannered *See* **polite**
well-off *adj* **= rich**, comfortable (*informal*), wealthy, affluent, prosperous, well-heeled (*informal*), well-to-do, moneyed
well-to-do *adj* **= rich**, comfortable (*informal*), wealthy, affluent, prosperous, well-heeled (*informal*), well-off, moneyed
well-versed *See* **experienced**
well-worn *adj* **= hackneyed**, stale, commonplace, overused, banal, trite, stereotyped
welt *n* **= mark**, streak, stripe, contusion, wale, weal
welter *n* **= jumble**, confusion, web, mess, tangle, muddle

DICTIONARY

westward *adj, adv* **westwards** *adv*
▶ **westerly** *adj* in, towards, or (of the wind) blowing from the west
▶ **western** *adj* 1 of or in the west ▷ *n* 2 film or story about cowboys in the western US **westerner** *n*
▶ **westernize** *v* adapt to the customs and culture of the West
▶ **West Coast** Pacific coast of N America

West *n* **Mae**. 1892–1980, US film actress

wet ⓣ *adj* **wetter, wettest** 1 covered or soaked with water or another liquid 2 not yet dry: *wet paint* 3 *informal* (of a person) feeble or foolish ▷ *n* 4 moisture or rain 5 *informal* feeble or foolish person ▷ *v* **wetting, wet** *or* **wetted** 6 make wet
▶ **wet blanket** *informal* person who has a depressing effect on others
▶ **wetland** *n* area of marshy land
▶ **wet nurse** woman employed to breast-feed another's child
▶ **wet room** waterproofed shower room with a drain in the floor
▶ **wet suit** close-fitting rubber suit worn by divers etc.

wether *n* castrated ram

whack ⓣ *v* 1 strike with a resounding blow ▷ *n* 2 such a blow 3 *informal* share 4 *informal* attempt
▶ **whacked** *adj* exhausted
▶ **whacking** *adj informal* huge

whale *n* large fish-shaped sea mammal
▶ **have a whale of a time** *informal* enjoy oneself very much
▶ **whaling** *n* hunting of whales **whaler** *n*
▶ **whalebone** *n* horny substance hanging from the upper jaw of toothless whales

wham *n* 1 sudden forceful blow or the sound produced by it ▷ *v* **whamming, whammed** 2 strike or cause to strike with great force

wharf ⓣ *n, pl* **wharves, wharfs** platform at a harbour for loading and unloading ships
▶ **wharfage** *n* accommodation at or charge for use of a wharf

Wharton *n* **Edith** (**Newbold**). 1862–1937, US novelist; author of *The House of Mirth* (1905) and *Ethan Frome* (1911)

what *pron* 1 which thing 2 that which 3 request for a statement to be repeated ▷ *adv* 4 in which way, how much: *what do you care?* ▷ *interj* 5 exclamation of surprise, anger, etc.
▶ **what for?** why?
▶ **whatever** *pron* 1 everything or anything that 2 no matter what
▶ **whatnot** *n informal* similar unspecified things
▶ **whatsoever** *adj* at all

wheat *n* 1 grain used in making flour, bread, and pasta 2 plant producing this **wheaten** *adj*
▶ **wheatear** *n* small songbird
▶ **wheatmeal** *adj, n* (made with) brown, but not wholewheat, flour

wheedle ⓣ *v* coax or cajole

wheel ⓣ *n* 1 disc that revolves on an axle 2 pivoting movement ▷ *v* 3 push or pull (something with wheels) 4 turn as if on an axis 5 turn round suddenly
▶ **wheeling and dealing** use of shrewd and sometimes unscrupulous methods to achieve success **wheeler-dealer** *n*
▶ **wheelbarrow** *n* shallow box for carrying loads, with a wheel at the front and two handles
▶ **wheelbase** *n* distance between a vehicle's front and back axles
▶ **wheelchair** *n* chair mounted on wheels for use by people who cannot walk

Wheeler *n* **John Archibald**. 1911–2008, US physicist, noted for his work on nuclear fission and the development (1949–51) of the hydrogen bomb, and also for his work on unified field theory

wheeze ⓣ *v* 1 breathe with a hoarse whistling noise ▷ *n* 2 wheezing sound **wheezy** *adj*

whelk *n* edible snail-like shellfish

THESAURUS

wet *adj* 1 = **damp**, waterlogged, moist, sodden, drenched, saturated, soaked • *Don't get your feet wet*. OPPOSITE: dry 2 = **rainy**, misty, humid, showery • *It was a miserable, wet day*. OPPOSITE: dry ▶ *n* 3 = **rain**, drizzle 4 = **moisture**, water, liquid, humidity, damp, condensation, dampness, wetness ▶ *v* 5 = **moisten**, water, spray, soak, dampen, irrigate • *Wet the edges and stick them together*. OPPOSITE: dry

whack *v* 1 = **strike**, hit, belt (*informal*), bang, thump, smack, wallop (*informal*), clobber (*slang*), thrash, thwack ▶ *n* 2 = **blow**, hit, stroke, belt (*informal*), bang, thump, smack, wallop (*informal*), thwack 3 (*Informal*) = **share**, part, cut (*informal*), bit, portion, quota 4 (*Informal*) = **attempt**, go (*informal*), try, turn, shot (*informal*), crack (*informal*), stab (*informal*), bash (*informal*)

wharf *n* = **dock**, pier, jetty, landing stage, quay

wheedle *v* = **coax**, persuade, entice, cajole, inveigle

wheel *n* 1 = **circle**, turn, spin, revolution, rotation, pivot, gyration ▶ *v* 2 = **turn**, swing, spin, revolve, rotate, whirl, twirl, swivel, gyrate, pirouette

wheeze *v* 1 = **gasp**, cough, whistle, hiss, rasp ▶ *n* 2 = **gasp**, cough, whistle, hiss, rasp 3 (*Brit slang*) = **trick**, plan, idea,

DICTIONARY

whelp *n* **1** pup or cub **2** *offensive* youth ▷ *v* **3** produce whelps
when *adv* **1** at what time ▷ *conj* **2** at the time that **3** although **4** considering the fact that ▷ *pron* **5** at which time
▸ **whenever** *adv, conj* at whatever time
whence *adv, conj obsolete* from what place or source
where *adv* **1** in, at, or to what place ▷ *pron* **2** in, at, or to which place ▷ *conj* **3** in the place at which
▸ **whereabouts** *adv* **1** at what place ▷ *n* **2** present position
▸ **whereas** *conj* **1** but on the other hand **2** considering that
▸ **whereby** *conj* by which
▸ **wherefore** *obsolete* ▷ *adv* **1** why ▷ *conj* **2** consequently
▸ **whereupon** *conj* at which point
▸ **wherever** *adv* at whatever place
▸ **wherewithal** *n* necessary funds, resources, etc.
whet Ⓣ *v* **whetting, whetted 1** sharpen (a tool) **2** increase (appetite or desire)
▸ **whetstone** *n* stone for sharpening tools
whether *conj* used to introduce an indirect question or a clause expressing doubt or choice
whey [**way**] *n* watery liquid that separates from the curd when milk is clotted
which *adj, pron* **1** used to request or refer to a choice from different possibilities ▷ *pron* **2** person or thing referred to
▸ **whichever** *adj, pron* **1** any out of several **2** no matter which
whiff Ⓣ *n* **1** puff of air or odour **2** trace or hint
Whig *n* member of a British political party of the 18th–19th centuries that sought limited reform
while Ⓣ *conj* **1** in the time that **2** despite the fact that **3** whereas ▷ *n* **4** period of time
▸ **whilst** *conj* while
▸ **while away** *v* pass (time) idly but pleasantly
whim Ⓣ *n* sudden fancy
▸ **whimsy** *or* **whimsey** *n* **1** capricious idea **2** light or fanciful humour
▸ **whimsical** *adj* **1** fanciful **2** full of whims
whimsicality *n*
whimper Ⓣ *v* **1** cry in a soft whining way ▷ *n* **2** soft plaintive whine
whin *n* gorse
whine Ⓣ *n* **1** high-pitched plaintive cry **2** peevish complaint ▷ *v* **3** make such a sound **whining** *n, adj*
whinge *v* **1** complain ▷ *n* **2** complaint
whinny *v* **-nying, -nied 1** neigh softly ▷ *n* **2** soft neigh
whip Ⓣ *n* **1** cord attached to a handle, used for beating animals or people **2** call made on Members of Parliament to attend for important divisions **3** politician responsible for organizing and disciplining fellow party members **4** whipped dessert ▷ *v* **whipping, whipped 5** hit with a whip **6** *informal* pull, remove, or move quickly **7** beat (eggs or cream) to a froth **8** rouse into a particular condition **9** *informal* steal
▸ **whipped** *adj* **1** having been whipped **2** exhausted
▸ **whiplash injury** neck injury caused by a sudden jerk to the head, as in an automobile crash
whippet *n* racing dog like a small greyhound
whir, whirr *n* **1** prolonged soft buzz ▷ *v* **whirring, whirred 2** (cause to) make a whir
whirl Ⓣ *v* **1** spin or revolve **2** be dizzy or confused **3** drive or move at high speed

THESAURUS

scheme, stunt, ploy, ruse
whereabouts *n* = **position**, site, situation, location
wherewithal *n* = **resources**, money, capital, means, funds, supplies
whet *v* **1** (*~ someone's appetite*) = **stimulate**, excite, stir, enhance, awaken, arouse, rouse, quicken, kindle **2** = **sharpen**, hone
whiff *n* = **smell**, hint, scent, sniff, aroma, odour
while *conj* **1** = **at the same time as**, during the time that, for the period that ▸ *n* **2** = **time**, period *or* period of time, space, stretch, patch, spell, interval (*informal*), stint
whim *n* = **impulse**, urge, fancy, fad, craze
• *We decided to go there more or less on a whim.*
whimper *v* **1** = **cry**, weep, whine, sob, moan, snivel ▸ *n* **2** = **sob**, whine, moan, snivel
whimsical *adj* = **fanciful**, odd, unusual, funny, curious, eccentric, playful, quaint, freakish
whine *n* **1** = **cry**, sob, wail, moan, whimper **2** = **complaint**, grumble, moan, gripe (*informal*), grouse, grouch (*informal*)
whip *n* **1** = **lash**, crop, scourge, cane, birch, cat-o'-nine-tails ▸ *v* **2** = **lash**, beat, paddle, cane, flog, birch, flagellate, strap, scourge, thrash, spank **3** (*Informal*) = **dash**, shoot, fly, rush, tear, dive, whisk, dart **4** = **whisk**, beat **5** = **incite**, drive, spur, stir, agitate, foment, goad, work up ▷ **whip up** *See* **incite**
whirl *v* **1** = **spin**, turn, roll, twist, swirl, revolve, rotate, twirl, pirouette **2** = **feel dizzy**, spin, reel ▸ *n* **3** = **revolution**, turn, roll, spin, twist, swirl, rotation, twirl, pirouette **4** = **bustle**, series, round, flurry, succession, merry-go-round **5** = **confusion**, spin, daze, dither, giddiness
whirlwind *n* **1** = **tornado**, waterspout ▸ *adj*

DICTIONARY

▷ *n* **4** whirling movement **5** confusion or giddiness **6** bustling activity
▶ **whirlpool** *n* strong circular current of water
▶ **whirlwind** *n* **1** column of air whirling violently upwards in a spiral ▷ *adj* **2** much quicker than normal

whisk Ⓣ *v* **1** move or remove quickly **2** brush away lightly **3** beat (eggs or cream) to a froth ▷ *n* **4** light brush **5** egg-beating utensil

whisker *n* **1** any of the long stiff hairs on the face of a cat or other mammal
▶ **whiskers 2** hair growing on a man's cheeks
▶ **by a whisker** *informal* only just

whisky *n, pl* **-kies** strong alcoholic drink distilled from fermented cereals
▶ **whiskey** *n* US or Irish whisky
▶ **whiskyjack** *n* Canada jay

whisper Ⓣ *v* **1** speak softly, without vibration of the vocal cords **2** rustle ▷ *n* **3** soft voice **4** something whispered **5** rustling **6** *informal* rumour

whist *n* card game

whistle *v* **1** produce a shrill sound by forcing breath through pursed lips **2** make a similar sound **3** signal by a whistle ▷ *n* **4** whistling sound **5** instrument blown to make a whistling sound **whistling** *n, adj*
▶ **blow the whistle on** *informal* inform on or put a stop to

Whistler *n* **James Abbott McNeill**. 1834–1903, US painter and etcher, living in Europe. He is best known for his sequence of nocturnes and his portraits

whit *n* **not a whit** not the slightest amount

white Ⓣ *adj* **1** of the colour of snow **2** pale **3** light in colour **4** (of coffee) served with milk ▷ *n* **5** colour of snow **6** clear fluid round the yolk of an egg **7** white part of the eyeball **8** **White** member of the race of people with light-coloured skin **whiteness** *n* **whitish** *adj*
▶ **whiten** *v* make or become white or whiter
▶ **whitebait** *n* small edible fish
▶ **white-collar** *adj* denoting nonmanual salaried workers
▶ **white elephant** useless or unwanted possession
▶ **white flag** signal of surrender or truce
▶ **white-hot** *adj* very hot
▶ **white-knuckle** *adj informal* causing fear or anxiety
▶ **white lie** see **lie**[1]
▶ **white paper** report by the government, outlining its policy on a matter
▶ **whitewash** *n* **1** substance for whitening walls ▷ *v* **2** cover with whitewash **3** *informal* conceal or gloss over faults
▶ **white water** rapids

White *n* **Gilbert**. 1720–93, English clergyman and naturalist, noted for his *Natural History and Antiquities of Selborne* (1789)

Whitehead *n* **Alfred North**. 1861–1947, English mathematician and philosopher, who collaborated with Bertrand Russell in writing *Principia Mathematica* (1910–13), and developed a holistic philosophy of science, chiefly in *Process and Reality* (1929)

whither *adv obsolete* to what place

whiting [**white**-ing] *n* edible sea fish

whitlow *n* inflamed sore on a finger or toe, esp. round a nail

Whitman *n* **Walt**(**er**). 1819–92, US poet, whose life's work is collected in *Leaves of Grass* (1855 and subsequent enlarged editions). His poems celebrate existence and the multiple elements that make up a democratic society

Whitsun *n* week following Whit Sunday, the seventh Sunday after Easter

Whittier *n* **John Greenleaf**. 1807–92, US poet and humanitarian: a leading campaigner in the antislavery movement. His poems include *Snow-Bound* (1866)

whittle Ⓣ *v* cut or carve (wood) with a knife
▶ **whittle down** *or* **whittle away** *v* reduce or wear away gradually

whizz, whiz *v* **whizzing, whizzed 1** move with a loud buzzing sound **2** *informal* move quickly ▷ *n, pl* **whizzes 3** loud buzzing sound **4** *informal* person who is very good at something

who *pron* **1** which or what person **2** used to refer to a person or people already mentioned
▶ **whoever** *pron* **1** any person who **2** no matter who

WHO World Health Organization

whoa *interj* command used, esp. to horses, to stop or slow down

THESAURUS

2 = **rapid**, short, quick, speedy, swift, hasty

whisk *v* **1** = **flick**, sweep, brush, whip **2** = **beat**, whip, fluff up ▶ *n* **3** = **flick**, sweep, brush, whip **4** = **beater**

whisper *v* **1** = **murmur**, breathe **2** = **rustle**, sigh, swish, hiss ▶ *n* **3** = **murmur**, undertone **4** = **rustle**, sigh, swish, hiss

white *adj* = **pale**, pasty, pallid, wan, ashen

white-collar *adj* = **clerical**, professional, salaried, nonmanual

whiten *v* **1** = **pale**, fade, lighten, blanch **2** = **bleach**

whitewash *n* **1** = **cover-up**, camouflage, deception, concealment ▶ *v* **2** = **cover up**, suppress, conceal, camouflage, gloss over

whittle *v* = **carve**, cut, shape, trim, shave, pare, hew ▷ **whittle down**, **whittle away** = **reduce**, consume, erode, eat away, wear away

DICTIONARY

whodunnit [hoo-**dun**-nit] *n informal* detective story, play, or film
whole Ⓣ *adj* **1** containing all the elements or parts **2** uninjured or undamaged **3** healthy **4** (of a number) not containing a fraction ▷ *n* **5** complete thing or system **wholly** *adv*
▶ **on the whole** taking everything into consideration
▶ **wholesome** *adj* physically or morally beneficial
▶ **wholefood** *n* food that has been processed as little as possible
▶ **wholehearted** *adj* sincere or enthusiastic
▶ **whole note** musical note four beats long
▶ **wholesale** *adj, adv* **1** of the business of selling goods in large quantities and at lower prices to retailers **2** on a large scale: *wholesale destruction of forests* **wholesaler** *n*
▶ **wholewheat** *adj* **1** (of flour) made from the whole wheat grain **2** made from wholewheat flour
whom *pron* objective case of **who**
whoop *n, v* shout or cry to express excitement
whoopee *interj informal* cry of joy
whooping cough *n* infectious disease marked by convulsive coughing and noisy breathing
whoops *interj* exclamation of surprise or apology
whopper Ⓣ *n informal* **1** anything unusually large **2** huge lie **whopping** *adj*
whore Ⓣ [**hore**] *n* prostitute
whorl *n* **1** ring of leaves or petals **2** one turn of a spiral **3** something coiled
whose *pron* of who or which
why *adv* **1** for what reason ▷ *pron* **2** because of which
WI *Brit* Women's Institute
wick *n* cord through a lamp or candle which carries fuel to the flame
wicked Ⓣ *adj* **1** morally bad **2** mischievous **wickedly** *adv* **wickedness** *n*
wicker *adj* made of woven cane
wickerwork *n*
wicket *n* **1** set of three cricket stumps and two bails **2** cricket pitch **3** small gate
wide Ⓣ *adj* **1** large from side to side **2** having a specified width **3** spacious or extensive **4** opened fully ▷ *adv* **5** to the full extent **6** over an extensive area **7** far from the target
widely *adv*
▶ **widen** *v* make or become wider
▶ **wide receiver** *football* player whose function is to catch long passes (Also **wideout**)
▶ **widespread** *adj* affecting a wide area or a large number of people
widgeon *n* same as **wigeon**
widow *n* woman whose husband is dead

THESAURUS

whole *adj* **1 = complete**, full, total, entire, uncut, undivided • *We spent the whole summer away.* **2 = undamaged**, intact, unharmed, untouched, unscathed, unbroken, in one piece ▶ *n* **3 = total**, all, lot, everything, aggregate, sum total, the whole schmear (*informal*), the whole enchilada (*slang*) • *the whole of Asia* **4 = unit**, ensemble, entirety, totality ▷ **on the whole = all in all**, all things considered, by and large; **= generally**, mostly, predominantly, as a rule, in general, in the main
wholehearted *adj* **= sincere**, enthusiastic, committed, dedicated, devoted, determined, zealous, unstinting
wholesale *adj* **1 = extensive**, mass, broad, comprehensive, wide-ranging, far-reaching, indiscriminate, sweeping ▶ *adv* **2 = extensively**, indiscriminately, comprehensively
wholesome *adj* **1 = beneficial**, good, healthy, nutritious, nourishing, salubrious **2 = moral**, decent, respectable, improving
wholly *adv* **= completely**, fully, totally, entirely, perfectly, altogether, thoroughly, utterly, in every respect
whopper *n* **1 = giant**, monster, mammoth, colossus, jumbo (*informal*), crackerjack (*informal*), leviathan **2 = big lie**, fabrication, falsehood, tall tale (*informal*), untruth
whopping *adj* **= gigantic**, big, great, huge, giant, massive, enormous, mammoth
whore *n* **= prostitute**, ho (*slang*), tart (*informal*), call girl, streetwalker
wicked *adj* **1 = evil**, bad, vicious, atrocious, sinful, depraved • *That was a wicked thing to do.* **2 = mischievous**, naughty, impish • *She always felt wicked when eating chocolate.*
wickedness *See* **evil, sin**
wide *adj* **1 = broad**, large, extensive, vast, immense, far-reaching, expansive, sweeping • *It should be wide enough to give plenty of working space.* OPPOSITE: narrow **2 = expanded**, dilated, distended, outspread, outstretched • *His eyes were wide with disbelief.* **3 = spacious**, full, loose, baggy, roomy, capacious, commodious **4 = distant**, remote, off course, off target OPPOSITE: narrow ▶ *adv* **5 = fully**, completely **6 = off target**, out, astray, off course, off the mark
See also: **thick**
widen *v* **= broaden**, extend, spread, expand, stretch, enlarge, dilate
wide-ranging *See* **broad**
widespread *adj* **= extensive**, common, broad, prevalent, rife, pervasive • *Food shortages are widespread.*
See also: **general, mass, universal**

DICTIONARY

and who has not remarried **widowed** *adj*
widowhood *n*
▶**widower** *n* man whose wife is dead and who has not remarried
width Ⓣ *n* **1** distance from side to side **2** quality of being wide
wield Ⓣ *v* **1** hold and use (a weapon) **2** have and use (power)
Wiesel *n* **Elie**. born 1928, US human rights campaigner: noted esp. for his documentaries of wartime atrocities against the Jews; Nobel peace prize 1986
wife Ⓣ *n, pl* **wives** woman to whom a man is married
Wi-Fi *n* system of wireless access to the internet
wig *n* artificial head of hair **wigged** *adj*
wigeon *n* duck found in marshland
wigging *n slang* reprimand
wiggle Ⓣ *v* **1** move jerkily from side to side ▷ *n* **2** wiggling movement **wiggly** *adj*
wight *n obsolete* person
Wigner *n* **Eugene Paul**. 1902–95, US physicist, born in Hungary. He is noted for his contributions to nuclear physics: shared the Nobel prize for physics 1963
wigwam *n* N American Indian's tent
Wilberforce *n* **William**. 1759–1833, British politician and philanthropist, whose efforts secured the abolition of the slave trade (1807) and of slavery (1833) in the British Empire
wilco *interj* expression in telecommunications etc., indicating that the message just received will be complied with
wild Ⓣ *adj* **1** (of animals or birds) not tamed or domesticated **2** (of plants) not cultivated **3** not civilized **4** lacking restraint or control **5** violent or stormy **6** *informal* excited **7** without reason or substance **8** *informal* furious **wildly** *adv* **wildness** *n*
▶**wilds** *pl n* desolate or uninhabited place
▶**wildcat** *n* **1** European wild animal like a large domestic cat ▷ *adj* **2** (of a strike) sudden and unofficial
▶**wild-goose chase** search that has little chance of success
▶**wildlife** *n* wild animals and plants collectively
Wilde *n* **Oscar** (**Fingal O'Flahertie Wills**). 1854–1900, Irish writer and wit, famous for such plays as *Lady Windermere's Fan* (1892) and *The Importance of being Earnest* (1895). *The Picture of Dorian Gray* (1891) is a macabre novel about a hedonist and *The Ballad of Reading Gaol* (1898) relates to his experiences in prison while serving a two-year sentence for homosexuality
wildebeest *n* gnu
Wilder *n* **Billy**, real name *Samuel Wilder*. 1906–2002, US film director and screenwriter, born in Austria. His films include *Double Indemnity* (1944), *The Lost Weekend* (1945), *Sunset Boulevard* (1950), *The Seven Year Itch* (1955), *Some Like it Hot* (1959), *The Apartment* (1960), and *Buddy Buddy* (1981)
wilderness Ⓣ *n* **1** uninhabited uncultivated region **2** state of no longer being in a prominent position
wildfire *n* **spread like wildfire** spread quickly and uncontrollably
wile *n* trick or ploy
▶**wily** *adj* crafty or sly
wilful Ⓣ *adj* **1** headstrong or obstinate **2** intentional **wilfully** *adv* **wilfulness** *n*
Wilhelmina I *n* 1880–1962, queen of the Netherlands from 1890 until her abdication (1948) in favour of her daughter Juliana
Wilkes *n* **Charles**. 1798–1877, US explorer of Antarctica
Wilkins *n* **Maurice Hugh Frederick**. 1916–2004, British biochemist, born in New Zealand. With Crick and Watson, he shared

THESAURUS

width *n* = **breadth**, span, extent, scope, compass, thickness, diameter, girth
wield *v* **1** = **brandish**, use, manage, handle, swing, employ, flourish, manipulate, ply **2** (~ *power*) = **exert**, have, exercise, maintain, possess
wife *n* = **spouse**, partner, mate, bride, better half (*humorous*)
wiggle *v, n* = **jerk**, shake, flutter, wag, squirm, twitch, shimmy, jiggle, oscillate, wave, writhe
wild *adj* **1** = **natural**, free, fierce, uncultivated, undomesticated, untamed • *a meadow of wild flowers* **2** = **stormy**, violent, rough, raging, howling • *They were not deterred by the wild weather.* **3** = **uncontrolled**, turbulent, boisterous, wayward, rowdy • *wild with excitement* **4** = **uncivilized**, fierce, ferocious, savage, primitive, barbaric, barbarous, brutish **5** = **excited**, crazy (*informal*), enthusiastic, hysterical, raving, wired (*slang*) ▶ *noun* ▷ **wilds** = **wilderness**, desert, wasteland, back of beyond (*informal*), middle of nowhere (*informal*)
See also: **fanatical, irresponsible, rampage**
wilderness *n* = **desert**, jungle, wasteland, wilds
wildness *See* **abandon**
wiles *pl n* = **trickery**, cunning, artfulness, chicanery, craftiness, guile, slyness
wilful *adj* **1** = **obstinate**, stubborn, determined, perverse, uncompromising, inflexible, intransigent, headstrong, obdurate, pig-headed **2** = **intentional**, deliberate, conscious, voluntary, intended, purposeful

W

DICTIONARY

the Nobel prize 1962 for his work on the structure of DNA
will[1] *v, past* **would** used as an auxiliary to form the future tense or to indicate intention, ability, or expectation
will[2] Ⓣ *n* **1** faculty of deciding what one will do **2** directions written for disposal of one's property after death **3** desire or wish ▷ *v* **4** try to make (something) happen by wishing for it **5** wish or desire **6** leave (property) in one's will
▸ **willing** *adj* **1** ready or inclined (to do something) **2** done or given readily
willingly *adv* **willingness** *n*
▸ **willpower** *n* ability to control oneself and one's actions
Willan *n* (**James**) **Healey**. 1880–1968, Canadian classical composer, choir master, and organist, born in England. He composed over 800 works, both secular and religious
William *n* **1** known as *William the Lion*. ?1143–1214, king of Scotland (1165–1214) **2 Prince**. born 1982, first son of Prince Charles and Diana, Princess of Wales
William I *n* **1** known as *William the Conqueror*. ?1027–1087, duke of Normandy (1035–87) and king of England (1066–87). He claimed to have been promised the English crown by Edward the Confessor, after whose death he disputed the succession of Harold II, invading England in 1066 and defeating Harold at Hastings. The conquest of England resulted in the introduction to England of many Norman customs, esp. feudalism. In 1085 he ordered the Domesday Book to be compiled **2** known as *William the Bad*. 1120–66, Norman king of Sicily (1154–66) **3** known as *William the Silent*. 1533–84, prince of Orange and count of Nassau: led the revolt of the Netherlands against Spain (1568–76) and became first stadholder of the United Provinces of the Netherlands (1579–84); assassinated **4** 1772–1843, king of the Netherlands (1815–40): abdicated in favour of his son William II **5** German name *Wilhelm I*. 1797–1888, king of Prussia (1861–88) and first emperor of Germany (1871–88)
William II *n* **1** known as *William Rufus*. ?1056–1100, king of England (1087–1100); the son of William the Conqueror. He was killed by an arrow while hunting in the New Forest **2** known as *William the Good*. 1154–89, last Norman king of Sicily (1166–89) **3** 1792–1849, king of the Netherlands (1840–49); son of William I **4** German name *Kaiser Wilhelm*. 1859–1941, German emperor and king of Prussia (1888–1918): asserted Germany's claim to world leadership; forced to abdicate at the end of World War I
William III *n* known as *William of Orange*. 1650–1702, stadholder of the Netherlands (1672–1702) and king of Great Britain and Ireland (1689–1702). He was invited by opponents of James II to accept the British throne (1688) and ruled jointly with his wife Mary II (James' daughter) until her death in 1694
William IV *n* known as the *Sailor King*. 1765–1837, king of the United Kingdom and of Hanover (1830–37), succeeding his brother George IV; the third son of George III
William of Malmesbury *n* ?1090–?1143, English monk and chronicler, whose *Gesta regum Anglorum* and *Historia novella* are valuable sources for English history to 1142
Williams *n* **1 Danny**. born 1950, Canadian politician, Premier of Newfoundland and Labrador (2003–07; 2007–) **2 Ralph Vaughan**. See (Ralph) **Vaughan Williams** **3 Robin** (**McLaurim**). born 1951, US film actor and comedian; films include *Good Morning, Vietnam* (1987), *Dead Poets' Society* (1989), *Mrs. Doubtfire* (1993), and *Insomnia* (2002) **4 Rowan** (**Douglas**). born 1950, Archbishop of Canterbury from 2002; formerly Archbishop of Wales (2000–02)
Williamson *n* **Malcolm**. 1931–2003, Australian composer, living in Britain: Master of the Queen's Music (1975–2003). His works include operas and music for children
willies *pl n* **give one the willies** *slang* make one nervous or frightened
will-o'-the-wisp *n* **1** elusive person or thing **2** pale light sometimes seen over marshes at night
willow *n* **1** tree with thin flexible branches

W

THESAURUS

See also: **obstinate, stubborn**
will *v* **1 = bequeath**, leave, pass on • *He had willed his fortune to his children.* **2 = wish**, want, prefer, desire, see fit ▸ *n* **3 = determination**, resolution, resolve, purpose, willpower • *the will to win* **4 = wish**, choice, mind, inclination, volition • *the will of the people* **5 = testament**, last wishes RELATED WORD *adjective*: voluntary
willing *adj* **= ready**, game, happy, eager, prepared, agreeable • *a willing helper* OPPOSITE: unwilling
willingly *adv* **= readily**, voluntarily, freely, happily, eagerly, gladly, cheerfully, by choice, of one's own accord
willingness *n* **= inclination**, will, agreement, wish, consent, volition
willowy *adj* **= slender**, slim, graceful, supple, lithe, svelte, sylphlike
willpower *n* **= self-control**, drive, resolution, resolve, determination, grit, self-discipline, single-mindedness

DICTIONARY

2 its wood **willowy** *adj* slender and graceful
Wills *n* **Helen Newington**, married name *Helen Wills Moody Roark*. 1905–98, US tennis player. She was Wimbledon singles champion eight times between 1927 and 1938. She also won the US title seven times and the French title four times
willy-nilly *adv* whether desired or not
Wilson *n* **1 (James) Harold**, Baron Wilson of Rievaulx. 1916–95, British Labour statesman; prime minister (1964–70; 1974–76) **2 John Tuzo**. 1908–93, Canadian geophysicist, noted for his pioneering work on plate tectonics **3 (Thomas) Woodrow**. 1856–1924, US Democratic statesman; 28th president of the US (1913–21). He led the US into World War I in 1917 and proposed the Fourteen Points (1918) as a basis for peace. Although he secured the formation of the League of Nations, the US Senate refused to support it: Nobel peace prize 1919
wilt Ⓣ *v* (cause to) become limp or lose strength
wimp Ⓣ *n informal* feeble ineffectual person
wimple *n* garment framing the face, worn by medieval women and now by nuns
win Ⓣ *v* **winning, won 1** come first in (a competition, fight, etc.) **2** gain (a prize) in a competition **3** get by effort ▷ *n* **4** victory, esp. in a game **winner** *n*
▸ **winning** *adj* **1** gaining victory **2** charming
▸ **winnings** *pl n* money won in gambling or in a competition
▸ **win over** *v* gain the support or consent of (someone)
wince Ⓣ *v* **1** draw back, as from pain ▷ *n* **2** wincing
winceyette *n* cotton fabric with a raised nap
winch *n* **1** machine for lifting or hauling using a cable wound round a drum ▷ *v* **2** lift or haul using a winch
wind[1] Ⓣ *n* **1** current of air **2** trend or tendency **3** breath **4** idle talk **5** flatulence **6** hint or suggestion ▷ *v* **7** make short of breath **8** make (a baby) bring up wind after feeding **windy** *adj*
▸ **windward** *adj, n* (of or in) the direction from which the wind is blowing
▸ **wind-chill factor** added chilling effect of wind on basic temperature
▸ **windfall** *n* **1** unexpected good luck **2** fallen fruit
▸ **wind farm** collection of wind-driven turbines for generating electricity
▸ **wind instrument** musical instrument played by blowing
▸ **windmill** *n* machine for grinding or pumping driven by sails turned by the wind
▸ **windpipe** *n* tube linking the throat and the lungs
▸ **windscreen** *n Brit* windshield
▸ **windshield** *n* front window of a motor vehicle
▸ **windsock** *n* cloth cone on a mast at an airfield to indicate wind direction
▸ **windsurfing** *n* sport of riding on water using a surfboard propelled and steered by a sail
wind[2] Ⓣ *v* **winding, wound 1** coil or wrap around **2** tighten the spring of (a clock or watch) **3** move in a twisting course ▷ *n* **4** winding **5** single turn or bend
▸ **wind up** *v* **1** bring to or reach an end **2** tighten the spring of (a clock or watch) **3** *informal* make tense or agitated
windlass *n* winch worked by a crank
window *n* **1** opening in a wall or vehicle

THESAURUS

wilt *v* **1 = droop**, sag, wither, shrivel **2 = weaken**, flag, fade, wane, languish
wily *adj* **= cunning**, sharp, tricky, crafty, shrewd, sly, astute, artful, guileful
wimp *n (Informal)* **= weakling**, mouse, loser (*slang*), drip (*informal*), coward, sissy, softy *or* softie
wimpy *adj (Informal)* **= feeble**, ineffectual, effete, weak, soft, spineless, weedy (*informal*), timorous
win *v* **1 = be victorious**, succeed, prevail, triumph, come first • *The top four teams all won.* OPPOSITE: lose **2 = gain**, get, secure, achieve, attain • *trying to win the support of the community* ▷ **win over = convince**, convert, influence, persuade, sway, bring round *or* talk round, prevail upon ▸ *n* **3 = victory**, success, triumph • *Last night's win was an important one.* OPPOSITE: defeat
See also: **earn**
wince *v* **1 = flinch**, start, shrink, cringe, quail, recoil, cower, blench, draw back ▸ *n* **2 = flinch**, start, cringe
wind[1] *n* **1 = air**, blast, draft, breeze, gust, zephyr **2 = breath**, puff, respiration **3 = flatulence**, gas **4 = talk**, bluster, babble, blather, boasting, hot air, humbug ▷ **get wind of = hear about**, notice, get an inkling of, hear tell of, learn of, find out about
wind[2] *v* **1 = coil**, roll, curl, twist, reel, spiral, loop, encircle **2 = meander**, turn, snake, twist, bend, curve, ramble, zigzag ▷ **wind up = end**, close, finish, settle, conclude, finalize, terminate, wrap up; **= end up**, be left, finish up
windfall *n* **= godsend**, find, jackpot, bonanza, manna from heaven
windy *adj* **= breezy**, wild, stormy, gusty, blustery, windswept, blowy, squally

DICTIONARY

containing glass, which lets in light or air **2** glass pane or panes fitted in such an opening **3** display area behind the window of a shop **4** area on a computer screen that can be manipulated separately from the rest of the display area **5** period of unbooked time in a diary or schedule

▸ **window-dressing** *n* **1** arrangement of goods in a shop window **2** attempt to make something more attractive than it really is

▸ **window-shopping** *n* looking at goods in shop windows without intending to buy

wine *n* **1** alcoholic drink made from fermented grapes **2** similar drink made from other fruits ▹ *adj* **3** of a dark purplish-red colour

▸ **wine and dine** entertain or be entertained with fine food and drink

Winehouse *n* **Amy** (**Jade**). born 1983, English rock singer and songwriter; her albums include *Frank* (2003) and *Back to Black* (2006)

wing Ⓣ *n* **1** one of the limbs or organs of a bird, insect, or bat that are used for flying **2** one of the winglike supporting parts of an aircraft **3** projecting side part of a building **4** group within a political party **5** *Brit* fender **6** *sports* (player on) either side of the field or ice **wings 7** sides of a stage ▹ *v* **8** move through the air **9** wound slightly in the wing or arm **winged** *adj*

▸ **winger** *n sports* player positioned on a wing

wink Ⓣ *v* **1** close and open (an eye) rapidly as a signal **2** twinkle ▹ *n* **3** winking **4** smallest amount of sleep

winkle *n* shellfish with a cone-shaped shell

▸ **winkle out** *v informal* extract or prise out

winnow Ⓣ *v* **1** separate (chaff) from (grain) **2** examine to select desirable elements

Winslet *n* **Kate**. born 1975, British film actress; her films include *Sense and Sensibility* (1995), *Titanic* (1997), *Iris* (2001), and *The Reader* (2008), for which she won an Oscar

winsome *adj* charming or winning

winter *n* **1** coldest season ▹ *v* **2** spend the winter

▸ **wintry** *adj* **1** of or like winter **2** cold or unfriendly

▸ **winter sports** open-air sports held on snow or ice

wipe Ⓣ *v* **1** clean or dry by rubbing **2** erase (a tape) ▹ *n* **3** wiping

▸ **wiper** *n* Also **windshield wiper** device that automatically wipes rain etc. from a windshield

▸ **wipe out** *v* **1** destroy completely **2** *slang* kill

wire *n* **1** thin flexible strand of metal **2** length of this used to carry electric current **3** fencing made of wire **4** telegram ▹ *v* **5** provide with wires **6** send by telegraph

▸ **wiring** *n* system of wires

▸ **wiry** *adj* **1** like wire **2** lean and tough

▸ **wire-haired** *adj* (of a dog) having a stiff wiry coat

wireless *n old-fashioned* same as **radio**

wisdom Ⓣ *n* **1** good sense and judgment **2** accumulated knowledge

▸ **wisdom tooth** any of the four large molar teeth cut usu. after the age of twenty

wise[1] Ⓣ *adj* possessing or showing wisdom **wisely** *adv*

▸ **wiseacre** *n* person who wishes to seem wise

▸ **wisecrack** *informal* ▹ *n* **1** flippant or sardonic remark ▹ *v* **2** make a wisecrack

wise[2] *n obsolete* manner

-wise *adv suffix* **1** indicating direction or manner: *clockwise; likewise* **2** with reference to: *businesswise*

THESAURUS

wing *n* **1 = faction**, group, arm, section, branch ▸ *v* **2 = fly**, soar, glide **3 = wound**, hit, clip

wink *v* **1 = blink**, bat, flutter **2 = twinkle**, flash, sparkle, gleam, glimmer ▸ *n* **3 = blink**, flutter

winkle out *v* **= extract**, dislodge, extricate, dig out, draw out, force out, prise out

winner *n* **= victor**, champion, conqueror • *The winners will be notified by mail.* OPPOSITE: loser *See also*: **success**

winning *adj* **1 = victorious**, successful, triumphant, conquering **2 = charming**, attractive, cute, engaging, pleasing, alluring, likable *or* likeable, disarming, enchanting, endearing

winnings *pl n* **= spoils**, prize, gains, proceeds, profits, takings

winnow *v* **= separate**, select, divide, sift, sort out

wintry *adj* **= cold**, icy, snowy, chilly, frosty, freezing, frozen

wipe *v* **1 = clean**, brush, rub, mop, swab, sponge **2 = erase**, remove ▹ **wipe out = destroy**, erase, massacre, eradicate, annihilate, obliterate, exterminate, expunge ▸ *n* **3 = rub**, brush

wiry *adj* **= lean**, strong, tough, sinewy

wisdom *n* **= insight**, reason, knowledge, judgment, discernment • *the wisdom that comes from experience* OPPOSITE: foolishness RELATED WORD *adjective*: sagacious *See also*: **sense**

wise *adj* **= sensible**, rational, informed, judicious, perceptive, shrewd • *a wise person* OPPOSITE: foolish *See also*: **logical, reasonable**

wisecrack *n* (*Informal*) **1 = joke**, quip, jest, jibe, witticism ▸ *v* **2 = joke**, quip, jest, jibe

W

DICTIONARY

wish Ⓣ *v* **1** want or desire **2** feel or express a hope about someone's wellbeing, success, etc. ▷ *n* **3** expression of a desire **4** thing desired
▸ **wishful** *adj* too optimistic
▸ **wishbone** *n* V-shaped bone above the breastbone of a fowl
wishy-washy *adj informal* insipid or bland
wisp *n* **1** light delicate streak **2** small untidy bundle or tuft **3** slight trace **wispy** *adj*
wisteria *n* climbing shrub with blue or purple flowers
wistful Ⓣ *adj* sadly longing **wistfully** *adv*
wit[1] Ⓣ *n* **1** ability to use words or ideas in a clever and amusing way **2** person with this ability **3** *sometimes pl* ability to think and act quickly **witty** *adj* **wittily** *adv*
▸ **witticism** *n* witty remark
▸ **witless** *adj* foolish
wit[2] *v* **to wit** that is to say, namely
witch Ⓣ *n* **1** person, usu. female, who practises (black) magic **2** ugly wicked woman **3** fascinating woman
▸ **witchcraft** *n* use of magic
▸ **witch doctor** (in certain societies) a man appearing to cure or cause injury or disease by magic
▸ **witch-hunt** *n* campaign against people with unpopular views
with *prep* **1** by means of **2** in the company of **3** possessing **4** in relation to **5** in a manner characterized by **6** because of **7** understanding or agreeing with
▸ **within** *prep, adv* in or inside
▸ **without** *prep* **1** not having, accompanied by, or using **2** *obsolete* outside
withdraw Ⓣ *v* **-drawing, -drew, -drawn** take or move out or away **withdrawal** *n*
▸ **withdrawn** *adj* unsociable
wither Ⓣ *v* wilt or dry up
▸ **withering** *adj* (of a look or remark) scornful
withers *pl n* ridge between a horse's shoulder blades
withhold Ⓣ *v* **-holding, -held** refrain from giving
withstand Ⓣ *v* **-standing, -stood** oppose or resist successfully
witness Ⓣ *n* **1** person who has seen something happen **2** evidence or testimony **3** person giving evidence in court ▷ *v* **4** see at first hand **5** give evidence **6** sign (a document) to certify that it is genuine
Wittgenstein *n* **Ludwig Josef Johann**. 1889–1951, British philosopher, born in Austria. After studying with Bertrand Russell, he wrote the *Tractatus Logico-Philosophicus* (1921), which explores the relationship of language to the world.

THESAURUS

wish *n* **1 = desire**, want, urge, hunger, longing, hankering • *She was sincere in her wish to make up with me.* ▸ *v* **2 = want**, long, desire, hunger, thirst, yearn • *We wished to return.* *See also*: **will**
wispy *adj* **= thin**, fine, delicate, fragile, frail, flimsy, attenuated
wistful *adj* **= melancholy**, thoughtful, longing, reflective, dreamy, meditative, contemplative, pensive
wit *n* **1 = humor**, banter, wordplay, badinage, drollery, jocularity, raillery, repartee **2 = humorist**, card (*informal*), comedian, wag, joker **3 = cleverness**, sense, wisdom, intellect, ingenuity, acumen, brains, common sense
witch *n* **= enchantress**, magician, crone, hag, sorceress
witchcraft *n* **= magic**, sorcery, wizardry, enchantment, necromancy, occultism, the black art, voodoo
withdraw *v* **1 = remove**, extract, draw out, take out • *I withdrew some money from the bank.* **2 = back out**, leave, retire, retreat, pull out • *They withdrew from the conference.*
withdrawal *n* **= removal**, extraction
withdrawn *adj* **= uncommunicative**, distant, shy, reserved, introverted, retiring, taciturn, unforthcoming
wither *v* **= decline**, fade, wilt, droop, shrivel • *Will the company flourish or wither?*
withering *adj* **= scornful**, hurtful, devastating, humiliating, mortifying, snubbing
withhold *v* **= keep back**, reserve, refuse, hide, retain, suppress, conceal, hold back
without charge *See* **free**
without delay *See* **now**
without doubt *See* **certainly**
withstand *v* **= resist**, bear, suffer, oppose, endure, tolerate, cope with, hold off, stand up to
witless *adj* **= foolish**, stupid, silly, senseless, idiotic, inane, moronic, halfwitted
witness *n* **1 = observer**, spectator, bystander, eyewitness, onlooker • *The police appealed for witnesses to come forward.* **2 = testifier**, corroborator ▸ *v* **3 = see**, watch, observe, be present at • *Anyone who witnessed the attack should call the police.* **4 = sign**, endorse, countersign
wits *pl n* **= intelligence**, reason, sense, understanding, comprehension, ingenuity, acumen, brains (*informal*), cleverness, faculties
witticism *n* **= quip**, pun, one-liner (*slang*), bon mot, riposte
witty *adj* **= humorous**, funny, brilliant, sparkling, clever, amusing • *He's so witty I could listen to him for hours.*

DICTIONARY

He was a major influence on logical positivism but later repudiated this, and in *Philosophical Investigations* (1953) he argues that philosophical problems arise from insufficient attention to the variety of natural language use
wittingly *adv* intentionally
wives *n* plural of **wife**
wizard Ⓣ *n* **1** magician **2** person with outstanding skill in a particular field
wizardry *n*
wizened Ⓣ [**wiz**-zend] *adj* shrivelled or wrinkled
Władysław II *n* original name *Jogaila*. ?1351–1434, grand duke of Lithuania (1377–1401) and king of Poland (1386–1434). He united Lithuania and Poland and founded the Jagiellon dynasty
Władysław IV *n* 1595–1648, king of Poland (1632–48)
WMD weapon(s) of mass destruction
wobble Ⓣ *v* **1** move unsteadily **2** shake ▷ *n* **3** unsteady movement **4** shake **wobbly** *adj*
Wodehouse *n* Sir **P**(**elham**) **G**(**renville**). 1881–1975, US author, born in England. His humorous novels of upper-class life in England include the *Psmith* and *Jeeves* series **Wodehousian** *adj*
wodge *n informal* thick lump or chunk
woe Ⓣ *n* **1** grief **woes 2** problems
▸ **woeful** *adj* **1** miserable **2** causing woe **3** pitiful **woefully** *adv*
▸ **woebegone** *adj* looking miserable
wok *n* bowl-shaped Chinese cooking pan, used esp. for frying
woke *v* past tense of **wake**[1]
▸ **woken** *v* past participle of **wake**[1]
wold *n* open downs
wolf Ⓣ *n, pl* **wolves 1** wild predatory canine mammal ▷ *v* **2** eat ravenously
▸ **cry wolf** raise a false alarm
▸ **wolf whistle** whistle by a man indicating that he thinks a woman is attractive
▸ **wolf willow** shrub with silvery leaves
Wolf *n* **1 Hugo**. 1860–1903, Austrian composer, esp. of songs, including the *Italienisches Liederbuch* and the *Spanisches Liederbuch* **2 Howlin'**. See **Howlin' Wolf**
Wolfe *n* **1 James**. 1727–59, English soldier, who commanded the British capture of Quebec, in which he was killed **2 Thomas** (**Clayton**). 1900–38, US novelist, noted for his autobiographical fiction, esp. *Look Homeward, Angel* (1929) **3 Tom**, full name *Thomas Kennerly Wolfe*. born 1931, US author and journalist; his books include *The Right Stuff* (1979) and the novels *Bonfire of the Vanities* (1987), and *A Man in Full* (1998)
Wolf-Ferrari *n* **Ermanno**. 1876–1948, Italian composer born of a German father, in Germany from 1909. His works, mainly in a lyrical style, include operas, such as *The Jewels of the Madonna* (1911) and *Susanna's Secret* (1909)
wolfram *n* tungsten
Wollstonecraft *n* **Mary**. 1759–97, British feminist and writer, author of *A Vindication of the Rights of Women* (1792); wife of William Godwin and mother of Mary Shelley
Wolsey *n* **Thomas**. ?1475–1530, English cardinal and statesman; archbishop of York (1514–30); lord chancellor (1515–29). He dominated Henry VIII's foreign and domestic policies but his failure to obtain papal consent for the annulment of the king's marriage to Catherine of Aragon led to his arrest for high treason (1530); he died on the journey to face trial
wolverine *n* carnivorous mammal of Arctic regions
woman Ⓣ *n, pl* **women 1** adult human female **2** women collectively **womanhood** *n*
▸ **womanish** *adj* (of a man) looking like a woman
▸ **womanly** *adj* having qualities traditionally associated with a woman
▸ **womanizing** *n* (of a man) practice of having casual affairs with women **womanizer** *n*
▸ **Women's Movement** movement for the removal of social and economic inequalities between women and men

THESAURUS

wizard *n* = **magician**, witch, shaman, sorcerer, conjurer, magus, necromancer, occultist, warlock
wizardry *n* = **magic**, sorcery, witchcraft, voodoo
wizened *adj* = **wrinkled**, dried up, gnarled, lined, shrivelled, shrunken, withered
wobble *v* **1** = **shake**, rock, sway, teeter, tremble, totter ▸ *n* **2** = **unsteadiness**, shake, tremor, tremble
wobbly *adj* = **unsteady**, shaky, uneven, rickety, teetering, tottering
woe *n* = **misery**, grief, distress, sadness, sorrow, anguish, gloom, agony, unhappiness, wretchedness
woeful *adj* **1** = **sad**, tragic, dismal, pathetic, miserable, deplorable, grievous, lamentable, wretched, distressing **2** = **pitiful**, bad, poor, sorry, pathetic, appalling, dreadful, deplorable, feeble, abysmal
wolf *See* **gobble**
woman *n* = **lady**, female • *The woman over there is my aunt.*
See also: **adult**
womanizer *n* = **philanderer**, Casanova, Don Juan, lecher, seducer
womanly *adj* = **feminine**, warm, female, tender, ladylike, motherly, matronly

DICTIONARY

womb *n* hollow organ in female mammals where babies are conceived and develop
wombat *n* small heavily-built burrowing Aust. marsupial
won *v* past of **win**
wonder ⓣ *n* **1** emotion caused by an amazing or unusual thing **2** wonderful thing ▷ *v* **3** be curious about **4** feel wonder ▷ *adj* **5** spectacularly successful: *a wonder drug* **wonderment** *n*
▸ **wonderful** *adj* **1** very fine: *a wonderful job* **2** causing surprise or amazement **wonderfully** *adv*
▸ **wondrous** *adj old-fashioned* **1** wonderful **2** strange
Wonder *n* **Stevie**, real name *Steveland Judkins Morris.* born 1950, US Motown singer, songwriter, and multi-instrumentalist. His recordings include *Up-Tight* (1966), "Superstition" (1972), *Innervisions* (1973), *Songs in the Key of Life* (1976), and "I Just Called to Say I Love You" (1985)
wonky ⓣ *adj* **-kier, -kiest** *informal* **1** shaky or unsteady **2** not working properly
wont ⓣ [rhymes with **don't**] *n* **1** custom ▷ *adj* **2** accustomed
won't will not
woo ⓣ *v* **1** try to persuade **2** *old-fashioned* try to gain the love of
wood ⓣ *n* **1** substance trees are made of, used in building and as fuel **2** *also pl* area where trees grow **woody** *adj*
▸ **wooded** *adj* covered with trees
▸ **wooden** *adj* **1** made of wood **2** without expression
▸ **woodbine** *n* honeysuckle
▸ **woodcock** *n* game bird
▸ **woodcut** *n* **1** engraved block of wood **2** print made from this
▸ **woodland** *n* forest
▸ **woodlouse** *n* small insect-like creature with many legs
▸ **woodpecker** *n* bird which searches tree trunks for insects
▸ **wood pigeon** large Eurasian pigeon
▸ **woodwind** *adj, n* (of) a type of wind instrument made of wood
▸ **woodworm** *n* insect larva that bores into wood
Wood *n* **1** Sir **Henry** (**Joseph**). 1869–1944, English conductor, who founded the Promenade Concerts in London **2 John**, known as *the Elder*. 1707–54, British architect and town planner, working mainly in Bath, where he designed the North and South Parades (1728) and the Circus (1754) **3** his son, **John**, known as *the Younger*. 1727–82, British architect: designed the Royal Crescent (1767–71) and the Assembly Rooms (1769–71), Bath
Woods *n* **Tiger**, real name *Eldrick Woods*. born 1975, US golfer: youngest US Masters champion (1997) and first Black golfer to win a major championship; in 2001 he became the only player to hold all four major titles at once
woodshed *n* shed made of or used for storing wood
▸ **take someone to the woodshed** *informal* reprimand privately
Woodsworth *n* **James Shaver**. 1874–1942, Canadian social democratic politician, social activist, and Methodist minister. He was an MP first for the Independent Labour Party and then for the Co-operative Commonwealth Federation, a party he led from its founding until his death
woof[1] *n* cross threads in weaving
woof[2] *n* barking noise made by a dog
woofer *n* loudspeaker for reproducing low-frequency sounds
wool ⓣ *n* **1** soft hair of sheep, goats, etc. **2** yarn spun from this **woollen** *adj*
▸ **woolly** *adj* **1** of or like wool **2** vague or muddled ▷ *n* **3** knitted woollen garment
▸ **woolgathering** *n* daydreaming
woozy *adj* **woozier, wooziest** *informal*

THESAURUS

wonder *v* **1** = **ask oneself**, speculate, puzzle, ponder • *I wondered what that noise was.* **2** = **be amazed**, marvel, boggle, be astonished • *He wondered at their sudden change of plans.* ▸ *n* **3** = **phenomenon**, miracle, spectacle, marvel • *one of the wonders of nature* **4** = **amazement**, surprise, awe, admiration, fascination, astonishment, bewilderment, wonderment
wonderful *adj* **1** = **excellent**, great (*informal*), tremendous, superb, marvellous • *It's wonderful to see you.* **2** = **remarkable**, amazing, incredible, magnificent, astounding • *The sunset was a truly wonderful sight.*
See also: **brilliant, grand, splendid**
wonky *adj* **1** = **askew**, crooked, awry, out of alignment **2** = **shaky**, unsteady, wobbly
wont *See* **custom**
woo *v* = **court**, pursue, cultivate, make a pitch for (*slang*)
wood *n* **1** = **timber** **2** = **woodland**, forest, grove, thicket, coppice, copse
wooded *adj* = **tree-covered**, forested, sylvan (*poetic*), timbered, tree-clad
wooden *adj* **1** = **woody**, timber, ligneous **2** = **expressionless**, lifeless, unresponsive, deadpan
wool *n* = **fleece**, hair, yarn
woolly *adj* **1** = **fleecy**, hairy, shaggy, woollen **2** = **vague**, unclear, indefinite, confused, hazy, ill-defined, indistinct, muddled

DICTIONARY

weak, dizzy, and confused

word Ⓣ *n* **1** smallest single meaningful unit of speech or writing **2** chat or discussion **3** brief remark **4** message **5** promise **6** command ▷ *v* **7** express in words

▸**wordy** *adj* using too many words **wordiness** *n*

▸**wording** *n* choice and arrangement of words

▸**word processor** keyboard, microprocessor, and VDU for electronic organization and storage of text **word processing**

wore *v* past tense of **wear**

work Ⓣ *n* **1** physical or mental effort directed to making or doing something **2** paid employment **3** duty or task **4** something made or done **5** decoration of a specified kind: *needlework* **works 6** factory **7** total of a writer's or artist's achievements **8** *informal* full treatment **9** mechanism of a machine ▷ *v* **10** (cause to) do work **11** be employed **12** (cause to) operate **13** cultivate (land) **14** manipulate, shape, or process **15** (cause to) reach a specified condition **16** accomplish ▷ *adj* **17** of or for work **workable** *adj* **worker** *n*

▸**work to rule** adhere strictly to all working regulations to reduce the rate of work as a protest **work-to-rule** *n*

▸**workaholic** *n* person addicted to work

▸**workhouse** *n hist* institution where the poor were given food and lodgings in return for work

▸**working class** social class consisting of wage earners, esp. manual workers **working-class** *adj*

▸**working party** committee investigating a specific problem

▸**workman** *n* manual worker

▸**workmanship** *n* **1** skill of a workman **2** skill exhibited in a finished product

▸**worktop** *n* surface in a kitchen, used for food preparation

world Ⓣ *n* **1** the planet earth **2** mankind **3** society **4** sphere of existence ▷ *adj* **5** of the whole world

▸**worldly** *adj* **1** not spiritual **2** concerned with material things **3** wise in the ways of the world

▸**World Wide Web** global network of linked computer files

THESAURUS

word *n* **1 = remark**, statement, comment, utterance • *I'd like to say a word of thanks to everyone who helped me.* **2 = chat**, talk, discussion, conversation • *May I please have a quick word with you?* **3 = message**, announcement, news, information, communication, intelligence, bulletin • *Since then we've had no word from them.* **4 = promise**, pledge, assurance, oath, word of honour • *He gave me his word that he would be there.* **5 = term**, name, expression **6 = command**, order, mandate, decree, bidding ▸*v* **7 = express**, say, put, state, phrase, utter, couch
See also: **bond, guarantee, rumour**

wording *n* **= phraseology**, language, terminology, phrasing, words

wordless *See* **silent**

word of honour *See* **word**

wordy *adj* **= long-winded**, windy, diffuse, rambling, verbose, prolix

work *v* **1 = labour**, slave, toil, slog away • *I had to work ten hours a day.* OPPOSITE: laze **2 = be employed**, be in work **3 = operate**, use, move, drive, control, manage, handle, manipulate **4 = function**, go, run, operate **5 = cultivate**, farm, dig, till **6 = manipulate**, form, fashion, shape, mould, knead ▷ **work out = solve**, resolve, calculate, figure out • *It took us some time to work out what was happening*; **= happen**, go, develop, turn out • *Things didn't work out that way after all.* ▷ **work together = co-operate**, unite, team up ▸*n* **7 = employment**, job, business, occupation, craft, profession, livelihood • *She's trying to find work.* **8 = task**, job, duty, assignment, chore • *Sometimes he had to take work home.* **9 = effort**, industry, sweat, labour, toil, exertion, drudgery, elbow grease (*facetious*) **10 = handiwork**, production, piece, creation, achievement, composition, opus
See also: **comprehend, crack, reckon**
See also: **act, behave, book, exercise, struggle, succeed**

workable *adj* **= viable**, possible, practical, feasible, doable, practicable

worker *n* **= employee**, labourer, craftsperson • *seeking a reliable research worker* ▷ **workers** *See* **labour, staff**

workforce *See* **labour, staff**

working *adj* **1 = employed**, active, in work **2 = functioning**, operative, going, running

workman *n* **= labourer**, worker, hand, employee, mechanic, operative, artisan, journeyman, craftsman, tradesman

workmanship *n* **= skill**, technique, expertise, artistry, craftsmanship, handiwork

workmate *See* **associate, colleague**

works *pl n* **1 = factory**, plant, mill, workshop **2 = writings**, output, canon, oeuvre (*French*) **3 = mechanism**, action, movement, machinery, parts, workings

workshop *n* **= workroom**, plant, factory, studio, mill

world *n* **1 = earth**, globe **2 = mankind**,

DICTIONARY

worm *n* **1** small limbless invertebrate animal **2** wretched or spineless person **3** shaft with a spiral thread forming part of a gear system **4** *computers* type of virus **worms 5** illness caused by parasitic worms in the intestines ▷ *v* **6** rid of worms **7** crawl **8** insinuate (oneself) **9** extract (information) craftily **wormy** *adj*
▶**wormcast** *n* coil of earth excreted by a burrowing worm
▶**worm-eaten** *adj* eaten into by worms
wormwood *n* bitter plant
worn *v* past participle of **wear**
worry *v* **-rying, -ried 1** (cause to) be anxious or uneasy **2** annoy or bother **3** (of a dog) bite repeatedly ▷ *n, pl* **-ries 4** (cause of) anxiety or concern **worried** *adj* **worrying** *adj, n*
worse *adj, adv* **1** comparative of **bad, badly** ▷ *n* **2** worse thing
▶**worsen** *v* make or grow worse
▶**worst** *adj, adv* **1** superlative of **bad, badly** ▷ *n* **2** worst thing
worship *v* **-shipping, -shipped 1** show religious devotion to **2** love and admire ▷ *n* **3** worshipping **4 Worship** title for a mayor or magistrate **worshipper** *n*
▶**worshipful** *adj* **1** worshipping **2** (in titles) honourable
worsted [**wooss**-tid] *n* **1** type of woollen yarn or fabric ▷ *adj* **2** made of worsted
wort [**wurt**] *n* infusion of malt used to make beer
worth *adj* **1** having a value of **2** meriting or justifying ▷ *n* **3** value or price **4** excellence **5** amount to be had for a given sum **worthless** *adj*
▶**worthy** *adj* **1** having value or merit **2** deserving ▷ *n* **3** *informal* notable person **worthily** *adv* **worthiness** *n*
▶**worthwhile** *adj* worth the time or effort involved
would *v* used as an auxiliary to form the past tense or subjunctive mood of **will**, express a request, or describe a habitual past action
▶**would-be** *adj* wishing or pretending to be
wouldn't would not
wound[1] *n* **1** injury caused by violence **2** injury to the feelings ▷ *v* **3** inflict a wound on
wound[2] *v* past of **wind**[2]

THESAURUS

man, everyone, everybody, humanity, humankind, the public **3 = sphere**, area, field, environment, domain, realm
worldly *adj* **1 = earthly**, physical, secular, profane, terrestrial, temporal **2 = materialistic**, selfish, greedy, grasping **3 = worldly-wise**, sophisticated, experienced, cosmopolitan, blasé, knowing, urbane
worldwide *adj* **= global**, international, general, pandemic, universal, ubiquitous, omnipresent
worn *adj* **= ragged**, shabby, frayed, tattered, tatty, the worse for wear, threadbare
worn out *adj* **1 = worn**, broken-down, tattered, threadbare • *These shoes are worn out.* **2 = exhausted**, tired, weary, fatigued, prostrate • *You must be worn out after the trip.*
worried *adj* **= anxious**, troubled, nervous, concerned, uneasy, bothered • *I'm worried about our lost dog.* OPPOSITE: unconcerned
worry *v* **1 = be anxious**, fret, brood, feel uneasy • *Don't worry, it's bound to arrive soon.* **2 = trouble**, plague, bother, hassle (*informal*), pester • *I didn't want to worry the kids with this.* ▶*n* **3 = anxiety**, concern, fear, apprehension, unease, misgiving • *a major source of worry* **4 = problem**, care, trouble, bother, hassle (*informal*)
See also: **agitate, burden, distress, disturb, sorrow, stress**
worrying *See* **serious**
worsen *v* **1 = deteriorate**, decline, degenerate, go downhill • *Their relationship worsened.* OPPOSITE: improve **2 = aggravate**, damage, exacerbate
worship *v* **1 = revere**, honour, venerate • *a place where people can worship* **2 = love**, adore, idolize • *She had worshipped him from afar for years.* OPPOSITE: despise ▶*n* **3 = adoration**, praise, homage, devotion, admiration, adulation • *Fans treated the home team with a respect close to worship.*
worth *n* **1 = value**, price, rate, cost, valuation **2 = merit**, value, quality, importance, excellence, goodness, usefulness, worthiness
worthless *adj* **1 = valueless**, poor, useless, meaningless, paltry, trivial, trifling • *a worthless piece of junk* OPPOSITE: valuable **2 = good-for-nothing**, despicable, lousy (*slang*), vile, contemptible, scuzzy (*slang*)
See also: **empty**
worthwhile *adj* **= useful**, valuable, productive, profitable, helpful, beneficial, constructive, expedient
worthy *adj* **= praiseworthy**, valuable, worthwhile, deserving, admirable, laudable, meritorious, virtuous, creditable
would-be *adj* **= budding**, unfulfilled, self-appointed, self-styled, wannabe (*informal*)
would like *See* **fancy**
wound *n* **1 = injury**, cut, hurt, trauma (*pathol*), lesion, gash, laceration **2 = insult**, slight, offence ▶*v* **3 = injure**, cut, hurt, wing, pierce, gash, lacerate **4 = offend**, hurt,

DICTIONARY

wove *v* a past tense of **weave**
▸ **woven** *v* a past participle of **weave**
wow *interj* **1** exclamation of astonishment ▷ *n* **2** *informal* astonishing person or thing
wpm words per minute
WRAC Women's Royal Army Corps
wrack *n* seaweed
WRAF Women's Royal Air Force
wraith *n* **1** apparition of a person seen shortly before his or her death **2** ghost
wrangle Ⓣ *v* **1** argue noisily ▷ *n* **2** noisy argument
wrap Ⓣ *v* **wrapping, wrapped 1** fold (something) round (a person or thing) so as to cover ▷ *n* **2** garment wrapped round the shoulders **3** sandwich made by wrapping a filling in a tortilla
▸ **wrapper** *n* **1** cover **2** loose dressing gown
▸ **wrapping** *n* material used to wrap
▸ **wrap party** party held by cast and crew to celebrate the completion of filming of a TV programme or film
▸ **wrap up** *v* **1** fold paper round **2** put warm clothes on **3** *informal* finish or settle (a matter)
wrath Ⓣ [**roth**] *n* intense anger **wrathful** *adj*
Wray *n* **Fay**. 1907–2004, US film and TV actress born in Canada. Best known for her performance as the heroine in *King Kong* (1933)
wreak Ⓣ *v* **1** inflict (vengeance) **2** cause (chaos)
wreath Ⓣ *n* twisted ring or band of flowers or leaves used as a memorial or tribute
▸ **wreathed** *adj* **1** surrounded (by): *wreathed in pipe smoke* **2** surrounded by a ring (of): *wreathed in geraniums*
wreck Ⓣ *n* **1** accidental destruction of a ship at sea **2** wrecked ship **3** remains of something destroyed **4** person in very poor condition ▷ *v* **5** cause the wreck of **wrecker** *n*
▸ **wreckage** *n* wrecked remains
wren *n* small brown songbird
Wren *n* Sir **Christopher**. 1632–1723, English architect. He designed St Paul's Cathedral and over 50 other London churches after the Great Fire as well as many secular buildings
wrench Ⓣ *v* **1** twist or pull forcefully **2** sprain ▷ *n* **3** forceful twist or pull **4** sprain **5** difficult or painful parting **6** adjustable spanner
wrest Ⓣ *v* **1** take by force **2** twist violently
wrestle Ⓣ *v* **1** fight, esp. as a sport, by grappling with and trying to throw down an opponent **2** struggle hard with **wrestler** *n* **wrestling** *n*
wretch Ⓣ *n* **1** despicable person **2** pitiful person
▸ **wretched** [**retch**-id] *adj* **1** miserable or unhappy **2** worthless **wretchedly** *adv* **wretchedness** *n*
wrier *adj* a comparative of **wry**
▸ **wriest** *adj* a superlative of **wry**
wriggle Ⓣ *v* **1** move with a twisting action **2** manoeuvre oneself by devious means ▷ *n* **3** wriggling movement

THESAURUS

sting, annoy, mortify, cut (someone) to the quick
wounded *See* **hurt**
wrangle *v* **1 = argue**, fight, dispute, row, contend, disagree, squabble, quarrel, bicker ▸ *n* **2 = argument**, dispute, row, altercation, squabble, quarrel, bickering, tiff
wrap *v* **1 = cover**, package, pack, bind, shroud, enclose, swathe, encase, bundle up, enfold ▸ *n* **2 = cloak**, cape, mantle, shawl, stole
wrapper *n* **= cover**, case, jacket, packaging, envelope, wrapping
wrap up *v* **1 = giftwrap**, package, pack, bundle up **2** (*Informal*) **= end**, conclude, terminate, finish off, polish off, round off, wind up ▷ **wrapped up** *See* **preoccupied**
wrath *n* **= anger**, rage, temper, ire, displeasure, resentment, fury, indignation
wreak *See* **bring**
wreath *n* **= garland**, band, ring, crown, festoon, chaplet
wreck *v* **1 = destroy**, break, devastate, smash, ruin, spoil, shatter, demolish ▸ *n* **2 = shipwreck**, hulk, sinking **3** *Also* **wreckage = remains**, debris, ruin, rubble, heap, fragments, pieces, rust bucket, remnants **4 = collision**, crash, accident, pile-up smash car crash, car accident
wrench *v* **1 = twist**, force, pull, tear, rip, yank, jerk, tug **2 = sprain**, strain, rick ▸ *n* **3 = twist**, pull, rip, yank, jerk, tug **4 = sprain**, strain, twist **5 = blow**, shock, upheaval, pang **6 = spanner**, adjustable spanner
wrest *v* **= seize**, take, win, force, extract, wrench
wrestle *v* **= fight**, battle, struggle, combat, grapple, scuffle, tussle
wretch *n* **= scoundrel**, worm, rogue, swine, rascal, miscreant, good-for-nothing
wretched *adj* **1 = unhappy**, hapless, depressed, miserable, dejected, downcast, disconsolate, forlorn, woebegone **2 = worthless**, poor, sorry, pathetic, miserable, paltry, inferior
wriggle *v* **1 = twist**, turn, jerk, squirm, jiggle, wiggle, writhe **2 = crawl**, snake, worm, slink, zigzag ▷ **wriggle out of = avoid**, dodge, manoeuvre, extricate oneself, worm out of ▸ *n* **3 = twist**, turn, jerk, squirm, jiggle, wiggle

DICTIONARY

wright *n* maker: *playwright*
Wright *n* **1 Frank Lloyd**. 1869–1959, US architect, whose designs include the Imperial Hotel, Tokyo (1916), the Guggenheim Museum, New York (1943), and many private houses. His "organic architecture" sought a close relationship between buildings and their natural surroundings **2 Joseph**, known as *Wright of Derby*. 1734–97, British painter, noted for his paintings of industrial and scientific subjects, esp. *The Orrery* (?1765) and *The Air Pump* (1768) **3 Wilbur** (1867–1912) and his brother, **Orville** (1871–1948), US aviation pioneers, who designed and flew the first powered aircraft (1903)
wring Ⓣ *v* **wringing, wrung 1** twist, esp. to squeeze liquid out of **2** clasp and twist (the hands) **3** obtain by forceful means
wrinkle Ⓣ *n* **1** slight crease, esp. one in the skin due to age ▷ *v* **2** make or become wrinkled **wrinkly** *adj*
wrist *n* joint between the hand and the arm
▸ **wristwatch** *n* watch worn on the wrist
writ Ⓣ *n* written legal command
write Ⓣ *v* **writing, wrote, written 1** mark paper etc. with symbols or words **2** set down in words **3** be the author or composer of **4** communicate by letter **writing** *n*
▸ **writer** *n* **1** author **2** person who has written something specified
▸ **write-off** *n informal* something damaged beyond repair
▸ **write-up** *n* published account of something
writhe Ⓣ *v* **1** twist or squirm in or as if in pain **2** be very embarrassed
WRNS Women's Royal Naval Service
wrong Ⓣ *adj* **1** incorrect or mistaken **2** immoral or bad **3** not intended or suitable **4** not working properly ▷ *adv* **5** in a wrong manner ▷ *n* **6** something immoral or unjust ▷ *v* **7** treat unjustly **8** malign **wrongly** *adv* **wrongful** *adj* **wrongfully** *adv*
▸ **wrongdoing** *n* immoral or illegal behaviour
wrote *v* past tense of **write**
wrought [**rawt**] *v* **1** *lit* past of **work** ▷ *adj* **2** (of metals) shaped by hammering or beating
▸ **wrought iron** pure form of iron used for decorative work
wrung *v* past of **wring**
WRVS Women's Royal Voluntary Service
wry Ⓣ *adj* **wrier, wriest** *or* **wryer, wryest** **1** dryly humorous **2** (of a facial expression) contorted **wryly** *adv*
wt. weight
Wu *n* **Harry**, real name *Wu Hongda*. born 1937, Chinese dissident and human-rights campaigner, a US citizen from 1994: held in labour camps (1960–79); exiled to the US in 1985 but returned secretly to document forced labour in Chinese prisons
Wu Di, Wu Ti *n* 156 BC–86 BC, Chinese emperor (140–86) of the Han dynasty, who greatly extended the Chinese empire and made Confucianism the state religion
wuss *n slang* feeble person
WWI World War One
WWII World War Two
WWW World Wide Web
wych-elm *n* elm with large rough leaves

THESAURUS

wring *v* = **twist**, force, squeeze, extract, screw
wrinkle *n* **1** = **crease**, line, fold, crumple, furrow, corrugation, crinkle, crow's-foot ▸ *v* **2** = **crease**, gather, fold, crumple, corrugate, pucker, rumple, furrow
writ *n* = **summons**, document, decree, court order
write *v* = **record**, compose, correspond, inscribe, take down • *Write your name and address on a piece of paper.* ▷ **write down** *See* **record**
writer *n* = **author**, novelist, hack, scribe, penpusher, scribbler, wordsmith
writhe *v* = **squirm**, struggle, toss, twist, thrash, jerk, wiggle, wriggle, thresh
writing *n* **1** = **script**, hand, scrawl, handwriting, scribble, calligraphy, penmanship **2** = **document**, work, book, publication, composition, opus
wrong *adj* **1** = **incorrect**, false, faulty, mistaken, untrue, unsound • *That was the wrong answer.* OPPOSITE: right **2** = **bad**, illegal, unfair, evil, immoral, unjust, crooked • *It's wrong to hurt people.* OPPOSITE: right **3** = **inappropriate**, unacceptable, incorrect, undesirable, unsuitable, unbecoming, unseemly, incongruous **4** = **defective**, faulty, awry, amiss, askew ▸ *n* **5** = **crime**, abuse, grievance, sin, injustice • *the wrongs of our society* ▸ *adv* **6** = **incorrectly**, badly, mistakenly, wrongly, erroneously, inaccurately **7** = **amiss**, awry, astray, askew ▸ *v* **8** = **mistreat**, abuse, hurt, harm, cheat, oppress, malign, dishonour, take advantage of
wrongdoer *n* = **offender**, criminal, culprit, villain, delinquent, lawbreaker, miscreant, sinner, evildoer, perp (*informal*)
wrongful *adj* = **improper**, criminal, illegal, evil, unethical, unlawful, wicked, immoral, unjust, illegitimate
wry *adj* **1** = **ironic**, dry, sarcastic, sardonic, droll, mocking **2** = **contorted**, twisted, uneven, crooked

W

X **1** indicating an error, a choice, or a kiss **2** indicating an unknown, unspecified, or variable factor, number, person, or thing
Xavier *n* **Saint Francis**, known as the *Apostle of the Indies*. 1506–52, Spanish missionary, who was a founding member of the Jesuit society (1534) and later preached in Goa, Ceylon, the East Indies, and Japan. Feast day: Dec 3
X-chromosome *n* sex chromosome that occurs in pairs in the females of many animals, and as one of a pair with the Y-chromosome in males
Xe *chem* xenon
Xenakis *n* **Yannis**. 1922–2001, Greek composer and musical theorist, born in Romania, later a French citizen. He was noted for his use of computers in composition; his works include ST/10-1, 080262 (1962) and *Doxorkh* (1991)
xenon *n* colourless odourless gas found in very small quantities in the air
Xenophanes *n* ?570–?480 BC, Greek philosopher and poet, noted for his monotheism and regarded as a founder of the Eleatic school
xenophobia [zen-oh-**fobe**-ee-a] *n* fear or hatred of people from other countries
Xerox [**zeer**-ox] *n* **1** ® machine for copying printed material **2** ® copy made by a Xerox machine ▷ *v* **3** copy (a document) using such a machine
Xerxes I *n* ?519–465 BC, king of Persia (485–465), who led a vast army against Greece. His forces were victorious at Thermopylae but his fleet was defeated at Salamis (480) and his army at Plataea (479)
Xmas ❶ [**eks**-mass] *n* Christmas
x-ray *n* **1** stream of radiation that can pass through some solid materials **2** picture made by sending x-rays through someone's body to examine internal organs ▷ *v* **3** photograph, treat, or examine using x-rays
Xuan Zong, Hsüan-tsung *n* 685–762 AD, Chinese emperor (712–56) of the Tang dynasty
xylem [**zy**-lem] *n* plant tissue that conducts water and minerals from the roots to all other parts
xylophone [**zile**-oh-fone] *n* musical instrument made of a row of wooden bars played with hammers

THESAURUS

Xmas *n* = **Christmas**, Noel, Yule, festive season, Yuletide
X-rated *adj* = **pornographic**, adult, dirty, graphic, obscene, hardcore (*slang*), scuzzy (*slang*)
X-rays *pl n* = **Röntgen rays** (*old-fashioned*)

Yy

yacht [**yott**] *n* large boat with sails or an engine used for racing or pleasure cruising **yachting** *n* **yachtsman** (**yachtswoman**) *n*
yahoo *n* crude coarse person
yak[1] *n* Tibetan ox with long shaggy hair
yak[2] *v* **yakking, yakked** *slang* talk continuously about unimportant matters
Yale lock *n* ® cylinder lock using a flat serrated key
yam *n* tropical root vegetable
Yamagata *n* Prince **Aritomo**. 1838–1922, Japanese soldier and politician. As war minister (1873) and chief of staff (1878), he modernized Japan's military system. He was premier of Japan (1889–93; 1898)
Yamani *n* Sheikh **Ahmed Zaki**. born 1930, Saudi Arabian politician; minister of petroleum and mineral resources (1962–86)
Yamasaki *n* **Minoru**. 1912–86, US architect. His buildings include St Louis Airport, Missouri (1953–55) and the World Trade Center, New York (1970–77)
yank Ⓣ *v* **1** pull or jerk suddenly ▷ *n* **2** sudden pull or jerk
Yankee, Yank *adj, n slang* (of) a person from the United States
yap *v* **yapping, yapped 1** bark with a high-pitched sound **2** *informal* talk continuously ▷ *n* **3** high-pitched bark
Yar'Adua *n* **Umara Musa**. born 1951, Nigerian politician; President from 2007
yard[1] *n* unit of length equal to 36 inches or about 91.4 centimetres
▸ **yardstick** *n* standard against which to judge other people or things
yard[2] *n* enclosed area, usu. next to a building and often used for a particular purpose: *builder's yard*
yarmulke [**yar**-mull-ka] *n* skullcap worn by Jewish men
yarn Ⓣ *n* **1** thread used for knitting or making cloth **2** *informal* long involved story
▸ **spin a yarn** tell an improbable story
yarrow *n* wild plant with flat clusters of white flowers
yashmak *n* veil worn by a Muslim woman to cover her face in public
yaw *v* (of an aircraft or ship) turn to one side or from side to side while moving
yawl *n* two-masted sailing boat
yawn *v* **1** open the mouth wide and take in air deeply, often when sleepy or bored **2** (of an opening) be large and wide ▷ *n* **3** act of yawning **yawning** *adj*
yaws *n* infectious tropical skin disease
Y-chromosome *n* sex chromosome that occurs as one of a pair with the X-chromosome in the males of many animals
yd. yard
YDT Yukon Daylight Time
ye [**yee**] *pron obsolete* you
yea *interj old-fashioned* yes
yeah *interj informal* yes
year *n* **1** time taken for the earth to make one revolution around the sun, about 365 days **2** twelve months from January 1 to December 31
▸ **yearly** *adj, adv* (happening) every year or once a year
▸ **yearling** *n* animal between one and two years old
yearn Ⓣ *v* (foll. by *for*) want (something) very much **yearning** *n, adj*
yeast *n* fungus used to make bread rise and to ferment alcoholic drinks **yeasty** *adj*
Yeats *n* **W(illiam) B(utler)**. 1865–1939, Irish poet and dramatist. His collections of verse include *Responsibilities* (1914), *The Tower* (1928), and *The Winding Stair* (1929). Among his plays are *The Countess Cathleen* (1892; 1912) and *Cathleen ni Houlihan* (1902); he was a founder of the Irish National Theatre Company at the Abbey Theatre in Dublin: Nobel prize for literature 1923
yell Ⓣ *v* **1** shout or scream in a loud or piercing way ▷ *n* **2** loud cry of pain, anger, or fear

THESAURUS

yank *v, n* = **pull**, snatch, hitch, jerk, tug, wrench
yardstick *n* = **standard**, measure, par, benchmark, criterion, gauge, touchstone
yarn *n* **1** = **thread**, fibre **2** (*Old-fashioned, informal*) = **story**, tale, anecdote, fable, cock-and-bull story (*informal*), tall tale (*informal*)
yawning *adj* = **gaping**, wide, vast, cavernous
yearly *adj* **1** = **annual** ▸ *adv* **2** = **annually**, every year, once a year, per annum
yearn *v* = **long**, desire, hunger, ache, covet, crave, itch, hanker
yearning *See* **desire, longing**
yell *v* **1** = **scream**, shout, howl, screech,

DICTIONARY

yellow *n* **1** the colour of gold, a lemon, etc. ▷ *adj* **2** of this colour **3** *informal* cowardly ▷ *v* **4** make or become yellow
▸ **yellow fever** serious infectious tropical disease
▸ **yellowhammer** *n* European songbird with a yellow head and body
▸ **yellow pages** telephone directory which lists businesses under the headings of the type of business or service they provide
yelp Ⓣ *v, n* (give) a short, sudden cry
Yeltsin *n* **Boris** (**Nicolayevich**). 1931–2007, Russian politician: president of the Russian Soviet Federative Socialist Republic (1990–91); president of Russia (1991–99)
yen[1] *n, pl* **yen** main unit of currency in Japan
yen[2] Ⓣ *n informal* longing or desire
yeoman [**yo**-man] *n, pl* **-men** *hist* farmer owning and farming his own land
▸ **yeoman of the guard** member of the ceremonial bodyguard of the British monarchy
yes Ⓣ *interj* **1** expresses consent, agreement, or approval **2** used to answer when one is addressed
▸ **yes man** person who always agrees with his or her superior
yesterday *adv, n* **1** (on) the day before today **2** (in) the recent past
yet Ⓣ *adv* **1** up until then or now **2** still ▷ *conj* **3** nevertheless, still
yeti *n* same as **abominable snowman**
Yevtushenko *n* **Yevgeny Aleksandrovich**. born 1933, Russian poet. His often outspoken poetry includes *Babi Yar* (1962), *Bratsk Station* (1966), and *Farewell to Red Banner* (1992)
yew *n* evergreen tree with needle-like leaves and red berries
YHA Youth Hostels Association
Yiddish *adj, n* (of or in) a language of German origin spoken by many Jews in Europe and elsewhere
yield Ⓣ *v* **1** produce or bear **2** give up control of, surrender **3** give in ▷ *n* **4** amount produced
▸ **yielding** *adj* **1** submissive **2** soft or flexible
yippee *interj* exclamation of joy or pleasure
YMCA Young Men's Christian Association
yodel *v* **-delling, -delled 1** sing with abrupt changes between a normal and a falsetto voice ▷ *n* **2** act or sound of yodelling
yoga *n* Hindu method of exercise and discipline aiming at spiritual, mental, and physical wellbeing
▸ **yogi** *n* person who practises yoga
yoghurt, yogurt, yoghourt *n* slightly sour custard-like food made from milk that has had bacteria added to it, often sweetened and flavoured with fruit
yoke Ⓣ *n* **1** wooden bar put across the necks of two animals to hold them together **2** frame fitting over a person's shoulders for carrying buckets **3** *lit* oppressive force: *the yoke of the tyrant* **4** fitted part of a garment to which a fuller part is attached ▷ *v* **5** put a yoke on **6** unite or link
yokel Ⓣ *n offensive* person who lives in the country and is usu. simple and old-fashioned
yolk *n* yellow part of an egg that provides food for the developing embryo
Yom Kippur *n* annual Jewish religious holiday
yon *adj old-fashioned, dialect* that or those over there
yonder *adv* over there
Yong Lo, Yung-Lo *n* 1360–1424, Chinese emperor (1404–24) of the Ming dynasty. He moved the capital from Nanjing to Peking (now Beijing), which he rebuilt (Also **Ch'eng Tsu**)
yoo-hoo *interj* call to attract attention

THESAURUS

shriek, holler (*informal*), squeal, bawl ▸ *n* **2 = scream**, cry, howl, whoop, screech, shriek
yell at *v* (*Informal*) **= criticize**, rebuke, censure, scold, tear into (*informal*)
yellow *adj, n*
yelp *v* **= cry**, yap, yowl
yen *n* **= longing**, desire, passion, hunger, ache, craving, thirst, itch, yearning, hankering
yes *interj* **= sure**, okay • *"Are you a friend of his?" "Yes."* OPPOSITE: no
yes man *n* **= sycophant**, brown-noser (*slang*), minion, timeserver, toady
yet *conj* **1 = nevertheless**, still, however, notwithstanding ▸ *adv* **2 = so far**, as yet, thus far, until now, up to now **3 = still**, besides, in addition, into the bargain, to boot **4 = now**, just now, right now, so soon
yield *v* **1 = produce**, give, return, provide, earn, net, bear, supply, generate, bring forth **2 = surrender**, resign, submit, bow, relinquish, succumb, capitulate, give in ▸ *n* **3 = profit**, return, income, revenue, output, earnings, takings **4 = produce**, crop, harvest
yielding *adj* **1 = submissive**, flexible, compliant, obedient, docile, accommodating, acquiescent, biddable, pliant **2 = soft**, elastic, spongy, supple, pliable, springy, unresisting
yoke *v* **= burden**, land, load, saddle, encumber
yokel *n* **= peasant**, countryman, rustic, redneck (*slang*), hick (*informal, chiefly US & Canad*), hillbilly, bumpkin *or* country bumpkin

Y

DICTIONARY

yore *n lit* the distant past
York *n* **1** the English royal house that reigned from 1461 to 1485 and was descended from Richard Plantagenet, Duke of York (1411–60), whose claim to the throne precipitated the Wars of the Roses. His sons reigned as Edward IV and Richard III **2 Duke of**, full name *Prince Frederick Augustus, Duke of York and Albany*. 1763–1827, second son of George III of Great Britain and Ireland. An undistinguished commander-in-chief of the British army (1798–1809), he is the "grand old Duke of York" of the nursery rhyme **3 Prince Andrew, Duke of**. born 1960, second son of Elizabeth II of Great Britain and Northern Ireland. He married (1986) Miss Sarah Ferguson; they divorced in 1996; their first daughter, Princess Beatrice of York, was born in 1988 and their second, Princess Eugenie of York, in 1990
Yorkshire pudding *n* baked batter made from flour, milk, and eggs and often eaten with roast beef
you *pron* **1** refers to the person or people addressed **2** refers to an unspecified person or people in general
young Ⓣ *adj* **1** in an early stage of life or growth ▷ *n* **2** offspring, esp. young animals **3** young people in general
▸ **youngster** *n* young person
Young *n* **1 Brigham**. 1801–77, US Mormon leader, who led the Mormon migration to Utah and founded Salt Lake City (1847) **2 Lester**. 1909–59, US saxophonist and clarinetist. He was a leading early exponent of the tenor saxophone in jazz **3 Neil** (**Percival**). born 1945, Canadian rock guitarist, singer, and songwriter. His albums include *Harvest* (1972), *Rust Never Sleeps* (1979), *Ragged Glory* (1990), and *Are You Passionate?* (2002) **4 Thomas**. 1773–1829, English physicist, physician, and Egyptologist. He helped to establish the wave theory of light by his experiments on optical interference and assisted in the decipherment of the Rosetta Stone
Younghusband *n* Sir **Francis Edward**. 1863–1942, British explorer, mainly of N India and Tibet. He used military force to compel the Dalai Lama to sign (1904) a trade agreement with Britain
your *adj* **1** of, belonging to, or associated with you **2** of, belonging to, or associated with an unspecified person or people in general **yourself** *pron*
▸ **yours** *pron* something belonging to you
youth Ⓣ *n* **1** time or condition of being young **2** boy or young man **3** young people as a group **youthful** *adj* **youthfulness** *n*
▸ **youth club** club that provides leisure activities for young people
▸ **youth hostel** inexpensive lodging place for young people travelling cheaply
Youville *n* St **Marie-Marguerite d'**. 1701–71, Canadian lay sister. She and four other women formed a group which in 1755 became the Sisters of Charity of the Hôpital Général,
yowl *v, n* (produce) a loud mournful cry
yo-yo *n, pl* **-yos** toy consisting of a spool attached to a string, by which it is repeatedly spun out and reeled in
YST Yukon Standard Time
YT, Y.T. Yukon Territory
yucca *n* tropical plant with spikes of white leaves
yucky, yukky *adj* **yuckier, yuckiest** *or* **yukkier, yukkiest** *slang* disgusting, nasty
Yugoslavian, Yugoslav *n* **1** person from the former Yugoslavia ▷ *adj* **2** of Yugoslavia
Yule *n lit* Christmas or the Christmas season
yummy Ⓣ *adj* **-mier, -miest** *informal* delicious
Yuppie *n* **1** young highly-paid professional person, esp. one who has a fashionable way of life ▷ *adj* **2** typical of or reflecting the values of Yuppies
YWCA Young Women's Christian Association

THESAURUS

young *adj* **1 = immature**, little, junior, infant, adolescent, youthful, juvenile • *young people* OPPOSITE: old **2 = new**, early, recent, fledgling, undeveloped ▸ *plural n* **3 = offspring**, family, litter, brood, babies, little ones • *The hen may not be able to feed its young.*
youngster *n* **= youth**, girl, boy, kid (*informal*), teenager, juvenile, lad, lass
youth *n* **1 = immaturity**, adolescence, boyhood, girlhood, salad days **2 = boy**, kid (*informal*), teenager, youngster, adolescent, lad, stripling, young man
youthful *adj* **= young**, juvenile, inexperienced, childish, immature, boyish, fresh-faced, girlish, rosy-cheeked
yummy *adj* (*Informal*) **= delicious**, good, edible, delectable, mouth-watering, tasty

DICTIONARY

Zz

zabaglione *n* Italian dessert of egg, sugar, and wine
Zaghlul *n* **Saad**. 1857–1927, Egyptian nationalist politician; prime minister (1924)
Zamboni *n* ® machine that repairs the surface of ice in a rink
Zamenhof *n* **Lazarus Ludwig**. 1859–1917, Polish oculist; invented Esperanto
zany ➊ [**zane**-ee] *adj* **zanier, zaniest** comical in an endearing way
zap *v* **zapping, zapped** *slang* **1** kill (by shooting) **2** change television channels rapidly by remote control **3** move quickly
Zapata *n* **Emiliano**. ?1877–1919, Mexican guerrilla leader
Zappa *n* **Frank**. 1940–93, US rock musician, songwriter, and experimental composer: founder and only permanent member of the Mothers of Invention. His recordings include *Freak Out* (1966), *Hot Rats* (1969), and *Sheik Yerbouti* (1979)
Zardari *n* **Asif Ali**. born 1955, Pakistani politician; President since 2009; widower of former Prime Minister Benazir Bhutto
Zátopek *n* **Emil**. 1922–2000, Czech runner; winner of the 5000 and 10 000 metres and the marathon at the 1952 Olympic Games in Helsinki
zeal ➊ *n* great enthusiasm or eagerness
▸ **zealot** [**zel**-lot] *n* fanatic or extreme enthusiast
▸ **zealous** [**zel**-luss] *adj* extremely eager or enthusiastic **zealously** *adv*
zebra *n* black-and-white striped African animal of the horse family
▸ **zebra crossing** pedestrian crossing marked by black and white stripes on the road
zebu [**zee**-boo] *n* Asian ox with a humped back and long horns
Zeffirelli *n* **Franco**. born 1923, Italian stage and film director and designer, noted esp. for his work in opera
Zemlinsky *n* **Alexander**. 1871–1942, Austrian composer, living in the US from 1938. His works include the operas *Es war einmal* (1900) and *Eine florentische Tragödie* (1917) and the *Lyric Symphony* (1923)
Zen *n* Japanese form of Buddhism that concentrates on learning through meditation and intuition
zenith ➊ *n* **1** highest point of success or power **2** point in the sky directly above an observer
Zeno of Citium *n* ?336–?264 BC, Greek philosopher, who founded the Stoic school in Athens
zephyr [**zef**-fer] *n* soft gentle breeze
zeppelin *n hist* large cylindrical airship
zero ➊ *n, pl* **-ros, -roes 1** (symbol representing) the number 0 **2** point on a scale of measurement from which the graduations commence **3** lowest point **4** nothing, nil ▹ *adj* **5** having no measurable quantity or size
▸ **zero in on** *v* **1** aim at **2** *informal* concentrate on
zest ➊ *n* **1** enjoyment or excitement **2** interest, flavour, or charm **3** peel of an orange or lemon
zigzag *n* **1** line or course having sharp turns in alternating directions ▹ *v* **-zagging, -zagged 2** move in a zigzag ▹ *adj* **3** formed in or proceeding in a zigzag ▹ *adv* **4** in a zigzag manner
zilch *n slang* nothing
zinc *n* bluish-white metallic element used in alloys and to coat metal
zing *n informal* quality in something that makes it lively or interesting
zinnia *n* garden plant with solitary heads of

THESAURUS

zany *adj* = **comical**, crazy, eccentric, goofy (*informal*), clownish, wacky (*slang*)
zeal *n* = **enthusiasm**, spirit, passion, zest, eagerness, gusto, verve, fanaticism, ardour, fervour, keenness
zealot *n* = **fanatic**, militant, extremist, enthusiast, bigot
zealous *adj* = **enthusiastic**, eager, keen, passionate, devoted, impassioned, ardent, fervent, fanatical
zenith *n* = **height**, top, summit, peak, crest, climax, pinnacle, apex, acme, apogee, high point
zero *n* **1** = **nothing**, zip (*informal*), nil, naught (*archaic or lit*), nada (*informal*), zilch (*informal*) • *I will now count from zero to ten.* **2** = **bottom**, nadir, rock bottom
zest *n* **1** = **enjoyment**, appetite, relish, zeal, gusto, keenness **2** = **flavor**, interest, taste, charm, spice, relish,

DICTIONARY

brightly coloured flowers

Zionism *n* movement to found and support a Jewish homeland in Israel **Zionist** *n, adj*

zip Ⓣ *n* **1** fastener with two rows of teeth that are closed or opened by a small clip pulled between them **2** *informal* energy, vigour **3** short whizzing sound ▷ *v* **zipping, zipped** **4** fasten with a zip **5** move with a sharp whizzing sound

zircon *n* mineral used as a gemstone and in industry

zirconium *n* greyish-white metallic element that is very resistant to corrosion

zither *n* musical instrument consisting of strings stretched over a flat box and plucked to produce musical notes

zloty *n, pl* **-tys, -ty** monetary unit of Poland

Zn *chem* zinc

zodiac *n* imaginary belt in the sky within which the sun, moon, and planets appear to move, divided into twelve equal areas, called signs of the zodiac, each named after a constellation

zombie, zombi *n* **1** person who appears to be lifeless, apathetic, or totally lacking in independent judgment **2** corpse brought back to life by witchcraft

zone Ⓣ *n* **1** area with particular features or properties **2** one of the divisions of the earth's surface according to temperature ▷ *v* **3** divide into zones **zonal** *adj*

zoo *n, pl* **zoos** place where live animals are kept for show

zoology *n* study of animals **zoologist** *n* **zoological** *adj*

▸ **zoological garden** zoo

zoom Ⓣ *v* **1** move or rise very rapidly **2** make or move with a buzzing or humming sound

▸ **zoom lens** lens that can make the details of a picture larger or smaller while keeping the picture in focus

zucchini [zoo-**keen**-ee] *n, pl* **-nis, -ni** small type of squash with green peel

Zulu *n* **1** member of a tall Black people of southern Africa **2** language of this people

zygote *n* fertilized egg cell

THESAURUS

piquancy, pungency, tang

zip *n* **1** (*Informal*) = **energy**, drive, zest, vigor, gusto, verve, liveliness ▸ *v* **2** = **speed**, shoot, fly, flash, zoom, whizz (*informal*)

zone *n* = **area**, region, sector, district, section, belt, sphere

zoom *v* = **speed**, shoot, fly, rush, flash, dash, pelt, hurtle, whizz (*informal*)

Reports and Presentations

Contents

Writing reports 2
Giving presentations 5

Writing reports

A report is a document that presents information about an investigation or a body of research. It should have a clear structure. This structure should enable specific pieces of information to be located easily by the reader. Reports are used in many areas of business, including accounting, finance, management, and marketing, as well as in scientific research work.

Initial planning

Before starting to write any report, there are a number of questions you need to be able to answer. The answers to these questions will largely define the approach you take when putting together the report.

▷ *what is the purpose of the report?*
Ideally, you should be able to summarize the purpose in one sentence
▷ *is there an outline or remit for the report?*
If there is, the purpose of the report should be clear
▷ *who will read the report?*
Reports can be written for internal and external office use, for professionals in a particular field, or for members of the public, for instance shareholders in a large corporation
▷ *will the report be formal or informal?*
This largely depends on who the report is written for
▷ *is there a timescale for completion of the report?*
▷ *is there a word limit for the report?*
▷ *are you the sole author of the report?*
▷ *how will you undertake research for the report?*
Research can take a number of forms: consulting reference sources, previous reports on the subject, and the internet; interviewing professionals in the area of research; asking colleagues for information; or undertaking new market research
▷ *how will the report be presented?*
The report could be for internal use only, or widely distributed inside and outside the work environment. The prospective readership will affect the design, approach, and style of the whole report.

When you have answered these questions, you will be in a position to organize the subject matter for your report into sections.

Organizing the report into sections

The organization or layout of the report must make it as easy as possible for readers to get to the information they need. By subdividing the report into sections, you should be able to accommodate all the information in a clear, straightforward fashion.

The following list covers all the section headings for a major report, but smaller or less important reports may not require all of them.

Title page

This page includes the report title, the author's name, and the date of completion or release. If the report has more than one author, consider putting the authors' names in alphabetical order. Alternatively, it may be more appropriate to place the main or most prestigious author first. Remember that, unless alphabetical, the order of names sends out messages about seniority or the level of contribution of each person.

Abstract

A short summary of the report, including aims, methods, conclusions, and any recommendations. Scientific research abstracts generally appear in library files or journals of abstracts. As they don't appear with the main report in these instances, they need to be comprehensible in isolation.

Contents

A list of the sections within the report, along with their corresponding page numbers.

Introduction

This explains the purpose of the report and the methods used in its background compilation. The introduction should be concise and explain:

- ▷ what the subject of the report is
- ▷ who commissioned the report
- ▷ what the background to the commissioning of the report is
- ▷ what the method of working in compiling the report was
- ▷ what the main sources are

Main body of the report

This contains the information you have collected for the report in a number of clearly headed sections. Ensure that each section is treated in a similar way and that the most important information always comes first within a section. See **Presentation** below for more details.

Conclusions

A brief, easy-to-understand section giving an overview of the results gained from the information given in the main body of the report.

Recommendations

A section detailing possible action points and strategies for improvement in the light of the conclusions.

Appendices

These contain additional information or samples omitted from the main body of the text but which are relevant to the report as a whole.

Notes

These give details that would be too cumbersome to include in the main text. Clear cross-reference superscript numbers should appear within the text, immediately after the information to which the note refers. The notes should appear in numerical order in the Notes section.

Bibliography

This is an alphabetical listing, normally by author, of all the sources used in the report. For example:

Stirling, E.Q., 2004. *Bovine Anatomy Revisited*. 2nd ed. Jersey: Hursto Press

Wilson, J., 2002. Better milking practices. *Farm and Field*, 24 (3), 36–38.

As you can see, each source should have the following information, though the order can be varied slightly but consistently, depending on the system used:

▷ the author's name
▷ the date of publication
▷ the title of the book, newspaper, or journal, or the website address
▷ the title of the newspaper or journal article, if appropriate
▷ any edition number, other than the first edition of a book
▷ the name of the publisher of the journal or magazine

Presentation

All reports need to be as clear as possible. If they are not, readers will lose interest in their contents. Ways of making information easily accessible include:

▷ Organizing information into different sections (see **Organizing the report into sections**), giving each one a clear heading.
▷ Breaking up larger sections into manageable subsections, each with its own subheading. Bear in mind that the longer a section is, the less likely it is that it will be fully read. Sections and subsections should be numbered as follows:

1. [section heading]
1.1 [subsection heading]
1.2 [subsection heading] etc
2. [section heading]
2.1 [subsection heading] etc

▷ Maintaining consistency in the presentation of similar information.
▷ Paying attention to the numbering of sections and appendices.
▷ If appropriate, adding simple graphs, tables, and illustrations. These break up the text and often provide a quick, easy-to-understand

overview of the information.
▷ Putting large and unwieldy amounts of data into appendices, so as not to interrupt the flow of the text.
▷ Using a clear typeface for all of the text in the report. The reader wants to take in the essential points of the report as quickly as possible.

SUMMARY

- ▷ **Know the subject and purpose of the report**
- ▷ **Know who is going to read the report**
- ▷ **Set out the report in clearly defined sections**
- ▷ **Make the essential points and conclusions as clear as possible**

Giving presentations

As with writing reports, one of the keys to giving a good presentation is organizing your material. Your subject should be clearly stated, logically thought through, and explained interestingly enough to hold your audience's attention.

Notes

▷ don't learn your presentation by heart or write it down word for word. Such strategies usually result in boring delivery. Instead, make notes to refer to during the presentation so that you have something to prompt you
▷ write the notes on numbered index cards. You can then move each card to the bottom of the pile when you have used it and will always keep your place

Content

▷ try to start with something exciting but relevant to make your audience sit up and take notice. A short, telling anecdote can be useful for this
▷ give an introductory outline of your presentation, and make sure you keep to this. Avoid introducing a completely new subject without warning halfway through, or changing the tone of your presentation
▷ use links to lead logically from one section to the next: *while we're on the subject of*; *in view of*; *as for*; *before moving on to*; *in spite of*

▷ provide specific examples. These give the audience something to think about, and can be a source for a later question-and-answer session

▷ if you are presenting an argument, build from the weakest point to the strongest

▷ include a few light jokes or puns, but always ensure that they are appropriate to the presentation subject and to the audience

▷ don't be afraid to express your opinions. When you are expressing opinion rather than stating facts, remember to make this clear by using expressions such as *I believe that*; *in my opinion*; *to my mind*. You can show how strong your beliefs are by slightly amending some of these expressions: *I firmly believe that*; *I strongly believe that*; *we are absolutely certain that*; *we are pretty sure that*

▷ consider including some aspect of audience participation. Some degree of interaction tends to make a presentation more interesting

▷ end the presentation with a brief recap of the main points and a strong, persuasive conclusion

Visual aids

▷ use visual aids to illustrate your presentation, but ensure that they are simple, useful and clearly visible from the back of the room. Well-explained, well-chosen and simple visual aids are more effective than under-explained, complicated visual aids. Avoid having too many visual aids since constant changes can be distracting. Be careful not to stand in front of any visuals

▷ if you have access to a computer, you might consider using a presentation program such as PowerPoint®. Keep the number of slides to a minimum, with no more than a few concise bullet points to each slide

▷ if you are providing handouts, ensure you have made enough copies for everyone beforehand. Remember too that you must allow some time for the handouts to be received and viewed before you continue your presentation

Practice and timing

▷ try recording your presentation beforehand. This will help you get your timing and pacing right. It will also allow you to check that you sound clear and confident, that you are not mumbling or talking too fast

▷ if you can enlist the help of a supportive friend or family member, try out your presentation in front of them and ask for comments on any distracting habits you may have, such as fiddling with your hair or endlessly repeating a particular expression

▷ before the event, make sure you run through your presentation exactly as you intend to do it on the day, complete with any visuals and handouts. Time how long it takes and tailor it as necessary to fit the time allotted for it. It is very important to ensure that it does not overrun

Venue

▷ if you are using a computer or overhead projector for your presentation, ensure that you have time to find out how to work it before the presentation
▷ make sure that there are enough seats for your audience
▷ familiarize yourself with the venue and its acoustics, to ensure that you feel comfortable speaking in it and that you are able to project your voice across the whole room

You, your body and your voice

▷ if you feel nervous before giving your presentation, practise deep breathing and rehearse your opening sentences
▷ if you are very nervous, standing behind a lectern may help you feel less vulnerable, as well as giving you something to lean on and somewhere to place your notes
▷ as you give your presentation, stand straight and keep you chin up as you speak. A strong, positive posture will both improve your confidence and convince the audience that you have something interesting to say
▷ look round all the faces in the audience with sweeping glances. Look members of the audience very briefly in the eye when you can, avoiding looking at any one individual for too long
▷ speak sincerely and with warmth
▷ subtly vary your tone of voice to add interest, but make sure that you do not overdo this
▷ vary your pace, but never talk too quickly as you may well lose your audience if you do
▷ pause slightly between points to show the audience when you are about to move on to a different subject. Allow pauses for audience reaction
▷ smile from time to time where appropriate. It will help you feel more relaxed and it will encourage a bond with your audience
▷ do not be put off if you make a mistake during the presentation. Apologize quickly and move on

SUMMARY

Three helpful steps to remember when planning your presentation:
▷ Say what you are going to say.
▷ Say it.
▷ Say what you've said.